Leaves Of Healing, Volume 15...

John Alexander Dowie

HE SENDETH HIS WORD

PATIENCE

AND HEALETH THEM

LEAVES OF HEALING

VOLUME FIFTEEN

FROM APRIL 23, 1904
TO OCTOBER 15, 1904

EDITED BY
JOHN ALEXANDER, FIRST APOSTLE
of the
Lord Jesus, the Christ, in the Christian Catholic Apostolic Church in Zion

ZION CITY, ILLINOIS
ZION PRINTING AND PUBLISHING HOUSE
1904

INDEX.

A WEEKLY PAPER FOR THE EXTENSION OF THE KINGDOM OF GOD
EDITED BY THE REV. JOHN ALEX. DOWIE.

Volume XV. No. 1. *ZION CITY, SATURDAY, APRIL 23, 1904.* *Price Five Cents*

April 25. 1816 **April 25, 1904**

Mother Stewart

Eighty-eight Complete Years

I WILL COME WITH THE MIGHTY ACTS OF JEHOVAH GOD:
I WILL MAKE MENTION OF THY RIGHTEOUSNESS, EVEN OF THINE ONLY.

Elder Mother Stewart came into Zion at the All-Night with God, 1901-2, having been baptized by Triune Immersion, August 11, 1901.

Our beloved General Overseer, the Rev. John Alexander Dowie, adopted her as his mother in the Christ, and she called him her son, and since that time the love of a mother and the devotion of a son have been most manifest.

His parting injunction to us as a people as he bade us good-by before leaving for the Around-the-World Visitation was, "Be good to Mother Stewart."

Her whole life has been a mission of love and good works for humanity.

She made herself a heroine during the Civil War; and, for meritorious service, the "boys in blue" named her Mother Stewart.

Her work for public charities, and her great leadership in the Crusade,

MOTHER STEWART.

followed by the early organization of the Woman's Christian Temperance Union, has so endeared her to the people that the sweet name, Mother Stewart, is her address the world around. Her immense correspondence is all thus addressed.

Since she has come into the Christian Catholic Church in Zion, her influence has gone out to all countries, and has helped largely to overcome the prejudice of people who knew us only through the misrepresentations of the press.

Her life, words, and example speak forcibly for any church or reform she adopts.

Though frail of body, and at present out of our City with her literary secretary in Hicksville, Ohio, her heart is with Zion, and she is looking with happy anticipation to the General Overseer's return, and expects to be in Zion City to greet him, if the Lord will.

Her many life-long friends, members of the press, soldier comrades, ladies' aid societies, her native state, and the societies of the Woman's Christian Temperance Union in different parts of the world, all join in honoring this noble woman's natal day. We feel that our City, most of all, should honor her noble life; and, in so doing, show our respect to our General Overseer, who has called her "Mother."

Letters of congratulation, or tokens of appreciation, will reach her if addressed: "Mother Stewart, Hicksville, Ohio, Box 391."

We take pleasure in giving this public recognition of our appreciation of the life and work of this dear old saint.

All Zion has learned to love her and, on behalf of the Christian Catholic Church in Zion, we will say to her:

Jehovah bless thee, and keep thee:
Jehovah make His face to shine upon thee, and be gracious unto thee:
Jehovah lift up His countenance upon thee, and give thee peace.

Would that God might raise up many other brave women to carry on the battle against the iniquitous liquor traffic. Unless the fight is prosecuted with renewed vigor, there is great danger that the drinking and selling of intoxicating liquors will become fashionable and reputable in the sight of the world, just as the abuse of medicine and poisonous narcotics has become universal.

Mother Stewart's heart went out for Zion because she saw in this great work the greatest organized opposition to the use of liquor that the world has ever seen.

Never before has she or the world had the privilege of seeing a whole City entirely free from its great curse.

No wonder that she has felt a great love for our beloved General Overseer.

She, too, has endured persecution for righteousness' sake.

We take pleasure in printing some of the letters that are being sent out by other organizations in honor of this great woman.

The Woman's Christian Temperance Union, the Grand Army of the Republic, temperance organizations, and others, are honoring her great name and work, by suitably celebrating the eighty-eighth anniversary of her birth with speech-making and programs of various kinds. The two following are but samples of a large number of circular letters being sent out:

SPRINGFIELD, OHIO, March 16, 1904.

MY DEAR FRIEND:

This letter is sent to remind you that "Our Beloved Mother Stewart," whom Frances Willard called "The Great Leader of the Crusade" and whom Philanthropy christened "The Mother of Reform," is nearing her eighty-eighth birthday, which will occur April 25, 1904. In her native state, "The Ohio Woman's Christian Temperance Union" have made this date a Red Letter Day for all local societies, and for years her birthday has been honored not only in her own state but in different parts of the United States and foreign countries. It occurs to us, her "Old Guard," (viz., her first vice-president, secretary and treasurer) that it is fitting that the celebration of this noble and heroic woman's natal day be as universal as the work of the White Ribbon Movement. She was a pioneer when it meant persecution, ridicule, scorn and calumny for woman to take the platform or even write against the social evils which menaced the home. But ever true to her watchword (when she started) "I will go in the strength of the Lord, God, I will make mention of Thy righteousness, Thine only," (Psalm 71-16) she dared all for the sake of the home and the death of the Liquor Curse. She was an agitator who plowed with truth, and planted with love, the seeds of sentiment that has grown legions of women and men who are in the arena of conflict, "For God and Home and Native Land." We trust that every one who receives this letter will constitute himself or herself a committee of one, to make this day one of love and honor, not only for Mother Stewart, but to forward the work which she traveled over lands and seas to organize.

A great general once said that the "strength of a nation is known by the loyal honor she pays to her heroes." May our loyal devotion to this "Great Leader" and any others who helped to blaze the trees and open the road of this Great Reform, prove that our strength is equal to the task she so heroically led.

Therefore we, her "Old Guard," as she lovingly calls us, have thought best to send out this letter, making Mrs. M. M. Farnsworth our corresponding secretary. Mother Stewart is at present visiting Mrs. Farnsworth, who is assisting her in finishing her Autobiography and preparing other manuscript for the press.

She will remain in Hicksville until the last of June. Physically Mother Stewart is very weak, but capacitated mentally to enjoy letters, company, books, papers, etc., etc. Let no one forget that Mother Stewart's work inaugurated the greatest society of temperance women the world has ever known. Let us fittingly celebrate, while the recipient is with us to SEE, HEAR and ENJOY.

Yours for true appreciation,

MRS. S. M. FOOS, Vice-president,
MRS. J. A. S. GUY, Secretary,
SARAH W. CATHCART, Treasurer.

Will Unions please ask notice in local papers?
M. M. FARNSWORTH, Secretary, Hicksville, Ohio.

HICKSVILLE, OHIO, April 4.

TO OUR FRIENDS, GREETING:

As we are desirous for the best interest of the temperance cause everywhere, and especially anxious for the growth and success of the Woman's Christian Temperance Union as combined in the local, state, national and world society; therefore we wish to do a little towards the celebration of Mother Stewart's birthday anniversary as ordered by the State Woman's Christian Temperance Union, which occurs April 25th, and we felt that this leaflet would reach more people and be of greater benefit to the cause than a banquet or entertainment. Mrs. Eliza D. Stewart, (known as Mother Stewart the world around,) began her temperance work in 1858. She organized a union of temperance women one hundred strong, at Osborne, Ohio, December 1, 1873, and all through the years she has labored to organize and spread the "Law of Prohibition and the Gospel of Christ" throughout the world. She probably organized her last union October 6, 19—. It is called the Mother Stewart Union, and this "Great Leader of the Crusade" was made honorary president for life. It had ten members, and we can only hope it may grow as the Scottish unions did. One at Paisley, Scotland, having one thousand workers, and the young woman's branch, five hundred. The one at Alloa, eleven hundred and thirty. We invite any or all persons who are not members of the Woman's Christian Tempe[illegible] in our ranks, and in honor of [illegible] the good of the cause we hope [illegible] sand strong. Sixty cents per y[illegible] and any person sending us that am[illegible] by vote of the society to *Ohio Stat*[illegible] one year. Address the president, M[illegible] Farnsworth, Hicksville, Ohio, Box 391. [illegible] ter we append speaks for itself and hope [illegible] be the inspiration to others it has been to us.

Yours for Temperance,

MOTHER STEWART UNION, Committee.

We are glad to know that the dear Elder will be with us during the Feast of Tabernacles, the Lord willing.

Her heart is still in the work.

Her great cry is that she might go out into the harvest field to bring in the precious sheaves for the Christ.

Her poor body is not strong enough, but her mind is strong and active as ever.

Her work will never die, but will be a source of inspiration to all who read the story of her life in the years to come.

May God grant that she shall still live to see a greater work wrought out in Zion.

J. G. S.

Zion Literature Sent Out from a Free Distribution Fund Provided by Zion's Guests and the Friends of Zion.

Report for the two weeks ending April 16, 1904:

4,458 Rolls to........Hotels in the United States
2,000 Rolls to Business Men in Brooklyn, New York, and Minnesota.
1,286 Rolls to........Various States in the Union
1,796 Rolls to Hotels in Europe, Asia, Africa, and to the Islands of the Sea.
1,675 Rolls to.........Various Foreign Countries
Number of Rolls for two Weeks. 11,215
Number of Rolls reported to Apr. 16, 1904, 3,116,284

EVANGELIST SARAH E. HILL,
Superintendent Zion's Literature Mission,
Zion City, Illinois.

MEETINGS IN ZION CITY TABERNACLES.

SHILOH TABERNACLE.

Lord's Day—Early morning service.. . 6:30 a. m.
Intermediate Bible Class.. 9:45 a. m.
Bible class, conducted by Deacon Daniel Sloan... 11:00 a. m.
Afternoon service........ 2:30 p. m.
Evening service .... 8:00 p. m.
First Lord's Day of Every Month—Communion service.
Second Lord's Day of Every Month—Baptismal service.
Third Lord's Day of Every Month—Consecration of children, 10:00 a. m.
Monday—Zion Restoration Host rally (Second Monday of every month).... 8:00 p. m.
Tuesday—Divine Healing meeting..... 2:30 p. m.
Tuesday—Adult Choir .... 7:45 p. m.
Wednesday—Baptismal service........ 7:00 p. m.
Wednesday—Citizens' rally............ 8:00 p. m.
Friday—Adult Choir.................. 7:45 p. m.
Friday—Officers of the Christian Catholic Church in Zion........ 8:00 p. m.
Saturday—Junior Choir . ... 1:00 p. m.
Meeting in the officers' room.

TWENTY-SIXTH STREET TABERNACLE.

Lord's Day—Junior service........... 9:45 a. m.
Lord's Day—Services (German)........10:30 a. m.
Tuesday—Services (German).......... 8:00 p. m.

ELIJAH THE RESTORER CONTRASTS THE NARROWNESS OF THE APOSTASIES WITH THE BROAD VIEW OF THE KINGDOM OF GOD.

A WEEKLY PAPER FOR THE EXTENSION OF THE KINGDOM OF GOD.

EDITED BY THE REV. JOHN ALEX. DOWIE.

Application for entry as Second Class Matter at Zion City, Illinois, pending.

Subscription Rates.		Special Rates.	
One Year	$2.00	100 Copies of One Issue	$3.00
Six Months	1.25	25 Copies of One Issue	1.00
Three Months	.75	To Ministers, Y. M. C. A's and Public Reading Rooms, per annum	1.50
Single Copies	.05		

For foreign subscriptions add $1.50 per year, or three cents per copy for postage.

Subscribers desiring a change of address should give present address, as well as that to which they desire LEAVES OF HEALING sent in the future.

Make Bank Drafts, Express Money or Postoffice Money Orders payable to the order of JOHN ALEX. DOWIE. Zion City, Illinois, U. S. A.

Long Distance Telephone. *Cable Address "Dowie, Zion City."*

All communications upon business must be addressed to
MANAGER ZION PUBLISHING HOUSE,
Zion City, Illinois, U. S. A.

Subscriptions to LEAVES OF HEALING, A VOICE FROM ZION, and the various publications may also be sent to
ZION PUBLISHING HOUSE, 81 EUSTON ROAD, LONDON, N. W., ENGLAND.
ZION PUBLISHING HOUSE, NO. 43 PARK ROAD, ST. KILDA, MELBOURNE, VICTORIA, AUSTRALIA.
ZION PUBLISHING HOUSE, RUE DE MONT, THABOR 1, PARIS, FRANCE.
ZIONSHEIM, SCHLOSS LIEBBURG, CANTON THURGAU, BEI ZÜRICH, SWITZERLAND.

ZION CITY, ILLINOIS, SATURDAY, APRIL 23, 1904.

TABLE OF CONTENTS.

LEAVES OF HEALING, SATURDAY, APRIL 23, 1904.

Notes From The Overseer-in-Charge.

"BRETHREN, BE YE FOLLOWERS OF ME, AND MARK THEM WHICH WALK SO, AS YE HAVE US FOR AN ENSAMPLE."

IT IS a great thing for a man to be able to say, "Follow me."

THE APOSTLE PAUL was not afraid to tell the Philippian brethren to follow him.

IT IS INTERESTING to note that the Revised Version uses the word "imitator" instead of "follower."

The original word has the meaning of imitation rather than merely following.

THIS WORD is used by Paul seven times in the epistles, and once by Peter. Peter refers to following Jesus. Paul is the only man in all the Bible Story who had the courage and the life to say, "Be ye imitators of me."

"BE YE imitators of me," is the exact meaning.

THIS DOES not include the idea of caricature, but is an exact copying or reproducing.

THERE ARE few men whose lives are so perfect as to make them fit for imitation.

OUR BELOVED LEADER, the General Overseer of the Christian Catholic Church in Zion, has been severely criticised and censured by those who oppose him because he has asked his people to take a vow which is called the Zion Restoration Host Vow.

A part of this Vow is as follows:

I promise to the fullest extent of all my powers to obey all rightful orders issued by him [the General Overseer] directly, or by his properly appointed officers.

THE GENERAL OVERSEER has always said, "Follow me only as far as I follow the Christ."

IN TIME of doubt and where the light is not clear, Zion has considered it safe to follow him whom God has so wonderfully used in leading forth His people out of darkness.

But never has it been taught in Zion that under all circumstances whatsoever, we must blindly follow our leader, whether he does right or wrong.

ZION ALWAYS puts conscience into her deeds.

The people of Zion are taught to exercise their consciences in all matters, and the right of individual thought has never been denied.

IT IS a great honor for any man to be the leader of any people and to have them follow him implicitly, but it becomes a still greater honor when this people in imitating a man's life become a pure, sober, industrious, God-fearing, self-reliant, healthy and happy people.

TRULY IT WAS well said, "By their fruits ye shall know them."

ZION IS PROUD of the leadership of such a man, of whom it can truthfully be said that in him is fulfilled the definition given by the Apostle James, of Pure Religion:

> To visit the fatherless and widows in their affliction, and to keep himself unspotted from the world.

IT IS BECOMING more and more noticeable that God is not choosing for His Great Leaders men who have had their lives burnt out in sin and shame before their conversion; that the strong men are not those who have been the deepest in sin; that the men whom God has ever used for His prophets and reformers are men who have been raised from childhood in purity and in the love and fear of God.

SUCH A MAN we have in our Leader.

NEVER HAS there been any reproach brought against him as to the purity of his life or character in all the world.

SUCH A MAN was Paul, whose conscience was "void of offense toward God and man."

OUR BLESSED SAVIOR did not take reformed drunkards and whoremongers and make apostles of them.

AND IT IS good that a man can say, "Be ye followers of me."

It is good for the people that there should be one in this degenerate age whom it is safe to follow.

THE TRUE LEADERS are becoming exceedingly scarce.

PRESIDENT JOSEPH SMITH cannot say, "Be ye followers of me." He must say, "Do not do as I do, but do as I tell you."

HE IS CARRYING the other side of the Race Suicide Question to a disgusting extreme.

THERE IS SCARCELY any wonder that the parents of today do not care to bear the responsibility of large families when it is considered how utterly reckless and disobedient the majority of American children are.

THE FLAT and tenement house problem is not a problem of large families, but it is a problem of disobedient and ungovernable children.

THE AVERAGE American child knows not what it means to obey.

And why should he know the meaning of obedience when his parents before him never knew what it meant to recognize authority?

UNGOVERNABLE PARENTS beget disobedient children, and today a few children, untrained and unrestrained, become a great curse in a flat building or a tenement house.

No wonder the owners of the buildings do not care to allow the children of drunken, riotous, vicious parents to be domiciled in their property.

THE QUESTION is not so much a question of Prevention of Race Suicide as it is of teaching the people the meaning of Government and Self-control.

WE TOOK occasion a few weeks ago, in speaking upon the serious question of marriage among our people, to declare that it is God's will and plan that every man and woman should establish a home and beget children; that marriage is not a matter or subject for levity; but that it is a serious matter to be fully considered and acted upon; that Zion encourages her young people to marry after a suitable age; and that celibacy is strongly discouraged; that Zion is proud of her large number of beautiful children, born in happy homes.

OVERSEER BRASEFIELD strongly supported this position last Lord's Day, and emphasized the necessity of having true homes; that the home is not merely a house where people live, but a home where there is a union of a man and woman in the sacred relations of husband and wife, around whom are gathered the beautiful lives of well-trained children.

AMERICA'S GREAT need today is godly homes.

IN THIS, again, Zion is in great contrast with the world.

The home life predominates in Zion.

We discourage everything that detracts from it.

THE EXTREME and unbounded selfishness of those who devote their whole lives simply to their own self-interests cannot be too strongly condemned.

IF EVERY MAN and every woman were to marry there would be no room for polygamy or prostitution.

THERE ARE just as many male children born as female.

The average length of life for the male is greater than that of the female.

THERE IS no excuse for men who are able-bodied not finding some suitable life companion.

ONE SERIOUS difficulty has been in the way, and is becoming more and more prominent, and that is that a great many women are unwilling to bear the responsibility of maternity, and will not marry until late in life because of this unwillingness.

THIS IS a great curse and blight upon humanity.

THE POSITION of the polygamists is absolutely unbearable, that one man should have a plurality of wives, while other men have none.

IF ALL MEN were married, there would be no unmarried women.

This is unquestionably God's order.

PRESIDENT SMITH cannot be followed in this matter, nor can he be followed in many other things.

IF THE PAPERS can be believed, the Mormons are farming out their grounds to liquor dealers, and are selling permits to sell intoxicating liquors to the people who come to their meetings.

UP TO THIS time there has not been one public declaration by our beloved General Overseer that has not been perfectly consistent and absolutely safe to follow.

WE DO NOT say that it is not right for President Smith to care for his wives and children, and to make the best of existing circumstances.

We believe that it is right.

We believe the same thing to be true in the far-off heathen lands.

A man who has a plurality of wives must care for them, but he must not enter into new relations of the same kind.

IT IS a terrible commentary on our boasted civilization that the more civilized the nations the more successful they become in destroying one another in war.

In a recent editorial in one of the Chicago papers it is said that "Russia and Japan are at war; Germany is fighting the Hereros; Great Britain is massacring the Tibetans; the United States is shooting Moros; Civilization is advancing with giant strides."

IT SEEMS that it is only a matter of a short time when our boasted civilization must break down of its own weight.

THE CIVILIZATION of Babylon was one of great culture (?) and refinement (?) externally, but how complete the overthrow!

IT SEEMS that we are in the beginning of the Great Tribulation.

AGES OVERLAP each other; and it must be that in the End of the Age, and in the rejection of the blessed truths of Christianity in the face of the wonderful testimony of Zion, utter ruin and destruction, suicide, anarchy and chaos will reign upon the earth.

THEN SHALL speedily dawn the Brighter Day, the Day of Hope, the Day of the Reign of King Immanuel, the Reign of Peace and Order; the Glorious Day of the RESTORATION OF ALL THINGS.

We are in the twilight of this Glorious Day.

The sun has not yet arisen, but we see the light that is breaking forth in the eastern sky.

The clouds will surely break away, and as the Night of Sorrow and Despair shall give way to the glorious sunrise, we shall rejoice that Zion has done what she could and has kept the Testimony of Jesus, and has been strong and pure in the midst of a wicked and adulterous generation.

THE FOLLOWING CABLEGRAM from the General Overseer received Friday morning makes us rejoice in the Lord:

COLOMBO.

SPEICHER, Zion City, Illinois.

Read the 48th Psalm. We have had a good voyage. All fellow passengers were respectful and agreeable. We were visited here by Zion people. Sail today. All are well. Hallelujah! Pray for us. Love to all Zion.

Mizpah DOWIE.

(Midnight.)

JOHN G. SPEICHER.

Around-the-World Visitation

of the

Rev. John Alex. Dowie

Elijah the Restorer
General Overseer of the Christian Catholic Church in Zion.

By ARTHUR W. NEWCOMB, Special Correspondent.

VISITATION AT SYDNEY, NEW SOUTH WALES, AUSTRALIA.

IN the last paper of this series, we closed with the sighting of the Australian shore from the deck of the Steamship Sonoma, on the early morning of Saturday, February 13, 1904.

Met by Dr. A. J. Gladstone Dowie, Overseer Voliva, and Deacons McCullagh and Hawkins in Sydney Harbor.

Soon after passing between the Heads into Sydney Harbor, we sighted, among the other crafts plying in all directions, a trim little launch, whose passengers were Dr. A. J. Gladstone Dowie, Overseer Wilbur Glenn Voliva, and Deacons J. S. McCullagh, of Sydney, and C. Friend Hawkins, of Adelaide.

The Sonoma was taken, first of all, to Watson's Bay, for the medical inspection, which proved to be quite a task, owing to the fact that smallpox had been reported in some parts of New Zealand, and all those who had booked at that port had to give an account of themselves.

As soon as this inspection was over, the launch containing the officers of Zion who had come out to meet us was permitted to come alongside, and our friends came on board. It was with great joy that the General Overseer and his son greeted each other, after nearly four months' separation, and there was a joyous reunion of all the party with the young man, and with Overseer Voliva, whom we had not seen for over two years.

TOWN HALL, SYDNEY.

Although none of us had met Deacons McCullagh and Hawkins before, it seemed like meeting old friends to see them, so much had we read about them, and so fully were they of the true Zion spirit.

As the ship was slowly steaming from Watson's Bay, just inside the Heads, to her wharf on Circular Quay, final preparations were made for going ashore, and farewells were said to the friends that we had made during the voyage. Among these were the Chief Officer, the Surgeon, and some of the other officers and stewards of the ship, who had been very kind to us all the way over.

Zion Friends and Others at the Wharf.

At the wharf, a goodly company of the members and the friends of Zion had gathered to welcome the General Overseer, and they greeted him with the same love that characterizes the people of Zion the world over.

There were present, also, a large number of curious ones, and of the notorious Sydney "larrikins," a very rough and dangerous element of that city.

These latter manifested that bitter hatred to which the Devil gives vent, in every age, when a Prophet of God appears. They hooted, called out impudently, insultingly, and profanely, and indulged in that peculiarly unmusical and senseless noise known in England and Australia as "boo-hooing."

They attempted to surround the General Overseer as he went to his carriage, but Zion Guard of the Sydney Branch and a few police kept them back, and the man of God was able to enter his carriage and drive away in safety.

He proceeded with his party to the Australia Hotel, where he entertained Overseer Voliva, Deacon and Deaconess McCullagh and their daughter, and Deacon Hawkins at luncheon.

Hostile Attitude of the Press.

The afternoon was spent in perfecting the arrangements for the mission and in giving the representatives of the afternoon press some promised interviews.

These interviews were treated in the most slipshod fashion; but a great deal of space was given to a rehash of a number of lies that had been worn out and discarded by the American press some time before.

Reporters for the Sydney Sunday papers also called, but were told that the General Overseer would not give interviews to papers published on the Lord's Day. This did not prevent some of them from publishing alleged interviews on the following morning.

Thus it was seen, at the very beginning of the mission, that the press could be counted on to show no spirit but that of uncompromising hostility.

It was encouraging to know that the Devil regarded the Visitation to Sydney as dangerous to him and his.

The newspapers were not content with mere hostility, however.

For Simon pure villainy, murderous malignity, amazing mendacity and ghoulish irreverence, they are unsurpassed.

It was some comfort for us, as American citizens, to know that, unspeakably vile as is the American press, there has been nothing tolerated there, since the death of the unlamented Chicago *Dispatch*, and the imprisonment of its editor and proprietor, so obscenely scurrilous as a monstrosity of journalistic degeneracy, impudently called *Truth*, and published in Sydney, Melbourne, Adelaide, Brisbane, and Perth, Australia, by a notorious person named John Norton.

On Lord's Day morning, the General Overseer conducted devotional exercises with the Zion party, in his rooms in the Australia Hotel.

In the afternoon, at half past two o'clock, the first service of the Visitation in Sydney was held in the Town Hall.

This is one of the most beautiful of the many public buildings in Sydney, splendidly situated on one of the principal streets of the city.

The auditorium of the building is a spacious one with a very high ceiling, and with seats for about three thousand four hundred people. Just outside this there is a large vestibule, which gave space for the Zion Literature tables and was also used as a prayer-room at the Divine Healing meetings.

The Lord's Day Afternoon Service.

There is no better way to describe the great crowds that thronged that hall on that first Lord's Day afternoon, than to say that they reminded one of the New York Visitation.

There had been five thousand tickets issued, all of which had been very eagerly taken up, and uncounted throngs who had no tickets tried to gain admittance.

Every chair was occupied, and the people would have filled all the aisles if they had not been prevented by Zion Guards.

Besides these, there was a constant stream of people coming, taking note of the crowds, and going away.

At this service, there was good order, for the most part, and the most intense interest on the part of the vast majority of the audience, who followed the General Overseer's every word, gesture and look.

They were very evidently heartily with him in nearly everything that he said, expressing their approval most enthusiastically.

At this meeting, the General Overseer, Overseers Voliva and Excell, and Deacons McCullagh and Hawkins appeared in the robes of their offices, Dr. A. J. Gladstone Dowie in his Doctor's robe and hood, and Colonel Carl F. Stern and Staff-captain Arthur W. Newcomb, of Zion Guard, in their uniforms.

---

*REPORTED BY E. W. AND A. W. N.

Town Hall, Sydney, Australia, Lord's Day Afternoon, February 14, 1904.

The meeting was opened by the General Overseer's pronouncing the

INVOCATION.

God be merciful unto us and bless us,
And cause Thy face to shine upon us;
That Thy Way may be known upon earth,
Thy Saving Health among all the Nations;
For the sake of Jesus. Amen.

PRAISE.

The Congregation then joined in singing Hymn No. 391:

Look, ye saints, the sight is glorious;
See the "Man of sorrows" now;
From the fight returned victorious,
Every knee to Him shall bow.
Chorus—Crown Him, crown Him, angels crown Him,
Crown the Savior, "King of kings."

The General Overseer then led the Choir and Congregation in the recitation of the Apostles' Creed:

RECITATION OF CREED.

I believe in God the Father Almighty,
Maker of heaven and earth;
And in Jesus, the Christ, His only Son, our Lord,
Who was conceived by the Holy Ghost;
Born of the Virgin Mary;
Suffered under Pontius Pilate;
Was crucified, dead and buried:
He descended into hell.
The third day He rose from the dead;
He ascended into heaven,
And sitteth on the right hand of God, the Father Almighty;
From thence He shall come to judge the quick and the dead.
I believe in the Holy Ghost;
The Holy Catholic Church;
The Communion of Saints;
The Forgiveness of Sins;
The Resurrection of the body,
And the life Everlasting. Amen.

READING OF GOD'S COMMANDMENTS.

The General Overseer then led the Congregation in repeating the Commandments, after which the words, "Lord, have mercy upon us, and write all these Thy Laws in our hearts, we beseech Thee," were chanted.

I. Thou shalt have no other gods before Me.

II. Thou shalt not make unto thee a graven image, nor the likeness of any form that is in heaven above, or that is in the earth beneath, or that is in the water under the earth: thou shalt not bow down thyself unto them, nor serve them: for I Jehovah thy God am a jealous God, visiting the iniquity of the fathers upon the children, upon the third and upon the fourth generation of them that hate Me; and showing mercy unto thousands, of them that love Me and keep My commandments.

III. Thou shalt not take the Name of Jehovah thy God in vain; for Jehovah will not hold him guiltless that taketh His Name in vain.

IV. Remember the Sabbath Day, to keep it Holy. Six days shalt thou labor, and do all thy work: but the seventh day is a Sabbath unto Jehovah thy God: in it thou shalt not do any work, thou, nor thy son, nor thy daughter, thy manservant, nor thy maidservant, nor thy cattle, nor thy stranger that is within thy gates: for in six days Jehovah made heaven and earth, the sea, and all that in them is, and rested the seventh day: wherefore Jehovah blessed the Sabbath Day, and hallowed it.

V. Honor thy father and thy mother: that thy days may be long upon the land which Jehovah thy God giveth thee.

*The following report has not been revised by the General Overseer.

VI. Thou shalt do no murder.

VII. Thou shalt not commit adultery.

VIII. Thou shalt not steal.

IX. Thou shalt not bear false witness against thy neighbor.

X. Thou shalt not covet thy neighbor's house, thou shalt not covet thy neighbor's wife, nor his manservant, nor his maidservant, nor his ox, nor his ass, nor anything that is thy neighbor's.

Hear also what our Lord Jesus, the Christ, the Son of God hath said, which may be called the Eleventh Commandment:

XI. A new Commandment I give unto you, that ye love one another; even as I have loved you, that ye also love one another.

The Choir then sang the

TE DEUM LAUDAMUS.

We praise Thee, O God; we acknowledge Thee to be the Lord.
All the earth doth worship Thee, the Father everlasting.
To Thee all Angels cry aloud, the Heavens and all the powers therein.
To Thee Cherubim and Seraphim continually do cry:
Holy, Holy, Holy, Lord God of Sabaoth,
Heaven and earth are full of the majesty of Thy Glory.
The glorious company of the Apostles praise Thee.
The goodly fellowship of the Prophets praise Thee.
The noble army of martyrs praise Thee.
The Holy Church throughout all the world doth acknowledge Thee,
The Father of an Infinite Majesty.
Thine Adorable, True and Only Son;
Also the Holy Ghost the Comforter.
Thou art the King of Glory, O Christ;
Thou art the Everlasting Son of the Father.
When Thou tookest upon Thee to deliver man,
Thou didst humble Thyself to be born of a Virgin.
When Thou hadst overcome the sharpness of death,
Thou didst open the Kingdom of Heaven to all believers.
Thou sittest at the right hand of God in the Glory of the Father.
We believe that Thou shalt come to be our Judge.
We therefore pray Thee, help Thy servants,
Whom Thou hast redeemed with Thy precious blood.
Make them to be numbered with Thy Saints in glory everlasting.
O Lord, save Thy people and bless Thine heritage;
Govern them and lift them up forever.
Day by day we magnify Thee;
And we worship Thy Name ever, world without end.
Vouchsafe, O Lord, to keep us this day without sin.
O Lord, have mercy upon us, have mercy upon us.
O Lord, let Thy mercy be upon us as our trust is in Thee.
O Lord, in Thee have I trusted, let me never be confounded.

The General Overseer then read from the Inspired Word of God the 35th chapter of the Book of Isaiah, and the 11th chapter of the Gospel according to St. Matthew.

Prayer was then offered by Overseer Voliva, at the close of which the Disciples' Prayer was chanted by the Choir and Congregation.

Greeting.

The General Overseer then said:

Before the offering is taken, I desire to speak a few words to you, thanking hundreds and even thousands of old friends in this great, broad Australian Continent, for their very kind welcome.

I am very deeply touched by the many private expressions, and also by some of the public expressions of welcome.

Some of these expressions are very funny.

Some people seem to take Zion as a huge joke, and do not understand that there is anything serious about it.

A Word as to the Press.

I do not want to have any fight, at the beginning, with anybody personally, but when a Sunday paper, today, says that I gave its representative an interview, I want to tell you that every word of that is a lie. The whole interview is an invention.

On principle, I would not give any interview to a Sunday newspaper. [Applause.]

Surely, there is one day in all the week, when the curs of an unbridled and licentious press ought to be kept away.

I trust that the legislature will see its way, some day, to suppress papers that are a menace to good order, although they bear high-sounding titles.

One is called the *Sun*, but it ought to be called something very different; for "if therefore the light that is in thee be darkness, how great is the darkness!"

Another is called *Truth!* [Laughter and applause.]

I have read that truth can be found only at the bottom of a well, but in Sydney you can find it only at the bottom of a literary cesspit. [Applause.]

It is time that such wretches as these feel the whip of some man of God.

I think that for villainy, the Sunday papers of this city have even excelled the yellow journals of New York and of Chicago. [Applause and laughter.]

It is considered a disgrace in America for a man to be seen reading a copy of any of the Hearst newspapers, such as the New York *Journal*, the Chicago *American*, or the San Francisco *Examiner*.

It is a reflection upon a man's character to be seen with a copy of such a paper in his hand—how much more to be seen with a copy of the Sydney *Sunday Times*, or—

A voice—"*Truth!*" [Applause.]

After Twenty-four Years.

General Overseer—But I am glad to be here among you again.

It is twenty-four years since I was a preacher in Sydney.

Some of these dear boys sitting at the press table were not born then—the new-born babes of the press.

Men and women have grown up since I was pastor at Newtown.

I am recognizing many of your faces. I find that you are not all dead.

It makes one feel that the years are rolling on, and the snows of winter are gathering on one's brow, and that we must so live that when the watchers say, "He is dead," it will be true that, being dead, we shall go on speaking to the generations yet to come.

God grant that we may speak for Him, for truth, and for humanity.

> Not myself, but the words that in life I have spoken,
> Not myself, but the deeds that in life I have done,
> Shall pass on to ages, all about me forgotten,
> Save the truth I have spoken, the good I have done.

I live to speak truth as far as I know it, to do good as far as I can, to live the words that my dear old friend, Thomas Guthrie, of Edinburgh, used to say:

> I live for those who love me,
> For those who know me true;
> For the heaven that smiles above me,
> And awaits my coming, too;
> For the wrongs that need resistance
> For the cause that needs assistance,
> For the future in God's distance,
> For the good that I may do.

I care not what any man, or any paper, or any pulpit may say, I live for God and for humanity, to speak truth and to do good! [Applause.]

Greetings From America.

I bring you loving greetings from the great people on the American Continent, where God is building up a vast commonwealth and empire, which is joining hands with our kin across the sea in Great Britain and in Australia.

These Anglo-Saxon nations are becoming closely knit in language, in literature, in religion, and in great political and national interests; and for all great practical purposes, today, in the Orient and everywhere, the American and the British people are one. [Applause.]

I am glad to know that I can bring to you, from so distinguished a man as the President of the United States, a word of greeting.

I had the pleasure of talking with him for an hour, on November 8th, in his private office in the White House.

When I said, "Mr. President, I shall not soon see you again, for I am going to Australia and around the world," he said, "Oh, I feel deeply interested in Australia; in that great, broad, beautiful land, and I should like to go and see its people."

I think you would like to see him.

He is a great, strong-minded, resolute, strenuous and godly man, a man after my own heart, I would say; for I know him to be good and true, a patriot, and to have the great Theocratic thought, that God rules this world, and that they that rule over men must be just, ruling in the fear of God.

Although I have no distinct, positive message to bring you from Theodore Roosevelt, President of the United States, I have this that he said: "I love that great people, and that great land, and I should like to see them."

Greetings From Zion Everywhere.

I bring the greetings of tens, yea hundreds of thousands of those who are gathered under the Banner of Zion in America, in Europe, in Asia, in Africa, in New Zealand, and in your own great land.

I ask you to receive me as your old friend, older by a good many years, and wiser, I hope, with the discipline of sorrow, the discipline of toil, the discipline of passing through the Valley of the Shadow of Death, the discipline of going out stronger than I was before, and ready to fight the great, good fight of Faith, and Hope, and Love. [Applause.]

To my own people, under the Banner of Zion, I bring greetings; to the friends of God and of truth, and the children of God in the Christ, by His Spirit I greet you, and ask that in these four days I may be able to be of some use in this city where my son was born, and where I spent many very happy years.

You will pardon this personal talk.

I think it would be unpardonable if I did not say something upon coming back and entering in by this, one of the Great Gates of Australia—the greatest and most beautiful Gate—that harbor which is the admiration of men everywhere.

May God bless Sydney, Australia! [Applause.]

"All Hail the Power of Jesus' Name," was sung, during which the offering was taken.

THE SONG OF SALVATION, HEALING, HOLINESS, AND TRIUMPHANT ENTRY INTO THE ZION ABOVE.

INVOCATION.

Let the words of my mouth and the meditations of my heart be acceptable in Thy sight, be profitable unto this people, and unto all to whom these words shall come, in this and every land, in this and all the coming time, Till Jesus Come.

TEXT.

And Jesus answered and said unto them, Go your way and tell John the things which ye do hear and see:

The blind receive their sight, and the lame walk, the lepers are cleansed, and the deaf hear, and the dead are raised up, and the poor have good tidings preached to them.

And blessed is he, whosoever shall find none occasion of stumbling in Me.

One of the greatest of all who ever lived upon this earth was, beyond all question, the son of Zacharias and Elizabeth, whom the angel Gabriel had said should be born, and come in the spirit and power of Elijah.

He did not understand his own mission at first.

Who does?

Difficulty of Understanding One's Own Mission.

How little Abraham Lincoln understood his mission, when he occupied the humble position which he did for so many years, never thinking that the mantle of the highest office in the United States would rest upon his shoulders, and that he should be the first Martyr-President!

Little did he know when, by a pine-knot in a little hut, he read his Bible and Shakespeare, that he was defining the great fundamental principles that one day would make him the restorer of the broken Union, the suppresser of a terrible Rebellion, the emancipator of millions of slaves, and the regenerator of his country; for it was the War of the Rebellion and its suppression, and the liberation of the slaves (which act of emancipation was the signing of his own death-warrant) that made him the great and mighty man that he was.

But it was there, at the fire, reading by a blazing pine-knot, that he got the solution for the whole question, so that in the debate with Douglas, he was able to say that it could not be that a great nation should continue to exist one-half slave and the other half free. "For," he said, "it is written, 'if a house be divided against itself, that house will not be able to stand.'"

It was in the Bible that he found the philosophy that made him the mighty leader of the people.

The Divine Principle of Unity.

That word went through the American nation, and they saw that it was not possible for the nation to be one-half free and one-half slave.

The Christ Himself said, "If a kingdom be divided against itself, that kingdom cannot stand."

You must learn that in Australia.

Divided interests are the destruction of a commonwealth, and a people divided against itself can never be strong, can never be great.

You must bury your differences and unite your interests, and make Australia to advance instead of making it a little pocket borough for a few politicians.

John the Baptist, Elijah.

John the Baptist did not understand his mission any more than Abraham Lincoln understood his. When the scribes and Pharisees came to him and said, "Art thou that prophet?" he said, "I am not;" "Art thou the Christ?" he said, "I am not;" "Art thou Elijah?" he said, "I am not."

But the Angel Gabriel said that he was Elijah.

When the Christ was asked, He said, "This is Elijah, which is to come."

After John had been put to death the Christ said that Elijah must come again.

I remind you that this wonderful word of Jesus to the Disciples of John the Baptist was the occasion on which He, Jesus, the Christ, the Son of God, made it clear for all time that Elijah the Tishbite had in spirit and in power reappeared in John, the son of Zacharias and Elizabeth.

The first Elijah, who came as the Destroyer, did his work.

He who came as the Preparer did his work.

God grant that the Restorer may do his work!

The Ministry of John the Baptist.

I speak of him who was Elijah the Preparer.

His ministry lasted only about eleven months; but, during those eleven months, while it was not his privilege to destroy much, or to restore much, it was his privilege, although he wrought no miracle, to be a great preacher of Repentance, and the Preparer, who opened the door for the Christ.

His mission was in an age when the system that God had established had become a mass of hypocrisy; when scribe and Pharisee alike had become so shamefully degenerate that their offices were like flesh sold in the shambles; when the high priest was merely a political officer in an ecclsesiastical position; when Herod, and other appointed high priests, had no qualification whatever for the office, from a spiritual point of view.

Notwithstanding all this, the services at the Temple were never more majestic.

The Temple itself had been rebuilt upon a magnificent scale; perhaps even greater than that of Solomon, but it had been rebuilt by Herod the Cruel, whose hands were imbrued with blood.

He had murdered his own mother, his own wife, his own son, and trod his way to empire through seas of blood.

John the Baptist was born at that time, a little before the Christ was born.

Training of John the Baptist.

John the Baptist was brought up, as indeed he only could be brought up, in the very best school, and under the best instructor.

He was not rude and rough, although he was a stern man.

He was the son of Zacharias, of the hereditary priesthood of Abijah, therefore he was educated for the priesthood.

John the Baptist was a man of profound learning.

He was brought up with the younger Herod, who afterwards, in a fit of drunkenness, permitted Herodias' daughter to dance off John the Baptist's head.

Herod afterwards grieved for that horrible crime.

Doubtless John was also educated with Manaen, the foster-brother of Herod, who afterward became one of the great men of the Early Church, joining in the ordination of Barnabas and Saul to the Apostleship.

Get away from the thought that John the Baptist was a rough man.

"Oh," you say, "he wore a garment of camel's-hair."

Yes, it was the most costly robe he could wear; it was a robe prepared, no doubt, by the sainted Elizabeth herself.

The fine camel's hair that is used in artists' brushes was the material of the robe that John the Baptist wore—a robe worth thousands of dollars, hundreds of pounds, even today.

He was no wild, half-naked man.

Culture and Power of John the Baptist.

He was one of the great cultured priests of his time.

He had the mightiest intellect, was the broadest thinker, the tenderest preacher, and the most powerful man of his time.

He had been in communion with God Himself.

He had received from God a wonderful communication that there should come a day when he should see the Messiah.

He who sent him said, "Upon whom thou shalt see the Holy Spirit descending, He is the Christ, He is the Messiah. Baptize Him and proclaim Him as the Lamb of God who taketh away the sin of the world."

No wild fanatic, no rude and impulsive man was John.

One of the things we know about him, outside of the words he spoke, is the wonderful fact, recorded by one of Jesus' disciples, who one day said to Him, "Lord, teach us to pray as John also taught his disciples."

He was a man who taught men how to pray, and how to get an answer from God.

A mighty teacher is he who can teach men and women how to pray, and how to get an answer from God.

John the Baptist had been such a teacher.

John Hated for Speaking the Truth.

When John had fulfilled his ministry and had gone back into the deserts, having proclaimed the Christ, he was arrested by the horsemen of Herod and taken to the dungeon of the Castle of Machærus.

Herodias hated him for the truth he had spoken.

That is why good men are hated—for speaking the truth.

He said that the divorce laws of Palestine, no matter what the king might say, would not justify divorce which had been granted by hypocritical priests to a woman who was his brother Philip's wife.

John the Baptist had therefore said, "It is written in the Law of God, Thou shalt not commit adultery; thou shalt not have her to wife."

He branded the woman who sat with Herod upon the throne, his guilty paramour, as a debased woman.

Murder of John by an Adulteress.

She never forgot it.

She did not dare to touch him, for all men counted John as a prophet.

When his work was done, however, she seized him, and then had her beautiful daughter, when Herod was drunk, dance off John the Baptist's head—to ask for his head in a charger as the greatest thing that she could have.

A woman whose sin has been made plain will hate the man that makes it plain, unless she repents and turns to God.

This evil woman would not turn to God; she chose to live with the adulterous king and adulterous women.

She sought John the Baptist's heart's blood for it.

I do not hesitate to say that no man can do his duty either as a statesman or Messenger of God without finding that there are those in this world ready to take his life.

Abraham Lincoln died a martyr.

William McKinley died a martyr, and many have died because they did right; for the forces of evil will seek the heart's blood of the man who does right.

What does it matter?

They sing in America, "John Brown's body lies moldering in the grave, but his soul goes marching on," and the spirits of those who have done right go marching on under the leadership of the Christ, the greatest of those who died for men.

John was arrested, placed in the dungeon of the Castle of Machærus, and there murdered.

John's Misery and Doubt in the Dungeon.

It is hard for one who has lived in the mountains and in the desert, to live in a prison.

He is like an eagle, beating its breast against the bars.

As John the Baptist lay in the Castle of Machærus prison, the Devil began to make him doubt.

Doubt!

Oh, the most terrible thing that can ever enter a human heart is doubt!

If a man once begins to doubt the purity and virtue of the wife whom he loves, and for whom he would give his life, that doubt is a hell until it is removed.

Doubt is hell.

It makes a hell of any heart into which it enters.

Doubting the Christ made a miserable man of that mighty prophet, as he lay there.

The Devil said to him, "John the Baptist, you made a terrible blunder when you proclaimed Jesus of Nazareth as the Christ.

"Do you not know, John the Baptist, that He is eating with the rich people, and that He is clothed in a purple robe?"

(The Christ wore the wonderful robes that the kings had brought to Him at Bethlehem. It had been kept all that time, the seamless robe, the robe which even the Roman soldiers would not tear up, but cast lots for. It was a beautiful robe.)

"John the Baptist," continued the Devil, "do you not know that the Christ, whom you proclaimed, goes about eating with centurions and with rich Pharisees, that He enters into rich people's houses, and, while He has done a great deal of good, yet He is hobnobbing with all the rich people of Galilee, of Samaria, and of Judea?

"John the Baptist, you blundered. Jesus is not the Christ."

Then his disciples came and told him of Jesus' mighty works.

The Devil said, "Yes, but if He were the Christ would He not set you free?

"Would He leave you here to die in this stinking dungeon?

"Would He leave you, He who can control the winds, and the waves, and raise the dead, and do all these things, would He leave you here to die?

"No, you made a blunder. John, He is a selfish man. He is not the Christ?"

John's Message of Inquiry.

John had only one way to solve the difficulty.

That is the only way for you and me when we are in difficulty.

Do not take it to man.

When you are in difficulty, you do not ask the editor of the *Truth* to help you, do you? [Laughter.]

When you are in difficulty you do not ask the press to help you.

Take the difficulty as John took it.

He sent the difficulty to the Christ.

He said, in effect, "O, Thou Christ of God, I am lying here in this dungeon; make the matter plain to me.

"Take from my heart the doubt as to whether You are the Christ!

"Art Thou He that should come, or look we for another?"

These travel-stained disciples of John went away from that castle of Machærus. They went up to Perea, possibly Samaria, they saw Jesus, they presented the Message, "Art Thou He that should come?"

Jesus' Reply to John's Question.

Jesus stopped.

He was preaching the Gospel.

He was healing the sick.

The blind were getting their sight, and the deaf were hearing.

The poor were rejoicing in the Glad Tidings of Salvation that the Christ of God was proclaiming.

All He said was: "Go your way and tell John the things which ye do hear and see: the blind receive their sight, and the lame walk, the lepers are cleansed, and the deaf hear, and the dead are raised up, and the poor have Good Tidings preached to them.

"Tell John that blessed is he, whosoever shall find none occasion of stumbling in Me."

Now, what would these men do?

The moment the Christ said that, the witnesses gathered around them.

The little girl, daughter of Rabbi Jairus, would tell the story of how she was dead, and the Christ had raised her up.

The widow of Nain's son would tell the story of how he was dead, and the Christ brought him back to life.

The deaf man of Bethesda would tell how the Christ had put His finger in his deaf ears and instantly he heard.

The blind would tell how He touched their eyes, and they were opened.

The leper who cried, "Lord, if Thou wilt Thou canst make me clean," would tell how the Christ touched him, and in a moment he was clean.

That was the proof.

When John received those testimonies, he was satisfied.

The Proof of a Living Christianity.

The proof of a living Christianity is of the same character.

If the Christ is not the same Savior, then He is not the Christ.

If He is not the same Healer, He is not the Christ.

If He is not the same Cleanser and Keeper, He is not the Christ.

"Jesus Christ is the same yesterday and today, yea and forever." And if He is not the present-day Healer of His people He is not the Christ.

But, Hallelujah! He is the Christ, "the same yesterday and today, yea, and forever."

That is my Message to Australia.

He will come and save you. Then the eyes of the blind shall be opened, and the ears of the deaf shall be unstopped. Then shall the lame man leap as an hart, and the tongue of the dumb shall sing.

He will come and cleanse you.

The wilderness and the waste shall be full of water.

The hills that are barren shall rejoice.

You shall walk in ways of holiness, and not of uncleanness.

The ransomed of Jehovah shall everywhere come to Zion with Everlasting Joy upon their heads.

This is the promise of the Latter Day.

The Promise of the Restoration.

This is the promise of "the Times of the Restoration of All Things, whereof God spake by the mouth of His holy prophets which have been since the world began."

These Times are here.

They have begun.

The present Dispensation, and the Dispensation that is to come, overlap.

I say to every minister in Sydney, to every minister in Australia, to every Christian teacher, listen, and listen very closely, to the questions which I now put:

Must not Elijah come again before the Christ can come?

Is it not the promise of God that he shall?

Brethren and sisters, open John Keble's "Christian Year," at "St. John the Baptist's Day," and read:

> Twice in her season of decay
> The Church has felt Elijah's eye.
>
> . . . .
>
> He comes again, his chariot wheels draw nigh.

Ask my friend, the greatest Rabbi of Sydney, "Must Elijah come before the Christ can come?" and the answer will be that which the Christ gave to His disciples when they said to Him, "How say the scribes that Elijah must first come?"

At that time Elijah the Tishbite had been in heaven for centuries.

Elijah the Preparer had been dead for months, and his headless body had been buried by his loving disciples.

But the Christ said, "Elijah has come; Elijah indeed cometh again, and I come."

The question is absolutely impersonal; it is apart from me altogether.

Testimony of Church Fathers and Commentators.

It is a theological question which no thinker can evade.

You know little about your Bible or your commentaries if you say that Elijah does not precede the Coming of the Christ.

All great commentators in the Early Christian Church—Chrysostum, Origen, Augustine and others—and all the middle-age fathers and the writers of the Pulpit Commentary of the Church of England declare that this is the theology of the Church, the Church as a whole, the Catholic Church.

I speak not of the Roman Catholic or of the Greek Catholic, or even of the Christian Catholic; I am speaking of the Holy Catholic Church, the General Assembly and Church of the First-born, whose names are written in heaven.

There has been no other theology; there is none except that Elijah shall come, and that the Word which is written, the last verse in the Old Testament, shall be fulfilled: "Behold, I will send you Elijah the Prophet before the Great and Terrible Day of Jehovah come. And he shall turn the heart of the fathers with the children, and the heart of the children with their fathers; lest I come and smite the earth with a curse."

Be thoughtful, be earnest, be prepared to study the matter.

You will see that the Word of God declares that, just as truly as Elijah the Tishbite came, whose name means "Jehovah is my God;" just as truly as Elijah the Preparer, John the Baptist, came, whose name also means "Jehovah is my God," so there must come one who shall proclaim the Supremacy of God and His Kingdom, and His right to reign, and the right to command all mankind to obey.

The Time Has Come.

Listen to me thoughtfully; then if you can reject my Message, and stand before the Judgment Seat, well and good; but if you cannot reject it, then you must accept it, and you must obey the Message that is ringing in your ears.

The time is very short; the Day of the Lord is coming.

The Thousand Years is at hand.

This century brings in the Day of the Lord, which Day is a Thousand Years—the Millennium, the Reign of our King.

All who believe that Jesus is coming again; and who desire to meet Him, pure in heart, and prepared for His Coming, stand and tell Him so.

All who desire God to bless them, and prepare them for the Coming of the King, stand and tell Him so. Do not be afraid.

[Several hundred rose.]

Now pray.

PRAYER OF CONSECRATION.

My God and Father, in Jesus' Name, I come to Thee. Take me as I am. Make me what I ought to be, in spirit, in soul, in body. Forgive my sin. Help me to do right to all against whom I have sinned; to repent, to restore, to do right in Thy sight, and to be ready for the Coming of the King. For Jesus' sake. Amen. [*Those standing repeated the prayer, clause by clause, after the General Overseer.*]

After the singing of the Doxology, the Service was closed by the General Overseer's pronouncing the

BENEDICTION.

Beloved, abstain from all appearance of evil. And may the very God of Peace Himself sanctify you wholly; and I pray God your whole spirit and soul and body be preserved entire, without blame, until the coming of our Lord Jesus, the Christ. Faithful is He that calleth you, who also will do it. The grace of our Lord Jesus, the Christ, the love of God, our Father, the fellowship of the Holy Spirit, our Comforter and Guide, one Eternal God, abide in you, bless you and keep you, and all the Israel of God everywhere, forever. Amen.

Communion of the Lord's Supper.

At the close of the afternoon service, the Ordinance of the Lord's Supper was administered by the General Overseer, assisted by the officers of the Christian Catholic Church in Zion present.

All Christians were invited to remain, and two or three hundred joyfully partook of the Sacred Emblems, distributed by the General Overseer and other Officers.

It was a time of great blessing spiritually, and a great delight to the members of the Church in Sydney, to have the privilege of sitting at their Lord's Table with him whom God had sent as His Prophet for the Times of Restoration which are precedent to the Coming to which this Ordinance ever looks forward.

It was also a delight for us of his party, after so long a voyage on a ship on which God was not recognized, to be able to meet together with His people and to break bread and drink wine with them in remembrance of our Lord.

It seemed a great privilege, too, to hear our Leader's earnest, loving, Post-Communion Family Talk, so like his talks in Shiloh Tabernacle at home, although we were so many thousand miles away from Zion City.

We realized, more and more, that Zion is one, the world over, and our hearts greatly rejoiced in that fact.

Lord's Day Evening Service.

The Town Hall was not yet empty after the afternoon service, when the people began to stream in to the evening meeting.

The attendance was fully as large as in the afternoon, and the order and interest even better. Never was man listened to with a more intense eagerness not to lose a word than was God's Prophet when he delivered his Message that Lord's Day evening.

That the churches of the city feared that they might be emptied that night was shown by the fact that, as the General Overseer drove by a little Baptist church near the Town Hall, on his way to the meeting, a brass band was playing outside to draw an audience.

It is an interesting fact that after they had finished playing, several members of the band came to the Town Hall, bringing their instruments with them.

Town Hall, Sydney, Australia, Lord's Day Evening, February 14, 1904.

The Service was opened by the Congregation's singing Hymn No. 116:

There's a royal banner given for display
To the soldiers of the King;
As an ensign fair we lift it up today,
While as ransomed ones we sing.

The General Overseer led the Congregation in the recitation of the Apostles' Creed, after which he read from the Inspired Word of God the last chapter of Malachi and the 1st chapter of the Gospel according to St. Mark.

Prayer was offered by Overseer Excell and the announcements were made.

The General Overseer then delivered his Message:

THE BEGINNING OF THE GOSPEL.

*REPORTED BY E. W. AND A. W. N.

INVOCATION.

Let the words of my mouth, and the meditation of my heart, be acceptable in Thy sight, be profitable unto this people, and unto all to whom these words shall come, in this and every land, in this and all the coming time, Till Jesus Come. Amen.

"The beginning of the Gospel of Jesus, the Christ, the Son of God"—what is that Gospel?

The first preacher of that Gospel was Elijah the Preparer, John the Baptist.

It was set forth by him as a Gospel of Repentance, a preparation.

Not the Gospel of a Church.

I think, tonight, not of the Gospel of the Church, for the Church has no Gospel.

The Church never had a Gospel.

It is the Gospel of God, the Gospel of the Kingdom of God, and not the Gospel of the Church.

Let me speak very plainly.

We have heard far too much about the word church.

In the Gospel according to St. John the word church is not once mentioned.

In the Gospel according to St. Mark the word church is not once mentioned.

In the Gospel according to St. Matthew, it is mentioned only twice.

First, with regard to the matter of discipline, the Lord says that if an offender will not hear the man he has wronged, or another who goes with him, it is to be told to the church.

The word church is *Ecclesia*, (ἐκκλησια) and it means, as every scholar knows, the gathering, that which is called out.

Whence is the Church called out?

The answer usually is, that it is called out of the world.

If it is only called out of the world, then you have the world in the Church.

"Ah, but," you say, "the Church is something greater than that; for the other answer is more sublime."

What is that answer?

It is the expression of the Christ, when Peter uttered his confession of Him.

When the Christ said, "Whom say ye that I am?" Peter said, "Thou art the Christ, the Messiah, the Son of the Living God."

Then the Christ said, "Flesh and blood hath not revealed it unto thee, but My Father which is in heaven . . . , and upon this Rock"—the Rock of His own Divinity—"will I build My Church."

The meaning is, I will make those whom I have called out from My Kingdom to be the Executive Force, as it were, of My Kingdom.

Limitation of the Word Church.

This word church is a very limited one. It has nothing to do with conversion.

You must be born into the Kingdom of God before you can ever rightly enter the Church.

When Jesus was speaking with Nicodemus, He said, "Except a man be born anew, he cannot see the Kingdom of God."

Nicodemus said, "How can a man be born when he is old? can he enter a second time into his mother's womb, and be born?"

Then the Christ said, "Except a man be born of water and the Spirit"—except he has a Real Baptism—"he cannot enter into the Kingdom of God."

*The following report has not been revised by the General Overseer.

There are two different statements in that passage.

First, there is being born of God that one may see the Kingdom, and then there is a Real Baptism that one may enter into the Kingdom of God.

That Baptism the church has lost.

A Real Baptism is by Triune Immersion into the Name of the Father, and of the Son, and of the Holy Spirit, the Baptism which is Death to Sin, Life in God, and Power for Service.

That Baptism brings one into the Kingdom that the Christ came to establish, not primarily into the Church.

Every one of the Christ's parables was concerning the Kingdom of God and the Kingdom of Heaven, not one of them concerning the Church.

It is immensely significant that, with the exception of these two passages, the word Church was never uttered by the Lord, so far as the record goes.

When He preached this Gospel, it was not the Gospel of the Church of England, or the Church of Rome, or the Presbyterian church, or any other *ecclesia*.

It was broader, larger than the churches—than all the little systems that have their day and pass away.

The Christ Came to Establish the Kingdom.

It is a Kingdom which He sends forth His people to establish.

It is the Kingdom, that is to rule over the earth.

God grant that it may be established soon!

Jesus shall reign where'er the sun
Does his successive journeys run;
His Kingdom spread from shore to shore,
Till moons shall wax and wane no more.

Every king, every autocrat, every limited monarchy, every republic, every form of human Government must go; the King will come, and He will reign.

I remind you that the Gospel is the Gospel of the Kingdom.

You make too much of the church.

You split it up, however, into so many petty sections that it is no church at all.

The Love of God is broader than that.

"The Love of God is broader than the measures of man's mind, and the heart of the Eternal" is so wonderfully kind that men who never heard of a church, and do not even know of the Christ, are blessed by Him.

Those Outside the Church Often in the Kingdom.

Will you ever get to the place where you will remember what Peter meant when in the house of Cornelius the Centurion he said, "Of a truth I perceive that God is no respecter of persons: but in every nation, he that feareth Him, and worketh righteousness, is acceptable to Him."

That was an eye-opener to that apostle, who was so narrow.

Oh, he was so bitterly narrow until he found that God had sent an angel to talk with the Centurion

That Centurion knew nothing of the Christ. He simply worshiped God as best he knew—gave alms and did good.

To Him God revealed Himself, and told him where to get the fuller revelation.

Do not forget that Cornelius was not a Christian, and yet God blessed him.

Do not forget that the Christ Himself blessed a man at the pool of Siloam who did not know that He was the Christ; for when he met the Christ in the Temple, after his eyes were opened, and Jesus said, "Dost thou believe on the Son of God?" he said, "Who is He, Lord, that I might believe on Him?" The Christ told him that He was the Son of God, and then he believed.

Have you no thoughts of a larger thing than the roll of the church to which you belong?

Have you no thought of a "General Assembly and Church of the First-born, whose names are written in heaven," but are written on no church book on earth?

Have you no thought that the Kingdom of God is broader, higher, deeper, greater than the petty little conventicles that we call churches?

Will you get it into your mind that the Christ did not come to establish a narrow, little sect?

He came to establish a Kingdom.

His Church should be a gathering of those who are in the Kingdom; a gathering of those who are lovers of Him, accepted with Him, and who will to do His work.

All-comprehensive Character of the Kingdom.

Oh, it is time, high time, that we realize that the Kingdom embraces everything!

It has been a criticism of Zion that Zion is engaged in business, and that spiritual men ought to have nothing to do with earthly concerns.

Pooh!

Men who talk like that are like the man who prayed concerning his minister—"O God, keep him humble, and we will keep him poor."

You have some ridiculous notion that earthly business is secular.

If God were not in the fish business, whence would your fish come?

If God were not in the coal business, and if He had not been in it for a great many centuries, from where would your coal come?

If God were not in the grain business, whence would you get grain?

If God were not in business, taking care of this world, and providing for us, we would quickly perish.

The Kingdom of Heaven is like unto a merchant seeking goodly pearls.

The Kingdom of Heaven is like unto a man building a house upon a rock.

The Kingdom of Heaven is like unto a woman hiding leaven in three measures of meal.

When the Christ desired to talk of the Kingdom He took business illustrations, yes, political illustrations, if you will, in the world.

When he spoke of the great nobleman who went into a far country to receive a kingdom and to return, he told of how he put his servants to business.

The words are "Trade ye herewith till I come."

They traded, and because one did not trade rightly for his master, but buried his pound in the earth, he was condemned. The man who had been diligent in his business was blessed, and not only were the five talents added to him but also the talent of the lazy man, and he had eleven.

It is time that the Church woke up to the fact that it is only a part of the Kingdom, and that the Kingdom is a far greater thing than the Church.

All-conquering Powers of the Kingdom.

The Kingdom covers everything Spiritual, everything Psychical, everything Physical, everything Commercial, everything Educational, everything Political, and the Kingdom must dominate this earth in every department of its activity.

The time will come when the Kingdom of God will own all the navies of the world, commercial and police; when the Kingdom of God will control the commerce of the world, regulate prices, and see that every man gets a fair recompense for his toil.

Then there will be no possibility of doing what I have seen done since I came here; that Standard Oil octopus has its tentacles around you, and the oil that is sold in America for twelve cents costs you sixty cents here.

In other words, what you can buy for sixpence in the way of gasoline in America you pay two shillings and sixpence for here, through the machinations of the trust and the supreme folly of your legislature.

It is time that the Kingdom of God had representation.

It is time that the Gospel were put before the world as something that enters into every relation of life.

I have no intention of preaching a Gospel of a church.

The Gospel of the Kingdom of God is the only Gospel that I know of or care anything about.

You have heard a great deal about the United Kingdom of Great Britain and Ireland, about the British Empire.

You have heard a great deal about the United States of America, and its great political power. You have heard about its commercial greatness, and about its agricultural and mining resources.

But the day is coming when you will hear of the Kingdom of God controlling everything; the Kingdom of God being a Kingdom within your hearts, within the home, within the schools, within the workshops, within the counting-house, within the city, within the state, within the nation, and controlling the world.

That is the Gospel that Zion brings.

The Church that I represent tonight, the Christian Catholic Church in Zion, is merely the Christian Catholic Church in the Kingdom of God.

Let us drop our foolish narrowness in talking about denominations.

Denominational Sects Not Scriptural.

Where do you read of the Baptist church in the Bible?

Where do you read of the Presbyterian church?

When did the Church of the Christ become the church of the *episcopi*, the Bishops?

When did it become the church of the Baptists only?

Was Cornelius baptized when God received him into His Kingdom?

No. It was after he had received the Holy Spirit that Peter said, "Can any man forbid the water, that these should not be baptized, which have received the Holy Spirit, as well as we?"

You miserable Baptists do not know anything about Baptism anyhow! You talk about one dipping when the Christ commanded three.

He said, "Baptizing them into the Name of the Father, and of the Son, and of the Holy Spirit."

You miserable Episcopalians have no Baptism at all!

You have a sprinkling of some water upon a baby's nose, and an abominable lie that the baby is thus transformed in spirit.

You know that is not true.

You know that these god-fathers and god-mothers are, for the most part, a set of hypocrites.

You have nothing in the Bible about the baptism of a baby. Those who were baptized first repented.

That brings me to the beginning of the Gospel.

Repentance the Beginning of the Gospel.

The beginning of the Gospel of Jesus, the Christ, the Son of God, is Repentance.

Repentance and not Faith is the first thing in the Kingdom of God.

This miserable teaching that if you believe, only believe, everything will be right, is a lie.

You cannot be saved by only believing.

"Oh, but, Doctor, did not the Apostle say to the Philippian jailer, 'Believe on the Lord Jesus, the Christ, and thou shalt be saved?'"

Yes, and he said more than that. He said, "Believe on the Lord Jesus, the Christ, and thou shalt be saved, and thy house."

But the Philippian jailer had already repented, saying, "What must I do to be saved?"

Repentance is the first thing.

When the Christ preached this Gospel, it is written that He preached the Gospel of the Kingdom of God, saying, "Repent ye and believe the Gospel."

The Unrepentant Not Converted.

The reason multitudes of people in the church are not converted is because they have not been born into the Kingdom dom of God.

They have not repented.

They have not brought forth "fruits meet for Repentance."

They have wronged a man, and have not confessed it.

They have wronged their neighbors, and have not restored.

You are condemned before God, with all your faith, if you have not brought forth "fruits meet for Repentance."

You must not only be sorry for sin, but you must make restoration for wrong.

You must make confession.

That is the Gospel that John the Baptist, Elijah the Preparer, preached. It was the Baptism of Repentance unto the remission of sins.

Jesus preached Repentance.

Paul preached Repentance toward God, and faith in our Lord Jesus, the Christ.

Faith that is not preceded by Repentance is no faith at all.

Large numbers of you are in the church who have not been born into the Kingdom of God.

I preach the Gospel of the Kingdom, the Gospel of Repentance, the Gospel of Faith, the Gospel of Jesus, the Christ, the Gospel of Holy Living, the Gospel that weighs sixteen ounces to the pound and measures thirty-six inches to the yard; the Gospel that means something, that is not a wretched emasculated thing that consists merely of singing a hymn, putting on your Sunday clothes, and doing the miserable "church work," as you call it.

Work for God All the Time.

Work for God in the heart. Work for God in the home. Work for God in the workshop. Work for God in the office. Work for God in the newspaper.

If you did work for God in the newspaper, there would be any amount of devil to turn out, would there not? [Laughter and applause.]

If there were not a great deal of devil in you, you would not lie as you do. [Laughter and applause.]

And you people will have a better press when you are worthy of it; when you live up to the truth we are talking about.

It is all very well to blame it to the press.

I wish that you would set to work to see that your heart is clean, and that your Repentance has been a Real Thing. See that, so far as it is in your power, there is no wrong that you have done that has not been confessed and put right.

It is utterly vain for you to say, "My God, I repent," until you say, "My brother, I confess; my sister, I repent and restore."

This is the Gospel that Zion preaches.

This is the Gospel that the Christian Catholic Church in Zion brings—the Gospel of the Kingdom.

The World Is Growing Old.

The world is growing weary; nothing human has ever satisfied the human heart; no human form of government can ever do it.

Oh, do not talk to me about the politicians!

Politicians are like cards, the more you shuffle them the dirtier they get. [Applause and laughter.]

You have been shuffling at politics in Australia until the poor fellow at the head of the commonwealth does not know what on earth to do with your last shuffle.

Do not talk to me about your politics.

You have not one man with a policy. If you have, where is he?

I have a Policy and I mean that you shall understand it.

My Policy is that the Lord Jesus, the Christ, shall be acknowledged as the King of kings, and Lord of lords in every heart, in every home, and in every part of the world. [Applause.]

The Laws that I should like to have you get are the old Laws of the Ten Commandments.

> In vain we call old notions fudge,
> And bend our conscience to our dealing;
> The Ten Commandments will not budge,
> And stealing will continue stealing.

Remember ye the law of Moses My servant, which I commanded unto him in Horeb for all Israel, even statutes and judgments.

What Do You know About the Eleventh Commandment?

The Ten Commandments never rose higher in the relation of man to man, than that you should love your neighbor as yourself; but there is an Eleventh Commandment:

A new commandment I give unto you, that ye love one another; even as I have loved you, that ye also love one another.

He loved us better than Himself.

For our sakes He became poor that we, through His poverty, might be made rich.

For our sakes, He left highest heaven to come down to earth, and then He descended into hell. There He led captivity captive, and preached to the spirits in prison who had disobeyed from the days of Noah.

The Eleventh Commandment is the Great Commandment.

It demands that you shall love your neighbor better than yourself; that you shall do for your fellow man what you would never expect your fellow man to do for you.

When you have done it, do not think that you will lose; for men will love you, men will pour into your bosom more and more, because you loved them before they loved you, because you loved them when they hated you, because you loved them and were willing to live and die for them.

The day will come when they will call you blessed; when God and the angels in heaven will unite with men on earth to bless the man who loves his neighbor better than himself.

That is the Commandment above all that we enforce in Zion.

The New York Visitation.

One day last year, I said to my people, "Come, ye members of Zion Restoration Host, how much have you for which to thank God?

"Can we not put our pennies together, and go down to New York and visit every house in that city?

"Can we not go to every house with this little picture of Holman Hunt's, 'The Christ Knocking at the Door,' and the Message, 'Behold, I stand at the door and knock: if any man hear My Voice and open the door, I will come in to him, and sup with him, and he with Me?'

"Let us put aside our prosperity and our toils in Zion City.

"Let us go to New York City."

Three thousand of us went with more than the precision of an army.

We had studied New York for months before we went, so that when we got there we could take that card and the Message to every district in that city, overlapping none, until we had visited every home with the Message, "Peace be to this house."

Down on the Bowery they received our people lovingly, and up on Fifth avenue the doors of the wealthy were open, and they received us lovingly.

Then they filled Madison Square Garden until there were twenty, thirty, fifty, a hundred thousand people outside who wanted to come in and hear the man who is talking to you now.

Every house in New York City was visited; every ship in the port and every business place.

We were received with the most perfect respect and love.

I feel debtor to New York for all the love they gave my people.

I desire to see a people here that will live the Eleventh Commandment.

God grant that the time may soon come when that which is the fulfilling of the Law—Love—shall be the ruling motive in Australia!

Love fulfils Law.

Love is greater than Law.

Love comes in, and Mercy and Peace get in, and Law is overcome.

We will fulfil the Law of Love.

We will live the Gospel of the Kingdom.

All who want to live that Gospel, stand and tell God so. [Many hundreds rose.]

PRAYER OF CONSECRATION.

My God and Father, in Jesus' Name I come to Thee. I want to live the Gospel. Give me Thy Spirit, a Real Repentance, a True Faith, that I may live the Gospel. For Jesus' sake.

The General Overseer led the Congregation in singing the Doxology, after which he pronounced the

BENEDICTION.

Beloved, abstain from all appearance of evil. And may the very God of Peace Himself sanctify you wholly; and I pray God your whole spirit and soul and body be preserved entire, without blame, unto the coming of our Lord Jesus, the Christ. Faithful is He that calleth you, who also will do it. The grace of our Lord Jesus, the Christ, the love of God, our Father, the fellowship of the Holy Spirit, our Comforter and Guide, one Eternal God, abide in you, bless you and keep you, and all the Israel of God everywhere, forever. Amen.

It is needless to say, after what we have already written concerning the Sydney press, that the two very successful meetings held on Lord's Day afternoon and evening were not fairly reported. The press simply reflected the sentiments of the very small element at both the services that seemed to be there for the purpose of creating disturbance, and failed because of the overwhelming weight of the majority who wished to hear and be enlightened.

The First Divine Healing Meeting.

On Monday morning, at half past ten o'clock, the first Divine Healing meeting of the Visitation was held in the Town Hall.

It was a service of great quietness, earnestness, and spiritual blessing.

About five hundred people were present, practically all of them seeking teaching, and many of them seeking healing of bodily ills.

The teaching of the General Overseer was simple, direct, practical, effective—the teaching that is so well known to thousands in Zion; the teaching to which so many owe, under God, their Salvation, their Healing, their Cleansing, their Prosperity, their Happiness.

It was strong meat for some of those who had been fed for years on the diluted, watery spoon-food of the apostasy; but most of them seemed to take it, and while they made wry faces over some of it, they were benefited.

---

*REPORTED BY E. W. AND A. W. N.

Town Hall, Sydney, Australia, Monday Morning, February 15, 1904.

The Service was opened by the singing of the Hymn, "Showers of Blessing."

In making the announcements the General Overseer said:

The Hot Sunday Dinner Condemned.

It is the wide-awake people we want, the people who do not eat hot Sunday dinners.

I think it is a disgrace to a man—I am going to say something dreadful now, look out!—I think it is a disgrace to a man to make his wife stand over a hot fire Sunday morning cooking for his dirty guts.

That is good old English.

It is a horrible thing, a shameful thing that a wife should be denied her Sabbath while she is preparing for his greedy, gluttonous belly.

In Zion I should admonish, and eventually discipline a man who insisted upon his wife's cooking a Sunday dinner.

I should say that there was no faith, no hope, no love, no wisdom in him; that he was no use in Zion.

We have cold Sunday dinners in Zion, even during the cold winter of a cold climate.

Women in Zion City can attend the early morning meeting, at half past six o'clock, the big Bible Class of two or three thousand, at eleven o'clock, and the Great General Assembly, of five thousand—and more sometimes—that meets at half past two.

There are large numbers of women that never have an opportunity to attend the House of God, simply because of the shameful gluttony of their gluttonous husbands.

The Time of Women Has Come in Zion.

We feel that women ought to be treated equally with men.

We educate our young women in that way.

We have coeducation in our college classes.

The young women even get ahead of the young men.

My own daughter was at the head of the mathematics class in college.

But I come back to the matter of these hot Sunday dinners.

A Glutton Has no Place in the House of God.

If a man will not make some sacrifices for his wife and children, for whom will he make sacrifices?

I say that the control of the body and its appetites is always the proof of a good Christian.

I should just as quickly believe a drunkard to be a Christian as to believe a glutton could be a Christian. Both are shameful; I do not know but that the glutton is the worse. He has a comparatively clear head, is a glutton with open eyes, and knows that he is a glutton; whereas the poor drunkard gets drunk, and knows nothing more about it.

I instruct you, Deacon McCullagh, to see that this is enforced in Zion in Sydney.

We will not have a Church of gluttonous beasts, who live for their bellies; "whose god is the belly, and whose glory is in their shame, who mind earthly things."

They are "enemies of the Cross of the Christ," even though they may call themselves Christians.

What we want in the Kingdom of God, and in the Church of God, is men and women that keep under their bodies, and bring them into subjection, and do not let the body rule.

Besides, you are healthier in doing it.

The strongest men, the strongest women, the cleanest thinkers, the hardest workers, do not eat much animal food.

I think I have eaten today perhaps about an ounce—perhaps two ounces—of meat, but I have eaten fruit, oatmeal, and bread and butter.

*The following report has not been revised by the General Overseer.

After prayer by Deacon J. S. McCullagh, and the singing of a hymn, the General Overseer delivered his Message:

THE SUPREMACY OF GOD THE FATHER.

INVOCATION.

Let the words of my mouth, and the meditation of my heart be acceptable in Thy sight, O God, and be a blessing to this people. For Jesus' sake.

Open your Bibles at the 8th chapter of the Gospel according to St. Matthew.

The Christian's Only Weapon.

Every one of you should carry a pocket Bible.

Why do you Christians not carry your Swords?

I have a Zion Guard of a thousand men.

When I say to them, "Draw Swords!" every man takes out his Bible from the sheath hanging at his belt.

That Guard knows its Bible.

If I say to Zion Guard, "Give me the Guard Psalm," they repeat the 20th Psalm.

Following Jesus.

When Jesus "was come down from the mountain, great multitudes followed"—Peter.

Is that right?

Voices—"No. Followed Jesus."

General Overseer—Now, whom do you follow?

Voices—"Jesus."

General Overseer—Are you quite sure, or are you a Methodist first, last, and all the time? Baptist first, last, and all the time?

Do you follow Martin Luther, John Knox, William Booth or anybody else, or even John Alexander Dowie? Follow men only as far as they follow Jesus.

He is the only safe Guide.

The great and mighty ones come and go.

God buries His workers, takes their spirits to Himself, but the Christ is with us All the Days, unto the Consummation of the Age.

Let us make a vow that, in this address, you will follow me as far as I follow Jesus.

All Agreed?

Voices—"Yes."

General Overseer—If you do not say yes, there is no use in your staying, because I intend to give you the Word of Jesus. That is the only Word that is worth having.

My words are powerful only in as far as I tell you what God says.

"Oh," you say, "we want to hear what you think."

I will not tell you my thoughts.

God's Thoughts All-Important.

The only thoughts that are worth anything are the thoughts of God.

If you do not think as God thinks you are wrong, because God's thinking is the Law of this Universe.

If you do not think as God thinks, you will get into trouble with God.

When He was come down from the mountain, great multitudes followed Him. And behold, there came to Him a leper and worshiped Him, saying—

Stop there.

That leper worshiped Jesus.

Jesus the Only Way to the Father.

Do you worship God in the Christ?

If not you might just as well call yourself a Brahmin as a Christian, as far as Salvation is concerned; for if you reject the Divinity of our Lord Jesus, the Christ, you cannot get to the Father.

Jesus said, "I am the Way, and the Truth, and the Life: no one cometh unto the Father but by Me."

If you say, "I can get to the Father without Jesus," then you and Jesus disagree.

There is the One Mediator between God and man, the Man Christ Jesus.

There is none other name given under heaven, among men, whereby we must be saved.

If you say there is, I am of no use to you, no apostle is of any use to you, and the Christ Himself is of no use to you.

You have carved out a way of salvation for yourself. You have forsaken Him, and have hewed broken cisterns that will not hold the Water of Life.

That leper was a Jew, and it was a very hard thing for a Jew to worship the Christ. It is a hard thing now.

God the Father in the Christ.

The great trouble with the Jew is, that he says he cannot worship a man.

I say to you, my Jewish friend, I do not want you to worship a man. I want you to worship God.

I do not say that Jesus was God; I say that God was in the Christ; that the Father was in the Christ.

I do not want you to worship Jesus. I do not want you to worship the Holy Spirit.

I want you to do what Jesus tells you.

I want you to do what the Holy Spirit tells you.

Jesus tells you, "When ye pray, say, Our Father."

The Holy Spirit says He comes into your heart, crying, "Abba, Father."

Neither Jesus nor the Holy Spirit ever told you to pray to either of them.

You have no right to pray to Jesus.

You have the right to worship God in Him.

I will tell you something that may surprise you.

Jesus Never Healed Any One.

Jesus said: "The words that I say unto you I speak not from Myself: but the Father abiding in Me, doeth His works."

He said: "My Father worketh hitherto and I work."

He declared that everything that He said was spoken by the Spirit of the Father within Him, and that everything He did was the work of the Father through Him.

Some of you do not understand that.

One goes into some of your prayer-meetings, and hears people praying, "My Dear Lord Jesus," and "Blessed Holy Ghost." Sometimes you will never hear the Father mentioned from the beginning to the end of the service.

Prayer Should Always Be Addressed to the Father.

When Jesus told you to worship the Father; when the Apostle says, "For this cause I bow my knees unto the Father of our Lord Jesus, the Christ," why do you not worship the Father?

Why do you not do what Jesus told you?

Why do you not worship God the Father, in the Name of Jesus, asking for the Power of the Holy Spirit to help you to do it?

Why do you not remember that the Christ came into this world to glorify the Father, to do the Will of the Father, to establish the Kingdom of the Father?

When He taught us to pray, did He teach us to pray to Him?

You have the Disciples' Prayer.

Can you find any passage in that teaching you to pray to Jesus?

It is Our Father who art in heaven, hallowed be Thy Name. (Father) Thy Kingdom come. (Father) Thy Will be done, on earth as it is in heaven (Father) give us this day our daily bread. (Father) forgive us our sins, as we forgive those who sin against us. (Father) let us not be led into temptation. (Father) deliver us from the evil one. (Father) Thine is the Kingdom, and the Power, and the Glory forever. Amen.

Is Jesus the Christ in that prayer?

Is the Holy Spirit in that prayer?

There is no one in that prayer but the Father. That is the prayer that the Christ taught us to pray.

God the Father was in the Christ, and when that leper worshiped the man Christ Jesus, he worshiped God in the Christ.

I wonder whether you do.

There is much that is hazy about Christian worship.

Why Many Prayers Are not Answered.

This is the reason thousands, yea millions, of prayers are not answered. They are not properly addressed.

Many letters lie in the dead-letter office because they are not properly addressed. By-and-by they are burned up.

Hundreds of millions of prayers go up to God, or are supposed to go up to God, that are never answered. They do not get higher than the roof.

That has gone on until the churches have got into the way

of never expecting an answer, and they are not disappointed. You can adore the Christ; you can worship Him in the sense of adoration, but when you pray, you must pray to God, the Father.

It was the Father in the Christ who spoke the words and did the work.

Do you not remember that when the Christ forgave a man his sins, He said, "Son, thy sins be forgiven thee?"

The Great Elder Brother was not talking. It was the Father in Him who said, "Son."

Who can say son but a father?

When a woman touched Him and was healed, He said, "Daughter."

It was the Father talking.

He said, "I can do nothing of Myself. Of Mine Ownself I can do nothing."

As the Man, Christ Jesus, He was just like any other man, only pure and holy; but when God, the Father, came into Him, when the Holy Spirit without measure came into Him, then the Spirit spoke, and the Father spoke.

Jesus Came as the Son of Man.

"Oh," you say, "but He was the Son of God."

Do you not know He laid aside His Power and Godhead?

Do you not know that when He came down to this earth He emptied Himself?

Do you not know that He did not come as the Son of God Himself?

He came as the Son of man.

He could not redeem us, as the Son of God.

It had to be a man who should die for man.

It would not have been an atonement that would have covered the case at all if He had been God, or an angel.

He had to be a man under the Law, with all the passions of a man, with all the sorrows of a man, with all the power to suffer as a man, the Man, Christ Jesus.

Then God entered into Him, the Father and the Spirit, and by-and-by He was declared to be the Son of God with Power, by His resurrection from the dead. Not till then did He tell us to ask the Father in His Name.

He said: "'Hitherto have ye asked nothing in My Name.' Now I am going to the Father, ask in My Name."

What I desire to point out to you is, that in worshiping, you must worship the Father, and in praying you must pray in the Name of Jesus, and in the Power of the Holy Spirit, but you must pray to the Father, and to the Father only.

Pray to no saints, to no virgin, to no apostles, to no man.

Trinity but not Equality of the Godhead.

I believe in the Trinity of the Godhead, but not in the equality of the Three Persons.

Did not Jesus say, "The Father is greater than I?"

I am a trinity. I have a spirit, a soul, and a body; but these three are not equal.

My spirit is eternal; it came from God.

My soul is mortal; it dies.

The soul of the Christ died. He poured out His soul unto death.

All souls die.

A beast has a soul, but it has not a spirit.

Spirits and souls are different.

Souls are the mere animal life.

The soul of a man and the soul of a beast are of the same nature.

The soul of the Christ was a mere animal soul, and it died.

The soul is all in the blood, but the spirit is something greater. That never dies.

If any of you believe in the immortality of the soul, any infidel can floor you; because there is no such thing as an immortal soul.

It is the spirit that is immortal.

I have a spirit, I have a soul, and I have a body. I am a trinity; these three are one; but they are not equal.

My body will molder into dust; my soul will die; but my spirit will return to God, who gave it.

God, the Father, God, the Son, and God, the Holy Spirit, are one God; but the time will come when the Christ shall "deliver up the Kingdom unto God, even the Father; . . . . that God may be All in All."

The Christ Is Subject to the Father.

The Apostle Paul, in arguing, says that the time will come when the Christ Himself shall be subject to the Father, who put all things under Him; when He shall deliver up the Kingdom to God, even the Father; when He shall recognize the supremacy of the Father before the whole Universe.

Get this fundamental thought, because it is the fundamental thought in prayer, that you are to pray to the Father.

A distinguishing thing in the Christ's teaching concerning prayer is that He revealed to us the Father.

Men do not know the Father, and men do not know the Christ.

A great majority of people have a man in front of them instead of God, the Father.

They forget that the man, Christ Jesus, is the Advocate with the Father, and that the Holy Spirit is the Advocate with us.

We Have Two Intercessors.

We have One who pleads with God for us, and we have One who pleads with us for God.

In both cases, however, the Intercessor, Jesus, and the Intercessor, the Holy Spirit, lead to the Father.

That is worship.

That is what the Christ taught.

When you read the bold word "He worshiped Him" you must remember that the Christ had been teaching them how to pray.

The chapter preceding this records the teaching.

You have the Disciples' Prayer in the Sermon on the Mount.

He taught them how to pray to the Father.

If you would make that plain to our Jewish friends they would understand better what Christianity is.

But you demand that they shall worship Jesus, the Christ. I do not.

I demand that they shall worship the Father in the Name of Jesus, and acknowledge Him as the Messiah, the Christ, the Intercessor.

They will understand you better.

The Jew will not have it; I will not have it, that I am to worship a man.

I will worship God.

I do not care whether the man is called Jesus, the Christ, or Saint Joseph, or Saint Paul, I will not worship a man.

I have not worshiped Jesus, the Christ.

I have not addressed a prayer to Jesus, the Christ, for twenty-five years.

It was only when I learned that lesson that I began to know how to pray and how to get an answer.

You Cannot Pray as You Like.

You say it does not matter so long as a man means it.

It does matter.

A man might mean all right, and address a letter to me as John Brown. The letter would never reach me.

You may mean all right, and pray in the way that the Christ told you not to pray. The prayer will never reach God.

You must pray as He says.

He said, "When ye pray say, Our Father," and I should like to know who you are that you think to change that?

I should like to know who I am, or who any one else is, to say that it does not matter.

It does matter.

The whole trouble with people is that they do not toe the line.

The Law of the Spirit of Life in the Christ, Jesus, demands that I shall do exactly what He tells me.

Law is supreme in the material world.

If I say, "Oh, it does not matter; I shall handle electricity as I like," electricity will handle me in short order.

The Law of the Spirit of Life in the Christ Jesus, is greater than any other law.

Do you think you can do as you like?

That is the trouble with you.

Most church members go as they like and do as they please, and you call that liberty.

It is not liberty at all.

"Oh," you proudly say, "I am an independent being."

False Idea of Liberty.

I once asked an engineer in my congregation, "How long have you been a locomotive engineer?"

"Forty years, Doctor," he replied.

"Suppose," I said, "that a number of men who have locomotives and trains under their control were to say, 'Now, you look out for yourself. We intend to run up and down the line on our own schedule time, just as we like.' What would you do?"

"I should take the first sidetrack and stay there. These fellows would smash me, and smash one another."

That is what you are doing, you churches!

You run up and down on your own schedule time, and no one can get through unless he smashes you.

And you are getting smashed, too.

Why are you not orderly?

Why do you not pray in an orderly way, you ministers?

Why do you not tell your people not to pray to Jesus, not to pray to the Holy Spirit, but to pray to the Father in the Name of Jesus and in the Power of the Spirit?

The Power and Effectiveness of Good Order.

I have been enabled to do a little work in this world, because I do not mix up things.

We have forty-two departments in Zion City, and forty-two departmental heads.

If any departmental head wants to mix up with some other department, I send him away.

I say, "No, you attend to your own business, run on schedule time, do your own work."

You have a great mixture in Australian politics now, have you not?

Poor Deakin, has he not a job with you?

You have shuffled your politicians so badly that he does not know what to do with the last shuffle.

He has shuffled himself, until no one knows what on earth to do with him.

Shufflers!

You need straight lines, straight policies, straight thinking, straight acting!

You need to know where to find a man, whether it is in religion or in education, or in business or in politics.

The trouble with the people is that they do not keep to straight lines.

No crooked ways will be blessed by God.

Those who turn aside to crooked ways, Jehovah will lead forth with the workers of iniquity.

Go straight! Make His paths straight!

The straight way to God is to pray to the Father, and the crooked way to the Father is to pray to the Virgin Mary, and to saints and angels, and to Jesus, and to the Holy Spirit.

God's Willingness to Heal.

Now, I will go back to that leper.

What did he say?

He said, "Lord, if Thou wilt, Thou canst make me clean."

Do not pray that prayer!

Do not say, "Lord, if Thou wilt, Thou canst make me clean."

The Christ answered the prayer for all time when He said, "I will. Be thou clean."

Did that leper continue to say, "If Thou wilt?"

Voices—"No."

General Overseer—If you ask me to do something, and I say I will, what is the use of your howling at me and saying, "O Dr. Dowie, if thou wilt, if thou wilt." [Laughter.]

Suppose I said, "I will see you at the Australia Hotel tomorrow morning at nine o'clock."

Suppose you came up into the hall and cried, "O Dr. Dowie, if thou wilt, thou canst see me."

I should say to my attendant, "Stern, who is that howling out there?"

"Oh, it is a man who says that you will see him at nine o'clock."

"If he has a card that says so, bring him in."

He comes to the door.

Then he says again, "O Dr. Dowie, I wish I could be quite sure. If thou wilt, if thou wilt."

"What is the matter with you? Why do you not come in?"

"If."

"Oh, because I am very humble. I always like to say if, if, if. I am not sure about you, Doctor. If you will only let me in, I will go out and tell everybody in the street that you let me in, that you kept your word."

"Bosh! I do not want you to go out on the street and tell that, because I am not in the habit of breaking my word. Come in."

"Oh, I wish I could believe it!"

"Colonel Stern, take that lunatic away."

That is what I should say.

Some of you have been praying to God with an eternal if, *if*, IF, "Lord if Thou wilt!"

Why do you not get rid of your if? Did not the Lord say, "I will?"

Did He ever say, "I will not," to any one who fulfilled the conditions?

What is the use to keep on praying the leper's prayer when that prayer has been answered?

That leper did not know the Will of the Lord fully.

He knew enough to get saved. So do you.

Many of you do not know enough to get healed.

God Does Not Heal by Means of Drugs and Knives.

Why?

There are many of you sucking at pills and medicine, and you cannot pray.

How can you pray when you are taking pills and medicine?

You are praying like this: "O Lord, if Thou wilt, heal me by means of Dr. Lancet and Dr. Squash."

Did the Lord ever promise to heal you by means of a doctor?

I know the Bible, and I know the doctors.

I had a narrow escape from being a doctor myself.

I walked the wards of the Edinburgh Infirmary, being honorary Chaplain.

I saw medical treatment.

I went into the operating theaters, and I saw butchery.

I saw and heard and knew men who were the best in their time, Sir James Young Simpson, the present Lord Lister, and others.

I found out that they were guessing in the dark.

They did not know what they were doing.

Medicine Not a Science.

The greatest lecturer of my time, in some respects, Professor Douglas MacClagan, the professor of Medical Jurisprudence in the University of Edinburgh, delivered the opening address to the medical session, in 1869.

Medical men and surgeons were seated all around.

The senatus in surgery, and the senatus in medicine were there.

Sir Archibald Grant was in the chair. MacClagan's lecture was upon "Medicine as a Science."

He looked at the audience.

They had come to hear a great man, and every one cheered.

He turned around to the senatus and said, "You will not cheer me long."

They cheered again.

He said, "You will not cheer me long. I intend to tell you God's truth."

I think that at that time he had been thirty years a professor of medical jurisprudence.

He then stood up and said these words:

"They have asked me to speak on medicine as a science. I warned them not to ask me.

"Gentlemen, the first thing I have to say to you is that medicine is not a science.

"It is purely empirical.

"From the days of Hippocrates and of Galen until now we have been stumbling in the dark, from diagnosis to diagnosis, from treatment to treatment, and we have not found the first stone that we can lay as a foundation for medicine as a science."

That statement has never been altered, and cannot be altered.

Scientia is accurate knowledge, and in medicine there is none.

The theories of medicine are changing every year, or every few years.

Theories of Medicine Ever Changing.

A few years ago, disease was all in the blood.

If you could do this and that, and the other thing, you could get healing.

Now they say it is all in certain little parasites, microbes, bacteria or something else.

All you must have now, in order to be healed is an "insect killer," a germicide, something that will kill the wretched creatures that make the trouble. These germicides are all humbugs.

Dr. Koch's lymph was lauded as a cure for consumption.

It did not cure the disease, however. Do you not remember

INTERIOR OF NEWTOWN CONGREGATIONAL CHURCH, NEAR SYDNEY, NEW SOUTH WALES.
The Rev. John Alex. Dowie was Pastor here 1876-1878. The Pulpit and Organ are new.

that Virchow, the great pathologist of Germany, held post-mortem examinations upon thirty to forty of Dr. Koch's patients?

Dr. Koch contended that his lymph drove the parasites out of the diseased tissue.

"Yes," said Dr. Virchow, "it is true that Dr. Koch's lymph drives the miserable parasites out of the tissues which are diseased, but it drives them into the healthy tissues and kills the man twice as quickly."

That is not my statement; that is Professor Virchow's.

Who uses Koch's lymph today?

What doctor would use it in his practice in Australia?

It is worse than a quack remedy. It is no remedy at all.

They have not found the germicide.

After relating the healing of Deliah King, of San Francisco, the General Overseer closed the Service with the following

PRAYER OF CONSECRATION.

My God and Father, in Jesus' Name I come to Thee. Take me as I am. Make me what I ought to be in spirit, in soul, in body. Give me power to do right, no matter what it costs. Give me Thy Holy Spirit, that I may trust Thee, that I may be saved by Thee through faith in Thy Son, the Lamb of God, who taketh away the sin of the world, who bore my sins and my sicknesses. For His sake, deliver me, give me power to put away all remedies, everything that would hinder, and to trust Thee alone. For Jesus' sake. [*Many repeated the prayer, clause by clause, after the General Overseer.*]

BENEDICTION.

Beloved, abstain from all appearance of evil. And may the very God of Peace Himself sanctify you wholly; and I pray God your whole spirit and soul and body be preserved entire, without blame, unto the coming of our Lord Jesus, the Christ. Faithful is He that calleth you, who also will do it. The grace of our Lord Jesus, the Christ, the love of God, our Father, the fellowship of the Holy Spirit, our Comforter and Guide, one Eternal God, abide in you, bless you, and keep you, and all the Israel of God everywhere forever. Amen.

At the close of this service, the General Overseer and other officers of the Christian Catholic Church in Zion met with a large number of those who were sick and desired prayer for their healing.

The prayer service was a very definite and practical one, as the General Overseer's always are, and there was great blessing.

Visit to the Old Church, the Newtown Congregational.

On the afternoon of this day, the General Overseer, with his son and members of his party drove out to Newtown, a suburb of Sydney, where the General Overseer had been pastor of the Congregational Church during the years 1876-1878, to visit his old church, Sunday-school room and manse.

The General Overseer found that the march of progress had left this beautiful suburb behind, and that the houses that had once been the homes of wealth and fashion were now either tenements or small shops for the sale of groceries, shoes, notions and other merchandise.

The church was very much the same, as to its exterior, but seemed to have been allowed to run down somewhat.

As soon as the General Overseer appeared in the suburb, a crowd began to gather, and before he could find some one to unlock the church for him, there were hundreds of people gathered in the streets.

At last a member of the church was found, near by, who had keys and kindly admitted us.

Within, the General Overseer found that there had been no change in the body of the church since he had preached there twenty-six years before; but an addition had been built for a small pipe organ, and a large, elaborately carved pulpit had replaced the one from which he had spoken.

"Why, how the place seems to have shrunk!" was his first exclamation.

He was reminded by one of the party that he had grown during the interval since he had last stood within these walls.

Some old residents of Newtown had come in, and the man of God spent some little time in inquiring for old friends and members of the church, taking keen interest in the information that he received.

Then he proceeded to the little Sunday-school room, near by, where he had held some of the liveliest of his Saturday night temperance meetings, during the days of his pastorate there.

All this time, old friends and others had been coming in until the visit was beginning to take the form of an impromptu reception.

We then took the carriage again, and drove to the site of the old manse, where Doctor A. J. Gladstone Dowie was born, in 1876. This also had fallen victim to the common lot of the residences in this street, and was hidden by a grocery that had been built in front of it.

The General Overseer and party then returned to the hotel to prepare for the evening meeting.

Monday Evening Meeting in the Town Hall.

For this meeting all the tickets had been taken early, and many more could have been given out had the hall been larger.

As the people entered, it was evident that the majority were quiet and thoughtful, desiring to hear for themselves what the

SCHOOLHOUSE OF NEWTOWN CONGREGATIONAL CHURCH,
Where Rev. John Alex. Dowie Held Saturday Night Temperance Meetings During His Pastorate There.

General Overseer had to say; but it was also very evident that there were a number who came for no other purpose than to disturb.

When the assembly began to fill the hall, there was a rattle above the hum of the thousands, that showed still more clearly that there were those in the congregation banded together in packs, like the cowardly wolves that they were, to drown out with their noise, the Voice of the Prophet, and to break up the meeting, if possible. As the time for the opening of the meeting drew near, that rattle grew to a roar, the disorderly element stamping their feet, pounding on the floor with their canes, clapping their hands, and otherwise exhibiting their impatience.

Then began the yelling that was like the howling of wild animals—yells of derision, impudence, and ribald irreverence.

The hall was crowded to the doors, and there were thousands outside, waiting for an opportunity to enter, when the General Overseer, accompanied by the members of his party, came upon the platform.

His appearance was greeted with a storm of friendly applause from thousands of right-minded people, and by a storm of howls from the Devil's Masonic mob.

The opening exercises were held, with considerable interruption.

Sydney Disgraced by a Lawless Mob.

Then the General Overseer began his Message: "The Coming of Elijah, the Restorer of All Things."

If any of us had entertained the slightest doubt as to the truthfulness of the claim of God's Prophet, up to this time, the scene that followed would have forever dispelled it.

The Devil was full of rage.

Men and women who showed in their faces that they were his miserable slaves, interrupted the speaker again and again.

Others whose countenances proclaimed them to be hypocritical pretenders to Christianity, joined in the disorder.

Thousands of people of all classes, with sincere, honest, thoughtful faces, desired to hear quietly and respectfully, and very heartily expressed their approval of the appeal of the man of God that the right of free speech be not denied.

The man of God spoke with power and was able to deliver the greater part of his Message.

When it was about half past nine or a quarter of ten, however, the mob broke all bounds. A crowd of those who held no tickets had rushed to the doors and entered in defiance of the guards. These were massed behind the regular seats.

Some one would cough, stamp his feet, or make some impudent remark.

This would be a signal for hundreds to stand upon their chairs and shout at the tops of their voices.

There were only two or three police officers inside the building, and these made no effort to keep order, declaring that they had no authority to act.

The Zion ushers did their best, but were too far outnumbered by the lawless element to accomplish much.

After a few moments of continuous disorder, the disturbers began to roar out songs of the street, drowning out all efforts of the speaker to be heard.

As the disorder was growing every moment, it was considered wise, in the interest of public safety, to close the meeting, which was done, amidst the hideous cries of the mob.

Even after the meeting closed, their diabolical hatred and fury was not to be restrained, but found vent in a perfect bedlam of shrieks, yells, ribald songs, and other disorder.

It was some time before the police and the attendants of the building could clear the hall.

In the meantime, the General Overseer and party had reached their hotel in safety, although thousands of rioters waited outside the Town Hall for him to come out.

Instead of going out by his accustomed door, he had quietly walked out by a door on the other side of the building, and driven away before the lawless element knew of his departure.

The following is a report of the Message of Elijah the Restorer:

Town Hall, Sydney, Australia, Monday Evening, February 14, 1904.

The Service was opened by the Congregation's singing Hymn No. 372:

> All hail the power of Jesus' Name!
> Let angels prostrate fall;
> Bring forth the royal diadem,
> And crown Him Lord of all.

The General Overseer then read the 3d chapter of Malachi; also from the Gospel according to St. John, in the 17th chapter beginning with the 9th verse.

Prayer was offered by Rev. C. Friend Hawkins, Deacon-in-charge, Adelaide, South Australia, after which the Congregation joined in singing Hymn No. 213.

The General Overseer then delivered his Message:

THE COMING OF ELIJAH, THE RESTORER OF ALL THINGS.

*REPORTED BY E. W. AND A. W. N.

INVOCATION.

Let the words of my mouth, and the meditation of my heart be acceptable in Thy sight, be profitable unto this people, and unto all to whom these words shall come, in this and every land, in this and all the coming time, Till Jesus Come. Amen.

Concerning the Declaration of June 2, 1901.

I stand, tonight, to repeat, in effect, a Declaration that I made first in the Chicago Auditorium, in the presence of seven thousand persons, on June 2, 1901.

That Declaration has become known in America, in Australasia, in Europe, in Asia, in Africa, and in the Islands of the Ocean, as the Declaration of Elijah the Restorer.

It was made without any previous consultation with any living man or woman; not even with my wife, my son, my daughter, my colleagues in the ministry, or the people to whom I ministered.

It is now many years since I was first informed, in a marvelous way, of my prophetic ministry.

At that time, I did what John the Baptist did when they came to him and said, "Art thou Elijah?" and he said, "I am not."

When I was hailed as Elijah, I said, "I am not."

But John the Baptist was wrong, for the Angel Gabriel had said to Zacharias, the priest, his father, in the Temple of God, before John was born; yea, before he was conceived in the womb of Elizabeth, an aged saint of God, that John should go forth to do his work, in the spirit and power of Elijah. But John the Baptist did not know, and did not believe that this was so, and when the Disciples asked Jesus about him, Jesus, the Christ, the Son of God, John the Baptist did not understand.

When he was in prison, he sent two disciples to Jesus with the question of doubt in his mind as to whether Jesus was the Christ.

After the Christ had given that wonderful answer, which satisfied John, then He spoke to the multitudes concerning John.

After putting those questions, beginning "What went ye out for to see?" He declared that John was not only a prophet, but much more than a prophet, saying:

> This is he, of whom it is written,
> Behold, I send My messenger before Thy face,
> Who shall prepare Thy way before Thee.

John had not feared the face of man, and they knew well he had not.

He was like one, who though he was not as great, was well nigh as great as he.

John Knox, an Example of Christian Fearlessness.

John Knox, of Scotland, the land where I was born, was that fearless man.

I was deeply thrilled, one day, standing, when the sun was setting, upon the western acropolis in Glasgow.

There I read—and it came with wonderful power—the words of Regent Morton of Scotland on the monument of John Knox.

The Regent said, as the body of that mighty man was being laid in the grave, "There lies a man who never feared the face of man."

By the grace of God, it shall be said, when my body lies in the grave, "There lies a man who never feared the face of man."

I do not understand what it means to be afraid.

Such conduct as this tonight makes me stronger.

I know my rights under the law. I keep to them.

I have fought for that which is right, and good, and pure, and true.

John the Baptist, as I have said, never feared the face of man.

Jesus asked, "Did you go out to see a reed shaken by the wind?"

No, indeed, he was no reed!

No wind of popular hatred, no wind of flattery, could shake John.

He was the Messenger of God.

Those were the days when men who spoke the truth had to go to the cross and to the dungeon.

*The following address has not been revised by the General Overseer.

There are some of you here who would like to send the man that speaks the truth to the cross and to the dungeon.

But, let me tell you, it is too late!

The Christ and His cross rule the world, and they will rule you. [Applause. Noises.]

The Messenger of the Covenant Not the Christ.

"But wherefore went ye out? To see a prophet? Yea, I say unto you," said the Christ, "and much more than a prophet. This is he of whom it is written, Behold I send My Messenger before Thy face."

Some people today try to make that passage refer to the Christ.

How can it refer to the Christ, when it is the Messenger of the Covenant, who comes before the Christ's face to prepare His way, to say, "Prepare ye the way of the Lord; make His path straight?"

John was a man that made things straight.

There was not an atom of crookedness about John.

He had the true Elijah spirit.

The first Elijah's name was probably not Elijah, because that name came to him simply because of what he said.

The name Elijah is not a proper name.

It was the name given to the prophet, who was a sojourner of Gilead, and who protested against the other prophets, who had gone into the worship of Baal.

He cried out whenever he was among them "*Eliyahu! Eliyahu!*" [Laughter. Cries of "Hoo! Hoo!"]

You do not know what you are laughing at.

That is a Hebrew word meaning, "Jehovah is my God." [Laughter, noises, shuffling, etc.]

You will have to hear that many times yet.

You will have to understand that the Elijah spirit always says, "Jehovah is my God."

The Christ Said that John the Baptist Was Elijah.

Jesus said of John, "This is Elijah which is to come;" but John, at that time, had been put to death.

He was not the Restorer. He was only the Preparer.

His ministry lasted only eleven months, but after he had been put to death the Christ said, "Elijah indeed cometh, and shall Restore All Things."

I have read, tonight, a passage which refers to that which is still the hope of all Israel.

Elijah the Hope and Expectation of the Jews.

Ask a Jewish rabbi, "Is the Messiah coming?" and he will say, "Yes."

Ask the rabbi what must happen before the Messiah comes, and he will tell you that Elijah must first come. [Laughter.]

You may laugh, but that shows your ignorance.

At every circumcision, a vacant chair is placed for Elijah.

At the Passover Feast, when the unleavened bread and the wine is set forth in a Jewish house, there is a chair set for Elijah.

The great rabbi of Vienna has recently written in that scholarly work, the Jewish Encyclopedia, that it is the conviction of every Jew that Elijah is the Messenger of the Covenant, and that he will appear before the Coming of the Lord; that the Messiah cannot come until the Elijah has been sent to prepare the way.

This is the Jewish faith, and hence it is that when those disciples came to Jesus, and said to Him, after John the Baptist was dead, "Why say the scribes that Elijah must first come?" [noises, yells, hoots] the answer of the Master was, "Elijah indeed cometh, and shall Restore All Things."

That cannot refer to the Tishbite, who, long centuries before, had passed away.

It cannot refer to the Baptist who had died. They had buried his body, and had come and told Jesus.

Theology of the Church Teaches That Elijah Must Come Again.

That answer referred to that which the whole Church, in its theology, confirms—that Elijah must come again.

I am making the declaration that even a Roman Catholic theologian must make, that Cardinal Moran cannot deny was the theology of the Church of Rome; for it was the teaching of the early fathers, down to the Council of Nicæa, without a single dissentient voice.

That teaching is, that before the next Coming of the Lord, Elijah must first come.

That was the teaching of Chrysostom, and of Augustine, the great and mighty author of "De Civitate Dei," that great work on the theology of the Church of God.

It has been the teaching of the theologians down to this day.

John Keble, in his "Christian Year," says that again the Elijah will come, and his chariot wheels are nigh.

The whole world, and the whole Church, will have to hear the Declaration from the Elijah's lips, that he has come to demand that the world shall bow to the Law of God given in Horeb, the Ten Commandments; that they shall bow to the Eleventh Commandment given by the Lord Jesus, the Christ, that you love one another as He loved you.

The whole earth will have to hear that all shall bow to God, and that no longer shall this world be under the sway of democracies or autocracies, or oligarchies, but that it shall become one great Theocracy; for the Christ shall be King.

The Message of the Restorer is to tell you that this shall be so, and to tell you to get ready for His Coming. [Applause, yells, noises.]

The Rule of God must be proclaimed.

I am not talking of a new thing.

I take the last one of the last commentaries, written by great theologians of the Church of England of today—the "Pulpit Commentary."

I find there the very teaching that I am giving now, in commenting upon this passage.

False Idea of Elijah's Coming.

Some of you imagine that when Elijah appears, he will drop down from the heavens.

He did not do that in the days of John the Baptist.

He was born, like any other man, and grew up ignorant even of his own calling.

Even as a great prophet, he would only say that he was "the Voice of one crying in the wilderness." If I had died five years ago, I should have died declaring that I was not Elijah.

But the time came when I was compelled to recognize my call; when I was compelled to bow and accept my office. There is no man with good sense who would want to assume an office like this, which means toil, self-sacrifice. [Laughter, noises, hoots and yells.]

Self-sacrifice! Such as you have never known!

You who smile at that, do as no man who knows me would do.

I have sacrificed my talent, all I have, upon the altar of God, and if my God has, in these Latter Days, entrusted me with large powers, it has been that I might fulfil my ministry, and make it possible to establish the Banner of the Kingdom of God in every land.

Not one man upon God's earth has ever made a charge against me that I have failed in sacrificing myself, my time, my toil. [Sneers.]

That sneer was utterly unworthy, uncalled for, and false.

The Consummation of the Age at Hand.

The time came when I was compelled to see that the General Overseer of the Christian Catholic Church in Zion had a divinely marked out place in the Christian Dispensation, which is hurrying to its Consummation, as every clear-thinking interpreter of the Word of God knows.

There can be no question at all that everything points to the fulfilment of the prophecy that "the Times of Restoration of All Things whereof God spake by the mouth of His holy prophets which have been since the world began," have begun.

I will tell you where it has begun. It has begun in Zion.

Zion's Message.

Zion has a Mission.

Zion has a Message which it is possible only for a man with Divinely-endowed Authority and with Prophetic Power to make known to the world.

It is a Message that covers the whole field; that brings a policy that is sufficient for the settlement of every difficulty in the Individual, in the Family, in the School, in Business, in the Church, in the State and in the World.

My Message is that the Law of God in the Ten Commandments, and the Law of Love which Jesus gave, must be put into operation, and prepare the world for the Coming of the King.

This is all that my Mission means.

I desire to say, however, continuing the Scriptural statements, that if you say, any of you, that Elijah is not to come you will find yourself opposed by overwhelming Scriptural and theological authority.

I am not speaking of myself; for this question of the coming of Elijah is absolutely impersonal.

Apart from personality altogether, get clear about the question that Elijah must come.

The scribes were right, and the Christ said it: "Elijah indeed cometh, and *shall* Restore All Things."

The Prophecy of the Apostle Peter.

Passing over many things, I desire to point out that this Declaration is connected with the sermon of the Apostle Peter, when he spoke, after the healing of the lame man at the Beautiful Gate of the Temple.

When the people came together, the Apostle Peter, as it is written at the close of the 3d chapter of the Acts of the Apostles, said:

Repent ye therefore, and turn again, that your sins may be blotted out, that so there may come seasons of refreshing from the presence of the Lord;

And that He may send the Christ who hath been appointed for you, even Jesus:

Whom the heaven must receive until the Times of Restoration of All Things, whereof God spake by the mouth of His Holy Prophets which have been since the world began.

Moses indeed said, A prophet shall the Lord God raise up unto you from among your brethren, like unto me; to him shall ye harken in all things whatsoever he shall speak unto you.

And it shall be, that every soul, which shall not harken to that prophet, shall be utterly destroyed from among the people.

Yea and all the prophets from Samuel and them that followed after, as many as have spoken, they also told of these days.

Ye are the sons of the prophets, and of the covenant which God made with your fathers, saying unto Abraham, And in thy seed shall all the families of the earth be blessed.

Unto you first God, having raised up His Servant, sent Him to bless you, in turning away every one of you from your iniquities.

Unto you first God, having raised up His servant—

It is not "His Son Jesus," as in the Old Version.

Apostasy of the Church.

Today, the church has lapsed into a condition of apostasy in which authority is not known, where authority is lost, where the idea is that the people shall rule the pulpit, and that the man who speaks there shall speak as the people will.

When that day comes, then Ichabod will be written over every church door and every pulpit. Then he who should be the messenger of God, becomes the prophet of a democracy.

The Messenger of God must be an officer in the Theocracy, in that government of God which permits none to interfere with His Divine right to declare the Law of God, and to enforce it.

Hence it is that I say tonight that unless the Reign of Law is established, then we shall have to face the coming of the Lawless One, whom the Lord Jesus, the Christ, shall destroy with the breath of His mouth at His Coming.

There is no question, that the prophet foretold by Moses was not Jesus, for that prophet was to be like unto Moses, and he was to be raised up as Moses was raised up. [At this point the interruptions were so loud and so prolonged that the General Overseer was unable to be heard.]

He closed his Message by saying:

I reaffirm my statement of June 2, 1901, as Elijah the Restorer.

The Doxology was then sung and the General Overseer pronounced the

BENEDICTION.

Beloved, abstain from all appearance of evil. And may the very God of Peace Himself sanctify you wholly; and I pray God your whole spirit and soul and body be preserved entire, without blame, unto the coming of our Lord Jesus, the Christ. Faithful is He that calleth you, who also will do it. The grace of our Lord Jesus, the Christ, the love of God, our Father, the fellowship of the Holy Spirit, our Comforter and Guide, one Eternal God, abide in you, bless you and keep you, and all the Israel of God everywhere, forever. Amen.

Notice to Officers and Members of the Christian Catholic Church.

Send all newspaper clippings concerning the General Overseer, the Elders, or any department of the work in connection with the Christian Catholic Church in Zion, to Deacon Carl F. Stern, Zion City, Illinois. Send as soon as possible after publication, and carefully mark *name and date of the paper clipped from* on each article. If this is not done, the clippings are absolutely useless.

GOD'S WAY OF HEALING.

BY THE REV. JOHN ALEX. DOWIE.

God's Way Of Healing Is a Person, Not a Thing.

Jesus said "*I am* the Way, and the Truth, and the Life," and He has ever been revealed to His people in all the ages by the Covenant Name, Jehovah-Rophi, or "*I am* Jehovah that Healeth thee." (John 14:6; Exodus 15:26.)

The Lord Jesus, the Christ, Is Still the Healer.

He cannot change, for "Jesus, the Christ, is the same yesterday and today, yea and forever;" and He is still with us, for He said: "Lo, *I am* with you All the Days, even unto the Consummation of the Age." (Hebrews 13:8; Matthew 28:20.) Because He is Unchangeable, and because He is present, in spirit, just as when in the flesh, He is the Healer of His people.

Divine Healing Rests on the Christ's Atonement.

It was prophesied of Him "Surely He hath borne our griefs (Hebrew, *sickness*), and carried our sorrows: . . . and with His stripes we are healed;" and it is expressly declared that this was fulfilled in His Ministry of Healing, which still continues. (Isaiah 53:4, 5; Matthew 8.17.)

Disease Can Never be God's Will.

It is the Devil's work, consequent upon Sin, and it is impossible for the work of the Devil ever to be the Will of God. The Christ came to "destroy the works of the Devil," and when He was here on earth He healed "all manner of disease and all manner of sickness," and all these sufferers are expressly declared to have been "oppressed of the Devil." (1 John 3:8; Matthew 4:23; Acts 10:38.)

The Gifts of Healings Are Permanent.

It is expressly declared that the "Gifts and the calling of God are without repentance," and the Gifts of Healings are amongst the Nine Gifts of the Spirit to the Church. (Romans 11:29; 1 Corinthians 12:8-11.)

There Are Four Modes of Divine Healing.

The first is the direct prayer of faith; the second, intercessory prayer of two or more; the third, the anointing of the elders, with the prayer of faith; and the fourth, the laying on of hands of those who believe, and whom God has prepared and called to that ministry. (Matthew 8:5-13; Matthew 18:19; James 5:14, 15; Mark 16:18.)

Divine Healing Is Opposed by Diabolical Counterfeits.

Amongst these are Christian Science (falsely so called), Mind Healing, Spiritualism, Trance Evangelism, etc. (1 Timothy 6:20, 21; 1 Timothy 4:1, 2; Isaiah 51:22, 23.)

Multitudes Have Been Healed Through Faith in Jesus.

The writer knows of thousands of cases and has personally laid hands on scores of thousands of persons. Full information can be obtained at the meetings held in the Zion Tabernacles in Chicago, and in Zion City, Illinois, and in many pamphlets which give the experience, in their own words, of many who have been healed in this and other countries, published at Zion Printing and Publishing House, Zion City, Illinois

"*Belief Cometh of Hearing, and Hearing by the Word of the Christ.*"

You are heartily invited to attend and hear for yourself.

ZION'S BIBLE CLASS

Conducted by Deacon Daniel Sloan in Shiloh Tabernacle, Zion City, Lord's Day Morning at 11 o'clock, and in Zion Homes and Gatherings throughout the World

MID-WEEK BIBLE CLASS LESSON, MAY 11th or 12th.

People to Shun and Beware of.

1. *The man who wants to run the affairs of God's House.*—3 John 1:5-11.
   He forms a ring to run things.
   He has the say about the preaching.
   He says who shall hold office.
2. *The man who does not live up to his profession.*—Matthew 10:16-24.
   He has a ravenous nature.
   He wants his own way.
   He has some greedy ambition.
3. *The man who is wicked and unreasonable.*—2 Thessalonians 3: 1-5.
   He does not believe in a man of God.
   He does not want the truth told.
   He is an infidel at heart.
4. *The man who lives after the flesh.*—Philippians 3: 1-4.
   He noses around to discover something wrong.
   He does more evil than good.
   He boasts of what he can do.
5. *The man who is obscene or dirty.*—Jude 1:17-25.
   He mocks at purity.
   He can see no harm in this or that.
   He is spotted with filth.
6. *The man who argues to prove he is right when wrong.*—2 Timothy 2: 14-23.
   He has premises to prove his position.
   He says things to hurt.
   He can ask many questions.
7. *The man who only makes a show of his religion.*—Matthew 16:6-12.
   Faith is not a vital part of it.
   He prays to be seen, not heard of God.
   He gives where men will observe it.

The Lord Our God is a Forewarning God.

LORD'S DAY BIBLE CLASS LESSON, MAY 15th.

Have No Fellowship With Evil Doers.

1. *You are not to shake hands with the man not sound in the Truth.*—2 John 1:4-11.
   The hand is related to the heart.
   The hand-shake means you are friends.
   Do not visit with those disloyal to God.
2. *The man who will not obey must be let alone.*—2 Thessalonians 3:6-15.
   He will talk but not work.
   He is impatient all the time.
   When you meet him reprove him.
3. *Shun the man who shows disrespect to those in authority.*—1 Timothy 6: 1-6.
   What a man says should help to make others godly.
   He thinks that gain is good evidence.
   He does not yield to the teacher.
4. *God does not believe in the sheep and the goats associating.*—Matthew 25:31-34.
   The sheep are for God's Fold.
   Goats do not follow the Shepherd.
   Goats are shut out of the Fold.
5. *The Name and Glory of the Lord must be the object of fellowship.*—Matthew 18:15-20.
   Some men will not repair a fault.
   Some will not listen to reproof.
   Some men must be let alone.
6. *It is not what men pretend or say but what they do that we are to observe.*—Ephesians 5: 1-12.
   They show the works of the flesh only.
   They do not live fruitful lives.
   They do things in underhanded ways.
7. *You cannot fellowship with evil doers without being partakers with them.*—Revelation 18:1-8.
   They are in league with the Devil.
   They are mixed up in uncleanness.
   Be with them and you will sin also.

God's Holy People are a Separate People.

LEAVES OF HEALING.

Two Dollars will bring to you the weekly visits of the Little White Dove for a year; 75 cents will send it to a friend for thirteen weeks; $1.25 will send it for six months; $1.50 will send it to your minister, or to a Y. M. C. A., or to a Public Reading Room for a whole year. We offer no premiums, except the premium of doing good. We receive no advertisements, and print no commercial lies or cheating enticements of unscrupulous thieves. LEAVES OF HEALING is Zion on wings, and we keep out everything that would detract the reader's mind from all except the Extension of the Kingdom of God, for which alone it exists. If we cannot send forth our Little White Dove without soiling its wings with the smoke of the factory and the dirt of the wrangling market-place, or compelling it to utter the screaming cries of the business vultures in the ears of our readers, then we will keep our Dove at home.

OBEYING GOD IN BAPTISM.

"Baptizing Them Into the Name of the Father and of the Son and of the Holy Ghost."

Eighteen Thousand One Hundred Sixty-one Baptisms by Triune Immersion Since March 14, 1897.

Eighteen Thousand One Hundred Sixty-one Believers have joyfully followed their Lord in the Ordinance of Believer's Baptism by Triune Immersion since the first Baptism in Central Zion Tabernacle on March 14, 1897.

Baptized in Central Zion Tabernacle from March 14, 1897, to December 14, 1901, by the General Overseer,	4754			
Baptized in South Side Zion Tabernacle from January 1, 1902, to June 14, 1903, by the General Overseer..	37			
Baptized at Zion City by the General Overseer........	583			
Baptized by Overseers, Elders, Evangelists and Deacons, at Headquarters (Zion City) and Chicago......	4940			
Total Baptized at Headquarters....................	—			10,314
Baptized in places outside of Headquarters by the General Overseer................................		641		
Baptized in places outside of Headquarters by Overseers, Elders, Evangelists and Deacons............		7084		
Total Baptized outside of Headquarters............		—		7,725
Total Baptized in seven years......................				18,039
Baptized since March 14, 1904:				
Baptized in Zion City by Elder Royall..............	63			
Baptized in Chicago by Elder Hall..................	1			
Baptized in Chicago by Elder Cossum................	12			
Baptized in Chicago by Evangelist Christie	3			
Baptized in Chicago by Deacon Matson..............	2			
Baptized in Chicago by Elder Kosch..................	6		87	
Baptized in California by Elder Taylor...............		4		
Baptized in Canada by Elder Simmons...............		5		
Baptized in Colorado by Deacon Cook...............		3		
Baptized in Illinois by Deacon Sprecher..............		1		
Baptized in New York by Elder Warszawiak..........		6		
Baptized in New York by Overseer Mason		10		
Baptized in Ohio by Deacon Arrington...............		2		
Baptized in Washington by Elder Simmons..........		1		
Baptized in Washington by Elder Ernst..............		3	35	122
Total Baptized since March 14, 1897......				18,161

The following-named three believers were baptized in Seattle, Washington, Lord's Day, April 3, 1904, by Elder August Ernst:

Kooken, James R	Marysville, Washington
McCormack, Henry Elmer	Everett, Washington
Ritchey, Mrs. C	2312 First avenue, Seattle, Washington

The following-named six believers were baptized in the South Side Zion Tabernacle, Chicago, Illinois, Lord's Day, April 17, 1904, by Elder Thomas Kosch:

Durchik, Mattus	832 Girard street, Chicago, Illinois
Kropp, Helene	Zion City, Illinois
Schmaltz, Elsie	3067 Broad street, Chicago, Illinois
Schmaltz, Martha	3067 Broad street, Chicago, Illinois
Schmaltz, Olga	3067 Broad street, Chicago, Illinois
Witt, Anna, Mrs.	442 West Twenty-third street, Chicago, Illinois

The following-named sixty-three believers were baptized in Shiloh Tabernacle, Zion City, Illinois, Lord's Day, April 17, 1904, by Elder F. M. Royall:

Asplin, Charlie	3021 Gabriel avenue, Zion City, Illinois
Austin, Edwin D.	3104 Eshcol avenue, Zion City, Illinois
Baker, Bessie	Boonville, Missouri
Bartholomew, Odias	2802 Elim avenue, Zion City, Illinois
Baughman, Mabel	3105 Emmaus avenue, Zion City, Illinois
Baughman, Pearl	3105 Emmaus avenue, Zion City, Illinois
Boyer, Erma	3200 Ezekiel avenue, Zion City, Illinois
Boyer, Maggie	3200 Ezekiel avenue, Zion City, Illinois
Boyer, D. G.	3200 Ezekiel avenue, Zion City, Illinois
Beatty, Nina	2107 Gabriel avenue, Zion City, Illinois
Border, Mary Elizabeth	2814 Gabriel avenue, Zion City, Illinois
Cameron, Jessie	1824 Gilgal avenue, Zion City, Illinois
Corney, Mrs. Fannie	3207 Gilboa avenue, Zion City, Illinois
Corney, Harry	3207 Gilboa avenue, Zion City, Illinois
DeJonge, Henry Richard	2809 Gilboa avenue, Zion City, Illinois
Gambee, Lloyd	2213 Elisha avenue, Zion City, Illinois
Gates, John	3202 Enoch avenue, Zion City, Illinois
Hagenender, Wendellena	3025 Gabriel avenue, Zion City, Illinois
Hanni, Rollin	3104 Ezra avenue, Zion City, Illinois
Hanni, Mabel	3104 Ezra avenue, Zion City, Illinois
Hansen, Richard	2917 Enoch avenue, Zion City, Illinois
Herrod, Jane	2314 Gideon avenue, Zion City, Illinois
Johnson, Ida	3112 Emmaus avenue, Zion City, Illinois
Koch, Edna	2719 Elizabeth avenue, Zion City, Illinois
Kreps, Hazel Victoria	2205 Ezra avenue, Zion City, Illinois
LaBelle, Calvin	1820 Gilgal avenue, Zion City, Illinois
LeRoy, Robert E.	2014 Hebron avenue, Zion City, Illinois
Lewis, Andrew	2321 Gideon avenue, Zion City, Illinois
McKenzie, Mrs. Agnes	2918 Enoch avenue, Zion City, Illinois
McNatt, Ruby	3212 Gideon avenue, Zion City, Illinois
Marpurg, Mrs. G.	Santee Thedinga, Amsterdam, Holland
Mayfield, Carrie	3112 Elizabeth avenue, Zion City, Illinois
Meredith, Myrtle	2106 Eshcol avenue, Zion City, Illinois
Meredith, Ralph	2106 Eshcol avenue, Zion City, Illinois
Morgan, Janet Mary	2905 Elizabeth avenue, Zion City, Illinois
Nowlan, Blanche May	2820 Ezekiel avenue, Zion City, Illinois
Nowlan, Frederica M	2820 Ezekiel avenue, Zion City, Illinois
Payne, Harry	3001 Gilboa avenue, Zion City, Illinois
Post, Mary	Marquis, Iowa
Pyle, Emma R.	2802 Emmaus avenue, Zion City, Illinois
Randall, Dorothy Elliott	3001 Eshcol avenue, Zion City, Illinois
Reed, Flood	2801 Enoch avenue, Zion City, Illinois
Robbins, George	2506 Elim avenue, Zion City, Illinois
Robbins, Francis	2506 Elim avenue, Zion City, Illinois
Rockafellar, Nellie	3110 Eshcol avenue, Zion City, Illinois
Sanders, Raymond Cliftondale	2809 Gideon avenue, Zion City, Illinois
Schertz, Florence Anna	605 Shiloh boulevard, Zion City, Illinois
Schertz, Irene Frances	605 Shiloh boulevard, Zion City, Illinois
Seamans, Mary M	3211 Elisha avenue, Zion City, Illinois
Shields, George Victor	3216 Ezra avenue, Zion City, Illinois
Shields, Joseph E.	3216 Ezra avenue, Zion City, Illinois
Shields, Louis Franklin	3216 Ezra avenue, Zion City, Illinois
Spellman, Edith Elliott	2901 Ezekiel avenue, Zion City, Illinois
Stevenson, Arthur	2912 Enoch avenue, Zion City, Illinois
Taylor, Emma	3022 Ezra avenue, Zion City, Illinois
Teeple, Florence	3023 Ezekiel avenue, Zion City, Illinois
Thorp, Frank Sidney	2907 Ezra avenue, Zion City, Illinois
Warner, Ebenezer Cox	Cape Colony, South Africa
Warner, Herbert Blackee	Cape Colony, South Africa
Watkins, Arthur Elmer	2502 Gideon avenue, Zion City, Illinois
Wesner, Elenora	3000 Enoch avenue, Zion City, Illinois
Wilcox, Emory	2704 Elim avenue, Zion City, Illinois
Young, Coyla	2910 Edina boulevard, Zion City, Illinois

CONSECRATION OF CHILDREN.

The following-named twelve children were consecrated in Shiloh Tabernacle, Zion City, Illinois, Lord's Day, April 17, 1904, by Overseer John G. Speicher:

Blankinship, Arthur Marshal	3104 Enoch avenue, Zion City, Illinois
Brown, Pansy Josepha	2709 Elizabeth avenue, Zion City, Illinois
Cedarstaff, Bertha Alexander	2600 Gideon avenue, Zion City, Illinois
Cedarstaff, Ernest John	2600 Gideon avenue, Zion City, Illinois
Cedarstaff, Victor Emmanuel	2600 Gideon avenue, Zion City, Illinois
Greer, Carrie Beth	3004 Ezra avenue, Zion City, Illinois
Greer, Charles Wesley	3004 Ezra avenue, Zion City, Illinois
Greer, Hattie May	3004 Ezra avenue, Zion City, Illinois
Greer, John Alexander	3004 Enoch avenue, Zion City, Illinois
Hosack, Clyde Raymond	2903 Gilboa avenue, Zion City, Illinois
Shaffer, Paul Eugene.	3115 Enoch avenue, Zion City, Illinois
Stocka, Walter Richard	Zion City, Illinois

ZION IN IOWA.

Rev. Charles A. Hoy, Elder in the Christian Catholic Church in Zion, Falls City, Nebraska, will hold religious services in the following places:

Marcus, May 2d, 3d and 4th; Dows, May 5th and 6th; Webster City, May 7th, 8th and 9th; Hubbard, May 10th; Ames, May 11th; Boone, May 12th and 13th; Des Moines, May 14th, 15th and 16th and Dedham, May 17th.

All friends or members desiring to obey their Lord in Baptism may arrange for the same with the Elder at the above places.

ZION IN ILLINOIS AND INDIANA.

Beginning about May 20th, Elder and Deaconess Lee will visit the following places in Illinois: Kankakee, Hoopeston, Danville. Also in Indiana as follows: Indianapolis, Noblesville, Logansport, Lafayette, and neighboring towns.

ZION IN ILLINOIS.

Deacon B. W. Brannen will visit and hold meetings in the following places: Ottawa, April 23d; Pontiac, April 24th; Odell, April 25th; Pekin, April 26th; Peoria, April 27th; Bloomington, April 28th; Paxton, April 29th; Champaign and Urbana, May 1st; Danville, May 2dr Hoopeston, May 3d.

A WEEKLY PAPER FOR THE EXTENSION OF THE KINGDOM OF GOD
EDITED BY THE REV. JOHN ALEX. DOWIE.

Volume XV. No. 2. *ZION CITY, SATURDAY, APRIL 30, 1904.* *Price Five Cents*

GOD'S WITNESSES TO DIVINE HEALING.

HEALED OF CONSUMPTION.

BUT IT SHALL COME TO PASS, IF THOU WILT NOT HARKEN UNTO THE VOICE OF JEHOVAH THY GOD, TO OBSERVE TO DO ALL HIS COMMANDMENTS AND HIS STATUTES WHICH I COMMAND THEE THIS DAY; THAT ALL THESE CURSES SHALL COME UPON THEE, AND OVERTAKE THEE. . . .

"Jehovah shall smite thee [that is, permit to be smitten] with consumption, and with fever, and with inflammation, and with fiery heat, and with the sword, and with blasting, and with mildew; and they shall pursue thee until thou perish. . . .

"Jehovah shall smite thee [permit to be smitten] with the boil of Egypt, and with the emerods, and with the scurvy, and with the itch, whereof thou canst not be healed."

Boils, felons, carbuncles, eczema, scrofula, consumption, cancer, these are some of the mongrel and monstrous offspring begotten by the Devil and conceived by impure blood.

This impure blood is largely caused by the eating of impure food.

The most common source of all the impure foods is in the various products manufactured from the carcass of the unclean hog.

It is impossible to destroy in any way the poison, or the impurity, or the bad effects of pork in its various forms. Cooking has no effect upon it whatever, with the exception that thorough heating in cooking will destroy trichinæ and will also in a large measure overcome any diseased condition which may have been in the animal.

MRS. ALICE SANDMYRE.

Large numbers of hogs when killed are suffering from various acute and chronic diseases, such as cholera, sore throat, parasites, skin diseases and trichinosis, and thorough heating for a long period of time will destroy the danger of contamination from these diseases, just as the cooking of tobacco will destroy any worms or insects or microbes that may infest the tobacco plant; but no amount of heat will destroy the nicotine poison contained in the tobacco itself.

Just so with pork. Cooking has absolutely no effect upon the essential and fundamental impurity of pork. In order to destroy the impurity of pork it would have to be converted into the flesh of some clean animal, and the hocus-pocus of a priest or the skill of a cook are merely a sham and a delusion.

There are three great diseases which are destroying more lives than any other ten diseases: cholera, cancer, and consumption; but the greatest of these is consumption. Unquestionably a large proportion of the deaths reported by physicians as pneumonia are nothing more nor less than pulmonary consumption. The atmosphere, the clothing, the dust of the streets, and the walls of the houses are saturated with the tubercular poison, and when the pulmonary organs are attacked by an inflammatory disease, how easily the bacillus of tuberculosis can find a breeding place and develop to the speedy destruction of the victim.

But the preachers still insist that it is the hand of God; that we must be patient; for His loving hand is destroying us for our own good; and they cite the book of Job and quote the words of Job:

The hand of Jehovah hath touched me.

It is exceedingly strange how credulous humanity is today, and how readily it believes the perverse teaching of the false shepherd.

Thank God that Zion is opening the eyes of the people, and making them see for themselves; opening their understanding and making them think for themselves!

This woman whose testimony we present could no longer be deceived. She saw plainly that her pastor was merely quoting the words of Job, who little understood, at the time that he uttered them, that it was Satan who was afflicting him.

This Job ascertained later on when God spoke to him, and revealed to him the fact that God is not the author of disease and of confusion; that Satan is going about "like a roaring lion," seeking "whom he may devour."

God permits it because of the sins of the people. He ever has permitted it, and ever must do so. For if the people will not seek His protection, how can He give to them the protection which He offers?

How important it is today that we know the author of any quotation from the Bible before we apply it to ourselves. A common quotation made by a large number of people is as follows:

Stolen waters are sweet, and bread eaten in secret is pleasant.

How many men and women would quote this familiarly if they remembered that these are the words of the harlot?

How many times the work of the Devil is laid upon the Lord!

Job said that God made him sick, but the record says it was the Devil's work. We are willing to accept the record.

There are but two sides to the picture, and the Devil's side is becoming blacker and blacker, and more and more terrible.

The side of God's eternal love is becoming more and more beautiful.

'Tis sweet to know that Jesus hears
Each simple, earnest, trusting prayer;
That in the hour of grief and pain
That He will hear, for He is near,
'Tis sweet to know that Jesus hears
And sweeter still that He is near.

J. G. S.

WRITTEN TESTIMONY OF MRS. ALICE SANDMYRE.

SPOKANE, WASHINGTON, March 2, 1904.

DEAR GENERAL OVERSEER:—I wish to add my testimony to those that have already been given through the pages of LEAVES OF HEALING, showing how the great white scourge, consumption, yields to the healing power of Jesus, the Christ.

Six years ago I was dying with that dreadful disease.

Five doctors had given me up, saying that I was beyond all hope of recovery.

My left arm, leg and side had become numb and the left lung was gone, leaving my chest sunken.

My little boy, aged nine, had inherited consumption from me and, oh, how much we had suffered from doctors and drugs!

Tongue or pen can in no way describe what we passed through.

After I was given up to die, two different Methodist ministers came to see me saying that I must be quiet and submit to the will of God.

They told me to read the book of Job and see how God afflicted him and how patient he was.

In my unconscious moments I would rave and say, "Oh! how can I possibly serve a God who makes me suffer this way?"

I read the book of Job, and when the ministers came back I said, "God never smote Job; it was the Devil."

Then they said that I did not understand it fully; that the Bible was written in parables.

But I praise God that LEAVES OF HEALING came to me, and through reading it I saw that Jesus is still the Healer of His people and Satan is the defiler.

How many false shepherds there are today who tell the poor afflicted ones that God afflicts them because He loves them so much!

Is it not ridiculous?

They must have overlooked, in some way, Psalm 107:17.

As soon as I saw the truth I put aside medicines of every kind and trusted God fully.

One evening when mother and I were alone in the room it seemed that Jesus must have come near and touched me. Such a wonderful power came over me that I almost felt as though I was in mid-air—so light—and a tingling sensation went through my body.

I seemed to feel a hand on my lungs.

I was healed, and felt well and strong in a moment of time.

My left lung came out as full as the other one, and my breathing was free.

I then took my boy to God, and he was perfectly healed also.

Since that time I have seen many raised up from the dying bed in answer to the Prayer of Faith.

After I was healed, my Methodist friends turned a cold shoulder to me, and said that I was losing my mind on religion.

I said, "Yes, I have lost my mind, and have been given the mind of the Christ."

I thought I could get the church to believe it, as they all knew how very sick I had been. But I had to get out.

I am now in the Christian Catholic Church in Zion, happy and healed by the power of God.

I am taking the glad Message to sick and sorrowing ones throughout the city.

To God be all the glory.

Yours for the Master.

(MRS.) ALICE SANDMYRE.

CONFIRMATION OF MRS. ALICE SANDMYRE'S TESTIMONY.

ZION CITY, ILLINOIS, April 6, 1904.

DEAR GENERAL OVERSEER:—I rejoice that I can say that the above testimony is positively true, as I am personally acquainted with Mrs. Sandmyre, and know that she is perfectly healed.

Any one who rides the bicycle must have a good pair of lungs, and, judging from the way she is able to ride, there certainly can be no weakness whatever left.

God's work is a perfect work.

(MRS.) LIZZIE LEE,
Deaconess in the Christian Catholic Church in Zion.

MEETINGS IN ZION CITY TABERNACLES.

SHILOH TABERNACLE.

Lord's Day—Early morning service.... 6:30 a. m.
Intermediate Bible Class.. 9:45 a. m.
Bible class, conducted by Deacon Daniel Sloan... 11:00 a. m.
Afternoon service........ 2:30 p. m.
Evening service......... 8:00 p. m.
First Lord's Day of Every Month—Communion service.
Second Lord's Day of Every Month—Baptismal service.
Third Lord's Day of Every Month—Consecration of children, 10:00 a. m.
Monday—Zion Restoration Host rally (Second Monday of every month).... 8:00 p. m.
Tuesday—Divine Healing meeting..... 2:30 p. m.
Tuesday—Adult Choir .... 7:45 p. m.
Wednesday—Baptismal service........ 7:00 p. m.
Wednesday—Citizens' rally............ 8:00 p. m.
Friday—Adult Choir.................. 7:45 p. m.
Friday—Officers of the Christian Catholic Church in Zion........ 8:00 p. m.
Saturday—Junior Choir................ 1:00 p. m.
Meeting in the officers' room.

TWENTY-SIXTH STREET TABERNACLE.

Lord's Day—Junior service............ 9:45 a. m.
Lord's Day—Services (German)........10:30 a. m.
Tuesday—Services (German).......... 8:00 p. m.

Zion Literature Sent Out from a Free Distribution Fund Provided by Zion's Guests and the Friends of Zion.

Report for the week ending April 23, 1904:
1,014 Rolls to Hotels in the United States and Canada.
2,172 Rolls to........Various States in the Union
1,300 Rolls to..............Hotels in Switzerland
1,304 Rolls to............Members of Parliament
Number of Rolls for the Week..............5,790
Number of Rolls reported to Apr. 23, 1904, 3,122,074

EVANGELIST SARAH E. HILL,
Superintendent Zion Literature Mission,
Zion City, Illinois.

BLESS Jehovah, O my soul;
And all that is within me, bless His holy Name.
Bless Jehovah, O my soul,
And forget not all His benefits:
Who forgiveth all thine iniquities;
Who healeth all thy diseases;
Who redeemeth thy life from destruction;
Who crowneth thee with lovingkindness and tender mercies:
Who satisfieth thy mouth with good things;
So that thy youth is renewed like the eagle.—*Psalm 103:1-5.*

IS ANY among you sick? let him call for the Elders of the Church; and let them pray over him, anointing him with oil in the Name of the Lord: And the Prayer of Faith shall save him that is sick, and the Lord shall raise him up; and if he have committed sins, it shall be forgiven him.—*James 5:14, 15.*

Daily Bible Study for the Home

By Overseer John G. Speicher

THE Daily Bible reading for the month of May begins with the Acts of the Apostles. As there are only twenty-eight chapters in the Acts, Paul's Epistle to the Colossians is added to complete the month.

SUNDAY, MAY 1ST.

Acts 1.—Ascension chapter.

Memory text—Verse 11. "This Jesus . . . shall so come in like manner."

Contents of chapter—Luke addresses his writings to Theophilus (meaning, lover of God); The Christ seen alive by the apostles forty days; Spoke concerning the Kingdom of God; His parting words to the apostles; His ascension; Angels assure disciples He will come again; Disciples return to Jerusalem; They gather in an upper room, with Jesus' mother and His brethren; one hundred twenty present; Peter tells necessity of ordaining one to take Judas' place; Lot falls on Matthias.

MONDAY, MAY 2D.

Acts 2.—Pentecost chapter.

Memory text—Verse 40. "Save yourself from this crooked generation."

Contents of chapter—Disciples all together; The place filled with the Spirit; Rests upon each of them like tongues; Disciples speak with other tongues; Devout men from every nation at Jerusalem at that time; Multitude astonished; Some mocked; Peter's sermon brings conviction; He commands them to repent and be baptized; Three thousand obey; Continued steadfastly; Many wonders and signs done; Things held in common; Possessions and goods sold; Distribution made; They continued daily praising and worshiping God.

TUESDAY, MAY 3D.

Acts 3.—Restoration chapter.

Memory text—Verse 23. "Harken to that prophet."

Contents of chapter—Peter and John going to Temple at hour of prayer; Lame man asks alms; They command him to rise in Jesus' Name; Man obeys and is immediately healed; Walks, leaps, praises God; Goes into Temple with them; People run together to see what has happened; Peter preaches to them; Says heavens must receive Jesus until the Time of the Restoration of All Things.

WEDNESDAY, MAY 4TH.

Acts 4.—Divine boldness chapter.

Memory text—Verse 13. "They had been with Jesus."

Contents of chapter—Priests, captains, and Sadducees troubled at the preaching of the resurrection of the Christ; Arrest Peter and John; Five thousand men converted; Brought before the rulers; Peter declares to them man was healed through the Christ; Their boldness indicated they had been with Jesus; Rulers charged them not to teach in Name of Jesus; Peter's reply; Further threatened; Apostles released; Go to their own company; Prayer; Filled with the Holy Spirit; Spoke the word with boldness; Held things in common; Believers sold land; Brought money to apostles.

THURSDAY, MAY 5TH.

Acts 5.—Ananias and Sapphira chapter.

Memory text—Verse 29. "We must obey God rather than men."

Contents of chapter—Ananias and Sapphira keep back part of price of the land; They lie about it, and immediately die and are buried; Many signs and wonders wrought; Sick carried on beds and couches into the streets and are healed; Apostles arrested and put into prison, but angel opens doors and brings them out; Rulers perplexed; Bring apostles before the council; Peter's words cut them to the heart; Tempted to slay them; Gamaliel's advice received and acted upon; Apostles beaten and commanded not to teach and preach Jesus, the Christ.

FRIDAY, MAY 6TH.

Acts 6.—Stephen's ministry chapter.

Memory text—Verse 10. "They were not able to resist the wisdom and the Spirit by which he spake."

Contents of chapter.—Grecians murmur because of widows being neglected; Apostles tell the disciples to select seven men of good report filled with the Holy Spirit, and with wisdom; These men set apart by laying on of hands by apostles; Word of God increased; Disciples multiplied; Priests obedient to the faith; Stephen's ministry especially blessed; Certain ones dispute with Stephen; Not able to withstand his wisdom; False witness brought in; Elders and scribes bring him to the council; Behold his face like that of an angel.

SATURDAY, MAY 7TH.

Acts 7.—Stephen's defense chapter.

Memory text—Verse 55. "Saw the glory of God, and Jesus."

Contents of chapter—Stephen points out the fulfilling of many things from Abraham to Jesus; Their rejection of the Divine order was like that of their fathers; They are cut to the heart and gnash on him; He sees the heavens opened and Jesus at God's right hand; They cast him out of the city and stone him; He commits his spirit to God and prays for his enemies; Falls asleep.

SUNDAY, MAY 8TH.

Acts 8.—Sorcerer and Ethiopian eunuch chapter.

Memory text—Verse 4. "They therefore that were scattered abroad went about preaching the word."

Contents of chapter—Saul consents to Stephen's death; Makes havoc of the Church; Disciples scattered; They preach everywhere; Philip's ministry blessed; Great joy in the city because of the sick healed; Simon, the sorcerer, believes and is baptized; Believers receive the Holy Spirit through laying on of hands of Peter and John; Simon offers money for the Holy Spirit; Peter rebukes him, tells him to repent; Simon asks them to pray for him; Philip sent by the Spirit into the desert; Told to talk to Ethiopian eunuch; He explains the Scripture; Eunuch believes and is baptized; Goes on his way rejoicing; Philip caught away by the Spirit; Preaches in many cities.

MONDAY, MAY 9TH.

Acts 9.—Conversion of Saul chapter.

Memory text—Verse 34. "Jesus, the Christ, healeth thee."

Contents of chapter—Saul, still persecuting the Church, goes to Damascus; A light from heaven stops him; Jesus speaks to him; He becomes blind; The Lord speaks to Ananias; Ananias goes to Saul; Saul receives his sight and is baptized; Tarries awhile with the disciples at Damascus, proving that Jesus is the Christ; Jews plot to kill him; Disciples let him down through the wall in a basket; Disciples at Jerusalem at first afraid of him; Barnabas tells of his faithfulness at Damascus; Paul disputes with the Grecian Jews; They seek to kill him; The Church has peace; Peter at Lydda; Æneas healed; People of two villages converted through this healing; Dorcas raised from the dead, at Joppa.

TUESDAY, MAY 10TH.

Acts 10.—Cornelius chapter.

Memory text—Verse 34. "God is no respecter of persons."

Contents of chapter—Cornelius' vision; He sends for Peter; Peter's vision; He goes to Cornelius' home; Peter preaches to Cornelius and his kinsmen and friends; Holy Spirit falls upon all who hear him; They of the circumcision astonished; Gentiles speak with togues and magnify God; Peter commands them to be baptized; They ask him to tarry.

WEDNESDAY, MAY 11TH.

Acts 11.—Gentile and Christian chapter.

Memory text—Verse 26. "And the disciples were called Christians first at Antioch."

Contents of chapter—Disciples in Judea hear of Gentiles receiving the Word; Circumcised Jews contend with Peter for going to the Gentiles; Peter relates the whole matter, and convinces them; Gospel preached by some to the Greeks; That ministry blessed; Barnabas sent out to exhort the brethren; He brings Saul to Antioch; They tarry there a year, teaching many; Disciples called Christians; Prophets come to Antioch; Agabus prophesies famine; It came to pass in the time of Claudius Cæsar; Disciples send relief to the brethren in Judea, by hands of Barnabas and Saul.

THURSDAY, MAY 12TH.

Acts 12.—Peter's deliverance and Herod's death chapter.

Memory text—Verse 23. "He gave God not the glory."

Contents of chapter—Herod kills James, and imprisons Peter; Prayer on behalf of Peter, by the Church; God delivers Peter from prison; Peter dazed; Goes to the home of Mary; Finds disciples praying for him; They are astonished; He tells them how the Lord delivered him; Then goes to Cæsarea; Herod seeks for Peter; Not finding him, commands keepers of the prison to be killed; Herod's death; Word of God grew and multiplied; Barnabas and Saul return to Jerusalem; Take Mark with them.

For we are a temple of the living God;
Even as God said,
I will dwell in them, and walk in them;
And I will be their God,
And they shall be My people.—*2 Corinthians 6:16.*

AND ye shall know the Truth,
And the Truth shall make you free.—*John 8:32.*

A WEEKLY PAPER FOR THE EXTENSION OF THE KINGDOM OF GOD.

EDITED BY THE REV. JOHN ALEX. DOWIE.

Application for entry as Second Class Matter at Zion City, Illinois, pending.

Subscription Rates.		Special Rates.	
One Year	$2.00	100 Copies of One Issue	$3.00
Six Months	1 25	25 Copies of One Issue	1.00
Three Months	.75	To Ministers, Y. M. C. A's and Public	
Single Copies	.05	Reading Rooms, per annum	1.50

For foreign subscriptions add $1.50 per year, or three cents per copy for postage.
Subscribers desiring a change of address should give present address, as well as that to which they desire LEAVES OF HEALING sent in the future.
Make Bank Drafts, Express Money or Postoffice Money Orders payable to the order of JOHN ALEX DOWIE, Zion City, Illinois, U. S. A.
Long Distance Telephone. *Cable Address "Dowie, Zion City."*
All communications upon business must be addressed to
MANAGER ZION PUBLISHING HOUSE,
Zion City, Illinois, U. S. A.

Subscriptions to LEAVES OF HEALING, A VOICE FROM ZION, and the various publications may also be sent to
ZION PUBLISHING HOUSE, 81 EUSTON ROAD, LONDON, N. W., ENGLAND.
ZION PUBLISHING HOUSE, NO. 43 PARK ROAD, ST. KILDA, MELBOURNE, VICTORIA, AUSTRALIA.
ZION PUBLISHING HOUSE, RUE DE MONT, THABOR 1, PARIS, FRANCE.
ZIONSHEIM, SCHLOSS LIEBBURG, CANTON THURGAU, BEI ZÜRICH, SWITZERLAND

ZION CITY, ILLINOIS, SATURDAY, APRIL 30, 1904.

TABLE OF CONTENTS.

LEAVES OF HEALING, SATURDAY, APRIL 30, 1904.

Notes From The Overseer-in-Charge.

"TEND THE FLOCK OF GOD WHICH IS AMONG YOU,
EXERCISING THE OVERSIGHT, NOT OF CONSTRAINT, BUT WILLINGLY,
ACCORDING UNTO GOD;
NOR YET FOR FILTHY LUCRE,
BUT OF A READY MIND."

THOSE TO WHOM authority is given, or who take upon themselves the authority of leadership in the Church of God, are expected at least to give their people good advice and safe counsel.

Every good shepherd will do the best he can to provide pure food and clean water for his sheep.

He does this because of his love for the sheep and not merely from a mercenary motive.

No man has a right to be a pastor or a teacher or a leader of any people who lacks the intelligence or the honesty to advise the people against the dangers that beset them on every hand.

It is the duty of a pastor to instruct the people in the proper care of their bodies as well as their spirits. It is a poor shepherd who would take no interest in the physical welfare of his flock.

If there is any article of food that is known to be injurious or adulterated, every true pastor will warn his people against it, and every honest Christian editor will publicly proclaim against that article of food.

He will go further and help the people to find that which is good, and wholesome, and beneficial.

THE SAME in the healing of disease.

Should the medical profession be so fortunate as to discover some safe and sure remedy for some disease, let the pastor see to it that his flock is properly supplied.

There are a few "sure cures" that are claimed by the physicians. One of these that has stood the test longer than any other of its kind is vaccination.

If this is such a good thing, let the pastors see to it that their people are all properly vaccinated. Let them begin with the baby, and go up through the household, and let not one member escape. It will not cost much to supply them with the vaccine virus. They can scratch themselves regularly once a month and insert the dirty smallpox poison.

THE NEXT FAD which has a great run at this time, especially in Chicago, is the so-called antitoxin treatment of diphtheria.

All you have to do is to take some of the diphtheritic poison and run it properly through the blood of the guinea pig, or some other unclean animal, and get a lymph full of unclean and poisonous material; and when the dear child is sick with diphtheria inject this into its veins. The child always gets well—if it does not die.

Let the pastor see to it that this remedy can be had at a reasonable price. If it is a good thing, why not push it? Let them see to it that the dear people are not imposed upon by the druggist.

ACCORDING TO the Chicago *Daily Tribune* of recent date, the druggists are the worst kind of wolves, and are literally tearing the wool from the dear sheep.

The following editorial was printed in the issue of April 22d:

GREED, POVERTY, AND ANTITOXIN.

Diphtheria is the disease of the poor. Antitoxin is the remedy of the rich. There you have the whole cruel situation. It could be mitigated if the Chicago druggist did not find that the expensive commercial antitoxin was superior to the economical health department antitoxin as a remedy for small profits.

A child is ill. The doctor is summoned. He says diphtheria. The family may not know that some of the health department antitoxin is kept for free distribution. Or it may think that it is not poor enough to be indigent. It orders antitoxin from the corner drug store. The druggist is sorry. He does not keep health department antitoxin. But he does keep a supply of the antitoxin manufactured by the big commercial houses. Won't some of that do? Naturally it will. The child's life has to be saved, and it has to be saved fast.

One thousand units of health department antitoxin cost 75 cents. One thousand units of commercial antitoxin cost $2. The profit for the druggist on 1,000 units of health department antitoxin is 7½ cents. The profit for the druggist on 1,000 units of commercial antitoxin is 66⅔ cents. A great many doses of 1,000 units each may be necessary for the preservation of one life.

Is it not possible in this matter that a great responsibility rests upon the medical profession? The "Hippocratic oath" elevates the doctor to a region where money-making, even if it has to be the ground, is no longer the sky. Is it not possible that the men who represent the ideals of the Hippocratic oath could bring such pressure to bear upon the druggists?

IT IS DEPLORABLE that the druggists are such unscrupulous scoundrels as the *Tribune* makes them out to be.

ZION HAS SAID something of the same kind for some time, and we are glad that the *Tribune* is beginning to agree with Zion in at least one particular. It must be reading LEAVES OF HEALING.

NOW COMES the London *Lancet*, (probably the foremost medical journal in the world) as quoted in the last issue of the *Literary Digest*, which declares that the dear people are consuming entirely too many drugs and medicines.

It contends that there is an increasing number of people, who "spend money and thought over the business of physicing themselves."

It gives "an account of an old lady who was in the habit of taking nightly 'nine compound rhubarb pills, several mixtures, four tablespoonfuls of senna, three tablespoonfuls of cascara, and a quantity of magnesia.'"

The *Digest* further quotes as follows:

The whole tendency of what may be called popular pharmacy during the last few years has been in the direction of introducing to the public a great variety of powerful medicines, put up in convenient forms, and advertised in such a manner as to produce in the unthinking a belief that they may be safely and rightly administered at all times and seasons, without any guidance from medical knowledge and without any reference to the actual state of the recipient, as remedies for the popular name of some real or supposed malady.

And then follows a dissertation upon the importance and necessity of knowing what drugs are consumed and the duty of the people going to physicians for advice instead of going to the druggists.

There always has been a great hue and cry with the physicians against the druggists and patent medicine men.

THE MEDICINE which the dear old lady is supposed to have taken in one evening, purchased at the drug store, cost her but a few cents. The same quantity and variety of medicines obtained from the physician would have cost her several dollars.

We have no doubt as to the consuming avarice of the majority of druggists, and that conscience never enters very largely into their dealings, but we cannot quite see that physicians are any less blamable; and the fight between the druggists and physicians is one of their own, not ours.

THE PHYSICIANS are rare who tell their patients that they are taking too much medicine, and who do not do all they can to induce their patients to come to them with every trifling ailment. The great majority are ready to prescribe freely and liberally whenever asked to do so.

This is their business, and they will treat their patients much in the same way that a grocer or a butcher will his customer. They can get what they want if they pay for it.

WE ARE GLAD to see in this connection the outspoken and bold statement of Mr. Edward Bok in the last issue of the *Ladies' Home Journal*. His bitter arraignment of what he calls "The 'Patent Medicine' Curse," is very strong and timely.

One cannot help thinking that he must have been reading the strong statements of our beloved General Overseer.

THE OPENING paragraph of his article is as follows:

Every year, particularly in the spring time, tens of thousands of bottles of patent medicines are used throughout the country by persons who are in absolute ignorance of what they are swallowing. They feel "sluggish" after the all winter in-door confinement; they feel that their systems need a "toning up," or a "blood purifier." Their eye catches some advertisement in a newspaper, or on a fence, or on the side of a barn, and from the cleverly worded descriptions of symptoms they are convinced that this man's "bitters," or that man's "sarsaparilla," or that "doctor's" (!) "vegetable compound," or So-and-so's "pills" is exactly the thing they need as a "tonic."

BUT IT IS hard to see why Mr. Bok should be so inconsistent as to antagonize and denounce so vehemently the patent nostrums and not to do the same against the druggists and doctors generally.

His youthful credulity seems to be unbounded. One would think from what he writes that every physician is to be fully trusted, or at least the majority. You must not purchase a patent proprietary medicine, but you must go and buy the same thing from your doctor.

We agree most heartily in all he says in his excellent article concerning the criminality of advertising and selling such accursed concoctions as "Whiskol," which is declared to be a "non-intoxicant stimulant," when it contains more than twenty-eight per cent. of alcohol, and "Schenk's Seaweed Tonic," which is pronounced to be "entirely harmless," and which contains nearly twenty per cent. of alcohol.

WE ARE advised by Mr. Bok that instead of going to the druggist and purchasing these concoctions we should go to "a reliable and intelligent physician."

Who and where is he?

Will Mr. Bok kindly rise and explain?

Will he kindly name a few for our information?

What about those who are not reliable and intelligent? Will he kindly give us a little light on this subject?

Is it not a fact that the majority of the medical profession are themselves taking alcoholic and narcotic poisons in excess?

What about the communities in which the physicians are not reliable?

What about the *doctor's* prescriptions?

How much strychnine, arsenicum, digitalis, morphine, cocaine, and other poisons are contained in *his* prescription?

How much of alcohol in the "drops" which the dear "intelligent physician" has prescribed for the little babe?

Will he kindly tell us how many people have been poisoned to death by *physicians* within the last year?

And from which school are the people to select? Surely they cannot all be the best. Which is to be trusted?

Will not Mr. Bok, who sets himself up as a teacher of the people and a leader, kindly advise us in this particular?

HE SAYS in closing his article:

Far better, ladies, that the contents of a bottle of champagne should go into the water, where it will do no one any harm, than that the contents of a bottle of "patent medicine," with forty per cent. of alcohol in it, by volume, should be allowed to go into the system of a child and strike at his very soul, planting the seed of a future drunkard!

MR. BOK, do you advocate the old maxim, "Of two evils choose the lesser?"

Why choose any evil?

Why trust in the mistakes of humanity at all?

Why not follow our Guide, who has given us a sure remedy and a safe treatment?

MR. BOK most severely arraigns the Women's Christian Temperance Union for their inconsistency, and well may he do so, but the inconsistency is more far-reaching than this.

As long as alcohol is a poison, it is injurious either in health or sickness.

On another page of the *Ladies' Home Journal* advice is given to the young women that "alcohol in any form is unnecessary in health. It is not a natural product."

Is it necessary in disease? When did God Almighty say that alcohol was necessary in disease?

It is the brew and spew of hell.

ZION IS MOST shamefully and abusively criticised and condemned because it declares that the Christ alone is the Healer, and that we must not take into our bodies these accursed poisons.

WHOSE POSITION is safe, that of Zion or that of the world?

CHRISTIAN PEOPLE generally are consuming alcoholic medicines in immense quantities, not only in patent nostrums, but through the prescriptions of the physicians.

Ministers are advocating it, and setting the example.

THE ARRAIGNMENT of Mr. Bok of the religious papers is none too strong.

We quote again:

Let the officers of the Woman's Christian Temperance Union look into the advertising columns of the religious papers of the country, and see how their columns fairly reek with the advertisements of these dangerous concoctions.

Yet in these very same so-called religious papers there are official Woman's Christian Temperance Union columns setting forth the "official" news of the organization and its branches.

A pretty consistent picture do these two portions of the average religious paper present—advocating, with one hand, alcoholic prohibition, or temperance, and receiving, with the other hand, money for advertising—and thereby recommending to their readers—preparations filled ten times over with more alcohol than the beer which fills them with so much horror in the editorial columns!

There are no papers published that are so flagrantly guilty of admitting to their columns the advertisements not only of alcohol-filled medicines but preparations and cure-alls of the most flagrantly obscene nature, as the so-called religious papers of this country. Unable, owing to their small circulations, to obtain the advertising of discriminating advertisers, they are all too ready to accept the most obscene class of advertising—business which the average second-rate secular paper would hesitate or refuse to admit into its columns.

I am speaking whereof I know in this matter.

Beside me, as I write, lie issues of some twenty different "religious" weeklies, the advertising columns of which are a positive stench in the nostrils of decent, self-respecting people.

IT IS a notorious fact that many of the religious papers have sold themselves to the Devil to advertise his nefarious business in the sale of these outrageous so-called medicines, in order that they may gain a few dollars and continue their petty publications.

Better a hundredfold that every such religious organ should be swept off the earth than that it should continue to deceive the people in the purchase of these accursed things.

THE MEN who advertise them are not honest.

The papers that publish them are not honest.

They know that they are deceiving the people.

WE APPEND the list in the *Ladies' Home Journal* as given by Mr. Bok of the so-called patent medicines, which contain large quantities of alcohol:

THE ALCOHOL IN "PATENT MEDICINE."

The following percentages of alcohol in the "patent medicines" named are given by the Massachusetts State Board Analyst, in the published document No. 34:

	Per cent. of alcohol (by volume)
Lydia Pinkham's Vegetable Compound	20.6
Paine's Celery Compound	21.0
Dr. William's Vegetable Jaundice Bitters	18.5
Whiskol, "a non-intoxicating stimulant"	28.2
Colden's Liquid Beef Tonic, "recommended for treatment of alcohol habit"	26.5
Ayer's Sarsaparilla	26.2
Thayer's Compound Extract of Sarsaparilla	21.5
Hood's Sarsaparilla	18.8
Allen's Sarsaparilla	13.5
Dana's Sarsaparilla	13.5
Brown's Sarsaparilla	13.5
Peruna	28.5
Vinol, Wine of Cod-Liver Oil	18.8
Dr. Peter's Kuriko	14.0
Carter's Physical Extract	22.0
Hooker's Wigwam Tonic	20.7
Hoofland's German Tonic	29.3
Howe's Arabian Tonic, "not a rum drink"	13.2
Jackson's Golden Seal Tonic	19.6
Mensman's Peptonized Beef Tonic	16.5
Parker's Tonic, "purely vegetable"	41.6
Schenk's Seaweed Tonic, "entirely harmless"	19.5
Baxter's Mandrake Bitters	16.5
Boker's Stomach Bitters	42.6
Burdock Blood Bitters	25.2
Green's Nervura	17.2
Hartshorn's Bitters	22.2
Hoofland's German Bitters, "entirely vegetable"	25.6
Hop Bitters	12.0
Hostetter's Stomach Bitters	44.3
Kaufman's Sulphur Bitters, "contains no alcohol." (As a matter of fact it contains 20.5 per cent. of alcohol and no sulphur)	20.5
Puritana	22.0
Richardson's Concentrated Sherry Wine Bitters	47.5
Warner's Safe Tonic Bitters	35.7
Warren's Bilious Bitters	21.5
Faith Whitcomb's Nerve Bitters	20.3

In connection with this list, think of beer, which contains only from two to five per cent. of alcohol, while some of these "bitters" contain ten times as much, making them stronger than whisky, far stronger than sherry or port, with claret and champagne way behind.

THINK OF Religious papers advertising such abominable stuff! The General Overseer has often arraigned the press because of its unscrupulous methods in advertising.

WE DESIRE to call attention to a few papers which are on our files.

THE *Southern Presbyterian* advertises the following:

Dr. Blosser Company, Catarrhal Cures. (Recommended by ministers, whose names are given.)
Dr. Marshal's Antiseptic Medicated Air Cure.
Acid Iron Mineral.
Dr. King's New Life Pills.
Vernal Saw Palmetto Berry Wine.
Free Medical Book from Dr. J. Newton Hathaway.
Hall's Catarrh Cure.
Electric Bitters.
Mozley's Lemon Elixir.
Mozley's Lemon Hot Drops.
Bucklen's Arnica Salve.
Piso's Cure for Consumption.
Dr. King's New Discovery for Consumption.
"S. S. S." for malaria.
Wine of Cardui.
"Baby Ease."

IT ALSO gives several most interesting testimonials of what certain "oil cures" have done for cancer, and so forth.

If the editor knows that this is true why does he not let poor, miserable, suffering humanity know that the "oil cure" will do all these wonderful things? It says: "The oil cure was discovered and perfected for the cure of cancer, bronchitis, catarrh, consumption, piles, fistula, eczema, diseases of the eyes, ears, nose, and throat, and in fact all chronic and malignant diseases."

Hallelujah! what a boon this is to humanity—at two dollars a boon!

This man who got up this "balmy oil" is blessed by old men and old women, according to the editor or the proprietor of the *Southern Presbyterian*, and he ought to know.

The *Christian Advocate*, of New York, April 21, 1904, advertises:

Brown's Bronchial Troches for hoarseness.
Hunyadi János for constipation.
Allcock's Porous Plaster for coughs.
Magic Foot Drafts for rheumatism.
Thompson's Eye Water for sore eyes.
Murray's Charcoal Tablets for stomach trouble.
Dr. J. M. Howe's Inhaling Tube for lung and throat disease—(as referred to by Rev. J. M. Buckley, D. D. Endorsed by Bishops Vincent, McCabe, Hartzel.)
Pond's Extract.

The *Christian*, of London, England, March 31, 1904, advertises on the second page—nearly a column display—amidst advertisements of Bibles and religious books:

Phosferine, for nervous dyspepsia, impoverished blood, rheumatism, etc.
Freeman's Chlorodyne, for coughs, colds, asthma, bronchitis.
Congreve's Balsamic Elixir, for asthma, bronchitis, consumption.
Potter's Asthma Cure, for asthma, bronchitis, croup, whooping-cough.

The *Missionary Review*, of New York and London, April, 1904, devotes one whole page advertisement to:

Dr. Sproule, of Boston, as a Catarrh Specialist.

The *Evangelical*, Harrisburg, Pennsylvania, April 21, 1904, advertises:

Dr. Peter's Blood Vitalizer, cures blood impurities and eruptions. Holds an unbroken record of success in treatment of these ailments.

Dr. Miles Grand Dropsy Cure, $3.75 worth sent free, from Elkhart, Indiana.

Christian Leader and *The Way*, of Cincinnati, Ohio, April 26, 1904, advertises:

Hood's Sarsaparilla, blood purifier.
Rheumatism Cure, of John A. Smith, Milwaukee, Wisconsin.

Cancer Cured, by soothing, balmy oils. Cancer, tumor, catarrh, piles, ulcers, etc., Dr. Bye, Kansas City, Missouri.

Mrs. Winslow's Soothing Syrup, for teething children; cures wind colic; best remedy for diarrhea.

Vernal Palmettona.

Vitæ Ore, for rheumatism, Bright's disease, blood poisoning, etc.

Whole page advertisement.

Alabama Baptist, Birmingham, Alabama, April 20, 1904, advertises:

Creath's Anti-Pain Elixir for headache, neuralgia, rheumatism, earache, etc.

Cuticura remedies—Testimony of a mother given, who says her child was healed fourteen years ago through using Cuticura Resolvent, Soap and Ointment.

Paracamph for babies, for croup, choking and strangling.

Capudine for ladies, relief from monthly headaches.

Vernal Palmettona.

Painkiller, for rheumatism.

Tape-Worm Expeller, Dr. M. Neysmith.

Morphine, Opium, and all Drug Habits Cure, Dr. B. M. Woolley, Atlanta, Georgia.

Tetterine, infallible for all Skin Diseases.

Dr. DeWitt's Electric Cure, "immediately relieves Muscular Rheumatism, Asiatic Cholera, Cholera Morbus, Dysentary, Cramps, etc."

Rev. Walker's Famous Dyspepsia Cure, for dyspepsia, nervous indigestion, constipation, and colic.

Xanthine, Prof. Hertz's Great German Hair Restorative.

The Keeley Cure for alcohol, opium, and drug habit.

Elixir Babek, for malaria, chills, fever, la grippe.

Allen's Lung Balsam, Cures Deep-seated Coughs.

The *Wesleyan Herald*, of Philadelphia, Pennsylvania, January 28, 1904, advertises, in editorials:

Radium.

On November 5, 1903, a large amount of space was given to

Radam's Microbe Killer; cure for eczema, bronchitis, consumption, Bright's disease, catarrh, cancer, etc.

MANY OTHERS COULD be cited. The *Baptist Standard* and *Baptist Sunday School Literature* have long been full of objectionable advertisements. There are a few notable exceptions, but there has never been a publication like LEAVES OF HEALING, which has continuously stood against all these advertisements and openly condemned them, and allowed none of them in its columns.

AND IF IT is right and proper to advertise these things in their so-called religious papers, why not advertise them also in the so-called Christian churches?

WE RECOMMEND to the indigent churches that if it is proper for their organs, the church papers, to advertise and get gain from the notorious patent medicine concerns, that they improve their opportunity and privilege in obtaining money in the same way. Let the space on the walls of the interior of the church buildings be advertised for rent and let these patent nostrums be properly set forth upon these walls.

If it is a good thing for the people to use these poisonous medicines, let your pastor become a committee of recommendation and let him provide for the people suitable information as to what is the best remedy for the various diseases with which members of his congregation are afflicted.

We would suggest that over the platform, back of the pulpit, these words be placed:

Ho, every one that thirsteth, come ye to the waters,
And he that hath no money; go ye buy—
Hood's Sarsaparilla is the best Spring tonic.

On the right of the pulpit might be this inscription:

Cursed is the man that trusteth in man and maketh flesh his arm. Dr. Cheatem's Cure Oil for sale at the Parsonage.

On the left side:

King Asa was diseased in his feet and he sought not to Jehovah but to the physicians and he died. Be wise today. Buy Dr. Cheatem's sure cure, Rheumatism Liniment.

So on throughout the building, until the walls are completely covered.

We expect to live to see this carried out, and why not? This would be just as reasonable as to have the preachers and the papers to publicly advocate to the people the use of all these quack remedies.

NO WONDER our beloved Mother Stewart, of Temperance Crusade fame, who has worked with the Woman's Christian Temperance Union and other organizations, in many parts of the world, had to come out of her Methodist Church and out of her organization and come into the Christian Catholic Church in Zion, for in it she found the only consistent opposition against the accursed traffic in alcoholic liquors. And as alcoholic medicines are being upheld by every Christian organization and by almost every Christian minister in all the land, she could no longer consistently remain with the organization in which she labored for so many years.

ZION ONLY is consistent. Our beloved General Overseer is the first and only man who has strongly opposed the use of alcoholic liquor in every form, and not only alcoholic liquors, but the use of poisons of every form for the human body.

THE MEDICAL profession is entirely too ready to accept any new or mysterious agent that may in any possible way be used in healing diseases, and takes for granted, without full investigation, any statement that any so-called scentists may make.

We have many examples of this. There have been hundreds of so-called remedies lauded to the skies at one time, which have since been proved to be useless.

At the present time the newly-discovered element of radium is being much talked about as a possible cancer cure. The idea is simply ridiculous.

The X-rays, and all the other rays, with the electric current and all the others, have had their day in the same way as radium will soon have. Already it is being discredited.

THE MINISTERS in the apostate churches are still more susceptible to this baneful influence of Sorcery. It does seem as though there is no class of people more easily humbugged and more prone to rely upon material remedies than that very class of men who as shepherds of the sheep and teachers of the people profess to put their whole, and sole, and entire reliance upon God.

No wonder the world has lost her confidence in the ministerial profession, and that the preachers have largely lost their influence over society.

The whole question of medical missions is an abominable delusion and a snare; the direct work of the Devil himself in deceiving otherwise good and capable men.

The following extract from the *Gospel Messenger* shows the absurdity of the whole thing:

FROM DAHANU, INDIA.

The month of February was the wedding month this year, but, notwithstanding the fact that the people do not come for medicine on account of our forbidding them the use of the "toddy" (of which they drink freely during their festivals) while we are treating them—we treated seven hundred seventy-eight cases at the Dahanu dispensary. This means an opportunity to touch over twenty-five souls a day, for which we praise the Lord.

Dr. O. H. Yeremian.

The natives do not need to drink their toddy when they come to the Free Dispensary, where they are given alcoholic medicines for the healing of disease, so that opportunity may be had to preach to them the Christ.

The only apology we have to offer for our extended notice of these matters in these Notes is because of their extreme importance.

It has been considered the rankest fanaticism to speak against the medical profession in any way whatever; but Zion has given a practical demonstration of the fact that the doctors are wrong and that the Christ is right, and that the Christ and the doctors do not go hand in hand.

Zion has proved that the only safe and consistent and honest course to pursue is the absolute disuse of so-called medical treatment, and the rational and reasonable and Scriptural use of good living, good food, good clothing, cleanliness, pure life and a trust in God in every time of need.

The truths of Zion are exceedingly beautiful, and the life in Zion is a great and increasing joy day by day.

With clear brains, clean hearts, willing hands, loving, helpful dispositions, and a Godly sentiment running through every department of the life in Zion, there is found in Zion the most full and complete Christian character that the world has ever seen.

The papers generally are calling attention to the continued prosperity of Zion City.

The following extract from the Chicago *Inter Ocean*, of Thursday, April 21, 1904, is a just and fair statement of facts:

THEY PAY THEIR TAXES.

The treasurer of Lake county certifies that Zion City is the only community on his books from which not one cent of taxes is due and unpaid. Probably it is the only community in the United States of anywhere near its size of which such a statement could truthfully be made. The fact that it can be made truthfully of Zion City is commended to the attention of those who see in John Alexander Dowie's ideas nothing but evil.

Mr. Dowie has, indeed, advocated some lines of conduct which do not appeal to common sense, and which at times become even a menace to the public safety. Above all, he would seem at times to have argued his cause with quite unnecessary violence, and to have forgotten that those who fail to agree with him in all things are not therefore necessarily the enemies of all good.

On the other hand, there is abundant testimony that Mr. Dowie's teachings have been beneficial to many of his followers in winning them from vices detrimental to themselves and to society. And in inducing his followers to pay their taxes promptly and in full he has caused them to set an example which shames many of their critics.

The primary duties of a citizen are three: To obey the laws of his country, to fight for his country when need comes, and to support the government which protects him and under which he lives.

How many of their critics equal the Dowieites in prompt and cheerful performance of these three primary duties? Above all, how many communities whose objection to Dowieism has taken the form of mob violence can show Zion City's clean tax record?

Let those who are without sin among us cast the first stone at Zion.

Actual work has begun on the new electric railway, and the prospects are exceedingly favorable for the successful progress of this undertaking.

There are new arrivals daily in our City; people who have come to make this their permanent home.

Inquiries are increasing in number, and the interest is growing at a constantly increasing rate.

One indication of the increased interest in Zion City is shown by the fact that since the 12th day of January, 1904, there has been added to the subscription-list of The Zion Banner one thousand five hundred twenty-one names. These are all regular subscribers who have paid for their own subscriptions.

Leaves of Healing subscription-list has not increased in the same proportion, but there has been a good healthy interest and a continuous growth.

The attendances at the tabernacle services in Zion City are continuously large. The interest is loyal and enthusiastic.

The General Overseer has arrived at Aden, Arabia. He is due to arrive at Marseilles, France, on May 6th. The following cablegram was received Thursday morning:

Aden.

Speicher, Zion City, Illinois.

Read in the 1st chapter of Revelation from the 4th to the 7th verse. Hallelujah. All are well. Love to Zion everywhere. Pray for us. Mizpah.

Dowie.

A cablegram from Overseer Bryant states that he and his party have arrived at Durban, South Africa, safe and well.

It is with rejoicing that the people of South Africa hail their Overseer.

May God graciously bless him, and give him a fruitful harvest is our earnest prayer.

Let Zion pray continuously for all the interests of Zion in Zion City and in all the world, and especially for our beloved General Overseer.

John G. Speicher.

ELIJAH THE RESTORER SHOWS THE VALUE OF AN EARLY START IN CHRISTIAN LIFE.

Around-the-World Visitation

of the

Rev. John Alex. Dowie

Elijah the Restorer
General Overseer of the Christian Catholic Church in Zion.

By ARTHUR W. NEWCOMB, Special Correspondent.

VISITATION AT SYDNEY, NEW SOUTH WALES, AUSTRALIA.

(CONCLUDED.)

THE last paper in this series closed with the report of the meeting held in Sydney Town Hall, on Monday evening, February 15, 1904.

Interview with Sydney Authorities.

On Tuesday, February 16th, Overseer Wilbur Glenn Voliva, in charge of the Christian Catholic Church in Zion in Australasia, accompanied by Dr. A. J. Gladstone Dowie, and Deacon J. S. McCullagh, in charge of the Branch of the Christian Catholic Church in Zion in Sydney, called upon Mr. Garvin, the Inspector-general of the Police of New South Wales, to learn whether the proper protection would be granted the General Overseer and the people who desired to attend the meetings in the Town Hall and listen quietly.

At first the Inspector-general declared that he could not send officers into the hall to keep order, his powers being only to arrest persons on the street, or on proper process served by a magistrate.

He said that he would guarantee that the life of the General Overseer should be protected, but would not make any definite promises as to what steps he would take to keep order and protect life and limb.

Upon being urged to make some definite promise, he became angry, and declared that he had nothing to add to what he had said.

Differing with him as to his statement that he had no power to act within the hall, Overseer Voliva, Dr. Gladstone Dowie, and Deacon McCullagh went to Sir John See, the Premier of New South Wales, and laid the matter before him in a very candid way.

The Premier expressed himself as being in sympathy, to the highest degree, with the desire to keep order in the meetings.

He then called in the Inspector-general of Police, directing him to conduct the party to a private interview with the Honorable B. R. Wise, Attorney-general and Minister of Justice of New South Wales, to get his ruling on the powers of the police in such cases.

The Inspector-general, however, instead of carrying out his orders to the letter, conducted the Zion party to a room by themselves, while he went in and talked with the Attorney-general, before permitting them to see him.

When at last they were admitted, and the matter was taken up, Mr. Wise was found to be in full accord with the Inspector-general, reading a typewritten statement of the law, which provided that an usher might remove from a public service any one who was making a disturbance; but the police had no right to interfere unless the one being removed assaulted the usher.

He was opposed in this ruling by Dr. A. J. Gladstone Dowie, of Zion Law Department, who, aided by the other members of the party, practically forced Mr. Wise to admit that the police had the power to remove, and to place under arrest, if necessary, any one whom the chairman should designate as a disturber of the peace of the assemblage, and to assist in keeping order, on their own motion; although this had not been the custom in Australia.

In accordance with this ruling, the Attorney-general published the following in one of the Sydney morning papers:

PUBLIC MEETINGS.

POWERS OF THE CHAIRMAN.

DUTIES OF CONSTABLES.

OPINION OF THE ATTORNEY-GENERAL.

The Attorney-general has given the following opinion regarding the powers of the chairman of a public meeting, and the duties of constables. In view of the Town Hall gatherings the opinion is important:

"The chairman of a public meeting is entitled by the common law to call upon any disorderly person to behave properly, or else to withdraw from the meeting. If such person refuses to leave when requested by the chairman, and continues to misbehave, the latter may direct the removal of such person from the meeting, using such force as may be reasonably necessary for the disorderly person's expulsion. If police constables are present, they are required to obey the direction of the chairman in this respect. Police constables are also required to act of their own motion to prevent a breach of the peace.

"If a person directed to be removed by the chairman from a meeting for disorderly conduct resists expulsion and lays hands on the person or persons who by the direction of the chairman are removing him, this is an assault which amounts to a breach of the peace, and which justifies such person being given or taken into custody. Mere disorderly conduct short of a breach of the peace, though it might justify ejection, will not justify a person being given into custody.

"The power of removal may be exercised by any persons, such as stewards or managers, who are acting as agents of the chairman for the purpose of maintaining order. But I advise that no police constable take action, except in the event of a breach of the peace, unless by the express direction of the chairman conveyed through his superior officer, and I advise that such officer of police should be stationed in the hall within earshot of the chairman.—B. R. WISE, February 17."

In view of this decision, the Rev. John Stephen McCullagh was appointed chairman of the meeting for that night, Tuesday, February 16, 1904.

The Inspector-general, apparently very much against his will, was obliged to order a large number of police to keep the peace within and outside the Town Hall. The action of the police on that night, however, was a reflection of the attitude of the mind of their chief, Inspector-general Garvin.

The Police of Sydney.

It may be said, in this connection, that the police of Sydney are not as large men physically, on the average, as the police of New York and Chicago, and that their authority seems to be very much less.

They carry no firearms and do not wear batons.

Most of them carry small sticks concealed about their clothing, but these are seldom used, and the larrikins have little fear of them.

The officials reap the reward of their supine policy in dealing with disturbers; for it is not uncommon for a crowd of these lawless ruffians to kick or trample an officer to death in the streets of Sydney.

Cowed by such outrages, and with insufficient backing by the law and their superiors, the police seem afraid to interfere in a disturbance that would quickly evaporate under the fierce glare of a Chicago police star, or a New York police shield.

It is also only too evident that many of the police share the prejudices and hatreds of the mob, being Roman Catholics or Freemasons first, and officers of the law afterward.

This characterization of the Sydney police should not be construed as including the entire force, as there are some strong, brave and conscientious men among them.

As for the rest, they can only escape the brand of "Coward" by admitting that they were in sympathy with the lawlessness that marked the meetings of the Around-the-World Visitation in their city. Even then there is a strong probability that both charges can truthfully be made against them.

But what is to be expected of the rank and file, when the

chief officers are cowardly, *ex-officio* members of the lawless mobs?

The Tuesday Divine Healing Meeting.

While the police matters referred to above were being attended to, the General Overseer was holding his second Divine Healing service in the Town Hall, and for a second time had a most quiet and attentive audience of about five hundred earnest people.

The teaching, as given in the report that follows, speaks for itself, but no words can convey the power with which this teaching came to the people who heard.

It was the Eternal Truth of the Ever-living God, interpreted by His Prophet for these very days, and brought down to an intense practicality of present-day application that was effectual.

Truth that affected the inmost secrets of the spirit, the privacy of the family, the conduct of business, the affairs of state, and the destiny of the world were forced home with a fearlessness and directness that admitted of no dodging the issue.

Purity in the spirit, Cleanliness of the soul, and Obedience to God must precede healing of the body.

There was no use in entering the prayer-room with a load of sin unrepented of, or with a proud rebellious spirit, and the teaching of the Messenger of God was for the purpose of making the conditions clear.

God fulfilled His promise and blessed His Word, and there was an incalculable spiritual refreshing for all who heard with a teachable spirit, whether they were seeking healing or not.

It was especially touching to see with what joy true people of God, both members of the Christian Catholic Church in Zion and friends of Zion, received the words of the Prophet.

Many had long been readers of LEAVES OF HEALING, some had heard the man of God years before when he had proclaimed the truth in Sydney as a Congregational minister and as an independent evangelist, many had heard and read much concerning this man; but all were astonished at his combined wisdom, love, power, knowledge of the Word of God, faith, and effectual fearlessness and earnestness.

"We loved the General Overseer," many said, "before we saw him, but now that we have seen him, we understand him still better, and love him still more. He is even more and better than we thought."

One said, "I had set my ideals of our Leader, God's Prophet, very high indeed; and have more than realized them."

God gave great blessing and victory to Zion in the evening meetings, when the enemy tried so hard to suppress the Voice of the Prophet, but it was in these quiet, deeply spiritual morning Divine Healing Meetings that the greatest individual blessings came to the few hundreds who gathered to hear God's Word proclaimed and His Work made manifest.

The following is a report of the service:

OBEDIENCE IN BAPTISM.

*REPORTED BY E. W. AND A. W. N.

Town Hall, Sydney, New South Wales, Australia, Tuesday Morning, February 16, 1904.

After singing, prayer, and announcements, the General Overseer said:

INVOCATION.

Let the words of my mouth and the meditation of my heart be acceptable in Thy sight, be profitable unto this people, and unto all to whom these words shall come, in this and every land, in this and all the coming time, Till Jesus Come. Amen.

God's Promised Blessings Conditioned on Obedience.

I desire to continue, a little further, the story of the leper, and speak to you briefly on the willingness of God to heal all who fulfil the Divine Conditions.

A great many people imagine that God will do things simply because they ask; that it does not matter about conditions being fulfilled on their part.

There is no such thing as unconditional Salvation, or unconditional Healing, or unconditional Cleansing—all are conditioned on your doing what God tells you.

Obedience is not only better than sacrifice, but the Obedience of Faith is absolutely essential to any Healing from God.

"Without Faith, it is impossible to please God."

Faith takes the form of Obedience, of doing what God says.

The faith that does not obey is no faith at all.

*The following report has not been revised by the General Overseer.

"Why call ye Me, Lord, Lord," the Master said, "and do not the things I say?"

The man that hears and does, is the man that founds his house upon a Rock.

The man that hears and does not, is the man that founds his house upon the sand.

Every one that cometh unto Me, and heareth My words, and doeth them, I will show you to whom he is like.

He is like a man building a house, who digged and went deep, and laid a foundation upon the rock: and when a flood arose, the stream brake against that house, and could not shake it: because it had been well builded.

But he that heareth, and doeth not, is like a man that built a house upon the earth without a foundation; against which the stream brake, and straightway it fell in; and the ruin of that house was great.

If you do not hear and do, you do not dig deep, and do not put your foundation on the Rock.

Your house will go.

Your whole Hope for Eternity will perish.

The willingness of God to heal is conditioned on Obedience.

Repentance.

The first thing that God demands is Repentance.

Repentance means that you shall confess to the extent of your power, not only to God, but to man, every wrong that has been done; that, if you have lied to any, if you have robbed any, whether it be a public or private robbery, you put that robbery right, restore, even if it beggars you, put the wrong right if it sends you to prison, and to the hangman's rope.

There is no use in talking about having Faith until you have repented; for Repentance is precedent to Faith, and essential to Faith.

Repentance is the foundation upon which Faith rests.

When the Christ preached, He said, "Repent ye, and believe the Gospel."

When the Christ preached, He preached "Repentance toward God, and Faith in our Lord Jesus, the Christ."

Some of you do not like to hear about Repentance. You do not want to do right.

You can get no blessing from God, and you have no Faith; for Faith is not born in an impenitent heart.

It cannot be.

Your Repentance must be Real.

Then your Faith must bring Obedience.

There are certain things that you have to do, if you are a Christian.

If you have truly repented and believed, you must be baptized.

Baptism Commanded.

On the Day of Pentecost, when they cried out under conviction, "Brethren, what shall we do?" Peter said: "Repent ye, and be baptized every one of you in the Name of Jesus, the Christ, unto the remission of your sins, and ye shall receive the Gift of the Holy Spirit."

When our Lord gave the Great Commission to His Apostles, He said:

Go ye therefore, and make disciples of all the nations, baptizing them into the Name of the Father and of the Son and of the Holy Spirit:

Teaching them to observe all things whatsoever I commanded you, and lo, I am with you all the Days, even unto the Consummation of the Age.

The command is, that when disciples are made, they are to be baptized.

There is no Baptism possible, therefore, for one that has not repented and believed.

Baptism Is Not An Ordinance for Babies.

A baby cannot repent.

Did you ever try to get one to?

I had dear babies—one of them now bigger than myself, who sits here.

When he was a little fellow, I used to lift him up, and he would make a dive for my hair, then for my beard, and then pull.

I would say, "You young sinner, repent."

He would only laugh at me, and take another handful.

Did you ever get a baby to repent of anything?

Babies do not repent. They do not know how to repent.

There are some of you who are worse than babies; you know how, and you will not. [Applause.]

You applaud that sentiment—is it not true?

It is a very sad state of affairs.

The Christ says that you must be baptized.

What Is Baptism?

It is an Ordinance for penitent sinners who believe, bring forth fruits meet for Repentance, and who are willing to obey.

You cannot find one instance in the Bible showing that a baby was baptized.

If you can, I will give it up, and acknowledge that babies may be baptized.

It is not in the Bible.

The Christ took the babies in His arms, laid His hands upon them and blessed them.

We have a service in Zion every month, called the Consecration and Presentation of Young Children to God.

I sometimes consecrate as many as two hundred babies on one Lord's Day morning.

Zion City is a great place for babies.

A paper in this city has said that the death rate among Zion City babies is very high.

That is a lie.

It was copied from some yellow journal in America.

In a recent six weeks in Zion City, during the coldest part of winter, when the thermometer was often below zero, we did not have one death in all our population of many thousands.

Could you say that of any ten thousand or even eight thousand people in one community in Australia?

You know you could not.

I consecrate these babies.

I like to lay my hands upon them, and bless them.

Children in Zion.

The mothers like to present them.

They are presented to God, and the Christian Catholic Church in Zion takes a great interest in its little children.

We have them trained from the beginning.

We have little children in Zion City, seven years of age, who read music.

Hundreds of them sing beautifully, step in time, and are a part of our great choir of six hundred voices.

I went out, with great love, to see the place where I once preached, the Congregational Church at Newtown.

I was very much interested, but as I looked at it, I said, "This place has shrunk." But it had not; I had expanded.

Our Choir in Zion City could not find room in that church.

You must obey; my people do; they were baptized properly.

Baptism Must Be by Three Dippings.

You may say, "I agree with you, Doctor, about immersion."

Zion's thousands were immersed three times, and you miserable Baptists have been dipped only once. [Laughter.]

"Oh, but that is enough," you say. "We were baptized into the death of the Christ."

Then you remain dead.

But that is not what the Christ said. He said, "Baptizing them into the Name of the Father, and of the Son, and of the Holy Spirit."

If I were to tell you to dip this handkerchief into the black, and the blue, and the yellow dye, how many times would you have to dip it?

Voices—"Three times."

General Overseer—And if I say to you, I baptize you into the Name of the Father, and of the Son, and of the Holy Spirit, do you not know that is a Triune Immersion?

Do you not know, you Church of England people, that there never was any other form of Baptism in your church until lately?

Take Smith and Cheetham's "Dictionary of Christian Antiquities."

Under the head of Baptism, Canon Marriot says in Volume I., page 161:

> Triple Immersion, that is thrice dipping the head while standing in the water, was the all but universal rule of the Church in early times. Of this we find proof in Africa, in Palestine, in Egypt, at Antioch and Constantinople, in Cappadocia. For the Roman usage, Tertullian indirectly witnesses in the Second Century; Saint Jerome in the Fourth; Leo the Great in the Fifth; and Pope Pelagius and Saint Gregory the Great in the Sixth. Theodulf of Orelans witnesses for the general practice at his time, the close of the Eighth Century. Lastly, the Apostolical Canons, so-called, alike in the Greek, the Coptic, and the Latin versions give special injunctions as to this observance, saying that any bishop or presbyter should be deposed who violated this rule.

There was not one church, in all the churches of Christendom, that broke this rule until, in the seventh century, the national Council of the Church of Spain, at Toledo, permitted one dipping and sprinkling because heretics were abusing the triune form.

Sprinkling and single immersion are innovations.

Take your Greek Dictionary, and you will see that the word *baptizo* (βαπτίζω), means to dip repeatedly, being the frequentative form of the simple word *bapto* (βάπτω), to dip.

The Greek church retains the form of Triune Immersion to this day, and they understand the Greek language better than you or I.

It is not the form that matters so much as what the form represents.

Signification of Triune Immersion.

It is not only being baptized into the Death of our Lord Jesus, the Christ; but those who are so baptized are to be baptized also into His Resurrection, and they are to walk with Him in Newness of Life.

These are the three things in Baptism: Death to Sin, Life in God, and Power for Service.

The difference between the Christian Catholic Church in Zion and other churches is that our people realize that when they are baptized they are to seek for Death from sin and Life in God—walking with Him in Newness of Life—and have Power for Service.

Repentance toward God, and Faith in our Lord Jesus, the Christ, brings us Death to Sin, Death to Self, Death to the World, Death to its Influences, and utter indifference to what it says, does, thinks, or threatens.

Life in God gives Power to serve Him, to use our bodies as well as our spirits for Him.

You had better get baptized properly, and you had better get baptized quickly. There is only one true Baptism.

We have "One Lord, One Faith, One Baptism."

That One God is in Three Persons, Father, Son, and Holy Spirit.

That One Faith covers Three things, Salvation, Healing, and Holy Living.

That One Baptism is a Triune Baptism, and into the Name of the Father, and of the Son, and of the Holy Spirit.

We have a Triune God, a Triune Faith, and a Triune Baptism.

Other baptisms are innovations.

I am an old-fashioned, conservative, old follower of the Lord.

Great Ecclesiastical Authorities Who Favored Triune Immersion.

I do not want a new Baptism.

I tell the Church of England people that there used to be a form of anointing for healing, and there used to be a form of Triune Baptism.

I tell you Methodists that John Wesley refused to baptize in any other way than by Triune Immersion.

It is in his own journals.

Luther, in the early part of his life, when he became a Reformer, was asked how people should be baptized. He said, "By Triune Immersion."

He directed that a Jewish convert, a woman, should be put in water up to her neck, and then dipped three times.

The Schaff-Herzog "Encyclopedia of Religious Literature" will confirm what I have said as to Triune Immersion being the one original, primitive form of Baptism.

The "Encyclopedia Britannica" will say the same thing, as well as "Chambers'."

You must toe the line and obey, and be baptized properly.

Obedience Not a Slavish Following of Example.

A Voice—"Was the Savior immersed three times?"

General Overseer—I am telling you what the Savior commanded. What He commanded is enough.

The Savior said "Baptizing them into the Name of the Father, and of the Son, and of the Holy Spirit;" and if the Savior had never been baptized, I should simply say, I do not care, He ordered us to be baptized in this way.

The Savior Himself was the Son of Man and Son of God.

There was a Triune Manifestation of God at His Baptism; for the Father spoke from heaven, and the Holy Spirit came in the form of a dove.

Possibly John the Baptist may not have immersed three times, but I think he did, because the word Baptize meant just the same thing there as it means in the Ordinance that the Christ commanded, and that is to dip repeatedly.

There is only One Baptism, and you are disobedient if you do not obey the Command to be baptized into the Name of the Father, and of the Son, and of the Holy Spirit.

Baptism Not Necessary to Salvation.

A Voice—"Is it necessary to Salvation?"

General Overseer—No, it is not necessary to Salvation.

The only thing that is necessary to Salvation is Repentance toward God, and Faith in our Lord Jesus, the Christ.

Baptism, however, is essential to Obedience and complete blessing. It is essential to power.

I lay stress upon it because the Lord laid stress upon it.

It is the command He gave. When He commands Baptism, you must obey.

Cornelius, the Centurion, was saved, and blessed, and the Holy Spirit had come upon him; but Peter said, "Can any man forbid the water, that these should not be baptized, which have received the Holy Spirit as well as we?"

Then he commanded Cornelius to be baptized.

This is a very important matter.

Multitudes of you Christians are unbaptized, and disobedient.

You are not getting power because you are not obeying.

The Diabolical Lie of Baptismal Regeneration.

Your baptism of babies is an abomination!

Your baptism of babies with your god-mother and god-father is a lie.

You know perfectly well that they take vows they never keep; that there are multitudes of men and women, who stand up half drunk and renounce the World, the Flesh and the Devil on behalf of the baby, when they are full of the World, the Flesh and the Devil themselves.

You know very well that there are people who take these vows in dozens in some churches, and if there is no god-father or god-mother present they get the janitor and his wife to come up and tell the lie.

It is an abomination!

It is a wrong!

It is a shame to say that the child's heart is changed by a little drop of water on its nose.

One reason men do not get blessing after they become Christians, is that they do not get properly baptized.

I am not saying that Baptism will make you a Christian.

I am not saying that Baptism is essential to Salvation.

I am not saying that the Lord's Supper is; for the Lord saved the penitent thief upon the cross, who was neither baptized nor tasted a Lord's Supper until he tasted it in paradise.

Loss of Blessing Through Disobedience.

If you are to be a real Christian, you must not stop at being saved; you must obey God.

One reason many of you do not get healing is because you do not obey God.

You do not get answers to prayers.

You do as you like, and you go as you please, and therefore you become useless.

You are not brave, you are not strong.

You do not master the Devil; the Devil masters you.

I believe that this Baptism in Zion counts for much.

Many have gone down into that Baptismal stream who were sick and dying, and there they have been healed.

Let us all promise to obey God.

Every one who intends to obey God stand and tell Him so.

[The greater part of the audience rose.]

PRAYER OF CONSECRATION

My God and Father, in Jesus' Name I come to Thee. Take me as I am. Make me what I ought to be in spirit, in soul, in body. Give me a True Repentance, a Real Faith, a Real Baptism, a Real Newness of Life in the Power of Thy Spirit. For Jesus' sake. [*All repeat the prayer, clause by clause, after the General Overseer.*]

BENEDICTION.

Beloved, abstain from all appearance of evil. And may the very God of Peace Himself sanctify you wholly; and I pray God your whole spirit and soul and body be preserved entire, without blame, unto the coming of our Lord Jesus, the Christ. Faithful is He that calleth you, who also will do it. The grace of our Lord Jesus, the Christ, the love of God, our Father, the fellowship of the Holy Spirit, our Comforter and Guide, one Eternal God, abide in you, bless you and keep you, and all the Israel of God everywhere, forever. Amen.

After the Benediction the Messenger of God prayed with many sick, with laying on of hands.

God greatly blessed.

On the afternoon of Tuesday, February 16th, a most delightful summer day, the General Overseer and party, accompanied by Overseer Voliva and Deacons McCullagh and Hawkins, went for a short trip in Sydney Harbor, seeing several places of interest, and enjoying the splendid view of Sydney and its environs.

There was a fresh breeze, and the little gasoline launch that had been engaged to carry the party, danced like a cork on the waves, but there was no danger, and the ride was an exhilarating recreation in the midst of the strenuous life that all had been leading since our arrival in Sydney.

The Tuesday Evening Meeting.

It was long before six o'clock that night when the people began to gather at the Town Hall for the evening meeting.

Sydney was stirred as it never had been before.

Every moment the crowds grew.

From all directions and from every class of people they came, and the same name was in every mouth.

The newspapers had pretended to describe the scenes of disorder of the previous night, attempting to make light of them, and to lay the trouble to the charge of the speaker and his people.

They had published garbled reports of his addresses of the Lord's Day and Monday, alleging that the voice of the speaker was thin and disagreeable, that the singing was weak and poor, and that the meetings were most dreary and uninteresting, causing a large part of the audience to leave early.

And yet, two and one-half hours before the service, here were thousands of people gathering to hear this "thin, disagreeable voice," this "weak, unmusical singing," and to attend these "dreary, uninteresting meetings!"

Why?

Whether they knew it or not, whether the papers would have them or not, and whether they themselves would or not, the people of Sydney were compelled to hear the Voice of the Prophet of the Restoration.

It was not anything that he had said, and it was not anything that he was reported to have said, that brought such multitudes together.

This same teaching had been given in Sydney again and again by officers of the Christian Catholic Church in Zion.

It was not mere curiosity to see and hear a man concerning whom they had read that made thousands stand, for hours, in a crush, at the doors of the Town Hall, sacrificing time, comfort, and even safety in order to get an opportunity to enter.

Many men of international reputation had visited and spoken in Sydney, and yet this scene was unprecedented.

It was because of what he *is*, that the people, consciously or unconsciously, were determined, some to see and hear John Alexander Dowie, others to prevent his voice being heard.

The hall was full to overflowing long before the time for the service to begin, and the police were compelled to close the doors in order to prevent serious overcrowding.

Then ensued a remarkable scene.

Thousands upon thousands of people surrounded the building, filling the great, broad steps on three sides, with a surging, impatient throng, against whom the few almost invertebrate police were practically powerless.

It was with the greatest difficulty that the General Overseer himself got into the building, having to pass through a great crowd of people packed so tightly together that it was only after hard work by the members of the party and a few police that a passage was forced through.

Among those who failed to get into the building that night, on account of the great crowds that surrounded it, was Deacon Ernest Williams, the General Overseer's special stenographer for the Around-the-World Visitation.

In consequence we have no stenographic report of that evening's service.

There was even wilder disorder than on the preceding evening, prior to the opening of the meeting, and it was evident that an organized mob was present, determined that God's Prophet should not be heard.

It was also very plain to be seen that there were many good, orderly citizens present, who desired to hear quietly, and who were highly indignant at the behavior of the mob.

On this night, as on the previous night, the police were almost useless, doing nothing on their own initiative to keep order, and acting with exceeding reluctance when called upon to do so by the deputies of the chairman of the meeting.

The General Overseer's Message was on the subject, taken from the question of Pilate, "What Shall I Do With Jesus?"

It was a powerful Message, full of love and the Spirit of the Christ.

It was a wonderful sight to see that great Prophet of God stand, with uplifted hands and calm, clear voice, and proclaim and enforce the Messianic Kingship of His Lord, in the face of that demoniac mob.

In the little lulls in the storm of yells, catcalls, stamping of feet, and other hideous noises, the man of God succeeded in uttering a Message of Truth which was heard by several thousands, who deeply sympathized with him in his declaration of his right to a hearing in a land that boasted its liberty, and held, as one of its most valuable heritages, the right of Free Speech.

The General Overseer not only delivered his Message, but warned the people of Sydney that this most precious freedom would be theirs no longer, once the mob was permitted to get the upper hand as it was in these meetings, through the cowardice or connivance of the police.

His Message made a profound impression, and has already borne fruit.

His warning was heard by thousands and read by many thousands more, and it will be remembered in the day when that irresponsible mob, flushed with a sense of its own power, drunken with lawlessness already committed, mad with a score of hellish lusts, and led by devils incarnate, shall bring in its Reign of Terror.

As the meeting progressed the disorder increased.

Every ejection of one of those who flagrantly disturbed the service brought forth a roar from the mob, all of whom would then stand on their chairs and make a hero of the one who was being removed.

The police did not assist in keeping out those who had no tickets, indeed, insisted that the doors should be kept open; thus those who were expelled at one door returned by another, to take still more active part in the disturbance, until pandemonium reigned all but supreme.

The General Overseer was able to close his Message and pronounce the Benediction upon a fairly orderly audience; but immediately afterwards, unbridled lawlessness took possession of the hall, which for many minutes, sounded as though filled with screaming demons.

Murderous Rioters Demand Their Prey.

Meanwhile, a still larger crowd gathered outside, watching every exit and howling like hungry wolves for the General Overseer to come out.

Instead of walking out into their midst, which would probably have meant another case of kicking and trampling to death, such as the larrikins deal out to the police who fall into their hands, the General Overseer passed quietly out by a little-used door, and was escorted thence to his cab by the members of his party and a squad of police and detectives.

In some way the mob got word that he had left the building, and immediately there was the rush of thousands of feet from the Town Hall to the Australia Hotel, and the hoarse cries of thousands of voices shouting, "We want Dowie!"

By the time his cab arrived at the hotel the street in front was crowded with a raging mob, shrieking over and over again their candid slogan, "We want Dowie!"

When the cab came up, the horse was seized by the bits and the vehicle by the wheels.

The cabman was brave and acted quickly, putting his whip to the horse; in a moment those who had made the attack were thrown back, and the cab, with its burden, was beyond their reach.

As the curtains had been drawn, they could not be quite sure that it was the General Overseer who had passed, so the crowd remained in front of the hotel howling, "We want Dowie," for about half an hour, when they were driven away from the door by the police. Even then they remained about half a block away, on each side, until far into the night.

Meantime, Dr. A. J. Gladstone Dowie, Overseer Voliva, and the other members of the party had reached the hotel in safety, and were discussing the probable movements of their beloved Leader.

It was decided that, since he had escaped the mob at the door, he was perfectly safe, and would either go to some other hotel until later, or to the home of some friend in the city.

Such proved to be the case, for it was not long before a telephone message was received from Colonel Stern, who was with him, stating that he had gone to the home of Deacon and Deaconess McCullagh, and would be at the hotel in the course of about three-quarters of an hour.

At the appointed time all was quiet, and the General Overseer and his personal attendant drove up and entered without incident, except that a reporter was there to tell of the return in the next morning's paper.

The Wednesday Morning Divine Healing Meeting.

Knowing that it was to be the last of the Divine Healing meetings in Sydney, a greater number of people than usual were in attendance on Wednesday morning, February 17, 1904, in the Town Hall.

They were well repaid for coming.

As on the other mornings of the Visitation in Sydney, the General Overseer threw his whole being into the teaching of God's Truth concerning the redemption of man's spirit, soul, and body.

Straightforward, unequivocal, and unmistakable was the teaching, and so simple that even a child could understand.

The sinful heard with conviction, and there were many that turned away from their sins and sought the Way to the Father by a True Repentance.

The sick heard with joy, for it was a Message of Hope in the midst of the pain, weariness and sorrow of their afflictions.

The children of God, who were well, heard with thanksgiving, for the Message was one of deep spiritual power, mighty for the upbuilding of stronger, more efficient Christian character.

The following is a report of the service:

Sydney Town Hall, Wednesday Morning, February 17, 1904.

After singing, the reading of the 8th chapter of Matthew by Deacon C. Friend Hawkins, prayer, and announcements, the General Overseer said:

THE HUMANITY OF THE CHRIST.

*REPORTED BY E. W. AND A. W. N.

INVOCATION.

Let the words of my mouth and the meditation of my heart be acceptable in Thy sight, and profitable unto this people, O Lord, my Strength, and my Redeemer.

You have had read to you that which I consider the most wonderful part of the New Testament in connection with the teaching of Divine Healing.

Divine Healing a Fact.

There was a time when the foolish press, and the still more foolish pulpit said that there were no healings, and that Divine Healing was a myth.

I will show them some witnesses.

I have not made any arrangement with you to testify this morning, but I ask every one in this assembly who has been healed through faith in Jesus, the Christ, to stand. [About one hundred stood.]

General Overseer—Did I ask you to come here to testify?

Witnesses—"No."

General Overseer—Did I ever charge you anything for any service I ever rendered you?

Witnesses—"No."

General Overseer—Did any member or officer of this Church?

Witnesses—"No."

General Overseer—Has this healing come to you through faith in Jesus, the Christ?

Witnesses—"Yes."

General Overseer—You give Him the glory?

Witnesses—"Yes."

General Overseer—You look to be a hundred sane persons.

I do not see any sign of insanity about you, or foolish fanaticism. You are quiet, good citizens, good-looking men and

*The following report has not been revised by the General Overseer.

women, some old, some young, some middle-aged, some only youths, but the majority are mothers and fathers.

I thank God that, without any previous arrangement, a hundred persons are on their feet this morning.

A lady told me yesterday, "General Overseer, I was healed by God, through your prayers, of disease of the kidneys, when dying, twenty-six years ago."

A Broken Elbow Instantly Healed.

I recognize the face of a sister here, whose boy had smashed his arm at the elbow, when delivering a telegram to Sir James Martin.

They could do nothing with it at the hospital.

It would not stay set and the boy was in pain night and day.

I prayed with him and he moved his fingers immediately. Then he moved his arm and carried a book in his hand.

He had his picture taken in a few days.

He came in to see me the other night with his mother, Mrs. Dillon.

Is that true?

Mrs. Dillon—"The splints were taken off before he went to the hall. I am glad that God healed him."

That testimony would be an impropriety in some meetings, but any Lord's Day in Shiloh Tabernacle, in Zion City, if I asked the healed to stand, they would stand in thousands to witness to Divine Healing.

You cannot pooh these facts away with a word.

The people are healed of all kinds of deadly diseases.

God is still the Healer, and God has still the glory.

When even was come they brought unto Him many possessed with devils and He cast out the spirits with a Word.

The Christ Did Not Cast Out Evil Spirits With His Own Word.

It was not His Word.

The Revision has it correctly with "a" Word.

It was the Word of the Father; for the Christ Himself said, "The words that I say unto you I speak not of Myself: but the Father abiding in Me, doeth His works."

This Word was the Word of the Father; and you will remember that the Christ always spoke the Paternal Word, the Father speaking in Him.

He said, for instance, when He healed the paralyzed man who was let down through the open roof, "Son, thy sins be forgiven."

That was the Father speaking.

When He healed the woman who touched the hem of His garment, He said, "Daughter." That was the Father speaking.

It was the Father speaking through the Christ, and the Father working through the Christ.

He said, "I can of Myself do nothing," not even one little thing.

It was the power of the Father, the Power of the Spirit within Him.

He had emptied Himself. He had laid aside His own power and Godhead.

The Christ Still Wears His Human Nature.

He came to us in His humanity, and He did not resume His Divine Nature, even when He rose from the dead, because He wears that human nature still.

He is a Great High Priest who wears a glorified human body.

He will come back in a glorified human body, and He will reign in a glorified human body.

Then, when the end is come, He will deliver up the Kingdom to God, even the Father, the Eternal Word.

For the purposes of Atonement, Mediation, and Restoration, the Christ retains a human nature.

Though now exalted up on high,
He bends on earth a Brother's eye.

It is the great High Priesthood, full of human sympathy that He exercises.

He is still compassionate to the ignorant, and He is still full of sympathy for the sinful and the suffering.

"We have not a high priest that cannot be touched with the feeling of our infirmities; but One that hath been in all points tempted like as we are, yet without sin."

It is a great thing to remember the humanity of the Christ, and that the Mediator that we have between God and man is the Man Christ Jesus, the Man of Sorrows, who is still the Man of Sympathies.

I am glad that He is a Man, and that I know something of what He feels, because I too am a man.

Though not as He, a sinless man, I am what He has made me. That brings me into sympathy with His humanity.

When He comes, we shall see the Son of Man in His glory.

He will sit upon the Throne of His Glory, and will rule this earth. There will be none in office anywhere, except those whom He appoints.

By-and-by, when the Millennium is finished, and the Last Conflict in the Millennium is fought, He will triumph.

The Millennium Not a Time of Perfect Peace.

But the Millennium is not to be a time of perfect peace, as some people imagine.

The Millennium, the Thousand Years of the Christ's reign, will undoubtedly be years of conflict, because it is only at the end that He finally triumphs.

You read in the Book of the Revelation, that the last great conflict, at the end of the Thousand Years, will be a most terrific conflict, and that then the Fire of God will come from heaven and destroy the adversary.

Then the Kingdom of God shall be established.

If any one is looking for a Millennium of perfect peace, he is mistaken.

The Peace will be in us, and in those who are with Him, and He will reign in Zion at Jerusalem.

But there will be multitudes of those who hate Him and hate His reign who will fight, and throughout the Millennium He will reign until He hath put all enemies under His feet.

He will continue to do so, until the Day is finished.

The Day of the Lord is a thousand years long.

That is the Millennial Day, and that Day is not far distant.

Its dawn is almost in the eastern sky.

The beginning of the Restoration of All Things is my ministry.

Overlapping of the Dispensations.

I desire to speak very plainly and simply, because the Dispensations overlap. They always have overlapped.

The Dispensation that is to come is now being overlapped in the approaching Consummation of All Things.

That is what I am here to talk about.

I remind you that, even now, our Lord speaks simply as a Man.

He pleads as a Man.

It is the Man Christ Jesus, who is the Mediator between God and man.

It is the Man Christ Jesus who comes to us today and says, "Wilt thou be made whole?"

It is the Man Christ Jesus "the healing of whose seamless dress is by all beds of pain."

It is He whom we can "touch in life's throng and press, and be made whole again."

It is the Man Christ Jesus who stands at the sinner's door and knocks, and "beneath the crowned hair, the patient eyes so tender, of Thy Savior waiting there," are the eyes of a Holy Man.

The pierced hand still knocks, and the Voice that once spoke from the cross and cried "*Tetclesti!*"—It is finished!—still speaks.

The Sympathetic Word of the Sympathetic Christ, by His Spirit is still heard everywhere.

The Christ Died for Our Sicknesses.

When the even was come, they brought unto Him many possessed with devils and He cast out the spirits with a word, and healed all that were sick: that it might be fulfilled which was spoken by Isaiah the prophet, saying, Himself took our infirmities and bare our diseases.

If this is true—and it is true—if the Bible is true, then the Christ died for our sicknesses.

If you say that He died for our sins only, you mistake, because it was prophesied of Him long ago: "With His stripes we are healed."

He came not only to save, but to heal, and He is just the same today as He was nineteen centuries ago.

He is the same Savior.

He is the same Healer.

He is the same Cleanser.

He is the same Keeper.

If He is not the same, then the Bible is a lie, and He tells us what is not true; for He says, "I am the Lord, I change not," and the Word of God declares that "Jesus, the Christ, is the same yesterday and today, yea, and forever."

He is present with us.

Some will tell you that He is not here.

If He is not here, He spoke falsely; for He said, "Go ye therefore, and make disciples of all the nations, baptizing them into the Name of the Father and of the Son and of the Holy Spirit: teaching them to observe all things whatsoever I commanded you: and lo, I am with you All the Days, even unto the Consummation of the Age."

If He is not with us All the Days, then He said what is not true.

But it is true, and He is with us.

> Where'er we seek Thee, Thou art found,
> And every place is hallowed ground.

So I desire to remind you that you cannot be where He is not.

> All scenes alike engaging prove
> To hearts now filled with God's own love;
>
> But regions none remote I call—
> Secure in finding God in all.

If we could be cast where God is not, then He would not be an Omnipresent God.

God's Presence Reaches Into Hell.

"Oh, He is not in hell," you say.

I am glad to know that He is.

I am glad to know that the Christ descended into hell.

I am glad to know that if a man make his bed in hell, even there shall His right hand find him.

There are multitudes in Sydney and in all great cities who make their bed in hell from night to night and from day to day; but the Hand of the mighty God is reaching down into the bed of the adulteress and the adulterer.

God is speaking to them in the depth of their sin and their wickedness.

God's Hand will reach you.

You will not go to heaven if you reject Him, but He will seek you until He finds you, until your heart submits to Him; for it is written, "He is the Savior of All men."

Oh the depths of the riches of His grace!

It is written, He "hath shut up all unto disobedience, that He might have mercy upon All."

"It is written, "I, if I be lifted up from the earth, will draw All men unto Myself."

It is written, "As in Adam all die, so also in the Christ shall All be made alive."

It is written that He will seek the lost until He finds them.

He will seek them through the darkest abysses of Despair.

He will never give up the search until the last is brought home; until Sin is destroyed, and Death and Hell are cast into the Lake of Fire.

Final Restoration of All Men to God.

I believe with all my heart, and without any hesitation whatever, that He is the Savior of All men, and that He who was lifted up will yet draw All men unto Him.

That Shepherd will seek the wandering and the lost, not only in earth and in time, but beyond the grave, in hell.

He who preached to the spirits in prison, to those who had rejected God in the days of Noah, will preach to the spirits in prison whither they go until He brings them back to God.

You can never get away from Him.

Prodigal child, you may go into the wilderness and try to eat the husks fed to the swine.

You may sin and be without hope, but the Mercy of Jehovah endureth forever, and He will seek His children until He finds them and restores them.

It is an awful thing that some people will go through hell to get to heaven. They do it now.

Instead of yielding to God they go into sin, and into shame, and into folly, and into drunkenness, and into infidelity, intemperance and impurity.

They go through hell, a living hell, and then at last they yield themselves to God.

But what do they bring to God?

They bring a withered life, a wasted body.

They bring to God an enfeebled mind; and although I am thankful that they are saved, they are not much when they are saved.

Bringing to God the End of a Worn-out Life.

There are a great many people who get Salvation after they have been living in a condition of damnation for years.

There are some who make a great to-do over these poor restored ones; but, my friends, let me tell you, it were better for you to have found God as a child, and to have lived and served Him, and never wandered from Him.

It were better for you to have resisted temptation, and to have walked in the ways of Wisdom and Salvation all your life.

I am glad I did not have to be saved when I became a man.

I gave my heart to God as soon as I knew Him.

I am glad I have loved Him and served Him all the way.

While I rejoice over those who have been saved after a wasted life, I tell you that it were far better for you never to have passed through that hell of sin and misery, and then come to God with withered powers, so that, even when you are saved, God Himself cannot make much of you.

Danger of Parading Past Lives of Sin and Shame.

I hear too much of this crying out about the prize-fighter and the drunkard and the harlot being saved.

Some of them make their testimonies so disgusting that they seem almost to glory in their shame.

It is a shame to speak of the lives that some of you have lived.

It is a shame to think of it; it is a disgrace to talk about it.

You should keep secret the great depths out of which God has taken you; for it pollutes people to hear the details of the shameless life of a harlot, of an adulterer, of a thief, and of a drunkard.

If you keep parading it, the probabilities are that you will go back to your sin, and have to be dragged out again.

Try to think pure thoughts, and get away from evil associations and then you will be more soundly saved.

May God prevent you from parading your old sores, and your old sins.

Be ashamed that you lived that life.

Be grateful that you are saved, but do not make a parade of the dirty cesspits from which you were taken, and all the filthy diseases which you contracted in your sin, and all the filthy thoughts that you thought then.

These are not profitable things.

I make this remark because through a very wide experience, and a long knowledge of humanity, I have found that the talking about past sins, the reading of these things, is liable to pollute the imagination, and injure those to whom these things are spoken.

Let us keep as clean as we can.

Let us speak the pure and good things.

The Christ does not want us to be eternally talking about how the Devil once used us.

Let us see that God uses us, and let others say it too, and walk humbly with God.

Be Not Many Teachers.

I like to see people who are not too eager to teach.

> Be not many teachers, my brethren, knowing that we shall receive heavier judgment.

A great many people stand up to teach who are not taught.

There is a great deal of misunderstanding and blundering because people who are not taught are attempting to teach.

It is one thing to testify to what God has done for you, and it is another thing to teach.

The man who has been saved can say, "I am saved, thank God," but when he attempts to teach, he is apt to blunder very seriously, because a witness is not always a teacher.

In order to be a teacher you must be a learner, and a learner must be obedient, and take a long time in preparation.

You may witness for God.

Be a sincere disciple and learner.

Some day God will give you a Word of Wisdom to utter, a word or two of clear teaching; but you will never be a power unless you are humble and learn.

My dear people I suppose are among the most active workers in the world.

They go forward and witness in thousands, spending their own money and their own time, but they never presume to teach, unless they are sent forth to teach.

The teaching is left to those who are teachers in the Church of God.

The teacher must be carefully taught, carefully selected, carefully ordained and carefully drilled.

Even then I sometimes have to bring back from the field teachers who have taught foolish things.

I say this because my heart is very sore when I see so much time wasted because of people pretending to teach.

It is right to testify to what God has done for you, but do not set up as teachers.

Teachers Are Very Few.

Whether it be in religion, education, commerce or politics, the great teachers are very few.

If the great teachers are really teachers, they have been for a long time learning; they have been for a long time testing their teaching, and are qualified to teach.

Those who are the least presumptuous in teaching, knowing that there is so much more to be learned than they know, are oftentimes the greatest.

When people say to me, "Do you know all about Divine Healing?" I say, "No. I leave that to be said by the people who know very little."

A woman came to me some time ago seeking healing. "O Doctor," she said, "I have all the faith in the world."

I said to my personal attendant, "Send for my photographer to take a photograph of the woman who has all the faith in the world; I want to preserve her picture."

She said: "What do you mean."

"Are you not very sick?" I asked.

"Yes," she replied.

"Have you had faith for your own healing?"

"No."

"Then I think that you lie when you say that you have all the faith in the world. What did you come to me for if you have all the faith in the world? I have not. I have a little faith."

I am like Sir Isaac Newton, who said, when somebody praised him for his profound knowledge, "I do not know what you say. I know that I am a little child who wanders by the seashore picking here and there a pebble on the sand while the great Ocean of Truth lies unexplored before me." The discoverer of many laws, and especially of the Law of Gravitation, humbly stated this of himself.

I have noticed, however, that people who are not teachers profess to know everything and know nothing.

I know some things, and I hope to know more, but I shall never know more unless I keep humble, strive to maintain a constant earnestness, and know that I do not know, and that there is more light to break out than I have ever known before.

There Are Some Things That We Do Know.

We do know that a truly penitent sinner, one whose Repentance is sincere, deep and true, who has put things right with God and man, who is desirous to do right in God's sight, who is willing to obey God in every Ordinance, to fall into line, and to humbly take his place in the Kingdom of God, will not miss the blessing of Divine Healing, if he turns aside from all others, and gives himself to God alone.

But the prating, impudent-talking, foolish people, who can guide their guides, and instruct their teachers, who go as they like and do as they please, and are not willing to be under any restraint whatever—these are the people who run amuck in the religious life.

They are like those who have engines on a railway and run upon their own schedule time.

They are a danger to themselves, and to all the trains that run upon that line.

The only thing to do is to arrest them and side-track every train, and make them stay there.

Order Essential in the Kingdom of God.

The Lord Jesus, the Christ, will not have you people running about and opening up Gospel shops wherever you like, and teaching just as you please, setting yourselves up as authorities.

You have to get into line, and be under rule, and be instructed.

You cannot undertake the bravest things in connection with life; you who are only just out of the depths of sin, and whose own lives are far from right.

Be instructed!

Be wise!

Be patient!

Get into line, and await God's time for you to be properly set apart for work by competent authorities.

God is the God of Order, and not of confusion.

He has established His Kingdom, and His Church.

In the Church there are first apostles, and then prophets; then teachers, then all the varied gifts as set forth in the first Epistle to the Corinthians, 12th chapter.

I plead with you, my brothers, and my sisters, get out of the disorderly ways into which some of you have been so long, and get into line.

Obey God, be truly baptized, and truly work for God.

I pray God that this morning you may believe that the Christ, who long ago healed men, is with us now to save, to heal, to cleanse and keep and guide.

Let those who desire His blessing stand. [Nearly all rose.]

PRAYER OF CONSECRATION.

My God and Father, in Jesus' Name I come to Thee. Take me as I am. Make me what I ought to be in spirit, in soul and in body. Give me power to do right to any whom I may have wronged, and in Thy sight give me true humility, simple faith and an obedient spirit that I may follow Thee. Take my spirit, my soul, and my body, and make and keep me clean. For Jesus' sake. [*All repeat the prayer, clause by clause, after the General Overseer.*]

BENEDICTION.

Beloved, abstain from all appearance of evil. And may the very God of peace Himself sanctify you wholly; and I pray God your whole spirit and soul and body be preserved entire, without blame, unto the coming of our Lord Jesus, the Christ. Faithful is He that calleth you, who also will do it. The grace of our Lord Jesus, the Christ, the love of God, our Father, the fellowship of the Holy Spirit, our Comforter and Guide, one Eternal God, abide in you, bless you and keep you, and all the Israel of God everywhere, forever. Amen.

After the Benediction, the General Overseer saw several hundred sick, and prayed with them, laying on hands in accordance with God's command.

The Wednesday Evening Service.

Their experience on Monday and Tuesday nights had evidently taught the officers of Sydney a lesson; and, besides, people from all over the city were demanding that the General Overseer be given an opportunity to be fairly heard.

As a result, permission which had been asked before but not granted, was given to close the gates of the grounds surrounding the Town Hall and make the only entrance by the small gate at the front, which would admit only one person at a time.

Larger crowds than ever before gathered in the streets early in the evening—indeed, the people began to come in the afternoon.

As the hour for the beginning of the meeting drew near, it was almost an impossibility for any one to get through the crowds to the little gate through which the people were being admitted by ticket.

The greatest care was taken to admit only those who seemed to be ladies and gentlemen, whether they had tickets or not; but subsequent events proved that it was not the larrikins of Sydney that were at the bottom of the trouble, but men who bore the external evidences of good standing.

When the meeting was begun, it seemed that at last a fairly orderly audience had been secured, and that the great majority of those present, who desired to hear, would be able to.

Deacon C. Friend Hawkins, in charge of the Branch of the Christian Catholic Church in Zion in Adelaide, South Australia, was appointed chairman of the meeting, and the opening exercises were conducted without serious interruption.

The General Overseer's subject was Zion City, and he spoke in his most interesting manner.

No sooner had he begun to speak, however, than the disturbance began.

A cough or a sneeze from some leader of the organized band of disturbers, (well-dressed men and women who had gained admission to the hall on the assumption that they were ladies and gentlemen,) would cause a roar of laughter, and it would be some seconds before the voice of the speaker could be heard.

Very gently and lightly, so as not to draw attention to himself, some one would begin pounding on the floor with his foot or a cane.

In a moment, hundreds would be doing the same, and it would be a minute before quiet could be restored.

Occasionally, when he thought he was not being watched, some ruffian would shout out some impudent remark, utterly void of wit, humor, or even sense. This would be a signal for more loud laughter, hand-clapping and feet-stamping.

Overseer Voliva, at the head of a little band of faithful Zion ushers, was acting as deputy to the chairman, and was designating to the police those who were the chief law-breakers, and demanding their removal.

Whenever the police took any one out, there was another great uproar, men and women standing on their chairs in all parts of the hall and yelling.

As time passed, the disturbance grew worse and worse, the fact that it was an organized effort, previously planned, becoming more and more evident.

One by one, young and middle-aged men were leaving their seats in various parts of the hall and congregating in the back of the room, until there were about two hundred gathered there.

A Riotous Member of Parliament.

At about this time a William Nicholas Willis, member of the Legislative Assembly of New South Wales, started an uproar by pounding heavily on the floor with his cane.

His action was detected by Overseer Voliva, who ordered him to leave the hall.

He angrily refused to do so, declaring that he had not caused any disturbance.

Instantly perceiving that the man was under the influence of alcohol, and had evidently come for the purpose of creating a disturbance, the Overseer quietly bade him keep silence, and dropped the matter.

Not so Mr. Willis, however.

He went to the police in the rear of the hall and made a charge against the Overseer, alleging that he had used threatening language, and asked that he be placed under arrest.

As the officers went up the aisle to where the Overseer stood to take him in charge, Mr. Willis went ahead of them, brandishing his cane and making a harangue upon his pretended wrongs.

All the men that had just gathered at the rear of the hall followed.

Arrest and Attempted Murder of Overseer Voliva.

When he reached the place where Overseer Voliva stood, this shining member of Parliament mounted a chair and began to roar out a speech, inciting the mob to take vengeance for the wrongs (?) that they had suffered at the hands of Overseer Voliva and the ushers.

Instantly there was a terrific rush.

Every possible effort was made by the mob to get the Overseer down and trample him to death, but God was with him.

He kept perfectly cool and calm, carefully watching his feet lest he stumble, and going over the chairs in the way, instead of tripping on them.

Even then, his escape from death or serious injury was miraculous.

As it was, he sustained slight strains in one shoulder and one knee.

As the rush continued, and the crowd kept increasing, the police, instead of taking the prisoner outside the hall, where his life would not have been worth a half penny in the hands of the mob, dodged into a side room of the building and locked the door until the crowd had been cleared out of the hall.

The Overseer was then taken to the police station, where he was very kindly treated.

He was allowed his liberty upon payment of a small cash bond, and his case was set for a hearing at ten o'clock the next morning.

The arrest of the Overseer caused such a terrible and prolonged disturbance that the meeting could not be continued, and it was brought to a close with the Doxology and Benediction, both of which were almost completely drowned out by the pandemonium of yells, catcalls, street songs and other noises that were being made by the male and female ruffians who had that night filled to the full the cup of Sydney's shame and disgrace.

The General Overseer immediately took his cab and drove to the Australia Hotel.

Inside the hall, the mob, believing that he was still there, made a mad rush for the platform, and the little room behind where they expected to find him; but he was gone.

Then a mob of many thousands surged through the streets running to interrupt God's prophet before he could reach the hotel, and screaming out their hideous threats.

It was a fearful sight, and a sad one.

Not one in a hundred among all those thousands could have given one clear, definite reason why he sought the life of the man whose name he was bellowing.

The leading spirit in that mob was the old enemy of Elijah, Baal, and his devotees were following as blindly and madly as in the old days.

Masonry, social impurity, and Labor Union tyranny are all rampant in Australia, and they are all forms of Baal worship, which will find their culmination in the coming of the Lawless One.

But God was good and saved His servant from the murderous hands of his enemies, the cab reaching the hotel a few moments before the advance guard of the rioters appeared.

They did not know that he had come, and so stood in the streets howling dismally and hungrily for a long time.

At last at the solicitation of the proprietor of the hotel the police cleared them away.

The following is the report of the Message of Elijah the Restorer delivered at this meeting:

---

*REPORTED BY E. W. AND A. W. N.

Sydney, Town Hall, Wednesday Evening, February 17, 1903.

Hymn No. 14 was sung, and prayer was offered by Overseer Voliva.

Rev. C. Friend Hawkins, chairman of the meeting, said:

"The General Overseer of the Christian Catholic Church in Zion, [applause, noises, yells] Rev. John Alexander Dowie, will now conduct the services, and I scarcely need ask that this audience will respectfully hear him, and will permit no interruption.

"I appeal to every good citizen of Sydney to help me to maintain perfect order in this meeting." [Applause.]

Introductory Remarks.

General Overseer—I am thankful for what I feel is a sympathetic chord in your hearts.

Twenty-five years ago, I gave seven or eight of the strongest years of my life to this city, and I should have been very sorry to have left it with the thought that my last meeting had been disturbed.

I intend to talk to you tonight, as I said, concerning the work of the Christian Catholic Church in Zion throughout the world, and especially concerning Zion City, and the policy of Zion in founding such cities.

I think the experiment, as men would call it, has now become so satisfactory, that it is really a successful working model that we have in Zion City, Illinois.

I will read to you a chapter that is very much in our hearts in Zion City. We often read it there.

It is the 60th chapter of the book of the Prophet Isaiah.

The General Overseer read the chapter, after which Hymn No. 32 was sung.

The announcements were made, during which there was considerable interruption.

The General Overseer then continued:

A certain amount of letting off of steam seems to be necessary, but do not let our brains be in our hands and in our boots merely. Let us— [Noises, yells, thumping of canes on the floor.]

I am very much obliged for what I feel is the intense desire of the vast part of this audience to hear what I have to say.

It is not very often that you will have the opportunity of hearing me, for I cannot very often visit these lands; probably this will be the last time.

ZION AND ZION CITY.

INVOCATION.

Let the words of my mouth, and the meditation of my heart be acceptable in Thy sight, be profitable unto this people, and unto all to whom these words shall come, in this and every land, in this and all the coming time, Till Jesus Come. Amen.

*The following report has not been revised by the General Overseer

I shall place in the front of all I have to say concerning Zion and her work throughout the world these words:

TEXT.

For Zion's sake will I not hold my peace,

[Noises and laughter.]

And for Jerusalem's sake I will not rest, until her righteousness go forth as brightness, and her salvation as a lamp that burneth.

[Noises, stamping and laughter.]

Warning to the Disorderly.

If I shall find that the organized opposition is going to be too troublesome I may close the meeting at once. I ask now— [Noises, pounding with canes, and laughter].

I will give this audience a certain length of time to get into order, and then if the police cannot keep order and put out the disorderly, I shall close the meeting. [Applause, and much disorder.]

I do not believe that you want to have this record, that the meeting shall be closed on account of a disorderly minority. [Noises and various interruptions, during which a number stood on the chairs. Interruptions, continued for considerable length of time, throwing the audience into confusion.]

"Jesus, Lover of My Soul," was sung while order was being restored.

The Christian Catholic Church in Zion.

The Christian Catholic Church in Zion is the outcome of my life and ministry.

It is now established on every continent of the world.

In the United States of America, we have our central headquarters which I shall describe later, and which is the outcome of the movement from a municipal, and political, and social, and educational point of view. [Noises, confusion, yells.]

I think it might be well for the intelligent to hear what has been done, how it has been done, and what is intended to be done.

I thank God for the privilege of speaking in this city tonight on that subject.

You will see that the Word of God points, in prophetic utterance to the time when there shall— [Noises and various interruptions, which continued for considerable length of time.]

Those that do that are very seriously injuring their own city. Let that stop. [Continued rioting ending by a large number in the rear singing a street song.]

The Christian Catholic Church in Zion has a very simple creed.

First, it demands that all members shall believe in the Inspiration, Infallibility and Sufficiency of the Bible as the Word of God.

Second, that they shall have repented of their sins, that through faith in Jesus, the Christ, they shall have entered by the Spirit into the communion of God, and know that they are children of God.

All matters of opinion are— [Laughter, interruptions of various kinds.]

There is no need to laugh. Those who do that are wasting their own time and mine. [Continued tumult.]

I did not come here for this kind of thing. [Prolonged interruption and confusion.]

I have traveled a long way to meet you, and I think I ought to be courteously treated. I am saying and doing nothing that can hurt the commonwealth. [Applause, hisses, stamping and general confusion, during which part of the audience stood upon chairs, joining in with the mob.]

Wide-spread Work of the Christian Catholic Church in Zion.

I desire to tell you, first of all, where the Church is established.

In the United States of America, in Europe, in Asia, in Africa, and in this country we probably have, with the adherents of the Church and their families, nearly one million souls under the Banner of Zion, and this within only eight years.

It is of some importance that a movement of this nature should be understood by the Christian Church.

Men come great distances to interview me and to see Zion City, and to understand the movement.

I have come tonight to say a few words to you, which, if you will listen, may help. [Noises.] It cannot hurt any— [General confusion, prolonged interruptions, singing and howling.]

Spiritual, Psychical and Physical Cleanliness in Zion.

In Zion, we demand and teach the Way to a Real Salvation.

There must be a Full Consecration to God.

The members of the Christian Catholic Church in Zion therefore are abstainers from everything that would defile the body, the soul or the spirit.

They are abstainers from all intoxicating drinks. Not one member uses tobacco.

They abstain from unclean foods, such as swine's flesh; for the pig is the scavenger of the land, as the oyster is the scavenger of the sea.

We do not have any desire to disobey the Word of God which says, regarding the swine, "Their flesh ye shall not eat, and their carcasses ye shall not touch; they are unclean unto you."

Moreover, God's people are directed, in His Word, not to eat anything from the sea which has not fins or scales.

We carefully abstain from these things that would be impure and hurtful; hence the people in Zion are free from many things that defile the body, and that, through the defilement of the temple of God, the body, defile the soul and the spirit.

Body, Soul, and Spirit—Distinct, yet United in Man.

We keep very clearly distinct the three parts of man's nature, spirit, soul, and body, differentiating between the spirit and the soul, the soul being the animal nature, [noises and interruptions of various kinds] and the spirit being the spiritual nature.

The soul is mortal.

The spirit is immortal.

Every soul dies, but the spirit cannot die.

The Christ poured out His soul unto death.

When we speak of the soul, we are speaking of the animal life.

When we speak of the spirit, we are speaking of that of which God is the Father.

God is not the Father of souls; He is the Father of spirits.

The spirit is eternal, and the soul is not.

We therefore make our people clearly to understand that everything in the way of a true and pure life begins in the spirit. [Noises, continuous interruptions.]

I will cast myself now, young men, upon your fair play.

I will ask you to stop this nonsense entirely, and let me go on with my discourse.

I will not keep you very long.

I have a few simple words to say.

There is one thing clear about our work; we understand where we are going, and what we are doing. [Interruptions.]

If people do not control their bodily appetites and passions, the soul will be destroyed and the spirit will be depraved.

The filthy blood of an unclean soul will go down through unclean bodies and be a great curse to generations that follow, while the spirit will go out of the body condemned.

We ask our people, therefore, to remember that if they are to maintain— [Interruptions and prolonged confusion.]

The Five Senses, the Gateways to the Soul and Spirit.

We very carefully impress upon our people the thought that the body is the gateway, through its five senses, into the soul and the spirit; that we must guard these gates, the five senses, for behind them there lie the five spiritual senses, of which they are the mere outward expression.

We are practical people.

My people have been trained carefully, and are now being brought together in cities.

I have already had the pleasure of founding the first Zion City.

It is situated forty-two miles north of Chicago, and forty-two miles south of Milwaukee.

It is upon that great chain of lakes which might be called the great unsalted seas of the Continent of America.

They are thousands upon thousands of miles in extent, beautiful lakes.

We have a lovely City, with two and one-half miles of lake front and stretching back four and one-half miles.

We have eleven square miles of land upon which we have established the first city.

Aims in Establishment of Zion City.

Let me endeavor to describe to you the aims we have had in establishing that City.

First, the aims are spiritual.

We aim at the salvation of the spirit, then of the soul, and then of the body.

We are gathering together in that City those who are like-minded.

We believe what God said concerning the land of Israel, when His people took possession of it: "The land is Mine. It shall not be sold in perpetuity."

It is not the Will of God that land shall be alienated from Himself, and therefore His Church, His Kingdom, must control the lands of the earth.

Hence, we sell no land. We lease the land for eleven hundred years under covenants, which must not be broken, or the lease will be canceled.

These leases are very carefully drawn up.

None need come to Zion unless they choose, but if they come they will find that the lease is in effect.

But it amounts to a fee simple as long as they do right.

I have been greatly pleased with the success of the City.

We have gathered together in that City many thousands of people in less than two and one-half years.

We have one large Central Tabernacle called Shiloh Tabernacle which seats seven thousand three hundred people, and is often too small for the congregation; so we are now building a tabernacle that will seat sixteen thousand.

Our intention is, later, to build the great Zion Temple to seat forty thousand. [Interruptions, confusion and excitement, during which a large portion of the audience stood on chairs, and joined with the mob in disturbing.]

Permit me to go on. I think there are thousands of people who want to hear what I have to say. [Cries of "Hear! Hear!" Applause, laughter, general confusion.]

Let me have the opportunity of speaking in a hall for which we have paid, and where we have invited you to come and quietly listen. [Hisses, exclamations and disorder.]

Theocratic Policy of Zion City.

God's people come to Zion City to coöperate in Industry, in Education, in Religion, in the Extension of the Kingdom of God, and in Political action; for, let me tell you, Zion is intensely political.

We have a Theocratic policy, the policy that God shall rule in His own world. [Interruptions extending over several minutes.]

Why should you trouble? They will soon be still; they will be indicated, and they may have to be removed. [Sudden outbreak of hostilities, shouts, hisses, stamping and yelling.]

The Christian Catholic Church in Zion carries its religion into Education, into Business and into Politics.

The people see no reason why religion should be separated from these things.

The man who separates God from any part of his life is not living, in that part, a Godly life.

We establish schools and institutions in connection with the Church, of a very practical character.

Zion Restoration Host.

For instance, there has been evolved what is known as Zion Restoration Host, a powerful Host of men and women under vow to obey God and serve Him everywhere, who have done a most remarkable work.

Another department is the women's work in Zion.

My own good wife, with her four hundred fifty Dorcas Deaconesses, with her forty-five— [Howls, shouts, stamping, interruptions of a varied character, coughing and laughing, which extended over several minutes, until the entire audience was in confusion.]

I ask you to kindly sit down. Let the disturber be removed quietly.

In the city of Chicago, last year, with the Dorcas Deaconesses Overseer Dowie relieved poverty and clothed no less than two thousand seven hundred families. [Uproarious noises, catcalls, interruptions.]

Zion is not living for herself.

Zion is living for God, and Zion is living for humanity, without any respect to nationality or creed.

Zion in the great cities is doing her work.

The New York Visitation.

For instance, lately, in the City of New York, three thousand members of Zion Restoration Host went down and held a Visitation with me.

They visited every house in New York City.

They visited every business house in that city and every ship in the harbor.

They distributed four million two hundred thirty thousand pieces of Zion Literature.

They left the Message, "Peace be to this house," everywhere they went.

I had the pleasure, in the great Madison Square Garden, of speaking, every night for two weeks, to no less than fifteen thousand persons, and God blessed that work.

[At this point the meeting was thrown into confusion and excitement by scuffling in the rear of the hall, yells, shouting, and a general uproar. It was several minutes before the General Overseer could be heard.]

I will continue my address, and endeavor to close in good time.

Zion's work is planted on every continent, and everywhere it is an evangelizing work, the first aim of which is the Salvation of men's spirits, through faith in Jesus, the Christ, our Lord, believing in Him as the Atoning Savior, believing in the Holy Spirit as the Regenerating Power, believing in our Father in heaven, whose Love has blessed the world.

The Theology of Zion Is Not Narrow.

We believe in the Ultimate Salvation of every man, of every spirit, although some may pass away into evil, and into evil places in the unseen world of spirits.

The Christ who went down into the deepest depths of Hades, and preached to the spirits in prison, to those who were disobedient in the days of Noah, will reach you, even if you make your bed in hell.

I thank God for the Words, "As in Adam all die, even so in the Christ shall all be made alive." [Applause and mocking laughter.]

The Theology of Zion is broad.

The Theology of Zion reaches out into Eternity, and preaches a Gospel of Eternal hope, and of Ultimate Restoration of mankind to God.

Zion Educational Institutions.

After the spiritual, we take up the educational, and we have already in our little City the first section of a College Building which has cost us one hundred fifty thousand dollars, and four large schools, so that in our little City we have over 1,700 attending the various schools from the kindergarten to the college.

We have an excellent staff of teachers, and a splendid college faculty.

Then we have our Commercial Institutions, concerning which there has been so much interest taken.

We aim to give every man in Zion City employment.

We think it is a foolish thing and a wicked thing if we have resources to let these resources stand unimproved.

Our people are eager to work.

I will explain to you some of the great institutions of Zion as commercial and manufacturing agents.

Zion Building and Manufacturing Association.

First of all, we built the City ourselves.

We have a Building and Manufacturing Association, tne capital of which has been subscribed by our wealthier people.

In that association, we find the capital to build the City.

We build the houses for those who want them built.

We take the contracts, we buy in the cheapest possible market, and we sell at the lowest possible price to our own people, making the contract as low as possible, so that the people may get their homes.

Ninety-five per cent. of the people, rich and poor, are living on their own land, and in their own houses in Zion City. [Continued disturbances and uproar, so that the General Overseer could scarcely be heard.]

That fact is of immense economic importance, and should make you see that he who speaks to you is the friend of the people. [Further disturbances of a threatening character shouting and yelling.]

I have never fought for myself

I am speaking now in the interests of humanity, and trying to bring to the people a Message that will be a blessing. [At this point the disturbances broke into a tumultuous uproar and confusion, and it was some considerable time before the General Overseer could be heard. After a hymn had been sung, the noise subsided sufficiently for the General Overseer to continue, although with much difficulty.]

The Workmen Share the Profits.

Some one might ask, "Do the profits of that association go into the pockets of rich capitalists?"

The stock which has been subscribed bears seven per cent. interest, and will bear eventually ten; but we have made an arrangement by means of which the more than one thousand men who are now employed share the profits.

After the proper percentage is paid out of the profits of the association to the shareholders, and a proper provision has been made for the wear and tear of machinery, the surplus profits are divided as follows: Ten per cent. to the Christian Catholic Church in Zion, twenty per cent. to the shareholders, pro rata, according to the number of their shares, and seventy per cent. to the employees, pro rata, according to their wages.

The profits are considerable, too.

That is a fair distribution of the surplus that I am sure must meet every one's approval.

Zion Lace Industries.

I looked around in the United States to see what great manufacturing industry was not represented, and I found that fine laces were not being made there.

I went into the whole matter of the lace industry, and saw that we had a duty of sixty-five per cent. in our favor if we made lace.

I took great pains.

I saw the Secretary of the Treasury of the United States, Mr. Lyman Gage, and I arranged with him for the importation— [Noises, general confusion lasting several minutes. After a hymn had been sung, it became sufficiently quiet for the General Overseer to proceed with his address.]

Do you want me to continue speaking?

[Cries of "No" and "Yes."]

Well, if you say no, why do you not go out? [Uproar and stamping.]

I should like to continue the statement as to the enterprises of Zion, and to show you how I was providing for the large population which is gathering there so rapidly. That large population— [Noises and shouts, singing of songs.]

I have some things to say that will be well for you to hear; for Zion is influencing the policies of the whole world. That is admitted.

Any one who does not know that, does not know the trend of thought, theologically, politically, educationally or commercially.

Zion has found a solution for the great social problems, and especially has she found a solution for God's own people. [Disturbances and interruptions.]

[At this point the noise and disorder was so great that the General Overseer was unable to proceed further with his address and so pronounced the Benediction, the meeting being broken up amidst much excitement and uproar.]

The Last Day in Sydney.

At nine o'clock on Thursday morning, February 18, 1904, the General Overseer met the members and friends of the Christian Catholic Church in Zion in Sydney and vicinity, in the pleasant little Zion Tabernacle in Queen's Hall, Pitt street.

It was a private meeting, in which many things of great importance in the Kingdom of God were discussed with great freedom.

Among these were Zion Cities in America, and the emigration of Australian Zion people to those cities.

The very deep and enthusiastic interest of the goodly company of people who had gathered was very encouraging, and it was evident that the great majority of Zion in Sydney had their faces set toward Zion City.

At the close of his talk, God's prophet gave opportunity for questions, and many were asked that showed a vital and intelligent interest in the ecclesiastical, educational, commercial and political departments of the Kingdom of God.

These the General Overseer answered with his usual keen discrimination and wit, much to the edification, instruction and delight of the assembly.

Applause and other expressions of approbation and joy were frequent and earnest, as point after point of the wonderful character of the Zion of these Latter Days was made clear.

This was indeed a delightful meeting, and showed among other things what we had noticed wherever we met with Zion people, that the Zion spirit is the same everywhere, and that Zion people are one people, whether we find them in Texas, California, New Zealand, Australia, or Zion City.

Norton and Willis, Partners in Iniquity.

While this meeting was in progress, Overseer Voliva was before the Central Police Court of Sydney, on a charge of using threatening language to W. N. Willis.

When the case was called, John Norton, the notorious editor of the filthy *Truth* was one of the most prominent figures in the court room.

He consulted with Mr. Willis and his attorney, and was continually running in and out of the room, talking with the witnesses and otherwise interesting himself in the case.

When first called, Mr. Willis asked for an adjournment until the following day, saying that he would have to serve papers on some of his witnesses in order to secure their attendance.

Overseer Voliva said that he was ready to proceed to trial and asked for an immediate hearing as he had taken passage for Melbourne on the express to go that evening.

The court refused to continue the case until the next day, ordering the parties to appear at two o'clock that same afternoon.

The case was called, therefore, at the time stated, and the testimony of Mr. Willis and his witnesses was taken that afternoon and the following day.

The gist of the testimony was that Overseer Voliva with his hat on, went about the hall insulting well-behaved, quiet and orderly people and having them thrown out by ushers who accompanied him; that he addressed respectable women by vile and obscene names; and that he "brutally and outrageously insulted" Mr. Willis, who had come there to be enlightened and was keeping perfect order, as became a highly respectable member of Parliament.

The testimony, as presented, was grotesquely contradictory and manifestly surcharged with bitter malice; but the above is the substance of it.

At the end of the second day's proceedings, the court adjourned the hearing until June 20, 1904, at the request of Overseer Voliva, who was needed in Melbourne for the next Lord's Day service.

When the case was thus adjourned, very much against the will of Messrs. Norton and Willis, Norton got down behind a bench, where he could see Overseer Voliva and made faces at him for five minutes.

What a spectacle!

A member of Parliament of the state of New South Wales, and editor of a paper claiming thirty-seven thousand circulation, making faces like a cowardly little street urchin, afraid to strike lest his precious skin suffer!

It is a significant fact that Mr. Willis is closely associated with this craven simulacrum of a man in the publication of *Truth*, falsely so-called; that both are Freemasons and bitter enemies of Zion, the General Overseer and Overseer Voliva.

The arrest of Overseer Voliva at the instance of Mr. Willis, the cowardly attempt upon his life by the mob that had gathered in the rear of the hall apparently for that purpose, and the close association of the Freemasons, Norton and Willis, at the trial, reveals the source of the disturbance in Sydney.

Masonic Baal-worshipers tremble in mortal terror lest the Voice of Elijah the Prophet be heard.

Many Good Citizens Protest Against Lawlessness.

It was like a gleam of light in the darkness to observe that thousands of the respectable citizens of Sydney bitterly regretted the lawlessness that disgraced their city.

At every meeting there were thousands who expressed themselves again and again as being indignant because of the riotous behavior of the mob.

At the hotel and elsewhere, there were many who verbally gave utterance to the General Overseer and members of his party, to sentiments of sympathy with him and disgust at the lawless element.

The General Overseer received many letters written in the same tone.

Among them were the two which we quote below:

"Ashamed of the People of Sydney."

PRATT & PRATT,
ACCOUNTANTS AND AUDITORS.
ESTATES ADMINISTERED FOR TRUSTEES.

VICKERY'S CHAMBERS, 76 PITT STREET, SYDNEY, February 18, 1904.
REV. DR. DOWIE, Australia Hotel, Sydney.

Dear Dr. Dowie:—Through your kindness, yesterday, in giving a ticket to my wife (*née* Barraclough), I was enabled the pleasure of hearing you speak at the Town Hall last night.

I was heartily ashamed of the people of Sydney not granting you a fair hearing.

We are ruled here by mob law—labor law.

The spirit of lawlessness is abroad, and is on the increase.

The people who do not reverence God are not likely to respect law and order.

The fault lies mainly with the parents bringing up their children in a Godless way, and without inspiring any respect for or obedience to themselves.

Disobedient parents produce disobedient children.

You will have a sorry tale to tell them when you get back to Zion, but I would beg you to believe that a large section of the community thoroughly sympathize with you in your efforts after righteousness, and protest against the rowdyism displayed at your meetings by a lot of irresponsible youths, and of ignorant men of no standing.

They strive here after a white Australia, but what we want is a civilized Australia.

My wife wishes me to thank you very heartily for LEAVES OF HEALING, which we receive regularly from Zion, and which are read by many of us with great interest.

Wishing you a prosperous voyage, and a safe return to your good work and beautiful home. I am, yours faithfully,

HENRY PRATT.

Cowardly Tactics of the Press.

SYDNEY, February 16, 1904.

REV. AND DEAR SIR:—I cannot refrain from writing to express the hope that you will believe that there are some in this large city who repudiate in the strongest possible manner the dastardly press tactics which have borne such disgraceful fruit at your Town Hall meetings.

I need hardly tell a man of your experience that the press throughout the world may be regarded as one great brotherhood, and when you attack any large section of this great brotherhood you do so at the risk of becoming a marked man from that day, subject to the vilest calumny and the most ingenious misrepresentation and *worse*.

How you have brought upon yourself the enmity of the press every one can see.

With honorable exceptions, the members of the press are a drinking, smoking, gambling body of men, and your unsparing denunciation of these vices has excited their enmity against you.

The press tactics that have been followed here have been very simple.

You have been held up to public ridicule both before and after your arrival in this city.

Every word spoken in heat, under justifiable excitement, has been recorded against you.

Your appearance has been laughed at, your mission misrepresented; and the one thing that would have set you fairly before the public—a fair and impartial report of your public utterances—has been carefully withheld.

The *suggestio falsi* and the *suppressio veri* have been potent weapons in the hands of our local press.

It should also be remembered that with practically no immigration, and a seriously declining birth rate, the authorities have felt that it would be a bad thing if you took away with you any of the inhabitants of this state, though whether that would be so, in view of our large number of unemployed, is a nice problem for the student of economic science.

The remedy for the pass to which you have been brought by an unscrupulous and smarting press is not easily pointed out.

The press is powerful, and having once excited a feeling against you will have no difficulty in keeping it up, and the very lawlessness of your meetings, which should be blamed against the press, will be blamed against you, and you will be held up—in fact you have been—as a disturber of the public peace.

In these circumstances you must meet the printing press with the printing press.

If it is put fully before our citizens in a pamphlet, that the religion you preach is a practical religion; that it offers not only food for the soul, but also for the body; that a man who has gathered together ten thousand people, among whom a high moral atmosphere is maintained, can neither be the feeble mountebank which one portion of the press represents him to be, nor the violent enemy to society which another portion holds him up to the world as, then I say you may get a hearing, if not in this state in others in which the true nature of your mission has been explained in advance by the means suggested.

Should you get a fair hearing, you are not the man I remember twenty-four years ago, if you do not succeed in your mission to an extent that will cause "weeping and wailing and gnashing of teeth" among the gentlemen who wield the pen, which is too often mightier than the sword when wielded by unscrupulous and mercenary hands.

Yours sincerely, —. —. ——.

P. S.—Do not forget that in speaking against that medieval relic, Freemasonry, you have committed the deadly sin. That brotherhood is antagonistic to the universal brotherhood preached by the Christ.

Many letters were sent to the local papers by persons not members or even friends of Zion, who protested against the flagrant denial of the right of Free Speech.

Among these, we reprint the following from among those that were published:

From the *Daily Telegraph:*

CIVILIZATION?

TO THE EDITOR.

Sir:—Some few days ago an old man arrived here from America. He has, or thinks he has, a mission to regenerate humanity. In speech, extravagant and extreme, but never offending the rules of decency. In character, so far as report goes, only guilty of eccentricity. This poor old man, the brave Sydney youths saw fit to hunt out of the city last night. In spite of the fact that he had paid for the Town Hall, and only wanted to hold what he, at any rate, considered a religious service, Sydney larrikins were allowed to turn the old man's meeting into a scene of riotous disorder, and to end their happy night by hunting the poor old fellow out to Coogee. In the name of all that is manly and decent, I protest against a cowardly pack of youths being allowed to make man-hunting a feature of Sydney life. Such a scene as last night's is a disgrace to any community, and the complacency of the press over the matter is regrettable indeed. A white Australia may or may not be desirable. A civilized Australia certainly is.

Yours etc., AUSTRALIAN

February 17th.

BRITISH FAIR PLAY.

TO THE EDITOR.

Sir:—I have no time for the Rev. J. Dowie, nor would I have his fads on my mind; consequently I have not occupied good room at his meetings. But surely it is a blot upon the fair fame of Sydney that he should be unable to enjoy the right of free speech in our civic hall, for which he has paid, and which to all intents and purposes is his during the period of his hire. British fair play in Australia will soon be the exception rather than the rule if tonight's proceedings are allowed to prevail, and our reputation abroad will not be improved. Surely all agree that conditions are such as not to court further hostile criticism. Yours, etc., W. W. CLARKE.

February 17th.

DR. DOWIE OUT-DOWIED.

TO THE EDITOR.

Sir:—I fear that we, the public, are in grave danger of reaching greater extremes of denunciation than Dr. Dowie himself is charged with. I am not what is called a Dowieite, nor do I hold any brief for our notable visitor, but I can claim the right, which I know your journal will be the last to impugn, to lift a voice in protest against a mode of treatment of a visitor that is flagrantly inconsistent with our claim to be Britishers who believe in fair play.

As a New South Wales born Australian, believing in freedom of speech to all who have a message that does not necessarily imperil public interests, I find myself at one with a respectable percentage of others, some of them, like myself, representatives of the Gospel ministry, who feel sorely that Sydney has been disgraced in recent days by a certain class of utterances that have appeared in the press, and certain talk and behavior that have been shamefully in evidence with the public on the streets and in the Town Hall in connection with Dr. Dowie and his propaganda.

Like many others, I personally differ widely from the visitor upon some points, perhaps, among the most salient of his teaching, as I understand it. But, without here discussing that teaching at all, I wish to emphasize the facts that the worst that have been alleged against Dr. Dowie are that (1) he differs from the bulk of the Christian Church in some—only some—of his theological views; (2) he adopts methods in his work and makes claims which, I suppose, most of us are thankful are uncommon in other branches of Christian enterprise; and (3) he is entrusted with large sums of money in connection with the Zion movement. The first allegation is, in a country of religious freedom, beneath criticism; the second is a question of taste; and if most of us do not admire Dr. Dowie's "taste" in his claims and methods, we at least must refrain from "going one worse" in misrepresentation and abuse of him and his methods, and boycotting his speech. Here we are in danger of doing, and sadly large crowds have done, precisely what we object to in Dr. Dowie. Whilst respecting the third, it may be argued that all large branches of Christian enterprise claim and expend large sums of money, so that Jesus, the Christ, through his organization, calls for and employs larger sums of money than any other in Christendom, and if Dr. Dowie is successful in persuading, as he does, large crowds that Zion has a legitimate, a Christian claim on their purses, it is but his and their business if they thus invest their money, and repose in him as their trustee.

But, so far as my twenty years' knowledge of Dr. Dowie as a public man goes, no charge has ever been laid against his moral behavior and character. As Britishers we boast of giving fair play to all, even to those who do not always give the same to others. We ought, therefore, without uproar and boycott of speech, without prejudiced and sneering misrepresentation, allow all with a message to state, and, as far as they can, substantiate that message, and then criticise and demolish if we can the arguments that have not carried our judgment. If addressing Christian folk, I would plead for charitable patience, even with those who may not be too patient with us. My plea with Britishers, who ought to be above prejudice, boycott, and riot, is what your columns contend for—fair play. With, I find, others who differ from Dr. Dowie, I protest he has not had fair play in Sydney, and our public cannot throw so many stones at him as he at them. There is a considerable amount of glass about where we live. Thanking you, Sir, Yours, etc.,

WILL H. SCURR.

Y. M. C. A. Rooms, City, February 17th.

P. S.—Since writing the above I have attended Dr. Dowie's last meeting. He was patience perfected, with a crowd who treated him barbarously.

W. H. S.

From the Sydney *Herald:*

MR. DOWIE'S MEETING.

TO THE EDITOR OF THE "HERALD."

Sir:—I desire as an Australian and a Britisher to protest most strongly against the indecent action of a mob of larrikins whose behavior last night at Mr Dowie's meeting at the Town Hall cast the greatest slur upon the city of Sydney. The very large audience assembled to hear what Mr. Dowie (be he an empiric or not) had to say for himself and his following. British fair play always grants a fair hearing, and I confess that I felt heartily ashamed last night of being amongst an Australian audience, many of whom, not content with demonstrating against Mr. Dowie, exhibited no sort of reverence for the Sacred Book—the Bible—from which he was attempting to read to his audience. It is the duty of the Mayor to see that such a disgraceful exhibition of "hooliganism" is prevented in future, and the delinquents, if it occurs, punished. I know neither Mr. Dowie nor his creed, but let us show him that we have forgotten neither decency nor reverance, or both, in this part of Australia. I speak, I am sure, for many hundreds who were present last night. I am, etc.,

WESTRALIAN AND QUEENSLAND MAGISTRATE.

February 16th.

TO THE EDITOR OF THE "HERALD."

Sir:—I quite agree with "Magistrate of W. A. and N. S. W." in the *Herald* of today. I was very much surprised and disgusted to think the police did not have the courage to do their duty. I do not know the Lord Mayor of Sydney, but think he as chief magistrate should have had the forethought to see that provisions were made to see that justice should be meted out to Mr. Dowie and his adherents.

I feel sure that our worthy Mayor of Adelaide will not allow such a stigma to be placed on fair Adelaide by such unseemly conduct being tolerated in the event of meetings being held in Adelaide. I am, etc.,

MAGISTRATE OF SOUTH AUSTRALIA.

Sydney, February 17th.

TO THE EDITOR OF THE "HERALD."

Sir:—I call it cowardice on the part of those who took part in the demonstration at the Sydney Town Hall last night. Though I am not a follower of the reverend gentleman, I look upon him as a very brave and fearless man—a man who has the courage to fight on for what he wants when he knows all the world is against him. Considering that free admission was given to all those present last night, I think that the least they might have done was to have given him a fair hearing. I always like to see fair play, and I think a great injustice was done to Mr. Dowie last night. I am, etc.,

ZION

Newtown, February 17th.

That public opinion regarding these outrages had reached such a point that even the press, which was, in a large measure, responsible for them, was compelled to protest in order to save its face, so to speak, is shown by the following editorial, published on Thursday morning, February 18, 1904, in the leading columns of the Sydney *Daily Telegraph:*

THE DOWIE DISTURBANCES.

The mighty disturbances at the Dowie meetings in the Town Hall, with their subsequent disorderly demonstrations in the streets, have now reached the stage at which they reflect discredit upon the city in which they are allowed to occur. It is quite immaterial whether the religious doctrines which Mr. Dowie has come here to expound are regarded as true or false. That is a matter for individual judgment, and while those who choose to reject Mr. Dowie's teachings have a perfect right to do so, the same liberty belongs, under the law, to such as elect to accept them. Nobody is compelled to attend the services or meetings, but whoever does go, no matter what his opinions may be, is under the common obligation of behaving himself, and not interfering with other people. Having rented the Town Hall for the holding of what he and his followers represent as genuine religious services, Mr. Dowie has as much right to be protected in the legitimate use of it as the clergyman officiating in a church or chapel. The law, which knows no sect or creed, cannot discriminate in matters of this kind, and allow one religious congregation to be violently disturbed while another is protected. Yet, night after night Mr. Dowie is rudely prevented from conducting his services, and his followers who go to peacefully participate in them, are not allowed to do so by a disorderly mob. The good name and fame of the city calls for the suppression of this at any cost. Free speech within the limits of the law must be upheld, and every law-abiding person protected from outrage and insult. So far Mr. Dowie has not had this protection, and it is time that some explanation was given of the reason why. The mistake seems to have been in the undue leniency shown to wanton offenders at the beginning. There was, perhaps, on the part of most of the disturbers no more malicious intent than that of amusing themselves at the Dowieites' expense, but this roused angry passions until the culminating point was reached in the mimic state of siege which prevailed in part of the city last night, while the police were escorting the preacher from the broken-up service to his hotel. It is intolerable that any mob should be allowed to repeat such conduct night after night, and the time has come when something more than mere ejectment from the meetings will have to follow in the case of those who make "push" heroes of themselves by getting expelled in this way. The matter has now assumed the seriousness of organized effort to disturb a religious congregation for which, in this land of unfettered judgment in theological affairs, there cannot be a moment's toleration. The matter has, therefore, reached a stage which demands more effective methods on the part of the authorities than those hitherto employed.

What childlike innocence!

Of course, this highly honorable editor knew nothing about the fact that the meeting held the night before was the last that the General Overseer was to hold in Sydney on this Visitation!

There is an excellent reason why this paper should cry "lock the barn-door!" after the horse was stolen.

It was one of the thieves.

Referring to the arrest of Overseer Voliva, editorially, another of the Sydney papers said:

ARBITRARY.

Some one, speaking of the late Mr. Foster, the biographer and critic, described him as being all that was excellent, but, nevertheless, as "a harbitrary gent." We fear that our esteemed friend Mr. Willis, member of the State Parliament for the Barwon, if he does not improve himself in certain small matters of conduct, will earn for himself hereafter the description given of Mr. Foster. Last night, so it is reported, two men connected with the mission which Mr. Dowie was holding at the Town Hall, were, on the direction of Mr. Willis, arrested by the police on the charge of having used threatening language towards him. Now, we have no desire to discuss the merits of the case, which was set down for hearing at the police court today. But, as to the arrest itself, we believe that it was rather in contravention of custom. When a policeman does not hear threatening language used, it is generally his rule to advise the party who represents himself as aggrieved to proceed by way of summons. And the same practice holds good in regard to an ordinary case of assault. But, in the case in question, unless report be incorrect, the police effected arrests on the mere word of a gentleman who happens also to be a member of Parliament. We have nothing to do with the merits or otherwise of Mr. Dowie's mission in this case. The subject with us is one of importance, as connected with the liberty of the person. Nor do we desire to lay too much stress on the fact that Mr. Willis is a member of the State Parliament. Our contentions would be just as good if Mr. Willis were not a legislator, and the persons of whom he complains were. Indeed, it may be here remarked that, judging from frequently reported proceedings of the State Parliament, no member of that body should be unused to hearing threatening language, and something worse, freely flung about during its deliberations.

At an enthusiastic meeting, held in Zion Tabernacle, Queen's Hall, Pitt street, on Lord's Day February 21, 1904, the following resolutions were unanimously adopted:

Resolutions Adopted by Three Hundred Eighty Sydney Citizens.

RESOLVED, That this gathering of citizens, numbering three hundred and eighty persons, assembled in the Queen's Hall, Pitt street, Sydney, Sunday, February 21, 1904, desires to express its profound sympathy with the Rev. John Alexander Dowie, in the barbarous treatment to which he was subjected, without the least provocation, by lawless mobs, whose demonstrations were a complete overthrow of every principle of responsible government, and of civil and religious liberty.

And, that we deplore with sorrow the apparent indifference of the powers that be, to control the mob violence that destroyed property, robbed Dr. Dowie of his right to freedom of speech and action in his own hired hall, and for which no redress could be secured.

And, further, that copies of this Resolution be forwarded by the chairman to the Honorable Premier Sir John See, the Attorney-general the Honorable B. R. Wise, and to the Rev. John Alexander Dowie by telegram.

CHAIRMAN.

Moved by PETER CLAYTON, Esq.; seconded by T. NEWTON, Esq.
Supported by telling addresses from Mr. Turnbull, and Mr. Creagh.
Carried unanimously.

On the same day, similar resolutions were adopted by a gathering of several hundred that met in the Domain, as the great park of Sydney is called.

On Thursday afternoon, February 18, 1904, the General Overseer, accompanied by the members of his party, took the Melbourne Express at the Redfern station of the New South Wales railway, leaving for Melbourne and Adelaide, where he was to meet his wife, Overseer Jane Dowie, whom he had not seen since she left Boston on Saturday, October 24, 1903.

As he left, there was a crowd of thousands at the station, many bidding him farewell with respect and love, others with senseless yells of foolish derision, and that diabolical noise called "boo-hooing."

That night was spent on board the train, and early the following morning, at Albury, we were compelled to change cars, because the roads in Victoria are of wider gage than those in New South Wales.

At noon of the following day, Friday, February 19, 1904, the General Overseer and his party arrived in Melbourne, the capital of the state of Victoria, and the temporary capital of the commonwealth of Australia.

Zion in Illinois and Indiana.

Beginning about May 20th, Elder and Deaconess Lee will visit the following places in Illinois: Kankakee, Hoopeston, Danville. Also in Indiana as follows: Indianapolis, Noblesville, Logansport, Lafayette, and neighboring towns.

A WEEKLY PAPER FOR THE EXTENSION OF THE KINGDOM OF GOD

EDITED BY THE REV. JOHN ALEX. DOWIE.

Volume XV. No. 3. ZION CITY, SATURDAY, MAY 7, 1904. Price Five Cents

GOD'S WITNESSES TO DIVINE HEALING.

HEALED OF HEMORRHAGE OF THE LUNGS.

MY MERCY WILL I KEEP FOR HIM FOREVERMORE, AND MY COVENANT SHALL STAND FAST WITH HIM.

The story as given in detail of the healing of this woman ought to put new life and courage into the hearts of those who are today without hope.

The story is a long one in print, but how much longer it was in fact!

How the weary hours of the night and day would drag on as she suffered with pain from her many ailments!

Just as a defective railway engine, with some parts of its machinery gone, wheezes and groans and labors on its way and finally comes to a stop—a "dead engine," as it is called—so the human machinery with some of its more important organs diseased is all thrown out of balance, and oftentimes there is scarcely an organ left in the body that is not suffering from the effects.

He is a poor engineer who will undertake to mend a broken wheel, or piston-rod, or air-brake while he is running on the track. At the first opportunity he will change engines and run the old and broken one to the repair-shop.

The most logical and reasonable thing for humanity to do is to take our bodily machinery to God's Divine workshop.

"The Prayer of Faith *shall* save the sick."

Elijah the Restorer has given back to the world the beautiful Covenant of Divine Healing.

MRS. LYDIA A. SHERLAND.

There is no secret about it. There is nothing new. There is nothing difficult.

It is easy and capable of application everywhere. God's mercies are boundless and His love is wider than the sea. They are deeper than hell and higher than heaven. God can be found everywhere and at all times.

How the hearts of the people glow with gratitude to God for His wonderful deliverance!

A recent letter from Mrs. Sherland confirms her testimony.

She has been at work with her husband making excellent maple sugar. She is able to do her housework and attend to her many duties.

She is no longer an invalid, but a healthy, strong and active Christian, doing what she can to build up the Kingdom of God.

The Devil's defeat has become the glory of God.

There is nothing that so sets forth His great and mighty Name as the deliverance of the people from the powers of death and hell.

Zion rejoices together in every new victory and in every case of deliverance from bondage.

They shall sing of the ways of Jehovah;
For great is the glory of Jehovah.
For though Jehovah be high,
Yet hath He respect unto the lowly;
But the haughty He knoweth from afar.
Though I walk in the midst of trouble,
Thou wilt revive me.

J. G. S.

WRITTEN TESTIMONY OF MRS. LYDIA A. SHERLAND.

LA PAZ, INDIANA, March 7, 1904.

DEAR GENERAL OVERSEER:—It is with a thankful heart that I write telling of the healing which God wrought in my body through your prayers.

I was a great sufferer from many diseases, and spent a great deal of money on physicians, but grew no better, but rather worse, until I realized that death was on my track.

My sickness was first brought on by measles. From that time on I took medicine, and was treated by five doctors, no two of whom agreed.

I went from worse to worse. Only God knows how I suffered.

I praise His Name that He did not permit the Devil to take my life, although I was a sufferer for seven years.

During this time other diseases set in.

I was taking medicine all the time, but became weaker and weaker.

My lungs became very weak, and at times I coughed up phlegm and blood. These hemorrhages would come on suddenly, and then I would be in bed several days.

I was losing flesh all the time.

I suffered very much from heart trouble, and the doctor gave me capsules for my heart, to stop it from beating so fast. This was to check the hemorrhages. I fainted away after taking them. I felt as if the life had gone out of my body.

My husband gave me one, and I fell over as dead. He and my sister rubbed me, and did all they could to restore circulation and enable me to rally.

At this time I was suffering from rheumatism. My feet were like puffballs, and my hands and fingers were all swollen out of shape. At times I placed my feet on a hot brick to get relief.

I was also suffering from stomach trouble, and had for years previously.

The pain in my stomach, when I ate anything, would frequently be so severe that I could scarcely endure it.

I had eczema on my right leg from my knee down to my ankle; and I doctored for that three years.

The doctor said that it was in my blood, and I could not be cured. He said that perhaps the bone would have to be scraped, as he thought it had become honeycombed; but, thanks be to God, I was healed inside of twenty-four hours after you prayed for me.

I was cleansed from the disease and have not had it since.

I praise the Lord for His cleansing power for spirit, soul, and body.

I was troubled with my eyes a great deal.

I went to South Bend to Dr. Shafer, an eye, ear and throat specialist. He said that my throat was very seriously affected, and that there were ulcers in my throat an inch long. He told me not to sing for two years.

He also said my eyes were in a dangerous condition, and that I was in danger of going blind.

He gave me some medicine to put into my eyes. It enlarged the pupil until I could not see.

I had to wear blue goggles and keep from the light.

I was troubled with constipation, bleeding piles and internal trouble; and I suffered from nervous prostration.

I had a lump in my right side as large as my fist.

My breast would swell and cause such intense pain that the doctor would give me morphine.

I wore a support for three years.

Doctor Hamilton, being our home physician and knowing all about my condition, told my husband that I was all broken down, and could not be patched up; but I might live till the leaves came out. This was in April, 1897.

He treated me for my lungs and throat, and had me come to his office.

He used a lung and throat spray. He would put a tube into my throat and then turn a wheel, and the spray threw the medicine in my lungs.

I was in his office one day when he used the lung spray and I came very near strangling to death. I had a hemorrhage.

I told him that I could not endure it, and he said that he had the medicine too strong.

I went home and spit blood all night.

I used a throat spray at home for three years, but it did me no good.

By this time I was becoming very weak.

I had taken all kinds of patent medicines, among them Dr. King's New Discovery for Consumption, but all these failed.

I was like a drowning person clutching everything I could get hold of with the hope of saving my life; but all in vain.

I then became discouraged and thought I would rather die than take all of this muck and then go at last.

One morning when thinking of my condition and crying, a copy of LEAVES OF HEALING was brought to me by one of our neighbors.

She had heard of my suffering and thought this would comfort me.

I read and studied the Word and found this to be a true Message.

I believed it was God speaking to me through you.

I studied and found that the Christ was my Healer, and that He was no respecter of persons.

I found that if I would do that which was right in His sight, obey Him in all things and keep His Commandments, I had a right to ask Him, and He would freely and abundantly bless.

While I was reading and crying my husband came in.

He said, "How do you feel?"

I replied, "No better."

"Are you taking your medicine?" he asked.

"No," I answered. "What is the use? I will not take any more."

"Are you discouraged? What shall we do?" he asked.

"We can do nothing; but I should like to go to Zion in Chicago," I said. "I believe that Dr. Dowie is a man of God or he could not do His work."

Through this, hope sprang into my heart.

I wrote a request for prayer, telling you of the hemorrhages, and asking you to pray that they should stop, as I was becoming very weak.

I sent this to you and received an answer that you had prayed, and that I should unite in prayer with you at half past nine.

I knew you had prayed, for the hemorrhages stopped.

At the time appointed I knelt in prayer. I received a wonderful blessing.

I began to get stronger. Then my husband assisted me to get ready, and went with me to Zion Home, Michigan avenue and Twelfth street, Chicago, Illinois.

This was June 13, 1897.

He left me there and went back home.

Monday morning following my arrival, those who were sick gathered in the assembly-room. It was there my eyes were opened to see the truth as never before.

With our Bibles in our hands, you led us from truth to truth.

As you taught us, I began to search my heart.

I realized that I had disobeyed God in many things.

I vowed I would obey Him and do right in His sight, no matter what the cost. And when you laid hands on me in the Name of the Christ, I was healed.

The blessing came. I could not but praise God, I was so happy. My heart was glad.

That night I slept all night.

I awoke in the morning feeling greatly changed. I had no pain. My lungs were healed, my cough was gone, my appetite quickened, my sore side did not pain, my eyes were all right, the eczema on my leg dried up and became like dead scales, and my bowels moved perfectly, and have ever since.

I could see clearly, and on the Friday following, the lump in my side commenced to discharge and a green fluid came from me. That was the last of the lump.

It came away without the least bit of pain, and there has not been the slightest sign of it since.

I have two little bony formations I coughed up out of my throat. These came out two or three days after I reached home. This was the last of the throat trouble.

I gained two and one-half pounds the week I was in Chicago, and in two weeks I gained eleven pounds. At this writing I am fleshier than I have ever been before in all my life.

I am in good health, doing all my housework—washing and all such heavy work.

I have not taken a drop of medicine, or eaten pork or anything cooked with lard, since.

I gathered all of the medicine, muck, and trash, with the throat spray and all the other things and put them into a market basket. When the basket was filled, I threw the whole thing out.

Thank God, His grace is sufficient in every time of need.

Thanking you for your prayers, and praying that God will long spare you and Overseer Jane Dowie for the good of humanity, I am,

Your sister in the Christ,

(MRS.) LYDIA A. SHERLAND.

TESTIMONY CONFIRMED BY HUSBAND.

LA PAZ, INDIANA, March 7, 1904.

DEAR GENERAL OVERSEER:—I can testify to my wife's testimony as being the truth.

She has been well ever since her healing in Zion Home in June, 1897.

She is always praising Zion and fighting for its cause, and sticking most tenaciously to the faith.

I am, kindly,

WILLIAM M. SHERLAND.

Zion Literature Sent Out from a Free Distribution Fund Provided by Zion's Guests and the Friends of Zion.

Report for the week ending April 30, 1904:

935 Rolls to........Various States in the Union
2,276 Rolls to......Hotels in the United States
1,515 Rolls to....Business men in New York City
2,648 Rolls to........................Switzerland
Number of Rolls for the Week..............7,374
Number of Rolls reported to Apr. 30, 1904, 3,129,448

EVANGELIST SARAH E. HILL,
Superintendent Zion Literature Mission,
Zion City, Illinois.

ELIJAH THE RESTORER

A WEEKLY PAPER FOR THE EXTENSION OF THE KINGDOM OF GOD.

EDITED BY THE REV. JOHN ALEX. DOWIE.

Application for entry as Second Class Matter at Zion City, Illinois, pending.

Subscription Rates.		Special Rates.	
One Year	$2.00	100 Copies of One Issue	$3.00
Six Months	1.25	25 Copies of One Issue	1.00
Three Months	.75	To Ministers, Y. M. C. A's and Public Reading Rooms, per annum	1.50
Single Copies	.05		

For foreign subscriptions add $1.50 per year, or three cents per copy for postage.

Subscribers desiring a change of address should give present address, as well as that to which they desire LEAVES OF HEALING sent in the future.

Make Bank Drafts, Express Money or Postoffice Money Orders payable to the order of JOHN ALEX. DOWIE, Zion City, Illinois, U. S. A.

Long Distance Telephone. *Cable Address "Dowie, Zion City."*

All communications upon business must be addressed to

MANAGER ZION PUBLISHING HOUSE,
Zion City, Illinois, U. S. A.

Subscriptions to LEAVES OF HEALING, A VOICE FROM ZION, and the various publications may also be sent to

ZION PUBLISHING HOUSE, 81 EUSTON ROAD, LONDON, N. W., ENGLAND.
ZION PUBLISHING HOUSE, NO. 43 PARK ROAD, ST. KILDA, MELBOURNE, VICTORIA, AUSTRALIA.
ZION PUBLISHING HOUSE, RUE DE MONT, THABOR 1, PARIS, FRANCE.
ZIONSHEIM, SCHLOSS LIEBBURG, CANTON THURGAU, BEI ZÜRICH, SWITZERLAND.

ZION CITY, ILLINOIS, SATURDAY, MAY 7, 1904.

TABLE OF CONTENTS.

LEAVES OF HEALING, SATURDAY, MAY 7, 1904.

Notes From The Overseer-in-Charge.

"AND JEHOVAH SPAKE UNTO MOSES, SAYING, SPEAK UNTO THE CHILDREN OF ISRAEL, SAYING:"

THE FIFTEENTH day of this seventh month
Is the Feast of Tabernacles for seven days unto Jehovah.

IT IS WITH joyful hearts that Zion looks forward to the coming Feast of Tabernacles.

ZION BELIEVES in the perpetuation of every good thing.

THE WISDOM of God is shown in the annual set Feasts of Israel.

THESE WERE times of gathering together of the people for instruction in the Word of God, and for inculcating the patriotism that has so deeply characterized the Jews to this day.

THE GOD of the Jew is a great God.

HIS ORDINANCES and Feasts are held most sacred; and to Zion the Feast of Tabernacles is a time of especial rejoicing in midsummer.

JUST AS the people are gathered together on the last night of the Old Year for an All-Night with God in Prayer, Praise, and Testimony, so at the Feast of Tabernacles the people come from the East and from the West, from the North and from the South, for a week or two to set forth the glories of God, and to hear the words of instruction and admonition of the Prophet of God.

ZION BELIEVES that he has a Message from God for the people—a Message of Restoration which will bring them into closer relationship with their God and Savior, and with each other, in the great work of establishing the Kingdom of God.

WE CALL especial attention to the excellent program for the coming Feast of Tabernacles, on pages 69-75, in this issue of LEAVES OF HEALING.

THIS PROGRAM was received late on Saturday, and in a private letter the General Overseer requested that an edition of twenty thousand copies with other matter, be printed in a sixty-four page booklet, and a large number of copies be sent to him in time for the Zion European Conference at Zürich, Switzerland, which will be held by the General Overseer from May 22d to May 29th.

IN ORDER to make it possible for the Programs to reach him during the Conference, they will have to be sent to him today, the 7th of May, as the last mail for Zürich leaves New York on Monday.

TO SHOW the excellent work which is being done in Zion Printing and Publishing House in Zion City, we take pleasure in saying that we are sending today a large number of these Programs to the General Overseer.

WHEN IT IS remembered that the program contains sixty-four pages, with a colored cover page, which requires four impressions, it is remarkable that in the short time of five or six days we have been able to prepare the first edition of this program. We sincerely believe that there is no other institution of the kind, perhaps, in the world, that can do better and quicker work.

Every employee of Zion Printing and Publishing House takes a deep and personal interest in the success of the Institution, and in getting out promptly any order that may be given to it.

WE ARE doing a large amount of outside work, and many are the commendations that are received from those who have had their orders filled.

WE CALL the attention of the Officers and Conductors in charge of Branches and Gatherings, and to individual members generally, that we desire them to send in orders at once for the number of copies of this beautiful program that will be required.

THE TIME is comparatively short, and what is done must be done quickly.

WE ARE anticipating a large attendance at the "Feast," not only from this country but from other countries in Europe and elsewhere.

A MOST NOTABLE and important conference is to be held by the General Overseer at Zürich, Switzerland, as mentioned in another column.

IN A RECENT letter sent by Elder Carl Hodler, to one of the officers in Zion City, he says:

Our headquarters' staff has now increased to five, and we are all kept very busy answering the many letters which pour in from all directions from those who desire information regarding the General Overseer's meetings.

We have to find accommodations for a great many people, and my time is fully taken up with the preparations for his coming.

We are looking forward to a time of great blessing and power, and great interest is being awakened throughout all Germany. Words fail to express the joy that fills our hearts at this time.

ELDER HODLER, Evangelist Hertrich, and others have been doing excellent work.

Even in Berlin, the capital of Germany, we now have a Gathering of the Members of Zion, with Brother E. Zimmerman in charge.

WE ARE proud of the fact that in the land of Luther, where the people have been so mightily blessed in accepting the Gospel that he preached, our beloved General Overseer, as Elijah the Restorer, is being received more kindly and heartily than perhaps in any other country in the world. We include, of course, with Germany, the delightful little country of Switzerland. May God bless her great, free, strong men and women.

AS THIS paper leaves the press our beloved General Overseer is probably reaching his port of destination, Marseilles, France, where he is due today.

AFTER FOUR months of journeying over land and sea, and after experiencing most distressing and annoying persecution by the "civilized" mobs of darker Australia, and after having been threatened with death and every cruel thing, God has gloriously brought him back almost within reach of his beloved City.

WITH HEARTS full of thanksgiving, Zion everywhere is singing, "Praise God from Whom all Blessings Flow."

WE AGAIN call the attention of the people of New York and vicinity to the meeting in Carnegie Hall, New York City, on Lord's Day, June 26th.

IMMEDIATELY AFTER this meeting our General Overseer will return to Zion City.

WE HAD occasion on last Lord's Day to speak to our people about visiting the World's Fair at St. Louis.

ZION HAS nothing in common with this "Vanity Fair!"

IT IS not an "affair" of the Kingdom of God, but it is an "affair" of the World, the Flesh, and the Devil.

LET THE people of Zion everywhere attend to their duties faithfully, and not be led astray by the temptation to spend their money and time where reign the powers of darkness.

AT ST. LOUIS will be gathered the scum and offscouring, the dregs of iniquity of all lands.

Here will be the disgusting effrontery of the harlot and the enticing wiles of the libertine serpent.

It will become a wild carnival of the flesh, and will be only an excuse for otherwise respectable people to associate themselves with the worst possible elements of society.

MRS. HELEN A. CHAPIN, President of the Woman's Foreign Missionary Society of the Methodist Protestant church of Missouri, writes a certain paper as follows:

MR. EDITOR: We wish your readers to know that the better class of people in Missouri strongly condemn certain men of Missouri who have pledged themselves to find fifty thousand virgins for immoral purposes at the World's Fair during the coming season, and we ask all parents to support us in our efforts to thwart their plot against the homes of the land.

HAS IT come to this, that a great commonwealth like Missouri has to advertise the fact that "the better class of the people strongly condemn" such an outrageous condition of affairs?

We should think they would "condemn," but it is probable that their condemnation will have very little effect. The iniquitous traffic will probably go on unhindered.

THE ONLY way for parents to protect their children is to keep them away from the fated city.

Let parents keep them out of danger by keeping them at home, and let them stay at home themselves.

ONE OF the greatest curses that can ever befall any city is the curse of a World's Fair.

"THE PIKE" is a Pike to hell, just as the Midway in Chicago was the Midway to hell.

AND YET the false shepherds will encourage their flock to participate in this "Vanity Fair"—the "blind leading the blind."

ZION WILL visit St. Louis just as Jonah visited Nineveh, as Jesus visited Jerusalem, and as Paul visited Ephesus.

ZION IS too busy with the work of the Kingdom of God, in getting men and women to live pure lives, and putting on the Robes of Righteousness, to run after the ways of the world in sight-seeing, merely for the temporary pleasure that it may give, and the excitement it may afford.

Zion will do what she can to preach the Gospel to the multitudes who will swarm around the poisoned honey of a World's Fair.

There is a Branch of the Christian Catholic Church in Zion in St. Louis in good working order. With the assistance of such Restorationists as will be sent from time to time, and with Zion Literature freely distributed, we shall be able to accomplish more good than would be possible in a promiscuous visitation by our whole people.

THE PEOPLE of Zion City are happy in their quiet, orderly and blessed surroundings.

LET EVERY faithful member of Zion make his own home a watch-tower and a beacon-light, a protection for himself and family and a warning against the sinner.

MAY GOD bless Zion in her Great Mission is our daily prayer! JOHN G. SPEICHER.

Publisher's Notice.

The remittance must accompany receipt of subscriptions at the Publishing House, no difference by or for whom or for whatever time they may be given, or whether forwarded through Ordained Officers, Branches, or Gatherings of the Christian Catholic Church in Zion. Accounts will be carried with Ordained Officers, Branches, or Gatherings, on quantity orders of periodicals consigned on sale for monthly settlement, but to include only such articles as bear the imprint of Zion. All orders for Bibles, books, buttons, pictures (except prints done by the Publishing House), lace souvenirs, etc., must be sent to the General Stores, Zion City, Lake County, Illinois.

Notice to Officers and Members of the Christian Catholic Church.

Send all newspaper clippings concerning the General Overseer, the Elders, or any department of the work in connection with the Christian Catholic Church in Zion, to Deacon Carl F. Stern, Zion City, Illinois. Send as soon as possible after publication, and carefully mark *name and date of the paper clipped from* on each article. If this is not done, the clippings are absolutely useless.

Daily Bible Study for the Home

By Overseer John G. Speicher

FRIDAY, MAY 13TH.

Acts 13.—First missionary journey chapter.

Memory text—Verse 49. "The word of the Lord was published abroad throughout all the region."

Contents of chapter—Prophets and teachers in the Church at Antioch; Barnabas and Saul separated for special work; They go to Seleucia; Thence sail to Cyprus; Preach at Salamis; Mark is with them; Paul speaks before the proconsul at Paphos; Elymas, the sorcerer, tries to hinder; Paul pronounces a curse upon him; He becomes blind; Paul and his company sail for Perga; Mark returns to Jerusalem, Paul and party to Antioch in Pisidia; Invited to speak in the synagogue; Gentiles pleased; Multitudes hear them next Sabbath; Jews filled with envy; Paul and Barnabas turn to the Gentiles, many of whom believe; Jews cast Paul and Barnabas out of the city; They go to Iconium; Disciples filled with joy.

SATURDAY, MAY 14th.

Acts 14.—First missionary journey chapter.

Memory text—Verse 22. "Through many tribulations we must enter into the Kingdom of God."

Contents of chapter—Paul and Barnabas speak in the synagogue at Iconium; Many Jews and Greeks believe; The Lord grants signs and wonders to be done; Apostles escape being stoned; Lame man healed at Lystra; Multitude seek to do sacrifice unto them, but they restrain them, telling them to turn from such vain things to God; Jews from Antioch and Iconium come and persuade the people against Paul and Barnabas; Paul is stoned; Dragged out of city as dead, but revives; Goes to Derbe with Barnabas; They return again to Lystra, Iconium, and Antioch, in Pisidia, confirming the souls of the disciples and ordaining elders; They also go to Pamphylia, Perga, Attalia; Thence to Antioch, where they tell the Church what God has done for them.

SUNDAY, MAY 15TH.

Acts 15.—Council chapter.

Memory text—Verse 18. "The Lord, who maketh these things known from the beginning of the world."

Contents of chapter—Certain men contending for circumcision cause dissension in the Church; Paul and Barnabas sent to Jerusalem to consult with the apostles; Preach at Phœnicia and Samaria; Received by the Church at Jerusalem; They tell what God did for them; Church called together to consider the question of circumcision; Peter preaches against circumcision; Barnabas and Paul tell of God's blessing to Gentiles under their ministry; James supports Peter's contention against circumcision; Apostles and elders send Judas and Silas to Antioch, with Paul and Barnabas; Write unto the brethren commending these men and commanding them to abstain "from meats offered to idols, and from blood, from things strangled, and from fornication;" Disciples at Antioch receive them and the epistle, and are much consoled; Judas and Silas exhort the brethren; Paul and Barnabas disagree.

MONDAY, MAY 16TH.

Acts 16.—Second missionary journey chapter.

Memory text—Verse 28. "Do thyself no harm."

Contents of chapter—Timothy circumcised; They go through the cities strengthening the churches; They pass through Phrygia and Galatia; Holy Spirit restrains them from preaching in Asia; pass Mysia; Hindered by the Spirit from going to Bithynia; Reach Troas; Paul interprets vision as a call to Macedonia; Sail to Samothrace; Next day to Neapolis; Thence to Philippi, in Macedonia; Lydia, of Thyatira, and her household baptized; Maid with spirit of divination is healed; Her masters angered, drag Paul and Silas before the magistrates; They are put in prison; At midnight Paul and Silas pray and sing; Prison shaken; Bands loosed; Jailer and his household converted and baptized; Magistrates give leave for Paul and Silas to go, but Paul refuses; Compels magistrates to come and fetch them out; Magistrates beseech them to depart out of their city.

TUESDAY, MAY 17TH.

Acts 17.—Unknown God chapter.

Memory text—Verse 28. "For we are also His offspring."

Contents of chapter—Paul and Silas pass through Amphipolis and Apollonia; Come to Thessalonica; Paul reasons three Sabbath days in the synagogue concerning the Christ; Many devout Greeks and chief women believe; Jealous Jews, with the rabble, make an uproar; Assault Jason at his home; Bring him before the rulers; Brethren send Paul and Silas away by night unto Berea; Many there believe; Jews follow Paul to Berea, stirring up the multitude; Brethren take Paul away, but Silas and Timothy remain; Paul taken to Athens; He sends for Silas and Timothy; Paul reasons in the synagogue, at Athens, with the Jews and with Epicurean and Stoic philosophers; Paul brought to the Areopagus; He makes a speech there, telling them of their superstitions, Some mock concerning the resurrection of Jesus; Others desire to hear again; Others believe.

WEDNESDAY, MAY 18TH.

Acts 18.—Corinth chapter.

Memory text—Verses 9 and 10. "Be not afraid . . . for I am with you."

Contents of chapter—Paul leaves Athens; Goes to Corinth; Meets Aquila and Priscilla; He abides with them, working as tent-maker; Reasons in the synagogue every Sabbath; Silas and Timothy come from Macedonia; Paul testifies to the Jews that Jesus is the Christ; They refuse to accept the teaching; He turns to the Gentiles; Ruler of synagogue believes with all his house; Many Corinthians believe and are baptized; Paul's vision assures him that God is with him; Paul brought before Gallio, the proconsul, who refuses to judge; Ruler of the synagogue beaten; Paul tarries awhile, and then sails for Syria; Priscilla and Aquila sail with him; Paul shaves his head in Cenchreæ for a vow; Goes to Ephesus; Teaches in the synagogue; Asked to tarry in the city, but refuses, promising to come again; Sails to Cæsarea and goes to Antioch; Goes also to Galatia and Phrygia; Apollos comes to Ephesus; He teaches carefully concerning Jesus, knowing only the baptism of John; Priscilla and Aquila expound the way more perfectly unto him; He is recommended to the brethren in Achaia; He goes there and helps them much.

THURSDAY, MAY 19TH.

Acts 19.—Uproar chapter.

Memory text—Verse 32. "The assembly was in confusion."

Contents of chapter—Paul comes again to Ephesus; Teaches concerning the Holy Spirit; Many rebaptized, having known only John's baptism; They receive the Holy Spirit through the laying on of Paul's hands; Speak with tongues, and prophesy; Teaches three months concerning Kingdom of God; Departs from them; Separates the disciples; Reasons daily in school of one Tyrannus two years; Many healed by the power carried away from his body through aprons and handkerchiefs; Exorcist Jews try to imitate the faith of Paul; Evil spirits turn on them, injuring them; Those who practiced curious arts bring books and burn them, confessing; Word of the Lord prevails; Paul sends two disciples into Macedonia; Tarries a while in Asia; Demetrius, the silversmith, stirs up an uproar; Gaius and Aristarchus, Paul's companions in travel, seized; Paul not suffered by his friends to go into the theater; Much confusion in the multitude; Will not allow Alexander, a Jew, to speak; Town clerk finally speaks and quiets the uproar and dismisses the assembly.

FRIDAY, MAY 20TH.

Acts 20.—Miletus chapter.

Memory text—Verse 35. "It is more blessed to give than to receive."

Contents of chapter—Paul goes to Greece; Continues there three months; Jews plot against him; Determines to sail for Syria, through Macedonia; Several brethren wait for him at Troas; Tarries there seven days; Preaches until midnight; Young man asleep falls from a window; Taken up apparently dead; Paul embraces him and assures them he will live; Continues breaking bread and preaching until morning; The young man is presented to them alive; Some disciples sail for Assos; Paul goes by land; They sail from there to Mitylene; Thence to Chios and Samos; Then to Miletus; Paul sends for elders at Ephesus; They come to him at Miletus; He exhorts them to faithfulness; Tells them they will see him no more; Prays with them; They weep and part from him.

SATURDAY, MAY 21ST.

Acts 21.—Vow chapter.

Memory text—Verse 13. "Ready not to be bound only, but also to die . . . for the Name of the Lord Jesus."

Contents of chapter—Paul and his companions sail for Cos, and thence to Rhodes; Thence to Patara; Next to Phœnicia; Cyprus sighted; Lands at Tyre; Tarries there seven days; Disciples and their families accompany Paul to the beach; They pray and bid farewell; Sails to Ptolemais; Remains there one day; Goes to Cæsarea next; Abides with Philip the evangelist; His daughters prophetesses; Agabus, a prophet from Judea, prophesies Paul's being bound and delivered; Disciples plead with Paul not to go to Jerusalem; He refuses to listen, saying not only willing to be bound, but to die for the Christ; Received gladly by the brethren at Jerusalem; They go to James and the elders; Tell what God has done for them; Paul is urged to take a vow and purify himself with some others, to please the Jews; He goes into the temple; Jews from Asia see him and stir up the multitude against him; Drag him out of the temple and beat him; Chief captain of the city comes with soldiers and stops them; Takes Paul away from them to the castle; Paul given permission to speak from the stairs.

The only thought that is worth anything is what God thinks. . . . If any of you think in any other way than the way God thinks, you will get into trouble. That is true even in material science. You must think as God thinks about electricity, or you will be electrocuted. You must think as God thinks about the law of gravitation, or you will get your head smashed. You must think as God thinks, and not run against His laws, or His laws will grind you to powder. If, on the other hand, you think as He thinks, you can use the great powers that He has given.

—*The Voice of Elijah the Restorer in Central Zion Tabernacle, Melbourne, Victoria, Australia, Monday Morning, February 29, 1904.*

ELIJAH THE RESTORER WARNS AGAINST SPIRITUAL ELECTROCUTION.

Around-the-World Visitation

of the

Rev. John Alex. Dowie

Elijah the Restorer
General Overseer of the Christian Catholic Church in Zion.

By ARTHUR W. NEWCOMB, Special Correspondent.

VISITATION AT MELBOURNE, VICTORIA, AUSTRALIA.

THE last paper of this series closed with the account of the journey of the General Overseer and his party to Melbourne, on Thursday and Friday, February 18 and 19, 1904.

Mob at the Spencer Street Station, Melbourne.

Upon our arrival at the Spencer Street Station, in the metropolis, we found the platform thronged with a crowd of several thousands of people, mostly young men, some of them loafers and professional "unemployed," of which Melbourne has thousands, the others, clerks who were out for their nooning.

As soon as the train came into view, these young exponents of lawlessness began shouting, hooting and "boo-hooing."

When the train came to a standstill, we saw that there was a squad of police on the platform trying to clear a little passageway through the crowd from the car-door to the carriage provided for the General Overseer, and a little later we observed a squad of Zion Guard—not uniformed, it is true, but with Zion buttons on their coats and the Zion light and courage in their eyes—preparing to act as an escort.

At last, after some difficulty, way was made and the General Overseer stepped from the car, and walked quietly and calmly to his carriage.

When the train stopped, he had been met by Elder Molly Voliva and Miss Sarah Booth, Overseer Voliva's private secretary, who introduced Deacons Moss and Carey, officers of the Branch of the Christian Catholic Church in Zion in Melbourne.

The two ladies and these two officers of the Church were therefore with him as he walked to his carriage.

When he appeared, such a howling and "boo-hooing" arose that it seemed as if all the wild animals from the Australian bush had been turned loose on the platform of Spencer Street Station.

A concerted rush was made for the General Overseer from all sides, and blows were rained upon the little escort formed of the members of his party and Zion Guard.

For a moment the mob brushed aside the police, and surged in a madly, roaring maelstrom about the Prophet of God and the little company around him. Then the police rushed in, and began striking and pulling right and left among the ruffians in an attempt to disperse them.

But, meantime, the General Overseer had entered his carriage and was driven away, thus suddenly removing the object of the wrath of the rioters, and, in a few moments all was quiet.

God had protected and none were hurt, although some had received painful bruises.

A Few Hours in Melbourne.

From the station the General Overseer drove at once to the Exhibition Building, where he was to open his Visitation in Melbourne, on Lord's Day afternoon, February 28, 1904. The secretary with whom he had some business, not being in his office, he drove to the Federal Palace Hotel, where he entertained the members of his party and the officers of the Church who had met him at the station, at a very pleasant luncheon.

When this was over, he drove again to the Exhibition Building, where he met Mr. Short, the Secretary, and also tested his voice in the auditorium of the place.

He then proceeded to the station and, with his son and personal attendant, took the express for Mount Lofty, near Adelaide, South Australia, where he expected to meet his wife, Overseer Jane Dowie, and her secretary, Deaconess Ida M. Stern. It was a happy reunion for both the General Overseer and his personal attendant, Deacon Carl F. Stern, when they arrived at the pretty little railway station up among the hills, at about ten minutes after nine o'clock the next morning.

A Week of Rest and Preparation.

The week following was spent in resting and work combined, at the beautiful summer home of Overseer Jane Dowie's parents, "Calton Hill," at Crafers Post-office, under the shadow of Mount Lofty.

In the meantime, Overseer Excell, Deacon Williams and the writer of these chronicles were left in Melbourne to assist Overseer Voliva in preparing for the Melbourne Visitation, and in preparing photographs and reports of the Visitation for LEAVES OF HEALING.

On Lord's Day, February 21, 1904, we had the privilege and pleasure of attending the afternoon and evening services in Central Zion Tabernacle, in Swanston street, near Latrobe street, Melbourne.

EXTERIOR, CENTRAL ZION TABERNACLE, MELBOURNE.
Formerly known as Hibernian Hall.

Central Zion Tabernacle, Melbourne.

This Tabernacle which was formerly known as the Hibernian Hall, is a large, brick and artificial stone building, at the top of one of the most prominent hills, and in one of the principal streets of the city.

It has a basement which is not used by the Branch.

The main floor has spacious offices, anterooms, and a beautiful assembly-room, which is used for Divine Healing meetings and other gatherings which do not need the space of the large, main auditorium, which is on the floor above.

This is equipped with large robing-rooms for choir and officers, a broad platform, a choir gallery, and seats for about fifteen hundred auditors—one thousand on the main floor and five hundred in the galleries. Inside, the entire building is beautifully painted and decorated.

Deacon Champe's design of the Zion Banner, with the Stars and Stripes, and the Union Jack, which appeared on the front cover of the first volume of THE ZION BANNER, is very cleverly reproduced, in enlarged form, over the proscenium arch.

Behind and above the choir gallery are the words, "I Am the Lord That Healeth Thee," and all about them are arranged, "Trophies Captured from the Enemy,"—crutches, high boots, plaster casts, surgical appliances, braces, drugs, Masonic and other Secret Order aprons and regalia, pipes, and cigar-holders, and other articles signifying bondage, for which their former slaves no longer have use.

Without, the building has been entirely repainted since it came into the hands of Zion, and over the front door, in large letters, is the legend, "Central Zion Tabernacle."

On either side of the building, which is high and has no other houses near it, is painted the word ZION, in great white letters eighteen feet high.

Thus Central Zion Tabernacle in Melbourne, the headquarters of the work of the Christian Catholic Church in Zion in Australasia, is set upon a hill and cannot be hid, the light of that great white word, ZION, shining in the sunlight all over the city of Melbourne.

A Delightful Zion Service.

The audience which gathered there on that lovely Lord's Day afternoon, was unmistakably a Zion audience, although there were also hundreds of outsiders present.

That the audience was somewhat larger than usual, owing to the approaching Visitation of the General Overseer, was no doubt true; but many of the members of the Church informed us that the Tabernacle services on the Lord's Day were usually attended by from eight hundred to a thousand people.

This is by far the largest audience that gathers at any Protestant church in the City of Melbourne.

On that very morning we had gone to one of the largest and most popular churches in the city, and had heard one of the most learned divines in all Australia speak to an audience of about two hundred.

The services on this afternoon began with the Processional of Zion White-robed Choir and Robed Officers.

It was very touching to us, so far away from home, to see the little girls come up the aisle, their bright eyes alight with the joy of leading that beautiful line, and their sweet faces grave with true worship as they sang the words of praise and adoration to God, just as we had seen the little girls lead the Processional so often in Zion City, in the Chicago Auditorium, and in the great Madison Square Garden, New York City.

It was very much like getting home again, to see the long line of singers, in their white vestments, slowly mount the platform and fill the gallery behind, the music of their consecrated voices growing in volume until the solemn Amen was sung, after the Robed Officers had taken their places on the platform.

The other exercises of the service were those to which we had become familiar in Zion, and which we had grown to love, the Choir singing the *Te Deum Laudamus* and an anthem in a manner that reflected great credit, not only upon them, but upon their Conductor, Deacon Harrison. The sermon of Overseer Voliva was a straightforward, fearless, simple, practical, and effective lesson from the Word of God on the subject of Repentance, and, like every true Zion sermon, was thoroughly up to date.

INTERIOR, CENTRAL ZION TABERNACLE, MELBOURNE.

The Overseer was listened to with quietness and respect throughout his discourse.

By patient and persevering efforts, and calm, courageous and unwavering determination, he has taught the larrikin element and the impudent, hypocritical questioners that in Central Zion Tabernacle, Melbourne, they cannot disturb religious meetings with impunity.

In the evening, Overseer Excell spoke from the following text:

> The voice of one that crieth, Prepare ye in the wilderness the way of Jehovah, make straight in the desert a highway for our God.

Every valley shall be exalted, and every mountain and hill shall be made low: and the crooked shall be made straight, and the rough places plain:
And the glory of Jehovah shall be revealed, and all flesh shall see it together: for the mouth of Jehovah hath spoken it.
The voice of one saying, Cry. And one said, What shall I cry? All flesh is grass, and all the goodliness thereof is as the flower of the field.

The Overseer's address was simple, clear and convincing, full of deep, spiritual truth and practical instruction for these Times of the Restoration of All Things.

On Friday morning, February 26, 1904, the General Overseer, Overseer Jane Dowie and Dr. A. J. Gladstone Dowie, accompanied by Colonel and Deaconess Carl F. Stern, arrived in Melbourne and proceeded at once to the home of Overseer and Elder Voliva, the Arlington, 43 Park street, St. Kilda.

St. Kilda is the most beautiful suburb of Melbourne, being situated on Hobson's Bay, near the great domain known as Albert Park.

All along the beach at St. Kilda, there is a beautiful esplanade overlooking the bay, and also St. Phillip's Bay, farther out.

On the beach there are several well-equipped bathhouses, which were very much appreciated by some of the General Overseer's party.

Overseer Voliva's pleasant home is situated only one block from the beach, two blocks from the Suburban Railway Station, and two blocks from the cable line that runs into Melbourne; so that it was a very convenient abiding place for the General Overseer and his family.

Zion in Melbourne Gives the General Overseer and Party a Pleasant Reception.

On Friday evening at eight o'clock, at Central Zion Tabernacle, a reception was held in honor of the General Overseer and party. Special tickets had been issued for the admission of the members of the Branch of the Christian Catholic Church in Zion in Melbourne, friends of Zion and of the General Overseer, and many members and friends of Zion from all parts of Australasia. Among those who were in attendance were Deacon and Deaconess J. Thomas Wilhide of Auckland, New Zealand, and Deacon Partridge, in charge of the Branch of the Christian Catholic Church in Zion in Kangaroo Island.

RESIDENCE OF OVERSEER VOLIVA.

The guests, of whom there were probably eight or nine hundred, were received in the handsome assembly-room, being presented to the General Overseer and the members of his party by Overseer Wilbur Glenn Voliva. As they passed through they were given a hearty hand clasp by the General Overseer and by those with him.

Among them the General Overseer found many who had been blessed through his ministry, when he was in Melbourne over sixteen years before, and many happy reminiscences were brought to mind.

When all had passed through, and had assembled in the auditorium of the Tabernacle, the General Overseer and his party took seats on the platform.

The room was very tastefully decorated with the Zion colors, gold, white and blue, foliage and cut flowers.

Over the platform in white and green were the words:

ZION WELCOMES ELIJAH THE RESTORER.

After the services had begun with a rousing Zion song and earnest prayer, in which all joined, three beautiful little girls dressed in white came up the aisle, each bringing with her a basket of flowers.

They were Miss Ruth Voliva, daughter of Overseer and Elder Voliva, and the twin daughters of Deacon Carey.

When they had reached the platform, they very sweetly presented a basket to the General Overseer, one to Overseer Jane Dowie, and one to Dr. A. J. Gladstone Dowie.

The exercises of the evening were in charge of the Overseer of the Christian Catholic Church in Zion for Australasia, the Rev. Wilbur Glenn Voliva.

In a very happy manner he presented the entire Visitation party to the people, and then introduced Overseer Jane Dowie.

The Overseer-in-charge of the Women's Work in the Christian Catholic Church in Zion Throughout the World, known and loved in Australia many years before, and now wherever the flag of Zion has been raised, was given a most hearty and affectionate greeting as she rose to address the little gathering.

Her words were brief but came straight from her heart, and were spoken with the gentle womanliness so well known to those who have heard the Overseer speak.

She expressed her pleasure at meeting the people of Zion, and so many old friends; also in seeing once more her dear father and mother and relatives, and the land of her birth.

She said, however, that she had also learned to love the land of her adoption, and especially Zion City, whither she urged them all to go.

She was followed by Dr. A. J. Gladstone Dowie, who upon introduction by Overseer Voliva, said that, inasmuch as he had talked to the people for an hour and thirty minutes on the previous Lord's Day week, he would be very brief on this occasion.

Having expressed his pleasure in meeting the people and assuring them of his prayers for them he closed.

Overseer J. G. Excell, General Ecclesiastical Secretary, and Deacon Arthur W. Newcomb, Secretary and Special Correspondent, spoke briefly.

Then that for which the people had been waiting, the address of the General Overseer, was given. Being introduced by Overseer Voliva, the man of God first of all gave hearty and loving greeting to all present. He then proceeded at once to an intensely earnest and practical discussion of his subject, "The Kingdom of God."

This address was most attentively listened to and enthusiastically received.

It was plain that God's Messenger was speaking to an audience in whose hearts were the highways to Zion.

On the following day, final preparations were made for the opening of the Visitation in Melbourne, in the Great Exhibition Building, on the afternoon of Lord's Day, February 28th

The City of Melbourne.

In order that the events of the next few days may be more thoroughly understood, it may be well to review a few points in the previous history of the General Overseer and of Zion in Melbourne.

Melbourne is the capital of the State of Victoria, and the temporary capital of the Commonwealth of Australia. It is also the metropolis of Australasia.

It is situated upon the Yarra River and St. Phillip's Bay.

It is one of the most beautiful cities in Australia, having very broad, well-paved, and well-kept streets, many handsome public buildings, parks and gardens, and being surrounded by a large number of very delightful suburbs.

Its climate is semi-tropical, and its trees, shrubs and flowers therefore, luxuriant and beautiful.

Nowhere can be seen brighter sunlight, bluer skies, or more wonderful starlight.

Its population, mainly emigrants from the British Isles, and their descendants, numbers between six and seven hundred thousand, it being but a very little larger than Sydney, New South Wales, the second city in the commonwealth.

A Bit of History.

It was in this city that the General Overseer labored as an independent evangelist of the Everlasting Gospel from 1880 to 1888.

During those eight years he not only taught and practiced Divine Healing through faith in Jesus, the Christ, the

Son of God, but preached Repentance with a terrible directness that made him hated and feared by the hypocrites in the apostate churches, the thieves, liars and oppressors high in official life, and by all the forces of evil in the city.

While the people heard him gladly and many were saved, healed and blessed, he was bitterly opposed by those whose craft he endangered, and whose sins he exposed.

As a result, he had many a fierce battle in Melbourne.

More than once attempts were made to take his life, and the whole colony rang with the noise of the conflict.

But he was always victorious there, as he has always been elsewhere.

For that reason he was even more bitterly hated, and more greatly feared by his enemies.

Needless to say that these old foes had not forgotten him.

Needless, also, to say that many of those who had been saved and healed and blessed through his ministry still remained and had not forgotten him.

Conditions in Melbourne at This Visitation.

And now he was returning to Melbourne, stronger and more powerful than ever; hating sin and loving God more than ever; more definitely and more effectively than ever the enemy of all hypocrisy and iniquity.

More than that, he came as Elijah the Restorer to herald the coming of the Christ to reign as King

Hence it was that, in addition to his old enemies, there arose against him every Masonic Baal-worshiper inside and outside of the denominational churches, every false shepherd of an apostate church, whose cloak of hypocrisy would be stripped from him by this mighty Prophet, and by every lawless larrikin in the city of Melbourne.

When he sent officers of the Christian Catholic Church in Zion to Melbourne several years before, a large number of the denominational ministers of the city met together and decided that they must not be permitted to obtain any foothold in that city.

As a result, the newspapers, the religious press, and many other influences in the city, were bound together against these Messengers.

Notwithstanding this opposition, as is well known, Zion obtained a foothold in Melbourne, and hundreds were saved, healed, blessed, and brought out of the apostasies and baptized by the officers of the Christian Catholic Church in Zion, as might be expected.

This only served to increase the bitterness of the hatred and the rage of the opposition.

When it became known that the General Overseer himself was to visit Melbourne, a crusade of the most diabolical lying was begun by the two morning papers of the city, the *Age* and the *Argus*, and by the so-called religious press of the city, chief among them, the *Southern Cross*, edited by Dr. W. H. Fitchett, a very prominent Methodist.

Every fiendish concoction of mendacity from the very worst of the gutter press of America was eagerly taken up, added to, and published in the columns of the *Age*, the *Argus*, the *Southern Cross*, and many other newspapers.

Everything possible was done by the press, by the pulpit, and in private conversation to fill the people with the belief that John Alexander Dowie, who was coming to Melbourne, was not only the prince of impostors, blasphemers and false prophets, but also the destroyer of domestic peace, the despoiler of widows and orphans, and the brutal, haughty, self-seeking oppressor of thousands of deluded, starving, freezing, dying victims in Zion City.

These attacks increased in frequency and in virulence as the time for the Visitation drew near.

Preparations for the Preservation of Order.

When the Masonic mobs of Sydney howled themselves hoarse in the Town Hall, and hunted the General Overseer for his very life in that city, the Melbourne *Age*, *Argus*, *Southern Cross*, and other newspapers, published accounts of the proceedings in such a manner that it could easily be read between the lines that this was the manner in which they wished Melbourne also to treat John Alexander Dowie.

This kind of journalistic incitement of mob violence had continued up to that very Saturday morning before the first meeting in the Exhibition Building.

Having seen something of the temper of the Melbourne mob, at the Spencer Street Station on the previous Friday week, the General Overseer determined that he would do all in his power to protect the people who might attend the services in the Exhibition Building, and give them an opportunity to listen quietly.

Accordingly he paid the police department of Victoria for twenty officers to be on duty inside the Exhibition Building on Lord's Day afternoon and evening, and secured the promise that thirteen more would be sent, making thirty-three in all.

The Exhibition Building is a very large structure, with a great deal of open floor-space, but is seated only in one wing, known as the Concert Hall.

This hall is provided with a great pipe-organ, choir gallery and platform, and about three thousand chairs. To the rear of these chairs the open floor-space of the building extends back for several hundred feet.

In a portion of this opens-pace four or five thousand more chairs had been placed, and behind them several screens to shut off the rest of the building. Chairs were also placed in the galleries nearest the platform.

Crowds at Lord's Day Afternoon Meeting.

On the Lord's Day afternoon, for several hours, all roads in Melbourne seemed to lead to the Exhibition Building.

Tickets were taken at the turnstiles, placed at gates in the iron fence surrounding the grounds in which the building stands.

Hour after hour these turnstiles whirled incessantly as the people passed through, and hour after hour the crowd of those who did not hold tickets gathered and grew in the streets outside.

By half past two o'clock, the time set for the beginning of the service, every chair was taken, while hundreds stood, so the turnstiles were closed and the doors shut.

Cowardly Action of the Police.

Before the audience had gathered, Overseer Voliva and Deacon A. J. Gladstone Dowie had placed the policemen, who had been hired for the day, at various points throughout the building, and had instructed them to remain there and keep order.

The Subinspector in charge, and many of his men, were loud in their boasts of the severe action that they would take with any one who attempted to disturb the meeting or enter without a ticket.

It is a significant fact that within a very few minutes after the opening of the service, only three of these boastful officers could be seen in the building, the rest having sneaked out with their tongues in their cheeks, as soon as the meeting was called to order.

For a few minutes after it had gathered, and before the General Overseer came upon the platform, the crowd seemed to be very orderly and quiet, making no disturbance whatever; so that Mr. Short, the secretary of the building, was led to assure the General Overseer that there would be no disturbance whatever.

The Beginning of the Disturbance.

But this exemplary orderliness was very short-lived.

A few minutes later there was a crash of heavily-booted feet on the floor, and a roar from hundreds of hoarse voices.

This had partially subsided when the General Overseer, accompanied by Overseer Jane Dowie, Dr. A. J. Gladstone Dowie, Overseer and Elder Wilbur Glen Voliva, and the other members of the Visitation party, in the robes and uniforms of their office, came upon the platform.

The enthusiastic greeting of thousands of friends was marred by the intermingling of yells, catcalls and imprecations from the organized mob.

The disturbers were not altogether quiet during the Invocation, and attempted, but were unable, to break up the singing of the hymn.

Several impudent and wicked men kept bawling out questions and comments, each of these being a signal for laughter, yelling, jumping on chairs, and other demonstrations by the larrikins and well-dressed ruffians that had entered the building.

All this the General Overseer endured with great patience and forbearance, waiting for the police to accomplish what they had so boastfully declared they would do, and for the sober sense of the thousands of law-abiding citizens who were present to assert itself and shame the interrupters into silence.

When, however, Overseer Jane Dowie rose and began to read the Scripture lesson from the 35th chapter of Isaiah, the insults which were heaped upon her became intolerable.

No sooner was her voice heard than several scores of young men began to mock, at which a large number of young women and others in the audience had the shamelessness to laugh.

The General Overseer stepped forward, and calmly but earnestly began to appeal to manhood, common decency, and reverence for the Word of God, that the disturbance might cease.

He had evidently appealed to qualities which these young men and women did not possess; for no sooner had the Overseer resumed reading than the disturbance was repeated.

Again, still calmly and quietly, but more earnestly, he made the appeal, and again it was shamelessly disregarded.

The General Overseer then announced that Overseer Dowie would read this chapter, and that the meeting would not proceed until she had been permitted to read it without interruption.

The audience was then comparatively quiet until she had finished the reading.

The offering was taken with considerable difficulty, owing to the very peculiar sense of humor of some of the audience, who seemed to regard it side-splittingly funny to take the collection boxes when they came to them and hide them under the chairs.

Some of the highly-cultured gentlemen of Melbourne in the rear of the hall conceived the brilliantly intellectual feat of breaking one of the boxes to pieces. It was too strong for them, however, and they succeeded only in smashing in the top of it.

And the three policemen who had remained in the building stood and looked on.

All this, the Melbourne *Argus* of the following day referred to as the rightful exercise of the prerogatives of British citizens.

An Organized Mob Breaks In.

Meanwhile, the crowds outside the building and outside the gates of the grounds had grown very restless.

Notwithstanding the presence of thirty-three of the brave, strong police officers of this order-loving (?) city an organized mob of some hundreds broke open one of the gates, and added themselves to the howling, stamping minority inside the building.

When the General Overseer rose to deliver his address, absolutely nothing had been said which could by the most severe stretch of the imagination be considered as offensive to the most sensitive of persons, nevertheless a howl of fear and rage greeted him from several hundred in that audience.

As he attempted to proceed with his address, it was clear as daylight that there were several thousand present who had come for no other purpose than to hear respectfully and quietly; but that the remainder of the audience, or rather assemblage, as this minority had no idea of hearing, had come fully organized with recognized leaders to prevent the Voice of God's Messenger from being heard, and to break up the meeting in disorder.

The Disorder Reaches Its Height.

The General Overseer could scarcely speak a single sentence without several minutes of yelling and stamping and singing of vulgar songs intervening between the subject and the predicate.

As he patiently attempted to continue his discourse, the disturbance grew worse and worse, until at last not a word could be heard above the uproar.

Hundreds were standing on chairs, screaming until they were red in the face, bawling out the choruses of vulgar songs, which some Australians are foolish enough to consider patriotic, and otherwise adding to the noise.

Personnel of the Mob.

Do not let any one for a moment lay this outrage to the charge of the Melbourne larrikins.

They were not the guilty parties, although a few may, perhaps, have been led on by others.

It is an absolute fact, and can be proved, that pastors of Melbourne churches, superintendents of Melbourne Sunday-schools, officers in the Salvation Army, members of the Young Men's Christian Association, the Epworth League, the Young People's Society of Christian Endeavor, and of many of the churches of the city, were among the most conspicuous of the disturbers of this meeting.

Besides these there were also cheap politicians, companions of John Norton, members of the Masonic order and other secret societies, and representatives of the saloon element.

It is not to be expected, of course, that any of these will deny their complicity in this disturbance.

They should rather glory in it, since the Melbourne *Argus*, that bulwark of Australian respectability (?), declared the next morning that they were only exercising their precious rights as British citizens.

The following is the report of the service:

Exhibition Building, Melbourne, Victoria, Australia, Sunday Afternoon, February 28, 1904.

The Service was opened by the Congregation's singing Hymn No. 46.

The Apostles' Creed was recited by the Congregation, led by Dr. A. J. Gladstone Dowie.

The 35th chapter of the Prophet Isaiah was read by Overseer Jane Dowie.

Prayer was offered by Overseer Voliva, at the conclusion of which Hymn No. 62 was sung from "Songs and Solos."

The General Overseer then read from the 11th chapter of the Gospel according to St. Matthew.

He then delivered his Message:

WISDOM JUSTIFIED BY HER WORKS.

*REPORTED BY E. W. AND A. W. N.

INVOCATION.

Let the words of my mouth, and the meditation of my heart be acceptable in Thy sight, profitable unto this people, and to all to whom these words shall come, in this great commonwealth, and in every land. For the sake of Jesus. Amen.

TEXT.

Wisdom is justified by her works.

It is not words, it is works that count.

I should like to have said something concerning the past, and regarding my Mission and Visitation in general, but casting myself upon the kind consideration of every Christian man and woman, and every good citizen present, I ask you to listen to the few words I have to say.

I am persuaded that those who are endeavoring to disturb this meeting, and who have dishonorably, and upon false pretenses, come in upon these tickets, are exceedingly few, and that the vast majority of this audience desires to hear respectfully and quietly. [Interruptions.]

"Wisdom," said Jesus, "is justified by her works."

Wisdom is the Principal Thing.

The House of Wisdom has Seven Pillars.

The Wisdom that is from above is first Pure, then Peaceable, Gentle, Easy to be Entreated, full of Mercy and Good Fruits, without Variance, without Hypocrisy. And the Fruit of Righteousness is sown in Peace for them that make Peace.

These are the Pillars of the House of Wisdom.

The Central Pillar is Purity.

John the Baptist, in his sublime character, stands as the great representative of Purity.

He demanded Purity from that king upon the throne.

He demanded, as the Prophet of God, that he should not have that adulterous paramour to wife; that she should be set aside, and that the Holy Land and the City of God should not be disgraced by an adulterer on the throne and an adulteress by his side.

He said, "She is your brother Philip's wife, and thou shalt not have her." [Interruptions.]

I dare say that those who interrupt would be very glad to close my mouth as Herodias closed John the Baptist's, but I thank God that He has not forsaken His world.

Purity is still the Central Pillar in the House of Wisdom.

John the Baptist was renowned for his Purity.

He was born under extraordinary circumstances, the son of Zacharias, the priest of the order of Abijah, and of Elizabeth, a holy woman, but past the age of child-bearing.

The angel Gabriel came, and in the Temple of God, told that aged priest that his wife should be a mother, and that the son who was to be born should be clothed with the power of God, and that he should come in the spirit and power of

*The following report has not been revised by the General Overseer.

Elijah to turn the hearts of the fathers to the children, and the children to the fathers to prepare the way of the Lord.

John the Baptist Fulfilled His Mission.

He was a splendidly-educated man, as was essential, because he was the son of a priest, and of the highest order of the priesthood. [Interruptions. Prolonged uproar.]

John had proclaimed the Christ at the Jordan.

He had said, "He that sent me to baptize with water, He said unto me, Upon whomsoever thou shalt see the Spirit descending, and abiding upon Him, the same is He that baptizeth with the Holy Spirit. And I have seen and have borne witness that this is the Son of God."

He also said of Him, "Behold, the Lamb of God, which taketh away the sin of the world!"

The Christ, from that day, went forth in His Mission, followed by many disciples of John, some of whom became His apostles.

But John himself retired into the wilderness.

His mission was accomplished.

"He must increase, but I must decrease," he said.

So he went back into the wilderness.

But the voluptuous and adulterous paramour of Herod seeing that opportunity, sent the soldiers down through Perea and arrested John in his solitude, carried him off, and plunged him into the dungeon of the Castle of Machærus.

There John the Baptist lay chafing like an eagle in a cage.

The restraint was severe upon him, who had lived on the mountaintop, and in the great wilderness; he who had—

[Interruptions. Prolonged confusion].

Doubt Assails John the Baptist.

John the Baptist lay in that dungeon, his heart sad.

He was not afraid to die, but doubt came to his heart. The great tempter came and tempted him with the thought that Jesus was not the Christ. [Interruptions, howls, laughter, singing of vulgar songs. Many stood upon chairs.]

Respectable citizens will have no part in this.

These are merely a small band, not of citizens, but of criminals.

Those who are making this disturbance are a band of criminals unworthy of citizenship. [Yells.]

John the Baptist had determined that he would put an end to his doubts.

These doubts had made him to question as to whether Jesus was the Christ; so from his prison he sent two of his disciples away up through Perea and Galilee, to Jesus, to ask Him the question as He stood there teaching vast multitudes and healing their sick:

Art Thou He that cometh, or look we for another?

The answer of the Christ is that upon which I shall now speak for a very few minutes.

Go your way, and tell John what things ye have seen and heard; The blind receive their sight, the lame walk, the lepers are cleansed, and the deaf hear, the dead are raised up, the poor have the Gospel preached to them.

[Interruptions.]

John the Baptist did his work. [Noises, shouts and prolonged uproar and confusion. It was some time before the General Overseer could be heard at all.]

The Destruction of Liberty.

This may be very interesting to these young men, but they should remember that they are destroying, by their action, one of the greatest gifts for which their fathers fought and bled —the gift of free speech in a free land.

The only thing that can be done— [Disturbances.]

I do not propose to break my voice speaking against that uproar.

I expect the authorities to do their duty.

I ask you to remember that the greatest heritage that you have, Liberty, is now being invaded and destroyed. [Continuous uproar.]

The day will come when you will bitterly regret allowing that band of criminals to disturb this meeting.

I pass away, but this lawlessness abides.

Unless you take care, all liberty will be gone, and then military power must come in.

Military power must sweep away your right of public meeting in order to maintain freedom. [Noises.]

John the Baptist had his answer.

The blind receive their sight, the lame walk, the lepers are cleansed, and the deaf hear, the dead are raised up, the poor have the Gospel preached to them.

Jesus had sent back His Message— [Disturbances, during which "Jesus, Lover of my Soul" was sung.]

I have many addresses to deliver before I again reach my home, and I do not intend to destroy my voice by speaking under such circumstances as these.

Will the entire audience stand with me and sing the Doxology?

After the Doxology had been sung, amid a pandemonium of yells, screams, ribald songs, and insulting epithets, the General Overseer closed the meeting by pronouncing the

BENEDICTION.

Beloved, abstain from all appearance of evil. And may the very God of Peace Himself sanctify you wholly; and I pray God your whole spirit and soul and body be preserved entire, without blame, unto the coming of our Lord Jesus, the Christ. Faithful is He that calleth you, who also will do it. The grace of our Lord Jesus, the Christ, the love of God, our Father, the fellowship of the Holy Spirit, our Comforter and Guide, one Eternal God, abide in you, bless you and keep you, and all the Israel of God everywhere, forever. Amen.

A Raging Mob Seeks the General Overseer's Life.

As soon as the General Overseer had left the platform, several hundred men made a rush for the rooms in the rear, searching for him.

Many of them were white and trembling with rage, breathing out the most terrible threatenings, as they ran, like a frantic pack of wild animals, from room to room, and through the galleries, seeking their prey.

And the police stood and looked on.

Meanwhile the General Overseer had retired to an anteroom in the rear of the platform which was either unknown to the ruffians or overlooked by them in their impotent fury.

There he was met by Mr. Short, secretary of the building, who apologized very humbly and with evident genuineness for the outrageous treatment accorded him.

Later the Subinspector of Police also came to interview the General Overseer.

After a conference, it was decided that unless an adequate number of foot and mounted officers could be supplied by the Chief Commissioner of Police for the evening service, it would be better, in the interests of public safety, to abandon it altogether.

The Subinspector and Overseer Voliva accordingly proceeded to the Chief Commissioner's office to find what protection could be promised.

Meanwhile the murderous shrieking of the demoniac mob could still be heard in various parts of the building, and especially around the little room where the General Overseer sat.

The full force of Zion Guard in Melbourne was present, and every avenue of entrance to the space behind the platform was carefully kept closed.

At last the majority of the audience having left the building, and the mob having grown appreciably smaller, the police began to sit up and take notice, as it were, and in a subdued manner to clear out the few remaining stragglers.

The Evening Meeting Abandoned on Account of Inadequate Police Protection.

By the time that quiet had been fully restored, word had come from the police headquarters that the greatest number of men that could be furnished for the evening meeting was sixty-eight officers on foot, and two mounted.

The experience of the afternoon had proved how absolutely inadequate any such force would be, and the evening meeting was accordingly abandoned.

During all the storm that followed the close of the afternoon meeting, the members of the Christian Catholic Church in Zion in Melbourne sat quietly in the choir gallery of the building.

They had expected to remain to the evening meeting, and had brought their dinners with them. When the time came, they gathered in little groups to partake of the meal.

When it had been decided, therefore, not to endanger the lives of good citizens and Christian people, by throwing open the building to a murderous mob, without adequate police protection, the General Overseer and the members of his party again came upon the platform, and the situation was explained to the people.

The little gathering was then dismissed, and the General Overseer drove to the home of Overseer Voliva, in St. Kilda.

That night a great crowd gathered at the Exhibition Building, but finding it dark and the gates closed, most of them dispersed disappointed.

Some young men, however, went to Central Zion Tabernacle in Swanston street, around which they skulked nearly all night long.

Another crowd of several hundred, following some leader, ran through the streets to the Federal Palace Hotel, where some of the members of the General Overseer's party were staying, apparently thinking that he himself was there.

For a few minutes they raged and stormed in the streets, but were evidently informed by some one that the General Overseer was not there, for they soon dispersed.

Later in the evening, another mob gathered in front of the hotel, but dispersed without much ado.

He whom they sought was not there.

Owing to the evident disinclination of the police to afford proper protection to him and his people, the General Overseer decided that the meetings to be held in Central Zion Tabernacle during the week should be in the mornings and afternoons instead of mornings and evenings, and that they should be open only to members of the Christian Catholic Church in Zion, their friends, and such other persons as he chose to admit.

The Chief Commissioner of Police Sides With the Mob.

On the Monday, the General Overseer interviewed Chief Commissioner of Police O'Callaghan, to ascertain what protection, if any, could be guaranteed him for the meetings in Central Zion Tabernacle, and especially the meetings to be held in the Exhibition Building on Lord's Day, March 6th.

He was coolly informed that he himself was to blame for the disturbances in the Exhibition Building on the Lord's Day afternoon, and that it would be impossible to guarantee him any protection whatever.

The Chief Commissioner stated, in fact, that if he had five hundred policemen, he could not control the mob, and advised the General Overseer to give up all meetings in Melbourne.

When Overseer Voliva carried the matter to Chief Secretary Sir Samuel Gillott, later in the day, he found that that officer was apparently in fullest accord with the position taken by Chief Commissioner O'Callaghan.

The Press of Melbourne on the Side of the Mob.

The attitude taken in the reports of the meeting in the *Argus* and the *Age* of Monday morning, February 29th, is also significant.

These reports were both of them outrageously false, justifying the mob in every particular, and declaring unequivocally that the General Overseer himself was wholly to blame for the disorder.

On Tuesday morning, March 1st, the Melbourne *Argus* appeared with a leading article, in which it declared that those who had disturbed the meeting in the Exhibition Building were only exercising the rights of free speech, and that it was the high privilege of the disturbers to prevent the General Overseer from being heard if they did not like what he had to say.

Indeed, they went so far as to say that unless the people took it into their own hands to silence any one who spoke in a way that they did not like, free speech would be entirely lost and public discussion would become pandemonium.

A more shameful prostitution of the press to the lawless desires and devices of Freemasonry we have never seen.

The *Argus* received a number of letters protesting against the treatment given God's Messenger in Melbourne, but was too cowardly to print them.

It had the effrontery, however, to print a short paragraph saying that it had received them, but would not print them, because the disturbances complained of were Dr. Dowie's own fault.

The Monday Morning Divine Healing Service.

At half past ten o'clock on Monday morning, February 29th, the General Overseer conducted the first Divine Healing meeting of the Melbourne Visitation in Central Zion Tabernacle.

This meeting was attended by several hundred people, all of whom were very quiet and attentive to the words of the speaker.

The General Overseer, notwithstanding the many other interests which were at that time pressing upon him, threw himself wholly into the teaching, and God greatly blessed his words to those present.

The following is the report of the service:

Central Zion Tabernacle, Melbourne, Victoria, Australia, Monday Morning, February 29, 1904.

After singing and the reading of the 8th chapter of Matthew, prayer was offered by Overseer J. G. Excell.

"The Great Physician" was sung and the General Overseer then delivered the address:

CONDITIONS OF THE COVENANT OF HEALING.

*REPORTED BY E. W. AND A. W. N.

INVOCATION.

Let the words of my mouth and the meditations of my heart be acceptable in Thy sight, be profitable unto this people, O Lord, my Strength and my Redeemer.

TEXT.

And when even was come, they brought unto Him many possessed with devils: and He cast out the spirits with a word, and healed all that were sick:
That it might be fulfilled which was spoken by Isaiah the prophet, saying, Himself took our infirmities, and bare our diseases.

With "a Word."

Not with His Word.

It Was the Word of the Father.

Jesus said, "The words that I say unto you, I speak not from Myself: but the Father abiding in Me, doeth His works."

Think into it.

The great trouble with the masses of the people is, they do not think.

It is an easy thing to talk, clatter, chatter and be impudent, but the thoughtful person is slow to speak.

Unthinking people say that Jesus healed the people.

But He did not; it was the Father.

He said, "Of Mine ownself I can do nothing."

"The words that I say unto you, I speak not from Myself: but the Father abiding in Me, doeth His works."

When He healed people, it was not the great Elder Brother, the Son of God, the Son of Man, talking; it was the Father.

When He forgave people, it was not the Son of God forgiving sins. It was the Father.

Jesus said, "Son, thy sins are forgiven thee."

A brother does not say, Son.

When the Christ said to the woman that touched the hem of His garment, "Daughter, be of good cheer, thy faith hath made thee whole," who was talking, our Brother or our Father?

Voices—"Our Father."

General Overseer—Do not forget that.

People talk about the Christ's saying this, and doing that; but it was not the Christ.

He had laid aside His power and Godhead, and emptied Himself and come into this world as a man.

Everything that He did was in the Power of the Spirit of the Father.

Everything that He said was spoken by the Father.

He said, "My Father worketh hitherto, and I work," but His work was to do the Will of the Father.

The Father's Will and Work were done through Him.

Never forget that point, because it is of the utmost importance.

He glorified the Father. He came to do it. He does it yet.

Jesus Teaches Us to Pray to the Father.

When He teaches us to pray, He never teaches us to pray to Himself.

He says, "When ye pray, say, Father."

When the Apostle Paul prayed, he said, "For this cause I bow my knees unto the Father."

Nowadays, when many people pray, they pray to the Holy Spirit, and they pray to Jesus, the Christ.

I shall do the same thing, if you will tell me where to get the command for it.

If you will tell me where Jesus ever taught me to pray to Him, I shall pray to Him.

*The following report has not been revised by the General Overseer.

If you will tell me where any apostle ever taught me to pray to Jesus, I shall pray to Jesus.

If you will tell me where the Holy Spirit ever taught me to pray to Jesus, I shall pray to Jesus.

But the Holy Spirit comes into our hearts crying, "Abba, Father," and teaching us how to pray.

Surely Jesus knew how to pray, and how to teach us how to pray!

When He Himself prayed, He said, "Father," and when He prays now He says "Father."

He is the Advocate with the Father.

Prayer Must Be in the Name of Jesus.

Do not pray to Jesus, the Christ, but pray to the Father in His Name, and for His sake, as He taught you.

He said, "Hitherto have ye asked nothing in My Name: ask, and ye shall receive, that your joy may be fulfilled."

But you are to ask the Father.

"If two of you," said the Christ, "shall agree on earth as touching anything that they shall ask, it shall be done for them of My Father which is in heaven."

At the very beginning, I tell you that a large number of you are blundering when you pray.

One would think that you had three Gods to whom to pray.

Sometimes you begin your prayer, "Blessed Lord Jesus." That is wrong.

Sometimes you begin your prayer, "Dear, blessed Holy Spirit." That is wrong.

You must say, "Father, I come to Thee in Jesus' Name, and ask the power of Thy Holy Spirit that I may know how to pray.

"Father, send the Spirit in power into my heart, that I may say, 'Abba, Father.'"

You see, that is a very important matter.

"Oh," you say, "it is all the same; it does not matter how we pray."

That is the reason you get into disorder.

It Does Matter How You Pray.

"Oh, but if we address Jesus, the Father will know that we mean Him, and if we address the Holy Spirit, the Holy Spirit will know that we mean the Father."

But He will do no such thing.

If you address a letter to John Brown, it will not go to Thomas Smith.

You must put the right name on it when you put it into the postoffice.

It will lie in the dead-letter office if you do not address it properly.

That is where a great many prayers lie—in the dead-letter office.

They are not offered as the Christ commanded.

Jesus said, "When ye pray, say Father," and you have no right to say, "I will pray as I like."

And when even was come, they brought unto Him many possessed with devils: and He cast out the spirits with a word, and healed all that were sick:

That it might be fulfilled which was spoken by Isaiah the prophet, saying, Himself took our infirmities, and bare our diseases.

Teaching With Authority.

I suppose that I can say, without any affectation or egotism, that I have delivered a larger number of Divine Healing addresses than any other man in the world; that I have given this matter more attention than any man now living on earth; that I now have hundreds of thousands of living witnesses who say that through my teaching, prayer and laying on of hands they have been healed of their sicknesses.

I have also the joy of knowing that vast multitudes of these were first of all saved through my agency, and received forgiveness of sins.

I speak, therefore, with authority.

I am not speaking controversially; what I am speaking is true.

It is not the discussion of the question as to whether it is true.

If I were teaching mathematics, I should not teach my pupils that certain propositions might be true; I should teach them that the thing was true.

If I were teaching any science, the basis of which was well-known and exact, I should speak positively.

I should not, for a single moment, take the position that it might be true, or it might not, leaving them to decide.

If I did that, my pupils would go uninstructed.

That was the case when I sat under great mathematical instructors. I believed that they were competent to instruct me, and I took the instruction.

I am telling you how I speak. Therefore, if you note in my positiveness something that you do not like, set it down to the fact that I know and you do not.

That is very strong, is it not?

But that is the master talking.

Do you not know that the true teacher always talks with authority?

He has no right to be a teacher, if he does not.

Jesus, the Christ, Ever the Same.

I know what I am talking about.

I know, for instance, that "Jesus, the Christ, is the same yesterday, and today, yea, and forever."

If He is the same, He is the same Savior.

If He is the same, He is the same Healer.

If He is the same, He is the same Cleanser and Keeper.

If He is not the same, the Bible is a lie, and we had better get some other text-book, and some other Savior.

If I were to ask you if He is the same, you would all say Yes; and yet some of you have medicine, perhaps, in your homes and even in your pockets.

While you would say He is the same Healer, with your lips, you would deny it in action, because you do not trust Him.

That is a terrible thing, is it not?

I will not ask you to say what you believe, because you might tell me a lie.

You might say, "I believe that He is the Savior, and the Healer, and the Cleanser, and the Keeper," yet there would be a great, doubting "but" in your heart.

BIRD'S-EYE VIEW OF THE CITY OF

But? But what?

"O Doctor, you know He is not here now," you might say.

Jesus, the Christ, With Us All the Days.

A minister a little while ago said, "Dr. Dowie talks as if Jesus, the Christ, were here, and we all know He is not."

The people looked at one another smiling.

They thought that the man had said a very clever thing.

He had shown that he was not a Christian, and they who approved it showed that they were not.

Did not Jesus say, "Go ye therefore, and make disciples of all the nations, baptizing them into the Name of the Father, and of the Son, and of the Holy Spirit: teaching them to observe all things whatsoever I commanded you: and lo, I am with you All the Days, even unto the Consummation of the Age?"

Is He with us All the Days?

People—"Yes."

General Overseer—Is He with us now?

People—"Yes."

General Overseer—Is He the same?

People—"Yes."

General Overseer—Then, is not He who took our infirmities and bore our sicknesses present with us?

People—"Yes."

General Overseer—Is He not now just as able, just as willing, just as ready to heal those who fulfil the Divine conditions as He was nineteen centuries ago?

People—"Yes."

If any of you think in any other way than the way God thinks, you will get into trouble.

That is true even in material science.

You must think as God thinks about electricity, or you will be electrocuted.

You must think as God thinks about the law of gravitation, or you will get your head smashed.

You must think as God thinks, and not run against His laws, or His laws will grind you to powder.

If, on the other hand, you think as He thinks, you can use the great powers that He has given.

If you obey the law and act in accord with it, then you will find that everything will go right.

We ask God to enable us this morning to think as He thinks.

Then we will think rightly.

I Am Not Talking to Infidels.

I never discuss matters with infidels; for I believe what the Word of God says:

> The fool hath said in his heart, There is no God.
> They are corrupt, they have done abominable works.

I do not trouble to argue with fools, and I do not trouble myself about the corrupt people who have done abominable works, except to reprove their works, and to demand that they shall do right.

I speak sternly to the people who call themselves infidels.

They are degenerate, vile, immoral wretches who are fighting

LBOURNE, VICTORIA, AUSTRALIA.

General Overseer—I am talking to my big class.

Oftentimes I have a great class of seven thousand, who are all just as quiet as this, sometimes ten thousand. Lately I have talked, in some cases, to fifteen or sixteen thousand.

Law and Order in America.

The mob is not allowed to rule in great American cities.

You may think different; you may hear different, but it is not.

I am not speaking of Southern lynchings.

In our great American cities, the riotous rabble are kept in perfect order. They have to be.

If it were not so, we should have our cities burned to the ground, our women ravished, and our banks and commercial institutions smashed.

The lawless people are there, but they have to be kept down. So they must be here.

We have all agreed upon the fact that Jesus, the Christ, is with us now; that He who took our infirmities and bore our sicknesses is with us now, and that He is doing the Will of the Father by the Spirit.

I trust that you will accept me as interpreting His Word.

I have no desire whatever to tell you what I think, because what I think is not worth a pin.

What you think is not worth a pin.

The Only Thought That Is Worth Anything Is What God Thinks.

Think as God thinks, and you will think rightly.

God, and trying to make a pretense that they do not believe there is a God, to cover up their own iniquities.

I never knew an infidel yet who was not an evil liver, even those of high literary rank.

You can be certain that they are men who trample under foot the Ten Commandments, every chance they get.

I have no time to talk with the infidel.

I do not trouble myself about him except to reprove him, and demand that he yield to God.

Many do yield to God. When they are commanded to repent, they repent.

But some of you preachers—and I see a few preachers here this morning—do not command the people to repent, and they do not repent.

They are allowed to go on in their sins without reproof.

When you make a pretense of reproving them, it is like sprinkling eau de Cologne!

You do not reprove them in a way they feel. I reprove them in a way they feel, and that is why they howled yesterday.

That is why they do not want to hear.

They think that they can stop my speaking, but they cannot; because if I were to die tomorrow, I have written enough to make it impossible to stop my voice.

I will be heard.

God's Promise to Heal Conditional.

We must understand that our Lord Jesus, the Christ, is not only able, and willing, and present to heal just as He was nineteen centuries ago, but that there are conditions that you must fulfil in order to get that healing.

You do not make the conditions, nor do I.

God makes them.

"Oh," you say, "If I ask Him He will do it."

If you ask in accordance with His Will, He will do it; but mark you, His Will makes clear the conditions.

You must ask in accordance with His Will; for it is written, "This is the boldness which we have toward Him, that, if we ask anything according to His Will, He heareth us: and if we know that He heareth us whatsoever we ask, we know that we have the petition which we have asked of Him."

But do you not see that the whole thing lies in that point—"according to His will?"

It is His will that makes the conditions.

Suppose that I left the vast property which I control, and which is supposed to be worth twenty-five million dollars, by a will which has conditions.

If the persons to whom I leave properties and powers do not fulfil these conditions, then they must stand aside and others must fulfil them.

They cannot claim what I have given them under the will unless they fulfil the conditions of the will.

God never, under any circumstances, uttered His will without conditions.

In connection with Divine Healing the conditions are perfectly clear.

The Conditions in the Covenant of Healing.

They are given to you in the very first Covenant of Divine Healing in the 15th chapter of the book of Exodus.

These are the words of the Covenant:

If thou wilt diligently harken to the Voice of Jehovah thy God, and wilt do that which is right in His eyes, and wilt give ear to His commandments, and keep all His statutes, I will put none of the diseases upon thee, which I have put upon the Egyptians: for I am Jehovah that healeth thee.

The conditions are put first: "If thou wilt diligently harken."

Is God the Healer of a brutal band of people who say, "I will do as I like, and go as I please?"

No. You must diligently harken to what He says.

The first thing that He says is, Repent!

That is what the Christ said when He preached the Gospel, after John the Baptist had been put into prison.

He came into Galilee, Mark says, preaching the Gospel of the Kingdom of God.

The Christ Made Very Little of the Church.

Throughout the Gospels of Mark, and Luke, and John He never once used the word Church.

It is only in Matthew that the word Church occurs, and then only twice; for the Church is simply those who are called out of something.

They are called out of the Kingdom of God, not out of the kingdom of this world.

People are born into the Kingdom of God, and from the Kingdom are called into the Church.

Those only who are saved can enter the Church.

If you have people in the Church who have not been born into the Kingdom of God, then they belong to the Devil.

The greater part of the mischief done in the Exhibition Building yesterday was done by professing Christians.

There is no question about that.

Our own people know how many professing Christians were there.

Many of them were Freemasons, who do not dare to name the Name of Jesus, the Christ, in their lodges.

The Bishop of Melbourne Rebuked.

The Bishop of Melbourne tells you that he will not hide his Masonry under his Episcopal garb.

When he delivers a sermon in the cathedral to the Masons, he does not dare to name the Name of Jesus, the Christ.

I have read two reports of that sermon, and the Name of Jesus, the Christ, is not in it from beginning to end.

Otherwise it would not have been a Masonic sermon.

He did not dare to stand in his own cathedral and preach a sermon to Masons that had the Name of Jesus, the Christ, in it; for that is contrary to Masonic teaching.

Go to the reports of that sermon, published in the *Age* and the *Argus*, and try to find the Name of Jesus. I will give you a twenty-dollar gold piece, an American coin, for every time you find the Name of Jesus, the Christ in the report of either the *Argus* or the *Age*.

It is not there.

You do not dare, if you are a Mason, to name the Name of Jesus, the Christ, to Masons.

The Name of Jesus, the Christ, cannot be mentioned in a Masonic Lodge.

Whenever the Masonic ritual quotes from the Scripture, where that Name occurs, it is cut out.

They do read the Scriptures, but with the Name of Jesus, the Christ, left out.

They do pray, but the Name of Jesus, the Christ, is left out.

They do exhort, but the Name of Jesus, the Christ, is left out.

That is not a mere assertion.

That is a fact.

Since I have come to this city, I have gone over these two reports of the sermon that Bishop Clark preached in his own cathedral, to Freemasons, and I do not find the Name of Jesus, the Christ, occurring in either of them. He did not dare to speak that Name.

He was a Mason in his cathedral, and a Christian nowhere.

The Masonic Order Responsible for Sydney and Melbourne Riots.

They talk about its being bosh and rot to say that the Masons are at the bottom of the disturbances in our meetings, but they are.

On the way here, I was told by a minister of the Gospel at Murray Bridge that a Freemason there had said that "the Masons of Australia would like to poleax Dr. Dowie," and they would do it if they could.

Perhaps they will be able to do it, if God permits them.

I am going on with my work, whether I am "poleaxed" or not. [Applause.]

That makes very little difference to me.

My great concern is to do my duty.

The Covenant of Healing stands. It is a Covenant of Jehovah, and Jehovah, in Hebrew, means the Coming One.

Jesus, the Christ, is the Coming One.

He came, and He is coming again; but He is also with us in Spirit.

The Covenant says that you are to ask, after you have done what God tells you.

The first thing is to Repent!

He preached the Gospel of the Kingdom of God.

The Kingdom is larger than the Church, because the Church is the mere expression of the Kingdom.

There are multitudes in the Kingdom of God who are not in the Church.

There are, alas! many in the Church who never were in the Kingdom.

Zion the Kingdom of God.

The Christ never spoke of the Gospel of a church.

All His parables are about the Kingdom of God.

All His teaching is about the Kingdom of God.

He came to establish a Kingdom.

The Kingdom of God is the principal thing, and that is what we are attending to in Zion.

This Church is the Christian Catholic Church in Zion.

Zion is the prophetic word for the Kingdom of God.

If you can find another church that is in Zion; that is in the Kingdom of God, that is all right. I am willing to acknowledge every one that is in the Kingdom of God.

I am a much broader man than you think in that matter.

I think that there are many in the Methodist church who are in the Kingdom of God, but some of you miserables hold the Methodist church first and belong to the Kingdom of God after.

You do not consider the interests of the Kingdom of God as supreme.

You oftentimes consider the interests of your little church as supreme.

That will not do.

It is the Kingdom of God that is to be considered.

If the Christian Catholic Church in Zion does not consider

the interests of the Kingdom of God as paramount, then it has failed in its duty, and ought to perish.

Every church ought to perish that does not maintain the broad and eternal interests of the Kingdom of God.

The Christ is working to establish the Father's Kingdom upon the earth, and when He has finished His work, He will deliver up the Kingdom unto God, even the Father, and God shall be All in All.

It is the Kingdom that is the great thing.

Repentance.

You must repent.

"Oh," you say, "I repented long ago, when I was saved."

There are many people who are saved and sin again, and they have to repent again, and repent thoroughly.

Some say that if a person is once saved, he does not have to repent any more.

Peter was saved, but he had to repent often afterwards.

"That was before Pentecost," it is objected, "and after Pentecost Peter was all right."

You are mistaken.

Twenty-five years after Pentecost Peter made the worst blunder of his life, except the awful blunder of denying the Christ, and I am not quite sure it was not as bad as his denying the Christ.

He separated from the gentile Christians because they were not circumcised, and he ate only with Jews.

Paul withstood him to his face, saying that he walked not uprightly according to the truth of the Gospel.

Paul pitched into him, laid him out on the anvil, made it hot for him, and hammered him out.

He put Barnabas there, too, and hammered him out.

After he got through, they acknowledged that Paul was right.

But they had a hot time while he was at it.

I have a number of Christians to put on the anvil.

I will warm them up and hammer them out until they get into good shape—into Zion's shape.

They must be hammered out.

Many of you professing Christians will have to repent.

Some of you have said ugly things about me.

What did you know about me?

You knew only what the papers said, and you took up the reproach against me upon the foundation of the most shameful lies.

The Lies of the American and Australian Press.

I have seen, since coming to this country, that the vilest contents of the literary sewers of America have been poured into your religious and secular papers.

The yellow journalism of New York has been repeated in your newspapers.

The American newspapers said that our people were poor and hungry, and without fire.

That was a lie.

There was not a family, and had not been a family, at any time, without food and fuel and clothing.

They published the story that there was no smoke coming from the chimneys, because there was no fire in the houses.

That is not only untrue but ridiculous.

The people would all have been frozen to death had that been true; because when the thermometer gets down to zero, and sometimes thirty degrees below zero, you freeze to death if you have no fire.

No one but a fool would have written that, because a man cannot live in a house without a fire.

That whole article is a lie from start to finish.

It is possible that they did not see much smoke coming from the chimneys of some houses.

They burn a superior kind of coal that does not make much smoke.

Some of you have taken up these reproaches and sent them around, and believed them, and taught them.

You have done what the Bible says you ought not to do.

You must repent of every wrong you have committed against me.

There is no use in my praying for you, unless you do.

If you are not saved, you must get saved through a True Repentance.

Repent toward God and man.

If you have lied to any one confess it.

If you have stolen from any one, restore what you stole. Confess the sin.

If you have done wrong, you must put that wrong right, if it costs you your life.

A True Repentance and What it Costs.

A man who had a good deal of money with him came to Zion City from Broken Hill, Australia.

He came to us representing himself as having been in the Church, in one of our Branches.

After a few days in Zion he began to get very uncomfortable.

Then he made the confession that he was a thief and a burglar, and an all-round bad man; that he had committed a great many crimes in America before he went out to Australia, and had committed some crimes in Australia.

We made him restore all the money he had stolen from the persons in Australia.

We started with the last stealing first, and the Australian people got their money, as far as we could give it to them.

Then we told him to go and give himself up to the authorities, and he did.

Now he is in the penitentiary in the State of New York, serving a long sentence.

There is some hope for that man, because he has repented; he has restored, he has taken the punishment due his crime.

When he comes out, if he has a good record in the prison, I shall receive him gladly, put him into fellowship and give him work, protect him, and do what I can to make a good man of him.

His heart was broken.

He said, "I will do whatever you tell me."

That is what they do throughout Zion everywhere.

You must repent, and you must put things right with God and man.

Your faith is not worth a snap unless you have truly repented.

You have not a Divine Faith at all, some of you.

You must confess what the real cause of your sickness is.

Sometimes young men and women suffer from sickness, and they do not tell the truth about it.

Some People Tempt the Devil to Tempt Them.

The fact is that it is not God's visitation, or even the Devil's. It is their own downright wickedness.

"Oh," they say, "the Devil tempted me."

Do not tell stuff and nonsense!

You tempted the Devil to tempt you.

I said to a man once, "Do not tell me that nonsense. The Devil never tempted you. You deliberately went out of Zion City into Waukegan. You went into a saloon there of your own accord. You went down where the Devil could tempt you. You stay out."

I kept him out for twelve months.

A man who has the appetite for alcohol and deliberately goes away from Zion City to a neighboring city where he knows he can get strong drink, cannot live in Zion City.

Should a man commit adultery in Zion City he cannot remain there.

Both adulterer and adulteress must go.

There is no place in Zion City for people who steal or lie, or will live bad lives.

They can go to the cities where such people are welcome.

They are not welcome in Zion City, and we clean them out.

"How do you clean them out?" some one asks.

We do not give them any work.

We remove them from fellowship.

We tell them that they have broken the conditions of their lease.

We demand them to give up their property.

We give them fair value for it, but we send them out.

We will not have a pack of dirty, filthy dogs, either men or women, living in Zion City.

There is one spot on God's earth that will be kept clean.

I thank you for listening; you have been very attentive.

Think over these things, and pray over them.

Every one who wants to do right, please stand and tell God so.

PRAYER OF CONSECRATION.

My God and Father, in Jesus Name I come to Thee. Take me as I am. Make me what I ought to be in spirit, in soul, in body. Give me power to do right, no matter what it costs. Give me Thy Holy Spirit. Help me to prepare myself for deliverance from sickness, and from all evil by examining myself, and by putting myself right with Thee, and with my fellow men. For Jesus' sake. Amen.

BENEDICTION.

Beloved, abstain from all appearance of evil. And may the very God of Peace Himself sanctify you wholly; and I pray God your whole spirit and soul and body be preserved entire, without blame, until the coming of our Lord Jesus, the Christ. Faithful is He that calleth you, who also will do it. The grace of our Lord Jesus, the Christ, the love of God, our Father, the fellowship of the Holy Spirit, our Comforter and Guide, one Eternal God, abide in you, bless you and keep you, and all the Israel of God everywhere, forever. Amen.

Zion in Canada.

Elder Brooks will visit the places in Ontario, Canada, mentioned below, during the months of May and June.

He will baptize, and consecrate children, in all these places where desired.

The halls in which the meetings will be held will be published in a later issue.

May 24th, Hamilton, Ontario, with a Zion Restoration Host party from Toronto—will visit the homes, and conduct services at 3 p. m.; May 25th, Kincardin; May 26th, Ripley—services at 3 p. m. and 8 p. m.; May 27th, Wingham—services at 3 p. m. and 8 p. m.; May 28th, Palmerston—meeting at 3 p. m.; May 29th and 30th, Chesley—Lord's Day services at 11 a. m., 3 p. m. and 8 p. m.; Monday at 3 p. m. and 8 p. m.; May 31st and June 1st, Wiarton—services at 3 p. m. and 8 p. m.; June 2d and 3d, Lion's Head—services at 3 p. m. and 8 p. m.; June 4th and 5th, Heathcote—Lord's Day services; June 6th and 7th, Meaford—services at 3 p. m. and 8 p. m.; June 8th and 9th, Waubaushene—services at 3 p. m. and 8 p. m.

Zion in Iowa.

Rev. Charles A. Hoy, Elder in the Christian Catholic Church in Zion, Falls City, Nebraska, will hold religious services in the following places:

Marcus, May 2d, 3d and 4th; Dows, May 5th and 6th; Webster City, May 7th, 8th and 9th; Hubbard, May 10th; Ames, May 11th; Boone, May 12th and 13th; Des Moines, May 14th, 15th and 16th and Dedham, May 17th.

All friends or members desiring to obey their Lord in Baptism may arrange for the same with the Elder at the above places.

Notice to Correspondents.

In writing to Headquarters it is *absolutely essential* that the writer give his full address.

Failure to comply with this request necessitates looking up or referring to the Church Records, which involves much time, and is very frequently fruitless.

Friends and members of the Christian Catholic Church in Zion everywhere will please bear this in mind, especially those in foreign lands.

Faithfully yours in the Master's Service,

J. G. Excell, General Ecclesiastical Secretary.

GOD'S WAY OF HEALING.

BY THE REV. JOHN ALEX. DOWIE.

God's Way Of Healing Is a Person, Not a Thing.

Jesus said "*I am* the Way, and the Truth, and the Life," and He has ever been revealed to His people in all the ages by the Covenant Name, Jehovah-Rophi, or "*I am* Jehovah that Healeth thee." (John 14:6; Exodus 15:26.)

The Lord Jesus, the Christ, Is Still the Healer.

He cannot change, for "Jesus, the Christ, is the same yesterday and today, yea and forever;" and He is still with us, for He said: "Lo, *I am* with you All the Days, even unto the Consummation of the Age." (Hebrews 13:8; Matthew 28:20.) Because He is Unchangeable, and because He is present, in spirit, just as when in the flesh, He is the Healer of His people.

Divine Healing Rests on the Christ's Atonement.

It was prophesied of Him "Surely He hath borne our griefs (Hebrew, *sickness*), and carried our sorrows: . . . and with His stripes we are healed;" and it is expressly declared that this was fulfilled in His Ministry of Healing, which still continues. (Isaiah 53:4, 5; Matthew 8:17.)

Disease Can Never be God's Will.

It is the Devil's work, consequent upon Sin, and it is impossible for the work of the Devil ever to be the Will of God. The Christ came to "destroy the works of the Devil," and when He was here on earth He healed "all manner of disease and all manner of sickness," and all these sufferers are expressly declared to have been "oppressed of the Devil." (1 John 3:8; Matthew 4:23; Acts 10:38.)

The Gifts of Healings Are Permanent.

It is expressly declared that the "Gifts and the calling of God are without repentance," and the Gifts of Healings are amongst the Nine Gifts of the Spirit to the Church. (Romans 11:29; 1 Corinthians 12:8-11.)

There Are Four Modes of Divine Healing.

The first is the direct prayer of faith; the second, intercessory prayer of two or more; the third, the anointing of the elders, with the prayer of faith; and the fourth, the laying on of hands of those who believe, and whom God has prepared and called to that ministry. (Matthew 8:5-13; Matthew 18:19; James 5:14, 15; Mark 16:18.)

Divine Healing Is Opposed by Diabolical Counterfeits.

Amongst these are Christian Science (falsely so called), Mind Healing, Spiritualism, Trance Evangelism, etc. (1 Timothy 6:20, 21; 1 Timothy 4:1, 2; Isaiah 51:22, 23.)

Multitudes Have Been Healed Through Faith in Jesus.

The writer knows of thousands of cases and has personally laid hands on scores of thousands of persons. Full information can be obtained at the meetings held in the Zion Tabernacles in Chicago, and in Zion City, Illinois, and in many pamphlets which give the experience, in their own words, of many who have been healed in this and other countries, published at Zion Printing and Publishing House, Zion City, Illinois.

"*Belief Cometh of Hearing, and Hearing by the Word of the Christ.*"

You are heartily invited to attend and hear for yourself.

PROGRAM...

The Set Feasts of Jehovah . . Ye shall proclaim to be Holy Convocations.
—Lev. 23:2.

Zion's Fourth Feast of Tabernacles

Will be held in Shiloh Tabernacle, Shiloh Park, Zion City, Illinois, from the Evening of Wednesday, July 13th, to the Evening of Lord's Day, July 24, 1904, and conducted by the

Rev. John Alexander Dowie
Elijah the Restorer

General Overseer of the Christian Catholic Church in Zion.

WEDNESDAY, JULY 13th

7:30 to 9 P. M.—Presentation and Consecration of the People to God.

Address by the General Overseer: "FOR ZION'S SAKE."

THURSDAY, JULY 14th

Fourth Anniversary of the Consecration of the Site of Zion Temple.

Public Holiday in Zion City.

Announcement of trains from Chicago will be made at a later date.

6:30 A. M.—Early Morning Sacrifice of Praise and Prayer.

The First of a Series of Twenty-Minute Addresses by the General Overseer on the Nine Fruits of the Spirit: "THE FIRST FRUIT OF THE SPIRIT: LOVE."

9:30 A. M.—First Convocation of Zion Junior Restoration Host.

Conducted by Overseer Harvey D. Brasefield.

2:00 P. M.—FULL PROCESSION of Zion Robed Officers, Zion White-robed Choir, and Zion Restoration Host will march around the Site of Zion Temple, and thence to the Site of Shiloah Tabernacle.

The Procession will then reform and take the seats reserved for them in Shiloh Tabernacle, where an Address will be given by the General Overseer on

"ZION: A CROWN OF BEAUTY IN THE HAND OF JEHOVAH."

Special Offerings will be received at the close of this Address for the building of Shiloah Tabernacle, which it is expected will cost $500,000, and seat about 16,000 people.

7:30 P. M.—Evening Sacrifice of Praise and Prayer.

FRIDAY, JULY 15th

A Half-Holiday in Zion City.

6:30 A. M.—Early Morning Sacrifice of Praise and Prayer.

Twenty-Minute Address by the General Overseer: "THE SECOND FRUIT OF THE SPIRIT: JOY."

9:30 A. M.—Second Convocation of Zion Junior Restoration Host.

Conducted by Overseer Harvey D. Brasefield.

10:30 A. M.—DIVINE HEALING MEETING.

Conducted by the General Overseer.

Address: "PRESENT YOUR BODIES A LIVING SACRIFICE, HOLY, ACCEPTABLE TO GOD, WHICH IS YOUR REASONABLE SERVICE."

At the close of this meeting the General Overseer, Overseer Jane Dowie, and other Overseers, Elders and Evangelists will pray with the sick who are seeking the Lord for healing.

The City Festal Day.

3:00 P. M.—A PROCESSION, headed by Zion Guard and Zion City Band, consisting of

The Municipal Officers of the City of Zion,
All Officers and Employees of the Legal, Financial and Business Institutions of Zion,
All Officers and Employees of the Educational Institutions of Zion, and
All Officers of the Political Institutions of Zion, will be REVIEWED BY THE GENERAL OVERSEER AT THE ADMINISTRATION BUILDING, and then proceed to Shiloh Tabernacle where a SERVICE OF THANKSGIVING will be held.

Those in the Procession, as they enter Shiloh Tabernacle, will take their places in the Choir and Officers' Gallery, and on the ground floor.

Spectators will occupy the remaining galleries.

7:30 P. M.—Evening Sacrifice of Praise and Prayer.

SATURDAY, JULY 16th

6:30 A. M.—Early Morning Sacrifice of Praise and Prayer.

Twenty-Minute Address by the General Overseer: "THE THIRD FRUIT OF THE SPIRIT: PEACE."

2:00 P. M.—Zion Athletic Association: Field Games on grounds at Northeast corner of Shiloh Park.

8:00 P. M.—Evening Sacrifice of Praise and Prayer.

LORD'S DAY, JULY 17th

6:30 A. M.—Early Morning Sacrifice of Praise and Prayer.

Twenty-Minute Address by the General Overseer on "THE FOURTH FRUIT OF THE SPIRIT: LONG-SUFFERING."

9:30 A. M.—Third Convocation of Zion Junior Restoration Host.
Conducted by Overseer Harvey D. Brasefield.

11:00 A. M.—The Rev. John G. Speicher, M. D., Overseer of the Christian Catholic Church in Zion of the City of Zion, will preach.

2:00 P. M.—GREAT GENERAL ASSEMBLY.
Procession of Zion's Robed Officers and White-robed Choir (probably One Thousand in line).
Elijah the Restorer will deliver a Message from God to Zion: "ARISE! SHINE! FOR THY LIGHT IS COME."
A Reception of New Members into the Communion and Fellowship of the Christian Catholic Church in Zion will be held at the close.

8:00 P. M.—Ordination of New Officers and the Celebration of the Ordinance of the Lord's Supper.

MONDAY, JULY 18th

6:30 A. M.—**Early Morning Sacrifice of Praise and Prayer.**
Twenty-Minute Address by the General Overseer: "THE FIFTH FRUIT OF THE SPIRIT: KINDNESS."

9:30 A. M.—Fourth Convocation of Zion Junior Restoration Host.
Conducted by Overseer Harvey D. Brasefield.

11:00 A. M.—THE ORDINANCE OF BELIEVERS' BAPTISM BY TRIUNE IMMERSION will be administered by Overseers Speicher, Mason, Brasefield and Excell, assisted by a number of Elders, Evangelists, Deacons and Deaconesses.

2:00 P. M.—A MEETING FOR ZION WOMEN ONLY will be addressed by the Rev. Jane Dowie, Overseer for Women's Work in the Christian Catholic Church in Zion Throughout the World.
This meeting will be strictly limited to female members of the Christian Catholic Church in Zion, and no children under twelve years of age will be admitted.

8:00 P. M.—A MEETING FOR ZION MEN ONLY will be addressed by the Rev. John Alex. Dowie, General Overseer of the Christian Catholic Church in Zion.
This meeting will be strictly limited to male members of the Christian Catholic Church in Zion above the age of twelve.

TUESDAY, JULY 19th

6:30 A. M.—**Early Morning Sacrifice of Praise and Prayer.**
Twenty-Minute Address by the General Overseer: "THE SIXTH FRUIT OF THE SPIRIT: GOODNESS."

9:30 A. M.—Fifth Convocation of Zion Junior Restoration Host.
Conducted by Overseer Harvey D. Brasefield.

11:30 A. M.—CONFERENCE OF WOMEN ELDERS, EVANGELISTS AND DEACONESSES OF THE CHRISTIAN CATHOLIC CHURCH IN ZION.
Conducted by Overseer Jane Dowie.

2:30 P. M.—CONFERENCE UPON THE WORK OF ZION RESTORATION HOST THROUGHOUT THE WORLD.

The General Overseer will preside, and at the close will administer the Restoration Vow to New Members of the Host, and Consecrate and Separate them to the Work of God in Zion by the Laying on of Hands.

8:00 P. M.—Evening Sacrifice of Praise and Prayer.

WEDNESDAY, JULY 20th

6:30 A. M.—**Early Morning Sacrifice of Praise and Prayer.**

Twenty-Minute Address by the General Overseer: "THE SEVENTH FRUIT OF THE SPIRIT: FAITHFULNESS."

9:30 A. M.—Sixth Convocation of Zion Junior Restoration Host.

Conducted by Overseer Harvey D. Brasefield.

11:00 A. M.—CONFERENCE OF MALE OFFICERS OF THE CHRISTIAN CATHOLIC CHURCH IN ZION.

Conducted by the General Overseer.

2:30 P. M.—THE ORDINANCE OF THE PRESENTATION AND CONSECRATION OF YOUNG CHILDREN TO GOD, will be conducted by the General Overseer.

He will deliver an Address on the Words: "WHAT THEN SHALL THIS CHILD BE?"

8:00 P. M.—Evening Sacrifice of Praise and Prayer.

THURSDAY, JULY 21st

6:30 A. M.—**Early Morning Sacrifice of Praise and Prayer.**

Twenty-Minute Address by the General Overseer: "THE EIGHTH FRUIT OF THE SPIRIT: MEEKNESS."

9:00 A. M.—Seventh Convocation of Zion Junior Restoration Host.

Conducted by Overseer Harvey D. Brasefield.

11:00 A. M.—EDUCATIONAL CONFERENCE.

Presided over by Overseer Brasefield.

Addresses by Members of the Faculty of Zion College, Zion Preparatory and Zion Manual Training Schools.

2:00 P. M.—A CONFERENCE ON ZION BUSINESS INSTITUTIONS will be conducted by the General Overseer, and Addressed by Managers of the Various Institutions.

The Meeting will be Strictly Limited to Investors in Zion Stocks.

8:00 P. M.—Evening Sacrifice of Praise and Prayer.

FRIDAY, JULY 22d

6:30 A. M.—**Early Morning Sacrifice of Praise and Prayer.**

Twenty-Minute Address by the General Overseer: "THE NINTH FRUIT OF THE SPIRIT: TEMPERANCE."

9:30 A. M.—Eighth Convocation of Zion Junior Restoration Host.

Conducted by Overseer Harvey D. Brasefield.

11:00 A. M.—A CONFERENCE CONCERNING DORCAS AND MATERNITY DEACONESS WORK IN ZION THROUGHOUT THE WORLD.

Conducted by Overseer Jane Dowie.

2:00 P. M.—A CONFERENCE ON ZION BUSINESS INSTITUTIONS will be Conducted by the General Overseer, and Addressed by Managers of the Various Institutions.

The Meeting will be Strictly Limited to Investors in Zion Stocks.

8:00 P. M.—Evening Sacrifice of Praise and Prayer.

SATURDAY, JULY 23d

6:30 A. M.—**Early Morning Sacrifice of Praise and Prayer.**

Twenty-Minute Address by the General Overseer: "THE NINE GIFTS OF THE HOLY SPIRIT."

2:00 P. M.—Zion Athletic Association; Field Games in the Northeast Corner of Shiloh Park.

8:00 P. M.—Evening Sacrifice of Praise and Prayer.

LORD'S DAY, JULY 24th

6:30 A. M.—**Early Morning Sacrifice of Praise and Prayer.**

Twenty-Minute Address by the General Overseer: "THE HOUSE OF WISDOM."

9:30 A. M.—The General Overseer will speak on "TRIUNE IMMERSION; GOD'S SEAL ON A LIVING CHURCH."

At the close of this Service the General Overseer, assisted by Overseers, Elders, Evangelists, Deacons and Deaconesses, will Administer the Ordinance of Believers' Baptism.

All persons desiring to be Baptized on this occasion must fill up their Application Cards for Baptism, and present them to the General Recorder, Deacon Andrew C. Jensen, and his Assistants, not later than 9 a. m.

2:00 P. M.—GREAT GENERAL ASSEMBLY.

FULL PROCESSIONAL of Zion Robed Officers, Zion White-robed Choir and all the members of Zion Junior Restoration Host, under their Leader, Overseer Brasefield.

The General Overseer will speak on "THE MINISTRY OF CHILDREN IN ZION." At the close of this Service he will Administer the Vow of Zion Restoration Host to New Members of Zion Junior Restoration Host.

8:00 P. M.—THE ORDINANCE OF THE LORD'S SUPPER will be Administered by the General Overseer and Ordained Officers of the Christian Catholic Church in Zion.

This Gathering will be open only to Members of the Christian Catholic Church. in Zion, and other Christians desiring to commune with them.

At the close the General Overseer will deliver the CONCLUDING ADDRESS OF THE FEAST.

REDUCED FARE—FEAST OF TABERNACLES.

ONE AND ONE-THIRD FARE FOR ROUND TRIP TO ZION CITY—CONDITIONS OF SALE OF TICKETS.

A reduction of fare to one and one-third on the certificate plan has been granted for those attending the meetings of the Christian Catholic Church in Zion, at the Fourth Feast of Tabernacles, in Zion City, Lake County, Illinois, between July 13 and July 24, 1904, inclusive.

The following directions are submitted for your guidance:

First—Tickets at full fare for the going journey, may be secured within three days, exclusive of Sunday, prior to and during the first three days of the meeting that is, July 11th, 12th, 13th, 14th, 15th and 16th.

The advertised dates of the meeting are from July 13th to 24th; consequently you can obtain your tickets not earlier than July 11th and not later than July 17th.

Be sure that when purchasing your going ticket you request a certificate.

Second—Present yourself at the railway station for ticket and certificate at least thirty minutes before departure of train.

Third—Certificates are not kept at all stations. If you inquire at your station you will find out whether certificates and through tickets can be obtained to place of meeting; if not, the Agent will inform you at what station they can be obtained. You can purchase a local ticket thence, and there take up a certificate and through ticket.

Fourth—On your arrival at the meeting, present your certificate to Deacon James F. Peters, Administration building, Zion City, Illinois.

Fifth—No refund of fare will be made on account of failure to have certificate validated.

Sixth—So as to prevent disappointment, it must be understood that the reduction on returning journey is not guaranteed, but is contingent on an attendance of not less than one hundred persons from all points throughout the United States and Canada, showing payment of full first-class fare of not less than seventy-five cents on going journey; provided, however, if the certificates presented fall short of the required minimum, and it shall appear that round trip tickets are held in lieu of certificate, that shall be reckoned in arriving at the minimum.

Seventh—If the necessary minimum is in attendance and your certificate is duly validated, you will be entitled up to July 26th, to reduced passage ticket to your destination by the route over which you made the going journey at one-third the limit fare.

This rate will apply to the entire United States and Canada.

SPECIAL TRAINS BETWEEN CHICAGO AND ZION CITY.

These trains will be arranged for and announcement will be made later.

CAMP HOLIDAY—1904.

REGULATIONS AND PROVISIONS FOR THE SEASON.

Persons desiring to spend a holiday or attend the great teaching meetings of Zion will find, either as individuals, families or parties, inexpensive tenting conveniences, with good water near at hand, in Zion's tents now in Service in Camp Holiday, Zion City.

The tents are made of heavy duck material, strongly stayed, with fly and are rainproof, being pitched above board floors.

The season's price for tents 9½x14, furnished, is $7; or unfurnished, $5 a month, when taken for two or more months, but not to be sublet.

Tents may be rented by the week at $4 for the first week and $2 a week thereafter.

The Feast of Tabernacles' rate is always $2.25 a person, four persons to a tent; otherwise the rate is double. Single cots for single nights, 25 cents: tent rates a day, $1.25.

All rentals payable in advance, in every case, whether by the month, week or day.

THE FURNITURE.

The furniture consists of the necessary cots, mattresses and chairs, one table, water-pail, tin cup, wash basin and slop-pail to a tent. The beddingincludes one white sheet, two light and one or two heavy blankets, and a pillow and pillow-slip to a single and two of each to double cots. Two-wick oil stoves may be rented for $1 a month, supplied with oil; and cooking utensils, including stew-pans, tin plates, cups, knives, forks and spoons, may be secured at a rental of 50 cents a month.

TENT PROVISIONS AND REGULATIONS FOR 1904.

Two tents may be required in some instances, and these will be cheaper than one large one. Then one can be used for sleeping, and the other for cooking purposes.

During the Feast of Tabernacles, tents will again be located in Camp Esther in Shiloh Park, for which a charge of $2.25 a person for the twelve days will be made; but persons leasing tents i.i Camp Holiday for at least a two months' period may obtain accommodations for the occasion at the season rental price.

Applications for such accommodations or conveniences should be addressed to Deacon James F. Peters, Administration building, Zion City, Lake County, Illinois.

THE RATES AT ELIJAH HOSPICE

NOW AND DURING THE FEAST OF TABERNACLES ARE AS FOLLOWS:

European Plan—One person in a room, $1.00 a day and up; two persons or more in a room, 50 cents a day and up; one person in a room, $6.00 a week and up; two persons or more in a room, $3.00 a week and up. These rates are for lodging only.

American Plan—One person in a room, $1.75 a day and up; two persons or more in a room, $1.25 a day and up; one person in a room, $10.00 a week and up; two persons or more in a room, $7.00 a week and up; single meals, 25 cents.

Children under twelve years old half rate.

The American Plan includes board and room.

Rooms will be charged for from the date reserved.

FRANK W. COTTON, Manager.

Notes of Thanksgiving from the Whole World

By J. G. Speicher, Overseer-in-Charge

Delivered From Nervous Prostration and Mental Exhaustion.

The God of Israel.
He giveth strength and power unto His people.—*Psalm 68:35.*

MARCUS, IOWA, December 22, 1903.

DEAR GENERAL OVERSEER:—It is with a grateful heart that I write to tell how I was delivered from nervous prostration and mental exhaustion.

I suffered intensely from the effects of a shattered nervous system.

I have prayed many times that I should not live to see another day; and, when life was spared, I believed that God was not through with me here, and that somehow, sometime, I should be well.

But I did not know God's way of healing, as I had always been taught to believe what I read in our own church papers, that we must "trust God, but keep on taking our medicine."

My sickness dates back ten years ago when I suffered from great loss of blood and mental shock.

Previously to this God had wonderfully delivered me in body in answer to my own prayer, when I saw I could trust in nothing else.

But I did not go on trusting Him as my only Healer, as I thought there must be a place for remedies, and that trust in God and medicines must be harmonized some way.

A doctor gave me bromid for my nerves.

This only quieted me so I could sleep; and of course was only temporary relief.

I kept this in the house almost constantly, and took a few doses whenever there was any special mental or physical strain to undergo.

As my family grew larger and the cares increased, my weakness increased, and I went to the doctor and got nerve tonics, after which I felt stronger, only to fall back into the same exhausted state.

I became very anxious about my health, and although I was saved in spirit the state of my health made me despondent.

I kept trying one remedy after another in hope of finding something life-giving, and at last tried "Oxine," advertised to make one strong.

This shattered my nervous system. After the effect of the medicine wore off, I was completely unstrung.

I was so weak both mentally and physically that I had to give up the care of my home.

About this time a dear old saint prayed for my healing; and in answer to her prayer I felt the touch of God in my body.

I had been taught that the day of miracles was over.

Up to this time I had never read LEAVES OF HEALING or had any teaching on Divine Healing.

I felt better after this prayer, and wondered if it was right to keep on taking my treatments.

I continued the treatments.

I resorted to bromids again, as my weakness reappeared; but it was losing its effect, and I asked the doctor for something stronger. That made me deathly sick.

I saw there was nothing left to do but trust God alone.

I have not taken any medicine since.

I became discouraged, and resolved to write to you in spite of all I had heard by false witnesses.

I believe the Spirit led me to make this decision, for after writing the letter I went to bed and slept like a child.

While awaiting your reply, I had more faith to overcome my weakness.

When I received your letter, your kindness, interest and spiritual understanding convinced me that you were a man of God.

About this time some Zion friends called and brought me LEAVES OF HEALING and some tracts.

The Devil tried to keep me from reading them. I thank God that I read them. I could not let them alone.

I found my healing rested not on my faith, but on the Christ's Atonement.

After reading "Jesus the Healer," I accepted Him as my Healer.

It was not until you prayed for me, November 4, 1903, that there was any permanent change in my body.

At that time I filled out a blank stating cause of sickness.

I noticed a change. I seemed to possess a new power. I felt natural, which, to a nervous person, is everything.

Two days from this time I received your reply, saying you had prayed very earnestly that God would cleanse me from sin and disease, and restore what the Devil had robbed me of.

I gained four pounds in flesh that month, and I have gained strength, until now I am stronger than for many years.

My conflict was largely a spiritual one, for it did not take long for God to restore what the Devil had stolen; but it took months to purge out false teaching, unbelief, and the "tradition of the elders."

I learned that the teachings of Zion were the old primitive Gospel, brought back to us. It was just what I was hungry for—a Triune God for a triune man.

God very clearly led me to see that He had healed me for Zion. He has been very good to me since coming into Zion. He has healed my family and me.

I thank you, dear General Overseer, for your prayers, counsel and patience.

I thank God who made it plain to me that you are the Messenger of the Covenant, Elijah the Restorer. I thank my Father every day that it is my privilege to have a part in the Restoration.

Praying God to bless and keep you till your work is done, I am,

Yours faithfully for God and Zion,

(MRS.) LILLIE PETERS.

Wife Healed of Affection of Throat—Husband Healed of Influenza.

Call unto Me, and I will answer thee.—*Jeremiah 33:3.*

GRAND FALLS, NORTH DAKOTA, February 25, 1904.

DEAR GENERAL OVERSEER:—I desire to testify to what God has done for us this winter.

My wife was taken sick with what we believe was diphtheria.

Her throat was swollen until she could hardly swallow. Water would come back through her nose.

Her tongue and throat were coated with white and yellow coating.

I prayed for her and she got well and is as well as ever.

We did not have to be quarantined, for which I thank God.

I was taken sick with influenza, which developed with a high fever.

We asked God to take it all away and heal me, making me able to go out to perform my duty on the railroad, and He did so.

Although I was weak, God gave me strength to go out and work.

I did not lose one day, for which I give God all the glory and praise.

Your brother in the Christ, NAT SPROUL.

Zion's Bible Class

Conducted by Deacon Daniel Sloan in Shiloh Tabernacle, Zion City, Lord's Day Morning at 11 o'clock, and in Zion Homes and Gatherings throughout the World.

MID-WEEK BIBLE CLASS LESSON, MAY 26th or 27th.

Slowness to Grasp the Word of God.

1. *God speaks in righteousness.*—Deuteronomy 32.1-6.
He points out the right way.
He shows the right things.
He wants people to do right.

2. *God speaks in truth.*—John 16:12-15.
He tells all the truth.
He tells it so people will hear it.
He leads into a fuller understanding of it.

3. *God speaks plainly.*—Isaiah 28: 9-13.
He points out a straight line.
He shows a narrow way.
He requires one to observe little things.

4. *God speaks fully.*—Luke 24 : 23-32.
He recalls the past.
He reveals the future.
He expounds the Scriptures fully.

5. *God speaks powerfully.*—1 Corinthians 1:18-27.
His Word is the Power of God.
It convinces of sins.
It confronts one with judgment.

6. *God speaks practically.*—Isaiah 28:22-29.
He illustrates how to come to know Him.
He shows that one must work and labor to know Him.
If one will do what He directs one cannot fail.

7. *God speaks patiently.*—Acts 28 : 23-31.
Early and late He seeks to win men.
He seeks until He finds.
He tries by repeated effort to get all to hear.

The Lord Our God is a Patient, Instructing God

LORD'S DAY BIBLE CLASS LESSON, MAY 29th.

The Unfolding of the Truth of God.

1. *Seek that which strengthens faith.*—1 Peter 2 : 1-6.
It empties one of petty meannesses.
It gives one a relish for good things.
It makes the Life to glow within one.

2. *Seek that which quickens conscience and makes one strong to resist evil and to do right.*—1 Peter 4:1-8.
The will of the flesh is broken by the hammer of Truth.
Self-denial must be a habit of daily practice.
We must become watchful and sober-minded.

3. *Seek that which inspires obedience and gives permanency to Christian experience and profession.*—Hebrews 10:21-31.
We must never draw back from God.
He draws near to us if we go forward.
We must never waver or look back.

4. *Seek that which gives discernment so that one may be safe as well as a help to others.*—Hebrew 5:7-14.
We must learn to cry in faith when in peril.
We suffer only to obtain a better view of God.
We grow strong by vigorous exercise.

5. *Seek that which prepares one for the greatest usefulness in service for God.*—2 Timothy 3:16, 17.
Reproof makes one more faithful.
Correction keeps one from going wrong.
Instruction shows how to do better work.

6. *Seek that which opens up the mysteries and makes hard things become easy.*—2 Peter 3.13-18.
We must see Him who is invisible.
We may understand the deep things of God.
He can see things to come

7. *Ever seek that which brings personal blessing from God and gives new views of the Christ.*—Revelation 1:1-3.
Jesus is better than things soon to come to pass.
The Christ is revealed only to God's servants.
Hear the Word and keep it and you will soon see the Bridegroom.

God's Holy People are a Growing People.

MID-WEEK BIBLE CLASS LESSON, JUNE 1st or 2d.

The Churches of Today Are Corrupt.

1. *They do not condemn sin. They tolerate it and practice it.*—Jeremiah 23:9-15.
A man may commit adultery and stay in most churches.
A man can swear and yet be a church-member.
They parade secret works in God's House.

2. *They are so mercenary and debased that they hinder people in getting God's blessings.*—Matthew 21:12-16.
They sell this and that to get money.
They allow indulgences to people who give them support.
They give socials the preference over prayer-meetings.

3. *Just look at the dishonorable things permitted to occur in God's House.*—Jeremiah 32:26-35.
They send children to destruction through their social agencies.
They have theatricals in their churches.
They try to copy after the world.

4. *Men whom God has never called are welcomed and praised as ministers.*—1 Samuel 2:27-32.
They take school-made preachers rather than God-called men.
These men always introduce some innovation.
They do not honor God and He will not honor them.

5. *They turn the House of God into a place of feasting and consorting with evil-doers.*—Ezekiel 23:36-44.
They win dimes, but not souls, with their socials.
They get up dainty dinners of unclean foods.
They have their children play the fool to amuse them.

6. *Real worship has no sense of satisfaction for them.*—Malachi 3:7-15.
They "get so tired going to church."
They say so many wicked things about God.
They say, "God does not help men; men must help themselves."

7. *The judgment now impending will come upon them first of all.*—1 Peter 4:12-19.
The world hates a true Christian.
The world will be harder, though, on a hypocrite.
The Devil, when he can no longer deceive, will try to destroy.

The Lord our God is an Evil-condemning God.

LORD'S DAY BIBLE CLASS LESSON, JUNE 5th.

Preaching Generally Heard Is Either False or Perverted Truth.

1. *Preachers preach to please the people.*—Jeremiah 5:25-31.
People pay for what suits them.
They make money in crooked ways and want crooked preaching.
They will not have their sins uncovered.

2. *They proclaim man's theories, ideas, or imaginings.*—Jeremiah 23: 25-32.
They have some place of redemption.
They offer some solution for every trouble.
Their plans tested prove to be chaff.

3. *They tell people that what God says will not occur as stated.*—Jeremiah 23:16-24.
They make people confident in danger.
God says, "Arouse ye!" they say, "Sleep on!"
God says, "Save yourselves!" they say, "Peace! Peace!"

4. *They cannot be the Christ's servants, for they do not bear His Message or do His work.*—Jeremiah 23.1-4.
They have not come to save.
Instead of pointing to the Christ they direct to physicians.
They are not out seeking for the lost.

5. *They argue that God is no longer the Healer, but advocate the cruelty of surgery.*—Ezekiel 34:1-6.
A minister should think of self last.
He should give rest and take little of it.
He should see that people get healing.

6. *They can preach questionable beliefs and yet be tolerated anywhere.*—2 Peter 2:1-9.
They make a very light thing of sin.
They make a nonentity of the Devil.
They make the Christ to be of no avail for the body.

7. *They do not care whether the people know God or not. They get people further from God.*—Jeremiah 2.5-8.
What ails the God of the Bible today?
Has He changed from former years?
They cannot tell you where God is.

God's Holy People are an Error-detecting People.

OBEYING GOD IN BAPTISM.

"Baptizing Them Into the Name of the Father and of the Son and of the Holy Ghost."

Eighteen Thousand Two Hundred Eighty-eight Baptisms by Triune Immersion Since March 14, 1897.

Eighteen Thousand Two Hundred Eighty-eight Believers have joyfully followed their Lord in the Ordinance of Believer's Baptism by Triune Immersion since the first Baptism in Central Zion Tabernacle on March 14, 1897.

Baptized in Central Zion Tabernacle from March 14, 1897, to December 14, 1901, by the General Overseer,	4754			
Baptized in South Side Zion Tabernacle from January 1, 1902, to June 14, 1903, by the General Overseer..	37			
Baptized at Zion City by the General Overseer........	583			
Baptized by Overseers, Elders, Evangelists and Deacons, at Headquarters (Zion City) and Chicago......	4940			
Total Baptized at Headquarters....................	——			10,314
Baptized in places outside of Headquarters by the General Overseer..............................		641		
Baptized in places outside of Headquarters by Overseers, Elders, Evangelists and Deacons...........		7091		
Total Baptized outside of Headquarters............		——		7,732
Total Baptized in seven years.....................				18,046
Baptized since March 14, 1904.				
Baptized in Zion City by Elder Royall..............	63			
Baptized in Zion City by Elder Hammond...........	36			
Baptized in Zion City by Elder Adams...............	40			
Baptized in Chicago by Elder Hall..................	3			
Baptized in Chicago by Elder Cossum...............	15			
Baptized in Chicago by Evangelist Christie..........	3			
Baptized in Chicago by Deacon Matson..............	2			
Baptized in Chicago by Elder Kosch................	6		168	
Baptized in California by Elder Taylor..............		4		
Baptized in Canada by Elder Simmons..............		5		
Baptized in Canada by Elder Brooks................		4		
Baptized in Colorado by Deacon Cook...............		3		
Baptized in England by Overseer Cantel............		5		
Baptized in Illinois by Deacon Sprecher............		1		
Baptized in New York by Elder Warszawiak..........		14		
Baptized in New York by Overseer Mason..........		19		
Baptized in Ohio by Deacon Arrington............		7		
Baptized in Pennsylvania by Elder Bouck...........		8		
Baptized in Washington by Elder Simmons..........		1		
Baptized in Washington by Elder Ernst.............		3	74	242
Total Baptized since March 14, 1897...............				18,288

The following-named five believers were baptized in Cincinnati, Ohio, Lord's Day, April 17, 1904 by Deacon A. E. Arrington:

Gray, Coneley F. Trigg....................................Blue Ash, Ohio
Gray, Mrs. Zenada Rebecca.................................Blue Ash, Ohio
Thompson, Edward Franklin.. ....Pleasant Ridge, Ohio
Thompson, Rodger Devissa.......................Pleasant Ridge, Ohio
Waller, Cladious Braxiton.............914 Findlay street, Cincinnati, Ohio

The following-named seven believers were baptized in Philadelphia, Pennsylvania, Lord's Day, April 17, 1904, by Elder R. N. Bouck:

Ahrens, Miss Annie..........924 Filbert street, Philadelphia, Pennsylvania
Bayley, Isaiah Gough..2509 N. College avenue, Philadelphia, Pennsylvania
Needs, Mrs. Julia B.................540 Carpenter street, Germantown, Ohio
Schuessler, Mrs. Friedericke K.
4318 Westminster avenue, Philadelphia, Pennsylvania
Scheussler, John.....4318 Westminster avenue, Philadelphia, Pennsylvania
Woodruff, Miss Henrietta, 1924 W. Passyunk av., Philadelphia, Pennsylvania
Woodruff, Mrs. Marie A., 1924 W. Passyunk av., Philadelphia, Pennsylvania

The following-named believer was baptized in Philadelphia, Pennsylvania, Lord's Day, April 24, 1904, by Elder R. N. Bouck:

Bayley, Clara L....2509 North College avenue, Philadelphia, Pennsylvania

The following-named three believers were baptized in the South Side Zion Tabernacle, Chicago, Lord's Day, April 24, 1904, by Elder W. H. Cossum:

Slyter, Beatrice.....................2643 Indiana avenue, Chicago, Illinois
Slyter, Mrs. Ella....................2643 Indiana avenue, Chicago, Illinois
Wilson, Mrs. Rose.....................6025 Peoria street, Chicago, Illinois

The following-named nine believers were baptized in New York City, Wednesday, April 27, 1904, by Overseer G. L. Mason:

Erkmann, Charles F.............78 Hutton street, Jersey City, New Jersey
Feigenbaum, Tobias.....................130 Norfolk street, New York City
Funk, Mrs. Caroline.........................60 King street, New York City
Leonard, Frank.......................803 Driggs avenue, New York City
McWaters, Mrs. Jane C................1489 Vyse avenue, New York City
MacDonald, Mrs. Mary E.,
282 New York avenue, Jersey Heights, Jersey City, New Jersey
Robertson, Mrs. Annie..............11 East Sixtieth street, New York City
VanderVoort, C. F................20 Church street, Patterson, New Jersey
Waterbury, William F..............................Stanford, Connecticut

The following-named eight believers were baptized in New York City, Wednesday, April 27, 1904, by Elder H. Warszawiak:

Erkmann, Miss Martha...........78 Hutton street, Jersey City, New Jersey
Erkmann, Mrs. Mina.............78 Hutton street, Jersey City, New Jersey
Gunzenhauser, Wm. O.........114 Chadwick avenue, Newark, New Jersey
Krukziener, Mrs. Annie..........218 East Eleventh street, New York City
Ohliger, William..............83 Twenty-first street, Irvington, New Jersey
Perkins, A. R...................237 Mohawk street, Herkimer, New York
Rosenberg, Joseph..................16 East Eighth street, New York City
Sleigh, William...............530 West Forty-sixth street, New York City

The following-named four believers were baptized in Toronto, Ontario, Canada, Thursday, April 28, 1904, by Elder Eugene Brooks:

Anderson, Mrs. Annie Clara....8 Fitzroy terrace, Toronto, Ontario, Canada
Anderson, George William.....8 Fitzroy terrace, Toronto, Ontario, Canada
Shields, Mrs. Eva B..........86 Maitland street, Toronto, Ontario, Canada
Smith, Robert......................Jane street, Toronto Junction, Canada

The following-named forty believers were baptized in Shiloh Tabernacle, Zion City, Illinois, Lord's Day, May 1, 1904, by Elder J. R. Adams:

Birsch, Paul Agustus..............3013 Gideon avenue, Zion City, Illinois
Bowers, Asa.........................1710 Gilgal avenue, Zion City, Illinois
Boyer, Mrs. Flora Catherine........3200 Ezekiel avenue, Zion City, Illinois
Boyer, Kervin......................3200 Ezekiel avenue, Zion City, Illinois
Bronson, Mrs. Frances......................................Pekin, Illinois
Broka, Miss Caroline L. ....1908 Horeb avenue, Zion City, Illinois
Cameron, Daniel....................1824 Gilgal avenue, Zion City, Illinois
Cameron, Miss Rhoda..............1824 Gilgal avenue, Zion City, Illinois
Crawford, Fred L.................3717 Emmaus avenue, Zion City, Illinois
Crawford, Mrs. Louise............3717 Emmaus avenue, Zion City, Illinois
Cutler, Miss Laura ....3106 Enoch avenue, Zion City, Illinois
Davis, Miss Ruth .... 3209 Ezra avenue, Zion City, Illinois
Dutch, Mrs. Elizabeth............2913 Gabriel avenue, Zion City, Illinois
Dutch, Miss Elizabeth............2913 Gabriel avenue, Zion City, Illinois
Dutch, William...................2913 Gabriel avenue, Zion City, Illinois
Ebert, Hattie.......................2812 Eshcol avenue, Zion City, Illinois
Gates, Miss Fay....................3202 Enoch avenue, Zion City, Illinois
Gates, Mrs. Jennie.................3202 Enoch avenue, Zion City, Illinois
Gates, Marion...................... 3202 Enoch evenue, Zion City, Illinois
Gates, Miss Nettie..................3202 Enoch avenue, Zion City, Illinois
Graves, C. F. ....2616 Elizabeth avenue, Zion City, Illinois
Griffith, Mrs. Ida C.................2927 Ezra avenue, Zion City, Illinois
Groot, John D. ....Zion City, Illinois
Hartman, Joseph E...............3116 Gabriel avenue, Zion City, Illinois
Herbold, Paul.... Gabriel avenue and Thirty-third street, Zion City, Illinois
Hoover, Carson Roswell............2800 Ezra avenue, Zion City, Illinois
Jenne, Miss Eva E.................3214 Gideon avenue, Zion City, Illinois
Johnson, Miss Bessie...............2913 Enoch avenue, Zion City, Illinois
Knepper, Mrs. Bessie..............1807 Hermon avenue, Zion City, Illinois
Lilly, Mrs. Mary E..................3010 Elim avenue, Zion City, Illinois
Moos, Miss Hannah.................1903 Horeb avenue, Zion City, Illinois
Moos, Miss Josephine...............1903 Horeb avenue, Zion City, Illinois
Moos, Miss Rosa May...............1903 Horeb avenue, Zion City, Illinois
Murray, Miss Alva....................2113 Elisha avenue, Zion City, Illinois
Raper, Miss Grace Edna.........1813 Hermon avenue, Zion City, Illinois
Schwerdt, Carroll....................2515 Gideon avenue, Zion City, Illinois
Sweeney, Miss Edith M.............2118 Elisha avenue, Zion City, Illinois
Thorpe, Miss Nellie..................2907 Ezra avenue, Zion City, Illinois
Waldron, H. S......................2919 Eshcol avenue, Zion City, Illinois
Waldron, Mrs. H. S.................2919 Eshcol avenue, Zion City, Illinois

Itinerary in Indiana.

Elder Abraham F. Lee will hold meetings in Indiana as follows: Lafayette, Sunday and Monday, May 22d and 23d, Indianapolis, Tuesday and Wednesday, May 24th and 25th; Noblesville, Thursday, May 26th; Walton, Friday, May 27th; Logansport, Saturday and Sunday, May 28th and 29th.

Zion in Iowa.

Rev. Charles A. Hoy, Elder in the Christian Catholic Church in Zion, Falls City, Nebraska, will visit the following towns in Iowa between May 7th and May 18th: Webster City, Hubbard, Ames, Boone, Des Moines, Dedham and Indianola.

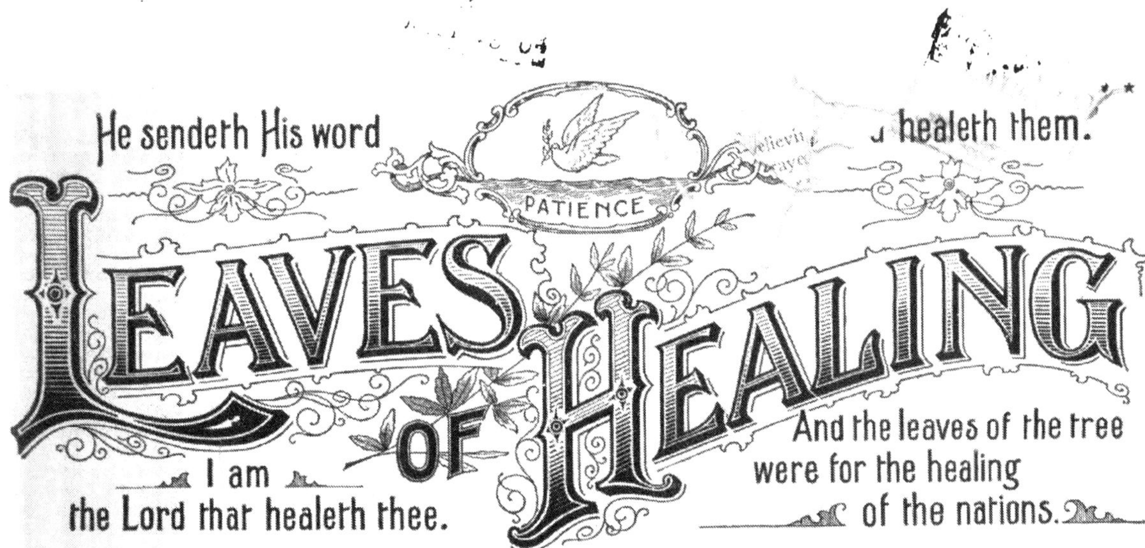

A WEEKLY PAPER FOR THE EXTENSION OF THE KINGDOM OF GOD
EDITED BY THE REV. JOHN ALEX. DOWIE.

Volume XV. No. 5. *ZION CITY, SATURDAY, MAY 21, 1904.* *Price Five Cents*

GOD'S WITNESSES TO DIVINE HEALING.

HEALED OF SERIOUS INJURY AND GENERAL WEAKNESS.

LOOK UNTO ME, AND BE YE SAVED,
ALL THE ENDS OF THE EARTH:
FOR I AM GOD, AND THERE IS NONE ELSE.

It is estimated that the most dangerous thing for a man to do is to take a walk.

The next most dangerous thing is to ride in a carriage or wagon.

It is safer far to travel by railroad, as in proportion to population there are less accidents.

The safest means of travel is by steamboat.

Every day, in Chicago, people are being killed or severely injured at the street crossings.

It is no rare thing to hear of death occurring during a carriage ride.

Nearly every one who has had occasion to drive continually has experienced a more or less serious accident.

Surely "a horse is a vain thing for safety."

The witness to Divine Healing who writes her testimony on the following page, tells of the serious accident which befell her and her companion in Kansas.

We remember the incident perfectly, for word was sent to Zion at the time, for prayer. Why was it that the one was healed and the other died? One of the natural circumstances against the old lady who died was her age; yet she lived long enough to have called upon God for deliverance. It is the temptation and tendency of those who are seriously injured to yield to the thought of death, instead of resisting the Devil with all their spiritual power and finding deliverance in God. The first thing to do in case of injury is to call mightily on God, and oftentimes this is all that needs to be done.

EVANGELIST MARY C. REED.

A severe concussion over the chest and heart is generally far more serious than a broken arm or broken leg. But no matter what happens, one ought to get into the habit of immediately calling upon God, and not give way to fear.

The secret of the healing of Evangelist Reed is that she had a hold on God and did not let go her hold. When we let go we fail.

She had long ago learned that God was her only help. She had heard the Voice of God:

> I said not unto the seed of Jacob,
> Seek ye Me in vain:
> I Jehovah speak righteousness,
> I declare things that are right.

Yet while she had her trust in God, and had learned that the arm of flesh cannot be relied upon, she felt it a privilege in other times of need to telegraph to her General Overseer, that he should unite in prayer with her, [illegible]ing that God heard and answered his pr[illegible]rs.

It is a good thing for Zion everywhere to know that in time of need they have access to the prayers of the General Overseer and those in charge at Headquarters, and they should more and more avail themselves of this privilege. For what one prescription of medicine would cost, a telegram can be sent in, and we are made acquainted with their need, and can unite our prayers with theirs.

Large numbers of telegrams have been received, and many are the notes of rejoicing that come to us, saying that God has heard and answered prayer, and delivered souls from death.

There is nothing that should not be taken to God.

In no case should hope be given up, but with a calm and steadfast trust in God and His willingness to deliver, we can go to the Throne of Grace and find sweet and full deliverance.

'Tis sweet to know that Jesus hears
Each simple, earnest, trusting prayer
And feel in every hour of need
His tender, watchful care.

'Tis sweet to know that Jesus cheers
The troubled soul by sin oppressed,
Forgives repentant hearts that ask,
And bids the weary seek His rest.

'Tis sweet to know that Jesus guides,
Though dark the night and long the way,
And that no harm can come to me,
Or aught my trusting heart dismay.

'Tis sweet to know that in that home,
That grand, eternal resting-place,
Our souls shall dwell in perfect peace,
When we shall see Him face to face.

J G. S.

WRITTEN TESTIMONY OF EVANGELIST MARY C. REED.

509 South Elizabeth Street,
Wichita, Kansas.

My Dear General Overseer:—After fully trusting God as my Healer for eleven years, I feel it my duty and a great privilege to send my testimony for Leaves of Healing, praying that some one may be strengthened and blessed by knowing something of what God, the Father, in His great love, has done for me.

When a child, I was always sick, having been afflicted with typhoid fever, spinal trouble, erysipelas, and a broken arm. It seemed as though the Devil was determined to destroy my life.

After I was married we moved from Canada to Douglas, Michigan.

God gave us children, but Satan destroyed the lives of two of them in one year.

Our little boy was killed by a dose of medicine given him by a physician who was drunk with morphine. He gave it to stop dysentery and it immediately threw him into cramps.

His limbs drew up and he screamed with pain until his spirit left his little body.

A Congregational minister came in just as he was passing away and hurriedly sprinkled a little water on his head for baptism. My husband was angry at the thought of a little water helping a pure baby into the Kingdom of God.

We were told that God took away our little ones to make us become Christians.

My husband became an infidel and for eight years declared that either the church people lied or the Bible was not true.

I repented of my sins and consecrated my life to God and for five years prayed for his redemption, but prayer was not answered in his behalf until my daughter and I erected the family altar.

My husband was brought to repentance and turned to God. From that time we obeyed God in bringing in the whole tithe.

We had spent hundreds of dollars on physicians.

I had suffered for about three years with female weakness.

Dr. Wilson, of Shelby, Michigan, told me that I had better not make a drug-store of myself any longer, and by that I saw he had no faith in drugs.

We saw the great need of spiritual power in the churches.

God revealed to us His will that we should leave all and follow Him in going out and preaching the Gospel.

On July 14, 1891, we withdrew from the Methodist Episcopal church and went into whatever church we were called, going from house to house into whatever city we entered, praying with the people and reading God's word to them.

We were greatly blessed in this work and many were added to the Kingdom, but we observed that the churches were fast losing their power.

God blessed me in spirit, soul and body, and added to our family two more children.

In 1894, I was again to become a mother, when I accidentally fell out of a rowboat into the lake. Fear entered my heart, and miscarriage followed.

Nearly all the blood left my body, and I was sinking very fast when my brother, who was not a Christian, sent for a doctor.

By this time my husband, who had been away from home, returned.

The doctor told him that I must have help soon from God or man. He replied that God would help us.

They were all crying around me. I had become very weak, and the hemorrhage still continued. I could not speak.

Mr. Reed told them all to go away, and leave him alone with me.

God wonderfully brought new life and strength to my body.

In about two years, I was again about to become a mother. While out selling *Salvation Heralds*, I fell on the ice, which caused another miscarriage.

The Devil said, "You will die this time."

Blood poisoning set in, and again my life-blood nearly left my body.

I became so helpless that my faithful daughter, now Mrs. McCreery, of Zion City, cared for me as if I were a little child.

I suffered from dropsy, rheumatism and consumption. At one time my husband laid me down, thinking I was dead.

I was restored but not healed.

We had read a few copies of Leaves of Healing, which gave us new light, and James 5:14-16 was before me all the time.

No healing came until I confessed all my faults.

Some persons to whom I made confession also confessed their faults to me, so I found it helped others to get right also.

Then I had confidence to come to God, and I knew God would heal me.

One of my legs was drawn up with rheumatism and I could not straighten it out.

"The joy of Jehovah is our strength."

There was great rejoicing when the children saw their mamma walking after three months of suffering.

Praise God! He again put the resurrection life within me, for I was like one raised from the dead.

How glad I was to speak to all I could of the glorious resurrection life of the Christ for spirit, soul, and body!

When we first came to Zion the Devil again tried to destroy my life with diphtheria, from which I nearly lost my voice.

When I fully accepted Zion teaching in everything, God restored me perfectly. Praise His Name!

While at Manchester, Kansas, we were driving to the meeting in a spring wagon, when suddenly the seat upon which I was riding was thrown backward, and an old lady, myself and little daughter fell to the ground.

I could not get my breath or speak for some time.

I felt as if my lungs were crushed and thought my back was broken, but I knew that God would heal me.

We sent a telegram to the General Overseer for prayer and in twenty-four hours I was on the train on my way to hold services at Delphos.

By afternoon I was able to conduct the service.

I walked several blocks, and talked for an hour.

The dear old lady who fell with me did not resist the Devil and in two days she was dead.

I thank God that we are now learning how to be kept by God, which is much more blessed than to be delivered from suffering.

Surely the Lord hath forgiven mine iniquities, and healed all my diseases; and renewed my youth like the eagle's; and satisfied my mouth with good things. My life is happy in carrying the Good News to suffering humanity.

If I had only been taught Zion truths earlier, I would have been kept from much suffering.

Oh, that all the world might taste and see
The riches of His grace!
The arms of love that compass me
Might all mankind embrace.

Thanking God for His great love in sending us Elijah the Restorer to teach the world the Full Gospel, I am,

In Christian love and fellowship,

(Mrs.) Mary C. Reed,
Evangelist in the Christian Catholic Church in Zion.

MEETINGS IN ZION CITY TABERNACLES.

SHILOH TABERNACLE.

Lord's Day—Early morning service.... 6:30 a. m.
Intermediate Bible Class.. 9:45 a. m.
Bible class, conducted by Deacon Daniel Sloan.. 11:00 a m.
Afternoon service....... 2:30 p. m.
Evening service......... 8:00 p. m.

First Lord's Day of Every Month—Communion service.

Second Lord's Day of Every Month—Baptismal service.

Second Lord's Day of Every Month—Consecration of children, 10:30 a. m.

Monday—Zion Restoration Host rally (Second Monday of every month).... 8:00 p. m.
Tuesday—Divine Healing meeting..... 2:30 p. m.
Tuesday—Adult Choir .... 7:45 p. m.
Wednesday—Baptismal service........ 7:00 p. m.
Wednesday—Citizens' rally. .... 8:00 p. m.
Friday—Adult Choir .... 7:45 p. m.
Friday—Officers of the Christian Catholic Church in Zion........ 8:00 p. m.
Friday—Junior Choir.................... 3:45 p. m.
Meeting in the officers' room.

TWENTY-SIXTH STREET TABERNACLE.

Lord's Day—Junior service .... 9:45 a. m.
Lord's Day—Services (German)........10:30 a. m.
Tuesday—Services (German)..... .... 8:00 p. m

ELIJAH THE RESTORER

A WEEKLY PAPER FOR THE EXTENSION OF THE KINGDOM OF GOD.
EDITED BY THE REV. JOHN ALEX. DOWIE.

Application for entry as Second Class Matter at Zion City, Illinois, pending.

Subscription Rates.		Special Rates.	
One Year	$2.00	100 Copies of One Issue	$3.00
Six Months	1.25	25 Copies of One Issue	1.00
Three Months	.75	To Ministers, Y. M. C. A's and Public Reading Rooms, per annum	1.50
Single Copies	.05		

For foreign subscriptions add $1.50 per year, or three cents per copy for postage.

Subscribers desiring a change of address should give present address, as well as that to which they desire LEAVES OF HEALING sent in the future.

Make Bank Drafts, Express Money or Postoffice Money Orders payable to the order of JOHN ALEX. DOWIE, Zion City, Illinois, U. S. A

Long Distance Telephone. *Cable Address "Dowie, Zion City."*

All communications upon business must be addressed to
MANAGER ZION PUBLISHING HOUSE,
Zion City, Illinois, U. S. A.

Subscriptions to LEAVES OF HEALING, A VOICE FROM ZION, and the various publications may also be sent to

ZION PUBLISHING HOUSE, 81 EUSTON ROAD, LONDON, N. W., ENGLAND.
ZION PUBLISHING HOUSE, NO. 43 PARK ROAD, ST. KILDA, MELBOURNE, VICTORIA, AUSTRALIA.
ZION PUBLISHING HOUSE, RUE DE MONT, THABOR 1, PARIS, FRANCE.
ZIONSHEIM, SCHLOSS LIEBBURG, CANTON THURGAU, BEI ZÜRICH, SWITZERLAND.

ZION CITY, ILLINOIS, SATURDAY, MAY 21, 1904.

TABLE OF CONTENTS.

LEAVES OF HEALING, SATURDAY, MAY 21, 1904.

Notes From The Overseer-in-Charge.

"SEEST THOU A MAN WISE IN HIS OWN CONCEIT?

"THERE IS MORE HOPE OF A FOOL THAN OF HIM."

WE HAVE taken occasion from time to time to refer in these columns to the opinions of men, both pro and con, in matters pertaining to Zion.

WE HAVE no intention of apologizing for or standing in defense of Zion.

Neither Zion nor her beloved founder, under God, the Rev. John Alexander Dowie, has any need for apology or defense.

The work of Zion and the beautiful character of her institutions is the only defense necessary.

THE REV. JOHN ALEXANDER DOWIE can claim more to his credit for the building up of an organization like Zion, with its thousands of strong, pure, godly, earnest men and women, than any other living man can for any work which he has done.

Yet there are men who admit that his work is a good one who have the audacity to speak against him, and make it an occasion for monetary gain, in trying to defame the fair name of our beloved General Overseer.

THE RECENT attempt of Dr. J. M. Buckley, in the Methodist Conference at Los Angeles, to crucify the Rev. John Alexander Dowie between two thieves, Christian Science and Theosophy, was a flat failure.

Letters just received from Los Angeles declare that those who paid the admission fee to his lecture regretted having done so.

The following are extracts from some of these letters:

Evangelist Sarah E. Hill says:

> The papers could not praise Dr. Buckley's address, and said that he showed evident want of preparation.
>
> People left the meeting, and Buckley told them to go if they were tired; that he would go himself if he were not the lecturer.

A letter from Deaconess Anna T. Reakirt says:

> A gentleman who was there said that he could not see that Dr. Buckley made any points, and that every one was disappointed.
>
> Two ladies expressed the same idea, and pronounced it flat; and one was sorry she had paid the money to hear it.
>
> The people went out in great numbers long before the lecture was over. He could not hold them with all his oratory.

WE SHOULD think that Dr. Buckley had all in hand that he could attend to to keep his church from going to the Devil—that little portion of it that has not already gone.

If he were to preach a little more of repentance and a little less against those who are bringing men to repentance, he would probably receive more commendation from God.

It is a poor thing to pull down those who advocate strong, rugged Christianity.

WHY DOES Dr. Buckley not raise his voice against men in the churches who are denying the fundamental truths of Christianity?

What about the tendency to do away with the Apostles' Creed?

Rev. Robert Russell Booth, Moderator of the Presbyterian General Assembly, and pastor emeritus of Rutger's Presbyterian church, New York City, declares that there are ministers who, instead of repeating the Apostles' Creed as we have it, read it as follows:

> "Jesus Christ, who, they say, was born of the Virgin Mary;" and "Jesus Christ, who, they say, was raised after the third day," and "they say" all the way through.

IT IS intimated by another minister that "the only refuge left today for those who would be faithful to the orthodox belief as expressed in the Apostles' Creed is to be found in the Roman Catholic church."

IF KING EDWARD is truly the "Defender of the Faith," let him see to it that the canons of Westminster Abbey are not permitted to belch forth their infidelity against the bulwarks of Christianity.

The silly vaporings of such men as H. Hensley Henson, who is attacking the resurrection of Jesus, and quotes largely from other infidel writers, reminds one of the crowing of a barn-yard fowl at midnight, upon being disturbed, whereupon all the neighboring cocks think dawn is at hand and begin to crow lustily also.

THERE IS another "Henson" who has been crowing particularly against Zion, and trying to belittle the testimony of the miraculous.

SUCH MEN do not believe in present day miracles, and their faith in biblical miracles will not bear investigation.

ZION DOES not depend upon historical evidence for the fact of the resurrection or the miraculous.

Her living witnesses in thousands can attest to the resurrection power in their own lives, and to their having been healed miraculously when they were without hope.

IT IS an easy thing for the jealous ministers to decry John Alexander Dowie and his work.

Some whose congregations numbered only hundreds to his thousands declared him to be mentally unbalanced, and the doctors, who are probably just a little more jealous of the success of the General Overseer than the preachers are, have taken up the cry.

ONE LITTLE fellow, by the name of "Brower," in Chicago, before a judge, the other day, declared that the General Overseer and Mrs. Eddy and Mohammed were all "paranoiacs," which, in plain English, means that their work is due to insanity.

We presume it is an insane thing to get people to give up employing Dr. Brower, and to trust in the Lord Jesus, the Christ, for healing, according to Dr. Brower's idea.

A number of papers have been commenting upon Dr. Brower's statements, and the Chicago *Chronicle* of May 11th, in an editorial, makes the following statement:

> Dr. D. R. Brower, as an expert physician with a reputation at stake, would never have gone out of the way to declare, as he did recently in Judge Honore's court, that Mrs. Mary G. Eddy and Dr. John A. Dowie were paranoiacs and irresponsible in anything they did, unless he meant what he said.
>
> His opinion on this subject would have been more valuable, perhaps, if both these public characters were not "healers," and therefore under the ban of the medical profession. But even without subjecting it to this discount, it will go for very little among reflecting people.

ANOTHER PAPER, which has never been very friendly toward Zion, but which is nearer home and probably knows as well what it is talking about as does Dr. Brower, (who in all probability has never met the Rev. John Alexander Dowie personally, and knows nothing about Zion, save that it opposes his abominable profession,) is the Waukegan *Daily Sun*, published in Waukegan, just six miles from Zion City.

In the leading editorial of recent date, commenting on Dr. Brower, is the following statement, the headline being in large capitals:

> DOWIE CRAZY? NO, BROWER.
>
> Dr. Brower, of Chicago, of whom we have kindly and benevolent recollections, is quoted as saying that John Alexander Dowie is crazy.
>
> He says: "It is not unusual for paranoiacs to transact their business for years with success; only in the enthusiasm with which they advance their delusions do they evince their insanity."
>
> A man who says Dowie is crazy, and means what he says, is worthy of careful watching by the authorities.
>
> Does this man Brower know what this man Dowie has done?
>
> Does Brower not know that Dowie is one of the most successful and really wonderful men of the century?
>
> Has Brower been so busy with his success (insanity), that he has failed to know of Dowie's accomplishments?
>
> Many of us, while not endorsing many things advocated by Dowie (no more than we do of many other men), believe that he is thoroughly sane and doing a great good, and hope that he will be spared to see his many laudable undertakings completed.
>
> Dowie crazy?
>
> No, Dr. Brower, you can every waking hour put your hand on one who is nearer an insane jury than he.

DR. BROWER is quoted as having said that either he or Dowie is insane.

We believe he is right.

THERE IS another Brower in Chicago who is an attorney, who tried to injure Zion, before a judge in Chicago, in a case in which both he and Zion are interested.

He declared to the judge that every man who joined the Christian Catholic Church in Zion was insane; therefore, the man whom he was opposing was insane, and was not in a condition to execute legal documents.

When we took him up on his own proposition that our client was just as insane as all the other people of Zion, he backea down and refused to proceed on that line.

THE BROWERS, the Hensons, and the Buckleys, the doctors, and the lawyers, and the preachers, are in a very bad state of mind against Zion.

But we have no fear.

We know we are right, because the evil hate us so.

We know we are right, because we are not working for self, but for humanity.

We know we are right, because God answers prayers.

We know we are right, for right wrongs no man.

AN EVENT of considerable interest to Zion and to the surrounding cities was the rendering of a large portion of "The Messiah" by Zion White-robed Choir, in Shiloh Tabernacle, last week Wednesday.

THE FOLLOWING is an outline of a report given in the Waukegan *Sun:*

FIVE THOUSAND ATTEND CONCERT IN ZION CITY

CHOIR OF THREE HUNDRED AND FIFTY VOICES, ASSISTED BY TWENTY-FIVE PIECE ORCHESTRA, RENDERS "THE MESSIAH."

PRESIDENT A. C. FROST RECEIVES OVATION.

MANY WAUKEGAN PEOPLE DRIVE TO ZION CITY AND ARE HIGHLY ENTERTAINED—VISITORS SHOWN MUCH COURTESY.

"Peace to Thee," are you a stranger?

Thus were the many visitors to Zion Tabernacle accosted last night, on the occasion of the immense White-robed Choir assisted by an orchestra of twenty-five pieces, singing "The Messiah." Five thousand people were in attendance.

Had the railroad provided accommodations, it is safe to say from the many inquiries at the *Sun* office regarding train service, that a thousand would have gone from Waukegan.

As it was two hundred fifty drove up.

VISITORS WELL PROVIDED FOR.

A detail of Zion Guard looked well after the numerous rigs.

The many ushers seemed to take especial pains that all out-of-town people were cared for.

A section immediately on the right of the rostrum and facing the section occupied by the Deacons had been reserved.

. . . .

The entire oratorio was not sung because of its length.

. . . .

Numbers twelve, twenty-three, forty-four and forty-five were especially well rendered.

The chorus throughout was of a high order and received hearty and deserved applause.

ZION CHOIR probably never did better than it did at this time. Deacon John D. Thomas deserves special mention and due credit for the admirable way in which he is keeping up the standard in Zion Choir.

THE ORCHESTRA is an excellent addition, and is giving excellent service.

AT THIS writing the General Overseer is in Zürich, preparatory to the beginning of his European Conference of the Christian Catholic Church in Zion, which begins on May 22d.

THE FOLLOWING cablegram was received from him last Lord's Day morning:

PARIS.

SPEICHER, Zion City, Illinois.

I send you Isaiah 61st chapter, 10th and 11th verses.

Spent five pleasant days in southern France. Some faithful friends of Zion are there.

Meet Paris members of the Christian Catholic Church in Zion here in my room at the Hotel Normandy this afternoon. Public meetings will be held Tuesday, in the Hall of Civil Engineers.

Leave for Zurich on Thursday.

Love to all Zion.

Pray.

Mizpah. DOWIE.

We can promise our readers a continuation of the excellent reports of the Around-the-World Visitation, from the General Associate Editor Zion Publications and Special Correspondent and Secretary, Deacon Arthur W. Newcomb.

We have copy enough on hand for several issues.

Within a week or two we hope to be able to give a number of most interesting pictures taken in Adelaide.

Photographs received this week show the General Overseer and Mrs. Dowie to be in excellent health.

WE DESIRE to keep the friends of Zion everywhere in remembrance of the coming Feast of Tabernacles, and to solicit their hearty coöperation.

We hope to have with us at that time more than a thousand visitors from various parts of this and other countries.

IT WILL be noticed that the Superintendent of the Transportation Bureau has arranged for at least one and one-third fare, and the probabilities are that we may be able to make the reduction to one fare for the round trip.

Read carefully the instructions on page 141 of this issue.

PROVIDE YOURSELVES with copies of the Feast of Tabernacles Program, which can be had at Zion Printing and Publishing House for the asking, and bring them with you.

PRAY FOR us that we may be able to acceptably prepare for the coming Feast. JOHN G. SPEICHER.

Daily Bible Study for the Home

By Overseer John G. Speicher

THE month of June will be devoted to the study of the Book of Romans, 1st and 2d Thessalonians, and 1st, 2d, and 3d John. There are many beautiful truths in Romans easy to be understood. Do not trouble yourselves with the hard things.

WEDNESDAY, JUNE 1ST.

Romans 1.—Gospel of the Christ versus Wickedness chapter.

Memory text—Verse 16. "I am not ashamed of the Gospel."

Contents of chapter—Paul's introduction concerning Jesus being the Christ, and their being called through Him; Their faith proclaimed throughout the world; Paul prays for them and longs to see them, to impart spiritual gift; Hindered in coming; Not ashamed of the Gospel; The power of God unto salvation to believers; Wrath of God against ungodliness; Invisible things understood through the things which are made; Those who glorify not God change the truth of God into a lie, worshiping the creature rather than the Creator; They were given up to evil deeds.

THURSDAY, JUNE 2D.

Romans 2.—True worship chapter.

Memory text—Verse 16. "God shall judge the secrets of men . . . by Jesus, the Christ."

Contents of chapter—He who judgeth against evil deeds must be free from them; Goodness of God leadeth to repentance; God will render to every man according to his works; No respect of persons with God; Judgment will be according to light and knowledge; Secrets of men will be judged; Teachers and leaders must be pure; True obedience and keeping of law is from the heart and not merely outwardly.

FRIDAY, JUNE 3D.

Romans 3.—Justification chapter.

Memory text—Verse 24. "Being justified freely by His grace through the redemption that is in Christ Jesus."

Contents of chapter—Jews were first entrusted with the oracles of God; Their unfaithfulness does not make God unfaithful; No man justified by works; Law brings knowledge of sin; Jesus, the Christ, is the righteousness of God; All have sinned and come short of the glory of God; Justified by grace, through the Christ; Glory in works of the law excluded by the law of faith; Circumcision and uncircumcision justified through faith.

SATURDAY, JUNE 4TH.

Romans 4.—Abraham's faith chapter.

Memory text—Verse 13. "For not through the law was the promise to Abraham, . . . but through the righteousness of faith."

Contents of chapter—Abraham justified by faith, not by works; Abraham by his faith accounted father of all, in circumcision and uncircumcision, who walk in the steps of faith; Promise given to Abraham not through works of the law but through the righteousness of faith; It is of faith, according to grace; Promise sure to all; Abraham considered condition of himself and wife, yet wavered not, believing God able to perform His promise.

SUNDAY, JUNE 5TH.

Romans 5.—Reconciliation chapter.

Memory text—Verse 17. "They that receive the abundance of grace and of the gift of righteousness reign in life through the One, even Jesus, the Christ."

Contents of chapter—Justified by faith, peace with God comes through Jesus, the Christ; Access to grace; Rejoice in hope and in tribulations; The Christ died for the ungodly; God's love manifested through the Christ; Sin, death and judgment came as the result of one man's transgression; Salvation, life, and righteousness came through the Christ.

MONDAY, JUNE 6TH.

Romans 6.—Influence of grace chapter.

Memory text—Verse 23. "For the wages of sin is death; but the free gift of God is eternal life in the Christ, Jesus, our Lord."

Contents of chapter—Must not continue in sin; Baptized into the Christ's death, His resurrection and newness of life; Our old man crucified with the Christ; We should no longer be in bondage to sin; Dead to sin, alive unto God; Sin shall not have dominion over us; Not under law but under grace; We are servants to him whom we obey; Our members to be presented as servants to righteousness; Wages of sin is death; Eternal life through the Christ, our Lord.

TUESDAY, JUNE 7TH.

Romans 7.—Use of the law chapter.

Memory text—Verse 22. "I delight in the law of God after the inward man."

Contents of chapter—Woman bound to her husband as long as he liveth; Death sets her free; So we are free from the law through the body of the Christ; Joined to the Christ to bring forth fruit unto God; Our service should be in the spirit and not in letter merely; The law was not sin, but brought knowledge of sin; Law is holy, and the commandment is holy; Law is spiritual; Humanity by nature carnal, preventing good deeds; The inward man delights in God's law; Only deliverance is through Jesus, the Christ.

WEDNESDAY, JUNE 8TH.

Romans 8.—Intercession of Spirit chapter.

Memory text—Verse 35. "Who shall separate us from the love of the Christ."

Contents of chapter—No condemnation to them that are in the Christ; Law of the spirit of life in the Christ makes free from the law of sin and death; Mind of the flesh is death; Mind of the spirit is life and peace; He that hath not the spirit of the Christ is none of His; Mortal body quickened through His Spirit dwelling in us; If we live after the flesh we die, but if after the Spirit, we shall live; Sons of God are led by the Spirit of God; We cry "Abba, Father!" through the spirit of adoption; Spirit witnesseth that we are heirs; Sufferings of this time not to be compared with the glory that shall be revealed; Whole creation waiteth for the full redemption; Spirit maketh intercession for us; All things work together for good to them that love God; God will freely give all things; Who or what can separate from the love of the Christ; We are more than conquerors through Him that hath loved us.

THURSDAY, JUNE 9TH

Romans 9.—Divine sovereignty chapter.

Memory text—Verse 26. "There shall they be called sons of the living God."

Contents of chapter—Paul sorrows for the Jews; The promises are to them, and also to all who are the seed of Abraham by promise; God's love manifested principally to the obedient; God not unjust or partial; The disobedient are rejected; A remnant of obedient ones to be saved; Gentiles to attain righteousness through faith; Israel seeking righteousness by works and fails; Righteousness of the Christ a stone of stumbling to the Jews.

FRIDAY, JUNE 10TH.

Romans 10.—Creating of faith chapter.

Memory text—Verse 17. "Belief cometh of hearing, and hearing by the Word of the Christ."

Contents of chapter—Paul's desire and prayer for the salvation of Israel; Their zeal not according to knowledge; Ignorantly seeking to establish their own righteousness, they did not submit themselves to the righteousness of God; With the heart man believeth unto righteousness; With the mouth confession is made unto salvation; Whosoever believeth shall not be put to shame; Whosoever calleth on the name of the Lord shall be saved; The gospel must be preached; Faith cometh through teaching and preaching of the Word.

SATURDAY, JUNE 11TH.

Romans 11.—Faithful remnant chapter.

Memory text—Verse 29. "The gifts and the calling of God are without repentance."

Contents of chapter—Elijah pleaded against Israel because of their wickedness; God answered that seven thousand had not bowed the knee to Baal; Remnant left who believed then; God overruled and sent salvation to Gentiles; Gentiles warned not to glory unduly, but to remember that the Root beareth them, not they the Root; Fear lest since God spared not the natural branches they might be cut off; A falling away until the fulness of the Gentiles shall come in; All Israel shall be saved; Gifts and the calling of God without repentance; God's riches of wisdom, knowledge, and judgments are of great depths.

SUNDAY, JUNE 12TH.

Romans 12.—Christian service chapter.

Memory text—Verse 9. "Let love be without hypocrisy."

Contents of chapter—Pleads for consecration of the body to God, and fashioning life after the will of God as reasonable; Sober thinking commended; Remembering the body of the Christ and our part in the same; Diligence and faithfulness in ministries; Loving the good; Abhoring the evil; In honor preferring one another; Not slothful in business, Hospitable; Rendering good for evil; Joyful and sympathetic; As far as possible living in peace with all men; Vengeance belongeth unto God.

For we are a temple of the living God;
Even as God said,
I will dwell in them, and walk in them;
And I will be their God,
And they shall be My people.—*2 Corinthians 6:16.*

ELIJAH THE RESTORER GOES STRAIGHT AHEAD BY USING BOTH OARS.

Around-the-World Visitation

of the

Rev. John Alex. Dowie

Elijah the Restorer
General Overseer of the Christian Catholic Church in Zion.

By ARTHUR W. NEWCOMB, Special Correspondent.

OUR last paper of this series closed with the report of the Message of Elijah the Restorer delivered in Central Zion Tabernacle, Swanston street, Melbourne, Australia, Tuesday afternoon, March 1, 1904.

Central Zion Tabernacle, Melbourne, Australia, Wednesday Morning, March 2, 1904.

The Service was opened with the singing of the Hymn, "I'm a Pilgrim."

The Rev. Stephen McCullagh, Pastor of the Branch of the Christian Catholic Church in Zion in Sydney, New South Wales, read the Scripture lesson from the Inspired Word of God, in the 15th chapter of Matthew from the 21st to the 31st verse.

The Rev. John Gabriel Excell offered prayer, the General Overseer praying for the sick, and closing with the Disciples' Prayer.

The General Overseer then delivered his Message:

THE STORY OF THE CANAANITISH WOMAN.

*REPORTED BY I. M. S. AND A. W. N.

INVOCATION.

Let the words of my mouth and the meditation of my heart be acceptable in Thy sight, and profitable unto this people, O Lord, my Strength, and my Redeemer.

Deacon McCullagh read to you, this morning, from the 15th chapter of Matthew.

I wish to talk to you a little about this.

Follow me, in your Bibles, while I read. If I make any mistakes in the reading, you may correct me.

Narrow Compass, Geographically, of the Christ's Earthly Ministry.

This is the story of the Christ departing into the coasts of Tyre and Sidon, and there having a very extraordinary experience with a woman of Canaan.

It may be well to remember that our Lord Jesus, when here on earth, confined His ministry to Palestine.

He went into the coasts and borders of neighboring countries, but it is questionable if He ever crossed the boundary line of the Holy Land.

It is wonderful that a life spent in such narrow limits should reach out through the whole world and through all the ages.

The whole of Palestine is not nearly so large as the State of Illinois, and it did not have as many people in it as that state has.

In that one State of Illinois alone, we reach more people than ever the Christ saw in Palestine.

It is wonderful that His life, lived in such circumscribed limits, should be the most important of all lives in the world.

A Beautiful Heathen.

I am glad that this story was written, and that the Christ went into this borderland between the Holy Land and the heathen lands.

The Tyrian and Sidonian women were traditionally beautiful, and I have no doubt they were; for, with all their evil practices, they were splendidly developed physically, and only the fittest survived.

It seems to me that this woman must have been a woman of considerable station.

Circumstances indicate it.

In the bold, free way of the Tyrian and Sidonian women, she comes straight to Jesus with her heart full of grief.

She has a demoniacally-possessed daughter, and the spectacle is a terrible one.

Her grief is ever with her.

She has heard of this great Prophet and kind and merciful Man who loves to relieve human misery.

*The following report has not been revised by the General Overseer.

She has either heard Him say or heard that He said, "Come unto Me, all ye that labor and are heavy laden, and I will give you rest. Take My yoke upon you, and learn of Me; for I am meek and lowly in heart: and ye shall find rest unto your souls."

The word souls there means lives.

It is the *psyche* (ψυχή) the animal life, not the spirit.

There is only one way in which the life can cease to be burdened, and that is by the spirit's coming to Jesus.

Futility of Long Prayers.

This woman came to Jesus with a long prayer, but He did not answer it.

Many of you have delivered long prayers that have never been answered.

You had better study why this woman's prayer was not answered.

Even the outline we have of it is long.

Everything in the New Testament is reduced to the smallest possible dimensions.

"Have mercy on me, O Lord, Thou Son of David; my daughter is grievously vexed with a devil."

He answered her not a word. He walked away.

What was the matter?

You have prayed and have not been answered, and there has been a good reason.

There was one in this case.

I suppose that she was greatly disappointed.

She began to wonder why He had not answered.

She thought that no doubt the reason was that He was too great a man altogether to take any notice of her.

She saw that he was surrounded by a party—James, John, Peter, Andrew and Philip—so she came to them and said, "O Peter! O holy apostle! (*Ora pro nobis!*) Pray for us."

Then she came to John, crying, "Pray for us; oh, go to the Master and ask Him; intercede with Him for me."

Futility of Prayer to Saints and Virgins.

That is just what many people do nowadays.

Instead of asking why it is that God does not answer them when they come to Him in the Name of Jesus, they say, "Oh, He is too great and good a God, let us go to the apostles, to the saints and angels. He will justify their praying for me. (*Ora pro nobis!*) Pray for us, saints and angels, pray for us!"

That is not the way.

If God will not answer you in the Christ's Name, there is no use in your howling to the Virgin Mary, or to Peter and James and John.

There is a reason why you are not answered.

It does not lie in Peter and James and John, and they know it too.

They saw the Master when He heard her prayer, "Have mercy on me, O Lord, Thou Son of David, my daughter is grievously vexed with a devil," and they saw that He walked on, so they did not dare to ask Him.

They did not dare; for, if He, the All-merciful and All-pitiful One walked away from her, He had a reason.

I am not much compared to Him, but if I will not answer a request and will say nothing, my men know that there is no use in talking to me about it. I have a reason.

I will attend to that matter at the proper time and when the conditions are fulfilled.

The Spirit of Prayer.

But this woman had the spirit of prayer in her heart.

That is one thing that she had.

She just kept after these apostles, although she was wrong.

Morning, noon and night they had no rest.

When they got up in the morning, it was, "O Peter, did you

talk to Jesus? O John, did you talk to Jesus for me? O James, O Andrew, will you not talk to Him?

"Pray for me.

"Get Him to do something for me."

"Go away," they would say, "He would not do it We do not know why, but there is no use in asking Him.

"He is infinitely wise, and you must put yourself right with Him There is something wrong."

She persisted, however, so they came to the Master and said, "Send her away, she is after us morning, noon and night."

He had gone away from her and not answered her, but He would not send her away.

I dare say she was right there at the time when they made that appeal to Him to send her away.

He looked at her and He looked at them, and smiled, I think, as He said, "I was not sent"—and she was listening to what He was going to say—"I was not sent but unto the lost sheep of the House of Israel;" and He walked away again.

Now she had no hope.

She was a Canaanite. That cut off all hope.

She might have drawn herself up in her heathen pride and said, "Ah, just as I thought! Narrow-minded, bigoted Jew! There is no help for me, because I am not an Israelite! I wish our fathers had cleaned them all out long ago."

She might have become angry.

Put it as you like, it was a hard answer.

She was pleading for her daughter, and was at His feet, but she was told that He was "not sent but unto the lost sheep of the House of Israel."

Look into that story and study it very closely so that you may understand it.

I have gone over it a great many times, and it almost seems to me that I was there and saw the incident, I see so many things about it.

Salvation Is from the Jews.

The Lord said that there was no Salvation outside of Israel.

Perhaps you do not see that.

Another woman of mixed race had to be taught that.

She had to be taught that Salvation is from the Jews.

Do you hear?

Get it right down into your heads and hearts.

It is a vile thing, this race hatred of the Jews.

Today Russia is suffering from it.

Russia, that great Colossus, has feet of clay. When she touched the warm waters of Asia the clay crumbled, and she fell on her face.

She is being smashed now, and by a stronger power than Japanese guns.

She is being smashed by the Jews, financially.

The Jew, who controls the money of Europe, is seeing to it that she can get no money.

In her stress, that murderer of the Jews, Russia, will be shut out of all the money markets of Europe.

She will put her back to the wall. Alexieff says that she is doing it now.

It is a significant thing to say, in the first few days of the fight, that she already has her back to the wall.

But it is true.

God Cares for His People.

He heard the cry of the Jew in bondage in Egypt, four hundred years ago, and He brought them out.

Although they have sinned and wandered, the Jew is an Israelite, and "all Israel shall be saved."

To me the vilest and most terrible thing is so-called race hatred.

There is only one race anyway.

It is the Adamic race, and every race, so-called, is from Adam.

Australia is going to pieces because of your contemptible race hatred.

You try to shut out the African because of the color of his skin. If you are so clever and powerful, why fear the African?

You have a color line in your hearts. If a man has a yellow skin, he has a right to be saved as well as you.

We are all one great race, with God.

You say that you cannot stand competition with the African.

We have eight millions of them in America and we can stand their competition. They do not hurt the prosperity of the American workmen.

We find them magnificent workmen in their sphere.

They grow cotton and many other good things.

You would do well to get a million of them to grow cotton in Queensland.

They are a most peaceful race.

They are the jolliest and happiest people in the world, with a very few exceptions.

They are the kindest and most faithful of servants.

They would die for those they love.

It is the lazy loafer who is afraid of the African.

Are you afraid of the Chinese?

They make magnificent servants.

Chinese servants are treasures.

The Motto, "Australia for the Australians," Properly Applied.

Did not the Christ die for every man?

"Oh, yes," you say, "but 'Australia for the Australians!'"

Very well, you all clear out of Australia and let the aborigines have it.

They were the original owners.

You say that you conquered it.

You never did.

There was nothing to conquer. You never fought a battle for it.

You got a great gift from God Almighty, and from a poor, ignorant, miserable people, who never charged you for it,

You have robbed them ever since, and never cared for them.

You oppress them and shoot them down in the interior.

The story of that has gone up to God. He knows about the blood that was shed.

Deacon Hawkins—"They are shooting them now in other parts of this country."

General Overseer—I plead for the whole race.

We belong to that portion of the human race called Israel.

I believe that I am an Israelite, every whit.

A part of the nation from which I came is pure Israelitish blood.

Gaelic, in Scotland, is a dialect of the Hebrew.

The customs are all Hebraic.

The Sabbath begins with the sundown and ends with the sundown in the Highlands of Scotland.

Throughout the Lakes of the South, when the sun sets Saturday night, the people put up their boats and stop fishing. When it sets on Sunday night, they get to work again.

It is a real fact that Salvation is from the Jews If you are to be saved, you must be saved by Jesus, the Christ, the Jew.

Get it down into your hateful hearts, any of you who have any hatred for the Jew.

I hope that there are none such here.

All Who Are Saved Must Be Ingrafted Into Israel.

The Christ wanted that woman to understand that truth.

He wanted her to know that she would have to be ingrafted into Israel, and that she would owe to Israel her Salvation and Blessing, and the Healing of her daughter; that she had to come, not as a proud Canaanitish woman, but to seek admission in the Covenant of God in Israel.

She did not know.

It could not be explained to her very easily in words.

There is something more emphatic than words, and that is deeds.

The Christ, after He said, "I was not sent but unto the lost sheep of the House of Israel," walked away.

I do not know how long it was after that until she went to Him again.

She had the spirit of prayer.

She had the grace of supplication.

This time she did something that brought a direct answer to her.

Look at the Bible and see what that something is.

But "she came and worshiped Him."

Now she has another prayer.

Why the Woman's First Prayer Could Not Be Answered.

That first prayer could not be answered.

It had many defects.

In the first place, she said, "Lord, Thou Son of David."

She did not see in Him any more than a man. He was simply the son of David, a mortal man.

That will not do at all.

If you think that the Christ is only a mortal man and not Immortal God, you will get no answer.

If there is a Unitarian here he may as well go home.

If you do not recognize Jesus, the Christ, as the Son of God, and the Father as in Him, you will get no answer.

He had claimed Divinity, and she had ascribed to Him only humanity in that prayer.

She had thought that He was a good man, a kind man, and had asked Him to have mercy upon her.

Second, all her cry was for her daughter.

She had not thought about herself.

Probable Lapse of Time Between Events of This Story.

I am of the opinion that several days passed while that story was being enacted.

Although you can read it in two minutes, I am of the opinion that this story lasted over, perhaps, a visitation of a week.

I think that the internal evidence would indicate that time elapsed in the various stages of this story--nights of weeping perhaps.

She had been receiving His teaching.

She had found that she had to be ingrafted into Israel.

She had found that she had to recognize that He is God, and that she had to worship God in Him.

God had been teaching her.

She had been hearing the Christ talk, and He had no doubt shown her the way to the Father.

She had received enlightenment, and what did she do?

Power of a Short Prayer.

She had a new prayer now.

It was very much shorter than the old one, and that made it more effective.

It was a prayer of three short words: "Lord, help me."

Her daughter was not in it this time.

What was the matter?

Had she forgotten her daughter?

Not a bit of it, but she had discovered that she was a sinner; she had discovered, in the light of His teaching, that she was responsible for her daughter's condition. That is my opinion.

She now remembered the time when the Bacchanalian mysteries were on, and when she went out into the woods, drunk, calling upon the Sidonian Venus, and worshiped the horrid Sidonian Baal, whose worship was enacted with the vilest prostitution.

That daughter was probably conceived at that time and born through the influences of that time with the Devil in her, because the mother had the Devil in her.

Why Some Children Are Born With Devils.

Some mothers are crying out for their children, wondering why their sons or their daughters have the Devil in them.

The Devil is in your son or daughter because the Devil was first in you.

Say, "Lord help me!"

That is where the help must begin.

The trouble begins with the mothers who read dirty books and think dirty thoughts, and then they have dirty-minded sons and daughters.

They go to theaters and see disgusting sights.

They do disgusting things, and talk filthy talk.

Do you wonder that their sons and daughters have devils in them?

Some women try to destroy their offspring before they are born.

They manage to do it sometimes, and sometimes they fail.

Child with a Murderous Devil—The Reason Why.

When they fail, they hate the little unborn baby, and when he comes into the world he is a hateful, diabolical little murderer.

I have known a child only two years of age so murderous in his spirit that he would break the legs of kittens, and take great delight in seeing them in pain.

When three years of age, he would capture flies and pull off their legs and wings, and take delight in seeing them live in torture.

He tried to strangle his little baby brother while lying in a baby carriage.

The mother brought him to me in great distress.

I said to her, "There is no use in your howling about this child; howl about yourself."

"What do you mean?" she said, "I am a Christian lady."

"You may be a Christian now," I said, "but I do not take much stock in your Christianity, coming to me and telling me that this child is afflicted with a devil, and not confessing your own sins."

"What sins?" she said.

"What sin?" I said, "did you not try to murder him before he was born?"

"How dare you talk to me like that?" was her first exclamation.

Then she broke down and said, "I did. I murdered several others, but I failed to murder him."

"Do you wonder," I asked, "that he was born into the world with a murderous spirit? Cry, 'Lord, help me.'"

Some of you here are howling, "O Doctor, pray for my sons, pray for my daughters."

I will pray for them at the right time, but look here, what about yourselves?

Begin at the proper place.

It was a different prayer that that Canaanitish woman offered last.

It is, in effect, "Lord, help me. I am the sinner; I am standing in the way of my son's or my daughter's healing. Lord, help me. Take my sin away; help me to understand Thee and to trust Thee, and to be Thine. Give me a new heart and a right spirit; cleanse me of the stain of my foulness that made my daughter the devil that she is."

Do you see?

The Husband Also Guilty.

Men, women, do you understand?

It hits the men as well as the women, because in the case to which I have just referred, the woman said, "My husband made me do it."

I said, "Bring the scoundrel in."

"Oh," she said, "he is a great man in the church."

"There are many devils in the church," I replied. "Bring him here."

She brought him.

He was a superintendent in a Sunday-school, and as brazen as you please.

I said to him, "You dirty murderer, you ought to be hanged if hanging is a good thing. Any man that connives at abortion ought to be hanged, if hanging is a good thing."

However, I do not believe that capital punishment is a good thing, or that it ever cures anything.

I said, "You had better get down on your knees and tell God what a murderous dog you are."

I knocked it into him until he did.

When we prayed for that child, after I had the father and mother right, the Devil went out of him, and he has grown up to be a beautiful boy.

The Devil stayed out of him, his mother says.

I give that story as an illustration of the crimes committed by tens of thousands of women.

Women become harlots.

Why?

Because their mothers had vile thoughts and filthy, adulterous passions even if they did not yield to them.

A woman can read dirty literature and instil into the heart of her unborn babe the vile influences of that demon passion.

You can trace them in the streets; you do not need to go far.

There they are, howling at me and wanting to kill me.

Why?

I never did them any harm.

I never did a working man or woman any harm willingly or unwillingly.

I have fought for what is right and good according to my light.

Why do they want to kill me?

Why do they insult my wife and son who never did them any harm?

Because they were born like that.

Their fathers and mothers were full of devils and their children are.

The wicked are getting worse and worse.

Get Down to Business in Prayer.

You see that this Canaanitish woman got down to business.

When you, too, get down to business, your prayers will be short, but they will be effective.

Long prayers are of no account. They never have been.

I do not believe in long prayers.

When I am with my people, I gather up their petitions and I lay my hand upon them and place them before God, but I try to be as brief as I can.

When I am praying directly for the sick, my prayer is very short.

It is often not more than these words, "Lord, help them by Thy Spirit's power and in Jesus' Name," and that is all there is to it.

I mean it, too.

When a person is drowning, he does not make long petitions, long, eloquent speeches, saying, "Great Architect of the Universe, Creator and Omnipotent Manufacturer, so mote it be."

They do not talk such nonsense as that.

In all cases of extreme necessity, people always say only one thing, "Help, *Help*, HELP! HELP!!!"

They had better get down to business. None of your long prayer-making!

A Severe Test.

When she prayed that short prayer, she got an answer.

But what was the answer?

When He heard the prayer, He looked at her and said, "It is not meet to take the children's bread and cast it to the dogs," and He went away.

How would you like to be called a dog?

Even after she had worshiped Him, He said that.

When you get to the right place, you will see that you are a dog.

Might not she have been indignant, and rose from her knees and said, "Well, I thought You were a gentleman, anyway? Here's a woman that comes to You and worships You, and, with a broken heart, sorry for her daughter, says, 'Lord, help me!' and You say to her, 'It is not meet to take the children's bread and cast it to the dogs;' and You pass on."

She might have said, "I should like to let You know that I am a Canaanitish lady. I will go back into my own country; I am disgusted with You."

That is the way that some people talk.

When I tell them they are stinkpots they squeal, "I am a Melbourne gentleman and not a stinkpot. I should like to knock you on the nose."

They go walking up and down at the end of a cigar like this—[illustrates]—puffing away like an engine. [Laughter.]

Some of them put tobacco in their mouths and squirt the juice about until it runs down their beards.

Ugh! Spewing buzzards!

They do not like to be called such names.

But they are stinkpots and dirty pigs.

Any man that fills himself up with whisky and smokes and chews, stinks.

That is all there is about it, whether you like it or not.

Some Truths About Tobacco.

I understand that a great deal of the noise we have had here is due to the fact that there is a tobacco factory close by; that it is the tobacco employees that object because I have called the people stinkpots.

They are fighting for their stink.

That is what the *Argus* is fighting for.

The *Argus* must fight for them, for have you not noticed how the Devil's tobacco is advertised in the *Argus?*

The *Argus* would lose considerable money if it did not advertise Havelock Tobacco.

Sir Henry Havelock would be ashamed to know that his name is being used in that way.

He was a great and good man; but that is the way they do. They take the names of good men and stick them on their dirty tobacco.

The best name I ever saw for tobacco was "Battle Ax." That is right; it splits your head open. [Laughter.]

Another good name is "Capadura"—hard head, indicated by a dog.

When people get convicted, they will either go away angry, or they will go on to Jesus.

What did this Canaanitish woman do?

Did she give up praying?

No. She went after Jesus again, saying, "Yea, Lord: for even the dogs eat of the crumbs which fall from their masters' table."

"Now," she said, in effect, "I come as a dog; a dirty, Canaanitish dog.

"I see that is all I am, and I ask You to help me.

"I ask the great, good Father, who is in You, to help me.

"I ask You to cleanse me.

"It is true that I am only a dog; but I want the crumb of mercy and life, and I want blessing for myself and my child."

What did the Christ say?

When a Person Gets to the Right Place He Gets Blessing.

"O woman, great is thy faith: be it done unto thee even as thou wilt."

She asked for a crumb and got a whole loaf.

Her daughter was made whole in that same hour. That was the beginning of a great and mighty work.

And Jesus departed thence, and came nigh unto the sea of Galilee; and He went up into the mountain, and sat there. And there came unto Him great multitudes, having with them the lame, blind, dumb, maimed, and many others, and they cast them down at His feet; and He healed them: insomuch that the multitude wondered, when they saw the dumb speaking, the maimed whole, and the lame walking, and the blind seeing: and they glorified the God of Israel.

Beyond question that case and that story was a mighty blessing to the whole multitude, because it was an object lesson.

There are some people who will never get blessing for themselves or for their children until they see that they are mere dogs, and dirty little dogs at that. You must face it.

You have been covering up your sins perhaps with a cloak of church membership, bazaars, tea-meetings and all kinds of abominations.

That will not take with God Almighty.

You cannot cover your sins with a Masonic apron.

You cannot cover your sins with church membership.

You must get right with God.

You will have to get away down, some of you.

Your prayers have not been answered, and they will not be answered until you get where you ought to be.

All who are determined to get where they ought to be, stand and tell God so.

PRAYER OF CONSECRATION.

My God and Father, in Jesus' Name I come to Thee. Take me as I am, and make me what I ought to be, in spirit, soul, and body. Give me power to do right, no matter what it costs. Lord, help me. Father, help me, for Jesus' sake, and by Thy spirit; help me to take the lowest place. May there be blessing today to every contrite heart. For Jesus' sake. Amen. [*The prayer was repeated, clause by clause, after the General Overseer, by nearly the whole company assembled.*]

The meeting was closed with the

BENEDICTION.

Beloved, abstain from all appearance of evil. And may the very God of peace Himself sanctify you wholly; and I pray God your whole spirit and soul and body be preserved entire, without blame, unto the coming of our Lord Jesus, the Christ. Faithful is He that calleth you, who also will do it. The grace of our Lord Jesus, the Christ, the love of God, our Father, the fellowship of the Holy Spirit, our Comforter and Guide, one Eternal God, abide in you, bless you and keep you, and all the Israel of God everywhere, forever. Amen.

Central Zion Tabernacle, Melbourne, Australia, Wednesday Afternoon, March 2, 1904.

The Service was opened with the singing of the Hymn, "God is Life, and Light, and Love."

Rev. C. Friend Hawkins, read the Scripture lesson in the Inspired Word of God, from the 12th chapter of 1 Corinthians.

Prayer was offered by Overseer Jane Dowie.

The free-will offering and tithes were received, while "The Great Physician," was sung.

Overseer Wilbur Glenn Voliva made the announcements.

The General Overseer then said:

THE GIFTS OF HEALING A PRESENT DAY REALITY.

*REPORTED BY I. M. S AND A. W. N.

INVOCATION.

Let the words of my mouth and the meditation of my heart be acceptable in Thy sight, be profitable unto this people, and unto all to whom these words shall come, in this and ever land, in this and all the coming time, Till Jesus Come. Amen.

I asked the Rev. C. Friend Hawkins, Deacon-in-charge of the

*The following report has not been revised by the General Overseer.

Branch of the Christian Catholic Church in Zion in Adelaide, to read to you from the 12th chapter of 1 Corinthians.

As he read the first verse, I thought of what I often say in introducing this subject, "The Gifts of Healing a Present Day Reality."

The first words that he read were, "Now concerning Spiritual Gifts, brethren"—the best thing for you is to be perfectly ignorant. Is that right?

Voices—"No."

General Overseer—"I would not have you"—

Voices—"Ignorant."

General Overseer—How many times have you heard that chapter read in the Christian churches?

Great Ignorance of the Spiritual Gifts in the Church.

How many times have you heard an address upon the Nine Gifts of the Spirit.

Up with your hands. [Two hands were raised.]

Where did you hear it?

Voices—"In Zion." [Laughter.]

General Overseer—That is right, but I meant outside of Zion. [Three hands were raised.]

General Overseer—Well, I am glad of that; but there are just three people out of about eight hundred here assembled who have ever heard an address on the Nine Gifts of the Spirit.

If the Apostles had written, Now, concerning spiritual gifts, brethren, the best thing for you is to be ignorant, it would have just suited the churches of today.

The Church of today never talks about spiritual gifts.

Yet how very important the subject is!

Our conception of the Gifts has been greatly limited.

The theological schools have evolved a theory that the Gifts of God were given for a time and then taken away.

Deacon Hawkins, turn to the 11th chapter of Romans and the 29th verse, and read it, please.

Deacon Hawkins—"For the Gifts and the Calling of God are without repentance."

General Overseer—Do you believe that is true?

Voices—"Yes."

General Overseer—If the Gifts and Calling of God are without repentance, is it possible that God could have repented of one of these Gifts?

There are Nine Gifts of the Spirit, according to the Apostle.

I venture to say that if you will ask ten Christian ministers to give you a list of the Gifts, in their order, offhand, nine of them will fail.

If any minister here, outside of Zion, can give me the list from memory, I should like to hear him do it.

I have tested that sometimes in ministerial conferences, and I have seen every one who tried break down.

The Nine Gifts of the Spirit.

The first gift is the Word of Wisdom, the next is the Word of Knowledge, then Faith, Gifts of Healings, Workings of Miracles, Prophecy, Discernings of Spirits, Divers Kinds of Tongues, and last, Interpretation of Tongues.

Then there is a Gift in the next chapter, which is really the Fruit of the Spirit, and that is Love.

The Nine Gifts of the Spirit have a specific service.

They have been entrusted to the Church, like a bride adorned for her husband.

"Oh, yes," says some person, "we agree to that, but they have passed away. We have medical science now."

Did ever any one hear of such humbugging?

Where is the science in medicine?

Medicine not a Science.

In 1869, thirty-five years ago, I sat in the University of Edinburgh as a student, and heard Professor Douglas Maclagan, who held the chair of medical jurisprudence in that University, declare, in the presence of all the medical and surgical senatus and hundreds of students, that the physicians had been groping in the dark from the days of Hippocrates and Galen until then, and had not found the first stone that could be laid as a foundation for medical science.

Scientia is a Latin word meaning certain, accurate knowledge, and there is nothing of the kind in medicine.

The homeopath says, *similia similibus curantur*, like cures like, and the allopath says, *contraria contrariis curantur*, the contrary cures the contrary.

The allopath says that the homeopath is a fool, and the homeopath says that the allopath is a fool. They are both right about that.

When Doctors Disagree.

Where is the science in medicine?

There are no two doctors who agree on a diagnosis.

Some time ago, in New York, a little lady, who worked on a newspaper, went to her editor and said, "Give me five twenty-dollar bills, and I will get you some astonishing information."

He gave them to her.

She went down Fifth avenue, and into the offices of five of the greatest doctors in New York City.

To each she said, "Examine me, tell me what is the matter with me, and give me a prescription."

One said she had a bad case of tuberculosis, wrote her a prescription, gave her some directions, and took a twenty-dollar bill.

Another said that there was no question whatever but that there were signs of Bright's disease of the kidneys. He gave her some medicine for that, and took a twenty-dollar bill.

Another said that surely there was something wrong with her liver; that was plain. [Laughter.]

He also gave her a prescription, and took a twenty-dollar bill.

The fourth said that she had heart complaint—she admitted that, because the little woman had a lover—and he prescribed for that. He also took a twenty-dollar bill.

The fifth one said that it was her stomach that had gone wrong.

They each prescribed for her, and told her what medicines would be good.

The prescriptions were all different and each diagnosis of her case was different, and there was nothing wrong with the girl at all.

She merely wanted to write an article for her newspaper.

Each in his turn had lied to her and pocketed the twenty-dollar bill.

I pour contempt upon the whole thing.

There is nothing more false than to say that medicine is a science.

God Has Not Substituted Medicine for Gifts of Healings.

What nonsense to suppose that God Almighty put us into the hands of doctors from the cradle to the grave!

Do you mean to say that God Almighty took away the Gifts of Healings and gave us all that muck of medicines instead?

If this is a railing accusation, then it is the railing accusation of the greatest physicians of today, not mine.

God never did any such thing.

The Gifts of Healings are a present day reality.

They are for us.

Is not the Word of Wisdom a present day reality?

Voices—"Yes."

General Overseer—As long as the Holy Spirit is in the Church, these things must be in the Church, because they are in the Holy Spirit. That is the declaration of the Apostle.

But, as John Wesley said, when commenting on James 5:14, 15:

> This single conspicuous gift, which Christ committed to His apostles, (Mark 6:13) remained in the Church long after the other miraculous gifts ceased. It seems to have been designed to remain always. St James directs the elders, who were the most gifted men, to administer it. This was the whole process of physic in the Christian Church, till it was lost through unbelief.

Because a Gift Is Not Exercised, It Does Not Follow That It Is Lacking.

Electricity was a fact before Mr. Edison or any other inventor applied it to lighting and other uses.

It had been there ever since the beginning.

Wireless telegraphy was a fact long before Marconi found it.

We do not invent anything. We merely discover, that is all.

Some of you Methodist parsons here note that.

The prophetic words of that apostolic man, John Wesley, are true.

It has been remarked by innumerable commentators that the Gifts were never taken away, but that the Church had got into a state of decay and degeneracy in which it was impossible to exercise them.

They know this.

Fitchett, the editor of the *Southern Cross*, knows it.

He came to me a number of years ago and asked me to pray for Father Wattsford, when he was lying sick with lumbago, and could not preach the following day unless he was healed.

When I prayed for the dear old father, he was healed and preached the next Sunday.

That lumbago never came back to him.

Facts Support the Word of God.

The Gifts of Healings are a present-day reality.

I know it because the Word of God says that they are permanent.

If I knew nothing about their being exercised I should declare it without any hesitancy because God says it.

I know that I have prayed the Prayer of Faith for hundreds of thousands of people, and they have been healed.

I believe that, even in this meeting, there are a number of people who have been healed.

All who have been healed through faith in Jesus in this meeting, up with your hands. [A number of hands were put up.]

In Shiloh Tabernacle in Zion City, which seats seven thousand two hundred people, if I ask those to stand who have been healed through faith in Jesus, there are from five to six thousand up in a moment.

Their testimony is true.

It is owing to unbelief and degeneracy that the Gifts of Healings are not exercised in the churches.

Any one who is a candid scholar will admit that the early Christians never thought of going to doctors or drugs for healing.

As John Wesley says, the Prayer of Faith was "the whole process of physic in the Christian Church till it was lost through unbelief"

The allegation that it was only in nervous diseases and things of that kind that Gifts of Healings were exercised is not true.

Nervous diseases are very real diseases, nevertheless.

They create very great mischief, and anything that would immediately take away a terrible condition of acute nervous disease would be a great blessing to humanity.

But organic diseases also are healed.

Gifts of Healings Exercised in the Healing of Cancers.

I see in front of me dear old mother Powell, who came to me one day with her daughter, who had cancer in her left eye and a terrible internal cancer.

She asked me to pray for her.

The doctors said that her babe could never be born because of the horrid cancer in the uterus.

When I prayed the Prayer of Faith, she was healed immediately.

She could see perfectly with her left eye, which had been blind as a result of the cancer.

The babe was born in due time, and he lives today, a young man twenty-one years of age.

The mother is well and keeps well.

That healing took place in this city, and it has been a well-attested case.

The doctors had seen the case, diagnosed it, and declared it cancer.

I remember well, dear Mother Powell, [addressing her in the audience,] that when your dear daughter, Mrs. Parker, was healed, she went home (she was a tailoress) took black cloth, closed the good eye and sewed with the sight of the one that had been blind and had had the awful cancer in it.

Mrs. Powell—"She did."

If the Church Exercised the Gifts.

Gifts of Healings are a reality for the Church of God.

If it would exercise those Gifts in the same degree which the man who stands before you has exercised them, there would not be a sick man in the world today.

I have figured that if twenty thousand persons had been healed through my agency, and I could count hundreds of thousands--if only twenty thousand persons had been healed through my agency, and if every Christian minister in the world had had the same experience, there would not be a sick man or woman or child in the world today.

The fact of the matter is that

When Divine Healing and Divine Salvation Go Hand in Hand, There is More Than a Pentecost.

At Pentecost there were three thousand saved, but when the lame man was healed at the Beautiful Gate of the Temple, the record is that there were five thousand men saved.

The sermon preached after the healing of that man at the Beautiful Gate awakened, impressed and aroused thousands of persons who never would have entered the common Salvation, which is always the case when Divine Healing and Divine Salvation is preached side by side.

I remember a case in this city where a woman who was dying was healed when I prayed for her.

She put on her clothes and came from her bedroom into the dining-room where her husband and family were eating.

The husband, a very ungodly and wicked man, fell on his face and worshiped God.

The whole family were brought into the Church through the healing of the mother.

I remember dear Father Wattsford's saying to me one day, "Mr. Dowie, if you would only preach Salvation as you preach the Gospel of Healing, how many would be saved!"

I asked, "How many have you had saved in your church this month?" and he said, "Two."

Then I said, "I have had one hundred eighty-three. I baptized one hundred thirty of them, and I received all of them into the Church."

Family after family were brought into fellowship through one or another of their number being healed.

They were awakened spiritually, repented of their sins, and sought God, in the Christ, for Salvation.

I tell you plainly that there is no healing for an unsaved man or woman.

You must first find Repentance and Salvation through our Lord Jesus, the Christ, and then you can seek for Healing.

What a farce it is to say that the Word of Wisdom remains, that the Word of Knowledge remains, and that the Gifts of Healings have gone, Workings of Miracles, Prophecy, Discernings of Spirits, Tongues and Interpretation of Tongues are all gone!

Who says so?

The Bible says that the Gifts and Calling of God are without repentance.

I am thankful to God for

A Clean-cut, Clear Gospel, and a Clean-cut, Clear Theology.

My theology is a very simple one. It is that no man can get Salvation who does not repent and bring forth fruits meet for Repentance.

You must put things right with God and man.

There is no use in your talking about being penitent while you have money in your pocket that you stole, while you are living with a wife whom you have wronged, while you are doing business in a way that is not right.

No matter what crime or offense you have committed, you must humble yourself and put it right, if it takes you to the prison cell or to the gallows.

It is better to go to prison or to the gallows than it is to die an unrepentant sinner and go to hell.

I will tell you who certainly will go to hell: the man who professes to be a Christian and knows he is not; who knows that he has not repented, does not believe, and is not born of God.

You have to repent of your sins, then believe in our Lord Jesus, the Christ, and know that, by the power of the Holy Spirit, your heart has been regenerated and that you have been born into the Kingdom.

You must know that God is in you.

You ought never to be in the Church unless you are first in the Kingdom.

The churches are full of people of the world.

No one has any right to enter the Church until he has been born into the Kingdom of God.

The Gifts the Adornment of the Church, the Bride of the Christ.

All these Gifts will be found to exist.

The time is fast coming, in the "Restoration of All Things,

whereof God spake by the mouth of His holy prophets which have been since the world began," when we shall see these Gifts developed.

Then the Church will come forth, like a bride adorned for her husband.

With what is she adorned?

She is adorned with the Gifts of the Bridegroom: she is adorned with the Gifts of Love, when she meets her Bridegroom.

God has given to His Church these Gifts, but the Church stands robbed of them today.

She is not ready for the Bridegroom; but God will make her ready. He will bring her out of all the apostasies, and every church is an apostate church which denies the permanence and perpetuity of the Gifts of God, the Gifts of Healings among them.

By a True Repentance, a Full Obedience and a Real Faith, the Church will get the Restoration of these Gifts.

All who desire to repent and trust and believe, stand and tell God so, and give yourselves, spirit, soul, and body, to Him. [A large portion of the congregation rose.]

PRAYER OF CONSECRATION.

My God and Father, in Jesus' Name I come to Thee. Take me as I am and make me what I ought to be, in spirit, soul, and body. Give me power to do right, no matter what it costs. Give me Thy Holy Spirit, that I may trust Thee, serve Thee and obey Thee, be a faithful member of Thy Church, and help Thy people to get back the lost Gifts. For Jesus' sake. Amen. [*All repeat the prayer, clause by clause, after the General Overseer.*]

General Overseer—Do you believe that?

Voices—"Yes."

General Overseer—Then live it.

If you are in a church where they deny these Gifts, get out of it; it is a good church to get out of.

May God bless you!

The Doxology was then sung, and the meeting closed with the

BENEDICTION.

Beloved, abstain from all appearance of evil. And may the very God of Peace Himself sanctify you wholly; and I pray God your whole spirit and soul and body be preserved entire, without blame, unto the coming of our Lord Jesus, the Christ. Faithful is He that calleth you, who also will do it. The grace of our Lord Jesus, the Christ, the love of God, our Father, the fellowship of the Holy Spirit, our Comforter and Guide, one Eternal God, abide in you, bless you and keep you, and all the Israel of God everywhere, forever. Amen.

The meetings of Thursday and Friday, morning and afternoon, were marked by an increased attendance, and an ever-growing spiritual power and blessing.

The General Overseer, since his arrival, had been studying Australia in all its aspects—political, economic, social, financial and religious.

With the results of this study, he combined his knowledge of the country, gained during his many years of former residence in it.

He came preaching the Gospel of the Kingdom of God, that Kingdom which deals with all departments of human life and interest.

Hence his Messages were Messages that dealt with conditions as he found them in the City of Melbourne in the Year of our Lord 1904.

It was for this reason that they fitted, with such amazing accuracy, into the lives of those who heard, and were so effective.

On Friday, March 4, 1904, at a private conference, the General Overseer restored to the offices of Elder and Evangelist, Deacon and Deaconess J. Thomas Wilhide.

As the week wore on, the question as to whether it would be wise to hold meetings in Melbourne on the Lord's Day was very carefully and prayerfully considered.

There was extreme reluctance on the part of God's Messenger to abandon meetings which he had announced, especially when there was such great need of a Voice to proclaim the truth in this wicked city.

On the other hand, there were many convincing indications that preparations were being made for extreme measures on the part of the lawless mob—acts of violence to be committed on the Lord's Day.

The General Overseer was compelled to consider the question as to whether it would be right to risk, not only his own life, but the lives of his wife and son, and members of his party, and the lives of many innocent men, women and children who would doubtless attend the service should it be held.

Supposing this to be the extreme danger of the situation, he had still to consider the fact that a well-organized and determined mob of several thousand could not fail, at the very least, to injure many people and destroy property.

When he considered, also, that all this risk would have to be taken with the probability that the rabble would make it impossible for even those who so desired to hear, he decided that it would be better not to attempt to hold any meetings on the Lord's Day.

As the last train for Adelaide, until the next Monday evening, left Melbourne at twenty minutes before five o'clock on Friday afternoon, and as there were no meetings announced for Saturday, the General Overseer, Overseer Jane Dowie, Dr. A. J. Gladstone Dowie, and the other members of the Around-the-World Visitation party, together with several of the officers and members of the Christian Catholic Church in Zion, drove directly from Central Zion Tabernacle to the Spencer Street Station on Friday afternoon, and took the Adelaide Express for Mount Lofty.

Arriving there on Saturday morning at about nine o'clock, the General Overseer and all his party spent the few days intervening, before the beginning of the final Visitation in Australasia at Adelaide, South Australia, on Lord's Day, March 20th, in rest and recreation, the preparing of reports, study, and preparation for future work.

The following are the reports of the meetings held in Central Zion Tabernacle, Melbourne, on Thursday and Friday, March 3d and 4th, 1904:

Central Zion Tabernacle, Melbourne, Australia, Thursday Morning, March 3, 1904

After singing, announcements, and prayer by Rev. C. Friend Hawkins, the General Overseer said:

THE BEAUTIFUL GATE OF DIVINE HEALING.

*REPORTED BY E. W. AND A. W. N.

I shall address you for a few minutes this morning on the story of the man who was healed at the Beautiful Gate of the Temple.

Important Events Witnessed by the Man at the Beautiful Gate.

He was about forty years old, and was, therefore, about seven years old when the Christ was born.

He must have heard the Wise Men, or heard of their sending their servants, doubtless, before them through the streets of Jerusalem, saying: "Where is He that is born King of the Jews? for we saw His Star in the East, and are come to worship Him."

"Where is He?"

That prayer was a very impressive one.

But the Christ disappeared, and the time of His birth was marked by a most horrible crime—the massacre of the innocents at Bethlehem.

This lame man must have remembered how, when he was a little boy, the mothers had wept and wailed, and how all Jerusalem was filled with horror and indignation that Herod should have murdered large numbers of young children, in the hope that he could murder the Christ.

I do not read that any priest of that time ever reproved Herod.

I do not read that he was ever shut out of the Temple.

The priests went on coöperating with that king who was a murderer.

What a terrible story that was for that child to hear!

When he was nineteen years of age, he lay daily at the Gate which was called Beautiful, a beggar, lame from his mother's womb.

He must have seen, or heard of, the little Boy, who had asked the doctors such questions that they could not answer, who had spoken to them words at which they wondered.

When John the Baptist came to preach, this man was seven years older than he.

He heard the wonderful stories of how the priests went out to see John the Baptist.

He knew that the minds of the people were stirred as to whether John was the Christ, or whether he was the Elijah.

*The following report has not been revised by the General Overseer.

REV AND MRS. J. THOMAS WILHIDE.

When John himself said, "I am not," it was a great dash to the hopes of multitudes, for he was Elijah, and he did not know it.

Jesus said, "This is Elijah," when He spoke of John the Baptist.

The Angel Gabriel said that he who was to come was to come in the spirit and the power of Elijah.

It is a very great mystery why John himself did not know it.

It seems to me a wonderful thing, but not more wonderful than many other things that have happened.

Ignorance of One's True Personality.

Many persons in their ignorance, have denied that they were this or that, not knowing any better.

Not many years ago, I knew personally of the following incident.

A certain young man was told that he was Earl of So-and-so.

He said, "You go away. Do not talk such nonsense to me."

The solicitor said to him, "You are the Earl So-and-so, and I am here to put you in possession of your estate."

"If you do not go away, I will knock you down," said the young man. And he looked as if he would do it.

The solicitor went away and brought with him a friend of his, saying once more, "You are the Earl of So-and-so, and I have come to put you in possession of your estate."

He said to his friend, "Take away that lunatic."

The friend said: "He is no lunatic. You are the Earl of So-and-so. Come to my house and examine the papers.

The young man came; they showed him proof of his paternity, and who he was.

It was with difficulty that he could believe them, and considerable time was spent before he could be convinced that it was not a conspiracy to make a fool of him.

At last, however, he believed what he did not know in any other way than by documents that were put before him, that his mother was the wife of a dead earl, and that he was the legitimate son.

He took possession of the estate, and sits today in the House of Lords.

John the Baptist did not know, but he did the work of Elijah up to his light and knowledge. He was Elijah the Preparer.

Elijah the Tishbite was Elijah the Destroyer.

This man at the gate heard how Herod's paramour had succeeded in getting John the Baptist murdered!

The Priests Afraid of John the Baptist.

The priests were, doubtless, very well pleased, that John was dead, because he had been preaching Repentance, and they were wicked.

They were afraid of him even after he was dead; because when Jesus, the Christ, said to them, "The Baptism of John, was it from heaven, or from men?" they reasoned, "If we shall say, From heaven; He will say, Why then did ye not believe Him? But should we say, From men—they feared the people: for all verily held John to be a prophet." So these cowardly priests, who in his day denounced John, were afraid of him when he was dead, afraid of the people, and afraid of the Christ.

They said: "We know not."

They lied!

They are not the only priests or ministers who have lied.

Time went on, and Jesus appeared.

This lame man, at the Beautiful Gate of the Temple, at last saw the Christ, whom John the Baptist had proclaimed.

He knew of His preaching, and knew of His healing; but he was not healed.

Why the Lame Man Was Not Healed by the Christ.

The Christ went in and out of that Beautiful Gate of the Temple, occasionally, for three years.

The blind were made to see, the lame walked, and the dead were raised, and this man knew it, but still he lay at the Beautiful Gate of the Temple unhealed.

Why?

One does not need to go far to see.

"Rabbi Eliezer," he would say, "tell me, is Jesus of Nazareth the Christ?"

"Jesus of Nazareth! The bastard! I hate Him!" said a rabbi in Sydney one day.

"He is no Christ," the rabbi would say to this lame man.

"But, rabbi," he would plead, "is it not written that a virgin shall conceive and bring forth a Son?"

Then they would say, in their Pharisaical pride, "Dost thou teach us?" and threaten to excommunicate him.

That was the way they tried to put down the Christ.

When a man received sight, and found Jesus in the Temple, he worshiped Him, but the Pharisees said, "Give God the glory; and as for this fellow, He is a sinner."

REV. WILBUR GLEN[...]
OVERSEER FOR AUS[...]

They lied!

They had tried to make out at first, that he had not been blind. But his parents had said, "This is our son, and he was born blind."

"How then is it that he now sees?" they ask.

"Ask him," said his parents, "he is of age."

He answered for himself.

When they said that Jesus was a sinner, he said:

We know that God heareth not sinners; but if any man be a worshiper of God, and do His will, him He heareth. Since the world began it was never heard that any one opened the eyes of a man born blind. If this Man were not from God, He could do nothing.

At that time he had not acknowledged Him as the Christ.

It was only afterwards that he did, but he was a brave, good man, and he would not deny the Christ.

Without any great stretch of the imagination, we may suppose that this man lay there at the Beautiful Gate of the Temple and asked the rabbis as to whether Jesus was the Christ, and they said, "No."

He knew, therefore, that if he acknowledged Jesus as the Christ, he would be flung out.

They had passed a decree that any one who acknowledged Jesus as the Christ would be excommunicated. It was after he was excommunicated that the blind man who had been healed met the Christ the second time.

When a man is a poor beggar, over forty years of age, and has never been anything but a beggar, he is likely to believe what the rabbis say, what the ministers say, so he said, "I repudiate the Christ."

He must have done so, because if he had cried to the Christ he would have been saved and healed.

The Conversion of the Lame Man.

The Christ was then crucified and buried, and it was reported that He had risen again.

This man was in great trouble about the matter.

He heard Peter preaching at Pentecost, and I think that was the time he was converted.

Multitudes were converted, and possibly this man, who may have cried, "Crucify Him," with the rest of the rabble, was among them.

At any rate, when Peter and John came up to the Temple at the hour of prayer, three o'clock in the afternoon, this man asked them for an alms.

My distinct conviction is that he knew who Peter and John were.

They were well-known men.

They had been going in and out with Jesus.

Peter had just preached that great Pentecostal Sermon.

Salvation Alone not Much Trouble to the Devil.

Up to that time, there is no record that there had been any preaching or practice of Divine Healing by the apostles.

Salvation only had been preached and realized.

The people were all rejoiced that three thousand had been baptized in one day, and they welcomed these apostles, everywhere. The Pharisees did not care much about that. Salvation does not bother the Devil.

If you get into a boat with one oar, and try to row you will go around in a circle.

The Church, likewise, does not make any very great progress, even where there is True Salvation by itself.

It reminds me of a one-legged, drunken man who got his wooden leg into a hole, and walked around it all night.

I do not know whether that story is true, or not, but I can see the churches walking around their wooden leg, Salvation.

Get Salvation for the spirit.

But is that all?

Have we not souls and bodies as well as spirits?

Is not the spirit in bondage, if the body is tied up with rheumatism?

When you put in both oars, the oar of Salvation and the oar of Healing, and pull, then you do not go around, you go ahead.

That day, at the Beautiful Gate, the oar of Divine Healing was put in.

That man was healed.

You know how simply the story is told.

The Apostles said that they had no money.

Money Spent in the Extension of the Kingdom of God.

You say, "That is not like you, Dr. Dowie."

I have oftentimes been without money.

A hundred times I have given, in Melbourne, my last shilling for the extension of the Gospel.

I have sold pictures, and books, and furniture to extend the Gospel.

Out of a million dollars, that is, more than two hundred thousand pounds, that I received in a given time, I spent nine hundred fifty thousand dollars—one hundred ninety thousand pounds—for the extension of the Gospel.

I did not spend fifty thousand dollars during those seven or eight years, on my family.

I did not spend five per cent.

"But," you say, "now you fatten on the tithes and offerings of the people."

I have not taken a penny from the tithes and offerings fund for several years, and give larger amounts to that fund than any other person in Zion.

I came to see that

Poverty Does not Glorify God.

I had always thought I could glorify God by being poor.

But I had not read rightly.

The Word of God says of the Christ, "Though He was rich, yet for your sakes He became poor, that ye through His poverty might become rich."

I came to the conclusion that my poor people ought to be saved, and healed, and blessed and shown how to make money. I set myself to it.

REV. CLEMENT FRIEND HAWKINS.

I coöperated with them; we have made money, and we are using it for God.

We used three hundred thousand dollars in one month, on the New York Visitation; that is over sixty thousand pounds.

We gave that out of our own pocket, and we are just as well-to-do now as ever, and a little more.

We give our tithes and offerings, and send the Gospel to all the world.

A Tribute to Overseer Voliva.

I sent Overseer Voliva here, paid all his expenses, and—I say it publicly—he has never cost me a dollar since

He is a man who knows how to do things.

He has not cost Headquarters a dollar since he came, and has been a blessing.

I have received about two hundred people from Australia, and I think I am likely to receive from four hundred to a thousand this year.

This racket that the priests and others are kicking up will send a great many people to Zion City. [Applause.] That is the only good thing there is in it.

Not one voice has been raised by a minister to demand that I shall have fair play.

The people will see that the ministers are on the side of the mob.

If this kind of thing goes on, they will see that Melbourne is a good kind of city to live outside of, and that Zion City is a pretty good place in which to live.

There we have never had disorder.

A Rich Man Without a Penny in His Pockets.

When the apostles said that they had no silver or gold, they did not mean that they were poor.

Baron Rothschild once got into an omnibus going along the Strand, in London.

The story is told that he fumbled everywhere for the coppers, but could not find them—had not a single copper with him.

He turned to the conductor and said, "I say, my good fellow, just excuse me, I have no money with me I will take your number, and see that you get the fare"

"You can't work me like that, you old Jew," said the conductor. "You will have to get out."

Just then one of the other passengers recognized the great banker and paid his fare.

It was not that the baron had not plenty of money. He simply was not carrying any with him. You might find me often in Zion City, without a penny in my pockets, because I do not need money there.

Not long ago, in fact, I took the train in to the city of Chicago.

I had only had a minute or two in which to get ready, and my carriage was driven at a great speed to the station.

When I was safely on board, I felt in my pocket to find if I had anything with which to pay expenses in the city.

I had not a cent.

I turned to my personal attendant, and asked him whether he had any.

"No," he said, "I have none."

"What shall we do? We are getting into town?"

"Oh, we can get money, General Overseer, many people around here would be glad to lend you money."

I found it so, for the conductor of the train readily let me have fifty dollars.

Because, therefore, the apostles had no money in their pockets it does not follow that they were poor.

REV. J. STEPHEN McCULLAGH, WIFE AND DAUGHTER.

Wealth of the Apostolic Treasury.

At that time the people were laying vast sums of money at the apostles' feet.

I have calculated what was put at their feet at about fifty million dollars

Whether they were poor or not, they had no money at that particular time, and for a minute they did not know what to say.

Perhaps they tried to find some money for the poor man; for Jesus had said that it was more blessed to give than to receive.

He was always giving to the poor, and they were accustomed to give in all these cities.

Zion is Giving to the Poor.

Mrs. Dowie works all day sometimes, and half the night in her department.

She has her secretary and stenographer at work too.

She is in charge of the Women's Work of the Christian Catholic Church in Zion Throughout the World. We have a Home of Hope for Erring Women, where we have as a rule from twenty to thirty erring women and their babies, numbering from fifteen to twenty.

Mrs. Dowie sees to this Home for me. I have never entered it.

The women have been blessed, saved, healed, baptized, and a very large proportion of the women who have entered that Home are in the Church today.

Mrs Dowie has something like six hundred fifty Dorcas women making garments for the poor under her direction.

She and the Dorcas women clothed about a thousand poor families, last year, in Chicago; many of them not connected with Zion at all.

We are always giving, and we love to give.

We have a corps of Maternity Deaconesses who have outfits for the mother and babe.

When we find women who have been abandoned by their husbands, we send Deaconesses who take care of them, bring the little one into the world, and clothe the babe and the mother until she is able to get about and help herself.

Mrs. Dowie receives vast quantities of goods.

Merchants in all parts of the country send her shop-worn goods, but warm and good articles. Last winter she received a whole case of boots and shoes for the little boys. That much for the poor outside of Zion.

Inside of Zion, everything has been looked after—clothing, food, and fuel—ever since the Church was organized. [Applause.]

A Methodist Minister's Shameful Lie Nailed.

Any statement to the contrary, such as that published by Mr. Fitchett in his *Southern Cross*, is an abominable and shameful lie.

A week or so ago he published one taken from an American newspaper in New York.

What do they know about Zion City, over a thousand miles away?

If the writer had been there, he was a liar, because he said that I had sixty thousand acres of land, and I have only six thousand seven hundred.

He said that the cemetery was away on the outskirts of that great tract of land, when the cemetery is only two miles and a half from the center of the City.

Instead of being in an obscure place, Mount Olivet is one of the highest points in the City of Zion.

We put it there purposely.

We intend to make it a very beautiful spot.

He says that we put it away back there for fear the people might know how many deaths there were.

That is all a lie, every word of it, and told by a Methodist minister, too!

A Good Thing to Put in Both Oars.

This poor man at the Beautiful Gate of the Temple received the healing instantly, and then how many people were saved?

A voice—"Five thousand."

General Overseer—Two thousand more than at Pentecost!

The Word says that Peter preached, and that the number of men that believed were five thousand.

I believe that there were at least as many women, because there are usually about twice as many women saved as men.

You see what a good thing it is to put in both oars.

Now, you Methodists, go and repent of all your naughtiness, and get the confidence to go in for Divine Healing.

All who desire to give themselves wholly to God stand. [Nearly all rose.]

PRAYER OF CONSECRATION.

My God and Father, in Jesus' Name I come to Thee. Take me as I am. Make me what I ought to be in spirit, in soul, and in body. Give me power to do right, no matter what it costs. Give me Thy Holy Spirit. Enable me to trust Thee, and serve Thee. Take away my sin. Give me grace to rest in Thee as that poor man did who had never walked; that in the Name of Jesus, in the power of the Spirit, and in accordance with the will of God my Father, I may get the blessing and glorify Thee. For Jesus' sake. Amen. [*All repeat the prayer, clause by clause, after the General Overseer.*]

The meeting was then closed by the General Overseer's pronouncing the

BENEDICTION.

Beloved, abstain from all appearance of evil. And may the very God of Peace Himself sanctify you wholly; and I pray God your whole spirit and soul and body be preserved entire, without blame, unto the coming of our Lord Jesus, the Christ. Faithful is He that calleth you, who also will do it. The grace of our Lord Jesus, the Christ, the love of God, our Father, the fellowship of the Holy Spirit, our Comforter and Guide, one Eternal God, abide in you, bless you and keep you, and all the Israel of God everywhere, forever. Amen.

Central Zion Tabernacle, Melbourne, Victoria, Australia, Thursday Afternoon, March 3, 1904.

The Service was opened with Hymn No. 9, Visitation Program, "The Morning Light is Breaking."

Rev. Clement Friend Hawkins read the 3d chapter of the Acts of the Apostles, beginning at the 11th verse.

The General Overseer said:

It has been a great pleasure to me to receive so very many of our friends, during the last few days, from different parts of the country.

The gentleman who has just read to you, the Rev. C. Friend Hawkins, is the pastor of the Branch of the Christian Catholic Church in Zion in Adelaide.

The Rev. J. Stephen McCullagh, who sits on my right, is the pastor of the Branch of the Christian Catholic Church in Zion in Sydney, and the Rev. J. Thomas Wilhide is the pastor of the Branch of the Christian Catholic Church in Zion in Auckland, New Zealand.

I am glad that so many have gathered from different parts, and only regret that we are unable to see a tithe of those who would like to be at these meetings.

Prayer was offered by the Rev. J. Thomas Wilhide.

The General Overseer then continued his discourse as follows:

THE TIMES OF THE RESTORATION OF ALL THINGS.

*REPORTED BY I. M. S. AND A. W. N.

INVOCATION.

Let the words of my mouth, and the meditation of my heart be acceptable in Thy sight, be profitable unto this people, and unto all to whom these words shall come, in this and every land, in this and all the coming time. Till Jesus Come. Amen.

I desire to call your attention this afternoon to a portion of the Scripture which Deacon Hawkins read to you, from the 3d chapter of the Acts of the Apostles.

I spoke to you this morning about the first part of that chapter, the healing of the lame man at the Beautiful Gate of the Temple.

*The following address has not been revised by the General Overseer.

I called your attention to the fact that the healing of that man and the discourse which followed were far more effective than the sermon that Peter preached at Pentecost.

The number saved on the Day of Pentecost were three thousand, while, on this occasion, it is written, "Many of them that heard the Word believed; and the number of the men came to be about five thousand."

A Review of Peter's Sermon at the Beautiful Gate.

I call your attention to that sermon which produced such great results.

It is very simple, of course.

Peter took occasion to call their attention to recent facts.

He told them that the man who had never before walked, who was about forty years old, had been healed by the Power of God, working through the Name of One whom they had rejected and crucified.

Speaking to them of their offenses, he called them murderers, which they were.

He said, "Ye denied the Holy and Righteous One, and asked for a murderer to be granted unto you."

When Pilate had said, "What then shall I do with Him whom ye call the King of the Jews?" they had cried "Crucify Him."

When he said, "I am innocent of the blood of this righteous Man," and washed his hands—he could not wash his heart—of the guilt, they cried, "His blood be on us, and on our children."

Peter reminded them of all these things.

He declared that God had glorified His Son Jesus, and that he and the other apostles were witnesses to the Resurrection; that they had seen Him and spoken with Him, and that He had ascended into heaven in their presence.

He went on to declare that there was Salvation in no other, and then he laid before them the great and beautiful Truths concerning final Restoration.

He spoke of Jesus as He "whom the heaven must receive until the Times of Restoration of All Things, whereof God spake by the mouth of His Holy prophets which have been since the world began."

The Times of the Restoration of All Things.

The Restoration of All Things has to be effected, in accordance with the Revelation of God, through the ministration of one whom the Christ Himself said would precede His Second Coming.

"Why then say the scribes that Elijah must first come?"

This was the question that the Apostles asked of Jesus when He came down from the Mount of Transfiguration, upon which He with James and Peter and John had met with Moses and Elijah.

They had seen Moses and Elijah speak with Jesus, and they knew who they were, for Peter had said, "It is good for us to be here: if Thou wilt, I will make here three tabernacles; one for Thee, and one for Moses, and one for Elijah."

Peter had not known what he was talking about. He had said it in his trepidation and confusion of mind.

If he had thought, he would not have said it, because to build tabernacles there for these three on the top of a mountain and make them a peep-show, would not have accomplished anything.

Coming down from the mountain, in their perplexity they put to the Master that question, "Why then say the scribes that Elijah must first come?"

The Scribes Were Right.

They were not always wrong; in fact, the scribes were good authorities upon these questions.

Their knowledge of the letter of the Word was excellent.

There were some of them who could have written the entire Scripture from memory, scarcely omitting a word or a tittle.

They were exceedingly able and intellectual.

There was almost nothing that could be added to their grasp of the letter of the Sacred Writings. They were right when they said that before the Christ should come, Elijah must first come.

The Christ said to them that Elijah had come.

He had declared, while John the Baptist was yet living, that he was Elijah.

John the Baptist had sent messengers to Him from the dungeon of Machærus, where he lay in a prison cell, on the eve-of his murder at the cruel hands of Herod, at the instance of the voluptuous and adulterous Herodias.

These messengers asked the question, "Art Thou He that should come, or look we for another?"

It scarcely seemed consistent to John that the Christ should have the power to raise the dead, and still the tempest, and heal the sick, and do the mighty works that He did, and yet that He did nothing to release him from prison.

John was perplexed.

It was probably on account of this perplexity that he sent these messengers with that question.

After the Christ had given His answer, He told the people that John the Baptist was Elijah.

John the Baptist was Elijah the Preparer, and he had done his work.

When a man's work is done, it does not matter how soon he goes to heaven.

If I knew that my work on earth were done now, I would be very glad to go to heaven, because that is the best land in which to dwell.

There are so many there that I love; but it will not be long until all who sleep in Jesus will return with Him.

Then the Day of the Lord Will Come—the Thousand Years.

Then, in glorified bodies, we shall come back, and we shall carry on the Restoration until it is finished.

What a wonderful thing it will be when the Lord comes back to this earth with those who have glorified bodies, like unto His body!

There will be a marked difference between those who have and those who have not the glorified body, as there is a marked difference now between a clean man and one who is not clean.

There is a great difference between those who keep their temples for God and have neither whisky, nor tobacco, nor pig, nor any filthy rubbish within them; who live clean lives and have clean thoughts and do clean things and fight the unclean and those who do not.

The man or woman who keeps clean carries on his or her face the light that never shone on sea or land. I thank God that there are many of those.

The man whose god is his belly, whose glory is in his shame, who minds earthly things, is an enemy of the Cross of the Christ.

Such men show it in their faces. Right between their eyes, God has put the brand, "Thou hypocrite!"

Worse than the lowest scum and the vilest rabble is the rabbi whom the Christ brands in the synagogue with the words, "Thou Hypocrite!"

The Millennium Not a Peaceful Reign.

Wonderful will it be, in the Restoration, to come back with Jesus to live and reign a Thousand Years, and carry out His purposes amid the conflict and the strife; for it will go on through the Thousand Years, through the Millennium.

He must reign until He hath put all enemies under His feet.

The fiercest fight will be at the end of the Thousand Years, when, as the Scripture declares, the enemies of God and of His Christ will gather together in almost countless numbers, and the fire of God will sweep them away.

Then will come the New Heavens and the New Earth, wherein dwelleth Righteousness.

Then all the kingdoms of this earth will have become the Kingdom of our God and of His Christ.

Just in passing, let me remind you that the Millennium is not a peaceful reign.

The Christ will go forth, conquering and to conquer. He will carry on His work for a Thousand Years, through the Holy Spirit.

Then the End will come, and the Kingdom will be permanently established.

The Restoration, therefore, goes on through the whole of the Day of the Lord—the Thousand Years.

Peter, in talking about these words, wants us to understand that the heavens must receive the Christ until that time, and that the Elijah must come again, because Jesus said, "Elijah indeed cometh and shall Restore All Things," after John the Baptist was dead.

The Overlapping of the Dispensations.

All students of the Word and of the Dispensations must know the remarkable fact that Dispensations overlap one another.

The beginning of a thing that is to be perfected and consummated in the Dispensation to come, is made clear in the Dispensation that is closing.

In connection with the matter to which I am now referring—"the Times of Restoration of All Things, whereof God spake by the mouth of His holy prophets which have been since the world began"—there is to be one, no matter who he is, who is to be the Elijah of that Dispensation.

When you say that there is no Elijah to come, you show your ignorance, because all Bible commentators are against you.

All the Early Fathers declare that before the Christ can come, the Elijah of the Restoration must come.

The first question is not as to whether I am he.

The most important question with Christians is, Must Elijah first come? And that was the question with these disciples.

Elijah the Tishbite had gone.

Elijah the Preparer, had come and gone, and after his death the Christ had said, "Elijah indeed cometh and shall Restore All Things."

Teaching Regarding Elijah the Restorer Not New.

I marvel that men who ought to be scholars, by their rank as ministers, talk about the Elijah matter as if it were something new.

It is the oldest thing in Christian theology.

You who are Episcopalians will remember that beautiful little volume of Christian verse, "The Christian Year."

On St. John the Baptist's Day, John Keble wrote:

> Twice in her season of decay
> The fallen Church hath felt Elijah's eye
> Dart from the wild its piercing ray;
> Not keener burns, in the chill morning sky,
> The herald star,
> Whose torch afar
> Shadows, and boding night-birds fly.
>
> Methinks we need him once again,
> That favored seer—but where shall he be found?
> By Cherith's side we seek in vain,
> In vain on Carmel's green and lonely mound:
> Angels no more
> From Sinai soar,
> On his celestial errands bound.

There were many years of my life in which I never failed to read one of John Keble's poems, every morning and every night.

I read them still.

That wonderful man of God has never been equaled in the Church of England. He still remains the great poet of the Church.

He goes on to say:

> And since we see, and not afar,
> The twilight of the great and dreadful day,
> Why linger till Elijah's car
> Stoop from the clouds? Why sleep ye? rise and pray,
> Ye heralds sealed
> In camp or field
> Your Savior's banner to display!

He sees that the Church is slumbering, and that it must get right before it can hear the Voice of Elijah calling them to awake and go and prepare the way of the King.

I think that his poems were written in the early decades of the last century.

Testimony of the Pulpit Commentary Regarding Elijah the Restorer.

Almost the latest commentary of the Church of England is the "Pulpit Commentary," written by canons and bishops of that church.

I ask you who are scholarly and doubtful to take the "Pulpit Commentary" and read Matthew 17th chapter, in connection with the coming of the Restorer.

You will find that the commentaries quoted—the "Pulpit Commentary" is a compilation of all the commentaries—declare that before the Lord comes again Elijah must first come, and that he is the prophet of the Restoration.

The theological question must be settled apart from my personality altogether.

Although I have the confidence that I am Elijah the Restorer, I do not believe that God would be very angry with me for endeavoring to do the work of the Restoration, if I were not.

No one need covet the work of Elijah the Restorer.

No man coveted the work of Elijah the Destroyer, or the work of Elijah the Preparer.

Some seem to think that when Elijah comes again he will not come as a man.

What nonsense!

Did not Elijah come as a baby when he was born of Zacharias and Elizabeth?

The Word says that even John the Baptist did no miracle.

Tens of thousands and hundreds of thousands have said that through my ministry aud through these hands, Miracles of Healings have been wrought and are being wrought.

There is no question about that. Any one who questions it questions facts that are indisputable.

A Methodist Minister Healed Through John Alexander Dowie's Prayers.

I would refer the Methodist ministers present (and I see there are a number of them here this afternoon) to the case of dear old Father Wattsford, and to Mr. Fitchett.

Mr. Fitchett once came to me in Fitzroy, and said, "Mr. Dowie, dear old Father Wattsford is in agony, and wants you to come and pray for him.

"He has lumbago and unless he is healed he cannot preach tomorrow."

I loved the dear old father, and I love him still.

He is a mighty man of God, and any one who knows his career will say that is true.

The man who walked ashore on that savage island and was welcomed as a god by the heathen of Fiji on that memorable day; the man who has lived, and loved and served God, is a good man, no matter what he may say about me now.

When Mr. Fitchett told me, over eighteen years ago, that the dear father was ill, I said, "All right, I will come to him immediately.

"Does he believe that God has given to me the Gifts of Healings?"

"He does," said Mr. Fitchett.

I questioned Mr. Fitchett as we went along, and came to the conclusion that he was not quite right with God, so, when we got there, I told him to stay outside, that I would see the father alone.

There he lay, the dear old man, agonizing in his lumbago.

I talked to him, and he listened earnestly.

I was just as plain with him as I am with every one else.

He had to preach the next day, and he could not do it unless he was healed.

I prayed with him, and he raised up and walked.

To this day, I have been told, that lumbago has never returned.

As he walked about, I could not help noticing what a magnificent personality he was.

He said, "I am well."

He knows that God used my hands.

What is the use in your talking?

God has witnessed to my ministry, and He witnesses still.

The Declaration of June 2, 1901.

For a great many years, I would become very angry when any one said that I was Elijah.

When I made the Declaration, on June 2, 1901, I had not consulted my wife, my family, or my colleagues, and I have a splendid set of men with me in the ministry.

They are scholars and gentlemen.

When I made my Declaration about the Elijah matter, about seven thousand people gathered together to hear me.

I did not know how it would be taken. I did not care.

I did it simply because I had to do it.

If I had opened Zion City without that Declaration, and had made it afterwards, many might have said to me, "If I had known that, I would not have come here."

Within one month of that time, however, we opened the Gates of Zion City, on July 15, 1901, and all the land we placed on the market was immediately taken up.

But when I had finished that Declaration, I asked all who believed it to stand, and that vast congregation rose as one man. There were not more than fifty that did not rise.

Many had said that they believed me to be the Restorer long before I thought of making the Declaration, and hailed it with great delight.

You make it a very difficult matter here. There is no difficulty there at all.

Belief of the Jews Concerning Elijah.

Not only do Christians believe in the Declaration, but Jews also.

You ask any Jew if Elijah must come before the Christ comes to reign as King, and he will say "Certainly."

Every Jew will tell you that a chair is placed for Elijah at every circumcision, and that the Mohel and all the officers appointed in connection with the circumcision will pray that Elijah may be present in spirit and take that chair.

He is supposed to be present there.

Elijah is looked for in person at every Paschal Feast.

A cup of unfermented wine, a plate of unleavened bread and an empty chair are set at the head of the table in every house at the Paschal Feast.

The father, if the priest is not there, will pray that he may take that place.

He says, "O Eli-ya-hu come!"

When he does not come, they often say with tears, "O God, for our sins his coming is delayed, and so the Messiah cannot come until he appears!"

Hard Problems Solved by Elijah the Restorer.

They will tell you that the mission of Elijah is a hard one and that he will have all the hard things to do and all the hard problems to solve.

I have had to face that.

You may ask, "Have you found a solution?"

Yes, I have.

We have solved the labor question, and I have over three thousand employees in Zion City, all my brethren in the Lord, and we have never had one strike.

We have solved the educational difficulty, and we have two thousand children to educate.

From the very beginning they get the Bible, and yet we give them a first-class education in science, and in all other useful knowledge.

We have a manual training school also.

We have solved the question of Christian coöperation without reducing it to the ridiculous nonsense of communism.

Every person in Zion City controls his own property, and his own money.

They have their accounts in Zion City Bank, and can draw upon them whenever they please.

All their stocks are safely guarded by law, and no person gives any money at all unless he chooses to make a free-will offering, and to pay his tithes.

If I were to say to my people, "Meet me, Zion Restoration Host, three thousand strong, in New York when I return from the Around-the-World Visitation next June," they would be there.

If I were to say to them, "Get ready, we will take ship across to England on such and such a date," they would be there if they had to sell their coats to do it, but they would not need to do that.

There are very few who do not have money available.

We Have no Committees in Zion.

A committee, in ninety-nine cases out of every one hundred, is a splendid illustration of how not to do it.

When I want a man to do a thing I appoint him.

I appoint every officer in Zion, and I have not yet had the first dispute on the question.

Zion Has Solved the Political Problem.

We are political to the finger-tips.

Our policy is Theocratic.

We believe in the Rule of God, in the Heart, in the Home, in the School, in the Church, in the Business, in the State, and in the Nation.

The Theocratic principle is injected into American politics to such an extent that if I want an interview with the President of the United States of America, he is exceedingly kind and considerate, and grants it.

Zion is a mighty political force.

There were years in Chicago when the votes that we controlled were the balance of power between the Democratic and the Republican parties.

The balance of power in Lake County, Illinois, where Zion City is located, is ours.

When we say that a man shall go in, belonging to either one of these two parties, he gets in.

We educate our children, and we train our people for God.

We are an industrious people.

No woman has ever been insulted in our streets.

No harlot has ever been suffered to live in Zion City. She would be sent out at once, either to Milwaukee or Chicago.

There is no place for the adulterer or the adulteress there.

The Leases and Their Covenants.

The land is leased and we never sell a foot of it.

If it is not rightly used, it reverts to us at once.

We buy back the leases of those who violate the Covenant, at the price for which they could sell it to any one else, and no person has ever lost any money in that way.

No one ever went away with less than he had when he came.

Any one that says the opposite, tells a lie.

I offered publicly, some time ago, to buy back all the land at the price the people gave for it, and to pay them for their houses at the price they built them for, and to pay them for their furniture what it cost them.

I said that if they would let me have it, I would make millions out of it.

There was not one willing to sell.

The land has increased in value, in many parts of the City, all the way from eighty-five to three hundred per cent.

There are people in Zion City who own thousands of dollars' worth of property, and there are people who own only their lots, who never owned anything in their lives before.

The Christian Catholic Church in Zion is a Reality.

Discipline is exercised.

There is not one person in the Christian Catholic Church in Zion who is living in even a doubtful condition, that we know of.

No person can be a member of the Church who drinks the intoxicating cup, or who smokes Satan's Consuming Fire, tobacco.

It is thus we solve the problems of life.

The results show the soundness of the solution.

The question is, therefore, first of all, whether the Restorer has to come, as the Scriptures say.

Then you must decide who is Elijah.

If I am not he, where is he to be found?

All who desire to know God's Will in this matter, stand.

PRAYER OF CONSECRATION.

My God and Father, in Jesus Name I come to Thee. Take me as I am. Make me what I ought to be, in spirit, soul, and body. Give me grace to understand Thy Will, and help me that whe In know it I may do it. For Jesus' sake. Amen. [*All repeat the prayer, clause by clause, after the General Overseer.*]

The meeting was closed with the

BENEDICTION.

Beloved, abstain from all appearance of evil. And may the very God of Peace Himself sanctify you wholly; and I pray God your whole spirit and soul and body be preserved entire, without blame, unto the coming of our Lord Jesus, the Christ. Faithful is He that calleth you, who also will do it. The grace of our Lord Jesus, the Christ, the love of God, our Father, the fellowship of the Holy Spirit, our Comforter and Guide, one Eternal God, abide in you, bless you and keep you, and all the Israel of God everywhere, forever Amen.

Central Zion Tabernacle, Melbourne, Australia, Friday Morning, March 4, 1904.

After the singing of Hymn No. 11, of the Visitation Program, "Hail to the Brightness of Zion's Glad Morning," Rev. C. Friend Hawkins offered prayer.

Overseer Jane Dowie then read the first seventeen verses of the 8th chapter of the Gospel according to St. Matthew.

The General Overseer then said:

DIVINE HEALING IN THE ATONEMENT.

*REPORTED BY E. W. AND A. W. N.

INVOCATION.

Let the words of my mouth, and the meditation of my heart, be acceptable in Thy sight, and profitable unto this people, and to all to whom these words shall come. For the sake of Jesus. Amen.

*The following report has not been revised by the General Overseer.

The last words that were read to you were these:

TEXT.

When even was come, they brought unto Him many possessed with devils: and He cast out the spirits with a word, and healed all that were sick: that it might be fulfilled which was spoken by Isaiah, the prophet, saying, Himself took our infirmities and bare our diseases.

I emphasize the correction in the Revision, namely; that it is not *His* word but *a* word.

You may ask, What is the difference?

The Difference Between His Word and A Word Is Very Profound.

It opens up a very great, and a very delightful fact, namely: that our Lord Jesus, the Christ, Himself never healed any one.

That is a very important matter; as a man He never healed any one.

We have this upon His own authority; for He said, "Of Mine Ownself I can do nothing."

That word nothing is very emphatic in Greek.

It is composed of three little Greek particles: *ou de hen* (οὐ δὲ ἕν), and means, not even one little thing.

Then who was it that did the mighty works?

He Himself can answer the question.

The words that I say unto you I speak not from Myself: but the Father abiding in Me doeth His works.

It is very important to remember that when the Christ came to this earth in great humility, He had laid aside His Divinity, His Power and His Godhead.

He had emptied Himself, and come to this earth, not as God but as man.

Remember that He continues His work as a man.

He is still the great and mighty Intercessor between God and man, the Man, Christ Jesus.

The Great High Priest whom we have is a sympathetic man.

Jesus' Words and Works were the Words and Works of the Father.

Since His words and works were the words and works of the Father, when He forgave sins He said, "Son." He did not say "Brother."

It was the Father speaking in Him who said, "Son, thy sins be forgiven thee."

When the Father in Him healed the woman, by the Spirit's power, the virtue went out of Him and He knew it.

He knew that the immeasurable power of the Spirit had moved through Him to the healing of that woman.

Then she told her story in the middle of the street.

There are some people who object to testimony about Divine Healing.

"It is not nice; it is not ladylike," they say.

I daresay the Devil told that woman, whom I always call Rebecca, "Now, Rebecca, it is not ladylike to testify in the middle of the road. There are a great many boys and girls and rough people here, and it is not nice for you to talk about having an issue of blood all these years."

But when the Master called her, she told it, and told it all.

She even reflected upon the doctors, because she told all the things she had suffered of many physicians, how she had spent all she had, but was nothing bettered, but rather grew worse.

The Devil perhaps told her to wait a week to be quite sure.

She did not wait a minute.

She told it all, and, after she had told it, the Master, in the plenitude of power, said, "Daughter, thy faith hath made thee whole; go in peace."

Who says daughter?

Is it not a father?

Who says son?

Is it not a father?

So it was the Father who healed His daughter.

It was the Father who healed His son.

It was the Father who gave that son and daughter the assurance of His Forgiving Love.

When You Pray, Pray Only to the Father.

When ye pray, say, "Our Father."

Never say, "Dear Lord Jesus," and, "Blessed Holy Spirit," because these are our Mediators.

The blessed Son of God, the Son of Man, the ever blessed Spirit, are our Mediators.

The One is our Mediator with the Father—Jesus, the Christ, the Righteous.

The Other is God's Mediator, who is pleading for God with us.

I believe in the Trinity of God with all my heart.

But the positions that the Son of God, the Son of Man and the Holy Spirit take in the Ever-blessed Trinity is distinctly defined.

The Holy Spirit helps our infirmities, and teaches us how to pray.

Jesus is our Mediator and presents our prayers; but we are to pray to the Father, and to the Father only.

If you pray in any other way you pray wrongly.

You had better learn to pray rightly.

This is a fundamental thing in prayer.

You must pray as God tells you to pray.

If you pray as you like, that is perhaps the way you live, and the way you think, and the way you act, and is the reason you do not get blessing.

You must pray as God tells you, think as He tells you, speak as He tells you, and act as He tells you, or you are wrong.

You are taught to pray to the Father, and to Him alone.

"For this cause," says the Apostle, "I bow my knees unto the Father."

You have no more right to pray to Jesus, the Christ, or to the Holy Spirit, than you have to pray to the Virgin Mary or St Joseph, because Jesus tells you to pray to the Father.

If Jesus had directed me to pray to Him, I should pray to Him.

If the Holy Spirit directed me to pray to Him, I should pray to Him; for the Holy Spirit is a faithful Guide, and Jesus, the Christ, is the Son of God.

But since both the Holy Spirit and the Son of God tell me to pray to the Father and to the Father only, I will so pray.

I believe that you are offensive to God when you know this and pray in any other way.

The Devil Is the Father of Liars.

When you pray, say "Our Father," and mean it and know it.

Some of you may belong to the Devil, as Jesus said to the Jews, when they said, "Our father is Abraham." He said:

If ye were Abraham's children, ye would do the works of Abraham.
But now ye seek to kill Me, a Man that hath told you the truth, which I heard from God: this did not Abraham.

. . . .

Ye are of your father the Devil, and the lusts of your father it is your will to do. He was a murderer from the beginning, and stood not in the truth, because there is no truth in him. When he speaketh a lie, he speaketh of his own: for he is a liar and the father thereof.

Every one that tells a lie is a coward.

A coward can never be a Christian; for the very essence of a Christian is to be truthful, and to be brave.

It must be remembered, however, that Jesus, the Christ, taught us prudence by withdrawing Himself into the wilderness, when the time came.

The Apostles have taught us prudence in doing wise things.

Cowardice Is a Crime.

You will remember that those who lead the procession to hell are, first of all, the cowards.

The order given in Revelation 21:8 is, "The fearful, and unbelieving, and abominable, and murderers, and fornicators, and sorcerers, and idolaters, and all liars, their part shall be in the lake that burneth with fire and brimstone; which is the second death."

That procession is led by the coward.

If a man is afraid to speak the truth and to do his duty he is fearful, he is a coward, he is no Christian, and he is leading the procession to hell.

In the churches today, there are vast numbers of cowards afraid to speak; afraid of their ecclesiastical superiors; afraid of public opinion.

That man can never be a helper or lover of his fellow men who is afraid of them.

You must love your fellow men too much to be afraid, and you must be careful that what you say is true.

When you know the truth, you must speak it, no matter what the results are to you or to any one else.

Passing from these thoughts, I come to the last words of the text: that the things the Christ did were simply the fulfilment of the prophetic Word spoken in the 53d chapter of Isaiah, by the prophet, when he said:

Surely He hath borne our sicknesses and carried our sorrows.

Every Hebrew scholar will admit that the word griefs is properly translated sicknesses, in the margin of the Revision.

Why they did not put it in the text I do not know.

Timidity of Translators of the Scriptures.

Our translators had begun to get afraid of Divine Healing.

It is a shameful confession to make, but all of us know how King James' translators were afraid of the King, and in various places they put in words that never were in the original.

They translated one passage, "Fear God and honor the king."

The word in the Greek does not mean king.

The word is ruler, and it would apply to a president, to a czar, or to an emperor.

I do not hesitate to say the translators were timid, if not afraid—we will call it timid—about Divine Healing.

Therefore in the 53d chapter of Isaiah and in the 4th verse in the Revision you will see that this word "sicknesses" is put in the margin.

He was despised, and rejected of men; a Man of Sorrows, and acquainted with griefs.

The marginal reference reads, "sicknesses. (Hebrew)."

We want the Hebrew. It is the Hebrew that is being translated.

Why did they translate the word "griefs" when it is "sicknesses?"

It ought to be put into the text.

With every respect to the great translators, I venture to say that what we were after was to get the Hebrew, and the Hebrew ought to have gone into the text, and not into the margin.

Surely He hath borne our sicknesses, and carried our sorrows: yet we did esteem Him stricken, smitten of God, and afflicted. But He was wounded for our transgressions, He was bruised for our iniquities: the chastisement of our peace was upon Him; and with His stripes we are healed.

God Is Not the Murderer of His Son.

I said, in a meeting in Timaru, New Zealand, a good many years ago—I think it was 1886, eighteen years ago—"Any of you who say that you are smitten and stricken of God, are lying.

"When you say that God afflicted His own Son, you are telling a lie against God.

"You are singing a lie when you sing that hymn:

Jehovah lifted up His rod,
O Christ—it fell on Thee;
Thou wast sore stricken of God—
There's not one stroke for me.

"God never struck His Son."

A man rose in the gallery.

His tall form stood up, and he raised his hand.

I whispered to a gentleman by my side, "Who is he?"

"The Rev. Dr. So-and-so," he replied.

"What kind of man is he?" I asked, because he had said, "May I speak?"

I said, "If he is a good man I will let him speak."

"He is a good man," my friend replied, "but he is against Divine Healing."

So I said, "Doctor, you may speak."

"Dr. Dowie," he said, "you are too much of a gentleman and scholar to be guilty of a wilful misstatement, but you have made a daring misstatement."

"All right, Doctor, go on and tell us where it is."

"You know well that the Scripture says that He was 'stricken, smitten of God, and afflicted.'"

"I know no such thing," I said. "Come down, Doctor, and read the passage from my Bible."

"All right," he said, "I will come down."

He came.

It was a very interesting scene.

It was in the theater in Timaru.

"Friends," he said, "I am sorry to put Dr. Dowie to shame, but I am bound to do it."

I said, "You go right ahead; that is all right."

"Now," he said, "here it is: 'Surely He hath borne our griefs'"—

I said, "Stop, Doctor, before you go any further, is that word not sicknesses?"

"Oh, yes," he said, "I admit what you said about it. The Hebrew is sicknesses. There is no getting around it."

"All right, Doctor," I said, "that is one thing in which you back me up. Now go on."

He read: "Surely He hath borne our sicknesses, and carried our sorrows."

"Now," he said, "Doctor, I have you: 'Yet we did esteem Him stricken, smitten of God, and afflicted.'

"Does not the Bible say that He was stricken, smitten of God and afflicted?"

I said, "No."

"Why?" he asked in astonishment.

"Why?" I said; "Doctor, do you not see that it says that 'we did esteem Him?'

"*We* said that He was stricken.

"*We* said that He was smitten of God.

"*We* said that He was afflicted of God.

"But He was not; for when He was stricken, it was the power of the Devil, as He Himself said: 'This is your hour, and the Power of Darkness.'

"It was the Devil who struck Him. It was the Devil's people, in priestly garb, who passed by and said, 'You are an imposter,' and wagged their heads and put out their tongues."

Unbelieving Israel "Esteemed" the Christ "Stricken, Smitten of God, and Afflicted."

The priests and Pharisees said to the Christ, "You are an imposter. You saved others, save Yourself. You cannot save. God has stricken You! God has smitten You. God has afflicted You.

"Come down from the cross, if You are the Son of God."

Who was it that flung that in His face?

Was it God?

Who said that He was stricken of God?

"We did esteem"—

Who are the "we?"

The unbelieving Israel.

Who are the "we" today?

The unbelieving Israel.

"We did esteem Him stricken, smitten of God, and afflicted," but He was not.

Every blow that fell upon Him was from the Devil's hand.

Did not Peter say that at Pentecost, when he said that He was crucified by the hands of wicked men?

He submitted, and endured the Cross for our sakes.

He despised the shame, because in doing this He bore our sicknesses, and carried our sorrows, and the chastisement of our peace was upon Him.

When the Christ Had Finished His Life in Mortal Flesh, He went Down into Hell For Us.

He went down into hell for those who had been disobedient in the days of Noah, and preached to them, and opened the Kingdom of God to them.

He went down to the deepest depths of hell, and led captivity captive.

He made it possible for these damned spirits, who had made their bed in hell, to find their way to heaven.

He is the same Mighty Savior, the same Mighty Healer today.

He died that He might do this. But it was not God who struck Him.

It was the Devil.

I have had many afflictions, but none of them came from God.

The Devil the Author of Disease.

When you say that diseases come from God, you lie.

You may not intend to do it, but you lie; because diseases cannot come from God.

Is there any disease in God?

There is not one of you who will say so.

How then can you get out of God what is not in Him?

If there is no impurity or corruption in God, how can you get impurity and corruption from Him?

There is no disease in heaven.

Naught that defileth can ever enter there.

If these things are true, you cannot get disease from heaven, and you cannot get it from God.

Whence are you to get it?

"Oh," you may say, "God gives it to us. He comes down to earth and hunts around the hospitals. He goes where He can find disease. Perhaps He goes down to hell and gets it."

Does God go around to the hospitals to get diseases for His children?

Is God the propagator of corruption; the corrupter of His own creation?

If He is the corrupter of His own creation, we do not want such a God.

That God cannot be our God.

He cannot be our Father.

There is no father who would hunt around for diseases to put upon his children.

You say it makes them better.

When did it make any one better?

How can making a man a sinner make him holy?

How can making a man sick make him strong and happy?

Sickness Cannot Make God's Children Better.

There is no sense in it.

"But God's saints have said so many times that it was good for them to be afflicted," says some objector.

Yes, it was good for one "saint" who said it—David.

He was a sinner.

He had been going after Bath-sheba and murdering Uriah.

He had been doing all kinds of dirty, bad things.

It was a good thing for him that he was afflicted; for he was a sinner arrested in the midst of his sin, and he says so.

But it was the Devil's work, and he was reaping the Devil's wages.

The affliction that he had in his family, and in his own body, was the result of his own unbridled lust, king though he was.

David, what is the use of talking nonsense?

"Job was a good man," you say.

Yes, but he talked nonsense for about twenty chapters. God said it.

God said, "Who is this that darkeneth counsel by words without knowledge?"

And Job said, "Therefore have I uttered that which I understood not, things too wonderful for me, which I knew not, . . . Wherefore I abhor myself, and repent in dust and ashes."

Job had talked nonsense.

Job said. "Have pity upon me, O ye my friends; for the hand of God hath touched me."

The hand of God had not touched him.

The Book itself says that it was the hand of Satan that smote him with sore boils from the crown of his head to the soles of his feet.

How can you make that out to be the hand of God?

Permission Not Commission.

"Ah, but God permitted it," you say.

Yes, and God permitted bad people to sell whisky last night.

God permitted them to knock one another on the head last night.

God permitted a man to draw a revolver and commit murder last night

God permits people who sin to live in this city—tricky politicians who lie and men who are afraid to do their duty.

He permits, for a time, the commissioner of police to live; but if I were premier he would live outside of the police department.

I should clean out the entire outfit that told me that they could not preserve order in your public building.

I should say that it was time for them to get out, and I should have men who would preserve order.

I cannot hold my meetings on the Lord's Day in the Exhibition Building because the chief secretary himself, and the commissioner of police tell me that they cannot insure my personal safety, and that they cannot insure the peace of the public who attend my meeting. They have practically given the whole thing over to the mob, and the mob rules! [Cries of "Shame!"]

It is a shame, an unutterable shame.

When I have left this city, you will begin to think about it.

Placing the Responsibility for the Exhibition Building Mob.

Did God do that in the Exhibition Building last Lord's Day?

Was that God's work?

No!

It was partly Mr. Fitchett's work.

He had helped to stir up the mob.

It was the *Age's* work; for it had helped to stir up the mob.

It was the *Argus*' work; for it had helped to stir up the mob.

It was the Devil's work.

The whole outfit were doing the Devil's work.

Do you mean to say that there was one true man of God that said that I should not be heard?

I am a careful speaker.

I speak a great many words, but I speak them very slowly and very deliberately. My stenographers all tell me that I am an easy man to report because I speak slowly.

The Size and Good Order of Zion Audiences.

I speak deliberately, and I am accustomed to speak to great audiences.

I have spoken for two consecutive years each Lord's Day afternoon in the Chicago Auditorium to several thousand people, and I was never interrupted one minute.

After we got out a few hoodlums in New York, I spoke to audiences of fifteen thousand with no serious interruption.

I am accustomed to speak in Shiloh Tabernacle, Zion City, which seats seven thousand two hundred.

I know very well what I am saying, when I say that, if I am spared to return to Zion City, I shall probably have to speak to over ten thousand persons every day for ten days; for it will be the time of our Fourth Feast of Tabernacles.

Our morning prayer-meeting, every Lord's Day morning at half past six o'clock in Zion City, is attended by from three to five thousand people.

All through the winter they come out in the darkness of the morning, bringing their lanterns to show them the pathway.

They are a very happy, healthy, well-fed, contented people, who have never missed a meal since they have been in Zion.

I am not telling you a cunningly-devised fable.

You have no letter from the City of Zion, signed by a Zion man, showing the opposite.

The Lies of the "Southern Cross"—Their Source.

You have the lies emptied into your religious papers by the yellow journals of America; papers so vile that decent people despise them, and are ashamed to be seen with them in their hands.

It is a reflection upon a man's moral character to be seen with some of the papers that Mr. Fitchett has quoted.

It is a well-known fact that these papers cannot tell the truth.

They are like the *Southern Cross*, they were born speaking lies.

That *Southern Cross*, from the beginning, has fought me and lied.

It lied before I came; it lies now.

Turn to the *Church Economist* of New York, edited under the supervision of Bishop Potter.

There is an article regarding myself and my ministry that could have been written by my warmest friend.

How is it Mr. Fitchett does not quote such things?

They can be found in hundreds.

Why is it that he does not quote LEAVES OF HEALING?

That tells the truth.

We certainly are much more to be considered than anonymous writers.

We say that none has ever suffered want either for fuel, food or clothing, at any time, in Zion.

We have always been able to relieve our poor.

I gladly give to my people, and to my work.

I have been the most generous giver to Zion's funds for seven years, and no greater joy has come into my life.

Why do they not tell the good work Zion does?

What is the use of piling up the lies of the yellow press?

Enemies of God Afraid of the Truth.

No more shameful thing has ever been done in this city than closing my mouth by means of an organized mob, and not permitting me to utter the truth.

It is a shame, an unutterable disgrace to the State and the Commonwealth!

So it was with our Lord Jesus, the Christ.

The more He told the truth, the more His following grew.

His enemies got together, and they said, "Do you not see that we prevail nothing? The world is gone after Him? The only way to shut His mouth is to kill Him."

They did it.

There is the same spirit now, because the world has gone after us.

Australia a Very Small Part of the World.

You are a very small part of the world here, you people in Australia.

You call yourselves four millions, but you are not.

I have been looking up your records.

You number only about three million eight hundred thousand.

With New Zealand you may be four and one-half millions.

Do you know what four and one-half millions is, compared to America?

There are five million people within one hundred miles of Zion City. You do not realize that, do you?

There are eight million people within one hundred fifty miles of Zion City.

When I go to New York, I can reach ten million people within fifty miles of the Town Hall of that city.

You do not realize how small a part of the world you are.

You are full of conceit and ignorance as a people.

Do you not know that your public debt, in this commonwealth of four million people, is bigger than the entire debt of the United States with its eighty millions of people?

Some Plain Truths for Australians.

You need to hear a Voice that will tell you people the truth, and that will bring you back to good sound sense, and let the people get the rule out of the hands of incompetent rulers.

You have not a financier worth talking about among you.

You have not a financier of any power in public life today.

Mr. Deakin, your prime minister, does not know what on earth to do with the extraordinary combination you have given him, you have shuffled the political cards so.

You have now given him three opposing parties to deal with, and a majority in none.

Do you not see how careless the people are about their political life?

Not one-fourth of all the voters of the commonwealth have voted. They do not care a snap about it.

They are weary of it; for your politicians are a weak, wicked lot.

You have a premier, in Victoria, whose name is Bent.

I think he is properly named, for he is one of the most crooked men I ever knew. [Applause.]

Every one laughs at Bent.

I know Bent. Any one of any sense in this country knows Bent, and knows how crooked he is.

He is so soft that you can bend him anyway, you have only to push him. He is one of the most amiable of men.

He got in by the votes of abstainers.

Now, he is telling the abstainers to make their peace with the publicans and do nothing for a while—but leave Mr. Bent in power!

You are not strong financially now, and you are getting into such a condition that it is not a question as to whether you will be able to pay your debt, but as to whether you will be able to pay the interest.

I would not take stock in your national debt for anything.

It will depreciate most surely, unless the British government does what it always does for you, stands back of you.

Then there is a possibility of more trouble; for consols have faults, and they will fall if you do not take care.

Of course the British Empire is strong, but great empires have rotted away, and it seems to me that you are suffering from rot.

You are rotten.

You have no religion.

You have no liberty.

You have no law in effect.

Your religion is in abeyance, your principles are trampled upon and your laws are broken.

There has not been one man who has made his voice heard in this city in protest against what was done last Sunday.

Our Lord Jesus, the Christ, Came to Protest Against All Disorder.

Order is heaven's first law.

Confusion is hateful to Christianity, and we must be careful to obey law.

One of my opponents stated some time ago, in an editorial note in a Chicago paper: "People wonder at Dr. Dowie's success, but there is no wonder about it. Dr. Dowie obeys the law, and his enemies do not; therefore, he is ten points ahead, and still gaining."

I am a stickler for law and order.

Law is maintained in Zion City.

We obey the laws of the State and Nation, not only in the letter, but in the spirit.

If there were a law that we could not obey, we would simply say, "We will not obey that," and fight it out until we got the law altered.

Zion City is ordered in accordance with the Constitution of the United States, and in exact compliance with the laws of the State of Illinois.

I am thankful for law.

Law Honored in Zion City.

But we do not need to bother about law in Zion City; for men do not commit assaults there.

No woman has ever been insulted.

We have never had a case of litigation among our people

They have submitted to arbitration in case of any dispute.

We are a peaceful people, a hard-working people, and a religious people.

We carry the Gospel to millions at our own cost.

Zion Restoration Host went down to New York at their own cost, and came back at their own cost.

I can get things done that you cannot.

For instance, I got the people down to New York and back, two thousand miles, for three pounds.

You do not know how to do things here.

I think that member of your federal parliament who said that the way to settle the question of the capital was to get me to come and build a city for you was about right.

But you do not want that, and I do not intend to come.

I have no time for these "peanut" politicians.

I grieve over his sins, but Sir Henry Parks was a great statesman.

When he offered me the portfolio of minister of education for New South Wales, I was strongly tempted to take it; especially as he pointed to the future of the commonwealth.

I said then, as I say now, "I am happier as a minister of the Gospel than I would be as a politician."

All of you who believe that Jesus, the Christ, is indeed what the Scripture says He is, the Savior and the Healer, the Cleanser and the Keeper, stand up and tell Him so. [Nearly all rose.]

PRAYER OF CONSECRATION.

My God and Father, in Jesus' Name, I come to Thee. Take me as I am. Make me what I ought to be in spirit, in soul, in body. Give me power to do right, no matter what it costs. Give me Thy Holy Spirit, that in spirit, soul and body I may be Thine. For Jesus' sake. Amen. [*All repeat the prayer, clause by clause, after the General Overseer.*]

After the singing of the Doxology, the meeting was closed by the General Overseer's pronouncing the

BENEDICTION.

Beloved, abstain from all appearance of evil. And may the very God of Peace Himself sanctify you wholly; and I pray God your whole spirit and soul and body be preserved entire, without blame, unto the coming of our Lord Jesus, the Christ. Faithful is He that calleth you, who also will do it. The grace of our Lord Jesus, the Christ, the love of God, our Father, the fellowship of the Holy Spirit, our Comforter and Guide, one Eternal God, abide in you, bless you and keep you, and all the Israel of God everywhere, forever. Amen.

Zion in Michigan.

Rev. G. E. Farr, Elder-in-charge of the branch of the Christian Catholic Church in Zion in Benton Harbor, Michigan, will visit the following towns in Michigan:

Kalamazoo, May 30th; Sturgis, May 31st; Three Rivers, June 1st; Moorepark, June 2d; Schoolcraft, June 3d.

Baptismal Services, Boston Branch.

Candidates for Triune Immersion, service to be conducted Lord's Day, June 5, 1904, should communicate with Overseer William Hamner Piper, 71 Perkins street, Jamaica Plain, Massachusetts.

Elder A. F. Lee's Itinerary.

Elder A. F. Lee will hold meetings in Indiana according to the following schedule:

Lafayette, May 22d and 23d; Noblesville, May 24th; Indianapolis, May 25th and 26th; Walton, May 27th; Logansport, May 28th, 29th and 30th; Auburn, May 31st and June 1st; Albion, June 2d; Lapaz, June 3d, Plymouth, June 4th; Valparaiso, June 5th.

Zion in Ohio.

Deacon Charles F. Kelchner, Deacon-in-charge of the Branch of the Christian Catholic Church in Zion in Cleveland, will conduct meetings in the following cities in Ohio:

Collins, May 18th; Oceola, May 19th; Mount Gilead, May 20th; Crestline, May 21st and 22d; Wooster, May 23d; Orrville, May 24th; Canton, May 25th; Akron, May 26th; Medina, May 27th.

Zion in Ohio.

Deacon A. F. Arrington, Officer-in-charge of the Branch of the Christian Catholic Church in Zion in Cincinnati, will conduct meetings in the following cities in Ohio:

Cedarville, May 23d; Columbus, May 24th and 25th; Plain City, May 26th; Dayton, May 27th; Middletown, May 28th; Germantown, May 29th; Eaton, May 30th; New Paris, May 31st.

Zion in Wisconsin.

Deacon B. W. Brannen of Zion City, Illinois, will conduct meetings in the following cities in Wisconsin:

Columbus, May 16th; Portage, May 17th and 18th; Hustler, May 19th and 20th; Bangor, May 21st; Viroqua, May 22d and 23d; Dodgeville, May 25th; Madison, May 29th and 30th.

Zion in Canada.

Elder Brooks will visit the places in Ontario, Canada, mentioned below, during the months of May and June.

He will baptize, and consecrate children, in all these places where desired.

May 25th, Kincardine, Town Hall, at 3 and 8 o'clock p. m.; May 26th, Ripley, Town Hall at 3 and 8 o'clock p. m.; May 27th, Wingham, in the Christian Workers' Mission Room on Victoria street, at 3 and 8 o'clock p. m.; May 28th, Palmerston, in the Anderson Hall, at 3 o'clock p. m.; May 29th, Sunday, in Chesley Town Hall, at 11 o'clock a. m., and 3 and 8 p. m.; May 30th, Baptism at 3 o'clock p. m. at the Leggett Farm, and services at the home of Allen Cross at 8 o'clock p. m.; May 31st, in Wiarton Town Hall at 3 and 8 o'clock p. m.; June 1st, in Wiarton at a private house; June 2d and 3d, Lion's Head, Public Hall, at 3 and 8 o'clock p. m.; June 5th, Heathcote, Sunday services in Grove near Woodhouse, Baptism in afternoon; June 6th, Meaford, Town Hall, at 8 o'clock p. m.; June 7th, Collingwood, at 3 and 8 o'clock p. m., possibly Town Hall; June 8th and 9th, Waubaushene, in Skating Rink, at 3 and 8 o'clock p. m.

Memorabilia of the New York Visitation

By Mrs. Emily Ware

BUT they that wait upon Jehovah shall renew their strength; they shall mount up with wings as eagles; they shall run, and not be weary; they shall walk, and not faint.—*Isaiah 40:31.*

MISS LUCY ORR, Zion City, Illinois.—I praise God for the part He allowed me to take in the work in New York City.

I did not lose one day during the entire time.

I received three ten weeks' subscriptions for LEAVES OF HEALING, one being from a Jewish lady.

She asked many questions about the General Overseer.

In the same house was a minister's wife who was deaf. To her we gave LEAVES OF HEALING and tickets for the meetings.

We did some work in the Bowery—some of the children kissed the card when we gave it to them.

One day, as our company was waiting for a car, a well-dressed gentleman came up and asked for one of the Messages that would tell him about the Clean City.

As we were talking to a policeman, we asked him if we should give the gentleman one, as we had had orders not to distribute the literature in the streets.

He said that it was all right; so we gave him one and also a copy of LEAVES OF HEALING.

I think New York should be proud of her policemen.

One noon, while in Brooklyn, we were invited into a home to a very nice lunch, which we enjoyed very much.

The lady asked us a great many questions, and we told her a great many things about Zion City.

We also gave them LEAVES OF HEALING, and tickets.

They were delighted to hear about a clean City.

They said that New York was such a hard place in which to do Christian work, that they were sorry for us.

In upper New York, a lady called us in and gave us a nice lunch.

She said that she wanted to do something for Zion Restoration Host, that came so far to help New York.

She said that the city was in great need of such work as we were doing.

In one home we found a gentleman reading a newspaper.

We invited him to come to the meetings and bring his wife.

He said that the world was too far gone to be helped, and that his wife was not able to go to the meetings.

We gave them LEAVES OF HEALING and before we left they had consented to have the General Overseer pray for the wife.

I am sure God prepared the hearts of the people to receive us.

I count those two weeks spent in Restoration work in New York City the happiest days of my life.

MRS. ELIZA WHEELER, Zion City, Illinois.—I thank God for the privilege of belonging to the Christian Catholic Church in Zion, and for the pleasure of going to New York with Zion Restoration Host.

I see as never before the power of being a united people; but the best of all is God was with us.

I thank God for the kindness shown us by the people of New York City. Those were the happiest days I have ever spent.

Although I was not in the house-to-house work, I gave out literature in the Garden three days, and the rest of the time I worked in the dining-room.

A number of people asked me if I had ever been healed of any disease.

I told them that I had been healed of many diseases and that God keeps me now day by day.

One day some ladies who were sitting near me said, "The papers have said that Dr. Dowie is having a great deal of trouble among his people, so we came to see for ourselves. We believe the papers have told wrong stories, and that Dr. Dowie is all right."

The lady with whom we roomed asked us for tickets to the meetings, and wished to know all about Zion City.

Another lady asked us for an application for fellowship.

When the Host goes again, I shall be with them, God willing.

LILLIE L. SPRAGUE, Zion City, Illinois.—It was a great joy to me to be permitted to go with the Host to New York, and carry to the people a Full Gospel of Salvation, Healing and Holy Living, through faith in the Christ.

It was also a joy to me to know that the Christ was received in New York, for the most part, for it is written, "He that receiveth you receiveth Me," and "He that receiveth a prophet in the name of a prophet shall receive a prophet's reward."

We were received among the poor, the working class and the rich, in the business places and in the homes.

One day we entered a bare and filthy home. The father and several of his brothers were smoking. The children were barefooted.

One of the brothers said that he once belonged to the Salvation Army, but had backslidden.

My companion asked him if he was not much happier then, to which he answered, "Yes."

The brothers promised to come to Madison Square Garden to the meetings.

We entered a carriage-shop, and at first did not seem to find any there desirous of having the literature, and we felt almost like giving up and going away to some place where we were wanted.

When about to leave, we came to a man who received us, and urged all his men to take the Messages, and took us in the elevator to other parts of the building.

They then invited us to go to the blacksmith shop, and there we found Elijah the Restorer's picture tacked on the wall, in full view, and all the men eager for LEAVES OF HEALING.

We went to great buildings filled with the offices of prominent business men, and were kindly received.

In the streets, policemen stopped the teams to allow whole companies of Restorationists to pass.

We realized so much the protecting care of our God, all the way through, and it gave us joy.

It was also a great joy to see the intense interest manifested at the evening services.

We met many Jews, who received the Messages after we had told them that the General Overseer is Elijah.

KARL STEINER, Zion City, Illinois.—As I read the many wonderful and most interesting testimonies of the members of Zion Restoration Host, each week in LEAVES OF HEALING, I feel it my duty to express my love and gratitude toward God and Zion that I was granted the privilege to have a part in the first great Visitation.

It was the greatest thing I ever witnessed in my life, and I can never forget it.

The night our beloved General Overseer so bravely and fearlessly thundered down upon Buckley and others, I was sitting in the first row of seats directly in front of the platform.

It was the night for our company to escort the General Overseer.

I could see how the Devil showed his teeth in fury against the man of God, but he could not prevail against the Power of God; yet I could see the possible danger of an outbreak into a riot.

I am glad to say that I was not afraid, for I knew when God was with us nothing could be against us.

As a member of Zion Guard I was not called to do any work outside of the building, but when at liberty we took some literature to different parts of the city, such as the navy-yard, Brooklyn bridge and other places.

Many came to us and asked for the literature, which we gladly gave them.

Many earnest inquiries were made about Zion, especially by the policemen in the Garden.

I believe that the half can never be told of the influence which that great Visitation had upon the people, nor of the blessings which came to the Host in thus sacrificing time, talent, and money.

It seems almost a miracle to me that such a great number of people could have made that journey, without the loss of one or injury to any.

I hope to witness more such Visitations.

IS ANY among you sick? let him call for the Elders of the Church; and let them pray over him, anointing him with oil in the Name of the Lord: And the Prayer of Faith shall save him that is sick, and the Lord shall raise him up; and if he have committed sins, it shall be forgiven him.—*James 5:14, 15.*

Program Zion's Fourth Feast of Tabernacles

Will be held in Shiloh Tabernacle, Shiloh Park, Zion City, Illinois, from the Evening of Wednesday, July 13th, to the Evening of Lord's Day, July 24, 1904.

WEDNESDAY, JULY 13TH.

7:30 to 9 P. M.—Presentation and Consecration of the People to God. Address by the General Overseer: "FOR ZION'S SAKE."

THURSDAY, JULY 14TH.

FOURTH ANNIVERSARY OF THE CONSECRATION OF THE SITE OF ZION TEMPLE.

Public Holiday in Zion City.

Announcement of excursion trains from Chicago will be made at a later date.

6:30 A. M.—Early Morning Sacrifice of Praise and Prayer.
The First of a Series of Twenty-Minute Addresses by the General Overseer on the Nine Fruits of the Spirit: "THE FIRST FRUIT OF THE SPIRIT. LOVE."

9:30 A. M.—First Convocation of Zion Junior Restoration Host. Conducted by Overseer Harvey D. Brasefield.

2:00 P. M.—FULL PROCESSION of Zion Robed Officers, Zion White-robed Choir, and Zion Restoration Host will march around the Site of Zion Temple, and thence to the Site of Shiloah Tabernacle.
The Procession will then re-form and take the seats reserved for them in Shiloh Tabernacle, where an address will be given by the General Overseer on "ZION: A CROWN OF BEAUTY IN THE HAND OF JEHOVAH."
Special Offerings will be received at the close of this Address for the building of Shiloah Tabernacle, which it is expected will cost $500,000, and seat about 16,000 people.

7:30 P. M.—Evening Sacrifice of Praise and Prayer.

FRIDAY, JULY 15TH.

A HALF HOLIDAY IN ZION CITY.

6:30 A. M.—Early Morning Sacrifice of Praise and Prayer.
Twenty-Minute Address by the General Overseer: "THE SECOND FRUIT OF THE SPIRIT: JOY."

9:30 A. M.—Second Convocation of Zion Junior Restoration Host. Conducted by Overseer Harvey D. Brasefield.

10:30 A. M.—DIVINE HEALING MEETING. Conducted by the General Overseer.
Address: "PRESENT YOUR BODIES A LIVING SACRIFICE, HOLY, ACCEPTABLE TO GOD, WHICH IS YOUR REASONABLE SERVICE."
At the close of this meeting the General Overseer, Overseer Jane Dowie, and other Overseers, Elders and Evangelists will pray with the sick who are seeking the Lord for healing.

THE CITY FESTAL DAY.

3:00 P. M.—A PROCESSION, headed by Zion Guard and Zion City Band, consisting of
The Municipal Officers of the City of Zion,
All Officers and Employees of the Legal, Financial and Business Institutions of Zion,
All Officers and Employees of the Educational Institutions of Zion, and
All Officers of the Political Institutions of Zion, will be REVIEWED BY THE GENERAL OVERSEER AT THE ADMINISTRATION BUILDING, and then proceed to Shiloh Tabernacle where a SERVICE OF THANKSGIVING will be held.
Those in the Procession, as they enter Shiloh Tabernacle, will take their places in the Choir and Officers' Gallery, and on the ground floor.
Spectators will occupy the remaining galleries.

7:30 P. M.—Evening Sacrifice of Praise and Prayer.

SATURDAY, JULY 16TH.

6:30 A. M.—EARLY MORNING SACRIFICE OF PRAISE AND PRAYER.
Twenty-Minute Address by the General Overseer: "THE THIRD FRUIT OF THE SPIRIT: PEACE."

2:00 P. M.—Zion Athletic Association: Field Games on grounds at northeast corner of Shiloh Park.

8:00 P. M.—Evening Sacrifice of Praise and Prayer.

LORD'S DAY, JULY 17TH.

6:30 A. M.—EARLY MORNING SACRIFICE OF PRAISE AND PRAYER.
Twenty-Minute Address by the General Overseer on "THE FOURTH FRUIT OF THE SPIRIT: LONG-SUFFERING."

9:30 A. M.—Third convocation of Zion Junior Restoration Host. Conducted by Overseer Harvey D. Brasefield.

11:00 A. M.—The Rev. John G. Speicher, M. D., Overseer of the Christian Catholic Church in Zion, of the City of Zion, will preach.

2:00 P. M.—GREAT GENERAL ASSEMBLY.
Procession of Zion's Robed Officers and White-robed Choir (probably One Thousand in line).
Elijah the Restorer will deliver a Message from God to Zion: "ARISE! SHINE! FOR THY LIGHT IS COME."
A reception of New Members into the Communion and Fellowship of the Christian Catholic Church in Zion will be held at the close.

8:00 P. M.—Ordination of New Officers and the Celebration of the Ordinance of the Lord's Supper.

MONDAY, JULY 18TH.

6:30 A. M.—EARLY MORNING SACRIFICE OF PRAISE AND PRAYER.
Twenty-minute Address by the General Overseer: "THE FIFTH FRUIT OF THE SPIRIT: KINDNESS."

9:30 A. M.—Fourth Convocation of Zion Junior Restoration Host. Conducted by Overseer Harvey D. Brasefield.

11:00 A. M.—THE ORDINANCE OF BELIEVER'S BAPTISM BY TRIUNE IMMERSION will be administered by Overseers Speicher, Mason, Brasefield and Excell, assisted by a number of Elders, Evangelists, Deacons and Deaconesses.

2:00 P. M.—A MEETING FOR ZION WOMEN ONLY will be addressed by the Rev. Jane Dowie, Overseer for Women's Work in the Christian Catholic Church in Zion Throughout the World.
This meeting will be strictly limited to female members of the Christian Catholic Church in Zion, and no children under twelve years of age will be admitted.

8:00 P. M.—A MEETING FOR ZION MEN ONLY will be addressed by the Rev. John Alex. Dowie, General Overseer of the Christian Catholic Church in Zion.
This meeting will be strictly limited to male members of the Christian Catholic Church in Zion above the age of twelve.

TUESDAY, JULY 19TH.

6:30 A. M.—EARLY MORNING SACRIFICE OF PRAISE AND PRAYER.
Twenty-Minute Address by the General Overseer: "THE SIXTH FRUIT OF THE SPIRIT: GOODNESS."

9:30 A. M.—Fifth Convocation of Zion Junior Restoration Host. Conducted by Overseer Harvey D. Brasefield.

11:30 A. M.—CONFERENCE OF WOMEN ELDERS, EVANGELISTS AND DEACONESSES OF THE CHRISTIAN CATHOLIC CHURCH IN ZION. Conducted by Overseer Jane Dowie.

2:30 P. M.—CONFERENCE UPON THE WORK OF ZION RESTORATION HOST THROUGHOUT THE WORLD.
The General Overseer will preside, and at the close will administer the Restoration Vow to New Members of the Host, and Consecrate and Separate them to the Work of God in Zion by the Laying on of Hands.

8:00 P. M.—Evening Sacrifice of Praise and Prayer.

WEDNESDAY, JULY 20TH.

6:30 A. M.—EARLY MORNING SACRIFICE OF PRAISE AND PRAYER.
Twenty-Minute Address by the General Overseer: "THE SEVENTH FRUIT OF THE SPIRIT: FAITHFULNESS."

9:30 A. M.—Sixth Convocation of Zion Junior Restoration Host. Conducted by Overseer Harvey D. Brasefield.

11:00 A. M.—CONFERENCE OF MALE OFFICERS OF THE CHRISTIAN CATHOLIC CHURCH IN ZION. Conducted by the General Overseer.

2:30 P. M.—THE ORDINANCE OF THE PRESENTATION AND CONSECRATION OF YOUNG CHILDREN TO GOD, will be conducted by the General Overseer. He will deliver an Address on the Words: "WHAT THEN SHALL THIS CHILD BE?"

8:00 P. M.—Evening Sacrifice of Praise and Prayer.

THURSDAY, JULY 21ST.

6:30 A. M.—EARLY MORNING SACRIFICE OF PRAISE AND PRAYER.
Twenty-Minute Address by the General Overseer: "THE EIGHTH FRUIT OF THE SPIRIT: MEEKNESS."

9:00 A. M.—Seventh Convocation of Zion Junior Restoration Host. Conducted by Overseer Harvey D. Brasefield.

11:00 A. M.—EDUCATIONAL CONFERENCE. Presided over by Overseer Brasefield. Addresses by Members of the Faculty of Zion College, Zion Preparatory and Zion Manual Training Schools.

2:00 P. M.—A CONFERENCE ON ZION BUSINESS INSTITUTIONS will be Conducted by the General Overseer, and Addressed by Managers of the Various Institutions.
The Meeting will be Strictly Limited to Investors in Zion Stocks.

8:00 P. M.—Evening Sacrifice of Praise and Prayer.

FRIDAY, JULY 22d.

6:30 A. M.—EARLY MORNING SACRIFICE OF PRAISE AND PRAYER.
Twenty-Minute address by the General Overseer: "THE NINTH FRUIT OF THE SPIRIT: TEMPERANCE."

9:30 A. M.—Eighth Convocation of Zion Junior Restoration Host. Conducted by Overseer Harvey D. Brasefield.

11:00 A. M.—A CONFERENCE CONCERNING DORCAS AND MATERNITY DEACONESS WORK IN ZION THROUGHOUT THE WORLD. Conducted by Overseer Jane Dowie.

2:00 P. M.—A CONFERENCE ON ZION BUSINESS INSTITUTIONS will be Conducted by the General Overseer, and Addressed by Managers of the Various Institutions.
The Meeting will be Strictly Limited to Investors in Zion Stocks.

8:00 P. M.—Evening Sacrifice of Praise and Prayer.

SATURDAY, JULY 23D.

6:30 A. M.—EARLY MORNING SACRIFICE OF PRAISE AND PRAYER.
Twenty-Minute Address by the General Overseer: "THE NINE GIFTS OF THE HOLY SPIRIT."

2:00 P. M.—Zion Athletic Association; Field Games in the northeast corner of Shiloh Park.

8:00 P. M.—Evening Sacrifice of Praise and Prayer.

LORD'S DAY, JULY 24TH.

6:30 A. M.—EARLY MORNING SACRIFICE OF PRAISE AND PRAYER.
Twenty-Minute Address by the General Overseer: "THE HOUSE OF WISDOM."

9:30 A. M.—The General Overseer will speak on "TRIUNE IMMERSION; GOD'S SEAL ON A LIVING CHURCH."
At the close of this Service the General Overseer, assisted by Overseers, Elders, Evangelists, Deacons and Deaconesses, will Administer the Ordinance of Believer's Baptism.
All persons desiring to be Baptized on this occasion must fill up their Application Cards for Baptism, and present them to the General Recorder, Deacon Andrew C. Jensen, and his Assistants, not later than 9 a. m.

2:00 P. M.—GREAT GENERAL ASSEMBLY.
FULL PROCESSIONAL of Zion Robed Officers, Zion White-robed Choir and all the Members of Zion Junior Restoration Host, under their Leader, Overseer Brasefield.
The General Overseer will speak on "THE MINISTRY OF CHILDREN IN ZION." At the close of this Service he will Administer the Vow of Zion Restoration Host to New Members of Zion Junior Restoration Host.

8:00 P. M.—THE ORDINANCE OF THE LORD'S SUPPER will be Administered by the General Overseer and Ordained Officers of the Christian Catholic Church in Zion.
This Gathering will be open only to Members of the Christian Catholic Church in Zion, and other Christians desiring to commune with them.
At the close, the General Overseer will deliver the CONCLUDING ADDRESS OF THE FEAST.

REDUCED FARE—FEAST OF TABERNACLES.

ONE AND ONE-THIRD FARE FOR ROUND TRIP TO ZION CITY—CONDITIONS OF SALE OF TICKETS.

A reduction of fare to one and one-third on the certificate plan has been granted for those attending the meetings of the Christian Catholic Church in Zion, at the Fourth Feast of Tabernacles, in Zion City, Lake County, Illinois, between July 13 and July 24, 1904, inclusive.

The following directions are submitted for your guidance:

First—Tickets at full fare for the going journey, may be secured within three days, exclusive of Sunday, prior to and during the first three days of the meeting; that is, July 11th, 12th, 13th, 14th, 15th, and 16th.

The advertised dates of the meeting are from July 13th to 24th; consequently you can obtain your tickets not earlier than July 11th and not later than July 17th.

Be sure when purchasing your going ticket to request a certificate.

Second—Present yourself at the railway station for ticket and certificate at least thirty minutes before departure of train.

Third—Certificates are not kept at all stations. If you inquire at your station you will find out whether certificates and through tickets can be obtained to place of meeting; if not, the agent will inform you at what station they can be obtained. You can purchase a local ticket thence, and there take up a certificate and through ticket.

Fourth—On your arrival at the meeting, present your certificate to Deacon James F. Peters, Administration building, Zion City, Illinois.

Fifth—No refund of fare will be made on account of failure to have certificate validated.

Sixth—So as to prevent disappointment, it must be understood that the reduction on returning journey is not guaranteed, but is contingent on an attendance of not less than one hundred persons from all points throughout the United States and Canada showing payment of full first-class fare of not less than seventy-five cents on going journey; provided, however, if the certificates presented fall short of the required minimum, and it shall appear that round trip tickets are held in lieu of certificate, that shall be reckoned in arriving at the minimum.

Seventh—If the necessary minimum is in attendance and your certificate is duly validated, you will be entitled, up to July 26th, to reduced passage ticket to your destination by the route over which you made the going journey at one-third the limit fare.

This rate will apply to the entire United States and Canada.

SPECIAL TRAINS BETWEEN CHICAGO AND ZION CITY.

These trains will be arranged for and announcement will be made later.

CAMP HOLIDAY—1904.

REGULATIONS AND PROVISIONS FOR THE SEASON.

Persons desiring to spend a holiday or attend the great teaching meetings of Zion will find, either as individuals, families or parties, inexpensive tenting conveniences, with good water near at hand, in Zion's tents now in service in Camp Holiday, Zion City.

The tents are made of heavy duck material, strongly stayed, with fly, and are rainproof, being pitched above board floor.

The season's price for tents 9½x14, furnished, is $7; or unfurnished, $5 a month, when taken for two or more months, but not to be sublet.

Tents may be rented by the week at $4 for the first week and $2 a week thereafter.

The Feast of Tabernacles' rate is always $2.25 a person, four persons to a tent; otherwise the rate is double. Single cots for single nights, 25 cents; tent rates a day $1.25.

All rentals payable in advance, in every case, whether by the month, week or day.

THE FURNITURE.

The furniture consists of the necessary cots, mattresses and chairs, one table, water-pail, tin cup, wash basin and slop-pail to a tent. The bedding includes one white sheet two light and one or two heavy blankets, and a pillow and pillow-slip to a single and two of each to double cots. Two-wick oil stoves may be rented for $1 a month, supplied with oil, and cooking utensils, including stew-pans, tin plates, cups, knives, forks and spoons, may be secured at a rental of 50 cents a month.

TENT PROVISIONS AND REGULATIONS FOR 1904.

Two tents may be required in some instances, and these will be cheaper than one large one. Then one can be used for sleeping, and the other for cooking purposes.

During the Feast of Tabernacles, tents will again be located in Camp Esther in Shiloh Park, for which a charge of $2.25 a person for the twelve days will be made; but persons leasing tents in Camp Holiday for at least a two months period may obtain accommodations for the occasion at the season rental price.

Applications for such accommodations or conveniences should be addressed to Deacon James F. Peters, Administration Building, Zion City, Lake County, Illinois.

THE RATES AT ELIJAH HOSPICE

NOW AND DURING THE FEAST OF TABERNACLES ARE AS FOLLOWS:

European Plan—One person in a room, $1.00 a day and up; two persons or more in a room, 50 cents a day and up; one person in a room, $6.00 a week and up; two persons or more in a room, $3.00 a week and up. These rates are for lodging only.

American Plan—One person in a room, $1.75 a day and up; two persons or more in a room, $1.25 a day and up; one person in a room, $10.00 a week and up; two persons or more in a room, $7.00 a week and up; single meals, 25 cents.

Children under twelve years old half rate.

The American Plan includes board and room.

Rooms will be charged for from the date reserved.

FRANK W. COTTON, Manager.

LEAVES OF HEALING.

Two Dollars will bring to you the weekly visits of the Little White Dove for a year; 75 cents will send it to a friend for thirteen weeks; $1.25 will send it for six months; $1.50 will send it to your minister, or to a Y. M. C. A., or to a Public Reading Room for a whole year. We offer no premiums, except the premium of doing good We receive no advertisements, and print no commercial lies or cheating enticements of unscrupulous thieves. LEAVES OF HEALING is Zion on wings, and we keep out everything that would detract the reader's mind from all except the Extension of the Kingdom of God, for which alone it exists. If we cannot send forth our Little White Dove without soiling its wings with the smoke of the factory and the dirt of the wrangling market-place, or compelling it to utter the screaming cries of the business vultures in the ears of our readers, then we will keep our Dove at home.

Notes of Thanksgiving from the Whole World

By J. G. Speicher, Overseer-in-Charge

As the Christ also is the Head of the Church,
Being Himself the Savior of the body.

. . . .

That He might present the Church to Himself a glorious Church,
Not having spot or wrinkle
Or any such thing;
But that it should be holy and without blemish.
—*Ephesians 5:23, 27.*

THE Christ came to establish His Church in the Kingdom of His Father; a Church which should feel the redeeming life and power that He brought to earth; a Church the members of which should develop in spiritual activity, mental power, and physical perfection, and regain their lost estate of Edenic purity of life, thus filling, as His Divine offspring, their places in the economy of God's creation.

He came and lived in the flesh that by His perfection and the example of His overcoming life, we might be free from the curse which fell upon the whole world as the result of the sins of our first parents.

He established a Church, the members of which should be a faithful and pure people, in which the Holy Spirit should dwell, and prepare them for the return of the Christ to earth to receive His own and to meet them in the air as His holy bride, "not having spot or wrinkle, or any such thing, but being holy and without blemish."

They must be holy vessels in which the holy light of His Divine love burns in preparation for His Coming.

It is these who have the quickening life of the Holy Spirit which shall return with Him to establish His Kingdom and rule the earth in godliness and equity.

These are to be the bride of the Christ.

It is not the desire of the Christ that His bride, the Church, shall be of those in which the lack of Godly harmony and the disorder of their association in so-called churches dwarf their spiritual natures and quench the light of Divine life, so that the body is limited in its power and is emaciated by the most violent afflictions which rob the mind of its vigor and sap the body of its vitality.

The Christ has come that His Church may have life and have it more abundantly.

He has promised to bless and heal all those who come to Him.

And having paid the price for their purification and cleansing from sin and its consequences, with His own blood, He will demand that His bride be of those whose vessels are cleansed and whose light is the effulgence of Divine light in them.

May God's faithful people ever realize that they should go from strength to strength, and prepare themselves by Godly living, Godly thinking and Godly working, for the return of the Christ as their Lord and King.

The following testimonies are from those who believe the words of the Psalmist:

No good thing will He withhold
From them that walk uprightly.

O. R.

Instantaneous Healing of Internal Tumors.

And Jesus went about in all Galilee, teaching in their synagogues, and preaching the Gospel of the Kingdom, and healing all manner of disease and all manner of sickness among the people.—*Matthew 4:23*

Jesus Christ is the same yesterday and today, yea, and forever.—*Hebrews 13:8*

STEINMETZSTRASSE 41,
BERLIN, GERMANY, FEBRUARY 3, 1904.

DEAR GENERAL OVERSEER:—Peace to thee.

I am glad to be numbered among those who can praise God for His wonderful healing power.

On May 16, 1903, I wrote to you, asking you to pray for me.

I had two internal tumors, and the suffering which I endured cannot be described.

I was about to undergo an operation by three physicians, when a dear sister, who is now a member of Zion, brought me a copy of BLATTER DER HEILUNG.

I gladly read it, and saw at once that it was God's will to heal me of my terrible disease.

Without hesitating, I abandoned doctors and drugs and turned to God.

I then sent a request for prayer.

About the time when my letter must have reached you, the Devil tormented me with such excruciating pain for three days in succession, that it seemed to become unbearable.

I could not take as much as a drink of water, and the lightest nourishment caused the pains to become more violent than ever.

On the third day the Devil said, "Now you have to send for a doctor."

But thanks be unto God, who enabled me to overcome the tempter and to cry to Him for help and deliverance.

While thus praying, I fell asleep.

I slept all night, and when I awoke, I felt like a different person. My body felt so light, all the terrible swelling having disappeared.

I was able to turn from side to side with the greatest ease, where previously I had not been able to move without suffering intense pain.

I asked for something to eat, for I was hungry.

To God be all the praise and glory for having heard and answered your prayers on my behalf. Surely His love is infinitely great.

It is my earnest prayer to be brought closer to God, and to be made useful in His service. May He give me daily grace and power to work for Him, and to let my light shine in my home, and wherever I am.

I pray God to bless you and to use you to prepare the way for the Lord, and to hasten His coming.

Praying that these words of testimony may be blessed of God, and that they may help poor sufferers to trust God, I am,

Your sister in the Christ,

(MRS.) ROSA SCHMIDT.

Healed of Diphtheria.

Pray one for another,
That ye may be healed.—*James 5:16.*

2911 GIDEON AVENUE, ZION CITY, ILLINOIS.

DEAR GENERAL OVERSEER:—It is with a heart full of gratitude to God that I write these few lines that they may be a help to some one.

I was taken very sick, with a high fever and sore throat, which developed into diphtheria, from which I suffered a great deal.

But God wonderfully heard and answered prayer and gave deliverance, for which we are truly thankful.

My sister and mother also took the diphtheria; but inside of four days they were both able to be about again. Thank God.

The first evening I was taken sick I had a very high fever; but when Deacon Johnson laid hands on me and prayed I felt better right away.

I went to sleep, and when I awoke I was much better.

We thank God for His goodness, and all He has done for us.

Yours in Jesus' Name,

BEATRICE GALLAUGHER.

Daughter Healed of Fever.

I have heard thy prayer,
I have seen thy tears:
Behold, I will heal thee.—*2 Kings 20:5.*

220 SYCAMORE STREET,
WATERLOO, IOWA, January 28, 1904.

OVERSEER SPEICHER:—It is with a very thankful heart that I write to tell you of the deliverance from the fever that little Ruth had.

She was a very sick child, and was very low when I wrote to you on Saturday, but on Monday morning she was very much better. The fever was gone, and she wanted something to eat.

She is as well as usual now, for which I praise the Lord.

I wish to thank you for your prayers in her behalf, and also for your prayers for me.

Respectfully, (MRS.) CHARITY MINIKUS.

God, the Great Physician.

To this end was the Son of God manifested,
That He might destroy the works of the Devil.—*1 John 3:8.*

WEST ALLIS, WISCONSIN, March 9, 1904.

DEAR OVERSEER SPEICHER:—I desire to let you know that when the dispatch was sent to you on February 21st to pray for me, that prayer was answered and God healed me.

I thank you, and give God all the glory.

May God bless you and Zion everywhere.

Your sister in the Christ,

(MRS.) ROSENA MAARKEE.

Zion Literature Sent Out from a Free Distribution Fund Provided by Zion's Guests and the Friends of Zion.

Report for the week ending May 14, 1904:

1,247 Rolls to.........Hotels in the United States
6,234 Rolls to.........Various States in the Union
1,796 Rolls to Hotels in Europe, Asia, Africa, and to the Islands of the Sea.
67 Rolls to..........................Germany
Number of Rolls for the Week............. 9,344
Number of Rolls reported to May 14, 1904, 3,145,770

EVANGELIST SARAH E. HILL,
Superintendent Zion Literature Mission,
Zion City, Illinois.

Zion's Bible Class

Conducted by Deacon Daniel Sloan in Shiloh Tabernacle, Zion City, Lord's Day Morning at 11 o'clock, and in Zion Homes and Gatherings throughout the World.

MID-WEEK BIBLE CLASS LESSON, JUNE 8th or 9th.

Judging Righteously.

1. *The judge's relation to God comes first.*—Micah 6:8, 9.
   Man sins first against God.
   Man must seek to do right in God's sight.
   He must show the mind of God.
2. *The Holy Spirit of God is necessary.*—Isaiah 11:2-5.
   God's Spirit brightens the thought.
   God's Spirit quickens the discernment.
   God's Spirit broadens the judgment.
3. *Use care in all you hear and observe before deciding.*—2 Chronicles 19:6, 7.
   One must be careful in judging.
   One must not make a mistake.
   One must be without partiality.
4. *Tact in questioning will reveal much.*—1 Kings 3:16-28.
   The spirit shown reveals the fault.
   The one questioned may show he does not care what happens.
   The heart is the cause of every action.
5. *The hearing of both sides must be gone into.*—Proverbs 18:10-15.
   No one must decide on hearsay evidence.
   Both sides must be heard.
   Care must be taken that the one first heard does not warp the judgment.
6. *Sift the aggressor thoroughly; he may be vindictive or guilty.*—Proverbs 18:16-24.
   A person may clamor loudly to justify self.
   The investigation must be searching.
   Men must watch lest they give offense.
7. *Be sure there is just cause for the action proposed.*—Proverbs 3:27-32.
   Do not contest over trifles.
   Do not be too sensitive.
   Do not be hasty or rash.
8. *Watch lest the advocates are too partisan or too zealous for their case.*—Proverbs 24:21-29.
   Do not make a construction to fit the case.
   Do not give an eye for an eye.
   Give a true answer to the question.
9. *There may be malice or revenge, and not a willingness to do good.*—Romans 12:17-21.
   Do not wrong a man because he wronged you.
   Compromise the case yourself.
   Blot out the offense by some good deed.
   The Lord Our God is a Righteously-judging God.

LORD'S DAY BIBLE CLASS LESSON, JUNE 12th.

Rules for Settling Differences or Enforcing Discipline.

1. *Offenses grow out of daily duties and relations.*—Luke 17:1-10.
   Some always blunder.
   Some give few offenses.
   Some love to make strife.
2. *The conscience should daily scan all events lest harm be done.*—Acts 24:10-16.
   Live to do no wrongs or harm.
   Do not let wrath find place within you.
   Learn to give the soft answer.
3. *When we know some one is offended we should seek reconciliation.*—Matthew 5:21-26.
   Do not expect the person to come to you.
   You must get forgiveness; then God is pleased.
   Give in; do not contend to the last.
4. *Be forgiving and merciful and you will obtain favor.*—Matthew 7:1-6.
   Do not condemn others for what you yourself are guilty of.
   Do not be hard on little sins when you commit big ones.
   Consider how merciful God has been to you.
5. *Be patient and reasonable and observe the Church rule.*—Matthew 18:15-22.
   See the person alone.
   Get one or two godly persons to go with you.
   Pray together as the Church advises.
6. *Do not resort to law to establish anything but legal rights.*—1 Corinthians 6:1-8.
   How shamefully Christians treat each other!
   Some are full of vengeance.
   Have you grace enough to take a wrong?
7. *Have no fellowship with wicked persons who will not be penitent.*—1 Timothy 5:20-25.
   Do not be afraid to warn sinners.
   Do not be partial to any man.
   Be sure you are right, then rebuke the sin.
8. *The law must be vindicated and honored in every serious breach.*—Romans 13:1-10.
   Law makes the earth habitable.
   The lawless break down all law.
   Uphold all officers who enforce law.
   God's Holy People are a Compassionate People.

OBEYING GOD IN BAPTISM.

"Baptizing Them Into the Name of the Father and of the Son and of the Holy Ghost."

Eighteen Thousand Three Hundred Seventy-nine Baptisms by Triune Immersion Since March 14, 1897.

Eighteen Thousand Three Hundred Seventy-nine Believers have joyfully followed their Lord in the Ordinance of Believer's Baptism by Triune Immersion since the first Baptism in Central Zion Tabernacle on March 14, 1897.

Baptized in Central Zion Tabernacle from March 14, 1897, to December 14, 1901, by the General Overseer	4754			
Baptized in South Side Zion Tabernacle from January 1, 1902, to June 14, 1903, by the General Overseer	37			
Baptized at Zion City by the General Overseer	583			
Baptized by Overseers, Elders, Evangelists and Deacons, at Headquarters (Zion City) and Chicago	4940			
Total Baptized at Headquarters				10,314
Baptized in places outside of Headquarters by the General Overseer		641		
Baptized in places outside of Headquarters by Overseers, Elders, Evangelists and Deacons		7091		
Total Baptized outside of Headquarters				7,732
Total Baptized in seven years				18,046
Baptized since March 14, 1904:				
Baptized in Zion City by Elder Royall	63			
Baptized in Zion City by Elder Hammond	90			
Baptized in Zion City by Elder Adams	40			
Baptized in Chicago by Elder Hall	5			
Baptized in Chicago by Elder Cossum	15			
Baptized in Chicago by Evangelist Christie	3			
Baptized in Chicago by Deacon Matson	2			
Baptized in Chicago by Elder Kosch	6		224	
Baptized in California by Elder Taylor		5		
Baptized in Canada by Elder Simmons		6		
Baptized in Canada by Elder Brooks		4		
Baptized in Colorado by Deacon Cook		3		
Baptized in England by Overseer Cantel		10		
Baptized in Illinois by Deacon Sprecher		1		
Baptized in Minnesota by Elder Graves		5		
Baptized in New York by Elder Warszawiak		14		
Baptized in New York by Overseer Mason		19		
Baptized in Ohio by Deacon Arrington		7		
Baptized in Ohio by Deacon Kelchner		2		
Baptized in Pennsylvania by Elder Bouck		11		
Baptized in Texas by Evangelist Gay		13		
Baptized in Washington by Elder Simmons		1		
Baptized in Washington by Elder Ernst		8	109	333
Total Baptized since March 14, 1897				18,379

The following-named believer was baptized at Vancouver, British Columbia, Canada, Lord's Day, April 10, 1904, by Elder R. M. Simmons:

Jorgensen, Hans Jorgen Christian, Hasting street, Vancouver, British Columbia, Canada

The following-named five believers were baptized at Caledonian Road Baths, London, England, Lord's Day, April 24, 1904, by Overseer H. E. Cantel:

Barnes, William Henry Francis, Claremont avenue, Guilford road, Woking, Surrey, England
Hubbard, Miss Amelia Ruth Rose, 14 Hillfield Park, Muswell Hill, N. London, England
Ilsley, Louis George . 98 Hemingford road, Barnsbury, N. London, England
Lancaster, Mrs. Emily ...... 73 Hoe street, Walthamstow, Essex, England
Schronfeld, Friedrick August, 2 Straud Green road, Finsbury Park, N. London, England

The following-named eight believers were baptized at San Antonio, Texas, Lord's Day, April 24, 1904, by Evangelist William D. Gay:

Anderson, Harvey .... Rural Delivery No. 8, San Antonio, Texas
Anderson, Mrs. I. V. .... Rural Delivery No. 8, San Antonio, Texas
Lee, Mrs. Annie .... 1114 Colorado avenue, San Antonio, Texas
Marshall, Miss Bertha .... 610 Day street, San Antonio, Texas
Marshall, Ollie Thomas .... 610 Day street, San Antonio, Texas
Miller, Mrs. S. .... 616 North Center street, San Antonio, Texas
Stanley, Mrs Lula .... Rural Delivery No. 8, San Antonio, Texas
Stanley, William Henry, Sr. .... Rural Delivery No. 8, San Antonio, Texas

The following-named believer was baptized at San Antonio, Texas, Wednesday, April 27, 1904, by Evangelist William D. Gay:

Davis, John Smith .... 2807 West Houston street, San Antonio, Texas

The following-named two believers were baptized in the West Side Zion Tabernacle, Chicago, Illinois, Lord's Day, May 1, 1904, by Elder Lemuel C. Hall:

Bolich, Mrs. Lillian .... 373 Cornell street, Chicago, Illinois
Schulz, Mrs. Wilhelmina .... 1506 North Ridgeway avenue, Chicago, Illinois

The following-named believer was baptized at San Francisco, California, Lord's Day, May 1, 1904, by Elder W. D. Taylor:

Schwobel, Marie Emilie .... 1623 Fruitvale avenue, Fruitvale, California

The following-named thirty-two believers were baptized in Shiloh Tabernacle, Zion City, Illinois, Lord's Day, May 8, 1904, by Elder Gideon Hammond:

Baker, Miss Rosa .... 2009 Horeb avenue, Zion City, Illinois
Balliet, Fred .... 2009 Hebron avenue, Zion City, Illinois
Boyce, Miss Ella .... 2307 Gilboa avenue, Zion City, Illinois
Boyer, Wade Nicholas .... 3200 Ezekiel avenue, Zion City, Illinois
Carey, Miss Mary May .... 2709 Elizabeth avenue, Zion City, Illinois
Elsworth, Mrs. Ida .... Edina Hospice, Zion City, Illinois
Farrell, Lizzie .... Edina Hospice, Zion City, Illinois
Hayes, Mrs. Adah .... 3112 Elizabeth avenue, Zion City, Illinois
Hayes, John .... 3112 Elizabeth avenue, Zion City, Illinois
Hubbi, Miss Florence .... 2703 Gilead avenue, Zion City, Illinois
Johnson, Margaret E. .... 3112 Emmaus avenue, Zion City, Illinois
Kirkendall, Miss Amy .... 3213 Elisha avenue, Zion City, Illinois
McGillivray, Miss Beulah .... 2003 Horeb avenue, Zion City, Illinois
Mudgett, Solon .... 1704 Hebron avenue, Zion City, Illinois
Orr, Martha B. .... 2816 Elizabeth avenue, Zion City, Illinois
Perry, Miss Martha C. .... South Wayne, Wisconsin
Plickle, Fredrick .... 3015 Emmaus avenue, Zion City, Illinois
Pyle, George W. .... 2802 Emmaus avenue, Zion City, Illinois
Raper, Merrill Arthur .... 2308 Hermon avenue, Zion City, Illinois
Raper, Wesley .... 1813 Hermon avenue, Zion City, Illinois
Richardson, Mrs. Ethel .... 2711 Enoch avenue, Zion City, Illinois
Schneider, Mrs. Mary .... 2712 Ezekiel avenue, Zion City, Illinois
Smith, Annie .... Edina Hospice, Zion City, Illinois
Stewart, Robert Clyde Hamilton .... 3001 Ezekiel avenue, Zion City, Illinois
Stow, Miss Bessie .... 2403 Gilboa avenue, Zion City, Illinois
Watson, Stanley .... 2806 Eshcol avenue, Zion City, Illinois
Watson, Miss Theresa Inez .... 2806 Eshcol avenue, Zion City, Illinois
Wehling, Frank .... 3214 Gabriel avenue, Zion City, Illinois
Wheelock, Miss Helen Louise .... 2819 Ezra avenue, Zion City, Illinois
Wheelock, Willie .... 2819 Ezra avenue, Zion City, Illinois
White, John Washington Mussle .... Bayou Labatre, Alabama
Wilson, Alexander Ford .... 3002 Gilead avenue, Zion City, Illinois

The following-named five believers were baptized at Seattle, Washington, Lord's Day, May 1, 1904, by Elder August Ernst:

Denniston, Clara Isaacson .... 717 East Pike street, Seattle, Washington
Denniston, Samuel Alexander .... Colby, Washington
Herzog, John Jacob .... 1617 South K street, Tacoma, Washington
Larsen, Miss Carrie May .... Tacoma, Washington
Waterson, Mrs. Christine .... Tacoma, Washington

The following-named four believers were baptized at San Antonio, Texas, Lord's Day, May 8, 1904, by Evangelist William D. Gay:

Conselman, Mrs. Cora .... 200 Cedar street, Montgomery, Alabama
Flores, Miss Martha .... 609 St. Mary street, San Antonio, Texas
Garretson, John Wesley .... 308 North Pine street, San Antonio, Texas
Ireland, Mrs. Jennie Warwick .... San Antonio, Texas

The following-named three believers were baptized at Philadelphia, Pennsylvania, Lord's Day, May 8, 1904, by Elder R. N. Bouck:

Ahrens, Mrs. F. Emily .... 924 Filbert street, Philadelphia, Pennsylvania
Creekmore, Mrs. W. E., 1154 North Thirty-second st., Camden, New Jersey
Deichert, Philip .... 545 North Vanango, Philadelphia, Pennsylvania

The following-named twenty-two believers were baptized in Shiloh Tabernacle, Zion City, Illinois, Lord's Day, May 15, 1904, by Elder Gideon Hammond:

Asplin, Miss Flora .... 3021 Gabriel avenue, Zion City, Illinois
Aznoe, Miss Nina .... 748 Carmel boulevard, Zion City, Illinois
Bell, Miss Nellie .... 2101 Emmaus avenue, Zion City, Illinois
Bowley, Miss Ethel .... 2209 Elisha avenue, Zion City, Illinois
Boyer, Della .... Lindsey, Ohio
Bozeman, Miss Alice .... 3105 Gilead avenue, Zion City, Illinois
Caldwell, Mrs. Alice .... Litchfield, Michigan
Carr, Alden .... 2409 Elisha avenue, Zion City, Illinois
Ferris, Herbert .... 3019 Gilead avenue, Zion City, Illinois
Fleming, David .... 2106 Enoch avenue, Zion City, Illinois
Hurlbut, Mrs. Ella .... 3117 Eshcol avenue, Zion City, Illinois
Hurst, Miss Minnie .... 2719 Elim avenue, Zion City, Illinois
Jones, Miss Naomi .... 2807 Ezra avenue, Zion City, Illinois
Markle, Miss Frances .... 2710 Eshcol avenue, Zion City, Illinois
Meloche, Villiars Wilson .... 3102 Enoch avenue, Zion City, Illinois
Pain, Mrs. Carrie .... Jackson, Michigan
Peterman, Pierre .... Mount Carmel, Zion City, Illinois
Rodd, Bruce W. .... 2604 Elim avenue, Zion City, Illinois
Walker, Miss Phœbe .... 2203 Gilead avenue, Zion City, Illinois
Whitrock, William F. .... Zion City, Illinois
Williams, Miss Leona .... 2802 Elisha avenue, Zion City, Illinois
Williams, Miss Neva .... 2802 Elisha avenue, Zion City, Illinois

The following-named five believers were baptized in Minneapolis, Minnesota, Lord's Day, May 15, 1904, by Elder F. A. Graves:

Fowler, Mrs. Maria H., 1778 Girard avenue South, Minneapolis, Minnesota
Hanson, Miss Anna Charlottie, 3427 Colfax avenue North, Minneapolis, Minnesota
Knowles, Lewis T., 2923 California street, N. E., Minneapolis, Minnesota
Mundem, Anna Serena, 338 East Fifteenth street, Minneapolis, Minnesota
Royse, Mrs. D. M. .... 2524 Fifth avenue South, Minneapolis, Minnesota

The following-named two believers were baptized in Zion Tabernacle, Cleveland, Ohio, Lord's Day, May 15, 1904, by Deacon C. F. Kelchner:

Schultz, Mrs. Delia .... 158 Alger street, Cleveland, Ohio
Schultz, T. Reinhardt .... 158 Alger street, Cleveland, Ohio

A WEEKLY PAPER FOR THE EXTENSION OF THE KINGDOM OF GOD

EDITED BY THE REV. JOHN ALEX. DOWIE.

Volume XV. No. 6. *ZION CITY, SATURDAY, MAY 28, 1904.* *Price Five Cents*

GOD'S WITNESSES TO DIVINE HEALING.

HEALED OF CHRONIC INTERNAL DISEASES.

ETHIOPIA SHALL HASTE TO STRETCH OUT HER HANDS UNTO GOD.

. . . .

FOR THEY SHALL HEAR OF THY GREAT NAME, AND OF THY MIGHTY HAND, AND OF THY STRETCHED OUT ARM, WHEN HE SHALL COME AND PRAY TOWARD THIS HOUSE;

HEAR THOU IN HEAVEN, THY DWELLING-PLACE, AND DO ACCORDING TO ALL THAT THE STRANGER CALLETH TO THEE FOR; THAT ALL THE PEOPLES OF THE EARTH MAY KNOW THY NAME, TO FEAR THEE.

There are at this time in the United States more than eight million Ethiopians.

It is estimated that there are in the world only eight to ten million Jews.

We have, then, at our very doors, more of the sons of Ham than there are children of Judah in all the world.

From about four million colored people in America in 1860, they have grown to more than eight millions, or double, in a little over forty years.

A mighty empire has arisen within our own borders. God is wonderfully blessing many of the so-called lesser peoples. Japan with a population of thirty millions in 1870 has today within her boundary more than forty-five million people; and this without any immigration to speak of. When we consider the fact that during the past year nearly one million of people have come into America from foreign countries, and that during the last twenty years there have come probably more than five million people from other lands, so that today it is safe to say that we have a population of which at least fifteen per cent. are either foreign-born or children of foreign-born parents, the growth of the colored population is phenomenal, for theirs is almost entirely an increase of native-born population.

MRS. SWEADIE TILLMAN.

No one who makes a study of the colored race can doubt for a moment that it has a great future and a mighty destiny before it.

Ethiopia will be heard, for God is with her.

She cannot be trampled under foot continuously with impunity.

The colored people will have to be recognized as human beings, by North and South alike.

It is no longer a question as to which section treats the colored race the better, but the question comes as to who will treat it fairly. We rejoice that in Zion there is a refuge for all the races, without distinction, and that as Ethiopia stretches out her hands to God she finds the same loving Father that all other nations and races are finding.

The once poor, miserable, sick, helpless, dying woman who tells the story of her wonderful deliverance is only one of hundreds of her race who have found the same deliverance in Zion.

The story of the healing power of God is one that is readily accepted by the mind of the colored people, who as a rule are intensely religious, but who have been heart-sore and hungry for many centuries, having turned away from the face of God, because of their sins, and finding no resting-place and no refuge in all the earth.

Being outcast and helpless they rejoice to find in God not a monster with a stern and hideous face, but a loving Father and Savior.

It is not enough that we should receive the light of a full salvation in this land. We must take it to the dying millions in heathen lands.

Let the word go forth, that God has promised the heathen for an inheritance for the Christ, and as His inheritance He has given His life for them, not only that they may be saved in spirit, and freed from their superstition and darkness, but that they may be healed of all their sickness.

Over the ocean's wave, far, far away,
There the poor heathen live, waiting for day;
Groping in ignorance, dark as the night;
No blessed Zion to give them the light.

Here in this happy land, we have the light,
Shining from God's own Word, free, pure and bright.
Shall we not send to them messengers true,
Teachers and preachers and all who will go?

Then while the mission ships tidings bring,
List as they, heaven bound, joyfully sing:
"Over the ocean wave, oh, see them come!
Bringing the Bread of Life, guiding us Home."

J. G. S.

WRITTEN TESTIMONY OF MRS. SWEADIE TILLMAN.

2503 GILBOA AVENUE, ZION CITY, ILLINOIS, April 24, 1904.

DEAR GENERAL OVERSEER:—I know that I have neglected writing my testimony too long.

I suffered for eight years with female weakness of the worst kind.

At times I would swell so large that I could not get my clothes on.

I could not let the doctors touch me at times because I was so sore.

There were days that I could not bear to have any one walk across the floor because it would cause severe pain.

I was in so much misery at times that I would walk the floor all night.

Like many others, I tried every doctor who came along and said that he could heal.

I took medicine and treatment from so many that I cannot remember their names.

I thought but little about God, because I thought he was a poor God to let His children suffer as I did.

I would only ask Him to let me die to be out of my misery.

I was like the woman spoken of in Mark 5:25, who had the issue of blood, and had suffered many things of many physicians.

My diseases were bleeding piles, indigestion, stomach trouble, eczema and female trouble.

The last severe spell I had was in September, 1900, in Chicago, Illinois.

I had made friends with my neighbor, whose two daughters had been healed of consumption through your prayers in Zion; but this dear old mother did not tell me of Zion at first.

I told her how sickly I was, and all she said to me was, "If you get sick, I will help you all I can."

So, sure enough, the Devil gave me one of those terrible spells, and, according to her promise, she came over.

She told me of you, dear General Overseer, and how you prayed for her daughter when she was dying of consumption, and how she was healed.

So I asked to see her daughter, Carrie Coleman, and she sent Carrie over to see me.

She told me that I must repent, turn to God, confess to my fellow men, and trust God, and He would heal me.

She told me how she had been healed.

She taught me for three days, and I made things right with God during that time.

On the third day I grew worse, and thought that I would die.

I sent for Miss Coleman, and when she came in I was covered with perspiration.

I told her that I would accept God as my Healer at that moment.

So she prayed the Prayer of Faith, and God heard and healed me in the selfsame hour.

All pain ceased, and about a cupfull of corruption passed from my body.

When my husband came in I was up cooking dinner.

He asked me if I was crazy, but I simply said that I had accepted God as my Healer and I was well.

I thank God that He healed me of that terrible sickness.

I have never been troubled with it from that day to this.

My weight then was about one hundred forty pounds, and now I weigh one hundred eighty-one.

I have been strong ever since.

I thank God that He raised you up, dear General Overseer, to lead us out of darkness into the light.

May God bless you and your family.

Trusting that my testimony may be a blessing to many who suffer, I am,

Your sister in the Christ,

(MRS.) SWEADIE TILLMAN.

Notes of Thanksgiving From the Whole World

By J. G. Speicher, Overseer-in-Charge.

Healed of Rheumatism and Measles.

The fear of Jehovah is a fountain of life.—*Proverbs 14:27.*

388 HOYLES AVENUE, AURORA, ILLINOIS, February 3, 1904.

MY DEAR OVERSEER SPEICHER:—I was taken very sick last week with rheumatism and measles.

I became worse, the rheumatism was very painful, especially in my chest, around my heart, and I had to lie in one position, on my right side. I suffered excruciating pain.

Then a telegram was sent to you to pray for me.

In a few hours I felt much better and soon I could turn myself over in bed.

I thank you very much, dear Overseer, for your kind interest and prayers.

Faithfully your sister in the Christ,

HELEN ZAISER,

Deaconess in the Christian Catholic Church in Zion.

Child Healed of Weak Eyes.

And Jesus, being moved with compassion, touched their eyes
And straightway they received their sight.—*Matthew 20:34.*

BLOOMINGTON, NEBRASKA, March 7, 1904.

DEAR GENERAL OVERSEER:—I have thought for some time that I ought to write this testimony and send it in, as it might be the means of helping some one else to trust God for healing.

I thank God that He sent you, Elijah the Restorer, to teach us the full Gospel instead of a part of it, and that Jesus is just as able and willing to heal now as when on earth in the body.

Our little boy, Dean, had complained so much of his eyes, saying that it was hard to study because he could not see well; there were big spots before his eyes.

In August, 1903, I took him to a specialist who was here from Kansas City.

He examined them and said that there was no help for him but to wear glasses.

I did not want my little boy only eight years old to wear glasses.

A dear friend, Mrs. Lake, of Republican City, Nebraska, had told us of many wonderful healings through prayer, and also gave us LEAVES OF HEALING to read

After reading it I said, "God will heal my boy's eyes, too."

I wrote to you for prayer. You prayed for him August 25th and his eyes were instantly healed.

We thank God for all He has done for us since.

We thank you for your teaching and prayers.

We have used no medicine since last August.

We became members of the Christian Catholic Church in Zion, in January, 1904, and expect to go to Zion City to live as soon as we can.

May God bless and keep you till your work is done.

Yours in Jesus' Name,

(MRS.) MARY E. MORSE.

Wife Delivered of Grip.

Surely He hath borne our sicknesses
And carried our sorrows.—*Isaiah 53:4.*

FOUNTAIN CITY, WISCONSIN, March 21, 1904.

DEAR OVERSEER SPEICHER:—Peace to thee.

Two weeks ago my dear wife was very sick with grip.

One night she had severe pain in her breast.

The next day I sent a request to you for prayer.

God heard and answered the prayer instantly.

The next night she had a good sleep and in the morning was able to do her housework.

We thank God, our Heavenly Father, and thank you, dear Overseer, for your kindness.

Your brother in the Christ,

GEORGE BAUMANN, SR.

ELIJAH THE RESTORER

A WEEKLY PAPER FOR THE EXTENSION OF THE KINGDOM OF GOD.

EDITED BY THE REV. JOHN ALEX. DOWIE

Application for entry as Second Class Matter at Zion City, Illinois, pending.

Subscription Rates.		Special Rates.	
One Year	$2.00	100 Copies of One Issue	$3.00
Six Months	1.25	25 Copies of One Issue	1.00
Three Months	.75	To Ministers, Y. M. C. A's and Public	
Single Copies	05	Reading Rooms, per annum	1.50

For foreign subscriptions add $1.50 per year, or three cents per copy for postage.
Subscribers desiring a change of address should give present address, as well as that to which they desire LEAVES OF HEALING sent in the future.
Make Bank Drafts, Express Money or Postoffice Money Orders payable to the order of JOHN ALEX. DOWIE, Zion City, Illinois, U. S. A.
Long Distance Telephone. *Cable Address "Dowie, Zion City."*
All communications upon business must be addressed to
MANAGER ZION PUBLISHING HOUSE,
Zion City, Illinois, U. S. A.

Subscriptions to LEAVES OF HEALING, A VOICE FROM ZION, and the various publications may also be sent to
ZION PUBLISHING HOUSE, 81 EUSTON ROAD, LONDON, N. W., ENGLAND
ZION PUBLISHING HOUSE, NO. 43 PARK ROAD, ST. KILDA, MELBOURNE, VICTORIA, AUSTRALIA.
ZION PUBLISHING HOUSE, RUE DE MONT, THABOR 1, PARIS, FRANCE.
ZIONSHEIM, SCHLOSS LIEBBURG, CANTON THURGAU, BEI ZÜRICH, SWITZERLAND.

ZION CITY, ILLINOIS, SATURDAY, MAY 28, 1904.

TABLE OF CONTENTS.

LEAVES OF HEALING, SATURDAY, MAY 28, 1904.

Notes From The Overseer-in-Charge.

"I HAVE SET THEE FOR A LIGHT OF THE GENTILES;
THAT THOU SHOULDEST BE FOR SALVATION UNTO THE UTTERMOST PART OF THE EARTH."

AND AS the Gentiles heard this they were glad,
And glorified the Word of God:
And as many as were ordained to eternal life believed;
And the Word of the Lord was spread abroad throughout all the region.

THESE WORDS were spoken by the Apostle Paul, to prove that the Christ had come for the salvation of the Gentiles as well as the Jews.

He quoted from the Prophet Isaiah, where we find these words:

I, Jehovah, have called Thee in righteousness;
And will hold Thine hand, and will keep Thee,
And give Thee for a Covenant of the people,
For a Light of the Gentiles.

THIS IDEA is repeated in the Gospel according to St. Luke, in the words of Simeon:

Mine eyes have seen Thy salvation,
Which Thou hast prepared before the face of all peoples;
A light for revelation to the Gentiles,
And the glory of Thy people Israel.

WHILE SALVATION is of the Jews, it is for the Gentiles and Jews alike.

CONFUCIANISM, BUDDHISM and the other allied religions of Asia, which hold in the bondage of heathenism more than six hundred millions of the human race, must be destroyed and the people set free by the preaching of the Gospel of the Lord Jesus, the Christ.

MOHAMMEDANISM, with its aggressive religion of sensualism, is doomed to decay, for the conquest of the Christ is coming, and Islam must yield to the sway of King Immanuel.

THE PAGANISM of darkest Africa, and of the Islands of the Sea, must clear away like the mists before the rising sun, in the light that is breaking forth from the Sun of Righteousness.

BUT THE first great work to be done is the work of Restoration of those who have a knowledge of the Christ, but who still are in the darkness of the apostasies.

Their light has been bedimmed by the superstitions and false theologies of their moss-bound sectarianism.

OF ALL the world the people most to be pitied are those who think they have the Gospel of the Lord Jesus, the Christ, and are deceived.

OF THE five hundred million nominal Christians, only a small handful have a living and abiding faith.

THE HEATHENISM in the church, the unbelief in the ministers, and the control of the whole system by the Baal worshipers—Freemasons—makes a picture that is dark indeed.

WERE IT not for our confidence in God, the task would seem almost hopeless.

WE ARE not among those artificial rain-makers, who expect to help out the work of Jehovah by patent means.

God has promised to water the thirsty earth, and He is able to do it.

He has promised that His Word should not return to Him void.

IT MAKES little difference as to whether the apostate denominations have failed or not—and they have failed to carry on the work of Jehovah to a successful issue—the church, as organized today, has had ample opportunity to prove its capability, and its almost utter failure to maintain the Gospel in its own organization is evident to all.

THE WORK must be done by new forces and new agencies.

GOD HAS called into existence the Christian Catholic Church in Zion to undertake the enormous task in which the churches have failed.

The wonderful work that has already been done in the few years of the history of this Church, and the wonderful interest manifested everywhere in our beloved General Overseer, is gratifying, to say the least.

ALTHOUGH HINDERED to a large extent in Australia, yet thousands gladly heard and received the Gospel, and are today enlisting under the Banner of Zion, and are accepting the New Covenant of a Full Salvation.

AND NOW as he begins his labors in Europe, still greater things can be hoped for.

THE FOLLOWING cablegram shows very briefly how God is blessing in Switzerland:

ZURICH.

SPEICHER, Zion City, Illinois.

Praise God for Pentecost.

The River of God is full of water.

We had a good week in Paris, much blessing in the meetings there.

Received a splendid reception last night in Zurich.

Members and friends of Zion from many nations are here.

About one thousand five hundred present at the opening of the Visitation this morning. Perfect order and intense earnestness prevails.

Love from Zion in Switzerland to Zion everywhere.

Overseer Jane Dowie is with son in France, she being compelled to rest.

Pray for them and us.

Mizpah. DOWIE.

UP TO the date of publication no word has been received of any disturbances of any kind.

THE ZURICH PAPERS have been anticipating the coming to Zürich of the General Overseer, by publishing accounts of his life and work. The following extracts are from a German paper, the *Zuricher Anzeiger*, translated by Elder John Dietrich, of Zion City. There are portions of the article which are omitted, as it is too long to publish here complete, and only a brief review is given.

THE PROPHET ELIJAH VISITS ZURICH, FROM 22d TO 29th OF MAY.

We are not advertising Dowie. It is not to be taken lightly, there is something behind it. Look out. Examine all things, keep the best. By shaking your heads you cannot contend with the facts. We say this without Dr. Dowie's side nor the contrary. He is not a stranger here, for he was here two years ago and preached mightily and not as the Pharisees. The press is against him. We found him not mild, but very severe and bold. We thought him gone and forgotten. We heard of a Zion City and thought it an American humbug; but perchance, there came a sketch of Zion City to our desk from a direct source, from a neutral writer, whose honesty we could not doubt. We became interested, still more interested by finding men of learning, without selfish interests, joining Dowie's followers; for instance, Mr. Clibborn, brother to the son-in-law of General Booth.

We find here in Zurich a gathering of about five hundred members under the leadership of Elder C. Hodler, who with his wife, has been in Zion City and become a convinced and strong follower.

We became more enlightened by reading Zion Literature and Dr. Dowie became something great in our eyes.

Then follows a brief history of the General Overseer, telling how he not only turned from business to preach the Gospel, but also refused the portfolio of minister of education offered him by Sir Henry Parks; how, after his remarkable healing in early life, he preached the Full Gospel for spirit, soul and body, eventually going to America where he encountered opposition but became victorious to such an extent that the Banner of Zion now floats over all the world.

Referring to Zion City, the writer makes mention of its bank, stores, Tabernacles, factories, power-house, beautiful homes, etc., its six thousand acres of land, thousands of inhabitants living without pork, tobacco, alcohol, medicines or theaters; eight-hour workday, and good wages.

He speaks of Zion as practical and Theocratic, and commends its apostolic teaching of holy living and healing through faith in God.

His comment concerning the General Overseer's meetings in Zurich is that he teaches with power.

The article closes with an emphatic protest against the narrow-mindedness of those people who withheld the Town Hall and Theater for the meetings in the free country of Switzerland.

IT REMAINS to be said that under the British flag there is less protection for a minister of the Gospel than under the flag of any of the other so-called civilized nations.

There is more downright disregard for law and order in the British possessions than in any other countries visited by the General Overseer.

ASIDE FROM the mean, petty, little, disgusting acts of a bum mayor of Chicago and his coterie of political henchmen, in trying to enforce an illegal ordinance upon Zion, the police and constabularies of the cities have done all they could to protect the life and property of our General Overseer, and nowhere has he been seriously disturbed in all America, but has been able to conduct every meeting in peace and order, with very few minor exceptions.

WE LOOK for no difficulty throughout Europe, save in London.

BUT THE Gospel must be preached, and as the Prophet Elijah the Restorer, he must open the Gates of all the world, that Zion may enter with her good news of the Coming of the King.

MANY THINGS of interest have come to us concerning the Around-the-World Visitation, besides those that are published from time to time in the printed reports of the General Associate Editor, Deacon Arthur W. Newcomb, who is the Special Correspondent for the Visitation party. We are sure all our readers have enjoyed the excellent reports received from him from time to time. His graphic and picturesque style of writing is very entertaining.

The following private letter was received from him a few days ago:

ON BOARD THE ROYAL MAIL STEAMSHIP MONGOLIA,
IN THE SUEZ CANAL,
ABOUT HALF-WAY BETWEEN SUEZ AND PORT SAID, EGYPT.
Monday, May 2, 1904.

REV. J. G. SPEICHER, M. D., Overseer-in-charge,
Zion City, Illinois, United States of America.

Dear Overseer:—As we expect to arrive at Port Said some time tonight, and as there is an express steamer taking the mails from there on to Europe and the United States, I take advantage of the opportunity to write you a few lines to let you and the people know a little of the details of our long voyage through the Indian Ocean, the Arabian Sea, the Gulf of Aden, the Red Sea, and the Suez Canal. I will write the full account as soon as I get to Zurich, and you will probably receive it in time to follow immediately after the account of our last few days in Australia.

We all agree that the voyage has been a most pleasant one; that the ship is a most excellent one, comfortable and seaworthy, and that, for the most part, the officers, crew and passengers have been very kind, respectful and friendly. Except for very severe heat from about April 18th to 30th, we have had exceptionally fine weather all the way, so that there has been no seasickness in the Zion party since the first day in the great Australian Bight, and no very serious cases even then.

The ship was comfortably filled when we left Adelaide. At Fremantle, Western Australia, a few disembarked, among them Deacon C. Friend Hawkins, who had accompanied us to Western Australia on Zion business. More joined us here, however, and still more at Colombo, where we took on passengers from Singapore, Japan and China, among them several British naval officers from the scene of hostility on the Yellow Sea. At Aden, we took on a large number of passengers from Bombay and other Indian ports and places, and now the vessel is very crowded.

There have been many games, concerts and other amusements to pass away the time quickly, en route, and we have participated in such of these as were innocent. We have also enjoyed the services of the Lord's Day, when all passengers have gathered in the first saloon, and the Church of England service has been read by the Captain and by Bishop Cassell, who is returning to England with his family, after fourteen years' work with the China Inland Mission. But we have greatly missed the privilege of assembling ourselves together, daily, to read the Word of God, to hear the teaching of our General Overseer, and to join together in prayer. Religion, on a P. & O. liner is fixed by rule at just so much, and no more is permitted.

At Fremantle, some of us visited Perth, the Capital of Western Australia; at Colombo, we took train to Kandy, the ancient capital of Ceylon, fifty-two miles inland, through most beautiful and interesting tropical scenery. Our party stayed two days in Ceylon. At Aden, which is a bare, forbidding, fortified rock, the party spent a few hours in visiting some great reservoirs, four miles from the city, said to have been built by King Solomon, and called, therefore, "Solomon's Tanks." None of us have been ashore at Suez or any point along the canal.

The Red Sea, of course, is as blue as any other part of the great, briny deep, and is so wide that we were out of sight of land, at times for more than twenty-four hours. Then, perhaps, we would see a barren island. We saw a range of mountains in which Mount Sinai is said to have a place, but it is doubtful whether we actually saw the mountain where the Law was given. There is also great doubt as to where the children of Israel crossed the Red Sea, especially on account of many changes that have taken place in the topography of the country since that time. We could see, nevertheless, that the place must have been very wild and barren, and that the ancient people of God must have been terribly thirsty when they reached Marah, after traveling three days and nights without water.

The Suez Canal runs through a very sandy, desert country, for the most part, and there is very little of beauty and not much of interest in the passage. The signal stations, that have been placed at frequent intervals along the canal, are very pretty and well kept, and the "sweetwater canal" that runs alongside the ship canal for several miles, is lined by palms and other verdure. Occasionally we pass dredges and their tenders working in the canal, and once we passed a place where a large force of men were working with camels and mules in widening the canal, or digging out sand that had blown in since it was dug. The camels sat down while the men filled the boxes that were slung on their backs, then rose, awkwardly, and walked further inland, where the boxes were dumped. The mules furnished the motive power for a narrow-gage railroad, equipped with small dump-cars.

We saw many interesting things at Colombo, Kandy and Aden, which I will describe more fully in the regular instalment of the story of the Around-the-World Visitation.

We all stood the journey and the heat very well, and are feeling delightfully healthy and strong and refreshed by the coolness of the day in the Suez Canal.

Our hearts turn very often to Zion City, which we hope to see in a little less than two months. We are especially reminded of the beautiful little Illinois City on the Lord's Day, when our longing to be with the people in their early morning, afternoon and other services is very strong.

We are looking forward to the Visitation in Zurich and London with earnest prayers that God will give His Prophet mighty words to speak, and that a great blessing may come to many nations and peoples through the Restoration Messages that he will proclaim in Switzerland and England. Then we look forward to a day in New York, and then our homecoming!

With love to you and all in Zion, I am

Yours faithfully in Jesus, ARTHUR W. NEWCOMB,
General Associate Editor and Special Correspondent.

JUST FOUR weeks and one day from the date of the publication of this issue of LEAVES OF HEALING, the General Overseer will conduct his meetings in Carnegie Hall, New York City.

On the following day he will return direct to Zion City.

WITH BUT a few days intervening, he will again enter upon a most important series of meetings in Shiloh Tabernacle, in Zion City—the Fourth Feast of Tabernacles.

WE REMIND our friends again of the program, which was published in the last issue of LEAVES OF HEALING, and will be published again next week.

Bear in mind the fact that the Feast of Tabernacles begins on Wednesday, July 13th, and continues until Sunday, July 24th.

FRIENDS DESIRING accommodations at Elijah Hospice will do well to write to Deacon Cotton at once.

ZION CITY is most beautiful at this time.

The weather is delightful, and there has been very little rain, and a great deal of sunshine.

SHILOH PARK is most beautiful in its carpet of living green and its budding trees.

Those who desire to take advantage of tenting can be nicely accommodated in this beautiful park.

THE PEOPLE of the City are making preparations to throw open their doors for the entertainment of their friends.

AND WHY not make it an object and definite purpose to come to Zion City and enjoy the good things of the Feast?

How much better than to spend time and money in going to St. Louis, where the memory will be full of unpleasant things, and the influence will be unwholesome and undesirable?

WE ARE preparing to send several earnest Restorationists to assist the Branch in St. Louis to distribute literature among the hundreds of thousands of people who are foolish enough to spend their time and money in seeking this vain diversion.

THE FRIENDS of Overseer Daniel Bryant will be glad to hear of his safe arrival in South Africa.

We take pleasure in publishing the following personal letter which was received a day or two ago:

UITENHAGE, CAPE COLONY, SOUTH AFRICA, April 21, 1904.

REV. J. G. SPEICHER, Overseer-in-charge,
Zion City, Illinois, U. S. A.

My Dear Overseer:—Peace to thee. Our little party of four has at last stepped out upon the shores of South Africa, the scene of our future labor. We left Southampton, England, March 19th, and although the passage through the Bay of Biscay was a little rough and produced slight unpleasantness, yet this was forgotten almost immediately as we entered the quiet waters and the sweet sunshine which characterized our journey throughout. We all four are agreed that our trip to South Africa was one of the most delightful experiences of our lives.

We were on a splendid vessel, which was more like a well appointed hotel than anything else I can describe. A very congenial lot of passengers, a good band, a well-furnished library, and many other blessings, made the trip one of great profit to us as well as pleasure. Best of all, God was with us. Each morning, immediately after breakfast, our little party met in our stateroom for communion and prayer.

We landed at Port Elizabeth on Tuesday, April 12th. We were met by our Conductor from Uitenhage, Mr. F. A. Magennis, and one of our loyal members, H. W. Bates. After going through the experience of customhouse rules and expense, we took the train at ten minutes past two in the afternoon for Uitenhage, the cleanest town with one exception I have ever been in. It has a population of five thousand and is called the garden-spot of South Africa.

On Tuesday evening the dear people, who, for months, had been looking and praying for us, gathered at the home of Mr. Bates, where Mrs. Bryant and I had been assigned. It is impossible to describe such a meeting, except to say that all our faces were beaming with love and gladness.

We have been holding meetings, getting Zion in Uitenhage on a thoroughly substantial basis. We have had the joy of receiving a number of applications and of baptizing thirteen, and above all, of seeing the people blessed with every spiritual blessing and a number of cases of distinct healing. Our joy in being actually at our work fills us to the uttermost. We are all as happy as we can be. I can hardly realize that ten thousand miles lie between us. The Word of God seems so fresh, so natural, and the Zion people here meet us exactly like Zion people everywhere that sometimes I wonder whether I am in Boston, London, or Cincinnati, or even Zion City.

We leave Port Elizabeth Friday afternoon for Durban where we shall hold meetings for a couple of days and move on towards Johannesburg.

Our work in Uitenhage has been one of great satisfaction. The gathering only numbers fifteen or sixteen, but after a week's careful teaching we have had the pleasure of getting eleven consecrated unwavering members into Zion Restoration Host. We have carefully arranged their work and Uitenhage will have Zion to deal with without question.

We all send you our heartfelt Christian Love, desiring to be remembered to Elder Speicher.

Your brother in the Christ, DANIEL BRYANT.
Overseer for the Christian Catholic Church in Zion for South Africa.

THERE IS a fellowship and love among true Christians in Zion that touches the heart with a thrill of joy wherever we meet with Zion.

HOW HAPPY were the people of Africa in welcoming their beloved Overseer and his party!

What a yearning the loved ones in Africa had for some one from Headquarters who could take charge of them and lead and direct them in a proper way!

Most of these faithful members have never seen an officer of Zion, and many of them have never seen any one from Headquarters.

THERE IS a glorious awakening on the Dark Continent, and we believe that God has chosen Overseer Bryant, and will abundantly use him in his great field.

IN THE great Empire of China, the work of Zion is of interest enough to cause a prominent journal, the *New People's Magazine*, to print a long article concerning Zion City. The following extract is translated by one of our Chinese young men, who is attending Zion College. There are many mistakes, but in the main it is a fair article:

ZION CITY.

A new city just opened. We saw a paragraph in Japanese newspapers, that the founder of socialism is Saint Simon, which he carried out and that his followers had come to America to open a new colony and came to one state and failed, then came to Illinois and succeeded, and intended to make a new heaven and earth. Afterward we came to America and to Chicago and heard of Zion City and said, "Oh! 'tis the one we read of, and said surely 'tis the socialistic city.

2. When we reached Zion City, we said "No, not socialism, but a Napoleon of religion opened it." This man's name is Dowie, from Australia. Thirteen years ago he came to the United States. His religion is not like the present day but is particular, and said he understands God's Word and others do not understand, and rebukes and curses all others with strong words. His plan is very strange, and says do not use medicine but pray and at once be made whole. He hates the doctors very much. We heard that he was indicted over a thousand times and imprisoned fourteen times, and when he began not one believer did he have—at this time seventy thousand and in every land. The church money is said to be more than ten million dollars. He is a hero and a wonderful man.

3. This City opened about two years, and it is his plan to collect all his followers and make a heaven on earth, and has chosen one place and paid a million for it and opened the City, and after two years twenty thousand inhabitants, and continually coming—so many that the toes of the people hit the heels of the others. Not able to build houses fast enough for the people, for tobacco and rum are not allowed--twenty-five dollars fine to use it, and people not allowed to work here who use it. There is one General Store and one Hotel--all business just one of each kind—to stop all competition, and all the people are controlled; and, in that respect, similar to socialism. Two factories and a bank and city site is the estate of Zion, and each one has his own possessions, in his own name. The only tax is income tax, and each person pays tithes into Zion, and Zion's money is very great.

4. In this teaches to love one another, peace, purity and virtue, and every one respects this at once when they come in the City. In the two years there have been no law suits of any kind among the people, and outside of this City cannot be said elsewhere.

5. Dr. Dowie has a very heavy beard; his eyes look like electric eyes, or balls of electricity. As soon as you see him, you know he is a great man, has a very strong voice, and is a man of very great ability. When he came from Australia he was a poor man, but now has great possessions. He teaches the sick people to pray and they will be healed. This specially concerns psychology. But if a person sincerely believes, there is always this healing. This is nothing great nor wonderful; philosophers say there is very much of this, but Dr. Dowie is the only one who can do it. He says the power is not in himself, but in God. His people must call him Elijah. In the City, working people are very many, but gentlemen and literary people not a few. If what he teaches were false the learned people would know it, for there is a teacher from Chicago University, also a juris doctor, a doctor of medicine, one from the Chicago National Bank, and these are not stupid people, and these all believe that he is far above the common people. He is planning to open a new city on the Pacific Coast, and in ten years his power will cover a great part of the United States.

6. His plans are very great and soon will cover the world. Now he is touring the world and will open a third city in Europe. The reason he loves China is he wants to carry his power to China and in ten years he will have a Zion City in China. His power is very great and what he says will be done. There are two great men in America, Dr. Dowie and Pierpont Morgan. What he preaches we much admire. Christians before have preached eternal punishment for the wicked, but he preaches that all people will at some time go to heaven. There is salvation for all. In this respect it is like Buddism, but Dr. Dowie is a second Martin Luther.

ALL IS joy and peace at Headquarters.

PEOPLE ARE coming into the City in increasing numbers.

LET THE prayers of Zion continually ascend to God on behalf of our beloved City and the great work of Zion everywhere throughout the world. JOHN G. SPEICHER.

Zion in Michigan.

Rev. G. E. Farr, Elder-in-charge of the Branch of the Christian Catholic Church in Zion in Benton Harbor, will conduct meetings in the following cities in Michigan:

Kalamazoo, May 30th; Sturgis, May 31st; Three Rivers, June 1st; Moore Park, June 2d; Schoolcraft, June 3d.

Baptismal Services, Boston Branch.

Candidates for Triune Immersion, service to be conducted Lord's Day, June 12, 1904, should communicate with Overseer William Hamner Piper, 71 Perkins street, Jamaica Plain, Massachusetts.

Zion in Canada.

Elder Brooks will visit the places in Ontario, Canada, mentioned below, during the months of May and June.

He will baptize, and consecrate children, in all these places where desired.

May 30th, Baptism at 3 o'clock p. m., at the Leggett Farm, and services at the home of Allen Cross at 8 o'clock p. m.; May 31st, in Wiarton Town Hall at 3 and 8 o'clock p. m.; June 1st, in Wiarton at a private house; June 2d and 3d, Southampton, Town Hall, at 3 and 8 o'clock p. m.; June 5th, Heathcote, Sunday services in Grove near Woodhouse, Baptism in afternoon; June 6th and 7th, Collingwood, at 3 and 8 o'clock p. m., possibly Town Hall; June 8th and 9th, Waubaushene, in Skating Rink, at 3 and 8 o'clock p. m.

The meetings in Lion's Head for June 2d and 3d have been postponed indefinitely; also the meeting in Meaford for June 6th.

General Letter from the General Overseer

ON BOARD STEAMSHIP MONGOLIA,
FREMANTLE, WEST AUSTRALIA,
April 2, 1904.

TO THE OVERSEERS, ELDERS, EVANGELISTS, DEACONS, DEACONESSES, ZION RESTORATION HOST, AND MEMBERS OF THE CHRISTIAN CATHOLIC CHURCH IN ZION THROUGHOUT THE WORLD, AND TO ALL LOVERS OF GOD.

Beloved Brethren and Sisters in the Christ:

Grace to you and Peace from God our Father, and from the Lord Jesus, the Christ.

May the comforts of the Holy Spirit abound in you, and may you be led by Him in all things.

Pray that I may be led, so that I may feed the flock over which the Holy Spirit has made me Overseer throughout the world, and that I may direct the affairs of Zion until God shall call me hence.

Our voyage from Adelaide, which city we left on Thursday, April 7th, was somewhat stormy, but we arrived here safely, by the goodness of God, this morning at half past eight o'clock.

I have had a very busy morning with our friends, and attending to correspondence here, and in giving instructions to the Rev. C. Friend Hawkins, Elder-in-charge of the Christian Catholic Church in Zion, whom I brought with me from Adelaide, and whom I leave in this state to deliver certain important Zion messages, which I have given him to convey to our friends in various cities of Western Australia.

I now take a few minutes before the vessel leaves to write to you all.

I will not attempt, in this Letter, to review the entire Visitation to Australia, which I still hope to be able to do on the voyage to Colombo, which is our next port of call.

It will be a great disappointment to many in India that I am not able to carry out my intentions of visiting that great empire this year; but I feel sure that I have been led of God to pass on to Europe at this time.

I am eagerly looking forward to the Mission in Zurich and to the Conference there, and also to meeting with our dear people in London; but I am still more eagerly looking forward to my return to America, to my brief visit to New York, and to my arrival at home in our beloved City of Zion not later than June 30th.

All the Visitation party are in excellent health, although we shall need the rest of the voyage to prepare us for our work in other lands, and for the work which awaits our return to our beloved City.

I am grateful to God for the enlightenment which He gives me by His Spirit from day to day, so that I may more fully follow our Master and our King, and prepare His way in these Times of Restoration, the dawning of which has so deeply aroused the hatred of all the powers of hell of every kind in the apostate churches, in the ungodly governments of the states of this Commonwealth, and in the pandemonium of the press, all of which conspire to keep the people in ignorance, and to stir up their hatred against Zion and myself.

But I am full of joy in the clearer understanding of God's purposes, and in a firmer grasp of the principles and methods of action demanded by my prophetic Mission.

I am Going Forward fearless of all consequences, but believing that God will see me safely through, and that I shall have the joy of meeting many thousands in the City of Zion on my return home at the end of June, and at the Fourth Feast of Tabernacles, which begins so soon after.

Pray for us.

God be with you till we meet again.

With love from every one of my party, I am

Faithfully your friend and fellow servant in Jesus, the Christ, our Lord,

John Alex. Dowie

General Overseer of the Christian Catholic Church in Zion.

ELIJAH THE RESTORER ARRAIGNS THE APOSTASY FOR ITS ABSURD SELF-COMPLACENCY.

Around-the-World Visitation

of the

Rev. John Alex. Dowie

Elijah the Restorer
General Overseer of the Christian Catholic Church in Zion.

By ARTHUR W. NEWCOMB, Special Correspondent.

THE last paper of this series concluded with the report of the Message delivered by Elijah the Restorer in Central Zion Tabernacle, Melbourne, Australia, Friday morning, March 4, 1904.

Central Zion Tabernacle, Melbourne, Australia, Friday Afternoon, March 4, 1904.

The Service was opened by the Congregation's singing Hymn No. 4, from the Visitation Program.

Prayer was offered by Rev. C. Friend Hawkins, after which Overseer Voliva read the 5th chapter of Galatians.

The General Overseer then said:

THE NINE FRUITS OF THE SPIRIT.

*REPORTED BY I. M. S. AND A. W. N.

INVOCATION.

Let the words of my mouth, and the meditation of my heart be acceptable in Thy sight, O Lord, my Strength, and my Redeemer.

The number three is not an accident.

The Triunity of God is the Essence of True Christianity.

The recognition of God the Father, and the Son, and the Holy Spirit, one God, is the Essence of a True and Orthodox Christianity.

The denial of the Divinity of either the Holy Spirit or the Son of God is a proof that the person so denying is not and cannot be a Christian.

He may be anything else he chooses to call himself, but he is not a Christian.

The declaration of the Christ Himself that He and the Father are One, and the declaration of the Apostles that in Him dwelt the fulness of the Godhead, is sufficient upon this point.

I always find in the number three a great deal to interest me.

It has had a great effect upon my life, and is connected with very many things in my life.

I was reminded just now that March 3, 1888, sixteen years ago yesterday, I left this country.

I considered the three--third day of third month—a very good omen, and it has been.

I have had a very delightful ministry in these sixteen years.

Although I have had many sorrows I gave them over to God, and He turned them into joy.

I have, and have had, many trials; they were but the purifying of my faith and life.

Although I have had many temptations, they have been overcome, and I have been enabled to preserve an equanimity of spirit which makes me able to say today, that notwithstanding all opposition and bitternesses I have no personal antipathy.

My heart has only been sad that in this city and land to which I gave sixteen years of the best of my life, I have not been permitted to speak to the vast multitudes who wanted to hear.

This place would easily be filled and overflowed at every meeting, if we were able to open the doors with the assurance that we should find protection.

I am glad, however, to be able to speak to even this limited audience.

I thank God that since March 3, 1888, I have been enabled to carry forward the work that He gave me, according to my light.

I seek your prayers, that, as the years roll on, with a Deeper Humility, a Purer Faith, a Brighter Hope, and a more Perfect Love, I shall fulfil my ministry.

I speak to you about a three times three.

*The following report has not been revised by the General Overseer.

If I shall be permitted of God, I shall return to the City of Zion, in Illinois, where my people are praying for me every day in a remarkable way.

Morning and Evening Prayer in Zion City.

Not only do they pray in their hearts, but every one of our departments of service, whether it be Ecclesiastical, Educational, Commercial, or Political, is opened with prayer.

Every morning, the workmen in the Building and Manufacturing Association gather in their departments for prayer ten minutes before they begin work.

At nine o'clock every morning three times three blasts come from the great power-house whistle.

These are heard all over the city.

Every one knows what that means. Every cart on the road stops, every machine in every shop stops, every workman lays down his tools, every clerk in the offices and stores closes his eyes and bows his head, everything is still, and, for one minute, Zion prays.

The same thing happens at nine o'clock at night.

No matter what our engagements are, when this signal is given there is perfect silence in every home, for the prayer is silent, inaudible.

Then business and social life, or whatever they may be engaged in, is resumed.

We value very greatly our three times three whistles, which call Zion to prayer.

Today, I am thinking of what I shall do when I return.

I am always thinking ahead.

I hope to send to Zion City, by the next mail, my program for the Fourth Feast of Tabernacles, at which we shall have vast numbers of people.

It is my purpose to deliver nine addresses, at the half past six o'clock meetings, on the "Nine Fruits of the Spirit," and in the afternoons, nine addresses on the "Nine Gifts of the Spirit."

Before I close this week of work, I desire to speak a few words to you concerning the Nine Fruits of the Spirit.

All Fruits of the Spirit Spring from Love.

They are all the outcome of the one great Fruit, out of which all the rest spring.

The Fruit of the Spirit, our brother read, is Love, and all the rest come from that.

Love, Joy, Peace!

Those are the first three.

Long-suffering, Kindness, Goodness!

Those are the second three.

Faithfulness, Meekness, Temperance, or, as the margin properly reads, Self-control!

There are the nine.

Indignation Swallowed up in Sorrow.

A friend said to me today, "I feel that I represent the feelings of a vast number of people who would be glad if I should express to you their intense sorrow, that through the supineness of the authorities, and their unwillingness to exercise their legal power, you could not speak to the great multitudes who want to hear. I desire also to express to you my love. You must be righteously indignant."

I said, "The indignation has all passed away in the feeling of intense sorrow for the multitudes who are deprived of any little help that I might be able to give, who, by their rulers, have been denied their common right.

"I do not know what will happen, but I have been hearing for some time the tramp, tramp, tramp of the Advance Guard of the Lawless One, and it has become very loud in these last weeks—louder and clearer than ever.

"The Man of Sin has been revealed, he who claims the

infallibility that belongs alone to God, and the Lawless One must follow.

"His coming makes the Coming of the Lord Jesus imminent.

"I see that the Lawless One has power in high places, and the end is not far.

"It seems to me that sorrow swallows up indignation.

"My heart is filled with love for this people to whom I gave sixteen years of my life."

I call your attention to these Fruits of the Spirit, which I hope have some embodiment and realization in me.

The Fruit of the Spirit Is Love.

Love is not the principal thing, but it is the greatest thing in the world.

The Principal Thing is Wisdom.

You must never forget that the Book says so.

Love itself, without Wisdom, would be a terrible thing.

You see how it is, when a mother or father has Love without Wisdom.

They love the child so much that they permit the child to be a little tyrant, to be selfish, and to be cruel.

That is want of Wisdom; and the love which they have for the child has gone into indulgence to such an extent that by-and-by that child will be a curse for want of Wisdom.

Wisdom Is the Principal Thing.

In the Gifts of the Spirit, the Word of Wisdom is the first thing.

The Wisdom that is from above is first pure, then peaceable, gentle, easy to be entreated, full of mercy and good fruits, without variance, and without hypocrisy.

Wisdom has built a House of Love.

Love, in its proper understanding, must be associated with Wisdom.

Love, even Divine Love, if it were devoid of Divine Wisdom, would be an awful curse.

First of all you must have the Heavenly Wisdom that always accompanies a really Divine Love.

That Love is pure.

It is unselfish.

It is without lust.

It seeks not its own, and it is not easily provoked.

It is the greatest of all the gifts that Wisdom's House contains.

As the Spirit gives us first the Word of Wisdom, it is the Spirit who gives us this Fruit of Love.

Love is no mere soulless clod,
But transfigured in the Light of God,
That Love, which makes this life so sweet,
Will render Heaven's joy complete.

God Is Love.

His word proclaims it, and we know it.

"Day by day the truth we prove."

It seems to me that all the heavens, and all the earth are telling that God is Life, God is Light and God is Love.

It seems to me that, above all things, we should seek for this.

We are so apt, in our poor human weakness, to be angry above measure.

We ought to be angry with sin; but let us not forget that the poor degenerate sinners are the victims of misrule, the victims of lust, the victims of the idleness even of the church which has not taken them in their youth and taught them and instructed them.

When we swept away denominational education in these lands, the ministers pledged God and one another that they would teach the children in the public schools, and I was associated with that movement.

It was a great delight to my wife and to me to teach in these public schools every Friday, and to have great classes who loved us.

Once, when our dear friend Rev. J. Wattsford, who had charge of one of these schools, told Mrs. Dowie to dismiss her class of little ones and come and take another, the children flatly refused to go.

Mrs. Dowie was their teacher. They cried over it, and sat there for twenty minutes waiting for her to come back, until the good brother sent his own daughter to sing for them.

It was the most beautiful thing to teach the Message of God's Love to the children in the schools, but it has been lost, and the children have not been taught.

They have not been brought up in the nurture and admonition of the Lord.

The Sunday-school has become a very weak institution, as you know.

The patient teaching of the Word of God to the Church has not been followed out.

The Preciousness of God's Word.

One great thing in my life for which I thank God is this, that I was taught the Scriptures, and that I could repeat, when a little child, the whole of the Gospel according to St. John.

As life went on, I became so fascinated with the Bible that I put it into my heart.

I have never failed to do that all my life.

The Word of God is the Word of Wisdom, the Message of Love.

Oh, it is such a good, pure, holy Love!

It is not a foolish love.

It is a Love that makes me see that God is very good in all that He gives.

The Love That Withholds.

It is still better, sometimes, when He withholds.

Our children have to be taught that it is Love that keeps back something that they want, and which they have not the Wisdom to use.

We should not put into their hands precious jewels or a fine watch, or something that is delicate and beautiful and valuable, until they have learned the value of things and how to use them properly.

Still more is it true that we cannot lead them into higher truths until they have learned that which is fundamental—Love, the Love that does not strike the blow, but gives the kiss instead; the Love that takes the wrong, and does not inflict it; the Love that does not live by gains but by losses; the Love that, at last, makes one to know that he that loses his life shall save it, and he that saves his life shall lose it; the Love that makes life one long sacrifice will one day—perhaps here, and surely hereafter—be rewarded by the richest reward.

Love Never Fails.

Prophecies are fulfilled, and pass away.

Tongues cease, and merge into the Universal Tongue.

Words pass and are changed.

But Love abides.

It never dies.

I cannot conceive of my daughters who are in Heaven ceasing to love me through all eternity.

I cannot conceive that I should ever cease to love them; but if I could conceive of that, I could not conceive that I should ever cease to love God; that I should ever cease to love the Christ who loved me ere I knew Him, and gave His life for me; who loved humanity, who loves it still, who is preparing, with Infinite Wisdom and Love and skill, for His people in the home above; and who is overruling everything that Love may reign.

A Canopy of Love

I say to thee, do thou repeat
To the first man thou mayest meet,
In lane, highway, or open street,
That he, and we, and all men move
Under a Canopy of Love,
Broader than that blue sky above;

That grief and sorrow, and care and pain,
And anguish, all, are shadows vain;
That death itself will not remain;
That weary deserts he may tread,
Life's dreariest labyrinths he may thread,
Through dark ways underground be led;

Yet, if he will the Christ obey,
The darkest night, the dreariest way,
Shall issue out in perfect day,
And we, on divers shores oft cast,
Shall meet, our perilous voyage past,
All in our Father's home at last.

And ere thou leave him, tell him this,
They only miss
The winning of that perfect bliss,
Who will not count it true that blessing, not cursing, rules above,
And that in God we live and move;
Whose Nature and whose Name is Love.

God's Nature and Name Is Love.

Love enables a man to tell the truth if he dies for it.

Love makes you love your neighbor too well to be afraid to tell him the truth.

Love loves the Truth it speaks.

Love is ever seeking to glorify the Lover; the Great Lover, the Lover of Humanity, the Lover of all beings throughout the universe with a Love that is a Consuming Fire, with a Love that ever consumes every unclean desire, and purifies us until we are pure, as God is pure.

Joy and Peace.

The Fruit of the Spirit is Love, and with that Love there comes the Joy and there comes the Peace.

These do not always come at once; for Love must weep, and Love must work, and Love must wait and toil while others sleep. But Love will get the Joy in the morning.

"Weeping may endure for a night," and Love may labor on in the darkness, but Joy cometh in the morning.

There is a Morning, and when that Joy comes it will never go.

The Fruit abides.

No sacrifice you ever made for humanity in Love, but brought you Joy.

It may have been Joy in your poverty as it was with me.

It may be Joy in your plenty, as it is with me; but whether it is poverty or plenty; whether it is want, or whether it is power, oh, it is the Joy of the Lord alone, that makes either the night or the day to be happy!

All other joys pass away. All other peace passes away.

If your Peace rests upon plenty, and your Joy rests upon the music of bliss, then it is of the earth earthy.

But, if the Kingdom of God is within you—His Righteousness, His Peace, His Joy—then all is well, and the other fruits will follow.

They cannot help following—Love, Peace, Joy, Long-suffering, Kindness, Goodness, Faithfulness, Meekness, and Self-control.

Self-control.

That is the hardest thing of all, perhaps.

Greater is he that controls his own spirit than he that takes a city, or that builds one.

It is better for me to have the Self-control of the Spirit than to have built a city, or ten of them.

Whatever others may say, I hope I say with a true humility, that I would rather have these Nine Gifts of the Spirit, the adornment which the Bridegroom gives to His Bride, than all that earth can give.

We brought nothing into this world, and it is certain we can carry nothing out.

"Put my hands outside my coffin, my dear," cried Alexander, the man who had won a world, "so that when I am carried to my grave, my soldiers, and all the world may see that Alexander, whose hands desired to grasp the world, went out without anything."

You brought nothing in.

You can take nothing out of all that the world has to give; but take care that when you go out you do not take with you an unbelieving heart and a loveless spirit.

"Yea, saith the Spirit, that they may rest from their labors; for their works follow with them."

May you be one of these.

Rise, and let us tell God that we shall. [Nearly all rose.]

PRAYER OF CONSECRATION.

My God and Father, in Jesus' Name I come to Thee. Take me as I am. Make me what I ought to be in spirit, in soul, in body. Give me power to do right, no matter what it costs; to repent, to restore to my fellow men, and to Thee, my God, by a True Repentance. Give me a simple faith in Jesus, the Lamb of God who taketh away the sin of the world. For His sake take away my sin. Heal my sicknesses. Purify my spirit, my soul and my body; and by Thy Spirit may I bring forth Fruits of Love, and Joy, and Peace. Give me Self-control. Control me by Thy Spirit, that I may obey Thee. Bless this City, and State, and Commonwealth. For Jesus' sake. Amen. [*All repeat the prayer, clause by clause, after the General Overseer.*]

BENEDICTION.

Beloved, abstain from all appearance of evil. And may the very God of Peace Himself sanctify you wholly; and I pray God your whole spirit and soul and body be preserved entire, without blame, unto the coming of our Lord Jesus, the Christ. Faithful is He that calleth you, who also will do it. The grace of our Lord Jesus, the Christ, the love of God, our Father, the fellowship of the Holy Spirit, our Comforter and Guide, one Eternal God, abide in you, bless you and keep you, and all the Israel of God everywhere, forever. Amen.

Two Views of "Calton Hill," Summer Residence of Mr. Alexander Dowie, where the General Overseer and Around-the-World Visitation Party Spent a Short Time in Rest.

VISITATION IN ADELAIDE, SOUTH AUSTRALIA.

The meeting held in Central Zion Tabernacle, Melbourne, Friday afternoon, March 4th, was the last meeting of the Melbourne Visitation.

From Melbourne the General Overseer and the members of the Visitation Party proceeded directly to Mount Lofty, which lies about ten miles southeast of Adelaide, South Australia.

A Fortnight of Rest, Prayer and Preparation Among the Hills.

Here is situated "Calton Hill," the summer home of Mr. and Mrs. Alexander Dowie, of Adelaide, the father and mother of Overseer Jane Dowie.

This beautiful place had been prepared for the occupancy of the General Overseer and Overseer Jane Dowie during their brief respite from the work of their missions while in Australia.

The house stands upon the crest of one of the hills of the Mount Lofty range, overlooking the lower hills, the plains, and the gulf of St. Vincent, twelve or fifteen miles away to the west; while on the east is the summit of Mount Lofty, two thousand five hundred feet in height.

Nowhere in the world, perhaps, are there any more beautiful sunsets than those which are to be seen as one looks out over the Gulf of St. Vincent from "Calton Hill." This is indeed an ideal place for peace, quiet, rest, meditation, prayer and conference. These hills are said to be among the most ancient on the earth's surface.

Among the Hills around Mount Lofty, South Australia.

View of the Hills near Mount Lofty, South Australia.

Formed principally of rock, they were, at the time when they were thrown up by the mighty terrestrial upheaval which gave them birth, perhaps higher than the Himalayas.

But as the centuries of centuries have rolled over their heads, the warring elements have ground away the sharp outlines, reducing the rocks to sand, and carrying the sand into the sea, until the eminences which, in the far remote ages, lifted their bold and rugged peaks far above the clouds, and into the crystalline blue of the sky, have become rounded, and covered with trees, shrubs and grasses.

The summer climate of these hills is incomparable.

The air is always cool, and of a fresh, light, sparkling purity that makes breathing a tingling delight.

The sky is usually so clear, and there is such an infinity of depth in its brilliant blue, that it seems higher than the sky of our northern latitudes, while at night the moon and stars rain down upon the earth a golden fire that touches tree and shrub, hill, valley, and plain with a strange magic that transforms them into a scene of indescribable, mystic beauty.

The spirit of a child of God as he stands upon these Australian hills and looks up into the glorious radiance of these summer skies at night cannot but be filled with awe and adoration for the great Father and Creator.

Again and again there comes to mind, like a strain of heavenly music, the inspired words of the great Israelitish poet:

> The Heavens declare the Glory of God;
> And the Firmament showeth His handiwork.

Climate and Flora of the South Australian Hills.

It is never too dry in these hills; it is never too hot; it is never too cold, and, in the summer time at least, it is never too wet.

Consequently almost anything can be grown here, and the gardens are almost of tropical luxuriance. The gardens at "Calton Hill" are not pretentious, but nevertheless have a richness and simple beauty that is a delight to the eye.

Tall pines surround the entire estate, while hedges and borders of laurel, thyme, box, rosemary and other handsome shrubs mark out the divisions of the grounds.

The house itself is built of stone, and has wide verandas on three sides. Its walls are vine-covered, making it a picture of coolness and homelike seclusion.

Near by is the quiet little hamlet of Crafers with its dozen or so of pretty stone cottages, its two churches and its schools.

It was in this beautiful spot that the General Overseer, Overseer Jane Dowie, Dr. A. J. Gladstone Dowie, and the other members of the Around-the-World Visitation party spent a delightful fortnight from the time of the close of the Melbourne Visitation to the opening of the Visitation in Adelaide.

Here they received delightful visits from relatives and old friends.

Among them were the venerable father and mother of Overseer Jane Dowie, and her two brothers, the Messrs. Norman and Stewart Dowie, two excellent young business men who are now managing the tannery, boot and shoe manufactory and salesrooms founded and conducted for many years by their father.

Adelaide, South Australia.

About ten miles to the northwest of Mount Lofty, and in plain view from its summit, lies the beautiful little city of Adelaide with its suburbs.

This city which has between fifty and sixty thousand inhabitants, is, in some respects, the most beautiful of the three capitals of the Australian states that we have seen.

The streets are broad and well paved, and there are many trees.

There is a park in the center of the city, and a series of parks lie between the city itself and the suburbs on all sides.

Here is the residence of Mr. and Mrs. Alexander Dowie, where they have lived forty-three years, and where Overseer Jane Dowie was born and spent her girlhood and young womanhood.

Here is the boot and shoe shop of her father, where John Alexander Dowie began his business career as a messenger boy.

Here are still to be seen the stores and offices of the firms with which he was afterward connected, and in whose employ he made a most excellent reputation for himself as a business man, before he was twenty-one years of age.

Here is the church in which he and Overseer Jane Dowie were married twenty-eight years ago.

Here is the little cottage where John Alexander Dowie and his family lived when they went into voluntary poverty for the work of the Kingdom of God and the uplifting of humanity.

It was in this city, known throughout all Australia as the "City of Churches," the city rich with so many associations of former years, that the Prophet of God was to hold the final mission of his present Visitation to Australia.

Arrangements for the Adelaide Visitation.

After the experiences with which Zion had met in Sydney and Melbourne, it was determined to take especial care in making the arrangements for the Adelaide Visitation, in order that the Message of God's prophet might be heard by all who wished to listen quietly.

Deacon C. Friend Hawkins (now Elder) who has for some time been in charge of the Branch of the Christian Catholic Church in Zion, in Adelaide, under the direction of Overseer Wilbur Glenn Voliva, and the General Overseer, was in active charge of all the preliminary arrangements.

Deacon Hawkins' headquarters in Adelaide were in Zion Tabernacle, in Federal Hall; but for the purposes of this Visitation he opened an office at the Town Hall.

The greatest possible care was taken in the distribution of tickets, none being issued except upon recommendation of the person receiving them by a member of the Christian Catholic Church in Zion, or some other person of repute.

Never were bits of cardboard sought after more eagerly than these which would give the bearer admission to the Exhibition Building and Town Hall during the Mission of Elijah the Restorer.

The pastors of the churches of the city were besieged by members of their churches, and friends, all clamoring for letters of recommendation, so that they might get tickets. It was a common saying, that the possession of a ticket to the "Dowie meetings" was a certificate of good character.

Concerning this the Adelaide *Register* said on Thursday, March 17th, three days before the opening of the Mission:

THE DOWIE MISSION.

TICKETS IN DEMAND.

The Rev. J. A. Dowie (General Overseer of Zion City), whose Adelaide mission is advertised to begin at the Jubilee Exhibition Building next Sunday, is taking special pains to ensure order in the meetings. On Wednesday, officers of the church attended at the box office in the Town Hall for the purpose of issuing free tickets for the various meetings. Applicants were required to produce introductions from members of the church or other reputable citizens of Adelaide, and to state the exact service to which they desired admittance. There was a crowd around the ticket office all day, and hundreds of people were turned away on account of not having the necessary introduction. One man on being told of the rule, sarcastically replied, "Will a letter from His Excellency the Governor do?" All that Mr. Dowie asks is that those who desire to attend the meetings shall satisfy the officers of their orderliness. There will be two gatherings in the Exhibition Building on Sunday at 11 a. m., and 3 p. m. No fewer than 2,000 tickets for the afternoon meeting had been distributed before the box office was opened on Wednesday.

The Police Promise Protection.

During the week previously to the opening of the meetings, the General Overseer visited the Honorable L. Cohen, Mayor of the City of Adelaide, and Colonel Madley, Commissioner of Police of South Australia, to inquire what aid might be expected from the authorities in maintaining order at the meetings, should there be necessity.

The General Overseer was received very cordially by both gentlemen, and treated with great consideration.

He was informed that there were persistent rumors to the effect that students of the University of Adelaide and others were planning to break up the meetings, and that there were other elements in the city that might possibly give trouble. He was confidently assured, however, that he would have the fullest and heartiest coöperation of the police in the maintenance of order, and in the protection of life, limb, and property.

In pursuance of this promise Colonel Madley, who is a brave and able officer, at once took action to forestall, if possible, any attempt at the repetition of the scenes which had disgraced Sydney and Melbourne.

In company with Overseer Voliva and Deacon Hawkins, he visited the Jubilee Exhibition Building and the Town Hall for the purpose of perfecting arrangements for the action of the police.

He also visited the University, and warned the young men there that the police authorities would not permit the State of South Australia to be brought into disrepute by the lawless denial to any one of the right of free speech.

In addition to this he also gave an authorized interview to the newspapers, w. ning all interrupters that the majesty of the law would be upheld.

This interview was published in the *Register* for Thursday, March 17th, as follows:

A WARNING TO INTERRUPTERS.

It has been whispered in various directions recently that an organized effort will be made by a section of the community to interrupt Mr. Dowie at his meetings, and if possible to prevent him from enjoying the right of free speech. It has come to the ears of the Commissioner of Police that such plans are on foot, and on Wednesday afternoon Colonel Madley made the following statement to a representative of the *Register:*

"It will be a sorry day for South Australia when a man shall not be allowed to exercise the liberty of free speech, and if a certain section of the community undertake to prevent Mr. Dowie from speaking, then any other section might organize and claim the right to stop other persons from giving expression to their views. Hitherto all public speakers who have come to South Australia have been allowed to speak without undue interruption. Those who disagree with the opinion of a speaker have a simple course to pursue: they need not attend his meetings. If any person interrupts a Sunday service the police will immediately take action. There is no place in the world where people have greater liberty in expressing their views than in South Australia, but once that practice is departed from then certain sections might organize to prevent Bishops from speaking, or stop the unemployed from holding their meetings. If people go to the meetings of Mr. Dowie with the object of interrupting him they will not get the slightest sympathy from me or the police."

It may not be generally known that interruption of a religious meeting may involve the culprits in a severe penalty. Clause 320 of the Criminal Law Consolidation Act of 1876, reads: "Whosoever shall wilfully interrupt or disturb any congregation, meeting, or assembly of persons assembled for religious worship, by noise, profane discourse, rude or indecent behavior, or by any unnecessary noise, either within the place where such congregation or such meeting is held, or so near thereto as to disturb the order and solemnity of such congregation, meeting or assembly, shall be guilty of a misdemeanor, and, being convicted thereof, shall be liable to be imprisoned for any term not exceeding two years, with hard labor."

MR. AND MRS. ALEXANDER DOWIE AND OVERSEER JANE DOWIE.

As will thus be seen that up to this time all signs seemed to indicate that the Adelaide Visitation would be the most quiet of all the Missions of the General Overseer in Australia on this tour.

A Voice from America.

On Saturday morning, just before the Lord's Day on which the Visitation was to be opened, there appeared in the Adelaide *Advertiser* the following long letter from the special correspondent of that paper in America, a young man whom we met in Los Angeles, who informed us that he was representing a large number of the principal Australian newspapers in a tour of the world.

AVENUE OF EUCALYPTUS TREES IN ADELAIDE, SOUTH AUSTRALIA.
RESIDENCE OF ALEXANDER DOWIE, ADELAIDE, SOUTH AUSTRALIA.

Members and friends of the Christian Catholic Church in Zion and readers of LEAVES OF HEALING will, of course, at once see many inaccuracies in the letter, and many opinions expressed by the correspondent which are not warranted by the facts.

Notwithstanding these, however, the letter is a very interesting one, and brings out many important facts in a striking way.

It was of especial interest to the people of Adelaide, appearing just at this time, and carrying with it the refutation of many false impressions concerning the General Overseer and his work, which were current among the people of Australia.

It need hardly be pointed out that the writer was most of all mistaken when he judged that the General Overseer's officers were his superiors by "immeasurable heights," and that his success was due not to his own ability but to theirs.

Such a proposition is, of course, illogical and absurd. No inferior man ever succeeds in gathering his superiors about him, and making them the foundation of his success.

The following is the letter referred to:

MR. DOWIE IN AMERICA.

(By our Special Correspondent.)

Los Angeles, California, February 6.

Whatever John Alexander Dowie is or is not, the fact remains that for over two years he has been the most spectacular figure of the public stage of America, and few men of any profession have succeeded in holding the public gaze so long in this sensation-loving country. Before this is read in Australia a considerable section of the people of the southern continent will have been given the opportunity of judging him for themselves, and their opinions of the man who claims to be Elijah reincarnated will have been delivered. Their verdict is looked for with some interest on this side of the Pacific, as thousands of interested eyes outside Zion City have followed the prophet over the ocean. The American press speculates with sensational prominence on the treatment likely to be meted out to him by the Australians, and many of the scribes express curiosity as to how Dowie will comport himself over there, and what tactics he will pursue to win his way into the confidence of the people he ministered amongst, as an ordinary mortal, many years ago. Even his most bitter traducers credit him with sufficient business acumen to know that his methods of oratory and the platform expressions with which he has entertained his American audiences of late will hardly gain him the respect of the more particular Australian. It will, perhaps, be interesting for residents of the Commonwealth who see and hear Elijah the Restorer to make a comparison of the methods used in attracting American and Australian crowds.

Character sketches written of Mr. Dowie twelve months ago, or even six months later, are today stale, and give no idea of the man at the present time. He has changed his methods and improved his personal appearance so many times since that night in Chicago, two years and more ago, so eventful in the history of some 5,000 Dowieites, when he declared himself to be the reincarnated Elijah, that the sensational press have found him to be a veritable gold mine, and discover something new and interesting in the man every few days. The prophet has no just complaint, or as the American patois has it, has "no kick coming with the Yankee reporter." It is a little over two years ago that Dowie stepped briskly to the proscenium of the public stage, and since that time the sensational reporter has kept him there. Other characters have appeared and said their lines, and made their exits with more or less applause, but Dowie has never budged, and the choicest hothouse bouquets have been handed up to him from the stalls, while turnips and carrots were flung from the gallery. One of the secrets of his success, or rather one of the principal reasons for it, for the secret is obvious, is that he reviled the reporter, and the reporter reviled again. Mr. Dowie informed me at Los Angeles, a few days prior to his departure for Australia, that for two years he had never given a newspaper an interview—in fact, was particularly careful to avoid doing anything that might be worked into one—and yet during that time his secretary had clipped from American newspapers, mostly of Chicago, no less than two thousand three hundred alleged interviews. It would be safe enough, therefore, to say that no man has ever before received such advertisement—cheap, persistent and effective. It was an unexpressed agreement between the prophet and the sensational press of America. He provided the sensation, and the press presented him with the publicity. So when he shook his fists at the reporters, and called them "vipers and dirty dogs" before the thousands in his audience, he may have been sincere, but his earnestness would scarcely be checked by a knowledge, which he must have had, that while so acting he was establishing himself before a sensation-loving people.

But the real secret of his administrative success lies not so much in the man himself as in the personnel of his advisory board—his cabinet officers—and it is inexplicable to the general public how he has managed to surround himself with such a coterie of brilliant, brainy men. I saw him and his chief officers in Los Angeles a few days before he sailed for Australia, and had exceptional opportunities of seeing "the man beneath the prophet," and of witnessing the manner in which he lived and moved amongst his staff. It was just after the bankruptcy proceedings in Chicago, from which Dowie had emerged triumphant, and, perhaps, a little arrogant. From that city he and his party took a trip to New Orleans, and worked up to Texas. In this state a site was inspected and approved of on which a new Zion settlement is to be established. It was explained to me that many Australians and Dowieites from other warmer countries suffered rather severely from the extreme cold of the Chicago district, and it was for such that the Texas settlement was to be established. A stay was made at Los Angeles, in Southern California, of several days, the Dowieites traveling up in a luxurious private car, besides which Madame Patti's and Mrs. Langtry's, which happened to be on the tracks at the same time, appeared humble and mean. The party consisted of ten of Zion's highest officers, including the prophet himself, the chief justice, the special correspondent and secretary, the chief ecclesiastical secretary, two financial managers, the personal attendant, a photographer and reporter for LEAVES OF HEALING, the official organ of Zion City, and two ladies. The ladies were left in Los Angeles to take charge of the local following. The others journeyed on to San Francisco with the leader, and, with two exceptions, returned to Zion to look after the city's affairs, when the steamer had left for Australia. The most fashionable tourist hotel in Los Angeles was selected for their stay there, and a handsome suite of apartments was reserved. On the first morning after the arrival of the party an audience was granted to the reporters of the city press, who had to content themselves with attending a reception rather than a special interview.

"Reporters are naughty boys, and sometimes I have to spank them," was the sum total of the interviews which appeared in the papers of the following day. It was on the same day that my card went up to the prophet's apartments. The card went up on the elevator, and Mr. Newcomb, the special correspondent, came down. He had to say that Mr. Dowie was entertaining some fifteen prominent business men to a private luncheon in his apartments, but would perhaps see me in a few minutes when the guests had departed.

In the meantime Mr. Newcomb took care of me, and it was not long before the discovery was made that I was being closely questioned and as closely watched by a remarkably clever man, and a well-groomed, good-looking fellow to boot, dressed in orthodox frock coat with silk facings, stove-pipe hat, with gloved hands, and hair parted within a hundredth of an inch of the center of his scalp. He might have been a banker, archbishop, or foreign ambassador, in fact anything but a newspaper man. He knew all about Australia, I discovered, but was not quite certain about the Australian he was talking with. Apparently satisfied, he disappeared upstairs and returned a few minutes later with another swellishly-dressed, but more elderly man, who was presented as Judge Barnes, Chief Justice of Zion City.

Then followed another cross-examination, and I commenced to wish myself well out of it. The questionings of the judge were rendered more disconcerting by the quiet, penetrating scrutiny of a pair of piercing brown eyes. There was no evading or avoiding them. The voice was kindly, the black-bearded, massive face was handsome and pleasant, and the generously proportioned figure breathed geniality. But those eyes! They searchlighted every nook and cranny of the mind relentlessly; they scorched flippant thoughts, and checked reckless words half expressed. I heard indistinctly a mellow voice explaining that there was no crime in Zion City, that no blows of anger were ever struck in its streets, that no cases had been brought before the supreme court, other than where a minor's interests were involved, since the establishment of the City, and I looked up into the eyes of its chief justice and understood the reason. Previous to throwing in his lot with Dowie this man was an eminent lawyer, a prominent politician, who had at one time been nominated for a state governorship. He was the officer who had arranged just previously an interview between the Prophet and Mr. Roosevelt, and he informed me that the American President had given unqualified approval of Zion City as at present constituted, and had declared that he would follow Dowie's tour of the world with special interest. And, indeed, why should he not? Whether he is a big prophet or a small human being, America can only receive benefits from Dowie's mission. Americans are not certain that Mr. J. A. Dowie is a good prophet, nor are they much concerned about it, so long as he continues to entertain them, but they realize fully that he is irreproachable as an immigration agent. He makes no charge for his services in this direction, and brings to their country none but sober, industrious people, who jingle plenty of money in their pockets and immediately become citizens.

As we ascended to the private apartments of the prophet the judge went on to tell how he had arranged with all the foreign embassies at Washington for permission for the doctor to visit their countries. In every case but one it had been freely given, and the exception was the Russian Embassy. The judge chuckled as he told how the ambassador had insisted on the prophet signing an agreement stipulating that he would make no attempt "to proselytise in large numbers in Russia." He himself considered it to be a nonsensical idea, but the leader called it a victory over Muscovite diplomacy. We entered the drawing-room, and Dowie walked into the center of the room, where he waited, and shook me ceremoniously by the hand. The ladies were presented and proved to be an "evangelist" and a "deaconess," and we sat down. Not so with the officers, however, who appeared to me to behave in a most extraordinary manner. Five men, of commanding stature, and garments of the latest New York cut, gentlemen who might have graced any European court, and have entertained the most exacting monarch without effort, stood at attention, and spoke to a little man of five feet stature, with flowing white beard and bald pate, and addressed him only in the most reverential tones. Before speaking they invariably saluted, and never addressed him other than as General Overseer. It was incongruously impressive, and Dowie's success seemed less marvelous, almost ordinary, with those handsome, alert, well-dressed gentlemen standing behind him. But every one of them looked to be his superior by immeasurable heights. A wave of his hand and they retired, leaving only the personal attendant to mount guard over him, and protect him from a possible onslaught of "one of those wretched vipers, a newspaper man."

The man before me, I realized, was the very latest edition of Dowie, the prophet, the one just out, flushed with his successes of the Bankruptcy Court. He was not the man who fifteen years before had left Los Angeles with nothing but empty pockets, and a burring Scotch accent; nor was he even the prophet of two years before, but Elijah the Restorer, clad in a light-gray tweed, built by a tailor who knew his business. He was the Elijah without maculations, with money to burn, setting out on a tour of the world to attract the superior man of money towards him. He was flushed, too, with his efforts at entertaining, which his guests had declared were attended with conspicuous success. "So you are from Australia, eh? Now, here is a message for Australia. I am going out there to preach the Gospel, and you will please tell the Australians that if I can do anything to create or promote a better feeling between Australia and America I shall devote my best services to furthering that end." The judge escorted me to the lobby of the hotel, and invited me to spend a couple of days as his guest in Zion City on my way through Illinois. The eyes were still as penetrating, but the voice held kindly, and besides I wanted to view this wonderful little City at close range, and I gratefully accepted the invitation.

Undoubtedly J. A. Dowie's genius is for financial affairs, and he has lately proved himself competent to cope with any complications or entanglements in money matters. The recent bankruptcy proceedings against the financial institutions of Zion City prove them to be sound and solvent, and that they were instituted by malicious men, who were personal enemies of J. A. Dowie.

The City was caught at a particularly unfortunate time, when considerable sums of money were tied up, and but for Mr. Dowie's extraordinary talent for unweaving financial tangles the plotters would have succeeded. Through these proceedings the City has received its soundest advertisement up to the present time. When a final settlement was made and the facts became known, with a single exception, the Chicago papers voluntarily published a full vindication of Mr. Dowie and a complete apology.

The writer then purports to give a report of the Los Angeles meeting. It was evidently clipped from a local paper.

Lord's Day Morning Meeting.

The first two meetings of the Adelaide Visitation were held in the Jubilee Exhibition Building on Lord's Day morning and afternoon, March 20th.

The Auditorium of this building is a large, bare room seated with chairs, and provided with a high but somewhat narrow platform.

There are galleries running all around the room. With these galleries the place will seat about four thousand five hundred people.

Admission to the building is gained through turnstiles placed in a gateway of the high iron fence which surrounds the grounds.

Although the morning meeting was held at eleven o'clock, an hour when all church members are supposed to be in their own churches, and although it had been raining all morning, the streets of Adelaide, in the neighborhood of the building, were alive with people for an hour before the meeting opened. All were hurrying through the rain to the Exhibition Building.

Some inkling as to who these people were may be gained from the fact that the *Christian Commonwealth*, the Methodist organ for South Australia, in its issue of that week complained bitterly that church-members, Sunday-school superintendents and teachers, and others whose religious duties should have kept them in their own churches, deserted them to attend this meeting.

When the General Overseer, accompanied by the members of his party, stepped upon the platform, he was enthusiastically received by an audience of about three thousand people.

This great audience was one of the most quiet and attentive that the General Overseer had addressed in the Commonwealth of Australia.

Every word of the speaker was followed with the most intense interest, every person in the audience seeming to be loth to miss one word that was said.

There was, accordingly, not the slightest interruption on the part of any one. On the contrary, there was frequent and enthusiastic applause, and apparently the most hearty agreement with all that the General Overseer said.

Stow Congregational Church, North Adelaide, South Australia, where John Alexander Dowie was Married May 26, 1876.

The man of God was in his best vein, and spoke with great freedom and power.

The following is the report of his address:

Exhibition Building, Adelaide, South Australia, Lord's Day Morning, March 20, 1904.

The General Overseer came upon the platform, accompanied by Overseers Jane Dowie, J. G. Excell, and Wilbur Glenn Voliva, Dr. A. J. Gladstone Dowie, Elder Milly Voliva and Deacons and Deaconesses C. Friend Hawkins, and J. S. McCullagh.

The audience rose, and the General Overseer pronounced the

INVOCATION.

God be merciful unto us, and bless us,
And cause Thy face to shine upon us;
That Thy Way may be known upon earth,
Thy Saving Health among All Nations;
For the sake of Jesus. Amen.

Hymn No. 20 in the Visitation Program, "We're Marching to Zion," was then sung.

The General Overseer read the 67th Psalm, and in the 14th chapter of the Gospel according to St. John, from the 1st to the 7th verse.

Prayer was offered by Overseer Jane Dowie, at the close of which the Disciples' Prayer was repeated.

The announcements were then made by Overseer Voliva, following which the tithes and offerings were received during the singing of the hymn, "Jesus Lover of my Soul." The General Overseer said:

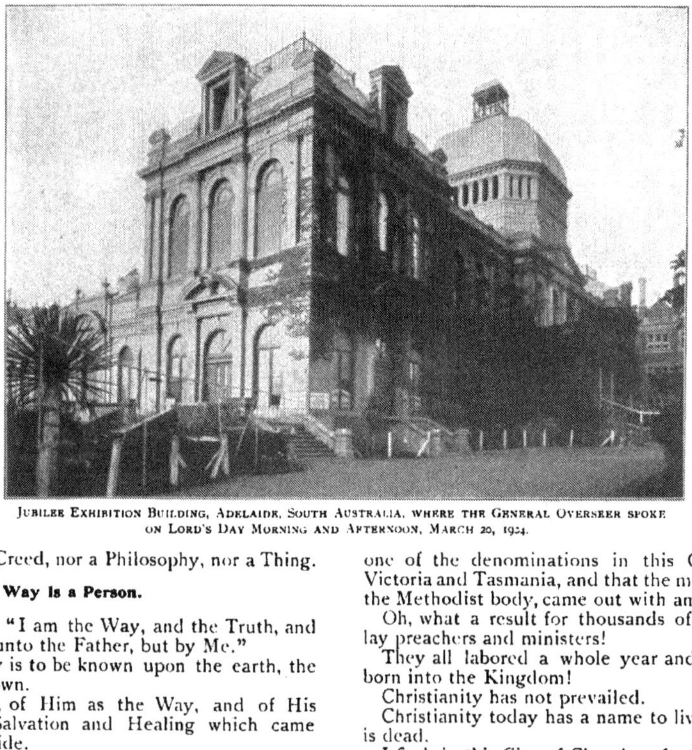

GOD'S WAY.

*REPORTED BY E. W. AND A. W. N.

INVOCATION.

Let the words of my mouth, and the meditation of my heart be acceptable in Thy sight, be profitable unto this people, and unto all to whom these words shall come, in this and every land, in this and all the coming time, Till Jesus Come. Amen.

TEXT.

God be merciful unto us, and bless us,
And cause His face to shine upon us;
That Thy Way may be known upon earth,
Thy Saving Health among All Nations.

I call your attention especially to the words:

That Thy Way may be known upon earth, Thy saving health among All Nations.

God's Way is neither a Creed, nor a Philosophy, nor a Thing.

God's Way Is a Person.

Jesus, the Christ, said: "I am the Way, and the Truth, and the Life: no one cometh unto the Father, but by Me."

Therefore, if God's Way is to be known upon the earth, the Christ of God is to be known.

I speak, this morning, of Him as the Way, and of His Saving Health—of the Salvation and Healing which came through Him, and still abide.

I speak that His Way may be known upon earth, and that His Salvation and Healing may be known among All the Nations.

That Way is not known.

Christianity, to Judge It by Its Present Condition, Is a Failure.

With one thousand millions out of the fifteen hundred millions of the world's population avowedly heathen—Mohammedans, Buddhists, anti-Christians—it is a farce to talk of Christianity's having prevailed.

Two-thirds of the human race are in open and avowed antagonism to Christianity.

The remainder are in such a condition, that to speak of them in general as Christian is folly.

To talk about the Christianity of the Greek church, notwithstanding the fact that there is much of the Christ in it, is a misnomer.

To speak of the Russian Empire as Christian, when it has a heathen priesthood bowing down to pictures, worshiping sacred icons, and leading the people to bow before these inanimate gods, is manifestly wrong.

Roman Catholicism, which has been the despair of a true Christianity for many years and centuries, is to be classed largely in the same category.

It is a screaming farce to talk about Baptismal Regeneration, the transformation and regeneration of a baby's spirit by the sprinkling of a little water upon its forehead.

It is a shame to suppose that any man, by a hocus-pocus, can transform a bit of wet dough into a Living God.

It is still greater folly to believe that Cardinal Sarto, who was a fallible man, became an infallible pope when he was elected by a college of fallible cardinals.

Many True Christians in the Roman Catholic Church.

I am thankful to say, however, that there are vast numbers in the Roman Catholic church in whom the Faith, and the Hope, and the Love that the Gospel engenders still find a place.

God forbid that we should say that the Christ is not in their lives! Who can forget the beautiful lives, and words, and the noble Christian thoughts, of even those of our own time; men like Faber and Newman?

It is also somewhat of a farce to talk of the Church of England as being Christian, when the so-called Defender of the Faith finds himself so very rarely inside the church, except at a formal service.

What a shame it is to speak of people as Christians who have no regeneration of spirit, and no entire consecration to the Christ!

JUBILEE EXHIBITION BUILDING, ADELAIDE, SOUTH AUSTRALIA, WHERE THE GENERAL OVERSEER SPOKE ON LORD'S DAY MORNING AND AFTERNOON, MARCH 20, 1904.

An Infinitesimal Increase.

How absurd it is, even in our Protestant Denominations, to talk of a Living Christianity, when I read in one Year-book that last year, after laboring all year, one of the denominations in this Commonwealth, covering Victoria and Tasmania, and that the most aggressive of them all, the Methodist body, came out with an increase of one member!

Oh, what a result for thousands of Sunday-school teachers, lay preachers and ministers!

They all labored a whole year and there was just one spirit born into the Kingdom!

Christianity has not prevailed.

Christianity today has a name to live, and nearly everywhere is dead.

I find, in this City of Churches, fewer people in the churches than there were thirty years ago.

I find, too, in the most aggressive of the churches, similar results to those I have indicated in the states of Victoria and Tasmania.

I bring no railing accusation, for the quotation is from their own Year-book.

Denominational Christianity Growing Weaker.

I look around the world today and see with an aching heart, that everywhere Christianity is weaker than it used to be; that in the church with which I used to be connected, the Congregational body, for instance, in sixteen states of the United States they lost nearly two thousand five hundred members last year, and that the entire increase was only on the average one-quarter of one per cent.

All the churches in the United States, Roman Catholic,

*The following address has not been revised by the General Overseer.

Greek Catholic, and Protestant, can show only a nominal increase of one per cent.

On the other hand Mohammedanism spreads rapidly in Central Africa.

Heathen tribes that were absolute idolaters a few years ago, are today, in millions, as in the Soudan, fanatical Mohammedans.

Something must be done.

There is no use in us who are Christians putting our heads, ostrich-like, in the sand, and imagining that the enemy does not see us.

We have to be up and doing if the prayer in my text is to be answered.

Truly God must be merciful to His Church.

Truly God must be merciful to us.

Truly God must bless us.

Truly God must shine upon us, if His Way is to be known upon earth, and His Saving Health among All the Nations.

That minister of God is not true to the Christ or to his conscience who does not speak out.

God help me so to speak!

Truth Must Be Spoken.

I have nothing to speak but that which is kind and good, so far as I know it; but if the truth hurts, then it can hurt only those who are opposed to it.

May God defend the right!

I will not, for any consideration whatever, keep back any part of my Message.

I will speak with the kindness and the love that I feel to all who name the Name of Jesus, by whatever name they are called.

It has been my joy that among the Roman Catholics, for instance, I have had the great privilege of baptizing, with these hands, several thousand who have come out of that church.

I am grateful to God for this. [Applause.]

I am the General Overseer of a Catholic Church.

It is not Roman Catholic, or Greek Catholic, or English Catholic; but it is Christian Catholic, and the Name of the Christ is better than all the other names.

I am in perfect love and amity with all who are willing to do right, and I am in antipathy against no man; for it is my aim to carry this Gospel to every land and every nation.

This Gospel Is the Gospel of the Kingdom of God.

It is not the Gospel of a church.

There is no such thing as a Gospel of a church.

It is the Gospel of the Kingdom of God. It was so called by Jesus, the Christ, Himself.

He never spoke of its being the Gospel of a church.

You can take the Gospels according to St. John, St. Luke, and St. Mark, search them from beginning to end, and you will not find the word church in any of them.

When you find that word in Matthew, you see at once its meaning, if you have any scholarship.

It is the *ecclesia* (εκκλησια), those who are called out of something, of which the Christ speaks when He says to Peter that upon this Rock, meaning Himself, the Rock of Eternal Ages, will I build My *ecclesia*.

On another occasion, He tells them that if a man has offended, they are to tell it to the *ecclesia*, the Church.

He does not say to take a vote on it and split the church.

The Church Not Properly a Voting Body.

The *ecclesia* is not a voting machine, and was not intended to be. One great trouble is that you vote.

In the Christian Catholic Church in Zion there has never been one vote taken, and we are in perfect love and amity.

Discipline is exercised by the properly-appointed officers, and the Church is merely "told," as the Christ directed.

The Church Gathered Out of the Kingdom.

The *ecclesia* is the "gathering-out" of something.

Gathered out of what?

They will tell you that it is the "gathering-out" of the world.

If that is true, then you have the world in the Church.

The Church of the Christ is gathered out of the Kingdom.

If you are not in the Kingdom of God; if you are not born of God into the Kingdom of God, you have no right, and no place in the Church.

Until you are born of God, and the Kingdom of God has come to be within you, you have no right to fellowship in the Church of the Christ.

The Church, therefore, is an assembly of those who have repented of their sins, have believed in our Lord Jesus, the Christ, and have obeyed Him.

They enter the Church, not to be converted, but because they are converted.

That is a definition of the Church that is wholly Scriptural.

It does not matter whether it is the common practice or not; it is the Scriptural practice.

The Church, which the Christ has purchased with His blood, important as it is, is composed merely of a number of those who are called out, having already come into His Kingdom. Therefore,

The Kingdom Is Larger Than the Church.

I thank God that Cornelius, the centurion, was in the Kingdom of God, although He did not know the Christ.

He was a man who prayed and gave alms and venerated God; but until the day when Peter, the Apostle, preached the Christ to him, he had not been a Christian.

But his prayers and his alms had come up with acceptance to God, and he was in the Kingdom of God, living up to all the light he had.

He was, therefore, rightfully brought into the Church of God.

I am grateful to think that there are vast numbers not in the churches who are in the Kingdom of God.

And there are vast numbers in the churches that never were in the Kingdom of God, but belong to the Devil. [Laughter.]

The Certain Effect of Sharp Discipline in the Churches.

I never speak but with respect of the Methodist Church.

Notwithstanding what has been printed about the matter in the secular and religious press, I never speak of that body, once so vigorous, but with respect.

Who that knows its history could but so speak?

Who that knows what John and Charles Wesley, and other wonderfully consecrated men of that period, did for true religion in England but would speak of them with the utmost respect?

But if they were to apply the discipline of John Wesley to that church today, there would be a mighty exodus.

No man, for instance, who makes, or sells, or takes that Liquid Fire and Distilled Damnation, called alcohol, can rightfully be a member of the Methodist church. [Applause.]

Apply the discipline, brethren, and you would cleanse the church, and get more converts than one per annum!

So with other churches.

Vigorous discipline would diminish the numbers, but it would increase the power and vitality of all the churches. If I can help to administer that discipline, God help me.

An Ecclesiastical Machine Has no Disciplinary Power.

You cannot get discipline administered inside a great, unwieldy ecclesiastical machine.

The machinery is oftentimes too much for the man who tries to operate it, and discipline has to come from without.

A mere ecclesiastical machine is a very hard thing to move; and when you have moved it, the result you get from it is very poor.

Individual Purity and Strength Necessary to Power Collectively.

The key to the power of the church is in the purity and strength of the individual.

Unless the individual components of a church are true to God, the church has no power.

A church is like an anchor chain of a thousand links; the strength of that chain is exactly the strength of its weakest link.

If that anchor is cast into the depths of the sea, and there is only one broken link, that broken link will sever the ship from the anchor, and let it go upon the rocks.

Likewise, if there be in the church one who is not right with God, the church will suffer.

Achan was the cause of the defeat of Israel at Ai.

Joshua commanded that they search through Israel until the offender was found.

He was only one man, but he had buried the Babylonish garments and the wedges of gold and silver in his tent, and for his sake Israel, which had prevailed at Jericho, was defeated in the conflict at Ai.

Therefore, I plead for a Christianity that is pure, where God's Way shall be known.

God's Way is the Christ.

The Christ will have no one in fellowship with Him who is also in fellowship with the World, the Flesh, and the Devil.

You have to decide on which side you will stand.

You can be a Christian all the time, or a Christian no time; but you cannot be a Christian on the Sunday, and something else on Monday, Tuesday, Wednesday, Thursday, Friday, and Saturday.

A Man Who Belongs to the Christ, Must Be a Christian at Home.

He must love and cherish his wife, as the Lord cherishes the Church.

An old grump, who is perpetually making trouble with his wife, may be called a Christian, but he is not a Christian.

A woman, who is perpetually making trouble with her husband, is not a Christian.

Children who fight with their parents, and are disobedient, are not Christians although their names may be upon the books of the church.

If you are not a Christian at home, then you are a devil all the time, although you may think that you are a saint in the church. Christianity begins at home; it begins in your heart.

It does not matter how high you stand on the rolls or in the offices of the church, your Christianity must be real or it does not count.

It must measure thirty-six inches to the yard, and weigh sixteen ounces to the pound.

Real Christianity means that when you are engaged to do work eight hours a day, you are not to put in a lick only now and then, and cheat your master out of three hours a day. [Applause.]

Christianity is an intensely practical thing.

When you have repented of your sins, you cannot go back to them and still be a Christian.

When you have exercised faith in the Christ, you cannot exercise faith in any other.

You cannot be a Christian during the day, and murder Hiram Abiff at night, singing your miserable Masonic "odes."

There Is No Christianity in Freemasonry.

A Christian is a Christian all the time.

He is not a man who at night strips off his clothes, puts on a dirty pair of drawers, an old shirt, and allows his eyes to be hoodwinked, and is led around the room with a tow-rope around his neck.

That man is not a Christian, he is a fool! [Laughter.]

He is murdered to represent the mythical Hiram Abiff, and then is raised by the mythical King Solomon, with the Lion's Paw, the grip of the Master Mason.

Then he hears the "omnific word," "Mah-hah-bone!" which always reminds me of Ma, have you got a bone?

Then he is supposed to come to life. He is no Christian.

He did not dare to name the Name of Jesus, the Christ, from the moment he entered that Lodge until he left it.

A Christian is a man who takes the Christ with him everywhere.

You cannot be a Christian and talk in a Cathedral about the "Great Architect of the Universe," and not mention the Name of Jesus from the beginning to the end of your discourse, as Bishop Clark did in Melbourne a short time ago.

A Bishop who is a Mason dares not name the Name of Jesus to his brother Masons, and he knows it; because a Jew may be a Freemason; a Mohammedan may be a Freemason.

The man who leaves out Jesus, the Christ, anywhere in his life, is not a Christian. [Applause.]

Chistianity means the Christ everywhere.

The Christ is All and in All.

If He is not so with you, then stand on the side to which you belong.

Do not call yourself a Christian in the morning, and call yourself something else at night.

Be a Christian All the Time.

Be a Christian with your wife, and with your family.

If you will put on an apron at night after supper, it is a good thing to put on an apron and help the wife clean up the dishes. [Applause and laughter.]

But it is not a good thing to put on an apron to go out and belong to the fools [laughter] and leave your wife, leave your family, leave prayer, and leave the loving association of family life.

If it is a good thing—come, I say, if it is a good thing, let us get the good thing into the light!

As for Jesus, the Christ, He said, when they charged Him with having said this and that:

I have spoken openly to the world; I ever taught in synagogues, and in the temple, where all the Jews come together; and in secret spake I nothing.

Christianity walks in the light as He is in the light.

Christianity has no fellowship with the Unfruitful Works of Darkness, but ever reproves them.

The Christ is God's Way.

The Christ is God's Truth.

The Christ is God's Life.

If the Church of God gets the Truth and hates the lie, and if the Church of God is filled with the Life of God, then we shall see the Christ triumph everywhere.

Growth of the Christian Catholic Church in Zion.

There has not been a day for the last seven years in which there have not been, on an average, seven persons baptized in the Christian Catholic Church in Zion.

I should want to say to my Overseers, Elders, Evangelists and Deacons who had no results, "Go and dig potatoes, or do some other work, but do not occupy the place of a Christian minister."

I am glad to tell you that

God Has Continuously Blessed This Australian Visitation.

When I closed my ministry in Sydney, Deacon McCullagh baptized eighteen.

When I closed my ministry in Melbourne, amidst all the hubbub, Overseer Voliva baptized thirty-four.

That makes fifty-two, exactly fifty-one more than all the Methodists got in a whole year in Victoria and Tasmania. [Applause.]

Since the Melbourne Visitation, the Overseer has received seventy-six applications for fellowship.

Talking like this stirs up things.

I came to stir up things. [Laughter.]

I did not come here for the purpose of doing nothing.

If I had had no Message to bring, I had better have stayed at home.

But I have a Message to bring; and I believe that the City of Adelaide will show itself to be the wisest and best of all the capitals of the states of the commonwealth and will hear me. [Applause.]

If any one differs with me, let him take this Exhibition Building, and show the people a better way.

I shall be delighted.

What is this Message?

This Gospel is, as I have said, not an Empty Creed, not a Pale Philosophy, not a gathering together of the thoughts of men; but this Gospel finds its impersonation in a Living Being.

Where is He? Where is He not?

The Christ Everywhere.

O Christ of God, if there were anywhere I could not find Thee, that would be the darkest spot in the Universe!

"Where'er we seek Thee, Thou art found," for Thou hast said, "Lo, I am with you All the Days, even unto the Consummation of the Age."

> The healing of Christ's seamless dress
> Is by all beds of pain;
> We touch Him in life's throng and press,
> And we are whole again.

There is no place where we cannot find Him.

Our Gospel is the Living Christ Himself, and He is with us everywhere, and All the Days.

I thank God that His Spirit is here; that His Spirit is in me, that His Spirit is in thee, and that His Spirit is in all who will receive Him, who will be brave and obey Him, speak His Truth, live His Life of Hope, and manifest His Love.

It takes more Love to speak the Truth than to conceal it.

It takes more Love to be brave and do the right than simply to pass on and let it go

This Gospel is therefore, as my text says,

A Gospel of Salvation and Healing.

"That Thy Way may be known upon earth, Thy saving" sickness, is that it? [Addressing Overseer Voliva.]

Overseer Voliva—"No, Sir."

General Overseer—Do you read it so? What is it? [Addressing Overseer Jane Dowie.]

Overseer Jane Dowie—"Saving Health."

General Overseer—"Oh," says some one, "do you not know that God saves us by sickness; that when He wants to be very kind, He makes us very sick, for 'whom the Lord loveth He chasteneth,' and that means, whom the Lord loveth He maketh sick?"

What do you do when the Lord loves you that way?

Do you say "O God, I am so thankful that You have sent me a fever. It is a token of love. Give me more, Lord. I am so glad that You have given me jaundice. Now give me something else of the same sweet kind; pile it on, O God!" [Laughter.]

You do not do it, you hypocrites!

You say that you believe that sickness is from God, but the first thing you do when you get sick is to cry, "Oh send for a doctor—Dr. Black, or Dr. Brown—to take it away."

Is that the way you do with gifts?

No, you hold on to them, and you would like another.

If God gives me a gift, I hold on to it; for all God's gifts are good. But, tell me, is smallpox good?

Do you like typhoid fever? [Laughter.]

Are you especially fond of measles? [Laughter.]

What nonsense this is!

Disease Is the Work of the Devil.

There never would have been Disease in this world but for Sin, and there never would have been any Sin but for the Devil.

It is a most shameful thing to talk about "saving disease," "saving sickness."

When the Christ came to preach the Gospel, He preached a healthy Gospel.

It was a Gospel for the spirit.

It was a Gospel for the soul.

It was a Gospel for the body.

It is the same old Gospel still. There is no change in it.

But the Church is changed.

It has gone into the Gospel of digitalis, nux vomica, arsenic, strychnine, Mother Siegel's Soothing Syrup, and Pink Pills for Pale People. [Laughter.]

That is a mighty gospel, is it not?

The Old Gospel said, Let a man repent, and let him believe and obey God, and he will get Salvation for his spirit, and for his soul, and for his body.

That is the Gospel that we bring, that Thy Way, the Christ, may be known upon earth, His Saving Health among All the Nations.

"O Dr. Dowie," says some objector, "do you not know that things have changed?

"Do you not know that now God has put aside the Gifts of Healings, and has given us doctors?"

What an exchange it would be if He had done it!

But when did He do it?

Medicine Not a Science.

"The Gifts of Healings are not in the Church now," they say; "we have the science of medicine!"

Well, which science is it, please? I ask.

Is it the allopathic science, which says *contraria contrariis curantur*, which tells us that the way to cure a disease is to put in an opposite one and knock the other fellow out?

If you put in a stronger poison to knock the poison of the disease out, what are you to do with the stronger poison you put in? Will that not do mischief?

"Oh, yes," says the allopath; "but by-and-by, if it does very much mischief, we get a still stronger one and knock that one out."

"But what do you do with the man?"

"Oh, at last we knock him out." [Laughter.]

That is true. So much for *contraria contrariis curantur*.

Then there is the homeopath.

His science is based on the proposition—*similia similibus curantur*; that is, like cures like.

That means that when you are sick, they give you the hair of the dog that bit you.

"When I desire to give a strong medicine," says the homeopath, "I give the 'infinitesimal potentiality.'"

The "infinitesimal potentiality!"

You could drink a bottlefull of it, and it would do you no harm. That is one thing in favor of the homeopath.

He fools you, but fools you with a thing that does not hurt you.

But which of them is the science of medicine that is to take the place of Gifts of Healings?

Is it the allopath, homeopath, psychopath, hydropath, isopath—which of all the paths that lead to the grave is the scientific thing that God gave?

He certainly did not give contradictory sciences.

If He has given us the science of medicine, it cannot be both *similia similibus curantur* and *contraria contrariis curantur*.

You cannot have it both ways.

Ask the doctors to agree.

The only thing they are good at is disagreeing.

The Disagreement of Doctors.

I knew of a naughty little girl, who wrote for the press in New York City.

She took five twenty-dollar bills and went into Fifth avenue, one of the best avenues of the city, where many noted doctors have their offices.

She went to five different doctors.

They all examined her.

One, after examining her, said that her heart was affected.

He gave her a diagnosis of her case and a prescription, and accepted a twenty-dollar bill as payment.

The next one told her that there was no doubt that her kidneys were badly affected.

He gave her a diagnosis and a prescription, and took the twenty dollars.

The third said that there were evidences of tuberculosis; that it would be very good for her not to apply herself too much to any hard work.

She got the prescription and the diagnosis, and paid the twenty dollars.

She went to another and another, and came back with five different diagnoses, and five different sets of prescriptions, none of which was correct; for the mischievous little girl was in perfect health.

Physicians Guessed Wrongly.

Some time ago, in the United States of America, a number of persons died in a small community.

They were all gravely buried after the doctors had given their certificates of death.

One said that it was heart failure—well, it is always heart failure, you know—another one said that it was fever, another one said it was senile decay, another said it was something else.

Investigation was made, and it was found that all these persons had partaken of a batch of baker's bread into which arsenic had been put.

Every one of these people, more than twenty in number, had died of arsenic poisoning, and not one of the ten or more doctors discovered it.

High Authority Against Medicine as a Science.

Professor Douglas Maclagan was the Professor of Medical Jurisprudence in the University of Edinburgh, and they often asked him to deliver the annual address.

He refused absolutely for more than twenty years.

At last he agreed to deliver it.

They gave him for a subject, "Medicine as a Science."

He said, "Do you want me to tell the truth about it?"

They said that they did. And they heard the truth.

I heard him say it myself.

I am not talking about what I do not know, because I had a narrow escape from being a doctor myself.

I wanted to see what there was in it, and I found that there was a great deal in it. The Devil was in it everywhere.

I found that the so-called science did not exist.

I was student of divinity and arts.

I was also honorary chaplain of the Edinburgh Infirmary, and went from bedside to bedside, ministering to the sick.

Oftentimes I was with them at the time of operation and investigation, and was with them in the hour and article of death. I saw many of them die as the result of operations.

The first words that Douglas Maclagan said were in substance:

"The noblest thing that God has made is an honest man.

"I have asked God to make me that.

"You have asked me to deliver this prelection upon "Medicine as a Science," and I intend to be honest.

"Gentlemen," he said, with his full, rich voice—which his son, the great Bishop of the Church of England, also had—"I tell you, as a professor in this University, and as a professor of medical jurisprudence for a quarter of a century, that medicine is not a science.

"It is purely empirical.

"From the days of Hypocrates and Galen until now we have been stumbling in the dark from diagnosis to diagnosis, and from treatment to treatment, and we have not found the first stone that we can lay as the foundation for medicine as a science."

Futility of the Germ Theory of Diseases.

How they groaned!

Some will say, "That was in 1869, but now medicine has become a science. We have a germicide to kill all the miserable microbes that infest humanity."

Have you?

Did not Professor Koch find a lymph that was exploited as a cure for consumption?

Did he not find something for which the German Emperor made him a Baron, somewhat hastily?

Professor Virchow examined his discovery and its effects.

The claim was that the lymph would drive the bacteria out.

"Yes," said Virchow, "I have examined thirty-nine of his dead patients, and it did so. It drove the parasite out of the diseased tissue into the healthy tissue, and killed the man twice as quickly."

Who will ûse Koch's Lymph now?

There is not a doctor of my acquaintance who will use it.

Many Ex-practitioners of Medicine in Zion.

I know a great many doctors, and am very friendly with them. I fight this matter out with them.

I have several doctors in Zion City who do not believe in medicine any more, do not take it, and do not administer it.

They are very useful citizens, excellent citizens.

I have left Zion City, at the present time, in the charge of the Rev. Dr. Speicher, who was a practitioner for ten years.

He was healed of cancer through faith in Jesus.

His father, also a doctor, died of the same disease.

All the good doctors agree with me, that there is no science in medicine; that there is no certainty in surgery.

Is There No Balm in Gilead?

Is there no physician who can heal?

Does not that Word mean what it says, that the Christ is God's Way, and that His Way of Salvation, and of Healing is to be known among all the Nations?

I know something whereof I speak.

For many years I have never touched drugs, or resorted to doctors.

I noticed the other day that one of the papers stated, among other lies, that seven hundred fifty of my people who went to New York with me, became sick, and went back home, and that I myself, had seriously thought of calling a doctor.

Not one of my people went back from New York on account of sickness.

Those who went back before the close of the Mission, were a small number who went back at the close of one week to take the places in Zion City of another number who were thus enabled to come to New York for the last week of the Visitation.

The whole thing, like a great many other things, was a lie.

So far, I have not much to complain about the Adelaide press, except that it copies into its columns statements that would be laughed at in America; things that are too ridiculous to talk about.

Indeed, you have only to compare them with other statements in their own columns to find the contradictions.

No Help Received from Pulpit or Press.

I have never had any help from either the press or the pulpit anywhere at any time, and yet I have preached to the largest congregations in the world, for the last ten years.

I am thankful to God for that.

I am thankful to God for the blessing that has accompanied my ministry.

I can live very well without the support of either the press or the pulpit.

I should be glad to get support from honest men in both professions.

I should be glad if my brethren in the ministry would deal fairly with me. I am in hopes that in Adelaide it will be so.

I have the desire that it shall be so.

I wish to treat the press and the pulpit with utmost courtesy, but if they need spanking, I can spank them at the proper time.

I do not intend to spank people who have done me no wrong—except the one for reprinting statements, things about which he had better have inquired.

But I cannot hold every editor responsible for that, because they have to fill up the columns of their papers, and make clippings from everywhere for that reason.

Free Advertising.

Next to thanking God I think I ought to thank the Devil; because the Devil has advertised the Christian Catholic Church in Zion and myself more effectually than I could have done if I had given a million dollars to the press.

I do not concern myself deeply about that, however.

The Word from which I am speaking tells you that God's Way is the Christ of God, Who is the Way of Salvation, and of Healing, and of Holiness, and the only Way to Heaven.

He is the Truth and the Life.

Salvation and Healing Go Hand in Hand.

Let me give you a very striking illustration of that.

A very distinguished and beloved Methodist minister for whom I have always had, and have today, the utmost respect and veneration, came to me one day. You all know him here.

He is known throughout the colonies—dear old Father Wattsford.

He had been healed through my agency of lumbago when he was a minister of the Brunswick Street church, Fitzroy.

He had been healed through my agency after Dr. Fitchett, editor of the *Southern Cross*, had come to ask me to pray for the aged man who was trying to lie on his back, but was rolling from side to side with his painful lumbago.

I have been told he has never had it since.

One day, shortly after his healing, he came to see me in my office in the Free Christian Tabernacle, Johnson street, Melbourne, not very far away from his own church.

We were friends.

He said, "Now, Mr. Dowie, if you would only preach the Gospel of Salvation as earnestly as you preach the Gospel of Healing, what wonderful results would come."

I said, "I do."

"Do you not preach more about Healing?" he asked.

"I tell the people who seek healing that they cannot be healed until they give up their sins," I replied.

"Then you preach Salvation first?" he asked.

I said, "I do."

"But," he said, "you give a great deal of time to Healing."

"I do; they come to me in thousands, and they are healed after they are saved."

"I believe in preaching the Gospel of Salvation," he said.

"You do it very eloquently," I replied, "but tell me, Father Wattsford, how many have joined your church through your preaching this last month?"

He scratched his dear old head for a minute, and then answered, "Two."

"Will you please look at my book?" I said; "I am to meet these candidates for fellowship tonight. Just read their names."

There were one hundred eighty-three.

"Why," he said, "how did you get them? Have you had a revival?" "We have that all the time," I replied.

Whole Families Led to the Christ Through Healing of One Member.

Then I pointed to whole families that were coming in through the healing of the mother.

Mrs. C—— was dying of cancer, and her husband was an ungodly man; her children were sinful.

After she was healed and raised up, able to return to her work, they all gave their hearts to God.

"Well," he said, "I am amazed."

Pentecost has been called the greatest day in the Church.

But it was not. At Pentecost, there were three thousand saved. Peter preached Salvation then.

A few days later, when Peter and John were the means of the Healing of the lame man at the Beautiful Gate of the Temple, there were five thousand men saved.

Brethren, beloved of God in all the churches, bear with me.

Take my Message, and do not attempt to row your boat with one oar.

If you do, you will go around and around, like a drunken man of whom I heard—I am not sure that this story is true—who got his wooden leg into a hole, and walked around it all night. [Laughter.]

I have seen some people like that. Ecclesiastically, they get their leg into a hole, walk around it for a whole year, and only get one convert.

Now, Divine Healing, and Divine Salvation go hand in hand.

The Savior who preached Repentance, and Faith, and Holy Living, healed the people.

The apostles who preached Repentance, and Faith, and Holy Living, were the means of healing to the people.

Bring this back, O God, to Thy Church, and then the world will be at Thy feet. [Applause.]

All who desire to live a good and holy life and to be God's children wholly, stand with me. [Many hundreds rose.]

Pray with me.

PRAYER OF CONSECRATION.

My God and Father, in Jesus' Name I come to Thee. Take me as I am. Make me what I ought to be in spirit, in soul, in body. Father in Heaven give us Thy Spirit, that we may be wholly Thine. For Jesus' sake. Amen. [*All repeat the prayer, clause by clause, after the General Overseer.*]

After the singing of the Doxology, the people were dismissed with the General Overseer's pronouncing the

BENEDICTION.

Beloved, abstain from all appearance of evil. And may the very God of Peace Himself sanctify you wholly; and I pray God your whole spirit and soul and body be preserved entire, without blame, unto the coming of our Lord Jesus, the Christ. Faithful is He that calleth you, who also will do it. The grace of our Lord Jesus, the Christ, the love of God, our Father, the fellowship of the Holy Spirit, our Comforter and Guide, one Eternal God, abide in you, bless you, and keep you, and all the Israel of God everywhere, forever. Amen.

At the close of the morning meeting, the General Overseer and the entire Around-the-World Visitation party, also Overseer and Elder Wilbur Glenn Voliva, went to the York Hotel, where they were very pleasantly and hospitably entertained during the remainder of their stay in Adelaide.

The rain had stopped before the morning meeting closed, and in the afternoon the sun came out, turning a wet day into a very beautiful one.

Lord's Day Afternoon Meeting.

No sooner had the morning meeting closed, than the people began to gather for the afternoon.

From every part of the City of Adelaide and its suburbs, from many neighboring towns and villages in South Australia, from Sydney, from Melbourne, from Perth and Fremantle in West Australia, in fact, from every part of the great island continent, the people had gathered for this Visitation to Adelaide, and presented themselves at the Exhibition Building in the afternoon.

Among the visitors were Deacon and Deaconess McCullagh (now Elder and Evangelist), formerly of Sydney, New South Wales, but now appointed to take charge of the work of the Christian Catholic Church in Zion in New Zealand.

In accordance with a suggestion from the police, the women who went to the building were given seats in the galleries, while the men were placed on the main floor.

Long before three o'clock, the hour for the beginning of the service, every available seat in the building was taken, and there were many who remained standing.

When the building was thus filled, about five thousand people being present, the police closed the turnstiles, and no more were permitted to enter.

Outside in the streets, thousands who had not been able to obtain tickets, and for whom there was no room in the building, stood quietly waiting for a possible opportunity to enter, while many others went away disappointed.

The largest audience that could be gathered in any building in Adelaide was present, and no one can estimate the number of thousands who came to the building and could not get in.

This meeting was, for the most part, a quiet one, although it was very plain that there were a few of the disorderly element present who would have broken up the meeting if they had dared.

At the slightest provocation they would laugh boisterously and senselessly, with the very evident purpose of disturbing and annoying the speaker and his hearers.

The General Overseer had not proceeded far with his discourse when there was a mysterious, sibilant, shuffling sound that seemed to come from nowhere in particular, that gradually grew in volume and then died away.

A few people stood up and attempted to see what the disturbance was, but they quickly resumed their seats, and order was restored.

It was not long, however, before the same sound was heard again, this time louder and more persistent than before, and resolving itself very certainly into a shuffling of a few score of restless feet.

The General Overseer was very patient and very calm, saying nothing at all about the matter, but proceeding quietly with his address. This interruption occurred several times, to the great annoyance of nine-tenths of the audience, until at last the police succeeded in partially locating the leaders, but not definitely enough to take action.

At last the General Overseer deemed it wise to remonstrate with the disturbers in behalf of good order.

That there was nothing fair or gentlemanly about them was proved by the fact that they paid not the slightest attention to his kindly-spoken and courteous remonstrances, but continued their ruffianly action.

It is sad to be compelled to say it, but this cowardly disturbance sometimes began in the galleries were the women sat.

Notwithstanding the shuffling and laughing, the General Overseer delivered an address, which was heard with deep respect by the great majority of the audience, and closed the meeting with good order.

His Message was delivered from a full heart, with great earnestness and convincing logic; so that his words were very effectual.

The following is the report of the service:

Exhibition Building, Adelaide, South Australia, Lord's Day Afternoon, March 20, 1904.

The Service was opened by the Congregation's singing Hymn No. 19 from the Visitation Program, "Jesus Shall Reign."

The Apostles' Creed was then recited, after which the General Overseer read the 35th chapter of the book of the Prophet Isaiah; also a part of the 11th chapter of St. Matthew.

Prayer was offered by Overseer Voliva.

After the announcements had been made, the tithes and offerings were received during the singing of the Hymn, "All Hail the Power."

The General Overseer then delivered the afternoon discourse.

JESUS' ANSWER TO THE QUESTION OF THE AGES.

*REPORTED BY E. W. AND A. W. N.

INVOCATION.

Let the words of my mouth, and the meditation of my heart be acceptable in Thy sight, be profitable unto this people, and unto all to whom these words shall come, in this and every land, in this and all the coming time, Till Jesus Come.

I desire to speak to you, this afternoon, from the 19th verse of the 11th chapter of the Gospel according to St. Matthew:

TEXT.

The Son of Man came eating and drinking, and they say, Behold, a gluttonous man, and a wine-bibber, a friend of publicans and sinners! And wisdom is justified by her works.

The last words of that verse, words spoken by our Lord Jesus, the Christ, are given differently in the Authorized Version: "Wisdom is justified of her children."

Practically, the meaning is the same.

Jesus was speaking, at this time, concerning that very wonderful man, the son of a priest of the order of Abijah, and of Elizabeth his wife.

I do not know of any one else in Scripture of whom it was ever said or written that they walked in all the commandments of Jehovah blameless, but it was said of Zacharias, the priest, and of Elizabeth, his wife.

John the Baptist was the son of that great priest, and was himself, of course, trained as a priest.

Wisdom the Principal Thing.

Wisdom is justified of her children.

It is of great consequence to remember that if Love is the Greatest Thing, Wisdom is the Principal Thing.

The Word of God, which declares Wisdom to be the Principal Thing, is indeed true; for even Love, without Wisdom, would mean irremediable misery to all concerned.

"Wisdom hath builded her house," the wise man says, and it has Seven Pillars.

It is the Apostle James who gives us the only definition of these Seven Pillars.

The Wisdom that is from above is first Pure, then Peaceable, Gentle, Easy to be Intreated, Full of Mercy and Good Fruits, Without Variance, Without Hypocrisy

The center of the House of Wisdom is the great Pillar of Purity.

Purity Is the Essential Thing in a Wise Man or Woman.

Impurity, Intemperance and Infidelity always go together.

But Purity is the Central Pillar in the House of Wisdom.

John the Baptist was essentially the champion of Purity.

He had seen it in the beautiful, saintly Elizabeth, his mother.

He had seen it in the lovely Mary, her cousin.

He had seen that Purity in Jesus, as He grew up in the house of Joseph in Nazareth; for he was closely related to Jesus.

He lived in an atmosphere of Purity. When the day came that he reached his priestly rank, and was then entitled to speak, he went forth to the fords of the Jordan, and there witnessed for Righteousness, Temperance and Judgment to come. He proclaimed Purity fearlessly.

He struck the foul king who sat upon the throne, and declared to her who sat at his side, that notwithstanding the Pharisees and priests had condoned her crime, and perhaps even agreed upon her divorce, she was an adulteress.

He did not fear to interfere in the affairs of state when the king was strangling the religious life of the nation.

He came in the spirit and power of Elijah, that Elijah who was not afraid to face Ahab and Jezebel.

He said to Herod, "Thou shalt not have her," and, of course, it was a dreadful offense.

She had married Herod according to the Herod-made law, but she was his brother Philip's wife.

John the Baptist was the Defender of family Purity.

Doom of the Impure.

Unless that is maintained, the nation must perish.

The nation that trifles with Purity is doomed.

The man who trifles with Purity will perish.

The woman who trifles with Purity must perish.

The first thing in Wisdom is Purity.

Over the fords of the Jordan, John rang out the word that reached the unclean paramour of Herod in her palace.

She said, "I will not rest until I have his heart's blood."

She felt as Jezebel felt against Elijah, and she acted like her.

Jesus was proclaimed to be the Christ by him who came in the spirit and power of Elijah, and whom the Lord declared was Elijah.

Having proclaimed the Christ, he said at the Jordan, "He that sent me to baptize with water, He said unto me, Upon whomsoever thou shalt see the Spirit descending and abiding upon Him, the same is He that baptizeth with the Holy Spirit."

He said, "I saw," and therefore He proclaimed Him to be the Messiah, the Anointed, the *Christos*, (χρίστος) the Savior of mankind.

He passed away with great humility, his work having been done. He retired into the deserts beyond Peræa or Galilee.

There the soldiery of Herod found him, arrested him, and took him to the dungeon of the castle of Machærus away down beyond the Dead Sea, and held him there.

The great purpose for which John was arrested was that he might be murdered.

It was not that he had done any wrong. He had merely maintained that law which exists and continues throughout all the ages.

The Ten Commandments Still in Force.

There are a great many people today who seem to imagine that the Ten Commandments have grown old, and are out of date.

In vain you call old notions fudge,
And bend your conscience to your dealing;
The Ten Commandments will not budge,
And stealing will continue stealing.

And lying will continue lying, and adultery will continue abultery, and murder will continue murder.

You cannot alter God's Law, and these Laws are written by His finger.

No matter what men may do, if for a moment they seem to suspend Divine Law, they can not alter it.

John, the wisest and best man of his time, was taken to prison.

Jesus said that among them that were born of women there had not arisen a greater than he.

He was taken to that dungeon, and cruelly treated, doubtless.

About the details of his imprisonment we know nothing, except the end of it all, when the voluptuous daughter of Herodias danced his head off.

Demoniacal Power of the Lustful Dance.

They say that a dance is a very simple thing, and is not to be spoken against at all.

But it has been always, in every age, the voluptuous dance that has been the cause of great misery and great war.

In this case it was the cause of John the Baptist's murder.

Before he was put to death, there came from him to the Christ a message.

It came through John's disciples to the Master, whilst He was preaching in Galilee.

This Message was in the form of the question: "Art Thou He that should come, or look we for another?"

John the Baptist's Temptation to Doubt.

It is very evident, therefore, that John the Baptist had begun to doubt; that in his mind there had arisen a question as to whether Jesus was the Christ. I know not how it came.

It is not surprising when you think of it.

It was exceedingly hard for a man who had lived in the open air on the mountain tops, and in the great broad plains beyond the Jordan, a man who had loved the mountain and the valley, a man whose heart was with nature in all her moods, to be imprisoned. Alone, and in that dungeon, he would feel the Tempter's power.

The Devil would probably put it this way: "If Jesus of Nazareth were indeed the Christ, would He leave you to die in this dungeon?

"You hear of His works; you hear that He controls the elements; you hear that He feeds people in the wilderness; you hear that He heals people, and that multitudes are blessed, and yet there He is, eating in the houses of the rich, and not caring for you, His forerunner, in this dungeon!"

So the temptation would come to wonder whether he had made a mistake—the temptation to doubt that Jesus was the Christ, and to wonder whether he had been proclaiming a selfish man.

These temptations would, probably, come to the great, strong Prophet as he lay in the dungeon of Machærus.

Doubt Is Most Miserable of All Torments.

When you doubt any one you love as to veracity, integrity, or purity, the torments of hell are yours.

That miserable spirit of doubt assailed John.

I do not think that he ever yielded to it; but perhaps some of his disciples said words that made him feel that it would be better to have this question answered authoritatively by the Christ Himself. He therefore sent two of them to Him.

When they found Jesus, the Christ, they found Him at work. They found Him teaching, and preaching, and healing. These were the three great features of His ministry.

[The General Overseer was interrupted by shuffling of feet.]

It is very surprising to me that so very simple a thing as that could cause some people to forget both the time and the occasion, and the nature of this work.

I hope it will not occur any more. [Applause. Shuffling.]

I am very quick to notice that there are a few persons scattered about this hall who endeavor to give a signal to others with their feet. I suppose all the brains they have are in their boots. [Laughter and applause,]

They are a very few, however, and we will be as kind to them as we can. [Applause.]

I suppose you have all read the passage, "Jehovah hath no pleasure in the legs of a man." I never knew before just why it was written.

The Question of All the Ages.

In John there seems to be doubt, but I think there was also great wisdom.

John wanted the answer authoritatively placed on record for every doubter in every age, "Art Thou He that should come, or look we for another?"

After all, that is the question of all the ages.

Was Jesus of Nazareth really the Son, the Christ, the Messiah of God? Does He still live, is He still King, and is He to come back to this earth to reign?

These are the central questions of the age.

They are the most important political questions; for religion always is the most potent power in social, educational, commercial and political life, and must ever be.

The way in which a man thinks determines the way he lives; for, "as a man thinketh in his heart so is he."

John therefore put that question to the Christ publicly, I think principally that he might get the answer of "Him who is made unto us Wisdom," who is Wisdom itself, personified, and who by His spirit of Wisdom is with us All the Days.

The answer of the Christ, therefore, is important.

The Christ looked at the messengers, and, lovingly thinking of His great, wonderful and mighty precursor, John, began to speak regarding him.

The Power of Testimony.

But first He gave the answer to John's question, and this was the answer:

Go your way and tell John the things which ye do hear and see; the blind receive their sight, and the lame walk, the lepers are cleansed, and the deaf hear, and the dead are raised up, and the poor have good tidings preached to them.

When He had said this, He began to talk about John.

John's disciples, no doubt, were immediately surrounded by the disciples of Jesus, the Christ, who began to tell them what Jesus had done. That is the greatest power after all, the power of testimony that cannot be assailed.

You can say that no one is healed, but I can say to the people in my own City, "Those who have been healed through faith in Jesus, the Christ, rise," and six thousand will rise. That is an unanswerable argument.

You can settle the question as to whether Jesus is the Christ, to this day, only by the justification which Wisdom gives of her works through faith in Him.

His answer, therefore, was "Go your way and tell John the things which you do hear and see."

Seeing and Hearing.

What you see is of less importance than what you hear; because, as a man hears, so will he understand.

There are many, of course, who have eyes and see not, ears and hear not, hearts and understand not, will not be converted and can never be healed.

These were the words of Jesus concerning the great priests of His own day. But it is not worthy of men that they should not open their ears and hear.

"Doth Our Law Judge Any Man Before it Hear Him?"

It is not Law that judges a man before it hears him; it is Lawlessness. Law never judges a man before it hears him.

That question was once asked by Nicodemus, the rabbi, in the Council of the Sanhedrin.

He said, in effect, "Doth our law judge any man before it hear him, and know what he doeth? You ought to have Jesus of Nazareth here. You ought to have His words and His works here." But that was the one thing His accusers did not want.

They did not want the people to hear the Christ.

They did not want the Council to hear the Christ.

But there were men like Nicodemus who were beginning to believe in Him, so that, in anger they rose up and asked him whether he were also of the Chiist.

Wise men will hear, and then if the matter is not right and will not stand the test of reason, and the test of fact, they reject it.

Listen, understand and then judge.

So the disciples of the Christ, as I have said, no doubt came around these disciples of John and said to them, "We want to show you some people who have been healed."

Some of the Christ's Witnesses.

So I think I see the dear little daughter of the Rabbi Jairus come up and say, "Go and tell John the Baptist that you saw me." "And who are you, little maid?" they would say.

Oh, she would be so glad to tell the story of how she was sick and dying, and Jesus was across the lake, but her father, the Rabbi of Capernaum, went and confessed the Christ openly at the side of the lake, and besought Him to come and see his daughter. But his daughter had died as they went.

Then she would tell the story of how she had heard the Master cry, "*Talitha cumi*—daughter arise," and grasp her hand, and her spirit came back, and she saw the face of Him she loved, and of those she loved, the father and the mother.

She perhaps said, "Go and tell John you saw me. I was dead, and He raised me."

Then a mother came up and said, "Now, wait a minute before you go. Tell John you saw me."

"Well, who are you, mother?"

Then, perhaps she said, "I am the widow of Nain. This is my son, and he was dead."

That poor boy had been lying dead, being carried to his grave, the people weeping as they went with the widow.

He was her only son, and perhaps he had not always been a very good boy. Perhaps she had much sorrow because of him, as your mothers may have because of some of you.

Perhaps she had had many a bitter cry because of her son's naughtiness, but she loved him. He was all she had.

She had been weeping and saying, "Oh, if the Christ were here, I would have asked Him to pray for my son."

The Christ made a journey across country, as you will see if you read the narrative.

He came there and met the funeral procession.

He touched the bier, saying to the woman, "Weep not," and to the young man, "Arise!"

The son himself perhaps said, as he stood by his mother's side, "Tell John the Baptist that you saw me, who was dead, and whom the Christ raised."

A Merited Rebuke.

These stories of the past have become idle fables to many of you; because you have never loved the Christ; you have never trusted Him; you have never seen what He has done, or felt in your hearts what He has wrought.

The blind came, and the deaf came, and the lame came, and they surrounded the disciples of John, and they said, "Go back and tell John that what Jesus says is true:

The blind receive their sight, and the lame walk, the lepers are cleansed, and the deaf hear, and the dead are raised up, and the poor have good tidings preached to them."

So John's Messengers went back to Jesus, and Jesus' Message rings down through the ages.

The Prophetic Proof of Jesus' Messiahship.

As he lay there in prison the great prophet would often think of one prophecy. He would think of Isaiah, 35th chapter.

He would see at once how it was being fulfilled in the Christ; how these desert places where the Christ preached were filled with joy and gladness; how the lame walked, deaf heard, and the Salvation of God came, and how they were being led into the King's Highway of Holiness. It is just the same story today.

I have no other Gospel to bring to you than the Gospel of Salvation, Healing, and the Cleansing Power of God through Faith in Jesus, the Christ.

My Message is being spoken that the ransomed of Jehovah may return, and come to Zion with songs and Everlasting Joy upon their heads, so that they may obtain Joy and Gladness, and that sorrow and sighing may flee away.

May this be your portion!

CLOSING PRAYER.

Father in heaven, for Jesus' sake, command Thy blessing upon this people in the Name, and for the sake of Him who sent this Message of Salvation, Healing, and Holy Living.

After the singing of the Doxology, the General Overseer dismissed the congregation with the

BENEDICTION.

Beloved, abstain from all appearance of evil. And may the very God of Peace Himself sanctify you wholly; and I pray God your whole spirit and soul and body be preserved entire, without blame, unto the coming of our Lord Jesus, the Christ. Faithful is He that calleth you, who also will do it. The grace of our Lord Jesus, the Christ, the love of God, our Father, the fellowship of the Holy Spirit, our Comforter and Guide, one Eternal God, abide in you, bless you and keep you, and all the Israel of God everywhere, forever. Amen.

A Mob at the York Hotel.

At the close of this service the General Overseer, Overseer Jane Dowie and Dr. A. J. Gladstone Dowie drove at once to the home of a friend in the suburbs.

The crowd in the street, however, anticipating that they would proceed to the York Hotel, gathered in the streets in front of this building.

In a very few minutes a mob of fully five thousand had formed. On the part of the great majority of them there seemed to be no especial animus, other than that of curiosity.

There were a few, however who showed the same diabolical hatred for the prophet of God that had marked the behavior of the well-dressed and apparently well-educated men and women who had disturbed the meetings of the Visitation of Sydney and Melbourne.

The General Overseer not appearing, they were obliged to content themselves with jeering and "boo-hooing" the other members of the party as they entered the hotel.

A large body of foot officers were on hand, but were apparently outnumbered by the mob, and the mounted police were ordered out.

Slowly and carefully, lest any one should be hurt, and yet firmly, the brave men on the splendidly trained white horses, pushed the crowd back until practically all the street in front of the hotel had been cleared. For some time, however, the crowd stood at a distance, kept back by the mounted officers.

At about half past five they at last quietly dispersed, so that when the General Overseer returned to the hotel at six o'clock, there were very few present to note his arrival.

The evening was spent quietly and peacefully at the hotel.

Unique Attitude of the Adelaide Press.

A very close acquaintance with the attitude of the secular press toward John Alexander Dowie as a man, as General Overseer of the Christian Catholic Church in Zion, and as Elijah the Restorer, during the last ten years, justifies us in according to the Adelaide *Register*, *Advertiser*, *Express*, and *Journal*, the unique distinction of having given the most complete and the most fair reports of his addresses that have ever been published by secular papers.

We are glad also to say that, with the exception of reprinting from the American press many ridiculous falsehoods, the treatment accorded the General Overseer previously to the opening of this Mission was, on the whole, better than that of the average secular paper. How these papers fell from their high estate will be developed in the course of the story of the few days' Visitation that will follow.

On Monday morning, March 21st, following the opening of the Visitation on the Lord's Day, the reports published in the *Register* and the *Advertiser*, the morning papers, were very fair, especially when contrasted with the reports in the Sydney and Melbourne newspapers.

The following is the report of the day's doings taken from the *Advertiser* of Monday, March 21st:

ELIJAH THE RESTORER.

A PEACEFUL BEGINNING.

SIGNS OF COMING TROUBLE.

The Rev. John Alexander Dowie, who claims to be Elijah the Restorer, inaugurated his mission in Adelaide on Sunday morning amidst peaceful surroundings. It was probably a disappointment to the prophet that at the morning service the Jubilee Exhibition Building was not filled—there was room for fully one thousand more hearers in the seats provided. Throughout the service perfect calmness reigned, and even when Mr. Dowie poured forth a vigorous attack on Methodists, Anglicans, Freemasons, doctors and other people, not a murmur rose from the large assembly. Mr. Dowie occupied an armchair on the platform, and lolled back in ease after carefully adjusting a large green plush cushion at his back. On his right hand were Overseer Jane Dowie, Dr. Gladstone Dowie, the Rev. C. Friend Hawkins, and Deaconess Hawkins. Sitting on the left were the Rev. Wilbur Glenn Voliva (Overseer for Australasia), Overseer J. G. Excell, Elder M. S. Voliva, Elder Stephen McCullagh, Evangelist McCullagh, and Deacon C. F. Stern. The deacons and deaconesses were attired in college robes, and wore mortar-board caps, but Colonel Stern wore the flashing uniform of the Chief of Police of Zion City. As soon as they had taken their seats Mr. Dowie lifted his hands above his head, and, stretching himself to his full height, said, "God be merciful unto us, and bless us, and cause Thy face to shine upon us, that Thy way may be known upon earth, Thy saving health among all the nations, for the sake of Jesus Christ. Amen."

Then he asked the people who had risen to be seated, and drank from a glass of mineral waters, with which Colonel Stern kept him liberally supplied throughout the meeting. A glance round the building showed that it was not the intention of Colonel Madley to allow any disturbance if he could prevent it. It was a strange sight at this religious meeting to see twenty stalwart policemen standing up in different parts of the hall, with their helmets on, and keeping a watchful eye on the congregation. There were also twelve detectives and plain-clothes constables engaged within the building.

The sweet, musical voice of Overseer Jane Dowie was heard leading the audience in prayer. Mr. Voliva then announced the various services to be held during the Adelaide Visitation, and stated that between twelve and one o'clock on Monday, the General Overseer would see all who were prepared to ask God for healing, through Christ. Mr. Dowie announced that free-will offerings would be taken up while hymns were being sung.

Then followed a lengthy report of the Message of the General Overseer.

THE AFTERNOON MEETING.

A SPLENDID AUDIENCE.

DISRESPECTFUL BEHAVIOR.

The audience which faced Mr. Dowie in the Jubilee Exhibition in the afternoon was of a character to inspire an orator with more than ordinary fervor. For an hour before the time (three o'clock) fixed for the beginning of the service, people were pouring in through the turnstiles, where attendants were placed to check the tickets. The women were for the most part sent by the courteous ushers at the doors into the balconies, which were soon crowded, although some women who were accompanied by their husbands were allowed to sit on the raised seats at the southern end of the hall, the male members of the congregation being massed together in the center. The accommodation there being too confined, they spread over into the spaces under the galleries, and even out into the annexes on either side. The dais was occupied by a piano and a number of ladies, and the narrow gallery at the north end also held many of the gentler sex. Before the prophet entered with his suite and occupied the seat prepared for him in the middle of the stage the hall was packed, over six thousand people probably being arrayed before him.

A broad band of ladies stretched round the building above the balcony railings, while the prospect along the auditorium showed one continuous sea of men's faces. A large proportion were young men, and some, it must be admitted, during the afternoon behaved themselves with execrable taste. Goldsmith, in the "Deserted Village," writes that "fools who came to scoff remained to pray," but history did not repeat itself on Sunday. The great majority of those present, however, were quite orderly. Many, no doubt, were attracted by sheer curiosity, but they evidently desired to hear what Elijah had to say, and they resented the disturbance created by an insignificant minority. Among those present were prominent business men, stockbrokers, and other hard-headed citizens. Sergeant Burchell and a number of police were conspicuous, but they had little to do during the service.

Punctually at the time appointed the prophet mounted the platform, attended by his suite. He was attired in a long, flowing black gown, with a white surplice and a beautiful purple stole, while his lawn sleeves were like those of a bishop. His high, round, shining forehead, his flowing hair, and his streaming grey beard gave him a patriarchal aspect, and it was manifest that he had spared no pains to dress his part effectively, and to look as much like the conventional idea of Elijah as possible. His attitudes in action and repose were all studied with equal care. On the right of the prophet were seated—in order from right to left—the Rev. C. Friend Hawkins, Overseer J. G. Excell, Dr. Gladstone Dowie and Overseer Jane Dowie. On the left of the chair, in order from left to right, were the Rev. W. G. Voliva (Melbourne), Mrs. Voliva, the Rev. S. McCullagh (Sydney), Mrs. McCullagh, Mrs. Hawkins and Colonel Stern, in a uniform of black and gold, with a resplendent gold belt.

The proceedings began with the singing of the hymn "Jesus shall reign where'er the sun doth his successive journeys run," which Mr. Dowie gave out with clear, resonant voice, and with good enunciation, verse by verse, in the old Methodist style. He then read two portions of Scripture from Isaiah and from Matthew, the latter chapter dealing with the dispatch of disciples to Christ by John the Baptist, and referring to the Elijah "which was for to come." During the reading the audience were very quiet, the only sounds other than the voice of the preacher being the occasional wail of a baby. In explanation of the verse "the kingdom of heaven suffereth violence, and the violent take it by force," Mr. Dowie remarked that the marginal reading "gotten by force" was preferable, and added that heaven was won by dynamic power, dynamic and dynamite being derived from the same word. "You can't fight evil with rose water," he said.

The Scripture having been read Dr. Gladstone Dowie recited the Apostles' Creed, Mr. Voliva offered up prayer, the prophet putting in a final sentence commending the petition to the notice of the Almighty, and then Mr. Hawkins made the business announcements, included among them being an information that Mr Dowie will, between twelve and one each day this week, see "all sick persons wishing to trust God for healing and pray with them." The hymn, "All hail the power of Jesus' Name," was sung while the freewill offering—apparently a very meager contribution—was collected, and then Mr. Dowie stood up to deliver his sermon, his text being Matthew 11:19, "Wisdom is justified of her children."

The address was of a purely evangelical character, and contained nothing objectionable to any one. For the most part it was listened to with attention, but occasionally there were rude and discourteous interruptions. None of these were vocal, if cheers and laughter can be excluded from that category, but they were none the less annoying to the preacher and the reputable section of the audience. A shrill cry from an infant caused the first diversion. It was recurrent and insistent, and at length Mr. Dowie turned to the northeastern corner of the gallery, and gave the direction, "Remove that child." There was a loud burst of laughter from the ribald few, and the prophet added, "There are some other children who may have to be removed." He was going on to speak of purity as the chief pillar of the house of wisdom, and to affirm that the Ten Commandments are not out of date, when a concerted shuffling of feet threatened to drown his words. This was followed by the agonized voice of yet another baby, with which the mother hurried to the door, but not without causing a great flutter in the audience.

"It is strange," said Mr. Dowie, "that you should forget the nature of this service because a little baby cries. In Zion we have a large baby-house, where all the infants are placed in good keeping and marked with checks, and the mothers go back after the service with the tickets and get the right babies." The shuffling beginning again, Mr. Dowie added: "In Chicago for two years I have preached regularly to seven thousand people, and have never been interrupted for a minute. There are people about the hall this afternoon trying to give the signal to others by shuffling their feet. All their brains are in their toes. I will try to be kind, but I must remind them that it has been written that 'Jehovah has no pleasure in the legs of a man.'"

The General Overseer went on to emphasize the power of unassailed testimony to the virtue of religion which was the most potent force in the social, political, commercial, and educational life of a community. When he called on those in Zion Tabernacle who had been healed by faith to rise to their feet, six thousand persons stood up. This was an up-to-date question, and they could prove the divinity of Christ today by such testimony. He referred to the healing of the centurion's servant and the raising to life of the son of the widow of Nain. A number of irreverent people in the audience, who had apparently never read the Bible, burst into loud laughter as the pathetic narratives were rehearsed; and Mr. Dowie said they treated the stories of the past as idle fables because of their ignorance of Christ and His teachings. Just here a policeman touched on the shoulder a man who was misbehaving himself, and a score of people stood up to see what was happening.

"Sit down! sit down!" expostulated the General Overseer. "Chairs were made for sitting on," and then he continued, more in sorrow than in anger:—"I have asked that no arrests should be made today. I should be glad if Adelaide proved itself the best behaved of all the Australian capitals in which I have spoken, and distinguished itself by its law-abiding qualities. My wife was born in this city, and I have many friends here. This is not the Adelaide I knew when I was here before, and which always knew how to conduct itself at a religious meeting. If all would behave as nineteen-twentieths of the audience want to behave there would be no trouble. The majority do not wish to countenance the interruptions. I have been a minister for twenty years, and I preached in Chicago—a very difficult center in which to hold an audience—for two years, and I was never interrupted there or met with such a great breach of courtesy as I have been subjected to in Australia."

With the solemn assertion that he preached no other gospel than that of salvation by the healing and cleansing power of God through Jesus Christ, the General Overseer concluded his discourse. After he had pronounced the benediction, the doxology was sung, and the congregation quietly dispersed. The service lasted exactly an hour.

A large crowd, largely composed of persons who had not gained admission to the building, waited outside for Mr. Dowie to come forth. He, however, left by the back entrance leading through the School of Mines' gate into Frome road. An outpost promptly apprised the crowd and they dashed in that direction. Mr. Dowie had intended to drive up to North terrace and thence to the York Hotel, where he is staying, but when he came in sight of the crowd the carriage was turned round and driven down Frome road, followed for a long distance by bicycles and traps. The crowd then surged towards the York Hotel, intending to lie in wait for the prophet. Soon between three thousand and four thousand men, shouting and singing, surrounded the hotel. The police-troopers, who had been warned to be in readiness, had thought that all danger of a disturbance was over and were unsaddling their horses. They were promptly called out and for a couple of hours were busily engaged in keeping the crowd back. An old gentleman with a long white beard happened to be on the balcony of the hotel. At once a cry was raised, "Here's Dowie, we've got him."

The gentleman pointed to himself and waved his hands in the air to explain that he was not the person sought, and soon the crowd were laughing heartily at their mistake. Forty policemen were engaged in maintaining order, but fortunately they had a good-humored crowd to deal with. Whenever a member of Mr. Dowie's band showed himself on the balcony the crowd made uncomplimentary remarks about his personal appearance, and called out, "Chuck Dowie down to us." Then the crowd sang lustily, "We'll hang old Dowie on a sour apple tree" and "Sons of the sea," of which Mr. Dowie has a special aversion. After an hour and a half the crowd gradually melted away without doing any damage, the news having been circulated that Mr. Dowie would not return to the hotel for tea.

We give also the following, from another column of the *Advertiser* of Monday, March 21st:

THE MODERN ELIJAH.

The Rev. J. A. Dowie conducted two services in the Jubilee Exhibition on Sunday, both of which were well attended. In the afternoon the audience was especially large, and for the most part those present behaved themselves like reputable Christians, although there was a disorderly element in the congregation, which covered itself with shame by its irreverence and lack of good manners. Those who composed the section of interrupters evidently forgot the respect due to Sunday as well as the character of the meeting. Mr. Dowie said nothing to provoke antagonistic feeling. He preached a gospel sermon, such as might have been delivered by the minister of any religious denomination in the city, without any abuse of other creeds or any assumption of special virtue for his own.

Whatever he may have said in the morning or in previous discourses, there was not a word to which any reasonable person could have taken exception on Sunday afternoon, and therefore there was absolutely no excuse for the senseless shuffling of feet and the loud outbursts of laughter which punctuated the prophet's utterances. The police exercised a wise discretion in refraining from interference, for any attempt at arrest would assuredly have caused a scene of wild disorder. Indeed they were asked to let the offenders alone. Mr. Dowie took matters very quietly and showed no sign of anger or excitement, although he manifestly felt annoyed and disappointed. It is asserted that there will be an organized attempt to break up Mr. Dowie's meeting in the Town Hall tonight, and that many bogus tickets have been printed in order to secure admission for the conspirators. For the credit of Adelaide, it is to be hoped that the persistent rumors to this effect, which have been in circulation for some days, are untrue.

"Freedom of speech" is a precious inheritance of the Britisher, and it should not be lightly interfered with in South Australia. Adelaide is wont to boast, with good reason, too, of its superiority to other Australian cities, and this particularly in regard to the fairness and courtesy with which it treats visitors, both in the field or on the platform. During the coming week it will have an opportunity of proving how much genuineness there is in the vaunt. Perhaps the reflection that Mr. Dowie will gain a greater degree of notoriety if he is made a martyr of than if he is listened to decorously and with patience will help the less orderly members of the community to behave themselves like intelligent human beings at his meetings. If they do not want to listen to him they can stay away. No one seeks to compel their attendance.

The report of the *Register*, concerning the Lord's Day afternoon meetings, was as follows:

ZION CITY MISSION.

OPENING IN PERFECT ORDER.

TWO SUCCESSFUL MEETINGS.

The complaint of some people that Zion City was putting a ring fence around itself so far as the Adelaide meetings were concerned, was not justified by the conditions at the Jubilee Exhibition building on Sunday. The Rev. John Alexander Dowie, General Overseer of the Christian Catholic Church, held two meetings on that day. The morning gathering, despite the rainy weather, was attended by about three thousand people, and in the afternoon the police closed the outer gates when five thousand persons had occupied all the available accommodation. The two addresses delivered by Mr. Dowie were in striking contrast to each other. The morning discourse, delivered with fine oratory, bristled with caustic criticisms on churches, doctors, and Freemasons, and the only interruption during the whole service was the frequent applause of the congregation. In the afternoon the address took the form of a simple gospel sermon, preached from Matthew 11:19, which was as colorless and temperate as anything to be heard in the nearest Sunday-school. Yet the peace and order of the morning had given place to a little impatience on the part of the people.

Probably they desired to hear an address of a more material description and to learn of the accomplishments in Zion City, for the slight interruption which took place was apparently due rather to impatience than to hostility. Certainly there was no provocation for it in anything that Mr. Dowie said, and it is his custom to give such addresses on Sunday afternoons. The police were in attendance in strong force, but there was nothing to call for their interference.

When Mr. Dowie had been speaking in the afternoon for about twenty minutes, a baby in the gallery—which had been entirely reserved for ladies—cried. Mr. Dowie requested the guardian to remove the child, whereat some people in the audience laughed. "I am afraid," remarked the General Overseer, "that there are some other children in the audience to whom I will have to speak. Let that suffice."

Later on another infant made itself heard, and more laughter followed. "Isn't it surprising," said Mr. Dowie, "that such a simple thing will cause some people to forget the time, the occasion, and the nature of this work? If we were in Zion we would hear no crying babies. There we have a baby-house, where, during services, the infants are cared for, checked, and returned to their mothers. If we had such a house here some of the older babies might go into it. [Laughter.] For two years I spoke in Chicago—admittedly one of the hardest cities in the world to speak in—to seven thousand people every Sunday afternoon, and I never knew what interruption was." [Applause.] The preacher proceeded, but a small section of the audience distracted the speaker by shuffling their feet, which caused others in the hall to stand up. "I notice a few people giving signals with their feet. I suppose all the brains they have are in their boots. There is a passage in the Scriptures which says that Jehovah hath no pleasure in the legs of man. I don't know what it means, I'm sure." Mr. Dowie continued in quietness, and said that at any meeting in Zion six thousand people would rise and testify to the reality of Divine healing. The shuffling broke out again. The interruption, in view of the evangelical nature of the discourse, was surprising. "Ah," remarked the General Overseer sorrowfully, "I am afraid that these grand old stories of the Bibles have become idle fables to you, because you have never loved Christ.

"I have asked the police to make no arrests on the Sabbath. I was in hopes that Adelaide would prove the one exception of the Australasian capitals in the matter of law-abiding and orderly people. [Cheers.] It would be very pleasing to Mrs. Dowie, who was born here, and to our many Adelaide friends, some of whom have been here over half a century. I am sure that nineteen-twentieths of this vast audience want to hear my message, and I hope that the well-behaved portion will not countenance disturbance. [Applause.] This is not apparently the Adelaide I once knew. I spoke in South Australia as a minister of the gospel for sixteen years without interruption. The few disturbers this afternoon sought my tickets on the agreement to be orderly, and, to say the least of it, they are guilty of a great breach of courtesy." [Applause.]

The General Overseer was permitted to conclude in quietness, but people wondered where the fire of his morning oratory had gone to. He spoke with studied calmness and clearness, every word being distinctly heard all over the building. The singing of the doxology closed a meeting which was over by four o'clock. It is stated that steps will be taken to prevent the baby nuisance at future meetings.

A large crowd awaited Mr. Dowie's return to his quarters at the York Hotel, but he had an engagement which kept him some time elsewhere, and a few in the crowd were discourteous enough to hoot the other unoffending American visitors as they entered the hotel. The platform on both occasions was occupied, among others, by Overseer Jane Dowie (who prayed in the morning), Dr. A. J. Gladstone Dowie, Overseer W. G. Voliva, Deacons A. W. Newcomb, C. F. Stern and C. F. Hawkins, Elders J. G. Excell, M. S. Voliva and Stephen McCullagh, Evangelist McCullagh and Deaconess Hawkins. All of them were robed except Deacons Stern and Newcomb, who appeared in gold-braided uniforms. Five thousand bulky programs were distributed in the hall, and the hymns were selected from them. Free-will offerings were taken up at each meeting.

Daily Bible Study for the Home

By Overseer John G. Speicher

MONDAY, JUNE 13TH.

Romans 13.—Rulers, Law and Gospel chapter.

Memory text—Verse 14. "Put ye on the Lord Jesus, the Christ."

Contents of chapter—Be subject to authorized rulers and powers; They are not a terror to those who do good; Render tribute, custom and honor to whom it is due; Owe no man anything; Love works no ill to neighbor; It is the fulfilling of the law; Cast off works of darkness; Put on armor of light; Careful and sober walking and living necessary; Put on the Lord Jesus, the Christ; Fulfil not the lusts of the flesh.

TUESDAY, JUNE 14TH.

Romans 14.—Duties to weaker brethren chapter.

Memory text—Verse 17. "For the Kingdom of God is not eating and drinking, but righteousness and peace and joy in the Holy Spirit."

Contents of chapter—The weak in faith to be considerately dealt with; Not to be despised; Each servant stands or falls to his own master; God able to uphold him; In matters of eating, or keeping of days, or other things, it is all before God, the Judge of all; He is Lord of living and dead; Every knee must bow to the Christ; Each one must give account of himself to God; Put no stumbling-block in the way of others; To those who hold things unclean it is sin to use them; Kingdom of God not meat and drink; Seek to do the things which edify; Whatsoever is not of faith is sin.

WEDNESDAY, JUNE 15TH.

Romans 15.—Gentile chapter.

Memory text—Verse 5. "Be of the same mind one with another according to the Christ Jesus."

Contents of chapter—Strong ought to help the weak; Scriptures written for our instructions and hope; With one accord glorify God; Gentiles to praise God for His mercy, believing that they may abound in hope, in the power of the Holy Spirit; Paul, as the minister of the Gentiles writes boldly to them, reminding them of their duties; Tells of his ministry to the Gentiles, where the Christ had not been preached; Writes of his coming to them, and asks prayers that he may be able to come in the joy of the Lord.

THURSDAY, JUNE 16TH.

Romans 16.—Salutation chapter.

Memory text—Verse 17. "Brethren, mark them which are causing divisions and occasions of stumbling, contrary to the doctrine which ye learned: and turn away from them."

Contents of chapter—Phœbe, a Deaconess, commended to their reception and assistance; Prisca and Aquila commended; Salutations to many others; Andronicus and Junias mentioned as "of note among the apostles;" The brethren are warned against those who cause divisions and occasions of stumbling; Their obedience known; Satan to be hindered shortly; Greetings from others; Benedictory words.

FRIDAY, JUNE 17TH.

1 Thessalonians 1.—Thanksgiving chapter.

Memory text—Verse 10. "Wait for His Son from heaven . . . even Jesus."

Contents of chapter—Greeting of Paul, Timotheus, and Silvanus to the Church of the Thessalonians; Assurance of their prayers for them; Remembrance of their faith, and love, and hope in the Christ; Gospel comes to them in the power of the Holy Spirit, although in much affliction; Their faith becomes known abroad; How they turned from idols to the true and living God; Their faith in the Second Coming of the Lord.

SATURDAY, JUNE 18TH.

1 Thessalonians 2.—Reminiscence chapter.

Memory text—Verse 12. "Walk worthily of God, who calleth you into His own Kingdom and glory."

Contents of chapter—Paul recalls the persecutions, and how with neither flattery nor covetousness he had ministered unto them; Not exalting himself or his office, nor making himself a burden upon them, he had preached the Gospel; Thanks God that they received the message as true and from God; They suffer persecution for doing so; Paul desires to see them again, but is hindered; They are his joy.

SUNDAY, JUNE 19TH.

1 Thessalonians 3.—Perfecting of faith chapter.

Memory text—Verse 10. "Perfect that which is lacking in your faith."

Contents of chapter—Timothy sent to establish and comfort them in their faith; His report of their love and faith comforts Paul; Paul prays that God might direct him unto them, and make them to increase and abound in love toward each other and toward all men, that they might be established, unblameable in holiness before God at the coming of the Lord Jesus, the Christ, with His saints.

MONDAY, JUNE 20TH.

1 Thessalonians 4.—Exhortation and Second Coming chapter.

Memory text—Verses 11 and 12. "Study to be quiet, and to do your own business, and to work with your hands. . . . Walk honestly toward them that are without."

Contents of chapter—Exhortation to be faithful to the charge given them; Will of God is sanctification, abstaining from fornication, having control over the passions, that no man wrong his brother; Exhortation to be quiet, to attend to their own business; Exhortation to work, that they might need nothing; Those who have fallen asleep in Jesus will God bring with Him; Dead in the Christ to rise first; Those that are alive will be caught up in the air to meet the Lord, and to be forever with Him.

TUESDAY, JUNE 21ST.

1 Thessalonians 5.—Admonition chapter.

Memory text—Verse 23. "May your spirit and soul and body be preserved entire, without blame at the coming of our Lord Jesus the Christ."

Contents of chapter—Day of the Lord to come suddenly; Children of the light need not be overtaken; Watch and be sober; Put on breastplate of faith and love, and the helmet of salvation; Not appointed to wrath but to salvation; Exhort and build one another up; Esteem highly in love those who labor for and are over the Church; Admonish disorderly; Encourage faint-hearted; Support weak; Long-suffering to all; None to render evil for evil; Rejoice always; Pray without ceasing; In everything give thanks; Quench not the Spirit; Despise not prophesyings; Prove all things; Hold fast the good, Abstain from every form of evil; God, who calls, is faithful, and will sanctify spirit, soul, and body.

WEDNESDAY, JUNE 22D.

2 Thessalonians 1.—Patient waiting chapter.

Memory text—Verse 11. "That our God may count you worthy of your calling, and fulfil every desire of goodness and every work of faith with power."

Contents of chapter—Greeting to the church; Thanks God because of their growing faith and abounding love; They were patient and faithful amidst persecutions and tribulations; God recompenses tribulation to the troublers; The troubled to rest; Waiting for the Coming of the Lord from heaven, with vengeance upon those who obey not the Gospel; Wicked will be driven from presence of the Lord when He comes to be glorified in His saints; Paul prays for them, that they may be accounted worthy of God's calling, and that He might fulfil in them all the good pleasure of His goodness; That the Name of the Lord Jesus, the Christ, might be glorified in them.

THURSDAY, JUNE 23D.

2 Thessalonians 2.—Signs of the End chapter.

Memory text—Verses 3 and 8. "For it will not be, except the falling away come first, and the Man of Sin be revealed. . . . And then shall be revealed the Lawless One."

Contents of chapter—Concerning the Coming of the Lord, minds to be stayed; Not shaken or troubled; Falling away must first be; Man of Sin and the Lawless One to be revealed; Lord Jesus will slay with breath of His mouth, at His coming; Those who receive not the truth given over to believing a strong delusion or lie; True disciples must stand fast and hold traditions which they have been taught; Hearts to be comforted and good works and words established.

FRIDAY, JUNE 24TH.

2 Thessalonians 3.—Warning against disorderly brethren chapter.

Memory text—Verse 6. "Withdraw yourselves from every brother that walketh disorderly."

Contents of chapter—Paul asks them to pray that he may be delivered from unreasonable and evil men; All have not faith; The Lord is faithful and will establish and guard from the evil one; Commanded to withdraw from those who walk disorderly; To imitate him; He had been an ensample to them, working night and day; Disorderly to work in quietness and eat their own bread; Brethren exhorted not to be weary in well-doing; Note the disobedient; Admonish him as a brother; Salutation.

SATURDAY, JUNE 25TH.

1 John 1.—Walking in the light chapter.

Memory text—Verse 7. "If we walk in the light . . . the blood of Jesus Christ His Son cleanseth us from all sin."

Contents of chapter—Jesus, the Word, was from the beginning, has been heard, seen, and touched by the Apostles; Fellowship with Him; His Message is that God is Light; No darkness at all in God; We cannot walk in darkness and be in fellowship with Him; The fellowship is in the Light; His blood cleanses from all sin; It is a lie to say that we have not sinned; He forgives and cleanses when we confess.

Memorabilia of the New York Visitation

By Mrs. Emily Ware

WHEN John the Baptist began his ministry, the Jews were looking for three persons—the Christ, the Elijah, and that Prophet.

In the 1st chapter of John, in the 19th verse, it is recorded that they sent the priests and the Levites out to ask John if he was not the Christ. He said that he was not.

Then they asked, "What then? Art thou Elias?" and he said, "I am not;" and again they asked, "Art thou that Prophet?" and again he answered, "No."

That he was one of the three, they were sure.

We know that he was Elijah, because it is recorded in Matthew 17:11-13 that the Christ told His disciples that John was Elijah.

With the Christ there was even greater doubt as to His identity.

Strange that those who had the world's greatest work to do, should have been surrounded with such mystery! Why was this?

It is because there are certain conditions to be met, before light comes on any subject.

Mathematics, chemistry, all sciences, are shrouded in mystery until certain steps are taken to unravel it all.

John the Baptist, (John 1:31,) said that he had come to baptize with water, so that the Christ should be made manifest to Israel; or, in other words, he had come to show them that they must repent of their sins and be baptized, before their eyes should or could be opened to know the Christ.

It is probable that not one person recognized Jesus as the Messiah save those who had obeyed John in repentance and baptism.

Will it be so again?

Many of the things seen today are beyond comprehension until the initial steps are taken. No stone must be left unturned; no light turned aside.

The times are as momentous as when the Christ made His first appearance.

New York certainly took the first step by turning an attentive ear, as is seen by all the testimonies given in the Memorabilia.

Many, and especially the Jews, dimly saw the prophet.

Let all who read these testimonies pray that each successive step may be taken by those who received the Messages so gladly and who listened to the words of the prophet with joy.

MRS. SARAH WILLIAMS, 189 Campbell avenue, Chicago, Illinois.—I thank God for the privilege of doing Restoration work every day during the New York Visitation.

We were met everywhere with the utmost courtesy and kindness.

Many who came to the meetings had evidently been studying the subject of the coming of Elijah.

One young man told me that as soon as he heard that the General Overseer was coming to New York he had taken his Bible and had satisfied himself that if the Bible was true the Elijah must come before the Christ.

I was much surprised when he told me that he had never been a professing Christian.

We met a young man on the street who recognized us as members of the Host. He was an Episcopalian, wore a St. Andrews' pin, and was evidently a church-worker.

He asked us where we found in the Bible that there was to be a work of Restoration.

We took out our Bibles and showed him Matthew 17:11 and Acts 3:22. He was much astonished and said that he had never heard it mentioned in the church.

He jotted down the texts in his note-book saying that he intended to go thoroughly into the subject.

Everywhere they had words of praise for the fearless way in which our dear General Overseer rebuked sin.

I am eagerly looking forward to our next Visitation.

MRS. MABEL BOCCASINI, Chicago, Illinois.—I wish to add my testimony to the memorabilia of the New York Visitation.

One afternoon, as I stepped out of the back entrance of Madison Square Garden, I met a lady carrying an oil portrait of a little girl.

As my husband is a portrait artist, I entered into conversation with her about the picture. I then told her of Zion.

She lived far out of the city, and was seldom in New York. She had heard of the meetings, but was not interested enough to attend.

I influenced her to remain to the evening meeting, and obtained a ticket for her.

After the evening meeting, as I came from the choir robing-room, she was looking for me.

When she caught sight of me, she came running to me, full of enthusiasm, saying, "You are the lady who gave me the ticket to attend this meeting. I thank you! From this night on, I am a 'Zionist!'"

She walked out of her way to accompany me to my room so that she could question me regarding the work of Zion.

This incident cheered me very much, and I was very grateful to God.

I thank God for using me to bring a blessing to, at least, this one.

MRS. MINNIE CUTHBERT, Zion City, Illinois.—It was very inspiring and interesting to me to see the way in which we were received by the people.

They were very glad to receive the Messages, and many asked for tickets of admission to the meetings.

In the Bowery I found many greatly interested, who wanted to know the truth about Zion.

I met a man one day on the street, who said, "Hallelujah, for John Alexander Dowie's Mission! Pray for my wife and daughter, they are reading and believing the lying press, but I know he is God's prophet."

Two ladies in Brooklyn asked us to pray that the way might be opened for them to attend the meetings. God answered prayer, and seeing them afterwards, I was told that they had received rich blessings.

One lady called her guests down to see us and introduced us as "Dowie's representatives," but we told her we were God's representatives, for we had a Message from Him.

They were deeply impressed, and took the Literature gladly.

I received many offers of hospitality, and the last Saturday of our stay, in which no regular Restoration work was done, I spent the entire day with a family who received quite a load of Zion Literature from us.

God greatly blessed our visit, and I thank Him for the great joy I had in the work with Zion Restoration Host.

MEETINGS IN ZION CITY TABERNACLES.

SHILOH TABERNACLE.

Lord's Day—Early morning service.... 6:30 a. m.
Intermediate Bible Class.. 9:45 a. m.
Bible class, conducted by Deacon Daniel Sloan... 11:00 a. m.
Afternoon service........ 2:30 p. m.
Evening service......... 8:00 p. m.
First Lord's Day of Every Month—Communion service.
Third Lord's Day of Every Month—Zion Junior Restoration Host rally.
Third Lord's Day of Every Month—Consecration of children.........................10:00 a. m.
Monday—Zion Restoration Host rally (Second Monday of every month).... 8:00 p. m.
Tuesday—Divine Healing meeting..... 2:30 p. m.
Tuesday—Adult Choir .... 7:45 p. m.
Wednesday—Baptismal service........ 7:00 p. m.
Wednesday—Citizens' rally............ 8:00 p. m.
Friday—Adult Choir.................. 7:45 p. m.
Friday—Officers of the Christian Catholic Church in Zion........ 8:00 p. m.
Friday—Junior Choir.................. 3:45 p. m.
Meeting in the officers' room.

TWENTY-SIXTH STREET TABERNACLE.

Lord's Day—Junior service............ 9:45 a. m.
Lord's Day—German service..........10:30 a. m.
Tuesday—German service .... 8:00 p. m.

Zion Literature Sent Out from a Free Distribution Fund Provided by Zion's Guests and the Friends of Zion.

Report for the week ending May 21, 1904:
2,925 Rolls to.........Hotels in the United States
6,000 Rolls to.....Business Men in Various States
559 Rolls.........................Miscellaneous
1,018 Rolls to.........................Switzerland
Number of Rolls for the Week.............10,502
Number of Rolls reported to May 21, 1904, 3,156,272

EVANGELIST SARAH E. HILL,
Superintendent Zion Literature Mission,
Zion City, Illinois.

How beautiful upon the mountains are the feet of him that bringeth good tidings, that publisheth peace, that bringeth good tidings of good, that publisheth salvation; that saith unto Zion, Thy God Reigneth!—*Isaiah 52:7.*

Zion's Bible Class

Conducted by Deacon Daniel Sloan in Shiloh Tabernacle, Zion City, Lord's Day Morning at 11 o'clock, and in Zion Homes and Gatherings throughout the World.

MID-WEEK BIBLE CLASS LESSON, JUNE 15th or 16th.

God's Light Shines Amid Darkness.

1. *The Light scatters darkness.*—John 1:4-13.
God said, "Let there be light."
He sent His Son who is the Way.
He enlightens every man.

2. *The Light comes in ever-increasing force.*—Ephesians 5:6-18.
God gives more and more Light.
God expects people to walk in the Light.
Men must not sleep when the Light shines.

3. *To have the Christ is to have no darkness.*—John 8:12-27.
One cannot follow Him and not have Light.
He gives more than Light to all who obey.
He gives assurance and strong consolation.

4. *The nearer we get to Him the more light we have.*—1 John 1:3-6.
God is Light.
All who know Him have Light.
Do the truth and you will get Light.

5. *The Light shows God's way out of darkness.*—Acts 26:13-20.
Only God can open blind eyes.
He turns from darkness to Light.
He shows men that they must repent.

6. *The dividing line between Light and Darkness is shown.*—1 John 2:7-11.
The Christ is the True Light.
A man cannot believe in the Christ and hate any one.
The darkness is the foe of righteousness.

7. *We are to carry the Light to all who sit in darkness.*—Luke 1:68-79.
We must send out the Light.
Some will not otherwise come to know it.
They find it hard to get out; seek them out.

The Lord Our God is a Light-manifesting God.

LORD'S DAY BIBLE CLASS LESSON, JUNE 19th.

Darkness of Ignorance now Envelopes the People.

1. *Property and success will blind their eyes.*—Luke 17:26-30.
Men plan big things in these days.
Business schemes go with a rush.
The love of the world blinds one to the plan of God.

2. *One cannot have light if engrossed with this world.*—Luke 12:31-40.
Some hold on to their property.
They will not give up houses and lands.
They will lose the Kingdom God offers.

3. *Half of those who profess our Lord will not see Him when He comes.*—Matthew 25:1-13.
The time of waiting makes some careless.
They neglect to have the Holy Spirit.
They only try to keep up appearances.

4. *No darkness will be in the hearts of those who fear God and obey Him.*—Isaiah 60:2-12.
Some can see God's plans plainly.
Some believe a great awakening is coming.
Things will turn in favor of him who serves God.

5. *That day comes upon the masses as a thief comes in the night.*—1 Thessalonians 5:1-11.
The masses do not practice self-denial.
They think no harm will come to them.
They believe what foolish preachers say.

6. *But a few, even in the churches, will be awake when Jesus comes.*—Revelations 3:1-6.
Most Christians live dirty lives.
They are mixed up in unclean practices.
But few will be saved.

7. *The people will be following their own vain imaginations and delusions.*—Psalm 2:1-12.
They rage at God's Prophets.
They hate to have the Christ come.
They will refuse to obey the Truth.

8. *The falling away from faith and vital godliness will increase.*—2 Thessalonians 2:1-12.
Various ways will be used to shake confidence.
The man who loves the truth will be saved.
The coming of the Lord is now near.

God's Holy People are an Expectant People.

OBEYING GOD IN BAPTISM.

"Baptizing Them Into the Name of the Father and of the Son and of the Holy Ghost."

Eighteen Thousand Four Hundred Fifty-five Baptisms by Triune Immersion Since March 14, 1897.

Eighteen Thousand Four Hundred Fifty-five Believers have joyfully followed their Lord in the Ordinance of Believer's Baptism by Triune Immersion since the first Baptism in Central Zion Tabernacle on March 14, 1897.

Baptized in Central Zion Tabernacle from March 14, 1897, to December 14, 1901, by the General Overseer,	4754			
Baptized in South Side Zion Tabernacle from January 1, 1902, to June 14, 1903, by the General Overseer..	37			
Baptized at Zion City by the General Overseer........	583			
Baptized by Overseers, Elders, Evangelists and Deacons, at Headquarters (Zion City) and Chicago......	4940			
Total Baptized at Headquarters..................	——			10,314
Baptized in places outside of Headquarters by the General Overseer..............................		641		
Baptized in places outside of Headquarters by Overseers, Elders, Evangelists and Deacons...........		7109		
Total Baptized outside of Headquarters............		——		7,750
Total Baptized in seven years....................				18,064
Baptized since March 14, 1904:				
Baptized in Zion City by Elder Royall...............	63			
Baptized in Zion City by Elder Hammond...........	90			
Baptized in Zion City by Elder Adams	40			
Baptized in Zion City by Evangelist Reder...........	24			
Baptized in Chicago by Elder Hall..................	9			
Baptized in Chicago by Elder Cossum................	19			
Baptized in Chicago by Evangelist Christie	3			
Baptized in Chicago by Deacon Matson............ ..	4			
Baptized in Chicago by Elder Kosch.................	6		258	
Baptized in California by Elder Taylor..............		5		
Baptized in Canada by Elder Simmons...............		6		
Baptized in Canada by Elder Brooks................		4		
Baptized in Colorado by Deacon Cook...............		3		
Baptized in England by Overseer Cantel............		10		
Baptized in Illinois by Deacon Sprecher.............		1		
Baptized in Indiana by Elder Osborn................		2		
Baptized in Minnesota by Elder Graves		5		
Baptized in New York by Elder Warszawiak..........		14		
Baptized in New York by Overseer Mason		19		
Baptized in Ohio by Deacon Arrington...............		14		
Baptized in Ohio by Deacon Kelchner...............		2		
Baptized in Pennsylvania by Elder Bouck............		13		
Baptized in South Africa by Overseer Bryant.........		13		
Baptized in Texas by Evangelist Gay................		13		
Baptized in Washington by Elder Simmons...........		1		
Baptized in Washington by Elder Ernst..............		8	133	391
Total Baptized since March 14, 1897......				18,455

The following-named eighteen believers were baptized in St. George's Hall, Newtown, Sydney, Australia, Tuesday, February 23, 1904, by Deacon J. S McCullagh:

Allen, Violet Harris ....George street, Canterbury, Sydney, Australia
Chapman, George Herbert........14 Buckingham street, Sydney, Australia
Cunliffe-Owen, Phillip Edward...........31 York street, Sydney, Australia
Devitt, Mrs. Sarah Jane,
66 Ashmore street, Erskinville, Sydney, New South Wales, Australia
Haines, Elizabeth Sarah........Wallerawang, New South Wales, Australia
Hunt, Percy Bordon........35 Terry street, Surrey Hills, Sydney, Australia
King, Catherine..Hillside, Catherine street, Leechhardt, Sydney, Australia
Kircher, August ......1 May and John streets, Newtown, Sydney, Australia
Newton, Blanche Lily, 55 King st., Newtown, New South Wales, Australia
Niness, Annie ....20 Neville street, Marrickville, Australia
Read, Miss Elizabeth Susanna,
38 Denmant street, Glebe, New South Wales, Australia
Ready, Joan.......38 Denmant street, Glebe, New South Wales, Australia
Rees, Ivor Hugh ....49 Victoria street, Ashfield, Sydney, Australia
Secky, Mary..25 Westbourne st., Petersborne, New South Wales, Australia
Sinfield, Ivy Josephine, 50 Mullens st., Balmain, New South Wales, Australia
Smith, Lilly..75 Foveaux street, Surrey Hills, New South Wales, Australia
Smith, Minnie, 75 Foveaux street, Surrey Hills, New South Wales, Australia
Walker, Alfred..................Bishop street, Peters, Sydney, Australia

The following-named ten believers were baptized at Uitenhage, Cape Colony, South Africa, Lord's Day, April 17, 1904, by Overseer Daniel Bryant:

Bates, Mrs. Clara Harriet, John street, Uitenhage, Cape Colony, South Africa
Bates, Henry William ...John street, Uitenhage, Cape Colony, South Africa
Dingle, Herbert S.....Young street, Uitenhage, Cape Colony, South Africa
Dingle, Mrs. Lillian A, Young street, Uitenhage, Cape Colony, South Africa
Edmunds, Gilbert B..Durban street, Uitenhage, Cape Colony, South Africa
Johnson, Mrs. Annie Hardysherer,
Baird street, Uitenhage, Cape Colony, South Africa
Johnson, John August...Baird street, Uitenhage, Cape Colony, South Africa
Magennis, Frederick A..Durban st., Uitenhage, Cape Colony, South Africa
Norton, David, 37 Sherlock street, Port Elizabeth, Cape Colony, South Africa
Rostel, Albert Gustav,
Lower Drosdty street, Uitenhage, Cape Colony, South Africa

The following-named three believers were baptized at Uitenhage, Cape Colony, South Africa, Tuesday, April 19, 1904, by Overseer Daniel Bryant:

Pannell, Mrs. Mariah..College Hill, Uitenhage, Cape Colony, South Africa
Smith, Campbell Martin..Caledon st., Uitenhage, Cape Colony, South Africa
Smith, Mrs. Johanna Cathleen Elizabeth,
Caledon street, Uitenhage, Cape Colony, South Africa

The following-named two believers were baptized at Barnard, Indiana, Saturday, May 7, 1904, by Elder S. B. Osborn:

Blaydes, Mrs. Linne Catherine ....Barnard, Indiana
Kelso, William Joseph.................................Barnard, Indiana

The following-named two believers were baptized in the South Side Zion Tabernacle, Lord's Day, May 15, 1904, by Deacon G. W. Matson:

Rogers, Dalma Walter.........290 East Sixty-third street, Chicago, Illinois
Washington, Leroy.................2948 Armour avenue, Chicago, Illinois

The following-named two believers were baptized at Philadelphia, Pennsylvania, Lord's Day, May 15, 1904, by Elder R. N. Bouck:

Deichert, Robert ....545 Venango street, Philadelphia, Pennsylvania
Woodruff, George Sydney,
1924 West Passyunk avenue, Philadelphia, Pennsylvania

The following-named five believers were baptized at San Antonio, Texas, Lord's Day, May 15, 1904, by Evangelist William D. Gay:

Kinman, Miss Victorienne..........Rural Route No. 8, San Antonio, Texas
Kontnik, Mrs. Fannie..........Number 9, Army Post, San Antonio, Texas
Redford, Mrs. Clara......610 Day avenue, West End, San Antonio, Texas
Stanley, Fred John................Rural Route No. 8, San Antonio, Texas
Stanley, William Henry, Jr........Rural Route No. 8, San Antonio, Texas

The following-named four believers were baptized in the South Side Zion Tabernacle, Chicago, Illinois, Lord's Day, May 15, 1904, by Elder W. H. Cossum:

Chobanian, Serope....................103 Austin avenue, Chicago, Illinois
Holwig, Emma....139 One Hundred Forty-seventh street, Chicago, Illinois
Narcissian, G.......................................Chicago, Illinois
Paterson, Mrs. Isabell,
136 One Hundred Forty-seventh street, Chicago, Illinois

The following-named four believers were baptized in the West Side Zion Tabernacle, Chicago, Illinois, Lord's Day, May 15, 1904, by Elder L. C. Hall:

Johnson, Mrs. Carl A. ......864 North Springfield avenue, Chicago, Illinois
Johnson, Carl A............864 North Springfield avenue, Chicago, Illinois
Schulz, Fred C. ....1506 West Ridgeway avenue, Chicago, Illinois
Thompson, Ross ....473 South Forty-second avenue, Chicago, Illinois

The following-named seven believers were baptized at Cincinnati, Ohio, Lord's Day, May 15, 1904, by Deacon A. E. Arrington:

Bang, Caroline Dorothea................316 Milton street, Cincinnati, Ohio
Coghill, Joseph B..........................30 Park avenue, Hartwell, Ohio
Devore, Mrs. Jennie...............302 Sycamore street, Cincinnati, Ohio
Obershine, Miss Julia.............1010 Rittenhouse street, Cincinnati, Ohio
Sayrs, W. C.. ....Wilmington, Ohio
Thompson, Emma. ....Pleasant Ridge, Ohio
Vandervoort, Miss Maud.............2123 Gilbert avenue, Cincinnati, Ohio

The following-named twenty-four believers were baptized in Shiloh Tabernacle, Zion City, Illinois, Lord's Day, May 22, 1904, by Evangelist E. W. Reder.

Baker, Mrs. Christine...............2009 Horeb avenue, Zion City, Illinois
Baker, Conrad.........................2009 Horeb avenue, Zion City, Illinois
Booth, Lawrence.......................3016 Elim avenue, Zion City, Illinois
Crawford, Graham.................3005 Gabriel avenue, Zion City, Illinois
Goodwin, W. N........................2604 Elim avenue, Zion City, Illinois
Hilyard, Joseph......................2606 Gilboa avenue, Zion City, Illinois
Innes, Harold......................2013 Gabriel avenue, Zion City, Illinois
Kesler, Paul Thomas..................2912 Elim avenue, Zion City, Illinois
Kruse, John..........................2903 Gilboa avenue, Zion City, Illinois
Leech, Porter.........................1707 Horeb avenue, Zion City, Illinois
McGillivray, Mrs Alice.............2500 Gideon avenue, Zion City, Illinois
Mentzer, Rachel ....2712 Emmaus avenue, Zion City, Illinois
Morris, Archie Lester...............2117 Gilead avenue, Zion City, Illinois
Morris, Mrs. Mary E.................2117 Gilead avenue, Zion City, Illinois
Morris, Wm. L....... ....2117 Gilead avenue, Zion City, Illinois
Nowlan, Edward ....2820 Ezekiel avenue, Zion City, Illinois
Puhl, Mrs. Katie.....................1910 Ezekiel avenue, Zion City, Illinois
Purvis, Emma........................2016 Hebron avenue, Zion City, Illinois
Oulman, Nellie.....................................Albert Lea, Minnesota
Rottmayer, Miss Lillian Mattie.......2617 Elim avenue, Zion City, Illinois
Rottmayer, William..................2617 Elim avenue, Zion City, Illinois
Saunders, Rubin I..............................Plankinton, South Dakota
Vanosdel, Elmer....................2907 Gilead avenue, Zion City, Illinois
Yenney, Walter.......................2314 Gilgal avenue, Zion City, Illinois

The following name was omitted from the list of names of children consecrated to God in Shiloh Tabernacle, Zion City, Illinois, Lord's Day, April 17, 1904, by Overseer John G. Speicher:

Campbell, Byron Frederick..........2803 Elijah avenue, Zion City, Illinois

A WEEKLY PAPER FOR THE EXTENSION OF THE KINGDOM OF GOD
EDITED BY THE REV. JOHN ALEX. DOWIE.

Volume XV. No. 7. *ZION CITY, SATURDAY, JUNE 4, 1904.* *Price Five Cents*

GOD'S WITNESSES TO DIVINE HEALING.

HEALED OF INFLAMMATORY RHEUMATISM.

IN ALL THEIR AFFLICTION HE WAS AFFLICTED,
AND THE ANGEL OF HIS PRESENCE SAVED THEM:
IN HIS LOVE AND IN HIS PITY HE REDEEMED THEM;
AND HE BARE THEM, AND CARRIED THEM ALL THE DAYS OF OLD.

It is a beautiful thought that the Christ knows all about every pain and sorrow that has ever come to humanity.

> Surely He hath borne our griefs,
> And carried our sorrows.

He has borne upon the cross every pain and every sickness, and every sorrow and pang of death. He has suffered them all.

Every temptation that has ever come to mankind it has been His to suffer and overcome.

He is "touched with the feeling of our infirmities."

He was "a man of sorrows, and acquainted with grief."

He is the great Burden-bearer of humanity.

No word comes nearer expressing the great heart of love and the boundless sympathy that He possessed, than the words of our text:

> In all their affliction He was afflicted.

Not one of God's children can suffer but what the Christ suffers with Him; the Head with the Body.

When we are wounded He is wounded.

When we are oppressed He is oppressed.

When we are in sorrow, He sorrows with us.

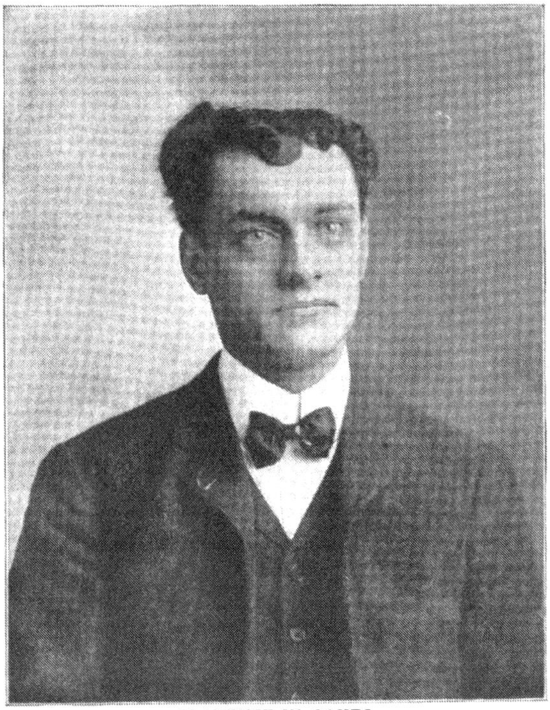

CLARENCE W. OAKES.

"What a balm for the weary!"

What a happy resting-place we have in Him!

We may not understand disease and its nature, but we can understand the wonderful love of God.

We may not know the cause of disease, but we know that the remedy is in God.

How little man has learned about the cause and nature of disease!

How little even is known of the more common component parts of the human system!

Who can describe a drop of blood and its formation?

Who can tell how one little corpuscle is made?

Where is the workshop from which is turned out the millions of little globular cells that go to make up the wonderful consistency of the human blood; the red corpuscles and the white corpuscles in just the right proportion; with just the right consistency of the fibrin and the fluids; with just enough iron to give it the proper tone; and the right shape and size of these corpuscles?

Where are the molds in which they have been fashioned?

Science is silent.

The young man who writes his testimony had inflammatory

rheumatism. Will the doctors please explain the cause of this destructive disease?

They talk learnedly about the uric acid in the blood. What is uric acid, and what causes its excess in the blood?

Why do the organs not eliminate the poison?

Why should the tissues of the joints be especially attacked?

Why is recurrence so likely, after having once suffered from the disease?

Why is the heart liable to suffer disease when the body is attacked with rheumatism?

Why does the sufferer need to undergo prolonged agony and generally remain sick for weeks, in spite of all the skill of the medical professsion?

Why has not some certain remedy been found for so common a disease?

Why?

But there is no end to the inquiry!

It is all mystery and all confusion.

The only certainty is in God!

There is no longer any doubt as to the love and mercy of God in healing disease.

Surely the Christ loves His own, and He will take care of them; His Church; His body. He has given His life that we might go free!

In the words of the Psalmist we can cry to God, "Thou art my Help and my Deliverer!"

O hear my cry, be gracious now to me,
Come, Great Deliv'rer, come;
My soul bowed down is longing now for Thee,
Come, Great Deliv'rer, come.

I have no place, no shelter from the night,
Come, Great Deliv'rer, come;
One look from Thee would give me life and light,
Come, Great Deliv'rer, come.

My path is lone, and weary are my feet,
Come, Great Deliv'rer, come;
Mine eyes look up Thy loving smile to meet,
Come, Great Deliv'rer, come.

Thou wilt not spurn contrition's broken sigh,
Come, Great Deliv'rer, come;
Regard my prayer, and hear my humble cry,
Come, Great Deliv'rer, come.

I've wandered far away o'er mountains cold,
I've wandered far away from home;
O take me now, and bring me to Thy fold,
Come, Great Deliv'rer, come.

J. G. S.

WRITTEN TESTIMONY OF CLARENCE W. OAKES.

2114 EMMAUS AVENUE,
ZION CITY, ILLINOIS, May 22, 1904.

DEAR GENERAL OVERSEER:—I feel it a duty as well as a pleasure to add my testimony to the many already given to God's power and willingness to answer prayer.

It is now over three years since my hardest attack of rheumatism, which I had had more or less since childhood.

I did not know what it was to trust God for my healing until December 9, 1899.

I was taken very ill with rheumatism on December 7, 1899.

At that time I had Doctor Becker, of Chicago, hired by the year.

I had not called the doctor yet when I sent for my mother, Mrs. L. E. Oakes, of 473 South Western avenue, Chicago, who had been healed by God.

She came and asked me if I was ready to trust God for my healing.

I told her I was, and asked her to send for an Elder of the Christian Catholic Church in Zion, which she did.

An Elder came and talked with me in regard to my spiritual condition, read the 5th chapter of James, and prayed with me.

When he left I went to sleep, and slept about an hour, which I had not done for two days and one night.

When I awoke, I was feeling very much better.

I asked for my clothes, and by the help of my wife, dressed and went out to supper.

By the time we finished supper I was able to get around very well, while before I went to sleep I had no use of my limbs at all, with the exception of three fingers on my left hand.

That evening I shaved myself.

The following day I went to Central Zion Tabernacle at Sixteenth street and Michigan avenue, a distance of over four miles; and the next day I went back to my work as a street-car conductor on Robey Street car line.

During the evening I lost sight of God and did not trust Him as I should and I became very sick again; but in a short time after I had made several restitutions I was restored to health.

On February 26, 1901, I was taken very suddenly ill while home at supper.

I received great blessing when an officer of the Church prayed with me, but I went out on a very stormy day and caught more cold and had a relapse.

I was then taken with chills and fever which ran into what Dr. Sayrs called rheumatic fever.

I then became partially paralyzed. My jaws would set at times so that I could not talk and I was not able to move.

During my illness different Elders came to see me.

I would receive a great blessing, but was not able to get up from my bed for some time, for I was too weak.

I had lost about fifty pounds. When I became sick I weighed one-hundred sixty-three pounds and when I was able to get up I weighed a little over one hundred pounds.

I tried to work in the month of May, but took another relapse. This time it went to my lungs and I had pneumonia.

May 28, 1901, it seemed that I could not live the night through, but God heard our prayers and next morning two Elders came, laid hands on me and anointed me with oil in the name of the Lord Jesus, and I received my healing at that very time and began to grow better and stronger.

I was soon able to go out, but my ankles were so weak I could not stand on them long at a time as they would turn over, and the bones became so out of place that they would come through the bottoms of my feet.

I still have a scar on the bottom of my foot where the bones came through.

Dr. Speicher and Dr. Ruby both examined me and said that I must take rest and keep off my feet.

I took a trip to the country and on my return I went back to work again on July 24, 1901.

I also thank God for many other blessings we received, and for taking away the appetite I had for drink, tobacco and snuff.

I also want to thank the many friends who were kind to me and my family during my illness.

I pray God that some other poor sinner will see the truth as I did and be saved before it is too late.

I am so glad I heard of our General Overseer and of his teaching. May God forever bless Him. I am,

Your brother in the Christ,
CLARENCE W. OAKES.

CONFIRMATION OF TESTIMONY BY DR. JOHN H. SAYRS.

ZION CITY, ILLINOIS, May 23, 1904.

BELOVED GENERAL OVERSEER:—I am glad to speak a few words confirming the testimony of Clarence W. Oakes, formerly of 273 Park avenue, Chicago, Illinois, now of 2114 Emmaus avenue, Zion City, Illinois.

I was sent to pray for him at the time he was most helpless, in March, 1901. He could not lift his head off the pillow. The paralysis was general, and, from a medical standpoint, all hope was shut out.

He was fully trusting God for blessings, and received much blessing when we prayed and laid on hands, and was soon out about his work. His was evidently a miracle of healing.

I thank God for having permitted me to see so many healings of the sick, in answer to prayer in Zion.

I pray God to bless your leadership as Elijah the Restorer.

Yours for our Master's cause,
JOHN H. SAYRS, M. S., M. D.
Registrar Zion Educational Institutions.

MEETINGS IN ZION CITY TABERNACLES.

SHILOH TABERNACLE.

Lord's Day—Early morning service.... 6:30 a. m.
Intermediate Bible Class.. 9:45 a. m.
Bible class, conducted by Deacon Daniel Sloan... 11:00 a. m.
Afternoon service........ 2:30 p. m.
Evening service......... 8:00 p. m.
First Lord's Day of Every Month—Communion service.
Third Lord's Day of Every Month—Zion Junior Restoration Host rally.
Third Lord's Day of Every Month—Consecration of children........................ 10:00 a. m.
Monday—Zion Restoration Host rally (Second Monday of every month).... 8:00 p. m.
Tuesday—Divine Healing meeting..... 2:30 p. m.
Tuesday—Adult Choir .... 7:45 p. m.
Wednesday—Baptismal service........ 7:00 p. m.
Wednesday—Citizens' rally............ 8:00 p. m.
Friday—Adult Choir.................. 7:45 p. m.
Friday—Officers of the Christian Catholic Church in Zion........ 8:00 p. m.
Friday—Junior Choir.................. 3:45 p. m.
Meeting in the officers' room.

TWENTY-SIXTH STREET TABERNACLE.

Lord's Day—Junior service............ 9:45 a. m.
Lord's Day—German service..........10:30 a. m.
Tuesday—German service .... 8:00 p. m.

Zion Literature Sent Out from a Free Distribution Fund Provided by Zion's Guests and the Friends of Zion.

Report for the week ending May 28, 1904:
1,000 Rolls to.........Hotels in the United States
373 Rolls........................Miscellaneous
5,000 Rolls to Business Men in Various States of the Union.
1,800 Rolls to Hotels in Europe, Asia, Africa, and the Islands of the Sea.
500 Rolls to. . Russia, Germany and Switzerland
Number of Rolls for the Week..............8,673
Number of Rolls reported to May 21, 1904, 3,164,945

EVANGELIST SARAH E. HILL,
Superintendent Zion Literature Mission,
Zion City, Illinois.

ELIJAH THE RESTORER

A WEEKLY PAPER FOR THE EXTENSION OF THE KINGDOM OF GOD.

EDITED BY THE REV. JOHN ALEX. DOWIE.

Application for entry as Second Class Matter at Zion City, Illinois, pending.

Subscription Rates.		Special Rates.	
One Year	$2.00	100 Copies of One Issue	$3.00
Six Months	1.25	25 Copies of One Issue	1.00
Three Months	.75	To Ministers, Y. M. C. A's and Public Reading Rooms, per annum	1.50
Single Copies	.05		

For foreign subscriptions add $1.50 per year, or three cents per copy for postage.

Subscribers desiring a change of address should give present address, as well as that to which they desire LEAVES OF HEALING sent in the future.

Make Bank Drafts, Express Money or Postoffice Money Orders payable to the order of JOHN ALEX. DOWIE. Zion City, Illinois, U. S. A.

Long Distance Telephone. *Cable Address "Dowie, Zion City."*

All communications upon business must be addressed to
MANAGER ZION PUBLISHING HOUSE,
Zion City, Illinois, U. S. A.

Subscriptions to LEAVES OF HEALING, A VOICE FROM ZION, and the various publications may also be sent to

ZION PUBLISHING HOUSE, 81 EUSTON ROAD, LONDON, N. W., ENGLAND.
ZION PUBLISHING HOUSE, NO. 43 PARK ROAD, ST. KILDA, MELBOURNE, VICTORIA, AUSTRALIA.
ZION PUBLISHING HOUSE, RUE DE MONT, THABOR 1, PARIS, FRANCE.
ZIONSHEIM, SCHLOSS LIEBBURG, CANTON THURGAU, BEI ZÜRICH, SWITZERLAND.

ZION CITY, ILLINOIS, SATURDAY, JUNE 4, 1904.

TABLE OF CONTENTS.

LEAVES OF HEALING, SATURDAY, JUNE 4, 1904.

Notes From The Overseer-in-Charge.

"HEAR, O ISRAEL; THE LORD OUR GOD, THE LORD IS ONE."

AND THOU shalt love the Lord Thy God with all thy heart,
And with all thy soul, and with all thy mind,
And with all thy strength.
This is the First Commandment.

THE TRUE relationship between man and God is one of absolute obedience and service.

THERE CAN be no allegiance to or alliance with any other power, or influence, or association.

IN MATTERS of morals the standard of God must be adhered to unswervingly.

IN MATTERS of business the whole aim and object must be the extension of the Kingdom of God.

THERE CAN be no other thought than that God is supreme, and that we live and move and have our being in Him; not for our pleasure, but for His Divine purposes.

MAN EXISTS for God and not God for man.

GOD HAS a right to propose and to dispose.
It is for man to hear and obey.

THE PEOPLE of Zion are learning this lesson, and are glad to know what God would have us do.

THE PEOPLE have been left so largely to seek out the truth for themselves that they become confused.

Zion has cleared the way and is setting forth the grand and perfect standard of Holy Living as the road to God.

BLESSED ARE the pure in heart,
For they shall see God.

THE STRONG denunciation of sin in every form by our dear General Overseer has brought forth a storm of hatred from the powers of hell in many lands.

The notable exception to this is in Switzerland, where he has been received most kindly, and where a most important work has been accomplished.

THE FOLLOWING cablegram was received from him on last Lord's Day:

ZURICH.

SPEICHER, Zion City, Illinois:

Read Psalm 113, first four verses.

Visitation to Zurich most successful.

Order is perfect and interest intense.

Results glorious.

Conducted sixteen meetings in eight days.

Have laid hands upon one thousand one hundred sick persons.

Baptized forty-one, and expect a very large baptism tomorrow morning.

Consecrated today one hundred ten children, and will ordain new officers.

Received large number of members, and will administer the Ordinance of the Lord's Supper this afternoon.

Have had two large church conferences, with good results.

Many are coming to Zion City.

The total attendance at the meetings has been more than thirty thousand.

Many have been saved, healed and blessed.

Close the Visitation tomorrow.

God willing, I shall visit Bern June 1st, Geneva 2d and 3d, Lausanne 4th, Neuchatel 5th, Liebburg 6th, Berlin 8th and 9th, London 12th and 13th.

Will sail for New York on the Lucania, by way of Liverpool, on the 18th.

Will be in New York 26th and 27th.

Home again on the 30th.

Love to Zion everywhere.

Pray.

Mizpah. DOWIE.

THE DIFFERENCE between the people of Zürich and elsewhere is that they are more noble, and their hearts more ready to receive the truth.

His denunciations against vice in all its forms are no doubt no less severe.

IN THE land where tobacco-smoking and beer-drinking are so common, it is encouraging to see how kindly they listen to his words, and how gladly they obey the commands of God.

IN ADDITION to the cablegram received on Lord's Day, we had the joy of hearing from the General Overseer, from Bern, Switzerland, on Wednesday of this week.

He begins his Message with the 19th chapter of Revelation, and the 6th verse, which reads as follows:

And I heard as it were the voice of a great multitude,
And as the voice of many waters,
And as the voice of mighty thunders, saying,
Hallelujah: for the Lord our God, the Almighty, reigneth!

Continuing his cablegram, he says:

Closing meetings of the Visitation in Zurich were full of blessing.

Immense audiences overflowed the building.

Received five hundred six members into fellowship Lord's Day.

Ordained thirty-two officers.

Administered Ordinance of the Lord's Supper to over one thousand.

Monday morning baptized one hundred twenty-five; during Visitation forty-nine; total (in Zurich) one hundred seventy-four.

Visited Rigi, Lucerne, Interlaken, Grindelwald yesterday.

Arrived at Bern today; will open Visitation by meeting tonight.

President of the Swiss Confederation will receive me tomorrow afternoon, and American Minister Saturday, at Lake Geneva.

Pray for the remainder of the Visitation in Europe.

Love to all in Zion.

Mizpah. DOWIE.

THESE SIGNAL successes in Switzerland mark a new era in the religious development in Europe.

There can be no doubt as to the meaning of the great movement in Zion.

The world is surely awakening to the fact that Zion is becoming a world-power in religion.

The empire of secretism long ago discovered it.

WE BELIEVE that the secret of this success in Zürich is that German peoples are not under the same domination of Freemasonry which exists in the English-speaking countries.

WHEREVER MASONRY and Rome control we are sure to find the most bitter opposition against Zion.

WE MADE mention in these columns, a short time ago, of the relations existing between Freemasonry and Methodism, and the influence Masonry has over the Apostasy in general.

The following item from *The Bookseller, Newsdealer, and Stationer*, of May 15th, shows how intimately they are connected:

The first number of a new monthly magazine—the *New Age*—is to appear this month in Nashville. It is to be published by the Supreme Council of the Thirty-third Degree Masons, and printed by the publishing house of the Methodist Episcopal Church, South. F. P. Elliott, recently associated with Harper & Brothers, of New York, is the managing editor, and George Flemming Moore, of Montgomery, Alabama, is Masonic editor. Henry W. Thayer, who designs the covers of the *Century Magazine*, has been engaged to design the covers of the *New Age*.

ZION'S GREAT opponent is to be found in the apostasy controlled by Freemasonry.

Freemasonry does not like purity of life, but it seeks license for indulgence of every form of evil.

Freemason banquets, as a rule, are nothing more nor less than hells of drinking, and carousing, and smoking.

IN THE midst of the common vice of filthy tobacco-using, it is refreshing to read an article like the following from the Chicago *Tribune* of May 17th:

MR. ROOSEVELT NEVER SMOKES.

ASSURANCE WINS ANTI-CIGARET LEAGUE FIFTY DOLLARS, PROMISED BY MRS. CARRIE NATION.

When Mrs. Carrie Nation visited the office of the Anti-Cigaret League, last week, she poked her umbrella through a picture of President Roosevelt. "He is a smoker and chewer," she said.

"The President is a nice man, and would not use the filthy weed," rejoined Miss Lucy Page Gaston.

"Prove it, and I'll give the league fifty dollars," said Mrs. Nation.

Yesterday, in Willard Hall, Miss Gaston exhibited this message, addressed to her from the White House:

The President does not, and never has used tobacco in any form.

Very truly yours, WILLIAM LOEB,
Secretary to the President.

"We will get a new picture with part of the fifty dollars," said Miss Gaston, cheerfully.

WE TAKE it for granted that this is true of President Roosevelt, and that he does not use tobacco in any form.

We take pleasure in recording this fact and presenting it to our readers.

We wish it could also be said that he never drinks; and if it can be shown that he does not use intoxicating liquors, we shall be glad to give space in these columns to this fact.

GOD HASTEN the day when the great men and rulers of this Nation shall be men who have but one God, the God of Israel, whom they love with all their heart, with all their soul, with all their mind, and with all their strength. Then and then only can they rule in righteousness. Then only can the Nation be fully blessed of God.

SEXUAL IMPURITY has become so common in society, among all classes of people, that today comparatively little is thought of the shocking condition of things that obtains, especially in the large cities.

There must be some reasons why impurity is so largely on the increase.

One of these reasons is undoubtedly the result of the practices of the medical schools, which admit to the dissecting-rooms men and women alike, where the nude and dead body is examined and cut up in the most shocking manner by both sexes, without any pretence whatever to modesty.

THE GENERAL freedom of the medical profession in examinations and operations upon women is disgustingly common, and must be exposed and denounced.

The shameful custom of the so-called local treatments is becoming a most distressing curse in all the land.

ANOTHER SOURCE of contamination comes through the so-called Art, which knows no sense of shame or modesty. The ungodly custom of having nude models before the class is dragging down the young men and young women to debasing immorality.

The following clipping from the Chicago *Tribune* of recent date, tells of this disgusting practice:

NUDE MODEL FOR MIXED CLASS SHOCK TO BOSTON.

WOMAN INSTRUCTOR INSISTS THAT THERE IS NO HARM AND MUSEUM TRUSTEES BACK HER—RULE FOR THIRTY YEARS.

BOSTON, MASSACHUSETTS, May 29th.—[Special.]—The good people of Boston, who have retained the sensibilities of their Puritan ancestors, were much shocked on learning recently that mixed classes in the Museum of Fine Arts study from undraped models.

The information given out by Miss Emily Danforth Norcross, the instructor, that such study has been the custom for years, has only increased the horror of her less artistic critics. It is doubtful, however, that there will be any change, as the board of twenty-eight trustees approves of her plan.

"The class is only a small one," explained Miss Norcross, "and is composed of advanced pupils studying for the Paige scholarship. There are two women to one man in the class, and none of them ever objected or gave evidence of being shocked."

The school was organized thirty years ago, and the practice of mixed classes prevailed almost from the start. The action of the executive council was not unexpected, as members expressed the fullest confidence in Miss Norcross, and are in sympathy with her conduct of the school. Several members of the board declared they look upon the criticism as an attempt merely to cause a sensation.

BUT THIS is not the worst.

In a certain art school in the City of Chicago, recently, there was brought before the class in drawing, consisting of twenty-five young men, a girl twelve years of age, for a nude model.

These boys themselves protested against such a shameful act, and the authorities had to furnish an older model.

BUT ALMOST anything passes, as long as it is done in the name of Science or Art, and the man who speaks against the disgusting custom of nude statues and nude paintings is called "prudish."

Thank God, Zion stands then for prudishness!

We shall ever raise our voice against these accursed customs which inflame the minds of men and women, and destroy all the sacredness of the human form, which is pronounced to be the "Temple of God."

THE ST. LOUIS exposition unblushingly exposes to the view of young and old alike the most obscene and disgraceful works of art, which would be prohibited from public view in all well-thinking communities, but because of this being a national affair, license is given for vice to run riot.

But as long as church-people give sanction and encouragement to the flesh shows of the theaters, there can be little hope of opposition by them to the impure in art.

IN A RECENT article in *Life* entitled, "A Catechism of Civics," as reprinted in *The Electric City*, of Chicago, a number of questions are asked concerning various topics and facetious answers are given in the following strain:

Where is the Corn Belt of the United States located?
It extends from the Chicago Exchange to Trinity Church in Wall street.
Does the climate vary much in different parts of the Union?
Yes.
What is the mean temperature?
Where Uncle Russell Sage happens to be.
What is considered to be the hottest region in the country?
Zion City.
And the coldest?
John D. Rockefeller's Safety Deposit Vault.

THE WORLD is getting an idea that Zion City is quite a hot place.

By the grace of God we will continue to make it a hot place for the sinner.

THE FIRE of God burns hotter than the Fire of Hell.

ELIJAH THE RESTORER has come, also, in the office of the Messenger of the Covenant, of whom it is said:

Who may abide the day of his coming, and who shall stand when he appeareth?
For he is like a refiner's fire, and like fuller's soap:
And he shall sit as a refiner and purifier of silver,
And he shall purify the sons of Levi,
And purge them as gold and silver;
And they shall offer unto Jehovah offerings in righteousness.

THE FIRE is melting out the dross and impurities, and only the pure metal is remaining.

WE SHALL let the Fire of God continue to burn, and we trust that it will ever be too hot in Zion City for the works of unrighteousness to continue.

Those who do righteousness have no fear in Zion.

Those who love evil cannot find a resting-place here.

WE FIND a source of encouragement in the words that come to us from all parts of the world.

Two letters in Thursday morning's mail, from Jamaica, were from persons rejoicing in the God of Zion, and asking our prayers in their behalf.

Others seeing the good work of Zion, "glorify their Father which is in Heaven."

THE FOLLOWING extract from a letter is interesting in its peculiarity, and in showing the earnestness of those who have come to see the safety of the position of Zion and the power of her publications:

Gate of the Rising Sun.
Plain of Jezreel.
Day of the Vengeance of our God.
The recompense for the Controversy of Zion.

The Least of the Flock of Judah unto John G. Speicher, Keeper of the House:

Peace to thee, and to the Flock in thy keeping.

Send by mail, to ————, West ————, New York, twenty-five to fifty assorted LEAVES OF HEALING of recent issues.

Send them with wrappers sufficient for remailing; for I propose to see what is the length and breadth of Jerusalem; and these rolls I am going to use for markers.

I sharpen one end and drive it in the ground at intervals along the straight lines, and a red one at every crook and angle; and I will drop one down the chimney of him that sweareth falsely by My Name, saith the Lord of Hosts, and it shall remain there until it shall consume the stones and the timber of that house; for I am jealous for Zion with great jealousy, and I am jealous for Jerusalem with the fury of a terrible King. And I will yet know who are Mine and who belong to the lawless one, saith the mighty Redeemer of Jacob.

WE THINK the idea is an excellent one.

LEAVES OF HEALING is marking the bounds of Zion—spiritual Jerusalem.

WHEREVER THE heart is true and pure in the sight of God, it is with rejoicing that LEAVES OF HEALING is received and the glorious Gospel of the New Covenant is accepted.

And wherever there is opposition to the work of God, LEAVES OF HEALING acts like dynamite in destroying the works and the kingdom of Satan.

MAY GOD bless the faithful ones who are doing so much in sending out the Literature of Zion, and bringing a knowledge of the Christ and His coming Kingdom into all the world.

WORD REACHES us from Vancouver, from Elder and Evangelist C. F. Viking, that they have arrived safely there, from Shanghai, China, after a voyage of twenty-five days.

Elder and Evangelist Viking have done excellent work in China during the last four years.

Their many friends will heartily welcome them as they return to Zion City.

WE ARE sending this week two members of Zion Restoration Host, John Taylor, and Gustav Sigwald, to St. Louis, to assist the Branch there, under the charge of Elder F. L. Brock, in distributing Zion Literature among the crowds who come to attend the Fair.

Mr. Taylor has been doing excellent work, recently, at Chattanooga, where he is much beloved by many for whom he has ministered.

WE BELIEVE the time is coming, and is probably near at hand, when the Seventies will be sent out two and two, throughout all the land, especially in the country districts, where meetings can be held in the schoolhouses and in the homes of the people, where they can gather together, and speak face to face, relating the wonderful stories of how God is miraculously saving and healing His people in Zion.

THERE IS not much to be expected from the old and almost obsolete methods of the apostasy, in planting a pastor in a locality where he has limited opportunities in reaching the people.

EVERY FAITHFUL servant of God must Go Forward and help in this great work.

There is no time for delay.

"The King's business requireth haste!"

ELIJAH THE PROPHET must go through the Gates, and prepare the Way for the people.

He must "cast up the highway," and "gather out the stones," and "lift up an ensign for the people."

THE BANNER OF ZION stands for Salvation and Healing and Holy Living.

WHO, WHO will go, salvation's story telling,
Looking to Jesus, heeding not the cost?

PRAY FOR more laborers for the harvest field.

Pray for greater resources, lest the harvest perish.

BRETHREN, PRAY FOR US.

JOHN G. SPEICHER.

GOD'S WAY OF HEALING.

BY THE REV. JOHN ALEX. DOWIE.

God's Way of Healing Is a Person, Not a Thing.

Jesus said "*I am* the Way, and the Truth, and the Life," and He has ever been revealed to His people in all the ages by the Covenant Name, Jehovah-Rophi, or "*I am* Jehovah that Healeth thee." (John 14:6; Exodus 15:26.)

The Lord Jesus, the Christ, is Still the Healer.

He cannot change, for "Jesus, the Christ, is the same yesterday and today, yea and forever;" and He is still with us, for He said: "Lo, *I am* with you All the Days, even unto the Consummation of the Age." (Hebrews 13:8; Matthew 28:20.) Because He is Unchangeable, and because He is present, in spirit, just as when in the flesh, He is the Healer of His people.

Divine Healing Rests on the Christ's Atonement.

It was prophesied of Him, "Surely He hath borne our griefs (Hebrew, *sickness*), and carried our sorrows: . . . and with His stripes we are healed;" and it is expressly declared that this was fulfilled in His Ministry of Healing, which still continues. (Isaiah 53:4, 5; Matthew 8:17.)

Disease Can Never be God's Will.

It is the Devil's work, consequent upon Sin, and it is impossible for the work of the Devil ever to be the Will of God. The Christ came to "destroy the works of the Devil," and when He was here on earth He healed "all manner of disease and all manner of sickness," and all these sufferers are expressly declared to have been "oppressed of the Devil." (1 John 3:8; Matthew 4:23; Acts 10:38.)

The Gifts of Healing Are Permanent.

It is expressly declared that the "Gifts and the calling of God are without repentance," and the Gifts of Healing are amongst the Nine Gifts of the Spirit to the Church. (Romans 11:29; 1 Corinthians 12:8-11.)

There Are Four Modes of Divine Healing.

The first is the direct prayer of faith; the second, intercessory prayer of two or more; the third, the anointing of the elders, with the prayer of faith; and the fourth, the laying on of hands of those who believe, and whom God has prepared and called to that Ministry. (Matthew 8:5-13; Matthew 18:19; James 5:14, 15; Mark 16:18.)

Divine Healing Is Opposed by Diabolical Counterfeits.

Amongst these are Christian Science (falsely so-called), Mind Healing, Spiritualism, Trance Evangelism, etc. (1 Timothy 6:20, 21; 1 Timothy 4:1, 2; Isaiah 51:22, 23.)

Multitudes Have Been Healed Through Faith in Jesus.

The writer knows of thousands of cases and has personally laid hands on scores of thousands of persons. Full information can be obtained at the meetings held in the Zion Tabernacles in Chicago, and in Zion City, Illinois, and in many pamphlets which give the experience, in their own words, of many who have been healed in this and other countries, published at Zion Printing and Publishing House, Zion City, Illinois.

"Belief Cometh of Hearing, and Hearing by the Word of the Christ."

You are heartily invited to attend and hear for yourself.

Memorabilia of the New York Visitation

By Mrs. Emily Ware

DOTH not wisdom cry,
And understanding put forth her voice?
. . . .
Unto you, O men, I call;
And My voice is to the sons of men.
. . . .
Hear, for I will speak excellent things;
And the opening of My lips shall be right things.
For My mouth shall utter truth.—*Proverbs 8.1-7.*

DEACONESS MARTHA WING, Zion City, Illinois.—During the New York Visitation, I acted as captain of a company, and thus I did not have the privilege of the house-to-house work, and did not come in as close contact with the people as I should have had great joy in doing.

However, I was not altogether denied opportunity of speaking a word directly now and then.

My experience in this surprised me, as I was continually accosted on the street by those who wished to learn of Zion, and while waiting for the members of my company to finish their blocks before I could assign them to new territory, I had many interesting conversations with inquirers, who were invariably courteous.

The first day I was out, a well-dressed, intelligent man stopped me, asking for Literature.

In the conversation that followed I learned that he was a traveling man whose route took him through Zion City, and he said that he had been watching Zion and Dr. Dowie "afar off" for two or three years.

He asked me a number of questions upon points of the teaching with which he disagreed, but after receiving a better understanding of these things expressed himself as being satisfied that Dr. Dowie was right.

In answer to my question as to whether he were a Christian, he said that he once called himself such, being a member of the Episcopalian church, but the hypocrisy he found had weaned him entirely from the church, and it was a number of years since he had attended a religious service.

"But I am going to hear Dr. Dowie," he said; "he is doing more practical good than all the churches put together."

I did not dwell upon any points of doctrine, but spoke to him directly about giving his heart to God.

"If I could be in Zion," he said, "I believe that I could serve God. But no one traveling as I do can be a Christian."

This point I contested, saying a Christian could carry his colors anywhere in an honest business, and if it were not honest he ought not to be in it.

Upon leaving he said, "Well, I don't know; I may find Zion to be the place for me. If I ever enter into fellowship with any church it will be that."

One evening, after service, Overseer Excell told the officers to return to the hall without disrobing, directly after the Recessional, in order to speak to the strangers.

We gladly availed ourselves of this permission, as most of the officers were, like myself, engaged in directing the work of Companies or Seventies, with little opportunity of coming in direct contact with the people.

Two ladies, evidently strangers, were looking about and I approached them.

They began at once eagerly to ask questions.

While we were talking, a third lady, well dressed and intelligent, asked permission to join us.

The two ladies first mentioned left after a little, but the third remained in conversation.

She asked many questions and was much interested.

She said, "I came through curiosity, intending to be amused, and perhaps disgusted, but I did not expect to be impressed; but I have been impressed very greatly. I have never heard a man speak like Dr. Dowie. He is very wonderful."

I asked if she were a Christian.

She answered, "Well, I am a church-member."

I told her that she had not answered my question.

She hesitated and laughed a little, and finally said, "I am an Episcopalian. I am not sure that I am a Christian."

It was the evening the General Overseer made mention of the Episcopalians grinding out the prayer, "We have done those things we ought not to have done, and have left undone those things we ought to have done, and there is no health in us," and when she named the church of which she was a member, we simultaneously recalled his remarks, and she laughed heartily.

"It is a ridiculous prayer," she said, "but really, I have said it hundreds of times, and have never given one thought to its meaning. Dr. Dowie makes things so plain. The idea! Suppose my cook should do that way? It is most absurd." Then she added, "I shall go over in the morning and tell my rector about it."

Knowing from experience how many whose faces have been turning Zionward have stumbled by seeking just such discussion and advice from their pastors, I told her her rector might not see as plainly as she did.

I went on to say that there were two classes of ministers who opposed Zion, one because of ignorance, the other because of prejudice and unwillingness to know the truth.

"Yes," she answered with conviction, "and because they are jealous of him. He is taking the sheep of their flocks, and I do not wonder he is," she added after a moment's reflection.

She then commented upon the choir service.

She told me that she had traveled considerably and had seen some of the finest and most beautiful services in Europe, "But never anything to compare with this" she said. "There is something about this—I cannot tell you how it made me feel.

"Have you ever seen a wheat-field swaying in the breeze?—that beautiful, slight, rhythmic undulation of the long white columns of the procession, and the sweet innocent faces and the little ones in front—Oh, I cannot tell you!

"Something came up into my throat; I could hardly keep from weeping.

"I have been used, you know, to the robed choir, and the Processional, but this impressed me differently from anything I have ever seen."

I said, "Do you know why? It is not merely the music and the rhythmical movement, the white robes and the sweet faces, but it is because the power of God is in that Processional."

The tears sprang to her eyes, and her voice broke. "I believe it," she said earnestly, "I believe it is. It was like that, as if God's presence was here; I never had a feeling like it before."

When she left I went to the door and selected Literature, which she insisted upon purchasing.

She promised earnestly to read it, and said that she would attend the meetings.

She thanked me for my interest, and commented upon the kindliness and courtesy of the Zion people.

She spoke several times of the intelligent faces, and expressed wonder at the falsehoods and misrepresentations of the press.

Many others expressed the same wonderment.

I took a party of ladies to the lace parlors, after sitting with them through a Divine Healing service, held by Overseer Mason.

They also came prepared to be amused, and laughed at everything at first, but one lady said, as soon as she saw Overseer Mason, "Oh, he has a good face; such a good, pure face!" As he talked, she commented frequently, "That is good! That is excellent! That is true Bible teaching!"

The other ladies soon became quiet and respectful and gladly accepted my offer after the meeting to show them the lace and candy exhibit.

They bought Literature, and as they were leaving thanked me, saying that they had an entirely different idea of the work and the people than before coming, and strongly condemned the press for its misrepresentations.

I was out every day but one on Restoration work, and felt stronger and in better physical condition upon my return than when I went.

God blessed me, and I am very thankful to have had my part in the first great Visitation of Zion Restoration Host.

MRS. C. S. COOK, Zion City, Illinois.—I am very thankful to our Heavenly Father that He permitted me to attend the New York Visitation.

For twelve days we did house-to-house Restoration work, were received very kindly, and had many good talks with the people.

One day, while on our work, we met a boy about fifteen years of age, to whom I gave a card, and soon afterwards, with a serious look on his face, he asked me, "Is it true that Jesus is knocking at the door of people's hearts?"

This gave us an opportunity to hold conversation with him, which, I trust, may prove helpful to him in opening his heart's door to the Christ.

On another occasion, after ringing the door-bell at a large hospital, and making known our mission, we were received very kindly by the superintendent, who sent an escort with us through the building.

We distributed the Literature very freely, and nearly all seemed anxious to receive it, especially the ones in charge, and as we were leaving some even called after us to give them copies of LEAVES OF HEALING.

MISS MATTIE MAYHAK, Zion City, Illinois.—I am grateful to God for the blessed privilege of going with our General Overseer on our first Visitation to New York City.

I fail to recall the many good things I heard spoken of our General Overseer and the Host.

Some ladies spoke very kindly of Overseer Jane Dowie.

My sister and I were talking to a mother and her daughter the last evening, and they said that they did not believe what the papers said and wanted us to write to them.

One policemen said, "I do not like some things the Doctor says, but I like and admire Him for he believes what he says."

The policemen said that they had no trouble with Zion people.

We were received kindly by nearly all, on our Restoration work.

I trust I may have the privilege of going again with our Leader.

THE TERROR OF THE MASONIC USURPERS AT THE HERALDING OF THE KINGDOM OF PURITY—THE THEOCRACY.

Around-the-World Visitation

of the

Rev. John Alex. Dowie

Elijah the Restorer
General Overseer of the Christian Catholic Church in Zion.

By ARTHUR W. NEWCOMB, Special Correspondent.

The last paper of this series closed with the account of the proceedings in Adelaide at the Exhibition Building and the York Hotel on Lord's Day, March 20, 1904.

The Monday Morning Meeting.

On Monday morning, March 21st, at half past ten o'clock, the General Overseer conducted the first of the series of Divine Healing meetings of the Visitation, in the Town Hall.

This hall is situated in King William street, Adelaide, and is one of the most conspicuous buildings in the city. Its architecture is of a pleasing character, and the auditorium of the hall, while not large, seating only about eighteen hundred people, is very handsome.

Immediately in the rear of the auditorium, there is a large banquet hall with a high ceiling. This was used, during the Visitation, for the display of Zion laces and lace curtains. A most interesting and beautiful display was prepared, by Colonel Carl F. Stern, with laces which had been brought with the party. Large numbers of ladies and gentlemen daily visited this room, and there were none who were not surprised and delighted with the excellent design, workmanship and quality of this Zion product.

The Divine Healing meetings were held in the Auditorium. These Divine Healing meetings, like all those of the Visitation in Australia, were attended by an ever-increasing number of most deeply interested people.

God's Prophet of the Time of the Restoration of All Things is, first of all, a great teacher; and it is in his capacity as a teacher that he is a means of spiritual, psychical, and physical blessing to many thousands throughout the earth. At the Divine Healing meetings he is at his best as a teacher. Here also he is seen especially in his prophetic office as Messenger of the Covenant—God's Covenant of Salvation, Healing and Holy Living.

In these meetings, the General Overseer also spoke to many who were suffering from various diseases, and in the quiet, earnest prayer services which were held at the close, the Spirit of God was present in power to heal, and many of God's children were able to date their deliverance from the oppression of the Devil, from the Adelaide Visitation.

The following is the report of the General Overseer's Message:

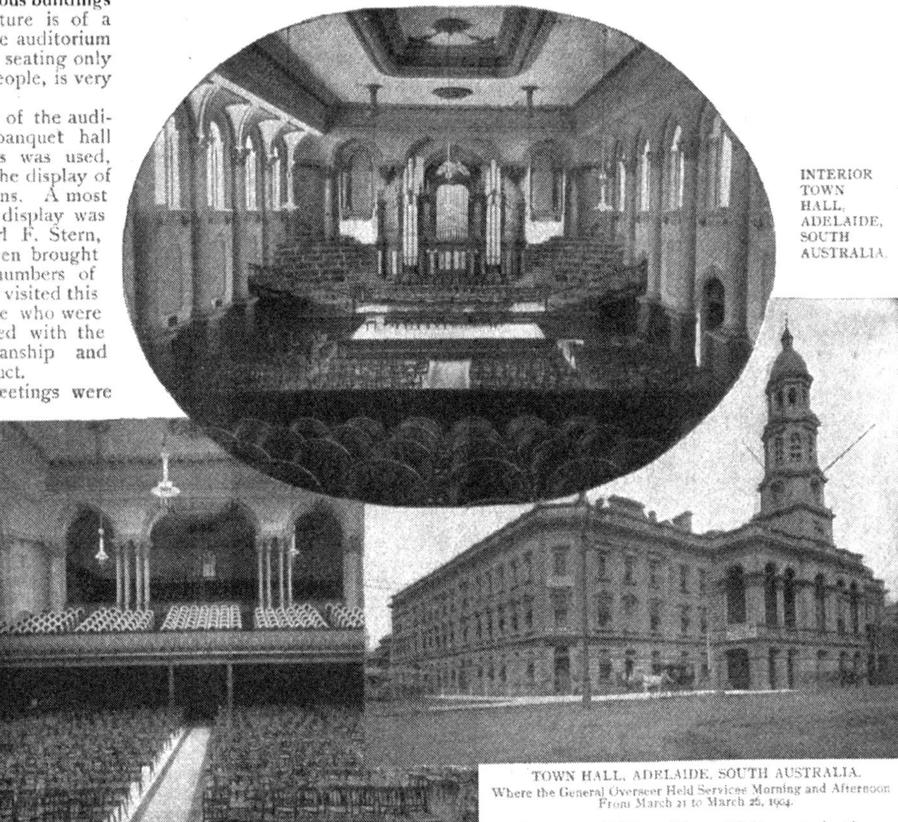

INTERIOR TOWN HALL, ADELAIDE, SOUTH AUSTRALIA.

INTERIOR TOWN HALL, ADELAIDE, SOUTH AUSTRALIA.

TOWN HALL, ADELAIDE, SOUTH AUSTRALIA.
Where the General Overseer Held Services Morning and Afternoon From March 21 to March 26, 1904.

Adelaide Town Hall, Monday Morning, March 21, 1904.

The meeting was opened with the singing of Hymn No. 32, in the Visitation Program, "Jesus, Lover of My Soul."

Overseer Jane Dowie read from the Inspired Word of God in the 8th chapter of the Gospel according to St. Matthew, the first seventeen verses.

The Rev. John Stephen McCullagh offered the general supplication, the General Overseer closing with prayer for the sick and sorrowing ones, whose petitions had been sent in

Overseer Wilbur Glenn Voliva made the announcements for the week.

The General Overseer then said:

THE STORY OF THE LEPER.

*REPORTED BY I. M. S. AND A. W. N.

INVOCATION.

Let the words of my mouth, and the meditation of my heart be acceptable in Thy sight, be profitable unto this people, and unto those who are seeking to understand Thy Will and Thy Way, that their spirits and their souls and their bodies may be made free from every defilement of the flesh. In Jesus' Name. Amen.

Following Jesus.

You people who have Bibles, please open them and see whether I read correctly from the 8th chapter of Matthew, beginning at the 1st verse.

*The following report has not been revised by the General Overseer.

"When He was come down from the mountain great multitudes followed"—whom, Peter?
Voices—"Him."
General Overseer—Followed John?
Voices—"No."
General Overseer—Followed John Wesley?
Voices—"Him."
General Overseer—Followed Martin Luther?
Voices—"Followed Jesus."
General Overseer—If I were to see all the apostles—Paul, and John, and James, and Peter, and even dear old Nathaniel—and Jesus were there, whom do you think I should like most to follow?
Voices—"Jesus."

The Apostles Fallible Men.

General Overseer—There are a great many people who live in the Epistles.
The Epistles are very good but they are the writings of fallible men.
Peter, as you know, was a very fallible man.
He fell, you remember. In fact, he cursed and lied about Jesus.
Jesus said:

I made supplication for thee, that thy faith fail not; and do thou, when once thou hast turned again strengthen thy brother.

Peter went to the devil nearly altogether, for a time.
He lied and cursed, and said that he did not know Jesus.
He was a coward.

The Coward Leads the Procession to Hell.

I will let you know a little of my private opinion about cowards.
The man I most detest and from whom I shrink is a coward!
The coward heads the procession to hell.

But for the fearful, and unbelieving, and abominable, and murderers, and fornicators, and sorcerers, and idolaters, and all liars, their part shall be in the lake that burneth with fire and brimstone; which is the second death.

He that heads that procession, you will observe, is he that is full of fear—the coward.
That was Peter's great fault.
He was very brave when there seemed to be little danger, and said, "I will never leave You," but he was the first to run.

Peter's Fall After Pentecost.

"But," you say, "He was not that way after Pentecost."
Was he not?
Long after Pentecost, the same mean devil possessed dear old Peter that had troubled him twenty-five years before.
Peter one day went to Antioch to see Paul, and Paul said, "Why, you dear old Peter! Come in, and let us have a good time."
They were eating and drinking together with the Gentile Christians.
One day a number of Jewish Christians came down from Jerusalem, and the next morning at breakfast Paul said, "Why, where is Peter?"
"Oh," was the reply, "he is eating with those who came down from Jerusalem yesterday."
"And where is Barnabas?" Paul asked.
"Well, he is eating with them, too."
"That is all right," said Paul, "perhaps he will come down to luncheon."
But when luncheon time came he was not there.
They went on with their conferences and church matters.
In the morning he was still missing, so Paul asked, "What is the matter?"
"Oh, you know those Jewish Christians, who came down from Jerusalem, have all been circumcised, and Peter does not want to make a fuss, and so he is eating with the circumcised only, for fear of trouble."
"I will make a fuss!" said Paul; and he did make a fuss.
You had better believe he did!
He went for Peter.
He said, "There is no difference; in the Christ Jesus there is no circumcision nor uncircumcision. You are an old coward, Peter!
"You are not walking uprightly according to the Truth of the Gospel."

Paul wrote afterwards concerning the controversy, "I resisted him to the face, because he stood condemned."
He hammered out dear old Peter in fine style, and Peter took it kindly.

Peter's Kindly Criticism of Paul.

In Peter's last letter he wrote very kindly of Paul, but he got in a dig at him when he wrote, "As our beloved brother Paul also, according to the wisdom given him, wrote unto you, as also in all his Epistles, speaking to them of these things, wherein are some things hard to be understood."
The fact of the matter is, that there are many things hard to be understood in the Epistles of Paul.
I wish myself that he had written a little more plainly, because theologians have flung texts at one another's heads for centuries from what Paul wrote.
Peter was great and Paul, perhaps, was greater, and John, perhaps, might be the greatest, but if all of them were here and Jesus also, whom do you think I should follow?
Audience—"Jesus."
General Overseer—Whom would you follow?
Voices—"Jesus."

Follow Jesus Regardless of the Cost.

General Overseer—If following Jesus meant to get into a rumpus with the Baptist church what would you do?
Audience—"Follow Jesus."
General Overseer—If it meant getting into a row with the Methodist church, or with the Congregational or the Presbyterian church, or with all the rest of them, whom would you follow?
Voices—"Follow Jesus."
General Overseer—It is a very hard thing sometimes to follow Jesus.
You lose friends, and get away from ecclesiastical associations that have been dear to you all your life.
You get away from churches where you have been so happy, because they have all been so soundly asleep. [Laughter.]

The Peacefulness of Death.

One minister said to me some time ago, "I do not know how you get on, Doctor. You have so much red pepper in you, and you are always stirring things up."
"I am glad of that," I replied.
He said, "My church is so quiet and so peaceable."
"I know that," I answered.
"Well," he said, "is that not nice?"
"No," I replied, "I have just been to see a church of twenty-five thousand members that is more peaceable than yours."
"Where," he said, "is there a church of twenty-five thousand members that is more peaceable than mine?"
"It is in the West Terrace Cemetery. They are all dead." [Laughter.]
He could never quite forgive me for that.
I do not care for a dead church.
I should rather be all alive and do something.
Even if people try to enlighten my understanding by throwing a brick at my head, I should rather have that than this miserable deadness.
Dead things ought to be buried.
The great trouble with some churches is that they were not buried long ago.
Before Jesus came down from the mountain, He had been teaching.
The 5th, 6th and 7th chapters say that He had been teaching.
In the 8th chapter, we are told that He came down from the mountain and "great multitudes followed Him. And behold, there came to Him a leper and worshiped Him."

Qualities of True Worshipers of the Christ.

That is the key to the whole thing.
If there are any Unitarians here, they may as well go home at once.
There is no use for people to try to get blessing unless they will worship Jesus.
Are you a true worshiper?
A true worshiper has repented of his sin, and has made restitution and confession to God and man.
A true worshiper believes in the Lord Jesus, the Christ, and is willing to do what He tells him.

It does not matter how stupid the thing may seem to be to him, he will obey orders.
A true worshiper is not one who is a worshiper only on Sunday.
He worships God on Sunday, Monday, Tuesday, Wednesday, Thursday, Friday and Saturday.
He is a worshiper all the time.
He worships when he works, when he sings, and when he writes.
He has God before him all the time.

Hard for a Jew to Believe in the Christ.

This man was a leper and he was a Jew.
It was hard for him to believe that Jesus, the Christ, was God Incarnate; because all the rabbis were saying that He was not.
They were all saying that He was merely an imposter, liar, and bastard.
Some of them say that to this day.
They were angry, and they are angry yet.
I have a great many Jewish friends.
I love them, and I have their friendship in business, in politics, in educational matters, and even in ecclesiastical matters.
But when it comes to the Divinity of the Christ they shrink.

Interest of the Jews in Zion.

Yet I have many converted Jews in Zion.
Certain Jews in New York have made a request to me that, when I return to America, I give one afternoon in the Carnegie Hall to Jews only.
There are half a million Jews in New York, and they are beginning to listen and to hear what Zion has to say.
The Elijah matter is one of intense interest to them.
They have been praying to God for the coming of Elijah.
They pray to God continually for his coming.
They believe that he must come before the coming of the Messiah, as Malachi said.
They are listening with intense interest and they are coming to the Christ now.
That is something that you denominations had better see to and think about.
It is a wonderful fact that Zion is reaching the Jews.
Zion is also reaching the Roman Catholics.
You must worship God in the Christ.
God was in the Christ, "reconciling the world unto Himself."
He was the "fulness of the Godhead bodily."
When the leper worshiped the Christ, he had become a Christian.

A True Jew Is a Christian.

A true Jew believes in the Messiah.
A true Jew believes the Prophet who said that a Virgin should conceive and bring forth a Son, whose Name should be called Emmanuel, which means God with us.
When you bring a Jew right up to it, he sees that the Messiahship of Jesus is Scriptural.
Give it to him in Hebrew. He loves to hear the Hebrew.
"Thank God!" he says, "where is the Virgin?"
We say "Mary."
"Where is the Son?"
We answer, "Jesus."
We show him all the Scriptures that bear on the question.
He sees it, and then he says, "Where is the Kingdom?"
We say "Zion;" for the word Zion merely means the Kingdom of God.
The Christian Catholic Church in Zion is the Christian Catholic Church in the Kingdom of God.
To be a true worshiper is the main thing.

Church-rolls Are Unreliable.

I do not believe much in your church-rolls, because they are padded and miserable things.
In the city of Chicago I twitted the churches and got them to examine their church-rolls.
The result of one man's examinations and investigations was that he found that more than one-half the members upon the roll of the church had either gone back into the world, were dead, or were not active members at all.
I care about the names that are enrolled in heaven; that is the principal thing.
The important point is not whether you are on the church-rolls, but whether you are in the Kingdom of God.
You must be born into the Kingdom and be born of God, before you have any right in the Church.
If you are in the Church without being born into the Kingdom, then you are a hypocrite, and have no place there.
The question is, "are you a true worshiper?"
You must get right on that question, because you will not receive healing until you do.
This leper would not have received the healing unless he had been a true worshiper. He came to the right conclusion as he heard the Christ.

How the Leper Heard the Christ.

I wonder how he heard Him.
I have often wondered about that, because leprosy is a contagious disease, and he would not be allowed to sit in the assembly of people because of it.
He probably hid behind a rock, where he was not seen, and yet could hear all that Jesus said.
Do you know why he was so anxious to speak to the Christ that day?
It was because He was going away across the lake, and it would be the only opportunity for the leper to see Him.

What Jesus, the Christ, Thought of Pigs.

Do you know what He went across the lake to do?
He went to kill pigs! [Laughter.]
Yes, he drowned two thousand.
That is what He thought of the pigs.
The only prayer of devils that He ever answered, was when they said to Him, "If Thou cast us out, send us away into the herd of swine."
To that prayer He merely answered, "Go," and they went. If He thought that a pig was a good place for a devil to live, do you think that pig is a food suitable for you to put into your stomachs? [Laughter.]
Voices—"No."
General Overseer—Concerning the swine, God said:

And the swine, because he parteth the hoof, and is clovenfooted, but cheweth not the cud, he is unclean unto you.
Of their flesh ye shall not eat, and their carcases ye shall not touch; they are unclean unto you

One of the Most Diseased, Dirty and Poisonous Creatures Is the Pig.

Even if bitten by a rattlesnake, the pig turns round and eats it up from tail to head.
There is a little island in the St. Clair river, between Canada and the United States, that used to be called Snake island, because it was so full of rattlesnakes.
No one dared to land on the island to fish, because the snakes were so numerous.
When they wanted to get rid of the snakes on the island, they did as St. Patrick did in Ireland. [Laughter.]
They turned a large number of pigs into the island, which ate all the snakes.
They had a glorious feast!
Then they were ready for the Australian market, or for some other market. [Laughter.]
Ugh! [Laughter.]
Just think of that, and you ate the pig! [Laughter!]
American ham!
Ugh! [Laughter.]
A pig is full of tuberculosis, trichinosis, cholera and cancer.
It is full of dirt and muck, and poisons more deadly than that of the rattlesnake.
If you can eat it with comfort after that, may the Lord have mercy upon you! [Laughter.]
The pork-packers will be after me. [Laughter.]
But there is no one who knows better than the pork-packer himself that what I say is true.
Do you know that

Cancer Is Not to Be Found Where Pigs Are Not Eaten?

There is not a case of cancer recorded throughout the Old and New Testaments.
There is no word in Hebrew for cancer.
The Christ never healed a case of cancer.

Why? Because the Jews did not eat swine's flesh.

The physicians of Owen College, Manchester, have declared that what I say is true; that there is not a case of cancer known among orthodox Jews.

But it is known everywhere among people who eat swine's flesh, because cancer is a scrofulous disease.

I hate to say it, because some of you may not relish your dinners after hearing it, that the word, scrofula, comes from the Latin word, *scrofa*, a breeding sow.

Scrofulae is the plural of the word meaning little pigs.

When you eat pig, you get little pigs in your stomach. [Laughter.]

That is true.

You get little scrofulous sores that vomit out their muck and filth! Ugh!

It makes me sick to think about it.

I have seen a little child in the stockyards district in Chicago with seventeen sores—open ulcerous sores—caused by eating pig. His little leg was all drawn up.

His story is told in LEAVES OF HEALING, Volume I, Number 1.

It is a wonderful story.

I have his crutches hanging on the walls of Shiloh Tabernacle.

He was not only bound in affliction, but also in iron; and I have his braces and his high-heeled boot.

Little Willie Esser got his healing, and is now a big, strong young man.

God can do wonderful things when you get the pig out of your system.

Some of you must give up some other things as well as pig.

A Word to Tobacco Users.

There are alcohol and tobacco.

Ugh, you stinkpots! [Laughter.]

You do not like that.

You do not want to be called stinkpots. They say that is "so vulgar."

It is Scripture, nevertheless.

Did not Martha say to Jesus, when her brother had been lying four days in the grave, "Lord, by this time he stinketh?" [Laughter.]

If a fellow has been guzzling whiskey and beer and chewing tobacco for forty years can I not call him a stinkpot?

You ask his wife if he does not stink. Ugh!

His throat is an open sepulcher.

You begin to stink the house at six o'clock in the evening and stink until twelve at night.

Then you stink your wife with your tobacco-saturated perspiration all night long.

Then you rise in the morning and you stink again.

When you have gone out, she opens all the windows and the doors, and says, "Phew! Let's have some air."

We have a right to say that you stink, because a man that smokes has a bad stomach and a bad breath.

He gets dyspepsia.

The tobacco dries up the gastric juices of the stomach.

Then the food that he eats goes down and tears the stomach and the bowels, so that they become diseased.

He gets cancer.

Is it worth your while to smoke like that?

If you do that, what right have you to ask God to heal your body?

Need for Hard-hitting Words.

I use that word stink because it hits hard, and the word, stinkpot, because that is all a fellow is who walks behind a pipe all day, or puffs at his cigar.

He may be a Christian but he smells like the Devil.

I think a Christian ought to be clean!

You have no right to stink your wife, and family, and house, and yourself.

This body should be the Temple of God.

God will not bless any stinkpot.

Mind you, I have known good men who have smoked and preached sermons, but they died long before their time.

They died of heart disease and other diseases caused by nicotine.

I have known magnificent men who have smoked, as they thought, with impunity, and they have shattered their nerves, and got tobacco heart.

There are some men who smoke until they are ninety, but are they any the better for it?

They live in spite of it, but the great majority die from it.

I have known good men to smoke and do much good; but they steadily reduced their influence until at last they were of no use for anything.

Have I not a right to ask you who want to come to God and ask Him for blessing to be clean before you come?

Ask God to make you clean.

That is the way to get Healing; to get God to cleanse you.

Worship God properly.

This leper no doubt had heard Jesus when He had ended His sayings, for this is the word in the 7th of Matthew:

> And it came to pass, when Jesus ended these words, the multitudes were astonished at His teaching:
> For He taught them as one having authority, and not as their scribes.

I am Teaching You With Authority.

I know what I am talking about.

I have the Authority of Knowledge, I have the Authority of Experience, and I have the Authority from God as His minister.

If I were teaching you mathematics, I should teach you with authority.

I should say to you that two times two make four.

If any one said that it made five I should keep at it until he understood.

I teach you authoritatively. If I were the master in a school I should teach with authority.

What is the use in teaching at all if you do not teach with authority?

If the child comes home from school and makes any complaint against the teacher, the parent should spank him and send him back to do what the teacher tells him.

I intend to teach you as the Christ taught you.

Human Opinions Valueless.

It does not matter what you think about it.

"Oh, it does," says some one, "I want my own opinion."

I have had to give up my own individual opinion many times.

Brothers, sisters, it matters not what you think; it matters not what I think, it matters not what any one thinks.

The one thing that does matter is what God thinks.

You must think as God thinks, or else you are wrong.

The leper said, after he worshiped the Christ, "Lord if Thou wilt, Thou canst make me clean."

Do not pray that prayer.

Other People's Prayers.

Much mischief is wrought by praying other people's prayers.

When I was a student in the University of Edinburgh, I was conductor of a prayer-meeting among a company of students for three months.

One morning, one of my classmates began to pray.

He was saying, "O Lord, cleanse Thou me from blood guiltiness."

I gave him a gentle kick, and said, "Get up! Why do you pray this kind of prayer?"

He said that David prayed it.

"Let David pray his own prayer," I said, "and you pray yours. Whom have you murdered? What blood have you on your hands and heart?"

"None," he said.

"Then," I replied, "why did you lie? If David was an adulterer and murderer, let him attend to that.

"If you are not an adulterer and murderer, do not tell lies to God Almighty about it, and ask Him to cleanse you from blood guiltiness."

"Oh," he said, "I did not see it like that before."

The Mistake in the Leper's Prayer.

The leper's prayer is not right.

A great many of you have been praying, "Lord, if Thou wilt, Thou canst make me clean," and have had no answer.

You ought not to have prayed it.

It was wrong, and will always be wrong.

The moment that the leper prayed that prayer, the Christ said, "I will, be thou clean."

Did not that reply take the "if" out of the man's prayer?

If, after He had said, "I will," the man had continued to say, "O Lord, it is too wonderful for me to believe, and oh, I cannot believe it," would he have been blessed?

Voices—"No."

General Overseer—If you were to ask me for something and I should say, "I will; come to my office in half an hour;" and you were to say, "O Dr. Dowie, if I could only believe you;" and after reaching my office were to continue to cry, "Oh, if thou wilt, if thou wilt, if thou wilt," would you not be very insulting to me?

Voices—"Yes."

The Sin and Futility of Doubt.

General Overseer—Then why do you everlastingly continue to say it to God?

Did that leper keep on saying, "If Thou wilt?"

He did not understand, at first, whether the Christ was willing to cleanse him; but the moment that the Christ said "I will, be thou clean," he was convinced,

Would he have been healed if he had continued to doubt?

Voices—"No."

General Overseer—Then let the "if" be cut out of your prayer, because Jesus said, "I will."

God said, "I am Jehovah that healeth thee."

When a man came to Jesus and said, "If thou canst do anything, have compassion upon us and help us," the Christ turned it upon him by saying, "If thou canst! All things are possible to him that believeth."

That is the point there.

The Christ said "If thou canst!" with an expression of intense surprise.

Get the If out of your prayers.

If means doubt and uncertainty.

The Christ Came to Earth to Heal.

The Christ said, "I will," and He has never said anything else; not to any one.

He has always said, "I will."

Why?

Because, He came to do that work.

He came to Heal.

It is written in Matthew 8, 17th verse,

That it might be fulfilled which was spoken by Isaiah the prophet saying, Himself took our infirmities, and bare our sicknesses.

That is plain, is it not?

Voices—"Yes."

General Overseer—That is as plain as words can put it, for the Christ not only died for our sins but also for our sicknesses.

Not only was "the chastisement of our Peace upon Him," but "with His stripes we are healed."

Divine Healing Is a Part of the Christ's Gospel.

If it is not, I should like to know any one who can prove that it is not.

The New Testament is full of Salvation and Healing.

They go hand in hand.

After people were saved, they were healed.

Multitudes were healed after they were saved.

Disease and death came into this world through sin.

Who is the author of sin?

Audience—"The Devil."

General Overseer—Who then is the author of disease?

Audience—"The Devil."

General Overseer—I call your attention, for a moment, to the 10th chapter of the Acts of the Apostles, and the 38th verse.

There was dear old Peter preaching this sermon to the household of Cornelius, and he was much surprised to find that God had blessed Cornelius before he was a Christian.

There will be some people very much surprised, when they get to heaven, just as Peter was very much surprised, when God heard a man, and sent an angel to him too, when he was not a Christian.

Disease the Work of the Devil.

Peter in preaching, said, "How God anointed Jesus of Nazareth with the Holy Spirit and with power; who went about"—making people sick—

Voices—"No, no."

General Overseer—What did he say, then?

Voices—"Doing good."

General Overseer—Who went about "doing good, and healing all that were oppressed of the Devil;" or healing all that God made sick?

Voices—"No, no."

General Overseer—Healing some that God made sick?

Voices—"No."

General Overseer—Healing some that the Devil made sick?

Voices—"No."

General Overseer—What is it then?

Overseer Excell—"'Healing all that were oppressed of the Devil; for God was with Him.'"

General Overseer—How many were oppressed by the Devil?

Voices—"All."

General Overseer—Were there not some whom God had oppressed?

Audience—"No."

General Overseer—Were they not His dear children to whom God had given a cancer because He loved them?

Audience—"No."

General Overseer—Who oppressed them?

Voices—"The Devil."

General Overseer—Do you believe that?

Voices—"Yes, sir."

General Overseer—Some of the ministers will tell you that you are very foolish to believe such stuff.

They say that God loves His dear people, and that He knocks them in the eye, and makes them half blind, strikes them in the solar plexus, then gives them cancer because He loves them, and then gives them jaundice.

That is what they say, in effect.

They lie.

No Disease in Heaven or in God.

Is there any disease in Heaven?

Voices—"No."

General Overseer—Can it come out of Heaven?

Voices—"No."

General Overseer—Is there any disease in God?

Voices—"No."

General Overseer—Can it come from God?

Voices—"No."

General Overseer—If it does not come from God and Heaven, whence does it come?

Does God come down here and go through the hospitals, hunting round for a disease to give you because He loves you?

Voices—"No."

General Overseer—I was in a certain church one day and the minister gave out this hymn:

God in Israel sows the seeds
  Of affliction, pain, and toil;
These spring up and choke the weeds
  That would else o'erspread the soil.

I felt like flinging my book at his head.

While they were singing it, I made up a parody on it:

The seeds in all the land
  Of poverty and pain,
Are sown by God's own hand,
  And bring forth heavenly grain.

Afterwards I gave it to the minister.

"Oh," he said, "I do not believe that."

"It means the same as your hymn," I said.

If God Made People Sick I Should Hate Him.

I should hate a God who went about sowing cancers and fevers and diseases.

I should hate a God who put consumption into a man to dig out his lungs.

That is the Devil's work, and God never did it!

It is very hateful to me to hear God praised for the Devil's work.

One reason God heals disease is because He hates it.

Rise and repeat with me the

PRAYER OF CONSECRATION.

My God and Father, in Jesus' Name I come to Thee. Take me as I am and make me what I ought to be, in spirit, soul and body. Give me power to do right, no matter what the cost. Help me to trust Thee with my spirit, my soul, and my body. For Jesus' sake. Amen.

The meeting was closed with the

BENEDICTION.

Beloved, abstain from all appearance of evil. And may the very God of Peace Himself sanctify you wholly; and I pray God your whole spirit and soul and body be preserved entire, without blame, unto the coming of our Lord Jesus, the Christ. Faithful is He that calleth you, who also will do it. The grace of our Lord Jesus, the Christ, the love of God, our Father, the fellowship of the Holy Spirit, our Comforter and Guide, one Eternal God, abide in you, bless you and keep you, and all the Israel of God everywhere, forever. Amen.

The Monday Night Meeting.

For several days previously to the opening of the Adelaide Visitation, and especially during Sunday and Monday, the firs two days of the Visitation, warnings poured in from many reliable sources to the effect that the students of the Adelaide University and others were planning to create a disturbance, and, if possible, break up the meeting in the Town Hall, Monday night.

It was asserted that the medical students would come armed with bottles of sulfureted hydrogen and other vile-smelling chemicals, and that an effort would be made to drive the audience out of the hall by means of them.

Inasmuch as it had been made evident, on Sunday afternoon, that many of those who had obtained tickets were unworthy of them it was determined that no tickets would be honored, especially when held by young men, unless the holder was accompanied by some well-known and reputable person or persons who would be responsible for his orderly behavior.

As early as six o'clock on this evening, great throngs began to gather in King William street, seeking admission to the Town Hall.

The main entrance to the Town Hall is guarded by a massive pair of iron gates, which, on this occasion, were closed and held by a number of Zion Guard, being opened to admit one at a time those who were to attend the service.

When the Hall was a little more than half-filled, however, a throng of disorderly young men gathered on the pavement and in the doorway, packing so densely all avenues of approach to the hall that no one could get within several yards of the door.

Thousands of Rioters in the Streets.

With every passing moment, the crowd in the street grew in numbers and increased in disorderliness until there was a mob of from fifteen to twenty thousand, howling and singing ribald songs.

Against this great throng, the comparatively small police force of the city, although acting with great bravery, coolness and judgment, were practically powerless, especially as they were not permitted to use their batons or weapons of any kind.

In the course of the evening, not only many of the constables were roughly handled by the crowd, but also the higher officials, including the Commissioner, Colonel Madley himself.

The cowards also broke several expensive window-panes in the Town Hall, for which, in accordance with his agreement, the General Overseer was obliged to pay.

Unable to obtain admittance with their stinking chemicals, the medical students broke the bottles containing them on the steps of the hall, hoping thereby to drive away those who desired to enter; but the sulfureted hydrogen argument is not a very convincing one, as the gas is light and quickly passes away.

Criminals in the Guise of Gentlemen.

A number of well-dressed and apparently well-educated young men, some of them business men, privileged on account of their supposed respectability and standing in the community, entered the Prince Alfred Hotel, which stands next to the Town Hall in King William street, and is connected with it by balcony and window, organized themselves into a band of housebreakers, smashed the window, and thus gained an entrance to the Hall in a lawless manner.

Their character was made manifest by the stench which filled the hall immediately after their arrival.

Through a side gate, guarded by an official of the corporation, the mayor of the city, Mr. L. Cohen, and a large number of the councilors, entered the hall.

Each of them was accompanied by two or three young men, for whose good character and orderly, law-abiding disposition they very glibly vouched.

It was evident, long before the hour for the opening of the service, that those who had broken into the hall, and had entered it under the protection and recommendation of city officials, were there for no other purpose than that of carrying out the plans which were reported to have been made some days before.

When the hour for the opening of the meeting drew near, it seemed almost an impossibility, considering the size and temper of the mob, for the General Overseer to get into the building or even to come near it without being seized and murdered by the mob.

The rioters were singing, "We'll hang old Dowie to a barb-wire fence," and they acted as if they would be delighted to do it.

Promptly on time, however, the General Overseer, Overseer Jane Dowie, and Dr. A. J. Gladstone Dowie, accompanied by Colonel and Deaconess Carl F. Stern drove down King Willliam street to the hall.

There was a howl from the mob as they rushed at the carriage, but the mounted troopers were there, and had cleared the little alley which leads to the rear entrance of the hall.

Into this, the carriage drove so quickly that the great iron gates had closed behind it before the mob could recover its breath.

The meeting was begun at once.

When the General Overseer entered the hall there were a few orderly people in the front seats, and a goodly number of ladies in the gallery.

The ground floor was a little more than half filled, principally with young men, and well-dressed, important-looking men of older years, some of them with hoary heads and gray beards.

Disorder Begins Without Provocation.

As the man of God walked upon the platform, accompanied by Overseer Jane Dowie, there was enthusiastic applause from the few orderly people present, and a chorus of jeers, yells, catcalls and "boohoos" from the contingent of well-groomed and well-fed human beings who had surreptitiously gained admission to the hall.

The General Overseer proceeded at once, very calmly and very quietly to open the meeting.

There was immediate and flagrant disorder.

The mayor of the city, who had himself very emphatically vouched for the gentlemanliness of some of those who were participators in the disturbance, sat on the front seat, wearing a smirk of self-satisfaction.

Although he was the chief executive of the city, and in active charge of its great hall, he did not by word, look or gesture attempt to prevent the disgraceful scenes of lawless disorder and criminal irreverence that followed.

On the other hand, his intense and joyful satisfaction with the mayor of Adelaide, and his apparent satisfaction with his friends in the hall did not for a moment leave him.

He appeared to be very happy and quite contented.

On account of the vast throng outside the hall and the limited number of policemen available, it was impossible to spare more than two constables for the keeping of order within. Even the action of these two seemed to have been utterly paralyzed from a higher source, and they made practically no move whatever to quell the disturbance or to arrest those who were clearly breaking the law.

As a result, the crowd seemed to throw off all restraint, growing worse and worse as the time went on.

That there was absolutely no excuse for such behavior in the alleged abusive remarks of the speaker, can be seen by reading the report of the sermon delivered.

A Scene of Disgraceful Disorder and Cowardly Fury.

They yelled, they sang ribald songs, and so-called patriotic songs; they sang offensive and insulting parodies on old familiar songs; they stood upon the chairs; they surged about the hall, at one time gathering in a turbulent, excited throng in front of the platform; they threw the programs at the platform; they hurled abuse and outrageously insulting epithets at the General Overseer, Overseer Jane Dowie, and others on the platform.

Well-known men stood up and openly insulted the General Overseer, and joined in the disturbance.

A young business man in Adelaide named Hogan, came to the platform, his face distorted with passion, and shaking his walking-stick in the General Overseer's face, shouted "Imposter! Liar! Fraud! Cheat! Humbug!"

The General Overseer stood calm and brave through all this uproar, although the infuriated criminals could have taken him from the platform and done as they wished with him, had they not been too cowardly.

Overseer Jane Dowie, Dr A. J. Gladstone Dowie, and the other members of the party were also unafraid.

The members of the local Branch were very courageous, behaving like veterans

Previously to beginning the meeting, the General Overseer had informed sub-Inspector Burchell, who was in charge of the police outside, that he would close the meeting promptly at nine o'clock.

When this time came, the Doxology was sung, and the Benediction pronounced, although the disorderly mob was singing some song which is supposed to give voice to British patriotism.

The General Overseer then turned and giving his arm to Overseer Jane Dowie walked calmly and slowly off the platform, amidst a perfect pandemonium of vile execrations, and a shower of Visitation programs, hurled at him by several hundred of the gentlemanly (!) citizens of Adelaide.

Adelaide Town Hall, Monday Evening, March 21, 1904.

The meeting was opened by the singing of Hymn No. 14, Visitation Program, "All Hail the Power of Jesus Name," amid wild interjections of whistling and other noises.

The General Overseer then read from the Inspired Word of God, in the Gospel according to St. Mark, the 1st chapter, from the 1st to the 15th verse inclusive.

Interruptions and Insults Begin without Provocation.

The General Overseer said:

My wife, Overseer Jane Dowie, who is the Overseer of Women's Work in the Christian Catholic Church in Zion Throughout the World, will pray.

I am very grateful to you for the very nice attention with which these meetings began [Applause, noises and interruptions by well-dressed men in the audience.]

I ask you to share with me my consideration for my wife who has been suffering very much in consequence of the death of our dear daughter by burning.

She has come to this land to see her mother and father after many years of absence—

[Interjection—"What did you come for?"]

General Overseer—I should not have come at this time, but for her sake.

I hope that, in her own native city, she will yet be able to say that the citizens of Adelaide, of whom she has boasted as being the most law-abiding people in the world— [Laughter, noises, hoots, and shuffling of feet.]

I am glad to hear you cheer her sentiment.

I hope that she will have reason to continue her boast.

I am glad to see so many young men present tonight. [Cheers, jeers, applause.]

I have the great joy, in Zion City, of educating over a thousand young people in our schools.

I am sorry that the large numbers of people who have tickets cannot get near the doors to get in.

[Interjections—"We will let them in for you." Laughter and uproarious noises.]

I am very sorry that they cannot get in, and I only hope that those who have— [Continued applause, noises, jeers, catcalls, whistling, etc., cries of "We'll let them in, Elijah."]

We should be very glad to let them in if it were possible, but they cannot get in. [Interruptions, cries, calls and various other noises to drown the voice.]

Now, gentlemen, that is all— [Scores take up the chorus of a vulgar song.]

Gentlemen, you know yourselves, that any one who does that is breaking the law.

Those who wish to maintain the law will see that this is not done. [Noises renewed.]

I have done my utmost to preserve peace, and hope to continue to do so. [Suppressed shuffles, etc.]

Mrs. Dowie will now pray. [Outbreak of noises, which were soon suppressed.]

An Outrageous Exhibition of Lawlessness and Cowardice.

Overseer Jane Dowie led in prayer, and at intervals was mocked and sneered at by male human beings who were dressed like gentlemen.

Immediately after she had finished, the noises were renewed with fresh energy.

Overseer Voliva, greeted with applaus and frequent interruptions, made the announcements.

The General Overseer then calmly proceeded with the discourse as follows:

THE GOSPEL OF THE KINGDOM OF GOD.

*REPORTED BY I. M. S. AND A. W. N.

INVOCATION.

Let the words of my mouth and the meditation of my heart be acceptable in Thy sight, and bless them to these people. For Jesus' sake. Amen.

I shall not speak at any very great length. [Interruptions, cries of, "We won't let you!" "Go on, Elijah." "Three cheers for Dowie." The song, "Sons of the Sea," was started in a very weak way but died out]

It does not seem to me that that was very much of a success. [Cries of "Hear, hear!"]

My text is in the 1st chapter of the Gospel according to St Mark, beginning with the 1st verse

TEXT

The beginning of the Gospel of Jesus, the Christ, the Son of God Even as it is written in Isaiah the prophet, Behold, I send My messenger before Thy face, who shall prepare Thy way; the Voice of one crying in the wilderness, Make ye ready the Way of the Lord, Make His paths straight; John came, who baptized in the wilderness and preached the baptism of repentance unto remission of sins.

In the 14th verse of that same chapter are these words:

Now after that John was delivered up, Jesus came into Galilee, preaching the Gospel of God, and saying,

[Interruptions.]

The time is fulfilled, and the Kingdom of God is at hand; Repent ye, and believe in the Gospel.

I speak tonight concerning the Gospel of the Kingdom of God.

A great deal too much has been made among Christians of the word church.

There Is No Gospel of the Church.

The Lord Jesus, the Christ, came into this world [laughter, noises, shuffling and thumping of canes and umbrellas] to preach the Gospel of the Kingdom of God. [Interruptions]

All His parables were concerning the Kingdom. [Interruptions, hurrahs, boohoos and foolish ejaculations. Some one in the audience said, "Dr. Dowie, 'Behold I stand at the door and knock.' They are knocking out there; why don't you open the doors and let them in?" Laughter, applause, continued noises, and bits of songs.]

General Overseer—I suppose that the gentleman who has spoken is aware that he has laid himself open to a charge under the Criminal Code, which may give him two years imprisonment with hard labor, during which his impertinent tongue will not be heard. [Catcalls, riotous noises and laughter.]

The officer in charge should certainly do his duty by taking notice of that man and dealing with him at the proper time [Interruptions.]

Our Lord Jesus, the Christ, mentioned the word church only twice in all His ministry. [Interruptions, applause, boohoos snatches of songs, "Sons of the Sea," and "Hang John Dowie on a sour apple tree," which died out after the first line or two]

It does not seem to be much of a success does it? [Voices—"No." Continued noises.]

Our Lord Jesus, the Christ— [Interruptions, loud and long.]

Of course, it is apparent that there is an organized band of disturbers here.

A Calm, Kindly Appeal for Order Shamefully Disregarded.

I have no doubt whatever that there are many well-behaved and earnest citizens here who feel that this is a great outrage. [Noises, shuffling.]

You came in here upon your honor on those tickets that you held, and you are acting without any honor at all. [Laughter and jeers.]

I, of course, have the power to order all the disturbers into custody— [Renewed and vigorous exercising of feet, and jeers and snatches of ribald songs.]

*The following address has not been revised by the General Overseer

I have a right to continue to speak— [Cries of "Hear, hear!" "Speak up Elijah!"]

The Gospel of the Kingdom of God— [Loud coughs and shuffling.]

If you do not want to hear me speak [boohoos, snatches of songs] you have a right to go out, but you have no right to stay here and prevent my speaking. [More lewd singing.]

Those who do not wish to hear me speak tonight ought not to have come into this meeting— [Shuffling of feet, getting upon seats, and songs, "Hang Old Dowie on a sour apple tree."]

If I had done you any wrong— [Singing of "Hang John Dowie on a sour apple tree," etc.]

God the Only Rightful Ruler of His People.

The Gospel of the Kingdom of God was the great theme of the Christ's life and teaching.

His intention [noises, shuffling] was to establish that Gospel and that Kingdom. [Shuffling, jeers.]

There is no difference between the Ancient and the New Dispensations in this matter. [Whistling.]

When God brought His people out of Egypt into the land of Canaan, He established a Kingdom of which He Himself was the King [whistling, noises and laughter], a Theocracy, the Government of the people by God, which is the only form of Government of which God has ever approved. [Noises.]

The Government of the people, by the people, or by military or monarchical tyrannies of any kind, is opposed to God's Word.

God has a right to govern His own world and His own creatures. [Coughs and interruptions.]

In every age, this has been the clear and unmistakable teaching of the prophecies, of the Christ Himself, and of all the apostles.

I am quite sure that every thoughtful man must see that

The Rule of the People Has Not Been a Success.

Democratic government has failed, for you see it here tonight. [Interruptions.]

Some of you who are the rulers of this land, by means of your votes, do not know how to rule yourselves, and the man that does not know how to rule himself can never be a wise ruler of the Nation! [Cries of "Hear, hear," boohoos, shuffling noises and demonstrations, singing "Boys of the Bulldog Breed," noises, jeers.]

Those who are doing this are breakers of the law, and are trampling upon the liberty for which their fathers bled and died; the liberty of free speech in every land. [Whistling, cries of "Hear, hear."]

In the land from which I have come, and of which I am a citizen— [Interruptions.]

I am not ashamed of America, and I have no need to be ashamed of it.

I have always spoken of this land with the utmost respect, [interruptions and catcalls] but I have spoken for many years in the great cities of America, and have never seen such scenes as those I have witnessed here tonight. [Shuffling of feet, noises and interruptions.]

This noise is not from the majority of the people, [rapping of canes and umbrellas on the floor] it is from the minority.

Every one now present knows that Law and Order are being trampled under foot.

The Kingdom of God is an Everlasting Kingdom.

It does not matter who lives or who dies, God lives on and His Kingdom lives on.

"God's Kingdom ruleth over all."

The Gospel that Jesus came to preach, is the Gospel of the Kingdom of God. [Interruptions.]

In preaching it, He said, "The time is fulfilled, the Kingdom of God is at hand, Repent ye, and believe the Gospel." [Interruptions.]

The Gospel is a Call to Repentance. [Interruptions and songs.]

A Solemn Call to Repentance.

I call you to Repentance! [Continued uproar.]

In the Name of Jesus, the Son of God, I command you to repent [boohoos], and if you do not repent you must perish. There is no possibility of your Salvation [interruptions] until you repent.

The beginning of the Gospel is Repentance towards God. [Interruptions, cries of "Three cheers for Dowie!" etc.]

The officers will please take note of that man who is endeavoring to lead the others.

Get his name and address, if he is so brave as to give it to you. [Cries of "Three cheers for Dowie!" a general scrambling upon chairs; songs, whistling, etc.]

I appeal to the men—[Boohooing; more people get up on chairs and sing ribald songs.]

Sit down; all good people sit down.

[Breaking of bottles containing offensive chemicals; General Overseer tries to speak, but voice is drowned by the opposition.]

Gentlemen, I think you will, upon reflection, see that it is a very cowardly thing for hundreds of men to speak against one man [continued riotous interruptions] who is speaking quietly and calmly.

I have a right to speak. [Catcalls.]

You have no right to interrupt me. [Interruptions continued.]

The Reign of the Christ as King Begins in the Heart.

The important matter in connection with the Gospel is [laughter] that the heart must be the seat of the King [Interruptions.]

The Kingdom of God [yells] must first be within you. [Cries of "Speak up!"]

I am speaking up very clearly, and am accustomed to speak to very large audiences.

I marvel that in this city, which had so good a reputation [cries of "Dowie, Dowie, Dowie!"] you should be so different from Chicago [interruptions and laughter,] where I spoke for many years without any interruption whatever except on one occasion. [Cries of "Dowie, Dowie!"]

Jesus said, "The Time is fulfilled, the Kingdom of God is at hand, Repent ye and believe the Gospel."

[Interruptions.]

These are the words of— [Interruptions.]

These are the words of Him who is the King of kings and Lord of lords.

These are the words of Jesus, the Son of God, and these words will be living when all you will be dead and have perished. [Uproarious noises, and ribald songs.]

These are the words— [Interruptions continued; people get on chairs.]

Let the friends sit down [Continued interruptions loud and long.]

Gentlemen obey the Law.

If you have no reverence for me, reverence the law, and sit down.

I desire to say— [Songs and interruptions.]

There is nothing brave in your doing that.

I do not think that, upon reflection, you will feel that it is brave for you hundreds of men to drown the voice of one man. [Stamping of feet, pounding with canes and noises.]

There is nothing manly about that. [Loud and continuous uproars, songs and other noises.]

The meetiug was closed with the Doxology and the

BENEDICTION.

Beloved, abstain from all appearance of evil. And may the very God of peace Himself sanctify you wholly; and I pray God your whole spirit and soul and body be preserved entire, without blame, unto the coming of our Lord Jesus, the Christ. Faithful is He that calleth you, who also will do it. The grace of our Lord Jesus, the Christ, the love of God, our Father, the fellowship of the Holy Spirit, our Comforter and Guide, one Eternal God, abide in you, bless you and keep you, and all the Israel of God everywhere, forever. Amen.

After a few minutes' waiting, until the police were quite ready, the General Overseer descended to the lane or alley in the rear of the Town Hall, and with his family and attendants entered the carriage.

This lane was shut off from the street by a high, strong, iron gate which the police were guarding.

Through a Murderous Mob.

Outside the gates was an angry throng of thousands of men and boys, and not a few women and girls, waiting for the carriage to come out.

The police cleared the way as best they could, and, escorted by mounted troopers, the carriage dashed out of the gates and through the mob.

As soon as it appeared there was a mighty surge toward it from all directions, accompanied by yells and screams of demoniacal hatred.

At the same time, a shower of stones and other missiles struck the vehicle, but fortunately none of them entered the window.

Before the mob could lay hold of it, the carriage had passed through their midst.

Several hundred ran after it until they were distanced, and many continued to throw stones, but none of them did any damage.

For several blocks the carriage was followed by bicycles; but these soon dropped the chase.

At one point, a woman ran out of a saloon and threw a stone at the carriage. It just missed the window.

Instead of going to the York Hotel, toward which the mob was already running, the General Overseer proceeded to the home of friends in the suburbs, followed shortly after, by a wagonette loaded with young men, which drew up in front of the house and watched for about a quarter of an hour, finally following one of the party who left the house and returned to the city.

Rioting at the York Hotel.

Meanwhile, there was a terrible scene at the York Hotel, where most of the crowd supposed the General Overseer to be.

Thousands upon thousands of men and women gathered about it shrieking, and singing, and cursing.

The two strongest emotions in the hearts of the mob seemed to be hatred and fear.

While they hated God's Prophet, and howled out their desire that he be delivered over to them that they might hang him, they feared the few police and the still fewer members of the household of the York Hotel too much to take any more aggressive action than yelling and throwing stones.

The few police acted with great bravery, although many of them were quite severely kicked and stoned.

The manager of the hotel, Mr. Sydney Ferry, a very able and courteous business man, and brave as a lion, stood in the doorway practically alone, although several members of his staff were bravely holding the fort at other points.

Mr. Ferry is of medium stature and slight build, but his lithe muscles are as strong as steel, and his small fists as hard as rocks.

At one time, a large company gathered, in close formation, and, with a rush, attempted to gain the entrance to the hotel.

The leader, a great hulking fellow, suddenly collided violently with Mr. Ferry's right fist, which flashed through the air and landed squarely on his jaw.

Down he went, limply falling across the feet of his comrades.

The rest of the crowd stopped, drew back, leaving their insensible companion to his fate, and stood howling like a pack of wolf whelps.

Mr. Ferry held the door alone, and the thousands of cowards were afraid to make another attempt to enter.

Cowardly Destruction of Property.

But hidden away among the throng of people about the hotel there were a few who were brave (?) enough to throw stones, smashing a glass out of a large lamp in front of the hotel and also some plate-glass windows.

All this time, the mounted police were busily engaged in attempting to push the crowd back, and finally succeeded in clearing quite a large space in front of the hotel.

The General Overseer Reaches the Hotel in Safety.

At about eleven o'clock, two hours after the close of the meeting, the crowd began to melt away, and before midnight the streets were comparatively quiet.

In the meantime, however, a large section of the mob had gone to the suburbs to search for the General Overseer.

They went first to the home of Alexander Dowie, Overseer Jane Dowie's father, but there were no lights burning there, so they concluded that he whom they sought was not there, and went on to the home of Hon. John Darling, Jr., Overseer Jane Dowie's brother-in-law.

There they yelled and sang, and demanded that the General Overseer be brought out to them.

Some also therw stones and a window-light in the conservatory was broken.

Mr. Darling told the crowd that if they had asked courteously whether his relative were there he would have told them, but since they had not, he refused to give them the desired information.

After a time, the police arrived on the scene and cleared away the rioters.

At about midnight the General Overseer returned to the Hotel with Overseer Jane Dowie, and Dr. Gladstone Dowie, and the rest of the night was spent in quietness.

All citizens of the place were united in declaring that never before had Adelaide been one-half so deeply stirred, and never in the General Overseer's experience had the opposition of the Devil and his children been so violent.

The Attitude of the Press.

An idea of how the occurrences of the night were viewed by the people of Adelaide may be gained from reading the following report of the events of the night, published in the Adelaide *Register* on Tuesday, March 22, 1904:

A LIVELY NIGHT FOR ZION.

STORMY SCENE AT THE TOWN HALL.

MR. DOWIE UNABLE TO GET A HEARING.

The peaceful opening which marked the visitation from Zion City gave place on Monday night to startling and unprecedented uproar, caused by a crowd of men. Mr. Dowie could not have wished for better order than that which prevailed at his morning meeting in the Town Hall, and although it was known that organized hostility would be shown at the night gathering, nobody dreamt that the proceedings would assume the alarming phase that they did. Zion's officers agree that the rioting was much more pronounced than it was in either Melbourne or Sydney, and not only are they disappointed, but they profess to be utterly at a loss to account for the extraordinary scene. Mr. Dowie is a fighter, and is still determined to deliver his message to Adelaide, although he has seen fit to rearrange his programme as indicated further on.

INSIDE THE HALL.

UNLIMITED DISORDER.

The discrimination which the Zion officers showed in selecting the evening audience by excluding even some of the ticket-holders, utterly failed in its object, and the meeting was marked by an hour's disorder. The stormy reception given to ex-Priest Slattery was a lullaby compared with Monday night's uproar. A crowd purely "out for fun" carried everything before them. Many people gained admission by breaking through the door of the Prince Alfred Hotel leading to the Town Hall balcony, although some who sought this way of entrance were thrown out by the police. Others who managed to pass through the outer gates were denied admission at the doors, but still a hundred or two of men, spoiling for mischief, found their way in. Ladies predominated in the back gallery and dress circle, while members of the Christian Catholic Church filled the organ galleries. The hall itself was only about half-filled, on account of the rigorous check imposed at the doors. The noisy portion of the audience sat chiefly on one side of the building under the dress circle, and although they were distinctly in a minority they simply did what they liked with the meeting.

REASON OF ADELAIDE VISIT.

When Mr. Dowie appeared on the platform with his wife and son and the Zion officers he was greeted with applause. In returning thanks he explained the reason of his visit to Adelaide. He would not have come personally at the present time but for Mrs. Dowie's sake. She was suffering very much over the decease of their only daughter, who had met her death from burning, and she wanted to see her mother and father in Adelaide after many years' absence. He still hoped to be able to speak to the citizens of her native town, of whom she had continually boasted as being the most law-abiding in the world. (Cries of "Oh!") He was very glad to see so many young men present that night. In his own city he was educating over two thousand children in his schools and three hundred sixty in his college. He was only sorry that there were a large number of ticket-holders outside who could not get in on account of the crowd around the gates.

A Voice—Let them come in if they have tickets. (Cheers.)

Mr. Dowie—I would be very glad to let them in if it were possible.

The noisy section here sang a few bars of "Sons of the Sea." Mr. Dowie reminded them that they were breaking the law, and he asked that the audience generally should insist on the maintenance of order. He had done his utmost to preserve the peace, and he hoped to continue to do so. He would ask Overseer Jane Dowie to pray.

MRS. DOWIE'S PRAYER.

Mrs. Dowie, who was almost overcome with emotion, then knelt and prayed, but some of the men in the audience subjected her to mockery, principally by loudly imitating the feminine voice. She concluded her prayer with the words—"Our hearts are broken today at these men who mock Thy word. Lord, touch their hearts." The answer from the audience came in the shape of jeering.

INTERJECTORS REBUKED.

Dr. Dowie then began his address. He remarked that he would not speak at length that night. The men joyfully greeted the announcement with three cheers and the singing of "For he's a jolly good fellow." The refrain broke down, and the General Overseer calmly observed, "It doesn't seem to add much to the success of the meeting." Strangely appropriate was the speaker's text, in which occurred the words, "The voice of one crying in the wilderness." "I want to emphasize," he said, "the fact that there is no gospel of the church, and that Jesus Christ came into the world to preach the gospel of the kingdom of God."

A Voice—Jesus Christ never spent as much money as you do. [Interruption.]

Mr. Dowie—You lay yourself open to a charge under the Criminal Code for which you can receive two years' imprisonment, during which period your impertinent tongue will not be heard. [Applause.] I hope the police will take notice of the interjector and deal with him at the proper time. [Hear, hear, and uproar, ending with the singing of "For he's a jolly good fellow."]

Mr. Abe Shannon next rose and addressed Mr. Dowie.

Mr. Dowie—Sit down, sir. You have no right to interrupt.

Mr. Shannon—I only want to point out that on the cover of your program appear the words, "Behold, I stand at the door and knock."

The point which Mr. Shannon wished to make was that a number of people were knocking at the Town Hall gates, but he could not obtain a hearing. Mr. Dowie appealed to the honor of the disturbers, who had sought his tickets in apparent good faith.

A Voice—There were three thousand tickets issued, but you won't honor them. Why not let the people come in?

Mr. Dowie—I have the power to order all you disturbers into custody.

This remark was followed by a verse of "Sons of the Sea" and a parodied refrain, "We'll hang old Dowie to a sour apple tree."

LIBERTY OF SPEECH A MISNOMER.

Mr. Dowie—I was satisfied before today that democratic government has not been a success. You who have votes cannot rule yourselves, and the man who cannot rule himself cannot be a wise ruler of a nation.

"Sons of the Sea" broke out again, and at its conclusion,

Mr. Dowie remarked—"Talk about liberty of speech in a free land! I am a citizen of the United States, and for years I have spoken of your land with great respect. I have never witnessed such a scene as there is tonight, and I have spoken in all the big cities of America. It shows what a minority can do in a meeting."

"WE ARE STINKPOTS."

The rioters changed their song to "Dolly Gray," and then Dick Stephens, the well-known ex-footballer, stood up and repeatedly led cheering for various persons. An officer of the church attempted to interfere, but without any good effect. The police, whose strength in the hall was weakened by the attention demanded by the crowd outside, looked on calmly, but did not stir themselves, nor did Mr. Dowie invite them to. The General Overseer shouted to the disturbers, "In the name of Jesus Christ I call you to repentance," and the uproarous ones answered, "No; we are stinkpots," and cheered "Hawkins" and "Voliva."

HOPELESS DISORDER.

The meeting was now completely out of the General Overseer's hands. The singing, shouting, cheering, and jeering were deafening, and Mr. Dowie stood on the platform calmly surveying the scene. The bulky programs were hurled at him in scores, but none struck him, although one hit Mr. Voliva on the chest. The rioting grew worse and worse. One of the most prominent interrupters was a leading Adelaide wine and spirit merchant. Some of his choicest expressions addressed to Mr. Dowie when comparative quietness occasionally reigned were—"Shut up," "Wash your mouth," "Flap your wings," "Get your hair cut," and "Don't point," and when Dick Stephens took around the collection box the merchant in question pretended to spit in it.

STINKPOTS IN REALITY.

The discomfort of the orderly portion of the audience was increased by the scattering about the hall of bisulphide of carbon. This vile-smelling chemical permeated the whole atmosphere, and nearly everybody held his handkerchief to his nose. "Three cheers for our smell," shouted one of the rioters, "and another one for Elijah."

A SHOWER OF PROGRAMS.

Those who were not engaged in the actual disturbance stood on chairs, and at last the General Overseer gave up the attempt to secure a hearing. He announced the doxology, but the crowd preferred the national anthem. Mr. Dowie offered his wife his arm, and left the platform amid a shower of programs and shrieks of laughter. As he was walking off a man advanced along the aisle and shouted at the General Overseer—"Fraud, liar, thief, humbug, hypocrite." The meeting was over in exactly one hour. One of the Zionites, referring to the proceedings, remarked—"The truest remark the General Overseer uttered this morning was 'The coward leads the procession to hell.'"

DISTURBANCE IN THE STREETS.

A NOISY CROWD.

Adelaideans have seldom behaved as they did on Monday evening in front of the Town Hall and the York Hotel. Before seven o'clock there was a noisy, surging crowd in front of the meeting place. What they wanted was plainly seen. Many had tickets, but the gates on all sides were shut, and the one definite answer was "No admittance." Earlier ones had got through before there was much sign of a row, but once the unruly element broke out the iron doors clashed, and the outsiders vainly appealed for an entrance. At all the side doors they were told to apply at the front, and before the iron gates at the main ingress there was soon after seven o'clock a seething mass of humanity. It struggled and pushed, and so great was the press that the massive iron bars creaked. Women screamed, their laces and ribbons were torn to shreds, hats were lost. At the time out in the street and on the footpaths the crowd was gathering in volume, until it reached from Pirie street to the Government offices. The cries of those caught in the crush at the gate was drowned in a volume of sound from outside. Songs of all kinds, sung by different bands with no idea of music, made night hideous. Cheers sounded above everything, but for whom and what no one knew or cared.

AMONG THE CROWD.

The men in the street seemed, from their dress, to belong to a fairly well-to-do section. There was a large sprinkling of people who had come with tickets in their hands to listen to Mr. Dowie. They slowly dispersed and went home, for by half past seven it was evident that there would be no entrance to the hall. By that time there were about ten thousand people in the street. It was plain many were there for one object.

ACTION OF THE POLICE.

A big array of troopers, with plenty of foot constables and private detectives, kept fair order until after nine o'clock. Those on the thoroughfare were kept moving, and two lanes were maintained for tram-cars and cabs to pass. So orderly then were the people that they obeyed without murmur the orders of the troopers to clear the way. At last the unruly element gained a chance. Right in front of the main entrance a tube of bisulphide of carbon was smashed on the footpath. Instantly there was a stampede. A fire could not have cleared the way faster. The crowd fled in all directions before the awful stench, and when it had passed away the troopers had taken possession of the sidewalk. From then on the people were kept on the move. "Here he comes," would be the cry from one side. Instantly there would be a rush to that quarter, but it was no one of importance. Just after half past seven there was a tremendous cry from Pirie street.

MR. DOWIE'S ARRIVAL.

The crowd, like sheep, rushed to the corner. At the same moment a mounted escort dashed around from Flinders street, scattered the people in front of it, and almost in a second followed by a closed carriage it swept into the lane between the Prince Alfred Hotel and the Treasury Buildings. Before any one knew it the iron gates at the end had sprung open and closed to again, and Mr. Dowie had gained an entry to the Town Hall. It was done so quietly that few people were aware he was inside. It was quite the talk that no meeting was being held, as Mr. Dowie had feared to face the ordeal. Those inside did not come out, and those in the street could not get in.

EFFORTS TO GET IN.

Some almost reached the desired place. An occupier of Gladstone Chambers allowed a few to pass through the passage which leads to the rear of the Town Hall. They were faced when they reached the other door by a number of constables. By-and-by their numbers increased, and then they were ignominiously led to the iron gates and cast out into the streets again. At that time the crowd was willing to enjoy anything. It laughed at the troopers, hailed every cart that passed with cries of "Here's Dowie," and the unfortunate occupant had to drive along a lane with a dense human fence on each side, to the accompaniment of ironical cheers. One instance seen by probably thousands of those present caused a howl of delighted amusement. The troopers had cleared a big space in the center of the road. Right under one of the electric lights an old man argued the point. He dodged around and around the horse, and the intelligent animal seemed to enter into the fun. At last the horse won. He got his chest against the man's back and slowly pushed him to the side of the road. It was an impromptu performance of the clown and Fitzgerald Brothers' famous pony, Commodore. The crowd enjoyed it immensely. Occasionally there was the possibility of accident. Generally the officers cleared a passage way for vehicles, but many times young women audaciously tried to drive through unprotected. The crowd cheered while the horses reared, and but for the rescue by the troopers some one would have been hurt.

SONGS FROM ABOVE.

The Prince Alfred balcony was guarded closely until about eight o'clock. Then it was rushed, and an unmusical crowd threw more discord into the air by trying to sing "Sons of the Sea," which chorus had been rendered hundreds of times by those below. "We'll hang old Dowie to a sour apple tree," and "Good by, Dowie, we must leave you," to the tune of "Dolly Gray." When the crowd recognized that Mr. Dowie must be inside or else not coming, they became noisier. There were shouts for "Dowie," and many coarse remarks. It was merely a vocal disturbance then, for there was little attempt at violence. Boys had clambered up the telegraph poles to the balcony of the hotel and gained the vantage ground. In a momentary lull there was a sound of falling glass. Something had been smashed. It was a tram-car window. Later a Town Hall window went, and for a while the crowd were silent. Then a new noise burst upon them. People kicked the tram-cars as they passed. The noise resembled the beat of a drum. Then the report was passed along that some one had been arrested. That quieted the men, and for half an hour the street was just as on an ordinary Saturday night. Then many of the people, tired of standing about, went home.

HUNTING FOR MR. DOWIE.

For awhile the tired crowd were sullenly quiet. They were doubtful whether the General Overseer of Zion was inside; but just at nine o'clock a new zest was added to the chase. The gates opened, and people came out. There had been a meeting, and Mr. Dowie was still inside. Men bragged of having assisted to upset the meeting. They inflamed those who were in the street into a fury, and the exits were watched. The troopers were still doing good, careful, humoring work, and they tried to put the people off the scent by not gathering at any entrance. Several times the crowd rushed to Pirie street, and on each occasion they were led away by the white horses. Finally there was almost a clear coast. However, a frantic cry broke out, "Here he comes." There was a stampede to Pirie street. Just as the crowd reached them the iron gates of Gladstone Chambers were thrown open. Two troopers dashed out; behind them was a closed carriage. The escort galloped out, and the coachman thrashed his horses into a gallop. Mr. Dowie was away, but at a dangerous rate. "Catch him, the swine," was called out. "Pull him out." "Turn him over." These expressions were heard as a crowd numbering some thousands ran down Pirie street after the carriage.

AT THE YORK HOTEL.

WOMEN STONED AND WINDOWS BROKEN.

The spectacle outside the Town Hall and the chase down Pirie street were mild in comparison with what took place at the York Hotel, where Mr. Dowie had been staying. If the police had been successful in preventing serious violence at the Town Hall, they failed at the York Hotel, where the roughs in the mob threw stones at inoffensive ladies and gentlemen to the danger of their lives, and did serious damage to property. The Rev. J. A. Dowie left the Town Hall at five minutes past nine. Ten minutes later there was an infuriated mob in front of the hotel. It had got quite out of hand. Howling, pushing, and struggling, it kept on calling for "Dowie." The adjoining footpath was kept clear, but the crowd pressed right to the curbstone. There were only a few police available to help the landlord (Mr. Syd Ferry) to prevent the place being rushed. From the street came all sorts of language and threats. Some were disgusting. They showed the class of people concerned. It was the rough, unruly element which is to be found in pushes, but for the time it was helped by youths and men whose training should have taught them better. Night was made a pandemonium. The faces of some of the roughs were distorted with fury.

Three well-dressed youths broke past the police and marched straight into the hall of the hotel, one behind the other. They came like soldiers. "The body-guard," was the cry. Their appearance deceived the outsiders, and with a yell there was a rush for the door. In the middle of it stood Mr. Ferry alone. The foot constables were tossed aside, and with a surge a thousand people rushed towards the landlord. The first to reach him went staggering back. He was struck by a good right arm fair in the face, and he did not want any more. The miserable wretches! It was one man against the crowd, and he quelled them. They stood hundreds deep right to within a yard of him and howled at him. A rush and he must have fallen, and the hotel would have been at their mercy; but Mr. Ferry's bold front awed them. A minute—it seemed longer—and then the police gained the upper hand for a time. The crowd, then about 5,000 strong, were thrust back to the center of the road. They should have been driven as far as Rundle street and the square, but they were left within a few yards of the building. By-and-by, amid cheers, an egg landed on the pavement. Then a hat struck one of the attendants, guarding the door, on the head. A storm was brewing. Mr. Ferry tried to speak to the besiegers from the balcony, but they could not see him and would not hear him.

A SHOWER OF STONES.

A cab bearing Overseer Voliva, Elder Excell, Mrs. Stern, and another lady drove up. The party alighted, and immediately they were out of the cab a shower of stones fell all around them. They dropped on the pavement, crashed on to the steps in the vestibule, and knocked holes in the cab. It was road metal. The Zionists hurried inside, and fortunately none of them was hurt.

A BOMBARDMENT.

When the carriage had passed away, the crowd were hustled back, but only as far as the opposite footpath. They should have been out of Pulteney street long before. Soon one of those in the door, standing behind a curtain, was hit by a rock, but the curtain had stopped its force. Then others came clattering into the vestibule. Smash! And windows were gone. The stones came from the other side of the road, and the police allowed the people to stay there. Then there were more crashes; over the heads of the police metal flew through the air, and broke some valuable stained glass windows which the late Mr. W. E. Ford brought from England, especially for the York. Soon it was plain that the stone-throwers wanted to put out the light in front of the main entrance. A stone fell now and again in the vestibule, and then there was a smash. One had gone to its mark, and the panes of the big lamp were knocked to pieces. "What have I done," said Mr. Ferry, "that they should break my property." Others looking on wondered what the police were doing. The smashing of the lamp was the signal for a terrific outburst of cheering. The strange part of the whole affair was that Deacon Newcomb, who could be picked out at once, walked into the hotel and out again without being noticed. Others coming in and going out were hooted. So the howling roughs continued for a couple of hours.

MR. DOWIE'S RETURN TO THE YORK.

The General Overseer returned to his headquarters at the York Hotel at ten minutes to twelve. The word was whispered through the throng outside shortly after eleven o'clock that Mr. Dowie had gone to sleep at the residence of a friend. This statement quickly spread, and the assemblage gradually dispersed. There were only a few stragglers in the street at half past eleven, and twenty minutes later, when the conveyance dashed up Rundle street from East terrace, there was scarcely a soul in the street beyond the members of the detective force. Mr. Dowie's staff were on the York balcony until a quarter to twelve, when they went downstairs. They rushed to the side entrance when the rattle of wheels was heard, and it was quite evident that this part of the evening's program had been prearranged. When the General Overseer and his party stepped from the carriage there was a body-guard of detectives handy. The instant Mr. Dowie entered the hotel he was warmly welcomed by his followers.

He walked up to Mrs. Ferry and said, "Good evening, Mrs. Ferry, I am sorry to hear they have been breaking the windows. Nothing very serious, I hope?" Turning to Mr. Ferry he said, "Well, will you still permit me to stay here, or would you rather I did not?" Mr. Ferry replied, "So long as you are satisfied to stay here, I am only too willing to accommodate you." Mr. Dowie thanked him for the assurance, and went on to say, "I intend to carry my mission through. But in future my meetings will take place in the mornings and afternoons, for you know some people like to cloak their deeds with the darkness. Good night, all."

FROM THE POLICE SIDE.

A BOY ARRESTED.

When the trouble at the Town Hall was at its height a trooper urged his horse towards a boy named Norman, whom he caught by the coat-collar and arrested. The constable saw a lad break the window of a passing tram-car, and is certain that he kept him in sight and made no mistake in the capture. Norman, however, affirms emphatically that he was not the offender, and states that several witnesses will be able to establish his innocence. A number of bystanders who witnessed the incident are confident that the constable captured the wrong lad. As the accused, who lives at Hindmarsh, is only seventeen years old, he will appear at the state children's department this afternoon.

POLICE KNOCKED ABOUT.

"Absolutely the worst night I ever remember," remarked Subinspector Burchell upon his return to the city watchhouse, and his opinion was shared by all the members of the police force who were "keeping order" outside the Town Hall. Almost every one of them had been badly knocked about; in fact, he was a lucky man indeed whose shins were not covered with bruises. There was ample evidence also that the stone-throwing had resulted disastrously. Sergeant Rose was hit in the face by three missiles, and was severely cut. He had the satisfaction, however, of leveling one of his assailants with a heavy fist. Just as the meeting closed and the people rushed downstairs a rough hurled a heavy stone, an inch or two over the heads of a number of policemen and private citizens. It crashed through one of the front windows of the building. Another blackguard threw an open knife at a detective, but luckily missed him. Subinspector Burchell received a number of bruises on the legs, and he was kicked on the thigh. When the force had compared notes it was generally agreed that never before had an Adelaide crowd been in such a pugnacious humor.

STATEMENT BY COLONEL MADLEY.

"The whole affair," remarked the Commissioner of Police (Colonel Madley) late on Monday night, "was absolutely disgraceful. The crowd inside was quite beyond our control; but what could you do in a case like that? The Zion people talked about using great discrimination in the issuing of tickets; but what was the result? There were any number of hoodlums, 'gentlemanly larrikins,' and University boys present. The meeting was utterly hostile to the speaker, and did not intend to give him a hearing, and any number of police could not have made any difference. The disturbance was a disgrace."

"But could not the outside disturbance be quelled?" "How could it? What can you do when thousands of youths, with all their larrikinish instincts worked up to the boiling point, misbehave themselves without committing any specific offense? We made every provision—there were at least fifty policemen outside the Town Hall—but although the crowd made a big disturbance, there was nothing to accuse them of individually."

ATTACK UPON MR. DARLING'S RESIDENCE.

Mr. Darling, M. P., telephoned to the *Register* office about eleven o'clock last evening, and said: "Whatever is Adelaide coming to? Just as I had put the lights out to go to bed, I heard a stone crash through the glass of my conservatory. Immediately there arose fearful howling from two or three hundred well-dressed 'respectable' larrikins, who were gathered in front of my house, and they made night hideous with their yelling." Mr. Darling said he presumed that as he was a relative of Mr. Dowie the crowd must have thought that the General Overseer was staying at his house. He telephoned to the watchhouse, and quickly two troopers and a couple of policemen were on the scene and dispersed the crowd.

ARRESTED FOR APPLE THROWING.

At twenty minutes past three o'clock on Monday afternoon Mr. Dowie came out of the York Hotel to enter his carriage, which was almost immediately surrounded by about two hundred people. The General Overseer was about to drive off when William Jones, aged twenty-one years, who is well known to the police, threw an apple at him. The offender was at once arrested by F. C. Naylon and conveyed to the watchhouse. The incident was also witnessed by Detective Mitchell, Colonel Holmes, and F. C. Ring. Jones was charged with having thrown in Pulteney street a certain missile, to wit, an apple, to the danger of persons passing therein, and he will appear at the Police Court this morning. The apple did not strike Mr. Dowie, but fell into his carriage, yet the report was spread all over the city that he had received a black eye.

ALTERATION OF THE PROGRAM.

AFTERNOON INSTEAD OF EVENING MEETINGS.

Deacon A. W. Newcomb, Zion's editor, informed us last night that owing to the disturbance Mr. Dowie had decided in the interest of public safety, and the preservation of life, limb, and property, to substitute afternoon for evening meetings. In accordance with this decision the meetings of the visitation which were announced for eight o'clock in the evening will be held instead at two o'clock in the afternoon. The tickets issued will stand good, although the General Overseer and his deputies reserve the rights, as stated on the tickets, to refuse admission to any one. The morning meeting announced for half past ten will now begin at ten o'clock, and from half past eleven to half past twelve Mr. Dowie will see all sick people "who are prepared to trust God for their healing."

As further evidence of the intense excitement which prevailed, a perfect shower of letters began to pour in to the General Overseer, some of them expressing sympathy, others offering criticisms and suggestions, while still others were simply the outpourings of spirits full of ferocity, fear and filth. Those who wrote the last named class of letters were usually too cowardly to sign their names.

But the General Overseer was not the only one who received letters from interested people.

Judging from their columns the newspapers were also in receipt of their share.

These letters expressed a great variety of opinions and emotions, showing that the citizens were divided, some saying one thing and some another.

The papers stated that they had received great quantities of letters that they could not publish, but they did publish a large number every day.

Some of these displayed rabid hatred, manifesting itself in violent, unjust and unreasonable criticism of God's Messenger; some displayed an almost incredible stupidity and asininity; some were calmly and more or less intelligently critical; some were impartial and strictly just in their temper; while others were clearly sympathetic with the General Overseer and indignant at his persecutors.

We publish below a few of the more interesting of the letters which commented upon the disturbances of Monday night.

In the Adelaide *Advertiser* for March 24th, there appeared the following:

Sir—The late disorderly conduct is a manifestation of the ignorance of the people who participate in such scenes. It proves conclusively that there is plenty of room for improvement of Adelaide people, intellectually and otherwise. Most assuredly there is an absolute necessity for the upholding of a high standard of religion and right living. Realizing the importance of the press in matters of this kind, I pen these few lines in the hope that they may cause many to stop and think, and thus take a more rational and humane attitude towards a man who, by his knowledge, is endeavoring to elevate the masses. I am, etc.,

WM. J. SHAW, Art Student.

Sir—The discreditable and unruly display by the disorderly section of the audience at the Town Hall on Monday evening calls for strong comment. It is to be hoped that in the future strong measures will be adopted to prevent the hoodlums of the city of Adelaide (whether rich or poor men's sons) doing exactly what they like. Here is an incident showing the great bravery (?) of the hoodlums who made a demonstration at the York Hotel: The landlord by a well-timed blow kept back an army of about 500 roughs. Those people who went to hear Mr. Dowie were entitled to hear him, without their rights being interfered with by the noisy portion of the assemblage. We boast of the liberty of the subject and freedom of speech, and then we deny it to those whose opinions we don't like. Every man, no matter what his nationality, his color, or creed, is entitled under the British constitution, freely to discuss any question, whether social or political, or religious, without let or hindrance.

Adelaide has always enjoyed a reputation for fairplay (otherwise the golden rule) and freedom from lawlessness, marred a few years ago by attacks on "ex-priest" Slattery, and by the doings of a one-eyed crowd on the present occasion. An important point is this, that the disorderly portion of the public, having taken the law into their own hands now, may do so again, unless strong measures are taken to deal with them in the future. It is no excuse to say that because Dowie spoke strongly that it is justifiable to damage the property of peaceable and unoffending citizens who had done the multitude no harm. Should a future display of rowdiness and damage occur it may result in the military being called out and hundreds of innocent persons being killed and wounded. Down with the mob; up with fairplay and justice. I am, etc.,

BILLY THE BUMPER.

Sir—Freedom of opinion is a great privilege allowed to people of every degree under the British flag, and it is most unfair to abuse that privilege, either through the press or orally. Mr. Dowie and his followers should be granted a fair hearing, and it says little for the Adelaide rabble that they should behave as they have done in denying the Zionites the utmost freedom of speech. We are looking for reform, and scorn it when it is offered freely. Britain's greatness has sprung from Britain's love of the Holy Bible, yet fair Australia is training our youthful citizens to impart Biblical knowledge to the Chinese, while our statesmen will not allow the young British Australian to enjoy the same blessing.

Can any God-fearing man or woman say we do not need a prophet from somewhere, and one not afraid to tell us our faults, who will help us to do better? We are all in the swim of a great nation's downfall. Neither can Britain's downfall be stayed unless we learn that our safeguard is a clean religion, pure living, and careful training of our youth. We, as a young country, are unfaithful to our trust. Our greatest blessings are repudiated by nearly all classes. The denominations we have are powerless to suppress the growing evils. Then why cannot a well-intentioned reformer speak of our infirmities, and why cannot we let those who so desire accept his teachings in peace? To an outsider it looks as though Adelaide is afraid of the truth, and Mr. Dowie is giving them too much of it. I am, etc.,

FRIAR BACON.

From a large number of letters, published in the same paper for March 25th, we reprint the following:

Sir—I trust the right of free speech will not be further violated in connection with the Dowie meetings. Dowie sometimes speaks strongly, and, perhaps intemperately, but if untruthfully or libelously, there is a civil law of punish, and to which his opponents should appeal. If Dowie is stopped because he displeases, where is it going to end? Continue violating the principle of liberty and we shall soon be back to the inquisition, the rack and the stake. I have heard it said, "Throw a club into a herd of pigs, and the one that squeals the loudest is the one most hurt." So it seems to me that Dowie's clubs "hurt" some wrongdoers, and consequently they are squealing, "suppress him." If Adelaide citizens suppress him, it will be at the peril of their good name in the eyes of all civilized people. I am not one of his followers, nor am I likely to be, and he has said some hard things of my people, but in view of it all I must add my protest against any unlawful means being used to prevent him speaking for the right. I am, etc.,

ELDER J. H. N. JONES.

Sturt street, Adelaide, March 24, 1904.

The following courageous and logical letter appeared in the *Advertiser* for Wednesday, March 23d:

Sir—It is hardly credible at this late day, and in South Australia, which boasts of its democratic tendencies, there should be any necessity for defining the right of "free speech." But thus the matter stands. Mr. Dowie had proposed—as under our laws he had a perfect right to do—to address his sympathizers in the Town Hall. Those who dissent from his spiritual pretensions had their course clearly marked out by common decency, to mention no higher consideration. It was to stay away. Others of a different mind were willing, and perhaps even anxious, to hear Mr. Dowie, and they surely had precisely the same right to have their wishes respected as we who differ from them. But the meeting, as your report shows, was thrown into utter disorder by an organized gang of disturbers. By tactics as disgraceful and degrading as have ever been witnessed in a public hall, the speaker was prevented from addressing his audience. I do not write this for the purpose of pointing out the obvious moral that the leading victors in scandalous scenes of the kind and their (often well-dressed) instigators should be exemplarily punished.

There is, I regret to note, even in intelligent quarters, some doubt as to how far those who dissent from the utterances of any speaker have a right to express their feelings. It is held that if you are entitled boisterously to signify your approval, you have logically the same right to express your feelings when they are of the opposite kind. But apart from the consideration that the one noise is objectionable and the other not, the question really is whether the interruptions are such as to render it impossible for a speaker to address his audience in an intelligent fashion, or even at all. If the matter were one that concerned the speaker and his disturbers alone, it is conceivable that the latter might have more to say for themselves than they can possibly have while their conduct interferes with the right of a third party, which in the case of Mr. Dowie was represented by the people who desired to hear him. It is really the right of this third element that should govern the situation. A man might possibly deserve little sympathy who persisted in addressing an audience entirely composed of persons who had no wish to hear him.

But while his audience includes a minority, however small, desirous to hear the speaker, our churches and schools and other agencies of enlightenment have surely been of small avail if they have failed to show that the proper course for the majority in such a case is to quit the building and leave those in it to the peaceful enjoyment of what they themselves refuse to hear. As for the suggestion that has been made that Mr. Dowie should be induced or compelled to refrain from holding meetings that fill the streets with a clamorous mob, the principle that should guide us here is no less simple. The presumption must always be in favor of liberty. The demand for the restriction of the liberty of A is not made out because it is understood that B has determined to assault A if he exercises his freedom. In such a case it is B, not A, who is a proper candidate for the notice of the police. I am quite certain that I express the view of every right-thinking person when I say that to hold otherwise would be to undermine the very foundations of democracy. I am, etc.,

JEANNE F. YOUNG.

Zion in Illinois.

B. W. Brannen, Deacon in the Christian Catholic Church in Zion, will conduct meetings in the following places in Illinois:

Grant Park, June 5th and 6th; Kankakee, June 7th and 8th; Watseka, June 9th; Hoopeston, June 10th; Champaign and Urbana, June 11th and 12th; Danville, June 13th; Paxton, June 14th; Melvin, June 15th; Roberts, June 16th; Pontiac, June 17th; Streator, June 18th and 19th; Ottawa, June 20th.

Zion in Ohio.

Rev. T. A. Cairns, Elder-in-charge of the Branch of the Christian Catholic Church in Zion in Detroit, Michigan, will make a trip through the northwestern part of Ohio, and hold meetings in the following towns:

Toledo, June 4th and 5th; Fremont, June 6th; Fostoria, June 7th; Bluffton, June 9th; Ada, June 10th; West Unity, June 11th and 12th.

Zion in Nebraska.

Elder Charles A. Hoy will conduct meetings in the following places in Nebraska on the dates given:

Bloomington, June 8th; Republican City, June 11th; Cambridge, June 14th.

Zion in Minnesota and South Dakota.

Elder F. A. Graves of Minneapolis, will conduct meetings of the Christian Catholic Church in Zion in the following places in Minnesota and South Dakota:

Janesville, Minnesota, June 6th; Blue Earth, Minnesota, June 6th; Worthington, Minnesota, June 8th; Centerville, South Dakota, June 10th; Brookings, South Dakota, June 11th; White, South Dakota, June 13th; Toronto, South Dakota, June 15th; De Smet, South Dakota, June 16th.

Notes of Thanksgiving from the Whole World

By J. G. Speicher, Overseer-in-Charge

Husband Delivered of Brain Trouble—Wife Healed.

Jehovah is my Strength and my Shield;
My heart hath trusted in Him, and I am helped:
Therefore my heart greatly rejoiceth;
And with my song will I praise Him.—*Psalm 28:7.*

ZION CITY, ILLINOIS, March 8, 1904.

DEAR OVERSEER SPEICHER:—Peace to thee.

I desire to thank God for His goodness to me.

Last November I became very sick, and was compelled to be in bed nearly a month.

I was sick with high fevers, and had delirious spells.

I thank God for victory over this, and I thank you and many dear ones who prayed for me in Zion City

We have had many things to thank God for during the last two years.

When we came here, my husband was in a serious condition.

He had kidney trouble, and it seemed he never would get well.

He also had brain trouble. When in sound sleep, it would seem as if his whole head were dead, and he would sit up and slap his head and cry for me to slap it.

It seemed terrible to see this.

I always prayed, and I thank God I never feared when we were alone, only God with us.

After a very severe spell like this, he would be afraid to go to sleep and I would have to keep awake to watch him.

He had severe pains in the top of his head for over two years before all this trouble came.

Too close application to office work caused it.

Thank God, it is gone.

It seems so good to see him go to sleep and wake up naturally.

Our united prayer to God is that he may be used anywhere, everywhere the Christ directs, Till He Come.

Pray for us.

Yours in His service, (MRS.) MARY MUNGER.

Healed in Answer to Prayer.

How precious is Thy lovingkindness, O God! And the children of men take refuge under the shadow of Thy wings. —*Psalm 36:7.*

MODESTO, CALIFORNIA, February 22, 1904.

DEAR OVERSEER-IN-CHARGE:—Peace to thee.

In answer to your prayer the Lord healed me sufficiently so that I was able to go to work before your letter reached me, for which I give God all the glory and thank you and the Elders of the Christian Catholic Church in Zion for your prayers in my behalf.

May the Lord bless you all is my earnest prayer.

Yours in the Christ, G. W. ANDREW.

Healed of Cold, Rash and Grip.

No good thing will He withhold from them that walk uprightly.—*Psalm 84:11.*

ZION CITY, ILLINOIS, March 18, 1904.

DEAR OVERSEER SPEICHER:—Peace to thee.

I desire to thank God that I am well again.

I caught a very severe cold.

It seemed from a human standpoint it would end in catarrh.

Just as I was getting over that I got the nettle-rash.

I thank God and all who prayed for me, it lasted only a few days.

The Devil thought that was not enough, so he gave me a touch of grip.

But those beautiful words, "Let not your heart be troubled, neither let it be fearful," were a great comfort to me.

I praise God every day that I am in Zion and in Zion City. It is such a blessed place.

By God's grace, I want to do all I can to bring others into the true light.

Praying for the dear General Overseer and Zion everywhere, I am,

Your sister in the Christ, Till He Come,

(MISS) MARTHA MAYHAK.

Healed of Colds.

Thou callest in trouble,
And I deliver thee.—*Psalm 81:7.*

2915 ENOCH AVENUE,
ZION CITY, ILLINOIS, January 18, 1904.

DEAR OVERSEER:—Peace to thee.

I give thanks to God for the healing of my little boy and for my own healing.

We were very sick with colds.

I am almost certain it was grip.

I was very sick last Wednesday.

My head felt as if it would burst, but we trusted God to give us the victory.

My little boy would say, "Come, Mamma, let us pray again."

We did pray and we were healed.

We thank God for all the blessings we have received since being in Zion.

May God bless and keep you, Till He Come.

(MRS.) SADIE HAMPSON,

Deaconess in Christian Catholic Church in Zion.

Saved and Healed Through Work of the Members of Zion Restoration Host.

He that was sown upon the good ground,
This is he that heareth the Word,
And understandeth it;
Who verily beareth fruit,
And bringeth forth, some a hundredfold, some sixty, some thirty.—*Matthew 13:23.*

144 EAST SEVENTH STREET,
HOLLAND CITY, MICHIGAN, February 22, 1904.

DEAR OVERSEER:—Peace to thee.

I thank God this morning for His healing power; and I am so thankful for Zion Restorationists, for through one of them I was brought to God.

I want you to pray for me that I may keep close to God and obey His Voice in all things.

I had been a terrible sufferer for four years.

God only knows how I suffered in body, and prayed to die.

I thought God was punishing me for my sins.

I am now healed through the blood of the Christ.

How thankful I am to God's faithful Restorationists in this town.

I remain, your sister in the Christ,

(MRS.) IDA TACKABURY.

Healed of Lung Fever.

O Jehovah my God,
I cried unto Thee, and Thou hast healed me.—*Psalm 30:2.*

ROSS, INDIANA, March 12, 1904.

DEAR OVERSEER SPEICHER:—Peace to thee.

I thank you for your kind and welcome letter.

We are the only Zion family here for many miles around, but God hears our prayers.

When I sent you the dispatch for my wife, she was suffering great pain and the children were standing around her bed, some weeping and begging her to have a doctor.

They told her that if she did not get one she would die; but she was firm and told them that in that case she would die without a doctor.

Then they telephoned to the doctor and asked him what her trouble was.

He said it was lung fever with other complaints, and a very sore eye.

She told me to telegraph to Zion for prayer and at once the pain in her body was taken away and she got strength from that time on.

She is up now and doing her work. For all His blessings we thank God and Zion.

Praying that God may bless you and yours and spare your life Till He Come, and thanking you for your sympathy and prayers, I am,

Yours in the Christ,

FREDERICK ROBERTSON.

Baby Healed at Hour of Prayer.

Now unto Him that is able to do exceeding abundantly above all that we ask or think,
According to the power that worketh in us,
Unto Him be the glory in the Church and in Christ Jesus unto all generations for ever and ever.—*Ephesians 3:20, 21.*

MONEE, ILLINOIS, March 5, 1904.

DEAR OVERSEER SPEICHER:—Our baby has been healed, and we thank you for your prayers and give God all the glory.

When she was sick two months ago I sent a request for prayer to you.

Bernice went to sleep at exactly nine o'clock on the 15th of January.

The next morning after eating nearly five ounces of food, more than she had eaten at one time for four days, she slept three hours, awoke laughing, and ate a hearty dinner.

We received your letter on the 19th, saying that you had prayed for her at nine o'clock, January 15th, the very hour she received healing.

I took a cold from being up nights. I was also healed that same day.

I want to recommend our Great Physician to all suffering ones.

Yours in His Name,

(MRS.) AMANDA DEUTSCHE.

Healed of Abscess on Shoulder.

I came that they may have life,
And may have it abundantly.—*John 10:10.*

NEW LISBON, NEW YORK, March 13, 1904.

DEARLY BELOVED OVERSEER-IN-CHARGE:—I write to testify to the healing of my six and a half months' old child of a terrible abscess on her shoulder, in answer to your prayers.

She could not raise her arm.

The swelling was as big as one's fist and very black.

I wrote you on March 4th for prayer for her, and I think about the time you prayed she received her healing, for on March 8th the abscess began to discharge; the pus would have filled a teacup. In three days it was healed over, and her shoulder is now as well as ever.

Through it all she did not suffer much pain, except about two minutes one evening.

Thanking you for your prayers, and the good Lord for the healing, I am,

Faithfully yours in Jesus' Name,

(MRS.) MYRTLE HINMAN.

Zion Restoration Host

Elder A. F. LEE, Recorder

I AM inquired of by them that asked not for Me; I am found of them that sought Me not: I said, Behold Me, behold Me, unto a nation that was not called by My Name.—*Isaiah 65:1.*

But God commendeth His own love toward us, in that, while we were yet sinners, the Christ died for us.—*Romans 5:8.*

He made of one every nation of men for to dwell on all the face of the earth, having determined their appointed seasons, and the bounds of their habitation; that they should seek God, if haply they might feel after Him, and find Him, though He is not far from each one of us: for in Him we live, and move, and have our being.—*Acts 17:26-28.*

IT may be interesting to the readers of LEAVES OF HEALING to know that the actual enrolment of Zion Restoration Host now numbers six thousand sixty.

This number is composed only of those who have subscribed their names to the Vow of Zion Restoration Host.

To these figures might also be added many thousand persons who are to all intents and purposes members of Zion Restoration Host, but who have not formally signed the Vow, but are and have been doing faithful work for the extension of the Kingdom of God in the circulation of Zion Literature as far as they have had the opportunity. Among these it is pleasing to state that we are able to include those of many nations.

It also gives us peculiar pleasure at this time, when the name of Japan figures so conspicuously in the affairs of the world, to present to our readers a group of faithful Japanese Restorationists.

This most excellent photograph reached us a few days ago, together with a very interesting letter from our Brother Tokida, who is so faithfully directing the work in that far-away land.

Feeling sure that the members of Zion Restoration Host will be interested in knowing something of what is being done by these faithful workers and the difficulties with which they have to contend, we print nearly in full our brother's letter.

It reads as follows:

YOKOHAMA, JAPAN, 1404 NAKAMURA,
March 29, 1904.

MY DEAR ELDER:—Your kind letter of February 2d, and the application forms, were received some time ago.

I thank you for your words of encouragement and the interest you express in our little flock in the far East.

We thank God that He has kept us and permitted us to do what we could to carry the Gospel to our countrymen, although we are only an insignificant little company of His children in His great Kingdom.

It was the first part of November, 1902, when we received orders from Elder Kennedy in Shanghai to go around from house to house and try to sell Zion Messages.

We had at that time the Message "He Is Just the Same Today" translated and printed.

Brother Kayeyema and myself obeyed the order and commenced the work on November 14, 1902.

It was a new experience to us, so we had some difficulty, but overcame the hesitating feeling and went out twice during each week visiting from house to house, explaining our aim and asking them whether they would not buy a pamphlet about Christian religion.

MEMBERS OF ZION RESTORATION HOST IN YOKOHOMA, JAPAN.

Most of the people received us kindly, but were surprised, for they had never received such a visitation before.

There were some, however, who received us coldly and refused to accept our Message.

The good-hearted people bought the tract from us.

We continued in this way week after week.

Last summer Mother Saito joined us, and has been my companion every Friday since.

She has been very faithful, and with her I have visited a great number of houses and sold many Messages.

Since last fall two more brothers and four sisters have participated in this work with us, and a brother who is not here at the present time sold hundreds of tracts in the city and in his home.

In this way we have visited about twenty thousand homes and sold about one thousand six hundred tracts since the beginning.

Two of the sisters visit the Yokohama penitentiary weekly and teach some of the female prisoners.

The picture which I send you shows those who are engaged in the work. Let me explain briefly about the picture.

The old lady in the center is our beloved Mother Saito who is about seventy years old, the mother of Brother Saito who is now with you in Zion City, and who is her only son.

The lady at her right is Miss S. Takagi who is well known in Zion, and who keeps a store here where Zion lace is sold.

She has charge of the work in the penitentiary with the help of Mrs. Saito; they go there every Lord's Day afternoon, and their work is very hopeful.

The lady next to her at the right is her sister, Mrs. Takabatake. The lady next to Mother Saito at the left is my wife. As she has three small children she is not able to go out regularly, but does so as often as she is able.

Mrs. Saito, the wife of the brother who is in Zion City, sits next my wife.

She goes to the penitentiary with Miss Takagi nearly every week, and when she does not go there she accompanies us in the house-to-house work.

At the left end of the line of gentlemen you will find me. The brother next to me is Mr. K. Kayeyema. He is my first companion and loves the work.

The next to him is Brother Masuda. He is the fruit of the labors of Evangelist Burkland, who is now with you in Zion City. He is one of those who were first baptized in Japan by a Zion Elder. He joined us last summer and removed from his former residence to this place. He is faithfully doing the work with us.

The tall young man next to him is our young Brother Uyeki.

He is a relative to Miss Tagaki and lives with her. Although he is yet young in the Christian life he gladly accompanies us when we go out on the work.

These nine are the working Restorationists in Japan.

I wish to tell you that we, the Restorationists of Japan, are in a far more disadvantageous situation than those in America and other Christian lands.

First of all, we have the disadvantage of not being able to use LEAVES OF HEALING and other Zion Literature which is the power in the work.

Second, we have not as yet a suitable Message for our people.

Third, the Zion salutation "Peace be to this house" cannot be translated into colloquial Japanese, and consequently we cannot use it in our house-to-house work.

Fourth, the word God conveys to the mind of the people a debased and ridiculous idea, and not the grand and sublime thought which is conveyed to those in Christian lands.

The word, Heavenly Father, carries no meaning to us at all.

The only word in Japanese which conveys to the mind any true idea of the Christian's God is the word which means Creator of heaven and earth.

Consequently, when we visit the people we have to explain briefly what Christianity is and then invite them to learn its teaching.

If we use the word repent to them, they do not understand what we mean; we must explain its meaning.

It is a very hard task, and we find we cannot do all this in our visitation, for many of the people are engaged in their work.

We need, therefore, literature which will help the people to understand plainly what Christianity is, and why we endeavor to preach it to them.

Before we can wake the common people to the truth, we are obliged to visit them many times and supply them with different Messages.

It is difficult in Japan to sell religious literature, for people expect to secure it free; besides, there are many religious beggars in our country, and we are often mistaken for some of these. When we offer our literature for sale, some of the people give us a copper coin, just as they give it to the beggars, without taking our papers.

Of course, we do not accept it, but tell them that we come not for money, but to tell them about the Christian religion, and then we give them a paper.

It is not altogether hopeless, however, but quite the contrary.

I also think it better to sell the papers than to give them freely, for what they buy they read, and too frequently what is given to them is thrown away.

We need to have, however, a supply of good, suitable Messages for free distribution to place in the hands of the common people of Japan and China, as the Restoration Messages which are commonly used are only suitable for those who are acquainted with the Christian religion.

The war is a great hindrance to the cause of the Christ here, for the people look upon Russia as a Christian nation, but which they consider is not working for the interests of humanity. This is another objection we have to explain away.

Pray for us all.

Hoping to hear from you soon again, I remain,
Very faithfully, yours in His Name,

D. TOKIDA.

Reports from Various Points.

Following is a tabulated report of the number of workers and the work done by them during the month of April, 1904, according to reports received to date from the various points named:

UNITED STATES.	No. of Workers	No. of Calls	Messages Given	Leaves Sold	Leaves Given
California—					
Fresno	6	850	848	163	12
Haywards	1	7	81	....	8
Los Angeles	16	2383	5455	140	380
Maxwell	1	40	900	...	20
Parlier	1	76	140	22	20
San Francisco	12	3000	3000	998	50
Santa Rosa	1	105	82	14	43
St John	2	....	135	...	43
Colorado—					
Trinidad	2	244	255	37	12
Connecticut—					
Danbury	1	6	11	....	29
Windsor	1	4	260	...	....
Illinois—					
Champaign	1	150	480	6	7
Chicago—Central Parish, Ger.	17	1386	1473	58	280
" South Side Parish	50	4490	4429	422	419
" Southeast Parish	21	1840	3910	715	185
" West Parish, Ger.	13	856	992	61	108
" North Parish	22	2433	2238	105	256
Deerfield Township	1	241	2350	81	...
Highland Park	1	...	230	....	11

UNITED STATES.	No. of Workers	No. of Calls	Messages Given	Leaves Sold	Leaves Given
Illinois—					
Lacon	1	15	....	....	14
Lyndon	1	7	20	....	9
Mazon	2	....	43	....	6
Odell	1	12	13	6	13
Vermilion Grove	1	80	60	7	13
Waukegan	137	3209	4172	685	405
Indiana—					
Hammond	4	25	....	78	69
Indianapolis	5	5	273	88	95
Lafayette	8	485	1500	105	141
Linn Grove	1	....	....	...	16
Logansport	3	350	365	216	210
Marion	2	133	381	7	16
Monon	2	68	71	....	4
Noblesville	1	....	200	....	10
Plymouth	3	4	54	1	24
Valparaiso	1	8	13	....	11
Walton	8	109	59	38	39
Iowa—					
Boone	2	114	228	....	11
Cedar Falls	1	....	....	42	30
Elberon	4	118	80	18	40
Forest City	2	69	254	48	34
Laporte	1	3	....	8	4
Marshalltown	1	30	50	....	15
Newton	3	251	981	....	225
Rock Valley	1	180	986	50	14
Tipton	3	4	64	....	40
Webster City	4	29	647	5	30
Kansas—					
Eskridge	1	33	103	28	12
Independence	4	80	259	6	15
Kansas City	14	1000	1200	227	182
Manhattan	2	12	20	5	....
Salina	1	22	25	....	20
Wichita	10	675	834	259	45
Kentucky—					
Danville	1	6	187	...	8
Massachusetts—					
North Duxbury	2	....	....	...	61
Worcester	1	76	206	64	4
Michigan—					
Grand Rapids	1	100	160	40	35
Manistee	2	40	42	....	63
Republic	1	....	....	13	2
Sault Ste. Marie	5	90	...	109	30
Minnesota—					
Delavan	1	24	80	....	25
Hector	3	....	1900	...	145
Minneapolis	9	1125	2035	278	127
Rushford	2	3	13	....	25
Missouri—					
Higginsville	2	226	222	32	11
Springfield	1	9	44	...	3
Montana—					
Havre	1	11	25	....	36
Nebraska—					
Inman	1	18	4	....	53
Omaha	2	350	1050	...	19
New Hampshire.					
Franklin Falls	2	...	70	.	15
New Jersey—					
Riverdale	1	....	....	....	9
Salem	1	...	....	36	37
New York—					
Bluff Point	4	....	6	..	29
Dundee	1	...	8	....	17
New York City	24	2238	20263	682	1760
Poland	1	2	2	..	1
North Carolina—					
Reidsville	1	45	50	...	....
Ohio—					
Ada	3	8	24	8	33
Akron	2	55	56	....	14
Alliance	1	...	173	..	18
Bluffton	3	...		59	6
Cincinnati	44	3441	6179	533	848
Cleveland	34	5980	7095	122	864
Dayton	3	107	631	49	12
Eaton	1	166	368	17	1
Fostoria	1	...	.	..	51
Germantown	1	428	459	24	25
Lancaster	1	100	724	8	1
Mansfield	1	..	98	.	8
Marion	1	...	63	22	134
Mifflin	1	4	40	..	3
Nevada	1	.	21	...	4
Oceola	2	2	69	.	27
Toledo	2	950	160	221	.
Oregon—					
Union	1	24	31	...	18
Pennsylvania—					
Philadelphia	41	4203	15573	699	402
Scranton	2	61	354	271	18
West Chester	1	175	207	11	6
South Dakota—					
Belle	1	...	..		60
Centerville	2	...	13	4	...
Summit	1	7	8	2	4
Tennessee—					
Chattanooga	6	986	3006	246	228
Memphis	1	9	98	1	42
Whiteside	2	42	47	.	86
Texas—					
Batson	1	...	24	2	19

UNITED STATES.	No. of Workers	No. of Calls	Messages Given	Leaves Sold	Leaves Given
Texas—					
Houston	1	7	105	....	43
Luling	1	11	21	....	5
Washington—					
Clinton	1	32	101	8	22
Easton	2	49	51	2	24
Everett	2	67	67	15	17
Garfield	1	....	200	....	75
Lynden	2	5	....	....	78
Seattle	29	1914	2078	476	57
Spokane	10	2225	1300	381	146
Tacoma	9	512	534	69	75
Wisconsin—					
Alma	2	11	3	3	26
Brookfield	2	20	20	....	8
Columbus	1	451	458	....	1
Maiden Rock	2	9	26	9	26
Milwaukee	10	949	3351	231	76
Minong	1	....	....	....	10
Omro	4	338	716	74	22
Racine	2	78	78	....	48
Viroqua	2	122	308	9	10
Wauwatosa	2	188	325	20	3
West Ellis	1	3	12	....	24
Total	753	55413	119704	9901	9988

DOMINION OF CANADA	No. of Workers	No. of Calls	Messages Given	Leaves Sold	Leaves Given
Canada—					
Berlin	2	....	423	....	27
Branchto	1	34	162	....	2
Elmira	1	16	16	....	9
Fredericton, N. B	1	....	300	120	25
Galt	1	70	124	....	...
Simcoe	2	80	97	75	....
Toronto	15	1658	2937	257	655
Vancouver	25	1764	1891	97	676
Victoria	2	519	387	143	83
Woodstock	3	136	120	53	61
Total	53	4277	6457	745	1537
Grand Total	806	59690	126161	10646	11525

Zion's Conflict with Methodist Apostasy.

This book of 200 pages, issued by Zion Printing and Publishing House, contains nine powerful discourses delivered in Central Zion Tabernacle by the General Overseer, in May, 1900, during a session of the Methodist General Conference. They are of especial value for the full and fearless exposure of Freemasonry.

"The Methodist Church the Property of the Masonic Order," "Freemasonry: A Heathen and Antichristian Abomination," and "Degrees of Masonic Devilry" ought to be read by every Lodge man. The iniquity of the Mystic Shrine is laid bare.

"The Christian's Duty in Breaking a Bad Oath" is the address which preceded the public working of Masonic and Odd-Fellow degrees in Central Zion Tabernacle, a full account of which is given.

Buy one of these books and keep lending it. No honest and intelligent man can read the book and still remain a Freemason.

Sent by mail, postpaid, for twenty-five cents.

Address

ZION PRINTING AND PUBLISHING HOUSE,
Zion City, Illinois, U. S. A.

IS ANY among you sick? let him call for the Elders of the Church; and let them pray over him, anointing him with oil in the Name of the Lord: And the Prayer of Faith shall save him that is sick, and the Lord shall raise him up; and if he have committed sins, it shall be forgiven him.—*James 5:14, 15.*

AND I WILL take you one of a city, and two of a family, and I will bring you to Zion: and I will give you shepherds according to Mine heart, which shall feed you with knowledge and understanding. —*Jeremiah 3: 14, 15.*

How beautiful upon the mountains are the feet of him that bringeth good tidings, that publisheth peace, that bringeth good tidings of good, that publisheth salvation; that saith unto Zion, Thy God Reigneth!—*Isaiah 52: 7.*

Program Zion's Fourth Feast of Tabernacles

Will be held in Shiloh Tabernacle, Shiloh Park, Zion City, Illinois, from the Evening of Wednesday, July 13th, to the Evening of Lord's Day, July 24, 1904.

WEDNESDAY, JULY 13TH.

7:30 to 9 P. M.—Presentation and Consecration of the People to God. Address by the General Overseer: "FOR ZION'S SAKE."

THURSDAY, JULY 14TH.

FOURTH ANNIVERSARY OF THE CONSECRATION OF THE SITE OF ZION TEMPLE.

Public Holiday in Zion City.

Announcement of excursion trains from Chicago will be made at a later date.

6:30 A. M.—Early Morning Sacrifice of Praise and Prayer.
The First of a Series of Twenty-Minute Addresses by the General Overseer on the Nine Fruits of the Spirit: "THE FIRST FRUIT OF THE SPIRIT: LOVE."

9:30 A. M.—First Convocation of Zion Junior Restoration Host. Conducted by Overseer Harvey D. Brasefield.

2:00 P. M.—FULL PROCESSION of Zion Robed Officers, Zion White-robed Choir, and Zion Restoration Host will march around the Site of Zion Temple, and thence to the Site of Shiloah Tabernacle.
The Procession will then re-form and take the seats reserved for them in Shiloh Tabernacle, where an address will be given by the General Overseer on "ZION: A CROWN OF BEAUTY IN THE HAND OF JEHOVAH."
Special Offerings will be received at the close of this Address for the building of Shiloah Tabernacle, which it is expected will cost $500,000, and seat about 16,000 people.

7:30 P. M.—Evening Sacrifice of Praise and Prayer.

FRIDAY, JULY 15TH.

A HALF HOLIDAY IN ZION CITY.

6:30 A. M.—Early Morning Sacrifice of Praise and Prayer.
Twenty-Minute Address by the General Overseer: "THE SECOND FRUIT OF THE SPIRIT JOY."

9:30 A. M.—Second Convocation of Zion Junior Restoration Host. Conducted by Overseer Harvey D. Brasefield.

10:30 A. M.—DIVINE HEALING MEETING. Conducted by the General Overseer.
Address: "PRESENT YOUR BODIES A LIVING SACRIFICE, HOLY, ACCEPTABLE TO GOD, WHICH IS YOUR REASONABLE SERVICE."
At the close of this meeting the General Overseer, Overseer Jane Dowie, and other Overseers, Elders and Evangelists will pray with the sick who are seeking the Lord for healing.

THE CITY FESTAL DAY.

3:00 P. M.—A PROCESSION, headed by Zion Guard and Zion City Band, consisting of
The Municipal Officers of the City of Zion,
All Officers and Employees of the Legal, Financial and Business Institutions of Zion,
All Officers and Employees of the Educational Institutions of Zion, and
All Officers of the Political Institutions of Zion, will be REVIEWED BY THE GENERAL OVERSEER AT THE ADMINISTRATION BUILDING, and then proceed to Shiloh Tabernacle where a SERVICE OF THANKSGIVING will be held.
Those in the Procession, as they enter Shiloh Tabernacle, will take their places in the Choir and Officers' Gallery, and on the ground floor.
Spectators will occupy the remaining galleries.

7:30 P. M.—Evening Sacrifice of Praise and Prayer.

SATURDAY, JULY 16TH.

6.30 A. M.—EARLY MORNING SACRIFICE OF PRAISE AND PRAYER.
Twenty-Minute Address by the General Overseer: "THE THIRD FRUIT OF THE SPIRIT: PEACE."

2:00 P. M.—Zion Athletic Association: Field Games on grounds at northeast corner of Shiloh Park.

8:00 P. M.—Evening Sacrifice of Praise and Prayer.

LORD'S DAY, JULY 17TH.

6:30 A. M.—EARLY MORNING SACRIFICE OF PRAISE AND PRAYER.
Twenty-Minute Address by the General Overseer on "THE FOURTH FRUIT OF THE SPIRIT: LONG-SUFFERING."

9:30 A. M.—Third convocation of Zion Junior Restoration Host. Conducted by Overseer Harvey D. Brasefield.

11:00 A. M.—The Rev. John G. Speicher, M. D., Overseer of the Christian Catholic Church in Zion, of the City of Zion, will preach.

2:00 P. M.—GREAT GENERAL ASSEMBLY.
Procession of Zion's Robed Officers and White-robed Choir (probably One Thousand in line).
Elijah the Restorer will deliver a Message from God to Zion: "ARISE! SHINE! FOR THY LIGHT IS COME."
A reception of New Members into the Communion and Fellowship of the Christian Catholic Church in Zion will be held at the close.

8:00 P. M.—Ordination of New Officers and the Celebration of the Ordinance of the Lord's Supper.

MONDAY, JULY 18TH.

6:30 A. M.—EARLY MORNING SACRIFICE OF PRAISE AND PRAYER.
Twenty-minute Address by the General Overseer: "THE FIFTH FRUIT OF THE SPIRIT: KINDNESS."

9:30 A. M.—Fourth Convocation of Zion Junior Restoration Host. Conducted by Overseer Harvey D. Brasefield.

11:00 A. M.—THE ORDINANCE OF BELIEVER'S BAPTISM BY TRIUNE IMMERSION will be administered by Overseers Speicher, Mason, Brasefield and Excell, assisted by a number of Elders, Evangelists, Deacons and Deaconesses.

2:00 P. M.—A MEETING FOR ZION WOMEN ONLY will be addressed by the Rev. Jane Dowie, Overseer for Women's Work in the Christian Catholic Church in Zion Throughout the World.
This meeting will be strictly limited to female members of the Christian Catholic Church in Zion, and no children under twelve years of age will be admitted.

8:00 P. M.—A MEETING FOR ZION MEN ONLY will be addressed by the Rev. John Alex. Dowie, General Overseer of the Christian Catholic Church in Zion.
This meeting will be strictly limited to male members of the Christian Catholic Church in Zion above the age of twelve.

TUESDAY, JULY 19TH.

6:30 A. M.—EARLY MORNING SACRIFICE OF PRAISE AND PRAYER.
Twenty-Minute Address by the General Overseer: "THE SIXTH FRUIT OF THE SPIRIT: GOODNESS."

9:30 A. M.—Fifth Convocation of Zion Junior Restoration Host. Conducted by Overseer Harvey D. Brasefield.

11:30 A. M.—CONFERENCE OF WOMEN ELDERS, EVANGELISTS AND DEACONESSES OF THE CHRISTIAN CATHOLIC CHURCH IN ZION. Conducted by Overseer Jane Dowie.

2:30 P. M.—CONFERENCE UPON THE WORK OF ZION RESTORATION HOST THROUGHOUT THE WORLD.
The General Overseer will preside, and at the close will administer the Restoration Vow to New Members of the Host, and Consecrate and Separate them to the Work of God in Zion by the Laying on of Hands.

8:00 P. M.—Evening Sacrifice of Praise and Prayer.

WEDNESDAY, JULY 20TH.

6:30 A. M.—EARLY MORNING SACRIFICE OF PRAISE AND PRAYER.
Twenty-Minute Address by the General Overseer: "THE SEVENTH FRUIT OF THE SPIRIT: FAITHFULNESS."

9:30 A. M.—Sixth Convocation of Zion Junior Restoration Host. Conducted by Overseer Harvey D. Brasefield.

11:00 A. M.—CONFERENCE OF MALE OFFICERS OF THE CHRISTIAN CATHOLIC CHURCH IN ZION. Conducted by the General Overseer.

2:30 P. M.—THE ORDINANCE OF THE PRESENTATION AND CONSECRATION OF YOUNG CHILDREN TO GOD, will be conducted by the General Overseer. He will deliver an Address on the Words: "WHAT THEN SHALL THIS CHILD BE?"

8:00 P. M.—Evening Sacrifice of Praise and Prayer.

THURSDAY, JULY 21ST.

6:30 A. M.—EARLY MORNING SACRIFICE OF PRAISE AND PRAYER.
Twenty-Minute Address by the General Overseer: "THE EIGHTH FRUIT OF THE SPIRIT: MEEKNESS."

9:00 A. M.—Seventh Convocation of Zion Junior Restoration Host. Conducted by Overseer Harvey D. Brasefield.

11:00 A. M.—EDUCATIONAL CONFERENCE. Presided over by Overseer Brasefield. Addresses by Members of the Faculty of Zion College, Zion Preparatory and Zion Manual Training Schools.

2:00 P. M.—A CONFERENCE ON ZION BUSINESS INSTITUTIONS will be Conducted by the General Overseer, and Addressed by Managers of the Various Institutions.
The Meeting will be Strictly Limited to Investors in Zion Stocks.

8:00 P. M.—Evening Sacrifice of Praise and Prayer.

FRIDAY, JULY 22d.

6:30 A. M.—EARLY MORNING SACRIFICE OF PRAISE AND PRAYER.
Twenty-Minute address by the General Overseer: "THE NINTH FRUIT OF THE SPIRIT: TEMPERANCE."

9:30 A. M.—Eighth Convocation of Zion Junior Restoration Host. Conducted by Overseer Harvey D. Brasefield.

11:00 A. M.—A CONFERENCE CONCERNING DORCAS AND MATERNITY DEACONESS WORK IN ZION THROUGHOUT THE WORLD. Conducted by Overseer Jane Dowie.

2:00 P. M.—A CONFERENCE ON ZION BUSINESS INSTITUTIONS will be Conducted by the General Overseer, and Addressed by Managers of the Various Institutions.
The Meeting will be Strictly Limited to Investors in Zion Stocks.

8:00 P. M.—Evening Sacrifice of Praise and Prayer.

SATURDAY, JULY 23D.

6:30 A. M.—EARLY MORNING SACRIFICE OF PRAISE AND PRAYER.
Twenty-Minute Address by the General Overseer: "THE NINE GIFTS OF THE HOLY SPIRIT."

2:00 P. M.—Zion Athletic Association; Field Games in the northeast corner of Shiloh Park.

8:00 P. M.—Evening Sacrifice of Praise and Prayer.

LORD'S DAY, JULY 24TH.

6:30 A. M.—EARLY MORNING SACRIFICE OF PRAISE AND PRAYER.
Twenty-Minute Address by the General Overseer: "THE HOUSE OF WISDOM."

9:30 A. M.—The General Overseer will speak on "TRIUNE IMMERSION; GOD'S SEAL ON A LIVING CHURCH."
At the close of this Service the General Overseer, assisted by Overseers, Elders, Evangelists, Deacons and Deaconesses, will Administer the Ordinance of Believer's Baptism.
All persons desiring to be Baptized on this occasion must fill up their Application Cards for Baptism, and present them to the General Recorder, Deacon Andrew C. Jensen, and his Assistants, not later than 9 a. m.

2:00 P. M.—GREAT GENERAL ASSEMBLY.
FULL PROCESSIONAL of Zion Robed Officers, Zion White-robed Choir and all the Members of Zion Junior Restoration Host, under their Leader, Overseer Brasefield.
The General Overseer will speak on "THE MINISTRY OF CHILDREN IN ZION." At the close of this Service he will Administer the Vow of Zion Restoration Host to New Members of Zion Junior Restoration Host.

8:00 P. M.—THE ORDINANCE OF THE LORD'S SUPPER will be Administered by the General Overseer and Ordained Officers of the Christian Catholic Church in Zion.
This Gathering will be open only to Members of the Christian Catholic Church in Zion, and other Christians desiring to commune with them.
At the close, the General Overseer will deliver the CONCLUDING ADDRESS OF THE FEAST.

REDUCED FARE—FEAST OF TABERNACLES.

ONE AND ONE-THIRD FARE FOR ROUND TRIP TO ZION CITY—CONDITIONS OF SALE OF TICKETS.

A reduction of fare to one and one-third on the certificate plan has been granted for those attending the meetings of the Christian Catholic Church in Zion, at the Fourth Feast of Tabernacles, in Zion City, Lake County, Illinois, between July 13 and July 24, 1904, inclusive

The following directions are submitted for your guidance:

First—Tickets at full fare for the going journey, may be secured within three days, exclusive of Sunday, prior to and during the first three days of the meeting; that is, July 10th, 11th, 12th, 13th, 14th, and 15th.

The advertised dates of the meeting are from July 13th to 24th; consequently you can obtain your tickets not earlier than July 11th and not later than July 17th.

Be sure when purchasing your going ticket to request a certificate.

Second—Present yourself at the railway station for ticket and certificate at least thirty minutes before departure of train.

Third—Certificates are not kept at all stations. If you inquire at your station you will find out whether certificates and through tickets can be obtained to place of meeting; if not, the agent will inform you at what station they can be obtained. You can purchase a local ticket thence, and there take up a certificate and through ticket.

Fourth—On your arrival at the meeting, present your certificate to Deacon James F. Peters, Administration building, Zion City, Illinois.

Fifth—No refund of fare will be made on account of failure to have certificate validated.

Sixth—So as to prevent disappointment, it must be understood that the reduction on returning journey is not guaranteed, but is contingent on an attendance of not less than one hundred persons from all points throughout the United States and Canada showing payment of full first-class fare of not less than seventy-five cents on going journey; provided, however, if the certificates presented fall short of the required minimum, and it shall appear that round trip tickets are held in lieu of certificate, that shall be reckoned in arriving at the minimum.

Seventh—If the necessary minimum is in attendance and your certificate is duly validated, you will be entitled, up to July 27th, to reduced passage ticket to your destination by the route over which you made the going journey at one-third the limit fare.

This rate will apply to the entire United States and Canada.

SPECIAL TRAINS BETWEEN CHICAGO AND ZION CITY.

These trains will be arranged for and announcement will be made later.

CAMP HOLIDAY—1904.

REGULATIONS AND PROVISIONS FOR THE SEASON.

Persons desiring to spend a holiday or attend the great teaching meetings of Zion will find, either as individuals, families or parties, inexpensive tenting conveniences, with good water near at hand, in Zion's tents now in service in Camp Holiday, Zion City.

The tents are made of heavy duck material, strongly stayed, with fly, and are rainproof, being pitched above board floor.

The season's price for tents 9½x14, furnished, is $7; or unfurnished, $5 a month, when taken for two or more months, but not to be sublet.

Tents may be rented by the week at $4 for the first week and $2 a week thereafter.

The Feast of Tabernacles' rate is always $2.25 a person, four persons to a tent; other wise the rate is double. Single cots for single nights, 25 cents; tent rates a day $1.25.

All rentals payable in advance, in every case, whether by the month, week or day.

THE FURNITURE.

The furniture consists of the necessary cots, mattresses and chairs, one table, water-pail, tin cup, wash basin and slop-pail to a tent. The bedding includes one white sheet, two light and one or two heavy blankets, and a pillow and pillow-slip to a single and two of each to double cots. Two-wick oil stoves may be rented for $1 a month, supplied with oil; and cooking utensils, including stew-pans, tin plates, cups, knives, forks and spoons, may be secured at a rental of 50 cents a month.

TENT PROVISIONS AND REGULATIONS FOR 1904.

Two tents may be required in some instances, and these will be cheaper than one large one. Then one can be used for sleeping, and the other for cooking purposes.

During the Feast of Tabernacles, tents will again be located in Camp Esther in Shiloh Park, for which a charge of $2.25 a person for the twelve days will be made; but persons leasing tents in Camp Holiday for at least a two months' period may obtain accommodations for the occasion at the season rental price.

Applications for such accommodations or conveniences should be addressed to Deacon James F. Peters, Administration Building, Zion City, Lake County, Illinois.

THE RATES AT ELIJAH HOSPICE

NOW AND DURING THE FEAST OF TABERNACLES ARE AS FOLLOWS:

European Plan—One person in a room, $1.00 a day and up; two persons or more in a room, 50 cents a day and up; one person in a room, $6.00 a week and up; two persons or more in a room, $3.00 a week and up. These rates are for lodging only.

American Plan—One person in a room, $1.75 a day and up; two persons or more in a room, $1 25 a day and up; one person in a room, $10 00 a week and up; two persons or more in a room, $7 00 a week and up; single meals, 25 cents.

Children under twelve years old half rate.

The American Plan includes board and room.

Rooms will be charged for from the date reserved.

FRANK W. COTTON, Manager.

LEAVES OF HEALING.

Two Dollars will bring to you the weekly visits of the Little White Dove for a year; 75 cents will send it to a friend for thirteen weeks; $1.25 will send it for six months; $1 50 will send it to your minister, or to a Y. M. C. A., or to a Public Reading Room for a whole year. We offer no premiums, except the premium of doing good. We receive no advertisements, and print no commercial lies or cheating enticements of unscrupulous thieves. LEAVES OF HEALING is Zion on wings, and we keep out everything that would detract the reader's mind from all except the Extension of the Kingdom of God, for which alone it exists. If we cannot send forth our Little White Dove without soiling its wings with the smoke of the factory and the dirt of the wrangling market-place, or compelling it to utter the screaming cries of the business vultures in the ears of our readers, then we will keep our Dove at home.

Notes from Zion's Harvest Field

By J. G. Speicher, Overseer-in-Charge

FIELD Notes from London, England—from London, the Metropolis of the world; from Great Britain, the mistress of the sea and a world-political power.

From Rome came Christianity to Great Britain.

It was as if the tiny ripple of influence and power of the tribes along the Tiber were beat into a mighty, restless wave by the breath of political ambition, thus sweeping all the earth, covering the known world, and uniting the separate and disjoined tribes and nations into one gigantic political unit, increasing the facility for travel, communication and speech, that the knowledge of the birth of the world's Savior might more readily be heralded to the ends of the earth.

Added to the unity of the governmental control and mingling of nations, the very persecution of the Imperial State served to scatter the good tidings into the more remote parts, where the sandal of proselyting zeal had not yet touched.

Rome was rising to her zenith. Her most illustrious son, Julius Cæsar, pressed northward through the warlike tribes of the Teutons, across the channel to the shores of Britannia.

Here, a half century before the Christ, he touched the soil which following his expeditions was to be prepared amid barbarians for the planting of the emblem of the cross of Jesus, the Christ, the Son of God.

Rome passed away with her glory and pride, weakened by the vice of a false moral life and a mythological religion.

In a remote corner of the Roman Empire, Britannia arose from the barbarism of Druidism and the cruelty and heathenism of her German and Danish invaders, through the political conquest of the Normans with their feudal morality, interspersed with mediæval fanaticism, into one of the world's most enlightened empires, owning the Name of God in her government.

It was in this chosen nation of His dispersed Israel that God raised up from among His people the prophet of the Last Days of the Dispensation, the days of preparation and of the Restoration of All Things.

In the power of his Mission, and with the seal of God's approval and favor, this prophet has gone to the center of the English-speaking world and boldly proclaimed the Times of the Age, and demanded the recognition of the Kingdom of God and preparation for the receiving of the Son of God as the coming King of kings and Lord of lords.

We print below testimonies from those who have been healed and blessed through the establishment of the Christian Catholic Church in Zion in Great Britain.

May God bless the people of this land and bring them to a sense of God's plan and purpose for them! O. R.

MY DEAR OVERSEER:—Peace to thee.

We herewith inclose a number of testimonies which were given at one of our testimony meetings, held once a month.

Trusting that you may be able to use them as a report of our work in London, believe me, with Christian greetings,

Faithfully yours in Zion's bonds,

H. E. CANTEL,

Overseer for the United Kingdom of Great Britain, and Ireland.

The following testimonies are the ones referred to in the above letter from Overseer Cantel:

ANTHONY C. HERRING-COOPER, 59 Drayton Gardens, South Kensington, S. W. London, England—I thank God with all my heart for the verification of the words in the last chapter of the Gospel according to St. Mark, "They shall lay hands upon the sick, and they shall recover."

I thank God for a perfect deliverance from constipation.

It is three years and one month ago since I gave up doctors and drugs and fully trusted in God.

I was under the care of the doctors for six years and during that time was taking their filthy poison and muck; but I found at the end of the six years that "I was nothing bettered, but rather grew worse."

Then I began to read LEAVES OF HEALING and the testimonies of those who had been healed of the same trouble, by trusting God absolutely.

Through reading these testimonies I was led to trust God, but I was not perfectly healed, although receiving a large measure of deliverance.

About three months ago, I asked Deacon Rush to pray for me, which he did, laying hands upon me, and I thank God that from that time I received a perfect healing.

I speak these words to glorify God.

I also praise God for healing me of chilblains, from which I suffered greatly.

This winter they came again, one on almost every finger.

Within three days after I asked Deacon Rush to pray for me, the deliverance came, and there is not one left. God has kept me.

I thank God that I know Jesus, the Christ, not only as my Savior, but as my Healer and Keeper. I can truly say, "The Lord hath done great things for me, whereof I am glad."

MRS. AGNES LUCAS, 14 Sussex street, Pimlico, S. W., London, England—I am very thankful to be able to testify to God's saving, healing and keeping power, and that He brought me into the Christian Catholic Church in Zion.

On January 16, 1904, I had a very severe hemorrhage of the nose, which lasted an hour. A week later, on the 22d, I had a similar attack, which lasted about five and one-half hours.

I nearly bled to death.

I sent requests for prayer both to Overseer Bryant and Deaconess Hurran; but my friends, who do not believe in Divine Healing, became so alarmed that they sent for a doctor.

Before the Overseer arrived the doctor came, and, after asking one or two questions, offered to give me something to stop the bleeding.

I declined his offer and informed him that I did not send for him, as I was looking to God for my healing.

He again urged me to take some remedy, and this further offer I declined, assuring him that I had not taken any medicine for two and a half years, and did not intend to do so now. I also pointed him to a copy of LEAVES OF HEALING which would explain the scope of my faith.

The indefatigable doctor still refused to accept my faith in God as sufficient, and tried to show me how God uses means in healing His people, instancing how God led Israel through the Red Sea dry shod by causing a wind to arise and divide the waters.

It is almost needless to say that the force of this illustration did not shake the foundations of my faith.

I am glad to say that before the doctor arrived in answer to the summons of my sister and my son, who were fearful lest I should pass away, God graciously answered prayer and the hemorrhage was stayed.

I afterwards ascertained that, as it had been with the nobleman's son for whom Jesus prayed, so too had been the manner of my deliverance, for at the very hour when Overseer Bryant prayed, God heard and answered, and to Him be all the glory.

MISS LIZZIE CHAPMAN, 114 Fortune Green Road, West Hampstead, N. W., London, England.—I thank God for healing me.

I was taken ill in September, 1903, before I was in Zion, and before my faith had risen to take the Christ as my healer

Dr. Harcourt Jervis was called in, who said I was suffering from muscular rheumatism.

He attended me for a fortnight, and then said that I was suffering from typhoid fever, and must go away to the fever hospital, Seagrave road, Fulham.

I went there the next day, and was treated as if I were suffering from typhoid fever.

But I gradually grew weaker, and after I had been there a month, the doctors said that I had not typhoid fever at all, but that they must keep me there until they had found out what I was suffering from.

When I had been in the hospital about six weeks, a lump arose in my side, which the doctors said was an abscess or some growth, and unless I were operated upon at once I should be dead in five hours.

They had to send for my sister's sanction and she would not give it, but instead she went to Deaconess Hurran, who prayed for me.

When the doctors came to examine me the next day they said that the lump had disappeared, and there was no sign whatever of it.

They were amazed at this miraculous evidence of God's power.

After this they continued to keep me in the hospital for some time, claiming that I must gain strength before leaving.

When they finally allowed me to go home, after some weeks, I was taken with typhoid fever and bronchitis, which went on for some time.

Here I must confess, with regret, that notwithstanding the marvelous manifestation of God's healing power when I was yet in the hospital, when I was unexpectedly stricken with the fever, not recovering at once, I turned to the arm of flesh and allowed some medicines to be given me by a doctor, a friend of the family.

Finally, however, throwing off their subtle power, I looked to God, and, in answer to the General Overseer's prayer, I obtained the needed deliverance.

I realize more clearly now that my deliverance might have been obtained more speedily, for this is surely God's will when we are willing to be raised to His gracious standard.

I heartily praise God for great and marvelous victories which He has given me, and I purpose to rest fully upon His keeping power henceforth.

Daily Bible Study for the Home

By Overseer John G. Speicher

SUNDAY, JUNE 26TH.

1 John 2.—Overcoming the world, and anti-Christ chapter.

Memory text—Verse 17. "And the world passeth away, and the lust thereof: but he that doeth the will of God abideth forever."

Contents of chapter—These things written that we sin not; Jesus, the Christ, is the Advocate with the Father; We know Him if we keep His commandments; If in Him, we ought to walk as He walked; Darkness is passing away; True light shining; He that hates his brother is in darkness; Fathers addressed because they knew Jesus; Young men written to because they were strong and overcame the evil one; Lust of the flesh and vainglory of life is not of God; Will pass away with the world; He that does the will of God abides forever; Those who go out are not of the faith; He is a liar who denies that Jesus is the Christ; That is anti-Christ; Whoso denies the Son has not the Father; Abiding in the Son; Not ashamed at His coming.

MONDAY, JUNE 27TH.

1 John 3.—Purifying and confidence chapter.

Memory text—Verse 3. "And every one that hath this hope set on him purifieth himself, even as He is pure."

Contents of chapter—What manner of love in calling us children of God; When the Christ appears we shall be like Him, and see Him as He is; This hope within purifies us; Sin is lawlessness; Righteous do righteousness; He that sins is of the Devil; Not strange that the world hates true Christians; They have passed from death unto life; Whosoever hates his brother is a murderer; Love of God not in him who shuts up his compassion for the needy; Boldness and confidence in God when our heart does not condemn us; We get that for which we ask, if we keep His commandments and please Him; Must believe in Jesus and love one another.

TUESDAY, JUNE 28TH.

1 John 4.—Perfecting of love chapter.

Memory text.—Verse 18. "There is no fear in love; but perfect love casteth out fear."

Contents of chapter—Believe not every spirit; Those which deny that Jesus, the Christ, is come in the flesh are not of God, but are spirits of anti-Christ; If we are God's, His power within us is greater than the powers of the evil world; True love is of God; God's love manifested in the Christ; Love one another; If we abide in God, His love is perfected in us; We know that we love Him, by the Spirit which He has given us; God is love; When we abide in love we abide in Him; No fear in love; Perfect love casts out fear; We love Him because He first loved us; Cannot love God and hate our brother.

WEDNESDAY, JUNE 29TH.

1 John 5.—Witnessing and overcoming chapter.

Memory text—Verse 8. "For there are three who bear witness, the Spirit, and the water, and the blood: and the three agree in one."

Contents of chapter—Whoso loves and believes in Him that is begotten, loves Him that begat; We know that we love the children of God when we love God and keep His commandments; Commandments not grievous; Our faith overcomes the world; He who believes in Jesus, the Christ, overcomes the world; The Spirit, the water, and the blood witnessing, agree in one, He that believes not God has made Him a liar; He that has not the Son has not life; Boldness in asking anything according to His will, knowing that He hears us; There is a sin unto death; All unrighteousness is sin; The begotten of God sins not; He is kept; The world lies in the wicked one.

THURSDAY, JUNE 30TH.

2d and 3d Epistles of John.—Full reward and hospitality chapters.

Memory text—Verse 8 (2 John.) "Look to yourselves . . . that ye receive a full reward." Verse 11 (3 John.) "He that doeth good is of God."

Contents of chapters—John writes to the elect lady and her children; Loved by those who know the truth; Exhorts her to love and to keep the commandments; Many deceivers gone forth into the world; Must watch that she receive the full reward; Not to greet or to receive into her house those who do not bring this teaching of the Christ; John writes to Gaius; Desires that he may prosper and be in health; Rejoices in knowing that he walks in the truth; Commands and exhorts him regarding his ministering to the brethren and strangers; Diotrephes rebellious; Hinders the ministry to John and the other brethren; Demetrius commended; Salutations to the brethren.

Zion's Bible Class

Conducted by Deacon Daniel Sloan in Shiloh Tabernacle, Zion City, Lord's Day Morning at 11 o'clock, and in Zion Homes and Gatherings throughout the World.

MID-WEEK BIBLE CLASS LESSON, JUNE 22d or 23d.

Good Morals.

1. *They make one live as the Christ lived.*—Ephesians 4:17-32.
Lying and anger must come out of the heart.
One must not fool with the Devil in any way.
Nothing filthy should be found about one.
2. *They lead one to avoid evil.*—1 Thessalonians 5:22-24.
One must not search for it.
One must not draw near it.
One must not inquire into it minutely.
3. *They prompt one to be obedient to the truth.*—Romans 2:4-16.
A man must love the truth.
Lying in business is devilish.
Men cannot cover up their rascality.
4. *They never provoke confusion or disorder.*—1 Corinthians 14:33-40.
Contentions do not come from God.
The Devil is the one who creates confusion.
God designs everything in an orderly way.
5. *They make a man honest, to mind his own business, and to work with his might.*—1 Thessalonians 4:6-12.
A man never has an excuse for cheating.
Some are always anxious about others' affairs.
The man who is honest and works will have plenty.
6. *They enable one to challenge any man to investigate one's doings.*—2 Corinthians 7:1-6.
Be able to say, "I have done no one any harm."
Be able to say, "No one is the worse for having met me."
Be able to say that you have never taken a dollar from any one without a just equivalent having been given.
7. *Good morals mean the elimination of sin from the life.*—Romans 6:13-23.
The practice of sin is immorality.
Immorality makes decent people ashamed.
Men should live and act to prolong life.
8. *Good morals keep one out of debt; make one do one's duty, and be an honor to society, not a person of base designs.*—Romans 13:6-14.
Debt leads to lying, deception, and fraud.
Dodging taxes or civil duties is stealing.
Be honest; do right; live happily.
The Lord our God is an Order-establishing God.

LORD'S DAY BIBLE CLASS LESSON, JUNE 26th.

Christian Conduct.

1. *The conduct of ministers.*—1 Timothy 3:1-13.
They must be wide-awake and faultless.
They must not be two-faced nor bent on money-getting.
They must be able to manage themselves and their families before they can manage the things of God.
2. *The conduct of husbands and wives.*—Ephesians 5:22-33.
Wives must do for their husbands what they would do for the Lord.
Husbands must do for their wives what the Lord has done for them.
They are to know each other well and be united in every effort.
3. *The conduct of children.*—Ephsesians 6:1-4.
Children must do things because they are right.
They must always respect their parents.
They cannot live long if they do not live happily.
4. *The conduct of servants and employees.*—Ephesians 6:5-9.
Servants must faithfully obey orders.
They must have a care lest they do not understand.
The work done must be from the heart.
5. *The conduct of mature men and women.*—Titus 2:1-3.
Mature men must give up vanities.
They cannot afford to be impatient.
Women must not fall into the habit of nagging.
6. *The conduct of widows.*—1 Timothy 5:3-13.
They should be on good terms with their relatives.
They should give themselves up to prayer and good works.
They should keep out of their heads a determination to remarry.
7. *The conduct of young men.*—Titus 2:6-8.
They must never try to play the fool.
They should improve every moment in good works.
They should never be mixed up in corrupt practices.
8. *The conduct of young women.*—Titus 2:4, 5.
They must be taught by their elders.
They must keep pure and never be indiscreet.
They must not gad, but find happiness in the home.
God's Holy People are a Christ-imitating People.

DO YOU KNOW GOD'S WAY OF HEALING?

BY THE REV. JOHN ALEX. DOWIE.

Let it be supposed that the following words are a conversation between the reader [A] and the writer [B].

A. What does this question mean? Do you really suppose that God has some one especial way of healing in these days, of which men may know and avail themselves?

B. That is exactly my meaning, and I wish very much that you should know God's Way of Healing, as I have known it for many years.

A. What is the way, in your opinion?

B. You should rather ask, WHO is God's Way? for the way is a Person, not a thing. I will answer your question in His own words, "I am the Way, and the Truth, and the Life: no one cometh unto the Father, but by Me." These words were spoken by our Lord Jesus, the Christ, the Eternal Son of God, who is both our Savior and our Healer. (John 14:6.)

A. But I always thought that these words only referred to Him as the Way of Salvation. How can you be sure that they refer to Him as the Way of Healing also?

B. Because He cannot change. He is "the same yesterday and today, yea, and forever." (Hebrews 13:8.) He said that He came to this earth not only to save us but to heal us. (Luke 4:18), and He did this when in the flesh on earth. Being unchanged He must be able and willing and desirous to heal now.

A. But is there not this difference, namely, that He is not with us now?

B. No; for He said "Lo, I am with you All the Days, even unto the Consummation of the Age;" and so He is with us now, in spirit, just as much as when He was here in the flesh.

A. But did He not work these miracles of healing when on earth merely to prove that He was the Son of God?

B. No; there was still a greater purpose than that. He healed the sick who trusted in Him in order to show us that He came to die not only for our sins, but for our sicknesses, and to deliver us from both.

A. Then, if that be so, the atonement which He made on the Cross must have been for our sicknesses as well as our sins. Can you prove that is the fact from the Scriptures?

B Yes, I can, and the passages are very numerous. I need quote only two. In Isaiah 53:4, 5, it is written of Him: "Surely He hath borne our griefs (Hebrew, *sicknesses*), and carried our sorrows: . . . and with His stripes we are healed." Then, in the Gospel according to Matthew, this passage is quoted and directly applied to the work of bodily healing, in the 8th chapter 17th verse: "That it might be fulfilled which was spoken by Isaiah the prophet, saying, Himself took our infirmities, and bare our diseases."

A. But do you not think that sickness is often God's will, and sent for our good, and therefore God may not wish us to be healed?

B. No, that cannot possibly be; for diseases of every kind are the Devil's work, and his work can never be God's will, since the Christ came for the very purpose of destroying "the works of the Devil." (1 John 3:8.)

A. Do you mean to say that all disease is the work of Satan?

B. Yes, for if there had been no sin (which came through Satan) there never would have been any disease, and Jesus never in one single instance told any person that sickness was God's work or will, but the very contrary.

A. Can you prove from Scriptures that all forms of sickness and infirmity are the Devil's work?

B. Yes, that can be done very easily. You will see in Matthew 4:23 and 9:35 that when Jesus was here in the flesh He healed "all manner of disease and all manner of sickness among the people." Then if you will refer to Acts 10:38 you will see that the Apostle Peter declares that He (Jesus) "went about doing good, and healing all that were oppressed of the Devil." Notice that all whom He healed, not some, were suffering from Satan's evil power.

A. But does disease never come from God?

B. No, it cannot come from God, for He is pure, and disease is unclean; and it cannot come out of Heaven, for there is no disease there.

A. That is very different from the teachings which I have received all my life from ministers and in the churches. Do you really think that you are right, and that they are all wrong in this matter?

B. It is not a question as between myself and them. The only question is, What does God's Word say? God has said in all the ages, to His Church, "I am Jehovah that healeth thee" (Exodus 15:26), and therefore it would be wicked to say that He is the defiler of His people. All true Christians must believe the Bible, and it is impossible to believe that good and evil, sickness and health, sin and holiness could have a common origin in God. If the Bible really taught that, it would be impossible to believe our Lord Jesus, the Christ, when He says: "A good tree cannot bring forth evil fruit, neither can a corrupt tree bring forth good fruit." (Matthew 7.18.)

A. But even if I agree with all you say, is it not true that the Gifts of Healing were removed from the Church, and are not in it now?

B. No, the "Gifts of Healing" were never withdrawn, and can never be withdrawn, from the true Church of God, for it is written: "The gifts and the calling of God are without repentance." (Romans 11.29.) There are nine gifts of God to the Church (enumerated in 1 Corinthians 12:8-11), and all these are in the Holy Spirit. Therefore, so long as the Holy Spirit is in the Church, all the gifts must be there also. If they are not exercised, that does not prove that they do not exist, but that the faith to exercise them is lacking in God's servants. The gifts are all perfectly preserved; for the Holy Spirit, not the Church, keeps them safely.

A. What should a Christian then do when overtaken with sickness?

B. A Christian should obey God's command, and at once turn to Him for forgiveness of the sin which may have caused the sickness, and for immediate healing. Healing is obtained from God in one of four ways, namely: First, by the direct prayer of faith, without any aid from the officers of the Church, praying as the Centurion did in Matthew 8:5-12; second, by two faithful disciples praying in perfect agreement, in accordance with the Lord's promise in Matthew 18:19; third, by the anointing of the Elders and the prayer of faith, according to the instructions in James 5:14 and 15; and fourth, by the laying on of the hands of them who believe, and whom God calls to that ministry, as the Lord commands in Mark 16:18, and in other places.

A. But are people healed in this way in these days?

B. Yes, in thousands of cases. I have myself laid hands upon many hundreds of thousands of persons, and I have seen the Lord's power manifested in the healing of great numbers, many of whom are living witnesses in many countries, who have testified publicly before thousands, and who are prepared to testify at any time. This ministry is being exercised by devoted Christians in many parts of America, Europe, Australasia, and elsewhere.

A. Is it not the same as Christian Science, Mind Healing, etc.?

B. No. Divine Healing is diametrically opposed to these diabolical counterfeits, which are utterly antichristian. These impostures are only seductive forms of Spiritualism. Trance Evangelism is also a more recent form of this delusion, and it deceives many.

A. But how shall I obtain the necessary faith to receive healing, which faith I am at present conscious that I do not possess?

B. It is written: "Belief cometh of hearing, and hearing by the word of the Christ." (Romans 10:17.) Our Missions are held for the express purpose of teaching fully the Word of God on this matter, and I very heartily invite you to attend the meetings which are announced for Zion Tabernacles in Chicago and other cities, and for Shiloh Tabernacle, Zion City, Illinois. All are welcome and there are no charges of any kind made, for all God's gifts are free gifts. Salvation is the first of these, without which you cannot be healed through faith in Jesus All the costs of this work are covered by the free-will offerings of the people who attend these meetings, and others whom the Lord leads to help, but the poorest, who have nothing to give, are as heartily welcome as the richest

A. Do you see the sick and lay hands upon them in this Mission?

B. Yes; after we feel satisfied that they are fully resting in the Lord alone for the healing, we see privately, so far as time permits, those who attend; but under no circumstances do we claim the power to heal any; for "power belongeth unto God."

A. Have you any writings upon this subject which can be purchased?

B. Yes, these can be obtained at the office of Zion Printing and Publishing House, Zion City, Illinois, and at any Zion Tabernacle. But the best book on Divine Healing is the Bible itself, studied prayerfully and earnestly.

We extend to you a hearty invitation to attend the meetings, which are free to all. Our prayer is that you may be led to find in Jesus, the Christ, our Lord and God your present Savior from sin, your Healer from sickness, your Cleanser from all evil, your Keeper in the way to Heaven, your Friend, and your All for Time and Eternity. We pray that these words may help many who read, and that our little conversation may bear fruit in leading many readers to look to Jesus only.

"The Healing of Christ's seamless dress
Is by all beds of pain:
We touch Him in life's throng and press
And we are whole again."

OBEYING GOD IN BAPTISM.

"Baptizing Them Into the Name of the Father and of the Son and of the Holy Ghost."

Eighteen Thousand Four Hundred Eighty-eight Baptisms by Triune Immersion Since March 14, 1897.

Eighteen Thousand Four Hundred Eighty-eight Believers have joyfully followed their Lord in the Ordinance of Believer's Baptism by Triune Immersion since the first Baptism in Central Zion Tabernacle on March 14, 1897.

Baptized in Central Zion Tabernacle from March 14, 1897, to December 14, 1901, by the General Overseer,	4754			
Baptized in South Side Zion Tabernacle from January 1, 1902, to June 14, 1903, by the General Overseer..	37			
Baptized at Zion City by the General Overseer........	583			
Baptized by Overseers, Elders, Evangelists and Deacons, at Headquarters (Zion City) and Chicago......	4940			
Total Baptized at Headquarters..................	—			10,314
Baptized in places outside of Headquarters by the General Overseer..................................		641		
Baptized in places outside of Headquarters by Overseers, Elders, Evangelists and Deacons............		7109		
Total Baptized outside of Headquarters............		—		7,750
Total Baptized in seven years......................				18,064
Baptized since March 14, 1904:				
Baptized in Zion City by Elder Royall........... ...	63			
Baptized in Zion City by Elder Hammond...........	115			
Baptized in Zion City by Elder Adams	40			
Baptized in Zion City by Evangelist Reder...........	24			
Baptized in Chicago by Elder Hall.....................	9			
Baptized in Chicago by Elder Cossum.................	20			
Baptized in Chicago by Evangelist Christie	3			
Baptized in Chicago by Deacon Matson...............	4			
Baptized in Chicago by Elder Kosch.................	6		284	
Baptized in California by Elder Taylor...............		5		
Baptized in Canada by Elder Simmons...............		6		
Baptized in Canada by Elder Brooks.................		7		
Baptized in Colorado by Deacon Cook...............		3		
Baptized in England by Overseer Cantel.............		10		
Baptized in Illinois by Deacon Sprecher...............		1		
Baptized in Indiana by Elder Osborn.................		2		
Baptized in Minnesota by Elder Graves...		5		
Baptized in New York by Elder Warszawiak..........		14		
Baptized in New York by Overseer Mason		19		
Baptized in Ohio by Deacon Arrington...............		14		
Baptized in Ohio by Deacon Kelchner...............		2		
Baptized in Pennsylvania by Elder Bouck............		13		
Baptized in South Africa by Overseer Bryant.........		13		
Baptized in Texas by Evangelist Gay...............		17		
Baptized in Washington by Elder Simmons...........		1		
Baptized in Washington by Elder Ernst.............		8	140	424
Total Baptized since March 14, 1897...............				18,488

The following-named four believers were baptized at San Antonio, Texas, Lord's Day, May 22, 1904, by Evangelist William D. Gay:

Abbott, Miss Mattie Dulcie......316 North Pine street, San Antonio, Texas
Dickens, Mrs. Bertha...............820 Dawson street, San Antonio, Texas
Heninger, Charles T.................212 State street, San Antonio, Texas
Heninger, Mrs. Elizabeth............212 State street, San Antonio, Texas

The following-named three believers were baptized at Toronto, Ontario, Canada, Lord's Day, May 22, 1904, by Elder Eugene Brooks:

Malloch, Joseph..............................Davenport, Ontario, Canada
Richards, Mrs. Emma ....Housey Rapids, Ontario, Canada
Willis, Mrs. Mary Lamperrey..........75 Niagara street, Toronto, Canada

The following-named believer was baptized in the South Side Zion Tabernacle, Chicago, Illinois, Lord's Day, May 22, 1904, by Elder W. H. Cossum:

Blossom, Frank L..............1701 Boston street, Michigan City, Indiana

The following-named twenty-four believers were baptized in Shiloh Tabernacle, Zion City, Illinois, Lord's Day, May 29, 1904, by Elder Gideon Hammond:

Armstrong, James..................3217 Eshcol avenue, Zion City, Illinois
Beem, Miss Twila..................2713 Elim avenue, Zion City, Illinois
Call, Charles Melvon.......................Elijah Hospice, Zion City, Illinois
Collett, Mrs. Paulina.............2810 Bethel boulevard, Zion City, Illinois
Gardiner, Miss Josephine Augusta ....Geneseo, Illinois
George, Mrs. Hattie ....2802 Elisha avenue, Zion City, Illinois
Goldschwitz, Miss Ledea............1911 Horeb avenue, Zion City, Illinois
Griffith, Miss Grace...................2803 Ezra avenue, Zion City, Illinois
Gurtler, Fred H....................1708 Hebron avenue, Zion City, Illinois
Kleinert, Miss Lydia..................3201 Ezra avenue, Zion City, Illinois
Lawrence, Miss Clara ....2809 Gideon avenue, Zion City, Illinois
Leetsch, W. C. Julius ....2612 Elim avenue, Zion City, Illinois
Leetsch, Mrs. W. C. Julius...........2612 Elim avenue, Zion City, Illinois
Mears, Miss Mary Margaret......2611 Elizabeth avenue, Zion City, Illinois
Melvin, Mrs. Eva Josephine..12006 Stewart avenue, West Pullman, Illinois
Mericle, Ross.......................2403 Gideon avenue, Zion City, Illinois
Meyer, Miss Rosa .... 3013 Gilead avenue, Zion City, Illinois
Newcomer, Mrs. Mayme............5802 Elisha avenue, Zion City, Illinois
Newcomer, Pearl B..................2802 Elisha avenue, Zion City, Illinois
Russell, Miss Gladys...............3210 Gabriel avenue, Zion City, Illinois
Urban, Frank W.....................2207 Enoch avenue, Zion City, Illinois
Welton, Harold D...................2205 Enoch avenue, Zion City, Illinois
Williams, Mrs. Mary Anna, 242 Eighth ave. South, Minneapolis, Minnesota
Zedicker, Miss Myrtle.............1905 Hebron avenue, Zion City, Illinois

CONSECRATION OF CHILDREN.

The following-named six children were consecrated at Eau Claire, Wisconsin, Lord's Day, April 24, 1904, by Rev. A. W. McClurkin:

Felton, Adelbert A..................................Eau Claire, Wisconsin
Felton, Sarah Almerta..............................Eau Claire, Wisconsin
Kingsland, Lysle Roland...........................Eau Claire, Wisconsin
Shaw, George William.........................Chippewa Falls, Wisconsin
Shaw, Miriam Augusta.........................Chippewa Falls, Wisconsin
Shaw, Wilbur Walter...........................Chippewa Falls, Wisconsin

The following-named child was consecrated at San Francisco, California, Lord's Day, May 1, 1904, by Elder W. D. Taylor:

Raymond, Lillian Maud ......1845 Market street, San Francisco, California

The following-named five children were consecrated to God at Chicago, Illinois, Lord's Day, May 8, 1904, by Elder C. R. Hoffman:

Schmidt, Annie ....2313 Avondale avenue, Jefferson Park, Illinois
Schmidt, Freddy............2313 Avondale avenue, Jefferson Park, Illinois
Schmidt, Herman...........2313 Avondale avenue, Jefferson Park, Illinois
Schmidt, Hulda.............2313 Avondale avenue, Jefferson Park, Illinois
Schmidt, Rosa..............2313 Avondale avenue, Jefferson Park, Illinois

The following-named two children were consecrated at the West Side Zion Tabernacle, Chicago, Illinois, Lord's Day, May 8, 1904, by Elder L. C. Hall:

Schulz, Nathalia............1506 North Ridgeway avenue, Chicago, Illinois
Schulz, George.............1506 North Ridgeway avenue, Chicago, Illinois

The following-named three children were consecrated to God, Wednesday, May 11, 1904, by Elder Charles A. Hoy:

Haven, Elizabeth Eunice............................ ......Hubbard, Iowa
Haven, Louis Damen.......................................Hubbard, Iowa
Heck, Nathan Daniel.. ....Boone, Iowa

The following-named eighteen children were consecrated to God in Shiloh Tabernacle, Zion City, Illinois, Lord's Day, May 15, 1904, by Overseer John G. Speicher:

Bintz, Grace........................2607 Gideon avenue, Zion City, Illinois
Cross, Eunice Belle...................2801 Ezra avenue, Zion City, Illinois
Hartong, John Gladstone............1909 Horeb avenue, Zion City, Illinois
Hartong, Julia Magdalene...........1909 Horeb avenue, Zion City, Illinois
Hartong, Odessa May...............1909 Horeb avenue, Zion City, Illinois
Hartong, Levi Adam.................1909 Horeb avenue, Zion City, Illinois
Hartong, Myrtle Elizabeth...........1909 Horeb avenue, Zion City, Illinois
Horney, Eunice.................3015 Elizabeth avenue, Zion City, Illinois
Griesheimer, Ruth ....2914 Elisha avenue, Zion City, Illinois
Johnson, Carl Alexander...........2806 Emmaus avenue, Zion City, Illinois
Klammer, Clarence Boortz..........3105 Eshcol avenue, Zion City, Illinois
McCormick, Alexander.............3103 Gideon avenue, Zion City, Illinois
Pyle, Edith Sharpless...............2901 Enoch avenue, Zion City, Illinois
Richardson, Ethel....................2811 Enoch avenue, Zion City, Illinois
Schneider, Ethel Matilda...........2712 Ezekiel avenue, Zion City, Illinois
Schneider, Bessie May.............2712 Ezekiel avenue, Zion City, Illinois
Schneider, Carrie Elizabeth.........2712 Ezekiel avenue, Zion City, Illinois
Spellman, Agnes Marie............2901 Ezekiel avenue, Zion City, Illinois

The following-named three children were consecrated to God, at Zion City, Illinois, Saturday, May 21, 1904, by Elder F. M. Royall:

Harvey, Percy Gladstone............2801 Elijah avenue, Zion City, Illinois
Harvey, Russel Earle................2801 Elijah avenue, Zion City, Illinois
Harvey, Shepherd Franklin ....2801 Elijah avenue, Zion City, Illinois

The following-named six children were consecrated to God at Chicago, Illinois, Lord's Day, May 22, 1904, by Elder C. R. Hoffman:

Scheel, Adela Emma Emila,
1833 Lorenz avenue, Jefferson Park, Chicago, Illinois
Scheel, Arnold Wilhelm Richard,
1833 Lorenz avenue, Jefferson Park, Chicago, Illinois
Scheel, Friederich Johann Carl,
1833 Lorenz avenue, Jefferson Park, Chicago, Illinois
Scheel, Maria Emma Elfrida,
1833 Lorenz avenue, Jefferson Park, Chicago, Illinois
Scheel, Otto Emil Erwig Friedrich,
1833 Lorenz avenue, Jefferson Park, Chicago, Illinois
Rosenthal, Fred Herman......1035 North Oakley avenue, Chicago, Illinois

The following name was omitted from the list of names of persons baptized in Shiloh Tabernacle, Zion City, Illinois, Lord's Day, May 15, 1904, by Elder Gideon Hammond:

Ingersoll, Euphrosyne..............2409 Gilboa avenue, Zion City, Illinois

AWAKE! AWAKE!

Isaiah 52

AWAKE, AWAKE, PUT ON THY STRENGTH, O ZION; PUT ON THY BEAUTIFUL GARMENTS, O JERUSALEM, *the* HOLY CITY: for henceforth there shall no more come into thee the uncircumcised and the unclean.

¶ 2. Shake thyself from the dust; arise, sit thee down, O Jerusalem; loose thyself from the bands of thy neck, O captive daughter of Zion.

. . . .

¶ 7. How beautiful upon the mountains are the feet of him that bringeth Good Tidings, that publisheth Peace, that bringeth Good Tidings of Good, that publisheth Salvation; that saith unto Zion, Thy God reigneth!

¶ 8. The voice of thy watchmen! they lift up the voice, together do they sing; for they shall see, eye to eye, when Jehovah returneth to Zion.

¶ 9. Break forth into joy, sing together, ye waste places of Jerusalem: for Jehovah hath comforted His people, He hath redeemed Jerusalem.

¶ 10. Jehovah hath made bare His holy arm in the eyes of all the nations; and all the ends of the earth shall see the salvation of our God.

WHAT CAN BE A MORE DIRECT FULFILMENT OF THIS SCRIPTURE THAN THE WORK *of* ZION AND THE REV. JOHN ALEXANDER DOWIE, WHO HAS BROUGHT GOOD TIDINGS, PUBLISHED PEACE AND SALVATION *and* DECLARES THE REIGN *of* GOD?

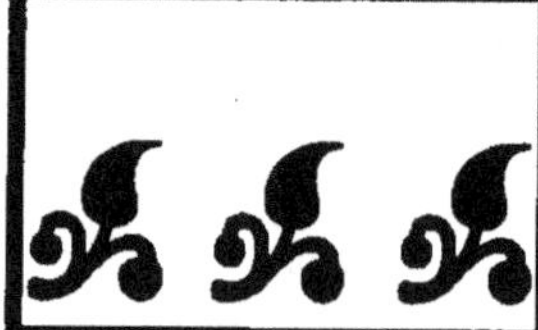

¶¶ LEAVES OF HEALING IS A MOST POWERFUL INSTRUMENT IN DOING THIS AND EXTENDING THE KINGDOM OF GOD.

¶¶ While hundreds and hundreds are being added to the host of God's workers every week, thousands and thousands are joining the ranks of Satan and going to destruction. LEAVES OF HEALING may be their only help for salvation.

¶¶ Is there not one or more whom you can reach through LEAVES OF HEALING? You are your brother's keeper. Give him an opportunity to know the Truth. Remember our inducement, "They that turn many to righteousness shall shine as the stars forever and ever."

¶¶ We cannot offer you cheap rates and premiums, as LEAVES OF HEALING is not a paying proposition. Our lowest rates are as follows:

One Year, ...	$ 2.00
Six Months, ...	1.25
Three Months, ...	.75

¶¶ Kindly let us have your co-operation for extending LEAVES OF HEALING. Address,

ZION PRINTING AND PUBLISHING HOUSE

ZION CITY, ILLINOIS

A WEEKLY PAPER FOR THE EXTENSION OF THE KINGDOM OF GOD
EDITED BY THE REV. JOHN ALEX. DOWIE.

Volume XV. No. 8. *ZION CITY, SATURDAY, JUNE 11, 1904.* *Price Five Cents*

Overseer Jane Dowie

Overseer in Christian Catholic Church in Zion for Women's Work Throughout the World

THE picture of Overseer Jane Dowie, presented to our readers on this page, was taken in Adelaide, South Australia, during the recent Visitation of the General Overseer and his party.

Adelaide is the birthplace of Mrs. Dowie. Her aged parents, Mr. and Mrs. Alexander Dowie, still reside there upon their beautiful estate.

It was near here, at Calton Hill, at the summer home of Overseer Dowie's parents, where she, with the General Overseer, spent a few weeks of rest and quiet.

We published, in the issue of two weeks ago, two views of the beautiful summer home referred to, as well as other views of beautiful Adelaide in that and other previous issues.

There is no more delightful land than South Australia in its wealth of natural products and beautiful scenery. Overseer Jane Dowie gave up much when she gladly and willingly accompanied the General Overseer to America on his evangelizing and Divine Healing Mission. She has been a close and constant companion of his in all his travels and in all his labors.

There are large numbers of people who testify to having been healed in answer to her prayers. There is no doubt that she is the foremost woman preacher in the world today. Her large and growing influence in connection with the oversight of the women's work in Zion throughout the World is attracting a great deal of attention.

To her excellent management was due largely the wonderful success of the Divine Healing Homes in Chicago.

Thousands of women await with loving hearts her return from Europe.

May God grant that the years before her shall be her best years and that the work, great as it is, may be but the beginning of a grand and universal work for the uplifting of womankind.

A WEEKLY PAPER FOR THE EXTENSION OF THE KINGDOM OF GOD.
EDITED BY THE REV. JOHN ALEX. DOWIE.

Application for entry as Second Class Matter at Zion City, Illinois, pending.

Subscription Rates.		Special Rates.	
One Year	$2.00	100 Copies of One Issue	$3.00
Six Months	1.25	25 Copies of One Issue	1.00
Three Months	.75	To Ministers, Y. M. C. A's and Public Reading Rooms, per annum	1.50
Single Copies	.05		

For foreign subscriptions add $1.50 per year, or three cents per copy for postage.

Subscribers desiring a change of address should give present address, as well as that to which they desire LEAVES OF HEALING sent in the future.

Make Bank Drafts, Express Money or Postoffice Money Orders payable to the order of JOHN ALEX. DOWIE, Zion City, Illinois, U. S. A.

Long Distance Telephone. *Cable Address "Dowie, Zion City."*

All communications upon business must be addressed to
MANAGER ZION PUBLISHING HOUSE,
Zion City, Illinois, U. S. A.

Subscriptions to LEAVES OF HEALING, A VOICE FROM ZION, and the various publications may also be sent to

ZION PUBLISHING HOUSE, 81 EUSTON ROAD, LONDON, N. W., ENGLAND.
ZION PUBLISHING HOUSE, NO. 43 PARK ROAD, ST. KILDA, MELBOURNE, VICTORIA, AUSTRALIA.
ZION PUBLISHING HOUSE, RUE DE MONT, THABOR 1, PARIS, FRANCE.
ZIONSHEIM, SCHLOSS LIEBBURG, CANTON THURGAU, BEI ZÜRICH, SWITZERLAND.

ZION CITY, ILLINOIS, SATURDAY, JUNE 11, 1904.

TABLE OF CONTENTS.

LEAVES OF HEALING, SATURDAY, JUNE 11, 1904.

LEAVES OF HEALING.

Two Dollars will bring to you the weekly visits of the Little White Dove for a year; 75 cents will send it to a friend for thirteen weeks; $1.25 will send it for six months; $1.50 will send it to your minister, or to a Y. M. C. A., or to a Public Reading Room for a whole year. We offer no premiums, except the premium of doing good. We receive no advertisements, and print no commercial lies or cheating enticements of unscrupulous thieves. LEAVES OF HEALING is Zion on wings, and we keep out everything that would detract the reader's mind from all except the Extension of the Kingdom of God, for which alone it exists. If we cannot send forth our Little White Dove without soiling its wings with the smoke of the factory and the dirt of the wrangling market-place, or compelling it to utter the screaming cries of the business vultures in the ears of our readers, then we will keep our Dove at home.

Notes From The Overseer-in-Charge.

"FOR MY THOUGHTS ARE NOT YOUR THOUGHTS, NEITHER ARE YOUR WAYS MY WAYS, SAITH JEHOVAH."

FOR AS the heavens are higher than the earth,
So are My ways higher than your ways,
And My thoughts than your thoughts.

FOR AS the rain cometh down and the snow from heaven,
And returneth not thither, but watereth the earth,
And maketh it bring forth and bud,
And giveth seed to the sower and bread to the eater;
So shall My word be that goeth forth out of My mouth:
It shall not return unto Me void,
But it shall accomplish that which I please,
And it shall prosper in the thing whereto I sent it.

FOR YE shall go out with joy,
And be led forth with peace:
The mountains and the hills shall break forth before you into singing,
And all the trees of the field shall clap their hands.

ZION HAS BEEN "led forth with peace," and she has gone "out with joy" continuously.

OUR CONFIDENCE has been in God, for He hath founded Zion.

He has never yet forsaken us, but has enabled us to triumph over every difficulty.

IT WAS extensively prophesied that Zion would not be able to meet the first payment due to her creditors; but when the time came we were more than ready and a prompt and full payment was made.

Again the time has come for the payment of a twenty-five per cent. instalment.

Nothing has been heard from the enemies of Zion. They seem to have taken it for granted that she would continue to meet her obligations, and they are not disappointed.

Today we send out the full twenty-five per cent.

It has all been done in a very quiet way, and without any difficulty on the part of Zion.

THERE IS no doubt in the mind of any one now that Zion will continue to do this and meet promptly all her obligations.

FOR MORE than half a year we have paid cash for all our purchases, so that at this time we are able to say that we are absolutely free from current accounts, with the exception of the balance due from last year, which is being met according to agreement.

THE WONDERFUL strength and prosperity of Zion is shown in these facts, and the world is being convinced that no power of earth or hell can destroy in any way or turn back the tremendously strong and powerful institutions of Zion.

If they had not been founded by God Himself and for God Himself, for the good of humanity, we might have doubt as to their stability.

But the world needs Zion, and will have to reckon with her more and more largely; and the world will have to come to the point of acceptance soon or late.

THE DESPICABLE and anarchistical action of some of the citizens of Tiffin, Ohio, are in keeping with the mob rule of Freemasons everywhere.

A dispatch from that city, to the Cleveland, Ohio, *Leader*, tells the following story:

DOWIEITE ESCORTED TO THE DEPOT BY ANGRY CITIZENS.

HE TRIED TO CURE A MERCHANT BY PRAYER WHEN HE WAS MARCHED OUT OF TOWN.

TIFFIN, OHIO, June 2.—The little village of Greenspring, this county, is all stirred up over the death of Squire Walter J. Merchant, a prominent citizen of that place, which occurred a few days ago. When Merchant was sick unto death, a Dowie elder was called, who attempted to cure him by prayer. The members of the different lodges to which Merchant belonged grew indignant over the treatment accorded him, and one evening in a body called at the Merchant home and escorted the elder to the depot and ordered him out of town. Merchant was taken to the home of friends, where he was properly attended to. A few days ago his death occurred.

THE FACTS in the case are entirely different.

When Mrs. Merchant saw that the doctors had given up hope of the recovery of her husband, she telegraphed Zion to send an Elder to pray for her husband; and an Officer of the Church was sent from Cleveland, Deacon C. F. Kelchner, who went in accordance with his duties as an Officer of this Church, and his privileges as a citizen of this country, and visited the home of the sick and dying man at the request of his wife.

But, hearing that a Zion officer was in the city, the Freemason mob, with no regard for law and decency, under threats of violence, compelled the Deacon to leave the city.

What were they angry about?

Were they afraid Mr. Merchant would get well?

What "treatment" did he offer?

He simply spoke words of consolation to the poor, heart-broken wife, and prayed that God might have mercy upon the dying man.

This is all the treatment that Zion offers any one.

No doubt the Freemason doctors saw that their craft was in danger and incited the mob to anarchy.

NOW THE sequel of the affair is dispatched to the Cincinnati, Ohio, *Enquirer*, of June 3d, as follows:

HELD TO DOWIE'S CREED.

TIFFIN, OHIO, June 2.—Clarissa Merchant, wife of Mayor Merchant, of Greenspring, was adjudged insane today and committed to the asylum. When Merchant became ill she refused to have a physician and called a Dowie Elder. Merchant died and his widow fled to friends of the Dowie faith until after the funeral.

IT IS a shameful lie that Mr. Merchant had no physician, for it was only after the physicians had given him up that Zion was called in, and even then we were not permitted to do anything.

Of course the man died.

And now, because the widow fled to the friends of Zion, she has been accounted insane by this sane (?) Masonic horde.

This man was not a member of the Christian Catholic Church in Zion. His wife merely demanded her right to trust in God for healing, and because of this demand she is to be incarcerated.

Would not such treatment be enough to drive a poor, weak, bereaved woman into insanity?

MORE AND more are the powers of hell driving those who would be true Christians into Zion City; for there is no safety outside.

No longer is there any liberty of thought or religion, but only persecution and destruction for those who oppose the powers that be.

ANOTHER SHAMEFUL lie is told by the *Daily Observer*, of Charlotte, North Carolina, in a telegram from Springfield, Ohio.

There is absolutely not one word of truth in the whole article.

HOPED DEAD WOULD BE RAISED.

DOWIE CONVERTS, DISAPPOINTED, WALKING HOME FROM CHICAGO TO WHEELING.

SPRINGFIELD, OHIO, May 31.

Weary and despondent, J. L. Hampton and his wife are walking from Chicago, where they were attracted by the promises of Dowieism, to their old home at Wheeling, West Virginia.

Their faith in the new creed was so firm that for two days they carried the bodies of their two dead children, believing that the apostles of the new faith could restore them to life. The children, aged three and five respectively, died of pneumonia, fifty miles from Crawfordsville, Indiana.

Walking, they carried the bodies to Crawfordsville, where kind strangers persuaded them to bury the children.

Hampton says that some months ago Dowie's missionaries were at Wheeling and picked up five couples, whom they engaged as a choir for the Dowie meetings throughout the country. He says he and his wife were engaged to cook for the party, and they traveled about the country until they reached Montana, where the party stranded. They finally reached Chicago, whence they started to walk to Wheeling on April 27th.

According to Hampton's story, the five men and five women who left Wheeling as a Dowie choir are also walking home.

DOES ANY one think for a moment that any sane community would allow people to carry for days through their streets the dead bodies of their children? It is simply unthinkable.

There never has been a man by the name of J. H. Hampton a member of this Church. It is a hoax all the way through.

Zion is not in the business of going about the country picking up members for the choir; neither have we a traveling choir going about the country.

IT IS probable that as our beloved General Overseer returns to America a flood of lies will again sweep over the country; and this may only be a sort of skirmish to show what is coming.

WE DO not mind such little squibs as this one from the Patterson, New Jersey, *Press*, which is more than half friendly:

JOHN A. D.-OWIE.

I know but little of ELIJAH'S claim,
For I am rusty on the-ol-o-gy;
But this I know, that formerly His name
Was written JOHN, way back in SIX B. C.
And so if now once more HE'S with us here,
This TISHBITE PROPHET of An-ti-qui-ty;
What likelier, than that again the SEER,
Assume the name of JOHN, and add A. D.

C. V.

THOSE WHO are not embittered against Zion because of her antagonization of their base appetites are inclined to be more and more friendly, and have many good things to say.

Even the Chicago *Inter Ocean* comments in a favorable way upon the relations existing between the Chicago & Milwaukee Electric Railroad and Zion as follows:

DOWIEITES TRAIN CONDUCTORS.

YOUNG MEN OF ZION CITY IN DEMAND ON ELECTRIC LINE.

"Peace to thee! I'll take your fare," may be the common salutation with which conductors of the Chicago & Milwaukee Electric railroad will collect fares soon, for Dowieites are to be extensively employed on the road henceforth.

Ever since President A. C. Frost negotiated a route for his road's extension through Zion City and let the work of construction to Zion men his relations with Dowie's followers have been getting closer.

A couple of Zion young men were recently hired as trainmen, and the result was so satisfactory that more are being sought. Zion young men do not drink, smoke, chew, or swear.

THE SECRET of the desirability of Zion men for train conductors and motormen, and for that matter all other positions of trust, lies in the fact that Zion men neither smoke nor chew nor drink nor swear; neither do they spend late hours at the lewd theater, or other places of immorality. They attend strictly to their own business, and make a business of attending to it. They are regular at their work, and rarely lose time because of sickness.

THE WORDS that we spoke recently concerning the St. Louis Exposition are bearing good fruit.

There is no longer any doubt as to the condition of affairs there.

How disgraceful to the fair name of the city, the state and the Nation, that in them five thousand people should be permitted to assemble on the Lord's Day to see a largely-advertised "Bull Fight," and then because it was not allowed to proceed, that these people should tear down the building and burn up the property!

UNDOUBTEDLY THE end of this Exposition will be the same as that of the World's Fair in Chicago—fire and death, destruction and degradation.

A MEMBER OF Zion Restoration Host recently sent to St. Louis writes as follows:

ST. LOUIS, MISSOURI, June 6, 1904.

BELOVED OVERSEER SPEICHER.

Peace to thee.

St. Louis is hell!

It seems that the dirtiest muck and filth that the Devil can scrape together out of all the nations under heaven is being dumped down here in St. Louis.

THE LATEST word from the General Overseer was received late Lord's Day afternoon, when the following cablegram reached us:

NEUCHATEL.

SPEICHER.

Jesus is conqueror.

Hallelujah!

Successful Visitation at Bern, Geneva, Lausanne and Neuchatel.

Zion Standard firmly planted in French Switzerland.

Much blessing along all lines.

President Comtese received me Tuesday at Federal Palace, in Bern.

He was much interested; conversed one hour; spent several pleasant hours with United States Minister Hill at Ny on Saturday morning.

Pray for special business conference of Zion friends at Zurich in the afternoon. Pray for Liebburg tomorrow night. Berlin, Wednesday and Thursday. Rotterdam, Friday. London, next Lord's Day.

Love.

Mizpah.

DOWIE.

WE PRAISE God and offer Him our heartfelt thanksgiving for His wondrous love and for the many blessed deliverances which He has given to Zion.

LET THE people rejoice everywhere in the God of Israel.

WE PRAY for Zion everywhere throughout the world, that she may be strong and ready for the Coming Battle.

BRETHREN, PRAY FOR US.

JOHN G. SPEICHER.

ELIJAH THE RESTORER

ELIJAH THE RESTORER REBUKES THE LIE THAT MAKES GOD THE AUTHOR OF DISEASE.

Around-the-World Visitation

of the

Rev. John Alex. Dowie

Elijah the Restorer
General Overseer of the Christian Catholic Church in Zion.

By ARTHUR W. NEWCOMB, Special Correspondent.

THE last paper of this series closed with an account of the meeting held in Adelaide Town Hall on Monday evening, March 21, 1904, the occurrences following on that night, and the comments of the press thereon.

On the following morning, Tuesday, March 22d, at half past ten o'clock, in the Town Hall, the General Overseer conducted the second Divine Healing Meeting of the Visitation.

These Divine Healing Meetings, like all those of the Visitation in Australia, were attended by an ever-increasing number of most deeply-interested people.

God's Prophet of the Time of the Restoration of All Things is, first of all, a great teacher; and it is in his capacity as a teacher that he is a means of spiritual, psychical and physical blessing to many thousands throughout the earth

At the Divine Healing Meetings he is at his best as a teacher.

Here also he is seen especially in his prophetic office as Messenger of the Covenant—God's Covenant of Salvation, Healing and Holy Living.

In these meetings the General Overseer also spoke to many who were suffering from various diseases, and in the quiet, earnest prayer services which were held at the close, the Spirit of God was present in power to heal, and many of God's children were able to date their deliverance from the oppression of the Devil, from the Adelaide Visitation.

Following is the report of the General Overseer's Message:

Town Hall, Adelaide, South Australia, Tuesday Morning, March 22, 1904.

The Service was opened by the Congregation's singing Hymn No. 11, in the Visitation Program, "Hail to the Brightness of Zion's Glad Morning."

The General Overseer then read the 53d chapter of the book of the Prophet Isaiah, after which Overseer Jane Dowie read the 8th chapter of Matthew.

The General Overseer said:

Prayer for the Disorderly People.

Let us pray about all this lawlessness and disorder in this city, and ask God for guidance and blessing in the meeting.

Rev. C. Friend Hawkins, the Pastor-in-charge of the Branch of the Christian Catholic Church in Zion in your own city, will pray.

He has been doing good work.

In his prayer, I desire him to pray as my officers and I prayed last night and again today, that the great God who sometimes permits the storms to sweep over the ocean, will now, in His infinite love and mercy, calm the tumults of the people.

In the meeting last night the disorder was distinctly and clearly defined as being the work, not of hoodlums from the lowest classes, but of persons who were well-dressed and probably in many cases well-educated.

Yet they behaved with an utter disregard of all propriety and of all decency, and put to shame the city and the state.

We will pray for them.

I Will Not Close This Hall.

I will hold every meeting that I have announced, but I will have no more night meetings.

We cannot again permit to be inflicted upon the city the disorder of last night.

Taking advantage of the darkness, these people who belong to lodges that do their work in the dark—that blind the eyes of those who take their oaths in the dark—sought our lives and destroyed property.

I will continue to fulfil the command in God's Word, "Have no fellowship with the unfruitful Works of Darkness, but rather even reprove them."

I will reprove, no matter what any one says.

It is my duty, and I will do it, temperately, but firmly and kindly

This Mission shall be carried on in the light

I pray God to bless the people.

Pray for us.

I do not need to tell you that it is quite a strain upon body, soul and spirit to have experiences such as those through which we have passed; but we are well, happy in God, and absolutely unhurt

One of the saddest things, last night, was that not far from here a woman came out of a public house, deliberately lifted a large stone, and flung it with great force at my face.

The carriage was moving rapidly, and the stone struck its side very violently, but we were not hurt.

If the stone had gone where she intended, I should have been struck in the face or on the head.

I Have Never Been Hurt.

I have gone through a great many things, and I am quite willing whenever God demands it to lay down my life for Him; but meanwhile I will keep life in my body as long as I can, and do all I can of good.

Even our bitterest enemies make no pretense that we said or did anything that could have provoked the riots of last night

I was patient with the young men, and stood here trying to make myself heard for an entire hour.

One man came right up to me here—I am told he is a Freemason—and shook a heavy stick in my face, calling me an impostor.

I said, "No, I do not need to be an impostor, and I am not."

That is such a foolish word!

No Need of Being an Impostor.

One of my sharpest critics in America, in an article in the *Century Magazine*, says that I am a man of such ability that if I had chosen to be a military man I should have been a great general; that if I had chosen to be a financier I should have been among the greatest; and that, if I had chosen to be a politician, I should have been at the head.

That is what Sir Henry Parks thought when he offered me the portfolio of Minister of Education of New South Wales.

He said, "If you choose to enter into my ministry, and go on in politics, when the Commonwealth is formed, you can be the Commonwealth Premier."

I said, "I should rather be a minister of Jesus, the Christ, than the Premier of Australia."

Why should I be an impostor if I have the ability to be all these things without being an impostor?

Why should I take all the trouble to be an impostor?

It is too silly!

Where is the imposture?

I have never seen it. My people have not seen it.

You never read a word of complaint from them in the papers.

You never have a line from Zion City saying that I have injured any one, or have been an impostor regarding any one or anything.

Who writes these things?

People who do not put their names to them.

They are so insignificant that you would not know them if they did sign their names.

Why are people so foolish as to believe a thing merely because it is written?

It all depends upon who writes it.

I do not blame the press of this city, except for what I have already blamed them, that in the past they have copied into their columns attacks upon us in which there was not a word of truth.

Some Lies Nailed Down.

There never has been any want, at any time, in Zion City.

No person has ever suffered from hunger in that City.

There never has been a person in that City cold for want of fuel, or for want of clothing.

Mrs Dowie is at the head of an organization of the Church that cares for the poor wherever there is a Branch of Zion, and not only for the poor among our people, although we care for them first. In Chicago she and her Dorcas and Maternity Deaconesses, last year, cared for and clothed the poor of thousands of families.

If we care for the poor of Chicago, who do not belong to us, do you think we would neglect our own poor?

The Poor Welcome at Zion City.

We have the poor with us always.

Poor people come to Zion City, and they are very welcome.

I welcome the man that comes to Zion City with an honest heart and strong hands, or even weak ones, and with a good purpose.

When he brings in children, I say, "The more the merrier."

I am glad to see the children.

No member of the Christian Catholic Church in Zion throughout the world is in prison for any offense.

We have not had one case of assault and battery before our courts.

We have not even had one case of a civil nature, except where the law requires a decree of the court, as in the case of minors, who cannot make a valid agreement of themselves in certain classes of cases. With that exception they are all settled by the judge of arbitration.

We are a peaceable, quiet, earnest people, but we fight against Sin and Disease, and the powers of Death and Hell, and we speak plainly. We do not beat around the bush.

I call a spade an old shovel if it is an old shovel.

I do not hesitate to speak so that you will understand.

On the other hand, I give every man the liberty I myself take, and I am respectful to all.

I Am Friendly to Those Who Disagree With Me.

I often have talks with Roman Catholic priests and bishops.

I have, indeed, among the list of my personal friends, one Roman Catholic cardinal in Paris.

I was once passing through the Rue Cambon, Paris, where the Paris branch of Zion Publishing House is located, and was very much struck, as I passed, with the nice way in which our manager had dressed the windows.

I stopped and looked at them.

As I looked, I became aware that a gentleman was standing by my side.

He was reading the words, *Crétienne Catolique*; that is Christian Catholic.

"*Très bien*," he said.

"Yes," I said, "that is a good name. Is it not better than Roman Catholic?"

He said, "Better."

"Pardon me," I said, "I do not speak French very well, but I think I understand what you are saying. Can you talk English?"

He talked English.

He looked at the picture in the middle of the window, and saw the words, Surintendant General; that is my title, in French.

Then he looked at me.

I lifted my hat, and he said, "I see," and presented me with his card.

It was the card of a Cardinal of the Church of Rome.

I said, "Come inside and talk with me."

We went inside, and I had one of the most charming conversations I have ever had in my life with a Christian gentleman.

Although I am opposed to many things in Rome, I never said, and I never thought, either regarding Rome or any other church, that there were not good people in it.

I value that man's friendship.

I think he greatly helped to put the present pope upon the throne.

He is a good man according to his light.

He said to me, "Your name is far better than ours; Christian is broader than Roman."

When the people get to understand the breadth and catholicity of Zion, this howling will pass away.

The Disturbers not of the Lower Classes.

Whence does it come?

It is not the working men.

It is not the lower classes.

Last night we had here three hundred intelligent men.

They were stock-brokers and merchants.

One of them, a capitalist, stood up here and insulted me. This man, Abe Shannon, disgraced his honored father's name and I was greatly grieved.

But it does not matter.

If I had died, it would have been all right, but my time has not come, and I do not fancy that it will come for a while.

A good soldier goes into battle every day, knowing that for him that day may end with a soldier's grave.

What do I care for the time?

I never did care; and if they think they can make me afraid, they are mistaken.

I Have Not Known What Fear Is.

When a man tells me he is afraid, I say to him, "How does it feel to be afraid?"

Had it not been for my wife and son, I should have felt like going into that crowd last night, but the crowd was intoxicated, partly with drink and tobacco, and partly with its passions, and it would have been unwise.

I Have No Revengeful Feeling.

Friends, I have no animus.

I have laid no charge.

A man was arrested last night who came up here and insulted me, and threw sulfureted hydrogen upon me, so that it made me horribly sick.

I said to an officer, "Take care of that poor fellow."

When they asked me, "Will you lay a charge against him?" I said, "No."

When they asked. "Shall we lock him up?" I replied, "No, he may have a wife; he may have a mother. Let him go, but take his name."

I have made no charges, and I do not intend to, so far as I can see just now.

If the police choose to make charges, they saw the disorder, that is their business, but I do not intend to press charges

I did not come to send citizens of Adelaide, naughty as they may be, to prison.

I came here to do some good.

I will do all I can, and I believe I have the prayers and the sympathies of all the law-abiding, good people. [Applause]

I believe that they far outnumber all the naughty people, because, you know, the naughty people make a big noise; but by-and-by the quiet people come up.

On Sunday, the shufflers exercised their feet.

I bore it patiently.

I know humanity, and I love my fellow men.

I have never hated any one, at any time, in any place.

Why should I?

How could I be the minister of God, and hate any one?

I speak the truth as I see it, and if some one else sees it more clearly than I, all right; let him speak.

I will have my little say, and you know there are many people in the world who want to hear it.

They say that I am no orator.

They declare that I am no speaker. It is wonderful, if I am no orator, how the people like to come and hear.

I have spoken to larger audiences than almost any man in the world, for ten years.

It is not an uncommon thing for me to speak in one Lord's Day to audiences that aggregate twenty thousand.

I spoke to thirty thousand in Madison Square Garden, New York, lately, fifteen thousand people at each meeting, and there was good order.

The police maintained order.

On more than one occasion it was estimated that there were a hundred thousand people outside who could not get in.

A Fair Proposal.

Beloved friends, bear with the naughty people.

Bear with even me.

I might say some things you do not like.

Will you not put up with it, and find out whether I am not right?

Perhaps I am right.

I think I am.

I have been over this ground a great deal, and I know the way.

If you know a better way, that is all right; go a better way, but it is right to listen respectfully and quietly, no matter what you think.

I hope that you will think well of me before I go.

Some of you think well of me now.

You are very kind and patient with me, and I need to be patiently dealt with, because I say things that at first sight seem very hard.

But then, if you take that medicine, it is very sweet when it gets down.

It may be a little bitter to the taste, but it works all right.

I Am Grateful to God for the Protection of Last Night.

I am sorry that the mob molested one of my distinguished relatives, a quiet gentleman in whose house I was not.

He was too brave to say whether I was there or not.

He told them that it was not their business.

He stands high in the world of business and politics.

I was sorry that his house was attacked last night, but then, that is one of the penalties of being related to me.

Such a thing has never happened before.

I never before had anything flung at me while in my carriage in any city in the world until yesterday.

When I was out driving with Mrs. Dowie and her mother yesterday, insults were hurled at these two good women, and at me.

In Melbourne, the vilest epithet that could be thrown at a woman was thrown at my wife.

Why?

For no reason except that the Devil was stirred up.

My ministry reaches down and it reaches up.

I am reaching the people very well; for that I am grateful.

I am willing to go on bearing the cross, enduring the shame, if shame there be.

Prayer was offered by Rev. C. Friend Hawkins, at the close of which the General Overseer also offered prayer, concluding with the Disciples' Prayer.

The General Overseer said:

---

*"I WILL; BE THOU CLEAN!"

*REPORTED BY E. W. AND A. W. N.

INVOCATION.

Let the words of my mouth and the meditation of my heart be acceptable in Thy sight, be profitable unto this people, and unto all to whom these words shall come, in this and every land, in this and all the coming time, Till Jesus Come. Amen.

My wife and I have read to you two passages from the Word of God, which I hope you will consider quietly in your own homes.

We Have Nothing New to Bring You.

That which is new is not true, and that which is true is not new.

It is the Old Time Religion.

It it were a new time religion, it would not be worth a snap.

I would not give a snap of my fingers for a merely twentieth century religion.

If any one imagines that I have a new Gospel to preach, he is mistaken.

The Gospel that I am preaching is the Gospel of Salvation, and Healing and Cleansing for spirit, soul, and body through faith in Jesus, the Christ.

That is older than the hills; because God has always been the Savior, the Healer, and the Cleanser of His people, whether they were angels in heaven or men on earth.

All good men and women have owed their Purity to God.

Even the angels might be charged with folly; but God is wise and always wise.

Angels may fall, but God never falls.

Angels may not keep their first estate, but God keeps His first estate.

Throughout all Eternity, He is Pure.

I am glad that this is the Gospel, the Glad Tidings, that God loves all that He has ever made, and hates nothing that He has made; that He never did anything that hurt His people; that, if they suffer, it is not God who makes them suffer.

*The following address has not been revised by the General Overseer.

I said, in expounding the prayer of the leper, that the words of the Master, "I will, be thou clean," accompanied by His touch, showed us the willingness of the Lord to heal.

God's Willingness to Heal.

I make the assertion and will prove that God must be willing to heal.

All His children who fulfil the Divine conditions, He must be willing to hear.

Must? Why?

Because, "Like as a father pitieth His children, so Jehovah pitieth them that fear Him."

"Who forgiveth all thine iniquities; who healeth all thy diseases."

He made our bodies, and only sin and disease, which are both the work of Satan, marred them.

You have been taught in the churches that God not only permits, but that He really sends sickness as a beneficent thing to make you better and to bring you to Himself.

I challenge that.

I say that it is not true.

Open your Bibles at the passage I gave you yesterday, the 10th chapter of the Acts of the Apostles, and the 38th verse.

Even Jesus of Nazareth, how that God anointed Him with the Holy Spirit and with power: who went about doing good, and healing all that were oppressed of the Devil.

Disease the Work of the Devil.

Every sickness and every disease that was among the people He healed, and all whom He healed were oppressed of the Devil.

Nineteen centuries ago all whom Jesus healed were oppressed of the Devil, but God oppresses today.

Overseer Voliva—"No, sir."

General Overseer—That is what you have been hearing in the churches.

Does God make people sick today?

Audience—"No."

General Overseer—A very healthy man named Job had no sickness until the Devil came up and touched him.

He was afflicted with boils from the crown of his head to the soles of his feet after the Devil touched him.

He was very ignorant.

He said, "Have pity upon me, O ye my friends! for the hand of God hath touched me."

It was not the hand of God at all. It was the hand of the Devil.

God rebuked Job.

Job said, "Therefore have I uttered that which I understood not, things too wonderful for me, which I knew not. . . . Wherefore I abhor myself, and repent in dust and ashes."

Job had said, "Jehovah gave, and Jehovah hath taken away."

Jehovah did give, but it was the Devil who took away.

Job had blessed the Name of Jehovah for all the bad things the Devil did.

The Good Things Come From God.

The Devil had taken away his cattle, horses, camels and other property.

The Devil had made his sons fools and drunkards, and then brought up a great wind from the wilderness, and pulled in the house about their heads, so that they were all killed.

It was the Devil's work from start to finish, and Job thought it was God's.

Who was right?

God said that it was not His work, and Job repented.

Then Job received healing, and he had better sons and daughters.

I believe that the old wife, who told him to curse God and die, died herself.

I believe that he got another wife, and good sons and daughters were born to them.

That is my opinion about it.

I do not see recorded in Scripture any signs of repentance in the old wife.

Any wife that tells her husband to curse God and die, deserves to die in Babylon, so that her husband may get well, get a new wife, and have better children.

I do not say that that is in the Bible. It is just my opinion.

Job was wrong, and you are wrong, if you say that disease comes from God.

I do not know exactly where the Devil obtained it.

It may have come from the fact that Adam and Eve fell and sin entered, and all disease came through them.

But poor old Adam and Eve are blamed for many things for which they ought not to be blamed.

One Prolific Source of Disease.

A man will go to a Masonic lodge, and go through thirty-three degrees of foolery, and get drunk about twenty times in doing it.

Perhaps the night he takes the thirty-second degree, he rolls into the gutter.

The policeman comes up and says, "This is a big Mason," and wants to take him home.

"Get away, I am comfortable here," he hiccoughs.

He thinks that the gutter is soft, and is trying to make a blanket of the paving stones.

The police officer says, "Excuse me, Mr. Jones, I must take you home."

"Get away, or I will report you."

At last the poor constable gets some sense into Mr. Jones, calls a cab, and takes him home.

But Mr. Jones gets a high fever.

They send for the doctor, and the doctor comes, but Mr. Jones does not get any better.

Then the papers say, "Our distinguished fellow citizen is dangerously ill."

The minister prays, "O God, remove Thine afflicting hand from Mr. Jones."

Is it God's afflicting hand?

Voices—"No."

General Overseer—Was it God who made him drunk?

Was it God who made him roll into the gutter?

At last they send for the minister, because Mr. Jones is dying.

But the minister comes too late, the undertaker has got in ahead of him.

They put upon his tomb, "The Lord gave, and the Lord hath taken away."

That is a big lie.

The Lord gave, and the Devil took away. [Laughter.]

Jones was a fool.

Another Common Cause of Disease and Death.

Here is a beautiful young girl.

Her father and mother want her to be introduced into society—into such society as we saw last night!

Some of these men who cannot control themselves, but can wear big diamonds in their shirts, and have big balances in the bank, are the pets and leaders of "society."

They never earned any of the money they spend.

It was their old fathers who earned it.

They never had grit nor brains enough to earn it; but they have foolishness enough to spend it, and to trample upon the liberties for which their fathers fought, and for which their great-grandfathers bled and died.

Here is a young girl, and a foolish father and mother say, "Now we must get Maggie fixed up, so that she can go to balls, dances, and parties; then she will get a rich husband."

Poor Maggie does not want to go to balls, but father and mother say she must.

At last she begins to go.

She gets excited.

She dances, and then her escort invites her to take champagne.

She takes it, and it is sham at night and pain in the morning.

When the morning comes, Maggie has a cold. Oh, she is coughing!

Her mother says, "Now, Maggie, you must stay in bed."

"But I want to see my lover," says Maggie; "he is coming today to see me."

She has a cold, but she sees her lover.

The next night she goes again to a ball.

A night or two later, she comes home, after naving had more champagne and more real pain.

Now, she has a very bad cold, and before the season is over Maggie is a consumptive.

Then they rush with her to France, and to other countries, but Maggie continues to cough.

The doctor comes, looks at her, and shakes his head.

There is nothing in it—I mean his head.

He knows that he cannot help her, but he gives her prescriptions.

He talks hopefully.

He gets big fees.

She is taken from doctor to doctor, and at last she is dying.

She dies, poor child, at twenty.

Then they write over her grave, "The Lord gave, and the Lord taketh away. Blessed be the Name of the Lord."

Did the Lord take her away?

Audience—"No."

General Overseer—The Devil took her away.

She danced her life out.

She might have lived to be a grandmother, but her parents were foolish, and so was she.

Inherited Disease Also Traceable to the Devil.

When you examine it, you will find that disease is always traceable to the Devil.

It is not always, of course, the fault of the sick man, woman, or child.

Sometimes the father eats pig. Then the sons get scrofula.

Sometimes the mother will be a fool, and instead of thanking God for the beautiful body that God gave her, she thinks her waist altogether too large, so she gets something that pinches her up.

She is really thirty-two inches around the waist, and she makes herself twenty-six, to have a nice wasp-like waist.

I think it is a wasp-like waist!

The woman who goes in for a wasp-like waist is a fool.

Sometimes she becomes a mother, and then—I do not like to talk about it—she gives birth to a poor misshapen monster instead of a sweet pretty baby.

His head and body have been injured.

He has had a fool for a mother.

Was that God's work?

Audience—"No."

General Overseer—The other day a woman with a wasp-like waist was prancing along in Buffalo, New York, with a prayer-book in her hand.

She was magnificently dressed.

All at once she fell.

They rushed to her.

She was dead.

A physician came and cut open her dress.

The dress bounded apart.

"Why," he said, "that woman has tight-laced herself to death; has crushed the life out of herself!"

She was vain, and crushed her heart so that there was a rupture of the aorta.

Take care what you do. Eat and drink and think, or you will get into the Devil's ways.

Disease never comes from God; but Healing does.

It is God's Will to heal, and if you will give up sin and do right He will heal you.

Rise and give yourselves to God. [Nearly all rose.]

Now, pray with me.

PRAYER OF CONSECRATION.

My God and Father, in Jesus' Name I come to Thee. Take me as I am. Make me what I ought to be, in spirit, in soul, in body. Give me power to do right, no matter what it costs, and to trust Thee with my spirit, my soul, and my body. For Jesus' sake. Amen.

The people were then dismissed by the General Overseer with the

BENEDICTION.

Beloved, abstain from all appearance of evil. And may the very God of Peace Himself sanctify you wholly; and I pray God your whole spirit and soul and body be preserved entire, without blame, unto the coming of our Lord Jesus, the Christ. Faithful is He that calleth you, who also will do it. The grace of our Lord Jesus, the Christ, the love of God, our Father, the fellowship of the Holy Spirit, our Comforter and Guide, one Eternal God, abide in you, bless you and keep you, and all the Israel of God everywhere, forever. Amen.

Tuesday Afternoon Meeting.

As a result of the terrible disturbances which marked the Monday evening service, the General Overseer decided that there would be too much danger for the police and for the people, as well as for himself and family, and that there would probably be too great a destruction of property if any more of the Visitation meetings were to be held in the evening.

Consequently, all the meetings which had been announced

for the evening were changed to the afternoon at two o'clock, the tickets which had been issued for the evening meetings being available for the afternoon of each day.

These afternoon meetings of the Visitation were attended by larger and larger numbers of quiet, orderly, attentive and intensely interested people.

The addresses were essentially Restoration Messages, and were received by practically all the hearers with thoughtful earnestness.

Their effectiveness and power were manifested not only in their effect upon hearers, who received them gladly, and made them a part of their lives, but also upon all the forces of evil.

Masons, hypocritical members of denominational churches, smokers, drinkers, impure men and women, and, indeed, all those whose dearest sins were mightily smitten by the hand of God's Prophet, became more and more bitterly malicious and murderous in their spirits as the week went by.

The subjects discussed at these meetings became subjects of the most lively discussions in the homes of the people, on the street, and in the public houses, shops, stores, and offices of the city.

Everywhere one went, could be heard discussions concerning the topics dealt with in Elijah's Restoration Messages.

It was reported to us that not even the Boer War, which had aroused enthusiasm to the highest pitch in Adelaide, created such a profound stir as the Visitation of Elijah, the Prophet of the Restoration.

Again and again the truth was brought vividly to mind that no one save the Prophet of these times could have created so great a commotion among the people of this usually quiet city.

The evils which he smote were the evils which every true minister of God who teaches the Ten Commandments decries without arousing the feeblest opposition.

But this time the words came with authority from a mighty Prophet of God.

That is the only explanation of the fierceness of the fire which he kindled.

The following is the report of the General Overseer's Message:

Town Hall, Adelaide, South Australia, Tuesday Afternoon, March 22, 1904.

The meeting was opened with the singing of Hymn No. 31, Visitation Program, "Zion Stands with Hills Surrounded."

The General Overseer said:

I shall read to you from the Gospel according to St. Mark, in the 1st chapter, the first fifteen verses.

The beginning of the Gospel of Jesus, the Christ, the Son of God.
Even as it is written in Isaiah the prophet,
Behold I send My Messenger before Thy face,
Who shall prepare Thy Way;
The voice of one crying in the wilderness,
Make ye ready the Way of the Lord,
Make His paths straight;
John came, who baptized in the wilderness and preached the Baptism of repentance unto remission of sins.
And there went out unto him all the country of Judæa, and all they of Jerusalem; and they were baptized of him in the river Jordan, confessing their sins.
And John was clothed with camel's hair, and had a leathern girdle about his loins, and did eat locusts and wild honey.

A Camel's-hair Robe.

I wonder if you all have the artists' idea of the camel's-hair robe.

It is painted oftentimes as a camel's skin in the roughest and most uncouth condition.

John the Baptist was not a rough and uncouth man.

He was the son of a priest who was at the head of the order of Abijah—Zacharias, who himself was a priest by heredity.

He was doubtless educated very carefully by his exceedingly pious mother, Elizabeth, of whom it is written that she and her husband walked blameless in all the Commandments of Jehovah.

He was a priest by heredity, and he would not be trained in any other way than in the best possible manner.

He would be brought up in the best rabbinical school, and when he went out into the desert to preach he would wear a very beautiful robe.

That robe of camel's-hair was exceedingly expensive.

It was not a camel's skin, but it was a robe woven of camel's hair.

I dare say many of you know how expensive good camel's-hair brushes are.

I do not know where the artists got their idea of a half-naked man in camel's skin, for it is perfectly absurd.

Even today, a camel's-hair robe, beautifully and finely made, such as John's mother would get for him, would be worth several hundred pounds.

It would be very strong and very useful for his work in the desert.

Refinement, Training, and Power of John the Baptist.

John was a refined man, splendidly born, and had a magnificent training.

He was a man of command and power, and the notion that people generally have about him is not true.

The man who taught his disciples to pray was essentially a teacher. A great part of his ministry was the training of people who would be prepared to follow the Christ when He came.

And He preached, saying, There cometh after me He that is mightier than I, the latchet of whose shoes I am not worthy to stoop down and unloose.
I baptized you with water; but He shall baptize you with the Holy Spirit.
And it came to pass in those days, that Jesus came from Nazareth of Galilee, and was baptized of John in the Jordan.
And straightway coming up out of the water, he saw the heavens rent asunder, and the Spirit as a dove descending upon Him.
And a Voice came out of the heavens, Thou art My beloved Son, in Thee I am well pleased.
And straightway the Spirit driveth Him forth into the wilderness.
And He was in the wilderness forty days tempted of Satan; and He was with the wild beasts; and the angels ministered unto Him.
Now after that John was delivered up, Jesus came into Galilee, preaching the Gospel of God,
And saying, The time is fulfilled, and the Kingdom of God is at hand; repent ye, and believe in the Gospel.

Overseer Wilbur Glenn Voliva offered the general supplication.

The free-will offerings and tithes were then received, during which a Hymn was sung.

The General Overseer then delivered his address:

THE KINGDOM OF GOD.

*REPORTED BY I. M. S. AND A. W. N.

INVOCATION.

Let the words of my mouth, and the meditations of my heart, be acceptable in Thy sight, and profitable unto this people and unto all to whom these words shall come. For the sake of Jesus, our Lord, our Strength and our Redeemer. Amen.

I call your attention to three verses in the passage which I read to you.

TEXT.

The beginning of the Gospel of Jesus, the Christ, the Son of God.

. . . .

Now after that John was delivered up, Jesus came into Galilee, preaching the Gospel of God,
And saying, The time is fulfilled, and the kingdom of God is at hand: Repent ye, and believe in the Gospel.

The Gospel of The Christ, of God, and of The Kingdom.

The 14th verse says, "Jesus came into Galilee, preaching," as the Old Version says, "the Gospel of the Kingdom of God."

The Revision says, "The Gospel of God."

The beginning of this chapter calls it, "The Gospel of Jesus, the Christ."

It is all the same thing.

The Gospel of Jesus, the Christ, is the Gospel of God, and the Gospel of the Christ and of God our Father is the Gospel of the Kingdom of God.

When Jesus came into Galilee, He began to preach, and He preached the Gospel of God, saying, "The Time is fulfilled, the Kingdom of God is at hand: repent ye, and believe in the Gospel."

It is of great importance, even in the very few days that I have remaining here, that we should get a clear foundation for all our teaching in connection with "the Restoration of All things, whereof God spake by the mouth of His holy prophets which have been since the world began."

The Beginning of the Gospel.

The Gospel of the Kingdom of God, the Gospel of God, the Gospel of the Christ must be understood.

First of all, the preaching of that Gospel began, not with Jesus, the Christ, but with John the Baptist.

John the Baptist was the porter, as the Christ said, and he opened the door.

*The following report has not been revised by the General Overseer.

He was the precursor, and he was the Messenger.

When, sometimes, people tell you that the Messenger of the Covenant was Jesus, the Christ, Himself, they are talking nonsense.

There is not a single reference Bible that I know of that has the reference to Jesus, the Christ, there.

That is quite a new theology, and it is not true.

The Messenger of the Covenant spoken of in Malachi 3:1 is undoubtedly the Elijah, first, of the Preparation, and then of the Restoration.

If you want confirmatory evidence of that, you have only to read the rabbinical comments upon it; and the rabbinical comments were commended by the Christ Himself, in a very famous inquiry concerning the Elijah question.

The rabbis were very learned, very able and very competent.

They answered questions very correctly.

When the question was put to them by Herod, "Where will the Christ be born?" they put their finger upon Bethlehem of Ephratah, and said, "He must be born there."

Zechariah Goldman—"No."

General Overseer—My friend must not interrupt.

I know that he is a Jew, and differs with me, but he must not interrupt.

He must take an opportunity of speaking elsewhere.

He will not interrupt any more, will he?

Mr. Goldman—"No."

General Overseer—According to the Gospel narrative which I am quoting, they gave the correct answer, and the wise men found Jesus at Bethlehem.

The rabbinical authorities of the Christ's time, like many now, were very learned.

Jewish Hope in Elijah.

I will quote from one that I have great pleasure in mentioning, the learned writer in the "Jewish Encyclopedia," which is in course of publication, in America, by Funk & Wagnells.

In his article upon "Elijah's Chair," he says, "The Messenger of the Covenant referred to in Malachi 3: 1, is Elijah.

"There is a chair set for him at every circumcision, and also at every Passover Feast."

Mr. Goldman—"Yes."

General Overseer—I am glad that my Jewish friend agrees with me now

That is the interpretation which the Jewish rabbis give to the passage referring to the Messenger of the Covenant.

They do the same thing in connection with this passage from Isaiah, that Mark does.

He says:

The beginning of the Gospel of Jesus, the Christ, the Son of God. Even as it is written in Isaiah the prophet, Behold I send My Messenger before Thy face, who shall prepare Thy Way; the Voice of one crying in the wilderness, Make ye ready the Way of the Lord, make His paths straight; John came, who baptized in the wilderness and preached the Baptism of Repentance unto remission of sins.

All Dispensations Heralded by Great Prophets.

At the beginning of every Dispensation, there has always been a great prophet.

The greater the prophet the humbler the man.

The greater the prophet the more he is persecuted, whether it is Moses at the beginning of the Dispensation leading the people out of Egyptian bondage or John the Baptist at the beginning of the Christian Dispensation.

John the Baptist, the First Preacher of the Gospel.

John the Baptist was the first preacher of the Gospel.

He preached that the Christ was coming and told the people to repent; for His fan was in His hand, and He would thoroughly purge His floor, and He would gather the wheat into the garner, and He would burn up the chaff with unquenchable fire.

John the Baptist told them that there was a hot time coming.

He was a very earnest preacher himself, but he was nothing compared with Jesus.

John had been in communication with God, and he did what God told him to do.

He said, "He that sent me to baptize with water, He said unto me, Upon whomsoever thou shalt see the Spirit descending and abiding upon Him, the same is He that baptizeth with the Holy Spirit."

John said that he saw the Spirit descend upon only one Man, and that He was "the Lamb of God, which taketh away the sin of the world."

John was the Preparer.

His ministry was short.

It lasted for only eleven months, and then Herodias, who had long threatened him, got him into her power.

In a short time she had his head cut off.

A Teacher of Purity Is Never Liked By an Impure Generation.

Impurity, intemperance, and infidelity always go together.

It is the fool that saith in his heart, "There is no God."

The fool is corrupt, as the Psalmist says, and has done abominable works.

Men who are impure are always intemperate, and often infidels.

One of the strikingly sad things about this generation is the abounding Impurity and Intemperance and consequent Infidelity,

The very center of all Wisdom is Purity.

When Wisdom builds her house, she puts Purity in the very center.

The Wisdom that is from above is first Pure, then Peaceable, Gentle Easy to be Entreated, Full of Mercy and Good Fruits, Without Variance Without Hypocrisy.

The Central Pillar is Purity.

They hated John because he said "You must be pure;" because he told Herod that he could not live that adulterous life in peace as long as he was about.

The principal opposition to me arises because I am determined, as far as lies in my power, to be pure, to be clean in spirit, soul, and body, and because I am determined to teach this generation that if they would be acceptable to God they must get clean in spirit, soul, and body. [Amen.]

I intend to keep at it, no matter what any one may say, or do, or threaten.

My business is to keep on preaching Purity.

The Kingdom of God was doubtless not understood in all its fulness by John.

He had a circumscribed ministry.

His ministry was to announce the coming of the Lord Jesus, to preach Repentance, to baptize the penitent and to prepare them for the coming of the Christ.

So, after John was put into prison, Jesus appeared upon the scene and began to preach.

He said, "The Time is fulfilled, and the Kingdom of God is at hand."

What does that mean?

There Is Always a Time.

That clock is marking time; that bell that has chimed is marking time.

Just as surely as that clock marks time and that bell chimes, so surely does the Word of God tell you what is coming.

God's clock never stands still.

The wheels of God are moving on; they grind slowly, but they grind exceeding fine.

There is no mistake about the clock of God.

The Time goes on, and events must take place.

They take place exactly on time, and there is no mistake about it.

When the Christ said, "The Time is fulfilled," He was right

The Time was fulfilled when the ignorance that was upon the earth, that God had winked at, was to pass away, and God was commanding men everywhere to repent.

The Christ came to fulfil the Law.

He came to do the Will of the Father and to establish the Kingdom of God.

The Gospel is not the property of any one man or of any one church.

It is not the church's Gospel at all; it is the Gospel of Jesus, the Christ: it is the Gospel of the Kingdom of God.

The Kingdom is bigger than the Church.

The Kingdom of God Is From Everlasting to Everlasting.

His Kingdom never changes.

There are changes among men only.

Empires rise and fall, republics rise and fall, commonwealths rise and fall, but there is no break in the Kingdom of God.

His Kingdom is an Everlasting Kingdom, and is dominant eternally.

The Christ was not preaching a new Gospel. There is no new Gospel.

The Christ came to preach the Everlasting Glad Tidings.

God did not begin to be kind to His people at the time when the Christ came.

In all their affliction He was afflicted, and the angel of His presence saved them: in His love and in His pity He redeemed them; and He bare them, and carried them all the days of old.

There never was a time when God did not love humanity; when He did not make a way by which His penitent, banished children might return to Him.

God's Mercy Endureth Forever.

There never was a time and there never will be a time when His mercy fails [Amen.]

His mercy endureth forever. It is an attribute of God always to have mercy for man.

Even if he will make his bed in hell, there is God's right hand to find him.

You will never get away beyond the Love, and the Mercy, and the Power of God.

You may sin, you may fall, but God will seek your miserable spirit, no matter how you sin and fall, until He finds you, until He restores you to the Gospel of Jesus, the Christ.

It is an everlasting Gospel.

As in Adam all die, so also in the Christ shall all be made alive.

Make no mistake about that.

It may be a long time before we get there, but we shall at last be restored to God.

There is no spirit of whom He is the Father whom He will not seek until He finds

The Gospel Is Infinite.

The Gospel of the Kingdom of God is a great and glorious Gospel.

It is not narrowed down to what some of you make it—the Gospel of the church.

You try to define it, and say exactly what it is and what it is not.

You cannot define the Infinite.

You cannot put bounds around the thing that is without bounds.

The Gospel is as Infinite as God's Mercy.

An Infinite God only can define the limits of His Gospel.

When any one tells you that he knows all about it, and just when God's Mercy will cease, tell him that His Mercy "endureth forever."

A Canopy of Love.

I say to thee, do thou repeat
To the first man, thou mayest meet,
In lane, highway, or open street,
That he, and we, and all men move
Under a canopy of Love,
Broader than that blue sky above;

That grief and sorrow, and care and pain,
And anguish, all, are shadows vain;
That death itself will not remain;
That weary deserts he may tread,
Life's dreariest labyrinths he may thread,
Through dark ways underground be led;

Yet, if he will the Christ obey,
The darkest night. the dreariest way,
Shall issue out in perfect day,
And we, on divers shores oft cast,
Shall meet, our perilous voyage past,
All in our Father's home at last.

And ere thou leave him, tell him this,
They only miss
The winning of that perfect bliss,
Who will not count it true that blessing, not cursing, rules above,
And that in God we live and move;
Whose Nature and whose Name is Love.

In God we live and move and have our being.

He loved all men, and loves them still.

He is not willing that any should perish.

The depth of His Mercy is so great that He has shut up all unto disobedience, that He might have mercy upon all.

This Gospel is too big to be the property of any little church, or any little company of men anywhere.

There is No Gospel of the Church Spoken of in the Bible.

I love the Epistles very much.

They are magnificent letters; but they are the writings of men who were fallible.

The Gospel is not in the Epistles.

The Epistles never pretended to be a Gospel.

They were merely letters to the churches that were of more or less importance, some of them purely local, and some of them permanently important.

The Gospel, as we have it, is all in these four books—Matthew, Mark, Luke and John.

Take the Gospel according to St. John, and try to find the word church there. If you can find it, I cannot.

After you are through with that book, take up St. Luke, and see whether you can find the word church there. If you can, I cannot.

I can find it neither in the English nor in the Greek.

Now, we will go to Mark.

I cannot find the word church in Mark, not from the first chapter to the last, and I know you cannot, because I have examined it most closely.

In Matthew I find the word church twice.

Once Jesus used it in speaking of a man who had been wicked and would not repent even when his friends told him his wickedness.

"Then," Jesus said, "tell it to the Church;" that is to say, "go and have a church meeting."

But He did not tell them to vote upon the subject.

Voting a Farce and a Failure.

That is all nonsense.

I take no stock in voting, and never did.

There never has been a vote taken in the Christian Catholic Church in Zion, since it has been established.

We get on very well without voting.

When I looked at the young men and others, making that disturbance last night, my heart was sore to think that these were the persons who vote for the members of Parliament who rule this nation.

They are not competent to rule themselves, and cannot rule others.

They who trample liberty under their feet and defy law, are not competent to vote for rulers.

Lawlessness is ascendent.

The only way to get back Law, will be for the Man on Horseback to do it.

It will be a poor thing for you to get into the hands of a military tyranny.

During the French Revolution, lawlessness grew worse and worse until society had to throw itself into the arms of a dictator to be saved from destruction.

If this kind of thing goes on in Australia, men openly defying law, the end of it will be that military power will have to put them down firmly, and rule every man who cannot rule himself.

Alas! that has been the end of nearly all the republics and commonwealths.

They have gone to seed.

The things for which their fathers bled and died, are trampled under their feet.

My friend, the Jewish gentleman, has a right to a platform where he may tell what he thinks is true; so has the Mohammedan, under the British law; so has the Buddhist, the Spiritualist, and the Infidel.

The truth will prevail.

There is no fear about the Truth's prevailing; but there must be free speech in a free country.

The Kingdom of God is different from your democracies

There is no voting in it.

When the Christ rules there will be no voting.

What do you want with voting? All you need is to get good rulers; and if you can get them without voting, that is a great deal better.

The Only Form of Government Approved by God Is a Theocracy.

God has established a Theocracy, a government in which *Theos*, (θεός) God, is the Ruler, God alone.

When the people cried to Samuel for a king, God said to him plainly, "Samuel, they have not rejected thee, but they have rejected Me, and desire a king to rule over them."

One of the prophets said that God permitted the people to have kings in His wrath.

Therefore, when He is pleased with us, He will take them away.

Kings are not of God's ordination. Saul was appointed King practically against God's will.

Although God permitted Saul to be king and Samuel to anoint him, what miseries came over them!

Misery after misery followed, until the nation perished and the last king tried to murder the Christ.

It was not a monarchy that God established, nor did He establish a republic.

I tell them that in America, and they listen to it.

There is one good thing about our big, broad United States, the people will listen, and if they are not of my opinion, some minister will have something to say about Dowie the next Sunday.

That is all right; I should like to go myself and hear him. [Interjection by Mr. Goldman.]

I desire to be good to this brother.

I like his face.

I am an Israelite myself.

I am glad to be an Israelite.

"Salvation is from the Jews."

Jesus, the Christ, said that to the woman of Samaria.

When some of you are talking contemptuously about the Jews, do not forget, please, that Jesus, the Christ, was a Jew, that Mary was a Jewess, and that all the religion we have came to us from noble prophets and great apostles and martyrs, all the first of whom were Jews.

God is no respecter of persons: but in every nation he that feareth Him, and worketh righteousness, is acceptable to Him.

God's Love Reaches Out to Those Who Do Not Know Him.

Jesus one day saw a man, blind from his birth.

He put clay on his eyes, and told him to go to the pool of Siloam and wash.

He went and washed and came back seeing.

He was not a Christian and did not know the Christ; for, when he was brought before the rabbis, and they asked him who had restored his sight, he said that he only knew that His Name was Jesus, and that He told him to go away and wash, and that he did so and came seeing.

They told him to curse Jesus, after they had said that they did not know anything about Him.

He answered, "Why, herein is the marvel, that ye know not whence He is, and yet He opened mine eyes. We know that God heareth not sinners: but if any man be a worshiper of God, and do His will, him He heareth."

He continued in effect, "God heard Him when He prayed for me. I will not curse Him."

Then they cursed the man and flung him out of the synagogue.

It is written that Jesus afterwards found him in the Temple, and said to him, "Dost thou believe on the Son of God?"

He said, "Who is He, Lord, that I may believe on Him?"

Jesus said, "Thou hast both seen Him, and He it is that speaketh with thee."

And he worshiped Him.

He had not known the Christ at all until then.

The Love of God reaches out to people who do not know Him.

If they will do right, according to their light, they are acceptable with Him.

Some of you miserable, narrow-minded people think that God Almighty will do nothing unless you are a Baptist, or a Congregationalist, or a Presbyterian, or a Methodist, or a miserable Episcopalian, who grinds out his prayers, "O Lord, have mercy upon us, miserable sinners, we have left undone all the things that we ought to have done and done all the things we ought not to have done, and there is no health in us."

Very poor prayer that!

If I had a clerk in my office who came to me every night, saying, "General Overseer, I have left undone all the things I ought to have done and done all the things I ought not to have done; I have smashed all the typewriters and upset all the ink, and there is no health in me, have mercy upon me, O General Overseer," I should say, "You are much too expensive to keep."

If some of you ladies had a cook in your kitchen, who would come to you every night and say, "O Mistress Jones, I have left undone all the things I ought to have done, and have smashed up all the dishes and pots, and there is no health in me, have mercy upon me, O Mistress," would you keep that cook? [Laughter.]

Miserable prayer that!

I always endeavor to do the things that I ought to do, and say the things that I ought to say, no matter what any one else says. [Applause.]

I will not stop until I am dead, and even then I will not stop.

I intend to keep right on talking, you may be sure about that.

The Effect of Elijah's Restoration Messages.

The things that I have spoken will go on and on, and will be read more after I am dead than while I am alive.

You will read LEAVES OF HEALING more in Adelaide when I am gone than you do now.

People everywhere want to know what I have to say, because what I have to say is beginning to affect the whole world and the whole Church.

It is simple truth but it is beginning to take effect everywhere.

It has affected one hundred thousand people who have come into fellowship with us in eight years.

It has affected people so that they are coming together to build cities, one of which is already well under way.

It has had such an effect that we turn out from Zion Printing and Publishing House many tons of Zion Literature every week, and it is only a beginning.

People everywhere want to hear.

What I say today will be heard by vast multitudes.

I am glad to have the joy of speaking, the joy of teaching, and the joy of upholding the Gospel of the Kingdom of God.

It is the Gospel of the Kingdom, do not forget that.

It is not a narrow church Gospel.

The Kingdom is Broad; It Includes Everything.

They say sometimes, "Dr. Dowie has his nose in everything"

I want to capture every good thing for the Kingdom of God.

The whole world is listening to what is now going on in Adelaide.

The press has followed this Around-the-World Visitation very earnestly.

There is not a newspaper in the United States or in England that is not interested.

We have twenty thousand newspaper clippings regarding the New York Visitation alone, and then we did not get a tithe of them.

"The Kingdom of God is not meat and drink; but Righteousness and Peace and Joy in the Holy Spirit."

All the other things are mere accessories, but there must be Righteousness.

Therefore we have a little City established, where God rules and Righteousness prevails.

We live right, and do right, and make money and spend it, too.

Some of you say, "What do you do with the money?"

I do all the good I can.

I get all I can, save all I can, and give all I can.

Some of you get all you can, but you give nothing and save nothing. [Laughter.]

I will guarantee that nine-tenths of the people who "boo-hoo" at me, never saved.

In Zion, the work of God is going on all the time, and I am grateful to God for it.

They attacked us in December last, but the receivers who had been appointed, walked into court and demanded their own dismissal.

I was indorsed at that time by all the papers of the city of Chicago, and practically the United States of America.

My enemies overshot the mark, and they are overshooting the mark here. [Cries of "Hear, hear!"]

Zion prospers because Zion walks with God.

A Man Must Be in the Kingdom Before He Can Come Into the Church.

Any man who does not know that he is converted has no business in the Church.

You ask a great many ministers where their members came from, and they say that they came out of the world into the Church.

That is the reason there is so much of the world in the Church.

They should be born into the Kingdom, and then come into the Church.

The only way to enter the Kingdom, is to enter in God's Way, by Repentance, Faith and Obedience.

Then God will bless you.

The Christ said, "Repent ye!"

That is what He says today.

If you will search your own hearts you will find that you have many things of which to repent.

It is the goodness of God that leads you to Repentance.

We have been miserable and narrow and blind, holding on to creeds and systems and men.

These little systems have ceased to be, and you ought to thank God when you get away from them.

The Way Into the Kingdom of God Begins With Repentance.

Repentance means that if you have lied to your wife or to your husband, you must face that, and tell her or him that you have been a mean liar.

You must account for the late nights that you have fooled away with Mah-hah-bone in the Masonic lodge, where you have banqueted and wined, and then lied to your wife about where you spent the time.

All the women are not angels. [Laughter. Applause.]

They, too, must repent properly.

You went to your husband's pockets and took out that sovereign, and then when he asked you for it, you pretended you knew nothing about it, and said, "Why do you not take care of your money?" [Laughter.]

A woman said to me one day, "Doctor, my husband is such a bad man that he will give me no money with which to pay the bills and buy food for the children, what shall I do?"

I said, "Take all the money you can get from him. Get it out of his pockets, but tell him you took it, and tell him what you did with it.

"Then if he growls, and tells you to pack up your things and get, you look sweetly at him, and say, 'All right, I have slaved and scrubbed and cooked and mended for you, and you have not given me a penny. I can earn wages elsewhere, and do what I like with them.' You go, and you will see how soon he will be after you, and ask you to come back and look after the children." [Laughter.]

Repent!

Get things straight.

There is a great deal of Repentance to be done.

There are many lies to be confessed.

Some of you have taken money from your employers that was not yours!

You must give back every pound of it.

I do not care what your confession may cost, you must confess.

God Blesses Those Who Repent, Confess and Restore.

A man said to me one day, "If I confess my sins and give back every dollar, I shall have to sell my house and property, and I shall be penniless."

"Well," I said, "do it. Tell your wife about it."

He did, and they are well-to-do today because they did right.

Another man came to me and said, "Doctor, I robbed a railway company, and if I confess it they will send me to prison."

I said, "You must confess it. If you do not, you will go to hell."

He restored the money, and the president of the company wrote to me and said that if all the thieves would confess and restore like this one, the company would be far richer.

We are doing things of that kind all the time, and God is blessing the people.

The work of Restoration is going on.

Repentance is not worth a fig if you do not restore and put things right.

A man once said to me, "O Doctor, if I do that, my brother will shoot me."

I said, "Go, and get shot, and go to heaven. If you will not do it, and go on in your sins, you will go to hell."

He said, "I will confess to my brother."

He confessed, and told his wife about it too, as there had been a double sin. His brother wept and said, "I have to confess, too."

Both of these brothers and their wives fell on their faces before God and asked for forgiveness.

It was one of the most touching scenes I have ever witnessed—these brothers and their wives asking God to cleanse their lives.

Robbers of God.

You are all thieves here!

Voices—"What's that?" [Laughter.]

General Overseer—You are all thieves!

Voices—"Prove it."

General Overseer—I will prove it to you.

All men and women here that never, no never, never, in all their whole lives took anything that did not belong to them, up with their hands! [Two hands were sheepishly raised. Laughter.]

Most of the people are honest about it, anyway.

Every one here who never, no never, in all his life told a lie, a big one or a little one, up with his hand! [No hands up. Laughter.]

You are all liars and thieves, according to your own confession! [Laughter.]

God says in His Word:

Will a man rob God? yet ye rob Me.
But ye say, Wherein have we robbed Thee? In Tithes and Offerings.
Ye are cursed with a curse; for ye robbed Me, even this Whole Nation.

Every one here who has given one shilling out of every ten to God, during all his life, up with his hand. [No hands up.]

You are all thieves! [Laughter.]

You have robbed God.

You had better cease robbing Him.

That is what has cursed the nation.

Read the 3d chapter of Malachi, and it will tell you what has cursed the nation.

In Zion, if we find any man that has not paid his tithes, we ask him to go.

You cannot live in Zion City and rob God.

The Gospel of the Kingdom of God begins with Repentance.

You must repent of every sin that you have committed and make wrongs right with God and man before God can bless you.

All who desire to be wholly God's, stand and pray with me.

PRAYER OF CONSECRATION.

My God and Father, in Jesus' Name I come to Thee. Take me as I am and make me what I ought to be, in spirit, soul, and body. Give me a True Repentance, and a simple Faith in Jesus, the Lamb of God, that taketh away the sin of the world. Take away my sin, and my sickness, and make me wholly Thine. For Jesus' sake. Amen. [*All repeat the prayer, clause by clause, after the General Overseer.*]

The meeting was closed with the singing of the Doxology, and the

BENEDICTION.

Beloved, abstain from all appearance of evil. And may the very God of Peace Himself sanctify you wholly; and I pray God your whole spirit and soul and body be preserved entire, without blame, unto the coming of our Lord Jesus, the Christ. Faithful is He that calleth you, who also will do it. The grace of our Lord Jesus, the Christ, the love of God our Father, the fellowship of the Holy Spirit, our Comforter and Guide, one Eternal God, abide in you, bless you and keep you, and all the Israel of God everywhere, forever. Amen.

Wednesday Morning Meeting.

On the following morning, Wednesday, March 23d, at half past ten o'clock, in the Town Hall, the General Overseer conducted the third Divine Healing Meeting of the Visitation.

On this morning, the Adelaide *Register* had appeared with the following lukewarm and, in some respects, very silly and illogical editorial or leader:

THE DOWIE DISTURBANCES.

An overwhelming majority of South Australians regret the riotous demonstrations, which in such an unpleasantly unusual manner diversified the experiences of citizens of Adelaide on Monday night. That, indeed, goes without the saying. The feeling of sorrow is probably shared even by many of those who took part in the disturbances, and who may not unnaturally experience also a sensation of shame. Shame, if only because of the reflection that—however greatly they may have been incensed by Mr. Dowie's indiscreet and pungent utterances—for one man to attack thousands with his tongue is in many respects a different thing from an attack upon that one man by scores among thousands with other things besides their tongues. This distinction is drawn for the reason that it would be preposterous to contend that, in any really aggressive sense, more than scores were concerned in the worse than foolish proceedings of Monday night.

Undoubtedly a number of the assailants attended at the Town Hall and its vicinity, and that of the York Hotel, with the deliberate purpose of committing violent assaults, and taking their risk of subsequent punishment. Road metal was provided beforehand by some of the cowardly fellows who threw it, regardless of whether it struck the person against whom they were exasperated or whether—as actually happened in some cases—it found a target in folk so innocent of offence as even to be sympathizers with the opponents of Mr. Dowie. In vast preponderance, however, the crowd struggled—each member of it—to obtain and maintain a footing, and to extricate himself or herself from the dangerous surge by which all were swayed in the prevailing agitation. Under such conditions—conditions to which was added an element of irritation through the abrupt exclusion of ticket-holders from the meeting to which they had been invited—malicious manifestations are apt to occur, through what has been called "mobbish magnetism," though the intentions of the crowd may originally be perfectly harmless. A multitude can rarely keep their heads in an emergency, and logic flies from them.

Still, between them all, their behavior on the occasion under reference was highly discreditable, and directly in defiance of the laws of manliness and the statutes of the country; and it is a pity that the police apparently could not manage to bring more of the offenders to justice. After all the bold rallying and challenging words of the commissioner, and the warnings which he had given of the appalling fate which would overtake any man who might dare to place himself in antagonism to law and order, the arrest of two youths during the whole day and night—and that for comparatively minor offences—surely seems like a ludicrous sequel.

It is somewhat strange that when one man has publicly committed an assault he is usually captured at once by a single constable; but that the chances of punishing offenders appear to decrease in due proportion to the number of assailants and official protectors of the people. In dealing with crowds, of course, much tact and judgment are required on the part of the guardians of the peace—whom the public never sufficiently assist—and in time of riot some offences must be passed over for obvious reasons; but the police could not have suffered more than they did on Monday night if they had arrested twenty able-bodied brawlers instead of one young lad.

Rightly, Commissioner Madley is enquiring into this matter, and the investigation ought to be thorough; for radical alterations in the police system will be needed if on any occasion of especial excitement the city may be left at the mercy of a mob, and if transgressions may with impunity be committed under the eyes of the police. The apparent breakdown of the constabulary was among the most disquieting features of the unworthy proceedings on Monday night. The Government, as well as the Commissioner, will presumably seek to ascertain the reasons for it; but, in expressing judgment upon their conduct, full allowance should in justice be made for the peculiar embarrassments and other difficulties of the position of the police.

Thus far the matter has been treated from one standpoint; now what of the other? If the immediate creators of disturbance should be denounced, ought Mr. Dowie himself to escape from censure as he did from the mob? Certainly not.

Without suggesting that, with a due appreciation of the value of advertisement, he may studiously court disturbances as productive advertising media, one may at least express the opinion that many of his methods are distinctly, if not deliberately, provocative of passion in the crowd. They appeal to prejudice and are meant to appeal to it. Freedom of speech, like freedom of action, is properly conserved and protected by the law; but liberty of movement, while it permits a man to enjoy a reasonable swinging of his arms in the street, draws the line at allowing him to brandish those arms to the detriment of the noses and eyes of passers-by. As a logical necessity, should not some parallel be established in relation to the abuse of language with similar general consequences, with due regard to the alleged fact that—

"Sticks and stones may break my bones,
But names will never hurt me."

At this point certain curious reflections are suggested. If Mr. Dowie or any one else were, with exciting gesticulations, to address one man in the street or in a public hall as "You stinkpot"—whether because he smoked tobacco or because he ate onions or Limburger cheese—and if the aggrieved person were to knock down Mr. Dowie or anybody else so offending, what would be the public verdict upon the occurrence? Would not even the ministers of the law decree that aggressors must not be prostrated with astonishment, as well as by something more substantial, if the use of words likely to provoke a breach of the peace is followed by hostile demonstrations? Yet, according to certain recent dicta, if hundreds of men are publicly denounced in the way indicated, the provocation must be ignored, and the thing provoked be alone dealt with by legal instruments. In other words, a lash from the tongue is no assault, though it may mutilate and lacerate and madden infinitely worse than a blow from the hand; but the flexible member of the body cannot easily bring its owner into trouble, while the other can do so with the greatest readiness.

The question of indulgence in certain habits in themselves is not now being discussed here, though it conceivably has indirectly had something to do with the cause of the trouble. The smoking of the narcotic tobacco—which Spurgeon said he did to the glory of God, but which Mr. Dowie denounces—may not be as innocuous as the drinking of the stimulating beverages tea and coffee, against which some doctors rail, while many social reformers bless them. In partaking of the drinks and bitterly decrying the narcotic, with alcohol and pork, Mr. Dowie may—in spite of Mr. Spurgeon—be rendering God service; but, if mere contemplation of what one man deems to be baneful habits on the part of other people who have not attacked his habits arouses his own anger, he must not be surprised if by their conduct they—after he has without provocation aroused them—resent his utterances, and strive to reply with their most effective weapon, just as he struck at them with his. Neither can they be blamed so long as they observe the law.

The question of what the law really requires in justice and in common sense should, however, be clearly settled, and its administration ought to reflect the settlement. That is more to the purpose than the utterance of the hint that men who set themselves on pedestals as moral exemplars—if not as mental geniuses—are expected rather to err on the side of rigid asceticism and irreproachable consistency than to evoke comment by the suspicion of a lack of either. What might be thought, for instance, if a man who led a crusade against the eating of bread lodged with a baker; if an apostle of alcoholic indulgence insisted on boarding at coffee palaces only; if a preacher of simplicity in life, and an avowed incarnation of a forerunner who was usually half-starved and half-clad, fared sumptuously every day, surrounded himself with princely luxury, and was arrayed more gorgeously than even Solomon in all his glory, not to include a greater than Solomon, "Who had not where to lay his head?" Still—as the question has been raised, and as it may affect popular incitements and excitements—what would be said if such things were done? Possibly that a man doing them has a perfect right in a free country to please himself—just as tobacco smokers have!

Town Hall, Adelaide, South Australia, Wednesday Morning, March 23, 1904.

Hymn No. 9, from the Visitation Program, was sung, after which Overseer Jane Dowie read the first seventeen verses of the 8th chapter of Matthew, and the first thirteen verses of the 12th chapter of Hebrews.

After the singing of another hymn the General Overseer said:

Thanksgiving.

I think it right to give praise to God before we pray.

I thank God for the good meetings of yesterday, and for blessing vouchsafed in answer to prayer.

I am thankful that the tumult of the people is being calmed, and that the foolish things that have been said and done are being repented of.

I have never for a single moment imagined that the tumult in any of the Australian cities was the work of the majority; because my eyes have seen, and my ears have heard that it was the work of a small minority.

During the Mission in Sydney, there were probably from two to three hundred who burst in upon the meetings by breaking open the door.

In the City of Melbourne, it was more distinctly so. While there were seven or eight thousand persons in the Exhibition Building, among them a small, noisy element at the beginning, perhaps fifty, that were gradually being got under control, a side door was broken in, and about two or three hundred organized, well-dressed disturbers broke in. I called them a band of criminals, because it is a crime to trample underfoot that most precious heritage, won by your fathers—the right of free speech in a free land.

All liberty would disappear if that were continued, and of necessity a nation would be compelled to throw itself into the arms of a military dictator to preserve life, liberty and property.

It behooves you all, in the Australian states, to let these recent events cause you to think a little.

I pass on my way in a few days, and it is not certain that I shall ever return to Australia.

Australia is a very important island continent, but it is very insignificant in point of population.

Australia has not been growing.

There should have been by this time, apart from immigration, nearly twice as many people in this country as there are now.

I think that the degeneracy which is visible, ought to be faced, and its causes dealt with vigorously.

We have much to grieve over in the United States, but there is one thing that makes me very grateful that I am a citizen of that country, and that is the absolute determination in every state, and in every city, without any exception, so far as I am personally acquainted, to maintain good order.

Australian Lawlessness the Work of a Minority.

I have never, for one single moment, imagined that the disorder in any of the cities was the work of a majority

It was the work of an exceedingly small minority of people

There were three thousand persons in the Exhibition Building last Lord's Day morning, who sat all through the service very attentively

In the afternoon, four thousand were present, and there were less than two hundred young men, in whose legs the Lord had no pleasure, who exercised their feet.

They were a little afraid, at that time, to exercise their tongues.

You also know, I suppose, that the leading disturbers, on Monday night, got in by windows.

They sneaked in at various points, until they numbered perhaps about two hundred.

Those who did this were well-dressed, and presumably well-educated, share-brokers, students of the University, and sons of respectable citizens.

I have, without question, spoken to the largest congregations in the world for ten years, and I have never before heard Mrs. Dowie insulted, as she has been in these states.

Mrs. Dowie during the sixteen years of my ministry in these states took considerable part in it.

A crusade work among the women, of which she was the leader, went on in Melbourne for years and at last took her into the saloons every Saturday night.

She was not insulted once.

My people, three thousand of them, reported that they visited every house in New York, rich and poor, every merchant's place, every ship, and delivered four million two hundred thousand printed Messages, and millions of spoken words: "Peace be to this house."

They practically visited New York twice, and none were insulted as we have been here.

It is very painful to come back to these lands, and find such an absolute disregard for the commonest decency.

The Menace of Lawlessness.

You who are thoughtful and earnest ought to pray and think into it; to remember that you have to live with lawlessness, and that, one of these days, it will take other forms.

The *Register* says this morning that it is very wrong to do what has been done, but that there is a question as to whether I have not given great provocation.

The article in the *Register* begins well, and ends badly.

I should think that it was written by two persons, and should be inclined to appeal from Alexander drunk to Alexander sober in that case.

If the gentleman who wrote that article somewhat inclines to the Melbourne *Argus'* view of it, that it is proper to insult a man and assault him whose opinions they do not like, then it would be proper for the populace, if they do not like the opinions of the *Argus* or of the *Register*, to go into these offices, and drive out the editors, assault the reporters, and smash the printing presses.

If it is proper to insult and assault a speaker, it would be equally proper to insult or assault a writer.

The fact is, it is not proper at all.

The fact is, too, that these gentlemen could not point to a single thing that I said that was a personal insult to any one.

It may hit hard to be called a stinkpot; but if Martha had a right to say, "Lord, by this time he stinketh," because her brother had been dead four days, I should just like to know, whether I have not a right to say regarding a man who has been smoking, and stinking, and drinking, and doing everything but thinking for five, ten, twenty, thirty, and forty years, "Lord, by this time he stinketh!" [Laughter.]

Do you not think he does?

Voices—"Yes."

General Overseer—If he is of a different opinion, that is because his sense of smell has been perverted.

The sense of smell can be entirely perverted in a person or in an animal.

Take, for instance, a vulture.

A vulture's sense of smell is very keen; but if you were to take a vulture, which loves carrion, and put it in a flower garden, it would be sick, because the odor of roses and of sweet-smelling flowers makes a vulture sick.

The Stinking Victims of Nicotine Poison.

I have no doubt that a large number of these gentlemen who smoke do not have any sense of smell left, except that they love stinks

I do not say "he smelleth," I say, "he stinketh."

It is a good old English word, and a Scriptural one.

God Himself uses it.

He says, concerning those who are wicked, that they are a stench in His nostrils.

It seems to me, concerning the poor victims of nicotine poison, that "the smoke of their torment ascendeth forever and ever."

It seems to me that they are tormented until they get a pipe or cigar in their mouths, set it on fire, and begin puffing. Then they are happy!

Then the Devil has his wage.

The poor man is spending his money, his strength, and his health, puffing them away!

It is not I, only, who says so.

If you will ask an insurance actuary, he will tell you that if that man applied for his life to be insured he would be loaded up with eight years, because tobacco brings a tobacco heart It creates amaurosis, paralysis, dyspepsia, ulcerations of the stomach and bowels, and cancer.

No insurance company will issue a policy on a smoker's life without loading it up with about eight years, because tobacco cuts short a man's life by eight years.

The same thing is true of alcohol.

Let a man drink alcohol, and his life is cut short.

There are a few men who survive and live to an old age, who both smoke and drink, but they are the exceptions.

With a few exceptions they are generally not very useful members of society.

Wherein is the wickedness of calmly and kindly stating my convictions regarding these matters?

If a man thinks that he is not a stinkpot, let him be of that opinion; but if I think he is—speaking without personal offense of the class—I have a right to say it.

I Do Not Understand This Nonsense and Noise.

It is a very silly thing.

How silly their letters to the press appear!

I cannot help smiling at the folly of an editor who would publish a letter in which the writer suggests that there should be a city meeting held to consider whether I should not be directed to leave Adelaide.

Perhaps the editor merely wanted to expose the folly of the writer.

If such a thing were to be done, they would have to get up a rowdy meeting, keep out all respectable people, vote out every one who wanted to do right, and leave the city and the land in the hands of these disorderly fellows.

It would then be very much worse than it was at the beginning, when the land was in the hands of black fellows and harmless kangaroos.

The generation of men whom I saw, when I landed here in 1860, were fine.

Their sons were strong and law-abiding citizens.

I spoke in these countries for sixteen years as an ordained minister and never had an interruption.

But there has been a terrible degeneracy in the last sixteen years.

You will have to face it and examine into it.

In the United States, the state legislatures have had to pass laws in an effort to stop minors from smoking tobacco in the form of cigarets.

In many of the states, it is a punishable offense on the part of a tobacconist to sell cigarets to any one under seventeen years of age.

These laws have been passed by legislators who, perhaps, are themselves smokers, because the young men of America, in many cases, were found to be smoking themselves to death.

If you cannot bear plain speech from a man who is most certainly your friend and not your enemy, who has not come here seeking anything, you are in a bad plight.

I have not come for money.

I am paying the expenses of my Visitation with much pleasure, and would pay them with more pleasure still if the people were to be more blessed.

Evidences of a Masonic Conspiracy.

I said at an early part of this Visitation in these states, that there was a conspiracy, an organized opposition to my being heard.

I repeat what I said.

I have seen abundant evidence of it since I came to this city.

The working classes are not in this trouble.

It is the men, not merely young men, but men as old as forty and fifty years, prominent Freemasons in this city, who are the cause of these disturbances.

They can howl if they like, but it is true.

I do not know how it is in this country; but in the United States of America, every other secret order besides Freemasonry, is presided over by a Freemason. The Freemasons direct all the secret orders, and control the labor unions.

They reach to the humblest and meanest man.

I will say a word or two about why I fight the Masonic Order.

It is a lawless order.

Any body of men which assumes to administer oaths and

to impose penalties and execute these penalties, is a body of anarchists, unless the man administering the oath is a magistrate or judge, unless the penalty is one prescribed by law, and unless the execution of that penalty is entrusted to the proper legal officer.

Just think of what I say.

It is a very serious thing.

The Lawlessness of Secretism.

The Masons administer an oath; they impose a death penalty, and they have it executed.

In the case of Captain Morgan there was not the slightest question, and in other cases that have been sheeted home.

I do not care what the order is, any order that administers an oath and imposes a penalty, whether it executes it or not, is an anarchistic society.

I do not care what you call it, whether it is Ali Baba and the Forty Thieves, or the Mafia, or the Clan-na-Gael, or the Masons—any organization that assumes the right to administer oaths and impose penalties is an association contrary to the law.

If any lawyer will stand up and argue that it is not, I should like to hear the argument.

I am very careful in my statements, and I know a little of law.

Because I do not know as much as I should like, I have a very good Law Department.

I never utter a legal proposition until I have examined it, and have had Zion Law Department examine it.

The statement regarding the lawlessness of secretism was affirmed by my General Counsel, Judge V. V. Barnes, than whom there is no abler judge in the United States, in my opinion.

He was a Probate Judge before he came to Zion, and he is now Judge of a Court of high jurisdiction; for he has been elected by his fellow citizens as Judge of the City Court of Zion City.

That Court has equal jurisdiction with the Circuit and Superior Courts of the State of Illinois.

There is no business before that Court in Zion City, except of the most formal kind, there being no cases to come before it in connection with criminal jurisdiction at all, because we have no crime in Zion City.

I am open to reason.

If a man wishes to convince me of something to the contrary of what I teach, he will have to find better reasons than those I adduce.

I say these things kindly, quietly and temperately, because I have no other desire than to speak temperately, kindly, and quietly. Of course, what I say is said plainly.

I am not afraid to speak what I think is right.

I do not care to say much regarding the editorial in this morning's *Register*.

The editor of the *Register* had a perfect right to write it, and it was his privilege to say all the ugly things about me he could say, if he liked to say them in the editorial or in any other columns.

Prayer was offered by Overseer Excell.

After the announcements had been made, the tithes and offerings were received during the singing of Hymn No. 31. The General Overseer then delivered the afternoon discourse:

CASTING OUT DEVILS.

*REPORTED BY E. W. AND A. W. N.

INVOCATION.

Let the words of my mouth, and the meditation of my heart be acceptable in Thy sight, O Jehovah, my Strength and my Redeemer. Amen.

TEXT.

And when even was come, they brought unto Him many possessed with devils: and He cast out the spirits with a word, and healed all that were sick: That it might be fulfilled which was spoken by Isaiah the prophet, saying, Himself took our infirmities, and bare our diseases.

You will see that He cast out the spirits with *a* word.

It was not His word.

The Words Spoken and Works Wrought by the Christ Were the Words and Works of the Father.

He said, "The words that I say unto you I speak not from Myself: but the Father abiding in Me doeth His works."

*The following report has not been revised by the General Overseer.

All the healings were the work of the Father.

All that Jesus did was done by the Spirit of the Father through Him.

He had laid aside His own Power and Godhead, and had come down to this earth in great humility as a Man.

He is a Man still.

The Advocate with the Father is the Man, the Christ, Jesus.

When He comes back to earth, you will see a Man.

He will not be a stinkpot, and He will not be a beerpot and a defiler; but He will be a Glorified Man in a Glorified Body.

If I should pass away before He comes, I should come back a man, and a better one than I am now, with a better body; with the body of this humiliation changed and fashioned like unto His Glorious Body.

When the saints come back, we shall have a glorious time. I know I shall be with the Lord, because He will come back and reign, and it will take a Thousand Years to put things right.

Something About the Millennial Reign.

The Day of the Lord is a Thousand Years.

If you will read your Bibles, you will see that the biggest fight comes at the end of the Thousand Years.

Then comes the end, and the Universal Triumph of the Christ, after which the Kingdom will be delivered up to God the Father.

When He comes back there will be a great conflict, because the world will not have Him to reign over it, any more than it would have Him before.

He will reign in great power from Jerusalem, until He hath put all enemies under His feet.

I do not care what king, or what president, or what people oppose Him, that king, or president, or people will perish.

He will bring back with Him those who have been glorified.

They will come back in new bodies which stones will not hurt, and which cannot be killed again, if they were killed before.

You will see something very wonderful when the Lord comes back.

He will rule and reign.

He will not have any voting either.

He will appoint the people whom He thinks best, and He will not consult your opinions either.

God does not consult human opinions.

The Word that was spoken by the Christ, was the Word of the Father.

He came to do the Will of the Father, and not to speak His own words.

And they brought unto Him many that were possessed with devils.

I Wonder How Many Here Are Possessed with Devils.

"Oh, Doctor, Doctor! None of us are possessed with devils!"

Are you not?

What kind of temper have you?

Most women are good compared to men, but some of them have a devil of a temper. [Laughter.]

It is a devil, an ugly, mean devil.

They torment themselves, and sometimes their husbands; but for every woman that is bad-tempered, I think there are ten men.

Men are a bad lot.

I am sorry that I cannot speak better of my own sex.

I feel humiliated personally, when I think of how bad men are, and how bad I should have been, but for the grace of God.

It is a terrible thing to see how men abandon their wives, and their own flesh and blood to poverty, shame, and misery, to ignorance and crime, utterly regardless of consequences!

What a horrible thing is the dreadful vice of Impurity, which throws upon the streets of the cities illegitimate offspring until this country is groaning under its blight!

Ten per cent. of those born in Sydney are illegitimate.

The birth-rate of this City of Adelaide is lower than that of any other city in the states because of the vices of the people.

I am not bringing a railing accusation against you.

That is the report of the commission, which says that the men and women of Australia are deliberately murdering their unborn offspring—a horrible crime!

Such people are possessed with devils.

They are full of uncleanness and lust.

They have the Devil of Murder in them.

A lady brought a little boy to me one day.

He was a pretty little fellow, with light, curly hair, bright blue eyes and a healthy color.

She said, "He has a devil."

"What does he do?" I asked.

She burst into tears as she told me that he took delight in torturing animals, and that he had tried to strangle his baby brother or sister.

A Reason Why Children Are Possessed of Devils.

"What is the cause?" I asked her.

"Oh," she said, "I do not know."

"That is a lie," I said, "a mean lie. You do know. It is not the child's fault."

"Oh," she said, "I am a Christian! I pray, and I do this, and that, and the other thing."

"I did not say that you do not pray, but your prayers will not be answered."

"Why?"

"Because," I answered, "you do not confess your sin. You cannot exercise faith unless you have repented."

"What shall I do?" she asked.

I said, "Tell the truth. You are a liar."

"What! Doctor!"

"You are a liar; I know it."

"How do you know it?"

"You cannot fool me about it. Did you not try to murder that child before he was born?"

She fell back fainting.

I let her faint, and waited until she regained consciousness.

"Doctor," she cried, "how did you find it out?"

"Find it out!" I said; "I have seen this hundreds of times."

"Oh! not only that," she confessed, "but I murdered three unborn children, and I tried to murder him and I did not succeed."

"Do you not see," I said, "that the devil that was in your heart got into him before he was born? He was a murderer in the womb, and he has been a murderer since."

She cried.

She said, "Yes, it is true."

How People Get Criminal Instincts.

Do you know how people become criminals?

They become criminals before they are born. They have the criminal and murderous instinct in them.

When a woman hates her own offspring, and wants to murder the unborn, the Devil gets into the child.

I know what I am talking about.

I have examined a large number of cases, and visited the jails, and I never found a case of a murderer who had committed many murders but that he was the offspring of a woman who wanted to murder him before he was born.

That is my experience and my experience goes for something.

It has been a very long one, and one of very close observation.

I said to that woman: "Get your husband. He is guilty, too."

"Yes," she said.

He came. He was a very fine man occupying a public position.

I said, "You murderer! You nearly murdered your wife, as well as your children. Get down upon your face before God, and confess your blood-guiltiness!"

A Plain-spoken Rebuke and Call to Repentance.

Every man or woman who hates the unborn child, and wants to murder him before he is born, is a murderer!

God dealt with those in the olden time on the ground that they were murderers.

You cannot do that with impunity.

You have no right to say that you will not be a mother if you are a wife.

You undertake the obligation when you become a wife.

You were told that marriage was ordained for the mutual care that the one should have of the other, and for the continuance and increase of the human race; that children should be brought up in the nurture and admonition of the Lord, to His praise.

If you do not want to undertake that obligation, do not marry.

If you do marry you ought to be joyful mothers of children.

If husbands and wives prevent conception they are murderers.

God dealt with Onan, who prevented conception.

God was angry with him and permitted him to be slain.

You do not know your Bible if you do not know that.

You had better read it.

It is a horrible story; but it is the story of how God punished, with death, a man who would not be a father.

The same law applies to a woman who will not be a mother, and this is a thing that must be dealt with.

If I were to be shot in the streets tonight I would say this.

This thing is a crime before high heaven, and it is the destruction of the State.

The population of this country is decreasing.

If it were not for the little immigration, it would decrease more rapidly.

Moreover, you are terribly afraid of immigration.

The Ridiculous Nonsense of Your "White Australia" Movement!

You say that you cannot have black men here, because the white men would not get on.

Bosh!

We have eight million black people in the United States, and we get on all right.

We are not afraid of the eight million blacks.

We love them and they do excellent work.

I do not say that the white man is not superior to the black. He is.

But there was a time when the black was superior to the white.

The valley of the Nile will show you that before the black man was oppressed and neglected in many ways, he had a magnificent civilization.

But Ethiopia has not been stretching out her hands to God in vain.

You say that you will not have any but white men in this country, and the whiter they are the better.

Let me tell you what God said about that.

God's Judgment Against Race Hatred.

Moses married a Cushite woman.

She was a black woman, and Miriam, his sister, turned up her nose.

She said that Moses ought not to have done it.

There are many sisters who try to rule their brothers in that way.

Aaron, Moses' brother, was against him, too; but God was angry with them.

He came down to the tent of the congregation and reproved Miriam and Aaron.

He defended Moses, who had a right to marry a black woman.

When Miriam came out of that tent—well, she was very white.

She belonged to the Lily-white Party.

She was a leper, as white as snow.

She would have died in her leprosy if Moses had not prayed, and God had not healed her.

You people who think you are superior persons because of the color of your skin, talk nonsene.

The Jewish people have a mixture of African blood.

The tribes of Ephraim and Manasseh were the sons of Asenath, a black princess, the daughter of Potiphera, priest of On, of the black belt of Egypt.

You have a devil in you when you have this color line, and this color cry.

It is nothing but a devil, this black spot upon the heart that cries out: "I will not have anything to do with a yellow man or a black man."

You send missionaries to them, but you will not have them.

I am thankful to say that we have many friends, personal friends, of all colors.

We have seventy nationalities in Zion City, and if you do not want to sit down at the Lord's Table with a black man, a Chinaman or a Japanese, do not come to Zion City, because they sit down at the Lord's Table.

I ordain them as officers of the Christian Catholic Church in Zion.

I have the honor of knowing some princes of China who have spoken from the platform of Shiloh Tabernacle.

You say that they belong to another race.
That is nonsense!

There Is Only One Race—the Children of Adam and Eve.

Some families are blacker, and some are yellower, and some are browner, and some are whiter; but there is more good blood in a brown man than there is in a white man, as far as blood is concerned.
The virility and strength of an Ethiopian is, for the most part, greater than the strength of a European, because the blood is there.
The whiter you are the less strong you are, as a rule.
It is a good thing to have some color.
Although the Caucasian family is a strong one, we have nothing to be proud of.
We are becoming degenerate, and if you do not take care we will die out.
The Africans have increased in America from four millions to eight millions within the last half century, and if it had not been for immigration from Europe the Americans would have almost died out in many places.
Not everywhere, however, because, thank God, there are a great many splendid American people who have always been true to the motherhood and fatherhood instinct and to the directions of the Word of God.
There are very large families, especially in the country districts of the United States, some of them having as many as nineteen children.
God wanted Mrs. Dowie and me, I suppose, to do His work, so He did not give us many children.
I am very fond of children.

The Consecration of Children.

Sometimes, when I consecrate babies, I consecrate two hundred at one service.
Zion City is a great place for babies.
It is a beautiful sight to see these babies and their mothers and fathers.
I get them on the platform and lecture the parents upon their duties and privileges.
I bless the babies.
I do not sprinkle water on their noses.
I bless them in the Name of the Lord.
They will get baptized properly when they are old enough.
But to return to my text.
"He cast out the spirits with a Word."
May God cast out these horrible lustful devils from all who have any of them!
May God cast out this Onan devil!
The father who tries to escape the consequences of fatherhood, and the woman who submits to it, has sinned.
I tell every woman throughout this country that if her husband will not fulfil his God-given office, she has a right to live away from him, and to no longer be the tool of his filthy lust.
I say it plainly, as far as my voice can reach, and the printed page can carry it.
Devils! Lustful Devils! Shameful Devils!
That will stir up some of them.
But that is the proper name for it.
I like to see my dear people in Zion present their clean, sweet babies, in which there is neither alcohol, nor tobacco, nor pig.
Let us go on to the next part of that verse.

And when even was come, they brought unto Him many possessed with devils: and He cast out the spirit with a word, and healed all that were sick: That it might be fulfilled which was spoken by Isaiah the prophet, saying, Himself took our infirmities, and bare our diseases.

Do you believe it?
Voices—"Yes."

Divine Healing a Part of the Atonement.

General Overseer—Then the Christ died for our sins, and for our sicknesses, and with His stripes we are healed.
Then what do you want with a doctor?
"Thou, O Christ, art all I want," you Methodists sing, but do you live it?
You do not, many of you.
You sing, "Thou, O Christ, art all I want," then say, "I have a pain; please send for a doctor."

Thou, O Christ, art all I want,
More than all in Thee I find;
Raise the fallen, cheer the faint,
Heal the sick, and lead the blind.

That is good Methodist theology.
It was John Wesley's theology.
The very first hymn in your Hymnal, "Oh for a Thousand Tongues to Sing," ends with the words:

Hear Him, ye deaf, His praise ye dumb,
Your loosened tongues employ;
Ye blind, behold your Savior come,
And leap, ye lame, for joy.

That is Divine Healing, is it not?
Audience—"Yes."
General Overseer—You Presbyterians, why are you kicking at Divine Healing?
Have you not another hymn in which are these words:

All thy iniquities, who doth
Most graciously forgive,
Who thy diseases all and pains
Doth heal, and thee relieve.

It is not "used to heal," but it is "doth heal."
Why are you kicking at Divine Healing?
Have you not another paraphrase that says:

As when the Hebrew prophet raised,
The brazen serpent high,
The wounded looked, and straight were healed,
The people ceased to die.
So from the Savior on the cross
A Healing virtue flows.

What are you kicking at? Why do you not live as you sing?
And you Congregationalists, do you not sing:

At even ere the sun was set,
The sick, O Lord, around Thee lay,
Oh, in what divers pains they met,
Oh, with what joy they went away.

Once more 'tis eventide, and we,
Oppressed with various ills, draw near;
What if Thy form we cannot see?
We know and feel that Thou art here.

Oh, Savior Christ, our wos dispel;
For some are sick, and some are sad,
And some have never loved thee well,
And some have lost the love they had.

And does it not end with the words:

Thy touch has still its ancient power;
No word from Thee can fruitless fall:
Here, in this solemn evening hour,
And in Thy mercy heal us all.

If you do not believe that He is the Healer, why do you sing that hymn, you hypocrites?
Be honest and say that you will not sing it; that you do not believe it; and do not read the Bible, which says, "I am Jehovah that healeth thee."
You had better alter it, and say that He used to be, but that He is not now.
If you do that, you will have to get a new Bible, edited, perhaps, by the editor of the *Register* and by the doctors. [Laughter.]

The Plain, Strong Speaking of the Christ.

As to plain speaking, I tell the editor of the *Register* that I am not nearly so blunt as Jesus, the Christ.
He said, "Ye serpents, ye offspring of vipers, how shall ye escape the judgment of hell?"
When He talked to them of their uncleanness, He said, "Ye are like unto whited sepulchers, which outwardly appear beautiful, but inwardly are full of dead men's bones and of all uncleanness."
Did I ever say anything harder? I can give you much more of that, if you want it.
It is all in the Bible.
He spoke plainly, and that is why they killed Him.
It was not that He did not tell them the truth, but because He told them the truth.
That is why John the Baptist lost his head.
It is a very serious thing to prevent your ministers from speaking plainly.
If they are afraid of you, the Lord have mercy upon you.

When your teachers are afraid; when they are dumb dogs (D. D's.) that do not bark nor do anything else, what is the use in feeding them?

I would not keep a dog that did not bark.

I would not keep a dog that would not bite if any one came along to do mischief.

What is the use in keeping a dumb dog?

It might do very well for a lady's lap as a poodle dog, but it is good for nothing else.

It might do very well for an afternoon tea.

Where is the fight in you?

Why do you not get up some fight?

"Oh, we have very nice, quiet churches!" you may say.

Yes, so has West Terrace Cemetery.

Is the Church to be quiet?

Is not the Church the fighting force of the Kingdom of God?

If it does not fight, who is going to fight?

If you do not fight the good fight of faith, who is going to fight it?

If you do not protest against sin, who is going to protest?

If you make war upon sin with lavender water or eau de cologne what good will that do?

The Way to Kill a Snake.

"Oh, but Doctor, you do not need to use such strong language," they say.

When I am hitting a snake, I do not consider what kind of stick I shall use. If it is a crooked stick, I do not mind.

The harder the stick the better I like it.

I have done some riding in this country when I was younger.

My horse would, at times, leap into the air, and nearly throw me off because there was an adder in the way.

Then I would tie my horse to the nearest fence and go after that adder.

I would smash its head, and then hang the snake up on the fence.

Then I would say, "Well done, John Alexander Dowie. That alone is a good morning's work, because the children coming along from school might have been bitten by it."

I paid my servant boy a shilling a head for snakes until he brought so many that I had to reduce it to sixpence.

Then he brought so many I had to reduce it to three pence.

I used to say, "Johnnie, how far did you go after these snakes?"

He was hunting the whole country over.

One day he came across one that was too big for him.

When we went down to kill that snake, we did not stand on ceremony.

When you are going to kill a thing that is going to kill the people, do not stand upon ceremony.

When I am fighting with the World, the Flesh, and the Devil, why do not some of you rise up and say, "Hallelujah! Amen! Back him up!"

Why do not some of you ministers do it?

You are afraid.

If you are to be healed you will have to fight sin.

You will have to get sin out of your heart.

Then God will hear your cry for healing, if you will give up doctors and drugs.

Doctors and Drugs Prevent God from Healing.

But you cannot have two physicians at one time—the Great Physician and an allopath or homeopath.

If you will trust Jesus, the Christ, as your Healer, leave the doctor alone.

If you do not, God will not hear you.

He will not undertake your healing in connection with doctors and drugs. He never promised that.

On the contrary, you cannot find one word in the Scripture that commends drugs.

"In vain shall ye use many medicines," God says.

The woman that touched the hem of the Christ's garment had suffered many things of many physicians, and had spent all that she had and was nothing bettered but rather grew worse.

That is the way with most of you.

You had better give them up, before they give you up.

They will never give you up while you have a dollar left.

They will never give you up while there is a chance of getting something out of you.

The doctor will be candid if you are poor.

He will say, "My dear madam, there is no use in my coming. It is only wasting money."

He knows that you have none.

Not that there are not some doctors who are kind, and will keep on treating people, even when they can expect no pay. There are many men who do their best, and are very kind-hearted.

But doctors do not have much faith in medicine.

The older they get the less faith they have in drugs.

One old physician said to me, "When I was a young doctor I had a hundred remedies for every disease. Now I am an old doctor, I have a hundred diseases without any remedy."

He was wise.

He was candid.

Let us trust God.

All who will do so stand. [Nearly all rose.]

PRAYER OF CONSECRATION.

My God and Father, in Jesus' Name I come to Thee. Take me as I am. Make me what I ought to be in spirit, in soul, in body. Give me power to do right, no matter what it costs. Give me Thy Holy Spirit that I may trust Thee fully for spirit, soul, and body. Amen. [*All repeat the prayer, clause by clause, after the General Overseer.*]

The people were then dismissed by the General Overseer's pronouncing the

BENEDICTION.

Beloved, abstain from all appearance of evil. And may the very God of Peace Himself sanctify you wholly; and I pray God your whole spirit and soul and body be preserved entire, without blame, unto the coming of our Lord Jesus, the Christ. Faithful is He that calleth you, who also will do it. The grace of our Lord Jesus, the Christ, the love of God, our Father, the fellowship of the Holy Spirit, our Comforter and Guide, one Eternal God abide in you, bless you and keep you, and all the Israel of God everywhere, forever. Amen.

Wednesday Afternoon Meeting.

Town Hall, Adelaide, South Australia, Wednesday Afternoon, March 23, 1904.

The meeting was opened with the singing of Hymn No. 11, in the Visitation Program, "Hail to the Brightness of Zion's Glad Morning."

Overseer Jane Dowie read from the 12th chapter of the Epistle to the Hebrews, the first thirteen verses.

After the singing of another hymn, the Rev. C. Friend Hawkins made the announcements.

Before the offerings were received the General Overseer said:

We are not here for money, or we would have made a charge for admission.

But I have never made a charge at any time in all my ministry.

Some of my friends, however, have asked for the privilege of being able to do something towards the expense of renting this hall and the Exhibition Building.

Paying for Damage Done by Well-dressed Criminals.

I have already paid the expenses of this Mission.

I have also had to pay today for the damages done by a band of lawless criminals.

They may call themselves what they please, but they are a band of criminals. They were not the low and poor of the city.

We had them at short range, and could see them well on Monday night.

They broke into this hall from the neighboring hotel and smashed the doors, and I am asked to pay for them.

They came in through windows and sneaked in without tickets, under the protection of aldermen and councilors of this city.

There was no mean way to get in which they did not try. They acted like devils when they got in.

I never before in all my life saw a more degraded and degenerate set of ruffians than the well-dressed men, apparently well-educated too, to the number of about two hundred, who disgraced this beautiful little city of Adelaide last Monday night.

I hope that some of them will yet see that they owe a public apology, not merely to me but to their fellow citizens, for their outrageous conduct.

I have refused personally to proceed against any of them.

I leave the police to do their duty.

They saw the outrages and they know the persons who committed them.

It is the duty of a public officer who sees a crime or a misdemeanor committed, to prosecute the misdemeanant, and not compel a private citizen to do it. [Amen.]

I therefore leave to the police the responsibility of doing their duty.

Let There Be One Law For All Offenders, Whether Rich or Poor.

It is a sham, a delusion and a snare for an officer to arrest a boy because he tossed a little bit of apple that struck me on the shoulder, and let a lawless stock-broker go free.

I did not give that boy into charge.

I would not have done it.

It is a farce to fine a poor boy who is a larrikin of the street, and to allow well-dressed ruffians, whom the police know well, to go unwhipped by justice. [Applause. Cries of "Hear, hear!"]

I have no desire to dictate to any one, but the government of this city and the gentleman responsible for the police department, the chief Secretary of State, ought to see that there is not one law for the poor boys who tossed a bit of apple at me, and who broke a window in a street car, and another for well-known stockbrokers and rich men's sons, who outrage all law and order. [Applause.]

I do not care if they are the friends of the government.

All the more ought these young men to be taught a lesson.

They are not fit to exercise the franchise and to rule this nation when they do not rule themselves.

I have no desire to interfere with police duty, but I make this observation because I think it wrong that two poor boys who belong to the lower classes should be punished and be in prison today as they are, and these wealthy young ruffians go free and unpunished.

Their names are known.

They could have been arrested the next morning, and they ought to be arrested.

I have no desire to punish them, and I should be very glad to forgive them, as far as I am personally concerned, upon an apology from them, yet I think there is a public duty that must be performed in this matter.

I think that this whole audience is of the same opinion.

All who are of that opinion say, Aye.

Voices—"Aye, aye."

General Overseer—I will not ask the Noes, because there ought not to be a No in this place.

If there were, it would be to the disgrace of the person who said it.

The outrages in the Australian cities have not been due to the poorer people.

The fight against Zion, since I entered Australia, has been made by well-dressed men, principally belonging to the Masonic body.

I have no malice against any one, but it is true that the leaders of the mob on Monday night were prominent Masons in this city, and of other secret societies directed by the Masonic Order.

They do not need to think they can frighten me, for I do not know what fear is.

I am ready to pass from this earth whenever God is ready to take me.

But I am not ready to hold my peace when I should speak. [Applause.]

With John Knox I say, "I am in the place where I am demanded of conscience and of God to speak the truth, and speak it I will, impugn it who so list."

After the tithes and offerings were received the General Overseer delivered his Message:

WHOM THE LORD LOVETH HE CHASTENETH.

*REPORTED BY I. M. S. AND A. W. N.

INVOCATION.

Let the words of my mouth, and the meditation of my heart be acceptable in Thy sight, be profitable unto this people, and unto all to whom these words shall come, in this and every land, in this and all the coming time, Till Jesus Come.

In the 12th chapter of the Epistle to the Hebrews, Mrs. Dowie read to you the passage of the Word of God concerning which I shall speak.

*The following report has not been revised by the General Overseer.

I shall repeat to you the special portion which I shall talk about as being misunderstood.

It is in the 6th verse:

TEXT.

For whom the Lord loveth He chasteneth and scourgeth every son whom He receiveth.

An Alleged Objection to Divine Healing.

Among the alleged objections to Divine Healing is one commonly put forward, namely, that disease is a means of Divine chastening; that when God wants especially to bless His children He chastens them with sickness, and scourges them with disease, and that this sickness and disease have a beneficent power to make them better.

So, when a minister comes to pray over the sick, he says, "I beseech you to receive from the chastening hand of God this sickness, which He has sent for your good, and to let it work for your good and to His glory."

That is, as nearly as I can express it in a few words, the commonly accepted mode of putting it.

The words are stronger in the Church of England Prayer-book. That goes to this length:

Dearly beloved, know this, that Almighty God is the Lord of life and death, and of all things to them pertaining, as youth, strength, health, age, weakness, and sickness. Wherefore, whatsoever your sickness is, know you certainly, that it is God's visitation. And for what cause soever this sickness is sent unto you; whether it be to try your patience for the example of others, and that your faith may be found in the day of the Lord laudable, glorious, and honorable, to the increase of glory and endless felicity; or else it be sent unto you to correct and amend in you whatsoever doth offend the eyes of your heavenly Father; know you certainly, that if you truly repent you of your sins, and bear your sickness patiently, trusting in God's mercy, for His dear Son Jesus Christ's sake, and render under Him humble thanks for His fatherly visitation, submitting yourself wholly unto His will, it shall turn to your profit, and help you forward in the right way that leadeth unto everlasting life.

It is thus positively stated, in the Church of England Prayer-book, that disease and death are from God.

I deny that.

I declare to you, in the Name of the Most High God, that it is an infernal and shameful lie to make our God responsible for the Devil's work!

Disease the Work of the Devil.

Open your Bibles and read, with me, a passage which covers all of the Christ's earthly ministry.

You will find it in the 10th chapter of the Acts of the Apostles, and in the 38th verse:

Even Jesus of Nazareth, how that God anointed Him with the Holy Spirit and with power: who went about doing good, and healing all that were oppressed of the Devil; for God was with Him.

It is a settled fact that Jesus healed every sickness and every disease among the people, and that nineteen centuries ago every sickness and every disease was the Devil's work.

The Apostle John declared in his first epistle, the 3d chapter and the 8th verse:

To this end was the Son of God manifested, that He might destroy the works of the Devil.

Did He come to destroy God's works?

Voices—"No."

General Overseer—If diseases were the work of God, would it not be the destruction of God's work to destroy disease?

Voices—"Yes."

General Overseer—I make the assertion, that is incapable of contradiction, that the Word of God nowhere says that disease is the Father's work.

The Two Chains; Good and Evil.

The Word of God distinctly makes Two Chains, the Chain of Good, and the Chain of Evil.

The Evil Chain is Satan, Sin, Disease, Death, and Hell; and the Good Chain is, Jesus, Salvation, Healing, Life, Heaven.

What connection is there between Jesus and the Devil; is there any?

Voices—"No."

General Overseer—What connection is there between Salvation and Sin?

Voices—"None."

General Overseer—What connection is there between Health and Disease; is there any?

Voices—"No, sir."

General Overseer—What connection is there between Life and Death? Is there any?

Voices—"No, sir."

General Overseer—What connection is there between Heaven and Hell? Is there any?

Voices—"No."

General Overseer—You cannot take one of the links in the Chain of Evil and put it into the Chain of Good.

You cannot take the Devil and make him God's executive officer.

Yet that is what men everywhere are trying to do.

Some Absurdities in Present-day Theology.

They say that God uses the Devil; and that disease comes from God through him.

Must not the Kingdom of God be in a very poor way when, in order to administer His Kingdom, God must use His worst enemy?

Is that sensible?

Is there any logic in that?

Look at the difficulty that God's children are put into if they are to believe that disease is sometimes the work of God for their good, and that at other times it is from the Devil.

We would get ourselves into a great puzzle.

We would have to say to God Almighty, "O God just tell us, or make the Devil tell us, whether he came on Your authority or on his own."

Would the Devil tell you the truth?

Voices—"No."

General Overseer—Is there any truth in the Devil?

Voices—"No."

General Overseer—Besides, look at the ridiculousness of our being left to such an investigation as that; that we should have to ask, "O Devil, have you come upon your own business or upon God's business?"

A young lady once said to me, "Doctor, I have come to ask you to pray for my dear mother, but I should not have come had she not sent me to you."

"Why?" I asked.

"Because I do not believe in what you have just been teaching," she replied, "that disease is the Devil's work. My mother is such a good woman, and is so saintly and so holy, that I cannot believe that it is the Devil that has made her sick.

"It is God who gave her that cancer. My dear mother reads Francis Ridley Havergal, and listens to the ministers. They all tell her that it is God who, in His Great Love, has laid His afflicting hand upon her.

"She has been so comforted, as she has sung, 'It is Thy hand, my Lord, my sickness comes from Thee,' and 'I take this pain, Lord Jesus, from Thine own hand.'

"O Doctor, do not go and see mother."

"Why?" I asked.

"Because," she said, "you will tell her that it is the Devil and will upset all her faith. Then she will be in a terrible condition." [Laughter.]

"She knows my teaching, does she not?" I asked.

"Yes, but do not go, Doctor."

I said, "I will go.

"I intend to tell her just how she got that cancer, for I know all about it."

Confusion Caused by False Teaching.

I said to her, "Down there, not far away from you, lives a woman who has been a drunkard and a very naughty woman.

"She has a cancer in her breast.

"She is very poor, and you are a good little girl and take nice things for her to eat. You pray with her and help her."

"Yes," she said.

"Now, tell me, Betty, if God sent the cancer to your mother, did He not send that cancer to the poor woman whom you are trying to help?"

"Oh, no," she said, "it was the Devil who did that."

"How did she get it?" I asked.

"She was in a fight and some one struck her in the breast, and then the cancer grew."

"Well," I said, "tell your mother that I will come down and see her."

I found her mother, a dear, sweet-faced, motherly woman, suffering great pain.

She told me very kindly to come in.

I pronounced the blessing, which I always do when I go to a bed which may be a bed of death:

Jehovah bless thee and keep thee,
Jehovah make His face to shine upon thee, and be gracious unto thee:
Jehovah lift up His countenance upon thee, and give thee peace.

She said, "That was so beautiful. I want peace; I am in such misery."

"That is not how a child of God should be," I said.

"Now listen, mother, you have been saying for years that this cancer came from God."

"Yes."

"You have been telling your daughter that?"

"Yes."

"Now," I said, "are you willing that I should tell you the naked truth?"

She looked at me for a moment, and her lips twitched.

Poor woman she was in great pain, and was in greater pain of mind than of body.

She wondered how much I knew.

She said, "Be tender with me, Doctor."

"I will," I said. "Will you tell me the truth?"

"Yes."

Horrible Story of Masonic Devilry.

"Go back sixteen years to the time when your husband, who was a Freemason, took a high degree one night, the Royal Arch degree.

"He did not come home until three o'clock in the morning, and you were beginning to be troubled about him.

"When he came in, you said, 'O John, I have been in such a terrible state of mind about you, fearing that you may have been hurt,' and you put your arms around his neck.

"What did he do?

"He was mad with drink, and looked at you like a demon.

"He grasped you by the throat and struck you blow after blow, on your face, neck, and breast; then flung you insensible to the floor.

"Then he stumbled into his own bed.

"When he awoke in the morning, he said, 'What a horrible dream I have had! I thought that I struck my wife whom I love so much.'

"He made his way into your room and saw you lying there with your head all bandaged, pale as death.

"He said, 'Betty, do not tell me that I did that!'

"'No,' you said, 'it was the Devil did it.'

"Now, is that story true?" I asked her.

"Yes," she said, "but I do not know how you know that."

"You forgave him," I continued, "and he died a Christian, five years ago."

"Yes," she answered.

"After a few years," I told her, "you began to feel this lump. It was just where he struck you."

"Yes," she assented. "I concealed it from him for years because I did not want him to think that he had been the cause of it."

"But," I said, "he knew about it before he died."

"How do you know?"

"Because he told me," I said.

"He told me how he was broken-hearted over it.

"He wanted you to come and hear me, and you would not do it then?"

Again she said "Yes."

"Now, from whom did that cancer come? Was it from God or from the Devil?

"Was it God who made your husband a Royal Arch Mason that night, and made him come home from that banquet drunk, so that he did not know what he was doing?

"Was it God who made him strike you, for whom he would have died?

"Was it God or the Devil?"

"Oh," she sobbed, "it was the Devil!"

"Then, you have been lying all the time.

"You have been telling your daughter and your friends a lie.

"You have been lying about God Almighty Himself in saying that God did it."

"I confess," she said. "I will tell my daughter."

I called the daughter into the room, and the mother told me to tell her the story.

I told it to her in a few words.

She said, "Then, mother, the Doctor is right. It is the Devil's work, and only the Christ can heal you.

"Mother, I am glad that you confessed it; I am glad that the Doctor is right, for in my heart I have always hated the thought that that cancer in the breast that nursed me when I was a child came from the hand of God.

"I hated the thought, but I fought the Doctor over it yesterday, because I believed you, mother."

You may not always be able to trace it, but disease is the Devil's work.

There would have been no disease in this world if there had been no sin, and there would have been no death but for disease.

"He that hath the power of death," is he that is the cause of sin and disease—the Devil.

The Christ of God came into this world to destroy the works of the Devil—Sin and Disease and Death and Hell.

He has not changed.

He is the same Christ.

Chastening Is Instructing, Training, Educating, Not Making Sick.

"But, Doctor, do you not think that the passage, 'Whom the Lord loveth He chasteneth,' means that whom the Lord loveth He maketh sick?" asks some one.

No. I do not. Let me tell you what that passage means.

The word chastening is a very simple Greek word.

There are some of you here who understand the original tongue in which the Scriptures were written, but even those of you who do not, can understand the very simple language that I shall use.

There is a little word in Greek, *pais* (παῖς) that means a child.

Paidos (παιδός) is the genitive form.

Paideia (παιδεία) means the instruction, education, and training of children.

Those of you who are scholars will remember the *Cyropaideia*, that was the training, educating and instructing of Cyrus.

The word *paideia* goes into our word Encyclopedia which means the circle of instruction.

In the expression "Whom the Lord loveth He chasteneth," the word chasteneth is translated from a part of the verb *paideuo* (παιδεύω) which means to instruct, to educate, to teach, to bring up, to train.

Whom the Lord loves He instructs and trains, and educates as a wise and good father educates and trains a son or daughter from the beginning.

A father teaches his children good habits; teaches them how to keep clean and how to exercise themselves; teaches them good things, and gives them a good education.

He trains their minds, their eyes, their hands, and trains them in many lines, especially those in which they have genius—music, painting, manufacturing, engineering or whatever it may be.

How does a wise and loving father train his child?

How does a wise schoolmaster train a child?

The Objection Reduced to an Absurdity.

When you send your children to school, do you say, "Now, Mr. President, I want you to take good care that my son and my daughter are properly trained, and that every quarter they get a fresh disease.

"Break their noses or give them black eyes.

"I hope you keep measles and other diseases on hand, because it is necessary to educate them by making them sick."

Would you send your children to a school where the president kept on hand a proper proportion of diseases, so all the children could get a fresh disease every quarter?

You would say, "That is absurd!"

Is God, then, more absurd than we?

Does He educate us and train us by defiling us?

Is it a part of God's plan to make your eyes dim and your ears deaf, or to make you lame or sick in some way? Is that God's plan of educating?

Or is our God like a father or mother who wants to keep the child well; who sees that it is well-fed and well-clothed and well-trained, and wants the youths and maidens to grow up with all their faculties alert and fully developed?

Is not that what you would expect of God?

Voices—"Yes."

General Overseer—What nonsense it is to interpret, "Whom the Lord loveth He chasteneth," to mean, "Whom the Lord loveth He maketh sick."

Yet that is the way it has been interpreted by the great majority of parsons and other Christians.

If People Really Believed That "Whom the Lord Loveth He Maketh Sick."

For a minute, suppose that that is the proper interpretation.

Pardon me if I make you laugh over it, and do not hold me responsible for it.

I desire to be very grave and earnest.

Let us believe, now, that there is a church near, where the minister believes that "Whom the Lord loveth He chasteneth," means, "Whom the Lord loveth He maketh sick."

We will go to find that church.

We can easily find it; for all the sick people are going to it.

When they get in, they all say, "How the Lord loves me today! Oh, how sick I am!"

One says, "How the Lord loves me in my feet! He has made me so lame!" and he comes along like this. [Illustrates Laughter.]

Another says; "The Lord loves me so much today that I have a bad eye; I'm almost blind." [Laughter.]

Then another is loved so much that she comes along all crippled up with rheumatism. [Illustrates. Laughter.]

Another has a boil here and a boil there, and can hardly sit down. [Laughter.]

They all come into the church and go into the pews.

They are all saying, as they come in, "Whom the Lord loveth He maketh sick."

The dear old elder at the door cannot show them to a seat, because the Lord loves him in his feet, and he cannot walk. [Laughter.]

There is another usher with a cramp in his toe, and he is disabled, too.

They all have to go in and sit down the best way they can.

The organist has had his fingers loved by the Lord and he cannot play at all.

The choir comes in, but they all have colds and cannot sing. [Laughter.]

Last of all the minister comes in.

He is the sickest of the lot, for the Lord loves him the most.

He creeps up the stairs like this. [Illustrates. Laughter.]

He is thin and pale and as he goes to his pulpit he says, "Whom the Lord loveth, He chasteneth; whom the Lord loveth He maketh sick, Oh, *Oh*, OH! Let us sing the Doxology"

They all try to sing, the best they can, "Praise God from whom all sickness flows." [Laughter, applause.]

That is the deduction, however absurd it may appear.

If a Thing Is True, You Cannot Make It Absurd.

If I am true you cannot make me absurd.

That is a thing that people have tried to do but they cannot do it.

After the cartoonists and the libelers have done their worst I stand the same.

I am quite well aware of the fact that I am not particularly beautiful.

I have great fun with the cartoonist.

But when they get through they have not made me absurd, because I am logical and reasonable,

The Contrast.

Now, I will put the other side.

Here is a congregation that believes that "Whom the Lord loveth He chasteneth," means "whom the Lord loveth He instructeth and traineth and saveth and healeth and bringeth up strong and well."

When you see that congregation coming in, you notice that they have some snap in their eyes and in their feet.

When the choir gets into its place, the singers sing like larks.

Zion has a Choir of seven hundred fifty voices.

This whole congregation is not so large as Zion White-robed Choir

Zion Choir and Officers would more than fill the Adelaide Town Hall.

We often put more than a thousand in line, and we sing the Processionals in beautiful order from the smallest child to the tallest youth or maiden.

Many a time in Shiloh Tabernacle in Zion City, which seats seven thousand three hundred, the Choir has come in singing the beautiful Processional:

Ten thousand times ten thousand
In sparkling raiment bright,
The armies of the ransomed saints
Throng up the steeps of light:
'Tis finished! all is finished,
Their fight with death and sin:
Fling open wide the golden gates,
And let the victors in.

We do not say that "Whom the Lord loveth He chasteneth," means "Whom the Lord loveth He maketh sick."

We teach, that whom the Lord loveth He maketh well and strong.

If we and our fathers have sinned and we have diseases, we go to God and ask Him to forgive the sin and heal the sickness.

We do not blame God for the disease which never came from His hands.

Our children may suffer, and we may suffer, but we never forget that the suffering is due to primitive sin; due, perhaps, to disease contracted through filthy living, that has passed down from generation to generation.

You cannot eat swine's flesh and smoke tobacco without getting disease.

You must eat what is good and drink what is good and set aside doctors and drugs, trusting in God alone, who is able and willing to heal.

He said, "I am Jehovah that healeth thee."

"I am Jehovah, I change not."

"Jesus, the Christ, is the same yesterday and today, yea, and forever."

He is the Healer still.

It is true that God has never forsaken His children.

He who said, "I am Jehovah that healeth thee," also said, "Lo, I am with you All the Days, even unto the Consummation of the Age."

He is with us now and here, and if you will do right He will heal you.

Many of God's Children Have Died Praising Him for the Devil's Work.

"Doctor," said a man to me the other day, "my dear mother died, and as she died she said, 'Jehovah gave and Jehovah hath taken away, blessed be the Name of Jehovah.'"

"Then," I said, "she talked the same nonsense that Job talked."

He was the first one to say that. He said that after the Devil had stripped him naked, killed all his cattle, and all his flocks, made all his sons and daughters drunkards, and had got his wife to say, "Curse God and die."

Poor Job was ignorant, so he said, "Jehovah gave"—that was true, "and Jehovah hath taken away"—that was a lie; for it was the Devil.

God Did Not Say Everything that is in the Bible.

I have been a very careful student of the Bible for a long time, and I know what I am talking about.

A man said, the other day, to a friend of mine, "You are sinning against God by saying that disease is not His work. The Word says, 'By the breath of God they perish, and by the blast of His anger are they consumed.'"

"Yes," said my friend, "but who says it?"

"Why, it is in the Book of Job," said the man, when he had found the passage.

"Yes," said my friend, "but it was Bildad the Shuhite who said it."

What became of him?

God was so angry with him and those two other friends of Job's that He said to them:

And it was so, that after Jehovah had spoken these words unto Job, Jehovah said to Eliphaz the Temanite, My wrath is kindled against thee, and against thy two friends: for ye have not spoken of Me the thing that is right, as My servant Job hath.

Now therefore, take unto you seven bullocks and seven rams, and go to My servant Job, and offer up for yourselves a burnt offering; and My servant Job shall pray for you; for him will I accept, that I deal not with you after your folly; for ye have not spoken of Me the thing that is right, as My servant Job hath.

These friends of Job's had talked about twenty-nine chapters of nonsense. They were reproved by God.

That is the way many people quote the Scripture.

They take a verse out of the Bible, no matter who said it, and declare that God said it.

Not long ago, in the United States, a distinguished lawyer rose and said, "The Word of God says, 'Skin for skin, yea, all that a man hath will he give for his life.'"

The opposing counsel replied, "If my most learned friend will consult the Bible he will find that it was the Devil who said that."

You have to be very careful in reading the Word of God, and very careful in disputing what one says who is certainly a teacher in connection with the Word of God.

I have taught you today what I want you clearly to understand, that no disease ever came from God; that Jesus, the Christ, is the same today; and that, if you will fulfil His conditions, you will find that the great and glorious Covenant of Divine Healing, which God gave thirty-four hundred years ago, at the Waters of Marah, will be found in your experiences.

And He said, If thou wilt diligently harken to the voice of Jehovah thy God, and wilt do that which is right in His eyes, and wilt give ear to His commandments, and keep all His statutes, I will [permit to be] put none of the diseases upon thee, which I have [permitted to be] put upon the Egyptians: for I am Jehovah that healeth thee.

He said, "I am Jehovah-Rophi," Jehovah the Healer.

He did not say, "I was the Healer," but "I am the Healer."

In all the ages, the Covenant reads, not "I was," but "I am" Jehovah that Healeth thee; I am Jehovah-Tsidkenu, Jehovah thy Righteousness, and so with all the other names of Jehovah, such as Jehovah-Jireh, Jehovah thy Provider.

Jehovah never changes.

He is still the Healer of His people.

Rise and give yourselves to God.

CLOSING PRAYER.

My God and Father, bless these people with Thy Spirit, and enable them to do Thy Will. For Jesus' sake. Amen.

The Doxology was then sung.

The meeting was closed with the Benediction and the Zion Salutation, "Peace to Thee," the audience responding heartily, "Peace to Thee be Multiplied."

Thursday Morning Meeting.

On the morning of Thursday there appeared in the columns of the *Advertiser* under the heading of "Topics of the Day," the following short paragraph to which the General Overseer referred in his Message:

A SHORT WAY WITH PROPHETS.

Nowadays, as in ancient times, self-styled prophets arise, and some are accepted of the people and "flourish as the green bay tree," while others are summarily rejected and wilt away like the product of seeds sown on stony ground. Taken altogether, the modern prophets who have managed to gain the ear of the public, have done better in a pecuniary sense and in the matter of home comforts than their predecessors of the olden Israelitish days, who led, for the most part, a hunted life. Brigham Young, for instance, did well, even if his colleague, Joseph Smith, fell into the hands of "violent and bloodthirsty men," and paid for his "revelation" with his blood. Other cases could be cited, however, in which latter-day prophets have done even better from a monetary point of view than the Mormons. Jeremiah, who is often quoted by them as giving support to their pretensions by his predictions, had little sympathy with the claims of some of his contemporaries, for he writes (chapter 29, verse 26)—"Every man that is mad and maketh himself a prophet, thou shouldest put him in prison and in the stocks."

The following is the report of the General Overseer's Message:

Town Hall, Adelaide, South Australia, Thursday Morning, March 24, 1904.

The Service was opened by the Congregation's singing Hymn No. 19, from the Visitation Program, "Jesus Shall Reign."

Overseer Voliva then read the first seventeen verses of the 8th chapter of Matthew, following which, prayer was offered by Deacon J. S. McCullagh.

During the singing of a Hymn, the offerings were received.

Overseer Jane Dowie then read from the 9th chapter of Matthew, and the first sixteen verses of the 5th chapter of St. Luke.

After the singing of another hymn the General Overseer delivered the following prelude:

SOME COMMENTS ON THE ADELAIDE PRESS.

*REPORTED BY E. W AND A. W. N.

I will take a little time, this morning, to deal with the press of the city.

I desire to do it in good temper, for I do not feel any other way.

It would be wicked to feel any other way.

I always conduct my Missions in good temper.

*The following report has not been revised by the General Overseer.

I Will Deal First With the "Advertiser."

The reports of the *Advertiser* have been excellent, and up until now their editorial articles have been fairly good.

They have been a credit to Sir Langdon Bonython and his young men.

I pay my respects to the gentleman who owns and edits the *Advertiser*, for the fair reports, and, up till this morning, the fair comments.

But it is evident that the editor has been letting one of his young men loose, and that young man has opened his mouth and put his foot into it very badly. I wish to read and explain to you a paragraph in this morning's *Advertiser*.

I shall keep the clippings from these papers with a great deal of interest.

They shall go into my scrap-books and into my library.

Some of the articles that appear are unique.

This paragraph is entitled,

A SHORT WAY WITH PROPHETS.

I do not know who wrote this, but I will give him a name: Shemaiah the Nehelamite.

The word Nehelamite means "the dreamer."

I will show you why I call him Shemaiah presently.

This young gentleman—I hope that he is young, because he has a chance to learn something before he is much older—writes a paragraph, under the heading, "The Topics of the Day."

He begins by saying:

Nowadays, as in ancient times, self-styled prophets arise.

I Was Called a Prophet Long Before I Made My Declaration.

I might stop here, for a moment, and say that the "self-styled" is not correct; because my people were demanding the Declaration for years before it was made.

I was very unwilling to make the Declaration until the time had come.

As far as the styling is concerned, I refer to the Australian press, which called me the "Prophet of Fitzroy," in the *Age*, for instance, long before I left Australia, sixteen years ago.

I believe that the first time the word prophet was applied to me was when the Melbourne *Age* used it.

That kept up until I left this country.

I think that this writer in the *Advertiser* might be a parson, or he might be a theological student, or he might be a man who knows something about the Bible, but very little.

It is a dangerous thing to have only a little knowledge.

Nowadays, as in ancient times, self-styled prophets arise, and some are accepted of the people and "flourish as the green bay tree," while others are summarily rejected and wilt away like the product of seeds sown on stony ground. Taken altogether, the modern prophets who have managed to gain the ear of the public, have done better in a pecuniary sense, and in the matter of home comforts, than their predecessors of the olden Israelitish days, who led, for the most part, a hunted life.

I do not care to say much about last Monday night, but I think that I was hunted then; for the mob went down to my brother-in-law's house and smashed his windows, they were so eager to find me.

I do not propose, however, to expose myself unnecessarily.

Neither did Elijah, the Tishbite. He kept out of sight for three and one-half years.

Brigham Young, for instance, did well, even if his colleague, Joseph Smith, fell into the hands of "violent and bloodthirsty men," and paid for his "revelation" with his blood.

That was the very thing that made Mormonism strong.

You Cannot Persecute Any Cause Without Helping It.

One of the things that is doing Zion the most good in Australia is all this persecution.

A gentleman sent a message to me yesterday asking to see me—a man of considerable means, a good citizen in this city, and a Christian man for many years.

He said, "The treatment accorded you convinces me that it is time for me to get out of this country."

He is going to sell his property, and bring his family to Zion City.

That is one of the immediate effects.

Mind you, some of these people have not hitherto been members of Zion.

Persecution does not hurt Zion.

Over one hundred persons came from Australia to Zion City last year.

There are now at least four hundred more whom we know to be coming.

If the foolish people will only howl a little longer, those coming will soon number a thousand.

One gentleman says, "I will take my family to Zion City because I cannot bring my children up in a city where there is such lawlessness as this."

That will be the result.

Other cases could be cited, however, in which Latter Day prophets have done even better from a monetary point of view than the Mormons. Jeremiah, who is often quoted by them as giving support to their pretensions by his predictions, had little sympathy with the claims of some of his contemporaries, for he writes (chapter 29, verse 26)—"every man that is mad, and maketh himself a prophet, thou shouldest put him in prison and in the stocks."

The "Advertiser's" Mistake as to Authorship of a Passage of Scripture.

Jeremiah never wrote that, Mr. *Advertiser*. [Laughter.]

Yet it is in the book of Jeremiah.

There are some things in the book of Job that were said by the Devil.

This young man—or old man—who writes this thing in the *Advertiser* must be corrected.

I do not like doing it; it is not nice to put a fellow over your knees and spank him, but I have to do it. [Laughter.]

Let us see who wrote this quotation from the book of Jeremiah.

Open your Bibles at the 29th chapter of Jeremiah, and we will get the whole story.

It is not often that I get such a good opportunity to expose a writer's ignorance.

We will begin at the 24th verse.

I will read the Revised Version.

And concerning Shemaiah the Nehelamite thou shalt speak, saying,

Thus speaketh Jehovah of hosts, the God of Israel, saying, Because thou hast sent letters in thine own name unto all the people that are at Jerusalem, and to Zephaniah the son of Maaseiah the priest, and to all the priests, saying,

Jehovah hath made thee priest in the stead of Jehoiada the priest, that ye should be officers in the house of Jehovah, for every man that is mad, and maketh himself a prophet, that thou shouldest put him in the stocks and in shackles.

It was Shemaiah, not Jeremiah, who wrote that letter.

Now therefore, why hast thou not rebuked Jeremiah of Anathoth, which maketh himself a prophet to you,

Forasmuch as he hath sent unto us in Babylon, saying, The captivity is long: build ye houses, and dwell in them; and plant gardens, and eat the fruit of them?

That was the letter of Shemaiah.

Mind that, Shemaiah, the Dreamer!

And Zephaniah the priest read this letter in the ears of Jeremiah the prophet.

You see now what happened after that.

Then came the word of Jehovah unto Jeremiah, saying,—

This is the word of Jeremiah.

Now Mr. *Advertiser* be fair.

Mr. *Register* you be fair too.

—Send to all them of the captivity, saying, Thus saith Jehovah concerning Shemaiah the Nehelamite (the dreamer.)

The man in the *Advertiser*, you know. [Laughter.]

Because that Shemaiah hath prophesied unto you, and I sent him not,—

Do you understand now?

—and he hath caused you to trust in a lie;—

That is Shemaiah, mind.

—therefore thus saith Jehovah, Behold, I will punish Shemaiah the Nehelamite, and his seed; he shall not have a man to dwell among this people, neither shall he behold the good that I will do unto My people, saith Jehovah: because he hath spoken rebellion against Jehovah.

Be sure to take that correctly.

It was not Jeremiah, it was Shemaiah, the Dreamer, who wrote those words about Jeremiah, saying that he was mad, and that he ought to be put in the stocks, and in prison.

It is a very dangerous thing for these fellows in newspaper offices to handle the Bible.

They do not read closely. It is a two-edged Sword.

I have caught that fellow this morning.

I recommend Sir Langdon Bonython to look after his young men who write "The Topics of the Day," and tell them that when they quote from the Bible, to be quite sure that they are quoting correctly, and that they do not get upset, as they have been this morning.

I am fifty-six years of age, and have read that Bible for fifty-two years, and you cannot fool me over a quotation.

You cannot make out that Jeremiah said a thing when Shemaiah the Dreamer said it.

Prophets Who Have Been Falsely Called Mad.

I may just as well pay my respects for a minute or two to this kind of thing.

Why should Jeremiah be counted mad, and put in the stocks and in shackles as Shemaiah wanted?

Who was the mad man? It was not Jeremiah.

It was Shemaiah.

Wherein am I mad?

If I am mad, let my insanity be inquired into, because no mad man ought to be at large.

If I am not mad, the question is, am I right?

Jeremiah was telling the truth.

Jeremiah told them that the captivity would last for some time, and that it would be better for them to build houses and plant vineyards until the time came when God would set His people free.

Shemaiah did not want that; he wanted to rebel against Jehovah.

It is a common thing, upon the part of people who do not like what a preacher says, to call him mad.

Do you not remember what they said of Jesus?

They said, "He is mad and hath a Devil. Why hear ye Him?"

Do you not remember what they said about the Apostle Paul?

The procurator upon the judgment seat said, "Paul, thou art mad; thy much learning doth turn thee to madness."

But Paul said: "I am not mad, most excellent Festus; but speak forth words of truth and soberness."

King Agrippa said, "With but little persuasion thou wouldst fain make me a Christian."

If I knew that I were mad, I should tell my wife to take care of me, to be kind to me, and to keep me from doing mischief, because it is a very serious thing to be mad.

But, as far as I know, and those about me know, my head is level, and I clearly understand what I am about.

Of course, I may not know so much as Mr. Shemaiah, the Dreamer of the *Advertiser*.

It is quite possible that Shemaiah knows more than I.

But Shemaiah had better quote the Scripture properly.

The Incompetency of My Critics.

The fact of the matter is that I am dealing with things that I understand.

Those who are criticizing me are not competent to do it, because a critic must know more than the man he criticizes.

If you are to criticize a poem, you ought to be a poet.

If you do not understand Hebrew, you had better not fight with a man who does.

A man who has been at a certain business all his life will know more about it than a man who never touched it.

I have never heard that Mr. Shemaiah, the Dreamer of the *Advertiser*, was a preacher or a Bible student.

If he is, trot him out, and let us know his name.

I have half a notion that that was written by a parson.

Let him put his name to that article; let him come out into the light.

What is the value of these anonymous articles? Just the value of the man who writes them.

Oftentimes the man who writes them knows a little less than nothing at all about the subject.

Now, Mr. "Register," Your Turn.

The *Register* criticizes, on page three of this morning's issue.

The editor, as he comes to my various points, puts in parentheses, into which he puts his answer.

I should like to have a good straight fight with a man who writes on the wrong side.

Quoting my words, the *Register* says:

> I do not deny the right of any editor to express his opinions, nor am I over-sensitive to criticism, but if I am to be subjected to insult and assault for expressing my views in a legal way, a crowd in antagonism to the *Register's* opinions might just as well enter the office, drive the editor out, assault his reporters, and smash the printing presses. That would be an intolerable proceeding; but what is sauce for the goose is sauce for the gander. If it is proper to insult a speaker, it is proper to insult a writer.

I commend the *Register* for very fairly quoting what I said.

This is the answer he makes:

> The whole question is one of reasonable provocation; that constitutes the difference.

I am amazed at the editor.

Does the editor not know that no provocation could justify a mob in rushing into his office and smashing him and his reporters and his printing presses; that no matter what he had written no provocation could justify a mob's doing that?

The law says distinctly that if any man violates the law he can be proceeded against.

He can be, if necessary, arrested, brought before judges and punished.

But does the *Register* really mean that the question is one of "reasonable provocation?"

Who Is to Be the Judge of "Reasonable Provocation?"

One man thinks that it is quite reasonable that he should insult his own father and mother. Some think that they have "reasonable provocation," for slapping their mother's face, for insulting her, and for even injuring her.

There are such cases. There are many of them, more than you think, perhaps, but does "reasonable provocation" justify a son in assaulting his mother?

Audience—"No."

General Overseer—No provocation justifies a mob in insulting or assaulting a speaker who is simply stating what he believes to be true, for the benefit of the people.

If I am doing wrong, let me be proceeded against.

I will answer any process that the Chief Justice, or any magistrate, may issue.

I am a law-abiding man.

If I am summoned for saying anything or doing anything wrong, I shall answer the summons, I shall plead, and I shall take the punishment if I am guilty.

It is right that I should submit to law.

If some one merely says, "Well, you are fighting Masonry," to him I reply,

I Have a Right to Fight Masonry if I Think It Bad.

Some people are fighting Christianity because they think it bad.

Would you like to have them put into prison simply because they are fighting Christianity?

There are Jews that deny the Divinity of our Lord Jesus, the Christ, and fight against it.

Am I to have them put into prison for that?

There are Spiritualists, Mohammedans and Buddhists all over the British Empire.

They have a perfect right to speak their own religious views, and the British power everywhere protects them.

I am saying nothing that a man may not say lawfully.

I am not injuring any one.

I am not naming individuals nor insulting them.

For instance, I am fighting liquor all the time, yet I am living in a hotel where liquor is sold, because I find that I cannot live in these temperance hotels.

They are miserable places; there is no proper provision for one.

One needs servants and telephones and telegraphic communication.

Moreover, there are few hotels that can accommodate all my party.

I have ten or twelve now in my party, and they require a good deal of room, so that usually I am compelled to stay in a hotel.

I am staying in a very nice hotel with an exceedingly good proprietor, and there are good servants, and good food, and very courteous treatment.

I never hear or see anything of drunken people about that hotel. It is kept with exceeding care.

I fight the liquor that my friend, Mr. Ferry, sells at his bar.

I told him this morning, "I wish, Mr. Ferry, that this hotel were a temperance hotel, and that you did not sell any liquor."

But because I fight liquor and call it liquid fire and distilled damnation do I cease to be a gentleman?

Can I not talk kindly to a man who differs with me?

I can talk to a Jew who differs with me.

I can talk to a Roman Catholic.

I can talk to an infidel, and I can talk to him as a gentleman, but, when I hit his infidelity, I hit it hard. And when I hit Shemaiah, the Dreamer, I hit him hard. [Laughter.]

When I hit Mr. *Register* Editor, I hit him hard.

An Old Fight With and Victory Over the "Register."

Thirty-five years ago, I wrote a certain report about the liquor traffic.

I was privately studying in this city for the ministry, in 1868, before I went back to Scotland.

I gave a little time to the service of the abstainers, and I took a great deal of pains to prepare a certain report for the anniversary meetings of the South Australian Total Abstinence Association, being secretary of the general committee.

My friend, the Honorable James Reynolds, was treasurer about that time, and my friend, Mr. Robert Kay, the secretary of the Institute, was very kind to me, and allowed me to go into the library and make research among the statistical registers and the documents of the government that were there.

I think I took about six months of my leisure time to examine thoroughly the cost of the wine, and the beer and the liquor that were imported into this country, and to make very careful quotations from the customs and excise returns.

I checked my figures with great care.

When a young fellow of twenty-one takes his evenings for six months to do that kind of thing he is very much in earnest, and I was very much in earnest.

I was known to be an accurate accountant, and I had my facts in fine order. I had agreed to become, for one year, an honorary secretary of the Alliance that I might produce these facts in a report.

Mr. Lawson, the editor of the *Register*, attacked that report.

He said, in an editorial paragraph, that I had guessed at the facts and multiplied my figures by two.

Mr. Nathan Forster, who was commonly supposed to be proprietor of the *Register*—he had been proprietor—and who certainly was very influential in its affairs, was angry about Mr. Lawson's editorial.

As a result, I was given an opportunity to write a reply to Mr. Lawson, which I did.

This was published in the editorial columns and was double-leaded, as editorial matter is.

The gentleman who set it up, told me that it was one of three letters, in the whole of his knowledge of the *Register* that had ever been set up in editorial style.

Shortly after that Mr. Lawson departed for Europe.

I know that he was censured in the office and out of the office for writing that very unkind and very improper article in which he reflected upon my veracity.

In my letter I gave the details, and columns of figures which I brought out with great pains, proving the correctness of the results that I had seen.

There was no contention about the figures after that.

I do not know Mr. Lawson personally, and only had a bowing acquaintance with that very good gentleman, the Honorable Nathan Forster.

He was a man of years and position, and I was only a young man.

I remember, as if it were yesterday, the indignation of the Honorable Captain Baget.

He said to relatives and friends of mine all over the city, that he had gone to the *Register*, and had given them a piece of his mind.

He was a very able man, and could speak very sharply and very powerfully.

Alexander Dowie—"He walked over from North Adelaide that very day that you wrote that letter, and spoke in the very highest terms of what you had done.

"He said that there could be no doubt that before you left the world, although you were then a young man, you would leave your mark in it." [Applause.]

General Overseer—I thank my wife's father for the words he has spoken.

It confirms what I say about the Honorable Captain Baget's position.

I venerate his memory.

He was a good and far-seeing man, and a member of the legislative council.

I do not make the editor of the *Register* responsible for Mr. Lawson's sins.

Mr. Lawson is the same man who is now the editor of the London *Financial News*.

He is an awful liar.

He attacked me again in 1900.

He said that Zion City was all in the air, and attacked it from a financial point of view very bitterly and falsely.

That Mr. Lawson is a very able man there can be no question, but he is a very wicked one.

He has not forgotten the trouncing he got that day from the young fellow who defended his figures.

Mr. Lawson's attacks in the *Financial News* passed away.

Zion City was and is established.

He poured contempt upon the possibility of my establishing Zion Lace Industries, but they are established.

It is just possible, of course, that, after many years, this or that little point may not be exactly remembered, but there is no question that Mr. Lawson wrote the article; that he was the editorial writer at the time; that he was severely censured for it; that my reply was placed in editorial style; that the reply can be found today in the files of that paper; and that the Honorable Captain Baget and others protested in the most vigorous language against Mr. Lawson's mode of writing concerning me.

[This statement was claimed to be inaccurate by the editor of the *Register*, but the General Overseer was able to substantiate every important point of it on the day that the criticism and allegation appeared.—A. W. N.]

Mr. Editor of the *Register*, just think it over again, whether any provocation justifies people in insulting or assaulting a lady?

Hatred Without a Cause.

What has Mrs. Dowie done?

Yet there is not a day when we are not insulted. We cannot come into this hall or go out of it without a number of people "boohooing."

A cow could do it better.

What are they "boohooing" at?

They do not know.

They are told that I say I am Elijah, so they say "boohoo!" [Laughter.]

That is what they said a long time ago when a man said he was Elisha.

There were fifty children who said, "Go up, thou baldhead!"

I am very bald. Some of these young men recommend me to cut my hair.

If I choose to wear my hair long, why should I cut it?

It is a matter of taste. I always wore my hair long.

Those of you who knew me thirty years ago must know I wore a long black beard, and long black hair.

To cut my hair hurts me. I hate to have it cut.

These wicked children said to Elisha, "Go up, thou baldhead."

Two bears came out of the wood and slew fifty of them.

The End of the Enemies of the General Overseer.

No man has ever insulted or assaulted me who has not suffered.

Every editor in Chicago that fought me in 1895, is dead or out of his editorial chair.

I had a tremendous fight with them for several years, and every one of those editors is dead, with one exception, and he sold his paper and got out. He was not very bitter against me.

I said to them, "Look out! You will die for that."

They laughed, but they are dead.

One day here, many years ago, on the banks of the Torrens, a man named Wright interrupted my meeting.

No one else did.

I said, "Wright, God Almighty will not stand you long."

"How long do you think He will stand me?" he asked, impudently.

"I think about a week, and if you do not take care you will die," I calmly replied.

He laughed, and they all laughed.

But the next Sunday morning he was found in the West Terrace Cemetery with a bullet through his head, and a revolver in his hand.

You can verify that from the public papers of the time.

I remember Mr. Tyreman, a famous lecturer on Spiritualism, who interrupted me in the Domain.

I said, "Tyreman, God Almighty is tired of you. I think you will die soon, and I think you will go to hell, because you are not going to heaven with such a spirit."

He laughed at me.

The following Sunday night a paper was handed to me, in which I read that Mr. Tyreman had died in the Darling House, a receiving-house for lunatics.

He had been taken there mad, and he had died.

I think I have at least some of the marks of a prophet.

One of them is:

Blessed are ye when men shall reproach you, and persecute you, and say all manner of evil against you falsely, for My sake.

Rejoice, and be exceeding glad: for great is your reward in heaven: for so persecuted they the prophets which were before you.

I know that the things that are said and written against me are false. All who know the facts know that they are.

God Cares for His Prophets.

What does God say about His prophets? "Touch not Mine anointed ones and do My prophets no harm."

When a man has a Message from God, God cares for that man, and He stands by him.

Wo to the man who touches a Messenger of God!

Jesus said regarding one of the little ones that believe in Him:

But whoso shall cause one of these little ones which believe on Me to stumble, it is profitable for him that a great millstone should be hanged about his neck, and that he should be sunk in the depth of the sea.

Wo unto the world because of occasions of stumbling! for it must needs be that the occasions come; but wo to that man through whom the occasion cometh!

You not only cannot insult a prophet with impunity, but you cannot insult a child of God with impunity.

You had better take care what you are about.

Concerning a Proposed Meeting of Protest in the Town Market.

I understand that there is a movement on foot to call a meeting in the Town Market to consider what is to be done with me.

I have no objection to their holding that meeting.

I do not know what the mayor will do, but if he were to ask my advice, I should be inclined to say, "Let them hold it, Mr. Mayor"

I should like to hear what they say.

If they will promise to take care of me, I shall go and listen to the speeches.

It would be very interesting to listen to the speeches of the people who would get together there.

If one should smell their breath, one would be able to say, "Lord, by this time he stinketh;" because I am quite sure one would find their breath befouled with both alcohol and tobacco, and the two together make an awful stink!

Let them meet together, and let them show good cause why a man who is doing his best to help his fellow men to be clean should be sent out of the state.

I am doing the best I can to get men and women clean.

Every one will admit that I am scrubbing them well. [Laughter.]

I get them into the tub here and scrub them just a little every day I hope to get them clean by-and-by

They are so dirty, however, that it seems to me almost as if I would need to take off their skin to get them clean.

I do not want to do that if I can help it.

I am using all the nice soap I can and being as tender as I can

. Let them meet in the market-place.

If the citizens of Adelaide want to distinguish themselves by passing a resolution that the mayor shall no longer open this hall to me, I do not think that I shall be the loser.

I am not gaining anything, pecuniarily, by this Visitation.

I am not asking any money from the citizens of Adelaide.

I am giving my time and my toil, when I could be resting.

Disgrace of Denial of Lawful Right of Free Speech.

If the Town Hall or the Exhibition Building were closed, it would go throughout the world that Adelaide is ruled by fools, by people who do not know the value of civil and religious liberty

I do not think Governor Le Hunte will find anything in his instructions which would warrant his acting in such a way

On the contrary, the instructions to a Governor are to maintain civil and religious liberty.

Mr. Mayor and the Chief Secretary of the State, Mr. Jenkins, will not find it in the laws that a man is to be denied freedom of speech because some people do not agree with him.

If this city and state are to be ruled by a mob in the market-place, instead of by the representatives of the Law, then they are a good city and a good state to live outside of.

It is a good place to get away from, because Law is not dependent upon what a mob in the market-place may say.

Law comes down to us through all the ages.

In the British Empire and America our Common Law rights are just the same.

There is no other Common Law in America than the British Common Law.

It is incorporated, by express statute, into the legislation of nearly every state.

I know the Common Law.

I am sufficiently a lawyer to understand the Common Law.

My son is a graduate in Law, a Doctor of Law.

He took his degree with honors.

I have a very strong Law Department, and a good law library, and many legal friends.

I think I understand Law, as far as the broad principles of Common Law are concerned.

I do not know of any country in which a man's right to speak is to be submitted to a howling mob in a market-place.

Do you remember reading of one scene in Ephesus?

Paul was preaching there, and there was a fellow named Demetrius who could lead a disturbance just like a fellow named Shannon here.

After Hymn No. 31 had been sung, the General Overseer delivered his Message:

THE POWER OF GOD TO HEAL.

INVOCATION.

Let the words of my mouth, and the meditation of my heart be acceptable in Thy sight, be profitable unto this people, and unto all to whom these words shall come, in this and every land, in this and all the coming time, Till Jesus Come. Amen.

You will find the subject of my brief address this morning, in the words which were read to you by my dear wife. They are in the Gospels according to St. Mark and St. Luke.

I will take the story from the Gospel according to St. Luke, the 5th chapter and the 17th verse:

TEXT.

And it came to pass on one of those days, that He was teaching; and there were Pharisees and doctors of the law sitting by, which were come out of every village of Galilee and Judæa and Jerusalem: and the power of the Lord was with Him to heal.

"The Power of the Lord was with Him to Heal."

The Healing Power of God flowed through our Lord Jesus, the Christ, whenever He so willed it, in immeasurable effectiveness; for God the Father, and God the Holy Spirit dwelt in Jesus, the Son of Man. and the Son of God.

It was not as the Son of God that He came. He came as Man.

The Power that was present to heal that day was the Power of God, our Father, by the Holy Spirit working through the Prophetic Man, the Christ Jesus.

He is God, but He is also Man.

It was as Man that He came, as Man that He reascended, and it is as Man that He now pleads; for we have "One Mediator between God and man, the Man Christ Jesus."

He is coming back as Man, and He will reign in this world a thousand years as a Glorified Man.

The Day of the Lord is a Thousand Years, and that is the Millennium.

On the day referred to in the text, He was teaching in what must have been a very large place

I do not know where it was.

It is probable that it was in a synagogue.

The place was a house, the roof of which opened, and through which a sick man was let down into the room below.

Size and Distinction of Jesus' Audiences.

The audience before Him was composed principally of the professed ministers of God, and the doctors of the law, the great leaders of thought in religious life.

And it came to pass on one of those days, that He was teaching; and there were Pharisees and doctors of the law sitting by, which were come out of every village of Galilee and Judæa and Jerusalem.

"Every village in Galilee" numbered hundreds: for at this time Galilee was exceedingly prosperous, and the Lake of Galilee was surrounded by numbers of little towns.

There were towns like Tiberia, Capernaum, Bethsaida, Magdala, and many others, all about.

At this particular time the shores of the Lake of Galilee were covered with beautiful Roman villas, and many rich Romans lived in these beautiful little cities, and in the country districts around.

Galilee was looked upon as a great health resort.

Not far away was Mount Carmel, where large numbers of persons go, even to this day. There are various Sanitariums on the slopes of the mountain, where people lie in the sun. Many persons think that they can be healed of consumption there, because the air is so clear.

This being the case, when Jesus taught, at this time, there would be hundreds of doctors of the law and rabbis there.

These doctors of the law and rabbis were the most learned men of their time.

Rabbis and Doctors of the Law in Jesus' Time Not All Hypocrites.

They were not all bad men, not all hypocrites.

There were men, for instance, like Nicodemus, who sat on the fence, just as a good many sit on the fence today.

One cannot tell where they are.

Many ministers will not denounce me, and will not approve me.

It does not matter whether they do or not, because they are of no consequence.

I venture to say that I have often addressed, on a Lord's Day, more people than gather in all the churches of Adelaide put together.

Ministers would better have listened to me while I was here.

It would have done them a great deal of good.

Even now, if they would listen, they might get a little information as to how I get the people, because I do get them everywhere.

It might be of some interest to you ministers, who sometimes sneak in and take a back seat, to take a front seat and get to know a little more about Zion, because Zion is going to make a deep inroad upon you.

Zion's Far-reaching Power.

There is not a church in this city that is not affected by Zion.

There is not a church in Australia nor one in America that is not affected by Zion.

If you think Zion is a little one-horse affair, you are mistaken. If I were to die now, Zion would go on.

There are hundreds of ministers and other able people, to carry on the work.

You might smite the shepherd, but the sheep would not be scattered.

They would gather together a little closer.

They are coming together; ten thousand of them have come to Zion City, within two years.

Three other cities are being planned.

These cities will be filled with inhabitants within a very few years of their founding.

We know what we are talking about. You do not.

In nearly every large city in the world there are some Zion people. They are in every country and under every flag.

In St. Petersburg they are very much afraid of us.

They would not visé my passport for Russia, because, they said, "that man will convert the people in masses."

The Russian government is always afraid, and people who are afraid go to pieces. The Russian Empire is going to pieces.

Whenever any city is afraid to hear the truth, that city will go to pieces.

If you are afraid to hear the truth in Adelaide, and are not strong enough to hear it, you will go to pieces.

If you are too weak to stand one man's lying, then you are exceedingly weak.

Much more are you weak if you cannot stand one man's telling the truth; and who convicts me of telling what is not true?

If there is anything that I have said that is not true, I will take it back. That is my duty.

If I have injured any man or any community, I hope I am a gentleman who would be willing to take it back immediately.

I would not be a Christian minister; I would not be a true child of God, if I had wronged any one and would not take it back.

They are not saying that I have wronged any one. They are only saying "boohoo!"

Foolish and Wicked Action of Many of The People of Adelaide.

One of the saddest things about this city has been the fact that a number of women have insulted Mrs. Dowie in the streets.

Mrs. Dowie was born in this city, and not a word has ever been said against her.

Our people have been in this city for fifty-three years.

I do not know that any one of them has ever been in prison.

I do not know that they have ever committed offenses.

One of them has been a justice of the peace for many years here, and in business for fifty-three years.

I do not know what is the sense in this thing.

There is no sense in it at all.

I lived in these states for sixteen years, and preached the Gospel in Adelaide, in Melbourne, and in Sydney.

I preached the same Gospel I am preaching now—preached against liquor and tobacco, and everything that is evil.

The difference is that my prophetic mission had not been so clearly established, at that time, and that is what they are afraid of now.

If a man is a prophet of God, you must listen to him and obey him.

These Jewish doctors of the law and rulers of whom I have spoken were listening to Jesus, the Christ.

They were learned men; many of them were honest men.

I believe that some of them were honest in putting the Christ to death.

I believe that some of them thought He was a malefactor.

I say that upon the ground of what Peter said, "Brethren, I wot that in ignorance ye did it, as did also your rulers."

I think that it was through ignorance that they did it, but

Ignorance Is a Terrible Thing.

The greatest crimes that have ever been committed upon this earth have been committed through ignorance.

The crucifixion of Jesus, the Christ, was the work of an ignorant mob, and of ignorant rulers.

Peter said that they did it in ignorance, and the Christ Himself said it.

Did He not say, "Father, forgive them, for they know not what they do?"

They were ignorant, but ignorance has to be removed.

A man may be wilfully ignorant.

That was the cry against these men.

Paul said of them:

Well spake the Holy Spirit by Isaiah the prophet unto your Fathers,
Saying, "Go thou unto this people, and say,
By hearing ye shall hear, and shall in no wise understand;
And seeing ye shall see, and shall in no wise perceive:
For this people's heart is waxed gross,
And their ears are dull of hearing,
And their eyes they have closed;
Lest haply they should perceive with their eyes,
And hear with their ears,
And understand with their heart,
And should turn again,
And I should heal them.

While the Christ was teaching these rabbis and doctors of law that He was the Son of God, they were very skeptical.

They would not believe it.

Then a man was let down into the midst and the Christ said to him, "Son, thy sins be forgiven thee."

They were shocked, and said in their hearts that He was a blasphemer.

He said:

Why reason ye these things in your hearts? Whether is easier to say to the sick of the palsy, Thy sins are forgiven; or to say, Arise, and take up thy bed and walk?

Then He said to him lying upon the bed, palsied, "Take up thy bed, and go unto thy house."

He got up, and the people glorified God.

But what did the Pharisees do?

They went away and consulted how to put Him to death

It is the old story.

You talk about the peace and gentleness of Jesus, and say that He did not make any trouble when He preached.

But He did. The first sermon that He preached was in Nazareth.

He told them that there was no faith among them.

They rose, and wanted to put Him to death; to cast Him down from the precipice upon which their city was built.

What had He done?

He had lived a good, blameless life, among them.

Hatred and Murder Without a Cause.

He told them the truth. That was the thing that made them want to murder Him.

That was the thing for which they eventually did murder Him.

Why did they murder Abraham Lincoln? Had he done any wrong?

No.

He had set the slave free, and that was enough to excite an intoxicated, vain, foolish, nicotine-poisoned man, an actor, to such a point that he took a revolver and murdered the President.

What did James A. Garfield do to be murdered?

Nothing, except that he would not give an office to a lunatic named Guiteau, a man of bad life.

Why did Czolgosz murder William McKinley?

Had he done any wrong?

Not at all.

I had the pleasure of knowing that President, and although I differed with him very strongly about his Masonry, a kinder gentleman never lived.

Czolgosz was a degenerate, profligate young man.

I do not think he was even a member of the Anarchists' society.

It was not proved that he was.

In fact the Anarchists did not care for him.

Wherefore did the Jews reject Jesus?

The people were glad that Jesus healed that man. But the Pharisees conspired to put Him to death.

The Christ forgives sin, and the Christ heals sickness still.

He is still the same Christ.

Trust Him.

PRAYER OF CONSECRATION.

Our God and Father, in Jesus' Name we come to Thee. Take us as we are. Make us what we ought to be in spirit, soul, and body. For Jesus' sake. [*All repeat the prayer, clause by clause, after the General Overseer.*]

BENEDICTION.

Beloved, abstain from all appearance of evil. And may the very God of Peace Himself sanctify you wholly; and I pray God your whole spirit and soul and body be preserved entire, without blame, unto the coming of our Lord Jesus, the Christ. Faithful is He that calleth you, who also will do it. The grace of our Lord Jesus, the Christ, the love of God, our Father, the fellowship of the Holy Spirit, our Comforter and Guide, one Eternal God, abide in you, bless you and keep you, and all the Israel of God everywhere, forever. Amen

---

Thursday Afternoon Meeting.

Town Hall, Adelaide, South Australia, Thursday Afternoon, March 24, 1904.

The meeting was opened with the singing of Hymn No. 9, Visitation Program, "The Morning Light Is Breaking."

Overseer Jane Dowie read the lesson for the afternoon from the Inspired Word of God, the 10th chapter of the Acts of the Apostles.

After another hymn, Overseer Wilbur Glenn Voliva offered prayer.

Deacon Clement Friend Hawkins, the General Overseer, and Overseer Wilbur Glenn Voliva made the announcements.

The General Overseer then delivered his Message:

SATAN THE DEFILER.

*REPORTED BY I. M. S. AND A. W. N.

INVOCATION.

Let the words of my mouth, and the meditation of my heart be acceptable in Thy sight, be profitable unto this people and unto all to whom these words shall come, in this and every land, in this and all the coming time, Till Jesus Come. Amen.

You will find my text in the 10th chapter of the Acts of the Apostles, from the 35th to the 38th verse.

TEXT.

But in every nation he that feareth Him, and worketh righteousness, is acceptable to Him.

*The following report has not been revised by the General Overseer.

The word which He sent unto the children of Israel, preaching Good Tidings of Peace by Jesus, the Christ, (He is Lord of all)—

That saying ye yourselves know, which was published throughout all Judæa, beginning from Galilee, after the baptism which John preached;

Even Jesus of Nazareth, how that God anointed Him with the Holy Spirit and with power: who went about doing good, and healing all that were oppressed of the Devil; for God was with Him.

I wonder if you think that Australia belongs to the Australians?

If you do, you are wrong.

"The Earth Is Jehovah's and the Fulness Thereof."

It belongs to God, every foot of it.

"Oh, but we possess it," you say.

For how long?

The earth laughs at you when you talk of possessing it.

It laughs at you louder and louder, the older you get.

At last you will fall into it and six feet of it will hold you, and it will fill your mouth.

What is the use of your talking about possessing it? It will possess you and very soon, too.

The earth will swallow you up, as far as your bodies are concerned.

The earth never belonged to any nation.

I wish you would get hold of the simple thought that there is not a foot of the earth that belongs to you or to me.

You say that Australia belonged to the aborigines.

How do you know?

There are some geologists who tell you that these hills around Adelaide were higher, at one time, than the Himalayas.

You cannot tell how many generations may have occupied these hills and plains before the aborigines.

What do you know about it?

You may ask, "What about Zion City?" Zion City belongs to God. You cannot alienate a single foot of that land.

It is the Lord's.

When we bought it we believed in the Word of God that said, "The land is Mine, it shall not be sold in perpetuity."

That is what God said to the Israelites when they got Canaan.

It was dear property when they began to sell it.

The word which He sent unto the children of Israel, preaching Good Tidings of Peace by Jesus, the Christ, (He is Lord of all)—

That saying ye yourselves know, which was published throughout all Judæa, beginning from Galilee, after the baptism which John preached.

The Truth About the Source of Disease.

Overseer Voliva, watch closely and see whether I read the last verse correctly.

I may make some mistakes purposely.

"How God anointed Jesus of Nazareth with the Holy Spirit and with power, who went about"—making people sick because He loved them—

Overseer Voliva—"That is wrong."

General Overseer—What did He go about doing?

Overseer Voliva—"'He went about doing good and healing—'"

General Overseer—Ah, I see! He went about doing good and healing all that God made sick.

Overseer Voliva—"That is wrong."

General Overseer—Well, what is right?

Overseer Voliva—"He went about healing all that were oppressed of the Devil."

General Overseer—That was nineteen centuries ago, but do you not know that it is not the Devil's work today?

Overseer Voliva—"No, sir, I do not."

General Overseer—Do you not believe in the Church of England Prayer-book which says, "Forasmuch as God Almighty hath laid His afflicting hand upon you?"

Overseer Voliva—"No, sir, I do not."

General Overseer—But many of the churches tell the people that these diseases come from a loving Father's hand.

If that is the case, then the hand must be a very dirty hand.

There is no disease in God and in heaven, and no disease can come out of Him if there is none there.

He is the Healer.

About "Luke, the Beloved Physician."

"But, Doctor," asks some one, "is there not a place which says that Luke was the 'beloved physician?'"

Oh, yes. We have John G. Speicher, the beloved physician,

who is the Overseer of Zion City now; but he does not take any medicines and does not give any.

He gave up that folly quite a number of years ago.

When he became afflicted with cancer, he came to me and asked me to pray for him.

God healed him, but He did not heal him until he gave up the practice of medicine.

He has been one of my colleagues for over eleven years, and the cancer has never returned.

Luke was a beloved physician; but do any of you know of his ever practicing?

We have some physicians in our Health Department.

We keep things clean, and sweet and nice in Zion City.

These are intelligent and good men who understand pathology, and who are well versed in hygiene.

We keep Zion City clean, but as for practicing physicians we have none.

Now I will go back to my text.

Peter was in the house of Cornelius, who was a wealthy man.

Just a word about this.

Jesus was often in the houses of very wealthy people.

The Bible says in the 9th chapter of Luke, that he was attended by noble women.

Among these women were princesses, such as Joanna the wife of Chusa, Herod's steward, the treasurer of the king, Susanna, and Mary of Magdala.

Women ministered unto Him of their substance.

I dare say that there were many women who said bad things about that, too.

I desire to say a few words about

Poverty and Riches.

It is a queer notion some folks have that in order to be Christlike you must be poor.

I once had that idea myself.

I reduced myself to voluntary poverty, but I learned that I could not get Salvation for the people by coming down to their level.

I had to get up higher and lift them up to a higher standard.

The Gospel says that the Christ bore our sins.

Did He bear them that we might sin? No, that we might not sin.

Did He bear our sicknesses that we might be sick? No, that we might have no sickness.

Did He bear our poverty that we might continue poor? No, "though He was rich, yet for your sakes He became poor, that ye through His poverty might become rich."

When I saw that, a number of years ago, I said, "Very good, my people shall be rich, and I will be rich.

"I will get as rich as I can," and I have been at it. [Applause.]

"But, Doctor," some one says, "you have not been preaching the Gospel."

Have I not? I have been preaching sometimes eighteen to twenty-one times a week.

If any parson in Adelaide does more than that, may the Lord bless him.

Send me his name.

I attend to business too, and do it properly.

We have forty-two great departments in the City of Zion, and not one of them is neglected.

The flag of Zion is on every Continent, and it is not neglected either.

I should not be able to do the work that I do if I did not have large resources.

The larger the resources I have, the better for the work throughout the world.

I need the largest resources I can get to smash up the Devil's work. [Applause.]

I am very glad to be in a position to personally extend the hospitalities of Zion to large numbers of people.

I should be very glad to extend Zion's hospitality to you all if you would all come to Zion City and see me there.

I could take care of you all at one time, too, for Zion has a Hospice where we can feed a thousand people at one time.

The Christ never wanted us to be sinful nor sick nor poor.

The Church of God cannot do this work in the world so long as it is poor.

Some of you miserable sinners here pray to God to keep your minister very humble, and then you see to it that he is kept very poor.

The Powerlessness of Ministers Who Depend on the Votes of their People.

The ministers themselves do not dare to say a word because you could make them go tomorrow.

No minister in Zion can be voted out; no matter what the people say about him.

The minister is not elected by the people.

The minister is sent out by the General Overseer, and is paid from Zion's Storehouse.

I myself am not paid from Zion's Storehouse.

I have not taken a dollar or a cent from the Tithes and Offerings of the Christian Catholic Church in Zion for over seven years.

I give the largest sums to the funds.

That fact has been again and again asserted by the General Financial Manager of Zion's Institutions and Industries and by the General Recorder of the Christian Catholic Church in Zion.

When a man's ways please God He sends him the resources.

It is a very bad state of affairs when the shepherd is ruled by the sheep; when the sheep say, "Now look you here, Mr. Shepherd, you must do this and thus and so, and if you do not do it, we will butt you out as we did the last shepherd."

Nice sheep these are!

My own opinion is that they are goats! [Laughter.]

The shepherd should be able to rule the sheep.

A general should be able to command his army.

You like voting.

The Value of Obedience to Rightful Authority.

Did you ever know of an army that voted for or against going into battle?

In an army, you cannot hold meetings and vote.

You have to obey.

The Church of God is a mighty army and some of you had better learn how to obey.

Some of you women promised your husbands that you would obey but you have not obeyed. [Laughter.]

I do not wonder much that some of you have not obeyed; because you promised to obey a husband and not a stinkpot. [Laughter.]

You did not promise to obey a fellow who neglects you.

You did not promise to obey a fellow who puts on an apron three or four times a week and goes around with the Ma-hah-bone fools riding a goat and doing all kinds of foolish things.

Such a man has failed to be a husband.

A true husband is a house band.

He keeps the house together, cares for the wife and children, prays with them and encourages them.

He does not go out and become a thirty-third degree fool

A man cannot do that and fulfil his duty as a husband, or as a member of the Church of God.

A true husband has no time for such things.

A Man of God Has No Time to Fool Away.

You cannot do these things in Zion, because we do not fool away time.

We do not walk behind a tobacco pipe all day like this, [illustrates]—puff, puff, puff. [Laughter.]

A man who does that is no man.

We have no time for people who lean against public-houses, chewing and squirting.

I once saw a man leaning against a building in Zion City.

I said to him "What is the matter with that wall?"

"Nothing, General Overseer," he replied.

"Why are you supporting it then?" I asked. "Can you not find something to do?

"Here, Mr. Jones, give this man a shovel. There is a pile of dirt in your back yard. Give him twenty-five cents an hour and let him shovel that out." [Laughter.]

What is the use of roaming around waiting for something to turn up?

I believe in people who believe that "God is no respecter of persons; but in every nation he that feareth Him, and worketh righteousness, is acceptable to Him."

You must fear God and work.

Some of you work mostly with your tongues.

You waggle, waggle, waggle, waggle. [Laughter.]

That is the only way you work.

If we find a man in Zion City who works mostly with his tongue, we send a message to him and ask him to stop, because he has spent one-half of his strength and time, for which Zion is paying, in waggling his tongue.

We have no place for that.

See that you fear God and work.

Work righteousness and righteously; then you will be acceptable to God.

Cornelius did not know the Christ, but God heard his prayer.

God sent an angel to him, and the angel told him to send down to Joppa for Peter.

He obeyed.

When Peter was in the way, in the house of one Simon, the tanner, some one neglected to get the dinner ready on time.

While they were making ready, he went up to the housetop to pray and fell into a trance.

I Believe in Having the Meals on Time.

You women, see that you have the dinner ready on time.

It is a sin for you to have breakfast late and half-cooked.

It gives people indigestion.

Many a wicked woman has killed her husband by not having dinner ready on time, and by having it badly cooked.

We had a case of this kind in the United States not long ago

She was a lovely woman, but she had had two husbands and now had the third one.

One day, shortly after their marriage, he said to her very sweetly, "Betty"—we will call her Betty—"what caused your other husbands to die?"

"Indigestion," she said. [Laughter.]

"Well," he said, "I think I shall die from indigestion, too."

I tell you, she was a limmer! [Laughter.]

A woman who does not have the oatmeal properly cooked, and serves all the potatoes with hard hearts, is a limmer. [Laughter]

Some of you women here have to learn that lesson.

Work righteousness and fear God, and see that you get your pies well cooked in good time for dinner.

Fear God, and keep things sweet and clean, and do not grumble at the old fellow, even if he does grumble at you. [Laughter]

Fear God and work righteousness, be kind and good, and God will send an angel to you some day.

He sent an angel to dear Peter when he was in a trance.

Mistaken Ideas about Peter's Vision on the Housetop.

Peter had a vision. A great many of you think far too much of that vision.

You have mistaken ideas about it.

You think, because God let down that sheet, in a vision, to Peter, wherein were all manner of four-footed beasts, creeping things, and fowls of the air, and because the Voice came to Peter, and said, "Rise, Peter, kill and eat," that the lesson of the vision makes it proper for people to eat all kinds of abominable things.

Do you not know what that sheet meant?

If you will read your Bible it will tell you.

While Peter was wondering within himself what this vision meant, the men who were sent from Cornelius inquired for Simon's house, and stood before the gate knocking

They asked for Peter, and the Spirit said unto him, "Arise, get thee down, and go with them, nothing doubting"

And Peter went down to the men who were sent to him from Cornelius, and went away with them.

God showed him what the vision meant; that the sheet represented all the nations of the earth.

All the nations are represented by either a bird or a beast: England by a lion, the United States by an eagle, Russia by a bear, France by a cock, Persia by a civet cat, China by a dragon, and so forth.

Peter, therefore, said, when he got to Cornelius, "Of a truth I perceive that God is no respecter of persons; but in every nation, he that feareth Him, and worketh Righteousness, is acceptable to Him."

God had shown him that he should not call any man common or unclean.

It was not a question of eating.

You Have No Right to Call Any Man Common or Unclean.

The earth is Jehovah's.

The earth was made for man of every tribe and nation, and the people of this land will always be miserable until they understand that fact.

"Oh," said a man to me the other day, "Doctor, you must not say anything in Australia about black labor or yellow labor. We could not tolerate the Africans or Chinese here."

We have eight million Africans in the United States, and I do not know of any one of sense who wants to part with them.

Although now and then there are a few illiterate and naughty ones among them, who do bad things, we need them in the cotton fields in the warm South.

We need their labor.

This great, broad Australian land is groaning for the want of inhabitants.

You are not only shutting out colored labor but you are shutting out white labor.

Unless you get a great immigration into this land, you will die out

You are dying out as it is.

The truth is that you are killing yourselves, and are being killed out.

The fact is already being deplored that there are such a large number of deaths in proportion to births in some states.

May God grant you the grace to see that the country needs population.

It is a beautiful land and needs development, with its mineral, agricultural, and pastoral resources, and land which could be developed and cultivated for coffee, rice, flax and a hundred other things.

May God break up your narrow-mindedness!

Zion City has seventy nationalities, and we live in perfect peace. Every man gets paid according to his work.

There are no labor troubles.

What is done on a small scale there can be done on a large scale anywhere.

Peter became enlightened and made that great statement, "God is no respecter of persons."

Then he told them:

Even Jesus of Nazareth, how that God anointed Him with the Holy Spirit and with power: who went about doing good, and healing all that were oppressed of the Devil; for God was with Him.

As every kind of sickness in the Christ's day was the work of the Devil, so it is today.

Wherein Can There Be Any Good in Disease?

"Oh, it makes one get closer to God," some people say.

Did you ever find that suffering and miseries brought you closer to God?"

Do you not find it hard to pray when you are sick?

Is there not much darkness all around you?

Disease is not a beneficent thing at all.

"While Peter yet spake these words, the Holy Spirit fell on all them which heard the Word," and he said:

Can any man forbid the water that these should not be baptized, which have received the Holy Spirit as well as we?

No man forbade the water, and therefore he commanded them to be baptized.

There Is No Such Thing as Baby Baptism.

I command you to be baptized, if you are true Christians, in the way that the Christ commanded.

He never commanded babies to be baptized.

He said:

And Jesus came to them and spake unto them, saying, All Authority hath been given unto Me in heaven and on earth.

Go ye therefore, and make disciples of all the nations, baptizing them into the Name of the Father and of the Son and of the Holy Spirit.

A disciple is a learner, and a baby cannot understand anything except to put things into its mouth.

You have to watch it and attend to it all the time.

A baby has no sense for a long time.

But you are to see that the babies are properly cared for and brought up, and then make disciples of them when they are old enough to understand.

When you have made them disciples then you are commanded to baptize them.

There is only one way to baptize and that is the Baptism that our Lord Jesus, the Christ, commanded.

He said, "Go ye therefore, and make disciples of all the nations, baptizing them into the Name of—

Voices—"The Father."

General Overseer—And of—

Voices—"The Son."

General Overseer—And of—

Voices—"The Holy Spirit."

General Overseer—Is that one act?

If I were to tell you to dip this handkerchief into blue, and yellow, and black dye, how many times would you have to dip it?

Voices—"Three times."

General Overseer—Could you do it by dipping it into the one vat?

Voices—"No, sir"

Triune Immersion the Primitive Mode of Baptism.

General Overseer—Triune Immersion was the only Baptism that the Church knew for Nine Centuries, except in the one case, that of a heretical bishop named Eunomius, in the fourth century, who baptized by one immersion because he denied the Triunity of God.

He was expelled from the Church.

That statement of mine does not rest upon my authority only.

It rests upon the authority that every scholar here will be compelled to accept—the latest and best work on Christian Antiquities, that of Sir William Smith and Canon Cheetham.

In an article upon Baptism, which was written by a Canon of the Church of England, Canon Marriott, we find that Triune Immersion was the original Baptism, and for nine centuries there was no other authorized by the Church. He declares that even the early popes said that they would expel from the church any presbyter or bishop who baptized in any other way.

There is only one God, but He is in three persons—Father, Son, and Holy Spirit.

There is only one Faith, but it covers Salvation, Healing, and Holy Living.

There is only one Baptism, but it is into the Three Names—the Name of the Father and of the Son and of the Holy Spirit.

The meaning of that Baptism is Death to Sin, Life in God, and Power for Service.

I command you to be baptized into the Name of the Father, and into the Name of the Son, and into the Name of the Holy Spirit.

Sprinkling Is Not Baptism.

Baptism means a repeated dipping.

The Greek word, *bapto* (βάπτω) means to dip.

Baptidzo (βαπτίζω) means to dip repeatedly.

The ending *idzo* gives the verb a frequentive force, signifying repeated action.

When a woman washes dishes, the verb used is *baptidzo*, that is to say, she dips the dishes repeatedly.

May God grant you to believe, and to receive Him as your Savior, as your Healer, as your Cleanser and as your Keeper.

May He lead you to obey Him in Baptism, and to follow Him in Newness of Life. For Jesus' sake. Amen.

PRAYER OF CONSECRATION.

Our God and Father, in Jesus' Name we come to Thee. Take us as we are and make us what we ought to be, in spirit, soul and body. Help us to repent, and to believe and to obey Thee. In Jesus' Name. Amen. [*All repeat the prayer, clause by clause, after the General Overseer.*]

The meeting was closed with the Doxology and the

BENEDICTION.

Beloved, abstain from all appearance of evil. And may the very God of Peace Himself sanctify you wholly; and I pray God your whole spirit and soul and body be preserved entire, without blame, unto the coming of our Lord Jesus, the Christ. Faithful is He that calleth you, who also will do it. The grace of our Lord Jesus, the Christ, the love of God, our Father, the fellowship of the Holy Spirit, our Comforter and Guide, one Eternal God, abide in you, bless you and keep you, and all the Israel of God everywhere, forever. Amen

Notice to Officers and Members.

Send all newspaper clippings concerning the General Overseer, the Elders, or any department of the work in connection with the Christian Catholic Church in Zion, to Deacon Carl F. Stern, Zion City, Illinois. Send as soon as possible after publication, and carefully mark *name and date of the paper clipped from* on each article. If this is not done, the clippings are absolutely useless.

GOD'S WAY OF HEALING.

BY THE REV. JOHN ALEX. DOWIE.

God's Way Of Healing Is a Person, Not a Thing.

Jesus said "*I am* the Way, and the Truth, and the Life," and He has ever been revealed to His people in all the ages by the Covenant Name, Jehovah-Rophi, or "*I am* Jehovah that Healeth thee." (John 14:6; Exodus 15:26.)

The Lord Jesus, the Christ, Is Still the Healer.

He cannot change, for "Jesus, the Christ, is the same yesterday and today, yea and forever;" and He is still with us, for He said: "Lo, *I am* with you All the Days, even unto the Consummation of the Age." (Hebrews 13:8; Matthew 28:20.) Because He is Unchangeable, and because He is present, in spirit, just as when in the flesh, He is the Healer of His people.

Divine Healing Rests on the Christ's Atonement.

It was prophesied of Him "Surely He hath borne our griefs (Hebrew, *sickness*), and carried our sorrows: . . . and with His stripes we are healed;" and it is expressly declared that this was fulfilled in His Ministry of Healing, which still continues. (Isaiah 53:4, 5; Matthew 8:17.)

Disease Can Never be God's Will.

It is the Devil's work, consequent upon Sin, and it is impossible for the work of the Devil ever to be the Will of God. The Christ came to "destroy the works of the Devil," and when He was here on earth He healed "all manner of disease and all manner of sickness," and all these sufferers are expressly declared to have been "oppressed of the Devil." (1 John 3:8; Matthew 4:23; Acts 10:38.)

The Gifts of Healings Are Permanent.

It is expressly declared that the "Gifts and the calling of God are without repentance," and the Gifts of Healings are amongst the Nine Gifts of the Spirit to the Church. (Romans 11:29; 1 Corinthians 12:8-11.)

There Are Four Modes of Divine Healing.

The first is the direct prayer of faith; the second, intercessory prayer of two or more; the third, the anointing of the elders, with the prayer of faith; and the fourth, the laying on of hands of those who believe, and whom God has prepared and called to that ministry. (Matthew 8:5-13; Matthew 18:19; James 5:14, 15; Mark 16:18.)

Divine Healing Is Opposed by Diabolical Counterfeits.

Amongst these are Christian Science (falsely so called), Mind Healing, Spiritualism, Trance Evangelism, etc. (1 Timothy 6:20, 21; 1 Timothy 4:1, 2; Isaiah 51:22, 23.)

Multitudes Have Been Healed Through Faith in Jesus.

The writer knows of thousands of cases and has personally laid hands on scores of thousands of persons. Full information can be obtained at the meetings held in the Zion Tabernacles in Chicago, and in Zion City, Illinois, and in many pamphlets which give the experience, in their own words, of many who have been healed in this and other countries, published at Zion Printing and Publishing House, Zion City, Illinois.

"*Belief Cometh of Hearing, and Hearing by the Word of the Christ.*"

You are heartily invited to attend and hear for yourself.

Zion's Bible Class

Conducted by Deacon Daniel Sloan in Shiloh Tabernacle, Zion City, Lord's Day Morning at 11 o'clock, and in Zion Homes and Gatherings throughout the World.

MID-WEEK BIBLE CLASS LESSON, JUNE 29th or 30th.

The Sin of Overwork.

1. *God warns against too much work.*—Exodus 20:8-11.
Labor must be confined to the daytime.
Night work is not in God's plan of labor.
A day of rest is a necessity from time to time.
2. *No one can work night and day and not find that it is vanity.*—Psalm 127:1-5.
A person can go to bed too late at night.
He can rise too early in the morning.
He can keep everlastingly at it and find sorrow.
3. *God-given wisdom shows that it is not necessary.*—Proverbs 16:8-16.
There are things better than gold.
Satisfaction comes from being right.
Do right, even if you do little.
4. *Satisfaction cannot come through overwork.*—Ecclesiastes 2:24-26.
Live for the true joys of life.
Work because you love to work.
Sinners always overwork.
5. *It is not necessary to overwork to succeed in the truest sense.*—Psalm 1:1-6.
God gives the increase.
God says you can prosper.
Do it by saving and trusting in God.
6. *Sometimes even in the Lord's work one is prone to work beyond one's strength.*—Philippians 2:19-30.
We must not worry because of the over-ripe fields.
One man can do the work of many men.
If the Devil cannot kill by sin he may by overwork
7. *The strain of effort upon the mortal body must be watched.*—2 Corinthians 4:5-16.
The body can stand just so much.
Be careful! It is an earthen vessel.
The power to do great things comes only from God.
8. *One must learn to rest in the midst of labors, and be composed, clear-headed, and always happy.*—Psalm 37:3-11.
Doing good comes before getting money.
Love God fully and He will bless you surely.
You shall inherit all things.

The Lord Our God is a Labor-limiting God.

LORD'S DAY BIBLE CLASS LESSON, JULY 3d.

Too Much Business.

1. *It keeps the mind in a whirl during the night.*—Ecclesiastes 5:3.
It produces sleeplessness.
It causes nervous prostration.
It robs the body of strength.
2. *A person should work up to the point of being tired, and then be quickly refreshed by sleep.*—Ecclesiastes 5:12.
Labor in such a way that you can sleep.
Some work so hard that they cannot sleep.
Night does not bring them refreshing sleep.
3. *To work for self or for selfish ambitions beyond one's necessities is a wrong.*—Ecclesiastes 5:13.
A man can be too rich.
He cannot make too much money.
He must use it for God and mankind.
4. *We come into the world and go out empty-handed, but God's Hand is always full of bounties.*—Ecclesiastes 5:14, 15.
How wealth does fly away!
Men make money, lose it, and die poor.
Some are born rich and die poor.
5. *God lavishly gives to all who trust Him, so one need not be afraid of not having enough.*—Ecclesiastes 5:9.
God gives enough for all.
God does not expect men to run corners on staple foods.
The rich must not deny help to the needy.
6. *Unless one labors for God one will find sorrow sitting in the lap of plenty.*—Ecclesiastes 5:16, 17.
Why are you working so hard?
What makes you see dark days?
Sickness will come with other troubles.
7. *Be happy in God with little or much; do not work and worry, but find joy in thy lot.*—Ecclesiastes 5:18-20.
Thank God for all that you get.
See how much good it will do you and others.
If you have power to make money, find those who have capacity to use it.

God's Holy People are a Moderate People.

Rev. John Alex. Dowie

General Overseer of the

Christian Catholic Church in Zion

ELIJAH THE RESTORER

Will speak in New York City on Lord's Day, June 26, 1904, at 10:00 o'clock a. m. and 2:30 o'clock p. m. Tickets of admission may be had on inquiry at the meetings now held every Lord's Day at 3 o'clock p. m., in Carnegie Chamber Music Hall, 154 West Fifty-seventh Street, near Fifty-eighth Street Station of the Sixth Avenue Elevated Railway. ∴ ∴

ZION CITY BANK

JOHN ALEX. DOWIE

ZION CITY, LAKE COUNTY, ILLINOIS, U. S. A.

Transacts a general Banking Business.

Issues Drafts payable in all the principal cities of the world.

Sells high-grade Securities bearing nine per cent. interest per annum. Particulars mailed on application.

Our Savings Department receives deposits from One Dollar upward, and pays interest at the following rates:

On all sums from $1 to $500, four per cent.

On all sums over $500, three per cent.

This Bank encourages thrift and economy among the people, and will assist them in their efforts to save money.

Our system of Banking by Mail has proved entirely satisfactory to thousands of persons living in different parts of this and other countries. It places everybody in close communication with the Bank and enables them to take advantage of the *excellent facilities* offered.

Correspondence from all parts of the world solicited.

Write for our booklet entitled, "Saving Money."

CHARLES J. BARNARD, Manager. WILLIAM S. PECKHAM, Cashier.
CHARLES H. IRISH, Assistant Cashier.

OBEYING GOD IN BAPTISM.

"Baptizing Them Into the Name of the Father and of the Son and of the Holy Ghost."

Eighteen Thousand Five Hundred Twenty-three Baptisms by Triune Immersion Since March 14, 1897.

Eighteen Thousand Five Hundred Twenty-three Believers have joyfully followed their Lord in the Ordinance of Believer's Baptism by Triune Immersion since the first Baptism in Central Zion Tabernacle on March 14, 1897

Baptized in Central Zion Tabernacle from March 14, 1897, to December 14, 1901, by the General Overseer,	4754		
Baptized in South Side Zion Tabernacle from January 1, 1902, to June 14, 1903, by the General Overseer..	37		
Baptized at Zion City by the General Overseer........	583		
Baptized by Overseers, Elders, Evangelists and Deacons, at Headquarters (Zion City) and Chicago......	4940		
Total Baptized at Headquarters....................	—		10,314
Baptized in places outside of Headquarters by the General Overseer................................		641	
Baptized in places outside of Headquarters by Overseers, Elders, Evangelists and Deacons.		7109	
Total Baptized outside of Headquarters............		—	7,750
Total Baptized in seven years....................			18,064
Baptized since March 14, 1904:			
Baptized in Zion City by Elder Royall.....	63		
Baptized in Zion City by Elder Hammond...........	115		
Baptized in Zion City by Elder Adams	40		
Baptized in Zion City by Evangelist Reder...........	24		
Baptized in Chicago by Elder Hall..................	9		
Baptized in Chicago by Elder Cossum................	20		
Baptized in Chicago by Evangelist Christie	3		
Baptized in Chicago by Deacon Matson...............	4		
Baptized in Chicago by Elder Kosch................	6		
Baptized in Chicago by Elder Hoffman...............	11	295	
Baptized in California by Elder Taylor............		5	
Baptized in Canada by Elder Simmons..............		6	
Baptized in Canada by Elder Brooks................		7	
Baptized in Colorado by Deacon Cook...............		3	
Baptized in England by Overseer Cantel............		10	
Baptized in Illinois by Deacon Sprecher............		1	
Baptized in Indiana by Elder Osborn................		2	
Baptized in Kansas by Elder Reed..................		3	
Baptized in Minnesota by Elder Graves..............		5	
Baptized in New York by Elder Warszawiak..........		14	
Baptized in New York by Overseer Mason		19	
Baptized in Ohio by Deacon Arrington..............		14	
Baptized in Ohio by Deacon Kelchner...............		2	
Baptized in Pennsylvania by Elder Bouck...........		13	
Baptized in South Africa by Overseer Bryant.........		29	
Baptized in Texas by Evangelist Gay................		19	
Baptized in Washington by Elder Simmons...........		1	
Baptized in Washington by Elder Ernst.............		8	
Baptized in Wisconsin by Elder McClurkin...........		3 164	459
Total Baptized since March 14, 1897...............			18,523

The following-named sixteen believers were baptized in the Public Baths, Durban, Natal, South Africa, Thursday, April 28, 1904, by Overseer Daniel Bryant:

Arrow, Mrs. Emma,
May's Cottage, Umgeni road, Durban, Natal, South Africa
Bath, Mrs. Mercy.........Clark road, Berea, Durban, Natal, South Africa
Benison, Thomas.........Cowey road, Berea, Durban, Natal, South Africa
Dimmig, George,
Zion Cottage, Harvey road, Stamford Hill, Durban, Natal, South Africa
Foxcroft, Arthur............................Durban, Natal, South Africa
Hillary, James............................Malvern, Natal, South Africa
Hillary, Mrs. Sarah........................Malvern, Natal, South Africa
Houghton, Arthur...........6 Umgeni road, Durban, Natal, South Africa
Kennedy, Donald..................Box 717, Durban, Natal, South Africa
Kennedy, Mrs. Margaret ....Box 717, Durban, Natal, South Africa
Larger, Edward
Zion Cottage, Harvey road, Stamford Hill, Durban, Natal, South Africa
Larsen, Mrs. Sarah..........549 Smith street, Durban, Natal, South Africa
Pleidrup, N. A.....................Box 717, Durban, Natal, South Africa
Roos, Mrs. Emma,
Zion Cottage, Harvey road, Stamford Hilll, Durban, Natal, South Africa
Roos, John,
Zion Cottage, Harvey road, Stamford Hill, Durban, Natal, South Africa
Staley, John,
Elijah avenue, The Oaks Ridge road, Berea, Durban, Natal, South Africa

The following-named three believers were baptized at New Auburn, Wisconsin, Friday, May 20, 1904, by Elder A. W. McClurkin:

Hagelberger, Mrs. Elizabeth ....New Auburn, Wisconsin
Hagelberger, Frank............................New Auburn, Wisconsin
Heyman, Eva ....New Auburn, Wisconsin

The following-named two believers were baptized at San Antonio, Texas, Lord's Day, May 29, 1904, by Evangelist William D. Gay:

Creswell, Miss Emma...........309 North Pine street, San Antonio, Texas
Flack Miss Lora...Evansville, Indiana

The following-named three believers were baptized at Wichita, Kansas, Friday, June 3, 1904, by Elder David A. Reed:

Speare, Miss Flossy Myrtle......................Antioch, Indian Territory
Speare, Mrs. Mary..............................Antioch, Indian Territory
Speare, Walter Richard........................Antioch, Indian Territory

The following-named eleven believers were baptized in the West Side Zion Tabernacle, Chicago, Illinois, Lord's Day, June 5, 1904, by Elder C. R. Hoffman:

Gaede, Miss Elma ....1043 North Oakley avenue, Chicago, Illinois
Hoffmann, Carl.............1006 North Spaulding avenue, Chicago, Illinois
Hoffmann, Mrs. Johanna....1006 North Spaulding avenue, Chicago, Illinois
Kasch, Miss Lucinda..................361 Orchard street, Chicago, Illinois
Scheel, Arnold...................1833 Lawrence avenue, Chicago, Illinois
Scheel, Otto.....................1833 Lawrence avenue, Chicago, Illinois
Stryker, Miss Elsie..................244 Fletcher street, Chicago, Illinois
Stryker, Mrs. Emilie.................244 Fletcher street, Chicago, Illinois
Stryker, John, Sr....................244 Fletcher street, Chicago, Illinois
Stryker, John, Jr.....................244 Fletcher street, Chicago, Illinois
Wolf, Mrs. Henrietta..............1000 Le Moyne street, Chicago, Illinois

CONSECRATION OF CHILDREN.

The following-named two children were consecrated to God in the Bohemian Zion Tabernacle, 722 West Nineteenth street, Chicago, Illinois, Lord's Day May 22, 1904, by Elder Thomas Kosch.

Witt, Anna M.......... ..442 West Twenty-third street, Chicago, Illinois
Witt, Karl..................442 West Twenty-third street, Chicago, Illinois

Warning.

I am directed by the General Overseer to warn our members and officers throughout the world against giving money to persons claiming to be members of the Christian Catholic Church in Zion. All benevolence must be given either from Headquarters or under the direction of same. Even though the applicant for benevolence be known to be a member of the Christian Catholic Church in Zion, financial aid must not be given except in extreme cases, and then only in small amounts Requests for help must be made to the officer-in-charge. In cases where there is no such officer, requests should be made direct to Headquarters, accompanied by recommendations from one or two members of Zion in good standing.

J. G. Excell,
General Ecclesiastical Secretary.

Publisher's Notice.

The remittance must accompany receipt of subscriptions at the Publishing House, no difference by or for whom or for whatever time they may be given, or whether forwarded through Ordained Officers, Branches, or Gatherings of the Christian Catholic Church in Zion. Accounts will be carried with Ordained Officers, Branches, or Gatherings, on quantity orders of periodicals consigned on sale for monthly settlement, but to include only such articles as bear the imprint of Zion. All orders for Bibles, books, buttons, pictures (except prints done by the Publishing House), lace souvenirs, etc., must be sent to the General Stores, Zion City, Lake County, Illinois.

Warning to Subscribers.

Scarcely a week passes that we do not have complaints about money having been sent to us in currency, stamps, or silver, in the open mails, for renewals of subscriptions or for other purposes, WHICH WE HAVE NOT RECEIVED AND WHICH NEVER REACHES US.

Therefore, we desire to warn every member and friend of Zion sending money to us, to always use some safe means, preferably a money-order, or bank-draft on New York or Chicago, or personal check on Zion City Bank.

In conforming to this notice you will save yourselves trouble and expense, and us much annoyance.

Zion Printing and Publishing House,
Zion City, Illinois.

A WEEKLY PAPER FOR THE EXTENSION OF THE KINGDOM OF GOD

EDITED BY THE REV. JOHN ALEX. DOWIE.

Volume XV. No. 9. *ZION CITY, SATURDAY, JUNE 18, 1904.* *Price Five Cents*

General Overseer, Overseer Jane Dowie and Other Officers of the Christian Catholic Church in Zion, at "Calton Hill," on the Occasion of the Ordination of Elders and Evangelists McCullagh and Hawkins

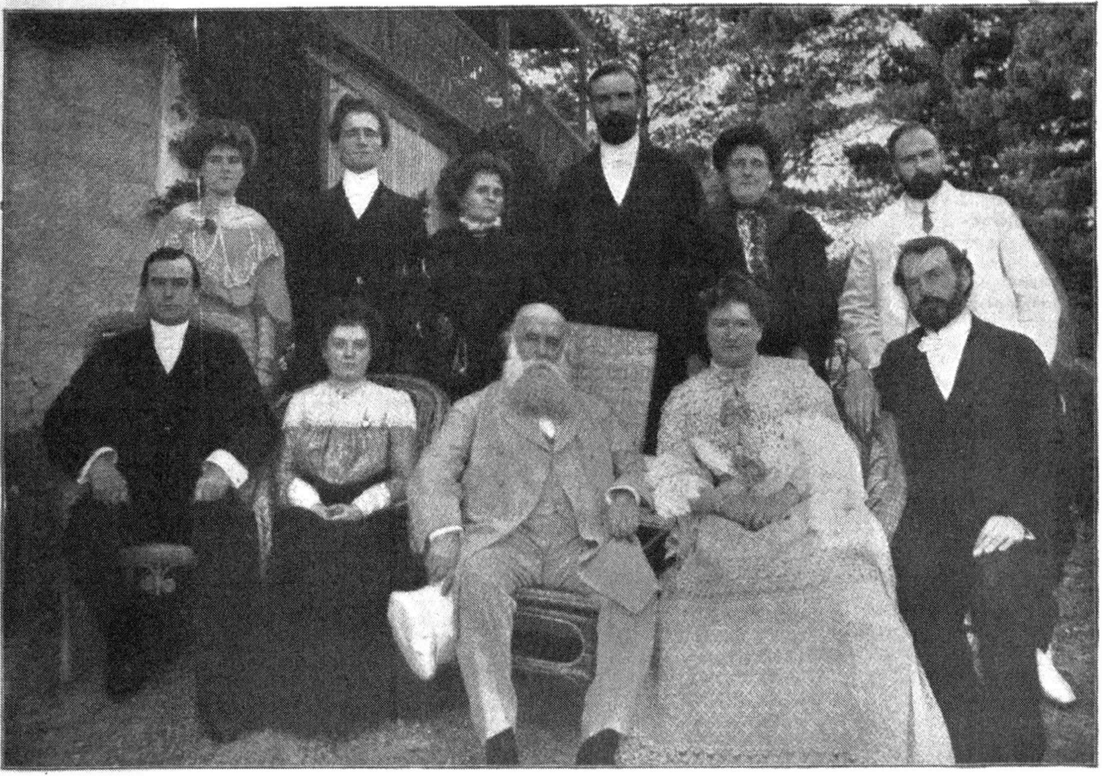

REV. JOHN ALEXANDER DOWIE,
General Overseer of the Christian Catholic Church in Zion.

Overseer Wilbur Glenn Voliva, Elder Mollie Voliva, Overseer Jane Dowie, Overseer John Gabriel Excell,
Miss Christobel McCullagh, Evangelist Hannah McCullagh, Evangelist Marion Eliza Hawkins,
Elder Stephen McCullagh, Elder Clement Friend Hawkins, Dr. A. J. Gladstone Dowie.

A WEEKLY PAPER FOR THE EXTENSION OF THE KINGDOM OF GOD.

EDITED BY THE REV. JOHN ALEX. DOWIE

Application for entry as Second Class Matter at Zion City, Illinois, pending.

Subscription Rates.		**Special Rates.**	
One Year	$2.00	100 Copies of One Issue	$3.00
Six Months	1.25	25 Copies of One Issue	.00
Three Months	.75	To Ministers, Y. M. C. A's and Public Reading Rooms, per annum	1.50
Single Copies	.05		

For foreign subscriptions add $1.50 per year, or three cents per copy for postage.

Subscribers desiring a change of address should give present address, as well as that to which they desire LEAVES OF HEALING sent in the future.

Make Bank Drafts, Express Money or Postoffice Money Orders payable to the order of JOHN ALEX. DOWIE, Zion City, Illinois, U. S. A.

Long Distance Telephone. *Cable Address "Dowie, Zion City."*

All communications upon business must be addressed to
MANAGER ZION PUBLISHING HOUSE,
Zion City, Illinois, U. S. A.

Subscriptions to LEAVES OF HEALING, A VOICE FROM ZION, and the various publications may also be sent to
ZION PUBLISHING HOUSE, 81 EUSTON ROAD, LONDON, N. W., ENGLAND.
ZION PUBLISHING HOUSE, NO 43 PARK ROAD, ST. KILDA, MELBOURNE, VICTORIA, AUSTRALIA.
ZION PUBLISHING HOUSE, RUE DE MONT, THABOR 1, PARIS, FRANCE.
ZIONSHEIM, SCHLOSS LIEBBURG, CANTON THURGAU, BEI ZÜRICH, SWITZERLAND.

ZION CITY, ILLINOIS, SATURDAY, JUNE 18, 1904.

TABLE OF CONTENTS.

LEAVES OF HEALING, SATURDAY, JUNE 18, 1904.

Notes From The Overseer-in-Charge.

"BLESSED IS THE MAN THAT WALKETH NOT IN THE COUNSEL OF THE WICKED,
NOR STANDETH IN THE WAY OF SINNERS,
NOR SITTETH IN THE SEAT OF THE SCORNFUL."

BUT HIS delight is in the law of Jehovah;
And in His law doth he meditate day and night.
And he shall be like a tree planted by the streams of water,
That bringeth forth its fruit in its season,
Whose leaf also doth not wither;
And whatsoever he doeth shall prosper.

JOHN ALEXANDER DOWIE, General Overseer of the Christian Catholic Church in Zion, and the organization which he represents, are entirely out of touch and out of harmony with the existing organizations and conditions of affairs in the world today.

He is ushering in a new régime, and is of necessity in conflict with the old.

THE EFFETE, obsolete, decaying systems, the social, theological and political conditions, are toppling to their fall.

They have become top-heavy with chicanery, debauchery and corruption.

Their foundations have been undermined by the Devil's trinity of Impurity, Intemperance and Infidelity.

NO WONDER that these organizations make a desperate fight for their existence!

WE MADE the statement a few weeks ago that we did not look for any difficulty throughout Europe, and that the only place where there would be any open and violent opposition to the work of the General Overseer would be in London.

This prediction has been fully met.

Throughout France, Germany, Switzerland, and Holland he has been received with an excellent spirit. While some of the papers have tried to discredit his work, others have been most fair. We quote from two of these. First, from the *Zuricher-Anzeiger* of May 28th. We omit several paragraphs which refer only to local conditions.

ONCE MORE: THE PROPHET ELIJAH IN ZURICH.

In publishing our first article, announcing the coming of Dr. Dowie, the founder of Zion City, to Zurich, on his "Around-the-World Visitation," we fully realized that it would arouse great indignation in the so-called Religious Circles.

To us it was no small surprise to find that since Dr. Dowie's first visit to Zurich in December, 1900, this Zion movement has spread itself to much larger circles than we, as close observers, had anticipated. It can be very clearly seen that his followers represent all classes of people—the laborers, organized and unorganized; the middle class, as well as the upper ten thousand, and the educated, as well as the uneducated.

The assurance of this we received from those who, encouraged by the publication of our article, came to us, to tell us and to prove to us that they were not only believers in Dr. Dowie's teaching, but that they were living witnesses to "Divine Healing." It is not our intention to enter again into this "Opposition Arousing" chapter.

Our chief reason for the publication of this second article is because of the conduct of the so-called Christians, who, in the *Protestant*, as well as in one of the daily papers, took pains to term our attitude to Zion "An Incomprehensible Puffery," and to warn, in tones of horror and lamentation, of this "Swindler Dowie."

Truly, we have felt ashamed, ashamed to the very depths of our hearts, at the laughable "Jeremiad" of S. . . r, (Pastor Serr), in the *Protestant* and the *Tageblatt*.

How Heaven sorrowing (Himmeltraurig) it must be to these servants of God, that whenever something contrary to their mock-philosophy is declared by some one else, they, with great lamentation, should fear the downfall of their whole work and system.

And then she wonders why her meeting-places are getting empty, and why her people turn to other teachings, where they find something better than mere promises of Heaven.

The Church has no right whatever to oppose the religious liberty of others, Dr. Dowie included. We do not ask for freedom and equality for ourselves only, but for people who think differently as well; and we protest against every kind of prejudice and every oppression executed in this respect.

And now another word. We are prepared to make the assertion that our knowledge of this Zion movement is just as impartial as that of the *Freitag's Zeitung*, and that it is founded on just as much careful study as that of Mr. Zurlinden.

The fact of the matter is, that the lamentations of the *Tageblatt* more than anything else induced us to go and hear Dr. Dowie's lectures, and we confess that we did not consider it a "sour task." On the contrary, we have not the least reason to take back anything that we said in our first article.

What wrong is Dr. Dowie doing? Is it the healing of more than one hundred people in Zurich alone? Or is the fact a crime, that in his Zion City, which was built by Architect Burkhardt, good wages are paid for eight hours a day labor?

But what about Dowie's jesting and vulgarity of speech on the platform? We admit that we have never before seen any public speaker of such liveliness and agility, and we would not take offense at any one for being that.

Furthermore, in the four lectures, which we successively attended, we noticed nothing whatever of "insolence" or "vulgarity," which is said to especially characterize him. That he does not handle with velvet gloves his opponents, who do their very best in slandering him, is easy to be understood. In all other things our attitude has been confirmed.

The petty conduct of certain circles have not in any way injured Dowie's Mission in Zurich. He could not have wished for better attendance, and the number of his adherents have no doubt grown to such extent that it will be impossible to get them out of the world by lamentations, cheap and base accusations, or by silence.

In another paper, the *Grus Gott*, an undenominational religious paper, published in Weinfelden, Switzerland, the description of the Praise and Testimony Meeting is refreshing:

We informed our readers a few weeks ago that Dr. Dowie would be in Zurich during the "Pfingstwoche" (Pentecost-week).

Opposed by the preachers of all denominations, he also has the state church against him, and very few of the political papers ever have a good word for him.

It is, therefore, difficult to get a personal conviction, and to get that you have to hear and see for yourself.

It was the last meeting, on the afternoon of May 29th, that the writer attended.

A venerable figure, this Dowie, and in spite of silver-white hair often eloquent to youthful fire. What he says, is clear, on the foundation of the Bible.

And the way he explains the "Coming of Elijah," whom he proclaims to be, is so clear, that you can only misunderstand him when you do not *want* to understand him.

Why are the churches empty? Every one who has read Kutter's "They Must" (we shall speak about that later on) admits gently that a revolution is taking place.

What is it that draws thousands and tens of thousands to Zion? Words alone are not sufficient, the deeds must confirm them.

A grand sight it was, when in that overflowing building, seating at least one thousand people, from one hundred to one hundred fifty testified to having been healed through faith, without the use of any drugs.

The Mission in Zurich was followed by meetings in Bern, Geneva, Lausanne, Neuchatel and Berlin.

BUT LONDON is one of the seats of the apostasy, and is also the world metropolis of Freemasonry.

King Edward, *ex officio*, is the "Defender of the Faith."

In all probability some one near the throne is at the head of Freemasonry everywhere.

It is here that we should expect the greatest opposition to the pure, clean, strong, abiding work of Zion.

THE FOLLOWING cablegram, received on last Monday, tells briefly the condition of affairs in London on the arrival of the General Overseer:

LONDON.

SPEICHER, Zion City, Illinois.

Read 105th Psalm, verses 12 to 15.

Have had most successful Visitation. On Monday, 6th of June, was at Liebburg; Lake Constance, Wednesday; Thursday, Berlin, Germany; Friday, Rotterdam, Holland.

Overflowing meetings, kind reception and perfect order everywhere.

Arrived in London Saturday morning.

Was excluded from Hotel Russell, and many other hotels.

Was received in the evening in Hotel Cecil, but must leave there today.

Delightful meetings yesterday in Zion Tabernacle.

Representatives of Zion from many parts of the United Kingdom, Ireland and the Continent were present.

Received fifty-seven new members into fellowship. Ordained Catherine and Arthur Booth-Clibborn Elders, also one Evangelist, and twenty-six Deacons and Deaconesses.

Held a large Communion Service.

There were violent demonstrations by a large crowd in Euston road, at the close of the services.

Shameful reports and attacks appeared in most of the London papers, the *Times* and the *Daily Chronicle* being excepted.

Pray for us.

Love.

Mizpah. DOWIE.

THE ENEMIES of God are determined that Elijah the Restorer shall not be permitted at this time to destroy the Priests of Baal.

They cannot endure his presence.

UNDOUBTEDLY there was a plot to take his life.

We have correspondence from Fremantle, Australia, proving that the assassins were prevented from taking his life at that place, and they no doubt have followed him to London.

It was apparently considered necessary, under the circumstances, to leave British soil.

EVERY TIME the General Overseer makes a move of any kind it is always the custom of the Devil's agents in the press to make it appear that Zion is about to go to pieces.

The Washington, D. C., *Star*, of the 9th inst., makes a disgustingly poor and weak criticism and prophecy.

Just as the Chicago papers a few years ago prophesied that Zion had gone to pieces because the General Overseer had gone to Europe, so now, because he is returning to America, they are saying that he has been driven out of Australia and Europe, and is going back to New York where, they allege, he met such a stupendous defeat before.

ZION HAS been accustomed to just this kind of defeats for ten years.

The beauty of it is that every "defeat" raises us higher in financial, numerical and spiritual strength.

ONE PAPER declares that the Visitation to Australia was an absolute failure.

Another states that of the four hundred eighteen passengers on the Steamship Minuka, which arrived from Australia, sixty-two were bound for Zion City.

The fact is that fifty-seven of them arrived here safely on Monday of this week.

On the very day of their arrival fifty others left Sydney, Australia, for Zion City.

This does not look like failure.

THE GENERAL OVERSEER ordained thirty-two officers in Zürich, received five hundred six members into fellowship and baptized by Triune Immersion one hundred seventy-four.

This does not look like failure.

HE ORDAINED twenty-nine new officers in London on last Lord's Day, among them Mr. and Mrs. Arthur Booth-Clibborn.

This does not look like failure.

THE GENERAL OVERSEER has met every engagement in every city, on the very date advertised, and has carried out his plan exactly as arranged months before he left America, with the exception of not visiting India.

This does not look like failure.

THE PAPERS generally are commenting upon the fact that Zion has promptly paid the second instalment of her outstanding indebtedness, amounting to twenty-five per cent.

This does not look like failure.

THE DEVIL of lust and gluttony does not like to be disturbed.

The antagonizing of wine drinking, tobacco using, sexual impurity, and the eating of unclean food touches a chord in the Devil's pneumo-gastric nerve which makes him howl with rage.

THE WEAK and insipid way in which the churches are fighting intemperance and impurity does very little to stir up the ire of the devil of gluttony; but when Zion comes and not only attacks all these in a most aggressive way, but also condemns that mass of disease-breeding uncleanness, the unspeakable hog, then there is gnashing of teeth.

THE BEER-GUZZLING, tobacco-soaked multitudes delight in their scrofula-breeding pork.

And how the terrible scourge is spreading!

New York City has again broken her record for the highest number of deaths from pulmonary diseases. The increasing impurity of the blood is largely the cause of this state of affairs.

ZION CITY is almost entirely free from pulmonary diseases.

WE EAT good food, and plenty of it; we live quiet, sober, godly lives; all of which is conducive to good health.

WE ARE ever watchful lest the pendulum be permitted to swing to the extremes and that the errors and fanaticisms of the world gain a foothold among us.

WHILE WE denounce the eating of impure food, and especially unclean animal food, we dare not go to the extreme of some and denounce all animal food as injurious.

DR. H. S. TANNER, who became famous for having fasted forty days, has not found many followers nor imitators in his fasting.

He may be able to find a larger number who are willing to agree with him that all animal food is injurious, and that a vegetarian diet is the only proper one.

But while Zion cannot agree with him in this, we do agree with all that he has said concerning the consumption of swine's flesh as a food.

We make some extracts from an excellent article of his, in a recent edition of a Pasadena, California, paper:

> One hundred fifty thousand persons die annually in the United States from tuberculosis, and there is a presumptive evidence to show that swine's flesh is the primary cause of this frightful mortality.
>
> The Jews eat no pork, and consumption is a disease almost unknown among them.
>
> The Bible student—the best book on hygiene extant—will not deny that swine's flesh was prohibited under the old Mosaic law, and severe penalties were visited upon the disobedient.
>
> Statistics show that the Jews, who eat no pork, are immune from cholera.
>
> There has not been a single case of cholera in Russia, its stronghold, among the Jews.
>
> In London, in the severe cholera epidemic of 1849, only two Jews died of the disease.
>
> Besides being immune from cholera, the Jews are singularly free from consumption and cancer.

OUR PEOPLE are a strong people physically, because they eat good, wholesome food and lead sober, godly lives.

DEMAND for our workmen is being increasingly made in surrounding cities.

BRETHREN, PRAY FOR US.

JOHN G. SPEICHER.

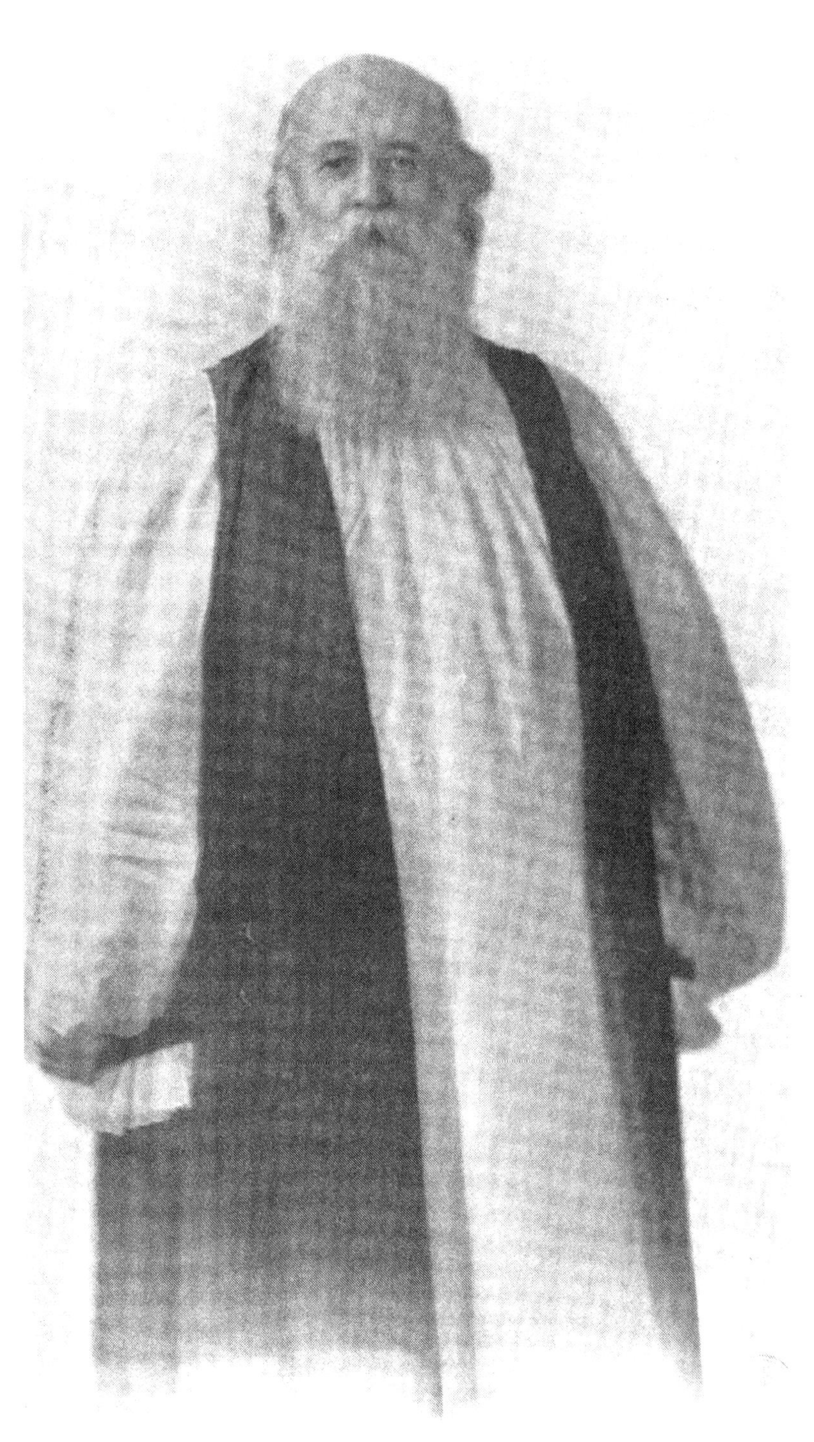

ELIJAH THE RESTORER

THE RIDE FOR A KNIGHTHOOD.

Around-the-World Visitation

of the

Rev. John Alex. Dowie

Elijah the Restorer
General Overseer of the Christian Catholic Church in Zion.

By ARTHUR W. NEWCOMB, Special Correspondent.

THE last paper of this series closed with the report of the General Overseer's Message delivered on Thursday afternoon, March 24, 1904.

On the following morning, Friday, March 25th, at half past ten o'clock, in the Town Hall, the General Overseer conducted the fifth Divine Healing Meeting of the Visitation.

These Divine Healing Meetings, like all those of the Visitation in Australia, were attended by an ever-increasing number of the most deeply interested people.

God's prophet of the Time of the Restoration of All Things is, first of all, a great teacher, and it is in his capacity as a teacher that he is a means of spiritual, psychical and physical blessing to many thousands throughout the earth. At the Divine Healing Meetings he is at his best as a teacher.

Here also he is seen especially in his prophetic office as Messenger of the Covenant—God's Covenant of Salvation, Healing and Holy Living.

In these meetings, the General Overseer also spoke to many who were suffering from various diseases, and in the quiet, earnest prayer services which were held at the close, the Spirit of God was present in power to heal, and many of God's children were able to date their deliverance from the oppression of the Devil, from the Adelaide Visitation.

The following is the report of the General Overseer's Message:

Town Hall, Adelaide, South Australia, Friday Morning, March 25, 1904.

The Service was opened by the Congregation's singing Hymns Nos. 12, 22 and 11, from the Visitation Program.

Following this the General Overseer said:

A Morning Prayer.

I ask your prayers, this morning, for an increased measure of the Grace of God, especially the Spirit of Wisdom, and of Understanding, and of a Sound Mind, that we may not judge after the seeing of the eyes, nor the hearing of the ears, but that we may have power to judge with a Spiritual Discernment, which is the only righteous form of judgment.

There is one little prayer that I offer every morning when the sun wakes me. I always awake with the rising sun.

I do not always get up, but I always awake.

I first pray that the Sun of Righteousness may rise that day upon me, and upon all to whom I minister, with Healing in His wings; that I may go forth to tread down wickedness under the soles of my feet until it is ashes.

I then pray: "Give unto me this day, O my Father, the Spirit of Wisdom, of Understanding, of Knowledge, and of the Fear of Jehovah, that I may be of quick understanding in the fear of Jehovah, not judging after the seeing of the eyes, nor the hearing of the ears."

The man who walks about through this life using only his natural senses will be saved from very much trouble.

Your nose will tell you when a thing is bad, unless you pervert your sense of smell.

Your tongue will tell you when a thing is bad, unless you pervert your sense of taste.

Your ears will tell you when a thing is bad, unless you pervert your sense of hearing.

But these natural senses are, after all, often deceptive.

You think that you see gold when you are looking upon brass, or something that is gold-lacquered.

You think that you hear truth when you are hearing cunningly devised fables or false teachings veiled under very beautiful phrases.

Sometimes you think that you are teaching what is good, when your are teaching what is evil.

We Need Our Spiritual Senses Wakened.

The Spiritual Sight, the Spiritual Hearing, the Spiritual Touch, the Spiritual Taste, and the Spiritual Smell should be acute.

There is a Spiritual sense of Smell, for God is Spirit, and He speaks of some things as a "stench in His nostrils, a fire that burneth all the day long."

He speaks of Himself as having senses of touch, and taste.

Pray that God may give me, and the people who are assembled here, the spiritual senses.

Prayer was offered by Overseer Voliva.

The General Overseer then said:

A BIBLE READING CONCERNING THE COMING OF ELIJAH THE RESTORER.

*REPORTED BY E. W. AND A. W. N.

We will now proceed with the Scripture reading, which will be, first of all, from the book of the Prophet Malachi.

Concerning the Prophet Malachi.

Except John the Baptist, Malachi was the last of the prophets of the Ancient Dispensation.

It is supposed that he wrote in the time of Simon the Just, who was the president of the Sanhedrin when the Sacred Canon was established, and that Malachi himself was a member of that great Council.

His were the last of the prophecies for nearly four hundred years.

The people had gone down into deep degeneracy, and God sent no prophet.

"Where there is no vision the people perish."

Malachi was the prophet who was to utter the last words of prophecy for nearly four hundred years, when Elijah the Preparer was to come.

Overseer Voliva will read the 3d and 4th chapters of that book from the Revised Version, because there is considerable difference between the Revised and the Old Versions, which is very important.

Overseer Voliva [reads]—

Behold, I send My Messenger, and he shall prepare the way before Me: and Jehovah, whom ye seek, shall suddenly come to His Temple; and the Messenger—

General Overseer—The Overseer is reading a word that is not correct according to the Old Version.

He is not saying "*even* the Messenger," but he is saying, "*and* the Messenger of the Covenant," a totally different person from Jehovah Himself.

The Messenger of the Covenant not the Christ.

Jehovah says that His Messenger will come. That does not refer to the Christ, because the coming of Jehovah was the coming of the Christ.

He is the Coming One.

He is God incarnate; but the Messenger of the Covenant is a different person.

It is now very foolishly stated by the churches, that the Messenger of the Covenant is Jesus.

Yet the reference Bibles issued by the Oxford press, all give the reference to John the Baptist, not to Jesus.

Overseer Voliva [reads]—

Behold, I send My messenger, and he shall prepare the way before Me: and Jehovah, whom ye seek, shall suddenly come to His temple; and the messenger of the covenant, whom ye delight in, behold, he cometh, saith Jehovah of Hosts.

But who may abide the day of his coming?

General Overseer—"Who may abide the day of his coming?" When Elijah the Preparer came, they did not stand.

They became angry and walked about, and they do not stand now.

A large number are kicking very hard.

Overseer Voliva [reads]—

*The following address has not been revised by the General Overseer.

But who may abide the day of his coming? and who shall stand when he appeareth? for he is like a refiner's fire, and like fuller's soap:
And he shall sit as a refiner and purifier of silver, and he shall purify the sons of Levi, and purge them as gold and silver; and they shall offer unto Jehovah offerings in righteousness.

General Overseer—Now if this refiner and purifier of the sons of Levi were the Lord Himself, it would read this way: And they shall offer unto Him (Jehovah) an Offering in Righteousness.

You can see that this refers to some one who does certain things, and is the means in God's hands of purifying the people, that they may offer unto God an Offering in Righteousness.

"An Offering in Righteousness."

One of the things for which this ministry is renowned is that we insist that people make an Offering to God in Righteousness; that is to say we have no member in our Church who does not pay tithes to God.

If they will not pay their tithes to God, we call them thieves who are robbing God.

They can go to the Methodists, Baptists, or Congregationalists and rob God, but they cannot stay in Zion and do it.

In Zion, we insist that the people shall not rob God.

We say that every penny out of ten, every dollar out of ten, every pound out of ten belongs to God, and must be paid to Him.

I make the charge against this Whole Nation that, for the most part, it robs God.

The prosperity of Zion is very largely due to the fact that her people do not rob God; that the humblest man in Zion pays his tithe, and he gets richer for it.

Zion herself is, beyond all question, notwithstanding all the cavil of the enemy, the richest religious institution in the world for the time it has existed.

Individually our people are better off for the time that they have been in Zion than any other people in the world proportionately.

One of the things that the Messenger of the Covenant, who is identical with Elijah, is to do, is to compel the people of God to make an Offering in Righteousness, as they are not to rob God, but to give Him His tithes and offerings.

Overseer Voliva [reads]—

Then shall the offering of Judah and Jerusalem be pleasant unto Jehovah, as in the days of old, and as in ancient years.
And I will come near to you to judgment; and I will be a swift witness against the sorcerers, and against the adulterers, and against false swearers; and against those that oppress the hireling in his wages, the widow, and the fatherless, and that turn aside the stranger from his right, and fear not Me, saith Jehovah of Hosts.
For I Jehovah change not; therefore ye, O sons of Jacob, are not consumed.
From the days of your fathers ye have turned aside from Mine ordinances, and have not kept them. Return unto Me, and I will return unto you, saith Jehovah of Hosts. But ye say, Wherein shall we return?
Will a man rob God? yet ye rob Me. But ye say, Wherein have we robbed Thee? In tithes and offerings.
Ye are cursed with the curse; for ye rob Me, even this whole nation.
Bring ye the whole tithe into the storehouse, that there may be meat in Mine house, and prove Me now herewith, saith Jehovah of Hosts, if I will not open you the windows of heaven, and pour you out a blessing, that there shall not be room enough to receive it.
And I will rebuke the devourer for your sakes, and he shall not destroy the fruits of your ground; neither shall your vine cast her fruit before the time in the field, saith Jehovah of Hosts.
And all nations shall call you happy: for ye shall be a delightsome land, saith Jehovah of Hosts.
Your words have been stout against Me, saith Jehovah. Yet ye say, Wherein have we spoken against Thee?
Ye have said, It is vain to serve God: and what profit is it that we have kept His charge, and that we have walked mournfully before Jehovah of Hosts?
And now we call the proud happy; yea, they that work wickedness are built up; yea, they tempt God, and are delivered.

General Overseer—Malachi is simply writing what these wicked men said.

He is not the author of these naughty things.

The Religion of Hypocrites.

They call the proud happy.

They serve God for nothing.

That religion is worthless.

Religion is of no use to you if you are only serving God mournfully.

There are a great many people who are exceedingly troubled because I laugh.

It is not written in the Bible, Thou shalt not laugh.

They seem to think that a minister ought not to laugh, nor to make people laugh.

Do you not know that God laughed?

The Word of God says, "He that sitteth in the heavens shall laugh; Jehovah shall have them in derision."

I think that God must laugh very heartily at the folly of the Devil.

I get more laughter out of the Devil than I do out of any one or anything else.

The Devil does look so foolish, and his people look foolish, too!

I do not know whether to laugh or cry sometimes.

One must cry for the sins of the people, and one must laugh at their foolish ways.

When you walk before God mournfully, you are not of much use.

If your religion is not a joy to you, it is a kind of religion you had better give up.

Overseer Voliva [reads]—

Then they that feared Jehovah spake one with another: and Jehovah harkened, and heard, and a Book of Remembrance was written before Him, for them that feared Jehovah, and that thought upon His Name.
And they shall be Mine, saith Jehovah of Hosts, in the day that I do make, even a peculiar treasure; and I will spare them, as a man spareth his own son that serveth him.
Then shall ye return and discern between the righteous and the wicked, between him that serveth God and him that serveth him not.
For, behold, the day cometh, it burneth as a furnace; and all the proud, and all that work wickedness, shall be stubble: and the day that cometh shall burn them up, saith Jehovah of Hosts, that it shall leave them neither root nor branch.
But unto you that fear My Name shall the Sun of Righteousness arise with healing in His wings; and ye shall go forth and gambol as calves of the stall.
And ye shall tread down the wicked; for they shall be ashes under the soles of your feet in the day that I do make, saith Jehovah of Hosts.

General Overseer—There are two important verses that sum up the whole matter. I ask you to listen very closely to the last verses in the Old Testament.

Overseer Voliva [reads]—

Remember ye the Law of Moses My servant, which I commanded unto him in Horeb for all Israel, even statutes and judgments. Behold, I will send you Elijah the Prophet.

General Overseer—You must remember that

The Ten Commandments Are Eternal.

They go on through all the ages.

Jesus said, "Whosoever therefore shall break one of these least Commandments, and shall teach men so, shall be called the least in the Kingdom of Heaven."

You shall not teach men to break one Commandment.

There are not only ten; there are eleven; for the Christ gave a New Commandment:

A New Commandment I give unto you, that ye love one another, as I have loved you.

Overseer Voliva [reads]—

Remember ye the law of Moses My servant, which I commanded unto him in Horeb for all Israel, even statutes and judgments.
Behold, I will send you Elijah the Prophet before the Great and Terrible Day of Jehovah come:
And he shall turn the heart of the fathers to the children, and the heart of the children to their fathers; lest I come and smite the earth with a curse.

General Overseer—The Scriptures are the court of final appeal in this matter.

First, I shall ask the Overseer to turn to the passage in Luke, in which is recorded the prophecy concerning the birth of John the Baptist.

Please read the 17th verse of the 1st chapter.

The Word of God is neglected so shockingly that you must read it carefully.

You cannot understand anything about Divine Revelation unless you read the revelation.

Overseer Voliva [reads]—

And thou shalt have joy and gladness; and many shall rejoice at his birth.
For he shall be great in the sight of the Lord, and he shall drink no wine nor strong drink; and he shall be filled with the Holy Spirit, even from his mother's womb.
And many of the children of Israel shall he turn unto the Lord their God.

General Overseer—Now, please listen very attentively, to the 17th verse.

Overseer Voliva [reads]—

And he shall go before His face—

General Overseer—Before whose face?

Overseer Voliva—"Before the Christ's face." [Reads]—

And he shall go before His face in the spirit and power of Elijah, to turn the hearts of the fathers to the children, and the disobedient to walk in the wisdom of the just; to make ready for the Lord a people prepared for Him.

John the Baptist Was Elijah the Preparer.

General Overseer—Did the Angel Gabriel know what he was talking about?

Voices—"Yes."

General Overseer—Did he not say that he came from God, the Eternal, with a Message, to say that John the Baptist should come in the spirit and power of Elijah?

Voices—"Yes."

General Overseer—Did he come in that spirit and power?

Voices—"Yes."

General Overseer—John did not think it himself. John made a big blunder about that.

Take the Gospel according to St. John, and read the 19th verse of the 1st chapter,

Overseer Voliva [reads]—

And this is the witness of John, when the Jews sent unto him from Jerusalem priests and Levites to ask him, Who art thou?

And he confessed, and denied not; and he confessed, I am not the Christ.

And they asked him, What then? Art thou Elijah? And he saith, I am not. Art thou the prophet?

General Overseer—Properly this should be "*that* prophet."

When they said, "Art thou Elijah?" what did he say?

Overseer Voliva—"He said, 'I am not.'"

General Overseer—Was he right?

Overseer Voliva—"No."

I Did Not Understand My Own Mission at First.

General Overseer—When they said I was Elijah, I said, "I am not," and I was angry. Your press speaks of me as the "self-styled prophet," but it is mistaken.

My people believed that I was a prophet.

They would come to me and say, "Doctor, you are the prophet who is to come in the spirit and power of Elijah. You are Elijah of the Restoration."

I would say, "Get away!" and would be angry.

I would not listen to it.

But the day came when I saw that I was the Messenger of God's Covenant; that I was the only man, perhaps, in the world who was proclaiming the great Covenant of Salvation and Healing and Holy Living all in one.

The 35th chapter of Isaiah prophesies, concerning the Christ, "He will come and save you."

"He will come and heal you."

"It shall be called the Way of Holiness."

There is the Covenant for spirit, soul and body; for Salvation, Healing and Holy Living.

I did not know any one but myself who was proclaiming it all in one.

Some were proclaiming it in pieces, but they were not as one.

I had to recognize that.

But they said,

"The Messenger of the Covenant is Elijah."

I would shrug my shoulders, and say, "Get away! Go on with your work. Do not bother me any more about Elijah."

I was angry, and I would not listen, but there came a day when I felt that I had to listen to God.

I well remember that day.

It was not in Australia, and it was not in America.

It was in Europe, where I was discussing this matter with some friends on the Continent.

One man was fighting my Declaration as Messenger of the Covenant.

He said, "You cannot be the Messenger of the Covenant, because the Messenger of the Covenant is Elijah."

"Well," I said, "I am Elijah." He started.

"Doctor," he said, "you are an apostle."

I said, "A prophet is less than an apostle; because in the 12th chapter of Paul's 1st Epistle to the Corinthians, 28th verse, it is written, "And God hath set some in the Church, first apostles, secondly, prophets."

An apostle is more than a prophet. I am merely claiming to be the prophetic Messenger of the Covenant."

"Then," he said, "you are Elijah."

"If the Messenger of the Covenant is Elijah, I am," I answered.

I had seen that before, only I would not say it.

When and Why the Declaration of Elijah the Restorer Was Made.

But I would not open the Gates of Zion City, and I would not lease land without making the Declaration, lest any one should say afterwards, "If you had made that Declaration before we took the lease, we should not have bought the land." I made the Declaration, therefore, when I fully believed it and knew it myself, and when God's time had come.

But I was just as honest as John the Baptist when he was asked, "Art thou Elias?" and he answered, "I am not."

But had not the Angel Gabriel said he was?

Audience—"Yes."

General Overseer—That is more important.

Overseer Voliva [reads]—

And if ye are willing to receive it, this is Elijah, which is to come.

General Overseer—While John was yet alive, Jesus declared that he was Elijah.

There is no question about that. It shows you that Elijah can come more than once.

Elijah is the prophet of All Time down to the End of the Dispensation.

He must come again and again in the spirit and power.

Whether I am or am not he, is not the question.

You understand that I am discussing the question as to whether or not he should come.

Overseer Voliva—"This is Matthew 11th chapter, 13th and 14th verses." [Reads]—

For all the prophets and the law prophesied until John.

And if ye are willing to receive it, this is Elijah, which is to come.

General Overseer—Who is speaking?

Overseer Voliva—"Jesus is speaking." [Reads]—

And if ye are willing to receive it—

General Overseer—That is the Revision, but is there not a marginal reading there?

Overseer Voliva—"Yes, 'If ye are willing to receive *him*.'"

General Overseer—John was in a dungeon, but the Christ said that he was Elijah, did He not?

Voices—"Yes."

General Overseer—Was he Elijah?

Voices—"Yes."

General Overseer—Yet his name was John the Baptist was it not?

Voices—"Yes."

General Overseer—My name is John Alexander Dowie—at least that is the name they gave me—and it is an honorable name in this city, I am thankful to say.

It is not the name I ought to have, but that is another matter.

A Scathing Rebuke to an Anonymous Letter Writer.

Some one has written an impertinent letter to my wife, wanting her to talk about our daughter's death.

She will not do it.

This writer, who signs the name "Jephtha's Daughter," says that Mrs. Dowie owes it to the women of Australia.

She owes no such thing to the women of Australia. Some of the women of this city have been more impudent than the men.

Some of the nastiest words she has ever received were in letters sent to her this week by women.

A most insulting letter was received from an apparently well-educated woman, who called Mrs. Dowie a coward, and was not brave enough to sign the letter.

There are women in this city who are incarnate devils.

I want to say that we owe nothing especial to the women, or the men either, of South Australia.

We owe it to all the world to say what is right.

We have said it.

If any one wants to know all the circumstances connected with our daughter's death, they can find them written in LEAVES OF HEALING.

They can go up to the office, and buy a copy for three pence.

Nothing is kept back in that story; it is all there.

We will not harrow our hearts and intensify our sorrow.

Mrs. Dowie has had enough of it, and we go on.

Our dear daughter is with the Lord, and we are going to meet her.

We had nothing to do with her death.

I thank God that she suffered no pain, and that she talked to us for nearly twelve hours, and then fell asleep.

But we do not deserve being insulted and having our hearts harrowed over it.

That letter, however, shows what fiendish women there are in this city.

I think the writer of that letter must be a daughter of Jezebel instead of Jephtha.

Death of John the Baptist.

We have been reading in the 11th of Matthew, and found there that Jesus said that John the Baptist was Elijah.

We will now read from the 14th chapter of Matthew, which gives an account of his death.

Herod was drunk, and Herodias' daughter danced before him.

He promised to give her anything that she might ask, even to the half of his kingdom.

He made a bad oath.

When she asked her mother what she should get, the mother told her to demand the head of John the Baptist, in a charger.

John the Baptist was put to death. What did they do?

Overseer Voliva [reads]—

And his disciples came, and took up the corpse, and buried him; and they went and told Jesus.

General Overseer—In the 11th chapter of Matthew, Jesus says that John is Elijah, and in the 14th chapter you have the account of his death.

They took up the corpse and buried it, and went and told Jesus.

Now, read the 17th chapter.

There was a Transfiguration on the Mount. As Jesus and the three disciples came down from the Mount, the following conversation took place.

Overseer Voliva [reads]—

And as they were coming down from the mountain, Jesus commanded them, saying, Tell the vision to no man, until the Son of Man be risen from the dead.

And His disciples asked Him, saying, Why then say the scribes that Elijah must first come?

And He answered and said, Elijah indeed cometh, and shall Restore All Things.

YORK HOTEL, ADELAIDE, SOUTH AUSTRALIA.

The Christ's Prophecy of a Future Coming of Elijah.

General Overseer—Did He say, "Elijah indeed came, and that is an end of it?"

Voices—"No."

General Overseer—What did He say?

Overseer Voliva—"'Elijah indeed *cometh*.'"

General Overseer—Did not Elijah the Tishbite pass away?

Audience—"Yes."

General Overseer—Was not John the Baptist dead?

Audience—"Yes."

General Overseer—But the Christ says, "Elijah indeed"—what?

Voices—"'Cometh.'"

General Overseer—"And"—what?

Overseer Voliva—"'And shall Restore All Things.'"

General Overseer—Elijah the Tishbite did not Restore All Things, did he?

Voices—"No."

General Overseer—Elijah the Preparer, John the Baptist, did not Restore All Things, did he?

Audience—"No."

General Overseer—His ministry was for only eleven months.

He simply proclaimed the coming of the Christ.

But I have been permitted to go on in this ministry of Restoration since June 2, 1901, and I hope I shall live to see June 2, 1904, 1905, 1906, 1907, 1908, 1909, 1910, and as much longer as the Lord wants me to live.

But there are a good many people in these countries who do not want me to live.

Do you not see that it is a very hard ministry?

When a man has the spirit and power of Elijah, every blow he gives tells.

No one takes any notice of a minister who has no prophetic authority.

No one cares what he says.

When I speak, it tells.

The words that I speak in public in the City of Zion, are repeated throughout the whole world.

LEAVES OF HEALING and other Zion Literature are being sent out from Zion Printing and Publishing House, by the tons every week.

You will have a gigantic task to cut out all the Elijah ministry.

It is going on.

"One drop of ink makes millions think."

As the Christ Is to Come Again, "Even So," Elijah Is to Come.

Overseer Voliva [reads]—

And He answered and said, Elijah indeed cometh, and shall Restore All Things: but I say unto you Elijah is come already.

General Overseer—Precisely. He wants them to understand that Elijah did come in the person of John the Baptist because He declared it before John died.

Overseer Voliva [reads]—

But I say unto you, that Elijah is come already, and they knew him not, but did unto him whatsoever they listed. Even so shall the Son of Man also suffer of them.

General Overseer—Did not the Christ die?

Audience—"Yes."

General Overseer—Will He come again?

Voices—"Yes."

General Overseer—"Even so," just in the same way they killed John the Baptist, and for the time being the spirit and power of Elijah went out of the world.

Does He not say the spirit and power of Elijah is to come back again the same way—"even so?"

Voices—"Yes."

General Overseer—Even so is *cathos* (καθώς) in Greek—just the same way as.

Overseer Voliva [reads]—

Then understood the disciples that He spake unto them of John the Baptist.

General Overseer—Do you not see that He was talking of John the Baptist, who had been put to death? Then He said that Elijah would come again, and Restore All Things.

He was pointing to His second coming.

Testimony of Church Fathers and Theologians Concerning Elijah the Restorer.

It is one of the most remarkable things in my own experience to find, when once I go into this matter, how ignorant I have been, and how ignorant the Church has been.

I mean the True Church, and its accepted teachers after the Apostles.

You have clearly the mind of the Church, as expressed by the early Christian Fathers, down to the days of the Council of Nice, in the fourth century, about 325.

There was not a dissentient, so far as I know, from the

statement that some one in the spirit and power of Elijah must come before the coming of the Lord.

That theological teaching has been continued down through the ages, and it is the teaching today of all the great commentators in the Church.

I challenge any minister to prove that it is not.

It was the teaching of Augustine, and Chrysostum and Origen, and all the other Great Fathers.

It has been the teaching of the Greek church and of the Roman Catholic church.

It is the teaching of the Protestant church.

It is the teaching of the Church of England.

The last great commentary that has come from the Church of England, the "Pulpit Commentator," has the most distinct and positive teaching that Elijah must come before the Lord comes again.

Altogether, apart from the question as to whether I am or whether I am not Elijah the Restorer, there is no question but that Elijah must come.

There is also no question but that this is the time for him to come.

No Wrong in Trying to do Elijah's Work.

If I am mistaken, and my people are mistaken—which we do not admit, not for a moment—do you think that God will be very angry with us for trying to do Elijah's work?

Voices—"No."

General Overseer—That work is to restore the hearts of the children to the fathers, the fathers to the children, and all to God.

If I am not he, and cannot do that work, all right, then I have undertaken something beyond my strength, and if God rebukes me, let Him rebuke me.

Thus far I have not failed to do the work, however.

I have kept everlastingly at it, and I feel very much like keeping at it still.

If Elijah is to come in some other church, then why do you not hasten him, you Methodists, or you Presbyterians, or you Congregationalists?

If you have Elijah among you, let him come forward.

What a time he would have in any of your churches if any minister should really be Elijah!

I am thankful that God led me out of denominational positions until He enabled me to establish the Christian Catholic Church in Zion.

Belief of the Jews Regarding Elijah.

Every Jew today believes that Elijah must come before the Christ comes as King.

They will tell you that they provide an empty chair for Elijah at every circumcision, and that they raise their hands and cry, "O Jehovah, send Eliyahu!" That is the Hebrew for Elijah.

The name Elijah means, Jehovah is my God.

That name was given to him because he protested against Baal worship, against the Masons of his day.

The Masonry of today is nothing but Baal worship. It is the old Phallic worship whose emblem is the point within the circle, which is the emblem of Masonry today.

I defy any Mason to stand up and say that in straight Masonry the Name of Jesus, the Christ, is ever mentioned.

I am not talking about Knight Templary; that is outside of Masonry, a side degree.

I am not attacking Masonry because I like to do it.

I do not like it at all.

It is a pretty hard thing to fight; but I am fighting it because it is right to fight it; because it belongs to the Devil, root and branch.

Every woman in the land ought to stand by me, because it is the foe of the Home, as well as of the Church and of the State.

These nine thousand Freemasons in South Australia think that they can run everything.

They have run a good deal; they are in the highest positions in the government.

The police are paralyzed, and I could tell you from where the stroke came. It came from Masons.

The Masons control all the smaller secret societies, because there is generally a Mason at the head of each.

If I were the ruler of Adelaide, I should take the citizenship away from members of oath-bound secret orders.

When the Lord Jesus, the Christ, comes, He will send rulers to every city.

He will not wait for you to vote.

He will send rulers, and when these rulers come, they will make you obey.

If I had my wish, I should like the Lord Jesus, the Christ, to send me to Chicago. I know that city well. I could keep that in order.

I believe this work of Elijah the Restorer goes on into the Millennium.

CLOSING PRAYER.

Our God and Father, bless this company, and let the Word which they have read and heard expounded be studied by them more and more until they understand fully what it means; so that they may obey the Voice of Thy servant, as far as he speaks in accordance with Thy Word, and that they may be saved in spirit, soul and body, for Jesus' sake. Come with us this afternoon, our Lord, in Jesus' Name, and bless us. Amen.

BENEDICTION.

Beloved, abstain from all appearance of evil. And may the very God of Peace Himself sanctify you wholly; and I pray God your whole spirit and soul and body be preserved entire, without blame, unto the coming of our Lord Jesus, the Christ. Faithful is He that calleth you, who also will do it. The grace of our Lord Jesus, the Christ, the love of God, our Father, the fellowship of the Holy Spirit, our Comforter and Guide, one Eternal God, abide in you, bless you, and keep you, and all the Israel of God everywhere, forever. Amen.

Friday Afternoon Meeting.

The last meeting of the week of the Adelaide Mission has perhaps caused more discussion and comment than any other service of the entire Australian Visitation.

The address was, in many respects, the most important of all the Messages of the General Overseer in Australia.

Not only was it a clear, logical, and convincing Declaration of his Prophetic Mission as Elijah the Restorer, the Messenger of the Covenant, the Prophet foretold by Moses, but it was also the most destructive blow that had ever been struck Freemasonry in the great island continent.

These two characteristics of the Message, while they were almost completely ignored in the newspaper reports of the service, were probably the cause of the commotion that followed, the noise of which has now been heard throughout the entire world.

This meeting was attended by the largest audience that gathered in the Town Hall during the week, the entire ground floor being filled, and there being no vacant seats left in the dress-circle and few in the gallery.

In all there were probably between twelve and fifteen hundred people present.

It was a quiet, orderly, and respectful audience, and the Message of the man of God was received in the most earnest and thoughtful manner.

Mayor Cohen, Chief Secretary Jenkins, and the Adelaide press, seized upon a very incidental and mild reference to the King of England, and made much of it as an alleged "insulting, vile, disloyal and seditious utterance."

That it was not considered so by the audience that heard it, is proved by the fact that it scarcely caused a ripple at the time.

One man objected mildly, but quickly subsided.

Other than that there was no demonstration on the part of any one, and the General Overseer spoke for about half an hour afterward, without the slightest interruption.

The following is the report of the Message:

Town Hall, Adelaide, South Australia, Friday Afternoon, March 25, 1904.

The Meeting was opened by Overseer Wilbur Glenn Voliva, awaiting the General Overseer's arrival.

Hymn No. 9, Visitation Program, "The Morning Light is Breaking," was sung.

Prayer was offered by the Rev. C. Friend Hawkins.

The announcements were made by Overseer Wilbur Glenn Voliva.

The free-will offerings were received while Hymn No. 19. "Jesus Shall Reign," was sung.

The Rev. C. Friend Hawkins read the 2d and 3d chapters of the Book of the Prophet Malachi.

Overseer W. G. Voliva then read in the Gospel according to St. Luke, the 1st chapter, from the 13th to the 17th verse; in the 11th chapter of the Gospel according to St. Matthew, the 13th and 14th verses; in the 17th chapter of Matthew from the 9th to the 13th verse, and from the 1st chapter of the Gospel according to St. John the 19th, 20th and 21st verses.

After the singing of another hymn, the General Overseer came upon the platform and delivered his Message:

THE PROPHET FORETOLD BY MOSES, THE MESSENGER OF THE COVENANT, ELIJAH THE RESTORER.

*REPORTED BY I. M. S. AND A. W. N.

INVOCATION.

Let the words of my mouth and the meditation of my heart be acceptable in Thy sight, be profitable unto this people and unto all to whom these words shall come, in this and every land, in this and all the coming time, Till Jesus Come. Amen.

We took perhaps an hour and a half this morning, to consider very attentively the passage of Scripture which Overseer Voliva and Deacon Hawkins read to you from the Book of the Prophet Malachi, written four hundred twenty years before the Christ.

You will notice that in the passages which Overseer Voliva read, you had first the declaration of the Angel Gabriel, who proclaimed that John was to be born of the childless Elizabeth and of the Priest Zacharias, and was to be born in the spirit and power of Elijah.

As I showed you this morning, Jesus said before John's death, that he was Elijah. That is recorded in the 11th chapter of Matthew.

The murder of John is recorded in the 14th chapter.

John the Baptist's Rebuke to the King.

While he was yet speaking to the people and proclaiming the great essential principle of Purity, he denounced the king upon the throne and said that he was a vile and wicked man, having broken the Law of God, and having placed by his side, as his queen, a vile and immoral woman, the wife of his brother Philip.

John believed that it was his business to denounce the king, and to say, "Thou shalt not have her."

He declared the marriage invalid and abominable.

That king and queen were very much like Ahab and Jezebel in Elijah the Tishbite's time.

They were really heathen.

No doubt that voluptuous paramour of Herod's whom John refused to recognize as queen registered an oath with the Devil (and every bad oath that a man or woman takes is an oath registered with the Devil and ought to be broken as quickly as possible, no matter what that oath may be), that she would have John the Baptist's heart's blood.

The story of how she succeeded in having him murdered is well known.

Herod murdered an absolutely innocent man, whom he himself used often to hear teach. He even did many things that John taught.

It is not at all unlikely that John the Baptist was educated with him, because John was the son of a priest of a very high order—the order of Abijah—and was himself a priest by heredity.

But Herod was so wicked that he kept his bad oath.

The Sin of Keeping a Bad Oath.

Every secret society oath is a bad oath.

It is a covenant with death and an agreement with hell.

The right thing to do with a bad oath is to break it.

But Herod would not break his bad oath, and rather than take back his drunken oath and words he ordered the death of John the Baptist.

When John the Baptist had been put to death in prison, his disciples tenderly took up the body, buried it, and went and told Jesus.

That is all in the 14th chapter of Matthew, and in the 11th chapter of Matthew you have the Declaration of Jesus that John the Baptist was Elijah.

In the 17th chapter of Matthew, you have the story of the Christ's answer to Peter, James and John, as they came down from the Mount of Transfiguration, months, probably nearly a year after John was dead and buried, when they asked Him, "Why say the scribes that Elijah must first come?"

He said, "Elijah indeed cometh, and shall Restore All Things."

The Restoration of All Things.

The Restoration of All Things seems to be a considerable puzzle to a great many people.

*The following report has not been revised by the General Overseer.

It was the teaching of the early Church that a prophet should be raised up who, before the Christ came, should be the Restorer; and Malachi had prophesied concerning that prophet.

That prophet could not possibly be either Elijah the Tishbite or Elijah the Preparer; for John's ministry lasted only about eleven months, and he did not restore anything except that by the grace of God, he restored people to good lives and made them penitent, and through baptism led them to be prepared for the Coming of the Lord.

As for the Restoration of the Kingdom and of All Things connected with the Kingdom of God, he was unable to do it and it was not his office to do it.

His office was merely to prepare for the Christ and then pass away.

Nor was it the office of the Christ to Restore All Things.

They asked Him at one time whether He would at this time restore the Kingdom.

He told them that it was not for them to know the times and seasons which the Father had put in His power.

But the Restoration was to come.

When John the Baptist had passed away and the Christ had passed away, then the Church looked forward to the Restoration, and it has been looking forward to the Restoration ever since.

Peter's Prophecy Concerning the Restoration of All Things.

Let me show you that this is true by the famous sermon of Peter after the healing of the lame man at the Beautiful Gate of the Temple.

> Repent ye therefore, and turn again, that your sins may be blotted out, that so there may come seasons of refreshing from the presence of the Lord;
> And that He may send the Christ who hath been appointed for you, even Jesus:
> Whom the heaven must receive until the times of Restoration of All Things, whereof God spake by the mouth of His holy prophets which have been since the world began.
> Moses indeed said, A prophet shall the Lord God raise up unto you from among your brethren, like unto me; to him shall ye harken in all things whatsoever he shall speak unto you.
> And it shall be, that every soul which shall not harken to that prophet, shall be utterly destroyed from among the people.
> Yea and all the prophets from Samuel and them that followed after, as many as have spoken, they also told of these days.
> Ye are the sons of the prophets, and of the covenant which God made with your fathers, saying unto Abraham, And in thy seed shall all the families of the earth be blessed.
> Unto you first God, having raised up His Servant, sent him to bless you, in turning away every one of you from your iniquities.

A prophet like unto Moses, is the meaning there.

The margin reads, "as He raised me up."

That cannot refer to Jesus; for Jesus was not raised up as Moses was.

Moses was a poor castaway waif, upon the waters of the Nile.

He was picked up out of the mud of the river by an Egyptian princess, and educated as a castaway.

He became nearer to her heart until he was made her adopted son and, in all probability, the heir to the throne of Egypt.

We know, as a matter of fact, that his story is partly told on the Egyptian monuments, his name being given as Osarsiph.

The story is told of his wonderful life and of his wonderful rescue.

He was the commander-in-chief of the armies of Egypt, up to the time when he murdered an Egyptian.

But Moses cannot for a single moment be compared to the Christ.

The prophet who was to be raised up, was to be "a prophet like unto me," said Moses; a mere mortal man, not an incarnate God, or the embodiment of God Himself, as the Christ was.

The Christ was conceived by the Holy Spirit, and born without earthly father of a virgin.

That was not the way Moses was raised up.

The Prophet Like Unto Moses.

This prophet, that is to be raised up in the Latter Times, is to be a man of prophetic power and authority, a law-giver and a leader, a man of affairs, a man raised up to bring out of bondage the oppressed of God's children and to prepare the way for the King.

I desire you to notice, therefore, that the interpretation that this refers to the Christ is entirely without foundation.

It most manifestly refers to the Messenger of the Covenant, who is the Elijah of whom Malachi speaks; for Malachi is not speaking concerning the same messenger of whom Isaiah speaks, the messenger who precedes the first Coming of the Christ.

It is clear that Malachi is speaking regarding the Restorer; that he is speaking regarding the coming of Elijah at the End of the Dispensation.

Every one will admit that, as a matter of mere scholarship.

I will read again this passage, which is so much misunderstood:

Moses indeed said, A prophet shall the Lord God raise up unto you from among your brethren, like unto me; to him shall ye harken in all things whatsoever he shall speak unto you.

You may just as well look at the full meaning of that.

And it shall be, that every soul, which shall not harken to that prophet, shall be utterly destroyed from among the people.

The people that would not believe Moses, died.

When Moses lifted up the serpent in the wilderness, all the serpent-bitten people that obeyed God, who gave His command through Moses, and looked, were healed.

They looked and lived; but there were some who did not obey and look, and they died.

That is all that this means.

It means that when a prophet speaks a Message from God, in the Name of God, that Message must be obeyed. It is not to be disputed.

It is a very simple thing.

When an army is in the field, and a commander-in-chief is appointed, he is appointed not to discuss the matter with officers, but to command them.

Any man who will not obey him can be shot.

There is no question at all about how to deal with him.

The same principle applies here.

When a prophet is sent from God, you must obey him or perish.

His Message, of course, must be a Right Message; it must be a Wise Message; it must be a Good Message.

It must bear upon its face the stamp of its Purity, the stamp of its Sincerity and of its Divinity.

It must not be a bad message.

No commander-in-chief has a right to give a bad and foolish order.

The Prophet of God Must Be Obeyed.

This is the Prophet of the Restoration, of whom Peter is speaking.

He is speaking of the Times of the Restoration of All Things when that prophet of whom Moses prophesied, when that prophet of whom Malachi prophesied, when that prophet whom the Christ Himself said should come and Restore All Things, should come.

He must be obeyed.

It is not a question as to whether I am he.

That is not the question that we are discussing.

The question is simply must Elijah come again before the Lord Himself comes?

The Book says that he is to be in command when the Christ comes.

Peter continued:

Yea and all the prophets from Samuel and them that followed after, as many as have spoken, they also told of these days.

He is talking about the Days of the Restoration, which shall begin previously to the second advent of our Lord Jesus, the Christ.

Ye are the sons of the prophets, and of the covenant which God made with your fathers, saying unto Abraham, And in thy seed shall all the families of the earth be blessed.

The next verse, which is the last verse I shall read in this connection, has a most shocking mistranslation in the Old Version.

Unto you first God, having raised up His *Son Jesus*, sent him to bless you, in turning away every one of you from his iniquities.

Unto you first God, having raised up His *servant*, sent him to bless you, in turning away every one of you from your iniquities.

The Revised Version of our English translators, you will notice, has, instead of "having raised up His Son Jesus," "having raised up His servant."

Elijah a Fallible Man, of Like Passions With Ourselves.

I humbly submit that a son is not a servant, and that the "servant" here has reference to the prophet, who will be a mere mortal man, and a humble servant of God—a fallible man; for Elijah was a fallible man.

He was a man of like passions with ourselves.

He could get very badly discouraged, and then lie down under a juniper tree.

He could howl, and say that he was the only fellow left who would do the right thing.

He was mistaken, because there were seven thousand who had not bowed the knee to Baal.

But I do not blame Elijah for thinking that he was the only one, because none of them appeared at Carmel when he had his great contest with the priests of Baal.

The Cowardly Silence of Some People.

If they did bow the knee to Jehovah, they were very quiet about it.

That is the way with a good many people.

They do not say much about their convictions.

They think that it is nice to be quiet.

I think you can be much too quiet.

You have been so quiet in Adelaide, that when a fact comes along and gives you a dig or two you get into a dreadful condition. [Applause. Laughter.]

You had not been much stirred up lately, and the whole community around believes that this is the greatest stirring-up you have ever had. [Amen. Laughter.]

I did not come to Adelaide with eau de Cologne.

I came with a hot poker, and I made it felt too.

There has been a good deal of jumping.

When I came here the place was dead.

Even the Devil did not bother about you.

The churches are all dead, and there was nothing for the Devil to make a stir about.

He goes after me.

You are pretty well handed over to him, and there is not much going on.

There are fewer people in the churches in Adelaide today than there were sixteen years ago.

Unto you first God, having raised up His servant, sent him to bless you, in turning away every one of you from your iniquities.

The Elijah to Turn the People from Their Sins.

God sent His servant, Elijah the Tishbite, to turn the people from their iniquities unto their God.

He sent His servant, Elijah the Preparer, to turn the people from their iniquities to God; and the promise is that He will send His servant in the Latter Times, before the Christ comes again, to turn the people to God; to turn the hearts of the fathers to their children, and the hearts of the children to their fathers, lest He come and smite the earth with a curse.

The Great and Terrible Day of the Lord was not when the Christ was born into this world.

The Great and Terrible Day of the Lord will come when He comes back and stands upon this earth, and when He abolishes all other forms of government.

Then kings will have to take a back seat, and very low down at that. [Laughter.]

King Edward VII. Has no Religion to Spare.

I do not want to say one disrespectful word, but no one can boast of King Edward's piety.

No one imagines that he has any religion to spare.

You hope that he has at least enough to get into heaven; if he does, it will apparently be by the skin of his teeth, because he has never been renowned for much religion.

Voice—"Let our king alone."

General Overseer—There is no use in howling about that.

I do not care if he is the king, I am standing in the place where John the Baptist stood.

If I get any more of this talk I will say more, not less. [Amen.]

You cannot keep me quiet with that kind of talk.

I am the servant of God.

John the Baptist did not care if Herod was king.

If you stir me up I will say more.

I will go after the king more severely.

But I do not want to talk about the king.

I merely wish to say that when the Christ comes, every king, every president and every potentate will have to take a back seat and go pretty low down, some of them. [Cries of "Hear, hear!"]

Some peasants will go higher than they.

"I perceive of a truth that God is no respecter of persons," and when the Christ comes, there will be many changes.

One thing is sure,

There Will Be no Other King When the Christ Comes to Reign.

God gave the people kings in His wrath. God said to Samuel, when the people demanded a king, "They have not rejected thee, they have rejected Me that I should not be King over them."

God has no use for republics either.

I say that, notwithstanding the fact that I am a citizen of a republican nation.

The rule of kings and emperors, oligarchies, or democracies is not God's purpose!

His purpose is to reign over the world Himself. [Cries of "Hear, hear!"]

When the Christ comes back, He will come as King of kings and Lord of lords. [Cries of "Hear, hear!"]

He will put down all other kings.

He will decide who shall be governor of South Australia.

He will say who shall be the mayor of Adelaide, and He will say who shall be king in England.

The Burden of Authority and Power.

I know enough of authority and power to be unwilling to have any more unless God gives me more strength for it.

It is no easy thing to rule ten thousand people, let alone a hundred thousand.

With all our adherents, and those under our influence in their families, Zion numbers now about a million, and it is not an easy task to rule Zion.

Real Authority and Real Rule is a tremendous responsibility.

No man who has ever felt the weight of that responsibility is very eager to have it.

Only when God imposes it upon a man; only when God gives him power to execute that authority, is it possible to bear it.

When the Christ comes there is to be a "fresh deal."

There has been a great amount of crooked dealing.

Politicians in this country, and in every country, are like a pack of cards; the more you shuffle them the dirtier they get.

They have been shuffled so confusingly that poor Mr. Deakin, the premier of the Commonwealth, does not know what on earth to do with the last deal you gave him.

You have given him three separate parties, not one of them with a working majority, and he does not know what to do with them.

The people do not know how to select their rulers. God only knows how.

The Theocracy, the rule of God, is the Divine intention.

The Rule of God must be in the Heart, in the Home, in the School, in the Business, in the Church, in the State and in the Nation.

This World Will Never Be Properly Governed Until God Rules.

When the Christ comes He will rule. [Amen. Applause.]

He will not ask you fellows for your opinions.

He will most surely shut up all the dark lodge rooms.

He will let out all the nasty goats.

He will make you Masons walk in the light as He is in the light.

Old Hiram Abiff will be buried forever, and no King Solomon will ever be able to resurrect his dirty old bones again. [Laughter.]

When the Christ comes there will be no secret societies, because He said, "In secret spake I nothing."

He walked in the light and told them that "every one that doeth ill hateth the light, and cometh not to the light, lest his works should be reproved."

I will go on with the Elijah question.

I have now demonstrated to you that there were two appearances of Elijah, and that there is to be a third appearance.

You say that this is a new doctrine.

Pardon me if I say that you show your ignorance if you say that, for if you were acquainted with the writings of the Church Fathers you would know that they speak of the return of Elijah before the Messiah comes again.

That is the testimony of commentators and theologians through all the ages to the present time.

John Keble, the great poet of the Church of England, and indeed the poet of the whole Church, for he was beloved by the whole Church, in his "Christian Year," on St. John the Baptist's Day, writes:

Twice in her season of decay
  The fallen Church hath felt Elijah's eye
Dart from the wilds its piercing ray:
  Not keener burns, in the chill morning sky,
The herald star,
Whose torch afar
  Shadows, and boding night-birds fly.

Methinks we need him once again,
  That favored seer—but where shall he be found?
By Cherith's side we seek in vain,
  In vain on Carmel's green and lonely mound:
Angels no more
From Sinai soar,
  On his celestial errands bound.

But wafted to his glorious place
  By harmless fire, among the ethereal thrones,
His spirit with a dear embrace
  Thee the loved harbinger of Jesus owns,
Well-pleased to view
His likeness true,
  And trace, in thine, his own deep tones.

And since we see, and not afar,
  The twilight of the Great and Dreadful Day,
Why linger till Elijah's car
  Stoop from the clouds? Why sleep ye? Rise and pray,
Ye heralds sealed
In camp or field
  Your Savior's banner to display!

Where is the lore the Baptist taught,
  The soul unswerving and the fearless tongue?
The much-enduring wisdom, sought
  By lonely prayer the haunted rocks among?
Who counts it gain
His light should wane,
  So the whole world to Jesus throng?

Personality of Elijah the Restorer a Spiritual Truth.

You may ask, "Are you he?"

I could not, by argument, make the natural mind comprehend a spiritual truth.

I could not make a person who does not understand the Christ, a Christian, could I?

I could not make a person who does not understand a word of Greek, know all about Greek.

I could not make a man to understand how to make brick if he never saw a brick.

I could not make an ungodly set of people, or even a godly set, understand a matter that they had not studied into.

I can show you what the Scripture is, however, and I can submit to you the fact that I did not call myself to this prophetic office.

I will ask the Overseers who are here and who were with me when I made the Declaration on June 2, 1901—Overseer Excell, is it not a fact that for years before I made the Declaration the people were demanding it of me?

Overseer Excell—"It is true."

General Overseer—I ask Overseer Voliva who was then at Headquarters, is that true?

Overseer Voliva—"Yes, sir, it is true."

General Overseer—The difficulty was in keeping the people back.

You say, "When did you become a prophet?"

My answer is that I have always been a prophet although I did not always quite know it.

I was a prophet, I think, when I was in Adelaide before.

John the Baptist was a prophet although he did not know it.

He knew he had some Message to deliver and he said, "I am the Voice of one crying in the wilderness."

I have been that for a number of years.

The Grave Possibilities of a Prophetic Mission.

I did not want to be Elijah, if I could escape the responsibility of the prophetic office.

It may not be understood by you, but the Elijah will probably be murdered; for "which of the prophets," said Jesus, "have ye not slain?"

No man can do the work of Elijah and not have women saying, "I will have his heart's blood," as Jezebel and Herodias did.

No man can do the work of Elijah and not hear a false priesthood say, "I will have his heart's blood," as the high priests did.

The man who tells you of your sins and exposes your iniquities, places himself in danger of his life.

The bullet has often passed by my ear.

The plot for my murder has often been laid.

If the men that made that noise here on Monday night, and those outside, had got me into their hands, how many minutes would I have lived? [Laughter from a few.]

You may laugh, but my wife would not have laughed had she received my dead body out of the streets.

My son would not have laughed.

My people would not have laughed.

Angels in Heaven would not have laughed.

The only ones who laugh at that are the Devil in hell and the man who has a devil in him. [Applause.]

It may be fun for you to think of my life being trampled out, but the thousands and tens of thousands to whom my ministry has been a blessing and who have been saved from sin and disease and set free from the powers of hell would not laugh.

When my body reached our little City they would not laugh as it was being carried through the streets and put where I told them the other night to put it; because I have never been nearer death than I have been in Adelaide. [Laughter from a few.]

The devils are laughing again. [Laughter.]

It is a shame!

Voices—"Shame!"

General Overseer—How would you feel if your father were trampled to death in the streets?

How would you feel if your mother or your brother or your sister were trampled to death in the streets?

I say to the poor, miserable, foolish ones that could find any satisfaction in the destruction of any life whatever, that it is a shame to laugh at murder.

The life of the poorest, humblest man in the city of Adelaide is precious to some one.

Some mother gave him birth, some daughter or brother or sister waits and watches for him.

I do not trouble about it, because I believe that God will not permit me to die until my work is done. [Amen. Applause.]

When that work is done—it matters not if it be tonight or in ten, twenty or thirty years—I shall be glad to go from a world of sin, suffering, sorrow, hypocrisy and wickedness, to a land where there is no sin and no sorrow, and no weeping and no night, and no secretism and no uncleanness, and no defilement of any kind.

I shall be glad to go.

I have many there whom I know, whose dying eyes I have closed, and with whom I have prayed in the long ministry that I have had.

I am not afraid.

There is one thing that you can never do, you can never make me afraid, for "Perfect Love casteth out Fear."

Zion's Acceptance of the Declaration of Elijah the Restorer.

My people, to whom I made that Declaration on June 2, 1901, had been eagerly looking for it for years.

I never said that I was a reincarnation of any one or anything.

I never use the word reincarnation.

John the Baptist was a separate being altogether from Elijah the Tishbite, and I am a separate entity also.

I do not understand it all, but I can only say that I had to declare that the spirit and power of Elijah was upon me and that I had to do his work.

I have been doing it and I continue to do it.

I continue to declare that the Time of the Restoration of All Things is coming.

I have been commanding men everywhere to repent, and I do it now.

I am here to say that the Christ is coming and that He is not far away.

When He does come, He will take out of the world those of His own who are prepared.

After the Rapture, He will come again with them and will reign for a Thousand Years, which is the Millennium.

At the end of that Thousand Years, He will have the hardest fight of all, as the Book of the Revelation shows, when Satan is let loose for a time, and "then cometh the end."

But the Restoration which begins now is the overlapping into this Dispensation of the Millennial Period.

All the Dispensations overlap one another.

John the Baptist, Elijah the Preparer, was the overlapping point of the Old Testament prophets, with the Christian Dispensation—the Dispensation of Grace.

The Elijah of the Restoration is the overlapping point of the return of the Christ and His reign.

My people received this Declaration on June 2, 1901, practically without a dissentient voice.

That was a marvelous thing!

Thousands rose and received that Declaration.

Ever since, the number has been growing.

I have formed Zion Restoration Host, which now numbers about ten thousand.

I took three thousand with me to New York, and they worked in perfect order.

We visited every house in that great city in two weeks, and delivered the Message of Peace.

The papers, both secular and religious, have been stuffing you with lies concerning that Visitation, but the people want the truth, and they will get the truth concerning Zion. [Applause.]

A Brief But Powerful Indictment of Freemasonry.

I have just seventeen minutes to deal with the Masonic Peacock, Sir Alexander Peacock.

That is perhaps seventeen minutes too much. [Laughter.]

I hold in my hand a pamphlet which has been in print for several years.

It is a simple and clear exposure of Freemasonry, especially as it is connected with the Methodist apostasy, and it is entitled "Zion's Conflict with Methodist Apostasy."

You will understand that when I quote from it I am quoting from my own pamphlet, and that I am also quoting from certain books of the Masonic Order from which I have taken excerpts.

I know everything in Masonry from the first to the thirty-third degree.

A man who signs his name W. J. Linegar, has sent me a letter and asked me to answer some questions today from the platform.

I will answer them.

He writes from Pivil street, Adelaide, and dates it March 23d.

He says:

TO THE REV. J. A. DOWIE.

Dear Sir:—Will you answer the following questions from the platform at your next meeting, on your honor?

Yes, on my honor, no doubt about that.

Have you ever tried to be initiated into any Masonic Lodge?

Never! [Laughter.]

Were you ever blackballed?

Never! No, sir, never! If I have never tried to be initiated, of course I could not have been blackballed.

Have you any Freemasons in Christian Zion who have violated their oaths and divulged the secrets of their Order, of your positive knowledge?

Yes, sir, hundreds of them.

Overseer Voliva—"We have them here." [Applause.]

General Overseer—They thought it was right to break a bad oath.

George Washington took an oath with uplifted sword, that he would be faithful and bear true allegiance to King George the Third.

THE OATH WHICH GEORGE WASHINGTON BROKE.

I, GEORGE WASHINGTON, DO TAKE ALMIGHTY GOD TO WITNESS, that I will be faithful and bear true allegiance to our most Sovereign Lord, King George the Third, and him will defend to the utmost of my power, against all conspiracies and attempts whatever, that shall be made against his person, crown and dignity: ***And I do faithfully promise***, to maintain, support and defend to the utmost of my power, the succession of the Throne in his Majesty's family, against any person, or persons whatsoever. Thereby utterly abjuring any allegiance or obedience to the person taking upon himself the style and title of Prince of Wales, in the lifetime of his father, and who, since his death, is said to have assumed the style and title of King of Great Britain and Ireland, by the name of Charles the Third, and to any other person claiming or pretending a right to the crown of these realms. ***And I do swear***, that I do detest and reject and detest as unchristian and impious, to believe that it is lawful to murder or destroy any person or persons whatsoever, for or under pretense of their being heretics, and also that unchristian and impious principle, that no faith is to be kept with heretics. ***I further declare***, that it is no article of my faith; and I do renounce, reject and abjure the opinion that Princes excommunicated by the Pope and Council, or by any authority of the See of Rome, ***or by any authority whatsoever***, may be deposed or murdered by their subjects, or by any person whatsoever; ***and I do promise***, that I will not hold, maintain, or abet any such opinion, or any other opinion, contrary to what is expressed in this declaration. *And I do solemnly, in the presence of God, and His only Son* JESUS CHRIST, *our Redeemer, profess, testify, and declare,* that I do make this declaration, and every part thereof, in the plain and ordinary sense of the words of this oath, without any evasion, equivocation, or mental reservation whatsoever, and without any dispensation already granted by the Pope, or any authority from the See of Rome, or any person whatsoever; *and without thinking that I am or can be acquitted before God or man,* or absolved of this declaration, or any part thereof, although the Pope, or *any other person or persons, or any authority whatsoever,* shall dispense with or annul the same, or declare *that it was null and void from the beginning.*

But the time came when he saw that it was right to break that oath and draw his sword against King George.

Eighty million Americans now think that he did right in breaking that bad oath.

He broke it rightfully.

Unlawful Character of Secret Order Oaths.

There is not a Mason who ever took an oath but committed an unlawful act.

There is no Mason who ever administered the Masonic oaths but committed an unlawful act by so doing.

Sir Alexander Peacock, that is the first of the feathers I shall pluck out of your tail.

You call yourselves a law-abiding organization.

I say, in the Name of the Most High God, that you are an Anarchistic Organization!

Any number of men or women, who gather themselves together and assume the right to administer oaths are taking into their hands a power which the law gives only to a notary, magistrate or a judge in open court.

The laws of the British Empire do not permit any one to administer an oath unless he is a properly qualified officer.

Moreover, any man who imposes a penalty upon his fellow men, especially a death penalty—as the Masonic Order does—or takes part in the imposition of a penalty, either voluntarily or otherwise, is guilty of an anarchistic act; for the only person who can impose a penalty, and a death penalty especially, is a properly appointed judge or a properly appointed officer of the highest courts.

I therefore say, as a matter of sound reason, that every secret society that assumes these powers is assuming them in direct violation of law. [Applause.]

I deny your statement that the Masonic Order is law-abiding.

I do not care who may belong to it, whether it is the chief justice or the governor or the president; for no good citizen has a right to subject himself or to be subjected to the judgment of a secret tribunal.

That is sound logic.

I should like to hear what the other side has to say, at the right and proper time.

I have never yet heard an answer to that argument.

Baby Masons.

There are very large numbers of Freemasons who are just baby Masons.

Any Mason who has gone through only the first three degrees of the Blue Lodge, knows very little about higher Masonry.

The taking of the first three degrees is like a child getting into the Third Reader in school and never going any further.

A man, however, who has been through all the thirty-three degrees has knowledge of the whole thing.

Sir Alexander Peacock was pleased to say that the Masons were not in a conspiracy against me.

Let me show you that the Masons are in a conspiracy against all religion.

I do not say that all Masons understand that conspiracy; because the rank and file of them do not.

A third degree Mason is a mere baby Mason and does not understand much.

I think that in this country you can not go beyond the Royal Arch degree, and you can only go higher when you go to England. I am not certain that this is true.

In America, however, we have Masons that have taken scores of degrees in associated orders, and in straight Masonry.

I say that Masonry is unchristian and anti-Christian because of the statements of the Masons themselves.

I hold in my hand my own pamphlet, and I read to you page 49, the title of the book that I held in my hand when I delivered this discourse.

It is entitled:

The Masonic Manual. A Pocket Companion for the Initiated: Containing the Rituals of Freemasonry Embraced in the Degrees of the Lodge, Chapter and Encampment; Embellished with Upwards of Three Hundred Engravings. Together with Forms of Masonic Documents, Notes, Songs, Dates, etc. Compiled and arranged by Robert Macoy, Past Master, Past Grand Secretary, Past Grand Commander, Grand Recorder, etc. Revised Edition. New York: Clark & Maynard, 5 Barclay street.

These manuals are in the hands of the Masons, and I have about a dozen copies.

The Name of Jesus, the Christ, Cut Out.

In this manual, on page 86, in connection with the charge at the opening of the lodge in the initiation of a Master Mason, a quotation is made from the New Testament.

Where the Name of Jesus, the Christ, should appear in the quotation, it is cut out, making it read as follows:

Wherefore, brethren, lay aside all malice, and guile, and hypocrisies, and envies, and all evil speakings. If so be ye have tasted that the Lord is gracious; to whom coming, as unto a living stone, disallowed indeed of men, but chosen of God, and precious; ye also, as living stones, be ye built up a spiritual house, an holy priesthood, to offer up sacrifices, acceptable to God—

That is found in the first Epistle of Peter, the 2d chapter and the first five verses.

At the opening of the Lodge of the degree of Royal Arch this portion of the Scripture is read:

Now we command you, brethren, that ye withdraw yourselves from every brother that walketh disorderly.

They leave out the words "in the Name of the Lord Jesus Christ."

That looks like Scripture, does it not? It is Scripture with something left out. Here is the Scripture:

Now we command you, brethren, *in the Name of the Lord Jesus Christ,* that ye withdraw yourselves from every brother that walketh disorderly.

But they cut that out.

Then in the same passage.

The Lord be with you all.

That is 2 Thessalonians 3. They omit there the words:

The grace of our Lord Jesus, the Christ, be with you all.

They leave out the Christ's Name everywhere it occurs. That is the fact throughout the whole of the ceremonies.

Then I quote from a book which deals with the first seven degrees of Masonry, by Jacob O. Doesburg, Past Master of Unity Lodge, No. 191, F. & A. M., Holland, Michigan.

He quotes from "Chase's Digest of Masonic Law," page 206, one of the accepted authorities among Freemasons:

To require that a candidate profess a belief in the Divine authenticity of the Bible, or a state of future rewards and punishments, is a serious innovation in the very body of Masonry. . . . It is antimasonic to require any religious test, other than the candidate should believe in God, the Creator and Governor of the Universe.

Any Chinaman or red Indian can say that. There is nothing of Christianity in that.

It is compatible with Unitarianism; it is compatible with Judaism; it is compatible with Shinto worship; it is compatible with fetish worship; it is compatible with all kinds of heathenism.

Quoting again from "Chase's Digest," which, mind you, is written in the interest of Freemasons, page 207:

The Jews, the Chinese, the Turks, each reject either the New Testament, or the Old, or both, and yet we see no good reason why they should not be made Masons. In fact, Blue Lodge Masonry has nothing whatever to do with the Bible. It is not founded on the Bible; if it was, it would not be Masonry; it would be something else.

There is no question at all that Macoy, Chase, and all well-known writers on Freemasonry distinctly agree that Masonry is not Christian, cannot be Christian, does not have any Christianity in it at all, and that the Name of Jesus, the Christ, is cut out of every quotation that is made from the Bible.

I wish to say to Sir Alexander Peacock that this, therefore, is an organization which supports murder.

I will tell you upon the authority of the Masons themselves, what their religion is.

When I quoted these words I held in my hand an "Encyclopedia of Freemasonry and Its Kindred Sciences: Comprising the Whole Range of Arts, Sciences and Literature as Connected with the Institution." By Albert G. Mackey, M. D.

It is brought down to date by Charles T. McClenachan, author of "The Book of the Ancient Accepted Scottish Rite of Freemasonry, Form and Ceremonies," etc.

This book is printed in Philadelphia by Louis H. Everts, and is the edition of 1898.

It is, therefore, a recent edition, and it is accepted by Freemasons as among their highest authorities, if not the highest, for Albert G. Mackey held one of the highest offices in the Masonic Order.

In the article entitled "Christianization of Freemasonry," on page 162, Dr. Mackey has these words:

It is true that it embraces within its scheme the great truths of Christianity upon the subject of the immortality of the soul and the resurrection of the body; but this was to be presumed, because Freemasonry is truth, and all truth must be identical. But the origin of each is different; their histories are dissimilar. The principles of Freemasonry preceded the advent of Christianity. Its symbols and its legends are derived from the Solomonic Temple and from the people even anterior to that. Its religion comes from the ancient priesthood; its faith was that primitive one of Noah and his immediate descendants. If Masonry were simply a Christian institution, the Jew and the Moslem, the Brahman and the Buddhist, could not conscientiously partake of its illumination. But its universality is its boast. In its language citizens of every nation may converse; at its altar men of all religions may kneel; to its creed disciples of every faith may subscribe.

The Buddist, the Brahman, the Moslem, and the Jew, who reject Jesus, the Christ, as the Son of God, the Savior of the World, can be Freemasons.

If you cannot understand the significance of that, you cannot reason at all.

What is this "religion" which embraces the foe of Christianity, which gives comfort to the impenitent Jew, whose fathers shed the blood of the Redeemer; which gives comfort to the Mohammedan, who believes that he is doing God's service when he imbrues his sword in the blood of the Christian today; which is open to the Brahman, who teaches a woman to sacrifice the fruit of her body for the sin of her soul, and throw her child into the Ganges that the crocodile may eat it—a woman who worships these horrid divinities of India, the trinity of Brahma, Vishnu and Siva, a religion which makes murder a part of its creed? Siva is the Destroyer.

But to what religion does it subscribe?

Masonry Is Phallic Worship.

I will tell you in Dr. Mackey's own words.

Dr. Mackey says:

FREEMASONRY CONTENDS FOR THE PURITY OF PHALLIC WORSHIP.

The Phallus was a sculptured representation of the *membrum virile*, or male organ of generation; and the worship of it is said to have originated in Egypt, where, after the murder of Osiris by Typhon, which is symbolically to be explained as the destruction or deprivation of the sun's light by night, Isis, his wife, or the symbol of nature, in the search for his mutilated body, is said to have found all the parts except the organs of generation, which myth is simply symbolic of the fact that the sun having set, its fecundating and invigorating power had ceased. The Phallus, therefore, as the symbol of the male generative principal, was very universally venerated among the ancients, and that too as a religious rite.

This is the symbol which is represented, he says, in Freemasonry by the "*point within the circle.*"

I always hate to read it, but now I ask you whether that is not the most degrading kind of worship that has ever been imposed upon humanity? [Cries of "Yes, yes!"]

Mackey says the same thing here in another form:

And here, I think, we undoubtedly find the remote origin of the point within a circle, an ancient symbol, which was first adopted by the sun-worshipers, and then by the ancient astronomers, as a symbol of the sun surrounded by the earth or the universe,—the sun as the generator and the earth as the producer,—and afterwards modified in its signification and incorporated into the symbolism of Freemasonry.

I am quoting from Masonic books.

It is a shame for Sir Alexander Peacock to attempt to impose upon us the notion that this is a very pure and good religious system when it is in its essence Phallic worship.

This was the horrible worship of the Canaanites of old, for which God threw them out of the Land of Canaan.

In the very last degree of Masonry in the Knights of Kadosh, all religion is thrown aside by the Masons.

I will read the words in the very last degree.

In this degree, no one can tell who the man is that gives it; for all that the candidates see of him is his hands outside of a tent or curtain.

Masonry the Foe of All Religions.

I am quoting now from one of their own great writers, who afterwards became a Christian man and rejected Masonry. It is entitled "Bernard's Light on Masonry."

These are the words:

Now, my brother, behold what you must fight against and destroy, before you can come to the knowledge of the true good and sovereign happiness. Behold this monster which you must conquer—a serpent which WE detest as an idol that is adored by the idiot and vulgar under the name of RELIGION!!! You must cast it forever aside.

That is the statement accepted in the Knights of Kadosh, where the very highest degree is taken.

You know nothing about it, because you have never got there, Sir Alexander, and there is not one of the Knights of Kadosh in this country.

Imagine now that every degree rules every lower degree, and that the Illustrious Grand Commander rules you all.

Do you, or does any man living, know who that Illustrious Grand Commander, who is the Supreme Head of all the Masons, is?

Do you know where he lives?

You know that you do not.

Yet you know that you are all bound to obey him in whatever he may say.

The Supreme Head of the Masonic Order is the Lawless One.

I tell you that he is the Lawless One.

When we have stripped the veil from him, the Lawless One will appear; because he is the head of the whole Secret Empire.

Sir Alexander does not know it, but this conspiracy has existed for years, and I have suffered from it for years.

I have suffered from it from the moment that I set foot in this country.

I will, however, exonerate all Masons of this city, who know nothing about it, and all the Masons generally, who know nothing about it.

They simply obey the orders they get.

These orders come to them, they know not whence.

I ask them to examine this matter.

I ask them to ask Almighty God to help them to understand this matter.

In all kindness I say to Sir Alexander Peacock, "You are a baby Mason yourself. You do not know anything about it except as the Grand Master of this jurisdiction.

"But you must know, if you know anything, that you are degrees and degrees below the high Masonry whose heads you do not know."

No Mason in the world, except perhaps three or four, knows who the supreme head of Masonry is.

No Animus But That of Love and Kindness in Attacking Freemasonry.

I have said nothing in anger; I have said nothing in malice.

I have nothing to gain by this fight against Masonry except to set you free, my brethren, so that, instead of wearing an apron to go out and be a fool, if you will wear an apron, you may wear it to help your wives in the kitchen, or for some other good purpose.

I should like to set you free from the folly of going through these silly degrees; to set you free, to be good fathers and good husbands, and good Christian men, and good loyal citizens.

I found a Mason only today who said to me, "I am a Mason."

"How long is it since you were in a lodge?" I asked.

"Oh," he said, "it is years."

I asked another one, "How long is it since you were in a Masonic lodge?"

He said, "Twenty-five years."

I find that nearly all the Masons in Adelaide are baby Masons.

They have never gone beyond the degree of Master Mason.

I have no anger or malice.

I have no hatred against any man.

I hate what I believe to be evil.

Let the Masons Show How Good Masonry Is.

I tell you what is the best thing for you to do: Take the Town Hall some night and show the people of Adelaide what Masonry really is, out and out.

Open it all out to them, from the beginning to the end.

If you do that, what will they see?

They will see you coming in with your eyes blindfolded and a tow-rope round your neck.

They will see you bow down, with only an undershirt and an old pair of drawers on, one shoe off and one shoe on, at the feet of the Worshipful Master, going from him in the east, to the south and then to the west, following the course of the sun, which you worship.

Then they will see you impersonate Hiram Abiff and be murdered and resurrected by the Worshipful Master, impersonating old King Solomon, with the lion's paw grip.

Then the people will hear the wonderful omnific word, Mah-hah-bone!

Then your wife will never respect you again when she sees you in that condition.

We know the secrets of Masonry, because we have hundreds and hundreds who have known it well and who have come out.

We have the whole story from A to Z.

One night in Central Zion Tabernacle, Chicago, we had a lodge upon the platform, and we had enough men to show us the whole thing.

Although I never was a Mason, never took their vows, and oaths, and so never broke any of them, I know the whole thing from beginning to end, and I have suffered for this knowledge, too.

The Beginning of My Fight Against Masonry.

I first became a foe of Masonry when I sat by the bedside of one who had been the Grand Secretary of a Masonic Lodge.

He cried when he was dying, and said to me "Mr. Dowie, would that I had never been a Mason!

"Then I would never have gone into these dreadful things; I would have been a faithful husband, a good man and a good citizen, but" he said, "the awful temptations in continuously meeting with Masons, and their dissipations after their initiations have ruined me bodily and well-nigh spiritually."

He died and the Masons would not bury him, because he had rejected Masonry before he died.

His wife could not get anything from them because he, on his deathbed, turned to God and became a Christian.

The Secretary of Zion Land and Investment Association, Deacon H. Worthington Judd, has been a Mason.

He took thirty-two degrees and was a Knight Templar.

I have scores of members of the Christian Catholic Church in Zion, who have rejected Masonry.

I have no hatred.

What I say I say as a minister of the Gospel, believing it to be my duty.

I say to Sir Alexander Peacock that when he says that I have some ulterior design, he is entirely wrong.

I am speaking for the good of all Masons.

CLOSING PRAYER.

My God and Father, in Jesus' Name I come to Thee. For Jesus' sake bless me, and bless this congregation. Be with us in our work for Thee. Help all people here, and all throughout this state to understand that we love Thee and love them, and have no desire but their good. If in anywise we have done them evil we regret it, but we do not know it. We have simply hated and fought against evil things. God bless these people. [Amen.] Make them sober, and industrious, and religious to a greater extent than they are now. We thank Thee for the good men there are in this state. We know there are many who are Masons, that have no other desire but that of doing right; they have long been away from Masonry. God bless them and bless those who are deeply in it. We pray this afternoon for all that have said bad words about us or done bad things to us. We ask Thee, for Jesus' sake to give them a True Repentance, and then all will receive full forgiveness. We ask it for Jesus' sake. Amen.

The meeting was closed with the

BENEDICTION.

Beloved, abstain from all appearance of evil. And may the very God of Peace Himself sanctify you wholly; and I pray God your whole spirit and soul and body be preserved entire, without blame, unto the coming of our Lord Jesus, the Christ. Faithful is He that calleth you, who also will do it. The grace of our Lord Jesus, the Christ, the love of God, our Father, the fellowship of the Holy Spirit, our Comforter and Guide, one Eternal God, abide in you, bless you and keep you, and all the Israel of God everywhere, forever. Amen.

Then followed the Zion salutation, Peace to thee! and the response, Peace to thee be multiplied!

Immediately after the close of this service, the General Overseer and all members of his party, except Deacon Ernest Williams, who remained in Adelaide in order to attend to some important matters, took carriages and drove quietly to "Calton Hill," Crafers, under the shadow of Mount Lofty.

The intention was to remain at "Calton Hill" Friday night and Saturday, and to return to Adelaide for the final public services of the Visitation to be held in the Exhibition Building on Lord's Day morning and afternoon, and the final farewell service for the members and friends of Zion on Monday afternoon, March 28th.

But it was not so to be.

Masonic Influence, Under Pretext of Loyalty to King, Refuses Use of Public Buildings.

The powerful Messages of Elijah the Restorer had been published very fully in the morning and afternoon newspapers of Adelaide, and the destructive sledge-hammer blows which had been struck Hypocrisy, Masonic Baal worship, Intemperance, Infidelity and Impurity had caused a terrific stir in the city.

"Wicked men and seducers" having grown worse and worse, and their wounds having become deeper and more inflamed, their pain and rage were checked in their murderous fury only by their cowardice.

Realizing the temper of this portion of the population of the city, the Inspector of Police had called upon the General Overseer and solemnly warned him that it would be almost if not quite suicidal for him to attempt to hold a meeting in the Exhibition Building on Lord's Day afternoon.

The General Overseer, however, had declared his intention of carrying through his Mission as announced, and was not willing to give up that service.

This was the situation, therefore, that the officials had to face.

The startling disclosures regarding the filthy, heathenish character of Freemasonry, made by the General Overseer in his Friday afternoon Message, apparently convinced the Masons that they would fare perhaps worse in the meetings on the Lord's Day afternoon.

Besides these considerations, it is well known that the self-satisfied Mayor of Adelaide, Mr. L. Cohen, is a very ambitious man, and has quite set his heart on being knighted by the King; so that he shall be no longer plain "Mr." Cohen, but "Sir" Lewis Cohen, Lord Mayor of the city of Adelaide, South Australia.

It is also quite generally thought that Mr. John Greeley Jenkins, the Chief Secretary of the State of South Australia, would be much pleased to receive that stroke from a sword which would entitle him to use the prefix "Sir" with his name.

The Mayor, the Chief Secretary, and those in control of the Adelaide daily papers, are all members of the Masonic Order.

As a result of the above combination of circumstances the afternoon papers of Friday, March 25th, appeared with startling headlines, among which are the following:

"ELIJAH AND THE KING."
"HIS MAJESTY ATTACKED BY DOWIE."
"THE KING'S PIETY IMPUGNED."
"KING EDWARD ATTACKED BY DOWIE."

Under these headings articles appeared in which the words of the General Overseer were wrested from their original meaning and character, and made as inflammatory as possible.

The following from the *Advertiser*, for Saturday, March 26th, is a sample:

Elijah the Restorer, otherwise the Rev. J. A. Dowie, at his meeting in the Town Hall on Friday afternoon made a malignant attack on his Majesty King Edward. He said with emphasis that when Christ came again He would take the rule into His own hands. King Edward would then have to take a back seat. Nobody could boast of his piety, and nobody imagined that he had much religion to spare. They only hoped that he would have enough religion to get him into heaven. If he did it would be only by the skin of his teeth.

On Saturday morning, March 26th, the following letter from Mayor Cohen was received by the General Overseer:

To the REV. J. A. DOWIE.

Sir:—I am sure that the Corporation of the City of Adelaide has never before permitted any one to use the Town Hall for the purpose of expressing disloyal sentiments towards our beloved King, and although you may be an American, yet a disgrace to your nationality, your utterances appearing in yesterday afternoon's press are an insult to every British subject of our Empire, and I enter my strongest protest against any further utterances of a disloyal character. If they should so occur I shall have no hesitation in instructing the police to eject you from the Town Hall.

Respectfully yours, L. COHEN, Mayor of Adelaide.

A Quixotic Quest for a "Knighthood."

But it was not consistent with the purpose of the Mayor to keep such a communication private; indeed, his action was taken for the express purpose of winning the applause of the populace and the favor of the Crown.

He was strapping on his spurs in preparation for a very hard ride after that coveted knighthood.

Therefore the letter was published in the Saturday morning papers, in connection with the highly colored reports of the General Overseer's attack on the King, before the letter was received by him.

The Mayor and his brother Masons and political henchmen took good care that there was a great deal of wild talk on the streets, Saturday morning, with the result that, by noon of that day, a large part of the populace were so wrought up that they were ready to tear the General Overseer to pieces if they could have laid hands on him.

The people of Australia have a reputation for being rabidly sensitive about their King and the royal family, although they cannot be said to have anything like a true love for the British government.

As for their own government, the majority of the people hold it in the greatest contempt—and rightfully.

But the self-satisfied Mayor and the severely wounded Masons had played upon this supersensitiveness about British royalty, and were trying to make it serve the double purpose of getting that coveted "Sir" for the Mayor and drawing people's attention away from the terrific exposure of the true character of Masonic Baal worship.

Another Seeker for Knightly Honors.

This was a hint to the ambitious Chief Secretary Jenkins.

It would never do to let the Mayor of Adelaide become "Sir" Lewis Cohen, while he, the chief secretary of a great state, remained plain Mr. Jenkins!

Hence the Saturday evening papers contained a letter from the Superintendent of Public Buildings, inspired by "the Government," that is to say, Mr. Jenkins, in which the Chief Secretary outdid the Mayor by absolutely refusing the General Overseer the use of the Exhibition Building for the two services announced for the Lord's Day morning and afternoon.

The following is the letter referred to:

OFFICE OF THE
SUPERINTENDENT OF PUBLIC BUILDINGS,
ADELAIDE, SOUTH AUSTRALIA, March 26th, 1904.
RE JUBILEE EXHIBITION BUILDING.

Sir:—I am directed by the government to inform you that in consequence of the disloyal utterances you are reported to have made yesterday in the Adelaide Town Hall in reference to His Majesty the King, you will not be allowed to again hold a meeting in any building under government control.

A cheque for one hundred twenty pounds, representing your deposit and rent for the Jubilee Exhibition Building for tomorrow, the 27th inst., is awaiting collection at this office.

I am, Sir, Your obedient servant, C. E. OWEN SMYTH,
Superintendent Public Buildings.

To Rev. J. A. DOWIE,
York Hotel, Adelaide.

The Mayor, finding himself thus left behind in the race, made his next move very quickly, and before night, Saturday, the following letter had found its way to the General Overseer, and, what was more important to "his honor," to the evening papers:

TOWN HALL, ADELAIDE, SOUTH AUSTRALIA, March 26, 1904.
REV. J. A. DOWIE,
York Hotel, Adelaide.

Sir:—I have the honor, by direction of the Right Worshipful the Mayor, to inform you that he has canceled the remainder of your engagement of the Town Hall. This action has been taken in consequence of your disloyal utterances concerning His Majesty the King, as reported in the press yesterday afternoon and this morning.

The balance of hire paid will be refunded to you on application at the city treasurer's office.

I have the honor to be, Sir, Your obedient servant, T. GEO. ELLERY,
Town Clerk.

The result of all this was that the narrow, insular prejudices of many people were so stirred that there were threats freely made that a mob would be organized to march out to "Calton Hill," and there wreak vengeance upon the man who had dared to "impugn the piety of the King!"

It was rumored on Saturday afternoon that three hundred cyclists had left Adelaide with this laudable patriotic purpose burning in their breasts.

It was also rumored that a petition was being circulated, praying Chief Secretary Jenkins to demand an apology of the General Overseer.

The three hundred cyclists did not arrive at Calton Hill, and the demand for an apology has not been seen, up to date.

Another rumor had it that the General Overseer was to be given twenty-four hours' notice to leave Australia, while another contended that he would not be allowed to leave until he had apologized.

Thus, for a day or two, public indignation seemed to run very high, and the self-satisfied little Mayor of Adelaide was hailed as the popular hero of the hour.

Had he not had the high courage (?) to assail a man whom he believed to be at the very depths of unpopularity?

Nor was Mr. Jenkins to be forgotten.

His action, while only imitative, was equally as brave.

Those knighthoods seemed almost within grasp.

The Tidal Wave Begins to Recede.

But the Australian people have a sense of humor.

It is true that it is, in most of them, dull, tardy and warped; but it is there, nevertheless, and the grotesque spectacle presented by Messrs. Jenkins and Cohen and their supporters soon began to make them laugh.

After all, what had the General Overseer said that was not true; and, indeed, might he not have said much more and still not have told all the truth?

Furthermore, how was it possible for an American citizen to be disloyal to the King of England?

It even began to be whispered that the very ferocity of the resentment of the Mayor and Chief Secretary was, perhaps, a graver reflection upon the piety of Edward VII. than the few calm, mild words that had aroused that resentment.

Thus the reaction set in.

The knighthood aspirants began to be laughed at.

This is evidenced by the following paragraphs from the weekly papers:

The Sydney *Bulletin*, for March 31, 1904, said:

In a wild moment Dowie said that when the Lord came to personally rule over the world Edward would have to take a back seat. This statement that Edward was less important than the Lord roused Adelaide to such anger that Dowie was refused the further use of the Town Hall.

The Adelaide *Quiz*, said, on April 1, 1904, in "A Girl's Letter:"

I hear on good authority that His Majesty is deeply relieved to hear that he has one loyal champion in Australia. Mayor Cohen is, of course, the hero of the hour, and King Edward is busily engaged looking over his stock of decorations to see which will best fit the vanquisher of Elijah. I did hear that the title was to be Sir Lewis Cohen, D. D., (which stands for Demolisher of Dowie, not Doctor of Divinity), or perhaps the Marquis of Loyalville, or may be the Earl of North Adelaide. In my opinion nothing short of an earldom could properly fit the case. It is rumored that His Majesty had just finished a game of baccarat with his friend Gordon Cumming, after having returned from Ascot, when the news was flashed across that his piety had been impugned by a Yankee in Adelaide. At first he imagined it was his friend Jenkins, but was deeply relieved to find that it was only Elijah Dowie, the Restorer.

Such an attitude of the public mind would never do for the lofty purposes of the would-be knights.

That wave of popular feeling, upon whose crest they had been so gaily riding on to their coveted haven, was very dangerously receding, and it seemed that they would be left high and dry on the treacherous sands.

Hence the doughty Cohen began to make speeches on every posssible occasion, toasting his "beloved king," and heaping imprecations upon the head of the man who had "impugned his piety."

The "impugning of piety" seemed to become a little tame, however, and it pleased the Mayor to refer, with sweeping generality, to the "vile and seditious utterances," the "ribald insults," and the "base slanders," of which the General Overseer had been guilty.

His Masonic friends and political toadies were whipped into line, and began to send him telegrams of congratulation upon his "courageous" action. Of course, these were all given prominent places in the Adelaide daily papers, which also tried to keep up the excitement by publishing fevered editorials.

But it was of no use.

The reaction had set in and was growing stronger every day.

The following, from the Adelaide *Register* for March 30, 1904, is a straw which shows something of the direction of the wind:

THE DOWIE INCIDENT.

The members of the Port Adelaide City Council, at the invitation of the Mayor (Mr. J. W. Caire), lunched at the Britannia Hotel on Tuesday. In proposing the loyal toast, the Mayor remarked: That visiting prophet, Dowie—the coming Elijah—has occasioned highly sympathetic feelings with reference to His Majesty the King, and I am sure every member of the council and the visitors present will show their loyalty to our sovereign by joining heartily in drinking the toast. I am sure you all regret that the situation should have arisen, and that the vile remarks were made. (Cr. Lundie—I was present at the meeting, and no vile remarks were made.) They were reported in the press, and were not refuted; and I am sure that you will agree with the action of the Chief Secretary and the Mayor of Adelaide in putting a stop to such proceedings. Cr. Lundie said he could not see that the remarks were offensive, as they were applied generally, and offense need not be taken. The toast was enthusiastically received, to the accompaniment of the national anthem.

Some Interesting Letters Published in the Adelaide Papers.

The following are from the Adelaide *Advertiser* for March 25th:

To the Editor.

Sir:—I went yesterday to the Town Hall to attend the service conducted by Mr. Dowie, but was not admitted. I was not surprised at my rebuff when I saw the mob that the police were keeping at bay. They put me in mind of the hooligans who rushed the doors of Victoria Hall when the Slatterys were here. Although I was brought up as a Roman Catholic, I have serious doubts that "we are the people, and wisdom will die with us." I am not like Artemus Ward's ancestors, who went to a country where they could not only enjoy their own religion, but they could stop others from enjoying theirs. The American rowdy detested abolitionists of negro slavery; the Adelaide rowdy is thirsting for Mr. Dowie's blood because he is an abolitionist of drink, tobacco, and what Wilberforce terms "everlasting cards." That is the head and front of his offending.

I am, sir, Michael D. Walsh.

Adelaide, March 24th.

Sir:—I have suffered a lot from living amongst smokers, and I don't wonder at Mr. Dowie calling them "stinkpots." I have been married twice. My first husband was a smoker, and I was nearly always ill. I suffered from most awful headaches and unendurable pain. The house was never sweet, but there was always a nasty musty smell, even when he was out all day. My second husband does not smoke, and I never have the awful headaches that I had with my first husband. Our house is always sweet and healthy. I am sure it is what God meant it to be. After my first experience, I have a perfect dread of smokers and drinkers, and I do thank God for my dear, clean husband whose mouth is so sweet it is a pleasure to kiss him. I am, A Lover of Truth.

The very well-written letter reprinted below is from the *Register* for March 25th:

To the Editor.

Sir:—I hold no brief for Mr. Dowie, neither am I numbered among his adherents; but I would point out that your correspondent "Stephen Page" misapplies the prophecies contained in the Book of Malachi. He erroneously asserts that these prophecies referred to John the Baptist, and quotes from Malachi 4 and Luke 1 and 2 to prove his assertion. The passages quoted from Luke 1 and 2 certainly refer to John the Baptist, who prepared the way for Christ's first coming. But the prophecies contained in the Book of Malachi refer to Christ's second coming. Part of Malachi's prophecy runs thus—"Behold, I will send My messenger, and he shall prepare the way before Me; and the Lord whom ye seek shall suddenly come to His temple, even the messenger of the covenant, whom ye delight in; behold, he shall come, saith the Lord of Hosts. But who may abide the day of his coming? and who shall stand when he appeareth? for he is like a refiner's fire and like fullers' soap."

This cannot be applied to John the Baptist. For all stood when he appeared, and the people did unto him whatsoever they listed," and finally he was beheaded at Herod's command after his mission had been fulfilled. But that mission was not to "restore all things," but to prepare the way for Christ's first advent. In fact "all things," or the full gospel, was not established till Christ had completed His work of redemption. When Malachi says (chapter 3:15)—"And now we call the proud happy; yea, they that work wickedness are set up; yea, they that tempt God are delivered," he gives a picture of this present time, when the commandments of men are taught instead of the doctrines of Christ, and the "church" is divided into numerous different sects. But he speaks of the time of the "restoration of all things" when he says (Malachi 4:1)—"For, behold, the day cometh that shall burn as an oven; and all the proud, yea, and all that do wickedly, shall be stubble." And when he says (verse 5)—"Behold, I will send you Elijah the prophet before the coming of the great and dreadful day of the Lord," he speaks of the prophet who shall prepare the way for Christ's second coming.

This is that prophet whom I understand Mr. Dowie claims to be. Whether Mr. Dowie is what he claims to be or not I do not know, and have no means of determining. His works alone must decide the question. In the meantime he deserves that respect and consideration that are due to a man who, so far as we know, has wronged no one. The Elijah spoken of by Malachi is represented as being a prophet of power who should carry everything before him. The Elijah mentioned in Luke 1, and Mark 9:13, is referred to as "The Voice of one crying in the wilderness, prepare ye the way of the Lord, make His paths straight." (See Isaiah 40:3, Matthew 3:3, Mark 1:3, Luke 3:4, John 1:23.) In Mark 9:12, Christ speaks of His second coming, and speaks of Elijah "who cometh first and restoreth all things" in the future tense. To prove this one has but to read the ninth and tenth verses, where Christ speaks of His resurrection, and His disciples wonder what the "rising from the dead should mean," and they put the question to Him, "Why say the scribes that Elijah must first come?" Christ explains that Elijah must come and restore all things, and then goes on to speak of John the Baptist, evidently teaching His disciples the difference between the Elijah of Malachi and John the Baptist. John was the prophet of the first coming of our Lord; the Elijah of Malachi is to be the prophet of the second coming of our Lord.

I am, Sir, Andrew P. Wauchope.

Narracoorte, March 23.

These significant letters appeared in the *Register* for Saturday, March 26th:

Sir:—If you throw a stone amongst a lot of dogs and one begins to yelp, you may be sure that the stone hit that dog. So it is with some of Dr. Dowie's utterances. We hear a yelp here and a yelp there, and we know they are hit somewhere. The Mason yelps, the brewer yelps, the smoker yelps, the parson yelps, the hypocrite yelps, etc., so that accounts for the mighty yelping on Monday night. Talk about "human beings"—inhuman monsters would be more appropriate. For could that "mob" have got hold of Dowie they would have torn every limb from his body. And why? For trying to get people to live clean, pure and holy lives. Oh, he makes money say some. Well, suppose he does. None of it came from you, so why worry? Oh, he calls us "stinkpots," say others. Well, isn't it true? Every smoker agrees smoking is a dirty habit. Then why should Christians indulge in such habits when the Bible says, "Be ye clean." Oh, he puts up at a public house, and he is against the liquor traffic. Yes; and after the display on Monday night I can quite see the wisdom of this, for what private house would shelter him, or what Coffee Palace in this city has all the requisites, such as being connected by telephone, etc., which are essential in his case? I am perfectly satisfied that Australia is persecuting a prophet of God, and very many will be sorry ere long for the part they have taken in these disturbances. I am, etc., Fairplay.

Knightsbridge, March 25, 1904.

Sir:—Mr. Dowie is not the only person the hoodlums have a set on. How about General Booth when the herd threatened to drown him in the Yarra, and skulls, windows, etc., were smashed nightly in Hindley street, flag-bearers were knocked down and left in the gutters? How about the Charlick riot, and the disgraceful treatment Wilson Barrett received when playing here? Mr. Dowie said on Sunday he came here to stir things up. The worst of it is he has stirred up the muck. Adelaide has got a name now she will not lose for many years. What Mr. Dowie says does not affect me one iota. I am no "stinkpot," "beerpot," "swine-eater," or that being who is screeching most at the present, the hypocrite. Do the drunkard and smoker ever think how unpleasant they make themselves to others, yet they can't stand Dowie's pin-pricks. I am, British Fair Play.

Park street, Hyde Park, March 25, 1904.

The *Register* for March 30th, published the following:

A KIND SUGGESTION.

From "Only a Woman"—How hard it must all be for Mrs. Dowie! An Adelaide girl, returned after long absence to the home of her youth, to her birthplace—and for this! A mother, suffering from a great grief—must she leave our shores with nought but miserable recollections? The present is, to some of us, known as Holy Week—a season when we are called upon to devote as much time as possible to the consideration of heavenly rather than of mundane matters. Daily during this Holy Week do we follow the story of One—a Man of Sorrows, and acquainted with grief—who suffered and was buried. From one of His great disciples we learn of that most excellent gift of charity that never faileth. Is not this a fitting season to exercise it? Shall we let an Australian native—a South Australian native—leave these shores without some evidence of gentler treatment than has hitherto been meted to her? A few kind words—some flowers even—from such as can spare them, from those who have the heart to spare them, might not be unwelcome to a daughter of South Australia revisiting her native land in such painful circumstances, and might even soften the asperity of the recollections she must needs bear away. What say the A. N. A.?

The following, from the *Advertiser* for March 30th, is clear and logical, and shows something of the sentiments aroused:

"A Seeker after the Truth" thinks it would be well to have some denial from the Freemasons in reference to Mr. Dowie's statements concerning them. "Mr. Dowie," he says, "is either telling lies or telling the truth. I refer to the statement that Mr. Dowie made in the Adelaide Town Hall on Friday, March 25th. He said: 'If a Freemason were charged with any criminal offence, no matter what the offence was, even murder, if the Freemason gave the Freemasonry sign to the judge on the bench it would terrorise the judge, so that the judge would be bound by oath to help his fellow Freemason in distress. In other words, the Freemason would escape punishment.' Now, either Mr. Dowie is right or he is wrong, and as there are always two sides to every question, those who are not Freemasons would like to hear the other side. I maintain, if Mr. Dowie is right in his statement, no judge should be allowed to sit on the bench if he is a Freemason. On the other hand, if Mr. Dowie has made a false statement, the Freemasons have their remedy by using constitutional means, not cowardly means such as Mr. Dowie has had to put up with. I, like many more, am waiting to see if the Freemasons will take up Mr. Dowie's challenge and prove to the public that Mr. Dowie has not told the truth. Until the Freemasons do this, I, for one, shall believe in what Mr. Dowie has made public, and shall watch coming events very closely.

An Ordination Service at "Calton Hill."

Owing to the action of the authorities, the General Overseer was unable to hold the meetings that had been announced for Lord's Day and Monday, and accordingly spent the day quietly with his family, the members of his party, and his household at "Calton Hill."

On Tuesday, March 29, 1904, Overseer and Elder Wilbur Glenn Voliva, of Melbourne; Deacon and Deaconess John Stephen McCullagh, and Miss Christobell McCullagh, their daughter, of Sydney; and Deacon and Deaconess Clement Friend Hawkins, of Adelaide; were guests at "Calton Hill."

In the afternoon of that day, in the midst of the beauty and quiet of the hills, the General Overseer administered the simple but solemn and impressive Ordinance of Ordination to the ministry of the Christian Catholic Church in Zion.

The following were the ordinations:—

To the office of Elder:

REV. JOHN STEPHEN McCULLAGH,
REV. CLEMENT FRIEND HAWKINS.

To the office of Evangelist:

REV. HANNAH McCULLAGH,
REV. MARION ELIZA HAWKINS.

Elder and Evangelist McCullagh were transferred from the charge of the Branch of the Christian Catholic Church in Zion in Sydney, New South Wales, to the charge of the work of the Christian Catholic Church in Zion throughout New Zealand.

Elder and Evangelist Hawkins will remain in charge of the Branch of the Christian Catholic Church in Zion in Adelaide, South Australia.

NOTES ON THE AUSTRALIAN VISITATION.

These brief notes are written on Wednesday, April 6th, on the eve of our departure from the shores of the great Island Continent of Australia.

All has been peace and quiet at "Calton Hill," since our coming hither from Adelaide, on Friday afternoon, March 25th, and the General Overseer and all the members of his party have had a refreshing rest and are prepared for the long sea voyage, which is to take us across the Great Australian Bight to Fremantle, West Australia; thence across the Indian Ocean to Colombo, Ceylon; thence across the Arabian Sea to the entrance of the Red Sea, at Aden; thence through the Red Sea and the Suez Canal, to Port Said, and thence to our destination, Marseilles, France, where we are scheduled to arrive on Lord's Day, May 8, 1904.

Although there have been many threatenings, there have been no acts of violence attempted since we left Adelaide, and our hearts are full of thanksgiving to God for His protecting care.

We feel that, if the Unseen Hosts had not encamped round about us, there could have been no power that would have saved our General Overseer from the hands of his evil and murderous enemies.

We have been vigilant, as our Lord commanded, and have been very ably and willingly assisted in this by the loyal members of the Branch of the Christian Catholic Church in Zion in Adelaide; but God's is all the glory.

As we look back over the nearly two months that we have spent in Australia we feel that the reports that we have been enabled to forward for publication in LEAVES OF HEALING have represented only faintly the true condition of affairs in the great Commonwealth, especially with reference to the Visitation of God's prophet, Elijah the Restorer.

Scenes like those through which we have passed since the 13th of February, when we landed at Sydney, can never be fully and fittingly described in words.

We can only give outlines of the events and leave our readers to read between the lines, something of the animus behind them.

There are many incidents which could not be incorporated in the reports, that are not only of great interest as a part of this Visitation, but are also of high significance as indications of the condition of affairs, and of the character of the people, in Australia.

It is our purpose, in these few Notes, to record some of these incidents which come to our mind as we write, praying God to bless them to those who may read.

THE MODERN ELIJAH RUNS AMUCK.

DOWIE'S GOSPEL OF PEACE.

—*Reproduced from the Adelaide "Express and Telegraph," Saturday, March 26, 1904.*

The Eagerness of the People to Hear God's Prophet.

In all three of the Australian cities where the General Overseer has held his Missions one of the most striking things in connection with the attitude of the people thereto has been their intense eagerness to see and to hear God's prophet.

It was repeatedly reported to us in all three of these cities that persons who came too late to secure tickets, or for some other reason failed to get them, were offering sums of from one shilling to five pounds in order to secure them.

It was also reported to us, upon good authority, that shrewd young speculators had, by hook or crook, obtained supplies of tickets and were disposing of them at rates varying from one to three shillings.

Not only was this true, but well-dressed business men, as well as young men and boys, and many women would stand for hours at points at which they expected the General Overseer to pass, waiting for an opportunity to see him.

The General Overseer and members of his party were daily in receipt of letters from people in all ranks and classes of society, most urgently and respectfully asking for tickets.

Fury of the Australian Larrikin.

We use the word larrikin here, not in the narrow sense that it is used in Australia, referring merely to rough, disorderly young roisterers, with no position and no responsibility, but as applied to any one, no matter what his position or responsibilities, that manifests the "larrikinish" instincts.

As a matter of fact, as the General Overseer remarked more than once, the principal trouble in all the Australian cities that we have visited has been caused by men of means, education and position, some of them even pastors of denominational churches; and, as might be expected, most of them Freemasons.

The bitter hatred and fury of these enemies of God's Messenger have been variously shown in the reports which have already been published; but there are other interesting incidents which are also indicative of the same fact.

They were business men, professional men and students, in Town Hall, Adelaide, who blasphemously mocked Overseer Jane Dowie while she knelt in prayer. The gentle voice never faltered in the midst of all the pandemonium, the Overseer praying earnestly for those who, at that time, so brutally insulted her.

But the Devil was in them, and all sense of manliness and decency seemed to have left; for they did not cease their vulgar and obscene interruptions.

Neither were they poorly-dressed, low skulkers, who threw a shower of heavy stones at the little party of Zion people who entered the York Hotel shortly after the close of the meeting on Monday night, March 21st.

It was a crowd of so-called respectable young men who pelted the unoffending members of Zion, including two ladies, Elder W. G. Voliva and Deaconess Ida M. Stern.

Another form that the persecution has taken is that of boycotting.

Not only members of the Christian Catholic Church in Zion, but even those who are brave enough to express any sympathy with the General Overseer, or with his teaching, have been exposed to the most unjust and cruel treatment. Zion servants have been discharged by their bigoted employers.

Zion employers have been deserted by their help.

Zion merchants have been notified that they need expect no more orders from certain of their customers.

In one case, a man who merely expressed sympathy with the General Overseer in a certain place of business, was informed that he could trade there no longer.

EXTERIOR AND INTERIOR VIEWS OF FEDERAL HALL, ZION TABERNACLE, ADELAIDE, SOUTH AUSTRALIA.

The son-in-law of a certain well-known and much-beloved minister, a business man in the City of Adelaide, said, on board of one of the suburban trains, that he could not see what Dr. Dowie had said about the King that was so terrible that such an uproar should be made about it.

His fellow passengers, who were business associates and life-long friends of his, told him that it was only their old friendship for him that kept them from smashing his face and throwing him from the train. He was completely dumfounded, and said in great perplexity, "Why, you must have all gone mad. I simply cannot understand it."

All of these things show how deeply the Devil has been stirred up in Adelaide, the "City of Churches," or, as it is sometimes called, "The Holy City."

Notwithstanding all this, however, there are many thoughtful people with broad views, in whose minds the reaction which set in a week ago has been steadily growing stronger.

Every day new friends are heard from, who declare that their sympathies are entirely with the man who had the courage to stand in the face of all his enemies and tell them the truth.

Why Many Australians Hate Zion.

One of the bitterest complaints that the Australian press and many of the Australian people have made against Zion is that she is taking her best people out of the country.

Australia has a most narrow-minded and short-sighted exclusion act, passed at the instance of the movers for a so-called "White Australia."

This act practically forbids any person with a dark complexion from entering the country.

As a result, their nation is in a terrible condition.

Nothing but black labor can endure the climate and develop the resources of the wonderful north country, and the rest of the Commonwealth is almost as much in need of such labor.

The "White Australians," most of them at least, would rather lean against the walls of the public houses than work on a farm.

Most atrocious misgovernment, bad financing and drouth has brought upon the Commonwealth a national debt of two hundred and twenty million pounds (£220,000,000—$1,100,000,000).

Australia is therefore not very attractive to immigrants.

The birth-rate of the present population has fallen off in a most appalling manner.

Hence it is with alarm that those whose capital is invested in Australia view the departure of any from her shores, and especially such industrious, sober, and prosperous people as the Zion people.

Leading articles have appeared in the papers, frightened people have written letters, and there has been a great deal of wild talk on the streets, deploring the departure of these people and urging them not to go.

At the same time the enemies of Zion are so illogical as to persecute the Zion people and make living there hard and unpleasant for them, in their efforts to prevail upon them to remain in the country.

It is hoped that by the time this paper is published, one hundred members of the Christian Catholic Church in Zion from Australia will have arrived in Zion City, leaving there by the May vessel.

During the Melbourne Visitation, while the General Overseer was holding private meetings in Central Zion Tabernacle, in

GENERAL OVERSEER AND AROUND-THE-WORLD VISITATION PARTY, AND MEMBERS OF ZION IN ADELAIDE, AT "CALTON HILL," CRAFERS, SOUTH AUSTRALIA, MONDAY, APRIL 4, 1904.

Swanston street, a Methodist minister, named Bailey, came into the meeting, being admitted on account of his clerical office.

During the meeting, he angrily and insolently interrupted the General Overseer several times.

A Speedy Execution of Judgment.

The General Overseer bore with him very patiently, but finally asked him to retire.

He refused to do so, saying that he would not leave that meeting until he had been put out forcibly, and that if he were removed by force, he would "take steps."

Seeing that the man had come for the express purpose of creating a disturbance, the General Overseer continued to bear with him patiently, and did not order him removed.

The wicked man mocked, with loud-spoken "Amens," during Deacon Hawkin's prayer.

At the close of the meeting, being disappointed that he had failed to create a disturbance, he tried to argue with some of the Zion people.

They, however, had no time to argue, and, going into the lower front vestibule, he began an harangue to the people who were going out.

As he was blocking the exit, Overseer Voliva requested him to be quiet and leave the place.

His retort was impudent and defiant.

Whereupon, the Overseer ordered several members of Zion Guard to remove him.

As soon as the Guards laid hold of him, he began to fight like a madman, while several Methodist ladies (?) who happened to be standing near, attacked the Guards from behind, striking and kicking them furiously.

Seeing the disturbance, two police officers, who were standing outside, came in and took charge of this clergyman, removing him from the building, and sending him about his business.

Almost exactly one month after this occurred, this wretched man was found dead—drowned in a lagoon near his home.

The coroner's jury brought in a verdict of accidental drowning, but it is not known exactly how the man met his death

"Vengeance is Mine; I will repay, saith Jehovah."

Service in Zion Tabernacle, Adelaide.

On Lord's Day, April 3, 1904, in Zion Tabernacle, Federal Hall, Adelaide, the Rev. C. Friend Hawkins delivered his first sermon as an Elder in the Christian Catholic Church in Zion.

Elder Hawkins spoke to a good-sized audience and was listened to with the most earnest attention.

As his sermon is a very clear and logical deduction from the events of the last few weeks in Australia, the General Overseer has directed that it be published.

The following is the report of the address:

Federal Hall, Adelaide, South Australia, Lord's Day Afternoon, April 3, 1904.

The Service was opened by the singing of Hymn No. 19, Visitation Program.

Elder C. Friend Hawkins read the Scripture lesson from the Inspired Word of God in the Gospel according to St. Luke, 7th chapter, closing with the 35th verse.

Prayer was offered and the tithes and offerings were received.

After the announcements were made Elder Hawkins delivered his address:

THE MARKS OF A TRUE PROPHET.

REPORTED BY I. M. S. AND A. W. N.

INVOCATION.

Our gracious Father, we pray Thee to bless us now as we speak to the people. May the words that are spoken be acceptable in Thy sight. For Jesus' sake. Amen.

TEXT.

Blessed are ye, when men shall hate you, and when they shall separate you from their company, and reproach you, and cast out your name as evil, for the Son of Man's sake.

Rejoice in that day, and leap for joy: for behold, your reward is great in heaven: for in the same manner did their fathers unto the prophets.

. . . .

Wo unto you, when all men shall speak well of you! for in the same manner did their fathers to the false prophets.

You find practically the same words in Matthew 5:11, 12:

Blessed are ye when men shall reproach you, and persecute you, and say all manner of evil against you falsely, for My sake.

Rejoice, and be exceeding glad: for great is your reward in heaven: for so persecuted they the prophets which were before you.

How many of you are looking for that kind of blessedness?

People Who Follow False Prophets.

These are the words of the Christ.

The sooner we get to see things as the Christ saw them the better.

If He says that a man is to count himself blessed when he is persecuted, reviled and despitefully used, you must believe Him.

If you believe that this is true, then why are you in the Methodist church, trying to be popular.

Why are you talking about how popular your minister is?

Why are you so satisfied to sit in a nice, cosy, fashionable church and listen to sermons that make your minister popular, and make all men speak well of him?

I know that "Beware of false prophets," is a very popular quotation, especially when the General Overseer of the Christian Catholic Church in Zion is being discussed.

That is about the only argument some people have.

They look very wise and say, "My friend, beware of false prophets," and then shake their empty heads.

They will then talk proudly of the fact that they are members of a popular church; that they have a popular minister; and that they have never heard one bad word against the man who occupies their pulpit.

Then you can turn round and say, "My friend, *you* beware of false prophets, for you have one in your church—a man of whom all men speak well."

We have had much sympathy wasted upon us during the recent Visitation.

Friends of mine have gone quite out of their way to sympathize with me, and to condole with me over the awful experiences through which we have passed.

I have had to say to them, "If you could only know the fun we have had out of it; how much we have laughed over it; and what a fool the Devil has made of himself, and of a lot of people too, you would not waste one word of sympathy on me.

"Do not weep for Zion.

"Weep for yourselves, for your children, and for your country."

God save this country!

I was born in Australia, but do not blame me for that.

I have been proud of it, but after this Visitation I can be proud of it no longer.

Australia Driving Out Its Best People.

I have had some sympathy with the dear sister who wrote from Zion City to Australia saying that when she received letters from her native land (Australia) she felt a little homesick, and sometimes shed tears.

Her mother writes back now and says, "My daughter no longer weeps for Australia, except for its sins." [Applause.]

The newspapers are doing a great deal of growling about the prospect of large numbers of people leaving Australia for Zion City.

They seem to be especially sore when they refer to the fact that these people are well-to-do, and are taking a great deal of money with them.

If they were some of the poor half-starved and unemployed, they would not mind if a ship-load or two of them left.

It would be one solution to the problem concerning the unemployed.

The newspapers say that the Zion people ought not to go; that they ought to stay here and develop this wonderful and beautiful country.

If they are sincere, and if they represent a constituency and a government which are sincere, why have they not treated the General Overseer better?

Why do they not treat members of the Christian Catholic Church in Zion better, instead of refusing us the use of all buildings controlled by the government, and by the municipality, and subjecting our people to all kinds of insults and petty boycotting?

Aspirants for Knighthood.

Knighthood ought to be quite an easy thing now for the Premier and the Mayor. [Applause.]

We almost find ourselves saying, "'Sir' Lewis Cohen," and "'Sir' John Greely Jenkins."

If Mr. Bastard, who refused us the use of the City Baths for our baptismal service, goes much farther with his "loyalty," we may soon be able to say "'Sir' Charles Bastard."

I need hardly remind you that Bastard has already aspired, once at least, to political honors, and was badly left in the old Wooroora electorate.

I am as loyal as any man in this country, and no one has ever heard me say, either publicly or privately, anything that would give a contrary impression.

But when it comes to denying Christian people—as Bastard happened to have the power to do—who have never offended any one, the sacred rite of Christian Baptism, and doing it in such a way, and under such circumstances as it was done, it seems to me like "loyalty" gone to seed.

If the government of this country wants us to live here, especially if it wants us to live here and deny ourselves the great privilege of living in Zion City, all it will need to do will be to close a few more halls against us; deny us a few more privileges; and heap a few more indignities upon us, and, of course we shall be happy to stay here for the term of our natural life. [Laughter.]

Many people have said to me, "Why does not the General Overseer establish a city in Australia? Why does he take the people away?"

Well, now, has he not been greatly encouraged to establish a city here?

Why did not the government of these States treat him as he was treated in the Southern states of America on his way here?

He and his party were treated royally throughout the South, and I should not wonder if the General Overseer were disposed to establish a city in that direction.

They know how to treat a man of God.

That is more than Australia knows how to do; although I who say it am an Australian, and an Australian who, up to within the last few months, was always proud of his country.

Australia has made herself ridiculous in the eyes of the whole world.

What has happened here has been cabled all over the world, and will subsequently be written up and published in the press throughout the world.

Do you not think that other people than Anglo-Saxons will sit down and have a jolly good laugh over the fools you have made of yourselves in Adelaide?

If we can laugh who are right on the spot, and have been through it all, people who read it afar off will simply have to rub their eyes and scratch their heads before they will be able to believe that it is true.

The foolery was not confined to one night only, either.

They are still keeping it up.

I do not know when it will die out. It seems to be a very malignant microbe. [Laughter.]

Wherever my poor head shows itself now, these wretched ribald songs and anything but gentlemanly epithets, are hurled at me.

Not that it troubles me very much.

I can stand a great deal of that kind of thing without fainting over it, but it does not make me feel any prouder of my fellow countrymen.

Only yesterday, on an up-country train coming to Adelaide for the races, a disgraceful scene occurred, described to me by two eye-witnesses.

At Gladstone an elderly gentleman with a long, white beard, got on the train.

About three hundred race-going hoodlums, supposing him to be John Alexander Dowie, tormented that poor old gentleman shamefully, treating him as they would like to treat the General Overseer. [Shame!]

The poor old man had to cling closely to a strong young man, who had compassion on him, throughout the journey; who spoke for him and kept these hoodlums off.

Does that not make you feel very proud of your country?

Such absolute stupidity and insanity!

That is all it is—insanity which comes from semi-stupefaction under the influence of tobacco, beer, whisky and everything else that defiles.

"They Know Not What They Do."

If you were to ask these people who sing or howl "We'll hang old Dowie on a sour apple tree," or "on a barb-wire fence," why they sing it, they would not know what to say.

If you were to ask them, "What harm has Dowie ever done you?" they would have to say, "None."

"What evil do you know that he has ever done any man or woman?"

"Oh, I do not know of any."

None of them know why they do it. One strong argument they have is the "false prophet" argument, and the other is, "boo-hoo-o-o!"

That is the entire sum of the evidence on the other side.

They simply cry "Away with him. Away with him. Let him be crucified."

A police officer said the other day that he could never believe that the people howled, when the Christ was on earth, "Crucify Him!" until he witnessed the scene outside the Adelaide Town Hall on Monday night, the 21st of March.

"Let Him be crucified," they cried after the Christ.

"Why, what evil hath He done?" asked Pilate.

"Let Him be crucified," was their only reply.

"What evil hath John Alexander Dowie done?" is asked.

"Away with him. Boo-hoo-o-o," is the only reply.

None of them know and none of them care what he has done.

These poor creatures have for so long swallowed whole the lies of the American press copied into both the secular and religious press of Australia that they have become absolutely mad.

They have made up their minds that no good thing can come out of Zion City.

The Results of the Australian Persecution.

What are the results, as far as Zion is concerned?

Let me name the first and most important of them all.

Every member of the Christian Catholic Church in Zion in Australasia, without a single exception, has come out of this Visitation with a stronger faith in God and a stronger faith in Zion than he has ever had before. [Applause.]

If we had had only a few more pieces of road metal and a few more bricks thrown at us, we all might have been even stronger in the spine than we are today.

As it is, I feel that my spine has stiffened up considerably during the last two or three months.

I notice that the same thing is true of many, if not all of our members.

Some of our members are such "fanatics" that they say that they would not have missed Monday night, March 21st, for a thousand pounds.

Yet there are some people who would have paid a thousand pounds to have been out of it.

There are one or two gentlemen whom I shall name some of these days, who would have paid a good deal more than that never to have been there.

Zion enjoys it all.

We thank God for it all.

What else could we have expected had we known how much Devil there was to the square inch in Adelaide?

People kept telling me that I was too hard on the people of this city; that they were not half so bad as I made them out to be.

Many very wise people have come to my meetings, and after they have heard what I had to say, have remarked to me or to my friends that I was altogether wrong; that people were not so bad as I made them out to be; and that things were not in such a desperate state as I assumed that they were.

I now acknowledge that I took too much for granted on the side of goodness.

Adelaide's Rejection of God's Prophet.

Things are ten times worse than I have ever represented.

Adelaide, with all its churches and with all its parsons, is on the highway to becoming like Sodom and Gomorrah.

The *Register* came out with an article on the "Rejection of the Prophet."

Do you remember what the Christ said about those who rejected His Word?

Do you remember what the Scriptures say about the cities that reject God's Message, and turn their backs on God's Prophet?

I almost wept when I opened the *Register* and read that leading article.

I thought to myself, "Oh, that Adelaide knew the day of her Visitation! Oh, that Adelaide understood the Message of Hope, and of Love that God has sent right into her midst!" But Adelaide knows it not; and Adelaide, according to the *Register*, rejects God's Prophet.

Surely I have underestimated the wickedness of this people!

I have revised all my estimates.

I intend to pitch in harder than ever at Adelaide's sins.

Look out from this time forward.

I now have my bearings better than ever I had before.

What else could you expect?

Have the masses of the people ever received a Prophet of God?

Have not God's Prophets always come to the few rather than to the many?

In this city there may be comparatively few who will hear, but when we get them together they make a fine, strong band, whose hearts God has touched.

When we get them ready to go to Zion City, we shall send out a clean set of godly people. [Amen.]

But when the salt has gone God help this city!

The people of God are leaving.

It does not matter how many leading articles are written in the papers, nor how many letters are published, God's people are going to get out of this city just as quickly as they can.

I will help them all I can.

When the General Overseer passes on to complete his Around-the-world Visitation, do you think Adelaide will be rid of him?

No!

He will have something to say a long time after he has gone.

Our people will have something to say, too.

What is better still, you will soon have LEAVES OF HEALING here with all his addresses printed in them.

When you see these things described in cold print, you will hardly be able to believe your eyes.

You will say to yourselves, "Did these things actually happen in bright, sunny Australia?"

Then, instead of singing the "Song of Australia" again, you will feel more like singing "We're marching upward to Zion, the beautiful City of God."

The Effect of Excellent Press Reports in Adelaide.

I think that it is generally admitted among Zion officials and members, and by the General Overseer himself, that, on the whole, the work done by the reporters on the daily papers here—I am saying nothing about the editorials or sub-editorials—was very good work; and, perhaps, in the experience of Zion, the best work done by the secular press throughout the world. [Applause.]

These reports have been telegraphed and cabled throughout the Commonwealth and New Zealand.

The words that the General Overseer has spoken in Adelaide have been read everywhere. The people have had to receive them without saying "boohoo."

Adelaide had one night of boohooing, but their plans were so badly upset by Zion's tactics that they did not have one hundredth part of the fun out of it that they had planned to have; and the General Overseer has spoken to the whole Commonwealth and New Zealand, besides speaking through cablegrams to all parts of the world.

They can do all the boohooing they like; they can close all the buildings they like, but without any building at all the General Overseer is in a position to speak to the whole world, and they must listen.

But after all the marvelous things that have been done in Australia; after the extraordinary antics of the Australian public and the many silly demonstrations that have been made, there is no question that the whole world will be extremely anxious to hear what the General Overseer is doing next, and what city will be the next to play the fool.

This is not the last sensation that the world is to have from Zion.

There are people in every land who are eager to hear Zion's Message, and willing to obey it, glad to share whatever there may be of sacrifice, persecution or shame in linking themselves with this work and coming into fellowship with the Christian Catholic Church in Zion.

The Devil Making a Fool of Himself.

Some poor silly fools think that they have put the quietus upon Zion, altogether.

They talk and write as if the General Overseer's doom were sealed; when, all the time, Zion is calmly, but surely, going ahead with her world-wide work, and smiling at the foolishness of the Devil.

The General Overseer has often said that he thinks of moving a vote of thanks to the Devil for the way in which he has helped Zion, by making a fool of himself so often that Zion has been able to win every time.

It is through persecution of this kind that Zion has been made strong, and has been given the spirit and courage to go on with this work.

The very blows, persecutions, and revilings with which the Devil attempts to crush Zion are the things that make Zion all the stronger and send her ahead all the faster.

What can her enemies do with an institution like that?

The best thing for the enemy to do is to keep quiet.

Hold your tongues.

Examine every thing closely.

Read your Bibles prayerfully, and see whether these things be true.

It is far better to read your Bibles and find out whether these things are true, than to keep on saying, "Boo-hoo-o-o."

You have before you what the Scriptures say about the false prophet and the true prophet.

If to have men revile you and persecute you and say all manner of evil against you falsely is any sign that you are associated with a true prophet, are you not pretty safe in being under the Banner of Zion?

Is there any name on God's earth today that will cause a greater fuss than the name of John Alexander Dowie?

The Terrible Commotion Caused by the Visitation of God's Prophet.

It is now freely admitted in Australia that there never has stepped upon these shores a man who has made such a stir.

John Alexander Dowie is the most hated man and the most loved man on God's earth today.

Those who know him best love him best.

Almost to a man or woman, they would lay down their lives for him.

That is true of Zion throughout the world.

The people who hate him most are those who know least about him.

All they know is what they have gathered from the lies of the press, and the pulpit—for you know that the parsons will have quite a harvest out of this Visitation.

They will have subjects to preach on for weeks to come. [Laughter.]

It will be "Dowie" for the morning service, "Dowie" for the evening service; the same for the prayer-meeting, and the same for the Christian Endeavor.

They will even have "Dowie" for the subject for the mid-week service.

One paper says, "Do let us try and forget Dowie; he is like an awful nightmare that has come over sleeping Adelaide." [Laughter.]

Many people are wishing that they could forget Dowie; but they cannot; some never will forget him.

No Marks of the False Prophet.

John Alexander Dowie has all the marks of a true prophet, and none of the marks of a false one.

Let us see if he has any of the marks of the false prophet.

Do all men speak well of him?

No.

All you have to do on a tram-car or railway train is to say a good word for Dowie, and the crowd will be ready to throw you off.

To say "Dowie" to an average Adelaide crowd is like holding up a red flag before a bull.

The spirit of anti-Christ, the false spirits that have gone out into the world to deceive people, deny that Jesus, the Christ, came in the flesh.

If you have listened to the General Overseer, or read LEAVES OF HEALING, you know perfectly well that in every discourse, in every Bible reading, in every prayer, he puts Jesus, the Christ, in the place God assigns Him in the Scripture.

He recognizes that in all things the Christ must have the preëminence.

I will not attempt to defend the General Overseer.

It would be foolish of me to do so.

I have made a few general remarks about him with an occasional reference to his work, but I will not be tempted into making any apologies for him, or ever attempting to defend his Mission.

He does not need it.

What I have said I have said to help you to understand the great work that Zion is doing throughout the world; and to show you that the dangers of being deceived by false prophets are not the dangers of Zion.

They are the dangers of the people in the churches.

The dangers of being deceived are not the dangers of the people who truly repent of their sins, who obey God, and seek to live clean lives.

God will not allow people of that kind to be deceived.

If God will allow me to be deceived after laying down my life for the truth, and sacrificing all I have ever had for it, then I want to know who ever is to get the truth, and what more is to be paid for it?

The Folly and Ignorance of Those Who Reject Elijah, the Restorer.

Some people come along and say, "I do not believe in Dowie's being Elijah; I do not believe any such nonsense."

You turn to such a one and say, "Do you believe what the Bible says about this matter?"

He replies, "Oh, I did not know that there was anything in the Bible about it;" and he looks very sheepish. [Laughter.]

You say to him, "To whom does Malachi refer in the 4th chapter, when he says, 'Behold, I will send you Elijah the Prophet before The Great and Terrible Day of Jehovah come?'"

He looks very silly, and says, "I do not know."

"When is The Great and Dreadful Day of the Lord coming?"

"I do not know."

"When is that prophecy of Malachi, concerning Elijah, to be fulfilled?"

"I do not know."

"What did the Christ say about the coming of Elijah?"

"I do not know."

"Well, what do you know?"

"I do not know."

That is about what it amounts to.

But that man will tell you just what the General Overseer ought to do, just how he ought to preach, just what he ought to say, just where he ought to live, and just how he ought to spend his money—that is, if he considers that he ought to have any.

It is marvelous how much wisdom these wise people have—who know nothing about the Bible—when it comes to minding some other man's business.

Zion Desires to Teach You What True Repentance Means.

What a marvelous reformation would be wrought in this city today if all the ministers were to begin teaching their people what True Repentance means.

What a clearing out and a cleaning up there would be!

Some poor persons would have only a wooden congregation next Sunday, composed of empty wooden seats and benches.

I am here to tell you what I know to be true, and to give you something that is thoroughly up to date—a living, present-day Gospel for body, soul and spirit.

May God help you and bless you.

The meeting was closed with the Prayer of Consecration, Hymn No. 45, "Sin no More," and the

BENEDICTION.

Beloved, abstain from all appearance of evil. And may the very God of Peace Himself sanctify you wholly; and I pray God your whole spirit and soul and body be preserved entire, without blame, unto the coming of our Lord Jesus, the Christ Faithful is He that calleth you, who also will do it. The grace of our Lord Jesus, the Christ, the love of God, our Father, the fellowship of the Holy Spirit, our Comforter and Guide, one Eternal God, abide in you, bless you and keep you, and all the Israel of God everywhere, forever. Amen.

An Informal Reception.

Monday, April 4, 1904, was Easter Monday, one of the greatest holidays in Australia.

One of the great curses of Australia is horse-racing, with its attendant evils, and Easter Monday is a holiday devoted especially to this so-called sport.

Probably the most notorious race-meeting of that day is held, every year, at Onkaparinga, about twenty miles southeast of Adelaide.

On this day, almost every man, woman and child in the City of Adelaide, and all the surrounding country, that can afford it, drives over the hills to Onkaparinga.

Those who cannot afford carriage hire, but can scrape together a few pence for excursion railroad fare, go out by train.

The main road from Adelaide to Onkaparinga runs within about two hundred yards of "Calton Hill," and, on Easter Monday, it was thronged with vehicles from early morning until noon, and from early afternoon until nearly midnight.

On that day, however, something very different from horse-racing was taking place at "Calton Hill."

About seventy-five members of the Branch of the Christian Catholic Church in Zion in Adelaide, accompanied by Elder and Evangelist Hawkins, came out to the neighborhood for a picnic, and on that afternoon were the guests of the General Overseer and Overseer Jane Dowie.

For the first time, these loyal and faithful Zion people were able to grasp the hand of their General Overseer, and to hear his hearty "Peace to thee. God bless you."

After this little informal reception on the veranda, the people gathered in front of the house, and were briefly addressed by the General Overseer and all the members of his party.

The General Overseer spoke especially of the advantages of Zion City, and at the close answered questions and gave practical directions for the journey thither.

Then the entire company adjourned to the tennis court for a picture, which we publish with these notes.

Farewell to Australia.

On Tuesday and Wednesday, April 5th and 6th, the entire party was working at high pressure, making the final preparations for leaving Australia.

Relatives and friends of the General Overseer and Overseer Jane Dowie, from Adelaide, were making their farewell visits, some of which were very touching.

And they were not all old friends who bade the General Overseer and his party good-by with tear-dimmed eyes.

God's Messenger always wins the love of every true heart that is given an opportunity to know him as he is.

It is now growing late on the night of Wednesday, April 6th.

Tomorrow morning we will embark on the Peninsular and Oriental Steamship Mongolia, in Largs Bay, and at two o'clock in the afternoon we are scheduled to sail out of St. Vincent's Gulf, on our long voyage to Europe.

Pray for us.

Baptisms in Missouri.

Persons living near the Kansas City Branch who are willing to obey their Lord in baptism, note that I will baptize in Kansas City on June 26th, and in Higginsville on June 29th. Bring robes. CHARLES E. ROBINSON, Deacon-in-Charge.

Notice to Officers and Members.

Send all newspaper clippings concerning the General Overseer, the Elders, or any department of the work in connection with the Christian Catholic Church in Zion, to Deacon Carl F. Stern, Zion City, Illinois. Send as soon as possible after publication, and carefully mark *name and date of the paper clipped from* on each article. If this is not done, the clippings are absolutely useless.

Notice to Correspondents.

In writing to Headquarters it is *absolutely essential* that the writer give his full address.

Failure to comply with this request necessitates looking up or referring to the Church Records, which involves much time, and is very frequently fruitless.

Friends and members of the Christian Catholic Church in Zion everywhere will please bear this in mind, especially those in foreign lands.

Faithfully yours in the Master's Service,

J. G. EXCELL, General Ecclesiastical Secretary.

Daily Bible Study for the Home

By Overseer John G. Speicher

FRIDAY, JULY 1ST.

1 Corinthians 1.—Preaching of the Christ versus world wisdom chapter.

Memory text—Verse 8. "That ye be unreprovable in the day of our Lord Jesus, the Christ."

Contents of chapter—Paul's apostolic greeting to the Corinthian Church, and to all Christians everywhere; Thanks God for the grace given to the Corinthians, in the Christ Jesus; Not lacking in the gifts; He exhorts to unity in speech; The Christ not divided; Effects of the preaching of the Cross; Unto the Jews a stumbling-block; Unto the Gentiles foolishness; God's choosings and callings; The Christ made unto us wisdom, righteousness, sanctification, and redemption; Let all glorying be in the Lord.

SATURDAY, JULY 2D.

1 Corinthians 2—Spiritual power chapter.

Memory text—Verse 5. "That your faith should not stand in the wisdom of men, but in the power of God."

Contents of chapter—Paul purposely uses simplicity of speech among the Christians; That their faith should stand in the power of God; Wisdom of God not understood by the rulers; The Christ crucified because of ignorance; Deep things of God revealed unto Christians by the Spirit; Natural man receives not the things of the Spirit of God, but the spiritual man does.

SUNDAY, JULY 3D.

1 Corinthians 3.—Christian glorying and building chapter.

Memory text—Verse 21. "Let no one glory in men."

Contents of chapter—Paul considers that divisions among the Corinthians indicate carnality; He feeds them with milk, not meat; To God is due all the glory for their conversion; Ministers through whom they believed simply His servants and coworkers; Jesus, the Christ, the One Foundation on which to build; Careful what we build thereon; Every man's work to be tested; Good will be rewarded; Bad will be burned; Our beings are God's temples; Wisdom of this world is foolishness with God; Let no one glory in men; All things are ours in the Christ, and He is God's.

MONDAY, JULY 4TH.

1 Corinthians 4.—Apostolic endurance chapter.

Memory text—Verse 7. "What hast thou that thou didst not receive?"

Contents of chapter—Paul directs the Corinthians to account him a minister and steward of the Christ; Not his own judgment of himself, or that of the Corinthians sufficient, but God's judgment of him; The Lord will come and bring to light the hidden things of darkness and true judgment will be given; Paul desires that they have an example in him and Apollos; Must not be puffed up against one another; Every grace and all else that they have is given to them; Apostles are set forth as fools; Apostleship leads to martyrdom; They become weak, suffer hardships and dishonor for the Christ's sake; Paul writes to the Corinthians as a father in the Christ.

TUESDAY, JULY 5TH.

1 Corinthians 5.—Christian purity chapter.

Memory text—Verse 7. "Purge out the old leaven, that ye may be a new lump."

Contents of chapter—Paul strongly condemns a fornicator among the Corinthians, and reproves those who have lightly passed the matter by; Delivers the guilty one to Satan for the destruction of the flesh, that the spirit may be saved; Old leaven of malice and wickedness is to have no part with the new leaven of sincerity and truth; Paul tells them not even to eat with the fornicator, covetous, idolator, reviler, drunkard, etc., but to put the wicked man away from among them.

WEDNESDAY, JULY 6TH.

1 Corinthians 6.—Christian arbitration chapter.

Memory text—Verse 2. "Do not ye know that the saints shall judge the world?"

Contents of chapter—Matters of difference between Christians should be arbitrated before a righteous man; Saints shall judge the world; They should find a wise man among themselves who can judge between brethren; Better that they should suffer wrong than have lawsuits with one another; Wicked shall not inherit the Kingdom of God; Some of the Corinthians saved from great sinfulness; The body is not for fornication, but for the Lord; The bodies are members of the Christ; He that is joined to the Lord is one spirit; The body the temple of the Holy Spirit; We are bought with a price, and should glorify God in our bodies.

THURSDAY, JULY 7TH.

1 Corinthians 7.—Concerning marriage chapter.

Memory text—Verse 31. "And those that use the world as not abusing it."

Contents of chapter—Paul advises marriage as a safeguard against fornication; Husband and wife must be faithful to each other; If the wife departs from her husband she must remain unmarried or be reconciled to her husband; Husband not to leave his wife; Believing husbands or wives not to leave unbelieving companion, if they be pleased to dwell with them; If the unbelieving depart, let them depart; Circumcision or uncircumcision is nothing, but the keeping of the Commandments of God; Each man to abide in the calling wherewith he was called; Paul desirous of their freedom from worldly cares; Things and conditions of this world must not be allowed to hinder spiritual life; Wife bound to husband as long as he lives; If he be dead, she may marry in the Lord.

FRIDAY, JULY 8TH.

1 Corinthians 8.—Eating meats offered to idols chapter.

Memory text—Verse 12. "And thus, sinning against the brethren, . . . ye sin against the Christ."

Contents of chapter—Knowledge without love is vain; Must possess humility with knowledge; Idols are worthless; There is one God, by whom are all things; One Lord, through whom are all things; All are not with full knowledge of the truth; Eating meats offered to idols will in itself neither commend nor condemn; But Paul warns them not to let their liberty in this matter become a stumbling-block to the weak, but to watch, lest what they do wound the consciences of the weak, and they be made to sin against the Christ; Paul determines not to eat flesh if it will make his brother to stumble.

SATURDAY, JULY 9TH.

1 Corinthians 9.—Christian ministers' rights chapter.

Memory text—Verse 14. "Even so did the Lord ordain that they which proclaim the Gospel should live of the Gospel."

Contents of chapter—Paul contends for his privileges as an apostle and servant of the Lord; He had sowed unto them spiritual things; It is right he should receive their material help, if he desires it; But he has not taken advantage of his rights in this matter; It is incumbent upon him that he preach the Gospel; He does it willingly and without price; He adapts himself to the circumstances and necessities, in order to win men to the Christ; He is in the race to win; He keeps his body under and watches, lest he fall.

SUNDAY, JULY 10TH.

1 Corinthians 10.—Admonition and warning chapter.

Memory text—Verse 12. "Let him that thinketh he standeth take heed lest he fall"

Contents of chapter—Paul declares that the fathers in Israel, under Moses, drank of the spiritual rock which followed them—the Christ; God not pleased with some of the Israelites, and they were overthrown in the wilderness because of their sins; The record of their sins is given as an admonition to the believers in the later ages; He that thinks he stands must take heed, lest he fall; Temptation will not be permitted above what we are able to bear; God will make a way of escape; Words concerning the sacredness of the communion, and having no fellowship or communion with devils; Directions concerning eating with unbelievers; Eating, drinking, and all else to be done to the glory of God.

MONDAY, JULY 11TH.

1 Corinthians 11.—Lord's Supper chapter.

Memory text—Verse 24. "This do in remembrance of Me."

Contents of chapter—Paul admonishes imitation of him as he imitates the Christ; Traditions to be held fast; Mentions various customs; Man created first, not woman; Man to have authority; Yet husband and wife are one; Customs spoken of not a question of fellowship, but local in their application; Divisions and heresies denounced; The Lord's Supper set forth in an orderly manner; The object of the Lord's Supper; Danger of eating it unworthily; Not a place for feasting.

Zion Literature Sent Out from a Free Distribution Fund Provided by Zion's Guests and the Friends of Zion.

Report for two weeks ending June 11, 1904:

1,300 Rolls to..........Hotels in New York State
1,690 Rolls to................St. Louis, Missouri
2,177 Rolls to........Various States in the Union
12,000 Rolls to. Business Men in the United States
2,132 Rolls to.............Germany and Scotland
1,797 Rolls to Hotels in Europe, Asia, Africa, and to the Islands of the Sea.

Number of Rolls for two Weeks............21,096
Number of Rolls reported to June 11, 1904, 3,186,041

EVANGELIST SARAH E. HILL,
Superintendent Zion Literature Mission,
Zion City, Illinois.

Han Er Den Selvsamme I Dag

Af John Alex. Dowie, (Elias Genopretteren.)

KÆRE LÆSER! Har du nogensinde hørt, hvorledes Frelseren før sin Korsfæstelse vandrede omkring og under Haandspaalæggelse velsignede og helbredte alle, som søgte Ham? Har du nogensinde hørt, hvorledes alle, som vare syge og sørgmodige, droge bort fulde af Fryd? O, hvor det glæder mig at kunne fortælle, at Han den Dag i Dag er den selvsamme. Ja, lad mig i simple og alvorlige Ord samt i al Inderlighed og Kærlighed fortælle dig om Jesus. Lad mig bringe dig det glade Budskab. "Kristus er uomskiftelig den samme," og som Han for Aarhundreder siden vandrede her paa Jorden, saaledes er Han uforandret endnu tilstede hos os. Det Ord, hvilket aldrig kan dø, er sandt, nemlig, at "Jesus Kristus er i Gaar og i Dag, ja indtil evig Tid, den samme."

Hans hele Liv og ypperstepræstelige Gerning har Apostelen Peter saa skønt beskrevet i disse Ord: "Gud salvede Jesus af Nazareth med den Hellig Aand og Kraft, hvilken drog omkring og gjorde vel og helbredte alle, som vare overvældede af Djævelen." Med aldrig svigtende Medfølelse vandrede Han omkring og lærte i Taalmod, prædikede uden Frygt og helbredte *al* Sygdom og *al* Skrøbelighed blandt Folket Han er i Dag den samme, som da Han betraadte det hellige Land og med Livets Ord velsignede Guds forkomne, adspredte og fortrykte Faar. Og endnu vandrer Han stedse omkring paa den ganske Jord og trættes aldrig i sin Kærlighedsgerning. Han læger endnu de blødende, sønderknuste Hjerter; Han udløser endnu af Tyrannens Lænker, medens den lægende Kraft endnu flyder ud fra Ham Selv, den Livsens Kilde. Med udstrakte Hænder staar Han stedse rede til at hjælpe dig, naar du anraaber Ham; Han er rede til at bortjage al din Kummer. Usynlig, men, som Han Selv har sagt: "Med eder alle Dage," staar Han ved Siden af dit Smertensleje. Kærlige Slægtninge og Venner kunne bøje sig over dit Leje og vise dig Medfølelse, men endnu nærmere staar dog Jesus, din Frelser og Helbreder. Den Haand, som rensede den Spedalske, den Haand, som bevirkede, at Døve hørte, Blinde saa, Halte sprang og Stumme talte; den samme Haand, som oprejste den Døde, er her tilstede. Kristus har ingenlunde forladt os. O, hvorfor tvivler du? Hvorfor søger du til andre; hvorfor søger du blandt Lægers Knive og Giftblandinger den Helbredelse, som Han ved Sin Død forskaffede dig, mig og den hele Menneskeslægt, i alle Lande og Zoner, nu og indtil evig Tid?

KRISTUS ER UFORANDERLIG DEN SAMME.

For seksten Aar siden sad jeg en Dag ved Middagstid i mit Studereværelse i Kongregationalisternes Præstebolig i Newton, en Forstad til den smukke By Sydney i Australien. Jeg var bedrøvet, thi jeg havde besøgt over tredive Syge og Døende i Menigheden og havde kastet Jord paa over fyrretyve Lig i Løbet af ganske faa Uger. O, hvor var Han henne, Han, som havde vandret omkring og helbredet alle sine syge og lidende Børn? Ingen Bøn om Helbredelse syntes at kunne naa Hans Øren, og dog var jeg forvisset om, at Hans Arm var ikke forkortet, endskønt den ikke nu udfriede fra Døden selv den, for hvem der var saa meget her i Livet, baade overfor Gud og Mennesker, at leve for. Kraftige Mænd, Fædre, ypperlige Borgere, og endnu mere, sande og trofaste Kristne, ramtes af en Slags Forraadnelsesfeber, hvilken medførte først frygtelige Kvaler med Fantaseren og undertiden Krampe og tilsidst Døden. O, hvilke smertelige Tomheder efterlodes ikke i mangen Enkes eller forældreløst Barns Hjerte. Desuden var der de talrige Hjem, hvor Smaabørn, saa vel som de unge Drenge og Piger, den ene efter den anden ramtes af Plagen og efter en haard Kamp med den afskyelige Sygdom maatte bukke under for Dødens kolde Haand.

Undertiden forekom det mig, som om jeg kunde høre Djævelens triumferende Spottelser lyde i mine Øren, naar jeg prædikede om den Kristnes Haab og Trøst for dem, fra hvem det Kæreste paa Jorden var borttaget Sygdom, Fader Satans og Moder Synds afskyelige Afkom, besmittede og ødelagde Guds Børns Legemer, hvilke ere den Hellig Aands Tempel, og tilsyneladende var der ingen Befrier.

Med Sorg for mit betrængte Folk sad jeg med nedbøjet Hoved, indtil bitre Taarer bragte Lindring til mit lidende Hjerte. Saa bad jeg om et eller andet Budskab, og o, hvor jeg længtes efter at høre blot et eneste Ord af Ham, den Sorgens Mand, som for længe siden havde grædt og sørget med de Betrængte.

Pludselig stode de af den Hellig Aand indgydte Ord i Apostlernes Gerninger 10:38 for mig i straalende Klarhed, aabenbarende mig Satan som Besmitteren og Kristus som Helbrederen. Taarerne aftørredes og Hjertet styrkedes; jeg saa Guds Maade at helbrede paa og Døren dertil stod vidt aaben, og jeg udbrød. "Gud hjælpe mig nu til herefter at prædike det Ord overalt og fortælle alle Døende, hvorledes det altid er Djævelen der besmitter, medens Jesus endnu befrier, thi Han er den selvsamme i Dag."

En heftig Ringen paa Dørklokken, en lydelig Banken paa Yderdøren, hurtige Fodtrin og to næsten aandeløse Sendebud viste sig i min Dør og sagde "O kom med os lige straks! Maria ligger for Døden. Kom og bed."

Besjælet af samme Følelse, som en Hyrde, der hører, at hans Faar sønderrives af den graadige Ulv, styrtede jeg ud af Huset, ilede uden Hovedbedækning ned at Gaden og traadte ind i den døende unge Piges Værelse. Der laa hun stønnende, og skar Tænder af Smerte under Kampen med Ødelæggeren, medens Fraaden, blandet med Blod, strømmede ud af hendes af Smerte fordrejede Mund.

Jeg betragtede hende i Tavshed, medens Harmen opblussede i mig. "O," tænkte jeg, "havde jeg blot et fra Himlen hærdet, skarpt Sværd, hvormed jeg kunde knuse denne frygtelige Fjende, der som en usynlig Slange stadig strammede sit Greb for den afgørende Sejer."

Paa en ganske vidunderlig Maade gik denne min Bøn i Opfyldelse Jeg opdagede, at jeg allerede holdt det forønskede Sværd i min Haand og jeg har det endnu og vil aldrig nedlægge det.

I dyb Medfølelse for Moderens Sorg og Smerte spadserede den gode kristne Læge lydløst frem og tilbage i Værelset, indtil han endelig standsede og tiltalte mig med disse Ord: "Hvor forunderlige ere ikke Herrens Veje, Hr. Pastor!" Straks blinkede Sværdet, det Aandens Sværd, hvilket er Guds Ord, i min Haand

"Guds Veje!" udbrød jeg. "Hvorledes tør De, Dr. K——, kalde dette Guds Maade at føre sine Børn fra Jorden hjem til Himmerig? Nej, nej, Hr. Doktor, dette er Djævelens Værk, og det er paa høje Tid, at vi paakalde Ham, som kom for at afskaffe Djævelens Gerninger og bede Ham tilintetgøre den dødelige onde Fjende og frelse Barnet! Kan De bede, Hr. Doktor? Kan De bede Troens Bøn, som frelser den Syge ud af Dødens Haand?"

En pludselig Forandring foregik hos min Ven, Lægen. Han følte sig fornærmet af mine Ord og udbrød, idet han forlod Værelset: "De er altfor ophidset, Hr. Pastor! Man gør bedst i at bøje sig under Guds Vilje."

"Ophidset!" Dette Ord formaar kun svagt at udtrykke mine Følelser. Nej, jeg var næsten ude af mig selv af guddommelig Harme og Had til denne afskyelige Ødelægger, denne Sygdon, som var of Satan. Den kan ikke være fra Gud, tænkte jeg, thi fra Ham kan saadan Grusomhed aldrig udgaa og jeg vil aldrig sige. "Din Vilje ske, Herre! til Satans Gerninger, hvilke Guds egen Søn kom for at afskaffe;" og visselig var dette Satans Værk.

O, hvor brændte ikke disse Herrens Ord I mit Hjerte: "Jesus af Nazareth . . . . . gik omkring og helbredte alle, som vare overvældede af Djævelen; thi Gud var med Ham."

Og var Gud ikke med mig ogsaa? Var Jesus ikke med mig ogsaa; og ere ikke alle Hans Forjættelser sande? Jeg havde en Forvisning om, at dette var Tilfældet og henvendt til Moderen spurgte jeg· "Hvorfor har De sendt Bud efter mig?" Hun svarede: "Bed, o bed for hende, at Herren maa oprejse hende!"

Vi bad. Hvori bestod min Bøn? Maaske kan jeg ikke nu genkalde de selvsamme Ord, men selve Ordene ere kun af ringe Betydning. Troens Bøn kan bedes i Tavshed. Den kan bestaa af ikkun et tillidsfuldt Suk fra Hjertet op til den forbarmende Gud. I et saadant Øjeblik bruger man kun faa Ord, men det kommer an paa med hvad Tro, de udtales, thi Gud ransager Hjerter. Dog erindrer jeg den Dag i Dag meget af den samme Bøn og med Guds Hjælp vil jeg forsøge at gentage den. Jeg bad.

"O, Fader, hjælp mig; o, Hellig Aand, lær mig at bede! Antag dig vor Sag, o Jesus, vor Frelser, Helbreder og Ven; vor Talsmand hos Gud, vor Fader. O evige Fader, bønhør os og giv Helbredelse Udfri dette dit blide Barn fra al Sygdom og fra Døden! Jeg stoler paa dit Ord. Bevis nu Sandheden of dine *Forjættelser*. Dit Ord er Sandhed: Jeg er Herren, som helbreder dig. Helbred hende saa nu! Dit Ord er Sandhed: Thi jeg, Herren, har ikke forandret mig. Uforanderlige Gud, o, bevis nu, at du er den, som helbreder! Dit Ord er Sandhed: Disse Tegn skulle følge dem, som tro: I mit Navn skulle de lægge Hænder paa de Syge og de skulle helbredes (Mark 16:18). Jeg tror derpaa og i Jesu Navn lægger jeg Hænder paa hende og gør Fordring paa dine Forjættelsers Fuldbyrdelse. Dit Ord er Sandhed: Troens Bøn *skal* frelse den Syge. I Tro til dig alene beder jeg: O, for Jesu Skyld, udfri hende nu, Amen."

Og se, Pigen laa stille hen og faldt i en saa dyb og tryg Slummer, at Moderen med sagte Stemme spurgte: "Er hun død?"

"Nej," svarede jeg, med endnu svagere Stemme. "Maria vil leve. Feberen har forladt hende og hun sover saa sødt som et lille Barn."

Idet jeg strøg hendes lange mørke Haar fra den blide Pande og hørte hendes Hjertes regelmæssige Banken samt følte Pulsen og den svale, fugtige Haand, følte jeg mig forvisset om, at Gud havde bønhørt os. Atter, som for mange Tider siden i Apostelen Peters Hus, kunde vi sige: "Han rørte ved hendes Haand og Feberen forlod hende."

Idet jeg henvendte mig til Sygeplejersken, sagde jeg, "Vil De være saa venlig straks at hente mig en en Kop Kakao samt et Par Skiver Smørrebrød?"

Vi sade stille og tavse ved Siden of den sovende Pige, til Sygeplejersken kom tilbage, saa bøjede jeg mig ned over hende og idet jeg snappede med Fingrene, raabte jeg: "Maria!" Hun vaagnede straks og spurgte smilende: "Men hvornaar er De kommen, Hr. Pastor? Jeg har sovet saa længe." Derpaa udstrakte hun Armene for at gengælde Moderens Favntag og vedblev: "Moder, jeg er saa rask." Og tillige sulten," tilføjede jeg, idet jeg hældte lidt Kakao ud i Underkoppen og rakte hende det efter at have ladet det afkøle lidt.

"Ja, jeg er ogsaa sulten," svarede hun smilende, og saa spiste og drak hun, indtil det hele var fortæret. Faa Minutter senere faldt hun atter i Søvn og aandede sagte og let. Med Tak til Gud forlode vi i Stilhed hendes Leje og traadte ind i Værelset ved Siden af, hvor en Broder og en Søster ogsaa laa syge of den samme Feber. Ogsaa for disse to bad vi og de bleve helbredte. Næste Dag vare de alle tre raske og en Uges Tid efter bragte de mig et kort Brev samt en lille Gave, bestaaende of et Par Guld—Manchetknapper, hvilke jeg brugte i flere Aar.

Da jeg forlod det Hjem, hvor Jesus havde vist sig at være den sande Helbreder, kunde jeg ikke andet end ligesom føle Genklangen of den Sejerssang, som nu uden Tvivl lød i Himlen, og dog var jeg samtidig ikke lidet forbavset over min egen besynderlige Handlemaade, men endnu mere over min Opdagelse, at

HAN ER DEN SELVSAMME I DAG.

Det var herved, at jeg kom til at prædike Evangeliet om Helbredelse ved Troen paa Jesus. Samme Dag kastede jeg Jord paa tre, som vare døde to Dage i Forvejen, men det glæder mig at kunne tilføje, at i de næste tolv Aar af min Præstegerning der i Australien, havde jeg kun fem Begravelser, endskønt jeg betjente flere Tusinder. Men jeg kunde ikke straks drage Nytte af den Lektie, jeg selv havde lært den Dag, og det var først seks Aar efter, at jeg tilfulde begyndte at prædike Helbredelse som en Del of Vorherres Jesu Kristi Evangelium, endskønt jeg i Aaret 1872 blev indsat som Forkynder deraf. I Løbet af de følgende Aar har jeg gaaet i Forbøn for og lagt Hænder paa mange Hundrede Tusinder Syge, af hvilke store Skarer have fundne Helbredelse. Disse Mennesker have vidnet i Tusindvis og deres Vidnesbyrd ere blevne udsente til mange Lande.

Vi have forladt Venner og vort Hjem i Australien for at bringe Helbredelsesblade fra Livets Træ til enhver Skabning i hver eneste Nation, vi kunne naa. Vi have aldrig, hverken i nogen By eller i noget Land, forkyndt dette Evangelium, hvor ikke ogsaa Gud har stadfæsted Ordet med medfølgende Tegn, endskønt det endnu, som for nitten Aarhundreder siden, kan siges om enkelte Steder: "Og Han gjorde ikke der mange kraftige Gerninger, formedelst deres Vantro."

Vi bringe dette Budskab til denne By og til dig, kære Læser, og vi ville med Glæde bringe det til alle, som ville modtage det: Saliggørelse og Helbredelse koste intet, thi Guds Gaver sælges aldrig.

Hvi betænker du dig længe?
Kom og køb foruden Penge.

Den Kristne Katolske Kirkes Hovedkvarter er i Zion City, Illinois, U. S. A., hvor Underretning om Zions Gerning kan erholdes.

Kirkedøren staar aaben for alle. Det er det samme gamle Evangelium og intet nyt, som prædikes. Det er Jesu Evangelium til Forløsning for Aand, Sjæl og Legeme, det bringer Frelse fra Synd, Helbredelse af Sygdom og Renselse fra enhver Art af baade kødelig og aandelig Besmittelse.

Indprent disse Ord dybt i dit Hjerte:

"Han er den selvsamme i Dag."

Og hvis du fuldtud stoler paa ham, først for Saliggørelse og dernæst for Helbredelse, saa vil du gaa fremad paa Kongevejen til Helligdommen, idet du paa Vejen gennem Jorderig til Himlen med bedre Forstaaelse kan synge de bekendte Ord:

"Du, o Krist, er alt jeg ønsker,
Thi i dig, jeg alt kan finde,
Rejs den Faldne, styrk den Svage,
Læg den Syge, led den Blinde."

Frelse Tilbydes Dig Nu Ojeblikkelig

Rev. John Alex. Dowie, (Elias Genopretteren.)

KÆRE LÆSER, jeg vil gerne sige dig nogle faa Ord angaaende din evige Velfærd, og maa Gud, som elsker dig, hjælpe mig.

Du er udødelig og et Barn af Aandernes Fader. Du er udødelig, thi Han er udødelig. Her paa Jorden i den synlige Skabelse er intet af en saa uendelig Vigtighed som en udødelig Aand, og du er just en saadan.

Solen er blot en Ildgnist, som en vis Tid viser sig paa Himmelen. Den har sin Tid og skal en Gang slukkes. Men den evige Aand skal aldrig slukkes aller dø.

Men Legemet er dødeligt; det er af Jord, er Jord og skal visne, dø og blive til Jord igen. Der er ingen Undtagelser. Betragt dit Legeme, føl din Puls, hør efter dit Hjertes Slag og sig, "Mit Legeme, nu er du livsvarmt, men du skal maaske inden ret længe ligge koldt i Døden: thi Sølvsnoren skal borttages, og du skal blive til Jord igen; men min frigjorte Aand skal atter vende tilbage til Gud, som gav den."

Stands derfor ved denne højtidelige Tanke og overvej den med dybt Alvor i dit Hjerte. Tal endnu en Gang og sig: "Men du min Aand er du bered at staa indfor Dommens "Hvide Trone," hvis du blev kaldet idag?"

Kære Læser, er du ikke frelst, saa er du fortabt. Har du nogensinde for Alvor tænkt paa Evigheden, hvorhen du kan blive kaldet inden ret længe, ja i dette Øjeblik? Hvis ikke, saa gør det, "Thi se, nu er den gode Tid, nu er Frelsens Dag."

Vent ikke, thi det kan blive skæbensvangert for dig. Faren er overhængende, og derfor er ogsaa middelbar Frelse nødvendig. Gud meddeler dig ogsaa som Følge deraf en øjeblikkelig Frelse. Lad mig helt enkelt og venligt sige dig, hvorledes du skal blive øjeblikkelig frelst.

DU MAA FØRST OG FREMMEST ANGRE DINE SYNDER OG DET STRAKS. Guds Hellig Aand har allerede overbevist dig om, at du er en Synder, du behøver en Frelser. Vend dig øjeblikkeligt bort fra din Synd med et oprigtigt Had mod alle dine onde Gerninger og Tanker med oprigtig Sorg og Længsel efter Barmhjertighed.

Syndens ivrige Orme have med sine døbringende Eddere forgiftet hele dit Væsens Livskilde. Du nærede disse Hugorme ved din Barm og gav dem den Kærlighed, som du var skyldig din Gud. Og selv om du ogsaa nu ved, hvorledes disse Synder bide dig ligesom Hugorme, saa er du dog mærkværdig nok, stadigt fortryllet af deres uhyggelige Tiltræknigskraft. Og rasende af utilfredstillet Begær, tillader du dem at slynge sig fastere om dig og klemme Livet ud af din stakkels Sjæl.

Vaagn op, døende Sjæl! Se op til Ham, som døde for at frelse dig, og du skal leve og blive lykkelig.

Ligesom Folket i Ørkenen blev helbredet, naar de betragtede Kobberslangen, som Moses oprejste, saa skal ogsaa du modtage en lægedomsbringende og livgivende Strøm, som udgaar fra Frelseren paa Korset. Hver og en som ser op til Ham med en levende Tro skal frelses fra al sin Sorg og al sin Elendighed.

DU MAA DERNÆST ØJEBLIKKELIGT TRO OG BEDE, TROENDE, AT GUD VIL HOLDE SINE LØFTER, SOM HAN HAR GIVET DIG.

Gud fordrer af dig, at du skal tro, (1) at Han elsker dig; (2) at Han kom for ved sin Søn at frelse dig, (3) at Hans Søn Jesus Kristus bar dine Synder, dine Sorger og døde for dig; (4) at Han opstod fra de døde og stadigt er din Fortaler, stedse rede til at tale for dig; (5) Hvis du virkelig beder Faderen i Jesu Navn og af Hjertet afstaar fra og bekender din Synd, saa skal du ogsaa blive frelst i samme Øjeblik, thi der staar skrevet (1 Joh. 1: 9) "Dersom vi bekende vore Synder, er han trofast og retfærdig, at han forlader os Synderne og renser os fra al Uretfærdighed."

Gør dette i simpel Tro og du er øjeblikkelig frelst.

Ikke at din Tro frelser dig, thi Tro har aldrig frelst nogen, og dog kan ingen blive frelst uden Tro.

Det er Guds Naade, Hans Kærlighed og almægtige Kraft som redder den Synder, som beder i Tro, thi der staar skrevet (Ef. 2: 5) af Naade ere I frelste, og atter i ottende Vers: "Thi af Naade ere I frelste formedelst Troen og det ikke af Eder; det er en Guds Gave.

Er dette vel saa svært at forstaa? Lad mig gøre det endnu mere tydeligt. Antag at du er fattig og i stor Pengeforlegenhed. En Person, som er er god og meget rig, giver dig alt hvad du ønsker. I Banken giver du Anvisningen i Tro, og din Tro belønnes med at du faar Summen udbetalt.

Men det var ikke din Tro, som forskaffede dig Pengene i Banken for dig. Det var Hans Naade, om jeg saa maa sige, som besvarede din Bøn, da du bad i Tro paa Hans skrevne Ord.

Saaledes er det med din Gud. Du stakkels fortærkede Sjæl, du faar Anvisninger paa den uendelige Kærligheds og Magts Bank. Anvisninger, som dække alle dine Behov til alle Tider. Tag denne: "Hvorfor han og kan fuldkommeligen gøre dem salige, som komme til Gud formedelst ham, efterdi han lever altid, til at træde frem for dem." (Hebr. 7: 25) Giv den nu i dette Øjeblik ved Naadens Trone og du skal blive frelst ganske og aldeles.

Evangelierne og andre Dele af det inspirerede Ord ere fulde af Beviser paa at Kristus frelser Syndere ØJEBLIKKELIGT. Næsten alle Hans Helbredelser vare øjeblikkelige, saaledes som de ere endnu idag. Den Spedalske, som kom i Tro, blev "straks ren." (Mark. 1: 40, 42) Peters Svigermoder blev "straks" rask, da Jesus rørte ved hende. (Luk. 4: 39) Kvinden som havde givet alt, hvad hun havde til Lægerne, blev efter tolv Aars Sygdom og tiltagende Lidelser "straks" rask, da hun i Tro rørte ved Hans Klædning. (Luk. 8: 43, 46). Manden, som havde ligget 38 Aar, "blev øjeblikkelig helbredet" ved Betesdas Dam (Joh. 5: 1, 9). Manden, som var over 40 Aar gammel og lam fra Fødselen, blev helbredet i Jesu Kristi Navn ved den skønne Port. "Straks fik hans Fødder og Ankler Styrke" (Ap. G. 3: 1, 11). Og mange andre bleve helbredede "straks" hvorom du kan læse i Skriften.

Og paa samme Maade tilgav Kristus angerfulde og bodfærdige Syndere, som f. Ex. den faldne Kvinde, som græd ved Hans Fødder i Farisæerens Hus: Han sagde til hende: "Dine Synder ere dig forladte," (Luk. 7: 48), og i Perlen af alle Lignelser lærte Han os, hvorledes den evige Fader gaar for at møde den tilbagevendende angrende Synder og redder ham "straks og for altid."

O! afgør Sagen nu, saa at Naadens Dag ej maa forsvinde og du blive dømt paa Dommens Dag. Gud kan, Gud vil redde dig, og, om du omkommer, saa er det kun derfor, at du ikke vil reddes.

"Hvorledes skal du undkomme, om du forsømmer en saa stor Frelse?"

Hvorledes? Hvorledes? Det er et Spørgsmaal, som ikke en Gang Gud kan besvare. Hvorledes? Hvorledes?

Tænk over. Forkast ikke Redningen, som tilbydes dig. Du kan dø allerede idag. Staa op, bestem dig. Se, din Frelser venter paa Dig!

Guds Laegedoms Maade.

Af Rev. John Alex. Dowie, (Elias Genopretteren.)

1. **Guds Helbredelsesmaade er en Person, ikke en Ting.**
Jesus sagde: "Jeg er Vejen og Sandheden og Livet," og Han har alle Dage aabenbaret sig for sit Folk under Pagtsnavent Jehovah-Rophi, eller, "Jeg er Herren, som læger dig." (Joh. 14: 6; 2 Mos. 15: 26.)
2. **Vor Herre Jesus Kristus er endnu vor Læge.**
Han forandrer ikke, thi "Jesus Kristus er i Gaar og i Dag, den samme, ja til evig Tid." Han er altid hos os, thi Han har sagt: "Se jeg er med Eder alle Dage indtil Verdens Ende." (Hebr. 13: 8; Matt. 28: 20.) Fordi Han er uforanderlig, og da Han endnu er nærværende i Aanden, som da Han var her i Kødet, saa er Han sit Folks Læge.
3. **Guddommelig Lægedom er grundet paa Kristi Forsoningsdød.**
Der var spaaet om Ham: "Visselig, han har taget vore Sygdomme paa sig og baaret vore Smerter og vi have faaet Lægedom ved hans Saar." Og det er klarligt lagt for Dagen, at dette blev opfyldt under Hans Lægedoms Gerning, som endnu stadig vedvarer. (Esaias 53; 4, 5; Matt. 8: 17.)
4. **Sygdom kan slet ikke være Guds Vilje.**
Det er Djævelens Gerning og en Følge af Synden og det er umuligt, at Djævelens Gerninger kunne være i Overenstemmelse med Guds Vilje. Kristus kom for at afskaffe Djævelens Gerninger, og medens Han vandrede her paa Jorden, helbredede Han al Sygdom og al Skrøbelighed og alle disse Syge erklæredes udtrykkeligt for at være overvældede af Djævelen. (1 Joh. 3: 8; Matt. 4. 23; Ap. G. 10: 38.)
5. **Helbredelsesgaven er vedvarende.**
Der staar udtrykkeligt skrevet—at "Naadegaverne, og sit Kald fortryder Gud ikke;" og Gaven til at helbrede er iblandt de ni aandelige Gaver til Kirken. (Rom. 11: 29; 1 Kor. 12; 8, 11.)
6. **Guddommelig Helbredelse kan erholdes paa fire Maader.**
Den første er den enfoldige Troens Bøn; den anden er Forbøn af to eller flere; den tredje er Salving af de Ældste under Troens Bøn; og den fjerde er Haandspaalæggelse af dem, som tro og hvem Gud har beskikket og kaldet til det Embede. (Matt. 8: 5, 13; 18: 19; Jak. 5: 14, 15; Mark. 16: 18.)
7. **Guddommelig Helbredelse modvirkes af Djævelske Efterlignelser.**
Blandt hvilke kunne nævnes "Christian Science" (Den falskeligen saakaldte Kristelige Kundskab, 1 Tim. 6: 20, 21-) Tanke Helbredelse, Spiritualisme og flere andre. (1 Tim 4: 1, 2; Esaias 51: 22, 23.)
8. **Mangfoldige have fundet Helbredelse ved Troen paa Jesus.**
Forfatteren kender Tilfælder i Tusindvis og har selv lagt Hænder paa flere Tusind Mennesker.

Fuld Underretning kan erholdes ved Gudstjenesterne i Zions Tabernakler. Desuden udgives i Zion Publishing House, Zion City, Illinois, U. S. A., mange Smaaskrifter, hvilke indeholde Vidnesbyrd af mange, baade i dette og andre Lande, som ere blevne helbredede.

Altsaa kommer Troen derved, at man hører, men at man hører, sker ved Guds Ord. (Romerbrevet 10: 17.)

Zion's Bible Class

Conducted by Deacon Daniel Sloan in Shiloh Tabernacle, Zion City, Lord's Day Morning at 11 o'clock, and in Zion Homes and Gatherings throughout the World.

MID-WEEK BIBLE CLASS LESSON, JULY 6th or 7th.

Ecclesiastical Rottenness.

1. *Faith alone can keep a man pure and holy.*—Jude 1:3-7.
When faith ceases to operate, men sin.
Faith alone can justify.
Faith keeps one pure and clean.
2. *False shepherds preach dreams which defile the flesh, instead of purifying the spirit*—Jude 1:8-11.
They dream of peace and plenty.
They dream of ease and comfort.
They dream that the world is getting better.
3. *They are fruitless and restless and wonder what is the matter that results do not come.*—Jude 1:12-16.
They have banquets for this and that.
They labor and toil but do not win souls to God.
They have the form, but the power of God is gone.
4. *They mock at the methods employed and at the results obtained in the early Church.*—Jude 1:17-25.
They mock at self-denial and holy living.
They are afraid of public opinion.
They are ruled by the spirit of the world.
5. *They try to get people into their churches instead of into the Kingdom of Heaven*—Matthew 23:13-15.
They call on new-comers to join their churches.
They pretend to pray and to be religious to carry out some plan.
They lead people to the Devil, where they themselves are going.
6. *They pervert the Scripture, twisting their own meaning into it.*—Matthew 23:16-23.
They are very strict on some things.
They say that the Bible means this and that.
They do not love to obey the truth.
7. *They are shocked at the name "stinkpot," and practice the habit of smoking, and others more defiling, perhaps.*—Matthew 23:24-28.
They are shocked if you call a man a "dirty dog."
They say, "Cover up all bad things."
At heart they are not righteous.
8. *They eulogize dead reformers and discredit and oppose those who are today doing similar work.*—Matthew 23:29-39.
They do not have the gentleness of the Christ.
They will not receive a prophet who condemns them.
The true prophet comes only in the Name of the Lord.
The Lord Our God is a Holy Ministry-demanding God.

LORD'S DAY BIBLE CLASS LESSON, JULY 10th.

The Reign of Lawlessness.

1. *Lawlessness begins in the Church.*—John 16:1-4.
Churches expel people who believe God is the Healer.
They shun people who contend that God insists upon godly living.
Persecution turns into wrath and murder.
2. *It breaks out in the home.*—Matthew 10:18-24.
The first murderer slew his brother.
One relative will consent to another's being killed.
The Christ's own would not receive Him.
3. *It spreads to the judiciary.*—Isaiah 59:1-8.
Justice is hard to get.
Judges are careful whom their decisions offend.
Thus they encourage evil-doers in doing evil.
4. *It permeates society today as in other days recorded in Scripture.*—Genesis 6:1-8.
The days of Noah are coming back on us.
Wickedness will be great in the earth.
The Spirit of God will find no place in men's hearts.
5. *You find the spirit of it in the preachers*—Ezekiel 34:1-6.
They think of their own gain.
They are oppressive and cruel.
They do not seek to save the lost.
6. *You find the practice of it everywhere and who is protesting against it?*—Malachi 3:1-6.
Doctors can kill with poisons and who cares?
Seducers get more bold and who pities the victims?
Men are cheated out of their due and who—except the lawyer tries to get it back?
7. *The bent of everything is on mischief, folly and filthiness.*—Psalm 53:2-6.
Who today is bent on seeking God?
Who is living only for the good he can do?
Pray that salvation may come speedily.
8. *The Devil will bring about the destruction of his own kingdom.*—Ezekiel 7:16-27.
The Devil will pull down the house upon himself and all in it.
Why this flood of iniquity which rushes in?
The rule of the mob will soon be stronger than that of the police and army, and what then?
God's Holy People are a Forewarned People.

OBEYING GOD IN BAPTISM.

"Baptizing Them Into the Name of the Father and of the Son and of the Holy Ghost."

Eighteen Thousand Six Hundred Seven Baptisms by Triune Immersion Since March 14, 1897.

Eighteen Thousand Six Hundred Seven Believers have joyfully followed their Lord in the Ordinance of Believer's Baptism by Triune Immersion since the first Baptism in Central Zion Tabernacle on March 14, 1897.

Baptized in Central Zion Tabernacle from March 14, 1897, to December 14, 1901, by the General Overseer,	4754		
Baptized in South Side Zion Tabernacle from January 1, 1902, to June 14, 1903, by the General Overseer..	37		
Baptized at Zion City by the General Overseer........	583		
Baptized by Overseers, Elders, Evangelists and Deacons, at Headquarters (Zion City) and Chicago......	5281		
Total Baptized at Headquarters....................	—		10,655
Baptized in places outside of Headquarters by the General Overseer................................		641	
Baptized in places outside of Headquarters by Overseers, Elders, Evangelists and Deacons...............		7311	
Total Baptized outside of Headquarters............		—	7,952
Total Baptized in seven years and three months....			18,607

The following-named two believers were baptized at Bervie, Ontario, Canada, Thursday, May 26, 1904, by Elder Eugene Brooks:

Monilaws, George................................Bervie, Ontario, Canada
Monilaws, Mrs. George..........................Bervie, Ontario, Canada

The following-named two believers were baptized at Wingham, Ontario, Canada, Friday, May 27, 1904, by Elder Eugene Brooks:

Lewis, Edwin....................................Wingham, Ontario, Canada
Lewis, Mrs. Mary................................Wingham, Ontario, Canada

The following-named ten believers were baptized in the Caledonian Road Baths, London, England, Lord's Day, May 29, 1904, by Overseer H. E. Cantel:

Adams, William Henry,
20 Carter lane, St. Paul's Churchyard, E. C., London, England
Black, Mrs. Fanny.............16 Burton street, W. C., London, England
Corrall, Alexander,
44 Cromer street, Gray's Inn road, W. C., London, England
Corrall, Mrs. Laura Albinia,
44 Cromer street, Gray's Inn road, W. C., London, England
Corrall, Miss Laura,
44 Cromer street, Gray's Inn road, W. C., London, England
Cumings, Harry Barter..........23 Charlotte street, N., London, England
Gordon, Frank......................8 Benson street, Cambridge, England
Ridgers, Miss Helena Mary,
12 Havelock street, King's Cross, N., London, England
Staples, Ernest Frederick......24 Harpour road, Barking, Essex, England
Staples, Mrs. Lucy Mary Ann...24 Harpour road, Barking, Essex, England

The following-named three believers were baptized at Malcolm, Ontario, Canada, Monday, May 30, 1904, by Elder Eugene Brooks:

Cross, Ralph Lionel.............................Malcolm, Ontario, Canada
Cross, Reuben...................................Malcolm, Ontario, Canada
McWhinney, James................................Hanover, Ontario, Canada

The following-named two believers were baptized at Wiarton, Ontario, Canada, Wednesday, June 1, 1904, by Elder Eugene Brooks:

Jasper, Ellen...................................Wiarton, Ontario, Canada
Clark, Mrs. Rachel Eugenia......................Wiarton, Ontario, Canada

The following-named three believers were baptized at San Antonio, Texas, Wednesday, June 1, 1904, by Evangelist William D. Gay:

Crago, Frank D..............226 South Alamo street, San Antonio, Texas
James, Miss Florence L......605 Pennsylvania avenue, San Antonio, Texas
Morgan, Mrs. Susie H.................821 Avenue B, San Antonio, Texas

The following-named two believers were baptized at San Antonio, Texas, Lord's Day, June 5, 1904, by Evangelist William D. Gay:

Miller, Mrs. Delphina,
Corner Mulberry and Howard avenues, San Antonio, Texas
Miller, Miss May,
Corner Mulberry and Howard avenues, San Antonio, Texas

The following-named seven believers were baptized at Heathcote, Ontario, Canada, Lord's Day, June 5, 1904, by Elder Eugene Brooks:

Croskill, Charles Clayton.......................Heathcote, Ontario, Canada
Hodge, James Hannah.............................Heathcote, Ontario, Canada
McDermid, Mrs. Frances Jane.....................Priceville, Ontario, Canada
McDermid, John..................................Priceville, Ontario, Canada
Shaw, Edward....................................Heathcote, Ontario Canada
Shaw, Miss Mabel................................Heathcote, Ontario, Canada
Shaw, Thomas William............................Heathcote, Ontario, Canada

The following-named three believers were baptized in the South Side Zion Tabernacle, Chicago, Illinois, Lord's Day, June 5, 1904, by Evangelist W. C. Christie:

Patterson, John Alexander...........137 East 147th street, Harvey, Illinois
Patterson, Robert Franklin..........137 East 147th street, Harvey, Illinois
Ward, Francis C.................14629 Kentucky avenue, Harvey, Illinois

The following-named four believers were baptized in the South Side Zion Tabernacle, Chicago, Illinois, Lord's Day, June 5, 1904, by Elder W. H. Cossum:

Arkama, Mrs. Clara................6017 Sangamon street, Chicago, Illinois
Hardin, Mrs. Addie.................3144 Armour avenue, Chicago, Illinois
Hardin, John.......................3144 Armour avenue, Chicago, Illinois
Monmouth, Newton......................3331 State street, Chicago, Illinois

The following-named two believers were baptized at the West Side Zion Tabernacle, Chicago, Illinois, Lord's Day, June 5, 1904, by Elder Lemuel C. Hall:

Anderson, Mrs. Annie........2953 South Fortieth avenue, Chicago, Illinois
Daniels, Herbert E.....................621 Fulton street, Chicago, Illinois

The following-named three believers were baptized at Collingwood, Ontario, Canada, Tuesday, June 7, 1904, by Elder Eugene Brooks:

Hollingshead, David Henry.................Collingwood, Ontario, Canada
Hollingshead, Miss Ida May................Collingwood, Ontario, Canada
Hollingshead, Miss Mary Caroline..........Collingwood, Ontario, Canada

The following-named four believers were baptized at Waubaushene, Ontario, Canada, Thursday, June 9, 1904, by Elder Eugene Brooks:

Arbor, Emily May..........................Waubaushene, Ontario, Canada
Baker, Frances Lucy.......................Waubaushene, Ontario, Canada
Boyd, Miss Fern Beatrice..................Waubaushene, Ontario, Canada
Boyd, Rachel Ethel........................Waubaushene, Ontario, Canada

The following-named thirty-seven believers were baptized in Shiloh Tabernacle, Zion City, Illinois, Lord's Day, June 12, 1904, by Elder A. F. Lee:

Allen, Miss Lizzie..................2914 Gilboa avenue, Zion City, Illinois
Allen, Thomas.......................1429 Gilboa avenue, Zion City, Illinois
Asbury, William....................3018 Gideon avenue, Zion City, Illinois
Augustiny, Philip..................2920 Gabriel avenue, Zion City, Illinois
Bailey, Mrs. Charlotte...............3003 Ezra avenue, Zion City, Illinois
Balliet, Emmanuel...................2009 Horeb avenue, Zion City, Illinois
Barber, Mrs. Anna.......................Elijah Hospice, Zion City, Illinois
Barber, John C..........................Elijah Hospice, Zion City, Illinois
Bohne, Miss Lillie...................2913 Ezra avenue, Zion City, Illinois
Brooks, Miss Mary Belle..............3017 Elim avenue, Zion City, Illinois
Brown, Miss Mabel....................3023 Elim avenue, Zion City, Illinois
Davis, Charlie A...................3003 Gideon avenue, Zion City, Illinois
Davis, Ernest......................3008 Gideon avenue, Zion City, Illinois
Densmore, Miss Veral...........................Zion City, Illinois
Franklin, Byron.................................Wilmington, Ohio
Granath, Edward.........................Elijah Hospice, Zion City, Illinois
Griffin, E. D......................3106 Ezekiel avenue, Zion City, Illinois
Griffin, John......................3106 Ezekiel avenue, Zion City, Illinois
Haynes, Mrs. Sarah..............................Fairmount, Indiana
Hershey, Mrs. Eleanor Gorham.......2813 Eshcol avenue, Zion City, Illinois
Hurlbut, Howard....................3117 Eshcol avenue, Zion City, Illinois
McCardell, Mrs. Mary C..............2703 Enoch avenue, Zion City, Illinois
Merrill, Louis......................3010 Enoch avenue, Zion City, Illinois
Miller, Mrs. Elizabeth..............2703 Enoch avenue, Zion City, Illinois
Miller, David John..................2703 Enoch avenue, Zion City, Illinois
Murrell, Sidney.........................Elijah Hospice, Zion City, Illinois
Neff, Alice..........................2605 Elim avenue, Zion City, Illinois
Noteboom, Miss Grace Loree...........2922 Ezra avenue, Zion City, Illinois
Pelton, Durward A..................2810 Eshcol avenue, Zion City, Illinois
Regier, Mrs. Maria D............................Denhoff, North Dakota
Sheller, Harry...................964 Twentieth street, Zion City, Illinois
Thompson, George.................3012 Elizabeth avenue, Zion City, Illinois
Wagner, Dorcas.....................2916 Elisha avenue, Zion City, Illinois
Wagner, Harry......................2916 Elisha avenue, Zion City, Illinois
Wangsness, Mrs. Marie...........................Zion City, Illinois
Westera, John......................2600 Gideon avenue, Zion City, Illinois
William, Harmon L...............................Zion City, Illinois

CONSECRATION OF CHILDREN.

The following-named child was consecrated to God in the South Side Zion Tabernacle, Chicago, Illinois, Lord's Day, June 5, 1904, by Elder W. H. Cossum:

Vaux, Mary Ruth..................1536 Michigan avenue, Chicago, Illinois

The following-named seven children were consecrated to God at San Antonio, Texas, Lord's Day, June 5, 1904, by Evangelist William D. Gay:

Hughes, Esther Elizabeth.........419 Sherman street, San Antonio, Texas
Morgan, Katie Bessie..................821 avenue B., San Antonio, Texas
Stanley, Lucy Alice..........Rural Route No. 8, San Antonio, Texas
Stanley, Josephine Emma......Rural Route No. 8, San Antonio, Texas
Stanley, Della Elizabeth.....Rural Route No. 8, San Antonio, Texas
Stanley, Lula Evaline........Rural Route No. 8, San Antonio, Texas
Stanley, Rosa Mary...........Rural Route No. 8, San Antonio, Texas

A WEEKLY PAPER FOR THE EXTENSION OF THE KINGDOM OF GOD

EDITED BY THE REV. JOHN ALEX. DOWIE.

Volume XV. No. 10. *ZION CITY, SATURDAY, JUNE 25, 1904.* *Price Five Cents*

Members and Friends of Zion, Herisau, Switzerland.

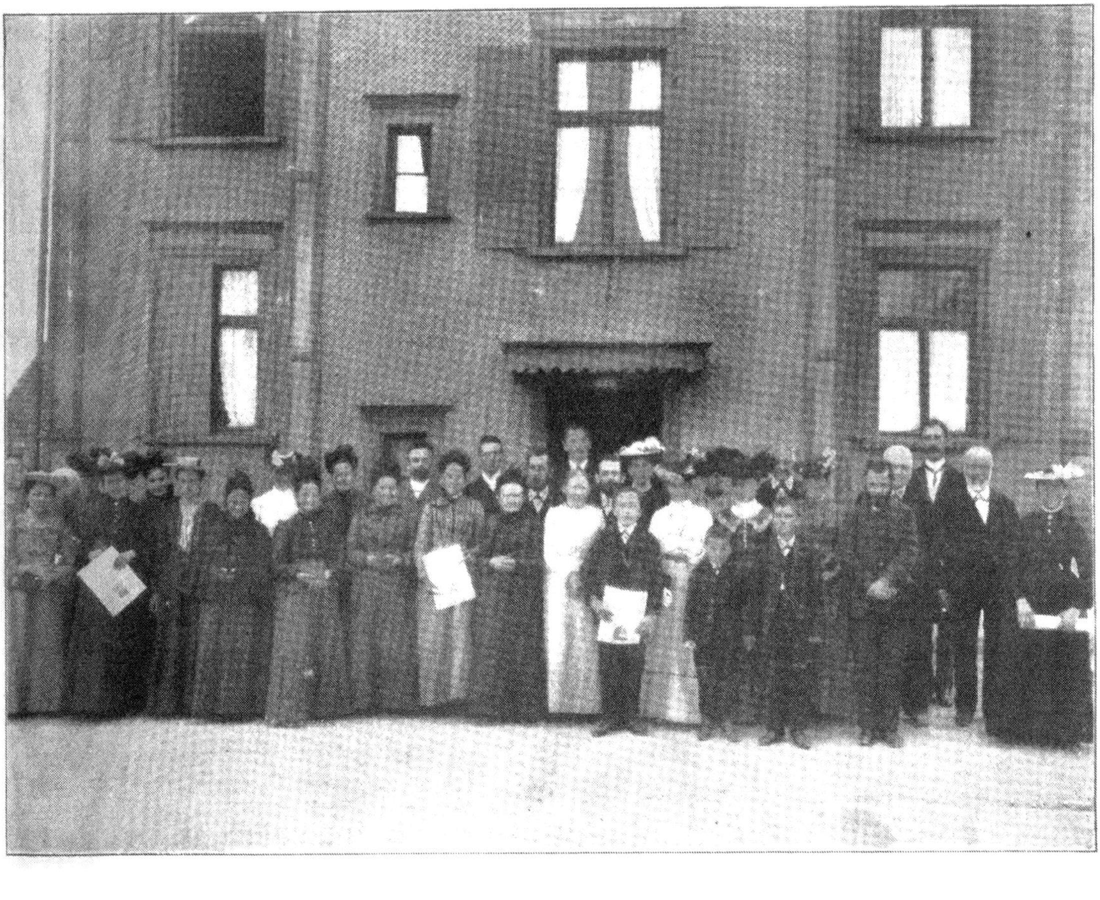

A WEEKLY PAPER FOR THE EXTENSION OF THE KINGDOM OF GOD.

EDITED BY THE REV. JOHN ALEX. DOWIE.

Application for entry as Second Class Matter at Zion City, Illinois, pending.

Subscription Rates.		Special Rates.	
One Year	$2.00	100 Copies of One Issue	$3.00
Six Months	1.25	25 Copies of One Issue	1.00
Three Months	.75	To Ministers, Y. M. C. A's and Public	
Single Copies	.05	Reading Rooms, per annum	1.50

For foreign subscriptions add $1.50 per year, or three cents per copy for postage.

Subscribers desiring a change of address should give present address, as well as that to which they desire LEAVES OF HEALING sent in the future.

Make Bank Drafts, Express Money or Postoffice Money Orders payable to the order of JOHN ALEX. DOWIE, Zion City, Illinois, U. S. A.

Long Distance Telephone. *Cable Address "Dowie, Zion City."*

All communications upon business must be addressed to MANAGER ZION PUBLISHING HOUSE, Zion City, Illinois, U. S. A.

Subscriptions to LEAVES OF HEALING, A VOICE FROM ZION, and the various publications may also be sent to
ZION PUBLISHING HOUSE, 81 EUSTON ROAD, LONDON, N. W., ENGLAND.
ZION PUBLISHING HOUSE, No. 43 PARK ROAD, ST. KILDA, MELBOURNE, VICTORIA, AUSTRALIA.
ZION PUBLISHING HOUSE, RUE DE MONT, THABOR 1, PARIS, FRANCE.
ZIONSHEIM, SCHLOSS LIEBBURG, CANTON THURGAU, BEI ZÜRICH, SWITZERLAND.

ZION CITY, ILLINOIS, SATURDAY, JUNE 25, 1904.

TABLE OF CONTENTS.

LEAVES OF HEALING, SATURDAY, JUNE 25, 1904.

Notes From The Overseer-in-Charge.

"THERE IS MESHECH, TUBAL, AND ALL HER MULTITUDE;
HER GRAVES ARE ROUND ABOUT HER:
ALL OF THEM UNCIRCUMCISED,
SLAIN BY THE SWORD;
FOR THEY CAUSED THEIR TERROR IN THE LAND OF THE LIVING."

AND THEY shall not lie with the mighty that are fallen of the uncircumcised,
Which are gone down to hell with their weapons of war,
And have laid their swords under their heads,
And their iniquities are upon their bones;
For they were the terror of the mighty in the land of the living.

THE SAD story of the Eastern War grows more and more terrible day by day.

THE RUSSIAN military peasant is compelled to leave his home and family and be driven across the dreary Siberian wilderness into a cruel war with which he has but little sympathy.

He is not fighting for his native land; neither is he fighting for the honor of his country.

Political aggrandizement in China finds no sympathetic chord in the hearts of the common people of Russia, but the autocratic and despotic government of Russia drives her populace like sheep to the slaughter.

JAPAN HAS some cause for the conflict.

Her claims appear more just, and instil a high degree of patriotism into her subjects.

She is fighting for that which is logically her own by right; for territory where her overflowing millions may find room for colonization.

IT SEEMS that the hour of Russia's humiliation has come.

She has long been the oppressor of many nations.

Poland, Finland and Bohemia are crying out unto God for deliverance.

BUT MORE cruel than all has been her bitter oppression and all but annihilation of the children of Shem.

RUSSIA TODAY is clearly the great representative of Japheth.

The sons of Japheth, Meshech (Moscow), Tubal (Tobolsk), Gomer, and Javan, are found largely in the nations of the Gaul and the Slav.

THE HEBREWS, who are the most notable descendants of Shem in the world today, are also found most largely in Russia.

The bitter race prejudice, which exists there, is probably deeper than can be found elsewhere in all the world, and the cry of the oppressed Jew has reached the ear of Jehovah Sabaoth.

The oppression cannot continue forever.

RACE HATRED is the most unreasonable and inexcusable thing imaginable.

God will recompense His people.

RUSSIA IS being weakened by this war with Japan, and whether she be victorious in the final outcome or not, her wealth and her prosperity will have been destroyed, and she will be in a very poor condition to meet the opposition of the great world-powers with whom she has been at enmity.

GREAT BRITAIN and America are undoubtedly more largely Semitic than Japhethic, and as blood is thicker than water, so the sympathies of England and America, especially Christian England and America, must be more largely with the Hebrews than with Russia as a government.

If there are any sympathies with Japan today, it is only because of the fact that she has been wronged, and that there is a desire in the hearts of the people to see justice meted out.

JAPAN WILL probably lose more than she can gain in the war, but God's purposes will be wrought out, and the wicked nations will be punished.

THE FINAL conflict is soon to come.

The oppression and persecution of Japheth against Shem and Ham cannot go on forever.

Although he is the oldest son, he cannot take the place of Cain without reckoning with God.

FRANCE IS largely allied with Russia, and has also shown her bitter spirit against the Hebrew.

THE ONLY place where he finds true liberty is England and America, and perhaps in a measure in Germany. And this is where all peoples find their greatest freedom.

BUT TRUE freedom is still unknown in these lands.

It remains for Zion, under God, to set the people free.

ZION KNOWS nothing of the meaning of race prejudice.

Zion owns one common flag, the flag for all the world, and that is the flag of Zion, the Banner of the Cross.

You ask a man in Zion City what his nationality is, and he will tell you that he is of the nation of Zion. He may have been born in England, but he is now a citizen of Zion.

You ask another who was born in America, "Which flag do you love the best?" and he will tell you "The flag of Zion."

While the American is loyal to the government under which he lives, he will be just as loyal to the government of England or Germany or China if he were sent to work for the Lord in these countries.

ZION'S FLAG is a universal flag; the Flag of Purity and Peace and Power.

THE FLAGS of the Nations represent but temporal Powers, and these Powers must be destroyed.

LET ALL the flags in all the world be brought down, and let the Flag of Zion be raised.

Let her folds be unfurled to the breezes of heaven.

WE ARE no less loyal to these temporal governments.

We are only more loyal to God.

WE RECOGNIZE the temporal authority of these governments, and that there are no powers but which are "ordained of God," and we are subject unto these higher powers as far as they are subject to God.

BUT THE governments will have to reckon with Elijah the Restorer.

His authority is higher than the authority of kings and potentates, for he has the Authority of God.

RUSSIA MAY close her doors temporarily to the Gospel of Zion, but she must be humiliated and brought low, and made willing to open her gates.

IT IS a mighty commentary upon the condition of affairs that in the French Republic, in the Swiss Republic, and in the American Republic, there is more religious liberty and greater freedom of speech than under any of the monarchical governments.

Where the people have done away with the rule of kings, which never has been pleasing to God, there religious and personal liberty is greatest and best.

THE FOLLOWING cablegram from the General Overseer, from Queenstown, gives us the last word before sailing for America, and concludes a most wonderfully interesting and important series of events in his World's Visitation:

QUEENSTOWN, IRELAND, June 19th.

SPEICHER, Zion City.

Read 34th verse of 50th chapter of Jeremiah.

The Christ is Conqueror!

The ignorant, degenerate, illiterate Tibetan warriors of the Babylonish London press howled against me for a week in every variety of animal disguise, stirring up a pack of human wolves last Monday, eager to murder and destroy.

I did not choose to be trampled to death in London gutters, and therefore crossed the channel and found protection, hospitality and rest in Republican France.

Returned Friday to London, boarded the Lucania at Liverpool the same night; sailed yesterday afternoon and arrived at Queenstown this morning with all the Visitation Party well and happy. Thank God!

Zion in Europe and around the world is a band of heroic Christian men, women, youths, maidens and children whose hearts God has touched with the fire of His love, faith and hope.

They are progressive, wise, intelligent, diligent, orderly, patient, ready for work or sacrifice, with faces set Zion Cityward.

I salute them with confidence and enthusiasm.

Peace to Zion in every land and nation!

Zion Restoration Host has begun the conquest of the world for the rejected Christ, who is the rightful Ruler of the kings of the earth.

God is hastening things—it is His time.

Pray for us.

Love.

Mizpah. DOWIE.

HE HAS already arrived in New York, where he speaks in Carnegie Hall on tomorrow, Lord's Day.

THERE IS great rejoicing among the hosts of Zion, and elaborate arrangements are being made for the reception of the General Overseer and Party on their return to Zion City on June 30th.

BRETHREN, PRAY FOR US.

JOHN G. SPEICHER.

GOD'S WAY OF HEALING.

BY THE REV. JOHN ALEX. DOWIE.

God's Way of Healing Is a Person, Not a Thing.

Jesus said "*I am* the Way, and the Truth, and the Life," and He has ever been revealed to His people in all the ages by the Covenant Name, Jehovah-Rophi, or "*I am* Jehovah that Healeth thee." (John 14:6; Exodus 15:26.)

The Lord Jesus, the Christ, is Still the Healer.

He cannot change, for "Jesus, the Christ, is the same yesterday and today, yea and forever;" and He is still with us, for He said: "Lo, *I am* with you All the Days, even unto the Consummation of the Age." (Hebrews 13:8; Matthew 28:20.) Because He is Unchangeable, and because He is present, in spirit, just as when in the flesh, He is the Healer of His people.

Divine Healing Rests on the Christ's Atonement.

It was prophesied of Him, "Surely He hath borne our griefs (Hebrew, *sickness*), and carried our sorrows: . . . and with His stripes we are healed;" and it is expressly declared that this was fulfilled in His Ministry of Healing, which still continues. (Isaiah 53:4, 5; Matthew 8:17.)

Disease Can Never be God's Will.

It is the Devil's work, consequent upon Sin, and it is impossible for the work of the Devil ever to be the Will of God. The Christ came to "destroy the works of the Devil," and when He was here on earth He healed "all manner of disease and all manner of sickness," and all these sufferers are expressly declared to have been "oppressed of the Devil." (1 John 3:8; Matthew 4:23; Acts 10:38.)

The Gifts of Healing Are Permanent.

It is expressly declared that the "Gifts and the calling of God are without repentance," and the Gifts of Healing are amongst the Nine Gifts of the Spirit to the Church. (Romans 11:29; 1 Corinthians 12:8-11.)

There Are Four Modes of Divine Healing.

The first is the direct prayer of faith; the second, intercessory prayer of two or more; the third, the anointing of the elders, with the prayer of faith; and the fourth, the laying on of hands of those who believe, and whom God has prepared and called to that Ministry. (Matthew 8:5-13; Matthew 18:19; James 5:14, 15; Mark 16:18.)

Divine Healing Is Opposed by Diabolical Counterfeits.

Amongst these are Christian Science (falsely so-called), Mind Healing, Spiritualism, Trance Evangelism, etc. (1 Timothy 6:20, 21; 1 Timothy 4:1, 2; Isaiah 51:22, 23.)

Multitudes Have Been Healed Through Faith in Jesus.

The writer knows of thousands of cases and has personally laid hands on scores of thousands of persons. Full information can be obtained at the meetings held in the Zion Tabernacles in Chicago, and in Zion City, Illinois, and in many pamphlets which give the experience, in their own words, of many who have been healed in this and other countries, published at Zion Printing and Publishing House, Zion City, Illinois.

"Belief Cometh of Hearing, and Hearing by the Word of the Christ."

You are heartily invited to attend and hear for yourself.

Around-the-World Visitation

of the

Rev. John Alex. Dowie

Elijah the Restorer
General Overseer of the Christian Catholic Church in Zion.

By ARTHUR W. NEWCOMB, Special Correspondent.

ONE MONTH ON AN OCEAN STEAMSHIP.

THE last paper of this series closed with the account of the last few days of the stay of the General Overseer and party in Australia.

On Thursday afternoon, April 7, 1904, the pilgrims went on board the Royal Mail Steamship Mongolia, lying in Largs Bay, near Adelaide, South Australia.

Embarking at Largs Bay, South Australia.

Repeated warnings having been received from authentic sources, that there would be an attempt at violence made when he embarked, the General Overseer, accompanied by all the members of the party, except those who had the baggage in charge, took a launch from Brighton, several miles down the coast from Adelaide, and were taken to the steamer in that way instead of coming off from the jetty at Largs Bay, where passengers usually take the launches.

Thus they were able to get on board without the slightest trouble or molestation, although a very considerable crowd had gathered at the Largs Bay Jetty.

The afternoon was a most beautiful one; the bay was quiet, so that there was not the slightest ripple on the glassy surface of the water, which is here so marvelously clear that the bottom can be seen very plainly even at a depth of fifty feet.

Many friends and relatives of the General Overseer and his family and party came out to the steamship to bid them good-by, and remained on board until the sailing of the vessel.

Elder C. Friend Hawkins took passage from Adelaide to Fremantle, Western Australia, whither the General Overseer had directed him to go on Zion business.

At half past three o'clock in the afternoon the last lingering visitor on board went over the side to the launch, lines were cast loose from the buoy, and our nine thousand three hundred ninety-three mile sea voyage was begun.

For some hours we sailed swiftly but quietly through the smooth, blue waters of the Gulf of St. Vincent, the city of Adelaide, with Mount Lofty towering behind, slowly sinking out of sight beneath the horizon.

As night came on we turned into the Great Australian Bight, reputed to be one of the roughest stretches of salt water in the world.

Be this as it may, several members of our party retired to their cabins that night with sad, pale faces.

The following day, April 8th, was a very beautiful one, as far as the sky was concerned, but several members of the party still found the motion of the vessel far from comfortable.

However, there were very few meals missed; and on Saturday, although the motion still continued, all were again in their wonted health and spirits.

By this time we had been able to take some account of the vessel which was to be our home for over four weeks, and of our fellow-passengers.

The Royal Mail Steamship Mongolia.

Our first impression was a very pleasant one. The Mongolia is a twin-screw Royal Mail Steamship, of nine thousand five hundred tons burden, being the newest and one of the largest and finest of the Peninsular and Oriental Steam Navigation Company's vessels.

We found her to be not only pleasing to the eye within and without but a very safe, steady, comfortable and convenient vessel to travel in.

The cabins are commodious, for cabins on a steamship, and very well equipped with convenient furniture. We found Commander C. F. Preston and his staff of officers exceedingly affable, courteous and obliging, and withal felt that our voyage would be as comfortable and pleasant as is possible on a great ocean liner.

Passengers had been taken aboard at Sydney, New South Wales; Melbourne, Victoria; and Hobart, Tasmania, before the Mongolia arrived at Adelaide, so that the vessel was very comfortably filled.

These passengers we found to be very genial, kind and respectful people for the most part, many of them treating us with marked friendliness and consideration from the very first.

As for the rest, they seemed to be watching to see whether the newspapers had been right in what they had said concerning the General Overseer.

In the course of a few days they had evidently come to the conclusion that the newspapers had shamefully lied, for they became very friendly.

As the days and weeks passed, the interest in Zion and Zion City became more and more intense on the part of our fellow passengers, and many on their way to visit America, declared their intention of seeing Zion City.

At Fremantle, West Australia.

Early on Monday morning, April 11, 1904, the Mongolia steamed into the harbor at Fremantle, West Australia.

No sooner had the first launch come out to meet the Mongolia than a reporter for the Fremantle *Daily News* approached the General Overseer and requested an interview.

After his experience in Australia, the General Overseer had very carefully and prayerfully considered the whole question of the attitude of the press, and of his policy in regard to this institution, and had fully determined that in future he would under no conditions make any communication to the press except on such rare occasions as circumstances might demand, and then only by a signed statement given upon written promise of the editor that it would be published verbatim.

Accordingly, when this young Fremantle reporter asked for an interview, the General Overseer's reply was, "I have nothing to say to the press."

Insolently ignoring this statement, the youth pressed the question. "How long do you expect to remain in Fremantle?"

Quietly but firmly the General Overseer said, "My words were perfectly clear; I have nothing to say to the press."

He then turned away.

Villainous Lie of Fremantle "Daily News."

It was with this foundation that the reporter, a son of a Methodist minister, wrote the following wicked and malicious falsehood which appeared in the *Daily News*, that afternoon, before we left Fremantle:

ELIJAH THE RESTORER.

REFUSES TO BE INTERVIEWED.

BUT THE "DAILY NEWS" SURPRISES HIM.

A VOLUME OF ABUSE.

"AUSTRALIA GOING TO DAMNATION."

"ALL THROUGH THE ROTTEN PRESS."

"THEY ARE SERVANTS OF THE DEVIL."

"A SPECIAL PLACE IN HELL."

A good deal of interest has been evinced in the movements of the Rev. J. A. Dowie, who styles himself "Elijah the Restorer," and the arrival of the Peninsular and Oriental Company's steamer Mongolia, on which he is returning to Europe, was awaited with a good deal of impatience by many. This morning a *Daily News* reporter boarded the vessel as she was approaching the river, and immediately set out in search of the notorious "Elijah." From the moment he stepped on board there could be noticed

SWITZERLAND RECEIVING THE PROPHET OF THE RESTORATION—DIVINE BLESSINGS POUR OUT.

AN AIR OF ALERTNESS

on the part of some dozen young men, dressed in light tweed suits, and white yachting caps. These, it afterwards proved, were Dowie's "Guards," and their duty it evidently was to warn off any enterprising pressmen. They all spoke with a pronounced "Yankee" twang, and did not by any means look like devout members of a religious sect. After dodging these gentry round the decks and behind sundry boats and fittings, our reporter managed to find the great man sitting with one "guard," closely examining the coast line with

A PAIR OF FIELD GLASSES.

Maybe he was mapping out in his mind the landing place for the one thousand Zion guards he has promised to invade Australia with, or perhaps he was on the lookout for his *bête noire*—pressmen.

"Elijah the Restorer" is a little man in stature. He has long white whiskers and small blue eyes. His face is of a peculiar whiteness, and to look at him one would think that he was an old decrepit gentleman on a health voyage. Today as he sat on deck he wore a Chesterfield overcoat and a white yachting cap.

"Good morning, Mr. Dowie, I represent the *Daily News*, and I—"

Dowie was instantly

A CHANGED MAN.

The languid look disappeared as by magic, and a look of dangerous anger took its place. With cutting emphasis he broke in, "I have nothing to say to the press."

"But may I not—"

"I tell you, I have nothing to say to the press. I think my language is perfectly clear."

As he said this Dowie flung down his glasses and sat bolt upright in his chair. His eyes flashed his anger, and his voice gradually rose in tone until it was nearly a scream.

"The press of Australia are liars, they are

VILLAINS AND PERJURERS.

Why can't they tell the truth? Australia is going to damnation, and all through the rotten press. Wherever I have been they have concocted lies and libels, and one wonders why decent, self-respecting people allow you to mix with them. You are rotten. You are servants of the Devil, and I am sure you will have a special place in hell. You ought not to be buried like ordinary, respectable people. Pooh! Even the worms would refuse to touch you all. And you smoke.

FILTHY, DISGUSTING STINKPOTS!

Go away, I tell you! go away. I have nothing to say to you."

With this, "Elijah" jumped up and disappeared down the adjacent companionway, and our representative withdrew to meditate on the villainy of pressmen.

This villainous lie was doubtless telegraphed over all Australia and no doubt believed by many of the citizens of that country who had previously been prepared to swallow it by being fed on many similar lies by the Australian press.

Their four days' association with him on board the boat, however, had taught the passengers of the Mongolia something of the personality of the General Overseer, and few if any of them believed that the alleged interview was genuine.

Crowd of West Australian Anarchists at the Wharf.

Soon after the Mongolia entered the harbor, a representative of the Fremantle police called upon the General Overseer and offered all the protection that his force could afford should the General Overseer desire to go ashore. The official stated, however, that there was a very rough element in Fremantle, and that threats had been more or less openly made, that if he came ashore he would be roughly handled.

The General Overseer assured the official that he had no business that called him ashore, and that there would be no necessity for his leaving the vessel.

The statement of the police proved to be correct, for a very large crowd had gathered at the wharf, and boohooed and shouted in the usual Australian manner when the vessel came alongside.

An old gentlemen, with a long gray beard, was mistaken by these anarchists for the General Overseer. He was jeered and struck with an egg before the mistake was discovered.

The other members of the party, however, went ashore at various times during the day, and some went to Perth, a capital of West Australia, about twelve miles distant. There is practically nothing of interest to be seen at either one of these places, both of them being very ordinary Australian cities.

On shore, however, a very large crowd waited all day for the General Overseer to leave the boat, and there is no doubt that had he done so these poor ignorant men, who had never seen him and to whom he could not possibly have done any wrong, would, if permitted, have handled him very roughly.

Such is the criminal effect of the lying religious and secular press of Australia.

While the vessel was tied up to the docks several friends of the General Overseer came on board and greeted him, so that the time passed very pleasantly until, having said farewell to Elder Hawkins and all other friends, at four o'clock in the afternoon we cast loose from the dock, and sailed out into the Indian Ocean, taking our last look at Australia, for this time at least.

The Mongolia turned her prow toward the northwest and began her ten days' journey to Colombo, Ceylon.

Beautiful Sunsets on the Indian Ocean.

This portion of our journey was marked by a delightfully quiet breeze, beautiful weather, and the most remarkably gorgeous sunsets that we had ever seen. Every evening, the ship's forward parts would be crowded with passengers watching for the going down of the glowing orb of day.

To those whose lives had been spent in high northern latitudes, the blending and commingling of many shades of red, blue, green, pink, violet, lavender, purple and gray; gold, silver, copper and other metallic tints, and many colors, tints and gradations of color that have no names, seemed beyond belief.

The whole vast vault of the heavens seemed fairly ablaze with multi-colored lights, and all the polished floor of the sea beneath reflected the glory.

Every moment it all changed, one matchless scene melting into another as the colors softened, and the approaching night began to throw the first gauzy veil of darkness over sky and sea.

But ere the brilliancy had departed, a pale slender crescent of silver was hung in the western heavens, and the jeweled lights of the stars gleamed out from the dome above.

One evening, just at this enchanted hour, a stately sailing vessel, with every inch of canvas spread to the light breeze, appeared off our starboard bow, completing a marine picture of rarest beauty.

As we saw these sunsets we felt that God was indeed the greatest lover of beauty in all the Universe.

Life on Board Ship.

The Mongolia was following the great ocean track between Australia and India, and there was hardly a day passed that we did not either meet or overtake some other vessel; so that there was a much greater interest in the sea around us than on our voyage across the Pacific.

The beautiful flying-fish were also very numerous, and we saw occasional porpoises, and two or three times the feathery spout of a whale.

On board the vessel there were numerous deck games, such as chess, checkers and halma, which helped to pass the time very quickly, especially as a very efficient sports' committee, organized among the passengers, conducted a series of tournaments, in which all members of the Zion party participated.

Occasional concerts were also prepared and given in the music saloon.

There were no facilities whatever, notwithstanding all these elaborate provisions for amusement, for any further religious activities than those afforded by the reading of prayers in the first saloon on Lord's Day morning and by private devotion.

Although large numbers of the passengers in both the first and second saloons, were exceedingly desirous of hearing the General Overseer speak; and, indeed, several times petitioned the captain to permit it, that very able official was bound by the rules of the Peninsular and Oriental Steam Navigation Company to permit no other religious services on board the vessel than the reading of prayers, Lord's Day morning.

In speaking of these facts to a party of friends, the General Overseer made a parody on the old hymn which begins:

Religion is the chief concern
Of mortals here below

He said that the rule of the company seemed to be:

Amusement is the chief concern
Of mortals here below;
May we its great importance learn,
And let religion go.

Notwithstanding the fact that he could not address the people publicly, the General Overseer was able to declare in private conversation, the essential Restoration Truths which he has been sent to preach.

In this way a very deep interest was created which increased to such an extent that many of our fellow passengers who were expecting to be in London at the time of the Visitation there, gave us their addresses and very earnestly requested that we send them tickets to the meetings.

Royal Mail Steamship Mongolia lying at Anchor in the Harbor at Colombo, Ceylon.

Royal Mail Steamship Mongolia.

Early in the morning of Wednesday, April 20, 1904, the dim outlines of the coast of the Island of Ceylon appeared.

Two Days in Colombo, Ceylon.

When the day broke and the sun came out, little fishing villages along the shore began to appear, while all about us we saw the fishing-boats and catamarans of the native fishermen.

Some of these were very crude and simple affairs, being constructed of a few hewn timbers lashed together with cords, and all were primitive and picturesque. Soon the spires, domes, minarets and towers of the city of Colombo were seen above the tree tops.

An hour later we had taken on board the pilot, and were entering the harbor.

As we came in sight, several scores of Cingalese boys and young men came paddling out on their catamarans and canoes to us.

When they were within hailing distance of the vessel, they began to shout, "A' right! A' right! A' right! Have a dive! Have a dive! di', di', di', di'!" a hideous clatter, which never ceased so long as there were any passengers at the rail of the Mongolia.

They were clothed only in breech-clouts, and their purpose was to inveigle the passengers to throw money into the water for the fun of seeing them dive for it.

When a bit of silver was thrown into the water, usually from eight to twelve of them dived with a great splashing, the result being a struggle under water, the wriggling brown bodies sinking lower and lower as they followed the coin downward, sometimes out of sight. At last they would begin to come up one by one, and strike out for their catamarans, one of them holding up the coin to show that it had not been lost.

Some of the more nimble of these little brown fellows climbed up the side of the ship, finding places to grasp with fingers and toes where the ship seemed to be almost smooth, until at last they were in the Mongolia's boat, nearly fifty feet above the surface of the water.

Standing in these they would urge the passengers to give them a shilling, or even a sixpence, for which they promised to dive from their high perch.

If they succeeded in getting the coin before they were driven off by the lascars (East Indian sailors and deck-hands, which are universally employed on steamers plying these waters), they dived head foremost, but when driven off they jumped striking the water feet foremost.

These lads seemed to be stronger, swifter, and more daring swimmers and divers than the Samoans, but had none of the grace of the South Sea Islanders.

One of the accomplishments of these youngsters, which they performed with great enthusiasm, was to stand on their catamarans, and, beating time on their sides with their elbows, sing "Ta-ra-ra-boom-de-a."

The water here was said to be infested with sharks, and some of the swimmers were minus an arm as the result of an attack of these voracious fish, but none were molested while we were there.

Conversational Powers of the Colomboites.

At last the Mongolia was anchored in the harbor, and the native craft began to swarm about begging to take passengers ashore.

Some of these were great clumsy, unwieldy boats, with three or four oarsmen as motive power. The oars that they used were very primitive, being long round poles, with flat discs of wood lashed to the end.

Others came in very narrow canoes, which stood high out of the water, and were kept upright by heavy outriggers.

Besides these, there were the boats of tradesmen, trying to sell their East Indian curios, and several barges loaded with coal, which was to be stored away in the Mongolia's bunkers.

All of these boats swarmed with native men and boys, and every individual among them seemed to be talking as fast as he could at the top of his voice in an attempt to make himself heard above all the rest. The maximum of talk with the minimum of work seems to have been reached by a large class of the natives of Colombo. Everywhere we went during the two days that we were on the island, we could hear the continual jabber.

After a great deal of talk, most of which came to nothing, we at last engaged boatmen to take us ashore.

Native Merchant, Colombo, Ceylon.

"Riksha" and Runners, Colombo, Ceylon; Bullock Team and Cart. A Dhow, Suez Canal.

When we arrived at the jetty, we were immediately besieged by a great throng of men and boys who wanted us to buy pictorial postal cards, knickknacks, newspapers, flowers, and other goods, and who offered themselves as guides, carriage drivers, and porters.

Beggars were also numerous.

How they did talk, plead, urge, demand, and lament!

They wanted us to buy their wares; they wanted us to engage them to lead to some wonderful sight; they wanted us to pay them for carrying our luggage, umbrellas, cameras, wraps, and, in fact, almost anything in sight that was portable.

It took a great many words for them to say this, and they said it over and over again as long as we were in hearing.

We finally succeeded in escaping from their blandishments, only to run into the arms of the "riksha" men.

Each of these enterprising coolies has a little two-wheeled covered carriage somewhat larger than a baby carriage which is drawn by means of shafts, somewhat similar to the shafts of a single buggy, except that they have a cross-piece fitted across the ends. These are jinrikishas, called "rikshas" for short.

Barefooted and dressed principally in a light cloth about the loins, these dark-skinned men trot at a good pace in the sun, mile after mile without apparent fatigue.

We finally engaged one of these "rikshas" for each member of the party, and were taken to the Galle Face Hotel, a very commodious and comfortable caravansary, with all modern conveniences, situated at the end of a very beautiful drive along the coast. Here we engaged rooms for the two days that we were in Colombo.

As we went, beggars and little brown boys with flowers to sell ran along beside us chattering faster than they ran.

Colombo an Interesting City.

The remainder of that day was spent in seeing the sights of this typical oriental city of the twentieth century, where the religion, costumes, manners, means of locomotion and speech of the Far East of centuries ago, and of the West of today, exist side by side.

The narrow, crowded streets, the small, dark, ill-smelling, block-shaped houses, the peculiar open markets, the great two-wheeled carts drawn by bullocks of all sizes, the many fakirs and beggars, some of them suffering from loathsome deformities and diseases; the many types of natives, the intermingling of British, German, French and American business men, tourists, and British soldiers, all combined to form a picture of the most intense interest.

The People of Colombo.

The human element, of course, is always the most interesting, so we first observed the people themselves. There are many different kinds of Malays in Colombo, but the most numerous are the Cingalese and the Tamils.

Cingalese men seem to make it their ambition in life to appear as much like women as possible, and indeed it was often very difficult to decide, on meeting them in the streets, whether they were men or women.

These men, some of them almost as light in color as Chinese, wear their hair long.

Occasionally we met one who wore his hair flying loose, like a schoolgirl.

Others gathered it in a knot at the back of their heads, wearing a peculiar horseshoe-shaped comb on top.

Some of them have very beautiful, glossy-black, wavy hair, of which any woman might be proud.

Their hands and feet are small and well cared for, and they wear skirts which come to the ankle.

The expression of their faces is serene and gentle, their large, dark eyes are very soft, and their voices are fine and smooth.

Many of the inhabitants of the city seemed to be beggars, beseeching the stranger at every few steps. Many of these were tiny children, wearing scarcely a stitch of clothing.

These beseech pedestrians and run along beside "'rikshas," chanting in mournful voices, "Oh, my papa, dear good papa; I got no papa, no mudder; all dead. You be my papa. Give me penny, papa;" or, "Master, good master, give me penny. Dear master, give me penny."

Their persistence is amazing, and their numbers are so great that even a penny to each would amount to a large sum.

A Travesty on Religion.

Scattered all about the city there are Buddhist and Hindoo temples, some of them very small, and others larger. The General Overseer, with his party, went into one of the Buddhist temples, where he was greeted by the priest in charge, and conducted to the altar. On the altar there were a number of flowers, and before it there knelt a weeping woman.

The priest evidently thought that she had been praying long enough, for he very peremptorily cleared her out.

"What are these flowers?" asked the General Overseer.

"That is the evening sacrifice," was the reply of the priest. "Have one."

Each of the party was presented with a flower, and some other parts of the temple were shown, after which the priest wanted to sell the General Overseer a leaf from some Buddhist book.

Some of the other members of the party visited a Mohammedan mosque, which they were permitted to enter after they had taken off their shoes.

BUDDHIST TEMPLE, COLOMBO, CEYLON.

Another place that we visited was the great washing place of the city. Here, on the banks of a large pond, there are several rows of large, flat stones. On these the clothes are laid and soaked in water taken from the pond, and then grasped in both hands and beaten upon the stones again and again.

At the water's edge there were other and smaller stones, which were being used in the same way. Above these stones for several hundred yards along the shore there was a perfect network of clothes-lines, all of them fluttering with clothes, which, notwithstanding the very primitive way in which they were washed, looked spotlessly clean.

In the water was a great throng of men and boys, bathing; also a number of bullocks and carts, which were also being washed.

Visit With Zion People in Colombo.

That evening, after dinner, we were very much pleased to receive a visit from a number of native Zion people, three very intelligent and well-educated sisters, their young brother, and others.

All spoke English very well, and were very much delighted to see the General Overseer, Overseer Jane Dowie, and the other members of the party.

After a very pleasant evening, closing with prayer by the General Overseer, these good people departed much refreshed spiritually, and more determined than ever to go forward with the work of Restoration in Ceylon. They were very desirous that the General Overseer hold meetings during his stay in Colombo, but the time was too short to perfect arrangements.

SCENE IN COLOMBO, CEYLON.

NATIVE CHILDREN, COLOMBO, CEYLON.

BANIAN TREE, CEYLON.

OUTRIGGER CANOE IN THE HARBOR AT COLOMBO, CEYLON.

That evening and the following day, the General Overseer was very earnestly besought for interviews by representatives of the Cingalese, the British, and the American press, but he continued his policy of "nothing to say to the press."

We slept that night with our windows open, and with the never-ceasing moan of the Indian Ocean sounding in our ears.

A Visit to Kandy.

Early the next morning, the General Overseer and five members of the party took the train for Kandy, the ancient capital of Colombo, situated fifty-two miles northeast of Colombo, in the interior of the island.

This railroad is the property of the Government of Ceylon, and is operated by the state. It is conducted on the same principles as are the railroads in England and Australia. Our little party was fortunate in securing a compartment to itself.

For several miles, our journey was across plains of tropical luxuriance, abundantly watered—almost too abundantly.

Soon, however, we began to climb the mountains.

Here the scenery became very beautiful and even grand.

On one side, the rocks towered precipitously above us, while on the other, we could look down thousands of feet, into the highly cultivated valleys below.

Beyond these, there were the mountains again—high, rugged, peculiar-shaped rocks.

The "Paddy Fields."

One of the most striking features of this part of our journey was the terraced "Paddy Fields."

These fields are on the slopes of the hills and mountains, the terraces, each about two feet high, extending from the very bottom of the valley, almost to the tops of the mountains.

Where the ascent is gentle, each terrace is broad, perfectly flat on top, with a very gracefully curved outline; but where the incline is sharp, the terraces are very narrow, still, however, preserving the undulating, irregular curve which makes them so much more picturesque than if they were all perfectly straight and rectangular.

These fields are watered from springs in the mountains, the water flowing from the highest to the one below, and then to the next, until all are watered. The crop grown is principally rice.

All along the way there were native huts, and the mansions and villas of wealthy Cingalese and foreigners.

Every few miles we passed through a native village.

All of these were full of scenes strange to our occidental eyes, and therefore deeply interesting.

The train wound in and out around the sides of the mountains and through tunnels; every turn bringing us within sight of some new scene of tropical beauty.

Drinking From Cocoanuts.

At every station there were boys and women with fruit, cakes and cocoanuts for sale. The fruit was very good, and incredibly cheap if you paid your own price for it; but if you gave these innocent natives what they asked for it, you paid about twice as much as the same fruit would cost in the United States.

The sale of a cocoanut was an interesting transaction.

It usually began by the boy merchant asking a rupee—about twenty cents—and ended by his selling it for ten Cingalese cents—about two cents of Uncle Sam's money.

When the bargain was struck, the boy took a strong, heavy knife, and with four or five skilful blows chopped the top off the cocoanut, which was always full of milk.

This the customer drank with great relish if it suited his palate, but somewhat dubiously otherwise, as this very popular beverage has a slightly acid taste.

SOLOMON'S TANKS, ADEN, ARABIA.

· One could be sure, however, that there were no typhoid germs in it.

The meat of these cocoanuts is not palatable, those that are eaten being of another species.

The weather in Colombo and on the plains that morning had been blistering hot, but when we got up into the mountains we found it delightfully cool and pleasant.

At Kandy we took "rikshas" to the Queen's Hotel where we were served a very delightful lunch, or "tiffin," as it is called throughout India.

We then took a carriage and drove about the city, which is remarkable for its beautiful little lake, its wonderful trees, its excellent roads, its ancient temples, and its handsome modern villas. It also has a Jesuit monastery.

At the Royal Botanical Gardens.

A drive of two or three miles in the direction of Colombo brought us to Peridiyna, where the famous Royal Botanical Gardens of Ceylon are located.

Here we were shown about by a very intelligent young native, who pointed out to us nutmeg, clove, cinnamon, allspice, bread-fruit, and other tropical trees and shrubs, among them the sacred lotus and the deadly upas, which last, however deadly it may be, is certainly a very handsome, innocent-looking tree.

At Peridiyna station we waited a few minutes for the train back to Colombo.

Here we saw tea growing, and on a large flat place near the railway station we saw a large quantity of it spread out to dry in the sun.

Rolling about in the cool, green leaves were two or three fat and happy brown babies. No doubt this particular brand of tea has a peculiarly rich flavor, much prized by its devotees in England and America.

Our return to Colombo was without special incident.

On the following morning, we returned to the Mongolia, and at eleven o'clock we steamed out of the harbor on our way across the Arabian Sea to Aden.

Notable Additions to the Mongolia's Passenger List.

At Colombo we had taken on board thirty-eight passengers from Singapore, China and Japan, among them several British Royal Navy officers on their way home from service in the Far East.

Some of these had been serving as naval attachés on the scenes of conflict of the Russo-Japanese war, and were able to give us much very interesting information concerning conditions and events there.

Our journey to Aden was marked by the hottest weather that we had experienced during the entire Visitation, but God gave us the strength to endure it without serious discomfort or any illness.

After leaving Colombo we either met or overtook steamers or sailing vessels of various kinds every day.

None were more picturesque, however, than the East Indian dhows which, although they are very small and very crude, fearlessly cruise in these waters, in the Red Sea, and in the Suez Canal.

They were formerly used in the slave trade, but now carry various tropical and semi-tropical products, as well as coal and manufactured articles on their north and east-bound trips.

On Tuesday, April 26th, we passed within sight of the rocky Island of Socotra in the Arabian Sea, and on Wednesday, the 27th of April, we sighted Cape Guardafui, the easternmost point of the great Continent of Africa.

At half past four o'clock on Thursday morning we arrived in the inner harbor of Aden, that British naval station and garrison which stands guard at the southern entrance of the Red Sea.

Aden.

Aden is a high, rocky promontory said to bear some resemblance to the Rock of Gibraltar, although its peaks are higher and more sharply defined. It is very strongly fortified.

The inhabitants are East Indians, Arabs, and Somali negroes.

About four miles from Aden are the wonderful tanks reputed to have been built by King Solomon to supply water for irrigating and drinking purposes for the country round about. They have not been full for twelve years. They were half full about six years ago, but are almost entirely dry now.

These tanks were visited by the General Overseer and his party, the journey being made by carriage.

The usual mode of transportation in Aden, however, is by means of camels, of which we saw many in the streets.

At about four o'clock on that same afternoon we left Aden, having taken on board sixty-eight new passengers from India and Somaliland, those from Bombay having arrived that afternoon by the Peninsular and Oriental Steam Navigation Company's Steamship Peninsular.

The Red Sea.

At half past nine o'clock that night we passed through the Straits of Bab-el-Mandeb, the lights of Perim Island gleaming a few hundred yards to our right as we entered the Red Sea.

Our journey through the Red Sea was marked by very hot weather at the south end, and by delightfully cool and pleasant weather as we approached the Gulf of Suez.

On Sunday, May 1st, the barren promontory of Ras-Mohammed appeared, and a little later we entered the Gulf of Suez, land being in plain sight on both sides of us.

That afternoon we sighted a range of mountains, one of which is said to be Mount Sinai.

There is great dispute as to where the children of Israel crossed this sea, so we did not know when we crossed their track.

Our hearts burned within us, however, when we thought that somewhere beyond that range of mountains was Marah, where the great Covenant of Divine Healing was given by God to His people nearly four thousand years ago.

The Suez Canal.

Monday morning at three o'clock we came to anchor in the harbor of the ancient city of Suez, Egypt.

At half past seven, we began our journey through the famous Suez Canal, which can be best described, perhaps, as a great ditch through the sandy desert, eighty-seven miles long, and filled with salt water.

CAMEL AND WATER CART, ADEN, ARABIA.

Here and there along the banks was a *gare* or station, surrounded by palm and other trees and beautifully kept.

At each of these stations there was a semaphore for display of signals.

Two or three times these signals warned the Mongolia to stop in a little widening of the Canal until another ship, coming from the north, could pass.

We passed through the Canal at the rate of about five or six knots an hour until we got into the Great Bitter Lake, through which we steamed at full speed.

A railroad runs along the Canal from Port Said to Suez, connecting also with a railroad to Cairo.

From Ismailia, situated about forty-three miles south of Port Said, to Suez, what is known as the Sweet Water Canal parallels the great waterway. It was built by the khedive of Egypt for the purpose of furnishing drinking water to the laborers who worked at the excavation of the Canal. Its water is from the Nile.

At one point on our journey, the banks of the famous waterway were being repaired, and we saw occidental and oriental methods in use side by side.

Here were camels upon whose backs were slung wooden hampers for carrying sand. The patient beasts would go to the place indicated by their drivers and kneel down while these hampers were being filled, then would slowly and awkwardly rise and patiently walk away to be unloaded. Here also was a narrow-gage railway, such as is used in America in construction work, equipped with dump-cars hauled by mules.

At many places Egyptian boys ran along the banks, shouting to the passengers to throw them money.

We were still creeping through the Canal when the sun went down and night came on, and it was after eleven o'clock when we reached Port Said.

There we discharged the mail for Europe and America, it being carried by a swift express boat to Brindisi, Italy.

About twenty of our fellow passengers disembarked here, some to go on in the express boat, and some to visit Egypt.

Forty passengers from Egypt, however, came on board, and the vessel was very crowded for the rest of the journey.

The Mediterranean Sea.

At five o'clock on Tuesday morning, May 3d, we departed from Port Said, and began our journey through the Mediterranean, that sea which was the Sea to the ancients; the Sea of which Moses wrote in the Book of Job; the Sea of which David wrote in the Psalms; the Sea on which the Prophet Jonah embarked, and into which he was thrown when he was swallowed by a great fish; the Sea on which Saint Paul was wrecked; the Sea concerning which the poets have sung from Homer and Virgil down to the present day.

We found it smooth and beautiful in the bright sunlight.

Early Wednesday morning, May 4th, we saw, north of us, the beautiful snow-capped mountains of the Island of Candia —ancient Crete.

All the lower part of these mountains was hidden in a mist, so that the peaks, gleaming in the morning sun, seemed almost to be floating on banks of feathery clouds.

A little later we passed the rugged southern promontory of the island.

Italian and Sicilian Shores and Straits of Messina.

Early the next afternoon, the southern shores of Italy were in sight, and some of us had our first glimpse of the great continent of Europe.

The shore here is very rugged and mountainous, but the valleys and lower hillsides are quite green.

Here and there on the seashore and far up among the mountains, we could see tiny Italian villages, their houses clustered closely together, presenting a very strange and picturesque sight, especially to those of us who had never before seen the Old World.

At other places were castles and chateaux.

Late in the afternoon the island of Sicily was sighted, with the famous volcano, Mount Etna, rearing its head into the very clouds.

We were then entering the Straits of Messina—the ancient Scylla and Charybdis.

As we approached these Straits, we began to understand better why they were so dreaded by ancient mariners.

The high precipitous shores on either side of the narrow passage seemed to act as a funnel for the winds, which came roaring through with almost incredible force.

So strong was the gale, that passengers, standing on the deck, were sometimes slid along before it.

The sea, however, was confined by the shores in such a way that the waves could not rise high, and the powerful engines drove the great vessel steadily, straight into the teeth of the gale.

A Thunderstorm on the Straits of Messina.

Soon after sunset a black thundercloud, which had been nursing its wrath and emitting threatening flashings of lightning high up in the mountains of Sicily, came sweeping down upon us, presenting a scene of awful grandeur as it flattened down the choppy waves and streaked the black waters with white ribbons of foam.

The Mongolia rode through it without the slightest difficulty.

When we had passed through the straits, however, into the broader waters of the open Mediterranean, we found the sea very rough, pitching and tossing the Mongolia with very little regard for the hearty dinners which the passengers had just eaten.

As a result, we regret to say, some of them were lost.

On the next morning the sea was again smooth, and no one seemed to be any the worse for the experience of the evening.

Arrive at Marseilles, France.

That afternoon, Friday, May 6th, at about sunset, we passed through the Straits of Bonifacio, between the Islands of Sardinia and Corsica, both of which were plainly visible from the decks of the ship, but neither of which presented anything of any very great interest.

When we awoke the following morning, the shores of Southern France were visible, and, at ten o'clock, we had entered the famous harbor of Marseilles.

We had been just one month on board the steamship Mongolia.

On the wharf, at Marseilles, we found Elder Percy Clibborn waiting to greet us and to deliver a great sheaf of letters, including a number for every member of the party. These were very welcome. Counting the month it takes for a letter to go from America to Australia, and the month we had been at sea, we had not heard from our relatives and friends for two months.

Hearty and sincere farewells were said to us by our fellow passengers, and we went ashore with many pleasant memories of our month's voyage across the seas from Adelaide to Marseilles.

Nevertheless we were very glad that it was over, and delighted to be on land once more.

ALONG THE RIVIERA AND IN PARIS.

Marseilles.

The port at which we landed has been a seaport for two thousand five hundred years, having been founded by the Phocæans, from Asia Minor, about 600 B. C.

Its ancient name was Massilia. It has figured prominently in French and European history and is the largest and most important seaport of France, having a population of nearly five hundred thousand.

Here the General Overseer took lunch and gave his attention to the very important correspondence and other business which he found awaiting him upon his arrival there.

At a quarter after six o'clock that afternoon, the entire party took the Paris-Lyon-Mediterraneé train for the Riviera, as the Southern coast of France is called.

At about half past eleven o'clock, the General Overseer, Overseer Jane Dowie, Dr. A. J. Gladstone Dowie and the writer, left the train at Cannes, that quiet and delightful little city at which Overseer Jane Dowie, her son and her secretary had spent a few weeks, on their way to Australia, last December.

The other members of the party, accompanied by Elder Clibborn, went on to Zürich, visiting at Nice, Monte Carlo, Genoa, Milan and Lugano on their way.

Arrival at Cannes.

At Cannes we found the *concierge* of the Hotel du Paradis, where rooms had been reserved for us, waiting at the station.

He very kindly looked after our baggage and placed us in a carriage, in which we were driven through the delightfully quiet streets to the hotel.

The proprietor welcomed us very heartily, remembering Overseer Jane Dowie and her son with great pleasure.

Soon we were off to dreamland, with the fragrance of roses and orange blossoms and the silver notes of nightingales floating in through the open casement.

The following morning, Lord's Day, May 9th, dawned wonderfully clear and bright, flooding the little niche in the hills in which Cannes rests, and the bright, blue waters of the Mediterranean, with Sabbath glory.

Cannes is distinctively an Old World city, with its quaint, old buildings, spotlessly clean, narrow, winding streets, its high walls and hedges, its picturesque little port, and its open-air cafés.

But Cannes is also a favorite winter resort for people from England, and many are the handsome villas that they have built here, and the hotels that have been built for their accommodation.

Hotel du Paradis is situated in the midst of a large and very beautiful garden, not far from the center of the city, and is a most delightfully quiet place.

We arrived there at the very end of the season, when all but very few guests had left, which made it almost as quiet and homelike as a private house. There we spent a very delightful six days.

The Scenery of Cannes.

Except for the seashore, Cannes is completely surrounded

MEETING PLACE OF ZION, HERISAU, SWITZERLAND.

by hills, some of them quite high, and all of them very rich in verdure and flowers.

Every available point of both hills and valleys is cultivated, the hillsides being terraced for the purpose.

The two principal crops are orange blossoms and roses, one of the chief industries at Cannes being the manufacture of perfumes.

The roses grown are of the rarest and most beautiful varieties, and being cultivated especially for their blossoms, every bush is fairly covered with them.

It was no uncommon sight to see a hedge or field of roses, such as sell readily on the Chicago market for from three to five dollars a dozen.

Another flower which is very much grown in Cannes, and which has been brought to a very high state of development, is the marguerite. The great bushes of this plant were white with splendid blooms when we were there.

Cannes abounds in delightful drives, each one of which has its own peculiar loveliness and interest.

One of these winds back and forth through the hills, climbing higher and higher, until it reaches the very summit of the highest hill in the neighborhood, La Californié.

The view from here is one upon which one could gaze with joy for days, finding new beauties every hour.

As we stood there, to the south lay that great glimmering sapphire, the Mediterranean.

Not far from the shore were the two beautiful and historic islands, St. Honorat and Ste. Marguerite, with their ancient fortresses and chateaux.

At our feet were the white houses and red tile roofs of the city of Cannes surrounded by its wonderful gardens and handsome villas, the purple hills forming a harmonious background to a picture of surpassing beauty.

Tucked away in the deep folds of the hills, we could see, here and there, the clustered white houses of an inland village.

To the southeast there stretched the curving shore of the Mediterranean, with its villages and hamlets, the view from La Californié ending with the city of Nice. Ancient towers, castles and fortresses abound, some of them in picturesque ruins.

Above and behind it all, to the northeast, rose the lofty, silent, white peaks of the Maritime Alps.

Visit to Nice, Monaco and Monte Carlo.

On Wednesday, May 12th, the General Overseer and the writer took an early train to Nice, where the General Overseer made some important calls upon members and friends of Zion.

We never before saw water such a wonderful, crystalline, brilliant blue as was the Mediterranean as we caught glimpses of it from the car windows, that morning.

One of the interesting sights was that of women washing clothes in the creeks and rivers, much as the natives did at Colombo. Indeed this seems to be a favorite mode of cleansing clothes all over southern Europe.

At midday, Overseer Jane Dowie and Dr. A. J. Gladstone Dowie came to Nice, where the entire party took luncheon, proceeding immediately after, by train, to Monte Carlo, which for many years has been the great fashionable gambling place of the whole world.

We spent a few hours here visiting the Casino, one of the most beautiful and at the same time one of the most hideous buildings in Europe, the Gardens, and other scenes.

Then we drove to Monaco and paid a brief visit to the royal palace.

Monte Carlo and Monaco are situated side by side, so close together that one does not perceive the dividing line between them, and are the two principal cities in the principality of Monaco, which is practically under the protectorate of the French government.

The people of the principality pay no taxes, the entire support of the government being derived from the income of the gaming tables at the Casino.

None of the residents of the principality are permitted to

ZION MEETING PLACE, ST. GALL, SWITZERLAND.

enter the doors of this building, but all others are welcome upon giving their names.

The tense, cold, desperate faces of the men and women around the tables, the calm, unimpassioned, monotonous voice of the *croupier*, as he coolly drew in, with his little wooden rake, the money that the players at his table had lost, and contemptuously threw the few coins to the occasional winners, made an impression upon our minds as if we had gone, like Virgil and Dante, down into Hell.

Monte Carlo and Monaco are very beautifully situated and have been very much beautified at great expense, but we could not greatly enjoy the beauty when we remembered that it had been paid for out of the income from that inferno, that place from which many a man and woman has gone with no other destination than a suicide's grave.

We were glad to leave Monte Carlo, feeling that nothing could have induced us to remain in the place over night.

Paris.

On Thursday afternoon, May 13th, we took train for Paris, where we arrived at the Paris-Lyon-Mediterraneé station at twenty-four minutes after nine on Friday morning.

We were met at the station by Mr. J. Rollier, the Manager of the Paris Branch of Zion Printing and Publishing House, 1 Rue Mont Thabor, Paris.

We found Mr. Rollier to be a very energetic, intelligent, young man, under whose management not only the Publishing House, but Zion's work in Paris is progressing.

After having secured rooms at the Hotel Normandy, on Rue de l'Echelle, not far from the great Avenue de l'Opera and within one-half block of the famous Louvre, we began our task of sightseeing in Paris, at which we worked faithfully, during all our spare time, seeing practically all the great historic and artistic places for which the city is famed.

Great Blessing in Zion Meetings in Paris.

The most delightful experiences during our visit to Paris, however, were the meetings of members and friends of Zion there.

On Lord's Day afternoon, at three o'clock, about twenty of these gathered in the General Overseer's drawing-room in the Hotel Normandy.

This meeting had no public announcement, the notices having been sent privately only thirty-six hours before by Mr. Rollier.

After the reading of the Scriptures and prayer, the General Overseer gave a very deeply spiritual and intensely practical address on "The Kingdom of God." This was very ably translated into French by Mr. Rollier.

The atmosphere of this little conference was profoundly spiritual, the people seeming to drink in these wonderful Latter Day Truths with great eagerness and earnestness.

At the close of his address, the General Overseer shook hands with all the people and talked with some of them privately, finding among them people of position and influence in Paris.

All expressed themselves very cordially, thanking God's Messenger for a great blessing.

On Tuesday afternoon, at three o'clock, in the Hall of Civil Engineers of France, 19 Rue Blanche, the General Overseer conducted a Divine Healing service, which was also privately announced.

This Hall is a very beautiful and well-furnished little auditorium, seating about three hundred people, with a very convenient room for a prayer-room in the rear.

The General Overseer's teaching was the plain, straightforward, bold proclamation of the Truth of Divine Healing, strongly and lovingly setting forth the conditions upon which God has promised to heal His people, and the never-failing validity of His Covenant.

Among those present were Roman Catholics, members of denominational churches, and earnest seekers for truth outside of all church fellowship.

The great majority of them were deeply sincere in their promises to surrender wholly to God and to meet His conditions when God's prophet prayed with them, with the laying on of hands. Among them were people of noble birth.

Several received great blessing in answer to the prayer of faith.

Good Attendance and Deep Interest at Public Service in Paris.

That evening, at eight o'clock, in the same place, the General Overseer delivered an address on the subject "The Story of the Founding of Zion City."

This service had been announced only the day before and then only in very modest cards in three of the Paris dailies.

Notwithstanding this, there were 175 or 200 persons present, and a more intelligent, respectful, interested and earnest audience one could not wish.

What a refreshing contrast to Australia!

There were present members and friends of Zion, not only from Paris, but also from England and the United States.

The General Overseer's address consisted not only of a very graphic and vivid account of the founding of Zion City and the City as it is today, sparkling here and there with wit and humor, that was heartily appreciated, but also a very clear and unmistakable setting forth of the Truths of the Everlasting Gospel of the Kingdom of God upon which it had been founded.

It was strong meat, but it was very kindly received by all and very gladly and eagerly received by many.

A large number came forward to greet the General Overseer after the meeting; to thank him for the privilege of hearing him; and to wish him Godspeed.

Many also commended Mr. Rollier for the fluency and accuracy of his translation.

During the remainder of the time that we were in Paris, there were several callers each day at the Publishing House in Rue Mont Thabor who came to express their regret that they had failed to see the announcement of the meeting, as they would have considered it a very great privilege to attend.

It was clear that if there had been sufficient time to announce the meetings in Paris, the General Overseer could have spoken to thousands.

However, very deep interest was created, the seed has been sown, and God will bless.

The Kingdom of God must come in France as well as in every other land and nation of the world, and the Gospel of the Kingdom has now been proclaimed in its greatest city.

VISITATION IN ZURICH, SWITZERLAND.

On Thursday evening, May 19th, at twenty-five minutes of nine o'clock the General Overseer, Mr. Rollier and the writer left Paris for Zürich, Switzerland, and on the following day Overseer Jane Dowie, who was compelled to rest, was accompanied by her son to Fontainebleau, near Paris.

The next morning, at about four o'clock, we entered the charming little Republic of Switzerland, and, when the sun arose, we found ourselves riding through scenery which poets have been trying to describe for centuries, and which has never yet been adequately described. Hence, the present chronicler can only hope that all his readers may some day see it for themselves.

At about half past six o'clock we arrived at the city of Bale, where we took breakfast and enjoyed a short walk through the picturesque streets.

At half past seven o'clock we were again on our way, the railroad running for many miles along the banks of the Rhine, that river so famous in history, story and song—certainly a noble stream, worthy of all that has been said, written and sung about it.

At Baden, we were delighted to find that Elder Carl Hodler, Overseer J. G. Excell and Deacon Carl F. Stern had come down from Zürich to meet the General Overseer.

When we arrived at the Hauptbahnhof or Central Railway Station, it was with great pleasure that we met Evangelist Hodler, Evangelist Hertrich, Evangelist Clibborn, Deaconess Baliff, and several members of Zion in Zürich, and Deacon Williams and Deaconess Stern of our party.

The General Overseer was greeted with great love and respect by all, and there was not one single word or utterance or gesture on the part of any one at the station, which even suggested the impudent, malicious, lawless spirit that inspired the boohooing and jeering of the people at the docks and railway stations and in all the streets of Sydney, Melbourne and Adelaide, Australia.

Immediately on his arrival, the General Overseer was presented with a magnificent span of black and white horses, by Elder and Evangelist Hodler in honor of the approaching fifty-seventh anniversary of his birthday.

As he drove through the streets to the Grand Hotel Bellevue,

HOTEL BELLEVUE, ZÜRICH, SWITZERLAND, THE GENERAL OVERSEER'S RESIDENCE DURING ZÜRICH MISSION.

where he had remained during his stay in Zürich over three years ago, it was evident that there was the most intense interest throughout the city, but it was also evident that the interest was respectful.

At the Bellevue, the General Overseer and party were very cordially and kindly welcomed by the proprietor and his staff, who had by no means forgotten their guest.

Shortly after noon the General Overseer entertained, at a very pleasant luncheon, Elder Hodler, and his ecclesiastical and clerical staff, several members of the Christian Catholic Church in Zion from distant places, and the members of his Visitation Party. During this luncheon it was found that there were ten nations represented among the twenty persons at the table. After luncheon, we had opportunity to look around us upon

The Beauties of the City of Zürich.

This is the capital of the Canton of Zürich and the largest and most important town in Switzerland, having over one hundred fifty thousand inhabitants.

It lies at the north end of the Zürich See, and on both sides of the swiftly-flowing green Limmat.

It is a very busy manufacturing town; silk and cotton mills, machine works and iron foundries being the principal industries.

It is one of the oldest cities in Europe, its site having been occupied in prehistoric times.

For centuries Zürich has been the intellectual center of Switzerland, and from 1519 to 1531 it was the home of Zwingli, one of the greatest leaders of the Reformation.

The scenery in and about Zürich is of surpassing beauty.

With the beautiful pale green lake surrounded by villages, chateaux, orchards, and parks; with the river and its handsome architectural bridges, and the combination of the quaint old houses and splendid modern structures along its banks, which are of solid masonry throughout the length of the city; with the Uitleberg and other hills, from one thousand to one thousand eight hundred feet high, shutting it in on either side; with its myriads of handsome trees, which at this season of the year are in the fresh fulness and beauty of spring verdure; and with the white peaks of the Alps gleaming through the haze, far off to the south, Zürich presents a scene of rarest loveliness.

The city is as spotlessly clean, even in the narrowest streets, as if every nook and corner of it were scrubbed and polished daily, and the shops and homes of the people present the same immaculate appearance.

The People of Zürich.

The people of Zürich are the strongest, healthiest, cleanest and most intelligent looking, that we have met since we left the United States.

Their physiques are straight, their bearing dignified, their complexions clear and their eyes straightforward and honest.

Theirs is no degenerate race.

A Reception to Zion in Zürich and Continental Europe.

On Saturday evening, May 21st, at eight o'clock, the General Overseer gave a reception to the members and friends of the Christian Catholic Church in Zion in Zürich and continental Europe, in the Velodrome, a large hall which had been very tastefully prepared for the meetings of the Zürich Visitation.

This hall seats about two thousand five hundred people.

On this occasion, although there had been only one day's notice, privately given, there were fully four hundred people present.

While the people were waiting, music was furnished by the Brass Band of the Zurich Branch of the Christian Catholic Church in Zion, numbering twenty-five pieces, which occupied a place in the rear gallery.

This band, which has been playing only about six months, is neatly uniformed, and renders excellent music very creditably.

When the General Overseer and party entered, the entire congregation rose and returned the General Overseer's hearty

VIEW OF MILAN FROM MILAN CATHEDRAL.

"Peace to thee," very enthusiastically, in both German and English.

Speaking in German, Elder Hodler then said a few very kind words in introducing the General Overseer and his party.

The General Overseer responded briefly, expressing his gratitude to God for a safe journey thus far, for the loving greeting of His people in Zürich, and for the wonderful work which He had wrought there in so short a time.

Those present then filed by the General Overseer and the members of his party, giving each a hearty hand-shake as Elder Hodler introduced them, giving the name of the place from which they came.

It was found that almost every nation in Europe was represented.

After this reception, the General Overseer took his place on the platform, and the formal service began.

Elder Hodler filled the very difficult part of interpreter very ably, and the General Overseer's eyes, head, hands, arms, feet—indeed, his entire body entered into his delivery, so that the people easily caught the spirit of the address and responded throughout most enthusiastically.

It was a most auspicious opening of a most important Visitation.

Velodrome, Zürich, Switzerland, Saturday Evening, May 21, 1904.

*REPORTED BY E. W. AND A. W. N.

The Congregation joined in singing in German "We're Marching to Zion."

Elder Hodler read the 67th Psalm.

The General Overseer then said:

Concerning Zion's Officers in Zürich.

Before we go to prayer, I wish to say a word or two concerning the officers of the Church and friends of Zion who are sitting upon this platform.

I delight exceedingly to be among you, and I praise God who has taken care of me, and of my Visitation Party, since we left Zion City on the first day of this year.

In December, 1900, I came among you a stranger, and, at the end of three days' work in this beautiful city, I had the joy of baptizing seventy-two persons, who professed to receive blessing for their spirits, their souls, and many of them for their bodies.

Since that time more than eight hundred have been baptized, and it is largely due to Elder Hodler, and especially to dear Evangelist Hodler, that Zion has made such strides here.

It is true that I had published a very few copies of BLÄTTER DER HEILUNG; but it was only when Madam Marie Brieger, now Evangelist Hodler, became my translator and the assistant editor of that paper that it became the power which it has been for more than four years.

"One drop of ink makes millions think."

Every drop of ink on the pages of BLÄTTER DER HEILUNG has made people think.

Wherever I have gone, I have found those whom God has blessed by the salvation of their spirits, of their souls, and of their bodies through the words printed in LEAVES OF HEALING.

The German edition has been a wonderful blessing to the Germans in every land.

I must give my gratitude to God and to the lady who toiled night and day to give you the first copies of BLÄTTER DER HEILUNG. Her name is written in heaven, and thousands have been blessed by her toil on earth.

Evangelist Hertrich has been with me for nine years in Zion.

I could very ill spare her, one of the most devoted women of Zion.

It is wonderful what God has wrought by her.

Beloved little Deaconess Baliff has been a wonderful help, and a great blessing.

We have Elder Clibborn, who came and stole one of my Deaconesses, and I had to let her go.

Deaconess Mabel Barnard is now Evangelist Mabel Clibborn.

When you grow, in Zürich, to be so big that you will need to have a baby-house, put her at the head of it.

I desire to introduce also, Fräulein Ruth Hofer, whose mother was the first conductor of a Gathering in Zürich.

I formed it in the Bellevue Hotel in December, 1900.

These two have done wonderful work. May God bless them.

Then there is this exile, who was banished to Zion City for eighteen months, Elder Jean Kradolfer.

I sent him a cablegram just two weeks ago, and he started for Zurich the next day, and here he is now, very happy. After prayer by Elder Kradolfer, the General Overseer delivered his discourse, saying, in part:

GENERAL OVERSEER ADDRESSING AUDIENCE IN VELODRO[ME]

THE KINGDOM OF GOD.

INVOCATION.

Let the words of my mouth and the meditation of my heart be acceptable in Thy sight, and profitable unto this people, and unto all to whom these words shall come, for the sake of Jesus, our Lord, our Strength and our Redeemer. Amen.

Elder Hodler then read the following telegram from Berlin:

Telegram to the General Overseer from Zion in Berlin.

BERLIN, May 21, 1904.

REV. JOHN ALEX. DOWIE, 76 Bahnhofstrasse, Zürich.

Willkommen, wack'rer Gottesmann,
Im schönen deutschen Schweizerland.
Die Gnade Gottes sei mit Dir!
Sein heiliger Friede für und für!

ZION IN BERLIN, SAUER.

*The following address has not been revised by the General Overseer.

Translation of the above into English:

BERLIN, May 21, 1904.

REV. JOHN ALEX. DOWIE, 76 Bahnhofstrasse, Zurich.

Welcome thou brave God's man,
Into beautiful German Switzerland.
The Grace of God upon thee be!
His Holy Peace abide with thee.

ZION IN BERLIN, SAUER.

The General Overseer then said:

I thank the friends in Berlin, and many others who have sent me loving letters from all parts of Europe.

I am glad to know that, although it was given out only yesterday that I would hold this reception tonight, no less than four hundred members and friends of Zion are present.

It is a wonderful thing that God is gathering into Zion, people from all the lands, from all classes, of all colors, and all languages.

God is fulfilling His Word.

ZURICH, SWITZERLAND, LORD'S DAY AFTERNOON, MAY 22, 1904.

The Little One shall become a Thousand, and the Small One a Strong Nation.

Zion City an Object Lesson to the Whole World.

All the rulers of the world are beginning to wonder whereunto this will grow.

It is very clear that in all the history of the world there has not been another organization of this nature.

The rulers of the world are beginning to see that Zion has a solution for all the difficulties in Church, in Business, in Education, and in Politics.

We are Theocrats.

We believe in the Rule of God.

We have a little model City, where "God rules" and "man prospers."

I have been around your beautiful Zurich today, and have seen the beautiful houses where the people make beautiful gardens, and then put high walls around them so that no one can see the garden except from the inside.

We have not a fence or a wall in Zion City.

Each house is in the midst of its own little garden, and everything is open. We are busy; we are happy, and we sing and pray while we work.

We are growing in grace.

When we are done with our work, in all its varied departments, we go to our beautiful homes, where children grow up for God.

God is making Zion City an Object Lesson to the whole world.

I am glad that all over the world the Gospel of the Kingdom of God is being preached.

It is more than the Lutheran church; it is more than the Romanist church; it is more than the English church; it is more than the Greek church; it is more than all the churches; it is the Kingdom of God.

Scope of the Kingdom of God.

First of all, the Kingdom of God must be in your heart, and the kingdom of the Devil cast out.

Then the Kingdom of God must be in your home and in your business.

We say to our people, "Get out of everything that is evil.

"It does not matter how poor you may become, you will be rich toward God."

We find our people blessed.

It is wonderful what God has done for that little people!

My dear people who were poor and sick and sad are strong, healthy, wealthy and using their money and their time for God, not afraid to spend all for Him.

Zion lives for the whole world to win all to God.

Thanks be to God, you have seen how Zion grows!

I came here, with my dear wife, less than four years ago; there were very few Zion people here.

Now my officers report to me that they have baptized eight hundred, and the lands are being filled with the Gospel of the Kingdom.

God is preparing a wonderful harvest.

But the apostate churches and the world are very much afraid of the teaching.

God's Blessing Upon the Elijah Declaration.

They say that Dr. Dowie has greatly erred in the Elijah Declaration.

Nevertheless, from the moment of that Declaration Zion sprang into a new life. Every year since then we have very greatly increased our membership, until we have tens of thousands.

Even in Germany they are afraid of Elijah, and have put two or three of my tracts upon the censor's list.

I want to know why the Kaiser is afraid of Elijah the Restorer?

Whether he likes it or whether he does not, Zion will fill Germany.

Zion will fill the world, for Zion is the Kingdom of God.

My Message is to kings and to presidents and to rulers.

The Devil is trying to keep me from delivering that Message.

The Possible Final Conversion of the Devil.

I am not afraid of the Devil.

Sometimes I think what a splendid thing it would be to get the Devil converted.

You think it is impossible?

He once was good.

Was he not once in heaven?

He fell. He must be very unhappy.

Perhaps the Devil can be saved some day.

First, however, we must defeat him.

First we must whip him on earth—drive him out of Zurich, out of Switzerland, out of Germany and out of your hearts, back to hell; bind him there for a thousand years, and then go down and fight the battle out there.

Death and Hell will be cast into the Lake of Fire.

I do not teach that hell will exist forever.

Did not Jesus go down to hell?

He descended into hell and preached to the spirits in prison.

If I am good enongh He may send me to hell to fight it out with the Devil there.

I should like to have the job.

Meanwhile I have the job of cleaning out hell here.

May hell be cleaned out of our hearts, out of our cities, and out of the world.

I thank God that, "as in Adam all die; so also in the Christ shall all be made alive."

Oh, the riches of God! the depths of His riches!

A Heavenly Restoration Host in Hell.

He has "shut up all unto disobedience, that He might have mercy upon all."

Perhaps some of us have dear ones who have gone to hell.

Do we not want them out of hell?

Mother! when you get to heaven, will you ever be perfectly happy when you know that your son is in hell?

Will you not be glad to see the day in heaven when the Restoration Host files through the Gates of the City, and millions go down to hell, to take the captives from the Devil, and bring them to God?

I believe in that.

Many will go to hell.

They cannot go to heaven, but by-and-by, when "He hath put all enemies under His feet," when Death and Hell have passed away and the great Lord delivers up the Kingdom to the Father, and "God shall be all and in all," then there will be no more hell.

Now we have to fight, and then we shall win.

The Master, the Lamb of God, who came to save all men, who said, "I, if I be lifted up from the earth, will draw all men unto Myself," will never be satisfied until He has drawn the last sinner to His heart.

I do not believe that I shall be satisfied until then; for I cannot rest now; I cannot give God any rest.

I have to remind Him of His Promises.

I must work, for the world is so full of Sin and Sorrow, War and Bloodshed, Tears and Groans and Sicknesses that I must work until He comes who wipes away every tear, and who will bring the last wandering sheep from the most remote wilderness, back to God.

Brothers, sisters, help me to extend the Kingdom of God until other kingdoms pass away, and we come back with Jesus and establish His Kingdom.

We are beginning to do it now.

This is the Time of the Restoration of All Things. It has begun.

Will you not get into line with me, and go forward to win men to God?

Meanwhile let us gather the people into cities where we can work together, and earn our bread, and earn a little bread for the people who have no bread, and make the people of the world to see how beautiful, how good the Zion of God is until they all want it.

Zion is reaching the thrones of Empires.

May Zion reach the beloved Kaiser, make him mighty for God, and a great war lord for the Kingdom of God.

May God grant it!

God bless beautiful Switzerland!

When I come here, and see that the snows of winter are melting on the Alps, and that the rivers are full of water, I look to the Eternal Hills beyond the skies, and say, "Father, all our sources are in Thee. All our springs are in Thee. Let Thy love send down the water. Oh make Switzerland a place where the waters shall flow to all Europe, and to all the world!"

May God bless you!

All pray.

PRAYER OF CONSECRATION.

My God and Father, in Jesus' Name I come to Thee. Take me as I am and make me what I ought to be, in spirit, soul, and body. Help me to do right and to give up all wrong; if I have wronged any to confess, to my fellow man; to restore whatever it may be I have taken wrongfully. For Jesus' sake help me to confess to Thee, my Father. Take away my sin. Give me power to trust Thee. Heal me. Cleanse me. Keep me. Help me. May tomorrow be a day of Pentecost to me. For Jesus' sake give Thy servant Power and Wisdom and Love, that Thy Kingdom may come, and Thy will be done in all our hearts, in all our homes, in all Switzerland, and in all the world. For Jesus' sake. Amen. [*All standing repeat the prayer, clause by clause, after the General Overseer.*]

BENEDICTION.

Beloved, abstain from all appearance of evil. And may the very God of Peace Himself sanctify you wholly; and I pray God your whole spirit and soul and body be preserved entire, without blame, unto the coming of our Lord Jesus, the Christ. Faithful is He that calleth you, who also will do it. The grace of our Lord Jesus, the Christ, the love of God, our Father, the fellowship of the Holy Spirit, our Comforter and Guide, one Eternal God, abide in you, bless you and keep you, and all the Israel of God everywhere, forever. Amen.

FROM MARSEILLES TO ZURICH.

BY DEACONESS IDA M. STERN

On arrival of the Royal Mail Steamship Mongolia at Marseilles, France, the Around-the-World Visitation Party separated, the General Overseer, Overseer Jane Dowie, Dr. A. J. Gladstone Dowie, and Deacon Arthur W. Newcomb going to Cannes, on the Riviera, and the other members of the party going to Zurich, Switzerland.

We left Marseilles at a quarter after six o'clock in the afternoon and went as far as Nice on the Paris-Lyon-Mediterraneé Railway, keeping close to the shores of the beautiful Mediterranean Sea all the way.

A railroad accident occurred at Saint Marcel, not far from Marseilles, which delayed us for over an hour.

Soon after, the night came on, and we were unable to see the many valleys and hills, rivers, glimpses of the sea, and picturesque cities and villages, which would otherwise have been visible from the car-windows on this trip.

We reached Nice about midnight, and were pleased to go at once to a hotel and find rest for the remainder of the night.

We arranged to have Elder Percy Clibborn with us, and found him an excellent guide and companion.

Nice.

Nice is a typical Old World city. It has a population of over eighty-eight thousand, and is built at the foot of a magnificent amphitheater of mountains, in the valleys and on the lower hills of the Maritime Alps, along the shores of the bright blue waters of the Mediterranean Sea.

It is one of the many delightful cities in the south of France to which the people from the north of Europe flock during the cold winter seasons.

It being situated in a niche sheltered by the mountains, and tempered by the Mediterranean Sea, the climate is mild even in midwinter.

It was at one time a favorite resort of the late Queen Victoria, of England.

We were delighted with the fragrance of the roses and other varieties of flowers, and the tasteful arrangement of them everywhere, so that even the most crude fence or rock seemed a beautiful picture.

We went together to the Terrace of the Chateau, from which point we were able to study the topography of the city, and were afforded a most magnificent view of the city, the sea, and the Alps in the distance, lifting their snowy peaks up into the very clouds.

Monte Carlo and Monaco.

From Nice we went to Monte Carlo, that most famous gambling resort of the world, where we spent only a few hours between trains, driving about the city, and to the palace of the Prince of Monaco, where we were delighted with the beautiful view of the city and its harbor, and the artistic arrangement of it all.

But our hearts were saddened as we lingered for a moment upon the thought that all that we saw was beautified from the revenues gained by the operations of the Casino, and we were relieved when we were again on our way out of this wicked place.

At Vintimiglia, on the Italian frontier, we had to change cars and have our baggage passed through the Italian customs.

After a short interval here, we boarded an Italian train.

Everywhere we saw Italian notices, etc., and passed our time very profitably in trying to puzzle out the meaning of these notices, and in looking at the Italian scenery.

There were pretty little villages in the hills, each clustered around a central cathedral or church; fertile valleys, and here and there, far below us, a rippling rivulet.

On the other side were ever the shores and the waters of the Mediterranean.

We had dinner on board the train, and arrived at Genoa (Genova) Italy, about half past ten o'clock p. m.

We went immediately to a hotel near the railway station and retired.

Genoa, Italy.

We rose early on the following morning, and were delighted to find the sunbeams streaming in at the open windows, and the soft, mild air bathing our faces.

After we had partaken of an Italian breakfast, composed of rolls, honey and coffee, which is the usual breakfast on the Continent, we took carriages and drove to the Cathedral of Saint John the Baptist.

Tradition says that here, in a marble tomb and casket, lie the bones and ashes of St. John the Baptist.

Our little party entered here while mass was being said, and a guide directed us to the tomb, which is in a little enclosure well towards the front on the left-hand side.

The gentlemen of our party entered, and the writer, as usual, followed.

But very soon a wild-eyed Italian worshiper came towards her, with many gestures and with excited talk, violently motioning to the gate.

It was learned, upon appeal to Elder Clibborn, that women are not permitted to enter the sacred place of the tomb, because it was a woman who caused the death of John the Baptist.

Of course, we quietly retired.

Any woman entering here is at once excommunicated from the church.

Here they also claim to have the chain with which John the Baptist was bound in the dungeons of the Castle of Machærus, and all the gentlemen were permitted to look at it closely and to touch it.

From here we drove about Genoa for a time, and then went to the other side of the city to the Genoa Cemetery.

This is one of the most beautiful and costly cemeteries in the world.

There are long lines of exquisite marble corridors containing the bodies of the dead, and handsome mythical and allegorical statues on either side.

The outer courts, which are reserved for the burial of the poorer classes, are full of the rarest and most beautiful roses and other flowers—roses especially—making it rich in appearance and very fragrant and refreshing.

Beyond these corridors are the handsome, beautifully carved tombs of the rich, built of the finest Italian marble, which tower above these other tombs and square corridors, being arranged on the sides of the hills beyond.

An interesting and intelligent guide directed us through numerous corridors into the mortuary chapel, a magnificent, dome-shaped sanctuary, of pure Italian marble, having an altar in the center, and in its walls numerous representations of important Biblical characters chiseled in marble.

The acoustics in this little place were most wonderful.

We had just time for luncheon at a restaurant on the summit of one of the hills, and for a little drive in the ancient part of the city and along the harbor, before leaving on the afternoon train.

Milan.

Here we left the Mediterranean Sea, and took an inland course to the ancient city of Milan, in northern Italy.

This is the capital of Lombardy, and one of the wealthiest manufacturing towns in Italy, having a population of about five hundred thousand.

We arrived here in good time for dinner, and after dinner went out to see some of the lofty arcades, handsomely frescoed, that are so numerous in large Italian cities.

On the following morning we went at once to the famous Cathedral of Milan, taking all our cameras with us.

This magnificent Cathedral is of Gothic construction and is one of the largest churches in Europe, built entirely of pure white marble, and adorned with ninety-eight turrets and two thousand statues.

It was begun in 1386, by Giangaleazzo Visconti, and continued with many interruptions until the end of the sixteenth century.

Its cost was over one hundred million dollars.

The interior, with its double aisles, flanked by fifty-two pillars, is very impressive, owing to the way in which the light falls through the richly-colored windows, which are representations of Biblical history, and tell many stories of the early Christians.

The two large windows immediately behind the altar tell the whole story of the Bible in picture, from Genesis to Revelation.

From the roof of this wonderful Cathedral we were able to get a beautiful view of the city of Milan, and of many little villages under the Appenine Alps.

The old city of Milan is surrounded by a wall over two hundred fifty feet wide, which was once used as a fortification, and now forming a beautiful boulevard, with large trees on either side.

Late in the afternoon, after seeing other points of interest in the city, we continued our journey.

Over the Plains of Lombardy and the Alps via the Saint Gothard Railway.

For some time we sped rapidly over the plains of Lombardy, and soon, in the distance, we could see the towering snow-covered peaks of the Alps.

The scenery became more and more beautiful, as we again entered the mountainous regions near Como, on the beautiful little inland Italian lake of the same name.

This lake is situated at the foot of rocky heights, dotted with villages and villas.

The express stopped here only long enough to take on and let off passengers, and we were again wending our way through mountainous scenery until we reached Chiasso, the Swiss frontier, where we had to change cars, and again get our baggage passed through the custom-house.

Lugano, Switzerland.

At about six o'clock in the afternoon we reached Lugano, the most important town in Italian Switzerland, which is situated on the bank of the extensive and picturesque Lake Lugano, in the very heart of incomparable landscape, and in a semicircular bay, which affords to the eye a scene of indescribable loveliness.

We had a very restful night in this quiet little city, and awakened early the following morning.

On every side we heard the rushing of waterfalls and the songs of the birds. The sweet, fresh air and aroma of rare flowers entered into our very spirits.

Immediately after breakfast we went out, unwilling to lose a moment when we might be feasting our eyes upon scenery more beautiful than ever the noblest and best painters have painted, more charming than the purest and most enchanted poetry.

In it we saw the riches of the glory of God, and our hearts were filled with praise to Him for the many beauties which He had permitted us, by His goodness, to see.

Here we separated from one member of our party, Deacon Ernest Williams, who could not be persuaded to leave as early as we had arranged to go, but remained behind another day to make pictures, and to visit Lucerne before coming to Zürich.

Through the Saint Gothard Tunnel.

We came on by the Saint Gothard express at eleven o'clock, a. m., having still before us the journey over the highest part of the Alps, Zürich lying on the other side.

This great international artery, the Saint Gothard Railway, is a wonderful piece of engineering, traversing the snow-peaks, dividing Central Europe from Northern Italy, piercing mountains, spanning chasms, bridging torrents, scaling heights—in its entirety, it is one of the greatest engineering triumphs of modern times.

There are innumerable spiral tunnels, and the great Saint Gothard Tunnel, from Goeschenen to Ariolo, is no less than nine miles long.

It took the train by which we came to Zürich exactly sixteen minutes to pass through it.

We felt that the scenery on the Italian side of the Alps was indescribably sublime, but when we came out of the Saint

Gothard Tunnel—the highest point which we reached—we opened our eyes to new grandeurs.

We felt it quite cold here, and found that we were above the snow-line of the Alps, and in the very clouds.

We were borne on over gorges, waterfalls, snowpeaks, wild ravines, peaceful, populous, fertile valleys, slumbering beneath the giant ranges, lakes of azure blue, fringed with clustered villages, wonderfully green verdure and rich vineyards, until at last Elder Clibborn said to us, "There you see the Zürich See, and at the end of it the city of Zürich."

This announcement was received with joy, and all attention was directed toward the beautiful little city.

A few minutes before we arrived in Zürich proper, we were met by Elder Carl Hodler, whom many of us had not seen for a long time, and we were delighted to meet him.

Arrival in Zürich.

Soon we were in the main railway station, called the Hauptbahnhof, and were met by Mrs. Percy Clibborn, Evangelist Hertrich, and several members and friends of Zion. It gave us very great joy to see these earnest colaborers in the Lord, and to be with them.

Overseer Excell and Deacon Williams, who arrived on the following evening, were entertained at the home of Elder Hodler, and the other two members of the party were taken to Zion Headquarters in Zürich, where a substantial dinner was prepared for all the party.

We were tendered a reception by Zion Band and officers at eight o'clock, with greetings and offerings of thanks to God for a safe journey.

The next morning, Thursday, May 12th, was Ascension Day—a public Holiday in Zürich—and services were held in all the churches.

Accordingly Zion in Zürich had arranged for two meetings.

All the members of the party then in Zürich attended the meetings in the new hall occupied by the Christian Catholic Church in Zion in Zürich for services, and upon request of Elder Hodler, gave very brief talks.

POST CARD SENT FROM SWITZERLAND BY THE GENERAL OVERSEER.

Visits in Vicinity of Zurich.

On Friday, Overseer Excell, Deacon Stern and the writer departed for Kreutzlingen, Schloss Liebburg, by a late afternoon train, and arrived there at about half past eight o'clock in the evening.

Our course was along the banks of the famous Rhine, via Schaffhausen and Stein am Rhein.

From the railway carriage window, not far from Stein am Rhein, we were delighted to see the wonderful Rhine Falls—the largest falls in Europe—and the beautiful scenery and great vineyards along its banks.

For some time we kept close to the shores of the Unter See before we reached Kreutzlingen.

We had some opportunities of making known the truths of God as they are preached in Zion to some of our fellow passengers, who apparently became very much interested.

At Castle Liebburg.

We were met at the railway station at Kreutzlingen by the coachman from Castle Liebburg, who had been sent down by Mrs. Hofer, and in about an hour we arrived at the Schloss, and were greeted by this dear sister in the Christ, and very hospitably entertained.

While here, Overseer Excell conducted a Divine Healing service and a Baptismal service, baptizing eight believers. He remained until Monday morning, when he went to the Rhine Falls to take pictures, and Deacon Stern and the writer remained only until the following morning, Saturday.

We visited Constance (Konstanz) on the beautiful Boden See—Lake of Constance—which is one of the largest lakes of Central Europe. The landscape is peculiarly charming, with its variety of scenery, its picturesque ruins, and the quaint, ancient houses, which dot the shore of the lake.

Constance is an old town, rich in history, having over twenty thousand inhabitants. It was the dwelling-place of the martyr, Huss, who was burned to death there.

We came on by an afternoon train, and arrived in Zürich again about half past seven o'clock.

The following day (Lord's Day) Deacons Stern and Williams accompanied one of the workers at Headquarters in Zürich to Herisau and St. Gall, two little villages in the vicinity of Zürich, and attended the meetings of the Branch of the Christian Catholic Church in Zion in each of these places.

The writer accompanied Evangelist Hertrich to Horgen and Thalweil, two delightfully pretty little villages on the banks of the Zürich See, where meetings were held.

In Horgen, Evangelist Hertrich consecrated one little infant to God at the close of the service.

The rest of the time in Zürich was spent principally in perfecting arrangements for the General Overseer's coming, a few days later. The Uitleberg and Rhine Falls, however, were visited by members of the party.

The Uitleberg is the finest and most interesting point in the neighborhood of Zürich.

It lies two thousand eight hundred eighty-seven feet above the level of the sea, and is reached without difficulty in one-half hour by rail from Zürich.

It commands a wonderful panorama of Zürich and its environments, the Rigi, and the Alps.

The General Overseer arrived on Friday morning, May 20th, and on Lord's Day, May 22d, was the first day of the Visitation.

VISITATION IN ZURICH, SWITZERLAND.

Lord's Day Morning Meeting.

Lord's Day morning, Pentecost, dawned clear and bright, God having sent what is well-known in Zion City as "General Overseer's weather" for the beginning of the regular meetings of the Visitation in Zürich.

Zürich is a great city for churches, and a great place for church-bells, many of the spires having very large and beautiful chimes.

On this Pentecostal morning, these were filling the air with deep-toned music; but the greatest throngs seemed to be going in the direction of the Velodrome, where the General Overseer was to speak.

As he drove to the place, he received most respectful greetings from great numbers along the streets, hundreds of men whom he had never seen before raising their hats to him.

At the building, there was a large concourse of people waiting outside to see the carriage drive up and to greet the General Overseer, among them the Zürich Zion Band, serving as a guard of honor.

The greeting which the General Overseer received was full of love on the part of Zion people and respectful on the part of all—in marked contrast to the chorus of impudent "boohoos" which came from Australian crowds that gathered on similar occasions.

The contrast is severe on Australia, but it is some comfort to remember that there are large numbers of good people in that unfortunate land, who very sincerely deprecate the lawless behavior of their fellow citizens.

The Velodrome, on this occasion, was filled to overflowing, many people standing outside, unable to find suitable seats within.

In his Message on this Lord's Day morning, and throughout the Visitation, the General Overseer gave the straightforward teaching of the Gospel of the Kingdom of God, which is so well known to all members of the Christian Catholic Church in Zion and to readers of LEAVES OF HEALING.

Although the truths have been so often repeated by him, they always come to his hearers with a newness and freshness and spiritual power that makes them oftentimes more effective the last time one hears them than the first.

Many of these truths have been published again and again in LEAVES OF HEALING, but the paper never loses its intense interest to its thousands of readers, nor its mighty power in the transformation of men's lives; for these Truths are the Truths of the Everlasting Gospel of the Kingdom of God and they do not grow old nor stale.

The Spirit of God is in them.

The Message on this Lord's Day morning was a great blessing to us, who had so often heard the General Overseer speak on the same subject, and it was received by the audience with an earnestness and sincerity of conviction that told of great blessings to flow from the Father at this Visitation.

Notwithstanding many severe things that God's Prophet had to say, the hearers received them in the same spirit of love in which they were given, and there was not a moment's interruption or disorder.

We regret that lack of space forbids our giving the reports of these Messages in full.

The music by the Band and the singing were full of the spirit of praise, and did our hearts good. Although the singing was in the German tongue, it had the same Zion spirit in it that characterizes the singing in English in the Zion meetings at home.

Zion is one the world over.

Elder Carl Hodler interpreted for the General Overseer at this meeting.

Velodrome, Zürich, Switzerland, Lord's Day Morning, May 22, 1904.
*REPORTED BY E. W. AND A. W. N.

The Service was opened by the General Overseer's pronouncing the

INVOCATION.

God be merciful unto us, and bless us,
And cause Thy face to shine upon us;
That Thy Way may be known upon earth,
Thy Saving Health among All Nations;
For the sake of Jesus. Amen.

After the singing of a hymn, Elder Kradolfer read the 24th chapter of Luke, from the 36th to the 53d verse; also the 1st

POST CARD FROM SWITZERLAND SENT BY DEACON ARTHUR W. NEWCOMB.

chapter of the Acts of the Apostles, the first fourteen verses.

Prayer was offered by Elder Carl Hodler, after which Hymn No. 20, was sung.

Gott, man lobt Dich in der Stille zu Zion!

Kommt, die ihr liebt den Herrn,
Laßt eure Freude seh'n
Laßt Gottes Volk von nah und fern
Mit uns nach Zion geh'n.

Wer unsern Gott nicht kennt,
Der mag ja stille sein;
Doch wer sich ein Kind Gottes nennt,
Der stimme mit uns ein.

Von ferne winkt uns schon
Der Glanz von Zions Höh'n,
Die Herrlichkeit von Gottes Thron,
Der Sieger Lobgetön.

Drum stimmt ein Loblied an,
Vergesset allen Schmerz;
Wir wandeln auf der Siegesbahn
Nach Zion himmelwärts.

TRANSLATION.

Come, ye who love the Lord,
And let our joys be known;
Join in a song of sweet accord,
And thus surround the Throne.

*The following report has not been revised by the General Overseer.

Let those refuse to sing
Who never knew our God;
But children of the heavenly King
Should speak their joys abroad.

The hill of Zion yields
A thousand sacred sweets
Before we reach the heavenly fields,
Or walk the golden streets.

Then let our songs abound
And every tear be dry;
We're marching through Emmanuel's ground
To fairer worlds on high.

After the tithes and offerings had been received, the General Overseer delivered his Message, saying, in part:

"IT IS NOT FOR YOU TO KNOW TIMES OR SEASONS."

INVOCATION.

Let the words of my mouth, and the meditations of my heart, be acceptable in Thy sight, and profitable unto this people and unto all to whom these words shall come, in this and every land, in this and all the coming time, Till Jesus Come. Amen.

TEXT.

And He said unto them, It is not for you to know times or seasons, which the Father hath set within His own Authority.

But ye shall receive power, when the Holy Spirit is come upon you: and ye shall be My witnesses both in Jerusalem and in all Judæa and Samaria, and unto the uttermost part of the earth.

It is not for you to know.

The glory of God is to conceal a matter; not only to reveal but to conceal; to hide it so deeply that not the angels in heaven, not the Son of God Himself, but only the Father in Heaven shall know. Jesus said that.

Wonderful it is to think that the Son of God Himself did not know, but the Father only.

I believe in the Triunity of God, but I believe and teach

The Supremacy of the Father.

Jesus said, "My Father is greater than I." "My Father is greater than all."

He taught us to pray not to Him, not to the Holy Spirit, but to the Father.

When He Himself prayed, He prayed to the Father.

He prays to the Father still.

He is the Advocate with the Father, Jesus, the Christ, the Righteous, the One Mediator between God and man, the Man Christ Jesus.

Oh, what a word is Father!

Do not pray to Jesus.

Do not pray to the Holy Spirit.

Do what Jesus tells you.

Pray to the Father, and when you pray say, "Father," and God will stop the stars in their courses rather than let you go unblessed.

We Have Two Intercessors, Two Mediators.

We have the Mediator with God, Jesus.

We have the Mediator within our own spirits, the Holy Spirit, who maketh intercession with our spirits, who teaches us how to pray, and who pleads with us for God.

"It is not for you to know," Jesus said, "Times or Seasons."

They wanted to know when the Kingdom would come.

Oh, how good it is for us to be willing not to know!

If we always knew the sorrow that awaited us, we could not live because of the shadow of that coming sorrow.

It was better for me not to know that our beloved daughter would part from us strong and well, and that we should look upon her dying body in a few hours.

It is always better to trust the Father, to go on doing your duty, walking with God, not seeking to know.

One step I see before me,
'Tis all I need to see.
The Light of Heaven more brightly shines
As earth's illusions flee.
And sweetly through the silence comes
His loving "Follow Me."

So on I go not knowing;
I would not if I might;
I'd rather walk in the dark with God
Than go alone in the light.
I'd rather walk by faith with Him,
Than go alone by sight.

"It is not for you to know."

He told the apostles that. He tells us that.

Go on.

Do your duty.

Be martyrs.

Lay down your lives for the Christ.

You must do your work and pass on.

The Kingdom will come.

The King will come again, and all the kingdoms of this earth shall become the kingdoms of our God and of His Christ.

What does it matter when it comes?

I Believe that the Kingdom of God Is Very Near at Hand.

I see the Signs of the Times.

I feel within my spirit that God has called me to be the preacher of the Restoration of All Things to all Nations, to prepare the people of God for the Coming of the King.

He is coming.

Before the Great and Terrible Day of Jehovah comes, He sends His Messenger to turn the hearts of the children to the fathers, and the fathers to the children, and all to God; for He does not want to come with a curse but with a blessing.

The heavens received Him, and His apostles had to go on and see Him no more until they had died for Him.

They knew not how to walk.

They were without Power.

While He was with them, they were strong, for He loved them, and the Power of the Most High was with them and the unerring Wisdom of God was with them; but He had gone.

Spiritual Dynamite.

Yes, but He said, "Ye shall receive Power," *dunamis* (δύναμις).

The Greek word for power is the same word from which we derive the word dynamite.

His meaning was, "I will put in your hands a Spiritual Dynamite, and you shall put it under the altars of the heathen gods, and they will go up and the false priests will flee."

He gives us dynamite, still.

The people say, "Doctor Dowie does not come to us with butter and honey. He does not come with eau de Cologne, but he comes with a stick of dynamite." [Laughter.]

I think it is time that we should use dynamite.

The false churches do not want dynamite. They say, "Do not put dynamite under our baptistry.

"Do not tell us that our baptism is of no value.

"Do not tell us that a little water on a baby's nose cannot change his heart."

God help us to use the dynamite; not to destroy good, but to destroy evil.

These apostles were very feeble men. They were poor fishermen. One of them was an honest tax-gatherer.

If you can find an honest tax-gatherer make him an apostle. A rare thing is an honest tax-gatherer.

Matthew was an honest tax-gatherer; therefore, Jesus made him an apostle.

The apostles, however, were mostly fishermen.

One of them came from the ranks of the rabbis, and another, Barnabas, came from the ranks of the rich, but it was later.

The first apostles were very humble men, and could have done nothing had they not used Spiritual Dynamite.

Peter had dynamite on the Day of Pentecost, when the Holy Spirit came upon them.

Then the poor coward, Peter, became brave.

He told them that they were murderers; that they had killed the Prince of Life, and had desired a murderer to be granted unto them.

He put in the dynamite, and it exploded in their hearts.

They cried out, "Brethren what must we do?"

God, who gives the dynamite, also gives the power to comfort, to lead, and to guide.

Peter said, "Repent ye, and be baptized every one of you in the Name of Jesus, the Christ, for the remission of your sins; and ye shall receive the Gift of the Holy Spirit."

Purity.

The Holy Spirit teaches you that you must put away uncleanness, no matter what it is.

There must be no impurity, no vice, no foolishness, but Joy, Peace, Purity, Heavenly Love, Wisdom, Kindness, Justice, and Sympathy to lift up your fellow men to God.

The Holy Spirit came and made these fishermen mighty men.

Humanity is crying out for help.

Do something.

Talk less; write less; do more.

Visit the widows and the fatherless.

They have the shadow of death; bring them the Light of Life.

Bring them bread.

Make the widow's heart sing for joy.

See that the children get bread, and clothing, and education.

Do something.

Lead men into a better place, where they can get power, and be a blessing; lead them into communion with God.

Our only purpose is to glorify God, and to help our fellow men that they may find God in their hearts, in their homes, in business, in the state, and in the whole world.

The Kingdom of God is at hand. Repent!

The Holy Spirit is speaking today!

May He come in power upon Zürich!

Repent!

Be Baptized!

Believe the Gospel!

All who desire to be right with God, stand with me, and tell Him so. [Apparently all rose.]

Now pray with me as I pray.

PRAYER OF CONSECRATION.

My God and Father, in Jesus' Name I come to Thee. Take me as I am. Make me what I ought to be for the sake of Jesus, the Lamb of God, who taketh away the sin of the world. Take away my sin. Cleanse my heart. Give me Thy Holy Spirit that I may truly repent. If I have wronged any man may I confess and restore, no matter what it costs; may I confess to Thee, and repent of my sin against Thee. Father, I have sinned against heaven, and in Thy sight. Forgive me. Make me Thy son. Give me Thy Spirit that I may follow Jesus, and do Thy Will, and be a blessing. I believe that Thou dost hear. By Thy Spirit bless me. For Jesus' sake. Amen. [*All repeat the prayer, clause by clause, after the General Overseer.*]

The Congregation then joined in singing the following *Gnade*, or Grace:

Die Gnade unsers Herrn Jesu Christi,
Und die Liebe Gottes,
Und die Gemeinschaft des heiligen Geistes,
Sei mit uns allen. Amen.

The translation of this old Grace is:

The grace of our Lord Jesus, the Christ,
And the Love of God,
And the Fellowship of the Holy Spirit,
Be with us all. Amen.

The meeting was then closed by the General Overseer's pronouncing the

BENEDICTION.

Beloved, abstain from all appearance of evil. And may the very God of peace Himself sanctify you wholly; and I pray God your whole spirit and soul and body be preserved entire, without blame, unto the coming of our Lord Jesus, the Christ. Faithful is He that calleth you, who also will do it. The grace of our Lord Jesus, the Christ, the love of God our Father, the fellowship of the Holy Spirit, our Comforter and Guide, one Eternal God, abide in you, bless you and keep you, and all the Israel of God everywhere, forever. Amen.

Lord's Day Afternoon Meeting.

The crowds at the Velodrome, long before three o'clock, the hour announced for the afternoon service, were even larger than those which had gathered in the morning, but there was the same tone and atmosphere of respect throughout.

The same spirit of honest seeking for the Truth of God, and of agreement with the teaching as it was proved from the Word of God, that had made the morning meeting such a blessing, was present in the gathering of the afternoon.

God gave His Prophet utterance with power, was with Elder Hodler in the interpretation, and applied the spoken Word to the hearts of the people.

It was a Service to be remembered, and we all praised God for it.

While the people were gathering, Zion Band rendered several splendid selections.

The General Overseer and ordained officers present were in the robes of their office, Colonel Stern and Staff-captain Newcomb of Zion Guard appearing in uniform.

When the General Overseer came upon the platform, the people rose, and stood reverently while he pronounced the

INVOCATION.

God, be merciful unto us and bless us,
And cause Thy face to shine upon us;
That Thy Way may be known upon earth,
Thy saving health among all the Nations;
For the sake of Jesus. Amen.

A hymn was sung in German, followed by the reading of the 35th chapter of Isaiah and the first nineteen verses of the 11th chapter of the Gospel according to St. Matthew, by Elder Jean Kradolfer.

Prayer was then offered by Elder Hodler, the General Overseer following with prayer for the sick and the sorrowing, requests from whom had been received in great numbers from all over Europe. The season of prayer closed with the Disciples' Prayer, in which the General Overseer led.

While the tithes and offerings were being received, a hymn was sung.

The General Overseer, after the usual Invocation, took his text from Matthew, the 11th chapter, and the 19th verse.

TEXT.

The Son of Man came eating and drinking, and they say, Behold a gluttonous man, and a wine-bibber, a friend of publicans and sinners! And wisdom is justified by her works.

In his Message, he showed how Jesus' answer to John the Baptist's question would show the captive Prophet that Jesus' ministry was in fulfilment of the prophecy in the 35th chapter of Isaiah, and that He was therefore "He that should come."

He also took occasion to give some very helpful teaching on the value and need of Wisdom—the Principal Thing—on the place of Purity in the House of Wisdom, and on the sinfulness and filthiness of eating swine's flesh.

He closed with a declaration that the work which the Christ did then, He was still doing, according to His promise, saying that there was no use in preaching a Gospel that only had power 1900 years ago; that he came to preach a Living Gospel, suited to the needs of the Twentieth Century, and efficient in bringing to the people the same blessings promised in that Song of Salvation, Healing, Holy Living, and Triumphant Entry into the Zion above—the 35th chapter of the book of the Prophet Isaiah.

His call to Repentance, Confession and Consecration brought apparently the whole congregation to their feet, with the earnest words of the Prayer of Consecration on their lips and in their hearts.

After the singing of the Grace, the meeting was closed by the General Overseer with the Benediction.

At the close of this Service, the General Overseer found the Zürich Zion Band waiting in double line to escort him to his carriage, which stood surrounded by a great throng of people.

There was a hearty "Peace to thee be multiplied," in good English in response to the General Overseer's salutation, and a general lifting of hats as he entered the carriage.

As he drove away, instead of unthinking jeers from those whom he had never harmed, such as he had been given in Australia, the General Overseer heard a hearty German "*Friede sei mit Ihnen*," (Peace to thee) and people ran after the carriage to give him flowers.

Along the streets there was the same interest and respect that we had seen in the morning.

Our hearts were full of thanksgiving to God.

Lord's Day Evening Service.

At eight o'clock the evening Service began.

It seemed to us that these meetings were already growing in power and blessing.

Once more the hall was filled to overflowing with an audience that heard the Message with an evident spirit of prayerful earnestness.

The General Overseer was in the Spirit, and his Message was a great blessing.

God was making it manifest that a great Baptism of the Holy Spirit would come upon the Zürich Visitation.

Velodrome, Zürich, Switzerland, Lord's Day Evening, May 22, 1904.

*REPORTED BY E. W. AND A. W. N.

The Service was opened with the Invocation by the General Overseer, after which Hymn No. 10 was sung.

The first fifteen verses of the 1st chapter of Mark were read by Elder Kradolfer.

The General Overseer said:

*The following report has not been revised by the General Overseer.

I give thanks to God tonight for the very beautiful day that we have had, and the very successful opening of the first meetings of the Visitation in Zürich.

I am delighted to meet the old friends whom I saw in my first visit when I was a stranger, and who so kindly received me.

Then I baptized seventy-two at the end of three days' Mission, and about eight hundred have been baptized since.

I trust to have the joy of seeing very large additions to our number during this Visitation.

I am grateful for all the good that has been done by the devoted people who have gathered around the banner of Zion.

Prayer was offered by Elder Hodler, also by the General Overseer.

During the singing of Hymn No. 11 the tithes and offerings were received, following which a solo was sung by Mrs. Jean Kradolfer, the people receiving much blessing from her deeply spiritual rendering of the beautiful words and music.

The General Overseer then said in part:

THE BEGINNING OF THE GOSPEL.

INVOCATION.

Let the words of my mouth, and the meditation of my heart be acceptable in Thy sight, be profitable unto this people, and unto all to whom these words shall come, in this and every land, in this and all the coming time, Till Jesus Come.

TEXT.

The beginning of the Gospel of Jesus, the Christ, the Son of God.
Even as it is written in Isaiah the prophet,
Behold, I send My Messenger before Thy face,
Who shall prepare Thy Way;
The Voice of one crying in the wilderness,
Make ye ready the Way of the Lord,
Make His paths straight.

Now after that John was delivered up, Jesus came into Galilee, preaching the Gospel of God,

And saying, The time is fulfilled, and the Kingdom of God is at hand, repent ye and believe in the Gospel.

After a very clear setting forth of Repentance as the beginning of the Gospel, the Prophet of God said:

Cowardice, Weakness, and Poverty of the Church.

Men do not like to hear about the Kingdom of God.

The Church has given way in the matter, has ceased to proclaim it, and has lain at the door of the rich man, and at the door of kings, like Lazarus, full of poverty, and misery, and sores, willing to take the crumbs that fall from the kings' tables.

The church has become a poor, weak, miserable and sick beggar, instead of being the representative of the Kingdom of God.

The Church will be Lazarus no more.

The Church will be healed and will kick against iniquity.

Lazarus is about to work.

God will raise up His people from their graves.

He is breathing upon them in the Valley of Dry Bones.

Come from the four winds, O breath, and breathe upon these slain, that they may live.

They are beginning to live.

Bone is coming to bone, sinews are forming on the bones and flesh upon the sinews.

They are beginning to realize strength, and the Breath of God is entering into them; they are standing upon their feet, an exceeding great army that has no bloody desires.

The Restoration Host of Zion has only one Sword—the Sword of the Spirit, which is the Word of God.

All that is great in Switzerland has come from that Sword, which never drew blood.

The Life of God, the Love of God, the Word of God, the Gospel of the Kingdom are working mightily, and

God's People Are Marching On.

I call upon God's people to rise and enter into association with one another.

Work together.

Pray together.

Use your talents together.

Till the fields together.

Grow the gardens together.

Work your workshops together.

Make money for God.

Care for the poor.

Zion awake!

God's people awake!

It is not a little church, but it is a mighty Kingdom into which God calls you.

The King is coming.

His chariot wheels are almost within hearing.

He is coming.

Let His people get ready by doing His Will, by uniting and carrying forward His Gospel.

Then you shall receive Salvation; you shall receive Healing; you shall receive the happiness which our Father in heaven sent His Son to bring.

Then His Kingdom shall be established in our Hearts, in our Homes, in our Cities, everywhere!

The Kingdom of God will rule over every other kingdom.

"Ah," they cry, "there is a man come to town who says there is another king, one Jesus. He is talking rebellion."

If it is rebellion to say that the Christ is the Ruler of the kings of the earth; to say that the Christ is the King of kings, that the Kingdom of God is above all, then I am a rebel, and I shall always be a rebel, for I say that God is supreme; that His Kingdom is the greatest, and that Jesus, the Christ, preached the Gospel of the Kingdom of God.

There will be no happiness, there will be no solution of the perplexities of humanity, unless the Christ reigns.

These questions are settled in Zion.

There is no contest there.

There are no strikes there, because we are one.

The rich use their riches for God, and the poor become richer.

Every man owns his own property, and uses it for God.

Will you not ask God to establish His Kingdom within your hearts?

Will you not ask God that by His Spirit His Kingdom will come into your hearts, and then to all the world?

All that want the Kingdom of God to come upon earth, stand up and tell Him so.

[Apparently all rose.]

Now pray with me.

PRAYER OF CONSECRATION.

My God and Father, in Jesus' Name I come to Thee. Father, I hallow Thy Name. Let Thy Kingdom come, bringing the Righteousness and the Peace, and the Joy of the Holy Spirit on this Pentecostal Night. I repent. Help me to do right to God and to man. Forgive me for the sake of Jesus who died for me, who pleads for me, who loves me, who wants to bring me into Thy Kingdom. For His sake take away every evil thing from my heart and life. Let Thy Kingdom come. Let Thy Will be done. May we all go home saying from this night, "I am in the Kingdom, the Kingdom is in me, and I will obey God always, everywhere, no matter what it costs." For Jesus' sake. Amen. [*All repeat the prayer, clause by clause, after the General Overseer.*]

Did you mean that? *Ja oder nein?* [Yes or no?]

Audience [very heartily]—"*Ja.*"

General Overseer—Will you live it?

Audience—"*Ja.*"

General Overseer—Then God will bless you.

BENEDICTION.

Beloved, abstain from all appearance of evil. And may the very God of Peace Himself sanctify you wholly; and I pray God your whole spirit and soul and body be preserved entire, without blame, unto the coming of our Lord Jesus, the Christ. Faithful is He that calleth you, who also will do it. The grace of our Lord Jesus, the Christ, the love of God, our Father, the fellowship of the Holy Spirit, our Comforter and Guide, one Eternal God, abide in you, bless you and keep you, and all the Israel of God everywhere, forever. Amen.

When the General Overseer left this Service there was only one man who jeered, and he was a poor drunken fellow who immediately subsided, evidently overcome by the attention he had attracted, as there was a general murmur of disapproval of his insolence.

And this was at night, under cover of darkness, when the Australian cowards would have been throwing stones.

Monday Morning Meeting.

Monday was a rainy day.

It was raining when we rose and continued raining, with scarce an interruption, all day.

It was also a holiday in Zürich, and accordingly three meetings were held.

Notwithstanding the rain and the many holiday attractions

and excursions the Velodrome was crowded at all three services, there being probably twelve thousand attendances in the aggregate during the day.

The wonderful story of the opening of the Beautiful Gate of Divine Healing was the subject of the morning's Message.

Velodrome, Zürich, Switzerland, Monday morning, May 23, 1904.
*REPORTED BY I. M. S. AND A. W. N.

The meeting was opened with the

INVOCATION.

God be merciful unto us and bless us,
And cause Thy face to shine upon us;
That Thy Way may be known upon earth,
Thy saving health among all the Nations.
For the sake of Jesus. Amen.

Hymn No. 20, "We're marching to Zion" was then sung, in German, with hearty, sincere spirit.

Elder Jean Kradolfer read the Scripture lesson from the 3d chapter of the Acts of the Apostles, closing with the prayer,

May God bless the reading of His Word.

Elder Carl Hodler, offered the general supplication, and the General Overseer offered prayer for the sick and sorrowing ones.

Another hynm was then sung.

The tithes and offerings were received, and the announcements were made by Elder Hodler, after which the General Overseer delivered his Message:

THE OPENING OF THE BEAUTIFUL GATE OF DIVINE HEALING.

And all the people saw him walking and praising God:
And they took knowledge of him, that it was he which sat for alms at the Beautiful Gate of the Temple: and they were filled with wonder and amazement at that which had happened unto him.

The Breadth of the Love and Mercy of God.

Do not be narrow.

Do not forget that the Father loves all His children.

He loves the ignorant and the wicked among them, as well as the good.

Sometimes a father or a mother on earth thinks a great deal more of the naughty children than of the good.

Parents pray for them still more than they do for the good, because the good are all right.

Our Father in Heaven loves us all.

He loves His own children that do good, but He loves His children that are naughty and wicked and ignorant, and is always seeking to bless them.

Do not forget that God is not so narrow as you would make Him to be.

Some people think that the only ones whom God loves are the Zwinglians, or the Calvinists, or the Roman Catholics, or the Lutherans, or those who are members of the English church.

They think that the only people who get blessing are those who are like themselves.

They pray something like this: "God bless me and my wife, my son John and his wife, us four and no more." [Laughter.]

Let us be broad and let us be kind.

Let us remember that "The Love of God is broader than the measure of man's mind," and that the heart of our Father is kind and good to all.

I think that the man at the Beautiful Gate of the Temple was a very wicked man.

He could often have touched the hem of the Christ's garment, as He went in and out of the Temple, and he did not.

Perhaps the rabbis had threatened him if he should, and he was afraid of them.

Perhaps they told him that Jesus was a bad man, and he believed them.

There are some rabbis of that kind in Zürich.

There are many who say, "Do not go to hear Dr. Dowie; he is a bad man. Have nothing to do with him."

They have never proved it of me, however, and they have never proved it of Jesus.

They simply lied then, and they lie now.

After speaking of witnessing to Divine Healing, the General Overseer said:

All who have been healed through faith in Jesus, rise.

*The following report has not been revised by the General Overseer.

[Fully five hundred persons, their faces shining with joy and thanksgiving, stood.]

Did God heal you?

People—"*Ja.*" [Yes.]

General Overseer—Through faith in Jesus?

People—"*Ja.*"

General Overseer—Did any man heal you?

People—"*Nein.*" [No.]

General Overseer—You are God's witnesses?

People—"*Ja.*"

General Overseer—Hallelujah! Hallelujah!

That is the way with Zion the world over.

I found scores and scores, on my Visitation to Australia, who had been blessed when I was there sixteen years ago.

They are God's witnesses, telling the story of God's blessing to them wherever they are.

The healing of the lame man was a very effective sermon.

Why did not the priests like it?

Because it was their own condemnation.

They had crucified Jesus.

Every minister of this city, and of this land who fights Zion and fights Divine Healing is fighting against God and against His Word; for the Covenant of Healing is as old as the Word of God. It is recorded back in Exodus 15:26.

Keep your hands off, you who do not understand Zion.

God will defend His work.

Be still if you do not understand it.

It does not pay to fight against God.

You reporters confine yourselves to what you understand, and keep your hands off Zion.

The meeting was closed with the call to Repentance and Consecration, responded to by practically the whole congregation, the Prayer of Consecration and the

BENEDICTION.

Beloved, abstain from all appearance of evil. And may the very God of Peace Himself sanctify you wholly; and I pray God your whole spirit and soul and body be preserved entire, without blame, unto the coming of our Lord Jesus, the Christ. Faithful is He that calleth you, who also will do it. The grace of our Lord Jesus, the Christ, the love of God, our Father, the fellowship of the Holy Spirit, our Comforter and Guide, one Eternal God, abide in you, bless you and keep you, and all the Israel of God everywhere, forever. Amen.

Monday Afternoon Meeting.

The meeting held by the General Overseer in the Velodrome, Monday afternoon, May 23, 1904, was the first of a series of Divine Healing services in which the Spirit of God was present in mighty power to heal.

In the prayer service after this meeting, the promise in Isaiah, 35th chapter, was abundantly fulfilled.

The blind actually and instantly received their sight.

The deaf heard.

The lame walked.

The sinful confessed and were delivered from the power of their sins and were healed.

The sorrowing received Divine consolation and cried for joy.

It was indeed a Pentecostal season—yea, more, for the Beautiful Gate of Divine Healing had been opened.

Velodrome, Zürich, Switzerland, Monday Afternoon, May 23, 1904.
*REPORTED BY E. W AND A W. N.

INVOCATION.

God be merciful unto us and bless us,
And cause Thy face to shine upon us;
That Thy Way may be known upon earth,
Thy saving health among all the Nations;
For the sake of Jesus. Amen.

Some Birthday Presents.

Elder Hodler spoke in German, making formal presentation to the General Overseer of a team of magnificent black and white horses, and of two large, beautiful books, illustrating Zürich, Switzerland, and Europe.

The General Overseer made response:

I have no doubt that Elder Hodler said very kind things, because he has been doing kind things ever since I came.

I had almost forgotten that my birthday came this week.

It has not come yet, and yet they begin to give me presents.

Elder Hodler and his beloved wife were determined to remember my birthday, and so they gave me two big horses.

They are black and white; because, I suppose, the Elder

*The following report has not been revised by the General Overseer.

knows that I love the black people, and I love the white people.

When the horses go along the street, the people will say: "Ah! that is just like the General Overseer. He believes in black and white being mingled together."

One day, when all the black and white, and all the yellow and brown, and all the races of the earth mingle together in purity in the Christ, we will get back the primitive man.

I do not think that the primitive man was as white as we are.

The good friends also gave me these pictures.

It is altogether unexpected, and it is exceedingly kind of you.

I will add these to my library, a little library of ten thousand volumes, in which I have a few books as big as these, but not many.

If you keep on giving them to me, I shall have to get another room and I shall have to get another stable.

I thank you very much.

May God bless you.

After the singing of a hymn, Elder Kradolfer read the 8th chapter of Matthew, the first seventeen verses.

Prayer was offered by Elder Hodler.

The General Overseer began his discourse by reading the 16th and 17th verses of the 8th chapter of Matthew, after which he said in part:

Our Bodies the Temples of God.

This gathering is especially for a little talk with those of God's people who have given their hearts to God, who are conscious that they are saved, and who now want to get healing for their bodies from God, believing as they do that their bodies were made by God to be a habitation for the Holy Spirit.

The Word of God has taught you that your bodies are the Temples of God, the Temples of the Holy Spirit; therefore you must ask God to cleanse this temple of all its impurities, that God may be satisfied and may possess it to use for His glory.

Our Lord Jesus, the Christ, had been teaching. You will find the teaching in the 5th, 6th and 7th chapters of Matthew.

This 8th chapter is a narration of events which immediately followed that sermon, or series of sermons, called the Sermon on the Mount.

Teaching Must Be With Authority.

He taught as one having Authority.

No one should teach unless he is quite sure of what he teaches.

You would not wish a professor of mathematics to stand in the university and to say that he did not know what he was talking about.

What a foolish thing for a minister of the Gospel to stand up and tell you that he does not know, and that no one else does!

I have no time to talk about things I do not understand.

I am a practical man.

I have nothing to do with theories unless they can be embodied in practice.

I have no use for a religion that belongs only to the grave, but I want a religion that materializes, and that gives effect to Faith.

Faith is the substance of things hoped for, and Faith gives the proof of the things that are not seen.

Faith must give substance and embody manifestation, or else it is not Faith at all.

This is true regarding other things.

When an architect draws a plan, it must be one that can be followed out in the erection of a building

So it is with true religion, you must be able to build.

The man who does the things that God tells him to do is like a man who builds upon the rock, and the result is a house which will not give way.

Faith Creates Mighty Things.

By Faith, God Himself made the world.

When He said, "Let there be light," they were Words of Faith.

All the forces of the Universe came into union, and brought the light. Faith is not a mere intellectual expression.

It is a spiritual power.

It saves the spirit; it saves the soul, and it cleanses the body from diseases that would kill.

May God give us back the Faith that Jesus preached!

When He came down from that mountain, the wondering multitudes followed Him.

God's Willingness to Heal.

A poor leper also followed after Him, and cried: "Lord, if Thou wilt, Thou canst make me clean."

Was that a good prayer?

No.

It was an ignorant prayer.

But God is so good; the Christ is so kind that even when we make an ignorant prayer, He looks in compassion upon us.

Do not pray the leper's prayer.

Do not say "If Thou wilt," because Jesus answered that prayer once for all.

He stretched forth His hand, and said, "I will. Be thou clean."

He touched the leper, and the leprosy passed away.

Has Jesus changed?

People—"*Nein.*" [No.]

General Overseer—Is He not the same yesterday, today, and forever?

People—"*Ja.*" [Yes.]

General Overseer—Does He not say, "Lo, I am with you All the Days, even unto the Consummation of the Age?"

People—"*Ja.*"

Then He is with us now

He is the same Savior, the same Healer, the same Cleanser, and the same Keeper, and is just as willing, or He would not be the same.

After dealing graphically and convincingly with several important truths bearing on the subject and presenting interesting illustrations of his points, the General Overseer made his call for Repentance, Confession and Consecration, to which, apparently, all present responded by rising and repeating the

PRAYER OF CONSECRATION.

My God and Father, in Jesus' Name I come to Thee. Take my spirit, my soul, and my body, and make me clean. Forgive all my sins, and give me power to do right. If I have wronged any, may I confess, restore, and do right no matter what it costs. Give me power to speak rightly, never to say that Thou dost make me sick; never to say that God made any one sick; but to say that God sent Jesus to make the people pure and healthy. For Jesus' sake help me to live a good life. [*All repeat the prayer, clause by clause, after the General Overseer*]

Do you believe what you have prayed?

People—"*Ja.*"

General Overseer—Will you live it?

People—"*Ja.*"

General Overseer—Then God bless you. May He bless you all.

BENEDICTION.

Beloved, abstain from all appearance of evil. And may the very God of Peace Himself sanctify you wholly; and I pray God your whole spirit and soul and body be preserved entire, without blame, unto the coming of our Lord Jesus, the Christ. Faithful is He that calleth you, who also will do it. The grace of our Lord Jesus, the Christ, the love of God, our Father, the fellowship of the Holy Spirit, our Comforter and Guide, one Eternal God, abide in you, bless you and keep you, and all the Israel of God everywhere, forever. Amen.

Monday Evening Meeting.

To put into words the Spirit that pervaded the evening service of that rainy Monday in the Zürich Velodrome, would be to define the Infinite; for it was the Spirit of the Living God.

The hall was again crowded, many standir[illegible]d many turned away because there were no seats for them, [illegible] even standing room

The General Overseer spoke with great boldness and power, and there was not one moment's waning of the intensity of interest with which he was heard.

The day closed with Zion in Zürich thanking God for the outpouring of His blessings upon the people.

We had expected great things during this Visitation, but God was exceeding our expectations.

Velodrome, Zürich, Switzerland, Monday Evening, May 23, 1904.

*REPORTED BY I. M. S. AND A. W N

The meeting was opened with the Invocation.

A hymn was then sung.

Elder Kradolfer read from the Inspired Word of God in the

*The following report has not been revised by the General Overseer.

Gospel according to St. Matthew, 9th chapter, and the first eight verses.

The tithes and offerings were received and the announcements were made, while a hymn was sung followed by a solo by Mrs. Kradolfer.

The General Overseer then delivered his Message, saying, among other things:

INVOCATION.

Let the words of my mouth, and the meditation of my heart be acceptable in Thy sight, be profitable unto this people, and unto all to whom these words shall come, in this and every land, in this and all the coming time, Till Jesus Come. Amen.

TEXT.

For whether is easier, to say, Thy sins are forgiven; or to say, Arise, and walk?

But that ye may know that the Son of Man hath power on earth to forgive sins (then saith He to the sick of the palsy), Arise, and take up thy bed, and go unto thy house.

The Character of Jesus' Audience.

The same story is told in the Gospel according to St. Luke, giving, in addition, the circumstances under which this miracle was wrought.

Luke tells us that it was on a certain day, when the doctors of the law and people of high station from all Galilee and from Judæa and Jerusalem gathered together to hear Jesus.

This audience was a very wonderful one, representing as it did, the most learned and the most reverend and powerful teachers of the time.

They must have numbered hundreds.

Why did they come?

Jesus was not a rabbi.

He had no degree from any university or from the rabbinic council.

He was an untitled man, known only as the son of the village carpenter.

He had no standing and no power as a teacher, according to them.

Perhaps they thought that He ought not to have taught at all.

But the people heard Him.

People of every degree in life, in Galilee, especially, followed Jesus.

The Jewish council of the Sanhedrin had evidently come to the conclusion that they must understand Jesus.

If they could capture Him and make Him one of themselves, they would do it; but if they had to fight Him they would kill Him.

They wanted to know.

It seems to me that this great delegation came together to hear His teaching; to understand, if they could, what His wonderful power was, why the people heard Him as they did not hear them; for the words in Luke 5:17 say:

And it came to pass on one of those days, that He was teaching; and there were Pharisees and doctors of the law sitting by, which were come out of every village of Galilee and Judæa and Jerusalem: and the power of the Lord was with Him to heal.

Not one of the doctors of the law, Pharisees or priests of high dignity was healed.

The only healing recorded is that of this poor palsied man, whom they let down through the roof in the midst of His teaching—a helplessly paralyzed man, who apparently could not walk.

The Power of the Lord was present to heal.

Jesus had been teaching things that they would not believe.

He taught them that He Himself was the Messiah; that He was the Wonderful, the Counselor, the Mighty God, the Everlasting Father, and the Prince of Peace.

They would not believe it.

They would not listen except to mock.

They said that He was a blasphemer, making Himself equal with God, saying that He had power on earth to forgive sins.

In the midst of all this, the man was put down through the roof.

Jesus looked at him and saw the Love, and the Faith, and the Confidence shining in his eyes.

He said:

Whether is easier, to say, Thy sins are forgiven; or to say, Arise, and walk.

That was

The Father Speaking in the Christ.

The Father did the work.

Jesus addressed this man as son.

He said "Of Mine Own Self I can do nothing."

These priests had said within themselves, "He is a blasphemer."

They were afraid to speak up.

That was the question—was God in Jesus, the Christ?

Jesus had understood the thoughts of their hearts.

The man rose and walked.

That was the answer to His question.

It did not change the attitude of the doctors of the law and of the Pharisees, convincing as it was.

You cannot convince some people.

While the Christ was on earth the people were healed in countless multitudes; but that did not convince the Pharisees.

When Lazarus was raised from the dead, it did not convince them.

Such is the condition of the Church even today.

Men are in the pulpits who never expect a prayer to be answered.

These men were not converted.

They went down to Jerusalem and conspired together how to murder the Christ.

It will always be the same.

Men who are hypocrites and bad at heart will never believe until they are converted.

They will fight the men of faith who do believe.

That man was healed.

That proved the Power of the Christ to forgive sins and to heal sicknesses.

Repentance Must Precede Faith.

You must restore and do right.

Your Faith must be based upon Repentance.

That is the only True Basis of Faith.

It is folly to say "I believe," until you have said from your heart, "I have done wrong, and I repent."

God is longing to bless you, but there is only One Way.

That is not your way, nor my way; it is God's Way.

It does not matter what you say or think; God's Truth is not changed.

After relating the facts concerning some wonderful cases of healing, through the Power of God, the General Overseer made the call to Repentance, Confession and Consecration, to which apparently all responded, repeating after him, very earnestly, the Prayer of Consecration.

The meeting was closed with the Grace, and the

BENEDICTION.

Beloved, abstain from all appearance of evil. And may the very God of Peace Himself sanctify you wholly; and I pray God your whole spirit and soul and body be preserved entire, without blame, unto the coming of our Lord Jesus, the Christ. Faithful is He that calleth you, who also will do it. The grace of our Lord Jesus, the Christ, the love of God, our Father, the fellowship of the Holy Spirit, our Comforter and Guide, one Eternal God, abide in you, bless you and keep you, and all the Israel of God everywhere, forever. Amen.

Tuesday Afternoon Meeting.

The second Divine Healing meeting of this Visitation fully redeemed the promise of the first.

The rain had ceased, and the sun was shining from a sky of wonderful depth of blue.

All nature was full of rejoicing in the freshness of springtime.

Zürich never looked fairer than on this day.

The meeting being held during working hours, there was not quite so large an attendance as at the previous services.

The Velodrome, however, was well filled, and, best of all, God was with the speaker and with the people.

Miracles of healing were wrought by the Power of God in the prayer service held after the teaching.

Velodrome, Zürich, Switzerland, Tuesday Afternoon, May 24, 1904.
*REPORTED BY E. W. AND A. W. N.

The Service opened with the Invocation.

A hymn was sung, after which prayer was offered by Elder Hodler.

*The following report has not been revised by the General Overseer.

The 8th chapter of Matthew was read by Elder Kradolfer.

After the General Overseer had made some announcements, the tithes and offerings were received, during the singing of a hymn by the congregation.

The General Overseer took as the text of his Message, Matthew 8:16, 17:

TEXT.

And when even was come, they brought unto Him many possessed with devils: and He cast out the spirits with a word, and healed all that were sick:

That it might be fulfilled which was spoken by Isaiah the prophet, saying, Himself took our infirmities, and bare our diseases.

He began his teaching with a clear declaration of the utter worthlessness of human opinion unless it be in accordance with what God thinks, illustrating his point in a manner that made the truth convincingly clear.

He then passed on to an examination of the theological lie, that God makes His people sick for their good and His glory.

This he demolished by appeal to the Authority of God's Word and to common sense, proving that disease is the work of the Devil.

He reduced to a ridiculous absurdity the teaching of the denominational ministers who thank God for disease—a token of His Love—and then send for the doctor to take it away.

He closed with a very helpful teaching on the subject of obedience to God and to those whom He has placed in authority.

He then said:

All who desire perfect Salvation for spirit, soul and body, stand. [Nearly all rose.]

Now pray.

PRAYER OF CONSECRATION.

My God and Father, in Jesus' Name I come to Thee. Take me as I am. Make me what I ought to be, in spirit, in soul, in body. I do repent. Help me to do right to any whom I may have wronged; to do right in Thy sight. Save me. Heal me. Cleanse me. Keep me. Give me strength to walk in the Way of God. For Jesus' sake. [*All repeat the prayer, clause by clause, after the General Overseer.*]

General Overseer—Beloved, do you believe what you have said?

People—"*Ja.*" [Yes.]

General Overseer—Are you determined, by God's grace, to live it?

People—"*Ja.*"

General Overseer—Then get together, keep together, and do not walk with those who would destroy your faith in God—in a Real Baptism, in a True Obedience.

Make your Vow to God, then God will bless you.

BENEDICTION.

Beloved, abstain from all appearance of evil. And may the very God of Peace Himself sanctify you wholly; and I pray God your whole spirit and soul and body be preserved entire, without blame, unto the coming of our Lord Jesus, the Christ. Faithful is He that calleth you, who also will do it. The grace of our Lord Jesus, the Christ, the love of God our Father, the fellowship of the Holy Spirit, our Comforter and Guide, one Eternal God, abide in you, bless you and keep you, and all the Israel of God everywhere, forever. Amen.

Tuesday Evening Meeting.

Continued good order, perfect attention, and an ever-increasing spirit of prayer marked the crowded meeting held by God's Prophet of the Times of the Restoration of All Things, on Tuesday evening, May 24, 1904.

This service, like all the services of the Zürich Visitation, was attended not only by the poor, the sick and the sorrowing, but by men and women high in social, financial, commercial and religious circles, from all parts of Europe.

But they were all as little children, as they sat learning the Truth of God from the lips of His Prophet.

Velodrome, Zürich, Switzerland, Tuesday Evening, May 24, 1904.

*REPORTED BY I. M. S. AND A. W. N.

A preliminary service was held before the General Overseer arrived, conducted by the Rev. Carl Hodler.

The General Overseer came upon the platform at half past eight o'clock, and pronounced the

INVOCATION.

Let the words of my mouth, and the meditation of my heart be acceptable in Thy sight, be profitable unto this people, and unto all to whom these words shall come, in this and every land, in this and all the coming time, Till Jesus Come. Amen.

*The following report has not been revised by the General Overseer.

He read from the Inspired Word of God, the 5th chapter of the Book of the Prophet Isaiah, and the 20th verse; also the 10th chapter of the Acts of the Apostles and the 38th verse.

He then delivered his Message:

THE TWO CHAINS, GOOD AND EVIL.

TEXT.

Wo unto them that call evil good, and good evil; that put darkness for light, and light for darkness; that put bitter for sweet, and sweet for bitter.

I desire to call your attention to the thought suggested by the two chains.

All good has its origin in God, and has its expression in Jesus, the Christ, the Eternal Word.

Through Him all things were made.

He is the Author of all Good.

On the other side, you have Satan the author of all evil.

The Age-long Conflict Between the Christ and the Devil.

If we believe the Word of God, we believe that it was Satan who came into this world and deceived mankind and taught men to sin against God.

This is the teaching of the Word of God, and of our Lord Jesus, the Christ.

When the Pharisees said to Him, "Our father is Abraham," He replied:

Ye are of your father the Devil, and the lusts of your father it is your will to do. He was a murderer from the beginning, and stood not in the truth, because there was no truth in him. When he speaketh a lie, he speaketh of his own: for he is a liar, and the father thereof.

He said in the plainest terms that the Kingdom of God and the Kingdom of Satan were in conflict, and must always be in conflict, until that Kingdom of Darkness, of Sin, of Disease, and of the powers of Death and Hell should be utterly destroyed by Him, through Salvation, through Healing, through Life and through the Powers of Heaven.

In the plainest of plain language He tells us that the conflict is between Good and Evil.

The Apostle Paul, in language that cannot be mistaken, says that our conflict or wrestling is not with flesh and blood, but is against principalities and powers, against the world-rulers of this darkness, against the hosts of spiritual wickedness in the upper air. That is the meaning of the expression "spiritual wickedness in high places." It is, literally, the "hosts of evil spirits in the upper air."

In the Book of the Revelation, the statement is made that at the end of the age, before the coming of the Lord, three unclean spirits will go forth out of the mouth of the Beast, out of the mouth of the false prophet, out of the mouth of the serpent, to deceive the rulers of this earth; to lead them to battle and to lead nations into conflict with one another, before the Great Day of God the Almighty.

This conflict between Good and Evil is the conflict in which you and I must take part.

We must rank ourselves either under the Banner of Jesus and fight for Good, or under the Banner of Satan and fight for Evil.

The Christ and Satan are two Unseen Powers, which are leading forward the hostile forces.

There is no possibility of making a treaty with the Devil.

The Kingdom of God must overcome the Kingdom of the Devil.

Sin Through Doubt; Salvation Through Faith.

When Satan came upon this earth, the first thing he did was to make man sin.

Sin came by Doubt, and the first work of the Christ when He came into this world was to bring Salvation, and Salvation comes by Faith.

Sin comes by Doubt.

The man who doubts must always be unhappy.

If he doubts his friend, friendship is destroyed, and he is miserable.

If a man doubts his wife or a wife doubts her husband there is misery.

Doubt is misery.

If a man doubts God there is misery.

Doubt is sin.

To doubt God is to sin against God.

Some people will tell you that doubt is an evidence of great intellectuality; that it is an evidence of a man's being a powerful, free-thinking man when he doubts God.

One of our English poets has said, "Believe me, there is more faith in honest doubt than in half your creeds."

I am not defending the creeds at this moment, although I have perfect confidence in the Apostles' Creed.

But there is no faith in honest doubt.

For this reason, no mortal man can ever honestly doubt God, our Father who is in heaven; He who made this beautiful world in which we dwell; He who sent His Son to Redeem us; He who loves us, and preserves us, and provides for us.

To doubt Him is sin.

Doubt is never honest.

How the Devil Finds Embodiment in People.

Satan was embodied in the serpent when he tempted Eve.

All that fell with Satan, when they were cast out of the heavens into hell, were disembodied spirits, seeking for embodiment.

The first embodiment by one of their number was in a serpent.

Their next embodiments were in the heart of a woman and then of a man because of sin.

Today there are multitudes of people on earth who are incarnate devils.

They give way to the Devil, and by means of sin the evil spirit enters in.

Let a man be tempted to be a thief, or an adulterer, or a murderer when he is sober, and he will say, "No."

But, put a quart of whisky into him, and he often becomes a liar, thief, adulterer and murderer.

The Devil gets into humanity through vanity, pride, envy, uncleanness, drunkenness, and eating filthy things.

The Devil gets in today just as he got in when Eve ate of the forbidden fruit and disobeyed God.

Take care what you drink.

Take care what you look at.

Take care what you hear; for every one of the Five Senses is a Gate by which God can enter, or a Gate by which the Devil can enter.

Danger of Questioning God's Commands.

When the Devil said to Eve, "Hath God said?" she discussed the matter with him, and reasoned it.

"Did God really say it?" she questioned.

She knew that God had said it. Why did she not say, "Yes, God has said it, and I will not reason about it!"

Whenever you begin to reason with the Devil, he has the better of you.

The moment you begin to question the commands of God, you are lost.

The man who hesitates when he hears the command of God saying, "Thou shalt not commit adultery," and begins to question the command, goes down.

After Eve had discussed the matter for awhile, she permitted the Devil to enter.

She thought that if she ate of the forbidden fruit she would become a goddess and would be like God Himself.

But sin entered and disease entered.

The very atmosphere became polluted.

Death came in through Sin.

God had said that in the day they disobeyed, dying, they should die.

Death began when sin entered.

The first-born, Cain, was an incarnate devil.

Before the birth of Abel, the mother's heart must have broken in penitence, and God came into her spirit again, for Abel had the Spirit of God in him when he was born.

Death Is of the Devil.

Death came by sin and disease, and it has continued to be so.

Many people will tell you that death is a gift from God.

Poets will write poems about death, as if it came from God.

What does God's Word say?

"The wages of sin is Death; but the free Gift of God is Eternal Life."

The Word of God says, "Him that hath the power of death, that is the Devil."

"Death and hell shall be cast into the lake of fire."

Death is God's enemy.

The Christ came, not only to take away our sins and our diseases, but to destroy Death.

He has said in His Word that He came for that purpose.

Death is as corrupt as hell, and it is hateful to God.

It is written, "O Death, where is thy sting?"

The Christ came to destroy death.

He said, "I am the Resurrection, and the Life: he that believeth on Me, though he die, yet shall he live."

Believest thou this?

People—"*Ja.*" [Yes.]

General Overseer—"He giveth His beloved sleep." Oh, I am so glad that it is not death.

> No man that breathes with human breath,
> Whatever crazy sorrow saith,
> Hath ever really longed for death.
> 'Tis life, not death, for which we pant;
> 'Tis life of which our nerves are scant.
> More life, and fuller, that we want.

Jesus said, "I came that they may have Life, and may have it abundantly."

Jesus and Salvation go together.

Satan and Sin go together.

Salvation and Healing go together.

Sin and Disease go together.

Disease and Death go together.

Health and Life go together.

Life and Heaven go together.

Death and Hell go together.

Do not forget it.

Disease is one of the links in the chain of evil, and the Christ came to break every link in that Chain; to set us free from Satan, free from Sin, free from Disease, free from Death, and free from Hell.

Oh, what a Power a Real Salvation is!

Oh, what a Blessing a Real Healing is!

Oh, what a Power a Divine Life is!

Oh, what a Glory to have the Christ within us, and then to have Salvation, Healing, Life and Heaven within us!

Do you want that?

Audience—"*Ja.*" [Yes.]

All who want that, stand up and tell God so.

[Apparently the greater part of the audience rose.]

The meeting was closed with the Prayer of Consecration, the Benediction, and the Zion Salutation, "Peace to thee!" from the General Overseer, the people responding heartily, "*Friede sei mit euch reichlich.*"

Deacon Charles F. Kelchner will conduct meetings in the following towns in Ohio on the dates given:

Collins, June 24th and 25th; Mount Gilead, June 27th; Marengo, June 29th; Wooster, June 30th; Orrville, July 1st.

Elder A. W. McClurkin will conduct meetings in the following places in Wisconsin:

Black Creek, Appleton, Omro, Ripon, Fond du Lac, Waupaca, Marshfield and Antigo.

B. W. Brannen, Deacon in the Christian Catholic Church in Zion, will conduct meetings in the following places in Illinois:

Mount Morris, June 25th and 26th; Rock Falls and Sterling, June 27th; Dixon, June 28th; Freeport, June 29th; Davis, June 30th; Belvidere, July 1st.

Elder Charles A. Hoy will conduct meetings in the following places in Nebraska, Iowa, and Illinois on the dates given:

Paul, Nebraska, June 24th; Omaha, Nebraska, and Council Bluffs, Iowa, June 25th and 26th; Des Moines, Iowa, June 27th, 28th and 29th; Boone, Iowa, June 30th; Newton, Iowa, July 2d, 3d and 4th; Washington, Iowa, July 5th and 6th; Muscatine, Iowa, July 7th; Geneseo, Illinois, July 8th; Cambridge, Illinois, July 9th and 10th.

Daily Bible Study for the Home

By Overseer John G. Speicher

TUESDAY, JULY 12TH.

1 Corinthians 12.—Gifts of the Spirit chapter.

Memory text—Verse 31. "Desire earnestly the greater gifts."

Contents of chapter—Paul desirous of their enlightenment concerning the Spiritual gifts; The Holy Spirit teaches men to witness that Jesus is Lord; Diversities of gifts, ministries, and workings, but the same spirit; Gifts of the spirit given in order; All Christians by one Spirit are baptized into one body; Importance and part of every member of the body working and coöperating together; There should be no schism in the body, but care, sympathy and rejoicing together; Order of the ministering offices which God has set in the churches.

WEDNESDAY, JULY 13TH.

1 Corinthians 13.—Love chapter.

Memory text—Verse 13. "The greatest of these is love."

Contents of chapter—Speech, prophecy, faith, gifts, bodily suffering, without love, profit nothing; Love's essential characteristics; The imperfect is now, but the perfect day is to come.

THURSDAY, JULY 14TH.

1 Corinthians 14.—Prophesying and tongues chapter.

Memory text—Verse 40. "Let all things be done decently and in order."

Contents of chapter—Paul considers that it were better for the Corinthians to seek to prophesy than to speak with tongues; Those who spoke with tongues should pray to be able to interpret so that others might understand; Tongues for a sign to the unbelieving; Prophecy a sign unto the believer; Effect of the church prophesying before an unbeliever; Instructions concerning speaking with tongues and prophecy in public; Paul's direction concerning women in the churches; All things to be done decently and in order.

FRIDAY, JULY 15TH.

1 Corinthians 15.—Resurrection chapter.

Memory text—Verse 22. "As in Adam all die, so also in the Christ shall all be made alive."

Contents of chapter (verses 1 to 26)—Paul reviews the Gospel which he preached to the Corinthians; The Christ's resurrection is proof that the dead will be raised; In Adam all die, in the Christ shall all be made alive, each in his own order; The Christ shall deliver up the Kingdom to God, when He has reigned and put all enemies under His feet; Death the last enemy to be abolished.

SATURDAY, JULY 16TH.

1 Corinthians 15, (remainder).—Victory chapter.

Memory text—Verse 54. "Death is swallowed up in victory."

Contents of chapter, (verses 26 to 58).—The Christ's subjection will be when He has put all things in subjection to the Father; Paul refers to his ministry at Ephesus as "with beasts at Ephesus;" If the dead rise not it profits him nothing; Influence of evil company; Sin not; Do righteousness; The manner of the resurrection; The different bodies; Not all sleep; All shall be changed; Death not victorious; Be steadfast; Abounding in the work of the Lord; Labor is not in vain, in the Lord.

SUNDAY, JULY 17TH.

1 Corinthians 16.—Direction, admonition, and commendation chapter.

Memory text—Verse 13. "Watch ye, stand fast in the faith, quit you like men, be strong."

Contents of chapter—Collections for the saints to be made on the first day of the week; Paul will send their bounty to Jerusalem; Desires to see them; An open door at Ephesus; Timothy commended to their loving reception and care; Apollos not able to go at that time; Exhortation to faithfulness and love in all things; Paul's joy in and commendation of Stephanas and Fortunatus and Achaicus; Salutation of the churches in Asia, and of Aquila and Prisca.

MONDAY, JULY 18TH.

2 Corinthians 1.—Comfort and deliverance chapter.

Memory text—Verse 5. "Even so our comfort also aboundeth through the Christ."

Contents of chapter—Paul gives thanks to God for the comfort given him by God, whereby he is able to comfort others; He had suffered much in Asia, even nigh unto death, but God delivered; His conscience witnesses that he behaved toward them in holiness and sincerity; His desire to come to them the second time not of fickleness; God establishes and seals; To spare them he had not come to Corinth.

TUESDAY, JULY 19TH.

2 Corinthians 2.—Suffering and sincerity chapter.

Memory text—Verse 14. "Thanks be unto God, which always leadeth us in triumph in the Christ."

Contents of chapter—Paul will not go to the Corinthians in sorrow; He writes to them with much affliction, anguish, and tears, that they might know the love which he has unto them; He who caused the sorrow injured all in part, and suffered consequently himself; They were to forgive if he had truly repented; Paul, troubled in spirit, had gone into Macedonia to meet Titus; Triumph in the Christ; His ministry a savor from life unto life to those who were being saved, and from death unto death to those who were perishing; Not corrupting the Word of God, he speaks sincerely in the Christ.

WEDNESDAY, JULY 20TH.

2 Corinthians 3.—Spirit ministry chapter.

Memory text—Verse 17. "Where the Spirit of the Lord is, there is liberty."

Contents of chapter—Paul refers to the Corinthians as his epistle in the Christ; His sufficiency of God, as a minister of the New Covenant; Letter killeth, but spirit giveth life; Ministry under Moses was with glory; That of the Spirit shall be with glory; Veil remain over the Jews that refuse to accept Jesus as the Messiah; Liberty where the Spirit of the Lord is; We are to reflect the glory of God.

THURSDAY, JULY 21ST.

2 Corinthians 4.—Overcoming and sustaining power chapter.

Memory text—Verse 11. "That the life also of Jesus may be manifested in our mortal flesh."

Contents of chapter—Paul sustained for his ministry; He renounces the hidden things of shame; In manifestation of truth commending himself in every man's conscience in the sight of God; If veil over his Gospel, it could only be to those whose minds the god of this world had blinded; His life kept in an earthen vessel, by the power of God; He is able to endure and overcome in all trials and persecutions; Temporal hardships will be overruled to our eternal good, if we are the Christ's.

FRIDAY, JULY 22D.

2 Corinthians 5.—Reconciliation and heavenly abode chapter.

Memory text—Verse 9. "Wherefore also we make it our aim, whether at home or absent, to be well-pleasing unto Him."

Contents of chapter—God has prepared in the heavens an eternal habitation for the spirit when this earthly house is dissolved; We long to be fitted into it; We must seek to be well-pleasing to God; All must be made manifest before the judgment seat of the Christ, where rewards will be given according to deeds done in the body; The fear of the Lord led Paul to persuade men; The Christ died for all; We should live for Him; In the Christ a man becomes a new creature; God was in the Christ reconciling the world unto Himself; Ambassadors for the Christ.

SATURDAY, JULY 23D.

2 Corinthians 6.—Faithful ministry and unequal yoke chapter.

Memory text—Verse 14. "Be not unequally yoked with unbelievers."

Contents of chapter—Paul warns the Corinthians not to receive the grace of God in vain; In God's accepted time is salvation; They were not to give occasion for stumbling; He reviews the nature of his ministries; Warns them against being unequally yoked with unbelievers.

SUNDAY, JULY 24TH.

2 Corinthians 7.—Godly sorrow chapter.

Memory text—Verse 10. "Godly sorrow worketh repentance unto salvation."

Contents of chapter—Paul exhorts to cleansing from the defilements of the flesh and spirit; Tells the Corinthians to open their hearts to him; He receives much comfort through Titus; He is glad that his epistle led to a sorrow unto repentance; Godly sorrow works repentance unto salvation; Sorrow of the world works death; Effects of the Godly sorrow on their part; Their actions won favor with Titus.

AND I WILL take you one of a city, and two of a family, and I will bring you to Zion: and I will give you shepherds according to Mine heart, which shall feed you with knowledge and understanding. —*Jeremiah 3: 14, 15.*

Zion Literature Sent Out from a Free Distribution Fund Provided by Zion's Guests and the Friends of Zion.

Report for week ending June 18, 1904:

1,097 Rolls to..........Hotels in the United States
2,200 Rolls........................Miscellaneous
2,286 Rolls to.....Business Men in Various States
1,005 Rolls to................The British Peerage
Number of Rolls for the Week..............6,588
Number of Rolls reported to June 18, 1904, 3,192,629

EVANGELIST SARAH E. HILL,
Superintendent Zion Literature Mission,
Zion City, Illinois.

Zion's Bible Class

Conducted by Deacon Daniel Sloan in Shiloh Tabernacle, Zion City, Lord's Day Morning at 11 o'clock, and in Zion Homes and Gatherings throughout the World.

MID-WEEK BIBLE CLASS LESSON, JULY 13th or 14th.

The Necessities of Life.

1. *God will never fail us.*—Matthew 6:24-34.
   We are His creatures.
   He never abandons His own.
   He has plenty for all.
2. *Live for a substance in Heaven.*—Matthew 6:19-23.
   The carnal nature is earthy.
   The spiritual nature is heavenly.
   The heart must always rule.
3. *God will supply food and raiment.*—1 Thessalonians 6:6-16.
   God's saints never starve.
   The love of God brings all things.
   One ought to find contentment in God.
4. *The Lord's pay-day is sure.*—Psalm 37:3-11.
   He will feed the men of faith.
   He will answer a righteous prayer.
   He will honor a devout trust.
5. *Bread and water are assured us.*—Isaiah 33:13-22.
   Sinners come to want and cry for bread.
   Prodigals subsist where swine feed.
   God's power is able to give an abundance.
6. *God provides plenty for all.*—Proverbs 30:5-14.
   God makes plenty.
   God never falls short.
   All who rely on Him bless Him for a sufficiency.
7. *God gives that for which one asks.*—Luke 11:5-13.
   Definite prayers get definite answers.
   He has the power to supply from His Kingdom when it is to His Glory.
   He gives what one asks for in faith.
   The Lord Our God is a Life-supplying God.

LORD'S DAY BIBLE CLASS LESSON, JULY 17th.

Pledges from an Unbroken Body.

1. *Christians must love and help.*—1 Corinthians 12:20-27.
   Those who suffer need for righteousness' sake.
   Those who suffer from the Devil's oppression.
   Those who give evidence of consistency.
2. *The first Christians did this.*—Acts 2:41-47.
   They had obedient spirits.
   They had joyful hearts.
   They had evidences of faith.
3. *The Christ pledges us all He has.*—1 Corinthians 3:18-23.
   A Kingdom awaits us.
   Mansions will be ours.
   Governments will be committed to us.
4. *There is power in deeds of love and mercy.*—Acts 4:31-37.
   Can you deny self?
   Are you willing to help others?
   Do you hoard all you get?
5. *We are not to offend one of the Christ's little ones.*—James 2:1-9.
   The poor must be clothed.
   The hungry must be fed.
   The oppressed must be set free.
6. *We cannot love God and see some brother in need without giving aid.*—1 John 4:11-21.
   Help your neighbor if you love God.
   Keep down your prejudices if you love God.
   Deeds alone can reveal love.
7. *We must clothe the naked and feed the hungry.*—James 2:13-22.
   Faith in God makes one work for others.
   Faith is an unselfish thing.
   Faith makes one deny self and live for others.
8. *We will go to hell if we do not do this.*—Luke 16:19-26.
   Living for self sends one to Hell.
   Neglecting the hungry brings death.
   God watches every motive that controls us.
   God's Holy People are a Love-fulfilling People.

LEAVES OF HEALING.

Two Dollars will bring to you the weekly visits of the Little White Dove for a year; 75 cents will send it to a friend for thirteen weeks; $1.25 will send it for six months; $1.50 will send it to your minister, or to a Y. M. C. A., or to a Public Reading Room for a whole year. We offer no premiums, except the premium of doing good We receive no advertisements, and print no commercial lies or cheating enticements of unscrupulous thieves. LEAVES OF HEALING is Zion on wings, and we keep out everything that would detract the reader's mind from all except the Extension of the Kingdom of God, for which alone it exists. If we cannot send forth our Little White Dove without soiling its wings with the smoke of the factory and the dirt of the wrangling market-place, or compelling it to utter the screaming cries of the business vultures in the ears of our readers, then we will keep our Dove at home.

OBEYING GOD IN BAPTISM.

"Baptizing Them Into the Name of the Father and of the Son and of the Holy Ghost."

Eighteen Thousand Six Hundred Fifty-three Baptisms by Triune Immersion Since March 14, 1897.

Eighteen Thousand Six Hundred Fifty-three Believers have joyfully followed their Lord in the Ordinance of Believer's Baptism by Triune Immersion since the first Baptism in Central Zion Tabernacle on March 14, 1897.

Baptized in Central Zion Tabernacle from March 14, 1897, to December 14, 1901, by the General Overseer,	4754		
Baptized in South Side Zion Tabernacle from January 1, 1902, to June 14, 1903, by the General Overseer..	37		
Baptized at Zion City by the General Overseer........	583		
Baptized by Overseers, Elders, Evangelists and Deacons, at Headquarters (Zion City) and Chicago......	5283		
Total Baptized at Headquarters....................			10,657
Baptized in places outside of Headquarters by the General Overseer................................		641	
Baptized in places outside of Headquarters by Overseers, Elders, Evangelists and Deacons............		7348	
Total Baptized outside of Headquarters............			7,989
Total Baptized in seven years and three months....			18,646
Baptized since June 14, 1904:			
Baptized in Chicago by Elder Hoffman...............	1		1
Baptized in Nebraska by Elder Hoy..................		6	6 7
Total Baptized since March 14, 1897................			18,653

The following-named two believers were baptized at South Carver, Massachusetts, Thursday, May 26, 1904, by Evangelist Helen A. Smith:

Andrews, Mrs. Lucinda......South Carver, Massachusetts
Tillson, Mrs. Lucinda W......South Carver, Massachusetts

The following-named three believers were baptized at San Francisco, California, Lord's Day, June 5, 1904, by Elder William D. Taylor:

Barron, Mrs. Leonor Geraldine...153 Day street, San Francisco, California
Hamilton, Harry......641 Commercial street, San Francisco, California
Trolson, Mrs. Rhoda Gean..546 Twenty-second street, Oakland, California

The following-named nine believers were baptized at Fostoria, Ohio Wednesday, June 8, 1904, by Elder T. Alexander Cairns:

Crandall, Itali Elizabeth......926 McDougall street, Fostoria, Ohio
Dicken, Mrs. Laura Elizabeth......941 North Union street, Fostoria, Ohio
Fox, Mrs. Annie Louise......823 North Main street, Fostoria, Ohio
Fox, Miss Dorothy Glen......823 North Main street, Fostoria, Ohio
Fox, Seymour Eland......823 North Main street, Fostoria, Ohio
Phillips, Gerald Arthur......239 East Crocker street, Fostoria, Ohio
Phillips, Miss Helen Eleen......239 East Crocker street, Fostoria, Ohio
Phillips, Miss Mabel Gay......239 East Crocker street, Fostoria, Ohio
Platner, Miss Florence Dot......134 Jackson street, Fostoria, Ohio

The following-named believer was baptized at Gladstone, Michigan, Saturday, June 11, 1904, by Elder A. W. McClurkin:

McKerlie, Robert......Gladstone, Michigan

The following-named two believers were baptized in the South Side Zion Tabernacle, Chicago, Illinois, Lord's Day, June 12, 1904, by Elder W. H. Cossum:

Brown, Mrs. Sarah......5547 Ada street, Chicago, Illinois
Mackie, Mrs. Anna......5704 Ada street, Chicago, Illinois

The following-named thirteen believers were baptized in the Charles river, Cambridge, Massachusetts, Lord's Day, June 12, 1904, by Overseer William Hamner Piper:

Berry, John......28 Washington street, Lawrence, Massachusetts
Borneman, Miss Jennie......117 Jackson street, Lawrence, Massachusetts
Britton, Mrs. T. B......302 Shawmut avenue, Boston, Massachusetts
Chamberlain, Herbert E...22 East Brookline street, Boston, Massachusetts
Dronsfield, Mrs. Alice.....28 Washington street, Lawrence, Massachusetts
Dronsfield, Charles......28 Washington street, Lawrence, Massachusetts
Dronsfield, Miss Elizabeth, 28 Washington street, Lawrence, Massachusetts
Griffith, Miss Mary Elizabeth..28 Washington st., Lawrence, Massachusetts
Mitchell, Mrs. Susan P......131 Falcon street, East Boston, Massachusetts
Savage, Miss Marguerite......63 Hawthorne street, Chelsea, Massachusetts
Seaman, Miss Ann......44 Rochester street, Boston, Massachusetts
Turner, Miss Alice......16 Crescent street, Newton, Massachusetts
Willis, Miss Edna......63 Newbery street, Lawrence, Massachusetts

The following-named nine believers were baptized at Paris, **Texas**, Lord's Day, June 12, 1904, by Evangelist William D. Gay:

Campbell, Mrs. Allie Annie......Paris, **Texas**
Campbell, William John......Paris, Texas
Clanton, Jesse Chalmas......Paris, Texas
Clanton, John James......Paris, Texas
Clanton, Miss Florence Olive......Paris, Texas
Clanton, Leroy......Paris, Texas
Clanton, Mrs. Susan Thomas......Paris, Texas
Vaughn, Mrs. Fronia......Brookston, Texas
Vaughn, George Washington......Brookston, Texas

The following-named six believers were baptized at Bloomington, Nebraska, Wednesday, June 15, 1904, by Elder Charles A. Hoy:

Gibson, Miss Nettie A......Republican City, Nebraska
Ingram, Adam......Bloomington, Nebraska
Ingram, Mrs. Minerva Jane......Bloomington, Nebraska
Lake, Calvin H......Republican City, Nebraska
Morse, Mrs. Mary E......Bloomington, Nebraska
Morse, William Walter......Bloomington, Nebraska

The following-named believer was baptized in the German North Parish, Chicago, Illinois, Saturday, June 18, 1904, by Elder C. R. Hoffman:

Klein, Mrs. Katharina Maria......134 Bissel street, Chicago, Illinois

CONSECRATION OF CHILDREN.

The following-named child was consecrated to God Wednesday, June 8, 1904, by Elder T. Alexander Cairns:

Platner, Esther Beulah......Fostoria, Ohio

The following-named child was consecrated to God, Saturday, June 11, 1904, by Elder T. Alexander Cairns:

Bressler, Valois M......1118 St. John's avenue, Lima, Ohio

The following-named three children were consecrated to God at Gladstone, Michigan, Saturday, June 11, 1904, by Elder A. W. McClurkin:

McKerlie, Cecil Roy......Gladstone, Michigan
McKerlie, Howard Goden......Gladstone, Michigan
McKerlie, Robert Emslie......Gladstone, Michigan

The following-named child was consecrated to God, Lord's Day, June 12, 1904, by Elder T. Alexander Cairns:

Merryfield, Gaylord Gilbert......West Unity, Ohio

The following-named four children were consecrated to God at Philadelphia, Pennsylvania, Lord's Day, June 12, 1904, by Elder R. N. Bouck:

Bayley, Clara Edith. 2509 North College avenue, Philadelphia, Pennsylvania
Bayley, Philip Edward. .2509 North College ave., Philadelphia, Pennsylvania
Naegele, Benjamin Thomas . .4543 Green st., Germantown, Pennsylvania
Zeeb, Martha Catherine, 339 Thompson street, Philadelphia, Pennsylvania

The following-named eight children were consecrated to God at Toronto, Ontario, Canada, Lord's Day, June 12, 1904, by Elder Eugene Brooks:

Bird, Ivan Eugene....276 Westmoreland avenue, Toronto, Ontario, Canada
Burgess, Eliza Louisa......265 Bartlett avenue, Toronto, Ontario, Canada
Burgess, Rossiter Alexander, 265 Bartlett avenue, Toronto, Ontario, Canada
Daniels, George Robert......250 Ontario street, Toronto, Ontario, Canada
Daniels, Grace Lillian......250 Ontario street, Toronto, Ontario, Canada
Daniels, Josephine Harriett Emaline,
250 Ontario street, Toronto, Ontario, Canada
Lock, Ernest William James...8 Fitzroy terrace, Toronto, Ontario, Canada
Marwood, Elizabeth Amy......8 Fitzroy terrace, Toronto, Ontario, Canada

The following-named ten children were consecrated to God at Paris, Texas, Lord's Day, June 12, 1904, by Evangelist William D. Gay:

Campbell, Clara Varna......Paris, Texas
Campbell, Florence Willie......Paris, Texas
Campbell, Myrtle......Paris, Texas
Campbell, Opal......Paris, Texas
Hinkle, William Warren......Paris, Texas
McReynolds, Mary Ruth......Paris, Texas
Vaughn, Arvin......Brookston, Texas
Vaughn, James Herbert......Brookston, Texas
Vaughn, Myrtle......Brookston, Texas
Vaughn, Pearl Vivian......Brookston, Texas

The following-named seven children were consecrated to God in Shiloh Tabernacle, Zion City, Illinois, Lord's Day, June 19, 1904, by Overseer H. D. Brasefield:

Abbott, Marion Clare......Zion City, Illinois
Abbott, Ernest Preston......Zion City, Illinois
Bailey, Lulu Frances......3003 Ezra avenue, Zion City, Illinois
Bailey, James Henry......3003 Ezra avenue, Zion City, Illinois
Divelbiss, Elsie May......2707 Emmaus avenue, Zion City, Illinois
Dreyer, James Wilbur......1712 Hermon avenue, Zion City, Illinois
Hauck, Harold Alexander......3002 Enoch avenue, Zion City, Illinois

A WEEKLY PAPER FOR THE EXTENSION OF THE KINGDOM OF GOD
EDITED BY THE REV. JOHN ALEX. DOWIE.

Volume XV. No. 11. *ZION CITY, SATURDAY, JULY 2, 1904.* *Price Five Cents*

View of Zurich, Switzerland.

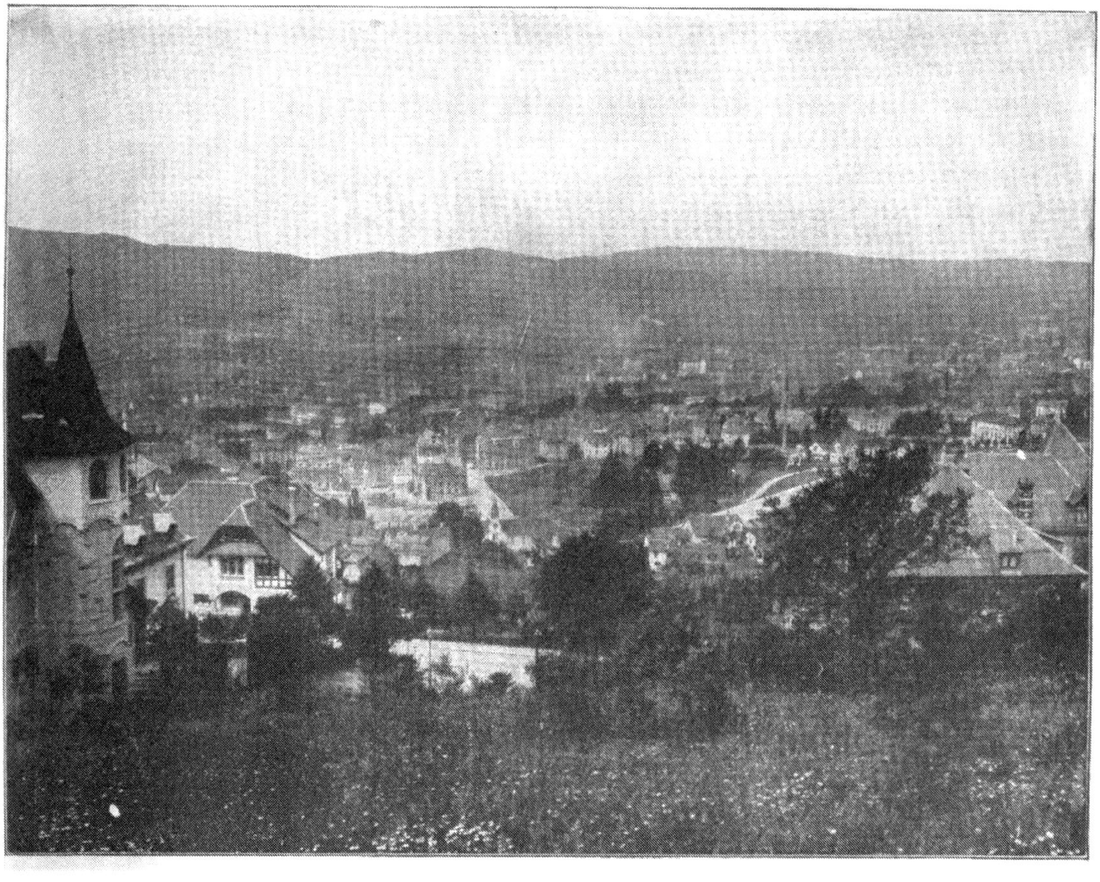

General Letter from the General Overseer

Administration Building,
Zion City, Lake County, Illinois, U. S. A.,
June 30, 1904.

To the Overseers, Elders, Evangelists, Deacons, Deaconesses, Zion Restoration Host, and Members of the Christian Catholic Church in Zion Throughout the World, and to All Lovers of God.

Beloved in the Christ, Our Lord and King:

Grace to you and peace,
From Him which is, and which was, and which is to come;
And from the Seven Spirits which are before His Throne;
And from Jesus, the Christ, who is the Faithful Witness,
The Firstborn of the dead,
And the Ruler of the kings of the earth.

With this beautiful salutation of John to the seven churches in Asia, (Revelation 1:4, 5,) I greet the Assemblies of the Christian Catholic Church in Zion throughout the world.

May you more and more fully understand the full import of these words and may they find more powerful realization in Zion throughout the whole world.

He who is the Ruler of the kings of the earth hath "made us to be a kingdom," and "to be priests unto His God and Father."

He hath "loved us and loosed us from our sins by His blood."

And joyfully do we say, "to Him be the glory and the dominion unto the ages of the ages, Amen."

Leaving this City, as most of you whom I now address are aware, on Friday, January 1st, upon a Visitation Around-the-World, we have by the goodness and mercy of God, been permitted to return today—which is exactly the day arranged in the program made for our tour.

We have traveled in all about Thirty-one Thousand (31,000) Miles by land and by sea, an average of Five Thousand Miles per month, and more than One Hundred Sixty-six Miles per day. The rate of traveling, however, has been very much more rapid than this average daily run would show, because we have tarried by the way, often for days, and sometimes for weeks.

Words are utterly inadequate to express our gratitude to our God and Father for His gracious protection, and for deliverances from dangers, seen and unseen.

Above all, we desire to record our gratitude to Him for the Innumerable Spiritual, Psychical and Physical Blessings which He has bestowed upon us, and upon the many tens of thousands of those to whom we have ministered.

It is not my purpose in this Letter to review the Visitation, which must be done more fully and more carefully than my time this evening permits.

My principal desire in writing this letter is to immediately record, for myself and my beloved companions of the Visitation Party, our thanksgiving to God and our grateful appreciation of the kindness of His people throughout all the lands.

Especially do we all appreciate the unfailing love and sympathy of all who are truly in Zion.

This stream has followed us every moment of our journeying, and it has found most touching expression in the delightful Reception which we received upon our arrival this morning in Zion City.

It was, indeed, a wonderful sight which met our wondering eyes as we stepped from our car this morning upon the platform of the railway depot in Zion City.

We beheld the perfect order of the numerous companies of uniformed Zion Guard, with their splendid Band; of the North American Legion of Zion Restoration Host; of the hundreds upon hundreds of the great Zion White-robed Choir and Orchestra; of the Legion of nearly two thousand members of Zion Junior Restoration Host; of the many hundreds of Robed Elders, Evangelists, Deacons and Deaconesses of the Christian Catholic Church in Zion; and of the vast throngs of the citizens of Zion City and friends of Zion from many near and some distant places.

All these constituted a vast and wonderfully impressive Assembly when, after we had passed between their ranks, they countermarched and gathered under the great Welcome Home Arch on Shiloh Boulevard, which bore the Words of Jesus which form the beautiful motto of Zion for 1904, (John 14:3,) "I Will Come Again."

The weather, which was delightfully mild and sunny, held out until we had spoken our words of response to the many greetings, formal and informal, of our beloved friends.

Then the rain clouds gathered over the dry and thirsty land, which had been without any considerable rain for many weeks, and after a few premonitory rolls of thunder, the heavens poured forth an abundant and refreshing rain, which has continued, with short intervals, in a warm, steady downpour up to the hour of writing.

The thirsty land is drinking in its Divinely-given refreshment, and all Zion City is rejoicing tonight in Showers of Blessing of every kind.

Our prayer is that over all the wide world, on every Continent and Island of the Ocean, wherever Zion is found, and upon those who are traveling to Zion by land or by sea, the many Blessings which we so richly enjoy tonight in Zion City, may abound, and that Peace, and Purity, and Power and Progress, along every line, may be experienced by Zion in every land.

I hope to meet, God willing, with the many thousands of Zion in Shiloh Tabernacle, Zion City, next Lord's Day, at the Early Morning Sacrifice of Praise and Prayer, and at the General Assembly in the afternoon, when we shall deliver the first of a series of discourses upon subjects especially suggested by our Visitation Around the World.

Your prayers for Divine Guidance in the preparation and delivery of these Addresses are most earnestly desired.

I will close this Letter by reminding you of Zion's Fourth Feast of Tabernacles, which will begin on Wednesday, July 13th, and continue until Lord's Day, July 24th.

The following Inspired Words in the Fiftieth Psalm have deeply impressed me today:

God, even God, Jehovah, hath spoken,
And Called the Earth from the Rising of the Sun,
Unto the Going-down thereof.
Out of Zion, the perfection of beauty,
God hath shined forth.
Our God shall come, and shall not keep silence:
A fire shall devour before Him,
And it shall be very tempestuous around about Him.
He shall Call to the Heavens above,
And to the earth, that He may judge His people:
Gather My Saints together unto Me;
Those that have made a Covenant with Me by Sacrifice.

Truly God hath spoken and "called the earth from the Rising of the Sun unto the Going-down thereof," through our lips and writings, to this Gathering of His Saints unto Himself, even those who have "made a Covenant with Him by Sacrifice."

It is impossible to make a Covenant with God without Sacrifice.

Fellowship and communion with God in Zion are ever accompanied by loving sacrifices for God and for Zion.

We earnestly call upon all who are willing to serve God by self-sacrifice, to gather together with us in Zion for this Feast beside the "River of God" which is "full of water," and receive from Him the Fruits of the Spirit from the Tree of Life, the Leaves of which are for the Healing of the Nations.

Let it be said in every land and nation, "Out of Zion, the Perfection of Beauty, God hath shined forth."

From this great Series of Gatherings at the Feast of Tabernacles it is our earnest prayer and confident expectation that a Glorious Company of Reconsecrated Children of God will receive fresh anointing, and that Zion City with its many thousands shall be blessed.

May Zion Restoration Host, which is God's "New, sharp threshing instrument having teeth," (Isaiah 41:15-16,) go forth to "thresh the mountains" of infidelity, intemperance, and impurity, "beat them small" and "make the hills as chaff."

May Zion deliver from the slavery of Satan and Sin, and from Disease and Death and Hell vast multitudes who are now groaning in darkness and despair, and cause them to rejoice, through Faith in Jesus, in the Saving-Health and Life, and Light and Love and all the temporal and eternal blessings of the Gospel of the Kingdom of God and of Heaven.

BRETHREN PRAY FOR US.

I am, your friend and Fellow Servant in Jesus, the Christ, our Lord,

General Overseer of the Christian Catholic Church in Zion.

A WEEKLY PAPER FOR THE EXTENSION OF THE KINGDOM OF GOD.
EDITED BY THE REV. JOHN ALEX. DOWIE.

Application for entry as Second Class Matter at Zion City, Illinois, pending.

Subscription Rates.		Special Rates.	
One Year	$2.00	100 Copies of One Issue	$3.00
Six Months	1.25	25 Copies of One Issue	1.00
Three Months	.75	To Ministers, Y. M. C. A's and Public Reading Rooms, per annum	1.50
Single Copies	.05		

For foreign subscriptions add $1.50 per year, or three cents per copy for postage.

Subscribers desiring a change of address should give present address, as well as that to which they desire LEAVES OF HEALING sent in the future.

Make Bank Drafts, Express Money or Postoffice Money Orders payable to the order of JOHN ALEX. DOWIE, Zion City, Illinois, U. S. A.

Long Distance Telephone. *Cable Address "Dowie, Zion City."*

All communications upon business must be addressed to
MANAGER ZION PUBLISHING HOUSE,
Zion City, Illinois, U. S. A.

Subscriptions to LEAVES OF HEALING, A VOICE FROM ZION, and the various publications may also be sent to

ZION PUBLISHING HOUSE, 81 EUSTON ROAD, LONDON, N. W., ENGLAND.
ZION PUBLISHING HOUSE, NO. 43 PARK ROAD, ST. KILDA, MELBOURNE, VICTORIA, AUSTRALIA.
ZION PUBLISHING HOUSE, RUE DE MONT, THABOR 1, PARIS, FRANCE.
ZIONSHEIM, SCHLOSS LIEBBURG, CANTON THURGAU, BEI ZÜRICH, SWITZERLAND.

ZION CITY, ILLINOIS, SATURDAY, JULY 2, 1904.

TABLE OF CONTENTS.

LEAVES OF HEALING, SATURDAY, JULY 2, 1904.

LEAVES OF HEALING.

Two Dollars will bring to you the weekly visits of the Little White Dove for a year; 75 cents will send it to a friend for thirteen weeks; $1.25 will send it for six months; $1.50 will send it to your minister, or to a Y. M. C. A., or to a Public Reading Room for a whole year. We offer no premiums, except the premium of doing good. We receive no advertisements, and print no commercial lies or cheating enticements of unscrupulous thieves. LEAVES OF HEALING is Zion on wings and we keep out everything that would detract the reader's mind from all except the Extension of the Kingdom of God, for which alone it exists. If we cannot send forth our Little White Dove without soiling its wings with the smoke of the factory and the dirt of the wrangling market-place, or compelling it to utter the screaming cries of the business vultures in the ears of our readers, then we will keep our D[illegible] at home.

Notes From the Overseer for Zion City.

"BE GLAD THEN, YE CHILDREN OF ZION, AND REJOICE IN JEHOVAH YOUR GOD."

FOR HE giveth you the former rain in just measure,
And He causeth to come down for you the rain,
The former rain and the latter rain, in the first month.

. . . .

And ye shall know that I am in the midst of Israel,
And that I am Jehovah your God, and there is none else:
And My people shall never be ashamed.

THE PROPHETS of God in Israel have always been mighty factors in the dealings of Jehovah with His people.

IT WAS through them that the message of peace or the coming of adversity was made known unto the people. And it has always come to pass according to the word of the prophet, whenever that prophet spake at the inspiration and direction of God.

WHEN GOD'S PROPHET declared that there should be no rain for the space of "three years and six months" it was fulfilled according to the Prophet's word.

Again when the Prophet spake, God sent the rain upon the thirsty land, but not until then.

Elijah had to return to Israel before the blessing of God was manifested in the bountiful rain.

GOD HAS again wonderfully shown to His people that the voice of His Prophet must be heard and obeyed in these last times, and has proved to the world that this is indeed Elijah who "is to come."

IT HAS long been prophesied by the daily papers of Waukegan and Chicago—perhaps in a mocking way—that when Elijah returned to Zion City there would be rain.

ALL THROUGH the beautiful spring months there has been a great lack of rain.

Time and again there would be threatenings, and it would seem as though there must be a great downpouring, but a a strong east wind would blow off the lake and beat back the coming shower, until the land has suffered from very serious drouth.

There had not been a good, heavy, soaking rain for

several months. The showers that have come have been exceedingly few and distressingly light. Even up to Wednesday night, when the whole sky was overcast with heavy thunder-clouds, and the thunder rolled and the lightning flashed across the heavens, and our hearts were rejoicing to think that at last the drouth was about to be broken, only a few drops of rain fell, and again the skies were cleared, and the morning broke into a most fair and beautiful day, bringing disappointment to thousands of waiting hearts.

BUT THE day of victory and deliverance came at last; Twenty-five representatives of the four great Councils of Zion—the Ecclesiastical, the Educational, the Commercial and the Political—left Zion City at seven o'clock, a. m., in a special car, to meet the General Overseer and his party in Chicago.

BY A TRIFLING delay in getting the General Overseer's private car across the city from the Nickel Plate depot to the North-Western station, the nine o'clock train was missed, and the program was disarranged to the extent of just one hour.

OTHERWISE the program, as arranged, was carried out to its minutest detail, up to the address of the General Overseer. The procession from the depot was headed by Zion City Band. Then followed, in order, the Staff Officers of Zion Guard, the Cabinet Officers, the General Overseer, Overseer Jane Dowie, Dr. A. J. Gladstone Dowie, the carriages of his Visitation Party and others; and by thousands of Zion Restoration Host, Zion White-robed Choir, Zion Robed Officers, and Zion Guard in uniform, in countermarch.

THE DAY was most beautiful and bright and fair—even up to the arrival of the General Overseer in Zion City the sun was shining brightly.

Clouds were scattered here and there, but there was no indication of rain, and up to the time the General Overseer began to speak to the thousands assembled around him, no one would have thought that in a few minutes there would be a heavy downpour of rain.

But the General Overseer had scarcely spoken fifteen minutes when it was noticed by many that the clouds were gathering from the east and from the west, from the north and from the south, and were accumulating directly overhead. A most peculiar phenomenon was seen: the clouds were actually coming from several directions at the same time.

THE RAIN began to fall, and before thirty minutes had elapsed there was a tremendous downpour, such as Zion City had not seen for many months.

THE RAIN WAS accompanied, in a short time, by a beautiful and nondestructive fall of hailstones. Rarely, if ever, have we seen the ground so thickly covered with the beautiful white globules of congealed water.

ACCOMPANYING THIS storm there was no wind to speak of.

No damage was done whatever; and while some of the people got considerably wet, no one was injured, and no one has taken sick because of the wetting. In fact, the people were glad for the rain, and willingly endured the slight inconvenience that resulted therefrom, for they saw in it the Hand of God in honoring His Prophet, and in proving to a scoffing age that God's presence goes before His servant.

IN THE Rally on Wednesday night we most seriously urged the people to carry their umbrellas the next day.

We felt confident that the rain would come when Elijah the Restorer returned to his own beloved City, but that we could not expect it before.

NO DOUBT, the long continued drouth is broken. Showers continued to fall during the afternoon and evening, so that today the land is refreshed, and the promise of a full and glorious harvest is assured.

THESE DEMONSTRATIONS began almost as soon as the General Overseer touched American shores.

In New York last Lord's Day there was the same heavy fall of rain during the afternoon service.

ONE BEAUTIFUL feature of the rain in Zion City was that there was no wind-storm and scarcely any electrical display which is so usual in a hail-storm. But the rain seemed to fall straight down, and while the fall of water was tremendous, the people were able to find places of shelter, without suffering any harm whatever.

IT IS likely that the papers will declare that it was simply a coincidence, but coincidences are in the Providence of God, and we believe and our hearts are assured that it all has been prearranged by God, and it was only at His bidding that this beautiful demonstration took place.

IT IS only fair to say that the General Overseer has not seen these Notes. Neither has he revised any parts of this paper save his General Letter to the Church, and perhaps one or two pages of the report.

THE HEARTS of the many thousands of the people of Zion City, as well as of all Zion in all the world, are rejoicing in the return of their beloved Leader and his entire Visitation party, all in good health and without one mishap through the more than thirty thousand miles of travel.

THE SIX MONTHS have seemed a long time, and it was only because of the good that he could do and of the demands that God has made upon him to carry the Gospel of Zion to every nation that it seemed possible for us to give him up for so long a time.

BUT GOD has blessed Zion City during his absence. It is no small compliment to the General Overseer, and a sure evidence that God is the Founder of Zion, that so great a work can be so thoroughly organized that for six months the City of Zion has prospered abundantly and has continued to go forward in many ways.

NOW, AS he takes up again the direction of affairs in Zion City and throughout the world, the influence of his mighty power and authority and love will be felt for good.

THE PLANS of the Evil One to prevent his return to the land of his adoption and to the City of his building have been thwarted.

THE PROPHECY of the press and the pulpit that he would never return has been put to the lie, and again he is here to face the great hosts of Satan, the powers of evil of this world.

ZION CITY is a happy place these days, and we praise God for His wonderful mercy and for the fulfilment of His Word,

Ye shall know that I am in the midst of Israel,
And that I am Jehovah your God, and there is none else:
And My people shall never be ashamed.

JOHN G. SPEICHER.

GOD'S WAY OF HEALING.

BY THE REV. JOHN ALEX. DOWIE.

God's Way of Healing Is a Person, Not a Thing.

Jesus said "*I am* the Way, and the Truth, and the Life," and He has ever been revealed to His people in all the ages by the Covenant Name, Jehovah-Rophi, or "*I am* Jehovah that Healeth thee." (John 14:6; Exodus 15:26.)

The Lord Jesus, the Christ, is Still the Healer.

He cannot change, for "Jesus, the Christ, is the same yesterday and today, yea and forever;" and He is still with us, for He said: "Lo, *I am* with you All the Days, even unto the Consummation of the Age." (Hebrews 13:8; Matthew 28:20.) Because He is Unchangeable, and because He is present, in spirit, just as when in the flesh, He is the Healer of His people.

Divine Healing Rests on the Christ's Atonement.

It was prophesied of Him, "Surely He hath borne our griefs (Hebrew, *sickness*), and carried our sorrows: . . . and with His stripes we are healed;" and it is expressly declared that this was fulfilled in His Ministry of Healing, which still continues. (Isaiah 53:4, 5; Matthew 8:17.)

Disease Can Never be God's Will.

It is the Devil's work, consequent upon Sin, and it is impossible for the work of the Devil ever to be the Will of God. The Christ came to "destroy the works of the Devil," and when He was here on earth He healed "all manner of disease and all manner of sickness," and all these sufferers are expressly declared to have been "oppressed of the Devil." (1 John 3:8; Matthew 4:23; Acts 10:38.)

The Gifts of Healing Are Permanent.

It is expressly declared that the "Gifts and the calling of God are without repentance," and the Gifts of Healing are amongst the Nine Gifts of the Spirit to the Church. (Romans 11:29; 1 Corinthians 12:8-11.)

There Are Four Modes of Divine Healing.

The first is the direct prayer of faith; the second, intercessory prayer of two or more; the third, the anointing of the elders, with the prayer of faith; and the fourth, the laying on of hands of those who believe, and whom God has prepared and called to that Ministry. (Matthew 8:5-13; Matthew 18:19; James 5:14, 15; Mark 16:18.)

Divine Healing Is Opposed by Diabolical Counterfeits.

Amongst these are Christian Science (falsely so-called), Mind Healing, Spiritualism, Trance Evangelism, etc. (1 Timothy 6:20, 21; 1 Timothy 4:1, 2; Isaiah 51:22, 23.)

Multitudes Have Been Healed Through Faith in Jesus.

The writer knows of thousands of cases and has personally laid hands on scores of thousands of persons. Full information can be obtained at the meetings held in the Zion Tabernacles in Chicago, and in Zion City, Illinois, and in many pamphlets which give the experience, in their own words, of many who have been healed in this and other countries, published at Zion Printing and Publishing House, Zion City, Illinois.

"Belief Cometh of Hearing, and Hearing by the Word of the Christ."

You are heartily invited to attend and hear for yourself.

ELIJAH THE RESTORER

SCENE AT THE WELCOME HOME OF THE GENERAL OVERSEER AND VISITATION PARTY

ZION CITY, ILLINOIS, JUNE 30, 1904.

Welcome Home to the General Overseer
and His Around-the-World Visitation Party.

Zion City, Thursday, June 30, 1904.

REPORTED BY S. E. C., A. C. R. AND E. S

LISTEN:—

A whistle sounds in the distance!

Ten thousand wait!

Expectation is soon to be realization.

The hum of conversation hushes.

Through the long lines of humanity stretching in double columns for nearly a mile there is a visible indrawing of the breath, the nervous tension tightens.

Away and away the living, breathing columns stretch!

Above is the blue of the sky. The sunlight strikes back from gold accoutrements, flashes against the brilliant coloring of myriad flags and uniforms and banners, and brings out, in strong relief, somber-garbed, stately clerical figures.

To the east lies the blue lake.

To the west they gather—this host of Zion; on, on, far away, the living columns extend.

Like multitudes of doves, the white robes of the great Zion Choir flutter and flash, their snowy whiteness gleaming against the background of flowered fields of green.

The Great Triumphal Arch.

Rising against the blue of the heavens is the great Triumphal Arch.

On its white pillars and across the top are inscriptions—the Promises of the Eternal Jehovah, which hath endured and shall endure, forever.

Here, too, are the names of the great cities which have been visited by the Prophet of God as he carried the Divine Message in his Around-the-World Visitation—four of these in red.

From its topmost pinnacles float the red, white and blue of the Flag of America, and the gold, white and blue of Zion.

Here, at the gates, the columns of the hosts mass, and, extending north and south, take the form of a cross.

On the other side, to the west, appears a sea—a sea of children's faces; instinct with life and grace and beauty, glowing with love and joy and happy expectancy.

And beyond, thousands of other faces, older, and with something in them absent from the first named; if one looks closely, too, tears are there. The children smile.

The air is perfumed with the odor of flowers. They are everywhere. They wreath the heads of the horses and festoon their silken coats. The children carry them. Their fragrance fills the air.

Welcome Home.

"Peace to thee!"

The first words of Zion's beloved Leader as he returns and views his own!

His own, by the grace of Jehovah, and by the abounding love in the hearts of Zion, as the hosts gather to welcome home that Leader—Friend; Father; Brother; Pastor; Shepherd of his Flock; Prophet; Priest; Servant and Friend of God!

And Zion gave of her best.

It was a royal welcome!

The General Overseer's carriage, drawn by the span of magnificent Russian stallions lately presented to him in Zurich, Switzerland, and wreathed in smilax and carnations, was in waiting at the depot, and soon he, accompanied by his wife, Overseer Jane Dowie, their son, Dr. A. J. Gladstone, and Overseer Speicher, were seated within.

This carriage was followed by others containing the other members of the Around-the-World Visitation Party, and the members of the Reception Party, who had met the Visitation Party at Chicago earlier in the morning and had returned with them.

Then began the ride from the station, up through the double columns of Zion Guard, Zion Restoration Host, and Zion Robed Officers, on either side of the road, all the way up to the Triumphal Arch.

At the station Zion City Band was in waiting and greeted the Party upon their arrival with a burst of sweet sounds, the Band then preceding the carriages and playing softly as the procession moved slowly on its way.

A Joyous Home-coming.

The General Overseer smiled to the right, to the left, to the east and west, north and south, to the rear and in front, and once or twice up--and would have smiled oftener had he not been struggling heroically with tears.

Overseer Jane Dowie looked fresh and rested and beautiful, and she, too, smiled and looked very happy.

Overseer Speicher fairly beamed.

The other members of the party reflected, in various degrees, the same happy emotions.

And the people—those who were not crying were smiling, and sometimes doing both at the same time.

Order of Exercises.

At nine o'clock the whistle blew for morning prayers.

Immediately after this the signal was given by the whistle, calling the people from all over the City, to gather at their various places, and arrange for position on Shiloh boulevard.

Zion Junior Choir was stationed immediately west of the Arch of Welcome.

Immediately back of them, and to the west, was placed Zion Junior Restoration Host, with their Zion badges. The Junior Choir and Junior Restoration Host were all supplied with American flags.

To the rear and to the west of Zion Junior Restoration Host was reserved space for visitors and others who did not take part in the procession and the exercises.

On the east of the Arch came first, the Senior White-robed Choir.

On either side of the Choir were stationed Zion Robed Officers.

To the rear and to the east came the great adult Zion Restoration Host, each member of which carried a Zion flag.

Surrounding the choir forces came Zion Guard in uniform.

Following the carriages, and on either side, came, first, in countermarch, staff officers of Zion Guard, Zion White-robed Choir, Robed Officers, and Zion Guard.

These continued their countermarch until they took their places with others of their class between Elijah avenue and the Arch.

As the band reached the Arch it ceased playing; and, as the General Overseer's carriage stopped, ten little girls, robed in white, with blue badges across their breasts, bearing the names in gilt letters of the ten principal countries visited by the General Overseer, pelted the General Overseer and party with bouquets of flowers, instead of the sticks and stones which he received in some of these countries. A little Swiss girl then extended a welcome to the General Overseer in verse, composed by herself.

Opening the Gates.

The gates of the Triumphal Arch were then unlocked by the Overseer-in-charge, and this key, together with the keys belonging to the General Overseer, which had been intrusted to him for six months, were presented to the General Overseer.

Two little girls in white opened the gates beneath the Arch, while the Junior Choir burst forth in singing:

Open Now Thy Gates of Beauty,
Zion Let Me Enter There.

As the Overseer-in-charge handed the keys to the General Overseer he said:

"Beloved General Overseer, I take great pleasure in returning to you the keys of Zion which you entrusted to my care temporarily.

"I thank God greatly that He has permitted you to return to this City that I may return them into your own hands."

In receiving the keys the General Overseer said:

My dear Overseer, I thank you for the safe return of the keys of Zion, which are symbolical of authority and trust.

I am glad once more to be permitted to be with my people and to lead them forward.

Rising, then, in his carriage and standing with outstretched hands and uncovered head, the General Overseer pronounced the

INVOCATION.

God be merciful unto us, and bless us, and cause Thy face to shine upon us; that Thy way may be known upon earth; Thy saving health among all the Nations. For the sake of Jesus. Amen.

He then said:

No words which human thought or tongue could frame would express the feeling of my heart at this moment. No words could possibly express my thoughts; they are too deep for utterance.

I am grateful beyond expression, first of all to my God and Father, who by the Eternal Spirit, through His Son, has heard my prayer and guided my way, and after more than thirty thousand miles of travel around the world, has brought me safely back. [Amen!]

Commends Overseer John G. Speicher.

I thank Overseer John G. Speicher, who has handed to me the keys, symbolically, of the City, and in reality of his office.

I thank him and thank my God for the good care that He has taken of the City in my absence. [Amen!]

I am glad to know that God has prepared him for the work, and that he did it so well.

I am glad to know that he preached to you so well and administered so well.

I feel concerning him as I do with Mrs. Dowie; when they tell me how well she preached and how well she did, I say, "I am grateful; I thank God; but I trained her;" and I can say of Overseer Speicher, "I trained him!"

He says, "Amen."

But you know it is not every one whom you can train.

I am grateful to God for all that He has wrought.

Of course, you will not expect me to speak at any great length, because it is difficult and almost impossible for a human voice to reach the many thousands whom I see around me on every side.

But next Lord's Day morning, at half past six o'clock, we shall all be in Shiloh Tabernacle at morning prayers.

It ought to be the best morning gathering for the Morning Sacrifice of Praise and Prayer that we have ever had.

I shall refrain from all public utterances, beyond these of thankfulness, until I can speak in Shiloh Tabernacle.

I am sure that the welcome which you are giving to me and to my dear wife and son is also, as is proper, given to the members of my Visitation Party.

They have done well, and I can say that I made no mistake when I selected them for my companions and helpers.

A Story That Cannot Be Told.

The story of our travel has been already read by you, in the pages of LEAVES OF HEALING, as far as it can be put into words.

But there are ten thousand things to tell that cannot be put into printed, or even spoken, words, and much that could not be understood were an attempt made to tell it in either way.

One thing I desire to say is this, that even where Zion was rejected you must never forget that she was rejected by only a noisy minority.

The vast majority, even in Australia, I believe, was in sympathy with me.

This I saw in the great Exhibition Building, in Melbourne, where eight thousand people were eager to hear, and two hundred were determined to interrupt.

Of course it is always possible in great cities, especially in London, to stir up the great rabble; [thunder rumbled] and the artillery of heaven is answering "Amen!" [Laughter.]

You have had God's blessing; you have been a united people.

If I had foreseen the trials which unexpectedly came to me and Zion in December, I possibly would not have prepared to go in January; but the victory which God gave us was so great and so complete, that I felt that Satan's arts to hinder my plans had all been employed in vain, and that it was best to go on with the Visitation. I am glad that I did.

Zion the Same the World Over.

I want to tell you, and all know it, that Zion in Australia is like Zion everywhere; loyal to God; loyal to the Christ; led by the Spirit; loyal to the General Overseer as the Prophet of the Restoration; and loyal to everything that is represented by the glorious word "Zion." [Applause.]

I am thankful for the sixty or seventy Australians who, since I saw them in Australia, have come ahead of me.

Deacon Partridge, I saw your face and many others of your number, as I came along the triumphal way to this Arch—faces which I saw in February and March last in South Australia.

I am glad to see you and I am glad to welcome all who have come to Zion from many other lands since I left.

Next week sometime, after we have unpacked our trunks and settled down a little, I shall have a reception, first of all for those who have come into Zion City since we left, and then for every one of you; but you must not all come at once. I hope to see you face to face, one by one.

Oh, how thankful we should be that there is one spot of God's green earth every inch of which belongs to Him!

There is no other place like Zion City in all the world; and I am grateful to God that I am home again.

I desire especially to thank these dear children who have been singing yonder, beyond the Arch, so beautifully. God bless the children of Zion! [Amen!]

I now wish to present to you Mrs. Dowie, and Dr. Gladstone Dowie. [Both rose amid the hearty cheering of the crowds.]

Overseer Jane Dowie then said:

An Inexpressible Joy.

"My heart is very full today, and it seems as if I could hardly speak a word.

"I am grateful to be again at home, and with you here.

"I am grateful to God that He has preserved the General Overseer's life, and our lives, amid the many perils through which we have passed.

"I rejoice with you all today in this beautiful City, the City of Zion, of which we have been speaking to the people in every part of the world in which we have been.

"We have told them of this beautiful, clean City, and of the people who have come together to lead good, clean, and holy lives, believing in the Full Gospel of Salvation, Healing and Holiness. As I look into your faces, I think that today, instead of having overdrawn our picture, we did not paint it beautiful enough; we have not given it half enough expression.

A Beautiful Contrast.

"The half was not told.

"We certainly told the people how good you all were to us, but it has not been fully told.

"Today we rejoice to see this beautiful company of fresh, healthy people.

"We know that the service of God is far better than the service of the Devil.

"As we passed through many cities, we had to endure the tobacco smoke and the filth; and as we looked upon the faces of many of the people that gathered around us in crowds as you have gathered here today, instead of seeing bright, happy, joyful faces, we looked upon cruel, wicked faces, expressive of every evil passion, and heard their horrible shouting and curses.

"It certainly is a beautiful, pleasing contrast to see the faces and hear the voices of our dear people.

"May God bless you all. Again, I say, I rejoice to see you.

"I think we certainly rejoice as much in seeing you all as you do in seeing us. We praise God for this Welcome Home."

Dr. Gladstone Dowie, being introduced, then said:

An Enthusiastic Audience.

"I feel very glad to be here today and to look again upon Zion City.

"It is especially pleasing to us to see this audience when we remember the audiences which we have seen in some parts of the world, who were not quite so enthusiastic.

"But still there are hundreds and thousands of Zion people, as the General Overseer says, all over the world, who are just as enthusiastic as this people.

"As it is beginning to rain, I shall not keep you longer, only to say that we are very glad to see you all again and to get back to Zion City."

Other Members of Visitation Party Introduced.

General Overseer—I wish to present to you, just for a word, in rapid succession, the members of the Visitation Party, to show you that I brought them all back.

Overseer John G. Excell—"I wish to say, dear friends, that I am very glad to be with you once more.

"I have enjoyed the trip with the General Overseer very much.

"I have received great blessing, and count it a great privilege to have gone with him on this trip.

"I am thankful to be with you and to greet you on his return."

Deacon Arthur W. Newcomb—"I praise God with all my heart for the beautiful sight which I see today.

"It is the most beautiful I have seen since I left Zion City.

"It has been a glorious thing to go around the world and to learn what is to be learned by traveling, but it is a more glorious thing to get back to Zion City and to God's people."

The General Overseer then introduced the remaining members of the Visitation Party, Deaconess Ida M. Stern, Deacon Carl F. Stern and Deacon Ernest Williams, who were welcomed with cheers by the assembled multitude, after which he pronounced the

BENEDICTION.

The grace of our Lord Jesus, the Christ, the love of God our Father, and the fellowship of the Holy Spirit be with you all, and keep you ever.

And then it rained!

The big drops had come pattering down, slowly at first, curtailing in a measure the reception program prepared, and then came a rush of summer rain such as Zion had been needing for weeks and asking God to send.

It soaked the earth, and sent the hosts of Zion helter-skelter, seeking for cover, and the General Overseer's carriage was driven rapidly to Shiloh House.

Notes of Thanksgiving from the Whole World

By John G. Speicher, Overseer for Zion City.

Girl Healed of Severe Cough and Pain.

He sendeth His word, and healeth them.—*Psalm 107:20.*

OCEOLA, OHIO, February 27, 1904.

DEAR OVERSEER:—Peace to thee.

I feel it my duty to thank God for His wonderful healing power and for His goodness in healing me.

I was very sick in February, 1903.

As I had no doctor, we could not tell exactly what the disease was.

It began with a severe cough. I was free from coughing scarcely a minute.

Deaconess Teeterick called and she, mamma and I knelt in prayer, expecting God to answer.

I received healing of the cough, but still had severe pains in my stomach, and was so sore I could not touch myself without causing pain.

As Elder Bouck was on business in our town, we requested him to come and pray with me, which he did.

I received a partial healing.

Once more Deaconess Teeterick prayed with laying on of hands and I received a perfect healing, for which we all praised God.

The symptoms were those of typhoid fever.

I want to thank my heavenly Father for a recent healing.

I had a breaking out on my side and felt very nervous.

We prayed, and I received some relief.

We then sent a request for prayer to you, and when you prayed I received a perfect healing.

I am now well and going to school.

I am ten years old and belong to the Christian Catholic Church in Zion.

Pray that I may grow up in the fear and love of God and be of some use in extending God's Kingdom.

May God use this testimony among many of His little children.

I remain,

Your little daughter in the Christ,

GRACE ESTHER YOST.

Healed of Violent Toothache.

Pray one for another
That ye may be healed.—*James 5:16.*

OCEOLA, OHIO, February 27, 1904.

DEAR OVERSEER-IN-CHARGE:—Peace to thee.

I am glad that I can confirm the testimony of my little daughter.

I wish also to add my own testimony.

On the 10th of February I was seized with a violent toothache which lasted for three days, during which time I was in constant pain.

I sent in a request to you for prayer, as I was nearly crazed with pain; and as soon as you prayed I received an instantaneous healing, for which I thank God, and also thank you for your prayers.

I cannot tell a tithe of the blessings which I have received since coming out of the apostasies and into the Christian Catholic Church in Zion.

The last two years have been the happiest of my life.

May God's richest blessings be upon you and your dear family and upon all Zion.

Faithfully yours in the Master's service,

(MRS.) ANNETTIE YOST.

Woman Ninety-two Years Old Healed of Wen.

He giveth power to the faint;
And to him that hath no might
He increaseth strength.—*Isaiah 40:29.*

3107 GILEAD AVENUE,
ZION CITY, ILLINOIS, February 28, 1904.

DEAR GENERAL OVERSEER:—I desire to give you a written testimony of the healing of my grandmother, Salome Wood, who is now in her ninety-second year.

She had a wen on her head for at least thirty-five years, and in the last six years it had grown larger, and at times was very painful.

She wrote to me just before the General Overseer left, and said, "I know that if the Doctor prays for me, I shall be healed."

The General Overseer prayed; and now I have word from her that the wen has entirely disappeared.

I thank God for the many blessings to my children and to me, and for a wonderful keeping power through this winter.

Yours in the Christ,

(MRS.) BLANCHE W. SPARROW.

Daughter Healed.

The joy of Jehovah is your strength.—*Nehemiah 8:10.*

QUEEN, PENNSYLVANIA, February 16, 1904.

DEAR DR. SPEICHER:—I am glad to tell you that my daughter, Rachel, for whom you prayed, is now well.

I wrote to you and she got well immediately and went to work as if nothing had been wrong.

(MRS.) M. M. CLAAR.

ELIJAH THE RESTORER REBUKES THE MINISTER WHO DEFILES HIMSELF WITH ALCOHOL AND NICOTINE POISON.

Around-the-World Visitation

of the

Rev. John Alex. Dowie

Elijah the Restorer
General Overseer of the Christian Catholic Church in Zion.

By ARTHUR W. NEWCOMB, Special Correspondent.

VISITATION IN ZURICH, SWITZERLAND.

THE last paper of this series closed with the report of the meeting held by the General Overseer in the Velodrome, Zurich, Switzerland, Tuesday evening, May 24, 1904.

Wednesday dawned bright, beautiful, springlike.

This day was the fifty-seventh anniversary of the General Overseer's birth, an anniversary remembered by Zion everywhere.

Many loving telegrams, cablegrams, and letters were received by the man of God, among which was the following from Zion at Headquarters, in Zion City:

All Zion in Zion City, and especially Zion Guard, send greeting and loving congratulations on the approaching fifty-seventh anniversary of your birth.
Zion Guard considers it an increasing honor to have you as its Commander-in-chief.
God bless you forever.
Mizpah.

To this the General Overseer replied:

Philippians, 1st chapter, 20th to 30th verses.
Thank Zion in Zion City and everywhere for loving congratulations on fifty-seventh anniversary.
Thank Zion Guard especially.
I salute them with Romans 16th chapter, verses three and four.
Splendid meetings in Zurich.
Many applying for Baptism.
Mizpah. DOWIE.

Besides the beautiful team of horses and the books already mentioned, the General Overseer received many gifts of flowers from members and friends of Zion in Zurich, and a topographic atlas of Switzerland from the members of the Around-the-World Visitation party.

At the Velodrome, a large floral piece with the figures "57" upon it, faced the platform, placed there by Zion in Zurich.

In the evening Zion Band serenaded the General Overseer at his hotel, and sent to his room a handsome sheaf of flowers.

This was a day of gladness for Zion in Zurich.

The brightness of the sun, the gleaming of the pale-green waters of the lake and the river, the fresh, cool breezes, the singing of the birds, the purple glow of the hills, and the snow-crowned heads of the distant Alps, all seemed to be in Divine harmony with the song of Love and Praise which filled the hearts of God's people as they dwelt upon His goodness and loving-kindness.

Again and again there came to mind that wonderful Truth, so often impressed upon us by the teaching of our General Overseer and by the daily gifts of our Father in Heaven: "The River of God is full of Water!"

Wednesday Afternoon Meeting.

It was in this joyous spirit that the thousands came together in the Velodrome on Wednesday afternoon, at the third Divine Healing meeting.

Under such conditions, there could not fail to be given a great blessing to the people.

God gave a very plain, practical and helpful Message to His Prophet, which was received with prayerful earnestness by nearly all present.

Again, in the prayer-room, God's spirit was present to bless, and many received healing.

Velodrome, Zurich, Switzerland, Wednesday Afternoon, May 25, 1904.
*REPORTED BY E. W. AND A. W. N.

The Invocation was pronounced by the General Overseer, after which, a hymn was sung.

Prayer was offered by Elder Hodler, also prayer by the General Overseer.

*The following report has not been revised by the General Overseer.

A hymn was then sung, during which the tithes and offerings were received.

The General Overseer then delivered the afternoon Message:

THE CANAANITISH WOMAN.

INVOCATION.

Let the words of my mouth, and the meditation of my heart be acceptable in Thy sight, be profitable unto this people and unto all to whom these words shall come. For the sake of Jesus. Amen.

TEXT.

And when even was come, they brought unto Him many possessed with devils: and He cast out the spirits with a word, and healed all that were sick:
That it might be fulfilled which was spoken by Isaiah the prophet, saying, Himself took our infirmities, and bare our diseases.

I am glad that this brief Visitation has already been blessed to so many sad, and sick, and suffering people.

A Man on Whom God Wrought a Miracle of Healing.

I am very happy to see a man sitting there beside his wife who sat in a chair like that yesterday, in just about that very position.

He had been in that chair, unable to walk, for four years.

I prayed to God for him, told him to rise, and he rose.

He was able to put his feet down, and walk up and down.

He has been able to walk ever since.

Stand up and let us see you.

[The gentleman referred to rose and walked up the aisle.]

Did God heal you?

Witness—"*Ja.*"

General Overseer—Thank God for that.

I expect to see him running up and down here before long.

I am very glad to hear that yesterday a good, honest German lady from Basel, who came in almost blind, received her sight.

She said, "Now I am going home. I can see you, and see my friends."

It seemed that she had received almost perfect sight.

I do not gather up the testimony at all.

I have not time to do that.

I have time only to preach and pray; I do not have much time to eat and sleep.

I am grateful that God has been blessing many of the six hundred fifty for whom I have prayed within the last few days.

We must go right on.

All of you who have been seeking healing should continue to seek until you find; keep knocking until it is opened unto you; keep asking until you receive.

"If ye then, being evil," Jesus said, "know how to give good gifts unto your children, how much more shall your Heavenly Father give the Holy Spirit to them that ask Him?"

I am glad to see that God is blessing many; but if there were not one person healed in Zurich, Jesus would still be the Healer.

If there were not one person saved in Zurich, Jesus would still be the Savior.

Such a lack of results would mean simply that the people had no faith, and would not obey Him.

Lack of Humility a Hindrance to Blessing.

That is the trouble with some of you—unwillingness to obey God.

You think that you know all about it.

You are quite content with yourselves; you have nothing more to ask for, and you have all the religion you care to have.

It does not do to have too much religion, because it might trouble you.

You do with just as little as you can.

You will have to get rid of the little you have, some of you, and start at the beginning.

If any of you imagine that you can become Christians by the

acts of a church, by the act of a minister putting water on your nose in your infancy, you are mistaken.

You must be born of God.

You must repent of sin.

You must believe in our Lord Jesus, the Christ.

You must be baptized as a true penitent, and a true believer.

You will not get the blessing of God unless you seek forgiveness by Repentance and by Faith, and unless you are determined, by obeying God, to be His acceptable child.

Divine Healing is not for the children of the Devil. It is for the children of God. It is the children's bread.

You must be His child and obey Him.

Then you can ask your Father to give you the bread that belongs to the children of God.

The Christ said, "I am not sent but to the lost sheep of the house of Israel."

The Canaanitish woman did not understand what the Christ meant.

Many of you do not understand it yet.

You fail to see that

Salvation Is From the Jews.

You fail to see that you cannot be saved unless you are saved by a Jew, by the Jew, Christ Jesus.

If there is anything that is hateful on this earth—if there is anything for which God will punish a nation, whether it is England, France, Germany or Russia, it is the oppression of God's people—the hatred of the Jew.

The Jews are God's people.

When the Christ sent His apostles to preach to the whole world, He said, "Begin at Jerusalem."

They were to preach to the people that crucified Him; to the Jew first, and the Gentile afterwards.

France, Germany, Russia, and every land that has hated the Jew will have to prostrate itself in sackcloth and ashes, and cry to God to forgive the sin of the nation that has hated the Jew because he is a Jew.

God will defend His people.

You cannot be saved except through Jesus, the Christ, the Son of David.

It is horrible to hear professed Christians cursing the Jews, when the mother of Jesus was a virgin Jewess.

She was pure; she was made holy by the Holy Spirit.

She was cleansed, and unless she had been pure in spirit, in soul and in body, she never could have become the mother of Jesus, the Christ.

If you have ever hated the Jew, if you have ever spoken against the Jew, ask God to forgive you, for you are a sinner; you are ungrateful.

One of the great sins of that great people, the Russian people, who have great powers, and who are loved by God, as all nations are, is their persecution of the Jews.

That people will never be delivered, and the Hand of God will be against them until they mourn for the murders of Kishinef; for the murder and cruelty that have been inflicted upon the Jews.

In Germany, and in France, the Jew holds on. His time comes.

It has come now.

Dreyfus is compelling France to put him back to his position.

It was only because he was a Jew that they degraded and imprisoned him.

God cares for His people.

Even if they have forgotten their Covenant with Him, He never forgets His Covenant with them.

He will seek them until He finds them.

The Jew will yet, with all Israel, seek the Lord.

It is the Jew first.

Afterwards, it is the Gentile.

The Folly of Pride of Birth.

There is no use in talking about your pride, your parentage, saying that you are a nobleman, or a noblewoman, and have come from a great family.

Bosh! Rubbish!

You came from Adam, from Eve—the gardener, Adam, and his wife.

Adam and his wife, Eve, look down upon you and laugh at your claim of long descent, at your claim of high birth.

They say, "After all, the highest emperor, and the greatest czar, and the greatest president, are only our children."

No matter what you say, you are all children of that wicked old Adam, and that naughty Eve who obeyed the Devil.

That is all your claim of high descent amounts to.

It is laughable, contemptible!

You must come to God as a humble, broken-hearted, sinful man or woman, willing to take even the place of a dog.

This woman of Canaan received the blessing when she took that place.

I have a number of very excellent people attending this Visitation who have "Von" and "De" before their names.

They are "noble."

I am afraid they will miss a blessing, because they think that they are so great.

Their father was a great nobleman—and an awful thief.

Their great-grandfather stole everything he could lay his hands on. He became a great nobleman.

Why do you not get rid of your nonsense?

Do you think that God will hear you because your great-great-great-grandfather killed a number of men in war, and stole all he could steal, for which they made him a great nobleman?

I know that you are angry with me, some of you. I do not care a pin about it. [Laughter.]

There is no use in being angry. You will have to take your medicine.

It may be bitter, but it will be good for you.

Perhaps you will have a vomit, and will vomit up your pride.

What a good thing that will be!

You will perhaps come to the Christ as a poor sick man or woman, poor sinner without any pride at all, coming as the humblest came, being like Jesus.

A Great Blessing Through Humbling of Pride.

A little while ago a lady of very high rank said to me:

"General Overseer, I should like to be baptized, but I do not like going into the baptistry with all these poor people. Will you please to baptize me alone in clean water?"

I said, "No. Jesus stood in the Jordan, with a crowd of sinners, to be baptized. If the King of kings and Lord of lords will stand amidst sinners, and if I will stand amidst sinners, it is good enough for you. If you will not be baptized there, you cannot be baptized at all."

Then she said, "Then will you please baptize me with the first lot, before the water gets dirty?"

"No," I said, "I will baptize you with the last lot; you shall have to wait until the water gets dirty; until two or three hundred have been baptized."

She went away very angry; but the next morning she came to me and said, "I cried very much; I thought you were very hard upon me; but you are right. I am willing to be the last."

"I will not make you the very last," I said, "because I have to baptize five people who have open cancers. I will keep them to the very end, but you shall come just before these five."

She was very thankful.

She was baptized, and the devil of pride that had always made her toss her head was cast out of her.

She said to me, "It is more than all the other blessings beside that that devil of pride is cast out."

Today she is not less a lady. She is more than ever a gracious lady; but she is humble, and she can go into the homes of her tenants and sit beside the sick, and read the Word of God.

She can kneel there and pray with them, and yet she can wear a coronet.

May God bless you!

God blessed her and took the pride out of her.

The Poor Often Very Proud.

May God take the pride out of you.

There are some poor people who have far more pride in them than even the rich and noble.

They have nothing to boast of, but they boast as if they were the greatest people in the world.

I have met many great people.

I was with the ruler of a great nation the other day, for an hour, in his private room.

I found him one of the humblest of men willing to kneel before God with a broken heart.

God will bless him.

He will always bless the humble, no matter what their station.

May God take the pride out of all of us, and make us willing to come to Him as the humblest sinner.

Then God will heal.

I believe that many of you will not be healed until you vow to God that you will be baptized.

I believe that some of you are afraid to set aside your infant baptism, which you know is of no use.

You have to come and be baptized, and be penitent.

Vow to God that you will.

He will accept that vow. See that you fulfil it.

If you will come and seek Baptism, then God will heal you.

Do not be afraid of any one.

Do right.

Are you willing to do right?

People—"*Ja.*"

General Overseer—When God shows you that you are to be baptized in a proper way, are you willing to obey?

People—"*Ja.*"

General Overseer—Every one that is willing to do the Will of God, in spirit, soul, and body, stand up and tell Him so. [Nearly all rose.]

PRAYER OF CONSECRATION.

My God and Father, in Jesus' Name I come to Thee. Take me as I am. Make me what I ought to be, in spirit, in soul, in body. Give me power to do right, no matter what it costs. Give me Thy Holy Spirit, that I may serve Thee, repent of all the wrong I have done my fellow men, and truly restore. May I repent in Thy sight, and be more desirous that my spirit be clean than even that my body be healed. My body will pass away; my spirit will never die. Save my spirit, and heal my body for Thy glory. For Jesus' sake. [*All repeat the prayer, clause by clause, after the General Overseer.*]

Now, did you mean it all?

People—"*Ja.*"

General Overseer—Are you going to live it?

People—"*Ja.*"

General Overseer—I have said some very hard things, perhaps, today.

You may think I am a hard man, but I am not harder than Jesus was. I simply told the truth, because my heart is filled with love for you.

I greatly delight in the thought that the result of this Visitation will be a blessing to many lands.

Some of you have come from the Mediterranean Sea; some from the Baltic Sea; some from the far-away western lands; some from England.

May God bless you all, and help you to carry back to your homes all the good that God has taught you.

I have no hatred against any one nor against any church.

I hate only what is evil.

May God cleanse all the evil out of all the people in all the churches in all the world!

That is all I ask.

I know that you will be happy when God is everywhere—in your heart, your spirit, your soul, your body, and in all your life.

BENEDICTION.

Beloved, abstain from all appearance of evil. And may the very God of Peace Himself sanctify you wholly; and I pray God your whole spirit and soul and body be preserved entire, without blame, unto the coming of our Lord Jesus, the Christ. Faithful is He that calleth you, who also will do it. The grace of our Lord Jesus, the Christ, the love of God, our Father, the fellowship of the Holy Spirit, our Comforter and Guide, one Eternal God, abide in you, bless you and keep you, and all the Israel of God everywhere, forever. Amen.

Wednesday Evening Meeting.

On Wednesday evening it was reported that the students of one of the universities in Zurich intended to attend the meeting in the Velodrome, and, perhaps, to make a disturbance.

The students evidently came; for there were several hundred young men at the meeting, many of whom could not find seats and stood in a body in the rear of the hall; but there was not a breath of disturbance.

As the General Overseer delivered his Message on the "Sanctification of Spirit, Soul, and Body," building up his argument step by step with the Living Rocks of Eternal Truth, there was a silence in that great audience room so intense that a breath could be heard.

It seemed to us that there could not be one in all that audience who could remain unconvinced of the truth of the Message, and leave without a blessing.

Velodrome, Zurich, Switzerland, Wednesday Evening, May 25, 1904.

*REPORTED BY I. M. S. AND A. W. N.

The meeting was opened by the General Overseer's pronouncing the

INVOCATION.

God be merciful unto us, and bless us,
And cause Thy face to shine upon us;
That Thy Way may be known upon earth,
Thy Saving Health among all the Nations;
For the sake of Jesus. Amen.

Hymn No. 24 was then sung:

Ein' feste Burg ist unser Gott.

Ein' feste Burg ist unser Gott,
Ein' gute Wehr' und Waffen,
Er hilft uns frei aus aller Not,
Die uns jetzt hat betroffen.
Der alt' böse Feind,
Mit Ernst er's jetzt meint;
Groß' Macht und viel List
Sein grausam' Rüstung ist,
Auf Erd' ist nicht sein's Gleichen.

Mit uns'rer Macht ist nichts getan,
Wir sind gar bald verloren,
Es streit't für uns der rechte Mann,
Den Gott hat selbst erkoren.
Fragst du, wer der ist?
Er heißt Jesus Christ,
Der Herr Zebaoth,
Und ist kein and'rer Gott;
Das Feld muß er behalten!

Und wenn die Welt voll Teufel wär
Und wollt' uns gar verschlingen,
So fürchten wir uns nicht so sehr,
Es soll uns doch gelingen.
Der Fürst dieser Welt,
Wie sau'r er sich stellt,
Tut er uns doch nichts,
Das macht, er ist gericht't;
Ein Wörtlein kann ihn fällen.

TRANSLATION.

A mighty fortress is our God,
A bulwark never failing;
Our Helper He, amid the flood
Of mortal ills prevailing.
For still our ancient foe
Doth seek to work his wo;
His craft and power are great,
And armed with cruel hate—
On earth is not his equal.

Did we in our own strength confide,
Our striving would be losing;
Were not the right Man on our side,
The man of God's own choosing.
Doth ask who that may be?
Christ Jesus, it is He!
Lord Sabaoth is His name,
From age to age the same;
And He must win the battle.

And tho' this world with devils filled,
Should threaten to undo us,
We will not fear, for God hath willed
His truth to triumph through us.
Let goods and kindred go,
This mortal life also;
The body they may kill;
God's truth abideth still,
His kingdom is forever.

Elder Jean Kradolfer read from the Inspired Word of God, the 5th chapter of the Epistle of Paul to the Thessalonians.

Prayer was offered by the Rev. Carl Hodler, Elder-in-charge of the Christian Catholic Church in Zion in Zurich.

The General Overseer said:

Gratitude for Kindness of Friends.

Before my friend, Elder Carl Hodler, makes the announcements tonight, I desire to thank the many friends for the exceeding kindness which they have shown to me this day.

I had almost forgotten that my birthday came this week, but the friends in Zurich had not forgotten it.

*The following report has not been revised by the General Overseer.

The first thing I received when I came to this city was a beautiful span of black and white horses as a birthday gift, and I have been receiving birthday gifts all week, and especially today—loving gifts of beautiful flowers. Our good friends of Zion Band came down to the Hotel Bellevue and serenaded me there tonight, and sent me a very beautiful bouquet of flowers.

I have been receiving telegrams from distant parts, especially a cablegram from Zion City.

I feel very grateful to God that all over the world, Zion has not forgotten that this is my fifty-seventh birthday. I thank you all here for the very kind way in which you have recognized that day.

May God bless you.

The announcements were made by Elder Carl Hodler, and the tithes and offerings were received, while a hymn was sung.

The General Overseer then delivered his Message:

SANCTIFICATION OF SPIRIT, SOUL, AND BODY.

INVOCATION.

Let the words of my mouth and the meditation of my heart be acceptable in Thy sight, be profitable unto this people and unto all to whom these words shall come, in this and every land, in this and all the coming time, Till Jesus Come. Amen.

You will find in the 1st Epistle of Paul to the Thessalonians, in the 5th chapter, and 22d and 23d verses, the following words:

TEXT.

Abstain from every form of evil.

And the God of peace Himself sanctify you wholly; and may your spirit and soul and body be preserved entire, without blame at the coming of our Lord Jesus, the Christ.

I have promised tonight to speak to you concerning the Sanctification of Spirit, Soul, and body.

Abstinence From Evil Must Precede Sanctification.

I desire to remind you that it is not possible for entire Sanctification to take place until the exhortation which precedes this 23d verse has been obeyed.

In the 22d verse, you have the key to Sanctification in the command, "Abstain from every form of evil."

The strength of a man is in exact proportion to his self-control.

By the grace of God, one is able to control the passions and to rise superior to the temptations which are to be found, on every side, warring against the spirit, fighting against the soul, and endeavoring to destroy the body.

The Devil attacks the outer fortifications first, endeavoring by means of defiling the body to destroy the soul, and to render ineffective and powerless all the powers of the spirit within.

The command of the Apostle is the command of God, "Abstain from every form of evil."

By means of these Gates out of which the spirit looks—the eyes—we can see the beauties of God's creation, and His wonderful works, but that same sense of sight can be made a degradation and a destruction by creating filthy imaginations in painting and in sculpture, in the creation of unclean gods and goddesses, which are simply the embodiment of foul passions.

By means of the eyes, the Devil is perpetually leading astray.

Yet God, by means of sight, brings the richest blessings to man's spirit.

There is not only animal sight.

Behind every animal sense there is a spiritual sense, which sees the Unseen, which hears the Inaudible, which touches the Immaterial, which tastes the Water of the River of God, yes, and which smells by spiritual smell, the glories of the garden, that garden in which God Himself walked at Eden.

The Devil, by degrading all natural senses, destroys our spiritual powers.

God Created Man to Be a Habitation for Himself.

"Abstain, therefore, from fleshly lusts which war against the spirit" and seek from God the spiritual desires and purity which raises you above the worldly, the sensual, and the devilish, and makes you long to be what God intended you to be.

When God made man He made him to be a habitation for God Himself, a temple in which God could dwell, and through which God could speak and live and work, and in which God delights to dwell.

But that temple must be pure.

"Abstain from every form of evil," and seek, with a devout earnestness and a continuous application, for those things that are pure; for the "Wisdom that is from above," which "is first Pure, then Peaceable, Gentle, Easy to be Entreated, Full of Mercy and of Good Fruits, Without Partiality and Without Hypocrisy, and the Fruit of Righteousness is sown in Peace of them that make Peace."

Abstain from evil and seek good.

Then you come to this glorious place where "the very God of Peace" can sanctify you wholly and make you clean in every part.

The prayer of the Apostle is, therefore, "I pray God your whole Spirit, and Soul, and Body, be preserved entire, without blame, unto the coming of our Lord Jesus, the Christ."

God Works from the Spirit, Outward.

The spirit is that which is within, invisible, but most real.

The soul is the animal life, and the body is that in which it is contained.

God begins with the spirit.

He always works from the center to the circumference, not from the circumference to the center; not from the outside, but from the inside.

When a doctor comes to his fellow man to diagnose a disease, he looks at the man's tongue, he feels the man's pulse, he takes his temperature, and wonders how he can get at the disease.

He looks very wise and shakes his head. There is nothing in it—I mean his head! [Laughter.]

He writes a prescription and tries to get at the disease by pouring something down the throat, or doing something to the body.

That is not God's Way.

God begins with the Spirit.

He says, "My son, My daughter, give Me thine heart."

God cleanses the spirit, then He cleanses the blood, and then He cleanses the body.

Therefore, the first thing that the Apostle prays for is the Sanctification of the Spirit.

Then he prays for the Sanctification of the Soul, and then of the Body.

Spirit and Soul Distinguished.

The great majority of people are constantly confusing Spirit and Soul.

Many talk of the Soul as if it were the Spirit.

It is not, for the Soul is a thing that dies.

There is no immortality of the Soul.

The Word of God has said, "The Soul that sinneth, it shall die."

That which dies is not immortal.

Our Lord Jesus, the Christ, said of His own Soul, "My Soul is exceeding sorrowful, even unto death."

The prophet in speaking of the Christ said that He would "pour out His Soul unto death."

There was nothing immortal in the Christ's soul.

His soul was His animal life. That was not His Spirit.

Every bird, every beast, and every fish has a soul.

Read in the 1st chapter of Genesis, the 20th verse:

And God said, Let the waters bring forth abundantly the moving creature that hath life, and let fowl fly above the earth in the open firmament of heaven.

The word "life" there is translated in the margin of our English Bible, "soul."

In the 30th verse we read,

And to every beast of the earth, and to every fowl of the air, and to every thing that creepeth upon the earth, wherein there is a living soul, I have given every green herb for meat: and it was so.

Man's Spirit the Offspring of God.

But man has a Spirit, while the fish and the fowl and the beasts have no Spirits.

They have Souls and Bodies, and both Souls and Bodies die.

The Christ's Soul died.

The animal life is contained in the blood, and when the blood is shed the Soul is dead.

With the Spirit it is not so.

God is the Father of our Spirits.

He is the Maker of the fowl, and the fish, and every animal, but He is the Father of our Spirits.

We share His nature.

We have His spiritual being.

Since He is the King Eternal, Immortal, and Invisible, the Spirits which come from Him are like Himself, Immortal. They cannot die.

The Body may die, the Soul may die, but the Spirit will return to God who gave it, and will be judged by God according to the deeds which that Spirit has done in the flesh.

The first thing, therefore, is the Sanctification of the Spirit.

The first thing is to awaken, in multitudes who know it not, the fact that they are Spirit; that that Spirit is from God; that they are children of God, and that God wants His child to be pure.

upon them, and today I prayed with one hundred seventy-two.

With those whom I prayed with privately, I suppose that I have laid hands upon eight hundred fifty sick people in Zurich.

Their bodies were diseased in many cases so terribly that their cry to God from their saved spirits came out of foul bodies.

People have been healed here in answer to prayer.

I have given God my Spirit, my Soul and my Body; and the Holy Spirit, who took possession of my Spirit, my Soul, and my Body, has flowed through my hands, and the power of God has come into the sick and they have been healed.

So will all be healed, whether it be through my agency or without my agency; for God is not limited by any agency.

Wherever you will call upon God and give Him your Spirit and your Soul and your Body, which He has made, He will accept it if you are honest and true.

MILAN CATHEDRAL, MILAN, ITALY.

Diseases Arise from Impurity of the Blood.

Therefore, ye who are Christians, surrender your spirits to God; seek that God shall take possession, and through your spiritual being there will flow into your blood the power of the Holy Spirit cleansing your blood.

This is the promise of God in the last words of the Prophet Joel.

It is written:

And I will cleanse their blood that I have not cleansed: for Jehovah dwelleth in Zion.

It is in Zion and through the power of His Kingdom that God wants to purify His people's blood.

It is the impurity of the blood which causes all the disease and all the misery and impurity that I have seen these last days in Zurich.

On Monday, I prayed with two hundred seventy-five, yesterday I prayed with three hundred forty and laid hands

He will cleanse that Spirit, He will cleanse that Soul, and He will cleanse that Body.

What a power the Ministers of God would be if they could all pray the Prayer of Faith and God would use their hands!

Then infidelity would disappear; for facts are the destroyers of foolish theories.

Those who say that the accounts of miracles of nineteen centuries ago are all false, cannot maintain that position when the miracles are repeated today.

This Church, which was founded only eight years ago, influences more than one million people, who are more or less under our ministry, and, through that million, millions more are influenced.

A Word to Ministers.

I say this, my brethren, to you who are ministers of God, that if you want God to use you, you cannot smoke tobacco and defile your bodies; you cannot drink intoxicating liquors and defile your bodies; for God will have your bodies clean.

Then He will flow through your body, and when you pray the Prayer of Faith, my brethren in the Christ, God will heal

VIEW OF HERISAU, SWITZERLAND.

you and answer your prayer for your sick people. Then they will rise up and bless you, and will praise God, whom you serve; for this is the Word of God.

"Faithful is He that calleth you, who also will do it."

The command is in the Epistle of James, 5th chapter, 14th, 15th, and 16th verses.

Is any among you sick? let him call for the elders of the church; and let them pray over him, anointing him with oil in the Name of the Lord:

And the Prayer of Faith shall save him that is sick, and the Lord shall raise him up; and if he have committed sins, it shall be forgiven him.

Confess therefore your sins one to another, and pray one for another, that ye may be healed. The supplication of a righteous man availeth much in its workings.

The Right of God's People When Sick.

Every one of you who is sick, in any church in this city, in accordance with that Word, has a right to call for the Elders of the Church—not to send for a doctor—and to demand that the Elders shall pray, and that they shall pray the Prayer of Faith.

If they cannot do it, then you can say to them, "You are not obeying the Word of God; you are not an Elder."

The best thing that you can do, is to get away from a church where the Elder will not obey the Word of God.

I challenge any Elder or minister of God to dispute that position.

There is the Word of God.

It is as plain as God's finger could write it.

You must believe it.

You must obey it.

If you do not, my brethren in the ministry, you may just as well confess that you are in the wrong place; that you have no faith at all; that you cannot pray to God and get an answer.

I should not pray at all, I should give up praying if God did not answer my prayers.

I should say, "There is something wrong with me. I cannot make connections with God and therefore I will quit. I will go and dig potatoes or do something else that is honest, but I will not preach any more."

What is the use in praying when there is no answer?

Give it up until you have learned how to pray.

Do not make a mockery of prayer that you never expect to have answered by God.

Let us pray the Prayer of Faith.

Let us give our Spirits, my brethren, and our Souls, and our Bodies to God. Then the Holy Spirit will take possession of them and will flow through them, and will bring Salvation through our words, that will get into the hearts of the people, and will bless men through our hands.

It is your privilege, my brethren and my sisters, every one of you, to make this consecration to God now, and God will accept it.

All who desire to make this consecration, rise and tell Him so.

All who want God to take possession of their Spirits, of their Souls, of their Bodies, rise and ask God to do it now.

Do not be afraid; rise up and ask God to do it.

Nearly the whole audience stood and reverently and solemnly followed the General Overseer, clause by clause, in the

PRAYER OF CONSECRATION.

My God and Father, in Jesus' Name I come to Thee. I am a poor sinner; I am nothing at all; but Jesus, the Christ, is my All in All. Jesus died for me, Jesus lives for me, Jesus pleads for me. My Father, I give to Thee my spirit; forgive my sins, give me power to do right to all whom I have wronged, to confess to my fellow men the wrong I have done them, to restore what is not mine. Father in Heaven, forgive my sin against Thee, that I have not loved Thee, that I have not served Thee, that I have not obeyed Thee as I ought to have done. For Jesus' sake, take away my sin, and make my Spirit clean. Now take my Soul, my poor defiled blood—defiled by many generations of sinners—defiled by my own sin—take my Soul, cleanse my blood, restore strength to my Body and health to every part. Help that I may serve Thee in a clean Spirit, in a clean Soul, in a clean Body, that I may be a blessing to humanity. For Jesus' sake. Amen.

Now, did you mean that?

People—"*Ja.*"

General Overseer—Live it and keep on praying until you get the blessing.

Keep on reminding God to keep you clean, then you will be a blessing to the world.

RHINEFALL, NEUHAUSEN, SWITZERLAND.

I am a poor weak man by nature.

I was dying when God healed me, over forty years ago.

I have been able to preach and to teach and to work and to help my fellow men, and so may you.

May God grant it! [Amen.]

There was not a stir in the whole vast audience until the very end of the Benediction.

The General Overseer pronounced the first part of the

BENEDICTION.

Beloved, abstain from all appearance of evil. And may the very God of Peace Himself sanctify you wholly; and I pray God your whole spirit and soul and body be preserved entire, without blame, unto the coming of our Lord Jesus, the Christ. Faithful is He that calleth you, who also will do it.

The *Gnade* was then sung, after which the General Overseer pronounced the latter part of the Benediction:

May the grace of our Lord Jesus, the Christ, the love of God, our Father, the fellowship of the Holy Spirit, our Comforter and Guide, one Eternal God, abide in you, bless you and keep you, and all the Israel of God everywhere forever. Amen.

The Service was closed with the Zion Salutation, "Peace to Thee," and the hearty response from the audience, "*Friede sei mit ihnen reichlich.*"

Thursday Afternoon Meeting.

The fine weather which had smiled upon the greater part of the Zurich Visitation up to that time, continued on Thursday.

The interest, attention, and consecration of the people were greater rather than less, and the consequent blessing was in proportion.

The Message which God gave His Prophet for the afternoon was a very solemn and important one, and greatly inspired and lifted up the spirits of the hearers.

Velodrome, Zurich, Switzerland, Thursday Afternoon, May 26, 1904.
*REPORTED BY I. M. S. AND A. W. N.

The Service was opened by the General Overseer's pronouncing the

INVOCATION.

God be merciful unto us, and bless us,
And cause Thy face to shine upon us;
That Thy Way may be known upon earth,
Thy Saving Health among all the Nations;
For the sake of Jesus. Amen.

After the singing of a hymn, Elder Jean Kradolfer read from the Inspired Word of God, the 35th chapter of the Book of the Prophet Isaiah, and the first eleven verses of the 11th chapter of the Gospel according to St. Matthew.

Prayer was offered by Elder Carl Hodler, Elder-in-charge of the Christian Catholic Church in Zion in Zurich, after which the General Overseer offered prayer for the sick and the sorrowing ones.

The announcements were made by Elder Carl Hodler and Elder Percy Clibborn, and the tithes and offerings were received while a hymn was sung.

The General Overseer then delivered his Message:

HEARING.

INVOCATION.

Let the words of my mouth, and the meditation of my heart be acceptable in Thy sight, be profitable unto this people, and unto all to whom these words shall come, in this and every land, in this and all the coming time, Till Jesus Come. Amen.

Please turn to the 11th chapter of the Gospel according to St. Matthew, and follow me in the reading of the 4th, 5th and 6th verses:

TEXT.

And Jesus answered and said unto them, Go your way and tell John the things which ye do hear and see:

The blind receive their sight, and the lame walk, the lepers are cleansed, and the deaf hear, and the dead are raised up, and the poor have Good Tidings preached to them.

And blessed is he, whosoever shall find none occasion of stumbling in Me.

The Word of God an Offense to the Disobedient.

There are a great many people who stumble at the Word of God.

It is a Stone of Stumbling, it is a Rock of Offense.

The Christ is a stumbling block to every one that wants to do wrong; to the disobedient, and to those that have made gods of their bellies, whose glory is in their shame, and who mind only earthly things.

You must not neglect earthly things, for God wants you to do them for His glory.

He put Adam and Eve in the garden and told them to till it and make it more and more beautiful, more and more fruitful.

The only command He gave them until after they fell into sin was, "Be fruitful, multiply, and replenish the earth."

I cannot help thanking you who came to me last night to the Hotel Bellevue with the excellent band that belongs to this Church, and serenaded me.

A dear little boy brought up a great bunch of beautiful white lilies. Attached to it was a broad streamer of blue, with a fringe of gold, inscribed with these words:

Thou hast multiplied the Nation:
Thou hast increased their Joy.

Fruitfulness.

The great purpose of our Lord Jesus, the Christ, was to increase the joy of humanity, to take away their sins; to take away their sicknesses and their sorrow, to take away the impurities of their lives, and to take away the pride and desert wilderness of their hearts by causing the Holy Spirit to flow like a River all through their beings.

"Herein is My Father glorified," He said, "that ye bear much fruit, so shall ye be My disciples."

That means fruitful in children, beautiful children, as well as in other things.

There is nothing more beautiful in the world than sweet, beautiful, healthy children.

Blessed are those to whom God gives the great privilege of being parents of such children.

"Happy is the man that hath his quiver full of them."

God wants us to be fruitful in our work, and we shall be when we do right, when we give to God our tithes and offerings.

When His people no longer rob God, then He fulfils His Word:

Will a man rob God? yet ye rob Me. But ye say, Wherein have we robbed Thee? In tithes and offerings.

Ye are cursed with the curse; for ye rob Me, even this Whole Nation.

Bring ye the Whole Tithe into the Storehouse, that there may be meat in Mine House, and prove Me now herewith, saith Jehovah of Hosts, if I will not open you the windows of heaven, and pour you out a blessing, that there shall not be room enough to receive it.

And I will rebuke the devourer for your sakes, and he shall not destroy the fruits of your ground; neither shall your vine cast her fruit before the time in the field, saith Jehovah of Hosts.

And All Nations shall call you happy: for ye shall be a delightsome land, saith Jehovah of Hosts.

Whatever other land does not get that blessing, Zion land gets it.

Zion's land has got it from the beginning. It has multiplied.

The Little One has become a Thousand, and the Small One a Strong Nation.

When I saw these words upon the blue sash yesterday—

Thou hast multiplied the Nation:
Thou hast increased their joy—

I felt that I ought to speak about it a little, and tell you how God has multiplied us; to tell you how He has taken a dollar and made it ten and a hundred; how He has enabled us to take three thousand people to New York, to give the Mesasge, "Peace be to this house" to every home in that large city.

Blessing Through Not Finding Offense in the Christ.

I cannot help feeling that the words which close the text that I have quoted, "Blessed is he who shall find none occasion of stumbling in Me," is a blessedness that we have.

We have not knowingly taken offense at any command that Jesus gave.

We have received the blessing that comes to those who obey God.

When these words were uttered, our Lord Jesus, the Christ, was teaching and preaching and healing.

You cannot get the healing until you know the preaching and until you get the teaching.

Therefore the Christ was first of all a Teacher, then a Preacher, then a Healer.

While He stood teaching, one day, there came up to Him the disciples of John the Baptist to ask of Him the question whether He was the Christ or "look we for another?"

The Way to Deal With Doubts.

You can see by the question that John wanted some reassurance.

Doubt had come whether Jesus was the Christ, and he could not bear that doubt.

When you have doubts, do not discuss them with the Devil, but take them at once to God, and say to Him, "O God,

*The following report has not been revised by the General Overseer.

doubt has come, and I cannot bear it, but I bring it to You to help me; give me the answer," and God will do it.

But He will not do it if you discuss the matter with the Devil.

There are multitudes today who doubt whether Jesus is the Christ.

This is the answer, not only to those disciples, but to those, in every age, who want to know if He is indeed the Christ:

And Jesus answered and said unto them, Go your way and tell John the things which ye do hear and see.

The blind receive their sight, and the lame walk, the lepers are cleansed, and the deaf hear, and the dead are raised up, and the poor have Good Tidings preached to them.

You notice that the word "hear" comes first, not "see."

Elder Hodler—"The German Bible has 'see' first."

General Overseer—I am very sorry to learn that. It is a wrong translation.

In no Greek text will you find the word "see" placed before "hear" in this quotation.

Hearing More Important Than Seeing.

You are to tell the things that you hear, and then tell the things that you see.

The most important thing is what you hear.

The most important thing is what the Christ said.

The things that they saw Him do were of far less importance than the things that He said.

The people whom He healed would pass away, but their testimonies would remain.

The most important thing that I can do in Zurich is to make the Word of God plain to you, so that you may hear and understand it and keep it in your hearts.

John's Messengers went back and told him the wonderful things that Jesus spoke, and then the wonderful things that He did

May God help you to carry with you the things you hear as well as the things you see.

How comforted John's heart was when he got that Message!

He knew that Jesus was the Christ, even though he could not understand why it was that He let him stay there to die.

Possible Message of Jesus to John the Baptist.

It is not written, but I think that the Christ spoke to these men that night and said, "Tell John that it is best that I should permit him to die, that he should seal his testimony with his blood. Tell him that it is best to die, tell him that I must die, that I must endure the Cross. It is best for Me to seal the Message of God with My blood, and it is best for you to seal your testimony with your blood."

It is always best to obey God.

I think that may have been among the things that He told those men to tell John.

It would have been easy to break the prison doors, but it was greater for the prisoner to die.

"It would be easy for Me," the Christ would say, "to bring legions of angels and scatter My enemies; but it is better for Me to die; because through death I shall destroy him that has th epower of death.

"Through death I shall descend into hell and shall set free millions who have been living in despair in the dark realms of hell, because of their disobedience to God in the time of Noah.

"Thousands of years they have been in hell.

"If I do not die, I cannot preach to the spirits in prison; but if I die I can descend into hell and set the prisoners free."

I should like to know all that Jesus said to John.

I feel sure that He said that.

It comes to my heart today, more than ever, that He told John that there was a time when it was best for men to die, when it was best for the witness, for the martyr, to seal his testimony with his blood.

Elijah the Preparer Seals His Testimony With His Blood.

How happy John was to get the Message!

Perhaps only a day or two after that, in the prison, he heard the tramp, tramp, tramp of the men coming down into the dungeon with the grim sword of the executioner.

But was John afraid?

With a smile of triumph he met it, and when Herodias saw that head, there were the open eyes and the smile of Elijah the Preparer.

He had died for his Lord.

He knew then that he was Elijah; Jesus had said it.

They had brought the message back to him that he was Elijah; that Gabriel, the angel, had made no mistake when he had said that the babe to be born would come in the spirit and power of Elijah.

So he who witnesses as Elijah, must always witness, if need be, by his own blood.

He must witness living or dying, it does not matter which.

I was fifty-seven years of age yesterday; and when my people in other lands sent me their loving greetings and congratulations, as you have done so many times in the last few days, I sent them back an answer which I think perhaps you too had better have:

According to my earnest expectation and hope, that in nothing shall I be put to shame, but that with all boldness, as always, so now also the Christ shall be magnified in my body, whether by life, or by death.

For to me to live is Christ, and to die is gain.

But if to live in the flesh,—if this is the fruit of my work, then what I shall choose I wot not.

But I am in a strait betwixt the two, having the desire to depart and be with the Christ; for it is very far better:

Yet to abide in the flesh is more needful for your sake.

And having this confidence, I know that I shall abide, yea, and abide with you all, for your progress and joy in the faith;

That your glorying may abound in the Christ Jesus in me through my presence with you again.

Only let your manner of life be worthy of the Gospel of the Christ: that, whether I come and see you or be absent, I may hear of your state, that ye stand fast in one spirit, with one soul striving for the faith of the Gospel;

And in nothing affrighted by the adversaries: which is for them an evident token of perdition, but of your salvation, and that from God;

Because to you it hath been granted in the behalf of the Christ, not only to believe on Him, but also to suffer in His behalf:

Having the same conflict which ye saw in me, and now hear to be in me.

John knew that it was gain to die. The time had come.

God Still Does the Works He Did through the Christ.

Do not forget that the thing that comforted John was to hear what Jesus said, and to know what Jesus did; because these things that Jesus did proved His Messiahship.

The things that God did through Jesus, the things that the Father did through His Son, He must do still.

And God is doing them.

He has done them here.

Every one that has been healed in this place, during this Visitation, through Faith in Jesus, stand. [About fifty rose.]

Every one here that desires to be free from the power of the Devil, and that wants God to deliver him perfectly, and all that desire more fully to be consecrated to God, stand and tell Him so. [With very few exceptions the whole audience stood.]

Repeat with the

PRAYER OF CONSECRATION.

My God and Father, in Jesus' Name I come to Thee. Take me as I am and make me what I ought to be, in spirit, soul, and body. Continue to give me power to do right to my fellow men, and in Thy sight, no matter what it costs. Give me Thy Holy Spirit this very day, that I may be cleansed in spirit, soul, and body. Help me to trust Thee, and to believe that, if I am faithful, God will use the General Overseer in giving me the desired blessing. Make me faithful, so that whether it be by his ministry or whether it be by direct answer to my prayer, the Christ may be glorified in my body, and in my spirit, which are Thine, O God. For Jesus' sake. Amen. [*All repeat the prayer, clause by clause, after the General Overseer.*]

Did you mean that prayer?

People—"*Ja.*"

General Overseer—Do you intend to live it?

People—"*Ja.*"

General Overseer—Will you ever turn aside from Jesus to man or means?

People—"*Nein.*"

General Overseer—Will you continue to be companions of those that fight this teaching?

People—"*Nein.*"

General Overseer—Do you intend to support churches that fight the Gospel?

People—"*Nein.*"

General Overseer—You had better get out quickly. They are Sodoms, spiritually dead. Get out quickly, because if you stay among the dead, you too are apt to die.

It does not do to stay out in the cold.

Get into Zion. That is my Message.

If the churches would preach the Gospel and defend it, I would say, stay there and do all you can, but while they fight the Gospel is it a good place for you to stay?

People—"*Nein.*"

General Overseer—I tell my people in Zion City that the

people that can say "*Ja*" like you say it, are the best people in the world next to those in Zion City.

I know that you can say it and I believe that you can do it too.

May God bless you!

The Services were closed with the singing of the *Gnade* by the audience and the

BENEDICTION.

Beloved, abstain from all appearance of evil. And may the very God of Peace Himself sanctify you wholly; and I pray God your whole spirit and soul and body be preserved entire, without blame, unto the coming of our Lord Jesus, the Christ. Faithful is He that calleth you, who also will do it. The grace of our Lord Jesus, the Christ, the love of God, our Father, the fellowship of the Holy Spirit, our Comforter and Guide, one Eternal God, abide in you, bless you and keep you, and all the Israel of God everywhere, forever. Amen.

Thursday Evening Meeting.

No more touching and effective Message was delivered by the prophet of God during the Zurich Visitation than that of Thursday evening, May 26, 1904, when he declared the Eternal and Infinite Love and Mercy of God the Father.

As usual, the Velodrome was crowded to its fullest capacity and the attention and interest were intense.

As usual in Zurich, there was not one moment's interruption or disorder.

Even the crowd from the street, that gathered around the General Overseer's carriage at the close of the meeting, was quiet and respectful, many giving a hearty greeting as he came out from his room to the vehicle, and an earnest "Peace to thee" in German as he drove away.

It developed later that there were a few apostate denominational people who would gladly have joined in a disturbance and a manifestation of disapproval, but that the public was so strongly in favor of the man of God, and against any such demonstration, that their craven hearts failed them and they had to stand back in the darkness and mutter their envious hatred to themselves.

The Truth was victorious in Zurich!

Velodrome, Zurich, Switzerland, Thursday Evening, May 26, 1904.
*REPORTED BY E. W. AND A. W. N.

The Service began by the General Overseer's pronouncing the

INVOCATION.

God be merciful to us, and bless us,
And cause Thy face to shine upon us;
That Thy Way may be known upon earth,
Thy Saving Health among all the Nations;
For the sake of Jesus. Amen.

After some announcements by Elder Clibborn, the third chapter of the Gospel according to St. John was read by Elder Kradolfer.

Prayer was offered by Elder Hodler and the General Overseer, after which the evening Message was delivered:

THE LOVE OF GOD FOR ALL MEN.

INVOCATION.

Let the words of my mouth, and the meditation of my heart be acceptable in Thy sight, be profitable unto this people, and unto all to whom these words shall come, for the sake of Jesus, our Lord, our Strength, and our Redeemer.

I desire to speak to you tonight concerning the Love of God in the Salvation, Healing and Cleansing which He has provided for us, and which will at last reach All Men.

In the 3d chapter of the Gospel according to St. John, the 16th verse, I read:

For God so loved the world, that He gave His only begotten Son, that whosoever believeth on Him should not perish, but have Eternal Life.

Also in the 22d verse of the 15th chapter of 1 Corinthians, I find:

For as in Adam all die, so also in the Christ shall all be made alive.

I desire you to believe that.

It is a very great Word.

False Teaching Limits God's Love.

The Love of God is limited by a great many preachers.

They do not tell you that God loved the whole world; that He sent His Son to save the whole world.

They tell you, on the contrary, that there are only a few who are to be saved; all the rest are going to be damned forever, and there is no help for them; that if they do not do what the church says now, they can never be saved throughout Eternity.

That is not the Word of God.

The Christ said:

I, if I be lifted up from the earth, will draw All men unto Myself.

The apostle says that He "is the Savior of All men, especially of them that believe."

Again he says that "God hath shut up All unto disobedience, that He might have mercy upon All."

God tells us that a time will come when all enemies shall be put under His feet; when Satan, and sin, and disease, and death, and hell shall pass away; for death and hell shall be cast into the Lake of Fire.

The Millennium is the Day of the Lord.

The "Times of Restoration of All Things, whereof God spake by the mouth of His holy prophets" have begun.

It will be sometime before the Restoration is complete; because, even when the Lord Himself comes back to reign, He will reign upon this earth a Visible Person, throughout the Millennium—that is the Thousand Years—and during that time, the Restoration will go on.

That Thousand Years is the Day of the Lord.

When that Thousand Years has been completed, the greatest fight of all will take place.

Satan who will have been bound, will be loosed for a time.

Then the Final Conflict will come, which the Book of the Revelation tells us will be closed only by the Fire of God coming down from heaven and destroying the bodies of those who fight against His Kingdom.

Then the earth will be God's.

Then there will be no more fighting, because the conflict will have ceased.

Final victory will have come.

All men will know the Lord, and the knowledge of the Lord shall cover the earth as the waters cover the sea.

The Preaching of the Christ in Hell.

Make no mistake about the teaching of the Word of God.

It is true that there will be a Judgment.

It is true that multitudes will find their way to hell; but the Christ went down to hell to find those who were disobedient, and hateful, and wicked away back in the days of Noah, when God could find only eight on all the earth who would believe.

At that time the whole race except those eight perished.

The wicked went into hell and remained there for the thousands of years until the Christ died, went down into hell, brought to nothing the power of him that had the power of death, and preached to the spirits in prison, as the Apostle Peter declares He did.

As truly as He took the penitent thief to Paradise, did He take those also who had dwelt in misery for thousands of years, and who believed His preaching—He led captivity captive.

Some will tell you that there is a parable which says that the rich man went to hell, and Lazarus went to heaven, and Abraham told the rich man, when he cried out of hell for Lazarus to come and touch his tongue to cool it, that there was a "great gulf fixed" which they that desired to pass from the one place to the other could not pass.

That was true; but did not the Christ bridge that gulf?

Did He not put the bridge across it, and did He not Himself go down into hell?

The Word of God says so.

You constantly repeat it in the Apostles' Creed: "He descended into hell. The third day He rose again from the dead."

He bridged that gulf.

Over that bridge, He brought multitudes from hell to heaven.

"Everlasting Punishment" is Age-long Pruning.

You tell me our Lord Jesus, the Christ, in His description of the Last Judgment, says to the righteous, "Come, ye blessed of My Father, inherit the Kingdom prepared for you from the foundation of the world," and to the wicked on the left hand, "Depart from Me, ye accursed, into everlasting punishment."

"He said that the righteous should go into Life Eternal, and

*The following report has not been revised by the General Overseer.

the wicked into Everlasting Punishment; that settles it," say some.

Why are not the preachers honest?

They tell you that the word, "punishment" means a hopeless misery.

It means no such thing.

Why do they not tell you that the word translated "everlasting" means age-long, and that the word translated "punishment" has no thought of misery; has no thought of separation from God.

The Greek word *koladzo* (κολάζω), used there, means to prune, as a gardener takes his knife and prunes the vine.

The word prune means not to kill the tree, but to make the tree bring forth good fruit; to make that which had been useless or fruitless worth something.

The meaning is the punishment of the offender for his betterment.

God does not hate any of His children, it matters not how much they have sinned.

God is not glorified by their destruction.

It is Impossible for God to Destroy His Own Offspring.

God is the Father of our spirits.

These spirits are immortal.

They cannot die, because our Father cannot die, and the spirit that He has given to us is indestructible.

It cannot possibly be that God would keep in misery, hopeless and endless, His own offspring.

No matter how grave their sins are, they are only temporal acts, finite acts, acts that have only a temporary life and power.

It would not be possible for God to make the punishment infinitely greater than the offense.

The great majority of those who are sinful are so because they are ignorant.

They do not know that they have been kept from knowledge.

Many wicked people have kept them from knowing God.

Even in Christian lands, multitudes have never really known the Love of God.

I remember how that fact went to my heart when a poor criminal, a murderer not twenty years of age, was hanged in Chicago.

He had committed two hundred crimes. He had been in the hands of the police for little crimes from the time of his childhood, and was continually at war with law.

Why was it?

He was the offspring of a harlot and a murderer.

His mother and father, after he was hanged, fought each other in the public streets over his coffin as his dead body was being taken from the jail.

He had lived in sin.

He had never known honesty.

He had been taught to be a thief and liar as soon as he could speak.

He was driven out, a drunken profligate, and nobody cared for him.

The churches did not seek him, and when he was about to be hanged, he lifted up his hands and cried, "I never had a chance!"

The First Impetus of Zion Restoration Host.

I said then that I would visit every home in Chicago, and take the Message to every sinner in every saloon, in every harlot's house.

Last year, through Zion Restoration Host, we visited every house in Chicago eight times.

I have determined that, as far as my power can extend, Zion Restoration Host shall carry the Message of God's Peace to every house in Zurich; to every mountain and valley in Switzerland; to every city in Europe; to every part of every continent.

Already I have reached one hundred twenty million of the world's inhabitants; because I believe that God loves every man, and wants to save every man, and will eventually do it.

Although many will go to hell, because they will not obey God, yet it is written by the Psalmist himself, who was inspired by God to write it:

> If I ascend up into heaven, Thou art there:
> If I make my bed in Sheol, behold, Thou art there.
> If I take the wings of the morning,
> And dwell in the uttermost parts of the sea;
> Even there shall Thy hand lead me,
> And Thy right hand shall hold me.

I believe it.

Restoration Work After We Get to Heaven.

A man said to me one day, "Well, what are you going to do when you get to heaven? It seems to me that your principal work will be over."

I replied, "No, when I get to heaven with God, and with the angels, and the redeemed of earth, and I meet my loved ones gone before and they who come in at the Gates of the City, one after another, the tens of thousands and hundreds of thousands of my own people, who will have served God, I shall ask God to let me go to preach to those in hell."

I hope He will forgive me if I do wrong; because He knows my heart, and I want my prayer to be right.

I know that I should have a hard fight, but I do not think it will be very much different from the fight I have here.

I have to fight the Devil all the time.

Sometimes I have to fight the Devil in solution; because when you see a bottle of whisky there is Devil in that.

I find a great deal of Devil in the churches here too.

They fight me as if I were the Devil himself, although I am fighting sin, and Satan, and disease, and death, and hell, and getting multitudes saved.

I do not do it their way, and the consequence is that they fight me.

I fight with the Devil now; it will not be much different when I get to hell, only now I have devils to fight who say they are Christians, and when I get to hell, the devils will admit that they are devils; and I will make no mistake about it.

God will follow the lost.

He has provided a way by which His banished may return to Him.

He is the Father of all spirits.

He mourns over the sinful and the lost, and He will seek them until He finds them.

He is the Shepherd who will seek in every street of every city of earth, in every valley, and in every mountain.

The Christ will send Zion to seek them, and we shall not rest until we have found them.

You will never get rid of me, you sinners.

I will follow you through earth, and I will follow you through hell, until I get hold of you and bring you back to God.

When I come down to hell and find some of you there you will say, "Well, you told us that in Zurich." [Laughter.]

That is my faith.

My Faith is that God means what He says.

My Faith is that the Christ means what He says; that God so loved the world that He sent His Son to save the world; to draw all men unto Himself.

Although some crucified the Christ, He did not say, "You go to hell," but He prayed to God, "Father forgive them, for they know not what they do."

The Same Christ is Pleading for All Men.

He is the Intercessor for all; not only for the good, but He pleads for the wicked.

His Love touches our hearts; because while we were yet sinners, and wicked, and far from God, He loved us, He died for us, He pleaded for us, He sent the Holy Spirit to us, and has raised up men to seek the lost and the perishing.

He has told them to tell men at the very margin of the grave when they are burying their dead—the words are there; they ring over the grave:

> As in Adam all die, even so in the Christ shall all be made alive.

I believe God's Word.

God will, at last, even if it takes Him a million years to do it, seek, and save unto the uttermost every poor, sinful spirit that in its folly, has gone to hell.

No One Would Want to Live in Hell, Even for a Short Time.

"Oh," some one says, "do not preach like that, because they will be sinful and wicked! If they know that they can get out of hell, they will not mind going there for a while."

That is not true.

Every man of common sense can see at once that it is far better to be good, to be saved, to be healed, to be cleansed, to be happy on earth, to obey God here and go straight to heaven when he dies, than to be wicked, sinful and hateful, and go to hell and live with devils and bad people, and find his way to heaven at last, after thousands of years, perhaps, in hell.

If you and I are traveling together to a beautiful city, and I show you a good road, and tell you that all along that road there are beloved friends who will entertain us, and cheer us and help us and make us happy, and take us straight to the city to which we desire to go, will we not go that way?

Or shall we go down into the valley, away down the dark river, into mud flats, and wallow in the mire, going ten thousand miles around about, miserable, hungry, naked, beset by enemies and surrounded by serpents that sting us and bite us?

I show you the pleasant way to go, and I tell you that although you take the other way God will follow you and will find you, but it may take long.

Will you go the right Way, the loving Way, the Way that the Christ opened up by His blood—the Way of Salvation, of Healing, of Holy Living?

Go the straight Way.

Our Father, if it takes Him a million years, must seek His sons and daughters, and He will, until at last He has brought them all home.

If any one tells you that the mercy of God is limited, tell him that God's mercy is above the heavens.

Tell him that the Word says it over, and over, and over again, that "the mercy of God endureth forever."

I Preach a Gospel of Hope.

I hate sin.

I hate disease.

I hate the powers of death and hell; but I tell you that Satan will be conquered by the Christ; that Sin and Disease, and Death and Hell will be conquered by Salvation, and Healing, and Life, and Heaven.

I know that God will win, for the Times of the Restoration of All Things have begun; and that work will go on until All Things are restored to God.

I love the Gospel.

It is a Gospel of Love, a Gospel of Life, a Gospel of Health, a Gospel of Heaven.

May God give you that Gospel and make your spirit happy while you live.

No pillow is so soft as that Gospel when you lay down your head to sleep and awake in Heaven.

All who desire the blessings of this Gospel rise and tell God so. [Nearly all rose.]

Now pray.

PRAYER OF CONSECRATION.

My God and Father, in Jesus' Name I come to Thee. I thank Thee that Thy love never fails, that Thy mercy endureth forever, that Jesus will draw All men unto Him, the most miserable on earth—yea, the most miserable in hell; that He came to seek and to save that which was lost. I thank Thee that He cannot stop seeking and He cannot stop saving until all the lost are found; until all who die in Adam are made alive in the Christ. Oh, help us to tell the story that God is Love; that He is good to all, and that He cannot limit His mercy, for it reaches all, and it endures forever. In Jesus' Name we pray Thee, give us a True Repentance; give us the True Faith; give us the True Obedience that we may obey Thee. If we have made bad vows to bad men, let us break the bad vows, and obey God, no matter what it costs. For Jesus' sake. [*All repeat the prayer, clause by clause, after the General Overseer.*]

Beloved, do you believe what you have prayed?

People—"*Ja.*"

General Overseer—Then do not be afraid to live it.

Do not be afraid to say it out, and unborn millions will bless you; for that Gospel will be a blessing to all the generations to come.

BENEDICTION.

Beloved, abstain from all appearance of evil. And may the very God of Peace Himself sanctify you wholly; and I pray God your whole spirit and soul and body be preserved entire, without blame, unto the coming of our Lord Jesus, the Christ. Faithful is He that calleth you, who also will do it. The grace of our Lord Jesus, the Christ, the love of God our Father, the fellowship of the Holy Spirit our Comforter and Guide, one Eternal God, abide in you, bless you and keep you, and all the Israel of God everywhere, forever. Amen.

Friday Afternoon Meeting.

On Friday afternoon, May 27, 1904, the General Overseer conducted the last of the Divine Healing meetings of the Zurich Visitation.

The audience was a representative one, there being present not only hundreds of sick who came to learn God's Way of Healing, but also many earnest seekers for the whole truth of God, and many who, having read of the General Overseer, came to hear and see for themselves whether indeed he were a man sent from God.

There was no spirit of mere light curiosity, but a deeply earnest and reverent attitude on the part of all those present.

Brave Words From a Prominent German Christian Worker.

Before the General Overseer delivered his Message, Mr. Manger of Frieburg, Germany, known in all the German-speaking countries of Europe, as an active Christian worker, delivered a short address to the people.

Mr. Manger and his daughters had been at every meeting of the Visitation, and had also been for a long time readers of BLÄTTER DER HEILUNG.

Mr. Manger's address was heard with enthusiasm by the great audience, practically all of whom expressed by rising, their sympathy with the sentiments he expressed.

The following is a report of Mr. Manger's talk. The translation was made by Evangelist Marie Brieger-Hodler:

Three years and a half ago I visited Zurich.

I left my home because I was longing to hear and see the man of whom I had heard so much from different parts.

I have been a Christian for a long time, and have taken part in the work of evangelization.

Many know me, perhaps some of you.

I have worked together with many in evangelistic work.

I am a layman, but I work for God, and am interested in everything that is connected with eternity and the truth of God's Word.

Hence I came here to know the Messenger of God.

I did not err when I heard him three and one-half years ago.

I have had many conflicts because of what I heard then.

I have swung the sword of God's Word because I found that some who love God, and are sincere, and whom I love, were persecuted and suspected.

That grieved me greatly.

When I heard the voices of the secular press and all the lies of the newspapers from New York, it did not affect me, except that I was grieved for humanity, seeing what great power the Devil had.

The time will come when all will be plain, my friends.

The work that God is doing is still in its infancy; it has only begun.

In a few years it will spread over all the world and will be a great power.

When one has been in the work of God for twenty-five or thirty years, and has found nothing but dirt, not only in the social democracy, but also in all religious communities, one is deeply grieved.

Now, behold this man of God!

I watched him yesterday.

How great is his love!

How he caressed and blessed the poor, little, sick children!

He was to me the image of Jesus as He did the same work.

He missed not one of the miserable ones in passing by.

My heart almost breaks when I see how he is persecuted.

I am glad that he does not well understand German and therefore does not know what I say, for he might think that I wished to flatter him.

He does not need that.

I have read BLÄTTER DER HEILUNG.

The lady who translated it and sent me the paper I knew well enough to be certain that what she wrote was truth.

Three years ago I met Mrs. Hofer.

She wrote to me long letters witnessing to the power and truth that is in Zion.

I wept in silence.

I heard from the General Overseer, and considered the matter.

The German needs much time to consider.

Some say that Dr. Dowie preaches too little of Jesus, the Savior.

That is not true.

I have attended all the meetings and seldom have I heard a man that was closer to Jesus and glorified Him more than he does.

Some people say that he is the Antichrist!

That is shamefully false!

What the Antichrist is, is found in 1 John 4:3:

"And every spirit which confesseth not Jesus is not of God: and this is the spirit of the Antichrist, whereof ye have heard that it cometh; and now it is in the world already."

All the General Overseer's preaching, and all his work, and all Zion, are for the Christ.

Some say of him that he is destroying all the denominations.

Of course he fights against apostasy!

Not only is the Roman Catholic church apostate, but all are apostate.

The apostasy grows worse from year to year.

Infidelity is not confined to the agnostics—it proceeds from the cathedral.

This man has the right to swing the Sword of the Spirit and rebuke the apostasies.

Dear friends, every one that is convinced, with me, that Dr. Dowie is the Messenger of God, an instrument in the hand of God, who is mighty, shall confess it in rising from his place.

[Apparently all rose.]

The General Overseer then invoked the blessing of God upon the Message he was about to deliver.

With Elder Hodler translating into German, he began his teaching.

In reply to a written question, he first took up the truth that God is not, and cannot be, the author of disease, and that the passage, "Whom the Lord loveth He chasteneth," could not possibly mean "whom the Lord loveth He maketh sick."

The original meaning of the Greek word, and the essential truth concerning God Himself are against that interpretation.

Answering another point in the same letter, the General Overseer showed that disease was always the result of sin; that it might not always be the sin of the sufferer, or even of his parents, but that if traced to its source it would always be found to be the result of some one's sin.

In illustrating this point the General Overseer related the story of a little girl born blind, with a marked depression of the eyeballs.

Investigation showed that, sometime before her birth, some wicked men had broken into the house in which her mother was lying alone

When at last they burst into the room where she lay, she had swooned, with her fingers pressed upon her eyes.

This little one was born blind, not as a result of her sin or the sin of her parents, but as a result of the sin of those who had broken into the house.

She was afterwards healed in answer to the General Overseer's prayers.

God's messenger closed with a few words about Obedience in Baptism, commanding all to repent and to be baptized.

At the healing meeting held afterwards, the General Overseer laid hands upon and prayed for a very large number of sick people, bringing the total of those for whom he had prayed during the Zurich Visitation to one thousand sixty, exclusive of the many for whom he prayed privately in his reception room at the Bellevue Hotel.

The Power of God was present to heal.

Many received great physical blessing and deliverance in the Name of the Christ.

Friday Evening Meeting.

On Friday evening, May 27th, in pursuance of his announcement, the General Overseer told the Story of Zion City, its conception, founding, wonderful growth, and present prosperity, happiness, and cleanliness.

The description was vivid, realistic and convincing.

The desire to become citizens of Zion City was already in the hearts of many.

At this meeting it was increased and strengthened, and was also born into the hearts of many more.

It was an enthusiastic service, and God greatly blessed to the very large and deeply interested audience, the discussion of the educational, commercial, and political features of His Kingdom as they have found their expression in the first Zion City.

Saturday Afternoon Conference.

Although he had been very hard at work practically every moment since he arrived in Zurich, pouring out his spiritual, psychical and physical strength in correspondence, in interviews, in prayer with the sick, and in many meetings, the General Overseer devoted almost the entire afternoon, Saturday, May 28, 1904, to a detailed, intimate, and confidential discussion of the work of the Kingdom of God in Zion City, for the benefit of the many members and friends of Zion who had come from nearly every country in Europe to attend this Visitation.

The General Overseer not only discussed this matter very fully, giving much valuable information, but also freely and fully answered a number of questions propounded by earnest inquirers.

Thus a deep impression was made upon many, their eyes being opened to the great truths that in Zion City is seen a successfully-working model of the Kingdom of God upon earth; that in Christian coöperation in Zion is the solution of the social, educational and economic problems that are vexing the world today.

A Day in God's Courts—Better Than a Thousand Years.

Eternity alone can ever disclose the full story of the last day of public services in Zurich during the Around-the-World Visitation.

On that day, for the first time on the Continent of Europe, Elijah the Restorer made the Declaration of his prophetic mission.

On that day, One Hundred Ten young children were presented to God by their parents, and consecrated and blessed by the laying on of hands by the General Overseer.

On that day, Five Hundred Six members of the Christian Catholic Church in Zion received the right hand of fellowship of their General Overseer, and his hearty, "May God forever bless you!"

On that day, three Evangelists, thirteen Deacons and sixteen Deaconesses were ordained to the ministry of God in the Christian Catholic Church in Zion, by the General Overseer.

On that day, God's Prophet administered the Ordinance of the Communion of the Lord's Supper to over one thousand Christians.

On that day, thousands heard with joy the simple truths of the Gospel of the Kingdom of God, and carried away the Message in their hearts.

By thousands of firesides, in hundreds of churches that have lost the foundation truths of that Gospel, and before hundreds of thousands of friends and acquaintances, the Power of that Message will find expression in simple, truthful, and effective testimony, and, best of all, in Holy Living, thus spreading the seed of God's Restoration Truth over all the continent of Europe.

That day was the crowning glory of seven days of ever-increasing spiritual power and nearness to God.

It was a day that can never be forgotten.

It dawned bright and beautiful; lovely Zurich smiling across her shimmering lake at the snowy Alps at its head, with a radiance that was in keeping with the joy and gladness that was in the hearts of the Around-the-world Visitation Party and the many Zion people in the city, as they gathered for the first service.

Lord's Day Morning Meeting.

The first sight that greeted the eyes of those at the Velodrome on Lord's Day morning, May 29, 1904, was a beautiful one.

Fairer than the rarest flowers were the sweet faces of the scores of happy, healthy, and intelligent children present.

They were well-behaved little ones, most of them in the care of their parents, to whom they were obedient and respectful, some of them—orphans—in the care of guardians.

Some of them were very young babies, lying on pillows in their mother's arms, others were almost as tall as their parents.

The Service was to be one of the Presentation and Consecration of these Young Children to God.

The audience that had gathered filled the Velodrome as the General Overseer opened the meeting with the Invocation.

After the very hearty singing of a hymn, the Rev. Jean Kradolfer read in the Inspired Word of God from the 10th chapter of the Gospel according to St. Mark, the 13th to the 16th verse, and in the 3d chapter of the Acts of the Apostles, from the 11th verse to the end of the chapter.

Prayer was offered by Elder Carl Hodler.

After the announcements and the taking of the tithes and offerings, the General Overseer, after asking God's blessings upon the words of his mouth and the meditations of his heart, discussed briefly the Scriptures which Elder Kradolfer had read, in regard to the "Times of Restoration of All Things, whereof God spake by the mouth of His holy prophets which have been since the world began."

The General Overseer pointed out that although the Times of the Restoration of All Things had been spoken of by God through the mouths of all His holy prophets since the world began, they were scarcely ever spoken of by denominational ministers of today.

The audience was questioned, and not one of all the three thousand present had ever heard a sermon on that subject, except in the Christian Catholic Church in Zion.

The man of God showed very clearly the reason for this strange silence.

The people would at once demand to know when the Times of the Restoration would begin, and where the Prophet of the Restoration could be found.

None of the denominational churches, he said, would desire to number a prophet amongst its ministers; because a prophet was a very uncomfortable person for the people to have around, unless they would obey God.

He then showed that the prophet raised up as Moses was raised up could not be the Christ, as the Christ was born of a sinless virgin, while Moses was raised up out of the slime and mud of the river Nile.

In speaking of the statement that all those who would not

obey "that prophet" should perish from among the people, the General Overseer pointed out that all those who would not obey Moses, and look upon the brazen serpent raised up in the wilderness, when they were dying from the poison of venomous reptiles, perished as the result of their disobedience.

So today he said, those who will not obey God's prophet, and look to Him for healing, must perish.

He did not say that they would not go to heaven if they took drugs, indeed, if they were children of God, they would get to heaven the more quickly.

Referring to the passage, "Unto you first God, having raised up His servant, sent him to bless you, in turning away every one of you from your iniquities," he pointed out the difference between "turning away," and "saving" people from their sins, declaring that Jesus came to save; but that the prophet referred to here came to turn away, according to prophecy in the last verse of the last chapter of the Prophet Malachi.

Following this brief address, the General Overseer proceeded to the Ordinance of the Presentation and Consecration of Young Children to God.

The parents brought their little children upon the platform, immediately around the General Overseer.

It was a beautiful sight—these scores of bright-faced, healthy children, gathered, with their parents, in the presence of God and of His Prophet and people, awaiting consecration and blessing.

One's heart filled with joy and thanksgiving at the thought of so great a number of strong, clean lives being trained, nurtured, and protected for the Master's use.

After prayer, God's Messenger spoke briefly concerning the significance of the Ordinance, and its difference from infant baptism, so-called, closing with a loving but solemn charge to the parents and guardians of the children.

Then the little ones were presented, the General Overseer consecrating each one in the Name of Jesus, in the Power of the Holy Spirit, and in accordance with the Will of God, the Father, and laying on his hands, blessing the child.

To all he gave a loving kiss, and the babies he took in his arms.

One hundred ten little ones were thus presented, consecrated, and blessed.

Lord's Day Afternoon Service.

On Lord's Day afternoon, May 29, 1904, for the first time on the Continent of Europe, indeed, for the first time in the Old World, Elijah the Restorer repeated the Declaration of his Prophetic Mission.

It was fitting that this wonderful truth of these Last Times should be proclaimed in this the largest and most important city in Switzerland, which is not only the topographic but the spiritual watershed of Europe.

It was fitting that it should be made, almost within a stone's throw of the place where the great Zwingli thundered forth the mighty truths of the Reformation; and in the presence of an audience of about three thousand people, gathered from nearly all the European nations.

The power of that Declaration, simply and humbly made, was manifested by the fact that at its close nearly all in that great audience rose to witness to their acceptance of its truth.

The Declaration was based upon the Sure Word of God in prophecy in the words of the Christ Himself, and in the words of the Apostle Peter.

As evidence of the fulfilment of these Divine and Divinely Inspired promises, God's Messenger pointed to the work done in Zion through his ministry—beyond question the work of Restoration.

Although the hall was crowded to its utmost capacity, hundreds standing throughout the service, there was the most earnest attention, from first to last, the entire people manifestly following the argument, step by step, and showing in their faces their acceptance of the clear, unanswerable logic of the Declaration.

At the close of this service, the General Overseer received into fellowship and communion of the Christian Catholic Church in Zion, giving them the right hand of fellowship, five hundred six members.

As each crossed the platform, he or she was introduced by Elder Jean Kradolfer, and received by the General Overseer with a hearty hand-clasp and a loving benediction.

Ordination of Officers in the Christian Catholic Church in Zion.

Then came the Ordination of New Officers.

The General Overseer first of all laid hands upon the kneeling candidates, for the reception of the Holy Spirit for the work of the ministry.

Then in brief, simple, but very solemn words, he ordained each in the Name of the Lord Jesus, in the Power of the Holy Spirit, and in accordance with the Will of God our Heavenly Father, to his or her respective office.

The following is a list of those ordained:

EVANGELISTS.

Arnold Muggli, Bahnhofstrasse 76, Zurich, Switzerland.
Mrs. Anna Kradolfer, Klausstrasse 44, Zurich, Switzerland.
Mrs. Anita Hofer, Schloss Liebburg bei Kreuzlingen, Canton Thurgau, Switzerland.

DEACONS.

Gottlieb Braun, Fürstenstrasse 95, Dresden, Germany.
Arnold Dünki, Kanzleistrasse 12, Zurich Switzerland.
Johann Emil, Fehr, Schanzengasse 12, Zurich, Switzerland.
Wilhelm Frey, Binningen, Schafmattweg, Basel, Switzerland.
Conrad Frischknecht, Spittel, Herisau, Switzerland.
Johannes Krahn, Nuremberg, Pomerania, Germany.
Ernst Liebe, Rossthalerstrasse 1, Dresden, Germany.
Alfred Mattenberger, Zehnderweg 16, Zurich, Switzerland.
Ludwig Merk, Bahnhofstrasse 76, Zurich, Switzerland.
Florentin Merk, Pfarrhofgasse 1, Schaffhausen, Switzerland.
Heinrich Reymund, Neusatz, Ungarn.
Hugo Ulrich, Anstätterstrasse 18, Erfurt, Germany.
Emil Zimmermann, Klausstrasse 44, Zurich, Switzerland.

DEACONESSES.

Miss Catharina Serene d'Acqueria, 4, Jernbanegade, Copenhagen, Denmark.
Mrs. Rosine Denzler, Grund Dübendorf, Canton, Zurich, Switzerland.
Mrs. Ida Dierauer, Schützenstrasse 25, Winterthur, Switzerland.
Mrs. Luise Ebner, Hegibach 25, Zurich, Switzerland.
Mrs. Lina Fehr, Schanzengasse 12, Zurich, Switzerland.
Mrs. Catharine Frischknecht, Spittel, Herisau, Switzerland.
Miss Ruth Hofer, Schloss Liebburg bei Kreuzlingen, Switzerland.
Mrs. Anna Höhn, Quellenstrasse 44, Zurich, Switzerland.
Miss Ottilie Kaufmann, Felzenbergstrasse, Seebach, Zurich, Switzerland.
Mrs. Hedwig Müller, Querstrasse 22, Limbach, Sachsen, Germany.
Mrs. Margareth Naumann, Dorfgasse, Horgen, Zurich, Switzerland.
Miss Frieda Seibt, Bahnhofstrasse 76, Zurich, Switzerland.
Mrs. Marie Steiger, Treuackerstrasse 30, St. Gall, Switzerland.
Mrs. Elise Thiele, Winkelriedstrasse 13, Zurich, Switzerland.
Miss Rosine Walz, Rohrdorf, Nagold, Württemburg, Germany.
Mrs. Anna Weber, Neufeldstrasse 15, Bern, Switzerland.

Communion of the Lord's Supper.

Then in the holy calm of the Sabbath evening hour, as the sun sank behind the beautiful Swiss hills, and the long twilight came on, over one thousand Christians gathered about the blessed Table of their crucified, risen, and coming Lord, partaking of the Sacred Elements in commemoration of His death, "Till He Come."

The General Overseer administered the Ordinance, assisted by the Ordained Officers of the Christian Catholic Church in Zion present.

When this service had closed, the General Overseer gave a very brief Post-Communion family talk, which was very enthusiastically received by his people.

It was then within a few minutes of the time for the evening service to begin.

But, although the people, many of them, had been steadily in attendance at the Tabernacle for ten hours, they entered into the evening service with all the zeal and joy of a people not weary, but refreshed.

Lord's Day Evening Service.

The General Overseer's address of the evening was on the subject of Baptism by Triune Immersion, in obedience to the command of our Lord Jesus, the Christ.

At the close of this meeting, the people joined very earnestly in the following

PRAYER OF CONSECRATION.

My God and Father, in Jesus' Name I come to Thee. I want to obey Thee, not from fear, but from Love, because I love Thee. It is best for me and it is best for all, and it pleases Thee. Thou hast been so good to me, so merciful to me, now help me to obey Thee, and to be baptized into the Name of the Father, and into the Name of the Son, and into the Name of the Holy Spirit. Amen. [*All repeat the prayer, clause by clause, after the General Overseer.*]

Did you mean that?

People—"*Ja.*"

General Overseer—You intend to do that, do you not?

People—"*Ja.*"

Even sweeter in the German tongue than in the English, was the parting song, so dear to all in Zion, "God be with You Till We Meet Again," or "*Gott mit euch!*"

Tenderly and with deep emotion, the people sang:

Gott mit euch, bis wir uns wiedersehn!
Uebergebt nun eure Wege
Seiner treuen Hirtenpflege.
Gott mit euch, bis wir uns wiedersehn!

Auf Wiedersehn, Wiedersehn
Hier auf Erden oder dort im Licht!
Auf Wiedersehn, Wiedersehn!
Unser Hüter schläft noch schlummert nicht.

Gott mit euch, bis wir uns wiedersehn!
Gottes Auge wird euch leiten
Und durch Freud und Leid begleiten.
Gott mit euch ꝛc.

Gott mit euch, bis wir uns wiedersehn!
Sollte Not und Schmerz euch schrecken,
Mög' sein Flügel euch bedecken.
Gott mit euch ꝛc.

Gott mit euch, bis wir uns wiedersehn!
Seine Gnade, Huld und Treue
Grüß' euch alle Tag aufs neue:
Gott mich euch ꝛc.

Then, his voice thrilling with love and earnest prayer, the General Overseer sang:

God be with you till we meet again!
Keep love's banner floating o'er you,
Smite death's threatening wave before you;
God be with you till we meet again!

The voice of God's prophet was then heard in those words of Divine Benediction, which have been an inspiration to so many thousands of God's children down through the centuries since the Apostle penned them by the inbreathing of the Holy Spirit:

Beloved, abstain from all appearance of evil. And may the very God of Peace Himself sanctify you wholly; and I pray God your whole spirit and soul and body be preserved entire, without blame, until the coming of our Lord Jesus, the Christ. Faithful is He that calleth you, who also will do it.

The people then joined in the singing of the sweet old German *Gnade* which had been used with such power throughout the Visitation, the General Overseer closing with the words:

The grace of our Lord Jesus, the Christ, the love of God, our Father, the fellowship of the Holy Spirit, our Comforter and Guide, one Eternal God, abide in you, bless you and keep you, and all the Israel of God everywhere, forever. Amen.

"Peace to thee," translated into the German, "*Friede sei mit euch*," received the hearty response, "*Friede sei mit ihnen reichlich*."

Thus the day came to an end, and with it the public meetings of the Zurich Mission of the Around-the-world Visitation.

BAPTISM OF ONE HUNDRED TWENTY-FIVE BELIEVERS.

Monday, May 30, 1904, was the last day of the General Overseer's stay in beautiful Zurich.

With the dawning of that morning, we heard the music of Zurich Zion Band under the General Overseer's window at the Hotel Bellevue.

It was appropriate music, well rendered, and the expression of a beautiful thought.

The man of God very kindly thanked the young men for their love and thoughtfulness.

At nine o'clock on that morning, at one of the city's baths, the General Overseer administered the Ordinance of Baptism by Triune Immersion to One Hundred Twenty-five Believers.

This, with forty-nine who had previously been baptized by Overseer J. G. Excell, made a total of One Hundred Seventy-four persons who thus obeyed God during this Visitation.

The service was a fitting close to the wonderful ten days' work in the metropolis of Switzerland.

The candidates were not only from Zurich and Switzerland, but from many other parts of the Continent of Europe, and God's Spirit was upon them in mighty power as they received the Ordinance which signifies Death to Sin, Life in God, and Power for Service.

The General Overseer was assisted by several of the Ordained Officers of the Christian Catholic Church in Zion.

At the close of the Ordinance, he addressed the people briefly, and then bade them good-by.

His parting with them was a very touching scene.

Hundreds were weeping, their faces shining with love as they returned his salutation.

The General Overseer had, by the Love of God implanted in his spirit, won the love of these excellent people, and they had won the hearts of the Around-the-World Visitation Party, for it was exceedingly difficult to leave Zurich, even with the prospect before us of a tour of the Bernese Alps.

We had indeed been among the people of God!

Notice to Correspondents.

In writing to Headquarters it is *absolutely essential* that the writer give his full address.

Failure to comply with this request necessitates looking up or referring to the Church Records, which involves much time, and is very frequently fruitless.

Friends and members of the Christian Catholic Church in Zion everywhere will please bear this in mind, especially those in foreign lands.

Faithfully yours in the Master's Service,
J. G. Excell, General Ecclesiastical Secretary.

Warning.

I am directed by the General Overseer to warn our members and officers throughout the world against giving money to persons claiming to be members of the Christian Catholic Church in Zion. All benevolence must be given either from Headquarters or under the direction of same. Even though the applicant for benevolence be known to be a member of the Christian Catholic Church in Zion, financial aid must not be given except in extreme cases, and then only in small amounts. Requests for help must be made to the officer-in-charge. In cases where there is no such officer, requests should be made direct to Headquarters, accompanied by recommendations from one or two members of Zion in good standing.

J. G. Excell,
General Ecclesiastical Secretary.

Street Addresses Are Necessary.

All Zion City Subscribers to *Leaves of Healing*, *The Zion Banner*, *Blätter der Heilung*, and *Voice from Zion*, whose correct street addresses are not positively known to be in our possession should send them to us AT ONCE. Please act upon this notice without delay as it is very important, now that we have postal delivery service, that the exact location of each and every subscriber be known to us. Write your name and address very carefully, designating also to what periodicals you are a subscriber and leave at your very earliest opportunity at our branch Publishing House on Elijah Avenue.

Very Sincerely Yours,
Zion Printing and Publishing House.

Warning to Subscribers.

Scarcely a week passes that we do not have complaints about money having been sent to us in currency, stamps, or silver, in the open mails, for renewals of subscriptions or for other purposes, WHICH WE HAVE NOT RECEIVED AND WHICH NEVER REACHES US.

Therefore, we desire to warn every member and friend of Zion sending money to us, to always use some safe means, preferably a money-order, or bank-draft on New York or Chicago, or personal check on Zion City Bank.

In conforming to this notice you will save yourselves trouble and expense, and us much annoyance.

Zion Printing and Publishing House,
Zion City, Illinois.

Memorabilia of the New York Visitation

By Mrs. Emily Ware

FOR He shall give His angels charge over thee, To keep thee in all thy ways.—*Psalm 91:11.*

EVANGELIST ANTONIUS DARMS, 2920 Emmaus avenue, Zion City, Illinois.—On September 14, 1903, our beloved General Overseer gave a most stirring discourse on Psalm 50:23, which gave a new turn to my Christian life in unfolding to me the true meaning of a sacrifice in the service of the Christ.

This spirit of true obedience to God's prophet and of a real sacrifice, willing to give up all for the salvation of others, was the secret of success in the work of the New York Visitation.

The Devil seemed determined that I should not go to New York, for I seemed nearly worn out by physical exhaustion.

I had vowed that I would obey the call of Elijah the Restorer, and so I went.

By the time I reached Buffalo, I had contracted such a cold that I was utterly unable to talk above the faintest whisper.

To aggravate matters still more, four German Reformed ministers of Buffalo had come down to Niagara Falls to inquire about Zion of me and to hear our General Overseer.

I was nearly unable to speak, and yet I felt I must use the opportunity.

I asked God for wisdom, and was thus enabled, from God's own Word, to show that Zion was the only organized work of God in this Latter Day approved of God, and that God dwelleth in Zion.

My dear brother, one of the ministers, after he had heard the General Overseer, said that he believed that Dr. Dowie indeed was a true man of God.

After leaving Niagara Falls my illness became very critical, and never was I nearer unto the gates of death.

Terrible agony suddenly seized me.

I was determined not to die, but to live and to do God's will and work.

Several brethren prayed for me, and soon I had deliverance.

My voice being speedily restored, I was enabled to do all my work as a captain in the German Seventy without the slightest interruption.

Our work among the German Jews was of special blessing.

Many boldly attested their love for Dr. Dowie.

One need only to see the many sweat-shops of New York to realize the need of Restoration in their homes and business.

One of the best experiences I had in New York was that of going through the great Mills hotel, which is over ten stories high, with over one hundred rooms on each floor, thus accommodating over one thousand poor, homeless men, at ten cents a night.

In order to reach as many of these as possible, I went down after the close of the evening meeting to the hotel and began at the top floor and, by the grace of God, was enabled to go through all the large halls and reading rooms and dispose of nearly a thousand cards and tracts.

One man asked me to come to his little room, where I found our little card with the picture of the Christ fastened to the wall.

We knelt down and I prayed for him and his separated family. He was deeply touched and manifested his kindness by directing me through the entire hotel, so that I was not detected by any watchman, till on the first floor, when the watchman violently seized me and put me out.

But praise God, many hundreds of men had already gladly accepted the tracts, and I heard many kind words about the dear General Overseer.

Once, when in Hoboken, a detective followed me and, showing his star, made me call in my company, because I had no written permit.

Going down towards the police station, I was given liberty to go on.

When I gave the policemen the beautiful card of the Christ knocking at the door, they put the cards inside their hats, as I saw many do at Madison Square Garden, and expressed their great appreeciation.

I had opportunity to go up to Union Theological Seminary, where I had been a student.

Dr. McGiffert expressed himself as glad to see me, invited me into his study, told me hewas much pleased with his visit at one of the public meetings in Madison Square Garden, and asked me many questions about the life of our Leader.

No word of criticism whatever came from him.

A Roman Catholic editor and the editors of the *Christian Herald* received me very kindly and believed that Zion is doing a great work in the world.

I spent the last two days in my old home in Philadelphia.

My former pastor was much stirred up that I should come among my acquaintances with Zion Messages.

The police gave me absolute freedom to give out Zion Tracts in factories and on the streets.

How my heart rejoiced that I could thus go to many hundreds of my friends with LEAVES OF HEALING and Zion Messages.

Never at any of my home visits had I been such a blessing to the community as during these few days.

God has been blessing me with ever increasing health and strength since the New York Visitation, so that I am stronger than at any former time and can work more for God in Zion than ever before.

Zion must go forward until not only America, but all the world becomes one great Zion City with the Christ ruling as King of kings and Lord of lords.

DEACON JAMES C. CUTLER, 2506 Gideon avenue, Zion City, Illinois.—It is with joy and praises unto God that through LEAVES OF HEALING I give thanks for the opportunity of having been with Zion Restoration Host on its great Visitation to New York City.

I give thanks, first, for the open way that God made for my going, for every way had seemed hemmed in, and the possibility only became a reality about twenty-four hours before time to leave with the members of the Host from St. Louis, Missouri, where I was living at that time.

I went prepared to work and endure hardship if necessary, for His Name's sake, feeling that on account of the work I was engaged in, having been a letter-carrier for over fifteen years, I was physically prepared to climb stairs for hours at a time.

But I was appointed captain of a ten and I can say that never did a company do better service, both men and women, climbing to four and five stories in most every case, to perhaps the poorest and most illiterate of New York and Brooklyn's mixed multitudes—Italians, Jews and others.

I can thank God that with one or two exceptions the poor people, as sheep without a true Shepherd, received the Host kindly, the women and children often kissing the picture of the Christ and showing true reverence and devotion. No doubt the picture at this time occupies a prominent place in many of the homes.

The police were kind and courteous and one officer told me that if they (speaking of janitors) would not allow the members of the company to come in their building he would go with them.

I ate my meals in Madison Square Garden, always having enough of pure, wholesome food.

Above all I thank God for my own personal experience during the Visitation compared with the experience of fifteen years ago, when as a member of Buffalo Bill's wild west show I ate and slept in Madison Square Garden, working night and day to make his show a success, and giving my spirit, soul, and body into the service of the wicked one.

I was then a cigaret fiend and a gambler, and vile in many ways, and here was an opportunity, fifteen years later, to stand in Madison Square Garden, a saved man, with clean hands and a pure heart, with a pure people, and with a Leader who had given his life to bring to this people the Kingdom of God.

So I again say that I am one who has much reason to be thankful to God for the New York Visitation.

DELLA D. GIBSON, Zion City, Illinois.—I praise God for the privilege of working with the host in New York.

The lady of whom we rented rooms was very much interested in the meetings at Madison Square Garden.

She said that she would rather have Zion people in her house than any other people.

She said that she would visit Zion City.

One day a Scotch lady said, "I thought that you had gone back to Zion City."

We replied, "No, only those returned who were in positions that needed them, and to let others come."

"Oh!" she said, "you cannot believe the papers; they do not tell the truth."

One day, on returning from our work, a gentleman stepped up to us and said that he had been to Madison Square Garden a number of times, to attend the meetings, but could not gain admittance, because the crowd was so great.

He said that he handed a prayer request to a Guard, to be given in to the General Overseer.

His knee which had been so sore and stiff for a number of years was healed. He also asked about Zion City and if he could live here.

He wished to bring his two boys here to be brought up in a clean city and he wished us to pray for him.

I could state many other pleasant instances and I can truly say that the work was an intense joy and blessing to me and will continue to be a pleasant memory.

Zion Literature Sent Out from a Free Distribution Fund Provided by Zion's Guests and the Friends of Zion.

Report for week ending June 25, 1904:

900 Rolls to.............. State of Washington
3,000 Rolls to..Business Men in the United States
2,500 Rolls to.........Various States of the Union
Number of Rolls for the Week..............6,400
Number of Rolls reported to June 25, 1904, 3,199,029

EVANGELIST SARAH E. HILL,
Superintendent Zion Literature Mission,
Zion City, Illinois.

Program Zion's Fourth Feast of Tabernacles

Will be held in Shiloh Tabernacle, Shiloh Park, Zion City, Illinois, from the Evening of Wednesday, July 13th, to the Evening of Lord's Day, July 24, 1904.

WEDNESDAY, JULY 13TH.

7:30 to 9 P. M.—Presentation and Consecration of the People to God. Address by the General Overseer: "FOR ZION'S SAKE."

THURSDAY, JULY 14TH.

FOURTH ANNIVERSARY OF THE CONSECRATION OF THE SITE OF ZION TEMPLE.

Public Holiday in Zion City.

Announcement of excursion trains from Chicago will be made at a later date.

6:30 A. M.—Early Morning Sacrifice of Praise and Prayer.

The First of a Series of Twenty-Minute Addresses by the General Overseer on the Nine Fruits of the Spirit: "THE FIRST FRUIT OF THE SPIRIT: LOVE."

9:30 A. M.—First Convocation of Zion Junior Restoration Host. Conducted by Overseer Harvey D. Brasefield.

2:00 P. M.—FULL PROCESSION of Zion Robed Officers, Zion White-robed Choir, and Zion Restoration Host will march around the Site of Zion Temple, and thence to the Site of Shiloah Tabernacle.

The Procession will then re-form and take the seats reserved for them in Shiloh Tabernacle, where an address will be given by the General Overseer on "ZION: A CROWN OF BEAUTY IN THE HAND OF JEHOVAH."

Special Offerings will be received at the close of this Address for the building of Shiloah Tabernacle, which it is expected will cost $500,000, and seat about 16,000 people.

7:30 P. M.—Evening Sacrifice of Praise and Prayer.

FRIDAY, JULY 15TH.

A HALF HOLIDAY IN ZION CITY.

6:30 A. M.—Early Morning Sacrifice of Praise and Prayer.

Twenty-Minute Address by the General Overseer: "THE SECOND FRUIT OF THE SPIRIT: JOY."

9:30 A. M.—Second Convocation of Zion Junior Restoration Host. Conducted by Overseer Harvey D. Brasefield.

10:30 A. M.—DIVINE HEALING MEETING. Conducted by the General Overseer.

Address: "PRESENT YOUR BODIES A LIVING SACRIFICE, HOLY, ACCEPTABLE TO GOD, WHICH IS YOUR REASONABLE SERVICE."

At the close of this meeting the General Overseer, Overseer Jane Dowie, and other Overseers, Elders and Evangelists will pray with the sick who are seeking the Lord for healing.

THE CITY FESTAL DAY.

3:00 P. M.—A PROCESSION, headed by Zion Guard and Zion City Band, consisting of

The Municipal Officers of the City of Zion,

All Officers and Employees of the Legal, Financial and Business Institutions of Zion,

All Officers and Employees of the Educational Institutions of Zion, and

All Officers of the Political Institutions of Zion, will be REVIEWED BY THE GENERAL OVERSEER AT THE ADMINISTRATION BUILDING, and then proceed to Shiloh Tabernacle where a SERVICE OF THANKSGIVING will be held.

Those in the Procession, as they enter Shiloh Tabernacle, will take their places in the Choir and Officers' Gallery, and on the ground floor.

Spectators will occupy the remaining galleries.

7:30 P. M.—Evening Sacrifice of Praise and Prayer.

SATURDAY, JULY 16TH.

6:30 A. M.—EARLY MORNING SACRIFICE OF PRAISE AND PRAYER.

Twenty-Minute Address by the General Overseer: "THE THIRD FRUIT OF THE SPIRIT: PEACE."

2:00 P. M.—Zion Athletic Association: Field Games on grounds at northeast corner of Shiloh Park.

8:00 P. M.—Evening Sacrifice of Praise and Prayer.

LORD'S DAY, JULY 17TH.

6:30 A. M.—EARLY MORNING SACRIFICE OF PRAISE AND PRAYER.

Twenty-Minute Address by the General Overseer on "THE FOURTH FRUIT OF THE SPIRIT: LONG-SUFFERING."

9:30 A. M.—Third convocation of Zion Junior Restoration Host. Conducted by Overseer Harvey D. Brasefield.

11:00 A. M.—The Rev. John G. Speicher, M. D., Overseer of the Christian Catholic Church in Zion, of the City of Zion, will preach.

2:00 P. M.—GREAT GENERAL ASSEMBLY.

Procession of Zion's Robed Officers and White-robed Choir (probably One Thousand in line).

Elijah the Restorer will deliver a Message from God to Zion: "ARISE! SHINE! FOR THY LIGHT IS COME."

A reception of New Members into the Communion and Fellowship of the Christian Catholic Church in Zion will be held at the close.

8:00 P. M.—Ordination of New Officers and the Celebration of the Ordinance of the Lord's Supper.

MONDAY, JULY 18TH.

6:30 A. M.—EARLY MORNING SACRIFICE OF PRAISE AND PRAYER.

Twenty-minute Address by the General Overseer: "THE FIFTH FRUIT OF THE SPIRIT: KINDNESS."

9:30 A. M.—Fourth Convocation of Zion Junior Restoration Host. Conducted by Overseer Harvey D. Brasefield.

11:00 A. M.—THE ORDINANCE OF BELIEVER'S BAPTISM BY TRIUNE IMMERSION will be administered by Overseers Speicher, Mason, Brasefield and Excell, assisted by a number of Elders, Evangelists, Deacons and Deaconesses.

2:00 P. M.—A MEETING FOR ZION WOMEN ONLY will be addressed by the Rev. Jane Dowie, Overseer for Women's Work in the Christian Catholic Church in Zion Throughout the World.

This meeting will be strictly limited to female members of the Christian Catholic Church in Zion, and no children under twelve years of age will be admitted.

8:00 P. M.—A MEETING FOR ZION MEN ONLY will be addressed by the Rev. John Alex. Dowie, General Overseer of the Christian Catholic Church in Zion.

This meeting will be strictly limited to male members of the Christian Catholic Church in Zion above the age of twelve.

TUESDAY, JULY 19TH.

6:30 A. M.—EARLY MORNING SACRIFICE OF PRAISE AND PRAYER.

Twenty-Minute Address by the General Overseer: "THE SIXTH FRUIT OF THE SPIRIT: GOODNESS."

9:30 A. M.—Fifth Convocation of Zion Junior Restoration Host. Conducted by Overseer Harvey D. Brasefield.

11:30 A. M.—CONFERENCE OF WOMEN ELDERS, EVANGELISTS AND DEACONESSES OF THE CHRISTIAN CATHOLIC CHURCH IN ZION. Conducted by Overseer Jane Dowie.

2:30 P. M.—CONFERENCE UPON THE WORK OF ZION RESTORATION HOST THROUGHOUT THE WORLD.

The General Overseer will preside, and at the close will administer the Restoration Vow to New Members of the Host, and Consecrate and Separate them to the Work of God in Zion by the Laying on of Hands.

8:00 P. M.—Evening Sacrifice of Praise and Prayer.

WEDNESDAY, JULY 20TH.

6:30 A. M.—EARLY MORNING SACRIFICE OF PRAISE AND PRAYER.

Twenty-Minute Address by the General Overseer: "THE SEVENTH FRUIT OF THE SPIRIT: FAITHFULNESS."

9:30 A. M.—Sixth Convocation of Zion Junior Restoration Host. Conducted by Overseer Harvey D. Brasefield.

11:00 A. M.—CONFERENCE OF MALE OFFICERS OF THE CHRISTIAN CATHOLIC CHURCH IN ZION. Conducted by the General Overseer.

2:30 P. M.—THE ORDINANCE OF THE PRESENTATION AND CONSECRATION OF YOUNG CHILDREN TO GOD, will be conducted by the General Overseer. He will deliver an Address on the Words: "WHAT THEN SHALL THIS CHILD BE?"

8:00 P. M.—Evening Sacrifice of Praise and Prayer.

THURSDAY, JULY 21ST.

6:30 A. M.—EARLY MORNING SACRIFICE OF PRAISE AND PRAYER.
Twenty-Minute Address by the General Overseer: "THE EIGHTH FRUIT OF THE SPIRIT: MEEKNESS."

9:00 A. M.—Seventh Convocation of Zion Junior Restoration Host. Conducted by Overseer Harvey D. Brasefield.

11:00 A. M.—EDUCATIONAL CONFERENCE. Presided over by Overseer Brasefield. Addresses by Members of the Faculty of Zion College, Zion Preparatory and Zion Manual Training Schools.

2:00 P. M.—A CONFERENCE ON ZION BUSINESS INSTITUTIONS will be Conducted by the General Overseer, and Addressed by Managers of the Various Institutions.
The Meeting will be Strictly Limited to Investors in Zion Stocks.

8:00 P. M.—Evening Sacrifice of Praise and Prayer.

FRIDAY, JULY 22d.

6:30 A. M.—EARLY MORNING SACRIFICE OF PRAISE AND PRAYER.
Twenty-Minute address by the General Overseer: "THE NINTH FRUIT OF THE SPIRIT: TEMPERANCE."

9:30 A. M.—Eighth Convocation of Zion Junior Restoration Host. Conducted by Overseer Harvey D. Brasefield.

11:00 A. M.—A CONFERENCE CONCERNING DORCAS AND MATERNITY DEACONESS WORK IN ZION THROUGHOUT THE WORLD. Conducted by Overseer Jane Dowie.

2:00 P. M.—A CONFERENCE ON ZION BUSINESS INSTITUTIONS will be Conducted by the General Overseer, and Addressed by Managers of the Various Institutions.
The Meeting will be Strictly Limited to Investors in Zion Stocks.

8:00 P. M.—Evening Sacrifice of Praise and Prayer.

SATURDAY, JULY 23D.

6:30 A. M.—EARLY MORNING SACRIFICE OF PRAISE AND PRAYER.
Twenty-Minute Address by the General Overseer: "THE NINE GIFTS OF THE HOLY SPIRIT."

2:00 P. M.—Zion Athletic Association; Field Games in the northeast corner of Shiloh Park.

8:00 P. M.—Evening Sacrifice of Praise and Prayer.

LORD'S DAY, JULY 24TH.

6:30 A. M.—EARLY MORNING SACRIFICE OF PRAISE AND PRAYER.
Twenty-Minute Address by the General Overseer: "THE HOUSE OF WISDOM."

9.30 A. M.—The General Overseer will speak on "TRIUNE IMMERSION; GOD'S SEAL ON A LIVING CHURCH."
At the close of this Service the General Overseer, assisted by Overseers, Elders, Evangelists, Deacons and Deaconesses, will Administer the Ordinance of Believer's Baptism.
All persons desiring to be Baptized on this occasion must fill up their Application Cards for Baptism, and present them to the General Recorder, Deacon Andrew C. Jensen, and his Assistants, not later than 9 a. m.

2:00 P. M.—GREAT GENERAL ASSEMBLY.
FULL PROCESSIONAL of Zion Robed Officers, Zion White-robed Choir and all the Members of Zion Junior Restoration Host, under their Leader, Overseer Brasefield.
The General Overseer will speak on "THE MINISTRY OF CHILDREN IN ZION." At the close of this Service he will Administer the Vow of Zion Restoration Host to New Members of Zion Junior Restoration Host.

8 00 P. M.—THE ORDINANCE OF THE LORD'S SUPPER will be Administered by the General Overseer and Ordained Officers of the Christian Catholic Church in Zion.
This Gathering will be open only to Members of the Christian Catholic Church in Zion, and other Christians desiring to commune with them.
At the close, the General Overseer will deliver the CONCLUDING ADDRESS OF THE FEAST.

REDUCED FARE—FEAST OF TABERNACLES.

ONE AND ONE-THIRD FARE FOR ROUND TRIP TO ZION CITY—CONDITIONS OF SALE OF TICKETS.

A reduction of fare to one and one-third on the certificate plan has been granted for those attending the meetings of the Christian Catholic Church in Zion, at the Fourth Feast of Tabernacles, in Zion City, Lake County, Illinois, between July 13 and July 24, 1904, inclusive.

The following directions are submitted for your guidance:

First—Tickets at full fare for the going journey, may be secured within three days, exclusive of Sunday, prior to and during the first three days of the meeting; that is, July 10th, 11th, 12th, 13th, 14th, and 15th.

The advertised dates of the meeting are from July 13th to 24th; consequently you can obtain your tickets not earlier than July 11th and not later than July 17th.

Be sure when purchasing your going ticket to request a certificate.

Second—Present yourself at the railway station for ticket and certificate at least thirty minutes before departure of train.

Third—Certificates are not kept at all stations. If you inquire at your station you will find out whether certificates and through tickets can be obtained to place of meeting; if not, the agent will inform you at what station they can be obtained. You can purchase a local ticket thence, and there take up a certificate and through ticket.

Fourth—On your arrival at the meeting, present your certificate to Deacon James F. Peters, Administration building, Zion City, Illinois.

Fifth—No refund of fare will be made on account of failure to have certificate validated.

Sixth—So as to prevent disappointment, it must be understood that the reduction on returning journey is not guaranteed, but is contingent on an attendance of not less than one hundred persons from all points throughout the United States and Canada showing payment of full first-class fare of not less than seventy-five cents on going journey; provided, however, if the certificates presented fall short of the required minimum, and it shall appear that round trip tickets are held in lieu of certificate, that shall be reckoned in arriving at the minimum.

Seventh—If the necessary minimum is in attendance and your certificate is duly validated, you will be entitled, up to July 27th, to reduced passage ticket to your destination by the route over which you made the going journey at one-third the limit fare.

This rate will apply to the entire United States and Canada.

SPECIAL TRAINS BETWEEN CHICAGO AND ZION CITY.

These trains will be arranged for and announcement will be made later.

CAMP ESTHER—1904.

Persons desiring to spend a holiday or attend the great teaching meetings of Zion will find, either as individuals, families or parties, inexpensive tenting conveniences, with good water near at hand, in Zion's tents, which will be in service during and after ZION'S FOURTH FEAST OF TABERNACLES. Tents will be erected in beautiful Shiloh Park, Zion City.

TENT PROVISIONS AND REGULATIONS FOR 1904.

Two tents may be required in some instances, and these will be more convenient than one large tent. Then one can be used for sleeping, and the other for cooking purposes, if desired.

The Feast of Tabernacles' rate is always $2.25 a person, four persons to a tent; otherwise than this tent rent when occupied by a less number of persons, single cots for single nights, 25 cents; tent rates a day $1.25.

The season's price for tent 9½x14, furnished, is $7.00; or unfurnished, $5.00 a month, Tent 14x20 furnished is $12.00, or unfurnished, $7.00. Small furnished tents may be rented by the week at $4.00 for the first week and $2.00 a week thereafter.

All rentals payable in advance, in every case, whether by the month, week or day.

THE FURNITURE.

The furniture consists of the necessary cots, mattresses and chairs, one table, water-pail, tin cup, wash basin and slop-pail to a small tent. The bedding includes one white sheet, two light and one or two heavy blankets, and a pillow and pillow-slip to a single and two of each to a double cot. Persons must furnish their own towels, soaps, brushes etc.

TENTS.

The tents are made of heavy duck material, strongly stayed, with fly, and are rain-proof being pitched above board floors.

Small tents 9½x14 will accommodate four (4) people, being equipped with four single spring cots with mattresses.

The large or family tents are 14x20, and may be equipped with four full-size beds with comfortable springs and mattresses, if so desired.

We would suggest that parties desiring to be accommodated with tents, write us full particulars as to the number of people and size of tent desired as early as possible, to avoid misunderstandings and delay.

Do not put off making your arrangements for tent service until you come, as it may be impossible for us to serve you then.

Applications for such accommodations and conveniences should be made at once to Deacon W. Hurd Clendinen, Manager Zion City General Stores, Zion City, Illinois

THE RATES AT ELIJAH HOSPICE

NOW AND DURING THE FEAST OF TABERNACLES ARE AS FOLLOWS:

European Plan—One person in a room, $1.00 a day and up; two persons or more in a room, 50 cents a day and up, one person in a room, $6.00 a week and up; two persons or more in a room, $3.00 a week and up. These rates are for lodging only.

American Plan—One person in a room, $1.75 a day and up, two persons or more in a room, $1.25 a day and up; one person in a room, $10.00 a week and up; two persons or more in a room, $7.00 a week and up; single meals, 25 cents.

Children under twelve years old half rate

The American Plan includes board and room.

Rooms will be charged for from the date reserved.

FRANK W. COTTON, Manager.

Zion's Bible Class

Conducted by Deacon Daniel Sloan in Shiloh Tabernacle, Zion City, Lord's Day Morning at 11 o'clock, and in Zion Homes and Gatherings throughout the World.

MID-WEEK BIBLE CLASS LESSON, JULY 20th or 21st.

Marks of a Good Soldier of Jesus, the Christ.

1. *He is inspired by a deep conviction of loyalty, duty and obligation.*—2 Corinthians 5:5-15.
   He is willing to do his duty.
   All he has and is belongs to God.
   He desires to live only for the Lord.
2. *He solemnly enlists, expecting the fight will be hard pressed.*—Genesis 17:1-8.
   He does not know where he will have to go.
   He is not concerned about events that may occur.
   He obeys orders and fights under command.
3. *He stands out-and-out under plain colors, and has no fellowship with the enemy.*—Ephesians 5:6-21.
   He does not listen to the reports of the enemy.
   He is against the enemy wherever found.
   He never shirks guard and picket duty.
4. *He obeys the command, is loyal to his superior, and observes military rule.*—Ephesians 5:1-5.
   He follows his commander wherever he leads.
   He does not consider warfare a picnic.
   He will preserve a soldier's honor.
5. *He reports and wants to see every coward and traitor disciplined and punished.*—Romans 2:1-11.
   He will excuse no one who fails in duty.
   Those who disobey and are insolent must be disciplined.
   Evil doers must be given a hard time.
6. *He does not think of the sacrifices he makes or the self-denial called for.*—2 Corinthians 4:7-18.
   He does not live in uncertainty, but in faith.
   He is willing to suffer loss that the cause may win.
   He knows that his losses will turn to gain.
7. *He enlists for life and will never surrender. Salvation must be cut off and strength fail before he gives up.*—Philippians 1:19-30.
   The enemy cannot terrify him.
   He knows that his life or death will count for the Christ.
   In faith he knows that all will end well.
   The Lord our God is a Fidelity-inspiring God.

LORD'S DAY BIBLE CLASS LESSON, JULY 24th.

Disloyalty to God's Call, Work, People, Church, City, Kingdom and Servant.

1. *He who questions God's promises and His power to fulfil them is disloyal.*—Isaiah 41:21-29.
   God has promised to raise up a mighty man of God.
   He has said that He will build a City.
   He purposes to purify unto Himself a people.
2. *He who gives way to doubts and fears and wants to make sure, is disloyal.*—2 Chronicles 20:5-13.
   Difficulties should never dishearten one.
   Faith overcomes every power in the world.
   Can you not trust God to work out His plans?
3. *He who criticises, complains, and murmurs at minor and temporary things is disloyal.*—Exodus 16:2-8.
   Murmurers are destroyed.
   Complain against God's men and you complain against Him.
   Some think there is but one way and that their way.
4. *He who becomes ambitious for self and impugns the fidelity of superiors is disloyal.*—Luke 12:13-21.
   "Money, money, money!" is the cry of some.
   Some cry for it; some strive and lay plans to get it.
   Some live only to make money, to spend it, and rob God.
5. *He who is afraid of want lest he lose all, is disloyal.*—Hebrews 13:5-18.
   He relies on dollars or property.
   He seems to think that when money fails God will also fail him.
   He fears some man will make him lose.
6. *He who consorts with critics or opposers, or who balks at discipline imposed, is disloyal.*—2 Thessalonians 3:6-14.
   When a man sins and will not repent, shun him.
   People are told what to do in Zion.
   If a man disobeys let him be marked and pointed out.
7. *He who is careless about churchgoing, does not work, and dishonors the Lord's Day, is disloyal.*—Hebrews 10:19-27.
   Some stay from meetings on very small excuses.
   They have half-hearted habits on the Lord's Day.
   They are not aggressive but have to be pulled into work for the Lord.
8. *He who does not act on reliable information, but on conclusions of what he sees, what he hears or thinks, and loses hope and expectation, is disloyal.*—John 21: 3-12.
   Some are ready to forsake God's Work.
   One man's influence leads another to follow him.
   Some act as though God would forsake His own cause or work.
   God's Holy People are a Strongly-assured People.

DO YOU KNOW GOD'S WAY OF HEALING?

BY THE REV. JOHN ALEX. DOWIE.

Let it be supposed that the following words are a conversation between the reader [A] and the writer [B].

A. What does this question mean? Do you really suppose that God has some one especial way of healing in these days, of which men may know and avail themselves?

B. That is exactly my meaning, and I wish very much that you should know God's Way of Healing, as I have known it for many years.

A. What is the way, in your opinion?

B. You should rather ask, WHO is God's Way? for the way is a Person, not a thing. I will answer your question in His own words, "I am the Way, and the Truth, and the Life: no one cometh unto the Father, but by Me." These words were spoken by our Lord Jesus, the Christ, the Eternal Son of God, who is both our Savior and our Healer. (John 14:6.)

A. But I always thought that these words only referred to Him as the Way of Salvation. How can you be sure that they refer to Him as the Way of Healing also?

B. Because He cannot change. He is "the same yesterday and today, yea, and forever." (Hebrews 13:8.) He said that He came to this earth not only to save us but to heal us. (Luke 4:18), and He did this when in the flesh on earth. Being unchanged He must be able and willing and desirous to heal now.

A. But is there not this difference, namely, that He is not with us now?

B. No; for He said "Lo, I am with you All the Days, even unto the Consummation of the Age;" and so He is with us now, in spirit, just as much as when He was here in the flesh.

A. But did He not work these miracles of healing when on earth merely to prove that He was the Son of God?

B. No; there was still a greater purpose than that. He healed the sick who trusted in Him in order to show us that He came to die not only for our sins, but for our sicknesses, and to deliver us from both.

A. Then, if that be so, the atonement which He made on the Cross must have been for our sicknesses as well as our sins. Can you prove that is the fact from the Scriptures?

B. Yes, I can, and the passages are very numerous. I need quote only two. In Isaiah 53:4, 5, it is written of Him: "Surely He hath borne our griefs (Hebrew, *sicknesses*), and carried our sorrows: . . . and with His stripes we are healed." Then, in the Gospel according to Matthew, this passage is quoted and directly applied to the work of bodily healing, in the 8th chapter 17th verse: "That it might be fulfilled which was spoken by Isaiah the prophet, saying, Himself took our infirmities, and bare our diseases."

A. But do you not think that sickness is often God's will, and sent for our good, and therefore God may not wish us to be healed?

B. No, that cannot possibly be; for diseases of every kind are the Devil's work, and his work can never be God's will, since the Christ came for the very purpose of destroying "the works of the Devil." (1 John 3:8.)

A. Do you mean to say that all disease is the work of Satan?

B. Yes, for if there had been no sin (which came through Satan) there never would have been any disease, and Jesus never in one single instance told any person that sickness was God's work or will, but the very contrary.

A. Can you prove from Scriptures that all forms of sickness and infirmity are the Devil's work?

B. Yes, that can be done very easily. You will see in Matthew 4:23 and 9:35 that when Jesus was here in the flesh He healed "all manner of disease and all manner of sickness among the people." Then if you will refer to Acts 10:38 you will see that the Apostle Peter declares that He (Jesus) "went about doing good, and healing all that were oppressed of the Devil." Notice that all whom He healed, not some, were suffering from Satan's evil power.

A. But does disease never come from God?

B. No, it cannot come from God, for He is pure, and disease is unclean; and it cannot come out of Heaven, for there is no disease there.

A. That is very different from the teachings which I have received all my life from ministers and in the churches. Do you really think that you are right, and that they are all wrong in this matter?

B. It is not a question as between myself and them. The only question is, What does God's Word say? God has said in all the ages, to His Church, "I am Jehovah that healeth thee" (Exodus 15:26), and therefore it would be wicked to say that He is the defiler of His people. All true Christians must believe the Bible, and it is impossible to believe that good and evil, sickness and health, sin and holiness could have a common origin in God. If the Bible really taught that, it would be impossible to believe our Lord Jesus, the Christ, when He says: "A good tree cannot bring forth evil fruit, neither can a corrupt tree bring forth good fruit." (Matthew 7:18.)

A. But even if I agree with all you say, is it not true that the Gifts of Healing were removed from the Church, and are not in it now?

B. No, the "Gifts of Healing" were never withdrawn, and can never be withdrawn, from the true Church of God, for it is written: "The gifts and the calling of God are without repentance." (Romans 11:29.) There are nine gifts of God to the Church (enumerated in 1 Corinthians 12:8-11), and all these are in the Holy Spirit. Therefore, so long as the Holy Spirit is in the Church, all the gifts must be there also. If they are not exercised, that does not prove that they do not exist, but that the faith to exercise them is lacking in God's servants. The gifts are all perfectly preserved; for the Holy Spirit, not the Church, keeps them safely.

A. What should a Christian then do when overtaken with sickness?

B. A Christian should obey God's command, and at once turn to Him for forgiveness of the sin which may have caused the sickness, and for immediate healing. Healing is obtained from God in one of four ways, namely: First, by the direct prayer of faith, without any aid from the officers of the Church, praying as the Centurion did in Matthew 8:5-12; second, by two faithful disciples praying in perfect agreement in accordance with the Lord's promise in Matthew 18:19; third, by the anointing of the Elders and the prayer of faith, according to the instructions in James 5:14 and 15; and fourth, by the laying on of the hands of them who believe, and whom God calls to that ministry, as the Lord commands in Mark 16:18, and in other places.

A. But are people healed in this way in these days?

B. Yes, in thousands of cases. I have myself laid hands upon many hundreds of thousands of persons, and I have seen the Lord's power manifested in the healing of great numbers, many of whom are living witnesses in many countries, who have testified publicly before thousands, and who are prepared to testify at any time. This ministry is being exercised by devoted Christians in many parts of America, Europe, Australasia, and elsewhere.

A. Is it not the same as Christian Science, Mind Healing, etc.?

B. No. Divine Healing is diametrically opposed to these diabolical counterfeits, which are utterly antichristian. These impostures are only seductive forms of Spiritualism. Trance Evangelism is also a more recent form of this delusion, and it deceives many.

A. But how shall I obtain the necessary faith to receive healing, which faith I am at present conscious that I do not possess?

B. It is written: "Belief cometh of hearing, and hearing by the word of the Christ." (Romans 10:17.) Our Missions are held for the express purpose of teaching fully the Word of God on this matter, and I very heartily invite you to attend the meetings which are announced for Zion Tabernacles in Chicago and other cities, and for Shiloh Tabernacle, Zion City, Illinois. All are welcome and there are no charges of any kind made, for all God's gifts are free gifts. Salvation is the first of these, without which you cannot be healed through faith in Jesus. All the costs of this work are covered by the free-will offerings of the people who attend these meetings, and others whom the Lord leads to help; but the poorest, who have nothing to give, are as heartily welcome as the richest.

A. Do you see the sick and lay hands upon them in this Mission?

B. Yes; after we feel satisfied that they are fully resting in the Lord alone for the healing, we see privately, so far as time permits, those who attend; but under no circumstances do we claim the power to heal any; for "power belongeth unto God."

A. Have you any writings upon this subject which can be purchased?

B. Yes; these can be obtained at the office of Zion Printing and Publishing House, Zion City, Illinois, and at any Zion Tabernacle. But the best book on Divine Healing is the Bible itself, studied prayerfully and earnestly.

We extend to you a hearty invitation to attend the meetings, which are free to all. Our prayer is that you may be led to find in Jesus, the Christ, our Lord and God your present Savior from sin, your Healer from sickness, your Cleanser from all evil, your Keeper in the way to Heaven, your Friend, and your All for Time and Eternity. We pray that these words may help many who read, and that our little conversation may bear fruit in leading many readers to look to Jesus only.

"The Healing of Christ's seamless dress
Is by all beds of pain;
We touch Him in life's throng and press
And we are whole again."

OBEYING GOD IN BAPTISM.

"Baptizing Them Into the Name of the Father and of the Son and of the Holy Ghost."

Eighteen Thousand Six Hundred Ninety-one Baptisms by Triune Immersion Since March 14, 1897.

Eighteen Thousand Six Hundred Ninety-one Believers have joyfully followed their Lord in the Ordinance of Believer's Baptism by Triune Immersion since the first Baptism in Central Zion Tabernacle on March 14, 1897.

Baptized in Central Zion Tabernacle from March 14, 1897, to December 14, 1901, by the General Overseer,	4754			
Baptized in South Side Zion Tabernacle from January 1, 1902, to June 14, 1903, by the General Overseer..	37			
Baptized at Zion City by the General Overseer........	583			
Baptized by Overseers, Elders, Evangelists and Deacons, at Headquarters (Zion City) and Chicago......	5283			
Total Baptized at Headquarters....................				10,657
Baptized in places outside of Headquarters by the General Overseer................................		641		
Baptized in places outside of Headquarters by Overseers, Elders, Evangelists and Deacons............		7375		
Total Baptized outside of Headquarters..............				8,016
Total Baptized in seven years and three months....				18,673
Baptized since June 14, 1904:				
Baptized in Chicago by Elder Hoffman...............	1			
Baptized in Chicago by Elder Cossum................	1		2	
Baptized in Nebraska by Elder Hoy..................		7		
Baptized in Ohio by Deacon Kelchner................		1		
Baptized in Ohio by Deacon Arrington...............		5		
Baptized in Wisconsin by Elder McClurkin...........		3	16	18
Total Baptized since March 14, 1897...............				18,691

The following-named twenty-seven believers were baptized in Johannesburg, Transvaal, South Africa, Lord's Day, May 8, 1904, by Overseer Daniel Bryant:

Clark, Mrs. Elizabeth,
48 Macintyre street, Jeppestown, Johannesburg, South Africa
Daniel, Mrs. Caroline Susan,
8 Biccard street, Braamfontein, Johannesburg, South Africa
Daniel, Miss Johanna Caroline Rhoda,
8 Biccard street, Braamfontein, Johannesburg, South Africa
Davey, Miss Adela Marguerite,
1 Jorissen street, Braamfontein, Johannesburg, South Africa
Langerhouw, Mrs. Magdalena,
1 Jorissen street, Braamfontein, Johannesburg, South Africa
Mackenzie, Mrs. Ellen Dora, 142 Marshall street, Johannesburg, South Africa
Mapstone, John Edwin,
Kitchener avenue, Bezuidenhout Valley, Johannesburg, South Africa
Opperman, Mrs. Isabella Maria Christina,
1 Jorissen street, Braamfontein, Johannesburg, South Africa
Opperman, Miss Kate,
1 Jorissen street, Braamfontein, Johannesburg, South Africa
Powell, Henry Modred.....228 Marshall street, Johannesburg, South Africa
Powell, Mrs. Mary..........228 Marshall street, Johannesburg, South Africa
Powell, Miss Jessie Nelly May,
228 Marshall street, Johannesburg, South Africa
Sheppard, Walter Cabell,
1 Jorissen street, Braamfontein, Johannesburg, South Africa
Sheppard, Mrs. Antoinette Elizabeth,
1 Jorissen street, Braamfontein, Johannesburg, South Africa
Thomson, John ....Natal Bank, Johannesburg, South Africa
Uyate, Henry Charles,
32 Wilhelmina street, Troyville, Johannesburg, South Africa
Uyate, Mrs. Lillie Amelia,
32 Wilhelmina street, Troyville, Johannesburg, South Africa
Uyate, William John......Postoffice box 1056, Johannesburg, South Africa
Van Aswegen, Peter Jacob Johannes,
42 Kock street, Johannesburg, South Africa
Van Rensburg, Phillip Nichloos Janse,
174 Marshall street, Johannesburg, South Africa
Van Wyk, Alfred Nicholas Smit, Bloomfontein, Orange River Colony, Africa
Watson, William Edward..174 Marshall street, Johannesburg, South Africa
Watson, Mrs. Marie Sophie Louise Henrietta,
174 Marshall street, Johannesburg, South Africa
Webb, Louis Pentecost,
28 Troyville Chambers, Troyville, Johannesburg, South Africa
Werth, Mrs. Sarah Maria,
Corner avenue and Crown road, Fordsburg, Johannesburg, South Africa
White, Mrs. Isabell Rhoda, Postoffice box 1766, Johannesburg, South Africa
White, Miss Ada Louisa.. Postoffice box 1766, Johannesburg, South Africa

The following-named believer was baptized at Cambridge, Nebraska, Friday, June 17, 1904, by Elder Charles A. Hoy:

Frank, Johann Fredrick..............................Farnam, Nebraska

The following-named believer was baptized in the South Side Zion Tabernacle, Chicago, Illinois, Lord's Day, June 19, 1904, by Elder W. H. Cossum:

Tinsley, Mrs. Alice.................181 Eighteenth street, Chicago, Illinois

The following-named believer was baptized in Zion Tabernacle, Cleveland, Ohio, Lord's Day, June 19, 1904, by Deacon C. F. Kelchner:

Treible, Miss Arminda......100 South Second street, Easton, Pennsylvania

The following-named five believers were baptized at Cincinnati, Ohio, Lord's Day, June 19, 1904, by Deacon A. E. Arrington:

Daniels, Mrs. Hattie Belle..............................Cedarville, Ohio
Daniels, Martin...Cedarville, Ohio
Epps, Mrs. Ellen.................627 West Fourth street, Cincinnati, Ohio
Gregg, Henry Clay........................53 Main street, Cincinnati, Ohio
Gregg, Margaret Eliza....................53 Main street, Cincinnati, Ohio

The following-named three believers were baptized at Marinette, Wisconsin, Lord's Day, June 19, 1904, by Elder A. W. McClurkin:

Bigelow, Abbie Irene............903 Terrace avenue, Marinette, Wisconsin
McClurkin, Miss Eleanor........903 Terrace avenue, Marinette, Wisconsin
Raue, Mrs. Effie J.................1141 State street, Marinette, Wisconsin

CONSECRATION OF CHILDREN.

The following-named five children were consecrated to God at Paris, Texas, Lord's Day, June 12, 1904, by Evangelist William D. Gay:

Riggs, George Record.................................... Paris, Texas
Riggs, Kate..Paris, Texas
Riggs, Ralph Smith..Paris, Texas
Williams, Alice Exenia.....................................Paris, Texas
Williams, Betsy Maria.....................................Paris, Texas

The following-named child was consecrated to God in the South Side Zion Tabernacle, Chicago, Illinois, Lord's Day, June 19, 1904, by Elder W. H. Cossum:

Wedekind, John George,
2320 Rinaldo avenue, Morgan Park, Chicago, Illinois

The following-named eleven children were consecrated to God in the North Side Zion Tabernacle, Chicago, Illinois, Lord's Day, June 19, 1904, by Elder C. R. Hoffman:

Baurle, Freddy.....................125 Webster avenue, Chicago, Illinois
Boeser, Elsie.............................79 Wisconsin street, Chicago, Illinois
Boeser, Emma...........................79 Wisconsin street, Chicago, Illinois
Boeser, Myrtle............................79 Wisconsin street, Chicago, Illinois
Boeser, Violet.............................79 Wisconsin street, Chicago, Illinois
Kasch, Lucinda..........................361 Orchard street, Chicago, Illinois
Kasch, Melinda..........................361 Orchard street, Chicago, Illinois
Kubans, Ella...............................19 Gardner street, Chicago, Illinois
Kubans, Ida................................19 Gardner street, Chicago, Illinois
Kubans, Max...............................19 Gardner street, Chicago, Illinois
Stryker, Elsie.............................244 Fletcher street, Chicago, Illinois

The following-named four children were consecrated to God at Bloomington, Nebraska, Monday, June 20, 1904, by Elder Charles A. Hoy:

Ingram, Belva Fern...............................Bloomington, Nebraska
Ingram, Urwin Clifford..........................Bloomington, Nebraska
Morse, Margaret Vera...........................Bloomington, Nebraska
Morse, Deane Woods............................Bloomington, Nebraska

Publisher's Notice.

The remittance must accompany receipt of subscriptions at the Publishing House no difference by or for whom or for whatever time they may be given, or whether forwarded through Ordained Officers, Branches, or Gatherings of the Christian Catholic Church in Zion. Accounts will be carried with Ordained Officers, Branches, or Gatherings, on quantity orders of periodicals consigned on sale for monthly settlement, but to include only such articles as bear the imprint of Zion. All orders for Bibles, books, buttons, pictures (except prints done by the Publishing House), lace souvenirs, etc., must be sent to the General Stores, Zion City, Lake County, Illinois.

Notice to Officers and Members.

Send all newspaper clippings concerning the General Overseer, the Elders, or any department of the work in connection with the Christian Catholic Church in Zion, to Deacon Carl F. Stern, Zion City, Illinois. Send as soon as possible after publication, and carefully mark *name and date of the paper clipped from* on each article. If this is not done, the clippings are absolutely useless.

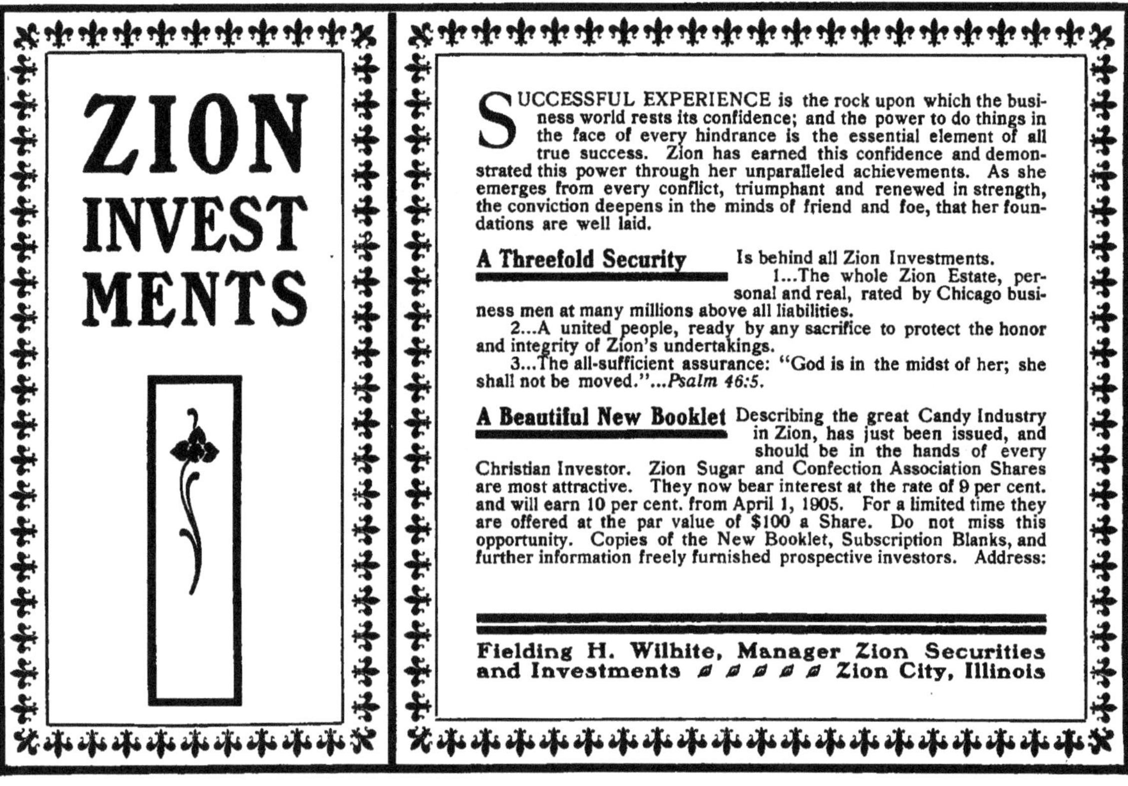

ZION CITY BANK

JOHN ALEX. DOWIE

ZION CITY, LAKE COUNTY, ILLINOIS, U. S. A.

Transacts a general Banking Business.

Issues Drafts payable in all the principal cities of the world.

Sells high-grade Securities bearing nine per cent. interest per annum. Particulars mailed on application.

Our Savings Department receives deposits from One Dollar upward, and pays interest at the following rates:

On all sums from $1 to $500, four per cent.

On all sums over $500, three per cent.

This Bank encourages thrift and economy among the people, and will assist them in their efforts to save money.

Our system of Banking by Mail has proved entirely satisfactory to thousands of persons living in different parts of this and other countries. It places everybody in close communication with the Bank and enables them to take advantage of the *excellent facilities* offered.

Correspondence from all parts of the world solicited.

Write for our booklet entitled, "Saving Money."

CHARLES J. BARNARD, Manager.

WILLIAM S. PECKHAM, Cashier.

CHARLES H. IRISH, Assistant Cashier.

LEAVES OF HEALING

Edited by REV. JOHN ALEXANDER DOWIE General Overseer of the Christian Catholic Church in Zion.

A 32-PAGE WEEKLY PAPER

For the Extension of the Kingdom of God. Contains Sermons, Addresses, and Editorial Notes by the General Overseer; Testimonies to Healing through Faith in Jesus, and Reports of Zion's Work Throughout the World.

Price, a year, $2.00

THE ZION BANNER

Edited by REV. JOHN ALEXANDER DOWIE General Overseer of the Christian Catholic Church in Zion

A WEEKLY NEWSPAPER

For the Extension of the Kingdom of God and the Elevation of Man. Deals with Social, Commercial, Political, and Industrial Problems. News from all over the World reliably reported. Notes on progress in the building up of Zion City. ***Subscription Price, 50c for 6 months.*** Address, General Manager Zion Printing and Publishing House, Zion City, Illinois, U. S. A.

Train Schedule Between Zion City and Chicago

Via Chicago & North-Western Railway.

Effective May 22, 1904.

Weekday Trains.

CHICAGO TO ZION CITY. Leave Chicago	Arrive Zion City	ZION CITY TO CHICAGO. Leave Zion City	Arrive Chicago
7.00 a. m.	8.25 a. m.	*6.45 a. m.	8.15 a. m.
*9.00 a. m.	10.13 a. m.	7.03 a. m.	8.30 a. m.
*11.30 a. m.	12.37 p. m.	8.22 a. m.	9.50 a. m.
2.00 p. m.	3.08 p. m.	*9.45 a. m.	11.10 a. m.
3.00 p. m	4.16 p. m.	*11.49 a. m.	1.15 p. m.
4.15 p. m.	5.39 p. m.	*‖1.18 p. m.	2.50 p. m.
*5.20 p. m.	6.50 p. m.	*†2.33 p. m.	4.00 p. m.
*8.00 p. m.	9.11 p. m.	5.05 p. m.	6.30 p. m.
		*7.59 p. m.	9.30 p. m.

Sunday Trains.

CHICAGO TO ZION CITY. Leave Chicago	Arrive Zion City
9.05 a. m.	10.18 a. m.
*10.45 a. m.	12.37 p. m.
2.15 p. m.	4.05 p. m.
*8.00 p. m.	9.11 p. m.

ZION CITY TO CHICAGO. Leave Zion City	Arrive Chicago
*8.29 a. m.	9.45 a. m.
5.05 p m.	6.40 p. m.
7.59 p m.	9.30 p. m.

Train leaves Waukegan at 12 28 p. m , arriving in Zion City at 12 37 p. m., daily, including Sunday.

* Signifies change train at Waukegan. † Train does not run South on Saturdays. ‖ Train runs South on Saturday only.

ZION'S TRANSPORTATION AND RAILWAY AFFAIRS (John Alex. Dowie), of Zion City, Illinois, supervises the railway ticket, steamship, excursion, freight, express and transfer business of Zion and her people everywhere. Direction as to railroad and steamship routes given upon request.

DEACON JAMES F. PETERS,
General Superintendent Zion Transportation.

A WEEKLY PAPER FOR THE EXTENSION OF THE KINGDOM OF GOD

EDITED BY THE REV. JOHN ALEX. DOWIE.

Volume XV. No. 12. *ZION CITY, SATURDAY, JULY 9, 1904.* *Price Five Cents*

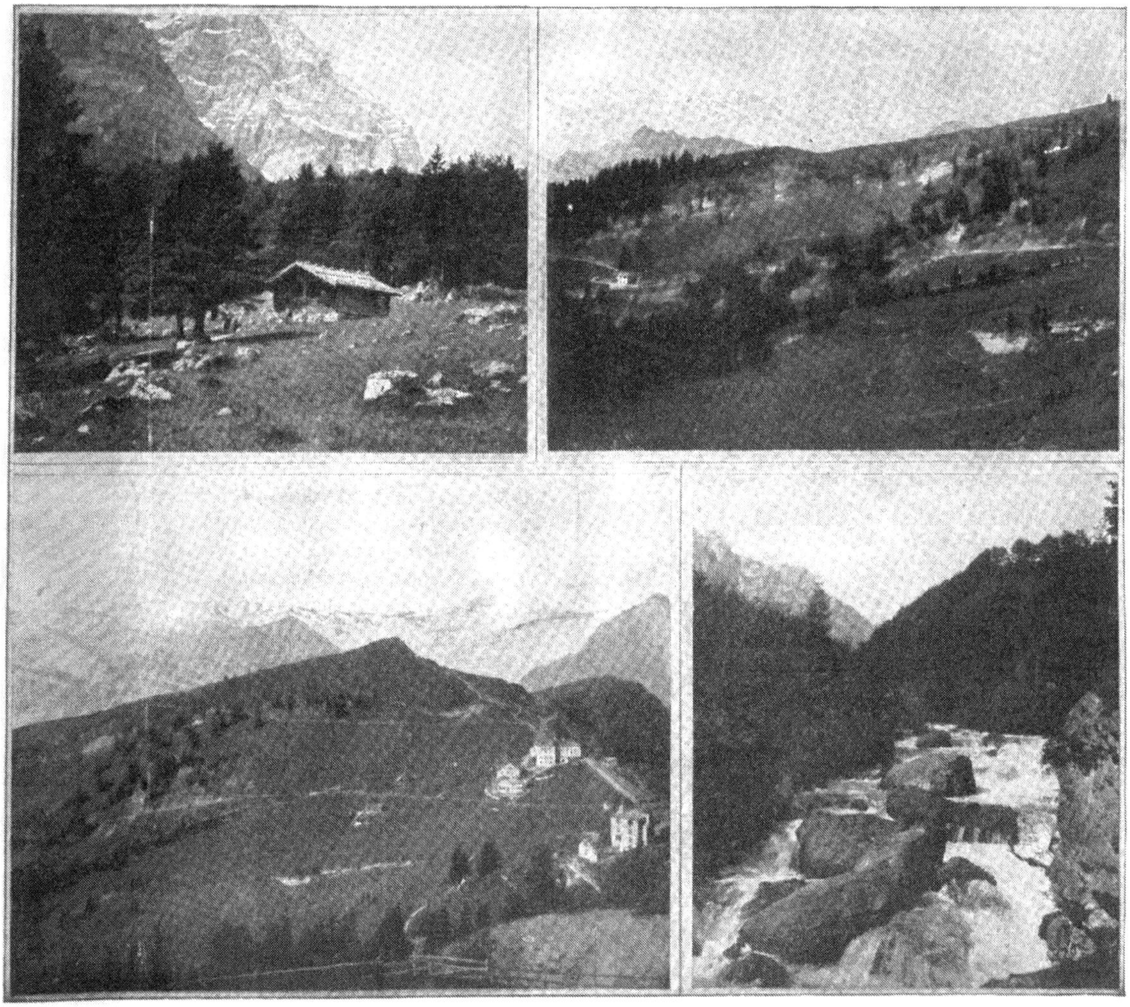

Swiss Chalet in Grindelwald.
View of Bernese Alps from Rigi-Kulm.

Mountain View from the Rigi.
The Black Lütschine, Grindelwald Valley.

SWISS MOUNTAIN SCENERY.

A WEEKLY PAPER FOR THE EXTENSION OF THE KINGDOM OF GOD.

EDITED BY THE REV. JOHN ALEX. DOWIE.

Application for entry as Second Class Matter at Zion City, Illinois, pending.

Subscription Rates.		Special Rates.	
One Year	$2.00	100 Copies of One Issue	$3.00
Six Months	1.25	25 Copies of One Issue	1.00
Three Months	.75	To Ministers, Y. M. C. A's and Public Reading Rooms, per annum	1.50
Single Copies	.05		

For foreign subscriptions add $1.50 per year, or three cents per copy for postage.

Subscribers desiring a change of address should give present address, as well as that to which they desire LEAVES OF HEALING sent in the future.

Make Bank Drafts, Express Money or Postoffice Money Orders payable to the order of JOHN ALEX. DOWIE, Zion City, Illinois, U. S. A.

Long Distance Telephone. *Cable Address "Dowie, Zion City."*

All communications upon business must be addressed to
MANAGER ZION PUBLISHING HOUSE,
Zion City, Illinois, U. S. A.

Subscriptions to LEAVES OF HEALING, A VOICE FROM ZION, and the various publications may also be sent to

ZION PUBLISHING HOUSE, 81 EUSTON ROAD, LONDON, N. W., ENGLAND.
ZION PUBLISHING HOUSE, NO. 43 PARK ROAD, ST. KILDA, MELBOURNE, VICTORIA, AUSTRALIA.
ZION PUBLISHING HOUSE, RUE DE MONT, THABOR 1, PARIS, FRANCE.
ZIONSHEIM, SCHLOSS LIEBBURG, CANTON THURGAU, BEI ZÜRICH, SWITZERLAND.

ZION CITY, ILLINOIS, SATURDAY, JULY 9, 1904.

TABLE OF CONTENTS.

LEAVES OF HEALING, SATURDAY, JULY 9, 1904.

EDITORIAL NOTES.

"BEHOLD, I HAVE SET BEFORE THEE AN OPEN DOOR,
AND NO MAN CAN SHUT IT."

A GREAT DOOR, and Effectual, is opened unto me,
And there are many adversaries.

MY SOUL doth magnify the Lord,
And my spirit hath rejoiced in God my Saviour.

GOD IS unto us a God of Deliverances;
And unto Jehovah the Lord belongeth the issues from death.

WE HAVE now been at home again for a week.

Despite the pressure of work in every department which has come upon us, we have found every moment of the time to be a delight.

We have realized that "He that is holy, He that is true, He that hath the Key of David, He that openeth and none shall shut, and that shutteth and none openeth," hath indeed set before us an Open Door which no man can shut.

OUR CRY to God our Father is, not that He shall take away our "many adversaries," but that He may enable us to overcome them and to make all the world to know that this "Great Door, and Effectual" is one through which we are entering into all the Nations of the Earth, with the Advance Guard of the Restoration Hosts of Zion.

As the Prophet of the Restoration, God has given us the honor of planting the Banner of Zion above every other flag on earth; for Zion is the Kingdom of God, and His Kingdom is over all.

THESE ARE still the Days of Small Things, comparatively, in Zion, when we consider the vastness of the task and the fewness of our numbers.

THIS SCRIPTURE comforts us:

The word of Jehovah came unto me, saying,
The hands of Zerubbabel have laid the foundations of this house;
His hands shall also finish it;
And thou shalt know that Jehovah of Hosts hath sent me unto you.

FOR WHO hath despised the Day of Small Things?
For they shall rejoice, and shall see the plummet
In the hand of Zerubbabel,
Even these Seven,
Which are the Eyes of Jehovah;
They run to and fro through the whole earth.

AS TRULY as God spoke these comforting words to His servant Zerubbabel, through the wonderful Prophet Zechariah, so truly does God speak to us today.

And so truly do "the Seven Spirits which are before the Throne rejoice" as they see "the mountains becoming a plain" and the day approaching when the Headstone of Zion shall be brought forth with "shoutings of Grace, grace, unto it."

WE HAVE once more taken up the Administration of Zion in all departments, aided by the efficient brethren to whom we committed the oversight during our six months absence in the Around-the-World Visitation.

IT HAS been our joy to speak within the last eight days, in Zion City, to audiences which have aggregated Forty-seven Thousand, as follows:

Welcome Home Celebration, Thursday, June 30th,	10,000
Closing Exercises of Zion Junior Schools, Friday, July 1st,	5,000
Lord's Day Morning Sacrifice of Praise and Prayer, July 3d,	5,000
Lord's Day General Assembly, Afternoon of July 3d,	6,000
Independence Day Celebration, Beulah Park, Zion City, Monday, July 4th,	9,000
Divine Healing Meeting, Shiloh Tabernacle, Tuesday, July 5th,	2,000
Mid-week General Assembly, Shiloh Tabernacle, Wednesday, July 6th,	5,000
Closing Exercises of Zion College and Preparatory Schools, Thursday, July 7th,	5,000
Total,	47,000

A FULL report of our First Fourth of July Oration as an American citizen has appeared in THE ZION BANNER of Tuesday, July 5th, and will be reprinted, God willing, in the next issue of LEAVES OF HEALING, as will also reports of the interesting College and School celebrations, etc.

THE NUMBER of students in attendance during 1903-4 in all departments of Zion's Educational Institutions is exactly one thousand nine hundred and four.

This is an increase of four hundred and ninety-one students over last year.

Four deaths have occurred during the year; three girls and one boy, all from Zion Junior Schools, which is only about two in a thousand of our total enrolment.

Of the four hundred and eighty-seven in the Preparatory, Ministerial and College Departments not one died.

The splendid order and excellent progress made by the students in all Departments has been of the most cheering and satisfactory nature.

The eminent services of Overseer Harvey D. Brasefield, Vice-president of Zion's Educational Institutions, and the splendid staff of Professors and Teachers in all Departments have been of a very high order.

Zion City has already become, within less than three years, a Powerful Center of Christian Education.

THE OUTPOURING of Love and Peace and Joy throughout these first days of our return to our beloved City has been of such a nature that we cannot put it into words.

But the Editor, on behalf of himself, and his wife and son, desires to record their appreciation of the innumerable attentions which have been showered upon them, not only by the citizens of the City of Zion, but also by cablegrams, telegrams, and letters from Zion all over America, and from Zion in many parts of the world.

ALTHOUGH WE have refused to give any interviews to the Chicago press, and although there have been some serious mistakes made, and some very unworthy reflections, yet we have to record the fact that the Chicago newspapers, for the most part, reported our Homecoming and Welcome, both by picture and letter press, in a more than ordinarily fair manner: for which we desire to thank them.

IN CONNECTION with the whole question of Interviews with Newspaper Reporters, we desire to say that we have not given any interview to any reporter since last February.

All statements to the contrary are false.

WE HAVE wondered whether it would be worth while to drag out of their obscurity the innumerable lies of the Press of the City of New York, published from the moment of our arrival from Europe, on Saturday, June 25th, to our departure for Zion City, on Tuesday, June 28th.

We have resolved to treat them with the contempt they merit, and shall for the present confine our remarks concerning them to the report of our Meetings in Carnegie Hall, New York City, on Lord's Day, June 26th, which will appear next week.

WE HAVE made a few important changes in connection with the Rearrangement of Work in many Departments of Zion, some account of which we propose to give in an early Issue.

MEANWHILE, WE know it will be glad tidings to the Christian Catholic Church in Zion throughout Great Britain and Ireland, and the Continent of Europe, for us to make the following announcements:

The Reverend John G. Speicher, M. D., an Overseer of the Christian Catholic Church in Zion, and his wife, Elder Abigail Thompson Speicher, will leave New York by the Cunard Steamship *Etruria* on Saturday, July 23d, and, after a brief visit to London, will proceed to Zurich, Switzerland, where he will take temporary charge of the work at our

European Continental Headquarters, No. 76 Bahnhofstrasse in that City.

Overseer Speicher will be likely to remain in Europe for several months, during which he will visit our Branches in Switzerland, Germany and Holland, and he will preside, God willing, at the Opening of a new Zion Tabernacle and Branch of Zion Publishing House, in Paris, France, early in October.

Elder Arthur S. Booth-Clibborn and his wife, Elder Catherine Booth-Clibborn, will remove from Brussels, Belgium, where they now are, to the charge of the work in Paris and throughout France, with residence, probably, at St. Cloud.

OVERSEER SPEICHER has labored most earnestly and successfully in Zion City during our absence.

We trust that the change and rest will be a great benefit to him and to his beloved wife.

We shall greatly miss him as the Overseer-in-charge of Zion City and the Commissioner of Health, but we have been convinced that it is our duty to spare him for awhile.

Let the friends in Europe know that he is sent by us as one of our most esteemed fellow laborers, and we charge all officers and members of the Christian Catholic Church in Zion, wherever he may go, to receive him, help him, and right heartily to love him for his work's sake, as a faithful Overseer in Zion.

Deacon John W. Innes and his wife, Deaconess Edith Kennedy-Innes, will proceed to England also by the Steamship *Etruria* in company with Overseer Speicher.

We have appointed Deacon Innes, who has been connected as Auditor and Special Financial Messenger, with the Financial Department for several years, to be the General Financial Agent for all Zion's Institutions and Industries in the United Kingdom of Great Britain and Ireland.

Deacon Innes is a thorough Christian gentleman and a most able business man. He is fully acquainted with the affairs of Zion, and we cordially commend him to the Overseer, Rev. H. E. Cantel, and to all Officers and Members of the Christian Catholic Church in Zion.

THE DUTIES connected with the business interests of Zion in Great Britain have become too numerous and onerous for our able and hard-working Overseer, and we have found the policy of appointing General Agents to be very successful both in Africa and in Europe, and we doubt not that it will be successful in Great Britain.

THE REV. FRED RICHERT and his wife, Evangelist Anna Richert, will also sail in the *Etruria* with Overseer Speicher, and strengthen our Ecclesiastical Staff in Switzerland.

They have done excellently in the Northwestern Parish of the City of Chicago.

The exact location of his labors will be left to the decision of Presiding Elder Carl Hodler, who will continue in charge of the Christian Catholic Church on the Continent of Europe until October 1st, when he will return to Zion City.

Elder Hodler will then take up work in offices of the General Overseer as Ecclesiastical Secretary for Europe.

A VERY able Zion business man, Deacon Max Koetz, who will soon take charge of a new and important department in Zion Printing and Publishing House, will also proceed with Overseer Speicher and his party by the Steamship *Etruria* on a visit to his mother and friends in Germany. He has been a most efficient deacon in one of our parishes in Chicago, and we desire for him a kind reception by Zion in Europe.

OUR READERS will be glad to know that our able and devoted Assistant Editor of the BLATTER DER HEILUNG, Evangelist Brieger-Hodler, is now on her way to Zion City, on the Steamship *Barbarossa*, which left Cherbourg, France, on July 3d, accompanied by her mother, Madame Brey, and by Mr. Joseph Rollier, who has been our representative in Paris, and who was in charge of the Branch of Zion Publishing House in that city for some time.

Mr. Rollier also acted as our French Secretary and Private Interpreter during our Visitation to Switzerland, and, under the direction of Elder Percy Clibborn, he did much to prepare our way, especially in the City of Bern, and in the French Cantons.

Evangelist Hodler is also accompanied by a lady member of Zion, who is coming to study, as we understand, in Zion College.

IT IS expected that the *Barbarossa* will arrive in New York not later than Tuesday, the 12th, and we shall hope that Evangelist Hodler and her party will be with us in Zion City, on our Anniversary Day, Thursday, July 14th, and throughout the Feast of Tabernacles.

AND NOW we, and all Zion, are looking forward to the Crowning Event of every year in Zion City, the Feast of Tabernacles.

This is our Fourth Feast.

The Program, which has appeared in nearly every issue of LEAVES OF HEALING for some time past, is too well known to our readers to need repetition in this issue, which has already exceeded our ordinary limits by an additional eight pages.

SUFFICE IT to say, that the Feast begins on Wednesday, July the 13th, and continues until Lord's Day, July 24th.

A BEAUTIFUL Program has been published, in pamphlet form, with a selection of fifty-three Hymns, and some very interesting information concerning Zion City, etc.

It will be forwarded without charge to those who desire it, upon application to Zion Printing and Publishing House.

BRETHREN, PRAY FOR US.

ELIJAH THE RESTORER.

TERROR FOR THE SHAKEN THRONE.

OF tremendous import were the words of the Prophet of God as he spoke before the thousands assembled in Shiloh Tabernacle, Lord's Day afternoon, July 3, 1904, to greet him upon his return from a tour embracing the Circle of the Earth, and extending over a period of six months.

The Nations of the Earth had been viewed from the standpoint of a Prophet sent by God with a Message to deliver, a work to accomplish.

It was merely a Reconnaissance—a preliminary examination or survey—a look, a skirmish here and there, yet what a commotion it had excited!

What will the Battle be when the Prophet of God, accompanied by the Legions of Zion Restoration Host, shall invade the kingdoms of the earth and wage the great War of Peace in the Name of Jehovah, King of all kings, Ruler of all rulers!

The great Tabernacle was filled to overflowing, many out-of-town strangers being present.

The day was a perfect one, and the sight of the slowly-moving columns of Zion Guard and Zion City Band, as they escorted the General Overseer from Shiloh House to Shiloh Tabernacle, formed a picture of rare beauty.

The summer breeze flung out the Flags of the Nations from the top of the big observatory in Shiloh Park, and the colors of the Zion Banner and of Zion Restoration Host touched with vivid hues the blue sky overhead as they were carried aloft by standard bearers.

Sweet strains of music filled the air as the escort moved slowly up Shiloh Boulevard.

A few moments, and inside the great, white building began that wonderful and indescribably beautiful procession of white-robed, chanting choristers and black-garbed, stately-moving clerics of the Church.

Orchestra, Band, Organ and human voices blend in a thrillingly beautiful burst of harmonious sounds.

A breathless silence obtains, save for this inspiring concourse of almost heavenly music; every eye is held, every ear strained.

Immovable stand the long lines of the uniformed Zion Guard, extending across the front and down the aisles, in double rows.

Through the open windows and doors the scene is pastoral—trees nod and bend their green branches almost within arm's length, the rustling of reeds can be heard as the wind sighs and ripples the surface of verdant fields.

The spectacle presented is brilliant, impressive, beautiful almost beyond belief.

At the Early Morning Service, the man of God spoke as a Pastor to his people.

At this Great General Assembly, he was the Prophet—the man of Divine Authority.

His words electrified the great audience.

For nearly four hours they listened spellbound, with scarcely a movement, and then the many thousands of Zion rose as one at his Call, and vowed they would follow him wherever he would lead them as Elijah the Restorer in the glorious work of the Restoration of All Things to God.

Shiloh Tabernacle, Zion City, Illinois, Lord's Day Afternoon, July 3, 1904.

The Service was opened by Zion White-robed Choir and Zion Robed Officers entering the Tabernacle, singing the words of the

PROCESSIONAL.

The Son of God goes forth to war,
  A kingly crown to gain;
His blood-red banner streams afar:
  Who follows in His train?
Who best can drink His cup of wo,
  Triumphant over pain,
Who patient bears His cross below,
  He follows in His train.

That martyr first, whose eagle eye
  Could pierce beyond the grave;
Who saw His Master in the sky,
  And called on Him to save;
Like Him, with pardon on His tongue,
  In midst of mortal pain,
He pray'd for them that did the wrong:
  Who follows in His train?

A noble band, the chosen few,
  On whom the Spirit came,
Twelve valiant saints, their hope they knew
  And mocked the torch of flame;
They met the tyrant's brandish'd steel,
  The lion's gory mane,
They bow'd their necks the stroke to feel:
  Who follows in their train?

A noble army, men and boys,
  The matron and the maid,
Around the throne of God rejoice,
  In robes of light arrayed.
They climb'd the steep ascent of heav'n
  Thro' peril, toil, and pain;
O God, to us may grace be giv'n
  To follow in their train.

At the close of the Processional the General Overseer came upon the platform, the people rising and standing with bowed heads while he pronounced the

INVOCATION.

God be merciful unto us and bless us,
And cause Thy face to shine upon us;
That Thy Way may be known upon earth,
Thy Saving Health among all the Nations,
For the sake of Jesus. Amen.

PRAISE.

The Congregation then joined in singing Hymn No. 19:

Jesus shall reign where'er the sun
Does his successive journeys run,
His Kingdom spread from shore to shore,
Till moons shall wax and wane no more.

The General Overseer then led the Choir and Congregation in the recitation of the Apostles' Creed:

RECITATION OF CREED.

I believe in God the Father Almighty,
Maker of heaven and earth:
And in Jesus, the Christ, His only Son, our Lord,
Who was conceived by the Holy Ghost:
Born of the Virgin Mary;
Suffered under Pontius Pilate;
Was crucified, dead and buried:
He descended into hell,
The third day He rose from the dead;
He ascended into heaven.
And sitteth on the right hand of God, the Father Almighty;
From thence He shall come to judge the quick and the dead.
I believe in the Holy Ghost;
The Holy Catholic Church;
The Communion of Saints;
The Forgiveness of Sins;
The Resurrection of the body,
And the Life Everlasting. Amen.

READING OF GOD'S COMMANDMENTS.

The General Overseer then led the Congregation in repeating the Commandments, after which the words, "Lord, have mercy upon us, and write all these Thy Laws in our hearts, we beseech Thee," were chanted.

I. Thou shalt have no other gods before Me.

II. Thou shalt not make unto thee a graven image, nor the likeness of any form that is in heaven above, or that is in the earth beneath, or that is in the water under the earth; thou shalt not bow down thyself unto them nor serve them: for I, Jehovah, thy God, am a jealous God, visiting the iniquity of the fathers upon the children, upon the third and upon the fourth generation of them that hate Me, and showing mercy unto thousands of them that love Me and keep My commandments.

III. Thou shalt not take the Name of Jehovah thy God in vain; for Jehovah will not hold him guiltless that taketh His Name in vain.

IV. Remember the Sabbath Day, to keep it holy. Six days shalt thou labor and do all thy work; but the seventh day is a Sabbath unto Jehovah thy God: in it thou shalt not do any work, thou, nor thy son, nor thy daughter, thy manservant, nor thy maidservant, nor thy cattle, nor thy stranger that is within thy gates; for in six days Jehovah made heaven and earth, the sea, and all that in them is, and rested the seventh day, wherefore Jehovah blessed the Sabbath Day and hallowed it.

V. Honor thy father and thy mother; that thy days may be long upon the land which Jehovah thy God giveth thee.

VI. Thou shalt do no murder.

VII. Thou shalt not commit adultery.

VIII. Thou shalt not steal.

IX. Thou shalt not bear false witness against thy neighbor.

X. Thou shalt not covet thy neighbor's house, thou shalt not covet thy neighbor's wife, nor his manservant, nor his maidservant, nor his ox, nor his ass, nor anything that is thy neighbor's.

Hear also what our Lord Jesus, the Christ, the Son of God, hath said, which may be called the Eleventh Commandment:

XI. A New Commandment I give unto you, that ye love one another; even as I have loved you, that ye also love one another.

The great Choir then sang the

TE DEUM LAUDAMUS.

We praise Thee, O God; we acknowledge Thee to be the Lord.
All the earth doth worship Thee, the Father Everlasting.
To Thee all Angels cry aloud, the Heavens and all the powers therein.
To Thee Cherubim and Seraphim continually do cry:
Holy, Holy, Holy, Lord God of Sabaoth,
Heaven and earth are full of the majesty of Thy Glory.
The glorious company of the Apostles praise Thee.
The goodly fellowship of the Prophets praise Thee.
The noble army of martyrs praise Thee.
The Holy Church throughout all the world doth acknowledge Thee,
The Father of an Infinite Majesty;
Thine Adorable, True and Only Son;
Also the Holy Ghost the Comforter.
Thou art the King of Glory, O Christ;
Thou art the Everlasting Son of the Father.
When Thou tookest upon Thee to deliver man,
Thou didst humble Thyself to be born of a Virgin;
When Thou hadst overcome the sharpness of death,
Thou didst open the Kingdom of Heaven to all believers.
Thou sittest at the right hand of God in the Glory of the Father.
We believe that Thou shalt come to be our Judge.
We therefore pray Thee, help Thy servants,
Whom Thou hast redeemed with Thy precious blood.
Make them to be numbered with Thy saints in glory everlasting.
O Lord, save Thy people and bless Thine heritage;
Govern them and lift them up forever.
Day by day we magnify Thee;
And we worship Thy Name ever, world without end.
Vouchsafe, O Lord, to keep us this day without sin.
O Lord, have mercy upon us, have mercy upon us.
O Lord, let Thy mercy be upon us as our trust is in Thee.
O Lord, in Thee have I trusted, let me never be confounded.

Prayer was offered by Overseer Speicher, after which the General Overseer prayed for the sick and sorrowing.

He then read in the Inspired Word of God, the 1st Psalm, commenting on first verse as follows:

A very Old Version, one that I read every morning, puts this first verse somewhat differently, and I think better. It reads thus:

Blessed is the man that *hath not walked* in the counsel of the wicked; nor stood in the way of sinners; and *hath not sat* in the seat of the scorner, but his delight is in the law of Jehovah, and in His law will he exercise himself day and night.

After concluding the reading of the 1st Psalm, the General Overseer read from the 13th chapter of the Gospel according to St. Matthew, beginning at the 24th verse and reading to the end of the chapter, closing with the prayer:

May God bless His Word.

After the announcements were made, the tithes and offerings were received while Zion White-robed Choir, accompanied by Zion City Band and Zion Orchestra, sang the "Gloria."

The General Overseer then delivered his Message:

THE PARABLE OF THE TARES OF THE FIELD.

INVOCATION.

Let the words of my mouth and the meditations of my heart be acceptable in Thy sight, be profitable unto this people, and unto all to whom these words shall come, in this and every land, in this and all the coming time, Till Jesus Come. Amen.

TEXT.

Then Jesus left the multitudes, and went into the house: and His disciples came unto Him, saying, Explain unto us the Parable of the Tares of the Field.

And He answered and said, He that soweth the Good Seed is the Son of man;

And the Field is the World; and the Good Seed, these are the Sons of the Kingdom; and the tares are the Sons of the Evil One.

And the enemy that sowed them is the Devil: and the Harvest is the Consummation of the Age; and the Reapers are messengers.—*Matthew 13:36-40.*

This afternoon and next Lord's Day, I shall deal as fully as I can with the wonderful thoughts that are suggested by this wonderful parable of the Kingdom of Heaven at the Time of the End, which it is our belief, and that of many of the most distinguished, and pious, and learned of Christian commentators all over the world, has now been reached.

The Consummation of the Age Cannot Be Far Away.

There is no such thing in the Scripture as the "End of the World." It should read the "Consummation of the Æon," or Age, a certain Divinely-fixed Period of Time.

Those words should never have been used there.

There is no such thing as the "end of the world," spoken of

in Scripture, but there is a declaration that the world shall be changed.

As a vesture it shall be folded up by God in the last Cleansing Fire, and a New Heaven and a New Earth shall evolve out of the chaos, and wreck, and ruin, as it would seem, of the old world.

A New Heaven and a New Earth shall be made wherein dwell the righteous ones.

We have to deal this afternoon especially with the Field of the World; yet one cannot reach that subject without dealing somewhat with the first portion of the explanation of the parable.

"Explain unto us," they said, and He did explain. The words of the Christ's Declaration are exceedingly clear, and I desire you to keep them in your memory.

The Sower of the Good Seed.

The sower of the seed is the Son of man and Son of God; but He is presented to us by Himself in His splendid and perfect humanity, the Son of man, and yet the Author of Life in all its forms—spiritual, psychical, physical and vegetable.

There is a deep underlying necessity for that expression which sets forth His humanity, for in this parable He is dealing essentially with the human nature of mankind.

He that soweth the good seed is the Son of man; and the field is the world.

It is not doctrines He is talking about; it is not theories; it is not a matter of words.

So you often hear people speaking of the "Seed of the Word," which the Lord gave as the explanation of the parables of the Sower and the Seed given in Matthew 13:3-9; Mark 4:3-20, and Luke 8:4-15.

That is all right; but it is not the Seed of the Word which is represented in this parable.

This is "another parable," and is so described in Matthew 13:24-30.

It is not words at all; it is not doctrine; it is human beings that are described by the word "Seed" in this Parable of the Tares of the Field.

The Good Seed are the Sons of the Kingdom; the tares are the Sons of the Evil One; the enemy that sowed them is the Devil. The harvest is the Consummation of the Age, and the Reapers are messengers, *angeloi* (ἄγγελοι) angels; not necessarily beings from another world, but messengers.

The word "angel" simply means a messenger, whether it be a heavenly messenger or an earthly messenger.

I believe that what is meant by the word *Angeloi* is the Messengers who shall be sent forth from Zion in these Latter Days, which are the beginning of the Times of the Restoration of all Things—the Consummation of the Age.

I desire to speak of the great field in which the Son of man is sowing, through His people, the Good Seed of the Sons of the Kingdom.

The field in which the Christ and the enemy, the Devil, are sowing, is the Field of the Whole World.

Countries Visited in the Around-the-World Visitation.

Very strikingly does this come to one who has been leading a Visitation like that which I have just closed.

Not that I visited the whole world; to make a ring around the world is not to visit all the world; it is simply to visit the countries through which that ring passes.

But, I have touched the great continents of the world, beginning with America, in which I journeyed with my party four thousand five hundred miles, from the 1st day to the 21st day of January—my journey from Zion City to San Francisco, by way of the Southern States.

In this four-thousand-five-hundred-mile journey we passed through a number of the States of this Union, and especially of the States of the Southland.

Then passing down through the Pacific Ocean we came to and passed through the beautiful Hawaiian Islands, and the Samoan or Navigator Islands.

Then in due season we reached New Zealand; then the Island Continent of Australia: and then the Island of Ceylon, which is almost the peninsula of India.

Then passing across a wide stretch of waters in very hot latitudes we came to Aden in Arabia, and sailed through the Red Sea.

Passing through the Suez Canal on the Northern Shores of Africa, we came to Europe.

Passing through a great part of France, and Switzerland, and Germany, and Holland, we reached the United Kingdom, and returned by way of New York to our home.

This was the ring that we made around the world; traveling somewhere between thirty and thirty-six thousand miles, in six months.

We tarried here and there for a day or two, in some places for one or more weeks, and in many places only for a few hours.

We met travelers at the Crossroads of the Pacific and the Indian Oceans; at Honolulu and in New Zealand, which might be called the Crossroads of the Pacific; and after leaving Australia, we came to the Crossroads of the Indian Ocean at Colombo.

Fellow Passengers.

We met many persons who had come down from various parts of the Indian, Chinese and Japanese Empires, to join the great ocean Steamer *Mongolia* by which we traveled.

Especially at Aden, we met the British from Bombay, India, and from Somaliland, Africa, where there had been war.

We also met many travelers from Syria and from Africa, at what might be called the Crossroads of the Mediterranean Sea, at Suez and at Port Said—the ports at either end of the Suez Canal. We also saw many interesting and intelligent persons of many nations and occupations in our journeys by railroad, or steamship—not least in interest were some of our fellow passengers across the Atlantic Ocean from Liverpool to New York.

Then we met in the great cities of Europe not only the inhabitants of those cities, but large numbers of persons from many parts of the world who, like ourselves, were traveling from one city to another upon some business.

Our one business was to look at the world and the Field of the World from the Standpoint of the Prophet of the Restoration.

My one prayer was that God would give me to understand as much as I could of the World's present condition.

Having been unable to visit India, China or Japan, I can only speak of these through distinguished men who have lived there, and whom I met and conversed with; indeed, one that could tell me of the first attack by the Japanese fleet upon Port Arthur; one who had been on board Admiral Togo's flagship when the first attack was made, and when so many Russian vessels (as I prophesied long ago would be the case) were reduced to scrap-iron by the Japanese fire.

A Prophecy Fulfilled.

Long ago I told you that the war between Russia and Japan would be a war between a Bear and a Swordfish, and that there was no question, whatever, that when the Bear put to sea to fight, the Swordfish would sail all around it, pierce it everywhere, and leave its blood upon the waters.

I told you that the great Tyrannical Colossus of Russia had feet of clay, and when it came down to the warm waters of Asia they would melt and that horrible Empire which has so cruelly oppressed God's people, the Jews, and denied civil and religious liberty to its own people, would fall upon its face, and eventually be dismembered and destroyed.

You heard me say that in this place many months before this war began; and I know that God guided me in making that statement.

It was made after very careful study of the situation, and especially a very careful study of the Prophetic Word of God.

Knowledge of the Eastern Situation Obtained by Careful Study.

I found that my reading for many years, and of nearly everything important in Slavonic and Oriental Literature up to date, and the special guidance of the Spirit of God, had wonderfully prepared me for the events of the war.

In talking with distinguished military and naval men and with missionaries, such as one Anglican Bishop, a very godly man who had spent much of his life far in the interior of China, I found that my careful reading of many years had enabled me to grasp the situation so intelligently that oftentimes my friends were kind enough to say, "Why, one would think that you must have been there and lived there!"

I had been asking God, as I continually ask Him, to help me

to understand the Situation All-over-the-World, by careful reading, and for that reason I keep up-to-date files of papers, magazines, statistical records, etc., from the principal parts of the world, and from many obscure parts.

I read also the most important works on the conditions of the governments and peoples of the nations as they are today, and all my life I have been a careful reader of ancient as well as modern history.

I also acquaint myself with the laws of nations, with international law, and with the main facts in the lives of kings, statesmen, literateurs, artists, builders, warriors, and leaders of the religious, political and reform parties and policies.

I have never been so busy as to neglect my Bible, and especially the Sure Word of Prophecy therein, which is indeed "a Light in a Dark Place."

Withal, I am a man of affairs, and attend to an immense number of details in the direction of the world-wide affairs of the Christian Catholic Church in Zion, and especially in all the affairs of Zion City, Illinois, and of the Zion Cities which are yet to be born all over the world.

I say these things with deep humility and regret that I have not been more worthy of the goodness of God, and with gratitude for His so graciously giving me the Key of Knowledge in so many directions.

Why the Visit to India Was Deferred.

It may be well to say here, for the sake of our friends in India who will read these remarks, that my inability to visit India was consequent upon several things.

First, the loss of about two weeks' time, owing to the breakdown of the Canadian Pacific steamer, which I thought I might be able to overcome, but in which I failed, as I could not make good connection.

Great care must be taken in traveling around the world in this manner to see that good connections are made.

We had to look far ahead and to see that this steamer would fit in with that steamer, and that this railway train would fit in with that railway train, and to see that every day's traveling was according to proper program.

In going around the world with a party all this is no very easy matter.

Owing to the detention made by the breakdown of the Canadian Pacific, I found that the hottest weather of the year would begin in India at about the time set for the beginning of my intended Visitation there—weather so hot that scarcely any one travels during that season.

There is still another reason why I did not visit India.

I am not quite sure but that I would have faced the hot weather, and given India what little time I could, had I not felt that Mrs. Dowie's condition of health must also be considered.

It was needful that she should reach the European continent, and as we found afterwards, she needed a place of rest much more than we knew.

I left her in France while I went on with my Visitation to Switzerland, Germany and Holland.

I regretted exceedingly my inability to visit India, but it was practically impossible, except at very considerable sacrifice of the time that I could give to Europe, and I felt that the field on the Continent of Europe was white unto the harvest, and that it would be well for me not to neglect France, Switzerland and Germany.

I have had no reason whatever to doubt that in that decision I was guided by God, as I was also in a subsequent decision to give to the French Cantons of Switzerland one week of the time that I had intended to give to London.

I am glad that I was permitted to visit those beautiful States of the Swiss Confederation.

I make this statement, because many throughout the world will read this address, and they will then know the reason why I gave up the brief Indian tour that I had planned.

I also find that India should be taken at a totally different period of the year—in November—and then one could do much and be of benefit not only in India, but also in the adjacent countries.

Making a Reconnaissance.

We have had exceptionally good opportunities to peep through into the great field of the world, and to see somewhat of it.

We were only making a Reconnaissance, not even a reconnaissance in force, for all I was doing was to lead a very small party principally for observation.

But it was remarkable how our presence drew the fire of the enemy.

Although I was only one man, with a very few companions, we had scarcely got sight of Australia before we heard the roar of the Disciples of the Lawless One.

It was very remarkable.

We found that when we touched the Masonic Baal, as we did at Auckland, when I spoke straight out regarding the godless Masonic captain of the Steamship *Sonoma*, who had stopped all open worship of God during the whole voyage, the sons of Belial in the pulpit and the press were sure to howl.

All other officers on board that ship were perfectly courteous.

The Wicked and Insulting Actions of the Captain of the Sonoma.

The captain took advantage of that which the law very properly gives every captain of a ship—the right to rule it.

But he did something that he had no right to do; he prevented nearly the whole ship's company from getting the desire of their hearts, namely, to hear the Word of God from our lips.

I spoke straight out; because he and those associated with him had held a mock lodge right under my cabin window, and I had heard them say, "We are all here, Most Worshipful Master," which are the first words in the opening of the lodge.

They acted like the Masons that they were, like the sons of Belial that they were, and when I got to Auckland and about seventy of my people filled the Social Hall, as the vessel lay at the wharf, I took advantage of the opportunity I then had to speak and complain that the captain had acted as an "infallible" pagan pope, and that there had been no voice of praise or prayer in that ship, so far as we knew, except when we sang our Morning Hymn, and when we met in our own cabins.

The only exception was that he twice gave permission to a Romish priest to offer the Idolatrous Sacrifice of the Mass—one of the growing proofs that Rome and Masonry are, at bottom, on very good terms.

Zion Directed Not to Take Passage by the Oceanic Steamship Company.

I protested against this especially in the interests of my people who were coming from Australia upon that line, and I directed that, until religious liberty, under proper regulations as to fitting time, place, etc., should be given by the Oceanic Steamship Company, not one Zion person should travel by that line. [Applause.]

That decision has already cost that company many thousands of dollars, and it will continue to cost them thousands of dollars if they continue to deny our people, as they cross the Ocean, the right to assemble and speak in the Christ's Name.

My words at Auckland, which were immediately cabled to Australia, several days' sail from Auckland, had done their work when I arrived there, and the Masons were thoroughly organized to fight me as a foe to the Masonic Baal, whom they vainly present as God.

Australia Sold Out to Freemasonry.

In looking at the field of the world, I found in that part of the field which I had loved, and which I still love, so well, the beautiful Australian Continent, that what I had so often said from this platform was true—the Secret Empire is aiming at the Control of the Whole World through secret Masonic influence.

I found in Australia that the ship captains, and the agents of great shipping companies were, with scarcely an exception, Freemasons.

I found that the editors and the managers of papers were, with scarcely an exception, Freemasons.

I found that many professed ministers of the Gospel had become Freemasons.

I found that the merchants, and especially all leading bankers, were Freemasons.

I found that the leading politicians, and every governor of every State in the Australian Commonwealth, were Freemasons.

I found that the premiers of nearly all the colonies, and the members of the state government, and the members of the Commonwealth government, with few exceptions, were Freemasons.

I found that the commissioners of police in nearly every state were Freemasons.

I found that the mayors in all the cities, with few exceptions, were Freemasons.

I found that the ruling powers in all the great affairs of the Australian Commonwealth were Freemasons.

I found, what I have so often told you, that the Freemasons were at the head of all the other secret societies, and that the most important officers in these societies, and always the leaders, were Freemasons.

Thus they could immediately reach down to the humblest member of every secret society, by the fact that the Freemasons were in control of these other secret organizations.

I saw in a moment that Australia had passed into the hands of the Secret Empire of Baal, and I knew that one of the greatest fights of my life was on.

I did not shrink from it, but, oh, how I did wish that I had my Zion City Legion of Three Thousand Zion Restorationists there!

I would have altered my program, and camped down in Australia for several months, and fought it out, and, by the grace of God, we would have won the Battle for Righteousness, and the Kingdom of God.

As it was, we won in a great measure; and there gave the Combined Powers of Darkness such a fight as they will never forget, and won many victories for God.

Size and Population of Australia.

With such a condition of affairs I was brought face to face with the fact that the great Island Continent, which is as large as the entire United States, was one of the Devil's most secure strongholds.

Do not forget the size of Australia.

It has only a small population.

It is a Magnificent Land, with a Little People.

With New Zealand, it is less than five million or thereabouts; but the continent of Australia, by the statistics for 1901 given in the Statesman's Year Book for 1904, is shown to have a population of three million seven hundred seventy thousand seven hundred fifteen. So many have been leaving Australia, and there has been such a falling off in the birth rate, that it is probable the present population is considerably less than four millions, with an area of nearly three millions square miles. The annual increase in 1861 was a little over eleven per cent., but it has fallen to less than two per cent.

Illegitimacy is frightfully on the increase, and, in several States, has reached the shameful rate of ten per cent. of all the births.

The Island of Australia is a little larger than the whole of the United States of America, leaving out Alaska.

This gives you an idea of the magnitude of that immense country.

It is a wonderfully rich Continent, but has the misfortune to be ruled by the Masons and by the most degenerate and conceited working class population to be found in the whole world—exception being made of hundreds of thousands of farmers, merchants, and working people of all occupations.

Only in a measure, however, does Baal rule, for let me tell you that, like all usurping secret powers, they are essentially weak; they are not strong; they are only strong in cunning; they are only strong in deceit; they are only strong in murderous violence, and in stirring up the mud and dirt of the two extremes of the classes, the rich and the poor.

The Middle Class a Sound Body of People.

They have no power over the great middle class in Australia, which is a sound, hearty body of people. Even the Masons in that class, and most of the Masons in other classes of society, have nothing to do with the murderous designs of the leaders of the Order.

This class may constitute even a majority of the Australian people, but they have been euchred out of their proper political power by the machinations of the Masonic body, which has so worked politics and municipal affairs as to control, to their own hurt and the nation's, the powers of the people.

But they have been able to control only by becoming the blind slaves of the most ignorant and violent working class population that has ever cursed the land.

I do not hesitate to say that a vast portion of the so-called Labor Party of the Australian Continent is lawless, ignorant, drunken, dissolute, unpatriotic, and utterly regardless of the interests of the whole Commonwealth.

But they control the majority of the votes.

They make these Masonic bankers and politicians tremble in their boots and make them carry out their will, which is the will of the anarchistic mob; for they know no rule, and will obey no orders, and will not recognize law, order, religion or anything else, unless it suits their whim.

The consequence is that

The Nation Is in a Storm on Its Beam-ends.

I do not know how it will ever weather it.

The Australian Commonwealth has a debt of more than one billion one hundred million dollars for four million people—an average debt of nearly three hundred dollars for every man, woman, child and baby in Australia.

The national debt is so great a weight around the necks of these people that they never imagine they will pay it.

They do not know how they will pay the interest, which now amounts to over forty million dollars every year.

In fact they have only paid the interest by borrowing more money and the consequence is that the nation is on its beam-ends in the midst of a terrific storm.

One significant fact as to the drinking and smoking habits of the people, or of many of them, in Australia, is the fact that *they expect to raise about Fifteen Million Dollars this year from customs duties on Intoxicating Liquors and Tobacco*, out of a Total Estimated Revenue of *Forty-five Millions*.

I told them that the labor party would get the extreme upper hand, and that then the nation would not be safe or weather the storm until after terrible consequences.

These consequences have already come.

These consequences will continue, and I warn Australia from this platform that their boasted "rejection" of God's Prophet has been their undoing.

Many see it.

Many saw it while we were there.

These are not fanciful words.

We know what we are talking about.

The statements that I have already made can have no other than an affirmative indorsement from all thoughtful, fair-minded and honest men in Australia.

The Sons of Belial who have wrecked Australia were afraid of my words; but they now pretend that their principal opposition was that I "insulted the king." That it is a mean and dastardly subterfuge, as those who fabricated and spread the lie, and every reader of LEAVES OF HEALING, know.

You know what I said about the king. The exact words are reported in LEAVES OF HEALING for June 18, 1904, page 257, and all may read who desire to be fair and honest.

God save the king! He needs saving. [Laughter.]

I said nothing in Sydney about the king.

I said nothing in Melbourne about the king; and I said nothing in Adelaide about the king until the very last day.

Then what did I say about the king?

King Edward, Defender of the Masonic Faith.

I had attacked Masonry, and said that the king had been a grand master of the English order, and had delegated his powers to his brother Arthur, Duke of Connaught, when he ascended the throne.

He is still the patron of the Masonic order, and is a Mason through and through, and a defender of the Masonic faith.

There is no question about that.

He is a defender of the Masonic faith, with its idiotic mummeries; with its bogus Hiram Abiff, and his bogus death and resurrection upon the five points of Masonry, by the Lion's Paw of King Solomon; with its bogus ceremonies, its countless lies, its drinking out of the skull of a dead man, its denial of all religion, and its absolute refusal to permit, in the straight Masonic order, the Name of Jesus, the Christ, to be used.

The Degrees of Knight Templarism are side issues.

They are not straight Masonry, but I have never yet found a Mason who would dare tell me that the Name of Jesus, the Christ, could be used in any lodge, for instance, of the thirty-three degrees of Scottish Rite Masonry.

It cannot be! Masonry does not acknowledge Jesus as the Messiah, Immanuel, God with us; nor believe that He is the Maker, the Savior, and the Judge of all mankind.

And so Albert Edward, late Prince of Wales, and now King

of England, is a defender of the Masonic faith, which is a mass of lies and shameful, bestial trash; the worship of the sun god; and of the organization of a number of men who agree that they will trample upon all rights except their own, and any other man's rights which they can steal.

They agree they will murder any one who violates their secrets, and they compel the poor wretches to take a vow that they will submit to be murdered, to have their tongues torn out, their hearts cut out, their throats cut, and their bodies dismembered, if they dare to give away their secrets which you can buy anywhere for a few shillings, and which you can read, at a cost of a few cents, in the Exposure of Masonry which I have long had in print.

A Murderous Power, That Fights Under Cover of the Night.

Oh, the anger of these Masons!

Oh, the bitterness of the press which they control!

Oh, the shameful lying of men like the Rev. W. H. Fitchett, Editor of the *Southern Cross*, published in Melbourne, who simply swept into the pages of his shameful semi-religious weekly, every lie that had ever been told by the gutter press of America, and all the shameless falsehoods that appeared in the so-called religious and secular papers of Australia!

The wonder was that I lived an hour!

The wonder was that I was not torn to pieces in broad daylight.

But they seldom fought me in broad daylight.

There were times, however, that they attempted violence even in the daylight and open street, especially one afternoon in Melbourne, outside of our own Tabernacle, when one of the most shameless and brutal mobs I have ever seen surrounded our carriage, used the most disgraceful language to Mrs. Dowie and to me, too shameful to utter, and then attempted to hold our horses' heads, to cut the traces and overturn the carriage and murder us in the streets.

But God was good to us, and our coachman had a whip which he used, and before they could organize we were out of the way.

The power of the Masonic order, organized as I have shown you in the first part of this address, was such that it was impossible for the great middle class and honest people of all classes to hear what I had to say, although they were eager to do so.

One afternoon, for instance, there were eight thousand people present in the large Exhibition Building, in Melbourne, and less than two hundred persons broke up that meeting, with the connivance of the police, who, to the number of thirty-three, deliberately walked out of the building and left us to the murderous mob, although twenty of them had been paid for their services.

After breaking up that meeting of eight thousand people, the mob dashed behind the platform endeavoring to find our rooms, openly saying that they intended to kill us.

Why the Australian Police Was Powerless Against the Mob.

The commissioner of police told me the next day that it was all right, that the mob had not exceeded their rights and the law, and that he could do nothing until some one was injured seriously or killed.

He said that then he would read the riot act—and, I suppose, permit my friends to bury my body.

I did not believe that that was what God intended, and so I went on and held two meetings daily for five days after that in our Zion Tabernacle, and did not again speak in the Melbourne Exhibition Building, where the state authorities simply intended to turn me over to their murderous supporters.

He said that each of his police officers was equal to only one of the mob.

That is not what I have seen in Chicago.

I have seen one police officer in Chicago give a good account of fifty or a hundred riotous persons.

I have seen a small company of police, just as many as one patrol wagon would hold, come out from Chicago to Oak Park, and take care of three hundred assassins belonging to the secret orders who were there that night, ready to murder us, and they melted like snow before Sergeant O'Brien and his little band.

I have seen the London police facing a mob of thirty thousand at Trafalgar Square, protecting us in our meeting in St. Martin's Hall.

Some of you perhaps thought that I was putting the figures too high when I said thirty thousand.

A few weeks ago, when in Notre Dame, Boulogne, Paris, in France, going over the cathedral, I stopped when I reached the high altar, and said, "God is love!"

I noticed my guide stop, and I asked, "Why are you looking so?"

He said, "Are you Dr. Dowie?"

I said, "Yes."

"Well," he replied, "I did not know you until I heard your voice. The last time I heard it was in St. Martin's Town Hall, London, when there were a hundred thousand in a mob in Trafalgar Square."

"I called that mob thirty thousand," I said, "and some of my critics—who were not here—thought that I overestimated it."

"There were one hundred thousand if there was one," he said again.

"I was an officer of a certain hotel near there, which I really am now, but I have a holiday and serve as a guide in the cathedral because I was born here. I knew your voice the moment you said, 'God is love.'"

Australian Government Guilty of Both a Lie and a Theft.

I have seen the police of London handle at least thirty thousand; and I have seen the police of Chicago handle at least ten thousand outside the West Side Tabernacle, and I know what police officers can do.

I saw the little police force of Adelaide, which did its best, and the mounted police there gave a good account of thousands. It is an excellent force.

The great railroad riots of Melbourne had been broken up by only a hundred officers when the mob was one hundred thousand strong, and I fling back their lie of inability to the commissioner of police, and to Sir Samuel Gillott, who was then the chief secretary.

There was also a crooked fellow there named Bent, who was premier at the time.

They are all "bent" into every variety of political trickery and crookedness.

I fling it back to the government of the State of Victoria, when they said they could not protect us in the city of Melbourne.

They knew that they could, but they were unwilling to do it.

They also stole our money by refusing to refund that which we paid for the hall: for it was government property.

Law in the Hands of Secret Societies.

That was the condition of Australia, at the time we were there to do the people all the good we could. The country is in absolute misery.

It was stated openly in Sydney—I think I have the quotation on file—that there were fifty thousand working men in that city who could not find two shillings and sixpence in their pockets.

What a state of things that is! Fifty thousand men that had not sixty cents each!

That fact was stated apropos of the arrest and fining of a man for this reason:

The Labor Unions have the thing in hand so completely, that they have had a law passed that if a man does not pay his dues to these semi-secret societies, he can be brought up by the police, and compelled to pay or go to prison.

This man said "I will go to prison. In the first place I have not the money, and in the second place I would not pay it if I could."

The papers, apropos of that decision, said that there was not half a crown each in the hands of fifty thousand working men.

Think of such a condition in a country that is literally flowing with milk and honey, whose hills are full of rich mineral, with coal and iron lying side by side.

Australia's Exclusion Laws a Curse to the Land.

Silver and gold and tin and copper may be mined there in vast quantities, and there is rich soil, but these lazy fellows who drink and stink in the cities, will not cultivate it, nor will they allow any one else to.

A crew of Asiatics was shipwrecked on a part of the Australian coast, while we were there.

The ship was lost, and the sailors, who were Japanese, came ashore: but they have a law there that no man, no matter whether he is a British citizen or not, who has a dark skin, shall be allowed to land.

And even white men are turned back at the behest of labor unions.

For instance, five hatters from the United Kingdom landed there, and were turned back, although they belonged to the same Empire.

They demand from every shipmaster who brings into port either an Indian or a Chinaman, though he may be a British citizen, a hundred pounds (five hundred dollars) guarantee that he will take him back.

These men who were shipwrecked landed, and the howl arose that they should be driven out.

One British officer of high position, writing about it, said that they were a degenerate set of inhospitable wretches that inhabited the Australian continent.

He went even further than I.

I found a great deal of hospitality and love.

I found in the midst of all this a splendid people who will one day wake up, and when Zion leads them into the right path they will realize what the power of truth and honesty is.

But for the time being that Commonwealth is degraded, degenerate, defiled and politically wrecked, and will continue to be so until the people do right.

But it was there I saw what the British Empire had become.

What Was Said About King Edward.

It was not until the last day of the Visitation there, when speaking to a large number of good people who filled the Adelaide Town Hall, that I ventured to say that a prophet of God who would do his duty would always be in conflict with the powers that were ordained by the Devil.

I said that Elijah the Tishbite was in conflict with Ahab; Elijah the Preparer, John the Baptist, was in conflict with Herod; and I should not wonder if one of these days I also should get into conflict with some king.

I did not imagine that the prophecy would be so quickly fulfilled.

I then said, "God sent His servant, Elijah the Tishbite, to turn the people from their iniquities unto their God.

"He sent His servant, Elijah the Preparer, to turn the people from their iniquities to God; and the promise is that He will send His servant in the Latter Times, before the Christ comes again, to turn the people to God; to turn the hearts of the fathers to their children, and the hearts of the children to their fathers, lest He come and smite the earth with a curse.

"The Great and Terrible Day of the Lord was not when the Christ was born into this world.

"The Great and Terrible Day of the Lord will come when He comes back and stands upon this earth, and when He abolishes all other forms of government.

"Then kings will have to take a back seat, and very low down at that. [Laughter.]

"King Edward VII. Has no Religion to Spare.

"I do not want to say one disrespectful word, but no one can boast of King Edward's piety.

"No one imagines that he has any religion to spare.

"You hope that he has at least enough to get into heaven; if he does, it will apparently be by the skin of his teeth, because he has never been renowned for much religion."

They all apparently agreed with me.

No one disputed the sentiment, because he is too notorious.

How English Kings Became Defenders of the Faith.

Let me tell you what was done just four weeks ago today, the Sunday before the Ascot Races, by "His Royal and Imperial Majesty, His Most Christian Britannic Majesty, Emperor of India and, by the grace of God, King of Great Britain and Ireland, and of all the dependencies and dominions of the British Empire; and also by the grace of God (which is an awful lie) Defender of the Faith."

Did I not show you, when I delivered my lectures upon the Church of England Apostasy, that the title, Defender of the Faith, was given by the Pope of Rome to King Henry VIII. for fighting Martin Luther the Reformer?

That is when the title was given.

It was given by the Pope of Rome to the then King of England, the dissolute and disgusting and murderous brute known as King Henry VIII., because of the book he wrote, violently opposing the Reformation, and Martin Luther especially.

That title was given not by the grace of God, but by the grace of His enemy, the so-called "infallible" Pope.

How the "Defender of the Faith" Spent the Lord's Day.

This is what this "Defender of the Faith" did four weeks ago. The London papers said that on Saturday night he went down to the Duke of Devonshire's estate, near to Beachy Head, and there some of his ministers preached to him, or "read prayers," the next morning.

In the afternoon His Majesty took an automobile and went out to see the racing stud of the Duke of Devonshire, and to look over the horses and get points, for some of these horses, it was alleged, were going to run at the Ascot Race-course in a few days.

That is how "His Most Christian Majesty" spent the greater part of his Sunday, and so *defended the Faith.*

He spent the whole of the next week at the race-course with blacklegs, gamblers and ruffians of the Continent and of England, titled scoundrels of all kinds, who were openly betting, lying, and stealing: for every man is a thief who is a gambler, since the money he gets, or tries to get, can never be honestly gotten.

Everybody knows that; but it must not be said when the king does it in England; so they say.

But I did say it; because, when I got to England, I saw that the fat was in the fire.

They were so afraid of me that even my shadow—the fear of my speaking in London—before I had crossed the channel, had come upon them as an appalling specter, and the consequence was that they turned Mrs. Dowie out of a first-class hotel, because they would not receive the truth.

She turned herself out,rather,b ecauseshe could have remained there if she would have stayed without me, but she would not do that—and I do not blame her. [Laughter.]

How scared and full of terror they were!

Service Held in Zion Tabernacle, London.

But I had one glorious day in Zion Tabernacle in London.

I kept out every reporter except one, who did so much better than the others that even we said it was a fair report.

But there were two women, by the way, whom we found there, and I got their names, which I very solemnly read, saying that they were wanted at the door.

They went to the door, and they never came back. [Laughter and Applause.]

It was very funny how those reporters made up speeches for me of the things they thought I might have said.

Some of them listened in a neighboring house; some were hanging by the clothes-line, on the roofs of stables, and on all kinds of things, endeavoring to hear.

Some of them heard a few words here and there, and then made up the rest.

Their lies were too numerous to mention.

Our beloved Zion people who were there represented all parts of England, Scotland and Ireland.

You will read what I said there in an early issue of LEAVES OF HEALING.

I said that if I were in America and standing on Republican soil, I might say this and thus and so about the king. [Laughter and applause.]

How frightened they were!

Why the People of London Were Troubled.

The few words concerning the king that I had spoken in the Chicago Auditorium on December 6, 1902, was what they were troubled about.

We found that men went around to the hotels with copies of LEAVES OF HEALING, specially the issues containing the words that I had spoken concerning the Defender of the Faith, falsely so-called, and said, "Look here, Mr. Manager, Dowie said thus and so about the king."

Then they read the words to these managers and said, "If you take Dowie into your hotels we will print these words, which will bring half of London around your doors, and they will take him out and hang him."

Some of these managers were frightened; and when they referred the matter to their directors, the directors wanted to stand in with the Court.

Some of the members of the board of directors were members of the government, or of families connected with the government, and some of them indeed were officers of the Court itself.

We had abundant reason to suspect that the Royal Court of England had directly, or at least indirectly, moved against us.

I could not hire a hall in London.

Albert Hall was taken by our Overseer in London, and then refused.

The Queen's Hall was taken, and paid for, and then refused.

I asked the manager of the Hotel Cecil if he was acting under orders and he said, "I am sorry to say that I am."

The manager of the Hotel Russell said the same.

Both of these men were most kind to us personally.

They said that they were acting under high orders.

The fact of the matter was this, that the Voice of Elijah the Restorer had already shaken the throne of the British Empire, and they feared the effects of further attacks upon the Royal Patron of Masonic Baal Worship. [Applause]

My opinion is that it will not take long to tumble it down.

They were afraid because they knew there were hundreds of thousands and millions of people in England who would have been glad to hear my voice, and would have shouted approval to the echo.

I think it well, ere I pass from the king, to repeat the words which I uttered concerning him when delivering a discourse entitled "Unveiling the Apostasy of the Church of England," in the Chicago Auditorium on Lord's Day, November 30, 1902, to an audience of fully four thousand persons. They are found in LEAVES OF HEALING for December 6, 1902, Volume XII, Number 7, pages 214-215, and are as follows:

DISSOLUTE CHARACTER OF PRESENT "HEAD" OF THE CHURCH OF ENGLAND.

Today a shameful spectacle is exhibited to the world. The present head of the Church of England was for many years a man of notoriously dissolute life as a prince, and has never repented.

If he has repented, he has never told his people of his repentance of the shameful life of abounding wickedness which made his good mother keep him and his set from her Court for many years.

I know whereof I speak.

All in England acquainted with the facts, however they may want to toady to King Edward VII., know that what I speak is true.

It is a shame and a scandal to think that a dissolute prince who has been an utter stranger to that Grace, and a trampler upon that Faith, should have been crowned the other day, in Westminster Abbey, with the title of "Defender of the Faith by the Grace of God."

If there were nothing else, this would be a proof of apostasy; for there is no other Head of the Church but Jesus, the Christ, Himself.

The making of all the chief ministers of that church dependent for their creation on that King who was for so long a dissolute prince, is a shame and disgrace intolerable to all true Christians.

But the Apostasy of the Church of England lies deeper than the Royal Supremacy.

I intend to take this matter up, and go into it thoroughly next Lord's Day without prelude of any kind.

I thank God for the splendid men who have lived, and loved, and served Him in the Church of England; and who have so stifled and strangled their consciences that they are dead to the sin they have committed in acknowledging any man or woman as the head of the Church.

No one, however, can look at that conglomeration of Latitudinarianism, Evangelical Christianity, Ritualism and Romanism in the Church of England, and not feel that the safety of true religion and the extension of Christianity in the great British Empire, which holds sway over nearly one-third of the population of the world, is dependent upon the destruction of the Church of England as an ecclesiastical and political organization.

ARRAIGNMENT OF KING EDWARD VII.

The Royal Supremacy which Henry VIII. established, Edward VII. maintains.

The present king is like his ancestor in many traits of character, as well as in physical appearance.

He dares not attempt, however, to do what Henry could do in a darker age, and perhaps has not the desire to do it.

There is no doubt but that the King is an amiable gentleman, personally, and very attractive in manner.

As a prince, however, he disgraced the good name that his father, the Prince Consort, Albert the Good, gave him.

I am glad he did not go on the throne as Albert.

Prince Albert was a true Christian, and a good husband, a Royal Consort such as the world never saw before nor has seen since.

Well might Queen Victoria mourn him in the eloquent ne[illegible]athetic language that came from her heart when he passed away, and that co[illegible]nued to come until she laid down her head to pass away, with the glad th[illegible]ught that she would join him.

I was a boy in Edinburgh at the time when the Prince, the Queen and the Royal Family used to spend some time nearly every year at the old Palace of Holyrood, Edinburgh, and, living near there and close to the Queen's Park where they frequently walked, I saw them often.

I frequently had the loving smile of that good Prince as he walked in that park with his sweet-faced little Queen, who was always literally compelled to look up to him all her life.

I can never forget how good and true and noble that Prince was, and the pride which the Scottish people and the entire Nation felt in his gentle and large Christian spirit, ever striving to please God and do the people good. It was a joy to salute him, and to see the smile of real happiness with which he responded, and, looking back, I think we boys put ourselves too often in his way. But he was ever the same. All England, and all Scotland, and all Ireland, and all the world knew him, not only for a noble, uncrowned King, but for a true husband and a wise father who trained his children well in paths of Divine wisdom and virtue. And when I returned to Edinburgh from Australia, years after his departure, I revisited the places where I had often seen him riding on horseback or walking—and it was a pain to think of him as gone.

We who were students in Edinburgh University and other schools of learning, who were desirous of living good lives such as God and all good men approve, all felt the burning sting of shame when the Prince of Wales was threatened by an outraged husband of high rank, at a London club, with horsewhipping, if he dared to continue his disgusting attentions to his wife, whom he and his set afterwards ruined and whose name they made a synonym with shame in all England. The Lady Mordaunt divorce scandal made every decent man's blood boil at the lecherous conduct of the Heir Apparent and his dissolute set, which was only aggravated by his probably compulsory appearance in the witness-box, to formally deny his guilt.

I never met a man who believed him to be innocent; for all the facts showed that he defied all decent conduct in the matter, and his many open *amours* were constant talk.

WARNING OF MR. GLADSTONE TO EDWARD WHEN HE WAS PRINCE OF WALES.

Every loyal heart responded to the closing words of an article in a great English newspaper, probably written by Mr. Gladstone, who was premier of the nation at that time. I committed the words to memory at the time, and, unless that memory fails me, they were to this effect:

"Let Albert Edward, Prince of Wales, remember that England will never tolerate another George IV. or Charles II. on the throne, and if he pursues his present dissolute course, it will become the duty of her majesty's ministers to propose to Parliament a change in the succession to the crown."

These brave words were written, and similar words spoken, by the greatest and best statesman of all the Victorian era, William Ewart Gladstone.

Oh, that God might give to that man who now nominally reigns as King Edward VII. a change of heart and a repentance before all his people for the seas of shame through which he dragged us all for many years!

May God, in His Infinite Mercy, destroy the Apostate Church that shamefully reverences him as "head," when its ministers well know that he is utterly incompetent to fill any such office.

These are words of one who has lived under the British flag for forty-one years of his life.

While I felt it hard, while the Queen lived, to renounce my allegiance to that flag, the moment that she departed I was ready to renounce allegiance to that dissolute king, and I did it gladly. It was good to be free.

SIN OF MINISTERS WHO PALLIATE KING EDWARD'S CRIMES.

I do not hesitate to say, although they have threatened me in Canada and England for speaking the truth concerning the King, that the minister of God who does not rebuke sin in high places is a traitor to his God. [Applause.]

Instead of rebuking his sin in the Church of England, they cover it.

Instead of dealing with him firmly, they have for many long years permitted him to do the things that are so shameful that, if I am provoked very much, I will drag out a great many facts concerning his past.

If I get any more impudence from Canada—let the words go across the border—if I get any more impudence from Ottawa, if I get any more impudence from London, from the Court, I will let fly, and I will tell the whole truth before I am through. [Applause.] I have been told that LEAVES OF HEALING will be denied transmission in the English Mails, unless I am silent. That does not cause me to fear for a moment, because the Little White Dove could get in by many other windows.

I do not want, for the sake of the amiable Queen who has borne with his shameful life, and of some noble spirits connected with his family and Court, to say all, but I am one, perhaps, of the few men who are able to say, and to say knowing them to be true, things that will help to shake that throne.

You may be startled at words like these from one who has all his life been under that flag till lately, but I am simply voicing in America that which is in the hearts of millions upon millions of honest, clean-living people throughout the British Empire. Alas! however, there are few brave enough to speak out.

As God's Messenger and Prophet, in the spirit and power of Elijah the Restorer, it is my Mission to put *everything* into the Crucible of Truth, and in the Fire of Love refine the Sons of Levi, until they offer unto Jehovah "Offerings in Righteousness."

I will obey God, and deliver His Message, until it reaches "every creature," and "makes disciples of all nations,"and leads them by Repentance towards God and by Faith in our Lord Jesus to obey the Christ, and receive that Triune Baptism which is the Seal of the Living God.

I UTTERED THIS ARRAIGNMENT ON BRITISH SOIL, IN LONDON.

You say, "It is all very well to say these things in America; why do you not say them in the king's domain?"

I did.

I said them in Melbourne.

I said them in Sydney.

I said them in Adelaide.

I said them in Auckland.

I said them in Wellington.

I said them in London two years ago, in St. Martin's Hall, Trafalgar Square, within a few blocks of Buckingham Palace.

That was partly the cause of the trouble there, too. [Laughter.]

I did speak the Truth concerning this Apostate and Corrupt Church of England, and its wickedness in proclaiming its degeneracy by lying at the feet of the monarch, who at that time was the world-honored and venerable Queen Victoria.

May God help me to speak it while I live. [Amen. Applause.]

Liberty of British and Australian People Destroyed by Organized, Lawless Ruffians.

We are not done with it yet. Of course we are not.

England will reap what she has sown.

Degenerate and profligate, the highest and lowest classes are phenomenally wicked, as the papers themselves admit.

All the papers throughout London described what I myself saw in 1900 when the City Imperial Volunteers came back from Africa—a horrible Saturnalia in the streets of London, the open profligacy of which was such as Heathen Rome in its worst days only could have excelled.

I found that Masonry was at the bottom of it, and I say to the British and Australian people that their liberties and their birthrights have been sold out to Baal, their legal protections destroyed, and a mass of lawless ruffians have organized themselves to steal the people's rights, and to fool them with the glittering baubles of royalty.

Every Masonic lodge is an anarchistic gathering, for this reason, which no one can ever dispute honestly, namely, that every organization, no matter how small or how large, that assumes the power to administer an oath, to formulate a penalty, to pronounce a sentence and execute that penalty—that organization is lawless.

Under every constitutional government the only person who may administer an oath is a properly-qualified judge.

The only persons who can try offenders are judges and juries properly qualified.

The only penalties that citizens can ever suffer are those which the law imposes.

The only men that can execute penalties under a constitutional government are constitutionally-appointed officers, and therefore secret societies, whether they are the Mafia, the Clan-na-gael, or Masons, are anarchistic organizations.

They must be suppressed, unless all law and order are to be absolutely lost.

Freemasons Who Desire To Be Honest and Law-abiding.

I know that there are vast numbers of Freemasons and persons in other secret societies who have no idea that they are promoters of, and partakers in, lawless assemblies and who do not have any desire to do that which is dishonest and unlawful. But such is the fact, and they will do well from henceforth to obey the apostolic injunction (Ephesians 5:11-12) "Have no fellowship with the Unfruitful Works of Darkness, but rather even reprove them: for the *Things which are done by them in Secret* it is a Shame even to speak of."

Many of my own personal friends in Australia, who were good citizens and sincere Christians, were Freemasons. They were amazed to find what the real nature of Secretism was.

When they refused to join the mob, their names were cast about as those of evil men, and their houses were assailed—men who had been for half a century good citizens and merchants of Adelaide, some of whom had in better days served South Australia in its government and in its magistracy.

I want to say that the reaction has come in Australia, and that the press was guilty of suppressing the manifestations of the reaction.

I challenge them today to poll either Adelaide, Melbourne, or Sydney and find one out of every ten decent men or women who would be in favor of the acts committed among the lower, disorderly classes.

Around-the-World Visitation Misrepresented by the Press.

In lands not Anglo-Saxon I found a great and wide-open door for Zion.

The Field is the World.

The press of London had its emissaries in Berlin and all over Europe, in Paris, in Zurich, in Bern, in Lausanne, in Neuchatel, and in Rotterdam.

They told the most shameful lies regarding the Visitation.

They said that I had been totally unable to get the people interested, and the fact was that the Velodrome in Zurich could not contain the crowds that came. A photo-engraving of one of these Gatherings appears in LEAVES OF HEALING for June 25th, pages 292-293.

It was the largest available building in the city.

In Rotterdam, with only one day's announcement, one of the greatest halls of that city was crowded before I could get to the meeting, and the streets were black with people who came to get in.

I was most amazed in Berlin.

There was perfect order, and very large meetings.

I was treated with the utmost consideration by all the authorities with whom we came in contact.

Two policemen in uniform sat on the platform at every meeting, one of them reporting and the other watching.

They treated me with great courtesy, and shook hands with me very warmly.

They told me that not one of the buildings in Berlin would have contained one-half of the people that wanted to come.

It was the same in London.

There was no question that we could have filled Albert Hall over and over again.

We filled all the largest buildings in Australia; and, with the exception of about three or four meetings, we carried out our program to the letter.

We carried it out in Sydney, without the loss of one meeting.

We carried it out in Melbourne, with a loss of only two.

We carried it out in Adelaide, with a loss of two meetings, but we had immense congregations and gatherings there to hear the Word of God.

The English and American papers lied about my Visitation in Europe.

The Loving Reception of God's Prophet in the Swiss Republic.

I was received heartily in Zurich, where we have our Headquarters, and where we are well known.

There the press and pulpit were against us, with one striking exception, of which you have read reports in LEAVES OF HEALING—the *Anzeiger*, of Zurich, which is edited by a member of the Zurich City Council.

That gentleman and others treated us with the utmost consideration, and the people in Zurich, as far as I know, almost without exception, were kind.

When we left for that city, I had been told by people from there, who were opposed to us, that there would be terrible rioting; but, instead of that, every one around was quiet, and even the local saloon-keepers near the Velodrome vied with one another to show us and our people consideration in that immediate neighborhood.

The children used to run to the side of the street and watch for us, to throw flowers into our carriage, and our rooms at the Bellevue Hotel were filled with flowers.

I have seen groups of as many as ten or twelve, in various parts of the city, on the way to and from the meetings, waiting for us, that they might respectfully salute us.

Bankers, merchants, lawyers, editors and even some ministers attended the meetings; and multitudes of the people were blessed.

I laid hands on one thousand three hundred people in Zurich and many were healed.

I received five hundred six members into fellowship at one meeting, and one hundred seventy-four were baptized.

All the expenses of the Zurich Visitation, and of the trip through Switzerland, were paid by the people themselves.

Received by Prominent European Statesmen With Great Consideration.

We touched Switzerland at every point.

President Comtesse of the Swiss Confederation, and other prominent European statesmen, received us with the greatest consideration.

The representatives of the United States in Germany, Switzerland, and elsewhere, treated us with consideration.

Whenever a Consul was seen, he was most kind.

I may say that we had most pleasant relations with some of these gentlemen, which, perhaps, I would better not go into at length.

Arthur S. and Catherine Booth-Clibborn Ordained Elders in the Christian Catholic Church in Zion.

When I got to Rotterdam, Holland, with which we had no connection, except through our friend, now Elder, Arthur S. Booth-Clibborn, who was there, I was amazed at the vast multitude of people that came out to hear us.

We ordained many important officers at our last Gathering in Zion Tabernacle, London, on Lord's Day, June 12th, among them Elders Arthur S. and Catherine Booth-Clibborn.

I may say now that I have it in charge from Elder Catherine Booth-Clibborn to say, that God had led her, as a distinct act of spiritual faith, to write to me the words, "I feel that I ought to and can accept you as Elijah, the Prophet and the forerunner, and this I do with all my heart. I offer myself to you for the Kingdom of God in Zion, with one prayer that His purposes may be accomplished in and through me."

I did receive her and her husband, and ordained them.

I believe that they not only will be, but that they already have been, eminently useful.

May God bless them.

That was one of the things that maddened many bitter foes of Zion in England.

The British Empire a Besotted Nation.

The Roman Catholic countries, yes, the infidel countries of the world are more open to receive the Gospel of the Kingdom of God than the besotted British Empire.

I use that word "besotted" as compared with the nations of Continental Europe, because I did not see a drunken man in Berlin, nor in Paris, save perhaps one, nor a drunken man or woman in a single city of Switzerland.

I did not see a drunken man or woman in the streets of Rotterdam, but you could scarcely take a few minutes' walk in any city of England without running against drunken brutes and hags of women staggering out of the gin-palaces, often pouring gin down the throats of their crying babies.

London is besotted and degenerate!

Liquor Traffic in Great Britain Controlled by the Clergy and the Nobility.

Nine-tenths of the clergy of England are directly or indirectly interested in breweries or liquor shops. More than that, the members of the government of Great Britain are interested in breweries.

Members of the present cabinet, noblemen in the House of Lords, and members of the House of Commons are interested in the liquor traffic.

They are now passing a bill the effect of which is to endow and make permanent that accursed business which has hitherto only existed upon the sufferance of an annual license, the renewal of which has never been guaranteed.

The best people in England will have to wake up, and wake up quickly, unless England is to go down; for physically, psychically, spiritually, and even financially, she is already going down.

Consols, that were one hundred thirteen before the Boer War, are eighty-five today. These "Consols" are Government Bonds, and are known as "the three per cent. Consolidated Annuities."

They have gone down twenty-eight points since the Boer War.

You know that Consols represent the public debt of Great Britain, and when they fall from one hundred thirteen to eighty-five, and stay there, you can see that that Empire is in a financial storm.

I may say that one reason why a vast amount of British capital is continually going to America and other countries for investment is that it cannot find safe and reliable investment in England.

The British people have lost confidence in even Government Securities, and are realizing their money by selling them at a great sacrifice. Some of that money has come, and more is coming, to Zion City for investment in Zion Stocks and Securities.

Many good people are coming out of England with their money, and many of them have come and are coming into Zion. [Applause.]

That is partly where the shoe pinches.

They wonder whereunto this will grow; and I sometimes wonder myself, as I look at this vast audience and think of the five thousand people who met me here at half past six o'clock this morning, and of the ten thousand who welcomed me upon my return a few days ago, and then remember that, less than three years ago, this City was an open prairie, without inhabitants, except here and there, at long distances, a farmhouse.

I have spoken to audiences aggregating more than twenty-one thousand people at three assemblies within three days since my return to Zion City.

You will find that God will make it more and more clear to the world that the Christ "has made us to be a Kingdom," as the Book of the Revelation says, and "to be priests unto His God and Father."

I am not a whit discouraged; I am greatly encouraged by my Around-the-World Visitation this year.

God's Prophet to Visit London With Ten Thousand Restorationists.

It will not be next year, and it may not be for a number of years, but when we have consolidated our City or Cities, and are able to do it in the way I want it done, I will have several Legions of Zion Restoration Host study a map of London until they know every street and lane in that Metropolis, and then I will cross the Atlantic Ocean in a Zion fleet for a Visitation to London, and possibly Edinburgh and Dublin.

I will send two Restorationists into every house in London, and, if we can get there, we will knock at the palace door of the king. [Applause.]

I have no hatred of the king, not a particle of personal feeling. It is against his sin, and the evil principles that he represents that I am contending in the Name of the Christ, the King of kings.

I say, "God save the king!"

May God save him! He needs saving, but the people that utter that prayer are often themselves half-drunk when they say it.

Church of England Threatened by the Brewers and Distillers.

There is no reality in the prayer of millions of those who shout and sing it. The king is to them a kind of political fetich.

In England they are afraid that the Church of England will come tumbling down one of these days.

The brewers and distillers of England have threatened the Conservative and Unionist parties that if they do not give them the license bill that they want, they will unite with the Liberals and the Disestablishment People to disestablish the Church of England, and take away its vast endowments, the origin of most of which is simply a story of legalized robbery—one of the worst kinds of robbery.

They are afraid, from the bottom of their poltroon hearts, from the Archbishop of Canterbury down, that the liquor dealers will join hands with the Liberals and Disestablishers, and destroy the Church of England.

How Zion Congregations Compare in Numbers With Those of the Various Churches.

The morning that I spoke in the City of London the papers themselves stated that in twenty-three of the largest churches of London, tall buildings with great towers, splendidly finished, with accommodations for perhaps from thirty thousand to forty thousand people, there were in all only about three hundred people in attendance at the morning services.

We had six hundred fifty people present, I was informed, in Zion Tabernacle, Euston Road, London, that morning, twice as many as all the twenty-three state-endowed churches; and because we had no more room, we kept out thousands who would have been glad to get in.

One of the largest of these churches had a congregation of only three persons. [Laughter.] Was the minister not ashamed?

A little while ago, I read that in the Cathedral of Canterbury, the canon in residence, at the head or at the tail of the procession of choristers and officers of the cathedral, went in and held a service, because the law said they must hold it, and there was only one man present as a congregation. [Laughter.]

Last Lord's Day, in New York City I preached in the morning and in the afternoon in Carnegie Hall, and although the heat was so intense as to be almost unbearable, I found hundreds waiting for me in the hall, and in the afternoon my congregation numbered from one thousand to one thousand two hundred people.

That was very small for us; but I was told by an officer of the Fifth Avenue First Presbyterian church that their congregation that morning numbered only fifteen.

They told me that they believed there were thirty of the central churches in New York that day that did not have anything like a thousand people all told.

So you see that, even in the midst of terrifically hot weather in New York, with the press lying about us, we had splendid congregations.

Glad To Be an American Citizen.

In looking over the field of the world I look at America, and thank God that He made me to stay in America, to plant the banner of Zion here, because in all the Field of the World there is no better land under the blue sky of heaven than America! [Applause.]

I am an American! [Applause.]

I am an American!! [Applause.]

I am an American!!! [Long and continued applause.]

I thank God that I cast my lot in with this Republic, and after all, although I have had my fights here, and although when I started there was more devil to the square acre in Chicago than almost anywhere else in the world, I thank God for the victory of Zion, and say that with all its faults the

United States of America Has the Best Government on Earth!

[Long applause.]

Moreover, we can help to make it better.

May God grant it!

Oh, what a great fight we will wage!

It is the Good Fight of Faith; and will bring the Blessings of Salvation, Healing, and Holy Living to many millions, preparing them for the Coming of the King of kings and Lord of lords, who shall reign forever, and ever, and ever—Amen!

When I go on a Visitation to London again, with a fleet, it will be to wage a peaceful war.

We shall carry the Christ's Message, "Peace be to this house!" to every home in London.

A Wonderful Scene!—Six Thousand Volunteers for the Legion of Zion Restoration Host to Invade London.

All that will go with me if you can, stand, and let me see you. [Thousands upon thousands eagerly rose.]

We must begin to prepare, because there are probably six thousand on their feet now of the ten thousand that I shall take.

All who will consecrate themselves to God, stand.

[There were few in the audience who were not already standing. Of these nearly all rose.]

PRAYER OF CONSECRATION.

My God and Father, in Jesus' Name I come to Thee. Take me as I am. Make me what I ought to be, in spirit, in soul, and in body. Give me power to do right, no matter what the cost. Help me truly to repent, fully to restore, and to confess, that I may be blessed by Thee in a pure and holy life. Give me this blessing, that I may be worthy to go forth with the Hosts of Zion Restoration Host, to live and love and serve Thee, and if need be to die for Thee. Bless the British Empire. God save the king, save the kingdom, save the empire, and save the people from their sins. Save Australia, and Europe, and Asia, and Africa, and America. Give us love. While we hate sin and fight it, help us to love the sinner, and to bring the seed of the evil one out of the field of the world, that Thou mayst grant Salvation to every spirit that ever came from Thee. Help us and him who speaks, and give us much wisdom and grace, that we shall be willing for service or sacrifice as Thou dost ordain. Amen. [*All repeat the prayer, clause by clause, after the General Overseer.*]

Did you mean it?

People—"Yes."

The General Overseer then led the congregation in singing "I Stand on Zion's Mount," the full words of which are:

I stand on Zion's mount,
And view my starry crown;
No power on earth my hope can shake,
Nor hell can thrust me down.

The lofty hills and towers,
That lift their heads on high,
Shall all be leveled low in dust—
Their very names shall die.

The vaulted heavens shall fall,
Built by Jehovah's hands;
But firmer than the heavens, the Rock
Of my salvation stands. Amen.

After the Benediction had been pronounced, those who wished retired, while about five thousand remained to gather around their Lord's Table.

COMMUNION OF THE LORD'S SUPPER.

After the General Overseer, assisted by the Officers of the Church, had administered the Ordinance of the Communion of the Lord's Supper, he addressed the people in his usual Post-communion Family Talk. He said:

Beloved friends, as we close this Communion, I feel so thankful for the opportunity of saying a few words to you in this Post-communion Talk, after a day that has been very long as regards hours, for some of us first came today into this Tabernacle a little over twelve and a half hours ago.

Some of you have been engaged in the many exercises connected with Zion Junior Restoration Host, others in the Intermediate Bible Training Institute, the Bible Classes, the Assemblies of German, Scandinavian and other Peoples in our four smaller Tabernacles in this City, and in the organization of this vast General Assembly with its opening Processional of nearly one thousand of Zion White-robed Choir and Church officers.

Urgent Need for Shiloah Tabernacle.

I can say truthfully that nowhere throughout the world have I seen so large an Assembly gathered for public worship as I have seen here today, except the assemblies that gathered in the Melbourne Exhibition Building, where we were unable to complete the service, and perhaps one service in the Adelaide Exhibition Building.

But there are no such orderly and thoroughly earnest worshipers anywhere else in the world, so far as I could see.

I am so glad to be back, but of course as you may suppose, something of the reaction from constant travel, and the strain of constant ministry, has come to me.

I ask you to pray for me that my bow may abide in strength, and that I may be able to discharge the important duties that devolve upon me in the many Departments of Zion here and in all the world, between this and the Feast, and then carry through, by God's grace, that great Fourth Feast of Tabernacles from July 13th to 24th.

Excellent Work Done by Choir, Band and Orchestra.

I feel especially thankful for this three-fold organization of musical powers—Orchestra, Choir and Band.

The blending of the instrument and the voice today has been a revelation.

I desire to say that while, of course, it would be folly for me to flatter you and speak of you as a perfect body, you are evidently on the road to perfection.

May you rise nearer still, and may all you do, all you sing, and all you think be pleasing in His eyes, who looks upon you, young men and young women, with such Infinite Love.

I know He does, for I look upon you with great love and affection, and it is but as starlight is to noonday in comparison with the full glory of His Boundless Love.

This Galaxy of Christian Song and Sound is only the nucleus of a still larger and mightier power with which we shall praise God, for after Shiloah Tabernacle, to seat sixteen thousand, has been built, filled and overflowed, then comes Zion Temple to seat forty thousand; and you are now preparing for that glorious Temple.

To Stay in Zion City Until Shiloah Tabernacle is Complete.

While I desire to make no rash statement, nor any statement whatever that may not be modified (because all I am saying is "as the Lord will, and as He shall direct"), as far as I can understand the mind of the Lord, I am able to make an announcement which I want you to remember, namely, that while I may be away for a few days or even weeks at a time, in various parts of this Continent, I shall stay in Zion City until Shiloah Tabernacle is built, furnished, paid for, and filled.

I pray that God will give me the realization of my heart's desire. [Applause.]

I shall call upon Zion City to give me at least a hundred thousand dollars towards this during the present year.

That is only a very small sum, comparatively, from each person.

Then I shall appeal to Zion and to the friends of Zion throughout the world for four hundred thousand more.

I desire to see this Tabernacle erected as soon as possible.

Hopes to Build Shiloah Tabernacle, as Far as Possible, of Material in Zion City.

While I have not yet fully consulted all my officers on this question, I may say that a great desire has come into my heart to construct Shiloah Tabernacle of the material that we have in Zion City; to take the sand and the gravel which is by our Lake Shore of two and a half miles, and, with the addition of Portland cement, to make a great Tabernacle for the Worship of God, and the Extension of His Kingdom.

I have become a convert, as I have gone through the world,

to concrete, and I am sure that we shall not have any trouble with contraction or expansion with that material.

But I am somewhat uncertain about the terrific effect of twenty-five degrees below zero outside when we make it seventy above inside; the contraction and expansion at the same moment of time will be a tremendous strain upon any metal, especially iron or steel.

I am feeling very desirous of using the material that God has given us so bountifully.

A great and beautiful building can be built of this material.

I was indisposed to make any effort to bring any outside people here today because I felt that within a few seats you would fill this Tabernacle which seats seven thousand three hundred—and you have.

I must tell you that the effect upon me of overflowing audiences in this Tabernacle will be very trying throughout the summer.

So you must give me this Shiloah Tabernacle for the next Feast of Tabernacles.

We must all pray about it, and ask God to show us what we can do.

How It Can Be Paid For.

If five thousand of us were to give God ten cents a day, what would that be?

Ten cents a day for five thousand people is five hundred dollars a day, and for three hundred sixty-five days in a year is one hundred eighty-two thousand five hundred dollars.

Of course we can ask the outside Zion to help, for it is for them also; it is for the whole world.

Another thing I wish to have by the fall is weekly editions, if they are only eight pages, of LEAVES OF HEALING in German and in French. [Applause.]

Then if some of you will give a few thousand dollars extra, I will put in a Danish and a Swedish edition.

They are crying out for them in Europe—the families of the earth that speak these languages.

I am so glad that God enables us to commune with one another at our Lord's Table once more, after long months of separation.

Let us keep close together and have confidence in God, in Zion and in one another.

May God bless every officer and member of the Christian Catholic Church in Zion everywhere.

You have all done so well, and the humblest is just as much to be thanked as the highest; for if the humblest had not done his duty, the highest would have been impeded.

May God bless you all, and always, in all places.

The Congregation and Choir sang the first stanza of the hymn, "God Be With You Till We Meet Again," after which the General Overseer sang the last stanza, the whole people uniting in the chorus.

The General Overseer then pronounced the

BENEDICTION.

Jehovah bless thee and keep thee.
Jehovah make His face to shine upon thee and be gracious unto thee.
Jehovah lift up His countenance upon thee,
And give thee peace.
The grace of our Lord Jesus, the love of God, and the fellowship of the Holy Spirit be with you ever. Amen.

Daily Bible Study for the Home

By Overseer John G. Speicher

MONDAY, JULY 25TH.

2 Corinthians 8.—Liberality in giving chapter.

Memory text—Verse 9. "That ye through His poverty might become rich."

Contents of chapter—Spirituality and liberality of the churches of Macedonia commended; Corinthians exhorted to liberality in giving; The Christ for our sakes became poor, that we might become rich; God accepts the readiness and willingness to give according to what a man hath; Paul desired a distribution from the abundance of the Corinthians, so that none should lack; Titus and another messenger of the churches commended to them.

TUESDAY, JULY 26TH.

2 Corinthians 9.—Cheerful giving chapter.

Memory text—Verse 7. "Not grudgingly, or of necessity: for God loveth a cheerful giver."

Contents of chapter—The Corinthian zeal in stirring up many at Achaia commended, Paul thinks best to send the brethren to them to get the bounty ready, that it might not appear as a matter of extortion; Reaping as we sow; Cheerful giving; God able to make grace abound unto all sufficiency in everything; God will multiply what we sow; Faithfulness in giving has good effect upon others.

WEDNESDAY, JULY 27TH.

2 Corinthians 10.—Warning against self-commendation chapter.

Memory Text—Verse 18. "For not he that commendeth himself is approved, but whom the Lord commendeth."

Contents of chapter--Paul desires not to have to speak boldly against some of them; His ministry while in the flesh not of the flesh; His weapons mighty in pulling and casting down every stronghold against God; Brings his thoughts into obedience to the Christ; His words to those who thought his letters strong, but his speech and bodily presence weak; Will not compare himself with some who ignorantly measure themselves by themselves; His desire to reach others beyond them; He is approved whom the Lord commendeth.

THURSDAY, JULY 28TH.

2 Corinthians 11.—Paul's apostolic boasting chapter.

Memory text—Verse 30. "I will glory in the things that concern my weakness."

Contents of chapter—Paul's desire for the purity of the Corinthians; Fears lest Satan beguile them from simplicity and purity; Questions whether he did not sin in abasing himself before them and letting the other churches support him; Determines that he will stand for his rights in Achaia; Satan fashions himself into an angel of light; No great thing if his ministers fashion themselves into ministers of righteousness; Paul recounts his reasons for glorying in the Christ.

FRIDAY, JULY 29TH.

2 Corinthians 12.—Vision and thorn in the flesh chapter.

Memory text—Verse 9. "My grace is sufficient for thee."

Contents of chapter—Paul refers to a vision in which he was caught up into the third heaven and into Paradise, but does not discuss it lest he be misunderstood; A thorn in the flesh given him lest he be unduly exalted; Prayer for its removal not answered; Is told God's grace is sufficient for him; He glories in his weaknesses for the Christ's sake; Apostolic signs wrought among the Corinthians, proving Paul's apostleship; Paul ready the third time to come to them; Not willing to burden them; He seeks not theirs but them; Neither he nor Titus takes advantage of them; He writes for their edifying, desiring that they and he should be without strife, jealousies, wraths, factions, etc., and that he need not mourn over any because of sin.

SATURDAY, JULY 30TH.

2 Corinthians 13.—Proving chapter.

Memory text—Verse 5. "Try your own selves, whether ye be in the faith."

Contents of chapter—Paul declares that in his third coming to them he will not spare those who have sinned; They seek a proof of the Christ speaking through him; Tells them to examine themselves whether they be in the faith; Prove themselves; Do no evil; Do that which is honorable; Nothing can be done against the truth; He rejoices when they are strong, and prays for their perfecting; Writes in authority, that he need not deal sharply when he comes to them; Apostolic benediction and salutation.

SUNDAY, JULY 31ST.

Philemon.—Love of the brethren chapter.

Memory text—Verse 6. "That the fellowship of thy faith may become effectual, in the knowledge of every good thing which is in you, unto the Christ."

Contents of chapter—Paul's salutation to the brethren; Thanks to God for the love and faith and good deeds of Philemon; Good words and recommendation of Onesimus; His confidence in Philemon; Salutations from the brethren with Paul.

Around-the-World Visitation

of the

Rev. John Alex. Dowie

Elijah the Restorer
General Overseer of the Christian Catholic Church in Zion.

By ARTHUR W. NEWCOMB, Special Correspondent.

VISITATION TO THE BERNESE OBERLAND AND FRENCH SWITZERLAND.

THE last paper of this series closed with the report of the Ordinance of Believers' Baptism administered in Zurich, Switzerland, by the General Overseer, at the close of his Visitation in, that city, on Monday morning, May 30, 1904.

Early that afternoon, the General Overseer, accompanied by members of the Visitation Party, Elder Carl Hodler and Elder and Evangelist Percy Clibborn, departed for a few days' Visitation to the Bernese Oberland and French Switzerland.

A number of Zion people in Zurich were at the station to bid the General Overseer good-by, happy in the thought that it was only for a few days this time, as he intended visiting Zurich once more on his way to Castle Liebburg and Berlin.

Along the Lake of Züg.

With the loving farewells of these earnest people still ringing in our ears, we began our journey, first of all skirting the western shores of the beautiful Lake Zurich, scene after scene of fascinating Old-world beauty spreading itself before our delighted eyes as we sped southward.

A little later we crossed the higher ground, which afforded tantalizing glimpses of more wonderful scenery, and then wound in and out among the hills, ravines and woods along the eastern shores of the Lake of Züg.

The shimmering loveliness of this little body of water, reflecting the green slopes, rugged cliffs, quaint villages, and picturesque castles which surround it, made us feel, for the moment, that this was the most beautiful sight we had yet seen; but one always feels that way about every view in Switzerland—they are all superlative.

As we glided along the shores of this lake, there was danger that we might, in our eagerness, break the excellent rule of the Swiss railways posted up in every car, in several languages, forbidding passengers to lean out of the windows—there was so much to see and so little time to see it.

Up the Rigi.

Upon reaching the little city of Goldau, lying a short distance beyond the head of the lake, and between it and Lake Lowerz, we changed cars to the Arth-Goldau-Rigi-Kulm inclined railway.

The train on this railway consisted of one car, which was pushed up the side of the mountain by a small, but stertorous locomotive, whose drive-wheel was a pinion working in a rack laid along between the rails.

The rate of speed of this peculiar railway train was leisurely, quite in accordance with our tastes.

We needed every moment of time for the use of our eyes upon the ever-changing scene that spread out before us as we climbed higher and higher.

It was worth days of study, instead of the very few minutes which we could give to it.

At one time we would cross a gently-sloping, elevated plain, covered with soft grasses and a dazzling profusion of Alpine wild flowers; then we would seem to crawl, like a great insect, along the side of some precipitous rock, towering hundreds of feet above our heads and dropping away thousands of feet into the valley below; the next moment we would find ourselves at the bottom of a great, jagged chasm, with titanic cliffs rising on both sides.

The most memorable of the scenes of that climb, however, were not those close at hand.

Farther and ever farther as we slowly went up, our eyes penetrated the distances to the north of us; broad plains, purple hills, silvery rivers, and placid lakes, reflecting the brilliant blue and snow-white of the summery sky.

In these rare settings were clustering villages, with their ancient churches, and their quaint, red-tiled dwelling-houses, and here and there the frowning old castles, mute but proud reminders of the "bad old times" of the robber barons and their feudal customs.

The Alps.

At last we passed the topmost barrier to the south of us.

Oh, the unspeakable majesty!

There, rearing their calm, cold, white heads into the molten glory of the sunset, we saw the Alps, a range of mighty kings among mountains, one hundred twenty miles long.

No words can describe the simplicity, silence, and grandeur of that scene, or give voice to the emotions that stirred our inmost spirits as we beheld it.

Far above the clouds; far above all the turmoil, dust, and clangor of puny man, these peaks seemed to annihilate distance and to crush, by the weight of their hoary age, the centuries into a moment.

We still had a mile or two to climb ere we reached the summit, and there were views of wondrous beauty to engage our attention and awaken our interest, but our eyes always returned to those silent, snowy Alps, and rested there.

The Rigi-Kulm.

We were still lost in the contemplation of these scenes when the brave little locomotive that had pushed us up so many thousand feet uttered a final snort and gasp, as much as to say, "There you are," and we were set down within a very few steps of the summit of that famous mountain known as the Rigi, which towers in almost solitary loftiness, five thousand nine hundred five feet above the level of the sea.

Some of our party suffered somewhat from the lightness of the atmosphere, as we climbed higher, having pain in their ears. This was not serious, however, and soon passed away.

It was somewhat of a jar upon our artistic and poetic sensibilities to find anything so prosaic at this enchanted eminence, but the long ride and the crystalline air of the mountains had whetted our appetites, so that, after all, we were quite pleased to find a large and comfortable hotel near at hand, art and poetry to the contrary notwithstanding.

Before dinner was served, however, we climbed to the very top and gazed about us in all directions, and then, as if the lightness of the atmosphere had affected our hearts and heads a little, some of us skipped down the mountainside to a snowbank and engaged in a brief, friendly snowball fight.

A moment later we were gathering cowslips and other Alpine flowers within a yard or two of the snow.

Sunset on the Rigi.

After dinner we had the privilege and joy of witnessing the sunset from the top of this mountain.

In the west, the glowing orb of day was sinking out of sight into a great splash of purple and golden fire.

From over two score lakes in view from this eminence, the reflections of the same regal colors shone through the softening haze that had begun to veil the landscape.

Far away to the north could be seen the Uitleberg, a sentinel wrapt in a cloak of glowing purple, standing guard over the beautiful city of Zurich.

The Jura mountains were just discernible through the haze, to the northwest, and in the same general direction lay the dark shadow of the Black Forest.

At the foot of the mountain, on the southwest, was the Lake of Lucerne, or the Vierwaldstätter See (Lake of the Four Forest Provinces), with the battlements and towers of the city of Lucerne gleaming in the ruddy glow, and grim Pilatus towering up behind.

To the east, at the foot of the mountain, was the little

Canal and Windmills, Rotterdam.
Fountain in Berlin.

Brandenburg Gate, Berlin.
Canal Scene, Rotterdam.

Reichstag (Imperial Parliament House), Berlin.
Palace Bridge and New Cathedral, Berlin.

SCENES IN BERLIN AND ROTTERDAM.

village of Goldau which we had just left, and beyond it the jewel-like little lake of Lowerz.

To the north, in the foreground, lay Lake Züg, a great natural mirror, framed in green velvet, studded with pearls and garnets.

As the sun set, and the long twilight came on, we could hear the murmur and splash of the brooks and waterfalls below us, to which the bells of unnumbered cattle rendered pleasing and harmonious accompaniment.

It was all very faint, for we were a long mile above the brooks and the rivers and the cattle, but by harkening for it, in the midst of the great silence of the mountains, we could hear it very plainly.

Long before the last glowing tint of the twilight had faded out of the sky, the moon, nearly at the full, had begun to shed her silvery radiance over the great panorama.

And then our eyes turned once more, irresistibly, to the Alps.

Serene, silent, profound with the unthinkable mystery of scores of centuries, they were lighted up by the Queen of Night with a strange, new beauty that was almost unearthly.

Prayer on the Rigi-Kulm.

Calmness and peace unspeakable entered our spirits as we gathered in the General Overseer's room for evening prayer.

He who does not behold the mountains with his heart open to the "still, small Voice," sees their real beauty not at all.

We all repeated together the 23d Psalm and then the General Overseer dwelt, with a simplicity and power that deeply stirred our hearts, on the blessed truth contained in the last few words, "And I shall dwell in the House of Jehovah forever."

The burden of his Message to us that evening was:

"These great mountains give one the idea of permanence and the poet has mistakenly called them eternal; but long after they have been removed into the midst of the sea, our spirits will dwell eternally in the House of Jehovah."

Sunrise on the Rigi.

Each member of the party offered prayer, and then we retired to rest, as all intended to rise at a very early hour on the next morning to see the sunrise from the Rigi, one of the most deservedly famous scenes in all Europe.

Although we rose at half past three o'clock the next morning, the light of the dawn was already in the sky, and it was beginning to bring out the striking features of the great panorama, three hundred miles in diameter, which was in view from this point.

As it grew lighter, we could see around us, below, the great white *nebelmeer*, or sea of fog, which rolled through the valleys.

It looked to our astonished eyes as if the depths of all the valleys had been filled, over night, with great, fleecy masses of new-fallen snow.

As it grew lighter, we could see that the sunrise was very near; for the lofty pinnacles of the Alps had already begun to catch the glorious beams that shot up from behind the great shoulder of the world.

Then, with a suddenness and brilliancy that flooded the whole landscape with an indescribable glory, the sun rose.

Our hearts overflowed with praise and thanksgiving to God for the marvelous wonder and inspiring beauty of His works.

With the sunrise came the awakening of life in the valleys, and up through the soft masses of fog came the faint tinkle of the bells of the cattle as they sought pasture for the day.

Little by little, as the sun grew warmer, the fog gathered itself into silvery clouds and sailed away.

Some of these clouds seemed to rest upon the somber sides of the lower mountains, shining scarfs of white that softened the forbidding grimness of these scowling cliffs.

The Mountains in Scriptural Poesy.

But, once more, it was the Alps upon which our eyes rested.

We seemed to hear, as we looked upon them, the Divinely Inspired poets and prophets of the Holy Scriptures:

Thy righteousness is like the Mountains of God;
Thy judgments are a great deep:
O Jehovah, Thou preservest man and beast.

God is our refuge and strength,
A very present help in trouble.
Therefore will we not fear, though the earth do change,
And though the Mountains be moved in the heart of the seas.
Which by His strength setteth fast the Mountains;
Being girded about with might.

The Mountains shall bring peace to the people,
And the hills, in righteousness.

Jehovah, Thou hast been our dwelling place
In all generations.
Before the Mountains were brought forth,
Or ever Thou hadst formed the earth and the world,
Even from everlasting to everlasting, Thou art God.

As the Mountains are round about Jerusalem,
So Jehovah is round about His people,
From this time forth and for evermore.

Praise ye Jehovah.
Praise ye Jehovah from the heavens:
Praise Him in the Heights.

Praise Jehovah from the earth,
Ye dragons, and all deeps.
Mountains and all hills;
Fruitful trees and all cedars.

Who hath measured the waters in the hollow of His hand, and meted out heaven with the span, and comprehended the dust of the earth in a measure, and weighed the Mountains in scales, and the hills in a balance?

Behold, I will make thee a new sharp threshing instrument having teeth: thou shalt thresh the Mountains, and beat them small, and shalt make the hills as chaff.

Sing, O ye heavens, for Jehovah hath done it; shout, ye lower parts of the earth; break forth into singing, ye Mountains, O forest, and every tree therein: for Jehovah hath redeemed Jacob, and will glorify Himself in Israel.

For the Mountains shall depart, and the hills be removed; but My kindness shall not depart from thee, neither shall My Covenant of Peace be removed, saith Jehovah that hath mercy on thee.

For ye shall go out with joy, and be led forth with peace: the Mountains and the hills shall break forth before you into singing, and all the trees of the field shall clap their hands.

A day of darkness and gloominess, a day of clouds and thick darkness, as the dawn spread upon the Mountains; a great people and a strong, there hath not been ever the like, neither shall be any more after them, even to the years of many generations.

The Mountains quake at Him, and the hills melt; and the earth is upheaved at His presence, yea, the world, and all that dwell therein.

The Mountains saw Thee, and were afraid;
The tempest of waters passed by:
The deep uttered his voice,
And lifted up his hands on high.

And every island fled away, and the Mountains were not found.

But, as the General Overseer has often taught us, we could not remain forever on the mountain, and in a very few minutes the inclined railway had lowered us, through scenes of striking beauty, to the beautiful little town of Vitznau, on the Lake of Lucerne.

Here again we were treated to an entirely new phase of the picturesqueness and beauty of the Swiss Lakes.

On one side the Rigi, where we had spent the previous night, lifted itself in lonely pride.

Pilatus and Its Legends.

On the other was that black, massive crag called Pilatus.

This mountain is so-called on account of the many legends connected with it, one of the most common of which is that Pontius Pilate, after the crucifixion of Jesus, was recalled to Rome, and from there sent to this part of Switzerland, which was then a Roman Province.

Overwhelmed by remorse on account of his part in the crucifixion, he threw himself from the top of this mountain.

Another legend says that he committed suicide in Rome and that his body, denied the honor of burial, was cast into the Tiber.

The Tiber, however, at once became so turbulent and destructive that the body, which was held to be the cause of the trouble, was taken up and carried to Lake Geneva, into which it was thrown.

The inhabitants around about the lake, however, were so much disturbed by the unbroken succession of storms and calamities that followed, that the body was again removed, this time being thrown into the lake at the foot of the mountain now called Pilatus.

For many centuries afterwards, the tradition goes, this lake was the scene of great elemental commotion until some brave and able scholar held an interview with the disturbed spirit of the former procurator of Palestine and persuaded him to rest quietly, with the exception of one day in the year.

In accordance with this agreement, the tradition runs, the

the spirit of Pontius Pilate troubles not the waters that lie at the foot of the mountain that bears his name, except on Good Friday.

Whether it is a meteorological fact that there is always a storm on this day, we were not informed.

While waiting for our steamer at Vitznau, we amused ourselves by throwing crumbs of bread into the clear water of the lake and watching the thousands of little fish, that apparently swim near the shore for this very purpose, tumble over one another in their eagerness to get them.

Our steamer, after crossing and recrossing the lake, in order to reach other stations on its route, finally landed us at the beautiful, historic city of Lucerne, where we spent an hour or two at lunch.

The Advantage of Knowing German.

It was here that the writer had a little experience that taught him the great value of knowing the modern languages, especially when traveling.

We wished to leave our baggage in the station, while we went to lunch, and it seemed best to obtain permission to do so and assurance that it would be perfectly safe.

We approached one of the porters and in our very best German very laboriously put the case before him.

Several simple German words necessary for a concise statement of the proposition had either temporarily slipped our memory or we had never known them, hence it was necessary to use considerable circumlocution in order to make ourselves perfectly understood.

As we worked and perspired at our task, the porter regarded us with solemn and unmoved countenance, giving no intimation as to whether he understood or not.

When, however, we at last stopped for breath, he said in excellent English, except for just a trace of Cockney accent, "You may leave your luggage here, sir, and it will be perfectly safe."

We gasped a few words of thanks and departed.

Through Brünig Pass.

It was nearly one o'clock when we took train for Brienz.

The scenery for the first few miles of our journey was through gently rolling country, somewhat swampy in places, which reminded us of that of Illinois, Wisconsin and Michigan.

There were, however, beautiful lakes, picturesque villages, swift rivers, with well-kept banks, and through it all the ever-present Old-World atmosphere that can never be mistaken.

A few hours brought us to the entrance of Brünig Pass, one of the most wonderfully and fascinatingly picturesque in all Switzerland.

We had afternoon tea at Brünig, but decided to wait for dinner until we arrived at Grindelwald, which we expected to reach at about eight o'clock.

To attempt to paint any word pictures of the scenery which delights the eye at every foot of the way through Brünig Pass is not within the poetic capacity of the chronicler of this tour. How can one describe it when one feels that not a tithe of all its glories were realized even when passing through it?

We must content ourselves by saying that we saw lakes, rivers, villages, castles, plains, mountains, precipices, torrents, waterfalls, winding roads, old stone bridges, and other beautiful things which God uses in composing His own Divine masterpieces upon the canvas of nature, combined in such a way that one could only look with his soul in his eyes and praise God for His beauty, glory, and power.

Alpine Waterfalls.

Here we saw the Alpine waterfalls in all their filmy grace.

Imagine a river leaping from the bare summit of a rocky precipice, thousands of feet high, and plunging down hundreds of feet to its first stopping place, there to gather itself quickly for another leap to the next and so on down until its waters are lost in the tree tops of the valley.

It looked not so much like a river as a veil of drifting mist.

Some of them were of considerable volume, others seemed like the thinnest and filmiest of silver threads on the gray mountainsides.

Here again we had a view of the snow-capped peaks of the Bernese Alps, the Wetterhorn, Mittelhorn and Rosenhorn being most prominently in sight. These mountains seemed to grow upon us and we never tired of looking at them and letting their great silent message sink deep down into our spirits.

We stopped for a few minutes at Meiringen, where there is a wonderful fall, and a little later left the train at Brienz, which lies at the head of the small but exquisite Lake of Brienz.

Here we took steamer for Interlaken.

Interlaken.

On our way there, we called for a moment at Giessbach, where the river comes tumbling down the mountain, hundreds of feet, directly into the lake.

We reached Interlaken from Lake Brienz by running a few hundred yards down the River Aare.

At Interlaken we found the solicitors for fifty hotels lined up on the wharf, but as our destination was Grindelwald we could bring joy to none of their hearts.

From Interlaken there is usually a splendid view of the three highest mountains among the Bernese Alps: Jungfrau, Eiger, and Mönch; but they were hidden from us by clouds on this occasion.

We took carriages for Grindelwald, which was said to be about an hour and one-half or two hours up the valley.

Measurement of Distances by Hours.

In Switzerland, distances are never measured by the mile, but by the hour.

Even on some of their maps, and in certain guide books, the distances are set down as two, five, six or twenty hours, as the case may be, instead of in miles or kilometers.

Just what means and speed of locomotion is the standard, it is not always clear, but in this case we were convinced, in the course of time, that the speed of a one-horse vehicle was not the standard from which it was reckoned that the distance to Grindelwald was one and one-half or two hours.

In the Midst of the Alps.

For the first few hours of our journey, however, this did not trouble us much, as we found ourselves ascending a valley amidst scenes of such grandeur, sublimity, beauty, picturesque charm, and simple loveliness combined, that the mere details of time, distance, speed, and the lateness of our dinner were completely forgotten.

On either side of the road the mountains rose to heights of from five to twelve thousand feet.

Never before had we been so near to such lofty mountains as these which seemed almost to meet in the sky above our heads.

On the left was the Faulhorn, eight thousand eight hundred five feet high, and to the right the three gigantic mountains, Eiger, thirteen thousand forty feet, and the Mettenberg, ten thousand one hundred ninety-three feet, forming the base of the Schreckhorn.

At the head of the valley could be seen the snow-white peak and the glacier-scored sides of the beautiful Wetterhorn, twelve thousand one hundred fifty feet high.

At last we were in the very midst of the Alps!

Through the narrow valley which we were ascending, roared and foamed the Black Lütschine, a typical mountain torrent fed by numerous glaciers.

The Swiss Chalets.

Here, also, we saw, for the first time, the quaintly beautiful Swiss chalets, looking just as if they had been transferred from the Alpine pictures that had delighted our eyes from our earliest childhood.

These broad, low houses with their heavy overhanging roofs, the great shingles of which are held in place by beams and stones; and with their many little windows, and queer little steps and porticos, had one strikingly pleasant characteristic in common—they were all spotlessly neat and clean.

Every separate little pane of glass shone with the high polish that only an industrious hand can give.

The simple curtains which were draped across them were snowy white.

Glimpses of the interior showed immaculate floors and unblemished furnishings.

The faces of the children shone with cleanliness, happiness and health.

The tireless energy and industry of the Swiss women that lived in these chalets were also shown by the fact that they not only kept their homes in such exemplary neatness, but could be seen rendering able assistance to their husbands and brothers in the fields.

As we ascended the valley, the mountains on either side drew closer and closer together, until it seemed almost as if the many waterfalls which leaped down their sides would drench us with their spray.

The Only Bad Weather Encountered During the Swiss Visitation.

As it began to grow dark, black thunder-clouds began to gather and chase one another up the valley along the faces of the mountains.

Our eyes had never before beheld such a sight.

It was worth the journey thither to see.

And then it began to rain.

At first it was only a very few small drops; but it continued to come down harder and harder, until we were climbing up the valley in the midst of a thoroughly soaking, all-night downpour.

Damp—water—wetness, seemed to be the keynote of the occasion.

Below us we could hear the complaining of the Lütschine as it fell from boulder to boulder; above us the rush of the many waterfalls, and all around us the patter and splash of the rain.

As the carriages were covered, most of the members of the party reached Grindelwald perfectly dry, but one—who shall be nameless—who in the exuberance of youth had gone ahead of the carriages to make the journey on foot, arrived at one of the hotels in Grindelwald almost as moist as if he had been dipped into the Lütschine.

Upon arrival at the hotel, he ordered the belated dinner for the other members of the party and, removing his saturated clothing, went to bed.

When the rest of the party drove up, about half an hour later, the porter at the door failed to make himself understood and they drove on to another hotel.

The pleasure and comfort of getting up from a warm bed and wriggling into clammy clothing, to countermand the order for dinner and join the rest of the party, need not be described.

An excellent dinner, served about three-quarters of an hour later, had the effect, in a large measure, of dispelling the memory of that experience.

The hotel where we were very delightfully entertained is known as the Bear Hotel, and is very excellently conducted by the Boss Brothers.

After a night of refreshing sleep we rose to find that it was still raining.

It might be well to note here that this was the only inclement weather that we experienced during all our Visitation on the Continent of Europe.

At all other times and places, oftentimes when it had been stormy before our arrival, we had nothing but "General Overseer's weather."

Visit to a Glacier.

Notwithstanding the rain, we took carriages, early in the morning, to the Upper Glacier, a very short distance from the hotel.

The drive was a very interesting one, a feature being a wooden schoolhouse, in the Swiss style of architecture, with mottos carved upon many of the timbers.

From a distance the view of the great "sea of ice" is a little disappointing, it looks so much like a mass of dirty snow.

When we had left the carriages and gone on foot to the place where a branch of the Lütschine flows out from under the foot of the glacier, and saw that it was a stupendous mass of clear blue ice, we had a great deal more respect for it.

Into this ice had been hewn a long grotto or tunnel ending with a circular chamber twelve feet in diameter, in which the keeper lighted a candle.

The walls of this grotto were of solid, transparent ice, a soft, radiant blue in color, and beautifully clean and clear, so that the light of the little candle could be very plainly seen, shining through a thickness of several feet of ice.

In this little chamber our party gathered, and the General Overseer offered a brief prayer for Zion in Zion City and throughout the world.

Our time here was very short, and we reluctantly left the glacier without further exploration.

On our way back to the hotel we were treated to a wonderful echo, sent back from the mountains to the note of an Alpine horn, a tremendous instrument about twelve or fourteen feet in length.

Its tone, however, was not unpleasing, and the echo very striking.

We felt that the laborer was worthy of his hire, and dropped a few coins into the outstretched hat of the weary-eyed man who furnished the lung power for the echo.

We returned to Interlaken by means of the inclined railway, and there took cars for Bern, the capital of Switzerland.

Bern.

Bern is one of the most picturesque of all the great cities in Switzerland, both on account of its striking situation, on a peninsula of sandstone rock formed by the Aare, the beautiful stream flowing one hundred feet below, and the many striking specimens of medieval architecture in the older portions.

The city is over eight hundred years old, and has been the seat of government of the Swiss Confederation since 1848.

An interesting feature of the ancient city is the arcades which flank the streets on both sides, forming a covered way for foot-passengers.

There is a beautiful view of the Alps from Bern, and here may also be observed the "Alpine glow," as the reflection of sunlight on the mountain peaks, after sunset, is called.

Here is also the Minster, the tower of which several of the members of our party ascended.

This tower is three hundred twenty-eight feet high and contains some very famous bells, one of them being one of the largest in the world, and another of them made of solid silver.

The Bears of Bern.

The meaning of the name Bern is "bears," and representations of bears in painting and sculpture are to be seen everywhere.

There is a tradition that the vicinity was infested with bears when the city was first established.

A family of real live bears, is kept by the city in a bear pit near one of the principal streets.

These bears and their predecessors are a very honorable institution in the city and own a very large estate.

We were told that many of the wealthy Bernese citizens, upon passing away, had bequeathed their entire property to these bears.

Notwithstanding their great wealth, however, these quadrupeds are very importunate beggars.

As soon as visitors appear at the railing overlooking their home, they approach, and either standing or sitting upright, beckon clumsily but imperiously with their heavy forepaws and gaping red mouths for carrots, rolls and other dainties, which are kept on sale near by, to be thrown to them.

While in Bern we were entertained at the Bernerhof, where we were joined by Evangelist Hodler and Deaconess Ruth Hofer.

Elder Jean Kradolfer, Evangelist Sophia Hertrich, Deaconess Sophie Baliff, Deaconess Seipt, and J. Rollier were also in Bern to attend the meeting of the General Overseer that evening.

Splendid Meeting Held in Bern.

This meeting was held in the *Salle Café des Alpes* at eight o'clock, on Wednesday evening, June 1, 1904.

The intense interest felt in Switzerland in the visit of the Prophet of God was shown by the fact that this hall, which seated about five hundred, was crowded to its utmost capacity, while many hundred more stood in the streets outside awaiting an opportunity to enter.

Elder Carl Hodler translated the Message of God's servant into the German language, the people listening with the closest attention and most absorbed interest for every word.

It is needless to say that the Message was straightforward, bold, unequivocal, but simple and truthful.

It was the proclamation of the Gospel of the Kingdom of God, made with all the power of the Prophet sent of God as the herald of the establishment of that Kingdom on the earth.

It was received prayerfully and thoughtfully by the majority of the audience.

At the close nearly all rose and earnestly and with apparent sincerity repeated the prayer of consecration.

Afterwards, several sick ones came to the General Overseer requesting prayer, and we rejoice to record that God answered immediately and with mighty power.

Members and friends of the Christian Catholic Church in

Zion in Bern, the officers of the Church present from Zurich, the members of the Visitation Party, and the General Overseer himself, all shared the feeling that if only there were time for more meetings God would work wonderful things for His glory and for the blessing of the people in Bern.

The following is a partial report of the General Overseer's address:

Salle Café des Alpes, Bern, Switzerland, Wednesday Evening, June 1, 1904.
*REPORTED BY I. M. S. AND A. W. N.

The meeting was opened with the singing of Hymn No. 3, "*Eine feste Burg ist unser Gott.*"

The Scripture lesson was read by the Rev. Jean Kradolfer, from the 35th chapter of the book of the Prophet Isaiah, and from Matthew 11:1-19, 14:1, 2, and 17:9-13.

Prayer was offered by the Rev. Carl Hodler, Elder-in-charge of the Christian Catholic Church in Zion on the Continent of Europe.

The General Overseer said:

Greeting.

I desire to thank God for the great privilege of speaking in the Capital of the Swiss Confederation.

This is my second visit to this beautiful land, and I am more than ever delighted with it.

I have only one night to talk to you in Bern, for my Around-the-World Visitation is drawing to a close.

I left Zion City on January 1st, and, when I get back there again, I shall have gone down one way and come back the other, around the world.

I am very grateful for this, which is my fourth journey around the world.

I ask your kind consideration, for, you see, I speak in English, which has to be translated into the German by our good Elder Hodler, and it is just possible that, while the Elder has a desire to translate correctly, he may not catch my exact meaning every time, and he may have a little difficulty in expressing, perfectly, my thought.

I am glad to have the privilege of speaking in the capital of the Swiss Confederation.

While I am not a Swiss citizen, I am one who has always looked upon Switzerland as the best governed country in Europe.

The tithes and offerings were received, while a hymn was sung.

The General Overseer then delivered his Message:

THE HOUSE OF WISDOM.

INVOCATION.

Let the words of my mouth, and the meditation of my heart be acceptable in Thy sight, be profitable unto this people, and unto all to whom these words shall come, in this and every land, in this and all the coming time, Till Jesus Come. Amen.

TEXT.

Wisdom is justified of all her children.

Purity the Central Pillar in the House of Wisdom.

In the House of Wisdom there are Seven Pillars, enumerated by the Apostle James as follows:

But the Wisdom that is from above is first Pure, then Peaceable, Gentle, Easy to be Intreated, Full of Mercy and Good Fruits, Without Variance, Without Hypocrisy.

Purity, therefore, is the Central Pillar in the House of Wisdom.

Jesus said, "Blessed are the pure in heart, for they shall see God."

Purity is necessary to Peace.

Peace cannot be gained without war upon impurity.

Men that are at peace are the men that make war on all that is impure.

John the Baptist was a preacher of Righteousness, of Purity, and he suffered death as the result of his boldness.

He maintained that adultery was against the commandment of God, although that stand got him into trouble with an adulteress who sat on the throne with king Herod.

The Prophet of God must fight impurity and the breaking of God's Commandments, even if that does bring him into conflict with kings and their paramours.

*The following report has not been revised by the General Overseer.

Speaking of his visit to the Rigi, the General Overseer said:

It is beautiful to be on the Rigi, beautiful to be on Mount Pilatus, but you cannot do your work there. You have to come down and fight in Bern, and in Zurich, and in Geneva, and in Paris, and in London, and help the people.

You never forget the sight, but you have to come down, just as Jesus and the three disciples had to come down from the Mount of Transfiguration.

The Dawn of the Restoration.

The Times of the Restoration begin with the dawn of the day, before the sunrise of the Lord's Coming.

On the Rigi there was a great deal of light before the sunrise—light everywhere, beautiful light.

I wondered.

The moon began to pale in the sky.

Still, there was no sun.

But the sun was really shining beyond these mountains—shining where we could not see it.

There is a long time sometimes in the dawn of the day.

The Christ's Day is a Thousand Years.

The dawn has been in the sky, and the Light will come suddenly.

I had my eyes turned to the Alps when suddenly I heard a cry: "The light has come!"

I turned and saw the sunrise.

The Christ has not come, but it will not be long.

Let us get ready for His Coming.

Rise and pray the

PRAYER OF CONSECRATION.

My God and Father, in Jesus' Name I come to Thee. Take me as I am. Give me sorrow for sin. May I hate sin for the sake of Jesus, the Lamb of God who taketh away the sin of the world, who is my Advocate with Thee. O Eternal Father, for His sake forgive my sins by Thy Spirit, give me a full Salvation for spirit, soul and body, here and now, and lead me to do Thy will and prepare for Thy coming. For Jesus' sake. Amen. [*The greater part of the audience followed the General Overseer very earnestly in the above prayer.*]

The meeting was closed with a short prayer by the General Overseer and the

BENEDICTION.

Beloved, abstain from every form of evil. And may the very God of Peace Himself sanctify you wholly; and I pray God your whole spirit and soul and body be preserved entire, without blame, unto the coming of our Lord Jesus, the Christ. Faithful is He that calleth you, who also will do it. The grace of our Lord Jesus, the Christ, the love of God, our Father, the fellowship of the Holy Spirit, our Comforter and Guide, one Eternal God, abide in you, bless you and keep you, and all the Israel of God everywhere, forever. Amen.

A Visit to President Comtese of the Swiss Confederation.

On Thursday, June 2d, at eleven o'clock in the morning, the General Overseer, and the members of his Visitation party, and several of the Officers of the Christian Catholic Church in Zion in Switzerland, also J. Rollier, his French interpreter, accompanied Mr. John Webber, Secretary of the American Legation at Bern, to the Federal Palace.

The General Overseer had an appointment to meet President Comtesse, of the Swiss Confederation.

The General Overseer and his interpreter, together with Mr. Webber, were almost immediately ushered into the President's private office, where they were in conference for about an hour.

During this interview the General Overseer found the President to be a very statesmanlike gentleman of keen perceptions and high ideals.

President Comtesse was very much interested in the story of Zion, the description of Zion City, and the outline of the teaching of the Christian Catholic Church in Zion, and closed the interview with a very hearty expression of his appreciation and friendship.

He then shook hands very cordially with each member of the party, who had been waiting in an anteroom, and the pleasant visit was at an end.

It was a significant and interesting fact that the only pictures on the walls of this anteroom, next to the President's private office, were those of George Washington and Abraham Lincoln.

Early in the afternoon of the same day, the General Overseer and his Visitation Party, accompanied by Elder and Evangelist Carl Hodler, Elder and Evangelist Percy Clibborn, Deaconess Ruth Hofer, and J. Rollier, departed for French Switzerland.

Beautiful Lake Geneva.

The first objective point was Geneva, lying at the foot of the lake of the same name, so famous in story and song.

The journey was a very delightful one, especially after reaching the shores of the lake at Lausanne.

Across the blue waters could be seen the mountains of Savoy and Valais, while smiling villages and picturesque cities dotted the shores on both sides.

This lake has been a favorite theme of writers of every nationality for centuries, and is perhaps the best known of all the lakes of Europe.

Geneva.

The sun was setting as we ran along the vine-clad hills on the shores of this beautiful body of water, into Geneva, one of the most historic cities in Europe.

Situated close to the border between France and Switzerland, on the shores of Lake Geneva and the Arve and Rhone rivers, Geneva is, in some respects, one of the most beautiful cities that we saw in all our travels.

On account of its being situated on the borders, it has become a great rendezvous for political offenders, adventurers, and rogues from all parts of the earth, so that the native Genevese are not proud of a large class of their fellow citizens.

Here we were guests at the beautiful Beau-Rivage Hotel, in front of which the late Empress Elizabeth of Austria was so cruelly stabbed by an anarchist, and in which she passed away.

First Zion Meeting in Geneva.

The meetings conducted by the General Overseer in Geneva were held in the *Casino de St. Pierre*, directly across the street from St. Peter's Cathedral, where John Calvin thundered forth the cheerless dogmas of his theology, and where his pulpit and chair are still to be seen.

This hall had a seating capacity of about six hundred fifty and was so crowded, when the first meeting was held, Thursday evening, June 2d, that many were turned away.

It was wonderful to see the intense earnestness and eagerness of these French-speaking people, who had never before heard the Zion Message, especially when one remembered that comparatively little Zion Literature had been published in the French language.

Many seemed led directly by the Spirit of God to His Prophet.

It is not to be wondered at that in this city, which is one of the greatest centers of infidelity in Europe, there were some who came to scoff, but it was wonderful to see how flat their scoffing fell, and how deeply and sincerely interested the great majority of the audience were.

It is always very difficult for a speaker of fire and force to make himself understood to his audience through a translator, but, on this occasion, the translations into French made by Elder Percy Clibborn seemed to convey to the hearers the spirit of the Message, and God greatly blessed the Word.

At no time during the meeting were there any signs of malicious disorder, the only demonstration of those who did not agree with the speaker, and were discourteous enough to manifest it, being foolish laughter.

Most of the people, however, had come to hear the Message honestly and in sincerity, and showed marked disapproval of the silly laughter of the scoffers.

In the audience were several members and friends of the Christian Catholic Church in Zion, who had been holding up the Banner of Zion in the beautiful but wicked city of Geneva.

It is needless to speak of their great delight in having the privilege of seeing and hearing their General Overseer.

The following is the report of the Message of the Prophet of God:

Casino de St. Pierre, Geneva, Switzerland, Thursday Evening, June 2, 1904.
*REPORTED BY E. W. AND A. W. N.

After the singing of a hymn, in French, the Scripture lesson was read by Elder Percy Clibborn from the 35th chapter of the Book of the Prophet Isaiah and from the 11th chapter of the Gospel according to St. Matthew.

Prayer was offered by Joseph Rollier.

*The following report has not been revised by the General Overseer.

A RESTORATION MESSAGE.

INVOCATION.

Let the words of my mouth, and the meditation of my heart be acceptable in Thy sight, be profitable unto this people, and unto all to whom these words shall come, in this and every land, in this and all the coming time, Till Jesus Come. Amen.

Greeting.

I thank God for my visit to Switzerland.

This is my first meeting in a French canton.

I spent a very pleasant hour, this morning, with the President of your Confederation, a courteous and able statesman, with whom I have had the pleasure of talking concerning many matters of interest.

I feel that he is a very noble representative of the French cantons as well as of the whole Confederation.

I come to you, praying that God may make this meeting a blessing to many.

I have many friends in and around this city, and some members of the Christian Catholic Church in Zion.

I bring you the greetings of my people in all the lands.

The General Overseer then spoke very carefully and thoughtfully of the coming of Elijah, the Prophet of the Restoration, and of the work that he was sent to do.

In discussing the work of the Restoration of God's Covenants to His people, and especially the Covenant of Divine Healing, he was enabled to make many telling points of intensely practical application for the transforming of the lives of the people.

While some laughed scornfully at his serious appeals for a holy life, the greater part of the congregation was deeply moved, joining heartily, at the close, in the

PRAYER OF CONSECRATION.

My God and Father, in Jesus' Name I come to Thee. Take me as I am. Make me what I ought to be, in spirit, in soul, in body. Deliver me from evil, that I may praise Thee in a clean body, in a clean soul, in a clean spirit. For Jesus' sake. Amen.

The General Overseer then pronounced the following

BENEDICTION.

Beloved, abstain from every form of evil. And may the very God of peace Himself sanctify you wholly; and I pray God your whole spirit and soul and body be preserved entire, without blame, unto the coming of our Lord Jesus, the Christ. Faithful is He that calleth you, who also will do it. The grace of our Lord Jesus, the Christ, the love of God our Father, the fellowship of the Holy Spirit, our Comforter and Guide, one Eternal God, abide in you, bless you and keep you, and all the Israel of God everywhere, forever. Amen.

Insolence and Impudence of Geneva Newspaper Reporters.

At the close of this service, the General Overseer was treated to an example of the supreme insolence and impudence of Geneva newspaper men.

Without invitation or permission, several of them boldly opened the door and walked into his dressing-room.

Notwithstanding this breach of good behavior on their part, the General Overseer treated them courteously and replied with great patience to their insolent inquiries.

When, however, one of them, with a leer on his filthy, sensual face, flagrantly insulted him, the General Overseer administered a sharp but perfectly courteous rebuke, and bade them all good evening.

As might be expected, the reports in their papers the following day were, for the most part, greatly distorted, and filled with an arrogant assumption on the part of the writers that they were perfectly competent to pass judgment and criticism upon spiritual matters.

Divine Healing Meeting in Geneva.

The following morning, Friday, June 3d, at ten o'clock, the General Overseer held a Divine Healing meeting in the *Casino de St. Pierre*.

At this meeting the attendance was large and the attention even more earnest than at the meeting of the night before.

There was a deep spiritual atmosphere in the gathering, which bespoke great blessing for the people.

The following is an outline report of the teaching:

Casino de St. Pierre, Geneva, Switzerland, Friday Morning, June 3, 1904.
*REPORTED BY I. M. S. AND A. W. N.

The meeting was opened by the General Overseer's pronouncing the

*The following report has not been revised by the General Overseer.

INVOCATION.

God, be merciful unto us and bless us,
And cause Thy face to shine upon us;
That Thy Way may be known upon earth,
Thy Saving Health among all the Nations;
For the sake of Jesus. Amen.

A Hymn was then sung:

A L'ŒUVRE!

Dès que l'aube dépose
Ses perles sur les fleurs,
Dès que s'ouvre la rose
Aux brillantes couleurs,
Dès que l'ombre s'efface
Devant le jour qui luit,
A l'œuvre! le temps passe,
A l'œuvre avant la nuit.

Work, for the night is coming,
Work thro' the morning hours;
Work while the dew is sparkling,
Work 'mid springing flow'rs;
Work, when the day grows brighter
Work in the glowing sun;
Work, for the night is coming,
When man's work is done.

Elder Percy J. Clibborn read from the Inspired Word of God the 8th chapter of Matthew the first seventeen verses.

Prayer was offered by the General Overseer, after which a Hymn was sung, and the announcements were made by Elder Clibborn.

JESUS THE PRESENT DAY HEALER.

The General Overseer pronounced the

INVOCATION.

Let the words of my mouth, and the meditations of my heart, be acceptable in Thy sight, be profitable unto this people and unto all to whom these words shall come, in this and every land, in this and all the coming time, Till Jesus Come. Amen.

TEXT.

And when even was come, they brought unto Him many possessed with devils: and He cast out the spirits with a Word, and healed all that were sick:

That it might be fulfilled which was spoken by Isaiah the prophet, saying, Himself took our infirmities, and bare our diseases.

Speaking on this text, the General Overseer laid the foundation for his teaching in the proclamation of the important truth of the supremacy of the Father.

The Word with which Jesus cast out the evil spirits he showed to have been the Word of His Father.

Proceeding to the great present-day work of Jesus as the Healer, the man of God pointed out and proved, on the testimony of the most noted of the world's physicians, the worse than uselessness of the so-called science of medicine as a means of healing.

Bringing the matter down to a present day practical reality, the General Overseer described, very vividly, some wonderful answers of God to the Prayer of Faith for the healing of the sick which had occurred in his own experience.

Passing on to the discussion of the origin and cause of disease, he spoke with convincing power upon the duty of God's people in the care of their bodies and of the sin of defiling them in any way, whether by filthy eating, drinking, living or thinking.

After a brief but very profitable discourse concerning the relative order of Teaching, Preaching, and Healing, the General Overseer dealt with some of the false teaching that was turning the people away from God.

Among other things he exposed the fallacies of Christian Science.

God's Messenger closed his teaching with a ringing call to Repentance, and then led the people in the following earnest

PRAYER OF CONSECRATION.

My God and Father, I come to Thee in Jesus' Name. Help me by Thy Spirit to confess my sin. Give me power to do right to any whom I have wronged, to my fellow men and to Thee my God. Give me faith to trust in Thee my Father, to trust Thee for deliverance in spirit, soul, and body. Give me power to live a good life, helping others, and living as Jesus would have me live. For His sake. Amen.

The Services were closed with the General Overseer's pronouncing the

BENEDICTION.

Beloved, abstain from every form of evil. And may the very God of Peace Himself sanctify you wholly; and I pray God your whole Spirit, and Soul, and Body, be preserved entire without blame, unto the coming of our Lord Jesus, the Christ. Faithful is He that calleth you, who also will do it. The Grace of our Lord Jesus, the Christ, the Love of God, our Father, the fellowship of the Holy Spirit, our Comforter and Guide, one Eternal God, abide in you, bless you, and keep you, and all the Israel of God everywhere, forever. Amen.

Prayer With Thirty Sick Ones in Geneva.

The General Overseer prayed with thirty sick ones at the close of this service, and God honored the Prayer of Faith, according to His Everlasting Covenants.

The afternoon was spent by the French-speaking members of our little party in Restoration work in the city, while those of us who did not know the language attended to some matters of business and took a number of photographs.

The last meeting of the Geneva Visitation was held that evening in the *Casino de St. Pierre*.

Once more the little all was full to overflowing, and again the Message of the General Overseer was received with earnestness of spirit on the part of the great majority of the audience.

Here, as in Bern, we all felt that it would have been a great blessing had the General Overseer had the time for a longer series of meetings.

We knew, however, that the precious Seed had been sown faithfully and lovingly, and we believed that God, in His Infinite Wisdom and Mercy, would give the increase.

Friends of Zion Made Everywhere by Zion Literature Mission.

These meetings in Geneva had greatly rejoiced our hearts and encouraged us by bringing out many true and strong friends of Zion, among them many of the English-speaking residents, who had been led to an interest in the work through reading LEAVES OF HEALING, sent to hotels by Zion Literature Mission.

It is with great joy that we record, in this connection, that throughout the world we found members and friends of Zion who had been led into the light of truth through Zion Literature sent out through this Mission.

The following is a partial report of the General Overseer's Message at the

Friday Evening Meeting in Geneva.

Casino de St. Pierre, Geneva, Switzerland, Friday Evening, June 3, 1904.
*REPORTED BY E. W. AND A. W. N.

The Services were opened by the Congregation's singing "Debout."

Debout, sainte cohorte,
Soldats du Roi des rois!
Tenez d'une main forte
L'étendard de la croix!
Au sentier de la gloire
Jesus-Christ vous conduit;
De victoire en victoire
Il mene qui le suit.

Prayer was offered by the Rev. Arthur S. Booth-Clibborn.

The General Overseer then proceeded, after the usual Invocation of God's blessing, to a clear statement of the truth that all sin, sickness, sorrow, misery and other evil were the work of the Devil, giving his unanswerable proofs from the Word of God.

Graphic and dramatic was the narration of the story of Job, as given by the speaker, and very convincing was his application of the truth contained in it to the subject.

The audience readily caught the idea, saw the logic of it, and showed their acceptance.

It was in response to a solemn Call to Repentance, Confession, and Consecration, that practically the entire congregation rose and repeated the

PRAYER OF CONSECRATION.

My God and Father, I come to Thee in Jesus' Name. Take me as I am. Make me what I ought to be, in spirit, in soul, and in body, For Jesus' sake.

The Service was closed by the General Overseer's pronouncing the

BENEDICTION.

Beloved, abstain from every form of evil. And may the very God of Peace Himself sanctify you wholly; and I pray God your whole spirit and soul and body be preserved entire, without blame, unto the coming of our Lord Jesus, the Christ. Faithful is He that calleth you, who also will do it. The grace of our Lord Jesus, the Christ, the love of God, our Father, the fellowship of the Holy Spirit, our Comforter and Guide, one Eternal God, abide in you, bless you and keep you, and all the Israel of God everywhere, forever. Amen.

*The following report has not been revised by the General Overseer.

On Saturday morning, June 4th, we found when we rose, that the clouds and haze that had veiled the mountains had cleared away, and we were treated to a magnificent view of Mount Blanc, fifteen thousand seven hundred eighty-two feet high, the most lofty of all the mountains in Europe. It was a wonderful sight, wrapped in its mantle of perennial snow.

Early that morning, all the members of our party except the General Overseer and his French interpreter, Mr. Rollier, embarked on the handsome lake Steamer *Lausanne* for a visit to Chillon Castle and the City of Lausanne.

A Visit to United States Minister Hill.

In the meantime, the General Overseer and his interpreter went by rail to Nyon, a very pretty suburb of Geneva, lying on the shores of the lake between that city and Lausanne.

Here the General Overseer visited the United States Minister to Switzerland, Mr. Hill, whose summer residence, "La Solitude," is in this place.

The General Overseer was very cordially received by the representative of the United States Government and very pleasantly entertained at luncheon.

The interview was most interesting and satisfactory.

Beauties of Lake Geneva.

Our trip up the lake was most delightful, the weather being perfect and the scenery full of the indescribable charm that has made Lake Geneva famous for centuries.

At the upper end of the lake the hills give way to towering mountains, a majestic setting for the great, white Dent du Midi, which gleams through the rugged opening at the south end of the lake.

Beside the many cities and villages along the lake, the names of which were almost as familiar to us, through literature, as the names of the towns along the shores of Lake Michigan, were the chateaux and villas of many famous people and families, some of them historic.

All these were very interestingly pointed out to us by Elder Percy Clibborn, who, for a number of years, carried on Salvation Army work in French Switzerland, and especially in the Swiss Riviera, as the northern shore of Lake Geneva is called

Among other distinguishing features of Lake Geneva, or *Lac Leman*, as the Swiss call it, are the bright blue color of its waters, contrasted with the pale green of the other Swiss lakes, and the very picturesque character of the two-masted barques that fleck its bosom with white.

The two slender, graceful sails of these barques are curved in opposite directions like the wings of a swallow, and make a most charming picture as they gleam in the sunlight against the green shores and are reflected in the quiet waters.

Visit to the Castle of Chillon.

Our visit to the Castle of Chillon was necessarily a very brief one.

We disembarked from the *Lausanne* at Territet, and there took an electric car to the castle.

As we had to return almost at once, we did not have time to enter, but were compelled to content ourselves with looking at the grim old walls of this famous castle and dungeon across the narrow stretch of waters that separates it from the mainland; for it is built on a rocky island, about twenty yards from the shore.

The story of this famous building goes back so far into antiquity that its beginning is lost. Historical mention is made of it as early as 830 A. D.

The Counts of Savoy often resided in this castle, and until very late years it was used as a State Prison.

It is now, after having been thoroughly restored and somewhat altered, used as a historical museum and a depository for archives.

The castle is chiefly celebrated, perhaps, by the poem of Lord Byron, "The Prisoner of Chillon," which was composed by him in the Anchor Inn at Ouchy, in 1817.

The prisoner described by Lord Byron is a myth.

The most celebrated of the historic prisoners of Chillon was Francis Bonivard who was confined there from 1530 to 1536.

During these six years he walked in a circle upon the stone pavement of his cell until his feet had worn a deep path in the rock.

Lausanne.

After a brief glimpse at this castle we returned to Territet, where we took the *Lausanne* to Ouchy, the port of Lausanne, which lies higher up on the hillside.

Lausanne is the capital of the Canton de Vaud, and is very beautifully situated on the terraced slopes of Mont Joret. Above the city are its cathedral and castle.

The newer parts of the city are very handsome, while the older parts, in the center, although not so prepossessing, perhaps, are exceedingly interesting on account of the hilly, narrow, twisting streets, and the peculiar architecture of the buildings.

Lausanne is a university town, and a great favorite of English people who desire to study the French language.

Our temporary home, while at Lausanne, was at the Hotel Gibbon, in the garden behind the dining-room of which, the historian, Gibbon, wrote the last part of his history of Rome, in 1787.

The first meeting conducted by the General Overseer in Lausanne was held in the *Maison du Peuple*, on Saturday afternoon, June 4, 1904.

As in Geneva, a large part of the audience was composed of thoughtful and earnest people, who desired to hear and learn.

There were present also a number of medical students, who disgraced themselves by making a slight disturbance.

God overruled all and there was much blessing.

The following is a report of the substance of the General Overseer's Message:

Maison du Peuple, Lausanne, Switzerland, Saturday Afternoon, June 4, 1904

*REPORTED BY I. M. S. AND A. W. N.

The Services opened with the singing of a hymn in the French language.

The General Overseer said:

Greeting.

I am glad to be in the ancient City of Lausanne, and to have an opportunity of speaking to you. [Some disturbances.]

I am sure that the young men now present will maintain the high opinion which visitors generally have, and which I certainly have, concerning the character and the conduct of all the congregations of Switzerland.

I have had nothing to complain of about the tens of thousands of people whom I have addressed in various parts of Switzerland since I came to this country.

Elder Percy Clibborn read from the Inspired Word of God, the first seventeen verses of the 8th chapter of the Gospel according to St. Matthew.

Prayer was offered by Joseph Rollier, and the announcements were made by Elder Clibborn.

THE WORKS OF THE FATHER THROUGH THE CHRIST.

INVOCATION.

Let the words of my mouth, and the meditation of my heart be acceptable in Thy sight, be profitable unto this people, and unto all to whom these words shall come, in this and every land, in this and all the coming time, Till Jesus Come. Amen.

TEXT.

And when even was come, they brought unto Him many possessed with devils: and He cast out the spirits with a Word, and healed all that were sick:

That it might be fulfilled which was spoken by Isaiah the prophet, saying, Himself took our infirmities, and bare our diseases.

He cast out the spirits with "a Word," not His word.

Jesus' Words and Works the Words and Works of the Father.

I desire to make a few remarks upon the alteration of that word and show you the difference between "a Word" and "His Word."

Jesus said "Of Myself I can do nothing." "The Father that dwelleth in Me He doeth the works."

The words that He spoke were the words of the Eternal Father, the Eternal Spirit speaking through Him.

Keep that always in mind.

It is not the Son of God, it is not the Son of Man, not our

*The following report has not been revised by the General Overseer.

Great Elder Brother, but the Father through Him that does the work.

When the woman touched the hem of His garment and was healed, He turned to her and said, "Daughter."

It is only a father who says daughter.

He said, "Daughter, thy faith hath made thee whole."

When the man who was paralyzed was carried in, Jesus turned to him and said, "Son, thy sins are forgiven thee."

It was the Father speaking.

Remember that our Lord Jesus, the Christ, never claimed that He did any works.

Prayer Must Be Addressed to the Father.

In that connection let me make another observation.

You who are Christians and pray to God, has it never impressed you sadly, that you get so few answers to prayer?

Does it never occur to you that your prayers may not be acceptable to God?

When Jesus was here He taught us to pray to the Father.

He said, "When ye pray, say, Our Father."

When the Holy Spirit comes into your heart He teaches you to cry, "Abba Father!"

Our Lord Jesus, the Christ, never taught us to pray to Himself.

His Name is not in the Lord's Prayer.

It was only at the end of His life that He said, "Hitherto ye have asked nothing in My Name, but now ask in My Name."

He is the Advocate with the Father, and the Holy Spirit is the Advocate with us.

You must pray to God, our Father, and you must pray in the Name of our Lord Jesus, the Christ.

There is no other name under heaven whereby you can be saved.

A vast majority of Christians are not praying as the Christ taught them to pray.

Remember that the Christ came to glorify the Father.

All His works, throughout all the ages, have been wrought for the one purpose of bringing the Kingdom to the Father, that God may be All and in All.

And when even was come, they brought unto Him many possessed with devils: and He cast out the spirits with a word, and healed all that were sick: That it might be fulfilled which was spoken by Isaiah the prophet, saying, Himself took our infirmities, and bare our diseases.

Jesus healed all that were sick.

He has not changed.

The General Overseer then proceeded to the teaching of the distinction between the spirit and soul; to the proclamation of a Full Redemption for spirit, soul and body; to the proof of Divine Healing as a present day reality; and to the setting forth of the logic of his contention that medicine is not a science.

Taking up the Christ's methods of healing, he directed attention to the necessity for Purity in all things, referring especially to the sin and folly of defiling the body with unclean food, such as swine's flesh.

This seemed to disturb the medical students very seriously, and there was some disorder.

The General Overseer held his audience, however, and proceeded with his discourse.

After a brief but pungent reference to the sin of tobacco smoking, the Messenger of God said:

Sin the Source of all Disease and Misery.

Sin is the transgression of the laws of God, the source of all disease, sorrow and misery in the world.

Sow to the flesh and you will reap corruption.

You and I have no right to sow evil.

You and I are God's children and we have no right to do evil.

We are responsible to God, and it is our duty to recognize that responsibility.

I venture to say that the man who puts these wicked things beneath his feet and does rightly, is the happiest man. He is acceptable to God and pleasing to his fellow man.

You must be that, or else you are a curse to your fellow men.

Our Lord Jesus, the Christ, demands that you shall be clean.

Disease never would have been in this world but for sin.

The miseries of humanity are always the Devil's work.

[Some of the medical students again interrupted.]

I do not think that these interruptions have been unkind; they have been simply inconsiderate.

May I remind you young men that when a stranger comes to your city to speak to you, who is not seeking or asking anything from you, but simply desires to speak quietly to you, that you at least owe to him and to yourselves the respect to receive him quietly? [Applause loud and long.]

I feel greatly indebted to the French people for the courtesy shown to me, ever since I landed.

I had a splendid hearing in Paris, and also for the last two days in Geneva.

I have heard so much about Lausanne, as a city of such intelligent people, that I thought I should like to speak here.

I never flatter people, but I like to be on good terms with them and to tell them the truth about themselves.

The Services were closed with the pronouncing of the

BENEDICTION.

Beloved, abstain from every form of evil. And may the very God of Peace Himself sanctify you wholly; and I pray God your whole spirit and soul and body be preserved entire, without blame, unto the coming of our Lord Jesus, the Christ. Faithful is He that calleth you, who also will do it. The grace of our Lord Jesus, the Christ, the love of God our Father, the fellowship of the Holy Spirit, our Comforter and Guide, one Eternal God, abide in you, bless you and keep you, and all the Israel of God everywhere, forever. Amen.

The Zion Salutation, "*La paix soir t'avec vous!*" was given by the General Overseer.

Saturday Evening Meeting in Lausanne.

On Saturday evening, June 4th, the *Maison du Peuple* was crowded to its fullest capacity with a very deeply interested audience.

There seemed to be a small element present determined to make trouble; but the sympathies of the great majority were strongly against these few, and they took pains to let them know it. Every outbreak of anything like disorder was met with expressions of the strongest disapproval on the part of nine out of every ten people present.

On one occasion, when some one had started a little disturbance by rising to his feet in the rear of the hall, and bawling out some insult in French, a gentleman of high standing in the city rose and addressed the disturbers in no gentle terms.

He laid it upon them, if they did not respect themselves and the city in which they were, at least to respect the gray hairs of the speaker and to give him the hearing which he deserved.

This speech was very warmly applauded, and the disturbers were shamed.

It is but fair to the city and people of Lausanne to say that most of the disturbers were not citizens of the place; but medical students from other European countries.

At this meeting, as in Geneva, we were surprised at the number of loyal and enthusiastic friends of Zion who came forward—friends gained through the work of Zion Literature Mission.

Many new friends were also made among the earnest people who, on this occasion, heard the teaching of Zion for the first time.

Again we felt the great need of further work in this overripe harvest field, and our hearts were raised in prayer to God that He would give to His Prophet the means for taking advantage, for His glory and the blessing of the people, of the splendid start that had been made in Lausanne.

The following is a résumé of the Message of the General Overseer:

Maison de Peuple, Lusanne, Switzerland, Saturday Evening, June 4, 1904.
*REPORTED BY E. W. AND A. W. N.

After the singing of a song in the French language, Elder Percy Clibborn read from the Inspired Word of God, from the 10th chapter of the Acts of the Apostles.

Prayer was then offered by Joseph Rollier.

The General Overseer, after the invocation of God's blessing upon his words, took as his text the 38th verse of the 10th chapter of the Acts of the Apostles:

Even Jesus of Nazareth, how that God anointed Him with the Holy Spirit and with power: who went about doing good, and healing all that were oppressed of the Devil; for God was with Him.

He then proceeded to show that the Son of God was made manifest that He might destroy the works of the Devil.

*The following report has not been revised by the General Overseer.

Taking up the objection of many, founded on the words of the Apostle, "Whom the Lord loveth He chasteneth," the man of God showed, from the Greek and by common-sense reasoning, how that could never mean, "whom the Lord loveth He maketh sick," but must mean, "whom the Lord loveth He instructeth, nourisheth, traineth and developeth," as a good, kind, loving father his child.

In the practical application of the truth of Divine Healing to present day necessities, he told the striking story of the miracle that God wrought in the healing of Deliah King, when she was dying of cancer at the age of sixty-eight years, at the same time proving the uselessness of physicians and surgeons from the similar case of Frederick William, Emperor of Germany, who died, although he had the very best medical skill that the world had to offer.

The General Overseer closed his discourse with a brief description of the City of Zion and of the work of God in founding and establishing that City; also an account of the blessings that have come to His children in and through that place.

The Service was closed by the General Overseer's pronouncing the

BENEDICTION.

Beloved, abstain from every form of evil. And may the very God of Peace Himself sanctify you wholly; and I pray God your whole spirit and soul and body be preserved entire, without blame, unto the coming of our Lord Jesus, the Christ. Faithful is He that calleth you, who also will do it. The grace of our Lord Jesus, the Christ, the love of God, our Father, the fellowship of the Holy Spirit, our Comforter and Guide, one Eternal God, abide in you, bless you and keep you, and all the Israel of God everywhere, forever. Amen.

That night was spent in Hotel Gibbon, which is on one of the principal squares of the city.

Orgies of a Company of Lausanne Students.

At five o'clock the next morning we were awakened by the singing of about forty or fifty students who had gathered in the square.

They were decorated with garlands and green caps and scarfs, while one of their number carried a huge basket of flowers, and was resplendent in a broad scarf that swept from his shoulders to his feet.

They had piled their coats, sticks and other impedimenta in a heap in the middle of the square, and were skipping around them in a circle, with joined hands, singing a French students' drinking song.

At the end of each stanza of their song, they would stop, let go hands, and waving their arms, chant their school cry, which probably is a first cousin to the American college yell.

Then they would join hands again and take up their song, which reminded us, more than anything else, of the chant of the naked Arabs at Aden, when they were importuning us to throw coppers to them.

We were informed that this was a club, of a musical or literary nature, and that the members had been manifesting their high artistic or literary attainments by drinking all night.

When this orgie in front of the hotel was over, most of the young men trooped off in response to the call of one of their number, in French, "Let's go to church!"

A little later in the morning we took train for our last stopping-place in French Switzerland, the quaint old city of Neuchatel, lying on the steep slopes of the Jura Mountains, on the northern shore of the Lake of Neuchatel.

The ride to this city from Lausanne was along the lake shore for about one half the distance, making the journey on this rare spring morning one of great pleasure and interest.

One of the first places through which we passed, after reaching the lake shore, was Grandson, the scene of several battles, the principal one of which was that fought on March 3, 1476, when twenty thousand Swiss, fighting for their independence, utterly defeated fifty thousand Burgundians under Charles the Bold, Duke of Burgundy.

Neuchatel.

At Neuchatel, we were very pleasantly received at the Grand Hotel Bellevue, on the lake shore, from which we had a magnificent view of Mont Blanc, the Jungfrau, Eiger, Mönch, and many others of the highest and most famous Alps.

On the hill above the city, we found a very interesting old castle or chateau, built in the twelfth, fifteenth and seventeenth centuries, in the prison of which Elder Percy Clibborn was once locked up for twenty-six days, on a charge of holding religious meetings after he had been expelled from the canton. Here, also, Elder Catherine Booth-Clibborn was once imprisoned.

Near by was the abbey church, built in the latter part of the twelfth century. In front of the church was a statue of the reformer, Farel, who lived and labored here in the cause of truth and righteousness in the sixteenth century.

Lord's Day Afternoon Meeting in Neuchatel.

The General Overseer held but one meeting in Neuchatel, that of the Lord's Day afternoon, in the *Salle de Conference* a large, well-lighted hall, seating about twelve hundred people.

The place was well filled, about a thousand people being present, and for the most part there was the most perfect order and the most respectful attention.

On the platform with the General Overseer, besides the members of the Visitation Party, and those who had accompanied him in the tour of French Switzerland, were ex-commissioner Arthur S. Booth-Clibborn, and the ex-Maréchale Mrs. Catherine Booth-Clibborn, formerly of the Salvation Army, but more recently in charge of the Christian Mission, in Amsterdam, Holland.

The translation of the General Overseer's Message into the French was done by Elder Percy Clibborn, and by Rev. (now Elder) Arthur S. Booth-Clibborn.

The audience was a very intelligent one, for the most part, and it was evident that many of them understood English.

The interest was intense, and there were many expressions of warmest approval as the Messenger of God proclaimed the Everlasting Gospel of the Kingdom.

It was glorious to see nearly the entire audience rise, at the close, and join, with deep sincerity, in the Prayer of Consecration.

The following is, in part, a report of the Message:

Salle de Conference, Neuchatel, Switzerland, Lord's Day Afternoon, June 5, 1904.
*REPORTED BY I. M. S. AND A. W. N.

The Services were opened by the spirited singing of a Hymn, *A L'œuvre* in the French tongue, the greater part of the audience joining.

The Rev. Arthur S. Booth-Clibborn read from the Inspired Word of God the 35th chapter of the Book of the Prophet Isaiah, and the 1st chapter of the Gospel according to St. Mark.

Prayer was offered by the Rev. Percy Clibborn, Elder in the Christian Catholic Church in Zion.

The General Overseer said:

Greeting.

Permit me to thank God for the privilege of speaking in this city, familiar as I am in some degree with its historical record.

I am glad to be here to deliver the first address in connection with the Christian Catholic Church in Zion, of which I am the General Overseer.

I had the joy, this afternoon, of meeting a few members of this Church who live in and around this city, and some who have done me the honor to come a considerable distance.

I shall close my brief tour in Switzerland with this address.

I have very greatly appreciated the kindness that has been extended to me in Zurich and in Bern, and in Geneva and Lausanne, and now in this city.

Permit me not only to thank my friends and people, but the authorities, and not least President Comtesse, who so kindly received me, and with whom I had a very long conversation.

It would be proper, also, for me to speak a word of thanks for the kindness of the American minister, Mr. Hill, and to thank all the friends everywhere for the many gracious courtesies they have extended to me.

I ask you to pray for me, as this is the twenty-sixth meeting I have addressed during the two weeks that I have been in Switzerland, with much traveling and correspondence and many interviews besides.

Kindly give me your consideration and bear with my translator in the address that I am about to deliver.

*The following report has not been revised by the General Overseer.

THE BEGINNING OF THE GOSPEL.

INVOCATION.

Let the words of my mouth and the meditation of my heart be acceptable in Thy sight, be profitable unto this people, and unto all to whom these words shall come, in this and every land, in this and all the coming time, Till Jesus Come. Amen.

TEXT.

Now after that John was delivered up, Jesus came into Galilee, preaching the Gospel of God, and saying, The time is fulfilled, and the Kingdom of God is at hand: repent ye, and believe in the Gospel.

The Christ's Work the Destruction of the Work of the Devil.

The Gospel sends you a Message to destroy the works of the Devil, who continues to sow disease, who is the enemy that sows tares in the field of the body, and in the field of the soul, and in the field of the spirit.

He is always sowing tares while the Church is sleeping.

Our business is to uproot them and prepare them for the Fire, that the wheat shall not utterly be destroyed.

The time of reaping has come.

The harvest is ready, and the Master will not take tares into His garner.

Oh, I want to see God's children saved!

How touching it is to see a Daniel praying, confessing the sins of God's people, and pleading with God that they may put their sins away by righteousness!

That was what Jesus did.

That is what Jesus is doing today, pleading for us that we may be wise, that we may be saved, that we may be healed and cleansed and kept and that we may obey Him, and be prepared for the Master's use, pure and good mothers and fathers and friends.

He pleads for us that we may have power to spread Purity and not Impurity.

The Gospel is the Gospel of Salvation from Sin, disease and Death, and from all the powers of Hell.

The Times of the Restoration of All Things Are Dawning.

Soon the Sun of Righteousness will rise.

A few mornings ago I was on the top of the Rigi.

It had been a delightful night.

It seemed as if I could scarcely sleep, it was so beautiful.

One felt as if one could almost touch the Alps all around.

The light came an hour or so before the sun rose, and everything that the darkness had concealed was gradually restored.

Then at last, suddenly, the sun rose, and three hundred miles of mountains and plains were revealed.

But I had seen the sunlight before the sun itself rose.

It touched the highest peaks of the Alps.

And so I see the Christ before He comes.

His Light has come.

When He comes it will be too late to get ready.

Beloved friends, get ready now; get ready now.

After we have prayed, my dear brother, Arthur S. Booth-Clibborn, and his beloved wife, whom you have always known as La Maréchale in the Salvation Army, desire to say something, and I have a letter in my hands which I will read to you.

Pray with me.

PRAYER OF CONSECRATION.

My God and Father, I come to Thee in Jesus' Name. Take me as I am and make me what I ought to be. Give me a True Repentance, a True Faith and a Real Obedience, no matter what it costs. Make me really one in Thy Kingdom, make me a true member of Thy Church, and give me power to serve Thee all the days until Thou dost come, till Thou dost take me to Thyself. For the sake of Jesus. Amen. [*The above prayer was repeated, clause by clause, by the greater portion of the audience.*]

Rev. Arthur S. Booth-Clibborn and Rev. Catherine Booth-Clibborn Received into the Christian Catholic Church in Zion.

I shall not pronounce the Benediction until after these statements are made. They are official, and, for certain reasons, are made in Neuchatel today.

The Church of which I am the General Overseer consists of about two equal portions.

One half, I suppose, have been won to God from the world and the other half have entered into fellowship with me from the churches, and a number from missions outside of the churches.

Eight years ago the Christian Catholic Church in Zion numbered four hundred fifty members.

Of actual members today we probably have one hundred thousand throughout the world, and with the families of the people and those who attend our ministry who are leaders everywhere we are probably ministering to a million people, and we influence many millions altogether.

God's Leading Shown.

My friend Arthur S. Booth-Clibborn was a reader of LEAVES OF HEALING while he was Commissioner in the Salvation Army, with his beloved wife, the leader of the Army in Holland and Belgium.

I knew him not, but he began to realize that in LEAVES OF HEALING there was a Message for him.

He was born a Quaker, and they are very conservative.

He had not entered into the Salvation Army without great consideration, and his wife had not married him without great consideration. [Laughter.]

But there they were fighting for God, for humanity, in the organization which they believed to be the best to fulfil the great purposes of God in the world.

My friend Arthur S. Booth-Clibborn quietly read LEAVES OF HEALING year after year, and eventually he and his wife paid me a visit in Zion City, two and one-half years ago.

They came into Zion and then they and I thought it best that they should step out for a while, anyway until they could be quite sure that they could enter and stay there.

I think they were right.

They have paid me another visit, after working in what they have termed "The Christian Mission," and in which I have no doubt God has greatly blessed them in Holland and Belgium.

But it seems to me as if the blessing was all sent to Zion, because I have the most of their officers in Zion City today, and quite a number of their members.

They were teaching—especially our brother—the things that God had taught him, not only through LEAVES OF HEALING, but by His Spirit.

In the wonderful way that God leads, they have now placed in my hands their applications for membership in the Christian Catholic Church in Zion.

My brother really has been in Zion all the time, and our sister has undoubtedly been getting there all the time.

She asks me to put him first, but I shall read her letter, and then state that a similar application has been made by my brother, Arthur S. Booth-Clibborn.

Letter From Mrs. Catherine Booth-Clibborn.

The General Overseer here read the following letter:

NEUCHATEL, June 5, 1904.

DEAR DR. DOWIE:—I feel that I *ought* to and can accept you as Elijah the Prophet and Forerunner, and this I do with *all my heart*.

I offer myself to you for the Kingdom of God in Zion, with one prayer that His purposes may be accomplished in and through me.

You understand my vocation received direct from God as a child.

The greatest grief of my life has been to find myself hindered in fulfilling it, but my faith in Him who has permitted the trial has never been shaken, and I am convinced that no human power can frustrate His purposes concerning those who have sacrificed all for His sake.

Yours to follow the Lamb whithersoever He goeth,

CATHERINE BOOTH-CLIBBORN.

I make the announcement now that I gladly receive them into the fellowship and communion of the Christian Catholic Church in Zion.

I shall hope to have the joy of ordaining them into our ministry in London, this day week.

May God bless them.

Arthur S. Booth-Clibborn spoke very earnestly, and with evident effectiveness, in the French language, relating, in brief, the story of his relations with the General Overseer, and some of the reasons that induced him to resign from the Salvation Army, in which he had served for many years as a commissioner, and become a member of the Christian Catholic Church in Zion.

He also referred to the causes that had led to his withdrawal, over two years before, and gave, with great force and clearness, the reasons why he now desired to again become a member of that Church and to devote his time, his talents, his life, his all, to the service of God under the direction of the General Overseer, whom, for years, he had thoroughly believed to be Elijah, the promised Prophet of the Restoration.

Mr. Clibborn's statements were made boldly, and without the slightest equivocation, and aroused the intense interest of the large audience that had remained after the regular service to hear him and Mrs. Clibborn.

The General Overseer then said:

It would be a very great favor to me, and also to La Maréchale, as she has been known to so many—and she never will be forgotten by the multitudes in Switzerland and France, to whom she has been known—if you will give her your kind attention and consideration for a few minutes.

I am glad that her conviction and her deep spiritual nature have arrived at the conclusions which make it possible to her, as well as to her beloved husband, to come into Zion.

Mrs. Catherine Booth-Clibborn gave her personal experience in reference to the work of the General Overseer and the Christian Catholic Church in Zion, explaining how the Spirit of God had led her, step by step, first to give up her connection with the organization which she had seen grow into being under the direction of her father and her sainted mother, and of which her father was still the head, and then, after long consideration and prayer, to accept John Alexander Dowie as Elijah the Restorer, and to become an obedient member of the Christian Catholic Church in Zion.

Her entire life, from this day forward, she said, would be devoted to the glorious work of the extension of the Kingdom of God, under the command of him whom she fully believed to be Elijah, the Prophet of the "Times of Restoration of All Things, whereof God spake by the mouth of His holy prophets which have been since the world began."

La Maréchale, as the people of this city loved to call her in the days when she and her husband were fighting the battle for religious liberty in the French cantons of Switzerland, was heard with the greatest respect by the audience, many of whom came forward to greet them at the close of the service.

The General Overseer closed the services with the usual

BENEDICTION.

Beloved, abstain from every form of evil. And may the very God of Peace Himself sanctify you wholly; and I pray God your whole spirit and soul and body be preserved entire, without blame, unto the coming of our Lord Jesus, the Christ. Faithful is He that calleth you, who also will do it. The grace of our Lord Jesus, the Christ, the love of God, our Father, the fellowship of the Holy Spirit, our Comforter and Guide, one Eternal God, abide in you, bless you and keep you, and all the Israel of God everywhere, forever. Amen.

Lord's Day night was spent in Neuchatel, and on the following Monday morning, the entire party returned to Zurich with the General Overseer.

A Successful Conference in Zurich.

On that afternoon, with very little notice, a conference of the members of the Christian Catholic Church in Zion in Zurich was held in Zion Tabernacle.

Between three and four hundred members were present, and a most encouraging and successful conference was held.

That evening, at six o'clock, the General Overseer, accompanied by Elder Jean Kradolfer, Evangelist Sophia Hertrich, Deaconess Ruth Hofer, Deacons Williams and Newcomb, and a Zurich business man, departed for the Castle Liebburg, near Kreutzlingen, on Lake Constance, in Canton Thurgau.

As this was the last visit of the General Overseer to Zurich, during this Visitation, there was a large company of members and friends gathered on the platform of the station to bid him farewell.

As they waved their good-bys, they sang the beautiful words of "*Gott mit euch!*" the German of "God Be with You Till We Meet Again!"

Some of them and some of us found difficulty in singing all the hymn, on account of the unbidden tears; for Zurich and Zurich people, and the General Overseer and his Around-the-World Visitation Party had become very warm friends, to whom parting was a sorrow.

Before our leaving, Elder Carl Hodler and Deacon Carl F. Stern had gone ahead of us to Berlin, to prepare for the Visitation of the General Overseer in that city, on Wednesday and Thursday, June 8 and 9, 1904.

Overseer Excell and Deaconess Stern remained in Zurich with Evangelist Hodler, and went on to Berlin later, joining the General Overseer and those with him en route.

The Beautiful River Rhine.

On the way to Liebburg, our enthusiastic admiration was particularly caught by the beauties of the Rhine, along which we traveled for many miles.

We began to understand why so much had been said, written and sung concerning this noble stream and its scenery.

The Hudson may be as beautiful in another way, and there are many larger rivers; but with its richly cultivated banks, its Old-World villages, its mystic old castles, its broad, glimmering expanses, reflecting the glories of the sky and the loveliness of its shores; its swift narrows and foaming falls, and its quaint river craft, the Rhine easily leads in picturesque charm, all the rivers that we have seen.

We were enchanted.

We add our feeble song to the great chorus of the lovers of Germany's greatest river.

Late Sunset and Long Twilight.

We were also impressed, during this ride, with the length of the day in Northern Europe.

It was nearly quarter after eight when the last rays of the setting sun gilded the battlements of a grim, old castle near our way, and the orb of day, that had thus kindly prolonged his shining on this pleasing landscape, sunk out of sight.

It was fully an hour later, although it had begun to rain, ere the last of the twilight glow had faded out of the sky.

This was in such marked contrast to the six o'clock sunset and swift darkness of the tropics that we began to realize that we were some hundreds of miles north of the latitude of Zion City. Later, at Berlin, and still later at Liverpool, when we were about six or seven hundred miles north of Zion City, the phenomenon was even more noticeable, it being light until about ten o'clock at night.

We were getting near to the land of the midnight sun.

We arrived at Emmishofen, where we left the train for Liebburg, at about half past eight in the evening, and there found the conveyances from the castle waiting for us.

Castle Liebburg.

After a drive of a few miles, we saw the welcome lights of Liebburg, and soon were being most heartily and hospitably welcomed by Evangelist Hofer and her household.

A bounteous and appetizing dinner with the guests added greatly to our comfort after the journey.

The Castle Liebburg is a most delightfully quiet place, and we all enjoyed a very refreshing sleep under its roof that night.

We were astir very early next morning, as there was too much in nature that appealed to eye, ear and spirit, and too many interesting old houses in the little villages all about to spend the precious hours of daylight sleeping.

The scenery in this neighborhood is what is generally termed rolling; but the Appenzell and the Vorarlberg Alps are in plain sight, forming a fitting background to a charming picture, in which the broad bosom of the Lake of Constance is a prominent feature.

The people in the neighborhood are chiefly agricultural.

Like the peasants of Germany, they do not live in widely separated farmhouses, but in little hamlets or villages.

In our morning excursion among them, with a camera, we found them delightfully simple, cordial and clean.

Nearly all greeted us with the beautiful salutation, "*Grüss Gott!*" for which there is no adequate equivalent in English, the meaning being somewhat the same as "God be with you!"

Castle Liebburg, formerly the home of a cardinal of the Church of Rome, is now the property of Evangelist Anita Hofer, and has been used by her for the last three and one-half years as a Divine Healing Home.

Evangelist Sophia Hertrich, who is one of the officers of the Christian Catholic Church in Zion in Europe, has spent a great deal of her time in the Home, teaching and praying with the sick.

God has greatly used this delightful place, which was consecrated wholly to His service, and many have here found their way to God, through Jesus, the Christ, not only as their Savior, but as their Healer, Cleanser and Keeper.

Hundreds throughout Europe and in other parts of the world, praise God from overflowing hearts for Castle Liebburg.

On this occasion, the General Overseer found about thirty guests, from all parts of the Continent, awaiting him.

Meeting With Thirty Guests at the Castle Liebburg.

He met them first of all at the breakfast table on Tuesday morning, June 7th.

There, after the meal, he spoke to them briefly, announcing the one meeting which he would be able to hold during his stay, at half past nine o'clock that morning.

Shortly after that hour, the meeting was held in the dining-rooms and drawing-room, which were thrown into one large assembly hall. Many members and friends of the Christian Catholic Church in Zion from the neighborhood were in attendance.

Deaconess Ruth Hofer interpreted into the German with fluency and clearness, the teaching of the General Overseer.

After the teaching, which was the effective proclamation of the truth of Divine Healing and the conditions of God's Covenants, the General Overseer prayed for the sick, with the laying on of hands.

The Spirit of God was present with Healing Power, and many received great blessings in spirit, soul, and body.

At three o'clock that same afternoon, we took carriages for Constance, which is partly in Switzerland and partly in Germany, where we were to take the train for Berlin.

Memorials of John Huss, Reformer and Martyr.

At Constance we visited the place where John Huss suffered martyrdom, now marked by a vine-covered boulder with a bronze tablet, and the Kaufhaus, erected in 1388, where the conclave of Cardinals met in the great council when Huss was condemned to death.

There we took train, at four o'clock, for Berlin, the Capital of Germany.

At Singen we changed cars, and there were joined by Evangelist Hodler, Deaconess Stern and Overseer Excell.

The ride from Singen to Stuttgart was full of interest; but there was one feature of the landscape that was full of pathetic significance.

Sad Results of Militarism in Germany.

All the fields and gardens along the way were very beautifully tilled, not a weed being allowed to show its disgraceful head anywhere; but we saw at what an expense this exemplary cultivation was effected.

Everywhere the workers were women, comparatively few men being seen, and, until the last glimmer of the long summer twilight had faded, these bent figures could be seen stooping to their heavy tasks.

The counterpart of the story was seen when we got to Berlin—tens, yes, hundreds of thousands of the flower of the young manhood of the country, taken away from the fields at the very time of the year when there was most work to be done, to do military duty.

At Stuttgart we left the compartment which we had occupied and took our berths on the *schlafwagen*, as the sleeping car is called.

Berlin, Germany.

We arrived in Berlin at about nine o'clock Wednesday morning, June 8th.

We were met at the station by Elder Carl Hodler, Deacon Carl F. Stern, and many members and friends of Zion in Berlin and in many other parts of Germany, some having come long distances to be present.

We were taken at once to the Hotel Bristol, on the famous avenue known as *Unter den Linden*, on account of the rows of lime trees that line it on both sides and down through the middle.

Berlin is too well known to need any description in these pages.

It impressed us as being a very beautiful city, in many parts, but its beauty was very much marred by the pall of black coal smoke from the many factories.

Drill of the Kaiser's Soldiers.

During our stay in the city, we saw practically all the places of interest, spending an hour or two one morning in watching the maneuvers of several regiments of the imperial army, stationed in the garrisons of the city.

It was very interesting, and it was wonderful to see the skill, accuracy, and harmony with which the difficult and complicated movements were executed, but it was a terrible thought that these thousands of young, strong, intelligent, capable men were being trained and perfected in the art of murder; that their talents, skill, and strength were far worse than non-productive.

We rejoiced that Zion's Message was a Message of Peace, and prayed God to hasten the day when the nations shall not learn war any more.

Wednesday Evening Meeting in Berlin.

The first meeting of the General Overseer in Berlin was held in the *Industrie Salle*, in Beuthstrasse, on Wednesday evening, June 8, 1904.

Absolutely no public announcement of the Service had appeared, private invitations having been sent out by Mr. Sauer, the very able Conductor of the Gathering of the Christian Catholic Church in Zion in Berlin.

All public meetings are very carefully supervised by the police in Germany, and it was necessary to obtain permission to hold this meeting.

This was readily granted, but the police took charge of the hall, and when it was full, shut the doors, permitting no more to enter.

What was our joy to find that there were present about eight hundred fifty friends of Zion or those interested in the teaching!

The interpreting into German was done on this occasion by Elder Carl Hodler, Evangelist Marie Brieger-Hodler, and Deaconess Ruth Hofer.

The solid, thoughtful character of the German people was well displayed in the intense interest with which they followed every word of the man of God, oftentimes expressing their approval of the bold, straightforward teaching of the Inspired Word and the Gospel of the Kingdom.

On the platform sat two uniformed officers of the Berlin police force, one of whom reported in full the entire service, the other taking copious notes of the salient points of the teaching.

It is needless to say that there was not the slightest attempt at disorder on the part of any one, neither in the hall nor on the streets.

The meeting was closed with a feeling on the part of all the Zion party and Zion in Berlin, that the Spirit of God had been present in power, and that Zion had made a great stride forward in this capital of the German Empire.

The following is the outline of the General Overseer's address:

Industrie Salle, Beuthstrasse, Berlin, Germany, Wednesday Evening, June 8, 1904
*REPORTED BY I. M. S. AND A. W. N.

The Services were opened by the singing of a hymn.

The General Overseer said:

Greeting.

Before we read the Word of God I desire to thank you very heartily not only for your kind reception tonight, but for the loving messages which you have so often sent to me, and especially for the greetings which you sent to me lately in Zurich.

I bring you the greetings of tens of thousands of members of the Christian Catholic Church in Zion throughout the whole world.

Germany's Splendid Character and History.

I thank God, in this the first meeting that I have ever held in Germany, for all that Deutschland has done and has been to the world.

It was the bulwark of Protestantism in the dark days, and it has been a wonderful inspirer of educational progress.

We are indebted to the earnest researches of great

*The following address has not been revised by the General Overseer.

theologians of Germany for many of our most priceless treasures.

Among my many books, and I have a library of over ten thousand volumes, the book that I prize most, next to the Bible, is "Lange's Bible Work," a German commentary.

I thank God for the great scholarship of that good man.

I have many other commentaries, some of them much later, but there are none that, in scholarship, surpass the German.

I express my indebtedness, and the indebtedness of Zion throughout the world, to Germany.

May God bless Deutschland! [Amen.]

May the Christian Catholic Church in Zion be a means of blessing in Germany in all things!

Zion's Reverence for Law.

Zion people are a law-abiding people, and there is no anarchy in Zion.

There is no foolish talk about destroying governments.

If a government can be made better, Zion will help to make it better, but Zion will never destroy; for government is essential to the protection of life, of property, of liberty and of progress.

I hope that there will be such a condition in Germany that there will be no hindrance to Zion's progress; for Zion will be a strength to the Emperor, and not a weakness.

However greatly we may differ in theories or governments, there is one thing that Zion stands for everywhere, and that is Good Order, Good Government, and Purity in all relations of life.

Zion has no sympathy with tyranny, but sympathy with strong government.

I thank God for this large gathering in Berlin.

Prayer was offered by Evangelist Marie Brieger-Hodler, closing with prayer for the sick and suffering ones by the General Overseer, and the chanting of the Disciples' Prayer by the assembly.

Deaconess Ruth Hofer read from the Inspired Word of God, the 67th Psalm and the 35th chapter of the book of the Prophet Isaiah.

The announcements were made by Elder Carl Hodler, after which a hymn was sung by Zion Choir in Berlin, small in number but exceedingly well organized and well conducted.

THE JOY OF THE RANSOMED.

The General Overseer pronounced the

INVOCATION.

Let the words of my mouth and the meditation of my heart be acceptable in Thy sight, be profitable unto this people, and unto all to whom these words shall come, in this and every land, in this and all the coming time. Till Jesus Come. Amen.

TEXT.

God be merciful unto us and bless us, and cause His face to shine upon us; that Thy Way may be known upon earth, Thy saving health among all the Nations.—*Psalm 67:1, 2.*

And the ransomed of Jehovah shall return, and come with singing into Zion; and Everlasting Joy shall be upon their heads: they shall obtain Gladness and Joy, and sorrow and sighing shall flee away.—*Isaiah 35:10.*

The ransomed of the Lord, those for whom God paid the wonderful price of the blood of His own Son, whom He ransomed from their sins, from their disease, from death and from hell, and gave His own Son to do it, shall return and come to Zion with songs, and Everlasting Joy shall be upon their heads.

God does not want His people to come home to heaven with groans.

They shall obtain Joy and Gladness, and Sorrow and Sighing shall flee away.

It has not fled away yet.

There Is Sorrow and Sighing Everywhere.

I have been around the world four times, and have traveled long distances enough to have gone around the world at least eight times, and I have not been anywhere that I did not find sorrow, that I did not find sighing, that I did not find the people mourning, like Rachel weeping for her children, and would not be comforted because they were not, like the women of Bethlehem, who mourned over their slain babies.

Oh, what a monster, far worse than Herod, is destroying the children, and not the children only, but youths and maidens, with the powers of disease and death, and is filling the graves! None are spared from this monster, Satan, the author of Sin, the author of Disease, the author of Death, and the author of Hell.

There would be no sin in this world were it not for Satan; there would be no Disease were it not for Sin, for all Disease is the result of Trangression of the Law of God.

There is another side.

Let me ask you to look at this side for a moment.

There are five links in the Chain of Evil: Satan, Sin, Disease, Death, Hell.

There are also five links in the Chain of Good: Jesus, Salvation, Healing, Life, Heaven.

There is the conflict between Good and Evil.

Jesus, from all eternity the Word of God, the Eternal Logos, the Word who became flesh, by whom all things came into being, is the Author of Good, and brings Salvation, Healing, Life and Heaven.

One of the most terrible blunders that Christians have made is to say that disease comes from God.

Disease is always the work of the Devil, and cannot be a link in the Chain of Good.

The General Overseer, after speaking strongly as to the diabolical source of all evil, including disease, told of the great work done by members of Zion Restoration Host in New York City, and of the wonderful way in which God kept them all in health and strength.

Speaking further on the origin of disease, he showed how cancer and other filthy diseases resulted from the eating of unclean swine's flesh.

He closed with a few convincing words on Divine Healing and a call to Repentance, Confession and Consecration.

The congregation responded, almost as one man, by rising and repeating the following

PRAYER OF CONSECRATION.

My God and Father, in Jesus' Name I come to Thee. Take me as I am and make me what I ought to be in spirit, soul and body. Give me power to do right. If I have wronged any man, give me power to confess and restore. Forgive me for my sins against Thee, for the sake of Jesus, the Lamb of God, who taketh away the sins of the world. Give me power that I may be saved and healed and cleansed, and kept for the use of God and for the use of my fellow men, that I may live a good life and come to Thee at last, in the land where there is no sin, no sorrow, no sickness, no death, no graves, no weeping and no night. For Jesus' sake. Amen. [*The above prayer was repeated by nearly every one in the audience.*]

Die Gnade was then sung.

The General Overseer closed the meeting by the pronouncing of the

BENEDICTION.

Beloved, abstain from every form of evil. And may the very God of Peace Himself sanctify you wholly; and I pray God your whole spirit and soul and body be preserved entire, without blame, unto the coming of our Lord Jesus, the Christ. Faithful is He that calleth you, who also will do it. The grace of our Lord Jesus, the Christ, the love of God, our Father, the fellowship of the Holy Spirit, our Comforter and Guide, one Eternal God, abide in you, bless you and keep you, and all the Israel of God everywhere, forever. Amen.

The Zion Salutation was given by the General Overseer and very heartily returned by the Congregation.

Thursday Evening Meeting in Berlin, Germany.

The second and last meeting of the Berlin Visitation was held in Germania Hall, in Chausseestrasse, a large, handsome auditorium, seating about twelve hundred people.

This also was filled to overflowing, so that the police closed the doors and would not permit any more to enter, and all seemed to be friends of Zion.

If the first meeting in Berlin was a feast of spiritual good things, this was a veritable banquet.

Seldom have we seen a meeting where the audience seemed more profoundly impressed with the Truth.

God was with His Prophet with power, and his Message was full of Restoration Truth, effectively proclaimed.

It was a great opportunity to address twelve hundred as intelligent and thoughtful people as these in the great center of the greatest Empire of Continental Europe, and the man of God was equal to it, by God's grace.

After the meeting, a large number of friends of Zion came forward, and for a few minutes the General Overseer was holding an informal reception.

One very intelligent lady, who had heard him for the first time that evening, begged him to accept the handsome bouquet which she carried, and was very much delighted when he graciously received the flowers.

Many expressed their intention of visiting Zion City in the near future.

The following is the report of the principal points of the General Overseer's Message:

words, that they might be profitable to all that should hear and read them, and proceeded with his Message.

It was the old but ever new teaching of the Covenants of God with His people, and especially that great Covenant made at the waters of Marah, "I am Jehovah that healeth thee."

It was also a heralding of the Coming of Jesus, the Christ, the Son of God, to reign as King over all the earth.

In the presence of two of the officers of his Majesty, Kaiser

Old Tower in Lucerne. Ancient Clock Tower in Neuchatel. Scene in Neuchatel.

Port of Neuchatel. Street in Old Lausanne. Square in Neuchatel.

Old Houses in Lucerne. Stairway of Chateau at Neuchatel. Example of Neuchatel Architecture.

VIEWS IN LUCERNE, LAUSANNE, AND NEUCHATEL, SWITZERLAND.

After the Invocation of God's blessing upon the Congregation by the General Overseer, all joined in the hearty singing of a hymn.

The first seventeen verses of the 8th chapter of Matthew were then read by Deaconess Ruth Hofer, after which Evangelist Marie Brieger-Hodler offered prayer.

The Prophet of God then invoked God's blessing upon his

Wilhelm's police, God's prophet declared that when the Christ came to rule, all other rulers, whether kings, emperors, princes, autocrats, or presidents, would have to give way to Him.

It was, in part, this same declaration, made in Adelaide, South Australia, that had created such a terrible stir in the British Empire; but evidently the throne of the German Empire is not so easily shaken as that of Edward VII., for the words were received very quietly and with apparent acquiescence by the large congregation present, and there was no trouble made about them afterwards.

The meeting closed with a very heart-searching Prayer of Consecration, in which the great majority of those present joined, the singing of the *Gnade*, and the General Overseer's pronouncing the Benediction.

At this meeting we were again treated to a very creditable production by the Zion Choir of the Berlin Gathering, very ably led by Karl Kaszemek.

In the course of the morning we changed cars four more times, arriving at Rotterdam about one o'clock.

We drove first to the *Groote Doelenzaal*, where the meeting was to be held that evening.

This we found to be a commodious hall, seating about twelve hundred people, and fronting on one of the principal streets of Rotterdam.

We then drove to the Maas Hotel, where we were met by Elder Percy Clibborn, Rev. and Mrs. Arthur S. Booth-Clibborn, and several of their children, and by a number of the members

Terraced Hillside on Lake Geneva. Scene in Geneva. Portion of City of Bern Scene in Bern.

SCENES IN SWITZERLAND.

Immediately after this service, the entire party proceeded to the Railway Station in Frederickstrasse, where the General Overseer and the members of the Around-the-World Visitation Party with him took the International Express for Rotterdam, leaving Elder and Evangelist Hodler and Deaconess Hofer to establish more firmly the work that had been done in Berlin.

From Berlin to Rotterdam.

We awoke early the next morning to change cars and get breakfast at Essen, where the famous Krupp Gun and Iron Works are located.

and friends of Zion in Rotterdam, several of whom could speak English very fluently.

As the meeting was to be held that evening, the afternoon was spent by the General Overseer and several of the officers in preparation, and by the rest of the party in taking photographs.

Picturesque Holland.

If Switzerland is the most beautiful of the European countries, Holland is the most picturesque.

This little kingdom near the sea has no lofty mountains to

give it grandeur, and not even hills high enough to be worthy of the name, but its canals, windmills, sailboats, homes, trees, fields, and people all have a quaint, quiet, restful, cleanly air, that is to be found nowhere else on earth.

Holland is a perfect paradise for painters and photographers.

Every acre of the country, and every nook and corner of every village, teems with scenes that have that rare, indescribable quality which is called pictorial.

We had always looked upon the paintings and photographs of Dutch landscapes as almost too good to be true, but found that the real was even more delightful than the picture.

The people we found to be simple, unaffected and courteous, with that true kindliness which comes from the heart.

Rotterdam.

Rotterdam itself we found to be hardly representative of Holland, being a great seaport town, and hence cosmopolitan in its character. On this account, perhaps, it is lacking in that air of immaculate cleanliness that characterizes other parts of the country. The city is nevertheless not without beauty and interest.

Favorable Article in a Rotterdam Paper.

We found that the meeting of the General Overseer had been announced but a day or two before, but that considerable interest had been created by an article from the pen of the Rev. Arthur S. Booth-Clibborn, published that day in the *Nieuwe Rotterdamsche Courant*, of which Elder Clibborn furnished us the following translation:

REV. JOHN ALEXANDER DOWIE AND HIS TEMPERANCE ZION CITY.

Having visited Zion City and spent two months there in the summer of 1902, I can speak from personal knowledge.

The great majority of the reports which reach Holland concerning Dr. Dowie and his work are erroneous, and many are deliberate falsehoods; others are caricatures.

History repeats itself.

Luther, Wesley, and the Salvation Army met with a similar reception and treatment in the beginning.

Zion City, founded three years ago, contains already a population of 10,000 people, peaceful, sober, religious and hard-working.

Strong drink, cursing and swearing, immoral men, women or literature are prohibited and excluded. Even smoking is forbidden, as being injurious to health and a bad example for children.

The sale of swinesflesh, as being a producer of disease, whose use was forbidden by God to the Jews on that account, is forbidden.

Zion City is beautifully situated on the shores of Lake Michigan, fifty kilometers from Chicago, and has a surface of eleven thousand acres.

The various valuable industries created there and the factories which are being erected give employment to an ever-increasing number of people who wish to do business on the most strictly truthful and honest principles, and to train up their children in the most pure and wholesome surroundings they can find.

Not a day passed when I was there when I did not notice some fresh and most encouraging feature of a great restoration.

The inhabitants are but human beings, subject to sins and mistakes, but taking them in an average, as citizens, as husbands, wives, brothers or sisters, masters or servants, they made a better impression upon me than any equal number I have ever met.

There is a strong, Christian, brotherly love among them which gladly makes sacrifices that none shall suffer the pinch of poverty.

The tone of the City and the assemblies in the Tabernacle, which seats seven thousand two hundred people, is not fanatical, but calm, strong and peaceful.

It is easy to make light of the doctrines of Christianity, but most will agree that true Christians have been the salt of the earth all through our "Christian era."

Zion City is a good City simply because it is a Christian City.

And now as regards the man, John Alexander Dowie.

Much evil is spoken of him, but is it logically probable that a bad man would build a good City?

We live in a time when facts have more influence than theories.

It is a *fact* that upwards of one hundred thousand people, members or friends of his Church, have not only a great love for Dr. Dowie, but an intense confidence in and respect for him. They testify that a closer personal acquaintance with him has ever increased their love and respect.

Their belief that he is the Elijah the Restorer of a complete Christianity before the return of the Christ to earth, is, after all, no more strange than other beliefs held by millions of Christians in all churches, such as the belief in the existence and mission of Noah at the time of the flood, of Moses at the time of the Exodus, or of John the Baptist at the time when Judaism was about to reject the Messiah.

The great majority of Christian chronologists are agreed that we are close to the end of the six thousand years since the creation of Adam—the six "days" of the world's labor, and that the seventh "day," the Sabbath or Millennium is at hand.

Hundreds of thousands of evangelical Christians believe that the Christ will return to earth at that time to reign as King.

But the Scriptures declare clearly that His coming must be preceded by that of a forerunner, as it was at His first advent, and that he will be a simple man and will do certain simple but thorough work to prepare the people of God for the coming of their Lord and to separate them from the world and its unbelief.

It may be conceded that after twenty-five years' study and work as a minister of the Gospel and a practical evangelist in various lands, I would not offer an opinion without careful examination, nor will the honesty of the opinion be doubted in this City.

The Elijah is to come when the time has come.

The Scripture leaves no doubt upon this question.

I believe Dr. Dowie to be the man, because the time has come and he is doing the work. ARTHUR S. BOOTH-CLIBBORN.

Crowded Meeting at Rotterdam.

With such short notice we were surprised to find that not only was the hall crowded with an audience of over twelve hundred people, but that the streets outside were black with a throng of some thousands.

The great audience inside was for the most part deeply attentive and sincerely respectful throughout, but there were a few, evidently foreign residents of the city, and some fellows of the baser sort who associated with them, who attempted to make a disturbance.

The great majority of those present being against them, however, their attempts fell flat, and the very best order was maintained throughout practically the whole meeting.

The General Overseer said by way of

Greeting.

I thank God for the privilege of delivering my first address in this important nation and in this ancient city.

I remember, with great gratitude to our Heavenly Father, how many mighty men of God have lived in this land.

I remember that this land has been a Bulwark of Liberty; that when darkness covered the earth, the Light of the Gospel shone here; and that the great principles of Liberty were maintained by heroic statesmen and great ministers of God I trust that God will use my humble words tonight to help in extending His Kingdom.

The 35th chapter of Isaiah was read by the Rev. Arthur S. Booth-Clibborn, following which prayer was offered by the Rev. Catherine Booth-Clibborn.

A Message of Truth and Power.

The General Overseer's Message which followed dealt first of all with the work of Jesus, the Christ, while here on earth in the flesh and the mighty significance of that work in view of His promise, "Lo, I am with you All the Days, even unto the Consummation of the Age," and in view of the Word of God, by His Apostle, "Jesus, the Christ, is the same yesterday and today, yea, and forever."

God's Messenger then passed on to very helpful and authoritative teaching on the vital subject of "How to Pray," closing with a bold, straightforward proclamation of the Kingdom of God, the Kingdom which should set aside and rule over all other kingdoms of the earth.

These strong Restoration truths were heard with the most thoughtful attention by the greater part of the audience, and it was clear that through the Spirit of God they were greatly blessed. Hundreds in that audience rose and joined in the solemn Prayer of Repentance, Confession and Consecration.

The interpretation of the General Overseer's Message into the Dutch language was by the Rev. Arthur S. Booth-Clibborn.

Thus ended the Visitation of Elijah the Restorer on the Continent of Europe.

This "Gospel of the Kingdom" had been proclaimed by him in the capitals and great cities of France, Switzerland, Germany and Holland.

During the five weeks on the Continent, he had addressed thirty-two public meetings, with an aggregate of perhaps ninety thousand attendances—people from all over Europe—had prayed with many hundreds of the sick, with laying on of hands had given private interviews to a very large number, and had attended to a great deal of correspondence, and other business besides.

In addition to all this work, the prophet of God had traveled two thousand four hundred sixty-six miles by railways, steamers and carriages, and had done a great deal of driving and walking about, sightseeing.

Not until the great Books of God are opened, will the results of these five weeks' work be known; but already a great song of praise is going up to God, from all parts of that broad Continent, for blessings in spirit, in soul, in body, in the home and in temporal affairs, as the result of the Visitation.

Notwithstanding all his toil and travel, the General Overseer was in supurb physical and psychical health, and in the very best of spirits, when on the night of Friday, June 10th, we took train from Rotterdam to the Hoek of Holland and there embarked on the Steamer Dresden to cross the German Ocean, or North Sea, to Harwich, en route for London.

Early Morning Meeting in Shiloh Tabernacle

REPORTED BY O. L. S., AND E. S.

LIKE the sweep of ocean billows came the "Peace to thee be multiplied!" from thousands of throats as the Prophet of God appeared upon the platform at the Early Morning Meeting, Lord's Day, July 3, 1904, and gave the old, familiar greeting, "Peace to thee!"

A sea of upraised, waving hands appeared for a moment, as the people's voices responded, like the sound of many waters —"Peace to thee be multiplied," and then perfect silence, perfect order, prevailed.

The scene presented was one never before witnessed.

Not a face in the great audience of five thousand that was not transfigured, aglow with Christian enthusiasm and deep inexpressible emotions. Here was depicted love, joy, devotion, consecration, forming an ensemble of spiritual power and beauty which, once seen, can never be forgotten.

Tears glistened in many eyes; but they were tears of gladness, of thanksgiving, of rejoicing.

In the service which followed, the Spirit of God was manifest as in a visible Presence.

As a Living Breath, He abode in the place.

Quiet, deeply convicting, solemn, earnest, intense was the Message given by the Prophet of God.

Yet it seemed but the preparation, the preface, to the Message delivered at the Great General Assembly in the afternoon.

THE LAND OF THE LIVING.

Shiloh Tabernacle, Zion City, Illinois, Lord's Day Morning, July 3, 1904.

The General Overseer opened the Service by asking the Congregation to sing Hymn No. 1, from the Special Song Sheet, to be used in the forthcoming Feast of Tabernacles:

Holy, holy, holy, Lord God Almighty!
Early in the morning our song shall rise to Thee!
Holy, holy, holy, merciful and mighty,
God in three persons, blessed Trinity!

Prayer was offered by the General Overseer, at the close of which he led the Congregation in chanting the Disciples' Prayer.

The General Overseer read the 27th Psalm, after which he pronounced the

INVOCATION.

Let the words of my mouth, and the meditation of my heart be acceptable in Thy sight, be profitable unto this people, and unto all to whom these words shall come, in this and every land, in this and all the coming time, Till Jesus Come.

The General Overseer then said:

I desire to read to you again the last two verses of the 27th Psalm:

I had fainted unless I had believed to see the goodness of Jehovah
In the Land of the Living.
Wait on Jehovah:
Be strong, and let thine heart take courage;
Yea, wait thou on Jehovah.

This Is the Land of the Dying.

The earth is full of graves.

Wherever we tread, yes, wherever we sail, the moldering bodies of almost countless generations lie under us.

The mold of the dead is beneath the rose.

The Earth is the Land of the Dying, for death hath passed upon all; for all have sinned.

I had fainted, unless I had believed to see the goodness of Jehovah
In the Land of the Living.

This is the Land of the Dying; yonder in the Heavens is the Land of the Living.

No clouds ever pass along that sky; no tear-drops glisten in the eye. Happy Land!

There are no graves there.

We shall not tread upon the dying when we walk the streets of gold; when we breathe the air of immortality not laded with disease, not burdened with the cries of the dying and the sighs of the living, who almost wish so often that they were dead too, that they are ready to say to the dead under them, "Make room for me."

Oh, Blessed Land of the Living, where Death never comes!

It is the contemplation of my living there that makes it possible to live here, for a little while, in the Land of the Dying.

A Parable of One Who Came from the Land of the Living to This Land of the Dying.

In the bazaars of the Orient, where the Arab story-teller entertains the curious people, and sometimes those that have been over-burdened, who sit in the market-place sleeping their life away, strange stories are told, and some of them with wondrous moral and spiritual effect.

In an ancient Eastern city this wondrous parable was told:

Suddenly, the story goes, there appeared one day on the streets of one of the great cities, a beautiful man.

He seemed to be neither very young nor old, but he had that in his face which made all the onlookers behold him with wonder, as he walked the streets of their city, filled with surprise at everything he saw, asking, in signs, the strangest questions, as if he had never lived in a City of Earth, asking also the simplest questions, that every little child could answer.

He asked what the intention of this, that, and the other thing was, and stood with amazement as he beheld the occupations of the people.

Then they began to ask him the question, "Where do you come from?"

But he did not know their language, so he did not understand what they were saying.

It seemed strange to see him walking up and down, clothed in beautiful garments, with a face neither young nor old, and with a look that caused those who beheld to say "He does not belong to earth."

At last he began to learn their language.

He was taken by good men to their homes, and was taught and kindly treated.

One night, under the starry skies, when he had acquired language enough to make himself understood, he said to his host, "I will tell you whence I came."

He then pointed to the star that had just issued forth in its beautiful light as the sun faded. It was the glorious Evening Star.

"I came from there!" he said.

"I had often observed this planet, and I said to my God, your God, the God of all the universe, 'Oh, let me go and visit that beautiful earth!' but I received no answer.

"I wept and said, 'Oh, I shall never be satisfied until I can get to that beautiful star!' pointing to this earth.

"Then I heard the message, 'You can go, but remember you can only return here by the pathway that all who live there tread!' Suddenly I awoke to find myself on the Earth."

Then the strange man turned to his host and said, "What does that mean? I have been wanting to know *the pathway that all tread.*"

The Pathway All Must Tread.

His host bowed his head and wept, and pointed to the earth.

But the stranger did not understand.

So the next day his host took him to the house of mourning, and there the dead lay; a beautiful young man in the very glory of his youth; suddenly the spirit had departed and his body lay dead, surrounded by weeping, wailing friends, some with broken hearts, which would never be comforted

The stranger looked long and earnestly and then said, "Why does he not awake? Why does he not speak? How deeply he sleeps!"

He went forward and touched him; then exclaimed, "How cold he is! My God! tell me what this is? Tell me what this is?"

"It is Death!" said his host.

"Death? Death?" he questioned. "What is Death?"

He was then led to the grave where he saw them put the dead into the ground.

"What is this? What is this place where all these monuments are?" again he questioned.

"The dead are here; this is the City of the Dead!" was the answer.

"My God!" he cried, "and can I live, as you live, if this is the path by which alone I can return to the heaven from which I came? Is this the *pathway that all who live on Earth must tread?*

"Shall I fool away the golden hours as you do here in pleasures, in visiting, in follies, in foolish sin and foolish words? Oh, I have drunk of a bitter cup! Your cup of pleasure is a Cup of Death!

"You have to die," he continued, "and you think of everything and talk of everything and prepare for everything except that which cannot be evaded. And this is the path by which alone I can reach the Land of the Living—the Land of the Living!"

When the Star rose that night, he knelt and cried, "O God, I have taken of the bitter cup of earthly pleasure and sin! Show me how my sin may be blotted out, and the stain that has come to my spirit be taken away! Show me how I may get back again to the Land of the Living, where they never sin nor sorrow, and where they never die!"

"That is how earth and its inhabitants appear to the heavenly beings," concluded the dark-skinned story-teller, and the tear-dimmed eyes of all the people fell, as they slowly went away from the market place, as the Evening Star appeared in the sky.

Will you not go away from this place with the thought that you shall more and more, through the Faith of God, live that life which, while it is happy and joyful and good, will be a life that will fit you for the Land of the Living?

I had fainted, unless I had believed to see the goodness of Jehovah
In the Land of the Living.

The Christ Leads the Way to the Land of the Living.

These six months that I have spent away from you, in the Land of the Dying, have made me more intensely earnest in preparing for the Land of the Living.

Do not be afraid!

Death! He is the King of Terrors, but he has no terror for him who has learned the pathway and has followed in the steps of Him who went before—the Christ our Champion—and died, showing us the Way of Life by which we, too, may pass through death and rise to endless life, as He rose! For He liveth!

He came not from the Evening Star, for He is the Bright and Morning Star.

He came from highest heaven, and He knew earth's sorrow, earth's sins, earth's sickness, earth's weariness, and tasted of the bitterness of death as He stood by Lazarus' grave, and wept, as He felt all the sympathy and love true friends feel when the lips are cold, when the tongue lies silent, when the hand that used to help is folded on the breast, and the last help it can give is over.

Oh, it was so bitter for Him to stand over Lazarus' grave!

But He showed by what He then said and did that every one that dies in Him shall come forth; that death cannot hold those to whom He hath given life, and that He is the Resurrection and the Life, and will lead us into the Land of the Living.

The Deathless Life.

So through all the months, the days, the hours, the nights, the triumphs, the trials, the storms, the sunshine, the expectations that were dashed and not realized, and the expectations that were more than fulfilled—through it all, whenever the time of trial has come, whenever the toil has been most severe, I have not fainted, because I have believed to see the Goodness of Jehovah in the Land of the Living.

Oft 'midst this world's ceaseless strife,
When heart and spirit fail me,
I stop and think of that better life
Where ills can ne'er assail me.
Where my wearied arm shall cease its strife,
My heart shall cease its sorrow;
And the night of life be changed
For the light of the endless morrow.

So I cannot faint while He is with me, for I believe that even in the Land of the Dying I shall see the goodness and the mercy of God, that I shall see many enter into God's Way in the Land of the Dying, and receive the Gift of God—Eternal Life—the Deathless Life—they who will never die.

I believe the Master's Word:

He that believeth on Me, though he die, yet shall he live:
And whosoever liveth and believeth on Me shall never die.

When He asks, "Believest thou this?" can we say that we do?

Let me ask you. The Master said:

I am the Resurrection, and the Life: he that believeth on Me though he die, yet shall he live;

And whosoever liveth and believeth on Me shall never die. Believest thou this?

People—"Yes!"

General Overseer—Is it from your heart?

People—"Yes!"

General Overseer—Then are you going to live as those that want to get back to the Land of the Living? Then

Wait on Jehovah!
Be strong and let thine heart take courage;
Yea, wait thou on Jehovah!

Be Patient.

Wait, Wait, Wait! "The Dawn is not distant, nor is the night starless."

Wait! the morning will come!

Wait! Work! Watch!

Labor on, labor on! But never fear!

Those in whose hearts the Good Seed is sown will "bring forth fruit with patience."

The Seed is sown by me, by you, today.

It may not grow tomorrow.

It may not all bear fruit this year nor the next, but it has been sown in a good honest heart, and by and by it grows, the fruit comes, we gather in the golden grain of a Deathless Life, and go on, patiently, ever sowing the seeds of Immortality.

Zion sows over all the earth the seeds of the Eternal Word that never dies.

I found the seed that I had scattered from this place.

I had sown it here in Zion City, and elsewhere, in the night, toiling and weeping, while others were sleeping; I sent it forth over the lands and seas on the wings of the Little White Dove, LEAVES OF HEALING, and I found where it had grown in distant isles and continents, in the hearts of thousands, yea, tens and hundreds of thousands.

So I go on, sowing and reaping, and sowing and reaping, and sowing what I reap over and over again.

Sowing now; weeping now; but reaping by and by, even on Earth, and by and by in the Land of the Living.

I believe that not one cup of cold water given in the Name of the Christ, not one kind thought offered in prayer to your Father, not one kind deed done, not one copy of LEAVES OF HEALING given with love, nor anything else that has in it the seed of the Kingdom will be lost; nothing will be lost.

We may not gather it here.

We do not know where to find it, but we shall gather it there; in the Land of the Living, the thing that endures, which is eternal, we shall find.

Let Us Sow for God and Live for Eternity.

Our eyes grow dimmer, for we weep.

Our eyes grow dimmer, for we toil.

Our bodies grow feebler, for their work is being done; and we pass on, but it is into the Land of the Living.

O Land of the Living! how we long to see thee, with the multitudes who from all the ages are there, and with our own who are there!

Land of the Living! Land of the Living!

We march on to thee through the Land of the Dying; for we, too, have the Life that gives us courage to labor and to wait.

Bring near Thy Great Salvation,
Thou Lamb for sinners slain;
Fill up the Roll of Thine Elect,
Then take Thy Power and reign;
Appear, Desire of Nations!
Thine exiles long for Home:
Show in the Heavens Thy promised Sign:
Thou Prince and Savior, come!

Pray with me.

[The people then stood and repeated, clause after clause, the Consecration Prayer.]

PRAYER OF CONSECRATION.

My God and Father, give me grace, by Thy Spirit, that I may receive the Word, and that I may bring forth fruit, no longer with impatience, but with patience, willing to wait; willing to work; willing to watch; willing to weep; but waiting for the harvest; working for the Master. Help us so to live. Forgive our sins, wherein we have failed to understand Thy will; wherein we have hurt one another by not understanding. Give to us all Thy pardoning Love. Bring us all into glorious communion with Thyself. Give us the strength to no longer faint, but ever to believe and to wait on Thee; to wait for Thee, and not be impatient. Help us to do Thy will; to suffer Thy will; and to go onward until we meet in the Land of the Living. For Jesus' sake.

The General Overseer sang the verses of Hymn No. 53 in the Feast of Tabernacles Program, "Arise and Shine," the Congregation joining with him in singing the chorus. It is as follows:

Lift up, lift up thy voice with singing,
Dear land, with strength lift up thy voice!
The kingdoms of the earth are bringing
Their treasures to thy gates—rejoice!

CHORUS—Arise and shine in youth immortal,
Thy Light is come, thy King appears!
Within the Century's glorious portals,
Breaks a new dawn—*the thousand years!*

And shall His flock with strife be riven?
Shall envious lines His Church divide,
When He, the Lord of earth and heaven,
Stands at the door to claim His bride?

Lift up thy gates! Bring forth oblations!
One crowned with thorns, a Message brings,
His Word a Sword to smite the nations;
His Name—the Christ, the King of kings!

He comes! Let all the earth adore Him;
The path His human nature trod
Spreads to a royal realm before Him,
The Light of Life, the Word of God!

The General Overseer then pronounced the

BENEDICTION.

Beloved, abstain from every form of evil. And may the very God of Peace Himself sanctify you wholly; and I pray God your whole spirit and soul and body be preserved entire, without blame, unto the coming of our Lord Jesus, the Christ. Faithful is He that calleth you, who also will do it. The grace of our Lord Jesus, the Christ, the love of God our Father, the fellowship of the Holy Spirit, our Comforter and Guide, one Eternal God, abide in you, bless you and keep you, and all the Israel of God everywhere, forever. Amen.

Expiration of Subscriptions.

On every subscriber's copy of LEAVES OF HEALING or THE ZION BANNER we attach a yellow label bearing his name, address, and two numbers, the figures referring to the volume and the number with which the subscription will expire.

Thus, should your label number happen to be 15—11, you may know that your subscription expires with Volume XV, Number 11, which will be July 2, 1904. Also take notice that LEAVES OF HEALING now completes a volume every six months, or twenty-six weeks, that being the number of papers which are put into a bound volume. Earlier in the life of the paper a volume contained fifty-two numbers, as LEAVES OF HEALING had fewer pages in those days.

By making yourselves familiar with these customs and remitting promptly you need never allow your subscription to lapse.

Send money only by Bank Draft, Postoffice or Express Money-order in favor of John Alexander Dowie, and address all letters intended for us to

ZION PRINTING AND PUBLISHING HOUSE,
Zion City, Lake County, Illinois.

DO YOU KNOW GOD'S WAY OF HEALING?

BY THE REV. JOHN ALEX. DOWIE.

Let it be supposed that the following words are a conversation between the reader [A] and the writer [B].

A. What does this question mean? Do you really suppose that God has some one especial way of healing in these days, of which men may know and avail themselves?

B. That is exactly my meaning, and I wish very much that you should know God's Way of Healing, as I have known it for many years.

A. What is the way, in your opinion?

B. You should rather ask, WHO is God's Way? for the way is a Person, not a thing. I will answer your question in His own words, "I am the Way, and the Truth, and the Life: no one cometh unto the Father, but by Me." These words were spoken by our Lord Jesus, the Christ, the Eternal Son of God, who is both our Savior and our Healer. (John 14:6.)

A. But I always thought that these words only referred to Him as the Way of Salvation. How can you be sure that they refer to Him as the Way of Healing also?

B. Because He cannot change. He is "the same yesterday and today, yea, and forever." (Hebrews 13:8.) He said that He came to this earth not only to save us but to heal us. (Luke 4:18), and He did this when in the flesh on earth. Being unchanged He must be able and willing and desirous to heal now.

A. But is there not this difference, namely, that He is not with us now?

B. No; for He said "Lo, I am with you All the Days, even unto the Consummation of the Age;" and so He is with us now, in spirit, just as much as when He was here in the flesh.

A. But did He not work these miracles of healing when on earth merely to prove that He was the Son of God?

B. No; there was still a greater purpose than that. He healed the sick who trusted in Him in order to show us that He came to die not only for our sins, but for our sicknesses, and to deliver us from both.

A. Then, if that be so, the atonement which He made on the Cross must have been for our sicknesses as well as our sins. Can you prove that is the fact from the Scriptures?

B. Yes, I can, and the passages are very numerous. I need quote only two. In Isaiah 53:4, 5, it is written of Him: "Surely He hath borne our griefs (Hebrew, *sicknesses*), and carried our sorrows: . . . and with His stripes we are healed." Then, in the Gospel according to Matthew, this passage is quoted and directly applied to the work of bodily healing, in the 8th chapter 17th verse: "That it might be fulfilled which was spoken by Isaiah the prophet, saying, Himself took our infirmities, and bare our diseases."

A. But do you not think that sickness is often God's will, and sent for our good, and therefore God may not wish us to be healed?

B. No, that cannot possibly be; for diseases of every kind are the Devil's work, and his work can never be God's will, since the Christ came for the very purpose of destroying "the works of the Devil." (1 John 3:8.)

A. Do you mean to say that all disease is the work of Satan?

B. Yes, for if there had been no sin (which came through Satan) there never would have been any disease, and Jesus never in one single instance told any person that sickness was God's work or will, but the very contrary.

A. Can you prove from Scriptures that all forms of sickness and infirmity are the Devil's work?

B. Yes, that can be done very easily. You will see in Matthew 4:23 and 9:35 that when Jesus was here in the flesh He healed "all manner of disease and all manner of sickness among the people." Then if you will refer to Acts 10:38 you will see that the Apostle Peter declares that He (Jesus) "went about doing good, and healing all that were oppressed of the Devil." Notice that all whom He healed, not some, were suffering from Satan's evil power.

A. But does disease never come from God?

B. No, it cannot come from God, for He is pure, and disease is unclean; and it cannot come out of Heaven, for there is no disease there.

A. That is very different from the teachings which I have received all my life from ministers and in the churches. Do you really think that you are right, and that they are all wrong in this matter?

B. It is not a question as between myself and them. The only question is, What does God's Word say? God has said in all the ages, to His Church, "I am Jehovah that healeth thee" (Exodus 15:26), and therefore it would be wicked to say that He is the defiler of His people. All true Christians must believe the Bible, and it is impossible to believe that good and evil, sickness and health, sin and holiness could have a common origin in God. If the Bible really taught that, it would be impossible to believe our Lord Jesus, the Christ, when He says: "A good tree cannot bring forth evil fruit, neither can a corrupt tree bring forth good fruit." (Matthew 7:18.)

A. But even if I agree with all you say, is it not true that the Gifts of Healing were removed from the Church, and are not in it now?

B. No, the "Gifts of Healing" were never withdrawn, and can never be withdrawn, from the true Church of God, for it is written: "The gifts and the calling of God are without repentance." (Romans 11:29.) There are nine gifts of God to the Church (enumerated in 1 Corinthians 12:8-11), and all these are in the Holy Spirit. Therefore, so long as the Holy Spirit is in the Church, all the gifts must be there also. If they are not exercised, that does not prove that they do not exist, but that the faith to exercise them is lacking in God's servants. The gifts are all perfectly preserved; for the Holy Spirit, not the Church, keeps them safely.

A. What should a Christian then do when overtaken with sickness?

B. A Christian should obey God's command, and at once turn to Him for forgiveness of the sin which may have caused the sickness, and for immediate healing. Healing is obtained from God in one of four ways, namely: First, by the direct prayer of faith, without any aid from the officers of the Church, praying as the Centurion did in Matthew 8:5-12; second, by two faithful disciples praying in perfect agreement in accordance with the Lord's promise in Matthew 18:19; third, by the anointing of the Elders and the prayer of faith, according to the instructions in James 5:14 and 15; and fourth, by the laying on of the hands of them who believe, and whom God calls to that ministry, as the Lord commands in Mark 16:18, and in other places.

A. But are people healed in this way in these days?

B. Yes, in thousands of cases. I have myself laid hands upon many hundreds of thousands of persons, and I have seen the Lord's power manifested in the healing of great numbers, many of whom are living witnesses in many countries, who have testified publicly before thousands, and who are prepared to testify at any time. This ministry is being exercised by devoted Christians in many parts of America, Europe, Australasia, and elsewhere.

A. Is it not the same as Christian Science, Mind Healing, etc.?

B. No. Divine Healing is diametrically opposed to these diabolical counterfeits, which are utterly antichristian. These impostures are only seductive forms of Spiritualism. Trance Evangelism is also a more recent form of this delusion, and it deceives many.

A. But how shall I obtain the necessary faith to receive healing, which faith I am at present conscious that I do not possess?

B. It is written: "Belief cometh of hearing, and hearing by the word of the Christ." (Romans 10:17.) Our Missions are held for the express purpose of teaching fully the Word of God on this matter, and I very heartily invite you to attend the meetings which are announced for Zion Tabernacles in Chicago and other cities, and for Shiloh Tabernacle, Zion City, Illinois. All are welcome and there are no charges of any kind made, for all God's gifts are free gifts. Salvation is the first of these, without which you cannot be healed through faith in Jesus. All the costs of this work are covered by the free-will offerings of the people who attend these meetings, and others whom the Lord leads to help; but the poorest, who have nothing to give, are as heartily welcome as the richest

A. Do you see the sick and lay hands upon them in this Mission?

B. Yes; after we feel satisfied that they are fully resting in the Lord alone for the healing, we see privately, so far as time permits, those who attend; but under no circumstances do we claim the power to heal any; for "power belongeth unto God."

A. Have you any writings upon this subject which can be purchased?

B. Yes; these can be obtained at the office of Zion Printing and Publishing House, Zion City, Illinois, and at any Zion Tabernacle. But the best book on Divine Healing is the Bible itself, studied prayerfully and earnestly.

We extend to you a hearty invitation to attend the meetings, which are free to all. Our prayer is that you may be led to find in Jesus, the Christ, our Lord and God your present Savior from sin, your Healer from sickness, your Cleanser from all evil, your Keeper in the way to Heaven, your Friend, and your All for Time and Eternity. We pray that these words may help many who read, and that our little conversation may bear fruit in leading many readers to look to Jesus only.

**"The Healing of Christ's seamless dress
Is by all beds of pain;
We touch Him in life's throng and press
And we are whole again."**

Zion's Bible Class

Conducted by Deacon Daniel Sloan in Shiloh Tabernacle, Zion City, Lord's Day Morning at 11 o'clock, and in Zion Homes and Gatherings throughout the World.

MID-WEEK BIBLE CLASS LESSON, JULY 27th or 28th.

Sorrow and Sadness Kill.

1. *God never shrouds one in gloom.*—Psalm 112:4-9.
Darkness comes to the ignorant.
There is no night where God is.
He is Light to all who fix their hearts on Him.
2. *Sorrow strikes at the heart's action.*—1 Timothy 6:6-12.
Some worry over the lack of this and that.
Some worry over the loss of this and that.
Sorrow pierces through every vital organ.
3. *Sorrow springs from earth's disappointments and losses.*—2 Corinthians 7:9-13.
The world is full of sorrow.
The spirit of the world brings sorrow.
Living after fleshly relations causes sorrow.
4. *The Christ came to heal hearts which the god of this world had broken.* --Luke 4:16-22.
The Devil first broke a wife's heart.
Then he sought to overthrow a family.
He will separate loved ones if he can.
5. *There is a better way to see things.*—Ecclesiastes 8:1-5.
God has a better way to live.
The spirit must lift one above earth's cares.
God can put in one's heart that which keeps out outside happenings.
6. *God's point of view must be taken to keep sorrow from racking the heart.*—Psalm 36:9-12.
Get His light and you see more light.
You see only lovingkindness.
He turns that which seems to harm into joy.
7. *Sorrow will change one's face.*—Nehemiah 2:1-4.
The face gets wrinkled by sorrow.
The hairs turn white through grief.
The shoulders stoop bearing earth's burdens of sorrow.
8. *God can bring victory and release from any seeming defeat and loss.*—Romans 8:24-30.
Hope saves one from grief and sadness.
Hope sees not loss but gain.
Hope sees God's hand working out His plan.

The Lord our God is a Succoring God.

LORD'S DAY BIBLE CLASS LESSON, JULY 31st.

Strength Comes from Joy.

1. *Be joyous when you eat.*—Ecclesiastes 2:24-26.
A mind free from trouble gives good digestion.
God does not want one to eat bread in sorrow.
One cannot thank God for food and be sad over it.
2. *Be joyous when you work.*—Isaiah 12:2-5.
We are to rejoice always.
God has a hand on earth's events.
We must labor in the spirit of joy.
3. *Be joyous while you live.*—Isaiah 29:18-22.
Sorrow with many increases with age.
God intends that joy shall increase.
Nothing should diminish one's joy.
4. *Be joyous whether at rising or bedtime.*—Psalm 127:2-5.
Get up happy and you may go to bed joyful.
Get your full quota of sleep.
The Devil robs some of rest day and night.
5. *There is comfort in joy.*—2 Corinthians 7:1-6.
One may be under trials and yet be joyful.
A person is to be joyful when persecuted.
The promises of reward is the basis of joy.
6. *There is deliverance in joy.*—Psalm 105:37-45
God's happy people are healthy.
God cannot bless a sad and sorrowful person.
If you seek God in prayer be glad and joyful.
7. *There is increase in joy.*—Joel 1:8-13.
Be happy and you will prosper.
Get disgruntled and who wants to help you?
God's people murmur and mourn and the Devil blights them.
8. *There is long life in joy.*—Isaiah 51:9-15.
Sorrow must cease with those who would live long.
Sighing severely shocks the heart.
Get the joy and comfort of faith.

God's Holy People are a Happy People.

OBEYING GOD IN BAPTISM.

"Baptizing Them Into the Name of the Father and of the Son and of the Holy Ghost."

Eighteen Thousand Seven Hundred Twelve Baptisms by Triune Immersion Since March 14, 1897.

Eighteen Thousand Seven Hundred Twelve Believers have joyfully followed their Lord in the Ordinance of Believer's Baptism, by Triune Immersion since the first Baptism in Central Zion Tabernacle on March 14, 1897.

Baptized in Central Zion Tabernacle from March 14, 1897, to December 14, 1901, by the General Overseer,	4754			
Baptized in South Side Zion Tabernacle from January 1, 1902, to June 14, 1903, by the General Overseer..	37			
Baptized at Zion City by the General Overseer........	583			
Baptized by Overseers, Elders, Evangelists and Deacons, at Headquarters (Zion City) and Chicago......	5283			
Total Baptized at Headquarters....................				10,657
Baptized in places outside of Headquarters by the General Overseer................................		641		
Baptized in places outside of Headquarters by Overseers, Elders, Evangelists and Deacons............		7376		
Total Baptized outside of Headquarters............				8,017
Total Baptized in seven years and three months....				18,674
Baptized since June 14, 1904:				
Baptized in Chicago by Elder Hoffman...............	1			
Baptized in Chicago by Elder Cossum................	1		2	
Baptized in Nebraska by Elder Hoy..................		7		
Baptized in New York by Overseer Mason............		9		
Baptized in Ohio by Deacon Kelchner................		1		
Baptized in Ohio by Deacon Arrington...............		5		
Baptized in Texas by Evangelist Gay................		11		
Baptized in Wisconsin by Elder McClurkin...........		3	36	38
Total Baptized since March 14, 1897................				18,712

The following-named believer was baptized at San Antonio, Texas, Lord's Day, June 19, 1904, by Evangelist William D. Gay:

Gage, Miss Kate Lois..........1126 Colorado avenue, San Antonio, Texas

The following-named four believers were baptized at San Antonio, Texas, Wednesday, June 22, 1904, by Evangelist William D. Gay:

Miller, John Martin
corner Mulberry and Howard avenues, San Antonio, Texas
Thomas, Mrs. Elizabeth Wilson..505 San Pedro avenue, San Antonio, Texas
Thomas, Miss Gladys ....505 San Pedro avenue, San Antonio, Texas
Thomas, Miss Mildred.........505 San Pedro avenue, San Antonio, Texas

The following-named three believers were baptized at San Antonio, Texas, Lord's Day, June 26, 1904, by Evangelist William D. Gay:

Garlinghouse, Miss Clara Belle.....204 Convent street, San Antonio, Texas
Heninger, Miss Florence..........1111 Crocket street, San Antonio, Texas
Sayers, Miss Georgia B. ....218 Nolan street, San Antonio, Texas

The following-named three believers were baptized at San Antonio, Texas, Monday, June 27, 1904, by Evangelist William D. Gay:

Robinson, Mrs. Hannah...........120 Mulberry street, San Antonio, Texas
Byrd, Miss Rose Cornelia............218 Nolan street, San Antonio, Texas
Stucky, Mrs. Maggie May............209 Idaho street, San Antonio, Texas

The following-named nine believers were baptized at New York City, Monday, June 27, 1904, by Overseer George L. Mason:

Allessandria, Louis.......................107 Prince street, New York City
Camus, Miss Georgette..............946 Columbus avenue, New York City
Hertz, Mrs. Sophie............115 Myrtle avenue, Jersey City, New Jersey
Hogg, B. Yorkston.........269 West Twenty-second street, New York City
Holton, Miss Linda............R. F. D. Number 18, Danbury, Connecticut
Shaffer, Mrs. Cora Janet ....Hillgirt, North Carolina
Simpson, John.......17 South Fifth avenue, Mount Vernon, New York City
Weitz, Oskar....................430 East Fourteenth street, New York City
Youngdale, Mrs. Augusta......301 East Forty-eighth street, New York City

The following name was omitted from the list of names of persons baptized in Johannesburg, Transvaal, South Africa, Lord's Day, May 8, 1904, by Overseer Daniel Bryant:

Watson, Ernest Alexander
174 Marshall street, Johannesburg, Transvaal, South Africa

Notice to Officers and Members.

Send all newspaper clippings concerning the General Overseer, the Elders, or any department of the work in connection with the Christian Catholic Church in Zion, to Deacon Carl F. Stern, Zion City, Illinois. Send as soon as possible after publication, and carefully mark *name and date of the paper clipped from* on each article. If this is not done, the clippings are absolutely useless.

WITH ILLUSTRATED SUPPLEMENT.

A WEEKLY PAPER FOR THE EXTENSION OF THE KINGDOM OF GOD
EDITED BY THE REV. JOHN ALEX. DOWIE.

Volume XV. No. 13. *ZION CITY, SATURDAY, JULY 16, 1904.* *Price Five Cents*

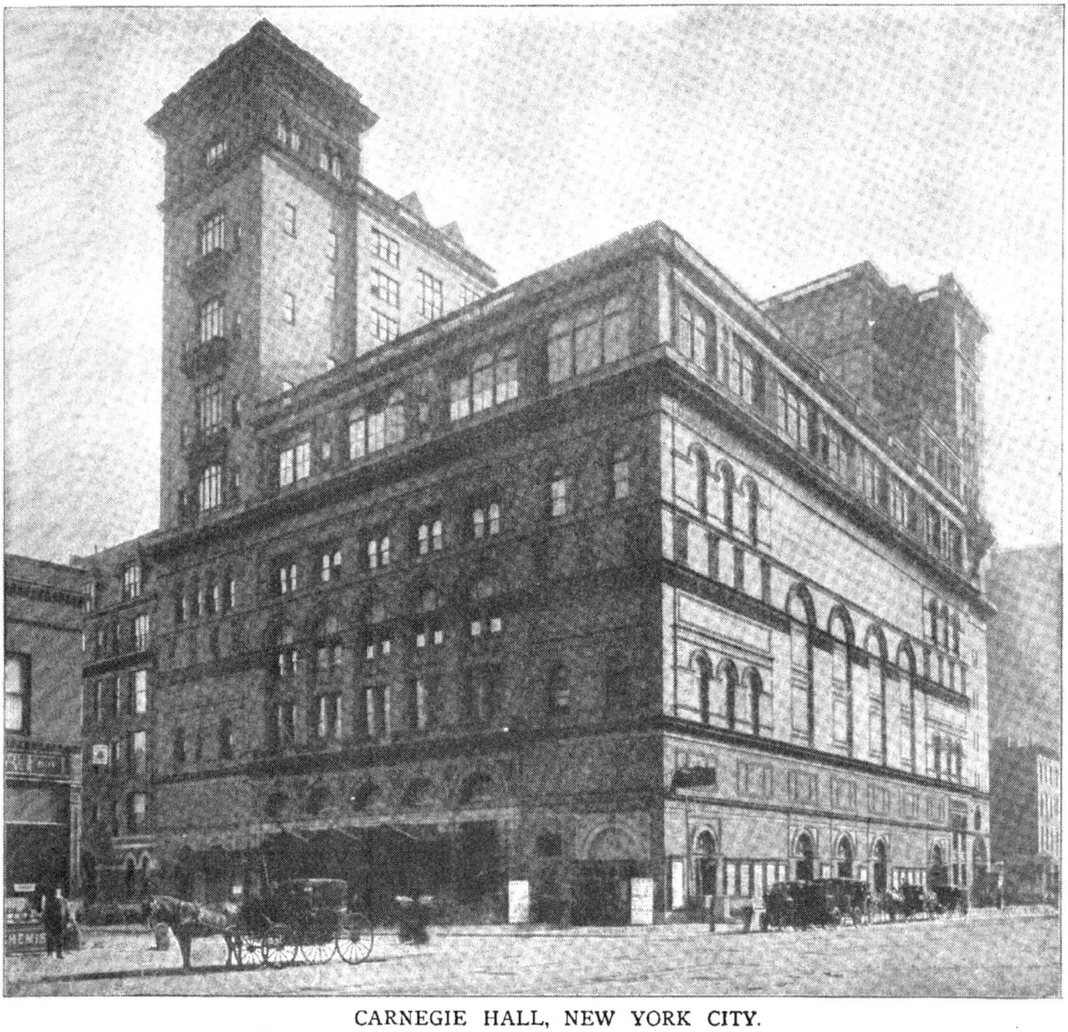

CARNEGIE HALL, NEW YORK CITY.

Where Meetings of the Around-the-World Visitation Were Held, Lord's Day, June 26, 1904

A WEEKLY PAPER FOR THE EXTENSION OF THE KINGDOM OF GOD.

EDITED BY THE REV. JOHN ALEX. DOWIE.

Application for entry as Second Class Matter at Zion City, Illinois, pending.

Subscription Rates.		**Special Rates.**	
One Year	$2.00	100 Copies of One Issue	$3.00
Six Months	1.25	25 Copies of One Issue	1.00
Three Months	.75	To Ministers, Y. M. C. A's and Public Reading Rooms, per annum	1.50
Single Copies	.05		

For foreign subscriptions add $1.50 per year, or three cents per copy for postage.

Subscribers desiring a change of address should give present address, as well as that to which they desire LEAVES OF HEALING sent in the future.

Make Bank Drafts, Express Money or Postoffice Money Orders payable to the order of JOHN ALEX. DOWIE, Zion City, Illinois, U. S. A.

Long Distance Telephone. *Cable Address "Dowie, Zion City."*

All communications upon business must be addressed to

MANAGER ZION PUBLISHING HOUSE,
Zion City, Illinois, U. S. A.

Subscriptions to LEAVES OF HEALING, A VOICE FROM ZION, and the various publications may also be sent to

ZION PUBLISHING HOUSE, 81 EUSTON ROAD, LONDON, N. W., ENGLAND.
ZION PUBLISHING HOUSE, NO. 43 PARK ROAD, ST. KILDA, MELBOURNE, VICTORIA, AUSTRALIA.
ZION PUBLISHING HOUSE, RUE DE MONT, THABOR 1, PARIS, FRANCE.
ZIONSHEIM, SCHLOSS LIEBBURG, CANTON THURGAU, BEI ZÜRICH, SWITZERLAND.

ZION CITY, ILLINOIS, SATURDAY, JULY 16, 1904.

TABLE OF CONTENTS.

LEAVES OF HEALING, SATURDAY, JULY 16, 1904.

EDITORIAL NOTES.

"WORSHIP THE KING, JEHOVAH OF HOSTS! AND KEEP THE FEAST OF TABERNACLES."

THESE WORDS are written in the 14th chapter of Zechariah and the 16th verse, concerning the time when "Jehovah shall be King over all the Earth."

AND IT shall come to pass, that every one that is left of all the Nations which came against Jerusalem shall go up from Year to Year to worship the King, Jehovah of Hosts, and to keep the Feast of Tabernacles.

THROUGHOUT THE Millennium, the Thousand Years of our Lord's Personal Reign on Earth, the Test of Loyalty to Him from all the lands will therefore be the going up to Jerusalem from Year to Year to worship Him, and the keeping of the Feast of Tabernacles.

TERRIBLE IS the Prophetic Declaration of "the Punishment of All the Nations who go not up to keep the Feast of Tabernacles."

WHEN WE established the First Feast of Tabernacles in Zion we did not realize as fully as we do now the importance of the Restoration of this "Holy Convocation."

But as we go forward in Zion from year to year, its importance grows; and God's blessing upon Zion is so great that this delightful annual festival has become the Crowning Glory of the Year.

THE FEAST opened on the evening of Wednesday, July 13th, at 7:30 p. m., by the Presentation and Consecration of the people to God.

We delivered an address entitled, "FOR ZION'S SAKE," to an audience of about Six Thousand people.

FOR SEVERAL days our beloved people from all parts of this and from many other lands have been pouring into the City in many hundreds daily.

They are coming especially from the Dominion of Canada, and from well-nigh every State in this Republic.

Many have come from Europe, Africa, Asia, and Australasia to this Feast, some of them with the intention of returning for a time at least to their distant homes, and others to make permanent residence here.

IT WOULD take many columns to give even a list of their names.

THERE HAVE been Wonderful Gatherings at the Early Morning Sacrifice of Praise and Prayer, at 6:30 a. m., where we have delivered the first two of a Series of Nine Addresses on "The Nine Fruits of the Spirit."

IT IS estimated that an attendance of between five and six thousand has been present at each meeting.

INTENSE INTEREST has been shown in the two great Anniversaries of Zion, which are always celebrated on the 14th and 15th of July.

The first of these was the Fourth Anniversary of the Consecration of Zion Temple Site.

The second was the Third Anniversary of the Opening of the Gates of the City.

THERE WERE probably nine thousand persons present on each occasion, and the great processions were very remarkable.

WE HOPE to be able to present our readers with large pictures of these Scenes, similar to the large photo-engraving of our Welcome Home, twenty-four inches by twelve inches, which we present as a Supplement this week.

THE PROCESSION of the Officers, Church, Choir, and Restoration Host, on the first of these Anniversaries; and the Procession on the second of all the Municipal Officers of the City, and the officers and employees of Zion's Legal, Financial, Commercial, Industrial, Educational, and Political Institutions, were each in their way, very wonderful scenes.

It is not possible for us to describe them in words.

EXCELLENT Daily Gatherings of Zion Junior Restoration Host, have been held, conducted by Overseer Brasefield.

A very largely attended Divine Healing Meeting was held yesterday, at the close of which hundreds who sought the Lord for Healing, were prayed with.

THE EVENING SACRIFICES of Praise and Prayer have been occasions of much blessing.

All in Zion City are looking forward to the Convocations of next week which, we doubt not, will be filled with blessing.

VISITORS CONTINUE to pour into the City every hour and already Edina and Elijah Hospices are filled to overflowing.

A large Camp containing many tents has been formed in Shiloh Grove, and is growing daily.

IT IS estimated that there have been Attendances of about Thirty-five Thousand people at the Gatherings in Shiloh Tabernacle during the last three days.

Including the Services of last Lord's Day, we have probably spoken to Audiences aggregating fully Forty-five Thousand during this week.

Within the last sixteen days we have spoken to Audiences in Zion City aggregating more than Ninety-two Thousand (92,000).

THESE FIGURES may help our friends at a distance to understand that, with all our other work as General Overseer, we have been "making history," and that we must be excused if we cannot find time to write it.

OUR PRIVILEGE, as God's minister, is indeed a great one.

We have the joy of ministering to God's children from all the world, and of sending the Record, in these pages, throughout the world.

REPORTS OF all the Convocations are being carefully prepared, and, with our address of last Lord's Day afternoon, will duly appear in future issues.

We felt, however, that, although we could not write the history fully, or even in outline, at this time, our readers would be glad to know concerning the Opening of Zion's Fourth Feast of Tabernacles.

THE WEATHER has been glorious.

None of the proceedings have been marred by rain or tempest.

Almost incessant rains had fallen for many days before the Feast.

They were greatly needed.

All Nature is rejoicing in the refreshing effects of these copious showers; and Zion City has never looked more beautiful than it does today.

THE BLESSING of God in Saving, Healing, and Cleansing Power is being continually manifested.

Especially is this Feast a season of spiritual enrichment and culture.

WE NOW ask the prayers of all our readers for ourselves and all our beloved Officers and people in the remaining Nine Days of the Feast which lie before us.

FROM ALL the earth encouraging tidings of Zion's Onward Progress come daily, and to All the Nations of the Earth we cry from the Watch Tower of Zion:

"THE RESTORATION OF ALL THINGS HAS BEGUN!!!"

CHRIST OUR King is preparing Zion and Zion Restoration Host, by rapid and solid extension, for the Conquest of every Nation, and Kindred and Tongue, and the Deliverance of this earth from the Destroying Powers of Satan and Sin, Disease and Death and Hell.

TRIUMPHANT ZION, lift thy head
From dust, and darkness! And the dead,
Though humbled long, awake at length,
And gird thee with thy Savior's strength.

No more shall foes unclean invade,
And fill thy hallow'd walls with dread:
No more shall hell's insulting host
Their victory and thy sorrows boast.

THE DAY has come for Zion to appear in Beauty, not in Sackcloth and Ashes.

SOME WOULD have us wear the Robes of Sorrow and Wo in delivering our Prophetic Messages.

WE DO NOT believe that we have any such ministry.

We do not identify our Message with that of the Two Witnesses in the 11th chapter of the Revelation, in the "Second Wo."

AS ELIJAH THE RESTORER, we proclaim the Gospel of the Kingdom of God, and, in the Name of the Christ our King—

To appoint unto them that mourn in Zion,
To give unto them a Garland for Ashes,
The Oil of Joy for Mourning,
The Garment of Praise for the Spirit of Heaviness;
That they might be called Trees of Righteousness,
The planting of Jehovah, that He might be glorified.

THEREFORE WE cry to Zion over all the earth:

Put all thy Beauteous Garments on,
And let thy Excellence be known:
Decked in the Robes of Righteousness,
The world thy glory shall confess.

WE ARE not a witness for God throughout "the Time of Tribulation."

But, by the grace of God, he who writes is the Prophet of the Restoration and of the Gathering of the people of God into Zion Cities all over the earth, where they shall be prepared as a mighty Evangelizing Host.

We go forth to restore millions to God.

We hope to build up Zion and to prepare the Temple of God at Jerusalem.

We hope to take part in building the Royal Palace for the Coming King.

We hope to make the Nations know "to earth's remotest bounds," that, after the "Tribulation" and the "Rapture," both periods are identical in duration, and are of brief time, our Lord will come again, and reign on earth for a Thousand years.

During that Time the Restoration will continue until "all enemies have been put under the Christ's feet," and until "all the Kingdoms of this world are become the Kingdom of our Lord and of His Christ."

OUR MESSAGE is not a Message of Sadness, Sorrow, and almost of Despair, to be trampled down in the streets of Sodom and Egypt, mingled with blood.

The "Two Witnesses" are prophets who witness throughout the "Tribulation."

Our Message precedes that time.

We expect, by the mercy of God, that we shall not be permitted to pass through that "Tribulation," which shall come "suddenly as a snare on all them that dwell on the face of the whole earth."

We do not intend to be numbered with the Foolish Virgins.

We shall obey our Lord's Command, "Watch ye at every Season, making Supplication, that ye may *prevail to escape all these things that shall come to pass*, and to stand before the Son of Man."

Having begun the glorious work of Restoration, we shall be permitted, by God's grace, to enjoy the Rapture of His saints in the glories of Heaven, and to be there prepared, as never before, for the Continuation of the Restoration during the Millennium in a glorified body.

We believe that we shall return with the Heavenly Hosts that will accompany Him when He finally returns to settle things with Satan.

We expect to retake possession in His Name of all the Zion Cities which will then be found all over the earth, and to behold His triumph in the glorious City on the Hill of Zion, at Jerusalem, where He shall reign as King of kings and Lord of lords throughout the Thousand Years.

THEN COMETH the End!

The Christ shall deliver up the Kingdom to God, even the Father;
He shall have abolished all rule,
And all authority and power,
For He must reign,
Till He hath put all enemies under His feet.
. . . .
THAT GOD MAY BE ALL AND IN ALL.

O ZION—

Arise, shine, for thy light is come, and the glory of Jehovah is risen upon thee!

Arise, and shine in youth immortal,
Thy Light is come, thy King appears!
Within the Century's glorious portal,
Breaks a new dawn—the Thousand Years!

OVER AND over again throughout this Feast we shall sing the beautiful words:

He comes! let all the earth adore Him;
The path His human nature trod
Spreads to a Royal Realm before Him,
The Light of Life, the Word of God!

AND SO we go forward joyfully, not in sackcloth and ashes. Let Zion everywhere put her Beauteous Garments on, and make God's Cities and Plantations and Enterprises pure, bright, rich, happy and contented, drawing to them from all the lands "the Wealth of the Nations, and their Kings led with them."

BRETHREN, PRAY FOR US.

Notes of Thanksgiving from the Whole World

By John G. Speicher, Overseer for Zion City.

THE following letters are from some who have received healing through faith in God, and who have written to us expressing their gratitude to God for His goodness and mercy.

Mother Healed—Daughter Healed of Severe Cough.

I trust in the mercy of God for ever and ever.—*Psalm 52:8.*

1420 WEST PETER SMITH STREET,
FORT WORTH, TEXAS.

DEAR GENERAL OVERSEER:—I had been a sufferer all my life.

Our family physician, Dr. J. H. Murphy, told me I had kidney and female trouble.

He treated me and I seemed to get worse, so my husband said that I must change doctors.

We sent for Dr. R. Chambers.

He examined me and said that I had a severe case of indigestion and female trouble.

I took his medicine as directed and was to make ready for an operation in the spring.

I worried about what would become of my children until I was nearly ready for the asylum.

But thanks be to God, the Little White Dove found its way to me from Clarendon, Texas, in January, 1902.

What a peace came to me! The more I read, the more I wanted.

I began to study my Bible and it became a new Book to me.

As I read LEAVES OF HEALING and compared it with the teaching of the Bible, I grew stronger, until I surrendered myself to God and sent a request for prayer to you.

I think it was in February, 1902.

I was instantly healed.

The next day I did a big washing.

Before that I could scarcely sweep my house and was very weak.

I am thanking the Lord day and night for our beloved General Overseer who taught us the way.

In June, 1902, my little daughter sent you a request for prayer for rain and God heard and answered your prayer.

My daughter was taken with a severe cough.

On the 28th day of April, 1903, I asked you to pray for her and she received healing and has not had any sickness since.

Praying that God will spare you and your dear wife and son Till He Come, I am,

Your sister in the Christ,

(MRS.) MATTIE WILSON.

Delivered in Childbirth—Healed of Severe Pain.

He giveth power to the faint;
And to him that hath no might
He increaseth strength.—*Isaiah 40:29.*

CITY POINT, VIRGINIA, March 1, 1904.

DEAR OVERSEER:—With gratitude to God, I send you this testimony, hoping it will help some one to trust the Lord.

In February, 1903, I wrote to Overseer Jane Dowie to pray for my safe delivery in childbirth, and, praise God, prayer was faithfully answered.

On March 29th my baby was born after a very short time of suffering.

The night baby was five days old I was taken very sick with a chill and violent pain in the left side.

All that night I had a raging fever.

The Devil tried to make me afraid, and I had a fierce battle all night.

In the morning my husband wrote to the General Overseer to pray for me, and, praise God, He healed me of that also; and in two weeks I was going about the house.

Pray for me, that I may be faithful.

Your sister in the Christ,

(MRS.) MATTIE F. BAILEY.

Mother and Daughter Healed of Grip.

Attend to My words;
Incline thine ear unto My sayings.

For they are life unto those that find them,
And health to all their flesh.—*Proverbs 4:20, 22.*

OMRO, WISCONSIN, March 14, 1904.

DEAR OVERSEER SPEICHER:—I write to give praise and thanksgiving to God for the healing and spiritual blessing that my dear aged mother and I have received in answer to prayer.

On the 15th of February I had a severe attack of grip, which continued until one o'clock in the afternoon on the 17th, at which time Deacon Brannen received my card asking for prayer; and when he prayed I had perfect deliverance.

At the hour of my healing, mother, who is eighty-five years old, was well and at work.

At half past two o'clock she was prostrate with a most severe attack of the same disease.

She soon became very sick, being only partially conscious much of the time, having a high fever and a numbness of her body, followed by cold sweat. Her appearance was as of one near death.

I wrote asking you to pray for us, and when you prayed she became better, but by carelessness she took more cold and again became very sick, becoming cold like a person soon to pass away.

Deacon Brannen visited us February 25th.

After he had prayed for her all sign of disease left her, and she ate and slept well, having received a great blessing.

She is now well.

We thank you and all the dear friends who prayed for us in our time of sickness.

Yours in the Master's service,

IDA E. LOCKE.

Delivered at Childbirth, Healed of Heart Trouble, Dyspepsia and Lung Disease.

Yea, though I walk through the valley of the shadow of death,
I will fear no evil; for Thou art with me.—*Psalms 23:4.*

ZION CITY, ILLINOIS, February 28, 1904.

DEAR OVERSEER SPEICHER:—I feel it my duty to send you my testimony to the blessings of God.

When our first Zion baby was born you prayed for safe delivery, and God wonderfully answered.

Our boy is now three years old, and plump and healthy.

On the 19th of November the Lord blessed our home with a ten-pound girl.

We praise God for the way He cares for His children when they trust Him.

We also praise God for Zion, and for our Leader, and for such a City as this in which to live.

We have six children.

When God saved me from sin, He healed my body of several diseases, such as dyspepsia, heart trouble, and lung and throat disease, from which I had suffered for about ten years.

May God greatly bless you and Zion in all the land Till Jesus Come.

Faithfully yours, (MRS.) M. L. RAY.

ELIJAH THE RESTORER.

Around-the-World Visitation

of the

Rev. John Alex. Dowie

Elijah the Restorer
General Overseer of the Christian Catholic Church in Zion.

By ARTHUR W. NEWCOMB, Special Correspondent.

VISITATIONS TO LONDON AND NEW YORK AND RETURN TO ZION CITY.

THE last paper of this series closed with the report of the meeting held by the General Overseer in the *Groote Doelenzaal*, Rotterdam, Holland, on the evening of Friday, June 10th, and his embarkation on the Steamer *Dresden*, for London, by way of Harwich, immediately after that service.

We were accompanied, on this journey, by Elder Percy Clibborn, and the Revs. Arthur S. and Catherine Booth-Clibborn.

The run across the German Ocean was made that night without special incident, and when we awoke the next morning, it was to look out upon the green shores of Old England, as the little steamer was making her way to the wharf in the harbor of Harwich.

There we found the train for London awaiting our arrival, which was a little late, owing to foggy weather during the night.

The English newspaper reporter is not as enterprising as the American, and our arrival at Harwich was evidently not expected by them, as none put in an appearance at the wharf.

English Rural Scenery.

In our short ride from Harwich to London, some of us had our first view of the charming scenery of rural England, so distinctive in its character, with its long, narrow lanes, bordered by green hedgerows, that one could never mistake it for scenery in any other part of the world.

Only when we passed through cities and villages did the landscape lose its beauty.

In these it seemed to us that nearly all the houses were designed by the same architect, or at least on the same lines, and the ubiquitous "chimney-pot" was not only hideous in itself, but very monotonous when multiplied by the thousand.

In about an hour we were running through the close, stifling ill-kept streets of London, and at about nine o'clock we arrived at the Great Eastern Railway Station in Liverpool street.

Even here the newspapers seemed to have missed the General Overseer, although they were so frantically eager to keep their readers informed as to his whereabouts.

In their noon editions, some of the newspapers stated that it was conjectured that Dowie was in London; some of them were even bold enough to hazard a guess that he was there, but none of them seemed to be quite sure

At the station, the General Overseer was met by Overseer Harry E. Cantel, Elder Ruth S. Cantel, and a number of the officers and members of the Christian Catholic Church in Zion in London.

He was at once escorted to the parlors of the Great Eastern Hotel, which is a part of the railway station in Liverpool street.

There he was met by Overseer Jane Dowie and Dr. A. J. Gladstone Dowie, who had very strange news for him.

Powerful Secret Influence Closes London Hotels Against General Overseer.

Overseer Dowie and her son had been in London for several days, and during that time had been guests at the Hotel Russell, one of the principal hotels in the city, and which had very cordially and hospitably entertained the General Overseer and his family during his London Mission, in October, 1900.

The manager of this hotel had very heartily and gladly received the Overseer and her son on this occasion; and had expressed himself as delighted to reserve rooms for the General Overseer.

On the previous day, Friday, June 10th, Overseer Jane Dowie and Dr. A. J. Gladstone Dowie had spent the day sightseeing at Oxford, not returning to the hotel until late in the evening.

Upon their arrival there, they had been waited upon by the manager, who was in a pitiable state of mind.

He informed them that, on account of the General Overseer's alleged attacks upon King Edward, the Directors had decided that he could not be entertained at the Hotel Russell.

It developed that an ill-favored individual, with red hair, who represented himself to be a reporter on the London *Daily News*, had called upon the manager with a copy of LEAVES OF HEALING, Volume XII., No. 7, containing the words of the General Overseer spoken in the Chicago Auditorium on Lord's Day afternoon, November 30, 1902, when he exposed the apostasy of the Church of England and its head, the so-called "Defender of the Faith."

After having called the manager's attention to these words, the professed reporter threatened him that if he gave shelter to the man who had said such terrible things, the *Daily News* would reprint the attack, and bring a mob of tens of thousands down upon the hotel.

The manager of the hotel had consulted with the directors regarding the matter, and evidently some hidden power had brought force to bear upon them, for the decision was that the Hotel Russell could not entertain John Alexander Dowie.

Cowardly Malice of the London Newspapers.

The generous self-restraint of the highly respectable *Daily News* in not reprinting the attacks which its editors professed to believe would set London ablaze with riotous, murderous patriotism and loyalty, was most admirable.

It is to be especially commended in view of the fact that every word of the attack was truth, and would have been recognized as such by every intelligent reader in London, and throughout England, to the shame and chagrin of the court, to the very great injury of the *Daily News*' standing with the sycophants to royalty, and to the great credit of the man who spoke the words, in the eyes of all good English people.

In this matter, not only the *Daily News*, but nearly all the other London newspapers showed the slimy depths of cowardly subserviency to which humanity can sink.

While they carefully refrained from printing what the General Overseer actually said, they all, with one accord, filled columns with cunningly-worded insinuations of terrible insults and seditious utterances, calculated to inflame the people, and with repeated and unmistakable suggestions of violence and murder, intended to point out to the rabble the way to give vent to their wrath.

There is no question that, from the time that it was announced that the General Overseer would visit London until he was on board the *Lucania* and out of the harbor of Liverpool, the London press made every possible effort to arouse the lowest and most lawless and dangerous elements of England's degenerate population to murderous fury against the Prophet of God.

If he had been murdered, as they hoped, his blood would have been on their craven heads and on the heads of the secret orders who inspired their utterances and urged them on in their diabolical conspiracy of lying.

Following the announcement that the General Overseer would be excluded from the Hotel Russell, Overseer Cantel and Dr. A. J. Gladstone Dowie had visited several of the other leading hotels of London in search of accommodations.

At every place, however, they had been either followed or preceded by the evil-visaged man who professed to be a reporter from the *Daily News*, and who, with threats and other means of influence, intimidated all the hotel managers, so that they with one accord refused accommodations.

This was the status of the case when the General Overseer arrived in London.

Calm, Fearless Reasonableness Shames an Insolent Coward.

Overseer Jane Dowie and her son had breakfasted at the Great Eastern Hotel, and Overseer Dowie was waiting in the parlor, as a guest of that hostelry. There she received the General Overseer.

He had not been there long, however, before the manager of the hotel entered, in a most pitiful state of mingled anger and terror, and very brutally and insolently ordered the General Overseer, Overseer Jane Dowie, Dr. A. J. Gladstone Dowie, and Overseer and Elder Cantel out of his house without a moment's delay.

The General Overseer, however, knowing his rights, was perfectly calm and courteous.

By showing the manager a little common sense and reason as well as ordinary civility, the man of God shamed him into something like his right mind, so that he very rapidly cooled down and humbled himself, ending the conversation by offering the General Overseer every possible courtesy and assistance, with the one exception of permitting him to remain in the hotel, which he could not do, on account of orders from a higher authority.

Then, although the hotel and its vicinity were infested with reporters, the General Overseer very quietly slipped out and drove away to the home of Overseer Cantel, in Muswell Hill, unobserved.

Posters Ask "Where Is Dowie?"

In a few hours the city was flaming with great posters, issued by the newspapers, with the words "WHERE IS DOWIE?" printed on them in large letters, while the newspapers themselves admitted in their columns that he had given their hounds the slip and had disappeared.

Some of them, of course, were not satisfied with the plain truth of the matter, but falsely stated that the General Overseer had gone to Zion Tabernacle, 81 Euston road, and there held a meeting.

Late that afternoon accommodations were found for the General Overseer, Overseer Jane Dowie, and Dr. A. J. Gladstone Dowie, and Deacon and Deaconess Stern, at the Hotel Cecil, where the General Overseer had been entertained for a few days, during his visit to London in the summer of 1900.

That evening they took possession of the rooms that had been engaged, and once more they were able to outwit the reporters, not a single paper in the city knowing where the General Overseer was until Sunday night.

In the meantime, however, with the possible exception of the *Daily Chronicle*, every newspaper in the city of London was filled with the most outrageous lies.

The meetings of the Lord's Day were held in Zion Tabernacle, 81 Euston road, a very handsome and well-equipped meeting-place as to its interior, although not strikingly prepossessing on the outside.

This is not unusual in London, however, as, with the exception of some of the public buildings, the idea of the architects seems to have been to make the city as hideous, gloomy, monotonous and depressing as possible. In this they are very effectively seconded by the weather.

Zion Tabernacle, however, while it is as bright and cheerful inside as a place could be in the dark gray compound that they call atmosphere in London, was entirely too small for the many thousands who desired to hear the General Overseer.

All London Halls Refused to the General Overseer.

With this fact in view, the General Overseer had written Overseer Cantel, from Australia, directing him, if possible, to secure the Albert Hall for his meetings in London, failing in which he was to engage the largest hall available.

In pursuance of these instructions, Overseer Cantel had labored almost incessantly for weeks, attempting to secure a suitable meeting-place.

He had found, however, that the proprietors, managers and directors of all large halls seemed to be in a conspiracy against the Prophet of God; for, beginning with the Albert Hall and continuing down through all the others, including practically every theater in London, all were refused, some of them with the most insulting language.

In the case of Queen's Hall the contract for the use of the hall had been made, and then apparently some influence was brought to bear, and the management canceled their agreement.

It was in consequence of this inability to secure a proper meeting-place in London that the General Overseer had decided not to hold meetings in that city during the week of June 5th to 12th inclusive and had visited French Switzerland, Germany and Holland instead.

It was also for this reason that the four meetings planned to be held in Zion Tabernacle on Lord's Day and Monday, June 12th and 13th, were strictly private, admission being granted only to members of the Christian Catholic Church in Zion and to their personal friends.

On Saturday, June 11th, a large number of the members and friends of Zion had come to London from the provinces, Scotland, Ireland, and Holland. Among these were a party of fifty from Leeds in charge of Deacon (now Evangelist) Robert McKell.

Lord's Day Morning Service in London.

The first service of the Lord's Day was held at ten o'clock in the morning.

The weather, according to Londoners, was unusually bright, although to us, whose eyes were accustomed to the crystalline purity and clearness of Zion City atmosphere, it seemed somewhat dull and gloomy.

Zion Tabernacle, in Euston road, was crowded to its utmost capacity with an audience whose faces glowed with joy at this privilege of meeting with and hearing the words of their beloved General Overseer, the prophet of God, in these Times of the Restoration of All Things.

Here, too, the members of the Around-the-World Visitation party who had been so long away from home, were delighted to see again the neat and handsome uniforms of Zion Guard and the beautiful white robes of Zion Choir.

The Choir here is under the able direction of Deacon E. A. Rush, whom we found to be a young Englishman of resourceful energy, and a great assistance to Overseer Cantel in the work at the offices of the Headquarters of the Christian Catholic Church in Zion in the United Kingdom.

After the Choir and Robed Officers had taken their places on the platform, the General Overseer came forward and pronounced the usual

INVOCATION.

God be merciful unto us, and bless us,
And cause Thy face to shine upon us;
That Thy Way may be known upon earth,
Thy Saving Health among all the Nations;
For the sake of Jesus. Amen.

Gift to the General Overseer.

When he had finished, two little bands were seen coming up the aisles—four little boys on one side and four little girls on the other.

They met on the platform, in front of the General Overseer.

The little girls carried a handsome bouquet of cut flowers, and the boys bore between them a beautifully-bound "Book of Remembrances."

This book was taken from the little boys by Overseer Cantel, who read the following address from the title page:

BELOVED GENERAL OVERSEER:—It is with hearts full of gratitude to our Heavenly Father and in loyal loving appreciation of your great Prophetic Ministry that we have prepared this Book of Remembrances.

We, who from its pages are now through the One Spirit in your Ministry bound into one volume, whose beautiful story written upon the tables of our hearts is that of the Gospel of the Kingdom of God.

Our earnest prayers are that we may have proof to be epistles known and read of all men and that with you, our Beloved Leader, we shall be increasingly used to add more Leaves of Healing to the volume of the book.

The book contained spaces for the signatures of three hundred four members and friends of the Christian Catholic Church in Zion, and was partly filled. The remaining space will be taken up by the signatures of residents of Zion City who were formerly members of the Branches of the Church in England.

The General Overseer was deeply moved by the presentation, and expressed his appreciation and gratitude in a few earnest, happy words.

In the service that followed, the man of God was full of joy and enthusiasm at meeting so many of his dear people in England, and at being able to address them in peace and quietness, notwithstanding the strenuous efforts of the newspapers to stir up disorder about the Tabernacle.

His persecution by the press, and his exclusion from the hotels, had not daunted him in the least, but had only fired his zeal, so that this meeting was one long to be remembered by the few hundred who were so fortunate as to be present.

The following is a condensed report of the service:

Zion Tabernacle, 81 Euston Road, London, England, Lord's Day Morning, June 12, 1904.
*REPORTED BY E. W. AND A. W. N.

After the singing of a hymn, Overseer Excell read from the 35th chapter of Isaiah and also the first nineteen verses of the 11th chapter of Matthew.

The General Overseer then spoke briefly concerning the false allegation that he had insulted King Edward VII., closing his reference to the subject with the words:

The pretense, the shameful, foolish, silly pretense, that I insulted King Edward will rebound with thousandfold power upon those who made it.

God's Protecting Care of His Prophets.

I should like to read to you some words which, as I approached London yesterday, were impressed upon my mind.

When they were but a few men in number;
Yea, very few, and sojourners in it;
And they went about from nation to nation,
From one kingdom to another people.
He suffered no man to do them wrong;
Yea, He reproved kings for their sakes;
Saying, Touch not Mine anointed ones,
And do My prophets no harm.

We have gone from nation to nation, from one country to another, and those who would have harmed us, have been reproved.

God has manifestly not permitted the Evil One to touch us.

Prayer was then offered by Overseer Cantel.

After the tithes and offerings were received, the General Overseer delivered the morning address, on the subject "Wisdom is Justified by her Works."

The Kingdom of God Proclaimed.

He opened with the story of John the Baptist, telling how that mighty prophet of God, at the cost of his life stood for Purity, which is the Central Pillar in the House of Wisdom.

The Gospel of the Kingdom of God, the Kingdom of which he was the Divinely-commissioned herald, was then declared in no uncertain tones.

Its imminent establishment, throughout the earth, and its supremacy over all other forms of government, was proclaimed.

Its beginnings, even now, in Zion, were shown, to the joy of the people of God present.

The Service closed with a solemn Prayer of Consecration, joined in by the entire congregation, and the General Overseer's pronouncing the Benediction.

Fruitless Efforts of London Reporters to Hear.

During both morning and afternoon services, there was the most vigorous work, on the part of a number of newspaper reporters, to hear the words of the speaker.

They climbed up to the roofs of the houses in the vicinity, they hung out of windows of buildings across the alley, they loitered about the entrance, hoping to get something from the people who came out, and two young women reporters attempted a trick that failed to work.

By hook or crook they had obtained admission to the Tabernacle, and were just beginning to think that they were about to outwit the vigilance of Zion Guard, when the General Overseer was informed of their presence and given their names.

With all solemnity, he read the name of the leader of the pair, and stated that she was wanted at the door.

After a moment's hesitation, she rose and made her way thither.

"Her friend is also wanted," said the General Overseer, and the friend followed.

They were not seen again, for, when they reached the door, they were very politely asked to retire from the hall.

Then the General Overseer delighted his audience by telling why the ladies had been called to the door.

Notwithstanding all their efforts, however, the reporters failed to get any account of what God's Messenger said. That being the case, they followed the example often set by Chicago and New York papers, and proceeded to manufacture reports of the day's services out of their own filthy imaginations.

*The following address has not been revised by the General Overseer.

Lord's Day Afternoon Meeting in London.

The afternoon service was, in reality, a continuation of the morning meeting, with a steady increase in spiritual power, from the Invocation to the Benediction.

It was a deep spiritual experience in the lives of the hundreds of God's children from all parts of Great Britain and Ireland, and from other lands, the flame of which will kindle lights in many dark places.

The service began with the Procession of the White-robed Choir of the London Branch, following which the Robed Officers and the General Overseer and Overseer Jane Dowie came upon the platform.

The following is a partial report of the General Overseer's Message:

Zion Tabernacle, 81 Euston Road, London, England, Lord's Day Afternoon, June 12, 1904.
*REPORTED BY E. W. AND A. W. N.

The General Overseer then pronounced the

INVOCATION.

God be merciful unto us, and bless us,
And cause Thy face to shine upon us;
That Thy Way may be known upon earth,
Thy Saving Health among all the Nations;
For the sake of Jesus. Amen.

The Choir and Congregation then joined in singing a hymn.

The General Overseer then said:

England's Boasted Liberty an Empty Name.

I would have been glad to have held this meeting in the Albert Hall, which we could have easily filled, or in the Queen's Hall, or in some other, but we have been refused these halls.

We have been told that there is "no room for us in the inn."

It is all right; God knows.

Strange, is it not, that there is less liberty in London than in Berlin; that in Berlin, without any difficulty, we spoke to many, many thousands!

Strange that there should be less liberty here than in Paris, or Bern, or Geneva, or Lausanne, or Neuchatel, or Rotterdam!

At the last-named place, with only twenty-four hours' notice, we spoke to people that filled one of the largest halls of the city, and the streets were black with people who could not get in.

In the City of London, with the single exception of this little hall, for which we pay rent, and which is our property while we do so, we have no place.

If it had been possible for the enemies of Zion to have kept us out of this Tabernacle today, they would have done it.

That is the boasted Liberty in England!

I say this by way of explanation that the meeting is not a public one.

It is a gathering of the members of the Christian Catholic Church in Zion, and of a few friends to whom tickets have been given on condition that they should come as friends.

Why is it that the newspapers strive so eagerly to get into our meetings, and to have interviews with us, and yet are exciting the people to do violence, and endeavoring to blacken our character? You can understand the reason why.

I have never been afraid of any report whether it was good or bad, but I have a right, as far as possible, to prevent misrepresentation by keeping those who do that outside the doors.

England's Wicked King Again Rebuked.

The man of God then made brief reference to the allegations that had been so freely circulated, that he had attacked King Edward VII. As this matter is dealt with in full in the reports of the General Overseer's Messages in Shiloh Tabernacle, Lord's Day afternoons, July 3 and 10, 1904, and published in LEAVES OF HEALING for Saturday, July 9th, and will be published next week, we omit the report of his remarks on this subject.

Suffice it to say that they were bold and fearless, and that the Prophet of God retracted nothing that he had said; on the contrary, emphasizing some of his rebukes to the King on account of his dissolute life.

Tremendous Effect of the Prophet's Words.

Among other things he said:

The day will come when London will be ashamed of its treatment of John Alexander Dowie today.

Small as he is, he is big enough to be a factor in the world. I never heard of so much trouble arising, from the Court down to the very last gutter paper.

I said that the Lord Jesus, the Christ, was a bigger Man than King Edward VII.

I say that with all love, but I am not disrespectful.

I am told that in private life he is a very much beloved man, but, if I may be allowed some day, when I get to America, to say what I think of him as Defender of the Faith, I shall say that I think he is doing mighty little on that line—but then, I should say that in America, you know. I do not know whether it is high treason here. [Laughter.]

I might even suggest—in America—that it was questionable whether he had any faith at all.

I do say, from my heart, "God save the King! God save the Queen! God save the Prince and Princess of Wales! Save them, spirit, soul and body, because they could be a mighty power if they were saved."

I do not know, some of them may be saved.

All of them may be saved for aught I really know.

I cannot positively tell, although I might have an opinion on the subject—in America.

The General Overseer then led the people in the recitation of the Apostles' Creed and the Eleven Commandments.

The 60th chapter of Isaiah was read by Overseer Jane Dowie.

Prayer was offered by Overseer H. E. Cantel.

After the announcements, the General Overseer invoked God's blessing upon his words, that they might be profitable to all that heard.

His address, which followed, was on "The Beginning of the Gospel."

Taking up first the story of the Philippian jailor, the man of God drew many spiritual and practical lessons from this account of the sudden conversion, the chief of them being that the man had repented before Paul said to him, "Believe on the Lord Jesus, the Christ, and thou shalt be saved, thou and thy house."

The General Overseer, after discussing, with great effectiveness, the true meaning of the Gospel Message, and showing how the principles of the Gospel were being applied to every phase of human activity in the City of Zion, called upon the people for consecration.

All in the Tabernacle rose, and, with joy and earnestness, repeated after the General Overseer, the following

PRAYER OF CONSECRATION.

My God and Father, in Jesus' Name I come to Thee. Take me as I am. Make me what I ought to be, in spirit, in soul, and in body. Give me power to do right, no matter what it costs. Give me strength to confess and to restore to my fellow men. Help me to do right in Thy sight; to obey Thee, to serve Thee, to love Thee, to do Thy Will. Take away my sin. Give me Thy Spirit. Make me clean and keep me clean. For Jesus' sake. Amen.

BENEDICTION.

Beloved, abstain from every form of evil. And may the very God of Peace Himself sanctify you wholly; and I pray God your whole spirit and soul and body be preserved entire, without blame, unto the coming of our Lord Jesus, the Christ. Faithful is He that calleth you, who also will do it. The grace of our Lord Jesus, the Christ, the love of God, our Father, the fellowship of the Holy Spirit, our Comforter and Guide, one Eternal God, abide in you, bless you and keep you, and all the Israel of God everywhere, forever. Amen.

ORDINATION OF OFFICERS.

After a few minutes' intermission, the General Overseer again came upon the platform and proceeded at once to the Ordination of Officers.

This Ordination was a very important one, as those thus consecrated to the work of the ministry of God in the Christian Catholic Church in Zion were set aside for service, not only in London and various parts of England, Scotland, and Ireland, but also in Holland and in France.

Among these were the Rev. Arthur S. Booth-Clibborn and his wife, the Rev. Catherine Booth-Clibborn, formerly high officials in the Salvation Army, who had been received into the fellowship of the Christian Catholic Church in Zion, by the General Overseer, at Neuchatel, Switzerland, just one week before.

By a strange coincidence, at the very moment when the General Overseer was laying hands upon these two for their ordination as Elders, a company of the Salvation Army began a meeting in the street outside, and the noise from their drums and tamborines floated in through the windows.

Among others ordained on this occasion were two Deacons and three Deaconesses from Rotterdam, Holland—earnest, efficient men and women, wholly devoted to the cause of the extension of the Kingdom of God in their country.

They had crossed the German Ocean, after the General Overseer's meeting in Rotterdam, on the previous Friday night, in order to be at the meetings in London.

Deacon Robert McKell, whom God has greatly used in the work of Zion in Leeds, England, and vicinity, and who has been much blessed to the sick and sorrowing, was ordained to the office of Evangelist.

Evangelist McKell, whom we had the pleasure of meeting for the first time at these services, after having read with great interest of his work in the North of England, is a splendid specimen of consecrated Christian manhood.

The Ordination Service was a very solemn and impressive one, the entire audience being in a spirit of earnest prayer throughout.

The following is a list of the Officers ordained by the General Overseer, with their present addresses:

ELDERS.

Arthur Sidney Booth-Clibborn, 147 Rue Tenbosch, Brussels, Belgium.
Mrs. Catherine Booth-Clibborn, 147 Rue Tenbosch, Brussels, Belgium.

EVANGELISTS.

Robert McKell, 3 Christ Church avenue, Armley, Leeds, Yorkshire, England.

DEACONS.

Fred Barlow, 46 Carlisle street, Kilnhurst, Rotherham, Yorkshire, England.
Richard Augustine Beetlestone, 153 Gwydir street, Cambridge, England.
John Cosgrove, 72 Fitzroy street, Ashton-under-Tyne, Lancashire, England.
Johan Georg Guttling, Oppert 28, Rotterdam, Holland.
John Hall, Albert House, Low Fell, Gateshead, Durham, England.
David James Herron, 6 Tennyson street, Morley, Yorkshire, England.
William George Humphrey, "Mount Villa," Cliff road, Leigh-on-Sea, Essex, England.
Thomas Jones, 39 Carrington street, Bradford, Yorkshire, England.
Frank Wenden Martin, Kuke's Farm, Birch, Colchester, Essex, England.
John Laurence Marwick, 133 Hilltown, Dundee, Scotland.
Arthur Richardson, 15 Pelham road, Wood Green, N., London, England.
Melchior Diederik Voskuil, 75 Agniesestraat, Rotterdam, Holland.

DEACONESSES.

Mrs. Annie Nicholson Angus, "Roseville," King's Kettle, Fifeshire, Scotland.
Mrs. Annie Beetlestone, 153 Gwydir street, Cambridge, England.
Miss Martha Elizabeth Fernley, 23 Cromack View, Waterloo road, Pudsey, Leeds, Yorkshire, England.
Mrs. Frederica Wilhelmina Guttling, Oppert 28, Rotterdam, Holland.
Mrs. Ann Hall, Albert House, Low Fell, Gateshead, Durham, England.
Mrs. Selina Hanson, 4 Upper Accommodation road, Leeds, Yorkshire, England.
Miss Johanna Petronella Hisschemoller, 176 Noordsingel, Rotterdam, Holland.
Miss Martha Jane Hodge, 45 Clarence street, Albert road, Morley, Yorkshire, England.
Mrs. Agnes Humphrey, "Mount Villa," Cliff road, Leigh-on-Sea, Essex, England.
Miss Elizabeth Louisa Mackay, 44 University avenue, Belfast, Ireland.
Mrs. Neeltje Clasina Ort, Oppert 28, Rotterdam, Holland.
Miss Mary Ann Sach, 255 Cauldwell Hall road, Ipswich, Suffolk, England.
Mrs. Mary Helen Westerman, 6 Ashfield Grove, Bridge street, Morley, Yorkshire, England.
Miss Martha Emma Woodhead, 6 Albury Terrace, Waterloo, Pudsey, Leeds, Yorkshire, England.

COMMUNION OF THE LORD'S SUPPER.

After the Ordination the General Overseer administered the Ordinance of the Lord's Supper to the six hundred Christians who remained in the Tabernacle.

It was a delightful and blessed privilege, in the midst of that great world-center of secret Baal-worship, in the midst of that great seething Babylon of all kinds of wickedness, while a murderous rabble waited outside, to gather, in the calmness of perfect faith and trust, around the Lord's Table, to eat of the emblems of His broken body and shed blood in remembrance of Him "Till He Come"—till He come, whose right it is to reign, and who, when He comes, will purify the great festering plague-spots of this earth with the Consuming Fire of God's Love.

At the close of this very precious season of communion, the General Overseer gave his "Family Talk," that little time of confidential heart-to-heart communion of the pastor with his flock, which has ever been full of the richest spiritual blessing.

He spoke with joyous, unfaltering tones, not knowing what might be the result of his drive along the streets of London immediately after the service, when he must pass through the midst of a mob roused and infuriated by the diabolical lies of a cowardly press.

Calmly, as if in his own Tabernacle in Zion City, he pronounced the Benediction, and then heartily gave the salutation, "Peace to thee!"

With a depth of love and prayer vibrating in their voices, the people responded, "Peace to thee be multiplied!"

All remained quietly in their seats, in order that the General Overseer and Overseer Jane Dowie might not be impeded in their way from the Tabernacle to their carriage, and also that the attention of the mob might not be drawn by people leaving the building.

A Murderous Mob Outwitted.

In Euston road, thousands of people had gathered on the curb opposite the Tabernacle, a large force of police being necessary to keep the sidewalk in front of the Tabernacle and the street itself clear.

As Euston road is one of the busiest streets in London, especially at this point, where many of the great railway stations are, it was absolutely necessary that it be kept open for traffic.

Hence, when the General Overseer's carriage drove up, there was no mob immediately surrounding it, so that, protected by a small company of Zion Guard, he was able to come down from the Tabernacle, and, with Overseer Jane Dowie and Dr. A. J. Gladstone Dowie, to enter the carriage without molestation.

As soon as the great mob across the street saw what was being done, they brushed aside the police and made a rush for the carriage "boohooing" and bellowing like the bulls of Bashan, and shouting "Hang him, hang him!"

The General Overseer had entered the carriage, which had driven away so quickly that it was almost immediately lost in the great procession of vehicles constantly passing by, and the mob was thrown off the scent.

Elder Booth-Clibborn Mistaken for the General Overseer and Assaulted.

Bewildered for a moment, they stood waiting.

Then they caught sight of Elder Arthur S. Booth-Clibborn, who had been one of the guards accompanying the General Overseer down to the carriage.

Some one in the mob mistook him for the General Overseer, and shouted, "There's Dowie!"

Instantly there was a rush made for him.

Elder Booth-Clibborn quietly stepped aside and, just in the nick of time, boarded a passing omnibus.

A pack of several hundred immediately set upon the vehicle in full cry.

Two policemen saw the trouble, and mounted the rear platform.

Their presence seemed to awe the crowd somewhat, but it did not prevent them from following the vehicle with howls of rage, and throwing into it the refuse of the streets.

Inside Elder Booth-Clibborn was having a very interesting time.

At first, the passengers seemed to take him for the General Overseer, and several expressed their sympathy with him, one woman saying that she honored him for his rebuke of the King on account of his gambling.

The Elder, of course, explained that he was not Dr. Dowie, but that he was one of his Elders.

He found that most of the passengers were very much interested, and several of them expressed their approval of the stand taken by the General Overseer in London, and their indignation that he should have been so wickedly treated.

A Strenuous Beginning of Work.

Elder Clibborn offered some subscriptions for LEAVES OF HEALING to some of his fellow passengers on the memorable ride, his first work as an Elder in the Christian Catholic Church in Zion. These were gladly accepted.

So persistent was the mob that they followed this omnibus several miles across the City of London to the Victoria Station, which was the terminus of its route.

By the time it had reached there, probably two thousand people surrounded the vehicle, yelling like incarnate devils.

Elder Clibborn expressed his intention of leaving the omnibus and going to Victoria Station to get a train back to his hotel.

Two policemen who had been standing on the rear platform warned him against attempting this, saying that he would surely be killed or very seriously injured once he fell into the hands of the mob.

He pointed out to them, however, that he would not be any safer if he remained much longer inside, as the crowd was rapidly growing in size and fury.

Accordingly with one officer on either side of him, the Elder stepped out and started for the station.

To the great and unwieldy size of the mob he probably owes his life, as they were not organized for attack and got in one another's way as they rushed for him.

As it was, he was quite severely kicked before he could get into the station.

Here a young man whom he had never seen before, who very indignantly resented the brutal treatment given him by the mob, stepped up to his side and volunteered to go with him and do everything in his power to protect him until he reached his hotel. This he very faithfully did.

In the meantime the General Overseer had reached his hotel in safety and was considering plans for the following day.

General Overseer Ordered to Leave the Hotel Cecil.

He had been notified that morning by the management of the Hotel Cecil that they had received orders from higher authority that forbade their entertaining him any longer.

They expressed themselves as being very sorry that such a step on their part had been necessitated, but declared that they could not do otherwise under the circumstances.

That same powerful, secret influence that had made itself felt in the other hotels of London had also entered the doors of the Hotel Cecil.

Relying upon his rights under the law, which compels every licensed victualer to provide entertainment, as far as his accommodations permit, for every orderly applicant who is able to pay for it, the General Overseer demanded that he be permitted to remain at least until the following day. To this demand the management acceded.

Although the danger to his life was imminent, especially as he now had nowhere to lay his head, except some private house, which would be very difficult to protect against the mob, the General Overseer was exceedingly loath to give up the meetings which he had announced for Monday, June 13th.

He therefore postponed final decision on the matter until the morning, in the hope that there might be some new development that would make it possible for him to hold these meetings without foolishly and wickedly exposing his life to danger.

When morning came, however, it was evident that there had been no change in the situation except for the worse.

The Monday morning papers all contained false accounts of his utterances of the Lord's Day, alleging that England's King had been again insulted, this time more flagrantly than ever before. They also printed many other lies.

From the tone of the papers, one would have imagined that some terrible danger threatened the very existence of their "beloved country," and that nothing could save it except the most summary action with the man who had thus villainously assailed the public weal.

A Sorry Day for London Newspaper Men.

One really could not help feeling a little sorry for the poor reporters and paragraphers, their situation was so desperate.

In the first place, the General Overseer had been so unmindful of the inalienable right of the London cur reporters to poke their ugly muzzles into every one's business except their own, as to absolutely refuse to say anything to them.

Then, adding insult to injury, he had left them for many hours yelping and whining about a lost trail, without even so much as a cold scent to appease their jaded nostrils, ending up by taking quarters in the Hotel Cecil, the very royal hotel of London, notwithstanding their utmost efforts that he should not find an abiding place in all the city.

It was a terrible blow to their "professional pride," which, pitiful as it is, is about the nearest approach to a decent feeling that the average London newspaper man ever has.

This same poor "professional pride" received another shock

when the General Overseer addressed two meetings in Zion Tabernacle, and they were able neither to hear what he said nor to pump one word out of the people who were there.

It had been a sad and inglorious day for the London reporters.

The wormwood and the gall had tinctured their reports, and the few leading paragraphs that appeared on that Monday morning.

Knowing that he had been ordered from the Hotel Cecil, a small pack of reporters hung about its several entrances all the morning, waiting for their quarry to emerge, that they might track him to his next stopping place.

General Overseer Decides to Cross to the Continent.

As every hotel in London had closed its doors upon him, leaving him no choice in the matter; as there was no certainty that hotels in other cities in England would dare to receive him, and as the doors of every hall in the city had been closed to him, so that he could not deliver his Message to the people, there was no course open to him but to cross the English Channel and spend on the Continent of Europe the few days before his sailing for America.

Moreover, he had already fearlessly delivered his Message, as far as the circumstances permitted, in Zion Tabernacle.

He accordingly decided to cross to Boulogne, France, and to spend three days under the protection of the French Republic.

Accordingly tickets were taken, and at ten minutes past two o'clock in the afternoon, the reporters, who had grown very weary with their long vigil, were at last rewarded by seeing the General Overseer, Overseer Jane Dowie, Dr. A. J. Gladstone Dowie, and Deacon and Deaconess Carl F. Stern leave the hotel and take their carriages.

Instantly there was a scrambling among the pack.

Cabs were quickly brought up and the trail followed.

It led to the Charing Cross Station, but, by the time the hounds came sniffing down the platform, the General Overseer and his party had taken the compartments on the train that had been reserved for them.

Those of the General Overseer's staff who had accompanied him to the station to complete arrangements about the tickets and baggage, were found to be very uncommunicative, and the reporters had to go hungry.

Of course the evening papers called it "flight."

But the passengers on board the Channel steamer to Boulogne were overheard to remark to one another that this was a very calm, serene, and happy man, although he had spoken words which he knew would put his life in jeopardy, and had been threatened with murder throughout the length and breadth of England.

Upon their arrival at Boulogne, the little party found that the London press had telegraphed to its representatives there to meet them.

From that time until he was on board the *Lucania*, at Liverpool, the General Overseer was shadowed by reporters practically all the time, except for a few hours, concerning which mention will be made later.

The party found very pleasant and quiet accommodations at the Grand Hotel, Wimeriux, a few miles down the coast from Boulogne, where they spent Tuesday, Wednesday, and Thursday, June 14th, 15th, and 16th, resting and attending to important business matters.

Elder Percy Clibborn, General Financial Agent of all Zion's Institutions and Industries on the Continent of Europe, went over from London to complete certain transactions, and a great deal of business was also done by telegraph, cable and mail.

Overseer Excell Holds Meetings in London.

Meantime, the meetings that had been announced for the Zion Tabernacle in London had not been abandoned.

Overseer J. G. Excell, General Ecclesiastical Secretary of the Christian Catholic Church in Zion, had conducted both the morning and the afternoon meetings.

In the morning, he gave very helpful teaching on Divine Healing and the fulfilment of conditions necessary to claiming the promises of God for blessing in spirit, soul, and body, after which he laid hands upon the sick, praying for their healing in the Name of the Lord Jesus, the Christ, in the Power of the Holy Spirit, and in accordance with the Will of God, the Father.

God was present with him, by His Spirit, and the people were blessed in answer to the Prayer of Faith.

In the afternoon, speaking again to an audience that crowded the Tabernacle, he told the story of the founding, growth, and present prosperity and happiness of Zion City, a story which was of the greatest interest to his hearers.

The people were, of course, very much disappointed in not having the General Overseer with them in these meetings, especially as they had been counting on it for so long, but they were comforted by the thought of the glorious seasons of refreshing of the Lord's Day, and by the very able manner in which the General Ecclesiastical Secretary had taken his place.

A Trip Up the Thames.

On Tuesday, June 14th, Overseer Excell, Deacon Williams and the present chronicler took the Thames steamer, *Queen Elizabeth*, for a trip up that historic stream to Hampton Court.

The first few miles of the journey were through the mud and filth of London, the only redeeming feature being several handsome bridges across the river.

As soon as we left the smoke and grime of the city behind, however, we began to enjoy ourselves.

There is a quiet, holiday, leisurely, almost sleepy beauty about the Thames that is very fascinating.

The broad, safe, comfortable rowboats and punts, filled with happy parties enjoying a restful outing; the drowsy houseboats that line its green banks; the slumbering, old, vine-covered villas, castles, and palaces that repose beneath its ancient oaks and elms, dreaming of the clash of arms and the flash and sparkle of courtly pageantry that was their life in the old days, now far in the distant past; the crumbling old churches and abbeys, relics of a religion that is now as lifeless as they; and the quaint, peaceful villages that blink across the tranquil bosom of the river, blend and harmonize into a picture of charming restfulness.

Even the fours and eights of racing oarsmen that skim swiftly along the stream, are representative of the slow, dignified old schools that doze beside the river.

The boating parties sitting in the shade of trees that lazily droop their branches into the water, eat their picnic lunches, or languidly scull or pole from place to place, having seemingly absorbed the summery relaxation of the scene.

The great onward rush of the world has left this little corner, so near its largest city, like an eddy beside a whirlpool, calm and unruffled by the noise, strife and turmoil of a commercial age.

We returned to London at about eight o'clock that evening, feeling that our day's outing had been well spent, and that, however depressing London might be, there was an escape from it in a trip up the river.

A Wednesday Night Rally in London.

On Wednesday evening, we were very pleasantly entertained at dinner at the comfortable and pretty little home of Overseer and Elder Cantel at Muswell Hill, a suburb of London.

After dinner we went to the Tabernacle, in Euston road, to attend the regular midweek rally of the London Branch.

It was a Zion City rally on a smaller scale, and with the General Overseer left out, which made a great difference, but not so great that it was not readily recognizable as a Zion rally.

Overseer Cantell presided in his usual happy style, and a very interesting program was provided, aside from the speeches which the members present of the Around-the-World Visitation Party were called upon to make.

The attendance was good, and the people entered into the spirit of the meeting with enthusiasm.

Off for Liverpool.

On the following afternoon, Thursday, June 16th, we gathered together our baggage and departed from London for Liverpool.

We were joined at the station by Deaconess Stern, who had come over from Wimeriux with the baggage belonging to the members of the party there.

Our journey to Liverpool was a very pleasant one.

We were glad to leave the reeking Babylon of London behind us and to get out upon the sweet, green fields of Old England, where nature, at least was pleasing.

Our way led through the old town of Rugby, the seat of the famous school of that name.

We were fortunate in having in the same compartment with us a former student at this school, a very pleasant young fellow, who kindly gave us much interesting information about the country through which we were passing.

We arrived at the Lime Street Station of the London and Northwestern Railway, in Liverpool, at about half past ten o'clock that night, and were glad to get to our beds in the Northwestern Hotel.

Our Impressions of Liverpool.

The next day, we found that we had time to take stock of the great English seaport.

It is hideous.

Grime, smoke, squalor, poverty, beggary, and wickedness make the place repulsive to all physical and moral senses.

If there are any beauty-spots to relieve this dark picture, we were not there long enough to find them.

In the afternoon, we took an electric car, and went as far out into the country as possible, in order to get away from the depressing influence of the city.

Outside the city, in the suburbs, the view is more pleasing.

During the day, Overseer Harry E. Cantel and Elder Ruth S. Cantel arrived in Liverpool, having come down for a final interview with the General Overseer.

That evening, Friday, June 17, 1904, the General Overseer, Overseer Jane Dowie and Dr. A. J. Gladstone Dowie, accompanied by Elders Percy Clibborn and Carl Hodler, Deaconess Ruth Hofer, Deacon Carl F. Stern and Deacon Henry Stevenson, General Manager of Zion Lace Industries, who had been summoned to England on business by the General Overseer, and had arrived in London on Wednesday evening, June 15th, reached the Lime Street Station, Liverpool.

From Wimerìux to Liverpool.

The General Overseer and party had left Wimeriux that afternoon and had gone to Boulogne, where they were joined by Elder Hodler and Deaconess Hofer. All the way they were followed by reporters.

ROYAL MAIL STEAMSHIP "LUCANIA."

At Boulogne they had taken the Channel steamer for Folkstone, and from there had gone on to London, where they arrived at the Charing Cross Station.

There they found Elder Percy Clibborn and Deacon Stevenson waiting for them with hired carriages.

As they drove away, they were followed by a persistent pack of newspaper hounds, hot on the scent.

But they were in cabs, and thereby came to grief.

The General Overseer and party having an hour or two before it was time to take the Northwestern train for Liverpool, decided to spend that hour driving in Hyde Park, being not unmindful of the fact that the police do not permit cabs in the park.

Forced to remain behind when the carriages passed through the gateway, the reporters could only fume in their rage, outwitted again.

They were not seen again as long as the General Overseer was in London.

Upon his arrival at Liverpool, however, the lost scent had been found, and the local reporters were on hand to receive him. There was no other crowd at the station.

It must be said for the Liverpool press, however, that it treated the General Overseer with very much greater respect and fairness than the London papers, its articles having but very little in them that was objectionable.

When they were told that it would be impossible to see the General Overseer, the reporters took it very good-naturedly, saying that they could hardly blame him for not wanting to talk to newspaper men after the treatment that he had received.

A Night on the "Lucania" in Port.

The General Overseer, Overseer Jane Dowie, and Dr. A. J. Gladstone Dowie went on board the Royal Mail Steamship *Lucania* immediately, and spent the night there.

They were enabled to do this, a very uncommon privilege, through the courtesy of the Cunard Steamship Company, its New York, London, and Liverpool officials coöperating to give the General Overseer and his Around-the-World Visitation Party every possible comfort and convenience.

That night was spent very quietly on board the steamship.

Farewell to Friends in England.

On the following morning, the General Overseer received Overseer Cantel, Elders Hodler and Clibborn, and Deacon Stevenson in the library of the ship, there giving them his final directions before leaving the Old World.

Early in the afternoon, the other members of the party went on board with the baggage, and at half past four o'clock lines were cast off, the bugle sounded, and the *Lucania* steamed away from the wharf.

The General Overseer and his Around-the-world Visitation Party were at last on their way across the three thousand one hundred miles of ocean that divided them from the great land that they called home, which had grown so dear to every one of them during the five months that they had been absent from it.

A great crowd stood on the pier waving and shouting good-by to friends on board, keeping it up as long as the ship was in sight.

The "Lucania."

The *Lucania* is one of the largest and fleetest of the ships of the Cunard Company, and is also a very steady, comfortable, and well-equipped home for the seven days of the voyage across the Atlantic.

Its average daily run during this trip was about five hundred ten knots.

We found the commander, Captain Watt, and all his staff, very able, courteous, and obliging, doing all in their power to make the voyage pleasant for us.

Saturday night, June 18th, we crossed the Irish Sea to Queenstown, where we arrived Sunday morning, after a very smooth and pleasant passage.

Here we took on board the American mail from London and in a few hours were plowing our way across the broad Atlantic.

Five Days of Dark, Stormy Weather.

The first five days of our voyage were very stormy, and the sea was sometimes rough, but the members of the Visitation Party were delighted to find that they were now hardened sailors, and that no amount of pitching and rolling of the ship could shake their internal equilibrium.

On Thursday, June 23d, the storm seemed to reach its height, and for several hours the gale lashed the sea into a seething caldron of foamy brine, great deluges of water being swept over the deck with every lurch of the vessel.

It was cold and disagreeable during all this time, so that overcoats were a comfort on deck.

Notwithstanding all this, our voyage was not at all unpleasant.

It seemed good to be at sea once more, breathing the invigorating salt air, and feeling in our pulses the powerful rush of the ship through the water.

Our fellow passengers, while few in number, were very quiet, respectable, well-behaved, courteous people, with whom it was a pleasure to travel.

Although the time of the voyage was so short, we made the acquaintance of several of them, who seemed to take a great interest in the General Overseer and the work of Zion.

Every morning and evening, the party would gather in the music saloon and join in singing a few Zion hymns, after which we went to one of the cabins and joined in the reading of the Word of God and in prayer.

A number of the passengers got into the habit of dropping into the music saloon at these times, and seemed to enjoy the singing.

Marconigrams.

One of the most interesting features of the voyage was the continual communication of the *Lucania* with either the land or with other vessels by means of ether waves, or "wireless telegraphy," as it is commonly called.

The following is a schedule of the Marconigrams received and sent during the trip:

Saturday, June 18th, 4:30 p. m.—In communication with station at Seaforth. Signals were exchanged until 9:30 p. m.

Saturday, 11:30 p. m.—In communication with Rosslare (County Wexford). Transmitting and receiving passengers' messages.

Sunday, June 19th, 4:30 a. m.—In communication with the Admiralty Station at Roches Point.

Sunday, 10:35 a. m.—Communication was established with Crookhaven. Transmitting and receiving passengers' messages until 5:30 p. m. One hundred twenty miles west of the station.

Monday, June 20th, 7:45 p. m.—Latitude 48:34 N., longitude 26:53 W. In communication with Company's Royal Mail Steamship *Carpathia*, bound East.

Tuesday, June 21st, 9:25 a. m.—Latitude 46:37 N., longitude 33:42 W. In communication with the French Transatlantique Steamship *La Gascogne*, bound East.

Tuesday, 8:10 p. m.—Latitude 44:55 N., longtitude 38:23 W. In communication with the Steamship *Moltke*, bound West.

Tuesday 10:00 p. m.—Latitude 44:37 N., longtitude 39:12 W. In communication with Company's Royal Mail Steamship *Campania*, bound East.

Wednesday, June 22d, 7:12 a. m.—Latitude 42:49 N., longtitude 40:20 W. In communication with the Atlantic Transport Line Steamship *Minneapolis*, bound East.

Wednesday, 11:00 a.m.—Latitude 42:20 N., longitude 44:29 W. In communication with the Red Star Line steamship *Zeeland*, bound East.

Thursday, June 23d, 8:30 a.m.—Latitude 40:52 N., longitude 54:18 W.—In communication with the Steamship *Kaiser Wilhelm der Grosse*, bound East.

Thursday, 2:30 p m.—Latitude 40:43 N., longitude 57:01 W. In communication with the Company's Royal Mail Steamhip *Saxonia*, bound East.

By Wireless Telegraphy from French Transatlantique Steamship *La Savoie*, June 24th, a long digest of the news of the world from the time of sailing of the *Lucania*.

Latest news from New York was received by wireless telegraphy from Nantucket Lightship, June 24th.

A Message from a Zion Deacon in Mid-ocean.

While the above was very interesting to us, it did not have the value of the following message, which had come across the waves from a vessel hardly in sight, and was handed to the General Overseer:

THE MARCONI INTERNATIONAL MARINE COMMUNICATION COMPANY LIMITED.

18 FITZ LANE, LONDON, E. C., LUCANIA STATION, June 24, 1904.

To JOHN ALEXANDER DOWIE, *Lucania*:

Peace to thee!
My wife and I are on *La Savoie* for Italy.
Very sorry to miss seeing you.
Pray for us.
God be with you. DEACON NATINO.

Deacon Natino is an Officer in the Christian Catholic Church in Zion in connection with the Branch in New York City, having been ordained by the General Overseer, at the close of the New York Visitation last fall.

In reply to this message the General Overseer sent the following:

TO DEACON NATINO, *La Savoie*.

Thanks for kind message.
Peace to Thee!
Zion and General Overseer send love to Italia.
God bless you and your dear wife!

JOHN ALEXANDER DOWIE.

One Day of Fine Weather on the Atlantic.

On Friday, June 24th, we all rejoiced in the change of the weather from storm to calm, from darkness and gloom to bright sunshine, and from chilling cold to genial warmth.

The General Overseer had said all the way that we would have fine weather as we approached the shores of our own beloved country, and his prophecy proved to have been true.

That night we made the final arrangements for landing, which, we were informed, would be at an early hour the next morning, and retired with happy hearts, rejoicing in the thought that on the morrow we should once more set foot upon the soil of the best country on earth.

It was some time during the wee small hours of the morning of Saturday, June 25, 1904, that we steamed through The Narrows into the New York Harbor and came to anchor at Quarantine.

We Rejoiced to See American Soil Once More.

When the sun rose we looked out and our hearts were filled with praise and thanksgiving to God, as we beheld the green shores of Long and Staten Islands, the Statue of Liberty, and the towering buildings of lower New York City, reflecting the glorious light of the sun.

We had a very enjoyable breakfast at half past six o'clock.

By seven o'clock the *Lucania* was threading her way, amongst the throng of other craft that dotted the harbor, to her wharf at the foot of Jane street.

As we approached the dock we could see the familiar faces of Overseer George L. Mason, Elder Warszawiak, Deacons James F. Peters, Frank W. Cotton, and George A. Corlette, and Michael J. Coffey among the crowd that had gathered to welcome the incoming ship.

Some of these reside in New York, the others had come down from Zion City to meet the General Overseer.

New York Reporters at Work.

Before we were brought alongside, a swarm of New York reporters came on board the vessel and attempted to interview the General Overseer.

He very courteously replied to one and all, "I have nothing to say to the press. Whatever I wish to say to the public I will say at Carnegie Hall tomorrow morning and afternoon."

Most of the reporters had the decency to leave him when he had thus expressed himself, but one or two persisted in their attemps to elicit answers to their impudent questions, with the result that the General Overseer finally had to speak to them very sharply in order to rid himself of their annoying attentions.

Finding themselves thus thrown upon their own resources for the sensational stories concerning the General Overseer's arrival, which they had been ordered to write, the whole company gathered together near by, and could be seen concocting the interviews which they would falsely claim to have had with the General Overseer, and the stories which they would write to go with them.

As the vessel approached the wharf, we could see a squad of photographers belonging to the New York press, waiting for an opportunity to get pictures of the General Overseer, his family, and some of the members of the party.

Some of these pictures were quite successful and some were very poor. Both kinds appeared in the papers the following day.

It seemed a very long time before the gangplank was at last secured, and we once more had the privilege of grasping the hands of our beloved friends, most of whom we had last seen in Zion City.

Deacon Peters, however, had been one of the last to wave his farewells to us as we steamed out of the harbor at San Francisco.

The General Overseer and Overseer Jane Dowie, accompanied by Deacon Carl F. Stern, drove at once to the Fifth Avenue Hotel, where they had the same rooms that they had occupied during the New York Visitation, the management giving expression to its sincere pleasure in having them again under its roof. This was in pleasing contrast with the attitude of the London hotels.

The rest of the party remained at the wharf to attend to getting the baggage through the hands of the United States Customs officials and on its way to the hotel.

Then we also took carriages for the Fifth Avenue Hotel.

"My Own, My Native Land!"

No words can express the emotions of joy, thanksgiving, and praise that filled our hearts as we felt ourselves once more on the soil of the United States of America.

It was like getting home again although a thousand miles still intervened between us and Zion City.

The afternoon was spent by the General Overseer in attending to important business matters, giving interviews to personal and business friends, and in a short drive in Central Park.

The other members of the party attended to private business, and also assisted in the arrangements for the meetings of the following day in Carnegie Hall.

Hot Weather in New York.

That night was one of the hottest we had encountered in all our journey, the heat seeming to be more debilitating and oppressive even than that of the tropics, on account of the great humidity of the atmosphere.

That night and the following morning, we had an opportunity to note again the extraordinary imaginative power of the New York reporter.

It is not necessary, perhaps would not be wise, to repeat here all the astounding lies that they told.

One of the most flagrant of these, however, was one upon which they had all evidently agreed during their conference on the deck of the *Lucania*, Saturday morning.

An Astounding Lie of the New York Newspapers.

This was to the effect that the General Overseer had gone into the smoking-room of the ship, on the way across, and there had heaped coarse and vulgar abuse upon the passengers who were smoking and playing cards, keeping up this tirade until they wearied of it and left the smoking-room, not because they were convinced of the evil of their ways, but in order to escape the tiresome diatribes of their assailant.

This lie was told by practically all of the afternoon and morning papers of the city.

There was a great difference among them as to details, however, some saying that the smokers and card-players had become so angry as to discuss the advisability of throwing the General Overseer overboard; some alleging that some of the men did seize him and throw him out upon the deck; and still others saying that he had been locked up in his stateroom during the latter part of the voyage.

It is needless for us to tell the readers of LEAVES OF HEALING that there is not one single word of truth in the story.

The General Overseer did not enter the smoking-room on the *Lucania*, during the entire voyage; did not even look into it, and did not know whether there was any card-playing going on there or not, although he might have surmised that there was, had he given the matter any special thought.

This is a fair sample of the many lies published in the New York newspapers, concerning the voyage and the arrival of the General Overseer at New York.

Lord's Day Morning Meeting in New York City.

The first meeting of this brief Visitation to New York was held in Carnegie Hall, on Lord's Day morning, June 26th, at ten o'clock.

The day was stiflingly hot, even the pavements seeming to throb with a burning heat.

Notwithstanding the very severe weather, there were probably nearly a thousand persons in the hall when the General Overseer began the service.

The congregation, although small, was composed of many members and friends of the Christian Catholic Church in Zion from the City of New York and vicinity, of a number of very influential men and women who were intensely interested, and of a sprinkling of the merely curious. These last were very respectfully attentive, and their curiosity, in many cases, turned to interest.

The General Overseer was in his happiest mood, rejoicing at being again on American soil, and glad to meet again with his spiritual children and friends in the City of New York.

The people were also very thankful to God to see their beloved Leader, safe from all the dangers that had threatened him.

Despite the intense heat, the meeting was a very enthusiastic one, and full of spiritual blessing.

The following is a partial report of the service:

Carnegie Hall, New York City, Lord's Day Morning, June 26, 1904.
*REPORTED BY I. M. S. AND A. W. N.

The Service was opened by the General Overseer's pronouncing the

INVOCATION.

God, be merciful unto us and bless us,
And cause Thy face to shine upon us;
That Thy Way may be known upon earth,
Thy Saving Health among all the Nations;
For the sake of Jesus. Amen.

He then said, "As I see so many faces of members and friends, I might properly begin with our Zion Salutation, Peace to thee!"

The people responded, "Peace to thee be multiplied!"

After the singing of a hymn, Overseer Jane Dowie read the 67th Psalm; also the first fifteen verses of the 1st chapter of Mark.

Prayer was offered by Overseer John G. Excell, the General Overseer praying for the sick and sorrowing, and leading in the Disciples' Prayer at the close.

After the singing of "Hail to the Brightness of Zion's Glad Morning," the General Overseer said:

Thanksgiving.

I wish first of all to record my gratitude to God for His great goodness to me and to all the members of this Visitation Party, some of whom left Zion City on October 14th last year.

Five of us left Zion City on January 1st and proceeded, after four thousand five hundred miles of railway travel in the Southern States, from San Francisco to Australia, thence back by way of Ceylon and the Suez Canal to Europe.

After a most delightful Visitation to France, German and French Switzerland, Germany and Holland, and a very unpleasant few days in England, we have arrived in New York.

I am glad to say that all have come back in perfect health and exceedingly happy, with our faces once more set toward the little City by the great Lake Michigan, where we find a place that we call "Home."

The announcements were made by Overseer Mason and the tithes and offerings were received, during which "Zion Stands with Hills Surrounded" was sung.

After invoking God's blessing upon his words and thoughts, the General Overseer delivered his Message—a Message proclaiming the Gospel of the Kingdom of God. The Gospel that the Christ came to give to the world, he said, was not the Gospel of a Church, but the Gospel of a Kingdom, the Kingdom of God.

The Kingdom of God is clearly defined by the words of Scripture as Righteousness, Peace and Joy in the Holy Spirit.

The Kingdom of God must therefore be, first of all, within.

But it will take the supremacy, also, in all things.

The Lord Jesus, the Christ, will come to reign.

All other powers and rulers will have to be subject to Him.

When He reigns, Intemperance and Impurity will have to be given up throughout the earth.

The Ten Commandments will then be the Supreme Law, and will have to be obeyed.

The greatest Commandment, however, is the Eleventh, that we love one another better than ourselves.

In order that the Kingdom of God may be within you, you must get clean in spirit, soul, and body, and keep clean.

Give up smoking and drinking.

These habits defile the body and create disease, and their cost to the American people is $1,500,000,000 annually.

Our Lord Jesus, the Christ, wants us to be good, and we cannot be good without getting away from sin, repenting of and forsaking it, and trusting and obeying Him.

All who desire to do this stand with me and pray. [Nearly all rose.]

PRAYER OF CONSECRATION.

My God and Father, in Jesus' Name I come to Thee. Take me as I am, and make me what I ought to be, in spirit, in soul, and in body. Give me power to do right, truly to repent of and forsake sin; to do right to any whom I may have wronged; to love Thee and to serve Thee and my fellow man. For Jesus' sake. Amen. [*Those standing repeated the prayer, clause by clause, after the General Overseer.*]

Did you mean it?

People—"Yes."

General Overseer—Then live it.

It is the ministry of Elijah the Restorer to restore men to God and to one another.

May God bless you.

The services were closed with the singing of the Doxology and the

*The following report has not been revised by the General Overseer.

BENEDICTION.

Beloved, abstain from every form of evil. And may the very God of peace Himself sanctify you wholly; and I pray God your whole spirit and soul and body be preserved entire, without blame, unto the coming of our Lord Jesus, the Christ. Faithful is He that calleth you, who also will do it. The grace of our Lord Jesus, the Christ, the love of God our Father, the fellowship of the Holy Spirit, our Comforter and Guide, one Eternal God, abide in you, bless you and keep you, and all the Israel of God everywhere, forever. Amen.

Lord's Day Afternoon Meeting in New York City.

At just about the time for the afternoon meeting in Carnegie Hall, a sudden thunderstorm struck the city, doing great damage in certain localities.

This, combined with the extreme oppressiveness of the heat, doubtless kept many thousands away who would otherwise have attended the meeting.

There were, however, between twelve and fifteen hundred people present.

This splendid audience was of intelligent, thoughtful people, who gave very earnest attention to the words of the speaker.

God gave His Prophet powerful utterance on this occasion.

The words that he spoke were effectual for the destruction of falsehood and evil, and for the building up of holy lives.

God's children present rejoiced in the bold, fearless Proclamation of Restoration, while many who had come either indifferent or prejudiced were convinced of the truth.

The following is a brief outline of the afternoon service:

Carnegie Hall, New York City, Lord's Day Afternoon, June 26, 1904.
*REPORTED BY I. M. S. AND A. W. N.

After the Invocation and the singing of a hymn, the General Overseer read from the Inspired Word of God, the 35th chapter of the book of the Prophet Isaiah; also part of the 11th chapter of the Gospel according to St. Matthew, from the 1st to the 19th verses, commenting briefly on certain portions of the lesson.

In the course of this exposition, he said:

A Few Burning Words to the New York Press.

The only people that can make peace are the people that go to war for God.

You must be a hater of sin if you would be a lover of God.

I should like to save every young fellow out of the dirty muck and mess of the literary scavengers. I feel like apologizing for hunting blowflies.

You always feel when you have caught them and killed them that they are nasty things.

I charge, in the plainest possible terms, the press of New York with a conspiracy.

They conspired together by their representatives to lie before I came, and they lied.

After I had come they lied harder than ever.

They got together upon the deck of the *Lucania* yesterday morning. Some of them came to me with honeyed lips.

"Doctor, welcome back to America!" they said.

"Yes?"

"Our editor's compliments! Will you please to give the

*The following report has not been revised by the General Overseer.

GENERAL OVERSEER AND PARTY WITH SPECIAL ENGINE AND CAR, ON TRIP OF BUSINESS AND PLEASURE, NEAR NEW YORK CITY, JUNE 27, 1904.

American Scavenger your opinions about King Edward and his patronage of the Salvation Army?"

I would not answer them, for I have nothing to say to the press; but I should think that the Salvation Army must be in a mighty bad way if it is dependent upon King Edward's patronage.

Although I had said, "I have nothing to say to the press," they asked me again, just as if they were deaf, and had not heard what I said. When they persisted, I said again, a little more emphatically, "I have nothing to say to the press."

Some Outrageous Lies Nailed Down.

The first lie they manufactured was, that on board the *Lucania*, I had gone to the smoking-room one day and had abused and railed at the gentlemen there playing cards.

There was not an item of truth in that. Nobody ever told them that.

They made it up themselves, these wretched, mean, little, scavenger liars. I do not know where the smoking-room on the *Lucania* is. I never was inside of it.

I never saw anybody smoking in it and I do not know whether they played cards or not. I never reproved them.

I had nothing to say on that subject during the entire voyage.

The whole of that mass of lies is a fabrication on the part of the press. They all got together to tell the same lie.

But if you examine the accounts, you will see that no two of them agree.

My fellow passengers on the *Lucania* and the officers know that I did not go to the smoking-room, or reprove them for playing cards. If they had asked me what I thought, I certainly would have said to them, "You are stinkpots."

A man has a right to go to the Devil if he likes, but I will do all I can to keep you from going there.

I remember that your dear old mother prayed over you when you were a sweet little baby and wanted you to be a good man, and if she is in heaven now she will say, "Thank God that Dr. Dowie is talking like that down there in New York. May God grant that my son will cease to be a stinkpot."

But the stories that you have been reading in the New York papers are all makeup on the part of these lying little dogs that I threw out last November.

They remember that I did it, too.

A Zion Daily Promised in New York City.

The next time I come to New York with Zion Restoration Host, I will have my own daily paper. [Applause.]

Voice—"We need one."

General Overseer—It is time that we had a daily ZION BANNER in New York.

Before God and all humanity I brand as lies the words of the press, without any exception, so far as I have been able to see them.

They were born in sin, conceived in iniquity, and brought forth by the Devil.

The General Overseer then devoted a few minutes to the discussion of his alleged insults to King Edward VII., but as that subject is dealt with elsewhere in this paper, we omit the report of the remarks of God's Prophet here.

Speaking again to the press, he said:

I say to you, Beware! Beware!

End of Methodist Minister Who Would Not Heed Warning of God's Prophet.

A mocking voice came up to me in Melbourne, Australia, in one of my meetings there.

It was that of a Methodist minister.

VIEWS OF PORTIONS OF THE PARADE AT WELCOME HOME OF THE GENERAL OVERSEER AND PARTY FROM AROUND-THE-WORLD VISITATION.

I warned him again, but was very patient with him.

He laughed.

Afterwards the police had to take him out of the vestibule of Zion Tabernacle because of his riotous conduct there.

In a few days his body, with his horse and buggy, was found in a pool of water near his house.

How he got into the water no one knew, but he was dead.

God Almighty had stopped his mouth.

Beware! God will stop your mouths.

"The mouth of them that speak lies shall be stopped!"

I will do my best to stop them.

I will warn you and God will see that it is stopped.

You cannot destroy Zion by these lies, for God hath founded her.

Prayer was offered by Overseer Mason, the General Overseer offering prayer for the sick and suffering, closing with the chanting of the Disciples' Prayer by the Choir and Congregation.

The announcements were made and the tithes and offerings were received.

During the taking of the tithes and offerings, Deaconess Harriet Ware sang, in her clear, sweet voice, and with deep feeling, the simple but beautiful old hymn, "I Gave My Life for Thee."

The General Overseer's Message was one especially to his people in the New York Branch and from the vicinity.

His subject was the "House of Wisdom."

Among other things, he said:

Purity.

The first of the Seven Pillars in the House of Wisdom is Purity.

In laying the foundations of a great building we lay a flawless stone; we see that the foundations are strong and sound throughout.

The great thing in connection with our lives is for us to see that, beyond all question, the foundation is laid upon the Rock of Eternal Purity.

Nothing will live that is not pure.

That which is impure will die.

Countless voices far and wide,
Sing beneath these skies:
All that is beautiful shall abide;
All that is base shall die.

That which is Divinely Pure is Divinely Beautiful.

God will judge, not by what seems to have been right, but by the Purity of our intent and of our desire.

The thing which is essentially pure is always Divine.

Every Word of God is Pure.

Whatever God has said is Pure and True.

You who are laboring in this city believe in the Christ.

You are just a little band, but God has blessed you.

Do not be discouraged.

The General Overseer then told of the hard conditions that marked the beginning of his work in Chicago, and recounted the glorious victories that God gave.

Purity Essential to Power and Progress.

He then emphasized more strongly the great essential character of Purity in this work.

"Purity," he said "is the essential link in the great chain that unites us with our anchor.

"Purity is a condition of Divine Progress."

He then showed how Divine Wisdom was absolutely opposed to earthly wisdom, and the friendship of the world was enmity with God.

He declared that all who followed the Christ would have persecution.

The marks of a True Prophet, he said, are not that all men speak well of him.

Elijah the Tishbite got into trouble with Ahab.

Elijah the Preparer got into trouble with Herod.

I am in trouble with King Edward.

If you do not believe that, go to London and you will soon find it out.

Stand in the middle of Euston road just for a minute and say, "Ladies and gentlemen I want to stand here and say that I am a friend of John Alex. Dowie, and believe every word that he says."

If you get to your hotel alive after that you will do well, and you will find you have a good deal of trouble on your hands.

No man can be a prophet of God, and permit the ruling powers to do evil with impunity.

Purity is demanded of the ministers of God.

When Ahab said to Elijah, "Art thou he that troubleth Israel?" he said, "No! but you and your father's house have troubled Israel."

Elijah had to stand alone, but the day came when God accepted his sacrifice.

Then, in one day, the altars of Baal were overthrown, the priests of Baal were destroyed, and the worship of Jehovah reëstablished.

The Worship of God Has to Be Re-established.

The iniquity which has cursed this world has to be overthrown, and God's righteousness must reign.

You can howl and hiss all you like, but there is one man who is entirely unaffected by it.

The worst that you could do would be to kill him, and that would be the best thing for him.

I will speak the truth, and let Heavenly Wisdom justify me by my works.

"Wisdom is justified by her works."

See to it that your works are pure.

Let the people be pure.

Let the officers be pure.

See to it that, above all things, you are pure.

May God bless you all.

All who want that Heavenly Wisdom stand and ask God for it.

[Nearly every one in the congregation rose.]

PRAYER OF CONSECRATION.

My God and Father, I come to Thee. Give me Wisdom—the Wisdom that makes me a truly penitent sinner, that makes me to right every wrong and to do what is right in Thy sight unto all men. Give me Thy Holy Spirit that I may be wise unto Salvation. Save me from sin and from self, from Satan and from disease, from all the powers of death and of hell. Give me Thy Salvation that Thy Healing Power and Thy Life and the Kingdom of Heaven may be within me. For Jesus' sake. [*All standing repeat the prayer, clause by clause, after the General Overseer.*]

I desire every one who is a child of God to stay to the Communion of the Lord's Supper.

One hundred twenty men and women moved Jerusalem.

If one hundred twenty men and women gather here around the Lord's Table and go out with Divine Unction, they can move New York.

Reception of New Members.

At the close of this service, the General Overseer extended the right hand of fellowship to fifty-seven new members of the Christian Catholic Church in Zion, welcoming each very cordially with an earnest prayer for God's blessing.

It was interesting to note that of this comparatively small number there were representatives, not only of several States in the Union, but of a number of foreign countries. Several also were Hebrews.

The General Overseer, assisted by Overseer Jane Dowie, and Overseers John G. Excell and George L. Mason, and by a number of the Ordained Officers of the Christian Catholic Church in Zion, administered the Ordinance of the Communion of the Lord's Supper.

It was a very delightful and blessed season of communion, and God greatly blessed the several hundred earnest Christians who participated.

When the Ordinance was over, the General Overseer gave a very brief but loving "family talk," and the public meetings of this short visit to New York were over.

A Delightful Trip, Combining Business With Pleasure.

On Monday, June 27th, accompanied by Overseer Jane Dowie, by the gentlemen members of his Visitation party, by those who had come from Zion City to meet him, by Deacon George A. Corlette, and by a number of the officials of a certain large railway running out of New York, the General Overseer made a business trip in the interest of Zion on a special train.

The journey was a very pleasant one, through some of the most picturesque scenery in the United States.

Everything possible was done by the railway officials to make the trip comfortable and pleasant.

Especially enjoyable was the privilege of riding on the observation engine that drew the special car.

For part of the journey our speed was about sixty miles an hour, over a road so smooth that there was scarcely any jar felt.

Tuesday, June 28th, was spent in the City of New York in attending to various matters of importance and in recreation.

Shortly after six o'clock that evening the General Overseer and his family and personal attendants boarded the very comfortable private car "Magnet," which had been kindly provided him by a great railroad company, and the last stage of the long journey around the world was begun.

The other members of the party, which by a curious coincidence numbered thirteen in all, the exact fortunate number with which we had started out, found accommodations in reservations which had been made in a Pullman sleeping-car.

On an American Railway Train.

It was a great joy and pleasure to the members of the Around-the-World Visitation Party to travel in an American railway train again.

The railway service in Australia, Ceylon, the Continent of Europe, and England, may possibly be comfortable and convenient, and our preference may be due to our American prejudice, but, for us at least, it was very much preferable to travel according to the American system.

At any rate, when we retired after evening worship in the private car, we slept more soundly than any of us remembered to have slept in any sleeping-car since we had left the United States, and rose very much refreshed the next morning.

We were in the City of Buffalo at rising time.

We ate our breakfast while speeding along the Southern shore of Lake Erie, on the way to Cleveland.

In the matter of dining-cars, at least, we do not think that any one would dispute the fact that, in point of comfort, convenience, equipment, service, and cuisine, America easily leads the world.

A Few Hours in Cleveland, Ohio.

We arrived at Cleveland, Ohio, at about noon, and the General Overseer's private car was placed on the side-tracks at the Euclid Avenue Station.

Here we were met by John Y. Calahan, a prominent railway official, who had charge of the General Overseer's train to New York and return on the occasion of the Visitation to that city last fall.

Mr. Calahan was very cordially welcomed by the members of the party, most of whom knew him personally, and at the invitation of the General Overseer joined the thirteen at lunch in the private car "Magnet."

After lunch, we spent several hours driving through the parks and along the principal boulevards of the City of Cleveland.

At an early hour that evening, the General Overseer's car was made a part of the fast train from Cleveland to Chicago.

Our prayer service that night was a season of joy and thanksgiving too deep for words, for were we not within one night's journey of Zion City?

When we awoke next morning, Thursday, June 30th, the train was running through the familiar sights, sounds and smells of the southern suburbs of the City of Chicago.

At about half past seven o'clock we arrived at the LaSalle Street Station.

Of course the General Overseer and the members of his party were at once besieged by a horde of Chicago newspaper reporters.

But the reply was courteous and firm in all cases, "I have nothing to say to the press."

The General Overseer and his family and personal attendants remained on the private car, which was switched around to the Chicago & North-Western Wells Street Station.

The other members of the party went on foot to a near-by restaurant for breakfast.

Enterprising Press Photographers.

While they were on the way, a swarm of about a dozen newspaper photographers fluttered about, taking pictures of the party as fast as they could load their cameras and press the botton.

A number of small boys created a diversion which, while it was very amusing to us, was probably quite the opposite to the enterprising camera men.

These lads, who evidently appreciated the humor of the situation, did their best to add to the gaiety of the occasion by dodging in front of the cameras, again and again, just as the photographers were about to make the exposure.

Meeting With Members of Zion General Business Cabinet.

After breakfast we proceeded to the Wells Street Depot where we found that a special parlor car had brought to Chicago, to meet the General Overseer, the members of his general business cabinet and their wives.

It was a great joy to behold the faces of these beloved brethren and sisters again, to grasp their hands and to hear their loving words of welcome and greeting.

A very delightful half hour was spent in visiting with these friends before the private car of the General Overseer arrived.

Then there was a very happy reunion, which lasted until the two cars, drawn by a special engine, furnished by the Chicago & North-Western Railway company, had arrived in Zion City.

End of Around-the-World Visitation.

The Around-the-World Visitation of the Rev. John Alexander Dowie—Elijah the Restorer, the General Overseer of the Christian Catholic Church in Zion—was at an end.

As we crossed the southern boundary, we were welcomed, first of all, by a joyous shrilling of every steam whistle in the City.

Welcome Home to Zion City.

At the railway station we were met by Zion City Band, whose music never sounded sweeter than on this glorious day.

The General Overseer, Overseer Jane Dowie, and Dr. A. J. Gladstone Dowie were escorted to their carriage, drawn by the handsome team of Russian stallions presented to him by friends in Zurich, Switzerland.

The vehicle itself was beautifully decorated with flowers and smilax.

The cabinet and the other members of the party were shown to other conveyances.

Then the procession was formed and we started up Shiloh boulevard with a mounted escort of the chief staff officers of Zion Guard, and a foot escort of Guards and the Zion City Band.

Along both sides of our way we found the Choir, in their robes of white, and the members of Zion Restoration Host, with their scarfs of Zion colors, drawn up to extend to the General Overseer and to his party their loving greetings.

All these countermarched as the cavalcade passed, and followed up to the corner of Elijah avenue and Shiloh boulevard.

Just beyond Elijah avenue, on Shiloh boulevard, we found that a beautiful arch and gateway, bearing appropriate mottos and watchwords from the Scriptures and the name of every city that we had visited inscribed upon it, had been erected.

Behind the gates could be seen the white surplices and bright, happy faces of Zion Junior Choir, every little tot in which was waving a small American flag in welcome to the General Overseer, with an intensity of enthusiasm that betokened a heart full of love.

Overseer Speicher unlocked the gates and formally handed the key to the General Overseer, but the portals were thrown open by two little girls, members of Zion Junior Restoration Host.

During this ceremony, ten little girls, dressed in white, bearing upon their sashes the names of ten different countries visited by the General Overseer on his Around-the-World Visitation, pelted him with roses, to emphasize the contrast between his welcome to Zion City and his treatment in certain parts of the world where they threw brickbats and stones at him.

The little Swiss girl who represented Switzerland then recited a poem of welcome to the General Overseer and his wife and son, which she herself had composed.

We give the mere outline of all this scene at the Welcome Home.

To portray the deep emotions which stirred the very depths of our spirits as we beheld once more the beauteous City which we had left just six months before, and to which God in answer to the prayers of hundreds of thousands of His children throughout the earth had brought us back in safety through many perils, would be beyond the power of written words.

Zion City and her people were, after all, the most beautiful sight that our eyes had beheld in six months.

The General Overseer, Overseer Jane Dowie, Dr. A. J. Gladstone Dowie, and some of the members of the party spoke very briefly to the people, expressing their joy and thanksgiving to God, but there was far more in their hearts than could ever be uttered by the lips.

Refreshing Rain in Answer to Prayer.

During all this time heavy rain clouds had been gathering and more and more threatening mutterings of thunder had been presaging the shower.

When the General Overseer had landed at New York, he had been informed that Zion City was in great need of rain. He had prayed at once, and that night there had been a light shower, which laid the dust.

The Waukegan papers ventured the assertion, however, that Zion City would not get a good rainfall until Elijah, the Restorer, himself returned to the City.

Their prediction was verified, for before the program of welcome which had been planned could be carried out, the windows of Heaven were opened and abundant showers of blessing were being poured out upon the earth.

Since that time there has been a splendid rainfall throughout all this vicinity.

Closing Words of Gratitude.

In closing this chronicle of the Around-the-World Visitation of the General Overseer, we rejoice to place on record the heartiest gratitude of the General Overseer and the entire party to those, at all points of our Visitation, who extended to us the true, hearty, loving hospitality that characterized the Zion people wherever we found them; to the officers and members of the Christian Catholic Church in Zion who so self-sacrificingly assisted in the meetings held, and in many other ways; to the brave members of Zion Guard who placed their own lives between the Prophet of God and danger; to hundreds of proprietors, managers and servants of liveries, hotels, steamship lines, railways, and other public utilities, who with sincere personal regard, went out of their way to add to our comfort and convenience; to the consular representatives of the United States of America and many public officials of the countries that we visited, for their many courtesies; to hundreds of thousands of people, in all of the places where meetings were held, who, notwithstanding the criminal action of a few in some places, heard with respect the Messages of God's Prophet and expressed their sympathy with him and their opinion on the side of law and order; and to the noble few newspaper editors and reporters who gave fair, unbiased reports of the Visitation.

We are especially and deeply grateful to the many thousands of members and friends of the Christian Catholic Church in Zion throughout the world, who followed us with their prayers, and above all to God our Heavenly Father who heard and answered the prayer of His people, giving us not only instruction, pleasure and profit all along the way, but glorious spiritual and material victories and deliverances, bringing His Prophet and his companions through dangers that at times seemed very threatening to human eyes, and returning all to their homes in Zion City in splendid health and without the slightest harm.

We indeed found the Word true:

When they were but a few men in number;
Yea, very few, and sojourners in it;
And they went about from nation to nation,
From one kingdom to another people.
He suffered no man to do them wrong;
Yea, He reproved kings for their sakes;
Saying, Touch not Mine anointed ones,
And do My prophets no harm.

The Keynote of the Visitation, is in two portions of the Word of God, which are of the most wonderful significance:

Go through, go through the Gates; prepare ye the way of the people: cast up, cast up the high way; gather out the stones; lift up an Ensign for the peoples.

Behold, Jehovah hath proclaimed unto the end of the earth, Say ye to the daughter of Zion, Behold, thy Salvation cometh; behold, His reward is with Him, and His recompense before Him.—*Isaiah 62:10, 11.*

And this Gospel of the Kingdom shall be preached in the whole world for a testimony unto All the Nations; and then shall the end come.—*Matthew 24:14.*

GOD'S WAY OF HEALING.

BY THE REV. JOHN ALEX. DOWIE.

God's Way Of Healing Is a Person, Not a Thing.

Jesus said "*I am* the Way, and the Truth, and the Life," and He has ever been revealed to His people in all the ages by the Covenant Name, Jehovah-Rophi, or "*I am* Jehovah that Healeth thee." (John 14:6; Exodus 15:26.)

The Lord Jesus, the Christ, Is Still the Healer.

He cannot change, for "Jesus, the Christ, is the same yesterday and today, yea and forever;" and He is still with us, for He said: "Lo, *I am* with you All the Days, even unto the Consummation of the Age." (Hebrews 13:8; Matthew 28:20.) Because He is Unchangeable, and because He is present, in spirit, just as when in the flesh, He is the Healer of His people.

Divine Healing Rests on the Christ's Atonement.

It was prophesied of Him "Surely He hath borne our griefs (Hebrew, *sickness*), and carried our sorrows: . . . and with His stripes we are healed;" and it is expressly declared that this was fulfilled in His Ministry of Healing, which still continues. (Isaiah 53:4, 5; Matthew 8:17.)

Disease Can Never be God's Will.

It is the Devil's work, consequent upon Sin, and it is impossible for the work of the Devil ever to be the Will of God. The Christ came to "destroy the works of the Devil," and when He was here on earth He healed "all manner of disease and all manner of sickness," and all these sufferers are expressly declared to have been "oppressed of the Devil." (1 John 3:8; Matthew 4:23 Acts 10:38.)

The Gifts of Healings Are Permanent.

It is expressly declared that the "Gifts and the calling of God are without repentance," and the Gifts of Healings are amongst the Nine Gifts of the Spirit to the Church. (Romans 11:29; 1 Corinthians 12:8-11.)

There Are Four Modes of Divine Healing.

The first is the direct prayer of faith; the second, intercessory prayer of two or more; the third, the anointing of the elders, with the prayer of faith; and the fourth, the laying on of hands of those who believe, and whom God has prepared and called to that ministry. (Matthew 8:5-13; Matthew 18:19; James 5:14, 15; Mark 16:18.)

Divine Healing Is Opposed by Diabolical Counterfeits.

Amongst these are Christian Science (falsely so called), Mind Healing, Spiritualism, Trance Evangelism, etc. (1 Timothy 6:20, 21; 1 Timothy 4:1, 2; Isaiah 51:22, 23.)

Multitudes Have Been Healed Through Faith in Jesus.

The writer knows of thousands of cases and has personally laid hands on scores of thousands of persons. Full information can be obtained at the meetings held in the Zion Tabernacles in Chicago, and in Zion City, Illinois, and in many pamphlets which give the experience, in their own words, of many who have been healed in this and other countries, published at Zion Printing and Publishing House, Zion City, Illinois.

"*Belief Cometh of Hearing, and Hearing by the Word of the Christ.*"

You are heartily invited to attend and hear for yourself.

Early Morning Meeting in Shiloh Tabernacle

REPORTED BY O. R., S. E. C., AND E. S.

THE Early Morning Meeting of Lord's Day, July 10, 1904, was a time of preparation for Zion's Fourth Feast of Tabernacles.

In the cool freshness of the summer morning the people gathered from near and far long before the time set for the service.

Approximately five thousand people returned the greeting of the General Overseer as he appeared upon the platform of Shiloh Tabernacle.

Shiloh Tabernacle, Zion City, Illinois, Lord's Day Morning, July 10, 1904.

The Service was opened by the singing of Hymn No. 6.

> Awake, and sing the song
> Of Moses and the Lamb,
> Wake ev'ry heart and ev'ry tongue
> To praise the Savior's Name.

The General Overseer then said:

Let us read from the Inspired Word of God, in the Book of the Revelation of Jesus, the Christ, in the 21st chapter.

And I saw a new heaven and a new earth; for the first heaven and the first earth are passed away; and the sea is no more.

And I saw the Holy City, New Jerusalem, coming down out of heaven from God—

Do not make any mistake about this City.

It is a City on earth, but it comes down from heaven.

There is a Glorious City above, but this is a City on earth.

Let us be common-sense people, and see that the City we are now reading about is a City that comes down to this earth from heaven.

And I saw the Holy City, New Jerusalem, coming down out of heaven from God, made ready as a bride adorned for her husband.

And I heard a great Voice out of the Throne saying, Behold, the Tabernacle of God is with men, and He shall dwell with them—

The literal reading is "He shall tabernacle with them."

He will be with us in our Feast of Tabernacles, for these are but tents in which we dwell as we tabernacle on.

This large temporary Tabernacle, I hope, will absolutely pass away within a year.

It shall have done its work.

It is only a tabernacle; but, however, with precious memories.

Even the new Shiloah will give way to Zion Temple.

Behold, the Tabernacle of God is with men, and He shall tabernacle with them, and they shall be His peoples.

I am glad to have that in the plural.

The Revised Version the Best Translation.

I am reading in the Revised Version.

I have great confidence that God will bless you more and more in the reading of His Word as it is translated in the Revised Version.

The last Version, if indeed it can be called one, authoritatively—the American version—is not of equal value with the revision in which both American and English, scholars of great piety and profound learning coöperated, which is commonly called the English Revised Version.

It is not strictly English because the Americans took a most important part in it.

I do not think that the Americans had any right to bring out another version without consultation with the scholarship of the whole world.

The so-called American Revision does not have the stamp of unchallenged authority and scholarship.

There is simply no question that the revision of 1881 of the New Testament and of 1885 of the Old Testament, which are bound up together and called the Revised Version, is, undoubtedly, of highest standard value, as the best English translation.

The Americans had no right whatever to dispute that and get out another one, because the combined translators put the renderings which were preferred by the Americans in a separate list at the end, giving them special consideration in this matter.

I hope that within a short time the Christian scholarship of the world will get together again and give us another revision of this revision; because discoveries have been made since 1881 and since 1885, which help us to get still better English renderings.

Moreover, the English language is continually altering in its force, and a number of expressions that even twenty-three years ago were considered proper, are today very far from expressing the real meaning of the original word.

Translations Not Inspired.

Let me remind you all that no translation is of absolute inspiration.

The inspiration attaches itself to the original and not to the translation.

That which is inspired is the Hebrew and Greek Scripture.

When I talk about the translations, I am not talking about the original inspiration.

The original inspiration is to be found in two languages that are not living languages.

There is a vast difference between the Greek of Modern Athens and the Greek of Ancient Athens.

There is also a vast difference between the Greek of Athens and the Greek of Alexandria, which is, for the most part, the Greek of the New Testament.

Some of you may have the silly notion that the English translation is an absolutely infallible inspiration.

It is no such thing.

Marked Changes in the English Language.

Because of the changes in our language, there are passages in the Scripture that, if read as they stand, are absolute nonsense.

A man said to me one day, "I do not believe that. I believe that the translation as it stands is authoritative and inspired."

Then I said, "Have you leased any land in Zion City?"

"Yes," he replied.

"Then you are a sinner," I said.

"How is that?" he asked, surprised.

"Because the Word of God speaks of them that are guilty of leasing as great sinners," I answered.

"Well," he said, "I got the lease from you." [Laughter.]

"And I do not think I was a great sinner in giving it to you either," I answered. "But the Scripture in King James' English version says that men that are guilty of leasing are great sinners."

"I did not know that. I never read that in my Bible."

"That is because you have not read your Bible carefully enough. Here it is in the 2d verse of the 4th Psalm: 'O ye sons of men, how long will ye turn My glory into shame? how long will ye love vanity, and seek after leasing?'

"That is serious, is it not, for a man who believes in the absolute inspiration of the translation?

"There is something wrong with that translation. At the time it was made the word leasing meant falsehood." It does not have that meaning now. The Modern English Revision translates the word:

Ye sons of men, how long shall My glory be turned into dishonor? how long will ye love vanity, and seek after falsehood?

The Revision is correct, and my friend said, "I give in."

I do not think that "leasing," as we use the word, is wicked.

When this translation was made in the days of King James of England, in the year 1611 or thereabouts, that is two hundred ninety-three years ago, that word "leasing" meant falsehood.

All Land Belongs to God.

I speak incidentally when I say leasing is a good thing, when the lease is one given by God.

"The land is Mine," saith God.

It is His, and I hold to it that there ought not to have been any selling of land upon this earth, until its Divine Maker and Owner had given permission.

It is God's land, and God should have had control of it from the beginning.

If God had had control of the land in America from the beginning, there would not be on it one grog-shop, one gambling-hell, not one harlot's house, not one place where God is dishonored at the hands of wicked people.

There are none of these things in Zion City, and there never shall be in any Zion City upon earth.

I want you to know that the inspiration does not extend to the translation, necessarily; although I thank God that the men that have translated, even in King James' day, with few exceptions, certainly were men of great reverence and of very high scholarship.

I give honor to those great and noble men of our own day who have made this magnificent translation.

There ought to be some authoritative printing of the Revised Version in this country, for some of the editions are full of blunders.

I very much question whether there is an absolutely correctly printed copy of the Bible in existence. It was supposed that there was, and the Oxford Press declared that they had at last a perfect copy without a printer's blunder, and that they would pay for every printer's blunder found.

The experts went into it and found scores of blunders in a week.

You would be surprised at the many blunders to be found in almost any printed matter.

Absolutely Perfect Printing Matter Almost an Impossibility.

Any one who knows anything about printing, how it is gotten up by fallible men, and read by fallible proof-readers, will know that there is no such thing as perfection.

I used to mourn greatly over the blunders that appeared in LEAVES OF HEALING.

Now I say, "Lord let no one be hurt by them," and go on. [Laughter.]

I do not believe that there is a perfectly printed copy of LEAVES OF HEALING in existence. Had I a mind to go into it, and should any good come of it, I could find very many blunders in the very best printed copy.

You do not know what a difficult thing it is to find a perfectly punctuated, perfectly spelled, perfectly printed copy of anything.

I say these things because I am asked to give an expression regarding these various versions of the Bible.

I do not dogmatize about this matter, but even the most carefully printed American Version seems to me to be gotten up, not for the people, but that it could be said, "Here is the latest edition."

It is of no standard value.

The alterations that are made have not received the impress of the best scholarship of our time, and some of them are questionable and more than questionable.

Therefore, until we get a better edition, I ask you to stand by the Revision of the New Testament of 1881 and of the Old Testament of 1885.

God Tabernacles With His People.

Behold, the Tabernacle of God is with men, and He shall tabernacle with them, and they shall be His peoples, and God Himself shall be with them.

It is so much better when you have that word "tabernacle."

When you say "God will dwell with them" it does not make the meaning clear; but when you say "God will tabernacle with them," it means that God will be in our moving tent, in our earthly home every day.

As we journey on and change our places, He is with us.

When we go from one place to another, He is with us all the way.

I am glad we have the word "peoples" in this verse for there are many peoples on this earth.

There is only one race.

There is no such thing as a black race, a yellow race, or a white race.

Only One Race.

There is only one race, and that is the Adamic race—the human race.

We had better get rid of this talk of separate races.

God has made all our bodies on the same general plan.

There is no difference between a black man and a white man as regards construction.

The difference is merely in the color of the skin.

I can put you under skies where you will get black enough.

If I had stayed much longer in Aden I should I think erelong have been as dark as any Arab, almost as black as a Somali.

That is the place to get black.

A great many of you are far too white.

There is not enough iron in your blood.

There is nothing especially beautiful or wonderful about a white skin.

White skin is oftentimes the evidence of disease.

The leper is as white as snow, but that is not beauty.

I have seen some very, very beautiful white faces; white, without color at all.

I have seen some very beautiful black faces.

They were majestic and beautiful in the black color.

I do not know which I like best.

I am very fond of the black color.

I am very fond of the cream color.

It is beautiful!

Some of these South Sea Islanders, especially the Samoans, are cream colored, and are splendidly formed people.

Their skins are a healthy, ruddy, copper color, and fairly shine.

I like to see the different families of the earth in their various colors.

There are people that live in the North, huddled under furs, who have to eat great quantities of fat.

There are people that are in the South Seas, who, if they ate fat, would die.

They eat fruits that are not fatty.

They eat those beautiful fruits, that grow there with very little labor.

Feed a Greenlander upon that and he would starve.

Let us remember that there are different peoples, but there are no distinctions of race.

There are not two distinct races upon this earth.

All Are Descendants of the Gardener Adam and his Wife.

There is only one race and that is the Adamic race.

All of us are descendants from the gardener, Adam, and his wife, Eve.

We are all children of that old gardener who sinned and was driven out of the garden by God because of it.

We are children of people who went to the Devil.

That is the reason poor sinners have to pray so hard to be forgiven.

You talk about your high birth.

I get so disgusted with people that talk about their high birth; and all the more that their claims are, in an offensive sense, true.

Yes, they are "high!"

Their pride stinks. They are a "stench in the nostrils" of God the Almighty.

The kings, princes, and high peoples of the earth must come down.

The common peoples in many countries also have a disgusting pride.

The pride of many of the common people of England is the most disgusting thing that I have ever met. "I am a true Briton!" and "I am a boy of the bulldog breed," are common expressions in word and in song.

I hate more than ever this color line.

May God take it out of all our hearts.

Let us deal with every man and every woman as they deserve to be dealt with, irrespective of color.

God Himself shall be with them and be their God:

And He shall wipe away every tear from their eyes; and death shall be no more; neither shall there be mourning, nor crying, nor pain, any more: the first things are passed away.

And He that sitteth on the Throne said, Behold, I make all things new. And He saith, Write: for these words are faithful and true.

And He said unto me, They are come to pass.

The Old Version reads, "And He said unto me, It is done," but the New Version has it correctly, "They are come to pass."

It is a more emphatic way of putting it.

Continual Weeping for the Departed, Selfish and Disgusting.

Yet every one does not realize that death is conquered.

Every one does not get every tear wiped away.

Many keep on weeping because they think it relieves them to cry.

What good in God's work are you who do that?

I wish you were in heaven.

"Why are you continually crying?" I once asked a man.

"Oh, I lost my Peggy," was the reply.

"Where did she go?"

"Heaven."

"What are you crying about then? She has gone to a good place, has she not?"

I have lost dear ones that have gone to heaven.

But if I kept everlastingly crying about it I would be of no use to God or to Zion.

My daughter is in heaven, but shall I continually cry about that?

I would not show my faith by my works.

It is not a good thing for you to show your faith by your waterworks. [Laughter.]

> Could my zeal no respite know,
> Could my tears forever flow,
> All for sin could not atone;
> Thou must save, and Thou alone.

Get saved from your waterworks!

Your son has had enough of them!

Your wife has had enough of them!

Some ask, "O please to pray for my eyes?"

"What have you been doing?" I ask.

"Crying."

"No, I will not! I will pray for you to stop weeping and sinning, then I will pray for your eyes.

"It is selfish to cry because your dear ones have gone to heaven and are happy.

"You are not crying for them at all. You are a miserable, selfish person, and are crying principally for yourself."

You miss your husband, do you?

Yes, and there are wives who gave their husbands a hard life of it while they had them—and some of you know you did.

You miss your wife?

Yes and she may now be very glad that she is missing. [Laughter.]

Why do you not stop this nonsense?

I do not take much stock in this perpetual crying, always going about with a mourner's face.

You are a hindrance to Christian progress and an intolerable abomination!

The Leaders in the Procession to Hell.

I am the Alpha and Omega, the Beginning and the End. I will give unto him that is athirst of the Fountain of the Water of Life freely.

He that overcometh shall inherit these things; and I will be his God, and he shall be My son.

But for the fearful—

Will you please to remember this is the 21st chapter of Revelation, 8th verse.

But for the fearful, and unbelieving, and abominable, and murderers, and fornicators, and sorcerers—

The word "sorcerer" is the plain word "pharmacist," *Pharmakoi* (φαρμακοί.)

You may as well read it in its original meaning—"a maker or seller of deadly drugs."

That is what the word "sorcerer" means.

It never meant anything else.

It meant the way the sorcerers in the olden times did.

These "sorcerers" were druggists, who drugged the people with deadly drugs, and put them under diabolical spells.

But for the fearful, and unbelieving, and abominable, and murderers, and fornicators, and sorcerers, and idolaters, and all liars, their part shall be in the lake that burneth with fire and brimstone; which is the second death.

Do you know who leads the procession to hell?

People—"It is the fearful."

General Overseer—It is the coward.

I pray more and more, "O God, convert the coward into a strong, brave man or take him out of Zion."

One Coward Is an Infection.

He is a deadly disease.

That cowardly woman or man in Zion is a contagious disease spiritually.

When you get cowardice into your heart, you had better get out of Zion; because Zion has no place for cowards.

The Methodists have plenty of room for them, as also have the Baptists, and all the Apostate Churches.

The denominations are full of them.

If you want fellowship with cowards, go to them.

They are cowards right down from the Archbishop of Canterbury to the humblest priest or curate in the Church of England.

The vast mass of apostasies are utter cowards.

They do not dare to tell the people the truth of God.

If they did dare, the king and the aristocracy would have been blessed; but they are cowards.

Cowards do not dare.

I have not heard of one Church of England archbishop or curate reproving the king for his gambling.

Zion has no place for cowards.

If You Are a Coward Get Out of Zion.

If you are afraid that Zion will go to pieces, get out quickly.

Do not stay in a ship if you think it is going to pieces.

I would not; I would get out.

I would get into one of the world's boats as quickly as I could.

But the fearful, and unbelieving, and abominable, and murderers, and fornicators, and sorcerers, and idolaters, and all liars, their part shall be in the lake that burneth with fire and brimstone; which is the second death.

That is an awful doom.

> There is a life above, unmeasured by the flight of years,
> And all that life is love.
> There is a death whose pangs outlast the fleeting breath;
> Oh, what Aeonian horrors hang around that second death!
>
> . . . .
>
> Lord God of truth and grace,
> Help us that death to shun,
> Lest we be banished from Thy face,
> Lest we be all undone.

The Congregation then sang, "I stand on Zion's Mount," after which they joined in the

PRAYER OF CONSECRATION.

Our God and Father, we come to Thee. We consecrate ourselves to Thee. Help us to make the consecration complete, in our spirits, our souls and our bodies. Take every sin out of our hearts. Take the horrible and awful sin of cowardice from every heart in Zion. Do not let it stay. O God, take it out, no matter how painful the operation. Let us be willing to risk bravely, if there be risks—to risk alike life, liberty, all our property and families in Thy Hands. We know that this is the best kind of happiness. O God, Thou hast taken a great risk in us, who are so poor, miserable and feeble by nature. Help many to get into Zion and stay in. Help us to be brave and true. If we are misunderstood in Zion, it is well that Thou dost understand us. Let us go on. Do not let us go out because some people misunderstand us. We are not judged by the people; we are judged by Thee. Help us to trust Thee, and even to be above the opinions of our dear ones. Do not let us make them our judges. Do not let us be our own judges. Judge Thou us, O God, and make us true. For Jesus' sake. Amen.

BENEDICTION.

Beloved, abstain from every form of evil. And may the very God of Peace Himself sanctify you wholly; and I pray God your whole spirit and soul and body be preserved entire, without blame, unto the coming of our Lord Jesus, the Christ. Faithful is He that calleth you, who also will do it. The grace of our Lord Jesus, the Christ, the love of God, our Father, the fellowship of the Holy Spirit, our Comforter and Guide, one Eternal God, abide in you, bless you and keep you, and all the Israel of God everywhere, forever. Amen.

Commencement Exercises of Zion Preparatory School

Held in Shiloh Tabernacle, Zion City, Illinois, Thursday Evening, July 7, 1904.

REPORTED BY S. E. C., O. R., AND E. S.

THE graduating exercises of Zion Preparatory schools, class 1904, were held in Shiloh Tabernacle, Thursday evening, July 7, 1904.

A scene of beauty presented itself in Shiloh Tabernacle, when, at eight o'clock, the General Overseer, preceded by the graduates and members of the faculty, took his seat upon the platform, which had been transformed into a bower of flowers and greenery.

Back of the stage was a representation of the House of Wisdom, each column entwined with evergreens, the middle one being surmounted by a miniature of the world, with the inscription, "In the beginning, God." Across the top of the pillars a scroll appeared, bearing the words, "The fear of Jehovah is the beginning of Wisdom."

A beautifully-modeled fountain basin, the work of the pupils in the plastic art class of the intermediate school, stood immediately below the center of the platform, the playing spray of water sparkling beneath a roseate light, created by crimson electric bulbs hidden behind a mass of ferns.

The thirty-five ushers were young women students; and to be shown into a seat by a graceful, white-robed, sweet-faced young woman, who, in softest tones, answered all inquiries, seemed a distinct advance over the regulation masculine usher.

OVERSEER HARVEY D. BRASEFIELD.
Vice-president Zion Educational Institutions.

Program.

The graduates are:

Academic—A. Laura Burnham, Clara E. Dietrich, Katherine Huntley, Clifford C. Meloche, Ethel Post.

Music—Lena E. Gallant.

Stenographic—Margaret Bailey, Oregon, Illinois; Lilly May Crawford, Daisy L. Wilcox.

After the Invocation by Professor Tindall and the reading of the 19th Psalm by Vice-president Brasefield, the following program was rendered:

Music—Trombone solo, "Stabat Mater"—*Rossini* (aria, "Cugus animam,") .... S. D. TUTTLE
Devotionals .... REV. H. D. BRASEFIELD, Vice-president
Recitation, "The Widow of Nain" .... KATHERINE HUNTLEY
Piano solo, "Caprice" (Op. 95)—*Raff* .... LENA GALLANT
Essay, Lowell's "Present Crisis" .... A. LAURA BURNHAM
Essay, "Success Waits at Labor's Gate" .... CLARA E. DIETRICH
Overture, "Poet and Peasant"—*Suppe* .... ZION CITY BAND
Essay, "Christian Education" .... ETHEL POST
Oration, "Farewell to the Preparatory School" .... CLIFFORD C. MELOCHE
Overture, "The Feast of Lanterns"—*Bennett* .... ZION CITY BAND
Address, with Presentation of Diplomas... REV. JOHN A. DOWIE, President

BENEDICTION.

MUSIC.

Presentation of Diplomas.

With the presentation of the diplomas by the President, some remarkable facts were brought out in the short address given by him.

The enrolment of Zion schools for 1904 is 1,904—which represents their growth since their establishment February 14, 1899.

There has been an increase of four hundred ninety-one the present year.

Out of the one thousand nine hundred four registered, only four have been lost by death.

In two years, only two have died out of nearly two thousand children and young people, for the kindergarten and junior schools are included in this number.

Fifty-one thousand dollars have been expended the present year for Zion Educational Institutions, this not including the cost of the Main Educational Building, which is estimated at one hundred fifty thousand dollars.

An event of considerable more than passing interest occurred when, answering to her name, there stepped forward to receive her diploma, a young woman, who had previously read an essay on the significant subject, "Christian Education," delivered in a clear voice, with perfect enunciation, and who proved to be the child, now grown into beautiful young womanhood, who, when dying of a malignant cancer of the mouth and throat, and given up by physicians, was healed instantly, in answer to the Prayer of Faith of the Prophet of God—who now, after seven years, as President of the school of which she is a graduate, handed her her diploma.

In his remarks, the President—which is one of the many titles of the General Overseer, by which name he is best known—touched on several lines of thought.

PRESIDENT'S ADDRESS.

The General Overseer said:

Before presenting the diplomas to the various graduates I have been asked to offer a few remarks.

I cannot, as President of Zion Educational Institutions, let this occasion close without calling especial attention to a number of things.

I cannot help calling attention to the fountain, in front of the platform, which has been made by pupils from fourteen to sixteen years of age, under the direction of Deacon Post, who is in charge of the Department of Art.

May God help you and them and me to see what a Fountain of Blessing we may be to all humanity.

The Fountain of Living Water is in ourselves if we will it.

We make a Fountain of Life to appear, by the grace of God, everywhere we go, if we are right with God.

A Beautiful Eastern Legend and Its Application.

An eastern legend says that once a mighty angel alighted from highest heaven upon a sandy desert on this earth.

Grieved was that being to behold the bones of travelers and of camels, and the rich burdens that were buried beneath the sands of the desert, because there was no water there.

With one touch of his shining wings he made a well in this desert; and that well had the property that, whoever took of its waters and was pure in heart, could conceal a little vial of it in his breast, so that if he were overtaken in a waterless desert anywhere, he could pour a drop from this vial upon the sands, and there a well would spring up.

But our Lord has come to this earth, and has created a Fountain of Living Water, and we may take of it until it becomes "within us" a Fountain "springing up into Everlasting Life."

Wherever we go we may drop a word of Kindness and Love—the Eternal Word of God, the Eternal Word of Life—and there a Flowing Well will be found.

I found, as I went around the world, wells of Living Water everywhere, that had spread from words that were spoken here, and carried by LEAVES OF HEALING, or by loving Zion hearts, over land and seas.

You can all carry words of Consolation.

I am glad tonight to look around upon this body of students.

Zion Educational Institutions Established February 14, 1899.

In February 14, 1899, it was my privilege to establish Zion Educational Institutions.

Now, in five and a half years, I have the joy of knowing that for this year, 1904, our enrolment is 1,904.

It is a peculiar coincidence that the year 1904 finds us with that exact enrolment.

The growth of Zion Educational Institutions has been very steady.

It has also been very rapid.

We have in our schools nearly five hundred more students this year than last year.

In a year of great difficulty it is wonderful to think that we have increased by that number.

The arrangement, also, of the entire educational system, has been more and more perfected.

But to perfection's sacred heights we would still nearer rise.

I congratulate the Vice-president and all the members of the faculty, not only of the College and Preparatory School, but of the Junior Schools, and not least, of the Kindergarten.

I thank you, in the Name of the Lord, for your devotion and earnestness, and for your intense determination that those committed to your charge shall not only have an education along intellectual and practical lines, but that there shall be a penetration, through all that education, of the Divine.

I thank God for this.

A Living Example of What God Hath Wrought.

The young lady who so eloquently addressed you on the subject of "Christian Education" is in herself an example of what God has wrought through a practical education.

As I sat listening to her I closed my eyes for a moment, and an interesting scene passed before me.

I saw, in the very depths of winter, a man, wrapped in furs, in a sleigh, driving across the deep snow which lay that day in Lincoln Park, Chicago.

Beneath his wraps on that cold day, he was praying earnestly that he might be used of God to kill a deadly disease that was killing one whom he was going to see.

I shall never forget that day, how I (for I was that man) entered into the room where Ethel Post lay dying of the horrible disease of cancer.

Oh, it was horrible!

She was scarcely able to speak even in the lowest whisper.

She was worn away, and near death, with the horrible disease, which not only filled all her mouth, but protruded from it.

It is a little over seven years since that horrible cancer was killed.

It is delightful to think that tonight she is one of the graduates from the Preparatory School into Zion College.

The education she has is above all an education in things of God.

She knows; she realizes; she understands, that God is a God of Deliverances.

Her story has gone throughout all the earth, on the wings of the Little White Dove.

Her father, who is a photographer as well as an artist, took those pictures of her at that time, which were reproduced in LEAVES OF HEALING for September 25, 1897, Volume III., Number 48.

I have also several dried pieces of the cancer.

Wonderful Preservation of Health and Life.

It is wonderful to know that the things of which we talk, and which have been so unreal to the Church for so many centuries, are real to the very humblest child in Zion; for the moment a child is sick, that moment he realizes his sin, and at once goes to God, and in nearly every case gets an answer of immediate healing through Faith.

Out of the one thousand nine hundred and four registered this year, we have lost only four by death, which is a very small percentage; so small that I do not think that another school in America can show it. It is only two in one thousand.

I am told that in Chicago many of the schools were closed during the winter because of contagious diseases.

This was also true of Milwaukee and other neighboring cities north and south of us.

The children died in many hundreds from throat and lung diseases.

But here in Zion City we were able to pray the Prayer of Faith, and, with the exception of four, all the children and young people enrolled have been kept.

I may say that these four were in the Junior School.

We have not lost one student from the College or Preparatory School.

We only lost two the previous year in the College.

Gratifying Reports of the Work of the School Year.

I have very able reports for the year from the Vice-president, and recommendations are made, which, of course, simply mean more money all the time.

I can say that there is no money of which I direct the expenditure in Zion with more pleasure than I do the money spent in the educational work.

We have not been dependent upon the rates of any county or any votes from the legislature, or any gifts from rich people.

We have educated our own children; taken care of all our poor; and done all the work that is commonly done by various agencies connected with the state or municipality.

This year let it be recorded to Zion's credit, I have been able to find fifty-one thousand dollars [$51,000] for Zion Educational Institutions. [Applause.]

Of course, that is in addition to the expense of the new building, which cost about one hundred fifty thousand dollars, [$150,000] and which is, I think, an exceedingly creditable beginning of our permanent Educational Buildings.

A Tithe of All Zion Children Claimed for God.

I say to Zion parents everywhere, that in the Name of the Lord I claim, as God's Messenger and Prophet, one out of every ten children for the Ministerial Training School, that they may be sent as Zion's Messengers to all the world.

I shall not be satisfied until I get my tithe of your children for God.

The world is crying out; the people of God are crying out for leaders, for helpers; and we could this day, if we had them, place not less than one thousand Elders and Evangelists throughout the world.

But I will not send forth those about whom I have any doubt.

Nor will I send out those who would cumber the ground.

I am glad to hear from the Vice-president that many of you young men and women, when you graduate from the preparatory schools, are setting your faces toward the Ministry of the Eternal Word of God.

I am glad also that at the same time you are taking a wide view of what that ministry means, and that you are realizing that all knowledge is helpful in the exercise of that ministry.

Zion is not merely a spiritual and ecclesiastical institution, but Zion is an educational, commercial, financial, manufacturing, and, by-and-by, in the not far distant future, will be a great transportation organization.

Zion's Political View.

It is a political force now, so that the word Theocracy is once more beginning to be understood.

It is well known that we stand apart from all the political parties, only giving our help to this or that one as we may find it will best help to maintain principles of righteousness.

I will never vote a ticket unless I have some hope that I can elect that ticket.

I do not think that it would be wise to estrange the most righteous of the two principal political parties, nor do I think it wise to lose our influence for good in connection with that party by voting for a man whom we know cannot be elected—a Prohibition Sacrificial Lamb.

Zion is a practical institution.

Zion will never do, knowingly, a foolish thing.

We are in the world, and we must act with great wisdom.

The power that we wield must be conserved and increased.

I could tell you very many striking things concerning Zion's political power and the way it has been wielded already for the advantage and extension of the Kingdom of God.

Because a man does not drink intoxicating liquors he is not necessarily a good man.

Some of the worst men I know in the world are abstainers.

Abstinence Does Not Necessarily Stand for Purity and Godliness.

The nation that abstains wholly from intoxicating liquors is not necessarily a good nation, for the Mohammedan religion teaches that the people shall never eat pork and shall never drink intoxicating liquors.

Throughout Persia, the greater part of India, and the Turkish Empire, the overwhelming majority of the people have never tasted intoxicants or pork, and yet they are degraded.

They are demoralized.

They are the most shameless, most wicked, most fanatical and murderous people in all the world.

I want you to understand that the mere abstinence from intoxicating liquors, while I consider it to be essential to a strong, pure, and fruitful Christian life, will not in itself make you a Christian, nor will it in itself make a nation strong, or great.

There is much nonsense talked about both personal total abstinence and national prohibition.

It is true that there are at least two hundred fifty million of our fellow creatures that never touch intoxicants, and for the most part it is true that men more miserable, poor, degraded, brutal, immoral and hateful in all their ways cannot be found upon all the earth. Of course there are many noble exceptions.

I say this with great sorrow, but it is a fact.

I want you to rise to a large conception of things.

I say this tonight, because I am continually asked why I do not vote the National Prohibition Presidential ticket.

I will never throw away the votes of Zion when they can be used to the furtherance of the Kingdom of God.

I should throw them all away, and do very much to smash all of Zion's industries, and the economic conditions that are so helpful to the United States at this moment, if I suffered that party, which is now meeting at St. Louis, to elect its candidates.

I say that without hesitancy.

I said, before I founded Zion, that if Mr. Bryan could win the support of the people and become President, I would cross the border and have done with the formation of Zion in the United States, for I never would support a government that endeavored to pay its national debt in a depreciated currency, and make fifty cents on a dollar sufficient payment for its obligations.

God's Law is "Thou shalt not steal."

God has vindicated what I said at that time, and eight years of great prosperity have followed the action that we then took.

A Word of Warning.

I desire the Preparatory School to repeat with me these words: "Be not deceived; Evil communications (or company) corrupt good manners" (or good habits). [*All repeat the words.*]

That is my admonition to you tonight.

The aim of your teachers has been to form good habits; to make it habitually easy to do right.

Among the very last things my dear daughter ever wrote was an essay which she had been asked to write for her class, while a student in the University of Chicago.

She was asked to write an essay upon the

"Aims and Objects of the Founder of Zion City."

They were eager, at the University, to know what my aims and objects were.

She wrote words like these at the beginning of her essay: "The object and aim of the founder of Zion is, first, to glorify God; second, to elevate man; and third, to make it easy to do right and difficult to do wrong."

She had caught my thought.

We have endeavored to make it easy for you to do right, and difficult for you to do wrong.

We have endeavored to make you see that to glorify God and to enjoy God forever, by elevating humanity, are the principal purposes for which God put us in this world.

You have been taught how to pray; and your prayer has become a good habit.

It has become natural for you to kneel and pray in the morning before you see the face of man.

I will tell you how you will lose it: by listening to evil communications; by going into evil company; by listening to evil suggestions; and by reading foolish and ungodly books, written by people who are not writing about Divine love, but about shameful lust and calling it love.

You will be degraded if you associate with wicked people in wicked literature, in wicked pictures, and even in the family life sometimes.

You must sometimes put your foot down and say, when asked to a card party, a dance, or a theater, "I will not be present at a function so foolish, so silly, and so ungodly."

"Evil Company Corrupts Good Habits."

You are set free for the long vacation after tonight.

The bright summer is with us.

You will have leisure and many opportunities of getting vigor and strength—spiritually, psychically and physically—but if you permit yourself to drift into evil association, and to listen to evil communications, you will be corrupted, and all that has been done will be undone, and you will be unfitted to resume your studies in Zion City.

I, therefore, warn you.

Evil communications and evil company corrupt.

Therefore, take care with whom you associate.

The moment you hear infidel, intemperate or impure suggestions, then part from that company immediately.

You cannot afford to take another step in company with such a person, for that step is downward, it leads to hell.

That person is walking with his back to the light; walking in his own shadow, and you are going with him when you keep his company.

Weary steps will have to be taken back.

You may be shown by some what seems to be a pleasant by-path, where the feet, which are so weary, may find refreshment, and that it is a good place to lie down and sleep.

But, if you go there, you will fall asleep, and Giant Despair will take you to Doubting Castle, and throw you into Dungeons of Darkness, and it will be by the mercy of God if you ever leave that giant's prison-house alive.

I want you to keep in

The Straight and Narrow Path Which Leads to God.

Steep and thorny it may sometimes be.

The old reformers sang:

> Steep and thorny is our way,
> Straight to heaven, our home, ascending;
> Happy he who every day
> Walks therein, for Christ contending,
> Happier when his journey's o'er;
> Conqueror he to Christ shall soar.

Keep under your bodies.

Bring them into subjection.

Quench not the holy fires that God has lit within you.

Gird your armor on; fight well and you shall find, after these wars, that your head wears sunbeams and your feet touch stars.

But you must fight.

Your enemy is oftentimes within you.

Yield not!

You have been taught good habits, good modes of living.

Do not go out and imitate the world.

I hope that there will not be one who will be deceived and keep company with those who are evil.

Young women, you cannot afford to keep company with one who is not a Christian, no matter what the circumstances may be.

You cannot be unequally yoked together with an unbeliever without disobeying God.

You cannot be acceptable to God, and be a companion to one who is walking the downward path.

No matter how pleasing, cultured, attractive, they may be, you must find a superior attraction in the Christ, our Lord, and refuse to keep the company of those who will not walk with the Christ, but who talk against God, and talk against Truth and Purity.

Young men, you cannot afford to keep company with young women who are frivolous and foolish.

We need all the common sense God gives us; and there is nothing so pleasant as doing right.

There is nothing pays so well in every way as doing right.

Visitors to our City say, "You have none of the things that the world thinks necessary to make one jolly and happy, and yet you are the jolliest and happiest people in the world."

We have better things.

We have the things that make us happy all the day and all the night.

World-wide Work of Zion Educational Institutions.

I am so glad of having this opportunity of meeting with you.

There are no such institutions in all the world as Zion Educational Institutions.

After having seen a good deal and heard a good deal about education throughout the world, and keeping up my reading upon that matter, I believe that, from every standpoint, the best education possible is being given in Zion City, and we shall improve it every year.

We shall do all we can to make this City a great Center of Christian Education, such as will be a blessing and an inspiration to Christians throughout the world.

I say further that I trust that we shall be able to educate in these schools and colleges those who will go out and found Zion Educational Institutions in all the world.

Zion City is really a large Preparatory School.

We are all learning how to build Zion Cities; how to build Zion churches; how to build Zion schools; how to build Zion commercial and manufacturing institutions, and how to build up the great policy of Zion, the establishment everywhere of the Kingdom of God.

It rejoices my heart to know that these things find an echo in the hearts of every one of you young people, and that you are earnest.

I do not want you to cease laughing with innocent mirth.

You all know that I can do that myself.

I do not want you to be unhappy.

Give free expression to everything that is pure and good. But I pray you to abstain from fleshly lusts which war against the soul, and to ask God to help you to abstain from all communications and company that will destroy or weaken your good habits.

It is my great delight to give these diplomas to the various graduates.

The General Overseer then presented the diplomas after which all joined in singing "I Stand on Zion's Mount."

BENEDICTION.

Beloved, abstain from every form of evil. And may the very God of Peace Himself sanctify you wholly; and I pray God your whole spirit and soul and body be preserved entire, without blame, unto the coming of our Lord Jesus, the Christ. Faithful is He that calleth you, who also will do it. The grace of our Lord Jesus, the Christ, the love of God, our Father, the fellowship of the Holy Spirit, our Comforter and Guide, one Eternal God, abide in you, bless you and keep you, and all the Israel of God everywhere, forever. Amen.

Street Addresses Are Necessary.

All Zion City Subscribers to *Leaves of Healing*, *The Zion Banner*, *Blätter der Heilung*, and *Voice from Zion*, whose correct street addresses are not positively known to be in our possession should send them to us AT ONCE. Please act upon this notice without delay as it is very important, now that we have postal delivery service, that the exact location of each and every subscriber be known to us. Write your name and address very carefully, designating also to what periodicals you are a subscriber and leave at your very earliest opportunity at our branch Publishing House on Elijah Avenue.

Very Sincerely Yours,
ZION PRINTING AND PUBLISHING HOUSE.

Warning to Subscribers.

Scarcely a week passes that we do not have complaints about money having been sent to us in currency, stamps, or silver, in the open mails, for renewals of subscriptions or for other purposes, WHICH WE HAVE NOT RECEIVED AND WHICH NEVER REACHES US.

Therefore, we desire to warn every member and friend of Zion sending money to us, to always use some safe means, preferably a money-order, or bank-draft on New York or Chicago, or personal check on Zion City Bank.

In conforming to this notice you will save yourselves trouble and expense, and us much annoyance.

ZION PRINTING AND PUBLISHING HOUSE,
Zion City, Illinois.

Notice to Officers and Members.

Send all newspaper clippings concerning the General Overseer, the Elders, or any department of the work in connection with the Christian Catholic Church in Zion, to Deacon Carl F. Stern, Zion City, Illinois. Send as soon as possible after publication, and carefully mark *name and date of the paper clipped from* on each article. If this is not done, the clippings are absolutely useless.

Notice to Correspondents.

In writing to Headquarters it is *absolutely essential* that the writer give his full address.

Failure to comply with this request necessitates looking up or referring to the Church Records, which involves much time, and is very frequently fruitless.

Friends and members of the Christian Catholic Church in Zion everywhere will please bear this in mind, especially those in foreign lands.

Faithfully yours in the Master's Service,
J. G. EXCELL, General Ecclesiastical Secretary.

Warning.

I am directed by the General Overseer to warn our members and officers throughout the world against giving money to persons claiming to be members of the Christian Catholic Church in Zion. All benevolence must be given either from Headquarters or under the direction of same. Even though the applicant for benevolence be known to be a member of the Christian Catholic Church in Zion, financial aid must not be given except in extreme cases, and then only in small amounts. Requests for help must be made to the officer-in-charge. In cases where there is no such officer, requests should be made direct to Headquarters, accompanied by recommendations from one or two members of Zion in good standing. J. G. EXCELL,
General Ecclesiastical Secretary.

Independence Day Oration

Delivered by the General Overseer in Beulah Park, Zion City, Illinois, July 4, 1904.

REPORTED BY A. C. R., S. E. C. AND E. W.

THE Fourth of July has come and gone, and while the world's newspapers are full of records of the loss of limbs, of life and of property, by those who have been having a "good time" with gunpowder, there is not one such item to enter into the columns of the weekly paper of Zion City, THE ZION BANNER, concerning her people.

No one spent a sleepless night in Zion City from the booming of cannons and anvils, from pistols and firecrackers and clanging bells.

A most delightful day was spent in Beulah Park by thousands who had congregated there for the purpose of celebrating the Fourth, and of taking a full day of rest in the cool shade.

To many who had not before visited it, the beauty of Beulah Park was a revelation.

Nothing could have been more delightful than its refreshing shade. Swings and hammocks had been provided, and also seats in plenty.

A platform had been built, and was decorated with flags.

At twelve o'clock, noon, the General Overseer, Overseer Jane Dowie and Judge Barnes took seats upon this platform.

Overseer Speicher offered the opening prayer, after which Judge Barnes read, in a voice to which it was a delight to listen: "When in the course of human events, it becomes necessary for one people to dissolve the political bonds which have connected them with another"—and on to the end of this wonderful document which we call the Declaration of Independence.

The General Overseer then stepped to the front of the platform and after pronouncing the Invocation delivered the following oration:

"LIFE, LIBERTY AND THE PURSUIT OF HAPPINESS."

I desire today, in delivering my first address as an American citizen, upon the Day of Independence, to record my gratitude to God for all that He has wrought in this great, broad American Continent, and especially in this portion during the last one hundred twenty-eight years.

The document which has just been so eloquently read by Judge Barnes, is one, the historic character of which is of the very greatest value.

I hold in my hand a facsimile copy of the original document written by Thomas Jefferson, with the alterations that were made, and one very striking paragraph, which was omitted, protesting against slavery.

But even as the document stands, it was a wonderful advance at that time upon everything that was known as a political and constitutional Declaration; Life, Liberty, and the Pursuit of Happiness were declared to be the inalienable, inherited rights, and that to secure these rights, the Declaration asserts, governments are instituted among men.

Inherited and Inalienable Rights.

Permit me, then, as this is the anniversary of the Declaration of Independence, to make a few remarks upon these rights, inherited and inalienable.

First, Life! How precious Life is!

What a wonderful gift is Life!

But Life itself would be almost worthless without Liberty; and Liberty which is directed in any other way than in the pursuit of that which is true happiness, becomes licentious, wicked and detrimental to human progress.

It is the duty of government to protect life; and therefore I stand here today and say that it is the duty of the Government of the United States to obey the Commandment, "Thou shalt do no murder." [Applause.]

No man on earth has the right to take human life.

I do not except the punishment for murder, for a state which can only punish murder by the *lex talionis*, the law of revenge, is not a state that has measured up to the full significance of the Declaration of Independence.

There are things contained in these three—"Life, Liberty, and the Pursuit of Happiness"—which admit of great expectation.

I believe that the act of our God and Father, who, in the cradle of our humanity, would not permit even the murderer, Cain, to be killed; that the act of the Christ who would not ask for vengeance upon His cruel murderers, but said, "Father, forgive them; for they know not what they do;" that the act of Stephen, who cried, "Lord, lay not this sin to their charge," blotted out forever the right of every man to take human life for any cause whatever.

Capital Punishment Increases Crime.

Let me say that the experience of this United States has proved that in such of the states where there is no capital punishment, there are fewer murders.

You only have to cross the lake to Michigan and compare their record with that of Illinois, and you will see at once, as in every other state in this country, and in every country in the world, where capital punishment has been abolished, most manifestly in Switzerland, that there are fewer murders.

The criminals are more afraid of solitude and imprisonment for life than they are of the gallows.

"Life, Liberty and the Pursuit of Happiness" implies that the state shall never take human life.

How often have men been executed for crimes that they have never committed?

One of the black spots upon this Flag is the readiness of the citizens of the United States, not only to kill, but to prevent the law from taking its proper course, and by lynching, by murderous mobs, to murder the law itself.

I claim that every black man, as well as every white man, is entitled to his life, and no matter that he has destroyed life, it is not the province of a Christian State to stamp out his life, but to remember the Command of God, "Thou shalt do no murder." [Applause.]

Thou Shalt Do No Murder.

I do not make this appeal on behalf of any one class in a community, although I might fairly make it today for the negro, who is so often charged with crime that he has not committed.

I have often stated it publicly, and I state it again, that more than once, women of the South have confessed to me that men were put to death cruelly, and burned by fire, who had not committed the crime upon them with which they were charged, but that they themselves were consenting parties to the alleged rape.

Many alleged crimes of murder have resulted in the execution of the wrong man, and under any circumstances I maintain that the Law of God, "Thou shalt do no murder," should be obeyed.

This has its extension to aggressive war.

No country has the right to assail the citizens of another country simply to extend its boundaries; to increase its commerce, or to add to its population by seizing upon the territory of any power.

I cannot but believe that the best way for this nation is to rule so justly, so majestically, that humble families of the human race now oppressed will gladly say, "Take us under this Flag and protect us and help us." [Cries of "Hear, hear!" Applause.]

I believe that the nations of the Orient and the multitudes of the Islands of the Sea, yes, and Canada on the north and the Mexicans on the south would by wise policy be led to say, "Let us get under this great Anglo-Saxon Flag.

But it will not be done by war.

"Wisdom is better than weapons of war," and the command, "Thou shalt do no murder," and the Declaration that has just been read, that the government exists for the protection of life, demands that the citizens of the United States shall see to it that its government does not at any time commit them to war's aggression under any circumstances, for God has said, "Thou shalt do no murder."

But there is something else.

Life Is a Large Word.

Life consists not in the abundance of the things that a man has; Life has three aspects—the Life of the Body, the Life of the Soul, and the Life of the Spirit, and the greatest of these is the Life of the Spiritual man.

The bodily life and the psychical life are but temporal.

The Declaration of Independence declares that it is the duty of the government to protect life, and that includes spiritual life; it includes spiritual liberty; it includes spiritual happiness.

It may not be that the government can teach the principle of Spiritual Life, Liberty or Happiness, but there is one thing that the government must do—it must protect every man in the exercise of his Spiritual Life, and let no hindrance come to the development of that life when it is consistent with the life, liberty and happiness of others.

Hence, I say that there is one thing which is harassing human life everywhere, and that is a press which is leading men into paths of Sin, Disease, Death, Bondage, Misery and Hell.

One of the great needs in protecting the Spiritual Life of the people of the United States is that, in their wisdom, the courts of this Nation should provide a muzzle for an unlicensed, brutal press.

It is worse than a million mad dogs being set at liberty among the people. [Applause.]

Liberty Destroyed by a Brutal, Degraded Press.

That muzzling will be done some day.

I claim that under the Declaration of Independence it is the duty of the Nation and of the State to defend life which is made unhappy, which is oftentimes circumscribed and deprived of liberty, and which is oftentimes, instead of being permitted to go on in the path of human and Divine happiness, arrested by a power which is now so well organized under the form of the associated press, that there are but few men in the United States, or in the United Kingdom, or in the world, who dare to stand up and meet this horrid monster; this brutal, ignorant, illiterate, licentious, degraded and fiercely hateful press, ready to destroy everything that is good.

As a maintainer of the Declaration of Independence I call upon the President, Congress, Governors, and State Legislatures to provide a muzzle for a mad and horrid press.

I declare further that liberty must be extended in many directions; that the Constitution of the United States shall not only give to the negro a right to cast his vote and maintain that right, even if it be necessary to send United States troops to stand around the ballot-box, but that they shall enforce the right to have that vote counted; that eight millions of our fellow citizens shall no longer be continuously deprived of that which the Constitution says that they shall have—the right to vote as citizens of the United States.

Liberty for the Afro-American.

They are deprived of this right in a large part of these United States by laws that are cunningly devised for the purpose of either preventing the Afro-American from voting, or taking good care that his vote is not counted when it is cast.

I ask, is it fair that those who come from Europe in hundreds, and thousands and millions, who know nothing of our language, who never have done anything to create liberty in this country, who have never borne any burdens at all, should be immediately enrolled as citizens, not only permitted to vote, but in every respect to have their votes protected, while the African, who has been here for more than two centuries, who has borne ages of oppression, and who is now rising up calmly to take a Christian, statesman-like, and citizen-like part in our Commonwealth, should be denied the right to vote?

They were born on this soil; their fathers fought for Liberty and helped the United States when, if they had been on the other side, there is no question that the War of the Rebellion would have had another termination. Why should they, who poured out their blood and lives for the independence and maintenance of the Union, be deprived of their votes, while illiterate foreigners in multitudes are enrolled and protected?

I claim Liberty for the Afro-American. [Applause.]

I claim Liberty for no illiteracy, but this government was not founded upon an educational basis.

Many of our forefathers who were supporters of that Declaration and went to war for us could not have passed through much of an examination.

Some of them could not write their names, but they were grand and holy men, for there is something better than mere intellectual scholarship.

There is the cultivation of a spiritual, moral and Divine nature, and while they were not expert scholars they were magnificent citizens.

If we are to apply an educational test to the ballot, then we had better start with Chicago, we had better apply it all over the Union, and not only upon an oppressed section of this people.

I claim Liberty! The principle given to us under the Constitution declares that the Declaration shall find its application, without exception, to eight millions of our dark-skinned brethren in the United States.

Let us have Liberty!

Let us have Life!

Let all engage in the Pursuit of Happiness.

The Pursuit of Happiness begins by your understanding what Happiness is, and the best definition that I can give is, "Happy is that people whose God is Jehovah." Happy is that people who love His Law! [Applause.]

Happy is that people where the Christ reigns in every heart —every home—every workshop—every office!

An Interpretation of the Declaration which Gives the Fullest Liberty.

I hold that in Zion we can show that a Theocratic interpretation of this Declaration gives us Life; gives us Liberty; gives us a Pursuit of Happiness far greater than any other interpretation, and I therefore declare under the Flag today that I am not a Democrat; that I am not a Republican, nor a Popocrat, nor a Plutocrat, but that I am a Theocrat, and that I believe in the Rule of God everywhere.

I hold that that declaration is in perfect accord with the Declaration of Independence, for I am simply declaring for Life, Liberty, and the Pursuit of Happiness, not only on earth, but throughout eternity. [Applause.]

I am an American! [Applause.]

I am an American!! [Applause.]

I am an American!!! [Loud and continued applause.]

I was only one-third of one when I left Zion City; when I reached Australia I became two-thirds, and when I reached England, I became an out-and-out American, and believed then in every line of the awful charges that Judge Barnes read out today against King George III., the great-grandfather of the present king. [Applause.]

Zion claims the right, under this Flag, to tell the peoples of the earth that a form of government which puts aside the king, and gives expression free and complete to the will of the nation, that respects Life, Liberty, Happiness and Purity, is one under which the nation will prosper.

I say that we have a right to tell them that it will be a good time when the Stars and Stripes extend their beneficent sway to all the kingdoms of the earth.

Zion's Flag will lead the way. [Applause.]

Zion's Flag will prepare the nations for that which is the best expression of government—a Theocratic form embodied in a democratic government, a government of the people, by God and for God. God grant us this. [Applause.]

We Look for a Greater Ruler.

Let me congratulate you that we who are loyal to that Flag also declare that there is another Ruler greater than the President of this Nation; another Ruler greater than the monarch of any nation, and gladly do we say that we believe that He is coming.

We carry His Cross, the Dove of Peace, and the Message of Peace on our Banner.

We carry the Crown of Life on our Banner; and the only weapon we carry there is the Sword of the Spirit, which is the Word of God.

I rejoice that the power of God has brought us into a nation where we are free to make such expressions, and gladly to declare our love and loyalty for this Flag and for this Constitution. We believe that a proper interpretation of the Declaration of Independence and of the Constitution is all that is necessary to make this Nation completely happy from a legislative point of view.

Our glad hearts go up to God, thanking Him that there is a larger Life, a larger Liberty, a larger Happiness than any that the Constitution has ever told.

All hail to these Stars and Stripes!

These Stars no less than Stripes lead after Him.

They that be wise shall shine as the brightness of the firmament; and they that turn many to righteousness as the stars forever and ever.

As I look at these Stripes and think how they have gone forth to heal many a wound, I thank God that by His stripes we are healed.

God bless the Stars and Stripes! [Amen.]

May God bless the United States of America! [Applause.]

May God bless the President, and may Theodore Roosevelt be made President again! [Applause.]

May God bless the Government, the Congress, the Judges, the Governors, and the Legislators! [Applause.]

May God bless every color and people from every country that are now assembled under this Flag, and make America an increasing blessing, spiritually, educationally, commercially, and politically, to every part of the wide world!

BENEDICTION.

Beloved, abstain from every form of evil. And may the very God of Peace Himself sanctify you wholly; and I pray God your whole spirit and soul and body be preserved entire, without blame, unto the coming of our Lord Jesus, the Christ. Faithful is He that calleth you, who also will do it. The grace of our Lord Jesus, the Christ, the love of God, our Father, the fellowship of the Holy Spirit, our Comforter and Guide, one Eternal God, abide in you, bless you and keep you, and all the Israel of God everywhere, forever. Amen.

Those assembled then joined in singing "America," after which they gave three cheers for the President, and again for the American Flag.

Expiration of Subscriptions.

On every subscriber's copy of LEAVES OF HEALING or THE ZION BANNER we attach a yellow label bearing his name, address, and two numbers, the figures referring to the volume and the number with which the subscription will expire.

Thus, should your label number happen to be 15—11, you may know that your subscription expires with Volume XV, Number 11, which will be July 2, 1904. Also take notice that LEAVES OF HEALING now completes a volume every six months, or twenty-six weeks, that being the number of papers which are put into a bound volume. Earlier in the life of the paper a volume contained fifty-two numbers, as LEAVES OF HEALING had fewer pages in those days.

By making yourselves familiar with these customs and remitting promptly you need never allow your subscription to lapse.

Send money only by Bank Draft, Postoffice or Express Money-order in favor of John Alexander Dowie, and address all letters intended for us to

ZION PRINTING AND PUBLISHING HOUSE,
Zion City, Lake County, Illinois.

Publisher's Notice.

The remittance must accompany receipt of subscriptions at the Publishing House, no difference by or for whom or for whatever time they may be given, or whether forwarded through Ordained Officers, Branches, or Gatherings of the Christian Catholic Church in Zion. Accounts will be carried with Ordained Officers, Branches, or Gatherings, on quantity orders of periodicals consigned on sale for monthly settlement, but to include only such articles as bear the imprint of Zion. All orders for Bibles, books, buttons, pictures (except prints done by the Publishing House), lace souvenirs, etc., must be sent to the General Stores, Zion City, Lake County, Illinois.

DO YOU KNOW GOD'S WAY OF HEALING?

BY THE REV. JOHN ALEX. DOWIE.

Let it be supposed that the following words are a conversation between the reader [A] and the writer [B].

A. What does this question mean? Do you really suppose that God has some one especial way of healing in these days, of which men may know and avail themselves?

B. That is exactly my meaning, and I wish very much that you should know God's Way of Healing, as I have known it for many years.

A. What is the way, in your opinion?

B. You should rather ask, WHO is God's Way? for the way is a Person, not a thing. I will answer your question in His own words, "I am the Way, and the Truth, and the Life: no one cometh unto the Father, but by Me." These words were spoken by our Lord Jesus, the Christ, the Eternal Son of God, who is both our Savior and our Healer. (John 14:6.)

A. But I always thought that these words only referred to Him as the Way of Salvation. How can you be sure that they refer to Him as the Way of Healing also?

B. Because He cannot change. He is "the same yesterday and today, yea, and forever." (Hebrews 13:8.) He said that He came to this earth not only to save us but to heal us. (Luke 4:18), and He did this when in the flesh on earth. Being unchanged He must be able and willing and desirous to heal now.

A. But is there not this difference, namely, that He is not with us now?

B. No; for He said "Lo, I am with you All the Days, even unto the Consummation of the Age;" and so He is with us now, in spirit, just as much as when He was here in the flesh.

A. But did He not work these miracles of healing when on earth merely to prove that He was the Son of God?

B. No; there was still a greater purpose than that. He healed the sick who trusted in Him in order to show us that He came to die not only for our sins, but for our sicknesses, and to deliver us from both.

A. Then, if that be so, the atonement which He made on the Cross must have been for our sicknesses as well as our sins. Can you prove that is the fact from the Scriptures?

B. Yes, I can, and the passages are very numerous. I need quote only two. In Isaiah 53:4, 5, it is written of Him: "Surely He hath borne our griefs (Hebrew, *sicknesses*), and carried our sorrows: . . . and with His stripes we are healed." Then, in the Gospel according to Matthew, this passage is quoted and directly applied to the work of bodily healing, in the 8th chapter 17th verse: "That it might be fulfilled which was spoken by Isaiah the prophet, saying, Himself took our infirmities, and bare our diseases."

A. But do you not think that sickness is often God's will, and sent for our good, and therefore God may not wish us to be healed?

B. No, that cannot possibly be; for diseases of every kind are the Devil's work, and his work can never be God's will, since the Christ came for the very purpose of destroying "the works of the Devil." (1 John 3:8)

A. Do you mean to say that all disease is the work of Satan?

B. Yes, for if there had been no sin (which came through Satan) there never would have been any disease, and Jesus never in one single instance told any person that sickness was God's work or will, but the very contrary.

A. Can you prove from Scriptures that all forms of sickness and infirmity are the Devil's work?

B. Yes, that can be done very easily. You will see in Matthew 4:23 and 9:35 that when Jesus was here in the flesh He healed "all manner of disease and all manner of sickness among the people." Then if you will refer to Acts 10:38 you will see that the Apostle Peter declares that He (Jesus) "went about doing good, and healing all that were oppressed of the Devil." Notice that all whom He healed, not some, were suffering from Satan's evil power.

A. But does disease never come from God?

B. No, it cannot come from God, for He is pure, and disease is unclean; and it cannot come out of Heaven, for there is no disease there.

A. That is very different from the teachings which I have received all my life from ministers and in the churches. Do you really think that you are right, and that they are all wrong in this matter?

B. It is not a question as between myself and them. The only question is, What does God's Word say? God has said in all the ages, to His Church, "I am Jehovah that healeth thee" (Exodus 15:26), and therefore it would be wicked to say that He is the defiler of His people. All true Christians must believe the Bible, and it is impossible to believe that good and evil, sickness and health, sin and holiness could have a common origin in God. If the Bible really taught that, it would be impossible to believe our Lord Jesus, the Christ, when He says: "A good tree cannot bring forth evil fruit, neither can a corrupt tree bring forth good fruit." (Matthew 7:18.)

A. But even if I agree with all you say, is it not true that the Gifts of Healing were removed from the Church, and are not in it now?

B. No, the "Gifts of Healing" were never withdrawn, and can never be withdrawn, from the true Church of God, for it is written: "The gifts and the calling of God are without repentance." (Romans 11:29.) There are nine gifts of God to the Church (enumerated in 1 Corinthians 12:8-11), and all these are in the Holy Spirit. Therefore, so long as the Holy Spirit is in the Church, all the gifts must be there also. If they are not exercised, that does not prove that they do not exist, but that the faith to exercise them is lacking in God's servants. The gifts are all perfectly preserved; for the Holy Spirit, not the Church, keeps them safely.

A. What should a Christian then do when overtaken with sickness?

B. A Christian should obey God's command, and at once turn to Him for forgiveness of the sin which may have caused the sickness, and for immediate healing. Healing is obtained from God in one of four ways, namely: First, by the direct prayer of faith, without any aid from the officers of the Church, praying as the Centurion did in Matthew 8:5-13; second, by two faithful disciples praying in perfect agreement in accordance with the Lord's promise in Matthew 18:19; third, by the anointing of the Elders and the prayer of faith, according to the instructions in James 5:14 and 15; and fourth, by the laying on of the hands of them who believe, and whom God calls to that ministry, as the Lord commands in Mark 16:18, and in other places.

A. But are people healed in this way in these days?

B. Yes, in thousands of cases. I have myself laid hands upon many hundreds of thousands of persons, and I have seen the Lord's power manifested in the healing of great numbers, many of whom are living witnesses in many countries, who have testified publicly before thousands, and who are prepared to testify at any time. This ministry is being exercised by devoted Christians in many parts of America, Europe, Australasia, and elsewhere.

A. Is it not the same as Christian Science, Mind Healing, etc.?

B. No. Divine Healing is diametrically opposed to these diabolical counterfeits, which are utterly antichristian. These impostures are only seductive forms of Spiritualism. Trance Evangelism is also a more recent form of this delusion, and it deceives many.

A. But how shall I obtain the necessary faith to receive healing, which faith I am at present conscious that I do not possess?

B. It is written: "Belief cometh of hearing, and hearing by the word of the Christ." (Romans 10:17.) Our Missions are held for the express purpose of teaching fully the Word of God on this matter, and I very heartily invite you to attend the meetings which are announced for Zion Tabernacles in Chicago and other cities, and for Shiloh Tabernacle, Zion City, Illinois. All are welcome and there are no charges of any kind made, for all God's gifts are free gifts. Salvation is the first of these, without which you cannot be healed through faith in Jesus. All the costs of this work are covered by the free-will offerings of the people who attend these meetings, and others whom the Lord leads to help; but the poorest, who have nothing to give, are as heartily welcome as the richest.

A. Do you see the sick and lay hands upon them in this Mission?

B. Yes; after we feel satisfied that they are fully resting in the Lord alone for the healing, we see privately, so far as time permits, those who attend; but under no circumstances do we claim the power to heal any; for "power belongeth unto God."

A. Have you any writings upon this subject which can be purchased?

B. Yes, these can be obtained at the office of Zion Printing and Publishing House, Zion City, Illinois, and at any Zion Tabernacle. But the best book on Divine Healing is the Bible itself, studied prayerfully and earnestly.

We extend to you a hearty invitation to attend the meetings, which are free to all. Our prayer is that you may be led to find in Jesus, the Christ, our Lord and God your present Savior from sin, your Healer from sickness, your Cleanser from all evil, your Keeper in the way to Heaven, your Friend, and your All for Time and Eternity. We pray that these words may help many who read, and that our little conversation may bear fruit in leading many readers to look to Jesus only.

"The Healing of Christ's seamless dress
Is by all beds of pain;
We touch Him in life's throng and press
And we are whole again."

Zion's Bible Class

Conducted by Deacon Daniel Sloan in Shiloh Tabernacle, Zion City, Lord's Day Morning at 11 o'clock, and in Zion Homes and Gatherings throughout the World.

MID-WEEK BIBLE CLASS LESSON, AUGUST 3d or 4th.

The Kings of the Earth Are the Foes of the Christ.

1. *They will combine to resist the preparation for the Christ's coming.*—Psalm 2:1-6.
   They stir people into a rage.
   They play on the prejudices of the people.
   They do not want any prophet to warn them.
2. *They will keep up the fight until smitten with judgment.*—Revelation 6:12-17.
   They will not always mock at God's truth.
   They are bringing destruction to their kingdom.
   They know they are wicked and reprobate.
3. *God has discarded so-called Christian nations, and is making of a people a nation which was not.*—Psalm 2:7-11.
   God's plan will carry to the end.
   God warns kings to be wise and surrender.
   A called, yet unfaithful people, are disowned.
4. *The kings and their kingdoms are so full of the Devil that they will continue to kill and destroy one another.*—Matthew 24:3-14.
   Their peace conference is hollow mockery.
   The Devil in them is a murderer from start to finish.
   The greed of conquest makes history black with horror.
5. *They will confederate with the harlot because they are so full of adultery.*—Revelations 18:1-11.
   What deviltry is not found in Rome?
   They are the outgrowth of Rome whether civil or religious.
   The kings of the earth are getting on good terms with the pope.
6. *They are organizing in combined strength to make war on the Christ and martyr Christians.*—Revelations 17:10-18.
   These kings will be swept to perdition.
   They are all being filled with the mind of the Devil.
   People must choose between the Christ and earthly monarchs.
7. *The work of reproving them may be a bitter one but they must be warned and the people delivered.*—Revelations 10:5-11.
   The end is at hand.
   God sends His prophet to kings.
   The Message is short but forceful.
8. *The called people of God, wherever they are, must get into Zion City and foreswear their allegiance.*—Jeremiah 3:12-18.
   People are called back by Elijah to the true God.
   Those who obey come to Zion, as God directs.
   Here they come to know God and make themselves ready.
   The Lord our God is a Monarchy-denouncing God.

LORD'S DAY BIBLE CLASS LESSON, AUGUST 7th.

A People Prepared for the King of Kings.

1. *God raises up a man to prepare the people for His coming.*—Isaiah 55:1-5.
   The deeply-convicted people act.
   They are told to obey God and live.
   They find God to be a Covenant-keeping God.
2. *The Gospel of the Kingdom must be preached to all nations.*—Matthew 24:4-14.
   The Christ is receiving a Kingdom.
   Other kingdoms perish. His will stand.
   His people alone will be in authority in that Kingdom.
3. *This Gospel compels radical changes, a repentance which precedes faith.*—Mark 1:1-15.
   One voice arrests the attention of the world.
   Men must repent in a godly way.
   The Kingdom is bursting in upon us.
4. *The people for the Lord must be cleansed from every defilement to be made ready.*—Revelation 1:4-7.
   Only regenerated and cleansed people will enter.
   God can do nothing until a person is fully clean.
   The spirit, the soul and the body must be cleansed.
5. *The call is to purity, for only those who obey from the heart will enter.*—Revelation 22:11-20.
   The wicked will speedily get more wicked.
   Persons cannot be partly good and partly bad at this time.
   Only the pure will find the life and city of God.
6. *So many who profess to be the Christ's followers are only workers of iniquity.*—Matthew 7:21-23.
   They cannot prophesy for they do not believe in prophets.
   They cannot cast out devils for they do not think people are demon-possessed.
   They lie and live in hypocrisy—lie even unto the Lord.
7. *God is calling out a people who fear no king, and who will do the will of God.*—1 Peter 2:5-17.
   The foundation stone of the Christ's Kingdom is laid in Zion.
   The Christ is so precious to those who know Him as a Savior, Healer, Keeper and Cleanser.
   They are not confounded when brought before rulers.
8. *The work of calling out is being hastened of the Lord and centers in one place.*—Isaiah 60:14-22.
   The tide of indignation will turn.
   Zion's strength will come from people not under monarchs.
   The wealth in these kingdoms belongs to God's Kingdom.
   God's Holy People are a Chosen People.

OBEYING GOD IN BAPTISM.

"Baptizing Them Into the Name of the Father and of the Son and of the Holy Ghost."

Eighteen Thousand Eight Hundred Eighty-nine Baptisms by Triune Immersion Since March 14, 1897.

Eighteen Thousand Eight Hundred Eighty-nine Believers have joyfully followed their Lord in the Ordinance of Believer's Baptism by Triune Immersion since the first Baptism in Central Zion Tabernacle on March 14, 1897.

Baptized in Central Zion Tabernacle from March 14, 1897, to December 14, 1901, by the General Overseer,	4754			
Baptized in South Side Zion Tabernacle from January 1, 1902, to June 14, 1903, by the General Overseer..	37			
Baptized at Zion City by the General Overseer........	583			
Baptized by Overseers, Elders, Evangelists and Deacons, at Headquarters (Zion City) and Chicago......	5283			
Total Baptized at Headquarters..................				10,65'
Baptized in places outside of Headquarters by the General Overseer..............................		641		
Baptized in places outside of Headquarters by Overseers, Elders, Evangelists and Deacons............		7517		
Total Baptized outside of Headquarters............				8,158
Total Baptized in seven years and three months....				18,815
Baptized since June 14, 1904:				
Baptized in Zion City by Elder Royall................	1			
Baptized in Zion City by Elder Hammond............	6			
Baptized in Chicago by Elder Hoffman...............	4			
Baptized in Chicago by Elder Cossum.	1			
Baptized in Chicago by Elder Keller.................	1		13	
Baptized in Canada by Elder Brooks.................		3		
Baptized in California by Elder Taylor..............		2		
Baptized in Minnesota by Elder Graves..............		5		
Baptized in Mississippi by Evangelist Gay...........		1		
Baptized in Missouri by Evangelist Gay.............		1		
Baptized in Missouri by Elder Brock.................		8		
Baptized in Missouri by Deacon Robinson............		1		
Baptized in Nebraska by Elder Hoy...................		7		
Baptized in New York by Overseer Mason............		9		
Baptized in Ohio by Deacon Kelchner................		3		
Baptized in Ohio by Deacon Arrington...............		5		
Baptized in Texas by Evangelist Gay................		11		
Baptized in Washington by Elder Ernst..............		2		
Baptized in Wisconsin by Elder McClurkin...........		3	61	74
Total Baptized since March 14, 1897..............				18,889

The following-named one hundred twenty-eight believers were baptized in the Wakkerstroom river, Wakkerstroom, Transvaal, South Africa, Wednesday, May 11, 1904, by Overseer Daniel Bryant:

Alexander, Booi	Wakkerstroom, Transvaal, South Africa
Butikati, Mrs. Jenetta	Wakkerstroom, Transvaal, South Africa
Duba, Mrs. Christian J	Wakkerstroom, Transvaal, South Africa
Duba, Esther H	Wakkerstroom, Transvaal, South Africa
Duba, Jim	Wakkerstroom, Transvaal, South Africa
Duba, Lukas	Wakkerstroom, Transvaal, South Africa
Dhladhla, David	Wakkerstroom, Transvaal, South Africa
Dhlamini, Mrs. Carolina	Wakkerstroom, Transvaal, South Africa
Fukuyane, Miss Corrie J.	Utrecht, Natal, South Africa
Fukuyane, Daniel	Utrecht, Natal, South Africa
Fukuyane, Mrs. Sarie	Utrecht, Natal, South Africa
Fukuyane, Thomas L.	Utrecht, Natal, South Africa
Hadebe, Albert	Wakkerstroom, Transvaal, South Africa
Hadebe, Mrs. Bellina	Wakkerstroom, Transvaal, South Africa
Hadebe, Mrs. Johanna	Wakkerstroom, Transvaal, South Africa
Hadebe, Koos	Wakkerstroom, Transvaal, South Africa
Hendriks, Harry	Wakkerstroom, Transvaal, South Africa
Hlapo, Mrs. Annet S.	Utretcht, Natal, South Africa
Hlapo, Joseph	Wakkerstroom, Transvaal, South Africa
Hlapo, Koos	Utrecht, Natal, South Africa
Hlatshwayo, Mrs. Carolina	Wakkerstroom, Transvaal, South Africa
Hlatshwayo, Hezekia	Wakkerstroom, Transvaal, South Africa
Hlatshwayo, Mrs. Laiza	Wakkerstroom, Transvaal, South Africa
Hlatshwayo, Miss Selina	Wakkerstroom, Transvaal, South Africa
Hliba, Miss Ettie	Utrecht, Natal, South Africa
Kanye, Miss Justina	Wakkerstroom, Transvaal, South Africa
Kubheka, Mrs. Dorothea	Wakkerstroom, Transvaal, South Africa
Kubheka, Miss Ellie	Wakkerstroom, Transvaal, South Africa
Kubheka, Miss Ellina	Wakkerstroom, Transvaal, South Africa
Kubheka, Jim	Amersfoort, Transvaal, South Africa
Kubheka, Mrs. Selfina	Wakkerstroom, Transvaal, South Africa
Kumalo, Andreas	Groenvlei, Utrecht, Natal, South Africa
Kumalo, Bessie	Wakkerstroom, Transvaal, South Africa
Kumalo, Jeremia	Wakkerstroom, Transvaal, South Africa
le Roux, Mrs. Adriana J	Wakkerstroom, Transvaal, South Africa
le Roux, Pieter L	Wakkerstroom, Transvaal, South Africa
Lutuli, Fred	Volksrust, Transvaal, South Africa
Mabuza, Ellina	Groenvlei, Utrecht, Natal, South Africa
Mabuza, Judida	Utrecht, Natal, South Africa
Mabuza, Miss Julia	Wakkerstroom, Transvaal, South Africa
Mabuza, Miss Lizzie	Utrecht, Natal, South Africa
Mabuza, Maria	Utrecht, Natal, South Africa
Mabuza, Mateu	Utrecht, Natal, South Africa
Mabuza, Mrs. Sarah	Wakkerstrom, Transvaal, South Africa

Madebele, Miss Lizzie..........Utrecht, Natal, South Africa
Madela, Mrs. Julia..........Wakkerstroom, Transvaal, South Africa
Makubane, Samuel..........Groenvlei, Utrecht, Natal, South Africa
Makubo, Alie..........Wakkerstroom, Transvaal, South Africa
Makubo, Miss Maria..........Wakkerstroom, Transvaal, South Africa
Makudulela, Miss Ellina..........Wakkerstroom, Transvaal, South Africa
Manana, Miss Ellina..........Wakkerstroom, Transvaal, South Africa
Masimula, Mrs. Anna..........Wakkerstroom, Transvaal, South Africa
Masimula, Mrs. Martha..........Wakkerstroom, Transvaal, South Africa
Masimula, Miss Paulina..........Wakkerstroom, Transvaal, South Africa
Masimula, Simon..........Wakkerstroom, Transvaal, South Africa
Mazibuku, Miss Eldia..........Utrecht, Natal, South Africa
Mazibuku, Jim..........Zandspruit, Transvaal, South Africa
Mazibuku, Johannes..Driefontein, Wakkerstroom, Transvaal, South Africa
Mbata, Christina..........Utrecht, Natal, South Africa
Mbata, Mrs. Emelina..........Groenvlei, Utrecht, Natal, South Africa
Mbata, Miss Emma..........Utrecht, Natal, South Africa
Mbata, Lina..........Utrecht, Natal, South Africa
Mbata, Maria..........Utrecht, Natal, South Africa
Meme, Andreas..........Wakkerstroom, Transvaal, South Africa
Meme, Mrs. Aggie..........Wakkerstroom, Transvaal, South Africa
Mfuzi, Esther..........Utrecht, Natal, South Africa
Mhlongo, Paulus..........Utrecht, Natal, South Africa
Mhlope, Petrus..........Graskop, Wakkerstroom, Transvaal, South Africa
Mnisi, Amon..........Driefontein, Wakkerstroom, Transvaal, South Africa
Mnisi, Solomon..........Wakkerstroom, Transvaal, South Africa
Msibi, Mrs. Jenetta..........Wakkerstroom, Transvaal, South Africa
Msibi, Jotham..........Wakkerstroom, Transvaal, South Africa
Mtembu, Amon..........Groenvlei, Utrecht, Natal, South Africa
Mtembu, Klaas..........Groenvlei, Utrecht, Natal, South Africa
Mtembu, Mrs. Rebecca..........Wakkerstroom, Transvaal, South Africa
Mtshali, Mrs. Anna..........Wakkerstroom, Transvaal, South Africa
Mzimela, Johannes..........Brereton, Wakkerstroom, Transvaal, South Africa
Ndaba, Benjamin..........Wakkerstroom, Transvaal, South Africa
Ndhlovu, Esther..........Groenvlei, Utrecht, Natal, South Africa
Ngobese, Jona..........Brereton, Wakkerstroom, Transvaal, South Africa
Ngobese, Muneli..........Zandspruit, Transvaal, South Africa
Ngomezuly, Paulus..........Wakkerstroom, Transvaal, South Africa
Ngwenya, Mrs. Anna M..........Wakkerstroom, Transvaal, South Africa
Ngwenya, Miss Julia..........Wakkerstroom, Transvaal, South Africa
Ngwenya, Miss Nesta..........Wakkerstroom, Transvaal, South Africa
Ngwenya, Saul..........Wakkerstroom, Transvaal, South Africa
Nkonyane, Daniel..........Wakkerstroom, Transvaal, South Africa
Nkonyane, Elias..........Wakkerstroom, Transvaal, South Africa
Nkonyane, Mrs. Elizabeth..........Wakkerstroom, Transvaal, South Africa
Nkonyane, Miss Ellina..........Utrecht, Natal, South Africa
Nkonyane, Mrs. Esther..........Wakkerstroom, Transvaal, South Africa
Nkosi, Isaya..........Wakkerstroom, Transvaal, South Africa
Nkosi, Miss Justina..........Wakkerstroom, Transvaal, South Africa
Nkosi, Mrs. Liza..........Wakkerstroom, Transvaal, South Africa
Nkosi, Mrs. Liza..........Charlestown, Natal, South Africa
Nkosi, Philip..........Wakkerstroom, Transvaal, South Africa
Nkosi, Miss Selina..........Wakkerstroom, Transvaal, South Africa
Nkwanyane, Elizabeth..........Groenvlei, Utrecht, Natal, South Africa
Ntsele, Simon..........Wakkerstroom, Transvaal, South Africa
Nxumalo, Abie..........Wakkerstroom, Transvaal, South Africa
Nxumalo, Jim..........Groenvlei, Utrecht, Natal, South Africa
Nxumalo, Joel..........Groenvlei, Utrecht, Natal, South Africa
Pitt, John H..........Wakkerstroom, Transvaal, South Africa
Pitt, Mrs. Sofie W..........Wakkerstroom, Transvaal, South Africa
Sangweni, Charlie..........Volksrust, Transvaal, South Africa
Sangweni, Johannes..........Volksrust, Transvaal, South Africa
Sengwayo, Mrs. Jessie..........Wakkerstroom Transvaal, South Africa
Shabalala, Mrs. Jessie..........Wakkerstroom, Transvaal, South Africa
Simelane, Mrs. Maggie..........Wakkerstroom, Transvaal, South Africa
Simelane, Mrs. Maria..........Wakkerstroom, Transvaal, South Africa
Sitole, Ananias..........Wakkerstroom, Transvaal, South Africa
Sitole, Miss Hessie..........Utrecht, Natal, South Africa
Sitole, Mrs. Roselina..........Wakkerstroom, Transvaal, South Africa
Stofberg, Mrs. Catrina J..........Wakkerstroom, Transvaal, South Africa
Stofberg, Hendrik J..........Wakkerstroom, Transvaal, South Africa
Tela, Mrs. Nellie..........Wakkerstroom, Transvaal, South Africa
Tshabalala, Miss Emily..........Wakkerstroom, Transvaal, South Africa
Tshabalala, Hendrik..........Wakkerstroom, Transvaal, South Africa
Tshabalala, Joseph..........Wakkerstroom, Transvaal, South Africa
Tshabangu, Mrs. Catrina..........Wakkerstroom, Transvaal, South Africa
Tshabangu, Mrs. Christina..........Wakkerstroom, Transvaal, South Africa
Tsnongive, Miss Bessie..........Wakkerstroom, Transvaal, South Africa
Twala, Mrs. Marie..........Wakkerstroom, Transvaal, South Africa
Vilakazi, Jona..........Wakkerstroom, Transvaal, South Africa
Viljoen, Miss Gesina M..........Waterval, Utrecht, Natal, South Africa
Xaba, Miss Sannie..........Groenvlei, Utrecht, Natal, South Africa
Zulu, Hezekia..........Glenfillan, Wakkerstroom, Transvaal, South Africa
Zungu, Lukas..........Wakkerstroom, Transvaal, South Africa

The following-named thirteen believers were baptized in the Wakkerstroom river, Wakkerstroom, Transvaal, South Africa, Thursday, May 12, 1904, by Overseer Daniel Bryant:

Budulwako, Miss Meta..........Wakkerstroom, Transvaal, South Africa
Kumalo, Mrs. Emma..........Wakkerstroom, Transvaal, South Africa
Kumalo, Johannes..........Wakkerstroom, Transvaal, South Africa
Kumalo, Mrs. Selfina..........Wakkerstroom, Transvaal, South Africa
Made, Moses..........Wakkerstroom, Transvaal, South Africa
Malinga, Lesaya..........Wakkerstroom, Transvaal, South Africa
Martin, Mrs Annet W..........Wakkerstroom, Transvaal, South Africa
Martin, Jim..........Wakkerstroom, Transvaal, South Africa
Martin, Miss Nettie..........Wakkerstroom, Transvaal, South Africa
Masimula, Mrs. Liza..........Wakkerstroom, Transvaal, South Africa
Mhlope, Johannes..........Wakkerstroom, Transvaal, South Africa
Ngwenya, Jotham..........Wakkerstroom, Transvaal, South Africa
Vilakazi, Philemon..........Wakkerstroom, Transvaal, South Africa

---

The following-named two believers were baptized at Seattle, Washington, Lord's Day, June 26, 1904, by Elder August Ernst:

Denton, John Ambrose..........Chehalis, Washington
Ritchey, Sanford H..........2312 First avenue, Seattle, Washington

---

The following-named believer was baptized at Kansas City, Missouri, Lord's Day, June 26, 1904, by Deacon Charles E. Robinson:

Massey, Mrs. Charlotte..........2534 Euclid avenue, Kansas City, Missouri

---

The following-named believer was baptized at Toronto, Ontario, Canada, Lord's Day, June 26, 1904, by Elder Eugene Brooks:

Bain, John..........259½ Yonge street, Toronto, Ontario, Canada

---

The following-named believer was baptized at Meridian, Mississippi, Wednesday, June 29, 1904, by Evangelist William D. Gay:

Canterberry, Mrs. Maggie E..........Meridian, Mississippi

The following-named two believers were baptized at Toronto, Ontario, Canada, Saturday, July 2, 1904, by Elder Eugene Brooks:

Trinier, Mary Jane..........Waubaushene, Ontario, Canada
Trinier, Richard..........Waubaushene, Ontario, Canada

The following-named believer was baptized in the North Side Zion Tabernacle, Chicago, Lord's Day, July 3, 1904, by Elder J. R. Keller:

Dittman, Mrs. Eunice Pearl..........3105 Enoch avenue, Zion City, Illinois

---

The following-named five believers were baptized at Minneapolis, Minnesota, Lord's Day, July 3, 1994, by Elder F. A. Graves:

Harlin, Mrs. A. M....805 Fifteenth avenue, South Minneapolis, Minnesota
Schaff, Mrs. Mary A..........Barronett, Wisconsin
Short, Mrs. Joseph, corner Rondo and Dewey avenues, St. Paul, Minnesota
Sutherland, Mrs. Anna Vilette..........Barronett, Wisconsin
Wigham, William Paul..........Newport, Minnesota

The following-named two believers were baptized at San Francisco, California, Lord's Day, July 3, 1904, by Elder William D. Taylor:

Barron, Charles Edmond..........153 Day street, San Francisco, California
Weir, Margaret C..........38 Oak street, San Francisco, California

---

The following-named eight believers were baptized in the Meramec River at Meramec Highlands, near St. Louis, Missouri, Monday, July 4, 1904, by Elder Frank L. Brock:

Ball, Allie..........1824 Morgan street, St. Louis, Missouri
Brock, Paul J..........3401 Morgan street, St. Louis, Missouri
Brock, Miss Ruth..........3401 Morgan street, St. Louis, Missouri
Gleghorn, Mrs. Catherine..1714 Newstead ave., North, St. Louis, Missouri
Moon, Mrs. Louise Anna..........1312 North Sarah street, St. Louis, Missouri
Pitman, Nora..........2650 Morgan street, St. Louis, Missouri
Taylor, Mrs. Mary..........2643 Lucas avenue, St. Louis, Missouri
Wells, Miss Flora........1714 Newstead avenue, North, St. Louis, Missouri

---

The following-named believer was baptized in Lake Michigan, Zion City, Illinois, Wednesday, July 6, 1904, by Elder F. M. Royall:

Wise, Elbirtes E..........Mason City, Iowa

The following-named six believers were baptized in Shiloh Tabernacle, Zion City, Illinois, Lord's Day, July 10, 1904, by Elder Gideon Hammond:

Brauckmann, David G..........1824 George avenue, Chicago, Illinois
Chase, Ernest Luverne..........Edina Hospice, Zion City, Illinois
Julian, Edmund Ralph..........1809 Hebron avenue, Zion City, Illinois
Paff, Adam..........3018 Gabriel avenue, Zion City, Illinois
McMertry, Susie..........917 North Cardinal avenue, St. Louis, Missouri
Williams, Miss Beulah..........2816 Emmaus avenue, Zion City, Illinois

---

The following-named two believers were baptized in Zion Tabernacle, Cleveland, Ohio, Lord's Day, July 10, 1904, by Deacon C. F. Kelchner:

Martin, Edward W. M..........92 Ontario street, Cleveland, Ohio
Splete, William..........105 Vergennes street, Cleveland, Ohio

---

The following-named three believers were baptized in the West Side Zion Tabernacle, Chicago, Illinois, Lord's Day, July 10, 1904, by Elder C. Hoffman:

Fischer, Johann Paulus..........100 Mohawk street, Chicago, Illinois
Rosenthal, Fred Herman..........1035 Oakley avenue, Chicago, Illinois
Voet, Mrs. Ida..........252 Orleans street, Chicago, Illinois

---

The following-named believer was baptized at St. Louis, Missouri, Lord's Day, July 10, 1904, by Evangelist William D. Gay:

Miller, David Suttle..........4034 Lincoln avenue, St. Louis, Missouri

HE-WORLD VISITATION.

WITH ILLUSTRATED SUPPLEMENT.

A WEEKLY PAPER FOR THE EXTENSION OF THE KINGDOM OF GOD

EDITED BY THE REV. JOHN ALEX. DOWIE.

Volume XV. No. 14. *ZION CITY, SATURDAY, JULY 23, 1904.* *Price Five Cents*

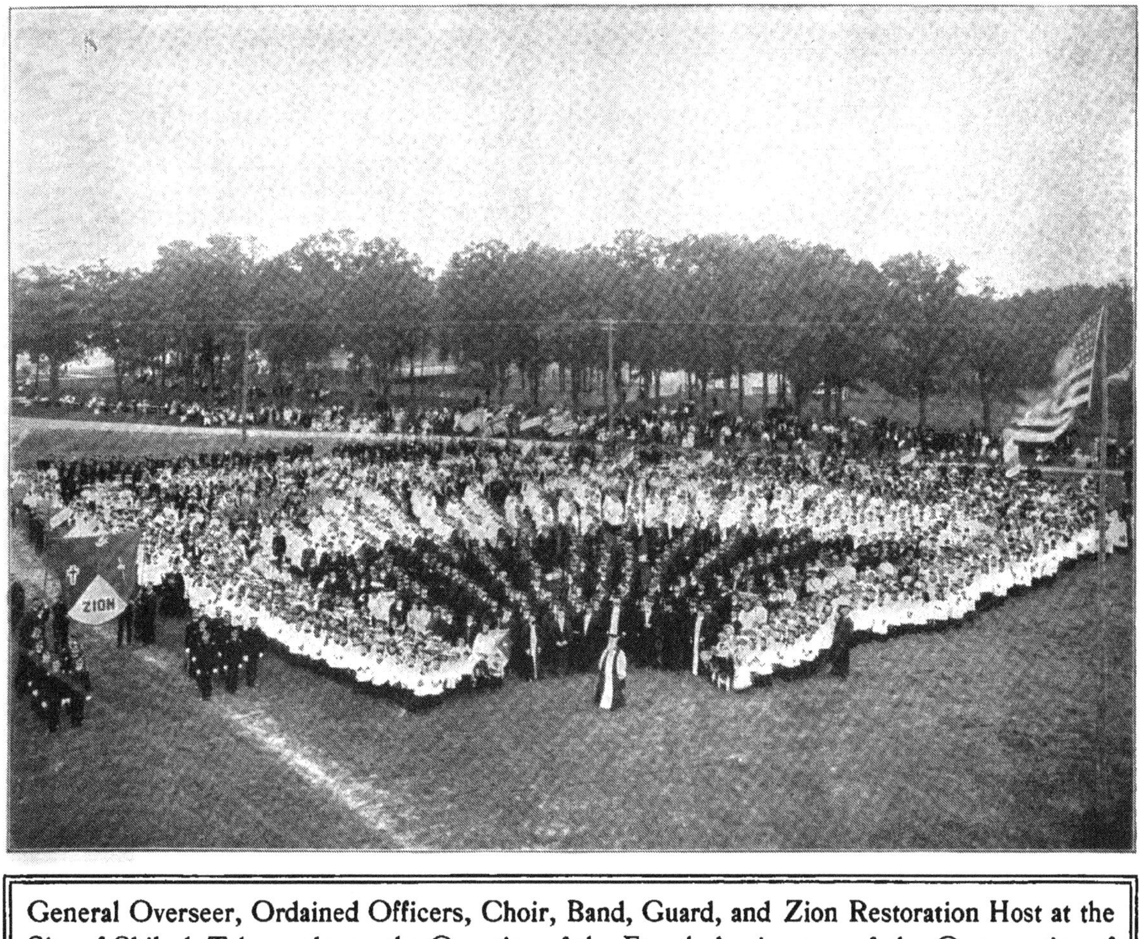

General Overseer, Ordained Officers, Choir, Band, Guard, and Zion Restoration Host at the Site of Shiloah Tabernacle, on the Occasion of the Fourth Anniversary of the Consecration of Zion Temple Site, During Zion's Fourth Feast of Tabernacles, Thursday, July 14, 1904.

A WEEKLY PAPER FOR THE EXTENSION OF THE KINGDOM OF GOD.

EDITED BY THE REV. JOHN ALEX. DOWIE

Application for entry as Second Class Matter at Zion City, Illinois, pending.

Subscription Rates.		Special Rates.	
One Year	$2.00	100 Copies of One Issue	$3.00
Six Months	1.25	25 Copies of One Issue	1.00
Three Months	.75	To Ministers, Y. M. C. A's and Public Reading Rooms, per annum	1.50
Single Copies	.05		

For foreign subscriptions add $1.50 per year, or three cents per copy for postage.

Subscribers desiring a change of address should give present address, as well as that to which they desire LEAVES OF HEALING sent in the future.

Make Bank Drafts, Express Money or Postoffice Money Orders payable to the order of JOHN ALEX. DOWIE, Zion City, Illinois, U. S. A.

Long Distance Telephone. *Cable Address "Dowie, Zion City."*

All communications upon business must be addressed to

MANAGER ZION PUBLISHING HOUSE,
Zion City, Illinois, U. S. A.

Subscriptions to LEAVES OF HEALING, A VOICE FROM ZION, and the various publications may also be sent to

ZION PUBLISHING HOUSE, 81 EUSTON ROAD, LONDON, N. W., ENGLAND.
ZION PUBLISHING HOUSE, NO. 43 PARK ROAD, ST. KILDA, MELBOURNE, VICTORIA, AUSTRALIA.
ZION PUBLISHING HOUSE, RUE DE MONT, THABOR 1, PARIS, FRANCE.
ZIONSHEIM, SCHLOSS LIEBBURG, CANTON THURGAU, BEI ZÜRICH, SWITZERLAND.

ZION CITY, ILLINOIS, SATURDAY, JULY 23, 1904.

TABLE OF CONTENTS.

LEAVES OF HEALING, SATURDAY, JULY 23, 1904.

EDITORIAL NOTES.

"WITH JOY SHALL YE DRAW WATER OUT OF THE WELLS OF SALVATION."

FROM DAY to day Joyful Hosts of the many Thousands of Zion have been gathering at the numerous Convocations of Zion's Fourth Feast of Tabernacles in Shiloh Park.

The Feast has continued throughout the entire week and will close tomorrow.

IT HAS been our Joy to conduct the Early Morning Sacrifice of Praise and Prayer at half past six o'clock for the last nine days, and to find an average of nearly five thousand devout and earnest worshipers in Shiloh Tabernacle at that hour.

WE HAVE now concluded our Nine Addresses upon the "Nine Fruits of the Spirit."

We have enjoyed our ministration.

The people have most earnestly and lovingly received our Message.

THE GATHERINGS of last Lord's Day were very large.

It was estimated that there were probably sixteen thousand attendances at the half past six o'clock Early Morning, half past two o'clock Afternoon, and eight o'clock Evening services.

With those present at the Convocation of Zion Junior Restoration Host at half past nine o'clock in the morning, and the sermon of Overseer Speicher at eleven o'clock in the morning, there were probably twenty-one thousand attendances in Zion Tabernacle throughout the day.

At the Communion of the Lord's Supper on that evening we ordained forty-two new officers, and received into fellowship four hundred twenty members.

THE ATTENDANCES at the various Convocations on Monday, July 18th, aggregated about fifteen thousand.

The ordinance of Believer's Baptism was administered to One Hundred Fifty-four persons.

The meeting for Zion Women only, conducted by Overseer Jane Dowie, was very largely attended, and very blessed in its results.

THE GATHERINGS on Tuesday, July 19th, continued to be very large, with an aggregate attendance of about fifteen thousand.

At the close of the Conference upon the Work of Zion Restoration Host throughout the World, we had the joy of administering the Restoration Vow and Consecrating and

Separating four hundred fifty-nine newly-enrolled members of the Host.

ON WEDNESDAY, July 20th, there was an aggregate attendance of more than ten thousand.

At the close of the afternoon address on the words: "What then Shall this Child be?" the Ordinance of the Presentation and Consecration of young children to God followed.

We then consecrated one hundred sixty-seven children to God.

ON THE EVENING of Wednesday, at eight o'clock, we conducted a brief Farewell Service to a Zion party which we have sent to Europe, consisting of Overseer John Gabriel Speicher, M. D., Elder Abigail Thompson Speicher, Master John Dowie Speicher, Elder and Evangelist Fred Rickert, Master Gottlieb Henry Rickert, Elder and Evangelist Thomas Kosch, Deacon and Deaconess John Innes, and Deacon Max Koetz.

These left Zion City for New York the following morning, and will sail today, God willing, by the Cunard Steamship *Etruria*, for Liverpool.

ON THE same evening, at forty-five minutes past eight o'clock, a magnificent audience of between six thousand and seven thousand persons, a large number of whom came in special trains from Chicago, Waukegan, etc., assembled in Shiloh Tabernacle to hear the Oratorio of "The Messiah."

It was presented in a marvelous manner by members of Zion Senior Choir and Orchestra to the number of three hundred fifty.

The four soloists belonged to Zion with one exception.

Competent musical critics declare that it was an almost faultless presentation of the glorious music and words.

We can witness, with the many thousands present, that the Oratorio was not only powerful musically, but also elevating and inspiring in its spiritual effect.

IT SEEMED almost incredible that three years ago there was only a wide prairie, with a few scattered farms, where Zion City now stands.

It was like a dream to think that we could gather together from all the world a Christian Choir and Orchestra which could so beautifully interpret one of the greatest and most complex of Christian musical compositions.

WE GIVE thanks to God that He has given us such a splendid Choir and Orchestra, every one of whom is a member of the Christian Catholic Church in Zion, and is living, so far as we know, a daily life which is worthy of his or her profession.

IF WE named one worthy of commendation, we should wish to name all.

Their service of Love to God and to his Eternal Son, Jesus, the Messiah, King of kings and Lord of lords, is recorded in Heaven.

ON THURSDAY, July 21st, there were Gatherings of about ten thousand attendances.

Overseer Brasefield conducted a very successful Educational Conference.

We also held the first of two Conferences on Zion's Business Institutions.

ON FRIDAY, July 22d, there were attendances of about twelve thousand persons.

Overseer Jane Dowie conducted a very large Conference concerning Dorcas and Maternity Deaconess work in Zion throughout the world.

Our second Conference on Zion's Business Institutions was also attended by many.

A MOST Important Conference of all the Officers of the Christian Catholic Church in Zion now in Zion City, will be held at ten o'clock today in Shiloh Tabernacle.

TOMORROW, LORD'S DAY, July 24th, will be the closing day of the Feast.

We believe that even as the Master on "that Last Great Day" of the Feast of Tabernacles long ago "stood in the midst," so He will reveal Himself gloriously in the many important Convocations of that day.

IN THE six days from the 17th to the 22d, which we noted above, there has been an aggregate attendance of about ninety thousand, which, with the thirty-five thousand mentioned in our last Notes, as present in the first four days of the Feast, gives a total aggregate attendance of about one hundred and twenty-five thousand, from Wednesday evening, July 13th, to Friday, July 22d.

OUR READERS will readily see that the work connected with these numerous gatherings makes it impossible for us to do more than record the simple facts contained in these Notes.

BRETHREN, PRAY FOR US.

LOVE—THE FIRST FRUIT OF THE SPIRIT.

Zion's Fourth Feast of Tabernacles

The Set Feasts of Jehovah . . .
Ye shall proclaim to be Holy Convocations.

BEAUTIFUL and bright dawned the day for which the people of Zion City, and many in Zion throughout the world, had long been looking and preparing with joyful expectancy.

It was Wednesday, July 13, 1904, the first day of the Fourth Feast of Tabernacles held in Zion City.

For days, the hosts of Israel had been gathering from every quarter of this and many other lands.

Elijah and Edina Hospices were full to overflowing, Camp Esther sheltered its hundreds, while every private residence in the City was generously hospitable, as Zion homes always are.

Besides all these, hundreds from nearby cities came for this particular service.

It was the largest and most representative attendance that had yet come up to keep the Feast of Tabernacles.

The City presented, in many respects, the same gala appearance that had greeted the eyes of the General Overseer and the members of his Party upon their glad return from the now famous Around-the-World Visitation.

The graceful arch of welcome stood intact, each tower surmounted by a flag waving its welcome to visitors, and from every staff on Zion City's public buildings floated either the national colors or the glorious Zion Ensign of Gold, White and Blue.

The hour for the first Holy Convocation is drawing near.

The many roads and paths that converge at Shiloh Tabernacle are traversed by a happy people wending their way to the House of God.

Within the park the scene is most animated and inspiring.

A holy, joyful calm seems to pervade the very atmosphere.

Zion City Band has just finished the first evening concert of the Feast, squads of uniformed guards are energetically drilling in the grove, vehicles of various capacities and kinds are quietly but swiftly moving to and fro, and the thick cluster of tents in Camp Esther adds novelty and suggestion to the scene.

How could one's thoughts help reverting to the earlier days —so long ago—when our fathers of "the tribes of Jehovah" went up from year to year to that holy, beautiful metropolis, Jerusalem, at His command, "to worship the King, Jehovah of Hosts, and to keep the Feasts of Tabernacles?"

How could one help being impressed by the deep significance of the fact, that of the several Feasts which the Prophetic Word declares shall be reëstablished in the Latter Days, the only one for failing to keep which judgment is predicted, is the very Feast which Elijah the Restorer has first restored to God's Covenant people now being regathered in Zion City?

But the hour of assembly has arrived, and the people wait upon God.

They gather, possibly with good reason, a little slowly at first, but soon a vast congregation of between five thousand and six thousand expectant people listen to the Voice of God's servant, and unite their voices in a mighty volume of Praise and Thanksgiving.

After the usual preliminary exercises, and a cordial welcome to those who had come to Zion City to keep the Feast, the prophet of God proceeded to speak upon the theme announced, "For Zion's Sake."

It was an address replete with interesting facts, relating especially to Zion City and the recent Around-the-World Visitation, both of which were "for Zion's Sake."

It was for this that he toiled and sacrificed—that God might be glorified in the building up of Zion in all the world.

He had found Zion well-nigh everywhere. The Little White Dove had dropped seeds of truth into the hearts of people all over the world.

Even in Colombo, he saw the longing look in the eyes of a group of women and men, as if the millions of India were looking through those eyes, longing for all that Zion stands for.

---

*REPORTED BY O. L. S., L. L. H., AND F. A. F.
Shiloh Tabernacle, Zion City, Illinois, Wednesday Evening, July 13, 1904.

The service was begun by the singing of Hymn No. 20 in the specially-prepared Program:

Come, ye who love the Lord,
And let our joys be known;
Join in a song of sweet accord,
And thus surround the Throne.

Prayer was offered by Overseer J. G. Speicher, after which the General Overseer prayed for the sick and sorrowing, the Congregation chanting the Disciples' Prayer at the close.

The General Overseer read the 62d chapter of Isaiah.

A Gift of Love from All the People.

He then said:

I desire a present of twenty-five cents from each person, so that I may have the great pleasure of giving it to Overseer Speicher as a little gift from you and from me to show our love for him.

You know how good and kind and diligent he has been during the six months of my absence.

I believe that the friends who have come in from distant places will feel that Dr. Speicher's editing of LEAVES OF HEALING and the Notes from the Overseer-in-charge have been a very valuable help, in many ways.

He has been very attentive in connection with correspondence.

We are sending the Overseer to Europe.

He will leave us on tomorrow week, and join the *Etruria* at New York City.

I have asked him to go into residence in Zürich for his headquarters; to get a little rest, and to do a little light work in Europe.

I expect him to get much benefit, with his beloved wife, who needs the rest even more than he.

General Overseer to Remain in Zion City Until Shiloah Tabernacle is Completed.

Tomorrow I may ask you to consider with me plans for raising the large sum of money necessary to build Shiloah Tabernacle.

I should like to have it ready this time next year.

We found it quite impossible to do it last year and this year; but we are addressing ourselves to it now.

I shall not leave this City, God willing (unless something occurs that I do not foresee now), on any lengthened absence, until that Tabernacle is built, is opened, and is paid for.

However, I desire to do some work elsewhere.

I am very much needed in parts that I have not visited, and I must go in a year or two, for a short time.

The fields in Europe are so white to the harvest, and the people are so receptive on the Continent!

We must also look at the field in China and Japan as soon as

*The following reports have not been revised by the General Overseer.

ELIJAH THE RESTORER.

possible, because the time has come for China, the land of Sinim, and Japan, the land of the Rising Sun, and Zion must do her work there.

Before I deliver my address I must say to you, friends, that have come from long distances, that I am very glad to see you.

In the Name of the Lord, representing the Christian Catholic Church in Zion, and all its officers, and the City of Zion especially, I heartily welcome you to Zion City and to Zion's Fourth Feast of Tabernacles.

May God bless you throughout the whole of the Feast.

FOR ZION'S SAKE.

Will you bow your heads with me and ask God for a blessing upon the address?

INVOCATION.

Let the words of my mouth, and the meditation of my heart be acceptable in Thy sight, and blessed to this people. For the sake of Jesus. Amen.

TEXT.

For Zion's Sake will I not hold my peace, and for Jerusalem's sake I will not rest, until her Righteousness go forth as brightness, and her Salvation as a lamp that burneth. And the Nations shall see thy Righteousness, and all kings thy Glory: and thou shalt be called by a New Name, which the mouth of Jehovah shall name.

"For Zion's Sake!"

Some might say, "No, let us say for the Lord's sake;" but the prophet says, "For Zion's Sake."

The Apostle Paul had a desire to "depart and be with the Christ; for it is very far better;" but, he said, "To abide in the flesh is more needful for your sake."

I am talking tonight "for Zion's Sake."

If I were to speak about my Lord and say what I should like to have, for my own sake, it would be that I should like to be with Him; to be where He is and to enjoy the felicity of heaven.

I should like to be independent of the conditions that now fetter us so much in spirit, in soul, and in body—the earthly conditions which continually prevent the uninterrupted exercise for God; of even the powers that we have here.

Zion Another Word for the Kingdom of God.

I shall say something of how I stand "for Zion's Sake," for the glory of God, for Zion is but another word for the Kingdom of God.

The Christian Catholic Church in Zion is the Christian Catholic Church in the Kingdom of God, and, although we for short say "Zion," we do not want you to think that Zion is to be found only in the Christian Catholic Church.

The Christian Catholic Church itself is but a gathering of God's people in His Kingdom, who take a step forward into His Church and into the hosts that are forming to carry on the Restoration work.

Around-the-World Visitation Made "for Zion's Sake."

I very gladly speak tonight "for Zion's Sake."

It was "for Zion's Sake," primarily, that I made the Visitation which has just closed; a Visitation which seems to have caused a great deal of commotion.

When you consider that the Visitation Party at no time exceeded eight members, and sometimes consisted of only five, and sometimes, at certain points of the Visitation, was even less than that, it really is very astonishing that so few could make such a tremendous commotion.

I must confess that there was one out of the eight who made more noise than all the rest.

Perhaps you may know who he was.

But the noise that he made was as nothing to the noise that was made in all the nations where we came.

I often thought of the verse that we have frequently sung:

> Each breeze that sweeps the ocean
> Brings tidings from afar,
> Of nations in commotion
> Prepared for Zion's War.

And they were prepared, too, some of them. [Laughter.]

They were prepared for war, but

We Had Not Gone Out for War.

We had gone out only upon a little reconnaissance, a little observation tour.

I told you that I was going for rest as well as for observation; but I need not tell you that we did not get much rest.

However we most certainly did some observing and we did some work.

But my tour was primarily "for Zion's Sake."

I wanted to see what degree of preparation there was among the nations for Zion's work, and what the condition was, especially of the English-speaking people, and then of the so-called Christian nations on the Continent of Europe.

I am glad "for Zion's Sake," that the journey was taken.

In the first place, we were able to help and strengthen our Overseers, Elders, Evangelists, Deacons, Deaconesses, Zion Restoration Host, and our people throughout the world.

It was interesting to see that we went nowhere without finding members of Zion, except at Aden, where we spent only a few hours on a very hot day, and at Suez and Port Said, where the vessel arrived during the night and sailed early in the morning, without giving us an opportunity to land.

We found Zion everywhere, and the work that God had done through us in this land represented everywhere.

The Little White Dove had dropped the seeds of Zion into hearts all around the world.

The Nations' Longing for Zion.

I remember sitting in the Galle Face Hotel in Colombo, Ceylon, with a few Cingalese and Tamil people.

They were nicely dressed; the gentlemen had come to meet me in full-dress evening clothes, and the ladies were dressed in the beautiful colored robes of their country.

They spoke in very pure English, their lovely Eastern faces aglow with delight that they had at last seen the General Overseer and were able to talk to him.

At first it seemed as if they were unable to talk; they just sat looking at me.

I thought as I sat there with these few representatives of India (which country I could not enter because of lack of time), that this little gathering was very suggestive. The longing look in their eyes I shall never forget.

They seemed to follow me, as if all India, with its hundreds of millions, was looking through the eyes of those beautiful young women and earnest young men.

I felt at once, when looking at that little number, what a longing there was in the hearts of these people for all that Zion stands for.

"For Zion's Sake," We Were Not Afraid of Any Consequences.

I was warned, for instance, not to set my foot in Great Britain.

I was told that there was a plot to take my life; and there is no doubt whatever that such a plot existed, for some of the London papers themselves said that if I had gone to the Euston Road Tabernacle on Monday I might never have left that place alive.

They knew what they were talking about, for they were among the leaders of the riotous proceedings.

But, as we went around the world, we felt more and more the need of the truths for which Zion stands.

Our Lord Jesus, the Christ's, whole mission and ministry was "for Zion's Sake."

He came to preach the Gospel of the Kingdom of God, and Zion is the Kingdom of God.

It was to proclaim the Gospel of the Kingdom of God that He came.

He made His Atonement that He might establish the Kingdom of God, for the Salvation of humanity; and the thought, "for the Kingdom of God's Sake," was ever in His heart.

We can best glorify God by extending His Kingdom, building up His Kingdom, by establishing His Kingdom in human hearts, and by giving His Kingdom a local name and habitation in the world, which today is everywhere under the power of the Prince of Darkness and Disorder and Despair and Doubt and Damnation.

The World Is Not Ruled by the Sons of Light.

The World is not ruled in such a way as to bring order; for confusion is everywhere.

The world is not ruled in such a way as to fill those who dwell in it with beauteous Divine Hope. Despair and Doubt, instead of Faith and Hope, rule everywhere.

Darkness has covered the nations, and gross darkness the peoples.

They live in the degradation of a horrible damnation, a

damnation which is the creation of their own shameless lusts and their own oftentimes wilful ignorance

I speak especially regarding Anglo-Saxon countries.

There is a condition of condemnation which makes the people to suffer and makes them ever restless, because they know that they are not doing the Will of God, and that they are condemned with a condemnation that is just.

The darkness that covers the heathen, and those who never heard of the Kingdom of God, is another thing.

With these people that dwell in darkness, we have greater sympathy still; for those that are dwelling in heathen darkness, in the midst of Christian Light and Revelation, cannot excite the sympathy which those who have never heard excite in our hearts, as we look at them bowing before the shrines of Buddha.

The Brutality and Mercilessness of Heathenism.

We saw the pitiful sight of one poor woman, at the shrine of her god, offering flowers that indicated a broken heart, when a cruel priest, thinking to get a few pennies from the white-faced visitors at the temple, looked at her, and said, "Get up, and get away."

He drove her away; and then we asked what those flowers were.

"An offering. Will you have them?" he asked.

He took them from the altar of the god and handed them to us.

When I thought of the ruthless, brutal, absolutely wicked nature of heathenism, that had no sympathy whatever with that sorrow-bowed, broken-hearted woman, who had laid her offering upon the altar, and was weeping there before an unknown god, seeking for help, and was ruthlessly pushed away, I felt deeply, and I still feel very deeply, for these nations that have never heard of Zion, and that know nothing about the Kingdom of God

I cannot help feeling angry, deep down in my heart, at those who talk of the Kingdom of God and do not for one moment live it.

When you tell them that that Kingdom is above all kingdoms, they get angry and proclaim the supremacy of their own king and their own kingdom.

One smart infidel paper said that "Dr. Dowie's offense in the British Empire" had been to say that the Lord Jesus, the Christ, was a bigger and better man than Edward VII. [Applause.]

And the infidel mocked at the so-called Christians who defended the piety and the beautiful, chaste, lovely character (!) of the present king of England.

"For Zion's Sake," I welcome you who belong to Zion and who now realize, what the world is beginning to realize, that

Zion City Is a Great Object Lesson.

"For Zion's Sake" I undertook the toil and the trial and faced the temptations and the trouble which were inevitable in the establishment of this City.

We went forward in simple Faith.

We have continued in simple Faith.

Unwavering confidence in God has met its glorious reward.

This little City of many thousand people, with its lovely homes and its industries, its great educational and ecclesiastical institutions reaching out all over the earth, sent forth one Legion last year to do what all the churches of New York in all their history had never done, namely, to visit every home in the city, carrying to the people a Message of Peace.

We did it within two weeks, and all the Christianity of New York has not done it in two centuries.

This little City has proved its peacefulness by the fact that there has not been an assault in its streets, that there has not been a person brought before its court for crime of that nature, and that the judge has never had to sit in criminal court since he was appointed.

Here National Differences Disappear.

This City stands as a representation of the great fact that when the people are united in God and to each other in Him, when in all their hearts are the Highways to Zion, you can bring a people together from all the nations of the earth and weld them into perfect Unity.

There are more than seventy nations of the earth represented in this City tonight; nations that are at almost constant strife with one another; that are always bickering with one another; and that are writing most insulting things about one another.

But there is no strife here.

The German and the Frenchman are one "for Zion's Sake."

They have Zion in their hearts, and the peace of God reigns there.

The Swede, the Norwegian and the Dane, whatever differences their fathers may have had in Europe, are one in Zion.

The English and the Irish, whatever differences they may now have (and they are many) have none in Zion.

The differences between the various nations of the earth are absolutely obliterated in Zion.

I have not heard of one quarrel in this City because of people belonging to different nations and wanting to fight the battles of their people.

Only One Fight in Which Zion Takes a Part.

The people in Zion have had only one fight; they have all been fighting the Good Fight of Faith.

They rejoice to help and love one another.

The only provocation they have given us has been to provoke to good works and to utter to one another good thoughts.

I know of no home, office, factory, or shop in Zion, where the morning salutation, "Peace to thee," from wife to husband and husband to wife, brother to sister and sister to brother, neighbor to neighbor, and fellow employee to fellow employee, and the loving response, "Peace to thee be multiplied," are not given.

In all languages they give the Salutation.

But I encourage our people everywhere to speak it in English; and it is now known in English all the world over.

Zion City is an object lesson.

We have not had one strike.

We have not had one disturbance that has paralyzed the wheels of industry for one moment in Zion, although we have come together from all parts of the earth.

The people have been brought together by God and "for Zion's Sake."

We have come together to build up Zion, through Zion to seek for the evangelization of the world, and by means of this and other Zion Cities to prepare for the King's Coming.

The Great Future Work of Zion.

If God continues to prosper us in the same ratio as in the past, and enables us to found the Cities that we contemplate, I have not the slightest doubt that the Christian Catholic Church in Zion will be able to go forth and, resting only upon God and herself, take up the task of making the City of Jerusalem the most beautiful city in all the earth, carrying, if necessary, soil to lay upon her rocks and stones, until it is terraced into beauty; until it, the Temple, and the Palace of the Great King are built.

"For Zion's Sake will I not hold my peace, and for Jerusalem's sake"—because the rebuilding of Jerusalem is one of the great objects of Zion—"I will not rest until her Righteousness go forth as brightness and her Salvation as a lamp that burneth."

Beloved, we are greatly privileged of God to be the citizens and the builders of the first Zion City in the world.

We are contemplating the building of others, but without sacrificing this City, for this City shall never be sacrificed.

I would have nothing to do with the building of any other city if it were to be at the cost of this City, for this City must go on and be built up.

Zion's Growth.

Let me tell you what I told a great financier who was speaking to me today in my office.

I said to him, "Between five and ten years from this time this City of Zion, with its great industries, and great schools and colleges, will have a population of one hundred fifty thousand people."

That, I believe, will be the case.

I am grateful to God that the rate of increase even now justifies me in saying that.

That which I now see, and that which Zion sees throughout the world is clear, namely, that as the people are brought out of the weary nations, and out of the apostate churches, into Zion, the very first thing they do is to look across the seas to Zion City, and say, "O, Lord, help me to get there."

These Cities of Refuge must be built all over the world, and from them will come the great Zion City builders, who will return to Jerusalem and prepare it for the Coming King.

All this must be done within a quarter of a century.

All this can be done in much less time; for these are the times in which men can do things quickly.

I do not want to speak boastfully, because I do not believe we have done an atom more than our duty; but our neighbor, Waukegan, has taken seventy years to be built, and I do not hesitate to say that Zion City in three years can raise her head and stand alongside of Waukegan, as a sister city.

In three years, we have been able to do that which Waukegan has not been able to do in seventy years; for Waukegan has not been able to make a clean city in all the years; she has to pay one hundred fifty thousand dollars, or thereabouts, a year to the sellers of Liquid Fire and Distilled Damnation.

Waukegan has to pay to the harlot, to the seller of Satan's Consuming Fire (tobacco), and to those that are gambling and sinning, a vast sum of money, equivalent probably to two hundred fifty thousand dollars a year, while this City stands clean and free.

If All the Cities of the World Had Been Built "for Zion's Sake."

You cannot find in all the story of the world another city built "for Zion's Sake" which has in anything like the same degree, within the same time, the same Message to give to the world.

If the whole world were a Zion City, then it would be a heaven compared to what it is!

Think of all the cities of the world as absolutely free from intoxicating drinks, from the presence of a known harlot or whoremonger, from the presence of a single gambler, from the stink of a smoker, from a hundred things that I could name, cities where there is Peace and Purity and Progress, and Power for God!

I say this "for Zion's Sake."

Zion City has been founded "for Zion's Sake."

To Zion throughout the world I say:

Come, Help Me to Build It up Quickly!

Help me to extend the manufacturing enterprises, which are already so successful, and which, developed to the extent of the business that we could do, can bring into Zion, in this City alone, an income of not less than from ten to twenty million dollars every year.

I know whereof I speak.

Those who know me know that I am not talking as a visionary, because I am a very practical man when it comes to figures.

Although I oftentimes startle my associates, I know I have never been caught napping.

This Feast of Tabernacles has been established "for Zion's Sake."

He who speaks to you has not rested, and day and night he has been the Lord's remembrancer in this matter.

Day and night he has worked for Zion all over the earth, and desires to work for Zion now, knowing that Zion is dear to the heart of our Lord; that Zion has been established by Him, and that

> The vaulted heavens shall fall,
> Built by Jehovah's hands;
> But firmer than the heavens, the Rock
> Of our Salvation stands.

Let us stand and consecrate ourselves to God.

PRAYER OF CONSECRATION.

My God and Father, in Jesus' Name I come to Thee. Take me as I am. Make me what I ought to be in spirit, in soul, and in body. Give me power to do right, no matter what it costs. Help me to do right to those whom I have wronged, to make confession and restitution, to do right in Thy sight, and to restore to Thee that of which I may have robbed Thee. O God, help Zion to be faithful to her trust at the End of the Dispensation, for the Consummation of the Age is drawing nigh. Give us grace to go forward in the preparation for the Coming of our Lord. For His sake.

BENEDICTION.

Beloved, abstain from every form of evil. And may the very God of Peace Himself sanctify you wholly; and I pray God your whole spirit and soul and body be preserved entire, without blame, unto the coming of our Lord Jesus, the Christ. Faithful is He that calleth you, who also will do it. The grace of our Lord Jesus, the Christ, the love of God our Father, the fellowship of the Holy Spirit our Comforter and Guide, one Eternal God, abide in you, bless you and keep you, and all the Israel of God everywhere, forever. Amen.

EARLY MORNING SACRIFICE OF PRAISE AND PRAYER.

REPORTED BY M. E. L., A. C. R., AND E. S.

The first Early Morning Meeting of Zion's Holy Convocation, Thursday, July 14, 1904, was a season of deepest spiritual power and blessing.

Approximately five thousand people were gathered in Shiloh Tabernacle at the early morning hour to hear the Message given by Jehovah through the mouth of His servant, the Prophet of the Restoration.

A consecrated feast, whose cup immortal Love's lip hath pressed was spread and all—the lowest, the humblest, the least in the Kingdom of God—were invited, nay, urged to partake thereof.

Love, the first of the Nine glorious Fruits of the Spirit, was the theme of the man of God.

Shiloh Tabernacle, Zion City, Illinois, Thursday Morning, July 14, 1904.

The service was opened by singing of Hymn No. 8, from the Program:

> When morning gilds the skies,
> My heart awaking cries,
> May Jesus Christ be praised!
> Alike at work and prayer,
> To Jesus I repair;
> May Jesus Christ be praised!

Prayer was offered by the General Overseer, after which he said:

Let us read from the Inspired Word of God in the epistle of Paul the Apostle to the Galatians, the 5th chapter and the 13th verse.

For ye, brethren, were called for freedom; only use not your freedom for an occasion to the flesh, but through Love be servants one to another.

For the Whole Law is fulfilled in one word, even in this; Thou shalt love thy neighbor as thyself.

That is the Law.

A Law That Reaches Higher Than the Ten Commandments.

I so often wish that you would remember that there is something better than the fulfilling of the Ten Commandments; that the Royal Law is not high enough for the Christian.

To love one another is good, to love as you expect to be loved is good, and the Law is fulfilled; but there is something better.

Love your neighbor better than yourself, that is the Gospel.

Remember the Eleventh Commandment.

That is better than all the Ten in regard to Love.

A New Commandment I give unto you, that ye love one another even as I also have loved you.

Did He love us as Himself, or did He love us better than Himself?

People—"Better."

General Overseer—"Thou shalt love thy neighbor as thyself," and "Whatsoever ye would that men should do to you, do ye even so to them," are very good, but do to men what you never expect them to do for you.

Pour out your life for them.

Love them.

Serve them.

That is better than loving them as yourself.

Love them better than yourself.

That is the best form of Love.

For ye, brethren, were called for freedom; only use not your freedom for an occasion to the flesh, but through Love be servants one to another.

For the Whole Law is fulfilled in one word, even in this; Thou shalt love thy neighbor as thyself.

I do not want to quarrel with the apostle, but I wish he had written that correctly.

That was the Law and the prophets, but the Gospel is bigger.

I think sometimes that the apostles and every one else forget how definitely Christ had given the Eleventh Commandment.

We do not always get even as high as the Royal Law, and therefore we do not see anything higher.

When you have fulfilled the Royal Law, and love your neighbor as yourself, you get to the place where you want to love your neighbor better than yourself.

Then there is nothing that you can do for humanity that you are not willing to do.

Your Only Measure of Service Is a Measure of Time and Opportunity.

You should never say merely, "Now I will do for that man what I should like him to do for me;" but "I will do for humanity what I never expect humanity to do for me."

That is the life that the Christ lived.

He never expected us to do for Him as He did for us, because we could not.

There are vast numbers of people who never can do anything for us, and to do something for them is the highest form of expression of Love.

For the whole Law is fulfilled in one word, even in this: Thou shalt love thy neighbor as thyself.

But if ye bite and devour one another, take heed that ye be not consumed one of another.

But I say, Walk by the Spirit, and ye shall not fulfil the lust of the flesh.

For the flesh lusteth against the spirit, and the spirit against the flesh; for these are contrary the one to the other; that ye may not do the things that ye would.

I call your attention to this better reading.

The old reading is, "So that ye cannot do the things that ye would."

A great many people say, "You know the Bible says that we cannot do the things we would. We are no better than Paul."

That was not what Paul wrote.

Paul did not write, "Ye cannot do the things ye would," but he wrote just the opposite.

He wrote as the Revision has it: "That ye may not do the things that ye would."

The flesh shall be so subdued; the spirit shall be so powerful, that the flesh will be overcome by the spirit, and that the evil things you otherwise would do, you will not do.

You cannot then do the things that you would in a state of sensual desire, which is not Love at all, but lust.

But if ye are led by the spirit ye are not under the Law.

You are above the Law.

If You Are Led by the Spirit the Law Is Beneath Your Feet.

You have triumphed over Law.

You are not bound by Law, but you stand on Law.

You are not lawless.

You obey the laws, and Law is the very foundation by which you walk.

But you are not under it; you are not carrying the load of the Law upon your shoulders.

Law is the strong foundation.

It is the rock. There is no slipping there.

You are standing on Law and that is liberty.

Now the works of the flesh are manifest, which are these, fornication, uncleanness, lasciviousness, idolatry, sorcery—

That word in the Scripture is always connected with drugs—sorcerer is the *pharmakos* (φαρμακός); *pharmakeia* (φαρμακεία) is the use of drugs to degrade and to pervert judgment and to get control over the spirit, soul, and body.

The sorcerer is the maker, vender, and user of deadly drugs.

Humanity is being poisoned at the fountain of all spiritual freedom by narcotics.

In hundreds of millions of men, the brain is never free, because it is controlled by narcotic poisons, lulled to sleep by tobacco, morphine, and deadly drugs.

The brain becomes inflamed, the will perverted, and the eyes do not see clearly.

They see strangely, and the heart utters perverse things under the power of sorcery.

The horror of universal drugging that goes on today!

Vast numbers of people are not free one hour from the influence of narcotic poisons.

The Word is clear on that.

Now the works of the flesh are manifest, which are these, fornication, uncleanness, lasciviousness,

Idolatry, pharmacy, enmities, strife, jealousies, wraths, factions, divisions, parties, or heresies.

Envy a Destructive Enemy of Humanity.

What a curse these party divisions are!

They are a curse in the church and in the state, where we find men striving, not for the supremacy of right, but for the supremacy of party.

What a horrid thing it is, striving after the supremacy of factional, denominational, and apostate things!

Envy! Envy!! Envy!!!

Envy has destroyed great cities, and uprooted mighty nations.

Envy has separated families, cities, states, nations, families of the race, until Envy is everywhere.

Because of Envy, men deliver one another to the Devil, as the Jews for Envy delivered the Christ to Pilate.

Envyings, drunkenness, revelings and such like: of the which I forewarn you, even as I did forewarn you—

The word "forewarn," really means, "tell you plainly."

Those Who Object to Plain Speaking.

We want plain speaking.

That is the thing the world objects to.

It does not like to get the plain truth.

That is the thing the church objects to.

They objected to the Christ because of His plain speaking.

There was no truthful man during my Around-the-World Visitation who said that I did not tell the truth.

They objected because I told too much truth, and told it in such a way that the whole world was listening to it.

According to them, that was the kind of thing I ought to have kept secret, or whispered where no one would hear it.

But, as usual, they were mistaken about what I would do or ought to do.

I will talk plainly until I am through, and I believe that Zion will keep on talking plainly.

We will not keep anything back that ought to be spoken.

I forewarn you even as I did forewarn you, that they which practice such things shall not inherit the Kingdom of God.

If you have practiced any of these things you are outside the Kingdom.

It does not matter what church you are in, you are outside the Kingdom of God, and the church that takes you in has gone to the Devil.

You will not inherit the Kingdom of God.

It is a question of practice.

"They which practice such things."

It is not a question of temptation.

It is not a question as to whether you have momentarily yielded to any of these things or not.

It is a question, however, as to whether you have repented of these things, have been forgiven, and your life is entirely changed.

If you continue to practice these things, you will not get into heaven. You must cease to be in any sense under the bondage of these works of the flesh.

The Fruits of the Spirit.

But the Fruit of the Spirit—

Paul speaks of the Fruit of the Spirit in those that do not practice these things.

It is impossible to practice these things and have any Fruit at all.

You have only Fruit of the Devil.

But the Fruit of the Spirit is Love, Joy, Peace, Long-suffering, Kindness, Goodness, Faithfulness,

Meekness, Temperance—

Temperance is Self-control, ἐγκράτεια—*engkrateia*.

Control of self by the power of the Spirit.

That is the highest, fullest manifestation of the Power of Love.

Not self-submission; but Self-control.

Meekness, Temperance, against such there is no law.

You are at the top of Law.

Law is under you.

Law is with you.

Law is not against you.

All Law in All the Universe is with you.

And they that are of Christ Jesus have crucified the flesh with the passions and the lusts thereof.

If we live by the spirit, by the spirit let us also walk.

Let us not be vainglorious, provoking one another, envying one another.

THE FIRST FRUIT OF THE SPIRIT: LOVE.

INVOCATION.

Let the words of my mouth, and the meditations of my heart, be acceptable in Thy sight, be profitable unto this people and unto all to whom these words shall come, in this and every land, in this and all the coming time, Till Jesus Come. Amen.

TEXT.

The Fruit of the Spirit is Love, Joy, Peace.

These are the first three in the triple trinity of the glorious Fruit of the Spirit.

Three Trinities Both in the Fruit and in the Gifts of the Spirit.

There are three times three.

Just as there are Nine Gifts of the Spirit, there are Nine Fruits of the Spirit.

The Nine Fruits of the Spirit have for their first trinity Love, Joy, Peace.

The second trinity is Long-suffering, Kindness, Goodness.

The third trinity is Faithfulness, Meekness, Self control.

A three-fold cord is not easily broken, but a three times three is more difficult to break.

When you have strong cords then there is great power.

In the Gifts of the Spirit you have the same order.

The Word of Wisdom, the Word of Knowledge, Faith: there is the first trinity.

As you go on, you find the trinity swells into Gifts of Healings, Workings of Miracles, Prophecies; there is the second trinity.

Then you have Tongues and Interpretation of Tongues; and with these you have the Discernings of Spirits.

That is the power to see not merely the corporeal but the spiritual nature of man; the eye to see not only the manifestation of the nature, but the inward spirit.

The spirit is that which we must see in order to understand.

Let me ask you to remember that in these talks I close with a little exposition of the Gifts of the Spirit; but do not imagine that the Fruits of the Spirit and the Gifts of the Spirit are the same things, for they are not.

The Fruits of the Spirit within us are very different from the Gifts which are without us, and which God gives to those who obey Him.

The Holy Spirit Has Never Come to the Disobedient.

He hath given His Spirit to them that obey, and it is a good thing for us when we consider the difficulties.

Have we received the Spirit since we believed?

There are many who have repented and believed, like those at Ephesus, who lived up to the light they had, but when Paul asked them, "Did ye receive the Holy Spirit when ye believed?" or, as it is more correctly translated, "Have ye received the Holy Spirit since ye believed?" they said they did not know anything about the Holy Spirit.

They did not know that the Holy Spirit had yet been given.

It was then that Paul went further than the teaching of Apollos, and showed these Christians that they might receive, humble as they were, the Indwelling Power of the Eternal Power; the Indwelling Purity of the Eternal Purity; the Indwelling Love of the Eternal Love.

Then they raised their hands and hearts, and said, "Come, Holy Spirit!" and the Spirit came.

"Have ye received the Holy Spirit since ye believed?"

By the Holy Spirit's Power you were led to believe.

He was with you.

He shall be in you.

Difference Between Dwelling In and Dwelling With.

Jesus said to His apostles when He spoke of the Spirit, and looked at their wavering and weak natures: "He dwelleth with you, but He shall be in you."

Oh, how weak they were until He dwelt within them!

He was with them as the Master was with them, but He was then outside them, as I would be outside a little child if I took his hand.

I should be with the child, but I should not be in the child.

The child of God, who may be led by the Spirit, is not necessarily indwelt by the Spirit.

These apostles did not have the Spirit within them.

Jesus said it. He said, "He dwelleth with you, but He shall be in you."

Is the Spirit in you, or is He only with you?

You cannot bear the Fruits of the Spirit if He is only outside you.

Have You a Temple in Which He Dwells?

Not in circling height,
Nor depth, but in the conscious breast,
Present to faith, though hid from sight—
There doth His Spirit rest.

It is not in Gerizim; it is not in Zion; it is not in Zion City that you may find Him.

The hour cometh; the hour now is when they that worship the Father shall worship Him in spirit and in truth, and it is not on this mountain nor that mountain.

The Water that I shall give him shall become in him a Well of Water springing up unto Eternal Life.

He that believeth on Me, as the Scripture hath said, out of his belly shall flow Rivers of Living Waters.

The Fruits of the Spirit are on the River of God, which is full of water, which bears along its beautiful course the Tree of Life which brings forth Fruit all the time.

The Spirit of Life waters the Tree of Life, and the Fruits are brought forth every month.

The Leaves of the Tree, the Words of God, are for the Healing of the Nations.

He sendeth His Word and healeth them.

So the Spirit nourishes the Tree all the way down the course of the River.

He shall be like a tree planted by the Streams of Water.
That bringeth forth its fruit in its season,
Whose leaf also doth not wither;
And whatsoever he doeth shall prosper.
The wicked are not so.

They only prosper for a time, but die shortly.

Then they sing as Byron sang before he was forty years old; when he was perhaps thirty!

My life is in the yellow leaf—
The care, the canker, and the grief,
Are mine alone.

When we have within us the Water of Life, then we bring forth Fruit.

Our leaf does not wither. Whatsoever we do, prospers; and as we go on in life we bear our best fruit in old age.

We Cannot Bear Fruit Without the Indwelling Spirit.

We must be quite sure, first of all, that we have the indwelling Power and Presence of the Spirit.

We have no right to expect fruit where nothing has been planted.

All I could do if I were Paul would be to plant.

All I could do if I were Apollos would be to water, and who gives the increase?

People—"God."

General Overseer—Who can bring forth fruit?

People—"God."

General Overseer—Very well, I will plant; I will water.

Pruning Necessary to Fruit Growing.

I will prune you, too.

I will use the knife.

I will use it unsparingly before I am through, but I shall take care of the tree.

I desire to see the tree grow.

The gardener goes into his garden to prepare the vine for fruit bearing.

He looks at it very lovingly, and says, "I am so thankful that these branches that are trailing up the trellis bore such beautiful fruit this year. We plucked it and stored it away. Thank God for that!"

Then he carefully looks at the vine, and deliberately calculates one knot from where it grew the previous year, and with a sharp knife cuts off the branch.

"O my God!" cries the Christian oftentimes, "is that the way You love me? O God, You cut off such a precious branch that bore fruit last year! Oh, do not cut any more!"

But the Father is the Husbandman, and He makes other cuts, until the vine stands there stripped of all its glory.

Is it right? Tell me?

People—"Yes."

General Overseer—Is it not right that God shall come and take away even a great part of a branch that bore fruit?

If He did not, our vine would go on growing merely wood, and the fruit would be less and less, until at last it would not be worth gathering.

It is Love that prunes.

It is Love that cuts away until all hope seems gone.

The Christ Entered the Valley of Death Alone.

In the darkness the Christ Himself cries, "*Eli, Eli, Lama sabachthani!*"—My God! My God! Why hast Thou forsaken Me?

It was not until He went down into the deeper darkness, that He was able to say, "*Tetelesti, tetelesti!*"—It is finished! I have conquered!

Oh, it was hard for that good, strong, beautiful Life to go down into death!

It was hard for Him, who, in sympathy with all life, rejoiced in the midnight and in the glories of the midday; on the mountain heights and in the sweetness of the valley; who lived and loved, and was strong because He was pure.

Oh, it was hard for Him!

He did not need to die unless He was going to submit to the Father, and let the Father take away everything.

Everything! Even His last breath! His last breath!

He gave up His Spirit, but He conquered.

Love was there.

Love gave His only begotten Son.

Love, in the embodiment of that Son, gave Himself.

The knife was there, but unless the very Christ Himself had suffered, being tempted; unless He had been made perfect by the suffering that Love prompted, He could not have accomplished His great work for humanity. Although He was the Son of God yet learned He obedience by the things that He suffered.

Love had gone down into the Christ-life itself, and given away everything.

He was left away out on the Sea of Death in the darkness, so that His humanity cried, for He felt alone!

For the first time in all the Eternal Story of His life, the first-born Son saw not the face of the Father, and out of the darkness He cried.

But it was Love that had taken the knife.

Not until we, too, have passed through our Gethsemane, our Golgotha, our Calvary, until we have been to the place of a skull, and seen the eyeless socket of death, and looked beyond the crashing, the chaos, the tempest, the wreck of all things, and gone out into the darkness with God alone shall we get the fulness of His Love.

Only Love Can Tread the Dark Valley Alone.

We will not have to drink that cup until the time comes.

Perhaps, some of us will never know much about it, because God sees how weak, how pitifully weak we are, and knows that we could not bear much.

But some of us will have to fill up the measure of the sufferings of the Christ, which is the very highest gift that Love can bestow.

Not to him who never treads the valley; not to him who always wants to live in mountain heights and there build tabernacles for the Christ and the prophets; not to him who always wants to be in the sunshine and above the clouds; but to him who can go down into the valley with the Christ and do His work in the darkness of the dark world, fight with devils, cast them out, and get close to the diseases of humanity, so that he may touch them, and the Spirit within him shall flow to their healing—will the Gifts of the Spirit be given.

It takes love, a great love, not to worry, but to go on through days and nights, where there is no inspiring audience to cheer by their faces and their interest, doing one's work in the darkness.

There is none to cheer, you are alone and it is dark, but you do not know it; for the Light is there and you are with Him who is the Inspiration.

When the Christ cried, then He found what He lets us always find.

He is with us, and He is Light.

There is no dark valley, for He is with us.

Though I walk through the valley of the shadow of death,
I will fear no evil; for Thou art with me.

The Shadow of Death! Where shall I meet it?

At the end?

No! No! I shall tread the vale many times.

The valley of the shadow of death was rightly put by Bunyan, in the middle of the Christian's journey; not at the end.

I shall never cry out unless I have sinned and gotten away from God: "My God! My God! Why hast Thou forsaken me?"

The Christ went through that.

He went through where there was no Light; but since He has gone, there has been Light always, and Love leads us there.

The Fruit of the Spirit is Love, the Love that lives for God and for others.

Real Love.

Real Love is not the mere sentimental expression which finds all its fulness in the adoration of an object of flesh.

That is not Love.

The pure are always quick to see the difference between Lust and Love.

Sometimes the Devil tricks people and makes them think that lust is love.

The World at large does not know any other kind of love than lust—the lust of desire, the lust which sees the beautiful face and form, and desires animal possession; the unclean passions seeking satisfaction and getting it for a time!

That is not Love; that is Lust!

Even though within that shrine of flesh there dwells a beautiful spirit, let us take care.

There is lust there as well as love, and you must distinguish.

Love that is true and pure will never seek her own, but will seek another's good.

Love, if it is Divine, will find expression, not in self-gratification, but in self-sacrifice; not in getting, but in giving; not in being, but in not being.

Love that pours out the soul unto death is the Love of God—the Love that was in the Christ: the Love of sacrifice, the Love of service, the Love that is willing to die, the Love that seeks not to save but to spare.

He That Loses His Life in the Service of His Love Shall Win It Unto Life Eternal.

Music breaks upon my ear! And what is it?

I want to know, O Music!

I am waiting for a note.

I do not often hear it.

Music, can you tell me what it is?

"Yes," says Music, "I am seeking a note to express Love."

Love! The Love of God; the Love that is Infinite; that Love I want to get into you.

O Music, come with it!

Perhaps it will not be a note at all; perhaps the Love will come by a look, by a thought, or perhaps by an act of sacrifice.

Whatever way it comes, Music, speak it; sound it in the hearts of this people today.

God is speaking it, but let us be quite sure that we are letting God say it.

God is speaking it through us.

We do not always have the same expression.

O Hand of God, take us and make us one harmonious Band of Love; one that shall tell the Story in unison!

We do not all have the same Gifts, but let us get together with the Gifts that we have.

O Love, as through the varied instruments the same breath breathes the sharp, shrill cry and the sweet, soft tone, use us, blend us all together in one, that the Music of Zion throughout the world may be the Music of Eternal Love!

PRAYER OF CONSECRATION.

My God and Father, in Jesus' Name I come to Thee. Take me as I am. Make me what I ought to be in spirit, in soul, and in body. Let the Love of God which was in the heart of the Christ, which is ever there, be with us and ever in us. Let that Love abound, and let us be willing, like a true vine, to bear the pruning, that we may bring forth more fruit. O God, forbid that we should cling to our dead past, even if it brought forth fruit. Let us be willing to be pruned so we may bring forth the fruits of Love. Then Joy will come; then Peace will come. Let us yield to Love, and let us be filled with Love that we may be patient, and pure, and perfect in Thy sight. For Jesus' sake.

Do you mean it?

People—"Yes."

General Overseer—Then, beloved, live it.

After the singing of Hymn No. 11 in the Program the General Overseer pronounced the

BENEDICTION.

Beloved, abstain from every form of evil. And may the very God of Peace Himself sanctify you wholly; and I pray God your whole spirit and soul and body be preserved entire, without blame, unto the coming of our Lord Jesus, the Christ. Faithful is He that calleth you, who also will do it. The grace of our Lord Jesus, the Christ, the love of God our Father, the fellowship of the Holy Spirit, our Comforter and Guide, one Eternal God, abide in you, bless you and keep you, and all the Israel of God everywhere, forever. Amen.

FOURTH ANNIVERSARY OF THE CONSECRATION OF THE SITE OF ZION TEMPLE.

REPORTED BY R. M. P., O. R. AND A. W. N.

Zion was indeed a "Crown of Beauty in the Hand of Jehovah," on the great Fourth Anniversary of that wonderful day, when ten thousand of her sons and daughters joined with the Prophet of God in the Consecration of that Sacred Site where, in years to come, the great Zion Temple will lift its pure white dome.

There was beauty in the sky, beauty in the broad, fertile fields and cool, peaceful groves, beauty in the shimmering, brilliant blue waters of the lake, beauty in the songs of the birds and in the exquisite harmony of nature, that marked this Crowning Day of Zion's year.

There was beauty in the clustered, clean, and happy homes of the people, in the scores of brilliant banners floating in the breeze, and in the animated but orderly scenes on the streets and in the parks.

But the brightest and most precious jewels in all this Royal Diadem were the thousands of men, women, youths, maidens, boys, and girls who, with songs of sweetest praise upon their lips, accompanied their beloved leader in a joyous march around the Site that had been consecrated four years before, and around that other site, where Shiloah Tabernacle will soon rise, that had been consecrated one year before.

As these thousands swept by, their faces aglow with health, vigor, purity, and happiness, they expressed infinitely more than mere component units in a great Festival Procession.

Each one was a living epitome of a special story of the Love, Mercy, Goodness and Power of God.

Here, with erect, powerful bearing, clear eye, and a steady, unfaltering step, there walks a man whom God, through Zion, has raised up from the very gutter of drunkenness, debauchery, and disease.

Beside him, his intelligent face alight with honesty and candor, is a man whom God's Hand lifted up from the terrible cowardice and degradation of that most despicable of sins—that sin which has honeycombed the churches—hypocrisy.

Next is a manly youth saved from the destruction that lay just a few steps ahead of him on the precipitous downward path along which he was swiftly rushing.

Singing from a full heart, in the white robe of Zion Choir, is a maiden saved from the awful peril of a life of the most insidious and subtle temptation.

There, marching side by side, are men and women in hundreds, whom Satan had dragged down to the very gates of death, by his filthy diseases, now walking with the elastic step which tells of abounding health.

Men and women from nations that have been implacable foes for so many generations that their children are born with a heritage of fierce, bitter hatred; men and women of different families or so-called races between whom the Devil has for centuries sowed the seeds of murderous prejudice and strife; men and women born into different religious, social, and political sects, classes, societies, and parties, between which there has been nothing but unyielding contention, all marched together shoulder to shoulder, heart to heart, in mutual love and with one common purpose.

Hundreds of the sweetest children under the broad blue sky, some of them saved from death, some of them delivered from life-long suffering and misery, some of them rejoicing in a reunited and reëstablished home, some of them instinct with life and happiness, who would never have been born at all but for the Power of God in Zion, all of them clean and pure, free from the terrible defilements of the flesh and spirit that are permitted to slaughter more innocents every year in every worldly city than shed their blood at the hand of the cruel Herod, form a most beautiful section of the procession.

In short, this procession of between two and three thousand, that encircled Zion Temple and Shiloah Tabernacle sites, on this glorious quadrennial, had been transformed, spirit, soul, and body, by the Power of God in Zion, and through the faithful ministry of God's Prophet.

But this great company signified even more than the work, wonderful as it was, done in their individual lives.

With their Leader, they represented a great, consecrated, united, compact force, that could move as one man, filled with the same Spirit, for the carrying out of the great purposes of God the Father in these days of the Consummation of the Age, for the Restoration of the world to Himself, and the establishment on this earth, in all its Beauty, Glory, and Power, of the Everlasting Kingdom of Jesus, the Christ.

The procession was formed of Zion Guard, handsome and effective-looking in their neat uniforms of black; of Zion Band, than which, for its size, there is none better for marching and concert music in the world; Zion Bugle and Drum Corps, khaki-clothed; Zion Junior Choir, in their little surplices of white; Zion White-robed Choir, with its hundreds of men and women singers; the Ordained Officers of the Christian Catholic Church in Zion; and thousands of members of Zion Restoration Host wearing their scarfs of gold, white and blue.

When the great procession had marched and countermarched, encircling the Temple and Tabernacle sites, presenting an indescribable scene of life, light, movement, color, music and rhythm, all combining in a Solemn Act of Praise and Worship, it entered Shiloh Tabernacle, and each section took the place allotted to it.

Besides all these, the Tabernacle was well nigh filled with thousands of people, from all parts of this and from many other countries, who entered heartily into the remaining exercises of the afternoon.

It was a wonderful service, every moment of which was replete with spiritual blessing.

But the great central feature was the Message of the Prophet of God on the subject, "Zion: a Crown of Beauty in the Hand of Jehovah."

Even for those who knew Zion best, new beauties flashed out as the man of God portrayed the potentiality of the organization for future work, taking his argument from the Word of God and from what had already been accomplished.

It was a wonderful exposition of Restoration Truth, full of deepest significance, and peculiarly befitting the occasion.

Thus another of Zion's great anniversary days passed into history, leaving Zion with a Purer Love, a Deeper Joy, a Brighter Hope, a Sweeter Humility, a Broader Sympathy, a more Perfect Knowledge, and a Mightier Power for the momentous work which God has given her to do.

Shiloh Tabernacle, Zion City, Illinois, Thursday Afternoon, July 14, 1904.

The service was opened by the Congregation's joining in singing Hymn No. 40, from the Program:

Blow ye the trumpet, blow,
  The gladly solemn sound!
Let all the nations know,
  To earth's remotest bound,
The year of jubilee is come!
Return, ye ransomed sinners, home.

Prayer was then offered by Overseer Jane Dowie, after which the General Overseer prayed for the sick and sorrowing.

Rev. William Hamner Piper, Overseer of the Christian Catholic Church in Zion for New England, read the Scripture lesson from the 62d chapter of the book of the Prophet Isaiah.

The General Overseer then delivered his Message:

ZION: A CROWN OF BEAUTY IN THE HAND OF JEHOVAH.

INVOCATION.

Let the words of my mouth and the meditation of my heart be acceptable in Thy sight, be profitable unto this people, and unto all to whom these words shall come, in this and every land, in this and all the coming time, Till Jesus Come. Amen.

TEXT.

For Zion's Sake will I not hold my peace, and for Jerusalem's sake I will not rest, until her Righteousness go forth as brightness, and her Salvation as a lamp that burneth.

And the nations shall see thy Righteousness, and all kings thy Glory: and thou shalt be called by a New Name, which the mouth of Jehovah shall name.

Thou shalt also be a Crown of Beauty in the Hand of Jehovah, and a Royal Diadem in the Hand of thy God.

These words are spoken prophetically concerning Zion's complete Restoration.

They cannot be applied to us fully in the beginning of the Times of the Restoration; but we can rejoice in that the beginning has come.

We can see signs of the glorious preparations for the Rapture, and for the Coming of the King in His beauty to reign.

The World Acknowledges Zion a Success.

I thank God that we are privileged to begin the Latter Day Zion movement, of which there have been so many shameful imitations.

I notice, however, that friend and foe unite in distinguishing this movement from all that have preceded it in modern times, and from all that are attempting to spring up around it.

I am glad, as the years roll on, to see what my tongue has prophesied, what my eyes have seen, what my ears have heard, and what the world has acknowledged—oftentimes grudgingly, but always more or less emphatically—that Zion is a success in many ways, and that the movement is one that not only challenges attention, but demands attention upon the part of every Christian, every social reformer, and every friend and lover of humanity, as the movement, which has within it, not only the glorious possibility for the future, but a wonderful present; and that here are seen models of a City and of a nation, which if adopted throughout the world, would result in the obliteration of crime and pauperism, and of a thousand evils from which the world is suffering.

The Beauty of Zion Is a Spiritual Beauty.

It is in the exact measure of our Holy Living—the Beauty of Holiness.

We should be exceedingly grateful, and we are, on this Fourth Anniversary of the Consecration of the Temple Site. As you will remember, that Site was consecrated a year before the first land was sold, when the City was not even laid out, or surveyed, nor were the plans ready, if I remember.

I say frankly and plainly, that the Crown will be woven not only by us in Zion, but by the many Zion Cities which are to follow this.

The Despicable Mark of Fear.

There are always some people who go about with a certain mark upon their faces that is the most detestable thing I know.

It is a Mark of Fear.

Some of them say, "Do you not think the General Overseer may weaken Zion City, Illinois, if he establishes a Zion City in Texas, or in Washington, or in New York, or perhaps one in England or Australia?" which means, "Do you not think that the few pennies I put into a lot might not grow as quickly if the Doctor establishes another City?" [Laughter.]

What splendid reformers you are!

How large your spirit is!

Oh, how magnificently you miserable creatures have understood the teachings of Zion, and the mind of God!

The General Overseer's Interests in Zion City.

Can you not see that the General Overseer has his interests in this City; that the General Overseer expects to build a home in this City for himself?

I have no house of my own yet.

Shiloh House is Mrs. Dowie's.

She owns all the houses I live in.

But one day I shall have a house upon Mount Carmel, Zion City, and it shall be my very own, and I shall do what I like in it. [Laughter.]

I shall run that in my way.

I shall be glad to entertain Mrs. Dowie there, too, and I want to entertain you all.

As I saw that countermarching today, I thought of Mount Carmel, and my three hundred forty-eight acres reserved, from the beginning, for that domain.

I thought how delightful it would be to entertain you all there.

But it does seem to me so foolish for some of you to talk about my weakening this City.

Who has a greater interest in the strength of this City than I?

Who has a greater interest in its progress than I?

Other Zion Cities, Each to Have Its Special Mission.

Who sees more clearly than I that this City has its own special mission, but that other cities will have their special missions, too?

Do we not want a City up there (I shall not say just where, somewhere about the Straits of Juan de Fuca) which will be the port both for the Orient—China and Japan—and the Occident? Do we not want a Zion City there?

People—"Yes."

General Overseer—Do we not want a City down on the warm waters of the Gulf of Mexico, perhaps in Mexico itself?—there! I am letting the cat out of the bag, as I usually do.

I may have a City in Mexico itself.

I have an offer now of a piece of land there, fifty miles long and thirty miles deep, and I can get the whole of that vast territory for a Mexican dollar an acre, which is less than half a dollar in American coin.

Just think of it!

It seems to me that I can see half a dozen places in the South where I can pick out sites.

I do not say that I have not already picked out one. I will not tell you anything about it. [Laughter.]

But you do not want me to tell, either.

You can trust me, because to tell you would be to injure Zion's business.

Message from Zion in South Africa.

Rev. Daniel Bryant, our dear Overseer in South Africa, sent me greeting last night by cable.

He also sends greetings from Zion in South Africa to Zion at Headquarters; and he tells me that he has baptized over three hundred since he went there. [Applause.]

Better still, he tells me in a note that there are thousands to be baptized, including our native converts.

When I read those words—"our native converts"—I remembered the good man, now associated with Zion, who has been used of God for many years in preaching to the Kafirs in South Africa, and that these Kafirs have come into Zion in hundreds.

Overseer Bryant very properly says that when the people come into Zion they long for a Zion City.

They want to go to some place in South Africa over which the Zion flag floats, and which is kept clean by strong Zion hands, and where white, black, and yellow alike can live and love one another, and labor in perfect peace together. [Applause.]

I have been thinking what a splendid thing it would be, if there were not enough Zion Africans available in Alabama, Mississippi, and other Southern States, for me to bring to Zion City, South, four or five thousand of our African converts from South Africa, where they have been cruelly and shamefully treated by the British government, forced out of the positions which they ought to occupy, and where the Chinese have been brought in in thousands to take their places.

I think the time has come to welcome both our brethren, the Boers and our friends in South Africa, to a City in a climate that is suitable to people who have been born and who have lived near the tropics.

How All the Zion Cities Can Coöperate.

Shall we not have that kind of City where we can bring the varied races of the earth to labor and work together?

There we could raise the cotton to be made into lace, and the things which we eat that do not grow here, and especially cannot grow during six months of the year when the ground is hard with frost.

We could make the ground in the South produce—as has been done, on land that I have been looking at—two hundred fifty dollars an acre, simply in tomatoes, in one year.

You poor, mean, miserable, wretched creatures, who fear for Zion City, had better hold your tongues! [Laughter.]

I will not say anything harder just now.

There Are Many Cities in Prospect.

I could electrify this country from end to end if I were to tell only the half I know regarding that.

Recently, I had offered to me in one part of this glorious country (I shall not say that it is east, west, north, or south; but it is in a nice spot and quite a distance from here) no less than ten thousand acres of land, which I can have when I want it.

Those who want to sell it to me are connected with great railways and things of that kind, and are looking forward to the possibility and the certainty, in their minds, not only of thousands of people settling there, but of thousands more coming to attend the services in the Tabernacle that will be built there.

Zion is not for Illinois, nor even for the United States of America.

Zion is the Kingdom of God, and it is an Everlasting Kingdom.

Therefore, Zion must plant her Cities on every Continent. [Applause.]

Every Zion City will have its own peculiar surroundings, its own peculiar institutions, and its own peculiar facilities for doing business, which will help this City.

I have looked forward to the day, within twenty years, when we can have our Zion Cities in China, in Japan, in the Islands of the Seas, India and Africa, as well as in Europe and America; and can be able to carry on all our financial business with our Bank branches everywhere.

Then we can do all our business and commerce with people who first grow the things we manufacture and then buy the things we have to sell to them.

An Offer of Land in China.

Already one man in China, who has been there a great many years, a Roman Catholic, has offered me land in a certain section.

With him is associated another gentleman whose name is known throughout the world.

He said, "Your project is the only real missionary project that can ever reach the Chinese, because you will take them and make use of them, coöperate with them and teach them how to help one another, and thus form a great Christian community.

"I am a Roman Catholic and I hate some of the things you say, but, after all, I must recognize that you are a Catholic, if not a Roman."

Broad-minded men in all the world recognize that fact.

Newspaper Editors, Themselves, Witness Against the Press.

I am not talking now of the pettyfogging press, with their little, miserable reporters, who are magnificently paid when they get twelve dollars a week, when they reach twenty dollars are supposed to be reveling in wealth, and are overpaid when they get twenty-five dollars.

The poor miserable creatures that write for the papers are absolutely beneath contempt.

The day has come when the editors themselves are witnesses against the press—men like Watterson of Louisville.

They say that the press has lost all power, and that the people have lost all respect for it.

Who can doubt it?

For instance, look at the flop of the Chicago *Chronicle* the other day.

In one day it turned Republican.

It was Democratic up to within two days of this week, and then it flopped around and said, "I am Republican."

My opinion is that that paper never underwent any change of heart at all, but that there were reasons of a financial nature which compelled its owner, John R. Walsh, banker, and, I understand, brother of Archbishop Walsh, of Dublin, to say that the financial interests of this country were in danger if the Democrats were in power.

Democrats Not to Be Trusted With Financial Policy of the United States.

However, he is right.

You cannot trust these Democrats with either the financial or the fiscal policy of the United States of America.

I thank God that there is very little danger of their winning.

I desire to say, under Theocratic direction, that the Theocrats of Zion City will cast their votes for the man who has been honest, true, and faithful to this country, and who loves his God, his wife, and his children, and is a straight, clean, honest man.

May God send Theodore Roosevelt back to the White House again! [Hearty applause.]

A Crown of Beauty at the Feet of Our Lord.

I trust we can say, humbly, that Zion, which is represented here today in its four great Departments—Ecclesiastical, Educational, Commercial and Political—is already a little Garland that we can lay as a Crown of Beauty at the feet of our Lord, and ask Him to accept from year to year as it grows in beauty: for it is He who has made it, and gives us power to do what little we have done.

I shall be so glad if I am permitted to see City after City come and lay garlands at the feet of our Lord.

When the right time comes I shall execute what I have already planned.

The Work of Preparing Jerusalem for the King's Coming.

I have thoughts concerning it that I know are right.

I believe that within twenty years, and perhaps long before that, I shall be able to say to the Cities that I have founded throughout the world, "Come, let us select from each City its best builders, and let us go and build the Temple for the King, in the City of the Great King.

"Let us build the Palace of the King.

"Let us terrace the City and cover its rocks with soil, and make it fragrant and beautiful with flowers.

"Let us build beautiful homes there, and pour into it the wealth from all our Cities and all our lands."

I shall never rest until God has made Jerusalem a praise in the earth. [Applause.]

But this City will not lack for progress.

I cannot afford to let it, neither shall I.

It has certain industries that belong to us, which we can well establish and work all the year round in this cold climate.

Zion City, Illinois, Strong in Manufactures.

We have no difficulty in making lace all through the winter, but we should find great difficulty in tilling the soil all the year round.

Other Cities could be established in the midst of agricultural, horticultural and pasture-land, where they would have totally different surroundings, and would be the Cities where raw material could be produced for us to manufacture in the North.

We have worked these lace machines twenty-one hours out of every twenty-four—running three shifts, and stopping just long enough to let them cool down and be oiled.

We have, in this industry, one of the most wonderful bonanzas, commercially, that any people have ever had.

It is only a question of money, of machinery and of men.

I sent for Deacon Henry Stevenson, manager of Zion Lace Industries, to come to England, and I may tell you that I have bought and made arrangements for very large increase of machinery.

Nothing Can Stop the Onward March of Zion.

The Devil has tried it in every way he can.

The last scheme he had was to kill me, but he is a bad shot and missed me, as he has every time. [Applause. Laughter.]

I know that God will make this a spiritually beautiful Zion, an educationally beautiful Zion, a commercially and industrially beautiful Zion.

We are learning by experience how to do it, and we could do it very much better if we had it to do a second time, then a third time, a fourth, a sixth, an eight and a tenth time.

I do not stop now at what I used to stop.

I believe that the Lord, in His infinite mercy, will make me ruler over Ten Cities before I die, and I ask God for the grace to do this, because I believe that it is connected with the upbuilding of this people. [Applause.]

These will be cities where families are educated and trained in a manner that is so delightful to us all; where prayer is not a pretense; where we live as we pray; where praise is not pretense; where we live as we sing; and where we are a happy people, enjoying all the blessings of this life, feeling that we are doing something to prepare for the Coming of the King.

What Will Be Accomplished Within the Next Ten Years.

I believe that God in His infinite mercy will enable me to train within this City's limits, between five and ten years from this time, a population of one hundred fifty thousand people.

It will be one of the most beautiful cities in the whole world.

I know what I am talking about, because I know what is within Zion.

I know that if I am eventually to supply the major part of the lace of the United States, that I have a trade of thirty millions of dollars within sight.

I believe that I can supply a greater part of the best candy for the United States, so that the children will not be poisoned.

I believe that by and by I shall have made in Zion City the sweetest-toned pianos and organs that were ever made anywhere.

We shall do everything we can to make Zion prosperous, by the establishment of profitable industries.

I can see things that we can do better than the world, and that will give this City, as I have said, at least one hundred fifty thousand inhabitants within ten years.

You will see that lake front covered with magnificent factories, reaching from the lace factory, now upon Deborah avenue, to the Port of Zion.

I believe that we shall see the cognate industries arise.

By faith I see them arising and other people are seeing them.

Large capitalists are looking at Zion, and seeing what every one else sees, that we have a community that is becoming wealthy by coöperation.

The Reason for No Strikes in Zion City.

We have a law-abiding, God-fearing and loving-spirited people, who work and have no place in their vocabulary for the word "strike."

That word means much—everything—to capitalists and people investing money, for all the United States of America today is dominated by the "delegoat" and the "Smoke-stack Gompers." [Applause and laughter.]

It is a burning shame, that men who want to work in the stockyards and elsewhere are compelled to walk out and be idle, and see their families suffer, at the bidding of demagogues and "delegoats."

I shall never hesitate to denounce the trades-unionism that has in it no Christian feeling for manhood.

Often before they go out they are offered arbitration; they could stop the strike, but they say that it has gone too far, that they must strike, after which they may arbitrate.

I cannot see on the horizon anywhere any thought of labor trouble here, for this reason: You who are here know what I say to be true, that the entire estate of Zion belongs to the people, with the exception of what I own privately; and that principally consists of the little piece of land of which I have spoken, of stocks in the Bank, and of shares in the Industries which God has graciously given to me, by making me the owner, and in some cases the trustee of people, who, when they pass away from this life, leave to me all that I represent as trustee.

I thank God that I have power, because I need power, having such tremendous responsibilities.

Each Individual Legal Owner of His Own Estate.

Although I am the legal owner of Zion's estate, you know that each one is the legal owner of his own estate; and that no person is ever asked to give up his own private fortune or estate.

All you are asked to do is not to rob God, but to give your tithes and offerings.

We do not expect all people to be alike rich or alike poor.

Money that has been honestly made at other times and places by your hard work or skill, or money that you may have inherited from your fathers, or lands that you have, you have a right to handle as you please.

God makes you responsible for the use you make of these things.

When you came into Zion and bought stocks and land and so on, you did not part with the control of your estate.

But, as you know, many of your estates have increased in value in your hands, and you still control, and have a right to control them, as individuals.

Now, in that way, individualism is very strong in Zion.

There are some shiftless people in Zion who never save a dollar.

Some Good Advice to Those Who Wish to Marry.

I had a case the other day of a young man and young woman who wanted to get married; at least the girl said so, and came and told me so.

I said, "I am against it."

When the young man came I was too angry to talk to him; I felt inclined to take a stick to him.

That young man may be here today.

He has been working for years and years at a fairly good salary and has not saved a dollar.

He has nothing in Zion.

He has nothing to show for his labor; but he has just fooled it away on little follies, none of them wickednesses particularly, but just buying things he did not need.

Some of you people need a stick instead of a wife, and a big one too.

The idea of talking about marrying a girl when you have not a dollar!

You want to make girls that have fairly good positions and are earning something, your wives and the mothers of your children.

They will have to slave on, and not get a dollar for themselves.

They will have to wash your shirts and sew on buttons, and put up with all your whims and nonsense; they can take care of your children, and then you never give them even a servant's wages, you dogs! [Laughter.]

They got three or four dollars a week as servants, but you never think of giving Peggy three or four dollars a week.

Oh, no; Peggy should be very thankful if she gets food and clothes for herself. [Laughter.]

I pity Peggy!

I cannot understand any man's denying his wife a proper proportion of his income.

She has a right to it.

If she stays at home and cares for you and the children, and makes a home for them, she is helping you to earn that income, is she not?

People—"Yes."

The Wife Entitled to a Proper Share of the Income.

General Overseer—See that she gets a share of it.

There was a time when I did not understand that, and God did not bless me as He would have blessed me if I had understood it.

But one day He showed it to me, and I say, before God, that I have never given Mrs. Dowie half of what she has been worth to Zion.

If you were to give to her a million dollars today, you would not pay what she has been worth to Zion or to me. [Applause.]

But I can say that I never gave her property or anything else but that I was blessed for it.

I am not in favor of men marrying who are not ready to support a wife in a proper manner.

Choose not only a proper mate, but a proper time to marry, and let both man and woman prepare for the marriage.

Some of you are married whose mothers are really dependent upon Zion.

You have abandoned the old mother and have ceased to support her.

You have a wife and children, and Zion must take care of your mother.

Is that right?

People—"No!"

General Overseer—It is not right, and I have a stick for you who have been doing that kind of thing.

I love to see people married in the Lord, at the right time.

Wise Economy Should Be Practiced by All.

Girls, you must save as well as the boys.

I do not care how small your salary is, you can always save a little, if you are careful and wise, giving to the Lord His tenth.

It is in the little things that you lose.

Economy and wise administration of money is a pro rata matter.

I could not do the work in Zion that I am now doing and live as I once lived.

I once thought it was right to deny myself everything, and reduce myself to voluntary poverty; but I found that I could do very little in such a position as that.

At last I saw that this was sin: that the Christ died to make us rich, as well as to make us good!

He not only bore our sins and carried our sicknesses, but He who was rich came down to this earth and bore our poverty, that we, through His poverty might be made rich.

I have come to the conclusion that God's poor people can be made rich; and we are making you rich.

Zion's Prosperity Means Prosperity for the Individual.

I desire to show you why there can never be a strike in Zion. The whole of Zion is enriched by everything that Zion wins.

My part of it is five per cent. of the increment of value; that is, of the increase of value.

Therefore it is very much to my interest to increase the value of the Zion estate.

Some people have said that I have been putting too high a value upon the Zion estate, and that the land inside of Zion City is not worth what we ask for it.

I want to ask you who bought it, if you think that the land in Zion City is worth what you paid for it?

People—"Yes."

General Overseer—Many of you know that your property has been and is worth from eighty to two hundred and three hundred per cent. more than you paid for it.

Many of you have sold your leases and many have made a good deal of money in selling both leases and houses.

There is only one way to tell the actual value of any city, and that is when land changes hands from the original owner to outside parties who want the land for such purposes as building a railway.

What Zion Land Was Worth to the Chicago and Milwaukee Electric Railroad.

Railroad men take big chances and fight to get through land, often forcing the matter into courts.

They never pay a dollar more for the land than they are actually compelled to.

I shall not speak of the gentleman who bought a right of way through Zion City as a gentleman whom we had to compel to do anything, because we did not.

He was interested in an attempt to get a railway alongside the North-Western, which I fought and fought hard.

At last he came to me and said, "I was interested in that project, Doctor, but I am convinced that it is not a right thing for your City; but I want to get through with the Chicago and Milwaukee Electric Railroad."

He is a very nice gentleman.

He saw me before I went away, and while I am willing to give Dr. Speicher credit for all that belongs to him, he had no credit for that deal, but merely carried out the details of the matter I had settled.

I may say that I had nearly an entire day with Mr. Frost, and I came to the conclusion that he was the kind of man I could let through, even at a lower price than I could let some one else through.

I told him, a few days before I left, that he could get land for his railway along Gilgal avenue; but that the lowest price he could ever get it for would be three thousand dollars an acre; and I added, "If you do not take it before I come back, Mr. Frost, it will be four thousand dollars; and if you do not take it quickly after that it will be five thousand dollars; for I am selling some land there now at the rate of seven thousand five hundred dollars an acre."

I have sold land in the woods at the rate of seven thousand five hundred dollars an acre, but I said I would let him through with a strip, one hundred feet wide, I think, and comprising thirty-three and two-thirds acres, at three thousand dollars an acre.

Remarkable Increase in Value of Zion's Estate.

I shall make a plain statement, on this Anniversary, as to the glorious success of Zion as a City.

I will own up to what I paid for this land.

I paid five thousand dollars for that thirty-three acres, and I sold it for one hundred one thousand dollars—twenty times what it cost. There were, in fact, a little more than thirty-three acres, so that it was one hundred one thousand dollars for thirty-three and two-thirds acres, and I did not pay five thousand dollars for that.

But Zion had increased the value of that land. Our skill and toil, and our laying out this beautiful City with all its possibilities of traffic, had made that land worth three thousand dollars an acre to that railroad man.

If you were to take the land of Zion City as originally costing one million and a quarter dollars for six thousand six hundred acres, and increase that twenty times, what is the entire value to Zion?

It is twenty-five million dollars ($25,000,000).

The value of Zion's land today, at the rate that Mr. Frost and his railway paid for it, would be twenty-five million dollars. [Applause.]

It is yours and mine—it is Zion's land.

I want to know why you should strike?

Look at the glorious heritage God has given you!

Is that all?

Is it merely Zion land?

Is it not something better than all that?

Has He not given you spiritual emancipation and spiritual satisfaction?

Has He not given you a good education for your children, and a spiritual coöperation in the Extension of the Gospel throughout the world?

People—"Yes."

General Overseer—God has made Zion a Diadem, a Crown of Beauty, even in its youth and childhood.

I am face to face with that which is a glorious opportunity and a great triumph.

Success Itself Demands Progress.

Zion today along all its lines—Spiritual, Educational, Commercial, and Industrial—must make rapid and yet steady and sure progress.

I have been around this world and I have talked with wealthy men in many lands.

I have talked with my own relatives, some of whom are owners of millions, and some of them would be very glad if their money were free to put into Zion.

One man, who owns several millions, and is a man of years, said, "If I were a young man, or even as young as my sons, I would sell off everything I have and come to Zion City.

"I believe that you are able to swing this thing as no man else in the world could."

I am not speaking egotistically when I say what the world everywhere admits, that the capacity of Zion is equal to carrying this matter through.

What we have done here we can do elsewhere; and what we have done here we can continue to improve.

With the help of God and a united people, we shall present a still more beautiful Zion to our Lord this day year.

But let us work and be faithful, and let there be no doubts and no secret doings.

Stand together, and do not put your money and your interests outside of Zion, and at the same time say that you trust God and trust me.

I Am Here to Answer to You and to the Law.

If I have done aught that is wrong, the law can reach me.

If I have done aught that is wrong, you have a right to redress.

I stand here innocent of conscious wrong of any kind, knowing that I have committed none, and knowing, that as far as I am aware, your investments in stocks, as well as in real estate, are a great and splendid success.

All I have on earth is in Zion, the solitary exception in the family being the little property that is held across the Lake.

I use that for Zion, by going there sometimes to get a rest when I am troubled with the Devil's people, and things of that kind.

Let us thank God that already the little Diadem and Crown of Beauty can be laid at our Lord's feet.

Beloved, I have a great desire to depart and to be with the Christ, which is far better

Earnest Preparation for the King's Coming.

I have an intense longing for the Lord to bring to an end this Dispensation, and to hurry forward the Consummation of the Age.

But that would only be for myself.

It is expedient both for you and for the world that a little time shall be given—time enough for the people of God to hear this Gospel in all the world, and to have an opportunity to gather into the Cities of Refuge before the Tribulation that will come upon all flesh.

Then when we are gathered together and have prepared the City for the King, at least in a measure, we shall be ready for the Rapture, for the speedy return of the Lord, and for the Continuation of the Restoration throughout the Millennial period.

We who have taken part in it at the close of this Age will, I trust, by the grace of God, be permitted to take a large part in the Coming Age, when we return with glorified bodies, having come back with the Lord.

That Thousand Years will be a thousand years of Conflict and Trial; but at the end of it there will be a Perfect and Complete and Permanent Victory.

Those of you who desire to stand with the Hosts of Heaven and sing "Hallelujah! for the Lord God Omnipotent reigneth!" rise and tell Him now.

PRAYER OF CONSECRATION.

My God and Father, in Jesus' Name I come to Thee. Take me as I am. Make me what I ought to be, in spirit, in soul, and in body. Give me power to do right, no matter what it costs. Make me true and pure, a true citizen in Zion, a true member of the Christian Catholic Church in Zion, and faithful to Thee, and to Zion under the General Overseer. For Jesus' sake. Amen. [*Congregation repeats the prayer, clause by clause, after the General Overseer.*]

Did you mean it?

People—"Yes."

General Overseer—Then live it.

The Congregation then joined in singing, "I Stand on Zion's Mount," after which the General Overseer pronounced the

BENEDICTION.

Beloved, abstain from every form of evil. And may the very God of Peace Himself sanctify you wholly; and I pray God your whole spirit and soul and body be preserved entire, without blame, unto the coming of our Lord Jesus, the Christ. Faithful is He that calleth you, who also will do it. The grace of our Lord Jesus, the Christ, the love of God, our Father, the fellowship of the Holy Spirit, our Comforter and Guide, one Eternal God, abide in you, bless you and keep you, and all the Israel of God everywhere, forever. Amen.

EARLY MORNING SACRIFICE OF PRAISE AND PRAYER.

REPORTED BY S. E. C., O. V. G. AND E. S.

Joy!—not mourning.

Rejoicing!—not fear, despair, death—was the Golden Truth brought out in the second Early Morning Sacrifice of Praise and Prayer in Zion's Fourth Feast of Tabernacles.

Following Love as the first Fruit of the Spirit, comes Joy.

These two are linked together and inseparable.

If Love is there, Joy, too, will be there.

Even a larger audience than on the preceding morning, listened to the words of the Prophet of God as he elaborated this thought and brought it out in all its fulness of rich beauty, applying it with the hand of a master—inspired by that Holy Spirit whose Fruit was his theme.

THE SECOND FRUIT OF THE SPIRIT: JOY.

Shiloh Tabernacle, Zion City, Illinois, Friday Morning, July 15, 1904.

The meeting was opened by singing Hymn No. 1, in the Program.

The General Overseer offered prayer.

Hymn No. 2, in the Program was sung.

Strange Ignorance of the Church Concerning Elijah.

The General Overseer then read a letter from one of the Elders, giving a long list of early Christian Fathers and later commentators who taught that Elijah must come as the forerunner of the Second Coming of the Christ.

He then said:

One of the strange things that comes to one more and more, is that the Church has been talking about the coming of the Lord, and failing to see that which the Lord Himself distinctly stated, that Elijah must precede Him; that Elijah the Prophet must come as the Restorer, in accordance with the prophecy of the Old Testament.

When Jesus' disciples said, "Why say the scribes that Elijah must first come?" His answer was, "Elijah indeed cometh, and shall Restore All Things."

"He came, and they killed him; I came, and they kill Me. He comes again, and I come again," is practically what He said.

This time, there will be no killing of the Christ, for even if the Prophet of the Restoration were to be killed, the Christ cannot be killed again.

He comes to die no more.

Sometimes I get a gleam of a possibility of outliving all the machinations of my enemies, and being one of those who shall be ready for the Lord at the Rapture.

I hope I shall.

At any rate, I know that the prophetic ministry which I have, closes the Dispensation and brings the Church up to the Consummation of the Age.

Christian Scholarship Beginning to Admit Elijah's Third Appearance.

Less and less does Christian scholarship fight the truth of Elijah's coming.

The only question they raise is as to whether such an insignificant person as I am could possibly be Elijah the Restorer.

He might be one of their great bishops or archbishops or theologians, but they have difficulty in believing that such a man as I should come in the spirit and power of Elijah.

They cannot think that Elijah would be such a terrible fellow, turning everything upside down.

If they could get together at their Methodist Conference and pass a resolution that Bishop So-and-So was Elijah, they might be satisfied.

But prophets do not come in that way.

God's Prophets Not Voted Into Office.

God sends the prophet absolutely apart from the Church.

A Prophet takes a position that is unique towards the Church, towards the State, towards the People.

You will all admit that I take a perfectly unique position.

I thank God that I have not for a single moment doubted my prophetic calling.

It was a long time before I would make the Declaration, and I was very unwilling to make it at the time I did, but it had to be made at that time.

Three years ago last June, I was within about a month of the opening of Zion City land.

I felt that the Declaration had to come, and come soon.

I made it then, so that no one could say, "I bought land in Zion City before you made the Declaration. If I had heard that Declaration, I would not have bought land."

Many persons said, "Dr. Dowie has killed the City. He will never get any one to rally around that standard."

You know the result of that Declaration.

The lots we had ready for the people were so largely taken up, that it was absolutely imperative upon me to get ready another section of ground, Section 17, for the working people especially.

I may say, in passing, that the people that have land in Section 17 have some of the most beautiful land in Zion City.

But, concerning the Declaration—it was simply a Declaration of what the people believed.

There had been no attempt upon my part to persuade any one, beyond expounding the Word of God concerning the Messenger of the Covenant.

I did not deliver a single discourse upon the Elijah question until June 2, 1901, when the Declaration was made.

It has consolidated us, and given to us the status that we ought to have in connection with so great a matter as the Restoration, which has, we believe, begun.

A Thinking Man's Position on the Elijah Question.

A New Yorker, who is not in Zion, said, the other day, "I am not yet in Zion. I am not good enough to ask them to receive me, but, when you say that Dr. Dowie is not Elijah, you must prove to me that he is not.

"Your Bible says, that a man is to come to Restore All Things.

"The Restoration must have a beginning; why not now?

"I have looked your Scriptures over; it seems to me that Elijah the Tishbite, and Elijah the Preparer, as Dr. Dowie calls them, did not have larger power with God or with humanity than he has.

"On the contrary, they were confined to a very small part of the earth, and their ministry was comparatively short, whereas he is moving the whole world.

"There is Zion City. Suppose that this City, and every city in the United States, and throughout the world, were as that City is, without drunkenness, without crime, and with all the blessings it has, would not things be pretty well restored?" [Applause.]

That man was a lawyer and looked at the thing in a logical way.

These great lawyers are coming into Zion.

All honest men who desire the coming of the Kingdom of God must see that there must be one Standard around which the people of God must rally, and that there must be some one with the Voice of Authority to lead the Hosts of Jehovah to victory.

The Heavy Burden of Authority and Responsibility.

The man with the Authority has also the responsibility, which is the heaviest end of the contract.

If it were not quite clear to me that God had called me to this office, I should very often want to lay it down.

Without disloyalty, without being a traitor to God, without being a traitor in the presence of the enemy, one cannot lay down his commission.

I will never lay mine down, while there is a lick of fighting to be done. [Applause.]

I am no coward in this matter, and you cannot make me one.

I am very grateful to God for this.

With the help of God's people, all being of one heart and mind, we have done something since June 2, 1901, the date of the Elijah Declaration.

These three years have been the most prolific of all my ministry in the Salvation, Healing and Cleansing of men, in the quickening and the gathering together of God's people.

These three years have been by far the most profitable period of all my life.

I could not begin to calculate what it all means.

I so often find what I found last night.

Remarkable Story of a Roll of "Leaves of Healing."

A man who had been twenty-one years in the British Royal Navy called upon me yesterday.

When I asked him, "How did you come into Zion?" he said, "I came into Zion through a Jewish peddler."

"How was it done?"

"Some one had thrust into her hands a roll of papers.

"She brought it into our house with her when she came in to sell my wife something.

"My wife began to talk to her about spiritual matters, which led the Jewess to show her the papers.

"After reading a little, my wife said, 'That is just what I have been looking for.'

" 'Then have them all,' said the Jewess; and she gave my wife four copies of LEAVES OF HEALING."

This good woman read them, and when her husband came home, she made him read them from A to Z.

Then they started off for Zion Tabernacle, in Euston Road, London. There they received a blessing.

After a brief attendance on the ministry of Overseer Cantel, the wife was to be baptized.

Her husband said, "Why should not I be baptized, too?"

"You are a stinkpot," they told him.

"I will be a stinkpot no more," he said.

That night he burned up his pipes and tobacco.

He and his wife were baptized upon the anniversary of their wedding-day.

It is beautiful to hear these things.

Our words, not only spoken here, but printed and sent abroad, have been more profitable than at any previous time in my ministry.

There has been some nonsense talked about my ministry being less efficient.

This is simply because people are either ignorant of all facts or wilfully wicked.

My ministry is more blessed than ever.

I thank God for these things.

Scripture Reading and Exposition.

Let us read in the Word of God, first in the 16th Psalm:

Preserve me, O God: for in Thee do I put my trust.
I have said unto Jehovah, Thou art my Lord: I have no good beyond Thee.

I call your attention to the proper rendering.

The Old Version had a very difficult rendering, and a very wrong one: "My goodness extendeth not to Thee."

That is a very peculiar rendering, and one that is not in accordance with the original.

I do not know how it got there, but the rendering in the Revision, which I am reading, is: "I have said unto Jehovah, Thou art my Lord: I have no good beyond Thee."

That means "All the good that I have is in Thee?"

Splendid Reputation of Zion People.

As for the saints that are in the earth,
They are the excellent in whom is all my delight.

It is a delightful thing to me to meet with the saints; with all the people of God in Zion whom I know better than any other people.

All over the earth everywhere, wherever we have met, we have seen the same spirit.

Even our critics acknowledge the excellence of Zion people.

For instance, in Australia, when it was announced in the papers that these good people that have come here, and others that are coming, would leave Australia, they declared that it was a great loss to Australia, for they were among the most respectable and desirable citizens.

Of course they are; Zion people always are.

As for the saints that are in the earth, they are the excellent, in whom is all My delight.

So it is all over the world.

In Germany, Switzerland, England, Canada, and elsewhere, they all admit that those that have come have been the good and excellent, those that want to do right, and are good citizens.

Their sorrows shall be multiplied that exchange Jehovah for another God.

Sad Downfall of Those That Leave Zion.

If you want your sorrows to be multiplied, go out of Zion, and you will not have to seek your troubles; they will come upon you in floods.

I do not want to speak sharply, but I do want to speak clearly, that you may be warned. I have known very few persons that have gone out of Zion who have not manifestly gone to the Devil.

They have gone to the Devil.

They have gone down, too, into deep depths of sin, and shame, and impurity, and infidelity, and intemperance, with very few exceptions.

Some, for instance, who went out of Zion a few years ago, are saying the most terrible and wicked things.

They are ministerial tramps, trying to tramp ahead of their reputation all over the world. But it catches up to them everywhere, and they go to pieces.

Zion is too strong to be affected by any one's going out.

You cannot affect Zion, but you can injure yourselves.

Of course, you can help Zion by being pure, and good, and helpful, but you cannot hinder Zion.

Their sorrows shall be multiplied that exchange Jehovah for another god:
Their drink offerings of blood will I not offer,
Nor take their names upon My lips.

It is the Christ talking; He will not plead; He will not intercede for those who will fight His Kingdom.

Jehovah is the portion of mine inheritance and of my cup:
Thou maintainest my lot.
The lines are fallen unto me in pleasant places;
Yea, I have a goodly heritage.
I will bless Jehovah, who hath given me counsel:
Yea, my reins instruct me in the night seasons.
I have set Jehovah always before me:
Because He is at my right hand, I shall not be moved.
Therefore my heart is glad, and my glory rejoiceth:
My flesh also shall dwell in safety.
For Thou wilt not leave my soul in Sheol;

That is the grave,

Neither wilt Thou suffer Thine Holy One to see corruption.
Thou wilt shew me the Path of Life:
In Thy presence is Fulness of Joy;
In Thy right hand there are Pleasures for evermore.

Let us read Galatians, the 5th chapter, and 22d verse:

But the Fruit of the Spirit is Love, Joy, Peace, Longsuffering, Kindness, Goodness, Faithfulness,
Meekness, Temperance: against such there is no Law.
And they that are of Christ Jesus have crucified the flesh with the passions and the lusts thereof.

Ministry of Elijah the Restorer and that of the "Two Witnesses" Not Identical.

There are some people who have a curious notion as to what my mission is in connection with the Elijah matter.

They are ready to identify me with the Two Witnesses spoken of in the Revelation.

I object to that identification.

In the first place, I am not two; I am one; and, in the second place, I am not the kind of prophet that these two prophets are. They prophesy in sackcloth and ashes.

"God's people are to rule this world.

"God has a right to rule this world.

"We will not answer to your whip.

"We will not dance to your piping.

"We will not work for you.

"We have worked for you long enough. We have toiled in the very fire for you, and our fathers did before us, piling up money for people who spent it in sin, who spent it in beer and skittles, and vanity, and affectations; piling up money for people who never worked at all. We will not do it.

"God's people are getting together, and they will work together.

"They will get the money, and own the whole earth one day." [Applause.]

There is no use in going about in sackcloth and ashes with such a Message as that.

PARADE OF ZION INDUSTRIES AND INSTITUTIONS DRAWN UP IN FRONT OF SHILOH TABERNACLE.
Third Anniversary of the Opening of the Gates of Zion City, Friday, July 15, 1904.

I am not clothed in sackcloth and ashes.

If I were to clothe myself as I would love to, I should be attired in lovely Oriental garb, and it would be as light as possible. I have no affinity with sackcloth and ashes.

I was not sent to prophesy in sackcloth and ashes.

I will let the other fellow have the sackcloth and ashes.

I am not a prophet of fear, or doubt, or despair, or death.

This is a Time for Rejoicing, not for mourning.

Triumphant Zion, lift thy head from dust, and darkness, and the dead.

We have been mourning long enough.

God's people have been afflicted long enough.

They have been under the rod of the World, the Flesh and the Devil long enough.

Zion's Joyous Defiance of the World, the Flesh, and the Devil.

Now I crack the whip over these vile oppressors and say: "Lie down there; keep still.

It is time enough to put on sackcloth and ashes when we are badly whipped, and have something to groan over.

Zion Triumphant, Therefore Joyous.

I do not feel that we have been whipped, do you?

People—"No."

General Overseer—It strikes me that my ministry, while it has been a very toilsome one, has been a triumphant one.

I am here today to tell you that the Fruits of the Spirit are Love and Joy.

Thou hast shown me the Path of Life.

Why should I groan and cry as if I were a prophet of death and despair, telling God's people that this is a time for crying and weeping?

It is no such thing. It is a Time for Rejoicing.

"Oh, but death has come, and I have lost my dear one," wails some mourner.

"Very well. She went to heaven; she is a great deal happier than she was when she was with you. What are you howling about? Why are you sorrowing as if you had no hope?"

Our dear children went to heaven.

We should like them to be here, and we are lonely oftentimes, but is there not something to do here?

Are there not others to care for?

Because my daughter has gone to be with God, shall I weep forever, and forget that there are daughters of Zion to help here?

Verily, no.

Our Lord Jesus, the Christ, did not establish a Gospel of Sorrows.

The Christ's Promise of Fulness of Joy.

He said, "If ye keep My Commandments, ye shall abide in My Love; even as I have kept My Father's Commandments, and abide in His Love. These things have I spoken unto you that My Joy may be in you, and that your Joy may be fulfilled."

If our Joy is to be full, shall we put on sackcloth and ashes to manifest it, and go through the world wailing?

I have no use for it, and I never will have.

I do not see what I have to do with it.

If I keep His Commandments, surely I can believe His Word:

If ye keep My Commandments, ye shall abide in My Love; even as I have kept My Father's Commandments, and abide in His Love.

These things have I spoken unto you, that My Joy may be in you, and that your Joy may be fulfilled.

"General Overseer," you may ask, "do you have no sorrow?"

Yes, a great deal of it!

But I buried the sorrows of yesterday right where they happened, at once.

I dug a pit for them and flung them in.

The Mistake of Allowing Wicked People to Break One's Heart.

Many people of God, good men, have broken their hearts over bad men.

One of my predecessors, Edward Irving—than whom a greater and mightier man of God never stood upon this earth—saw the whole truth as to the Restoration of the Apostolic Church, but he let sinners get into the Christian Catholic Apostolic Church, who said that they were prophets, and this and that and the other thing, and they broke his heart.

He went down to his grave a young man, because he allowed these miserables in Zion to break his heart.

I will not allow such people to break my heart.

By the grace of God, I will break their hearts. I will bring them to Repentance, or else they will have to get out.

I am not a prophet in sackcloth and ashes

I am one man, not two.

If you think that Moses is coming, as well as Elijah, I say you have nothing in Scripture for it.

There is nothing said about either Moses or Elijah in that connection.

I am a Prophet of Love, of Joy, and of Peace.

It Takes a Great Deal of Love to Be Firm in Doing Your Duty.

It takes a great deal more love to do that than it does to do as Edward Irving did, to mourn, and break his heart and die.

I have often wished that he could have lived out the beautiful life that he began.

If you desire to have the Strength of Jehovah, you must get the Joy.

God has shown me the Path of Life.

Love proceeds from Life.

No Love can ever come from death; no Love can ever come from corruption; no Love can ever come from Impurity, Intemperance or Infidelity.

Damning lust, hell-born, can come from that, but no Divine Love, that is heaven-born, can come from these things.

In the Path of Life there is Love, there is Joy, there is Peace, and all the Fruits of the Spirit, until you get to the summit of them all—Temperance or Self-control.

When you are completely under the control of God, He can hand you the reins and say, "Now, drive on. Drive on."

He can trust you, and give you the control of yourself.

We had better consider something of the Joy of the Lord.

Joy Does Not Mean a Giggling, Silly, Foolish Mirth.

There is no joy in that.

The laughter of fools is like the crackling of thorns under a pot.

It endures for only a moment. It is brilliant and bright, but it goes out.

It does not make the pot boil.

The laughter of fools never made a pot boil yet.

It never did anything for the world.

The laughter of fools is folly, and utterly fruitless.

The saddest thing upon God's earth is the witty fool.

A man came to a physician in Paris, and said:

"Help me, for if I do not get help, I die."

"What is the matter with you?" said the doctor.

"I am suffering from melancholia so intense that if I do not get relief from the constant sorrow I must take my life," he replied.

The doctor suggested various remedies. He found that his patient was acquainted with drugs, but, after they had talked them all over, the man said:

"I have had all these, and they have done me no good. I have been told that you are a man of very great skill, and I thought, perhaps, you might have something better for me."

"Well," said the doctor, "I will tell you of something better. Last night I went to hear Grimaldi, the clown, and I have been laughing ever since. Go and hear his jokes and look at his face."

The man stepped back, with the question, "Is that all you have to offer?"

"Yes," said the doctor.

"Then," he said, "there is no hope for me, for I am Grimaldi."

The man who was setting all Paris laughing night after night, as the greatest clown, the greatest mirth-producer of Europe, was consumed by melancholia.

There was not a bit of real fun or happiness in his heart.

Unutterable Sadness Beneath the Glitter of the Comic Stage.

Do you know anything at all about the people that appear before the footlights, making people laugh?

They are the saddest, the most broken-hearted people upon God's earth.

They weep many bitter tears.

The woman who dances there knows that her husband has gone to the Devil.

They are tempting her to go, too. She does not know what to do; for she has babies to take care of, and her husband has gone off with some other woman.

While she is dancing there, she is thinking of it all, and the seducer is there, offering her pearls and diamonds, if she will only tread his path.

Oh, what a broken heart; a blighted life is oftentimes there!

If godliness were only for this life, it would be profitable to be good; because there is no Happiness, no Purity, no Joy, in evil; there is no Strength in it.

We have spent three years in Zion City very happily, have we not?

People—"Yes."

General Overseer—We have not had a single theatrical performance.

Zion City Joyous and Happy Without the Theater.

We have got on splendidly without the theater.

We have not needed the clown to make us happy.

We have not found it necessary to pay out our money to poor, fallen women to dance for us, to make us happy.

We have not found it necessary to pay out money to poor, fallen men to make jokes for us, to make us happy.

We have not found it necessary to get joy out of liquor, or out of tobacco, or any other narcotic poison.

The greatest Joy we have is in filling our hearts with Divine thoughts and our dear singers with Divine music.

They are looking forward to next Wednesday night with intense Joy.

That evening they will sing "The Messiah" for us. They are preparing it prayerfully and carefully.

There is an immense amount of toil in the preparation for it.

I know that the singing of that "Messiah" will bring joy to our hearts.

I believe that oratorio after oratorio will roll out from Zion.

The day will come when we shall strike a new note in music,

for God's Love is always seeking for a new note in music, and this note is a note of Joy.

The "Joy of the Lord," not the sorrow of the world, "is strength." "The Joy of Jehovah is strength."

There Is No Strength in Sorrow.

It dims the eye with weeping.

It palsies the hands and makes feeble the knees.

It takes you from duty, and you care less for the living, because your heart is with the dead.

There is no Joy, until you lift up your eyes, and "sorrow not as those without hope," but learn to sing the Song of the Fulness of Life, and to believe what I have read this morning: "In Thy Presence is Fulness of Joy; at Thy right hand there are Pleasures forevermore."

One would really think, from the way some Christians live, that heaven must be a very miserable place.

You weep so bitterly because your friends have gone to heaven, that one would think that at God's right hand there were sorrows forevermore.

I call that downright hypocrisy

If you believe, in your heart, that there is "Fulness of Joy" in heaven, and that at God's right hand there are "Pleasures forevermore," then you should not weep for your loved ones that have gone there.

They do not wish you to keep on weeping.

They are not in the grave. They are up yonder, "forever with the Lord."

Dry your tears.

Work for God.

Weeping will not save you.

Weeping will not help you, but weeping will hinder you.

"Weeping may endure for a night." I do not say that there will not come some nights when there will be weeping, but

Even When Weeping, Work; Even When Weeping, Rejoice.

When my daughter was taken, I sat down that night, and wrote the story of her death; I prepared LEAVES OF HEALING.

Although there were bursts of tears, and, every half hour, my heart would seem to break, yet I would go on, and that issue of LEAVES OF HEALING was all written, before I came to Zion City to put her body into the grave.

When I went back, I finished my task. I spoke some words into the phonograph, my Message to you, as I left you for a few days.

"Weeping may endure for a night," but, even then, we will work; even then, we will rejoice; even then, through the tears, there shall be the Light shining, the rainbow will span our heaven, and we will be rejoicing.

Then, when time has softened our grief for the dear one who has passed away, we think of the Joy of her two years with God in heaven.

God taught her the Path of Life, and she is now in the "Fulness of Joy," and at His right hand, where she has pleasures forevermore.

Do not let us only talk these things, but let us live them.

The Strength of Zion is its Joy.

Let us sometimes sing a song that will carry our hearts into sympathy with the mourners, for this is right.

It is oftentimes better to go to the house of mourning, than to the house of rejoicing and feasting, because there you can carry the Joy and comfort where it is needed.

If I could do all that I should like to do this morning, I should visit every home that has been afflicted.

I should love to sit down and talk to every one of you, but I can only talk to you in this way, for I cannot come to every one of your homes.

Go to the house of mourning, but carry with you Joy.

> Go bury thy sorrow,
>   The world hath its share;
> Go bury it deeply,
>   Go hide it with care;
> Go think of it calmly,
>   When curtained by night,
> Go tell it to Jesus,
>   And all will be right.

Bury it deeply, and never resurrect it.

Some of you are digging up your past sorrows.

Some of you are carrying around with you a skeleton; some of you are carrying around with you the dead, and you have the weight upon you, yet you say you believe that the dead are not dead, but living with God.

Then act as you talk.

The Strength of Zion is its Joy, not the laughter of fools.

There is a place for laughter, but it is the laughter of the wise. I dare say there is more laughter in Zion Tabernacle than there is in any other religious meeting-place in all the world, yet there is more earnestness—yet there is deeper feeling.

There are sometimes tears that mean very much sympathy for those that mourn, but they are wiped away.

Zion goes forth with quick, happy steps, to work for the redemption of the world.

Zion People Recognized by Their Calm Joyousness.

One of the things in Zion Restoration Host work in New York that was constantly spoken of to me, and to others all over the city, was that the people of New York knew members of the Host everywhere.

They said, "There is something about them that makes you know them before they speak the word to you, 'Peace to thee.' You see they have the Peace, they have the Joy, they have the Love."

If you have the Love, you also have the Joy.

It was Love that took us down to New York.

We went joyfully to our work.

The Love and Joy was followed by Peace, and that was the Message that we carried, "Peace be to this house."

We could not have carried it, if the Love and the Joy had not been in our hearts.

No one can ever make a good Zion Restorationist who has sorrow filling his heart, making him look doleful and miserable; because the Fruit of the Spirit is Love, Joy.

When a general wants to get his soldiers into good order for a big fight, he gives them a hearty meal.

One of the things he does is to give orders that his men be rested, that they get sleep, and that they get the inspiration of music.

When they march into battle, then rings out the song, and then the Scotch with their pibroch, and their hurrah, dash to battle, under the inspiration of music, and with joy in their hearts.

That is what they do in the world, to win a battle, and cannot we see that there is a great deal of wisdom in the world's way?

The people of God must be well fed, and well nourished. They must be strong.

There is no use in sending a man into battle drunk. No general would think it a good thing to fill his men up with whisky.

The alcohol would be a whip that would be taking the strength out of them every minute, and when they went into battle they would be quickly weakened.

Good Lessons Can Be Learned From the Devil.

Beloved, let us learn from the world. There are many good things that we can learn from the Devil.

The Devil knows a good many things, and while we are not going his way, yet, we can oftentimes get a lesson from the persistence with which he pursues his plans.

But if you feed an army and rest it, and strengthen it by music, and then only stand still, you waste all your preparations.

We are not an army fighting a battle once or twice, but we are fighting battles every day.

The Path of Life is the path we must tread to get Love.

Walk in the Path of Life.

It leads upward, not downward, and away from the Path of Death.

Seek out the Path.

Ask God to show you everything that will make you strong in spirit, in soul, and in body, and put away everything that means sin and disease and death, for they mean hell.

On the other hand, see that you get a Full Salvation; that Salvation which, in the Path of Life, is flowing in streams of Goodness and Mercy, by your side every day.

You have not to go far to seek it.

The River of God Is Full of Water.

You are sailing, not over a salt sea, but you, my brethren, are sailing down the River of God, which is full of water.

It is ever so broad. You cannot see the shore, but, as in the mouth of the Amazon, put down your bucket, and you will find the water sweet.

Put down your bucket, and you can get fresh water, for the fresh water goes far out to sea.

If you will read Ezekiel very carefully, you will see that this River flows right through the sea, right through the land, and that wherever that River flows, everything lives.

I put down my bucket in the middle of the Atlantic and found the Water of Life.

I put down my bucket in the middle of the Pacific and in the middle of the Indian Ocean, and I found the Water of Life there.

I found God there. I found rest there. I found strength there. It is not merely to be found in big meetings, or in homes. It is here.

Remember that the River of God is not only outside you, but it is in you, and that within you there flows, and through you there shall flow, because of the Fountain of Life that is within you, Rivers of Living Water.

Thou hast shown me the Path of Life.

And what a wonderful Path it is!

And in Thy presence is Fulness of Joy.

Joy of Jehovah Here and Now.

You say, "That is all very well when you get to heaven."

Have we to wait until we get to heaven to realize the presence of God? What kind of Christians are they that talk like that?

We believe that He is with us every day, everywhere; that He is here, now.

"In Thy presence," now, this morning, "there is Fulness of Joy."

Must we wait until we get to the right hand of God in Heaven before we find the pleasures?

Audience—"No."

General Overseer—The right hand of the Lord is here as as well as there.

He is bestowing blessings upon us, and cheering us, and lifting us up with His own right hand.

Do not always look away up.

Look around you.

How many servants there are that wait on man of which he takes no notice—servants that spring up from the very ground.

Things provided for man, serve him, satisfy him. Fruits and flowers are all around him.

In the sea, fishes wait for him to take them for food.

The bees make honey for him.

All over the world God is providing pleasures for the spirit, for the soul, for the body—endless pleasures. They are coming from His right hand.

Thou openest Thy right hand and satisfiest the desires of every living thing.

I am so glad this morning that I do not have to wait for Heaven to get the Fulness of Joy, and the things that come from God's right hand.

I know that in some things there will be a fuller Joy there than there is here.

Poor Reward of Those Who Bury Their Talents.

I do not know that for some of you there will be a fuller Joy there.

I think that, when He comes and finds that some of you have not been working for God, and have buried your talent in land, in this or that or the other state, or in investments in the world, He will say to you, "I gave it to you that you might invest it where it would bring forth for Me."

"Oh, yes, but we were afraid, and we thought it might not be best to invest it in Zion, and so we dug a hole, and put it in a field in such a county, in such a state, for we thought it would be safe there," or, "We put it into stocks in the world, where we thought it would be safer, and here it is. It has not grown any."

"Thou wicked and slothful servant!"

At the Restoration, when the Master comes, He will take your talent, and will give it to some who have the ten talents.

Do you know, that is the reason why I get so much?

I get the lazy man's talent, and, as there are so many lazy men, Zion grows by two thousand per cent.

No Joy in Divided Interests.

Some of you are thinking, "I am not sure but that Manitoba is a good place, and so is Ohio. I know I have lands that are rich. They bring up lots of pigs there. California is pretty good, and we will keep one leg over in Gadara and the other in Zion, and we will wait awhile. We are not ready to take this leg out of Gadara, and put both into Zion."

The Lord have mercy on you!

You have no Joy.

You cannot have any Joy with one leg in Gadara and a pig-pen, and the other in Zion; one leg in towns where they are selling Liquid Fire and Distilled Damnation, and the other in Zion.

There is Fulness of Joy in Zion, if you will walk her Path.

There is Peace in Zion, but I do not see how you can manage it with one leg in Zion, and the other in Gadara.

What a spectacle you are to men and angels! But when you have both feet here in Zion, then it is all right.

I can call you who have been associated with me through these long years to witness that

I Have Not Failed to Sympathize With You in Your Sorrows.

I wanted to lift you out of sorrow into Joy.

I have not been able to do all I wanted to do.

I could not do the work of all the years in one month, or one year, but I will do all I can every day, and every week, in every year.

I am so glad that we are marching to the Joy-bells, the Joy-bells that are ringing every day in heaven, because spirits are being emancipated on earth by the words that go forth from Zion; by the women and men that go forth from Zion; by those that are toiling in the hard places of the field; that are toiling in the high places of the field.

It is a glorious fight, and the Joy of Jehovah is Strength.

So we go forward with the Joy of Jehovah in our hearts.

There is weeping, there is darkness; it is not for ourselves, but it is for others.

"Weeping may endure for a night, but Joy cometh in the morning."

The night may seem long, but the Joy will come, and then you will get to that place where you will have

Songs in the Night.

Paul and Silas were in the innermost prison, with their feet fast in the stocks, their backs bleeding from the cruel and unmerited scourges.

Yet Paul and Silas were thinking of those whose faces were shining, who had been delivered from the power of sin and disease.

They are in prison.

They sing and God hears them.

The earthquake comes, and the very man who cruelly flogged them is at their feet, saying, "What must I do to be saved?"

Oh, it was Joy in the hearts of these men, on that dark night, that sent a thrill through heaven which made an earthquake shake the prison and open the doors!

Paul and Silas came out with Joy to a feast spread for them by their enemy, who washed their stripes and brought all his house to hear them.

Before the morning had come, they had the Joy of baptizing all his household.

"Joy cometh in the morning!"

Sing on, O Zion, sing on!

Let the Love that is ever searching for the Joy- Love- and Peace-note in Music, be found.

Sing on! Sing on, as you march through the night, into the Light!

"Joy cometh in the morning!"

PRAYER OF CONSECRATION.

My God and Father, in Jesus' Name I come to Thee. Take me as I am. Make me better from day to day. Make me ever what I ought to be. For Jesus' sake, forgive my wavering, my inconsistencies. Help me to consecrate myself, my time, my talent, my family, my money, all that I have, to Thy service; to gather in with Thy people into the City of Zion, into the continuation of Thy work throughout the world, that I may have the Joy of marching with Zion through the darkness into the Light, and to enjoy communion in the days that are to come, preparing for Thy coming; to enjoy Thy presence, having done what I could to prepare for Thy coming; to bless the world of weary, sin-stricken, disease-smitten, heavy-laden, tormented, demon-possessed and oppressed people. O God, Thou hast set me free; help me to set others free. Give me Thy Joy. May it remain. May I bring forth Fruit in Joy. For Jesus' sake. [*All repeat the prayer, clause by clause, after the General Overseer.*]

The Congregation then joined in singing the Consecration Hymn:

It may not be on the mountain's height,
Or over the stormy sea;
It may not be at the battle's front,
My Lord will have need of me;
But if by a still, small voice He calls,
To paths that I do not know,
I'll answer, dear Lord, with my hand in Thine,
I'll go where You want me to go.

REFRAIN—I'll go where You want me to go, dear Lord,
Over mountain, or plain, or sea;
I'll say what You want me to say, dear Lord,
I'll be what You want me to be.

Perhaps today there are loving words,
Which Jesus would have me speak,
There may be now in the paths of sin,
Some wanderer whom I should seek.
O, Savior, if Thou wilt be my guide,
Tho' dark and rugged the way,
My voice shall echo Thy Message sweet,
I'll say what You want me to say.

There's surely somewhere a lowly place,
In earth's harvest field so wide,
Where I may labor through Life's short day
For Jesus, the Crucified;
So, trusting my all to Thy tender care,
And knowing Thou lovest me,
I'll do Thy will with a heart sincere,
I'll be what You want me to be.

The General Overseer then brought the meeting to a close by pronouncing the

BENEDICTION.

Beloved, abstain from every form of evil. And may the very God of Peace Himself sanctify you wholly; and I pray God your whole Spirit, and Soul, and Body, be preserved entire without blame, unto the coming of our Lord Jesus, the Christ. Faithful is He that calleth you, who also will do it. The Grace of our Lord Jesus, the Christ, the Love of God, our Father, the fellowship of the Holy Spirit, our Comforter and Guide, one Eternal God, abide in you, bless you, and keep you, and all the Israel of God everywhere, forever. Amen.

Expiration of Subscriptions.

On every subscriber's copy of LEAVES OF HEALING or THE ZION BANNER we attach a yellow label bearing his name, address, and two numbers, the figures referring to the volume and the number with which the subscription will expire.

Thus, should your label number happen to be 15—11, you may know that your subscription expires with Volume XV, Number 11, which will be July 2, 1904. Also take notice that LEAVES OF HEALING now completes a volume every six months, or twenty-six weeks, that being the number of papers which are put into a bound volume. Earlier in the life of the paper a volume contained fifty-two numbers, as LEAVES OF HEALING had fewer pages in those days.

By making yourselves familiar with these customs and remitting promptly you need never allow your subscription to lapse.

Send money only by Bank Draft, Postoffice or Express Money-order in favor of John Alexander Dowie, and address all letters intended for us to

ZION PRINTING AND PUBLISHING HOUSE,
Zion City, Lake County, Illinois.

Publisher's Notice.

The remittance must accompany receipt of subscriptions at the Publishing House, no difference by or for whom or for whatever time they may be given, or whether forwarded through Ordained Officers, Branches, or Gatherings of the Christian Catholic Church in Zion. Accounts will be carried with Ordained Officers, Branches, or Gatherings, on quantity orders of periodicals consigned on sale for monthly settlement, but to include only such articles as bear the imprint of Zion. All orders for Bibles, books, buttons, pictures (except prints done by the Publishing House), lace souvenirs, etc., must be sent to the General Stores, Zion City, Lake County, Illinois.

DO YOU KNOW GOD'S WAY OF HEALING?

BY THE REV. JOHN ALEX. DOWIE.

Let it be supposed that the following words are a conversation between the reader [A] and the writer [B].

A. What does this question mean? Do you really suppose that God has some one especial way of healing in these days, of which men may know and avail themselves?

B. That is exactly my meaning, and I wish very much that you should know God's Way of Healing, as I have known it for many years.

A. What is the way, in your opinion?

B. You should rather ask, WHO is God's Way? for the way is a Person, not a thing I will answer your question in His own words, "I am the Way, and the Truth, and the Life no one cometh unto the Father, but by Me." These words were spoken by our Lord Jesus, the Christ, the Eternal Son of God, who is both our Savior and our Healer (John 14:6.)

A. But I always thought that these words only referred to Him as the Way of Salvation. How can you be sure that they refer to Him as the Way of Healing also?

B. Because He cannot change. He is "the same yesterday and today, yea, and forever." (Hebrews 13:8.) He said that He came to this earth not only to save us but to heal us. (Luke 4:18), and He did this when in the flesh on earth. Being unchanged He must be able and willing and desirous to heal now.

A. But is there not this difference, namely, that He is not with us now?

B. No; for He said "Lo, I am with you All the Days, even unto the Consummation of the Age;" and so He is with us now, in spirit, just as much as when He was here in the flesh.

A. But did He not work these miracles of healing when on earth merely to prove that He was the Son of God?

B. No; there was still a greater purpose than that. He healed the sick who trusted in Him in order to show us that He came to die not only for our sins, but for our sicknesses, and to deliver us from both.

A. Then, if that be so, the atonement which He made on the Cross must have been for our sicknesses as well as our sins. Can you prove that is the fact from the Scriptures?

B. Yes, I can, and the passages are very numerous. I need quote only two. In Isaiah 53:4, 5, it is written of Him: "Surely He hath borne our griefs (Hebre[illegible], *sicknesses*), and carried our sorrows: . . . and with His stripes we are healed." Then, in the Gospel according to Matthew, this passage is quoted and directly applied to the work of bodily healing, in the 8th chapter 17th verse: "That it might be fulfilled [illegible]h was spoken by Isaiah the prophet, saying, Himself took our infirmities, and bare our [illegible]seases."

A. But do you not think that sickness is often God's will, and sent for our good, and therefore God may not wish us to be healed?

B. No, that cannot possibly be; for diseases of every kind are the Devil's work, and his work can never be God's will, since the Christ came for the very purpose of destroying "the works of the Devil." (1 John 3:8.)

A. Do you mean to say that all disease is the work of Satan?

B. Yes, for if there had been no sin (which came through Satan) there never would have been any disease, and Jesus never in one single instan[illegible] told any person that sickness was God's work or will, but the very contrary.

A. Can you prove from Scriptures that all forms of sickness and infirmity are the Devil's work?

B. Yes, that can be done very easily. You will see in Matthew 4:23 and 9:35 that when Jesus was here in the flesh He healed "all manner of disease and all manner of sickness among the people." Then if you will refer to Acts 10:38 you will see that the Apostle Peter declares that He (Jesus) "went about doing good, and healing all that were oppressed of the Devil." Notice that all whom He healed, not some, were suffering from Satan's evil power.

A. But does disease never come from God?

B. No, it cannot come from God, for He is pure, and disease is unclean; and it cannot come out of Heaven, for there is no disease there.

A. That is very different from the teachings which I have received all my life from ministers and in the churches. Do you really think that you are right, and that they are all wrong in this matter?

B. It is not a question as between myself and them. The only question is, What does God's Word say? God has said in all the ages, to His Church, "I am Jehovah that healeth thee" (Exodus 15:26), and therefore it would be wicked to say that He is the defiler of His people. All true Christians must believe the Bible, and it is impossible to believe that good and evil, sickness and health, sin and holiness could have a common origin in God. If the Bible really taught that, it would be impossible to believe our Lord Jesus, the Christ, when He says: "A good tree cannot bring forth evil fruit, neither can a corrupt tree bring forth good fruit." (Matthew 7:18.)

A. But even if I agree with all you say, is it not true that the Gifts of Healing were removed from the Church, and are not in it now?

B. No, the "Gifts of Healing" were never withdrawn, and can never be withdrawn, from the true Church of God, for it is written: "The gifts and the calling of God are without repentance." (Romans 11:29.) There are nine gifts of God to the Church (enumerated in 1 Corinthians 12:8-11), and all these are in the Holy Spirit. Therefore, so long as the Holy Spirit is in the Church, all the gifts must be there also. If they are not exercised, that does not prove that they do not exist, but that the faith to exercise them is lacking in God's servants. The gifts are all perfectly preserved; for the Holy Spirit, not the Church, keeps them safely.

A. What should a Christian then do when overtaken with sickness?

B. A Christian should obey God's command, and at once turn to Him for forgiveness of the sin which may have caused the sickness, and for immediate healing. Healing is obtained from God in one of four ways, namely: First, by the direct prayer of faith, without any aid from the officers of the Church, praying as the Centurion did in Matthew 8:5-13; second, by two faithful disciples praying in perfect agreement, in accordance with the Lord's promise in Matthew 18:19, third, by the anointing of the Elders and the prayer of faith, according to the instructions in James 5:14 and 15; and fourth, by the laying on of the hands of them who believe, and whom God calls to that ministry, as the Lord commands in Mark 16:18, and in other places.

A. But are people healed in this way in these days?

B. Yes, in thousands of cases. I have myself laid hands upon many hundreds of thousands of persons, and I have seen the Lord's power manifested in the healing of great numbers, many of whom are living witnesses in many countries, who have testified publicly before thousands, and who are prepared to testify at any time. This ministry is being exercised by devoted Christians in many parts of America, Europe, Australasia, and elsewhere.

A. Is it not the same as Christian Science, Mind Healing, etc.?

B. No. Divine Healing is diametrically opposed to these diabolical counterfeits, which are utterly antichristian. These impostures are only seductive forms of Spiritualism. Trance Evangelism is also a more recent form of this delusion, and it deceives many.

A. But how shall I obtain the necessary faith to receive healing, which faith I am at present conscious that I do not possess?

B. It is written: "Belief cometh of hearing, and hearing by the word of the Christ." (Romans 10:17.) Our Missions are held for the express purpose of teaching fully the Word of God on this matter, and I very heartily invite you to attend the meetings which are announced for Zion Tabernacles in Chicago and other cities, and for Shiloh Tabernacle, Zion City, Illinois. All are welcome and there are no charges of any kind made, for all God's gifts are free gifts. Salvation is the first of these, without which you cannot be healed through faith in Jesus. All the costs of this work are covered by the free-will offerings of the people who attend these meetings, and others whom the Lord leads to help; but the poorest, who have nothing to give, are as heartily welcome as the richest.

A. Do you see the sick and lay hands upon them in this Mission?

B. Yes; after we feel satisfied that they are fully resting in the Lord alone for the healing, we see privately, so far as time permits, those who attend; but under no circumstances do we claim the power to heal any; for "power belongeth unto God."

A. Have you any writings upon this subject which can be purchased?

B. Yes; these can be obtained at the office of Zion Printing and Publishing House, Zion City, Illinois, and at any Zion Tabernacle. But the best book on Divine Healing is the Bible itself, studied prayerfully and earnestly.

We extend to you a hearty invitation to attend the meetings, which are free to all. Our prayer is that you may be led to find in Jesus, the Christ, our Lord and God your present Savior from sin, your Healer from sickness, your Cleanser from all evil, your Keeper in the way to Heaven, your Friend, and your All for Time and Eternity. We pray that these words may help many who read, and that our little conversation may bear fruit in leading many readers to look to Jesus only.

"The Healing of Christ's seamless dress
Is by all beds of pain;
We touch Him in life's throng and press
And we are whole again."

ZION BAND IN ZURICH, SWITZERLAND

From a Photograph by Deacon E. Williams, May 29, 1904

THE GENERAL OVERSEER AND MEMBERS OF HIS VISITATION PARTY

And Officers of the Christian Catholic Church in Zion Including Those Ordained in Zurich, Switzerland, Lord's Day May 29, 1904

Zion Restoration Host

Elder A. F. LEE, Recorder

THEY therefore that were scattered abroad went about preaching the Word.—*Acts 8:4*.

ALL efforts of the Devil to smother Divine Fire in the hearts of men by means of persecution have resulted in the more rapid spread of that which he attempted to destroy.

As it was in the early days of the Church so it is today; the more persistent and desperate the Devil becomes in his efforts to retard the work of God, the more determined and aggressive the true children of the Kingdom become in their efforts to extend the Kingdom of the Christ.

Because of bitter persecution, large numbers of God's children have come to Zion City from all parts of the world, having sold their possessions in the world, and invested their money in Zion, where both money and life are consecrated to the service of God.

Having established homes here and received proper training, God is by various means now causing them to go out into the world, as members of Zion Restoration Host, to carry the Gospel of the Kingdom everywhere.

Some have returned to their former homes on matters of business only, to do more earnest work for their King, which has resulted in awakening great interest and leading many into the Light.

Others as salesmen and salesladies are now going from place to place doing most successful Restoration work, bearing their own expenses, God wonderfully prospering them also in material things.

One of these faithful workers writes in a letter dated June 13th, as follows:

I gave out one hundred Messages here today and twenty-seven LEAVES OF HEALING; made ten special calls on sick people with the result that one lady and her daughter consecrated themselves to God and gave me their medicine, declaring that they would use no more.

They have also given up eating swine's flesh.

We had a good talk and a season of prayer, after which I came away leaving them three copies of LEAVES OF HEALING, for which paper they are going to subscribe.

The profits of my sales today, in the face of the fact that I spent many hours in work for God, amounted to —— dollars and the profits of five days' work this week have amounted to —— dollars. So you see it is wonderful how God provides, for which I thank Him.

Work in Ireland.

The following very interesting letter was received recently from Deaconess Elizabeth S. Gaston, who returned to Europe last January with Overseer Cantel and party to do some special Restoration work in Ireland:

44 UNIVERSITY AVENUE, BELFAST, IRELAND.

MY DEAR ELDER:—It affords me great pleasure to be able to tell you of the splendid work that is being done by the Restorationists. God is wonderfully blessing us, and we praise Him.

We also thank the dear ones in Zion City who are daily praying for us.

The first Sunday in March we went out two and two.

We were organized as a company; there were just seven of us in all.

Since then four new workers have joined, and are enjoying the work very much.

Deacon Cooper was then sent from the London Branch to take charge of the work in this city.

He is doing excellent work. God is answering his prayers for the sick, which has been the means of interesting many people in Zion.

The first Saturday in March, Miss Mackay and I did the first saloon Restoration work in Belfast.

The next Saturday night, Deacon Cooper and Mr. Mackay joined us. Now there are seven of us to do this Saturday night work.

We sometimes sell as many as seventy-five LEAVES in a night.

I spent one week in Derry and enlisted two workers and took them out with me one at a time; now, in my absence, they go out together. Overseer Cantel has directed me to visit the Branch again.

Most of my time has been given to Belfast, as this, we believe, will be the center for Ireland.

I know that it will interest you to know that God is prospering His work in the Emerald Isle.

You will please continue to pray for us. We pray for Zion City and her people every day.

I am so glad that it has been my privilege to live there, and I can tell the people of the things I have seen and heard there, and that they disagree with the press reports.

One gentleman said to me just today, as I was telling him about Zion as she really is, "Do you blame me for believing the newspapers, for until this time I had had no other source of information?"

He bought a copy of the LEAVES, saying, "This may, with what you have already told me, convert me; I hope it will."

Many people have thanked me for taking the trouble to tell them the truth about Zion. I love to do it. It is a great joy to do this work.

Yours in His Service,

ELIZABETH S. GASTON.

The statement of the gentleman referred to by Deaconess Gaston, that the newspapers had been his only source of information up to the time that she presented him with a copy of the LEAVES, ought to arouse every Restorationist to the importance of diligently scattering Zion Literature, so as to counteract the evil influence of the newspaper press.

While we have great occasion for rejoicing over all that has been and is still being accomplished by the faithful efforts of Zion Restoration Host in the circulating of LEAVES OF HEALING and Restoration Messages, there is no question but with a little more effort and earnest consecration on the part of each one, we should see even greater results than those which have already gladdened our hearts.

Scarcely a day goes by but that scores of letters are received at Headquarters bearing testimony to the fact that the marvelous growth of Zion, and the great blessings which have come to our people, are principally due to the wide circulation which has been given LEAVES OF HEALING.

Work in India.

Again there comes to us a letter from a faithful member of Zion Restoration Host, who, after spending several months in Zion City, returned to her home in India last December. It reads as follows:

CAWNPORE, INDIA.

DEAR BROTHER:—Your kind letter, together with a roll of Messages, reached me soon after my return to India in December last.

I had brought quite a little supply of Literature with me which I gave out on the steamer and elsewhere, but kept no account of it.

I gave a package of tracts to a man interested in Zion to distribute among Europeans, as he went out in the district on business.

As to LEAVES OF HEALING, I am sure single papers have passed into many hands.

I cannot give you exact figures.

My supply is not yet gone.

I have been asked as to the meaning of Zion Restoration Host, and could tell you of some very interesting conversations I have had with missionaries, telling them of what I have learned and seen in Zion City.

I have given them Literature which, I am sure, has been a revelation to them, and some, going home, have said that they hoped to visit Zion City.

It is wonderful how the newspapers have succeeded in poisoning the minds of the people even at this great distance.

God has opened the way for us, so that we are leaving India at an early date, and hope to make Zion City our future home.

I had no idea that this would be brought to pass so soon when I returned from America, but God has heard prayer.

A great many are interested here, and are eagerly reading and getting information concerning Zion, and our going to Zion City, I believe, will have the effect of leading others at least to investigate.

My heart continues to rejoice that God has led my husband with me to a people who are united in their service for Him.

May God bless you greatly in your important work, and believe me, sincerely,

Yours in the Christ, (MRS.) M. B. BOND.

Work in China.

The following letter will show some of the faithful Restoration work which has been done in Shanghai, China:

MY DEAR BROTHER:—Peace to thee.

Below please find the last report of Restoration work in Shanghai before we start for Zion City. We are hoping, God willing, to arrive early in July of this year.

This Literature was distributed from the 1st of January, 1904, to the 31st of March, 1904, in all three months.

The work has been done by Elder Kennedy and me.

LEAVES OF HEALING distributed........... 1,259
VOICE FROM ZION distributed 121
Restoration Messages distributed............1,380
Sent by mail LEAVES OF HEALING.......... 200
Sent by mail THE ZION BANNER........... 90
Sent by mail VOICE FROM ZION 50
Total pieces of Literature put in circulation..3,100

Trusting to see you soon, I am

Yours sincerely, C. F. VIKING.

Work in Australasia.

Overseer Voliva, who has been so exceedingly busy in connection with the Visitation of the General Overseer, encloses the following report in a recent letter, in which he says:

I regret exceedingly that I have been unable to send you regular reports of the work of the Restorationists in Australia.

I herewith inclose you a partial report of the work done.

This report does not include much of the work done by the Branches in Adelaide and in Sydney.

I hope to have these reports complete by the next mail.

Number of calls made.................... 60,294
Number of Messages given.............. 27,310
Number of copies of LEAVES OF HEALING given 917
Number of subscriptions to the LEAVES... 26
Number of copies of LEAVES sold......... 13,217
Number of copies of THE ZION BANNER given away.......................... 48
Number of copies of the THE ZION BANNER sold............................ 825
Number of copies of VOICE FROM ZION sold................................ 175
Number of persons prayed with........... 553
Number of persons helped in various ways................................ 120

Reports from Various Points.

Following is a tabulated report of the number of workers and the work done by them during the month of May, 1904, according to reports received to date from the various points named:

UNITED STATES.	No. of Workers	No. of Calls	Messages Given	Leaves Sold	Leaves Given
California—					
Fresno	6	290	311	49	7
Haywards	1	7	153	...	5
Los Angeles	15	2258	4845	115	441
Maxwell	2	12	27	2	13
St. John	2	20	60	....	37
San Francisco	12	3000	3000	1100	50
Santa Rosa	1	50	35	15	47
Colorado—					
Durango	1	....	386	..	29
Trinidad	2	296	308	50	27
Connecticut—					
Danbury	1	35	60	....	27
Meriden	1	135	140	....	3
Illinois—					
Champaign	1	180	670	5	39
Chicago—Central Parish, Ger.	22	1531	1577	30	374
" South Side Parish	63	....	3765	470	1427
" Southeast Parish	21	2310	4200	700	80
" North Parish	30	4376	5412	77	413
" North Parish, Ger.	14	484	487	18	394
" West Parish, Ger.	12	831	1070	59	101
" Northwest Parish	14	454	477	19	141
Illinois—					
Highland Park	2	299	1810	4	5
Lyndon	1	10	28	....	5
Mazon	2	....	65	....	....
Odell	1	14	11	...	12
Paxton	2	15	15	....	15
Vermilion Grove	1	134	146	9	11
Waukegan	138	2734	2756	728	176
Indiana—					
Hammond	5	37	30	79	150
Indianapolis	9	180	1041	119	182
Lafayette	4	243	701	58	79
Linn Grove	1	..	4	....	14
Marion	2	112	148	18	28
Monon	3	112	199	....	38
Noblesville	1	....	105	6	31
Plymouth	3	4	3	...	37
Valparaiso	1	9	14	...	10
Walton	6	127	42	43	66
Iowa—					
Council Bluffs	3	22	1114	...	6
Cedar Falls	2	42	58	25	27
Dunkerton	1	74	87	8	25
Elberon	3	63	80	15	37
Forest City	2	61	341	42	44
Laporte City	1	6	3	9	3
Rock Valley	1	144	757	44	17
Tipton	4	38	105	....	30
Webster City	5	297	1043	14	40
Winterset	1	3	21	7	21
Kansas—					
Eskridge	1	65	90	38	15
Independence	3	50	521	....	16
Kansas City	5	450	492	54	43
Manhattan	2	21	95	14	...
Mound Valley	1	.	126	....	....
Salina	2	....	85	...	35
Wichita	5	455	565	250	31
Kentucky—					
Danville	1	4	343	...	6
Louisville	1	150	500	...	70
Massachusetts—					
Boston	23	4702	2861	1681	816
Lawrence	12	1105	1000	300	600
North Duxbury	2	....	....	...	51
Michigan—					
Bay City	3	612	556	48	139
Coldwater and Detroit	1	...	115	....	20
Manistee	1	...	10	...	9
Port Huron	5	278	479	141	....
Sault Ste. Marie	5	100	...	90	95
Minnesota—					
Delavan	1	27	27	...	38
Moorhead	1	3	20	...	2
Rushford	1	5	10	...	38
Missouri—					
Higginsville	1	200	200	26	8
Springfield	1	5	45	..	15
St. Louis	17	1321	1030	320	60
Nebraska—					
Falls City	3	168	900	123	25
Inman	1	1	8	..	8
Omaha	2	22	1115	....	7
Republican City	1	...	...	....	20
New Jersey—					
Salem	1	...	....	16	19
New York—					
Bluff Point	1	2	6	...	6
Dundee	1	...	11	....	20
New York City	30	3965	11038	471	3028
Syracuse	4	185	225	6	153
Ohio—					
Ada	3	5	43	9	15
Alliance	1	100	536	....	38
Cincinnati	45	4036	6241	422	857
Cleveland	32	4812	6789	234	502
Columbus	3	190	202	32	6
Dayton	2	44	324	13	23
Germantown	1	54	60	19	13
Lancaster	1	9	58	9	18
Mansfield	1	..	103	4	....
Nevada	1	....	10	..	4
Oceola	2	7	113	.	16
Toledo	2	1000	400	222	
Urbana	3	8	23	...	16
Oregon—					
Union	1	16	7	.	27
Pennsylvania—					
Downington	1	...	260	..	27
New Brighton	1	39	99	...	55
Philadelphia	49	5811	24095	516	601
Pittsburgh	8	469	102	..	398
Scranton	2	68	200	106	35
West Chester	3	402	1646	86	7
South Dakota—					
Belle	1	....	....	..	77
Brookings	2	90	80	7	18
Centerville	2	23	42	..	15
Summit	1	26	32	10	4
Tennessee—					
Memphis	2	6	158	...	20
Whiteside	2	.	75	..	30
Texas—					
Batson	1	2	28	1	39
Dallas	1	12	51	...	9
Houston	1	12	93	.	53
Luling	1	13	28	6	2
Paris	1	3	28	.	15
San Antonio	17	850	334	81	409
Washington—					
Clinton	1	23	163	17	22
Easton	1	134	137	16	26
Everett	2	284	357	38	74
Lynden	3	7	....	....	72
Seattle	32	3032	2995	792	188
Spokane	13	3147	3940	366	563
Tacoma	8	627	495	96	96
Wisconsin—					
Alma	2	19	11	....	18
Black Creek	1	150	300	....	20
Brookfield	1	3	34	....	7
Columbus	1	30	35	....	....
Maiden Rock	2	20	86	7	45
Marinette	4	472	1963	50	66
Milwaukee	8	926	2069	207	46
Minong	1	4	16	...	22
Omro	3	133	246	18	39
Racine	4	307	480	....	249
Viroqua	3	171	465	41	54
Wauwatosa	2	30	30	4	...
West Ellis	1	....	....	...	25
Total	851	62568	135740	11022	15157

DOMINION OF CANADA AND CONTINENTS.	No. of Workers	No. of Calls	Messages Given	Leaves Sold	Leaves Given
Australia—					
*Sydney	30	2936	209	503	51
Canada—					
Elmira	1	....	15	....	2
London	1	62	72	3	17
Simcoe	2	123	82	76	1
Toronto	18	1903	3221	184	1002
Vancouver	21	1676	1415	56	569
Victoria	2	261	198	55	64
Winnipeg	1	....	....	25	5
Woodstock	1	76	30	30	46
Total	77	7037	5242	932	1757
Grand Total	928	69605	140982	11954	16914

*Work done in month of April.

MEETINGS IN ZION CITY TABERNACLES.

SHILOH TABERNACLE.

Lord's Day—Early morning service.... 6:30 a. m.
Intermediate Bible Class.. 9:45 a. m.
Bible class, conducted by Deacon Daniel Sloan... 11:00 a. m.
Afternoon service........ 2:30 p. m.
Evening service......... 8:00 p. m.

First Lord's Day of Every Month—Communion service.

Third Lord's Day of Every Month—Zion Junior Restoration Host rally.

Third Lord's Day of Every Month—Consecration of children .... 10:00 a. m.

Monday—Zion Restoration Host rally (Second Monday of every month).... 8:00 p. m.

Tuesday—Divine Healing meeting..... 2:30 p. m.

Tuesday—Adult Choir .... 7:45 p. m.

Wednesday—Baptismal service........ 7:00 p. m.

Wednesday—Citizens' rally............ 8:00 p. m.

Friday—Adult Choir.................. 7:45 p. m.

Friday—Officers of the Christian Catholic Church in Zion........ 8:00 p. m.

Friday—Junior Choir.. .... 3:45 p. m.
Meeting in the officers' room.

TWENTY-SIXTH STREET TABERNACLE.

Lord's Day—Junior service........... 9:45 a. m.
Lord's Day—German service..........10:30 a. m.
Tuesday—German service .... 8:00 p. m.

IS ANY among you sick? let him call for the Elders of the Church; and let them pray over him, anointing him with oil in the Name of the Lord: And the Prayer of Faith shall save him that is sick, and the Lord shall raise him up; and if he have committed sins, it shall be forgiven him.—*James 5:14, 15.*

How beautiful upon the mountains are the feet of him that bringeth good tidings, that publisheth peace, that bringeth good tidings of good, that publisheth salvation; that saith unto Zion, Thy God Reigneth!—*Isaiah 52:7.*

By Evangelist Sarah E. Hill.

BEHOLD I SEND My messenger, and he shall prepare the way before Me; and Jehovah, whom ye seek, shall suddenly come to His Temple; and the messenger of the Covenant, whom ye delight in, behold, he cometh, saith Jehovah of Hosts—*Malachi 3:1.*

GOD, through the Prophet Malachi, here tells us of a man who is to do a wonderful work in the Consummation of the Age. God calls him His messenger or forerunner.

It was the custom in Eastern countries for a messenger to run before the king, when he went forth on a journey, and prepare the way before him.

The coming of the king was never very far behind that of his messenger.

The Prophet foretells the coming of the messenger, describes his work, and finally announces him as Elijah. (Malachi 3; 4.)

Through the Prophet, God commands the people, saying: "Remember ye the law of Moses My servant, which I commanded unto him in Horeb for all Israel, even statutes and judgments." (Malachi 4:4.)

This is the Covenant which the Messenger comes to present to the world.

It is through the Covenant that the Rule of God is to be reëstablished in the Spirit, Soul and Body of man, that he may be restored to his original relations with God.

Elijah is declared to be not only a Prophet, but much more than a Prophet, because he is the forerunner of the Lord.

When he came as John the Baptist, his father, Zacharias, prophesied of his future coming, and that he should be called the Prophet of the Most High, saying, "For thou shalt go before the face of the Lord, to make ready His ways." (Luke 1:76.)

Whenever the Lord Jesus spoke of Elijah He said that he *had* come as John the Baptist, and also spoke of a future coming when he should Restore All Things. (Matthew 17:10-14; Mark 9:11-14.)

John the Baptist declared himself to be the forerunner of the Lord. (Matthew 3:1-4.) But he did not Restore All Things.

The world was not ready for the Restoration.

John could not come as the Messenger of the Covenant because the Lord Jesus, the Lamb of God, had not yet taken the place of the sacrificial lamb in the Old Covenant, thus making it the New Covenant.

The Apostle Peter tells us that the Lord Jesus is to come in the Times of the Restoration of All Things. (Acts 3:20, 21.)

He also speaks of a prophet like unto Moses who is to come in the Times of the Restoration. (Acts 3:22.)

The Lord tells us that Elijah is this prophet of the Restoration.

We see also that his work, as described by the Prophet Malachi, is Restoration.

The Apostle Peter tells us: "It shall be, that every soul, which shall not harken to that prophet shall be utterly destroyed from among the people." (Acts 3:23.)

This is because the Messenger brings to the world the Covenant which is to establish the reign of the Christ in man's spirit, soul and body, and thus take his entire being out of the hands of the Devil.

As a result of the teaching of the Covenant, the Sun of Righteousness shall again arise, with Healing in His wings, after the world has for centuries turned away from the Lord, who declares Himself to be their Healer. (Malachi 4:2; Exodus 15:26.)

One sign of the Messenger of the Covenant is that his people shall delight in him. (Malachi 3:1.)

This is necessary because of the character of the work which he is sent to do.

God will use him to shake the heavens and the earth, that the things which are not of God may be shaken out. (Haggai 2:21-24. Hebrews 12:25-29.)

The people must be willing to submit to his authority in order that he may form them into a nation for God—a Theocracy. He is to come in the Latter Days, when the world will have become very corrupt.

As in the days of Noah, the people will be absorbed in "eating and drinking, marrying and giving in marriage."

As it was then, lust is to be the culminating sin of the age. (Matthew 24:37, 38.)

With fiery words, filled with the Holy Spirit, he is to burn up the sins of the people, and wash away their filthy habits as with "a refiner's fire and with fullers' soap."

He attacks sin of every kind, and in all places, so that the question is asked, "But who may abide the day of his coming, and who shall stand when he appeareth?" (Malachi 3:2.)

Those who harken to this Prophet shall receive the power to turn to God and live clean, Christian lives, and help to extend the Kingdom of God.

God tells us that He witnesses through His Prophet, and that He uses him as a battle-ax to break in pieces conditions which are not according to His Will. (Malachi 3:5; Jeremiah 51:20-27.)

God says that He will be a swift Witness against the sorcerers *(kashaph)*. These are the makers and venders of drugs.

God through Elijah was a swift Witness against King Ahaziah when that king sent to Baalzebub, the god of Ekron, in his sickness.

God sent him a message through Elijah, saying: Thus saith the Lord, forasmuch as thou hast sent messengers to inquire of Baalzebub, the god of Ekron, is it because there is no God in Israel to inquire of His Word? Therefore thoushalt not come down from the bed whither thou art gone up, but shalt surely die. So he died according to the word of the Lord which Elijah had spoken. (2 Kings 1:2-18.)

Elijah's work is to witness against the adulterers, though it should cost him his life, as it did John the Baptist. (Malachi 3:5; Matthew 14:1-13.)

He must also witness against false swearers. (Malachi 3:5.)

Other portions of prophecy show that this refers chiefly to oaths in Secretism.

This brings on the old fight which Elijah had with Baal worship, the worship of the sun. (1 Kings 18:16-41.)

God will also witness through Elijah against those who oppress the hireling in his wages, the widow and the fatherless, and that turn aside the stranger from his right, and fear not God. (Malachi 3:5.)

A most important part of Elijah's work is the Restoration of God's law in regard to the paying of tithes and offerings.

This is of the greatest importance, not only because they are necessary for the support of the work of God and the extension of His Kingdom, but also, because failure in this withholds Heaven's blessings from the people. (Malachi 3:7-13.)

Wherever the work of Elijah in the Latter Days is described in the Scriptures, there is usually some reference to the Temple or to God's house. (Malachi 3:1.)

This probably refers not only to his building a Temple in which God's people shall worship Him, but it has also reference to man's body, which God says was created to be His Temple. (2 Corinthians 6:16, 17.)

A part of Elijah's work as it is described in prophecy is to cleanse the temple of man's body that it may be a fit dwelling-place for God.

This is the result of the teaching of the Covenant which establishes the Rule of God in man's entire being, and brings God into every department of daily living.

The work of John Alexander Dowie in Zion is that which God, through the Prophet Malachi, said He would send Elijah to do before the Great and Terrible Day of Jehovah.

The Literature of Zion all relates to the Covenant and the Restoration of the world to its right relations with God.

The distribution of this Literature is one of the greatest works of this period.

Zion Literature Mission needs your help, dear reader, in sending this Literature over the world.

Zion Literature Sent Out from a Free Distribution Fund Provided by Zion's Guests and the Friends of Zion.

Report for the three weeks ending July 16, 1904:
32,679 Rolls to Business Men in the United States
2,368 Rolls to Hotels in Europe, Asia, Africa, and the Islands of the Sea.
476 Rolls to.........Various Foreign Countries
Number of Rolls for three Weeks..........35,523
Number of Rolls reported to July 16, 1904, 3,244,325

Zion's Bible Class

Conducted by Deacon Daniel Sloan in Shiloh Tabernacle, Zion City, Lord's Day Morning at 11 o'clock, and in Zion Homes and Gatherings throughout the World.

MID-WEEK BIBLE CLASS LESSON, AUGUST 10th or 11th.

Opposers of the Truth.

1. *Such are sometimes converted.*—1 Timothy 1:12-20.
   A man may blaspheme and persecute, and then be saved.
   How easy it is for the Devil to deceive!
   There are ways to keep in touch with God's Truth.
2. *Pray in faith that they may all be saved.*—2 Timothy 2:1-8.
   Kings have to be prayed for always.
   They make the men of their kingdom sin.
   They drag men down to hell with themselves.
3. *They must be taught to realize how much good they might do.*—2 Timothy 3:1-14.
   They must be won to the Christ.
   They must be approached with discernment.
   The work of the Devil must be destroyed; and men saved.
4. *They are so-called Christians who kick at plain preaching.*—2 Timothy 4:1-5.
   They do not like to be reproved and rebuked.
   They do not want to know God's Way more perfectly.
   They do not love the truth.
5. *They are the wolves which would devour God's lambs.*—Matthew 10:16-25.
   Men are ready to devour God's servants.
   Men in high places and low places.
   Kings always stoop to the level of the Devil's work.
6. *Some profess friendliness, but at heart resist the truth.*—Titus 1:7-16.
   They will preach and prophesy for gain.
   They get people to believe their errors.
   They must be resisted with the truth.
7. *Even a disciple will prove to be a veritable enemy.*—Matthew 26:14-25.
   Persons can fall from their steadfastness.
   They may have something in their hearts that will undo them.
   What watchfulness it requires to live right in God's sight!

The Lord our God is a Truth-vindicating God.

LORD'S DAY BIBLE CLASS LESSON, AUGUST 14th.

A Heroic Stand for God's Truth.

1. *A man must have convictions which move others.*—Matthew 11:7-15.
   Many come to hear out of curiosity.
   They watch to catch at something false in others.
   The man who stirs up such people does God's work.
2. *Many will not stand true under severe tests.*—2 Timothy 4:9-18.
   Those who love the world go back into it.
   Those who love evil will do evil.
   Those who are cowards will run from battle.
3. *Preachers of the Truth are called evil-doers sometimes.*—2 Timothy 2:1-12.
   A man must not wantonly stir up strife.
   He must preach God's Word and stand by it.
   He is a flame of fire and people do not like it.
4. *A man who uncovers wickedness is not always welcomed.*—Matthew 10:26-34.
   Uncover sin and men will want to kill you.
   You must expose every evil-doer.
   You must not be anxious for the outcome.
5. *A man must never be dismayed under opposition.*—2 Timothy 1:9-18.
   The Lord must be your Keeper and Defense.
   You must give up nothing.
   Never become cast down over those who surrender.
6. *The "Cry aloud and spare not" preaching must come.*—Isaiah 58.1-7.
   The sins of God's people are the worst of all sins.
   It is better not to have known the way of righteousness.
   Some appear religious but are full of hypocrisy.
7. *Many think the midnight cry so strange and uncalled for.*—Matthew 25:1-13.
   How foolish some act at the plain truth of God!
   How careless some are in obeying God's commands!
   Each must stand and give an account of himself.

God's Holy People Are a Truth-heralding People.

LEAVES OF HEALING.

Two Dollars will bring to you the weekly visits of the Little White Dove for a year; 75 cents will send it to a friend for thirteen weeks; $1.25 will send it for six months; $1.50 will send it to your minister, or to a Y. M. C. A., or to a Public Reading Room for a whole year. We offer no premiums, except the premium of doing good. We receive no advertisements, and print no commercial lies or cheating enticements of unscrupulous thieves. LEAVES OF HEALING is Zion on wings, and we keep out everything that would detract the reader's mind from all except the Extension of the Kingdom of God, for which alone it exists. If we cannot send forth our Little White Dove without soiling its wings with the smoke of the factory and the dirt of the wrangling market-place, or compelling it to utter the screaming cries of the business vultures in the ears of our readers, then we will keep our Dove at home.

OBEYING GOD IN BAPTISM.

"Baptizing Them Into the Name of the Father and of the Son and of the Holy Ghost."

Nineteen Thousand Fifty-six Baptisms by Triune Immersion Since March 14, 1897.

Nineteen Thousand Fifty-six Believers have joyfully followed their Lord in the Ordinance of Believer's Baptism by Triune Immersion since the first Baptism in Central Zion Tabernacle on March 14, 1897.

Baptized in Central Zion Tabernacle from March 14, 1897, to December 14, 1901, by the General Overseer,	4754		
Baptized in South Side Zion Tabernacle from January 1, 1902, to June 14, 1903, by the General Overseer..	37		
Baptized at Zion City by the General Overseer........	583		
Baptized by Overseers, Elders, Evangelists and Deacons, at Headquarters (Zion City) and Chicago......	5283		
Total Baptized at Headquarters....................			10,657
Baptized in places outside of Headquarters by the General Overseer..................................		641	
Baptized in places outside of Headquarters by Overseers, Elders, Evangelists and Deacons............		7517	
Total Baptized outside of Headquarters............			8,158
Total Baptized in seven years and three months....			18,815
Baptized since June 14, 1904.			
Baptized in Zion City by Elder Royall...............	1		
Baptized in Zion City by Elder Hammond............	6		
Baptized in Zion City by Overseer Mason............	59		
Baptized in Zion City by Overseer Excell............	55		
Baptized in Zion City by Overseer Piper.............	40		
Baptized in Chicago by Elder Hoffman	4		
Baptized in Chicago by Elder Cossum...............	6		
Baptized in Chicago by Elder Keller................	5	176	
Baptized in Canada by Elder Brooks.................		4	
Baptized in California by Elder Taylor..............		2	
Baptized in Indiana by Elder Osborn................		2	
Baptized in Minnesota by Elder Graves..............		5	
Baptized in Mississippi by Evangelist Gay..		1	
Baptized in Missouri by Evangelist Gay.............		1	
Baptized in Missouri by Elder Brock................		9	
Baptized in Missouri by Deacon Robinson............		1	
Baptized in Nebraska by Elder Hoy..................		7	
Baptized in New York by Overseer Mason............		9	
Baptized in Ohio by Deacon Kelchner...............		3	
Baptized in Ohio by Deacon Arrington..............		5	
Baptized in Texas by Evangelist Gay		11	
Baptized in Washington by Elder Ernst.............		2	
Baptized in Wisconsin by Elder McClurkin...........		3	65 241
Total Baptized since March 14, 1897................			19,056

The following-named five believers were baptized in the South Side Zion Tabernacle, Chicago, Illinois, Lord's Day, July 10, 1904, by Elder W. H. Cossum:

Boyd, Miss Goldie.........318 West Sixty-fifth street, Chicago, Illinois
Boyd, Mrs. Harriett ....318 West Sixty-fifth street, Chicago, Illinois
Boyd, Vincent................318 West Sixty-fifth street, Chicago, Illinois
Early, Mrs. Mary ....318 West Sixty-fifth street, Chicago, Illinois
Scott, John.........................2819 Dearborn street, Chicago, Illinois

The following-named believer was baptized at Toronto, Ontario, Canada, Lord's Day, July 10, 1904, by Elder Eugene Brooks:

Wilkins, Edith...............................Branchton, Ontario, Canada

The following-named two believers were baptized in Columbian Park, Lafayette, Indiana, Lord's Day, July 10, 1904, by Elder S. B. Osborn:

Bates, Mrs. Alice Ellen............643 Alabama street, Lafayette, Indiana
Bates, Mary Ann..................643 Alabama street, Lafayette, Indiana

The following-named four believers were baptized in the North Side Zion Tabernacle, Chicago, Illinois, Lord's Day, July 10, 1904, by Elder J. R. Keller:

Kaufman, Earl O................2204 Emmaus avenue, Zion City, Illinois
Phelps, Miss Carrie ....Goshen, Indiana
Roy, John William ....535 Burling street, Chicago, Illinois
Swanson, Mrs. Carolina Sophia...242 Belle Plaine avenue, Chicago, Illinois

The following-named believer was baptized in the Merimec river, St. Louis, Missouri, Monday, July 11, 1904, by Elder Frank L. Brock:

Gill, Sherman ....2643 Lucas avenue, St. Louis, Missouri

The following-named fifty-nine believers were baptized in Shiloh Tabernacle, Zion City, Illinois, Monday, July 18th, 1904, by Overseer G. L. Mason:

Allen, Mrs. Elizabeth.................................Thawville, Illinois
Ay, Mrs. Louisa......................355 Bristol street, Buffalo, New York
Bailey, Mrs. Elizabeth Jane...........................Dodgeville, Wisconsin
Balliet, Miss Ruby.......................................Mansfield, Ohio
Barnes, Evans Paul...................2304 Elisha avenue, Zion City, Illinois
Berryhill, Mrs. Annie L...................................Streator, Illinois

Bishop, Mrs. Alice Hulbert....Alma, Nebraska
Christ, Mrs. Elise....Woodmere, Long Island, New York
Crary, Mrs. Minnie....Trippville, Wisconsin
Daniel, H. L....Traer, Iowa
Ellingson, Elling M....Des Moines, Iowa
Ferges, Mrs. Luella....920 State street, Trinidad, Colorado
Filion, Mrs. Mary A....Filion, Michigan
Fox, Charley H....823 North Main street, Fostoria, Ohio
Friend, James....Viola, Illinois
Grahlow, Miss Helen....612 Lafayette avenue, Racine, Wisconsin
Grahlow, Mrs. Louise....612 Lafayette avenue, Racine, Wisconsin
Hanna, L. G....Logansport, Indiana
Harlin, Harry Hugo...805 Fifteenth avenue south, Minneapolis, Minnesota
Hire, Mrs. Edith....3006 Gabriel avenue, Zion City, Illinois
Hog, Mrs. Sarah S....3000 Elim avenue, Zion City, Illinois
Howell, J. M....Henleyville, California
Hull, John Wellington....Connersville, Indiana
Keller, John Emil....Elijah Hospice, Zion City, Illinois
Kohr, Mrs. Hettie....Pueblo, Colorado
Laing, Mrs. Catherine....2606 Elim avenue, Zion City, Illinois
Lake, William Henry....Omro, Wisconsin
Lamberger, Oscar I....Elijah Hospice, Zion City, Illinois
Lavarnz, Matilda....2712 Gabriel avenue, Zion City, Illinois
Lawson, Mrs. Hattie....Indianapolis, Indiana
Leitch, Mrs. Sarah F....Maiden Rock, Wisconsin
Mayhak, Mrs. Matilda....Spencer, South Dakota
Maynard, Edward Alphonso....Viola, Illinois
Nagle, Miss Ruby....Auburn, Indiana
Neff, Miles W....3117 Enoch avenue, Zion City, Illinois
Peet, Miss Martha E....Delphos, Kansas
Price, Mrs. Lutitia E....North Yakima, Washington
Putnam, Frank L....506 Franklin street, Decorah, Iowa
Reinecke, Meta Margreta....Roberts, Illinois
Roberts, Miss Ethel....2911 Emmaus avenue, Zion City, Illinois
Rodda, Miss Ruth Mildred....318 Forest avenue, West Detroit, Michigan
Schmidt, Carl....2920 Enoch avenue, Zion City, Illinois
Schwalm, J. H....Yates Center, Kansas
Sengewald, Miss Josephine....Geneseo, Illinois
Shaw, Miss Margaret....Collins, Ohio
Smith, Miss Lottie Jane....Plymouth, Indiana
Smith, Miss Pearl....Ivanhoe, Illinois
Snider, Miss Sarah Ann....Drysdale, Ontario, Canada
Spooner, Mrs Mary E....Havana, North Dakota
Stanley, Mrs. O. L....122 Fourth street, Waukegan, Illinois
Swanson, Mrs. J. P....Shabbona, Illinois
Tarbox, Thomas N....Cedarville, Ohio
Tessmer, Metha....2712 Gabriel avenue, Zion City, Illinois
Thurlow, Miss Gladys....2816 Elizabeth avenue, Zion City, Illinois
Turner, Mrs. Emmeline....Viroqua, Wisconsin
Varnum, Mrs. Susan....Centerville, South Dakota
Weller, Mrs. Mary E....Streator, Illinois
Williams, Mrs. Benjamin F....West Pullman, Illinois
Wyrick, Mrs. Swereldia....Knobnoster, Missouri

The following-named fifty-five believers were baptized in Shiloh Tabernacle, Zion City, Illinois, Monday, July 18, 1904, by Overseer J. G. Excell:

Alexander, Mrs. Eunice Maria....Winnebago, (State omitted)
Asplin, Chester....3021 Gabriel avenue, Zion City, Illinois
Bailey, Miss Susie....Dodgeville, Wisconsin
Bishop, Mr. C. R....Conklin, Michigan
Bishop, Mrs. C. R....Conklin, Michigan
Blanks, Miss Annie Elizabeth....2114 Enoch avenue, Zion City, Illinois
Boal, Miss Esther Carrie....Hobart, Indiana
Boggan, Miss Hattie....Tupelo, Mississippi
Brodt, Mrs. H. M. W....Davenport, Iowa
Clark, Miss Mary M....Cambridge, Illinois
Copeland, John W....Zion City, Illinois
Cowing, Mrs. Delcena....Winnebago City, Minnesota
Crouch, John G....Side View, Kentucky
Erdman, Friedrich W. A....Abrams, Wisconsin
Escher, Mrs. Marie Elizabeth....Zion City, Illinois
Eyre, Miss Jane....Darlington, Oklahoma Territory
Farrer, Samuel....2915 Gilead avenue, Zion City, Illinois
Fox, Miss Florence Anna....Fostoria, Ohio
Freeman, Florence....3212 Gabriel avenue, Zion City, Illinois
Fuller, Miss Lee Aura....2202 Emmaus avenue, Zion City, Illinois
Gilbert, Miss Laura E....2712 Gabriel avenue, Zion City, Illinois
Grout, Miss Pearl....3103 Eshcol avenue, Zion City, Illinois
Gubser, Robert A....Gering, Nebraska
Hammond, Miss Lizzie....Viroqua, Wisconsin
Hoodelmier, Howard C....Auburn, Indiana
Ickowsky, Jakob P....173 East Ninety-sixth street, New York City
Jasper, Miss Ethel M....Wiarton, Ontario, Canada
Kendrick, Miss Gladys....St. John, California
Lamberger, Mrs. Georgia....Elijah Hospice, Zion City, Illinois
Lindem, Mrs. G. O....Marinette, Wisconsin
Loucer, Mrs. Rachel....Streator, Illinois
Low, George....Dundee, Scotland
(Now 150 Tenth avenue, Camp Esther, Zion City, Illinois.)
McDuffie, Mrs. M....1007 Bartlett street, Milwaukee, Wisconsin
McGinnes, Mrs. Eliza....Elwood, Indiana
Matson, Jerome....3000 Elisha avenue, Zion City, Illinois
Nagle, Miss Ada....Auburn, Indiana
Nagle, Mrs. Mary....Auburn, Indiana
Narber, Mrs. Sarah....Sturgis, Michigan
Neff, Miss Ada B....3117 Enoch avenue, Zion City, Illinois
Neff, Miss Chloe M....3117 Enoch avenue, Zion City, Illinois
Neff, S. M....3117 Enoch avenue, Zion City, Illinois
Neff, Miss Zella May....3117 Enoch avenue, Zion City, Illinois
Nichols, Mrs. Hulda E....Cambridge, Illinois
Noomen, Miss Cornelia Viola....Orange City, Iowa
Rebmann, Christian....23 Cherry street, Buffalo, New York
Rofka, Fred....Zion City, Illinois
Sepin, Mrs. Anna....Connersville, Indiana
Stevens, Mrs. Minnie....Bingham, Michigan
Swihart, Mrs. Anna....Brighton, Indiana
Tarbox, Mrs. Maggie....Cedarville, Ohio
Tessmer, Gustav....2712 Gabriel avenue, Zion City, Illinois
Trask, Mrs. E. G....Quitman, Louisiana
Underwood, James Robert....Hoisington, Kansas
Warszawiak, Miss Evelyn....Elijah Hospice, Zion City, Illinois
Woodworth, William Potter....Bristow, Iowa

The following-named forty believers were baptized in Shiloh Tabernacle, Zion City, Illinois, Monday, July 18, 1904, by Overseer W. H. Piper:

Allen, Miss Maggie....Sheridan road, Zion City, Illinois
Back, William....Napoleon, Ohio
Bevitt, Miss Henrietta J....Madison, Wisconsin
Callow, Mrs. Lou....Cobb, Wisconsin
Cameron, Mrs. Martha....423 Hawley avenue, Syracuse, New York
Cole, Mrs. Betsie....Northwood, Iowa
Crooks, Mrs. Alice....Pekin, Illinois
Doneth, Mrs. Emma Caroline....2114 Eshcol avenue, Zion City, Illinois
Ellingson, Mrs. Mary....Des Moines, Iowa
Froos, Mrs. Johanna Christina....6131 Wilson avenue, St. Louis, Missouri
Hann, Mrs. Adah Z....Farnam, Nebraska
Hay, James....Gabriel avenue, Zion City, Illinois
Hire, Linval Justen....3006 Gabriel avenue, Zion City, Illinois
Howell, Mrs. Elizabeth....Henleyville, California
Hull, Mrs. Mariah F....Connersville, Indiana
Jackson, Von Cortland Columbus....Marquis, Georgia
James, John W....2710 Emmaus avenue, Zion City, Illinois
James, Mrs. Lula....2710 Emmaus avenue, Zion City, Illinois
Johnson, Mrs. Martha....McFarland, Wisconsin
Kelchner, Deacon C. F....229 Hodge avenue, Cleveland, Ohio
Lawrence, Miss Bessie....Thornton, Iowa
Miller, Mrs. Candice C....Ames, Iowa
Moller, George P....Hagerstown, Maryland
Morris, Mrs. Rebecca A....Porter, Indiana
Neff, Mrs. Josephine....3117 Enoch avenue, Zion City, Illinois
Neff, Roy....3117 Enoch avenue, Zion City, Illinois
Northcutt, Mrs. Frances R....New Trenton, Indiana
Phillips, Hubert....Marengo, Ohio
Plumb, Charles F....Clarkston, Michigan
Plumb, Mrs. Mary E....Clarkston, Michigan
Powell, Mary....2700 Ezekiel avenue, Zion City, Illinois
Rowland, Mrs. Genevieve....512 West Main street, Madison, Wisconsin
Shaw, Mrs. Almina B....Collins, Ohio
Tessmer, Karoline....2712 Gabriel avenue, Zion City, Illinois
Tessmer, Richard....2712 Gabriel avenue, Zion City, Illinois
Thurlow, Mrs. Addie....2816 Elizabeth avenue, Zion City, Illinois
Tigner, Charles F....Cambridge, Ohio
Tudor, Roy E....DeKalb, Illinois
Wagner, Miles....Bradford, Pennsylvania
Woodworth, Mrs. Jane....Bristow, Iowa

CONSECRATION OF CHILDREN.

The following-named twenty-eight children were consecrated to God, at Wakkerstroom, Transvaal, South Africa, Friday, May 13, 1904, by Overseer Daniel Bryant:

Alexander, Dorie....Wakkerstroom, Transvaal, South Africa
Alexander, Izak....Wakkerstroom, Transvaal, South Africa
Alexander, Piet....Wakkerstroom, Transvaal, South Africa
Hadebe, Joseph....Wakkerstroom, Transvaal, South Africa
Hlatshwayo, Essie....Wakkerstroom, Transvaal, South Africa
Hlatshwayo, Jeanie....Wakkerstroom, Transvaal, South Africa
Hlatshwayo, Solomon....Wakkerstroom, Transvaal, South Africa
Hlatshwayo, Thomas....Wakkerstroom, Transvaal, South Africa
Hlatshwayo, Zebedia....Wakkerstroom, Transvaal, South Africa
Kubheka, Naphthali....Wakkerstroom, Transvaal, South Africa
Kumalo, Willie....Wakkerstroom, Transvaal, South Africa
Mabuza, Jael....Wakkerstroom, Transvaal, South Africa
Mabuza, Maria....Wakkerstroom, Transvaal, South Africa
Mabuza, Merika....Wakkerstroom, Transvaal, South Africa
Masimula, Bella....Wakkerstroom, Transvaal, South Africa
Masimula, Essie....Wakkerstroom, Transvaal, South Africa
Masimula, Jacob....Wakkerstroom, Transvaal, South Africa
Masimula, Nellie....Wakkerstroom, Transvaal, South Africa
Masuku, Lina....Wakkerstroom, Transvaal, South Africa
Mtembu, Andrina....Wakkerstroom, Transvaal, South Africa
Ngomezulu, Julia....Wakkerstroom, Transvaal, South Africa
Nkonyane, Jeanie....Wakkerstroom, Transvaal, South Africa
Nkonyane, Josina....Wakkerstroom, Transvaal, South Africa
Nkonyane, Mateu....Wakkerstroom, Transvaal, South Africa
Nkonyane, Stefane....Wakkerstroom, Transvaal, South Africa
Seagwayo, Jessie....Wakkerstroom, Transvaal, South Africa
Sitole, Esther....Wakkerstroom, Transvaal, South Africa
Tshabalala, David....Wakkerstroom, Transvaal, South Africa

The following-named three children were consecrated to God in the North Side Zion Tabernacle, Chicago, Illinois, Lord's Day, July 3, 1904, by Elder J. R. Keller:

Dittman, Clarence W....3105 Enoch avenue, Zion City, Illinois
Mifflin, Royal Herr Smith....509 Webster avenue, Chicago, Illinois
Reis, Grace E....470 Berwyn avenue, Chicago, Illinois

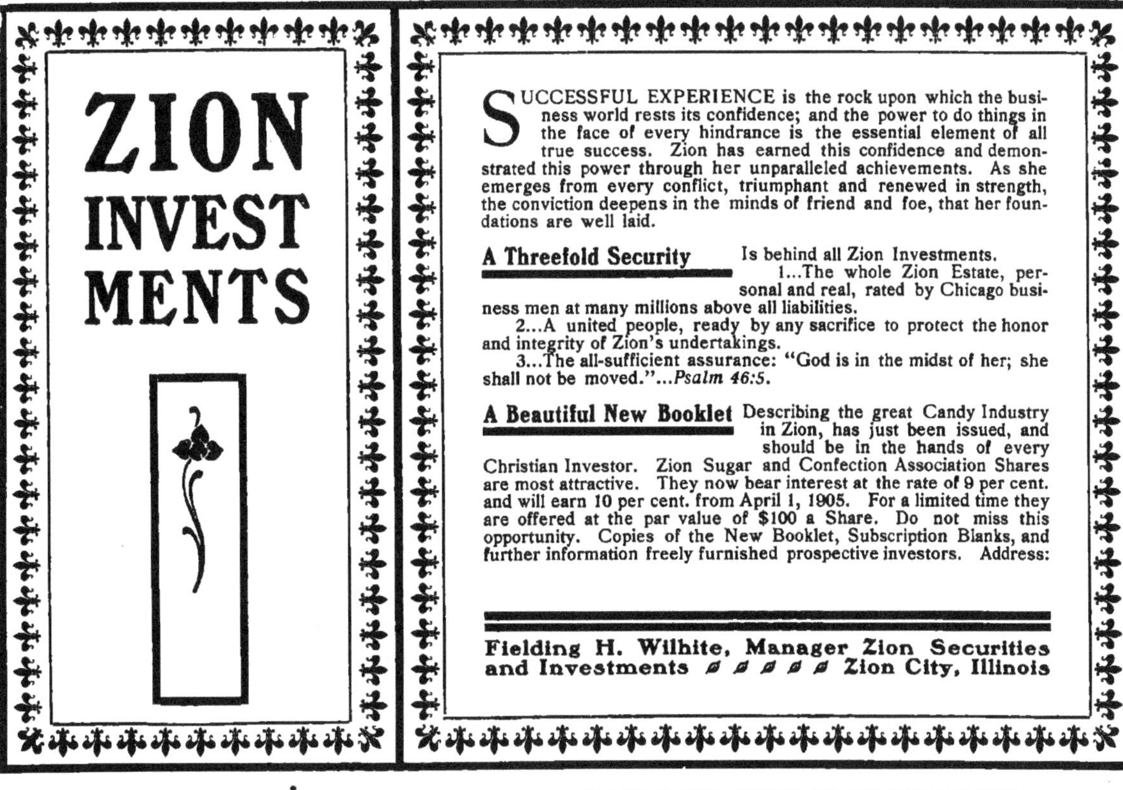

ZION CITY BANK

JOHN ALEX. DOWIE

ZION CITY, LAKE COUNTY, ILLINOIS, U. S. A.

Transacts a general Banking Business.

Issues Drafts payable in all the principal cities of the world.

Sells high-grade Securities bearing nine per cent. interest per annum. Particulars mailed on application.

Our Savings Department receives deposits from One Dollar upward, and pays interest at the following rates:

On all sums from $1 to $500, four per cent.

On all sums over $500, three per cent.

This Bank encourages thrift and economy among the people, and will assist them in their efforts to save money.

Our system of Banking by Mail has proved entirely satisfactory to thousands of persons living in different parts of this and other countries. It places everybody in close communication with the Bank and enables them to take advantage of the *excellent facilities* offered.

Correspondence from all parts of the world solicited.

Write for our booklet entitled, "Saving Money."

CHARLES J. BARNARD, Manager.
WILLIAM S. PECKHAM, Cashier.
CHARLES H. IRISH, Assistant Cashier.

LEAVES OF HEALING

Edited by REV. JOHN ALEXANDER DOWIE General Overseer of the Christian Catholic Church in Zion.

A 32-PAGE WEEKLY PAPER

For the Extension of the Kingdom of God. Contains Sermons, Addresses, and Editorial Notes by the General Overseer; Testimonies to Healing through Faith in Jesus, and Reports of Zion's Work Throughout the World.

Price, a year, $2.00

THE ZION BANNER

Edited by REV. JOHN ALEXANDER DOWIE General Overseer of the Christian Catholic Church in Zion . . .

A WEEKLY NEWSPAPER

For the Extension of the Kingdom of God and the Elevation of Man. Deals with Social, Commercial, Political, and Industrial Problems. News from all over the World reliably reported. Notes on progress in the building up of Zion City. *Subscription Price, 50c for 6 months.* Address, General Manager Zion Printing and Publishing House, Zion City, Illinois, U. S. A.

Train Schedule Between Zion City and Chicago

Via Chicago & North-Western Railway.

Effective May 22, 1904.

Weekday Trains.

CHICAGO TO ZION CITY. Leave Chicago	Arrive Zion City	ZION CITY TO CHICAGO. Leave Zion City	Arrive Chicago
7.00 a. m.	8.25 a. m.	*6.45 a. m.	8.15 a. m.
*9.00 a. m.	10.13 a. m.	7.03 a. m.	8.30 a. m
*11.30 a. m.	12.37 p. m.	8.22 a. m.	9.50 a. m.
2.00 p. m.	3.08 p. m.	*9.45 a. m.	11.10 a. m.
3.00 p. m	4 16 p. m.	*11 49 a. m.	1.15 p m
4.15 p. m.	5.39 p. m.	*‖1.18 p. m.	2.50 p. m.
*5.20 p. m.	6.50 p. m.	*†2.33 p. m.	4.00 p. m.
*8.00 p. m.	9.11 p. m.	5.05 p. m.	6.30 p. m.
		*7.59 p. m.	9.30 p. m.

Sunday Trains.

CHICAGO TO ZION CITY. Leave Chicago	Arrive Zion City
9 05 a. m.	10.18 a. m.
*10.45 a. m.	12.37 p. m.
2.15 p. m.	4.05 p. m.
*8.00 p. m.	9.11 p. m.

ZION CITY TO CHICAGO. Leave Zion City	Arrive Chicago
*8.29 a. m.	9.45 a. m.
5 05 p. m.	6.40 p. m.
7.59 p. m.	9.30 p. m.

Train leaves Waukegan at 12.28 p. m., arriving in Zion City at 12.37 p. m., daily, including Sunday.

* Signifies change train at Waukegan. † Train does not run South on Saturdays.
‖ Train runs South on Saturday only.

ZION'S TRANSPORTATION AND RAILWAY AFFAIRS (John Alex. Dowie), of Zion City, Illinois, supervises the railway ticket, steamship, excursion, freight, express and transfer business of Zion and her people everywhere. Direction as to railroad and steamship routes given upon request.

DEACON JAMES F. PETERS,
General Superintendent Zion Transportation.

Whose Fan is in His Hand!

I INDEED baptize you with water unto repentance: but He that cometh after me is mightier than I, whose shoes I am not worthy to bear: He shall baptize you with the Holy Spirit and with fire: **Whose fan is in His Hand,** and He will thoroughly cleanse His threshing-floor; and He will gather His wheat into the garner, but the chaff He will burn up with unquenchable fire.—*Matthew 3:11, 12.*

Whose fan is in His Hand, thoroughly to cleanse His threshing-floor, and to gather the wheat into His garner; but the chaff He will burn up with unquenchable fire. With many other exhortations therefore preached He Good Tidings unto the people.—*Luke 3:17, 18.*

AS WE look at the photograph of the Fan, consisting of the ORDAINED OFFICERS, WHITE-ROBED CHOIR, ZION BAND, ZION RESTORATION HOST and ZION GUARD, led by our **BELOVED GENERAL OVERSEER,** *how forcibly this prophecy of John the Baptist concerning the Christ comes to us, as we see the wheat separated from the chaff as a result of the work done in His Name by His united force! The threshing-floor is being cleansed, the chaff burned, and the wheat prepared for use.*

Leaves of Healing Causes a division at once between those who will serve God and those who will not, and is a great dynamic force for publishing the Good Tidings and extending the Kingdom of God.

Those who are most successful in garnering the wheat, send forth the ***LEAVES OF HEALING*** *and* ***THE ZION BANNER*** *most freely.*

How much can the Christ use you in this work?

The Subscription rates to Leaves of Healing are:

One Year,	*$2.00*	*Three Months,*	*$0.75*
Six Months,	*1.25*	*Single Copies,*	*.05*

For Twenty-five Cents

We will send a Trial Subscription to "Leaves of Healing" for Ten Weeks.

Our Inducement

"They that turn many to righteousness shall shine as the stars forever and ever."

WITH ILLUSTRATED SUPPLEMENT.

A WEEKLY PAPER FOR THE EXTENSION OF THE KINGDOM OF GOD
EDITED BY THE REV. JOHN ALEX. DOWIE.

Volume XV. No. 15. *ZION CITY, SATURDAY, JULY 30, 1904.* *Price Five Cents*

GOD'S WITNESSES TO DIVINE HEALING.

HEALED WHEN DYING OF SEVERE STOMACH TROUBLE AND OTHER DISEASES.

GOD BE MERCIFUL UNTO US, AND BLESS US, AND CAUSE THY FACE TO SHINE UPON US; THAT THY WAY MAY BE KNOWN UPON EARTH, THY SAVING HEALTH AMONG ALL NATIONS.

With these beautiful words the General Overseer of the Christian Catholic Church in Zion has invoked the blessing of God upon the services which he has conducted in many parts of the world.

Thousands can testify that God has most surely poured out His blessings upon these services.

From every continent, and from almost every nation, the witnesses have come to Zion.

They declare that God has been merciful, and caused His face to shine upon them.

They know that God's Saving Health has been given for the body as well as His Salvation for the spirit.

God's Way is being made known upon the earth.

The mercy of God, manifested to the witnesses in Zion, is a mercy which has touched the whole being. It has saved them from sin, healed them from diseases, and given them power to live Godly lives.

They have been taught how to pray. They have found The Way. What the world needs to know is God's Way. Multitudes think that either there is no God or that He cares nothing for them, but it is simply because they have not been taught how to find Him. In their ignorance, and darkness, and sin men are seeking after they scarcely know what. Really, they seek Divine help, but how to get it they do not know:

Oh, how shall I, whose native sphere
Is dark, whose mind is dim,
Before the ineffable appear,
And on my naked spirit bear
That uncreated beam?

MR. AND MRS. ALBERT BARY.

Unless God had provided the Way, and sent men filled with the Spirit to plead with men to turn to the Way, it would certainly be dark. But the beautiful words are true:

There is a way for man to rise,
To that sublime abode,
An offering and a sacrifice,
A Holy Spirit's energy,
An advocate with God.

Jesus said, "I am the Way, the Truth, and the Life."

Zion has found it true.

It is recorded that He is "touched with the feeling of our infirmities."

Zion has experienced His sympathy.

It is also written, "Jesus, the Christ, is the same yesterday, and today, and forever."

In Zion, the witnesses rise and say, "It is true."

But the apostate churches have been almost altogether declaring the gospel of "saving sickness," and not until God sent His Messenger of the

Covenant and the Restorer, did the light begin to dawn in any great measure as to the fulness of the Atonement and the completeness of the Gospel.

God has wonderfully used John Alexander Dowie in declaring the Gospel of "Saving Health," and the people of God have arisen with new faith and hope and trust in their Heavenly Father.

In reading the testimonies of the two witnesses whose stories follow these words, we get a little glimpse of how God used His servant, John Alexander Dowie, when he was in Switzerland in 1900.

He faithfully declared the Everlasting Covenants of God, and the people were blessed, and went out and told others.

The story is as usual—sick, dying, trusting doctors, and believing that was God's way.

But, "nothing bettered," at last they are given the Word of God as it has come from God's servant, Elijah the Restorer. It brings them to the Way, and they get the blessings of God in spirit, soul, and body.

Now they write the words, which tell another story. They are saved, healed, and, the husband says,

I have not touched any medicine since then, and I am in good health and working hard.

Once more the servant of God has proclaimed the Messages God has given him in Switzerland, and who can tell how far-reaching will be the truth which has been sent forth?

Will not the Church of the Living God pause in its forgetfulness, and listen to the Messages God is giving in these Latter Days?

Will she not repent and declare the Full Salvation and the "Saving Health" there is in God?

Whether the apostate churches receive the Messages of truth or not, let all true Christians in and out of the churches glorify God for His revelation and His love and mercy manifested in these "Times of the Restoration of All Things."

Let us seek the face of God and live for Him, and seek to know His will, so that in spirit, soul, and body we shall be prepared for the Coming of our Lord and King.

Little White Dove, hasten on with your Messages, that the "knowledge of Jehovah may cover the earth as the waters cover the sea."

That Thy Way may be known upon earth,
Thy Saving Health among all nations.

J. G. S.

WRITTEN TESTIMONY OF ALBERT BARY.

285 First Avenue, Milwaukee, Wisconsin,
April 25, 1904.

Dear General Overseer:—In gratitude to God for what He has done for my wife and me, I desire to send you my testimony.

I feel that I should have done so sooner, but there was a little fear in my heart that the extremely cold climate of this country would cause my troubles to return.

I thank God that at the close of this severe winter, the coldest that I have ever experienced, I am in excellent health.

It is now almost four years since, in answer to your prayer, God instantaneously healed me of a terrible bladder disease and stomach trouble, from both of which I had suffered for eleven years.

In the year 1889, I was appointed assistant manager of a large machine shop in Budapest, Hungary.

I was so zealous in my work that I neglected to take proper care of my body.

Soon I complained of stomach trouble and pains all through my internal organs.

I consulted a number of the best physicians, obeying their instructions, as well as trying many other remedies.

Not one of the many doctors who treated me did me any good; and one of them succeeded in persuading me to have an operation performed.

After the operation, I was at the point of death.

My wife came to see me, and became so frightened that she fainted.

For a few moments the nurses did not know which of us needed the more care.

God in His great mercy spared my life, and some time after the operation I was able to resume my work.

However, I was far from being well, and I kept on taking medicine.

I did all I could to recover, and we prayed to God as well as we knew how; but it was all in vain; and in 1896 I consented to have another operation.

I told my wife to prepare for the worst. I thought that it could not be any harder for her to have me die under the operation than to see me suffer continually. I said that such a life was not worth living.

To be sure that the physician, who performed the operation, should do all he could to save my life, my wife offered him more money than he asked.

He refused, saying that I was beyond all human help.

After the operation was performed, my wife took me home that I might die there and not at the hospital.

As I lay on my bed of suffering, we read in the Bible of the wonderful things God had wrought through the hands of the apostles.

I wept until my pillow was wet, and I said, "Why have we not believers today, who can pray the Prayer of Faith for the sick?"

It was at this time that a friend gave my wife a copy of Blätter der Heilung.

She said to me, "Mrs. N—— has brought us a Catholic paper, which contains testimonies of Divine Healing. Do you think these things can be really true?"

I replied, "If it is a Catholic paper, you must not read it, because it cannot be true."

She obeyed and laid it aside.

But she picked it up the next day, and did her best to draw my attention to what she was reading.

We rejoiced to find that it was not a Roman Catholic paper, but Christian Catholic, and we read it from cover to cover.

Then we went to our Bible and compared very carefully to see if it was really true.

Our hearts and minds were convinced of the truth that sickness is the work of the Devil, and that we were apostate Christians, our pastors included.

We were at that time members of what was considered the most spiritual church in Budapest—the Evangelical Reform church.

Our minister had always consoled us with the words, "Whom the Lord loveth He chasteneth."

I went to church whenever I was able, and I was sometimes proud at the thought that the Lord still loved me and sent me sickness.

But now, after reading that copy of Blätter der Heilung, we saw that God would heal me if I had faith.

God used our old friend, Professor W. Möse, (now living in Zion City) to teach us how to get this faith.

I gave up doctors and drugs, and he wrote to you to pray for me.

God heard and answered your prayer, and He healed me of my diseases.

I have not touched any medicine since then; and I am in good health and working hard.

Luther and Spurgeon were great and good men, but they could not give as much light on the Word of God as we get from you, dear General Overseer.

I thank God for bringing me back from the verge of the grave, and for counting me worthy to become a member of the Christian Catholic Church in Zion. I believe that He will let me live long that I may be a living witness to His saving, healing and keeping power.

Praying God to spare your life for many years to come, and thanking you for your prayers, I am,

Your brother in the Christ, Albert Bary.

WRITTEN TESTIMONY OF MRS. KAROLINE BARY.

285 First Avenue, Milwaukee, Wisconsin,
April 25, 1904.

Dear General Overseer:—It is with joy and gratitude that I take the opportunity to add my testimony to that of my husband.

God has done great things for me, and with the Psalmist I can say, "Bless the Lord, O my soul, who forgiveth all thy iniquities, who healeth all thy diseases."

Since we have been reading Blätter der Heilung, the Bible has become a new Book to us.

It is true that we both had godly parents, who brought us up in the fear of the Lord, and as far as they understood, taught us to pray.

But whenever one of the family became sick, we went to the doctor, and looked to him for help.

I had a great deal to do with doctors and drugs, being weakly from childhood, and suffering from enlarged tonsils.

The doctors wanted to cut them out, but I never consented, because I had a horror of the thought of an operation, and could not endure the sight of blood.

I had attacks of sickness very often, and each time the tonsils would swell up, which brought on a high fever.

I suffered more than I am able to tell.

It is now three years since I had the last attack.

It was the worst one I ever had, but I did not send for the doctor, as usual.

A brother from the Baptist church, who had attended your meetings in Zürich during your mission there in December of 1900, came and prayed for me.

I was relieved from pain at once, but during the night I grew much worse.

Then my husband prayed for me, but we received no answer from God, because there was fear in my heart.

My throat was practically closed up, and in my anguish I yielded to the Devil, and reached for the glass of vinegar to gargle my throat.

In doing so, I upset the glass and spilled its contents.

Not being able to utter a sound, I could not tell my husband that I wanted him to pray for me again. I took hold of his arm and shook it hard.

He understood, and immediately got on his knees.

Very earnestly he asked God to forgive me, and to deliver me from the power of the Devil.

While he was yet praying, I started to cough, and at the same moment my swollen tonsils broke open.

All pain was gone, and my throat was perfectly clean. I was able to eat at once. For two weeks previously milk had been the only thing I was able to swallow.

To the glory of God I can say that since that time I have not had the slightest return of this disease.

God has also healed me of bowel trouble.

For eighteen years I suffered beyond description, and often in my anguish I sinned by saying, "If God is a God of Love, why does He send me such a terrible disease?"

Oh how blind we were to believe that God makes sick those whom He loves!

We praise God for having sent us His prophet to teach us the Full Gospel, and to show so clearly that God is not the Author of sickness and disease.

Through this glorious teaching God has saved us from the verge of the grave, and we thank you, dear General Overseer, with all our hearts, for your prayers on our behalf.

I pray that this testimony may help many suffering ones to turn to God for help and deliverance, and that it may be a blessing to all who shall read it.

Your sister in the Christ,

(MRS.) KAROLINE BARY.

IS ANY among you sick? let him call for the Elders of the Church; and let them pray over him, anointing him with oil in the Name of the Lord: And the Prayer of Faith shall save him that is sick, and the Lord shall raise him up; and if he have committed sins, it shall be forgiven him.—*James 5:14, 15.*

How beautiful upon the mountains are the feet of him that bringeth good tidings, that publisheth peace, that bringeth good tidings of good, that publisheth salvation; that saith unto Zion, Thy God Reigneth!—*Isaiah 52:7.*

Notes of Thanksgiving From the Whole World

By Overseer J. G. Excell, General Ecclesiastical Secretary.

Healed of Severe Burn.

The exceeding greatness of His power to usward who believe, according to that working of the strength of His might.—*Ephesians 1:19.*

LEEDS, YORKSHIRE, ENGLAND.

DEAR GENERAL OVERSEER:—Peace to thee.

With gratitude to God and to you for the teaching I have received through LEAVES OF HEALING, I send you my testimony.

I was a member of the Methodist church for twenty-two years, but for some time was dissatisfied on account of the worldliness which had crept in, and for the lack of spiritual food therein.

I praise God for the blessings and healings I have received during the two years I have been in the Christian Catholic Church in Zion.

It has been the most blessed period of my Christian life.

A short time ago I scalded my finger in boiling fat.

The pain was almost unbearable.

I asked God to forgive me and take away the pain and heal my finger.

He did.

In four hours there was not a mark to be seen on it.

I give God all the praise.

Praying that God will continue to bless you in your labor of love for suffering humanity, I am,

Yours in the Master's service,

(MRS.) CATHERINE HOWARD.

Delivered in Childbirth.

Commit Thy way unto Jehovah,
Trust also in Him,
And He shall bring it to pass.—*Psalm 37:5.*

SAN FRANCISCO, CALIFORNIA,
1845 MARKET STREET, March 28, 1904.

DEAR OVERSEER SPEICHER:—I feel that I must write to give my testimony to the wonderful deliverance through the mercy of our dear Father in heaven.

On March 13th I was delivered of a beautiful ten-pound Zion girl.

I was awakened at fifteen minutes past one in the morning, and the babe was born at three.

I was alone with my mother at the time of the birth.

God wonderfully cared for the bowels in answer to prayer; also in blessing and keeping us.

My husband and I join in giving God all the honor and glory.

I sincerely hope this testimony will be a blessing to other mothers, and help them to trust God.

Your sister in the Christ,

(MRS.) JULIA RAYMOND.

Little Boy Healed of Growth on Neck.

O fear Jehovah, ye His saints:
For there is no want to them that fear Him.—*Psalm 34:9.*

6097 LOOMIS STREET,
CHICAGO, ILLINOIS, March 27, 1904.

DEAR OVERSEER SPEICHER:—Some time ago I wrote you asking you to pray for my little boy and me.

He had a growth on his neck about the size of a goose egg.

At times he could hardly get his breath.

The growth was hard and solid.

It was not sore to the touch, but at times it would pain him badly in the night, causing him to cry.

A doctor who saw the child, said we ought to send him to the hospital; that the growth was a collection of matter, and would have to be cut out.

He said it was his only hope, and that he was too fine a boy to neglect that way.

We told him that we did not neglect him; that we had him in the best of hands, and we feared no evil.

He asked, "Whose hands?"

I said, "In God's."

He became angry and said that he was going to have us arrested if we caused that child to die.

We agreed to write and ask you to pray and ask God to destroy the works of the Devil, and he was instantly healed.

The growth is gone, and he breathes freely.

Thank God for that!

(MRS.) JENNIE ROGERS.

Prayer Answered for Temporal Blessings.

But seek ye first His Kingdom,
And His righteousness
And all these things shall be added unto you.—*Matthew 6:33.*

305 AUGUSTA AVENUE,
DEKALB, ILLINOIS, April 5, 1904.

DEAR OVERSEER SPEICHER:—I write to tell you that your prayers are answered.

Our boarding-house is full of roomers and every seat at the tables is taken by the finest lot of students we have ever had.

We thank you so much for the interest you have taken, and we give God all the glory.

How wonderful is His condescending love and His care for our minutest affairs!

Pray for us that our influence may be just what it should be in this place.

Your sister in the Christ,

(MRS.) ANNA A. DORWIN.

Healed of Swelling on Side of Face.

O Jehovah, my God, I cried unto Thee, and Thou hast healed me.—*Psalm 30:2.*

ROSECRANS, ILLINOIS, April 1, 1904.

DEAR OVERSEER SPEICHER: I thank you for praying for me.

I was healed of a swelling on the side of my face and neck.

It was very painful and it made me very sick. I could not eat anything.

Mamma sent in a request asking you to pray for me, and in the afternoon the swelling began to go down.

I praise God for healing me, and thank you for your prayers.

Yours in Jesus' Name,

MARGARET NESMITHE.

Daughter Healed in Answer to Prayer of Faith.

Fear thou not, for I am with thee;
Be not dismayed, for I am thy God:
I will strengthen thee;
Yea, I will help thee;
Yea, I will uphold thee with the right hand of My righteousness.—*Isaiah 41:10.*

BOX 161, LAKE FOREST, ILLINOIS,
April 6, 1904.

DEAR OVERSEER SPEICHER:—I received your letter yesterday stating that you had prayed for our little daughter, Myrtle.

God has heard and answered, and to Him be ascribed all the praise and glory forever.

Thanking you for your prayers, I remain,

Your brother in the Christ,

ARTHUR WAGTAFF.

A WEEKLY PAPER FOR THE EXTENSION OF THE KINGDOM OF GOD.

EDITED BY THE REV. JOHN ALEX. DOWIE.

Application for entry as Second Class Matter at Zion City, Illinois, pending.

Subscription Rates.		Special Rates.	
One Year	$2.00	100 Copies of One Issue	$3.00
Six Months	1.25	25 Copies of One Issue	1.00
Three Months	.75	To Ministers, Y. M. C. A's and Public	
Single Copies	.05	Reading Rooms, per annum	1.50

For foreign subscriptions add $1.50 per year, or three cents per copy for postage.

Subscribers desiring a change of address should give present address, as well as that to which they desire LEAVES OF HEALING sent in the future.

Make Bank Drafts, Express Money or Postoffice Money Orders payable to the order of JOHN ALEX. DOWIE, Zion City, Illinois, U. S. A.

Long Distance Telephone. *Cable Address "Dowie, Zion City."*

All communications upon business must be addressed to
MANAGER ZION PUBLISHING HOUSE,
Zion City, Illinois, U. S. A.

Subscriptions to LEAVES OF HEALING, A VOICE FROM ZION, and the various publications may also be sent to

ZION PUBLISHING HOUSE, 81 EUSTON ROAD, LONDON, N. W., ENGLAND.
ZION PUBLISHING HOUSE, NO. 43 PARK ROAD, ST. KILDA, MELBOURNE, VICTORIA, AUSTRALIA.
ZION PUBLISHING HOUSE, RUE DE MONT, THABOR 1, PARIS, FRANCE.
ZIONSHEIM, SCHLOSS LIEBBURG, CANTON THURGAU, BEI ZÜRICH, SWITZERLAND.

ZION CITY, ILLINOIS, SATURDAY, JULY 30, 1904.

TABLE OF CONTENTS.

LEAVES OF HEALING, SATURDAY, JULY 30, 1904.

EDITORIAL NOTES.

"ARISE AND THRESH, O DAUGHTER OF ZION."

FOR I will make thine Horn iron,
And I will make thy Hoofs brass:
And thou shalt beat in pieces many peoples:
And thou shalt devote their Gain unto Jehovah,
And their Substance unto Jehovah of the whole earth.

BEYOND ALL question, the Threshing of the Harvest of all the Nations has begun.

FOR OUT of Zion shall go forth the Law,
And the Word of Jehovah from Jerusalem.
And He shall judge between many peoples,
And shall reprove strong nations afar off;
And they shall beat their swords into plow-shares,
And their spears into pruning-hooks:
Nation shall not lift up sword against nation,
Neither shall they learn war any more.
. . . .
For all the peoples will walk every one in the name of his god,
And we will walk in the Name of Jehovah, our God, forever and ever.

THESE BLESSED times of Universal Peace shall come; but the threshing must first come, and God is preparing His thresher.

FEAR NOT, thou worm Jacob,
And ye men of Israel;
I will help thee, saith Jehovah,
And thy Redeemer is the Holy One of Israel.
Behold, I will make thee a New Sharp Threshing Instrument having teeth;
Thou shalt thresh the mountains, and beat them small,
And shalt make the hills as chaff.
Thou shalt fan them, and the wind shall carry them away,
And the whirlwind shall scatter them:
And thou shalt rejoice in Jehovah,
Thou shalt glory in the Holy One of Israel.

ZION, REFRESHED and strengthened by her glorious Fourth Feast of Tabernacles, is going forth into the Harvest Field of the World.

Glorious will be the Reaping in many parts of the earth.

ZION HAS obeyed the command of her King, and has been diligently taking out the tares, binding them in bundles, and casting them into the Fire of Divine Indignation.

Zion has not spared any known evil, nor shunned to declare the whole counsel of God.

WE ARE conscious, therefore, of a great increase in Divine Equipment for Service.

The "teeth" of the "threshing instrument" are sharp, and the Harvest is, in many places, almost overripe.

IT BEHOOVES all in Zion, therefore, to "arise and thresh." The great Harvest of Golden Grain is ready to be winnowed from the chaff and straw, and gathered into the Threshing Floor of God.

SINCE THE closing of Zion's Fourth Feast of Tabernacles, last Lord's Day evening, we have been engaged, day and night, in cleaning up the Threshing Floor.

TRULY THE Master's "Fan" is "in His hand," and He will thoroughly cleanse His Threshing Floor.

All that is unclean must be taken away from the Threshing Floor ere the Precious Grain, which has just been threshed out, is harvested therein.

NEW CONVERTS never can be blessed in an unclean church.

The ecclesiastical weevil has eaten out the spirituality of the Apostasies, and utterly corrupts the new harvest.

All the destroying parasites must be taken away.

THE PROCESS of Purification in Zion still continues.

It will also continue throughout all the days and years to come; for "the price of safety is eternal vigilance."

WE ASK the earnest prayers of all everywhere who are true to God, that we may be able to keep the Christian Catholic Church in Zion clean from all known pollution, in all its Branches throughout the world, and especially at its Headquarters in Zion City.

IT MIGHT be well for us at this point to note the Closing Assemblies of the Feast of Tabernacles, on Saturday, July 23d, and Lord's Day, July 24th.

THE MORNING SACRIFICE of Praise and Prayer, on Saturday, was attended by an immense audience, which listened with great interest to our address on "The Nine Gifts of the Spirit."

A pleasant and enjoyable day was spent by many thousands of Zion at the beautiful Lake Front, and in visits to the delightful Parks of the City.

In the afternoon, the healthful, happy games of Zion Junior and Senior Athletes, on their grounds on the northwest corner of Shiloh Park, afforded much innocent enjoyment.

AT TEN o'clock in the morning of that day we had a continuation of a most important Conference of the Ordained Officers of the Church, at which hundreds were present, and at which matters of the greatest importance to the welfare of the Church were most earnestly discussed.

The Conference, after remaining in session more than four hours, was adjourned to Monday, July 25th, at ten o'clock in the morning.

ACCOMPANIED BY Zion Band and the Staff Officers of Zion Guard, we paid a delightful visit on Saturday evening to Camp Esther, where we were very enthusiastically received by the many hundreds camping there, under the shade of the beautiful trees of Shiloh Grove.

BUT LORD'S DAY, July 24th, was truly the Crowning Day of the Feast.

FULLY SIX THOUSAND most earnest Worshipers were assembled in Shiloh Tabernacle at half past six o'clock in the morning, when we delivered our address on "The House of Wisdom."

AT HALF PAST nine o'clock in the morning we spoke on "Triune Immersion; God's Seal on a Living Church," and at the close we baptized one hundred sixty-five believers.

AT TWO O'CLOCK in the afternoon, the last great General Assembly of the Feast was held, when a full Processional of Zion Robed Officers and Zion White-robed Choir, and all members of Zion Junior Restoration Host, under their leader, Overseer Brasefield, gathered in the Grove, and were received by us at the door of the Tabernacle.

The sight was most inspiring.

When, after following at the end of the Processional, we stood upon the platform of the Tabernacle, facing the audience, we found there were more than seven thousand people present.

God greatly blessed us in the delivery of our address on "The Ministry of Children in Zion," and in the administration of the Vow of Junior Restoration Host to many new members.

IN THE evening, at eight o'clock, came the closing scenes of the never-to-be-forgotten Zion's Fourth Feast of Tabernacles.

WE ADMINISTERED the Ordinance of the Lord's Supper, and delivered the final address to a gathering of many thousands, and, at the end, we sang for our Closing Song the glorious words:

I stand on Zion's Mount,
And view my starry crown;
No power on earth my hope can shake,
Nor hell can thrust me down.

The lofty hills and towers,
That lift their heads on high,
Shall all be leveled low in dust—
Their very names shall die.

The vaulted heavens shall fall,
Built by Jehovah's hands;
But firmer than the heavens, the Rock
Of my Salvation stands.

"THE HALLELUJAH CHORUS," from Beethoven's "Mount of Olives," was then sung by the Choir, the Benediction was pronounced, and the Feast was ended.

IT IS probable that the aggregate attendances on the Closing Day were more than Twenty-one Thousand.

The aggregate for the entire Feast, from the 13th to the 24th of July, was about One Hundred Fifty-three Thousand.

FROM EVERY side we heard, during the Feast, in its closing hours, and during the five days which have followed, the declaration, "*It was the best of all the Feasts.*"

And we believe it was, from every point of view.

IT WILL be impossible, in any reports of it, to convey to our distant readers the Holy Calm, the Intense Earnestness, and the Constant Growth of these Wonderful Days.

But these blessings abide with us, and, by the Grace of God, they will continue.

ON MONDAY MORNING, the adjourned Conference of the Ordained Officers of the Christian Catholic Church in Zion was held at ten o'clock, and continued until three o'clock in the afternoon.

The final conclusions of the Conference were absolutely unanimous.

But for the present, until the time comes to publish the whole matter in proper order, the proceedings remain private.

We were deeply impressed with the high plane upon which all the discussions were conducted at these Three Conferences upon the great themes that were placed before the gathering.

These Conferences will lead to great results; greater, perhaps, than any which have yet gone forth from us as a Church of the Living God.

AND NOW we once more inform our readers that there are many things we would like to say, but it is impossible to say them in these Notes.

Attending diligently to the business of the Ecclesiastical Work, especially, and also to the other great departments of Zion, we have, without any cessation, labored on throughout the entire week.

IT IS our purpose, early next week, to cross the Great Unsalted Sea of Lake Michigan and rest for a few days, with our beloved wife and son, beside our little Galilee, White Lake, Michigan.

FROM THERE we hope to send forth an important General Letter to the Church, upon the great work which now lies before Zion in the construction of Shiloah Tabernacle, and the fuller organization of the Church for the accomplishment of her Divine Mission.

BRETHREN, PRAY FOR US.

Warning.

I am directed by the General Overseer to warn our members and officers throughout the world against giving money to persons claiming to be members of the Christian Catholic Church in Zion. All benevolence must be given either from Headquarters or under the direction of same. Even though the applicant for benevolence be known to be a member of the Christian Catholic Church in Zion, financial aid must not be given except in extreme cases, and then only in small amounts. Requests for help must be made to the officer-in-charge. In cases where there is no such officer, requests should be made direct to Headquarters, accompanied by recommendations from one or two members of Zion in good standing. J. G. EXCELL,

General Ecclesiastical Secretary.

ELIJAH THE RESTORER.

While speaking of a certain Russian lady whom he met in Zurich the General Overseer said: I told her that Russia was treading in the Path of God's Wrath in this War where He was permitting her to be punished for her transgressions. I also told her that until the Czar and his Government, and the Greek Orthodox Church, fell upon their faces in penitence before God for the cruel treatment of their own people in depriving them of Civil and Religious Liberty, and especially for the hatred and murder of God's people, the Jews, the face of God would continue to be against the Nation. . . . What I said years ago is coming true. I prophesied that if Russia came into conflict with Japan it would be a bear putting to sea to fight a sword-fish, and that the sword-fish would pierce the bear and that his life-blood would flow out into the waters of the Sea . . . and the horrible Power that is against all real Christianity would fall on its face into the Sea. I believe that this is indeed the case. The result will be the break-up of the Russian Empire, and the restoration of their stolen liberties to many oppressed and conquered peoples, both in Europe and Asia.—The Voice of Elijah the Restorer in Shiloh Tabernacle, Zion City, Lord's Day Afternoon, July 17, 1904.

THE "BEAR" AND THE "SWORD-FISH."

Zion's Fourth Feast of Tabernacles

The Set Feasts of Jehovah . . .
Ye shall proclaim to be Holy Convocations.

DIVINE HEALING MEETING.

*REPORTED BY O. R., O. L. S., AND E. W.

IT is almost always said by those who attend all of the meetings conducted by the General Overseer, that at the Divine Healing meetings he is at his best.

If this is true, it is probably because of his joy in knowing that he is the messenger bringing such real blessings to those in sorrow, and to those who are oppressed.

Shiloh Tabernacle, Zion City, Illinois, Friday Forenoon, July 15, 1904.

The service was opened by the singing of Hymn No. 32, in the Program.

In looking over the papers and prayer requests which had been given to him at the hour of the meeting, the General Overseer found a few lines of testimony from a lady who had been healed of cancer.

The lady who had written this testimony also had with her a small medicine glass which she handed to the General Overseer.

The General Overseer said:

This little glass has quite a history.

The lady to whom it belongs, says that she has taken one hundred seventy-seven quarts of medicine from it.

She had cancer of the stomach, bowels, and the left breast, and many other diseases.

She lived in Salem, Oregon, and when I prayed for her, the Lord heard me for her, although she was two thousand three hundred miles from here, and she was healed.

I would like her to give her testimony.

Remarkable Testimony to God's Healing Power.

Mrs. Minerva Sutton—"My name is Mrs. Minerva Sutton, and I lived formerly in Salem, Oregon.

"I now live at 2217 Gilgal avenue, Zion City, Illinois.

"I had a cancerous tumor of the stomach, and cancer in the left breast. I was treated by Dr. J. F. Cook, only, of Salem, Oregon, as the other doctors that examined me said that they could not understand my case.

"Dr. Cook told me that it was cancer of the stomach, and we afterwards found that he was right, for when the roots decayed and broke, the cancerous tumor fell down to my bowels, and was as hard as bone. The cancer had eaten through the lining of the stomach down to the bowels.

"When I received my healing it just disappeared; we never knew what became of it.

"The cancer in the left breast was about the size of this glass.

"I was led to seek the Lord for healing through LEAVES OF HEALING.

"I was an invalid, lying perfectly helpless, when I received a ten weeks' subscription to LEAVES OF HEALING.

Way to Divine Healing Made Plain by "Leaves of Healing."

"I learned through the LEAVES that it was not God's will that I should die, although the preachers had told me to get ready for death. But LEAVES OF HEALING told me to get ready to live.

"I then wrote to you to pray that I might have confidence in God to heal me.

"You prayed, and I began right away to get better, so that I could move my body.

"My internal organs seemed like a mass of jelly; the cancer had eaten the tissues so that they would fall from one side to the other as I turned my body.

*The following reports have not been revised by the General Overseer.

"We wrote for prayer in July, but I did not get my healing until August, because I did not give up everything until I received your reply.

Complete Healing Conditioned Upon Absolute Obedience.

"I had given up medicine, but the doctor said that the pus must be removed from the stomach and bowels, or else gangrene would set in, so I went on with the operations.

"However, after your reply came, I gave up the operations, and have not used any human remedies since.

"On the 9th day of August we received a letter from the General Overseer, saying that we must give up all drugs and medicines, because God would not give His glory to another.

"I obeyed, and today, two years later, you see the consequence of that obedience.

"I also had paralysis of the bowels for eleven years.

"Dr. S. A. Davis of Salem, Oregon, had performed an operation.

"Immediately after my healing my bowels began to move naturally, and have continued to do so to this day

"I at once began to eat five hearty meals a day, and sometimes between.

"My hands were then like birds' claws, but now I am healthy and well, and all my diseases are completely gone."

General Overseer—I am so glad to see your face; and may God bless you.

I am so glad that in Salem, Oregon, He answered my prayer for you.

A Physician Who Heals Without Money and Without Price.

You who are seeking healing ought to receive great encouragement from the facts she has given you.

Out of this glass she has taken one hundred seventy-seven quarts of medicine—a barrel and two-fifths of medicine.

She received no benefit from the operations.

The poor woman had drunk large quantities of medicine, for which she spent large sums of money, and it was all fruitless.

Then God healed her without money and without price, and without my being there.

If you would all get the healing which the Lord wants you to get now, you would get it immediately without my laying hands upon you.

That would save much time and strength.

I am glad to see a number of doctors in the meeting who are seeking the Lord for healing.

No one knows better than they that the whole so-called science of medicine is an unmitigated humbug.

There is nothing in it—yes, there is; there is lots of Devil in it.

There are a great many doctors who are doing the best they can; but they have got into a bad business.

They cannot diagnose clearly, and they cannot find a remedy when they have diagnosed.

There is no Human Remedy for Cancer.

Neither surgery nor medicine affect cancer.

If you will make an entire consecration of yourselves to God, before we utter a word of teaching, you ought to get your healing.

Let us pray.

The General Overseer then offered prayer, leading the Congregation, at the close, in chanting the Disciples' Prayer.

Scripture Reading and Exposition.

Let us read from the Word of God, in the 12th chapter of the Epistle to the Romans.

If I make any mistakes as I read, I should like you to correct me.

"I beseech you, therefore, brethren, by the mercies of God,

to present your bodies"—to the best doctor you can find in town?

People—"The Bible does not say so."

General Overseer—"I beseech you therefore, brethren, by the mercies of God, to present your bodies"—to the best surgeon you can find in town?

A Reasonable Service.

People—"'Present your bodies a living sacrifice, holy, acceptable to God.'"

General Overseer—"Your bodies a living sacrifice, holy, acceptable to God, which is"—a most unreasonable thing to do, because you ought to go to a doctor?

That is what some people read there.

They say, "It is a most unreasonable thing to suppose that God Almighty will hear you, and look after you; for you must go to the doctor with your body!"

But the Bible has no use for doctors.

If you can find one passage, from Genesis to Revelation, that says that we are to go to doctors, I should like to have you tell me now, because I do not know where to find it.

You may say, the Christ said that "they that are whole have no need of a physician; but they that are sick."

Of course He said it; but did He not say at the same time that He was the Physician?

Did He not declare that God, the Eternal Father, had given them a Covenant at the waters of Marah, where He said:

If thou wilt diligently harken to the Voice of Jehovah thy God, and wilt do that which is right in His eyes, and wilt give ear to His Commandments, and keep all His statutes, I will (permit to be) put none of the diseases upon thee which I have (permitted to be) put upon the Egyptians: for I am Jehovah that healeth thee.

Churches Filled with So-called Elders Who Have no Faith.

Again, we read in James, the 5th chapter and the 14th and 15th verses:

Is any among you sick? let him call for the Elders of the Church; and let them pray over him, anointing him with oil in the Name of the Lord:
And the Prayer of Faith shall save him that is sick, and the Lord shall raise him up; and if he have committed sins, it shall be forgiven him.

He says, "The Prayer of Faith shall save," and that is the rub.

What is the use in calling the elders? They have no faith.

When you call for them to see a sick person they are frightened, and usually say, "Send for the doctor!"

An officer—"I know of one woman that sent for an elder of a church."

General Overseer—What happened?

The officer—"He told her that God would have to heal her on her own faith, that he did not have any. He was an elder in the Presbyterian church."

General Overseer—But was he an elder?

The officer—"No."

General Overseer—If the so-called "elder" cannot pray the Prayer of Faith he is not an elder.

He has no right there, and should step down and out.

The Word of God expects an elder to be a man of faith who can pray the Prayer of Faith.

Present Your Bodies as Well as Spirits.

I beseech you therefore, brethren, by the mercies of God, to present your bodies a living sacrifice, holy, acceptable to God, which is your reasonable service.

People have been presenting their spirits, or what they call their souls, but they have not been presenting their bodies.

The beast has a soul; the fish has a soul; every living thing has a soul.

The spirit is not the soul.

The soul is the animal life, and the spirit is that which comes from God—the spiritual being.

You have presented your bodies to man long enough, and have drunk barrels of drugs, many of you, and spent your money and your time, and are "nothing bettered," but have rather grown worse.

Is it not time to quit?

The doctors are here themselves.

They have quit.

There are four or five doctors here this morning, and I am glad to see them.

I am going to pound them hard! for you cannot do anything with a doctor until you have knocked all the medicine out of him!

I do not think it is hard for some of them, though.

Physicians Without Faith in One Another or in Themselves.

I read a little while ago of a very fashionable doctor in London, Dr. Bellegravie.

He came home very sick.

He put his finger on his pulse.

His lady came in and said, "What shall I do, Sir Joshua? Shall I send for Dr. Squills?"

"Oh, no!" said the doctor.

"Shall I send for Dr. Leech?"

"Oh, no!"

"Shall I send for Dr. Lancet?"

"Oh, no!"

"For whom shall I send?"

"Do not send for any one! We are all humbugs, and we all know that we are!"

These doctors do not drink their own drugs, nor do they have confidence in one another.

I beseech you therefore, brethren, by the mercies of God, to present your bodies a living sacrifice, holy, acceptable to God, which is your reasonable service.

You Must Get New Minds.

And be not fashioned according to this world: but be ye transformed by the renewing of your mind.

May God give you a new mind.

That ye may prove what is the good and acceptable, and perfect will of God.

I want you to "prove" in your spirit, soul, and body, by "the renewing of your mind," "what is the good and acceptable, and perfect will of God;" because you will not receive healing for your bodies, nor power to present your bodies unto God, until you get a new mind. Many of you have bad minds.

The old minds of many of you are worthless.

The Work of the Devil Can Never Be the Will of God.

In that old time, the preachers told you that you were to say, "I thank Thee, Lord, for Thy loving, chastening hand, and that Thou hast laid me on my bed in sickness, and that Thou hast laid Thy loving hand upon me, for my good and Thy glory!"

That is an awful, shameful lie; one of the biggest lies they could have told you.

The first thing I shall show you is that disease is not, never has been, and never can be the will of God.

That is not what you have been taught.

In the first place, there would have been no disease in this world had there been no sin.

Then who is the author of sin?

People—"The Devil."

General Overseer—Through sin disease has come.

If the Devil is the author of disease, can the work of the Devil ever be the Will of God?

People—"No."

General Overseer—Get that into your mind.

The Christ Came to Destroy the Devil's, not God's Work.

When Jesus came to this world, He came to destroy the works of the Devil.

He "went about doing good, and healing all that were oppressed of the Devil, for God was with Him."

We find that statement in the 10th chapter of the Acts of the Apostles, the 38th verse.

Did He heal every kind of sickness and every manner of disease among the people?

People—"Yes."

General Overseer—Did He ever say that any of the sicknesses was the work of God?

People—"No."

General Overseer—He came to do the Will of God, and in doing that Will could He have destroyed the work of God?

People—"No."

General Overseer—When He destroyed disease, was He doing the work of God?

People—"Yes."

General Overseer—Is He the same?

People—"Yes."

Why They Thought the Christ Was Not in Chicago.

General Overseer—But He is not with us now, is He?

A minister in Chicago said that Dr. Dowie was a very

powerful and fascinating speaker, "but he talked as if the Lord Jesus, the Christ, were actually in Chicago, and we all know He is not."

I wondered that the people did not laugh; but they did not.

They said, "That is one on Dowie."

They had never seen any evidence of the Christ's being in that church.

No one had ever dreamed that Jesus, the Christ, had ever been there.

That was a church where they had all kinds of bazaars; it was a great society church.

It was full of doctors and druggists.

Is Jesus, the Christ, in Chicago?

People—"Yes."

General Overseer—Is He in Zion City?

People—"Yes."

General Overseer—Is He the same Jesus and is He with us now?

People—"Yes."

General Overseer—It is the Will of God that you should believe that disease is the work of the Devil.

How could it be the work of God?

How could it come from heaven?

Where do you read in the Bible that when you get to heaven you will be sure to find disease waiting there, to keep you good? [Laughter.]

A "Gift of God" That Is Never Coveted.

Parsons tell you that disease is necessary to keep you good, and that you would never have been good if you had not been sick.

But they are very inconsistent, for when they get sick they send for the doctor to take away the Good Gift of God.

Oh, how ready they are to get rid of the Good Gift of God!

They say that disease is the Loving Hand of God.

If my hand laid upon you communicated disease to you, would not the disease be in me?

If God's hand communicates disease to you, is not the disease in Him?

If disease comes from heaven, must not there be disease in heaven?

If it comes from God, must not God be responsible for it?

Could you believe that God is the corrupter of His own creation?

If I believed that, I should hate God; and I should say, "You are not a good God. You brought me into being, and gave me a diseased body, for which I am not responsible, and yet You make me more miserable by sending me more disease than that which I inherited. You are not a good God. How can You expect me to be a good man, when You send me dirty and foul diseases? You are not kind; You are not a good Father."

If you parents were in the habit of inoculating your children with disease, would you be good fathers? Would you be good mothers?

Is not disease a foul and filthy thing?

Is it not the destruction of your body?

Is it not the beclouding of your mind and spirit?

Does it not keep you back in everything that is good?

It makes you fretful, and peevish, and selfish.

Disease Develops Selfishness.

Gradually the persons that are always sick get their minds concentrated on self.

They cannot help it; they cannot help thinking about the poor brain that is in pain all the time, their miserable squeamish stomachs, their nasty catarrh, and other internal miseries.

Then the rheumatic devil keeps them thinking.

Even the people who love and care for them think about it.

They hate to see their loved one afflicted, and they think about it when they are at work, think of what they can do, think of getting holidays to hunt up the latest patent medicine and the newest doctors, until at last they begin to get a little weary.

The daughter finds it hard to be lifting mother all the time and carrying to her, a little at a time, quarts upon quarts of medicine.

It is hard for the father to find the money for it all.

It is hard for the children and hard for every one.

But at last the invalid grows quite content with her position, and she becomes one of those people that "enjoy" poor health—but no one else enjoys it.

People Who Enjoy Poor Health.

I know that there are some people that positively enjoy poor health.

There are some people that would be very frightened to get well.

I once went to see a bed-ridden man who had rheumatism.

It was a kind of rheumatism that did not bring much pain, but fossilized him in body, and spirit as well.

He looked so amiable, and they told me that he was such a saint!

He made little watch-guards worth about twenty-five cents, and sold them to the people that came to see him.

He talked about "Whom the Lord loveth He chasteneth," and said, "It is God's hand of chastisement that is upon me; I am very happy in my sickness."

The mayor of that city was a friend of mine, and he told me about this man.

I said, "I will go and see him."

You should have seen that man.

He was quite content to be sick, and he did not want to see me.

I said, "If you will do this, and thus, and so, God will heal you."

"I do not agree with you, Doctor," he answered.

"You must agree with God," I said, "and He said that Jesus was sent to take our infirmities and our sicknesses, and it is written, 'With His stripes we are healed.'"

I said, "It is written, 'The Prayer of Faith shall save him that is sick, and the Lord shall raise him up; and if he have committed sins, it shall be forgiven him.' Now, if you will repent and believe, I will pray with you."

"Oh," he said, "I do not want you to pray with me."

He really was frightened lest he would be healed and would have to get up and work.

It was very much easier to make little guards worth twenty-five cents and sell them for two dollars and fifty cents, than to be healed and get to work.

The mayor, who was with me, said to him, "Why do you not want the Doctor to pray for you? He has prayed for a great many other people and they have been healed."

For reply he again insisted, "I do not want him to pray with me; and I want you to take him away."

When we got outside the mayor laughed loud and long, and said, "I never expected I would live long enough to see a man afraid to be healed."

But this man was.

I often see people who enjoy poor health.

They hold on to it.

If you tell them that they can be healed, it becomes dreadful to them to think of it.

They fear that they might have to get up and go to work.

When they are sick they get everything done for them.

I have little sympathy for some sick people.

Content to Remain Invalids at the Cost of Their Loved Ones.

They are very selfish.

They forget that children have a right to play ball and get some life in them.

They wear them out by keeping them at work at home until the daughters are old before they are young, and the sons are broken-hearted with the continuous demands of peevish, selfish sick people. I do not say that all are like that.

There are a great multitude, like many here today, no doubt, who say, "I wish I could rise and work; I only wish I could!"

These earnestly seek God that they may get well.

But there are many others, and do not make any mistake about it, who are afraid to be healed.

They can get bread without earning it, and they are lazy and selfish down to the heart's core.

The building of many of the hospitals is a great curse.

A large number of persons get into them who want to stay there.

They believe that God meant them to be sick, and they sing

My willing soul would stay
In such a frame as this,
And sit and sing itself away
To everlasting bliss.

What they need is a stick.

What they need is to get wakened up and to be told the truth: that their sickness is an offense to God.

God does not want one of His children to be sick this morning.

He does not want one of us to be sinful.

Do you want any of your children to be sinful? Do you want any of them to be sick or miserable?

People—"No."

General Overseer—Are you kinder than God?

An Infamous Lie Told in Church of England Prayer-book.

The word "chastening" never meant what the parsons say it means.

They lie if they say that you should be sick. The Church of England has put into the prayer-book:

Wherefore, whatsoever your sickness is, know you certainly, that it is God's visitation.

God Almighty never gave any one cancer or consumption, or any other disease

These prayers are wicked, shameful lies.

There is no use glossing over the matter.

There is no use saying soft words about it.

They are downright lies that the Devil has in these prayer-books.

There are men, for instance, who are great joiners; they join every lodge in town.

They join the Maccabees, the Elks, and the Goats.

They become Redmen and Woodmen.

They join the I. O. O. F.

I used to wonder what that was; I wondered if it was 100 fools—I. O. O. F.

When I was talking about that one day, a man came up and tore off his lodge emblem from his watch-chain and said, "Doctor, it is no longer a hundred fools; it is only ninety-nine now. Take my emblem! I will not be one of the hundred fools any longer."

A Lie the Parsons Tell at Which the Devil Laughs.

Here is a man who goes into all the abominable, silly lodges that he can, and at every degree there is a dinner, for which he often has to pay—and in many ways.

He eats great messes of indigestible stuff, and by the time he has reached his thirty-third degree of deviltry, he has got into the habit of eating and drinking so gluttonously that he is sick half the time.

At last we find him coming home, singing, "We won't go home until morning," and it is morning then.

He lies down and tries to make a blanket of the paving-stone, and says, "Oh, isn't this fine!"

He rolls into the gutter and the policeman finds him and takes him home.

It had rained in the meantime and he gets a splendid attack of rheumatism; then the Devil grips him everywhere.

He gets very sick.

His wife sends for the doctor—not the minister; the minister comes last of all.

The minister gets there about the time the undertaker does.

The doctor comes, and the woman gets alarmed.

She is afraid that he may die, so she sends for the minister.

He comes, and he says, "Forasmuch as it hath pleased Almighty God to lay His afflicting hand upon you—"

That fellow lying there may be a drunkard, he may be a glutton, he may be a thirty-third degree Masonic devil; but he is not a fool.

He knows that the Lord had nothing to do with his being sick.

He knows that all his sickness came from his own sin, and that in getting drunk of his own accord, and rolling into that gutter while the rain was coming down, he was a fool.

He knows that the raging fever that set in was the result.

When that parson says, "O brother, remember, I beseech you, that it is the hand of the Lord God Almighty," he laughs at him and says, "Get away! you do not know what you are talking about. It is my own sin. It is not God's hand. It is the Devil's hand giving me what I deserve."

What downright wickedness to have this lie told all over the world!

The parsons are telling the people that God Almighty does the things that the people are doing themselves.

I want you to clearly understand that every disease, directly or indirectly, is the work of the Devil.

You must trust God, for you cannot ask Him to destroy the Devil's work while you hold on to drugs and doctors.

You Can Have Only One Doctor at a Time.

Suppose you were to say, "I believe in having several doctors. I shall have Dr. Jones, the allopath, in the morning at eight o'clock; at eleven I shall have Dr. Smith, the homeopath; in the afternoon at two o'clock I shall get Dr. Brown, the electropath; and in the evening I shall have Jenny Sawbones, the anything-you-like—the eclectic."

How long would it be before you were dead, if you took four doctors' remedies?

Would you think you were sensible to take four separate systems of treatment?

People—"No."

General Overseer—Can you take two at the same time?

People—"No."

General Overseer—Then if you are going to trust the Lord, can you depend upon doctors and drugs also?

People—"No."

General Overseer—If God said that doctors and drugs were a part of His system, I should say, "Yes;" but they are not.

Did the Christ ever send any of His people to doctors?

People—"No."

General Overseer—"But once He took some clay and put it upon the eyes of a blind man," you may say.

Must Be Healed Alone by Faith.

The Lord Jesus, the Christ, wanted that man to go and get healing at Siloam, without seeing, and, as a test of his faith, He sent him to the place called Siloam—which is really Shiloh—to get washed, and he came away seeing.

There was nothing more in that act of the Christ's than in what I do when I lay hands upon a blind person.

I often touch my finger to my tongue and then touch the eye.

Do you think I believe that that has any healing power?

It is merely easier to put the finger on the eye if there is a little moisture on it.

Do you imagine that I believe for a moment that water has ever opened blind eyes?

The Lord Jesus, the Christ, never used means.

He taught His people that faith alone was the thing essential to healing.

You must make up your mind to be done with doctors and drugs when you take the Lord Jesus, the Christ, for your Doctor, and when you take His Word instead of drugs.

The Whole System of Drugging Is an Unmitigated Curse.

We do without it in Zion, and as a result we have the highest birth rate and the lowest death rate in the country

Our statistics show that during the present year we had one thousand nine hundred four young people being educated here.

Strange to say, it is the exact number of the year, 1904.

Out of all that number we lost only four.

That is just about two in a thousand.

That is quite good, is it not?

A doctor in the audience—"Yes, that is good."

General Overseer—And this was in a year when all around us they were dying of pneumonia and of various lung diseases, in thousands and thousands.

It is often the fault of unwise parents.

You let your childnen run out in the cold winter, without seeing that they are properly clothed.

You know that you can get help if you are too poor to care for their feet.

We have cared for every child in this place whose parents were too poor to buy.

We have seen that they were kept warm.

You cannot expect the children to run out from a warm house into weather twenty-five degrees below zero and not get cold.

I know that most of the deaths of mothers in confinement have been entirely due to gross carelessness upon the part of the women themselves.

In some cases the nurses pleaded with them not to open windows and have drafts upon their bodies shortly after the birth of the children; but they would insist upon it, and the consequence was that they caught cold and died.

We must be wise.

We Must Take Care of the Earthen Vessel.

There is no use talking nonsense; we cannot use the vessel unwisely.

When the weather is cold, wear warm clothes.

When it is warm, wear light clothes.

Adapt yourself to climate, and take pains to do so.

It is cheaper for you to clothe the children than to bury them.

It is cheaper for you to take care of yourselves than to kill yourselves.

Be careful.

Because you get healing of the Lord is no reason why you should fling it away.

First Salvation, Then Healing.

The Lord is the Healer, and the Lord is present to heal.

You cannot get healing in body until you have given the Lord your spirit; there is no use asking for it.

You must get Salvation first; Healing next.

What right have you to go to Almighty God, the Father, and say, "I do not want to be saved; I do not want to give You my spirit and be a servant of Yours; but I will think about it. Meanwhile I bring to You my body; here is my old carcass; heal it. I will think about salvation afterwards."

Will God hear that kind of prayer?

Ought He to hear that?

People—"No."

General Overseer—What is the use healing your miserable old carcass if you intend to serve the Devil; if you will still be a selfish man and go your own way and not God's way?

Yet you want God to heal you!

I will be no party to that.

I do not want to see you healed, if that is your attitude.

I tell you plainly that I have no interest in the healing of the children of the Devil.

I do not want to see them healthy, and rich, and strong, and powerful.

I have no satisfaction in seeing them efficient and devilish!

If you will serve the Devil, (I am going to say a dreadful thing,) for the next ten or twenty years, I wish you were with the Devil, in another world, because you will be a curse here!

I am not on the side of the Devil's army; I am on the side of God's army.

I have no particular desire to see the children of the Devil strong and fighting the army of the Lord and winning battles from God.

No Sympathy With the Army of Rebels.

If I were General Grant on one side of the war, with General Lee's forces on the other side, I should not be sorry if the latter all had the dysentery.

I should capture them all the quicker.

I should not send doctors into their camp.

If I am right in putting down a rebellion, I shall not be particularly troubled if all the rebels are sick.

I will put down that rebellion!

I am on God's side in this matter, and I am not on the Devil's side.

You may just as well know it.

I am not on the rebel side at all.

I have no interest whatever in the healing of the rebel.

I would have had much interest, during the war, in the healing of the Southerners, because many of them were gentlemen who acted according to their light; and I do not think they were nicely treated by the North.

Putting aside the illustration, I am on the side of the government of God, and if you are on the side of the government of the Devil, I am against you.

I am not foolish enough to ask God to heal you, when you rebel against Him.

God Almighty can do it if He pleases, but I have no right, and He does not ask me to pray for the healing of those who rebel against Him.

He asks me to pray for those who are His children.

Divine Healing Belongs to the Children of God.

I have no interest in the healing of people that are determined to serve the Devil.

I am interested in their Salvation, and I would like to knock the Devil out and get them saved, and then healed, but I cannot pray for their healing until they are saved.

They must come over on God's side.

They must give up rebellion and get under the Flag of God's government.

They must be children of God.

That is good, sound, common sense.

Kind Words for the People of the South.

When I used that illustration just now about the Rebellion I meant no reflection against the South.

I believe that the old rebellious feelings against National Unity and the Flag have long gone out of their hearts, with the exception of a very few who would like to keep it up.

They would like to have the old rebel flag flying still, and they have no right to it.

They have no right to call themselves good citizens of the United States and want that flag to float over the buildings in their cities.

Put that flag away and put the Stars and Stripes there.

I was very pleased to see that down South the Stars and Stripes was floating over the cities.

The people have put away the old flag, and they want to be good, loyal citizens.

They are a magnificent people; and if they would only not eat pig they would be far more healthy.

They are far more chivalrous than the people of the North.

I am inclined to think that they believe in the Bible more than a good many people in the North.

I noticed when I spoke in San Antonio, that if I gave them Bible they had nothing to say; and I gave them Bible, too.

God Will Not Heal Those Who Love Evil.

I have come to the conclusion that I had better spend my time, my talents, and my energies with the people of God.

I have no right fooling around with the people that belong to the Devil.

There are people who will belong to the Devil.

They do not want to obey God.

They do not want to be Christians.

They do not want to go to God for anything.

They hate Divine Healing, and they hate Divine Salvation.

They hate Purity of life.

They hate the things that God loves.

There is no use pretending that they are not lovers of disease and of their wickednesses.

If there are any such here, I say that you must repent.

You must find Salvation through Repentance and Faith.

Then God will hear you.

But you must quit fighting God.

You must quit fighting God's truths.

You must quit fighting me, because you know what it costs to fight me.

I do not care how many are against God; God will surely win.

The time has come to tell to the world, and that not with bated breath, that they need no longer talk as if they were the masters of the situation.

We are the masters of the situation.

God Is Master of the Situation.

The Christ is coming, and He has put His armies in the field.

He is telling us to take the tares out; to take out the "things that cause stumbling," and bind them into bundles, and throw them into the fire.

The time has come for that.

Make no mistake about it.

I will bind up all that array themselves against God's Word.

I will take out of the Church of God, as far as I can, everything that offends.

Drink offends; it causes people to stumble.

Tobacco offends; it causes people to be sick.

Filthy eating offends; it causes people to be full of disease.

Eat pig, and you get trichinosis, tuberculosis, cholera, cancer, and other dirty diseases.

I want to take out everything that causes people to offend.

If I find any one in Zion who is doing iniquity, I will take him or her out.

I will have this part of the harvest-field clean, so that when at last the Reaper comes, He will find wheat here, and not tares.

My business is to do that all over the world.

The people who hold on to doctors and drugs, and all kinds of dirt and muck do not like it.

They say, "He has no right to talk like that! God uses doctors and drugs!"

He never used them; and never promised to use them.

Instead we read, "In vain shalt thou use many medicines."

God can do without knives.

You make men miserable; and I am against the whole thing, root and branch.

"What are you not against?" you may ask.

I tell you, there is nothing evil that I am not against.

Just show me that a thing is bad, and I will take a lick at it.

I will get at it, if I can.

I want to have the Church clean.

A Fight Against King-craft.

I see some dear, good people here, who were very angry with me last year because I said that Jesus, the Christ, was a much better man than Edward VII., and also because I said what I repeated lately, and what I repeat now, that God hates monarchy, and that when God permitted Israel, after four hundred years of judges, to have a king, He said to Samuel, "They have not rejected thee, but they have rejected Me, that I should not be King over them."

As I have gone through the world, I have seen nothing but misery and wretchedness resulting from kingcraft.

I passed through Germany, and I saw several women to one man working in every field.

I found the women on the highways and in the trams, with poles, dragging carts as if they were horses.

Where were the men?

When I got to Berlin I saw many thousands in the neighborhood of Berlin marching up and down, and teaching one another how to kill, while their wives were working like cattle in the fields.

Is it right?

It is wrong!

It is sinful!

When I met some of these women, I found they were suffering from diseases consequent upon doing the work of men, and upon working out in the harvest fields when about to bear children; they ought to have been at home.

I say that military tyranny is cursed!

I am against kings, and against kingcraft.

"What right have you to talk like that?" some may say.

I Am God's Prophet. I Have a Right to Talk.

I have a right to talk to the whole world; and I will talk! [Applause.]

My Message is not only for the United States.

My marching orders are, "Go ye into all the world and preach the Gospel to every creature."

I go to preach the Gospel of the Kingdom, but not the kingdom of man who gets on a throne, merely because he is his mother's or father's son.

No one imagines that Great Britain would ever have selected Edward VII. to be the leader of the nation because of his great virtues and capacity.

If any of you have hard feelings against me for saying that, you will have to get over it.

God Alone Heals.

I shall pray for you all as I kneel here, and then for as many as I can see in the prayer-room.

Do not depend upon my hands.

If I find you leaning upon me for healing I will not pray for you.

I cannot carry all you people on my back.

I love you, and will help you all I can; but you must stand on your own legs.

PRAYER OF CONSECRATION.

My God and Father, in Jesus' Name I come to Thee. Take me as I am. Make me what I ought to be. Make me honest; make me willing to give up my own will, my own way, my old practices; and help me to trust Thee, and Thee alone for a complete Salvation. Give me a True Repentance and power to do right to all whom I may have injured. No matter what it costs, help me to do right in Thy sight; and to put myself right with Thee. Help me to do right; to repent, and to "bring forth fruits meet for repentance." Help me to trust in the "Lamb of God who taketh away the sin of the world;" who Himself took our infirmities and bore our sicknesses." I Come to Thee with my spirit; cleanse my spirit. I come to Thee with my soul; cleanse my blood. I come to Thee with my body. I present it unto Thee. Receive me; heal me; and help me to prove this day in my own experience that Thou art the Healer. Help me to prove it now. I bring to Thee my body now. I give it to Thee. Stretch forth Thine hand to heal; and give me the grace to persevere until the healing is perfected. For Jesus' sake. Amen.

BENEDICTION.

Beloved, abstain from every form of evil. And may the very God of Peace Himself sanctify you wholly; and I pray God your whole spirit and soul and body be preserved entire, without blame, unto the coming of our Lord Jesus, the Christ. Faithful is He that calleth you, who also will do it. The grace of our Lord Jesus, the Christ, the love of God, our Father, the fellowship of the Holy Spirit, our Comforter and Guide, one Eternal God, abide in you, bless you and keep you, and all the Israel of God everywhere, forever. Amen.

THE CITY FESTIVAL DAY.

REPORTED BY M. E L., A. C. R., AND E. S.

"Thanks be unto God, who giveth us the victory! We say with all our hearts, Thine, O Jehovah, is the Kingdom, and the power, and the glory forever."—*General Overseer.*

Zion's Third Home Festival, held Friday, July 15, 1904, surpassed all previous ones in its excellence.

In the numbers taking part, in the originality and elaboration shown in the floats, in the general beauty of scene and setting, and in the almost military order and precision obtaining throughout the great parade, Zion City almost outdid herself.

Rather the three-year-old City measured up to herself on this occasion—no more.

And when one remembers the First Festival, then the Second, and then witnessed the display of Friday, July 15th, the mind is filled with wonder, the imagination leaps forward to other thanksgivings yet to come, and with bowed heads and reverent lips, the words of the founder and head of the City, as quoted in the paragraph above, become the speech and prayer of Zion.

Approximately three thousand people were in the great Procession, commemorating the Anniversary of the Opening of the Gates of Zion City.

Probably six thousand spectators, men, women and children, viewed the parade along the line of march, Shiloh Tabernacle later being filled with those taking part, citizens and outsiders —many out-of-town visitors being present—when the man of God, the founder, under God, of the City, the Prophet of the Restoration, addressed the people assembled.

It took one and a half hours for the Procession, which was two miles in length, to pass a given point.

Two hundred fifty vehicles, many of them being beautiful and artistically designed floats, depicting the various industries of Zion as engaged in their separate work, were in line, while six hundred horses stepped to the music of Zion's incomparable Military Band.

The marchers proceeded four abreast, each department being distinguished by a banner with name and motto inscribed in black lettering, held aloft, the marchers themselves adding no little to the picturesque and beautiful panorama.

Many of the various costumes worn had been especially designed for the occasion. Nearly all wore the Zion sash of blue, white, and gold.

At the very head of the Procession, borne by the Ecclesiastical department, was the great silken shield known as Zion's flag, or banner. Surrounding this emblem of Power, Purity, and Progress were the flags of the nations, conspicuous among them being that of America; but high over all towered this great shield of Zion.

The General Overseer, Overseer Jane Dowie, and Dr. A. J. Gladstone Dowie occupied seats in the alcove built above the porch of the Administration Building fronting Elijah avenue, from which point of vantage they viewed the Procession, manifesting the liveliest interest in each and all, often rising and saluting the marchers.

Overseer Jane Dowie looked very beautiful in a gown of Zion lace, and her smiling face indicated a joy and pleasure equal to that of the General Overseer's—though perhaps scarce so exuberant in expression!

As the marchers passed this reviewing point, heads were bared, and many a glance of love and reverence bespoke the perfect sympathy and unity existing between them and these two, who are best known and loved as the General Overseer and Overseer Jane Dowie.

The day was perfect; a cloudless summer sky canopied the brilliant scene with its kaleidoscopic change and hue, the green of field and forest rimming the whole as a jewel is set in a band of gold.

Following was the order of march:

Colonel C. F. Stern and Staff.
Police Department.
Zion Band.
General Overseer's Ecclesiastical Staff.
Educational Department.
Law Department.
Bank and Financial Department.
Land and Investment Association.
Transportation Department.
Hospices.
Lace Industries.
General Stores.
Fresh Food Supply.
Candy Department.
Printing and Publishing House.
Bureau of Employment.
Building and Manufacturing Association.
Laundry.
Photograph Gallery.
Wagon and Blacksmith Shop.
Dental Department.
Horticultural Department.
Soap Factory.
Broom Factory.

VEHICLES.

Fire Department.
Live Stock Department.
Livery.
Land and Investment Association.
General Stores.
Fresh Food Supply.
Laundry.
Bakery.
Building and Manufacturing Association.

Conspicuous among the exhibits of the industries of Zion City appeared the new ones established during the year.

Many of the smaller industries were unable to make a representation; but a few, though so young, took their places with the older ones, and suffered nothing by the contact.

Conspicuous among these was the Transportation Department, with its many employees. A street-car, well conceived, and constructed, and flower-trimmed, whose conductor rang up innumerable fares, collected from the childish passengers who filled every inch of space, standing-room and all, was delightful to view.

A long line of dirt-shovels and brawny, bare-armed men following in the wake of this modern civilizer—the street-car—bespoke eloquently the stride forward Zion City has taken in the acquisition of the new electric railway, in the construction of which, incidentally, employment is given to many of her working men.

The Soap Factory—the youngest of Zion's industrial progeny—was most creditably represented by a huge dray supporting two bars of soap, each weighing four hundred pounds, besides pyramids of the daintier kinds.

The broom float, following close after, depicted the manufacture of this homely but honored article of well-ordered homes.

A unique feature of the parade was the representation of the box factory, with its many young women employees wearing box hats, tasseled in gold, the unusual head-gear as worn by the pretty young women, proving exceedingly becoming,

Most artistic in conception of all the floats was that of Zion Printing and Publishing House. Even startling in its beauty was the picture, presented in form and reality, of the figure of Zion, so familiar to all readers of LEAVES OF HEALING, as appearing in the work of Zion's cartoonist, Deacon Charles Champe.

Resting on a foundation of bound volumes of LEAVES OF HEALING, appeared a scroll bearing the names of Zion publications. Surmounting this stood the figure of a beautiful woman --the wife of the artist—in a flowing white garb, with a Greek border of blue, wearing on her head the Helmet of Salvation, bearing in her hand the Shield of Faith, girt with the Girdle of Truth, having on the Breast-plate of Righteousness, and carrying the Sword of the Spirit—the figure of Zion.

Fluttering at the ends of many white ribbons, extending from the front of the scroll, were white doves—the whole forming a picture, in the brilliant sunlight, of striking beauty.

Another exhibit which called forth much comment was the miniature, in cardboard, of Shiloah Tabernacle, as contemplated, this belonging to Zion Building and Manufacturing Association.

The float of Zion Lace Industries presented an airy, elusive picture of white woven web and seemingly inextricable confusion of thread as nimble-fingered, white-garbed girls, half hidden by hanging curtains of lace, engaged in all the various handiwork of the lace industries as carried on in the big building of brick and stone.

Every department, as represented, showed a distinct advance over last year's exhibit.

Each and all reflected the greatest credit upon the men and women, from the highest to the humblest, engaged in doing the great, every-day work of Zion City, and in this annual festival presenting, in pictorial form, the City as she exists today in her varied industries and occupations.

Seated upon the platform of Shiloh Tabernacle, with the General Overseer, his wife and son, were Zion's Overseers and the Business Council.

After devotional exercises and the recitation by the audience of that great song of Salvation, of Healing, of Holy Living, and of a Triumphant Entrance into the Zion above—the 35th chapter of Isaiah—the General Overseer addressed the audience, being followed, briefly, by Overseer Jane Dowie, Dr. A. J. Gladstone Dowie, and Judge Barnes.

In his address, which was extemporaneous, the General Overseer dwelt upon the wonderful increase which the present year has seen in Zion Land values, and demonstrating that Zion's estate is not less, at the present time, than fifty millions of dollars—although, as he slyly remarked, with an apprehensive look in the direction of the county tax assessor, this was not its taxable value.

He reviewed, briefly, the progress made in the various departments, and paid deserved tributes to the men whom he had placed at the heads of Zion's institutions and who had so faithfully and ably coöperated with him in the upbuilding of the City.

Overseer Jane Dowie, in the course of her brief address, paid a tribute to her son which found an echo in many a heart in the audience.

Dr. Gladstone responded, when called upon for a speech by his father, in a few words aptly put, after which came Judge Barnes—the unreportable.

As a fitting finale to this great annual thanksgiving, the audience sang, in closing, Zion's grand hymn:

I stand on Zion's mount
  And view my starry crown,
No power on earth my hope can shake,
  Nor hell can thrust me down.

The lofty hills and towers
  That lift their heads on high
Shall all be leveled low in dust,
  Their very names shall die.

The vaulted heavens shall fall,
  Built by Jehovah's hand,
But firmer than the heavens, the Rock
  Of my Salvation stands.

What a wonderful Baby City this is!

It grows more wonderful every year!

And this Procession today!

As I watched it, I thought of what a good, old friend of mine said to me one day when I asked him what he thought of Zion City now.

"What do I think of it, sor? It bates the world!" was his enthusiastic reply.

But to his surprise I said, "It does more than that."

"What then does it do?" he asked. "Surely if it bates the world that is enough?"

"Oh, no," I said, "that is not nearly enough for me."

"Well, what more do you want?" he questioned.

SCENES IN PARADE OF ZION INSTITUTIONS AND INDUSTRIES.
Third Anniversary of Opening of the Gates of Zion City, Friday, July 15, 1904.

Shiloh Tabernacle, Zion City, Illinois, Friday Afternoon, July 15, 1904.

The meeting was opened by the singing of Hymn No. 11, in the Program, "Hail to the Brightness of Zion's Glad Morning."

Overseer Jane Dowie offered prayer.

The 35th chapter of Isaiah, the Song of Salvation, Healing, and Holy Living, was then repeated by the entire audience, after which all joined in singing "We're Marching to Zion."

The General Overseer then said:

The Remarkable Growth of a Baby Three Years Old.

I had a baby born to me three years ago called Zion City, and I have been looking at that baby today.

"Well," I replied, "Zion City not only beats the World, but also the Flesh and the Devil." [Applause.]

I believe that Zion City has overcome the World, has overcome to a large extent the Flesh and for the most part the Devil.

A Service of Thanksgiving.

I am so thankful today!

This is a thanksgiving meeting, and I did not prepare any program, because I thought the program would make itself.

It was enough for us to see the City in all its varied institutions, represented by the workers, all of whom, however, were not there.

There were reasons, no doubt, why some could not be in the

Procession; but next year, God willing, I shall see that they are all there, for I think that we can provide for some that cannot walk.

I think that I of all men should lead the thanksgiving, and all I can say is, Thanks be unto God who giveth us the victory through Jesus, the Christ, our Lord.

We give the glory to God.

We say that all that has been wrought has been done by His grace, and although it is manifest to all men that He has been willing to use us, and has graciously used us, yet we say with all our hearts, I and all my colleagues of the Ecclesiastical, Educational, Commercial, Industrial, and Political Departments, Thine, O Lord, is the Kingdom, and the Power, and the Glory, forever. [Amen.]

We do not merely utter words; we mean it, because we have realized that all "power belongeth unto God."

There never has been a moment when we have been willing to take glory to ourselves.

The Indisputable Value of Zion City Today.

I will not attempt at this time to give you figures and facts connected with the City.

Figures and statistical facts are not needed with such a representation as you have had today.

I may say this, however, illustrative of the increase in the value of land in Zion City.

We paid for this entire tract one million two hundred fifty thousand dollars.

If you apply the rate of increase to the entire tract that is represented by the amount paid by the Chicago and Milwaukee Electric Railroad for its right-of-way through the City, namely, twenty times the cost, that would make what Zion holds, and what the people hold, worth twenty-five million dollars.

But it is more than that, and I will tell you why.

We are leasing land at the rate of seven thousand five hundred dollars an acre.

We have leased land on this boulevard near-by at the rate of nearly twelve thousand dollars an acre.

Some Future Developments.

Two years ago, we leased some at the rate of nine and ten thousand dollars an acre.

When you talk about this land, you must think of the tremendous value of that untouched Lake Front; for one day we shall have a beautiful harbor dug out there and a pier. A charming promenade will lead to it from the center of the City, and Zion will be one of the shipping ports of the Great Lakes. [Applause.]

God willing, we shall have a beautiful drive along the whole of the two and a half miles of Lake Shore, and connect it with the continuous drive all through the parks and around the City, making twelve to fifteen miles at least.

The future, and even the present, is worth talking about.

We could easily double the value of the entire tract, and I will tell you how I know that.

Did we not lease our first land at the rate of three thousand dollars an acre, and has it not changed hands over and over again at the rate of six and seven thousand dollars an acre?

Is it not a fact, as I have said, that on the boulevard we have been paid from nine to twelve thousand dollars an acre?

Elijah avenue has been reserved, because there are millions of dollars in that.

Can any one estimate the development of that land on the west side of the City?

I might speak also of the development of the lovely south and north tracts.

One day we shall suck the sand in from the lake and bring it into a good bottom and make that half of the lake front flats, north of Shiloh Boulevard, a magnificent place for the very finest residences.

What will be the value of this vast estate as Zion Lace Industries develop?

I reeeived a letter this morning showing how successful the policy I pursued in Europe was, and how rapidly we are arranging for machinery and everything of that kind.

The Riches of the Nations Have Begun to Flow Into Zion.

As regards investments, there is no question whatever that this City is a Crown of Beauty in the hands of Jehovah.

He has blessed us, and this sacred soil of Zion City, which the people hold and which we hold, is worth much more than the actual money value.

I believe that this City of Zion, its land, its homes, its factories and all that we have here and hold for the Lord is worth not less than fifty million dollars.

I do not mean that this is its taxable value, Mr. Assessor. [Turning to Deacon Sloan. Laughter.]

We are one body and we have one spirit.

Speaking of us as one people, although we each hold our own separate interests in the whole body, I have not exaggerated when I say that this great estate is worth fifty million dollars.

But Who Can Tell Me What it Will Be Worth in Three More Years?

Who can tell me, with the rapid development of the now established factories, what its value will be?

Who can tell me how much candy Deacon Rodda will turn out in three years?

In the City of Chicago itself we could sell a hundred thousand dollars' worth a year if we could make it fast enough.

We have such purity, originality, and workmanship in candy, that perfectly impartial people say, "I do not know anything about Dowie or his doctrines, but his candy is all right."

I am told by one of our officers in New York that there was a Roman Catholic gentleman of great wealth there who said that the candy had so impressed him with its purity, its originality, and its workmanship, that he wanted to know more about the place in which such candy was made.

He is in this City investigating Zion, and may be in the meeting today for all I know.

Some of the Unsurpassed Products of Zion.

We certainly are manufacturers of beautiful lace.

The beautiful lace dress which Mrs. Dowie wears today is all Zion lace, made in Zion Lace Industries.

Wherever Mrs. Dowie went, she often wore Zion lace.

She likes it and so do other people.

We have given presents of it to our beloved friends throughout the world, many of whom are quite important and wealthy people.

We have shown the lace in the great cities of the world.

We did not have enough candy with us on our Around-the-World Visitation. Whenever we got a consignment it seemed to disappear instantly.

We should have had a ton with us.

Such beautiful boxes as the Box Factory is making for this candy!

Look at those girls, with their beautiful boxes for hats. [Turning to the box factory department.]

Talk about originality!

I never saw prettier girls with prettier candy-boxes.

We also had today a beautiful representation of LEAVES OF HEALING.

Deacon Champe certainly dressed his wife in a wonderful fashion. [Applause.]

She was a very beautiful impersonation of Zion, the picture of which is so well-known.

But I cannot mention all the different departments represented.

I can only say that I am very happy, and that I praise God for what He has wrought in Zion.

Look at the vast business being done at Zion City General Stores--one of the most remarkable businesses in the world.

Look at Zion Printing and Publishing House!

Is there anything like it, for its age, in the world? and it is nothing compared to what it will be.

Safety in Zion's Investments.

There are Zion Stocks and Securities, of which Deacon Wilhite is Manager.

He represents the most valuable paper in the world.

While the three per cent. consolidated annuities of Great Britain have fallen from one hundred thirteen to eighty-five since the Boer war, Zion has never sold a share of her Stock, in Bank, Land, Lace, Store, Candy, or anything else, under par—one hundred dollars—and today Zion Lace Industries stand at one hundred ten, as does also the Bank Stock.

The day will soon come when Zion Sugar and Confection Stock and the Building and Manufacturing Stock will be worth one hundred ten.

We have never gone below par, but instead have advanced.

I should not wonder to see Zion Industry Stock quoted at two hundred, in ten years.

That is a great deal to say, but I know what I am talking about.

There are stocks worth far less in reality that are quoted in the market today at two hundred.

I am giving you some little business points, because I want to tell you that one of the great triumphs of Zion is, that God has given to us such business capacity that, in the face of the fiercest fighting that was ever made against any institution,

God Has Given Victory to Zion Against Bitterest Foes.

Zion has had to fight the press of the world.

She has had to fight the apostate churches and the politics of the world.

She has had to fight the people who were misled by the press, the pulpit, and the Devil.

She has had to fight commercial foes.

She has had to fight the concentrated hatred of the powerful and rich Masonic order throughout the world.

She has to fight foes of every kind, a few of them within our borders, whom we have had to get out.

But there has been no foe that Zion has had to fight that she has not overcome.

In the face of difficulties that it is admitted would have smashed any bank in existence, or any commercial institution, our friends stood like a solid wall behind us, not moving one step, but they were always ready to move, waiting for direction; exactly as I said.

Thus I was actually able to control all the indebtedness of Zion.

Zion has never paid one cent less than one hundred cents on the dollar, and Zion never will. [Applause.]

Men Who Have Helped to Fight the Battles.

As I look at the triumphs of last year, and at the men who have been with me through it all, my heart is filled with gratitude to God.

I look at the men who have had no easy task, the Cashier of Zion City Bank, Deacon Peckham; the General Financial Manager, Deacon Barnard; and, coöperating with him, the splendid head of our Law Department, Judge Barnes; God bless them!

Then, when I needed some one to leave in charge of all Zion City, I knew where to find him.

I had watched my man, and I had trained him, too.

I had to knock many things out of him and get a great deal into him.

I knew him better than any of you did.

None of you knew what splendid material there was in Overseer Speicher, until after he had taken charge, and then you learned that he was a magnificent man. [Applause.]

There may not be very much of him, but, like Deacon Peckham, there is much in him.

God has given me splendid men.

Look at the man whom He has given me for the Educational Institutions, Vice-president Brasefield, who, following up the splendid work of Overseer Piper, has, in one or two years, made these Educational Institutions such that I venture to say there are none of their age in America with a higher and better standard. [Applause.]

Mrs. Dowie's Value to Zion Inestimable.

As I pass from one to the other of my splendidly equipped helpers I come to Mrs. Dowie, and I ask, What is she worth in Zion? [Prolonged applause.]

I did not know how valuable she was until I was in danger of losing her; then I knew that I could not do without her, and I told God so.

I had come to see how much more valuable she was to me and to Zion then even I had known, and I asked God to give her back to me, and He did.

Then you know Dr. Gladstone Dowie, who is here, there, and everywhere, but is yet an unknown quantity. [Applause.]

May God bless my son!

I think that he is rather uncertain as to what department he belongs.

But he will go on and take his place in the Law Department.

The Overseers All Doing Excellent Work.

Then there is Overseer Mason.

He has had rather a large field in New York; but he has held the fort and increased a little.

I do not know but that he has felt half the time that he ought to be in China, and I believe that we will have to send him there.

Among the Overseers, we have one who is not present today, a magnificent and splendid little man whose stature is gigantic from an organizing point of view, a kind of Napoleon—Wilbur Glenn Voliva.

I shall make him Overseer for New York as soon as Australia can spare him.

All the Overseers are pegging away.

There is Overseer Piper pegging away in Boston.

He tells me that they recently had two thousand at an open-air meeting on Boston Common.

That is very good, but we had a larger open-air meeting in Australia. [Laughter.]

You must wake up the people of Boston.

If I come down to Boston, they will not simply sit and smile; they will howl.

Here is Overseer Excell, who has had quite a hard row to hoe.

He has been a very efficient and excellent companion.

I must say a few words about Deacon Newcomb, General Associate Editor of Zion Publications and General Manager of Zion Printing and Publishing House.

He has proved himself a prince of correspondents, has he not?

People—"Yes." [Applause.]

General Overseer—He has grasped the situation with a large mind.

Every line in his correspondence and his introductions to all my various Visitations have been his own without dictation by me of a single sentence or word.

He is entitled to all the credit.

May God bless him and give him a splendid wife. [Applause.]

The Business Cabinet.

Our Deacon Anderson has been an excellent colleague and helper, who like many you know, does not appear very much to the public eye, but his work tells.

Then there is Deacon Judd.

It is right that I, as the General Overseer, knowing these gentlemen and knowing that you all in the various deparments respect them, should speak of them.

Deacon Judd has been the Manager and Secretary of Zion Land and Investment Association from the beginning. He still holds that place, and he will continue to hold it.

He will help me launch some very big things, presently.

I will tell you one thing about Deacon Sloan, who now occupies the position of Inspector-general of all Zion Institutions in this City.

In that most important position, in which he is directly responsible to me, he is my eye and my tongue.

When he speaks, remember that I put him there to speak and to see.

He is also my Auditor-general.

Deacon Judd will bear me out that he has given splendid service.

I must also mention the Department of Stocks and Securities, which Deacon Wilhite now so ably manages, and who was an assistant of Deacon Judd, following Deacon Sloan.

These three men represent the kind of service to Zion that can never be measured by dollars and cents.

Like Deacon Barnard and Deacon Peckham, they have given themselves to their departments until their departmental work has become a part of them.

These brethren have been men after my own heart.

President Roosevelt said to me when he saw them, "Dr. Dowie, you have a Business Cabinet that looks to me so clean, so fresh, so strong, so manly, that any one might envy you such associates. I compliment you upon your selection of men." [Applause.]

I said to him, "Mr. President, I am indebted to God for these men; I did not select them. God gave them to me. God brought them to me, and I could not help seeing them as the right men."

Deacon Judd left a good little business in Englewood, where

he pottered around with real estate, and suddenly found himself at the head of a vast real estate concern, such as he had never dreamed of being manager of.

It was just as if you were to take a captain of a company and make him the commander of an army.

But Deacon Judd measured up to it.

I thank him here today for the tenacity, the sagacity, and the perseverance with which he has handled the entire landed interest of Zion.

I thank Deacon Sloan, Deacon Wilhite, and all associated with him.

God bless the manager of Zion Land and Investment Association, and all working with him.

I am perfectly willing to continue the work with these men; are you?

People—"Yes."

General Overseer—Without any desire to praise you unduly, I thank all Zion for the splendid backing that you have given to your leaders.

It Is Sometimes the Humblest Man Who Is the Key of the Situation.

Sometimes it is the faithfulness of a messenger like Mr. Tebbe, who is a splendid messenger; God bless him!

Sometimes it is the faithfulness of a Zion's special messenger of finance, of whom we have a number.

Sometimes it is the faithfulness of a young man like Deacon

SCENES IN ZION INSTITUTIONS AND INDUSTRIES' PARADE.
Third Anniversary of the Opening of the Gates of Zion City, Friday, July 15, 1904.

Corlette, who occupies a very important position in New York and represents Zion magnificently there.

May God bless him!

Good as the men that will follow may be, I can scarcely expect ever to have in Zion better men than I now have around me.

I hope they will be with me (most of them are younger than I) until they assemble around my tomb.

Then if they can only say, "He did what he could; he never feared the face of man, but he loved God and lived for Zion," that will be enough.

But I do not want to make a valedictory, because I feel as if I were going to live quite a while. [Applause.]

I think I may yet live twenty years.

Zion Law Department.

I thank God today for the men I have around me, not the least of whom is the splendid head of the Law Department.

Zion Law Department is a great help and inspiration to me.

I believe that we are getting hold, not only of the law as it bears on Zion, but of those great underlying principles which we are studying in Law and Gospel, so that we shall never be found unprepared.

I thank God for the splendid men whom He has given me.

I must say of Judge Barnes, without any offense to his predecessor, that he has proved himself to be not only not inferior to that splendid lawyer, but also a great Judge.

May God bless Judge Barnes. [Applause.]

Around-the-World Visitation a Wonderful Inspiration.

It is a wonderful inspiration for a man to pass through such experiences as the Around-the-World Visitation and live.

It was a reconnaissance.

I drew the fire of the enemy and I found out just how weak they were.

I now know where to strike.

It has not been without much thought that I have entered upon this tremendous strike against monarchy and all its devilish works.

God help me! [Amen.]

They have been trying to laugh at it, but it is no laughing matter.

They have come to see that the words that I say are dangerous to monarchy. They may try to keep LEAVES OF HEALING out of England, Germany, Austria-Hungary, and other empires and monarchies.

"Leaves of Healing" Cannot Be Kept Out of Empires and Monarchies.

But the very fact that they want to keep it out will make the people of the world eager to get it by hook or by crook.

We know how to help them in that.

They may keep it out of the postoffice, but they cannot keep it out of Zion's express and Zion's underground railway.

I will get it into Europe if I have to send special messengers across the continent with every issue. [Applause.]

I have many people in Europe who will take it from town to town and from city to city and risk their lives in doing it.

They will be willing to go to prison, if need be, for distributing LEAVES OF HEALING. LEAVES OF HEALING from the Tree of Life, which is for the healing of the nations, will yet be known to all the world.

The terror that it inspires in the Devil's lieutenants will make the whole world more and more determined to read it.

The best thing that could happen to us would be for it to be shut out of the mail in England.

But it will not be shut out of the mail in America.

We will do nothing whatever to break the Law, and I believe that America, if she does not forget what the Declaration of Independence means, will be with me, and is with me, in my fight against monarchical tyranny and military oppression.

I have not said all I should like to say; but I shall now ask Mrs. Dowie to say a little.

A Mother's Tribute to Her Son.

Overseer Jane Dowie—"I thank God for bringing us back in safety from our journey.

"I know that the journey has been a blessing to many thousands.

"Today I thank you for your love and for the kind expression of it that you have given.

"I notice that the one man upon the platform who had the least said about him was the General Overseer's son.

"I desire to say a few kind words about him, and then I will sit down.

"He was my companion, as you know, on the journey, and he was an excellent son to his mother. [Applause.]

"I was not well when I started on that journey, as many of you know, and I should never have continued if I had not had my son with me.

"He took every care of me on the way.

"During the time of which the General Overseer spoke, when I was nearly away from this earth, my son stayed by me, and was a great blessing and help to me. [Applause.]

"He has been very good to his mother."

General Overseer—I did not say that he was bad, I only said that he was an unknown quantity.

He himself cannot yet tell how the Lord will lead him.

He himself does not know, if he will continue in that department, after he has taken his bar examination and becomes able to represent us as council.

I ask you to pray for him.

I have confidence that the prayers which his mother, his father, and all of you offer for him, will be answered.

A Life Without Fear and Without Reproach.

He has been able to live a life which, I might say, has been without fear and without reproach; a life that, thank God, has been with such credit, that when I asked the acting president of the University of Chicago about him, and whether he had passed, he said to me some words concerning his high esteem for my son, which I have never told any one.

Then he added these words: "Dr. Dowie, do not be troubled about your son's passing and taking his degree of Juris Doctor. His scholarship, his character, and his capacity are such that there is no question that he has qualified for his degree;" and I found it was true.

I want you to pray for him; he is all we have.

We want him to be the very best he can be for God and for Zion.

I believe that all Mrs. Dowie said is true, and I shall add something more: in the dangers and trials through which we have passed, while all were brave, none were braver in standing by his father, than Alexander John Gladstone Dowie. [Applause.]

I think that we might hear a word or two from him.

Dr. A. J. Gladstone Dowie—"The question under discussion seems to belong to Professor Brasefield's department—the solution of unknown quantities.

"I shall not take up the matter at this late hour.

"I think we had better let the proposition lie over until Professor Brasefield's department and some of the other departments can, in the future, furnish you with the right solution." [Applause.]

General Overseer—With the permission of the departmental chiefs, I shall ask for the one who always remembers something, to represent them all—Judge Barnes. [Applause.]

Judge Barnes—"Beloved General Overseer, and Christian friends in Zion: I remember reading some time ago an incident of a very learned and distinguished divine, who took for his subject on a memorable occasion, 'The Major and the Minor Prophets.'

"After talking for an hour and a half about the major prophets, he came to another branch of his subject and said, 'I now come to the second branch of my subject: the Minor Prophets. What place then shall we give to Hosea?'

"A tall person in the back part of the house rose and said, 'If you please, sir, he can take my place; I am going home.' [Laughter and Applause.]

Words of the General Overseer Always an Inspiration.

"After having listened to our beloved General Overseer, who is certainly a great prophet, you will not care to hear from one of the 'minor prophets' on this occasion.

"I was interested in listening, as I always am, and as I know all the members of Zion are, to his words of friendship and love and kindliness of heart as well as of wisdom, given to us, as I believe, from God as an inspiration in carrying on the great work of Zion.

"I believe the Irishman to whom he referred spoke wisely when he spoke of the work of Zion. You remember the anecdote told by the General Overseer near the beginning of his address.

"It reminds me of a remark of another Irishman who took a friend of his to see a vast cathedral that had been constructed in a certain city in New England.

"After examining it, he said to his friend, 'What do you think of it?'

"'Phwhat do I think of it? It bates the Divil,' was his reply.

"His friend answered, 'Thot was the intintion.'

"It is the intention of Zion to destroy the works of the Devil, and all of us must be very faithful and earnest.

"I believe that that cathedral was located in the City of Boston, and you know Boston is a most wonderful city.

"It is called the Athens of America, and we have a very distinguished representative of Zion in Boston here on the platform, our beloved Overseer Piper.

"I read not long ago about a Philadelphian who went to visit a friend living in Boston. He said to his friend, 'I understand you said once you thought so much of the City of Boston that you believed that heaven must be such a place as Boston is.'

"'Well,' said his friend, 'I believe I did say that some years ago, but Boston has improved considerably within the last few years.'

"It seems as though Zion City is the one place on earth that is nearest like heaven.

"I believe our experiences will warrant us in saying this.

A Bond of Love and Unity.

"We are all bound together in a spirit of love and unity.

"We have that unity and peace which comes to us through the Holy Spirit, purchased for us by the Son of God, and we do well to be faithful.

"No man has prospered who has been disloyal to the General Overseer or untrue to Zion.

"Every man will receive his reward if he has been faithful and true to the principles of Zion.

"But it will not do to loiter.

"It will not do to lose faith.

"It will not do to be in doubt.

"We must keep up with the procession.

"I have noticed frequently that those who have misunderstood and occasionally have been untrue to Zion—a very small minority—have not come in contact with the spirit of the institutions.

"They have wandered away and got on the outside, and have forgotten many things they once knew.

"The clouds have risen before their eyes and concealed the facts from them.

"When we once get into Zion, we must remain loyal and perform our duty as it arises.

"Occasionally my attention is called to some of our friends for whom I can have nothing but the greatest sorrow.

Expedient to Keep Up With Zion.

"They remind me of two Norwegians waiting for a train out in Minnesota.

"The train stopped for a few minutes at the station, and these two Norwegians did not get on promptly.

"They were watching something else and not giving enough attention to the train, and finally it moved out.

"They ran at great speed and overtook the train.

"One climbed up on the rear platform and the other had hold of the railing, increasing the length of his steps as he went.

"The one on the rear platform yelled to him, 'Yump, Ole, yump, yump!'

"'Yiminy, how can I yump when every time I yump I fall down?'

"Those who do not keep up with Zion, but watch the train, are very likely to get left upon the platform or somewhere else.

"My friends, it certainly would not be my place to undertake to make a lengthy speech upon this occasion after the words of our beloved General Overseer, Overseer Jane Dowie, and Dr. Gladstone Dowie.

"I feel that I am among friends, and such friends as I have never been among before.

"I have never for a single moment regretted having come into Zion to become a part of it.

"It is a continual inspiration, and I thank God today that I am in Zion.

"I have the unspeakable pleasure every day of grasping by the hand those who are here, and listening to the salutation, 'Peace to thee,' and 'Peace to thee be multiplied.'

"I thank God for the General Overseer and for the rank and file of Zion.

"I thank Him for the privilege of standing in your presence and expressing my thanksgiving and praise upon this great day in Zion.

"Certainly it was a wonderful inspiration to see the magnificent product of the work done under the General Overseer during the last three years.

"My friends, I know that more is due you than I have said, but in response to the invitation of the General Overseer, I join with all others today in the expression of gratitude and praise, thanking God for him and for you, and for the spirit that is continuously the inspiration of Zion here and throughout the world.

"May God bless you."

The Reward of Patience and Honest Labor.

General Overseer—Young people and those of all ages in Zion's Institutions: Napoleon once said to one of his armies, "Be diligent, be attentive to duty, be brave, be obedient, work on, and you will find, it may be, a marshal's baton in your knapsack."

What he meant by that was that every man that did his duty had promotion in store, for his was an army that well-nigh conquered Europe.

You have, it may be, a general manager's baton in your knapsack.

We have many general managers; we will have more, and if you are diligent and attentive to duty, who can tell but that you may be one of them?

The officers of the new Zion Cities will naturally come from this City, at first, and the Elders, Evangelists and Overseers of the future will naturally come from this City.

You may have a very humble position, but do your duty.

I have a hundred eyes, because I take a keen interest in every department; in all its submanagers and in all its help.

When recommendations for promotion come to me at the right time, I am glad to advance you.

Be not impatient.

The man who wants to get everything, to grasp promotion quickly, is the man who we think is desirable to get rid of as soon as possible, because if he cannot wait he will never be able to rule.

The only one who can ever rule is the man who knows how to obey.

The trouble with some splendid men and women is that they do not know how to obey.

They obey just as they like and when they like.

These are the people that, no matter how talented, we never can make permanent use of.

In closing, I say, be of hope. Zion has possibilities for all her workers, but you must be patient.

I had long, long, long years of toil and patience ere I came to be the General Overseer of the Christian Catholic Church in Zion, and I have to be more patient now than ever.

May God bless you!

I cannot talk about you all, but as I look at you, I see an army of Zion workers—merchants, bankers, lawyers, manufacturers, artists, great thinkers and writers, men and women of affairs.

Zion, I salute you.

God bless you!

All joined in singing, "I Stand on Zion's Mount," after which the General Overseer pronounced the

BENEDICTION.

Beloved, abstain from every form of evil. And may the very God of peace Himself sanctify you wholly; and I pray God your whole spirit and soul and body be preserved entire, without blame, unto the coming of our Lord Jesus, the Christ. Faithful is He that calleth you, who also will do it. The grace of our Lord Jesus, the Christ, the love of God our Father, the fellowship of the Holy Spirit, our Comforter and Guide, one Eternal God, abide in you, bless you and keep you, and all the Israel of God everywhere, forever. Amen.

EARLY MORNING SACRIFICE OF PRAISE AND PRAYER.

REPORTED BY R. M. F., O. R., AND E. S.

The third day of the Holy Convocation was the rounding out of a week full of blessings and mercies.

The day was a perfect one, with its beautiful sunshine after the refreshing and copious rain which had renewed the earth and brought life to all growing things.

In the early morning hour, as the people of God gathered in Shiloh Tabernacle, Sweet and Perfect Peace lay like a benediction over the earth, and abode in the hearts of His children.

The third Fruit of the Spirit—Peace—seemed embodied, on this morning of perfect beauty, in the little City and its inhabitants.

Shiloh Tabernacle, Zion City, Illinois, Saturday Morning, July 16, 1904.

The service was opened by the singing of Hymn No. 9, in the Program.

Prayer was offered by the General Overseer, at the close of which the Congregation joined in chanting the Disciples' Prayer

The General Overseer then said:

Letter Concerning Plot Against the General Overseer's Life in London.

I have a letter from London which tells of the plot against my life, which would have been carried out had I not retired to France.

It is becoming clearer and clearer.

The writer, Mr. William Parker, 120 Pelham road, London, one of Zion Guard, writes to Mr. Wallis of this City.

Mr. Wallis says among other things:

I enclose a letter I received today from one of our Guards in London, showing how completely the plot to take your life in our beautiful Tabernacle at Euston road, June 13th, would have been carried out, had you not retired to France. I thank God for the wisdom He gave you to do this. I rejoice to tell you that your words on the Lord's Day were a blessing to my brother-in-law.

In the letter from London, which accompanies Mr. Wallis' letter, details are given of that plot.

It tells how a stranger came upon some of the details of this plot by mixing up with the men who were in it.

They were medical students, and expected that I would be in Zion Tabernacle, Euston road.

They were armed, and one of them fired his pistol into the Tabernacle, even though I was not there.

Several of them were arrested, and were put under bonds by the magistrate. We knew about that before.

Even the newspapers in London intimated that if I had entered Euston Road Tabernacle that day there is little probability that I would have come out alive.

There is no way to get a carriage to the door.

There is no side or back door, and it would have been exceedingly easy for the mob to have trampled me in the streets.

Why the General Overseer Crossed Over Into France.

I did not believe that God wanted me to be trampled in the gutters of London.

I did not believe that He wanted my life trampled out by a band of vile medical students, who had tried to murder me before.

As the police probably would not have been there in force, and as the whole arrangements of the Hall were absolutely opposed to my being able to get away quickly at the close of my work, I did the wisest thing.

I went across the Channel; and when I was ready I came back.

I did not think it would be fair or right to you and Zion to throw away my life in the gutters of London.

Are you with me in that matter?

People—"Yes."

I do not feel that I showed any fear, because I was warned of this plot before I went to London.

We found every evidence of it after reaching there

We tried to get large halls and could not.

Persons in authority prevented us after Overseer Cantel had engaged halls and paid for them.

Albert Hall was refused.

Queens Hall was actually paid for and arrangements made, and then it was refused.

We tried for weeks to get a large place where we could speak to multitudes.

I was only prudent and took shelter in France from the storm; but even before it had passed I came back to England and went through the midst of it.

I went openly through London and right across England, from the Channel to the Irish Sea.

The details of this letter I do not care to read. I have a great many letters to the same effect.

The Bravery and Faithfulness of Zion Guard.

Pray that we may be spared to carry out the great purposes for which God has put us here.

I thank Zion Guard in London and everywhere for their excellent care of me.

Wherever I may be, loving hearts gather around me—strong men who would get between me and the bullet if they knew it was coming, and gladly give their lives to save mine.

I know that is the case with Zion Guard in Zion City, to a man.

May God bless them! [Amen.]

I know that their wives, too, have oftentimes said, "If the Doctor is in danger, get between him and the bullet."

We have been in danger much oftener than we have told you.

Cowardly Mobs Hunt Their Prey Like Wolves.

If I can get into a carriage and have good horses and a good driver, I am never troubled about getting away, for even when there are tens of thousands wanting to stop me, the cowardly mob is afraid when the horses plunge and strike out with their feet.

You should see the cowards scatter.

They fly on every side.

They are only brave, like wolves, when they hunt in packs.

God has been wonderfully good to us, and I desire you to praise Him with me.

I want to go on with my work.

I believe it will be a number of years before I take up that Visitation to London, but if I live ten years I want to take ten thousand Restorationists to London with me.

We will get them from the Continent, as well as from America, and we will have a glorious time. [Applause.]

I did not have a sufficient army on my late Visitation.

The Devil was in force, and I had only an observation party.

I know that God was with me and protected me.

Only Kindness and Love Shown on Continent of Europe.

What a wonderful thing it is that on the Continent of Europe, in all the lands which we visited, the people were so kind and so ready to receive us, while the great Anglo-Saxon people howled with passion!

They felt the Masonic whip, and it was that which aroused the classes and masses.

The great multitude between was friendly.

I could have filled the largest hall in London twenty times over with people who were eager to hear me.

I am very grateful to them for the kind words and good wishes which were expressed to me in so many ways before I left London.

Let us now read in the 14th chapter of the Gospel according to St. John, the first three verses and also the 25th, 26th, and 27th verses:

Let not your heart be troubled: ye believe in God, believe also in Me.

In My Father's House are many mansions; if it were not so, I would have told you; for I go to prepare a place for you.

And if I go and prepare a place for you, I come again, and will receive you unto Myself; that where I am, there ye may be also.

These things have I spoken unto you, while yet abiding with you.

But the Comforter, even the Holy Spirit, whom the Father will send in My Name, He shall teach you all things, and bring to your remembrance all that I said unto you.

Peace I leave with you; My Peace I give unto you: not as the world giveth, give I unto you. Let not your heart be troubled, neither let it be fearful.

The General Overseer then delivered his Message:

THE THIRD FRUIT OF THE SPIRIT: PEACE.

INVOCATION.

Let the words of my mouth and the meditation of my heart be acceptable in Thy sight, be profitable unto this people, and unto all to whom these words shall come, in this and every land, in this and all the coming time, Till Jesus Come. Amen.

TEXT.

But the Fruit of the Spirit is Love, Joy, Peace, Long-suffering, Kindness, Goodness, Faithfulness,

Meekness, Temperance: against such there is no law.

The third Fruit of the Spirit is Peace.

Peace Is the Product of Power.

Peace is only possible in a sin-distracted, sin-smitten, and disease-smitten world, when the Power of God has subdued and destroyed the power of sin, disease, death, and hell, and broken the power of the Devil.

There is no Peace, saith Jehovah, unto the wicked.

You can get no Peace without good order.

Confusion and strife and every evil work go together.

The First Law of Heaven is Order.

Order must prevail throughout the entire Church of God, or there is no Peace.

Peace does not mean the surrender of Purity, of Liberty, or of any right which God has given you.

It means the complete subjugation of the individual by the Power of God, that the discontent and native arrogance that are in our hearts by nature, and the determination to run our engine up and down the line on our own schedule time, may be lost entirely in God's Will.

I remember one day, in Central Zion Tabernacle, asking a brother, who had been a locomotive engineer for some forty years, "What would you do if you knew that there were a number of men on the line who had powerful engines, and who said they did not care what the manager said about the time-table; they were going to run up and down that line on their own schedule time?"

"What would I do?" he answered; "I would run my train on the first side-track and stay there until they got the fellows off."

Peace and real progress can only come into our disordered beings by power, working there for righteousness, calling out the things that defile, and making strong and sound the track along which the engine of power runs, so that when you need to put on pressure and go fast eveything is in good order.

Then you can work your minds upon such occasions and come out just as strong as before.

Peace the Legacy of the Christ.

Peace is the result of power.

If it were not for the Power of our Lord Jesus, the Christ, who gave Himself a sacrifice for us, and became our Peace; if it were not for His Power which overcame the World, the Flesh, and the Devil, and made Atonement for our sins and for our sicknesses, and made the track clear, we could make no progress.

There would be no Peace, but disorder at every step, and probable wreck.

The Fruit of the Spirit is Peace.

The greatest legacy that the Christ left us was the Legacy of Peace.

It is a Pearl of Great Price, so great that we may well part with everything else to possess it

Peace! Peace! Peace!!

He who is the Prince of Peace lived in the midst of confusion, and strife, and every evil work.

But He obeyed Law.

He could say, "I delight to do Thy Will, O My God; Yea, Thy Law is within my heart."

That is why He was at peace.

There was no conflict between Him and Law.

There was perfect harmony.

The Will of God, the Father, was supreme.

He delighted to do it.

He taught us that the Path of Peace was in absolute obedience to the Word of God.

The Fruit of the Spirit is Love, Joy, Peace.

Peace Does not Consist in Idleness.

There is no doubt that large numbers of Christians have a sentimental notion about Peace, as if it consisted in folding their hands and swinging in a hammock, and being at perfect rest, physically, and enjoying the physical and psychical condition of absolute laziness.

To me, constituted as I am, knowing something of the Peace of God, I do not imagine that you could describe a state of misery for me more complete than a prolonged physical and psychical rest.

There would be no spiritual rest for me in it.

I would have no rest, for I, as one of God's remembrancers, give God no rest and I take no rest.

There is not an hour in the twenty-four when the cries of the sick and sorrowing are not coming to me, by telegram, by cablegram, by telephone, and by message.

When I absolutely close down and say that there are none to be delivered for a certain length of time, until I get a little sleep, I know they are there, nevertheless.

I know that they are piling up.

I remember the promises that I have made to God to pray for my people.

All over the world they are calling on me, even when I sleep, to remember them.

One peculiar thing is that I will oftentimes awake and be led to pray for some one I have not particularly thought of for a long time; and often I will find that the telephone message, cablegram, telegram, or letter is at the door, and God had caused me to offer the prayer.

To some people I suppose it would be simply intolerable if they could never know a time when they could rest or expect to rest; but to me it is not so.

I have the intense joy of mental and spiritual activity, and find a perfect Peace in the midst of the most intense activity.

God is supremely and constantly active.

He is always working in nature, working in grace, working in myriad forms of life, and working out designs that reach unto the ends of the Universe.

He cares for this great Universe, with suns and systems so numerous that we cannot count them; and yet with what perfect order, perfect power, and perfect harmony the Divine Government is conducted, and in what Perfect Peace!

There is Perfect Peace for the man who is in communion and union with God.

There Is No Unrest in God.

Where there is unrest, and doubt, and fear, and questioning, there is no Peace.

Then the Love and Joy that you have, in some degree, is quickly destroyed, or rendered ineffectual.

One can pour Love and Joy into you, but when you are fretful and impatient, and not at Peace, it is like pouring water into a vessel that has a bottom full of holes.

You can pump into that vessel all night, a full and gloriously beautiful supply, and in the morning you find it as dry as ever.

That is the way with a great many people.

They have little troubles, and they are quarrelsome and fretful, and want things their own way.

Then the Love and Joy that have been poured into them these last two morning meetings are gone, because they have the pin-pricks of unrest and have run dry.

Perfect Peace Is Possible Only to the Perfectly Controlled Nature

He who brings Peace, and is its Author, must be its Preserver.

The Faith, the Hope, the Love, the Joy which He brings must be preserved by Peace.

The Unity of the Spirit must be bound together by Peace.

Unrest, discontent, rebellion, and disorder are the destruction of the individual, the business, the home, and the nation.

Peace is the product of the Spirit of God operating in power, keeping you perfectly calm.

One of the curiosities of nature is that the center of a flame is perfectly cool.

Inside each jet of gas that is burning so brightly and hot, there is a point that is perfectly cool.

It is one of the strange things of nature that in the midst of a cyclone there is a center that is perfectly calm.

Amidst the innumerable activities and in the tremendous velocity of the world, whirling through space at a speed that is incalculably quick, there is Perfect Peace in God.

Peace is not allied with indolence.

In God's Great Economy Peace Is Connected With Progress.

It is deepest often when the darkness is deepest, when the impending suffering is most inevitable; when the cup of death itself must be drunk to the deepest dregs, as when the Redeemer took it in His Gethsemane.

It was then that He spoke of Peace; it was then that He gave us Peace.

> Peace I leave with you; My peace I give unto you: not as the world giveth, give I unto you. Let not your heart be troubled, neither let it be fearful.

He left Peace! It is here!

It is in the Holy Spirit, the Spirit of Peace.

He left the Comforter!

He came to us and He never leaves us!

He will be with us all the way, a Comforter Divine!

He Gives Peace, He Never Sells It.

You cannot buy Peace.

All your toil for God can never be exchanged for Peace.

If you offer God your services, as an exchange for Peace, He refuses it.

You trafficker, how dare you think you can buy that which God only gives!

The King of kings never sells.

He is no trafficker.

You cannot traffic with God.

"My Peace I give unto you."

The Gifts of the Spirit are not purchasable.

They cannot be obtained by clamor and demand for them.

The Gifts of God are given where the preparation is acceptable to God.

He will not pour the beautiful Water of Life into an unclean vessel.

He will not give the Peace in its fulness to those who are unclean in spirit, soul, or body.

You must get clean.

You must be healthy, and then in the cleansing power of God be made fit for the Peace of God to flow into the reservoir of your whole being, calming your spirit, your soul and your body, making every nerve to be perfectly still, and every fiber of your being to be at rest.

That is only possible when you are wholly God's.

He will not sell Peace, He gives it to you.

The Divine Peace of the Christ of God is not purchasable.

Peace Is Not Given as the World Gives.

When the world gives, it often repents almost as quickly as it has given, and wants to take it back, and sometimes does.

The love that was offered you and assured you forever was a lie; it was only dirt and unclean lust, and you did not know it.

Perhaps the man who offered it did not know it.

He thought it was Divine, but shortly you find that it was not.

The world gives its own, but it does not give in perpetuity.

Everything that belongs to the world is hard to get, it is harder to keep, and must at last be given up.

You brought nothing into the world, and you can carry nothing out that belongs to the world.

You came into the world a naked spirit, embodied for a time in a temple of flesh, with a living soul.

This spirit oftentimes is trammeled by the flow of filthy blood, and by the inheritance of shattered nerves and weakened brain.

Then only God Himself can restore your being until there is Peace, and He will.

All that can ever be given to us by the world is unrest, for there is simply no peace in humanity that can be extended beyond a very limited area, the boundaries of which we very quickly see.

The Difference Between the World's Peace and God's Peace.

The Gift of Peace is not hard to get, for it is freely and lovingly bestowed.

It is not hard to keep, for He keeps us in Perfect Peace.

It is never taken away, for God never repents of His own work.

I know that, whatsoever God doeth, it shall be forever.

God's work is not transient, and His gifts are not repented of.

The Gifts and calling of God are without repentance.

Peace is not hard to get, not hard to keep, and never to be given up.

That is the difference between the World's Peace and God's Peace.

But God's Peace will only be continued, and only perfected, by your continuing in God, for the Peace is not in yourself, but in Him.

Perfect Control by God Brings Perfect Peace.

The Peace is in Him, but it is only while you are in accordance with Him, and He is in accordance with you, that His Peace is yours.

"If a man love Me, He will keep My words," Jesus said, "and My Father will love him, and We will come unto him, and make Our abode with him."

A Triune God is needed to satisfy the nature of a triune man, who is made in the image of a Triune God.

Peace is always imperfect until God perfectly takes and keeps the control of our being.

That can only be by the absolute surrender of your being to Him, or your will to His Will; then God can use you.

I care not to speak much of myself, but I have enjoyed Perfect Peace, for the most part, during a great many years of Christian life.

If I erred, I always found that the Holy Spirit led me, through goodness, into repentance, and through repentance into a Perfect Faith, where Hope shone brightly, where Love was given freely, and where Joy came in the morning.

I desire to say, to the glory of God, that I do not know what this unrest is, from which so many suffer.

Perfect Peace in the Midst of the Storm.

I see it just as I would watch, from a strong castle-window, a storm at sea, with the waves lashed into fury, while the cries of those that were on the deep came up to me.

But I do not know anything about the distress of mind experienced by others in such a storm.

"You have never been in a storm?" you ask.

Yes, I have; but that is when I am most at peace.

I believe that those who have traveled with me will be able to bear me out in saying that a peculiar thing in connection with my physical constitution, as well as my psychical and physical condition, is this: that when the winds are howling most fiercely, the lightnings flashing, the thunder rolling, the sea rising until it sweeps over the highest decks, and even strikes the masts—when the vessel begins to pitch, and toss, and roll, and almost turns over, I have a kind of delirium of joy.

I feel so happy, and my stomach, which may have been a little fitful and uncertain, becomes ravenously hungry.

I go where I can see the storm, and I rejoice.

When the storm is greatest, I am most happy.

I enjoy life at sea best, and am never sick in the tossing of water.

But as soon as I get to land I begin to realize that there is such a thing as bile, and in a day or two I vomit.

I land at some port and smell the disgusting odor of filthy nicotine and stinking beer and wine and whisky; I see the selfish, beastly natures of men and women hunting for one another's flesh, until it makes me sick.

It is the land that makes me sick, not the sea.

Beloved, in the heart that is at Peace with God, the Peace is deepest, purest and sweetest, most satisfactory, most stirring, enlivening, quickening and impelling to work, when the storms are greatest.

Sweetest Peace Born of Deepest Suffering.

It was so with Paul, when he sang in the prison.

It was so with the Christ, when the darkness was deepest, and there burst from His heart the last prayer: "Father forgive them, for they know not what they do."

When His agony, physical and psychical, was most intense, His union with God, the Father, was most perfect, although the darkness hid Him, and the loving, joyful cry burst from His lips—the prayer of love for the murderers, for those who hated Him, and of joy in the hour of His agony; for it was during the agony of the Redeemer that our Peace was born.

The sweetest Peace in our life has been born in our deepest suffering.

The Holy Spirit will never impart the Peace of God to the fretful, lazy, skulking, cowardly, wretched creature, who is always seeking for a soft place, light work, and an easy time.

I could have stayed here; I did not need to go out and face the World, the Flesh, and the Devil.

I could have stayed in many places and not have done what I did; but it was the Peace of God within my heart that impelled me to carry the Message of Peace to others.

Zion's Salutation of Peace a Great Blessing.

The Third Fruit of the Spirit is especially the Gift of God to Zion, and unless our words are a mockery and our morning salutation is a sham, a delusion, and a snare, then the salutation God has given to Zion must be a great reality: "Peace to thee!"

There are those in this loud and stunning tide
  Of human care and crime,
With whom the melodies abide
  Of the everlasting chime;
Who carry music in their heart
Through dusty lane and wrangling mart,
Plying their daily task with busier feet,
Because their secret souls a holy strain repeat.

You can tell those who are at Peace, when they say, "Peace to Thee." Peace flows from them like a river.

I would rather you would not say it than to say and not mean it.

Take time to say it.

When you get the Salutation, look back at him from whom it comes—he may be wanting help—and say, "Peace to thee be multiplied."

In all parts of the world the people love our Salutation, because it comes from hearts that are at Peace with God.

Let the Peace of God rule in your hearts.

PRAYER OF CONSECRATION.

My God and Father, in Jesus' Name I come to Thee. Take me as I am, and make me what I ought to be, in spirit, in soul, and in body. Give me a full redemption—the Love, the Joy, and the Peace—that it may abide;

that the Fruits of the Spirit may increase, until by Thy grace, I reach a Self-control that is all Divine, because of Thy control. Be in me a Power that makes Peace, that subdues all that is evil and that keeps in Perfect Peace. For Jesus' sake. [*Congregation repeated the prayer, clause by clause, after the General Overseer.*]

The service was closed by the General Overseer's pronouncing the

BENEDICTION.

Beloved, abstain from every form of evil. And may the very God of Peace Himself sanctify you wholly; and I pray God your whole spirit and soul and body be preserved entire, without blame, unto the coming of our Lord Jesus, the Christ. Faithful is He that calleth you, who also will do it. The grace of our Lord Jesus, the Christ, the love of God, our Father, the fellowship of the Holy Spirit, our Comforter and Guide, one Eternal God, abide in you, bless you and keep you, and all the Israel of God everywhere, forever. Amen.

EARLY MORNING SACRIFICE OF PRAISE AND PRAYER.

REPORTED BY I. M. S. AND E. S.

The Fourth Fruit of the Spirit—Long-suffering—was the theme of the Man of God at the Fourth Early Morning Sacrifice of Praise and Prayer of the Holy Convocation.

Long-suffering—a large-hearted generosity, a large capacity for forgiveness, a large patience, long patience, long-suffering!

How beautiful and to be desired became this Fruit of the Spirit, as revealed by the Prophet of God!

Approximately, six thousand people listened to the Message given at this meeting.

The day, even at this early hour, was oppressively warm, yet the vast audience gave the closest attention throughout, the entire number, so far as observed, rising at the close and consecrating themselves to God and His service.

Shiloh Tabernacle, Zion City, Illinois, Lord's Day Morning, July 17, 1904.

The services were opened by the singing of Hymn No. 4, Special Program, after which prayer was offered by the General Overseer, closing with the chanting of the Disciples' Prayer by the Congregation.

Hymn No. 53 was then sung.

The General Overseer said:

THE FOURTH FRUIT OF THE SPIRIT: LONG-SUFFERING.

INVOCATION.

Let the words of my mouth and the meditation of my heart be acceptable in Thy sight, be profitable unto this people, and unto all to whom these words shall come, in this and every land, in this and all the coming time. Till Jesus Come. Amen.

Now read with me in the Second General Epistle of Peter, and the 3d chapter:

TEXT.

This is now, beloved, the Second Epistle that I write unto you; and in both of them I stir up your sincere mind by putting you in remembrance.

"Putting You in Remembrance."

That is what we must continually do, put ourselves in remembrance of God's Will.

Whenever you have a minute or two, be ever ready to find your Bibles, and put yourselves into remembrance of God's Word.

That ye should remember the words which were spoken before by the holy prophets, and the commandment of the Lord and Savior through your apostles:

Knowing this first, that in the last days mockers shall come with mockery, walking after their own lusts.

One of the most extraordinary signs of these times is the cartoonist and the mocker.

It has often been said that William McKinley was murdered by William R. Hearst, the editor of a number of villainous newspapers, which kept up a mockery of Mr. McKinley, both editorially and in silly cartoons.

If one tithe or one hundreth part of what is charged against W. R. Hearst in his race for the Democratic presidential nomimation is true, he ought to be put behind prison-bars for bribing delegates.

I should like to see a law passed in the United States of America, making it a penal offense for anybody to bribe a delegate to a political party convention.

I am inclined to think that the jails would be filled if such a law were enforced.

"Mockers" in Modern Journalism.

As I have said, one of the great signs of the times is the mocker.

Chief among these are the *Examiner*, the *American*, and the various other papers controlled by Mr. Hearst.

That man gets villains to write for his papers, and then gets foolish people, of supposedly good character, to write pious articles, that will carry the vileness of the rest of the paper into decent homes, there to do its deadly work of defilement and destruction.

What a farce it is for a professed minister of the Gospel to have his name signed to an article on one page, while the filthiest society muck and the lowest sporting gossip appears on the next page!

One of the "attractions" of these vile papers are the cartoons that make fun of the very best men in the community.

I am not complaining on my own account, because I have never paid the slightest attention to these cartoons.

They do not hurt me, because I rose above that long ago.

I only grieve that the common people may think or imagine that I am such a man as the cartoonists sometimes draw.

I was recently cartooned in New York in the act of picking the pockets of Father Knickerbocker.

I could have turned upon that editor and prosecuted him, and perhaps could have recovered heavy damages.

I very much question, however, whether he had not protected himself in such a way as to make it exceedingly difficult to hold him responsible for what he did.

Besides, I have no time for getting into lawsuits with people.

But it was a shameful thing!

Sometimes you see the greatest and best men in the country maligned in this way.

Assassination of President McKinley Result of Newspaper Mockery.

For years, the late President William McKinley was represented as a miserable little boy with a cocked hat, playing at being President, and altogether under the power of a big, black, ugly-looking woman whom they called Mark Hanna.

That got into the public mind, until the able President was held in the utmost contempt by a vast number of people, who were very ignorant and could not read much—foreigners who could not understand our language, but who could understand a cartoon like that.

They mocked at the President and they mocked at Roosevelt, and from among the mockers came the poor, miserable wretch that assassinated President McKinley.

Thousand of mockers are to be found connected with the press in this land.

Not merely do they mock at good men and good institutions, but they mock at all good.

They often mock at God.

Some of them call Him the Weather Man.

They mock at God until even Christians sometimes take up the words, and say, "I wish the Weather Man would give us better weather."

You are mocking at God when you say that.

The weather is in God's control.

I warn you lest you should take up the mocking words.

There is nothing so foolish as the would-be wit of today.

There is nothing so cheap, there is nothing that degrades more, than the mockery of the press of today.

Certainly, there never has been a period in the world's history when the mockery of God was so prevalent.

Surely these are the Last Days!

Knowing this first, that in the Last Days mockers shall come with mockery, walking after their own lusts.

Degenerate and Filthy Character of Press "Mockers."

These mockers, the so-called comic artists, with scarce an exception, are drunkards, tobacco fiends and immoral, utterly without principle.

They are like the prostitutes of the streets—they can be hired and made, and all their talents and powers can be bought for the vilest purposes.

Knowing this first, that in the Last Days mockers shall come with mockery, walking after their own lusts,
And saying, Where is the promise of His coming? for, from the day that the fathers fell asleep, all things continue as they were from the beginning of the creation.

"All things continue as they were from the beginning of the Creation."

That is not true.

Everything is not as it was.

There have been some very wonderful things since the beginning of the Creation, and the most wonderful of them all was the Coming of the Lord Jesus, the Christ, and His Crucifixion and Resurrection.

For this they wilfully forget, that there were heavens from of old, and an earth compacted out of water and amidst water, by the Word of God.

Wilful Forgetfulness.

There are people that "wilfully forget." They put the thing aside, put it out of their minds.

People shut their eyes, and stop up their ears and harden their hearts.

They will neither see nor hear, nor yet understand.

They plunge themselves into things that obliterate, for the time being, memory itself.

For this they wilfully forget, that there were heavens from of old, and an earth compacted out of water and amidst water, by the Word of God;
By which means the world that then was, being overflowed with water, perished:
But the heavens that now are, and the earth, by the same Word have been stored up for fire, being reserved against the Day of Judgment and destruction of ungodly men.

"Stored Up for Fire."

The heavens are full of fire and the earth is full of fire.

Sometimes there is more fire where it is cold then where it is warm. The most terrific volcanic eruptions take place in the coldest regions.

Being reserved against the Day of Judgment and destruction of ungodly men.

Just as surely as God's Word is written, it is true that ungodly men will be destroyed.

If they will be ungodly, let them be ungodly still.

I will draw the line very sharply between the good and the wicked. May God help us to draw it sharply!

But forget not this one thing, beloved, that one day is with the Lord as a thousand years, and a thousand years as one day.

When the world is ready there will be a work of Salvation wrought which otherwise would take a thousand years.

Go to a place where LEAVES OF HEALING has been, and there you will find a people ready.

One day, when we have sown the world with the Truth, and it keeps on growing and growing, we will be able to do the work in One Day that would take ordinarily a Thousand Years.

The Lord is not slack concerning His promise, as some count slackness; but is long-suffering to youward, not wishing that any should perish, but that all should come to repentance. . . . .
Wherefore, beloved, seeing that ye look for these things, give diligence that ye may be found in Peace, without spot and blameless in His sight,
And account that the Long-suffering of our Lord is Salvation; even as our beloved brother Paul also, according to the wisdom given to him, wrote unto you.
As also in all his epistles, speaking in them of these things; wherein are some things hard to be understood, which the ignorant and unsteadfast wrest, as they do also the other Scriptures, unto their own destruction.
Ye therefore, beloved, knowing these things beforehand, beware lest, being carried away with the error of the wicked, ye fall from your own steadfastness.
But grow in the grace and knowledge of our Lord and Savior Jesus the Christ. To Him be the glory both now and forever. Amen.

The Congregation then repeated with the General Overseer, Galatians 5:22, 23:

But the Fruit of the Spirit is Love, Joy, Peace, Long-suffering, Kindness, Goodness,
Faithfulness, Meekness, Temperance: against such there is no law.

"He Is Long-suffering over Them."

"Long-suffering!"

The first thought that came to me this morning was just as if I heard a voice saying, "Though He bare long with them."

I turned these words over in my mind, thinking that perhaps I could go to sleep again.

I found that I could not, and I thought these words over and over: "Though He bare long with them."

Then I knew that they were the words of our Lord Jesus, the Christ:

And shall not God avenge His elect, which cry to Him day and night and He is Long-suffering over them?

That is the way it is put there by the Lord Himself in

The Parable of the Unjust Judge.

This judge had wronged the woman who cried after him.

He was in collusion with the trustee of the estate, and had wronged the widow.

He had received a part of the plunder.

Perhaps he said at last, "The plunder I got is not worth the misery I suffer.

"This woman comes after me day and night.

"When I rise in the morning, I hear her cry, 'Avenge me of mine adversary.'

"When I go out for a drive, there she stands with her children, at my door, and she cries, 'Avenge me of mine adversary.'

"They turn her away, but she returns.

"When I sit on the judgment seat, she says again, 'Judge, avenge me of mine adversary.'

"She stands there with her poor, orphan children and looks at me, and she will not go away.

"She follows me.

"When I go home at night, I hear her cry, 'Avenge me of mine adversary.'

"In the middle of the night I hear her cry, 'Avenge me of mine adversary.'"

Day after day and week after week she goes on with this, and at last the judge says:

Though I fear not God, nor regard man;
Yet because this widow troubleth me, I will avenge her, lest she wear me out by her continual coming.

Our Lord says:

And shall not God avenge His elect, which cry to Him day and night, and He is Long-suffering over them?

Oh, How God Has Borne With Us!

How long He has borne with His own elect—with His own children!

How long He has borne with you!

What Long-suffering!

Oh, how wonderfully long has been the Long-suffering of God!

How patient He has been, and how willing He has been not to execute Law and demand its full penalty!

If there has been True Repentance, no matter how grievous the offense, He has always been willing to forgive.

The fruit of the Spirit is Long-suffering.

I was meditating this morning upon that word, Long-suffering, which is, in the Greek, *makrothumia* (μακροθυμία).

θυμία means "spirit." Its principal meaning is very clear—large-hearted generosity, large-hearted capacity for forgiveness.

A Large Capacity for Suffering.

Beloved friends, we not only need to have Long-suffering, but we need to have large suffering, a large capacity for suffering, a large capacity for exercising forgiveness even when the person who commits the offense is not entitled to an atom, because God is Long-suffering towards us.

Oh, how wonderful is the Long-suffering of God!

How He bore with the people who wilfully and wickedly sinned, led by God's High Priest, when Moses was up in the mountain receiving the Law from God!

He had brought them out of Egyptian slavery and bondage by His great Love, yet while Moses was getting the Law from God, that wretched Aaron made a calf out of the gold that they had stolen from Egypt, and the people worshiped it with disgusting, filthy, heathen orgies.

When Moses came down from the Mountain of God, he heard the music and singing of Baal worship.

He knew it. "My God! Can it be true?" he thought.

He looked over the heads of the people, and there stood the golden calf shining in the bright sunlight.

They were singing the lustful, damning songs that they had sung in Egypt.

He rushed forward, and there was his own brother, the High Priest of God, leading in the singing.

Then he took the tables of stone and dashed them down at his feet and broke them.

"My God, cut off these people," was almost the cry in his heart.

Moses Pleading for His Sinful People.

Yes, and God was about to do it, too.

But a cry went up. Moses loved that people.

That cry went up from Moses' heart.

Although he saw that they deserved judgment, indignation, wrath, and to be cut off, he cried, "O God, spare them! Remember their ignorance, remember that they were in bondage four hundred years, and learned nothing!

"Remember that the iron entered into their souls.

"Do not forget, O God, that they were despised, degraded and debased!

"O God, spare them!

"If You will not spare them, blot me out of Your Book. I do not want to live if they do not."

"He endured as seeing Him who is Invisible."

Have you Long-suffering in your hearts?

Are you willing to suffer?

God saw how He could easily mend matters temporarily by cutting everybody off, and yet, that would not be a permanent remedy.

It might do for the present, but if you kill a man in this world, you have to deal with him in the next.

You Have Not Settled the Question of a Murder When You Have Hanged the Guilty Man.

That man goes out into the life beyond, to where the murderers and the devils are, and God has to deal with him.

He is still in God's Universe.

Oh, brothers, sisters, have we been patient enough?

How ready some men are to send a man into eternity!

I think we should do with the man that has committed crime as God did with Cain.

God saw that murderer at the moment when he killed his brother.

God said, "Where is Abel, thy brother?"

"Am I my brother's keeper?" asked the insolent Cain.

"The voice of thy brother's blood crieth unto Me from the ground."

Ah, his blood speaks!

Cain never forgot the look of Abel's face.

He never forgot the blood that was shed. Day and night and day and night he would rise up, and he would hear his dying brother's imploring cry, "O God, forgive Cain!"

"Being dead he yet speaketh."

Does not the blood of the Christ cry, being dead yet speaking?

But God would not let Cain be killed.

Jesus would not let the Pharisees be killed.

Blood never wipes out blood.

Murder, legal or otherwise, never wipes out murder.

No crime can ever be wiped out by another crime.

God steps in and says, "Thou shalt not kill."

Give the murderer forty or fifty years' imprisonment, or give him a life sentence, but remember that you did not help him to be better.

Remember that you did not teach him that the Fruit of the Spirit was Love, and Joy, and Peace; that you never came to him or helped him.

I am so glad for the Long-suffering of God!

Let it be mine, let it be yours today.

We Must Bear Long With Offenders.

We must sometimes punish severely, but we must bear long with them.

Remember how Long-suffering God has been with them.

Let our Love and Joy, let the Peace of God, find expression in making us more patient with humanity.

Do not forget, when insult is flung into your face, that the offender has something perhaps to be said for him, that he was, perhaps, shamefully neglected, and never had the love of a mother or father.

Do not forget that the poor sinner has to be patiently dealt with.

Be Long-suffering!

A Tradition of a Lesson God Taught Abraham.

"Abraham, Abraham!" says a Voice.

Abraham answers, "Yes, Lord."

"There is a stranger coming. Take care of him."

So runs an old rabbinical tradition.

Abraham turned and saw at the door of his tent a poor, dirty, old, wayfaring man.

"Come in," he said.

He took the stranger in, washed his feet, and called for Sara, his own princess, to bring food.

Sara, the princess, waited upon the beggar.

Abraham said, "God sent you to me—eat."

There was rich food and beautiful fruits; for Abraham was a rich man and a great one.

The man devoured the food.

As Abraham looked at him, he became more and more angry.

He wondered if the man was ever going to thank anybody.

He had not thanked God, and he had not thanked Abraham.

Abraham was boiling with indignation.

Presently, when he had finished, the beggar rose and walked away.

Then Abraham's indignation burst forth.

He rushed out and called to the man, "Stop, ungrateful wretch! I did not grudge to give you food, but you did not thank God and did not thank me."

He heaped upon him maledictions, and the poor wretch slunk away.

Abraham came home, thinking that he had done a great thing, and lay down to sleep.

"Abraham, Abraham, Abraham!" called a Voice. He listened.

"How long did I bear with you in the long night of your heathen darkness, when you never thanked Me for anything?

"O Abraham! I bore with you all those years, and you never thanked Me for anything! Now I have enriched you and sent you this poor man, whom you gave only one meal, and because he did not thank Me, and because he did not thank Abraham, you did not teach him anything else, but went after him and cursed him."

"Oh, what shall I do?" Abraham cried in his penitence, bowing his face in the dust.

"How Long-suffering Thou hast been with me, Jehovah! Tell me what to do."

"Go after him," said the Lord, "and fall at his feet and ask him to forgive you."

Abraham overtook the man, put his arm around him and said, "Forgive me. Come back. I ought to have taught you how to thank God. God was patient with me for a long time, and I was not patient with you for one hour. Forgive me! forgive me!"

"Lest We Forget."

Some of you forget how patient God has been with you.

Let your wife say one single thing that you do not like, and you forget her long years of love; you forget how faithful a mother and how good and kind a wife she has been, how she nursed you when you were sick and almost dying.

You rail at her and curse her, or you break her heart.

Some of you women forget the long days of patient toil that the man who loves you has given for you, how patient he was with you when the baby was sick, how he bore his part and cared for the baby all night, and then went to work the next morning.

Just for one little thing you screech at him in anger.

Where is the Fruit of the Spirit?

Where is the Love?

Where is the Joy?

Where is the Peace?

Where is the Long-suffering?

You have none of them.

They are gone.

Why?

Because you were impatient, and because you did not suffer long.

You were not willing to wait and to say, "I will think of all the good things in life."

Instead of this, you are so ready to fight and to snarl.

The Fruit of the Spirit is withered. The Love is withered, the Joy is withered, the Peace is withered.

They are blighted. They are dead, because you did not suffer long, and were not willing to suffer even a minute.

God forgive us and give us Long-suffering Grace.

PRAYER OF CONSECRATION.

My God and Father, in Jesus' Name, and for His sake, take away the sin of impatience; forgive, restore Love, Joy, and Peace, and give unto us the grace to suffer long, and to be kind and to be patient. Amen. [*All repeat the prayer, clause by clause, after the General Overseer.*]

Do you intend to live that?

People—"Yes."

The Consecration Hymn was then sung.

The General Overseer closed the services with the following prayer:

CLOSING PRAYER.

Father bless us, and give us more of the Spirit of Love, Joy, Peace and Long-suffering. Master, how Thou hast borne long with us! Thou didst not put any away until it was absolutely needful. Thou wilt not sweep any away that are wicked, unless it is impossible to do anything else. Oh, still bear with us, Thy people. We have borne so little Fruit compared to what we might have borne had we been more Loving, more Joyful, more Peaceful, more Patient, more Long-suffering. Oh, bear with us! For Jesus' sake.

The General Overseer then pronounced the

BENEDICTION.

Beloved, abstain from every form of evil. And may the very God of Peace Himself sanctify you wholly; and I pray God your whole spirit and soul and body be preserved entire, without blame, unto the coming of our Lord Jesus, the Christ. Faithful is He that calleth you, who also will do it. The grace of our Lord Jesus, the Christ, the love of God our Father, the fellowship of the Holy Spirit our Comforter and Guide, one Eternal God, abide in you, bless you and keep you, and all the Israel of God everywhere forever. Amen.

GREAT GENERAL ASSEMBLY.

REPORTED BY L. L. H., O. L. S., AND A. W. N.

How glorious the prophetic vision of that ancient man of God, who, upon the impulse of Divine Inspiration wrote that wonderful rhapsody which begins with the thrilling words, "Arise, shine; for thy Light is come, and the Glory of Jehovah is risen upon thee!"

How his own spirit must have been exalted and filled with unspeakable Joy as he beheld, by Divine Revelation, the future glory of his beloved Zion!

How the spirits of multitudes in the true Israel of God, in all the centuries that have passed since that wonderful chapter was written, have rejoiced in the prophecy, looking into the future with eager eyes for the first faint glow of the coming of that Light and the arising of that Glory!

How many of "God's remembrancers," lying upon their face before Him, have besought Him for the day when Zion should come forth in the Perfection of Beauty in obedience to that call, "Arise, shine!"

Upon us these times have come!

To us is given the Solemn Joy of hearing, at last, that Divine call, "Arise, shine!"

To us God has vouchsafed the crowning privilege of all the ages, that of beholding the arising of His Zion and the effulgence of her Divine Light.

It is we who are to see the fulfilment of this sublime prophecy, who indeed see, even now, the beginning of that fulfilment.

Such were the joyous and yet deeply solemn thoughts that were awakened by the Message of the General Overseer, the Prophet of God, in Shiloh Tabernacle, Lord's Day afternoon, July 17, 1904.

It was the fourth day of Zion's Fourth Feast of Tabernacles.

On the three previous days, and especially on Thursday and Friday, something of the brightness of Zion's rising had been seen in the great Anniversary processions, parades, and exercises.

Hence it was that the momentous prophetic Message, founded upon the 60th chapter of Isaiah, came with such irresistible power to the thousands upon thousands who gathered on that occasion in Shiloh Tabernacle.

Notwithstanding the sultry and exceedingly oppressive heat of the day, seven hundred fifty visitors had come out from Chicago on the special excursion in the morning, in addition to several hundred who had come out the night before.

The City was full of visitors from distant parts, and hundreds had driven to the meetings from neighboring cities and districts.

Six thousand five hundred people witnessed the beautiful procession of Zion White-robed Choir and Robed Officers, heard the splendid music of Zion Band, Zion Orchestra and Zion Choir joining together in the production of the "Gloria," from Mozart's "Twelfth Mass," and listened with deep feeling to the Message of God's Prophet.

At the close of this Message, the man of God pronounced the Benediction and dismissed the greater part of the audience, those who wished to receive the right hand of fellowship remaining, together with a goodly number who desired to attend that ordinance.

Four hundred twenty-two people from twenty-seven states of the Union and from ten foreign countries were taken by the right hand and welcomed into the fellowship and communion of the Christian Catholic Church in Zion, by the General Overseer, with a fervent prayer for God's blessing upon them.

It was a deeply impressive service.

Shiloh Tabernacle, Zion City, Illinois, Lord's Day Afternoon, July 17, 1904.

The service was opened by Zion White-robed Choir and Zion Robed Officers entering the Tabernacle, singing the words of the

PROCESSIONAL.

Open now thy gates of beauty,
Zion, let me enter there.
Where my soul in joyful duty
Waits for Him who answers prayer;
Oh, how blessed is this place,
Filled with solace, light and grace.

Yes, my God, I come before Thee,
Come Thou also down to me;
Where we find Thee and adore Thee,
There a heaven on earth must be.
To my heart, oh, enter Thou,
Let it be Thy temple now.

Here Thy praise is gladly chanted,
Here Thy seed is duly sown;
Let my soul, where it is planted,
Bring forth precious sheaves alone,
So that all I hear may be
Fruitful unto life in me.

Thou my faith increase and quicken,
Let me keep Thy Gift Divine,
Howsoe'er temptations thicken:
May Thy Word still o'er me shine,
As my pole-star through my life,
As my comfort in my strife.

Speak, O God, and I will hear Thee,
Let Thy will be done indeed:
May I undisturbed draw near Thee,
Whilst Thou dost Thy people feed.
Here of life the fountain flows,
Here is balm for all our wos.

At the close of the Processional the General Overseer came upon the platform, the people rising and standing with bowed heads while he pronounced the

INVOCATION.

God be merciful unto us and bless us,
And cause Thy face to shine upon us;
That Thy Way may be known upon earth,
Thy Saving Health among all the Nations,
For the sake of Jesus. Amen.

PRAISE.

The Congregation then joined in singing Hymn No. 11:

Hail to the brightness of Zion's glad morning,
Joy to the lands that in darkness have lain!
Hush'd be the accents of sorrow and mourning,
Zion in triumph begins her mild reign.

The General Overseer then led the Choir and Congregation in the recitation of the Apostles' Creed:

RECITATION OF CREED.

I believe in God, the Father Almighty,
Maker of heaven and earth:
And in Jesus, the Christ, His only Son, our Lord,
Who was conceived by the Holy Ghost:
Born of the Virgin Mary;
Suffered under Pontius Pilate;
Was crucified, dead and buried:
He descended into hell,
The third day He rose from the dead;
He ascended into heaven.
And sitteth on the right hand of God, the Father Almighty;
From thence He shall come to judge the quick and the dead.
I believe in the Holy Ghost;
The Holy Catholic Church;
The Communion of Saints;
The Forgiveness of Sins;
The Resurrection of the body,
And the Life Everlasting. Amen.

The General Overseer then led the Congregation in repeating the Commandments; after which the words, "Lord, have mercy upon us, and write all these Thy Laws in our hearts, we beseech Thee," were chanted.

READING OF GOD'S COMMANDMENTS.

I. Thou shalt have no other gods before Me.

II. Thou shalt not make unto thee a graven image, nor the likeness of any form that is in heaven above, or that is in the earth beneath, or that is in the water under the earth; thou shalt not bow down thyself unto them nor serve them: for I, Jehovah, thy God, am a jealous God, visiting the iniquity of the fathers upon the children, upon the third and upon the fourth generation of them that hate Me, and showing mercy unto thousands of them that love Me and keep My commandments.

III. Thou shalt not take the Name of Jehovah thy God in vain; for Jehovah will not hold him guiltless that taketh His Name in vain.

IV. Remember the Sabbath Day, to keep it holy. Six days shalt thou labor and do all thy work; but the seventh day is a Sabbath unto Jehovah thy God: in it thou shalt not do any work, thou, nor thy son, nor thy daughter, thy manservant, nor thy maidservant, nor thy cattle, nor thy stranger that is within thy gates; for in six days Jehovah made heaven and earth, the sea, and all that in them is, and rested the seventh day, wherefore Jehovah blessed the Sabbath Day and hallowed it.

V. Honor thy father and thy mother; that thy days may be long upon the land which Jehovah thy God giveth thee.

VI. Thou shalt do no murder.

VII. Thou shalt not commit adultery.

VIII. Thou shalt not steal.

IX. Thou shalt not bear false witness against thy neighbor.

X. Thou shalt not covet thy neighbor's house, thou shalt not covet thy neighbor's wife, nor his manservant, nor his maidservant, nor his ox, nor his ass, nor anything that is thy neighbor's.

Hear also what our Lord Jesus, the Christ, the Son of God, hath said, which may be called the Eleventh Commandment:

XI. A New Commandment I give unto you, that ye love one another; even as I have loved you, that ye also love one another.

The great Choir then sang the

TE DEUM LAUDAMUS.

We praise Thee, O God; we acknowledge Thee to be the Lord.
All the earth doth worship Thee, the Father Everlasting.
To Thee all Angels cry aloud, the Heavens and all the powers therein.
To Thee Cherubim and Seraphim continually do cry:
Holy, Holy, Holy, Lord God of Sabaoth,
Heaven and earth are full of the majesty of Thy Glory
The glorious company of the Apostles praise Thee.
The goodly fellowship of the Prophets praise Thee.
The noble army of martyrs praise Thee.
The Holy Church throughout all the world doth acknowledge Thee,
The Father of an Infinite Majesty;
Thine Adorable, True and Only Son;
Also the Holy Ghost, the Comforter.
Thou art the King of Glory, O Christ;
Thou art the Everlasting Son of the Father.
When Thou tookest upon Thee to deliver man,
Thou didst humble Thyself to be born of a Virgin;
When Thou hadst overcome the sharpness of death,
Thou didst open the Kingdom of Heaven to all believers.
Thou sittest at the right hand of God in the Glory of the Father.
We believe that Thou shalt come to be our Judge.
We therefore pray Thee, help Thy servants,
Whom Thou hast redeemed with Thy precious blood.
Make them to be numbered with Thy saints in glory everlasting.
O Lord, save Thy people and bless Thine heritage;
Govern them and lift them up forever.
Day by day we magnify Thee;
And we worship Thy Name ever, world without end.
Vouchsafe, O Lord, to keep us this day without sin.
O Lord, have mercy upon us, have mercy upon us.
O Lord, let Thy mercy be upon us as our trust is in Thee.
O Lord, in Thee have I trusted, let me never be confounded.

The General Overseer then read from the Inspired Word of God, the 62d chapter of the Book of the Prophet Isaiah.

Overseer Piper led in the general supplication, after which the General Overseer prayed, presenting the requests from the sick and distressed, praying for Zion throughout the world, and leading in the chanting of the Disciples' Prayer.

The announcements were then made by the General Overseer, after which the tithes and offerings were received, during which Zion White-robed Choir, accompanied by Zion Orchestra and Band, rendered the "Gloria," from Mozart's "Twelfth Mass."

The General Overseer then delivered his Message:

ARISE! SHINE! FOR THY LIGHT IS COME.

INVOCATION.

Let the words of my mouth, and the meditation of my heart be acceptable in Thy sight, be profitable unto this people, and unto all to whom these words shall come, in this and every land, in this and all the coming time, Till Jesus Come. Amen.

TEXT.

Arise, Shine; for thy Light is come, and the Glory of Jehovah is risen upon thee.—*Isaiah 60:1.*

Perhaps the word "shine" might be better translated, "be enlightened."

Arise, *Be Enlightened;* for thy Light is come, and the Glory of Jehovah is risen upon thee.

The call, "Arise, Be Enlightened; for thy Light is come," is the call of God now.

Surely the Glory of Jehovah Has Risen Upon Zion.

We shone like a little candle in a great, dark place, when Zion opened her first Tabernacle.

The denominations made a great deal of fun of the new-born Church.

When we at last, in 1896, entered into fellowship with one another, four hundred fifty in number, it did not seem as if the new Church would make a very great impression.

But when that Church became a thousand within a week, when the enrolment was nearly three thousand within a month, when hundreds upon hundreds were saved and healed and blessed, and the roll of the baptized began to swell into thousands, when tabernacle after tabernacle proved too small, and when at last the greatest buildings in Chicago were too small, and one of the largest in the world, was overflowed, and that almost continually, then the Organization began to be something that was seen and heard.

Then we made a new Tabernacle out of an old church, and spent thirty thousand dollars in transforming it.

But we were forced to leave this because it could not contain us.

Upon my return from Europe early in 1901, the great building known as the Chicago Coliseum could not contain the people.

Twelve thousand five hundred people were within the building, and the Chief of Police asserted that more than twenty-five thousand were outside.

The Little One Had Become a Thousand.

The Church continued to move forward, and at last moved out of Chicago to this City.

Then some of our adversaries thought this Congregation could never keep up its large numbers forty miles from Chicago.

But they were made to see their mistake when, four years ago, we consecrated Zion Temple Site, with probably more than ten thousand present; when we opened the City three years ago, with vast concourses of people; when Shiloh Tabernacle was built, holding five thousand, and had to be increased to its present capacity of seven thousand three hundred.

The world saw that these Feasts of Tabernacles were attended by such vast numbers of people, that there were weeks in which we spoke to thirty, forty, and fifty thousand, until at last, we could say that we had talked to audiences of well-nigh one hundred thousand people within a period of ten days.

Then Zion Restoration Host, which no one seemed to know anything about, was suddenly found to be an active power for evangelization. It was found that we had visited every house in Chicago eight times in one year. It was found that we had visited in the neighboring cities and towns, that the work of the Host was rapidly spreading throughout the world, that Branches of the Christian Catholic Church in Zion were being established upon every continent, and that Overseers, as well as Elders and Evangelists, had to be sent to take care of the work. Then the people began to think that Zion was somewhat of a world-power.

The World Surprised at the Work of Zion Restoration Host.

Then we went to New York City three thousand strong, having thoroughly studied the city until Zion Restoration Host knew every street in New York City, and could go, when it landed there, to the places provided for its accommodation.

We showed the world an Organization so perfect that every man knew his place, not only on what train he would go, but the very seat on that train.

It was found that this first reconnaissance in force went to New York City "like a mighty army."

Then suddenly it dawned upon some that this was an Organization that could reach every man, woman, and child in New York City, and we did reach them.

We distributed the Literature of Zion to the number of four million two hundred thousand pieces, in more than a million homes and in the shops and factories, as well as in almost every ship in port.

The people came continuously in such vast numbers to Madison Square Garden, that night after night our audience was fifteen thousand, with tens of thousands outside, the average being at least thirty thousand who could not get in, and on one occasion more than one hundred thousand stood patiently outside.

It was found that despite the falsehoods of the press this work went on, and Zion Restoration Host did its work.

Vast multitudes of people were reached, so that everywhere the Salutation of "Peace to thee" became so universally known, that you would hear the cabmen, and the drivers of carriages, and the people everywhere saying it, more or less seriously, to one another.

Not long since, a relative who bears the same name that I do, received some merchandise from some part of America, and found that on the boxes the words, "Peace to thee," had been painted.

They had not forgotten the Salutation in New York, and the merchant shipping the goods thought it was proper, when they went to a Dowie, to say, "Peace to thee!"

When our Messengers are found to be in every land, and the numbers continuously growing, it begins to dawn upon the world that something has come; that down in the darkest places of the great cities a Power has come that shines as a Bright Light.

But Greater Things Than These Are Being Wrought.

The vast amount of Literature that has been sent throughout the world, it may be properly calculated, has reached the people in all the lands, to the number of more than two hundred millions.

Then, through the press giving more or less garbled statements, doubtless the news that this New Power has arisen, has reached perhaps two-thirds of the human race.

We find that in Arabic, in Tamil, in Cingalese, in many comparatively unknown tongues of almost unknown tribes, statements have been made concerning the establishment of the Christian Ca holic Church in Zion, and concerning the Declaration of Elijah the Restorer.

And so we can say, truthfully, that we have been obeying this command, and have risen, and gone forth.

Zion's Work in South Africa.

The last Overseer sent out, Overseer Daniel Bryant, who went to South Africa, where perhaps there are not ten people who have ever seen our face, has already baptized between three and four hundred people, and has made the statement, in his own writing, that there are several thousands in South Africa awaiting to be baptized when he can get to them. [Applause.]

This is the case in all the world.

If we had enough Elders and Evangelists we could find work for them in more than one thousand fields of labor.

The Cry Coming From All Parts of the World.

The General Ecclesiastical Secretary, Overseer Excell, will please tell me if he thinks I am right.

Overseer J. G. Excell—"Certainly!"

General Overseer—I think that that is the minimum number of places from which the cry, in one form or another, is reaching us.

I am no sooner home than I find it expedient to send Overseer Speicher to Europe, both that he may get a little rest and that he may do some official work.

He has instructions to open a new Zion Tabernacle in Paris and install Elder Arthur Booth-Clibborn, and his wife, Elder Catherine Booth-Clibborn, in charge of the work there.

Others will be ready for ordination as Deacons.

I venture to say that he will find, when he takes Elder Kosch and Evangelist Kosch, who have been studying here for some years, down to Budapest to place them in charge of their station, that the largest place will not hold the congregations.

The work demands our sending additional help to Great Britain, to Switzerland, to Austria-Hungary, and we would be glad to send to hundreds and thousands of places.

Zion Preparing for the Future.

One of the things that is showing the whole world, and all that are true to God, that we are looking to the future, is the building of the beautiful new Educational Building, of which you see the first section now, which cost one hundred fifty thousand dollars.

It is, thank God, like every building and institution in Zion City, without a penny of indebtedness or mortgage of any kind. [Applause.]

That section of the College Building is already too small, so Overseer Brasefield, who has the active charge of Zion Educational Institutions, tells me.

All our beautiful school buildings are almost bursting now.

We have had the joy of educating many youths and maidens.

This year, 1904, by a peculiar coincidence, the number enrolled is exactly 1,904.

Our beautiful Zion Printing and Publishing House, which we thought was large, they tell me now is too small, and that I will have to give them more room, because the vast amount of printing that is now done calls for enlargement.

I mention these things because we have been reading this 60th chapter of Isaiah closely for years, and for years I have been saying to you every year at this time, "Arise, shine!"

We have risen, and have been doing some shining.

The Nations Stirred by the Around-the-World Visitation.

Eight of us just returned from a tour around the world, and you would have thought, from the noise that the enemy made, that we were eight hundred thousand at least.

One dear old Scotchman, in Australia, who had known me all my life, nearly, looked at me and said, "I dinna understand, John Alexander; you have moved, you have shaken, you have stir-r-r-red this Commonwealth of Australia from its center to its circumference, again and again, until it is all stirred! It seems to me as if you have also stirred the whole world!" [Applause.]

It seemed so.

It seemed that the presence of one man, with seven companions, was enough to stir and move the nations.

It seems very clear that it shook them to such an extent that you would have thought there had been an earthquake under the coronation chair in Westminster Abbey, for the throne seemed to be reeling.

Here we are at home again, thankful to God that this center of the work is, after all, a center which reaches every land and every nation.

We have officers and members of the Church throughout the great Australian Island Continent.

We have them in Asia and in Africa.

From Zürich as a center, away up near the Alps, we are sending the Water of Life down, as the rivers flow on every side from these Alps, into every part of Europe.

The work is becoming known from the frozen north to the sunny south of Europe.

Russian Empire Trembling With Fear at Zion's Power.

The Russian Empire was so afraid of my presence that not only did Baron Schlippenbach refuse to visé my passport, that I might visit Russia, but while I was in Zürich I had one of the most singular visits that I have ever had in my life.

I will not give the name which the lady sent up on her card, and which was undoubtedly correct, for the gentleman who owns the hotel said, with a shrug of his shoulders and a smile, that it was all right, she was the Baroness ——.

When she came all the way from St. Petersburg, with a princess in her company, to see me, I was on my guard.

Was She a Russian Spy?

After a great many honeyed compliments, the lady, who spoke beautiful English, said, "Now, my dear General Overseer, I am very much interested in your work in Russia."

I said, "Madam, this is the first I have heard of your interest!"

"Oh," she hastened to reply, "I assure you that I have been very attentively considering it for some time!"

"The Madam has not informed me of her interest," I answered, "nor have any of my friends told me anything about your Ladyship's being interested."

"Oh, but—but—I have," she stammered; then, collecting herself, she said, "I should very much like to know who your correspondents are in St. Petersburg and Moscow."

"If you are very much interested, you must know my people," was my reply.

"You have them in the Court," she said. "I know you have them in the Imperial Court, and in the Czarina's household, but will you please give me their names, that I may have the pleasure of calling upon them?"

I looked at her, and she read my look perfectly well. as I said, "The Madam would know very well who they were if she were a friend of Zion! Why does your Ladyship want names?"

"You do not think that I am a spy, do you?" she said.

"I did not say so," I replied.

"But do you think it?" she insisted.

"Madam," and I looked squarely at her, "the very suggestion that it was possible for you to be a spy may have confirmed me in some impressions that were growing."

"Oh," she exclaimed, "do not think that!"

"I cannot ask the Madam to be troubled about my thoughts, but I wish to say that you cannot have the names!" I said, firmly. That was enough; all her great interest in my Mission evaporated.

She attended one meeting, during which I managed to get in some good advice to the Czar and the "Holy Office."

It was quite a hot day, and the Baroness grew very, very warm; she became so warm that at last she had to go.

Russia Punished for Her Great Transgressions.

I told her that Russia was treading in the path of God's wrath in this war, where He was permitting her to be punished for her transgressions. I also told her that until the Czar and his government, the Greek Orthodox church, fell upon their faces in penitence before God, for the cruel treatment of their own people, in depriving them of civil and religious liberty, and especially for the hatred and murder of God's people, the Jews, the face of God would continue to be against the nation.

I said that unless they did, their fleet would be reduced to scrap-iron, their armies would be overcome and practically annihilated; Manchuria and the Asiatic provinces would be torn from their grasp; that rebellion would rend the empire asunder, and that the Colossus would fall. [Applause.]

She sat with a pale face, that Russian noble lady, who, as far as I could see, was the spy of the state and of the church.

But in Cæsar's household we still have those who love God and Zion.

We are getting petitions for prayer even from Russia.

During last week I had petitions presented in this place from one of the northern provinces, where large numbers of people have been getting the Literature since the Zürich Mission.

These are earnestly seeking God, and are being led by a pastor who may, perhaps, find his home in Siberia soon.

But never mind, he is facing the dangers and the possibilities, and he is doing the work of God.

May God bless him in Russia.

People—"Amen!"

General Overseer—But I must not talk too much about Russia, for I might say some things that the Russian spies, who are all over the United States, would pick up and send to Russia.

Then there would be a police visitation in the dead of night, the man would be torn from his family, and in a few days a dead body would be secretly buried, as hundreds have been recently buried in Moscow and St. Petersburg, where thousands have been arrested.

Common People of Russia Not in Sympathy With Present War.

The Czar and his ministers know well that the whole people of Russia are against this war, and that the soldiers, instead of fighting with patriotism and earnestness, must be whipped into the cars that transport them to the field of action.

Some break their hands and fingers that they may not be able to handle a gun.

Large numbers of them are being deported, shot, and treated horribly, because they do not want to fight.

Prophecy Made Some Years Ago Now Being Fulfilled.

What I said years ago is coming true.

I prophesied that if Russia came into conflict with Japan, it would be a bear putting to sea to fight a sword-fish, and that the sword-fish would pierce the bear, and his life blood would flow out into the waters of the sea.

I said that the Russian fleet would be reduced to scrap-iron every time the Japs hit them; and it is so.

I said that when the Colossus with its feet of clay, touched the warm waters of the Asiatic Seas the feet would be washed away, and that the horrible power that is against all real Christianity would fall on its face into the sea.

I believe that this is indeed the case.

The result will be the break-up of the Russian Empire, and the restoration of stolen liberty to many oppressed and conquered peoples, both in Europe and in Asia, from whom it has been stolen by the Russians.

It may mean the restoration to Finland of its own rights, to Poland, to many other places in Europe, and to Manchuria.

The restoration may reach through the lines of communication between Vladivostock and Moscow, to numerous nations that have never been united to Russia, but were cruelly treated—their people murdered, their women treated so shamefully that no words can express it.

They have been wrongfully tied to Russia; but the knot is slipping, and will at last be cut by the sword of the conquering Oriental Power, that is doing it now most efficiently. [Applause.]

Present War Forced Upon the Japanese.

War is horrible!

I hate to think of it!

But if ever a war was forced upon an empire, if ever a people were compelled to fight for their very national existence, it was the Japanese, who saw that they were the only power in Asia that could meet that horrid power that knows no liberty except the liberty of obeying an apostate church and a cruel autocratic tyrant.

The Japanese had no alternative between national extinction and fighting, and they had to fight.

It was forced upon them.

If they delivered the first blow, it was because it was merely a question as to which of the two fighters would strike the first blow.

They struck it, and struck it effectively.

God, who does not love war, has at the same time prophesied the downfall of the Prince of Meshech, and Tubal, and Rosh.

Rosh is clearly Russia.

Meshech is clearly Moscow.

Tubal is the name given to a city.

These are the three principal points, and the Word of God says, that God is against that cruel prince, and that his empire shall fall.

"Blätter der Heilung" a Mighty Power for God.

I was surprised to find that the light which comes from Zion had shone into the Imperial Court so much that both the Court and the apostate church were afraid, not only to let me into Russia, but were afraid of those who had been won to God through LEAVES OF HEALING, and especially BLÄTTER DER HEILUNG.

The lady who is my Assissant Editor on BLÄTTER DER HEILUNG, Evangelist Marie Brieger-Hodler, came from one of the northern provinces of Russia, where she had lived for many years, although a German brought up in Austria.

I thank God for the work she has done, in assisting me in getting LEAVES OF HEALING into places where it seemed impossible to get it.

I thank God that she is sitting in this building this afternoon, having come from Zürich on the *Barbarossa* late last week.

May God bless her! [Applause.]

BLÄTTER DER HEILUNG has been the principal means of blessing the people, both in Russia and in Austria-Hungary, as well as in Switzerland, because it has been the principal minister to the German-speaking and German-reading people.

I have brought over my French interpreter, Mr. Rollier, who has been our agent in Paris, and also some others, and have determined that we shall, by the grace of God, shine brighter this year in these lands.

By the fall we shall have a weekly paper in German and a paper in French, that can be sent throughout the whole of Europe.

May God give me the help that will enable me to do this!

People—"Amen!"

The North is Crying Out.

The light has come to Denmark.

I had the great joy in Zürich of ordaining a lady of noble station in Denmark, Mademoiselle d'Acqueria, to be a Deaconess in the Christian Catholic Church in Zion.

I long to be able to send a number of our beloved Scandinavian Deaconesses to carry Zion's Message into Scandinavia. [Applause.]

I may also say to you that the work is spreading in every part of Europe; even in Rumania, in Bulgaria, and in the Turkish Empire.

The Nations Coming to Zion.

May God grant that the little beginnings that are being made in India and China may speedily increase, and that the dear ones who are holding up the Banner of Zion in Japan may be blessed.

Let Zion never forget for a moment that her work is to all the world.

Arise, shine! for thy Light is come; and the Glory of Jehovah is risen upon thee.

That gross darkness is covering the earth and the peoples, is beyond all question.

The darkness is deepest and most horrible and hateful in professing Christian countries, where there is Light.

The promise is that nations shall come to see the Light that Zion is sending.

We are told to "lift up thine eyes round about, and see, they all gather themselves together, they come to thee: thy sons shall come from far, and thy daughters shall be carried in the arms."

All in this Tabernacle that have come to Zion City from across the seas stand. [Hundreds stood.]

I am glad to see such a large number standing.

We found, some time ago, upon examination, that there were about seventy nationalities in this City.

I believe we have more today.

We lift up our eyes and we see you.

You have come from far.

Thy sons shall come from far, and thy daughters shall be carried in the arms.

Many little babes have been carried here in the arms.

I saw yesterday no less than five hundred new inhabitants of this place, most of whom had come from across the seas.

The Word says, that when this takes place we shall see and we shall "be enlightened," and our hearts "shall tremble and be enlarged."

They Are Bringing the Wealth of the Nations.

Because the abundance of the sea shall be turned unto thee, the wealth of the nations shall come unto thee.

I believe that God will send, not only the people, but the "wealth of the nations;" and that all over the world it will be seen that this City and the Zion Cities that will follow when this is fully and strongly established, are a mighty power in the hands of God.

But I shall take no steps that will weaken the Zion City in which we live.

Every step that shall be taken shall be to increase the strength of this City.

These Cities shall stretch hands across the seas and the boundaries of all the nations, and prepare the way for the Coming of the King.

We must work in every nation, and found strong centers in Cities from which, by and by, I shall be able to summon a portion of each to go with me, if I am spared to live, and build up the ruined walls of the Great City.

We will terrace its hills, if we must carry the earth from distant places by ship.

We will build there a Palace for the King and a Temple for God, so that when the King comes, He will find Zion ready.

May God help us in these things.

The Word says that the Little One shall become a Thousand.

We became that.

Zion a Nation Within the Nations.

We also read that "the Small One shall become a Strong Nation."

Without any desire to interfere with the governments of the nations by their lawfully constituted authorities, Zion is and must be everywhere, a people who, while they obey every good law and are good citizens, are a nation within the nations, as Israel is Israel wherever it is found.

Now may God help us to continue to shine, each of us doing his or her work.

Much of the very best work that has been done in Europe, in this land and elsewhere, has been done by humble people, individually.

Many have written letters to friends, telling of the blessings that they have received in spirit, soul, and body; telling what their eyes have seen and their ears have heard, and sending LEAVES OF HEALING.

Your individual work as members of the Christian Catholic Church in Zion, and as members of Zion Restoration Host, has done much.

But it is the organization of the individual into an exceeding great army that is doing the work.

While we will never stop doing what we can individually, I thank God that this people has learned that while individual effort is good, it must be organized and directed so that it shall not be wasted.

It must be instructed, and cared for, and supported in such a manner that the whole world shall feel its power.

Within ten years I believe God will enable me to throw a Host on London, on Dublin, on Edinburgh, and on Belfast, of not less than ten thousand Restorationists.

God grant it! [Applause.]

I have been making my reconnaissance.

I ask this audience, composed almost entirely of Zion people, are you willing to follow Elijah the Restorer, the man that talks to you?

If you are willing, stand up and let him see you. [The people rose in thousands.]

Are you willing to go anywhere for God?

People—"Yes."

General Overseer—All who desire to consecrate themselves to God, stand. [With few exceptions the entire Congregation rose.]

Now pray.

PRAYER OF CONSECRATION.

My God and Father, in Jesus' Name, I come to Thee. Take me as I am. Make me what I ought to be, in spirit, in soul, and in body. Give me power to do right, no matter what it costs. Give me Thy Holy Spirit. Purify my spirit, my soul, and my body, and make me a true citizen of Zion, a true member of Zion Restoration Host, determined to do Thy Will, to serve or to sacrifice, wherever I may be directed. Bless Zion in all the earth, and all that are praying for us this day especially. For Jesus' sake. Amen. [*All repeat the prayer, clause by clause, after the General Overseer.*]

Did you mean that?

People—"Yes."

General Overseer—At the close of this meeting I shall give the right hand of fellowship to all who desire to enter into the fellowship of the Christian Catholic Church in Zion.

The Congregation then sang with the General Overseer the beautiful Consecration Song.

After the Recessional had been sung, the General Overseer pronounced the

BENEDICTION.

Beloved, abstain from every form of evil. And may the very God of Peace Himself sanctify you wholly; and I pray God your whole spirit and soul and body be preserved entire, without blame, unto the coming of our Lord Jesus, the Christ. Faithful is He that calleth you, who also will do it. The grace of our Lord Jesus, the Christ, the love of God our Father, the fellowship of the Holy Spirit, our Comforter and Guide, one Eternal God, abide in you, bless you and keep you, and all the Israel of God everywhere, forever. Amen.

RECEPTION OF NEW MEMBERS.

The Congregation sang Hymn No. 12, from the Program.

The General Overseer then offered prayer; after which he said:

I will address you very briefly this afternoon, in receiving you, from the words found in the 2d chapter of the Acts of the Apostles, and the 42d verse.

They are written concerning those who were saved on the Day of Pentecost, who received the Word and were baptized.

And they continued steadfastly in the apostles' teaching and fellowship, in the breaking of bread and the prayers.

Beloved friends, it would be better for you never to enter into our fellowship if you are not to be steadfast, for of all the curses that can ever come to a body of believers, the worst is that those who come into fellowship should be feeble, unstable, unreliable, and unfruitful.

Christians of that kind I cannot consider to be Christians at all.

Instability Is an Evidence of Insincerity of Character.

Above all things a Christian must be sincere.

Unsteadfastness also indicates that you do not possess the root of the matter, for if you were rooted and grounded in love it would be impossible for you to be easily moved.

I therefore earnestly exhort you to be quite sure that you are standing fast.

I know that you may be conscious of weakness, but you must also be conscious of the determination, by the grace of God, to hold fast and to be steadfast.

These early Christians were not only steadfast, but they were, as the Word says, steadfast believers in the "apostles' doctrine."

If you have received the teaching in the Christian Catholic Church in Zion and believing it, are steadfast in the doctrine, you will be strong.

Weakness arises from being steadfast only up to a certain point.

People enter into the Church without a knowledge of the teaching, and the consequence is that they do not go forward and do not grow.

These early Christians continued steadfastly in the apostles' doctrine—that is, in the apostles' teaching.

That is the first necessity.

The apostolic teaching was the teaching of the Gospel of the Kingdom.

The apostles taught those fundamental truths concerning the existence of God the Father, Son and Holy Spirit.

They taught the need that man had for a Savior, and that God had sent His Son to redeem mankind.

They taught that God loved us, and gave His Son, and that the Christ loved us and gave Himself to die in our place.

He made an Atonement for our sins, our sicknesses, and all our necessities.

They not only continued steadfast in the doctrine, but

They Continued Steadfast in Fellowship.

My brothers and sisters, you will not be strong if you do not continue steadfast in fellowhip.

You may be a long way, some of you, from the Headquarters or the meetings of this Church, but you must continue in fellowship by correspondence.

Take up your fellowship as an active member of the Church, and it will soon be seen that your faithfulness will result in blessing to, and the ingathering of, many others.

The Result of One Woman's Faithfulness.

I know of one place in the neighborhood of this City where nearly four hundred members of this Church have been gathered together, and the first beginnings were those of a very humble woman, who had no sympathy from her husband, her sons, her daughters, nor her friends.

She had been reproved severely by her pastor.

She turned upon him with a loving and yet very firm spirit, and said, "Sir, I may need that reproof, but you cannot give it to me! You visit in my home, you drink, and smoke, and talk scandal to my husband, you play cards, you talk about politics, and about business, but you have never prayed with me, sir!

"You have never helped me to be a better woman!

"You have left me lonelier in this house when you have gone; because I cannot bear tobacco smoke, nor liquor, and often when you have left, my husband has been much under the influence of liquor!

"You are telling me that Dr. Dowie is a very bad man, but he has prayed with me, and my horrible tumor is gone!

"He has helped me! You have never prayed the Prayer of Faith for me."

She turned away, saying, "I do not know what my husband will say."

Immediately the pastor began to storm at her; but her husband quietly rose up and said to the minister:

"I have been thinking. You have been a curse to me! You have often left me nearly drunk, and I have never received any good from your company. You never have prayed with me or with my family! Go!"

The pastor, overwhelmed with surprise, asked, "Where are you going?"

"I am going with my wife to see a man to whom I owe her life, and whom I have not thanked," he quietly answered.

They came to me, and now he is a Deacon and she is a Deaconess in this Church.

The work began to open up there, and within two or three years there were about four hundred members gathered into this Church, humanly speaking, all because of one woman's faithful work.

Be faithful, and God will bless you.

You may be able to do only a little, but you can remain in our fellowship only while you are working for God.

We Have No Fellowship With Dead Members.

We do not reach down into graves and grasp their hands.

We have no fellowship with people who as far as their usefulness is concerned, are in their graves.

You must do something.

You can do it in your own home and in your own neighborhood.

It does not matter what husband or wife or any one else says; you are free.

You are free in a free land; free to serve God, free to talk, and free to spread the Literature.

You can be enrolled as a member of Zion Restoration Host and become an active member.

We have thousands of members of this Church throughout the world.

The work in nearly every country has been due to the faith of one man or woman.

True fellowship means fellowship in service, not merely in name.

These early Christians continued steadfast.

They were fellow laborers.

Many of them were very ignorant, but they did what they could, and they were a magnificent generation.

The Word also says that they continued steadfast "in the breaking of bread and in prayers."

Never miss an opportunity of Communing.

All Can and Must Be Faithful in Prayer.

One thing in which all can be faithful is prayer.

At nine o'clock every morning and nine o'clock every night, Zion is praying for Zion in all the world and for all the world.

You may be in sympathy with us here, and allowing for the change of time in the various places where you live you can be in prayer at nine o'clock in the morning and at night, or at a corresponding time in your town.

We are always in touch with you in prayer, because we are always praying for our people.

We *never* forget them.

We cannot always help others, but we obey the injunction:

So then, as we have opportunity, let us work that which is good toward all men, and especially towards them that are of the household of the faith.

One reason why this Church is so strong is that while we do much good to people outside, our first business is to take care of one another.

We do not believe in taking care of all the loafers in the town, and letting God's people be neglected.

We care for our own poor.

We care for our own sick.

We care for our own people, in distress and sorrow.

We do our utmost to do all we can to help them live purer and holier lives, and to help them in any distress, or in any necessity.

This has always been the case.

You can always be in fellowship with us in prayer.

I trust you will remember this verse; it is very comprehensive.

I beg of you as you enter into our fellowship to continue steadfast in the doctrine of the apostles, as taught in the Word of God—the teaching of our Lord Jesus, the Christ.

That is the teaching of Zion—the exposition of the Word of God—and we live it.

We have no new Bible.

And they continued steadfastly in the apostles' teaching and fellowship, in the breaking of bread and the prayers.

After asking the usual questions of the candidates for fellowship and receiving their satisfactory answers, the General Overseer gave the right hand of fellowship to four hundred twenty-two persons, representing twenty-seven states and two territories of the United States of America, and twelve foreign countries.

All present then rose and sang the Doxology, after which the General Overseer pronounced the

BENEDICTION.

Grace, mercy and peace, from God, the Father, Son and Holy Spirit, be with you ever, and with all those received into fellowship, and may they be blessed, and be a great blessing. For Jesus's sake. Amen.

ORDINATION AND COMMUNION.

REPORTED BY M. E. L., A. C. R. AND A. W. N.

At eight o'clock in the evening of Lord's Day, July 17, 1904, three or four thousand of God's children gathered again in Shiloh Tabernacle to attend the Ordination of officers in the Christian Catholic Church in Zion and the Communion of the Lord's Supper.

The General Overseer prefaced the Ordination service by an informal but deeply spiritual and intensely practical talk on Consecration.

This was followed by a Consecration service of unusual power, in which all the people joined.

As they knelt, in that solemn evening hour, brief prayers of consecration were offered by a large number, and all joined with the General Overseer in a very earnest prayer at the close.

The whole course of many lives was changed in that brief season.

This service was a peculiarly fitting prelude for the Ordination service, in which forty-two Elders, Evangelists, Deacons and Deaconesses registered their vows and were definitely set aside and consecrated for the work of the ministry of God in Zion.

The sacred and blessed Table of our Lord was then spread; and thousands gathered around, on the sacred Sabbath Night, to partake of the Communion.

The General Overseer administered the Ordinance, assisted by several hundreds of Overseers, Elders, Evangelists, Deacons and Deaconesses.

The services of this never-to-be-forgotten day were closed by a brief but very profitable Post-communion Family Talk by the General Overseer, the singing of Zion's parting song, "God be With You Till We Meet Again," the Benediction, and the Salutation.

Shiloh Tabernacle, Zion City, Illinois, Lord's Day Evening, July 17, 1904.

The service was opened by the Congregation's singing Hymn No. 48, in the Program:

At even, ere the sun was set,
The sick, O Lord, around Thee lay;
Oh, in what divers pains they met!
Oh, with what joy they went away!

The General Overseer read from the Inspired Word of God, in the 22d chapter of Luke, beginning at the 7th verse.

The Congregation was led in prayer by Overseer Mason.

The General Overseer then said:

Beloved friends, I am grateful for the joy given me this afternoon of receiving into fellowship four hundred twenty-two. [Applause.]

There are more than twenty-seven states, as well as many foreign countries, represented in this Feast of Tabernacles.

An Illustration of the Catholicity of Zion.

Nothing more fully illustrates the catholicity of Zion than a reception of members at such a time as this.

I do not believe that the world has ever seen a similar spectacle continuously going on.

It is not as if it were an occasional thing.

Here is an organization born into existence, brought into being by God, and from the very beginning a world-wide organization.

It is an organization that reaches out to all the world, and all the world has come to see.

We are very young yet.

Do not let us forget how young.

The City is only a Baby City of three years, and the Church is only a stripling.

One of the great triumphs of Zion is that people who belong to nationalities who are opposed to one another, and have strong prejudices against one another, are living here in perfect harmony.

There is no South and no North in Zion.

There is no color line in Zion, for no shade of color can make any difference.

The children of God of every language, and of every race, and of every color, are one in Him who tasted death for every man.

I am so glad for this broad catholicity; and for the sweet simplicity with which people that have had the so-called race prejudice, now live here in perfect unity.

There is no such thing as race difference.

There is only one race, and that is the human or Adamic race.

There are many families of that race, with different shades of color and different modes of living, because they have lived so much apart.

A Universal Language to Be Restored to the Peoples of the Earth.

While talking to President Comtesse in the Federal Palace at Bern, Switzerland, I said, "There must be one language by and by in the Restoration, and, of course, there is no question as to what that language will be. It will not be French and it will not be German; it is sure to be English." [Applause.]

He smiled a little, and came to the conclusion that I was not very far wrong, because today the language that we speak is the ruling language.

It is the official language in countries, including the protectorates, occupied by nearly six hundred million people—not far from one-half of the human race.

The Strength of the English Language.

It is wonderful to think how the language is spreading.

Of course it has its strength in that it is a composite language.

The language is married, and very much married.

It is married into all the nations, and has absorbed from all the nations the most forcible words and forcible modes of expression.

I venture to differ with those who believe that they have a grammar that is an adequate expression for the English language.

When the Restoration reaches the schoolhouse more fully, we will make an awful mess of the grammar, because it seems to me that language is enfeebled oftentimes by this splitting of hairs.

You all know that I take great liberties with the English language.

While I am thankful for all that Lindley Murray ever taught me, and for grammarians since, I am glad that the day of building scaffolds is over.

I call grammar scaffolding.

When you have the house built you take down the scaffolding and diligently forget your grammar.

Sometimes if you hold to your grammar too closely, you make mistakes.

You must be sure and get hold of the language and use it in such a way that your words will be like explosive bullets; they will not only strike, but explode when they get there.

Of course, there is a time when your language must be tender, pathetic, and very expressive, going into the heart with comfort.

I sometimes wonder what the grammarians really think of me.

They have been kindly saying, however, that the language which we will call the Zion language does not err in distinctness, in want of forcibleness, or in clearness.

I pray God that all the nations coming together in Zion may give us the best that belongs to us.

There are a great many things to be seen in traveling, even among nations that are semi-civilized.

They can teach us a great many things.

Familiarity With All Countries and Their Peoples Obtained Through Careful Reading.

The world is perhaps different to me than it is to some of you.

I have been around the world four times, and have traveled a great deal besides.

To me the world is a place I know.

I know the various lands, and even though I have not been in China or Japan, persons who have been in these countries many years have often said to me, "Why, Doctor, you must have been there."

I have not been there, but I have read nearly everything on China that I could get to read.

So you, by means of books, can keep yourself well informed.

Some day this City must possess one of the finest libraries in the whole world. [Applause.]

We will wait until we can make it a good one; but we will not ask Andrew Carnegie to provide it. [Applause.]

I am very happy tonight in thinking how the nations are coming into Zion.

Yet do not let us forget that we are only a small people among the nominal tribes of Israel.

We are a very little tribe, but it was the little tribe that did the work.

Out of Benjamin and Judah the mighty ones came.

Great tribes were almost without representation in the heroic history of Israel.

The Power of a Work Never Lies Merely in Its Numbers.

You may add cipher to cipher, but the strength of these ciphers is still a cipher unless you have a unit to place before them.

A strong unit of power must be linked to any organization which is simply an aggregation of weakness.

You may have a great name, but the whole thing lies in that organization's being a living thing, led to victory by some unit of power at the head of it.

The great weakness of this country was that for a long time there was no man who could be found to step into the breach and win his way to the White House, wield a pen that could strike the fetters from the slaves, and break down every opposition, making one flag and one nation.

But when that one man came, then all behind him united, and he was a mighty power and did the work.

All Israel together would have been ineffectual without Moses.

In the time of Ahab, how could that great reformation have been wrought unless God had raised up one man who, with fearless and unyielding persistency, refused to have anything to do with the mixed religion of Baal and Jehovah?

He iterated and reiterated the words, "Eliyahu! Eliyahu! Jehovah is my God!" until in mockery, I think, they called him, Eliyahu—Elijah.

The day came when the mockery changed to fear.

The Fire of God came down and the sacrifice was accepted.

Then the whole people cried, "Eliyahu! Jehovah is my God!" and adopted the name of the prophet.

The Work of Destruction and Restoration Must Be Pushed Forward Rapidly.

I believe the time is coming again when the nations will cry, "Eliyahu! Jehovah is our God!"

Then the temples of Baal and all the apostasies will fall and be swept away.

We have a great work to do, and we have little time in which to do it.

Everything must be done quickly, for the pressure of events is rapid, and the pace at which the nations are going is rapid.

The destruction of old-time monarchies will go on rapidly, until crash after crash will take place, and revolution after revolution will upset the whole order of things.

While that is going on, Zion will have to be ready to step into the breach and say, when people are looking around for a government, "Let God govern, for where God rules, man prospers."

May God grant that the ordinations that are to follow may be the means of imparting, by the Holy Spirit's Power, such gifts that, when you enter the ministry after tonight, you will realize that there is something in you that is stirring you up.

No Idleness Tolerated in Zion.

There is no credit due me for activity.

I must be active.

I began with a certain work for God and He gave me more and more to do, until at last He has given me the world-wide work of the beginning of the Restoration.

Hence, I need to have my hand in everything where Restoration is to be accomplished.

Members of Zion who do not work have no right to eat, and neither shall they eat.

I pray God that drones shall not eat in Zion.

I should like to see them all in Heaven.

They are of no value on earth nor in Zion.

Let us pray God tonight that we shall all get such a blessing this week that is now upon us so auspiciously, that there will come the impelling Power which will make effective the vast amount of knowledge that you possess, because Zion possesses a vast amount of real practical knowledge, and you have to make that knowledge a power.

It seems to me that the Holy Spirit must teach us how to become concentrated spiritual forces, that when we direct our attentions to any particular thing, something will be accomplished.

It will not be us doing the work, but the Power of God working through us, will be such that nothing can stand before us.

That is how I feel about all the powers of earth and hell and the apostasy that stands before Zion; they are as nothing.

They must go.

May God help me to make you a people that make things go.

The Reward of True Humility.

I should rather say something about Overseer Speicher in his absence than in his presence; but perhaps, it is only right for me to say to you, that when we took Dr. Speicher from the ranks of the Overseers and suddenly gave him the tremendous responsibilities, both of the teaching office and of the care and oversight of the work in the City, and, to a considerable extent, throughout the world, this man, whom the Baptists never honored with more than a fragmentary kind of honor, became a wonderful power in the hands of God.

When I found him, he was an assistant pastor to a feeble man and a feeble church.

I realized that he was willing to be turned inside out and upside down.

God had healed him of cancer, a disease of which his father died.

He had come with all his heart into Zion, and there is that grand thing about him, as well as about many others, thank God, that when he came into Zion, he came in with both feet, and brought in as quickly as possible everything connected with him, until at last he was wholly in Zion.

Then he was willing to do the humblest work.

He had such humble work that he was really a baggage man, carrying baggage up and down in Home No. 3, and doing all kinds of humble tasks as house-master in a very small house.

But I watched him closely, so that the thing that surprised many did not surprise me, namely, when the responsibility came, he rose right up to it, and God took this thin, wiry man, and made him faithful as a teacher, and a mighty power and help to you.

Was he not?

People—"Yes." [Applause.]

General Overseer—He knows that I am not given to flattery, and I say that there is not a fiber or nerve in him that does not tingle at the word Zion.

He has the go-forward in him, and he will go if he dies.

I do not want him to die, but I should rather he would die fighting than die rusting.

"O, Dr. Dowie, you will work yourself out if you work on in this way."

They have said that to me for twenty or thirty years, and I have out-worked them and am all right yet.

I Never Measure the Work that is Before Me with My Strength.

I call upon God for strength, and the Dynamic Powers of the Holy Spirit are always sufficient to energize the weary body and nerves, to make the blood flow, to make the digestion perfect, and to make one grow young, which makes it possible for one to sleep whenever one desires.

I can sleep any minute I desire, and can work any minute I desire.

To do this you must be wholly God's.

Do not be half-and-half.

A man's greatest usefulness in God's service depends upon his being entirely consecrated.

Such a wholly consecrated people as I pray this Zion may be has never yet been seen.

Zion's Advantages.

She is already a conquering power that can stand before anything.

The generations that came out of Egypt are not to be compared with Her.

They were ignorant.

They had been brought up out of Egypt, where they had had no books and no schools.

They did not have wise parents.

They did not have good homes.

They had none of the tremendous facilities and forces of this twentieth century.

They were honest and true, and God could make much of them.

Above all things, that first generation that came up out of the desert were always ready for a fight, and they always won, except at Ai.

Taking them as a whole, they were a conquering generation; but we ought to be a thousand times stronger than they.

Here we are with all the wealth of experience of the centuries, and living in the best and freest and strongest nation in the world.

If we, with all the facilities that we have—and, may I not say, with the Leader that you have?—if we cannot do the work that God calls us to do, we had better tell God Almighty that we will not make any pretense of doing His business.

I do not believe in pretense.

We must do Zion's work, and that work is to conquer the World, the Flesh, and the Devil, and to plant the Standard of God over all humanity.

It must be done, and we must do it.

Teaching Fundamental Truths, Not Balloon Theories.

I say these few practical words tonight instead of delivering a regular address, because I want to break away from my usual mode of speech.

There is danger of a man's getting into a rut with his own thoughts, and I ask God, if I am getting into ruts, to get me out.

Of course, you cannot travel away from certain fundamental truths, and there is no use in bothering about balloon theories and that kind of things.

I have come to the conclusion that it is quite probable that some day we may be able to go from country to country by air-ships; but meanwhile it does not seem to be practical, and I shall not bother about them.

I will cross the sea by steamer, and the land by rail, and not spend my time in theorizing about air-ships.

Let us keep on solid land, and we will wait for the balloon to be perfected.

I have lost faith in the balloon theories of political economists and theologians.

Zion City Built Contrary to All Theories of Political Economists.

This City has risen up and has become a tremendous power in the world, and not one thing has been done properly, according to the political economist.

But we did it, and leave the political economist to wonder how on earth was it done.

They always tell you that the demand creates the supply, but here, on this tract of six thousand six hundred acres there was no demand.

The cows and the pigs, who were the principal inhabitants, with a few dozen farmers, never demanded anything.

The Chicago & North-Western Railway had run through this land for many years, and they never saw a future city on this site.

They never expected that we would be able to create a place out of which they could get five hundred thousand dollars in gold in a little over two years.

And not a theory of the political economist as taught in any university or school has been complied with in building up this wonderful City.

I did not ask the political economist for his opinion.

I Had the Conviction that the Supply Would Create the Demand.

I demanded from God a piece of ground, and I got it.

Then I demanded from my people that they bring in money, and they brought it.

Then I said, "Come in yourselves," and they came.

Then we built up industries that even our bitterest enemies say are a bonanza.

But the best of all is that we are building up human lives, human character, a strong people—people who have a real aim in life.

They determine to do things.

If they do not accomplish it the first year or the next, they keep everlastingly at it until they do.

Some of them keep at it until they become excellent preachers—better preachers than I am, for I never was a preacher.

I never preached as the schools told me to preach.

Why the General Overseer Does Not Deliver "Beautiful" Sermons.

Once I tried and I made a magnificent and beautiful sermon, fearfully and wonderfully made. [Laughter.]

When I got through and sat down, the people said, "Was that not magnificent?"

They went home and ate their dinners, and never changed at all.

It did not do them any good.

I was a great orator.

You might not think so now, but I was then a Congregationalist in Australia, and large numbers came to hear me preach.

I would preach—but I did not accomplish anything.

The time came when I saw what had to be done.

I loved my people.

I wanted to be wise.

The day came when I saw that I had to tear the rags of

Congregationalism from their backs, and leave them naked, as it were, and I did it.

I have told you a little about that night.

I loaded up with buckshot, and I shot to kill.

I wounded them everywhere, and I had them crying out to God for mercy.

It was a wonderful night.

It was one of those nights when I talked just as I am talking now.

I flung everything in the way of the professionalist aside and took for my text, "Who slew all these?"

Before I got through I told them "It was you! you! you!—deacons and members—you did it!

"You went in for that infernal liquor—Liquid Fire and Distilled Damnation.

"You are a mass of goats! I will not preach to you any more unless you will do right."

I made them weep. [Applause.]

But that did not amount to much.

As time went on, I found that the only thing that told was organization of force.

Divine and Human Sympathy.

I shall pray God the Almighty that, as we sit at the Lord's Table and take the bread and wine, that Sustenance Divine will come into us—the Enthusiasm of Divinity and the Enthusiasm of Humanity.

We want them both.

We want the Divine Sympathy and the human sympathy to come into us—the God-inspired, Divine side, that depends wholly upon God, and the God-inspired, human side, that depends upon our united effort under God.

It is this united effort that I am looking for.

We shall win anywhere, under God, if you will be good captains, and all of you true soldiers.

This Zion army will knock everything of the World, the Flesh, and the Devil to pieces, and prepare the way for the Coming King by overturning until He shall come whose right it is to reign.

Meanwhile, in the midst of it all, we are to have a beautiful, calm, peaceable home life in our own City.

Presentation and Consecration to God.

Before we touch this evening Feast and before we come to the Ordination, let us consecrate ourselves to Him.

Let us ask God to empty our spirits of everything, that He may fill them afresh with Living Water.

I believe that sometimes even the Living Water stagnates in us.

We must work!

Do not let us make idols of our mental and spiritual instruments.

Do not let us lean upon the splendidness of our City or the Leader or the industry of our people. Let us be thankful for these.

Beloved friends, let us get into touch with God so that even our good things will be replaced by better things.

Pray God to take away any dross we may be in danger of having in ourselves.

God will not suffer us to give His glory to another or to human instrumentalities.

You must not forget that any power that has ever come into this work has come from God, and that my instrumentality is nothing.

He could have taken many much better and greater instruments than I.

I do not want you not to love me and trust me and back me up, but do not lean upon me.

Let us all lean upon God.

Let us pray.

The Congregation united in a Consecration Prayer, after which a number of short prayers were offered by various officers and those who were to be ordained.

Ordination Service.

The following persons were then ordained to office:

ELDERS.

Arrington, Deacon Archibald Evans, Fourth and Johns streets Cincinnati, Ohio.

Brasefield, Evangelist Mary Elizabeth, 3009 Eshcol avenue, Zion City, Illinois.

Excell, Evangelist Marie Anna, Elijah Hospice, Zion City, Illinois.

EVANGELIST.

Arrington, Mrs. Fannie Amelia, Cincinnati, Ohio.

DEACONS.

Benckendorf, Louis, 2404 Elisha avenue, Zion City, Illinois.
Blanks, John H., 2114 Enoch avenue, Zion City, Illinois.
Burnley, Alfred Benjamin, Patterson, Louisiana.
Green, Alfred Marion, 401 Millard, East Toledo, Ohio.
Hammock, August, 901 East Front street, Cincinnati, Ohio.
Kerkhecker, Frederick, 2719 Elim avenue, Zion City, Illinois.
Lauder, Charles Edward, 2114 Elisha avenue, Zion City, Illinois.
Marpurg, Albertus E., Elijah Hospice, Zion City, Illinois.
Möse, Wenzel, 3012 Gideon avenue, Zion City, Illinois.
Polman, Gerrit Roelof, Elijah Hospice, Zion City, Illinois.
Rank, Caleb A., 14633 Kentucky avenue, Harvey, Illinois.
Taylor, Andrew, 2115 Eshcol avenue, Zion City, Illinois.
Thomas, Guston David, 401 Juanita Building, Dallas, Texas.

DEACONESSES.

Barron, Miss Alice Elsie, 619 Michigan street, Port Huron, Michigan.
Buettner, Mrs. Emma, 619 East Fifty-fifth street, Chicago, Illinois.
Corlette, Mrs. Harriette, 419 Flatiron Building, New York City.
Cornwall, Mrs. Eliza Catherine, 358 St. Aubin avenue, Detroit, Michigan.
Davis, Miss Johnnie, 2807 West Houston street, San Antonio, Texas.
Grossenheider, Mrs. Amalie, 4725 Evans avenue, Chicago, Illinois.
Heath, Miss Laura Luella, Elijah Hospice, Zion City, Illinois.
Hill, Mrs. Emma Eva, 190 Campbell avenue, Detroit, Michigan.
James, Mrs. Mabel Shatt, 605 Pennsylvania avenue, West End, San Antonio, Texas.
Landphere, Mrs. Mary, Mazon, Illinois.
Lauder, Mrs. Harriet Frances, 2114 Elisha avenue, Zion City, Illinois.
Lee, Mrs. Annie Maria, 93 Twenty-third street, Detroit, Michigan.
Lewis, Mrs. Anna White, Twelfth street and Twenty-fourth avenue, Meridian, Mississippi.
Locke, Miss Ida Elizabeth, Omro, Wisconsin.
Lindblad, Dagmar J., 268 Willis avenue, New York City.
McBean, Mrs. Sarah Harrison, South 314 Monroe street, Spokane, Washington.
Mangold, Mrs. Katherine, 2902 Elisha avenue, Zion City, Illinois.
Marpurg, Mrs. Gesena, Elijah Hospice, Zion City, Illinois.
Miller, Mrs. Caroline, 2204 Enoch avenue, Zion City, Illinois.
Oberholtzer, Miss Maud E., 1129 South Eighth street, Minneapolis, Minnesota.
Polman, Mrs. Wilhelmina, Elijah Hospice, Zion City, Illinois.
Rather, Mrs. Martha Louena, Luling, Texas.
Sayers, Mrs. Mollie Amelia, 218 Nolan street, San Antonio, Texas.
Seger, Mrs. Margaret Ames, 606 Spofford avenue, Spokane, Washington
Tarbox, Mrs. Mattie Hart, Cedarville, Ohio.
Ward, Mrs. Mary A., North Harvey, Illinois.

COMMUNION OF THE LORD'S SUPPER.

Following the Ordination of Officers the General Overseer, assisted by the Officers of the Church, administered the Communion of the Lord's Supper to thousands who remained for that Service.

The General Overseer then said:

Thanksgiving for Peculiar Blessings in Zion's Fourth Feast of Tabernacles.

Before I retire from this platform and you from this gathering at this the first Ordinance of the Feast, I thank God for a peculiar kind of blessing that is coming at this Feast.

It is not like any previous Feast. In its outward form it is just the same to many of us, and the program runs along the same line, but, beyond all question, in this present Feast there are many remarkable differences.

Zion has gathered in larger numbers than ever, and in better order than in the first three Feasts.

The City now has so many comfortable homes, that large numbers of our beloved friends find accommodation and loving hospitality.

Our Hospices, filled to overflowing, have become more comfortable.

We are thankful to God for the communion of many that have come for the first time.

One man said to me, the other day, "As I walk about the streets, I see many calm, strong-looking men and women of all ages; and many bright youths and maidens.

"Having been here at two previous Feasts, I can see that the entire tone of the community is lifted; that there is on the part of the citizens a calm, strong look, the look of veterans who have been to war, and have won the fight, and are at home.

"But they are ready to go again."

He said, further, "I also see among those that are coming

to the Feast, large-brained men, broad-gaged men, that are warmly appreciating everything connected with Zion and your ministry. You ought to be a happy man," or words to that effect.

I said, "I am exceedingly happy, but I am not satisfied."

I think that this Feast will mean great things for us spiritually, and a wonderful preparation for the building of Shiloah Tabernacle, and for the gathering together of vast multitudes next year.

I really was almost tempted to fear a greater multitude than we have now, because when you get seven thousand five hundred persons in a place like this, with a comparatively low roof and very primitive ventilation, it causes suffering to some of you, and a tenfold greater trial to the man who has to conduct the proceedings, and who has to spend the strength that I have to, to carry this through on the lines that I have laid down.

Twenty-three Thousand Attendances in One Day.

I am grateful, almost, that we have not exceeded, at any one time during this Feast, the capacity of the Tabernacle.

When you think of today's gatherings, the record is wonderful.

Six thousand were at the Early Morning Sacrifice of Praise and Prayer.

Overseer Speicher spoke to an audience of three thousand, which would make it nine thousand.

The afternoon audience was between six and seven thousand; that would be fifteen thousand five hundred.

If you place tonight's attendance at forty-five hundred, you have twenty thousand, and if you add to that about twenty-five hundred juniors at their morning convocation, and the German meetings, we have had not less than twenty-three thousand attendances in Zion City today.

Where would you find a population anywhere else on earth that would make such a record, after having been at it every day for three days before that?

I think we have, by the goodness of God, been feasting today.

The audience then sang the first verse of "God be With You Till We Meet Again," and the General Overseer sang the last.

BENEDICTION.

Jehovah bless thee and keep thee, Jehovah make His face to shine upon thee and be gracious unto thee, Jehovah lift up His countenance upon thee and give thee peace. May Grace, Mercy and Peace from God the Father, Son and Holy Spirit abide in you and keep you ever. May He bless you, spirit, soul and body, and all Israel everywhere, forever. Amen.

Publisher's Notice.

The remittance must accompany receipt of subscriptions at the Publishing House, no difference by or for whom or for whatever time they may be given, or whether forwarded through Ordained Officers, Branches, or Gatherings of the Christian Catholic Church in Zion. Accounts will be carried with Ordained Officers, Branches, or Gatherings, on quantity orders of periodicals consigned on sale for monthly settlement, but to include only such articles as bear the imprint of Zion. All orders for Bibles, books, buttons, pictures (except prints done by the Publishing House), lace souvenirs, etc., must be sent to the General Stores, Zion City, Lake County, Illinois.

GOD'S WAY OF HEALING.

BY THE REV. JOHN ALEX. DOWIE.

God's Way Of Healing Is a Person, Not a Thing.

Jesus said "*I am* the Way, and the Truth, and the Life," and He has ever been revealed to His people in all the ages by the Covenant Name, Jehovah-Rophi, or "*I am* Jehovah that Healeth thee." (John 14:6; Exodus 15:26.)

The Lord Jesus, the Christ, Is Still the Healer.

He cannot change, for "Jesus, the Christ, is the same yesterday and today, yea and forever;" and He is still with us, for He said: "Lo, *I am* with you All the Days, even unto the Consummation of the Age." (Hebrews 13:8; Matthew 28:20.) Because He is Unchangeable, and because He is present, in spirit, just as when in the flesh, He is the Healer of His people.

Divine Healing Rests on the Christ's Atonement.

It was prophesied of Him "Surely He hath borne our griefs (Hebrew, *sickness*), and carried our sorrows: . . . and with His stripes we are healed;" and it is expressly declared that this was fulfilled in His Ministry of Healing, which still continues. (Isaiah 53:4, 5; Matthew 8:17.)

Disease Can Never be God's Will.

It is the Devil's work, consequent upon Sin, and it is impossible for the work of the Devil ever to be the Will of God. The Christ came to "destroy the works of the Devil," and when He was here on earth He healed "all manner of disease and all manner of sickness," and all these sufferers are expressly declared to have been "oppressed of the Devil." (1 John 3:8; Matthew 4:23; Acts 10:38.)

The Gifts of Healings Are Permanent.

It is expressly declared that the "Gifts and the calling of God are without repentance," and the Gifts of Healings are amongst the Nine Gifts of the Spirit to the Church. (Romans 11:29; 1 Corinthians 12:8-11.)

There Are Four Modes of Divine Healing.

The first is the direct prayer of faith; the second, intercessory prayer of two or more; the third, the anointing of the elders, with the prayer of faith; and the fourth, the laying on of hands of those who believe, and whom God has prepared and called to that ministry. (Matthew 8:5-13; Matthew 18:19; James 5:14, 15; Mark 16:18.)

Divine Healing Is Opposed by Diabolical Counterfeits.

Amongst these are Christian Science (falsely so called), Mind Healing, Spiritualism, Trance Evangelism, etc. (1 Timothy 6:20, 21; 1 Timothy 4:1, 2; Isaiah 51:22, 23.)

Multitudes Have Been Healed Through Faith in Jesus.

The writer knows of thousands of cases and has personally laid hands on scores of thousands of persons. Full information can be obtained at the meetings held in the Zion Tabernacles in Chicago, and in Zion City, Illinois, and in many pamphlets which give the experience, in their own words, of many who have been healed in this and other countries, published at Zion Printing and Publishing House, Zion City, Illinois.

"*Belief Cometh of Hearing, and Hearing by the Word of the Christ.*"

You are heartily invited to attend, and hear for yourself.

By Evangelist Sarah E. Hill.

HE THAT overcometh shall inherit these things; and I will be his God, and he shall be My son.—*Revelation 21:7.*

GOD promises wonderful things to those who overcome.

They are to have a new earth.

When our first parents allowed themselves to be overcome by the Devil, through temptation, evil not only entered into them, but into the earth and everything on it. (Genesis 3:17, 18.)

As man overcomes evil in every form, in the strength of the Christ, he is to be restored to his original condition and his right relations with his Heavenly Father.

In order to be an Overcomer, he must be able to overcome every temptation and every difficulty that presents itself.

This is a work of training.

The School of the Overcomers is the most wonderful school in the world.

It is the only school that can develop man's powers, and bring forth the wonderful being which lies enfolded within him.

It is the school of being and doing—the wonderful school of experience into which all may enter and overcome, because Jesus, the Captain of our Salvation, has overcome for us.

He says: "If a man love Me, he will keep My Word: and My Father will love him, and We will come unto him, and make Our abode with him."

He and the Father will live in him. (John 14:23, 20.)

He tells us to be of good cheer, because He has overcome the world for us. (John 16:33.)

It was because of this that Paul said: "Wherefore I take pleasure in weaknesses, in injuries, in necessities, in persecutions, in distresses, for the Christ's sake: for when I am weak, then am I strong." (2 Corinthians 12:10.)

It was because Paul caught sight of the glory which is to be revealed to those who overcome, that he was able to count as light affliction his cruel scourgings and imprisonments, and even the loss of all things. (2 Corinthians 4:17; 11:23-33.)

God permitted the apostle John to see the New Heaven and the New Earth.

He saw also the Holy City, the New Jerusalem, coming down out of heaven from God. (Revelation 21:1-6.)

He saw, too, that in this beautiful City of pure gold, with its gates of pearl, no sin, or sickness, or sorrow, could enter.

Only the pure and the good can enter there, and dwell in the light of God's countenance.

It is the Overcomers who are to inherit "these things."

The Overcomers are to be made pillars in the Temple of God.

Pillars must be strong and upright.

God will write His Name upon them, showing that they belong to Him, and the name of the New Jerusalem, showing that they dwell in the City of Peace, where there is no sin nor sickness, no death and no crying. (Revelation 21:4; 3:12.)

Little children may belong to the Army of the Overcomers—God's Army.

Very early in life they may be taught to overcome the difficulties and trials which they daily meet.

To them these trials and temptations are as great as those of their elders.

See the joy of a little child when he has overcome some difficulty.

Perhaps it was only a successful effort to climb upon a chair, after numerous failures.

To him it is a great achievement.

He has a feeling of triumph, and his overcoming power has been strengthened.

So it is when a sensible mother talks with her child about overcoming a bad habit.

It may be a strong temper which she talks over with him and tells him how to control. Then she observes and encourages his efforts to control the temper or break the habit until he has it well in hand.

She is training a soldier for God's great Army of the Overcomers.

On the other hand, children can be reproved for their faults before others until they lose their self-respect; or they can be found fault with and told how bad they are until they become reckless and do not care to be better.

These are almost sure to get into the Army of the Overcome—the Devil's army.

The Apostle John saw these two armies side by side—the Army of the Overcomers who will inherit all things, and the Army of the Overcome. (Revelation 21:7, 8.)

In the latter he saw a procession headed by the fearful.

And yet there are parents who, instead of teaching their children to be brave and to fear nothing but to do wrong, try to rule them through fear, and thus make them cowards.

John saw in this army the unbelieving, and abominable, and murderers, and fornicators, and sorcerers, and idolators, and all liars.

He said of all these, "their part shall be in the lake that burneth with fire and brimstone; which is the second death. (Revelation 21:8.)

Yet God wills not that any shall be overcome.

He has done all that He can to save man, and still permit him to be a free agent. (Revelation 22:17.)

The Church in Philadelphia, about which John writes, is peculiarly the Church of the Overcomers, because it is the Church of the world's great hour of trial or temptation which is to come upon the whole world, to try them that dwell upon the earth. (Revelation 3: 7-13.)

This church may expect to be tried in every way, and to be put into the furnace heated seven times hotter than is wont.

If they look to God they will see the form of One like unto the Son of Man walking beside them, and they will have no hurt; but their bands will be loosed and they will walk in freedom. (Daniel 3:25.)

The Christian Catholic Church in Zion corresponds to this Church in Philadelphia about which John writes.

The teaching of God's Prophet in this Church, which is sent out in the Literature of Zion, is to educate soldiers for the Army of the Overcomers.

It has taken many from the Army of the Overcome and helped them to repent and break off evil habits, get healed and step into the Army of the Overcomers.

We invite all who read this Literature to help send it over the world that multitudes may learn how to be Overcomers.

Zion Literature Sent Out from a Free Distribution Fund Provided by Zion's Guests and the Friends of Zion.

Report for the week ending July 23, 1904:

3,375 Rolls to....... Business Men New York City
2,666 Rolls to.. Hotels in United States and Canada
5,200 Rolls to..... Business Men in Various States
1,223 Rolls to.......... Various Foreign Countries
Number of Rolls for the week.............. 12,464
Number of Rolls reported to July 23, 1904, 3,256,789

Notes of Thanksgiving from the Whole World

By Overseer J. G. Excell, General Ecclesiastical Secretary.

THEY shall see the glory of Jehovah,
The excellency of our God.

And the ransomed of Jehovah shall return,
And come with singing unto Zion;
And everlasting joy shall be upon their heads:
They shall obtain gladness and joy,
And sorrow and sighing shall flee away.—*Isaiah 35:2, 10.*

ZION stands between the cycles of all the past ages, and the onward sweep of the imminent future, and of eternity.

Each day adds to the chronicles of the earth's historical record of the deeds of men and nations and of God's overruling power and Divine guidance; and each day lessens the intervening time between the Consummation of the Age and the sure approach of the Days of Prophecy.

The very forces of the Universe are in subservience for the fulfilment of the conquest of the world for God; the overthrow of the rulers of darkness and the enthronement of the Monarch of the Kingdom of God.

Through God's prophet the door toward this consummation is opened, showing the position of Zion in the events of that consummation; and through his guidance "The ransomed of Jehovah are returning, and are coming with singing unto Zion;" and with a sober, intelligent and God-fearing zeal are preparing themselves and their families for the further and more rapid spreading, among their cities and the nations of the world, of the knowledge of the Good Tidings of the Gospel of the Christ and of His coming to reign.

It is God's work.

His Divinity and Power are back of every pure thought, every pure desire, and every pure act for the furtherance of His Kingdom; and hence He has promised to give life, strength, and a holy calmness and happiness to His children, and to cleanse their spirits, and their souls, and their bodies from the damning blight of sin and the defiling control and power of Satan.

Thousands in Zion have already learned to control their entire beings through their spirits, which are from God, and then to consecrate their spirits to Him, and thus in their whole nature to abide under His guidance and His Divine Will.

It is thus that the destiny of the individual, the state, the nation, the continent, and the whole world is feeling the hand of God's work in Zion.

If this is Zion's morning, what shall be the day, when the consummation bursts into midday, and the King, the Christ, appears in the clouds of glory, and the emotions of the millions of human beings—the offspring and partakers of Divine nature—swell to meet the Lord toward whom the hands of time, history and the religion of the true God through all the ages have pointed, and with whose impulse the world itself exists?

God has promised every good and perfect gift to His children.

He sent His own Son to seal His Covenent with His blood.

He has sent His Holy Spirit to plead with us to accept the love of an Eternal God, and to empower us against the wiles of the Adversary.

Let none, therefore, reject the fulness of God, and fail to accept the regeneration for their bodies and souls which will enable a freer and broader exercise of their spiritual natures, in anticipation of the preparation for the coming of the Christ, their King and of the Salvation of the world. O. R.

Blessed in Zion.

Jehovah shall bless thee out of Zion.—*Psalm 128:5.*

2809 EMMAUS AVENUE,
ZION CITY, ILLINOIS, April 3, 1904.

DEAR OVERSEER SPEICHER:—My heart has been filled with joy today, the anniversary of the resurrection of the Son of God, at the remembrance of the great sacrifice He made for us, that we might be saved from our sins, and all the sicknesses and diseases, which are the oppressions of the Devil.

God has often delivered me from sickness; and the year ending the last day of March, 1904, has been the best year of my life.

I have not missed half a day's work by sickness in the year.

I cannot remember another year in all my life before that has equalled this one.

It has been filled with blessing.

My spiritual life has been widened also, and the constant prayer of my heart is that I shall be pure in heart that I may see God, and that the Restoration of All Things shall speedily be fulfilled.

Praying God's blessing upon you and your work, I am,

Your sister in the Christ,
(MISS) ELLA V. CLARK.

Healed of Symptoms of Appendicitis.

Pray one for another, that ye may be healed.
The supplication of a righteous man availeth much in its working.—*James 5:16.*

2614 EDINA BOULEVARD,
ZION CITY, ILLINOIS, March 5, 1904.

BELOVED OVERSEER:—I thank God for His great mercy to me, and I wish to thank Him especially at this time for graciously sparing my life and healing me during the month of October, 1903.

Wednesday night, September 30, 1903, I was taken suddenly and severely ill.

There is little doubt that I had a severe attack of what is commonly known as appendicitis.

It seems to me that one must have had this terrible affliction of the enemy to fully realize the intense suffering this disease causes.

When suffering, it seemed almost beyond endurance.

I received instantaneous relief in answer to the prayers of Elder Dinius, whose wise counsel, also, encouraged me very much.

A little later, directly after the General Overseer had prayed, the high fever broke, and a few hours thereafter the trouble in the region of the appendix was removed.

This was the third day of my sickness.

There is no doubt in my mind now that if I had immediately sought God for healing, when the symptoms first manifested themselves, as earnestly as I did for relief from the intense pain, I should have escaped much suffering.

I wish to thank the General Overseer, Overseer Jane Dowie, Overseer Speicher (the latter kindly coming and praying with me, at which time I received much blessing and encouragement), and the many in Zion City who knew of my illness, together with the loved ones of my own household, who earnestly prayed at this time for my healing, which God graciously granted.

To Him we give all the glory; and in closing can yet say, "The half has not been told."

Trusting this testimony will be used to the glory of God and the extension of His Kingdom on earth, I am,

Faithfully yours, Till He Come,
(MRS.) BURTON C. DINIUS.

Healed of Blood Poisoning.

Blessed be Jehovah, who daily beareth our burdens.—*Psalm 68:19*

FRAUENFELD, CANTON THURGAU,
SWITZERLAND.

DEAR GENERAL OVERSEER:—My heart is filled with praise and thanksgiving to God for the many blessings which He bestowed upon me during my stay at Castle Liebburg.

For many years I had been afflicted with a chronic disease in my back and in my head.

Twice I suffered from blood poisoning in my hands.

Five years ago I was also severely ruptured.

I was a constant sufferer, and had to wear a truss, which did not bring me any relief, but only increased the pain.

The physician told me that I was too weak to undergo an operation, and therefore I would have to get a new truss every year.

Added to my misery was remorse of conscience, from which I suffered night and day.

I felt that I was suffering the consequences of my sin (the sin of grumbling); but I did not find forgiveness and peace, although I asked God earnestly to forgive all my sins.

I did not know anything about Zion and I had no Bible.

My brother who had been to Castle Liebburg, and received great blessing, sent me BLÄTTER DER HEILUNG.

God then led me to go to Liebburg to seek healing.

After prayer was offered for me at the close of the meeting, I felt a change come over me; and I realized that God was performing a miracle.

I confessed my sins, gave myself fully to God, and was prayed with once more, with the laying on of hands.

God heard and answered prayer.

I could feel the goiter, from which I had suffered for many years, disappear, and my weak stomach was better at once.

I trusted God for perfect deliverance, and I was not put to shame.

The following morning my disease and all the other ailments were entirely gone, and I returned home a well woman.

I am growing stronger every day, going to my work at the factory joyfully and gladly every morning.

May God spare your life many more years to come, and may He use you to the salvation and healing of many.

I give God the glory for what He has done for me in spirit, soul and body.

I am happy and glad to be in Zion.

Yours truly, (MRS.) LÜTHI-NATER.

Healed of Weak Eyes.

Jehovah openeth the eyes of the blind.—*Psalm 146:8.*

9 TENNYSON STREET, MORLEY,
YORKSHIRE, ENGLAND, April 1, 1904.

DEAR GENERAL OVERSEER:—Peace to thee.

I send you my testimony to God's power to heal the body, as well as to save the spirit. I have been a Christian for twenty-one years, and was a member of the Salvation Army for nearly nineteen years.

I knew that the Army did not teach the Full Gospel, but did not think that I could make a change for the better, so I staid there, feeling I was compelled to disobey God, as the Army has set aside Baptism and the Lord's Supper, and is disobedient in other things.

But, praise God, I came across LEAVES OF HEALING, and began to read.

I became very much interested, and was delighted to find that Jehovah had founded Zion as a refuge for the afflicted of His people.

About a year and seven months ago, I became a member of the Christian Catholic Church in Zion, together with my wife, who was also a member of the Salvation Army for about fourteen years.

About one year ago, I obeyed the instruction given by the Apostle James, "Is any among you sick, let him call for the elders of the church."

I might say that ever since I can remember anything, I have had exceedingly weak eyes, which were always a great trouble to me.

I never tried many remedies to heal them as I had very little faith in medicine.

They did not improve.

About a year ago in a meeting, when Overseer Cantel visited Ardsley, he laid his hands on me and prayed for me.

I did not see any visible results that day (Tuesday), but on Thursday morning there was a very wonderful change, and the healing has continued until today, and still they are getting stronger.

I never remember a time in all my life when my eyes were so strong and well as they are at this present time.

To God be all the glory.

I thank Overseer Cantel, you, and all Zion friends for prayers on my behalf.

I also thank God for our General Overseer's teaching through LEAVES OF HEALING. I am,

Faithfully yours in Zion's bonds, till the Coming of the King, DAVID J. HERRON.

Healed of Severe Pains.

For I Jehovah thy God will hold thy right hand, saying unto thee, fear not; I will help thee —*Isaiah 41:13.*

15 DAISY VALE TERRACE, THORPE,
YORKSHIRE, ENGLAND, March 7, 1904.

DEAR GENERAL OVERSEER:—Peace to thee.

It is with a heart full of praise and thanksgiving to God that I write this short testimony.

I thank God for the many blessings and healings I have received since I first heard of Zion, about four years ago. It has been the best four years of my life.

The Sunday Elder Clibborn was at Leeds, I set out early in the morning to take one of the announcement cards to one of our members.

After leaving his home I had not very much time to get down to the meeting and I walked very fast, as it was raining heavily.

On getting into the meeting I was taken with severe pains in the body, the results of overexertion.

I was in pain the remainder of the day, and during the evening meeting I was obliged to go outside and walk about.

After the meeting was over I went out, with several others, to be prayed with.

Elder Clibborn prayed and laid his hands on the exact spot where the pain was. I did not, however, get relief just then.

When I went to bed the pain was very severe; but I retired, trusting God; and the next morning, when I awoke, I was perfectly healed; for which I praise God.

I have many causes for which to praise God.

My earnest prayer is that God will bless the work of Zion here in this dark place.

I remain, yours in Zion's bonds,

WILLIAM G. SINGER.

Healed of Pains at Heart.

Whoso putteth his trust in Jehovah shall be safe.—*Proverbs 29:25.*

9 TENNYSON STREET,
MORLEY, YORKSHIRE, ENGLAND,
April 11, 1904.

DEAR GENERAL OVERSEER:—Peace to thee.

I desire to give testimony to God's power to save the spirit and to heal the body.

About sixteen years ago I was saved in spirit, but did not know God's way of healing for my body until I read our General Overseer's teaching in LEAVES OF HEALING.

Since then I have had many healings, but I wish here to tell you of a particular one.

Some time before this healing I received a severe shock through the sudden death of a dear friend, and after that I had a very severe pain at my heart.

On one occasion, I went to our united rally at Leeds, and just as the Host was preparing to go out I had a very severe attack. I thought I was going to die.

Request was made for prayer and the pain ceased instantly and has not returned.

I went out with the Host, and I could not help praising God, as I went from door to door, for the glorious deliverance He had given me.

To Him I give all the praise and glory.

I thank you and Zion for prayers. I am,

Sincerely yours in the bonds of Zion,

MAGGIE J. HERRON.

Healed of Tonsilitis.

Bless Jehovah, O my soul, and forget not all His benefits; Who forgiveth all thine iniquities; Who healeth all thy diseases.—*Psalm 103:2,3.*

ORRSTOWN, PENNSYLVANIA,
March 18, 1904.

DEAR OVERSEER SPEICHER:—Peace to thee.

I have felt it my duty as well as a great privilege to add my testimony to the many that are being printed from week to week.

I have received many answers to prayer since I have been in the Christian Catholic Church in Zion, and have learned to pray the Prayer of Faith.

I thank God for a dear Zion baby boy who is nearly seven months old, and also for the healing of tonsilitis I received this winter through prayer.

It was almost an instantaneous healing.

If I were to tell of all the healings and answers to prayer which I have received it would make a very long letter.

I thank and praise God that it is my privilege to live in this Time of the Restoration of All Things.

May God bless and keep you and all Zion Till He Come, is my prayer.

Your sister in the Christ.

(MRS.) MARTHA M. KILLIAN.

Healed of Sore Throat, Deformity, and Pebble in Ears.

Surely He hath borne our griefs, and carried our sorrows; yet we did esteem Him stricken, smitten of God, and afflicted. —*Isaiah 53:4.*

3216 EZRA AVENUE,
ZION CITY, ILLINOIS, February 27, 1904.

DEAR OVERSEER:—I praise God for healing me, and desire to thank you and those connected with you for the prayers that have been offered for my family and me since I came from Toronto in the fall.

My baby Joseph was very sick with a sore mouth and throat.

Deacon Williams prayed, and the child began to improve from that moment, and was soon entirely well.

My second boy was healed of a deformity in answer to the General Overseer's prayer the last Sunday in November.

My oldest son, Edwin, was healed of a severe attack of dysentery and great pain, in December.

My third son, Louis, got a pebble the size of a pea in his ear last May.

We came to Zion City in September.

I went to a Divine Healing meeting in October.

Elder Brock took the meeting.

He prayed for the boy, and the following Monday the pebble came out.

It was in so far you could not see it, and at times he could not hear with that ear.

I consider this last case a miracle.

I also received a marked blessing at the All-Night meeting, in body as well as spirit.

I also thank God for bringing me to Zion City, and many other things.

Hoping these lines may be the means of helping some poor sufferer to trust God, and praying for Zion to go forward, I am,

Yours Till He Come,

(MRS.) HATTIE SHIELDS.

Rejoices in God, Savior, Healer, and Keeper.

I will instruct thee and teach thee in the way which thou shalt go:
I will counsel thee with Mine eye upon thee.—*Psalm 32:8.*

MINONG, WISCONSIN, April 3, 1904.

DEAR GENERAL OVERSEER:—I wish to add my testimony to those of the many thousands who have learned, "what a wonderful Savior is Jesus our Lord."

I sincerely thank our Heavenly Father for the many answers to prayer He has given me and those who are near and dear to me.

I thank you, Overseer Jane Dowie, and Overseer Speicher, for your prayers offered for us in several instances.

It is so blessed to feel that we may take our Heavenly Father as an Adviser and Helper in all matters in our lives, be they ever so small and commonplace; and He is ever ready to help if we will let Him.

I praise His holy Name.

Very sincerely yours in the love of the Christ.

JULIA L. LEWIS.

Form of Application for Membership in the Christian Catholic Church in Zion

To all who are desirous of entering into Fellowship with the Christian Catholic Church in Zion.

MY DEAR BROTHERS AND SISTERS:—The Principles of the Christian Catholic Church in Zion have been fully set forth in the Reports of Two Conferences on Organization, held in Zion Tabernacle No. 2, which are fully reported in LEAVES OF HEALING for January 31 and February 7, 1896. The Basis of Fellowship is set forth in the Second Section of the Resolution passed on February 5th (see LEAVES OF HEALING, Volume II, Number 17, Page 267):

First—That we recognize the infallible inspiration and sufficiency of the Holy Scriptures as the rule of faith and practice.

Second—That we recognize that no persons can be members of the Church who have not repented of their sins and have not trusted in Christ for Salvation.

Third—That such persons must also be able to make a good profession, and declare that they do know, in their own hearts, that they have truly repented, and are truly trusting Christ, and have the witness, in a measure, of the Holy Spirit.

Fourth—That all other questions of every kind shall be held to be matters of opinion and not matters that are essential to Church unity.

All who are conscious of fulfilling these conditions, no matter where they may reside, are invited to fill up the following blank and answer all the questions contained therein.

I am, faithfully yours in Jesus,

John Alex. Dowie

General Overseer of the Christian Catholic Church in Zion.

AS FAR AS POSSIBLE THE APPLICANT HIMSELF SHOULD FILL OUT THIS BLANK. WRITE PLAINLY AND WITH INK.

Address..............................

Date.............................. PLEASE BE SURE TO FILL IN

TO THE REV. JOHN ALEX. DOWIE, General Overseer of the Christian Catholic Church in Zion,
Zion City, Lake County, Illinois, U.S.A.

I hereby make application to be received as a member of the Christian Catholic Church in Zion, and declare my agreement with the Basis of Fellowship agreed upon at a Conference held February, 5, 1896, as set forth in your Circular Letter of February 7, 1896.

What is your full name?..............................

Where is your residence?.............................. PLEASE GIVE FULL POSTOFFICE ADDRESS

What is your age last birthday?.............................. ALSO GIVE DATE AND YEAR OF BIRTH

Are you married, unmarried, widowed, or divorced?..............................

How many children have you living?..............................

What is your occupation, profession, or trade?..............................

What nationality are you?.............................. *Where were you born?*..............................

What language or languages do you speak?..............................

How long have you lived in America (or the country where you are now living)?..............................

When and where were you converted to God?..............................

....

Are you conscious that you are saved through faith in Jesus?..............................

When and where were you immersed by TRIUNE Immersion?..............................

By whom were you immersed?..............................

With what religious organization were you formerly connected?..............................

Recommended by..............................

Signature of Applicant.............................. WRITE VERY PLAINLY

REMARKS

....

....

Extra Copies of this Form will be sent to intending members on application to the General Recorder of the Christian Catholic Church in Zion, Zion City, Lake County, Illinois, U.S.A.

STIRRING TRUTHS FOR WIDE-AWAKE CHRISTIANS

Present Day Themes of REV. JOHN ALEXANDER DOWIE,
General Overseer of the Christian Catholic Church in Zion

The following list of Pamphlets, Books, and Tracts, supplied on receipt of price by
ZION PRINTING AND PUBLISHING HOUSE
ZION CITY, LAKE COUNTY, ILLINOIS, U. S. A.

Zion, Her Organization, Truths, and Leader.

	Vol.	No.	Price
Zion's Answer to the Messenger of the Nation	3	8	$0.05
Organization of the Christian Catholic Church	2	2	.10
Principles, Practices and Purposes of the Christian Catholic Church in Zion, and The Everlasting Gospel	4	8	.05
Conquests for Christ in America: Past, Present, and to Come	4	5	.05
By What Authority Doest Thou These Things? and The Voice of One Crying in The Wilderness	4	4	.05
Elijah the Restorer and General Letter from the General Overseer	5	7	.05
The Times of Restoration	5	8	.10
The Beatitudes	4	10	.05
The Kingdom of God is Come, Suffering on Behalf of Christ, and Let Not Your Heart be Troubled	4	9	.05
Repentance	3	11	.05
Ye are Come Unto Mount Zion. Will a Man Rob God?	3	2	.05
The Love of God in the Salvation of Man	4	11	.10
The Christian Ordinance of Baptism by Triune Immersion	1	12	.05
The Ordinance of Christian Baptism (18 centuries of proof)	5	10	.05
Organization of Zion Restoration Host	6	12	.05
The City of God; and What Shall This Child Be?	7	2	.05

Zion's Replies to Her Enemies and Critics.

	Vol.	No.	Price
Zion and Her Enemies	3	12	$0.05
Fighting Blackmailers	3	3	.05
Estimates and Realities: Reply to Baptist Ministers	2	11	.05
Reply to D. L. Moody and the *Ram's Horn*	3	10	.05
Reply to *Ram's Horn* of March 3d	4	3	.05
"You Dirty Boy," Reply to Rev. P. S. Henson, D. D	2	3	.05
Reply to Dr. Hillis	1	3	.05
Christ's Methods of Healing: A Reply to Rev. J. L. Withrow, D. D	2	5	.05
Reply to Dr. Gray	3	9	.05
Reply to Ingersoll's Lecture on Truth	1	4	.05

The Evils Zion Exposes and Condemns.

	Vol.	No.	Price
Doctors, Drugs, and Devils; or, The Foes of Christ the Healer	1	10	$0.05
Secret Societies: The Foes of God, Home, Church, and State	1	8	.05
Zion's Protest Against Swine's Flesh as a Disease-Producer	2	6	.05
Tobacco, Satan's Consuming Fire	2	7	.05
The Press: The Tree of Good and Evil	2	10	.05
Ethiopia Stretching Out Her Hands to God	1	11	.05
False Christian Science Unmasked	2	8	.05
Christian Science Exposed as an Anti-Christian Imposture	3	5	.05
Diabolical Spiritualism Unmasked	2	12	.05
The Man of Sin Revealed; or, An Exposure of the Blasphemous Claim of the Pope of Rome to be the Infallible Head of the Church of Our Lord Jesus Christ	3	7	.05
Ingersoll Exposed	3	4	.05
Spurious Holiness Exposed	5	3	.05

Divine Healing and Its Truths as Taught in Zion.

	Vol.	No.	Price
Jesus the Healer and Satan the Defiler	4	2	$0.05
Do You Know God's Way of Healing? and He is Just the Same Today	4	1	.05
Reasonings for Inquirers Concerning Divine Healing Teaching	4	7	.05
Divine Healing Vindicated	2	9	.05
Lessons on Divine Healing, from the Story of the Leper	4	12	.05
Job's Boils; or, Objections to Divine Healing Considered	3	6	.05
What Should a Christian Do When Sick?	2	1	$0.05
"I Will"	1	9	.05
Permission and Commission	1	2	.05
How Jesus Heals the Little Ones	5	2	.05
Talks with Ministers	1	6	.05

Prayer and Its Conditions as Realized in Zion.

	Vol.	No.	Price
How to Pray	2	4	$0.05
If It Be Thy Will, Like a Shepherd, and How I Came to Speak for Jesus	4	6	.05
A Woman of Canaan	1	1	.05
The Disciples' Prayer, a series of Morning Discourses at Shiloh Tabernacle	7	3	.10

Zion Standard of Consecration and Sanctified Living.

	Vol.	No.	Price
Sanctification of Spirit, Soul, and Body	1	7	$0.05
The Seal of the Living God	5	4	.05
The Baptism of Fire, and The Cup of Suffering	5	5	.05
Ye are God's Witnesses, and The Power of Passive Faith	5	6	.05
The Chains of Good and Evil, and Sanctification of Triune Man	5	1	.05
Redemption Draweth Nigh	1	5	.05
Zion's First Feast of Tabernacles	5	9	.10
Zion Bible Calendar	3	1	.05
Four Addresses: — Love Fulfils Law; The Zion of the Holy One of Israel; The Wages of Sin; and Seest Thou This Woman?	6	4	.05
The Leaven of the Kingdom	7	4	.05

Devotional and Inspirational Zion Tracts.

Two Cents Each.

How I Came to Speak for Jesus.
If It Be Thy Will.

One Cent Each.

Do You Know God's Way of Healing?
If It Be Thy Will.
Jesus the Healer.
Satan the Defiler.
How I Came to Speak for Jesus.
He is Just the Same Today.

Suitable for enclosing in envelopes.

Special Books.

	Price
Zion's Conflict with Methodist Apostasy	$0.25
Zion's Holy War	.35

Tracts of Zion in Foreign Languages.

	Price
German:	
I Will	$0.05
How to Pray	.05
Permission and Commission	.05
A Woman of Canaan	.05
The Ordinance of Christian Baptism	.05
Organization of the Christian Catholic Church	.10
What Shall a Christian Do When Sick?	.05
Christian Science Exposed as an Anti-Christian Imposture	.05
Reasonings for Inquirers	.05
Sanctification of Spirit, Soul, and Body	.05
How I Came to Speak for Jesus	.02
How Jesus Heals the Little Ones	.05
Do You Know God's Way of Healing?	.01
He Is Just the Same Today	.01
How I Came to Speak for Jesus	.01
Elias	.05
Divine Healing Vindicated	.05
Zion's Protest Against Swine's Flesh	.05
French:	
How I Came to Speak for Jesus	.02
How Jesus Heals the Little Ones	.05
Danish:	
He is Just the Same Today	.02
Do You Know God's Way of Healing	.02
Norwegian:	
If It Be Thy Will	.02
Holland:	
Divine Healing Vindicated	.05

Rates for Quantity Orders.

Charges Prepaid.

Kinds at 35 cents:	$3.75 a dozen.
Kinds at 25 cents:	2.75 a dozen.
Kinds at 10 cents:	1.00 a dozen or $6.00 per 100
Kinds at 5 cents:	.50 a dozen or 3.00 per 100
Kinds at 2 cents:	.75 for 50 or $1.25 per 100.
Kinds at 1 cent:	.60 for 100.

Elijah's Restoration Messages.

	Vol.	No.	Price
Five Messages:—The Purifying Word; Purification by Obedience; The Purifying Water of Life; Purification by the Word of Wisdom; and Purification by Penal Fire	6	1	$0.05
Two Messages:—Christ, the World Conqueror; and Hear What the Unjust Judge Saith	6	2	.05
Five Messages:—Zion's Star of Hope and Peace; Thy God Reigneth; Peace Passing All Understanding; Then Peaceable; Sowing Peace	6	3	.05
Two Messages: — Until Shiloh Come; delivered at the consecration of Shiloh Tabernacle, Zion City, Illinois, March 31, 1902. Theocracy Contrasted with Democracy and Plutocracy, Chicago Auditorium, April 23, 1902.	6	5	.05
Two Messages, at Chicago Auditorium:—Power Belongeth Unto God; The Power and the Wisdom of God	6	6	.05
Two Messages, at Chicago Auditorium:—The Power of Divine Faith; and The Power of Christ's Resurrection	6	7	.05
Two Messages, at Chicago Auditorium:—The Power of a Living Faith; and The Power of the Word of God	6	8	.05
Two Messages, at Chicago Auditorium:—Awake; and The River of God is Full of Water	6	9	.05
Two Messages, at Chicago Auditorium:—The Power of Sacrifice; and Power of the Covenant, and Elijah the Restorer	6	10	.05
Three Messages, at Chicago Auditorium:—On the Purification of The Temple	6	11	.05
One Message, at Chicago Auditorium:—Saved Whole	7	1	.05

Zion's Second Feast of Tabernacles.

A book of over 300 pages, nicely bound in cloth, 30 cents. By mail, 10 cents extra. Should be in the libraries of all Zion people.

Leaves of Healing

A weekly paper for the extension of the Kingdom of God: Containing accounts of Miracles of Healing; Stenographic Reports of Sermons by the Editor; with Testimonials of Blessing realized by God's people through the ministry of the Christian Catholic Church in Zion, of which the Rev. John Alexander Dowie is the General Overseer.

Subscription price, $2 per year; $1.25 for six months; $0.75 for three months. Clubs of ten, $15. To ministers and Public Libraries, $1.50 per year. Foreign subscriptions, $3.50 per year.

Bound Volumes I, II, III, IV, V, VI, VII, VIII, IX, X, XI, XII and XIII, $3.50 per Volume. Three or more Volumes, $3.00 each. Entire set, $32.50. Carriage on bound volumes always to be paid by purchaser.

Blätter der Heilung.

German Edition of Leaves of Healing. Monthly, $0.50 per year. Foreign, $0.75 per year.

The Zion Banner.

A weekly semi-secular paper devoted to the extension of the Kingdom of God and the Elevation of Man, containing the news of Zion City, brightly and interestingly told; the news of the world up to within a few hours of its publication, and editorials on current events from a Zion standpoint. Edited by the Rev. John Alexander Dowie.

Subscription price, $0.50 for six months; $0.30 for three months. Sold for three cents a copy.

A Voice From Zion.

Monthly. Containing leading Sermons by the Rev. John Alexander Dowie. $0.50 per year. Foreign, $0.75 per year.

Bound Volumes I, II, III, IV, V, VI and VII Voice from Zion, may be secured at $1 per Volume; the complete set for $6.10, F. O. B. Zion City.

All orders for above publications except those quoted at other prices in the foregoing lists, under 25 copies, 5 cents per copy; exceeding 25 copies, 4 cents per copy; 100 or more copies, 3 cents per copy. If mailed to a foreign address, add 3 cents per copy for additional postage.

Trial subscriptions (new), Leaves of Healing, 10 weeks for 25 cents each; Blätter der Heilung, 10 months for 25 cents each. Foreign 55 cents.

Make All Remittances Payable to the Order of John Alex. Dowie.

Zion's Bible Class

Conducted by Deacon Daniel Sloan in Shiloh Tabernacle, Zion City, Lord's Day Morning at 11 o'clock, and in Zion Homes and Gatherings throughout the World.

MID-WEEK BIBLE CLASS LESSON, AUGUST 17th or 18th.

Unflinching Confidence in God.

1. *We must live without fear.*—2 Timothy 1:7-13.
   Fear is not from God's Spirit.
   The calling of God is without alarm.
   Suffering for His sake must become a joy
2. *What can make us afraid?*—Psalm 46:1-11.
   He helps in time of trouble.
   We are never to fear the outcome.
   God is near to help us.
3. *We are to say boldly, "God is for us."*—Hebrews 13:5-6.
   There is salvation in being content.
   He never leaves nor forsakes one.
   Why not live without fear?
4. *When all seems lost, what then?*—Job 2:7-13.
   Health may fail, but what then?
   Property may go, but what then?
   Is there not a double portion to come back?
5. *There are scenes that try one's soul.*—Acts 27:19-31.
   Storms arise to terrify one.
   Be calm in every adversity.
   You are God's and He is for you.
6. *God can keep amid perils.*—1 Peter 3:8-16.
   Men may threaten, but do not fear.
   Follow the Christ without thought of harm.
   God sees you and will hear you.
7. *Some people are easily frightened.*—Luke 21:8-19.
   Wars will frighten some.
   Commotions will frighten some.
   Earthquakes will alarm some.
8. *Trouble need never swerve one.*—2 Corinthians 1:5-12.
   Find consolation in the Christ.
   Trust in God, who has all power.
   He has, does, and will deliver you.

The Lord our God is a Confidence-imparting God.

LORD'S DAY BIBLE CLASS LESSON, AUGUST 21st.

The Sacrifices of Pioneer Effort.

1. *The loss of position, friends and property must not move one.*—Acts 20:17-27.
   The Kingdom is yours with all the Christ has.
   Let even persecution or loss be a joy.
   Some hesitate to be plain for fear of the cost.
2. *There can be no losses for the Christ's sake—it is all gain.*—Matthew 19:27-30.
   If you forsake all you will get all.
   The Christ did. Will you follow Him?
   Make the Christ more than all else.
3. *We will never inherit unless we sacrifice.*—Luke 12:31-40.
   Only those who seek first the Kingdom get it.
   Are you afraid to sell your property?
   If you do not you love this world more than the next.
4. *Losses to those in deep consecration become a joy to Christ.*—Hebrews 10:30-39.
   God repays every loss for His sake.
   Are you joyful when losses come?
   Be patient, hold on to the promise.
5. *God can bring good out of everything hard to bear.*—Romans 8:28-39.
   Are you ignorant of God's plan of recompense?
   Did He not freely give you the Christ?
   Does He not promise freely to give you?
6. *God feels keenly all we feel and suffer.*—2 Corinthians 6:1-10.
   Can you suffer and He not suffer?
   If you go to prison is He not there also?
   If you are hungry does He not hunger?
7. *One must be willing to die that others may live.*—Romans 9:1-8.
   Forget yourself for the Christ's sake.
   Give up your possessions for the Christ's sake.
   Wisely sacrifice all for the Christ's sake.

God's Holy People are a Daily-dying People.

LEAVES OF HEALING.

Two Dollars will bring to you the weekly visits of the Little White Dove for a year; 75 cents will send it to a friend for thirteen weeks. $1.25 will send it for six months; $1.50 will send it to your minister, or to a Y. M. C. A., or to a Public Reading Room for a whole year. We offer no premiums, except the premium of doing good. We receive no advertisements and print no commercial lies or cheating enticements of unscrupulous thieves. LEAVES OF HEALING is Zion on wings, and we keep out everything that would detract the reader's mind from all except the Extension of the Kingdom of God, for which alone it exists. If we cannot send forth our Little White Dove without soiling its wings with the smoke of the factory and the dirt of the wrangling market place, or compelling it to utter the screaming cries of the business vultures in the ears of our readers, then we will keep our Dove at home.

DO YOU KNOW GOD'S WAY OF HEALING?

BY THE REV. JOHN ALEX. DOWIE.

Let it be supposed that the following words are a conversation between the reader [A] and the writer [B].

A. What does this question mean? Do you really suppose that God has some one especial way of healing in these days, of which men may know and avail themselves?

B. That is exactly my meaning, and I wish very much that you should know God's Way of Healing, as I have known it for many years.

A. What is the way, in your opinion?

B. You should rather ask, WHO is God's Way? for the way is a Person, not a thing. I will answer your question in His own words, "I am the Way, and the Truth, and the Life: no one cometh unto the Father, but by Me." These words were spoken by our Lord Jesus, the Christ, the Eternal Son of God, who is both our Savior and our Healer. (John 14:6.)

A. But I always thought that these words only referred to Him as the Way of Salvation. How can you be sure that they refer to Him as the Way of Healing also?

B. Because He cannot change. He is "the same yesterday and today, yea, and forever." (Hebrews 13:8.) He said that He came to this earth not only to save us but to heal us. (Luke 4:18), and He did this when in the flesh on earth. Being unchanged He must be able and willing and desirous to heal now.

A. But is there not this difference, namely, that He is not with us now?

B. No; for He said "Lo, I am with you All the Days, even unto the Consummation of the Age;" and so He is with us now, in spirit, just as much as when He was here in the flesh.

A. But did He not work these miracles of healing when on earth merely to prove that He was the Son of God?

B. No; there was still a greater purpose than that. He healed the sick who trusted in Him in order to show us that He came to die not only for our sins, but for our sicknesses, and to deliver us from both.

A. Then, if that be so, the atonement which He made on the Cross must have been for our sicknesses as well as our sins. Can you prove that is the fact from the Scriptures?

B. Yes, I can, and the passages are very numerous. I need quote only two. In Isaiah 53:4, 5, it is written of Him: "Surely He hath borne our griefs (Hebrew, *sicknesses*), and carried our sorrows: . . . and with His stripes we are healed." Then, in the Gospel according to Matthew, this passage is quoted and directly applied to the work of bodily healing, in the 8th chapter 17th verse: "That it might be fulfilled which was spoken by Isaiah the prophet, saying, Himself took our infirmities, and bare our diseases."

A. But do you not think that sickness is often God's will, and sent for our good, and therefore God may not wish us to be healed?

B. No, that cannot possibly be; for diseases of every kind are the Devil's work, and his work can never be God's will, since the Christ came for the very purpose of destroying "the works of the Devil." (1 John 3:8.)

A. Do you mean to say that all disease is the work of Satan?

B. Yes, for if there had been no sin (which came through Satan) there never would have been any disease, and Jesus never in one single instance told any person that sickness was God's work or will, but the very contrary.

A. Can you prove from Scriptures that all forms of sickness and infirmity are the Devil's work?

B. Yes, that can be done very easily. You will see in Matthew 4:23 and 9:35 that when Jesus was here in the flesh He healed "all manner of disease and all manner of sickness among the people." Then if you will refer to Acts 10:38 you will see that the Apostle Peter declares that He (Jesus) "went about doing good, and healing all that were oppressed of the Devil." Notice that all whom He healed, not some, were suffering from Satan's evil power.

A. But does disease never come from God?

B. No, it cannot come from God, for He is pure, and disease is unclean; and it cannot come out of Heaven, for there is no disease there.

A. That is very different from the teachings which I have received all my life from ministers and in the churches. Do you really think that you are right, and that they are all wrong in this matter?

B. It is not a question as between myself and them. The only question is, What does God's Word say? God has said in all the ages, to His Church, "I am Jehovah that healeth thee" (Exodus 15:26), and therefore it would be wicked to say that He is the defiler of His people. All true Christians must believe the Bible, and it is impossible to believe that good and evil, sickness and health, sin and holiness could have a common origin in God. If the Bible really taught that, it would be impossible to believe our Lord Jesus, the Christ, when He says: "A good tree cannot bring forth evil fruit, neither can a corrupt tree bring forth good fruit." (Matthew 7:18.)

A. But even if I agree with all you say, is it not true that the Gifts of Healing were removed from the Church, and are not in it now?

B. No, the "Gifts of Healing" were never withdrawn, and can never be withdrawn, from the true Church of God, for it is written: "The gifts and the calling of God are without repentance." (Romans 11:29.) There are nine gifts of God to the Church (enumerated in 1 Corinthians 12:8-11), and all these are in the Holy Spirit. Therefore, so long as the Holy Spirit is in the Church, all the gifts must be there also. If they are not exercised, that does not prove that they do not exist, but that the faith to exercise them is lacking in God's servants. The gifts are all perfectly preserved; for the Holy Spirit, not the Church, keeps them safely.

A. What should a Christian then do when overtaken with sickness?

B. A Christian should obey God's command, and at once turn to Him for forgiveness of the sin which may have caused the sickness, and for immediate healing. Healing is obtained from God in one of four ways, namely: First, by the direct prayer of faith, without any aid from the officers of the Church, praying as the Centurion did in Matthew 8:5-13; second, by two faithful disciples praying in perfect agreement, in accordance with the Lord's promise in Matthew 18:19; third, by the anointing of the Elders and the prayer of faith, according to the instructions in James 5:14 and 15; and fourth, by the laying on of the hands of them who believe, and whom God calls to that ministry, as the Lord commands in Mark 16:18, and in other places.

A. But are people healed in this way in these days?

B. Yes, in thousands of cases. I have myself laid hands upon many hundreds of thousands of persons, and I have seen the Lord's power manifested in the healing of great numbers, many of whom are living witnesses in many countries, who have testified publicly before thousands, and who are prepared to testify at any time. This ministry is being exercised by devoted Christians in many parts of America, Europe, Australasia, and elsewhere.

A. Is it not the same as Christian Science, Mind Healing, etc.?

B. No. Divine Healing is diametrically opposed to these diabolical counterfeits which are utterly antichristian. These impostures are only seductive forms of Spiritualism. Trance Evangelism is also a more recent form of this delusion, and it deceives many.

A. But how shall I obtain the necessary faith to receive healing, which faith I am at present conscious that I do not possess?

B. It is written: "Belief cometh of hearing, and hearing by the word of the Christ." (Romans 10:17.) Our Missions are held for the express purpose of teaching fully the Word of God on this matter, and I very heartily invite you to attend the meetings which are announced for Zion Tabernacles in Chicago and other cities, and for Shiloh Tabernacle, Zion City, Illinois. All are welcome and there are no charges of any kind made, for all God's gifts are free gifts. Salvation is the first of these, without which you cannot be healed through faith in Jesus. All the costs of this work are covered by the free-will offerings of the people who attend these meetings, and others whom the Lord leads to help; but the poorest, who have nothing to give, are as heartily welcome as the richest.

A. Do you see the sick and lay hands upon them in this Mission?

B. Yes; after we feel satisfied that they are fully resting in the Lord alone for the healing, we see privately, so far as time permits, those who attend, but under no circumstances do we claim the power to heal any; for "power belongeth unto God."

A. Have you any writings upon this subject which can be purchased?

B. Yes; these can be obtained at the office of Zion Printing and Publishing House, Zion City, Illinois, and at any Zion Tabernacle. But the best book on Divine Healing is the Bible itself, studied prayerfully and earnestly.

We extend to you a hearty invitation to attend the meetings, which are free to all. Our prayer is that you may be led to find in Jesus, the Christ, our Lord and God your present Savior from sin, your Healer from sickness, your Cleanser from all evil, your Keeper in the way to Heaven, your Friend, and your All for Time and Eternity. We pray that these words may help many who read, and that our little conversation may bear fruit in leading many readers to look to Jesus only

"The Healing of Christ's seamless dress
Is by all beds of pain;
We touch Him in life's throng and press
And we are whole again."

OBEYING GOD IN BAPTISM.

"Baptizing Them Into the Name of the Father and of the Son and of the Holy Ghost."

Nineteen Thousand Two Hundred Fifty-eight Baptisms by Triune Immersion Since March 14, 1897.

Nineteen Thousand Two Hundred Fifty-eight Believers have joyfully followed their Lord in the Ordinance of Believer's Baptism by Triune Immersion since the first Baptism in Central Zion Tabernacle on March 14, 1897.

Baptized in Central Zion Tabernacle from March 14, 1897, to December 14, 1901, by the General Overseer,	4754			
Baptized in South Side Zion Tabernacle from January 1, 1902, to June 14, 1903, by the General Overseer..	37			
Baptized at Zion City by the General Overseer........	583			
Baptized by Overseers, Elders, Evangelists and Deacons, at Headquarters (Zion City) and Chicago......	5283			
Total Baptized at Headquarters.....................	—			10,657
Baptized in places outside of Headquarters by the General Overseer..................................		641		
Baptized in places outside of Headquarters by Overseers, Elders, Evangelists and Deacons..............		7535		
Total Baptized outside of Headquarters............		—		8,176
Total Baptized in seven years and three months....				18,833
Baptized since June 14, 1904:				
Baptized in Zion City by the General Overseer........	64			
Baptized in Zion City by Elder Royall...............	6			
Baptized in Zion City by Elder Hammond............	6			
Baptized in Zion City by Overseer Mason............	90			
Baptized in Zion City by Overseer Excell............	87			
Baptized in Zion City by Overseer Piper.............	79			
Baptized in Chicago by Elder Hoffman.......	4			
Baptized in Chicago by Elder Cossum.	6			
Baptized in Chicago by Elder Keller.................	5		347	
Baptized in Canada by Elder Brooks.................		4		
Baptized in California by Elder Taylor..............		2		
Baptized in England by Overseer Cantel.............		12		
Baptized in Indiana by Elder Osborn................		2		
Baptized in Minnesota by Elder Graves..............		5		
Baptized in Mississippi by Evangelist Gay...........		1		
Baptized in Missouri by Evangelist Gay.............		1		
Baptized in Missouri by Elder Brock.................		9		
Baptized in Missouri by Deacon Robinson...........		1		
Baptized in Nebraska by Elder Hoy..................		7		
Baptized in New York by Overseer Mason............		9		
Baptized in Ohio by Deacon Kelchner................		3		
Baptized in Ohio by Deacon Arrington...............		5		
Baptized in Texas by Evangelist Gay................		11		
Baptized in Washington by Elder Ernst..............		3		
Baptized in Wisconsin by Elder McClurkin...........		3	78	425
Total Baptized since March 14, 1897................				19,258

Note.

Several of those who were baptized on the following dates had previously received the ordinance at the hands of Officers of the Church, afterward proving themselves to have been apostate, and in one case, the person was not ready spiritually for baptism, and as these names were published at the time, they are omitted from the following list.

The following-named four believers were baptized in the Local Swimming Baths, Bloemfontein, Orange River Colony, South Africa, Monday, May 23, 1904, by Overseer Daniel Bryant:

Miller, Cowan, Fountain Villa, Douglas street, Bloemfontein, Orange River Colony, South Africa
Moore, John Henry, St. George's street, Bloemfontein, Orange River Colony, South Africa
Richardson, Mrs. Sarah, Erin Cottage, Hoop street, Bloemfontein, Orange River Colony, South Africa
Swanepoel, Mrs. Maria Levina, Cumnor Postoffice, Bushmanskop, Orange River Colony, South Africa

The following-named fifteen believers were baptized in Liverpool Road Baths, N. London, England, Monday, June 13, 1904, by Overseer H. E. Cantel:

Arme, Mrs. Agnes Fanny......30 Fairview, Heanor, Nottingham, England
Donaldson, Thomas Chalmers......11 Argyle terrace, Edinburgh, Scotland
Garner, John.......39 Stanford street, Old Trafford, Manchester, England
Hartley, Israel............Orchard House, Heywood, Lancashire, England
Hill, Mrs. Christianna.............Tattingstone, Ipswich, Suffolk, England
Jackman, Arthur.......3 Plasket Grove, Upton Park, E., London, England
Jackman, Catherine Sophia S., 3 Plasket Grove, Upton Park, E., London, England
Jackman, John ....3 Plasket Grove, Upton Park, E., London, England
Kingaby, Ivy Maude Ellen, 95 St. Thomas road, Finsbury Park, N., London, England
Kingaby, Percival Frederick, 95 St. Thomas road, Finsbury Park, N., London, England
Moody, Charles. ..12 Havelock street, King's Cross, N., London, England
More, Mrs. Clementina ....54 Dallfield walk, Dundee, Scotland
Morris, George Henry......105 Bridge street, Swinton, Yorkshire, England
Osborne, Albert....................28 Duncairn Gardens, Belfast, Ireland
Whitaker, Mrs. Rebecca, Croftfield, Littleborough, near Manchester, England

The following-named twelve believers were baptized in the Caledonian Road Baths, N. London, England, Lord's Day, June 26, 1904, by Overseer H. E. Cantel:

Clarke, Isobel Winifred, 151 Ashmore road, Paddington, W., London, England
Constant, Emma......123 Kensal road, Paddington, W., London, England
Costa, William, 61 Elsden road, Bruce Grove, Tottenham, N., London, England
Dawson, Mrs. Annie B. S., 45 Gildersome street, Woolwich Common, S. E., London, England
Dawson, Thomas J., 45 Gildersome street, Woolwich Common, S. E., London, England
Deeprose, Mrs. Florence Emily, 56 Cambrian road, Grosvenor Wood, Tunbridge Wells, Kent, England
Deeprose, John Edward, 56 Cambrian road, Grosvenor Wood, Tunbridge Wells, Kent, England
House, Edith Gertrude...92 Brewery road, Islington, N., London, England
Levell, Mrs. Mary Ann, 101 Kensal road, Paddington, W., London, England
Sanders, Miss Milly..............109 Elgin avenue, W., London, England
Tanner, Miss Ellen, 4 B, Montague Mansions, Baker street, W., London, England
Turpin, Edwin H......7 Rostrevor road, Fulham, S. W., London, England

The following-named believer was baptized at Seattle, Washington, Lord's Day, July 3, 1904, by Elder August Ernst:

Case, Mrs. Catherine..2318 North Fifty-seventh street, Seattle, Washington

The following-named sixty-four believers were baptized in Shiloh Tabernacle, Zion City, Illinois, Lord's Day, July 24, 1904, by the General Overseer:

Bishop, Arthur J......................2314 Gilboa avenue, Zion City, Illinois
Bliss, Percy Parker..................3019 Enoch avenue, Zion City, Illinois
Boldt, Mrs. Louisa.................6746 Sangamon street, Chicago, Illinois
Bouck, Drew.....................3101 Elizabeth avenue, Zion City, Illinois
Bresler, Russell Owen.................1118 St. Johns avenue, Lima, Ohio
Butcher, Mrs. Emily Magdelene..2905 Elizabeth avenue, Zion City, Illinois
Carson, Mrs. Belle....................2806 Ezra avenue, Zion City, Illinois
Cathers, Albert William..............................Syracuse, New York
Chenoweth, Arthur................ ..1350 Montana street, Chicago, Illinois
Christ, Peter...........................Woodmere, Long Island, New York
Christiansen, A...............735 North Campbell avenue, Chicago, Illinois
Christiansen, Mrs. R.........735 North Campbell avenue, Chicago, Illinois
Clarke, Miss Flossie M................Elijah Hospice, Zion City, Illinois
Cooper, Jerold...................................Aldesburg, Pennsylvania
Cressy, Morton Starr..Zion City, Illinois
Dalgity, Anna M.....Moose Jaw, Assinaboia, Northwest Territory, Canada
Dalwood, Mrs. Emma ....3011 Emmaus avenue, Zion City, Illinois
Dike, Mrs. A..Woodstock, Illinois
Eckels, Miss Annette Florence ....Washington, Iowa
Eliason, Mrs. Alice..Twenty-seventh St. and Hebron Ave. Zion City, Illinois
Estrem, Laura ....Easton, Washington
Fraser, Mrs. Anna P..........224 West Seventeenth street, New York City
Galloway, Miss Lottie J...............2903 Eshcol avenue, Zion City, Illinois
Gilbert, Jessie Irene ....207 Hanover street, Milwaukee, Wisconsin
Hartman, Gustav Carl.......................................Clarendon, Texas
Haumont, Mrs. Mary F....................... ......Broken Bow, Nebraska
Holiday, Anna......................3406 Patrick avenue, Omaha, Nebraska
Hoover, Charles E.....................................Plattsburg, Missouri
Hosken, Mrs. Rhoda..................3116 Enoch avenue, Zion City, Illinois
Huntley, Raymond D....... ... 1811 South Sixth street, Des Moines, Iowa
James, Owen......................2710 Emmaus avenue, Zion City, Illinois
James, Wilhelmine...............2720 Edina boulevard, Zion City, Illinois
Jamowneau, Lavinia E........... ....Newark, New Jersey
Kerfoot, Mrs. Isadore...................63 Pearson street, Chicago, Illinois
Kewley, William Henry....................................Piper City, Illinois
Kisor, Miss Osie Ora.......................................New Sharon, Iowa
Knatt, Henry N... ....Oxford, Michigan
Leech, James B......................1719 Horeb avenue, Zion City, Illinois
Logan, Ava E..Cedar Falls, Iowa
McClintock, Miss Lida M..................Sprenkle street, Canton, Ohio
Martin, Miss Ella Viola ....1408 North street, Logansport, Indiana
Mather, Mrs. Louisa..................1004 Center street, Racine, Wisconsin
Monteath, Mrs. Isabella.. Butte, Montana
Olling, Grace.......................1913 Horeb avenue, Zion City, Illinois
Patterson, Margaret W..............2106 Enoch avenue, Zion City, Illinois
Peterman, William..........................R. R. Number 1, Zion City, Illinois
Peterson, Dagmar ....1904 Hermon avenue, Zion City, Illinois
Pittaway, Master Edwin............2603 Gideon avenue, Zion City, Illinois
Populorum, Francis................2809 Gabriel avenue, Zion City, Illinois
Richardson, Mrs. Elizabeth..........................Salem Center, Indiana
Rinker, Miss Marie Adams.......22 East Terrace, Chattanooga, Tennessee
Ross, Harry Fenton................ ......Elijah Hospice, Zion City, Illinois
Robinson, James Sylvester........ ....Parrott, Ohio
Roulo, Adele Gilberta.............2513 Elizabeth avenue, Zion City, Illinois
Toggenburg, Miss Mathilda A.. 660 South Halstead street, Chicago, Illinois
Tomlin, Mrs. Ellen... .... 2919 Eschol avenue, Zion City, Illinois
Thompson, Mrs. Albert .... 6824 Lafayette avenue, Chicago, Illinois
Wheeler, Mrs. Janet.........342 Webster avenue, Jersey City, New Jersey
White, M. E ....Boone, Iowa

Wilcox, Mrs. R. A....................Fitzgerald, Georgia
Williams, Mrs. Lena A....................North avenue, Chicago, Illinois
(Former address 780 Jackson boulevard.)
Wilson, Miss Margaret Locke....................Chattanooga, Tennessee
Winnie, Miss Maud I....................1907 Asylum avenue, Racine, Wisconsin
Yonker, Mary....................Joliet, Illinois

The following-named thirty-nine believers were baptized in Shiloh Tabernacle, Zion City, Illinois, Lord's Day, July 24, 1904, by Overseer William Hamner Piper:

Bond, Miss Daisy B....................West Unity, Ohio
Boroff, Lucinda Frances....................Hamilton, Missouri
Corson, Miss Helen....................2806 Ezra avenue, Zion City, Illinois
Chesney, William James....................Baxter Springs, Kansas
Copeland, Margaret....................3004 Gilgal avenue, Zion City, Illinois
Flaglore, Mrs. Hannah Malinda....................Pontiac, Illinois
Fox, Diah....................(postoffice omitted) Virginia
Gannaway, John Houston....................Chattanooga, Tennessee
Goodwin, Eliza J....................Mound Valley, Kansas
Hicks, Henry G....................Box 679, South Bend, Indiana
Hoskin, Mary A....................3114 Enoch avenue, Zion City, Illinois
Huntley, Mrs. Persis....................1811 South Sixth street, Des Moines, Iowa
Jepson, Mrs. Maggie V....................Mineral City, Ohio
LeRoi, Mrs. Tillie Holmberg....................2606 Elisha avenue, Zion City, Illinois
Long, Willie Christian....................Keokuk, Iowa
Maddox, William Santford....................930 Kingdom avenue, Danville, Illinois
Mather, Elsie May....................1004 Center street, Racine, Wisconsin
Maxwell, Willard A....................22½ Walnut street (State not given)
Milloy, Master Walter....................66 St. Johns place, Chicago, Illinois
Olson, Mrs. Lena....................Evanston, Illinois
Olsson, Mrs. Charlotta....................1807 Horeb avenue, Zion City, Illinois
Pike, Mrs. Etta V....................Binghamton, New York
Reeves, Mrs. M. A....................Valley Junction, Iowa
Riggins, Mrs. Florence A....................3203 Gabriel avenue, Zion City, Illinois
Ritchey, Earl Alexander....................3106 Ezekiel avenue, Zion City, Illinois
Schneider, Charles F....................2712 Ezekiel avenue, Zion City, Illinois
Scott, Miss Gertrude....................224 West Seventeenth street, New York City
Sears, Mrs. Almira Lavinia....................St. Croix, New Brunswick, Canada
Siepman, William....................Brazil, Indiana
Silvey, Benjamin....................Helmer, Indiana
Stauffer, John P....................Wakarusa, Indiana
Svanson, Elma....................2313 Hermon avenue, Zion City, Illinois
Thompson, Wallace....................Danville, Illinois
Unruh, Mrs. Mary....................Kouts, Indiana
Van Zandt, William Wesley....................Zion City, Illinois
White, Loyd....................Boone, Iowa
Wilson, Miss Orpha....................Muncie, Indiana
Yonker, Jacob....................Joliet, Illinois
Zederstaff, Mrs. A. C....................2202 Gilead avenue, Zion City, Illinois

The following-named thirty-two believers were baptized in Shiloh Tabernacle, Zion City, Illinois, Lord's Day, July 24, 1904, by Overseer John G. Excell:

Arnley, Mrs. Ermina....................Waterville, Michigan
Bolinger, Mrs. Sadie....................Huntington, Indiana
Bosworth, Maibelle....................2810 Elisha avenue, Zion City, Illinois
Bowen, Mrs. Sarah E....................Jonesville, Michigan
Brown, Mrs. Edith....................2810 Elisha avenue, Zion City, Illinois
Burrell, Mrs. Margaret....................3106 Emmaus avenue, Zion City, Illinois
Chappell, Alfred Charles....................3016 Gilboa avenue, Zion City, Illinois
Clark, Alvin George....................2925 Gideon avenue, Zion City, Illinois
Crawford, Miss Alice....................3108 Elisha avenue, Zion City, Illinois
Frederickson, Harry B....................3000 Elisha avenue, Zion City, Illinois
Gourlay, Mrs. Margaret....................3203 Eschol avenue, Zion City, Illinois
Grey, Miss Violet....................207 South Broom street, Madison, Wisconsin
Hershey, Carl Gorham....................2813 Eshcol avenue, Zion City, Illinois
Hosken, Albert....................3114 Enoch avenue, Zion City, Illinois
Jones, Nellie....................2804 Elizabeth avenue, Zion City, Illinois
Leavitt, Mrs. Catherine Louise....................2809 Emmaus avenue, Zion City, Illinois
Morton, Miss Clara....................3101 Elizabeth avenue, Zion City, Illinois
Ortwig, Charles....................3108 Gideon avenue, Zion City, Illinois
Peterman, Mrs. Christina....................R. R. Number 1, Zion City, Illinois
Peterman, Wesley L....................Mount Carmel, Zion City, Illinois
Reebel, Perry Daniel....................Sault Ste. Marie, Michigan
Reeve, Master Rex W....................2509 Elizabeth avenue, Zion City, Illinois
Robinson, Mrs. Mary E....................Parrott, Ohio
Roulo, Wellington James....................2513 Elizabeth avenue, Zion City, Illinois
Schwenck, Ella....................Grand boulevard, Grossdale, Illinois
Schwenck, Miss Clara....................Grossdale, Illinois
Sharp, Lorien E....................417 Ingram street, Bay City, Michigan
Shreffler, Mrs. Opal....................2810 Elisha avenue, Zion City, Illinois
Sorenson, Elsworth....................2713 Gilboa avenue, Zion City, Illinois
Thresher, Charles C....................Marshfield, Wisconsin
Weaver, Mrs. Minnie C....................Wakarusa, Kansas
Wilson, Mrs. Thomasina Wilder....................3000 Elim avenue, Zion City, Illinois

The following-named thirty-one believers were baptized in Shiloh Tabernacle, Zion City, Illinois, Lord's Day, July 24, 1904, by Overseer George L. Mason:

Alexander, Merla H....................1908 Gideon avenue, Zion City, Illinois
Anderson, John....................2702 Elizabeth avenue, Zion City, Illinois
Bloomfield, Ethel C....................Valley Junction, Iowa
Bowen, Elsie Bernice....................14618 Green street, Harvey, Illinois
Campbell, Mrs. Julia A....................Hamden Junction, Ohio
Chappell, Miss Agnes Beatrice....................3016 Gilboa avenue, Zion City, Illinois
Fowler, Mrs. Sarah....................2911 Gabriel avenue, Zion City, Illinois
Hall, Henry Horace....................1727 Horeb avenue, Zion City, Illinois
Hammond, John, Jr....................Viroqua, Wisconsin
Hibbets, Jennie....................2816 Edina boulevard, Zion City, Illinois
Hildyard, Bennie Monroe....................2606 Gilboa avenue, Zion City, Illinois
Hosken, Stanley....................3114 Enoch avenue, Zion City, Illinois
Hosken, Rhoda Evelina....................3114 Enoch avenue, Zion City, Illinois
Hurlbut, Allen Jonathan....................312 East Eighth street, Muscatine, Iowa
Jackson, Miss Mabel....................Concord, Indiana
Johnson, Maggie....................2815 Elizabeth avenue, Zion City, Illinois
King, Ruth....................3000 Enoch avenue, Zion City, Illinois
Leech, Miss Winona....................1707 Horeb avenue, Zion City, Illinois
Long, Ethel....................R. R. Number 1, Keokuk, Illinois
Mayfield, Thomas A....................2702 Elizabeth avenue, Zion City, Illinois
Olling, Marie....................1913 Horeb avenue, Zion City, Illinois
Peterman, Clinton Elihu....................R. R. Number 1, Zion City, Illinois
Sears, Joseph....................St. Croix, New Brunswick, Canada
Sorenson, Roy....................2713 Gilboa avenue, Zion City, Illinois
Stieglitz, John....................Muscatine, Iowa
Swank, Vergil....................2404 Gilboa avenue, Zion City, Illinois
Tennyson, Arthur Ake....................Danville, Kentucky
White, Reevie....................Boone, Iowa
Woelke, Florence....................3212 Gilead avenue, Zion City, Illinois
Woelke, Ethel....................3212 Gilead avenue, Zion City, Illinois
Wolcott, Mrs. Kate....................Summit, South Dakota

The following-named five believers were baptized in Shiloh Tabernacle, Zion City, Illinois, Monday, July 25, 1904, by Elder F. M. Royall:

Butler, Charles Walter....................Elijah Hospice, Zion City, Illinois
Cameron, Erwin....................Camp Esther, Zion City, Illinois
Gaston, Stewart H....................3119 Elijah avenue, Zion City, Illinois
Olinger, Harley S....................Madison, Wisconsin
Sayrs, Francis Penn, Sr....................Reesville, Ohio

CONSECRATION OF CHILDREN.

The following-named twelve children were consecrated to God, at Heathcote, Ontario, Canada, Lord's Day, June 5, 1904, by Elder Eugene Brooks:

Crosskill, Charles Clayton....................Heathcote, Ontario, Canada
Crosskill, Emma....................Heathcote, Ontario, Canada
Crosskill, Rosetta....................Heathcote, Ontario, Canada
Shaw, Ada....................Heathcote, Ontario, Canada
Shaw, Alice....................Heathcote, Ontario, Canada
Shaw, Laura Pepper....................Heathcote, Ontario, Canada
Shaw, Lillie....................Heathcote, Ontario, Canada
Shaw, Mabel....................Heathcote, Ontario, Canada
Shaw, Pearl....................Heathcote, Ontario, Canada
Shaw, Stephen....................Heathcote, Ontario, Canada
Woodhouse, Annie Cora....................Heathcote, Ontario, Canada
Woodhouse, Wesley....................Heathcote, Ontario, Canada

The following-named four children were consecrated to God at Collingwood, Ontario, Canada, Tuesday, June 7, 1904, by Elder Eugene Brooks:

Hollingshead, Ida May....................Collingwood, Ontario, Canada
Hollingshead, George E....................Collingwood, Ontario, Canada
Hollingshead, Mary Caroline....................Collingwood, Ontario, Canada
Hollingshead, Victoria....................Collingwood, Ontario, Canada

The following-named ten children were consecrated to God at Waubaushene, Ontario, Canada, Thursday, June 9, 1904, by Elder Eugene Brooks:

Boyd, Clarence Gordon....................Waubaushene, Ontario, Canada
Boyd, Fern Beatrice....................Waubaushene, Ontario, Canada
Boyd, Leafy Tressa....................Waubaushene, Ontario, Canada
Boyd, Loy Mildred Frances....................Waubaushene, Ontario, Canada
Boyd, Myrtle Evelyn....................Waubaushene, Ontario, Canada
Boyd, Wilma Margaret....................Waubaushene, Ontario, Canada
Hambley, Fuchsia Louise....................Lovering, Ontario, Canada
Hambley, Maxwell Dowie....................Lovering, Ontario, Canada
Hambley, Raymond Baker....................Lovering, Ontario, Canada
Hambley, Violet Olla Bessie....................Lovering, Ontario, Canada

The following-named four children were consecrated to God in the North Side Zion Tabernacle, Chicago, Illinois, Lord's Day, July 10, 1904, by Elder J. R. Keller:

Jessen, Elsie Grace....................815 Sheffield avenue, Chicago, Illinois
Jessen, Everett Charles....................815 Sheffield avenue, Chicago, Illinois
Jessen, Myrtle May....................815 Sheffield avenue, Chicago, Illinois
Jessen, Walter Frank....................815 Sheffield avenue, Chicago, Illinois

The following-named three children were consecrated to God at Newport, Minnesota, Lord's Day, July 10, 1904, by Elder F A. Graves:

Wigham, Margaret Viola....................Newport, Minnesota
Wigham, Paul W....................Newport, Minnesota
Wigham, Wilma Nellie....................Newport, Minnesota

The following-named two children were consecrated to God at Zion City, Illinois, Tuesday, July 19, 1904, by Elder Eugene Brooks:

Crary, Esther Maria....................Trippville, Wisconsin
Crary, Geraldine Monta....................Trippville, Wisconsin

The following-named one hundred sixty-seven children were consecrated to God, in Shiloh Tabernacle, Zion City, Illinois, Wednesday, July 20, 1904, by the General Overseer:

Aikin, Mildred Pearl......3530 West Sixtieth street, Chicago, Illinois
Anderson, Edgar Nathaniel..........2318 Elisha avenue, Zion City, Illinois
Anderson, Eloise Blanche...........2318 Elisha avenue, Zion City, Illinois
Axton, Alice Luetta.........Mount Morris, Illinois
Barber, John Woodward.............2312 Gilead avenue, Zion City, Illinois
Beck, Theodore Morton...........2012 Hermon avenue, Zion City, Illinois
Bennewate, Ruth Evilene...........2701 Gideon avenue, Zion City, Illinois
Berger, Arthur Glenn..............1709 Hermon avenue, Zion City, Illinois
Berger, Gladys Irene...............1709 Hermon avenue, Zion City, Illinois
Berger, Grace Carroll..............1709 Hermon avenue, Zion City, Illinois
Biddle, Bernice........5618 East Seventeenth street, Kansas City, Missouri
Biddle, Earl Franklin..5618 East Seventeenth street, Kansas City, Missouri
Blanks, Marguerite.................2114 Enoch avenue, Zion City, Illinois
Bolinger, Dale L.........Huntington, Indiana
Bolinger, Morris Gladstone.........Huntington, Indiana
Bosworth, Vernon...............2807 Emmaus avenue, Zion City, Illinois
Bosworth, Vivien Estella..........2807 Emmaus avenue, Zion City, Illinois
Bouck, Martha A................3101 Elizabeth avenue, Zion City, Illinois
Bouck, Mary M.................3101 Elizabeth avenue, Zion City, Illinois
Bouck, Stacy P................3101 Elizabeth avenue, Zion City, Illinois
Boyer, Faith Idella.................3009 Gideon avenue, Zion City, Illinois
Boyer, Flora Elizabeth............2506 Edina boulevard, Zion City, Illinois
Boyer, Paul Brasefield............2506 Edina boulevard, Zion City, Illinois
Brander, Curtis Archibald..........3108 Emmaus avenue, Zion City, Illinois
Brander, Esther Mildred.........3108 Emmaus avenue, Zion City, Illinois
Brander, Mamie Vielda............3108 Emmaus avenue, Zion City, Illinois
Branson, Arthur Elwood............406 Beal avenue, Hammond, Indiana
Branson, Edgar....................406 Beal avenue, Hammond, Indiana
Brister, Margaret..............1902 Ezekiel avenue, Zion City, Illinois
Brock, John Russell...............2103 Ezekiel avenue, Zion City, Illinois
Brown, Arlas Emmanuel...........2811 Ezekiel avenue, Zion City, Illinois
Buffa, Emma Marguerite............Elijah Hospice, Zion City, Illinois
Borkenhagen, Ruth Eleanor....632 Second avenue, Milwaukee, Wisconsin
Busch, Lodema Dorothy.........St. Louis, Missouri
Butcher, Ivan John Tennyson.....2905 Elizabeth avenue, Zion City, Illinois
Butcher, Owen Edgar Frank.....2905 Elizabeth avenue, Zion City, Illinois
Carmer, Esther Lenore..........Auburn, Indiana
Chambers, James Henry.............2457 Ontario street, Chicago, Illinois
Chambers, Thecla Marie..........Zion City, Illinois
Clark, George Hyde...............2002 Hebron avenue, Zion City, Illinois
Cook, Maude Ethel..................2508 Gilboa avenue, Zion City, Illinois
Corson, Ruth Naomi.........Pueblo, Colorado
Crane, Eugenia May...............2708 Eshcol avenue, Zion City, Illinois
Crooks, Mary M..........Pekin, Illinois
Cutts, Ruth.........................2914 Elim avenue, Zion City, Illinois
Dalwood, Alfred.................3011 Emmaus avenue, Zion City, Illinois
Dalwood, Doreen Amy Matilda....3011 Emmaus avenue, Zion City, Illinois
Dehner, Clifford Clarence............Lexington pike, Covington, Kentucky
Dehner, George Carl...............Lexington pike, Covington, Kentucky
DeJonge, John Edward..............2809 Gilboa avenue, Zion City, Illinois
Densmore, Ruth S..........Zion City, Illinois
Dermot, Frederic...................2457 Ontario street, Chicago, Illinois
Doll, Amelia..........Marshfield, Wisconsin
Ellis, Calvert Nice...............653 Carmel boulevard, Zion City, Illinois
Falkner, Charles E..........Tiffin, Ohio
Fisher, Lemuel James...........2817 Emmaus avenue, Zion City, Illinois
Fox, Esther Elizabeth..........1611 Prairie avenue, Chicago, Illinois
Ganz, Lilly Ruth......................98 Le Moyne street, Chicago, Illinois
Graf, Harold.......................3019 Gideon avenue, Zion City, Illinois
Gee, Ruth Luise..........Dahoga, Pennsylvania
Greener, Marjorie Phillips..........Missal, Illinois
Greener, Louise Victoria..........Missal, Illinois
Greenfield, Leslie Excell..........3104 Eshcol avenue, Zion City, Illinois
Griswold, Julia R..................2621 Gilboa avenue, Zion City, Illinois
Hall, Elmer Gladstone.............1727 Horeb avenue, Zion City, Illinois
Hall, Milton Frank.................1727 Horeb avenue, Zion City, Illinois
Hammon, Ziona Lydia...............1713 Horeb avenue, Zion City, Illinois
Hancock, Florence Gertrude.........2611 Gilboa avenue, Zion City, Illinois
Hanson, Harold Albert.........742 Carmel boulevard, Zion City, Illinois
Harkness, Elnora Louise............5706 Indiana avenue, Chicago, Illinois
Hartsfield, Albert..................3110 Gideon avenue, Zion City, Illinois
Hartsfield, Joseph N..............3110 Gideon avenue, Zion City, Illinois
Hire, Richard Fielden.............3006 Gabriel avenue, Zion City, Illinois
Hoffman, Sherman Francis..........Knox, Indiana
Holtz, Esther.......................3065 Lock street, Chicago, Illinois
Howard, John Robert...............2706 Enoch avenue, Zion City, Illinois
Inman, Jean Esther.................3216 Gilboa avenue, Zion City, Illinois
Inman, Sarah Bell...................3216 Gilboa avenue, Zion City, Illinois
Johnson, Abigail Dette.............2916 Enoch avenue, Zion City, Illinois
Johnson, James Raymond.........2815 Elizabeth avenue, Zion City, Illinois
Jones, Harry Perry..................2807 Ezra avenue, Zion City, Illinois
Kile, Helen Verna..................3013 Gabriel avenue, Zion City, Illinois
Kleinert, Ruth Augusta..............3201 Ezra avenue, Zion City, Illinois
Kinsman, Chester James...........3300 Ezekiel avenue, Zion City, Illinois
Koetz, Lester Irvin.................2310 Elisha avenue, Zion City, Illinois
LaBelle, Rachel Irene.............1807 Hebron avenue, Zion City, Illinois
LaBelle, Russell E..................1807 Hebron avenue, Zion City, Illinois
LaBelle, Sylvia May.................1807 Hebron avenue, Zion City, Illinois
Lamberger, Eva Alla-bena..........Elijah Hospice, Zion City, Illinois
Lavin, Myrtle Ruth..................713 Artesian avenue, Chicago, Illinois
Lawrence, Otto.....................2809 Gideon avenue, Zion City, Illinois
Lee, Cecil Francis................3212 Emmaus avenue, Zion City, Illinois
Lee, Ida May......................3212 Emmaus avenue, Zion City, Illinois
Lee, Merwin Hugh...................3009 Elim avenue, Zion City, Illinois
Lippold, Edith May................3106 Gabriel avenue, Zion City, Illinois
Luce, Grace Lowene...............3015 Eshcol avenue, Zion City, Illinois
McClurkin, Anna Alberta.......903 Terrace avenue, Marinette, Wisconsin
McKenzie, Eleanor Sarah M.........2918 Enoch avenue, Zion City, Illinois
McKoon, Nita Bell..........Washington, Iowa
McKoon, Irwin C..........Washington, Iowa
Maltby, Ivan Leroy...............3106 Edina boulevard, Zion City, Illinois
Maltby, Jessie May...............3106 Edina boulevard, Zion City, Illinois
Marshall, Dorothy Bernice..........3201 Eshcol avenue, Zion City, Illinois
Mercer, John Theodore..............2202 Ezra avenue, Zion City, Illinois
Mill, Ethel Marie....................2917 Enoch avenue, Zion City, Illinois
Miller, Edna Avis....................1819 Gilboa avenue, Zion City, Illinois
Miller, Eva Frances.................1819 Gilboa avenue, Zion City, Illinois
Miller, John Morris.................1819 Gilboa avenue, Zion City, Illinois
Mitchell, Beulah June...............2310 Gideon avenue, Zion City, Illinois
Morgan, Dora Elizabeth............2903 Eshcol avenue, Zion City, Illinois
Morrisse, Julia Anna..............Lexington Pike, Covington, Kentucky
Morrison, Lilly.................6238 Aberdeen avenue, Chicago, Illinois
Mudgett, Daniel Alexander.........3117 Gabriel avenue, Zion City, Illinois
Murray, Joseph Alexander..........3021 Gilead avenue, Zion City, Illinois
Newland, Elizabeth Allison......2620 Elizabeth avenue, Zion City, Illinois
Noland, Amy Ruby.................1903 Horeb avenue, Zion City, Illinois
Nooman, Elizabeth Dorothy..........Orange City, Iowa
Norton, Ralph Lester..........Hustler, Wisconsin
Oakes, Mary Magdalene.........2114 Emmaus avenue, Zion City, Illinois
Peterman, Catherine..............Mount Carmel Farm, Zion City, Illinois
Peterman, Milton M...............Mount Carmel Farm, Zion City, Illinois
Peterson, Paul Herman..............2112 Elim avenue, Zion City, Illinois
Pierce, Horace Howard..............3022 Ezra avenue, Zion City, Illinois
Puhl, Girdon........................1910 Ezekiel avenue, Zion City, Illinois
Rathjen, Ruth Evelyn...............1801 Hebron avenue, Zion City, Illinois
Reninger, Mary Elizabeth..........2105 Ezra avenue, Zion City, Illinois
Richey, Ziona Faith...............3106 Ezekiel avenue, Zion City, Illinois
Riggins, Ruth Leona...............3203 Gabriel avenue, Zion City, Illinois
Robinson, Dorothy Elizabeth.......1812 Hebron avenue, Zion City, Illinois
Rose, Anna Louise....................2801 Elim avenue, Zion City, Illinois
Sallberg, Paul Fredrick.............2308 Gideon avenue, Zion City, Illinois
Schultz, Samuel Gladstone...........3003 Elisha avenue, Zion City, Illinois
Sefton, Sarah Ellen..................2106 Enoch avenue, Zion City, Illinois
Sefton, Willie........................2106 Enoch avenue, Zion City, Illinois
Short, Doris Barbara...............2016 Hebron avenue, Zion City, Illinois
Speare, Walter Richard..........Antioch, Indian Territory
Speare, Flossie Myrtle..........Antioch, Indian Territory
Springer, Beulah Christina..........Knowlton, Wisconsin
Springer, Joseph Oliver..........Knowlton, Wisconsin
Smith, Lillian..........Danville, Illinois
Sourby, Albert Hubbard............2207 Gabriel avenue, Zion City, Illinois
Stange, Pansy Sarah......140 Belvedere street, Oak Park, Chicago, Illinois
Stanley, Mary Catherine...........1329 North street, Logansport, Indiana
Stevens, Percy Cecil Gladstone..........Bingham, Michigan
Stockstill, Fred Arthur..........Springfield, Missouri
Stockstill, Irwin Lewis..........Springfield, Missouri
Stockstill, Lawrence Webster..........Springfield, Missouri
Stoyke, Walter Richard..........2917 Emmaus avenue, Zion City, Illinois
Stuck, Celia Alide..........Zion City, Illinois
Stuck, Gerhard Folkert D..........Zion City, Illinois
Stuck, Herman Friedrich Wilhelm..........Zion City, Illinois
Stuck, Theodor Diedrich..........Zion City, Illinois
Taylor, Harry Cantel...............2115 Eshcol avenue, Zion City, Illinois
Taylor, Ruth Jane...................2918 Gabriel avenue, Zion City, Illinois
Turner, Dowie Otto..........Viroqua, Wisconsin
Viking, Carl John..........Elijah Hospice, Zion City, Illinois
Villiger, Herman Joseph...........1718 Horeb avenue, Zion City, Illinois
Wall, Arthur Edward...............2019 Joanna avenue, Zion City, Illinois
Wall, Esther May...................2019 Joanna avenue, Zion City, Illinois
Welti, John Emmel.................3013 Emmaus avenue, Zion City, Illinois
Wertz, Orvil Percy...................2303 Elisha avenue, Zion City, Illinois
Wertz, Esther Mabel................2303 Elisha avenue, Zion City, Illinois
Wertz, Herbert Charles.............2303 Elisha avenue, Zion City, Illinois
Wertz, Ralph Waldo..................2303 Elisha avenue, Zion City, Illinois
Wilder, Jesse Noble...................2705 Ezra avenue, Zion City, Illinois
Young, Lois Ruth...................2910 Edina boulevard, Zion City, Illinois
Young, Loyla Marie..................2910 Edina boulevard, Zion City, Illinois

Notice to Officers and Members.

Send all newspaper clippings concerning the General Overseer, the Elders, or any department of the work in connection with the Christian Catholic Church in Zion, to Deacon Carl F. Stern, Zion City, Illinois. Send as soon as possible after publication, and carefully mark *name and date of the paper clipped from* on each article. If this is not done, the clippings are absolutely useless.

Notice to Correspondents.

In writing to Headquarters it is *absolutely essential* that the writer give his full address.

Failure to comply with this request necessitates looking up or referring to the Church Records, which involves much time, and is very frequently fruitless.

Friends and members of the Christian Catholic Church in Zion everywhere will please bear this in mind, especially those in foreign lands.

Faithfully yours in the Master's Service,

J. G. EXCELL, General Ecclesiastical Secretary.

Train Schedule Between Zion City and Chicago

Via Chicago & North-Western Railway.

Effective May 22, 1904.

Weekday Trains.

CHICAGO TO ZION CITY.		ZION CITY TO CHICAGO.	
Leave Chicago	Arrive Zion City	Leave Zion City	Arrive Chicago
7.00 a. m.	8.25 a. m.	*6.45 a. m.	8.15 a. m.
*9.00 a. m.	10.13 a. m.	7.03 a. m.	8.30 a. m.
*11.30 a. m.	12.37 p. m.	8.22 a. m.	9.50 a. m.
2.00 p. m.	3.08 p. m.	*9 45 a. m.	11.10 a. m.
3.00 p. m	4.16 p. m.	*11.49 a. m.	1.15 p. m.
4.15 p. m.	5.39 p. m.	*‖1.18 p. m.	2.50 p. m.
*5.20 p. m.	6.50 p. m.	*†2.33 p. m.	4.00 p. m.
*8.00 p. m.	9.11 p. m.	5.05 p. m.	6.30 p. m.
		*7.59 p. m.	9.30 p. m.

Sunday Trains.

CHICAGO TO ZION CITY.	
Leave Chicago	Arrive Zion City
9.05 a. m.	10.18 a. m.
*10.45 a. m.	12.37 p. m.
2.15 p. m.	4.05 p. m.
*8.00 p. m.	9.11 p. m.

ZION CITY TO CHICAGO.	
Leave Zion City	Arrive Chicago
*8.29 a. m.	9.45 a. m.
5.05 p. m.	6.40 p. m.
7.59 p. m.	9.30 p. m.

Train leaves Waukegan at 12 28 p. m., arriving in Zion City at 12.37 p. m., daily, including Sunday.

* Signifies change train at Waukegan. † Train does not run South on Saturdays. ‖ Train runs South on Saturday only.

ACLE.

A WEEKLY PAPER FOR THE EXTENSION OF THE KINGDOM OF GOD

EDITED BY THE REV. JOHN ALEX. DOWIE.

Volume XV. No. 16. *ZION CITY, SATURDAY, AUGUST 6, 1904.* *Price Five Cents*

Commemoration of the Consecration of the Temple Site

ZION GUARD, ZION BAND, ZION RESTORATION HOST, ZION WHITE-ROBED CHOIR AND ORDAINED OFFICERS FOLLOWED BY THE OVERSEERS AND THE GENERAL OVERSEER MARCHING AROUND THE TEMPLE SITE WHICH WAS DEDICATED JULY 14, 1900 :: ::

A WEEKLY PAPER FOR THE EXTENSION OF THE KINGDOM OF GOD.

EDITED BY THE REV. JOHN ALEX. DOWIE.

Application for entry as Second Class Matter at Zion City, Illinois, pending.

Subscription Rates.		Special Rates.	
One Year	$2.00	100 Copies of One Issue	$3.00
Six Months	1.25	25 Copies of One Issue	1.00
Three Months	.75	To Ministers, Y. M. C. A's and Public Reading Rooms, per annum	1.50
Single Copies	.05		

For foreign subscriptions add $1.50 per year, or three cents per copy for postage.

Subscribers desiring a change of address should give present address, as well as that to which they desire LEAVES OF HEALING sent in the future.

Make Bank Drafts, Express Money or Postoffice Money Orders payable to the order of JOHN ALEX. DOWIE, Zion City, Illinois, U. S. A.

Long Distance Telephone. *Cable Address "Dowie, Zion City."*

All communications upon business must be addressed to
MANAGER ZION PUBLISHING HOUSE,
Zion City, Illinois, U. S. A.

Subscriptions to LEAVES OF HEALING, A VOICE FROM ZION, and the various publications may also be sent to

ZION PUBLISHING HOUSE, 81 EUSTON ROAD, LONDON, N. W., ENGLAND.

ZION PUBLISHING HOUSE, NO. 43 PARK ROAD, ST. KILDA, MELBOURNE, VICTORIA, AUSTRALIA.

ZION PUBLISHING HOUSE, RUE DE MONT, THABOR 1, PARIS, FRANCE.

ZIONSHEIM, SCHLOSS LIEBBURG, CANTON THURGAU, BEI ZÜRICH, SWITZERLAND.

ZION CITY, ILLINOIS, SATURDAY, AUGUST 6, 1904.

TABLE OF CONTENTS.

LEAVES OF HEALING, SATURDAY, AUGUST 6, 1904.

EDITORIAL NOTES.

"BEN MACDHUI," WHITE LAKE, MONTAGUE,
MICHIGAN, U. S. A.,
August 4, 1904.

"BE SOBER, BE VIGILANT."

BECAUSE YOUR Adversary, the Devil, as a roaring lion,
Walketh about, seeking whom he may devour:
Whom withstand steadfast in your faith.

TWO DAYS ago we arrived here at our little Galilee for a few days' rest, during which we hope to give attention to much correspondence, and to write our General Letter to the Christian Catholic Church in Zion throughout the world.

THE SOLEMN WARNING of the Apostle Peter, with which we begin these Notes, is one which we ever have need to emphasize.

When Zion is most peaceful and prosperous, then Satan is most angry.

"Roaring like a lion," in his mad rage he endeavors to make timorous and unstable hearts afraid, and to drive them, panic-stricken, out of the fold of Zion into the world, where he can most easily devour them.

SIGNS THAT the Devil is again plotting to instill these fears are again apparent, both in the press and otherwise.

We once more warn our friends against the avalanche of lies which are usually poured upon Zion at this season of the year.

They began in the false reports of last Monday's Chicago papers, concerning which we made the following statement at the Weekly Rally in Shiloh Tabernacle last Wednesday:

OFFICE OF
THE REV. JOHN ALEXANDER DOWIE,
General Overseer of the Christian Catholic Church in Zion.

"BEN MACDHUI," MONTAGUE, MICHIGAN,
August 2, 1904.

REV. J. G. EXCELL, *Acting Overseer for Zion City,*
Zion City, Lake County, Illinois.

MY DEAR OVERSEER:—I wish you to read to my people at the Rally, on Wednesday night, the following:

BELOVED IN THE CHRIST:

I was greatly grieved to read, in the Chicago papers of Monday, a shameful misreport of my discourse, in Shiloh Tabernacle, Zion City, on Lord's Day afternoon, in which it was alleged that a number of the higher Officers of Zion City were under censure or under suspicion of having embezzled the funds of Zion.

I wish to say that the allegation is wholly false, and that no Officer of Cabinet rank has ever been suspected of misappropriation. I do not believe there ever existed a more honorable and reliable company of men than those to whom I have entrusted large powers and given large responsibilities, and whom God has enabled me to choose for the important offices which they fill.

I think it is right, also, to remove every vestige of suspicion from any of the under managers or Heads of Departments in all the Institutions and Industries; for they, too, are a splendid body of men and women of high Christian integrity, and worthy of my confidence.

I have felt the attack upon my brethren most painfully, and I directed Judge Barnes, my General Counsel, to call up all the newspaper offices of Chicago and, in my name, contradict the statement in the most forcible terms, which was done, and of which the Judge will himself give you some little account tonight in the Mid-week Citizens' Rally.

I am compelled, however, to make the sad admission that there has been stealing, principally from the General Stores, by a number of thievish boys, and in one case a clerk misappropriated the sum of ninety-two dollars, which he confessed, and which his father, a most excellent man, was permitted to restore.

All these offenders have been disciplined and dealt with as seemed right, and, so far as I am aware, there is not at present one shadow of reflection upon the honesty and honor of any of Zion's employees, in any Department, and I wish to say this in the most emphatic manner.

At the same time, beloved friends in the Christ, I desire to warn you that the enemy—the Great Enemy of mankind—who defiled man in the Garden of Eden, is still very much alive, and that, as I warned you on Lord's Day, "perpetual vigilance is the price of safety."

God has given to us all in Zion City a solemn charge and responsibility, and each and all in their station have their portion of that Divinely-imposed duty which must be fulfilled if we would be acceptable to Him and do the work that He has given us to do.

I solemnly and earnestly charge all parents to rule their households well. I earnestly desire all wives and mothers to maintain respect and reverence in the family for the father as the head of the household, and not to interfere unduly with proper discipline of unruly children, but to aid in every way, so that where sharp restraint is needed it shall be supplied.

I urge at the same time upon all fathers that they shall not discourage their children by undue severity, but, treating them with love, and patience, and consideration, win them closer to themselves and to God, making the ties of family life to be strong in Love, in Faith, in Hope, in Wisdom, and in all Purity, so that home-life may be made delightful and attractive.

To that end Morning and Evening Sacrifice of Praise and Prayer must never be neglected, and parents must see that their children attend with them the means of grace which God has so abundantly supplied in Zion City.

I especially charge all parents to accompany their children to the services in Shiloh Tabernacle at half past six o'clock in the morning and half past two o'clock in the afternoon on the Lord's Day. The Early Morning Sacrifice of Praise and Prayer is especially important, and is, as we all know, a delightful occasion. The richest blessings in all our lives in recent years have been obtained at that gathering.

I am looking forward to a noble generation—a Royal Generation—from our young people, of whom it is my delight to say that, for the most part, they have been a great comfort to my heart. But I have observed a slackening of interest on the part of many young people, and many older people who fail to set a good example, and, although our morning meetings are probably the largest and best in the world, there are those who do not attend them as they might; and so, with all the means of grace, there are those who neglect the "assembling of themselves together," and, upon the most paltry excuses, leave the meetings. These readily fall into sin, both on the Lord's Day and at other times, and a few of these have been recently expelled from our fellowship and sent from the City, because of their falling into very deep sin.

Looking forward, as I am, to a Glorious Harvest this year, I am determined that the Threshing-floor shall be absolutely clean, and I believe that you, my beloved people, will help me in this task.

Purer, and purer, and purer must we be!

Let "the River of God," which is "full of water," flow through your hearts and homes and be ever flowing through you in all your daily life; for the River of God is the Spirit of God—the Spirit of Purity, and Peace, and Progress!

It is my joy to say that, after closest investigation on the part of myself and officers, we have every reason to believe that we can report that the moral and spiritual atmosphere of Zion is becoming, as a whole, increasingly *clean* and *pure*. But if there are hidden sins and hidden iniquities, I charge you, who may know of them, that, if you do not report such things, *you are partakers of their sins who do them*, and *will be so judged should we find that you have neglected to do your duty* in making known anything which would imperil the purity and progress of Zion.

I sustain every Officer in every Department in their arduous duties. But if this people is to be trained, as I trust they will be, for world-wide blessing, then all must co-operate and patiently and perseveringly Go Forward as God shall direct.

I earnestly desire your prayers for my guidance and for blessing upon my beloved wife and son, and that we may be still better fitted to help you all on your Heavenward way.

Mizpah!

Faithfully your Friend and Fellow Servant in Jesus,

John Alex. Dowie

General Overseer of the Christian Catholic Church in Zion.

"THE SEASONS of Refreshing from the Presence of the Lord," which accompany "The Times of the Restoration of All Things," have been most abundant during the past month.

THE FOURTH FEAST OF TABERNACLES has brought spiritual strength, and refreshment, and joy in no ordinary degree, to all our people and to the many thousands who have come from all parts of this Continent, and from every Continent, to attend the Annual Convocations of God's people at this Feast.

BLESSINGS, ALSO, of every kind are being bestowed upon us, and this is sufficient reason for the Adversary to be particularly angry.

THE APOSTATE CHURCHES, and the Powers of Hell which control them, have been grievously disappointed that the murderous designs of our enemies were not accomplished during our recent Around-the-World Visitation.

BUT ZION is triumphant, and will continue to be triumphant, notwithstanding all the attacks which may be made upon us; for "Jehovah hath established Zion."

BRETHREN, PRAY FOR US.

Expiration of Subscriptions.

On every subscriber's copy of LEAVES OF HEALING or THE ZION BANNER we attach a yellow label bearing his name, address, and two numbers, the figures referring to the volume and the number with which the subscription will expire.

Thus, should your label number happen to be 15—11, you may know that your subscription expires with Volume XV, Number 11, which will be July 2, 1904. Also take notice that LEAVES OF HEALING now completes a volume every six months, or twenty-six weeks, that being the number of papers which are put into a bound volume. Earlier in the life of the paper a volume contained fifty-two numbers, as LEAVES OF HEALING had fewer pages in those days.

By making yourselves familiar with these customs and remitting promptly you need never allow your subscription to lapse.

Send money only by Bank Draft, Postoffice or Express Money-order in favor of John Alexander Dowie, and address all letters intended for us to

ZION PRINTING AND PUBLISHING HOUSE,
Zion City, Lake County, Illinois.

Street Addresses Are Necessary.

All Zion City Subscribers to *Leaves of Healing*, *The Zion Banner*, *Blätter der Heilung*, and *Voice from Zion*, whose correct street addresses are not positively known to be in our possession should send them to us AT ONCE. Please act upon this notice without delay as it is very important, now that we have postal delivery service, that the exact location of each and every subscriber be known to us. Write your name and address very carefully, designating also to what periodicals you are a subscriber and leave at your very earliest opportunity at our branch Publishing House on Elijah Avenue.

Very Sincerely Yours,
ZION PRINTING AND PUBLISHING HOUSE.

LEAVES OF HEALING.

Two Dollars will bring to you the weekly visits of the Little White Dove for a year; 75 cents will send it to a friend for thirteen weeks; $1.25 will send it for six months; $1.50 will send it to your minister, or to a Y. M. C. A., or to a Public Reading Room for a whole year. We offer no premiums, except the premium of doing good. We receive no advertisements, and print no commercial lies or cheating enticements of unscrupulous thieves. LEAVES OF HEALING is Zion on wings, and we keep out everything that would detract the reader's mind from all except the Extension of the Kingdom of God, for which alone it exists. If we cannot send forth our Little White Dove without soiling its wings with the smoke of the factory and the dirt of the wrangling market place, or compelling it to utter the screaming cries of the business vultures in the ears of our readers, then we will keep our Dove at home

GOD'S WAY OF HEALING.

BY THE REV. JOHN ALEX. DOWIE.

God's Way of Healing Is a Person, Not a Thing.

Jesus said "*I am* the Way, and the Truth, and the Life," and He has ever been revealed to His people in all the ages by the Covenant Name, Jehovah-Rophi, or "*I am* Jehovah that Healeth thee." (John 14:6; Exodus 15:26.)

The Lord Jesus, the Christ, is Still the Healer.

He cannot change, for "Jesus, the Christ, is the same yesterday and today, yea and forever;" and He is still with us, for He said: "Lo, *I am* with you All the Days, even unto the Consummation of the Age." (Hebrews 13:8; Matthew 28:20.) Because He is Unchangeable, and because He is present, in spirit, just as when in the flesh, He is the Healer of His people.

Divine Healing Rests on the Christ's Atonement.

It was prophesied of Him, "Surely He hath borne our griefs (Hebrew, *sickness*), and carried our sorrows: . . . and with His stripes we are healed;" and it is expressly declared that this was fulfilled in His Ministry of Healing, which still continues. (Isaiah 53:4, 5; Matthew 8:17.)

Disease Can Never be God's Will.

It is the Devil's work, consequent upon Sin, and it is impossible for the work of the Devil ever to be the Will of God. The Christ came to "destroy the works of the Devil," and when He was here on earth He healed "all manner of disease and all manner of sickness," and all these sufferers are expressly declared to have been "oppressed of the Devil." (1 John 3:8; Matthew 4:23; Acts 10:38.)

The Gifts of Healing Are Permanent.

It is expressly declared that the "Gifts and the calling of God are without repentance," and the Gifts of Healing are amongst the Nine Gifts of the Spirit to the Church. (Romans 11:29; 1 Corinthians 12:8-11.)

There Are Four Modes of Divine Healing.

The first is the direct prayer of faith; the second, intercessory prayer of two or more; the third, the anointing of the elders, with the prayer of faith; and the fourth, the laying on of hands of those who believe, and whom God has prepared and called to that Ministry. (Matthew 8:5-13; Matthew 18:19; James 5:14, 15; Mark 16:18.)

Divine Healing Is Opposed by Diabolical Counterfeits.

Amongst these are Christian Science (falsely so-called), Mind Healing, Spiritualism, Trance Evangelism, etc. (1 Timothy 6:20, 21; 1 Timothy 4:1, 2; Isaiah 51:22, 23.)

Multitudes Have Been Healed Through Faith in Jesus.

The writer knows of thousands of cases and has personally laid hands on scores of thousands of persons. Full information can be obtained at the meetings held in the Zion Tabernacles in Chicago, and in Zion City, Illinois, and in many pamphlets which give the experience, in their own words, of many who have been healed in this and other countries, published at Zion Printing and Publishing House, Zion City, Illinois.

"Belief Cometh of Hearing, and Hearing by the Word of the Christ."

You are heartily invited to attend and hear for yourself.

ELIJAH THE RESTORER.

ELIJAH THE RESTORER SHOWS THE FOLLY OF TRYING TO CARRY CROSSES OTHER THAN OUR OWN.

Zion's Fourth Feast of Tabernacles

The Set Feasts of Jehovah . . .
Ye shall proclaim to be Holy Convocations.

EARLY MORNING SACRIFICE OF PRAISE AND PRAYER.

*REPORTED BY S. E. C., O. V. G. AND E. S.

As an exquisite chain of jewels, each perfect in itself, each possessing its own peculiar beauty, yet not one to be spared or separated from the beautiful whole, seemed the Early Morning Meetings of the Holy Convocation.

Each seemed more beautiful than the preceding one; richer, deeper, more glowing, purer, with an ever-increasing spirituality and power, until these meetings, more than any others, were the expression of Zion, in her purest, highest, best form.

Next to Long-suffering, the fourth Fruit of the Spirit, there was linked Kindness, or Gentleness.

The meaning of the word was brought out by the man of God with a wonderful clearness and simplicity of words.

This being set forth, the thought was then elaborated, enriched, and applied in a practical manner, as befitted the spiritual needs of the people to whom he ministered.

The word, he said, indicated a benignity, a majesty, a splendor, of one great and mighty; a sweet condescension of one possessing power, yet being loved for the gentleness, not the power.

The word also, in the original, he said, indicates a usefulness, a willingness to do any good thing possible.

This Gift of Gentleness is not an affectation of superiority, a condescension, but is inborn, and is a characteristic of the Royal Generation which God is creating in Zion.

Shiloh Tabernacle, Zion City, Illinois, Monday Morning, July 18, 1904.

The service was opened by the singing of Hymn No. 4 in the Program.

The General Overseer then offered prayer, at the close leading the Congregation in the chanting of the Disciples' Prayer.

After Hymn No. 4 had been sung, the General Overseer presented Overseer Speicher, who with his wife was soon to leave for Europe, with a check for one thousand dollars—a gift from the General Overseer and the people of Zion.

Overseer Speicher then said: "Beloved General Overseer and beloved people, I thank you most heartily this morning for your very kind gift to me.

"I am not worthy of all that has been said in praise of me, concerning my work during the General Overseer's recent absence, because

A Man Does Not Deserve Credit for Doing His Duty.

"I do not know that the General Overseer deserves credit for all that he does; he simple cannot help it.

"How can he help being Elijah the Restorer?

"I desire to say, General Overseer, that notwithstanding the duties and responsibilities of the last winter and spring, I am stronger today than I have been for twenty years.

General Overseer—Thank God!

Overseer Speicher—"I have never been rugged, and strong, and hearty as some people, but in Zion I am getting stronger every day.

"What the General Overseer said last night is true—that, as far as I know my heart, there is not a fiber or chord in my being that does not vibrate for Zion.

"You will bear me out in saying that I have not sought my own interests, but I have been loyal and faithful to God, to Zion, and to our General Overseer.

"God has given me ten years of life, because of the teaching that I heard from our beloved General Overseer.

"I do not deserve credit for belonging to God after He has healed me; God and our beloved General Overseer deserve the credit.

"All I am today, I am through what He has done for me.

"Beloved General Overseer and friends, I should be doing a great wrong if I were to selfishly use this gift, which you have given me today, for myself only; but I will use it for Zion and for God. I want to do a little good.

"I am glad of the opportunity of going away.

"I want to get broader, for I am narrow. I have not had the advantages of travel.

"May God help to broaden me, that I may come back and be of still more use to Zion, and in some way help to lighten the burdens of the General Overseer.

"May the Lord bless you!"

General Overseer—I trust the Overseer will come back stronger and broader.

We shall hope to see him somewhat as I am said to be, as broad as I am long; and he is certainly very long.

After the announcements were made, the General Overseer delivered his Message:

FIFTH FRUIT OF THE SPIRIT: KINDNESS.

TEXT.

Thou hast also given me the Shield of Thy Salvation:
And Thy right hand hath holden me up,
And thy Gentleness hath made me great.—*Psalm 18:35.*

Let us now repeat together the 22d and 23d verses of the 5th chapter of Galatians:

But the Fruit of the Spirit is Love, Joy, Peace, Long-suffering, Kindness, Goodness, Faithfulness,
Meekness, Temperance: against such there is no law.

The Word Gentleness a Better Translation Than the Word Kindness.

In the Revision, the Fruit of the Spirit which is called "Gentleness" in the Old Version, is translated "Kindness."

I am almost sorry that that alteration was made.

Of course, none of these words in English can represent the full meaning of the word in the original, because it is a very wide-embracing word.

So, if you will allow me, I shall use instead of the word "Kindness," the word "Gentleness," which is the old rendering for the Fifth Fruit of the Spirit.

But the fruit of the Spirit is Love, Joy, Peace, Long-suffering, Gentleness, Goodness, Faithfulness,
Meekness, Temperance: against such there is no law.
And they that are of Christ Jesus have crucified the flesh with the passions and the lusts thereof.

Sometimes we think a passion or an evil tendency is crucified and dead when it is not.

It is only scotched, not killed; but may God grant that the Fruit may abound by the works of the flesh being destroyed.

The Fruit of the Spirit concerning which we are to speak this morning is Gentleness.

The Original Meaning of the Word Translated Gentleness.

That word, in the original, has a deep root.

The root is *chrao* (χράω), which was originally applied to the heathen gods.

The highest conception the heathen had of God was put into that verb *chrao*.

It had the idea of benignity, majesty, splendor and the great and mighty condescension and love of a great God.

*The following reports have not been revised by the General Overseer.

That was their idea of *chrestotes* (χρηστότης), translated for us in the 5th chapter of Galatians gentleness or kindness.

There was always connected with it the thought of a gift, given through the sweet condescension of one possessing great power, who knew he had power, but who was so gentle that he was loved, not for his greatness, but for his gentle benignity.

The word, of course, became degenerated as the centuries passed, and there are now all kinds of meanings connected with it.

There is no doubt that the original word had, from the very beginning, a Divine idea, and came to mean, not only Kindness and Gentleness, but, essentially usefulness, a kindness and gentleness which made the bestower useful.

The old mythological heroes were a strange combination of strength, wisdom, and lustful wickedness, and yet, humanity was drawn to them by many qualities which they were supposed to possess.

Hercules, that great hero and god, was a strange combination of tremendous power and great attractiveness in his personality.

He did the most cruel things, as well as the most kind things, but an essential of his nature was his innate gentleness.

So Homer sketches many of the heroes as great and powerful, ruthlessly cruel at times, but afterwards gentle.

The thing that brought the idea of these gods close to humanity, was the fact that they were gentle and generous in their relations to man, loving him, being useful to him, and giving gifts to him.

Knowledge of Original Language Essential to a Scholarly Comprehension of the Bible.

I should like to say here that it is impossible for one to have a scholarly comprehension of the Bible and not understand how these words were used in the ancient religions of the people.

Although it is a very unpleasant task to wade through the mythology of Greece, Rome, and other nations, yet those who are to be the teachers of humanity, and who are to preserve the original teaching of the Word of God, must be students, not only of the original language in which the Bible was written, but of the nature of that language as derived from heathen thought or from historic facts.

The study of the word Gentleness, this Great Fruit of the Spirit which follows Long-suffering, is very delightful.

I say to the Elders and others who have a knowledge of the original languages, that it would be very well for them to study all these words in the original tongue; to get down to their roots, and to realize what the Holy Spirit intended these words to convey.

God, the Holy Spirit, used the historic errors of the people as well as the historic goodness of the people, to embody in words that which dwelt especially in the Greek mind.

There are many words that do not have much effect upon us, because we do not think as the Greeks used to think.

We do not think as the ancient world used to think, and I am glad that we do not.

We do not have to arrive at the purity of Christianity through words that were connected with the impurity of heathenism.

Let me try to tell you what it seems to me the Holy Spirit intended us to understand by this Fruit called Gentleness.

As I said, from the beginning it had the idea of Divine condescension and love, and the gentleness and kindness of a superior power that made it pleasant for men to be associated with that power.

God, when He gives us His Spirit, sets us free.

He makes us His children, and endows us with Divine Love, Divine Joy, Divine Peace, and Divine Grace.

He puts the beautiful Fruit of Long-suffering between the third Fruit, Peace, and this Fruit of Gentleness, which is the Fifth.

Long-suffering and Gentleness Must Be Joined Together.

One of the characteristics of the old gods, was their impatience.

Any one who did not do what they wanted him to do was persecuted, hated, and followed to his death by the malignity of the gods.

You have, therefore, the very reverse in the attributes of God.

He is very Long-suffering, but it is His Gentleness that leads us to repentance.

The wonderful thing about God's Love is that it is not like our poor ordinary human nature.

Our poor human nature seeks to get something in loving, to get some gratification mentally, spiritually, psychically, or physically through association with some other being.

But the Love of God is absolutely unselfish.

The Love He puts into our hearts is absolutely unselfish.

Anything that is selfish is not of God.

This Love that He gives seeks not its own.

It does not seek for the gratification of self, but for a blessing to the person upon whom the love is bestowed.

True Gentleness Has None of the Spirit of Condescension.

The idea in this Fruit is that we are to be gentle, but not with a contemptible affectation of superiority, bestowing gifts upon people as if we were made of better clay than they, as if we were so majestic and so tremendously far above them in every way that our gentleness was a great act of condescension.

Humanity, if it has the love of God in it, has no use for that kind of thing.

Anything like that in exercising Gentleness or Kindness will make you offensive.

There is nothing more offensive to my mind than what one sees in England so often, the affectation of great condescension upon the part of people of noble rank who condescend to ally themselves with certain causes.

No woman of aristocratic rank can be much, unless she breaks away entirely from the horrible and disgusting idea that a woman or a man is something because some ancestor of hers or his was a favorite harlot of the king's, as is the case with many of the ducal houses.

The Duke of St. Albans is directly descended from that harlot of Charles II., Nell Gwynn.

A great many of the aristocracy of today are the offspring of the vilest kind of men.

This so-called pride of birth is simply disgusting.

It is offensive to me.

I never was more inclined to wish to see this prophecy fulfilled than I am now:

> The lofty hills and towers,
> That lift their heads on high,
> Shall all be leveled low in dust,
> Their very names shall die.

The quicker they die the better.

There is a gentleness on the part of those who are really great, whom God has made great, that is delightful.

I mean great in the sense of good, for

The Only Greatness Is Goodness.

That is the true Greatness.

The only thing that makes me realize the Greatness of God is His wonderful Goodness and Gentleness.

We who receive the Fruits of the Spirit must all be true, Gentle men, and true, Gentle women.

Every Zion man and every Zion woman should be essentially a Gentle man and a Gentle woman.

I desire to warn you against something.

You must not imagine that you can copy me when I become angry with sin, and say hard things instead of gentle things.

I sometimes have to put on all my paint and feathers to go after the enemy.

You must not copy that, because I do not act or speak in a private capacity.

That is not the way I do in private life.

I have to smite iniquity in high places, and I have to use hard language.

I have to use clubs sometimes, and even put in dynamite charges and explode them.

That is a part of my work that must be done.

Those who are best born oftentimes have the greatest fight, because they not only have the goodness and the powerfulness of their heritage, but they have the dangers of it, among which are fierce tempers and dreadful passions.

We must remember that God wants us to be entirely without these things that mar great lives, and which have destroyed many in the past.

God is creating a Royal Generation in Zion, and we who are part of it, and leading, must, by the grace of God, be completely emancipated.

Wonderful Changes That Accompany the Rapture.

I know that great changes must come in the Restoration, and we must not anticipate these changes.

We cannot realize in their fulness what we shall be when we come back after the Rapture, in glorified bodies, purified, without animal life.

Our souls will die, and will never be resurrected. All that will ever be resurrected and reëmbodied will be our spiritual being, and that not in a body such as we now wear, but in a body such as God will give us.

He will give us a body that is incorruptible, that does not need blood for its sustenance.

It will be bloodless, and yet animated with a power greater than blood can bestow, for our regeneration is not of the will of the flesh, not of blood, and not of man

We are born of God.

The old man passes away, and is to be entirely crucified.

When we come back after the Rapture we shall not bring with us the same hellish passions that cursed our race here, and which we inherited from our ancestors

These passions will be gone with the blood in which they were transmitted.

I am thankful that there will be neither blue blood, nor white blood, nor any other kind of blood in us, but the bodies we shall have will be the kind of body the Christ had, who, when He rose from the dead said, "A spirit hath not flesh and bones, as ye behold Me having." He had flesh, but it was pure flesh.

He had bones, but there was no need of sustenance of the flesh or of the bones by blood.

His blood had all been shed.

It was a bloodless body that reascended into heaven.

Moreover, it had been transformed, and our bodies are to be transformed, like unto His glorious body, so that the Gentleness of God will by and by be wonderfully manifested in the children of God, when they come back to this earth, where there will be so many people left who will be continually growing worse and worse, because humanity's muddy stream of dirty blood is getting filthier and filthier as time goes on.

When we come back, we shall be absolutely different from the people among whom we shall dwell, for we shall be bloodless, and we shall have pure spirits and pure bodies.

If you have been following my words, you will get into your mind what God really means by this word Gentleness.

Only Divine Purity Can Do God's Work Amidst Impurities.

We must be kind in being useful.

We must be kind in bringing down from the lofty height of the Divine nature our whole being into works of Salvation for those that are in the humblest places.

But we cannot do it without Purity, for Purity alone can make it possible for us to work to any purpose amidst impurity.

It is not possible for Purity to be preserved amidst impurity unless it is Divine Purity, for contact with, and living amidst, iniquity must degenerate, for evil communications, evil associations, always corrupt good habits, good manners and good living. I desire to remind you that God, while He calls upon His people to minister to the vilest and humblest, does not call upon them to live with them.

ZION GUARD AND BAND ESCORTING THE GENERAL OVERSEER FROM SHILOH HOUSE TO SHILOH TABERNACLE, ZION CITY, ILLINOIS, JULY 3, 1904.

He does not call upon you to work for the harlot by living in her house.

You are not called upon to work for a drunkard by living in a saloon.

You are not called upon to work for unclean people by living with them.

You cannot help them one-half as much by living with them as you can by living with those who are good and pure, and in an atmosphere of Purity.

Purity the Power of the New York Visitation.

That was the power of our Visitation in New York City.

We came from good homes all over the land, and especially did we come from a good, pure City.

We were able to help the impure in all classes of society, because we were associated with Purity.

They realized that the stamp of Gentleness and Kindness was upon our faces in the fact that not with an affectation of descent, but in reality, we had come down from the Hill of Zion to the foul, filthy streets of the City of the Devil. But we must not stay in the cities of the Devil.

That is why I cry to my people all over the world: "Get out! Get out! Gather into the Cities of Zion!"

A Horrible, Unspeakable Vice That Must Be Throttled.

But it is not only in the cities that you find impurity, for I sometimes think that the country districts are more impure than the cities.

Associations in many country districts are oftentimes very bad, because not only are ordinary vices practiced, but there is one most horrible vice, that I do not know how to mention without shame—the horrible vice of bestiality, which must be throttled.

Young people, and especially boys, in country districts, become associates not only of vile men and women, but, in the most horrible manner, become the associates of beasts. That crime, under the Ancient Law, caused a man to be stoned to death.

In Zion, by the grace of God, we are living lives that are good and pure.

The Essential Fruit of the Spirit that we speak of this

morning, can only be manifested by a pure man or woman, or one that is becoming pure, in winning hearts by gentle, sweet ways, loving-kindness and gentleness.

Beloved, I am trying to make you understand something which no words can really express.

Those Who Attempt to Imitate the General Overseer Hinder Zion.

Some of you are very offensive.

I shall talk plainly.

You hinder Zion.

You think that you can ape and imitate the General Overseer, but you cannot do it.

That is impossible.

There is only one man like me in the world, and that is myself.

I am thankful to God that you will never have any success in trying to imitate me.

I do not want any one else to bear the burdens I have borne.

I do not want any one else to pass through the afflictions through which I have passed.

I do not want any one else to win the successes I have won at the price I have paid; and yet I am not sorry for any price I have paid for them, or for any path I have had to tread.

You must understand that you cannot under any circumstances be the General Overseer.

Imitation may be the sincerest form of flattery, but the General Overseer does not appreciate your imitations of him.

They are very poor imitations.

There are some Elders, indeed some Deacons, as well as others that want to be like the General Overseer in talking.

Do you not know that you irritate, rather than help, because you are affecting something that does not belong to you?

There is only one man, as far as I know, that has my commission, and that is myself.

This warning does not apply to the people in general, because they do not attempt to imitate me.

The General Overseer Uses a Weapon Which You Cannot Carry.

Sometimes I say to a man, "You dirty dog! You filthy stinkpot! How do you dare to call yourself a Christian? You mass of corruption!

"You a gentleman—and puff your tobacco smoke in your wife's face?

"You a Christian—smoking, stinking, drinking, chewing? You dirty dog, give it up!"

That man becomes as angry as he can be.

He turns white and then red; he feels in his hip-pocket for his revolver, and would like to shoot me.

But I keep on. "You must have some nice qualities, or else the woman who married you would not tolerate you, but you stink her, and defile the house in which you live. Now, give it up!"

Somehow, he looks at me and says, "Why does that man say that?"

He begins to understand two things—first, that I have the authority to say it. God backs me.

Second, that I have the Kindness and Love that makes me win that man, and eventually makes him do what I say.

He does not forget it.

He goes home and fumes and fusses, and says to his wife, "Dowie calls me a stinkpot. Betty, do you think that I am?"

She replies, "Just settle it yourself with God."

He finds she, too, thinks he is a stinkpot.

He gets angry, and he says, "You can never go and hear that fellow again. No gentleman would talk in that way. He is no Christian, but a coarse, vulgar man."

But, somehow, he comes the next night to hear the coarse, vulgar man, and, somehow, after about two weeks, he says, "Got any LEAVES OF HEALING?" although he has sworn that he will not look at it again.

How is it that I can say things that no other man has ever said, not even Paul?

Why is it that I can say these things, and make the world listen until they get angry and whole communities are stirred?

In Adelaide, when I said: "Gentlemen, gentlemen," they would say, "We are not gentlemen; we are stinkpots."

They knew it.

What is the effect?

The effect will be in Australia what it has been here.

You sometimes forget that, in this land, we passed through persecutions as severe as in Australia.

We were arrested in Chicago a hundred times, and had to pass through great tribulation; but today, Chicago has a kind of sneaking, universal love for me.

They feel that I belong to Chicago, and they back me.

They now know that I love them, and that I want only to smash dirty, stinking, filthy, costly habits, that God's children may be pure and clean.

"Leaves of Healing" a Power in the Hands of Every Member of Zion.

But you cannot say these things in exactly the same words I use.

If they say to you, "Do you believe the horrible things Dr. Dowie says?" you answer, "Yes."

If they say, "Then you are just as bad as he is," you can reply, "You read what he says," and give them a copy of LEAVES OF HEALING.

It will soak into their minds and hearts, and they will think about it.

Thousands of you were Methodist, Baptist, Episcopalian, or some other kind of stinkpots, but you were made to see that I was right.

That is what I think God means by linking Long-suffering with Gentleness—Gentleness associated with Power.

You must remember that all have not the same gift.

Some of you try to use my forcible language without having back of it the kind spirit and the Gentleness.

I do not know how to speak of it myself, because it might appear like egotism.

A Severeness Actuated by the Spirit of Kindness.

I never speak with a manuscript in front of me.

When I speak I look for your spirits.

I search down into your hearts, and try to bring blessing to you.

Some of you use my words, but you do not use them as they are in my spirit.

You do not have the Kindness, the Gentleness back of them.

I desire to be a Gentle man everywhere, but when I stand upon this platform and speak, not only to you, but to the whole world, I must speak in such a way that the whole world will hear, and obey the voice of God's servant, who sends forth God's Message.

You are not placed in the position that I am.

I do not want you to attempt an imitation.

You have a great advantage over me in the fact that you can put into the hands of the people my words, printed in LEAVES OF HEALING, and can carry this blessed Fruit of Kindness, Usefulness, Gentleness with you as you go into your work.

In your private life you must be extremely patient, not harsh and rash.

Sometimes people will not understand, not because they do not want to, but because they cannot.

You sometimes come at them with a bludgeon, when you ought to come at them with a kind word.

My manner upon the platform is so different from that of my private life that people cannot believe that both are a part of the same man.

But I am the same man all the time, and the same spirit is within me.

Sometimes I have to blow a trumpet that almost wakes the dead, but when I am at home I do not care to use that trumpet, because the house is not big enough for it.

In my office, as you who have been there know, I speak in a very low tone.

I do not like any one to use noisy language.

Danger of So-called Gentleness Becoming Familiarity.

I do not like unnecessary noise, and vulgarity is very disgusting to me, as well as affected familiarity.

I am willing to be your servant, for the Christ's sake; but when a man comes up to me, and slaps me on the back, and says "Hello, how are you, Brother Dowie, how are you?" I do not like that.

There are not very many men who do that, but, when a man does that to me, I become the General Overseer, every inch of me, and he knows it.

Do not be familiar with one another.

The best of us will be tempted above that which we will be

able to bear if we allow the so-called gentleness to grow into familiarity.

May God keep you from familiar spirits of every kind.

I do not think that I need to reprove the people of Zion City for that, for I have noticed, and all have noticed, that this is a City of gentle men and gentle women, from the highest down to the humblest.

Thanks be to God!

I want you to have the Gentleness that will make you great.

Gentleness in the Southland.

One of the things that is charming in the Southland, is the exceeding gentleness of the people.

Their very tone of voice is delightful.

There is a mellifluous gentleness about those that come from New Orleans.

I wish I could roll the Southerner and the Northerner into one, or give to the Southerner something of the strength and force of the Northerner, and to the Northerner the gentleness and beautiful manners which make a visit to a Southern home, or to a Southern city, so delightful.

I said exactly the same things in San Antonio, Texas, that I say here, only I was careful to say them there in language something like that which the Southerner uses, because I was among Southerners.

I found that I was dealing with persons with whom I could deal with gentleness.

The Northerner is a fellow into whom you cannot get anything until you have knocked him down, morally, as it were.

He does not appreciate anything until you make a football of him for a while.

The Northerner does not know he is licked until he is properly licked.

The Southerner is a different kind of man.

You must adapt yourselves to the different people as you pass through the world.

You must be gentle with the Mohammedans.

They do not fight the Christ because they know Him, but because they do not know Him.

You must be gentle with the Roman Catholics.

They do not fight the Christ.

They love the Christ according to their light, and many of them have a sweet piety and gentleness of spirit which often times the Protestant lacks very much.

Be gentle!

If you know some truth they do not know, be gentle in communicating it.

Do not Reject the Virgin Mary.

Take her to your heart, and love her.

Say to these Roman Catholics that you believe what the Word of God says, that she is the holy, blessed virgin mother, and do not be too harsh with them if they make her their intercessor.

Do you not know that they do not know any better?

She must have been a very sweet intercessor while she lived.

Oftentimes, no doubt, she led the way to Jesus by her love.

Oftentimes, she would sympathize with women.

Can you imagine a more beautiful and sympathetic life than hers who went about after His death, having the memory of the Cross ever with her?

The story is not written of how the blessed Son of God, when He rose from the dead, went to see His mother, and comforted her.

It is not written—it could not be written; but did you ever try to imagine it?

Did you ever try to imagine how, when He rose from the dead with the marks of the nails in His hands and in His feet, He went, in His gentleness, to comfort His mother?

There are many parts of that story left unwritten, because no words could express them.

Let us have the Spirit of the Master, for that is what true Gentleness is.

If you want to find the perfect, gentle man, you must find the Christ Jesus.

He showed the Spirit of Gentleness.

PRAYER OF CONSECRATION.

Our God and Father, in Jesus' Name, we come to Thee. Take us as we are. Take away from us the gentleness which makes us partakers of sin. Give us a Gentleness that hates sin, but is kind to the sinner, loving to brother and sister no matter whether Mohammedan or Pagan; no matter how apostate they may have been. Let us be kind. May the fruit of the Spirit in Love, Joy, Peace, Long-suffering, and Gentleness be our portion. Make us truly gentle. Thy Gentleness will make us great. Make us great in a deep humility. For Jesus' sake. Amen. [*All repeat the prayer, clause by clause, after the General Overseer.*]

The Congregation joined in singing, "I Stand on Zion's Mount," after which the General Overseer prayed as follows:

PRAYER BY THE GENERAL OVERSEER.

O God, our Father, we cannot be Gentle and Long-suffering, nor be at Peace, nor can we have Divine Joy or Love unless Thou dost impart it. Oh, by Thy Holy Spirit, impart this gracious Fruit.

Preserve and increase within us Thy gifts, and help us to develop them in one another by all the love that Thou wilt give us. O Father, make Zion everywhere so large and kind and gentle and sympathetic that we shall win all men in all conditions, even, by and by, the corrupt kings. God bless these men who occupy positions which are so dangerous; and let us be gentle with them, personally, while we fight bad principles. Take us into Thy care and give us a good day. For Jesus' sake. Amen.

BENEDICTION.

Beloved, abstain from every form of evil. And may the very God of Peace Himself sanctify you wholly; and I pray God your whole spirit and soul and body be preserved entire, without blame, unto the coming of our Lord Jesus, the Christ. Faithful is He that calleth you, who also will do it. The grace of our Lord Jesus, the Christ, the love of God our Father, the fellowship of the Holy Spirit, our Comforter and Guide, one Eternal God, abide in you, bless you and keep you, and all the Israel of God everywhere, forever. Amen.

EARLY MORNING SACRIFICE OF PRAISE AND PRAYER.

REPORTED BY L. L. H., O. L. S., AND E. S.

Goodness, the Sixth Fruit of the Spirit, was the theme taken by the Man of God on Tuesday morning, July 18, 1904, of the Holy Convocation.

Between five and six thousand people had assembled at this early hour of the morning to praise God in his Temple and to listen to His Message as given through the mouth of His own Prophet.

Hearts were drawn irresistibly toward this beautiful Fruit—Goodness—as it was held up by the Man of God, and an intense longing created for its possession.

At the close of the address, the entire audience rose and joined in the Prayer of Consecration.

Shiloh Tabernacle, Zion City, Illinois, Tuesday Morning, July 19, 1904.

The service was opened by the Congregation's singing hymn No. 27, in the Program.

Prayer was then offered by the General Overseer, closing with the chanting of the Disciples' Prayer by the Congregation, the General Overseer leading.

Hymn No. 18 was sung, after which the Congregation repeated in concert the 23d Psalm.

The General Overseer called upon the Congregation to read with him the 19th verse of the 33d chapter of the book of Exodus.

He then asked the people to turn to the 5th chapter of Galatians and read with him the last four verses of that chapter.

The Message was immediately preceded by the General Overseer's pronouncing the usual

INVOCATION.

Let the words of my mouth and the meditation of my heart be acceptable in Thy sight, be profitable unto this people, and unto all to whom these words shall come, in this and every land, in this and all the coming time, Till Jesus Come. Amen.

The General Overseer said:

We have reached this glorious Fruit of the Spirit, which is, as it were, a fountain out of which the wonderful blessing that we were talking about yesterday morning—the Life of Usefulness—may be supplied.

You see that the Sixth Fruit of the Spirit is Goodness.

The Origin of the Word "Goodness."

I am impressed to again deliver a little disquisition upon the origin of that word.

It is always exceedingly interesting to trace the origin of words, and to get the fundamental idea that suggested them.

For instance, this is a peculiar word, which originated away back in the idea of Nobility and Majesty, as well as in the thought of Sympathy and Benignity coming down from a very high source.

Now the expression which is translated "Goodness" has for its origin the Goodness, the Nobility, the High Birth, as it were, of the source from which Goodness flows.

It is not merely a Goodness that means good gifts, although it includes that; but it is a Goodness which implies Gentleness, Nobility, and Goodness, primarily in reference to birth.

We are born of God; we are reborn; we are regenerated; and the idea of this Goodness is a goodness peculiar to the New Birth.

It is a Goodness that we get by virtue of the fact that we receive it by Divine heredity.

It is an inhate quality inseparable from the noble, gentle, Divine, and Pure Nature which is imparted to us by Regeneration.

That is the meaning of the original word.

It is not merely the simple Latin *bonus*, good, although that is a wonderful word; but it is the original *agathos* (ἀγαθός) of the Greek, which has that meaning, and more than that.

It is *agathosune* (ἀγαθωσύνη) which is a compound word meaning a Goodness with you—the idea expressed by *sun* (συν) —making it to be a Goodness inseparable from union with a Source of Goodness.

In fact, it is a Goodness and Mercy which, to be good, has to be all the time flowing.

There Is a Kind of Goodness that Stagnates.

It is a most offensive quality.

There are many people that are good, but it is hard to get along with them.

They are so good; they are so sweet; they are so conscious of their goodness; and they never seem to be human!

They are, if you were to take their own estimate of themselves, so superlatively pious and good that they lack everything that makes you feel that they are human.

They never get angry—never!

They are not capable of getting angry!

As far as they are concerned, the Devil can do anything he likes.

He can destroy humanity; he can make wars and strife; he can destroy the Church; he can do anything he likes; but these people are so good that nothing vexes them.

I wish I could wake them up.

They are offensively good.

You cannot find any particular fault with them; you almost wish that you could, because then you would feel that they are human; but they are so absolutely inhumanly good that you wish that they were somewhere else.

They are no help to you; they are not much help to humanity.

That kind of piety has no place in Zion.

This Goodness of which God is here speaking—the *agathosune*—is the Gentleness and Nobility, the Stream of Beneficent Power, that flows through an active, and holy, and loving, and joyful, and yet peaceful, and patient, and gentle, and beneficent nature; a Goodness which is always in operation.

It is a Goodness and Mercy which is always flowing.

There is a great deal of the so-called piety of which I have spoken that has actually stagnated.

That kind of goodness is a poor thing.

It is a grace that those who possess it received long ago.

They were molded into that particular Quaker-like shape, and they have retained it, and all that they possess is the same old thing.

They do not understand moving along and applying the Goodness of God to the conditions in which they live. To them it is enough that they are at peace and that they have the goodness and the mercy of God.

Having these, they are selfishly at rest.

That is not the Divine conception of Goodness.

The Divine Conception of Goodness.

The thought of the inspired writer is that the Goodness of Jehovah shall be in you an Ever-flowing Spring—a Spring of Water which cannot be confined, or a spring which bursts the barriers that confine it and then flows through the earth, and keeps flowing.

I want you to get the idea that this water, even at the very lowest level, has its Inspiration in the High Mountains from which it descends, and that it again springs up in the place to which it falls. The idea of *agathos* (ἀγαθός), in the early times, signifying Good, and Gentle, and Noble, in reference to birth, will give you the idea.

It is our Birthright.

Our Springs are in God!

This Goodness is not at all an apathetic virtue.

It is a most active and Purifying Power, and makes the recipient of it a very Active Christian.

Divine Goodness Includes Bravery.

It also has the idea of Bravery, Courage.

The good were brave; the good were fighters for the right; the good were never at peace with evil or wrong.

They were determined to live purely, to see that the oppressed were set free, and to see that the dignity of their heritage was marked by hatred of oppression and a strife to make all things around them good and pure.

After the thought of Courage and of the essential transformation of the Moral Nature, there comes the idea that is particularly expressed in the *agathosune* (ἀγαθωσύνη) of the New Testament Greek—the thought that there is in us, as well as above us, by virtue of this Birthright, a Power constantly operating.

The Love, the Goodness of God is leading us—leading us according to Paul's expression, "The goodness of God leadeth thee to Repentance." This goodness extends to all the saints that are on the earth, "in whom," as the Psalmist says, "is all My delight."

If I can get you to understand, from the origin of the word, something of its meaning, you will begin to know what God desires us to possess in this grace of Goodness.

I say again that one of the distressing things in the past record of the church, even among the most evangelical of Christians, has been that their goodness has really been of such a quality that it was not serviceable.

It could not come down and find practical expression in the brickyard and in the workshop.

It did not come into touch with men's difficulties as they labored for their daily bread.

It did not help them to meet daily trials.

It was an abstract quality, which seemed to be so wonderfully beautiful that it did not belong to this workaday world at all.

I want to get into your minds and mine, increasingly, the thought that

This Goodness of God Flows by Our Side in Streams of Constant Blessing.

It follows us, too, in thousands of forms.

Angelic beings, filled with the Goodness and the Purity of Life, are our ministers, servants; not always by our knowledge or will; but they are sent forth to "do service for the sake of them that shall inherit Salvation."

The Angel of Jehovah, unseen and unrecognized, is with us all the time.

Around us are the Good Spirits, the Spirits that are filled with this Goodness, of which we know comparatively so little.

All their varied powers are good.

They are untouched by evil.

Impurity has no place in their Purity.

Infidelity and doubt have no place in their Perfect Faith, their Perfect Hope.

Their whole being is good.

They cannot do evil, because evil is not in them.

They are so absolutely good, so tender and so sympathetic, that they are the servants of the Good and Holy God.

We should recognize that the Goodness of God and the Mercy of God flow together.

The Goodness is shown in the Mercy and the Mercy is shown in the Goodness.

It is infinitely merciful of God to take such pains to make us good.

I am endeavoring, in the words that I am saying, to give expression to that of which I am always conscious that speech cannot clearly state, that which really can only be expressed in Living.

I want you to recognize the Source of this Goodness, and how it is flowing.

I presume you all realize that "every Good Gift and every Perfect Boon is from above, coming down from the Father of lights, with whom can be no variation, neither shadow that is cast by turning," and are the purchase of the Savior's Atoning Sacrifice, coming to us through Him and by the Holy Spirit.

Fruits of the Spirit Indigenous to the Soil of the Regenerate Heart.

You know that these beautiful Fruits of the Spirit of which we are talking these morning hours, are from God; that they are not indigenous to the soil of our unregenerate nature; but that they belong to the Soil of a Regenerate Heart —a good, honest heart, into which the Good Seed of the Word of God may be put, and where these seeds will grow.

God's people are a garden in which each fruit and flower has its own distinct characteristic, and these fruits and flowers combined, make the variety which constitutes a beautiful garden, orchard, or field.

There are some people that are content to have quite a little garden; they do not want one on a big scale.

They are small people, and they do not want to see their farms very big.

If they have five acres, and a cow, that is enough.

I want a million acres and a million cows!

I want to see this Goodness prevail to such an extent that the Knowledge of Jehovah shall cover the earth as the waters cover the sea. I want all to realize that the Goodness that God gives is so great, that if we carefully preserve the Seed, we may eat of the Fruit every year and yet have left Seed to sow over and over again, until the whole earth is filled with the Goodness, with the Gracious Sweetness of the Divine Life, full of Fruit, full of Beauty.

Get this thought, realizing that Goodness is all around us; that Goodness is constantly flowing to us; and that every Good and Perfect Gift that we can use is waiting for us.

Divine Goodness Must Be Broad, Reaching Out to All.

Men are so limited, so narrow, and so miserably small, that really a great many people have not got away from that miserable prayer, "Lord, bless me and my wife, my son John and his wife; us four and no more. Amen." [Laughter.]

That is the miserable thing.

You concentrate your prayer and thought upon the narrow circle of yourself, your family, and a few odd friends here and there.

God sees that you have no thought—at least no dominating thought—for the salvation of a whole world that must yet be redeemed.

This Goodness, therefore, must be the brave, great, benignant, majestic quality that comes to us with the High Birth that we have as Regenerated Beings, made new, born again, born of God, born into the majesty of a Divine Life—a life in which He has made us to be a Kingdom and Priests unto His God and Father.

This is the object of our Lord, that He shall create a Generation that is altogether Royal.

Understand, get hold of the truth that the Generation that God creates in His Zion is to be altogether a Royal Generation, conscious of its Kingly descent, in the best sense; with a deep humility, and never forgetting that the King of kings has given to them, no matter what their color or their degree of intelligence, the majesty of a Divine Birth.

This Goodness, which He gives us by a Divine generation, should take us, as it took the Redeemer, into the humblest and lowliest walks, sympathizing with and helping the meanest, and attracting to us, as many were attracted to Him, the very humblest, by reason of the Real, Practical Goodness—the bravery, the courage, the separation from evil that must make us a Power.

We cannot all be equally good, or even be good in the same way.

Goodness Will Find Expression in a Natural and Right Way.

The goodness of a pure, good, sweet woman, will find expression in tenderness of love for her husband; in reverence for all that is really Divine in him; in the thought that God has given her a husband through whom, by the great Goodness of God, there may come into this world in Purity, good, and noble, and pure children.

A wife has a right to expect Real Goodness in a Divinely-born man, and she has a right to expect that the offspring shall be the Seed of Real Goodness.

With this come all the sweet thoughts that gather around the Good Gift of God, as He bestows the Heritage of Jehovah.

Lo, children are an Heritage of Jehovah:
And the Fruit of the womb is His reward.
As arrows in the hand of a mighty man,
So are the children of youth.

That takes us back to the Parable that I considered in the first two discourses after my return—the Parable of the Tares of the Field.

In that Parable, the Good Seed are the Sons of the Kingdom, and the Evil Seed are the Sons of the Wicked One.

A Man's Goodness Manifested in His Offspring.

We have a right to expect that in this, the most important thing in life in connection with the extension of the Kingdom of God, we shall have good children, and that these children shall carry down to posterity good living; that there shall arise a Seed that shall be Good Seed, and that shall be worth cultivating; and that it shall be in strong contrast with the tares, the darnel, the ζιζάνια—the horrible, wretched weeds that have been sown in the field by the Devil, the children of God giving proof of the Goodness of God in themselves by the Goodness of their offspring

That is one of the ways in which this Goodness is manifested.

It is manifested in the transformation of the spiritual, the psychical, and the physical nature, so that the thoughts that dominate father and mother, thoughts of Purity, Peace and Power, shall go into the composition of the unborn babe, and produce a babe, a youth, a woman, a man, that shall be Royal.

That is the idea, and it must take practical embodiment in our children.

Goodness shuts out pestiferous things.

Goodness is not always happiness in the worldly sense.

Sometimes, real goodness involves anything but happiness

The maintenance of the Purity and Nobility of this Grace often entails much pain.

In fact, to be good is not merely to be good, but to embody Goodness.

I am speaking of the Grace that is capable of embodiment.

I do not care for Grace that is impossible of embodiment.

A mere abstract thing that cannot find embodiment in practice has no attraction for me.

A philosophy that is away up in the air is a cold philosophy.

It is a philosophy of death!

You can go up so high as to get into an atmosphere where the blood will start from your nose and ears, and you will die.

Elevation Does not Mean Strength.

The higher you get in the Alpine regions, the more difficult it is to breathe.

The heights where there are eternal snows is no place for habitation.

God Almighty never intended us, in this life, to live there.

If you will live away up there amid the eternal snows, because you love to see the great mountain heights, you will find it is not a healthy place in which to live.

The valley of the Engadine, away up in the Alps, for instance, produces misshapen and physically weak people.

I want to point out to you that there is a so-called elevation which is destruction.

I am not speaking about abstract philosophy. I have seen too much of it.

I am not speaking about an abstract sentimentality in religion

I am speaking about Graces which find embodiment and which bring forth Fruit; "for," said Jesus, "herein is My Father glorified; that ye bear much Fruit."

I am now speaking about the practicality which brings this Goodness into every-day life, into the life of the family, where a good man and a good woman establish a good home and bring forth Good Seed; where they bring forth children of God, who are good, and sweet, and pure, and brave, and powerful, and righteous, filled with real capacity; with clean, sweet-thinking, strong brains, well-developed bodies, and strong nerves, and who have not a trace of the coward's blood in all their composition.

Now that is a good thing to have, is it not?

People—"Yes."

General Overseer—It is this Good Seed of the Kingdom that is to be the Power in these Latter Days.

Lest We Fail to Enter the Promised Land.

In the olden days, when God gave to Israel the Promised Land, the fathers did not realize in full the blessing of God

They did not realize how good God was in bringing them out of Egyptian slavery; and they went back to it, back to the heathenism and to the slavery of their own will, until God had to bury that whole generation in the sands of the desert.

It was the new generation, the Royal Generation that had learned to trust God in the wilderness, that entered into and possessed the Promised Land and realized the larger blessing.

And so it is with us; unless we are to fall by the way, unless we are to miss the entering in, we must have so complete a transformation in our nature that we can be classed with the Calebs and the Joshuas, so that not merely shall our children enter in, but that we shall enter in with them.

I think that no more majestic figures can be imagined than Caleb and Joshua.

They seem to have been wonderfully faithful.

There is scarcely a shadow upon their names.

There is scarcely a shadow upon the simplicity, and majesty, and courage of their good, strong lives.

They were among the very few of those who came out of Egypt that entered into the Promised Land.

In this Goodness there is no slipping back.

You must not be good in spots, or in streaks, and you must not be good just here and there, and then slip back into your old Egyptian ways.

If you are going to get this Grace you must be good all the time.

Goodness Does Not Always Mean Happiness.

I say that Goodness is not always connected with happiness, because in separating one's self from the friends of one's whole life, family ties, which are sacred and beautiful, have to be broken.

The Christ did not come to send peace on earth, but "a sword," and that sword is an exceedingly sharp one, and it severs ties.

It severs the ties of blood, when these ties would drag you down or keep you down, or keep you away from the Inheritance of God in Zion.

That idea of religion which supposes that it does not separate is wrong.

The other day I saw a letter written in Europe to one in this City, saying that the writer had no respect for a religion that broke up families, that separated people one from another; and the letter spoke of me in very severe and extremely wicked language.

The writer belongs to a class of people who are absolutely without religion, that live only for themselves.

One, however, had broken away and was determined to live a pure and holy life, having entirely consecrated that life to God.

Her associates could not help admiring her beautiful character and her Divine consecration, but when it came to the point of separation from them, and separation from her native land, and from a wide range of friends, then their indignation knew no bounds.

They were angry that religion would take one away from the old pigsty and the mess and muck of the worldly ways.

They are not only indignant, but dreadfully indignant; so indignant that their "goodness" finds expression in a declaration that they will embarrass that person as much as they can, and see that she does not get what is her rightful dues, by keeping back the estate that belongs to her.

Divine Goodness Separates.

You will find that Divine Goodness separates; that the Sword of the Spirit will cut family ties; that father will rise up against mother, and that wives will rise up against husbands; that sons, and daughters, and daughters-in-law, and all degrees of relationship will be plunged into strife and confusion: yea, "a man's foes shall be they of his own household."

This Goodness will take you through a path which, for the time being, seems a thousand times worse than death; for you love those that are dear to you by the ties of consanguinity.

You cannot help it.

It is born in you.

It is in your blood.

You played with those from whom you are now compelled to separate, when you were children; you wept together; you loved one another, and you found the boys and girls such dear companions!

The people to whom I have referred prefer to go on in the old, worldly, formal way, with a religion that means nothing more than mere verbal expression.

But you have come out, and you are walking with God.

You are walking in the pathway of His Goodness and Mercy; and all at once you wake up to find that that makes you hateful to your family, to your friends, to your town, to your acquaintances, and you are held in absolute contempt.

You are used in a most shameful manner, and are robbed

One of the things noticeable in connection with this is that relatives and friends proceed to show how much they love you by trying to steal everything that belongs to you.

Do not make any mistake.

You will find that that kind of happiness which consists in agreeable association with even blood relatives and old friends, is not Goodness.

But when you receive this Goodness, this High-birth Goodness, and go forth to be the Children of God, Sons of the Kingdom, then you will find that those who are the Tares are among your very dearest

Divine Goodness Meant Separation in Jesus' Life.

It is the story told in all ages

Even when the mother of the Lord Himself, with the Lord's own brothers and sisters by birth, stood outside the crowd, and the Lord was delivering His Divine Message, they saw on the faces of these Pharisees the hate which that Message inspired as He exposed their wickedness.

The Pharisees had brought, with pious hypocrisy, a woman taken in adultery, and said, "Master, Moses said that she should be put to death."

Then He wrote on the ground—I wonder what He wrote!

Perhaps they were words in the Hebrew tongue; it may have been just the one word, "Purity."

But presently He rose and said in effect, "Yes, all right' but Moses' law demands that the executioner shall not be a party to the crime; therefore, go ahead, let him that is without sin among you cast the first stone."

Their faces changed.

They were afraid, every one of them, to cast the first stone: for they were all guilty!

Those accusers could not execute the law; for they were partakers in the accursed crime; and so they went out one by one.

Mary saw their faces.

Jesus' disciples saw their evil faces on that and on many other occasions.

They did not dare to lift the stone, because they had learned that this Man had wonderful knowledge, and in a moment He would say, "You cannot throw the stone, because you were guilty, here and there."

He could name day, and date, and place and woman; and they were afraid, because He knew their hearts.

He knew their lives; and His Divine omniscience would track them, and His eye would pierce through the darkest shades of night.

So they went away.

They were not going to be good.

They were sons of the Devil.

They were Tares.

They were not children of God at all.

They were the worst kind of Tares, and the Christ told them to their faces, "Ye are of your father the Devil."

Purity of Love Destroyed by Fear.

Mary and Jesus' brothers did not like the thought of the Christ's getting into trouble with the rulers.

It meant death by stoning or crucifixion.

Mary stood outside; and her love, her great love, sent in the message beseeching Him to come away, to talk no more, not to aggravate those Pharisees any more, lest He should suffer.

Was she faithful?

Verily, no!

She permitted fear to destroy the Purity of her Love, and for the time being she was an ally of the Devil, so that the Christ had to lift His hands, and the warning Voice went to her heart, "Who are My mother and My brethren?"

"Whosoever shall do the Will of God, the same is My brother, and sister, and mother!"

Away above all unbelieving brethren, and even a doubting, sainted mother, He had to tread the Path of Goodness and Purity that led to Death.

If we are called to tread that Path, shall we not tread it, despite what even the sweetest mother and the kindest brethren and sisters may say?

We shall find the relationship that is higher than these.

"Whosoever shall do the Will of My Father which is in heaven, the same is My brother, and sister, and mother!"

Have you that Goodness that rises above the things of earth, and that places them in their proper place?

Do not forget that even His brethren did not believe on Him.

It was not until after His death that they openly entered into fellowship with Him.

It took the agonies of the Cross to bring them to realize the Goodness, and Sublimity, and Purity of their Brother, of Mary's Son, and of their Redeemer.

By and by, however, they trod the Path of Faith, and by and by they walked with Him.

But there were bitter tears that they had not been in sympathy with Him when He passed through the "Valley of the Shadow of Death;" that they had not been in sympathy with Him when He fought His Good Fight; but all their tears could not take away the memory of their faithlessness when they should have been faithful.

Work on!

Live on!

Pray on!

By and by, your dear ones will reach the place where they can understand you and where they can sympathize with you.

But do not go back to them.

Do not submit to the world's fears.

Let your Goodness be such that you are willing to dispense with happiness, for it is better to be good and weep with the Christ, than to be happy with the world and not follow the Master.

PRAYER OF CONSECRATION.

My God and Father, in Jesus' Name I come to Thee. Take me as I am. Make me what I ought to be, in spirit, in soul and in body. Give me power to do right, to realize the Divine birth within and never to degrade my Regeneration. Help me, my Father, to walk, if need be, the path alone. For Jesus' sake, let the Fruits of the Spirit, which are planted within me, grow in Love, in Joy, in Peace, in Long-suffering, in Gentleness and Goodness, and in all the other gifts. For Jesus' sake. Amen.

Now, do not be content with praying it, but live it.

The service was closed by the General Overseer's pronouncing the

BENEDICTION.

Beloved, abstain from every form of evil. And may the very God of Peace Himself sanctify you wholly; and I pray God your whole spirit and soul and body be preserved entire, without blame, unto the coming of our Lord Jesus, the Christ. Faithful is He that calleth you, who also will do it. The grace of our Lord Jesus, the Christ, the love of God, our Father, the fellowship of the Holy Spirit, our Comforter and Guide, one Eternal God, abide in you, bless you and keep you, and all the Israel of God everywhere, forever. Amen.

CONFERENCE ON THE WORK OF ZION RESTORATION HOST THROUGHOUT THE WORLD

REPORTED BY M. E. L., A. C. R., AND E. S.

Perhaps the most important of all the conferences and meetings of the Holy Convocation was that held the afternoon of Tuesday, July 19, 1904, on the Work of Zion Restoration Host Throughout the World.

This force known as Zion Restoration Host, pushing out in the front of the Church, has been called the Battle-ax of the Prophet of the Restoration.

Certainly it is the pulse of the Church; and if judged by the number of those taking the Restoration Vow, thus consecrating themselves to this work, at the close of the address given by the Man of God, then never was the great heart of the great Organization in better condition—never were its pulsations stronger, steadier, calmer.

Four hundred fifty-nine enrolled themselves in the great and growing Zion Restoration Host.

This in a time of seeming inactivity—a time of training, drilling, and preparation for the work to come!

The magnitude of this work, its rigid requirements, its exalted character and peculiar part in the Restoration and preparation for the reign of the Christ upon the earth, was put before those assembled, in words whose plain meaning none could doubt.

Yet gladly they responded. With holy enthusiasm they took upon themselves the Vow which means absolute Obedience, absolute Consecration, and recognition of the Prophetic Mission of the Man of God.

Throughout the meeting the closest interest was displayed, and the words of the Man of God were listened to with deepest interest by the five thousand present.

Preliminary to the address, a review, or rather view, of the nations of the earth, as they are grouped today in their relative positions, was given, showing that, while Zion is preparing for her work among the peoples of the earth, they, too, are getting ready, in the Divine order of things, for Zion and her War of Peace.

At the close of the address, Overseer Speicher spoke a few words of farewell to the audience, as he was to depart soon for Europe.

The Vow, Consecration and Separation to the Work of the Host, then followed

---

Shiloh Tabernacle, Zion City, Illinois, Tuesday Afternoon, July 19, 1904

The service was opened by the singing of Hymns Nos. 7 and 5, in the Special Program.

The General Overseer then said:

Beloved, I desire you all to realize that this is the most important meeting of the entire Feast.

I Look Upon Zion Restoration Host as My Battle-ax.

I look upon the force that is here represented in this Host as especially mine; that is to say, while the Church is a great and mighty institution, this Host has a right to be looked upon as not only a part of a Church, but a part of the Church that has taken a step ahead, and is an effective army.

Never before, in the history of the world, could there have been organized a Host on such lines as Zion Restoration Host has been organized.

The Vow is to God.

It contains a recognition of my Prophetic Mission and a positive Vow that you will obey orders and go where you are sent.

I have not found any considerable misunderstanding upon this matter. However several persons have thought that, notwithstanding their Vow, there was no necessity for obeying when the time came to obey.

These persons were removed at once from the roll of members of Zion Restoration Host.

We had no use for them.

We cannot retain those that are hesitating as to whether they will perform their promise and as to whether they will show that they believe in my Prophetic Mission.

We have now had enough experience with the Host to warrant us in getting to more perfect organization.

I shall tell you some things in connection with this matter, that have come to me more and more clearly.

I greatly rejoice to see so many this afternoon who are about to take the Vow and to be set apart.

Let us all pray with the Holy Spirit's power.

May God bless us in a very remarkable manner.

I do not ask for visible and emotional results.

I Have Very Little Confidence in the Mere Physical Expression of Emotion.

We must be exceedingly careful about that.

Our emotions may be played upon by the Devil, and tears and fears can be excited, as well as laughter, by simply getting at a proper part of the brain and tickling it.

There is nothing in that which of necessity indicates real spiritual work.

You no doubt know that the brain is so constituted that if you were to lift off the scalp, you could touch a certain part of the brain and the person would laugh; he could not help it, because that is the convolution which controls laughter.

If you were to touch that part of a dog's brain he would have to bark.

The mere expressions of emotion are often created by false sentiments.

Oftentimes people will weep over the sorrows of the heroine in a theater, although they have never wept over their own sins, and, after the play is over, forget all about it.

They laugh and weep, and become indignant, or angry, all in the same moment, and none of it amounts to anything.

It is all forgotten after the play.

They are rather ashamed that they laughed or cried; but for the time being there was a play upon the emotions.

While I know that sometimes emotions can be legitimately excited by tender associations and loving remembrances of our Lord and of His wonderful love to us and of His gracious deliverances, yet I do not care very much to live in an atmosphere of mere emotional excitement.

We are reasonable beings, and the more solid our happiness, the more solid is our reason.

God's Service Is a Reasonable Service.

That which pleased me most about the Host that went with us on the New York Visitation was that the people there said that they were sympathetic, kind, and gentle and did not fly off into emotions

To the surprise of the people there, they were not denunciatory nor were they beseeching with theatrical effect.

Our people were sensible.

When they said, "Peace be to this house," the people knew that they meant it.

They talked in such a sensible way that they won New York City

I ask you to pray God to bless us abundantly during this year, which is the year of the continuation of the Organization rather than of its full development.

We are getting the soldiers together and drilling them.

We are not doing a tithe of what we expect to do when we get ready for work, because just now we might be premature if we undertook any long Visitation.

For instance, I think it would be very premature if we were to undertake London this year.

I think it desirable to let London wait a while; to let London get ready for us, as well as for us to get ready for London.

There will be great changes of sentiment in Great Britain before we go to London.

Many Important Changes Seem Imminent.

No one can tell what a day may bring forth at the present time.

One thing has happened recently which any man who has a keen eye for important news will see is a very serious matter.

Under a commercial flag the Russians have been sending vessels through the Black Sea into the Mediterranean, which they have a right to do only under a commercial flag.

These vessels were disguised war-ships, and passed through the Mediterranean, and through the Suez Canal, still under a commercial flag.

When these vessels reached the Red Sea they unfurled the fleet flag of Russia, and began to search British, and German, and American ships.

If they do not stop, there may be a Declaration of war between Great Britain and Russia, which would be one of the most terrible of things.

America might be brought into it.

Russia is utterly beside herself; she has no good counselors.

The great Colossus is beginning to lose her head since she lost her feet in the warm waters of Asia, as I said she would.

If there should be war (which God forbid), it could only terminate one way: in a more complete destruction of the monarchical principle, because just as sure as Russia goes to pieces, the old nationalities will resume, more or less, the semi-republican form.

Russia is honeycombed with republican ideas, and once they again begin to spread, as at the opening of the last century, you will see a tremendous upheaval.

I should not be surprised if inside of ten years, when we are ready to go to London, we should find that Great Britain was no longer the United Kingdom of Great Britain, but the United States or Republic of Great Britain and Ireland.

In that case, I believe that they would be more disposed to listen to me, because I had prophesied it.

I know that I am speaking under Divine guidance.

I can see clearly that God is restoring things, by first destroying.

The Time of the Drying Up of the Euphrates.

And the sixth (angel) poured out his bowl upon the great river, the River Euphrates; and the water thereof was dried up, that the way might be made ready for the kings that come from the sunrising.

And I saw coming out of the mouth of the dragon, and out of the mouth of the beast, and out of the mouth of the false prophet, three unclean spirits, as it were frogs·

For they are the spirits of devils, working signs; which go forth unto the kings of the whole world, to gather them together unto the war of the Great Day of God, the Almighty.

That takes place at the time of the drying up of the Euphrates—the Turkish power—in Europe and Asia, which certainly is being dried up very rapidly.

Then comes the time for the military power in the Land of the Rising Sun—Japan.

So it will be with the spiritual power.

We shall come from the East and West and from the North and South, but we shall come as the children of Light, in this glorious Restoration Host.

Multitudes are looking for us, longing for us, and getting ready for us.

We must get ready for them.

I desire you to be all that you vow to God.

Therefore, I ask you to pray that God will make you to see and know what His Will is.

Scripture Reading and Exposition.

Prayer was then offered by Overseer Speicher, after which the General Overseer said:

Let us read from the Inspired Word of God, first, in the 10th chapter of the Gospel according to St. Luke:

Now after these things the Lord appointed seventy others, and sent them two and two before His Face into every city and place whither He Himself was about to come.

And He said unto them, The harvest is plenteous, but the laborers are few: pray ye therefore the Lord of the harvest, that He send forth laborers into His harvest.

Go your ways: behold, I send you forth as lambs in the midst of wolves.

Carry no purse, no wallet, no shoes; and salute no man on the way.

And into whatsoever house ye shall enter, first say, Peace be to this house.

I hope that you will always be very careful as members of Zion Restoration Host, to say, very clearly and very plainly "Peace be to this house." "Peace to thee" is not the proper salutation, and thereby hangs a tale.

In the Bowery District of New York, in a certain saloon in that low district, two of our Restorationists entered and said to the proprietor, "Peace to thee."

The Proper Salutation of Zion Restorationists.

"Ladies," he asked, "are you members of Zion Restoration Host?" and they answered in the affirmative

"Please step out, then," he said, "and come in with the proper salutation."

The one said to the other, "Why, did I make a mistake?"

"I do not know," the other replied, "I believe you said it correctly."

Then suddenly she saw the mistake, and said, "Thank you, sir. Peace be to this house."

"Now," he said, "you have given me the proper salutation; I was waiting for it.

"You shall go through this house and deliver your Messages, and I will protect you, but there is no Peace in this house; it is the Devil's own. But you bring a Message of Peace, and may God bless you!"

That man was not far from the Kingdom, and you cannot wonder that today his saloon is closed."

I had the pleasure of meeting one saloon-keeper in New York City who had given up his saloon.

Overseer Mason—"He is in Zion City now."

General Overseer—Are you here this afternoon, you old sinner?

A voice—"Yes, sir."

General Overseer—You must never forget that when you come to a house, you must not say, "Peace to thee," but "Peace be to this house."

Do not mumble it, do not be ashamed of it, do not fail to say it emphatically.

And if a son of Peace be there, your Peace shall rest upon him; but if not, it shall turn to you again.

You may find an opponent there who will answer you very wickedly, but that will not lessen your Peace.

Your Peace shall return to you, and God will increase it in your heart.

Do Not Go From House to House for Entertainment.

And in that same house remain—

This evidently refers to persons in the scattered districts.

Today our Restorationists have to labor, and with difficulty.

I have known of some in districts in Africa and Australia, where houses were many miles apart, to journey perhaps fifty miles to visit five or six houses.

In such cases they are entertained, and this passage would apply to them

And in that same house remain, eating and drinking such things as they give for the laborer is worthy of his hire. Go not from house to house.

This means that if you have been entertained nicely at a certain home continue to go there. Do not go to other houses.

And into whatsoever city ye enter, and they receive you, eat such things as are set before you.

And heal the sick that are therein, and say unto them, The Kingdom of God is come nigh unto you.

God's Indignation upon Those Who Make Miserable Excuses.

Let us now read in the 14th chapter of Luke, beginning at the 15th verse:

And when one of them that sat at meat with Him heard these things, he said unto Him, Blessed is he that shall eat bread in the Kingdom of God.

But He said unto him, A certain man made a great supper; and he bade many·

And he sent forth his servant at supper time to say to them that were bidden, Come; for all things are now ready.

And they all with one consent began to make excuse.

How many people who profess to love their Lord are doing the same thing!

When they get the command to go, they begin to make excuses.

They say, "O Lord, not just now; I have some things I must attend to. I will obey you by and by."

"I will do it when I have everything so arranged that I can obey without injury to myself, to my fortune, or to my family."

"I will do it when it will not inconvenience me."

"I will go when my husband goes with me," or "when I can have the people of the church, to which I belong, go with me."

That miserable excusing of yourself is the most accursed thing, and brings down God's indignation upon you.

When you have a distinct command to go, go.

If you do not go, wo unto you who have vowed that you will go where you are sent and obey the voice of His servant who is speaking to you now.

Excuses Which Must Also Have Been Lies.

And they all with one consent began to make excuse. The first said unto him, I have bought a field, and I must needs go out and see it: I pray thee have me excused.

And another said, I have bought five yoke of oxen, and I go to prove them: I pray thee have me excused.

And another said, I have married a wife, and therefore I cannot come.

These excuses that we have just read were lies; I do not believe that one of them was true.

The first said, "I have bought a field, and I must needs go and see it. I pray thee have me excused."

I do not believe that any Jew ever bought a field without seeing it, do you?

I do not think you can find many Americans who have been so foolish as to buy a field without seeing it.

Another said, "I have bought five yoke of oxen, and I go to prove them; I pray thee, have me excused."

He would be an exceedingly foolish farmer to buy oxen without first proving them.

I believe that that was a lie.

At the most it was a contemptible excuse.

The last excuse given was most certainly a lie.

"I have married a wife, and, therefore, I cannot come."

If you understand this to be the Gospel Invitation, you know that that was a lie, because the wife also was invited.

If the wife objected to his going, he should have gone without her.

If he disobeyed God because of his wife, he was of no account.

He was a rebel against God.

But this disgusting business of excusing has only one result:

And the servant came, and told his lord these things. Then the master of the house being angry said to his servant, Go out quickly into the streets and lanes of the city, and bring in hither the poor and maimed and blind and lame

And the servant said, Lord, what thou didst command is done, and yet there is room.

I am so glad that heaven cannot be overcrowded!

There is room for all.

There is no possibility of overcrowding heaven.

And the lord said unto the servant, Go out into the highways and hedges, and constrain them to come in, that my house may be filled.

For I say unto you, that none of those men which were bidden shall taste of my supper.

None of them shall taste of the Supper of the Lord.

They will never know the enjoyment of communion with God.

Those who have been guilty of these paltry excuses will not drink the wine anew in the Father's Kingdom.

When We Should Hate Those Dear to Us.

Now there went with Him great multitudes and He turned, and said unto them

If any man cometh unto Me, and hateth not his own father, and mother, and wife, and children, and brethren, and sisters, yea, and his own life also, he cannot be My disciple.

Does that mean that we are really to hate our own fathers, mothers, brothers, wives, and children?

Are we to hate our own life?

Yes.

In the true sense we must look upon every obstacle as hateful and detestable, and not to be tolerated if it interferes with our obedience to God.

You understand?

If my own soul cries out, "I will not bear this cross! I will not carry it; I have done enough! It is time for me to rest and enjoy leisure," then my life is my enemy.

I must hate it.

I must say, "Life, you will not rule me in this way. I hate a life that is not willing to pour out the last drop of blood for the Lord."

It is a hateful thing to yield to the flesh when the flesh lusts against the spirit.

You must hate the flesh and give it the whip.

Many a time I have been so tired that I might have said, "Lord, I have done all I can; and I really cannot face that appointment; I have not any strength;" but I have never yielded to the flesh.

I have never in all my life failed to keep an appointment with God, although I sometimes have flogged myself, as it were

If my wife, my child, my brother, or friends should get between me and duty, I should say, "You are hateful to me. You are detestable to me. I detest you at this moment as much as I detest my own life when it cries out for gratification."

I Hate and Count Despicable Anything That Comes Between Me and Obedience to God.

When you are given a command, be sure it is from the Lord.

Some of you say, "The Lord told me to do so and so."

He never told you to do any such fool things as some of you imagine.

On the other hand, if you receive an order from qualified authority in any position where you have taken the place of a servant and you do not obey, you must get out.

He who gives you the order is responsible for the results.

When the first Legion of the Host was about to go to New York City, a woman came to me and asked what she should do.

"Did I not give orders that the entire Host go?" I asked.

"Oh, yes," she replied, "but I have a baby."

"I have provided nurses for that baby," I replied, "who will take good care of it, over there in Elijah Hospice."

"Oh, but I cannot leave it," she insisted.

I then said, "Get out of Zion Restoration Host quickly, if you love your baby more than you do Obedience to God."

"But I do not want to do that," she said.

"Then put your baby into the hands of Deaconess Irish. My opinion is that your baby will be much better cared for than it would be in your hands."

"Oh," was all she said.

"I do not think you take very good care of the baby."

I had my own opinion about her.

I had seen how that baby was cared for, and I knew that Deaconess Irish would care for it better than she did.

God Blesses and Provides for Those Who Obey.

She went away crying, and said that the General Overseer was very hard, and would not listen to anything that she had to say.

Time went on; still they could not consent to leave the baby.

At last they wrote me a pathetic letter, and said that they did not have enough money to go, to which I answered that I did not say they had to have money, I merely told them to go.

"But how can one go without money?" they asked.

"You can sell something and get the money," was all I would say.

I was not going to give them the money.

I could have done it, as I did to many, but I thought it best not to.

Subsequently I saw the woman and her husband

I had said something about the way they were keeping their children, and I saw that they were much better kept.

They came to me with bright faces and said, "General Overseer, we had some correspondence with our brother, who is not a Christian, and we said how sorry we were that we had not the money to go with the Host, and he sent us the money."

"What about the baby?" I asked.

"O Doctor, we will leave the baby," and the baby was left.

They left not only the baby, but three or four other children, who were quite young.

None of them were old enough to take care of themselves.

I saw these people going about New York; their faces shone, they were so happy.

They were having the first real holiday they had had in all their married life, and they were enjoying it.

They were also beginning to understand.

Overseer Speicher—"Not one of the babies left by mothers with the nurses provided had any evil thing happen to them, but two babies died whose mothers remained with them at home."

General Overseer—Is not that remarkable?

All That Was Asked Was Obedience.

I should hate the life that I could save only by skulking from duty.

The Lord does not mean that you should hate your own flesh and blood, but that you are to hate any obstacle that comes between you and obedience.

I should have been deprived of at least four or five hundred of my best workers in New York City if they had said, "I cannot leave my baby."

I took care of the babies.

They were in splendid condition when the mothers came back.

One person said to me, "I cannot leave my old mother."

I said, "I will take care of your mother."

I was willing to provide the means, but I did not need to, because later the young lady said, "It was so very kind of you, General Overseer, to say that you would do it, but you do not need to

"A sister of mine, who is not in the Host, nor even a member of Zion, said, 'If you would like to go to New York, I will come and take care of mother,' and she did."

A great many people who helped this Host go to New York were not members of Zion.

Zion Children Filled With the Spirit of Sacrifice.

I could tell you of many outside people who admired the pluck of Zion, and who knew that there were poor people here.

I took up a big collection here one day, and I think I got several thousand dollars.

Gifts were offered that were afterwards sold, and the proceeds used to defray the expenses of the poorer people

People came with rings and all kinds of things, and one little girl brought her doll.

I saw her look at it longingly, so I bought the doll myself, and to her surprise she found it at home that night.

In another case, I did not buy the old doll, but I gave it away, and I had the joy of sending another doll to the little girl, who said, when she saw it, "Oh, I gave my dolly, but God sent me another!"

We got the Blessing.

If there were any that went down to New York in the wrong spirit, they did not get much blessing, but I do not believe there were many who went in the wrong spirit.

I emphasize this at this conference, because willingness to sacrifice is the essence of the whole matter.

On the other hand, Zion must be strong enough to do what is properly and rightfully undertaken by the Storehouse.

I should never think of sending Overseer Speicher and his dear wife to Europe without seeing that the proper provision was made for their children.

Zion Provides for Her Own.

Overseer Speicher—"If we never come back, you may conconsider that I have given the children to you."

General Overseer—In that event I will be a good deal richer than I am now.

I will take care of those children, and, if I am taken away, I will see that they are taken care of.

Zion proposes to take care of all her children, without any distinction as to parentage.

We have never yet handed over an orphan child to a public institution, and, thank God, we never shall! [Applause.]

We have never handed over an old mother to be cared for in a poorhouse.

Zion takes care of the old mothers. My good wife has a fund on which she draws for this purpose.

It is God's business to take care of His own poor, and in such a way that the flush of shame shall not be upon their faces.

I do not want any one to neglect his duty.

I want you all to be able to say, "God will provide; if not in one way He will in another. The General Overseer will not give me an order to do something and then let my children suffer and starve."

We cannot afford to lose a child.

We cannot afford to lose one of our old people.

We want them to live out their lives.

There are some dear old people that are worth a dozen of some of you young people.

They are a benediction and a blessing.

Grumblers Had Better Go to Heaven.

Of course, when they grumble and find fault, I am apt to say, "May that old mother go to heaven. It is time she was there."

When people begin to grumble, I shall pray that they may get to heaven quickly.

I want to have pleasant memories of you all after you are gone; so, if anybody grumbles, I shall pray, "God Almighty, take this dear child home before we have too many memories of her grumbling."

Sometimes I wish all the murmurers were in heaven; every one of them is an awful curse here.

The point I wish to emphasize is that no matter who the person is, he must not be allowed to stand between you and Obedience to God.

A Cross That Looks Beautiful But Which Is Very Heavy.

I once asked a person, "What are you doing?" and he replied, "O Doctor, I am bearing a heavy Cross."

"But what are you doing in the way of work?" I persisted.

"O Doctor," he complained, "the Cross is so heavy that I can only stay at home."

Why do you not get up and carry the Cross as the Lord commanded? Now look at it: "Whosoever doth not bear his own cross and come after Me, cannot be My disciple."

God does not want you to lie at home, bearing your Cross.

I suspect that you are bearing no Cross whatever.

"O Dr. Dowie," some say, "if we were all like you, and had the kind of Cross you have, we should like to carry it."

Would you? I will give you my Cross.

How many could stagger under it for only twenty-four hours?

You think my Cross is so beautiful and so jewelled, but do you know the weight of it?

If God did not increase my strength to correspond with the increasing weight of the Cross I should fall under its weight.

But I have never fainted under it.

I know that God would not give me the Cross without also giving me the necessary strength to carry it.

Some of You Bear Crosses That Are Not Your Own.

That is your trouble.

Some of you have gone away and adopted children that God Almighty never told you to adopt, and you have a hard cross, because you did something that you ought not to have done.

I once saw a woman wreck her home by adopting a child that was a poor child of shame, with a bad inheritance.

Her husband said, "God did not put that child in our home."

"But I feel so sorry for the child," she replied, "and I must adopt it."

Although the husband did not want the child, she was put in the home in spite of him.

She was a little thief, and a liar, and a dirty little thing, and vexed that man's soul.

She had not been with them two years before she was put in prison.

Over and over again she got into trouble, until at last she well-nigh broke his heart; she caused his name to be branded with shame in the city where before he had stood so well.

That wife gave him a Cross that God Almighty had nothing to do with.

The Devil gave it to him.

Be very sure that God gives you the Cross.

Others Carry Burdens That Never Had Existence.

Your business is to carry the Cross that God permits.

Some people say, "I am bearing a heavy burden for Zion."

To some of these I have asked, "What are you bearing for Zion?"

One replied, "Oh, my heart is oppressed, because there are so many things that are not right in Zion."

"When did God give you the Cross of taking care of Zion?" I asked.

"Oh, but He has laid it upon me."

"The Lord have mercy upon you; you are a fool; you are trying to carry my Cross."

"But I have made it mine."

"No wonder you are down in the dust. You are attempting to carry something that belongs to me."

It was some time before I could make that man see that he was very foolishly trying to carry my burden, and that nine-tenths of the burden he did carry was all bosh.

He said to me in deep compassion, "A young man was cruelly turned out of Zion by Dr. Speicher while you were away, because he was outspoken and would tell the truth about things."

I called up those who could give me information concerning this young man, and I found that fellow had committed adultery, had stolen, had lied, and was a child of the Devil through and through.

He would not repent, but kept on lying, and the Overseer did the only thing he could.

The man of whom I am telling you, was carrying the burden of this wicked young man.

I asked him how he knew about this alleged injustice, and he said that the young man himself told him.

I talked with this man again yesterday, and heard more trash and nonsense.

I let him talk on, for I wanted to hear the whole thing.

I found that he was carrying all kinds of burdens that never existed.

There are some of you who undertake to carry burdens other than your own, because you are meddlesome and intrude yourselves into business that does not concern you

When Punished, People Tell Their Own Stories.

He had heard it all "from the party himself"—from the young man who is being punished for his sins.

Did you ever visit a prison and speak to the prisoners?

One day after making such a visit in a certain prison, the governor said to me, "Well, Mr. Dowie how did you get on?"

"Why, Governor ——," I exclaimed, "this prison is filled with honest people; not one of whom has committed a single crime." [Laughter.]

It was perfectly laughable.

They had all told me that they were innocent, and had been put there by trickery on somebody's part.

One fellow was a cruel murderer, and he told me that he was perfectly innocent.

If you are going to take the word of the guilty party that has been punished, you will have to believe that at least four-fifths of the people in prisons never committed any crime.

Did you ever go into a lunatic asylum?

I used to often visit lunatic asylums, and it was very seldom I found any one that was insane.

Every one of them could tell me that they were wrongfully held there.

One little woman came to me one day and said, "O Doctor, can you not liberate me?"

She was a very sweet little woman and was dressed in a very simple, but nice way.

We found that she belonged to a good family, and they allowed her to dress as she had been accustomed to.

She began to talk so sensibly that it seemed impossible that she was insane.

But very soon she gave herself away.

She said, "I suppose you know who I am?"

"No," I answered, "I have not that pleasure."

"I am Queen Victoria," she said, "and they are keeping me here in this asylum."

A little nun stepped up just then, dressed in black robes, and said, "Do not believe her, I have seen Queen Victoria, and she is not a bit like her."

Here and there in that asylum I would find one who would admit that he or she had periods of insanity, but there was no indication of mental disease during the conversation.

For instance, a lady said to me, "I am perfectly sane today, Dr. Dowie; I know I am; but I know that I ought not to be liberated from this place, because I never can count upon a day's sanity. When I least expect it, darkness comes over me, and for weeks at a time I do not know what happens."

During those periods she would curse, and lie, and cheat, and steal, if left to herself, and would commit the most terrible and cunning assaults.

I say this to you to show that you are in a world where, if you believe everything that you hear, you will load yourself with needless anxieties and swallow countless lies, compared to which the lies of Hearst's *American* are nothing.

You Are not Responsible for the Administration in Zion.

In the work of Restoration you cannot be gossipers.

In Zion City you are not to spend your time in listening to stories; you have something better to do.

You have nothing whatever to do with the Administration of Zion City.

You may rest assured that we are after the things that are evil, and we will find them out very quickly.

Your business is to carry the Peace of God, and to deal with the individual; but if you take the burden of these long, foolish stories, you will never get around your district.

Be quick and bright about your work.

Leave the Message in the heart.

Leave it with a bright smile.

If some future work is needed at any home in your district, note the name and address, and hand it to some Elder or Overseer or some other officer, and they will look up the case; but you pass on with your Message from house to house.

You do not have to undertake all the minute work of relieving poverty.

Do Not Talk About What You Do Not Understand.

For instance, if some one says to you, "I should like you to give me the Scriptural proofs for Triune Immersion and for the Elijah position," remember that that is not your business.

You can get the proofs for Triune Immersion in two tracts that I have had published.

You also can find the Elijah question discussed in the various issues of LEAVES OF HEALING, in a much clearer and more scholarly way than you could ever discuss it.

You have a large supply of Literature to draw upon—you have all Zion's publications.

It will cost you but a few cents, and if you cannot afford that, Zion's Free Distribution Fund will supply you with Literature with which to help others.

But if in reply to inquiries you say that you fully understand the matter, when you do not, and attempt an explanation, you will get involved in difficulties, and your questioner will see that you do not understand the subject.

Is not that stupid?

I do not myself discuss with every one who desires me to do so.

I say to them, "There is what I have written and said about it; read that.

Greatest Troubles Those That Never Happen.

Take care that you do not assume Crosses that God never laid upon you. Half of your trouble is caused by thinking of what may happen.

Remember that good old man who, although he had been very cheerful and bright all his life, called his sons around his bedside and began to mourn.

"Father, are you sick?" they asked in surprise.

"No, I am not sick."

"Why, then, should you call for us?" they asked.

"I am going to die. I am weary of this body and I think it time that I should have some rest.

"Boys, I do not want to bother you to come to me at a time of the year when it might not be convenient to you, and so I thought I would call you now, in view of the possibility that I may pass away.

"I am pretty well worn out," he continued, in a complaining voice; "I have had a lot of trouble in this life."

They were very much amused, because he had passed through life very cheerfully.

"But, father," they said, "you never told us about it."

"Oh, boys," he said again, "I have had lots of trouble in this life," and then added, with a twinkle in his eye, "but, boys, the most of it did not happen."

That is what he wanted to show them.

Nine-tenths of the troubles that some people fear will come upon them never happen.

Do not carry that Cross of troubles that may not happen.

If they do happen, will it give you any strength to make a great cross of them?

It may be that there will be real trouble, "but sufficient unto the day is the evil thereof."

Do Not Bear Crosses That God Does Not Give You.

Take up "your own Cross," daily, and follow the Christ.

I met a lady some years ago in one of the western cities, who said, "Oh, my dear Doctor, I am so grieved for you. I am carrying a heavy burden on my heart for you."

"Why do you carry burdens for me?" I asked.

"You have so much persecution, that I have been weeping all night about it"

"You are a goose," I said, "I have not been weeping all night; I have been sleeping."

"Well," she said, "I love you so, and I would do anything for you."

"Are you sure you would do anything for me?" I asked.

"Can you show me something I can do for you?" she said.

"Yes, do not exercise your waterworks; then you will be of considerable use. If you wear a smiling face, you will be able to reach people's hearts with the Truths of God."

"Now go home and get a good dinner and a good sleep, and let me see you tomorrow."

I saw her the next day, and it was a joy to see her happy face.

I never saw her again exercise her waterworks for me.

I do not want you to weep for me.

I carry my own Cross, and without weeping.

Worry Is Selfishness.

I have been disgusted, not comforted, by hearing that a few foolish people were lying awake at night, crying, because they feared I might be killed.

That is very selfish of you.

If I had not come back, I would have gone to heaven, would I not?

"Oh, but you are needed here," you say.

Ah, the cat is out of the bag.

You were weeping, not because I would go to heaven, but because I would not be here to help you.

I never lost any sleep over any of my troubles.

My Visitation Party will tell you that on the night of one of the worst of these troubles, I went to sleep while the enemy were still howling in the street—about twenty or thirty thousand people.

I told the Lord that if he permitted them to come into the hotel and choke me it would be all right; but any way I was going to have a sleep before being choked. [Laughter.]

I remember that I laughed just as you are laughing now.

I went to sleep laughing.

Bury your sorrows and give others the sunshine.

If you have a sorrow, hide it with care.

Do not tell it to any one except God, and go on and do your work.

As you go about your work, you have only to carry your own Cross.

Do not let others see you are carrying a burden.

So therefore whosoever he be of you that renounceth not all that he hath, he cannot be My disciple.

Renounce All You Have in God's Favor.

You must say to God, and mean it, "O God, all that I have is Thine; I renounce the right to call it mine.

"Show me how to use it, and grant that I may never call it my own. I renounce it in Thy favor and I will use if for Thee."

That is what is meant by the words that I have just read.

Let the Lord have the control.

All these instructions are given in connection with the parable of going out into the streets and lanes of the cities, and into the highways and hedges.

The only man or woman who is a true disciple of the Master, and who can go forth and do this work, is the one who will obey these instructions.

As God's Prophet, I am dealing with vastly important matters when I plan and work to set you free from your burdens.

God Will Supply Strength and Wisdom for the Work He Assigns You.

Go on with your work and God will give you strength for it.

I get strength for my work.

I do enough work to kill half a dozen men, but I have passed through it.

I do not burden myself about it, I only do my best.

Do your work and renounce all you have in God's favor.

I want you to be ready to obey the orders of the Lord, which will be given you through the General Overseer.

We will take very great care that he does not issue orders that are not sensible.

Some people imagine I do things very rashly.

On the contrary, I act very deliberately.

It takes me a long time to make up my mind to certain courses of action.

If I had been rapid in deciding these things I should have done great damage.

I am slow in coming to a decision; but when I have decided, I go ahead and do the work.

If you have come to a decision, then you can work for God in Zion Restoration Host under my direction.

I want you never to waver, but to stand by that determination

I now ask you at this point to make a Solemn Declaration to God that you will put aside every Cross except the one that God gives you—your own Cross.

There are people that sometimes think they have to carry the Cross of Jesus; they say that and they sing it.

Do you imagine for a moment that you can carry the Cross of Jesus?

Overseer Speicher—"No, not even one little end of it."

General Overseer—Do you imagine you can carry my Cross? You cannot, not even for one moment

Jesus Carried His Own Cross.

There is no need that another should carry it.

It was carried to Victory.

Do we continue to carry it?

Verily, No. The Book says that every man must carry his own Cross.

We glory in the Cross of Jesus, but we do not carry it.

Who gave you the Cross of Jesus to carry?

Have you to do the work of Jesus over again?

He could carry it only because He was the Son of God, with Power.

I am carrying my Cross to Victory.

You cannot take any bit of it from me; you make it heavier when you attempt to take it.

I emphasize this today as one of the principal things in connection with this teaching.

Carry your own Cross, but do not attempt to carry the Cross of Jesus.

Glory in the Cross of Jesus.

Do not Inflict Your Sorrows upon Others.

Let us ask God to make us a practical people, and instead of carrying imaginary crosses and burdens, let us so conceal even our own Crosses that others will think that we have none.

Many times I have stood upon this and other platforms with a tremendous responsibility, with a tremendously heavy cross to bear; with a sad heart.

But I have knelt and left my burden with the Lord, and I gave you nothing but brightness, and joy, and blessing.

It was not for me to load my sorrows upon you.

You could not bear them; you had no right to bear them.

I want real Restorationists, bright and happy, carrying smiles and sunshine.

There may be a time when, as a preacher, I have to do things that are hard; but, oh, when I carry the Message of God to the fainting heart, I want to carry it with a joyful spirit.

All present then joined in silent prayer, after which the General Overseer said:

Let us have a word or two from Overseer Speicher before I administer the Vow.

The Host Cannot Rest Upon Its Past Work.

Overseer Speicher—"Beloved General Overseer: It seems to me that there is scarcely room for anything more to be said.

"I have great regard for the future of Zion Restoration Host.

"I heartily agree with the General Overseer, that it is his Battle-ax

"The work that has been done by the Host has been most precious, I believe, in the sight of God, and it is only the beginning of what will be done if the Host is faithful.

"We cannot rest upon what has been done

"I especially like the thought that has been expressed that we should leave the past behind us

"We can go forward and do something better than that which has been done.

"We are only getting to where God can fully use us.

"It is with a great deal of joy and anticipation that I go to Europe and there look into the faces of Zion Restoration Host at the various Branches of Switzerland, Germany, Austria-Hungary, and perhaps other countries.

"I wish I could carry them a report of this meeting in their own language.

"They can read it in BLÄTTER DER HEILUNG and in LEAVES OF HEALING.

"The people are so good, so loyal, and so faithful, especially in these far-away lands.

"I wonder how it can be that through the reading of the printed page, Restorationists, who are glad to go into the field, are springing up everywhere.

"I rejoice today in the prospects of Zion Restoration work.

"May God bless you, and may every one be faithful and willing to fulfil the Vow already taken and to carry out the Vow that shall be taken.

"This is my prayer."

General Overseer—Candidates for membership in Zion Restoration Host, who have not yet been set apart, please to stand [Candidates stand.]

It is a wonderful sight to see this vast company, composed very largely of people living outside of Zion City, who are about to take the Vow.

I am so glad to see you, dear Southern people, and you who have come from across the ocean, and you dear Canadian people, and those from all the States.

A Vow, a Declaration, and a Promise.

The Vow will be read to you by Elder Abraham F. Lee, and you will be asked to repeat it, clause by clause.

I wish to point out to you that the Vow is made in the Name of the Triune God, that you will be a faithful member of Zion Restoration Host.

The Declaration is that you recognize John Alexander Dowie, General Overseer of the Christian Catholic Church in Zion, of which you are a member, in his three-fold prophetic office, as the Messenger of the Covenant, the Prophet foretold by Moses, and Elijah the Restorer; these three offices being combined in the same officer.

Sometimes an officer in the Church of God may have thirty offices.

For instance, the President of the United States is not only the President, but he is Commander-in-chief of the Army; he is the Admiral of the Navy; he is the Head of the Police Force of the country; he is the Chief of the Treasury; and he has scores of other positions

He is President of the United States, but he has many other offices.

There are three offices here that we believe are combined in the one man.

I believe that you all understand, because you are a well-instructed people, and have read LEAVES OF HEALING and know all about it.

A Promise to Obey Only Rightful Orders.

The Promise is that, to the fullest extent of all your power, you will fully obey all rightful orders

That does not mean wrong orders.

If I should be so misled by myself or by the Devil (which God forbid) as to give you orders to do something which the Word of God forbids, you would be under no obligation to obey that, because it would not be a rightful order.

Should I command you to steal, or to murder (which God forbid), it would be a wicked and unrighteous order, which you must not obey

I call your attention to this, because there are some persons that have asserted that you promise to obey all orders.

That is not the promise, but a promise to obey all "rightful orders issued by him directly, or by his properly appointed officers."

I call your attention to the clause: "and to proceed to any part of the world, wherever he shall direct, as a member of Zion Restoration Host."

Some of you may hesitate and say, "I am too old to cross the ocean"

Do you think that the General Overseer, as Elijah the Restorer, would be so foolish as to ask you to do something that was impossible for you to do?

I want you to trust me in that matter, because in our first Visitation to New York City, I told the entire Host that if there were any who could see any just reason why they should be excused from going to New York City, I should be glad to hear it.

I did excuse a large number who could not have gone without sin.

It would have been wicked for them to have gone.

Some of these were able to do splendid work for the Host by giving money to others who could not have gone without that assistance.

If I command the Host to cross with me to London, I shall make this exception: Any persons who can show me just and proper reasons why they should not go, will be excused.

This Vow is reasonable; it has the qualifications which good sense and the Spirit of God imposes.

A Clause of the Vow Which Will Cause Trouble.

I also mention this clause: "And that all family ties and obligations, and all relations to all human government shall be held subordinate to this Vow, this Declaration, and this Promise."

I must tell you that this clause will surely get you into

trouble; and if you want to escape trouble, do not enter Zion Restoration Host.

If you say, "I will not bear any tribulation for the Lord," then keep out of Zion Restoration Host, because Jesus said, "In the world ye shall have tribulation: but be of good cheer; I have overcome the world."

If you say, "I will place my family ties and obligations above this Vow to God, this Declaration, and this Promise," then you are not fit for Zion Restoration Host.

I will not send you out of the Church, but we will not have you in the Host.

We must have a Host, with the exceptions I have made, that I know I can depend upon to rise and go in a moment, at the word of command.

That is the great power of this Host.

I shall give you an illustration.

Suppose I should believe that it was the right thing for me to go down to St. Louis (which I do not believe) with a Legion of this Host.

I should not hesitate to give that order within three days of my going, and expect the Host in Zion City to obey it.

Would you do it?

Restorationists—"Yes."

General Overseer—You might be called upon to go into a country that says that if any person obeyed the orders of Elijah the Restorer, he shall be fined ten dollars or fifty dollars; would you obey the orders even if you were fined?

Restorationists—"Yes."

General Overseer—That law would be illegal in the sight of God, and I believe illegal under all their constitutions.

If I were claiming to direct you in matters that would involve your disloyalty to government, it would be another thing.

I do direct my people to pray in all parts of the world that monarchy may fall; but while they are under the monarchy, and while the laws exist, I direct them to obey these laws, if they are not inconsistent with the Law of God.

I know that one day this may possibly be a difficulty in foreign countries.

I want you to understand that this Vow and Declaration and Promise in the Kingdom of God takes you above family, business, and state—it means that you will obey God first, last, and all the time.

If any of you do not want to take that Vow, after having heard this brief exposition, and after having heard it read by the Recorder, then I should like you to step out of the ranks.

It is a very grave matter.

The gravest thing I have ever done in my life was to form this Host.

This Host stands upon a basis different from any organized effort that has ever existed.

The Power as Leader of Zion Restoration Host Used Only for God's Glory.

It will be two years next September since the Host was organized, and during that time we have had some interesting experiences.

I will ask the Overseers and Elders present whether any member of the Host has ever had any rightful reason to say that I used my power in a tyrannical way—a way that would not extend the Kingdom of God? [Answers, "No, No!"]

I have been careful to see that the power to direct you, which you by your Vow give me, has not been misused.

I have asked God to keep me from ever giving a command in this Host that should not be for His glory.

Much more could be said, but I shall say only this one thing in closing: Zion Restoration Host has already been a power throughout the whole world, such as the Christian Catholic Church in Zion has never seen.

The World-wide Work of the Host.

If it continues to grow in the same ratio as in the last two years, it can be said, in a few more years, that this Host is carrying the Gospel directly to one-third of the human race.

In twenty years I believe that I shall be able to say, if I stand on the earth, that this Host has been able to carry the Message of the Christ's Peace to every human being in the whole world. [Amen.]

I am planning that, inside of twenty years, there shall not be a human being of any tongue or nation upon God's earth who shall be able to say, "I never heard the Message of Peace."

This is my expectation and my ambition, if I may so put it.

Then cometh the End, for this Gospel of the Kingdom will then have been preached as a witness to every creature on the earth.

You may think that it cannot be done.

But it can be done.

Inside of ten years I will be able to cover the City of London with ten thousand people working under my direction.

We know what we are talking about.

Brothers and sisters, you and I are being summoned by God to the greatest work of all the ages.

There are many other things that the Host will do besides carrying the Message.

Out of this Host will be taken Deacons and Deaconesses, Evangelists and Elders, and mighty workers for all the institutions.

This Host is merely being organized; what it will do only God can tell.

The Power of the Host Limited Only by the Earth's Bounds.

The power of this Host in the work for the Christ is limited only by the size of the earth itself, for I see no reason why I should not carry this Host to the furthermost bounds of human habitation—North, East, South, and West.

With these explanations I say again that if any feels he cannot take a Vow like this, after it has been read let him retire.

Elder Lee then read the Vow while the candidates, with uplifted hands, solemnly repeated it after him, clause by clause

The General Overseer then said:

In the Name of the Lord Jesus, the Christ, in the Power of the Holy Spirit, and in accordance with the Will of God, our Eternal Father, I receive your Vow, your Declaration, and your Promise, and pray that you may keep it, not only in the letter, but in the spirit.

I pray that you and I, when earth is passed, shall meet in the Rapture, and by and by, when that is over, come back with the Christ to carry on the Restoration throughout the Millennium.

Clearer and clearer do we see that this is but the beginning.

While we believe that it will be a glorious beginning, and while we believe that God will enable us to gather into Cities many of His people; and while we believe that much good will be done and vast areas covered, and the whole earth witnessed to, yet we believe that it will not be until we come back with the Christ that the work will be finished.

I believe that if I am faithful now, the Lord will, in His infinite love and mercy, give me grace to carry forward, as the Prophet of the Restoration, under His own Divine direction, the work that will be needful in the Consummation of All Things.

The Consummation of This Age Is Rapidly Approaching.

Beloved, let us be as if we had no other business in the world, except to do the Will of God.

Let us do the Will of God in all the work that we have in the world.

May God bless you!

It is a great trust that you have put into my hands—the trust of your direction.

I know that never before in the world have the people of God been willing to put the concentrated powers of their office and all they have under the direction of any prophet in any age

Therefore, next to putting yourself into God's own hands, this is the greatest proof of your affection, and your absolute conviction that the prophetic power and right is mine.

I take it as a great blessing from God, and I know that He who has given me grace to use this power somewhat in the past, will give me grace to use it still better in the future.

My brethren and my sisters, I depend, under God, upon your loyalty and your prayers.

As your leader, you must hold me up before God.

Unless God lead me, I cannot lead you successfully.

Unless God gives me the resources, I cannot do the work effectually.

If I am led by God, I shall surely be provided with the resources necessary to carry out the work.

With me there is no fear, no doubt, and I hope no impatience.

I am determined to secure every step I take, and to take no step forward that I will afterward have to retrace.

I thank God that I have never turned my back to the foe.

The General Overseer then laid hands upon and consecrated to God four hundred fifty-nine persons for Zion Restoration Host.

BENEDICTION.

Beloved, abstain from every form of evil. And may the very God of Peace Himself sanctify you wholly; and I pray God your whole spirit and soul and body be preserved entire, without blame, unto the coming of our Lord Jesus, the Christ. Faithful is He that calleth you, who also will do it. The grace of our Lord Jesus, the Christ, the love of God, our Father, the fellowship of the Holy Spirit, our Comforter and Guide, one Eternal God, abide in you, bless you and keep you, and all the Israel of God everywhere, forever. Amen.

EARLY MORNING SACRIFICE OF PRAISE AND PRAYER.

REPORTED BY S. E. C., O. V. G., AND E. S.

As sublime, as far reaching as Faith itself, was the Message.

Long before the hour set for the service, the people wended their way from every point of the little City whose very existence was the expression of that Fruit of the Spirit which was the theme of the Message delivered by the man of God.

So simple that the veriest child might understand was the beautiful lesson given at the Early Morning Meeting of Wednesday, July 20, 1904, on "Faith, the Seventh Fruit of the Spirit."

Shiloh Tabernacle, Zion City, Illinois, Wednesday Morning, July 20, 1904.

The service was begun by the singing of Hymn No. 35, in the special Program.

The General Overseer then offered prayer, concluding by leading the Congregation in the chanting of the Disciples' Prayer.

The announcements were then made.

Referring to the approaching rendition of "The Messiah" by Zion White-robed Choir and Zion Orchestra, the General Overseer remarked concerning the Choir:

A Wonderful Combination.

This Choir is a wonderful combination.

It combines, first of all, the Zion people in it—our own young people.

Many of these fresh, young voices are the voices of those whose parents have been in Zion, and who themselves have been in Zion, since 1890, 1891, 1892, 1893, 1894, and right on.

Little children, who came into the Divine healing meetings and were healed in 1893, 1894, 1895, 1896, etc., are now grown into young men and women, and are singing in our Choir.

They are singing with an Inspiration and a Power that we know has a tremendous spiritual quality in it, because they are the children of Zion singing the songs of Zion.

Indeed, many in our Junior Choir were born since their parents came into Zion.

Their voices have the peculiar sweetness incident to a life that has been in touch with Zion all the time.

Still more wonderful than that, however, is the fact that in the Band and Orchestra connected with this Choir we have musicians who seem to unite the whole world.

From the Sunny South we have our brother, Deacon Bosworth, from Fitzgerald, Georgia.

He brings to us, in his splendid instrumentation, the inspiration of the Southland, and blended with it we have the strength of the Northland.

We have those who have been trained in Northern latitudes.

And we have the rich tones of the loving Germans, Mr. Möse and Mr. Burkhard, while our young Americans have the dash of the American people.

Preparation for Shiloah Tabernacle.

As I look at that Choir—I think it is the largest choir in the world; if there are any larger, I do not know of them; but there are none better, although it is only a beginning—I realize that it is not only a preparation for Shiloah Tabernacle, in which we hope they will sing next year, but for the worship of God in the glorious Temple which some day we hope to erect, and in which probably forty thousand people will unite in praise to God.

I am glad to know that the songs that these loved ones will sing tonight will draw the people from all parts, and I fear that the Tabernacle will be too small.

I ask you to pray for the Choir.

I want you to pray for those that will be present.

There is always a process of elimination in a great choir, and some step out because they find they are scarcely up to the required standard.

The standard is rising all the time.

It is becoming what I prayed and directed that it should be—a Choir that has in it the Desire and the Power to create Musical Inspiration in those that do not have much.

I am thankful that it will be a great instrument in leading the praises of God.

Pray for the Choir, that, as it goes on from year to year and from generation to generation, it may become one of the mighty powers of God in reaching the hearts of men.

I wish more and more that I could put into music the thoughts of Zion.

The Music of Zion.

I am praying that God will raise up poets and composers who will be able to compose an Oratorio—one that will give expression to our aspirations.

Such an Oratorio can be written.

I have been thinking about it.

I have been almost wishing that I had the power to write it, and the time to take some part in it.

But this morning an Oratorio has been in my thoughts which I wish I might be able to put into words.

It might be called "Zion!"—simply "Zion!"

That Oratorio might become a mighty power.

We will sing "The Messiah" and other oratorios, and other Divine songs, until we have our own Oratorio—original, and yet not original, for, after all, it can be only a compilation of the glorious promises of God concerning Zion.

May God bless you!

Come tonight with glad hearts.

Do not come as to a mere concert.

It is to be no such thing.

It is to be Religious Worship.

If it were not to be an Evening Sacrifice of Praise and Prayer, I should have nothing to do with it; but to me the occasion will be worship, because I can pray through every line of the Oratorio.

Come in a prepared spirit; and pray for this Choir; and help me to make it what God wants it to be.

The General Overseer then said:

Let us read in the 11th chapter of the Epistle to the Hebrews

Faith.

Now Faith is the giving substance to the things hoped for.

This is the best rendering that we can get for that verse.

It is not simply the substance, but it is the ground, the confidence, the assurance, the embodiment, the giving substance to, and the making substantial; in other words, the embodiment to us of Spiritual Power in a psychical and physical form, thus making that Faith to take embodiment in everything that is good.

Sometimes Faith takes embodiment in a song that never dies; in a poem that is never forgotten; in a building that is the expression of the Faith of the builder.

It takes expression, in our case, very manifestly, in a City.

This is an act of Faith.

Because God gave me Faith this City came to be.

Because God gave you Faith to come and to help me secure the land, and to build the City, it has come to be.

Get that thought as we begin thinking about Faith this morning.

Divine Faith an Operative Power.

By Faith you test the promises of God.

You test me, and rightfully, by the standard, not of promises, but of performance.

You test one another by that standard.

Faith is the proving of things not seen.

The Unseen Powers are tested by Faith.

Faith proves the existence of that which you do not see.

I made the declaration, that a City could be established where alcohol, nicotine, doctors, and drugs should find no place, and that such a City would be a power.

That was a declaration.

We got together and proved that the Unseen Truth could find embodiment in visible manifestation.

That definition of Faith is tremendously far-reaching!

Faith toward God and toward man!

Faith toward those we love!

Faith!

It never can be lost, because it is Divine!

We are not talking about a human virtue, but one that is Divine. The Divine Power, the Divine Faith, is an operative, and tremendously operative, Power.

It is not quiescent.

As we continue to read we shall see that

Faith is the giving substance to things hoped for, the proving of things not seen.

For therein the Elders had witness borne to them.

By Faith we understand that the Worlds have been Framed by the Word of God.

There was the Word that said, "Let there be light!" and instantly there was light.

There was the Word that commanded Life by means of that Word, and all things came into being.

In Him was Life, and that Word, the Word of God, is the Christ.

It is the Christ of God that is spoken of here.

In the beginning was the Word, and the Word was with God, and the Word was God.

The same was in the beginning with God.

All things were made by Him; and without Him was not anything made that hath been made.

In Him was Life; and the Life was the Light of men.

And the Light shineth in the darkness, and the darkness apprehended it not.

The Word of God!

That is His Name.

We are not now speaking simply of some words that came from God.

The Word of God means, in the passage which we have quoted, the Eternal Word that was manifested in the flesh.

It was through Him and by Him that all things were created.

He had given Him the Power to Create, as well as to Redeem.

The Power was given Him, and He has that Power still.

He said Himself:

All Authority hath been given unto Me in Heaven and on Earth.

. . . .

By Faith we understand that the Worlds—

Not only this world, but the Worlds,

—have been framed by the Word of God, so that what is seen hath not been made out of things which do appear.

The Visible Is an Embodiment of the Invisible.

The wood, the timbers, of which this building is constructed, are all embodied sunbeams.

The light shone upon a little seed, and that seed grew into a tree; and the winds, and the rains, and the things which we do not see coöperated all through the generations to make successive generations of forests.

The visible has been created by the Invisible.

This order has always been observed.

Things that do appear are made of the things that do not appear.

The Spiritual and the Invisible are the Inspiration, and, indeed, the Constructive Power, of the things which are seen, so that:

What is seen hath not been made out of things which do appear.

By faith Abel offered unto God a more excellent sacrifice than Cain, through which he had witness borne to him that he was righteous, God bearing witness in respect of his gifts: and through it he, being dead, yet speaketh.

The Most Eloquent Voices Are Silent Voices.

They speak with the majesty of a Divine Silence.

We think of Moses and Daniel, men of might, and the Christ, whose human voices are silent, but who still speak.

Paul speaks.

John speaks, and his words reach down into the heart.

All the good and great lives of the past speak.

All that is good about men lives.

All that is base dies.

A man may even be on the wrong side of a question, and still be a majestic and beautiful character.

Robert E. Lee, doing his duty on the wrong side of the Civil War, was, in my judgment, a chevalier; but there were men on the right side of that war who had base, brutal passions.

They passed away, but the great and beautiful lives of men like Robert E. Lee and Stonewall Jackson, are still with us.

They were faithful according to their light, but, although on the wrong side, they loved God and their fellow men.

It is the love that lives after all the passion is gone.

All the mistakes die, and the great and good life lives in the historical records of humanity.

It is not always the best man who wins.

The best man may be mistaken, but he lives, for he is honest and true.

It is the man who lives, and the essential Purity of that life goes on.

I want to apply this thought to some noble persons who have lived in the past.

Men in Whom God's Faith Was Embodied.

We do not know much about Abel, but we begin with him because we know that he lives in that he was faithful to God.

When there were only two men in the world, he was the faithful one.

The other belonged to the Devil.

"By Faith," with a Faithless brother, a Godless brother, a perfect demon in human form, Abel still speaks.

We do not read of words of Faith that were uttered, but by Faith, Abel, second son—"vanishing breath," that is what his name means—still speaks.

By Faith Enoch was translated that he should not see death; and he was not found, because God translated him: for before his translation he hath had witness borne to him that he had been well-pleasing unto God.

This is a second character of which we know very little, but both are placed in the very front of all.

Enoch, the seventh from Adam, was, humanly speaking, a flawless character.

He was well-pleasing to God.

Therefore, he was translated, and did not see death.

Oh, one wishes so much that one had the full record of these lives.

A Wonderful Library Is Awaiting Students of History in the Life to Come.

In some form that story will be preserved.

I do not think it will be preserved with printers' ink.

I am glad to think that there will be no printers' ink in heaven.

I am glad to think that in heaven we will get away from the mechanical.

I have a belief that all these historical records will be preserved in a form akin to that of the record of the phonograph.

Sweet and beautiful voices will have recorded stories to which we can listen as they are spoken out from the records of the Glorious Land.

How glorious it will be to have all this thinking and beautiful expression come down to us in forms that are Divine!

Sometimes I think that some of the beautiful records of the past, which will be an inspiration even in heaven, will come to us in the beautiful harmony of music; that there will be Divine poetical expression, and a glorious cultivation, in heaven, of reverence and delight in God's wondrous ways.

Perhaps the story of Enoch will be told by Enoch himself, and the story of Abel will be told by Abel himself.

We may listen to the spirit that records the story, if we do not see the very man; or, still better, perhaps to some angelic spirit who is the historian of the man.

Do you not know that we have historians that are writing our lives as we never could write them?

Do you not know that these ministering spirits who minister unto them that are heirs and shall be heirs of salvation, are recording angels?

Do you not know that God has the record of the good that we have done and that we sometimes carefully conceal, or that is concealed from us?

Perhaps we never knew that we did it; we never knew that it came to pass.

God Keeps a Diary of Our Lives.

Do you not know that there is nothing in connection with these lives of ours that is not faithfully recorder?

I do not need to keep a diary.

God keeps it; the angels keep it—the record is there.

There are no mistakes in such records.

If I have done evil, the evil is recorded; unless by the infinite mercy of God it is repented of, and put away, and blotted out.

The page which the Blood of the Christ has washed will present no unclean record.

There is a Record that God Himself loves to preserve, the Record of the Lives of His Saints who are faithful; faithful in the dark and obscure places.

There are people that have maintained a Light in the window.

That was all that they could do.

They are poor men, poor women, uncultured, but they have loved God and lived the Life of God.

They had nothing that recommended them to man, but they were highly esteemed by God.

Who would not have the record of some of these obscure lives that were so great?

Who would not have the life of the poor African upon whom was laid the cross of the Christ; or the life of some of those whom the Christ healed, whose after-life was so full of beauty, but the record of which is lost?

I want you to remember that the record of these lives is lost only to our sight—that your record and mine, and the good that you have done, is not forgotten.

God has not forgotten.

There Is a Book of Remembrance

before Him for them that think upon His Name.

God never forgets.

There is a faithful record, and the story of Enoch will one day be known.

It was his Faith that was again embodied in the person of Noah.

Enoch was the ancestor of Noah, and the record that we have—fragments of the Book of Enoch—show that.

I suppose that some day we will have the book itself.

I suppose that no Bible author had so perfect a knowledge of the story of man's fall and the story of the angels that kept not their first estate, as Enoch.

He seems to have been the historian of the antediluvian period.

Oh, how wonderful it will be to read the life of the man who was so pleasing to God that he never saw death!

Without Faith it is impossible to be well-pleasing to God, for he that cometh to God must believe that He is.

God the I AM.

He says I AM.

That is His Name.

All other Names are simply additions to that one.

The Name of God is I AM.

It is the Name of the Christ.

"I AM the Way, the Truth, and the Life."

"I AM the Good Shepherd."

"I AM the True Vine."

"I AM!"

"Before Abraham was, I AM!"

"What is His Name?" said Moses at the burning bush.

"When I go back an exile to Egypt, whom shall I say sent me?

"Forty years have I wandered in this wilderness; forty years have I fed sheep in this mountain of God.

"I am only a shepherd, obscure and far away.

"They will say, 'Who sent you?'

"What shall I say, O Thou, who art within the bush that is never consumed?"

The answer came clearly: "Say, I AM THAT I AM."

"I AM hath sent Me."

Do you not know that that is the only Name by which God reveals Himself?

You can only say, "He is!" But He is because He says "I AM."

I believe God is because He said, "I am the Resurrection and the Life: he that believeth on Me, though he die, yet shall he live: and whosoever liveth and believeth on Me shall never die. Believest thou this?"

Yes! I say I believe He is the Resurrection and the Life!

HE IS! He lived; He loved; He died; He rose again!

HE IS! HE IS the Advocate!

And when He says, "I am the Advocate," I say, "Thou art!"

That is Faith; Faith that believes that God is.

I AM! There is no possibility of getting beyond those words.

Everything else is superfluous, because everything else is more or less an explanation of the Eternal, Self-existing God, and faith finds its fundamental expression and its fundamental power in the continuous consciousness of an ever-existing God.

He says, I AM! We say, "Thou art! HE IS!"

We tell the world that HE IS!

HE IS coming!

> With joy we tell this scoffing age,
>   Christ that was dead has left the tomb;
> He lives above men's utmost rage,
>   And we are waiting Till He Come.

He is coming.

He said, "I come again."

He is coming, and we say HE IS.

God Is the Rightful Ruler.

He says, I AM!

We say that he that cometh unto God must believe that HE IS; and when we say, "Thou art," we believe it, or else our declaration is an awful mockery.

Without Faith it is impossible to please God—to be well-pleasing to God—for he that cometh unto God must believe that HE IS, and that He is what He says He is.

All His Covenants are preceded by that I AM!

I AM Jehovah-Tsid-kenu, Jehovah Thy Righteousness!

I AM Jehovah-Jireh, Jehovah thy Provider.

I AM Jehovah-Rophi, Jehovah thy Healer.

I AM Jehovah-Shammah, Jehovah thy Banner.

I AM Jehovah-Nissi, Jehovah thy Victory.

You always have to read I AM before the Covenant.

In connection with the Christ's assertions it occurs repeatedly.

"I AM the Living One; and I was dead, and behold, I am alive forevermore."

"I AM the Alpha and the Omega."

"I AM the Beginning and the End."

I AM! HE IS! THOU ART!

That is Faith.

Faith there finds its expression in naked confidence.

At the request of the General Overseer, the Congregation read with him, in unison, from the 22d verse of the 5th chapter of Galatians to the 26th verse of the same chapter.

The General Overseer then delivered his Message:

THE SEVENTH FRUIT OF THE SPIRIT: FAITHFULNESS.

INVOCATION.

Let the words of my mouth, and the meditation of my heart be acceptable in Thy sight, be profitable unto this people, and unto all to whom these words shall come, in this and every land, in this and all the coming time, Till Jesus Come. Amen.

TEXT.

But the Fruit of the Spirit is Love, Joy, Peace, Long-suffering, Kindness, Goodness, Faithfulness,
Meekness, Temperance: against such there is no Law.

I am glad that we have been able to consider these Gifts of the Spirit so far as to reach the Seventh Fruit of the Spirit.

In the Old Version that Gift is translated "Faith," but in the New Version it very properly reads "Faithfulness," because it is the Fruit of the Spirit and Embodiment of Faith that is especially meant here.

Faithfulness means full of Faith—full of Faith, with no degree of doubt.

I do not like to speak of my virtues, but, although as a teacher I am sometimes compelled to find an illustration of something in the lives of others that indicates doubt, I can truthfully say of myself that which, perhaps, not very many nowadays are able to say, that

I Never Doubted God.

I marvel that so few are able to say that they never doubted God.

I have never drawn a doubting breath—not one!

I never saw the day, or the hour, or the place, or the circumstance, where doubt of God had a moment's place in my heart

I give Him the glory for that, because He made me so.

I could not have made myself so.

I never thought there was anything wonderful about it.

I thought that everybody who knew God would never doubt Him.

How could they?

I was amazed when I found that there was such a thing as doubt in the world.

Doubt God!

Was not He my Father?

Had not He made me?

Was not everything that existed from His hands?

Had not He power to take care of me, and to eternally told me in His good and Eternally-loving Heart?

How could I doubt Him?

I could not understand.

When I came to the knowledge that there was such a thing as doubt, I could not understand it.

I could understand sin; I could understand how people might be overcome by temptation.

I could understand conflict with the powers of evil, but I could not understand a man or a woman who could doubt God.

Oh, that seemed such a desperately wicked thing!

I never doubted my mother.

I could not doubt her—she loved me so.

Doubt her!

It never entered my mind.

It does not enter into the mind of a child to doubt a true mother—one who is not a liar or a cheat; but mind you, there are many mothers that are liars

The Awful Sin of Parents' Lying to Children.

Think of a mother, a sweet mother, lying to her child!

I was visiting a gentleman one night, several years ago, and said, "We had better be going. We have hardly time to get to our destination."

His wife was to go with us.

"Oh," he said, "she is just lying down in the bedroom of our little baby boy, pretending that she is going to sleep there, and when he falls asleep she will get up, finish her dressing, and come."

"Oh," I replied, "if that baby boy wakes up and does not find his mother there, he will say, 'Mother lied; she pretended that she was going to stay with me in the room;' and he will say, 'Mother! Mother! Mother!' She will not be there, and he will cry, and then he will say, 'She lied to me; she just pretended, and she left me.' Do you know you and your wife are making that child a liar? You are making that child doubt everything you say."

How Doubt Is Sown in the Human Heart.

I suppose it is in this way that doubt is sown in the human heart, in the very earliest stages of life, because the children are deceived.

"Just amuse that child."

"How are you going to amuse her?"

"Just tell her the story of 'Jack, the Giant Killer;' or 'Jack and the Beanstalk.' You know the whole story.

"Tell a story from 'Mother Goose;' tell the story of 'Mother Hubbard.'"

You miserable liar!

You have told that child a whole mass of lies, and the child talks about 'Mother Goose,' and 'Jack and the Beanstalk,' and how Jack killed the Giant, and suddenly one day you have to say, "Now, stop that!"

The little girl replies, "Why should I stop?

"Mother, you told me those stories.

"You told me that fairy tale about Santa Claus.

"You told me that lie."

Yes, your mother made you a liar.

Your mother told you lies, and now you doubt, and you do not know that the Bible is not a story on an equal footing with the Santa Claus pretense.

That is how people are filled with lies.

One day a very sweet, little girl friend of mine came to me, and said, "Johnnie, come," and I went with her.

I was very susceptible to her influence.

I remember how she led me by the hand, and took me to a picture shop where Mother Goose stories were displayed.

Perhaps I might have been five years of age, and she a little older.

We read together.

"Oh!" I said, "come away; come away, Marjorie, come away!"

"Why?" she replied.

"It is all Lies," I said, "it is all Lies about 'Jack and the Beanstalk!'"

I am so glad that I never believed these things!

The daily tale of lies that the so-called reading public demands is largely responsible for the fact that there are so many infidels in the world today.

Readers of the papers demand a serial novel—a whole mass of abominable lies, concocted in the brain of some man or woman

They must have their cartoonist and their joker, telling lies

They have to joke, and therefore they have to imagine things.

They have to make out that Dr. Dowie went into the smoking-room in the *Lucania*, and that there was an awful row; that they have puffed tobacco smoke in his face, and that at the las got out. The whole thing never happened.

Lies! Why, the world is full of lies.

The Lies of the Religious Press.

Religious papers lie.

They copy into their papers lies concerning me which they know are lies.

They print advertisements that they know are lies. Among them are advertisements of drugs of all kinds, and of spurious investments that are cheats.

Vast numbers of people have been made absolutely poor by believing advertisements of religious papers.

Just now, I had a cry put into my hands which reads something like this:

"Pray God, Doctor, that what little Faith I have may not be absolutely swept away. I believed an advertisement guaranteed by the editor of a certain religious paper, and I took all the money I had and invested it.

"That advertisement was a lie! That editor was hand and glove with a scoundrel, and my money is gone!"

Faith is lost through the telling of lies by liars.

Sometimes these liars are women who are exceedingly sweet in appearance.

They are unmarried, perhaps, but when they get married, out comes the Devil.

Then there are the men.

You would think to hear them talk that butter would not melt in their mouths.

Oh, they are so loving!

If only they can get you to marry them, what will they not do?

Liars! The moment they get married, they say, "Excuse me, I cannot help it. I must go back to my smoke."

The stinkpots!

The beerpots!

The cheats!

The liars!

They said that they would help you to live a holy life, and they nearly wrecked you in time and for eternity, because you believed them as you believed God.

It is Impossible For God to Lie.

Is it not good to know that?

You can say that about no one else.

Peter, the President of the Apostolic College, when he was hard put to it, lied.

"Peter, you are an Apostle?"

"I am not."

"I saw you with Jesus. I heard you say you believed He was the Son of God."

"It is a lie! You did not!"

And he uttered oaths and curses, because he was afraid he would be arrested; he was afraid he would be flogged; he was afraid he would be crucified.

A coward is always a liar.

I do not want to speak about myself, but I have to do it

Do you know why Faith has always been in me?

It is because I never was afraid.

Faith will exist only, and Faithfulness toward God is possible only, if you are not afraid; but if you have once been afraid, it is easy to be afraid again.

The army that has once retreated, can be kept running.
The Japanese have licked the Russians again and again.
They will keep licking them, until they destroy their armies, because the Russians have cowardice in their hearts.
They are afraid of these little Japs, who are afraid of nothing.
The Japs do not care if they die.
They are going to get the Russians out of Port Arthur if they lose fifty thousand men in the effort.
Fear has entered into these big Russians, and they are more than licked before the last battle is fought.

The Men That Never Fear Always Win.

Do you hear that?
The Japs have faith—a human faith, it is true; but they have faith.
Oh, if it only was Faith in God! [Amen.]
Oh, if they only were fighters for God!
How I covet them for a Legion of Zion Restoration Host:
There is fine material in them.
They are brave through and through, and when they become Christians they will be the leaders in the Orient, because they do not know fear.
They do not know it now.
They love the Mikado.
The Mikado and his family have been longer on the throne than any other ruling family in the world—more than two thousand five hundred years.
The Japs love their land, they obey orders, and they have faith.
I have so much of the man of Peace in me that I am a good fighter.
I should have been in war long ago, fighting, had it not been that I had this big war for God on my hands.
I am so glad that that quality of courage is essential to Faith.
Do you not know that many people have lost faith because they first lost courage?
"Oh," they say, "I am not sure about going to Zion and backing up Dr. Dowie. I have fifty cents, and I might lose it." [Laughter.]
It makes me laugh.
"I have a little bit of land, and although I know that the General Overseer's work is a good work, and that I ought to trust God, I am sure of getting something out of the pigs, and I might lose it in Zion."
There is nothing of Zion in such a man.
You might whip out the Devil, and get the Zion in, after a time, but there is no Zion there now.

The Grace That Keeps a Man Faithful.

We are talking this morning of the Grace of Faithfulness—the Grace that keeps a man Faithful.
To whom?
Faithful to God!
If it were faithfulness to his brother only, or to his wife, or to his friends, that were a small thing.
A man does not need to be a Christian to be faithful to his word as a merchant.
In fact, many worldly merchants are more faithful than some professed Christians.
Wordly men are often faithful because they know perfectly well that there will be no progress in business unless they possess the confidence of the business community in which they dwell.
When once that confidence is gone, the man might just as well shut up shop, for the possibility of being a successful man is gone.

When the World Loses Confidence in a Man His Strength Is Gone.

Therefore, many men, through policy and good, moral principle have become strong men, with an honorable standing.
They never fear; they go right on, doing right according to their light.
But that does not make them Christians.
A man may be good to his wife, but that does not make him a Christian.
I do not doubt that some of those Pharisees had great love for their wives, and for their children, for the Christ said:

If ye then, being evil, know how to give good gifts unto your children, how much more shall your Father which is in heaven give good things to them that ask Him?

A man was arrested the other day for a horrible, brutal murder.
He was a member of a union, and killed another man because the latter would not work for the union.
That man was visited in prison by his wife, and she put his baby in his arms.
He took it and kissed it, and wept over it.
Oh, he loved his baby, but he was a cruel murderer, a wilful murderer, and he did not hesitate to use a pair of knuckles to smash the face and head of an innocent man who was working for his bread, and who also had a wife and family.
That murderer was an incarnate devil, and yet he loved his baby.
Do you not know that that man manifested no Faith in God?

Faith Not Necessarily Beautiful.

A man may be a very loving man and a very bad one at the same time.
The Faith of God is a quality that, while it finds expression in all kinds of beautiful, loving actions, is independent of them.
How shall I put it?
I will put it this way.
Let the stars be blotted out; let the sun never shine again; let my eyes never again see the faces of loved ones; let my ears never hear the voice of sympathetic friendship, or the sound of sweet music; let there be nothing that can slake my thirst or feed my hunger; let me be absolutely desolate and alone in a dark world where light has disappeared, and where life has been effaced.
Faith says, "My Father loves me; my Father knows," and Faith cries out, "Father, take me out of this abyss, and give me what I need."
At once I am where there is no need of the sun, for God is there; where there is no longer any need of human speech, for I am where the tongues of angels are speaking, and where there are songs of heaven.
Faith takes us out of the darkest night and the most abject misery, and transports us at once where all is light, because we believe God Is.
The day may come when the light is a burden, and the sunshine pain; when no food or drink can satisfy, for the body is dying, and you are going down into the deepest darkness.

The Christ's Work Was Accomplished Through Faith.

O Christ of God, You have descended into depths deeper than any that we have ever sounded!
You went where the darkness was so great that You did not see the Face of the Father.
You were the Author of Faith, and You have gone down into death for us.
By Faith You lived, and loved, and died, and were buried, and by Faith the Spirit of God reanimated You, and You ascended to heaven.
By Faith You sent out poor, weak fishermen to win a world to God.
By Faith You went back to heaven, and by Faith You plead for men.
By Faith You inspire with love for You those who never saw Your face, and millions of these would die for You, O Christ of God.
You are the Author of Faith and by Faith You will bring us out into perfect Light, if we have Faith.
Faith which never doubts is the dynamic Power which removes mountains with more than volcanic and earthquake energy; which removes from the Path of Progress great and powerful barriers.
If we are faithful to God and do not doubt, my brothers—I speak to Zion everywhere now—this generation of Zion shall do what no preceding generation has done.
We will never fear.
We will never tremble.
We will never falter.
All things may pass away, but we have the Divine Confidence that gives substance to the Invisible, and makes real the Promises of God.

We see a heaven and an earth in which dwells Righteousness, and there we shall enter.

By and by we who are faithful witnesses shall stand with Him who is the Word of God, before the Great White Throne when earth and the seas are fled, and hear the Judge pronounce our names with blessings on our heads.

Be Faithful.

Be Faithful in the little things.

Be Faithful in the little things in your home and in your business, in the little while between this and the time when you shall see God.

Trust Him with everything.

Obey Him everywhere.

Love Him constantly, unswervingly, without any turning or changing

Go on! It does not matter whether it is night or day; whether you are surrounded by those who are hunting for your blood,—they know not why—or by those whose every look is Love.

Go on, being Faithful, Loving, Kind all the time.

Then God shall bless you, and

> The darkest night, the dreariest way,
> Will issue out in perfect day.

And we, no matter how widely we may have been severed, shall meet in the Land where Love, and Joy, and Peace abide for those who have been Long-suffering, Patient, Gentle, Good, and Faithful.

Without Faith it is impossible to please God.

The Reward of Faith Is Sure.

Do not think you can please Him with an atom of doubt in your heart.

The men and women who are well-pleasing to God are those who, without a fear, and without a doubt, enter into the ark, after which the door is shut, while the tempest is howling, the rain falling, the lightnings flashing, and the boat sailing out beyond the mountains, into the wide ocean.

Day by day there is no change.

The howl of the tempest still resounds throughout the lost world, mingled with the cries of the miserable, sinking and lost humanity, fighting for life with the wild beasts and the serpents that at last are to be hushed.

The ark is floating where it is dark.

When, after that long period of rain and tempest, Noah and his family saw for the first time the bow that spanned the sky, they remembered that God had said He would set that bow in the Heavens as an earnest that the earth would no more be destroyed by water.

By Faith a great multitude of those living today, may be translated, that they shall not see death.

> Oh, joy! oh, delight! should we go without dying,
> No sickness, no sadness, no dread and no crying,
> Caught up through the clouds with our Lord into glory.

The translation of Enoch will be as nothing compared with the translation of the Faithful in that Day.

By Faith every story of the Faithful in all the ages is more than repeated, and we, upon whom the ends of time and of the world have come, must be Faithful unto death.

Go on having confidence in God, in Zion, in your leader, and in one another, and Faithfulness will find its reward in Fruitfulness, Joy, Abiding Strength; and, if not here, it will find its reward in heaven.

PRAYER OF CONSECRATION.

My God and Father, in Jesus' Name I come to Thee. Take me as I am. Make me what I ought to be. Forgive me if I may have wavered, fainted, doubted, murmured, or wandered. Let me trust Thee, and without doubt or fear, go on to live, and love and serve Thee, and if need be die for Thee. For Jesus' sake. Amen.

BENEDICTION.

Beloved, abstain from every form of evil. And may the very God of Peace Himself sanctify you wholly; and I pray God your whole spirit and soul and body be preserved entire, without blame, unto the coming of our Lord Jesus, the Christ. Faithful is He that calleth you, who also will do it. The grace of our Lord Jesus, the Christ, the love of God, our Father, the fellowship of the Holy Spirit, our Comforter and Guide, one Eternal God, abide in you, bless you and keep you, and all the Israel of God everywhere, forever. Amen.

PRESENTATION AND CONSECRATION OF YOUNG CHILDREN TO GOD.

REPORTED BY O. R., R. M. P. AND E. S.

"What, then, shall this child be?"

How often the words have fallen upon the ears of Zion fathers and mothers!

Yet never did they possess a deeper, sweeter significance than on the morning of Wednesday, July 20th, of the Holy Convocation, when, at the close of an address by the General Overseer on the words quoted above, one hundred sixty-seven young children were presented and by him consecrated to God

No more beautiful sight can be imagined than the scene as these many little ones, the greater number of whom were babes in arms, were presented by parents or guardians, and the Ordinance performed.

God had given them and now they are consecrated—regiven—to Him.

A bright and useful future for these Zion babies was pictured by the General Overseer, as he looked forward and saw the Zion schools, the college, industrial training, technical and business schools developing together with the industrial conditions obtaining in Zion, which make it possible for men and women to earn their living, and lead useful and good lives, free from the strife and warfare which obtains everywhere in the world

Shiloh Tabernacle, Zion City, Illinois Wednesday Afternoon, July 20, 1904.

The service was opened by the singing of Hymn No. 52, in the Special Program, after which Elder F. A. Graves read from the Gospel according to St. Luke, beginning at the 57th verse of the 1st chapter

The General Overseer then delivered his address:

WHAT, THEN, SHALL THIS CHILD BE?

INVOCATION.

Let the words of my mouth and the meditation of my heart be acceptable in Thy sight, be profitable unto this people, and unto all to whom these words shall come, in this and every land, in this and all the coming time, Till Jesus Come. Amen.

That question was asked concerning a little baby, whom, at the circumcision they wanted to call Zacharias.

The mother knew better

The father was dumb.

He could not speak.

Why?

A Result of Incredulous Laughter.

Because he had laughed.

He had laughed in the Temple of God when the Angel told him that his wife would be a mother.

It seemed incredible, and he almost disputed the Message of the Angel.

The Angel declared that he would give a token that it was so, and said in substance, "You shall be dumb until the day of his circumcision;" and he was.

When they were about to call him Zacharias, his mother said, "Not so; but he shall be called John."

That is a very good name—John, the gift of God.

Do Not Give Your Children Absurd Names.

I hope none of you will bring your children to me with some very absurd name.

One good father asked me what I thought about calling his son Abednego.

I answered, "Certainly not.

"When he goes to school, some youngster will say, 'Into bed you go,' and make great fun of him."

Abednego, as a Hebrew name, was all very well.

It had great meaning, in the time of Daniel, for Shadrach, Meshach and Abednego were great and mighty witnesses for God.

They were cast into the fiery furnace, and I should like very much to preserve their names, if we could do so without exposing children to mirthful allusions which would follow them through life.

I have known names much more absurd than that, but Abednego is not a pleasant name for a man to write; and it is not suitable.

A member of our literary staff says that John is the name that she has most frequently had to write in filling cards.

I do not object to it; it is a good name.

I hope there are not too many John Alexanders, but you are perfectly free to choose any name.

"Zacharias" was a good name, but God had chosen the name "John."

Zion's Answer to An Important Question.

The angel had said so.

There were so many remarkable things connected with his birth, that they could not help saying, "What shall this child be?"

I have just been looking at this little assembly. In some instances I know neither the parents nor the child, and the question has been in my mind, "What shall this child be?"

An unknown future lies before each one, but one thing is certain, that by the grace of God a child born in Zion City, brought up in Zion City, protected in Zion City, and instructed in Zion City, ought to be a beautiful man or a beautiful woman.

These children have, beyond all question, greater opportunities than any I ever had, if the parents and those connected with their training in Zion, especially in this City, are faithful.

I know of no place upon earth where I would so heartily have wished my son and daughter to have been born, had it been possible, as in this City.

Blessing Should Be Expected at Consecration.

What shall these children be?

In the first place, they are, even now, very much what the lives of their parents have made them.

But if, through hereditary transgression, some of them are weak, there is no reason, beloved, why you should not ask God as you present them today, not only that a general blessing may come to them, but that a specific blessing may come; and that they may be healed.

Above all, pray that a spiritual blessing may come, and that the gift which God bestows through the laying on of hands may be a Divine Reality.

You know that they brought young children to Jesus that He might touch them; and the disciples were grieved with the parents, and said in effect, "Take them away. The Master is too great a man to be troubled with a lot of babies. There are a great many men and women here who want to see Him. Take those children away."

That is the way they talked.

But Jesus was not only displeased, but very much displeased.

He said, "Suffer the little children (the babies) to come unto Me, and forbid them not, for of such is the Kingdom of Heaven."

One thing is certain, that these children should be

Sons and Daughters of the Lord God Almighty.

God called them "Sons of the Kingdom."

It seems to me that the highest ambition that you can have for these children is that they shall be Children of God; that they shall know that this Consecration was made; that you presented them to God; and that I, as God's Minister, took them and laid my hands upon them, and consecrated them to God; and that they belong to God.

They belong to His Church.

They belong to Zion.

I do not say that they are regenerated and made entirely new in their spiritual natures; but I do say this, that if they are really presented by you in Faith, and consecrated by me in Faith, they are covered by the blood of Jesus, by the Atoning Sacrifice; and, should they die, there can be no question that the Atonement covers them, and that they are saved.

They should be so brought up that their conversion should be accomplished ere they have a knowledge of wilful transgression.

Their conversion and regeneration should go on from the very moment of their consecration.

We should expect them to receive that which we implore for them—that the Holy Spirit may abide in them, a Living Reality, and that, as you continue to maintain the presentation, and God continues to accept the consecration, the Sanctifying Power may come to the consecrated thing.

Consecrated Children Should Not Know the Bitterness of Sin.

I want to say that I believe that these children should never know the bitterness of sin; that they should so early, consciously, and of their own volition, give their hearts to God, that they, shall be children of God from the very moment of consciousness of their independent existence, spiritually.

I think it was you, Elder, [addressing Elder Graves] who said to me that your little twenty-months' old child—perhaps you will tell the story in your own words, that I may not make a mistake.

Elder Graves—"Our little twenty-months' old boy, Carl, just about the time that our General Overseer was in greatest danger—it might have been the exact day of the riots and mobs—was found kneeling in a room, no one knowing previously that he was in there, and saying: 'Fader 'n He'v'n, bless D' Dawie.'"

General Overseer—Is not that a sweet story?

As the children get early into sympathy with the General Overseer, and into sympathy with the Church and its work, they will insensibly realize that they are a part of it; and very quickly recognize the fact that the Church has a place for them.

I believe that I am the first minister who ever built a Baby House. [Laughter.]

I do not know for a certainty.

I delight to think that the mothers of the babies that are now present have been able to attend Divine worship in this place up to within a few weeks of the baby's birth; and that, in many cases, they had other babies cared for in the Baby House.

Zion Babies Carefully Cared For.

We have cared for the other little ones, and we will care for these.

This Church is in full sympathy with me in saying that we make the children our care.

It has been done practically with the very poorest as well as the richest.

It has made no difference in Zion.

The question of riches or poverty makes no difference as regards the Church's care, only that we care a little more for the children of the poor, because they need the care.

I have been so thankful that they have been cared for in cases where such care was helpful.

But in Zion City there is very, very little poverty, comparatively.

What is here came here; it was not created here.

But poverty has here been done away with very largely.

I think that as we look forward into the future and see Zion Junior Restoration Host, Zion Junior schools, the training schools of the technical education, Zion Preparatory schools and College, and the opportunities for even the humblest to get a good living—I say, as I look forward and see the provision that God is enabling us to make for the children of Zion, we have a right to say that these children shall be God's, and shall be blessed and be a power in the world for God.

It depends upon you who will make your vows, as to whether you, father and mother, will unite in holding sacred the promises which you publicly make today.

May God grant it.

[All the parents having brought children to present to God rose and took the Vow of Responsibility, after which the General Overseer consecrated one hundred sixty-seven children to God by the laying on of hands.]

The service was then closed with the

BENEDICTION.

Beloved, abstain from every form of evil. And may the very God of Peace Himself sanctify you wholly; and I pray God your whole spirit and soul and body be preserved entire, without blame, unto the coming of our Lord Jesus, the Christ. Faithful is He that calleth you, who also will do it. The grace of our Lord Jesus, the Christ, the love of God, our Father, the fellowship of the Holy Spirit, our Comforter and Guide, one Eternal God, abide in you, bless you and keep you, and all the Israel of God everywhere forever. Amen.

RENDITION OF HANDEL'S ORATORIO, "THE MESSIAH."

REPORTED BY S. E. C. AND A. W. N.

Shiloh Tabernacle, Zion City, Illinois, Wednesday Evening, July 20, 1904.

"On behalf of the audience," said the General Overseer, "I wish to thank this wonderful Choir—"

Then his voice broke.

He could go no further.

The silence was more eloquent than any words that he could have spoken.

It expressed what was in the hearts of the more than six thousand people present in Shiloh Tabernacle, Wednesday evening, July 20, 1904, when Zion White-robed Choir and Zion Orchestra rendered Handel's inspired Oratorio, "The Messiah."

That wonderful production is the story of the Christ, as expressed in the prophetic Gospel and apocalyptic Scriptures set to Divine music.

Throughout, it breathes the spirit, not only of the great work of Salvation, Healing, Cleansing and Keeping through the Atonement of the Messiah, but also of the Restoration of All Things and the establishment of the everlasting Kingdom of God.

Zion Choir and Zion Orchestra are the only musical organizations in all the wide world today that can interpret that great theme with the spirit and the understanding.

Song that to the Singers Was Glorious, Divine Truth.

These sweet-voiced singers and skilled players can send forth the flood of melody, harmony, and sublimity that there is in "The Messiah" from their inmost spirits, because they all have actually lived many of these truths, and all believe the prophetic words that they sing.

And they were singing from their own hearts straight into the hearts of their audience.

The hearers had also lived these truths, and were looking forward with the clear eye of Faith to the consummation of these glorious, Divine plans.

For this cause, the singing of "The Messiah" was a sacrament, an exalted act of worship, a mighty spiritual inspiration, which swept all in that holy place into the very presence of the Living God.

Hearts and eyes overflowed with inexpressible joy when the truths that had become so infinitely precious through experience were caught up by hundreds of voices, echoed by a score of instruments, and translated into sweetest music.

Love, Joy, Peace, Hope, and Faith, which could never be put into words, seemed to have found their interpretation in exquisite harmony.

A Triumph Won by Sincere and Happy Toil.

As solo after solo, chorus after chorus, overture, symphony, and accompaniment rolled forth in high technical excellence, as well as a sincere spirit of interpretation, amazement and admiration filled the thoughts of the hearers.

This was a Choir of young men and women, for the most part, who came to Zion City a few months or years ago, with no special musical training; this was an orchestra that had no existence, a year ago, many of the members of which had learned to play within that time!

This triumph told of hours, days, weeks, months, of the hardest and most conscientious toil on the part of every one who took part in it.

But it told also of incessant, faithful, earnest prayer, which was ever a part of the work; indeed, the very spirit of it.

This was the second time that the Choir and Orchestra had rendered this Oratorio, the first being on the evening of Wednesday, May 11, 1904.

All who had heard that first production agreed that the second was better, although the singers and players had had very little time for practice, and had been hard at work for a week, furnishing the music for the meetings of the Feast of Tabernacles.

Excellent Work of Soloists.

Great credit is due Conductor Deacon John Thomas, who had given his time and talents, night and day, in the preparation of the Choir for this work; also to Professor Möse, the Conductor of the Orchestra.

Tenor solos were sung by Deacon H. Worthington Judd, whose rare, sympathetic voice has been a joy, comfort, and inspiration to thousands at Zion Headquarters for years.

Deaconess Carrie L. Bradley-Higley, also well known to Zion at Headquarters, who sang the soprano solos, was in splendid voice, and seemed to her hearers to outdo any of her previous excellent performances. Her "I know That My Redeemer Liveth," was perhaps the best of her work on this occasion. It was beautifully rendered.

The pure, liquid tones of the voice of Deaconess Harriet Ware were heard in the contralto solos. It was a voice vibrant with sincere feeling, heard to best advantage, in some respects, in the air "He Was Despised and Rejected of Men."

Conductor Deacon John Thomas and Mr. Jacob Ickowsky, of New York City, rendered the bass solos. Deacon Thomas' rich, smooth, melodious voice was especially effective in the recitative and air "For, Behold, Darkness Shall Cover the Earth," and "The People That Walked in Darkness."

Mr. Ickowsky has a rotund, resonant bass, that is especially adapted to the solemn recitatives of this Oratorio, of which "Thus Saith the Lord of Hosts," may be given particular mention, although Mr. Ickowsky's work was conscientious throughout.

Choruses Wonderful in Perfect Harmony and Inspiration.

The choruses were rendered with a vigor, sharpness and cleanness of attack, exquisite delicacy of harmony, and unity of tempo, that bespoke an assurance and accuracy that comes only with long, hard, conscientious work. The volume and balance of parts were very effective. "And the Glory of the Lord," and the "Hallelujah Chorus," were perhaps the best of the work of the Full Choir, although the singing of the last chorus, "Worthy Is the Lamb!" was well-nigh faultless.

Of the Orchestra, nothing but praise is to be said, especially with regard to their accompaniments of the solos, which was of the very highest quality.

The harp, played by Mrs. Linval Hire, was a valuable addition.

The audience, over six thousand in number, was composed for the most part, of citizens of Zion City and those members and friends of the Christian Catholic Church in Zion who had come from other places to attend the Feast of Tabernacles, but there were also several hundred who came out on a special train from Chicago, and many who came in for this evening's services from other cities and towns in the vicinity.

The General Overseer, Overseer Jane Dowie, members of the ecclesiastical and business cabinets, and a few invited friends occupied the band platform in the west gallery.

The members of the Colonel's staff of Zion Guard were the ushers for the evening, performing their duties quietly, unostentatiously, but effectively.

Bid God-speed to Party Who Sail for Europe.

After the audience had gathered, but before the Choir and Orchestra had entered and taken their places in the choir loft, the General Overseer stepped upon the platform, accompanied by the party who were soon to sail for Europe, and said:

I have ascended the platform tonight to say a few words while we wait for the special train from Chicago which is to bring out hundreds who desire to hear the rendition of Handel's glorious Oratorio.

I have just been informed that eight coaches have started and are expected here within five or ten minutes.

I desire to present to you tonight a little party who are going to Europe by the *Etruria*.

I have thought it well to insist upon Dr. Speicher's taking a vacation, and with his dear wife and their little son (neither of whom are on the platform tonight) he will start tomorrow morning, accompanied by Deacon John Innes, General Financial Agent for Zion Industries and Institutions, and Deaconess Kennedy-Innes, his wife; Elder Fred Rickert, wife, and son, who have been with us several years, and have been doing excellent work in Chicago, on the North Side; and Elder Kosch and his wife, who came to us from Budapest, and who will go back there, to carry on the work for God.

I shall not ask all to speak, because there is not time; but I shall ask Dr. Speicher to say a few words.

He will be back before the end of the year.

May God bless him!

I know that you would like to hear him before he goes. [Applause.]

Dr. Speicher—"Beloved friends, this is a very happy day to me.

"It has been exceedingly kind of our dear General Overseer to arrange for me such a pleasant trip.

"I look forward with a great deal of pleasure to our going to Europe at this time.

"I do not feel that I need a vacation, as far as my physical condition is concerned, and yet I believe it will be for my good and for the good of Zion that I go away for a little time from the continuous routine of office work.

"I only regret that my dear wife is not stronger.

"I beg of you to pray that her journey to Europe may be a great blessing to her.

"Many of you have been exceedingly kind in expressing your love and sympathy for her and for me.

Mizpah.

I want to thank you, dear friends, for your kindness to me.

"I have no words of farewell to say.

"I say to you, Mizpah—Jehovah watch between me and thee, while we are absent one from another.

"I am sure that God's blessing is upon Zion.

"God has wonderfully poured out His blessing upon us through this Feast of Tabernacles.

"How can one doubt that God has established Zion, when we feel the glow of Love and Power, as we hear our dear General Overseer speak, and as we see the people's hearts overflowing with Sympathy and Love and a determination to go forward and do the work of God better?

"Pray for me, that I may be of some service to God and to Zion while I am away; and pray for these, my brethren, who are going with me.

"May God's blessing rest upon all Zion."

General Overseer—[Turning to those with him upon the platform.] In behalf of all Zion, I bid you all Godspeed.

Mizpah—Jehovah watch between thee and me, and this people, while we are absent one from another.

The party then retired to seats in the gallery.

After the hymn, "God be With You Till We Meet Again," had been sung, the General Overseer offered the following

PRAYER:

Our Father, grant that through all our hearts tonight Handel's wondrous Oratorio may come with Divine and Mighty Power. Bless all who shall hear. May we get from the hearing of it, life for better and purer service. For Jesus' sake. Amen.

Notice to Officers and Members.

Send all newspaper clippings concerning the General Overseer, the Elders, or any department of the work in connection with the Christian Catholic Church in Zion, to Deacon Carl F. Stern, Zion City, Illinois. Send as soon as possible after publication, and carefully mark *name and date of the paper clipped from* on each article. If this is not done, the clippings are absolutely useless.

GIVEN THE RIGHT HAND OF FELLOWSHIP.

The following-named four hundred twenty-one persons were given the right hand of fellowship, as members of the Christian Catholic Church in Zion, by the General Overseer, Lord's Day Afternoon, July 17, 1904, in Shiloh Tabernacle:

Alexander, Miss Annie Belle........1908 Gideon avenue, Zion City, Illinois
Alexander, Ferdinand..............1908 Gideon avenue, Zion City, Illinois
Anderson, Mrs. C. M..............................Custer, Washington
Anderson, Mrs. Susan.................................Canby, Minnesota
Aring, Edward Ernest Henry.......2922 Gabriel avenue, Zion City, Illinois
Aring, Miss Eleanora A... ... ...2922 Gabriel avenue, Zion City Illinois
Armstrong, Mrs. Emeline E..........................Lafayette, Indiana
Asplin, Miss Laura ....3021 Gabriel avenue, Zion City, Illinois
Axton, Mrs. May Ada...................................Mount Morris, Illinois
Ay, Mrs. Louisa ....355 Bristol street, Buffalo, New York
Aznoe, Nina..... ....3104 Eshcol avenue, Zion City, Illinois
Back, William ....Washington street, Napoleon, Ohio
Baker, Mrs. Carrie A............North Michigan street, Plymouth, Indiana
Baker, Miss Rose......................1126 Hull street, Dennison, Texas
Barber, Mrs. Annie.................2312 Gilead avenue, Zion City, Illinois
Barber, John C......................2312 Gilead avenue, Zion City, Illinois
Beatty, Nina.........................2107 Gabriel avenue, Zion City, Illinois
Beckman, E. P. ....Lake Villa, Illinois
Beem, Mrs. M. E......................2713 Elim avenue, Zion City, Illinois
Benckendorf, Edith ....2404 Elisha avenue, Zion City, Illinois
Benckendorf, Mrs. Hermine ....Streator, Illinois
Benckendorf, Louis.................2404 Elisha avenue, Zion City, Illinois
Benckendorf, Myrtle................2404 Elisha avenue, Zion City, Illinois
Benckendorf, Miss Phronia E........2404 Elisha avenue, Zion City, Illinois
Berryhill, Mrs. Annie.............611 East Wilson street, Streator, Illinois
Bliss, P. P............................3019 Enoch avenue, Zion City, Illinois
Boal, Esther Carrie...... ....Hobart, Indiana
Bobb, Edward Reuben ....1809 Horeb avenue, Zion City, Illinois
Boggan, Miss Hattie.......... . ...Tupelo, Mississippi
Bohl, Jacob F.......................3119 Gideon avenue, Zion City, Illinois
Boroff, Miss Lucinda F...............................Hamilton, Missouri
Boyer, Erma.........................2506 Edina boulevard, Zion City, Illinois
Boyer, Kerwin......................2506 Edina boulevard, Zion City, Illinois
Boyer, Miss Maggie...............2506 Edina boulevard, Zion City, Illinois
Bozeman, Miss Alice...............2310 Gilboa avenue, Zion City, Illinois
Branson, Mrs. Ida M...............406 Beal avenue, Hammond, Indiana
Broka, Miss Caroline L............ .1908 Horeb avenue, Zion City, Illinois
Brown, Lucile ....3016 Emmaus avenue, Zion City, Illinois
Brown, Miss Minnie.................................Bangor, Wisconsin
Brown, Mrs. Sarah ....5547 Ada street, Chicago, Illinois
Buckman, Miss Maud...............2806 Eshcol avenue, Zion City, Illinois
Burgess, Miss Marie ....2601 Elim avenue, Zion City, Illinois
Burnley, Alfred B..................................Patterson, Louisiana
Burris, Mrs. Mattie B.............2617 Elizabeth avenue, Zion City, Illinois
Bussey, Celia...Omro, Wisconsin
Bute, Delila...Stanhope, Iowa
Cahee, Miss Irene...................2917 Enoch avenue, Zion City, Illinois
Cameron, Sadie A.............................Ezra avenue, Zion City, Illinois
Chapman, Julia M.......1129 Eighth street South, Minneapolis, Minnesota
Chappell, Agnes Beatrice...........3016 Gilboa avenue, Zion City, Illinois
Chappell, Alfred Charles............3016 Gilboa avenue, Zion City, Illinois
Chappell, Charles Dickens..........3016 Gilboa avenue, Zion City, Illinois
Chappell, Lizzie Eliza...............3016 Gilboa avenue, Zion City, Illinois
Chase, Ernest L.. ....Edina Hospice, Zion City, Illinois
Christenson, Miss Mary............1807 Hebron avenue, Zion City, Illinois
Clark, Mary M..Cambridge, Illinois
Clark, Ophelia Price ... .Dearborn street, Chicago
Clark, Mrs Rachel E.................................Wiarton, Ontario, Canada
Clemens, Pearl Dorothy......626 West Sixty-ninth street, Chicago, Illinois
Cleveland, Mrs. Emma... ....1701 Lucas avenue, St. Louis, Missouri
Coghill, J. B...............................30 Park avenue, Hartwell, Ohio
Coghill, Mrs. J. B..........................30 Park avenue, Hartwell, Ohio
Cole, Betsie............ ....Northwood, Iowa
Cooper, Jerald......................................Hollidaysburg, Pennsylvania
Corder, Mrs Lizzie..... ....3014 Edina boulevard, Zion City, Illinois
Corder, Robert.....................3014 Edina boulevard, Zion City, Illinois
Cowhick, Hazel...... ....Elijah Hospice, Zion City, Illinois
Cowhick, Marion ....Elijah Hospice, Zion City, Illinois
Cowing, Mrs. Delcena..............................Winnebago City, Minnesota
Cowles, Mrs. Lena...... ....San Antonio, Texas
Crary, Mrs. Minnie.......................................Tripville, Wisconsin
Crawford, Mrs. Eva......320 Heatly avenue, Vancouver, British Columbia
Crosby, Mrs. Mattie.. ... ...921 University Place, Evanston, Illinois
Crouch, John G............... . ...Side View, Kentucky
Davis, Grace.........................3209 Ezra avenue, Zion City, Illinois
Davis, Miss Johnnie........2401 West Houston street, San Antonio, Texas
Dean, Eliza V............ ....Elberon, Iowa
Dehner, Mrs Anna K... ....Lexington Pike, Covington, Kentucky
Dittman, Elias A.......... .... 3105 Enoch avenue, Zion City, Illinois
Dittman, Eunice Pearl...............3105 Enoch avenue, Zion City, Illinois
Donath, Mrs. Emma Caroline.......2114 Eshcol avenue, Zion City, Illinois
Eckels, Miss Annetta F......... ....Washington, Iowa
Eitnier, Mrs. Mary............ 616 Honeywell avenue, Hoopeston, Illinois
Eliason, Mrs. Alice L.,
Hebron avenue and Twenty-seventh street, Zion City, Illinois
Ellingson, E. M. ....1521 Pleasant street, Des Moines, Iowa
Ellingson, Mrs. Mary..............1521 Pleasant street, Des Moines, Iowa
Epley, Hannah L.....................2320 Gilboa avenue, Zion City, Illinois
Escher, Mrs. Marie E...Zion City, Illinois
Eyre, Miss Jane.................... ....Darlington, Oklahoma Territory
Farnum, Esther...... .... 1819 Hebron avenue, Zion City, Illinois
Fairlie, James .... Cambridge, Illinois

Fairlie, Mrs. Mary A....Cambridge, Illinois
Falch, Fred....3116 Ezra avenue, Zion City, Illinois
Farrar, Samuel....2915 Gilead avenue, Zion City, Illinois
Farrar, William H....2915 Gilead avenue, Zion City, Illinois
Ferges, Mrs. Luella....920 State street, Trinidad, Colorado
Fisher, Mrs. Mary A....Elijah Hospice, Zion City, Illinois
Forrest, Miss Martha. Gilgal avenue and Salem boulevard, Zion City, Illinois
Fox, Mrs. Anna L....823 North Main street, Fostoria, Ohio
Fouke, Mrs. Elizabeth....Mount Morris, Illinois
Franklin, Byron....Camp Esther, Zion City, Illinois
Fraser, Mrs, Anna P....2207 Ezra avenue, Zion City, Illinois
Freeman, Miss Florence....2816 Ezekiel avenue, Zion City, Illinois
French, Joshua Lewin....Edina Hospice, Zion City, Illinois
Frisbie, Miss Lula S....3209 Elisha avenue, Zion City, Illinois
Froos, Mrs. Johanna C....6135 Wilson avenue, St Louis, Missouri
Fry, John....3004 Ezekiel avenue, Zion City, Illinois
Fryett, Mrs. Myrtle C....7550 Parnell avenue, Chicago, Illinois
Funk, Riley....3009 Ezra avenue, Zion City, Illinois
Gaede, Miss Elma....1043 North Oakley avenue, Chicago, Illinois
Gage, Mrs. S. R....Hustler, Wisconsin
Galloway, Miss Lottie J....2903 Eshcol avenue, Zion City, Illinois
Ganz, Alfred A....98 LeMoyne street, Chicago, Illinois
Ganz, Mrs. Bertha A....98 LeMoyne street, Chicago, Illinois
Ganz, Will H....98 LeMoyne street, Chicago, Illinois
Gay, Mrs. W. D....Montgomery, Alabama
Gellinger, Dora E....3007 Elim avenue, Zion City, Illinois
Gibbons, Mrs. Alice....Valton, Wisconsin
Goetz, Emily....2927 Shields avenue, Chicago, Illinois
Goetz, John....2927 Shields avenue, Chicago, Illinois
Gould, Mrs. Sarah M....11 Breckenridge street, Detroit, Michigan
Graber, Mrs. Tillie C. 221 West Chestnut street, Westchester, Pennsylvania
Grandy, Mary S....Hicksville, Ohio
Grannemann, Mrs. Jennie..315 Willow street, Central Covington, Kentucky
Grant, Mary O....R. R. Number 3, Newton, Kansas
Griffin, E. D....Edina Hospice, Zion City, Illinois
Griswald, Mrs. Sophia....Valparaiso, Indiana
Gubser, Robert A....Gering, Nebraska
Gurtler, Fred....1709 Hebron avenue, Zion City, Illinois
Gurtler, Mrs. Margaret A....1709 Hebron avenue, Zion City, Illinois
Hale, Miss Josephine....Zion City, Illinois
Hann Mrs. Ada Z....Farnam, Nebraska
Hansen, Richard....2917 Enoch avenue, Zion City, Illinois
Hardin, Addie L....3144 Armour avenue, Chicago, Illinois
Hardin, Alexander....3144 Armour avenue, Chicago, Illinois
Hardin, Delila....3144 Armour avenue, Chicago, Illinois
Hardin, Gussie....3144 Armour avenue, Chicago, Illinois
Hardin, Henry....3144 Armour avenue, Chicago, Illinois
Hardy, Miss Anna M....2902 Elisha avenue, Zion City, Illinois
Harlin, Harry....805 Fifteenth avenue, South, Minneapolis, Minnesota
Hartong, Mrs. Laura E....1813 Hermon avenue, Zion City, Illinois
Haumont, Mrs. Mary F....Broken Bow, Nebraska
Haven, Abbie Elizabeth....Main street, Hubbard, Iowa
Hendricks, Frances....3007 Elizabeth avenue, Zion City, Illinois
Hendricks, Oliver....3007 Elizabeth avenue, Zion City, Illinois
Herrod, Miss Jane....2314 Gideon avenue, Zion City, Illinois
Hildyard, Benjamin M....2606 Gilboa avenue, Zion City, Illinois
Hildyard, Mrs. Carrie B....2606 Gilboa avenue, Zion City, Illinois
Hildyard, G. B....2606 Gilboa avenue, Zion City, Illinois
Hildyard, Joseph A....2606 Gilboa avenue, Zion City, Illinois
Hill, Mrs. Emma Eva....190 Campbell avenue, Detroit, Michigan
Hire, Mrs. Edith....3006 Gabriel avenue, Zion City, Illinois
Hire, Linval J....3006 Gabriel avenue, Zion City, Illinois
Hitchman, Mrs. M....4366 Vista avenue, St. Louis, Missouri
Hollingshead, Mrs. Abbie....3007 Gideon avenue, Zion City, Illinois
Holmes, Miss Mary M....623 Shiloh boulevard, Zion City, Illinois
Hosken, Mary Ann E....3114 Enoch avenue, Zion City, Illinois
Hosken, Mrs. Rhoda....3114 Enoch avenue, Zion City, Illinois
Hosken, William....3114 Enoch avenue, Zion City, Illinois
Hotopp, Ludwig....310 Lake street, Waukegan, Illinois
Hull, Mrs. Maria....Connersville, Indiana
Hull, J. W....Connersville, Indiana
Ingram, Eli....3014 Edina boulevard, Zion City, Illinois
Ingram, W. R....3014 Edina boulevard, Zion City, Illinois
James, Carey Roy....2710 Emmaus avenue, Zion City, Illinois
James, Owen....2710 Emmaus avenue, Zion City, Illinois
James, Miss Wilhelmine....1720 Edina boulevard, Zion City, Illinois
Jenkins, Mrs. Kate O....1525 Fourth avenue, Rock Island, Illinois
Johnson, Carl A....864 North Springfield avenue, Chicago, Illinois
Johnson, Jennie....2915 Elisha avenue, Zion City, Illinois
Johnson, Mrs. Margaret E. L....3112 Emmaus avenue, Zion City, Illinois
Johnson, Rachel....2715 Elizabeth avenue, Zion City, Illinois
Jones, Irvin....3205 Ezra avenue, Zion City, Illinois
Julian, E. Ralph....1809 Hebron avenue, Zion City, Illinois
Kegg, Mrs. Ella V....702 Monroe street, Chicago, Illinois
Keller, John Emile....Elijah Hospice, Zion City, Illinois
Keller, William G....3105 Enoch avenue, Zion City, Illinois
Kesler, Paul Thomas....2912 Elim avenue, Zion City, Illinois
Ketchum, Mrs. F. C....109 West Wilson street, Madison, Wisconsin
Kippie, Mrs. Alice....3218 Elijah avenue, Zion City, Illinois
Kirkendall, Amy....3213 Elisha avenue, Zion City, Illinois
Kitchen, Mrs. Martha....3331 State street, Chicago, Illinois
Kohr, Michael....1640 Cedar street, Pueblo, Colorado
Kohr, Mrs. Michael....1640 Cedar street, Pueblo, Colorado
Krebs, Genevieve....Zion City, Illinois
Kreiter, Charles....Webster, South Dakota
Kreiter, Mrs. Julia....Webster, South Dakota
Kruse, Miss Anna....227 Clifton avenue, Cincinnati, Ohio
Kuhn, Lizzie....601 Crescent avenue, Covington, Kentucky
LaBelle, Mrs. Sylvia....1807 Hebron avenue, Zion City, Illinois
Lackey, Gertie O....Barnard, Indiana
Lackey, J. W....Barnard, Indiana
Lackey, Mrs. Lucy E....Barnard, Indiana
Ladley, Mrs. D. B....1339 Meier avenue, Mount Lookout, Cincinnati, Ohio
Lake, Calvin H....Republican City, Nebraska
Lake, Mrs. Florence S....Republican City, Nebraska
Lake, Master Leonard....Republican City, Nebraska
Lake, William....Omro, Wisconsin
Lamberger, Oscar I....Elijah Hospice, Zion City, Illinois
Lamberger, Mrs. Oscar I....Elijah Hospice, Zion City, Illinois
Lantzer, Mrs. Rachel....216 South Shabbona, Streator, Illinois
LaRose, Paul....3102 Ezekiel avenue, Zion City, Illinois
Larson, Mrs. Sarah Maria....Clintonville, Wisconsin
Lathrop, Alvin H....Hampshire, Illinois
Lawrence, Hattie B....Thornton, Iowa
Lawson, Mrs. Hattie....1008 Zenith avenue, Indianapolis, Indiana
Lee, Willis Fred....3009 Elim avenue, Zion City, Illinois
Leech, Miss Myrtle....1700 Horeb avenue, Zion City, Illinois
Leitch, Mrs. Sarah F....Maiden Rock, Wisconsin
Leetsch, Mrs. Elizabeth....2610 Elim avenue, Zion City, Illinois
Leetsch, W. C. Julius....2610 Elim avenue, Zion City, Illinois
Logan, Louise....6720 Parnell avenue, Chicago, Illinois
Logan, Mrs. Tillie....6720 Parnell avenue, Chicago, Illinois
Long, Miss Ethel....Keokuk, Iowa
Lorenz, Robert....2720 Edina boulevard, Zion City, Illinois
Love, Grace H....2810 Elizabeth avenue, Zion City, Illinois
Lowe, John....Petersburg, Missouri
McBean, Mrs. Sarah H....314 South Monroe street, Spokane, Washington
McCann, Mrs. Susan A....5829 Jackson avenue, Chicago, Illinois
McCardell, Mrs. Mary C....2708 Emmaus avenue, Zion City, Illinois
McClain, Mrs. Rose....3108 Gilboa avenue, Zion City, Illinois
McClay, Clyde Frisbie....3209 Elisha avenue, Zion City, Illinois
McCumber, Miss Louise....Victor, New York
McDowell, Minnie....R. R. No. 6, Logansport, Indiana
McGee, Mrs. Hattie....Dahoga, Pennsylvania
McGill, Hugh....2707 Gabriel avenue, Zion City, Illinois
McGinness, Mrs. Eliza....Elwood, Indiana
McKim, Miss Abbie....3202 Ezra avenue, Zion City, Illinois
McMertry, Mrs. Susie....917 North Cardinal avenue, St. Louis, Missouri
McNatt, Mrs. Lucy E....3212 Gideon avenue, Zion City, Illinois
McNatt, Thomas R....3212 Gideon avenue, Zion City, Illinois
Maddox, W. S....930 Kingdom avenue, Danville, Illinois
Main, Madison....3003 Elim avenue, Zion City, Illinois
Mapes, Charles....3213 Gilgal avenue, Zion City, Illinois
Mapes, Stewart....3213 Gilgal avenue, Zion City, Illinois
Marpurg, Mrs. Gesina....Elijah Hospice, Zion City, Illinois
Mayhak, Mrs. Matilda....Spencer, South Dakota
Maynard, Edward Alfonso....Viola, Illinois
Melvin, Mrs. Eva....12006 Stewart avenue, West Pullman, Chicago, Illinois
Meredith Mrs. Mary....2106 Eshcol avenue, Zion City, Illinois
Mill, Herbert C....2917 Enoch avenue, Zion City, Illinois
Mill, Mrs. Jennie....2917 Enoch avenue, Zion City, Illinois
Miller, Amy M....1819 Gilboa avenue, Zion City, Illinois
Miller, Edna....1819 Gilboa avenue, Zion City, Illinois
Miller, David John....2703 Enoch avenue, Zion City, Illinois
Miller, Mrs. Elizabeth....2703 Enoch avenue, Zion City, Illinois
Miller, Miss Elsie....1 Washington street, Bradford, Pennsylvania
Miller, John M....1819 Gilboa avenue, Zion City, Illinois
Miller, Mrs. Marguerite....946 Twentieth street, Zion City, Illinois
Miller, William....946 Twentieth street, Zion City, Illinois
Miller, Mrs. Laura....66 St. John place, Chicago, Illinois
Mills, Mrs. Ruby....East Canal street, Portage City, Wisconsin
Moore, Miss Josie....2013 Elizabeth avenue, Zion City, Illinois
Moos, Mrs. Anna....1903 Horeb avenue, Zion City, Illinois
Moos, Miss Hannah....1903 Horeb avenue, Zion City, Illinois
Moos, Josie....1903 Horeb avenue, Zion City, Illinois
Moos, Miss Rose....1903 Horeb avenue, Zion City, Illinois
Moller, G. P....612 Potomac avenue, Hagerstown, Maryland
Mories, Mrs. M. H....2602 Elim avenue, Zion City, Illinois
Morisse, Mrs. Kate M....Lexington pike, Covington, Kentucky
Morlock, Mrs. Henrietta....2902 Elisha avenue, Zion City, Illinois
Morris, William L....2117 Gilead avenue, Zion City, Illinois
Murrell, Hina....Elijah Hospice, Zion City, Illinois
Murrell, Miss Stella....Elijah Hospice, Zion City, Illinois
Mutch, Mrs. Sarah....Elroy, Wisconsin
Naden, Mrs. Harriet....Orchard, Iowa
Naden, Samuel J....Orchard, Iowa
Narber, Mrs. Sarah....Sturgis, Michigan
Neff, Ada B....Enoch avenue, Zion City, Illinois
Neff, Alice....Elijah Hospice, Zion City, Illinois
Neff, Chloe M....3117 Enoch avenue, Zion City, Illinois
Neff, Mrs. Josephine....3117 Enoch avenue, Zion City, Illinois
Neff, Miles W....3117 Enoch avenue, Zion City, Illinois
Neff, Roy B....3117 Enoch avenue, Zion City, Illinois
Neff, S. M....3117 Enoch avenue, Zion City, Illinois
Neff, Zella M....3117 Enoch avenue, Zion City, Illinois
Nelson, Eugenia E....New Auburn, Wisconsin
Nelson, Gust N....21 West Twenty-fourth place, Chicago, Illinois
Nelson, Mrs. Mary J....612 Leonard street, Chattanooga, Tennessee
Newcomer, Mrs. Mayme....Zion City, Illinois
Nichols, Mrs. Hulda....Cambridge, Illinois
Noomen, Mrs. Dorothy....Orange City, Iowa
Norton, Mrs. F. M....Hustler, Wisconsin
Nowlan, Frederica....2820 Ezekiel avenue, Zion City, Illinois
Oberholtzer, Miss M. E....1129 Eight street South, Minneapolis, Minnesota
Orcutt, Mrs. Emma....Union Mills, Indiana
Palmer, Mrs. Laura....Mount Morris, Illinois
Pardoe, H. W....Newton, Iowa
Parton, Mrs. Mary....2620 Elim avenue, Zion City, Illinois
Parton, William....2620 Elim avenue, Zion City, Illinois
Patterson, Mrs. Mattie Elizabeth..2807 Elizabeth avenue, Zion City, Illinois

Paulsen, Mrs. Maria........... 3016 Gabriel avenue, Zion City, Illinois
Peet, Miss Martha E.. .....Delphos, Kansas
Peterman, C. E....................R. R. Number 1, Zion City, Illinois
Peters, Eleanor Young..................Main street, Watervliet, Michigan
Phelps, Carrie..................Division street, Goshen, Indiana
Phillimore, Miss Carrie
care of Deacon Sloan, Gilgal avenue, Zion City, Illinois
Polman, Gerdin A....................Elijah Hospice, Zion City, Illinois
Polston, Mrs. N. A................2109 Gabriel avenue, Zion City, Illinois
Pooley, Miss Lottie................2203 Elisha avenue, Zion City, Illinois
Pooley, Robert................2203 Elisha avenue, Zion City, Illinois
Pooley, Mrs. Robert................2203 Elisha avenue, Zion City, Illinois
Potter, Miss Bertha................3212 Gabriel avenue, Zion City, Illinois
Potter, Flossie................3212 Gabriel avenue, Zion City, Illinois
Prescott, George................1813 Horeb avenue, Zion City, Illinois
Price, Laura O.....................North Yakima, Washington
Price, Mrs. Letitia E.....................North Yakima, Washington
Price, Mrs. Sarah A................3011 Gilead avenue, Zion City, Illinois
Puhl, Sadie S................1910 Ezekiel avenue, Zion City, Illinois
Purdy, Miss Emily................2808 Elisha avenue, Zion City, Illinois
Purvis, Emma................2016 Hebron avenue, Zion City, Illinois
Raper, Miss Mabel................2306 Hermon avenue, Zion City, Illinois
Raper, Mrs. Rosa................2306 Hermon avenue, Zion City, Illinois
Rather, Mrs. Martha Louena.....................Luling, Texas
Rebman, Christian................23 Cherry street, Buffalo, New York
Reeve, Master Rex W................2509 Elizabeth avenue, Zion City, Illinois
Reynolds, Mrs. M J................4325 Gibson avenue, St. Louis, Missouri
Rice, Mrs. Emily................3214 Ezra avenue, Zion City, Illinois
Richey, Miss Roxanna................3106 Ezekiel avenue, Zion City, Illinois
Riggins, Mrs. Florence A................3203 Gabriel avenue, Zion City, Illinois
Rinker, Miss Marie A................22 East Terrace, Chattanooga, Tennessee
Ripley, Anna V................1809 Horeb avenue, Zion City, Illinois
Roberts, Ethel................2911 Emmaus avenue, Zion City, Illinois
Robbins, A. W................3107 Gideon avenue, Zion City, Illinois
Robbins, Francis................3107 Gideon avenue, Zion City, Illinois
Robbins, George................3107 Gideon avenue, Zion City, Illinois
Rockafellar, Ephraim K................3110 Eshcol avenue, Zion City, Illinois
Rockafellar, Miss Nellie................3110 Eshcol avenue, Zion City, Illinois
Ross, Harry Fenton....................Elijah Hospice, Zion City, Illinois
Rowley, L. C....................Darlington, Wisconsin
Rowley Mrs. L. C....................Darlington, Wisconsin
Russell, Edwin................3210 Gabriel avenue, Zion City, Illinois
Russell, Ruth................3210 Gabriel avenue, Zion City, Illinois
Russell, Samuel Clarence A................3210 Gabriel avenue, Zion City, Illinois
Sayers, Mrs. Mollie................218 Nolan street, San Antonio, Texas
Scales, Mrs. Maria................499 State street, Chicago, Illinois
Schindler, Miss Paulina................2712 Elizabeth avenue, Zion City, Illinois
Schmidt, Carl................2920 Enoch avenue, Zion City, Illinois
Schmidt, Charles................2920 Enoch avenue, Zion City, Illinois
Schmidt, Frank................2920 Enoch avenue, Zion City, Illinois
Schmidt, Luise................2920 Enoch avenue, Zion City, Illinois
Schmidt, William................2920 Enoch avenue, Zion City, Illinois
Scott, Gertrude................2207 Ezra avenue, Zion City, Illinois
Sechrist, W. H................751 Carmel boulevard, Zion City, Illinois
Seger, Mrs. Margaret A................606 Spofford avenue, Spokane, Washington
Sell, Mrs. Martha....................Fairmount, Indiana
Sengewald, Miss Josephine....................Geneseo, Illinois
Sepin, Mrs. Annie....................Connersville, Indiana
Shaw, Margaret....................Collins, Ohio
Shaw, Mrs. Mina H....................Collins, Ohio
Shields, Louis................3216 Ezra avenue, Zion City, Illinois
Short, Eliza F....................Pocahontas, Illinois
Short, Leila Perley....................Pocahontas, Illinois
Sims, Miss Pearl................207½ Hanover street, Milwaukee, Wisconsin
Smith, Mrs. Lottie................3211 Gideon avenue, Zion City, Illinois
Smith, Miss Lottie....................Box A, Plymouth, Indiana
Smith, Mrs. Mary Stevens................210 Reid street, Jackson, Tennessee
Snyder, Edith L................159 North Fifty-first court, Chicago, Illinois
Speare, Flossy Myrtle....................Camp Esther, Zion City, Illinois
Speare, Mary Catherine....................Camp Esther, Zion City, Illinois
Speare, Walter Richard....................Camp Esther, Zion City, Illinois
Spellman, Miss Edith................2901 Ezekiel avenue, Zion City, Illinois
Spindler, Edward....................Wooster avenue, Akron, Ohio
Spooner, Mrs. Mary E....................Havana, North Dakota
Steel, Ralph M................614 West Sixtieth street, Chicago, Illinois
Steel, Mrs. Ralph M................614 West Sixtieth street, Chicago, Illinois
Stevens, Mrs. Minnie E....................Bingham, Michigan
Stockstill, Mrs. Anna................1817 Benton avenue, Springfield, Missouri
Stone, Mary A....................Omro, Wisconsin
Stow, Bessie Louisa................2403 Gilboa avenue, Zion City, Illinois
Stow, Ethel Martha................2403 Gilboa avenue, Zion City, Illinois
Stuck, Richard................3104 Gilboa avenue, Zion City, Illinois
Sweeney, Edith M................2118 Elisha avenue, Zion City, Illinois
Sweeney, Florence E................2118 Elisha avenue, Zion City, Illinois
Swihart, Mrs. Anna....................Brighton, Indiana
Sydelott, L. C....................Converse, Indiana
Tate, Abbie J....................Effingham, Illinois
Tate, Andrew R....................Effingham, Illinois
Thompson, Mrs. Elizabeth....................Hobart, Indiana
Thorpe, Miss Nellie................2907 Ezra avenue, Zion City, Illinois
Thurlow, Mrs. Addie................2816 Elizabeth avenue, Zion City, Illinois
Tillman, Miss Carrie................2503 Gilboa avenue, Zion City, Illinois
Toop, Mrs. Sara A....................Ulysses, Nebraska
Trask, Mrs. E. J....................Quitman, Louisiana
Treible, Miss Arminda................229 Hodge avenue, Cleveland, Ohio
Turner, Mrs. Emmeline....................Viroqua, Wisconsin
Umbarger, Jennie....................Walton, Indiana
Underwood, James R....................Edina Hospice, Zion City, Illinois
Upp, Mrs. Mary A................2116 Enoch avenue, Zion City, Illinois
Van Gieson, David E................184 Franklin street, Brooklyn, New York
Van Hoesen, Miss Marietta................1726 Horeb avenue, Zion City, Illinois
Varnum, Mrs. Susan....................Camp Esther, No. 84, Zion City, Illinois
Barrowcliff, Mrs. Rebecca................1007 Ludlow avenue, Cincinnati, Ohio
Vetter, Mrs. Amelia................3002 Ezra avenue, Zion City, Illinois
Wagner, Miles L................1 Washington street, Bradford, Pennsylvania
Wait, Miss Sarah J................2543 Columbus avenue, Minneapolis, Minnesota
Warner, H. B................3108 Ezekiel avenue, Zion City, Illinois
Weathers, Mrs. Nettie....................Cloverdale, Indiana
Weaver, Mrs. Minnie C....................Wakarusa, Kansas
Wesner, Eleanora................3013 Ezekiel avenue, Zion City, Illinois
West, Daisy................5948 Parnell avenue, Chicago, Illinois
West, Harry E................5948 Parnell avenue, Chicago, Illinois
Whipple, Lucy Adelle....................Madison, Ohio
Whitrock, Melissa B................3020 Enoch avenue, Zion City, Illinois
Wigham, William....................Adrian, Minnesota
Wilkins, Mrs. Jessie O................1819 Gilboa avenue, Zion City, Illinois
Williams, Albert George................174 West boulevard, Chicago, Illinois
Williams, Mrs. Anna M....................West Pullman, Chicago, Illinois
Williams, H. L................2316 Elijah avenue, Zion City, Illinois
Williams, Mrs. Mary................3110 Emmaus avenue, Zion City, Illinois
Williams, Mrs. Sarah N....................Dodgeville, Wisconsin
Wilson, Hyland Fm................3000 Elim avenue, Zion City, Illinois
Wilson, Miss Margaret................221 Prospect street, Chattanooga, Tennessee
Wilson, Mrs. T. W................3000 Elim avenue, Zion City, Illinois
Wiseman, Miss Anna................6889 Hamilton avenue, Pittsburg, Pennsylvania
Wood, Elizabeth................2412 Elisha avenue, Zion City, Illinois
Wood, Gertrude Willard................2820 Enoch avenue, Zion City, Illinois
Wyrick, Mrs. S....................Knobnoster, Missouri
Yenny, Fred................2314 Gilead avenue, Zion City, Illinois
Yenny, Walter John................2314 Gilead avenue, Zion City, Illinois
Zediker, Miss Myrtle................1905 Hebron avenue, Zion City, Illinois

Zion in Missouri.

Deacon Charles E. Robinson, Deacon-in-charge of the Branch of the Christian Catholic Church in Zion at Kansas City, will conduct services in the following cities in Missouri on the dates given:

Independence, August 20th; Pleasant Hill, August 21st; Warrensburg, August 22d and 23d; Knobnoster, August 24th and 25th; Sedalia, August 26th; Higginsville, August 27th and 28th; Lexington, August 29th and 30th; Orrick, August 31st; Liberty, September 1st.

All members and friends desiring baptism will please communicate with Deacon Robinson at once.

Let all having friends in these cities or in their vicinities notify them of the proposed meetings, and send their names and addresses to Deacon Charles E. Robinson, 2112 North Fourth street, Kansas City, Kansas.

EXCURSION TO ZION CITY

REV. H. D. BRASEFIELD,

Overseer in the Christian Catholic Church in Zion, will preach on

Lord's Day Afternoon, August 7th

REV. JOHN ALEXANDER DOWIE

will return to Zion City and preach, God willing,

AUG. 14TH,

and expects to preach every Lord's Day thereafter until further notice.

Special trains will be run each Lord's Day until Christmas, leaving the Chicago & North-Western Depot at 11:30 and 11:45 a. m. and will return about 6:30 to 7:30 p. m.

Notes of Thanksgiving from the Whole World

By Overseer J. G. Excell, General Ecclesiastical Secretary.

Little Girl Healed of Fever.

Surely He hath borne our griefs,
And carried our sorrows:

The chastisement of our peace was upon Him;
And with His stripes we are Healed.—*Isaiah 53:4, 5.*

1209 OAK STREET,
MUSCATINE, IOWA, April 3, 1904.

DEAR GENERAL OVERSEER:—As you know, we sent in a request for prayer for our little girl, who was very sick.

The next morning between eight and nine o'clock the change came and she began to get better and the fever abated, for which we praise God.

Today she has been up and has eaten with us.

I praise God for the wonderful deliverance He gave her, and also thank you for your kindness in helping us.

It is good that we have a Physician in heaven who asks for no money and gives no poison.

It is so wonderful when we read in LEAVES OF HEALING and in other Zion Literature of the great and wonderful works of God.

Your brother in the Christ, JOHN STIEGLITZ.

Little Boy Healed.

The works of Jehovah are great, sought out of all them that have pleasure therein.—*Psalm 111:2.*

2915 ENOCH AVENUE, ZION CITY, ILLINOIS.

DEAR OVERSEER:—I praise God for His goodness and wonderful works to the children of men.

Last week, May 26th, my little boy was taken very sick. He began to vomit, and he could keep nothing on his stomach.

He had been jumping, and said that he hurt himself; so I told him he must ask God to forgive him, and God would make him well again.

He asked God to forgive him.

He had eaten nothing for four days, and was therefore very weak.

We called for the Deacon-in-charge, and he prayed for him.

I read from my Bible Matthew 21:22; I said to my husband, "We believe that; let us kneel and pray, expecting the blessing."

Our little boy went to sleep, and, when he wakened, he said, "I am all well, and I thank God for making me well."

Being hungry he ate something, and went to play.

We thank God for all the blessings we have received from Him, and pray God to bless and keep you.

Till He Come.

MR. and MRS. E. J. HAMPSON.

Healed of Sore Throat.

All things whatsoever ye pray and ask for, believe that ye have received them, and ye shall have them.—*Mark 11:24.*

2816 ELIZABETH AVENUE,
ZION CITY, ILLINOIS, May 6, 1904.

DEAR GENERAL OVERSEER:—I praise my Heavenly Father for all His goodness to me. Blessed be God who hath not turned away my prayer nor His mercy from me.

I was taken with a very sore throat on the 3d of May, and left my work at noon for a day and a half.

I did not eat anything, but drank some grape juice which I could scarcely swallow.

My throat was swollen and very sore.

On the 5th, a few minutes after the hour of prayer, I was healed instantly.

All soreness and the lump disappeared, and I ate an orange and some crackers.

I returned to my work on the 6th.

This was the first sickness I have had since my conversion, nine years ago.

I am so thankful that we have a Physician that never fails us.

As our days, so shall our strength be.

I am thankful that LEAVES OF HEALING ever came to me. Oh, what darkness would envelop us had not God sent Elijah the Prophet!

I am thankful for the privilege of living in Zion City, and to be one of the children of God.

Praying God's blessing upon our Leader and Zion everywhere, I am,

Yours in the Lord's work,

(MRS.) MARY L. FREAS.

Healed of Grip—Family Blessed.

He sendeth His Word, and healeth them.—*Psalm 107:20.*

PIERPONT, SOUTH DAKOTA, May 29, 1904.

DEAR GENERAL OVERSEER:—I feel that I ought to write and testify to God's goodness to myself and family.

We have trusted God for healing for about three years, and I can truthfully say that they have been the most healthful years of my life.

A week ago, I was very sick with grip, having terrible pains in my head and back, which lasted about forty-eight hours.

We prayed and looked to God.

The pains left, but I had a bad cough and very sore lungs, and felt weak.

We asked a Zion lady living in town to pray with us, and today I am perfectly healed, for which I truly thank God.

God has been good to us.

Our children have been healed many times.

Once our little girl had a high fever; we prayed for her, and the fever was gone in fifteen minutes. Praise God!

May God bless you and all Zion is my prayer.

H. A. HARDER.

Healed of Swollen Eye.

Delight thyself also in Jehovah;
And He shall give thee the desires of thine heart.—*Psalm 37:4.*

JAMESTOWN, PENNSYLVANIA, April 9, 1904.

DEAR GENERAL OVERSEER:—I feel it my duty to give a written testimony of what God has done for me in regard to my healing.

I had the grip, and it settled in my eye, which was swollen as large as a hen's egg, and was very badly inflamed.

We wrote to Zion for prayer, putting our whole trust in God to heal my eye.

He healed it at the time the request reached you.

I am well and trusting in God.

I am nine years old.

Your little son in the Christ,

WILLARD N. VANZANDT.

Healed of Nervous Weakness.

For Thy loving-kindness is better than life;
My lips shall praise Thee.—*Psalm 63:3.*

LEEDS, YORKSHIRE, ENGLAND.

DEAR OVERSEER:—I am thankful for the light and blessing I have received through LEAVES OF HEALING.

For years I suffered much from nervous weakness, and spent all the money I could get for medicine; but now I seek God, and He always hears and answers prayer.

Praying God's richest blessing on our dear General Overseer, I am,

Yours in Christian love,

(MRS.) M. A. PINDER.

Healed of Swelling in Face and Neck.

Heaven and earth shall pass away, but My Words shall not pass away.—*Luke 21:33.*

MARCUS, IOWA, June 17, 1904.

DEAR OVERSEER:—I wish to thank you for prayer in my behalf, and to render praise to our Heavenly Father for speedy healing of a very sore and painful ailment, caused by suppuration of the gum of right lower jaw.

The swelling extended over the entire side of face and neck, and the soreness to the cords in shoulder, and to the top of the head.

With praise to God for the faithful ones in Zion who have taught us the way to trust and to find relief, I am, Yours in His service,

C. E. AUSTIN.

Child Healed of Scarlet Fever.

So he enquired of them the hour when he began to amend. They said therefore unto him, Yesterday at the seventh hour the fever left him.—*John 4:52.*

BURR OAK, KANSAS, April 18, 1904.

DEAR BROTHER IN THE CHRIST:—We sent a telegram about the 3d of March, asking you to pray for our children.

Our youngest girl had scarlet fever.

About the time you prayed the fever left her and there seemed to be no sickness after that.

The other little girl improved, and did not have the fever.

We give God all the glory, and wish to thank you for your prayers.

Your brother and sister in the Christ,

(MR.) AND (MRS.) WALTER OAK.

Delivered in Childbirth.

But she shall be saved through the childbearing, if they continue in faith and love and sanctification with sobriety.—*1 Timothy 2:15.*

2911 BLAKE STREET, DENVER,
COLORADO, May 10, 1904.

DEAR OVERSEER:—I write to tell you of the wonderful blessings we have received in answer to prayer.

About February 4th of this year, I wrote you a letter, telling of an expected baby at our house.

I also sent you a request to pray for my wife, as she was in very poor health, and could hardly get around.

We received a very prompt reply, stating that you had laid our petition before God, asking Him in Jesus' Name to bless her in spirit, soul and body, to take away her affliction, to restore her to health, and to be with her at the time of confinement

You also gave us the advice we asked for.

My father, Elder J. R. Keller, of Chicago, has also prayed for her.

On Monday, May 2d, one week ago last night, we received the warning, and I sent a telegram to Elder Keller to pray, and at nine o'clock in the evening our home was blessed with a little daughter.

There was no one with my wife but my mother (Evangelist Keller) and myself. We prayed for her at the time, but four or five minutes intervened between the time she lay down and the birth of the baby.

From the time you prayed for her, she began to improve in health and strength; she has an excellent appetite, which continued through her confinement.

When I see her looking so bright and happy, I cannot help praising God for Zion and the teaching of our beloved General Overseer.

This experience is in striking contrast with the awful time we had when our other baby was born, before we came into Zion.

My wife was in bed for over three weeks.

She had nervous prostration, and what the doctor called a complication of other diseases, for which he made an "extra charge."

He nearly killed both wife and baby with strong medicine.

But this time, thank God, we knew better than to poison her with any of the "concoctions of the sorcerer."

We also have had many other healings and blessings since we came into Zion and accepted God's way.

Asking you to accept our thanks for your prayers and advice, I remain

Your brother in the Christ,

J. ELMER KELLER.

Healed of Congestion of Liver, Chills, and Fever.

In Him we live, and move, and have our being.—*Acts 17:28.*

WEST UNITY, OHIO, May 6, 1904.

DEAR GENERAL OVERSEER.—It is with a heart full of thankfulness and praise to God, my Heavenly Father, for His goodness and mercies to me, that I send my testimony, praying it may go forth in the Little White Dove and be a blessing to those who read it.

On March 4, 1904, I was taken very sick with congestion of the liver, having chills and fever at the same time.

The chills lasted from two to three hours.

My condition was very serious, and my friends thought I could not live; but a brother and sisters in the Christ came and prayed earnestly to God for me; and God heard and answered our prayers, and healed me just as He has promised to do when we come in the right way.

Deacon R. W. L. Ely, of Zion City, came and prayed and laid hands on me, and I received a complete healing.

I thank my dear Father in heaven for healing me.

Praying God's blessing upon Zion, I am your sister in the Christ,

Till He come, (MRS.) HANNAH A. COLEMAN

Hemorrhages Stopped in Answer to Prayer.

Jehovah is good,
A strong hold in the day of trouble;
And He knoweth them
That put their trust in Him.—*Nahum 1:7.*

ZÜRICH, SWITZERLAND, May 26, 1904.

DEAR OVERSEER:—It gives me great joy to say that in God and through Jesus, the Christ, I have found healing.

From April 18th to the 28th, I had hemorrhages, and raised blood day and night.

The doctor, after having tried every known remedy to stop the bleeding, said that nothing more could be done for me.

He gave hypodermic injections, but the more he did to stop the bleeding the worse I bled.

I also gave up all hope of recovery, for the great loss of blood made me so weak that I was unable to move myself in bed.

For a whole week, my mother had to feed me with a spoon.

The doctor said that he had never seen such a case before, and he thought that I would bleed to death. But I did not.

Like many others, as a last resort I turned to the Great Physician, Jesus, the Christ, and He heard our prayers, and He has healed me.

On May 15th, from Neupest, Hungary, where I I am living, I sent a cablegram to Zion City, asking you to pray for me.

With the help of God, and by trusting Him fully, I was able to undertake the long journey to Zürich.

It took me two days and two nights to get there, but, thank God, I reached that city in safety.

I am now here to listen to the sermons and talks of the General Overseer.

He has laid hands on me, and I feel very happy.

To Him Who has made me well, be all the glory.

May He bless you, and may He grant answers to your prayers in behalf of many thousands for healing of spirit, soul, and body.

Respectfully, your brother in the Christ,

JOSEF ZSAN.

Boy Healed of Dysentery.

Jesus, the Christ, is the same
Yesterday and today,
Yea and forever.—*Hebrews 13:8.*

WISANGER, KANGAROO ISLAND, SOUTH AUSTRALIA, April 16, 1904.

DEAR GENERAL OVERSEER:—Peace to thee.

I feel it my duty to tell how God has wonderfully kept us through these last few years.

We were truly converted to God four years last November, and since that time God has richly blessed us.

February last, our oldest boy was suddenly taken very ill with dysentery We had Deacon Partridge come and pray for him, and he seemed to be a great deal better after prayer. Then he would become worse again.

We felt very anxious about him. He became so ill, that we sent a request for prayer to Overseer Voliva; and that same day he commenced to improve. The next day he was asking for food.

I am thankful to say that God heard and answered prayer.

Both my dear husband and myself have been wonderfully healed in answer to prayer.

I earnestly pray that God will spare our dear General Overseer for many years to finish this glorious work, and that we may be kept faithful to our God.

Faithfully yours in the Christ's service,

(MRS.) EMMA MARY BELL.

Abscess in Throat and Neck Removed through Faith in God.

And all the multitude sought to touch Him; for power came forth from Him, and healed them all.—*Luke 6:19.*

DELPHI, INDIANA, June 13, 1904.

DEAR BROTHER IN THE CHRIST:—I write to inform you that your prayers have been answered.

The abscess in my little boy's throat and neck has disappeared, and he is sound and well.

I am growing stronger spiritually, and have more faith.

God bless you for your willing service.

Your brother in Jesus, MANSON N. SIBERT.

Daughter Healed Through Faith in God.

Commit Thy way unto Jehovah; trust also in Him, and He shall bring it to pass.—*Psalm 37:5.*

HOBART, INDIANA, May 18, 1904.

DEAR BROTHER IN THE CHRIST:—You will remember my asking you to pray for the healing of my daughter.

Praise God, He has healed her and blessed her wonderfully.

It has been a great trial of my faith. Many times I came near giving up and turning to remedies of some kind.

God blessed her whenever any in Zion prayed.

It seemed beyond me to make some things right, but God has made them right.

I give God all the glory.

I was afraid Ruth would die of dropsy, but God was with me in my trouble.

Both the girls have been sick, and God has healed them.

God said the children He has given should be for a sign in Israel.

Thanking you and all Zion for prayers, I remain,

Your sister in the Christ,

(MRS.) M. C. BOAL.

Healed of Grip and Cold.

Blessed are all they that put their trust in Him.—*Psalm 2:12.*

2813 ELIZABETH AVENUE, ZION CITY, ILLINOIS, April 16, 1904.

DEAR OVERSEER:—It is with a heart filled with gratitude to God that I write my testimony and tell of God's love and mercy toward me, His child.

Through your prayers I was healed of grip and a very severe cold, for which I give God all the praise.

When I was taken sick you prayed for me, and about eight hours later the answer came, while I was lying down.

I involuntarily arose, and felt so much better that I said, "Oh, I believe the Doctor is praying for me."

I grew better from that time on, and thank God for that healing and for many other healings.

I thank Him, too, for the blessed privilege of living in Zion City.

Pray for me. Pray that I may be more faithful, more like Jesus, and that I may be readv when Jesus comes.

I am, faithfully yours Till He Come,

(MISS) STELLA RUSSELL

Restored to Health in Answer to Prayer.

Glorify God, therefore, in your body.—*1 Corinthians 6:20.*

EATON, OHIO, April 13, 1904.

DEAR BROTHER:—I want to testify to God's goodness to me in restoring my health and strength in answer to your prayer.

I thank you, and may God ever keep you. Thank you for your kind letter.

Glory to God! Praise His Holy Name!

Yours until He Come, SARAH GRIFFIN.

Healed of Wound Caused by Nails.

..e healeth the broken in heart, and bindeth up their wounds.—*Psalm 147:3.*

UREAL SPRINGS, ILLINOIS, May 15, 1904.

DEAR OVERSEER:—I praise God that through your prayers my little boy, Scott, was healed. Two nails were accidently stuck in the bottom of his foot, on May 7th.

I wrote at once for prayer.

Tuesday morning, May 10th, at nine o'clock, you prayed for him, after which he walked naturally, and soreness entirely disappeared.

I am so thankful that there is a Church that is trusting God for spirit, soul, and body.

This is just one testimony among many which can be given to the honor of God since I joined the Christian Catholic Church in Zion, in 1899.

God has healed other members of my family.

Your sister in the Christ,

(Mrs.) ROBERT A. FERRELL.

By Evangelist Sarah E. Hill.

AND THE Voice which I heard from heaven, I heard it again speaking with me, and saying, Go, take the Book which is open in the hand of the Angel that standeth upon the sea and upon the earth.—*Revelation 10:8.*

THIS Angel or Messenger of the Latter Days, which John saw in vision on the Isle of Patmos, had a Message from God for the whole earth.

It was to go over land and water.

The Little Book above referred to was a part of God's Message to the whole world.

It was one of many books containing the Message.

God says of this Messenger: "I will raise them up a Prophet from among their brethren, like unto thee (Moses). (Deuteronomy 18:18.)

Peter tells us that this Prophet shall come in the Times of the Restoration of All Things, when the Lord is to come. (Acts 3: 19-24.)

The Lord, Himself, tells us that Elijah is the Prophet who is to come and Restore All Things. (Matthew 17: 10-14.)

He is to come before the Great and Terrible Day of the Lord. (Malachi 4:5.)

As of old, in Elijah's time, there shall be a famine in the land. (1 Kings 17:1-16.) Not a famine for bread nor a thirst for water, but of hearing the Word of God.

It is a time when the people shall travel from sea to sea, and from the North even to the East, as they are doing today.

The Prophet Amos speaks of the Latter Days, when the earth shall tremble and shake, and when there shall be signs in the heavens. (Amos 8:8, 9.)

God also says that many shall run to and fro to seek the Word of Jehovah and they shall not find it. (Amos 8:11, 12.)

There shall be a famine of the Word of God, because false teaching of every kind shall abound.

The Devil, knowing that his time is short, shall revive the false religious systems of the past ages, to draw the people away from the Full Gospel teaching that God sends to the world through His Messenger.

These errors are presented to the world under new forms, and with a mixture of various degrees of truth.

Some of these errors are so subtle, and seem so much like truth, that multitudes of earnest people are being deceived by them.

The Devil understands mankind too well to think for a moment that they will accept any religious teaching that is all error.

The teaching that he gave Mother Eve was not all a lie, for God confirmed the truth of a part of what he said to her. (Genesis 3:4, 5, 22.)

God does not want us to go to the mixed Tree of the Knowledge of Good and Evil to get our spiritual food. (Genesis 2:17.)

He wants us to go the Tree of Life, Jesus, the Christ, who says that His words have in them His Spirit and His Life. (John 6:63; Revelation 22:2, 14.)

It is of the greatest importance that all the world shall be able to understand the Message which the Little Books carry forth.

The Apostle Peter tells us that every soul which shall not harken to this Prophet shall be utterly destroyed from among the people. (Acts 3:23, Deuteronomy 18:18, 19.)

This is because the Message which God sends is able to prepare a people for His Coming and preserve others from destruction during the Times of the Great Tribulation.

It is the Message of the Messenger of the Covenant, Elijah the Restorer, who has established the Christian Catholic Church in Zion.

This is not a denomination nor a sect.

It is the Restoration of the Primitive Apostolic Church, and is represented by the Church of Philadelphia, which John saw in his vision of these Latter Days. (Revelation 3:7-13.)

This Message must be forcible and denunciatory, striking blows that shall shake the world to its foundations.

It is spoken of as the seven thunders, because it is such a strong denunciation of seven great evils.

Under these seven heads may be classified all the sins of the world.

The several classes that are to be purged are: 1. The churches and their priests (Malachi 3:3, 4); 2. The sorcerers (*pharmakos*), pharmacists, or makers or venders of drugs; 3. The adulterers; 4. The false swearers (members of secret societies); 5. Those who oppress the hireling in his wages; 6. Those who oppress the widow and the fatherless; and, 7. Those who turn aside the stranger from his right (Malachi 3:5).

The Message must be expressed in language so simple that the most ignorant can understand, and so powerful as to command the attention of the most learned.

It must go forth in the Power of the Holy Spirit, in order that it may do the work which God says it shall do.

The Message of Elijah the Restorer, which goes over all the earth in the Literature of Zion, meets all these requirements.

It goes into the homes, and transforms the lives of the people.

Wherever its teaching is lived out, it gives the Power to break sinful habits, and to live pure, good lives in the fear of God and in a love for mankind.

The Messenger referring to the Little Book, said to John, "Take it, and eat it up; and it shall make thy belly bitter, but in thy mouth it shall be sweet as honey." (Revelation 10:9.)

This command is for all the world.

The entire Message must be eaten.

No part must be rejected.

It is bitter when it goes into man's inmost being and is being digested and lived out in his daily life.

Many who receive the Message with joy find it sweet to the taste at first, afterward "when tribulation or persecution ariseth because of the word, straightway" they stumble. (Mark 4:16, 17.)

These have no depth of earth in which the truths may take root.

They like to take life easy, and refuse to endure hardships as good soldiers of the Christ. (2 Timothy 2: 3.)

The hardships of life are needed to break up our hard, stony, human nature.

These hardships are like the storms, and cold, and heat, which break in pieces the stones and rocks of the earth, pulverizing them into soil in which vegetable life finds root and opportunity for growth.

This Message which comes to the world in these Latter Days is not like the message of any other man.

Those who try to mix with it other religious teaching will fail.

It is the New Wine which refuses to mix with the old wine of denominational teaching.

All this must be emptied out, and the man or woman must become a new being through Zion truths.

Multitudes are needed to take the Little Book from the hand of the Messenger, and send it through the world.

John caught a glimpse of the wonderful harvest that is to come from scattering this Message.

He saw it as "a great multitude which no man could number, out of every nation, and of all tribes and peoples and tongues, standing before the Throne and before the Lamb, arrayed in white robes, and palms in their hands." They come up out of the Great Tribulation. (Revelation 7:9, 14.)

Dear reader, are you standing idle while the fields of the world are white to the harvest?

Will you not take a part in Gathering this Harvest and have a share in the Harvest Home?

God calls you to work, and Zion Literature Mission needs your help.

Zion Literature Sent Out from a Free Distribution Fund Provided by Zion's Guests and the Friends of Zion.

Report for the week ending July 30, 1904:

19,782 Rolls to.. Business Men in the United States
4,646 Rolls to Hotels in United States and Canada
203 Rolls to........................ Germany
1,661 Rolls to.............. Hotels in Switzerland
7,212 Rolls to........................ Denmark
Number of Rolls for the week.............. 33,504
Number of Rolls reported to July 30, 1904, 3,200,203

Zion's Bible Class

Conducted by Deacon Daniel Sloan in Shiloh Tabernacle, Zion City, Lord's Day Morning at 11 o'clock, and in Zion Homes and Gatherings throughout the World.

MID-WEEK BIBLE CLASS LESSON, AUGUST 24th or 25th.

A Christian's Duty to Every Man.

1. *Show moderation to them.*—Philippians 4:4-7.
   Never act rashly with them.
   Never fly in a rage at them.
   Display a conservative demeanor.
2. *Honor them.*—1 Peter 2:13-24.
   Honor them for the worth they possess.
   Honor them for the good they might do.
   Honor them for what they really are.
3. *Be meek before them.*—Titus 3:1-7.
   Do not assume to be a lord over them.
   Remember your faults and failings.
   Think of your wicked past.
4. *Be peaceable with them.*—Hebrews 12.11-15.
   Do not give way to quarrels.
   You can not exercise Holiness and not possess Peace.
   You must be at peace with men before being at peace with God.
5. *Do good to them* —Galatians 6:9-10.
   Seek opportunities to do good to men.
   Pray that you may have eyes to see opportunities.
   Help the men you associate with.
6. *Love them.*—1 Thessalonians 3:8-13.
   Can you love the unlovable?
   God loves those who do not love Him.
   God can make you love others.
7. *Teach them.*—2 Timothy 2:22-26.
   Teach them the right way.
   Aptly show them the evil way.
   Be patient until they see it.
8. *Pray for them.*—1 Timothy 2:1-8.
   Pray for all classes of men.
   Pray for the masses of men.
   Pray for the worst and the best.

The Lord Our God is an Obligation-imposing God.

LORD'S DAY BIBLE CLASS LESSON, AUGUST 28th.

God's Alternatives to Men.

1. *They must die to sin or die in sin.*—Romans 6:16-18.
   Sin brings death.
   Righteousness brings life.
   Not serving sin is living without sin.
2. *They must abstain from evil or yield to it.*—1 Thessalonians 5:16-25.
   The spirit of evil must be shunned.
   They must refrain from evil habits
   They cannot justify themselves by evil doings.
3. *They must come out from wicked associates or be partakers with them.*—Revelation 18:2-8.
   The congregation of the wicked is very large.
   The wickedness of the masses is great
   God demands separation of his people.
4. *They must work for the Lord or serve the Devil.*—Matthew 6:19-26.
   So few know what it is to serve the Lord.
   They are such faithful servants of Mammon.
   They try to live with divided hearts.
5. *They must forget self or become sensual slaves.*—Matthew 16:24-28
   Self is alive to sin and its demands.
   Living for self is yielding to the Devil.
   The Devil puts self in the place of God.
6. *They must yield to God's will or be seduced by the Devil.*—Romans 6:19-23.
   Persons living in sin first become unclean.
   Then they are given to iniquity.
   Then they add iniquity to iniquity.
7. *They must forsake the world or perish with it.*—Matthew 3:7-12.
   The world is reserved unto fire.
   A baptism of fire is coming.
   A new heaven and a new earth will appear.

God's Holy People are a Whole-hearted People.

DO YOU KNOW GOD'S WAY OF HEALING?

BY THE REV. JOHN ALEX. DOWIE.

Let it be supposed that the following words are a conversation between the reader [A] and the writer [B].

A. What does this question mean? Do you really suppose that God has some one especial way of healing in these days, of which men may know and avail themselves?

B. That is exactly my meaning, and I wish very much that you should know God's Way of Healing, as I have known it for many years.

A. What is the way, in your opinion?

B. You should rather ask, WHO is God's Way? for the way is a Person, not a thing. I will answer your question in His own words, "I am the Way, and the Truth, and the Life: no one cometh unto the Father, but by Me." These words were spoken by our Lord Jesus, the Christ, the Eternal Son of God, who is both our Savior and our Healer. (John 14:6.)

A. But I always thought that these words only referred to Him as the Way of Salvation. How can you be sure that they refer to Him as the Way of Healing also?

B Because He cannot change. He is "the same yesterday and today, yea, and forever." (Hebrews 13.8.) He said that He came to this earth not only to save us but to heal us. (Luke 4:18), and He did this when in the flesh on earth. Being unchanged He must be able and willing and desirous to heal now.

A. But is there not this difference, namely, that He is not with us now?

B. No; for He said "Lo, I am with you All the Days, even unto the Consummation of the Age;" and so He is with us now, in spirit, just as much as when He was here in the flesh.

A. But did He not work these miracles of healing when on earth merely to prove that He was the Son of God?

B. No; there was still a greater purpose than that. He healed the sick who trusted in Him in order to show us that He came to die not only for our sins, but for our sicknesses, and to deliver us from both.

A. Then, if that be so, the atonement which He made on the Cross must have been for our sicknesses as well as our sins. Can you prove that is the fact from the Scriptures?

B. Yes, I can, and the passages are very numerous. I need quote only two. In Isaiah 53:4, 5, it is written of Him: "Surely He hath borne our griefs (Hebrew, *sicknesses*), and carried our sorrows: . . . and with His stripes we are healed." Then, in the Gospel according to Matthew, this passage is quoted and directly applied to the work of bodily healing, in the 8th chapter 17th verse: "That it might be fulfilled which was spoken by Isaiah the prophet, saying, Himself took our infirmities, and bare our diseases."

A. But do you not think that sickness is often God's will, and sent for our good, and therefore God may not wish us to be healed?

B. No, that cannot possibly be; for diseases of every kind are the Devil's work, and his work can never be God's will, since the Christ came for the very purpose of destroying "the works of the Devil." (1 John 3.8.)

A. Do you mean to say that all disease is the work of Satan?

B. Yes, for if there had been no sin (which came through Satan) there never would have been any disease, and Jesus never in one single instance told any person that sickness was God's work or will, but the very contrary.

A. Can you prove from Scriptures that all forms of sickness and infirmity are the Devil's work?

B. Yes, that can be done very easily. You will see in Matthew 4:23 and 9:35 that when Jesus was here in the flesh He healed "all manner of disease and all manner of sickness among the people." Then if you will refer to Acts 10.38 you will see that the Apostle Peter declares that He (Jesus) "went about doing good, and healing all that were oppressed of the Devil." Notice that all whom He healed, not some, were suffering from Satan's evil power.

A. But does disease never come from God?

B. No, it cannot come from God, for He is pure, and disease is unclean, and it cannot come out of Heaven, for there is no disease there.

A. That is very different from the teachings which I have received all my life from ministers and in the churches. Do you really think that you are right, and that they are all wrong in this matter?

B. It is not a question as between myself and them. The only question is, What does God's Word say? God has said in all the ages, to His Church, "I am Jehovah that healeth thee" (Exodus 15:26), and therefore it would be wicked to say that He is the defiler of His people. All true Christians must believe the Bible, and it is impossible to believe that good and evil, sickness and health, sin and holiness could have a common origin in God. If the Bible really taught that, it would be impossible to believe our Lord Jesus, the Christ, when He says: "A good tree cannot bring forth evil fruit, neither can a corrupt tree bring forth good fruit." (Matthew 7:18.)

A. But even if I agree with all you say, is it not true that the Gifts of Healing were removed from the Church, and are not in it now?

B. No, the "Gifts of Healing" were never withdrawn, and can never be withdrawn, from the true Church of God, for it is written: "The gifts and the calling of God are without repentance." (Romans 11:29.) There are nine gifts of God to the Church (enumerated in 1 Corinthians 12:8-11), and all these are in the Holy Spirit. Therefore, so long as the Holy Spirit is in the Church, all the gifts must be there also. If they are not exercised, that does not prove that they do not exist, but that the faith to exercise them is lacking in God's servants. The gifts are all perfectly preserved; for the Holy Spirit, not the Church, keeps them safely.

A. What should a Christian then do when overtaken with sickness?

B. A Christian should obey God's command, and at once turn to Him for forgiveness of the sin which may have caused the sickness, and for immediate healing. Healing is obtained from God in one of four ways, namely: First, by the direct prayer of faith, without any aid from the officers of the Church, praying as the Centurion did in Matthew 8:5-12; second, by two faithful disciples praying in perfect agreement, in accordance with the Lord's promise in Matthew 18.19; third, by the anointing of the Elders and the prayer of faith, according to the instructions in James 5:14 and 15; and fourth, by the laying on of the hands of them who believe, and whom God calls to that ministry, as the Lord commands in Mark 16:18, and in other places.

A. But are people healed in this way in these days?

B. Yes, in thousands of cases. I have myself laid hands upon many hundreds of thousands of persons, and I have seen the Lord's power manifested in the healing of great numbers, many of whom are living witnesses in many countries, who have testified publicly before thousands, and who are prepared to testify at any time. This ministry is being exercised by devoted Christians in many parts of America, Europe, Australasia, and elsewhere.

A. Is it not the same as Christian Science, Mind Healing, etc.?

B. No. Divine Healing is diametrically opposed to these diabolical counterfeits, which are utterly antichristian. These impostures are only seductive forms of Spiritualism. Trance Evangelism is also a more recent form of this delusion, and it deceives many.

A. But how shall I obtain the necessary faith to receive healing, which faith I am at present conscious that I do not possess?

B. It is written: "Belief cometh of hearing, and, hearing by the word of the Christ." (Romans 10:17.) Our Missions are held for the express purpose of teaching fully the Word of God on this matter, and I very heartily invite you to attend the meetings which are announced for Zion Tabernacles in Chicago and other cities, and for Shiloh Tabernacle, Zion City, Illinois. All are welcome and there are no charges of any kind made, for all God's gifts are free gifts. Salvation is the first of these, without which you cannot be healed through faith in Jesus. All the costs of this work are covered by the free-will offerings of the people who attend these meetings, and others whom the Lord leads to help; but the poorest, who have nothing to give, are as heartily welcome as the richest.

A. Do you see the sick and lay hands upon them in this Mission?

B. Yes; after we feel satisfied that they are fully resting in the Lord alone for the healing, we see privately, so far as time permits, those who attend; but under no circumstances do we claim the power to heal any; for "power belongeth unto God."

A. Have you any writings upon this subject which can be purchased?

B. Yes; these can be obtained at the office of Zion Printing and Publishing House, Zion City, Illinois, and at any Zion Tabernacle. But the best book on Divine Healing is the Bible itself, studied prayerfully and earnestly.

We extend to you a hearty invitation to attend the meetings, which are free to all. Our prayer is that you may be led to find in Jesus, the Christ, our Lord and God your present Savior from sin, your Healer from sickness, your Cleanser from all evil, your Keeper in the way to Heaven, your Friend, and your All for Time and Eternity. We pray that these words may help many who read, and that our little conversation may bear fruit in leading many readers to look to Jesus only.

"The Healing of Christ's seamless dress
Is by all beds of pain;
We touch Him in life's throng and press
And we are whole again."

OBEYING GOD IN BAPTISM.

"Baptizing Them Into the Name of the Father and of the Son and of the Holy Ghost."

Nineteen Thousand Two Hundred Seventy-eight Baptisms by Triune Immersion Since March 14, 1897.

Nineteen Thousand Two Hundred Seventy-eight Believers have joyfully followed their Lord in the Ordinance of Believer's Baptism by Triune Immersion since the first Baptism in Central Zion Tabernacle on March 14, 1897.

Baptized in Central Zion Tabernacle from March 14, 1897, to December 14, 1901, by the General Overseer,	4754			
Baptized in South Side Zion Tabernacle from January 1, 1902, to June 14, 1903, by the General Overseer..	37			
Baptized at Zion City by the General Overseer........	583			
Baptized by Overseers, Elders, Evangelists and Deacons, at Headquarters (Zion City) and Chicago......	5283			
Total Baptized at Headquarters....................	——			10,657
Baptized in places outside of Headquarters by the General Overseer................................		641		
Baptized in places outside of Headquarters by Overseers, Elders, Evangelists and Deacons............		7535		
Total Baptized outside of Headquarters............		——		8,176
Total Baptized in seven years and three months....				18,833
Baptized since June 14, 1904:				
Baptized in Zion City by the General Overseer........	64			
Baptized in Zion City by Elder Royall.........	11			
Baptized in Zion City by Elder Hammond...........	6			
Baptized in Zion City by Overseer Mason...........	90			
Baptized in Zion City by Overseer Excell...........	87			
Baptized in Zion City by Overseer Piper............	79			
Baptized in Chicago by Elder Hoffman............ .	4			
Baptized in Chicago by Elder Cossum.	6			
Baptized in Chicago by Elder Keller	5			
Baptized in Chicago by Elder Hall..................	3		355	
Baptized in Canada by Elder Brooks................		4		
Baptized in California by Elder Taylor..............		4		
Baptized in England by Overseer Cantel............		12		
Baptized in Indiana by Elder Osborn................		2		
Baptized in Minnesota by Elder Graves.............		5		
Baptized in Mississippi by Evangelist Gay............		1		
Baptized in Missouri by Evangelist Gay.............		1		
Baptized in Missouri by Elder Brock................		9		
Baptized in Missouri by Deacon Robinson...........		1		
Baptized in Nebraska by Elder Hoy.................		7		
Baptized in New York by Overseer Mason......		9		
Baptized in Ohio by Deacon Kelchner...............		3		
Baptized in Ohio by Deacon Arrington..............		5		
Baptized in South Africa by Overseer Bryant		10		
Baptized in Texas by Evangelist Gay...............		11		
Baptized in Washington by Elder Ernst.......... ..		3		
Baptized in Wisconsin by Elder McClurkin...........		3	90	445
Total Baptized since March 14, 1897......				19,278

The following-named ten believers were baptized in the Public Baths, Pretoria, Transvaal, South Africa, Lord's Day, July 3, 1904, by Overseer Daniel Bryant:

Hutchinson, Frank Oliver..........Johannesburg, Transvaal, South Africa
Leopold, Anna Catherine ..Rosenekal, Orange River Colony, South Africa
Mare, Paul ....Pretoria, Transvaal, South Africa
Rose, Ernest Andrew .. .. Pretoria, Transvaal, South Africa
Rose, Louis Henry .... Pretoria, Transvaal, South Africa
Sales, Sarah Elizabeth .... Pretoria, Transvaal, South Africa
Spuy, Ellen van der.............. . Pretoria, Transvaal, South Africa
Spuy, Hubert Arundel van der..... .. ..Pretoria, Transvaal, South Africa
Spuy, Kennith Reid............. ...Pretoria, Transvaal, South Africa
Spuy, Ursula Grace van der ....Pretoria, Transvaal, South Africa

The following-named two believers were baptized at San Francisco, California, Lord's Day, July 17, 1904, by Elder W. D. Taylor:

Ball, Helen.............. 14 Montezuma street, San Francisco, California
Woods, Miss May Violet, 436½ Clementine street, San Francisco, California

The following-named five believers were baptized in Lake Michigan, Zion City, Illinois, Saturday, July 30, 1904, by Elder F. A. Royall:

Chapman Mrs. Emily..............................Devoe, South Dakota
Cooper, Mrs. Margaret R.........................Spearfish, South Dakota
Frauzier, Felix..Dana, Indiana
Frauzier, Mrs. Talitha..................... ....Dana, Indiana
Mosher, Mrs. Mabel E...... . ...Sisseton, South Dakota

The following-named three believers were baptized in the West Side Zion Tabernacle, Chicago, Illinois, Lord's Day, July 31, 1904, by Elder L. C. Hall:

Estabrooke, Mrs. Martha.......................... Copemish, Michigan
Craig, Miss Agnes............... .....2025 Adams street, Chicago, Illinois
Williams, Miss Adaline........669 Washington boulevard, Chicago, Illinois

CONSECRATION OF CHILDREN.

The following-named child was consecrated to God, Wednesday, June 22, 1904, by Elder C. A. Hoy:

Young, May Esther........... ....Falls City, Nebraska

The following-named child was consecrated to God, Lord's Day, June 26, 1904, by Elder C. A. Hoy:

Willeford, Samuel..............918 Harmony street, Council Bluffs, Iowa

The following-named two children were consecrated to God at St. Louis, Missouri, Monday, July 4, 1904, by Elder F L. Brock:

Moon, James Wright................1312 Sarah street, St. Louis, Missouri
Moon, Ruth..........................1312 Sarah street, St. Louis, Missouri

The following-named child was consecrated to God in Zion City, Illinois, Lord's Day, July 24, 1904, by Overseer G. L. Mason:

Schmidt, Esther Ida Martha, Broadway ave., North, Fond du Lac, Wisconsin

The following-named two children were consecrated to God, in the West Side Zion Tabernacle, Chicago, Illinois, Lord's Day, July 31, 1904, by Elder L. C. Hall:

Bartholomee, Lemuel Alexander.......313 Cornell street, Chicago, Illinois
Bolich, De LaVerne................170 Potomac avenue, Chicago, Illinois

Warning.

I am directed by the General Overseer to warn our members and officers throughout the world against giving money to persons claiming to be members of the Christian Catholic Church in Zion. All benevolence must be given either from Headquarters or under the direction of same. Even though the applicant for benevolence be known to be a member of the Christian Catholic Church in Zion, financial aid must not be given except in extreme cases, and then only in small amounts. Requests for help must be made to the officer-in-charge. In cases where there is no such officer, requests should be made direct to Headquarters, accompanied by recommendations from one or two members of Zion in good standing. J. G. EXCELL,

General Ecclesiastical Secretary.

Notice to Correspondents.

In writing to Headquarters it is ***absolutely essential*** that the writer give his full address.

Failure to comply with this request necessitates looking up or referring to the Church Records, which involves much time, and is very frequently fruitless.

Friends and members of the Christian Catholic Church in Zion everywhere will please bear this in mind, especially those in foreign lands.

Faithfully yours in the Master's Service,

J. G. EXCELL, General Ecclesiastical Secretary.

Warning to Subscribers.

Scarcely a week passes that we do not have complaints about money having been sent to us in currency, stamps, or silver, in the open mails, for renewals of subscriptions or for other purposes, WHICH WE HAVE NOT RECEIVED AND WHICH NEVER REACHES US.

Therefore, we desire to warn every member and friend of Zion sending money to us, to always use some safe means, preferably a money-order, or bank-draft on New York or Chicago, or personal check on Zion City Bank.

In conforming to this notice you will save yourselves trouble and expense, and us much annoyance.

ZION PRINTING AND PUBLISHING HOUSE,
Zion City, Illinois.

SUCCESSFUL EXPERIENCE is the rock upon which the business world rests its confidence; and the power to do things in the face of every hindrance is the essential element of all true success. Zion has earned this confidence and demonstrated this power through her unparalleled achievements. As she emerges from every conflict, triumphant and renewed in strength, the conviction deepens in the minds of friend and foe, that her foundations are well laid.

A Threefold Security Is behind all Zion Investments.

1...The whole Zion Estate, personal and real, rated by Chicago business men at many millions above all liabilities.

2...A united people, ready by any sacrifice to protect the honor and integrity of Zion's undertakings.

3...The all-sufficient assurance: "God is in the midst of her; she shall not be moved."...*Psalm 46:5.*

A Beautiful New Booklet Describing the great Candy Industry in Zion, has just been issued, and should be in the hands of every Christian Investor. Zion Sugar and Confection Association Shares are most attractive. They now bear interest at the rate of 9 per cent. and will earn 10 per cent. from April 1, 1905. For a limited time they are offered at the par value of $100 a Share. Do not miss this opportunity. Copies of the New Booklet, Subscription Blanks, and further information freely furnished prospective investors. Address:

Fielding H. Wilhite, Manager Zion Securities and Investments Zion City, Illinois

ZION CITY BANK

JOHN ALEX. DOWIE

ZION CITY, LAKE COUNTY, ILLINOIS, U. S. A.

Transacts a general Banking Business.

Issues Drafts payable in all the principal cities of the world.

Sells high-grade Securities bearing nine per cent. interest per annum. Particulars mailed on application.

Our Savings Department receives deposits from One Dollar upward, and pays interest at the following rates:

On all sums from $1 to $500, four per cent.

On all sums over $500, three per cent.

This Bank encourages thrift and economy among the people, and will assist them in their efforts to save money.

Our system of Banking by Mail has proved entirely satisfactory to thousands of persons living in different parts of this and other countries. It places everybody in close communication with the Bank and enables them to take advantage of the *excellent facilities* offered.

Correspondence from all parts of the world solicited.

Write for our booklet entitled, "Saving Money."

CHARLES J. BARNARD, Manager.
WILLIAM S. PECKHAM, Cashier.
CHARLES H. IRISH, Assistant Cashier.

LEAVES OF HEALING

Edited by REV. JOHN ALEXANDER DOWIE General Overseer of the Christian Catholic Church in Zion. . .

A 32-PAGE WEEKLY PAPER

For the Extension of the Kingdom of God. Contains Sermons, Addresses, and Editorial Notes by the General Overseer; Testimonies to Healing through Faith in Jesus, and Reports of Zion's Work Throughout the World.

Price, a year, $2.00

THE ZION BANNER

Edited by REV. JOHN ALEXANDER DOWIE General Overseer of the Christian Catholic Church in Zion . . .

A WEEKLY NEWSPAPER

For the Extension of the Kingdom of God and the Elevation of Man. Deals with Social, Commercial, Political, and Industrial Problems. News from all over the World reliably reported. Notes on progress in the building up of Zion City. *Subscription Price, 50c for 6 months.* Address, General Manager Zion Printing and Publishing House, Zion City, Illinois, U. S. A.

Train Schedule Between Zion City and Chicago

Via Chicago & North-Western Railway.

Effective May 22, 1904.

Weekday Trains.

CHICAGO TO ZION CITY. Leave Chicago	Arrive Zion City	ZION CITY TO CHICAGO. Leave Zion City	Arrive Chicago
7.00 a. m.	8.25 a. m.	*6.45 a. m.	8.15 a. m.
*9.00 a. m.	10.13 a. m.	7.03 a. m.	8.30 a. m.
*11.30 a. m.	12.37 p. m.	8.22 a. m.	9.50 a. m.
2.00 p. m.	3.08 p. m.	*9 45 a. m.	11.10 a. m.
3.00 p. m	4.16 p. m.	*11.49 a. m.	1.15 p. m.
4.15 p. m.	5.39 p. m.	*‖1.18 p. m.	2.50 p. m.
*5.20 p. m.	6.50 p. m.	*†2.33 p. m.	4.00 p. m.
*8.00 p. m.	9.11 p. m.	5.05 p. m.	6.30 p. m.
		*7.59 p. m.	9 30 p. m

Sunday Trains.

CHICAGO TO ZION CITY. Leave Chicago	Arrive Zion City
9.05 a m.	10.18 a. m.
*10.45 a. m.	12.37 p. m.
2.15 p. m.	4.05 p. m.
*8.00 p. m.	9.11 p. m.

ZION CITY TO CHICAGO. Leave Zion City	Arrive Chicago
*8.29 a. m.	9.45 a. m.
5.05 p. m.	6.40 p. m.
7.59 p. m.	9.30 p. m.

Train leaves Waukegan at 12.28 p. m., arriving in Zion City at 12.37 p. m., daily, including Sunday.

* Signifies change train at Waukegan. † Train does not run South on Saturdays. ‖ Train runs South on Saturday only.

ZION'S TRANSPORTATION AND RAILWAY AFFAIRS (John Alex. Dowie), of Zion City, Illinois, supervises the railway ticket, steamship, excursion, freight, express and transfer business of Zion and her people everywhere. Direction as to railroad and steamship routes given upon request.

DEACON JAMES F. PETERS,
General Superintendent Zion Transportation.

Come From The Four Winds O Breath

AND

Breathe Upon These Slain

That They May Live.

This Prophecy or declaratory prayer recorded in the 37th Chapter of Ezekiel is being fulfilled to-day. The Breath which is the Holy Spirit is coming into those who have obeyed the command

"O, ye Dry Bones, Hear the Word of the Lord"

An exceedingly great army will hear and stand up and live, even the whole House of Israel and those who are engrafted. The Holy Spirit is doing this work through the spoken words of Rev. John Alexander Dowie and his Sermons and Editorials and the testimonies recorded in . . . .

LEAVES OF HEALING

Is this prayer in your heart and work?

Can you expect the commendation that the woman received of whom the Christ said "She hath done what she could?"

Do all you can by sending out **LEAVES OF HEALING, THE ZION BANNER, BLATTER DER HEILUNG** and other Zion Literature, and be sure that no one whom you can reach will have a chance to say they have never had an opportunity to know the Word of the Lord.

REMEMBER THE INDUCEMENT:

"They that turn many to righteousness shall shine as the stars forever and ever."

SEND ALL ORDERS TO

ZION PRINTING AND PUBLISHING HOUSE, ZION CITY, ILL.

A WEEKLY PAPER FOR THE EXTENSION OF THE KINGDOM OF GOD
EDITED BY THE REV. JOHN ALEX. DOWIE.

Volume XV. No. 17. ZION CITY, SATURDAY, AUGUST 13, 1904. Price Five Cents

GOD'S WITNESSES TO DIVINE HEALING.

HUSBAND SAVED FROM UNBELIEF AND HEALED OF INSANITY—WIFE HEALED OF INTERNAL TROUBLES, SINKING SPELLS, AND OTHER DISEASES.

IF I MAKE MY BED IN HELL, BEHOLD, THOU ART THERE!

God sets no limits upon His Love, Mercy and Power. It is man, in his presumption, that has attempted to put metes and bounds upon God.

The conceit and folly of puny man has led him to attempt the obvious impossibility of defining the Infinite.

"Fools rush in where angels fear to tread," and we find intellectual and spiritual degenerates and pygmies glibly and oracularly telling where God's Love stops short, where His Mercy ends, and where His Power fails.

It is man, not God, who judicially pronounces the sentence, "a hopeless case."

It is man, not God, who says that a human being can sink so deep into sin and unbelief that there is no hope for him.

It is man, not God, who says that one can be so wasted and defiled by disease that there is no hope of recovery.

In God, there is Eternal Hope.

He is Love.

HE IS always and everywhere.

Therefore there is no time and no place where His Love can ever fail—it is as Infinite as Himself. And His Mercy—hear the words which He Himself inspired, sung over and over again in sweetest music, "For His Mercy endureth FOREVER!" He is the Father of all spirits, and never, in all the endless cycles of eternity can His ear be deaf to the penitent cry of any of His children.

GEORGE W. COSPER.

His Word says of Him:

> All things were made by Him; and without Him was not anything made that hath been made.

Surely the Creator has Power over His Creation!

Surely He who is the Father of man's spirit and the Maker of his soul and body has Power to save that spirit and cleanse and heal that soul and body!

The man and wife whose portraits and testimonies appear on these pages, are Witnesses to the glorious truth that God's Love, Mercy, and Power reach down into the lives of His children today.

The husband had made his bed in a hell of unbelief, doubt, and fear.

No hope for this life, spiritually, psychically or physically, and no hope for the life to come, brightened the deep darkness of that inferno.

The deadly despair of such a life, coupled with disease, gave the Devil power over his mind.

From deepest melancholia, he became the victim of the most horrible hallucinations.

His mental and spiritual agony became so great that, bereft of sleep, he paced the floor in an ecstasy of shuddering horror, night after night, for weeks.

Again and again, his mania drove him to the very verge of murder and suicide.

Such was his condition—a man past middle life, deep in infidelity and insanity!

There were many to pronounce the verdict, "a hopeless case," upon him.

His good wife, in addition to all the care, anxiety, and sorrow caused by her husband's condition, suffered severely from many diseases.

Internal troubles, affection of the stomach, extreme prostration and sinking spells, and, worse than all, a terrible difficulty in her head, made it seem almost as if she, too, had made her bed in Hell.

There God's Love found them.

There they learned that with God there is no such thing as "a hopeless case."

The simple, straightforward, truthful story written by Deaconess Cosper, and confirmed by her husband, tells how God, in His Infinite Love, brought to them the Message of Hope, founded upon His Divine Word.

She tells how, in His Infinite Mercy, He heard the very faint cry of penitence that went up from the insanity-fettered spirit of the husband, and freely forgave him all his years of unbelief and rebellion.

She tells how the Illimitable Power of God restored the forgiven sufferer to sanity and health, and how that Power, in answer to the Prayer of Faith, healed her of all her terrible afflictions, so that she is the strong, well, capable woman of God and Deaconess in the Christian Catholic Church in Zion that we see pictured here.

All glory and praise to God!

Suffering, sinning, doubting, despairing one, we bid you be of hope!

Sick, weary, weak, dying one, we bid you be of hope!

Loving, yearning, sorrowing one, whose loved one is far from God, we bid you be of hope!

God Lives!

God Loves!

God's Mercy endureth Forever!

God's Power, in all its Irresistible Might, is at your behest, if you trust and obey.

A. W. N.

WRITTEN TESTIMONY OF GEORGE W. COSPER.

318 WASHBURN AVENUE,
SISTERSVILLE, WEST VIRGINIA,
April 28, 1904.

DEAR GENERAL OVERSEER:—It is with deep gratitude to God, that I add my testimony to the many thousands in LEAVES OF HEALING, telling what God has done for me, in and through Zion.

The extent of this can never be told, but I can enjoy it, and thank God and Zion.

I regret to say that, until nearly fifty-four years of age, I lived without God, and to some extent, a life of sin.

Failing to give my heart to God in early life, when it would have been comparatively easy, in later life I became skeptical, a disbeliever in the Word of God, in the Divinity of our Lord Jesus, and in the entire Plan of Salvation.

Then, when my mind became clouded, growing worse and worse, my case seemed indeed hopeless.

DEACONESS MARIETTA COSPER.

Yet, God did not let me go, and in His Love and Mercy sent me deep conviction.

I knew not how to find God.

Meantime, doctors and a hospital failed to help, and my mind continued to grow worse.

At last, in answer to prayer, God opened the way and my wife took me to Divine Healing Home No. 1, Chicago.

This was much against my will, but she persisted.

The first two weeks of my stay I heard the Bible read and taught until the very foundations of my skepticism and unbelief were shaken.

I was in despair and deep melancholy.

There were "fightings within and without"—mostly within.

My sufferings were indescribable.

I constantly expected to be killed, and thought horrible plans were being devised for my torture and death.

My wife, too, was in some danger from me; but she did not know it, and God stayed my hand.

During our stay I received much blessing and help, but on leaving that place of Christian love and harmony and coming to our friends here, I refused to obey, and went back on such consecration as I had made.

The Devil took a greater hold on me than ever before.

For months I was hopeless, and believed myself doomed to hell.

But my wife continued to request prayers, without my knowledge; and at last the Light of Salvation and Healing broke in upon me.

Since that time my Light and Joy have increased, my Faith has grown stronger, my Love deeper, my Hope brighter.

For all this, I thank God.

I wish to express my deep Love and Gratitude to our dear General Overseer, his good wife, and to all who gave a helping hand in that time of darkness.

I have been healed many times in these years; twice of a very severe attack of grip, the last quite recently.

Although sixty-three years of age, and feeling the loss of youthful vigor, my general health is better than in my early life.

I long to live and see Zion triumph, and greet the Coming of the King.

But greatly as I value my healing, far more do I prize the spiritual blessing which God has given me.

I praise Him that He has enlightened my darkness.

I rejoice to be able to say spiritually, with the blind man, "Whereas once I was blind, I now see."

I remain, faithfully in Jesus' Name,
GEORGE W. COSPER.

WRITTEN TESTIMONY OF DEACONESS MARIETTA COSPER.

318 WASHBURN AVENUE,
SISTERSVILLE, WEST VIRGINIA,
April 28, 1904.

DEAR GENERAL OVERSEER:—It is with gratitude and pleasure that I write my testimony, recording, in some measure, what God, through Zion, has wrought in us.

In the spring of 1893, not having been well for many years, I suffered an almost entire breakdown.

I will not speak at any length of my diseases, as to tell of my healing is by no means the leading purpose of this testimony; but, rather, that I may describe the wonderful conversion and healing of my dear husdand.

I had been ill for two years previously to his terrible affliction, and through all that time God had been calling me to Zion.

But my "eyes were holden," and I did not understand.

Therefore, my going at last with him to Zion Home was but a later step in what seems one story, that cannot well be separated.

Concerning my diseases, I will simply say that they were many, among which were severe internal trouble, great prostration with sinking spells, stomach trouble, and a terrible difficulty in my head, which was far worse than all.

During the summer of 1893 I was forced to spend much time in bed.

At this time I received my first literature on Divine Healing, which was brought to me by an earnest lady whom God had interested in me.

I read the tracts and leaflets which she brought, but without special interest.

I failed to see God's leading. Yet it was my aim to live a close, consecrated life, and I had been a very earnest church worker for years.

I spent a most miserable winter, with greatly increased suffering.

The trouble in my head became so annoying, that on one occasion, while writing a letter, I suffered an almost entire collapse of mind and body.

In the Spring of 1894, we removed from our old home near Bradford, Pennsylvania, to Indiana, a short distance south of Fort Wayne.

Here our troubles increased.

I saw that my husband was in a bad way, very despondent, and at times almost desperate; but I attributed it to other causes, and did not realize that his mind was affected

As winter approached, I became much worse.

Sinking spells were more frequent.

Sometimes I staggered and well-nigh fell.

At this time, while Satan seemed attacking on all sides, the truth came to me, that I had failed to follow God.

I began to see His leading, and turned to Him in repentance.

One day I asked God, if He was leading me to Divine Healing, to save my husband, and make him a believer; for, although skeptical on all points, he was especially bitter in his opposition to Divine Healing.

In my weakness it seemed that I could not take another step alone.

How God answered that prayer, the remainder of this testimony tells.

Soon LEAVES OF HEALING came; three copies of Volume I.

They had been first sent to my sister in Pennsylvania, who sent them to me.

One contained the story of the Healing of Willie Esser; another the account of the raising of Mrs. S. A. Kelley.

I read with great interest, and from that time longed to go, and prayed that the way might be opened.

Next, grip attacked us, making three of us its victims.

While I was confined to my room, however, God blessed in lifting me to a place of spiritual rest, such as I had never known.

This prepared me, in a great measure, for the terrible scenes through which I had yet to pass.

My husband seemed to recover at first, but was immediately taken worse, with what the physician called "effects of grip."

At times, we would both be lying in bed. I was scarcely able to rise often enough to give him his medicine.

We were also in the depths of financial difficulty.

It was a dark time, the one ray of light being the spiritual blessing God had given me, which was exceedingly precious, and which kept me calm and restful.

At this time, I asked God for my husband's salvation, and almost at once, found that he was trying to pray.

I tried to help him, little realizing the mighty power which must be manifested before he could "see Jesus."

He continued to grow worse.

He would throw his body into the most terrible contortions, spring from the floor, strike his hands together, and rush out of the house like a madman.

The physician seemed perplexed, and wished that he might be sent to a hospital.

We secured another physician, who thought the same.

One day, my husband asked me to have the gun put away, saying he had bad spells, and though he tried to pray, he could not tell what might happen.

He has since told me that he rose three times and took the gun, and it seemed as if a voice spoke, and told him not to do it.

I told the physician, who said it showed momentary insanity, which might become permanent, and strongly advised a hospital.

We took him to Fort Wayne and placed him in a hospital (I think St. Joseph's) under the care of one of the best physicians in the city, Dr. Rosenthal.

I visited him there, and conversed with his physician, who told me he was suffering from neurasthenia, and that he might lose his mind unless he grew better, but that they were trying to build him up.

He returned home with me, the physician thinking the change might do him good, but we sent him back in a few days.

Here he was taken much worse, and almost in spite of them, left the hospital and came home to us. He was wild and worried for a few days, then he seemed to take a turn for the better, and for two weeks seemed almost well, even caring for me.

Subsequently, I suddenly came upon him, and saw him slipping a cartridge into his gun.

At first, he evaded my question, then told me that persons would soon be there to arrest him, and said this was the easiest way out.

I sat and held the gun and prayed, until I succeeded in sending him out to dinner; then ran out at a back door, and carried the gun to the home of his brother, who lived near.

Then began a most terrible time of watching.

For four weeks, he paced the floor almost day and night, hat in hand, peering from the window, in the most terrible fear and excitement, constantly expecting arrest, torture and death.

We could scarcely prevail on him to take food, or to lie down, in that time.

It was, indeed, terrible.

We had sent a telegram to his nephew, in West Virginia, Mr. J. R. Griffith, and his mother (both now of Zion City).

They came at once, but his sister could scarcely endure the strain, and stayed away much of the time.

I was marvelously sustained.

His sister went to Fort Wayne, to see the physician, who said they could do no more, and suggested a specialist, saying it would take some money.

I then told her of my wish to go to Zion for myself, and that my husband had once expressed a desire to go.

Preparations were begun at once.

I wrote to and received a reply from Mrs. Dowie.

I wrote again asking if we could come, and then, without waiting for a reply, started.

The four weeks past had been weeks of waiting, —no light, no money, no open door; but the moment our faces were turned Zionward, there came a wondrous change.

The way opened and cleared, money came from different sources, and in five days from the time I first wrote we started, at midnight, our nephew going with us.

We arrived in the morning, and found Edgerton avenue.

I was taken to Divine Healing Home No. 3, and introduced to the steward.

Upon hearing of my husband's condition, he was quite doubtful about receiving him.

I told him that I knew God had sent me, and promised that if my husband made trouble I would take him away.

We were finally installed in Divine Healing Home No. 1.

It was the summer of 1895—the year of the persecution.

We arrived on a Saturday morning, about the last of June.

We attended the meeting for the guests in the afternoon, and the next day, Lord's Day, I had the pleasure of hearing him who is now our beloved General Overseer, recount how God had enabled him to triumph over his enemies.

As he led in the recital of the 91st Psalm, the reality of that glorious Word appealed to me as never before.

I was also present, on a Lord's Day, later, when he was twice arrested on the platform, and went with the officer, leaving the meeting in charge of his wife.

Never can I forget the matchless courage he displayed, as well as his justice and kindness to the officer who made the arrest.

My own healing was wonderful, and began, I believe, before leaving home.

The sinking spells disappeared, and have never returned.

My husband, however, progressed but slowly.

In two weeks his skepticism had disappeared, but he was in despair.

His case was very trying, and seemed, indeed, well-nigh hopeless.

I had great difficulty in getting him to the meetings, especially at the Tabernacle.

On one occasion he seemed taken, and almost shaken, by some invisible power, reminding me strongly of the young man whom the evil spirit tore so severely while on the way to Jesus.

Besides his constant fear, he felt that the Tabernacle, and especially the healing-room, were too sacred for him to enter.

Once, I think, the fight lasted about two hours before he yielded and went into the healing-room.

Sometimes one, sometimes another, sometimes a number, came to the rescue, and once Dr. Dowie came up to him, took his hand, and, with kindness I can never forget, said to him, "If you were the Devil's castaway, you would be the very man we want up there," and sent Captain (now Colonel) Stern to take him up-stairs.

Though he had no ill-will toward any of the guests, what I passed through in our room none but God will ever know.

He has since told me that he once had his hand on my throat to choke me, but *something* had prevented him.

It was a long fight, but gradually he grew calm, gentle, and kind; and when we left, on the first of October, and came to our friends here in West Virginia, the victory seemed well-nigh won.

But on coming into an atmosphere of unbelief, and among wicked men, Satan reasserted his power.

My husband rebelled, and refused to obey God.

The result was terrible.

It was a clear case of "and the last state of that man becometh worse than the first."

He became fierce and wicked; and when we came into our little home by ourselves, he was almost uncontrollable.

It was pitiful to see him pace the floor, and declare he was going to hell. This was the greatest trial of all. I had not expected it, and was unprepared.

The battle seemed lost.

His friends, who had stood by us so faithfully, thought the time had come to send him to an asylum, as they feared that our lives were in danger.

Leaving him with our son, I went to his sister.

Together we prayed, and I wrote to Dr. Dowie before coming home.

It seemed as if the turning point hung on that decision.

He began at once to be better, perhaps before I reached home, and continued better.

A few months later, I sent another request, and the result was marvelous, many times greater than I had ever seen when we were in Zion Home.

So marked was it that, though for months he had steadily refused even to take a short walk or scarcely to leave the house, he began at once doing these things; and in a few days he went twenty-eight miles from home and worked more than a week.

Later, I wrote once more, and he received the assurance of his Salvation as well as more perfect healing.

I sent these requests (three in all) without his knowledge, and God answered.

Still later, he came into great spiritual blessing, and for seven years he has been a strong, fearless Christian, growing ever more loyal to God and to Zion.

These years have tested the permanency of his healing, as he has been often under the greatest mental and physical strain.

He has been healed in answer to his own prayers, and has been healed of two severe attacks of grip, one but a few weeks ago, which I am sure would have proved fatal had we not received direct answer from God, which came at Zion's hour of prayer.

In conclusion, I wish to express my deep gratitude and love to our beloved General Overseer, his dear wife, Overseer Speicher and wife, Elder J. Thomas Wilhide, Colonel Stern and all others who, by their sympathy and prayers, helped in fighting the terrible battle; and, above all, to praise God, who saved and restored my dear husband, and caused him to be found "sitting, clothed, and in his right mind, at the feet of Jesus."

Hoping and praying that this testimony may bring courage and hope to other poor sufferers, and cause decision and obedience on the part of some halting child of God, I remain,

Faithfully Till He Come,

(MRS.) MARIETTA COSPER.

A WEEKLY PAPER FOR THE EXTENSION OF THE KINGDOM OF GOD.
EDITED BY THE REV. JOHN ALEX. DOWIE

Application for entry as Second Class Matter at Zion City, Illinois, pending.

Subscription Rates.		Special Rates.	
One Year	$2.00	100 Copies of One Issue	$3.00
Six Months	1.25	25 Copies of One Issue	1.00
Three Months	.75	To Ministers, Y. M. C. A's and Public Reading Rooms, per annum	1.50
Single Copies	.05		

For foreign subscriptions add $1.50 per year, or three cents per copy for postage.

Subscribers desiring a change of address should give present address, as well as that to which they desire LEAVES OF HEALING sent in the future.

Make Bank Drafts, Express Money or Postoffice Money Orders payable to the order of JOHN ALEX. DOWIE, Zion City, Illinois, U. S. A.

Long Distance Telephone. *Cable Address "Dowie, Zion City."*

All communications upon business must be addressed to
MANAGER ZION PUBLISHING HOUSE,
Zion City, Illinois, U. S. A.

Subscriptions to LEAVES OF HEALING, A VOICE FROM ZION, and the various publications may also be sent to

ZION PUBLISHING HOUSE, 81 EUSTON ROAD, LONDON, N. W., ENGLAND.

ZION PUBLISHING HOUSE, NO. 43 PARK ROAD, ST. KILDA, MELBOURNE, VICTORIA, AUSTRALIA.

ZION PUBLISHING HOUSE, RUE DE MONT, THABOR 1, PARIS, FRANCE.

ZIONSHEIM, SCHLOSS LIEBBURG, CANTON THURGAU, BEI ZÜRICH, SWITZERLAND.

ZION CITY, ILLINOIS, SATURDAY, AUGUST 13, 1904.

TABLE OF CONTENTS.

LEAVES OF HEALING, SATURDAY, AUGUST 13, 1904.

LEAVES OF HEALING.

Two Dollars will bring to you the weekly visits of the Little White Dove for a year; 75 cents will send it to a friend for thirteen weeks; $1.25 will send it for six months; $1.50 will send it to your minister, or to a Y. M. C. A., or to a Public Reading Room for a whole year. We offer no premiums, except the premium of doing good. We receive no advertisements, and print no commercial lies or cheating enticements of unscrupulous thieves. LEAVES OF HEALING is Zion on wings, and we keep out everything that would detract the reader's mind from all except the Extension of the Kingdom of God, for which alone it exists. If we cannot send forth our Little White Dove without soiling its wings with the smoke of the factory and the dirt of the wrangling market-place, or compelling it to utter the screaming cries of the business vultures in the ears of our readers, then we will keep our Dove at home.

GOD'S WAY OF HEALING.

BY THE REV. JOHN ALEX. DOWIE.

God's Way of Healing Is a Person, Not a Thing.

Jesus said "*I am* the Way, and the Truth, and the Life," and He has ever been revealed to His people in all the ages by the Covenant Name, Jehovah-Rophi, or "*I am* Jehovah that Healeth thee." (John 14:6; Exodus 15:26.)

The Lord Jesus, the Christ, is Still the Healer.

He cannot change, for "Jesus, the Christ, is the same yesterday and today, yea and forever;" and He is still with us, for He said: "Lo, *I am* with you All the Days, even unto the Consummation of the Age." (Hebrews 13:8; Matthew 28:20.) Because He is Unchangeable, and because He is present, in spirit, just as when in the flesh, He is the Healer of His people.

Divine Healing Rests on the Christ's Atonement.

It was prophesied of Him, "Surely He hath borne our griefs (Hebrew, *sickness*), and carried our sorrows: . . . and with His stripes we are healed;" and it is expressly declared that this was fulfilled in His Ministry of Healing, which still continues. (Isaiah 53:4, 5; Matthew 8:17.)

Disease Can Never be God's Will.

It is the Devil's work, consequent upon Sin, and it is impossible for the work of the Devil ever to be the Will of God. The Christ came to "destroy the works of the Devil," and when He was here on earth He healed "all manner of disease and all manner of sickness," and all these sufferers are expressly declared to have been "oppressed of the Devil." (1 John 3:8; Matthew 4:23; Acts 10:38.)

The Gifts of Healing Are Permanent.

It is expressly declared that the "Gifts and the calling of God are without repentance," and the Gifts of Healing are amongst the Nine Gifts of the Spirit to the Church. (Romans 11:29; 1 Corinthians 12:8-11.)

There Are Four Modes of Divine Healing.

The first is the direct prayer of faith; the second, intercessory prayer of two or more; the third, the anointing of the elders, with the prayer of faith; and the fourth, the laying on of hands of those who believe, and whom God has prepared and called to that Ministry. (Matthew 8:5-13; Matthew 18:19; James 5:14, 15; Mark 16:18.)

Divine Healing Is Opposed by Diabolical Counterfeits.

Amongst these are Christian Science (falsely so-called), Mind Healing, Spiritualism, Trance Evangelism, etc. (1 Timothy 6:20, 21; 1 Timothy 4:1, 2; Isaiah 51:22, 23.)

Multitudes Have Been Healed Through Faith in Jesus.

The writer knows of thousands of cases and has personally laid hands on scores of thousands of persons. Full information can be obtained at the meetings held in the Zion Tabernacles in Chicago, and in Zion City, Illinois, and in many pamphlets which give the experience, in their own words, of many who have been healed in this and other countries, published at Zion Printing and Publishing House, Zion City, Illinois.

"Belief Cometh of Hearing, and Hearing by the Word of the Christ."

You are heartily invited to attend and hear for yourself.

General Letter from the General Overseer

"Ben MacDhui," White Lake,
Montague, Michigan,
U. S. A.,
August 11, 1904.

[By Special Messenger.]

To the Officers and Members of the Christian Catholic Church in Zion, and of Zion Restoration Host, and to All who Love Our Lord Jesus, the Christ, in Sincerity, Throughout the World:

Beloved Brothers and Sisters in Jesus, the Christ, Our Lord and Coming King:

"GO FORWARD!"

Beside the Sea, "When Pharaoh drew nigh, the children of Israel lifted up their eyes, and, behold, the Egyptians marched after them; and they were sore afraid: and the Children of Israel cried out unto Jehovah."

And in the same breath they bitterly and unjustly reproached their Leader, ending with the bitter cry, "It were better for us to serve the Egyptians, than that we should die in the wilderness."

That mighty Leader and Prophet whom they thus reproached, knowing that he had obeyed the command of God in leading the people, replied:

Fear ye not, *stand still*, and see the Salvation of Jehovah,
Which He will work for you today:
For the Egyptians whom ye have seen today,
Ye shall see them again no more forever.
Jehovah shall fight for you,
And ye shall hold your peace.

MOSES' MISTAKEN ORDER—STAND STILL!

These were, for the most part, brave and true words, and yet Moses erred in one thing.

It was not wise to say, "Stand still!"

Victories are never won by the army that "stands still."

In the Far East, today, the world is looking upon two great Armies fighting for Oriental supremacy.

All thoughtful observers say that it is not the lethargy of the Russian Slav, but the persistent energy of the Japanese Mongolian, which is winning in the mighty conflict.

AN UP-TO-DATE ILLUSTRATION.

Never *Standing Still*, but ever *Going Forward*, the Armies and war-ships of the numerically smaller Nation are proving the stronger, by the persistency with which they press onward every hour and every day.

Going Forward, and keeping on going, never resting, ever thinking and ever acting, the Japanese advance, until the awful spectacle is seen of a Giant Empire in its death throes, whose Naval power is broken, and whose Armies are fleeing before the foe which encompasses them on every side.

This great object lesson of human warfare between the Children of Darkness is full of instruction for Zion and all the Children of Light everywhere, in this time as in Moses' Day.

The Army which "stands still," and waits for the Foe to come up, is easily overtaken and destroyed.

GOD'S REBUKE TO MOSES AND ISRAEL.

God rebuked Moses for that foolish command to the Hosts of Israel, "*Stand still!*"

It was right to say, "Fear ye not, ... and see the Salvation of Jehovah," but it was not right to say, "Stand still," even although God would fight for them.

Hence the rebuke when the Lord said unto Moses:

Wherefore criest thou unto Me?
Speak unto the Children of Israel,
That they Go Forward.
And lift thou up thy Rod,
And stretch out thine hand over the Sea, and divide it:
And the Children of Israel shall go into the midst of the Sea on dry ground.

ISRAEL AGAIN BESIDE THE SEA.

Once more the Israel of God stands beside the Sea.

The many thousands of Zion, who have come out of the Bondage of Apostasy in the Church, and out of Pollution in the World, are *crying* unto Jehovah.

But they are not *obeying* as they could and ought the command of their Leader under God, the Prophet whom He hath raised up, "as He raised up Moses."

Many are more disposed to "*stand still*" than to obey the voice of Elijah the Restorer, which rings out to the people of God in this Dark Night of the World's Terror, "GO FORWARD."

We do not desire to reproach any, much less to reproach all, in the Christian Catholic Church in Zion.

We gratefully record the fact that "Hitherto hath Jehovah helped us," and that the people of God in Zion have gone forward.

ZION'S DANGER IS IN STANDING STILL

But six months of "standing still" on many lines, and of a little *going backward* in some things, during our absence on our Around-the-World Visitation, has given to some in Zion, and more especially to those outside of

Zion City, the thought that it might be well to continue to "*stand still*" for a time, and thus repeat the mistake which Moses made, and for which God rebuked Moses, bidding him to see that it was vain for either him or the people to be continually praying for a salvation which would never come while they *stood still*.

GOD'S COMMAND TO ZION!

"Wherefore criest thou unto Me?" was God's Rebuke.

"Speak unto the people that they *Go Forward*," was God's Command.

Let the Rebuke come with power to those in Zion who are waiting for a deliverance which only comes to those who *Obey* and *Go Forward*.

All over the earth today there are thousands and tens of thousands of those in Zion who are "standing still."

Long ago we uttered the Command to Zion in all the world, in the Name of Jehovah, "*Go Forward!*"

Year after year we have "lifted the Rod of Faith" and "stretched out our hand over the Sea."

And God has divided it, and the pathway of deliverance has always been to those who have boldly advanced on "dry ground in the midst of the Sea."

Part of the Host of Zion have crossed between the "walls of water," and part are crossing now.

But a timorous multitude still stand, some in distant lands and some in this land, hesitating, and therefore hindering, the onward march, the complete deliverance, and the triumphant victories of Zion.

God has brought you all, my beloved brethren and sisters, out of a worse than Egyptian Bondage, the Bondage of Satan, and sin, and disease, and death, and hell.

But your deliverance is not complete, and cannot be completed, whilst you cling to Egypt and fear to go out with Israel, and journey with those who have advanced onwards through the deserts, through the seas, between the mountains, and along the valleys, until you cross the Jordan and enter into the "Land of Promise."

THE PATH OF FAITH IS THE PATH OF VICTORY.

God is calling out His people, as He has called you, in these Latter Days, to follow in the Path of Faith, in which His people have ever trod when they have been victorious.

The Apostasy never leads the people of God out of Bondage to the World, but bids them remain the social, commercial, and political slaves of the Pharaohs who oppress God's people.

The ministers of the Apostasy bid God's people stay in cities which are ruled by the World, the Flesh, and the Devil.

In these Cities of Destruction, corruption and blasphemy in the rulers, and intemperance, impurity, and infidelity amongst the people, are so general that anything else is only an exception to that terrible rule.

ZION DEMANDS SEPARATION AND CO-OPERATION.

Zion demands that God's people shall come out and be separate, leaving the swine-steeped lands and Gadarene conditions, leaving the Sodoms and Gomorrahs, to enter into loving association and co-operation with each other in establishing a City of Zion where God rules and men prosper.

Zion demands that God's people shall unite all their spiritual, psychical, physical, material, and financial powers and efforts to Go Forward into the securing of virgin soil and fertile lands, where cultivation should yield most proftable results, and into the formation of Cities where industries and businesses, schools and colleges will flourish.

Zion believes that by these, and by a true Church unity, and by the Blessing of God upon prayerful, intelligent, and faithful work, Powerful Centers for the training of men and women, youths and maidens, into a Zion Restoration Host, shall be established, from whence shall continually proceed Evangelizing, Educating, and Quickening Power into all the World, rapidly fulfilling the Divine Purposes in these "Times of the Restoration of All Things," which have so gloriously begun.

The curse of Israel in ancient days was that it entered into the land "flowing with milk and honey," and then "*stood still*."

ISRAEL "STOOD STILL," "WAXED FAT AND KICKED," AND FELL INTO THE NATIONAL SIN OF MONARCHY.

Israel grew as a Theocracy for Four Hundred Years, but failing to fulfil her Mission of carrying the Light of God to all the Nations of the Earth, she became selfish, "waxed fat, and kicked," fulfilling the prophecy of Moses concerning Israel in his Dying Song, recorded in Deuteronomy 32d chapter:

Jehovah's Portion is His People;
Jacob is the Lot of His Inheritance.
He found him in a Desert Land,
And in the Waste Howling Wilderness;
He compassed him about, He cared for him,
He kept him as the Apple of His Eye:
As an eagle that stirreth up her nest,
That fluttereth over her young,
He spread abroad His wings, He took them,
He bare them on His pinions:
Jehovah alone did lead him,
And there was no strange god with him.
He made him ride on the High Places of the Earth,
And he did eat the Increase of the Field;
And He made him to suck Honey out of the Rock,
And Oil out of the Flinty Rock;
Butter of kine, and Milk of Sheep,
With fat of Lambs,
And rams of the breed of Bashan, and goats,

With the fat of Kidneys of Wheat;
And of the Blood of the Grape thou drankest Wine.
BUT JESHURUN WAXED FAT, AND KICKED:
Thou art waxen fat, thou art grown thick, thou art become sleek:
Then he forsook God which made him,
And lightly esteemed the Rock of his Salvation,
They moved Him to jealousy with strange *gods*,
With Abominations provoked they Him to anger.
They sacrificed unto Demons, *which were* no God,
To *gods* whom they knew not,
To New *Gods* that came up of late,
Whom your fathers dreaded not.
Of the Rock that begat thee thou art unmindful,
And hast forgotten God that gave thee birth.

And so the Theocracy faded away, and the Rule of God was followed by the Rule of the Belly, that basest of all forms of heathenism; and Israel, forsaking the Theocracy, rejected God, and desired a King to rule over them, and God, "in his anger," permitted the curse of Monarchy to come upon them.

"Waxing fat," Israel "kicked" against the Law and the Rule of God, and would not have Him to reign over them.

THE AWFUL STORY OF MONARCHY FROM SAUL TO HEROD.

Hence Israel fell, and through long centuries of degeneracy, lit up here and there for a brief period by the faith of a David and the wisdom of a Solomon, and the warnings of prophets, only to fall again through David's shameless crimes, and by Solomon's unspeakable follies, idolatries and vices, and to go astray with the prophets and priests into the sensuous and disgusting worship of Baal.

Kings, wise men, priests, and prophets, with but few exceptions, failed, and became cruel oppressors and idolators, dragging God's people down into the deepest depths of moral and spiritual degeneracy—a degeneracy that was at its lowest depths of hypocritical religious pretense when the Christ was born in Bethlehem amidst a Monarchy whose King sought to murder Him when a babe, amidst a priesthood who hated Him from His cradle, until at last they rolled His dead body from a Roman cross into the sepulcher of the Arimathean.

Israel failed to live for God and for humanity, failed to carry His Message to those that lay in darkness and in the shadow of death; and hence the Glory of the Theocratic Principle, that God was the Only Rightful Ruler, established when Israel was given the Land of Promise, faded away in these less than five centuries.

THE RESTORATION OF THE THEOCRACY HAS BEGUN.

It has never been restored until this "Time of the Restoration of All Things," when God has now established the Christian Catholic Church in Zion, and the Restoration of the Theocracy has begun, with Zion City for its first political embodiment—"a Day of Small Things," which none but malicious enemies of God, or ignorant fools, despise.

APOSTATE CHURCHES ARE THE TOOLS OF OPPRESSORS.

Satan rules the Apostate Churches; makes them tools of kings, and politicians, and priests; makes them the homes of the sorcerers, the adulterers, the false swearers—those that oppress the hireling in his wages, the widow, and the fatherless, and that turn aside the stranger from his right, that neither fear God, nor serve Him. (Malachi 3:5.)

The Apostate Churches demand that their people shall continue in association with cities and communities in which they know that Satan reigns, and that a godly life is a practical impossibility for all who will remain in association with the "World-rulers of this Darkness," as Paul the Apostle calls the Demons who possess so many of the men who control human governments.

Zion declares that the time has come for God's people to come forth out of these political and social "graves" in which they are now buried, out of these "charnel houses" of death called Churches, which are, like the great Cathedrals of the Apostasies in Europe and elsewhere, tenanted by the bodies of the dead, and which have no Christ to offer but a dead Christ, and no hope on earth but a grave.

Zion demands that God's people shall hear the Voice of God and shall come forth out of these "graves," these "valleys of dry bones," and shall live where they and their children shall grow in Purity, in true Prosperity, and, controlled by the Holy Spirit, shall Go Forward, ever progressing, ever fighting the Hosts of Hell, and ever conquering, following Him who is still the Leader of His people, the Savior, the Healer, the Cleanser, the Keeper, the Author and Finisher of their Faith—Jesus, the Messiah, the Son of God.

ZION, ARISE, FOR THY LIGHT IS COME!
It shines upon thy Pathway through the Sea!
GO FORWARD!

There is no escape from Egyptian bondage, but by following where God leads, and where His Prophet commands!

Yea, more; forget not, O Zion, that the Church is on a Pilgrimage!

ZION'S RESTORATION WORK A PREPARATION.

Although we build Cities for God, establish Industrial Institutions for God, Educational, and Commercial, and Financial Institutions for God, work mines for God, till fields for God, grow flowers for God, build Tabernacles for God, yet we are but dwellers in Tents and Temporary Institutions and Enterprises, needful for the present security, and purity and progress of God's people. but which are all Preparatory to the Coming of the King and His Personal Reign on Earth for One Thousand Years. Grander Organizations will precede His ultimate triumph over all the enemies of God and Man, in the destruction of the powers of Satan and Sin, and Death, and Hell, and in the making of a "New Heavens" and a "New Earth, wherein dwelleth Righteousness."

But meanwhile God's Kingdom of "Righteousness, and Peace, and Joy in the Holy Spirit" must be established in the hearts, and lives, and cities, and occupations of His people, under His Rule; for the Time has come when there shall be "One Flock and One Shepherd."

Godless States and fallen Churches, godless rulers and apostate priests and ministers, under the rule of Satan, divide, and destroy, and proclaim the vile principle of the Separation of Government, People and True religion

But Zion everywhere protests that God must rule in all

DIVINE UNITIES ARE TRIUNITIES.

Jehovah our God is One God, the Faith of God is One Faith, the Baptism of God is One Baptism.

And yet our God is One in Three and Three in One, Father, Son, and Holy Spirit; and that Faith is one in three, and three in one—the Faith which brings Salvation, and Healing, and Holiness; and that Baptism is into the three names of the Triune God, as a Baptism of Death to Sin, Life in God, and Power for Service.

The Unity is everywhere a Triunity in God, and is only complete when it is "a Three-fold Cord" of Eternal Life, and Love, and Light.

Zion proclaims that the Time has come when, loving all men and doing all the good within her power, she must be separate from all fellowship with faithless apostasies, and have no fellowship in any form with the "Unfruitful Works of Darkness (the Secret Empire), but rather reprove them."

"GOD IS LIGHT, AND IN HIM IS NO DARKNESS AT ALL."

This, then, is the Call which in this General Letter we first address to all who are now in fellowship with us in the Christian Catholic Church in Zion,—

GO FORWARD!

Beloved, you have "come out," but you must not "stand still"

Pharaoh's cruel host is behind you, seeking to drag you back into bondage; the desert is around you, and *there is only danger and disaster in delay.*

Go Forward! O Zion, join the hosts that are passing through, join the hosts that are now gathering in the City of Zion here, and that are gathering in the City of Zion above

DANGER, DISASTER, AND DEATH IN DELAY.

To "*stand still*" is to fall into the hands of the cruel Enslaver, who would drive you into his Army and push you forward as his soldiers into the Valley of Death.

Pharaoh's Army could not cross where Israel passed in safety, for it is written: "By faith they (God's people) passed through the Red Sea as by dry land: which the Egyptians, assaying to do, were swallowed up."

Zion must not be entangled with Alliances of which God disapproves.

JOSEPH, AND JESUS, AND MARY IN BUSINESS AT NAZARETH.

Whilst in the world, Joseph and Jesus wrought as carpenters for faithless Nazarenes; Peter caught fish for faithless Galileeans, and Paul made tents in heathen Corinth (Acts 18:3), yet neither Joseph nor Jesus, nor Peter nor Paul, were "of the world."

And now in the End of this Dispensation, in the gathering of God's people together as He hath commanded, we cannot divest ourselves, nor would we if we could, from lawful and Divinely-approved labor, the products of which must be, for the present, largely sold to the world.

PAUL, PRISCILLA, AND ACQUILA IN BUSINESS AT CORINTH.

Yet, as Paul the Apostle "came unto" Aquila and Priscilla in Corinth, "because he was of the same trade, he abode with them, and they wrought, for by their trade they were tentmakers," so we, in Zion, should follow this example of these three, who evidently went into business as tentmakers, possibly as the firm of "Paul, Aquila & Priscilla;" and we should labor together who are of the same trade in making good things, even for those who continue in the world.

Doubtless this Christian firm of tentmakers in Ancient Corinth made good tents, and had many opportunities of preaching the Gospel, through their superior and honestly-made tents, to many heathen customers.

And so Zion makes good lace, good candies, good soap, and other things, and, by reason of the superior excellence of its products, has many opportunities of preaching the Gospel to its customers all over the world.

ZION'S BUSINESSES ARE GOD'S BUSINESSES.

Zion's Business Messengers are God's Messengers; Zion's businesses are God's businesses; Zion's Cities are God's Cities; and Zion's Agricultural Colonies and Mining, and Shipping, and other Enterprises will be God's, and God's alone; for Zion everywhere demands that every one within her borders shall belong to God, spirit, soul, and body, and that their business shall belong to God, and that all we have and are shall belong to Him and be fully consecrated to His service.

Zion, therefore, must Go FORWARD on the line of an

Entire Consecration to God, whilst each one shall personally be free to control his individual life and properties in such ways as shall not interfere with his individual responsibilities, nor be inconsistent with his individual duties to God and to Zion.

The Pauls, and the Aquilas, and the Priscillas, and their trade must get together in Zion, and do things better than they are done by those who dwell in the cities of the world, or who cultivate, mine, or manufacture under the direction, and for the profit, largely, of men of the world.

Zion must Go Forward, and leave behind all servitudes to those who serve not God.

Zion, in things temporal, as well as in things eternal, must serve God and co-operate only with each other.

A COMMAND.

THEREFORE, IN THE NAME OF JEHOVAH, the ONE AND ETERNAL GOD, WE COMMAND THE MEMBERS OF THE CHRISTIAN CATHOLIC CHURCH IN ZION EVERYWHERE *to Go Forward* INTO UNION WITH EACH OTHER IN ALL THINGS, IN THE SERVICE OF GOD.

YET THERE IS A GREATER DUTY WHICH GOD LAYS UPON ME.

But our duty is still greater and wider than to those who are in our Fellowship in the Christian Catholic Church in Zion

"I have a Message from God to thee," O, my brother and sister in the Christ, wherever you may be; to you who, whether members or ministers in apostate Churches, or outside of all Churches, love our Lord Jesus, the Christ, in sincerity

I gladly recognize the fact that God's people are to be found in all the Churches and outside of all the Churches.

There are many in the Apostasies who love our Lord in sincerity, even although they, as I believe, sinfully continue to follow the leadership of men who have departed from God and to be parts of Ecclesiastical Institutions which are directed in ways that are contrary to Cod's Will

AN EXHORTATION TO ALL CHRISTIANS.

As Elijah the Restorer, the Prophet of the Restoration, I call upon you everywhere to obey the Command of God given through the Prophet Isaiah in the 52d chapter, 11th verse:

Depart ye, depart ye, go ye out from thence,
Touch no Unclean Thing;
Go ye out of the midst of her; be ye clean,
Ye that bear the vessels of Jehovah.

This Command is also repeated by the Apostle Paul in the 6th Chapter of Second Corinthians, the 17th and 18th verses:

Wherefore come ye out from among them,
And be ye Separate, saith Jehovah,
And touch no Unclean Thing;
And I will receive you,
And will be to you a Father,
And ye shall be to me Sons and Daughters, saith the Lord Almighty.

The Time has come, beloved in the Christ, to speak very plain words to you, who in hundreds of thousands are consciously dwelling in the midst of Shameful Apostasies, and making no effort to get away.

There has been some excuse in the past, and, perhaps, some good reason for your present condition, in the fact that there was no place to go, if you were to remain in organized church life, except from one Apostasy to another

This has led in many thousands of cases to the sin of denying the "body of the Christ," the Unity and Catholicity of the Church of the Living God, and to serious divisions amongst those who have been born into the Kingdom of God.

Large numbers of earnest Christians seek to escape from the bondage of organizations where they are deprived of all Christian liberty, and are, by their membership obligations, compelled to support Institutions and Ministrations which are doing the Devil's work.

ORGANIZATIONS WITHOUT SCRIPTURAL AUTHORITY OR ORDINANCES.

Separations which seem to be forced upon earnest Christians have led to the formation of organizations which have no Scriptural basis.

These are very numerous.

Sometimes they take the form of such organizations as the Salvation Army, where two of the Ordinances which our Lord Himself instituted are ignored and practically denied to His people, namely: the Ordinance of Believers' Baptism by Triune Immersion, and the Ordinance of the Communion of the Lord's Supper.

It seems incredible that those who seem to be preaching "repentance toward God and faith in our Lord Jesus, the Christ," should fail to preach Obedience to Christ in Baptism, since the cry at Pentecost, "Men and brethren, what shall we do?" was answered by Peter under the inspiration of the Holy Spirit, "*Repent and be Baptized every one of you.*"

The Salvation Army, and other organizations of that theologically slip-shod character, practically say to penitents seeking restoration to God, "Repent, and pay no heed to Baptism."

Yet over and over again the Spirit teaches in the Acts of the Apostles that Baptism, as our Lord commanded in Matthew 28:19, 20, immediately followed Repentance and was the Seal of Discipleship.

Baptism by Triune Immersion was, and is, an Act of Obedience. It immediately made a most pronounced separation between the world and the Apostate Judaism of that day on the one side, and a true Christianity on the other

The consequences of such Obedience, while they were glorious, in that the Gifts of the Holy Spirit came upon those who obeyed, were made the occasion for severe persecution, because of its bold avowal that previous ordinances, such as Circumcision, etc., were of no value.

A REAL BAPTISM IS A SEAL OF A LIVING CHURCH.

The Salvation Army has no Baptism of any kind, and therefore, no Seal as a Living Church.

Pretending to be an Army apart from the Church, it fails to be acceptable to God, as an organization, since it does not gather the disciples into Church Fellowship and teach them Obedience to all the Christ's Ordinances.

Christian effort, in the form of many thousands of large and small Missions, throughout the world, belong to the Salvation Army class.

Some of these are full of hypocrisy and sins of many kinds, while they are pretending to be Christian and Missionary Alliances.

They are utterly without Spiritual Power, as organizations, without a single element of permanence, and without Authority from God.

Some of these organizations have been established by men of great sincerity and true Christian spirit, such as some of those which have been founded by the people called "Brethren," etc.

But God does not permit His people to disobey His commands with impunity: for these Disorderly Missions fail to satisfy the revealed requirements of God in the organization of His people into the Kingdom as well as into the Church.

Never forget, my brethren and sisters in the Christ who are outside of the Christian Catholic Church in Zion, that God has "called you to Liberty," but it is a "liberty" which is thus expressed in the Book of the Revelation of Jesus, the Christ, 1st chapter, 5th and 6th verses:

> Unto Him that loveth us, and loosed us from our sins by His blood;
> And He made us to be a Kingdom,
> To be Priests unto His God and Father;
> To Him be the Glory and the Dominion forever and ever. Amen.

WHERE IS THE KINGDOM?

Where is the "Kingdom" to be found in Armies, Missions, Crusades, and Institutions which deny all Divinely appointed officers to administer Church Discipline and to exercise Scriptural Rule and Authority? Where is the rule and authority of a Kingdom, if equal powers are declared to exist in every member?

The Kingdom of God is no more to be found in such chaotic disorganizations than it is to be found in an organization of so-called spiritual Military rule which has no rebuke for sin in high places, and which has recently, through its General, accepted the Patronage of a Monarch who was renowned for his godless and unclean life as a Prince, and who openly continues to be a pleasure-loving King, a companion of race-track men, etc.

A SHAMEFUL SPECTACLE.

The shameful spectacle of William Booth glorying in quoting the patronizing words of a Royal Defender of the Faith, who has never manifested any Divine Faith, and making Edward VII. practically the patron saint of the Salvation Army, has filled every true Christian heart throughout the world with intense disgust.

Thousands and tens of thousands of Christian people tolerated the Salvation Army in its unspiritual vagaries and crudities, in its illogical positions, in its shameless beggaries on every highway, for the sake of the "good" that it was supposed to be doing, and undoubtedly in a measure did, for the poor and fallen.

But the time has come to denounce with unsparing severity an organization which has become renowned for the tyranny, and untruthfulness, and dastardly cowardice of some of its principal leaders.

It is as little entitled to respect as the Jesuit Order of the Church of Rome.

These words must, of necessity, at first awaken still more bitter feelings of antagonism in those who have, publicly and privately, shamefully misrepresented me and the work which God has given me to do.

A great number of the most efficient officers and members of the Salvation Army have already come out from its ranks, and are now in the Christian Catholic Church in Zion, where they find Means of Grace which qualify them more fully for God's service, and which satisfy more fully the hunger of their spirits, souls, and bodies, which could not find bread in a stone, or an egg in a scorpion, or a fish in a serpent.

Children of God in all the apostasies, Missions, Armies, Crusades, etc., remember that the Christ came to establish a Kingdom!

THE KINGDOM IS GREATER THAN THE CHURCH.

Remember that this Kingdom is greater than any Church, however great it be, even although it were founded by God Himself.

All Churches and Gatherings, in ancient and modern times, including the Church which I represent at this moment, are but associations of those who are born into the Kingdom of God.

The True and Holy Catholic Church is "the General Assembly and Church of the First Born, whose names are enrolled in Heaven," and wherever that Church is found, it is ever seeking to promote the establishment of the Kingdom of God.

Zion is but another name for the Kingdom of God.

The Gospel is the Gospel of the Kingdom of God.

The whole Aim, and Mission, and Purpose of the Christ was, and is, to establish the Kingdom of God.

We bid you come out of the Kingdom of Darkness and Error.

Come out of organizations which are establishing improper relations with the kingdoms of this world, all of which must fade away, and become the "Kingdom of our God and of His Christ."

So far as I know, in all the world, the Christian Catholic Church in Zion is the only organization which maintains this truth of the Gospel of the Kingdom, in practical form.

God has made this Church a means, is making it a means, and will make it a means, through all its varied organizations, Ecclesiastical, Educational, Industrial, Commercial, and Political, for the upbuilding of the Kingdom of God, and for the Preparation of His People for the Coming of the King.

A DECLARATION BY THE PROPHET OF THE RESTORATION.

Hence I proclaim, as Elijah, the Prophet of the Restoration, that it is your absolute and immediate duty to enquire "the Way to Zion, with your faces thitherward."

You are not at liberty, and, if you are truly honest, God will show you this, to refuse Obedience to this Call.

If you close your eyes, shut your ears, and harden your hearts, and refuse to hear the Voice from Zion which speaks with Apostolic and Prophetic Authority from God, then you will have to answer to God for this, both in Time and in Eternity

I have written these words with much natural unwillingness.

They may seem to many to savor of tyranny, absurdity, and even of blasphemy.

But they are none of these three.

Without affecting a false humility, I can say truly that these words come from a thoughtful mind, an experienced spirit, and a loving heart.

They come from one who despises tyranny, as he despises the Tyrant who rules over Hell and over the greater part of this earth, Satan himself.

They come from one who from a child has known the Scriptures, and who loves to see God's people free, and enjoying the fulness set forth in the promises of God.

They come from one who has known, loved, and served God, with many conscious shortcomings, sometimes with many tears, but always without fear, all the days of his life, and who has risked that life continually for God and for humanity.

I would say to all who read these words as did the great Apostle Paul:

Having therefore these Promises, beloved,
Let us cleanse ourselves from all defilement of flesh and spirit,
Perfecting Holiness in the fear of God.
Open your hearts to us: (Greek, *Make room for us*)
We wronged no man, we corrupted no man.
We took advantage of no man.
I say it not to condemn you;
For I have said before,
That ye are in our hearts to die together and live together.
Great is my boldness of speech toward you.
Great is my glorying on your behalf:
I am filled with Comfort,
I Overflow with Joy in all our Affliction.

I can find no better words than these to express my present thoughts.

They are true in me as in Paul the Apostle.

I "glory on your behalf," who have been true to God and to conscience, and have lived up to your light in all the churches and organizations with which you have been connected.

But the Time has come when there can no longer be Separation from each other without Sin among those who are really in the Christ.

Separation from Apostasy, Impurity, and Worldliness are essential to individual and to organic progress in the Church of God, and to the Salvation of a perishing world.

VICTORY MUST BE ORGANIZED.

It cannot be secured by disorderly units, or by disorderly masses, or by co-operation with those who call themselves Christians, but who are co-operating with the Enemy in many directions.

Victory for God can only be permanently won by those who are obedient to God and who have been *Set Free* "by the Law of the Spirit of Life in Christ Jesus, from the Law of Sin and of Death."

THE CHRISTIAN CATHOLIC CHURCH IN ZION IS ORGANIZED CHRISTIAN LIBERTY.

The Apostasies and Disorderly Organizations hinder growth, promote impurity, destroy liberty, and decoy the people of God into the hands of the Devil, who conquers and destroys, as Napoleon did, by pursuing, as his continuous policy, the maxim, "Divide and Destroy."

I know not, nor is it my concern too much to consider, how these words may be received throughout the world, whither they are going.

I pray that they may be understood by those who are honest and true-hearted.

The dishonest and the false, who turn aside into "crooked ways," I can never influence so long as they are of that mind.

But God will deal with such: for it is written:

As for such as turn aside unto their Crooked Ways,
Jehovah shall lead them forth with the Workers of Iniquity.
Peace be upon Israel.

And so, with this Invocation of Peace, I close this portion of my Appeal to my brethren and sisters in the Christ, and to every Lover of God throughout the world, with the words:

Come thou with us and we will do you Good,
For Jehovah hath spoken Good concerning Israel.

THE IMPORT OF THIS LETTER.

It will be seen that the foregoing Statement, which I have made after much prayerful deliberation, embodies Two Exhortations:

The first is addressed to those who are now in the Christian Catholic Church in Zion and in Zion Restoration Host; and the Second is to those who are in the Kingdom of God in All Lands, whether members of Ecclesiastical Organizations or not.

But I have written enough for one *General Letter*, or one *Catholic Epistle*, as it would have been called in ancient times, and of which we have no less than seven in the New Testament, written by the Apostles James, Peter, John, and Jude.

It is not merely the Church in Zion City, or the Church in London, Zurich, or Melbourne, which I address, but I am now speaking with a consciousness of Divine Authority to the whole Church in all the World.

ANOTHER LETTER ON THE RESTORATION OF THE APOSTOLIC OFFICE.

In another General Letter I will set forth a Plea for the speedy Restoration of the Apostolic Office to the Church, so that she may accomplish her Divine Mission in the establishment of the Kingdom of God upon earth.

This I shall do, God willing, in my next General Letter, which I trust I shall be able to prepare for the next issue of LEAVES OF HEALING.

Meanwhile, I earnestly request the prayers of every reader of this Catholic Letter, that I may be sustained amidst the toils, and trials, and temptations which beset me on every hand in the fulfilment of my Apostolic and Prophetic Mission.

Were it not that I believed with Paul that God has also said to me, "My grace is sufficient for thee," I should utterly despair of being able to fulfil my Divinely-appointed task.

But I have been prepared for this by my work as Elijah the Restorer, in this beginning of the "Times of the Restoration of All Things, whereof God spake by the mouth of His holy Prophets which have been since the world began."

The Question rings down through nineteen centuries—

And who is Sufficient for These Things?

Most sincerely can I reply, as Paul did:

We are not Sufficient of ourselves,
To account anything as from ourselves;
But our Sufficiency is from God;
Who also made us Sufficient as Ministers of a New Covenant;
Not of the letter, but of the Spirit.
For the letter killeth, but the Spirit giveth Life

I trust I write these words in a spirit of deep and true humility, not "putting a veil upon my face," "not corrupting the Word of God," but "as of sincerity," "as of God," in the sight of God, speaking in the Christ.

Working together with Him, we "entreat also that ye receive not the grace of God in vain."

Let all to whom these words shall come, consider prayerfully what I say.

Be fully persuaded in your own minds, ere you reject or accept the Message which I know that I have brought to you from God.

Let us, therefore, as many as be perfect, be thus minded:
And if in anything ye are otherwise minded,
Even this shall God reveal unto you:
Only, whereunto we have already attained,
By that same Rule let us walk.

With earnest prayers for your guidance by the Holy Spirit in all things pertaining to the knowledge of the Will of God, our Father, I am,

Faithfully your friend and fellow servant in Jesus our Lord and Coming King,

General Overseer of the Christian Catholic Church in Zion.

Warning.

I am directed by the General Overseer to warn our members and officers throughout the world against giving money to persons claiming to be members of the Christian Catholic Church in Zion. All benevolence must be given either from Headquarters or under the direction of same. Even though the applicant for benevolence be known to be a member of the Christian Catholic Church in Zion, financial aid must not be given except in extreme cases, and then only in small amounts. Requests for help must be made to the officer-in-charge. In cases where there is no such officer, requests should be made direct to Headquarters, accompanied by recommendations from one or two members of Zion in good standing. J. G. EXCELL,
General Ecclesiastical Secretary.

By Evangelist Sarah E. Hill.

AND JEHOVAH said unto him (Moses) What is that in thine hand? And he said a rod.—*Exodus 4:2.*

THE great Israelitish Leader and Lawgiver was pursuing his daily occupation as a shepherd when God manifested Himself to him in the Burning Bush.

The cry of His people in Egypt had entered the ear of the Most High; and when He saw that they were weary of their bondage to the flesh, He knew that they had reached the place where He could deliver them. (Exodus 2:23, 25.)

Many years He had been training Moses as a Leader who should bring them from the bondage of Egypt to the freedom of the Holy Land.

He had preserved Moses in infancy, when the cruel king had passed a law commanding the destruction of all the male children who should be born among the Israelites. Exodus 1:22.)

God had also caused that king to receive the boy into his own household, and to educate him to take his place as a great leader when the right time should come.

Even his work in the wilderness in taking charge of the flocks of sheep bore a part in the training which fitted him to lead Israel like a flock.

If he had not done his humble work as a shepherd faithfully, God could not have trusted him to lead Israel to Horeb that they might receive the Law from His hands on Sinai. (Luke 16:10.)

On the day when Moses led his sheep to Horeb, the Mount of God, and God manifested Himself to him in the Burning Bush He spoke with him face to face, as he did later on Sinai. (Exodus 3:2; Isaiah 63:9.)

In this scene God gave him an object lesson of man indwelt by God.

It showed Moses his work.

He was to bring a people out of Egypt, where they had been ruled by the flesh, and from among a people who worshiped the flesh as a god in the form of a calf or bull.

He was to teach the Israelites the Everlasting Covenant which should establish the Rule of God in the spirit, soul, and body of man, and save him, and heal him, and keep him whole (holy).

To him was given the great work of forming the people into a Theocratic nation.

God gave them at the waters of Marah the Covenant in which Divine Healing was formulated into a law. (Exodus 15:26.)

When God appeared to Moses in a bush He chose a very humble place to fill with His presence.

In the Scriptures a tree is often used to represent man. (Psalm 1:3; Isaiah 61:3.)

The Covenant which God gave to Moses for ancient Israel is the same Covenant which Elijah, the Messenger of the Covenant, brings to the people today. (Malachi 3:1; 4:5.)

He is that Prophet of whom God spoke to Moses, saying,

"I will raise them up a prophet from among their brethren, like unto thee; and I will put My Words in his mouth, and he shall speak unto them all that I shall command him." (Deuteronomy 18:18; Acts 3:22, 23.)

This Prophet, John Alexander Dowie, is today leading a people out from the bondage of the flesh, and teaching them the Covenant through which the Rule of God may be established in the spirits, souls, and bodies of the people.

He is forming a Theocratic Nation of Zion.

Moses knew the condition of the Israelites, because he had lived in Egypt with them.

He knew that although they had become weary of serving flesh, they were still in bondage to it.

It was then as it is today, when persons turn from the service of the flesh, and through repentance and faith get a new heart, they have a hard task in bringing the flesh into subjection to their spirits under God.

This was the task which Moses had before him.

When he stood before God at the Burning Bush, listening to His Message, he held in his hand his shepherd's rod or crook which he used with his flock.

This rod suggested these animals; and God used it to represent human nature, which is animal nature.

Jehovah said unto him, What is that in thine hand? And he said, a rod. And He said, Cast it on the ground. And he cast it on the ground, and it became a serpent; and Moses fled from before it. (Exodus 4:2, 3.)

So human nature if uncontrolled seeks the earth and makes crooked paths, and stings its owner like a serpent.

Many a man has in dismay desired to flee from his animal nature, when it has grown strong by indulgence.

But when it is held in the firm grasp of a man who is ruled by God, it becomes a rod of support and strength to him.

When Moses looked at the weakness of his human nature, and measured it with the work which God called him to do, he faltered and shrunk from the task with dread.

And although God promised to be with him, he still looked at his own weakness, and plead his slowness of speech. (Exodus 3:11, 12; 4:10-17.)

Moses found, when he held his rod firmly in his hand, that through it God enabled him to do mighty deeds in Egypt, and bring deliverance to Israel.

Although the Israelites were afflicted in Egypt and their lives made bitter by service to the flesh, yet when God delivered them from it they complained against Moses and Aaron in the wilderness.

The flesh, when it rules, is never satisfied.

If we study the history of their lives in the wilderness we have an object lesson which helps us to understand the nature of the flesh.

They murmured and they criticised Moses.

God sent them bread from heaven to eat but they longed for the leeks, and the melons and cucumbers of Egypt instead. (Numbers 11:4-11.)

To bring the flesh in subjection to God is the problem of life.

The Covenant which God gave to Moses became a new Covenant when the Lord Jesus, the Lamb of God, took the place of the sacrificial lamb in it.

It is through Him that man is able to keep the Covenant.

He cannot do it in his own strength.

The teaching of Zion all relates to the Covenant.

This teaching shows the right relations of the spirit, soul, and body of man to each other, to God and to the world.

All are important in their way, but the soul and body, which are made servants, must not be the masters.

Then material things take their proper place and assume their right value.

It teaches how to live pure, honest, practical lives, carrying the fear of God into business, education, and daily living in every form.

When the world accepts the teaching of Zion it will become a new world.

The mountain of evil which destroys mankind will become a plain, and the Kingdom of God will be established upon the earth.

Reader, will you help to sow this teaching broadcast over the Earth?

The time is short, and we need your help.

Zion Literature Sent Out from a Free Distribution Fund Provided by Zion's Guests and the Friends of Zion.

Report for the week ending August 6, 1904:
6,800 Rolls...to Business Men in the United States
4,517 Rolls..............to Hotels in United States
1,796 Rolls to..............................
Hotels of Europe, Asia, Africa and the Islands of the Sea
279 Rolls to..............................India
1,749 Rolls to.........Various States of the Union
Number of Rolls for the week..............15,141
Number of Rolls reported to Aug. 6, 1904, 3,305,434

ELIJAH THE RESTORER.

Zion's Fourth Feast of Tabernacles

The Set Feasts of Jehovah . . .
Ye shall proclaim to be Holy Convocations.

EARLY MORNING SACRIFICE OF PRAISE AND PRAYER.

*REPORTED BY M. F. L., A. C. R., AND E. S.

"The Eighth Fruit of the Spirit: Meekness," was the subject of the Early Morning Meeting of Thursday, July 21, 1904.

The distinction between Meekness—the Fruit of the Spirit—and Weakness—which comes from the Devil—was brought out most forcibly by the man of God.

Practical application of this Fruit, in daily life, was made, the great assembly rising, at the close, to indicate that they accepted the teaching as laid down so unequivocally in God's Word.

Shiloh Tabernacle, Zion City, Illinois, Thursday Morning, July 21, 1904.

The meeting was opened by the singing of Hymns Nos. 8 and 27, in the Special Program.

Overseer Excell conducted a short Bible Reading on the subject of the morning, "Meekness."

Prayer was offered by the General Overseer.

Many People Are Suffering for Want of Training.

The General Overseer then said:

Many people are suffering today for want of training.

They were never trained at all.

They were not brought up; they were dragged up.

Some were kicked up, and oftentimes kicked out.

They were brutally trained.

They were trained as if they were so many beasts of burden.

I never was so astonished in my life as when I came to this country and found large numbers of young men in debt.

I asked, "To whom are you in debt?"

"To my father."

"To your father? What for?"

"Oh, for my education."

"For your education?"

"Yes, my father has my notes," they said, "and I am burdened in paying them."

What kind of a father was that, to put the burden of a note upon his son?

"Oh, well, you know, my father thought he ought to do so to protect himself, and that it was my duty to care for him."

Parents Must Care for the Children.

The Scripture says that it is the duty of the parents to lay up for the children, and not the children to lay up for the parents.

You have a wrong idea.

Some wretched farmers treat their sons as if they were so many hogs, because these fathers themselves are hogs.

They lay burdens upon their children.

I want some of these old hogs on the farm to read this, and to groan and growl, and say, "There is the Doctor off the line again."

Yes, I am off the pig line, but I am on the line of Righteousness and Truth.

The first duty of the parent is to care for his children.

Paul, writing to the Christians of his day, said that he was their father, and that he would most gladly spend and be spent for them, although they were very ungrateful.

He said that it was the duty of the parents to lay up for the children, and not the children for the parents.

You and Paul can have it out, if you think that you know better than Paul, you old American hog, wherever this finds you.

I also met young ministers in this country who could not come into Zion because they were indebted to some denomination.

They had given notes to the church for their education, and the church had thus bound them hand and foot.

There is a church for you!

Large numbers of ministers in the denominations today are in the hands of the church authorities, and if there is a difference the church comes down upon them and sells them out.

Zion Keeps Its Young Men and Women Free from Burdensome Responsibility.

In Zion, I have never allowed a young man or woman, who was poor, to sign a note, or to be indebted to the Christian Catholic Church in Zion.

If they could not pay for their education, and they were worthy of being educated, I saw that they had the education, and the food, too; and I did that without laying any burden upon them, believing that the Church that was generous to its young men and women would reap as it had sown.

Do you not think that is right?

Audience—"Yes."

General Overseer—If any father or mother holds notes against their sons or daughters, let them cancel those notes.

Take the son or daughter into your room.

Kiss them and kneel down and pray with them, and say, "I was an old hog for getting that note from you; here it is; you are free." [Applause.]

Perhaps the elder brother, who is in the field, will murmur, "O father, you have given Bobbie back that note and you have killed the fatted calf for him; I will not sing; I will not pray."

Let him growl!

Let the American hog's oldest son growl!

Hear what I say!

Cancel the note, and if you do not, I think you are not a good member of the Christian Catholic Church in Zion, nor a good father.

Do you think that you can train a tree by hanging weights upon it?

Will it grow up straight, and strong, and symmetrical by weighing down the little branches?

Audience—"No."

General Overseer—Then take the weights off, you old hog!

The General Overseer's Auditors are Only a Part of His Congregation.

I am really talking to the fellow who is not here. [Laughter.]

I fancy there are not any such here, but I often talk on this platform to the fellow that is not here as well as to the one that is here.

There may be some here.

If so, take your medicine properly.

It is good medicine, and you will have a cheerful heart after taking it.

If you remove the burden from your children, they will study all the harder to prove themselves worthy of your kindness.

When father gets old they will say, "I will never forget how father and mother helped me get an education when I was young."

You will get far more from them because of your goodness than you would have got from that note.

If you insist upon their paying, some day they will rebel.

I recommend them not to pay it.

"Oh," you say, "that is dishonorable."

It is no such thing.

The dishonor was in father's executing that ungodly note.

No gift of love to your children will ever be lost.

Attend this Education Conference today, and get interested as to how your children are being educated.

We want to make this City a great educational center.

---

*The following reports have not been revised by the General Overseer.

Some of the Things in Which Zion Trains Her Children.

There is an interesting exhibit at the College Building which is well worth seeing.

We are teaching our children to use their fingers—to get their brains into their fingers.

In some kinds of modeling, one needs all the fingers.

We teach our children stenography.

Everybody ought to learn stenography.

One can write letters in stenography to another who knows stenography.

One can write a stenographic letter in one-fifth the time that it takes to write it in longhand, and it is useful in taking notes at a meeting.

It is a good thing to know.

So we are teaching all our children, as far as they care to learn it, stenography, typewriting, modeling, and other such practical things.

Dimension is an unknown quantity to many people.

They do not understand the very first principles of algebra or mensuration; they do not understand how to calculate, which is very necessary and interesting.

If they owned a piece of land, they would not know how to measure it properly.

Some of those whom we may send as messengers to distant lands may find such knowledge very useful.

We are teaching our children so that they may find their way into all kinds of electrical engineering, into the workshops, and to be skilful; and, above all, teaching them how to live and how to pray.

Overseer Brasefield, and the teachers and professors have a right to your support in these things.

Then stretch your lazy legs this morning and get here by eleven o'clock.

The Importance of a Cheerful Countenance.

Do not look as if you had had a cup of vinegar for breakfast.

Brighten up! If you do not, I will give you a stick!

You dear old people look fine when you smile, but when you do not, you look like the portrait of some crabbed old ancestor.

Some people are spoiled by the pictures on their walls.

"Whose picture is that?" I once asked.

"Oh, that is my mother."

"Turn her face to the wall, will you?

"Surely, she never looked as ugly as that."

The person looked at me and said, "My mother was a real pretty woman."

"Then that is a real disgrace; take it away; that cannot be like your mother. I am sure she was never like that. No woman ever had such a wooden face as that, or such cork-screw curls."

I wish some of you would get rid of your pictures.

I wish you would study to get pictures of your loved ones that are really like them; if you cannot do this, turn their faces to the wall.

Put them out of sight.

Let the memory carry the face.

Some of you have pictures in your houses that make your children miserable.

They have been taught to believe that the originals were the very pink of perfection.

They look at the picture, and they are glad that their grandfather is in heaven.

That is a fact. [Laughter.]

How is it that some of you, when you have your pictures taken, put on most ridiculous looks?

You seem to say, "I am sitting for my picture!"

Look natural.

I insist upon the photographer taking me like a flash.

I will not have the nonsense of posing and all that kind of thing, with two sticks at the back of my head.

Do not let them do it.

How a Favorite Picture of the General Overseer Was Taken.

I will tell you how that picture of me that so many love was taken.

I went into a room and I told the photographer that when I came to a certain spot I would say, "The Voice of one crying in the wilderness, Prepare ye the Way of the Lord," and that when I came to the words, "Make His paths straight," he was to take my picture.

That picture was natural.

Some of you prepare by dressing yourself in a way that is painful to behold.

Everything is exact; not one hair out of place.

You say, "Oh, look at my cares."

I have more cares than you all, and one of my cares is you.

I speak these things, because I have been thinking over and over again in my heart these words:

Ten thousand thousand precious gifts,
My daily thanks employ;
Nor is the least a cheerful heart
That tastes those gifts with joy.

I feel so sorry when I see those who look as if they might sing:

Nor is the least a grumbling heart
That never tastes those gifts with joy.

It is a thousand times better to get a laugh into such people.

A lady said to me one day, "Oh, what a delightful meeting we would have had, had not the General Overseer made us laugh."

Do you not know that God laughs?

He laughs at the foolish and the wicked.

"He that sitteth in the heavens shall laugh, Jehovah shall have them in derision."

The Lord has a great deal of fun, and of laughter.

I should think He would.

The Folly of Those Who Array Themselves Against Their Superiors.

He cannot help laughing at the mouthings of a poor little infidel, microscopic in size compared with the immensity of God.

Get something to smile over all the time and be glad, and you will be far better able to help others.

What I have said arises out of my reference to Overseer Brasefield's meeting.

Why Some Teachers Fail.

Some teachers are not much good, because they and their schoolrooms look too proper.

Children know when one is natural and cheerful.

Teachers, upon entering the schoolroom, should look cheerful and say, "Peace to thee, children."

They will brighten up and say, "Peace to thee, teacher."

It makes a difference how you say it.

You say, "Oh, my children were so cross today; I could do nothing with them."

How did you meet them?

"Oh, well, I had something that did not agree with me."

Yes, and you looked it; and you let them have all your indigestion and all your misery.

The world is like a six-foot looking-glass.

Go up to that looking-glass, and say, "Peace to thee," and smile, and the fellow in the glass will smile.

That is yourself.

Do the same thing with the school, and it will respond; but go before a class and frown and scowl, and it will do the same thing.

That advice is not in your curriculum, but it is proper.

What a glorious inheritance God has given us!

What a wonderful estate!

In the midst of all the persecutions and fighting, Zion Stocks have never gone down!

Do you not know that the British stocks have gone down?

They fell yesterday five, six, and ten points.

Why?

Because of the rumor that there would be war with Russia.

Russia's Folly in Her Desperate Strait.

England has sent an ultimatum to Russia.

Russia has been smuggling vessels through the Dardanelles, as commercial vessels, and afterwards arming them as privateers.

She seized the British vessel *Malacca*, in the Red Sea, and had the impudence to put on board a prize crew and take it to Port Said, but the British would not let them get any farther.

Admiral Fremantle said, "If I were in charge, I would blow those Russian privateers out of the water."

Russia is also in trouble with Germany.

Russia wants to make war all over Europe.

She is beaten by Japan, and she is making a last desperate effort.

She has a treaty with France, and she is trying to embroil England with France, because England has a treaty with Japan.

She is also trying to embroil America, for America has a treaty with Japan.

We are nearer an European and Asiatic war than we have ever been at any time, and what is the consequence?

A Good Time to Realize on English Securities.

I sent Deacon John W. Innes today to my people in Great Britain to tell them to sell their stocks, and to do it quickly, for they had tumbled from one hundred thirteen to eighty-five.

Now they are tumbling to seventy-five.

They practically tumbled about thirty-eight points, having dropped from one hundred thirteen to seventy-five.

I think these are good stocks to sell.

Zion Stocks, with all her fighting and trouble, have never sold under a hundred dollars, and both our Lace and Bank Stocks are now one hundred ten.

Some of you put your money into Bank Stock at a hundred, and it is now one hundred ten.

I intend to keep it up; God intends that it shall be kept up.

You ought to be grateful to God that there is a firm hand at the head of Zion affairs, because it preserves the strength of your investments.

I want you to pray for me and to back me up.

Those who do right will be helped along, but let them enter into a business fight with Zion, and it will be the bear putting to sea against a swordfish.

There is not as much chance as there would be for the bear, because we know how to deal with these things better than our adversaries, and we occupy a strong position.

I could refund the whole of your investments in Zion Lace Industries.

I could give you notice that I would take up those shares in a year and pay you six per cent., and I believe I could get the whole of the capital for Zion Lace Industries at four and a half per cent., or, at the most, five and a half per cent., and save money on you.

If you are very wicked, I will do it; but I do not intend to do it, because you are not going to be wicked.

You have helped me establish these Industries, and they will be and are one of the wonders of the industrial world.

THE EIGHTH FRUIT OF THE SPIRIT: MEEKNESS.

INVOCATION.

Let the words of my mouth, and the meditation of my heart be acceptable in Thy sight, be profitable unto this people, and unto all to whom these words shall come, in this and every land, in this and all the coming time, Till Jesus Come. Amen.

Read again with me the 5th of Galatians, the 22d, 23d and 24th verses. [The congregation repeated these verses in unison:]

TEXT.

But the Fruit of the Spirit is Love, Joy, Peace, Long-suffering, Kindness, Goodness, Faithfulness,

Meekness, Temperance: against such there is no law.

And they that are of Christ Jesus have crucified the flesh with the passions and the lusts thereof.

The Fruit that we are to consider this morning is Meekness.

Some of my critics have said that I am distinguished by my lack of that Grace.

Perhaps I am, but I do not think so.

Meekness Does Not Mean Weakness.

Some people have an idea that a Meek man is a Weak man—a man who washes his hands in invisible soap and water.

"Truly, beloved, how humble I am!"

Watch out for that man!

Never let him have your pocket-book; never take his note; never do business with him.

When a man tries to pose as a meek man, watch him.

Our Lord Jesus, the Christ, was meek and lowly in heart, but when He went into the Temple, He entered with a whip.

When He laid it on the backs of those wretches He said, "Take these things hence; make not My Father's House a house of merchandise."

He laid the stick on them, kicked over the tables, and threw them out.

The word in the Greek is *exebalen* (ἐξέβαλεν.)

He threw them out.

That word is used in connection with a military engine which throws a heavy stone against a wall.

"Oh, but that was the temple—a great occasion; if it had been a house of death He would not have been violent," you say.

Do you not remember how He went into a house where the mother was crying for her sweet little daughter, twelve years of age, who lay dead?

The professional mourners and the friends of the mother were around, and some of them were saying, "Oh, if this child had not trusted Jesus! If this child had only taken medicine and not insisted upon her father's, Jairus, going for Jesus!"

They howled because they were paid for howling; they were professional mourners and it was necessary for them to howl.

When Jesus came to the door, they howled worse than ever.

Jesus Mingles Sternness With Meekness.

What did Jesus do?

He went in and—the same word is used, ***ekbalon***, (ἐκβάλων)—threw them out.

The grip that He had on their shoulders was not a gentle one.

Then He took the mother and the father into the silent room.

Is He the same man?

His eyes are dimmed with tears; His heart is sad.

He looks at the Fruits of Sin and Disease, the works of the Devil.

The sweet child whom He had seen in so many of His assemblies and who loved Him so well, was dead—cold in death.

Although He knew He was going to raise her, I think He, too, wept.

I think that He wept many tears that are not recorded.

It is only once recorded that He wept where people could see Him.

I see Him standing there.

It is the same Man who threw these howling mourners out, "Meek and lowly in heart."

He raises His eyes to heaven.

Then He takes the hand of the child, both hands I think, and says, *Talitha cumi*.

The spirit comes back and the maid arises.

He could not have done that if He had not thrown out these people.

The Strength of Moses' Character.

Moses was the meekest man in all the earth, but he took the tables of stone and broke them; and he ground the golden calf, and made the people drink it.

Moses preserved Israel by punishing crime, and by being an agent in God's hands for the punishment of crime.

He was Meek, but not Weak!

He married an Ethiopian woman, a Cushite; and his sister, Miriam, who thought he ought to have married a white woman, was angry about it, and so was Aaron.

They went for Moses.

I think he expostulated with them, and warned them of their danger in fighting him in a matter in which he had a right to do as he pleased.

You talk about different races; that is a lie.

There is only one race, and that is the race that sprang from Adam and Eve.

There are many families, and some of them are very degraded; but you and I belong to a family that has come up from degradation.

When our fathers were savages in the forests—brutal heathen—the African was a civilized man.

He built the pyramids; built the great temples on the Nile.

The Africans were great mathematicians, great philosophers, and great builders.

That family of the human race was wonderful, although it is now degraded.

When Moses exercised the right that was his, his brother and sister murmured. What happened?

God Will Settle Every Wrong That Is Left With Him.

Moses was Meek, and he left it with God.

When you leave things for God to settle, He settles them quickly.

When you try to force an issue with your brother because he does not do what you want him to do, God will settle that question with you.

Take care what you do.

God sent for Moses, and Aaron, and Miriam.

Miriam was a good woman; she had done wonderful things; she had saved Moses' life when he was a child, and she had been faithful.

At the crossing of the Red Sea, she led the song of the ransomed on the other side, but she thought that because she had been used, she could be impudent to her greater brother.

Some of you who happen to be the brother, or the sister, or the wife of some one higher in authority, think you can presume upon that relationship and be impudent—look out!

When God was through with Miriam that day she was white enough.

She was a leper, as white as snow, because she had sinned against God and against her brother.

God permitted the Devil to smite her.

Moses was a Meek man, and when Aaron said, "O Moses, pray for our sister," Moses prayed.

God was very angry.

"Moses," He said, "If she had sinned against her father only, he would have spit in her face and put her outside for seven days.

"I will hear your prayer, but I will spit in her face, and I will put her outside, and all generations shall see that it does not pay to fight because one wants his brother's wife to be white."

A Story That Has Been Forgotten.

That story has been forgotten, both South and North, and the negroes themselves are very much surprised when it is told them.

They did not know it was in the Bible.

A little while ago I talked with an African gentleman, cultivated, and, in some respects, better educated than I am.

He owns large properties on the Gold Coast, and was trained in English schools, being a member of the English bar.

He said, "I do not like to come to America. I am insulted at every step in the North as well as in the South.

"In the South they want me to ride in a particular part of the car, or in a special car, and insist that I shall so ride.

"I am, surely, an equal of that workman or workwoman who rides to and from the factory; but I am insulted if I endeavor to enter a car.

"The Southern people are nice to you, sir; but I am black in color, and they will not let me eat in a hotel; they will not let me sleep there, but drive me to a poor lodging, although I am a Christian gentleman.

"In the North there are many hotels where I am told, 'We cannot receive you. If we did, our white guests would leave.'"

I met a titled Jew the other day, a thorough gentleman, who said that he had been turned away from a hotel for no other reason than that he was a Jew.

Race Prejudice Contemptible and Abominable.

There is nothing more contemptible and abominable than that.

I never was guilty of the nonsense of saying that everybody should eat at the same table; no more than that everybody should do the same work.

You might as well tell me that everybody should work a typewriter or everybody should do business in this, that, or the other way, and that everybody was entitled to an equal salary, without reference to capacity or intelligence.

God has made the so-called whites the ruling race.

Therefore, let us be Gentle; let us be Kind; let us be Meek; let us be considerate, and treat our brother as an equal when he is our equal.

Treat him as a superior, if he is superior.

Treat him as an inferior, if he is inferior.

> He that would rise to be the highest
> Must first come down to be the lowest,
> And then ascend to be the highest
> By keeping down to be the lowest.

Some of you would never know how to eat with Jesus, the Christ.

He was very kind when He ate with people who, perhaps, ate with their fingers.

I believe that it is our duty to help those that have not learned.

A Man Must Be Adapted to the Work He Has to Do.

Today I have sent a gentleman to represent us as General Financial Agent in Great Britain and Ireland; that gentleman knows how to eat with a prince; he knows how to behave like a gentleman anywhere.

Would I have been wise in sending an uncultivated man?

Audience—"No."

General Overseer—Would I have done well by Zion had I sent a man who would drink from a finger-bowl or eat with a knife?

Audience—"No."

General Overseer—Of course not.

Some of you err in your judgment of others when they are severe.

You do not know the Master.

You do not know Moses.

You do not know me.

I am meek and lowly in heart.

No poor man or woman can justly complain that I have not treated him or her lovingly and in humility.

I love to lift my hat and salute the humblest member of this Church, and you know I do.

It is a pleasure to grasp the hand of an honest farmer who loves me and who has brought his riches into Zion, when some who are more intelligent, as they think, do not love me.

Our children are acquiring the Gentleness and the Good Sense that comes with increased cultivation.

A gentleman who is a stranger said to me, "I went amongst your people and found splendid men in your officers and thorough gentlemen in your workmen."

He said, "One thing was very noticeable; they would not stop working to talk with me."

Perhaps some of you saw an article in the *Inter Ocean*, giving an account of his experience in this City.

He inquired of a workman who was digging in the soil. "Where are all the people?—everything seems so quiet in Zion City."

The fellow kept on digging and replied, "Out earning a living."

That man would not stop to talk, and, although he was perfectly gentlemanly, he gave the man to understand that he was working for Zion, and that he would not steal Zion's time by standing and talking.

A Zion Workman Knows How to Be Both Stern and Meek.

This writer said that he was impressed by that workman's gentlemanliness and his meekness; but when he purposely uttered an offensive remark about me, the workman drew himself up with manifest indignation and said, "You cannot talk like that to me. Dr. Dowie laid his hands upon me when I was dying. God heard his prayer, and I am here.

"I tell you," continued the workman, "that the word you spoke concerning the Doctor is a shameful lie. I am sorry to have to speak like that. You will please go away and leave me, for I once was a man who could swear, and I once was a man that would knock down a man who insulted any one that I loved, and I do not know what might happen if the Devil got in again. Excuse me, sir, you must go and talk to the Overseers."

"I felt so ashamed," said the gentleman, "that I had to turn to him and say, 'Well, now, I just said that to test you, and I very humbly beg your pardon;' but he replied, 'Excuse me, you lied to me once, and I cannot tell whether you will lie to me a second time; you tricked me with a lie. Excuse me, I am busy.'

"I was sent about my business," he said, "by a man who was earning perhaps twelve dollars a week, while I, with an income of nearly a hundred dollars a week, felt that he was the real gentleman."

What the Word Meekness Means.

That workman was Meek in his answer; and he was Meekest, perhaps, when he was boldest for the truth.

I want you to understand what that word Meekness means.

It is a very peculiar word.

Praotes (Πραότης), has a very peculiar derivation; it comes from the word *Praos* (Πρᾶος), and is used to express two different qualities.

It is used with reference to people of high birth, who are gentle and meek.

It is used with reference to high-bred horses that are full of life, but so gentle that a little child is able to lead them.

Through the kindness of some of our beloved people in Zürich, I have received a splendid pair of horses of combined Arabic and Russian strain.

I was driving behind these horses in Zürich, when a newspaper, caught by the wind, was blown directly in front of them and struck their breasts.

They looked at it as much as to say, "You cannot scare us; you are only a bit of paper," and then went on.

That is the idea of Meekness in the original—a Gentleness and a Meekness.

Which is the meeker horse in your stable, the well-bred or the poorly-bred?

Surely the well-bred, if it has been well treated.

If you have not treated it properly, it will be a kicker, sure.

It will not stand any nonsense.

We Have to Show That We Are Sons of God.

We have to combine our Divine heritage and show that we are the Sons of the Kingdom—Sons of our Father in Heaven—who do not prance, and snort, and kick, at every bit of paper that falls in our way.

We will not be afraid to grasp the hand of a black man or woman, and we will not think that the whole world is going to pieces because our brother married a very nice African lady.

Some of the most beautiful people that I saw while abroad were very black, and there were some that were copper-colored, and some that were just like the delicate hue of coffee with rich cream in it.

I have been giving you a talk about manners.

Well, manners are good, but I want you to have a large conception of what a child of God should be.

I have yet much to learn.

But there is one thing I will never learn.

I will never learn to have contempt for a man because he is poor, because he is ignorant, or because he has a colored skin.

I sympathize with those who have been so trained that they do not know better, and I want to lift them up.

I would love to be able to say today, that every man and woman, no matter how humble, in Zion, is a true Christian gentleman and gentlewoman, with the Meekness and yet the Courage of a noble Christian.

PRAYER BY THE GENERAL OVERSEER.

Our God and Father, in Jesus Name, take us as we are, make us what we ought to be, give unto us this Grace of true Meekness, for Jesus' sake.

The service then closed with the

BENEDICTION.

Beloved, abstain from every form of evil. And may the very God of Peace Himself sanctify you wholly; and I pray God your whole spirit and soul and body be preserved entire, without blame, unto the coming of our Lord Jesus, the Christ. Faithful is He that calleth you, who also will do it. The grace of our Lord Jesus, the Christ, the love of God, our Father, the fellowship of the Holy Spirit, our Comforter and Guide, one Eternal God, abide in you, bless you and keep you, and all the Israel of God everywhere, forever. Amen.

EARLY MORNING SACRIFICE OF PRAISE AND PRAYER.

REPORTED BY S. E. C. AND O. V. G.

Shiloh Tabernacle, Zion City, Illinois, Friday Morning, July 22, 1904.

The service was opened by the singing of Hymn No 22 in the Special Program, after which the General Overseer offered prayer, leading the Congregation, at the close, in the chanting of the Disciples' Prayer.

After the singing of Hymn No. 13, the General Overseer, in announcing the meetings of the day, spoke as follows concerning Zion Dorcas Work:

Excellent Management of Zion Dorcas Work.

I desire to say a few words concerning the close of the Program.

We have reached the last full day of work of this week.

It is not my purpose to flatter any one, but Mrs. Dowie, like myself, is exceedingly gratified with the way in which Elder Speicher, who, with her husband, is now on the way to Europe, and Elder Brasefield, the wife of Overseer Brasefield, have conducted the Dorcas and Maternity Deaconess Work during Overseer Dowie's absence.

I think the people scarcely understand how much that work is.

I take a great interest in it, and I back Mrs. Dowie.

Whenever she is short of money she comes to me, and she gets some; but I very rarely have an appeal from her.

She has managed that fund in such a way, and God has so abundantly blessed her, that she is nearly always in funds.

Sometimes, at the beginning of her winter's work, she will remind me that I have to give her a check; but after a year of considerable toil, she left the funds in pretty good order.

The Magnitude of Zion Dorcas Work.

She told me yesterday that fifteen thousand garments have been supplied to the poor.

Deaconess Thomas is at the head of the workers who get the garments together.

When you go home, before winter comes, will you not look over your things?

Do not send us little trifling things that may be worn only on a summer day.

Look over your winter garments, and say to yourself, "I expect to have some new winter clothing; I will send the old ones for the Dorcas work."

Do not send us old boots that are unfit to shield one from the cold.

As a rule we give the poor new boots, because they need them.

Do not give us something that is worn out, and no good.

You have much serviceable clothing lying about that is of no use to you.

The moths are getting at it.

Our workers can take coats that you are through with, and make little coats of them for children.

Ladies' dresses can be converted into little dresses for children, and it is done nicely and quickly.

Two hundred fifty Zion women are working for the poor of other cities as well as the poor of this City.

They do it very willingly.

Our districts in Chicago are crying out for help.

The Folly of Industrial Strikes.

There has been a strike down in the Stockyards.

That strike has already cost Chicago two million dollars.

Not only those employed in the Stockyards have suffered, but also those employed on the railroads.

Two hundred fifty thousand people, mostly those who live from hand to mouth, have been deprived of the money needful to keep the house going nicely.

They pawn their furniture, and then they begin drinking.

They get drunk and smash the men who take their places, especially if they are negroes.

One of the men said yesterday, "We had very little to gain; all that we could have gained was a cent or so an hour."

In fighting for cents, they have lost dollars.

Our people have nothing to do with strikes.

These labor leaders nearly always enter upon a strike at the beginning of winter, and when cold weather comes, the poor are unprepared.

These men do not think about that.

Some of the women are just as careless; but for the most part they are thoughtful, begging the men to resume work.

They would clothe their children if they could, but they cannot do it, and we help clothe them.

Every Need of Zion City's Poor Supplied.

Then we have our poor here.

You have heard ridiculous things about the suffering of our people.

I know that not a single person in Zion City has been obliged to go without fuel, food, or clothing.

This is one of the great works of the Church.

Jesus said, "Ye have the poor always with you, but Me ye have not always;" and again, "Blessed is he that considereth the poor."

I never forget the poor, and the poor never forget me.

There are some people that are shiftless.

All the shiftless people are not in the South, although many that come from the South are shiftless.

Good people with their children, that come from the warm states, where only the minimum of clothing is required, are not prepared for the cold winters of Zion City.

Some of these, who are the most sweet-tempered and nicest people that you can imagine, forget that it gets cold in Zion City.

Healthfulness of Zion City Climate.

The climate of Zion City is healthful—make no mistake about it.

Last year, out of one thousand nine hundred four pupils in our schools, we lost only four—about two in a thousand.

In Chicago, at one time, they lost thirty or forty in a thousand.

The difference is accounted for, partly, by the fact that Mrs. Dowie and her colleagues—the loving-hearted Deaconesses and Dorcas Workers, were caring for the poor.

They had provided before the winter came.

If you wish to clothe the poor in the winter, you have to start in the fall, in September or October, for the cold comes suddenly.

Even as early as November, we have to cover the little bodies and the little feet; and we aim to do that.

Mrs. Dowie does not give them old boots.

She gives them new boots and arctics.

Their little feet are covered, they go to school with a jump and a hop; and they are well.

There are some shiftless mothers.

I declare to you, before God, it is a wonder to me that God entrusts you with children.

You do not look after them.

You do not care for them.

You wait until they get cold and are coughing before you clothe them properly.

We aim to preserve our children; and, while we are willing to do good to all men as far as we have opportunity, we begin at home.

We do not look after the heathen in Africa until the poor at home are cared for.

The poor in Zion City are the best cared for of any in all the world. [Applause.]

They shall be.

Do you imagine, for one moment, that I will let the people in Zion City go without food while I have food?

Verily, no!

So far as I know, there is not one Zion man or woman in prison.

Folly of Presuming Upon the Generosity of Zion.

There is not one Zion man or woman in the poorhouse.

There is not one Zion man or woman that needs bread.

Some people have to be watched.

"Why," they say, "Mrs. Dowie will look out for us this year," and the consequence is they do not look out for themselves.

They may look out for a stick, because those that are guilty will get it.

We are willing to help those in need, but when one wants to acquire money by neglecting the children and throwing them on the Dorcas fund, that won't do.

The poor we will have always with us, in a measure; and, whether it is through the shiftlessness of the parents, or their inability to understand this climate, we have to clothe them throughout, and sometimes to keep it up.

I want you to help Mrs. Dowie.

I make this appeal without her knowledge, but I want to give expression to my indebtedness to Mrs. Dowie and to the Woman's Work.

I believe there is no better work being done in all the world than that which is being accomplished under her direction.

The Charity of Zion Not Confined to America.

In Australia, and in Europe, our people are caring for the poor there, as we are caring for the poor here—for the poor who belong to other churches, and for those who belong to no church.

I want you to help.

There may be another severe winter.

I cannot tell, but we have to start early to prepare for it.

The work is tremendous, and money is required to do it.

I shall be glad if you will pray God to help you to assist.

How One Boy Obtained a Situation.

A boy said to his mother, "Mother, I could get a nice place down-town if I had better clothes."

She had been abandoned by her husband, and was left with six children, for whom she was obliged to work at the wash-tub, and this boy, who had a fairly good education, was not suitably clothed.

"Oh," she said, "I will tell Mrs. Dowie."

She told Mrs. Dowie, and we clothed that little chap from head to foot.

When he walked into that merchant's office and doffed his cap, he secured that situation. He has it still.

His employer is so well pleased with him that he practically furnishes about two-thirds of the family living.

God bless the boy!

That suit of clothes did it.

We never have very much in our treasury with which to face the New Year.

Mrs. Dowie will tell you that her fund now amounts to about five hundred dollars.

What is five hundred dollars in the face of so great need, with perhaps twenty thousand garments to be made?

Now, pray and help her.

Read in the 2d epistle of Timothy, the 2d chapter:

> Thou therefore, my child, be strengthened in the grace that is in Christ Jesus.
>
> And the things which thou hast heard from me among many witnesses, the same commit thou to faithful men, who shall be able to teach others also.

Zion Training a Royal Generation of Teachers.

That is just what we are doing.

We are training children, youths, maidens, and young men and women, that we may be able to commit to others the things that we have taught before many witnesses.

> Suffer hardship with me—

Or it might be read—

> Take thy part in suffering hardship with me, as a good soldier of Christ Jesus.
>
> No soldier on service entangleth himself in the affairs of this life; that he may please him who enrolled him as a soldier.

I want to see in Zion a concentration of all our monetary interests, so that we may be able to make as large an income as possible for all our people, that they may not be entangled with the outside World, the Flesh, and the Devil.

We are creating a monetary interest in Zion such as the world has never seen.

We pull together.

Our Stocks are being bought freely.

The Prophet of God Utters a Note of Warning.

You had better get in quickly; get in out of the Tribulation.

Here is a letter that I received this morning from a woman.

It has just come to my mind:

"I wish you to pray for my son."

She is a poor widow.

This poor widow lent her son three hundred dollars.

This is not along the line of what I said yesterday morning.

I talked about parents being mean to their children; but here is a poor widow who lends, out of her hard earnings, to her son.

Ten years ago she lent it; and now she needs it.

She says, "He does not pretend to want to pay me. He has always paid me the interest, but he has not renewed the note. I have not needed it until now, but I believe he does not intend to pay me, because I have come to Zion City to live. He is a Freemason, and he seemingly hates the things of God."

A Freemason, even the son of a widow, has such hatred of the things of God, that he would let his mother starve.

He knows that she will not starve in Zion.

He knows that we will take care of her.

Come in, and thank God Almighty that you have a place into which you can come.

While I do not want you to come in foolishly, and not without arranging your matters wisely, yet be careful.

Do not let the Devil trick you, and keep you out too long.

Do not entangle yourself with affairs of this world.

If you get into Zion you will have this joy, that your affairs are in the hands of good men, who will not steal a dollar.

All Zion Institutions are absolutely free of incumbrances.

There is not a dollar of bond on this City.

We are not entangled with the world.

Will you not help us keep free?
Pray about it.

And if also a man contend in the games, he is not crowned, except he have contended lawfully.
The husbandman that laboreth must be the first to partake of the fruits.
Consider what I say; for the Lord shall give thee understanding in all things.
Remember Jesus, the Christ, risen from the dead, of the seed of David, according to my Gospel:
Wherein I suffer hardship unto bonds, as a malefactor; but the Word of God is not bound.

The Word of God Cannot Be Bound.

What a grand word that is! "The Word of God is not Bound."

The Word that we have sent from this place cannot be bound.

It has gone all around the world, and it keeps on going all the time.

The word of the Devil dies, and the Word of God goes on growing.

It is the Seed that every year is being sown, and the sowing and the reaping is going on.

What a glorious possibility we have in Zion of reaching the whole world, and of doing something to prepare for the Coming of the King!

How my heart goes out to the nations that sit in darkness!

How I long to see Zion colonies for them!

I really believe I will have to buy that land in Mexico, fifty miles by thirty miles; for the colored people, especially, and for the white people that will not be afraid to go down amongst them.

I will not be afraid.

If you make much noise, I will go down there altogether; but I tell you, I am not afraid to say that the union of all the families of the race is something that God wants.

The Word of God is not bound:
Therefore I endure all things for the elect's sake, that they also may obtain the Salvation which is in Christ Jesus, with Eternal Glory.

Faithful is the saying:

For if we died with Him, we shall also live with Him:
If we endure, we shall also reign with Him.

You have to die with Him—be dead to self and sin; and you have to endure with Him if you are to reign with Him.

Why do you shrink from losses and crosses on the Way to Triumph?

If we shall deny Him, He also will deny us:
If we are faithless, He abideth faithful; for He cannot deny Himself.

THE NINTH FRUIT OF THE SPIRIT: SELF-CONTROL.

INVOCATION.

Let the words of my mouth and the meditation of my heart be acceptable in Thy sight, be profitable unto this people, and unto all to whom these words shall come, in this and every land, in this and all the coming time, Till Jesus Come. Amen.

In Galatians, the 5th chapter, repeat with me:

TEXT.

But the Fruit of the Spirit is Love, Joy, Peace, Long-suffering, Kindness, Goodness, Faithfulness,
Meekness, Temperance: against such there is no law.
And they that are of Christ Jesus have crucified the flesh, with the passions and the lusts thereof.
If we live by the Spirit, by the Spirit let us also walk.
Let us not be vainglorious, provoking one another, envying one another.

Temperance People the Narrowest People in the World.

The word in the Greek for Temperance means more than our word Temperance.

I am convinced that the narrowest people in the world are to be found amongst the "temperance" people.

They imagine that if you do not take alcoholic liquors you are a saint.

Bah! I have seen races where no intoxicating liquors are drunk!

If you want to see the dirtiest, meanest kind of people on God's earth, look at the Mohammedans.

There are two hundred fifty millions of them that never touch liquor.

It is against the law of the Mohammedans.

Liquor is left for the white man.

The white man gets drunk.

They leave the pig to him, too.

But they are not good, clean people, for all that.

I am an abstainer.

I have been all my life.

That is why I have some strength left to do the work God calls me to do.

I have neither smoked nor drank, all my life.

I once had some alcohol poured into me.

My mother said I went mad.

I am glad I did.

They never tried it again.

I cannot imagine, however, that the whole meaning of Temperance would be giving up liquor, tobacco, or any other thing of that kind.

Temperance is a larger thing than that.

Let me give you the real meaning of the word.

Temperance Means More Than Self-control.

The word *engkrateia* (ἐγκράτεια) comes from the word *kratos* (κράτος), which means strength, and originally meant Divine strength, the strength of the gods—a Greek idea.

It is not only strength, but the first idea was the strength of the gods.

The next idea was that of absolute mastery, rule; and there you get the verb *krateo*, (κρατέω), to rule; and from it you have the words Democrat, Theocrat, Plutocrat.

Democrat would mean, the people rule.

Theocrat would mean, God rules.

Plutocrat would mean, money rules.

The word has the idea of strength, power, rule.

It also has the meaning of absolute mastery; and then, as it comes down, it means as a Fruit of the Spirit in the Christian, Self-control—absolute Self-control of every power, and every passion.

It means that you shall be master, under God, of yourself.

Master of the Mind, and master of the World, the Flesh, and the Devil.

I strive for mastery, and I intend, God helping me, to put the Lord Jesus, the Christ, in control of just as many men, and just as many women, and just as many cities, and just as many nations, as I can.

I strive, with the hosts of Zion, for mastery over Satan, and sin, and disease, and death, and hell. [Amen. Applause.]

You must be master, every one of you, of yourself.

If we do this, the men and women in Zion must get this last Fruit of the Spirit, mastery, the power to rule.

The Christian Must Be Master Everywhere.

You must be master, my brother, in your own Home.

You must be kind, considerate, gentle, loving, and full of all these other Fruits; but you must be master.

You can be master only by the first Fruit, Love; and you can be master only by going through the whole gamut of the Nine Fruits, until you reach Self-control.

How can you be master, in the best sense of the word, of your wife, when you have neither Love nor Self-control?

You are not master.

She cannot obey you; she cannot serve you; she cannot bear your rule, or your presence.

You must have Love!

Control yourself, and then the woman will wear you in her heart, and wear you there forever.

If you do not love, and you have no Self-control, you are a mere beastly creature of Passion.

How can you wonder that every day the poor woman shrinks from you, loving you less and less, until at last she thinks only of the day when death will set her free.

I tell you, my brothers, have the Love, have the Joy, have the Peace, have the glorious Grace of Long-suffering; have the Goodness, and the Gentleness, and the Kindness, and the Meekness; but, listen—have the Self-control.

Do Not Be Discouraged if Sometimes You Fail.

Sometimes the best man will fail.

Sometimes, under the oppression of the world, and the unsatisfied longings of his heart and nature, he will lose control.

Do not throw the man aside because he lost it once.

Do not forget that Self-control may, for a moment slip from a man's fingers.

But do not let it slip, my brothers.

When you fall, make confession with deep humility, and ask for forgiveness where you have failed to exercise Self-control.

I said, "I strive for mastery."

I do.

I have never made a mock of it, and pretended that I did not want to rule.

I have to rule.

I must rule.

I cannot do the work in Zion if I do not rule, and Zion would never be what it is if, under God, I did not rule.

I must rule with diligence; but, my brothers, and my sisters, do you not know that it is the man that rules who has to exercise the greatest amount of Self-control?

It is easier for you who have a small sphere to exercise Self-control, than it is for me.

I have to exercise Self-control when I am attacked from every side; when the World, the Flesh and the Devil, and my own inherited nature, are against me.

A Man of Like Passions with Others.

I did not inherit a nature free from sin.

I inherited a sinful nature, a strong nature, a nature that came down to me from those that had ruled for centuries, and that rule now.

Unless God had had mercy upon me, and had made me what little I am for God, I would be one of the worst men in the world—perhaps the very worst.

As I grow in power to rule, as I look at the World, the Flesh, and the Devil everywhere, I say, "You shall not master me."

I say to the Masonic order, "You shall not master the Christian Catholic Church in Zion." [Applause.]

"You have mastered the Methodist Episcopal church.

"You have mastered the Presbyterian church.

"You have mastered the Baptist church.

"You have mastered the Congregational church.

"You have mastered the politicians, the bankers, the merchants and the newspaper editors; but you cannot master me!

"You cannot master Zion!" [Applause.]

I said, "No, we will master you, for we are the Children of God." [Applause.]

A man once said of me, "He does not speak as if he wanted to persuade the people to do anything. He speaks as if he wanted to master them."

Exactly so.

I do not want you to be without reason.

I will master you by reason, by the Word of God, by Love, by the things I want to make you master of.

Make no mistake!

We Have Either to Master the Devil, or He Will Master Us.

We have either to defeat that army that is marching upon us, and which surrounds us everywhere, or it will overwhelm us.

This is true in all our affairs.

It is more true than you realize.

Every apostate church in existence would send up a shout of triumph if they could hear that John Alexander Dowie was dead and Zion City destroyed.

The world that lies in sin—the poor masses of the people outside the churches—might shed a tear. I think that they would.

They might utter a sigh and say, "We had hoped that he and Zion would show us a way out."

But the apostate churches would rejoice.

That shows you where the Devil is in force.

The Devil is in force today in the apostasies.

He has mastered the churches.

He has mastered their resources.

Those that hunted for my life in Australia were led on by ministers.

They were people that had been brought up in Sunday-schools.

This Self-control includes the Grace of Joy.

The Happy Man Is Strong.

It is the happy man that is strong, not the miserable man.

People who go about with long faces, complaining of everything, may be splendid people, but their miserable faces undo all the good they ever did.

Why cannot you be bright?

Are you not a son or daughter of God?

If you suffer, smile as you suffer.

"Oh, it's all very well to talk, General Overseer, but do you suffer?"

Yes, and smile; and I have sometimes come to you with a broken heart.

But I gave you all the light I had; all the strength I had; all the brightness I had; and God healed my broken heart while I did it.

Give to others.

Pour out your life for others.

Set to work to do something, and turn off the water-works!

Turn off those tears!

Your face would look so sweet if it did not have furrows that the tears have made!

Your eyes would look so bright, if you did not weep out their brightness!

I say this because you have no Self-control.

Get the Love!

Get the Joy!

Get the Peace!

Get the Long-suffering!

Get the Kindness!

Get the Goodness!

Get the Faithfulness!

Get the Meekness!

The proof that you have them will be *engkrateia* (ἐγκράτεια)—the Self-control.

"There is no use talking, General Overseer, is it not God who has the Control?"

We Have to Work Out What God Puts Within.

Yes, but listen!

> Work out your own salvation with fear and trembling;
> For it is God which worketh in you both to will and to work, for His good pleasure.
>
> . . . .
>
> Cleanse your hands, ye sinners; and purify your hearts, ye double-minded.

Throw out every controlling power and passion that belongs to the Devil, and let your whole spirit, soul, and body come under the Control of God.

Where God has complete mastery, He puts the reins in your hands, and says, "Drive on for Me; work for Me."

"O Master," we sometimes cry, "You do it all. You just let me go into the traces, and be a horse, and You drive me."

But we are not horses.

We are men.

We are men and women endowed with a large degree of liberty, and with large capacity for independent thought.

I am glad of that.

I never wanted to crush out independence in Zion.

You know that.

If you mean by independence, to go as you like and do as you please, that is not independence.

That is folly.

That is running up and down the railway track on your own schedule time, and everybody is afraid of you.

Run on schedule time.

Run with us.

Work with us.

There Is Large Room in Zion for the Exercise of One's Individuality.

There is more individuality in Zion than anywhere else.

On this platform, the other day, I asked Judge Barnes, who, as you know, is a man of strong individuality, how much of his individuality he had lost since he came into Zion.

Judge Barnes, how much have you lost?

Judge Barnes—"I never was so free before."

General Overseer—Not even when you were Prohibitionist candidate for Governor?

Judge Barnes—"No, General Overseer."

General Overseer—Is Evangelist Gay, from Alabama, here?

Evangelist Gay—"Yes, sir."

General Overseer—How much of your individuality have you lost?

Evangelist Gay—"Not a bit, sir. I wish I could lose a little more."

General Overseer—You are willing to be controlled a little more, are you?

Evangelist Gay—"Yes."

General Overseer—Look at the men I have around me!

I cannot understand how the world keeps up that chatter about everybody who comes into Zion having to give everything they have to Dr. Dowie.

A little while ago some one said, "I took forty thousand dollars to Zion City."

He was asked, "Well, has Dowie got it all?"

"No," he said.

"Well, has he not made money out of you?"

"I do not know," he replied, "but one thing I do know—I have made money out of him." [Laughter.]

"How was that?"

"Well," he said, "I reckon my forty thousand dollars is now worth eighty thousand."

"You do? Now, don't you imagine that?"

"No," he said, "because, the other day, land that I bought for five hundred dollars I refused to sell for two thousand dollars. Now," he continued, "I reckon it is not what he has made out of me, or what Zion has made out of me, but what I have made out of Zion that merits consideration."

What Lack of Self-control Cost One Man.

One man left us a little while ago.

Reporters gathered around him.

He had had no trouble with me, or with Zion, but he had got into a quarrel with his brother.

He was very naughty, and struck his brother.

"Well," his brother said, "I shall have to report that, because some day you might do your wife an injury."

"If you do," he replied, "I will leave Zion."

He sold his property, and was sorry for it within twenty-four hours, although he got about two and one-half times what he paid for it.

He loaded up his furniture, and had it down to the depot before I heard about it.

When I sent for him, he said, "I am sorry, but I have sold my property; I guess I would better go away, because I have no Self-control."

"Will you learn it better on the frontier?" I inquired.

"If you do not have Self-control, some fellow may put a bullet into you."

He went to the frontier; and one day he lost his temper, and got a blow from which he has not yet recovered.

Before he received that blow the reporters got around him in Chicago, and said, "Now, tell us, how Dowie robbed you."

"Bless your life, what do you mean?"

"Did you not take a lot of money into Zion?"

"Yes."

"Did you not give it all to Zion?"

"No," he said, "I gave no money. I was a bad member. I did not pay my tithes."

That was how he got into trouble with his brother.

His brother told him he ought to pay tithes.

"Well," they said, "did Dowie not get any of it?"

"No."

"Well, are you not poorer?"

"No," he said, "I have two and a half times as much money as I had when I went there."

One of The Newspaper Lies Again Refuted.

You might just as well put that down, because it is one of the lies about Zion that may as well be knocked in the head once more.

Did I take your money?

People—"No."

General Overseer—Did I make you give up everything to me when you came into Zion?

People—"No."

General Overseer—Have you still the control of your estate?

People—"Yes."

General Overseer—I have the responsibility and the care.

I have to see that you get the interest.

I have to exercise great Self-control when these lies are told about me all over the world.

The temptation is to smash these things, and to a certain extent we do.

Last February I came to a conclusion from which I have not deviated.

I had come to the same decision before, but I afterwards thought that I might glorify God by letting the newspapers have an occasional interview.

After landing in Australia, where I had expected fair treatment and kindness, I was thoroughly disgusted.

Every interviewer, from the time I landed in Sydney, received fair treatment, and every one of them lied.

Every interview was distorted.

Those who failed to get interviews manufactured them.

Every report of our meetings was garbled and full of misrepresentation.

They published things I never said.

I then resolved that I would never, God helping me, lose another minute's time over the press.

I shall never give them an interview, and I shall not, for one moment, lose my Self-control over anything that they may write. [Applause.]

It required a good deal of God's grace to make this decision, and it will require a good deal of grace to keep to it.

Will you pray for me?

Audience—"Yes."

The General Overseer Has to Control His Appetite for Work.

General Overseer—The snows of winter are on my brow, and although at fifty-seven I possess a marvelous power of endurance, I know I stand very close to the shadows, and that I need to control myself, and not do as much work as I have done during this Feast of Tabernacles.

I need to control my enormous appetite for work.

I love work.

I work all day, and sometimes all night.

Will you ask God that I shall have sufficient Self-control to get enough sleep and to get enough time to eat; and will you help me by not bothering me?

Audience—"Yes."

General Overseer—I ask you to help me, because I need help.

If I fall, it will be from inability to control my appetite for work.

We do not always know just what the measure of our strength is, and we go right on, for the work is so great.

We must have enough food, we must have enough sleep, and we must have enough time for quiet reflection, and study, else we will never be any good.

A Wide Range of Knowledge Has to Be Acquired.

I am a student.

I must be.

I have the files of all the principal papers and magazines of the world.

I have all the latest literature, and have had for many years.

I keep myself so well informed, that when I meet prince or peasant in any country, I know about that country.

I know its affairs; I understand its difficulties.

I must keep myself abreast the times in architecture, and in manufacturing, and in things of importance to Zion.

I have a builders' library, an engineers' library, an architects' library, an artists' library, an historians' library, a theologians' library, and the library of a man of affairs, who keeps in constant touch with all the world.

What you get from me is the result of study and toil, as well as the Gift of God in Inspiration.

Genius Is a Capacity for Taking Pains.

The only thing that constitutes genius is the capacity for taking pains.

Some of you preachers who do not do much for God are lazy.

You do not study your Bible.

You do not study historical facts.

You do not take the time that you might.

"Oh, well, General Overseer, we would have to take the time out of the work."

No such thing.

I never take time out of the work.

I take time out of the night.

While I am pleading for you not to overwork, I also say, do not underwork.

Do not overfeed and underwork.

There are some who overfeed and underwork, and they go to pieces, for they have no Self-control.

It would be better for you to overwork and underfeed.

Do neither.

Let us all ask God to give us grace to do what is right, and to work as much as we can, and to sleep as much as is necessary.

There are a thousand ways in which to talk of this Self-control.

The time to control yourself is when you have that headache; when you have that tired, weary feeling; when you cannot be bothered, and you are almost ready to say so; when the child comes to you with a joyful run, and you are sick.

"O mamma, what is the matter?"

The child sees it.

The little child's exuberance is checked.

How much better it would have been if you had just stifled that little pain, even if it was only to put on a smile, and get the joy of the Lord in your heart, and met the little one with a smile.

Then she would not have known that mamma was tired.

She would have loved you, and she would have petted you.

Then you could have said, "Pray for mamma," and the little one would have prayed.

You would have gotten the joy and the strength, because you exerted yourself.

If I preached the way I felt sometimes, you would get some awful things.

I should cry when my people needed light and strength.

We All Have to Control Ourselves.

Do not let even your dearest ones know the weight of your care, of your trial, of your sorrow.

Take it to God, and before you salute your wife in the morning with the kiss of peace; before you see your servants in the morning, and before you see the face of man, look upon the face of God.

Seek the face of God, and ask for all these precious Fruits, and say, "Lord, at the top of this glorious bouquet of Divine flowers I see Self-control.

It is such a beautiful flower!

Love is its root.

Love is all around it.

Love is there twining through it, but at the top is Self-control.

In the forests of Mexico, where magnificent trees raise their heads—giants of many centuries—there is a beautiful creeper to be found around the base.

Every Mexican, when he passes one, takes his knife and cuts it down, if he can spare the time.

What is he cutting down?

He is cutting down the matador.

It grows around that tree, winds around it so beautifully, and, twining itself around it, climbs away up, hanging in graceful festoons, until it reaches the top; then it bursts into horrid red flowers, and the Mexican passes the tree, looks at it and says, "Matador! Matador! Murderer! Murderer!"

The tree is dead.

That murderous plant has strangled it.

If you do not take care, sensual desires and earthly lusts will grow around the tree of your life.

If they be laziness, follies, sensuality, uncleanness, even though they look graceful, they are deadly flowers.

Matador! Murderer!

They will strangle you!

But here is another plant representing a glorious Self-control. We see it winding itself around the Tree of Life, on which are the Fruits of Love, Joy, Peace, Long-suffering, Gentleness, Goodness, Meekness, Temperance.

As you look at these, you say, "Blessing! blessing!"

Not murderer!

You cry, "Savior, Healer, Cleanser, Keeper, Strengthener."

And the highest flower of them all is the White Lily of Purity, Self-control.

May God give us that increasingly.

PRAYER OF CONSECRATION.

My God and Father, in Jesus' Name I come to Thee. Take me as I am, but make me what I ought to be; and take out of me everything that could offend, and give me these graces, and the white Purity of perfect Temperance, perfect Self-control. Give me this, O God, that I may be a blessing to others. For Jesus' sake. [*Congregation repeats prayer clause by clause, after the General Overseer.*]

Did you mean it?

Audience—"Yes."

General Overseer—Will you live it?

Audience—"Yes."

The service was closed by the Congregation's joining in singing, "I Stand on Zion's Mount," after which the General Overseer pronounced the

BENEDICTION.

Beloved, abstain from every form of evil. And may the very God of peace Himself sanctify you wholly; and I pray God your whole spirit and soul and body be preserved entire, without blame, unto the coming of our Lord Jesus, the Christ. Faithful is He that calleth you, who also will do it. The grace of our Lord Jesus, the Christ, the love of God our Father, the fellowship of the Holy Spirit, our Comforter and Guide, one Eternal God, abide in you, bless you and keep you, and all the Israel of God everywhere, forever. Amen.

EARLY MORNING SACRIFICE OF PRAISE AND PRAYER.

REPORTED BY M. E. L. AND A. C. R.

Shiloh Tabernacle, Zion City, Illinois, Saturday Morning, July 23, 1904.

The service was opened by the singing of Hymn No. 6, in the Program, "Awake and Sing."

Prayer was offered by the General Overseer, after which Hymn No. 16, "Come, Let us Join our Cheerful Songs," was sung.

The General Overseer said:

Pray for Russia.

I should like to ask you to pray with me for many in distant lands who are looking Zionward for help.

I especially ask you to pray at this time for Russia. I hope that you understand that in speaking severely concerning Russia, I am not antagonistic to the Russian people.

I am antagonistic to the Russian apostasy, and to the Russian autocracy, and bureaucracy, and military tyranny.

The Russian people are very dear to my heart.

I have a profound conviction that the Slavonic race will be a great power in the world when the monarchy is smashed, when that bad government is destroyed, when that corrupt church is disrupted.

It were infinitely better, even for those in authority, that such a government should be destroyed.

I have a great many private letters from various parts of Russia, written in English.

As one travels around the world, one increasingly sees that this confusion of languages is one of the great reasons for the continuance of national strife.

The masses of the people are unable to read any language but their own, and the consequence is that they are deceived easily by the lies of their preachers, by the lies of their editors and teachers, by the lies of others who know that they are lying.

There are liars everywhere, but in official circles in Russia it might almost be said that they are all liars. Very few among them speak the truth.

God save the Russian people. [Amen.]

Zion's War Is a War of Peace.

You can see that

> Each breeze that sweeps the ocean
> Brings tidings from afar,
> Of nations in commotion
> Prepared for Zion's war.

Zion's war is a War of Love, a war at strife only with that which is wicked and all that is bad.

Keep watch of the signs of the times.

In order to do so, you must keep well informed.

You cannot get good, clear information out of the muck of the daily papers.

A Zion Daily Paper.

I believe that the people of Zion throughout the world will have to get their news of the day from a Zion newspaper. And we can only do it by being in touch with our Zion correspondents throughout the world. [Applause.]

We are in touch with every land on earth.

If you will help me, I will get for you, within this next year, a Zion morning paper. [Applause.]

I will see that the news which is collated is, as nearly as we can find it, reliable.

I want to send out a clean paper, cutting down all the

crime and that kind of thing to a few lines, and getting all the good that I can get and keeping you well informed.

I would like to be able to say that I shall write or dictate a daily article in that paper.

I talk half a dozen articles every day, and I might as well talk them for the paper.

I can plead for the Negro; I can plead for the Chinese; I can plead for the oppressed of all classes and conditions, in the pages of that paper.

I can send the news to you every day, no matter in what part of the world you are.

It is an agony to take these five morning dailies and these three or four evening papers published in Chicago and try to pick out the facts.

You can trust scarcely anything you read until it has been sifted for a day or two.

Interesting Incident Showing Power of "Leaves of Healing."

Pray that God will give me the staff and give me the means to establish a daily paper.

I have just engaged, after a good deal of careful investigation, a first-class man to take a most important place in connection with Zion Printing and Publishing House.

He was wonderfully saved after being a Methodist for many years.

Some one handed him a copy of LEAVES OF HEALING, on a railway train.

As a printer, he was attracted by the appearance of it.

If it had been printed on a poor, dirty sheet, he would have flung it aside.

He read it, and before he got through he went back to the gentleman who gave it to him and had a talk with him.

That night he took the paper home to his wife.

The result was that they were soon out of the Methodist Church, whose apostasy they had seen before this, and became members of the Christian Catholic Church in Zion.

He is giving up a splendid position to come into Zion.

I believe that you can help us build up a secular daily paper which, while it would never supersede LEAVES OF HEALING, would give you the news of the day and facts concerning daily life and good information on various subjects and take the muck away that curses your family now when you bring a daily paper into the house.

I believe that we have to produce a Daily Zion Banner, and you must help us do it. Will you help us?

People—"Yes."

General Overseer—Pray about it.

I shall probably appeal to you through the pages of the weekly BANNER and LEAVES OF HEALING some time in the Fall, towards this end; for Zion Printing and Publishing House must Go Forward.

May God in His infinite mercy help us so to live that we may be a blessing to all the nations, and that as they are being disrupted and rended, Zion may watch her opportunity, and pass in through the Gates that even war has opened.

May God grant it. (Amen.)

THE NINE GIFTS OF THE SPIRIT.

INVOCATION.

Father, let the words of my mouth, and the meditations of my heart, be acceptable in Thy sight and profitable unto this people, for Thou art in the Christ, our Lord, our Strength and our Redeemer.

The General Overseer then read from the 1st epistle of Paul to the Corinthians, the 12th chapter:

"Now concerning Spiritual Gifts, brethren," it is an excellent thing to be ignorant—is that it?

People—"No."

General Overseer—"Now concerning Spiritual Gifts, brethren, I would not have you ignorant."

Extent of Ignorance of Gifts of the Spirit.

There is nothing of which the Church is more profoundly ignorant than the truth concerning the Gifts of the Holy Spirit.

Even Christians who have been used of God, and who have many precious Fruits of the Spirit, do not know anything about the Gifts of the Spirit.

Gifts of the Spirit and Fruits of the Spirit are entirely different.

Fruits of the Spirit are growths of the Holy Spirit's planting upon earthly soil.

The Gifts of the Spirit are growths of the Spirit's Life in heaven and are brought down to us on earth.

They are not the same.

Oranges grown in Canada are different from oranges grown in Florida.

Fruits that grow from the same seed are very different in different soil.

An Illinois Concord grape, with its thick skin, is very different from the grapes of Spain and Italy, or of France, or of many other parts of the world, with their delicate skin and their delicious flavor.

The difference between the things that God sends us from heaven and things grown on earth is much greater than that between the products of Illinois and of the sunny South.

But the Gifts of the Spirit are more than fruits; they are specific Powers—great Divine Powers for service, which make it possible for us to employ the Fruits of the Spirit in the service of God.

Dumb Idols.

The apostle goes on to say:

Ye know that when ye were Gentiles, ye were led away unto these Dumb Idols.

I wonder if you have got away from Dumb Idols.

Idolatry is deeply rooted in the heart of humanity.

"What is that?" you ask a lady.

"That is my old grandfather's sword. Ah, I tell you, we are somebody. My grandfather used that sword in the War of the Revolution, and I am a Daughter of the Revolution."

Do you not know that there are women who worship their grandfathers' swords, their old caps and coats and any old thing that belonged to their grandfathers?

Idols, Dumb Idols!

Idolatry of old clothes, of old sword—relics!

You have no idea, perhaps, some of you, how they are worshiped, especially in the old countries; but by no means are you without that kind of idolatry here.

Old notions have become Idols.

Old habits have become Idols.

Old associations have become Idols.

Dumb Idols!

The idolatries are innumerable.

Many are guilty of the idolatry of money. That is a Dumb Idol.

Property is a Dumb Idol.

I know many in Zion now who were idolaters, but their Idols were not quite dumb.

They were squealing pigs.

They did like to see the pig get fatter and fatter, and nastier and nastier, until the dirty thing could scarcely walk.

Some make idols of their horses. They almost get as far as Caligula, a Roman emperor, who, when his horse died, had a golden replica made of it, worshiped it, and declared it had been deified, and was now among the stars.

The Dumb Idol of Venus, in Corinth, took horrible form in the ministry of vice of the most unutterable debasement.

Wherefore I give you to understand that no man speaking in the Spirit of God saith, Jesus is anathema.

Meaning of "Anathema Maranatha."

I heard a man say the other day, "It is a terrible thing to say, '*Anathema Maranatha.*'"

I said, "No. It is a terrible thing to say Anathema against the Christ, but there are some things against which you ought to say Anathema.

"You ought to pray that the curse of God may destroy bad things.

"But," I said, "what do you mean by *Maranatha?*"

"I do not know," he replied.

"*Maranatha,*" I explained, "is a Hebrew word for, 'The Lord is at hand,' and it is not a curse at all. It is a blessing. It is an invocation."

The Christians used the word among themselves.

When they met they would say, "*Pax Tibi,*" and add, "*Maranatha*"—The Lord is at hand; He is coming.

It is a happy word. It is a bright word.

Let us get *Maranatha* into our hearts.

Do not let us think that it is a wicked thing to say.

You are not to call Jesus, the Christ, Anathema.

Any one that reviles Jesus, the Christ, is not speaking under the direction of the Spirit of God, nor is any one who reviles one who faithfully serves Jesus, the Christ

No man can say, Jesus is Lord, but in the Holy Spirit.

You can only say that Jesus is Lord when God gives you power to do it.

You may say it with the lips, but there is no power in it.

But when you say it in the Power of the Spirit, then there is Power.

Now there are diversities of Gifts, but the same Spirit.
And there are diversities of Ministrations, and the same Lord.
And there are diversities of Workings, but the same God, who worketh all things in all.
But to each one is given the manifestation of the Spirit to profit withal.

The thought is that these things are given that they may be reproductive; that they may produce a Divine profit; that the man himself may profit; that the Church may profit by the Gifts.

For to one is given through the Spirit the Word of Wisdom; and to another the Word of Knowledge, according to the same Spirit:
To another Faith, in the same Spirit; and to another Gifts of Healings, in the one Spirit;
And to another Workings of Miracles; and to another Prophecy; and to another Discernings of Spirits: to another Divers kinds of Tongues; and to another the Interpretation of Tongues:
But all these worketh the one and the same Spirit, dividing to each one severally even as He will.

I might just as well try to pour Lake Michigan into a teapot, as to try to give you a full explanation of these Gifts this morning.

No Gifts of the Spirit Unless Fruits of the Spirit Are Brought Forth.

I desire to call your attention to the truth that God will not bestow these Gifts of the Spirit upon any who do not bring forth Fruits of the Spirit.

The very first Fruit of the Spirit is Repentance toward God, which finds expression in Love—the Love that cries "I will lovingly obey Thee, and I will bring forth 'Fruits meet for Repentance,' no matter what it costs."

People sometimes say, "Will you pray for me that I may receive the Gifts of Healings?"

The worst possible thing for you would be a Gift that you could not employ.

Nothing more disastrous can happen to young people than to give them money that they cannot use wisely.

If you were to receive Gifts of Healings without first receiving the Word of Wisdom, and the Word of Knowledge, and Faith, you would be in the possession of something that would be an embarrassment to you.

You would dash about the world—if it were possible to do it, as it is not—healing people who ought to go to hell.

I have learned that there are a great many people with whose going to hell you ought never to interfere.

I mean exactly what I say.

Our Lord Jesus, the Christ, did not put a straw in Judas Iscariot's path.

Some People Must Be Allowed to Go to Hell.

"What thou doest," He said, "do quickly."

"Betray me and go to hell," was His meaning.

He had done everything for him that He could.

He had made him an apostle.

He had made him Treasurer of the Apostolic College.

He had given him the powers of an apostle, and Judas had used that power.

Probably he was faithful at one time, but he deliberately and of set purpose became a thief, a liar, and a betrayer.

He went to the Last Supper, having arranged for the Christ's murder that night.

The Christ would not put one straw in his way.

The Devil had entered into him; the Devil was in full possession, and all that the Christ said was, "What thou doest, do quickly."

There are people that are wicked.

I would not put a straw in their way to hinder their going to hell. Not one.

You can do nothing for them.

They are like Judas Iscariot.

He knew all about it; you could tell him nothing.

He knew nothing about Salvation.

He was an apostle; but he was a wicked, wilful thief; a liar, a murderer, a betrayer, and full of the Devil.

Hell was the best place for him, and he went to his own place.

I do not propose to try to be better than the Christ.

I do not imagine that I am.

I propose to be as commonsense as the Christ.

Good Wrought for Zion Through Urging on a Wicked Man.

When Samuel Stevenson threatened Zion and said that he would do this and that, and that I would be afraid to have the affairs of Zion go before a court, I said, "Go ahead. Do it! Do all you can, and if Zion and I have anything to be afraid of before a court, then we ought to be smashed now. Go ahead!"

It was a very good thing for Zion that I urged him to go ahead.

If I had put a straw in his way, multidudes would have said "Dr. Dowie is afraid of Samuel Stevenson. He can tell things."

I said, "Tell them, you traitor, you liar, you thief, you murderer!"

I called him all that in open court, and he was all that.

He went before an unjust judge, a judge who called him a liar; a judge who in his own words condemned him; but he got at that judge somehow.

I never did a better thing for Zion than when I let that apostate, that thief, that liar, that cheat, that murderer do his work.

We won!

And today he sneaks into dark corners.

He tried to get a Nottingham lace machine maker to make lace machines for him, the other day.

The man, a man of the world, said, "No, I won't make a machine for him."

I blasted, and blighted, and destroyed his reputation. He can do Zion no harm.

God blasted, and blighted, and destroyed forever the reputation of Judas Iscariot. His lies can do no harm.

A Waste of Time to Preach to Some Men.

You have to get Wisdom enough to see that there are some men to whom you have to stop preaching. You cast your pearls before swine. They will trample them under their feet and turn again and rend you.

"He that is righteous let him be righteous still: he that is filthy let him be filthy still."

Sometimes Christian people spend their lives trying to scrape a black man white.

Some men take an incarnate devil and try to make a Christian out of him.

Some women hold on to a filthy adulterer when they ought to get a divorce.

I know a fine Christian lady who is suffering from a third attack of syphilitic poison, from a dirty dog of a husband.

I say that she sins in living with him for an hour.

She has no right to make her body a temple of disease.

It is her duty to go before a magistrate and before her God and get freed from such a dirty, filthy dog.

I insult the dogs by saying that. He is worse than a dog.

Take your boys and bring them to Zion, and have done with that dirty devil. Do you hear?

That is a Word of Wisdom. It is a Word of Knowledge; a Word of Faith.

Let him alone!

Let him go down to hell if he will.

If he will repent and return to God and be saved, that is all right; you have a right to receive him again, if you choose, but wait until he gets right with God.

Take no more promises. Let the devil alone.

That is my answer to that lady and hundreds of others.

If that good woman had the Gifts of Healings, perhaps she might say, "O God, use me in healing," and, if it were possible, heal that dirty dog, that he might go on in his sin.

The first thing is to get the First Gift, the Word of Wisdom.

Jesus knew that the Pharisees had made up their minds to murder Him.

He let them alone.

More than that.

He told them the parable of the vineyard, in doing which He drove them to kill Him.

He knew that they knew the right, but that they wilfully did the wrong.

They were children of the Devil, and nothing could be done with them.

God puts such men and women into hell, where they can hurt humanity no more; where they can, in a disembodied state, make their Repentance and get to heaven.

Having made their bed in hell, even there His right hand shall find them.

The way to start your prayer to God is to say, "O God, give me the Word of Wisdom!"

Wisdom the Principal Thing.

The Second Gift is the Word of Knowledge.

"O God, give me the Word of Knowledge!"

I have been doing all I could to get some Wisdom into you, and more Knowledge into you, and more Faith into you.

The Gift of Teaching that God has given me has been a Word of Wisdom, a Word of Knowledge, and a Word of Faith.

I have prayed earnestly, and large numbers of you have been healed through the ministration of the Gifts of Healings and the Prayer of Faith.

Greater than all the Healings, and the Workings of Miracles, the Principal thing is Wisdom.

Do not crave prophetic power.

Do not crave the Workings of Miracles or the Gifts of Healings; do not crave Discernings of Spirits, and Tongues, and Interpretation of Tongues.

You will not get them if you do crave.

God is too wise to fling out His Gifts in a disorderly manner.

All these Gifts are put in their exact order.

They are given in that order.

That is one reason why some of you who have been crying for Gifts of Healings and Faith do not get them.

You cannot get them until you get the Word of Wisdom; until it dwells in you richly.

I am here to endeavor to get some Wisdom into you.

I thank God that I have been successful, to some extent.

Still, there are some of you who have been very slow.

When the floods come, it is a good thing to get in out of the rain, out of the flood, out of the tempest.

Pray God that the Word of Wisdom, the Word of Knowledge, Faith, and all these Gifts, shall be more and more manifested in Zion. [Amen.]

I would that all the Lord's people were prophets; but I know that they are not.

A prophet is very close to an apostle; it is the next office.

A prophet must certainly be a teacher, because the greater includes the less, and a prophet must have certain Gifts.

"My brethren, be not many teachers, knowing that ye shall receive the greater condemnation."

Can you not take the Teaching from authoritative lips, and no longer hesitate?

God has given me the Word of Wisdom, that I might give it to you.

God has given me the Word of Knowledge, and I am here to give it to you.

He has given me Faith—and you all say that He has—then I am here to impart it to you.

If He has given me Gifts of Healings, and Prophecy, and other Gifts, I am here to give them to you.

But, are all Apostles?

People—"No."

General Overseer—Are all prophets?

People—"No."

General Overseer—Are all teachers?

People—"No."

General Overseer—Have all Gifts of Healings?

People—"No."

General Overseer—Have all the Word of Wisdom?

People—"No."

General Overseer—Have all the Word of Knowledge?

People—"No."

General Overseer—Have all Faith?

People—"No."

General Overseer—God has put these Gifts in the Church, and He has put them in the Divine order.

None in Zion Have the Gifts in All Their Fulness.

I do not suppose, for a moment, that this Church has one in it who possesses them in all their fulness.

I certainly do not.

I know something of all of them, but of some of them I know very little.

I know but little about Tongues or Interpretation of Tongues, but I know a little.

I know but little of Discernings of Spirits, but I know a little.

Many of you know nothing about these things, and how can you be expected to know?

I would like to see God's people filled with the Spirit of Wisdom, of Knowledge, and of Faith.

When you get these first three Gifts, then, if you bring forth the Fruits of the Spirit, God will give you more.

My brothers, my sisters, let us be wise in these things.

There were long years in which I knew very little about preaching the Word of Wisdom.

I preached as well as I knew; but Wisdom comes gradually.

Wisdom Comes by Following Wisdom's Way.

Knowledge comes, and grows more and more, by doing as God says.

Faith comes as a Specific Gift only to the spirit, soul, and body that is purified; for God does not allow the Water of Life to flow through a dirty vessel.

Unless we are clean—clean in spirit, soul, and body—God can never use us in Gifts of Healings.

Therefore, I say to you who bear the vessels of the Lord, be clean, be clean!

O God, make us clean! [Amen.]

Let us ask for the first of all the Gifts—the Word of Wisdom, and be patient.

A Library on the Gifts of the Spirit.

I will tell you where to get a library on this subject.

There are Fourteen Volumes of LEAVES OF HEALING printed; thirteen are bound.

Why do you not buy?

If you cannot buy the whole fourteen, buy one volume at a time, and put them on your shelves and read them.

It is not that I wrote them; it is not that our people gave their testimonies in them; but these Fourteen Volumes are the story of how God has been restoring, in these Last Days, the Gifts of the Holy Spirit. [Amen.]

Read these volumes through, during the long winter nights.

Read ten pages a day, and twenty pages a night, and you will read two hundred pages a week, and in four weeks you will read a volume.

Zion ought to read the story of how God has been restoring His Gifts to the Church.

You will never understand Zion, some of you who have come in only lately, until you go back to the Little Wooden Hut; until you go back to the story that precedes it, too.

Keep your volumes.

Do not lend them.

Tell people that they can come to your house and read them; but do not give them away.

You would not give up your Bible, would you?

You would say, "Come here and I will read to you, or I will buy you one; but I will not give up my Bible; it is very precious to me."

Make your LEAVES like your Bible.

I make it a rule not to lend books.

I find that most people who borrow books are very good bookkeepers, and many of them are very careless with them.

There is only one way to get the Word of Wisdom—that is to have it from the Bible, and from some authoritative interpretation.

Surely, God has been interpreting the Bible.

Has He not been interpreting it in my life and work, and in the lives of our many godly Overseers and Elders?

People—"Yes."

General Overseer—Has He not been interpreting it in your lives?

People—"Yes."

General Overseer—Get the record, and you will be able to answer the adversary.

When a man says to you, "I would like to know what Dr. Dowie teaches upon such a point," these volumes being indexed, you can find what I say and then say to him, "Come to my house, and I will read it to you."

He may come and bring his wife with him.

Then he may buy for himself.

May God bless you!

Let us consecrate ourselves to God.

PRAYER OF CONSECRATION.

Our God and Father, for Jesus' sake, make us wise; give us thy Word of Wisdom, Thy Word of Knowledge; give us the indwelling consciousness of the Indwelling Christ, who is made unto us Wisdom, Righteousness, Knowledge; who is the Author of our Faith, and of Love, and Hope; and who will lead us by the Spirit into the Way of All Truth. Oh, give us humble hearts, unwilling to go unless Divinely directed. For Jesus' sake, Amen. [*All repeat the prayer, clause by clause, after the General Overseer.*]

After the singing of the Consecration Hymn, the General Overseer closed the meeting with the

BENEDICTION.

Beloved, abstain from every form of evil. And may the very God of Peace Himself sanctify you wholly; and I pray God your whole spirit, and soul, and body be preserved entire, without blame, unto the coming of our Lord Jesus, the Christ. Faithful is He that calleth you, who also will do it. The grace of our Lord Jesus, the Christ, the love of God our Father, the fellowship of the Holy Spirit, our Comforter and Guide, one Eternal God, abide in you, bless you, and keep you, and all the Israel of God everywhere, forever. Amen.

BAPTISMAL SERVICE.

REPORTED BY S. E. C., O. V. G., AND A. W. N.

Obedience to God in all things, and especially to His command "Repent ye, and be baptized," was the theme of the General Overseer's address in the meeting held in Shiloh Tabernacle Lord's Day morning, July 24, 1904, at 9:30 o'clock.

An audience of about three thousand people had gathered and listened most attentively while the man of God expounded the Divine Word relating to this Christian Ordinance.

At the close of his brief but effective Message, the General Overseer called upon all who had obeyed God in Baptism by Triune Immersion to stand.

Nearly the entire audience rose.

But there were some who remained seated, among them something over a hundred candidates for Baptism, who had gathered in the front seats of the central section of the ground floor of the Tabernacle.

The General Overseer then very emphatically commanded all those who remained seated in other parts of the house to come forward and take their places with the candidates for Baptism.

Several obeyed, but there were others who did not.

To these God's Messenger gave the choice of either coming forward at once or leaving the building.

He declared that he would not have any present who were not in full sympathy with the Ordinance.

This declaration he carried out by the aid of officers of the Christian Catholic Church in Zion and members of Zion Guard.

As a result, many more joined the candidates for Baptism, and a number of the disobedient left the building.

It was with one hundred sixty-five earnest candidates before him that he delivered the Charge impressively and heart-searchingly.

When the candidates had taken their Vows, all those present were asked to rise and renew their Baptismal Vows, which they did with sincerity and joy.

The people experienced a rich spiritual blessing, and felt that the General Overseer had been right in narrowing down the attendance at this service to those only who had obeyed God in Baptism, or were ready to go forward in that obedience immediately.

The General Overseer, assisted by Overseers Piper, Mason, Excell, and Brasefield, then proceeded with the baptism of the one hundred sixty-five candidates. This, with the one hundred fifty-four baptized on the previous Lord's Day, made a total of three hundred nineteen baptized during Zion's Fourth Feast of Tabernacles.

Shiloh Tabernacle, Zion City, Illinois, Lord's Day Forenoon, July 24, 1904.

The meeting was opened by the singing of Hymn No. 42, in the Special Program.

The General Overseer then said:

I shall read a very short passage, and preach a very short sermon, and make a very short declaration, and get right to the Baptism.

Let us read in the Gospel according to St. Matthew, the 28th chapter, the 18th, 19th, and 20th verses.

Authority and Power Distinguished.

And Jesus came to them and spake unto them saying, All Authority--

Not merely power, as the Old Version has it, but as this Revision has it.

"Authority," which is more than power.

Sometimes power is in the hands of evil persons who, for a time, override law, and have the power of life and death

Power is not itself a sign of goodness, or righteousness, or justice.

Power may be in the hands of oppressors, and it is very largely in the hands of the wicked.

Power is only good when it is lawfully used; but Authority, even if you have no power for the time being, is in itself the Greatest Power.

To have a Divine Commission, even if one has not an atom of power, is to have Divine Authority.

That is all I had when I entered upon this work.

When Jesus said "All Authority," He meant not only power but Rightful Power.

He had Authority.

"All Authority."

Not Some, but All.

All Authority hath been given unto Me in heaven and on earth.

The Christ's Authority Was Derived From the Father.

It was not His own; it was given; and it was given to Him, the Eternal Son, by the Father; God, the Father, gave it.

He is the only Supreme Authority.

No matter what government you live under, that government is under Him; and if it does not acknowledge Him, so much the worse for that government.

The people among whom you dwell are under Him, and if they do not acknowledge Him so much the worse for that people, because All Authority hath been given unto Him in heaven and on earth.

Go ye therefore, and make disciples of all the nations.

"Make disciples of all the nations—make them to learn of Me."

Make them!

It is not a question as to whether they want you or not, usually they do not, but go and make them by the Imperative Power of the Divine Message and the Divine Love accompanying it.

Go ye therefore, and make disciples of all the nations.

A True Baptism the Seal of Discipleship.

What is to be the Seal of Discipleship?

Baptizing them the moment they become Disciples.

Command them to be baptized!

"Baptizing them into the Name of"—whom?

Audience—"The Father."

General Overseer—And of—

Audience—"The Son."

General Overseer—And of—

Audience—"The Holy Spirit."

General Overseer—Did He speak that about babies?

Audience—"No."

General Overseer—About those that were made—what?

Audience—"Disciples."

General Overseer—Disciples. I now call your attention to the text.

I will say a few words about it presently.

I want you to understand as we go.

Make disciples of all the Nations, baptizing them into the Name of the Father, and of the Son, and of the Holy Spirit.

Triune Baptism Illustrated.

If I gave Overseer Excell a handkerchief, and put three vats of dye here, and said, "Now, dip that into the black, into the yellow, and into the blue"—[Overseer Excell illustrates]—how many times would he dip it?

Audience—"Three times."

General Overseer—If I am to Baptize you into the Name of the Father, and of the Son, and of the Holy Spirit, how many times am I to dip you?

Audience—"Three times."

General Overseer—Is it once?

Audience—"No."

General Overseer—No honest scholar would for a moment deny that Triune dipping was the method of Baptism practiced in the Early Church.

That fact is settled.

Nor would he deny that the Early Church, with a single exception—and that in the Fourth Century—in unbroken continuity, baptized by Triune Immersion.

That is historically true.

It is not a new view.

It is the other fellows that are doing something new.

We are going right back to Primitive Baptism.

"Baptizing them," Jesus said, "into the Name of the Father, and of the Son, and of the Holy Spirit, teaching them to observe"—how many things?

Audience—"All things."

General Overseer—"All things."

Surely this Baptism is one of the things.

The Christ Himself, after He had risen from the dead and before He ascended into heaven, made it a part of His Commission.

Teaching them to observe all things whatsoever I have commanded you: and lo, I am with you All the Days, even unto the Consummation of the Age.

The World Never Has Been, and Never Will Be, Destroyed.

It is not, "Alway, even unto the end of the world," because the world will never end.

You say, "The world was destroyed by the flood."

No such thing, if you mean by the word "destroyed" that the world was blotted out of existence.

It was simply turned over, and the dry land became the sea, and the sea became the dry land.

That was the destruction of the world by the flood, and when the world is destroyed by fire—and it will be—there will be no other destruction than this—that everything will be melted, and you will not be able to find your corner lot.

You will not be able to distinguish your gold from that of others.

Everything will be melted, the world will be changed, and it will come out a new and beautiful world.

Certain parts of the world have been devastated by fire.

The lava has burst out and the mountain has become a plain, literally.

A lake has sometimes emptied into a cavern of molten lava, and the great mountain, full of fire, has burst and scattered its contents over the country.

Lava Fields Exceedingly Fruitful.

The change is so great, that we speak of the country as having been destroyed, but some of the most fertile soil in the world is found where volcanoes have poured out lava.

The lava beds that are found on the slopes of Vesuvius are most fruitful.

Look at the fruitfulness of Southern France and Italy, where there is lava soil, and where they grow the sweetest roses, as in Cannes and Nice.

It is fertile everywhere.

They scrape a little soil on the rocks, and then grow roses—literally hundreds of square miles of roses, from which the fragrant essences are taken.

When this world is burned up, and reconstructed, I think the soil will be most fruitful.

There will be a New Heaven and a New Earth, wherein dwelleth Righteousness.

New Heavens and New Earth Will Follow Consummation of the Age.

When the Age has reached its Consummation, and the world has been destroyed, as we call it, by fire, the New Heavens and the New Earth will come out just as they came out of the flood.

Meanwhile, if we are to enter the New Heaven, the Heavenly City, if we are to stand upon the New Earth, wherein dwelleth Righteousness, we must do right, now.

We must obey God, now

Is not that clear?

Audience—"Yes."

General Overseer—Can you expect to dwell with the righteous by and by if you will not do right, now?

Audience—"No."

General Overseer—You have to be baptized if you are a Christian; and if you are not a Christian you will have to go out, presently, for this place is to be occupied by Christians only in a little while.

Overseer Brasefield then offered prayer, at the close of which the General Overseer led the Congregation in chanting the Disciples' Prayer.

Hymn No. 46, in the Program, was sung, and the General Overseer delivered his Message.

TRIUNE IMMERSION: GOD'S SEAL ON A LIVING CHURCH.

INVOCATION.

Let the words of my mouth and the meditation of my heart be acceptable in Thy sight, be profitable unto this people, and unto all to whom these words shall come, in this and every land, in this and all the coming time, Till Jesus Come. Amen.

The General Overseer then said:

I will read to you two passages, one in the Epistle of Paul to the Ephesians, the 1st chapter, and the 13th verse:

In whom ye also, having heard the Word of the Truth, the Gospel of your Salvation,—in whom, having also believed, ye were sealed with the Holy Spirit of Promise.

Triune Immersion the Seal of the Living God.

What was the Seal?

Audience—"The Seal of the Holy Spirit of Promise."

General Overseer—In the 4th chapter, the 30th verse:

And grieve not the Holy Spirit of God, in whom ye were Sealed unto the Day of Redemption.

The 7th chapter of the Book of the Revelation, the 2d verse:

And I saw another angel ascend from the sunrising, having the Seal of the Living God.

I could speak for hours on this large subject, but it is not necessary.

We have carefully prepared Literature that you may read.

We have a carefully prepared synopsis, from a scholarly point of view, which I directed Elder Kennedy to make.

He was a Presbyterian minister before coming into Zion.

After being baptized, there crept into his mind doubts as to whether Triune Immersion was, after all, the mode of Baptism which God required.

He came to me and said, "I want to be more firmly established."

Triune Immersion Established by Historica Evidence.

Well, I said, I will give you leave of absence.

Go to the great libraries and search for everything bearing on the question of Baptism.

If, with the solitary exception of the heretical bishop, Eunomius, in the fourth century, who was a bad man, and denied the Divinity of the Holy Spirit and of the Christ, the Son of God, and who was baptized by one immersion, simply because he rejected the triunity of God, and was expelled from the Church both for that and for bad living you can find a single occasion in the Early Church on which Baptism was by any other mode than Triune Immersion, I will renounce Triune Immersion as the only right mode of Baptism.

I would not give it up on account of the Church's failing, but I am so sure that you cannot find it, that I will agree to give it up.

He searched everywhere, and has compiled the result.

If you want the historical facts, you will find them in Elder Kennedy's pamphlet, entitled: "The Ordinance of Christian Baptism," which can be obtained from Zion Printing and Publishing House.

Now I shall show you what the command of God is, and then direct you to obey it.

The Disobedience of the Disobedient Emphasized.

Every one that does not obey it will have to leave this Tabernacle and this park, and go home, saying to themselves, "I have been driven out because I would not obey."

I will have no unbelievers left here. I intend to have Baptisms where only believers will be present.

At the Lord's Table I want only those who partake.

I send out all the worldlings.

I have decided that when I baptize I will send out all the disobedient.

Go! Reflect upon your disobedience.

The Question of Obedience Not Debatable.

The command is that when a man, or woman, or child of sufficient age to understand, becomes a disciple, they shall be baptized.

It is not debatable.

When an order is given on a battlefield, it is treason to disobey.

Baptism is not for unbelievers; it is for believers.

It is not for babies.

The Master said that we were first to make disciples, then baptize.

You cannot make a disciple of a baby.

A baby can be a disciple of its mother only.

As for baptizing a baby, and getting some man and woman who are half drunk to say that they renounce the World, the Flesh, and the Devil for the baby, or that they will be its sponsors, it is wickedness.

It is not Baptism at all, for Jesus taught, and the Apostle Peter taught, that you must Repent and be Baptized.

A baby does not want to repent.

It does not know anything about repentance.

The only ground of repentance that many babies have is that they have such foolish fathers and mothers.

If they could only repent of that it would be a good thing, but they cannot.

Infant Baptism a Shameful Farce.

Many babies have water sprinkled upon them and then are told that they are children of God.

That is one of the meanest and most shameful of lies.

It causes more infidelity in Europe than anything that I know.

Men say, "A priest said that I had a change of heart when I was sprinkled with water.

"In the first place, the ruffian himself did not have a change of heart.

"In the second place, I did not have a change of heart.

"In the third place, my godfather and godmother lied—they had no change of heart, and they never fulfilled their vows."

Christianity has been trodden under foot and in the mire by the shameful lie of baby baptism.

There is no such thing in that Bible.

Show me where in the Bible it says that one baby was baptized, and I will recall all the babies I have consecrated and have them baptized.

You cannot find one instance.

The Command of the Christ Is to Baptize Believers, Only.

If you have repented of all your sins, if you believe in our Lord Jesus, the Christ, if you have the witness within you that you love and serve Him, then you are a Christian; and to you only I utter the command to be baptized.

Be baptized, and be baptized now.

Peter was in the house of Cornelius, who knew nothing about the Christ.

He knew nothing about the Holy Spirit, but while Peter spoke in the house of that captain of the Italian band, the Holy Spirit fell on them that heard the Word.

Then Peter said, "Can any man forbid the water, that these should not be baptized, which have received the Holy Spirit as well as we?"

You who say, "I have been blessed by the Holy Spirit and I do not need to be baptized," do you not see that Peter, speaking by the Holy Spirit, had a different opinion?

The Reception of the Holy Spirit Does not Take the Place of Baptism.

Baptism does not make you a Christian.

You are to be baptized because you are a Christian.

When you have received the Spirit of God, you will obey, for the Spirit of God is a Spirit of Obedience to God, and if you are not willing to obey God, go back to Gadara and your pigs.

You are not obedient to God, and you are no Christian.

If you were a Christian, you would obey.

Obedience must be immediate, even if you do not understand.

Peter did not say, "Think about it for a week or two."

The Book says, in the 10th chapter of the Acts of the Apostles—you had better read the words, that you may be sure what it does say—the 47th and 48th verses.

Overseer Piper, read it.

Overseer Piper—[reading] "Can any man forbid the water, that these should not be baptized, which have received the Holy Spirit as well as we?"

General Overseer—Nobody said "No." What did Peter say next?

Overseer Piper—"And he commanded them to be baptized in the Name of Jesus, the Christ."

General Overseer—Did he persuade them?

People—"No."

General Overseer—Did he reason with them?

People—"No."

General Overseer—What did he do?

He commanded them to be baptized.

What must I do?

Must I spend an hour or two with you rebels to persuade you?

What is my duty?

People—"To command."

General Overseer—What is your duty?

People—"To obey."

The General Overseer Exercises Authority.

General Overseer—Every one who has already obeyed the Command of God, and has been baptized by Triune Immersion, stand. [Numbers rose.]

General Overseer—Look around and find any who are sitting.

If you are a Christian, come and be baptized, instantly.

You must come, or go out.

All who have been baptized, sit down.

All Christians who have not been baptized by Triune Immersion, stand! [Several rose in various parts of the Tabernacle.]

In the Name of the Most High God, in the Name of Jesus, the Christ, His Son, in the Power of the Holy Spirit, I command you to come and be baptized!

You will not?

Then get out!

After some time had been spent by the General Overseer in warning the people of the consequences of disobedience, and in lovingly, but firmly and solemnly, commanding those who were Christians, but had not obeyed God in Baptism by Triune Immersion, to obey God or leave the building, the Tabernacle was cleared of all except those who had obeyed in Baptism, and those who were candidates for Baptism.

The General Overseer then said:

Beloved friends, I have come to the point where I am determined that Baptism shall not be a peep-show for unbelieving, godless people, and disobedient and almost godless so-called Christians.

I am determined to have this Sacred Ordinance witnessed only by people who are sympathetic, and who can pray for the candidates, for I am persuaded that great blessing is lost in these ordinances by the presence of unbelieving spectators.

My heart has been nearly broken by the great crowd of godless people that have crowded around the baptistry, whose presence was prompted only by the meanest kind of curiosity.

They have gloated over poor candidates who happened to choke with a little water, and the power of the Ordinance has been largely lost to many dear Christians.

My action this morning has been prompted by no mere desire to have my own way.

Baptisms in the Early Church Conducted Privately.

I realize more than ever the solemnity of this Ordinance.

I think that Baptisms in the Early Church were private.

I think these three thousand mentioned in the Acts of the Apostles were baptized privately—possibly in the public baths in Jerusalem in the presence of fellow Christians.

There were many hundreds of baths in the houses of the rich

people, and thirty people baptized in each one of a hundred would make the three thousand.

Let us have the Ordinance where God, the Holy Spirit, will be present in Power; where our Lord will be present in Spirit, and look with approval; and where our Father will say, "These are my beloved sons and daughters, in whom I am well pleased." May God grant it.

I long to see Baptisms witnessed by thousands of those who have been baptized and who can pray for those that are being baptized.

I long to get rid, forever, of the simply curious crowd at these baptisms that have been annoying and vexing my soul for years.

I am sorry to speak thus, but I know no other way of getting what is right.

Charge to Candidates for Baptism.

Beloved candidates, will you please stand?

In the 2d chapter of the Acts of the Apostles and the 42d verse, we read,

And they continued steadfastly in the Apostles' teaching and fellowship, in the breaking of bread and the prayers.

Candidates Act Freely, Gladly, and From Conviction.

I believe that you have received my word and this teaching gladly, and are presenting yourselves for Baptism from deep conviction. Can you say "Yes?"

Candidates—"Yes."

General Overseer—It is not because of being pressed, is it? Is it because you want to obey God?

Candidates—"Yes."

General Overseer—I wish to say to you that this first three thousand, baptized on the Day of Pentecost, were examples of what I pray you to be.

Having gladly received the Word, and having gladly obeyed in Baptism, they continued steadfastly.

My beloved brothers and sisters, young and old, Steadfastness is the glorious privilege of Zion—rooted, grounded, established, firm.

I pray God to make you steadfast.

Let nothing shake you; let no man take your crown; be faithful; be steadfast; be unmovable; always abounding in the work of the Lord, and you will be a blessing to the Church.

Tearing up one's religious life by the roots, every now and then, is not conducive to growth in spiritual life.

Do not be childish.

A Conscientiousness That is Foolish.

Some Christians are so conscientiously foolish, that they sometimes examine themselves by tearing themselves up, and looking at the roots.

You can do that once too often.

You can injure yourself very seriously, so that you will not grow; you will die.

It is not conscientiousness; it is folly.

Do not forget that steadfastness, continuous growth in grace, depends upon your keeping strictly, solidly, in one place.

God has put you in the Christian Catholic Church in Zion; grow there.

When you have to go away from Zion City, you are not transplanted; you are still in Zion; grow there, but do not tear yourself up.

Continue steadfastly in these things.

First, in the Apostles' Doctrine.

Beloved, I beseech you—I, who realize the Apostolic Commission—that you continue steadfastly in the doctrine that you have received.

Let no man shake you.

You have received it from God, from His Word, from these first Apostles, and now you receive it from me.

Hold fast to the Teaching.

God has blessed it.

Do not allow any man to shake you from it.

When you cannot explain it say, "Well, I have good reasons for holding on to it."

The man who wants to shake you in it is surely your enemy.

All Zion Should Keep in Touch With Headquarters.

Keep in Fellowship, wherever you may live.

Keep in touch with Zion.

If sometimes you feel downhearted or troubled send in a request for prayer, not only when you are sick, but when you are weary, and when your heart is oppressed, and when you are alone.

Write and say, "General Overseer, pray for me. I want quickening," and we will pray for you.

Keep in Fellowship by works—by keeping in touch with Zion Printing and Publishing House, with the Recorder of Zion Restoration Host, with the General Recorder, and with the Storehouse by constantly sending your Tithes.

Keep in touch with us when you go out to Work for God in some of the great Visitations, when you will be called upon to coöperate.

Keep in touch and in Fellowship by keeping in Fellowship with God.

Our Fellowship is with the Father, and with His Son.

Keep in Fellowship with God, the Father, and the Son, and the Holy Spirit, and then you will always be in Fellowship with us.

They continued steadfastly in the Apostles' teaching and Fellowship, in the breaking of bread.

Sometimes I am asked if it is right to commune with other Christians.

Yes, you can go to the Lord's Table anywhere, but you must not forget that you cannot partake of the evil deeds of those that are there.

Christians Should Not Sit at the Lord's Table Where the Ordinance is Administered by Ungodly Ministers.

I would say to you, that if you know that the man that administers that Ordinance is an ungodly man, you should not go.

If the man is godly, I know of nothing in the Word of God which forbids your communing with him.

Do not wait until every member of his Church is a saint.

If you wait until every member of this Church is a perfect saint, ready for the highest place in heaven, you will never commune with us.

There are many that are weak in the faith.

Be kind, and constantly commune with God.

You are not responsible for their weakness unless you are the cause of it; then you have to get forgiveness.

Keep in the Breaking of the Bread, the Communion of the Lord's Table, if you are far away from this Church; but seek communion especially with those who are in communion with us.

Do not forsake the daily reading of the Bible.

Those that do are always the weakest type of Christians.

They continued steadfastly in the Apostles' Teaching and Fellowship, in the Breaking of Bread and the Prayers.

There is one thing in which you, and I, and the whole Church can keep in close Fellowship.

At nine o'clock every morning and nine o'clock every night the whistle sounds here in Zion City, and all Pray.

Pray one minute at the corresponding time wherever you may be.

You can pray anywhere.

You can keep in touch with us in Prayer.

This Fellowship of Prayer Around-the-World is a Wonderful Blessing.

I thought of that wherever I went; if I forgot, God let me know the Hour of Prayer.

Often when I have been on board ship and seemed to have forgotten it, I had not forgotten; I was praying at the minute, because, in a measure, I am praying all the time.

I have often wondered why the Spirit of Prayer had come especially upon me, and, looking at my watch, I have found that it was nine o'clock in the morning, or evening, at Zion City.

Pray with us at all times, but especially at nine o'clock, morning and evening.

Will you please go over the points with me?

They continued steadfastly in the Apostles' Teaching and Fellowship, in the Breaking of Bread and the Prayers.

These are the four things that the early Christians did.

God grant that you may, my brothers and sisters.

Do you know that by Grace you are saved, through Faith?

Can you say, I do?

Candidates—"I do."

General Overseer—Are you determined to Obey God in All Things? Can you say I am?

Candidates—"I am."

General Overseer—Will you obey those who have the rule over you, in the Christ? Can you say I will?

Candidates—"I will."

General Overseer—All who desire to renew their Baptismal Vows stand and pray with me.

PRAYER OF CONSECRATION.

My God and Father, with these candidates, we renew our Baptismal Vow. We Vow to Thee that by Thy Grace we will follow where Jesus leads; we will do what He bids us do; say what He bids us say; we will be what He bids us be. Keep us faithful; and now, today, let the Blessing of Death to Sin, Life in God, and Power for Service come upon these Candidates, and upon us all in increasing measure. For Jesus' sake. Amen.

This is Glorious!

I realized, while we were praying, that there was no one here to say No to that prayer—that everybody was of one heart and mind.

We will have a Pentecost here some day!

May God grant it!

The Candidates and Officers then prepared for the Baptism.

The General Overseer prayed as follows:

PRAYER BY THE GENERAL OVERSEER.

Father, for Jesus' sake, command Thy Blessing upon these Candidates. Let the Holy Spirit's Power descend. Let all here hope in Jesus, the Christ, and grant that the Spirit's Power may rest upon every one of these to be baptized, and give unto them that Joy which no water can ever give. Grant that they may be Dead to Sin, Alive unto God, and Endowed with Power for His Service. We ask this in the Name and for the Sake of Jesus, the Christ, our Lord. Amen.

The Ordinance of Baptism was then administered by the General Overseer and Overseers, after which the General Overseer said:

I have the joy of telling you, brothers and sisters, that one hundred sixty-five persons have just been baptized.

May God bless them!

A few days ago one hundred fifty-three were baptized, making three hundred eighteen during the Feast of Tabernacles.

It is so pleasant to feel that I have not a single unsympathetic listener or observer.

BENEDICTION.

Beloved, abstain from every form of evil. And may the very God of Peace Himself sanctify you wholly; and I pray God your whole spirit, and soul, and body be preserved entire, without blame, unto the coming of our Lord Jesus, the Christ. Faithful is He that calleth you, who also will do it. The grace of our Lord Jesus, the Christ, the love of God our Father, the fellowship of the Holy Spirit, our Comforter and Guide, one Eternal God, abide in you, bless you, and keep you, and all the Israel of God everywhere, forever. Amen.

Notice to Officers and Members.

Send all newspaper clippings concerning the General Overseer, the Elders, or any department of the work in connection with the Christian Catholic Church in Zion, to Deacon Carl F. Stern, Zion City, Illinois. Send as soon as possible after publication, and carefully mark *name and date of the paper clipped from* on each article. If this is not done, the clippings are absolutely useless.

Zion in Missouri.

Deacon Charles E. Robinson, Deacon-in-charge of the Branch of the Christian Catholic Church in Zion at Kansas City, will conduct services in the following cities in Missouri on the dates given:

Independence, August 20th; Pleasant Hill, August 21st; Warrensburg, August 22d and 23d; Knobnoster, August 24th and 25th; Sedalia, August 26th; Higginsville, August 27th and 28th; Lexington, August 29th and 30th; Orrick, August 31st; Liberty, September 1st.

All members and friends desiring baptism will please communicate with Deacon Robinson at once.

Let all having friends in these cities or in their vicinities notify them of the proposed meetings, and send their names and addresses to Deacon Charles E. Robinson, 2112 North Fourth street, Kansas City, Kansas.

DO YOU KNOW GOD'S WAY OF HEALING?

BY THE REV. JOHN ALEX. DOWIE.

Let it be supposed that the following words are a conversation between the reader [A] and the writer [B].

A. What does this question mean? Do you really suppose that God has some one especial way of healing in these days, of which men may know and avail themselves?

B. That is exactly my meaning, and I wish very much that you should know God's Way of Healing, as I have known it for many years.

A. What is the way, in your opinion?

B. You should rather ask, WHO is God's Way? for the way is a Person, not a thing. I will answer your question in His own words, "I am the Way, and the Truth, and the Life: no one cometh unto the Father, but by Me." These words were spoken by our Lord Jesus, the Christ, the Eternal Son of God, who is both our Savior and our Healer. (John 14:6.)

A. But I always thought that these words only referred to Him as the Way of Salvation. How can you be sure that they refer to Him as the Way of Healing also?

B. Because He cannot change. He is "the same yesterday and today, yea, and forever." (Hebrews 13:8.) He said that He came to this earth not only to save us but to heal us. (Luke 4:18), and He did this when in the flesh on earth. Being unchanged He must be able and willing and desirous to heal now.

A. But is there not this difference, namely, that He is not with us now?

B. No; for He said "Lo, I am with you All the Days, even unto the Consummation of the Age;" and so He is with us now, in spirit, just as much as when He was here in the flesh.

A. But did He not work these miracles of healing when on earth merely to prove that He was the Son of God?

B. No; there was still a greater purpose than that. He healed the sick who trusted in Him in order to show us that He came to die not only for our sins, but for our sicknesses and to deliver us from both.

A. Then, if that be so, the atonement which He made on the Cross must have been for our sicknesses as well as our sins. Can you prove that is the fact from the Scriptures?

B. Yes, I can, and the passages are very numerous. I need quote only two. In Isaiah 53:4, 5, it is written of Him: "Surely He hath borne our griefs (Hebrew, *sicknesses*), and carried our sorrows: . . . and with His stripes we are healed." Then, in the Gospel according to Matthew, this passage is quoted and directly applied to the work of bodily healing, in the 8th chapter 17th verse: "That it might be fulfilled which was spoken by Isaiah the prophet, saying, Himself took our infirmities, and bare our diseases."

A. But do you not think that sickness is often God's will, and sent for our good and therefore God may not wish us to be healed?

B. No, that cannot possibly be; for diseases of every kind are the Devil's work and his work can never be God's will, since the Christ came for the very purpose of destroying "the works of the Devil." (1 John 3:8.)

A. Do you mean to say that all disease is the work of Satan?

B. Yes, for if there had been no sin (which came through Satan) there never would have been any disease, and Jesus never in one single instance told any person that sickness was God's work or will, but the very contrary.

A. Can you prove from Scriptures that all forms of sickness and infirmity are the Devil's work?

B. Yes, that can be done very easily. You will see in Matthew 4:23 and 9:35 that when Jesus was here in the flesh He healed "all manner of disease and all manner of sickness among the people." Then if you will refer to Acts 10:38 you will see that the Apostle Peter declares that He (Jesus) "went about doing good, and healing all that were oppressed of the Devil." Notice that all whom He healed, not some, were suffering from Satan's evil power.

A. But does disease never come from God?

B. No, it cannot come from God, for He is pure, and disease is unclean; and it cannot come out of Heaven, for there is no disease there.

A. That is very different from the teachings which I have received all my life from ministers and in the churches. Do you really think that you are right, and that they are all wrong in this matter?

B. It is not a question as between myself and them. The only question is, What does God's Word say? God has said in all the ages, to His Church, "I am Jehovah that healeth thee" (Exodus 15:26), and therefore it would be wicked to say that He is the defiler of His people. All true Christians must believe the Bible, and it is impossible to believe that good and evil, sickness and health, sin and holiness could have a common origin in God. If the Bible really taught that, it would be impossible to believe our Lord Jesus, the Christ, when He says: "A good tree cannot bring forth evil fruit, neither can a corrupt tree bring forth good fruit." (Matthew 7:18.)

A. But even if I agree with all you say, is it not true that the Gifts of Healing were removed from the Church, and are not in it now?

B. No, the "Gifts of Healing" were never withdrawn, and can never be withdrawn, from the true Church of God, for it is written: "The gifts and the calling of God are without repentance." (Romans 11:29.) There are nine gifts of God to the Church (enumerated in 1 Corinthians 12:8-11), and all these are in the Holy Spirit. Therefore, so long as the Holy Spirit is in the Church, all the gifts must be there also. If they are not exercised, that does not prove that they do not exist, but that the faith to exercise them is lacking in God's servants. The gifts are all perfectly preserved; for the Holy Spirit, not the Church, keeps them safely.

A. What should a Christian then do when overtaken with sickness?

B. A Christian should obey God's command, and at once turn to Him for forgiveness of the sin which may have caused the sickness, and for immediate healing. Healing is obtained from God in one of four ways, namely: First, by the direct prayer of faith, without any aid from the officers of the Church, praying as the Centurion did in Matthew 8:5-13; second, by two faithful disciples praying in perfect agreement in accordance with the Lord's promise in Matthew 18:19; third, by the anointing of the Elders and the prayer of faith, according to the instructions in James 5:14 and 15; and fourth, by the laying on of the hands of them who believe, and whom God calls to that ministry, as the Lord commands in Mark 16:18, and in other places.

A. But are people healed in this way in these days?

B. Yes, in thousands of cases. I have myself laid hands upon many hundreds of thousands of persons, and I have seen the Lord's power manifested in the healing of great numbers, many of whom are living witnesses in many countries, who have testified publicly before thousands, and who are prepared to testify at any time. This ministry is being exercised by devoted Christians in many parts of America, Europe, Australasia, and elsewhere.

A. Is it not the same as Christian Science, Mind Healing, etc.?

B. No. Divine Healing is diametrically opposed to these diabolical counterfeits which are utterly antichristian. These impostures are only seductive forms of Spiritualism. Trance Evangelism is also a more recent form of this delusion, and it deceives many.

A. But how shall I obtain the necessary faith to receive healing, which faith I am at present conscious that I do not possess?

B. It is written "Belief cometh of hearing, and hearing by the word of the Christ." (Romans 10:17.) Our Missions are held for the express purpose of teaching fully the Word of God on this matter, and I very heartily invite you to attend the meetings which are announced for Zion Tabernacles in Chicago and other cities, and for Shiloh Tabernacle, Zion City, Illinois. All are welcome and there are no charges of any kind made, for all God's gifts are free gifts. Salvation is the first of these, without which you cannot be healed through faith in Jesus. All the costs of this work are covered by the free-will offerings of the people who attend these meetings, and others whom the Lord leads to help; but the poorest, who have nothing to give, are as heartily welcome as the richest.

A. Do you see the sick and lay hands upon them in this Mission?

B. Yes, after we feel satisfied that they are fully resting in the Lord alone for the healing, we see privately, so far as time permits, those who attend, but under no circumstances do we claim the power to heal any; for "power belongeth unto God."

A. Have you any writings upon this subject which can be purchased?

B. Yes; these can be obtained at the office of Zion Printing and Publishing House, Zion City, Illinois, and at any Zion Tabernacle. But the best book on Divine Healing is the Bible itself, studied prayerfully and earnestly.

We extend to you a hearty invitation to attend the meetings, which are free to all. Our prayer is that you may be led to find in Jesus, the Christ, our Lord and God your present Savior from sin, your Healer from sickness, your Cleanser from all evil, your Keeper in the way to Heaven, your Friend, and your All for Time and Eternity. We pray that these words may help many who read, and that our little conversation may bear fruit in leading many readers to look to Jesus only.

"The Healing of Christ's seamless dress
Is by all beds of pain;
We touch Him in life's throng and press
And we are whole again."

Notes of Thanksgiving from the Whole World

By Overseer J. G. Excell, General Ecclesiastical Secretary.

JESUS ANSWERED and said unto her, Every one that drinketh of this water shall thirst again:
But whosoever drinketh of the Water that I shall give him shall never thirst; but the Water that I shall give him shall become in him a Well of Water springing up unto Eternal Life.—*John 4:13, 14.*

UPON every side we see the restless search for life, health, and satisfaction.

Men are on fire.

There is a burning within them—the insatiable fire of their calorific passions.

Thousands and millions of men and women are rushing down the Broad Way to Destruction, their tongues parched with the passing of vile calumnies and unholy words; their bodies and souls scorching, burning Saharas, crying out for water.

Frantically they drink deep drafts from the fountains of learning, art, philosophy, ambition, glory; from the troughs of base amusements and licentious revelry; or, for their physical woes, at the bowl of diabolical sorcery, to which they go anon to draw; or else to some salt well of vanity in a Ponce de Leon quest for a fountain of happiness and youth, until they take a draft from that which may prove in a moment what they will all mean in time—the cup of hemlock to their hopes, their happiness, and their life!

It may be that in going from font to font, there will be found pleasing and beautifully carved fountains; bearing in bold relief, a name—"church"—which will cause many to sup of the anodyne solution which perchance will quiet conscience for a time; but the craving, continuous thirst cannot thus be quenched.

Satisfaction is not found in the "mountains" of learning and philosophy, nor in inordinate indulgence, nor in the "Jerusalems" of false creeds; but in the Christ of God.

In Him are the Springs of perennial hope, happiness and health. He is the Way, the Truth, and the Life. In Him there is plenteous redemption for spirit, soul, and body.

With a Divinely-powerful and beautiful melody, Zion sings to a restless and thirsty world the words of hope from the Author of Life, Christ our Lord:

Blessed words, in sweet refrain,
Drink and never thirst again,
Water from the Fount of Love,
From the crystal streams above.

Gushing streams that never cease,
Bringing ecstasy and peace,
Through the vale of tears and woe,
Healing streams that ever flow.

Let the sick and weary and heavy-laden come, and, as the woman of Samaria came, and as these have come whose testimonies appear in this paper, ask of Him, "Lord, give me this Water," and the Water of Life will spring up in them and become in them a Well of Water unto Eternal Life.

O. R.

Praises God for Keeping Power and Zion City.

The Name of Jehovah is a Strong Tower
The Righteous runneth into it, and is safe.—*Proverbs 18:10.*

2818 GABRIEL AVENUE,
ZION CITY, ILLINOIS, June 6, 1904.

DEAR OVERSEER:—I wish to thank God for the way in which I have been kept during the last winter.

I have not been sick in bed one day.

Twice Satan tried to thrust grip upon me, but I looked to God and obtained victory at once, by claiming the promise in Psalm 91:15.

I have also been delivered from severe colds.

It has been my blessed privilege to sit under the teaching of God's Prophet, in Zion City, for three years.

I feel as if I never could thank Him enough for help and deep spiritual blessings I have received during this time.

Praying for God's blessing upon Zion everywhere, I am, Your sister in the Christ,
(MISS) BESSIE FULLER.

Little Daughter Healed of Pneumonia.

Jesus, the Christ, healeth thee.—*Acts 9:34.*

3004 ENOCH AVENUE,
ZION CITY, ILLINOIS, May 31, 1904.

DEAR OVERSEER:—I feel grateful to our dear Father for keeping me until now, that I may write this testimony to His glory.

He miraculously healed our little daughter when life was almost gone, after being ill with pneumonia for six days. The sixth day, you called at noon and prayed for her, and your prayer was answered.

I will praise His Name forever.

Your servant in the Christ,
(MRS.) M. GERTRUDE MEHAFFER.

Healed Through Faith in God.

And all things, whatsoever ye shall ask in prayer, believing, ye shall receive.—*Matthew 21:22.*

CEDAR FALLS, IOWA, May 25 1904.

DEAR BROTHER IN THE CHRIST:—Yours of the 26th at hand.

Thanking you for your prayers, I am rejoiced to tell you that before my letter had time to reach you, I felt the healing power.

I am free from all pain.

My whole trust is in God, who is so faithful to hear and answer our prayers.

Thanking you for your prayers, I am,
Faithfully yours in the Christ,
(MRS.) M. A. COOK.

Little Girl Healed of Pain at Time of Prayer.

Like as a father pitieth his children, so Jehovah pitieth them that fear Him.—*Psalm 103:13.*

CRYSTAL, NORTH DAKOTA, May 23, 1904.

DEAR OVERSEER:—About the last of April, our little girl, three years old, became sick with pains in her bowels.

For ten days she was so ill that she could stand on the floor but for a short time without crying out in pain.

The third day, I sent for you to pray for her.

The morning our letter arrived, she got down off my knee and began to play as if nothing had been the matter with her. She was perfectly healed at the time you prayed for her.

Thanking you for your prayers, and giving God the glory, I remain,
Your sister in the Christ,
(Mrs.) ALEX. ROBERTSON.

Strength Increased, Child Healed.

For the Lord shall be thy confidence.—*Proverbs 3:26.*

ZION CITY, ILLINOIS, June 17, 1904.

DEAR OVERSEER:—I desire to give my testimony to blessings which God has bestowed upon me.

At the time our little boy was born, God wonderfully blessed me. I was sick only a short time, and had a very easy time, for which I praise God. When my little boy was a month old, and once after that, he was very sick, but he was healed in answer to prayer.

My health has been poor for many years, but I thank God I am stronger than I have been for a long time.

I praise God for this teaching, and for His many blessings to us.

Your sister in the Christ, (Mrs.) E. KELLOG.

Instantly Healed of Disease.

Jehovah hath been mindful of us;
He will bless us.—*Psalm 115:12.*

SPANAWAY, TACOMA, WASHINGTON,
April 14, 1904.

DEAR BROTHER IN THE CHRIST:—I feel impressed to write to you, thanking you for the prayer that was offered for my sister, and giving God all the glory for His answer to prayer.

She was wonderfully and instantly healed of her disease, for which she is very thankful to the Lord.

She gave her heart to the Lord, and is a member of Zion, as well as I.

We are expecting to be baptized at the first opportunity.

I thank God for leading me and teaching me to trust Him as my Healer.

I have received many blessings in answer to prayer for my little ones.

I receive so much blessing through reading LEAVES OF HEALING.

I remain your sister in the Christ,
(MRS.) C. C. WATSON

Healed of Rheumatism.

Your Father knoweth what things ye have need of.—*Matthew 6:8*

TE KUITI, AUCKLAND, NEW ZEALAND.

DEAR GENERAL OVERSEER:—I sent a request a few days ago that you would pray that I might be healed of rheumatism.

In the evening I asked God to answer your general nine o'clock prayer for the sick and heal me, as my pain was very severe.

God in mercy and love fulfilled His word: "And it shall come to pass, before they call I will answer." Praise God!

I also thank you for all you and LEAVES OF HEALING have been to me and mine.

Yours Till Jesus Come, I. NICHOLS.

STIRRING TRUTHS FOR WIDE-AWAKE CHRISTIANS

Present Day Themes of REV. JOHN ALEXANDER DOWIE, General Overseer of the Christian Catholic Church in Zion

The following list of Pamphlets, Books, and Tracts, supplied on receipt of price by
ZION PRINTING AND PUBLISHING HOUSE
ZION CITY, LAKE COUNTY, ILLINOIS, U. S. A.

Zion, Her Organization, Truths, and Leader.

	Vol.	No.	Price
Zion's Answer to the Messenger of the Nation	3	8	$0.05
Organization of the Christian Catholic Church	2	2	.10
Principles, Practices and Purposes of the Christian Catholic Church in Zion, and The Everlasting Gospel	4	8	.05
Conquests for Christ in America: Past, Present, and to Come	4	5	.05
By What Authority Doest Thou These Things? and The Voice of One Crying in The Wilderness	4	4	.05
Elijah the Restorer and General Letter from the General Overseer	5	7	.05
The Times of Restoration	5	8	.10
The Beatitudes	4	10	.05
The Kingdom of God is Come, Suffering on Behalf of Christ, and Let Not Your Heart be Troubled	4	9	.05
Repentance	3	11	.05
Ye are Come Unto Mount Zion, Will a Man Rob God?	3	2	.05
The Love of God in the Salvation of Man	4	11	.10
The Christian Ordinance of Baptism by Triune Immersion	1	12	.05
The Ordinance of Christian Baptism (18 centuries of proof)	5	10	.05
Organization of Zion Restoration Host	6	12	.05
The City of God; and What Shall This Child Be?	7	2	.05

Zion's Replies to Her Enemies and Critics.

	Vol.	No.	Price
Zion and Her Enemies	3	12	$0.05
Fighting Blackmailers	3	3	.05
Estimates and Realities. Reply to Baptist Ministers	2	11	.05
Reply to D L Moody and the *Ram's Horn*	3	10	.05
Reply to *Ram's Horn* of March 3d	4	3	.05
"You Dirty Boy," Reply to Rev. P S Henson, D.D	2	3	.05
Reply to Dr. Hillis	1	3	.05
Christ's Methods of Healing: A Reply to Rev J. L. Withrow, D D	2	5	.05
Reply to Dr Gray	3	9	.05
Reply to Ingersoll's Lecture on Truth	1	4	.05

The Evils Zion Exposes and Condemns.

	Vol.	No.	Price
Doctors, Drugs, and Devils; or, The Foes of Christ the Healer	1	10	$0.05
Secret Societies: The Foes of God, Home, Church, and State	1	8	.05
Zion's Protest Against Swine's Flesh as a Disease-Producer	2	6	.05
Tobacco, Satan's Consuming Fire	2	7	.05
The Press: The Tree of Good and Evil	2	10	.05
Ethiopia Stretching Out Her Hands to God	1	11	.05
False Christian Science Unmasked	2	8	.05
Christian Science Exposed as an Anti-Christian Imposture	3	5	.05
Diabolical Spiritualism Unmasked	2	12	.05
The Man of Sin Revealed; or, An Exposure of the Blasphemous Claim of the Pope of Rome to be the Infallible Head of the Church of Our Lord Jesus Christ	3	7	.05
Ingersoll Exposed	3	4	.05
Spurious Holiness Exposed	5	3	.05

Divine Healing and Its Truths as Taught in Zion.

	Vol.	No.	Price
Jesus the Healer and Satan the Defiler	4	2	$0.05
Do You Know God's Way of Healing? and He is Just the Same Today	4	1	.05
Reasonings for Inquirers Concerning Divine Healing Teaching	4	7	.05
Divine Healing Vindicated	2	9	.05
Lessons on Divine Healing, from the Story of the Leper	4	12	.05
Job's Boils; or, Objections to Divine Healing Considered	3	6	.05

	Vol.	No.	Price
What Should a Christian Do When Sick?	2	1	$0.05
"I Will"	1	9	.05
Permission and Commission	1	2	.05
How Jesus Heals the Little Ones	5	2	.05
Talks with Ministers	1	6	.05

Prayer and Its Conditions as Realized in Zion.

	Vol.	No.	Price
How to Pray	2	4	$0.05
If It Be Thy Will, Like a Shepherd, and How I Came to Speak for Jesus	4	6	.05
A Woman of Canaan	1	1	.05
The Disciples' Prayer, a series of Morning Discourses at Shiloh Tabernacle	7	3	.10

Zion Standard of Consecration and Sanctified Living.

	Vol.	No.	Price
Sanctification of Spirit, Soul, and Body	1	7	$0.05
The Seal of the Living God	5	4	.05
The Baptism of Fire, and The Cup of Suffering	5	5	.05
Ye are God's Witnesses, and The Power of Passive Faith	5	6	.05
The Chains of Good and Evil, and Sanctification of Triune Man	5	1	.05
Redemption Draweth Nigh	1	5	.05
Zion's First Feast of Tabernacles	5	9	.10
Zion Bible Calendar	3	1	.05
Four Addresses: — Love Fulfils Law; The Zion of the Holy One of Israel; The Wages of Sin; and Seest Thou This Woman?	6	4	.05
The Leaven of the Kingdom	7	4	.05

Devotional and Inspirational Zion Tracts.

Two Cents Each.

How I Came to Speak for Jesus.
If It Be Thy Will.

One Cent Each.

Do You Know God's Way of Healing?
If It Be Thy Will.
Jesus the Healer.
Satan the Defiler.
How I Came to Speak for Jesus.
He is Just the Same Today.

Suitable for enclosing in envelopes.

Special Books.

	Price
Zion's Conflict with Methodist Apostasy	$0.25
Zion's Holy War	.35

Tracts of Zion in Foreign Languages.

	Price
GERMAN:	
I Will	$0.05
How to Pray	.05
Permission and Commission	.05
A Woman of Canaan	.05
The Ordinance of Christian Baptism	.05
Organization of the Christian Catholic Church	.10
What Shall a Christian Do When Sick?	.05
Christian Science Exposed as an Anti-Christian Imposture	.05
Reasonings for Inquirers	.05
Sanctification of Spirit, Soul, and Body	.05
How I Came to Speak for Jesus	.02
How Jesus Heals the Little Ones	.05
Do You Know God's Way of Healing?	.01
He Is Just the Same Today	.01
How I Came to Speak for Jesus	.01
Elias	.05
Divine Healing Vindicated	.05
Zion's Protest Against Swine's Flesh	.05
FRENCH:	
How I Came to Speak for Jesus	.02
How Jesus Heals the Little Ones	.05
DANISH:	
He is Just the Same Today	.02
Do You Know God's Way of Healing	.02
NORWEGIAN:	
If It Be Thy Will	.02
HOLLAND:	
Divine Healing Vindicated	.05

Rates for Quantity Orders.

Charges Prepaid.

Kinds at 35 cents:	$3.75 a dozen.
Kinds at 25 cents:	2.75 a dozen.
Kinds at 10 cents:	1.00 a dozen or $6.00 per 100
Kinds at 5 cents:	50 a dozen or 3.00 per 100
Kinds at 2 cents:	.75 for 50 or $1.25 per 100.
Kinds at 1 cent.	.60 for 100.

Elijah's Restoration Messages.

	Vol.	No.	Price
Five Messages:—The Purifying Word; Purification by Obedience; The Purifying Water of Life; Purification by the Word of Wisdom; and Purification by Penal Fire	6	1	$0.05
Two Messages:—Christ, the World Conqueror, and Hear What the Unjust Judge Saith	6	2	.05
Five Messages:—Zion's Star of Hope and Peace; Thy God Reigneth; Peace Passing All Understanding; Then Peaceable; Sowing Peace	6	3	.05
Two Messages: — Until Shiloh Come; delivered at the consecration of Shiloh Tabernacle, Zion City, Illinois, March 31, 1902. Theocracy Contrasted with Democracy and Plutocracy, Chicago Auditorium, April 23, 1902.	6	5	.05
Two Messages, at Chicago Auditorium:—Power Belongeth Unto God; The Power and the Wisdom of God	6	6	.05
Two Messages, at Chicago Auditorium:—The Power of Divine Faith, and The Power of Christ's Resurrection	6	7	.05
Two Messages, at Chicago Auditorium:—The Power of a Living Faith; and The Power of the Word of God	6	8	.05
Two Messages, at Chicago Auditorium:—Awake; and The River of God is Full of Water	6	9	.05
Two Messages, at Chicago Auditorium:—The Power of Sacrifice; and Power of the Covenant, and Elijah the Restorer	6	10	.05
Three Messages, at Chicago Auditorium:—On the Purification of The Temple	6	11	.05
One Message, at Chicago Auditorium:—Saved Whole	7	1	.05

Zion's Second Feast of Tabernacles.

A book of over 300 pages, nicely bound in cloth, 30 cents By mail, 10 cents extra. Should be in the libraries of all Zion people.

Leaves of Healing

A weekly paper for the extension of the Kingdom of God: Containing accounts of Miracles of Healing; Stenographic Reports of Sermons by the Editor; with Testimonials of Blessing realized by God's people through the ministry of the Christian Catholic Church in Zion, of which the Rev. John Alexander Dowie is the General Overseer.

Subscription price, $2 per year; $1.25 for six months, $0.75 for three months. Clubs of ten, $15. To ministers and Public Libraries, $1.50 per year. Foreign subscriptions, $3.50 per year.

Bound Volumes I, II, III, IV, V, VI, VII, VIII, IX, X, XI, XII and XIII, $3.50 per Volume. Three or more Volumes, $3 00 each. Entire set, $32.50 Carriage on bound volumes always to be paid by purchaser.

Blätter der Heilung.

German Edition of LEAVES OF HEALING. Monthly, $0.50 per year. Foreign, $0.75 per year.

The Zion Banner.

A weekly semi-secular paper devoted to the extension of the Kingdom of God and the Elevation of Man, containing the news of Zion City, brightly and interestingly told; the news of the world up to within a few hours of its publication, and editorials on current events from a Zion standpoint. Edited by the Rev. John Alexander Dowie.

Subscription price, $0.50 for six months; $0 30 for three months. Sold for three cents a copy.

A Voice From Zion.

Monthly. Containing leading Sermons by the Rev. John Alexander Dowie. $0.50 per year. Foreign, $0.75 per year.

Bound Volumes I, II, III, IV, V, VI and VII Voice from Zion, may be secured at $1 per Volume; the complete set for $6.10, F. O. B. Zion City.

All orders for above publications except those quoted at other prices in the foregoing lists, under 25 copies, 5 cents per copy; exceeding 25 copies, 4 cents per copy; 100 or more copies, 3 cents per copy. If mailed to a foreign address, add 3 cents per copy for additional postage.

Trial subscriptions (new), LEAVES OF HEALING, 10 weeks for 25 cents each; BLÄTTER DER HEILUNG, 10 months for 25 cents each. Foreign 55 cents

Make All Remittances Payable to the Order of John Alex. Dowie.

Form of Application for Membership in the Christian Catholic Church in Zion

To all who are desirous of entering into Fellowship with the Christian Catholic Church in Zion.

MY DEAR BROTHERS AND SISTERS:—The Principles of the Christian Catholic Church in Zion have been fully set forth in the Reports of Two Conferences on Organization, held in Zion Tabernacle No. 2, which are fully reported in LEAVES OF HEALING for January 31 and February 7, 1896. The Basis of Fellowship is set forth in the Second Section of the Resolution passed on February 5th (see LEAVES OF HEALING, Volume II, Number 17, Page 267):

First—That we recognize the infallible inspiration and sufficiency of the Holy Scriptures as the rule of faith and practice.

Second—That we recognize that no persons can be members of the Church who have not repented of their sins and have not trusted in Christ for Salvation.

Third—That such persons must also be able to make a good profession, and declare that they do know, in their own hearts, that they have truly repented, and are truly trusting Christ, and have the witness, in a measure, of the Holy Spirit.

Fourth—That all other questions of every kind shall be held to be matters of opinion and not matters that are essential to Church unity.

All who are conscious of fulfilling these conditions, no matter where they may reside, are invited to fill up the following blank and answer all the questions contained therein.

I am, faithfully yours in Jesus,

John Alex. Dowie

General Overseer of the Christian Catholic Church in Zion.

AS FAR AS POSSIBLE THE APPLICANT HIMSELF SHOULD FILL OUT THIS BLANK. WRITE PLAINLY AND WITH INK.

Address..........

Date..........
PLEASE BE SURE TO FILL IN

TO THE REV. JOHN ALEX. DOWIE, General Overseer of the Christian Catholic Church in Zion, Zion City, Lake County, Illinois, U.S.A.

I hereby make application to be received as a member of the Christian Catholic Church in Zion, and declare my agreement with the Basis of Fellowship agreed upon at a Conference held February, 5, 1896, as set forth in your Circular Letter of February 7, 1896.

What is your full name? ....

Where is your residence? ....
PLEASE GIVE FULL POSTOFFICE ADDRESS

What is your age last birthday? ....
ALSO GIVE DATE AND YEAR OF BIRTH

Are you married, unmarried, widowed, or divorced? ....

How many children have you living? ....

What is your occupation, profession, or trade? ....

What nationality are you? .... *Where were you born?* ....

What language or languages do you speak? ....

How long have you lived in America (or the country where you are now living)? ....

When and where were you converted to God? ....

....

Are you conscious that you are saved through faith in Jesus? ....

When and where were you immersed by TRIUNE Immersion? ....

By whom were you immersed? ....

With what religious organization were you formerly connected? ....

Recommended by ....

Signature of Applicant ....
WRITE VERY PLAINLY

REMARKS

....

....

Extra Copies of this Form will be sent to intending members on application to the General Recorder of the Christian Catholic Church in Zion, Zion City, Lake County, Illinois, U.S.A.

Zion's Bible Class

Conducted by Deacon Daniel Sloan in Shiloh Tabernacle, Zion City, Lord's Day Morning at 11 o'clock, and in Zion Homes and Gatherings throughout the World.

MID-WEEK BIBLE CLASS LESSON, AUGUST 31st or SEPT. 1st.

Wholesome Discipline for Children.

1. *The Word of God must be the basis of all such.*—Proverbs 5:1-14.
   Appeal to God in prayer in such a time.
   Show where His truth has been disregarded.
   Point out the particular sin done.
2. *They must be taught what to do and what not by choice.*—Proverbs 3:21-35.
   Show where an evil course leads to.
   Do not simply say, "You must not do it."
   Tell them specific things to do and not to do.
3. *The rod is an important factor if used rightly.*—Proverbs 13:18-25.
   You cannot stand it to whip your child, you say.
   You are no true parent to say this.
   But do not be always whipping; occasionally give good ones.
4. *Some things are corrected only by the rod.*—Proverbs 22:15.
   A rod drives foolishness out of the heart.
   When the rod is not used foolishness gets bound there.
   It is wholesome to prayerfully use the rod.
5. *The rule is, Great good comes out of chastening.*—Hebrews 12:5-11.
   Love must wield the rod.
   Sentimentality must be put aside.
   Never must it be done except the cause is good.
6. *Sometimes it will do no good at all; some will be wicked.*—Proverbs 27:17-23.
   Sometimes it will not be effective.
   You can tear a body to pieces and not get the demons out of the spirit.
   Your child may be a fool-child of sin through your folly.
7. *The law of life gives fruit always like the planting.*—Ezekiel 16:44-54.
   A daughter is so much like the mother.
   Daughters make the kind of wives their mothers are.
   Sisters copy after sisters, and both after mothers.
8. *The agonizing cry of faith alone will change and correct some.*—Matthew 15:21-31.
   Inbred demons come out by prayer.
   The prayer must be that of Faith.
   If parents do not pray the Prayer of Faith the Devil gets the child.
   The Lord our God is a Discipline-imposing God.

LORD'S DAY BIBLE CLASS LESSON, SEPTEMBER 4th.

Parental Safeguard of Children.

1. *Children are not liable to go right.*—Proverbs 22:5, 6
   Outside pressure makes them go wrong.
   Inside inclinations make them crooked.
   A crooked sprout can, with care, be grown straight.
2. *They have dispositions and tendencies to evil.*—Genesis 49:3-7.
   Children are not what they are by accident.
   Some have no stability in them.
   Some are full of self-will and cruelty.
3. *They must be admonished by the Truth of God.*—Ephesians 6:1-4.
   The truth of God must be taught.
   They must be admonished by sound words.
   They must be fed the sincere milk of God's Word before being admonished.
4. *If left to choose their ways they will grievously sin.*—1 Samuel 2:27-36.
   Some say, "Boys will be boys;" yes, and more.
   Parents know plainly what they should do.
   The Devil ruins boys and girls when parents are not awake.
5. *Prenatal influences curse almost every child.*—Psalm 51:5-11.
   The mother does not love truth in her heart.
   The father is full of evil seed.
   This bad seed grows in bad soil and brings forth wild oats.
6. *Children cannot do right amid evil associates.*—Psalm 144:9-15.
   Children are imitators of what they see and hear.
   One child acts strange, another tries also.
   See what associates your children have.
7. *Constant vigilance is necessary lest they get deeply into sin.*—Job 1:1-5.
   If you fear God you are on your guard lest your children do evil.
   Evil creeps into them through their pleasures.
   Are you alive to the sins that may be done in secret?
8. *The follies of youth should give parents deep anxiety.*—Ecclesiastes 11:9-10.
   Children are bent on having fun.
   They get wilful in having their kind of fun.
   They cannot see the harm to which their actions lead.
   God's Holy People Are a Vigilant People.

OBEYING GOD IN BAPTISM.

"Baptizing Them Into the Name of the Father and of the Son and of the Holy Ghost."

Nineteen Thousand Six Hundred Forty-eight Baptisms by Triune Immersion Since March 14, 1897.

Nineteen Thousand Six Hundred Forty-eight Believers have joyfully followed their Lord in the Ordinance of Believer's Baptism by Triune Immersion since the first Baptism in Central Zion Tabernacle on March 14, 1897.

Baptized in Central Zion Tabernacle from March 14, 1897, to December 14, 1901, by the General Overseer,	4754			
Baptized in South Side Zion Tabernacle from January 1, 1902, to June 14, 1903, by the General Overseer..	37			
Baptized at Zion City by the General Overseer........	583			
Baptized by Overseers, Elders, Evangelists and Deacons, at Headquarters (Zion City) and Chicago......	5283			
Total Baptized at Headquarters....................				10,657
Baptized in places outside of Headquarters by the General Overseer..................................		765		
Baptized in places outside of Headquarters by Overseers, Elders, Evangelists and Deacons............		7732		
Total Baptized outside of Headquarters............				8,497
Total Baptized in seven years and three months....				19,154
Baptized since June 14, 1904:				
Baptized in Zion City by the General Overseer........	64			
Baptized in Zion City by Elder Royall................	11			
Baptized in Zion City by Elder Hammond............	6			
Baptized in Zion City by Overseer Mason............	90			
Baptized in Zion City by Overseer Excell............	87			
Baptized in Zion City by Overseer Piper............	79			
Baptized in Zion City by Elder Mercer..............	2			
Baptized in Chicago by Elder Hoffman..............	4			
Baptized in Chicago by Elder Cossum..............	6			
Baptized in Chicago by Elder Keller..............	5			
Baptized in Chicago by Elder Hall................	3		357	
Baptized in Canada by Elder Brooks................		4		
Baptized in California by Elder Taylor..............		4		
Baptized in England by Overseer Cantel............		13		
Baptized in Indiana by Elder Osborne..............		2		
Baptized in Michigan by Elder Reed................		4		
Baptized in Minnesota by Elder Graves............		5		
Baptized in Minnesota by Elder Simmons..........		3		
Baptized in Mississippi by Evangelist Gay..........		1		
Baptized in Missouri by Evangelist Gay............		1		
Baptized in Missouri by Elder Brock..............		9		
Baptized in Missouri by Deacon Robinson..........		1		
Baptized in Nebraska by Elder Hoy................		7		
Baptized in New York by Overseer Mason..........		9		
Baptized in Ohio by Deacon Kelchner..............		3		
Baptized in Ohio by Deacon Arrington..............		5		
Baptized in South Africa by Overseer Bryant		49		
Baptized in Texas by Evangelist Gay..............		11		
Baptized in Washington by Elder Ernst............		3		
Baptized in Wisconsin by Elder McClurkin..........		3	137	494
Total Baptized since March 14, 1897..............				19,648

The following-named nineteen believers were baptized at Stettin, Germany, Wednesday, February 17, 1904, by Elder Carl Hodler:

Braun, Gotthilf ....Kaiser-Wilhelmstrasse, 15, Stettin, Germany
Braun, Mrs. Helene ....Kaiser-Wilhelmstrasse, 15, Stettin, Germany
Brink, Mrs. Auguste ....Muhlenstrasse, 7, Stettin, Germany
Brink, Herbert........................Muhlenstrasse, 7, Stettin, Germany
Dreesen, Heinrich ....Kaiser-Wilhelmstrasse, 25, Stettin, Germany
Dreesen, Mrs. Lina ....Kaiser-Wilhelmstrasse, 25, Stettin, Germany
Feldt, Christian ....Konstantinopel, Pommern, Germany
Gaede, Hermann..........................Wallstrasse, 16, Stettin, Germany
Herzog, Christian..................Scharnhorstrasse, 15, Stettin, Germany
Hilgendorff, Paul..............................Zullchow, Stettin, Germany
Koepke, Mrs. Marie...............Scharnhorststrasse, 15, g Stettin, Germany
Koepke, Miss Elfriede..........Scharnhorststrasse, 15, g Stettin, Germany
Renn, Mrs. Wilhelmine..............Politzerstrasse, 42, Stettin, Germany
Schiemann, Miss Mathilde ....Frankenstrasse, 5, a Stettin, Germany
Stabow, Mrs. Auguste................Konstantinopel, Pommern, Germany
Thomas, Carl ....Kaiser-Wilhelmstrasse, 25, Stettin, Germany
Waldow, Mrs. Ida..............................Erichstrasse, 5, Stettin, Germany
Reproeger, Miss Margarethe....Scharnhorststrasse, 15, g Stettin, Germany
Hilgendorff, Mrs. Helene ....Zullchow, Stettin, Germany

The following-named three believers were baptized at Lubeck, Germany, Friday, February 19, 1904, by Elder Carl Hodler:

Fries, Miss Katherina....................................Lubeck, Germany
Krutzfeldt, Friedrich...................Johannesstrasse, 2, Lubeck, Germany
Rohlff, Miss Elisabeth.............Kuthorstrasse, 1, Oldenburg, Germany

The following-named twenty-seven believers were baptized at Berlin, Germany, Lord's Day, February 21, 1904, by Elder Carl Hodler:

Abraham, Mrs. Christian............Buschingstrasse, 9, Berlin, Germany
Barthel, Miss Margarethe...........Annenstrasse, 42, Dresden, Germany
Beeskow, Carl..................Parkstrasse, 22, Pankow, Berlin, Germany
Beeskow, Hermann............Parkstrasse, 22, Pankow, Berlin, Germany
Beeskow, Mrs. Mathilde...........Parkstrasse, Pankow, Berlin, Germany
Eck, Hermann ....Blumenthalstrasse, 13, Berlin, Germany
Fischer, Miss Auguste...........Blumenthalstrasse, 27, Berlin, Germany
Fritsch, Theodor.....................Stargardersrasse, 63, Berlin, Germany
Hagen, Miss Amalie..................Akazienstrasse, 20, Berlin, Germany
Hallwass, Mrs. Mathilde...........Munchenerstrasse, 53, Berlin, Germany
Kaphammel, Heinrich.........Weissenburgerstrasse, 36, Berlin, Germany
Karig, Miss Auguste................Steinmetzstrasse, 30, Berlin, Germany
Kaszemek, Carl..............Kaiser-Wilhelmstrasse, 17, Berlin, Germany
Kaune, Wilhelm.........................Yorkstrasse, 84, d Berlin, Germany
Klahn, Heinrich.........................Bussestrasse, 10, Berlin, Germany
Kruger, Mrs. Emilie................Friedrichstrasse, 234, Berlin, Germany
Marquardt, Mrs. Emilie.................Hasenheide, 56, Berlin, Germany
Merk, Joseph..........................Lutzowstrasse, 74, Berlin, Germany
Mohnke, Albert..........................Goltzstrasse, 48, Berlin, Germany
Monien, Miss Martha.................Blumenstrasse, 62, Berlin, Germany
Richter, Mrs. Lina.............Kurfurstenstrasse, 99, Berlin, Germany
Rindt, Ludwig..................................Frankenfelde, Berlin, Germany
Schroder, Mrs. Luise............Koniggratzerstrasse, 107, Berlin, Germany
Wiechert, Miss Anna....................Fidioinstrasse, 32, Berlin, Germany
Wieske, Franz.....................Bismarckstrasse, 23b, Berlin, Germany
Wieske, Mrs. Marie.................Bismarckstrasse, 23b, Berlin, Germany
Magnus, Mrs. Amalie..............Schellingstrasse, 14, Berlin, Germany

The following-named four believers were baptized at Dresden, Germany, Thursday, February 25, 1904, by Elder Carl Hodler:

Barthel, Mrs. Margarethe............Annenstrasse, 42, Dresden, Germany
Geyer, Alfred...............................Seidenberg, Schlesien, Germany
Schwab, Mrs. Auguste.............Schaferstrasse, 61, Dresden, Germany
Zimmerman, Miss Hulda............Furstenstrasse, 95, Dresden, Germany

The following-named six believers were baptized at Castle Liebburg, Switzerland, Wednesday, March 2, 1904, by Evangelist Sophia Hertrich:

Ilitis, Nickolaus....................................Bacs-Szt-Tamas, Hungary
Kessler, Miss Marie..........................Binningen Basel, Switzerland
Kunzli, Xaver....................Steckborn, Canton Thurgau, Switzerland
Kuster, Miss Babette..............Altstatten, Canton St. Gall, Switzerland
Singer, Mrs. Margarethe.........Mammern, Canton Thurgau, Switzerland
Ulmer, Miss Nannette............Steckborn, Canton Thurgau, Switzerland

The following-named twelve believers were baptized at Zurich, Switzerland, Lord's Day, March 6, 1904, by Elder Carl Hodler:

Amberg, Mrs. Barbara...............Langstrasse, 239, Zurich, Switzerland
Furrer, Mrs. Marie..................Josephstrasse, 25, Zurich, Switzerland
Hurliman, Albert.......................Fehraltorf, Canton Zurich, Switzerland
Konig, Miss Hermann..................Langstrasse, 65, Zurich, Switzerland
Konig, Miss Marie.......................Langstrasse, 65, Zurich, Switzerland
Ruchti, Friedrich........................Oberrieden, Canton Zurich, Switzerland
Ruchti, Mrs. Karoline............Oberrieden, Canton Zurich, Switzerland
Rupp, Mrs. Ida.........................Hildastrasse, 12, Zurich, Switzerland
Schaffner, Miss Marie..................Horgen, Canton Zurich, Switzerland
Steiner, Mrs. Luise..................Kradolf, Canton Thurgau, Switzerland
Wuest, Gottfried...................Bruttisellen, Canton Zurich, Switzerland
Zuberbuhler, Ulrich................Burglistrasse, Winterthur, Switzerland

The following-named five believers were baptized at Castle Liebburg, Switzerland, Saturday, March 26, 1904, by Elder Carl Hodler:

Fulleman, Ida, Miss..............Ermatingen, Canton Zurich, Switzerland
Gsell, Heinrich.....................Ober-Uster, Canton Zurich, Switzerland
Keller, Anna, Mrs.....................Ronifirst, Canton Aargau, Switzerland
Muller, Bertha, Mrs........St. Margarethen, Canton Thurgau, Switzerland
Neuhauser, Conrad.................Altnau, Canton Thurgau, Switzerland

The following-named twenty-eight believers were baptized at Zurich, Switzerland, Lord's Day, April 3, 1904, by Elder Percy Clibborn:

Brunner, Albert..............................Thalwil bei Zurich, Switzerland
Dunner, Adolf...................Dufourstrasse, 133, Zurich, Switzerland
Ehrat, Miss Margarethe...............................Winterthur, Switzerland
Ehrat, Miss Anna.......................................Winterthur, Switzerland
Guhl, Miss Eurica................Clausiusstrasse, 42, Zurich, Switzerland
Haemig, Miss Rosa....................Kochlistrasse, 22, Zurich, Switzerland
Hess, Mrs. Kreszencia...............Frankengasse, 16, Zurich, Switzerland
Hirt, Mrs Regula............Ober-Wenningen, Canton Zurich, Switzerland
Hohl, Miss Marie........................Hintern-platz, Aargau, Switzerland
Hollenstein, Eugen.....................Neustadtgasse, 1, Zurich, Switzerland
Hollenweger, Mrs. Lisette...........Wagnergasse, 6, Zurich, Switzerland
Huber, Mrs. Albertine................Wagnergasse, 6, Zurich, Switzerland
Honegger, Albert......................Wagnergasse, 6, Zurich, Switzerland
Kradolfer, Mrs. Anna....................Clausstrasse, 44, Zurich, Switzerland
Krebser, Theodor ....Neustadtgasse, 8, Winterthur, Switzerland
Krebser, Mrs. Karoline.........Neustadtgasse, 8, Winterthur, Switzerland
Lehle, Miss Justine....................Motorenstrasse, 4, Zurich, Switzerland
Marti, Miss Fany.........Wasserfurristrasse, 39, Winterthur, Switzerland
Meier, Mrs. Mathilde...............Schienengasse, 20, Zurich, Switzerland
Meierhofer, Mrs........................Mullerstrasse, 87, Zurich, Switzerland
Muhlibach, Philip ....Frauenfeld, Thurgau, Switzerland
Muhlibach, Mrs. Anna..................Frauenfeld, Thurgau, Switzerland
Muller, Miss Emilie..........Niedersteinmaur, Canton Zurich, Switzerland
Nortz, Mrs. Lydia..........................Frauenfeld, Thurgau, Switzerland
Rutschmann, Mrs. Louise ....Dienerstrasse, 28, Zurich, Switzerland
Schulthess, Miss Bertha.......................Thalwil bei Zurich, Switzerland
Vollenweider, Mrs. Bertha ....Bremgarten, Canton Aargau, Switzerland
Walder, Robert.......................Baretsweil, Canton Zurich, Switzerland

The following-named six believers were baptized at Berlin, Germany, Monday, April 4, 1904, by Evangelist Sophia J. Hertrich:

Hanf, Mrs. Henriette..............Krummstrasse, 7, Hof Berlin, Germany
Heinrich, Miss Elisabethe..............Langstrasse, 31, Berlin, Germany
Kohring, Miss Elisabethe ....Gitschinerstrasse, 87, Berlin, Germany
Leepa, Johann......................Landbergstrasse, 48, Berlin, Germany
Meier, Otto.........Radenaustrasse, 22, Schonweide bei, Berlin, Germany
Schmid, Mrs. Rosa ...Steinmetzstrasse, 41, Quergebaude, Berlin, Germany

---

The following-namod six believers were baptized at Castle Liebburg, Switzerland, Saturday, April 2, 1904, by Elder Percy Clibborn:

Brosamle, Miss Martha..............Betzingen bei Reutlingen, Germany
Neuwiller, Mrs. Adelheide......Kreuzlingen, Canton Thurgau, Switzerland
Schellenberg, Emil.............Walzmuhlstrasse, Frauenfeld, Switzerland
Spring, Oskar......................Rheinstrasse, Frauenfeld, Switzerland
Spring, Christian..........................Stocken, Thurgau, Switzerland
Vogel, Miss Pauline........................Kradolf, Thurgau, Switzerland

---

The following-named thirteen believers were baptized at Zurich, Switzerland, Lord's Day, May 1, 1904, by Elder Percy Clibborn:

Dunki, Mrs. Ana....................Kanzliestrasse, 12, Zurich, Switzerland
Hartmann, Adolf....................Josephstrasse, 141, Zurich, Switzerland
Matzinger, Mrs. Bertha.............Anwandstrasse, 57, Zurich, Switzerland
Muggli, Rosa.....................Baretsweil, Canton Zurich, Switzerland
Notz, Anna.........................Lavaterstrasse, 77, Zurich, Switzerland
Scheller, Mrs. Johanna..............Mullerstrasse, 46, Zurich, Switzerland
Schmidt, Mrs. Karolina..............Josephstrasse, 29, Zurich, Switzerland
Sprecher, Mrs. Elise.................Lagerstrasse, 35, Zurich, Switzerland
Schwank, Mrs. Josephine..........Clausiusstrasse, 3, Zurich, Switzerland
Temperli, Mrs. Bertha..............Weststrasse, 116, Zurich, Switzerland
Temperli, Jakob....................Weststrasse, 116, Zurich, Switzerland
Weber, Franz.....................Wartegg bei Fehring Steiermark, Austria
Witzig, Johann.....................Kanzleistrasse, 190, Zurich, Switzerland

---

The following-named twelve believers were baptized at Limbach, Germany, Lord's Day, May 8, 1904, by Evangelist Sophia Hertrich:

Aurich, Mrs. Fanny..........................Limbach, Sachsen, Germany
Gruntz, Hugo..............Querstrasse, 22, Limbach, Sachsen, Germany
Gruntz, Mrs. Mina.........Querstrasse, 22, Limbach, Sachsen, Germany
Gruntz, Otto.................Querstrasse, 3, Limbach, Sachsen, Germany
Muller, Paul ....Kreuzstrasse, 1, Limbach, Sachsen, Germany
Muller, Mrs. Hedwig........Kreuzstrasse, 1, Limbach, Sachsen, Germany
Petzold, Theodor............................Limbach, Sachsen, Germany
Petzold, Mrs. Auguste.......................Limbach, Sachsen, Germany
Turschmann, Theodor.......Bergstrasse, 17, Limbach, Sachsen, Germany
Turschmann, Mrs. Ida.......Bergstrasse, 17, Limbach, Sachsen, Germany
Schmidt, Mrs. Emilie...Leipzig, Germany
Schurer, Mrs. Franziska......Bergstrasse, 17, Limbach, Sachsen, Germany

---

The following-named eight believers were baptized at Castle Liebburg, Switzerland, Saturday, May 14, 1904, by Overseer J. G. Excell:

Burkhardt, Mrs. Hermine.............Bruggen bei Saint Gall, Switzerland
Fischer, Miss Elisabeth.....Meisterschwanden, Canton Argau, Switzerland
Frey, Mrs. Sophie..............Dornstetten, Canton Thurgau, Switzerland
Greminger, Mrs. Elisabeth........Dodtnach, Canton Thurgau, Switzerland
Helk, Miss Emma.......................Kandel Bay, Rheinpfalz, Germany
Rudt, Mrs. Marie..................Lengweil, Canton Thurgau, Switzerland
Zwahlen, Miss Anna...Burg bei Weinfelden, Canton Thurgau, Switzerland
Warther, Miss Katherine...Wildberg bei Nagold, Wurttemberg, Germany

---

The following-named twenty-three believers were baptized at Zurich, Switzerland, Tuesday, May 24, 1904, by Overseer J. G. Excell:

Abt, Mrs. Marie...............................Binningen bei Basel, Switzerland
Brunner, Miss Mathilde..............Muhlethal, Schaffhausen, Switzerland
Brunner, Miss Mina..................Muhlethal, Schaffhausen, Switzerland
Brunner, Miss Dorothe...............Muhlethal, Schaffhausen, Switzerland
Brunner, August.....................Muhlethal, Schaffhausen, Switzerland
Eberhardt, Andreas.........................Dornstettin, Wurttemberg, Germany
Fiechter, Mrs. Elise.........................Binningen bei Basel, Switzerland
Franke, Miss Selma..........Querstrasse, 22, Limbach, Sachsen, Germany
Furrer, Miss Elise.......................Lausen, Canton Basel, Switzerland
Feldt, Franz..................................Konstantinopel, Pommern, Germany
Glaser, Martin ....Reichenbrandt bei Leipzig, Germany
Hitz, Heinrich..................Schonenberg, Canton Thorgau, Switzerland
Metzler, Mrs. Katharina...............Thal, Canton St. Gall, Switzerland
Muchenberger, Mrs. Cathanna..........Binningen bei Basel, Switzerland
Meier, Mrs. Agate......................Tagerig, Canton Argau, Switzerland
Ruegger, Mrs. Luise.......................Binningen, bei Basel, Switzerland
Schick, Miss Luise..........................Laufen, Wurttemberg, Germany
Scheideger, Fritz............................Junkergasse, 17, Bern, Switzerland
Schneider, Mrs. Hermine..............Altnau, Canton Thurgau, Switzerland
Schnetzle, Christian.........................Dornstetten, Wurttemberg, Germany
Staub, Mrs. Verena,..........................Brittnau bei Zofingen, Switzerland
Waltz, Mrs. Philippine.......................Rohrdorf, Wurttemberg, Germany
Weinstein, Miss Frieda ....Josephstrasse, 25, Zurich, Switzerland

---

The following-named eighteen believers were baptized at Zurich, Switzerland, Friday, May 27, 1904, by Overseer John G. Excell.

Albrecht, Karl........................Eisengasse, 10, Zurich, Switzerland
Baumann, Mrs. B.................................Uzwil, Saint Gall, Switzerland
Krahn, Johann.....................................Noerenberg, Pommern, Germany
Kuder, Jakob ....Stammheim, Wurttemberg, Germany
Maute, Miss Luise.............................Thailfingen, Wurttemberg, Germany
Meier, Mrs. Lisette...........Wazmuhlenstrasse, Frauenfeld, Switzerland
Pedrazzi, Miss Albertine.........................Uzwil, Saint Gall, Switzerland
Pfister, Mrs. Susanna................Militarstrasse, 98, Zurich, Switzerland
Rehorn, Mrs. Susanna.............................Nemei, Slavonien, Hungary
Reymund, Heinrich..Neusatz, Hungary
Rieger, Jakob...............................Bottmingen bei Basel, Switzerland
Ruf, Mrs. Elise.....................Murgenthal, Canton Aargau, Switzerland
Schonfeld, Friedrich........Zscheilaerstrasse, Meissen, Sachsen, Germany
Schulz, Andreas.................................Mondgasse, 4, Budapest, Austria
Suter, Miss Elisabeth...............Hintere Vorstadt, Aargau, Switzerland
Wahl, Karl...Nemei Slavonien, Hungary
Waller, Heinrich..Nemei Slavonien, Hungary
Wursten, Mrs. Elisabeth...............Neustadt, 17, Lucerne, Switzerland

---

The following-named one hundred twenty-four believers were baptized at Zurich, Switzerland, Monday, May 30, 1904, by the General Overseer:

Aqueria, Miss Gerhardine...................Irnlaneg, 4, Copenhagen, Denmark
Albrecht, Mrs. Barbara.................Eisengasse, 10, Zurich, Switzerland
Bader, Miss Anna........................Birchstrasse, 4, Zurich, Switzerland
Bachofner, Alfred ....Langstrasse, 65, Zurich, Switzerland
Baumann, Fritz ....Schaffisheim, Canton Aargau, Switzerland
Baumann, Mrs. Bertha..............Honggerstrasse, 27, Zurich, Switzerland
Baur, Lorenz ....Langnau bei Zurich, Switzerland
Berchtold, Mrs. Dorothea...................Seebach bei Zurich, Switzerland
Beuerlein, Mrs. Luise.................Ramistrasse, 44, Zurich, Switzerland
Billweiler, Mrs. M...................Plattenstrasse, 34, Zurich, Switzerland
Bollinger, Mrs. Elisabeth..................Erlenbach bei Zurich, Switzerland
Bosshardt, Mrs. Franziska............Rieterstrasse, 67, Zurich, Switzerland
Brand, Miss Martha ....Nieder-Oenz, Canton Bern, Switzerland
Bar, Miss Emile............................Dubendorf bei Zurich, Switzerland
Brandli, Mrs. Eliese..........................Thalwil bei Zurich, Switzerland
Brandli, Mrs. Marie..........................Thalwil bei Zurich, Switzerland
Brunner, Otto.......................Bahnhofstrasse, 76, Zurich, Switzerland
Brunner, Mrs. Emma..............Blumenbleiche, Winterthur, Switzerland
Collatz, Mrs. Mina..Nemitz, Pommern, Germany
Deack, Mrs. Eva.......................Sommergasse, 97, Neu-Pest, Hungary
Denzler, Johannes..........................Dubendorf bei Zurich, Switzerland
Dingemann, Wilhelm.............................Buchum, Westphalia, Germany
Eber, Mrs. Magdalena...............Plattenstrasse, 50, Zurich, Switzerland
Egli, Mrs. Elise......................Schweizergasse, 8, Zurich, Switzerland
Eich, Mrs. Anna..................................Horgen bei Zurich, Switzerland
Fausch, George...........................Weststrasse, 116, Zurich, Switzerland
Fehr, Jakob...........................Culmannstrasse, 8, Zurich, Switzerland
Fey, Albert.......................Unterthorgasse, 32, Winterthur Switzerland
Fischer, Mrs. Marie...................Uetlibergstrasse, Zurich, Switzerland
Frey, Karl...................................Dornstetten, Wurttemberg, Germany
Frick, Miss Emilie......................Steinstrasse, 65, Zurich, Switzerland
Furter, Rudolph....................Staufen, Canton Aargau, Switzerland
Gerber, Mrs. Elise...................................Freiburg im Alsace, Germany
Gluckler, Natalie..............................Thalwil bei Zurich, Switzerland
Graff, Miss Amalie..........................Seebach bei Zurich, Switzerland
Grampes, Mrs. Pauline..............Grunhofstrasse, 6, Zurich, Switzerland
Greuter, Mrs. Luise.........................Rumlang bei Zurich, Switzerland
Griesser, Miss Bertha........................Oerlikon bei Zurich, Switzerland
Gut, Mrs. Rosine..............................Langnau bei Zurich, Switzerland
Haberlin, Mrs. Catherine...........Schreinergasse, 62, Zurich, Switzerland
Haueter, Miss Elise..........................Route de chene 2 Genf, Switzerland
Hauser, Mrs. Thorodea..............Quellenstrasse, 37 Zurich, Switzerland
Hausammann, Miss Amalie......Romanhorn, Canton Thurgau, Switzerland
Hartmann, Mrs. Rosa ....Thalwil bei Zurich, Switzerland
Hedinger, Mrs. Bertha ....Dietlikon bei Zurich, Switzerland
Holtmann, Mrs. Gustav..........................Bochum, Westphalia, Germany
Hochstrasser, Mrs. Magd..........Limmatstrasse, 317, Zurich, Switzerland
Holder, Miss Ida.........................Rigistrasse, 52, Zurich, Switzerland
Hollenweger, Mrs. Rudolf............Wagnergasse, 6, Zurich, Switzerland
Humm, Miss Lisette ....Hunzenschwil, Canton Argau, Switzerland
Inne, Mrs. Karolina ....Schwarzenberg, Canton Bern, Switzerland
Isler, Mrs. Bertha ....Oberthor, 22, Winterthur, Switzerland
Isler, Miss Bertha.......................Oberthor, 22, Winterthur, Switzerland
Kagi, Miss Anna ....Stafa, Canton Zurich, Switzerland
Keller, Mrs. Anna........................Marienstrasse, 14, Bern, Switzerland
Kellenberger, Mrs. Gertrude......Herisau, Canton Appenzell, Switzerland
Kradolfer, Miss Jenni..................Klausstrasse, 44, Zurich, Switzerland
Kradolfer, Miss Mimi...................Klausstrasse, 44, Zurich, Switzerland
Langer, Eduard..............Niedersteinmaur, Canton Zurich, Switzerland
Landis, Mrs. Barbara....................Pfaffikon, Canton Zurich, Switzerland
Lechner, Mrs. Pauline.....................Lagerstrasse, 69, Zurich, Switzerland
Leeman, Mrs. Barbara............Mannedorf, Canton Zurich, Switzerland
Leuthold, Miss Anna..............Obernieden, Canton Zurich, Switzerlaad
Lopresti, Mrs. Adele...Torre-Pellice, Italy
Luthi, Mrs. Freida..................Frauenfeld, Canton Thurgau, Switzerland
Mack, Mrs. Babette........................Oberuzeil, Saint Gall, Switzerland
Mack, Adolf.....................................Oberuzeil, Saint Gall, Switzerland
Mack, Johann.................................Oberuzeil, Saint Gall, Switzerland
Manger, Martin......................................Freiburg im Alsace, Germany
Meier, Albert...........................Dolderstrasse, 9, Zurich, Switzerland
Meier, Miss Elise.....................Laurenzstrasse, 12, Zurich, Switzerland
Meierhofer, Mrs. Sophie................Weiach, Canton Zurich, Switzerland
Mettler, Mrs. Barbara........................Stafa, Canton Zurich, Switzerland
Moerker, Mrs. Marie.....................Ramistrasse, 44, Zurich, Switzerland
Mohnke, Mrs. Emma......................Goltzstrasse, 47, Berlin, Germany
Moos, Mrs. Elise ....Irgenhausen, Canton Zurich, Switzerland
Moser, Mrs. Anna.........................Horgen, Canton Zurich, Switzerland
Muller, Mrs. Margareth.....................Dubendorf bei Zurich, Switzerland
Mussig, Mrs. Rosa...........................Josephgasse, 28, Neu-Pest, Hungary
Peter, Jakob..............................Gibswell, Canton Zurich, Switzerland
Pfenninger, Mrs. Amalie....................Stafa, Canton Zurich, Switzerland
Pfenninger, Miss Anna......................Stafa, Canton Zurich, Switzerland
Pommerning, Mrs. Johanna.......................Nemitz, Pommern, Germany

Quadri, Mrs. B. M.............Schaffhauserstrasse, 75, Zurich, Switzerland
Rathgeb, Johannes.................Rothelstrasse, 107, Zurich, Switzerland
Ruckstuhl, Mrs. Regula..............Ackerstrasse, 35, Zurich, Switzerland
Rupflin, August.......................Langstrasse, 65, Zurich, Switzerland
Rupflin, Mrs. Agatha...................Langstrasse 65, Zurich, Switzerland
Sauter, Mrs. Anna................Herisau, Canton Appenzell, Switzerland
Siegfrid, Mrs. Barbara.....................Thalwil bei Zurich, Switzerland
Sourbeck, Adolf.......................Langstrasse, 65, Zurich, Switzerland
Sourbeck, Mrs. Emma................Langstrasse, 65, Zurich, Switzerland
Susser, Mrs. Emilie.............Eschwiesenstrasse, 33, Zurich, Switzerland
Schaffner, Mrs. Anna......................Horgen bei Zurich, Switzerland
Schaffner, Mrs. Anna................Josephstrasse, 29, Zurich, Switzerland
Schaffitz, Mrs. Rosa............Rheinstrasse, 5, Schaffhausen, Switzerland
Schatti, Mrs. Albertine.............. Redlikon am Zurichsee, Switzerland
Schelling, Mrs. Gottliebe...........Vorstadt, 51, Schaffhausan, Switzerland
Schmidt, Jakob..........................Steinstrasse, 8, Zurich, Switzerland
Schmittseifer, Christian.................... Bochum, Westfalen, Germany
Spring, Lina......................... Stocken, Canton Thurgau, Switzerland
Schuder, Martin....................Marktgasse, 22, Winterthur, Switzerland
Schuder, Mrs. Marie...............Marktgasse, 22, Winterthur, Switzerland
Schulze, Mrs. Antonie Gutacherstrasse, 16, Hornberg, Schwarzwald, Germany
Schulze, Friedrich..Gutacherstrasse, 16, Hornberg, Schwarzwald, Germany
Schurter, Mrs. Barbara..............Wulfinge bei Winterthur, Switzerland
Schweizer, Miss Anna................Wollishofen bei Zurich, Switzerland
Steffen, Miss Elise........................Affoltern bei Zurich, Switzerland
Stida, Miss Gertrud.....................Schillerstrasse, 5, Erfurt, Germany
Tanner, Mrs. Elisabeth.................Utzenstorf, Canton Bern, Switzerland
Temperli, Miss Frieda............Wolfbachstrasse, 35, Zurich, Switzerland
Tobler, Miss Emma...........Schaffhauserstrasse, 144, Zurich, Switzerland
Uster, Mrs. Marie..................... Feldstrasse, 61, Zurich, Switzerland
Vollmer, Miss Julie..........................Weesen St. Gall, Switzerland
Weber, Miss Lisette................Baretsweil, Canton Zurich, Switzerland
Weber, Gottfried..........................Niederuzwil St. Gall, Switzerland
Wenziker, Mrs. Susanna.............................Winterthur, Switzerland
Wepf, Mrs. Anna................Steckborn, Canton Thurgau, Switzerland
Wieland, Mrs. M.........................Horgen am Zurichsee, Switzerland
Winkler, Mrs. Eliese................Wulflingen bei Winterthur, Switzerland
Witt, Mrs. Minna.......... Bergstrasse, 69, Stargard, Pommern, Germany
Wuest, Albert.................. Niederlentz, Canton Aargau, Switzerland
Zahnler, Jakob........................Degersheim, St. Gall, Switzerland
Zahnler, Mrs. Annette.......................Degersheim, St. Gall, Switzerland

---

The following-named seven believers were baptized at Kimberley, Cape Colony, South Africa, Lord's Day, May 29, 1904, by Overseer Daniel Bryant:

Bernhard, Carl Philip, P. O. box 20, Kimberley, Cape Colony, South Africa
Bernhard, Fanny Ada, P. O. box 20, Kimberley, Cape Colony, South Africa
Cook, Mrs. Emma B., Thornhill, Belmont Station,
Grigualand West, South Africa
Farrel, Charles Christopher, 22 Innes street, Kimberley,
Cape Colony, South Africa
Gregory, Mrs. Ann, 60 Warren street, Kimberley, Cape Colony, South Africa
Trusckky, William, 22 Innes street, Kimberley, Cape Colony, South Africa
Ward, Mrs. Elizabeth Russell, 66 Warren street, Kimberley,
Cape Colony, South Africa

The followfng-named thirty-nine believers were baptized in Pretoria, Transvaal, South Africa, Lord's Day, June 19, 1904, by Overseer Daniel Bryant:

NOTE—In the list of names of those baptized in Pretoria, Transvaal, South Africa, Lord's Day, July 3, 1904, by Overseer Daniel Bryant, and published in LEAVES OF HEALING, issue of August 6, 1904, there is an error in the surname which appears as Spuy. It should be *Van der Spuy.*

Armstrong, Isabella Joplin,
Care T. J. Armstrong, Natal Bank, Pretoria, Transvaal, South Africa
Armstrong, John Ord,
Care T. J. Armstrong, Natal Bank, Pretoria, Transvaal, South Africa
Armstrong, Thomas Joplin,
Care T. J. Armstrong, Natal Bank, Pretoria, Transvaal, South Africa
Basson, Mrs. Susan......Church avenue, Pretoria, Transvaal, South Africa
Bosch, Willem Johannes..P. O. Box 869, Pretoria, Transvaal, South Africa
Brooks, James.....P. O. Box 3074, Johannesburg, Transvaal, South Africa
Buchanan, Mrs. Isabell.......................Pretoria, Transvaal, South Africa
Buchanan, Miss Margaret..................Pretoria, Transvaal, South Africa
Cornell, Cyril Frederick George Hudson, P. O. Box 386,
Pretoria, Transvaal, South Africa
Cornell, Mary Elaine St. Patrick .... Pretoria, Transvaal, South Africa
Cornell, Frank Ernest Morkel, Hamilton street, Arcadia,
Pretoria, Transvaal, South Africa
Flood, Thomsa Lystra 149 Schoeman's street,
Pretoria, Transvaal, South Africa
Fouche, Barend Hercules, 35 Skinner St., Pretoria, Transvaal, South Africa
Gatzke, Elizabeth Jane.................... Pretoria. Transvaal, South Africa
Hattingh, Christiaan Pieter, 21 Bloed St.,...Pretoria, Transvaal, South Africa
Hattingh, Mrs. Maatji Maria, 21 Bloed St.,.Pretoria, Transvaal, South Africa
deJager, Petrus Jacobus, 120 Struben St.,..Pretoria, Transvaal, South Atrica
Jubber, Alfred James, Hamilton St., North, Pretoria, Transvaal, South Africa
Jubber, Mrs. Martha Elizabeth Jane,
Hamilton street, North, Pretoria, Transvaal, South Africa
Kerner, John.............P. O. box 878, Pretoria, Transvaal, South Africa
Lombard Jr., Johannes Petrus, La Grange, P. O. box 389,
Pretoria, Transvaal, South Africa
Muloch, Mrs. Catherina Magdelene, Villieria,
Pretoria, Transvaal, South Africa
Passmore, Eddy George Tillerton........Pretoria, Transvaal, South Africa
Passmore, Sarah Christina..... ....Pretoria, Transvaal, South Africa
Passmore, Lilly Violet Sales .... Pretoria, Transvaal, South Africa
Passmore, William James Sales..........Pretoria, Transvaal, South Africa
Rowing, Mrs. Maria, Hamilton St., North, Pretoria, Transvaal, South Africa
Rose, Maurice Samuel, 82 Van der Walt St., Pretoria, Transvaal, South Africa
Rose, Elizabeth...82 Van der Walt street, Pretoria, Transvaal, South Africa
Roos, Teileman Francais, Wonderboom Spruit,
Pretoria, Transvaal, South Africa
Sales, Mrs. Ellen..........................Pretoria, Transvaal, South Africa
Sussens, Mrs. Elizabeth, Hamilton street, North, Arcadia,
Pretoria, Transvaal, South Africa
Sussens, Jessie Alvina, Hamilton street, North, Arcadia,
Pretoria, Transvaal, South Africa
Sussens, Julien Victoria, Hamilton street, North, Arcadia,
Pretoria, Transvaal, South Africa
Townsend, Lloyd Arthur...Villieria Dist., Pretoria, Transvaal, South Africa
Watson, Mrs. Susana Gertrude, Corner Vermeulen and Prinsloo streets,
Pretoria, Transvaal, South Africa
Sussens, Lucy Victoria, Hamilton street, North Arcadia,
Pretoria, Transvaal, South Africa
Armstrong, Richardson Joplin, Care T. J. Armstrong, Natal Bank,
Pretoria, Transvaal, South Africa
Townsend, Martin........ P. O. Box 487, Pretoria, Transvaal, South Africa

---

The following-named believer was baptized at Caledonian Road Baths, London, North, England, Lord's Day, June 26, 1904, by Overseer H. E. Cantel:

Neuendorf, Mrs. Julia, 65 Cleveland street, Fitzroy Square, West,
London, England

The following-named four believers were baptized at Shelby, Michigan, Lord's Day, July 31, 1904, by Elder David A. Reed:

Fox, Miss Anna Elizabeth..............................Shelby, Michigan
Fox, Nicholas Joseph ....Shelby, Michigan
Fox, Cornelius Leo.......................................Shelby, Michigan
Fox, Frank Samuel ....Shelby, Michigan

The following-named three believers were baptized at Royalton, Minnesota, Monday, August 1, 1904, by Elder R. M. Simmons:

Gray, Miss Eda Viola...................................Royalton, Minnesota
Gray, Henry C.......................... ......Royalton, Minnesota
Gray, Mrs. Mary A......................................Royalton, Minnesota

---

The following-named two believers were baptized at Zion City, Illinois, Wednesday, August 10, 1904, by Elder Frank A. Mercer:

Lusk, Mrs. Lucetta,......................................Gray's Lake, Illinois
Proctor, Mrs. Agnes,..................3208 Ezra avenue, Zion City, Illinois

---

CONSECRATION OF CHILDREN.

The following-named two children were consecrated to God at Zion City, Illinois, Tuesday, July 19, 1904, by Overseer H. D. Brasefield:

Varnum, Paul Ayer ....Centerville, South Dakota
Varnum, James Eugene.......... ....Centerville, South Dakota

---

The following-named three children were consecrated to God, at Royalton, Minnesota, Tuesday, August 2, 1904, by Elder R. M. Simmons:

Hughes, Claud Lester.....................................Royalton, Minnesota
Hughas, Mable Lillian................................. Royalton, Minnesota
Hughes, Myrtle May.. Royalton, Minnesota

Expiration of Subscriptions.

On every subscriber's copy of LEAVES OF HEALING or THE ZION BANNER we attach a yellow label bearing his name, address, and two numbers, the figures referring to the volume and the number with which the subscription will expire.

Thus, should your label number happen to be 15—11, you may know that your subscription expires with Volume XV, Number 11, which will be July 2, 1904. Also take notice that LEAVES OF HEALING now completes a volume every six months, or twenty-six weeks, that being the number of papers which are put into a bound volume. Earlier in the life of the paper a volume contained fifty-two numbers, as LEAVES OF HEALING had fewer pages in those days.

By making yourselves familiar with these customs and remitting promptly you need never allow your subscription to lapse.

Send money only by Bank Draft, Postoffice or Express Money-order in favor of John Alexander Dowie, and address all letters intended for us to

ZION PRINTING AND PUBLISHING HOUSE,
Zion City, Lake County, Illinois.

Train Schedule Between Zion City and Chicago

Via Chicago & North-Western Railway.

Effective May 22, 1904.

Weekday Trains.

CHICAGO TO ZION CITY.		ZION CITY TO CHICAGO.	
Leave Chicago	Arrive Zion City	Leave Zion City	Arrive Chicago
7.00 a. m.	8.25 a. m.	*6.45 a. m.	8 15 a. m.
*9.00 a. m.	10.13 a m.	7 03 a. m.	8 30 a. m.
*11.30 a. m.	12.37 p. m.	8.22 a. m.	9.50 a. m.
2.00 p. m.	3.08 p. m.	*9.45 a. m.	11 10 a. m
3.00 p. m	4.16 p. m.	*11.49 a. m.	1.15 p. m.
4.15 p. m.	5.39 p. m.	*‖1.18 p. m.	2.50 p. m.
*5.20 p. m.	6.50 p. m.	*†2.33 p. m.	4 00 p. m
*8.00 p. m.	9 11 p. m.	5 05 p. m.	6.30 p. m.
		*7.59 p. m.	9.30 p. m.

Sunday Trains.

CHICAGO TO ZION CITY.	
Leave Chicago	Arrive Zion City
9.05 a. m.	10.18 a. m.
*10.45 a. m.	12.37 p. m.
2.15 p. m.	4.05 p. m.
*8.00 p. m.	9.11 p. m.

ZION CITY TO CHICAGO.	
Leave Zion City	Arrive Chicago
*8.29 a. m.	9.45 a. m.
5.05 p. m.	6.40 p. m.
7.59 p m.	9.30 p. m.

Train leaves Waukegan at 12.28 p. m., arriving in Zion City at 12.37 p. m., daily, including Sunday.

* Signifies change train at Waukegan. † Train does not run South on Saturdays. ‖ Train runs South on Saturday only.

A WEEKLY PAPER FOR THE EXTENSION OF THE KINGDOM OF GOD

EDITED BY THE REV. JOHN ALEX. DOWIE.

Volume XV. No. 18. *ZION CITY, SATURDAY, AUGUST 20, 1904.* *Price Five Cents*

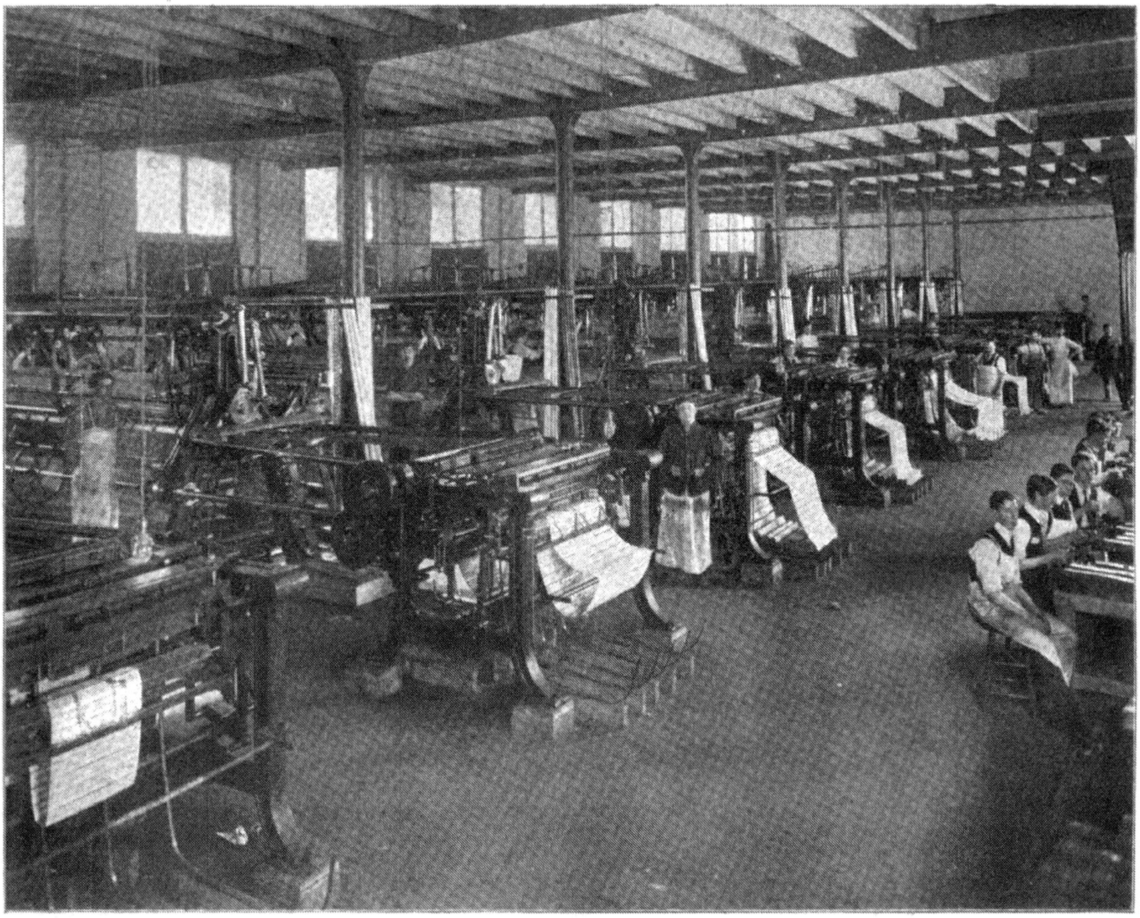

Portion of Zion Lace Industries, Interior View, Showing Levers Lace Machines

A WEEKLY PAPER FOR THE EXTENSION OF THE KINGDOM OF GOD.

EDITED BY THE REV. JOHN ALEX. DOWIE.

Application for entry as Second Class Matter at Zion City, Illinois, pending.

Subscription Rates.		Special Rates.	
One Year	$2.00	100 Copies of One Issue	$3.00
Six Months	1.25	25 Copies of One Issue	1.00
Three Months	.75	To Ministers, Y. M. C. A's and Public Reading Rooms, per annum	1.50
Single Copies	.05		

For foreign subscriptions add $1.50 per year, or three cents per copy for postage.

Subscribers desiring a change of address should give present address, as well as that to which they desire LEAVES OF HEALING sent in the future.

Make Bank Drafts, Express Money or Postoffice Money Orders payable to the order of JOHN ALEX. DOWIE. Zion City, Illinois, U. S. A.

Long Distance Telephone. *Cable Address "Dowie, Zion City."*

All communications upon business must be addressed to

MANAGER ZION PUBLISHING HOUSE,
Zion City, Illinois, U. S. A.

Subscriptions to LEAVES OF HEALING, A VOICE FROM ZION, and the various publications may also be sent to

ZION PUBLISHING HOUSE, 81 EUSTON ROAD, LONDON, N. W., ENGLAND.
ZION PUBLISHING HOUSE. NO. 43 PARK ROAD, ST. KILDA, MELBOURNE, VICTORIA, AUSTRALIA.
ZION PUBLISHING HOUSE, RUE DE MONT, THABOR 1, PARIS, FRANCE.
ZIONSHEIM, SCHLOSS LIEBBURG, CANTON THURGAU, BEI ZÜRICH, SWITZERLAND.

ZION CITY, ILLINOIS, SATURDAY, AUGUST 20, 1904.

TABLE OF CONTENTS.

LEAVES OF HEALING, SATURDAY, AUGUST 20, 1904.

EDITORIAL NOTES.

"OCCUPY, TILL I COME."

"TRADE YE herewith, till I Come."

"DO BUSINESS, till I Come."

THESE THREE lines are three translations of the Command given in the Parable of the Ten Pounds. [Luke 19:11-27.]

THE FIRST TRANSLATION is that of the Common Version.

The Second is that of the Revised Version.

And the Third is that of the eminent Christian scholar, Dr. Robert Young, in his "Translation of the Holy Bible, according to the letters and idioms of the original languages."

We prefer, as a translation, the last of the three:

DO BUSINESS, TILL I COME.

THIS ISSUE of LEAVES OF HEALING is largely devoted to the presentation of Zion's Business Interests.

WE GIVE on Pages 583 to 605, full Reports of the Two Business Conferences, which were held during Zion's Fourth Feast of Tabernacles, in Shiloh Tabernacle, Zion City, on Thursday, July 21st, and Friday, July 22d.

THE GENERAL REVIEW of Zion's business for the Year is contained in our Address on Pages 583 to 593.

Each separate Enterprise is dealt with on pages 595 to 605, in the Addresses of the General Managers and Chiefs of each Institution.

WE PRESENT to our Readers very excellent portraits of those who took part in these Business Conferences, and a few other photo-engravings, which explain themselves.

THE INFORMATION contained in the Reports of these Conferences covers the entire Field of the Financial, Commercial, and Industrial Institutions of the City of Zion.

WE TRUST that every Reader of LEAVES OF HEALING will give very earnest attention to this careful presentation of Facts.

EVERY MEMBER of the Christian Catholic Church in Zion is, or ought to be, deeply interested in the Progress of Zion City and its Business Institutions.

CONSTANT ATTACKS have been made, from the very beginning, upon the building up of the City and its Business Institutions, and these Attacks will possibly never cease until the last hypocrite and liar has gone from this earth to his place in hell.

THE STATEMENTS, officially made at these Conferences, are absolutely reliable, no matter what the supporters of Apostate Churches, Secret Societies, or the Enemies of Zion may say.

ZION WOULD not be of God if she did not have Enemies who are inspired by envy and hatred: for Zion's success is the despair of Satan and his friends.

WE HAVE withheld the Reports of these Conferences until we had time to revise them carefully, and to send them forth to all in Zion, and to all who are lovers of God and of that which is good, in all the world.

AND NOW we exhort, in the Name of the Lord, the Officers and Members of the Christian Catholic Church in Zion everywhere, carefully to read and to remember "what God hath wrought," so that they may have answer to give to those who inquire concerning God's Business in Zion.

ZION LACE INDUSTRIES and Zion City Bank Stock are now at a premium of ten per cent., at which price they have been selling freely up to this very moment of writing.

These stocks are paying respectively Ten Per Cent. and Nine Per Cent. per annum.

We are now addressing ourselves to the increase of the Capital of both Institutions.

ZION LACE INDUSTRIES have now been fully established upon a profitable basis, of which we have spoken fully in our Address. (See Page 587.)

This Stock will next year earn Eleven Per Cent.

Therefore, it will soon be advanced to One Hundred Fifteen Dollars per One Hundred Dollar Share, a premium of Fifteen Per Cent.

The following year it will yield twelve per cent., when the stock will be advanced to a premium of Twenty Per Cent., namely, One Hundred Twenty Dollars for each One Hundred Dollar Share.

We now offer Ten Thousand Shares of Zion Lace Industries Stock at the present price of One Hundred Ten.

When this is subscribed for, we shall probably at once advance the price to One Hundred Fifteen.

CONCERNING ZION CITY BANK STOCK, we now offer Five Thousand Shares at the present price of One Hundred Ten.

When these Shares are subscribed for, the Bank Stock, which yields Nine Per Cent. per annum, will be advanced to One Hundred Fifteen.

ZION SUGAR AND CONFECTION ASSOCIATION Stock now earns Nine Per Cent. per annum, and we offer for sale Five Thousand Shares at par—One Hundred Dollars per share.

When these are subscribed for, the price will at once be advanced to One Hundred Ten Dollars per share.

ZION BUILDING AND MANUFACTURING ASSOCIATION Stock, now earning Nine Per Cent. interest, with contingent benefits as set forth in the Agreement, is a stock of great value, which will soon be at a considerable premium.

We now offer Twenty-five Thousand Shares of this stock at Twenty Dollars per share, par value.

This Stock has been very eagerly sought by families; as it can be issued in certificates of one share of Twenty Dollars each, it furnishes a favorable opportunity of investment for young people who have saved that sum.

Splendid work has already been done by the Association, and which there is no doubt can be well continued, and we are justified in speaking of this important Stock in the very highest terms.

ZION CITY GENERAL STORES Stock, now earning eight per cent., is a First-class Security.

We now offer Five Thousand Shares at the par value of One Hundred Dollars per share.

It is our intention to begin the construction of new and permanent stores for this great Institution, which is now doing an immense cash business, upon a strong and profitable basis.

FOR THE present we shall not offer any stock in Zion Land and Investment Association, which is now an Eight Per Cent. Stock.

We are more inclined to retire the balance of the Stock, which has always been exchangeable for land, than we are to increase it.

The splendid position which this Association has attained, and the magnificent work which it has done, are well known; and on pages 586 to 587 facts are given, which prove that the value of the land in Zion City has increased to *more than twenty times its original cost.*

This is not a mere allegation, but is proved by the fact that Thirty-three and Two-thirds Acres, which cost us less than Five Thousand Dollars, were sold for One Hundred One Thousand Dollars to the Chicago & Milwaukee Electric Railroad Company.

Lands west of that new line of Railway, and further from the present center of population, have already been disposed of, in some cases, at *more than twice that rate of increase.*

ALL LANDS already occupied or unoccupied have risen very largely in value.

As the area of the City is limited, it is of the utmost importance to the present holders of Zion Land and Investment Association Stock, that they should exchange their Certificates for land.

That exchange will be much more profitable to them than the eight per cent. which they are now receiving on their Stock.

We, therefore, most heartily advise our friends who hold this Stock, to take advantage of the offer contained in a letter, which is about to be issued by Deacon H. Worthington Judd, General Manager and Secretary of Zion Land and Investment Association, which reads as follows:

H. WORTHINGTON JUDD, Secretary and Manager. — Zion City Real Estate and Improvements.

GENERAL OFFICES OF

ZION LAND AND INVESTMENT ASSOCIATION

John Alex. Dowie

ADMINISTRATION BUILDING

ZION CITY, ILLINOIS, August 19, 1904.

BELOVED SHAREHOLDER:—It is not expected that any new subdivisions will be placed in the market this year, and understanding that many of our shareholders have delayed making lot selections in order that they might get the benefit of the ten per cent. discount usually allowed shareholders when new subdivisions are placed on the market, this Association has decided to make a special offer to all original shareholders, which is as follows:

Beginning with September 1, 1904, and extending to November 1, 1904, each shareholder of Stock in this Association will be given the privilege to select a lot, or lots, in any of the last three subdivisions made by this Association in Sections 16, 17, 20, and 21, in Zion City, and will be allowed a discount of ten per cent. from the original published rentals.

This is an exceedingly liberal offer, when we consider the fact that the new Chicago & Milwaukee Electric Railroad, now in course of construction, and extending North and South through the center of this City, paid on an average about as much for the leasehold of their right of way as our published lot rental list calls for.

It must be understood that this is not done because of any shrinkage in the rental value of properties in Zion City. On the contrary, we can truthfully say that our Real Estate market was never in a firmer and healthier condition than at this time. Our lots are steadily increasing in value, and must inevitably continue to do so, as the population increases.

These Subdivisions are attractive, high, and well-located, and no better home sites can be found in Zion City, and shareholders in this Association have never had an opportunity to secure a more desirable investment in some of the choicest residence property in Zion City—property which, we are safe in saying, will increase in value at least fifty per cent. within the coming two years.

Rentals of lots adjacent to this New Railroad must advance as soon as the line is in operation, and the latter is expected to take place within the next few months. Then it will not be long before the cross-town lines will be constructed and put in operation, bringing all of these lots within from five to ten minutes' ride of the center of the City.

It has already been proved that there are no investments more safe and more profitable than the Real Estate investments in Zion City. Hundreds of lot investors realized one hundred per cent. profit on their investments, and some two hundred per cent. within the first year. We again emphasize the fact that there never has been any shrinkage in land values in Zion City, and we have every reason to believe that there never will be. Our General Overseer has declared that this City will, within a few years, have a population of at least one hundred fifty thousand people; that being the case, early investors will easily realize a profit of from three hundred to five hundred per cent. on their investments within that time.

All shareholders in this Association who are not entirely dependent upon the annual income derived from their Stock investments should take advantage of what we believe to be the best offer that has ever been made by this Association.

Payments for lots can be made as follows: All cash, or one-third of the rental down—the balance, one-third in one year and one-third in two years, with interest at the rate of six per cent. per annum, payable semi-annually.

The following rules are to be observed in the allotment of lots to shareholders:

First, Shareholders should make a choice of several lots—first choice, second choice, third choice, etc., as indicated on the application accompanying this letter, and sign their name to the application and send it in to this Association.

Second, In order to facilitate matters, Stock Certificates should be assigned to John Alex. Dowie by the shareholder (see form on back of Certificate), and sent in with the list of lots selected.

Third, The choice of selection will be given to the shareholders according to the date each application and Certificate of Stock is received, each application being numbered when received by this Association.

Fourth, the Secretary of this Association will act, without compensation, as proxy for any shareholder who desires to accept his services in the selection of desirable lots.

We trust that every shareholder will take advantage of this liberal offer, and thus enable himself or herself to secure most desirable home sites which must prove exceedingly profitable investments, at exceptionally low rentals.

Praying God for the future prosperity of Zion, as well as of every Zion Investor, and believing you will readily see the great advantage of sending in your application at once, I am

Faithfully yours in the Lord's Service,

H. WORTHINGTON JUDD,
Secretary and Manager.

COPIES OF the above excellent Letter, with the papers referred to therein, will be at once mailed to every Zion Land and Investment Association Shareholder.

We trust that there will be few, if any, who will fail to take advantage of the excellent offer which it contains.

Shareholders in Zion Land and Investment Association, however, do not need to wait for the reception of the Official

Letter, if they desire the General Manager to select lands for them in exchange for their Stock.

They may communicate with him at once.

AND NOW we commend this whole matter to God and to His people in Zion.

We have made proposals, which all who are able and who desire to make Investments of Great Value, should at once accept.

THE REPORTS of the Conferences, published in this issue, confirm this assertion.

We are sure also, that there is no truthful, competent, and unprejudiced person, who has ever visited Zion City, but will say, that which all such visitors say every day, that "the half has not been told," and that, far from any exaggeration, the progress of Zion's Business Institutions is even more wonderful than it has been declared to be.

IT IS self-evident why we are not willing to disclose fully the Large Profits that are now beginning to be made by Zion's Institutions, and which have justified us in paying the large annual interests that we have paid, even when these Institutions were in their infancy.

ALL THAT is now needed, both for investors and for Zion generally, is that we shall receive a large and immediate increase to our capital.

In urging this we are not asking for gifts.

We are only asking for that which it is in the interest of those whom we now address to supply.

We ask that they shall quickly realize money by the sale of their properties and stocks in outside Institutions, and invest in Zion City, which God has so abundantly blessed, and where we are so manifestly able to protect and increase the value of our investments.

The Security for these Investments is not merely the immensely valuable properties now established on Zion City soil, upon which there is not a dollar of mortgage; but they are represented by our own Personal Estate to the last cent, and by all that we represent as the legal owner and proprietor of the vast Zion Estate, here and elsewhere, amounting to Many Millions of Dollars in excess of all liabilities.

Ninety-five per cent. of that vast Estate, at our departure from this life, is absolutely *willed in perpetuity*, to the Christian Catholic Church in Zion.

WE VENTURE to say that *there are no Investments in the world better secured than those in Zion.*

We therefore confidently expect that our Friends all over America and the world, who are in fellowship with us in the Christian Catholic Church in Zion, or who are in active sympathy with us, will quickly subscribe for the Stocks which we have now offered for sale.

Full particulars of Forms of Agreements between ourselves and our investors, and all necessary papers, can be had immediately upon application to Deacon Fielding H. Wilhite, Manager of Zion Stocks and Securities, Administration Building, Zion City, or from our Special Agents abroad, who are mentioned on page 584 of this issue.

Special Zion Financial Messengers can also be sent to intending investors, if thought desirable. These Messengers will explain the nature and value of Zion's Stocks, and give counsel and help where needed.

AND NOW, in closing these Notes, let us remark that the Story of the Triumph of Zion's Business Institutions over assaults of every kind proves incontestably that *God is with us.*

The Blessing of God has been upon us also in the Spiritual and Educational Work of Zion in an extraordinary manner.

Ten years' Records, in Fifteen large Volumes of this paper, LEAVES OF HEALING, have placed the facts, as far as they can be stated, before the world, from week to week.

Only Envy, Malignity, and all Uncharitableness could deny the fact that God has abundantly blessed us in all Zion's Business undertakings.

THESE ARE destined, like Zion's Spiritual Operations, to be of a World-wide nature.

But the same Conservative, as well as Progressive, Spirit which has guided us in the past will continue to guide us in the future.

WE ARE not speculators with God's money, entrusted to us by God's people.

We are, by the grace of God, intelligent and industrious users of every talent thus entrusted to our care.

IN THIS sense of responsibility all our people in Zion City join us.

The Unity, the Love, the Peace, the Purity, and the Energy of Zion City was never greater than it is at the present moment.

We feel that God has not only saved us, and healed us, but that He is cleansing us.

A Powerful and Progressive People have been raised up, and the Banner of Zion is now floating over Zion in many nations and cities on every Continent.

WE CANNOT do without the prayers and sympathies, and co-operation of our people.

Our very successes call for larger capital and increased production.

We have never made an article that we could not sell.

We are careful to produce only those things that are good and profitable.

IT IS our delight and our duty to praise God for the Wonderful Business Year through which we have passed.

And this we gratefully, and most sincerely, and humbly do, ascribing unto Him in the Christ our Lord, all the Glory, since from Him has been all the Power.

Without God's blessing and protection we could have done nothing.

OUR GENERAL LETTER upon the Apostolic Organization of the Church has been held over until our next issue.

MAY WE *not ask every one of our friends in Zion to do us a little special personal favor?*

We ask that every one will send twenty-five cents to the General Manager of Zion Printing and Publishing House, and a list of ten persons, to whom, for that sum, we may send ten copies of this Issue.

This will entail an immense amount of work, but we know that we can easily get Five Hundred of our young men and women to volunteer to address the wrappers and prepare the papers for mailing.

If the papers are for foreign countries, an extra sum of thirty cents for every ten copies must be sent.

TWO HUNDRED Fifty Thousand (250,000) copies of this issue of LEAVES OF HEALING should go forth from Zion City.

We ask as a personal favor that this shall be done.

Some of our friends may be able to send ten or twenty such twenty-five cent subscriptions.

Let them do so.

But, above all things, let what is done, be done quickly.

BRETHREN, PRAY FOR US.

Notice to Officers and Members.

Send all newspaper clippings concerning the General Overseer, the Elders, or any department of the work in connection with the Christian Catholic Church in Zion, to Deacon Carl F. Stern, Zion City, Illinois. Send as soon as possible after publication, and carefully mark *name and date of the paper clipped from* on each article. If this is not done, the clippings are absolutely useless.

GOD'S WAY OF HEALING.

BY THE REV. JOHN ALEX. DOWIE.

God's Way of Healing Is a Person, Not a Thing.

Jesus said "*I am* the Way, and the Truth, and the Life," and He has ever been revealed to His people in all the ages by the Covenant Name, Jehovah-Rophi, or "*I am* Jehovah that Healeth thee." (John 14:6; Exodus 15:26.)

The Lord Jesus, the Christ, is Still the Healer.

He cannot change, for "Jesus, the Christ, is the same yesterday and today, yea and forever;" and He is still with us, for He said: "Lo, *I am* with you All the Days, even unto the Consummation of the Age." (Hebrews 13:8; Matthew 28:20.) Because He is Unchangeable, and because He is present, in spirit, just as when in the flesh, He is the Healer of His people.

Divine Healing Rests on the Christ's Atonement.

It was prophesied of Him, "Surely He hath borne our griefs (Hebrew, *sickness*), and carried our sorrows: . . . and with His stripes we are healed;" and it is expressly declared that this was fulfilled in His Ministry of Healing, which still continues. (Isaiah 53:4, 5; Matthew 8:17.)

Disease Can Never be God's Will.

It is the Devil's work, consequent upon Sin, and it is impossible for the work of the Devil ever to be the Will of God. The Christ came to "destroy the works of the Devil," and when He was here on earth He healed "all manner of disease and all manner of sickness," and all these sufferers are expressly declared to have been "oppressed of the Devil." (1 John 3:8; Matthew 4:23; Acts 10:38.)

The Gifts of Healing Are Permanent.

It is expressly declared that the "Gifts and the calling of God are without repentance," and the Gifts of Healing are amongst the Nine Gifts of the Spirit to the Church. (Romans 11:29; 1 Corinthians 12:8-11.)

There Are Four Modes of Divine Healing.

The first is the direct prayer of faith; the second, intercessory prayer of two or more; the third, the anointing of the elders, with the prayer of faith; and the fourth, the laying on of hands of those who believe, and whom God has prepared and called to that Ministry. (Matthew 8:5-13; Matthew 18:19; James 5:14, 15; Mark 16:18.)

Divine Healing Is Opposed by Diabolical Counterfeits.

Amongst these are Christian Science (falsely so-called), Mind Healing, Spiritualism, Trance Evangelism, etc. (1 Timothy 6:20, 21; 1 Timothy 4:1, 2; Isaiah 51:22, 23.)

Multitudes Have Been Healed Through Faith in Jesus.

The writer knows of thousands of cases and has personally laid hands on scores of thousands of persons. Full information can be obtained at the meetings held in the Zion Tabernacles in Chicago, and in Zion City, Illinois, and in many pamphlets which give the experience, in their own words, of many who have been healed in this and other countries, published at Zion Printing and Publishing House, Zion City, Illinois.

"Belief Cometh of Hearing, and Hearing by the Word of the Christ."

You are heartily invited to attend and hear for yourself.

Zion Restoration Host

Elder A. F. LEE, Recorder

WE are pleased to introduce to readers of this issue of LEAVES OF HEALING a group of faithful Zion Restorationists who are working in Belfast, Ireland.

The picture which appears herewith, together with a very interesting account of their work, prepared by Deacon Cooper, the Officer in charge, was forwarded to us by Overseer Cantel.

Mr. Cooper's report reads as follows:

26 MALONE AVENUE, BELFAST, IRELAND,
April 15, 1904.

MY DEAR OVERSEER:—Peace to thee be multiplied.

As you have asked me to give you a résumé of the work done since coming here on the 12th of March, I now take much pleasure in doing so.

Before I begin, let me say that Miss E. L. Mackay, who started the meetings here fifteen months ago, carried on a real "work of faith and labor of love;" and, notwithstanding the fact that she suffered much opposition, abuse, persecution, and great sorrow, she held the fort nobly and well; and, in the midst of all these discouragements, she kept the Banner of Zion waving all the time.

If I were asked to preach a sermon on her, I would take for my text, "Many daughters have done virtuously, but thou excellest them all."

I was delighted to find a very loving, loyal, and faithful, though little, band of workers here, "full of faith and of the Holy Spirit," and "prepared unto every good work," for which I thanked God, took courage, and went forward.

I may say, as Paul said at Corinth, I came here "in weakness, and in fear, and in much trembling;" "but God has marvelously stood by us and strengthened us for good," confirming the Word by signs that followed.

After the second Lord's Day evening meeting, a young woman who suffered greatly from fits asked for prayer.

When she determined to abandon doctors and drugs altogether, and trust in God alone, we laid hands on her in the Name of Jesus, and in answer to "the Prayer of Faith" she has been wonderfully delivered, and kept by the power of God ever since. Truly, "the power of the Lord was present to heal." Others also have received the healing touch, for which we thank and praise God.

ZION RESTORATION HOST IN BELFAST, IRELAND.

We are glad to notice a steady increase in attendance at the meetings, and the interest which has been aroused for sometime deepening.

Most of all, we praise God for the sweet influence of the Holy Spirit at all the services, without which we could do nothing.

The Host work has been very encouraging, indeed; and, with very few exceptions, we have been well received at the homes of the people, and have had some very interesting interviews.

We find this work the most important of all, as

it is the only way to let the people know the truth about our beloved General Overseer, and the mighty work that God is doing through Zion's far reaching ministry; for, I am ashamed and sorry to say, the papers here, with one or two exceptions, have followed in the wake of the *American Cess-pool*, and misreported and misrepresented this good work in a shamefully wicked way, as will be seen by what Deaconess Gaston related to us, and which we quote here as an illustration of how the people are being deceived by a lying, secular, and so-called "religious" press:

"I called on Mrs. M——, who had known my parents and myself when I was a child.

"She was very glad to see me, and asked if I was taking a vacation.

"I replied, 'that had been my intention until I found that many of the people of this and other cities and towns, where I have been, are believing the newspaper reports about Zion and our beloved General Overseer. This being the condition of affairs, I feel that I must do something to reach as many people as possible and enlighten them as to the truth of this glorious work of God in Zion.'

"She became very much interested as I told her of the beautiful, happy City where I had spent one year and seven months, and of my relatives and friends, and of their happy homes and sweet, pure surroundings.

"She said, 'I am so glad to know that you have been well and happy, for I used to read the reports in the papers and think of and pity you, and wonder why you did not come back to your home, and get away from that place where the people are having to endure starvation and many other hardships. Now,' she said, 'I do not wonder at your wishing to get back to a City with such happy and prosperous surroundings.'

"She took a copy of the LEAVES, and asked me to be sure and call before returning to Zion City.

"This is one of scores of similar cases.

"This house-to-house visitation is a glorious work. God has wonderfully used our testimony to change the minds of the people regarding Zion, and they will not believe the newspapers any more."

We wish to say that Deaconess Gaston has been a very great help, and we thank God for sending her to Belfast.

The only thing we have to complain of is that her visits, like those of the angels, have been few and far between.

She is off again to Glarryford, her home, and we pray that God may greatly use her there in extending His Kingdom.

A little item regarding her work there will be of interest:

"A gentleman at whose home I called, by special invitation from his wife, who came several miles to see me, has since my visit to their home given up the use of tobacco and also intoxicating liquor. They are now arranging to sell their property and come with their children to Zion City."

The work in the saloons has been exceedingly interesting.

One man, whom I asked to buy a copy of LEAVES OF HEALING, said he believed "that Dr. Dowie was the biggest impostor that God ever put on this earth."

When asked, could he tell of one person upon whom he had imposed, he had to admit, after a few moments of dead silence, with shame and confusion of face, before them all, that he knew of none.

Another man told us that he heard Dr. Dowie in Madison Square Garden, and bought a copy of LEAVES OF HEALING.

On Easter Monday, five of us visited Lurgan, a town of nearly fifteen thousand inhabitants, ten miles from here, where there is a very strong feeling against our work, principally because of a modern Demetrius, who preaches to the Orangemen against Dr. Dowie, for he is greatly enraged at the way in which he speaks against secret societies, thereby bringing their craft into danger.

Notwithstanding all this, we had a very pleasant and profitable time.

Miss Mackay relates the following: "Deaconess Gaston and I had some very interesting experiences. The people on whom we called received us gladly, and thanked us as we gave the sweet salutation 'Peace be to this house.'

"One lady, who had read the LEAVES before, was delighted to see us, and bought a copy. She invited us in to have some refreshments, but we could not accept the invitation, as our time was limited. At parting, she asked us to call again the next time we visited Lurgan, as she would like to know more of Zion.

"We afterwards met a gentleman who had heard our beloved General Overseer in America, and was very much interested in the work. He was anxious to know if there was any truth in the newspaper reports about the bankruptcy of Zion. Deaconess Gaston, having been there during the difficulty, told him the truth, which he was pleased to hear. He bought three copies of LEAVES OF HEALING, and promised to come to our meetings in Belfast.

"In our visitation, we met many who were thirsty for the Full Gospel as it is taught in Zion. Truly, 'the harvest is great, but the laborers are few.' God is blessing our work and giving us great and lasting joy, for which we thank Him daily."

There was one street in particular which we were warned not to visit, as the residents were nearly all Roman Catholics, but we knew that that was the very place where we should go, so we did not heed the warning.

After two hours' work in a certain place, I discovered it was the very street we were told not to visit. I had a very profitable time in it.

One gentleman who came to the door said he objected to Dr. Dowie. When asked, Why? he replied, "Come in." After a twenty minutes' interview, in which his objections were stated and answered, a smile lit up his face, and he invested in a copy of LEAVES OF HEALING, and then we knelt in prayer.

In the same street that Satan did not want us to visit, a policeman and his wife, who are earnest Christians, asked me in, and showed me their baby boy, who was dying. After telling them that it was not God's will that the child should die, and reading a portion of the Inspired Word, we knelt at the bedside in prayer and laid on hands. Three days later I received a letter saying the baby was "improving every day," to the great delight of the parents.

There are many other tokens of God's blessing that we could record, but I am afraid we must put on the brake, or you will never ask me to write another account.

While writing this, another letter has come, saying the "baby is all right again."

In four weeks, with an average of six workers, we have visited one thousand one hundred forty-six homes, given eight hundred thirteen Messages and eighteen copies of LEAVES OF HEALING, and sold three hundred twenty-six copies of LEAVES OF HEALING.

In the same time, with an average of four workers, we have visited eighty-five saloons, given eleven copies of LEAVES OF HEALING, and sold two hundred eighty-two.

We pray that God may greatly bless this good seed that has been sown.

We are sure of a great harvest; already there have been showers of blessing, and "there is the sound of abundance of rain."

All this is the outcome of our General Overseer's visit to this city, three years and six months ago.

With a heart overflowing with joy and gratitude to God for sending me to this corner of His vineyard, and with best Christian love and greetings, I am, faithfully yours in the everlasting bonds of Zion,

ANTHONY C. HERRING COOPER,
Deacon in the Christian Catholic Church in Zion

Restoration Work in Switzerland.

The following report, recently received from Deaconess Baliff, of Zürich, proves that faithful work is being done by members of Zion Restoration Host in that part of the Master's vineyard.

The report reads as follows:

SWITZERLAND.	No. of Workers	No. of Calls	Messages Given	Leaves Given
February	49	3792	4180	157
March	41	3365	3354	106
April	36	2420	2639	122
May	35	2250	2739	64
Total	161	11827	12912	449

Restoration Work at World's Fair, St. Louis, Missouri.

About the first of June, Messrs. John Taylor and Gustav Sigwalt were sent from Zion City to St. Louis, Missouri, where they were assigned to special Restoration work among the visitors at the Exposition.

Vast quantities of literature have been sent them, and they report that it is being most eagerly sought for by the people, who are very desirous of getting the facts concerning the work of Zion. Many have since visited Zion City, and have expressed their surprise and delight at what they have seen.

Following is a tabulated report received from these workers, telling of the amount of literature distributed during the month of June:

ST. LOUIS, MO.	Houses Called at	Messages Given	Leaves Given	Leaves Sold	Banners Given	Other Literature Given
June	2974	11680	2586	60	435	821

Reports from Various Points.

Following is a tabulated report of the number of workers and the work done by them during the month of June, 1904, according to reports received to date from the various points named:

UNITED STATES.	No. of Workers	No. of Calls	Messages Given	Leaves Sold	Leaves Given
California—					
Fresno	6	397	397	47	20
Haywards	1	3	4	....	8
Los Angeles	13	1000	2636	63	334
Maxwell	2	....	5	....	20
Parlier	1	123	165	21	18
San Francisco	16	3000	3000	1050	20
Santa Rosa	1	51	21		64
St. John	1	37	60	...	32
Colorado—					
Durango	2	177	177	....	16
Trinidad	2	145	177	17	13
Connecticut—					
Danbury	1	30	42	....	35
Meriden	1	70	72	2	9
Illinois—					
Chicago—South Parish	43	3700	3520	492	1318
" Southeast Parish	21	2463	6110	520	224
" North Parish	39	2572	2604	151	401
" West Parish	30	2794	2941	215	456
" West Parish, Ger.	13	619	671	50	94
" Northwest Parish	11	447	477	19	122
Clyde	2	50	63	9	44

UNITED STATES.	No. of Workers	No. of Calls	Messages Given	Leaves Sold	Leaves Given
Illinois—					
Evanston	2	108	14	18	143
Highland Park	2	260	1987	5	11
Libertyville	1	...	122	2	4
Mazon	1	4	16	...	4
Odell	1	11	5	1	14
Pontiac	3	240	....	55	374
Richmond	1	26	36	4	7
Vermilion Grove	1	100	114	....	20
Waukegan	224	4026	4392	436	191
Indiana—					
Albion	2	2	5	....	43
Indianapolis	6	228	1035	90	63
Lafayette	4	203	676	39	59
Linn Grove	1	5	....	...	20
Monon	1	185	259	....	20
Plymouth	3	5	39	....	11
Sweetser	1	....	33	....	9
Walton	8	217	83	62	75
Iowa—					
Cedar Falls	2	98	267	33	11
Elberon	2	36	31	13	23
Forest City	1	...	370	37	38
Laporte City	1	9	1	6	5
Newton	1	25	25	25	....
Rock Valley	1	148	660	41	28
Tipton	4	26	72	...	54
Washington	3	....	241	....	14
Webster City	4	58	96	4	53
Kansas—					
Eskridge	1	52	14	30	10
Independence	4	50	130	11	38
Manhattan	2	26	85	10	13
Salina	4	50	340	....	25
Kentucky—					
Danville	1	1	67	...	9
Massachusetts—					
Boston	23	4287	3218	1876	445
Lawrence	12	600	610	276	470
North Duxbury	2	....	....	..	50
Michigan—					
Benton Harbor	7	407	425	200	100
Detroit	8	900	988	161	124
Ingalls	1	7	28	2	.
Manistee	1	...	7	....	11
Port Huron	6	100	249	62	21
Republic	1	4	7	18	3
Sault Ste. Marie	4	226	188	93	38
Minnesota—					
Delavan	1	20	17	....	26
Minneapolis	6	589	1266	194	59
Moorhead	1	18	38	....	1
Missouri—					
Higginsville	2	599	631	97	38
Montana—					
Havre	1	9	9	...	29
Nebraska—					
Falls City	1	...	18	42	10
Inman	1	5	22	....	1
Republican City	1	8	110	....	20
New Jersey—					
Salem	1	75	85	16	66
New York—					
Bluff Point	1	3	8	....	8
New York City	30	1987	11388	415	923
Poland	1	...	10	....	10
Ohio—					
Ada	3	38	15	7	3
Akron	3	30	132	61	120
Alliance	1	....	187	..	28
Bluffton	2	80	166	43	4
Cincinnati	41	2477	4627	414	1154
Cleveland	25	2798	4401	140	363
Dayton	3	82	416	22	24
Germantown	1	132	172	29	19
Lancaster	1	1	193	7	2
Lebanon	1	150	....	37	2
Mansfield	1	....	89	...	4
Nevada	1	....	13	..	7
Oceola	1	4	95	..	16
Urbana	1	3	8	....	6
Oregon—					
Astoria	1	....	33	2	31
Pennsylvania—					
Coatesville	2	...	590	32	....
New Brighton	1	14	14	....	13
Philadelphia	34	3783	20662	330	859
Souderton	1	...	82	...	24
Turtle Creek	2	2	618	79	22
West Chester	2	635	1030	106	....
South Dakota—					
Belle	1	....	..	....	60
Brookings	1	90	79	20	11
Summit	1	19	25	5	2
Tennessee—					
Memphis	1	7	142	....	14
Texas—					
Austin	1	80	122	12	37
Dallas	2	81	84	167	29
Houston	1	8	73	..	31
Luling	1	4	14	....	6
Paris	1	2	6	.	6
San Antonio	....	600	66	104	358
Washington—					
Badger	2	....	....	....	40
Clinton	1	51	158	9	31
Easton	1	138	138	23	25
Everett	2	192	192	32	39
Garfield	1	...	624	....	25
Lynden	3	11	....	....	70
Seattle	22	1958	1927	569	155
Spokane	9	2325	2015	287	176
Tacoma	....	367	....	42	60
Wisconsin—					
Alma	1	6	2	1	10
Black Creek	1	31	75	....	14
Kenosha	12	697	1717	183	77
Maiden Rock	2	13	38	12	28
Marinette	11	829	2700	111	184
Milwaukee	9	745	1940	191	100
Omro	3	148	153	16	80
Racine	2	36	67	10	20
Viroqua	3	70	132	23	10
West Ellis	1	....	25	....	41
Total	841	52458	100336	10138	11500

DOMINION OF CANADA AND CONTINENTS.	No. of Workers	No. of Calls	Messages Given	Leaves Sold	Leaves Given
Australia—					
Sydney	30	4086	337	66	76
Canada—					
Galt	2	37	45	....	38
Simcoe	2	97	83	87	4
Toronto	17	3143	7782	362	927
Vancouver	20	875	976	69	450
Victoria	2	243	179	65	60
Woodstock	1	104	69	39	37
Total	74	8585	9471	688	1592
Grand Total	915	61043	109807	10826	13092

NOTES OF THANKSGIVING FROM THE WHOLE WORLD

By OVERSEER J. G. EXCELL.

Saved of Drunkenness, Murder, and Suicide Through "Leaves of Healing."

I have blotted out, as a thick cloud, thy transgressions, . . . return unto Me; for I have redeemed thee.—*Isaiah 44:22.*

2 AZAMOR STREET, SHANKILL ROAD,
BELFAST, IRELAND, March, 1904.

DEAR GENERAL OVERSEER:—Peace to thee.

In spite of home influence, where the Bible was read, I was early found in sin, and grew up into infidelity and all its accompanying evils.

I was converted in 1893, through the Faith Mission, in Scotland.

Previously to this I had become connected with secretism, in the form of the Loyal Orange and Royal Black Institutions.

I left them at my conversion, but was induced to rejoin some eight months later, after the occurrence of one of their great annual processions.

It was then that I was led away by their influence into a path which almost landed me into death and hell.

On one occasion we drove eight miles to the "Black" Lodge, and, when half way there, a halt was called at a public house.

As I still kept up a profession of Christianity, and took no strong drink, I joined the company with what was called a temperance beverage—a sort of bitters.

This gave me cramp, and, when we arrived at the lodge, which was in a room above a public house, I was induced to "take a little wine for my stomach's sake."

The so-called wine given me was brandy, the distilled fire of wine.

I reached home on Sunday morning, almost helplessly drunk.

From this time I dropped all profession of Christianity, and went headlong into sin.

I became a Freemason through the influence of some companions of the Black Institution, and it was just a step deeper.

I found these three institutions followed each other in order of depravity.

I pursued this course from July, 1894, to some time in 1900 (in addition to almost two years before my conversion) and during those last six years the spirit of immorality gained its utmost possession of me.

In 1900, I learned of an affair which made me indulge in most intense hatred to a certain person, whom I determined to murder, and then to commit suicide.

I carried a revolver in one side pocket, a bottle of poison in the other, and a bottle of whisky in my breast pocket, in order that I might carry out my determination.

In this condition, when on the verge of despair, I came across LEAVES OF HEALING. I read it and was convicted of my sins.

A strong desire to repent and be saved was awakened within me, but Satan worried me with a terrible sense of wrong and kept suggesting revenge.

I had not obtained the spirit of readiness to forgive, though I wanted to be forgiven.

I wrote a full confession to you, and asked you to pray for me.

Gradually the battle became a victory for God.

I am now ready to forgive.

I saw you in the Ulster Hall some time after I had written to you, in 1900, but had not an opportunity of saying who I was, or how I was progressing.

In 1902, I accepted fully your Declaration that you came as Elijah to restore All Things.

In fact I saw it before the Declaration was made, and I was glad that you took your stand so firmly. It encourages us to go on.

I wish to state that all you have said about Freemasonry and other forms of secretism is true.

I have also been healed of disease. I got a troublesome ringworm from some cattle. It grew the size of the palm of my hand. I was told it would spread over my whole body if I did not get something to rub on to kill it.

I wrote to Evangelist (now Overseer) Cantel for prayer.

God heard and answered. My skin, where the ringworm had been, soon became as clean as an infant's.

I rubbed nothing on it, not even oil to soothe the itch. A clean linen cloth to keep it from infecting my clothes, was all I put over it.

I give God all the glory.

Thanking God with all my heart for the great blessing He has made you and LEAVES OF HEALING to me, I remain,

Faithfully yours in Christ Jesus,
ARCHIBALD MCKANE.

Healed of an Attack of Quinsy.

Fear thou not, for I am with thee; be not dismayed for I am thy God: I will strengthen thee; yea, I will help thee.—*Isaiah 41:10.*

CEDAR FALLS, IOWA, June 22, 1904.

DEAR OVERSEER:—Peace to thee!

It is with a grateful heart that I write these few lines to tell of the blessing I received June 7th, after we had sent a telegram, asking prayer for myself, for I was very sick with quinsy.

My body had begun to grow cold at the time we sent the dispatch.

One-half hour later, I felt a sensation of life flow through my body, and I began to perspire very freely, and a little later the gathering in my throat broke.

June 9th, I was well enough to do my Restoration work, walking a distance of four miles.

I thank you for your prayers, and praise God and give Him all the glory.

May God bless you and yours, and Zion throughout the world.

I am, faithfully yours for the Master's use,
(MRS.) M. LARSON.

THE REV. JOHN ALEXANDER DOWIE,
General Overseer of the Christian Catholic Church in Zion.

Zion's Fourth Feast of Tabernacles

The Set Feasts of Jehovah . . .
Ye shall proclaim to be Holy Convocations.

ZION'S ANNUAL BUSINESS CONFERENCES.

REPORTED BY A. C. R., O. R., S. E. C., O. L. S., AND F. A. F.

Thursday Afternoon Conference.

A Conference of Zion's Business Institutions was conducted by the General Overseer on Thursday and Friday, July 21 and 22, 1904—the Great Annual Business Conferences that are now recognized as such a valuable part of the Program of Zion's Feast of Tabernacles.

On the first occasion, the General Overseer occupied about three hours with a very frank, and careful, yet enthusiastic description of Zion's financial resources and prospects.

But in the midst of it all, there were frequent outbreaks of his consuming zeal for the spiritual advancement of Zion, and of that larger view which, while conserving the interests of the first Zion City, looks beyond to the establishment of other Zion Communities and Cities, as well as to the Restoration of the City of the Great King—Jerusalem—the Future Capital on Earth of the King of kings in Person, throughout the Millennium.

The Second Meeting was addressed by several of the General Managers of the great Financial, Commercial, and Industrial Enterprises of Zion.

Much of what was said, naturally enough, was not intended for publication.

But it is an open secret that the "inside information" is of such a nature as to warrant the most optimistic expectations for future successes and growth.

The attendance at both these conferences was very large, the interest intense, and the enthusiasm of the people keen.

The splendid progress and prospects of the material side of the Kingdom of God rejoiced the hearts of all the many thousands of Zion who know the truth that "Where God rules, man prospers."

Shiloh Tabernacle, Zion City, Illinois, Thursday Afternoon, July 21, 1904.

The service was opened by the singing of Hymn No. 31, in the Special Program:

Zion stands with hills surrounded
Zion, kept by power Divine;
All her foes shall be confounded,
Though the world in arms combine:
Happy Zion,
What a favored lot is thine.

The General Overseer then offered prayer, closing by uniting with the Congregation in chanting the Disciples' Prayer.

He then called upon Deacon William S. Peckham, Cashier of Zion City Bank, to read the 60th and 61st chapters of Isaiah.

Before the reading, the General Overseer said:

I will have him read the two chapters, as they should go together.

They are the Glory Chapters in the Prophetic Vision of Zion.

They show us what Zion is going to be in these Latter Days.

I love to read them.

Sometimes, when I am in the darkness or traveling, I repeat them from beginning to end.

It is a good thing to have the cashier of Zion Bank read the Bible. He knows a good deal about it.

He is also an eloquent reader of the Bible.

Zion's Blessings for "The Peoples" of the Earth.

Deacon Peckham then began the reading of the chapters mentioned. When he came to the words:

For, behold, darkness shall cover the earth, and gross darkness the peoples,

The General Overseer said:

I want you to grasp the fact that in the Revised Version it is "the Peoples."

It is such a grand thing to feel that while "darkness covers the earth," it is to all "the Peoples" of the earth that Zion's blessings are coming,

The Deacon then read without comment the remainder of the two chapters.

A GENERAL VIEW OF ZION'S BUSINESS PROGRESS AND PROSPECTS.

The General Overseer then pronounced the

INVOCATION.

Let the words of my mouth and the meditation of my heart be acceptable in Thy sight, and profitable unto this people, O Lord, my Strength and my Redeemer.

Beloved friends, I suppose that the best way for us to open this Conference is for me, as General Overseer, and the one legally responsible for everything in Zion, to make a General Statement to you.

I have been thinking a good deal about this Conference, and it seemed to me that if we were to endeavor, even, to read to you figures in detail, we would drive you away; because they are so enormous in extent.

Moreover, we still pursue the policy that we inaugurated at the very beginning—that of assuming the responsibility of not making statements that might embarrass Zion.

It is very desirable for us to keep some things, at least for a time.

I am bursting with desire to let you know all that is wise for you to know, and my danger is that I might say, in some things, too much, not too little.

I shall, however, keep back nothing that your interest requires me to speak.

Gratitude for Confidence of Investors.

I thank God, I thank you, and I thank the thousands of investors who are not here for the confidence reposed in me.

We carry in the Bank no less than Seven Thousand Accounts.

ADMINISTRATION BUILDING ZION CITY, ILLINOIS.

If we were to show a banker the growth of this Bank, he would scarcely believe it; and if I were to prophesy to you what this Bank will be at some time in the future you would scarcely believe it.

I have a large interest in the Bank, because, as it happens,

I hold a very large portion of the stock, personally, or as Trustee.

I am thankful that I hold a great amount of personal stock in the Bank, and that I have perfect confidence in this Institution.

I have a larger interest in the Bank than any fifty of you, and that is one of the foundation features of the work.

I would like to see the Bank strengthened.

It needs capital.

The work is growing at such a rate that it requires larger capital to do the rapidly growing business properly.

The Beginnings of Zion Business Institutions.

Zion City Bank and Zion Land and Investment Association were the first Institutions that we established.

We established them simultaneously in March, 1899.

These accounts are from San Francisco to New York, and not only in this country, but from Canada; and there are people in many countries in Europe, in India, and in many other parts of the world who have open accounts with us.

Zion Financial Institutions for All the World.

On my Around-the-World Visitation, in many places the question was asked, "General Overseer, are you going to establish Financial Institutions in Australia, in India, and in Europe?"

I answered, "Yes, they are coming." And I may add that we now have sent Financial Agents from Headquarters to Europe and Africa.

Deacon John W. Innes left only this morning to be Financial Representative of all Zion's Institutions in Great Britain and Ireland, with Headquarters in London. Elder Percy Clibborn

SHILOH HOUSE, PRESENT RESIDENCE OF THE GENERAL OVERSEER IN ZION CITY.

This house was designed by Zion Architects and built, throughout, by Zion Construction Department.

Five years and four months ago I gathered together a few thousand dollars and made my deposit.

I was the first depositor, Mrs. Dowie was the next, and my family and many dear personal friends in Zion followed.

From the day that our Bank was established, in March, 1899, until now, we have handled many millions of dollars.

You can well imagine that there has been some business done.

We have, of course, had a constant flow of business, and the fact that we now have seven thousand accounts will show you something of the proportions of that business.

similarly represents us on the Continent of Europe, with Headquarters at Zürich, Switzerland. Deacon Nicholas B. Rideout represents us in Africa, with Headquarters at Johannesburg, Transvaal. Deacon George A. Corlette is Special Agent for the Eastern States, with Headquarters at the Fuller Building (known as the Flatiron Building), corner of Fifth avenue, Broadway, and Twenty-third street, in the City of New York.

All these have my fullest confidence, and intending investors can be assured that these brethren are finely-trained business men, with personal knowledge of Zion's affairs, competent to give information and good counsel and such help as is within their power, in connection with local estates, etc.

This system will be extended all over the world in due time, and, probably, Zion Banks will be established on every Continent as one result of the labors of these Financial Agents.

A very bright banker in Zürich, whose father had been a banker, attended all my meetings in Zürich.

He was one of those bright, big-brained business men that one likes to see in a meeting—clean-cut, with the look of generations of honest Christian business men in his face.

He was a good man, too, for his father was as pious as he was shrewd, and carried a Bible in his pocket.

He was not ashamed to have it by his side in the bank.

This gentleman attended our meetings in Zürich.

There were more people present at the Business Conference in Zürich than there are here today.

That, in one way, is a compliment to us, for the people at our Headquarters here in Zion City say, "Oh, well, it is all right; the Financial Institutions are in good hands; we can go on and attend to our work;" and they do not bother about coming in large numbers to these Business Conferences.

If my people in Zion City experienced any anxiety, this place would be crowded.

Large Values in Zürich Conference for Investment in Zion.

I convened a Business Conference in Zürich on June 6th last—just about six weeks ago.

I felt, from what they told me, that the time had come for a very plain talk about finance.

The hall was nearly filled, as Evangelist Hodler, who is present here today, knows: for she was one of my translators on that occasion.

The banker of whom I have spoken came to me at the close.

He knew Zürich from A to Z.

He said, in effect, words like these, "There is a wonderful power about you and Zion! Why," he continued, "this afternoon you have had four hundred fifty people, of whom at least three hundred fifty have risen up to say that they will put all their investments in Zion, whether they come to Zion City or not."

He told me that these people represented considerable values.

Of course it will take a little time for those people to realize on their properties.

Thanking you, thanking Zion everywhere, and thanking the thousands of investors in the Land and Investment Association, in the Bank, and in the Industries, for the confidence reposed in me, I will now say something about the General Business of Zion City since we met here one year ago.

Enormous Demand for Building at the Beginning of the Year.

The business of the last year began very well; but we had been building at such a tremendous rate that we scarcely knew where we were. We had to build.

People came in upon us and demanded houses.

Some were able to pay for them at once; others, who were not able, we had to help.

One of our difficulties was that we had just inaugurated a new Building Association and that private contracting had been done away with by common consent, after full consideration.

We are very well satisfied with the principles upon which that Association was established. We organized it in April, last year, a few months before the Feast of Tabernacles.

We called it Zion Building and Manufacturing Association.

The Building and Manufacturing Association appeals to those who can think deeply into things.

The stock now pays eight per-cent. dividend; next March it will begin to pay nine per cent., and we hope very soon that we shall be able to divide a surplus of profits amongst the workmen and the investors, in accordance with the Agreement into which I have entered with the shareholders.

At the beginning, there is naturally a little difficulty in adjusting some things, but we have found this Association to be a complete solution of the Contractor Difficulty.

Contractors who had very little interest in Zion and very little capital, came in here, and we had practically to carry them by using the funds of the Bank.

SOME ZION CITY RESIDENCES.

I need not remind you at any length of the painful incident that caused me to call the people together.

They were all of one heart and mind in settling forever the petty contractors who were underbidding, and scheming, and "cutting each other's throats" in a business way, and often doing poor work.

Houses were built by contractors that looked very well, but when we had to finish them, as we often did, we found that the contractor, if he had made any profit, made it at the expense of our people—in bad material and bad workmanship.

Difficulty Caused by an Unexpected Rush of Business.

The work of the Association became something tremendous.

I have not the figures here, but, literally, within the first two or three months, hundred upon hundreds of houses, and extensions, and finishings, came into Deacon Harper's hands, so that we had something over five hundred contracts upon our hands within a very short time.

That, with the tremendous amount of general business, came upon us, and we had a little difficulty in being able to stagger along under such an unexpected increase—the prosperity of our business as builders was a burden almost too great for our strength and immediate resources.

One of the difficulties was that such large numbers of people wanted to build at once.

They came down upon our Cashier, Deacon Peckham, for half a million of United States gold coin per month; and any banker will tell you that such a sum is a big business in a little town like this.

We certainly did some splendid building, and some of our public buildings show it.

We finished four school buildings, and later the first section of Zion College Building and other important buildings, such as Zion Printing and Publishing House, were begun.

There are very few places three years old that can show accommodations for two thousand pupils, which is the number we have on the roll of our Educational Institutions, and few that can show so fine a plant, and so good a building, as we can in Zion Printing and Publishing House.

That Building and Manufacturing Association is a wonderful Institution.

Zion Civic Parade each year is the best demonstration of Zion as a Business Institution.

It is a Panorama! It was a wonderful sight which was shown here a few days ago.

I want to get you interested, because many of you are representative people from many parts of the land.

Zion Building and Manufacturing Association the Key to Many Industries.

It requires a little time to get an Association of this kind well established.

There is no question, however, that the principles upon which this Association has been established are so sound, that they will constitute the Key with which we shall be able to unlock door after door of more Industries for Zion.

We do all the Construction of the City streets.

We do the building of the Public Institutions, and of all private houses.

We make brick.

We make doors and sash, fine book-cases, etc.

We make soap, and a great variety of things.

Some day, not far distant, we will have a Zion Piano and Organ Factory, and the music of Zion will float over the world.

Of course, we have to prepare carefully for these things.

The True Value of Zion City Real Estate.

I go back for a few minutes to the Land and Investment Association.

After all, the true test of the value of land, whether it be a farm or city property, is what it is worth after sufficient time has elapsed to remove it from the possibility of boom.

You can boom agricultural land far above its value, and you can boom city land far above its value, by processes that are shameful and illegitimate.

Zion has done none of these things.

We have never had land sales, with brass bands, and liquor flowing.

We have never given premiums to people to induce them to buy.

We have said, "There it is! 'You can take it or leave it!

"We have named the price It is God's land 'in perpetuity,' and we shall only lease it to you for a century and a millennium—eleven hundred years—and only upon condition that you, and those who follow you, keep the covenants."

I remember when the land was first offered, some of our friends, not seeing what Zion was destined to become, thought it was pretty stiff for the General Overseer to ask at the rate of three thousand dollars an acre—and a little more, perhaps.

It had cost me two hundred dollars, on the average.

I said to them, "Think what we are doing; we are giving you streets, parks, and sidewalks; and we are planning schools and advantages."

Still it looked to be a high price.

I said again, "The land that you buy now at three thousand dollars an acre is dirt cheap.

"It is cheap dirt, and if you do not take it you will regret it; because it will be gone, and you will not be able to get it."

It was gone in a week!

"Oh, but that was a boom!"

Was it a boom?

Then the boom has gone on.

Elder Dinius is an investor in Edina boulevard.

He paid six hundred dollars for a lot

Now, I will take an honest man like him and appeal to his knowledge of his own locality.

Elder Dinius, for what sum have you known land to sell, near you, that cost five hundred dollars?

Elder Dinius—"From one thousand two hundred dollars to one thousand four hundred dollars. They are now asking one thousand five hundred fifty dollars."

General Overseer—The fact of the matter is, that land which we sold at the rate of three thousand dollars an acre has risen to more than six thousand dollars an acre.

Tremendous Permanent Increase in Land Values.

How about the whole City?

The ratio of increase has not everywhere been the same, but Deacon Judd informs me that the average of increase is fully eighty per cent., although some portions have reached two hundred per cent.

Elder Dinius—"A man bought a lot just off the playground of the schoolhouse for four hundred fifty dollars, and he refused two thousand three hundred fifty dollars for it."

General Overseer—Well that was four hundred per cent. increase—five times as much as he paid for it. Now, I do not want to say that all the land could be sold at an increase like that.

I am talking about the general value of the land; and I want to tell you that the value of the land that you bought, and that I hold for Zion, has increased to such an extent, that the price we received from the Chicago & Milwaukee Electric Railroad Company a few months ago is a fair test

Mr. Frost, its president, is a shrewd and able business man

He is the possessor of a large capital, and he is backed by Canadian capitalists.

They do not pay more for land than it is worth.

A railway company has great powers.

A railway company can force a sale.

The courts are always more or less favorable to the railways.

They say that their action is in the interests of the people.

After consulting all the land records, and consulting with his friends, and looking into the matter, Mr. Frost paid, for thirty-three and two-thirds (33⅔) acres, one hundred one thousand dollars ($101,000); and I am bound to tell you that it did not cost us five thousand dollars ($5,000).

The price we charged was really one-half the present value of some of the land in that locality, although it was twenty times more than we paid for it.

Deacon Judd, have we not leased some land in that neighborhood at the rate of seven thousand dollars an acre?

Deacon Judd—"Yes, and it was quarter of a mile west of the land we sold to Mr. Frost."

General Overseer—I will admit that I have leased some land on one of the big boulevards of Zion City at the rate of ten thousand dollars an acre.

I let Mr. Frost through at three thousand dollars an acre.

What for?

Because the railway is going to develop that land.

I believe that the land west of that railway to the City

boundary is now worth many hundreds of dollars an acre more than it was—in fact, thousands.

I believe that every acre of that land has an average value of four thousand dollars.

Resources of Zion City Lake Front Land.

Now come to the East Side.

The Golden Cup of Zion is in the Lake Front.

That is our Bonanza.

It is bigger in value than all the rest; and we have not tried to dispose of a foot of it.

One of these days we will bring in the sand-sucker and cut a hole, a thousand feet in diameter, in the Lake Front.

We will suck out the sand and run it over into the other side, thus bringing it up to datum.

Perhaps we will take out the peat first and make, some say, a million dollars out of that.

We are now making experiments with it.

We have a vast amount of peat there, which will make magnificent fuel.

We have many good things hidden in this soil.

For instance, in places underneath the white sand of the Lake Front we have a deposit of iron sand of considerable depth.

No man knows how much there is; there may be more than a million dollars' worth there.

We have black sand containing, perhaps, twenty-five per cent. iron.

Just think of every pound of that sand containing a quarter of a pound of iron.

I do not know how many pounds there are; no one can tell, but you may depend upon it, that if there is any money to be got from it, we will some day get it for God and Zion.

One of these days we will build a pier into Lake Michigan and bring our ships into Zion City harbor.

We have deep water within three hundred feet of the shore, making it possible to construct piers between which the largest lake craft can float into our port.

Potential Value of Zion City Lake Front Real Estate.

We also have hundreds of thousands of dollars' worth of torpedo sand along our Lake Front of two and a half miles, that we can dispose of.

We have to watch now to keep pirates from stealing it.

They have come in the night with steam tugs and taken a whole barge full and sneaked off with it.

I do not think they do that as much as they used to, but they did it at the beginning.

Let me tell you that that Lake Front south of the Boulevard is for our manufactories and industries, and by and by that portion north of the Boulevard will be occupied by residences.

If we build it up to good datum and build a lake shore drive, and connect it with our park system, we will very soon make that Lake Front, which is now such a desert, and for which we paid only five hundred dollars an acre, worth more than ten thousand dollars an acre very soon.

I would not begin to think of parting with it at that price, and, in fact, it is not for lease at all. Zion will need it all one day.

I want to show, by these few words and facts, that if you were to correctly estimate the present value of the land which you helped me buy and which I hold for Zion—after taking out the streets, and alleys, and other reservations for public uses—you would find that the land remaining is worth at least twenty-six million dollars.

Cut that amount fifty per cent., and consider it as being worth only thirteen million dollars. What a tremendous increase it is!

A Gain of Two Thousand Per Cent.

We made two thousand per cent. on one strip!

All that the Parable promises is that the one talent shall become ten, but God has been so good to us that in three years this one land talent has become twenty.

That does not take into consideration the value of Zion's other estates.

I do not hesitate to say that Zion Lace Industries are worth at the present moment more than five million dollars.

But there is scarcely any price that could be offered that would buy them.

All the initial difficulties have been overcome, and it is admitted by experts that we are up to the standard of any lace factory of its kind in the world.

We have done better—we have outdone the Nottingham lace manufacturer at his own business.

I could list Zion Lace Securities on the market as an Incorporated Industrial Stock; but I do not wish to do so; we have never placed any Zion Stocks on the Stock Market.

Nobody can play "battledore and shuttlecock" on the Stock Exchanges with Zion Stocks.

Nobody can "bull" or "bear" them.

Not one dollar's worth of Zion Stock has been sold at a discount.

Not one has been sold for less than its face value of one hundred cents on the dollar.

Two Zion Stocks Being Sold at a Premium.

Two Zion Stocks are now one hundred ten.

Lace Stock is one hundred ten and Bank Stock is one hundred ten; that is to say, we are getting one hundred ten dollars for each hundred-dollar share.

The people are buying it at that price.

Look at the price of National Bonds on the British Stock Market, today.

Why, the tumble is tremendous!

Three per cent. Consolidated Annuities, generally called Consols, were quoted at one hundred thirteen, before the Boer War.

Recently they were quoted at eighty-five. (On August 17th they were quoted by cable from London at a fraction above eighty-eight.)

That is a pretty big tumble.

I have just sent Deacon John Innes, one of our bright financiers, to England, as agent of Zion Financial and Commercial Institutions, to advise my people in Great Britain to get out, and to get out quickly.

I think I am right.

Look at the difference in conditions between this little Zion's Stocks, and the Consols of the mighty British Empire.

We have been battered and fought, and everything possible has been done to break us down, both in England and America.

What is the result?

Today we stand stronger than ever before.

British Consols have fallen twenty-eight—Zion stocks have never fallen a cent, and some have risen to a premium of ten per cent.

I am grateful to God for His goodness.

A Review of the Present Condition of Zion Lace Industries.

Let me, in this review, touch upon the present condition of Zion Lace Industries.

I hope you have been down to look at that factory.

You ought to go before returning home, that you may be able to confirm what even our British friends themselves admit—that while ours is far ahead of the ordinary factory, the very best and most recent factories are not better than ours.

You will ask, "how could you get ahead of those countries that have been so long at it?"

Because God has blessed us with ability to put together a factory where we have everything under one roof, and with good workmen and workwomen, and up-to-date methods.

In Nottingham it takes three, four, and sometimes five or more roofs to cover one plant.

They have been clever and bright, but not large enough in their conceptions.

Then we do by electricity what they do by steam.

We make a surer twist, break fewer threads, and produce better work.

I know these things because I have been personally submitting our lace to tests in England, France, Switzerland, and Germany.

I took it with me around the world during this year, submitting it to bright people, who have been selling laces all their lives.

Wanted to be Zion's Industrial Agents.

You should have seen the eagerness of a member of one of the largest firms of lace importers in Australia, when he and his principal buyer had seen our beautiful display of Zion Laces.

He wanted his firm to be our Australian agents.

"No," I said, "we cannot supply even the American market.

"Whenever we have supplied that, we will come to you."

When we showed our laces in the banqueting-room of Adelaide City Hall, we covered the walls of that room with our laces, and I watched the people as they looked at them.

The Australian people understand laces, because they wear them. The ladies were enraptured with them.

These laces were submitted to experts all over the world.

ZION LACE INDUSTRIES' BUILDING.

Amongst these was one of the most famous dressmakers in Paris.

She is a personal friend and a good woman.

She was charmed with our lace, and said to me, "Doctor, you have a gold mine there! I do not know how you could have such excellent designs without being in touch with us in Paris."

Zion Lace Industries Running Three Shifts Each Day.

Some machines in Zion Lace Industries run more than twenty hours every day, with three shifts of workmen.

Is not that proof enough that Zion laces are being sold?

We do not sell to the wholesalers. We sell to the big retailers and save that profit.

We offered it to the wholesale trade, and they insulted us by offering a ridiculous price.

We sell laces from San Francisco to New York, and from New Orleans to the borders of Canada.

When we get into Canada we have to deal with Great Britain.

Elder Simmons—[From Vancouver, British Columbia.] "General Overseer, in Vancouver, we get lace curtains from Zion City."

General Overseer—I am glad to hear that they sell even there, where there is no protective duty.

Let me further say that the future of Zion Lace Industries means that if we can capture one-half of the lace trade of the United States, it will probably be necessary to make twenty or thirty million dollars' worth a year.

SAMPLES OF ZION LACE PATTERNS.

Large Profits in Lace Making.

"What is the profit?" Well, I will not give the figures publicly, for that would not be good policy; but I will say that the percentage of profits is such that I believe that, if we can secure the necessary capital, etc., before very many years have passed, Zion Lace Industries will be making for Zion ten million dollars a year.

Would not that give us money for God's work for building up Zion and extending the Kingdom of God over all the earth?

You had better help me to get machinery enough to make that ten million dollars a year.

I cannot make it now—I have not the machinery.

But we know we can do it; for we are doing a splendid business now.

Zion has to get the best, and we are getting the very best machines that can be made.

Many New Machines Contracted For.

I may say that this year we are contracting for twelve new machines, and that we are already running eighteen machines; so that this year we shall hope to either set up, or have on the way to be set up, thirty machines, thus nearly doubling the output.

Some of the new machines will make lace very much wider than that made by those we now have.

We have been using machines that make lace one hundred eighty-two inches wide; some of the new machines will make a width of two hundred twenty-two inches.

Our manager says that we have practically doubled the output during the past year.

Then give me more capital and I will make more lace, pay our people a large return, and make millions for God.

I shall, God willing, nearly double the output this year, and I want to double that next year.

I want to have sixty machines by this time next year, either in or on the way.

The following year I want one hundred twenty machines; following that, two hundred forty.

I want to build factory after factory until I reach that Lake Shore.

That will require a population in Zion City of over one hundred thousand people. After paying interest on the capital we will be able to make for Zion millions of dollars a year.

God's Guidance Recognized in Zion's Commercial Affairs.

I believe that God guided me in establishing these Industries

We have a tariff of sixty-five per cent. in our favor.

We also can save all the expense of sending buyers abroad

Take ten dollars' worth of lace made in Europe and you can easily add one hundred fifty per cent. to cover duties and charges.

The wholesaler has to pay sixty-five per cent. duty, a large sum to his buyer, a large sum for getting the lace together, and packing it, and taking risks, so that you could not put the additional cost to the wholesaler at less than one hundred per cent.

I believe from what I have been told that it is one hundred fifty per cent., but call it one hundred per cent. and then we are a long way inside the mark.

That ten dollars' worth of lace, purchased in Nottingham, would cost the wholesaler in America twenty dollars.

The wholesaler usually loads up his lace with seventy-five to one hundred per cent. profit, because he has to cover such contingencies, for instance, as patterns left on his hands because they do not sell.

We will call it seventy-five per cent.

Twenty dollars' worth of lace, with seventy-five per cent. added is thirty-five dollars.

That is the wholesale dealer's price.

How much profit does the retailer get?

Put it at the very low figure of fifty per cent.

When it gets into the hands of the lady who buys it at the store, she has paid fifty-two dollars and fifty cents for lace that cost ten dollars in Europe.

Have I stated the facts correctly?

A Voice—"Yes, that is right."

That is the weak kind of competition that we have

We can make laces nearly as cheaply as they can in England.

Suppose, however, that the ten dollars' worth of lace had cost us fifteen dollars to manufacture.

We have no duty to pay, no wholesalers' profit, and no buyers' salaries to pay.

We are the manufacturers, and we go directly to the big retailer.

When he gets it, he booms it, and advertises, "Zion Lace has reached us! Come and see it!"

The whole town knows it.

Suppose that lace cost us fifteen dollars. Suppose we took only fifty per cent. profit.

Then we receive twenty-two dollars fifty cents.

The retailer adds fifty per cent. for his profit, so that the consumer gets that lace for thirty-four dollars.

That is thirty-four dollars against fifty-two dollars fifty cents.

We undersell the foreign maker by over fifty per cent. and make at least fifty per cent. profit.

I am talking to investors.

I want more money, and I am showing you that your investments will be safe.

The more money you give me the more I can get for you and for Zion.

I have in view schools, and colleges, and messengers of Zion, and LEAVES OF HEALING, and getting at the nations of the earth with the Everlasting Gospel.

GENERAL OVERSEER AND OVERSEER JANE DOWIE IN GARDEN OF MR. ALEXANDER DOWIE, "CALTON HILL," MOUNT LOFTY, SOUTH AUSTRALIA.
(Overseer Jane Dowie Is Wearing Dress of Zion Lace.)

Zion Industries Pay Better Than Farming.

You have been down in Kansas [addressing Deacon Clendinen]. Do they make eight per cent. on their farm property?

Deacon Clendinen—"Some do, now and then, on wheat farms."

General Overseer—That is the highest.

Elder Ropp made a statement last year. What was it Elder?

Elder Ropp—"I said, I could not make six per cent."

General Overseer—Elder Ropp has been a farmer, on a large scale, in Illinois and is now an Elder in this Church; he says he could not make six per cent. I ong to get a thousand of those money-making lace machines.

I am buying twelve, but I want to buy thirty next year, and the following year I want to buy sixty, and the year after that I want to buy one hundred twenty, and the year after that I want to buy two hundred forty.

Then I can turn out money for God and Zion, and send Zion's Message over all the world.

Do you not think you had better help me more than you have been doing?

Do you not think you had better sell that old farm, which stinks of pig, and get the proceeds into Zion?

Large Financial Resources in Sight.

I am told that there is a man sitting in front of me who has six thousand dollars in his pocket, and will now invest that sum in Zion Lace Industries.

I could tell you of one that has ninety thousand dollars.

I could tell you of two or three persons who represent three hundred fifty thousand dollars; they are thinking of investing it, but are waiting to hear what I have to say today.

You have now heard what I have to say, and, as far as I know, I have told you the truth, although it is not the whole truth: for the whole truth is *better* than I have told you.

What do you think, General Financial Manager?

Deacon Barnard—"That is correct."

General Overseer—What do you think, Cashier Peckham?

Deacon Peckham—"Yes; right."

General Overseer—What do you think, Manager Stevenson?

Deacon Stevenson—"Yes, that is right."

General Overseer—Here is Deacon Rodda, the General Manager of Zion Sugar and Confection Association, who is looking at me so earnestly, and I can see that he is wanting me to talk about candy.

Deacon Rodda—I am interested in lace, too, Doctor; I could ell you something. We sent a candy salesman out West. He met an Eastern representative selling English laces, who said, after examining the quality of Zion lace, that one thousand machines would not supply lace for this country!"

General Overseer—Do you not see that I was right in telling you that I wanted a thousand machines?

They are very costly, but we take care of them and they last for years.

Our machines are all working beautifully.

We have no strikes amongst our employees; the causes of strikes do not exist in Zion City.

Resources Needed for the Evangelization of the World.

I have taken pains about this, because I want the Overseers, and Elders, and Evangelists, and Deacons, and Deaconesses, who have been here today to get a grasp of these facts.

I will tell you what I, as God's Minister, see in them.

I see the extension of the Gospel of the Kingdom of God throughout the world, with all the Blessings that accompany it in Zion.

That is what I am aiming at.

Why should I care for making money?

I do not personally need more than I have.

If I cared, I could keep the profits, after paying what I agree to pay to the shareholders.

You know, Judge Barnes, that no one could prevent me.

Judge Barnes—"You might easily do it."

General Overseer—I could pocket the whole thing after paying interest. But I am true to God and to Zion, and without an iota of selfish motive in my toils for this people and God's Kingdom.

I put all I have into Zion; and I never fear nor falter, by God's grace.

Why do not you follow me fully, up to the measure of your ability, in this?

Can you tell me where you can get a safer investment and larger returns?

As a Financial Proposition Zion Stands Without Fear of Competition

Mothers, sisters, daughters, is not this a good place in which to live?

Ladies—"Yes!"

General Overseer—Then why not get away from that pig-soaked farm?

Every acre of it smells with pig!

Why not turn the farm into money?

Zion wants you and Zion wants to employ your money.

I am not asking for selfish purposes, nor am I asking money as a gift to Zion, I am only asking that you shall trust Zion which stands before you fair, and beautiful, and strong, with a splendid record for her three years' work, and let Zion earn for you splendid returns on the money which you lend her and me.

Every one in Zion has full control of his or her individual estate.

I said at the beginning that I would ask for only five per cent. of the increment of the value, and the right to take five per cent. of the land, at cost.

I have taken that.

About five per cent. of the land is in my hands, and I will not lease it, but use it as I believe God would approve.

EAST WING OF ZION MAIN EDUCATIONAL BUILDING.

No Mortgage on Zion Properties.

There is not one dollar of indebtedness in the way of bonding or mortgaging upon one single Institution in Zion.

That is a great thing to say.

We have not borrowed a dollar upon the Industries—not a dollar. All I owe in connection with these Industries is simply to the stockholders, and I am well able to pay that when it becomes due.

You will not find a place in the world, where so much has been done in so short a time, free of debt.

We have not bonded the city for a dollar, have we, Mr. Mayor?

Mayor Richard H. Harper—"No."

General Overseer—We have not bonded ourselves for a dollar upon any of our buildings.

Judge Barnes—"All taxes of the people are paid, and the City has the highest record, in respect of prompt and full payment of taxes, of any in the United States." [Applause.]

General Overseer—Now then, if you are Christians, get into Zion, and let Zion employ your money and yourselves. Zion has room for millions of God's people and millions of God's money.

I feel I have a right to plead with you, in the Name of the Christ, our King.

One thing more. I do not want to borrow from the world.

Do you want Zion to get into the hands of the world?

Audience—"No."

General Overseer—I will sell Stocks, but I will sell them with fifty times more pleasure to Zion men than to those outside.

We sell next to nothing to outside men.

We have sometimes refused to sell to persons who were willing to trust us, but who refused to trust God.

Some of you know that the world came to me through you and offered me large sums of money, and I refused to take it.

But I think the time has come to say that if we can get clean money we will sell Stocks to outside parties of good reputation.

Clean Money for Clean People.

They must be clean people whose dividends will not be used for drunkenness and revelry.

I hate the thought of Zion working for people who spend their money on theaters, gambling hells, horse races, harlots, alcoholic liquors, and upon such dirty practices as smoking and spewing tobacco.

I want the money that we earn to be used for the glory of God, and the happiness of man.

I am glad to tell you of another thing.

Mr. Barnard and I have had very little chance to talk together since my return from the Around-the-World Visitation, because I have had to attend to many things, and I have not been able to tell him some things I am going to say now.

He and I once made a list in which we found that there was from fifty to one hundred million dollars' worth of property in the hands of Zion people, which they were endeavoring to turn into money; it was on its way, and would come in perhaps during five years.

Since then I have been around the world, and I have seen our people in many places.

I have listened and I have looked at the whole situation, and my conviction is that one hundred fifty million dollars will flow into Zion within five years.

That is a tremendous thing!

"What are you going to do with it?" you say.

I am going to have those machines with which to make lace, and coin money for God to be used in the Evangelization and Restoration of multitudes in all the Nations of the World.

I am going to make the best candy for all the children, old and young, of the United States, if I can, and use the profits in Zion for God.

Would it not be a grand thing if the greater part of the candy that is eaten had the Zion label?

Zion Exists for the Welfare of All.

I believe we can develop these and many other Industries for which we have been planning.

We cannot stop at that!

We cannot stop with the success of this City.

Do you think that God Almighty would bless us if we should say, "Oh, we will just confine everything in one spot?"

No!

Moreover, I do not think that this City would be really I have invested here, the money with which God has personally entrusted me and it would be the height of folly for me to reduce the value of my estate in this City, even if there were no other reason.

The Interests of Zion City to be Conserved.

I will do nothing that will damage this City or lessen the value of the investments, but I will go on with my work, and plant other Cities when I can do so without injuring this City.

Is not that right?

Audience—"Yes."

General Overseer—The land that I have referred to is in a magnificent country.

We can raise cattle for about twelve dollars that we have to pay forty dollars for here.

We can grow cotton, rice, and other grains; and several crops of tomatoes and other garden truck in a year; and semi-tropical fruits of every kind, much of which could be shipped to the north and sold.

Of course such a colony and City would help us, and so will every Zion City which God leads us to build on this and every Continent.

ELIJAH HOSPICE.

successful, if we, after founding it and strengthening it, were to say, "Now we will live for ourselves."

We cannot do it. We must live for God and for humanity.

There are many Zion people throughout the world who could not live in this climate all the year: for whilst the winters are healthful to many, they are too severe for some.

For these people we must have some place farther south.

The Possibility of a Southern Colony.

I have been offered a tract of land in Mexico, thirty miles deep and extending fifty miles along the shores of the Gulf of Mexico.

On that million acres I could colonize our colored people from the South, from Africa, and perhaps some of our Chinese and Indian people.

I could buy that land for fifty cents an acre.

Just think of it! [Laughter.]

I should be recreant to God if I talked about this City being the end of all our thoughts.

I should be recreant to this City if I established any other city that would in any way injure it.

I will not do it!

Why should I?

We have to consider those that are even now coming from other lands.

We will grow cotton, and one day we shall clean it and spin it, and not buy yarn for our Lace Industries.

We will have our own sea-island cotton before we are through, and what we cannot use we will sell.

There is no greater expert in the making of cotton-seed oil than that little man down there. [Referring to Deacon Lewis.]

He can show us how to make cotton-seed oil.

I have not given up a Zion Plantation and City in Texas, or in some other of the Gulf States that is nearer than this Mexican proposal. But I must be led of God most clearly ere I come to any decision.

This Work Is God's Zion.

Pray for me, and pray that God will lead His people.

He has promised that the wealth of the nations shall flow into Zion, and, if this is not Zion, what is it?

What is it?

Is it the Devil's work?

Audience—"No."

General Overseer—Does the Devil make people sober and virtuous, and make them love one another?

Audience—"No."

General Overseer—It is an awful blasphemy to say it is the Devil's work. He never designed a Zion City, where it is easy to do right, and difficult to do wrong.

It is God's work.

We are poor and imperfect people at the best, and we are not saying that we are incapable of sin.

We leave that for the liars in certain churches.

We say that we are very imperfect, and that we need th Mercy of God all the time.

But we do say this, that we do not sin wilfully, and that we are a people who are determined to do right according to our light.

With all our faults, this Zion City is the best spot on all the earth in which to live. [Applause.]

If, in view of what God has done for Zion, we have no gratitude to Him, we are the most ungrateful people on God's earth; but I believe we have gratitude.

We have committed to us a solemn, Divine trust, for which we have to answer to God.

I Care to Live only that I May Fulfil the Mission God Has Given Me.

I cannot do it better than by establishing prosperous communities, where we can get tens and hundreds of thousands of people to love and serve God and be kind and good to each other.

Help build up Zion, so that when the time comes to send a contingent from each of these Zion cities, we shall build the City of the great King, and rebuild the Temple which God said must be rebuilt, and perhaps the Palace for the King.

Then it will be time for the Rapture—for us to go home, and come back, and repossess all that belongs to God and to us in this world, and to live on in the Millennial Glory with the King until He rules over all, and the Restoration of All Things has been fully accomplished.

I praise God for that Prospect of Working with the King of kings in the Thousand Years of Restoration, until that work is done, and then to serve and love God and His children through the Endless Ages to come.

It will be a happy time when I shall have finished my labors in the flesh, when I shall have done my part, and gone to God, and come back with Jesus in a glorified body, to go on with Him throughout the Millennium, until the Restoration is perfectly accomplished.

May God grant it.

PRAYER OF CONSECRATION.

Our God and Father, we thank Thee for all the blessings Thou hast given to Zion spiritually, educationally, commercially, and politically. We thank Thee for the solid foundation that has been laid, and we ask Thee to help us build strongly and more quickly upon this foundation; that we may have more money with which to spread the Gospel; more money for the poor; more money for the sorrowing; more money for educating the children; more money for sending forth the Messengers and the Literature to all the world. For Jesus' sake. Amen.

BENEDICTION.

Beloved, abstain from every form of evil. And may the very God of Peace Himself sanctify you wholly; and I pray God your whole spirit and soul and body be preserved entire, without blame, unto the coming of our Lord Jesus, the Christ. Faithful is He that calleth you, who also will do it. The grace of our Lord Jesus, the Christ, the love of God our Father, the fellowship of the Holy Spirit, our Comforter and Guide, one Eternal God, abide in you, bless you, and keep you, and all the Israel of God everywhere, forever. Amen.

FRIDAY AFTERNOON CONFERENCE.

REPORTED BY S. E. C., O. R., L. L. H., AND F. A. F.

Shiloh Tabernacle, Zion City, Illinois, Friday Afternoon, July 22, 1904.

The service was opened by the Congregation's joining in singing Hymn No. 29.

The General Overseer then said:

Pray that the proceedings of this afternoon may be glorifying to God.

Deacon Daniel Sloan then offered the general supplication, after which the General Overseer prayed for the sick, and the Congregation joined in chanting the Disciples' Prayer.

"WHERE GOD RULES MAN PROSPERS."

INVOCATION.

Let the words of our mouths, and the meditations of our hearts be acceptable in Thy sight, O Lord, our Strength and our Redeemer.

I came to open the meeting this afternoon, and then to place Judge Barnes in the chair, and have you hear what all these powerful Departmental Chiefs have to say to you regarding the business that I have entrusted to them—the Business of Zion.

I can trust them so well, that I do not have to stay here and watch them. I trust them all the time and very gladly.

If I did not, they would hear about it.

Last Fiscal Year Best Zion Has Ever Had.

There are some people who say that there was not a great deal of progress in Zion City during the last year. That is one of the lies, and one of the foolish things, because the progress has been tremendous. It has been a good year all around, has it not Deacon Barnard?

ZION CITY POSTOFFICE.
(This building has been much enlarged since this photograph was taken.)

Deacon Barnard—"Yes, sir, the best year we have had."

General Overseer—We have put up a great many more houses than you think, because we have been filling up the vacant lots between houses already built. But we have done many things of still greater importance.

It has been a wonderful year.

The General Overseer then spoke at length on the growth of United States Postal Business in Zion City, commenting upon it as an indication of the City's progress.

He took, as the basis of these remarks, the following report:

Stamp sales for month of June, 1903, amounted to	$ 1,130 10
Stamp sales for month of June, 1904, amounted to	1,602 05
Number of pieces of registered mail received June, 1903	217
Number of pieces of registered mail received June, 1904	251
Number of pieces of registered mail dispatched June, 1903	239
Number of pieces of registered mail dispatched June, 1904	206
Number of pieces of special delivery mail received June, 1903	70
Number of pieces of special delivery mail received June, 1904	54
Three hundred eighty-five money-orders issued June, 1903, amounting to	$3,031 40
Three hundred sixty-nine money-orders issued June, 1904, amounting to	3,208 41
Six hundred fifty-two money-orders paid June, 1903, amounting to	5,296 62
Eight hundred thirty-four money-orders paid June, 1904, amounting to	7,260 40
Total money-order business transacted June, 1903, amounted to	8,328 02
Total money-order business transacted June, 1904, amounted to	10,477 81
Total postal business transacted in 1903	13,159 13
Total postal business transacted in 1904	21,994 11
Total gain over the previous year	8,834 98
Total money-order business transacted in 1904	131,578 87
Grand total postal and money-order business transacted in 1903	107,171 36
Grand total postal and money-order business transacted in 1904	153,572 98
Total gain over one year previous of	46,404 51
Total money-order transactions during the year	15,257

Unseen But Important Work.

He then said:

Pray for our Postmaster.

He has a great work.

I oftentimes think that he is one of our many officers in Zion hose work is fully recognized only by God.

Many of us have to do publicly work that may be seen, but ally the most, and perhaps the best, of our work is unseen.

When you see an iceberg floating in the ocean—not that Zion an iceberg, or that I am an iceberg—you see only a small action of it: for more than two-thirds are concealed beneath e waters of the sea.

When you look at Zion and the visible work of the workers ou see, at the very best, only about one-tenth of it.

Nothing that you can say or that we can tell you of Zion ity shows it to you, because the greatest work is accomplished elow water, as it were.

For instance, I do not suppose that the majority of people ave any idea what Zion Printing and Publishing House has do.

There are very few nights when they do not have to work te.

The Commercial Printing Department has grown so fast that e have to work very late, and in getting out LEAVES OF EALING we have to work all night over and over again.

Deacon Newcomb, my General Associate Editor, and anager of Zion Printing and Publishing House, with whom have been working this morning, is one of the workers ho does an immense amount of unseen work.

Need of More Capital for Zion City Bank.

I will leave the meeting to these men, and to the only oman who is a member of my Business Council—Overseer ne Dowie.

I want Deacon Peckham to plead eloquently for more capital r Zion City Bank.

We really ought to have a capital of a Million Dollars for the ank.

We have so many attractive Stocks that you have been neglecting the Bank Shares.

The Bank Stock is a magnificent stock, that has gone to a premium of one hundred ten dollars.

I like it, and I have a good big share of it, personally.

I wish you would help me increase the capital.

It is now nearly five hundred thousand dollars; but to handle our increasing business we ought to have a million dollars.

All the other Stocks are very powerful, but they represent property values.

I have not pushed the Bank Stock, because all our people who are depositors in the Bank know very well that we have these great values behind us, and they have nobly stood by the Bank when it has been attacked.

We have what is better than gold coin.

We have Productive Industries which produce wealth.

The General Overseer then left the platform, leaving the meeting in charge of the Honorable V. V. Barnes.

ZION PRINTING AND PUBLISHING HOUSE.
(Now in Course of Construction.)

Judge V. V. Barnes Takes Charge of the Conference.

Judge Barnes—"Christian friends, we regret that the General Overseer has to retire at this time.

"Overseer Jane Dowie would, of course, preside, but she had a very long meeting, and a very fine meeting, this morning, occupying several hours, and, of course, she is wearied with the great amount of work.

"The heads of the various business departments find themselves better able to present the facts pertaining to their various departments, without the embarrassment of being in the chair.

"Therefore, I have come to receive this position by the appointment of the General Overseer, an honor which I highly esteem, though I feel very greatly the loss of his presence on the platform.

"Deacon Charles J. Barnard, General Financial Manager of all Zion Institutions and Industries, needs no introduction to the people of Zion, and is as widely known throughout the United States as almost any financier in the country."

ELIJAH THE RESTORER DIRECTS THE INVESTMENT OF GOD'S MONEY IN ZION.

Deacon Charles J. Barnard, General Financial Manager of All Zion Institutions and Industries.

Deacon C. J. Barnard—"Christian Friends, the General Overseer, in referring to the opening of Zion Financial Institutions, took us back to a very important period in their history.

"At that time there were two employees.

"Now, taking in all the Institutions and Industries of the

DEACON ARTHUR W. NEWCOMB,
General Associate Editor of Zion Publications and General Manager of Zion Printing and Publishing House.

Christian Catholic Church in Zion, there are nearly two thousand.

"Five years ago, it meant a great deal more than it does now, for men and women to come forward with their money, place it in Zion City Bank, or invest it in Zion securities.

"I look back on that period of Zion's history, and remember the men and women who came forward and placed their money in the hands of our beloved General Overseer, with a great deal of satisfaction and gratification

Confidence in the Face of Bitterest Opposition.

"Then remember that this was done in the face of terrific opposition.

"All the papers in Chicago, and the religious papers everywhere, were attacking the General Overseer, showering upon him all kinds of vile names—fraud, cheat, liar, hypocrite.

"Yet Zion men and women came with their money and made it possible for our beloved Leader to establish two Financial Institutions: namely, Zion City Bank and Zion Land and Investment Association.

"Later on, came the establishment of Zion Lace Industries and the other Industries.

"The full history of Zion can never be written.

"The meetings held by our beloved Leader and his Business Cabinet, and the way in which he planned, always giving us clear and definite instructions, never hesitating even in the face of opposition, but always giving us a clear note of 'Go Forward,' were a wonderful revelation and inspiration.

"He could see what none of us could see. He told us very plainly of the establishment of Zion City.

"Now, we have a City well established, with Industries, with Institutions, with thousands of godly men and women.

"What of the future?

General Overseer's Great Grasp of Detail.

"The General Overseer, although he may never have mentioned this, is quite familiar with everything in connection with Zion.

"I have often been asked the question, 'How is it possible for one man to conduct such vast enterprises?'

"There is only one John Alexander Dowie in all the world, and, with all my experience as a banker and business man, I have never seen his equal.

"There is not a subject that is presented to him by his Business Cabinet that he is not familiar with, and upon which he cannot give good, sound advice.

"That is one reason why men and women have so implicitly confided in him and trusted him.

"All along the way it has been a question of confidence in the management of Zion's affairs.

"Confidence lies at the foundation of all business, and it is especially essential in making investments.

"No one has ever lost a cent of an investment in Zion.

"On the other hand, they have all received good rates of interest.

"If so much has been accomplished in the past, what may not be accomplished in the future?

"There must be a standing together of all the people.

Plan for Extending Zion Commercial Institutions.

"Much can be done, in various ways, by those of our people who live outside of Zion City, by speaking a word in behalf of the Institutions, not only the Financial, but the Commercial.

"Take, for instance, the question of our Products.

JUDGE V. V. BARNES,
General Counsel of Zion Law Department.

"We have just inaugurated a system whereby we shall notify all members of Zion and all readers of LEAVES OF HEALING, that certain merchants in certain places keep Zion products, requesting them to go there and purchase goods of those merchants.

"They may keep only a few of the articles. Ask them if

they have Zion soap, Zion candy, Zion flavoring extracts, Zion shortening, or Zion brooms.

"Let one merchant in a town of three or four thousand people understand that we are advising our people to come and buy Zion products of him, and he will carry those products.

DEACON CHARLES J. BARNARD,
General Financial Manager of all Zion Institutions and Industries.

"You will soon be able to get Zion products, no matter where you live.

The One Grand, Supreme Purpose of All Zion Activities.

"There are many ways in which you can help Zion along commercially; and by helping in these ways you help in the work of Restoration, because from the sale of our products God's Prophet will receive money to be used in effecting the Evangelization of the World.

"We are working here for this purpose.

"That is what our beloved Leader is pouring out his life for; that is what all these men and women who are on Zion's payroll are working and laboring for—the Evangelization of the World.

"I wish to say that every word which our beloved Leader uttered yesterday is true.

"May God bless you." [Applause.]

Judge Barnes—"I have the pleasure now of introducing to you the Cashier of Zion City Bank, Deacon William S. Peckham.

"I can personally testify, as a great many of you can, to Deacon Peckham's work, not only in the Bank, where he is faithful and loyal, but everywhere.

"He lives in my neighborhood, and wonderful cases of healing take place in answer to Deacon Peckham's prayers, which fact I believe to be the seal of God's blessing upon his work in the Financial as well as other Departments of Zion." [Applause.]

Deacon William S. Peckham, Cashier of Zion City Bank.

Deacon Peckham—"Beloved brothers and sisters, as Cashier of Zion City Bank, I am very glad to stand before the people whom I serve, and express my gratitude to Almighty God for the wonderful way in which He has guided us, protected us, delivered us, and prospered us during the last year.

"We have had that Faith which is a consciousness of an ever-existing God, and we were able to go calmly, quietly, strongly through all our trials.

"God brought us out, and gave us Victory.

"Zion City Bank is the center of the great Financial Work of Zion.

"It must be kept strong; it must be able to care for all these vast interests.

Great Need of a Bank in Doing Zion's Work.

"It would be utterly impossible for us to do the work of Zion without a Bank.

"I am very glad that God put it into the heart of the General Overseer to establish Zion City Bank so early, and that He also put it into his heart, as I believe He did, to call me to work in that Institution.

"It is the joy of my heart to serve Him anywhere, but perhaps most of all in Zion City Bank.

"It is a service of love, a service which no money could buy, and a service which we most gladly give, because it is a service for our Lord and for the extension of His Kingdom.

"It is necessary that we have large sums of money to carry on the business of a great City, and of a great people.

"We have been enabled, many times, to help not only those who are residents of Zion City, but those who are away, by clearing matters up, and getting them ready to come to Zion City, and helping them out of difficulties in many ways.

"Our Commercial and Industrial Institutions sometimes save a great deal of money through the Bank's furnishing them cash for timely purchases.

"Moreover, it will be seen that it will be wise to centralize all the vast banking interests of Zion in this City, even after we have established branches in other cities.

Zion People Can Help Zion Bank.

"You, here and everywhere, can help Zion very much by being faithful in your deposits in Zion City Bank.

DEACON WILLIAM S. PECKHAM,
Cashier Zion City Bank.

"If it should be a little inconvenient to you, and should occasion you some trouble and delay, remember that you are helping the great work of Zion, and be willing to sacrifice, if it is necessary, in that direction.

"I believe we are generally able to serve you very acceptably, no matter where you live.

"Now there are some people who think that when they put money into the bank it is simply that it may be put in the safe and locked up, and that is all there is to it. But the money must be put to some use where it can earn something, in order that we may pay you interest on your deposits.

"The deposits in the savings banks alone in this country amount to more than the entire money issued by the United States government; so that if these savings banks had all the money in their safes that has ever been issued by the United States Government, they could not pay off all their depositors.

"I want to thank this people for their kindness, patience, and faithfulness; but you can be more faithful.

The Great Importance of the Habit of Saving.

"I believe that the deposits in Zion City Bank could be increased a million dollars this year if every one would begin systematic saving.

"Many people have been enabled, by getting into a systematic habit of saving, to get their lots and build their homes in Zion City.

"As our beloved General Financial Manager has said: 'Pray for us.'

"It is not an easy task to swing great enterprises, and establish them, and push them forward, with limited means.

"The man who has money has the advantage in any business, in any place, anywhere in all the world.

"So we must have the money.

"It belongs to God.

"You and everything you have belongs to God.

"By and by you will be very glad if you have given it to Him and had it used in His service.

"I believe that every man will have to give an account of every dollar bill he ever received.

"Zion will go forward whether you do your duty or not; whether I do my duty or not.

"But if we do not do our duty, God will sweep us out of the way.

Excellence of Zion City Bank.

"We ought to have ten thousand open accounts in Zion City Bank; and we ought to have them before this year closes.

"We can have them if each one does his or her duty.

"We have a well-equipped Bank, as well-equipped as any bank of its size that I know of.

"All its appointments are first-class.

"All its bookkeeping and systems are up to date.

"I praise God for the faithful President, the Manager, the Assistant Cashier, and all those associated with me in the Bank.

"I believe that you have found them gentlemen, kind and courteous in all the dealings which you have had with them.

"We have the commercial deposit and savings departments, and a well-equipped safety-box department.

"We are prepared to take care of any line of business; to give you drafts payable in any part of the world.

"We are prepared to serve you in anything that pertains to the banking business.

"I think you will bear me out that we have not been misleading you. We have not been unfair with you; but in all our work we have striven to do that which we believe God would have had us do.

"It is necessary for the Bank to make some charges for its work, or else it could not exist.

"You must all recognize that and help us in that matter, and be willing to bear the necessary expenses attending the transaction of the banking business.

Zion City Bank Rates Low.

"Our rates for the transfer of money, however, are lower than for the same amount of money by any other mode.

"We are also safer and better, I believe, than postoffice orders or express orders.

"Our drafts go in all directions, and are taken everywhere, with rare exceptions.

"We have been able, this year, to make the best of connections in Chicago.

"Our business is handled there most acceptably by the Western Trust and Savings Bank.

"I praise God for the wonderful year which He has given us in Zion in the Financial Institutions, and especially in the Bank.

"You cannot get the blessings of Zion unless you give unto God all that you have; surrender to Him fully, completely, wholly, spirit, soul, and body—your time, talents, earthly store, everything for the Master's service; and there is no place where we can serve God so well as in Zion.

"There is no other place where money deposited in the bank is not used for ungodly purposes; is not loaned to ungodly men, and does not go into channels that are working against the Kingdom of God, and hindering and keeping back the preparations for the Coming of the King.

"In Zion we are preparing for the Coming of the King; and, it sometimes seems to me, so near, and we have so little time in which to do this work! Very soon we shall not want the money we are now holding.

The time will be gone, the opportunity will be gone!

Prophetic Character of Zion.

"The power, the glory, the majesty of the great work of God in Zion can never be separated in any way from the Prophetic Office of our General Overseer.

"We must see in a larger measure what God is doing in these Last Days of this Dispensation, and get away from the littleness, the narrowness which makes us love our money better than we love the Kingdom of God.

"Every succeeding day, in its mighty power, is swinging us further on to Victory and to the Grand Day that is coming—the Rapture, and the return with our Lord, to take rule over all these Cities, and over all the great work of God in the Kingdom which He is now establishing.

"We have our part in it.

"Let us be faithful." [Applause.]

Judge Barnes—"I now have the pleasure of introducing to you the gentleman who is at the head of the Department that, from a business standpoint, has been very aptly called the Mother of the Institutions of Zion.

"Deacon H. Worthington Judd will now address you." [Applause.]

Deacon H. Worthington Judd, Secretary and General Manager Zion Land and Investment Association.

Deacon H. Worthington Judd—"Friends and fellow Christians in Zion, honor must be given to God and to our beloved Leader for the privilege that has been given me to have a part in this very important work in connection with the land interests of Zion.

"Some might think there could be little to say at this time, because there is no great boom on, but we are in the midst of a legitimate, substantial boom, although there may be a lull.

"It is a good thing to have a lull sometimes.

"It has usually been the case that in the presidential election year, real estate generally stands still.

"I have carefully gone into this, and feel that it has been a good thing for Zion.

"We have had an opportunity to stand still and look around, and see what has been accomplished.

"God has been talking to us, and we have seen these wonderful developments.

"We have seen wonderful progress.

"Perhaps some of you may think that we have been doing very little in the last six months; but we have done wonderful things.

No Shrinkage of Values of Zion Real Estate at Any Time.

"We have never seen any shrinkage of values in Zion City real estate.

"That is a wonderful thing in itself

"I know that there is not one disgruntled one that has ever left Zion City with less than he had when he came into it, especially those who have made land investments.

"Some of you may not consider the new railroad of as great importance as it is; but I know something about what has happened in other places, when such an improvement as this has gone through.

"They are building one of the best railroad beds that has ever been made.

"And their object is to give rapid transit.

"With the splendid equipment that they are to operate with, and the extensive improvements at different points in our City, their willingness to locate stations wherever we say, is bound to enhance the value of the property on both sides of these lines. I am satisfied that within twelve months that property will be

DEACON H. WORTHINGTON JUDD,
General Manager Zion Land and Investment Association.

increased in value at least twenty-five per cent. over and above the present rentals.

Expressions of Onlookers as to Zion's Financial Soundness.

"If you knew of some of the expressions that have come to me within the last few days in regard to the future outlook of this City, by people who are not interested in the work of Zion from a spiritual standpoint, but are merely worldly people, onlookers, it would astound you.

"Only a day or so ago I met a gentleman from the State of Washington.

"He came in to see if he could induce us to buy additional land on our borders; and he informed me that in his section those who engaged in industrial pursuits were seriously looking to the wonderful solution of the labor question in this City. He told me that one responsible man who has an establishment worth a hundred thousand dollars, said that he would give all that it would require to move his whole establishment here, if he could have the privilege of locating his plant in Zion City, for he believes he would get it all back inside of two years.

"Such things should stimulate us and should encourage us to put our shoulders to the wheel, to put our money in Zion City real estate—the cleanest, safest land investment you can find in the world today. It is customary to hold land ten and fifteen years to get profits out of the investment, but how much more quickly you have realized here!

"I was satisfied in saying, at the beginning, that you would double your money inside of three years, and I thought that was doing wonders; but you have doubled your money in hundreds of instances inside of twelve months, and there is no shrinkage in values.

"I feel grateful to God for what He has enabled us to accomplish in the last six months.

"We have acquired full title to nearly one thousand acres more land, and that some of the most valuable that we had to purchase.

"We have paid off nearly sixty thousand dollars of indebtedness upon land not yet occupied or even subdivided.

"Zion Land and Investment Association never was in better condition than it is today.

"We need not only your prayers, but a closer and more devoted interest in connection with the land interests of our City.

"I wish we could all realize, inside of Zion, the confidence which the commercial and industrial world has in us.

"I think it would stimulate our interest a little, and we would get a little more backbone than we have.

"You are not doing your whole duty, if you have land outside that you are holding on to, waiting to get a big price for it.

"There is a shrinkage going on outside, and it will continue to go on.

"God will favor this district right here, when the outside land will be filled with disease and disaster.

"I have never had any doubt in my heart as to the outcome of this work."

Judge Barnes—"On behalf of Zion, I have the pleasure of presenting to you Deacon Henry Stevenson, who has just returned from an important business trip to Europe.

"He is at the head of Zion Lace Industries as General Manager."

Deacon Henry Stevenson, General Manager Zion Lace Industries.

Deacon Stevenson—"Christian friends, in the running of Zion Lace Industries we have found that we can make very handsome profits. Last year's report, you will remember, was very gratifying.

"There is a great deal of the trade which we cannot touch, simply because we have not the machinery to make the goods.

"We could nearly sustain this City, if we could put fifty machines into that factory.

"The increase of work and trade we have had is forty per cent., and we have done it with ten per cent. less cost on wages, not through cutting down wages, but by better system.

DEACON HENRY STEVENSON,
General Manager Zion Lace Industries.

"As we increase the plant, we will produce lace to the value of many more thousands of dollars, and pay less money for it.

"The scope of activity for our expert and highly paid labor is too limited.

"A man who looks after two or three or four or five machines now, could look after twenty-five.

"I do not think that it needs any words of mine to convince you that God is really in this business.

"He gives the skill.

"He teaches the people. It is not because I am better, or because our people are better workmen.

"One of the Englishmen said to me: 'I am surprised at myself that I do such work as I do today.'

"An experience of twenty-five years teaches me that the splendid working of the machines, the evenness of the fabric, and the small amount of accident and loss all go to prove that God is really in Zion Lace Industries.

"I thank God, dear friends, for Zion and the General Overseer, and for the wonderful way in which he has been led and used of God.

DEACON FIELDING H. WILHITE
Manager Zion Stocks and Securities.

"The reports of the buyers of very large institutions, who have seen our laces, are very gratifying.

Trade for Zion Lace Industries Opening up Everywhere.

"I have a letter in my pocket that came today from San Francisco, wanting us to put our lace curtains into that part of the country. They are short of lace curtains and are asking us to send our products there.

"The General Overseer was inside the mark, yesterday, when he told you of the wonderful possibilities.

"I have the greatest confidence in Zion Lace Industries.

"I think it will be the greatest Industry of its kind in the world.

"We have the expert opinion of very large factory holders in England, which I know to be true, that we have one of the finest factories in the world.

"I think that the time has come for us to establish firmly these great institutions, so that they will crowd out the people who do not extend His Kingdom." [Applause.]

Judge Barnes—"We have on the platform today one who has rapidly risen in Zion, until he is now at the head of Zion Stocks and Securities—Deacon F. H. Wilhite, Manager of Zion Stocks and Securities."

Deacon Fielding H. Wilhite, Manager Zion Stocks and Securities.

Deacon Wilhite—"Dear Friends in the Christ, I am very glad to talk to you about Zion Securities and Investments.

"With all my heart I believe that Zion Securities are the Securities of a Nation, because Zion is a Nation.

"Just as the Securities and the Bonds of the Government are better than those of any private corporation, so are those of Zion better than any mere business institution.

"We have back of our investments millions of dollars in the various assets of Zion.

"This is not merely our opinion, but it is the opinion of all hard-headed business men of the city of Chicago, who sent a committee out here to look over our affairs at a time, when, to people who had not the Faith of God, it looked very dark.*

"They stated that our assets were worth many millions of dollars over all our liabilities, even including those of our securities, which mature some twenty years hence.

Zion's Great Wealth-Creating Power.

"We have not only these assets to back up the securities of Zion, but in my opinion we have a thing that is much greater; and that is the ever-present power in Zion to create wealth.

"In the city of Chicago, land has been selling within the last twelve months at the rate of five to eight million dollars an acre.

"I have in mind now, as I have followed these transactions in the city of Chicago, one particular lot on one of the leading streets, but not the most important street in the city, eighty feet front, which sold last year for about one million dollars.

"That lot, about sixty years ago, was bought for about one thousand two hundred dollars, and was turned over to the Archbishop of the Roman Catholic Church of the City of Chicago.

"It had been held by that denomination ever since.

"What has made that great increase?

"It has been the concentration of great interests there and the population around it.

"That is precisely what we are doing in Zion City, except that these interests in Chicago were in the hands of thousands of different persons, while in Zion City they are in the hands of one man; and the power of that concentration is not to be estimated.

"We know very well that there is in the world today a great population crying out for God. They want clean lives; they want a clean place to live. They desire to see Purity and Righteousness established; and they will come to Zion Cities.

"Thousands upon thousands of people could be brought here, had we our Industries established to give them all employment.

"Our Securities are now bearing interest at the rate of nine and ten per cent., and they are backed up by all this vast, ever-increasing estate.

"We know that God is with us in this matter.

"As we have overcome one difficulty after another, even our foes have come to see that God is with us.

"We have made thousands and thousands of friends by overcoming the various obstacles and hindrances which have been in the way.

A Good Time to Sell Farm Land.

"The Bureau of Securities and Investments desires to aid you in the matter of the sale of your properties.

"Now is a good time to sell farm land. You have crops growing on them, and this is the time of the year when men are looking about to buy.

"We feel that it is better for you to sell now, even at a sacrifice, and let the money flow into Zion, and thus help lay the foundations of this City, so that the great population desiring to come to Zion may get employment.

DEACON R. E. RODDA.
General Manager Zion Sugar and Confection Association.

"May God help you to do this.

"In anything that we can do to help you, command us freely." [Applause.]

Judge Barnes—"We come now, my friends, to one who is designated by Deacon Barnard as the silver-tongued orator—I suppose because of his eloquence in presenting the claims of candy.

"If we are not careful, and do not impose some restriction upon him, he may occupy all the space of the Lace Industries for the purpose of making candy."

Deacon Roscoe E. Rodda, General Manager of Zion Sugar and Confection Association.

Deacon Rodda—"The demand for Zion Candy is increasing very rapidly, and we find no trouble in disposing of all the candy which Zion can make, at a good price.

---

*The following is the document, to which Deacon Wilhite referred. It was presented to the Federal Court, and published at the time in all the Chicago Daily Papers, at the request of those who signed it. They represented business interests valued at hundreds of millions of dollars:

The following Resolution was unanimously adopted at a Meeting of the Creditors of the Rev. John Alexander Dowie, held in Zion City, Illinois, December 7, 1903:

After a thorough and exhaustive canvass of the situation, it was the unanimous sense of the meeting that the Rev. John Alexander Dowie was more than solvent by many millions of dollars; and that his intentions and ability to pay one hundred cents to each and every Creditor is above question.

In view of this conclusion, a Petition was signed to the Honorable C. C. Kohlsaat, Judge of the United States District Court, asking the immediate dissolution of the Receivership, and the restoration of all the property to the possession and management of the Rev. John Alexander Dowie, believing that only under his skilful management can the best results be accomplished.

The creditors present were:

HIBBARD, SPENCER, BARTLETT & COMPANY,
WESTERN STONE COMPANY,
J. L. MOTT IRON WORKS,
F. BAIRSTOW,
WILLIAM J. WAGSTAFF,
MCNEIL & HIGGINS COMPANY,
L. GOULD & COMPANY,
AMERICAN BOOK COMPANY,
CHICAGO & NORTH-WESTERN RAILWAY CO.
and J. V. FARWELL COMPANY.

WILLIAM E. MUSE, Chairman.

Large Dealers Are After Zion Candy.

"They have confidence in the purity of Zion candy.

"Our salesmen are treated most courteously, and dealers are waiting for them to come back.

"Some of the largest dealers in the country say to them, 'When you come back I will place my largest Christmas orders with you, and give you an order for a thousand pails.'

"We have orders on our books at the present time for many tons of candy.

"My good assistant, Deacon Cook, came to me this morning, and wanted to know if he could not be excused from coming here this afternoon, as the orders were pressing.

"We are on a more solid foundation than we have been, and today everything connected with our business is paid for.

"I go to Deacon Barnard, and say, 'I want a hundred barrels of sugar.'

"He says, 'All right,' calls in an assistant, and makes out a check for one thousand eight hundred dollars; and I go down and pay for it.

"We are getting special discounts, and our credit and the credit of Zion is established more firmly than ever.

"The General Stores were established three years ago last March, in a small way.

"They have grown to be quite a large Institution, as you all know; and I can say that the last year of business, covered by twelve months between July 1, 1903, and July 1, 1904, was the best we have had.

"The General Stores in a City like this is a necessity.

"It is, as its name indicates, a storehouse to supply the needs of the people.

"Occupying the position that we do, we are feeling more and more the responsibility that rests upon us, in seeing that the people get proper goods at proper prices.

"There are many things that we are not permitted to do in the General Stores that we might do in Chicago.

"It becomes our duty, under God and the direction of the General Overseer, to see that the people get good goods as far as it is within our power to do so.

"Some one has said, 'Tell me what you eat, and I will tell you what you are.'

"We are obliged to give a great deal of attention to the line of foodstuffs, and we are sorry that we cannot give more.

ZION CITY GENERAL STORES.

"Deacon Cook and myself are known almost from one end of this country to the other as candy makers.

"When our representatives go on the road and show their samples, they are greeted with, 'Why! is Rodda making candy for Dowie?' 'Have you Horace Cook there?' 'How did Dr. Dowie come to get those men?'

"Well, he has them; and they are making the candy.

"If you want to make good investments, now is your time.

"Put your shoulder to the wheel; put your money into Zion Bank; and help us make pure candy and fine lace."

Judge Barnes "A man who is as deep in the candy business as Deacon Rodda, has a right to feel stuck up. [Laughter.]

"I now have the pleasure of introducing to you Deacon W. Hurd Clendinen, the head of Zion City General Stores."

Deacon W. Hurd Clendinen, General Manager Zion City General Stores.

Deacon Clendinen—"Dear brothers and sisters, these men who have been addressing you make the goods and I sell them to you.

"I can recommend them, and I have been recommending them; and I believe that you are all pleased with them.

"The history of Zion City General Stores is along the same line of progress as the history of Zion City.

The People Need Help in Selecting Pure Foods.

"The carelessness of the people with respect to what they eat is appalling.

"In Zion we are taught that we must eat pure food, properly prepared, and in the General Stores we seek to supply this kind of goods.

"We exercise all possible precautions to see that nothing that is unfit to eat is sold.

"We manufacture baking powder and tooth powder; we are packing our own starch, laundry starch, and soda; and we are also buying our coffees in the green, and having them roasted, blending them ourselves and putting them in packages.

"We are just beginning the packing of teas, and we expect to extend this to other lines of goods.

"We also, in a small way, manufacture special articles in the way of furniture, of which we have a sample on the platform here today.

"Deacon Sloan is now occupying one of our chairs."

Deacon Sloan "To demonstrate its strength."

The General Stores Have a Bright Prospect.

Deacon Clendinen "The prospects of the General Stores are certainly bright.

"They cannot be otherwise with a people that are united, a people that love God and want to build up Zion's Institutions.

"I thank God that they will continue to grow as the City grows.

"To those who are living outside, I wish to say that we thank you for your loyalty, because we know that many of you have sent us orders for merchandise that you possibly could have bought a little more conveniently elsewhere.

DEACON W. HURD CLENDINEN,
General Manager Zion City General Stores.

"As suggested by Deacon Barnard, we are establishing agencies for all Zion City products as rapidly as possible.

"We need more capital in the General Stores, as they do in the other Industries.

"While we are enabled at the present time to buy many things from the manufacturers, we would be in a better position if we had more capital.

"We might possibly, ourselves, import some lines of goods.

The Extension of the Trade of Zion General Stores Desirable.

"We desire to extend this business to every Zion Gathering in the country.

"There may be some delay in receiving your goods, as the railroads are rather an uncertain quantity; but, with the help of Deacon Peters and the Transportation Department, we hope we may be able to improve upon our present service.

"We believe that some day we will have Zion General Stores in every nation under the sun.

"We do not think it at all impossible that we may be able to make a tour of the world and ride on Zion Railways, stop at Zion Hospices, and buy Zion Merchandise at every place at which we stop." [Applause.]

Judge Barnes—"I wish to present to you the gentleman who is at the head of Zion Hospices, and who had very great success in feeding three thousand Restorationists, last October, in the City of New York.

"I can, as on a former occasion, very truthfully say of that gentleman, that he is all Cotton and a yard wide."

Deacon Frank W. Cotton, General Manager Zion Hospices.

Deacon Cotton—"Dear friends, I do not know what I shall say to you, unless I invite you all down to the Hospice to take a meal with us.

"You would, of course, pay for it. [Laughter.]

"We are serving from thirteen hundred to fifteen hundred meals every day.

"We find that it is quite a task, but we are doing the very best we can." [Applause.]

Judge Barnes—"I desire to present to you Deacon J. F. Peters, head of Zion Transportation Department, one of the most useful departments we have.

"So long as he is at the head of that department, it can never be said that the transportation department 'peters' out.

Deacon James F. Peters, Superintendent of Zion Transportation and Railway Affairs.

Deacon James F. Peters, after speaking of better local train service, said:

"The General Manager of the Chicago & North-Western Railroad told me a few days ago that he was very seriously considering asking the General Overseer if they could establish a portion of their shops in Zion City.

"Do you realize what that means?

"I suppose in their shops at Fortieth street in Chicago they employ perhaps five thousand or six thousand men.

"Multiply that by five and you have a population of twenty-five thousand people.

"He also said, that while he supposed he would be compelled to bring some of his skilled labor here, that just as fast as the General Overseer could furnish the men to operate the machines in this shop, he would employ Zion men. [Applause.]

"Now I come to our new friends, the Chicago & Milwaukee Electric Railroad.

"One of the officials, who has been loyal and true to Zion, and who believes in our beloved General Overseer and in his teaching, has said to me frequently, 'Deacon, nothing on earth can stop that movement in Zion City. It is bound to be the largest city between Chicago and Milwaukee.'

"He called me up on the long distance telephone the other

DEACON FRANK W. COTTON,
Manager Zion Hospices.

day and said, 'Deacon, I want to congratulate you on the road-bed and construction, as far as you have gone.

"'It is the best that I have ever had built.'

"I want, first of all, in connection with that, to give God the glory; and then the laboring men.

Zion Transportation Bureau To Be a Great Institution.

"Zion Transportation and Railway Bureau is a small department at present, but by the grace of God I believe that it will be one of the biggest departments in Zion, because naturally it will have to reach out all over the world.

"We now have daily correspondence from every country on the earth, asking what we can do for Zion people, in bringing their goods and themselves to this City.

DEACON JAMES F. PETERS,
General Superintendent Zion Transportation and Railway Affairs.

"It must necessarily have a part in every City that is built.

"I am sorry that Zion does not own the Chicago & Milwaukee Electric Railroad between Chicago and Milwaukee, because in the future it will be a gold mine.

"Will you invest in that property about which Deacon Judd has asked you?

"We have been promised the contract for constructing the road between here and Kenosha next year; and where we are now working one hundred and fifty men, I believe that we will be working three hundred next summer.

"I asked you two months ago to pray for that little portion of the line out there, which Zion is constructing under contract.

"I know you have prayed, and God has blessed us with good weather.

"Not a man or animal has been injured, and I know in my heart that it is all God's work, in answer to your prayers." [Applause.]

Judge Barnes—"I now come to the gentleman of whom I must speak with very much respect, since he has power over my department as the Inspector—Deacon Daniel Sloan, General Inspector of Zion Institutions.

"I know you will all want to hear Deacon Sloan."

Deacon Daniel Sloan, Inspector-General of Zion.

Deacon Daniel Sloan—"I was assured at the beginning of the meeting this afternoon that I was to have an hour and a half.

"I suppose that refers to the hour and a half I have had sitting in that chair. [Laughter.]

"If you want to get real comfort out of a chair, visit the Furniture Department of Zion City General Stores.

"I have inspected that chair, and can highly recommend it."

Judge Barnes—"I do not want you to inspect me in the same way." [Laughter.]

Deacon Sloan—"I was thinking, this afternoon, of a passage of Scripture: 'Thou shalt remember all the way in which the Lord thy God hath led thee.'

"We are so liable to forget.

"God has wrought a wonderful work in the midst of this people.

"The forcible presentation of the various Zion Institutions, to which you have listened this afternoon, has undoubtedly awakened in you intense interest.

"These Institutions are simply the beginnings of many others.

"Deacon Rodda's declaration, that he could make a profit of ten per cent. and turn his goods six times a year, thus making sixty per cent. is nothing.

"We have an Institution under consideration that will enable us to turn the capital six times a year, and yield one hundred per cent. each time, a Paint Factory.

"Everybody is wanting the goods, and when we get that thing started, which we hope with the blessing of God to do, we can paint the town red." [Applause.]

Judge Barnes—"I will introduce to you Deacon George E. Wiedman, properly speaking the Postmaster-general of Zion City."

Deacon George E. Wiedman, Postmaster of Zion City.

Deacon George E. Wiedman—"Beloved friends, the postoffice is an indispensable institution.

"We had, probably, a population of between three and four thousand people before the Department at Washington would consider giving us a postoffice.

"One reason for this delay was its peculiar name.

"There is Zion, Illinois, in Carroll County.

"People sometimes wonder why they do not hear from their letters.

DEACON DANIEL SLOAN,
Auditor General and Inspector General of all Zion Institutions and Industries.

"The reason is that they have written to Zion, not to Zion City.

"This will be a good fact to remember.

"This similarity of names necessitated a visit to Washington by the General Overseer, who got everything that he wanted —even to a Postmaster.

"When unconsciously preparing for this work by eight years' experience in the Chicago postoffice, I had no thought that I should reach this position.

"The first year's business, as you know, amounted to ten thousand seven hundred dollars.

"Think of it!

"I did not think that it would amount to five thousand dollars.

"The first order for postage stamps amounted to thirty dollars.

"I sold that in two days.

"I had to go to the neighboring cities and ask them for stamps until I could make the Department understand how large Zion City really was.

"Our order to Washington for stamps now frequently amounts to three thousand dollars.

"The first day's business amounted to nineteen dollars and nineteen cents.

"Now we do a daily business of between one hundred and three hundred dollars in the sale of postage-stamps alone.

DEACON GEORGE E. WIEDMAN
Postmaster, Zion City.

"When the office was one year old, I made application for free delivery, and it took about twenty-four pages to give the department the facts.

"They sent a man to inspect the City.

"He was agreeably surprised, and although a worldly man, he said, 'Surely, this is not of man.'

"When he wrote to the department, verified my statements, and recommended free delivery throughout the City, he incorporated in his letter a description of the character of the people, told how clean the City was, and that it was void of all the stench and filth of the world.

"This made a great impression upon the postoffice department at Washington, and from that time on, I have had very little difficulty in getting what I have asked for.

"Zion City Postoffice has flourished wonderfully.

"Two years ago there were but two employees in the postoffice—a postmaster and his assistant; today I have a corps of fifteen.

"Sixty years ago, Waukegan was a small city; today in postal revenues and in postal work they do not exceed us; we are very nearly equal.

"I predict that within two years we shall be far above our neighboring cities.

"The marvelous thing to the postoffice officials who have come to investigate Zion City Postoffice Department, is the very small degree of illiteracy on the part of the people.

"Last year we did ten thousand dollars' worth of postal business.

"This entitled us to free delivery.

"I mean by postal business the sale of postage-stamps.

"The aggregate business is the sale of stamps and money-orders.

ZION CITY PLANING MILL.

"This year we did twenty thousand dollars' worth, and next year, as the General Overseer predicts, we will probably do thirty thousand or forty thousand dollars' worth.

"Many friends outside of Zion City have had trouble with their postmasters, and as a last resort, they have referred the matter to the Postmaster at Zion City.

"In that way I have been enabled to remedy many grievances.

"If any of you have trouble with your postmasters, in the way of delivery or the receipt of your mail, write to the Postmaster at Zion City, and he will rectify that error.

"In closing, I wish to remark that within the last six months we have had but forty complaints concerning the loss of mail.

"When one considers that we have a population of many thousands of people, that fact is marvelous."

Judge Barnes—"Some years ago a person in Great Britain—Edward VII., then Prince of Wales—offered a prize in the shape of a gold medal to the one having the highest rank in scholarship in one of the great universities of Canada.

"We are very glad that the man who captured that gold medal, and who still possesses it, became the first, and present, and only Mayor that the City of Zion has ever had, Honorable Richard H. Harper, our beloved Mayor, who will now address you."

Deacon Richard H. Harper, Mayor of Zion City, and General Manager of Zion Building and Manufacturing Association.

Deacon Richard H. Harper—"The golden-tongued orator at the power house reminds me that I must be exceedingly brief.

"Nature has made me that.

DEACON R. H. HARPER,
General Manager of Zion Building and Manufacturing Association.

"I am only about five feet one inch and a half in height, and I will make my speech something like myself.

"Zion Building and Manufacturing Association, which I

represent, is one of the latest of the business children of Zion, but not one of the least.

There are about a dozen departments, and although it is only about sixteen months old, it has been able to do considerable business.

"Looking over our records, before coming to this meeting, I found that during those sixteen months, we have, in the Building Department alone, done about seven hundred fifty thousand dollars' worth of work.

"In addition to that, we have had the work of the Bakery, with sales amounting to four thousand dollars each month.

"We have had the Power House, sending out bills amounting to from twenty thousand to thirty thousand dollars a month.

"We have the Box Factory, with its immense business at the present time.

"We have a Lumber Yard, a Planing Mill, a Tin Shop, and various other Institutions.

"The combined business of these departments, in sixteen months, has amounted to about nine hundred thirty thousand dollars.

"This, with the work which is partly finished, including the Chicago & Milwaukee Electric Railway, which is a part of the work of the Building and Manufacturing Association, combined with the Zion City Railroad and Transportation business, makes a total of over a million dollars.

"Do you not think that is pretty good for an infant?

"One word as to the needs of Zion Building and Manufacturing Association:

Possibilities of Zion Laces.

"I told you before I left here that I was going to wear Zion lace, and I did so.

"I had a number of garments made up here, and I took some lace with me and had it made up while I was in Paris, so that I might be able to have it done in the nicest possible way, and that it might show to the best advantange.

"A lady in Paris is very much interested in Zion City, and in the work of Zion.

"She has been reading LEAVES OF HEALING for many years.

"She has a large dressmaking establishment.

"While Deacon Stevenson was in Europe this time, he visited her, and was very much delighted with what she was able to tell him about the various fabrics that would be used with the different laces, and how they combined them.

"Among the things she showed him was a beautiful lace dress.

"My Zion lace garments were very much admired, and great interest was taken everywhere in the samples that I carried with me.

Zion Products Open the Way for Zion's Message.

"Showing these samples would lead many to ask questions, thus giving us an opportunity to tell them about the work that was being done.

"I was able to tell them that we gave good prices to our working people, that we sold our goods at a good profit, that it was a religious work, and that we did not cheat.

ZION SUGAR AND CONFECTION ASSOCIATION BUILDING
(As Planned)

"About fifty thousand dollars was required for warming the people the past winter.

"That was included in the work of the Building and Manufacturing Association.

"We urgently need capital to enable us to build economically, and to carry on the work of the Building and Manufacturing Association." [Applause.]

Judge Barnes—"Before I call upon the last speaker, our beloved Overseer Jane Dowie, I wish to say that I do not feel justified in inflicting any speech of my own upon you this afternoon, owing to the lateness of the hour.

"I present to you our beloved Overseer, Jane Dowie, the woman who, I believe, occupies the most exalted position of any woman in the world."

Rev. Jane Dowie, Overseer of Women's Work in the Christian Catholic Church in Zion Throughout the World.

Overseer Jane Dowie—"I thank Judge Barnes for his kind words. I believe we have a great future before us, not only in Zion City, but in all the world, if God gives us the strength that we expect Him to give for the future.

"In our visit around the world, we were able to tell a great many people about Zion and the wonderful work God has been doing here through His people.

"It seemed to some people as though we were telling them idle tales, which they could scarcely believe.

"I was pleased to be able to tell them that the people got good value for what they bought; that we were not expecting to get more for our products than they were really worth because we were a religious community.

"They had always supposed that a religious community extorted great sums for almost nothing at all.

"I told them we had no sales and no bazaars, and none of these things that bothered the people in the churches so much.

"I said that we took our religion into our business, and our business into our religion.

"They would listen and say, 'Well, that is good common sense, and it is all right, and we wish there was more of it.'

"All this they would get because they looked at a few little pieces of lace, and every one that saw our laces was delighted.

"We had the same experience with Zion candy.

"We did not taste better candy anywhere; in fact, none that was nearly as good as the candy we got from Zion City.

"In Australia we added to our enemies another class of people.

"We have had against us the ministers, whose people we have taken out of the churches.

"We have had against us the doctors, whose patients we have delivered from their hands, and who now do not take drugs or medicines.

"We have had against us the publicans, or saloon-keepers as we call them in America.

"We have had against us the people who sell the pig, and all these things.

"But during the last meetings we held in Australia, we found we had to add another class of people to the list of our antagonists, and that was the stockbrokers.

"They were afraid the people would realize on their stocks and investments there and put their money into Zion Stocks.

"Now we have the King of England against us.

"However, we have not only enemies, but we have friends

OVERSEER JANE DOWIE,
Overseer in the Christian Catholic Church for Women's Work in Zion Throughout the World.

that are really true and godly, and who are desiring to do right.

"There are many loving hearts all over the world that are turned toward Zion.

"We were told by many who had invested in Zion, how they were able to live better, because they had so much higher percentage on their investments.

Purity and Wholesomeness of Zion Candy.

"My young brother, about three years older than my son, said, when I came away, 'Jeanie, if you will send me some of that candy when you get back I will be glad to pay for it at its full price, and pay the duty and the freight.'

"He said all the other candies he had eaten were not good for his stomach, and that he had been injured by eating them; but that he could eat this candy and not feel distressed.

"Of course I told him that it was because it was wellmade, and because of the workmanship and purity.

"In talking about that, we were able to tell the people that they should eat clean things, and not take dirty tobacco; so we were enabled to bring in a little talk on tobacco.

"I do not know why I have been asked to speak today, but I am usually asked to speak at business meetings.

"I am not at the head of any of the Business Institutions.

"Although I am one of the Business Cabinet, and occasionally attend their Cabinet Meetings, I have nothing to do with the actual workings of the business.

"My real business today is that of being a lace exhibit.

"It is not so terribly unpleasant to be a lace exhibit, when it is for Zion.

"I thank God that we have done as much good work as we have.

"We do not say that we have yet everything perfect in Zion; but we are going on to get things more nearly perfect.

"Money makes money if it is properly handled; and it is very apparent, after all, that with a city growing as our City is growing, and with the necessity for growth being forced upon us, that it is needful for God to send us plenty of money.

"I believe that this will come.

"I know that God will give great wisdom to all our workers.

"If here and there we all have had a little hardship and pressure, it is nothing more than we might have expected if we intended to be good soldiers for the Christ.

"Some of our people do have hardships, even when they go out upon a pleasure trip, to have a rest or carry the Gospel. We cannot have it pleasant all the time.

"Our trip was a very profitable one to us all.

"I am thankful that we were brought back again to Zion City, whole and well, the entire party, not one being left.

"Every one felt better for having taken the journey.

"We have a happy people and a happy City.

"We ask God to bless you and give you the joy of the Lord, which is His strength.

"I wish to thank you for the way you have listened to our talk.

"We trust we will have many happy days together here.

"We were able to speak to many thousands of people in many nations.

"My son, Dr. A. J. Gladstone Dowie, addressed large gatherings before the General Overseer came, in Melbourne and Adelaide.

"I also addressed people there. At that time my son was able to give the people a good deal of information on these subjects, and they were greatly interested.

"I believe that the results of that Visitation will be far more manifest in the future than they are now.

"The visit we paid to Europe some years ago, has brought great and good results, that were unexpected.

"It looked at the time, from a financial standpoint, as if it was a failure; but it was not, for large investments came to Zion through our European visit of 1900-1, and it certainly has been a blessing to thousands and thousands of people there.

"God is blessing the work everywhere, in all the various agencies that have been established and that are being established.

DR. A. J. GLADSTONE DOWIE.

"They all work together to bring about a more perfect whole.

"May God bless you!"

Judge Barnes—"I now take pleasure in surrendering the chair to Overseer Jane Dowie, who will close the meeting."

The Congregation then sang one stanza of "I Stand on Zion's Mount," after which Overseer Jane Dowie pronounced the

BENEDICTION.

Beloved, abstain from every form of evil. And may the very God of Peace Himself sanctify you wholly; and I pray God your whole spirit, and soul, and body be preserved entire, without blame, unto the coming of our Lord Jesus, the Christ. Faithful is He that calleth you, who also will do it. The grace of our Lord Jesus, the Christ, the love of God, our Father, the fellowship of the Holy Spirit, our Comforter and Guide, one Eternal God, abide in you, bless you, and keep you, and all the Israel of God everywhere, forever. Amen.

EARLY MORNING SACRIFICE OF PRAISE AND PRAYER.

*REPORTED BY O. R.

Shiloh Tabernacle, Zion City, Illinois, Lord's Day Morning, July 24, 1904.

The service was opened by the singing of Hymn No. 1, in the Program.

Prayer was then offered by the General Overseer, at the close of which the Congregation joined in chanting the Disciples' Prayer.

Hymn No. 4 was then sung.

The General Overseer then said:

THE HOUSE OF WISDOM.

INVOCATION.

Let the words of my mouth and the meditation of my heart be acceptable in Thy sight, be profitable unto this people, and unto all to whom these words shall come, in this and every land, in this and all the coming time, Till Jesus Come. Amen.

We will read first in the book of Proverbs, the 4th chapter, the 7th verse.

I intend to talk about the House of Wisdom.

Wisdom is the Principal Thing.

Will you not repeat these words, please? [All repeat them.]

It Is Good Sense to Get Wisdom.

Therefore get Wisdom.

That is good sense, is it not?

Do not be like Solomon, and lose it, and become a fool.

That is one of the things that always pains me when I read this book.

There is a good deal of God-given Wisdom; but it was the wisest man of his time who got these wise words from God, and then became a fool, a brute, a beast, a bad man—going away after idols, wine, women, whoredom, horses, and idolatry.

He had seven hundred wives and three hundred concubines.

There is no question about God having given him Wisdom; but he threw it all away.

Not only get it, but keep it.

And with all thy getting, get understanding.

The Revised Version says:

With all thou hast gotten get understanding.

In the 9th chapter, first verse:

Wisdom hath builded her house,
She hath hewn out her Seven Pillars.
She hath killed her beasts; she hath mingled her wine·
She hath also furnished her table.
She hath sent forth her maidens, she crieth
Upon the highest places of the city,
Whoso is simple, let him turn in hither:
As for him that is void of understanding, she saith to him,
Come, eat ye of my bread,
And drink of the wine which I have mingled.
Leave off, ye simple ones, and live;
And walk in the way of understanding.

Wisdom is here represented as a beautiful, gracious, and benign woman, who makes a feast for all the foolish; who sends out her beautiful maidens to bring them in; and who spreads a table with good things, that the foolish people may be made wise, and live.

That might be a good figure of the Church—the Church of God, the Bride of the Christ, the Lamb's Wife—sending forth her maidens, her wise maidens, to bring in the people to the Feast of Tabernacles, and into the House of Wisdom.

The House of Wisdom Has Seven Pillars.

"Wisdom hath builded her house, she hath hewn out her Seven Pillars."

Suppose we go to the epistle of James for the Pillars, and read in the 3d chapter of the epistle, beginning with the 13th verse:

Who is wise and understanding among you? Let him show by his good life his works in meekness of Wisdom.

But if ye have bitter jealousy and faction in your heart—

Stop here a minute.

Whenever I find an officer of this Church who takes delight in underrating another officer, I mark that man and I warn him.

I am almost certain that I will have to get rid of him, because, no matter how able he may be, he has a factious and quarrelsome spirit.

He is always ready to find out how many mistakes somebody else makes, and to tell all about it.

If he had loved that brother officer, he would have gone to him and would have shown him what he thought was his mistake.

Sometimes an investigation proves that there has been no mistake, and that the critic has been nosing into his brother officer's business, instead of attending strictly to his own.

His own business has been neglected while he has been attending to another's affairs.

Every Man's Cause Seems Good in His Own Eyes.

There are people, and some of them are in Zion City, who listen to every person who comes along with a tale regarding some supposed wrong that So-and-so has suffered.

"They were sent away, and they were so good!"

A person came to me, the other day, and said that a man was sent out of this City because he was a fearless, truth-speaking man.

I went after the officer that had to do with this case, because if an innocent person had been sent out of the City, he would get back in a hurry, and the person who sent him out would get a leave of absence for a long time.

When I went into the matter, I found just what I had expected to find—that the criticism was all a lie.

I asked the person who complained, where did you get that information?

He replied, "From the person who was sent out."

"Did it never strike you that it might be a lie?" I asked.

"Oh, no; he was so sincere!" he replied.

"You have swallowed that man's lies," I said.

"That man was sent out of this City for adultery, for stealing, and for lying; and perhaps he ought to have been sent to the penitentiary, only we were compassionate."

The faultfinder was amazed at the facts in this affair.

I cite another case, in which a lady supposedly had been wronged.

I folded a letter that I had received from that lady in such a way as to show only one paragraph, which read:

"I have deeply sinned; my punishment is just; I pray for your forgiveness and that of the Church."

Sin and Folly of Listening to Gossip.

The person opened her eyes.

"Why, that isn't what I heard."

No! what business have you to go about hearing?

It is our business, not yours, to see that justice is done.

You foolish people, going about and judging matters that you have nothing to do with, and that have been judged!

You damage Zion, and you talk nonsense, just because you are foolish.

Get wise, and attend to your own business!

I love you very much, but I think I will ask some of you to come and visit me in my office, and I will have you put out your tongues, and let me clip a little off the end. [Laughter]

The amount of energy that you waste in attending to matters that do not concern you!

You ought to be wise, and not listen to gossips.

You that listen to them are worse than those who talk.

If there were no receivers of stolen property, there would be no thieves.

If there were no listeners, there would be no gossipers.

True Christians Have no Time nor Ears for Gossip.

If a gossiper begins to talk to you, say, "I have no time for that; I have no ears for that."

If you know of any wrong that has been done, write to the General Overseer, and put your name to your letter. Send

*The following address has not been revised by the General Overseer

the complaint to him, and he will investigate it; and if you are wrong, you will get the stick.

Attend Diligently to Your Own Heart.

Make it clear to your own minds, that your business is to attend diligently, first of all, to your own heart.

During the lunch hour, do not fill your mind with all the gossip that may be around.

If you have any time to spare, take out your Bible and say: "Look here, Brother Jones, I do not want to hear that gossip about Brother Smith or Sister Johnson. Get out your Bible and we will read a little, sing a hymn and pray.

"If you have any complaint to make, make it to the Deacon or the Elder in charge of that district, and let it get up to the General Overseer, if it is important enough. But let us enjoy the dinner hour."

Exaggeration a Cause of Stumbling.

I was very angry yesterday when a complaint was sent in to me by a woman about her husband, and I gave sharp directions.

I learned, during the course of the afternoon and evening, that the woman had grossly exaggerated; in fact that she had shamefully lied, and that three-fourths of the fault was hers, and not her husband's.

I telephoned Overseer Excell, directing him to give her words of rebuke. I threatened that if she again wrote me such a mass of lies I would send her out of the City, and that her husband would have to go with her.

She had exaggerated a trifling incident until she had made a mass of lies out of it.

The story that she wrote me was so shameful that I directed Overseer Excell that if he found it to be true he was to get that man out of the City at once.

It was not true.

Many a woman would be glad to have a husband as good as that man is.

Nine-tenths of the mischief arises from exaggeration—shameful exaggeration!

Who is wise and understanding among you? let him shew by his good life and works in meekness of Wisdom.

Now, show if you have understanding, by your good life, by your works, in meekness and wisdom; but if you have bitter jealousy and faction in your heart, glory not.

When a man gets a factious spirit in him, he not only glories in the defects of his brother, but he puts his finger in them and tears the holes open, until at last he begins to lie against the truth.

This wisdom is not the Wisdom that cometh from above.

It is a wicked kind of wisdom.

It is earthly.

It is sensual.

It is devilish.

The word sensual there is animal—not spiritual--but earthly, animal, demoniacal, devilish.

For where jealousy and faction are, there is confusion and every vile deed.

The Spirit of Jealousy and Faction Must Be Kept Out.

If we permit the spirit of jealousy and faction to get into Zion City affairs, there will be "confusion and every vile deed."

This is true with respect to every Institution—especially with respect to the Church of God.

Envy has destroyed great cities, and uprooted mighty nations.

Envy was the cause of the Crucifixion of the Christ, our Lord.

Pilate, it is written, knew that for envy they had delivered Jesus.

Some of you who are poor may say, "Oh, I havn't this, and I havn't that, and I havn't the other thing."

If you had it, you would not know what to do with it.

It is a good thing that you don't have it.

If you had large means you would probably waste it.

I remember being in Victoria, British Columbia, a number of years ago.

The Indians had been very successful that year, as they often are, in spearing salmon in the Fraser River.

One Indian came down in his canoe, with his squaw and his children, with fifteen hundred dollars that he had made that year by spearing salmon.

I happened to see him after he came in with the canoes.

Somebody called my attention to him.

The manner in which that man spent his money was ridiculous.

He kept his wife and daughters barefooted, but he clad all his boys in boots—some of them in top-boots; and he himself was arrayed in the most absurd style.

I really could not take the time to tell you, if I could remember, of all the things that he bought.

But I know that he bought a kettle-drum, or something of that kind.

I happened to see him the day after, coming from town to his canoe with the purchases of that day.

There were trumpets and all sorts of things piled upon his back—ridiculous things, of which he could make no permanent use, while his family needed blankets and other good things which would be serviceable to them.

He began to drink fire-water, and when he went out of Victoria he had to sell his drums and trumpets for what he could get.

I think he went out of Victoria with not more than two or three blankets to show for the one thousand five hundred dollars that he had spent.

Wisdom is Needed in the Use of Riches.

Some people in and out of Zion have not much better judgment than that poor Indian in the spending of money.

If they were rich, they would not know how to use their riches.

They could not use them in extending the Kingdom of God.

They would not know how.

It seems to me, that we all could learn how to do without many things.

Do you not know that it is sometimes a great burden to have so many things?

In my work I require so many things that I am sometimes burdened with them.

Zion Printing and Publishing House has been my personal care all these years; and I have had to throw out all the old machinery and get the newest and best.

The progress that is constantly being made requires frequent changes in, and additions to, the plant.

After building the house and making many additions to the machinery, I find that the requirements of this year will necessitate the addition of department after department, and the purchase of more machinery to do work that has not been done hitherto.

But what could you do with all the money that will be necessary to make these changes?

You could not buy that machinery, and you would not know how to manage that house if it were given you to manage.

God Will Give Us All We Can Wisely Use.

Do not you trouble about it.

If God sees that you can use money, He will give you the power to make it.

But you will never make it by grumbling.

You will never make it by envy.

You will never get power in Zion, or a better position, by being a grumbler.

Some grumble themselves into their graves when they might have risen to be powerful, and strong, and a blessing to Zion.

They were impatient, and they wanted it all done in a day.

A little while ago, a poor fellow said, "I want what Dr. Dowie has."

Well, how long has it taken Dr. Dowie to get it?

How many long years have I had to be deprived of everything that I might do the work?

I do not know now but that I would rather, if I had my pleasure in the matter, just have my belongings in a trunk, and go and evangelize the world, if that were the best thing.

But in order to build up Zion and to do the work here, I require to establish a home, and all the surroundings necessary for building up Zion.

Why do you grumble?

One Who Would Be a Leader Must First Learn to Follow.

There are not many who grumble, but that infernal spirit of envy gets into people!

If you want to be a great leader, learn to be a good follower.

That is the way to learn to be a great leader.

Do your work, you young people!

The other morning I called up Zion Printing and Publishing House, and a young man answered me.

He told me who he was.

I said, "I am glad that you have been a good boy. When I put you in that position years ago, with a rag and some oil, I told you to clean that machine. I said to you, some day you will understand that machine if you study it by oiling it properly; and you may work that great machine."

He was only a little chap, then. He looked at me with a bright face, and said, "I will do it, Doctor."

Every now and then I said to him, calling him by name, "Well, Bobby, how are you getting on with oiling that machine?"

He would reply, "First class. I am beginning to understand it, Doctor."

Faithfulness Rewarded.

He went on, and we kept him oiling the machine—under it and over it, and he kept every bit of it perfectly oiled and cleaned.

He was studying it.

Now he has charge of several machines, bigger and better than the one he used to oil.

In talking to me over the telephone he said, "Thank you for your encouragement when you told me to take a rag and clean and oil that machine. I am glad you made me study it."

Some of you will have to take your oil and rags and rub, if you would understand. [Laughter.]

I began my life with a currycomb, currying horses, cleaning out stables, sweeping out the shop, and getting everything ready for the other employees.

I got my breakfast after that was done, and received only two dollars a week.

But I never grumbled.

I went at it, and I cleaned that horse properly.

I cleaned out that stable properly; and then I went down to the store, and I cleaned that properly.

Some Do Not Begin Humbly Enough.

Some of you have no sense.

You did not begin humbly enough.

I kept doing my work; and it was not many years before I could get almost anything I wanted, because I did my duty.

I was good, and I obeyed.

I want you to be strong; but attend to your own business, and attend to your duty.

Today I have the love and respect of the people for whom I worked when a little boy.

They have opened their homes, and treated me with the highest honor.

You will rise if you are wise.

Some of you foolish people throw yourselves out in the very beginning, and then you are nothing but tramps!

You never will rise.

The only thing that can be done with you is to attach you to a pole, and make you grind around and around like an old blind horse. [Laughter.]

The General Overseer then read the 17th and 18th verses:

But the Wisdom that is from above is first Pure, then Peaceable, Gentle, easy to be Entreated, full of Mercy and Good Fruits, without Variance, without Hypocrisy.

And the Fruit of Righteousness is sown in Peace for them that make Peace.

The House of Wisdom.

Wisdom hath builded her House.

Each one of you has a house.

"No, General Overseer," you say, "I have no house."

Then you are the first man I ever saw without a house.

[Turning to a boy in the orchestra.] Have you a house?

Answer—"No, sir."

General Overseer—But you have. You have a house; stand up and I will show you your house.

I should think your house was about four feet high. [Laughter.]

It is your body.

It is not only a house, my son, but it is a temple.

You have a house with a brain that can do what I never could do. I never could fiddle.

We all have houses, and each has a dome; do you see? [Pointing to his head. Laughter.]

The House that God Builds Has a Dome.

Every house that God builds has a dome, the dome of one's head.

Some people do not take care of their domes.

Others are afraid too much might be thought of their domes, and they adorn them with hair, that they buy. [Laughter.]

Why can you not let the dome of your head appear?

I will give the ladies permission, at all services today, to take off their hats; I am half inclined to give you the command to do it. [Applause.]

People behind you can then see the speaker.

I give that little hint, because I think that the dome of the head is beautiful!

Many of you have beautiful heads—magnificent heads; but you have bonnets stuck upon them.

I cannot tell what nice heads you have; I guess at it; but I never did see any sense in expecting a man to remove his hat and allowing a woman to wear her bonnet.

I know it may be a little trouble to take off this great creation, and undo it, but if I were you, at the next Feast of Tabernacles, I would buy a very simple hat to wear to the meetings, and then tuck it under the chair. [Applause.]

That is a little thing, you say; but there is Wisdom in that.

How nice it is, since the women have taken off their hats!

I am now looking at such a number of nice heads!

"Wisdom hath builded her house."

We Are Builders With God.

Do you know that we have the building of a beautiful house entrusted to us?

Oh, if we only could talk about it with Real Purity!

What a wonderful thing it is that man and woman have the building of a house!

Oh, how beautiful the little house is when it comes into being!

How many say, "What shall this child be?"

The child will be, under God, just what you make it.

If you will take care of that little house that God has given you, the little house will grow, because it is not like other houses.

When we make a house, it stands as it was built until we pull it down, or until we build additions.

I am talking about the house of the body.

What a beautiful thing is a well-born child, from a clean, wholesome mother, with sweet, pure thoughts; and with a good, clean, wholesome father, who is a true man, gentle and loving.

I saw babies the other day that were really beautiful; and some that were not so beautiful.

I looked at the faces of some, and I thought I saw some reason why they were not beautiful; it was not their fault.

An Accursed Heredity.

They were badly born.

They were the offspring of some wretched drunkard or foolish woman.

I tell you, I watch the babies.

I receive hundreds of them in my arms every year.

I have taken more interest in these babies whom I have consecrated than perhaps any of you have.

I thank God for the way in which the house grows—the House of Wisdom.

How beautiful it is to see the child, full of Faith and Heavenly Wisdom, wanting to help brother and sister, and saying, "how can we help baby?" and, "how can we help mamma?" and, "how can we love God?"

Some of you have old houses, but they can be made clean.

The House of Wisdom has Seven Pillars.

The first great Pillar in Wisdom's beautiful house is Purity—Divine Purity—pure as the Great White Throne.

The Great White Throne.

Oh, what is the Great White Throne?

I know not what else it is, but it is Purity.

You find a gem that is beautifully pure, and you find a gem that has streaks in it; you put the two together, and you want to put the latter aside.

You want the beautiful gem!

Oh, what a beautiful gem a pure diamond is! A beautiful ruby is like a drop of heart's blood.

Sometimes a ruby looks like a drop of the cup of the beautiful red wine, without any base and intoxicating power in it, that we shall drink one day in our Father's Kingdom.

Gems are wonderful things!

They are from the hand of God.

Some of you poor, wretched creatures are always envious against the Pure in Heart, and thinking what a wicked thing it is to have diamonds.

Do you not know that when God established His Church in the wilderness, amongst the poor slaves that came out of Egypt, He clothed His High Priest in garments of beauty and glory, with twelve gems upon the breast, one for each of the Twelve Tribes of Israel?

The Perfect City that God is to build will have twelve precious stones, one thousand five hundred miles in length, for foundations.

Gems From the Foundations of Heaven.

It seems almost as if all our precious stones upon earth were just little chips from the Foundations of Heaven.

God is desirous that the House of Wisdom which He is constructing—the great Spiritual Temple—shall be built of Living Stones.

One day, this great Living Temple of His Living Church will stand in the world, and it will be like the Zion of today.

The strength of Zion is the Central Pillar of Purity—Purity of Spirit, Soul, and Body; Purity in Commerce, Purity in Business, and Purity in Love.

When Zion Sugar and Confection Association came to me with their motto, I said, "That is all right: Purity, Originality, and Workmanship."

The people believe that Zion candy has those qualities.

The Church that God is building is to be a House of Wisdom.

It has pillars, and pillars that we must fight for if necessary; pillars that we must cleanse our hands for, and do everything to seek.

The Wisdom that is from above is first Pure, then Peaceable, Gentle, Easy to be Entreated, full of Mercy and Good Fruits, Without Partiality, Without Hypocrisy.

And the Fruit of Righteousness is sown in Peace for them that make Peace.

May God grant that we shall realize that we are ourselves the Temple of God, and that the Temple of God should be Holy; that from the center to the circumference of our being, we should be clean and pure in every way, spirit, soul, and body; clean in our houses, clean in our back yards, and clean in our front yards; clean in the humblest places.

Keep things clean.

Then you will have Power; for Purity is Power.

Purity is Peace. Purity is Progress. Purity is Divine.

May God make us Pure.

PRAYER OF CONSECRATION.

Our God and Father, in Jesus' Name we come to Thee. Take us as we are, make us what we ought to be, in spirit, in soul, and in body. Forgive our transgressions, our impurity of thought, or word, or deed. Cleanse us by the blood of the Messiah who died for us, who lives for us, who loves us, who will bring us out into Perfect Purity. Give us this blessing now. For Jesus' sake make us wise. Amen

The Congregation then joined in singing, "They that be Wise shall Shine," and the General Overseer pronounced the

BENEDICTION.

Beloved, abstain from every form of evil. And may the very God of Peace Himself sanctify you wholly. And I pray God your whole spirit, and soul, and body be preserved entire, without blame, unto the coming of our Lord Jesus, the Christ. Faithful is He that calleth you, who also will do it. The grace of our Lord Jesus, the Christ, the love of God, our Father, the fellowship of the Holy Spirit, our Comforter and Guide, one Eternal God, abide in you, bless you and keep you, and all the Israel of God everywhere, forever. Amen.

Publisher's Notice.

The remittance must accompany receipt of subscriptions at the Publishing House, no difference by or for whom or for whatever time they may be given, or whether forwarded through Ordained Officers, Branches, or Gatherings of the Christian Catholic Church in Zion. Accounts will be carried with Ordained Officers, Branches, or Gatherings, on quantity orders of periodicals consigned on sale for monthly settlement, but to include only such articles as bear the imprint of Zion. All orders for Bibles, books, buttons, pictures (except prints done by the Publishing House), lace souvenirs, etc., must be sent to the General Stores, Zion City, Lake County, Illinois.

DO YOU KNOW GOD'S WAY OF HEALING?

BY THE REV. JOHN ALEX. DOWIE.

Let it be supposed that the following words are a conversation between the reader [A] and the writer [B].

A. What does this question mean? Do you really suppose that God has some one especial way of healing in these days, of which men may know and avail themselves?

B. That is exactly my meaning, and I wish very much that you should know God's Way of Healing, as I have known it for many years.

A. What is the way, in your opinion?

B. You should rather ask, WHO is God's Way? for the way is a Person, not a thing. I will answer your question in His own words, "I am the Way, and the Truth, and the Life: no one cometh unto the Father, but by Me." These words were spoken by our Lord Jesus, the Christ, the Eternal Son of God, who is both our Savior and our Healer. (John 14:6.)

A. But I always thought that these words only referred to Him as the Way of Salvation. How can you be sure that they refer to Him as the Way of Healing also?

B. Because He cannot change. He is "the same yesterday and today, yea, and forever." (Hebrews 13:8.) He said that He came to this earth not only to save us but to heal us. (Luke 4:18), and He did this when in the flesh on earth. Being unchanged He must be able and willing and desirous to heal now.

A. But is there not this difference, namely, that He is not with us now?

B. No; for He said "Lo, I am with you All the Days, even unto the Consummation of the Age;" and so He is with us now, in spirit, just as much as when He was here in the flesh.

A. But did He not work these miracles of healing when on earth merely to prove that He was the Son of God?

B. No; there was still a greater purpose than that. He healed the sick who trusted in Him in order to show us that He came to die not only for our sins, but for our sicknesses, and to deliver us from both.

A. Then, if that be so, the atonement which He made on the Cross must have been for our sicknesses as well as our sins. Can you prove that is the fact from the Scriptures?

B. Yes, I can, and the passages are very numerous. I need quote only two. In Isaiah 53:4, 5, it is written of Him: "Surely He hath borne our griefs (Hebrew, *sicknesses*), and carried our sorrows: . . . and with His stripes we are healed." Then, in the Gospel according to Matthew, this passage is quoted and directly applied to the work of bodily healing, in the 8th chapter 17th verse: "That it might be fulfilled which was spoken by Isaiah the prophet, saying, Himself took our infirmities, and bare our diseases."

A. But do you not think that sickness is often God's will, and sent for our good, and therefore God may not wish us to be healed?

B. No, that cannot possibly be, for diseases of every kind are the Devil's work, and his work can never be God's will, since the Christ came for the very purpose of destroying "the works of the Devil." (1 John 3:8.)

A. Do you mean to say that all disease is the work of Satan?

B. Yes, for if there had been no sin (which came through Satan) there never would have been any disease, and Jesus never in one single instance told any person that sickness was God's work or will, but the very contrary.

A. Can you prove from Scriptures that all forms of sickness and infirmity are the Devil's work?

B. Yes, that can be done very easily. You will see in Matthew 4:23 and 9:35 that when Jesus was here in the flesh He healed "all manner of disease and all manner of sickness among the people." Then if you will refer to Acts 10:38 you will see that the Apostle Peter declares that He (Jesus) "went about doing good, and healing all that were oppressed of the Devil." Notice that all whom He healed, not some, were suffering from Satan's evil power.

A. But does disease never come from God?

B. No, it cannot come from God, for He is pure, and disease is unclean; and it cannot come out of Heaven, for there is no disease there.

A. That is very different from the teachings which I have received all my life from ministers and in the churches. Do you really think that you are right, and that they are all wrong in this matter?

B. It is not a question as between myself and them. The only question is, What does God's Word say? God has said in all the ages, to His Church, "I am Jehovah that healeth thee" (Exodus 15:26), and therefore it would be wicked to say that He is the defiler of His people. All true Christians must believe the Bible, and it is impossible to believe that good and evil, sickness and health, sin and holiness could have a common origin in God. If the Bible really taught that, it would be impossible to believe our Lord Jesus, the Christ, when He says: "A good tree cannot bring forth evil fruit, neither can a corrupt tree bring forth good fruit." (Matthew 7:18.)

A. But even if I agree with all you say, is it not true that the Gifts of Healing were removed from the Church, and are not in it now?

B. No, the "Gifts of Healing" were never withdrawn, and can never be withdrawn, from the true Church of God, for it is written: "The gifts and the calling of God are without repentance." (Romans 11:29.) There are nine gifts of God to the Church (enumerated in 1 Corinthians 12:8-11), and all these are in the Holy Spirit. Therefore, so long as the Holy Spirit is in the Church, all the gifts must be there also. If they are not exercised, that does not prove that they do not exist, but that the faith to exercise them is lacking in God's servants. The gifts are all perfectly preserved; for the Holy Spirit, not the Church, keeps them safely.

A. What should a Christian then do when overtaken with sickness?

B. A Christian should obey God's command, and at once turn to Him for forgiveness of the sin which may have caused the sickness, and for immediate healing. Healing is obtained from God in one of four ways, namely: First, by the direct prayer of faith, without any aid from the officers of the Church, praying as the Centurion did in Matthew 8:5-13; second, by two faithful disciples praying in perfect agreement, in accordance with the Lord's promise in Matthew 18:19; third, by the anointing of the Elders and the prayer of faith, according to the instructions in James 5:14 and 15; and fourth, by the laying on of the hands of them who believe, and whom God calls to that ministry, as the Lord commands in Mark 16:18, and in other places.

A. But are people healed in this way in these days?

B. Yes, in thousands of cases. I have myself laid hands upon many hundreds of thousands of persons, and I have seen the Lord's power manifested in the healing of great numbers, many of whom are living witnesses in many countries, who have testified publicly before thousands, and who are prepared to testify at any time. This ministry is being exercised by devoted Christians in many parts of America, Europe, Australasia, and elsewhere.

A. Is it not the same as Christian Science, Mind Healing, etc.?

B. No. Divine Healing is diametrically opposed to these diabolical counterfeits, which are utterly antichristian. These impostures are only seductive forms of Spiritualism. Trance Evangelism is also a more recent form of this delusion, and it deceives many.

A. But how shall I obtain the necessary faith to receive healing, which faith I am at present conscious that I do not possess?

B. It is written: "Belief cometh of hearing, and hearing by the word of the Christ." (Romans 10:17.) Our Missions are held for the express purpose of teaching fully the Word of God on this matter, and I very heartily invite you to attend the meetings which are announced for Zion Tabernacles in Chicago and other cities, and for Shiloh Tabernacle, Zion City, Illinois. All are welcome and there are no charges of any kind made, for all God's gifts are free gifts. Salvation is the first of these, without which you cannot be healed through faith in Jesus. All the costs of this work are covered by the free-will offerings of the people who attend these meetings, and others whom the Lord leads to help; but the poorest, who have nothing to give, are as heartily welcome as the richest.

A. Do you see the sick and lay hands upon them in this Mission?

B. Yes; after we feel satisfied that they are fully resting in the Lord alone for the healing, we see privately, so far as time permits, those who attend; but under no circumstances do we claim the power to heal any; for "power belongeth unto God."

A. Have you any writings upon this subject which can be purchased?

B. Yes; these can be obtained at the office of Zion Printing and Publishing House, Zion City, Illinois, and at any Zion Tabernacle. But the best book on Divine Healing is the Bible itself, studied prayerfully and earnestly.

We extend to you a hearty invitation to attend the meetings, which are free to all. Our prayer is that you may be led to find in Jesus, the Christ, our Lord and God your present Savior from sin, your Healer from sickness, your Cleanser from all evil, your Keeper in the way to Heaven, your Friend, and your All for Time and Eternity. We pray that these words may help many who read, and that our little conversation may bear fruit in leading many readers to look to Jesus only.

"The Healing of Christ's seamless dress
Is by all beds of pain;
We touch Him in life's throng and press
And we are whole again."

Zion's Bible Class

Conducted by Deacon Daniel Sloan in Shiloh Tabernacle, Zion City, Lord's Day Morning at 11 o'clock, and in Zion Homes and Gatherings throughout the World.

MID-WEEK BIBLE CLASS LESSON, SEPTEMBER 7th or 8th.

God's True Servant's Course.

1. *He is a flame of fire.*—Hebrews 1:1-9.
He warns sinners of hell.
He imposes judgment on sin.
He impresses the terrors of the Lord.
2. *He is wise above his enemies.*—Matthew 10:16, 17.
He sees their designs
He knows no fear of them.
He does not unnecessarily provoke them.
3. *He is a debtor to all men.*—Romans 1:13-20.
He prays for all men.
He does good to all men.
He offers salvation to all men.
4. *He has a Message of Salvation, Healing, and Holy Living to declare.*—Mark 16:15-20.
He goes where the people are.
He sees that they get where he is.
He has something that attracts people.
5. *Whether he lives or dies, he must be true to the Lord.*—Acts 20:17-27.
There is not a sin that he shrinks from uncovering.
There is not a truth that he will not declare.
He gives to all their meat in due season.
6. *He strikes at lawlessness and every work of the Devil wherever he finds it.*—1 John 3:4-13
The work of the Devil must be undone.
He destroys it with salvation and judgment.
He uses the truth to do this work
7. *He refuses to compromise at any cost, for the work must be done.*—Romans 8:31-39
His life is not safe.
He is a sacrifice unto God.
He is not easily moved on earth or from earth.
The Lord our God is a Ministry-inspiring God.

LORD'S DAY BIBLE CLASS LESSON, SEPTEMBER 11th.

The Ministry Chosen of God.

1. *It calls for patience.*—2 Timothy 2:23-26.
Some who have eyes will not see.
Some are charmed by sinful ways.
The Devil has them bound.
2. *It calls for afflictions.*—2 Timothy 4:5-8.
They do not last long.
They bring rich rewards.
They come to all who prove their work.
3. *It calls for privations.*—1 Timothy 6:5-9.
The food may be coarse.
The clothes may become worn.
Be poor for the Christ's sake, but be happy.
4. *It calls for hardships.*—2 Timothy 2:1-5.
You may have to go through storm.
You may become weary through toil.
You may have nights of watchfulness.
5. *It calls for seclusion.*—1 Timothy 4:12-16.
Have your time for reading.
Get into your closet for prayer.
Think in silence before you appear publicly.
6. *It calls for undesirable repute.*—2 Timothy 2:6-12.
You will be told you are doing evil to men.
You must endure contradiction of sinners.
Send out the lighted Truth of God.
7. *It calls for much sadness.*—Luke 12:48-53.
You have a baptism that makes hard things a delight.
Opposition from your relatives will arise.
The fire of Truth stirs up the fires of Hell.
8. *It calls for self-sacrifice.*—Matthew 16:24-28.
Deny self; reckon it dead.
Do not spare self; spend and be spent.
They that wait on God obtain renewal of strength.
God's Holy People are a Ministry-fulfilling People.

LEAVES OF HEALING.

Two Dollars will bring to you the weekly visits of the Little White Dove for a year; 75 cents will send it to a friend for thirteen weeks; $1.25 will send it for six months; $1.50 will send it to your minister, or to a Y. M. C. A., or to a Public Reading Room for a whole year. We offer no premiums, except the premium of doing good. We receive no advertisements, and print no commercial lies or cheating enticements of unscrupulous thieves. LEAVES OF HEALING is Zion on wings, and we keep out everything that would detract the reader's mind from all except the Extension of the Kingdom of God, for which alone it exists. If we cannot send forth our Little White Dove without soiling its wings with the smoke of the factory and the dirt of the wrangling market place, or compelling it to utter the screaming cries of the business vultures in the ears of our readers, then we will keep our Dove at home.

OBEYING GOD IN BAPTISM.

"Baptizing Them Into the Name of the Father and of the Son and of the Holy Ghost."

Nineteen Thousand Seven Hundred One Baptisms by Triune Immersion Since March 14, 1897.

Nineteen Thousand Seven Hundred One Believers have joyfully followed their Lord in the Ordinance of Believer's Baptism by Triune Immersion since the first Baptism in Central Zion Tabernacle on March 14, 1897.

Baptized in Central Zion Tabernacle from March 14, 1897, to December 14, 1901, by the General Overseer,	4754			
Baptized in South Side Zion Tabernacle from January 1, 1902, to June 14, 1903, by the General Overseer..	37			
Baptized at Zion City by the General Overseer........	583			
Baptized by Overseers, Elders, Evangelists and Deacons, at Headquarters (Zion City) and Chicago......	5283			
Total Baptized at Headquarters....................				10,657
Baptized in places outside of Headquarters by the General Overseer..................................		765		
Baptized in places outside of Headquarters by Overseers, Elders, Evangelists and Deacons............		7732		
Total Baptized outside of Headquarters............				8,497
Total Baptized in seven years and three months....				19,154
Baptized since June 14, 1904:				
Baptized in Zion City by the General Overseer........	64			
Baptized in Zion City by Elder Royall..............	11			
Baptized in Zion City by Elder Hammond..........	6			
Baptized in Zion City by Overseer Mason....	90			
Baptized in Zion City by Overseer Excell......... ..	87			
Baptized in Zion City by Overseer Piper....	79			
Baptized in Zion City by Elder Mercer..........	2			
Baptized in Zion City by Elder Dinius........ ..	2			
Baptized in Zion City by Elder Cossum......	5			
Baptized in Chicago by Elder Hoffman.....	4			
Baptized in Chicago by Elder Cossum.	7			
Baptized in Chicago by Elder Keller	5			
Baptized in Chicago by Elder Hall.....	3		366	
Baptized in Chicago by Elder Hammond...... ...	1			
Baptized in Canada by Elder Brooks..........		4		
Baptized in California by Elder Taylor......		9		
Baptized in England by Overseer Cantel......		41		
Baptized in England by Deacon Hall.........		1		
Baptized in Indiana by Elder Osborn........		2		
Baptized in Michigan by Elder Reed........		4		
Baptized in Minnesota by Elder Graves............ .		5		
Baptized in Minnesota by Elder Simmons....		3		
Baptized in Mississippi by Evangelist Gay......... ...		1		
Baptized in Missouri by Evangelist Gay.....		1		
Baptized in Missouri by Elder Brock...		9		
Baptized in Missouri by Deacon Robinson...........		1		
Baptized in Nebraska by Elder Hoy............		7		
Baptized in New York by Overseer Mason....		9		
Baptized in Ohio by Deacon Kelchner.......		3		
Baptized in Ohio by Deacon Arrington......		5		
Baptized in South Africa by Overseer Bryant		49		
Baptized in Tennessee by Elder Hall..........		2		
Baptized in Texas by Evangelist Gay........ ...		11		
Baptized in Washington by Elder Ernst.......... .		11		
Baptized in Wisconsin by Elder McClurkin...........		3	181	547
Total Baptized since March 14, 1897...............				19,701

The following-named twelve believers were baptized at Felixstowe, Suffolk, England, Saturday, July 23, 1904, by Overseer H. E. Cantel:
Aldous, Mrs. Elizabeth.........38 Borough road, Ipswich, Suffolk, England
Aldous, Samuel...................38 Borough road, Ipswich, Suffolk, England
Arnold, Mrs. Charlotte.............Dove street, Ipswich, Suffolk, England
Foster, Albert................Coggeshall road, Kelvedon, Essex, England
Foster, Mrs. Ellen.............Coggeshall road, Kelvedon, Essex, England
Foster, John..................Coggeshall road, Kelvedon, Essex, England
Gilbert, William Robert...105 Woodbridge road, Ipswich, Suffolk, England
Gillings, Miss Elizabeth ..105 Woodbridge road, Ipswich, Suffolk, England
Hewitt, Miss Ethel Kate, 35 Garfield Villas, York road, Ipswich, Suffolk, England
Hewitt, George V...............35 York road, Ipswich, Suffolk, England
Hill, Thomas George, "The Kennels," Woolverstone, Ipswich, Suffolk, England
Hill, Mrs. Emma, "The Kennels," Woolverstone, Ipswich, Suffolk, England

The following-named believer was baptized at Low Fell, Gateshead-on-Tyne, Sussex, England, Monday, July 25, 1904, by Deacon John Hall:
Pettersson, Adolf Fredrik..............................Rää, Raus, Sweden

The following-named sixteen believers were baptized at Caledonian road Baths, North, London, England, Lord's Day, July 31, 1904, by Overseer H. E. Cantel:
Arnold, Mrs. Lillie, 117 Harrison street, Gray's Inn road, W. C., London, England
Berridge, Richard, 18 Sheldon road, Silver street, Edmonton, N., London, England
Berridge, Mrs. Sophia, 18 Sheldon road, Silver street, Edmonton, N., London, England
Bush, Elizabeth Mary, 132 Crowther road, South Norwood, S. E., London, England
Church, Mrs. Sarah, 117 Harrison street, Gray's Inn road, W. C., London, England
Corrall, Montague Leykauff, 44 Cromer street, Gray's Inn road, W. C., London, England
Croker, Miss Helen, 21 St. Thomas road, Old Kent road, S. E., London, England
Deeprose, Miss Eva Florence, 56 Cambrian road, Tunbridge Wells, Kent, England
Haourt, Mrs. Edith, 44 Gloucester street, Theobalds road, W., London, England
Hern, John............. ..2 Longfield road, Ealing, W., London, England
House, Arthur..........92 Brewery road, Islington, N., London, England
House, Miss Ethel ......92 Brewery road, Islington, N., London, England
Kirk, Cecil Edward Isaac, "Bungalow," Rail's Farm, Pirbright, Surrey, England
Miller, Miss Emma Elizabeth, 45 Lanark Villas, Maida Yale, W., London, England
Moore, Miss Gertrude Miriam, 58 Wellesley road, Croydon, Surrey, England
Mumford, Mrs. Susan, 117 Harrison street, Gray's Inn road, W. C., London, England

The following-named two believers were baptized in Lake Michigan, Zion City, Illinois, Tuesday, August 2, 1904, by Elder W. O. Dinius:
Reichert, Fred.... ....Flint, Michigan
Sedina, Miss Frances...........509 Grand street, South Lansing, Michigan

The following-named believer was baptized at South Side Zion Tabernacle, Chicago, Illinois, Lord's Day, August 7, 1904, by Elder W. H. Cossum:
Doods, Mrs. R. C............519 East Forty-fourth street, Chicago, Illinois

The following-named believer was baptized at South Side Zion Tabernacle, Chicago, Illinois, Lord's Day, August 7, 1904, by Elder Gideon Hammond:
Robinson, Elizabeth..............1904 Dearborn street, Chicago, Illinois

The following-named five believers were baptized at San Francisco, California, Lord's Day, August 7, 1904, by Elder W. D. Taylor:
Newcomb, Mrs. Mildred Agnes, 3366 Nineteenth street, San Francisco, California
Quinly, Edward E.. ....Fruitvale, California
Reeves, John Thomas........11 Hickory avenue, San Francisco, California
Tate, Herbert Clifton......419 Fourteenth street, San Francisco, California
Taylor, Harold Ross.......1350 East Sixteenth street, Fruitvale, California

The following-named two believers were baptized at Chattanooga, Tennessee, Monday, August 8, 1904, by Elder Lemuel C. Hall:
Brown, Mrs. Kate Colburn........535 Vine street, Chattanooga, Tennessee
Grange, Dr. James............Lookout Mountain, Chattanooga, Tennessee

The following-named eight believers were baptized at Spokane, Washington, Wednesday, August 10, 1004, by Elder August Ernst:
Haney, Miss Agnes G.........1826 E. Sixth avenue, Spokane, Washington
Hill, Mrs. Mary..................725 Walnut street, Spokane, Washington
Haney, Mrs. Almira M........1826 E. Sixth avenue, Spokane, Washington
Jayne, Mrs. Clara Agnes........711 Pittsburg street, Spokane, Washington
Mack, William.................1718 E. Riverside, Spokane, Washington
Martin, Mrs. Sarah E...........701 Pittsburg street, Spokane, Washington
Pease, Mrs. Sidney L...............S. 127 G street, Spokane, Washington
Sandmire, Mrs. Alice...........603 Crestline street, Spokane, Washington

The following-named five believers were baptized at Shiloh Tabernacle, Zion City, Illinois, Lord's Day, August 14, 1904, by Elder W. H. Cossum:
Barney, Miss Rosa.................2212 Gideon avenue, Zion City, Illinois
Flickinger, Mrs. Annie S..1229 West Nineteenth St., Indianapolis, Indiana
French, Joshua Lewin...................Edina Hospice, Zion City, Illinois
McClain, Mrs. Rose ....3108 Gilboa avenue, Zion City, Illinois
Williams, W. C.......................Fire Department, Zion City, Illinois

CONSECRATION OF CHILDREN.

The following-named twenty children were consecrated to God, at Zion Tabernacle, in Pretoria, Transvaal, South Africa, Thursday, June 16, 1904, by Overseer Daniel Bryant:
Barrett, Alvi Elizabeth Rhodes....... ..Pretoria, Transvaal, South Africa
Barrett, Eunice Lillyean............ ..Pretoria, Transvaal, South Africa
Barrett, Evereld Mary Rhodes....... ..Pretoria, Transvaal, South Africa
Gatzke, Gladstone Charles Willard ...Pretoria, Transvaal, South Africa
Gatzke, James Raymond Hugh... ...Pretoria, Transvaal, South Africa
Gatzke, Louis Osborne Baldwin, ...Pretoria, Transvaal, South Africa
Gatzke, Robert Victor Edwin... . . Pretoria, Transvaal, South Africa
Muloch, Mary Elizabeth....... Pretoria, Transvaal, South Africa
Jubber, Bryant................ . ....Pretoria, Transvaal, South Africa
Reed, Hyacinth Francis........... Pretoria, Transvaal, South Africa
Roos, Tieleman Francois.... ..Pretoria, Transvaal, South Africa
Rose, Azariah Claudia...... ... ..Pretoria, Transvaal, South Africa
Rose, Ernest Andrew......... .Pretoria, Transvaal, South Africa
Rose, Henrietta............ .. Pretoria, Transvaal, South Africa
Rose, John Alexander...... . . Pretoria, Transvaal, South Africa
Rose, Maurice Samuel......... . . ....Pretoria, Transvaal, South Africa
Rose, Norval...................... ....Pretoria, Transvaal, South Africa
Sussens, Clarence.......... ....Pretoria, Transvaal, South Africa
Sussens, Elton Clyde..... ... .Pretoria, Transvaal, South Africa
Watson, Baby ....Pretoria, Transvaal, South Africa

The following-named child was consecrated to God, at Zion Tabernacle, 117 Anderson street, Johannesburg, Transvaal, South Africa, Lord's Day, June 26, 1904, by Elder Emma D. Bryant.
Thomson, Emma Mary Annie Gwendaleen Bryant, Johannesburg, Transvaal, South Africa

WEEKLY PAPER FOR THE EXTENSION OF THE KINGDOM OF GOD
EDITED BY THE REV. JOHN ALEX. DOWIE.

·lume XV. No. 19. ZION CITY, SATURDAY, AUGUST 27, 1904. Price Five Cents

GOD'S WITNESSES TO DIVINE HEALING.

·EALED OF CHRONIC CONSTIPATION AND EPILEPSY IN ANSWER TO THE PRAYER OF FAITH.

·ND I WILL BE A SWIFT WITNESS AGAINST ·HE SORCERERS.

Many good people stumble ·er the title of one of the ·essages of God's Prophet of ·e Restoration, "Doctors, ·rugs, and Devils."

They declare it a wicked ·lumny upon a noble profes- ·on.

Yet sorcerers are always ·ssed among the evil-doers · the Word of God.

And sorcerers are those who ·ake, sell, or administer poi- ·ns.

The Hebrew word used in the ·d Testament is *Kashaph*, and ·s just that meaning.

The Greek word used in the ·w Testament is *pharmakoi* (·αρμακοί), and is the parent of ·r modern English word, ·armacist.

It occurs in the following ·ssage in the Revelation:

But for the fearful, and unbelieving, ·d abominable, and murderers, and ·nicators, and sorcerers, and idola- ·s, and all liars, their part shall be in · lake that burneth with fire and ·mstone; which is the second death.

"But," the defenders of the ·rcerers of the Twentieth ·ntury say, "that refers to · ignorant, superstitious, and

G. M. STAUFFACHER

wicked sorcerers of the olden times; now we have medical science."

But no well-informed and honest physician will contend that medicine is a science.

The wisest and best of them unite in declaring that it is not a science; indeed, is far from being a science.

One of these, Dr. James Mason Good, said:

"The effects of our medicines are in the highest degree unsatisfactory except, indeed, that they have destroyed more lives than war, pestilence, and famine combined."

The strangest part of it is, that the very people who profess to be so deeply offended at this title know that doctors do not and cannot heal.

They laugh at and make jokes about the doctors' patients being killed by the treatment.

They see all around them, every day, evidences of the worse than useless treatments given in accordance with the precepts of so-called medical science.

They suffer from it themselves and experience it in their own families.

"But," begging the question,

and quietly dropping their first contention, they say, "the doctors are good, self-sacrificing men, and do the best they can."

We gladly acknowledge that there are a few such.

But what of the great majority?

Figures, most carefully collected during nine years' research, by Dr. Crother, of New York, himself a physician, showed that twenty per cent. of the large number of physicians under observation were victims of narcotic and alcoholic poisons.

Dr. Crother also stated that the effect of these poisons was to deaden or warp moral sensibility.

Statistics prove that doctors of medicine are guilty of suicide and murder in larger proportion than members of any other profession.

Overwhelming and incontrovertible testimony, much of it from the lips of surgeons themselves, goes to show that they carelessly and often criminally cause death by needless operations, performed as a result of a kind of "knife-madness."

Those preparing for medical and surgical careers in the professional schools are notoriously wild and wicked, as a class, although there are some God-fearing youths among them.

The truth of the matter is, that the medical and surgical craft of the Twentieth Century is a cruel, exacting, murderous hierarchy—deluding, robbing, and killing the people, as did the horrid system of ancient sorcery, from which it is the direct lineal descendant.

Ancient sorcery was, professedly, of the Devil.

Modern sorcery strives to conceal its parentage, but by its fruits it may be known.

One of the characteristic sins of ancient sorcery was the sale of spells, potions, philters, and charms—some harmless and some noxious—that were supposed to work certain results, but which were worse than frauds.

People of today laugh at the ignorance and superstition of those who paid for such things; but they pay thousands of dollars to physicians for treatments that result only in suffering and death.

Physicians everywhere treat diseases which they know to be incurable by any human means, and exact large sums for the treatment.

Volumes could be written about the physical agony and death, and the material ruin, of hundreds of thousands, through the villainy of doctors.

The clean, intelligent young man, who witnesses to God's healing power on this page, was robbed of hundreds of dollars by physicians who professed to cure him of epilepsy.

They knew that they could do nothing for that terrible affliction.

No physician can cure it except the Great Physician; for it is possession by an evil spirit, and no drug can cast out a devil.

God Himself is the only Healer of this and all other diseases.

He has said, "I am Jehovah that healeth thee."

Of Him the Psalmist said, "Who healeth all thy diseases."

He sent His only begotten Son, Jesus, the Christ, who "went about doing good and healing all that were oppressed of the Devil."

That same Jesus is with us today, for He said, "Lo, I am with you All the Days, even unto the Consummation of the Age."

He is still the Healer Divine, for God's Word says of Him, "Jesus, the Christ, is the same yesterday and today, yea, and forever."

After suffering many things of many physicians, and being nothing bettered, but rather growing worse, and having spent a great deal of his money, this young man turned to God, in the Name of Jesus.

He tells, simply and truthfully, how his Heavenly Father healed him, in answer to the Prayer of Faith.

That is God's Way of Healing.

It has nothing whatever to do with diabolical sorcery, which, even in the hands of the very best of men, and practiced with the very best of intentions, is, in the majority of cases, more harmful than beneficial, and in all cases useless.

The title, "Doctors, Drugs, and Devils," was inspired by God's Spirit.

It contains a most important truth for God's people.

No wonder the Devil hates it!

No wonder he howls about it, and deceives even some very good people, causing them to stumble over it!

May God grant that, through the simple testimony of this young man, His Spirit may open the eyes of many who are being thus deceived. A. W. N.

WRITTEN TESTIMONY OF G. M. STAUFFACHER.

ZION CITY, ILLINOIS, July 19, 1904.

DEAR GENERAL OVERSEER:—With thankful heart I desire to tell some of the many blessings God has given me.

I thank God for the privilege of living in these Latter Days, under the ministry of Elijah the Restorer, the man of God who brought to us the Gospel of Salvation, Healing, and Holy Living in its fulness.

Many are the blessings I have received since leaving the apostate church and coming under your ministry, which is in accordance with the Word of God.

In 1891, I was afflicted with chronic constipation and epilepsy, the result of disobeying the laws of God.

The church with which I was connected did not teach that God was the Healer of His people, and that Jesus, the Christ, died for our diseases as well as for our sins; but taught the people to trust in man, and were in favor of doctors and drugs, from which I earnestly sought relief, but without good results.

In August, 1896, I took a treatment in the Dr. Hartman Medical Institution, of Columbus, Ohio, which cost me nearly three hundred dollars.

I only grew worse.

Eight months later, still trusting in the arm of flesh, I took a treatment from a so-called specialist, from Chicago, who guaranteed to cure me.

He charged me ten dollars for every visit I made him, but was unable to help me.

A few months later another so-called specialist, late of Berlin, Germany, visited our city.

My first visit to him cost me fifty dollars, and he promised to cure me in five months, but was unable to do so.

Later he wrote me that if I would come to Milwaukee he would give me a treatment free of charge.

I did not go, for I had begun to believe that doctors and drugs were a farce, which I soon learned was true.

In January, 1899, being almost in despair, I decided to go to Zion Home, on Twelfth street, Chicago, having heard about your ministry, and read the tract, "Jesus, the Healer," which my brother brought to our home.

I thank God for putting it in my heart to go.

After staying at Zion Home two weeks, and attending the meetings at Central Zion Tabernacle, I was convinced that this work was of God, and that there was healing for me.

The kindness shown me by the brethren, and their willingness to help and give council, had greatly impressed me.

During these two weeks I received a wonderful blessing and was healed of constipation by the laying on of hands by Overseer Jane Dowie.

I was not delivered from the evil spirit until about two and a half years later.

Some of the reasons were that I had fear in my heart and did not trust God fully, but believed things that the Devil told me.

I thought that if I asked God to forgive me my wrong-doings, that was all that was needed.

But that would not work.

I had to make confessions and restorations, which was a new doctrine to me, and hard to do.

After making things right as best I knew, and trusting God fully, and giving myself entirely over to Him, I was completely delivered from the evil spirit which, the Christ said, goeth not out but by prayer and fasting.

It is over three years since, and God has by His mercy wonderfully kept and blessed me, for which I give all the glory to the Father of mercies, and God of all comfort, Who giveth us the victory through our Savior and Coming King, Jesus, the Christ.

I believe, had it not been for Zion, that I would today be in the grave.

I also wish to thank God for the many blessings received in attending Zion Educational Institutions, for the last two years, where so valuable instruction is given.

May God's richest blessing rest upon you and Overseer Jane Dowie in this glorious work of Restoration, "Till He Come."

G. M. STAUFFACHER.

By Evangelist Sarah E. Hill.

THEN lifted I up mine eyes, and saw, and behold, there came forth two women, and the wind was in their wings; now they had wings like the wings of a stork: and they lifted up the ephah between the earth and the heaven.—*Zechariah 5:6.*

WOMAN has always been a great power in the world, for good or for evil.

It was woman who first led the world away from God, and she is to be a mighty factor in leading the world back to Him, in the Consummation of the Age.

The Psalmist refers to these Latter Days when he writes, "Jehovah giveth the Word: the women that publish the tidings are a great host. Kings of armies flee, they flee: and she that tarrieth at home divideth the spoil." (Psalm 68: 11, 12.)

In these Latter Days, Jehovah *has* given the Word. He has raised up the "Prophet like unto Moses," and He has put His Words into his mouth. (Deuteronomy 18:18.)

His Message is going forth today over the world, on the pages of Zion Literature.

This Message is to bring about the Restoration of All Things. (Acts 3:21.)

Multitudes of women are keeping step with their brothers in Zion Restoration Host, and helping to publish the Word.

The Prophet Zechariah, in his vision of the Latter Days, saw first God's Literature going over the face of the whole land. (Zechariah 5:3, 4, 6.) Then he saw the ungodly teaching going forth.

God did not say of this as he had said of the former, that He sent it forth.

Referring to the ungodly teaching which was shown the prophet by the symbol of a measure, an ephah, in which sat a woman called Wickedness, Luther's German translation of the Bible says, *Das ist die gottlose Lehre*—"This is the ungodly teaching." (Zechariah 5:8.)

It is sad, but true, that women are leaders in teaching the isms of the day.

Mrs. Eddy, the "mother of Christian Science," and Madame Blavatsky, the leading exponent of modern Theosophy, are two typical women.

They may fittingly be represented by the two women which the prophet saw carrying the ephah.

Between Christian Science and Theosophy may be classed all of the false systems of the world; for all are founded on the same general principles, and originate in a desire of the flesh to save itself and to rule. They reject the Atonement of the Lord Jesus.

The ungodly teaching is a mixture of truth and error.

To meet the needs of this period of confused teaching, this Babylon Age, God has sent to the world Elijah, the Messenger of the Covenant, to call the world to enter into Covenant relations with our Father in Heaven, and to let Him rule in our spirits, souls, and bodies, that God's Kingdom may displace the Devil's kingdom on earth.

The Christian Catholic Church in Zion, established by John Alexander Dowie, Elijah the Restorer, is the Restoration of the Primitive Apostolic Church and of its teachings as promulgated by our Lord.

It is opposed to Christian Science as an anti-Christian imposture, and to all teaching that does not agree with the teaching of our Lord Jesus, the Christ.

Zion Literature must be scattered over the world, that the nations may have the light of the Full Gospel.

All who desire to hasten the dawning of this glad day, are called on to assist us in scattering the Literature of Zion over the earth.

Pundita Ramabai, the learned Hindu lady, so well known in the United States, on visiting this country in 1898, said: "I am surprised and shocked to find that ancient philosophies are making their appearance in the United States under the guise of Christian names. It is a sad sight to one acquainted with the results of heathen philosophy and superstition, to see educated people, who enjoy the privileges of a Christian civilization, being deceived by a new name.

"I was told, on my arrival in New York, that a new philosophy was being taught in the United States. The philosophy was called Christian Science, and when I asked what its teaching was, I recognized it as being the same philosophy that had been taught among my people for four thousand years.

"It has ruined millions of lives and caused immeasurable suffering and sorrow in my land; for it is based on selfishness, and knows no sympathy or compassion.

"As I was born and educated in the philosophy, having taken my degree of Pundita in it, I am both acquainted with its literature and its influence upon my people; and I want to witness to its degradation.

"To study Indian philosophy, one must go to India and see its results, and learn to read the *Shaster* in the original.

"It is all very nice to read pretty translations, where much that is base and degrading is expurgated; but the original is quite another thing.

"They tell me they found so many grand things in the Hindu religion.

"The grandeur and beauty of that philosophy must be judged by its fruit. *It is the philosophy of nothingness.*

"You are to take the whole universe as nothing but a lie. You are to think it does not exist. You do not exist. The birds and beasts that you see do not exist.

"Christian people are a people of some feeling. Everything is real. They feel that when other people are starving they ought to give them something to eat; but in our late famine, our philosophers felt no compassion for sufferers, and did not help the needy.

"Why should they help when they claim the suffering was not real, neither were the dying children real?

"The people of India and the philosophers never show a particle of kindness to the women, and their lives are made so unbearable that they want to kill themselves. These philosophers have established hospitals for animals, but none for women.

"The preachers who have come to America to preach Buddhism to the American people, have established a hospital for animals in Bombay, where there is a ward devoted to bugs. A man is hired to feed those bugs on his blood every night.

"They never take any thought of the women who are dying under the weight of this philosophy, but they just show their charity toward the bugs.

"The Hindu women have been made slaves, and it is Christian people who bring them the liberty of Christianity. Our philosophers have never established schools for our women and girls, but they have taught that it was a religious duty to burn thousands of widows alive.

"Now (1898) the women are taught to cast themselves into the sacred river, or take opium, and go to heaven, where they may find their husbands. They are taught that in heaven they must be the servants of their husbands the same as on the earth.

"The third place open to her is hell.

"This religion says women are naturally wicked, and if they get any knowledge they become worse and worse.

"The Hindu woman's religious duties consist in household cares and the worship of her husband.

"They are taught, also, that woman is naturally unholy, and that nothing cleanses her from all sin but drinking the dirty water in which she has washed her husband's feet.

"I wonder how many of the American disciples of Hinduism would like to realize that religion?"

Zion Literature Sent Out from a Free Distribution Fund Provided by Zion's Guests and the Friends of Zion.

Report for two weeks ending August 20, 1904:
5,098 Rolls.....to the Hotels of the United States
1,661 Rolls..........to the Hotels of Switzerland
14,527 Rolls..to Business Men in the United States
14,251 Rolls........................Miscellaneous
Number of Rolls for two weeks 35,537
Number of Rolls reported to Aug. 20, 1904, 3,340,971

A WEEKLY PAPER FOR THE EXTENSION OF THE KINGDOM OF GOD.
EDITED BY THE REV. JOHN ALEX. DOWIE.

Application for entry as Second Class Matter at Zion City, Illinois, pending.

Subscription Rates.		Special Rates.	
One Year	$2.00	100 Copies of One Issue	$3.00
Six Months	1.25	25 Copies of One Issue	1.00
Three Months	.75	To Ministers, Y. M. C. A's and Public Reading Rooms, per annum	1.50
Single Copies	.05		

For foreign subscriptions add $1.50 per year, or three cents per copy for postage.

Subscribers desiring a change of address should give present address, as well as that to which they desire LEAVES OF HEALING sent in the future.

Make Bank Drafts, Express Money or Postoffice Money Orders payable to the order of JOHN ALEX. DOWIE, Zion City, Illinois, U. S. A.

Long Distance Telephone. *Cable Address "Dowie, Zion City."*

All communications upon business must be addressed to
MANAGER ZION PUBLISHING HOUSE,
Zion City, Illinois, U. S. A.

Subscriptions to LEAVES OF HEALING, A VOICE FROM ZION, and the various publications may also be sent to
ZION PUBLISHING HOUSE, 81 EUSTON ROAD, LONDON, N. W., ENGLAND.
ZION PUBLISHING HOUSE, No. 43 PARK ROAD, ST. KILDA, MELBOURNE, VICTORIA, AUSTRALIA.
ZION PUBLISHING HOUSE, RUE DE MONT, THABOR 1, PARIS, FRANCE.
ZIONSHEIM, SCHLOSS LIEBBURG, CANTON THURGAU, BEI ZÜRICH, SWITZERLAND.

ZION CITY, ILLINOIS, SATURDAY, AUGUST 27, 1904.

TABLE OF CONTENTS.

LEAVES OF HEALING, SATURDAY, AUGUST 27, 1904.

EDITORIAL NOTES.

"JEHOVAH WILL CREATE OVER THE WHOLE HABITATION OF MOUNT ZION,"

**AND OVER her Assemblies, a cloud and smoke by day,
And the shining of a Flaming Fire by night:
For over all the Glory shall be spread a Canopy.**

THESE BEAUTIFUL words concerning the glory of Zion, in the "Times of Restoration of All Things, whereof God spake by the mouth of His Holy Prophets which have been since the world began," will be found in the 4th chapter of Isaiah, 5th verse.

They are a part of a Wonderful Prophetic Song concerning the glory and beauty of Zion, the Kingdom of God, at the Times of the End of this Dispensation.

THE PROMISE is that the Canopy of Jehovah's Love will cover "every Dwelling Place" of Mount Zion.

Not only upon the homes and habitations of the people, but upon the Assemblies of Zion, the Glory of God will come.

AS IN the Days of Old, by day and by night, the conscious Presence of God in the homes of Zion is to be realized, as if it were a Divine Canopy spread over every bed.

The words in the Original for "canopy" are used only twice in the Ancient Scriptures, and in both cases mean "a bridal chamber, and a bridal canopied bed." [Psalm 19:5; and also Joel 2:16.]

THIS BEAUTIFUL passage shows the tender love and care which our God and Father has for the domestic interests of His people, and especially for their physical, psychical, and spiritual Purity.

DURING THE late Feast of Tabernacles, we had the joy of ministering to many thousands of those in Zion, in Special Addresses for Zion Women and for Zion Men only, on July the 18th.

The first of these Addresses was delivered by our dear wife, Overseer Jane Dowie, in the afternoon of that date, in Shiloh Tabernacle; and the second by ourself in the evening.

THESE ADDRESSES are reported in this Issue, on pages 621 to 629, and we trust they will be a blessing in the homes of Zion everywhere.

IT HAS been our custom in these private meetings to speak in greater detail than we have in these Discourses.

But "the Wise shall understand."

It is not wise to speak in too great detail regarding the Evils that are wrought in secret, much less to publish such details.

WE TRUST, however, that all our Readers will be enabled to realize somewhat of the Real Purity that Zion is contending for, and which is so beautifully set forth in the Chapter from which our opening Note is quoted.

IN THAT Day the Men of Zion are to be called "Holy," and Jehovah shall have "washed away" the uncleanness of the Daughters of Zion.

THAT WORK of Purification cannot be done without the exercise of great Spiritual Energy.

The Spirit, or *blast*, of Judgment, and the Spirit, or *blast*, of Burning, will be God's means of purification.

Then every Dwelling Place of Zion shall be filled with the Glory of God, and every bed shall be canopied by His glory and purity.

WE EARNESTLY desire that Zion everywhere will give heed to the instruction of God in this matter, and press forward to the Millennial Day, when the Branch of Jehovah shall be beauteous and glorious, and the Fruit of the Land "majestic and comely."

WE HAVE labored, with intense earnestness, to make the City of Zion a Habitation of Purity, of Peace, of Power, and of Divine Progression.

THE SUCCESSES with which God has thus far blest us, have been most wonderful, and have given us great joy.

The Homes of Zion are increasingly happy and good—filled with the Joy of Jehovah.

We have not been without our Trials.

The Spirit of Judgment and of Burning has had to be exercised, or the Purity of the City of Zion could never have been preserved.

Had we failed in this, no other kind of success would have been of any consequence.

THE DISCIPLINE of Zion has been immediate and thorough.

We, and all associated with us in the Spiritual and Moral direction of Zion, have most earnestly coöperated in producing the delightful conditions which now exist in the City of Zion.

LARGER, BROADER, wiser, and purer conceptions of the Social Life of the Zion of God are being unfolded to us continually, as we Go Forward *doing* His Will.

BUT THERE are many things which must be said, and many things which must be done, that can only be spoken and wrought under the still Purer Conditions of Thought and Life which are being produced as the glorious Work of the Restoration continues.

MEANWHILE, IT is our joy and duty to maintain the Standard of Purity, and to unfold the Will of God at the right time and in the right way, doing the Will of God from a pure heart.

WITH THESE observations, we again commend to Zion in all the Lands, the consideration of the Special Addresses to which we have referred.

OUR READERS are doubtless looking in this Issue for the promised "General Letter upon the Apostolical Constitution of the Church," to the preparation of which we have given very much prayer and careful thought.

WE HAVE, however, now determined that it will be best to publish at the same time, the Reports of Three most important Conferences of Ordained Officers of the Christian Catholic Church in Zion, which were held in Zion City on Wednesday, July 20th, Saturday, July 23d, and Monday, July 25th.

THE PUBLICATION of these reports, and of other matter of a kindred nature, will enable our Readers more clearly to understand our General Letter.

Therefore, we have directed that the stenographic Reports of the Conferences shall be most carefully prepared and published, with the General Letter, God willing, in our Issue of September 10th.

WE SHALL, at the same time, give Full Announcements concerning the DECLARATION OF APOSTOLIC OFFICE AND AUTHORITY, which we shall make, God willing, in Shiloh Tabernacle, Zion City, on the Afternoon of Lord's Day, September 18th.

BRETHREN, PRAY FOR US.

Warning to Subscribers.

Scarcely a week passes that we do not have complaints about money having been sent to us in currency, stamps, or silver, in the open mails, for renewals of subscriptions or for other purposes, WHICH WE HAVE NOT RECEIVED AND WHICH NEVER REACHES US.

Therefore, we desire to warn every member and friend of Zion sending money to us, to always use some safe means, preferably a money-order, or bank-draft on New York or Chicago, or personal check on Zion City Bank.

In conforming to this notice you will save yourselves trouble and expense, and us much annoyance.

ZION PRINTING AND PUBLISHING HOUSE,
Zion City, Illinois.

Street Addresses Are Necessary.

All Zion City Subscribers to *Leaves of Healing*, *The Zion Banner*, *Blätter der Heilung*, and *Voice from Zion*, whose correct street addresses are not positively known to be in our possession should send them to us AT ONCE. Please act upon this notice without delay as it is very important, now that we have postal delivery service, that the exact location of each and every subscriber be known to us. Write your name and address very carefully, designating also to what periodicals you are a subscriber and leave at your very earliest opportunity at our branch Publishing House on Elijah Avenue.

Very Sincerely Yours,
ZION PRINTING AND PUBLISHING HOUSE.

Notice to Correspondents.

In writing to Headquarters it is *absolutely essential* that the writer give his full address.

Failure to comply with this request necessitates looking up or referring to the Church Records, which involves much time, and is very frequently fruitless.

Friends and members of the Christian Catholic Church in Zion everywhere will please bear this in mind, especially those in foreign lands.

Faithfully yours in the Master's Service,
J. G. EXCELL, General Ecclesiastical Secretary.

GOD'S WAY OF HEALING.

BY THE REV. JOHN ALEX. DOWIE.

God's Way of Healing Is a Person, Not a Thing.

Jesus said "*I am* the Way, and the Truth, and the Life," and He has ever been revealed to His people in all the ages by the Covenant Name, Jehovah-Rophi, or "*I am* Jehovah that Healeth thee." (John 14:6; Exodus 15:26.)

The Lord Jesus, the Christ, is Still the Healer.

He cannot change, for "Jesus, the Christ, is the same yesterday and today, yea and forever;" and He is still with us, for He said: "Lo, *I am* with you All the Days, even unto the Consummation of the Age." (Hebrews 13:8; Matthew 28:20.) Because He is Unchangeable, and because He is present, in spirit, just as when in the flesh, He is the Healer of His people.

Divine Healing Rests on the Christ's Atonement.

It was prophesied of Him, "Surely He hath borne our griefs (Hebrew, *sickness*), and carried our sorrows: . . . and with His stripes we are healed;" and it is expressly declared that this was fulfilled in His Ministry of Healing, which still continues. (Isaiah 53:4, 5; Matthew 8:17.)

Disease Can Never be God's Will.

It is the Devil's work, consequent upon Sin, and it is impossible for the work of the Devil ever to be the Will of God. The Christ came to "destroy the works of the Devil," and when He was here on earth He healed "all manner of disease and all manner of sickness," and all these sufferers are expressly declared to have been "oppressed of the Devil." (1 John 3:8; Matthew 4:23; Acts 10:38.)

The Gifts of Healing Are Permanent.

It is expressly declared that the "Gifts and the calling of God are without repentance," and the Gifts of Healing are amongst the Nine Gifts of the Spirit to the Church. (Romans 11:29; 1 Corinthians 12:8-11.)

There Are Four Modes of Divine Healing.

The first is the direct prayer of faith; the second, intercessory prayer of two or more; the third, the anointing of the elders, with the prayer of faith; and the fourth, the laying on of hands of those who believe, and whom God has prepared and called to that Ministry. (Matthew 8:5-13; Matthew 18:19; James 5:14, 15; Mark 16:18.)

Divine Healing Is Opposed by Diabolical Counterfeits.

Amongst these are Christian Science (falsely so-called), Mind Healing, Spiritualism, Trance Evangelism, etc. (1 Timothy 6:20, 21; 1 Timothy 4:1, 2; Isaiah 51:22, 23.)

Multitudes Have Been Healed Through Faith in Jesus.

The writer knows of thousands of cases and has personally laid hands on scores of thousands of persons. Full information can be obtained at the meetings held in the Zion Tabernacles in Chicago, and in Zion City, Illinois, and in many pamphlets which give the experience, in their own words, of many who have been healed in this and other countries, published at Zion Printing and Publishing House, Zion City, Illinois.

"Belief Cometh of Hearing, and Hearing by the Word of the Christ."

You are heartily invited to attend and hear for yourself.

ELIJAH THE RESTORER.

ELIJAH THE RESTORER SHOWS HOW TO OVERCOME AN EVIL HERITAGE.

Zion's Fourth Feast of Tabernacles

The Set Feasts of Jehovah . . .
Ye shall proclaim to be Holy Convocations.

A MEETING FOR ZION WOMEN ONLY.

REPORTED BY I. M. S. AND E. S.

Crowned with a mature, sweet and gracious womanhood, holding in her hand the Word of God, and speaking by its precepts and drawing from a ripe experience, Overseer Jane Dowie addressed, on Monday afternoon, July 18, 1904, the women of Zion gathered in Shiloh Tabernacle at the Holy Convocation.

With a dignity and simplicity peculiarly her own, the words she spoke seemed, even more than on previous like occasions, inspired by a Divine Love and a Sweet Humanity, which, blended, gave to her Message a tenderness, a fulness of sympathy, and a sweetness, which touched and won every heart.

Her subject, Woman, was handled with a delicacy of expression and feeling—yet losing nothing of strength or directness by reason thereof—which in itself was the strongest expression of that combination of Purity, Sweetness, Delicacy, Strength, and Nobility, which we call Womanliness.

The great lesson deducted was that the daughters of Zion are the daughters of a King; theirs is a royal heritage, by reason of their birth into the Kingdom of God.

And as Eve, the first mother, brought with Adam, her husband, sin and sorrow to the race of men, it is for the daughters of Zion to restore, to rehabilitate, to renew, that Eden whence they were banished because of their disobedience to God's laws.

OVERSEER JANE DOWIE.

After a song and prayer for God's blessing on the words she should speak, the Overseer read the story, as recorded in Genesis, of the Creation of the first man and woman; then of the Temptation as it came to Eve, of the Yielding, of the Fall, and of the Banishment.

When the sad, old story was ended, the reverse side of the picture was quickly shown—the Redemption side to this Great Drama of humanity, whose close is drawing near.

Shiloh Tabernacle, Zion City, Illinois, Monday Afternoon, July 18, 1904.

The service was opened by the singing of Hymn No. 20 in the Special Program.

Prayer was offered by Overseer Jane Dowie, after which she read the Scripture lesson from the Inspired Word of God, beginning with the 1st chapter of Genesis and the 26th verse, continuing to the 2d chapter and the 9th verse, reading also the 15th verse; and in the 3d chapter of Genesis from the 1st to the 19th verses, and from the 22d verse to the end of the chapter; also from the 1st epistle of Paul to Timothy, 2d chapter, 5th and 6th verses, and the 13th, 14th, and 15th verses.

Hymn No. 19 was sung, after which Overseer Jane Dowie pronounced the

INVOCATION.

Let the words of my mouth, and the meditation of my heart be acceptable in Thy sight, be profitable unto this people, and unto all to whom these words shall come, in this and every land, in this and all the coming time, Till Jesus Come. Amen.

The wonderful story of the birth of our first parents, Adam and Eve, which I have just read to you, is told so beautifully and so simply in these first few chapters of the Holy Scriptures!

God made man after He had made all other creatures.

He prepared the earth for man and gave him everything in it for his use, giving him dominion over the fish of the sea, over the fowl of the air, over the cattle, and over every creeping thing that creepeth upon the earth.

Then, after God had made man, He made woman, whom He gave to the man as "a help meet for him," a companion, one who was prepared for him.

Then God looked upon everything that He had made and saw that it was good.

God never created evil; all that He made was good.

Sin did not come by the Will of God, nor did God cause man to sin.

Sin Came by Disobedience to God's Laws.

We cannot make God responsible for man's disobedience.

God had told Adam and Eve that they were to use everything that He had given them, but that there was one thing which he had not given them—the fruit of the Tree that was in the midst of the garden.

There have been a great many opinions as to what that tree was.

We may guess at it, but we have no certain knowledge concerning it.

However, it is not essential for us to know.

The Scriptures say that it was the tree of the Knowledge of Good and Evil, and that is sufficient for us.

Man was made innocent at the beginning, but he chose to take the knowledge of evil.

The serpent entered into the Garden of Eden and began to speak to Eve.

Eve listened to his voice, which was really the voice of Satan speaking through the serpent, and he said, "Yea hath God said?" making Eve to doubt.

She was not at that time as old as Adam; we must make that little excuse for poor Eve, for we cannot but feel a tender, daughterly sympathy for our first mother, since she was so very young at that time.

Adam had been on the earth for some time before she was created. He therefore had more understanding and knowledge than Eve.

She listened to the voice that spoke to her through the serpent.

She had looked at the Tree of Knowledge of Good and Evil, and as she listened to the seductive voice which said that it was good for food as well as pleasing to the eye, he made her believe that the fruit would make her wise.

The serpent talked to her and argued about it, saying, "Yea hath God said, ye shall not eat of any tree of the garden?" until, as she continued to listen, he got her to doubt that God had said it.

The Devil Begins His Work by Causing Doubt.

"Hath God said?"

That is the way in which a great many people are tempted to do evil.

They are ignorant and do not quite understand; but instead of going to those that have knowledge, they will argue with the Devil about the matter

Then Eve said, "Of the fruit of the trees of the garden we may eat: but of the fruit of the tree which is in the midst of the garden, God hath said, Ye shall not eat of it, neither shall ye touch it, lest ye die."

She knew perfectly well that God had said it; but the serpent then put his statement against God's statement, and said to the woman:

For God doth know that in the day ye eat thereof, then your eyes shall be opened, and ye shall be as God, knowing good and evil.

Is not that just the way the Tempter does today?

He puts into the mind the thought that God may not have said some things.

He gets people to doubt, and then he contradicts God and says, "It will do you no harm if you do it, because God will not keep His Word, and you will not 'surely die.'"

He tells them that instead it will be a great benefit—that they shall be able to discern between good and evil and be as gods.

As things are now in this world, with the Satan usurping God's power, it seems to be necessary that we should be informed about the evil; that we should know of it, and be able to discern. For God afterwards said, "in sorrow shalt thou eat of it all the days of thy life."

Adam Sinned Deliberately.

After Eve had eaten she also gave of the fruit unto her husband, and he ate.

In Paul's 1st Epistle to Timothy, 2d chapter, and the 12th, 13th, and 14th verses, we find that the man knew that it was wrong, and therefore he deliberately sinned.

We are told that the woman was beguiled by Satan and fell first into transgression, but that Adam was not beguiled; he acted with his eyes open; he was not deceived.

He desired, no doubt, to go with his companion, Eve.

Fear Ever Follows in the Wake of Sin.

What were the consequences of that fall?

After they had sinned, their eyes were opened, and they knew that they were naked, and they were afraid.

The first thing we see is that fear entered into them and their simplicity and faith were cast aside.

They were afraid of the Voice of God.

Fear always enters immediately after sin.

When a young man or woman sins, the first persons they fear will know about it are the ones that love them most—their mother and father.

So Adam and Eve, our first parents, were afraid to hear the Voice of God their Father.

God used to talk to them in the Garden of Eden, in the cool of the day; and when He came to speak with them, after they had sinned, they were afraid, and hid themselves from His presence among the trees of the garden.

Oh, what folly! To think that they could hide themselves from the presence of God!

What folly for people to think that they can hide their sins from God! They cannot escape from the all-seeing eye of God.

Adam and Eve hid themselves behind the trees in the garden, but the all-seeing eye of God penetrates everything.

God called Adam and said to him, "Where art thou?"

Then Adam answered, "I heard Thy Voice in the garden, and I was afraid, because I was naked; and I hid myself."

Fear follows in the wake of sin all through the generations, and in the Revelation we find that "the fearful" head the procession to hell.

God asked Adam who had told him that he was naked. Had he eaten of the tree whereof he was commanded not to eat?

He tried to put the responsibility of his sin upon the woman and said, "The woman whom Thou gavest to be with me, she gave me of the tree, and I did eat."

God asked the woman what she had done, and the woman said, "The serpent beguiled me, and I did eat"

Then God said to the serpent:

Because thou hast done this, cursed art thou above all cattle, and above every beast of the field; upon thy belly shalt thou go, and dust shalt thou eat all the days of thy life:

And I will put enmity between thee and the woman, and between thy seed and her seed: it shall bruise thy head, and thou shalt bruise his heel.

Unto the woman He said, I will greatly multiply thy sorrow and thy conception; in sorrow thou shalt bring forth children; and thy desire shall be to thy husband, and he shall rule over thee.

And unto Adam He said, Because thou hast harkened unto the voice of thy wife, and hast eaten of the tree, of which I commanded thee, saying, Thou shalt not eat of it: cursed is the ground for thy sake; in toil shalt thou eat of it all the days of thy life;

Thorns also and thistles shall it bring forth to thee; and thou shalt eat the herb of the field;

In the sweat of thy face shalt thou eat bread, till thou return unto the ground; for out of it wast thou taken: for dust thou art, and unto dust shalt thou return.

God's Love Provided a Way of Redemption.

God in His great mercy immediately provided a way by which all flesh should be saved. The seed of the woman was to bruise the head of the serpent. And in 1 Corinthians 15:22 we have the beautiful promise: "As in Adam all die, so also in the Christ shall all be made alive."

The redemption that was given through the Christ covers all our necessities for spirit, soul, and body.

God will reclaim this earth.

We know that His mercy endureth forever, and that at the end He shall be All in All.

When that time comes, it will be the time of the Final Restoration of All Things.

But that time has not yet come.

We are at the Beginning of that Restoration.

Humanity has had to suffer, not only for Adam's sin, but for its own sins.

People are too ready to blame Adam for what they have done themselves.

We are apt to dwell too much on the thought of Adam's sin and the fall, and not look enough at our own transgressions.

There was a redemption promised through the Man Christ Jesus, who was to be the Intercessor and Mediator between God and men.

He has prepared for us, in Himself, a Full Redemption.

Men Sin Because of Ignorance of Right and Wrong.

Today many are led into error because of ignorance of right and wrong.

In many cases people do not know the difference between good and evil.

If a thing looks good to the eye, they immediately desire it.

If it looks as if it might taste good, they have the idea that it must be good.

You must learn to make a clear distinction between the things that are good and the things that are evil.

God has provided a way for the banished ones to return.

Many people suffer in their bodies because they have been badly born.

They suffer from the sins of past generations just as we all have had to suffer from the sins of our first parents.

People have been growing weaker throughout the generations.

Adam lived for nine hundred thirty years; so you can imagine what a strong man he must have been.

If people in this generation live threescore years and ten, they do well.

It is estimated that not one-half of the human race live to be fifty years of age.

As we grow into maturity, we see many that we have known in youth pass away.

When a man lives to be over seventy years of age, he finds that nearly all the people of his own age that he has known have passed away.

We then begin to feel that this is not the Land of the Living, but the Land of the Dying.

We greatly desire to be redeemed from sin and all its consequences.

May God help us to receive and retain these blessings for spirit, soul, and body through the power of the Lord Jesus, the Christ!

He who was the Seed of the woman and the Son of God said, "I Am the Way, and the Truth, and the Life; no one cometh unto the Father, but by Me."

Thus, when we are asked, "What is the way?" we say, "The Christ is the Way. Redemption comes only through obeying Him."

Your body must be a fit temple of the Holy Spirit, if you are to be kept free from sin.

You must consecrate yourselves wholly to Him as a Living Sacrifice.

"How can we do that?" you may ask.

You can have your bodies cleansed by the blood of Jesus, the Christ, and then you must do your part.

You must give yourselves to God and ask Him to keep you from sin.

You cannot keep yourselves; you must be kept by the Power of God.

We are so often asked, "Why is it that I am not healed? Why is it that I do not get this blessing from God?

"God promised that when Jesus came He would set us free from sin.

"The Christ has come, and still there are so many suffering from all kinds of sickness!"

Your sufferings continue, first, because of the imperfect condition of your bodies when you first sought God for healing.

People ask God to heal them, and He does; but they do not obtain in a day the strength which it has taken years to destroy.

If you go back to your sin, and do the things which harm the body, how is the restoration of the body to continue?

Those Seeking Healing Must Be Honest With God.

You must continue in The Way if you would keep what He has given unto you.

There are many persons who ask God for healing who do not confess even to themselves what it is that is causing the sickness.

They not only do not confess it to the one whom they asked to pray for them, but they are not even honest with themselves.

You must make a clean breast of this both to yourself and to God.

Today we ask God to help all who have been guilty of secret sin and to give them power to overcome it.

You must give your bodies to God, and fully consecrate yourselves to Him, that He may put His Holy Spirit in vour hearts.

Accept the Blessing by Faith.

When you do not have the victory, do not sit down and mourn and fret over it, saying that you have been supplicating God to help you; but determinedly ask God to give you the help that you need, and then believe that you will receive the blessing.

Does not God promise to give you this blessing and the faith with which to come and ask?

The one who knocks and seeks will receive, because God is not unwilling to help you.

Then, after you have turned your face to God, and have asked Him to help you and to keep you from these sins, do something for Him.

Find something to do for some one else that will keep you occupied and your mind busy, so that it will not be left an open blank, ready for the Devil to come in at any moment and again tempt you to sin.

The Command to "Be Fruitful and Multiply," Given Before the Fall and Again After the Fall.

You will notice that among the things that God commanded before the fall was that they should increase, and multiply, and replenish the earth.

When Eve was given to Adam, he said, "This is now bone of my bones, and flesh of my flesh."

There are some foolish people who say that the sin of Adam and Eve was in their having children.

That cannot be, because the command was given before the fall.

Please remember that.

When any one suggests to you that that was the sin of Adam and Eve, tell them that God gave the command to be fruitful and multiply when they were yet in Paradise, before the fall.

That command was not only given in the beginning—in man's innocency—but it was also given after the flood, to Noah and to his sons and daughters.

Every living thing was swept off the face of the earth with the exception of the one family, and then the same command was given—"Be fruitful and multiply upon the earth."

One of the Greatest Sins of the Present Time

is the prevention of increase.

The more degenerate a people become the smaller is the number of children that are born among them.

God's Word says:

Lo, children are an heritage of Jehovah:
And the fruit of the womb is His reward.
As arrows are in the hand of a mighty man,
So are the children of youth.

So we in Zion teach our people not to prevent the birth increase; it is a sin.

Children are not a curse; they are a blessing.

We tell the people of Zion that with the children which God gives them they will have blessings from God; and that God will give them the strength, to labor for their children and to care for them.

There are some women who believe that they are not strong enough to bear children.

That teaching is not of God; the doctors are largely responsible for that.

I believe that I am right when I say that there are many thousands of women all over the lands whom doctors have told that they must not bear any more children, and who have helped to prevent births.

Instead of this having the effect of making the women stronger, it has an exactly opposite effect.

They become weak and nervous, and are unfitted for the duties of wifehood and motherhood.

We say to the mothers in Zion,

Bear Your Children and God will Take Care of You.

We find that those who have children are usually stronger than those who have not.

When a man depends upon his daily work for his living, he knows that he must work, or his children will be cold and hungry.

The responsibility is good for both the father and the mother.

A man and a woman who have the responsibility of bringing up their little family, and who love their sweet, little children, will not do the things that some foolish people do—create strikes and spend money in foolish and unprofitable ways.

Very often the preference of employment is given to a man who has a family, because it is reasonably thought likely that his responsibility will make him steadfast.

When we look over the story of the lives of great men in the past, we find that many of the greatest men have come from large families, and have had to endure hardships in their youth.

It is not always best for people to have everything they want.

God will take care of you and help you to take care of your children, if you do what is right and live in a temperate and sensible manner.

This teaching has been emphasized in Zion so much that I do not believe that there are any mothers here who need to be warned against the destruction of the unborn.

The Duties of the Wife Include Those of the Mother.

If you young women undertake to become wives, you must also expect to become mothers.

You must not say that you will marry but will not be mothers, or that you will have just as many children as you choose to have, or that you will wait a few years until you are better able to take care of them.

This is a sin that you must guard against.

You must put aside the thought at once when it comes, and not question and say, "Yea, hath God said?"

Marriage was ordained, first, for the mutual help of the one to the other; but it was also ordained for the increase of the human race, and that children should be brought up in the nurture and admonition of the Lord.

In many places the marriage service has been largely set aside, and many people are married by a registrar or justice.

Many Protestant clergymen marry people without going through the form of a marriage service.

The Church of England marriage service is a very good one.

It is taken from the Scriptures.

If you have not taken these vows and you think that you are exempt from them because you did not go through the marriage service, you are mistaken; because marriage was ordained by God, and if you take the Word of God for your guide, you must follow the teaching of the Holy Scriptures.

When People Should Not Marry.

One of the reasons why young married people get these strange ideas is because they do not begin rightly.

Some young people think that all that is necessary is to want to get married, and so, without any proper preparation, they marry.

Young men who have made no preparation at all, who have earned from eight to ten dollars a week and have saved nothing, have no right to marry.

Let them show that they can save, and then they may ask the girl to marry.

It is not best for girls to marry at the age of sixteen, eighteen, or even nineteen.

A woman should be mature before she marries.

"Our grandmothers did it," you may say.

We should profit by the too often bitter experiences of our grandmothers.

We see that it is far better to be careful and to wait a few years; then, when you begin your married life, you will be better fitted for it.

Do not encourage your children to marry too young.

Begin in the right way.

Neither do I think it is well for you to wait before marrying until you become too old.

It is well to marry young, but not too young.

"Children of the youth" are spoken of with commendation, but these are the children of youthful men and youthful women, not children of those who are themselves still children.

A great deal of sorrow would be avoided if people would be more careful and marry only when they are older and better prepared.

It is a mistake for very old men to marry young women and for old women to marry young men.

It does not matter if the one or the other is rich.

You never know when the riches may take wings and fly away.

But when you have married at a suitable age and without that great difference in years, you will sympathize with each other, and in case of any calamity you will be able to strengthen and help each other.

I entreat you, be careful with your children and keep them from marrying too young.

Thoughts of Matrimony Conflict with School Work.

Young girls who are getting an education should not accept attentions from young men while they are attending school.

The conditions now are different from those of the olden times.

It seems almost as if then they had nothing else to think about or to do; so they got married.

I want to emphasize the fact that you cannot attend to your lessons and at the same time give time to young men.

Give time and attention to your studies; and, when you have finished your school work, you will be better prepared for the duties of life.

I believe that all teachers will agree with me in this.

Some of you may say that if you do that you will lose all your chances of marrying.

You are mistaken about that.

Young men like to do their own choosing, and they will be more likely to desire a girl who does not put herself in their way.

A girl who is a flirt may have a great many men admiring her, but she will not be likely to have many sensible men wanting to marry her.

Do not choose a man merely because he has money.

But on the other hand a man has no right to ask a girl to marry him unless he has saved something.

If he has saved something before his marriage, he will be more likely to be provident after marriage.

Your tastes should be somewhat similar.

You should be attracted to each other personally.

A man and his wife should be congenial to each other.

Otherwise, although both may be very nice persons, yet, each may be better suited for some one else.

I have been talking to the young people; but there are many who are unhappily married, but who now cannot get out of it; and they must not get out of it.

Having once voluntarily accepted each other they should always thereafter make the home life as pleasant as possible.

The Curse of the Divorce Laws.

You must make the best of it, because the Word of God does not allow persons to separate and get divorces merely because they are not congenial to each other.

You did the thing yourself, with your eyes wide open.

You may say, "We were like Eve, we were deceived."

Perhaps that is true.

Perhaps you did your best, and still you did not get the right person.

In that case you must still keep the marriage vow.

You must make the best of it, for you have no right to be divorced except for the one cause named in Scripture—adultery.

How much misery has been caused through people's taking advantage of these lax divorce laws, both among the lower and the upper classes!

We read every day of married people taking a dislike to each other and liking some one else, and then going to some other state and filing a petition for a divorce on the ground of desertion or incompatibility of temperament, or anything else that they may choose as a reason, which is no reason whatever.

What are the results?

You sometimes hear of women who have been divorced from two husbands coming back and asking to be married again to the first husband, and then leaving him again and wanting the second.

What a mix-up of families.

For instance, a woman marries three times and has children by the three husbands, and then these children grow up together in the same house—boys and girls, who are half brothers and half sisters; and sometimes there are some who are not related at all.

Such a state of affairs often leads to a low and immoral condition in the home.

A woman has no right to marry the second time, unless her husband has been an adulterer and she has obtained a divorce from him; because in taking the marriage vow, they vowed that they would never leave nor forsake each other as long as life lasted, except for this one cause.

A woman has a right to forgive a man for his sin if she

chooses, and to continue to live with him as his wife if she believes that he will do right.

These loose divorce laws have been the cause of much misery in the family life.

If you give up sin in every form, you have healthier and purer bodies.

We have had the experience of many years, having heard the sad stories of many sinful and sorrowful lives.

In getting down to the root of evils, we have found where the difficulties and dangers were, and we have been able to show others the dangers that are to be avoided.

The Future Generation in Zion.

In Zion City, instead of a weak and sickly people, we will have a generation growing up to maturity who will bring forth the Fruits of the Spirit.

They will be able to receive from God the Gifts of the Spirit, even if some have to die, as the children of Israel died, in the wilderness, because they grumbled against Moses and God.

We know and believe that God will here raise up a Royal Generation, who will do their part in bringing about the Restoration of All Things.

I believe that God is not only willing to benefit future generations, but that we will make our people strong, with pure bodies and pure spirits, and through obedience obtain increasing purity; so we will each do our part lovingly and faithfully.

All of you who desire to live clean and holy lives, to have pure bodies as well as pure spirits, to be the temples of the Holy Spirit, stand and give yourselves to God.

PRAYER OF CONSECRATION.

My God and Father, I come to Thee in Jesus' Name. Take me as I am and make me what I ought to be—clean in spirit, clean in soul, and clean in body. Help me to do right. Forgive my sins. I give myself to Thee, spirit, soul, and body. Sanctify me now. For Jesus' sake. Amen. [*All repeat the prayer, clause by clause, after Overseer Jane Dowie.*]

Beloved, if you have given yourselves to God and have confessed your sins and have asked Him to help you so that you may put them away, God has forgiven your sins and will cleanse you from all unrighteousness.

PRAYER BY OVERSEER JANE DOWIE.

Our Father, grant that we may have a clean people who will live clean and holy lives in this clean City. Help us each to do our part. Let us all help each other in love. May we take the burdens cast upon us and lay them down at the feet of the Great Burden-Bearer, who came to take our sins and carry our sorrows. Our Father, we thank Thee for Jesus, our Savior. We thank Thee for the many thousands of spirits who have come and have been cleansed; and we ask Thee to take away not only the sin and the disease, but all the marks that have been made by the sin. Help us to live a humble, clean, and holy life. For Jesus' sake. Amen.

Overseer Jane Dowie then pronounced the

BENEDICTION.

Beloved, abstain from every form of evil. And may the very God of Peace Himself sanctify you wholly; and I pray God your whole spirit, and soul, and body be preserved entire, without blame, unto the coming of our Lord Jesus, the Christ. Faithful is He that calleth you, who also will do it. The grace of our Lord Jesus, the Christ, the love of God, our Father, the fellowship of the Holy Spirit, our Comforter and Guide, one Eternal God, abide in you, bless you, and keep you, and all the Israel of God everywhere, forever. Amen.

A MEETING FOR ZION MEN ONLY.

REPORTED BY R. M. P., O. R. AND F. A. F.

The meeting in Shiloh Tabernacle for men only, announced for Monday evening, was attended by a large audience.

It was one of the most profitable and deeply interesting of the series of meetings of the Feast thus far held.

The General Overseer was in a specially tender mood, and the whole audience seemed to be prepared, by the Spirit of God, to receive his solemn Message of Truth.

The address was profound in thought, at times eloquent, and hopefully inspiring to all who heard it.

It was delivered in a calm, earnest, but, for the most part, unimpassioned manner, which was thoroughly in keeping with the deeply spiritual thought and utterances of God's inspired prophet.

There were no horrible disquisitions on impurity, such as some might possibly have expected, but rather a strong, convincing appeal for Purity and Self-control.

Although women and young boys were properly excluded from the meeting, yet, so pure and spiritual was every sentiment, that not one word was spoken that might not have been listened to by the most sensitive person in a mixed audience.

His reasoning along the line of thought, that knowledge is sometimes the most disastrous of things; that the glory of God is often in the concealment of a matter; and that to know before God's time is like eating unripe fruit, was exceedingly instructive and suggestive.

One thing that gave the meeting a specially sympathetic and serious character at the very beginning, was the reading by the General Overseer of a request for prayer, without name, from a young man who was suffering from a wicked inheritance transmitted to him by an ungodly parent.

The father, at the age of thirty-six years, had committed suicide, and on the day of the funeral the wife had given birth to their ninth child.

The man of God appeared to be deeply moved by the incident, and, in connection with a very earnest Prayer of Faith for the sufferer, made the request a text for a few intensely practical and telling comments on the awful consequences of a lustful life.

Zion Band was present and rendered a few choice selections.

The meeting closed at a comparatively early hour, but the words and truths uttered by God's servant will forever live on in the lives of those who heard them.

Shiloh Tabernacle, Zion City, Illinois, Monday Evening, July 18, 1904.

The service was begun by the General Overseer's pronouncing the following

INVOCATION.

God be merciful unto us and bless us,
And cause Thy face to shine upon us;
That Thy Way may be known upon earth,
Thy Saving Health among all the Nations;
For the sake of Jesus. Amen.

This was followed by the reading of the 5th chapter of Galatians, beginning at the 16th verse.

In commenting on the word fornication, in the 19th verse, the General Overseer said:

The word fornication must be held to include adultery, but it has a wider meaning than adultery, which is only one form of fornication.

After the Scripture reading, the General Overseer said:

A Cry From One Cursed With an Inheritance of Wickedness.

I have been handed a request for prayer tonight—of course I shall not read the name of the person who sends it—that I want to make the text of a few remarks.

He says:

Please pray for me. I have inherited some of my father's wickedness, who, at the age of thirty-six got a young lady into trouble and then in a state of depression committed suicide, leaving a family of eight children. The ninth was born upon the day of his funeral. The oldest was fourteen years of age at the time.

What a volume of sin, and wickedness, and sorrow is comprised in that petition! The man, who must have married at about the age of twenty or twenty-one—it might have been later—was the father of nine children.

Not satisfied with a virtuous and manly life, he seeks and finds the way of death, shamefully and without cause, as is apparent from the fact that he already had nine dear children.

He plunges into vice, ruins a young woman's life, throws upon the world her offspring—his offspring—and then, like the coward that he is, commits self-murder, and leaves a broken-hearted widow, about to become a mother, who upon the day that his body is buried gives birth to her ninth child!

His son, conscious of inherited wickedness, cries out from the depths of his heart.

He is right.

God can and will remove the curse. [Amen.]

I bid the brother be of Good Hope, and of Confident Faith that if he will but make the surrender of all his being to God, the Father will, for the Christ's sake, by the Holy Spirit, take away the brutal inheritance of lust and crime, and give him the victory.

There may be many here, who, though their fathers did not commit suicide, have an inheritance of lust and sin.

May God give you grace tonight to cast this burden upon Him. He ever loves and feels for us, and is our Burden-bearer. Let us pray. [Amen.]

PRAYER BY THE GENERAL OVERSEER.

Our Father who art in the Heavens, we hallow Thy Name, and bless Thee tonight for this day. Although the weather has been hot and trying, many of us have been able to accomplish a good day's work. We thank Thee for all Thy continued blessings during the Feast. We pray Thee to grant blessing to all the women who were gathered here this afternoon to hear Overseer Jane Dowie speak. Grant, O God, that they may retain the blessing; and that the wives, and mothers, and maidens may be purer and better for the meeting. [Amen.]

And now, Father in Heaven, give us a good night. Bless the sick ones, and those that are conscious of an inheritance of vicious passion and tendency to crime; and give unto them, the innocent victims, indeed, of paternal transgressions, the grace to cast themselves entirely upon Thee. We thank Thee, O God, for the thousands in Zion who have been delivered from the power of the Enemy; who have been brought out of deep sin, from the pollution of themselves and others, and the degradation of their nature. We thank Thee for the deliverance and the transformation which Thy Holy Spirit has wrought in the spirits, souls, and bodies of so many here. And now, hear us, as with one heart and voice we pray as our Lord hath taught us.

The Congregation then joined with the General Overseer in chanting the Disciples' Prayer, after which two appropriate selections were sung by the manly voices of the Zion Male Chorus.

The General Overseer then delivered his address:

PURITY THROUGH FAITH.

INVOCATION.

Let the words of my mouth, and the meditation of my heart be acceptable in Thy sight, be profitable unto these, my brethren, and unto all to whom these words shall come. For Jesus' sake.

The works of the flesh are manifest. I have read to you that awful catalog. Let me read it to you again, in the Epistle of Paul to the Galatians in the 5th chapter, nineteenth to twenty-first verses:

Now the works of the flesh are manifest, which are these, fornication, uncleanness, lasciviousness,

Idolatry, sorcery, enmities, strife, jealousies, wraths, factions, divisions, heresies,

Envyings, drunkenness, revelings, and such like: of the which I forewarn you, even as I did forewarn you, that they which practice such things shall not inherit the Kingdom of God.

When we have read it, we seem to hear the cry of another Apostle, Peter. "I beseech you to abstain from fleshly lusts, which war against the life."

Earthly desires and sensual lust
Are passions springing from the dust,
They fade, they die.
But in the life beyond the tomb,
They seal the immortal spirit's doom.

You will pass either into the felicity, and joy, and beauty, and glory of Heaven, where the Divine satisfaction for every pure and holy power and passion will be complete; or you will pass into hell, where the rich man, and the poor man, and men of all ranks find themselves in the company of demons, and of the spirits of unclean men and women, who cursed one another while they lived, and in whom the hellish passions still continue without the possibility of satisfaction—no, the debauchee and drunkard shall find no paramour, nor even a drop of cool water to quench his thirst.

Torture of Disembodied Lust.

If the consequences of transgression were limited to this life, it were terrible to contemplate the results of a life of sin, which is the transgression of Law.

It were terrible to contemplate it, if it were only for time; but the results are more terrible when they reach out into the Dark Regions of Hell—when those who would be unclean are unclean still, when those who would be unrighteous are unrighteous still, and when those who would be unholy are unholy still.

What an awful thought! Disembodied spirits, feeling all the hellish passions that have dragged them down to damnation—with these unholy desires intensified, it may be, and yet with no power of gratification!

Add to that the horrible torture of memory, the constant ringing through the spirit of the words, "Son, remember, remember!" and the thought that the poor lost one might have been in heaven, in the Purity and the Perfect Love of God, in the companionship of the pure, and holy, and noble of all the ages.

Tonight I warn you who are with me in the Land of the Dying, lest, peradventure, some of you may reach the Land where their worm dieth not, where the fire is not quenched—the miseries of Gehenna, or Hell.

I speak to you also of those who hope.

Hope Through Jesus, the Christ.

I would fain hope that every one would reach Heaven.

There the blessed consequences of that highest and last Fruit of the Spirit, Self-control, are realized.

Heaven is attained through the subjection of the body.

This body is by nature an inherited body of death, to which through succeeding generations has been transmitted the physical, psychical, and spiritual corruption of an ancestry reaching back to the horrible transgression of our first parents.

You will find that He who has taken away your sins has given you the power of the Spirit within.

He has steadily increased the capacity for controlling self, for binding self, for laying self at the feet of the Christ, and at the feet of the Father; for making self a subject and not a master.

The sphere of Self-control lies even higher, to where Self can be trusted; to where the Control is Divine.

It were vain for me to talk to you as if I could, in any one address, embrace the whole subject of spiritual, psychical, and physical Purity.

But one thing that I shall begin with and emphasize is—

Wisdom is the Principal Thing in Life.

Love may be, and is, in one sense, the greatest thing, but Wisdom is the Principal Thing.

The Pillar of Purity is the greatest thing in the House of Wisdom, where the man of Self-control lives; the house within, not made with hands; the temple, the outer courts of which we see in the physical nature; the inner courts of which we see in the warm life's blood—the soul—that flows through it; the innermost shrine of which has become the holy of holies, because it is the spirit in which God dwells.

Divine Control brings into perfect harmony every power of spirit, soul, and body, cleanses the entire being, and creates conditions of Purity which are accompanied by Peace, and where the Fruits of the Spirit can abound; where Love, Joy and Peace; where Long-suffering, Kindness, Goodness, Faithfulness, Meekness and Self-control are Triumphant Powers.

The greatest thing is to be wise; and "the Wisdom that is from above is first Pure."

Purity is a priceless gem, worth your paying everything for—even life itself.

If you possess Purity of Motive, Purity of Thought, Purity of Intention, Purity of Speech, and a simple and firm determination that impure thoughts shall have no place in your life, that impure ends shall have no place in your purpose, then you have Power.

Power! The Power of a Divinely Emancipated Being!

A consequence of that is the transmission of Power; for the Power of which I speak is never quiescent; can never be limited to yourself.

You carry with you an atmosphere, an influence, which makes your presence mean Purity.

Those who know nothing about you will look at you and feel that they cannot say an unclean or filthy thing.

Divine Certainty of Freedom From Unclean Inheritance.

I am glad that in the Christian Catholic Church in Zion we are getting to understand better and better that there is not only a possibility, but a Divine Certainty that even here and now we shall be free from the unclean inheritance that clings to every part of our being, and which, even when sins are forgiven, remains until the Spirit's work is accomplished, until the Regeneration is complete, and the Restoration entire.

Then, and not until then, can we be perfectly free.

By the Grace of God, if we will do His Will, we shall be free. [Amen.]

In the beginning, the evil powers which burst into the world ɔm hell, took the shape of the most beautiful and subtle of the beasts of the field, and became the tempter of woman, so at she fell.

She, in her turn, became the tempter of man and he fell.

That fall came through doubting as to whether God's Word, ıich had declared a blessing for obedience, and the awful nalty of death for disobedience, was true.

Doubt lay at the foundation of the inclination in man to ten to the tempter, to obey him, and to seek gratification for ameless appetite in direct disobedience to God's command.

The Sin of our First Parents.

There is no need to discuss the question as to whether there ıs or was not a veritable apple.

It is of no consequence at all.

I do not care to discuss it.

The Word speaks of evil and immoral practices as fruits of e spirit of lust and sin; and of Love, Joy, Peace, and the ner gloriously powerful graces of the Spirit, as the Fruit of e Holy Spirit.

There is no question whatever, that there was forbidden a mething of which woman first partook, and of which man his turn partook.

The sacred historian, by Divine Inspiration, speaks of the ee of the Knowledge of Good and Evil as the Forbidden ee.

God meant that we should never know evil; at least not in a rm by which we should be partakers of it.

You will notice that the Tree was planted by God, but that, the infancy of humanity, its fruit was forbidden.

ıere Are Times When Knowledge Is the Most Disastrous of Possessions.

If we would all remember that it is "the glory of God to conal a thing," we should be much more blessed than we are ıen we foolishly suppose that we must know the evil as well the good.

It is impossible, in the opinion of foolish humanity, to know il without partaking of it.

Awful consequences ensue when you forget that there is rtain knowledge that, when you get it, results in death.

I do not doubt that such knowledge may be had and that, art from criminal participation, it may be useful; but the ansgression lay in the partaking of the Tree of Knowledge d of the fruit, which, being forbidden to man at that time, it as death to eat.

Pause for a moment and think of how many things it is sirable that we should be ignorant until we attain a period life and degree of knowledge when knowledge of those ings may be acquired without sin.

If it were good and evil of which I am speaking, I should e sinning even to suggest that we could ever partake of evil.

I am speaking of the knowledge of evil without doing evil.

I believe that God would never have planted that Tree of nowledge of Good and Evil unless it had been essential for an's good that it should have been there.

Although it is often fatal to eat fruit when it is unripe, yet, ıen one patiently waits for maturity, one finds it the most licious and most abundantly satisfying of foods.

You must remember that knowledge, which at one time will a power for God, would, in the untrained and undisciplined ind, and heart, and hands of untutored youth, be destructive.

Sin in Disobediently Anticipating God's Time.

It seems to me clear, beyond all question, that the entire nge of knowledge, both of evil and of good, was, so to speak, be provided for us at the right time.

But the man and woman sinned when they listened to the ice that said, "Yea, hath God said," and discussed the quesɔn as to whether God's Word was really God's Word.

They sinned in continuing to listen, even after the Serpent d boldly declared, "Ye shall not surely die: for God doth ow that in the day ye eat thereof, then your eyes shall be ened, and ye shall be as God, knowing good and evil."

They sinned in seeking by disobedience to anticipate God's ne.

The Tempter often puts within man the thought that there is tremendous satisfaction to be gotten by deliberate and wilful sobedience to God's Law.

Herein lies the whole matter.

Divine Law is perfect.

"The Law of Jehovah is perfect," converting, renewing, the life.

All things connected with that Law are perfect.

"The Fear of Jehovah is clean, enduring forever. The Judgments of Jehovah are true and righteous altogether."

Sweeter than the sweetest honeycomb is the sweetness of obedience to God.

But the converse is just as true—that disobedience is more bitter than tongue can express.

It is the bitterness of the intense concentration of every disease, moral, spiritual, and physical.

The Two Rivers.

A very Ocean of Damnation, a very River of Death, the black waters of which boil up from Hell itself, flows through this earth, bearing upon its bosom every pollution, every horrible consequence of transgression, every disease and every horrible consequence of every disease, until that river is blacker than night, and more horribly filthy than imagination could conceive or words express.

Laden with every iniquity and pollution, it flows on.

These evils came from the first transgression.

I have emphatically laid down these premises, because I wanted to call attention to the other side.

Just as truly as this River of Disease and Death forces itself up into this world from Hell, flowing constantly, so "there is a River, the Streams whereof make glad the City of God."

It flows from the Throne of God and of the Lamb; and in the midst of it, on either side of the River, is the Tree of Life.

The Fruit of that Tree is yielded every month.

The Leaves of that Tree are for the Healing of the Nations.

The River is full of Water, and is forever flowing.

I believe that there never has been a time, except in the Christ's earthly ministry, when Pure Doctrine and insistence upon Purity of Life has been more clearly preached and more consistently practiced than since God founded the Christian Catholic Church in Zion.

The Time Has Come for Driving Out the Demons of Impurity.

I believe that the terror of evil beings in human form and of demons that possess them, when the words "Zion" and "Dowie" are mentioned, provokes, as in the days of our Lord, these demons to cry out, "What have I to do with thee?"

"O Zion, what have I to do with thee? O Prophet of God, what have I to do with thee? Art thou come to torment us before the time?"

We say, "No! We have come just at the right time, and we are determined either to convert you or to drive you out!"

"Oh, we cannot convert the Devil," you say.

But God can deliver the demon-possessed man. We can, by God's help, turn him to God.

I rejoice that the River is flowing, and that the Leaves of the Tree, which are the Eternal Words of God, are being sent forth.

"He sendeth His Word and healeth them."

LEAVES OF HEALING, to which we boldly gave that title, has proved to be indeed inspired of the Divine Spirit, for it has done the very work that the Word is sent forth to do.

Like the Sword of the Spirit, it is "death to sin."

It is "Life to him that mourns for sin;" it "maketh and it endeth strife."

It makes strife with evil; it makes peace with God.

I will not enter into any horrible disquisition concerning sin.

You and I have to face not only the fact of the hard fight that we have had, but of that which all of us may still have.

The Never-ending Fight Against Temptations.

Do not forget that, even though saved, you have to be saved to the uttermost before the fight within shall cease.

Temptations will never cease.

It was not at the beginning only of His earthly ministry that the Master was tempted, but surely the tempter was present at Gethsemane, when He prayed with such intensity and agony that His sweat was blood, and when, in the garden, He triumphed over the Tempter.

He said, "The Prince of this world cometh, and hath nothing in Me."

There was nothing which the Tempter, the Prince of this world, could work upon.

There was nothing in the Christ to coöperate with him.

Alas, we cannot say that of any being beside the Christ, for we have inherited that which belongs to the Devil.

The Mysterious Power of Heredity.

Besetting sins come down to us by hereditary transmission.

The faculties, and powers, and tendencies that make each of us powerful in some directions, that give to our whole lives tone and character, and to our minds a trend, and to our operations a clear distinctness, have often come to the front when we did not know that we possessed such powers.

We know nothing even as to how they came.

We simply find ourselves possessed of both good and evil powers, that are inheritances.

They have come down to us in our psychical nature, from the natures of our ancestry; in a direct line from distant fathers and mothers, who were great or who were wicked, who were good and powerful for good, or who were evil and powerful for evil.

Characteristics that have come down to us find expression even in the very formation of our bodies.

The compactness or looseness with which we are put together is often the result of heredity.

We inherit the tendencies that make us. It may be, perhaps, an organizing power, that makes it easy for us to do certain things without knowing where we got the capacity; easy to grasp mathematical problems; easy to grasp great moral and social problems; easy to see at one glance the field of battle and to know where to fight, and how to win that fight.

These things come down to us.

Heredity is responsible for much; do not forget it.

The tendencies, the powers, and the purities and impurities of our ancestry come down in straight family lines.

Hence it is that many of us are the possessors of a shameful inheritance; an inheritance of sin that has come down to us, perhaps, from the woman who permitted the Devil to poison all her beautiful nature, and made her the tempter and defiler of him whom God had made her leader and her head.

The Hereditary Power of a Pure Mother.

The Virgin Mary presented unto God a body that had been preserved in its virginity, although it cannot be held that she was herself an immaculate conception, or absolutely and personally sinless, since she, in common with all others on earth, had to be saved from sin.

But she was saved and glorified, being sanctified in spirit, soul, and body, so that the curse that had been brought upon humanity was through her canceled by God, and taken away in her Sinles Son, Jesus, the Christ.

God made, by His grace and her willingness, a virgin to be a mother without being the wife of a mortal man.

She was willing to take upon herself the degradation in men's eyes.

Therefore glorious and absolutely unspeakably sublime was the beatification of her nature when God dwelt in her, and overshadowed her, and so perfectly purified her, that, when the Christ was born, He was a "Holy Thing."

We, my brothers, may one day, in a body of Purity, be the procreators, and holy women the mothers, of holy beings, in whom there shall be no sin.

God hasten that day! [Amen.]

Our Inheritance Not All Bad.

Meanwhile, no matter what we may have inherited, it has not all been bad.

Thank God it has not all been bad, because humanity is never altogether and irremediably hopeless.

Deep as has been the degradation of humanity, the Star of Hope has never been extinguished.

When God had to sweep the whole world into an awful hell, there was a Star of Hope.

The Seed of the woman would one day bruise the head of the Serpent; one day that Seed would enter the gates of Hell, having died for men, open the dark gates of misery, and lead captivity captive—lead the lost out of the despair and the miseries of their condition.

Never has Hope been taken away.

It never can be taken away, for that which is Divine can never lose the attribute of unchangeableness which belongs to all that comes from God.

That which is Divine, and which is the offspring of God's own essential being, can never lose wholly and forever the imprint of its Divine Paternity.

Away down deep it may be buried beneath sin and iniquity, but Hope will exceed all the years of Time—it is Eternal.

When the penalty has come, Hope will say, "He hath made a way by which His banished may return."

Our Spirits, Souls, and Bodies Intended to Be Habitations of God.

Although you may be the inheritor of evil, remember that even if it be the leper's taint that has come down in your blood; even if it be the syphilitic poison that has been your inheritance; even if it be the horrible and unmerited disease which flowed as the consequences of prenatal immorality, and of impurity of every kind; even if these inheritances are in your blood, and you possess horrible tendencies to indulge in these sins, it is the Will of the God who has saved in all the ages, and who has made pure these temporal bodies which once were the temples of the Devil, that your bodies should be the temples of God—Holy Habitations for Himself through the Spirit. [Amen.]

Never forget that the great design of this body, this soul, this spirit, made in the triune nature of God and in the triune image of God, was that one day the Word that the Master spoke should be fulfilled, "If a man love Me, ... My Father will love him, and We—Father, Son, and Holy Spirit—will come unto him and make Our abode with him."

This is the highest possibility of our being—the complete possession at all times, under all circumstances, and in every place, by the Indwelling of a Triune God.

The Christian's Armor Cannot Be Laid Down.

In addition to our inheritance, we have our own transgressions.

"Let him that thinketh he standeth take heed lest he fall."

It is the unexpected that happens.

The Devil is too wise in evil, too subtle, always to attack you where you are strongest; nor is he so foolish as always to attack you where you are weakest.

Sometimes, having overcome him again and again, when he has attacked you where you have been weak, you fail to guard that part of your nature where you have been strong.

Suddenly he makes a dash, and fills with consternation your whole being, by getting in where you were strongest.

My brothers, do not forget these simple words:

Oh, watch, and fight, and pray!
  The battle ne'er give o'er;
Renew it boldly every day,
  And help Divine implore.

Ne'er think the victory won,
  Nor lay thine armor down:
Thy arduous work will not be done
  Till thou obtain thy crown.

Be on your guard perpetually.

I cannot promise that you can ever lay your armor down.

Even when you slumber, you will have to take the Shield of Faith for your pillow.

You can never take from your head the Helmet of Salvation; nor can you ever afford to lose the Girdle of Truth, nor, day or night, to lie down without the Breastplate of Righteousness; nor dare you ever leave your feet unprotected; for the Gospel of Peace must be that with which you are shod.

Even when you are sleeping, your hand must grasp your Sword.

Pillowing your head upon your Shield, you must be ready in a moment to leap up, fully armed, ready for the Good Fight of Faith.

Leave no unguarded place.

There must be no weakness of the spirit, soul, or body.

Take every virtue, every grace that God gives you, and, possessing them, you will be strong at every point.

These are Realities; they are not sentimental abstractions.

Divine Faith is the Faith that never doubts; Divine Hope is the Hope that is never dimmed and never despairs.

Divine Love is the Quenchless Fire—the All-consuming Fire of a Purity that can never be destroyed.

Life in the Christ is a Life that never dies; it is Eternal.

Knowledge and Wisdom are Real Powers in the Glorified Nature, in which animal passions are completely transformed, and are no longer mere lusts, but the agents of Divine and Self-denying Love.

Every part of the being is purified and made the agency of Purity, of Power, and of Eternal Peace.

May God give you these Eternal Possessions.

Seek for them now. Pray this

PRAYER OF CONSECRATION.

My God and Father, in Jesus' Name I come to Thee. Take my spirit; take my soul; take my body, as once again I lay it upon the altar of an entire consecration. Make me Thine in every part, and help me to fulfil Thy Will; to be pure in thought; to be pure in word; to be pure in action; to treat every woman as if she were my mother, except the sweet wife whom Thou hast given to be with me, one flesh. But let every other woman be to me as my mother, as my sister, whose Purity it is mine to preserve, and never to destroy by word, or thought, or unclean gesture, or suggestions. Make me the maintainer, not only of my own Purity, but the preserver of the Purity of all around me; of the chastity of every wife and the Purity of every maiden. Give me the grace that I may love Thee; trust Thee; serve Thee; be possessed by Thee. Clothe me with the Whole Armor of God. Place upon my brow the Helmet of Salvation. Place over my heart the Breastplate of Righteousness. Gird my loins with the Girdle of Truth. May my feet be shod with the Preparation of the Gospel of Peace. May I firmly grasp the Shield of Faith, which will quench all the fiery darts of the Evil One. Give me the Sword of the Spirit. Help me better to know how to use it—the Word of God—the Spirit of God; the Word that is Spirit, the Word that is Life, by means of which I can thrust the tempter and destroy the evil power. For Jesus' sake. [*All repeat the prayer, clause by clause, after the General Overseer.*]

Did you mean it?

MEN—"Yes."

The audience then joined in singing, "I Stand on Zion's Mount," after which the General Overseer pronounced the

BENEDICTION.

Beloved, abstain from every form of evil. And may the very God of Peace Himself sanctify you wholly; and I pray God your whole spirit, and soul, and body be preserved entire, without blame, until the coming of our Lord Jesus, the Christ. Faithful is He that calleth you, who also will do it. The grace of our Lord Jesus, the Christ, the love of God, our Father, the fellowship of the Holy Spirit, our Comforter and Guide, one Eternal God, abide in you, bless you, and keep you, and all the Israel of God everywhere, forever. Amen.

DORCAS AND MATERNITY DEACONESS WORK IN ZION.

REPORTED BY I. M. S. AND F. S.

Could any one thing be separated from the great body of the Christian Catholic Church in Zion and designated as happiest in all its component parts, it would be that quiet, deep, far-reaching, though largely unseen, force following, and often going in the front of the Church, known as Zion Dorcas and Maternity Deaconess Work.

Cold figures can give no adequate conception of the great work being done, under this name, and under the direction of Overseer Jane Dowie, who is at the head of Zion work for women throughout the world.

The Conference concerning this work, belonging peculiarly to the women of Zion, was held Friday forenoon, July 22, 1904, and was largely attended.

Besides the interesting and instructive addresses given by the Overseer, Elder Brasefield, and Deaconesses Thomas and Paddock, there was an exhibit of samples of the work done during the past winter in the way of making new garments out of old, which was as mystifying as it was admirable.

The little coats, trousers, dresses, hats, caps, cloaks, leggings, underwear, muffs, slippers, bootees, hoods, and all the other things necessary to clothe the little bodies, were most beautifully made and showed consummate skill in an art which has, in these days of cheap, ready-made clothing, been all but lost.

The wisdom displayed in the management of the finances is shown in the single fact that after this enormous output of the Dorcas work, there remains in the treasury, at the close of a winter of unusual severity, five hundred dollars.

In her address, the Overseer, after reviewing the work done during her six months' absence, expressed her appreciation of the ability and faithfulness shown by those in whose hands she had placed the active management, and thanked the workers everywhere for their part in this great work.

A happy and heartfelt welcome home was extended the Overseer by Deaconess Thomas, on behalf of all the workers, to which the Overseer responded in the same happy vein, taking the occasion to thank the ladies for their gift of beautiful floral decorations in Shiloh House which greeted her upon her return home.

The work for the year has shown a distinct advance over all the previous ones, and after a few weeks' interim, the work of the coming winter will be begun in the same spirit of consecration and devotion to God which has characterized it from its inception.

Shiloh Tabernacle, Zion City, Illinois, Friday Forenoon, July 22, 1904.

The meeting was opened by singing Hymn No. 25.

Overseer Jane Dowie read from the Inspired Word of God, in the 9th chapter of the Acts of the Apostles, from the 36th verse to the end of the chapter, after which she offered prayer.

She then said:

Our Conference this morning is concerning the Dorcas, the Maternity Dorcas, the Deaconess' Work and Women's Work in general, in the Christian Catholic Church in Zion throughout the world.

Progress of Women's Work in Zion.

We are delighted with the progress that has been made during the last year, especially with the Dorcas, and Maternity Dorcas Work in the City of Zion.

When I left here nine months ago, I divided oversight of the work between the wives of two of the Overseers in Zion City.

The care of the Maternity Dorcas Work was given into the hands of Elder Speicher, and the General Dorcas Work to Elder Brasefield.

After the General Overseer left on his Around-the-World Visitation we had a very cold winter, and the necessity for the Dorcas Work was even greater than usual.

It has been very gratifying to me in looking over the reports to know that even in the severest and coldest weather, the workers came out to the meetings and did their work.

Our good Deaconess Thomas, who is the deaconess in charge of the Zion City branch has been at all the meetings.

I especially commend her today for the faithful work that she has done.

We rejoice that God has given her power to do it.

She has shown much wisdom in the direction of the details.

At the beginning of her work in Zion City, she became very ill, but God heard prayer for her and raised her up. She seems to have been stronger and better than ever, and has not flinched from any of the hard work.

We also thank the noble band ot women workers whom she had with her and who have done so well.

Report of Elder Abigail T. Speicher, in Charge of Zion Maternity Dorcas Work.

I will first read to you Elder Speicher's report. She is not with us this morning, having left with her husband and son for a visit to Europe.

She says:

I am grateful to God for the part He has enabled me to do, and for the willing coöperation of all those who have so faithfully assisted me; also for the many kind words which have been spoken and written concerning this work.

Praying God's continued blessing upon you and trusting that, as you again take up the work among us, your health and strength may be renewed.

I am, faithfuly yours in the Master's service,

ABIGAIL T. SPEICHER.

The report which she has sent me in addition to her letter is as follows:

Garments made	826
Garments given out	682
Number of hours' work	1,940

This covers the period beginning November, 1903, to end of June of this present year.

Zion Maternity Dorcas Work.

Perhaps some of you may not quite understand what this Maternity Dorcas Work is.

It is a department which we started two years ago.

We found that some women who had come to Zion City and were becoming mothers had neglected to get ready what was necessary for the little newcomers; also, that some of our poorer women dreaded having children because they did not have proper clothing for them.

Then we also find women who do not understand what a little child needs.

We decided that we would not have any women in Zion City who could truthfully say that they would not have a child because they could not clothe the little one.

All those who have little children coming and cannot get the clothing ready for them can apply to the Maternity Dorcas Department of the work.

Elder Speicher is a young married woman, who has a little family herself and understands the needs and cares of women at such times.

Now that she is absent, I give Elder Brasefield that department of the work.

She also is a young mother, and she too knows what is necessary for a little baby, from personal experience.

Report of Elder Elizabeth Brasefield, in Temporary Charge of Zion Dorcas Work.

Elder Brasefield writes regarding the General Dorcas Work:

OVERSEER JANE DOWIE,

Shiloh House, Zion City, Illinois.

My Dear Mrs. Dowie:—The following is a general report of the work done in connection with the Dorcas work during the months of November, December, January, February, March, and April.

In order that you may have a general report of the work done during your absence, without having to refer to the files, I now give you a brief summary.

The workers have been for the most part very faithful and earnest in doing their part of the work in all the Branches.

In many of the outside branches the workers have had to be changed, owing to the changes in Elders. This has somewhat impeded the work, as has also changes that have had to be made in places of meeting.

Some of the outside Branches report little need for the Dorcas Work in their localities; others expect to be able to do more during the coming year. Of these I can speak to you in detail if you wish to know more of them.

For the outside Branches the total number of Articles received, is	2,173
Articles given out	2,113
Number hours' work	1,507

showing an increase of 1,105 hours' time over the work of last year.

In some of the Chicago Branches there has been an urgent demand for sewing classes.

The workers have found, in visiting the homes, many mothers who were very ignorant, especially in the sewing line, and who were very desirous of knowing how to make their children's dresses.

The total number of articles received in the Chicago Branches, is	3,427
Given out	3,398
Number hours' work	3,259

The work done by the visiting Deaconesses has been of very practical value.

Deaconess Munger reports sixty-two people whom she has visited regularly for the last four months during which she has been at work.

She has been able to effect some very permanent changes in many of these homes in the way of house cleaning and cleanliness in general.

By patient effort and perseverance, she has been able to work her way into the hearts of the people with whom she has dealt, and made them feel her kindly, Christ-like interest in them and their welfare, and has ministered to both their physical and spiritual needs in a most helpful way.

Of the work over which Deaconess Thomas has had supervision, I cannot speak too highly.

The total number of articles received from November, 1903, to June, 1904, is	6,057
Given out	7,509
Number hours' work	7,639

These numbers alone are sufficient to indicate the faithful and efficient service that has been rendered by the Deaconess and her willing corps of assistants and helpers.

This is especially remarkable when one considers the very severe cold of the winter months.

The report of attendance during the coldest winter months shows scarcely any decrease in numbers.

The Shoe Department has had a large output during the last six months.

The total number of pairs of shoes, rubbers, slippers, and hose given out amounts to one thousand three hundred twenty-seven.

The grand total for the six months of work in the outside Branches, and the eight months of work in Zion City Branch, is as follows:

Number articles received	11,657
Number articles given out	14,347
Number hours' work	12,405

I am now preparing a list of those who, during the last winter, have received assistance from both the Dorcas and the Poor Fund of the Church, so that if you wish to use the list in the future, it will be at hand.

In a few cases, articles donated to families have been disposed of; in others they have been refused because not good enough. These people we have felt to be totally unworthy of any further aid, and we are awaiting your decision in the matter of dropping them from our list

I am grateful to God for the little part He has enabled me to have in this work and only regret that it has not been more efficient.

I pray God's blessing upon you, and trust that your strength may be greatly renewed, and that we may be able in the future to give you much more efficient, though it could not be more willing, service in this branch of the Master's vineyard.

Sincerely yours in God's service, ELIZABETH BRASEFIELD.

The garments referred to in this report have been cleaned, renovated, made over, put into good order, and given out; so that there has been given out, altogether, fourteen thousand three hundred forty-seven.

Add to this the articles given out by the Maternity Dorcas Work, six hundred eighty-two, and we have a grand total of fifteen thousand twenty-nine.

That represents only the work that has been done during the term just closed, during my absence.

Finances of Zion Dorcas Work.

I left a thousand dollars, to be divided between the Dorcas and the Maternity Dorcas, giving seven hundred dollars for the general Dorcas Work and three hundred dollars for the Maternity.

We have received, in donations and collections since then, $671.47 for the General Dorcas Work; adding that to the $700 which I left, makes $1,371.47.

We spent on shoes in Zion City $376.09, and for flannel and dress-goods only $47.79.

We sent to the outside Branches $413.10, making a total expenditure of $836.98.

This still leaves us a balance of $534.49.

Our previous year's record shows expenditures amounting to $923.19 for Zion Dorcas Work; so you see we spent less money, and have done more work.

Zion City's little children were properly clothed and taken care of, all through that severe winter.

In all the cold parts of America, there is always more or less suffering among the working classes.

There is always a dearth of work, and if the man who is at the head of a family is not able to lay up any store for the winter, it is often very trying for the wife and the little people in the home.

We cannot do everything at once, but we do hope, in time, to be able to arrange and plan so that everybody in Zion City will have work all the year through.

A Wicked Lie Nailed Down.

Among the wicked stories that the newspapers sent all over the world were falsehoods concerning the condition of our poor in Zion City. We do have some poor. Christ said, the poor ye have always with you.

They usually select stories of this kind to send around the world.

When we were in Australia, a Methodist minister in Melbourne published them in his paper, trying to impress upon the people the idea that the poor people in Zion City were starving and freezing, while we were traveling around the world in affluence and luxury.

Some people were foolish enough to publish the statement that you were entirely without fuel in Zion City.

We pointed out to them that, if you were without coal in this cold northern climate with the thermometer twenty degrees below zero, there would not be one left to tell the tale.

If that had been the case, I think the facts would have been very widely published all over the world, giving a list of the number of corpses that were found in the houses where the poor people had frozen to death, because they had had no fuel for fires.

They knew better; but they invented these stories to inflame the people against God's Prophet.

All they wanted to do was to invent something sensational to catch the eye of the public and make their papers what they considered sensational and saleable.

Just at the time when these reports were published, I received some letters from America, and among them was a very sweet little letter from our Deaconess Thomas, telling about the Dorcas Work.

I was able to say that I had a letter in my hand telling about the good work that was being done, and that no one in Zion City was suffering from cold, or hunger, or insufficient clothing.

They had another wicked story, which they circulated very widely, saying that our little children died in great numbers and that our cemetery was filled with the dead.

Just at that time, very fortunately, Overseer Speicher

published in LEAVES OF HEALING the facts about the very low death rate in Zion City.

Encouragement for Mothers in Zion.

We encourage our mothers to have their little children joyfully, without care and sorrow.

They are out of the hands of the physicians, and we do not want them to get into the hands of the Devil through fear.

It means a great deal of patient work and a great deal of toil, but our beloved sisters do it cheerfully and lovingly, illustrating, in their work, the words of the Master, "it is more blessed to give than to receive."

They have more joy in giving than many of the people have in receiving.

We ask God to give our beloved sisters insight to give the right things to the right people, and to do it in the right way.

This Dorcas Work is one of the most blessed departments of women's work in Zion.

It has always been a great joy to me.

Our workers open all meetings with praise to God, reading of the Scripture, and prayer.

Many of the Deaconesses who are at the head of the work in the different branches, come hours before the time announced, to prepare and arrange the work, so that there shall be no time lost when their helpers come.

A Contrast.

During my tour I was told by a lady who has quite a large family of children, and who has always been helpful to the poor wherever she has had opportunity, that she had read the articles on Zion Dorcas Work in LEAVES OF HEALING, at various times, and that she was pleased to know that there was a work of this kind.

She said that she had attended some Dorcas meetings in connection with a denominational church, but she found that it was not a profitable use of time.

She could do far more by taking the things home and sewing on them, and giving her money to the poor directly.

The trouble was want of system, and too much talk, criticism, and gossip.

I do not want any of our Dorcas meetings to degenerate into gossip, or meetings where people go simply to pass away time.

Painstaking and Efficient Character of Zion Dorcas Work.

I am glad that the number of hours' work reported, twelve thousand four hundred five, were hours of good, solid work, put in by people who were competent to do it.

When Deaconess Thomas speaks to you, she will show you work that has been done, and you will see that it is not rough, slipshod work.

The poorer children are not all dressed up in one pattern so that they will be known everywhere as "little Dorcas children."

On the contrary, our little Dorcas girls and boys are often better clothed than they would be if they were clothed by their own mothers, because many do not know how to do the work so carefully and nicely as our Dorcas women.

The hours spent in this work count for more than mere money value, because the clothing is carefully prepared, cleaned, turned, and made over into beautiful little things which Mrs. Thomas will show us presently.

Zion City People Well Dressed.

You may ask why we have such a demand for clothing in Zion City when the people are not poor.

None of our people are paupers; but they all attend church.

Many a poor man's family cannot go to church or anywhere else because they are not decently dressed.

In Zion City, all the people come to church and they all look decent and clean.

The little children do not run about with bare feet and with just a little bit of rag around them.

We have, in this part of the world, four distinct seasons, spring, summer, autumn, and winter.

We cannot wear the same clothing in these different seasons.

Some people who come from more equable climates do not realize this.

Many of our working people have had all they could do to get here.

Some of them have been persecuted in the places from which they came because they were Zion people. Some of them have been turned out of work; and others have left good employment, but have not saved much.

We like to help these people, especially for the first year or two, with clothing and to minister, in every way that we can, to both their physical and spiritual needs.

They have to be cheered, and comforted, and helped in every way to make them feel that they have not come into a city of strangers, but that they have come to a City where the people are children of God who want to be helpful and loving one to another.

That is the work that our Dorcas women do.

The Poor Fund of the Church, from which we provide food and fuel, is in Overseer Speicher's Department; but the clothing is attended to by our Women's Department.

It is gratifying to know that during the unusually severe and cold winter there has been very little suffering.

I have not heard of any one that has been in any way injured by the cold.

God has given these comforts and blessings to the people.

We do not say that everybody is equally well provided for.

There are some people to whom you may give all the time, and still they never have anything. They are improvident and lazy.

But we have had good reports from our visiting Deaconesses about the improvements that have been made in many of the households.

I will call upon Elder Brasefield to say a few words.

Elder Elizabeth Brasefield Speaks on the Culture of Motherhood.

ELDER ELIZABETH BRASEFIELD—"Dear Overseer and dear friends: I am grateful to God for the return of our dear Overseer.

"I am glad that she has come back strengthened for the work.

"I am glad to shift the responsibility that she gave me back to her.

"I did the very best I could and I left the rest with God.

"I am grateful for the high ideal of an exalted and cultured motherhood which she has kept before us, and the high standard of the Women's Work in Zion which she has given us.

"I thank God for the beautiful motherhood that our Overseer illustrated in her living.

"It is not merely the putting together of stitches to cover the bodies of the people, but it is the Culture of Motherhood which seems to me to be the supreme work which belongs to us as women, if we would fulfil our mission as such mothers, as God meant us to be.

"Froebel said: 'The world's destiny lies in the hands of our women, the mothers. If the coming generation is to accomplish its work we must educate the mothers.'

"To us this means the work of Restoration.

"I will gladly take the Maternity Dorcas Work, which has been given me, and do it faithfully.

"I love the little ones, and I trust that God will give me the strength and wisdom to bring many of them into the world and train them for His Kingdom.

"I thank you all for your prayers during the time of the Overseer's absence, and I trust that together we may go forward gladly and lovingly in the work of the future."

[Elder Brasefield then opened the box of infant garments which had been sent down to be shown to the people, unfolding each garment and telling about its uses, and exhibiting the splendid workmanship.]

She said: "The women put so much love into this work that it is a great joy to them, I know, to make these beautiful garments which you see."

OVERSEER JANE DOWIE—I will now call upon Deaconess Thomas and ask her to speak.

Deaconess Rachel Thomas, in Charge of Zion Dorcas Work in Zion City.

DEACONESS THOMAS—"Dear Overseer and sisters in the Christ: I believe that this day is the happiest day for the Dorcas women in Zion City, for we have received our dear Overseer back. [Hearty applause.]

"I am glad and thankful to say, dear Overseer, that we were good children when you were away. [Laughter.]

"We made the most of our time.

"I am thankful, dear sisters, that you have never wearied of coming to the work, and I believe you were looking forward every week for the Dorcas day to come.

"It was a delight and a blessing for us to meet together.

"Some of us would leave our homes very early and get ready for the workers who would come about ten o'clock.

"Then we would have a little season of prayer, reading of the Word of God, a hymn of praise, and often just a little time for testimonies.

"There was not a morning passed when we met that we did not have requests for prayer presented.

"God blessed us, and we would go on in His strength.

"I am glad, dear Overseer, to be able to give the answer firmly that there was no gossipping in our Dorcas meetings.

"The women came in a loving way for the purpose of working for the poor and needy.

"The people have been kind in sending us very good clothing.

"Some of the things which we have received, however, would have been all the better if they had been first put through the water.

"We would like to have the people remember that we have no laundry, nor rag shop, connected with our Dorcas work. We want clean things, and good things.

"We can use things, even if they are partly worn, if they are clean. Deacon Mason at Zion City Laundry, has been very good in helping us.

The Great Resources of an Old Coat.

"We received many coats during the winter.

"Those that we did not think worth while to renovate, we would rip apart.

"Of the larger good pieces we would make little boys' coats; of the next in size, trousers; of the next, leggings; of the next, mittens.

"Then we would have the small pieces to make quilts and comforters.

"The pieces next in size we would have for rugs, such as I will show you presently; and then we would have nothing left but rags.

"These we sold and with the money bought thread.

"We made some of the little girls' dresses of several pieces so carefully that the pieces could not be distinguished; and trimmed them nicely.

"Everything that came in that was partly worn we used in that way, so that nothing was wasted.

"We got many bolts of goods from the Stores to make new dresses.

"We received two hundred twenty-eight dresses, having to make over most of them; made one hundred fifty-one new ones; and gave out three hundred seventy-nine.

"We made one hundred eight little boys' coats out of old garments.

Some Examples of Zion Dorcas Tailoring and Needlework.

"Here is a little coat and a pair of trousers for a little boy, which was made out of a pair of sleeves taken from a lady's jacket—old-fashioned, leg-of-mutton sleeves.

"We made one hundred seventy-seven of these trousers out of the best pieces of partially worn coats and jackets."

[Deaconess Thomas exhibited a beautiful, well-made, and prettily lined little coat and a pair of trousers for a little boy, which exhibit was received with prolonged applause by the audience.]

OVERSEER JANE DOWIE—That is a beautiful little suit.

You can see what can be done with material that would be just lying in your houses and getting moth-eaten.

DEACONESS THOMAS—"We have quite an extensive tailoring department, and many women take to their own homes little trousers and make them for us.

"Some are very industrious, and it is a pleasure to see their happy faces as they come to our meetings and ask us to give them something to take home.

"Some of the mothers to whom we have given garments also take them home to make over for themselves and for their children. They know how to do it, and do not want everything done for them.

The Improvident and Ungrateful Taught.

"Then there is another side. The more we give to some people the more they want.

"We are sometimes grieved to give out our little things, and see them handled in the way they are.

"We do the best we can to teach these mothers to be careful with what they have, and to keep their children clean.

"We are sad to have them come to us with their hands and faces unwashed; and good work has been done by our visiting Deaconesses in this line.

[Deaconess Thomas then exhibited little caps, which were made out of the smaller pieces of a garment, the larger pieces of which were used to make a little suit, and again there were expressions of great satisfaction from the audience.]

"We are thankful to say that we have able Deaconesses who help in our tailoring department.

[Deaconess Thomas then exhibited some very beautiful and well-made leggings, collarets, mittens, etc., the high standard of the work of which was clearly shown by the hearty appreciation of those present.]

"Here is an overcoat, which is made out of twenty-eight pieces. We put them all together, and you can hardly see that there are any more pieces than it ordinarily takes to make such an overcoat. [Applause.]

"This is a quilt, which is made up of the smaller pieces. It is nice and warm made up of the pieces that are too small to make mittens of.

"We made eighty comfortables last term, received seventeen and gave out ninety-seven. [Applause.]

Organization of the Work.

"Our work is divided into different branches, with a Deaconess at the head of each branch.

"Deaconess Clendinen is at the head of the millinery department. We make use of all the trimming we can, clean the straw, and trim our hats nicely.

"When a hat goes out, you could not tell that it did not come direct from a store. [Appause.]

"The old felt hats that we have left over from the winter which we cannot make use of in any other way, we cut up and make up into little babies' bootees, like these. [Illustrating.]

"They are cleaned nicely, and made up with silk and little baby-ribbon. Are they not beautiful?"

AUDIENCE—"Yes." [Applause.]

OVERSEER JANE DOWIE—That is very clever.

DEACONESS THOMAS—"We also make rugs."

[Deaconess Thomas displayed a large and very prettily designed, well-made, and original rug. She also exhibited various other rugs of different styles and sizes, which brought forth enthusiastic appreciation and applause from the audience.]

"I will now show you some little girls' dresses, which have been made out of two or three different kinds of material. [A number of beautiful, prettily trimmed children's dresses were shown by the Deaconess.]

"We make use of the trimmings, velvets, and silks, used on ladies' jackets which are sent us to make up hoods.

"We made three hundred seventy-three of these beautiful hoods and hats. [Deaconess Thomas then exhibited some of the little hoods referred to, and a number of collarets, also made up of trimmings taken from jackets.]

"Here is a whole dress—an entire suit for a little girl. which has been made out of a lady's skirt. You see it is very beautiful; and nice enough for any little girl to wear on Sunday —fit for a little princess.

"Deacon Stevenson very kindly sends us remnants of laces and things of that kind, which we use for trimming dresses and other things." [Applause.]

OVERSEER JANE DOWIE—I have been very much interested in this display, and I am very well pleased that our good Deaconesses are able to do such excellent work.

Splendid Economy in Management.

In addition to the work in our Zion City Branch, we send out materials and money to the different outside Branches as they need it.

I commend our Deaconess Thomas especially for the care that she has taken in using up materials that she had on hand.

Her total expenditure for new material has not been more than forty-seven dollars and seventy-nine cents. I call that good management. [Applause.]

Our good sister, Deaconess Jennie Paddock, has used the same kind of management and skill with the work.

Deaconess Thomas informed me that in addition to all the work that they have done for Zion City they have sent out things to seven different States.

We want you all to go and do likewise.

You ought to be encouraged to send your materials and garments by seeing this work made up so carefully and so beautifully.

Need of Proper Domestic Training for Women.

I think that these industrious workers and mothers of Zion are a great object lesson to others.

I say to those who have homes and are heads of families, and have young people under their care, that proper domestic training for the women is one great lack in the world.

If you would carefully teach your daughters and those that you have under your care, and yourselves also, to become more and more perfect in your domestic arrangements and work, it would be very much better, both for your homes, and also for the daughters who will have to make homes in the future.

I think that mothers sometimes neglect to teach their daughters what they know themselves.

Some mothers really do not know themselves, and cannot teach their daghters.

I have in mind at present a case where the mother is such a poor manager and such a poor housekeeper that it is perfect misery to go into her home, and in that home is a girl of about sixteen years of age, who does not know how to do anything; whereas, if she had been trained properly, she could herself be a manager and remedy the defect in the home.

What kind of a home will she make in the future?

Somehow it seems to be women of this kind that get husbands.

Some poor, unfortunate creature takes pity on them.

This is the kind of woman that good men often marry, and not always the most shiftless men.

How a Daughter Should Be Trained.

Teach your daughters to pay much attention to domestic work.

Teach them to do all the necessary things first, and the little *et ceteras* after.

Cleanliness is the first thing.

The beautifying can be done afterwards if there is to be a dividing line.

There are many of our young people now employed in the factories and industries of Zion City

Sometimes, when a daughter who has been working in an office or a factory, comes home at night, her mother seems to think, "The poor child is tired," and does everything for her, although she, herself, has had a heavy day's work, and is weary.

It would be a far better plan, and would not make a great deal of extra labor if the daughters were taught to do for themselves—taught the habit of self-helpfulness, of picking up their own clothes, washing the dishes in the evening and other things.

It would be helpful for the daughters, giving them change of employment, and restful to the mothers. They would not have so much idle time, for "Satan always finds some work for idle hands to do."

You are not doing your daughters an unkindness by teaching them to do domestic work.

A Training School for Women.

It is our intention to have in Zion City, as soon as we can arrange it properly, a good Training School for Women, teaching every department of domestic work.

We need funds to build a Home for Aged Women, and for a new Home of Hope for Erring Women, in large grounds, a little out of the City.

We are looking forward to the time when God will enable us to do all that He wants us to do; and will give us the resources with which to do it.

We find it most difficult to get people to handle food carefully and wisely, and to cook it nicely.

This is a lack not only in Zion City but in all the world—a lack of knowledge of the preparation of foods in a palatable way, and without waste.

These things we want to remedy.

I have not yet found one that I could be sure I could entrust with the work.

There may be many of our people who can do it.

There are some that know how to do these things themselves, but they have not the power to teach others.

Many Departments of Women's Work in Zion.

We have our women teachers and Zion Restorationists in the Church.

Zion aims to have women and men work together in every department.

There must be unity in the home, and unity in the Church. One must help the other.

If, in the home life there were true love, and unselfishness on the part of the mothers, and the fathers, and the children, many of these difficulties that we are asked to solve, and that so many people are puzzled about in the home relationships, would be avoided.

If our women were better able to make things comfortable in the homes, the husbands would be better, and the children would be better, and the wife would be better herself; because not only do the husband and the children suffer from inefficiency and mismanagement, but the wife also.

The General Overseer has so often said, "Oh, you dreadful women, you do not cook your oatmeal properly, and your poor husbands have to cook their oatmeal in their stomachs and get indigestion!"

What about the poor woman herself? She eats the same stuff. [Laughter.]

I look at the woman's side, and the General Overseer speaks from the men's standpoint. [Laughter.]

A good many people suffer from indigestion, not because their food is not properly cooked, but because they eat too much of it.

Sometimes you see a person who is very thin, so that when you look at him you feel as if you would like to give him something to eat. Then you meet a stout and comfortable-looking person, who, you would think, would be better if he did not eat so much; but when you see the two eating you find that the thin person eats a great deal more than the stout person.

The most miserable man I ever knew in my life was a gluttonous dyspeptic.

The General Overseer said that we could take up an offering for the Women's Work in Zion, this morning.

Just as I left today I received a check for Ten Dollars for the Dorcas Work; then I also had put into my hands by one who came into the house—a young woman, who has worked for her living and has done so for many years—One Hundred Dollars in Gold, which she had carefully saved.

This she gave me for Women's Work in Zion, as a thank-offering for blessings received the past year.

Go ye all and do likewise.

The offerings were then received, and a hymn was sung.

A Warning to Mothers.

OVERSEER JANE DOWIE—I have just received a letter which says:

DEAR OVERSEER—Please warn mothers against their little girls, carrying large babies, lest one or both be injured. I was injured by carrying my baby sister, and I wish to warn others.

I think that is a very good warning note. It is not right to let little children carry babies, and mothers should see that it is not done.

We cannot let this meeting close without hearing a few words from Deaconess Jennie Paddock, who is in charge of Zion Home of Hope for Erring Women.

Deaconess Jennie Paddock, Matron of Zion Home of Hope for Erring Women.

DEACONESS PADDOCK—"First of all I thank God for our noble leader, Overseer Jane Dowie.

"My heart is filled with joy, and love, and gratitude to God that He has so loved us in this country as to send us such noble teachers as our General Overseer and his dear wife.

"I thank God for the interest our Overseer has in the mothers and in the dear little children.

"How my heart was filled with joy when she was speaking to the young girls!

"I often think what a great mistake mothers make in training their young girls, and not teaching them how to cook and how to do housework.

"How my heart goes out to an untrained young woman

who is about to be married and go into her own home! Although she may be able to hire servants, yet she cannot give a girl any instruction; she does not know how to get a meal.

"She does not know how to save the little things.

"God's Word teaches us that by being faithful over a few things, He will make us ruler over many things.

"I have taken special care to teach my dear women in Zion Home of Hope to be saving.

"In the making of their own clothing, we teach them to save the little pieces.

"We make these up into little rugs and quilts.

"I have often taken the large sleeves of a waist to make dresses for the dear little babies in Zion Home of Hope.

It Is Idleness that Drives Many a Girl into Sin.

"There is a work for every one of us.

"Let us work, sisters.

"I thank God that I have a part in Zion Dorcas Work, besides my Home of Hope work.

"I have a very large family.

"Sometimes I have had as many as twenty-eight children in the Home, but I thank God that I have not missed three days from the Dorcas Work.

"This last winter I have missed only one day on account of sickness.

"There is no better Work in the world than Zion Dorcas Work.

"My heart was so filled with joy when I saw the beautiful little garments that had been made here, in Zion City, by these good women.

"We have done a great deal.

"As you know, a mother with such a large family as I have needs a great many things to clothe them, and I do not have very many things to show, because we have used them all.

"I thank God for the wisdom that He has given me to teach others.

Character of the Work in Zion Home of Hope.

"The poor women come into the Home dirty, filthy, and ragged.

"Many of them do not know even how to take a bath.

"It is not an easy task to take women, some of whom are older than myself, who do not know how to do anything, and teach them. They have to be taken as little children and taught with patience, firmness, and diligence.

"They are more to be pitied than blamed. Their mothers never taught them.

"But I thank God for the noble, godly women that He has given me in the Home of Hope—for they are such after we have taught them.

"There are diamonds in the rough among erring women.

"They can be polished and made to shine brighter than the stars.

"Twenty-seven women from Zion Home of Hope have married and have good homes, and are splendid housekeepers. It is a beautiful work.

Good Counsel to Women.

"Christians should not be dirty; they should be clean.

"I tell women if they have only one calico dress to get it cleaned, and keep it clean.

"There is plenty of water and soap to be had here, surely.

"If you have no carpets, keep your floors clean.

"What is prettier than a spotless, white floor?

"Have your table clean, if you have nothing but a piece of white muslin cloth to put upon it.

"Be cheerful.

"Do not get disheartened and discouraged because you are poor.

"Make the best of everything.

"If you have only a little to eat you have only a little to cook.

"God will give you the strength; our strength comes from Him.

"There is no use in spending everything you have in eating. There is something more needed than eating.

"There is no use in spending all your money on trimmings; have the plain things first, and then if you have something extra you can get the trimmings.

"The most beautiful dresses I have ever seen have been plain dresses.

"We must live economically, and ask God to help us and to train us. We ask Him for wisdom.

An Incident in the Chicago Zion Home of Hope.

"I was all dressed and ready to go out of the house, on my way to New York, for the Visitation last fall, when I happened to go to the back door, and there sat a poor, young girl, ready to become a mother, wretchedly dirty.

"I said to her, 'Dear, what's the matter?'

"She said that she was tired and sick, and was hunting for a place to stay while her child was born.

"I asked her to come in, and found that she was already in the agonies of labor.

"In about half an hour her dear little babe was born. It was a beautiful little boy.

"I said to the girl, the morning that she came in, 'Now, dear, will you give your heart to God and become a Christian, and sin no more?'

"She agreed that she would, and I had her promise me that she would train this little one for God.

"At the end of ten days my daughter, who was left in charge during my absence, let her sit up.

"When my daughter returned to her room, some time later, she found that she had gathered together all her clothing and had gone, leaving her little babe.

"We have seen and heard nothing of her since.

"The little baby who was thus deserted by his mother is a bright, smart little fellow, healthy and clean, and now we have him in the home, and we would like some good Zion woman to give him a home.

"I believe that God can cleanse the hearts of these little children. I do not limit God's power. He is no respecter of persons, and He pities these dear little ones.

"May God give us a greater love for fallen humanity.

"These six years have been the greatest experience of my whole life.

"These dear women that have been blessed and healed are as dear, devout Christian women as you would find anywhere. God has cleansed them.

"Some dear women come to us who never knew what Purity was until they came to Zion Home of Hope.

"Let us have Christ-like love.

"Let us work while it is yet called today, for the night cometh when no man can work." [Applause.]

About the Adoption of Children.

OVERSEER JANE DOWIE—One word about these little babies.

I went to visit this Home just after my return from Europe, and I found more there than there ought to be with present accommodations. We have made some changes since then.

We want to let some of these little ones go into homes where we are sure they will be taken care of. We will not give them to people who are not Christians, and we will not give them to unmarried women. It is embarrassing, and not good for the child or woman.

It is not best for you to apply for a little boy if you have little girls in your family. If you have a number of boys, take another boy, and if you have a number of girls, take a little girl.

It is best for some family in which there are no children to take one of these dear little babies.

I saw the little baby that Mrs. Paddock has told about, whose mother deserted him when he was only a week old, and my heart went out in sympathy for him. His mother, who deserted him, has now no legal claim upon him, and therefore he can be given to any one who wishes to take him and give him a good home.

Rise and receive the Benediction.

Overseer Jane Dowie closed the meeting by pronouncing the

BENEDICTION.

Beloved, abstain from every form of evil. And may the very God of Peace Himself sanctify you wholly; and I pray God your whole spirit, and soul, and body be preserved entire, without blame, unto the coming of our Lord Jesus, the Christ. Faithful is He that calleth you, who also will do it. The Grace of our Lord Jesus, the Christ, the love of God, our Father, the fellowship of the Holy Spirit, our Comforter and Guide, one Eternal God, abide in you, bless you, and keep you, and all the Israel of God everywhere, forever. Amen.

FIRST ANNIVERSARY OF ZION JUNIOR RESTORATION HOST.

*REPORTED BY L. L. H., O. L. S., AND A. W. N.

The deep, quiet, spiritual power of Zion's Fourth Feast of Tabernacles, which had been steadily increasing throughout the eleven days, came to a fitting climax in the glorious services of Lord's Day, July 24th, the Last Great Day of the Feast.

From the Early Morning Sacrifice of Praise and Prayer, in the cool freshness of the perfect summer morning, to the last exulting, triumphant notes of the "Hallelujah Chorus" from Beethoven's "Mount of Olives," sung by the hundreds of consecrated voices in Zion's White-robed Choir at eleven o'clock that night, it was, indeed "a day in the Courts of Jehovah."

In addition to the thousands already in Zion City, nine hundred came out from Chicago on two special trains, to attend the meetings.

The great service of the day, and perhaps the most largely attended of any during the Feast, was the Great General Assembly in Shiloh Tabernacle beginning at two o'clock in the afternoon, at which there were fully seven thousand people, filling all but the very least desirable seats in the Tabernacle.

This wonderful service marked the First Anniversary of the formation of Zion Junior Restoration Host.

As the Feast of Tabernacles came to an end, God's people instinctively looked into the future.

Spiritual refreshing and nourishment had been received, Knowledge had been increased, better methods of work had been learned, Wisdom had been gained, Love was purer, Hope was brighter, Faith was stronger, Humility was deeper, Courage was firmer, and Consecration was more complete.

And so, as these eleven days on the mountaintop passed, the hearts of the people were filled with thoughts of the work, in the valleys, of the next day, the next year, the next decade, indeed of all the "Little While Between," ere the King come.

Through all this thought of the work of the future there ran the inseparably associated thought of the children of Zion.

It was therefore peculiarly fitting that the principal service of this last great day of the Feast should have been devoted to Zion Junior Restoration Host.

Beautiful! Wonderful! Inspiring! Overwhelming!

Adjectives are weak and language is meager when one attempts to describe the procession on this occasion.

It was not in the clean, white raiment of the children and their scarfs of gold, white and blue, although these made a spectacle pleasing to the eye; it was not in the splendid music of Zion Band to which they marched, although music and marching were remarkable in their excellence; it was not in the orderly massing of the hundreds of children in the places assigned them in the great Tabernacle, although this was most artistic and effective; it was not in the clear, sweet ringing of a perfect flood of beautiful, childish voices in song, although this was sweetest music to the ear; it was not in any of these things, although they had their part in the great general effect, that this procession had the power to stir the hearts of that great audience so strangely and bring quick unbidden tears to so many eyes.

It was the unspeakably glorious promise shining out from the clean, clear, honest, intelligent eyes, and fresh, rosy faces, and expressed in the strong, erect, purposeful bearing of these hundreds of little ones.

As one looked at them, a mental vision of their homes—peaceful, clean, happy—where the Word of God and the Voice of Prayer were heard morning and evening, seemed to form a part of the picture.

With it, one could also see the schools in which they were trained—schools in which God is first, and from which all that debases and defiles is rigorously shut out.

Then one saw the City in which they live—a City whose spiritual, moral, and material atmosphere is pure and clean.

This was a Royal Generation!

What capacities, talents, and powers for God and humanity were latent but potential in this Host, no man could foresee; for the world has never before known such a generation.

Some of the possibilities of Zion's children were revealed, and many were suggested, in the Message of God's Prophet on the subject of "The Ministry of Children in Zion."

The chief thought in this Message, which was founded on the story of the child Samuel, was that one child out of ten—the brightest of the ten—should be consecrated especially to the work of the ministry of God and especially trained, from the age of responsibility, for work as a messenger of Zion.

At the close of this Message, the General Overseer administered the Vow to a large number of new members of Zion Junior Restoration Host.

The service closed with a recessional and the pronouncing of the benediction by the General Overseer.

Shiloh Tabernacle, Zion City, Illinois, Lord's Day Afternoon, July 24, 1904.

The service began with the Processional, led by Zion Junior Restoration Host, as it came marching into the Tabernacle to the music furnished by Zion City Band.

The Junior Restoration Host was followed by Zion Junior White-robed Choir, and they were followed by the Senior Choir.

As the Senior Choir entered the Tabernacle, the Band and the Orchestra struck up the Processional, in which the Choir joined:

O Zion, haste, thy mission high fulfilling,
To tell to all the world that God is Light;
That He who made all nations is not willing
One soul should perish, lost in shades of night.

REFRAIN—Publish glad tidings, tidings of peace,
Tidings of Jesus, redemption and release.

Behold how many thousands still are lying
Bound in the darksome prison-house of sin,
With none to tell them of the Savior's dying,
Or of the life He died for them to win.

Proclaim to every people, tongue, and nation,
That God, in whom they live and move, is Love:
Tell how He stooped to save His lost creation,
And died on earth that man might live above.

Give of thy sons to bear the Message glorious;
Give of thy wealth to speed them on their way;
Pour out thy soul for them in pray'r victorious;
And all thou spendest Jesus will repay.

He comes again: O Zion, ere thou meet Him,
Make known to every heart His saving grace;
Let none whom He hath ransomed fail to greet Him,
Thro' thy neglect, unfit to see His face.

The General Overseer, upon ascending the platform, pronounced the

INVOCATION.

God be merciful unto us and bless us,
And cause Thy face to shine upon us.
That Thy Way may be known upon earth,
Thy Saving Health among all the nations,
For the sake of Jesus. Amen.

Hymn No. 41 in the Program was then sung:

Oh, wondrous Name, by prophets heard,
Long years before His birth;
They saw Him coming from afar,
The Prince of Peace on earth.

CHORUS—The Wonderful! The Counselor!
The Great and Mighty Lord!
The everlasting Prince of Peace!
The King, the Son of God!

Oh, glorious Name, the angels praise,
And ransomed saints adore,
The Name above all other names,
Our refuge evermore.

*The following reports have not been revised by the General Overseer.

Oh, precious Name, exalted high,
To Him all power is given;
Through Him we triumph over sin,
By Him we enter Heaven.

Overseer Brasefield then led the Congregation in reciting the Apostles' Creed and the Commandments.

This was followed by the Choir's chanting the words, "Lord, have mercy upon us, and write all these Thy Laws in our hearts, we beseech Thee."

Zion Junior Choir then chanted the Te Deum, and Overseer Jane Dowie read the Scripture lesson from the 1st book of Samuel, the 3d chapter.

Prayer was offered by Overseer Mason, followed by the General Overseer in special supplication for the sick. He also led in the chanting of the Disciples' Prayer, after which Hymn No. 12 was sung.

The General Overseer then said:

I want you to pray for the words that have to be spoken today.

I thank God that our City has been so remarkably healthful during all the time of the Feast, and that we have had such delightful and enjoyable weather.

Let the free-will offerings and the tithes be received, and while that is being done, the Junior Choir will sing one of the songs of Zion, and then the Junior Restoration Host will sing.

The Junior Choir and Host are really one, because I think all the Choir is in the Host, although all the Host is not in the Choir; but they are getting there.

The Junior Choir then sang an anthem.

After the offering had been received, Overseer Brasefield said, "The Junior Host and Choir will now sing their rallying song. The Branches will rise at the same time with the members of the Junior Choir."

The Juniors then sang a very beautiful song.

THE MINISTRY OF CHILDREN IN ZION.

The General Overseer pronounced the

INVOCATION.

Let the words of my mouth, and the meditations of my heart, be acceptable in Thy sight, and profitable unto this people and unto all to whom these words shall come, in this and all the coming time; in this and every land, Till Jesus Come. Amen.

In the 3d chapter of the 1st Book of Samuel, the last three verses, and the 1st verse of the following chapter, we read:

And Samuel grew, and Jehovah was with him, and did let none of his words fall to the ground.

And all Israel, from Dan even to Beersheba, knew that Samuel was established to be a prophet of Jehovah.

And Jehovah appeared again in Shiloh: for Jehovah revealed Himself to Samuel in Shiloh by the Word of Jehovah.

And the Word of Samuel came to all Israel.

Little Samuels in Zion City.

Once more God is revealing Himself in Shiloh.

The little Samuels are here.

I gratefully acknowledge to-day the goodness of God to us in the establishment of this Host, and also of the Intermediate Bible Training Institute in this City.

Statistics of Zion Junior Restoration Host.

The number of Zion Junior Restoration Host is as follows: Six hundred nineteen males, and seven hundred seventy-two females; making one thousand three hundred ninety-one.

The number enrolled in the Intermediate Bible Institute, which consists of young men and women between the ages of sixteen and twenty-one years, and which is under the Honorable Judge Barnes, is one hundred twelve males and two hundred sixty-three females; making three hundred seventy-five.

Then we have eight hundred ninety-seven in the Junior Host, who have signed the Vow.

Two hundred one of the Juniors were baptized this year, and a number had been already baptized.

The number of Juniors who have become members of the Church is no less than one hundred seventy-two—seventy-six males and ninety-six females.

Zion Junior Work Flourishes in Other Places.

This work extends to other places; we have just begun to make it extend.

We have no less than one hundred fifty Branches in connection with this Zion Junior Restoration work.

We are communicating with one hundred fifty Branches of this Church, in regard to the work; and we have already found, from one hundred twenty-four of these Branches replying to communications, that there are one thousand fifty children enrolled as members; that twenty-one Branches of this Host have been organized during the last year, and that six hundred sixty-two children have been enrolled; that there are thirty-three Branches in course of organization, and that the children already enrolled in these Branches number two hundred seventy-seven; so that we have something like nine hundred thirty-nine in outside Branches, which would make, with our number here, something like two thousand three hundred.

One little thing will interest you.

The general offerings from these children connected with the Branches in Zion City have been no less than five hundred one dollars and forty-one cents; and the offerings since April, from the Branches outside, amount to thirty-two dollars.

The offering for Shiloah Tabernacle Fund, by the Branches, has been two hundred sixteen dollars, and outside Branches of this little Junior Restoration Host have contributed two hundred twenty-two dollars. The children always tithe money that they receive, and they send it with great delight.

They ask their parents, "Now, how much of this is to go in for tithes?"

In addition to their tithes, the children have given offerings amounting to seven hundred fifty-seven dollars.

That is a beautiful illustration of their Faith.

A Vast Congregation.

I know how difficult it is for this vast Congregation to hear me.

This Tabernacle will seat seven thousand three hundred people, and, as far as I can see, there are not three hundred empty seats, so that there are now about seven thousand people present.

It is very delightful for me to say to you, as I stand here, that this Feast has far exceeded what we might have expected, under all the circumstances.

It has been a wonderful Feast for order and the earnestness with which the people have got into line in everything.

I cannot tell exactly, but we estimate that this morning there were between five thousand and six thousand people present to hear the Word of God and to offer Praise and Prayer.

Something like two thousand or three thousand were here again at the Baptismal service, making between seven thousand and eight thousand; and now we have seven thousand present—making fifteen thousand; and I reckon that tonight, for the closing, we shall have not less than five or six thousand; so that the total attendances for the day will be not far from twenty thousand people.

What a wonderful thing, that in a City where three years ago there was only an open prairie, we should now have this great audience, in this great Tabernacle!

It is, however, only the day of small things in Zion City.

I gladly record my gratitude to God, and feel that this Junior Restoration Host present today is most delightful to me, and to all the people; for they are the hope of Zion in all its Glorious Future.

The Ministry of Children in Zion.

I have been very much struck, over and over again, with this story of Samuel in Shiloh.

I cannot feel that it is an accident that this Tabernacle is called Shiloh.

I have felt that Shiloh—or that wonderful Shiloah, where two great streams flowed—has its counterpart in these Latter Times in the Shiloh Tabernacle of today, and in the Shiloah Tabernacle, where, I very earnestly hope, I shall meet you a year hence.

If you will help me, certainly I shall.

There was a little boy named Samuel, and he was the son of a woman whose name was Hannah.

There is not very much said about his father, whose name was Elkanah.

Now there was a certain man of Ramathaim-zophim, of the hill country of Ephraim, and his name was Elkanah, the son of Jeroham, the son of Elihu, the son of Tohu, the son of Zuph, an Ephraimite.
And he had two wives;
The name of the one was Hannah,
And the name of the other Peninnah:
And Peninnah had children,
But Hannah had no children.

Hannah's Importunity in Prayer.

And she was troubled that she had no children.

She went to the Temple, where she used to pray about it.

God answered her prayer and gave her the boy, Samuel.

The next time Eli saw her, he was the high priest, and she came and gave the boy into his hands.

She said, "I asked him from God, and I said that when He gave me the boy, I would bring him to you, God's high priest, and lend him to you as long as he lived."

Eli was very much delighted; for his sons were very wicked.

This little boy was girded with an ephod, and he became servant to the great and old high priest whose heart was broken by the sins of his two sons, Hophni and Phinehas.

They were wicked, but this was a good little boy.

He did things about the Temple, keeping the lights burning in the Temple of God through the long, dark night.

God Speaks to Little Samuel.

God was watching over him, but as yet he had never heard the Voice of God.

One night the Temple lights burned dimly, and he heard a Voice, "Samuel!"

Samuel said, "That's the dear high priest. He wants me;" and he went to Eli, and said, "Here am I, for thou calledst me."

"I called thee not, my son," replied Eli, "Go, lie down, it is a mistake;" and he lay down, and the little fellow went to sleep again.

He heard the Voice again, "Samuel! Samuel!" and he went to Eli saying, "Now, I am sure of it this time."

But Eli said, "I called thee not, my son, lie down again."

Samuel came to Eli once more, for there was a Voice again, "Samuel! Samuel!"

Then Eli perceived that Jehovah, God, had called the child, and said, "Lie down again, but if you are called, stand up, and bow thyself before God, and say, 'Speak, Jehovah, for Thy servant heareth.'"

When he went back, the Voice came again, "Samuel! Samuel! Samuel!"

He rose, and said, "Speak, Jehovah; for Thy servant heareth."

Then God made a wonderful communication to that child, which he hid in his heart until Eli demanded that it should be told.

It was an awful thing.

It was to tell of the ruin of Eli's family, and that God had anointed the child to be the Prophet of God for that Great Dispensation; to be a Great Judge, and, as it turned out, to be the Last Judge in the Theocracy of Israel.

It is a wonderful story.

He grew, and he was in favor with God and with man.

But he began to minister when he was a child.

I am so glad that you, like myself, are beginning to minister to God.

Listen to the Voice of God.

You may hear it through mine—"John," "Thomas," "Mary."

Listen; God will talk to you.

An Interesting Story of Early Childhood.

I remember a little story about myself.

I have told it partly, and it has always been difficult to tell it wholly, because I am not a visionary man. I am not given to imagination in dreams and visions.

I have to be a very practical man; and yet, all the great events of my life have been in connection with distinct and audible calls.

I was a little fellow, and I was feeling my way into spiritual work for God.

I knew God, and I loved Him.

I knew Him to be my Savior in the Christ; and I was very earnest in those days in an organization which we called the British League of Juvenile Abstainers.

I had no wealthy friends, and my entire income for a whole week often would not exceed four cents; sometimes, for a full week, it was six cents.

I began to look about for some way to invest that income for God.

I belonged to this league of little fellows, and bigger fellows, too; but I was at that time six years old. I remember I used to be trusted to go to that meeting.

The league was formed by a godly man who got the children to abstain from alcohol, opium, and tobacco. His name was John Hope.

Whenever I saw him I had a feeling that I would like to hold on to his coat tails.

Perhaps it was because he carried candy in his coat; he never was without it.

The children loved him, not merely for his candy, but for his great loving-kindness; and he got them to sign that pledge.

The General Overseer a Missionary in His Youth.

In 1853, I signed that pledge against tobacco, alcohol, and opium; and I have kept it.

That man, who was at the head of the branch in Davie Street Lancastrian School, Edinburgh, rose up and said, "Boys, you could double the attendance at this meeting next Saturday, if you liked; if you prayed to God first, and then went to the boys in your neighborhood and asked them to come with you."

I thought it out, and it was my opinion that the boys in my neighborhood would roll me into the gutter if I went to them about any such matter.

That day he said, "Will you tell God you will do it?" and I replied, "Yes."

Then I thought of the poor boys not far from the quarter of the city where I lived.

There were many very poor children, who were very rude and very uncultivated.

They threw stones at well-dressed boys who came into their neighborhood.

I was kept clean.

I thought, "Oh, how can I do it?"

The Saturday morning following that I got to thinking and troubling myself about what the meaning of my name was.

I think it must have been from something that was said about the name.

Samuel meant, "Asked of God." Other names also meant something.

Names That Mean Something.

I wish that we would have more names that mean something.

The other day, when I was consecrating the children, one of my assistants made a mistake, and when I was going to consecrate the child, gave me his name as "Lexington Park."

I refused to give that name to the child.

I said, "No, I won't do it; you must get a better name than that. "Lexington Park" won't do."

It turned out that that was the parents' address, and the child's name was Daniel.

I have seen children who were loaded with even worse names.

However, I was thinking that morning about names, and I remember I was praying.

I never was ashamed to pray, and I never saw why I should be.

I had a little corner, given me by my mother, where I would be out of the way of everybody, and have my books; for, at the age of six years, I could read very well.

I did not make great progress, but I remember that I was reading Latin at the age of seven.

I felt that I wanted to know what my name meant; and I said to my mother, "What is it?"

She replied, "I do not know what you mean."

I said, "I want to know what 'John' means, and I want to know what 'Alexander' means."

Well, she could not tell me; but there was an old Bible in my corner that had the meaning of names, and I went there and searched.

I found that "John" meant, "By the grace of God." and "Alexander" meant "A helper of men."

Preparations for Youthful Missionary Work.

I knelt and prayed, with my heart full, that God would, by His grace, make me a helper of men.

I must have prayed very earnestly.

I cannot remember all the details, but I remember getting inspiration before I got up.

I went out, and spent three pennies for candy.

I went to a poor little shop, where I knew I could get an extra large quantity for each penny, and bought a number of sugar balls.

First, I wrapped each separately; then I rolled them into fours; and then I tucked each four under my pinafore, until I had about twenty-four.

I acknowledge that I kept eight for myself, two of them being the biggest.

One of these two I ate, the other I kept in reserve.

The rest I had under my pinafore.

I went down where the naughty boys were.

I did not know how to address them.

I remember they were playing with cherry stones, and each four, I think, was called a "caddle."

They were groveling in the dust and playing for cherry stones, and fighting over the result.

They were pretty rough; and some of them were playing "top," or something of that kind.

I did not know how to go at it, but I got down amidst this crowd and said, "Laddies, will you gang wi' me to the Davie Street Lancastrian school and sign the pledge? I will gie ye four sugar bools each."

I remember that they laughed, and had me repeat the speech to various groups.

They just laughed at me and guyed me; and one led me all around to show off my "spotless purity"—the pinafore—and suggested that now that they had had fun with me, they had better roll me in the dust.

Laughter Is Followed by Success.

That is just what they have wanted to do with me, lately.

I was not afraid of being rolled in the dust, but I did want them to come to school.

One big fellow, just as they were going to seize me, rose up and said that if they struck me, he would give it to them.

He seemed a great big fellow to me.

He asked where the candy was.

I said, "Here!" and I brought out four candy balls.

He said, "Gie me my four now."

"No," I said, "I will gie you one now, and I will gie you the rest after you come oot."

He laughed, and said, "Gie me ane, and I'll gang wi' ye."

The rest said, "We'll roll him in the gutter and take them frae him."

"No," he said, "we'll keep faith wi' him."

"Will ye all come?" I asked.

"Yes," was the reply.

I gave him one, and tucked away the other three.

Soon I had that draggle-tailed little mob on the way.

All the clothing that some of them had was an old, dirty shirt, one suspender, and a pair of breeches.

They were "holely" all around; and some of them had no caps; but they followed me, laughing and joking about it.

I was as happy as a prince.

I was leading them on; and when I got to the school I dashed in at the door and said, "I have got ten of them."

I took them in, marshalled them, and got them all to sign that pledge against tobacco, liquor, and opium.

I do not know how many I got after that—I did not keep account; but I never gave the same ten any more sweets, although they helped me in my work.

The Beginning of the General Overseer's Great Mission.

Now I want to say that I believe that that little affair was the beginning of my Mission for God in the world.

That little band grew, and one day we followed John Hope to Dalmeny Park, Lord Rosebery's father's park, five thousand strong.

Thousands of the boys that signed the pledge at that time kept it, and are today working in the front ranks for humanity.

They are preachers; they are teachers; they are statesmen; they are men of power.

Now, children, your work will come on very soon.

I only regret that in that institution they did not ask us to give our hearts to the Christ, and did not ask us to seek the help of the Holy Spirit; but those who conducted it were mostly good Christian men. It was liquor, tobacco, and opium that they fought.

In Zion, we fight everything that is bad.

"The Child is the Father of the Man."

Some of you boys will never hear the Voice of God, because you are not quiet enough; you do not get away into a quiet place with God.

I know that concentration—that is a big word for you children; it means the bringing of all your mind upon a thing—is needful to make you great and strong.

Wandering eyes, wandering thoughts, wandering fingers, wandering feet will do nothing.

Be in earnest!

I was in earnest that day.

To part with those few pennies meant a great deal to me; they were all I had.

I saved them for various purposes and gave a little portion on the Lord's Days.

I used to change my pennies into bright, new farthings that a groceryman had; and those farthings I put on the plate.

I loved to give.

I loved to do something.

I loved to see the Army of God marching to overcome the power of the Devil.

That is what I love now, and that is why I want you to be girded with your ephod, and to serve in the Temple of God.

Zion Has a Wondrous Ministry for Her Children.

You will not be children long.

I looked at you, as I stood at the door to receive you, and I saw a little girl who was once sick and dying.

When I looked into her face, it seemed impossible that she could be the same person; but we each smiled in recognition, and I saw my little child of long ago grown up, just verging into womanhood.

I want you to be happy while you are children; but on occasions like this, when good order should be maintained—and there is something to be done by good order—maintain it.

When you play, play!

When I play, I play!

When you are in the House of God, remember that fact.

You are being trained in the Word of God to be Messengers of Zion, whether you all become ordained officers or not.

The Brightest Child Out of Every Ten for God's Ministry.

I feel in my heart to say to the parents now what I have said before, that I demand of you a tenth of your children for God.

I want one out of every ten to be educated as perfectly as we can educate man or woman, to be an Officer in the Christian Catholic Church in Zion and in Zion Restoration Host, who can be sent at the head of a great band of men and women to foreign lands and to other parts of this country.

Out of two thousand that you have in the schools and college, I want two hundred; and I want volunteers.

I want you, children, to come to me some day, when I call for volunteers, and to stand up and say, "Here am I, General Overseer; take me; train me."

The Folly of Giving the Poorest to God.

I want your fathers and mothers to stand up by your side, and pick out the brightest of the children.

I do not want the fool of the family—there was too much of that in the old country.

They used to say, "Now, we will make Jimmy a soldier, and we will make Tommy a sailor, and we will make Fred a doctor, and what shall we do with this little fool of a John? We will make him a minister."

These children, consecrated to God's ministry, I will put in a class by themselves.

They will be marked. They will gird themselves with their little ephods; and they will serve in the Temple of God.

They will have no other work in life but to be trained to be God's servants.

That does not mean that they shall not work in the garden; but it means that at a certain age we will take them from their homes and put them into dormitories, and train both boys and girls with a view to their being our Messengers in the future.

We will allow them to go to their homes, and to be with their parents at times; but their home shall be in the training-house of Zion, and their work shall be in the Temple of God. May God grant it.

AUDIENCE—"Amen!"

Zion's Parents Record a Promise.

GENERAL OVERSEER—I have this intense desire.

Parents, do you not think it right that, in the Name of the Lord, I should have one-tenth of all the children in Zion, to be wholly consecrated to God; yes or no?

PARENTS—"Yes."

GENERAL OVERSEER—Will you give me them?

PARENTS—"Yes."

GENERAL OVERSEER—I am not ready yet; but I shall build, if I live; and I shall start as soon as I can.

I am perfectly convinced that I shall never be able to move this world for God with a ministry that has been educated elsewhere.

With a few exceptions they are not effective.

We must raise our own prophets in Shiloh. May God grant it! [Amen.]

I think that the bringing up of a band like that, from the very beginning, will be one of the great things in Zion—one of the greatest things in the world.

I shall hope, within a few years, to see at least a thousand being rightly trained.

I have not yet determined the age.

I should say that at about ten years of age their characters would be sufficiently established for us to be able to see whether they have mental, moral, spiritual, physical, and psychical capacity to be strong and powerful men and women.

That does not mean that the Host shall not go on as now, but it means that those who are trained, and their children, shall be the little Captains of a glorious Restoration Host for the Salvation of the whole world.

A Favored Generation of Children.

I believe, my dear children, that you are the most favored children in all the world.

You are kept from all the temptations that curse children in the cities of the world--the liquor, the tobacco, the blasphemy, the oaths and curses of bad companions, and the teaching of vice and wickedness.

May God help you and bless you; and may there be a glorious ministration of children in Zion!

PEOPLE—"Amen."

GENERAL OVERSEER—Overseer Brasefield, please step forward.

OVERSEER BRASEFIELD—"Those who have not taken the Zion Junior Restoration Host Vow, please stand. The first division does not sign it; but all above seven years of age, who have not taken the Vow, and who desire to take it, come down here and stand before the General Overseer."

Hundreds of Children Take the Junior Restoration Host Vow.

GENERAL OVERSEER—Do you know what the Overseer is about to do? What is he about to read to you?

CHILDREN—"The Zion Junior Restoration Host Vow."

GENERAL OVERSEER—Do you understand that?

CHILDREN—"Yes, sir."

GENERAL OVERSEER—Do you want to take it?

CHILDREN—"Yes, sir."

GENERAL OVERSEER—Do you want to be good little soldiers for God?

CHILDREN—"Yes, sir."

GENERAL OVERSEER—Do you want to be good at home?

CHILDREN—"Yes, sir."

GENERAL OVERSEER—Now, then, right hands all up; and faces toward the Overseer.

Overseer Brasefield then read the Vow:

In the presence of God, I vow to love and obey Him, as my Father in heaven, believing in Jesus, the Christ, as my Savior, and in the Holy Spirit as my Guide.

I promise to read His Holy Word, and pray every day.

I promise to love His Commandments, and obey them, with His gracious help

I promise to keep from evil words and deeds, and to do all the good I can.

So far as I understand, I believe that the General Overseer, John Alexander Dowie, is Elijah the Restorer; and I desire to be a member of Zion Junior Restoration Host, so that I may follow him in doing good, wherever he shall direct me, in the Lord, all over this world.

The Children Affirm Their Sincerity.

GENERAL OVERSEER—All who have taken the Junior Restoration Vow, stand. [Hundreds of children stood.]

Do you mean to keep this Vow, by the grace of God?

CHILDREN—"Yes."

GENERAL OVERSEER—Will you pray to God that you may be able to keep it every day?

CHILDREN—"Yes."

GENERAL OVERSEER—Then you will be my strong Host, by and by.

I charge you, before God, to keep the Vow.

The General Overseer then prayed, as follows:

Father, bless these dear children, and grant to them grace to keep this Vow. For Jesus' sake, by Thy Spirit.

GENERAL OVERSEER—Overseer Brasefield will arrange for your signing the Vow; and you must take it to your parents, and they must agree. We will not have you sign the Vow without their agreeing; but there is no parent in Zion who ought to keep you back, unless you are very wicked little children and tell lies.

May God bless you.

All the people present may now rise with me and consecrate themselves to God.

PRAYER OF CONSECRATION.

Our God and Father, in Jesus' Name we come to Thee. Take us as we are; make us what we ought to be in spirit, in soul, and in body. Give us power to do right, no matter what it costs; to trust Thee, to love Thee, to serve Thee. Help us to help these dear children, and to consecrate some of our children, until the General Overseer gets His tenth for God, of all the children in Zion. O God bless them. And now, for Jesus' sake, help us in what remains of this day, that we may get the strength we need for the work that lies before us Amen. [*All repeat the prayer, clause by clause, after the General Overseer*]

The beautiful Recessional, "The Son of God Goes Forth to War," was then sung.

Standing upon the platform, after the Recessional, the General Overseer said:

Beloved, you have seen the order of Zion, how the people are forming themselves into these Hosts, until we are like an army.

"Like a mighty army moves the Church of God."

I am thankful, not only for the good order, but for the Divine enthusiasm that has made this people so mighty a power for God.

I pray you who are strangers here that you will exercise a Divine charity, and remember that this is only a representation, in a feeble way, of the good order that characterizes Zion everywhere throughout the world and in every department of her work.

May God bless you and Zion everywhere in the whole wide world, and bring all everywhere to find in the Christ a perfect Salvation, and Healing, and Cleansing.

The General Overseer then pronounced the usual

BENEDICTION.

Beloved, abstain from every form of evil. And may the very God of Peace Himself sanctify you wholly; and I pray God your whole spirit, and soul, and body be preserved entire, without blame, unto the coming of our Lord Jesus, the Christ. Faithful is He that calleth you, who also will do it. The grace of our Lord Jesus, the Christ, the love of God our Father, the fellowship of the Holy Spirit, our Comforter and Guide, one Eternal God, abide in you, bless you, and keep you, and all the Israel of God everywhere, forever. Amen.

The usual salutation between the General Overseer and the people was then exchanged.

COMMUNION OF THE LORD'S SUPPER.

REPORTED BY M. E. L., A. C. R., AND A. W. N.

At 8 o'clock in the evening of Lord's Day, July 24, 1904, the General Overseer conducted the closing service of Zion's Fourth Feast of Tabernacles.

It was a most delightful gathering of the Zion family throughout the world; for those present felt a great spiritual nearness to the many thousands in all the lands, who could not be there, but whose hearts were lifted to God in prayer for Zion at Headquarters, especially at this time.

Not only was the great Zion family there at that Table, but also the loving Heavenly Father, and the kind, sympathetic

Elder Brother, in the Spirit, according to Their precious promises.

The Message of the General Overseer was a very spiritual and helpful exposition of the last verses of the Gospel according to St. Luke.

After this, assisted by Overseers, Elders, Evangelists, Deacons, and Deaconesses, he administered the Communion of the Lord's Supper.

The music by Zion Choir, Orchestra, and Band on this occasion, was of an unusually high order.

Early in the evening they rendered "The Heavens Are Telling," from Haydn's oratorio, "The Creation," Deaconess Chamberlain and Messrs. Eugene Huyck and Lehman Peckham singing the trio.

At the close of the service, the spirits of all that audience were borne up in praise and thanksgiving to God, on the wings of Divine music, as the Choir sang Beethoven's "Hallelujah Chorus," from "The Mount of Olives."

Shiloh Tabernacle, Zion City, Illinois, Lord's Day Evening, July 24, 1904.

The service was begun by the Congregation's singing Hymn No. 7 in the Special Program.

The General Overseer then read from the Inspired Word of God, in the Gospel according to St. Luke, the 24th chapter, beginning at the 36th verse:

And as they spake these things, Jesus Himself stood in the midst of them, and saith unto them, Peace be unto you.

But they were terrified and affrighted, and supposed that they beheld a spirit.

And He said unto them, Why are ye troubled? and wherefore do reasonings arise in your heart?

See My hands and My feet, that it is I Myself: handle Me, and see; for a spirit hath not flesh and bones—

Jesus Died of a Broken Heart.

Not flesh and blood; His blood was all shed, His body had died; the heart had been ruptured, where the spear had pierced Him; He had died, pathologically speaking, of a broken heart.

That rupture was caused by sorrow, the awful strain of all that was involved in Human Redemption by His death.

When He arose from the dead, He stood before them in flesh and bone.

Remember that flesh and blood can never enter into the Heavenly Kingdom.

His bloodless body stood upon this earth; but that body is now glorified; it is no longer a body of humiliation.

It is a Body of Glory, Transformed and Glorified.

The only description we have of it is that in the Revelation, and there it is represented as being so majestic in appearance that John fell at His feet as one dead.

It is the same body glorified; the same kind of body that we shall wear; for we shall be like Him.

A Transformed and Glorified Body.

Our bodies will be no longer bodies of humiliation; but they will be transformed like unto His glorious body.

Jesus' body had not yet been transformed.

He had not yet ascended into heaven.

He was still in the human body that He wore on the earth; as He said, "I am not yet ascended unto the Father: but . . . . I ascend, unto My Father and your Father, and My God and your God."

When He ascended, the glorious transformation took place.

Previous to His ascension, however, He said:

See My hands and My feet, that it is I Myself: handle Me, and see; for a spirit hath not flesh and bones, as ye behold Me having. And when He had said this, He showed them His hands and feet. And while they still disbelieved for joy—

There is a kind of disbelief for very joy.

He gave them a very practical illustration.

He said, "Have you anything to eat," and they gave Him a piece of broiled fish; and He took it and did eat before them.

That is the second time that He is spoken of as eating after He arose from the dead.

There is a third time, when He went into Galilee.

They found that He had made a fire, and had fish there, and He ate with them, no doubt, at morning breakfast.

He ate at Emmaus with the Disciples, and He ate here again with His Apostles.

I do not know that the glorified bodies of the Redeemed will need to eat fish; because, as I have already said to you, this body had not yet ascended—had not yet been glorified.

It may be, and I think it likely, that the bodies of the Redeemed will experience the changes through which our Lord's own body passed when He went into the heavens.

While I do not think there are fish in that "glassy sea," that does not alter the fact that it is a very good thing to eat fish on earth; for the Redeemer ate broiled fish and pieces of honeycomb; and He ate lamb. Therefore I feel myself perfectly at liberty to eat fish, and honeycomb, and lamb.

The General Overseer Not a Vegetarian.

I want all to eat only that which is good and which will nourish.

If any one tells me that I cannot eat lamb or fish, I say, "Jesus ate it and I may."

I am not a vegetarian.

Whatever you eat, however, you must eat in moderation.

It is such a delightful thing to think that our Lord proved His bodily presence by eating.

There was always that about the Lord which was genial and kind, even at the most sacred times.

This question, "Have ye anything to eat?" was the same that revealed His identity at the Sea of Galilee, while Peter was wondering whether that was the Christ who was walking by the seashore.

He said, "Children, have ye any meat?"

He was so kind, and so condescending, and so loving, that He ate freely with them.

He will eat with us tonight, thank God!

May God grant us to realize His kind presence!

And He took it, and did eat before them.

And He said unto them, These are My words which I spake unto you, while I was yet with you, how that all things must needs be fulfilled, which are written in the Law of Moses, and the Prophets, and the Psalms, concerning Me.

It Is a Good Thing to Have the Mind Opened.

Then opened He their mind—

What a glorious thing that was!

Oh, it is a good thing to have one's mind opened by the Christ Himself!

May our Father, by the Holy Spirit, open our mind.

The mind is so closed, but if our hearts are right with Him, He will open our mind!

Then opened He their mind, that they might understand the Scriptures:

And He said unto them, Thus it is written, that the Christ [the Messiah] should suffer, and rise again from the dead the third day;

And that Repentance and Remission of Sins should be preached in His Name unto All the Nations, beginning from Jerusalem.

Ye are Witnesses of these things.

And behold, I send forth the promise of My Father upon you; but tarry ye in the city, until ye be clothed with Power from on high.

And He led them out until they were over against Bethany: and He lifted up His hands and blessed them.

And it came to pass, while He blessed them, He parted from them, and was carried up into heaven.

And they worshiped Him, and returned to Jerusalem with great joy:

And were continually in the Temple, blessing God.

We have been in this Tabernacle, blessing God, from early morn till night, since the 13th of this month; and now, tonight, on the evening of the 24th, we are still joyfully blessing God.

We cannot always be in the Feast of Tabernacles.

We have to go and fulfil our part in the great mission in these Latter Days.

We Have to Fulfil Our Part in the Times of the Restoration.

What a wonderful privilege is ours!

This people are growing in numbers; but, best of all, in deepening Spirituality, in Sincerity, in Humility, in Purity, in Faith, in Wisdom, in Knowledge, in the capacity which makes even a Zion child grasp a world-wide promise, so that we are thinkers along great lines.

We have to study geography, because we have, as a people, to follow in Love and Faith, and intelligently, the Messengers who are going out, and those who have gone out, to the ends of the earth.

A lady of great intelligence was among the nine hundred from Chicago who visited us today.

She had never been here before.

She had heard me when I spoke in Tabernacles Nos. 1 and 2 and in the Central Tabernacle, but further opportunity had been denied.

Today, she came and walked around our home and made herself known; and when we gave her a few minutes, she said, "Oh, it would be unbelievable were it not so real. I walked about this City today. I entered that vast Tabernacle and saw a larger congregation than I have ever seen elsewhere. There is nothing that approaches it in Chicago. Seven thousand people! And to see what has been wrought! Such beautiful order and harmony! Then the Power of it all on one's heart, and the thought that if all the world were like Zion City this earth would be heaven! It seems to me as if it would be very close to it, anyway; a place where not an oath is heard; where no drunkard or filthy tobacco-spitter is in the streets; where no woman need fear insult or assault; and where people love each other, and greet each other with that sweet salutation of Peace that comes from the lips and hearts, so that the whole atmosphere seems to be redolent with Peace."

No Assistance or Resistance from the Press.

Beloved, this is indeed a glorious opportunity of meeting you who belong to Zion from distant parts and others who have never known us.

That lady is like some who are here tonight.

You heard of the City, but you never entered it; you never saw it before; and now, you know that we have had no assistance from the press, and that we have had no resistance from the press during this Feast.

I do not know quite what to make of it.

The press is perfectly quiet on my return. With very little exception it is perfectly respectful in its attitude.

I can only say this, that I am done with the press and everything connected with it, having finally determined that it is my duty to spend no time in chasing its lies or in defending myself against it.

It seems to me that whatever we need to do in that way can be left for our own secular paper.

I am delighted, as we go to prayer, to ask you to help me praise God for a calm, beautiful, even, all-prevading sense of continuous blessing.

I will not say that it has come in showers that we could not contain it; but it has come all the time, continuously, like a gently flowing river that is filled with water—flowing silently, because the river is deep; and flowing Purely, because the river is Clean.

I am glad that we have been drinking with Joy out of the Wells of Salvation—yea, out of the River of God, which has been Full of Water in this beautiful Feast.

May God now help us to pray and to get to His Table, and to seek the presence of our Master. Then let us pass to our daily work, thanking Him for this Festival and looking forward to Festivals of the Church, which are becoming very clearly marked as we go on.

We Have Festivals Ahead of Us.

We have the great Festival of the Anniversary of Zion Restoration Host, on September 21st; and we have, with intervening minor festivals, the glorious All-Night, which closes the Old Year and opens the New Year.

There has been no day during this Feast of Tabernacles that this Tabernacle could have contained the people had they all come together at one time.

We saw this enlarged Tabernacle occupied within three hundred, or thereabouts, of its utmost capacity.

There have been seven thousand people here today; and those seats that were not occupied were in the blazing sun, and were most undesirable.

We may truthfully say that we have reached the point of overflowing.

We must ask God, as we kneel here tonight, to give us Wisdom and Grace in connection with the raising of half a million dollars for the building of Shiloah Tabernacle.

I have thought it best not to make an appeal to you for money at this time.

I want to perfect my plans before I make this appeal, and I know that I shall not lose any money that you would give me by delaying a little while.

I shall soon be able to give you more information than I can now give.

The New Shiloah Tabernacle Being Planned.

I specially desire to be quite sure that I can build this Tabernacle of concrete, with some pleasing facing.

I want the Tabernacle to be absolutely beyond dangers that arise in this country from the expansion and contraction of steel frame buildings.

Then, again, I know that should a steel frame building take fire, it is gone. The steel gets so heated at last that it warps and falls down like a house of cards.

I want something more substantial than that.

But my mind goes beyond the Tabernacle.

I see that Tabernacle overcrowded with our regular congregations in three years.

Mark what I say.

I have been right in all other statements, and I am right in this one.

I want you to help me pray that the rate of progress in the City, great and wonderful and without precedent of its kind as it has been, shall be accelerated.

Zion Faces Great Undertakings of the Future with Courage.

As we close tonight, we shall thank God for the past and courageously face these great undertakings.

The development of our Industries is being arranged for very much more rapidly, now that we know that our manufactures are acceptable, and that they are profitable, and that God has given us great opportunity.

We can go forward with great confidence.

I want this Note of Praise from every side to go into our prayer.

I want to ask God, that, as we approach His Table tonight with Joy and Unspeakable Gratitude, we may vow that we will go forward, and go into all the world until we have Preached the Gospel to Every Creature.

In Zion, we have never theorized on this matter.

We have shown how three thousand people can reach four million in ten days, by doing it in the City of New York.

London contains not more than eight million people.

If three thousand can reach four million, then ten thousand can very easily reach London's eight million, and have a large contingent to spare for Edinburgh, Dublin, Glasgow, and Belfast.

Six thousand will be ample to cover London in ten days, and the other four thousand will be enough for these other four cities.

Zion can reach the whole world within a measurable length of time, if we continue to increase at the present rates.

Zion's Breadth of Mind Recognized.

We will go forward to do it, and God will bless us.

I am glad that even the poets have given up their satirical effusions, and that one of them has been kind enough to refer to "Elijah Dowie's breadth of mind."

I am glad that even the world recognizes our breadth of mind, our catholicity.

I want you all to rise with me to this great opportunity.

Bend your energies to the work, working steadily, bravely, lovingly, uncomplainingly, assured that victory is waiting upon us at every step of the way.

I have never taken a backward step in leading Zion, and I never shall, God helping me.

That must stand for all the sermon that I shall deliver tonight.

Those who do not partake of the Communion must retire after prayer; but I do not want one here to fail of consecration to God at this moment.

I ask that Overseer Piper and my son, Dr. Gladstone Dowie, engage in prayer.

Prayer was then offered by Overseer Piper, followed by Dr. A. J. Gladstone Dowie, after which the General Overseer prayed for the sick, closing with the Congregation's chanting the Disciples' Prayer, led by the General Overseer.

Zion White-robed Choir then sang "The Heavens Are Telling."

Last Communion Service of the Feast.

The Communion Service was begun by singing Hymn No. 4 in the Program.

It was administered by the General Overseer, assisted by

Overseers, Elders, Evangelists, Deacons and Deaconesses present, and was a season of deep spiritual blessing.

The General Overseer then said:

Beloved in the Christ, our Lord and King, we now come to the last moment of this Feast; and, as we began it with thanksgiving unto God for the past, we rejoice tonight in the fulness of present blessing

I am glad that such rich, full, and satisfying abundance from God should come to us in the quiet, still, strong, and gloriously satisfactory way in which the blessing has come at this Feast.

It has been a subject of much comment, even by outsiders and strangers, that there has been such evident happiness, and yet so orderly a manifestation of it.

Few men have survived such demonstrations of lawlessness as have been made against me.

I have been touched with many things in this meeting today, but, most of all, by the expression of gratitude to God, by my son, for deliverance from the perils through which I had passed, and from which I had been so gloriously delivered.

He was with me through them all, and bore his part bravely, as did all my companions, not the least of whom was my beloved wife.

May God give her increasing strength!

I give thanks tonight for deliverance from peril.

I have found, as the Apostle Paul found, that the greatest perils that I have met, have been perils amongst false brethren, those who have professed the Name of the Christ, but whom He has so manifestly set aside.

Lying of the Meanest Kind.

The champion enemy of Zion was supposed to be a distinguished minister of the Methodist Church—an old personal friend, by the way, who could not keep from lying of the meanest kind.

There was no difficulty in understanding his position.

He was bereft of spiritual power.

All the Methodist bodies of Australia came into union—Primitive Methodists, Methodist New Connection, Bible Christians, and Wesleyan Methodists.

They gloried that Methodism would now prove itself the evangelizing power of Australia, and that all Dr. Dowie's previous statements would be shown to be utterly false.

They selected the leader of the prevailing enmity against Zion for their standard-bearer, and made him president of the conference of the States of Victoria and Tasmania.

They gave him the standard of a united church to lead them on to victory.

He had talked so much about it that they thought they must be a spiritual force.

When he talked so in Australia I said, Let the man who has done something talk to me and to Zion.

Let not the man talk to me who is bereft of spiritual power, and who has no right to speak for God.

I pointed to the results of the year before, when he was the standard-bearer of Methodism in Australia.

I pointed to their own statistics, which proved that in the whole of that year of united labor in Melbourne they had lost four hundred members, or thereabouts.

They had lost hundreds in their principal circuits.

Some country circuits had revivals and gave them a balance; but when the whole conference report was made up, the gain for the entire year was only one person.

Hundreds of ministers had preached; hundreds of local preachers, and thousands of Sabbath school teachers, exhorters, and class leaders had labored, and all that this false leader was able to show was a gain of only one.

Fabricated Gains.

Thousands of voices responded "Amen," when I said that even that one was a sham and a lie; for I knew, by statements made by my friends, of large numbers of circuits where they had claimed a gain, but where there had been a real loss.

Zion has never gone a step backward, and today Victory is on our banner, everywhere.

The World, the Flesh, the Devil, and the apostate church recognize the fact that all the powers of hell combined have not been able to keep back the Restoration; and that Elijah the Restorer has returned to his Headquarters, victorious all around the world. [Applause.]

We give God the Glory.

At the close of this Feast of Tabernacles, which has followed so rapidly upon my return, you will not wonder if I need rest.

I beg of you, that my strength may be equal to the duties that devolve upon me, that you will not plague my life with unnecessary appeals and long letters asking me to go into minute details.

I received one letter, today, of fourteen pages, which I may read next week.

I have received thousands of letters that were unworthy of the expenditure of my time or strength.

Some of them relate to the most paltry things, that can easily be attended to by the Overseers, Elders, business men, and the Law Department.

You surely do not want me to break down under the terrific strain of a mass of minute details, do you?

AUDIENCE—"No, sir."

A Serious Question.

GENERAL OVERSEER—Then pray, and I will do my part.

It is mine to work out the great policies of Zion.

It is mine to help in providing the vast sums of money needed for Zion; but you must leave me to be the judge as to whether I consider your individual cases of sufficient importance to justify me in setting aside the whole business of Zion that you may have your petty little matter attended to.

I say that lovingly.

You think your matters of vast importance; but let me ask if all your little affairs were attended to, and the result of it should be my breakdown, would it have been worth while?

AUDIENCE—"No, sir."

GENERAL OVERSEER—Then leave me to attend to the vast business, and the general policies, of Zion, and these labors will reach all individuals.

Quiet, calm, and restfulness are essential to success in thinking out and working out these problems.

You must not attempt to make me the investigator of every little thing.

You must spare me; for I am needed by you, and by Zion throughout the world, now and in the coming years.

I should be just as foolish if I let you wear out my life in these details as I would have been if I had walked into the trap that they set for my murder in London last month.

I beg of you, and I beg of you officers and members, to remember that it is a physical impossibility for me to give minute personal attention to everything.

I will oversee.

I will see that no wrong is done; and if wrong is done by my highest officer, appeal to me; I will see that it is set right.

But do not give me any hocus-pocus stories of wrong that do not exist, when you simply want to reverse a just decision.

Such words as these can apply only to a few.

Take Your Burdens to the Lord.

Pray for me, and bravely bear your own burdens.

Carry them to the Lord, with your wife, children, or friend; gather around the mercy seat, leave your burden there, and go on. God will see you through.

No necessity will be overlooked, so far as I can help it.

If there be poverty, the Storehouse is at your disposal.

But you must be wise, and you must remember that Zion will not be imposed upon.

That which is put into the Storehouse by all the people and ourselves must be administered wisely, lovingly.

We are glad to help when brethren are in distress.

My business next week will be to continue what I have been doing—making arrangements for large accessions to our machinery and large accessions to our capital that will enable me to go forward with work that we have to do, without borrowing from the world, looking only to God and to the coöperation of His people.

God is seeing us through gloriously.

I say to you who are outside, why are you not in?

Why do you not come, you and all your house, into Zion?

Why do you not realize upon your estates and come in?

Will not God hold it against you that you are helping promote the prosperity of Godless Institutions and Ungodly cities when Zion offers you a Home, Happiness, and Prosperity?

If you are waiting to get the good price that you want, you are waiting for something that will never happen.

You will not get it; you cannot get it.

You will have to sacrifice.

It is better for you to come into Zion, even at a sacrifice of fifty per cent., than to remain outside.

The reward in Zion will compensate you, both in financial prosperity and in blessing to your family.

You who are waiting, thinking the sacrifice for God and Zion is too great, will find one day that God will say, "Too late; too late."

He will put you aside, and you will never be a citizen of Zion.

You will die, as so many have died, outside the City that you love.

You will die within sight of the Promised Land.

Zion has a right and God has a right to demand the realization of all properties outside, and the concentration of all our powers within Zion.

If you delay, in consideration of good that may be done in the cities in which you live, remember that Zion will reach these cities better from a strong central point than by scattered effort.

I say this boldly.

When you come into Zion, another will arise to take your place, and then follow you, leaving another to continue the succession; for nothing is more effectual in the awakening of a community than the leaving of good people from religious convictions.

Multitudes will follow your example and carry on the work.

Do your duty.

The people in the cities, and towns, and country districts where you live know that while you say you are Zion through and through, that you are no such thing.

You are half baked; you are only half in earnest.

They see it, and they have a contempt for you.

I have issued the command that God's people are to come into Zion with all that they have.

Had I the right to issue it?

AUDIENCE—"Yes, sir."

GENERAL OVERSEER—Then you must obey, and obey quickly.

I thank you for closely listening to the reiteration of that command.

I know that the future of yourself, in every respect, and that of your family, and of the Kingdom of God, lies in the Concentration in this City of Money, of Men, of Women, Children, and of Talent.

We can use, profitably, all who come.

I never was a party to the writing of a single letter which said, to anybody, stay back.

If you are the poorest man on God's earth, come; because your labor, your toil and your presence is an inspiration and a blessing.

God will not bring into Zion more than He will enable us to use profitably.

This word I utter not alone to you who are here, but to all Zion throughout the world.

The time has come when you must come out of Apostate Churches, and Anarchistic Government, and come into Zion, under the Banner of Zion, and live in Peace, Purity, and Progress, and prepare to go out with us to do battle on the high places of the field, and to win battles everywhere for God.

This is our belief.

Is it yours?

AUDIENCE—"Yes, sir."

GENERAL OVERSEER—Is it your conviction that I am right?

AUDIENCE—"Yes, sir."

GENERAL OVERSEER—Then live it.

And now, beloved, stand and sing with me, "I Stand on Zion's Mount."

After the singing of this hymn, by the Congregation, the Choir then sang the "Hallelujah Chorus" by Beethoven, and the General Overseer pronounced the

BENEDICTION.

Beloved, abstain from every form of evil. And may the very God of Peace Himself sanctify you wholly; and I pray God your whole spirit, and soul, and body be preserved entire, without blame, unto the coming of our Lord Jesus, the Christ. Faithful is He that calleth you, who also will do it. The grace of our Lord Jesus, the Christ, the love of God our Father, the fellowship of the Holy Spirit, our Comforter and Guide, one Eternal God, abide in you, bless you, and keep you, and all the Israel of God everywhere forever. Amen.

DO YOU KNOW GOD'S WAY OF HEALING?

BY THE REV. JOHN ALEX. DOWIE.

Let it be supposed that the following words are a conversation between the reader [A] and the writer [B].

A. What does this question mean? Do you really suppose that God has some one especial way of healing in these days, of which men may know and avail themselves?

B. That is exactly my meaning, and I wish very much that you should know God's Way of Healing, as I have known it for many years.

A. What is the way, in your opinion?

B. You should rather ask, WHO is God's Way? for the way is a Person, not a thing. I will answer your question in His own words, "I am the Way, and the Truth, and the Life: no one cometh unto the Father, but by Me." These words were spoken by our Lord Jesus, the Christ, the Eternal Son of God, who is both our Savior and our Healer. (John 14:6.)

A. But I always thought that these words only referred to Him as the Way of Salvation. How can you be sure that they refer to Him as the Way of Healing also?

B. Because He cannot change. He is "the same yesterday and today, yea, and forever." (Hebrews 13:8.) He said that He came to this earth not only to save us but to heal us. (Luke 4:18), and He did this when in the flesh on earth. Being unchanged He must be able and willing and desirous to heal now

A. But is there not this difference, namely, that He is not with us now?

B. No; for He said "Lo, I am with you All the Days, even unto the Consummation of the Age;" and so He is with us now, in spirit, just as much as when He was here in the flesh.

A. But did He not work these miracles of healing when on earth merely to prove that He was the Son of God?

B. No; there was still a greater purpose than that. He healed the sick who trusted in Him in order to show us that He came to die not only for our sins, but for our sicknesses, and to deliver us from both.

A. Then, if that be so, the atonement which He made on the Cross must have been for our sicknesses as well as our sins. Can you prove that is the fact from the Scriptures?

B. Yes, I can, and the passages are very numerous. I need quote only two. In Isaiah 53:4, 5, it is written of Him: "Surely He hath borne our griefs (Hebrew, *sicknesses*), and carried our sorrows: . . . and with His stripes we are healed." Then, in the Gospel according to Matthew, this passage is quoted and directly applied to the work of bodily healing, in the 8th chapter 17th verse: "That it might be fulfilled which was spoken by Isaiah the prophet, saying, Himself took our infirmities, and bare our diseases."

A. But do you not think that sickness is often God's will, and sent for our good, and therefore God may not wish us to be healed?

B. No, that cannot possibly be; for diseases of every kind are the Devil's work, and his work can never be God's will, since the Christ came for the very purpose of destroying "the works of the Devil." (1 John 3:8.)

A. Do you mean to say that all disease is the work of Satan?

B. Yes, for if there had been no sin (which came through Satan) there never would have been any disease, and Jesus never in one single instance told any person that sickness was God's work or will, but the very contrary.

A. Can you prove from Scriptures that all forms of sickness and infirmity are the Devil's work?

B. Yes, that can be done very easily. You will see in Matthew 4:23 and 9:35 that when Jesus was here in the flesh He healed "all manner of disease and all manner of sickness among the people." Then if you will refer to Acts 10:38 you will see that the Apostle Peter declares that He (Jesus) "went about doing good, and healing all that were oppressed of the Devil." Notice that all whom He healed, not some, were suffering from Satan's evil power.

A. But does disease never come from God?

B. No, it cannot come from God, for He is pure, and disease is unclean; and it cannot come out of Heaven, for there is no disease there.

A. That is very different from the teachings which I have received all my life from ministers and in the churches. Do you really think that you are right, and that they are all wrong in this matter?

B. It is not a question as between myself and them. The only question is, What does God's Word say? God has said in all the ages, to His Church, "I am Jehovah that healeth thee" (Exodus 15:26), and therefore it would be wicked to say that He is the defiler of His people. All true Christians must believe the Bible, and it is impossible to believe that good and evil, sickness and health, sin and holiness could have a common origin in God. If the Bible really taught that, it would be impossible to believe our Lord Jesus, the Christ, when He says: "A good tree cannot bring forth evil fruit, neither can a corrupt tree bring forth good fruit." (Matthew 7:18.)

A. But even if I agree with all you say, is it not true that the Gifts of Healing were removed from the Church, and are not in it now?

B. No, the "Gifts of Healing" were never withdrawn, and can never be withdrawn, from the true Church of God, for it is written: "The gifts and the calling of God are without repentance." (Romans 11:29.) There are nine gifts of God to the Church (enumerated in 1 Corinthians 12:8-11), and all these are in the Holy Spirit. Therefore, so long as the Holy Spirit is in the Church, all the gifts must be there also. If they are not exercised, that does not prove that they do not exist, but that the faith to exercise them is lacking in God's servants. The gifts are all perfectly preserved; for the Holy Spirit, not the Church, keeps them safely.

A. What should a Christian then do when overtaken with sickness?

B. A Christian should obey God's command, and at once turn to Him for forgiveness of the sin which may have caused the sickness, and for immediate healing. Healing is obtained from God in one of four ways, namely: First, by the direct prayer of faith, without any aid from the officers of the Church, praying as the Centurion did in Matthew 8:5-12; second, by two faithful disciples praying in perfect agreement, in accordance with the Lord's promise in Matthew 18:19; third, by the anointing of the Elders and the prayer of faith, according to the instructions in James 5:14 and 15; and fourth, by the laying on of the hands of them who believe, and whom God calls to that ministry, as the Lord commands in Mark 16:18, and in other places.

A. But are people healed in this way in these days?

B. Yes, in thousands of cases. I have myself laid hands upon many hundreds of thousands of persons, and I have seen the Lord's power manifested in the healing of great numbers, many of whom are living witnesses in many countries, who have testified publicly before thousands, and who are prepared to testify at any time. This ministry is being exercised by devoted Christians in many parts of America, Europe, Australasia, and elsewhere.

A. Is it not the same as Christian Science, Mind Healing, etc.?

B. No. Divine Healing is diametrically opposed to these diabolical counterfeits, which are utterly antichristian. These impostures are only seductive forms of Spiritualism. Trance Evangelism is also a more recent form of this delusion, and it deceives many.

A. But how shall I obtain the necessary faith to receive healing, which faith I am at present conscious that I do not possess?

B. It is written: "Belief cometh of hearing, and hearing by the word of the Christ." (Romans 10:17.) Our Missions are held for the express purpose of teaching fully the Word of God on this matter, and I very heartily invite you to attend the meetings which are announced for Zion Tabernacles in Chicago and other cities, and for Shiloh Tabernacle, Zion City, Illinois. All are welcome and there are no charges of any kind made, for all God's gifts are free gifts. Salvation is the first of these, without which you cannot be healed through faith in Jesus. All the costs of this work are covered by the free-will offerings of the people who attend these meetings, and others whom the Lord leads to help; but the poorest, who have nothing to give, are as heartily welcome as the richest.

A. Do you see the sick and lay hands upon them in this Mission?

B. Yes; after we feel satisfied that they are fully resting in the Lord alone for the healing, we see privately, so far as time permits, those who attend; but under no circumstances do we claim the power to heal any, for "power belongeth unto God."

A. Have you any writings upon this subject which can be purchased?

B. Yes; these can be obtained at the office of Zion Printing and Publishing House, Zion City, Illinois, and at any Zion Tabernacle. But the best book on Divine Healing is the Bible itself, studied prayerfully and earnestly.

We extend to you a hearty invitation to attend the meetings, which are free to all. Our prayer is that you may be led to find in Jesus, the Christ, our Lord and God your present Savior from sin, your Healer from sickness, your Cleanser from all evil, your Keeper in the way to Heaven, your Friend, and your All for Time and Eternity. We pray that these words may help many who read, and that our little conversation may bear fruit in leading many readers to look to Jesus only.

"The Healing of Christ's seamless dress
Is by all beds of pain;
We touch Him in life's throng and press
And we are whole again."

Early Morning Meeting in Shiloh Tabernacle

*REPORTED BY S. E. C., O. L. S., O. R., AND E. S.

"FOR there is the sound of abundance of rain."

Elijah the Tishbite said it.

The heavens were as brass.

The people did not hear.

But the prophet heard the sound of the falling rain.

Again a prophet, with ear attuned, speaks.

And again come the words:

"For there is the sound of abundance of rain."

The prophet of old spoke of the rain which falls from the heavens upon the earth, refreshing and giving life to it.

The Prophet of the Restoration, with vision widened by the years, speaks of the things today which God has given him to know and speak.

To all the world he says it.

To the Ahabs on thrones, to the people in the streets, to the children of God, to men everywhere, the word goes forth.

"For there is the sound of abundance of rain!"

The time is at hand!

Though across the red sky there is visible but one little cloud, no larger than a man's hand, the downpour of God's blessing is near.

Shiloh Tabernacle, Zion City, Illinois, Lord's Day Morning, July 31, 1904.

The service was opened with the singing of Hymn No. 94, in Gospel Hymns Nos. 5 and 6.

The General Overseer then led in prayer, after which Hymn No. 95, in Gospel Hymns, was sung:

> There is a Name I love to hear;
> I love to sing its worth;
> It sounds like music in mine ear—
> The sweetest Name on earth.

The General Overseer read the verses of this Hymn and commented upon the 3d verse as follows:

The Undefinable Cry of the Human Heart.

Oh, there comes to one so often the feeling, "The nearest and dearest to me cannot understand me."

It is not given to us to understand one another.

We cannot get from humanity a full understanding; because we do not understand ourselves, and we do not really know what we want.

We are like babies—crying, and we do not know what we are crying for.

Babies cannot tell; they have no language with which to tell.

Is it not good to know that the good God knows?

When the baby cries, the mother searches to see if there is a pin pricking it.

Baby is crying, and baby is in trouble; and the good, loving mother hunts for the trouble, and if she finds it is not a pin, then she wonders, "What is the trouble?"

What am I, what are you, but infants crying in the night, infants crying for the light? for that is what the baby sometimes cries for.

It is dark, and baby wants to see the face it loves; and it cannot, because it is night.

I once was where a little one was crying, and we could not make out what it was crying about.

The mother went into the room, but she could see nothing wrong.

I noticed that when she turned on the light that the baby did not cry, and that when the light was turned out it again cried.

*The following address has not been revised by the General Overseer.

I said, "Why, don't you see?

"The baby is crying for the light! It wants to be where it can see something. Bring it out here, and it will crow; there is nothing on earth wrong with it."

The baby was brought into the light, and was happy.

Sometimes We Want to See.

It was a very inconvenient time to care for baby, because the father and mother wanted to converse with me; but baby wanted to see, and to be where it could hear my voice and see who it was that was talking.

Sometimes we are only crying because it is dark—because we want to see.

> It tells of One whose loving heart
> Can feel my smallest wo—
> Who in each sorrow bears a part
> That none can bear below.

There is great comfort to me in that verse.

I do not know why we have not sung it oftener; we seem to have missed it; but it is a wonderfully simple hymn, and it has wonderfully simple lines.

The Father and Mother Love of God can find out what is wrong with us.

Oftentimes we cannot tell anybody, because we do not know we are just feeling our way out of the dimness, and the darkness, and the narrowness.

It is hard, sometimes; for we have not yet become adjusted to the new conditions in which we find ourselves, and the old conditions have such attractions for us, because they fitted like an old shoe, and now we have a new shoe; somehow it is hard to walk in it.

Little Things Often Worry Big Men.

We have many small woes—none of them very big—and sometimes they make us very unhappy.

Be determined that you will take all the little things to God—the little things that worry a big man, and that one feels ashamed to acknowledge are a cause of worriment.

There is One who has not forgotten that we are children.

He was big, and He was good, and He was kind, and He was patient.

This hymn

> Tells of One whose Loving Heart,
> Can feel my smallest wo,
> Who in each sorrow bears a part
> That none can bear below.
>
> It bids my trembling soul rejoice,
> And dries each rising tear;
> It tells me in a "still, small voice,"
> To trust, and not to fear.

Read with me in the 18th chapter of the first book of Kings, beginning at the 31st verse.

I want you to read with me this story.

There is a great deal in having one's eyes upon the passage and reading it word for word.

I sometimes get hungry for the Word of God; and I say, "O God, I want some bread."

My body is not hungry; but my appetite for the Word of God is good.

I have much of the Word in my heart, and I can repeat it without reading; but there is much in the Bible that I do not understand.

I have read it, thought about it, and preached about it.

I have sometimes, in times past, preached about a thing, and, at the end, known less about it than when I started.

My text was bigger than my conception of it.

We Cannot Know All That Is in the Bible.

The Bible has heights and depths, mountains and streams, and all kinds of beautiful things.

It is like a big world—you never get to know all that is in it.

. You may have the letter of it in your hearts, and be able to repeat it from beginning to end, but you do not know it all.

A little tot recently repeated to me the names of all the Presidents, from Washington to Roosevelt.

The child did not have a ghost of an idea who George Washington was, nor did he have the ghost of an idea who John Quincy Adams was.

Do you not know that the people of the United States know but little about him?

John Quincy Adams was the ablest President that ever sat in the Presidential Chair.

He was a fine man; a man of the highest integrity, and scholarship.

Do you know why they do not talk about him?

It is because he was against Freemasonry and slavery.

He was against slavery long before Abraham Lincoln came to the front.

If his advice had been taken, there would have been no war between the North and the South.

Oh, that horrible war!

John Quincy Adams a Man of Varied Talent.

I have been studying John Quincy Adams.

He was a poet, a splendid literary man, and a splendid ambassador.

He was the son of President John Adams.

He was a patriot, a magnificent speaker, and a thinker; but because he was opposed to Freemasonry and slavery, they snubbed him and tried to keep the people from knowing anything about him.

When the names of many of the presidents are forgotten, the name of John Quincy Adams will shine.

Abraham Lincoln acknowledged that he received his best inspiration in politics from John Quincy Adams.

Many of you who have Bibles say things, the meaning of which you know no more than that little child knew about the men whose names he had recited.

You in this City know much about the Bible, but you do not know anything compared with what you might know, because you forget to bring your Bibles to the meetings.

We will read in the 18th chapter of 1 Kings, beginning with the 31st verse:

And Elijah took twelve stones, according to the number of the tribes of the sons of Jacob, unto whom the Word of Jehovah came, saying, Israel shall be thy name.

And with the stones he built an altar in the Name of Jehovah; and he made a trench about the altar, as great as would contain two measures of seed.

And he put the wood in order, and cut the bullock in pieces, and laid it on the wood. And he said, Fill four barrels with water, and pour it on the burnt offering, and on the wood.

And he said, Do it the second time; and they did it the second time. And he said, Do it the third time; and they did it the third time.

Elijah Would Have no Secrecy.

Elijah was a fellow who used to get things done over and over again.

He wanted to be sure, and make everybody else sure, that there was no trick about this altar.

In that time, the priests often concealed fire below the altars, and made pretense that the sacrifice was consumed from above.

Elijah made them build their altar in front of him that day, and there was no way by which they could sneak their fire in.

He built his altar in their presence, cut the bullock in pieces, and poured water into the trench.

And the water ran round about the altar; and he filled the trench also with water.

And it came to pass at the time of the offering of the evening oblation, that Elijah the prophet came near, and said, O Jehovah, the God of Abraham, of Isaac, and of Israel, let it be known this day that Thou art God in Israel, and that I am Thy servant, and that I have done all these things at Thy word.

There were three things in that prayer:

Let it be known this day that Thou art God in Israel,

That I am Thy servant, and

That I have done all these things at Thy Word.

There is concentration in that prayer.

Many times I have prayed that prayer.

Hear me, O Jehovah, hear me, that this people may know that Thou, Jehovah art God, and that Thou hast turned their heart back again.

Then the Fire of Jehovah fell, and consumed the burnt offering, and the wood, and the stones, and the dust, and licked up the water that was in the trench.

And when all the people saw it, they fell on their faces: and they said, Jehovah, He is God; Jehovah, He is God.

An Instance in Which a Knowledge of the Hebrew Is Essential.

We miss a good deal because we have not the Hebrew of this passage.

When the people fell upon their faces they cried, "Eliyahu! Eliyahu!"

That was the name of Elijah.

Elijah is not a common name.

It probably was not the prophet's name.

It might have been a nickname that they gave him.

He was always saying, "Eliyahu! You may have Baal, and Moloch, and Ashtaroth, and all these accursed heathen divinities for your gods, and mix heathenism with the worship of Jehovah, but as for me, Eliyahu!—Jehovah is my God!"

Therefore, they called him "Eliyahu."

There was no other way to say "Jehovah is my God" than to repeat Elijah's name.

It is grand to have a man's name stand for what he is.

When this name, "Eliyahu," was thrown at him in derision, Elijah answered, "The day will come when the Sword of God will be in my hands. It will fall upon you wretches; and I will clean you out, to the last man."

He warned them. He afterwards did clean them out to the very last man.

If ever righteous judgment came upon a mass of wretches that had misled the people and the whole nation, it was that.

And Elijah said unto them, Take the prophets of Baal; let not one of them escape. And they took them: and Elijah brought them to the Brook Kishon, and slew them there.

That tells a big story in very few words.

"Take the prophets of Baal," and they took them.

"Take them down to that Brook Kishon, and settle it there. They have murdered God's people, and they would have murdered me if they could. They have destroyed the worship of Jehovah. They have cursed this nation, and brought three years of famine upon it. Take these wretches down to the Brook Kishon, and put an end to them."

That was a horrible thing to do, and I am glad that we do not have to do that in this Dispensation.

A Fearful Prediction.

However, the time will come when we will have to say, "If you do not obey God, you shall die."

Then the people in the churches that will not obey God, will fall dead.

The time will come when the Ananiases, and the Sapphiras, and the hypocrites will die like flies.

It will come to that, in the Restoration, when the Christ comes.

He will not stand it.

I can see it plainly.

In the Restoration, our Message will be, "You just believe God and do what he tells you, or die. That is the only alternative!"

God will rid this earth of liars, cheats, and humbugs—of those in His Church especially.

When judgment comes to this world, it will begin at the House of God—with the people that are Christians only in streaks, and hypocrites all the time.

Got will get at the bottom of everything.

We must be a people that are out-and-out.

There is no room in Zion for anything else.

And Elijah said unto Ahab, Get thee up, eat and drink.

Elijah Not Wise in His Treatment of Ahab and Jezebel.

I do not see why Elijah said that.

I differ with him.

Ahab was the fellow that had done more wickedness than all others.

I would have said, "Take Ahab and Jezebel to the borders of Tyre and Sidon, and fling them over among the heathen muck from whence they came."

I would have said, "If you come back we will kill you. We will have the Theocracy now."

I wish Elijah had been wiser in his time.

I do not see why those priests should have been killed, and their master have been told to eat and drink.

I think I have learned something.

So Ahab went up to eat and to drink.
And Elijah went up to the top of Carmel;
And he bowed himself down upon the earth,
And put his face between his knees.

Remember that he bowed himself down upon the earth, and that he put his face between his knees.

The man who had lifted his face before God and man, when praying in secret has his face to the very earth.

Elijah Suffers for His Cowardice.

Elijah! Elijah! No wonder that you had your face to the earth; you did not fulfil your mission properly, and you suffered for it.

You became a coward, because you did not clean out Ahab and Jezebel.

Jezebel made you a coward, that very day!

She said she would have your life, and then you began to be afraid!

And he said to his servant, Go up now, look toward the sea. And he went up, and looked, and said, There is nothing.

"You are praying in vain, Elijah! There is nothing! The heavens are just as they have been for three years and six months! They are like brass! The sun is shining down upon that Mediterranean Sea, and it is just like a sheet of fire and flame. Although the people have said, 'Jehovah is God, Jehovah is God;' although you have said, 'There is a sound of abundance of rain,' there is not; there is nothing!"

And he said, Go again seven times.

And it came to pass at the seventh time, that he said, Behold, there ariseth a cloud out of the sea, as small as a man's hand. And he said, Go up, say unto Ahab, Make ready thy chariot, and get thee down, that the rain stop thee not.

And it came to pass in a little while, that the heaven grew black with clouds and wind, and there was a great rain. And Ahab rode and went to Jezreel.

And the hand of Jehovah was on Elijah; and he girded up his loins, and ran before Ahab to the entrance of Jezreel.

With my present light, I would not have run before Ahab down to Jezreel.

I think the hand of the Lord was on Elijah.

The Lord never sent him to be the footman of that miserable, wretched king.

Perfection Is Not to Be Found Among Men.

May God bless that Word.

I have been thinking much about it this morning.

I want you to read more about this prophet, so mighty in his day.

It did not make him less a prophet that he made mistakes.

Every prophet has made mistakes, except the Lord Jesus, the Christ.

He never made a mistake.

Every rose has a thorn, except the Rose of Sharon.

Every lily has a blemish except the Christ, the Lily of the Valley.

Every sun has spots, except the Sun of Righteousness.

Every man has his wicked spots.

The only One that was pure from the cradle to the grave was the Son of God.

You cannot find infallibility in Peter and John.

You cannot find it in Elijah.

You cannot find it in any man.

You will find infallibility only in God.

Our Lord Jesus, the Christ, the one Perfect Man, was the only Infallible Man.

Remember how fallible, how very imperfect, you are.

Now read in the 5th chapter of James.

Is any among you suffering? let him pray. Is any cheerful? let him sing praise.

Is any among you sick? let him call for the elders of the church; and let them pray over him, anointing him with oil in the Name of the Lord.

Numbers of you have not called for the Elders when you failed to get the blessing.

Elders are for service.

That is also what the Deacons and Deaconesses are for; they were ordained for that.

If you do not get the blessing, call.

You have a right to their services.

They promised to serve you and to serve God, in this ministry.

And the Prayer of Faith shall save him that is sick, and the Lord shall raise him up; and if he have committed sins, it shall be forgiven him.

Confess therefore your sins one to another, and pray one for another, that ye may be healed. The supplication of a righteous man availeth much in its working.

"Elijah was a man of like passions with us"—that is, of like nature. He had just the humanity that you and I have.

Praying That Is Real Prayer.

And he prayed fervently that it might not rain.

The Greek is peculiarly expressive. "He prayed with prayer." He prayed with real prayer; not with something that was not prayer.

Many people pray with something that is not real prayer.

They say the first thing that comes into their stupid heads.

They think they will be heard for their much speaking.

They are like the heathen—they think their long prayers will pull them through.

Your long prayers are a curse to you!

Elijah did not pray a long prayer, and he got that rain.

In fact, you have no record of what he prayed.

All that you see is a man on the top of a mountain, perhaps in the cave of a rock; he says nothing; but he is praying for rain.

He is asking the good God that this drouth may break up, and that the famine may stop, and that He may save His people.

There Is a Time to Pray For Judgment.

He prayed first that it might not rain—"O God, keep back the rain, and make this people know that You are the Giver of rain. They say that Baal, the Sun-god, is the god that gives them good crops, and sends rain. O God, withhold the rain. Make the people know that You, not Baal, give the rain."

There comes a time when all that you can pray is that God will come in judgment to the land.

This land of ours has been so wonderfully blessed that if it continues in its ungodliness, eating up the harvests without thanking the Giver of the harvest, it will suffer the penalty.

One day there will be judgment.

Elijah was a man of like passions with us, and he prayed fervently that it might not rain; and it rained not on the earth for three years and six months.

And he prayed again; and the heaven gave rain, and the earth brought forth her fruit.

My brethren, if any among you do err from the truth, and one convert him;

Let him know, that he which converteth a sinner from the error of his way shall save a soul from death, and shall cover a multitude of sins.

SOUND OF ABUNDANCE OF RAIN.

INVOCATION.

O God, bless Thy Word! And let the few words that we shall now say, be blessed to this people.

Beloved friends, it is far better for us to read the words and have you understand them, than for me to speak to you; because what I say is of less importance than the Word, understood.

There is a sound! "There is a sound of abundance of rain!"

Will the rain come?

There Is Sound of Abundance of Rain.

I say this morning to this people, and I say it to all Zion, throughout the world, "there is a sound of abundance of rain."

I say it to Ahab on the throne.

I say it to the people in the streets.

I say to the world, that the Great, and Good, and Holy God, has blessed this land ever since Zion came into existence; that He has blessed this land ever since we started to pray for the blessing of the land and people; that He has given us the rain; that He has given us blessings; that He has piled upon America a succession of magnificent harvests, and of riches in every direction such as no nation has ever seen in the same time.

Statistics show that since the days of the formation of the Christian Catholic Church in Zion in February, 1896, to this time eight years and six months, there has been more blessing, agriculturally and horticulturally; more blessing in the digging of gold and silver out of the mines; more blessing in manufactures and exportation; more blessing in the wealth of the people, than has ever been in this nation at any preceding time, or that has ever been given to any nation in the whole history of the world.

I do not hesitate to say that.

You may say that these blessings sustain no particular relation to the Christian Catholic Church in Zion, and that they have nothing to do with the prayers that I have offered; but I believe they have.

I believe that the mightiest thing that has happened in these eight years, is that a people has been called out to live a godly life and to follow Elijah the Restorer.

I believe that the Restoration of All Things, in the beginnings of which we are now, is the mightiest factor in the history of the world today.

Zion Has Her Own Beginning of the Year.

I am talking at the end of the Feast, and at the beginning of our working year.

The end of the Feast has come to be the beginning of the year to us.

"There is a sound of abundance of rain."

I heard it last night, and I said, "There will be much rain."

I have been praying that after the Feast closes, as quickly as God sees that we can do well with it, He may give us abundance of rain.

I am asking God to make this land rich and prosperous, and to give good harvests, that we may be able to bring our brethren out of all the lands into these Zion Cities, and to do the work that God will enable us to do.

That will bring us the still better rain.

I heard the pouring rain fall this morning—it seemed as if God had opened my ears at four o'clock to hear—and I said, "Lord, am I wrong, or do I hear behind this material blessing the sound of abundance of spiritual rain?"

I do not know whether you got any of it; but I got it.

It fell upon my farm.

It fell upon my garden.

It fell upon my heart.

It fell upon my spirit.

The dawn came before I could see any light in the skies.

We Must Pray Even Though We Hear the Sound.

Although the spiritual skies may seem to many people to be like brass, I hear the "sound of abundance of rain!"

Because I hear the "sound of abundance of rain," is that any reason why I should not pray for it?

Is that any reason why I should not ask you to pray for it?

Elijah, though he heard the "sound of abundance of rain," kept on praying when he told Ahab to "get up and eat and drink."

That was about the only thing that Ahab could do.

I think he did not ask Ahab to go and pray, because he knew Ahab could not pray.

Perhaps Ahab said to him, "Elijah, what shall I do?".

"Oh, go! Eat and drink! That is all you can do!"

I do not know whether Elijah said that in contempt, or not. But I have a notion that Ahab asked the question when frightened.

He saw the dead bodies, and in his fright he said, "O Elijah, what shall I do?"

"You miserable dog, go, and eat, and drink!"

That was the only thing he was fit to do.

Many people have been praying long years for a revival.

The good people in all the churches have been praying for a revival, but they have been praying for a revival of their own kind; and when the revival came, in 1896, in the formation of the Christian Catholic Church in Zion, many persons said, "There is the revival; there is the revival, in Zion."

Others said, "Why, there is nothing to be seen there except a man who is laying hands upon the sick. And do you mean to say that that man's hands are the revival?"

"Yes! Yes!" many people cried, "It will spread along the skies, until it covers the whole heavens."

Have you not seen it?

The Devil Revives When God's People Revive.

Have you not seen the clouds that came over Australia? There was a rumble and a flash. Did you hear it?

Did it not roll across the Pacific and come to you here, and in England?

There was a revival!

The Devil howled!

Overseer Voliva is having a revival.

Do you not know that our Tabernacle in Melbourne canno contain the people, and that they crowd the streets?

The crowds are so great that Overseer Voliva can get out only by the aid of an escort of police

It is a revival so great that his life is in danger.

That is a fine sign!

The Devil is getting revived.

I always know that there is a revival, when the Devil revives.

Some people say that the absence of activity by the Devil is a sign of a revival.

That is a mistake.

The revival of the Devil is the sign of a spiritual revival.

There are no signs of a revival in the Salvation Army.

Why?

Because the Devil is patting the Salvation Army on the back, and King Edward has become its Patron Saint.

General Booth is speaking of the king in terms of the highest admiration.

General Booth knows, as well as I know, that King Edward VII. has been a dissolute Prince; that there is not a bit of piety in him; that he is not a converted man; and that he is going from race-course to race-course.

Talk about that being a revival!

I had a revival when I got there.

The Devil was stirred up, and the court was almost like Ahab, searching for Elijah.

"Wherever you find him, kill him, kill him!"

But they could not kill him.

God's Prophet Gets Out of Danger.

Some of the papers say, "How is it that that fellow gets out of everything?

I use my good judgment.

Before they knew where I was, I was in France; and then, before they knew where I was, I was in England; and I drove through their streets in an open carriage, from Charing Cross to Hyde Park, and took a fine ride with the nobility around the Park, leaving the reporters in cabs outside.

I went openly.

But there was a revival!

There was a revival all through the three years and six months in which there was no rain.

The Devil was hunting for Elijah everywhere, and on the day that God blessed them and the fire came down, there was a revival.

There is a revival, and the revival is coming!

We received glorious and copious showers of blessing during the Feast, did we not?

AUDIENCE—"Yes."

President Roosevelt Commended.

GENERAL OVERSEER—God will give us prosperity this year.

He will again give us the good man who occupies the presidential chair.

If you wait to vote for a president who has no blemishes, you will have to wait until you get to heaven; you will never find him on earth.

I do not say that Roosevelt has not some spots; but I tell you that he wants to do right as in the sight of the Most High God.

I believe that if this nation sends him back to the White House, God will bless this nation.

You do not know how much the United States owes to that man.

When McKinley lay dead, and it was known that the reins of power were in the hands of Theodore Roosevelt, the nation felt contentment in the conviction that there would be good government.

The world manifested its confidence in that the stocks of the United States did not fall a point.

The murder of Von Plehve last week, in Russia, made Russian stocks fall fifteen or twenty points.

That horrible government is breaking up.

This whole nation ought to be grateful to God that when William McKinley fell under the assassin's bullet, there was a man ready to take up the reins; and, if only out of gratitude, they ought to send that young man back to the White House! [Applause.]

Pray about it.

I shall start upon my political campaign when I come back from Ben MacDhui.

I wonder at the audacity of the Democrats putting up a

candidate for the Presidency of the United States who has never ruled a county, who has never ruled a state, who has never been a legislator; who has never been a man of prominence, and who knows nothing about rule.

He is simply a political lawyer who is acceptable to the political elements of the Democratic Party.

There Will Be Rain in This County if We Do Right.

There are things that keep back blessing; and if I do hear the sound of abundance of rain, I have to get up to Mount Carmel and pray.

Some of you people who do not see the skies black with clouds, say, "Oh, I am going away."

Go away quickly; because the rain will come sooner if you go.

If you do not go, you may suffer; for when this spiritual revival comes, it will burn like a fire.

It will be a very powerful fire.

I believe that the cloud about which some people contemptuously said in 1896, "Why, the whole thing is no bigger than Dowie's hand," has covered the sky.

That hand has written words that are going all over the world.

Zion is the only source from which this blessing can come.

It will come only through the faithfulness of Elijah the Restorer, and through the faithfulness of his people.

Tell me where I can find men full of faith and full of the Holy Spirit who are holding prayer-meetings, and who are not mere ranters, and talkers, and howlers.

I have no use for mere howlers; but if you can find men anywhere whom God is blessing in conducting prayer-meetings, I will make a bee-line for that prayer-meeting.

I shall not find it at Desplaines.

I shall not find it in the Holiness Band on the other side of the river.

Do you know why?

Because that Holiness Band has lied about John Alexander Dowie.

There was a cartoon in their paper the other day, representing me and all my people as in hell.

I observed that my beard and robes were in fine order, that my people were with me, and that the Devil had taken a back seat.

I said to myself, "That is true; when I go down to hell the Devil will have to take a back seat."

The Christ Had a Front Place in Hell.

I had a front place in hell.

The Christ had a front place when He went down to hell.

He went down to hell.

Do you not know that?

I wonder if there is any chance of converting the Devil?

I wonder if any of you have ever prayed for the conversion of the Pope?

Why not?

He is a man with an immortal spirit, that has to be saved.

Do you ever pray for the conversion of the saloon-keepers, or do you only curse them?

There is no use in my fighting Edward VII., if I do not pray for him.

I do; and when they sing, "God save the King," I sing it louder than anybody.

Some one heard me singing, "God save the King," and they said, "We thought you were against him!"

I replied, "No, I want him saved. He needs saving."

God save the Czar!

God save every sinner!

There will be no revival in a Methodist camp-meeting.

They will not get a revival in the Church of England as long as they grind out that miserable prayer:

> Lord, have mercy upon us, miserable sinners; for we have left undone the things we ought to have done, and done the things we ought not to have done; and there is no health in us.

Is that the church in which you expect to find a revival?

Do you expect Bishop Potter to lead a revival in New York?

Nor will you find it among the Presbyterians.

They have no religion to spare.

Think of a Presbyterian minister setting America on fire! He hasn't enough fire to boil his own teakettle.

Will you get it from the Baptists?

They have water; lots of water, although very few are getting into it.

It is very muddy!

There Are Good Men in All the Churches.

There are good men in all the denominational churches; good men in the Salvation Army; and good men in the Church of Rome.

There is no place where God has not left His representatives.

God does not desert His world, nor His people.

There are people who want to do right in all the churches.

But the churches, as organizations, with the Salvation Army, have gone to the Devil.

They are not going—they have already gone.

Do you think you will get the rain through their instrumentality?

If it were to fall in the churches, it would stink within a week, because of the rottenness of everything inside the church.

What could Bishop Potter do with a revival?

He would not know how to handle it if it came.

What could the Presbyterians do with a revival?

There was a revival in the Presbyterian Church in John Knox's time, but the Presbyterians of the present day have never seen a revival.

Some of you professed ex-Methodists here are Methodists yet.

Do you know how I can tell?

I can tell as I tell that a chicken has just come out of an egg-shell.

"How do you know that?"

By a bit of shell that is sticking to its back.

There is a bit of Methodism sticking to some of your backs!

And some of you Hard-shell Baptists have some of the shell sticking to your backs.

I wish you would get rid of that shell.

The Revival Will Come Through the Intercession of Elijah.

Where are we to get the revival, if it does not come through the intercession of Elijah to God, the Almighty?

I believe that the only way that the revival can come in this world is for me to get where I can pray to God.

You will not get the blessing if you keep on saying, "There is nothing."

Say, "God's promises are with us, and God will bless His Prophet, and bless His people."

Has He not blessed us in the past?

PEOPLE—"Yes."

GENERAL OVERSEER—Who have been blessed more than this people in three years?

There is not a line in which we have not been blessed. Have we not been blessed in spirit?

PEOPLE—"Yes."

GENERAL OVERSEER—Have we not been blessed in the educational sphere?

PEOPLE—"Yes."

GENERAL OVERSEER—Have we not been blessed in our Commercial and Industrial activities, and in standing up as a great Theocratic and Political force in the world?

PEOPLE—"Yes."

GENERAL OVERSEER—What have we not been blessed in?

We have not been blessed in not getting off all of that old shell that is sticking to your backs.

We have not been blessed in not getting rid of the wretched grumbling spirit that is in some of you.

The Grumbling Spirit Is a Curse.

A man on the Pacific coast said recently, "There is nothing to Zion!"

The man to whom he said it began to inquire of him as to why he had left Zion.

After a little while he admitted that he had been expelled from Zion, because he had sinned.

"But," he said, "there is nothing in Zion."

Then the gentleman, who knew a little about him, turned around and said, "Look here, did you invest in Zion?"

"Yes."

"How much money did you put in?"

"I took with me a few hundred dollars, and I bought a little land and a house. But then I got out! I couldn't stand Dowie!"

No! Dowie could not stand him; that was the trouble!

"How many dollars did you take in with you?" he was asked.

"About six hundred dollars."

"And, I say, friend, how much did you bring out?"

"Oh, well," he said, "I brought out over a thousand dollars."

Where did he get it?

He got it in Zion; the liar! That was saying there was nothing in Zion!

He had lived in Zion.

He received blessing in Zion, in many ways; and he had taken out nearly twice as much money as he brought in.

The Christ's Hand Is to Be Seen in Zion.

There is another hand to be seen in Zion; it is the hand of the Living Christ; the hand of the Living God.

If you cannot see that hand, it is because you have no eyesight.

I am inclined to think that that cloud as big as a man's hand was in the sky all the time; only Elijah's servant could not see it.

He was looking for some great movement, such as you sometimes see on the Mediterranean when there is to be a change in the weather. The whole horizon has a long, low cloud upon it; and as you look at it through marine-glasses, you will see the sea foaming in the distance.

He was not looking for a cloud that was only the size of a man's hand; and that is the trouble with some of you.

If God will only show us today His Hand in the sky, is not that enough?

PEOPLE—"Yes."

GENERAL OVERSEER—All right. I tell you there is the "sound of abundance of rain."

Do you believe it?

PEOPLE—"Yes."

GENERAL OVERSEER—Do you believe it is coming?

PEOPLE—"Yes."

GENERAL OVERSEER—And you are holding on?"

PEOPLE—"Yes."

GENERAL OVERSEER—I believe I have a people who are holding on; and I am not sorry that I have not the people who do not believe.

Let us make our consecration to God.

I believe we have an earnest people.

All the people that believe there is a "sound of abundance of rain," and who want to pray God that we shall not fail God in this matter, stand and tell Him so.

PRAYER OF CONSECRATION.

My God and Father, in Jesus' Name, I come to Thee. I believe that there is "a sound of an abundance of rain," and that Thou who hast blessed Zion in these three years, and who hast blessed us in the late Feast, wilt give us showers of blessing; blessing in every department in Zion; blessing in finance, blessing in business, blessing in the schools, blessing in the politics of Zion, and blessing, above all things, in the spirits of the people. Give us this blessing! Give it now! Give us the faith to believe that, though sometimes the sky seems like brass, that the rain will come. For Jesus' sake. Amen. [*All repeat the prayer, clause by clause, after the General Overseer.*]

Beloved, I am so thankful, for I believe you meant that prayer. Keep at it, and never let the element of doubt enter in.

The service was closed by the General Overseer's pronouncing the

BENEDICTION.

Beloved, abstain from every form of evil. And may the very God of Peace Himself sanctify you wholly; and I pray God your whole spirit, and soul, and body be preserved entire, without blame, unto the coming of our Lord Jesus, the Christ. Faithful is He that calleth you, who also will do it. The grace of our Lord Jesus, the Christ, the love of God, our Father, the fellowship of the Holy Spirit, our Comforter and Guide, one Eternal God, abide in you, bless you, and keep you, and all the Israel of God everywhere, forever. Amen.

LEAVES OF HEALING.

Two Dollars will bring to you the weekly visits of the Little White Dove for a year; 75 cents will send it to a friend for thirteen weeks; $1.25 will send it for six months; $1.50 will send it to your minister, or to a Y. M. C. A., or to a Public Reading Room for a whole year. We offer no premiums, except the premium of doing good. We receive no advertisements, and print no commercial lies or cheating enticements of unscrupulous thieves. LEAVES OF HEALING is Zion on wings, and we keep out everything that would detract the reader's mind from all except the Extension of the Kingdom of God, for which alone it exists. If we cannot send forth our Little White Dove without soiling its wings with the smoke of the factory and the dirt of the wrangling market-place, or compelling it to utter the screaming cries of the business vultures in the ears of our readers, then we will keep our Dove at home.

Every Reader of Leaves of Healing Should Also Read The Zion Banner.

The cost is too small to be worth mentioning, being fifty cents for six months.

LESS THAN TWO CENTS A WEEK!

If you will put in a few hours' work among your friends, and obtain THREE NEW SUBSCRIBERS TO THE ZION BANNER, we will send you your own copy free.

YOU CAN GET THEM EASILY!

Just give it a trial.

Scarcely any news in THE ZION BANNER is reprinted in LEAVES OF HEALING.

Many people will read THE ZION BANNER who might not be interested in our other publications.

Resolve today that you will do this for the extension of the Kingdom of God.

ZION PRINTING AND PUBLISHING HOUSE,
Zion City, Illinois

Expiration of Subscriptions.

On every subscriber's copy of LEAVES OF HEALING or THE ZION BANNER we attach a yellow label bearing his name, address, and two numbers, the figures referring to the volume and the number with which the subscription will expire.

Thus, should your label number happen to be 16—1, you may know that your subscription expires with Volume XVI, Number 1, which will be October 22, 1904. Also take notice that LEAVES OF HEALING now completes a volume every six months, or twenty-six weeks, that being the number of papers which are put into a bound volume. Earlier in the life of the paper a volume contained fifty-two numbers, as LEAVES OF HEALING had fewer pages in those days.

By making yourselves familiar with these customs and remitting promptly you need never allow your subscription to lapse.

Send money only by Bank Draft, Postoffice or Express Money-order in favor of John Alexander Dowie, and address all letters intended for us to

ZION PRINTING AND PUBLISHING HOUSE,
Zion City, Lake County, Illinois.

Warning.

I am directed by the General Overseer to warn our members and officers throughout the world against giving money to persons claiming to be members of the Christian Catholic Church in Zion. All benevolence must be given either from Headquarters or under the direction of same. Even though the applicant for benevolence be known to be a member of the Christian Catholic Church in Zion, financial aid must not be given except in extreme cases, and then only in small amounts. Requests for help must be made to the officer-in-charge. In cases where there is no such officer, requests should be made direct to Headquarters, accompanied by recommendations from one or two members of Zion in good standing. J. G. EXCELL,
General Ecclesiastical Secretary.

Notice to Officers and Members.

Send all newspaper clippings concerning the General Overseer, the Elders, or any department of the work in connection with the Christian Catholic Church in Zion, to Deacon Carl F. Stern, Zion City, Illinois. Send as soon as possible after publication, and carefully mark *name and date of the paper clipped from* on each article. If this is not done, the clippings are absolutely useless.

Zion's Bible Class

Conducted by Deacon Daniel Sloan in Shiloh Tabernacle, Zion City, Lord's Day Morning at 11 o'clock, and in Zion Homes and Gatherings throughout the World.

MID-WEEK BIBLE CLASS LESSON, SEPTEMBER 14th or 15th.

Events Preceding the Christ's Reign.

1. *Society will get more and more corrupt.*—2 Timothy 3:13-27.
Sin is getting more subtle.
Iniquity is getting more brazen.
Deception is getting to be more easy.
2. *Hypocrisy will take the place of true faith.*—Matthew 23:27-33.
Men cover up their sins.
They appear outwardly righteous.
They serve the Devil, not God.
3. *People will condemn the thing they take pleasure in doing.*—Romans 2:1-10.
They condemn tobacco, yet use it.
They condemn liquor, but drink it.
They condemn lust, but yield to it.
4. *Signs of famine, wars, and pestilences will appear.*—Matthew 24:3-13.
Peace will be taken from the earth.
Epidemics will be more common.
Commotions will be more shocking.
5. *The kings of the earth will resist the Christ's coming.*—Psalm 2:1-6.
The Devil wants to reign.
He will reign through men.
He masters the hearts of earth's monarchs.
6. *Social pleasures will more and more dominate people.*—Matthew 24:36-43.
Having a good time is the spirit of the age.
Some want banquets and others want something else.
They are not watching the signs of the times.
7. *Adultery is becoming the one corrupting sin.*—Mark 8:34-38.
The sin of lust is damning people.
Adultery is in the forefront.
Married people are given to it.
8. *Selfishness will make people blind to opportunities to do good.*—Matthew 25:41-46.
People do not care for their neighbors.
They do not inquire into how people are getting along
The Christ lives on earth yet today.
The Lord our God is an Event-predicting God.

LORD'S DAY BIBLE CLASS LESSON, SEPTEMBER 18th.

The Millennial Reign of the Christ.

1. *It will be given over to the destruction of evil.*—Matthew 13:36-43.
Everything that offends must come out.
His pure eye sees every sin.
The Devil will not then hold sway.
2. *The Word of Power will smite evil-doers.*—2 Thessalonians 1:6-12.
Sinners will then be judged.
Nations will also be judged.
The Wicked will be smitten with Truth.
3. *The City of God will be no place for evil-doers.*—Revelation 21:22-27.
No wicked thought will enter there.
No unrighteous deed can there be done.
Every hateful thing will be shut out.
4. *The time will be taken up with judgment and subduing enemies.*—1 Corinthians 15:24-28.
Every enemy must be put down.
His reign is for this purpose.
He has power to enforce righteousness.
5. *All who love iniquity will fall.*—Psalm 45:1-11.
The Sword of Truth will rule.
Sinners will fall under the sway of Truth.
Men must worship only God.
6. *The people who then fall into sin will be cursed for it.*—Isaiah 65:17-25.
Men cannot sin and escape.
People who live right will not die.
All who persist in sin will find no mercy.
7. *The confederated kings and their subjects will fight against the Lord.*—Zechariah 14:1-11.
The nations will fight the Christ.
The Lord will dash nations to pieces and make a new nation.
The Christ will then be supreme.
8. *Everything must yield to the Christ, and those who kiss Him will find salvation.*—Revelation 11:15-18.
Every Kingdom shall be the Christ's.
His power enables Him to take all His own.
He will then give honor to all who serve Him.
God's Holy People are a Sin-destroying People

EXCURSION TO ZION CITY

REV. JOHN ALEXANDER

DOWIE

(Elijah the Restorer)

General Overseer of the Christian Catholic Church in Zion, will preach, God willing,

Lord's Day Afternoon, August 28

At 2:30 o'clock in Shiloh Tabernacle

And expects to preach every Lord's Day thereafter until further notice

Special trains will be run each Lord's Day until Christmas, leaving the Chicago and North-Western Wells Street Depot at 11:30 and 11:45 a. m. and will return about 6:30 to 7:30 p. m.

OBEYING GOD IN BAPTISM.

"Baptizing Them Into the Name of the Father and of the Son and of the Holy Ghost."

Nineteen Thousand Seven Hundred Forty-two Baptisms by Triune Immersion Since March 14, 1897.

Nineteen Thousand Seven Hundred Forty-two Believers have joyfully followed their Lord in the Ordinance of Believer's Baptism by Triune Immersion since the first Baptism in Central Zion Tabernacle on March 14, 1897.

Baptized in Central Zion Tabernacle from March 14, 1897, to December 14, 1901, by the General Overseer	4754			
Baptized in South Side Zion Tabernacle from January 1, 1902, to June 14, 1903, by the General Overseer	37			
Baptized at Zion City by the General Overseer	583			
Baptized by Overseers, Elders, Evangelists and Deacons, at Headquarters (Zion City) and Chicago	5283			
Total Baptized at Headquarters				10,657
Baptized in places outside of Headquarters by the General Overseer		765		
Baptized in places outside of Headquarters by Overseers, Elders, Evangelists and Deacons		7732		
Total Baptized outside of Headquarters				8,497
Total Baptized in seven years and three months				19,154
Baptized since June 14, 1904:				
Baptized in Zion City by the General Overseer	64			
Baptized in Zion City by Elder Royall	11			
Baptized in Zion City by Elder Hammond	6			
Baptized in Zion City by Overseer Mason	90			
Baptized in Zion City by Overseer Excell	87			
Baptized in Zion City by Overseer Piper	79			
Baptized in Zion City by Elder Mercer	2			
Baptized in Zion City by Elder Dinius	4			
Baptized in Zion City by Elder Cossum	5			
Baptized in Zion City by Elder Gay	2			
Baptized in Chicago by Elder Hoffman	4			
Baptized in Chicago by Elder Cossum	7			
Baptized in Chicago by Elder Keller	5			
Baptized in Chicago by Elder Hall	3			
Baptized in Chicago by Elder Hammond	1		370	
Baptized in Canada by Elder Brooks		6		
Baptized in Canada by Elder Simmons		5		
Baptized in California by Elder Taylor		9		
Baptized in England by Overseer Cantel		41		
Baptized in England by Deacon Hall		1		
Baptized in Indiana by Elder Osborn		2		
Baptized in Iowa by Elder Hoy		2		
Baptized in Michigan by Elder Reed		4		
Baptized in Minnesota by Elder Graves		5		
Baptized in Minnesota by Elder Simmons		3		
Baptized in Mississippi by Evangelist Gay		1		
Baptized in Mississippi by Elder Hall		3		
Baptized in Missouri by Evangelist Gay		1		
Baptized in Missouri by Elder Brock		9		
Baptized in Missouri by Deacon Robinson		1		
Baptized in Nebraska by Elder Hoy		7		
Baptized in New York by Overseer Mason		9		
Baptized in Ohio by Deacon Kelchner		3		
Baptized in Ohio by Deacon Arrington		5		
Baptized in South Africa by Overseer Bryant		74		
Baptized in Tennessee by Elder Hall		2		
Baptized in Texas by Evangelist Gay		11		
Baptized in Washington by Elder Ernst		11		
Baptized in Wisconsin by Elder McClurkin		3	218	588
Total Baptized since March 14, 1897				19,742

The following-named twenty-five believers were baptized at Johannesburg, Transvaal, South Africa, Lord's Day, July 17, 1904, by Overseer Daniel Bryant:

Benton, Ostle Boaz, 15a Nursery road, Fordsburg, Johannesburg, Transvaal, South Africa
Bold, John Hurst, Doornfontein Station, Doornfontein, Johannesburg, Transvaal, South Africa
Butler, Arthur Charles, 49 Macintyre street, Jeppestown, Johannesburg, Transvaal, South Africa
Cowie, Isabella, corner Marshall and Eloff streets, Johannesburg, Transvaal, South Africa
Daly, Friedrich Henri, National Bank of South Africa, Limited, Johannesburg, Transvaal, South Africa
Daniel, Caroline Susan, 8a Biccard street, Braamfontein, Johannesburg, Transvaal, South Africa
Daniel, Estella Hilda, 8a Biccard street, Braamfontein, Johannesburg, Transvaal, South Africa
Gault, James.....Postoffice Box 92, Johannesburg, Transvaal, South Africa
Hendricks, James Charles, No. 3 Error street, Doornfontein, Johannesburg, Transvaal, South Africa
Lamb, Walter, California House, Frederick street, Johannesburg, Transvaal, South Africa
Mackenzie, Sophia Louisa, 128 Eloff street, Johannesburg, Transvaal, South Africa
Magagula, Samuel,....................Swaziland, Transvaal, South Africa
Masimula, Aaron..............Wakkerstroom, Transvaal, South Africa
McLoughlin, Rosetty Elizabeth, 49 Macintyre St., Jeppestown, Johannesburg Transvaal, South Afzica
McNeilage, Mrs. S. M., 195 Main street, Johannesburg, Transvaal, South Africa
Nkosi, Solomon..................Walkerstroom, Transvaal, South Africa
Sangwayo, Josia..................Walkerstroom, Transvaal, South Africa
Sangweni, Abel........................Volksrust, Transvaal, South Africa
Smith, Thomas Charles, 106 Anderson street, Johannesburg, Transvaal, South Africa
Thomson, James, 128 Marshall street, Johannesburg, Transvaal, South Africa
Thomson, Mrs. Janet, 128 Marshall street, Johannesburg, Transvaal, South Africa
Uridge, Harry A. U., 24 Bergsma building, Johannesburg, Transvaal, South Africa
Uridge, Mrs. May Violet Daisy, 24 Bergsma building, Johannesburg Transvaal, South Africa
Van Aswegen, Ada Margaret, 42 Kock street, Doornfontein, Johannesburg, Transvaal, South Africa
Van Aswegen, Marguarite Louisa, 42 Kock street, Doornfontein, Johannesburg, Transvaal, South Africa

The following-named two believers were baptized at Rock Creek, Tipton, Iowa, Monday, August 1, 1904, by Elder Charles A. Hoy:

Brown, Mrs. Ella V.......................................Tipton, Iowa
Brown, Hamlin C...Tipton, Iowa

The following-named believer was baptized at Nelson, British Columbia, Canada, Friday, August 12, 1904, by Elder R. M. Simmons:

Cranston, James R......................Nelson, British Columbia, Canada

The following-named four believers were baptized at Albert Canyon, British Columbia, Canada, Monday, August 15, 1904, by Elder R. M. Simmons:

Brill, Richard Samuel...............Revelstoke, British Columbia, Canada
Carlson, Mrs. Ida Charlotte.........Revelstoke, British Columbia, Canada
McIntosh, Donald.................Revelstoke, British Columbia, Canada
McMahan, Mrs. Henrietta.........Revelstoke, British Columbia, Canada

The following-named two believers were baptized at Toronto, Ontario, Canada, Wednesday, August 17, 1904, by Elder Eugene Brooks:

Shields, Louis Franklin.......86 Maitland street, Toronto, Ontario, Canada
Wilkins, William.............................Branchton, Ontario, Canada

The following-named two believers were baptized at Zion City, Illinois, Wednesday, August 17, 1904, by Elder William D. Gay:

Saller, Henry.........................2719 Elim avenue, Zion City, Illinois
Williams, Miss Mary...................................Lost Nation, Iowa

The following-named three believers were baptized at Meridian, Mississippi, Lord's Day, August 21, 1904, by Elder Lemuel C. Hall:

Glenn, William Washington, Paulding and Forty-fourth avenue, Meridian, Mississippi
Newman, Mrs. Mary Ann, Sixteenth avenue and Fourteenth street, Meridian, Mississippi
Newman, William Anderson, Sixteenth avenue and Fourteenth street, Meridian, Mississippi

The following-named two believers were baptized in Lake Michigan, Zion City, Illinois, Tuesday, August 23, 1904, by Elder W. O. Dinius:

Gratz, Charles...Noel, Missouri
Gratz, Mrs. Eliza..Noel, Missouri

CONSECRATION OF CHILDREN.

The following-named thirteen children were consecrated to God, at Spokane, Washington, Lord's Day, August 7, 1904, by Elder August Ernst:

Beckett, Alice..................709 Pittsburg street, Spokane, Washington
Beckett, Isabelle Serena........709 Pittsburg street, Spokane, Washington
Beckett, Mary...................709 Pittsburg street, Spokane, Washington
Hill, Freiddi ....725 Walnut street, Spokane, Washington
Hill, Daniel ....725 Walnut street, Spokane, Washington
Hill, Albert......................725 Walnut street, Spokane, Washington
McKee, Glenwood Fey........317 Fairview avenue, Spokane, Washington
Miloradovich, Emily Frieda .....1129 Third avenue, Spokane, Washington
Pease, Mary Ellen..................S. 127 G street, Spokane, Washington
Pease, Grace Mary..................S. 127 G street, Spokane, Washington
Pease, Gladstone Leonard ....S. 127 G street, Spokane, Washington
Pease, Virginia Esther.............S. 127 G street, Spokane, Washington
Pease, Francis See.................S. 127 G street, Spokane, Washington

The following-named child was consecrated to God, Lord's Day, August 7, 1904, by Elder C. A. Hoy:

Stried, Gladstone Oscar ....Marcus, Iowa

The following-named child was consecrated to God, Monday, August 15, 1904, by Elder R. M. Simmons:

McMahan, Lloyd..................Revelstoke, British Columbia, Canada

The following-named two children were consecrated to God, in Chicago, Illinois, Lord's Day, August 21, 1904, by Deacon B. W. Brannen:

Johnson, Hilda Josephine......864 N. Springfield avenue, Chicago, Illinois
Johnson, Lillian Gertrude......864 N. Springfield avenue, Chicago, Illinois

A Man's Hand

Was about the size of the cloud first seen coming out of the west when Elijah the Tishbite prayed after three and one half years of drouth. It spread and increased and there was sound of abundance of rain.

Only a short time ago a real hand was seen coming up out of the west and there began to be sound of abundance of rain again.

This hand also grew in its far-reaching influence and the showers of blessing have been falling.

The deaf hear, the blind see, the lame walk, the poor hear good tidings of the Savior and the coming of God's Kingdom, all in answer to the definite prayer, "In the Name of the Lord Jesus, in the Power of the Holy Spirit, in Accordance with the Will of God our Heavenly Father."

Through this hand showers are refreshing and bringing life into business industries and institutions which are a blessing to all the earth.

These copious, Spiritual showers are collecting and uniting in their onward flow and we behold the streams of Shiloh flowing.

These streams are flowing to the uttermost parts of the earth, and wherever

Leaves of Healing

go, and the voice of Rev. John Alexander Dowie is heard, those who are glad recipients are cleansed in these streams and receive grace to be good, and obtain peace and joy in their hearts, which is the Kingdom.

We desire that **Leaves of Healing,** and other Zion literature, be rapidly extended. We therefore wish to draft in every reader of this page to help extend the circulation. Can you send us one new subscription for one year for $2.00, six months for $1.25, or three months for 75 cents? If you will, next week our readers will number twice the present list.

Remember Our Inducement—They that turn many to righteousness shall shine as the stars forever and ever. . . . .

What can we depend on you for today

ADDRESS ALL ORDERS TO

Zion Printing and Publishing House, : : Zion City, Illinois

A WEEKLY PAPER FOR THE EXTENSION OF THE KINGDOM OF GOD
EDITED BY THE REV. JOHN ALEX. DOWIE.

Volume XV. No. 20. *ZION CITY, SATURDAY, SEPTEMBER 3, 1904.* *Price Five Cents*

GOD'S WITNESSES TO DIVINE HEALING.

HEALED WHEN DYING; ALSO HEALED OF RUPTURE OF THIRTY-ONE YEARS' STANDING.

CONFESS THEREFORE YOUR SINS ONE TO ANOTHER, AND PRAY ONE FOR ANOTHER, THAT YE MAY BE HEALED.

God's Covenant of Healing is unmistakable in its straightforward plainness.

He says, "If thou wilt diligently hearken to the Voice of Jehovah thy God, and wilt do that which is right in His eyes, and wilt give ear to His commandments, and keep all His statutes, I will (permit to be) put none of the diseases upon thee which I have (permitted to be) put upon the Egyptians: for I am Jehovah that healeth thee."

Upon certain conditions, God Covenants to keep His people free from disease.

These conditions are expressed in four clauses, every one of which signifies Obedience to the Law of God.

And every sickness and every disease is traceable to disobedience.

Sometimes the obedient have to suffer as the result of the sins of the disobedient; but failure to keep the Law of God is always the cause of bodily affliction.

Disobedience to God is Sin.

Every intelligent and logical person will agree that the way to remove any effect is, first of all, to remove its cause. The way to get rid of disease is to get rid of its cause—Sin. Sin is put away by Repentance, Confession, and Forgiveness. The natural inclination of every human heart that seeks to be rid of sin is to repent, confess, and ask forgiveness. This is also the teaching of the Word of God.

MRS. HEDWIG ALBACH.

The teaching of the Apostle James is therefore the logical conclusion of God's Covenant of Healing.

He says, "Confess therefore your sins one to another, and pray one for another, that ye may be healed."

Sin having been put away by Repentance and Confession, healing comes from God in answer to prayer.

God is the Creator of the human body.

He alone understands it.

He alone can heal it when it becomes diseased.

He not only is able to heal; but He is willing.

In the Covenant which we have quoted, He says, "I am Jehovah that healeth thee."

He also says, "I, Jehovah, change not."

When He was on earth in the flesh, in the person of Jesus, the Christ, He "went about . . . healing all manner of disease and all manner of sickness among the people." When the leper said to Him, "If Thou wilt, Thou canst make me clean," His reply was, "I will; be thou made clean."

That "I will," is His reply to every one who fulfils the conditions of the Covenant, and forever settles the question as to His willingness to heal.

He "is the same yesterday and today, yea and forever."

He is with us "All the Days, even unto the Consummation of the Age;" for that is His promise.

Hence, "the healing of His seamless dress is by all beds of pain," and we may "touch Him in life's throng and press, and be made whole again."

We rejoice that this is true.

It is a joy to know that it is not a mere theory; but that it is the precious experience of tens of thousands of God's children who are very real, healthy, present-day facts.

The aged but very happy and bright saint of God whose face smiles out from our first page, tells a wonderful story of the Healing Power of God in her body.

At the age of seventy-six years, she was dying.

She made Confession, in Repentance.

She looked to God in Faith.

God's minister prayed for her "in the Name of the Lord Jesus, in the Power of the Holy Spirit, and in accordance with the Will of God, her Heavenly Father."

God's conditions were fulfilled.

There could be no failure on His part.

She was immediately healed.

At another time, God quickly healed a rupture from which she had been suffering for thirty-one years.

It is a simple, straightforward story.

It is told with a ring of absolute truthfulness, and yet without the slightest trace of cant or fanaticism.

It is like the stories of healing as told in the New Testament.

There is no loud acclaim, such as a sensation-loving world might expect in the recounting of the working of a miracle.

The promise of God is so sure, and the conditions are so plainly set forth, that it seems nothing wonderful when the miracle follows the fulfilling of the conditions.

It is accepted with joyous gratitude; and yet with the perfect, quiet simplicity of a child who receives a promised gift from a loving father.

Oh, that thousands of God's children, now in the horrid, galling bondage of disease, would learn, from the story of this Witness, to look, in childlike, confident Faith, to their Heavenly Father, who has promised the blessing, and longs to bestow it!

A. W. N.

TESTIMONY OF MRS. HEDWIG ALBACH, WRITTEN BY HER DAUGHTER.

2819 EMMAUS AVENUE,
ZION CITY, ILLINOIS, August 4, 1904.

BELOVED GENERAL OVERSEER:—Two years ago, mother came to Zion City to live.

She came into fellowship with the Christian Catholic Church in Zion three and a half years ago.

She said that she could not help but trust Jesus as her Healer when she saw what He did for me almost six years ago, when He healed me of a tumor and of nervous prostration.

Mother is seventy-six years old.

She was raised a Lutheran, but did not know Jesus as a personal Savior until fourteen years ago, when she was converted at home.

She then associated herself with the Methodist Episcopal Church at Asbury, near Carbondale, Kansas.

One false teaching we received in the Methodist Church was that God sent diseases upon us for our good and chastening, and to draw us nearer to Him.

This was one hindrance to mother's faith.

But the first time she had to go to God for healing after her arrival in Zion City, she learned by her own personal experience, as well as from God's Word, that the Devil, not our kind and loving Heavenly Father, is the author of sickness and disease.

Although receiving the light in her old age, mother has a spiritual insight into God's Word which has enabled her to step out on His promises and to obey joyfully as the light has come to her.

Her life is a joy and blessing to us, and her heart is full of praise to God that He has led her to see the glorious truths of the Gospel, for spirit, soul, and body.

She loves you, General Overseer, for helping her to understand the Scriptures and for leading people out of their ignorance of God's Word into the blessed Light.

She longs to see every one forsaking sin and accepting Jesus as his Healer, Keeper, and Cleanser, especially those near and dear to her

It is with this desire in her heart that she wishes to give her testimony to help others to know God, our Father, as she knows Him to be a God of love, able and willing to look after our bodily as well as our spiritual needs.

She has learned how closely these are associated. When we are right with God, and living up to our privileges in the Christ, our bodies are sound.

Last Autumn, mother allowed Satan to get in by making her angry with one whom she knew had sinned against God.

She had not then learned to distinguish between the sin and the sinner.

We are taught in Zion to love the sinner and hate his sins.

Because she was angry, she went by herself and sat in a room where there was no fire.

She took a cold.

It kept growing worse until she became bedfast.

By the end of a month of illness, she and we saw that healing must come speedily, or she would pass away.

During this time prayer was answered to the extent that she was relieved from pain each time, but complete deliverance did not come.

From a human standpoint, mother could not live much longer.

She made all arrangements she thought necessary for her burial.

She preferred to be laid away in Mount Olivet, Zion City cemetery, although in Kansas there is a tombstone erected to father's and her memory, and a place for her remains beside his.

Her reason for this was because this ground has been consecrated to God.

Through sadness at the thought of losing our dear mother, Satan succeeded a number of times in making me look away from God.

But I soon saw through his device and knew I must never give up, if I would be any help to mother in getting the victory.

Satan tried to make mother think she had lived out her life, and it was all we could do to help her get rid of such thoughts; for we knew, and finally she saw, that if God wanted her to come home to Him, He would not use the Devil's methods, by making her sick, but it would be her privilege to fall asleep as when taking her rest.

When we had done all we could in pointing her to God, I sent a message to you to come if you could to see mother, and pray for her.

Then mother began to search her heart, for she knew that she would be healed when you prayed for her if there was no hindrance in her own life.

She said to me, "Louisa, I know of only this that could stand between me and God." Then she related how she had become angry with the one who had done wrong and was unkind at times.

She was repentant.

I told her that this was enough to hinder the blessing, and that since she now repented and vowed to ask forgiveness, that God would accept that until she had the opportunity to make things right.

I assured her that the General Overseer was praying for her.

It was then that she could rest in God.

The healing came at once.

Our hearts were filled with joy, and together we praised God for what He had done.

We thank you now for praying for her at that time.

The next day she was up, and regained her strength rapidly.

Just a month ago mother was healed of rupture of thirty-one years' standing.

Elder Adams was used of God in helping her to see that she was not too old to be healed of that.

When he prayed the Prayer of Faith, and laid hands on her in Jesus' Name, she was healed.

We rejoice in God for that.

In her old age she is bringing forth fruit unto righteousness.

Mother sends out this testimony with a prayer that God may be glorified in it, and that your life may be spared in this work of Restoration, until He comes.

Gratefully yours in the Christ,
DEACONESS LOUISE ALBACH,
for MRS. HEDWIG ALBACH.

ELIJAH THE RESTORER.

A WEEKLY PAPER FOR THE EXTENSION OF THE KINGDOM OF GOD.

EDITED BY THE REV. JOHN ALEX. DOWIE.

Application for entry as Second Class Matter at Zion City, Illinois, pending.

Subscription Rates.		**Special Rates.**	
One Year	$2.00	100 Copies of One Issue	$3.00
Six Months	1.25	25 Copies of One Issue	1.00
Three Months	.75	To Ministers, Y. M. C. A's and Public Reading Rooms, per annum	1.50
Single Copies	.05		

For foreign subscriptions add $1.50 per year, or three cents per copy for postage.

Subscribers desiring a change of address should give present address, as well as that to which they desire LEAVES OF HEALING sent in the future.

Make Bank Drafts, Express Money or Postoffice Money Orders payable to the order of JOHN ALEX. DOWIE, Zion City, Illinois, U. S. A.

Long Distance Telephone. *Cable Address "Dowie, Zion City."*

All communications upon business must be addressed to
MANAGER ZION PUBLISHING HOUSE,
Zion City, Illinois, U. S. A.

Subscriptions to LEAVES OF HEALING, A VOICE FROM ZION, and the various publications may also be sent to

ZION PUBLISHING HOUSE, 81 EUSTON ROAD, LONDON, N. W., ENGLAND.

ZION PUBLISHING HOUSE, NO. 43 PARK ROAD, ST. KILDA, MELBOURNE, VICTORIA, AUSTRALIA.

ZION PUBLISHING HOUSE, RUE DE MONT, THABOR 1, PARIS, FRANCE.

ZIONSHEIM, SCHLOSS LIEBBURG, CANTON THURGAU, BEI ZÜRICH, SWITZERLAND.

ZION CITY, ILLINOIS, SATURDAY, SEPTEMBER 3, 1904.

TABLE OF CONTENTS.

LEAVES OF HEALING, SATURDAY, SEPTEMBER 3, 1904.

EDITORIAL NOTES.

"MANY SHALL RUN TO AND FRO,
AND KNOWLEDGE SHALL BE INCREASED."
(Daniel 12:4.)

THIS ISSUE OF LEAVES OF HEALING is sent forth at the beginning of the Eleventh Year of the establishment of Zion Printing and Publishing House.

WE CELEBRATED our Tenth Anniversary last Wednesday evening, August 31st, in Shiloh Tabernacle, Zion City.

A report of the proceedings appears in our issue of this date, pages 683 to 688, to which we direct the attention of our readers.

"WHAT HATH GOD WROUGHT?"

NO EARTHLY pen can write; no human tongue can ever tell the Workings of God all over the earth through the four hundred thirty-nine million ten thousand (439,010,000) pages of Zion Literature which have gone forth to every Continent of the earth during the last ten years.

ON JULY 18, 1894, we had less than Three Hundred Dollars ($300) in hand for printing purposes.

Six weeks after that date, on August 31, 1894, we had purchased and paid for a small plant costing Three Thousand Dollars ($3,000).

Ten years have passed away, and we now have a Plant acknowledged to be among the best of its kind, completely paid for, worth Two Hundred Fifty Thousand Dollars ($250,000).

It will be seen, therefore, that the Value of the Plant in Ten Years has increased by Eighty Times—from Three Thousand Dollars ($3,000) to a Quarter of a Million Dollars ($250,000).

THE GROWTH of Zion Printing and Publishing House during the last three years has been very great.

THREE YEARS ago we told the story of Zion Printing and Publishing House at very considerable length, in Volume IX., Number 19, dated August 31, 1901, on pages 582 to 606.

COMPARISON OF our Editorial Notes of that date, and of the facts set forth in the Special Article to which we have just referred, with the statistics herein given, will show the wonderful progress made within the three years.

AT THAT DATE, about One Hundred Fifty Million (150,000,000) pages of Zion Literature had been sent forth within the previous Seven Years.

At this date, three years later, nearly Four Hundred Fifty Million (450,000,000) pages have been sent forth—an increase of Two Hundred per cent.

OUR GERMAN EDITION, BLATTER DER HEILUNG, has now a very large circulation in America, and in German-speaking countries.

OUR FIRST issue of a French Edition, FEUILLES DE GUERISON, is now being prepared, and we hope to publish it on Saturday, October 1st.

MUCH PRINTING has been done in many languages, and Special Editions of Zion Messages, etc., are now being prepared for Europe and other Continents.

THE TOTAL number of Separate Pieces of Zion Literature sent out in these Ten Years is at least Twenty-five Million.

These have probably reached more than Two Hundred Million (200,000,000) people.

ZION RESTORATION HOST has gratuitously distributed within two years Seven Million Three Hundred Sixty-eight Thousand Four Hundred Forty-seven (7,368,447) Pieces of Literature, each accompanied with the spoken words of the Restorationist: "Peace Be to This House."

THE ZION SEVENTIES, which preceded the organization of the Host, distributed an immense number of pieces, probably bringing up the entire distribution of these organizations to at least Nine Million pieces, in the homes of the people all over the world.

IT IS probable that not far from a Hundred Million people were reached by these pieces of Literature left in the homes.

WHO CAN TELL what God hath wrought by these agencies?

The pages of LEAVES OF HEALING, from week to week, during the ten years of its existence, record that many tens of thousands of persons were blessed in spirit, soul, and body, through the agency of the LEAVES.

A mighty work of Salvation, Healing, and Holy Living has resulted all over the earth; and it continues to go on in ever-widening cycles of Divine Power.

WE EARNESTLY desire our friends in all the lands to redouble their exertions in getting annual subscriptions for LEAVES OF HEALING.

If all were to do this, by simply either increasing their own subscriptions to two copies yearly, or getting a friend to subscribe for another copy, we could easily reach a Subscription List of One Hundred Thousand Copies a Week, within the present year.

This, by the blessing of God, we hope to do.

BRETHREN, PRAY FOR US.

Warning to Subscribers.

Scarcely a week passes that we do not have complaints about money having been sent to us in currency, stamps, or silver, in the open mails, for renewals of subscriptions or for other purposes, WHICH WE HAVE NOT RECEIVED AND WHICH NEVER REACHES US.

Therefore, we desire to warn every member and friend of Zion sending money to us, to always use some safe means, preferably a money-order, or bank-draft on New York or Chicago, or personal check on Zion City Bank.

In conforming to this notice you will save yourselves trouble and expense, and us much annoyance.

ZION PRINTING AND PUBLISHING HOUSE,
Zion City, Illinois.

Street Addresses Are Necessary.

All Zion City Subscribers to *Leaves of Healing*, *The Zion Banner*, *Blätter der Heilung*, and *Voice from Zion*, whose correct street addresses are not positively known to be in our possession should send them to us AT ONCE. Please act upon this notice without delay as it is very important, now that we have postal delivery service, that the exact location of each and every subscriber be known to us. Write your name and address very carefully, designating also to what periodicals you are a subscriber and leave at your very earliest opportunity at our branch Publishing House on Elijah Avenue.

Very Sincerely Yours,
ZION PRINTING AND PUBLISHING HOUSE.

ELIJAH THE RESTORER SHOWS A PHASE OF THE CHRISTIAN FIGHT.

ABOVE all the crashing tumult and turmoil of strife between nations, races, and classes; above the shrieks of the wounded and the groans of the dying on international and industrial battlefields, and the wailing of countless widows and fatherless, in palace, cottage and hovel, the Prophet of God hears one clear, unmistakable "still, small Voice."

Outshining all the false lights of man-made theology; brighter than the feeble phosphorescence of decay emitted by the fallen church; and clearer than the lurid flames of the torches of organized lawlessness, he sees in the heavens the pure, serene ray of the Promised Sign.

That Voice declares the approaching Consummation of the Age

That Promised Sign signifies that the Day of Full Redemption draweth nigh.

With a deep humility but unfaltering courage, the Prophet, standing where his voice rings forth to all the ends of the earth, proclaims that the King is at the very doors, and warns all His people to be ready to meet Him.

It is a call to wakefulness and vigilance.

It is a call to righteousness and purity.

It is a call to work.

About six thousand people had gathered in Shiloh Tabernacle Lord's Day afternoon, July 31, 1904, when the Prophet of God uttered this momentous Message.

It was Scriptural, spiritual, and intensely practical.

It reached up to the very Throne of the Most High for its inspiration.

It reached around this world and into eternity in its scope, and it reached down into the common affairs of every day life in its application.

Speaking from the text, Luke 21:28, "But when these things begin to come to pass, look up, and lift up your heads; because your Redemption draweth nigh," God's Messenger declared that only the wakeful, the watchful, the pure, the active, would be ready when that Day of Redemption dawned.

He struck the keynote of the high importance of that preparation when he declared that he would rather lose all the choir, officers, and people that had gathered around him, and begin anew, than to go into the coming fight with an army of slothful, cowardly, unclean, and unprepared soldiers.

There was a triumphant note of certain victory in his voice, however, as he expressed his belief that he did have an army, most of whom were ready for the conflict.

His warnings to any who might not be ready, however, were very severe, but, by the power of the Spirit, very effective.

It was with very deep earnestness and sincerity that the thousands present stood and repeated the solemn, heart-searching prayer of consecration.

A wonderfully moving part of this never-to-be-forgotten service was the humming of "Bethany," by Zion White-robed Choir, with harp accompaniment by Mrs. Linval Justen Hire.

As the well-known strains of the beautiful music of the hymn, "Nearer, My God to Thee," went up like the breathing of a prayer, a deep hush fell over the great congregation, and many eyes filled as from their spirits there went up that petition—"Nearer to Thee."

Although the day was peculiarly oppressive, and notwithstanding the fact that no excursion had been advertised, a goodly number of people came out from Chicago and from other cities to attend this service.

Shiloh Tabernacle, Zion City, Illinois, Lord's Day Afternoon, July 31, 1904.

The services were opened by Zion White-robed Choir and Zion Robed Officers entering the Tabernacle, singing as they came the words of the

PROCESSIONAL.

Go forward, Christian soldier,
  Beneath His banner true;
The Lord Himself, thy Leader,
  Shall all thy foes subdue.
His love foretells thy trials;
  He knows thine hourly need;
He can with bread of heaven
  Thy fainting spirit feed.

Go forward, Christian soldier,
  Fear not the secret foe;
Far more o'er thee are watching
  Than human eyes can know.
Trust only Christ, thy Captain;
  Cease not to watch and pray;
Heed not the treach'rous voices
  That lure thy soul astray.

Go forward, Christian soldier,
  Nor dream of peaceful rest,
Till Satan's host is vanquished
  And heav'n is all possessed;
Till Christ Himself shall call thee

*The following report has not been revised by the General Overseer.

To lay thine armor by,
And wear in endless glory
The crown of victory.

Go forward, Christian soldier,
Fear not the gathering night;
The Lord has been thy Shelter;
The Lord will be thy Light.
When morn His face revealeth,
Thy dangers all are past:
Oh, pray that faith and virtue
May keep thee to the last!

At the close of the Processional the General Overseer came upon the platform, the people rising and standing with bowed heads while he pronounced the

INVOCATION.

God be merciful unto us and bless us,
And cause Thy face to shine upon us;
That Thy Way may be known upon earth,
Thy Saving Health among all the Nations,
For the sake of Jesus. Amen.

PRAISE.

The Congregation then joined in singing Hymn No. 207:

The Lord's my Shepherd, I'll not want
He makes me down to lie
In pastures green: He leadeth me
The quiet waters by.

The General Overseer then led the Choir and Congregation in the recitation of the Apostles' Creed:

RECITATION OF CREED.

I believe in God, the Father Almighty,
Maker of heaven and earth:
And in Jesus, the Christ, His only Son, our Lord,
Who was conceived by the Holy Ghost:
Born of the Virgin Mary;
Suffered under Pontius Pilate;
Was crucified, dead, and buried:
He descended into hell,
The third day He rose from the dead;
He ascended into heaven,
And sitteth on the right hand of God, the Father Almighty;
From thence He shall come to judge the quick and the dead.
I believe in the Holy Ghost;
The Holy Catholic Church;
The Communion of Saints;
The Forgiveness of Sins;
The Resurrection of the body,
And the Life Everlasting. Amen.

The General Overseer then led the Congregation in repeating the Commandments; after which the words, "Lord, have mercy upon us, and write all these Thy Laws in our hearts, we beseech Thee," were chanted.

READING OF GOD'S COMMANDMENTS.

I. Thou shalt have no other gods before Me.

II. Thou shalt not make unto thee a graven image, nor the likeness of any form that is in heaven above, or that is in the earth beneath, or that is in the water under the earth; thou shalt not bow down thyself unto them nor serve them: for I, Jehovah, thy God, am a jealous God, visiting the iniquity of the fathers upon the children, upon the third and upon the fourth generation of them that hate Me, and showing mercy unto thousands of them that love Me and keep My commandments.

III. Thou shalt not take the Name of Jehovah thy God in vain; for Jehovah will not hold him guiltless that taketh His Name in vain.

IV. Remember the Sabbath Day, to keep it holy. Six days shalt thou labor and do all thy work; but the seventh day is a Sabbath unto Jehovah thy God: in it thou shalt not do any work, thou, nor thy son, nor thy daughter, thy manservant, nor thy maidservant, nor thy cattle, nor thy stranger that is within thy gates; for in six days Jehovah made heaven and earth, the sea, and all that in them is, and rested the seventh day: wherefore Jehovah blessed the Sabbath Day and hallowed it.

V. Honor thy father and thy mother; that thy days may be long upon the land which Jehovah thy God giveth thee.

VI. Thou shalt do no murder.

VII. Thou shalt not commit adultery.

VIII. Thou shalt not steal.

IX. Thou shalt not bear false witness against thy neighbor.

X. Thou shalt not covet thy neighbor's house, thou shalt not covet thy neighbor's wife, nor his manservant, nor his maidservant, nor his ox, nor his ass, nor anything that is thy neighbor's.

Hear also what our Lord Jesus, the Christ, the Son of God, hath said, which may be called the Eleventh Commandment:

XI. A New Commandment I give unto you, that ye love one another; even as I have loved you, that ye also love one another.

The great Choir then sang the

TE DEUM LAUDAMUS.

We praise Thee, O God; we acknowledge Thee to be the Lord.
All the earth doth worship Thee, the Father Everlasting.
To Thee all Angels cry aloud, the Heavens and all the powers therein.
To Thee Cherubim and Seraphim continually do cry:
Holy, Holy, Holy, Lord God of Sabaoth,
Heaven and earth are full of the majesty of Thy Glory.
The glorious company of the Apostles praise Thee.
The goodly fellowship of the Prophets praise Thee.
The noble army of martyrs praise Thee.
The Holy Church throughout all the world doth acknowledge Thee,
The Father of an Infinite Majesty;
Thine Adorable, True, and Only Son;
Also the Holy Ghost, the Comforter.
Thou art the King of Glory, O Christ;
Thou art the Everlasting Son of the Father.
When Thou tookest upon Thee to deliver man,
Thou didst humble Thyself to be born of a Virgin;
When Thou hadst overcome the sharpness of death,
Thou didst open the Kingdom of Heaven to all believers.
Thou sittest at the right hand of God in the Glory of the Father.
We believe that Thou shalt come to be our Judge.
We therefore pray Thee, help Thy servants,
Whom Thou hast redeemed with Thy precious blood.
Make them to be numbered with Thy saints in glory everlasting.
O Lord, save Thy people and bless Thine heritage;
Govern them and lift them up forever.
Day by day we magnify Thee;
And we worship Thy Name ever, world without end.
Vouchsafe, O Lord, to keep us this day without sin.
O Lord, have mercy upon us, have mercy upon us.
O Lord, let Thy mercy be upon us as our trust is in Thee.
O Lord, in Thee have I trusted, let me never be confounded.

The General Overseer read the Scripture lesson, in the Gospel according to Luke, the 21st chapter, beginning with the 1st verse:

And He looked up, and saw the rich men that were casting their gifts into the treasury.

And He saw a certain poor widow casting in thither two mites.

And He said, Of a truth I say unto you, This poor widow cast in more than they all:

For all these did of their superfluity cast in unto the gifts: but she of her want did cast in all the living that she had.

God Blesses Every Act of Consecration.

I wonder if any of us imagine that she lost anything; if the God, who saw her loving gift, suffered her to want?

Certainly not.

I never knew one to consecrate all to God without sooner or later receiving back in abundance all that was needed.

The General Overseer then read on through the 24th verse, and commented as follows:

Notice that it is just at this point that the whole scene changes.

And they shall fall by the edge of the sword, and shall be led captive into all the nations: and Jerusalem shall be trodden down of the Gentiles, until the times of the Gentiles be fulfilled.

The Christ, who has been talking about events that were to occur prior to and at the time of the siege of Jerusalem, and the destruction and scattering of the nation, which happened within forty years after the time at which He was speaking, now utters another and totally different prophecy.

It is a Latter Day Prophecy.

He had spoken of events that were to happen in the immediate future, within the lifetime of the people to whom He was talking; and now He begins to forecast the Times of the End—the Times in which we live, the Times in which the "Times of the Gentiles" shall be fulfilled, when the Times of the Restoration of All Things shall have come.

And there shall be Signs in sun and moon and stars; and upon the earth distress of Nations, in perplexity for the roaring of the Sea and the Billows;

Men fainting for fear, and for expectation of the things which are coming on the world: for the powers of the heavens shall be shaken.

The Hosts of Evil Spirits Are to Be Shaken.

It seems to me that that has reference to the powers of which e apostle speaks when he says, "our warfare is not against sh and blood, but against the principalities, against the wers, against spiritual wickedness in high places"—which is ore properly translated "against the hosts of evil spirits in e upper air," or in the heavens.

The "hosts of evil spirits" shall be shaken.

There is no doubt that the elemental power of the Devil and his angels is very, very great.

It seems to me as if this earth, for a number of hours, had en whirling through an exceedingly unhealthy and miserable ne—as if we had come for a few hours, where there was considerable amount of Devil around.

There were hours today, and on each of the last few days, en there was a stifling condition of air that rendered it rrible to breathe—conditions that were exceedingly trying health.

Evil Atmospheric Conditions from the Devil.

These conditions are not from God.

These conditions are from the Devil.

Every evil and every bad thing is from the Devil.

You may see from the book of Job what a tremendous emental power the Devil had when he brought that storm om the wilderness—that stifling heat, and awful gloom, and ror.

The lightnings flashed, the thunders rolled, and the tempest ote the house, and brought it down; and all Job's family re crushed to death beneath it.

The Bible says distinctly that it was the Devil who got up at storm.

Jesus, the Christ, recognized that the Devil was the origi-tor of disastrous storms.

Once, when on the sea, a great storm arose while He was eeping; the Devil being determined, if it were possible, to nd Him and all the apostolic college to the bottom of the a.

The Christ continued to sleep; the storm continued to rage; d these men who were accustomed to the sea became rrified.

It took a good deal to terrify fishermen that were customed to that little inland sea; but they were terrified.

The Master was in danger, and they were going to the ttom.

Surely the boat could not live.

They woke Him and said, "Master, carest Thou not that perish?"

He told them that they had very little faith to think that ey could be with the Christ in the boat, and perish.

Jesus Rebukes the Winds and the Waves.

You remember what He did?

He rose and said, "Peace! be still!"

He rebuked them.

He would never have rebuked the winds and the waves if ey had been doing God's Will.

He rebuked the winds and the waves, because they had been ing the Devil's work; and He stopped it!

Many a time I have been at sea and I have prayed that the ord would kindly step in and rebuke the waves, or that He ould step in and lift the fog, lest our vessel should run the rocks that were near; and again and again there has en immediate deliverance from danger.

The elemental conditions are oftentimes so terrible that they ive people to insanity and to suicide.

It is not altogether a question of oppressive atmospheric nditions.

It is a question of penetration into the body of minute and numerable evil influences that pertain to the atoms that nstitute the air.

The heart gives way, and men faint or expire from very fear, d from horror of the conditions that surround them.

Think of these conditions as continuing for a little while, d you can easily see that all inhabitants of the earth might sappear.

The Master is saying that there will also be "Signs in the n, and moon, and stars; and upon the earth Distress of ations, in perplexity for the roaring of the Sea and the llows."

Striking Fulfilments of Prophecy.

In recent times, in the Island of Martinique and down in the Caribbean Sea, the sea has been stirred up and vessels have been lost; hurricanes have come, and tidal waves, and even fire has burst from volcanic mountains, utterly destroying them; perhaps in half a minute the whole population of a large city and an island has been destroyed.

The Master is speaking about such events as these.

> And then shall they see the Son of Man coming in a cloud with Power and Great Glory.
>
> But when these things begin to come to pass—

That is, before they have come to pass.

When you see the beginning of these things—"distress of nations" and "perplexity for the roaring of the sea and the billows"—look up! Look beyond them! "Lift up your heads; because your Redemption Draweth Nigh."

The very thing that shall be the terror of the heathen and the ungodly, and of those that have no confidence in God, shall cause you to say "Hallelujah! The Lord is at hand! Redemption draweth nigh!"

May God bless His Word!

The General Overseer then continued:

A Zion Messenger from China Welcomed.

During the Feast we had many brethren and sisters from many parts of the earth, and we had some of our own people who had come home from distant fields of ministry. Among these was the Rev. Carl F. Viking, who had been our Messenger, with his good wife, in Shanghai, China, about four years.

I know that we shall all say from the heart, "Welcome, in the Name of the Lord."

PEOPLE—"Welcome in the Name of the Lord!"

GENERAL OVERSEER—I ask him to pray.

We are delighted to see him.

He has done very excellent work; work of a kind that we have not been willing to talk very much about; because, in regard to the Chinese and Japanese work we are pursuing, I hope, a Divine policy, and preparing for that work in a careful manner.

I am very glad that Elder Viking has been preserved amid the perils of residence in those countries where so often disease abounds; where the native population is so horribly poor and disgustingly dirty that working amongst them is a very serious matter.

Our brother inhaled the bad air of closely-confined rooms in Shanghai, and now and then we had to send him off to Japan, to rest.

Pray this afternoon for Elder Kennedy and Evangelist Kennedy, who are holding the fort in Shanghai.

Preparations for Larger Operations in China.

I pray God to bless our brother in his rest, and that you will all pray for him that he may get strong again.

He is very eager to get to work.

Some of our people need the bridle, and others need just a little of the whip.

I would not wish to sit behind a horse that had to be whipped all the time.

I do not want to be associated with people who have to be whipped into service.

Prayer was offered by Elder Viking, the General Overseer following with special prayer for the sick and leading in the chanting of the Disciples' Prayer.

After the announcements and the singing of an Anthem by the Choir while the tithes and offerings were being collected, the General Overseer delivered his Message:

"YOUR REDEMPTION DRAWETH NIGH."

INVOCATION.

> Let the words of my mouth and the meditation of my heart be acceptable in Thy sight, be profitable unto this people, and unto all to whom these words shall come, in this and every land, in this and all the coming time, Till Jesus Come. Amen.

The words about which I wish to speak are in the 21st chapter of the Gospel according to Saint Luke, the 28th verse:

But when these things begin to come to pass, look up, and lift up your heads; because Your Redemption Draweth Nigh.

An Eventful Week.

The week which has just closed has been one of the most eventful weeks of this year.

As far as I can see, the prophecy which I delivered sometime before the beginning of the war between Russia and Japan, is coming to pass with a rapidity and an exactness which is very marvelous.

The downfall of the empire may take place, literally, in a day.

When the second French empire fell, in our own time, it was literally in a day.

When the Battle of Sedan had been fought, and the French Emperor, Napoleon III., with a great army had surrendered, the empire fell in Paris with a crash.

I foresee that the rapidity with which the dissolution of the Russian empire is taking place is one of the Signs of the Times of which we have been reading in those solemn words of the Lord.

Surely these things have begun to come to pass, and are coming to pass with terrible rapidity.

A Terrible Retribution.

Last week, in St. Petersburg, Von Plehve, the minister of the interior—the man next in power to the Emperor of all Russia—was assassinated while on his way to the Peterhof palace, to report to the Emperor.

It is asserted that on Wednesday night last some one said to him, "You are looking very serious."

"Yes," he replied, "I am thinking of my visit to the Emperor tomorrow. On other days of the week the assassin can not be sure where to find me; but on that day I drive publicly through the streets to the Peterhof, and they know where to find me."

Although surrounded by his body-guard, and followed by secret service officers on bicycles, he was killed.

Even though he is dead, let the truth be spoken.

When I talked with the Russian noble lady of whom I spoke to you a week or so ago, I told her to tell Mr. Von Plehve, that the facts were now too well known to allow of any doubt as to who was at the bottom of the Kishinef massacres, and that God would require it at his hands.

Those horrible massacres in Bessarabia!

Those horrible things that have been done to those in Russia, besides the Jews, that wanted civil and religious liberty!

I said to her some very plain words.

The assassin threw his bomb, and the poor wretch, Von Plehve, was ushered into eternity in a moment.

His horses, wounded and bleeding, dashed off, only to fall dead a few steps distant.

His coachman was shattered to pieces; and he himself, with face mutilated beyond recognition, and limbs torn from his body, lay in a pool of blood on the street.

A Tragedy that Shocked Europe.

That tragedy has shocked Europe; and the Empire of Russia has received a heavy blow.

It followed many assassinations of Governors of Provinces in Russia.

The Nihilists followed one statesman to Bern, where he was murdered in the streets.

Within an hour or two after Von Plehve was murdered, Muravieff, the minister of Justice, driving to the Peterhof, to officially inform the Emperor of the death of Von Plehve, was stoned in his carriage and narrowly escaped with his life.

I have often asserted that the people of Russia are against that war with Japan.

This military and ecclesiastical autocracy has shadowed the world, and has made men to fear and dread its increasing power.

I knew that when Russia reached the warm waters of Asia, the feet of clay would be washed away, and that the Colossus would fall on its face; and it has.

To vary the figure, the Bear put to sea and the Swordfish stabbed him everywhere; and the blood of that Bear is crimsoning the ocean and dyeing the Peninsula of Liaotung.

Men's Hearts Failing Them for Fear.

The hearts of men that are at the head of government a failing them for fear, and the Sea and the Billows are roarin

The people will stand it no longer to be driven as dur cattle to fight over quarrels that are not their own, and to d on a thousand battlefields.

We look with horror upon a Von Plehve lying dead in t street; but do not forget the Jews who lay murdered in t streets of Kishinef, in Bessarabia.

All over the earth thrones are reeling.

The German emperor can keep his throne only by practica having an army in Berlin.

It is not possible for any king or emperor today to be su whether the morning may not show a revolution.

If the endeavor of Russia to embroil France, Englan Germany, and perhaps other nations in one common war, whi is perilously near, is effective, the people will have somethi to say about it.

We are living in perilous times.

These are the times when Zion's War must go forward.

> Each breeze that sweeps the ocean
> Brings tidings from afar,
> Of nations in commotion,
> Prepared for Zion's War.

An Able Business Man's Testimony.

My Message to you and to Zion this afternoon is, Prepar

I was speaking yesterday to a gentleman who is said to many times a millionaire.

He was kind enough to make certain very large busine proposals to me, and, after he had finished, I spoke to hi very earnestly on getting ready to meet God.

He spoke very loving words concerning Zion.

That man has been a citizen of Chicago for more than fif years, and in business for nearly half a century.

He is a man of great intellectual vigor, and spends a gre part of every year in foreign lands.

Looking at me very intently, yesterday, he said, "Wh peace! What good order! What a wonderful City! I trav all over the earth. I see great cities and little ones; bu Doctor," he continued, "there is no city like this."

Referring to the economic conditions of the City, he sai "It seems to me that you have solved every problem. Th happy faces and lives of your people is evidence that you ha solved the problem of religion. The economic problem fin solution in a well-ordered series of factories, where you simp have to go forward on the lines that you have established, an you will be able, in some things, to command almost the who trade of the land." Continuing, he said, "I feel that it is th work of a master mind, and I congratulate you."

The Kingdom and the Glory Are God's.

I immediately responded, "The Master Mind is not mine. am the servant of the Master Mind. The Master Mind God's, and it is He that hath wrought this, and it is He alor that can give me strength to maintain it, and purify it, an keep it, and do all that you say. But the Master Mind is God

If our Redemption in Zion is nigh, and if we are to be fitte for the translation to that City beyond the sky, it will only b by the Master Mind of the Master Himself—by His Spi giving us the Mind of Himself, the Christ.

God only can help us overcome, and enable us to be amo those that stand in the white garments of Purity and Holines having our loins girded and our lamps burning, wakeful, an bright, whether He comes at morning, noon, or night; an ready for the Master's Call.

That Call is not far away.

It may be that the twenty years for which I have asked w not be granted; I cannot tell.

Coming Years Will Pass Quickly.

If the twenty years are granted, they will pass quickly.

The work to be done in these twenty years is so great th one might think of it as the work of two hundred years, an more.

It can be done; but it can be done only by a people who a pure in spirit, soul, and body, redeemed, and waiting for th fulness of their redemption.

If the midnight cry were to come tonight, would you b ready?

I regret to think that even in Zion City there may be five foolish and five wise; that half of this people may be left to pass through the Tribulation.

I shall not hesitate to do my duty.

I shall do my duty if I have to strip the robes off half my Officers and half my Choir, and purge the roll of members.

I am not a shepherd of goats.

God made me a shepherd of sheep, and I refuse to shepherd goats.

The General Overseer Is Not Faint-hearted, and Will Go On.

I do not despair.

I never despair.

You may go out of Zion, or you may have to be put out, but I cannot go out.

I have to stand here.

Whoever may leave, I dare not leave.

I will not leave.

I go on, for all the responsibilities of this work find their center in myself.

Prosperity is the hardest of all things to bear; and I warn you not to think that because God has blessed you, and has given you great spiritual and other privileges, that now you can afford to be careless.

I tell every mother; I tell every father; I tell every youth; I tell every maiden; I tell every singer and player on instruments; I tell every officer that "Perpetual Vigilance is the price of safety."

Above all things, Watch!

Watch, lest you stumble and fall.

I say this, because it is given me to lead a little band to victory.

I will not have a band with cowards, thieves, sloths, harlots, whoremongers, and other wicked people in it.

"Redemption Draweth Nigh!"

Now, brace up; clean up; get vigilant; clean up everything, from your front teeth to your back yard.

That is a comprehensive injunction.

Clean Up If It Costs You Your Life.

Clean up, and keep clean.

I do not want to see Shiloah Tabernacle built, if unclean hands are to build it.

I do not want to see Zion City grow, if it is to be a compound of half Devil and half God, which means almost wholly Devil.

I did not come to do that work.

I came to have a place, every foot of which should be for God.

Stop your wicked gossiping!

Stop your criticisms of one another!

Stop your jealousies!

God's "fan is in His hand, and He will thoroughly purge His threshing floor."

He will make ready for the harvest that is to come in, and to be threshed out.

"Redemption Draweth Nigh"—I wish it would come!

I could wish, but for your sakes, that I might now pass into the fulness of that Redemption; but it cannot be so.

I have to bear my share in this great Restoration.

I cannot throw it off; and I have nothing to live for but the Restoration of All Things.

The Nations are "in perplexity." The churches have failed.

Their prayers are not answered.

They are singing Te Deums, and each asking the same God to help them cut one the other's throat successfully.

Zion the Only Hope of the World.

Zion, with her Message of the Gospel of Peace, and her declaration that the King is coming, and the getting of His people together for His coming, is the only Power and Hope there is in the world for its Redemption.

I begin to see these things, and already I look up.

I lift up my head, and I say, "Hallelujah! My sorrow will soon be gone!

"Hallelujah! The night is far spent!

"The day is at hand!

"Hallelujah! Redemption Draweth Nigh!"

I am glad that it is near, and that the day is coming when—

> My wearied arm shall cease its strife,
> And my heart shall cease its sorrow,
> And the night of life be changed
> For the night of the endless morrow.

Master, I look up!

Master, I lift up my head!

Master, the Redemption is drawing nigh.

Get my people ready, that when it comes they shall not be shut out.

PRAYER OF CONSECRATION.

My God and Father, in Jesus' Name, I come to Thee. Take me as I am. Make me what I ought to be in spirit, in soul, and in body. Give me power to do right. Take every bit of falsehood out of my heart; every impurity; all laziness; all cowardice; all meddlesomeness. Help me to be a true man; a true woman; a true youth; a true maiden; a true child of God; and give to the General Overseer the strength that he needs; the grace that he needs, to lead on in the Restoration until the Redemption is complete. For Jesus' sake. Amen.

GENERAL OVERSEER—Did you mean that?

PEOPLE—"Yes."

GENERAL OVERSEER—Then live it!

After the Recessional, the General Overseer offered the

CLOSING PRAYER.

Our Father, in Thy great compassion, bend a pitying eye upon us. Thou knowest that we are dust; and Thou dost not forget these bodies; but we are Thy children—Thine offspring. We belong to Thee, O God. We came from Thee. Redemption is our portion. Oh, continue that redeeming work in us all, until spirit, soul, and body are redeemed; until the fulness of Redemption shall be our portion. And let us be ready. Bless these words to earth's remotest bounds. For Jesus' sake. Amen.

The service was closed with the

BENEDICTION.

Beloved, abstain from every form of evil. And may the very God of Peace Himself sanctify you wholly. And I pray God your whole spirit, and soul, and body be preserved entire, without blame, unto the coming of our Lord Jesus, the Christ. Faithful is He that calleth you, who also will do it. The grace of our Lord Jesus, the Christ, the love of God, our Father, the fellowship of the Holy Spirit, our Comforter and Guide, one Eternal God, abide in you, bless you, and keep you, and all the Israel of God everywhere, forever. Amen.

RESTORATION MESSAGE NO. 94.

*REPORTED BY S. E. C., O. R., A. C. R., AND A. W. N.

It was a glimpse of the Unseen World that God's Prophet gave his audience in Shiloh Tabernacle, on Lord's Day afternoon, August 14th, 1904.

Unseen but very real; more real than the seen!

The Message was not that of a fanatic, a mystic, a visionary dreamer, or a Spiritualist.

While deeply spiritual, and while dealing with matters which were hidden from all but those whose spiritual eyesight was keen, the General Overseer was calm, practical, sane, and logical.

The Message, like all his utterances, was based upon the plain teaching of the Word of God, delivered under the guidance and inspiration of the Holy Spirit, in answer to prayer.

The Messenger of God spoke with the assurance and confidence born of rich personal experience.

To him, again and again, in his life of sacrifice, toil, and danger, the Unseen Legions of the Heavenly Hosts, and the Warning Voices of Ministering Spirits, had been intensely real in their presence and protection.

While portions of the Message were to be understood more from the spirit of the speaker than from the words that he spoke—for the thought that he wished to convey was too deep for words—there were other passages that were clear and simple; so plain that even the little children could understand and receive blessing from them.

There were words, also, that were full of the deepest and tenderest pathos, melting all hearts in sympathy and love.

As a whole, the Message was powerful in drawing the people of Zion together and toward God, awakening in many a heart a more earnest desire to become spiritually purer and stronger

*The following report has not been revised by the General Overseer.

that the Unseen World—that which is the most important and the most real, especially in these closing days of the Dispensation—might be more clear to their spiritual vision.

The General Overseer made, as a prelude to this Message, a brief appeal to Zion for increasing honesty and courage in dealing with the Word of God, calling particular attention to the fact that, contrary to the evident opinion of the majority of Christians, the lives of the Bible characters were not recorded as examples of infallible virtue and wisdom.

He also contended that the epistle to the Hebrews, from which he read, was not written by the Apostle Paul, and that, while it was an Inspired Writing, and full of beauty and power, it was not necessarily of Apostolic Authority.

In these matters the man of God was followed closely by the people, who heartily accepted his teaching.

The day was a perfect one except for a trifle too much heat, and a large number of people from Chicago and other cities were present.

During the offering, Deaconess Harriet Ware sang very effectively, the beautiful old hymn, "I Love to Tell the Story."

Shiloh Tabernacle, Zion City, Illinois, Lord's Day Afternoon, August 14, 1904.

The service was opened with the Processional, sung by Zion White-robed Choir and Zion Robed Officers.

At the close of the Processional, the General Overseer came upon the platform, the people rising and standing with bowed heads while he pronounced the

INVOCATION.

God be merciful unto us and bless us,
And cause Thy face to shine upon us;
That Thy Way may be known upon earth,
Thy Saving Health among all the Nations;
For the sake of Jesus. Amen.

The Congregation then joined in singing Hymn No. 128, in Gospel Hymns, "Hark, hark! my soul! angelic songs are swelling," after which the General Overseer led the Congregation in the recitation of the Apostles' Creed, the Choir singing the responses.

The General Overseer then read, very impressively, the Eleven Commandments, the Choir and Congregation reverently singing the response "Lord, have mercy upon us, and incline our hearts to keep this law."

This was followed by the singing by the Choir of the glorious "Te Deum Laudamus."

The General Overseer then said:

Let us read in the Inspired Word of God, in the epistle to the Hebrews, the 1st chapter.

Paul Did Not Write the Epistle to the Hebrews.

I think I ought to say something concerning the erroneous title of this epistle.

It is headed, "The Epistle of Paul the Apostle to the Hebrews."

There is not a fragment of authority for that heading.

All the epistles of Paul have the opening salutation, "Grace to you and Peace from God the Father and our Lord Jesus, the Christ."

If you look over the epistles, you will find that that is, in substance, almost without exception, the salutation.

That salutation is not in this epistle, nor is there a single reason to suppose that Paul wrote it.

His name does not appear in one of the ancient manuscripts.

I think that no manuscript of this epistle of earlier date than the thirteenth century bears his name.

The great commentators have been divided in opinion as to who wrote this epistle.

Among the most learned of these, in recent times, is Dean Alford, and he is in doubt as to its authorship.

He suggests, I think, five or six different possible authors, and, while he closes by saying that in all probability Apollos was the author, his opinion is simply speculation.

It is a great epistle, but it is not written in Paul's peculiar style of writing.

Paul was especially the Apostle to the Gentiles, not to the Jews.

The writing of this epistle would have been foreign to his great ministry and work.

The Epistle to the Hebrews Not of Apostolic Authority.

This epistle ranks very high in the glorious measure of its inspiration; but I will say now what I believe and what I have believed for many years, that it is not an Apostolic Epistle.

It has no Apostolic Authority, and one may safely differ from some statements of the author.

In the Gallery of Faith, for instance, after naming many noble men of faith, he says:

Time will fail me if I tell of Gideon, Barak, Samson, Jephthah; of David and Samuel, and the prophets.

I am very glad time did fail him, because I have the most supreme contempt for the character of Samson—a dirty, vile dog of a man who went into that "Valley of Sweet Wine" and disgraced his God by becoming drunk, and laying his head upon the lap of an adulterous woman.

Well did he deserve that his hair should be cut off, and that he should lose his strength and be forsaken of God.

I do not see why he should have been put into this Gallery of Faith.

We do well not to discuss David; because, while he was a good young man, he was a very bad king.

He did some of the vilest and most shameful things.

I venture to say that we have a right to judge men by their records.

This epistle is essentially a Hebrew production, and the writer thought every man that was great and powerful ought to go into that Gallery of Faith.

I am glad he did not discuss some of them.

Abraham Not Always an Example of Honorable Conduct.

It is he that makes the assertion that it was God who directed Abraham to murder his own son, which statement, as you know, I have controverted.

If God did that, He broke His own commandment, which says, "Thou shalt do no murder."

If He told Abraham to commit a cruel and shameful murder and then told him not to do it, as many believe, He repented between the bottom and the top of a hill.

God did no such thing.

If God told Abraham to kill his own son, He meant him to do it.

Abraham was living in bad company at that time.

He had been doing bad things.

He had been telling shameful lies.

He had been telling King Abimelech that Sarah, his wife, was his sister, in order to save his own skin.

He had said, "You are so beautiful, Sarah, that Abimelech will murder me if he thinks you are my wife."

Sarah was taken to the harem of the king because of Abraham's cowardice.

She very nearly fell into the hands of Abimelech, and it was not Abraham's interference that saved her from being defiled.

I have a very poor opinion of Abraham for that.

A man that would sneak behind his wife's petticoats to save his life is no man at all.

The Bible Records Much That Is Nonsensical.

There are many things in the Bible that I do not believe.

I read chapter after chapter containing conversations between Job and his three friends.

It is one mass of nonsense.

God rebuked Job for what he said.

Who is this that darkeneth counsel
By words without knowledge?

Job put his hand upon his mouth and said:

I have uttered that which I understood not,
Things too wonderful for me, which I knew not.

As for his three friends, they talked nonsense in a score of chapters.

God, the Almighty, said that they would have to repent of it and get Job to pray for them; that he was right with Him.

Why were these things written?

For our instruction.

There is no more instructive book in the Bible than the nonsense of Job and his three friends.

It is the kind of nonsense that people utter in all ages, and for which God has to rebuke them: the nonsense of trying to make God the Author of their miseries, when the Devil is responsible for all evil.

That is the point in the Book of Job.

Prophetic and Apostolic Authority Are to Be Accepted.

Wherever God speaks by prophet or apostle, it is your duty and mine to receive it, and obey.

Many things that are not of apostolic authority are a great blessing; and this epistle, in many parts, is able, pious, and wonderful in its inspiration.

In no part is it more beautiful than in the words that I shall read.

It is conceived in the highest style of Grecian thought, mingled with all the majesty of the Hebrew mind.

I am charged by many with being unorthodox in this matter.

I believe in the Inspiration and Infallibility of the Word of God, but I do not believe that we should talk of something as the Inspired Apostolic or Prophetic Word of God which has no such authority.

Bibliolatry Not a Part of Zion's Creed.

If any one believes that the Bible is to be treated as if it were a book to be worshiped, then I am not with him.

Bibliolatry never formed a part of my creed.

Much of its history has a use, but it is not profitable for continuous reading.

We have the clear Inspiration of the New Testament, and we do not need to stumble along in the darkness and semi-darkness of the Old Testament.

I do not worship the Truth of God.

I worship the God of Truth.

I will not pin my faith to books or words.

We are not saved by believing that this epistle was written by Paul; and we are not saved by believing that the Gospels were written by the men whose names are attached to them.

In reading the Word of God we must be honest with ourselves, with our consciences, and with God.

God does not want us to believe lies.

That Bible was not written to praise Abraham, David, or Solomon.

It tells when they were good, and when they were bad.

I am required only to accept the facts and the truth as they are presented, and I do accept them.

The Abomination of Hero Worship.

The Lord Jesus, the Christ, is the only man that, from the cradle to the grave, was Infallible.

The time has come to talk straight out against ridiculous hero worship.

It has become such an abomination that one cannot talk truthfully regarding any man without getting into trouble.

If I were to tell you the truth about George Washington—even what he says about himself in his diary—I would be considered unpatriotic.

He was nearly always in trouble with Congress about his wine bill or something of that kind.

George Washington bought and sold slaves, but he was a a great man; and God made him a mighty deliverer of this country.

Let us have sound sense.

This Bible has passed through many hands in coming to us down through the ages, and there are necessarily some errors.

I greatly love this epistle, and while it is not Paul's writing, and not apostolically or prophetically canonical, it is a great epistle and has great truths in it.

I think these first chapters are wonderfully beautiful.

Let us read the first chapter:

And of the angels He saith—

One of the great beauties of this epistle is the stringing together of pearls taken from the Word of God—these beautiful quotations.

The General Overseer then read, without further comment, to the end of the chapter.

Prayer was then offered by Elder Dietrich, followed by the General Overseer in supplication for the sick, after which the Choir and Congregation joined with him in chanting the Disciples' Prayer.

Deaconess Harriet Ware then gave an effective rendering of "I Love to Tell the Story."

The General Overseer then delivered his Message:

MINISTERING SPIRITS.

INVOCATION.

Let the words of my mouth, and the meditation of my heart, be acceptable in Thy sight; be profitable unto this people; and unto all to whom these words shall come, in this and every land, in this and all the coming time, Till Jesus Come. Amen.

The General Overseer then said:

It is written in the 11th verse of the 91st Psalm:

TEXT.

He shall give His angels charge over thee.

In the Epistle to the Hebrews, the 1st chapter, and the 14th verse, it is written:

Are they not all ministering spirits, sent forth to do service for the sake of them that shall inherit Salvation?

The Holy Spirit the Only Safe Guide.

I am opposed to modern Spiritualism.

I am opposed, also, to putting myself under the guidance of any other spirit than the Spirit of God.

I believe that modern Spiritualism is diabolical, for the most part.

It is genuinely wicked, in many cases.

Often it is shameful imposture.

But I have seen, and know, too much of what may be called spiritual phenomena not to be deeply impressed with the fact of its reality.

At one period of my life I gave this subject much attention.

It is a subject which, if touched at all, requires an exceedingly careful use of language, lest there be misunderstanding.

I therefore introduce what I have to say by these explanatory words.

Evil Spirits Control Many Rulers of Empires.

I believe, in fact I know, that large numbers of potentates of the world are being led by evil spirits.

Those who know anything of Oriental lands, understand that the potentiality of evil spirits is a very direct factor in all Oriental governments, especially in those among the Mongolian peoples.

The governments of China, Japan, Korea, and other countries of the Mongolian tribes, are absolutely controlled by alleged revelations from spirits.

The late Emperor Napoleon III., like his great uncle, Napoleon I., was continually misled by spirit mediums.

In this country there has been so much of this wickedness that godly men are unwilling to speak concerning Angelic Ministrations lest they be classed with Spiritualists.

Great and glorious truths have often been lost or put aside, because of wicked perversions of truth.

I plead guilty, in common with others, to the fact that I have said much less concerning Angelic Ministration than I would have said had it not been for the danger of seeming to give countenance to modern Spiritualism.

There Are Many Kinds of Spirits.

In speaking of the Ministration of Spirits, one has to remember that there are many kinds of spirits in the spirit world, as there are many kinds of spirits on this earth.

Doubtless spirits in heaven are as diverse in individuality as we are upon earth.

They are led and guided by God Himself into fellowship with each other, very much as we are.

God, who has redeemed our spirits by the precious blood of Jesus, the Christ, His Son, is bringing into union with each other in Zion at this period of the world's history, large numbers of earnest people of the same spiritual affinities.

They are in accord with the spiritual nature of their leader.

That, of course, is to be expected, because the Holy Spirit works in an intelligent and orderly manner.

Even the Rebellious and Sinful in Zion Have no Quarrel With the General Overseer.

The trouble is their sinfulness.

I often notice how willing they are to obey even when the penalty of disobedience comes sharply upon them.

Some of these spiritual beings kept their first estate, and never fell.

Some lost their first estate, and fell.

Some spirits of men on earth have been redeemed from the power of sin, and disease, and death, and hell, and are now glorified beings in heaven.

These spirit beings include those Seven Spirits before the Great White Throne, of whom we know so little.

Possibly the perfect number seven, as applied to them, represents very exalted spiritual nature.

What a great place these Seven Spirits have!

John to the seven churches which are in Asia: Grace to you and peace, from Him which is and which was and which is to come; and from the Seven Spirits which are before His Throne.

And from Jesus, the Christ, who is the Faithful Witness, the Firstborn of the Dead, and the Ruler of the Kings of the Earth.

The remarkable thing about this prelude is that the Seven Spirits are placed around the Eternal God.

They are not spoken of as being partakers of His Godhead.

They are clearly spoken of as being partakers of the Divine Nature, as we all are who are the offspring of the Father of Spirits.

But they are, in a very high degree, partakers of the Divine Purity and Power, being the immediate Ministers of the Eternal God.

It Is Easier to Understand Than to Explain Spiritual Realities.

How little we know of these Seven Spirits!

It is almost impossible to put into words the little that some of us know.

It is much easier to understand it without words than with words.

We have no words to express the psychical embodiment of beings who have Spiritual and Celestial Bodies, and who need no clothing, either of earthly garments, or of flesh.

They are clothed with bodies that are incorruptible; that are spiritual; that are celestial; that are like unto the Christ's glorious body, which is a pattern of ours that shall be.

That I may put in order some thoughts on this subject, I remind you that the Bible is full of instances of Angelic Ministration.

I use the word "angelic" in a Scriptural sense. The angels are messengers of God.

These messengers may be embodied as we are, or they may be embodied in spiritual bodies.

This afternoon I feel led by God's Spirit, to talk to you, and to those to whom these words may come, concerning the great part that spirits from God's presence have always taken in the affairs of men, and which they will take increasingly as the Dispensation closes.

The Chariots of Heaven are Swinging Low.

The Hosts of Heaven are very near.

They are coming nearer all the time, ready to take their part in the Consummation of the Age.

It is for this reason that I deliver this first discourse upon the "Ministration of Spirits."

When the world was born, the Morning Stars sang together and all the Sons of God shouted for joy.

In these words there is a glorious and wonderful thought regarding heavenly music.

What a wonderful Oratorio!

An Oratorio by angels from all the heavens!

The first thing we hear about them is that they came with songs.

So many times in this world's history, have they come with songs!

When the Christ was born at Bethlehem, there was one that led a Heavenly Host in song.

There was a great company of the Heavenly Host to sing, "Glory to God in the highest: on earth Peace to men of good will."

That was a glorious song.

It seems to me that the language of the Heavenly Host is music.

I know it is, for I have heard it.

No words that you may utter, no song that you may sing, no chord that you may strike, in this life, can equal in inspiration the music of that Heavenly Choir.

A Beautiful, Illustrative Legend.

The ancients had a legend that when Orpheus played, all nature gathered around him, and was at peace, while his beautiful song floated over the mountains, and rivers, and valleys.

Stone came to stone, and great and majestic temples were built under the inspiration of his songs.

The fact is greater than that.

When men have reached an understanding of the tongues of angels, they will find that these Angelic Voices have no such clumsy modes of expression as human language.

They will find that the deep things of God, the things that touch the deepest springs of the human heart, are the songs without words.

I have long thought, and I think now, that the Zion of God should be filled with the spirit of Divine song.

Not until the King has come and the Thousand Years of the Restoration have begun, will we fully understand the power of song.

But even now, if these lips and these vocal chords are touched with Holy Fire, the songs of Zion will do something that has not yet been done.

I have seen some signs of this, already.

The Power of Spiritual Services in Zion Illustrated.

During the New York Visitation a very worldly but very beautiful and highly educated society lady begged to see me.

She burst into tears and said, "Oh, I want to see your face. Your words have come into my heart. I do not think I would have listened to them had not a friend asked me to come and see your children."

Then she described how sweetly they behaved.

"And then I thought I would like to hear them sing, and I came last night. O Doctor," she said, "there is something about your Choir, there is something about that Processional, that takes hold of one's heart. I could do nothing but cry."

She continued, "If all New York and America could see and hear you and your Choir, you would win, hands down."

There was something in our music that she could not express in words.

She said, "I found myself singing 'Ten Thousand Times Ten Thousand,' over and over again last night.

The power of our songs was such that one of the most cultivated ladies in this country has not been able to get away from it.

"They that Be Wise Shall Shine as the Stars."

These morning stars that sang together were spiritual beings, for "they that be wise shall shine as the brightness of the Firmament; and they that turn many to Righteousness as the Stars forever and ever."

In this world great prima donnas are called "stars."

In some instances, they are stars of great brilliancy.

There is no mistaking them.

They may be naughty and sinful, but there is a diamond-like purity about their music that makes one know that they are indeed stars.

Oh, that we might win them for God!

How often have I coveted the musical stars!

Not that we are without those that can sing, for we have the Spiritual Song in Zion.

Music does not appeal to some people.

They have no ear for music.

Color does not appeal to some people.

They are color-blind.

Red, green, and other beautiful shades of color have no attraction for them.

I am not one of that kind.

The tones in music, and shades in color, and brilliancy in jewels have a wonderful power over me.

The City of God has Twelve Precious Stones for foundations.

The walls are of jasper; the streets are of gold; and the gates are of pearl.

You may say, "Oh, that is figurative."

Then the reality must be even better and more magnificent than precious stones.

The Brilliancy of Person of Spirits.

One of the beautiful things about spiritual beings is that the brilliancy of their person is in the blending of all the colors, which makes a pure white.

A pure white is the blending of every color.

If we were to make this Tabernacle dark, and let light pass into it through a prism, you would see the many colors, separated by the prism, of which white light is composed.

One star differs from another star in color.

The metal that predominates in any star may be determined by the color of the light from that star.

There is something in spiritual bodies which answers to these colors.

The blending of all colors means pure, dazzling white.

The Great White Throne is a combination of all colors.

The nature, the robing, the living, and the expression of these spiritual beings, is like the glorious majesty of Him who is the embodiment of all Beauty, of all Purity, of all Glory, and of all Power.

Let the Beauty of God be upon us as we contemplate this wonderful theme of spirit life!

Mind and Thought May Have Spiritual Color.

What is it that makes it possible for me to impress humanity and to get people all over the world to think as I think?

It is because rays of spiritual color reach the thought and the mind of the people.

It is the spiritual power in the words that makes them attractive.

A man said, "I don't like Doctor Dowie; I don't like his teaching; I am opposed to him, because I am an infidel. But," he continued, "if I listen to him he encircles me with light and color, like a rainbow, and I have to listen; I have to look; I have to think; I have to reason; and, therefore, I read LEAVES OF HEALING; and I see life! life!! life!!!"

When God made this world, He made it beautiful. Color is essential to the highest beauty.

That which is all white or all black, is not particularly beautiful.

Zion has not yet put on her Beautiful Garments.

She is not ready to wear them.

It would be very foolish for us to put on the garments of beauty until we had the beauty in our spirits.

A Wonderful Display of Color.

During our recent journey, when we were passing from Colombo to Aden, there was a succession of sunsets that elicited the admiration of every man, woman, and child on the boat, even the most careless.

From every view point the people would crowd to look at them.

It was a wonderful sight to see those colors chase each other and blend until the western sky was one mass of ever-changing glory.

There were thrones, palaces, and towers—majestic in proportion and indescribable in color.

OVERSEER EXCELL—"It seemed as if we were sailing directly into heaven."

GENERAL OVERSEER—It seemed, as the Overseer has said, when our prow was pointed in the direction of the sunset, as if we were sailing into heaven itself.

You do not know what color is until you have been in the Orient.

If you are very good, I may take you some day.

But God will certainly take you to the better scenes.

Spirits Are More Than Ordinary Embodiments.

When you think of these spirits, you must not think of mere embodiments.

You must think of them as I want you to think of me, as I want you to think of yourselves—as Spiritual Majesties, spiritual beings possessed of tremendous possibilities.

Some of you are very little spirits.

Some people in Zion are mostly belly—mostly passion—mostly of the earth, earthy.

Their spiritual being is comparatively small.

Some of you are all spirit.

I am not speaking of those nervous creatures who are all nerves.

There is no special power in such, unless it be the power of a wicked spirit who plays upon the nerves.

When we are pure—when our eye is single—our bodies will be full of that Light of God which is all Spirit.

An Instance of Spiritual Ministration.

When John, and James, and Peter were on the mountain, the Inner Light shone out, and for a moment they were permitted to see the Transfiguration of the Christ, with Moses and Elijah.

The brightness was so great that they were afraid.

That was spiritual ministration.

That was a manifestation of the Spirit's Power in such a degree that the bodies on that Mount of Transfiguration were full of Light, because they were bodies that could be full of Light.

The Angelic Hosts that are nearing us have never left us.

The angels that sang when the earth was born have been watching over a poor, lost humanity, mourning over its degeneracy and its depravity, and as the appointed ministers of God, ever seeking to guide it.

What wonderful patience they have shown!

I firmly believe that a spirit watched over the embodiment of the spirit of every little child who listens now, and over that of every man and woman here, when they came into the world.

When the Master was on earth, sick children were brought to Him, and He not only suffered them to come, but He said that they were more like the Kingdom of Heaven than any other thing on earth.

Those sweet, little, innocent babes were unconscious of sin.

When speaking of them He said:

> But whoso shall cause one of these little ones which believe on Me to stumble, it is profitable for him that a great millstone should be hanged about his neck, and that he should be sunk in the depth of the sea.

The Angels Grieve Over Sin in This World.

What did He further say?

> Their angels do always behold the Face of My Father which is in heaven.

"Their angels"—the angels that belong to them.

Have you ever thought, dear children, that when you are naughty, you have not only grieved God, but that the beautiful angel who came into mamma's room when God gave you to mamma, and whom God the Father sent to watch over you, is also grieved?

My little daughter, when very young, was once frightened by a naughty servant, and we heard her cry.

The servant had told her that a black man and a dog would go for her if she did not put the blanket over her head and go to sleep.

Then that naughty nurse went away, and when we returned and heard her cry, I said, "Esther, take down the blanket and let me see your face."

"I cannot, papa, there is a black man and a dog there, and wicked spirits."

"There are not," I said; "Papa is here; Jesus is here; and the holy angels are here; take that down."

Presently she took it down.

"There are none, papa?"

"None, dear; it was a wicked lie, Esther. A shameful lie. There are no wicked spirits here; there is no wicked white man nor black man, nor a dog of any kind here; but, Esther, this room is filled with God's Spirit, and with the angels, and with Jesus. He is here."

The tears went, and she looked up and said, "Ah! then that was a wicked lie, was it?"

The tear-stained face brightened, and all the tears were wiped away as we talked to her.

Assurance Inspired by Angels' Presence.

"The angels are looking at me," she said. "Jesus is looking at me. Put out the light, papa;" and out went the light.

She repeated, "Angels are looking at me! Angels are looking at me!" and fell asleep.

The next day the little tot was found searching under the bed, and here, and there; and mamma said to her, "What are you looking for, Esther?"

"I am looking to see if I can find the angels. I can't find Jesus. But I saw angels last night; I saw Jesus."

She sees them now.

She did see them then.

Her eyes were opened, and that room was full of the Light of God; she could tell you about them, too.

Have you ever seen the angels?

Oh, perhaps you have grieved them so that they could not let you see them!

I wonder how many have seen them?

Dear children, this is a very practical thing.

It seems to me that the angels weep when the little feet go astray, and the little hearts are perverse.

As we go away when older, how the angels weep!

Angelic Intervention Has Preserved Life.

I say that it is a very deep conviction of mine, yes, it is within my absolute knowledge, that I have been indebted many times to angelic interventions when I would have been killed.

During storms at sea, many times, I have prayed, and God has sent His angel; and there was peace.

We know not the value of angelic ministration in our ministry of healing.

I know not.

I can only tell you that many of the wonderful healings of which I have known have been in assemblies where some one received the Light, and Life, and Love, and suddenly felt a touch; and all the disease was gone!

Who shall say that that was not an angelic touch—that God did not heal by means of angelic healers?

It would seem that they, through the Holy Spirit in them, became the media of healing power.

At Pentecost, they appeared as Tongues of Fire—thousands upon thousands of holy, angelic ministers.

The Ministry of Angels Will Continue to the End.

My desire is to make clear that ministration by angels, which began at the creation, will go on to the end; and that the hosts of ministering spirits in heaven will attend the Lord, when He descends from heaven with a shout, with the trump of the archangel, and with the Voice of God.

We will need them.

We have hosts of devils to fight—demons in the upper air.

Disease, death, and the powers of hell are all linked together.

Science, falsely so-called, is trying to account for disease by ascribing it to little parasites and microbes.

Lately these scientists have raised the cry that many of these microbes should not be killed, because they are good microbes.

What a farce to pretend to find in minute parasites—unintelligent, wretched, little, filthy parasites—the whole secret of disease!

One might ask the question, "Who gave these parasites birth; and what, after all, are these parasites?"

Everything that is at war with Purity is from the Devil.

Everything That Is at War with Life Is from the Powers of Death.

Everything that is at war with God's creation is the offspring of Evil.

You may call them parasites or demons, but you have practically the same thing.

You have something that takes embodiment in a filthy, and diabolical, and wicked, and diseased body.

Ministering Spirits, also, take embodiment.

The Spirit that was in the Christ Jesus, the Spirit that was in Elijah, the Spirit that was in John the Baptist—that Spirit, that Mind, is here today, a reality.

The Holy Spirit Himself is pleading to get possession of your spirit, your soul, and your body; and myriads of spirits from God are waiting to attend you and bless you.

These ministering spirits are seldom seen, because it takes the spiritual eye to see a spiritual being.

The natural eye cannot see them.

Natural sense cannot perceive their presence.

Behind each one of our natural senses there lies a supernatural sense, a supernatural power to see, to hear, to touch, to feel, to taste, to take.

O taste and see that Jehovah is good.

We have the power to become wholly spiritual beings.

We have an undeveloped spiritual existence, but the spiritual nature is so weak in some people that they do not know that they have spirits.

They know only that they have souls and bodies.

They do not know that the spirit is not the soul and that the soul is not the spirit.

They never knew it, and outside of Zion it is seldom talked about and very seldom understood.

Spiritual Realities Are Not Understood by Many.

Nine-tenths of the people do not understand the things about which I have been talking.

To understand them one must be spiritually acute and have the spiritual senses awakened.

If you are a mass of flesh, and bones, and nerves—simply animal—you cannot understand.

May God help you, and may God help me, and may God help each of us to be a spirit embodied with flesh, and bone, and blood, all of which shall be permeated by the Spirit of God from center to circumference.

Then we will be a power, a wonderful power.

We will be such a power that when people speak of us they will say, "That man, that woman, impresses me. I cannot get away from the glance of that eye; from the word of that tongue; from the impression of that spiritual being."

God grant that we may realize the awakening of our own powers to be in sympathy with this host of blessed spirits that are all around us, and that are ministering to us.

God grant that we may enter into such close alliance with them that, by the Grace and Power of the Spirit of God, we shall be able to battle with the hosts of hell and sweep them before us, everywhere.

I am aiming at that.

Here is an illustration.

How One Young Man's Eyes Were Opened to See.

Elisha, walking up and down the battlements of the little City of Dothan, was apparently utterly regardless of the fact that a vast Syrian host was all about him, thirsting for his blood.

"Alas!" cried his servant; "my master, how shall we do?"

"How is that?" said Elisha.

"Look at the host and look at this little city. Why, they will take us and massacre every one of us!"

"Well," said Elisha to his servant, "do you not know that they that be with us are more than they that be with them?"

I believe the servant thought that Elisha was a little daft, for possibly, there were as many hundreds in the Syrian host as there were persons in Dothan.

"Where are they?" he said, "I do not see them. I cannot understand this kind of talk, my Lord Elisha. I see a great host, and they will murder every one of us."

Great Prayers Are Brief.

Miserable prayers that are not worth a snap of the finger, are lengthy.

They are the prayers of people that howl all night on one subject.

I do not mind all-night prayers if the subject is changed, but some of you have all-night prayers over your own carcasses.

You howl, you do not pray at all.

I have great contempt for that kind of prayer.

Elisha prayed:

Jehovah, I pray Thee, open his eyes, that he may see.

That was all.

That prayer went straight to God, and God gave His prophet what He has so often given to His prophets, a direct answer.

In a moment the natural eyes of the servant were rolled back, and the spiritual eyes saw hosts of chariots and horsemen trooping over the plain, and sweeping around the little City of Dothan, ready to fall, with uplifted sword, upon the Syrian host.

The vision was over in a moment, but the man never forgot it.

People have said, "I cannot understand Doctor Dowie. He does not seem to mind how many are howling in the streets."

No, because I have seen the unseen, and I never trouble.

The innumerable hosts of heaven are with us, as Zion marches forward.

Are they not all Ministering Angels?

What thankfulness we should have to our Father in heaven, and to our Redeemer, who won our Redemption by His blood, that the Gift of the Holy Spirit Himself is ours—that He has opened to us more and more the secrets of the Invisible, and revealed the hosts of heaven!

Have you seen them?

Have you heard them?

No?

Then, beloved, ask God to make you so Pure, so True to Him, that sometime you may see them; that sometime you may hear them.

If you see or hear you will not forget that experience.

All the powers of hell will not efface it.

I pray God that the veil which hides the hosts of ministering spirits shall be removed from before every one of you.

All who desire this stand and join with me in the Prayer of Consecration.

The Congregation rose and joined with the General Overseer in the

PRAYER OF CONSECRATION.

Our God and Father, in Jesus' Name we come to Thee. Take us as we are. Make us what we ought to be in spirit, in soul, and in body. Give to us by Thy grace Purity of being, that lust may be driven away, and that lust may give place to Love that is pure as God is pure; that the powers of hell may give way to the powers of heaven; and that we, led by the Holy Spirit, may see Jesus; may see God in Him; may see the holy angels. In the times of peril, when we know not who is helping us, may we be quite sure that God is helping us, that the holy, ministering spirits are helping us, and that we are protected; that the angels of Jehovah encamp around about us day and night, on sea and on land; in perils known and unknown. We ask this for Jesus' sake. Amen.

The Recessional, "Ten Thousand Times Ten Thousand," was then sung, and the service was closed by the General Overseer's pronouncing the

BENEDICTION.

Beloved, abstain from every form of evil. And may the very God of Peace Himself sanctify you wholly; and I pray God your whole spirit, and soul, and body be preserved entire, without blame, until the coming of our Lord Jesus, the Christ. Faithful is He that calleth you, who also will do it. The grace of our Lord Jesus, the Christ, the love of God, our Father, the fellowship of the Holy Spirit, our Comforter and Guide, one Eternal God, abide in you, bless you, and keep you, and all the Israel of God everywhere, forever. Amen.

Warning.

I am directed by the General Overseer to warn our members and officers throughout the world against giving money to persons claiming to be members of the Christian Catholic Church in Zion. All benevolence must be given either from Headquarters or under the direction of same. Even though the applicant for benevolence be known to be a member of the Christian Catholic Church in Zion, financial aid must not be given except in extreme cases, and then only in small amounts. Requests for help must be made to the officer-in-charge. In cases where there is no such officer, requests should be made direct to Headquarters, accompanied by recommendations from one or two members of Zion in good standing. J. G. EXCELL,

General Ecclesiastical Secretary.

Publisher's Notice.

The remittance must accompany receipt of subscriptions at the Publishing House, no difference by or for whom or for whatever time they may be given, or whether forwarded through Ordained Officers, Branches, or Gatherings of the Christian Catholic Church in Zion. Accounts will be carried with Ordained Officers, Branches, or Gatherings, on quantity orders of periodicals consigned on sale for monthly settlement, but to include only such articles as bear the imprint of Zion. All orders for Bibles, books, buttons, pictures (except prints done by the Publishing House), lace souvenirs, etc., must be sent to the General Stores, Zion City, Lake County, Illinois.

Notice to Officers and Members.

Send all newspaper clippings concerning the General Overseer, the Elders, or any department of the work in connection with the Christian Catholic Church in Zion, to Deacon Carl F. Stern, Zion City, Illinois. Send as soon as possible after publication, and carefully mark *name and date of the paper clipped from* on each article. If this is not done, the clippings are absolutely useless.

DO YOU KNOW GOD'S WAY OF HEALING?

BY THE REV. JOHN ALEX. DOWIE.

Let it be supposed that the following words are a conversation between the reader [A] and the writer [B].

A. What does this question mean? Do you really suppose that God has some one especial way of healing in these days, of which men may know and avail themselves?

B. That is exactly my meaning, and I wish very much that you should know God's Way of Healing, as I have known it for many years.

A. What is the way, in your opinion?

B. You should rather ask, WHO is God's Way? for the way is a Person, not a thing. I will answer your question in His own words, "I am the Way, and the Truth, and the Life: no one cometh unto the Father, but by Me." These words were spoken by our Lord Jesus, the Christ, the Eternal Son of God, who is both our Savior and our Healer. (John 14:6.)

A. But I always thought that these words only referred to Him as the Way of Salvation. How can you be sure that they refer to Him as the Way of Healing also?

B. Because He cannot change He is "the same yesterday and today, yea, and forever." (Hebrews 13:8.) He said that He came to this earth not only to save us but to heal us. (Luke 4:18), and He did this when in the flesh on earth. Being unchanged He must be able and willing and desirous to heal now.

A. But is there not this difference, namely, that He is not with us now?

B. No; for He said "Lo, I am with you All the Days, even unto the Consummation of the Age;" and so He is with us now, in spirit, just as much as when He was here in the flesh.

A. But did He not work these miracles of healing when on earth merely to prove that He was the Son of God?

B. No; there was still a greater purpose than that. He healed the sick who trusted in Him in order to show us that He came to die not only for our sins, but for our sicknesses, and to deliver us from both.

A. Then, if that be so, the atonement which He made on the Cross must have been for our sicknesses as well as our sins. Can you prove that is the fact from the Scriptures?

B. Yes, I can, and the passages are very numerous. I need quote only two. In Isaiah 53:4, 5, it is written of Him: "Surely He hath borne our griefs (Hebrew, *sicknesses*), and carried our sorrows: . . . and with His stripes we are healed." Then, in the Gospel according to Matthew, this passage is quoted and directly applied to the work of bodily healing, in the 8th chapter 17th verse: "That it might be fulfilled which was spoken by Isaiah the prophet, saying, Himself took our infirmities, and bare our diseases."

A. But do you not think that sickness is often God's will, and sent for our good, and therefore God may not wish us to be healed?

B. No, that cannot possibly be; for diseases of every kind are the Devil's work, and his work can never be God's will, since the Christ came for the very purpose of destroying "the works of the Devil." (1 John 3:8.)

A. Do you mean to say that all disease is the work of Satan?

B. Yes, for if there had been no sin (which came through Satan) there never would have been any disease, and Jesus never in one single instance told any person that sickness was God's work or will, but the very contrary.

A. Can you prove from Scriptures that all forms of sickness and infirmity are the Devil's work?

B. Yes, that can be done very easily. You will see in Matthew 4:23 and 9:35 that when Jesus was here in the flesh He healed "all manner of disease and all manner of sickness among the people." Then if you will refer to Acts 10:38 you will see that the Apostle Peter declares that He (Jesus) "went about doing good, and healing all that were oppressed of the Devil." Notice that all whom He healed, not some, were suffering from Satan's evil power.

A. But does disease never come from God?

B. No, it cannot come from God, for He is pure, and disease is unclean; and it cannot come out of Heaven, for there is no disease there.

A. That is very different from the teachings which I have received all my life from ministers and in the churches. Do you really think that you are right, and that they are all wrong in this matter?

B. It is not a question as between myself and them. The only question is, What does God's Word say? God has said in all the ages, to His Church, "I am Jehovah that healeth thee" (Exodus 15:26), and therefore it would be wicked to say that He is the defiler of His people. All true Christians must believe the Bible, and it is impossible to believe that good and evil, sickness and health, sin and holiness could have a common origin in God. If the Bible really taught that, it would be impossible to believe our Lord Jesus, the Christ, when He says: "A good tree cannot bring forth evil fruit, neither can a corrupt tree bring forth good fruit." (Matthew 7:18.)

A. But even if I agree with all you say, is it not true that the Gifts of Healing were removed from the Church, and are not in it now?

B. No, the "Gifts of Healing" were never withdrawn, and can never be withdrawn, from the true Church of God, for it is written: "The gifts and the calling of God are without repentance." (Romans 11:29.) There are nine gifts of God to the Church (enumerated in 1 Corinthians 12:8-11), and all these are in the Holy Spirit. Therefore, so long as the Holy Spirit is in the Church, all the gifts must be there also. If they are not exercised, that does not prove that they do not exist, but that the faith to exercise them is lacking in God's servants. The gifts are all perfectly preserved; for the Holy Spirit, not the Church, keeps them safely.

A. What should a Christian then do when overtaken with sickness?

B. A Christian should obey God's command, and at once turn to Him for forgiveness of the sin which may have caused the sickness, and for immediate healing. Healing is obtained from God in one of four ways, namely: First, by the direct prayer of faith, without any aid from the officers of the Church, praying as the Centurion did in Matthew 8:5-13; second, by two faithful disciples praying in perfect agreement in accordance with the Lord's promise in Matthew 18:19; third, by the anointing of the Elders and the prayer of faith, according to the instructions in James 5:14 and 15; and fourth, by the laying on of the hands of them who believe, and whom God calls to that ministry, as the Lord commands in Mark 16:18, and in other places.

A. But are people healed in this way in these days?

B. Yes, in thousands of cases. I have myself laid hands upon many hundreds of thousands of persons, and I have seen the Lord's power manifested in the healing of great numbers, many of whom are living witnesses in many countries, who have testified publicly before thousands, and who are prepared to testify at any time. This ministry is being exercised by devoted Christians in many parts of America, Europe, Australasia, and elsewhere.

A. Is it not the same as Christian Science, Mind Healing, etc.?

B. No. Divine Healing is diametrically opposed to these diabolical counterfeits, which are utterly antichristian. These impostures are only seductive forms of Spiritualism. Trance Evangelism is also a more recent form of this delusion, and it deceives many.

A. But how shall I obtain the necessary faith to receive healing, which faith I am at present conscious that I do not possess?

B. It is written: "Belief cometh of hearing, and hearing by the word of the Christ." (Romans 10:17.) Our Missions are held for the express purpose of teaching fully the Word of God on this matter, and I very heartily invite you to attend the meetings which are announced for Zion Tabernacles in Chicago and other cities, and for Shiloh Tabernacle, Zion City, Illinois. All are welcome and there are no charges of any kind made, for all God's gifts are free gifts. Salvation is the first of these, without which you cannot be healed through faith in Jesus. All the costs of this work are covered by the free-will offerings of the people who attend these meetings, and others whom the Lord leads to help; but the poorest, who have nothing to give, are as heartily welcome as the richest.

A. Do you see the sick and lay hands upon them in this Mission?

B. Yes; after we feel satisfied that they are fully resting in the Lord alone for the healing, we see privately, so far as time permits, those who attend; but under no circumstances do we claim the power to heal any; for "power belongeth unto God."

A. Have you any writings upon this subject which can be purchased?

B. Yes; these can be obtained at the office of Zion Printing and Publishing House, Zion City, Illinois, and at any Zion Tabernacle. But the best book on Divine Healing is the Bible itself, studied prayerfully and earnestly.

We extend to you a hearty invitation to attend the meetings, which are free to all. Our prayer is that you may be led to find in Jesus, the Christ, our Lord and God your present Savior from sin, your Healer from sickness, your Cleanser from all evil, your Keeper in the way to Heaven, your Friend, and your All for Time and Eternity. We pray that these words may help many who read, and that our little conversation may bear fruit in leading many readers to look to Jesus only.

"The Healing of Christ's seamless dress
Is by all beds of pain;
We touch Him in life's throng and press
And we are whole again."

Early Morning Meeting in Shiloh Tabernacle

*REPORTED BY S. E. C., A. C. R., O. R., AND F. A. F.

THE Early Morning Sacrifice of Praise and Prayer on Lord's Day morning, August 14, 1904, was one of unusual length and blessing. For nearly three hours God's Prophet held the closest attention of a vast audience of at least five thousand people.

After prayer, the man of God read from the Inspired Word of God the Master's parable of the importunate widow and the one that follows, illustrative of the Divine Master's injunction, that men ought always to pray and not to faint.

He did not read continuously, but interjected his address between the sentences of the parable and uttered a modified invocation so near to the benediction that it had to deal more with what had been than that which was to be.

By means of argument and illustration, and flashes of wit and sarcasm, the man of God unfolded and applied his theme, until after quarter past nine o'clock.

The General Overseer thought it must be past eight o'clock!

But there were some who had not thought so.

What are three hours when one is brought face to face with Zion's need, and Zion's conflict, and Zion's God?

Shiloh Tabernacle, Zion City, Illinois, Lord's Day Morning, August 14, 1904.

The meeting was opened by the singing of Hymn No. 1 in the Special Leaflet of Songs prepared for the Feast of Tabernacles.

This was followed by prayer by the General Overseer, closing with the chanting of the Disciples' Prayer, in which he led the Congregation.

After the singing of one verse of "What a Wonderful Savior," and Hymn No. 309 in Gospel Hymns, the General Overseer said:

In the Gospel, according to St. Luke, 18th chapter, 1st verse, we read:

And He spake a parable unto them to the end that they ought always to pray, and not to faint.

Men Ought Always to Pray.

It is a good thing to have head-lines to important statements, and this parable has this head-line: "They ought always to pray, and not to faint."

When one faints, you may set it down that that person does not pray; for the people that faint do not pray, and the people that pray do not faint.

You tell me you faint? Then you do not pray.

"Oh, but I do."

You may talk; you may chatter; you may howl; but you do not pray.

Get that head-line into your minds this morning!

"And He spake a parable unto them to the end that they ought always to"—what?

PEOPLE—"Pray."

GENERAL OVERSEER—How often?

PEOPLE—"Always."

GENERAL OVERSEER—Always to pray.

Some of you pray only when you get into a tight place.

You are like those sailors who were shipwrecked and did not know how to pray.

One of them, so the story goes, said, "Let's take up a collection!"

Ah, how much more do you know about it than they?

There are worse ways of praying than taking up a collection.

That fellow had this thought—that he ought to do something.

He did not know much about faith, but at the bottom of his suggestion there was the thought that doing something went with praying.

Praise Should Accompany Prayer.

The most effective thing connected with prayer is praise.

With thanksgiving let your requests be made known to God.

But do not forget that those that pray do not faint.

The Early Christian Church was renowned for its spirit of prayerfulness, although it had very few advantages.

There was not such a thing in the early Church as a complete Bible.

In fact, the first martyrs had a part in making the Bible.

Stephen had no such help as we have in the stories of the completed Gospel.

He had not the Beautiful Story of the Revelation of Jesus, the Christ, which John saw on the Island of Patmos.

He did not have the story of the grand Hallelujah, that the Kingdoms of this world had become the Kingdom of our God and of our Lord Jesus, the Christ.

A Bible in those days would have cost a fortune.

But they had God.

They Had Faith, and They Prayed.

They prayed, and they triumphed, and they died.

They crucified the flesh.

The mother surrendered her babe, went to the stake, and died.

She was torn in pieces by wild beasts rather than deny her Lord.

Husbands left wives and families; and they prayed, and saw their Master in the skies.

The heavens were opened to them.

They conquered.

Oh, what a poor, pitiful thing it is that in this day of the fulness of God's grace, people should cease to Praise and Pray, or find it hard to do it.

No wonder they faint.

He spake a parable unto them to the end that they ought always to pray, and not to faint;

Saying, There was in a city a judge, which feared not God, and regarded not man:

And there was a widow in that city; and she came oft unto him, saying, Avenge me of mine adversary.

"Do Me Justice of Mine Adversary!"

That is a better rendering; it is the rendering of the margin of the Revision.

The General Overseer then read through the 6th verse:

Avenge me of mine adversary.

And he would not for a while: but afterward he said within himself, Though I fear not God, nor regard man;

Yet because this widow troubleth me, I will avenge her, lest she wear me out by her continual coming.

And the Lord said, Hear what the unrighteous judge saith.

And shall not God avenge His elect, which cry to Him day and night—

If an unrighteous judge, moved by the importunity of a widow, who was wronged, will do justice, shall not God the Righteous Judge, avenge—do justice to His own elect?

The elect cry unto Him day and night.

The non-elect find it hard to pray to Him at all,

They would rather play.

They would rather grumble.

They would rather gossip.

They would rather make money.

They would rather do anything than pray.

Their trousers never wear out at the knees.

They wear out at the seat.

They are so tired!

They are so weary!

They lie back—and they backslide.

*The following report has not been revised by the General Overseer.

They are stiff-necked!
They are grumblers!
They are murmurers!
They are lazy!
Do you know them?
Have any of you personal acquaintance with them?

God Almighty Is Tired of Prayerless People.

Some of you might look into a looking-glass, when you get home, and see a life-size picture of one.

I am tired of you!

God Almighty is tired of you, you prayerless people!

Some of you need much stirring up.

I will stir you up as an eagle stirs her nest.

I will throw you out, and if you do not fly you will fall.

You had better learn to fly.

It is time to stir up these nests!

It is not the young birds only that need stirring up.

Some of you old birds do not like to fly.

The eagle stirs up her nest, and throws out her young.

They scream and say, "Oh, I will fall!"

The old eagle gets below them, lets them fall a little distance, and then takes them up and says, "Now, you little fool, do not do that again!"

The eaglet cries, "Oh! I do not like this. You bring up here the chickens that you steal in the valley. It is so nice to eat them, mother! Don't throw me out again!"

The mother brings another chicken, and next morning she throws them out again.

Even the Elderly Must Learn to Fly.

Some of you old people have not learned to fly!

You have no wings.

You had better grow wings, because I will have people in this Church who can fly.

I will not have people sit and sing, "Fly, Mighty Gospel, Fly."

You will have to fly with the Gospel.

I once said, "Zion is on wheels."

I now say, "Zion is on wings."

If Zion had not been on wings and gone to the uttermost parts of the earth, there are thousands and tens of thousands today who would be in darkness and in the shadow of death.

Some lands have been so stirred that they will never forget it.

You have no idea how they have been stirred.

Last night I received a letter from Dr. Speicher.

He arrived in London Lord's Day, two weeks ago, and spoke in the Tabernacle that evening.

He registered at a nice hotel, "The Kenilworth:"

John Gabriel Speicher, Zion City, Illinois.
Abigail T. Speicher, Zion City, Illinois.
John Dowie Speicher, Zion City, Illinois.

That last name cost him his place in the hotel [laughter], for when he came back from the Tabernacle he had notice to get out.

John Dowie was there!

He received a letter addressed, "John Dowie, Esq.," which read, "Get out of this place on Monday."

Dr. Speicher said, "This is a mistake."

"No, it is on the register."

"Why, it is John Dowie Speicher."

"Well," they said, "anyhow, you will have to go."

"How is that?"

"Oh, well, the fact that you came from Zion City is enough."

Don't you think London must be considerably stirred?

It must be stirred when a little boy, eight years of age, because he is called Dowie, has to be sent away from a hotel.

Will You Ever Stir the World Like That?

I hope you will, and I want you to stir it.

But you must first stir up the Gift that is in you—the Gift that God gave you, beloved.

Oh, what a Gift it is—the Gift of Prayer!

Let us get hold of this parable.

Let it get hold of us!

Let this thought come into your hearts— if an unjust judge, because of a widow's importunity, will say, "I will avenge her lest she wear me out by her continual coming," shall not the Just Judge, who loves us, do justice to His own elect, which cry to Him day and night?

He is long-suffering, for many are crying as the people of Israel cried at the Red Sea; as Moses himself cried when in his folly he said, "Stand still."

I am tired of these "stand-still" people.

Get out, and go forward, and do something!

The Russians Stood Still, and Were Defeated.

Oh, they thought the Japanese were not going to do anything to them, and so they had a good time at Port Arthur.

It was full of wine and women, and there was a circus performance at the time that the Japanese sank two of their ships.

When the Russian vessels went out, the Japanese sank another, and the Russians suddenly awoke to the fact that war was real and pretty serious business.

Do you not know that the Japanese never forgot that experience?

They kept at it.

The Russian fleet ventured out the other day, and the Japanese smashed it, and sent four or five of the battle-ships back into the harbor at Port Arthur, battered having sunk the fleet's greatest battle-ship.

These men won because they kept at it.

They go forward; they never stop.

They do not howl day and night; but they work day and night.

The Army of the Living God Must Be Everlastingly at It.

The children of darkness are wiser in their generation than the children of light.

If I had you working as these Japanese have been working at this war, we would have beaten the Devil a hundred times harder than we have.

You are not ready to whip the Devil.

The Japanese were the best drilled soldiers in the world.

When they went out to battle, they were not food for powder, for they had been drilled practically, and they had borne hardships.

They had been drilled while the weather was more disagreeable than that of summer.

Summer maneuvers of the National Guard!

That makes me smile!

They do not think of venturing out to drill unless the skies are bright and the winds are gentle, and they can make a holiday of it.

Hardness Essential to Good Soldiership.

If I were a military general, and wanted to drill an army, I would drill them when the thermometer registered thirty-two degrees below zero.

That is the time to make a fellow march!

He will march then!

He will get warm!

That is the time to make him hard!

The idea of drilling soldiers in summer maneuvers! The Japanese did not do that.

I have followed them for years in their military training.

I admire their methods.

They train their soldiers principally in the winter.

They make them go up mountains covered with snow.

They send them to build bridges across rivers.

They make them go into swamps and fight imaginary enemies.

They drill them and make them efficient.

I will drill you.

I will have some real fighting.

If you think that the whole thing consists in "Feast of Tabernacles," in summer time, you are mistaken.

It is time to get into the fall fighting; time to get ready for winter.

The Japanese won because they were thoroughly drilled.

They did not have an ounce of superfluous flesh upon their little bodies, and they could shoot straight.

Oh, how much the children of darkness in their generation can teach us!

How much wiser they are in their generation than the children of light!

Jesus said it, and He was right.

He was always right.

Oh, if we had followed Him more closely!

He was always at it.

Mrs. Edna Sheldrake
News Editor The Zion Banner

Evangelist Sarah E. Hill
Supt. Zion Free Literature Mission

Evangelist Marie Brieger-Hodler
Assistant Editor Blätter der Heilung

Rev. Jane Dowie
Contributor on Women's Work

REV. JOHN ALEX
Editor and Prop

General

THE EDITOR AND EDITORIAL, LITERARY, BUSINESS AND MEC

Deacon B. F. Morris
Assistant Manager

Deacon M. N. Price
Superintendent of Printing

Deacon O. W. Davis
Superintendent of Circulation

thur W. Newcomb
ad General Associate Editor

Deacon Charles Champe
Artist

J. B. Coghill
Manager Printing Department

AL FORCES OF ZION PRINTING AND PUBLISHING HOUSE

What a Loss the Church Has Suffered Through Its Summer Maneuvers!

I cannot say that we have always been like that, because we have done much winter fighting; but some of you have been skulkers.

We cannot afford to have any in Zion who are not willing, day or night, not only to cry to God, but to go forward.

I say unto you, that He will avenge them speedily. Howbeit when the Son of man cometh, shall He find the Faith on the earth?

If you speak of the next coming, I would say, "Yes, Lord, when You come in the clouds with Power and great Glory, You will find the Faith on the earth; but if You speak of the coming to reign, after the Rapture, I think You will not find it."

I will tell you why.

Because those that will have been left to pass through the Tribulation, will be the Foolish Virgins, and the Faith will not be in them—the Faith in all its fulness.

They will be lazy.

They will not rise and trim their lamps.

"It is a cold morning," they will say, "I have had a long week's work. I will sleep."

Why don't you get to bed about eight o'clock on Saturday night, so that you may get enough sleep, if you will have a long sleep, and not sleep away the first hours of the Sabbath?

Let us get hold of this.

It Is the Men That Rise in the Darkness and Fight That Win Battles.

I have been watching every move in this Russian-Japanese war.

I have studied war all my life.

I suppose it is in my blood to do so.

If I had not been a Soldier of Peace, at war with the Devil, at war with sin, I believe I would have gone into military warfare.

I have learned not only from the past, but from the present.

Warfare has changed.

Just think!

A vessel may be so far away from its enemy as to be scarcely seen, and send its great shells with such mathematical precision as to strike a vessel and sink it!

Seven, eight, nine, and ten miles away!

In olden times, in order to kill a man, one had to be near him.

Nearly all the ships that were battered the other day were struck from a distance of three thousand five hundred yards to five thousand yards.

May God make us long-range fighters! I have been studying long-range fighting, and I have sent quite a number of bombs into England, so that a little boy, only eight years of age, could not stay in a London hotel because his name was Dowie.

Is it not astonishing?

Fear in the Enemy Does Not Hurt Zion.

Those bombs must have hit hard; but do you think that fear in the enemy is injuring Zion?

Not at all.

The people of London are eager to read LEAVES OF HEALING.

The people of Melbourne and Adelaide are eager to read LEAVES OF HEALING.

I dare say some of you who came from Australia yesterday will confirm the statement that I have received from Adelaide, that although large numbers have come to this country from that city, the Tabernacle in Adelaide is more largely attended than ever; and as for Melbourne, our last advices were that the very street in front of it was crowded.

It was needful that some one should suffer that they might be stirred.

I had no idea that we would hit so hard.

Admiral Togo's guns were not in it with us.

He could hit at a distance of only eleven miles.

We hit at a distance of three thousand miles and more!

We Must Be Up-to-Date Fighters for God.

Let us realize what a glorious fight is ours!

What a magnificent fight it is!

We have to be up-to-date warriors.

The old style is ineffective.

If you depend upon old style fighting, you will be killed before you get anywhere.

Today we have to fight the good Fight of Faith with up-to-date methods!

The old methods will not do. The old Spirit will do however.

Get the Old Spirit, but use up-to-date methods.

And He spake also this parable unto certain which trusted in themselves that they were righteous, and set all others at nought—

O God, forbid that this spirit which makes us trust in ourselves and sets all others at nought, should be in Zion.

Let me give you a passage which comes to mind whenever I read these words, "He that trusteth in his own heart is a fool."

The Folly of Self-dependence.

How many here are fools?

Whenever I hear any one say, "I can do this," or "Depend upon me, I can do that. Though all should leave you I shall not leave you; you can depend upon me," I fear that that person is trusting in himself or in herself.

I watch a little, and I find that some of these people set others at nought.

"Why, Elder So-and-so doesn't know how to do that."

They do!

"Deacon So-and-so doesn't know how to do that."

They do!

"Overseer So-and-so doesn't know how to do it."

They do!

It is a little risky to say anything about the General Overseer, but they say, "Oh, if the General Overseer only knew. If he only knew!"

The General Overseer Knows.

You would be surprised to know what the General Oversee does know.

It might very much surprise you to learn that the General Overseer knows that the people who say, "Oh, if the General Overseer only knew," are just the people that are a hindrance.

We do know, and we know better than you know, because you see only one little point; but I stand where I see the whole work.

I have not the disproportionate view of things that you have.

The one thing that you see is magnified out of all proportion in your mind, because you continually dwell upon it.

That is why the Devil is able to inspire fear in you.

Do you not know that the reason why a little child can guide a horse is because its great, flashing eyes magnify, and the horse sees that child as a giant?

Perhaps you did not know that.

Do you not know that it is the big-eyed brutes that do not see?

Some of you have awfully big eyes. [Laughter.]

Do you not know that it is these little Japanese, with small eyes, that shoot straight?

One of my adversaries said, "I expected to see Doctor Dowie as a man of very noble presence, and I saw a little round fellow, with small, beady eyes."

I do not bother about how my eyes look.

I only say that I am glad I have not eyes like a horse.

Some of you have tremendously big eyes. You see something, and you say "Oh, what is the matter? Things are going to smash in Zion. I got ten cents less than usual last week."

Christians Should Learn to Look Upon the Things of Others.

May God heal that disease in your eyes—that disease that causes them to magnify.

I will tell you why you have it.

It is because you trust in your own heart.

You are a fool!

It is because you are looking only at your own things, and at the things that concern yourself.

You are praying nearly all the time, "Lord, bless me and my wife; my son John, and his wife; us four and no more."

You are everlastingly murmuring about yourself.

You are always thinking about your head or your stomach.

You are thinking about your immediate surroundings.

It is all very well to do that sometimes, but you are everlastingly doing it, and you keep looking at them until you see nothing else.

If you were standing where I stand; and if you saw this City as I see it; and this State as I see it; and this Nation as I see it; and this world as I see it, you would see things more proportionately, and you would not so tremendously overestimate your own importance, and that of your house, and of your son John and his house.

Do Not Trust in Yourselves.

Trust in God, and let God elevate you until you are able to take part with Him in His great, Universal Work.

Let your own individuality sink; and be willing to suffer, and, if need be, to die.

These Japanese have the eye of empire.

They sail those seas as no warrior of ancient Viking days ever did.

They face odds!

Just think of their facing that mighty Russian empire and smashing it.

They have dug into its very vitals, until blood is covering the warm waters of Asia, as I told you long ago it would.

These men are teaching us, children of darkness though they be, how real Children of Light should work.

I am greatly stirred when I think how Zion's fleet ought to be in every Ocean; how the Church of God, instead of being the miserable thing that it is, should be a power.

The Salvation Army today has Edward VII. for a Patron Saint.

Think of it!

William Booth reads speeches to the Salvation Army, in which that dissolute and vile king is made to appear as its distinguished protector.

Distinguished protector!

Some of the greatest criminals of Europe are to be found on and near thrones.

If the nations of the earth will not rid themselves of these kings, the fires of hell will burst out and burn up the whole monarchical system.

The Fires of Revolution Are Everywhere.

Von Plehve was blown in pieces in the very center of St. Petersburg, on his way to the Emperor.

"Oh," you say, "the people were horrified. They all deplored such an act."

Not a bit of it!

Within two hours afterwards, the Minister of Justice drove along the same road on his way to the Emperor, to report Von Plehve's death, and his carriage was attacked.

Two prominent officers, although the papers have not made much of it, have since been murdered.

Russia is full of revolution.

Germany is full of revolution.

The Kaiser can keep peace in his own Capital only by keeping there an army of many thousands of men.

London is kept in peace only by great bodies of police and military right in the center of it, ready to pour out at any moment; ready to shoot.

There is not a capital in Europe, with the possible exception of Bern and Paris, capitals of republics, that can trust its citizens.

There are very few in this country.

Chicago cannot be trusted, and that is why Fort Sheridan has its small army, ready to rush in and do what it did in 1894.

If God does not stir us up to do His work, a Great and Terrible Day is not far away.

Let us get stirred.

Do not trust in yourselves, but trust in God; "for the Lord Jehovah is an Everlasting Rock."

In Us Is Everlasting Weakness.

That is all we are.

And He spake also this parable unto certain which trusted in themselves that they were righteous, and set all others at nought.

Two men went up into the Temple to pray; the one a Pharisee, and the other a publican.

These two men are in this Tabernacle.

These classes are represented in all such assemblies as this.

Wherever God erects a House of Prayer, the Devil always places a chapel. It will be found upon examination that sometimes Satan has the larger congregation.

Even amongst God's own people it will be found that Satan's chapel is largely attended, because the Devil gets God's people to trust in themselves, and to make pharisaical prayers.

All are not so candid as this Pharisee was.

I would rather they would be candid; but the worst of it is, some of the biggest hypocrites are those that wash their hands in invisible soap and water and are so humble, so gentle!

They could wish that the dear General Overseer was a little more gentle.

I feel such a contempt for those Christians who never had one straight fight with the Devil!

They are a curse.

They are self-righteous because they are so good. They are so sweet! They are so humble!

Two men went up into the Temple to pray; the one a Pharisee and the other a publican.

The Pharisee stood and prayed thus with himself,—

The Hypocrisy of Praying With One's Self.

That is it.

He never prayed with God.

He never had God with him.

He prayed with himself.

That was his god—himself.

That has been the trouble with God's people.

"I am something. I will do what I like. I will think as I like. I will obey the General Overseer and all the commandments of God when I get ready, and just to the extent that I please."

If you who thus think imagine for one moment that you are a Christian, get rid of that imagination at once.

You are a first-class devil.

"The Pharisee stood and prayed thus with himself, God, I thank Thee"—for what?

For saving me, a poor sinner?

Oh, no!

"I thank Thee that I am not as the rest of men!"—

I thank Thee that I am not as the rest of men, extortioners, unjust, adulterers, or even as this publican.

How blest that man would have been if he had been like that tax-gatherer, that publican!

What a blessing some of you would be with the experience of a broken-hearted penitent!

I fast twice in the week; I give tithes of all that I get.

A Danger That Zion Must Avoid.

You are fasting, you are tithing, but your praying is all a part of your hypocrisy.

Tithing with you is not tithing at all.

Zion is in danger of that very thing.

It is right that in Zion City tithing should be compulsory. We shall most certainly look upon the man or woman that does not tithe as a thief and a robber. We do not want such a person in Zion's employ.

I am somewhat inclined to think that some of you tithe, not because you want to, but because you have to.

If you are tithing because you have to, you are a hypocrite.

If you fast because you want others to know it, you are a hypocrite.

I wish all would ascertain what motives underlie their actions, for God is judging motives.

"Man looketh on the outward appearance, but God looketh on the heart!"

God Is Able to Penetrate Every Deception.

But the publican, standing afar off—

The tax-gatherer, standing afar off in the Temple court of the Gentiles, could not get into the court of the Jews.

He could not see the Mercy Seat.

That Pharisee, with his broad phylacteries and outstretched arm; with his elevated, majestic appearance, was in the way of his seeing.

He could not see the Cherubim and Seraphim.

He could not see the Holy Place.

He could not see inside the veil—the priest barred the way.

He could not see the Ark of the Covenant.

He believed it was there, and he sought the God of the Covenant.

Though he was afar off, and though he would not lift up so much as his eyes to heaven, he smote upon his breast and said, "O God, be merciful to me a sinner!"

I wonder if any of you pray, "God bless me, because I am a first-class saint; because I am a very good fellow. O God, bless me, because I am a very good woman. Bless me; I am no ordinary person; I belong to a fine family. Bless me, O God, because You know I make great sacrifices for You."

You hypocrite!

"Faithful is the saying, and worthy of all acceptation, that the Christ Jesus came into the world to save sinners; of whom I am chief!"

The chief of the apostles wrote that.

The Chief of Sinners, the Chief of the Apostles.

Though he was less, in his own eyes, than the least of all saints, and not worthy to be called an Apostle, he knew that, humanly speaking, he stood superior to any of them.

Yet he was the chief of sinners.

All his hope and all his plea were that he was a poor sinner who was trusting in the mercy of an Infinite Savior.

The chief of saints knew that he was the chief of sinners.

The Light of Glory shone in and he saw, in that light, the Incorruptible Crown.

He looked at himself. Oh, he was such a poor object!

So am I; so little; so insignificant.

Jesus said about that man who said he was a sinner:

I say unto you, This man went down to his house justified rather than the other: for every one that exalteth himself shall be humbled; but he that humbleth himself shall be exalted.

INVOCATION.

Father, let these words be of value; and let the words which I shall now speak be of value, for the Christ's sake. Amen.

We have golden weeks and golden moments before us, but they are very short.

There are yet three months, and then cometh winter.

The Reaper whose name is Death, may reap some of you in this congregation of thousands before the winter comes.

There are far worse things than dying.

Death of Some People Would Be a Blessing.

There are some people so wicked that if they should die it would be a great blessing to their families.

They are so cross; they are so perpetually finding fault; they make life such a heavy burden.

That applies to some of you.

The wife that loved you and gave you all her youth, the mother of your children, has been caused many a sigh, many a tear.

She would like to die; she is tired of you, you wretch!

And the death of some of you women will occasion no loss, you everlasting naggers!

Nag, nag, nag, nag!

You never open your mouth without a complaint.

It would not be a very great sorrow to me to hear that certain people had died.

I will have no goats in this flock.

I am no shepherd of goats, and I never undertook that charge. Never! I am the shepherd of God's sheep, and the goat that will pollute the flock and gore the sheep, has to go.

Some people have said to me, "Suppose that young man who has been sent out into the world should go deeper into sin, and die?"

I should thank God that such a hypocrite, thief, adulterer, liar, and breaker of his father's and mother's heart, was where he could do no more harm.

Elijah Must Take Forth the Precious from the Vile.

The Elijah who prayed for rain prayed also that it might not rain; and three years and six months of famine meant, not only the death of the cattle and the withering of the grass of the field, but it meant, also, plagues, and pestilences, and death to thousands and hundreds of thousands in Israel.

Nevertheless it was the only thing that would bring the people to Carmel, and decide the question as to who was God.

If I sin by failing to take forth the precious from the vile, I shall be responsible before God for the corruption that follows.

Would you farmers knowingly put wheat into a storehouse that was full of weevil that eat the kernel of the wheat?

VOICES—"No."

GENERAL OVERSEER—Tell me, you good housewives, who look at your apples every now and then to see how they are getting on, when you see a great, big apple that has become corrupt, can you afford to let it stay?

VOICES—"No."

GENERAL OVERSEER—In order to save that which you have harvested, you must throw away that apple and clean out the place where it was, that the infection and corruption may not spread.

It is the business of the officers of the Christian Catholic Church in Zion, from the highest to the lowest, to help me keep this City clean.

It is the business of all to see that we are pure, because the battle in which we are engaged can be won only by those who have clean hearts.

Qualifications of Zion Restorationists.

You have come out, and I have come out; but how are we benefitted by coming out if we tolerate impurity; if we are content with crying to God for Purity and do not go forward?

This people must be clean.

This people must be thoroughly drilled.

This people must be thoroughly imbued with the tremendous realities and responsibilities of the work they have vowed to do.

This people must get rid of the last vestige of worldly sorrow, and have the Joy of the Lord, which is strength.

I want this people to be rich, and not poor.

I want them to be healthy, and yet free from bestial passion.

I want them to be strong, but with something more than the strength of an ox.

I want them to have more angelic Purity.

I want that we shall learn how to use up-to-date weapons.

I want you who are teachers to become skilful instructors.

I want you who are being taught, to learn all that your instructors can teach you, and seek for more.

I want you to take the one Great Book, the Book of all books, and get it into your inmost heart, until something can be said of you greater than that you possess the Truth—that the Truth possesses you.

A Mistaken Conception of the Holy Spirit.

Some years ago a sanctimonious hypocrite came to me and said, "Doctor Dowie, do you think you ever had the Holy Spirit?"

"No, Madam. Never!"

"I thought so!" she said.

"Madam, have you the Holy Spirit?" I asked.

"Oh, I have Him!" she said.

"What is the size of Him?" I queried.

"Oh, He fills my heart," she gushed.

"How much does it take to fill your heart? About a thimbleful?

"Madam, I was perfectly candid when I said that I did not have the Holy Spirit, but the Holy Spirit has me.

"I cannot put my arms around the Infinite God, nor can I ever possess Him; but listen, Madam, He possesses me. He has me. He controls me."

I do not believe that woman was possessed of the Holy Spirit.

We must be practical Christians.

The work of God must be a reality.

We must obey Him, love Him, serve Him, be controlled by Him, and be organized into a force through which the Holy Spirit can work.

I want Zion to be a mighty power.

But I would rather have Zion on her back, sick; I would rather have Zion so poor that we would have to live on bread and water; I would rather see Zion in the deepest depths of the valley of humiliation than that we should be healthy, and wealthy, and strong materially, and be spiritual pigmies, spiritually corrupt, and spiritually fruitless.

Material Success of Zion not the First Thing.

If you imagine for one moment that I suppose the material success of Zion is the first thing, you are greatly mistaken

But I do not pretend that we shall be sick or poor or powerless.

I pray God that we may see something that the world has not yet seen; for there has not yet been seen in this world a strong, powerful community of men and women, healthy and vigorous in spirit, soul, and body, and full of progressiveness, that has at the same time been such a mighty spiritual power as we are at this time.

But we must be clean.

If you do not deal with that little rebel of a child in your home, if there is one there, you are countenancing rebellion in Zion against God.

If you have a lustful boy or girl in your home, you are responsible for their conduct to me, as the Spiritual Health Officer of Zion; and I will hold you responsible if I have to send you back where you belong—into the World, where the Flesh and the Devil hold sway.

I cannot do and will not attempt to do more than a certain amount of disciplining.

When discipline is ineffective, the only remedy is separation.

The Devil Will Try to Destroy Zion from Within.

The Devil fights hard, because he sees that to injure Zion he has to secure a foothold within; for he knows that he can never destroy Zion from without.

Every attack that has been made upon Zion from without has only united and strengthened her.

The Devil who, as a serpent in the Garden of Eden, tempted Adam and Eve, and dragged them down to sin and death, wants to destroy this first City of Zion.

But he will have to kill me first!

My heart cries out for every beloved father and mother; for every true, pure sister and brother; for every sweet girl, who are mourning today some loved one's banishment; for every wife that is mourning a husband's banishment.

But it is better that you should mourn than that Zion should die.

My mourning brother and sister, pray that those that have been disciplined shall accept the discipline and go.

Then God will deal with them in the wilderness and in the darkness.

They were not worthy of living in Light, and Peace, and Purity.

They are in the outer darkness.

There is weeping, there is wailing, there is gnashing of teeth.

Pray God that the Repentance may be sincere and complete.

Do not forget that if it is, that God, who hath made a Way that His banished may return, knows my heart when I say that the door of Zion shall never be shut perpetually against those that have sinned and that have been disciplined, if they truly repent and "bring forth fruits meet for Repentance." [Amen.]

But the door shall be shut and kept shut until we are sure of that.

Some ask, "Why not keep them in Zion City and make them good here?"

Why not keep that diseased apple with the sound ones and make it good there?

Zion City Is Not a Reformatory for Criminals.

This City was built for God, and for the people of God.

It was built that there might be one clean spot upon God Almighty's earth where we would not have a harlot, a thief, a liar, a cheat, an adulterer, or a false swearer, as far as we can know.

I will take the stand of the chief of apostles and the chief of sinners, and say that but for the grace of God I would have been, though I never was, the vilest among men.

I thank God that, while I am conscious of many imperfections and of many transgressions, there never has been in my heart for one single moment any peace with the Devil, or any desire for sin.

I have been sometimes "overtaken in a fault."

God has sometimes shown me that there was a better way than the one in which I was going, and I have quickly changed my way, and have lain down at peace with God.

I early determined that I would not rise one day without first talking to God; that, even before I opened my eyes to see the morning light, I would be awake and seek for that "Light that never shone on Sea or Land."

This morning, when I woke, a long time before the day broke, I sought God and sought Him for this people.

Every night in my life that I can remember I have knelt and prayed, and been at peace with God as far as I knew how to be.

But you cannot pray and live in sin.

As a Christian, you cannot pray and faint.

If I had ceased to pray I would have ceased to fight, and I would have gone down.

I Desire the Greatest Happiness for the People of Zion City.

No one more than I wants you to be happier, and purer, and to make your life a more continuous joy.

I love to see the sunny faces of the innocent and sweet children, and youths, and maidens that are seeking for and enjoying life and all its blessings.

I love to see the faces of men and women who seek the Face of God and whose faces shine.

It is worth the toil.

I pray God that you and I may be faithful to this trust, so that this City's foundations shall be laid so strongly that there shall be no cracks in the walls; that there shall be no need to take down the walls some day, because of faulty construction.

We must be a people who shall be a model of all the peoples that are to follow.

We must be happy in doing it.

There is no Happiness in sin.

The only Happiness is in God and in Salvation.

All who believe that stand.

The congregation rose and repeated the following prayer, clause by clause, after the General Overseer.

PRAYER OF CONSECRATION.

Father, our Father, Thou art in the heavens and Thou art in the earth, and Thou art away far off upon the sea. There is no place where Thou art not; for even those that have made their bed in hell find that Thou art there. Father, help us in this City of Zion to be a pure people. Help me to be clean in spirit, soul, and body. Help me to be unselfish; help me to be out-and-out, not half-and-half. May my spirit, as well as my soul and body, and all that I have, and am, or ever shall have, be Thine; my family, my life, my all. Make Thou each of us to be true to Thee. Make us pure, make us peaceable, make us watchful; make us to be our brother's keeper, our sister's keeper. For Jesus' sake. Amen.

My brothers and sisters, remember that the life of the Leader is bound up with the Purity of this people.

After the singing of "I stand on Zion's Mount," by the Congregation, the General Overseer closed the meeting by pronouncing the

BENEDICTION.

Beloved, abstain from every form of evil. And may the very God of Peace Himself sanctify you wholly; and I pray God your whole spirit, and soul, and body be preserved entire, without blame, unto the coming of our Lord Jesus, the Christ. Faithful is He that calleth you, who also will do it. The grace of our Lord Jesus, the Christ, the love of God, our Father, the fellowship of the Holy Spirit, our Comforter and Guide, one Eternal God, abide in you, bless you, and keep you, and all the Israel of God everywhere, forever. Amen.

EARLY MORNING SACRIFICE OF PRAISE AND PRAYER.

*REPORTED BY A. C. R., O. R., AND F. A. F.

Christianity is Discipleship.

To be a Christian is to be a Learner.

Zion is an organized body of learners of Jesus, the Christ—the God Man—with the Prophet of the Restoration as Interpreter of His Words.

As represented in Zion City, at least, Zion is beginning to understand many things, among them the rich significance of the Lord's Day and of the Early Morning Sacrifice of Praise and Prayer held on that day.

Zion not only looks forward to this day and this service as occasions of great spiritual refreshment, but she makes preparation.

Zion retires early Saturday night that she may rise early Lord's Day morning—she is learning to live for God.

Next to the notable cessation of all activities at the appointed hours of prayer, one of the most beautiful sights in Zion City is the streams of people—young and old—flocking early to the House of God.

No loitering gait may be seen; but an eager, alert, forward movement of the body that is, perhaps unconsciously, a reflection of the spirit's hard following after God.

The service, Lord's Day morning, August 21, 1904, drew together an unusually large number of worshipers; and they were rewarded with unusual blessing.

*The following report has not been revised by the General Overseer.

When the Lord makes the wine, the last is always the best.

The service was one of teaching, from first to last—there was little preaching.

The words selected for consideration were the first ten verses of the 5th chapter of 2d Corinthians.

Although the reading and the address were separated by the usual Invocation, they were both one in spirit, in purpose, and in inspiration.

The teaching was almost wholly on the relation that spirit sustains to body, both in the seen and in the unseen world.

Many erroneously think of the prophets of old as dealing almost wholly with predictive prophecy, and this view in a measure, hinders their acceptance of the Prophet who speaks today.

The Prophet declares the Will of God, lifts the curtain that hides the unseen, and reveals things to come as far as God sees fit to lay bare the secrets of the future.

The veil was certainly drawn aside on Lord's Day morning, and God's people were permitted to catch an inspiring and suggestive view of things revealed in the Word of God that only a prophet-teacher could make plain.

The teaching was an inspiration to holy living as well as to study, prayer, and meditation with reference to the secrets that are revealed only to those who fear God.

Shiloh Tabernacle, Zion City, Illinois, Lord's Day Morning, August 21, 1904.

The service was opened by the singing of Hymn No. 307:

In the heavenly pastures fair,
'Neath the tender Shepherd's care,
Let us rest beside the living stream today;
Calmly there in peace recline,
Drinking in the truth divine,
As His loving call we now with joy obey.

CHORUS—Glorious stream of life eternal,
Beauteous fields of living green
Though revealed within the word
Of our Shepherd and our Lord,
By the pure in heart alone can they be seen.

Prayer was offered by the General Overseer, after which the Congregation joined in singing Hymn No. 312.

The General Overseer then said:

Scripture Reading and Exposition.

Let us read in the Inspired Word of God in the 2d epistle of Paul to the Corinthians, the first ten verses of the 5th chapter:

For we know that if the earthly house of our tabernacle be dissolved, we have a building from God, a house not made with hands, eternal, in the heavens.

For verily in this we groan, longing to be clothed upon with our habitation which is from heaven.

Demons Are Disembodied Spirits.

Devils are disembodied spirits—spirits without embodiment.

The doom of Satan and fallen angels was, among other things, disembodiment.

They are spirits without embodiment, but always longing for it; and so eager are they to be reëmbodied that they would rather be embodied in a pig—in a snorting, unclean sow—than not be embodied at all.

Their prayer to the Master, when He cast a legion of them out of one man, was, "If Thou cast us out, send us away into the herd of swine."

Oh, in what misery, filthiness, and despair these disembodied and naked demons must be, that they are so willing to be embodied in a serpent, or in a herd of swine!

How horrible the condition of a disembodied spirit!

Its condition is the very opposite of that of the ministering spirits that are clothed with heavenly bodies.

Its condition is the very opposite of that of saved spirits, which are clothed upon with a house from heaven.

I emphasize that contrast.

If so be that being clothed we shall not be found naked.

For indeed we that are in this tabernacle do groan, being burdened; not for that we would be unclothed, but that we would be clothed upon, that what is mortal may be swallowed up of life.

We do not want to be without bodies, but to be clothed upon with our habitation—our house, more properly, as the Revised Version has it—which is from heaven.

Now He that wrought us for this very thing is God, who gave unto us the earnest of the Spirit.

Being therefore always of good courage, and knowing that, whilst we are at home in the body, we are absent from the Lord.

(For we walk by faith, not by sight);

We are of good courage, I say, and are willing rather to be absent from the body, and to be at home with the Lord:

Wherefore also we make it our aim, whether at home or absent, to be well-pleasing unto Him.

For we must all be made manifest—

"Made manifest" means, literally, that we all must be made to stand out in the light—the light of the Great White Throne, before which we shall stand, and in the light of which and by the light of which we shall be tested.

God a Judge from Whom Nothing Can Be Hidden.

The impurity, the uncleanness, the motives that have been wrong will then stand out like so many dark and horrible stains.

If our spirits are unclean when they go out of this life—make no mistake about it—the uncleanness will be manifest to God.

Our moral condition will then be just what it is here.

No words of ours can change it.

No concealment will be possible, for we will all stand in the light before the Judgment-seat of the Christ.

He will judge us.

The perfectly Pure Man will judge us.

He will make no mistake.

He is infinitely merciful, and will give consideration to earth's failings and to the temptations and trials that we have had; but He will make no peace with sin.

For we must all be made manifest before the Judgment-seat of the Christ; that each one may receive the things done in the body, according to what he hath done, whether it be good or bad.

In whatever degree we may receive His mercy, He will make no compromises with sin; each one will receive according to the things done in the body.

That does not mean His body, but your body—every one's body.

An Individual and Unerring Judgment for Every Person.

You will get according to what you did here.

You will not be condemned before God for Adam's sin; you will be condemned for your own sin.

Every man shall bear only his own burden, not Adam's burden.

Adam will bear his own burden.

David will bear his own burden.

Every man will bear his own burden.

We must all stand out in the light, before the Judgment-seat of the Christ, each one separately.

We are not judged collectively; there is an individual and unerring judgment for each.

Not only is an absolutely infallible record made in heaven, but it is carried with you.

A man, while standing near a tree, the other day, was struck by lightning, and when his unconscious form was taken up the exact image of the tree was found on his back.

Every Deed Is Photographed.

Everything we ever did is photographed upon our spirits.

It is there.

It is a scientific fact that the very rocks reveal the action that was committed upon them centuries ago.

It was recorded.

Sometimes in the eyes of a murdered man the face of the murderer as he was looking at his victim may be seen.

It had been photographed upon those eyes.

So every deed is photographed upon the body.

Let a man be a drunkard—the fact is photographed upon his nose.

That is color photography.

A mean and miserly person's character is photographed upon his face.

The character of a man who is right with God, and who is happy and bright, is photographed upon his face.

Moreover, if you go with a bright, happy face to others you photograph yourself upon them, and they carry your face of love down the busy street and through the dusty lane.

You photograph yourself upon your wife's heart if the last thing you say in the morning is "Ugh! this breakfast was horrid. Everything is all wrong!"

The Photograph Remains when the Personal Presence is Removed.

You go out but you have left the photograph.

Your wife, perhaps, has been thinking—

"How different from what he used to be!

"He used to say, 'O Betty, you are such a dear, little woman. Never mind if things have gone wrong.'

"He makes no allowances now."

But if you say, "Well, Betty, never mind; I know you could have had an excellent breakfast if things had not gone wrong," and kiss her before you go, she has a photograph of a loving heart and a kind, considerate man.

Remember that life is being photographed upon life, action is being photographed upon action, and that everything that we do is photographed.

We remember these assemblies. They are photographed upon our memories.

Story after story is being photographed upon our memories.

I see something that takes me away back to Australia.

The photograph was taken in the garden at the very time when the mob was howling for our lives.

We were so happy in that dear, little garden up in the mountains.

The memory of it comes back to us, and we think of the love that surrounded us, and of the hate.

There is a photograph of both.

The photograph is something more than mere words; it is a picture of the thing itself.

You Cannot Hide from God.

The darkness will not hide you.

The spiritual photograph taken in the darkness is just as accurate as that taken in the light.

The sunlight was not needed to take it.

Get the thought that we must all be made to stand out in the light "before the Judgment-seat of the Christ, that each one may receive the things done in the body."

One of the Books that will be opened is the record of our own lives, of our own hands, and our own bodies—of each one, separately and individually.

Wife, you will be judged for your own sins; not for your husband's.

Husband, you will be judged for your own sins; not for your wife's.

Brother, you will be judged for your own sins; not for others'.

Consider yourself. You will not be judged for another's follies, unless you are a partaker.

Each one will be judged for deeds done in the body, "according to what he hath done, whether it be good or bad."

I am so glad that was written.

In the judgment of our deeds God will remember the good as well as the bad.

He will not forget the work of faith, and labor of love.

He will not forget the nights of toil, the weeping, and the striving, the self-repression, and the self-abnegation that made it possible to do the work.

O God, You will not forget!

It is all in Your Book.

Things that never were written upon man's book, and that we would not like to tell, are all in God's Book, whether they be good or bad.

May God bless His Word.

After the singing of Hymn No. 304, the General Overseer delivered his address.

THE HEAVENLY BODY.

INVOCATION.

Let the words of my mouth and the meditation of my heart be acceptable in Thy sight, be profitable unto this people, and unto all to whom these words shall come, in this and every land, in this and all the coming time, Till Jesus Come. Amen.

The General Overseer then read from the 2d epistle of Paul to the Corinthians, in the 5th chapter, 9th verse.

TEXT.

Wherefore also we make it our aim, whether at home or absent, to be well-pleasing unto Him.

"Wherefore also we make it our aim," or, still more clearly as in the Greek, "We are Ambitious, whether at home or absent, to be well-pleasing unto Him."

The Christian Walks by Faith.

The apostle says, before speaking the words of my text:

Being therefore always of good courage, and knowing that, whilst we are at home in the body, we are absent from the Lord

(For we walk by faith, not by sight);

We are of good courage, I say, and are willing rather to be absent from the body, and to be at home with the Lord.

Therefore, it is our ambition that, whether at home in the body with the Lord—that is, standing in the very presence of the Lord—or absent from the body in the Lord—that is, absent by sight, for we walk by faith, not by sight—we may be acceptable and well-pleasing to Him.

May we live, work, and do everything so that we shall be acceptable unto Him, for the very good reason, if there were no other, that we must stand before the Judgment-seat of the Christ.

This morning I have been very much impressed with the thought that was in my mind when I lay down last night, thinking of this morning meeting.

I was somewhat uncertain as to what I would speak to you about, and after I had retired to rest I was moved to leave my room and go to my study and look up this entire passage.

I was very much impressed with it.

That is a beautiful passage in Paul's writings in which, with an apostolic, prophetic, and didactic power—the power of an apostle, a prophet, and a teacher—he gives us some insight into things relating to the heavenly body, so that, if we occupy his standpoint we may, by the Holy Spirit's power, see more than he saw.

We ought to be wiser than he, after nineteen centuries.

Spiritual Law in the Natural World.

But to some these things are enveloped in mists more dense than ever, because they do not look at the natural, physical body from a spiritual standpoint.

They are always talking about Natural Law in the Spiritual World, forgetting the more important thing—which our dear friend, Henry Drummond, forgot—the operation of "Spiritual Law in the Natural World."

That is the most important.

If we will only be careful to stand where Paul stood, and not move from that point, we shall see all of which he speaks, and more.

If you stand at certain points you will get correct perspectives, you will get a correct understanding of that at which you are looking.

If you approach closely to a great mountain, you will see only a very small part of it; you must stand at a distance to see the whole mountain.

Alpine scenery illustrates that.

Beauties Not Always Seen from an Exterior Viewpoint.

Go up the Grindelwald to the glacier of the Wetterhorn, and you will see very little: a mass of ice and debris, covered with mud and dirt that has come down from the mountain.

You cannot see that it is a body of pure ice.

But go up to the point where it has been tunneled into. There you may get right into the very heart of that body of ice.

Then, if you enter, you will understand what the glacier is, because you have gone into it. The debris, and the dirt, and the muck that have come down from the mountain—the skin—you do not see, because you are beneath the skin.

Some people never see what a glacier is, because they look only on the outside of it.

I can imagine a person living in the Grindelwald Valley, looking at the Wetterhorn Glacier and saying, "That is nothing but a heap of muck, and dirt, and debris, and stones. There is nothing beautiful about that ice."

Why do you stand there looking at the skin of it?

Why do you not go up a little higher and follow your guide inside of that great, beautiful glacier and see its glories, where millions of tons' pressure has solidified the snows of the mountain into pure, crystal ice?

Look beyond the mere skin of things.

Paul looked beyond the mere skin of things.

The great majority of Christians are simply looking upon the mere outward appearance.

If you look upon the mere outward appearance of humanity, you will see little that is good.

Only Despair Would Attend a Mere Outward View of Humanity Today.

I am sure that it must be exceedingly disappointing to every student of life, to see this twentieth century open with wars of the most horrible description.

You talk about the progress of humanity, but the Christian powers of Europe have been teaching the Asiatic powers how to make war, how to kill, how to destroy; and they have learned the lesson.

It is a terrible thing that the Japanese have learned; and once the Chinese learn it as the Japanese have learned it, and they flow over the world with their four hundred millions, the Christian powers will regret the day they taught the Chinese and Japanese how to shoot straight.

They will regret the day when they armed them with guns and gave them the idea of drill and of how to fight, murder, and destroy.

If, in viewing the world today, I were to look only at the skin of things, I should fling up my hands in disgust and despair, and say, "I despair of the world! I despair of the world!"

But Paul did not look at the outside of things, and I must not.

The great River of God which is full of Water may be like that imprisoned glacier—there is dirty debris upon the skin of it, but inside there is the Sure Word of Prophecy.

Paul gives us one of these inside views of humanity, as it were; but if you look only at the dirty outside of humanity you will get sick at heart.

All Humanity Is Not an Utter, Complete, and Permanent Failure.

There is the inside.

There is the inside of the Divine Life in humanity.

God has never left Himself without witnesses.

Much of our trouble arises from the fact that we are simply looking at ourselves as bodily beings, and the Apostle wants us to look at things from the standpoint of him who, though he is in the flesh, has a sure and a certain hope of another embodiment.

Our spirits are groaning in these bodies, which at their very best—even when they are pure, and strong, and healthy—subject our spirits to limitations which hinder the working out of those higher and holier purposes and powers that are within the spirit.

For this cause the wise man groans many times in this earthly tabernacle.

The Apostle begins this beautiful chapter by speaking of this body as an earthly house, but as one that will be dissolved.

He says that he will be glad when it is dissolved, because there is waiting for him a building of God—a house not made with hands, eternal in the heavens.

He says that we groan, but not because we would be unclothed.

We do not want to be without a body, but we want a better body.

This body has been spoiled to a large extent, and even though redeemed by the precious blood of the Christ, it cannot immediately be what it was at the beginning.

But the redemption of our Lord Jesus, the Christ, has provided for these saved spirits of ours a better body; a body like unto His Body—all glory.

What is that body?

It certainly is not a corruptible body; it is incorruptible.

It is not a different kind of body.

The Human Body, in Its Original State, Was Perfect.

There was nothing wrong with this body in its original state.

It was all right, and it is wonderful how, even in its decay, caused by sin, this body has much of the very image of God.

Make no mistake about that.

I do not say that God is confined to any particular form of embodiment; but this body must not be spoken of as if it were an utterly contemptible thing.

The words, "Who shall change our vile body," is not in the Scriptures.

That is a shocking mistranslation.

You will see, if you look up that passage in the Revision, that the correct translation is, "Who shall fashion anew the body of our humiliation, that it may be conformed to the body of His glory."

This body is very humble.

Appetite Must Not Be Allowed to Master the Body.

Oh, what a humble body it is in which man dwells—a body that craves a master—and that not a human master, nor a Divine master; but a dirty, filthy master!

I believe there is in this room this morning one man, at least, who is thinking of his body.

I know that there is a man here this morning who has a fight on, and if he does not today settle that fight for good he will go out of the City tomorrow, and that is a fight with the dirty, stinking, vile tobacco.

He goes out and smokes outside of the boundary of the City.

He is a dirty dog.

He goes to Winthrop Harbor, and sits on a log just outside of this City that he may not break the letter of the law.

I caught sight of him a little while ago, and he was yawning—he opened his mouth wide enough to enable one to walk right into it, and that is why I am walking into it now!

That man's body is a nicotine-soaked body.

He has allowed himself to become the slave of a dirty bit of tobacco.

He lies awake nights thinking about it.

He wants to chew it; he wants to suck it; he wants to stink himself and everything about him.

That cannot continue in this City.

We will not have it.

We will not let you stink any one here, not even yourself.

One thing we are teaching, is the mastery of passion, and the keeping under of the body; bringing it into subjection, and saying that this body shall be God's body, and in it we shall do God's Will.

That is Purity.

Paul Possessed Great Purity, but Not Without a Fight.

The Apostle takes us into the region of Absolute Purity when he tells of what is coming to him.

He does not say that he does not have a fight.

If you imagine that he did not have a fight you are mistaken.

The Apostle Paul was a strong man, in every way.

He was just as hard as nails, and had a disciplined mind and a disciplined body.

He was a man who, even before he became a Christian, had his body washed with pure water.

He was one of those men whom you cannot imagine as being dirty.

He was a gentleman.

He was a rabbi.

He was a scholar.

He was a Hebrew of the Hebrews.

Before he was a Christian he stood with the dignity and the majesty of a man that kept his body under.

But oh, what zeal for God!

It was a great and holy zeal, but he was wrong.

He thought that he had to kill Christians.

But he was a clean, strong man, and when he became a Christian he was ten-fold cleaner.

He had a religion which did not say that cleanliness was next to godliness, as if dirt could ever be a part of godliness; but one which said that Cleanliness was Godliness.

He was a clean, strong man, with all the virility and purity of a man who had kept under his body.

He had been a Pharisee, but never a dirty, vile man.

He was one of the men who, when they do become Christians, make finer, stronger, and purer men.

But as he went on in life, his very virility, his very strength, his very manhood was a temptation, and he had to keep under his body and bring it into subjection.

He had to fight with it, so that he cried out, "O wretched man that I am! who shall deliver me out of the body of this death?"

He cried hourly to be delivered from it, and yet he could not be delivered.

"He could have been delivered if he had cut his throat, or if he had drowned himself," you say.

No, no! You cannot be delivered from the body of death by being a suicide, a self-murderer.

You will go to hell if you do that.

You will become a disembodied spirit, and go to the Devil, and you will not get a heavenly body, not for awhile, at least.

You will have to go where they have no bodies; only shadows of bodies.

The Horrible Plague of the Evil Spirits.

It is there the evil spirits are whose horrible plague it is to continue with all the passions of a vile, horrible, sinful, lustful body, but which cannot be gratified.

The rich man goes to hell, but he cannot find a drop of water much less whisky, wine, or opportunities for gratifying the gluttony in which he indulged here.

But he has an appetite, and passions, and he would like to eat and drink, but he has the torture of the damned.

He is like Tantalus, who was plunged up to the chin in water with the finest fruits hanging over his head, but both water and fruit retreated whenever he attempted to partake of them.

This is a story of the voluptuous Tantalus, who, having lived for his body, after death was tortured with both thirst and hunger while the means of gratifying both were apparently within his reach.

That is an illustration of the condition of the damned.

Satan, a fallen angel, who was cast out of heaven, and the spirits of those who kept not their first estate, are in this place and condition of torment.

Satan and all evil spirits have no bodies.

One of the distinguishing characteristics of an angel of darkness is his disembodiment, while the angel of light is embodied.

The angel of darkness pretends that he has a body but he has none.

He cannot touch you with a physical touch.

He may pretend that he is some one who has died, and he may imitate your mother's or your father's voice; or, if youy ourself die, he may imitate your voice; but he is a liar; he is not the person he pretends to be.

He cannot have a body.

God's Angels Have Bodies.

One of the most extraordinary things in connection with the whole realm of the spirit life, is that the angels have bodies.

An angel, a young man in shining garments, sat by the sepulcher.

The angels that came to Abraham to warn him of the destruction of Sodom and Gomorrah appeared as majestic men, and they ate and drank with Abraham in his tent.

They had bodies that ate and drank.

When the Lord Jesus, the Christ, Himself, rose from the dead, did He not eat at Emmaus?

Did He not say to His disciples, "Children have ye any meat?" Did He not provide a fire for them, possibly assisted by angelic hands, and broil fish that they might eat when they had come in from their boats in answer to His call, after they had been toiling all the night in vain, and had not got a draft until He told them to put down their net on the right side?

These heavenly bodies, these resurrection bodies of the saints, are glorified bodies.

They have all the powers of this body, which God made in His own image; but they are better by reason, in part, of their bloodless condition.

And yet some are boasting of this blood, which at its best, as we now know it, is vile and dirty.

They say, "I have good blood."

Have you ever found any good blood?

Will you tell me where you found it?

Heredity Imparted Through the Blood.

I do not say that there is not a strain of blood that imparts to men and women, to an extent, certain powers, certain dignity and other relatively good inheritances.

There is no use in saying that there is not.

You might as well say that not all horses were finely-bred horses.

Blood will tell, they say; and that is true.

It tells in the horse, dog, cat, and in the man and woman.

I will not say that there is nothing in heredity, because there is.

There comes down to us through the ages—we do not know exactly from whence—not only thes piritual, but the psychical and the physical heredity.

If you are to be fathers and mothers this is one consideration why you should seek to have your bodies clean.

The transmission of our own nature, our own life, is of the utmost importance.

Many children are born who are children of dirt and muck, from the very beginning.

Their fathers and mothers were ignorant, beastly gluttons and drunkards, and nothing less than thieves, liars, cheats, and brutes.

Look at those poor people down at the Stockyards!

They went on a strike, but they do not know why.

Their leaders got them to strike.

Now they are starving and shooting the police.

They steal the cattle, jumping upon the poor beasts and killing them with knives;-before the police get there they have cut up and disappeared with the carcass.

Do you say that men who do such things have good blood?

What about the South today?

Two men in Statesboro, Georgia, were sentenced to be hanged for crime.

The law was about to take its course, when, with the brutal instincts of a white mob, hundreds rushed upon the court house, and, not content that the poor wretches should be hanged, they took them out, tied them to a stake, poured kerosene over them, and burned them to death, with all the horrors and tortures that Apache Indians are supposed to be capable of inflicting.

Is that fine blood?

Is that fine training?

Is that not something of which to be ashamed?

Horrible!

The brother of the man who was murdered plead with the mob to let the poor wretches die at the hands of justice, and to let them have a few hours to repent, and make confession more fully of their crimes.

But, no; this brutal mob would not listen.

Unwillingness to Let Divine or Human Justice Take Its Course.

There is no doubt that we all have this savageness by nature—the unwillingness to let Divine or human justice take its course.

We want to be the brutal settlers of our own quarrels, just as the nations are that are murdering each other today.

Neither the Japanese nor the Russians have any right in Manchuria or Korea.

Those that are fighting this battle in the East have no right in either place.

The Koreans should have Korea; the Manchurians should have Manchuria, and the Chinese should have China.

But two thievish nations that want Korea and Manchuria are fighting upon Manchurian and Korean soil for lands that are not theirs.

They are murdering each other in tens and hundreds of thousands on sea and on land, just to get their neighbor's property.

The Apostle saw all that, but knew it to be only the skin of things.

He saw something better.

He said as I say this morning, that I am glad to know that you and I who are the children of God, are not far away from that better body.

I am glad that the Consummation of the Age is at hand.

I am glad that the Restoration of All Things is begun.

I am glad that among the Things to be restored is our body.

Then Our Bodies Will no Longer Be the Slaves of Passion, of Sin, and of Uncleanness.

Lift up your heads, redemption is nigh, for our Lord will take us to Himself and change this body into a glorious body like unto His body of glory.

We shall then be free from many things with which we now have to battle.

We can then make full use of our powers, for we cannot exercise our very best powers, in many respects, because of the limitations of this body.

I cannot do half that I would do in this life if I did not have to sleep or eat.

I should be very glad if I did not have to sleep or eat.
I could work twenty-four hours every day.
Sometimes I work more than that.
While I am not indifferent to food and to sleep, I should be glad if the hours I have to give for eating and sleeping could be used for God.
I am glad to think that in the new body if we have to rest it will not be by sleep.
Perhaps you cannot understand rest without sleeping.
When I have had a long, busy day laboring over Zion's business I rest by going into my library and reading.
I roam over the histories of the past, and the facts of the present.
I go to my Bible and feed in the heavenly pastures green, under the Shepherd's tender care, and the guidance of the Holy Spirit.
Thus I turn from the business of Zion to the spiritualities of Zion, or perhaps to writing an apostolic letter which is very important.
I rest by change of occupation.
Some of you will rest far more if you will not look forward to holidays in which you can lie on your back.
Some of you sleep far too much.
I am also convinced that many eat too much, and that is why their spirits are not more wide-awake.
If they cultivated more and more the habit of eating and sleeping less, their spirits would be purer and soar higher, reaching the high and pure things of God.
But do not eat too little.
You must eat enough to have a good, strong body, and sleep enough to keep that body in a fairly good condition.
But you can eat so much that your body will become weak, and you can sleep so much that your body will always be tired.

No Habitation Awaiting the Child of the Devil.

The Apostle Paul does not want to be a naked spirit, but a spirit with a heavenly body, with a house that is from God.
It is awaiting us in the measure created by us.
When a person, that is a child of the Devil, leaves this body, he does not get a heavenly body, but goes to hell where there is no house, no habitation.
When you go to hell and dwell with devils you go a naked spirit.
That is what the devils are aiming at.
You will see in the 16th chapter of the Revelation, that these unclean spirits, like frogs, go out of the mouth of the beast and of the false prophet and of Satan himself.
They go out to take hold of men and women to deceive them and strip them naked, so that they shall stand before the Judgment-seat of the Christ disembodied and timid spirits.
Children of the Devil will have no spiritual embodiment until they repent, and until God, in His infinite mercy, takes them out of hell.
When you come before God to be judged according to the deeds done in the body, and your record is a bad one, you liars, you hypocrites, will stand out in the light of God, disembodied spirits.
Your spirit will have upon it a spiritual brand of hypocrite, liar, unclean, filthy, that every eye shall see.
Oh, how deformed and horrible that spirit will be to the spiritual eye!
You had better get rid of these evils now by repenting and by getting right with God.

Some to Receive a Dwarf's Body.

Others of you, when you get your heavenly bodies, will be about a foot high, because you are spiritual dwarfs now, and all the body you can get will be a dwarf's body.
I hope it will grow through eternity.
Some of you will not need a large body, because you have a small spirit.
Yes, you will get into heaven, but you will have a dwarf's body as it were.
Why not get into heaven in such a way that you will get a body of glory that will be large, majestic, and beautiful.
The body that you will have will be dependent entirely upon how you live, for we must all stand out in the light before the Judgment-seat of the Christ, and receive from Him according to the deeds done in the body, whether these deeds were good or bad.

The Body Dies and the Reward Will Be Entirely Proportionate to the Way We Have Lived.

Seeing that is true, should we not take care of this earthly body, and see that it is a pure and clean temple of God?
Ought we not to take care that our thoughts and lives are clean, and that we do not allow this body to be dragged down into the mire, and dirt, and muck of a tobacco fiend; of a whisky fiend; of the house of her whose house is the gate of hell?
Surely we are not Christians while we waste our bodies in filthy uses, and make wives or husbands mere tools of debauchery.
Have you no restraint?
Have you no Purity?
Have you no desire that your body shall be the temple of God?
Talk about the bodies of some of you being the temples of God!
Do you think that God Almighty will dwell in that filthy, dirty tobacco shop of yours?
Do you think that God Almighty will live in that dirty body, that is full of unclean thoughts, and greed, and dirt, and muck?
The Holy Spirit will never live in such a mass of dirt as that.
But, beloved, if we are seeking that every power in this body, every drop of blood, and every organ shall be used for God and by God, then, when the time comes for us to leave this body, we shall find waiting for us a glorious body—a body of glory.
You want to read of a body of glory?
Then read the description in the 1st chapter of the Revelation.
May God grant us the desire to have our earthly tabernacle clean, that when the last breath goes out of it, the beautiful body that is being prepared and fitted for us as we live will be waiting for us.

God Is Building Our Glorious Body.

I think that we ourselves are doing something in the building of it.
All through this earthly life it is being built.
There are beautiful bodies waiting for some who shall go, not with disembodied devils, but embodied angels, to our Master, and when He comes back they shall dwell with Him, in a body celestial and pure.
May God make us worthy of such a body.
Those who want it stand and pray.

PRAYER OF CONSECRATION.

My God and Father, in Jesus' Name I come to Thee. Take me as I am. Make me what I ought to be in spirit, in soul, and in body. By Thy Spirit give me power to abstain from every form of evil. Give me power to keep under my body and to bring it into subjection, that I may live a spiritual life, and obey the spiritual laws in my earthly and natural body, so that when I leave this body, I shall enter into the habitation which Thou hast prepared —the body which Thou hast prepared for those that are Thine, and that are prepared to enter into the pure and holy life. Help me so to live that I may be prepared for a pure body. For Jesus' sake. [*All repeat the prayer, clause by clause, after the General Overseer.*]

Now did you mean it?
PEOPLE—"Yes."
GENERAL OVERSEER—Live it, beloved friends, and all will be well.
The service was closed by the Doxology and the

BENEDICTION.

Beloved, abstain from every form of evil. And may the very God of Peace Himself sanctify you wholly; and I pray God your whole spirit, and soul, and body be preserved entire, without blame, unto the coming of our Lord Jesus, the Christ. Faithful is He that calleth you, who also will do it. The grace of our Lord Jesus, the Christ, the love of God, our Father, the fellowship of the Holy Spirit, our Comforter and Guide, one Eternal God, abide in you, bless you, and keep you, and all the Israel of God everywhere, forever. Amen.

Notice to Correspondents.

In writing to Headquarters it is *absolutely essential* that the writer give his full address.
Failure to comply with this request necessitates looking up or referring to the Church Records, which involves much time, and is very frequently fruitless.
Friends and members of the Christian Catholic Church in Zion everywhere will please bear this in mind, especially those in foreign lands.
J. G. EXCELL, General Ecclesiastical Secretary.

Tenth Anniversary of Zion Printing and Publishing House

*REPORTED BY S. E. C., O. R., AND A. W. N.

Shiloh Tabernacle, Zion City, Illinois, Wednesday Evening, August 31, 1904.

ON August 31, 1894, in the City of Chicago, Illinois, the wheels and levers of a small printing-press moved for the first time, and a "weekly Paper for the Extension of the Kingdom of God" was quietly born into the world.

In the ten short years that have sped away into eternity since that day, that paper, LEAVES OF HEALING, has gone out to all the ends of the earth.

As it has gone, it has overturned, and overturned, and overturned in men's hearts, in their homes, in their workshops and offices, in their schools and churches, in their societies, in states and nations, until the whole world has been shaken by its power; for it has carried upon its pure-white pages the Messages of the Living God.

It has been the Messenger that has carried the words of Elijah, the Prophet of the Restoration.

That Prophet's work precedes the coming of Him who will reign supreme over all the earth, and this paper has been his mightiest instrument in the work of preparation.

The sinful have been saved and cleansed, the sick have been healed, the sad have been comforted, the weary have found rest, the desolate have found love and shelter, the poor have found profitable employment, the despairing have found a blessed hope, families have been reunited, homes have been made happy and prosperous, and tens of thousands have consecrated themselves wholly to God and to His work, as the result of the dynamic force of the millions of papers that have followed the first one printed on August 31, 1894.

The strongholds of Evil have been shattered until the walls are undermined and crumbling.

The massive structure of apostasy has been dealt blow upon blow until the whole rotten fabric is tottering to its fall.

"This Gospel of the Kingdom" has been preached by LEAVES OF HEALING in well-nigh every nation, and the End is very near at hand.

The Christian Catholic Church in Zion has been founded.

A City has been built, and ten thousand of the people of God have gathered within its walls, from all the corners of the earth.

Great Educational, Financial, Commercial, Industrial, and Political Institutions have been set on foot and are succeeding.

Many other Cities, Institutions, and Industries, of world-wide scope, are being planned, and the plans will be successfully carried out.

LEAVES OF HEALING has been and is the instrument in God's hands for more than nine-tenths of all this work.

LEAVES OF HEALING is the chief product of Zion Printing and Publishing House, which Institution celebrated its Tenth Anniversary on Wednesday, August 31, 1904.

This Anniversary was appropriately observed by a very busy and productive day's work in all departments of the plant, at the corner of Deborah Avenue and Shiloh Boulevard, and by a special program at the regular Citizens' Mid-week Rally, in Shiloh Tabernacle, that evening.

While the people were filling the great auditorium, Zion City Band entertained them royally with a number of very excellent selections, which showed that this organization—the admiration of people and musical critics in Chicago, New York, and other cities—since last October, has been steadily growing and improving, until, today, it stands the peer of any professional band of its size in the country.

On the platform, with the General Overseer, were seated Overseer Jane Dowie, Dr. A. J. Gladstone Dowie, Deacon Arthur W. Newcomb, General Associate Editor of Zion publications and General Manager of Zion Printing and Publishing House; Deacon B. F. Morris, Assistant Manager; Evangelist Marie Brieger-Hodler, Assistant Editor of BLÄTTER DER HEILUNG; Evangelist Sarah E. Hill, Superintendent Zion Free Literature Mission; J. B. Coghill, Manager of the Printing Department; Deacon M. N. Price, Superintendent of Printing; Deacon O. W. Davis, Superintendent of Circulation; Miss Lydia V. Stauffacher and Mrs. Emily Ware, of the Editorial Staff; Deacon Theodore R. Becker, Foreman of the Composing Room, and Christopher Hendricks, Foreman of the Press Room.

Distribution of Prizes for Flower Gardens.

On this occasion, Overseer Jane Dowie and Dr. A. J. Gladstone Dowie distributed the prizes to those who had won in the annual flower competition.

These prizes are given by the General Overseer, Overseer Jane Dowie, and Dr. A. J. Gladstone Dowie for excellence of flower gardens in the City of Zion.

Dr. A. J. Gladstone Dowie made the address of presentation.

During the course of his remarks, he took occasion to compliment the prize-winners, and many of those who did not win prizes, upon the general excellence of the gardens of the City this year, especially in view of the lateness and unfavorableness of the season.

He stated that, notwithstanding this handicap, the gardens in Zion City were fifty per cent. better this year than they were last.

He also expressed the hope and expectation that next year would see another fifty per cent. of improvement.

He offered many practical suggestions to gardeners and property owners for the improvement of the appearance of their grounds, and the city as a whole.

The following is the list of prize-winners in the order named:

S. E. Yonkers, 2812 Elizabeth avenue, first prize, $75.

Charles Miell, 2113 Enoch avenue, second prize, $50.

Mrs. O. W. Farley, 3016 Enoch avenue, third prize, $35.

Mrs. R. S. Osburn, 3001 Elizabeth avenue, fourth prize, $20.

A. J. Thompson, 3012 Elizabeth avenue, fifth prize, $15.

A. E. Simons, 3006 Elizabeth avenue, Deacon J. Vinnedge, 3014 Enoch avenue, and J. Granstrom, 3027 Gilead avenue, $10 each.

C. Caldwell, 2512 Gideon avenue, Mrs. D. D. Hotchkiss, 3002 Edina boulevard, Mrs. V. J. Gurtler, 1709 Hebron avenue, Mrs. M. Oberholtzer, 1821 Hebron avenue, and Mrs. L. A. Bierthaupt, 2911 Ezra avenue, $5 each.

While the checks for the prizes were being distributed by Overseer Jane Dowie and Dr. A. J. Gladstone Dowie, a very delightful harp solo was rendered by Mrs. Linval J. Hire of Zion Orchestra.

It was also very appropriate to the occasion, as its title was "A Flower Song."

In honor of this distribution of the flower prizes, the platform of the Tabernacle was very handsomely decorated with cut flowers and floral pieces, most of the blooms being furnished by the several prize-winners.

A very unique and tasteful feature of this decoration was a great blaze of Golden Glow all along the railing immediately behind the platform and in front of the Choir gallery.

*The following reports have not been revised by the General Overseer

Immediately after this part of the program, the General Overseer introduced the members of the staff of Zion Printing and Publishing House present on the platform, very generously and kindly complimenting and praising his fellow workers on the Editorial, Business, and Mechanical staffs.

He spoke very briefly of what God had wrought during the ten years of the existence of this Institution, but said that he would keep his principal address on this subject until the last.

He then introduced Deacon Arthur W. Newcomb, General Associate Editor and General Manager, who spoke as follows:

Address by Deacon Arthur W. Newcomb.

"General Overseer, dear brothers and sisters—First of all I desire to thank Overseer Jane Dowie, Dr. A. J. Gladstone Dowie, the Horticultural Department, and the other friends who have decorated this platform so beautifully in honor of the Tenth Anniversary of Zion Printing and Publishing House.

Place of Zion Printing and Publishing House in History of These Times.

"I wonder if you all realize just how important Zion Printing and Publishing House is.

"I firmly believe that God, our Heavenly Father, had Zion Printing and Publishing House at heart when, by His Holy Spirit's inspiration, printing from movable types was invented about four hundred fifty years ago.

"The invention of printing was followed by the discovery of America, and by an era of progress along mechanical lines, especially in the development of means of communication and travel.

"With the invention of the steam engine and the discovery of some of the laws of electricity, this development took a great onward stride about a century ago.

"It has gone forward with an ever-accelerating pace, until the present time, when we have trains that run seventy miles an hour all over the world, with experimental trains that rush along as rapidly as two hundred fifty miles an hour; when we have ships that steam from five hundred to five hundred fifty miles in twenty-four hours; when we have cables and telegraphs that flash the thought of man around the world in a few seconds; marconigraphs that send messages through the ether without wires; telephones, phonographs, biographs, engraving processes, and many other inventions and improvements that make communication and travel in this, the beginning of the twentieth century, something that was not even thought of, and scarcely imagined, only fifty years ago.

"I believe that all these inventions are a part of the plan of God in the bringing of the Age to its Consummation.

"It is only the development of the art of printing and the perfecting of the means of bringing information and thought from all the ends of the earth to the printing press, and of carrying it again therefrom on the printed page to all parts of the world, that has made it possible for the Prophet of God to send forth the Messages of the Restoration of All Things to every creature.

"And in that plan Zion Printing and Publishing House occupies a central position next to the Prophet of God himself.

"It is therefore with a sense of great unworthiness, and yet great joy and thanksgiving, that I find myself representing, on this its Tenth Anniversary, this most wonderful printing plant in all the world, and in all the history of the world.

Unique Character and Purpose of Zion Printing and Publishing House.

"It is the only printing plant I know anything about that has ever been used for the dissemination of a Prophetic Message from God; and of course the only printing plant that has ever been used for the sending forth of the Messages which are to prepare this world for the coming of Jesus, the Christ, to reign as King.

"I have prepared a few statistics concerning some of the work which has been done during the ten years' existence of Zion Printing and Publishing House.

"I might have prepared a great many more; but my experience as a reporter has always been that the spreading out of a table of statistics by a speaker is the signal for every one to go to sleep.

"I have, therefore, made mine as short as possible.

"I hope that in view of the importance of the work you will find them interesting.

"The first and most important product of Zion Printing and Publishing House, as you all know, is LEAVES OF HEALING.

"Here are a few figures about the number and amount of LEAVES OF HEALING produced in ten years.

Some Statistics of "Leaves of Healing."

"There have been nearly Fifteen Volumes of LEAVES OF HEALING, of which there have been thirteen thousand ninety-seven (13,097) separate and distinct pages.

"The total number of pages of LEAVES OF HEALING, counting all the copies that have been printed, up to the present time is two hundred thirty-four million four hundred sixty thousand (234,460,000); that is nearly a quarter of a billion.

"In the printing of these pages were consumed one thousand one hundred fifty-two (1,152) tons of paper.

"If you were to take the sheets on which these LEAVES OF HEALING were printed, twenty-eight inches one way and forty-two inches another, and pile them up in a single column, they would reach a height of two thousand three hundred ninety-five feet; that is to say, nearly a half mile high; in other words, about four and a third times as high as the Washington Monument at Washington, D. C.

"If you were to take these sheets of paper and spread them out with the edges touching, just one thickness, they would cover four hundred sixteen million eight hundred ninety-six thousand (416,896,000) square feet, or fifteen square miles. That is to say, these papers, if spread over the site of the City of Zion would cover it all and have enough left to cover half as much area again.

"When LEAVES OF HEALING was started by the General Overseer, the number of weekly subscriptions was about two thousand (2,000).

"Today our subscription list for all Zion publications, amounts to fifty-one thousand (51,000) weekly, making the number of pieces sent out each year at the present rate, two million six hundred fifty-two thousand (2,652,000).

Twenty-five Million Pieces of Zion Literature.

"The total number of separate pieces of Zion Literature, counting all the Messages, LEAVES OF HEALING, BANNERS, BLÄTTER DER HEILUNG, BLADEN DER HEELING, A VOICE FROM ZION, and all the tracts sent out in ten years, is twenty-five million (25,000,000), or one piece, nearly, for every fifty persons now living on the face of the earth.

"If we suppose that ten people, on an average, read every piece of Zion Literature sent out, then there are not enough people living now to have done all that reading.

"The number of pages of Zion Literature, LEAVES OF HEALING and others, combined, is four hundred thirty-nine million ten thousand (439,010,000).

"Zion Literature has been printed in English, German, French, Dutch, Italian, Danish, Swedish, Bohemian, Arabic, Chinese, and Japanese.

Some Comparative Statistics.

"Zion Printing and Publishing House started with one printing-press; today we have eleven.

"Zion Printing and Publishing House began with five employees.

"Today we have on our pay-roll one hundred eighty-two; and besides those we have a number of contributors to the pages of LEAVES OF HEALING, THE ZION BANNER, and other Zion Publications.

"When Zion Printing and Publishing House started, the capacity was five hundred LEAVES OF HEALING an hour.

"Today we are able to print and complete ten thousand five hundred an hour for twenty-four hours each day, if necessary; and it is sometimes necessary.

"Two compositors began to set up Volume I., Number 1, of LEAVES OF HEALING.

"Today it takes thirty compositors to set up the different publications of Zion Printing and Publishing House, and the job printing that comes in from the City of Zion and the world outside.

"Zion Printing and Publishing House, on August 31, 1894, covered six hundred square feet of floor space.

"Today Zion Printing and Publishing House is so crowded it

seems to us sometimes it surely must burst the walls, yet it covers forty thousand square feet.

"We want more room.

"As nearly as we have been able to estimate, Zion Printing and Publishing House, ten years ago, was begun with three hundred dollars, and cost complete between eight and ten thousand dollars.

"The value of Zion Printing and Publishing House, including the building, machinery, fixtures, and our electrotype plates, which are invaluable, and, in one sense, cannot be estimated in dollars and cents, is two hundred forty-eight thousand ninety-nine dollars and eighty-nine cents ($248,099.89).

"An average of these different increases, shows that Zion Printing and Publishing House of today is thirty-four and one-tenth times as large as Zion Printing and Publishing House of ten years ago.

Fifteen Million Pieces of Zion Literature Given Away.

"I have a very interesting letter from Elder Lee, who is the Recorder of Zion Restoration Host.

"Zion Restoration Host gets its ammunition from Zion Printing and Publishing House; and, therefore, the work that has been done by that Host is of vital interest in this connection.

"This letter reads as follows:

ZION CITY, ILLINOIS, U. S. A., August 31, 1904.

REV. JOHN ALEX. DOWIE,

General Overseer of the Christian Catholic Church in Zion, Zion City, Illinois.

My Dear General Overseer:—In compliance with your instructions, I submit to you the following report of Literature which has been distributed by members of Zion Restoration Host since the date of organization.

I regret to say that we have no record of the vast quantity of Literature which was distributed by Zion Seventies prior to September 21, 1902, so that the figures given below represent only the work of the last two years, from September, 1902, to September, 1904.

Total number of pieces of Literature, including LEAVES OF HEALING, THE ZION BANNER, A VOICE FROM ZION, Penny Tracts, and Restoration Messages, seven million three hundred sixty-eight thousand four hundred forty-seven (7,368,447).

Of this number one million two hundred fifty-five thousand four hundred forty-one (1,255,441) pieces were distributed by members of the Host during the Chicago Visitation from September, 1902, to June 1, 1903, while four million one hundred thousand two hundred fifty (4,100,250) pieces were distributed by the Host during the New York Visitation in October, 1903.

The balance, two million twelve thousand seven hundred fifty-six (2,012,756) pieces, have been distributed by members of the Host in various parts of the different continents of the world.

These figures give us some little conception of what a mighty factor Zion Printing-presses are in the work of evangelizing the world.

With a heart full of thanksgiving to God for giving me a small part in this great work, and earnestly praying that He may spare your life to direct these great agencies for many years to come, I remain,

Most faithfully, Your humble servant in Jesus, the Christ,

ABRAHAM F. LEE,
Recorder of Zion Restoration Host.

"In addition to the distribution of Zion Restoration Host, there is another department of Zion which always gets its ammunition from Zion Printing and Publishing House.

"Zion Restoration Host might be compared with the infantry, which has a short sword and goes into the fight hand to hand and face to face.

"We furnish them the sword.

"Zion Free Literature Mission might be compared with the artillery, which is able to hit the mark ten thousand miles away, or any distance to which it is sent.

"The number of rolls sent out by Zion Free Literature Mission since its inception is three million three hundred sixty-nine thousand five hundred eighty-nine (3,369,589).

"This, added to that given out by Zion Restoration Host makes the recorded number of pieces of Zion Literature that have been given away during the last ten years, ten million seven hundred thirty-eight thousand thirty-six (10,738,036).

"Of course, that does not count the number of pieces that a great many of you and other people all over the world have given away individually, not as members of Zion Seventies, or of Zion Restoration Host.

"Neither does it count all the Messages and LEAVES OF HEALING that were given away by Zion Seventies in the four years of their existence before the organization of Zion Restoration Host.

"It seems to the General Overseer, and I heartily agree with him, that if we add all those given away by Zion Seventies, and those given away by private individuals, the total number of pieces of the product of Zion Printing and Publishing House given away throughout the world during these ten years would reach the sum of fifteen million (15,000,000).

"If we estimate that ten people read every piece—and we know of many copies of LEAVES OF HEALING that have been read by hundreds—that means that one hundred fifty million (150,000,000) people have read Zion Literature, as a result of these agencies.

"That does not include the number that has been sent out from Zion Printing and Publishing House on subscription or the number that has been sold in our various retail branches.

Some New Departments of Zion Printing and Publishing House.

"On January 1st of this year we opened Zion Printing and Publishing House to commercial printing.

"It was a new feature to us.

"Zion Printing and Publishing House, as an institution, had been a heavy financial loser up to that time.

"Every institution of Zion, from the Christian Catholic Church in Zion down to the least and most unimportant, had been a gainer by that loss.

"We thought that the time had come, with all the splendid equipment of the plant, to make money for God.

"The General Overseer, therefore, finally gave his consent for us to take in commercial printing.

"We have had many things to learn; but I am very glad to report to you that the venture has been a successful one, and that Zion Printing and Publishing House is making a splendid reputation for its products in the business world.

"Soon after the first of the year, the Department of Office Specialties and Supplies was added.

"This department manufactures blank books of all kinds and for every proper purpose, stationery, commercial forms, and other printed matter for use in offices, and does a general jobbing business in office supplies.

"We now have several very successful salesmen on the road, and we want as many more good salesmen as we can get.

"Through an oversight, E. C. Fish, the excellent superintendent of this department, is not on the platform tonight.

"During the last few months a bookbindery has been added to our equipment, so that we now bind LEAVES OF HEALING, and other books under our own roof.

"We have also added an electrotyping plant within the year.

"Zion Printing and Publishing House made all its plates in the beginning; but when the plant was moved to 1300 Michigan avenue, we had no room for the electrotype plant, and it had to be sold.

"When we moved to Zion City, a little over a year ago, we installed the best and most modern machinery and equipment for making electrotype plates, so that we are able to do very rapid and very perfect work.

"In addition to our own work we are doing a very good business in the making of plates for outside firms.

"We are now going forward in the establishment of an engraving plant, which we hope to have running in a few weeks.

"We will then be able to make all the pictures and cartoons, and all the other classes of engraving you see in LEAVES OF HEALING, THE ZION BANNER, and other Zion publications, and will also be able to do some for the outside world.

Commercial Advantages of a Plant in Zion City.

"We have wonderful advantages in Zion City in being free from strikes and labor union tyranny.

"We are in our own building and have no heavy rent to pay, and have many other advantages.

"We hope to be able to produce engravings of all kinds at prices and at a profit that will enable us to compete successfully with the largest engraving plants in the cities of Milwaukee and Chicago.

"We are also preparing, slowly but surely, for the instalment of a lithographic plant, for the printing, on stone, in colors, the beautiful pictures, advertisements, cards, labels, checks, letter-heads, fine stationery, stock certificates, and other products of the lithographer's art.

"This plant will be installed in the next few months.

"We are preparing to extend and push forward.

"Leaves of Healing," the First and Highest Consideration.

"But especially, night and day, week in and week out, month in and month out, year in and year out, we are everlastingly pushing the subscriptions to LEAVES OF HEALING.

"That is the direction in which we desire to expand most of all.

"In view of the great importance of the work in which we are engaged, we feel it right to call upon every member of Zion Restoration Host, every member and friend of Zion, and every friend of Righteousness and Purity on this earth, to join with us, heart and soul with all the energies they have, in pushing up the subscription list of LEAVES OF HEALING." [Applause.]

The General Overseer then called upon Overseer Jane Dowie to say a few words, which she did very graciously, but very briefly, thanking God for His goodness in connection with Zion publications.

Addresses by Members of the Staff.

Evangelist Marie Brieger-Hodler, Assistant Editor of BLÄTTER DER HEILUNG, then gave a very bright and interesting talk on the work that God had wrought in German-speaking lands through the German edition of LEAVES OF HEALING, and giving praise to Him for great personal blessings.

Evangelist Sarah E. Hill, Superintendent of Zion Free Literature Mission, spoke briefly, but with that great earnestness and absolute conviction that always make her addresses a power.

Mrs. Emily Ware gave thanks to God for the high honor and great privilege of being a member of the Christian Catholic Church in Zion and Zion Restoration Host, of being a citizen of Zion City, of being permitted to work with the Host during the New York Visitation, and of having been given the work of writing and editing the Memorabilia of that Visitation.

Miss Lydia V. Stauffacher, in a few happily-chosen words, told of her joy and gratitude in the doing of editorial work on Zion publications.

Deacon B. F. Morris spoke with great earnestness and zeal on the high privilege and important duty of every member and friend of Zion to assist, to the utmost extent of his or her power, in the extension of the circulation of LEAVES OF HEALING.

Joseph B. Coghill, after a few witty opening remarks, seconded Deacon Morris' plea by telling how one copy of LEAVES OF HEALING, placed in his hands by a faithful Zion Restorationist on a railroad train, brought him and his family into Zion and wrought great blessing in their lives.

Deacon M. N. Price told briefly of his experience in Zion and his gratitude for the privilege of having a part of the work in Zion Printing and Publishing House.

Deacon O. W. Davis told what God had done for him through LEAVES OF HEALING, and brought the matter down to a practical application by calling attention to the fact that a large number of subscription blanks had been provided for the occasion and could be had immediately after the meeting.

Deacon Thepdore R. Becker and Christopher Hendricks gave joyous testimonies to the great blessings wrought in their lives by the power of God through the teaching and prayers of the General Overseer and gave thanks to Him for Zion Printing and Publishing House and the honor of having a part in its work.

The General Overseer then said:

I feel tonight that all my toil in keeping this great work going during these long ten years has not been too much.

I am glad for these ten years of work.

A Work That Will Not Pass Away.

If I had nothing else by which to be remembered, should I pass away tonight, these fifteen volumes of LEAVES OF HEALING would be enough.

They will stand while the world stands.

They will talk when you and I, perhaps, have passed away.

I believe that they will have a part in the Millennial glory.

There is a record in them that God will not suffer to die.

It is the record of work wrought.

The whole Bible does not contain forty detailed cases of healing.

You will find forty detailed cases of healing, on an average in every four issues of LEAVES OF HEALING, and sometimes in one issue alone you will have almost that number.

The work goes on and on, and the testimonies in hundreds of thousands of those who have found Salvation, Healing, and Cleansing stand unimpeached and unimpeachable.

The Whole Life of This Movement Depends Upon an Energetic Pushing Forward.

Thus far the Russians have lost in Central Asia because they are dealing with a little nation that will never spell the word "defeat" until the last man is killed.

They know nothing about going backward.

That is the kind of people we want.

Do they not grow tired?

Yes.

Recently they fought a battle against Kuropatkin who had all his forces concentrated; and they made little progress.

But they slept on their arms; they bivouacked on the battle field.

At daylight they were at it again, and they will keep everlastingly at it until they drive the Russians out of Manchuria back into Russia.

I want to see that spirit here.

The children of darkness are more than equaled by the children of light.

I want to see a people that keep at it and at it.

No matter how dark it may be, no matter how hard the path never let the foe see your back.

But you cannot succeed in that unless you are awake.

How Each One Can Have a Part in the Work.

There is one thing you all can do.

It is a little thing for you to spend a few extra cents each week in sending out LEAVES OF HEALING.

If all would do it, what wonderful results might be accomplished!

Suppose that in this City of ten thousand inhabitants, five thousand of you sent out this month a hundred copies each that is three copies a day for the month we are now approaching.

That would amount to five hundred thousand copies.

There is scarcely a boy or girl who could not send out one hundred copies during the month.

I know that a great deal can be done.

I also know that it is the humblest and poorest people in Zion who do the most, proportionately; but I am thankful for those of larger means who do so much.

My strength in the world has always lain in the great masses of the poor who have been with me.

I have never bothered myself about the very rich.

I thank God for those who have brought means and who have had some considerable portion of this world's goods; and we want more; but the strength of Zion has been in the comparatively poor.

This Tenth Anniversary of the establishment of Zion Printing and Publishing House ought to be signalized by every one of you voluntarily and heartily filling out a subscription blank of LEAVES OF HEALING.

I want two hundred fifty thousand copies of Volume XV, No. 18, containing reports of the Business Conferences, to be sent out.

It contains the answers to hundreds of thousands of questions that are being asked in America.

Only the Cheerful Giver Receives a Blessing.

But if you do not do this because you love to do it, do not do it at all.

I do not believe that the Lord cares for your giving if it is not done cheerfully.

The great power in my work has been that by the grace of God I have been a cheerful giver.

I give that for which no money could ever repay me.

I pour out my very life into every page of LEAVES OF HEALING.

Then that life comes back to me; for even when I read these pages myself, I get a blessing.

Then when I hear from all over the world what has been done, I feel that God has made them wonderful words of life; and God blesses them.

I know that there is no other paper that has ever been produced that God has so greatly blessed to the Salvation and Healing of multitudes.

Just now you are not being called upon to do much work.

I am calling upon you to get into training.

If you all worked as hard as the General Overseer does, and as many hours, a great deal more would be done.

I do not expect it of you.

The reason why I am so strong today is because I do so much work and have so little sleep.

I believe that God has blessed me because I have unselfishly poured out my life.

He that findeth his life shall lose it; and he that loseth his life for My sake shall find it.

My heart is filled with gratitude, first to God, and second to the good and earnest people that have rallied around me and enabled me to do this work.

Personal Sacrifices.

I do not want to talk much about the personal sacrifices that created Zion Printing and Publishing House; but there have been personal sacrifices.

They have been personal burdens.

There have been personal toils.

I have been the personal worker in connection with the financial work of this Institution.

God had to give me money in order to do this work; and only now and then have I appealed to the people.

I have had to appeal to God, and He has sent me the resources from all over the world.

If He had not, I could not have done this work.

The plant is now worth at least a quarter of a million dollars.

It is a plant that has turned out in these ten years four and one-half hundred million pages.

It is a plant that has awakened the world, by firing shots that have gone all around the world.

Realize That "Leaves of Healing" Is Zion on Wings.

If you want to develop the City; if you want to see capital pour into our enterprises so rapidly that Zion Lace Industries will be extended to the lake, and the Zion Sugar and Confection Association will grow proportionately, send out this quarter of a million copies, and who can tell what the result will be?

One copy may fall into the hands of a godly man who has large capital; and he will come and look, and then say, "Doctor, here is a million dollars that I desire to invest."

I ask you to pray especially that LEAVES OF HEALING may bring Salvation, Healing, Cleansing and Quickening to multitudes.

We must remember that we have to be up to date.

There is no profit in the production of these two hundred fifty thousand copies of LEAVES OF HEALING, which I have asked you to send out.

"Leaves of Healing" Channel Through Which Wealth Flows Into Zion.

I have known of one copy being the means of bringing into Zion one hundred fifty thousand dollars, for investment.

I believe that I could put my hand upon twenty men in this place who through one copy of LEAVES OF HEALING have brought into Zion two hundred thousand dollars, for investment.

If we want the wealth of the world to flow into Zion we must dig channels for it.

Do you think that the wealth will flow over the hills?

We dug channels this last year in Australia and in Europe.

We dug channels in England; and there have been great results.

The world talks about our losses, but we have been gaining all the time.

We did not lose one member in Australia, but we gained hundreds, and we are gaining thousands.

Did we lose one member in England? Not one.

Did we lose one in Europe? Not one.

We gained everywhere; and we are still gaining.

Let us send forth the vital truths which LEAVES OF HEALING, THE ZION BANNER, and other publications contain, not spasmodically, every now and then getting up fresh enthusiasm, but let us keep at it continuously.

I venture to say that it is within your power, in this City alone, to increase the output of Zion Printing and Publishing House by five hundred thousand copies a month.

Then I should have to get in fresh machinery, and add a new wing.

Zion's Battle-ax.

I should be glad to do it, and God would send me the resources with which to do it.

I believe that in Zion Printing and Publishing House lies our greatest power.

It is Zion's battle-ax.

Let every one help in this work.

I have never complained of the ten years I have bowed my head over my work, sometimes for twenty-seven consecutive hours.

I have often worked thirty-two successive hours.

Deacon Newcomb has worked with me, as have many others.

My printers have worked; and they have never grumbled.

We cannot do this work without tremendous sacrifices.

If you had a little realization of the strength it costs to do this work, you would better understand what God has given to us.

He has poured in a fresh supply of strength as we have given it out.

I find that it has been so with all of us.

None of these workers are weaker than they were ten years ago; they are even stronger.

The world is longing for our Message in every language, and we have been able to print it in only a very few.

We must print LEAVES OF HEALING in every tongue.

There are, perhaps, two hundred forty-five languages and dialects, and I shall never rest until every language and dialect in the world has Leaves of Healing from the Tree of Life.

The power of this work is already being seen.

The denominations say, "You cannot get away from Dowie. You meet him in Japan, in China, in Egypt, in Paris, on hotel tables all over the world, and in the great ships that sail from port to port.

How Zion Printing and Publishing House Was Established.

When I determined to establish Zion Printing and Publishing House I had only three hundred dollars; but I never doubted for a moment that God would give the needed amount.

I had contracted to buy a new printing plant, paying one-third of it when I gave the order; another one-third when it was delivered, and another one-third inside of sixty days.

By God's help, I paid for it all, and produced the first copy of LEAVES OF HEALING.

I look back with delight to my little baby Publishing House.

We had only three men in the establishment.

A lady who was blind, said of my first issue: "LEAVES OF HEALING did you say? Bring it to me."

They brought it to her as she lay in bed, and as she passed her hand over it she exclaimed, "Oh, how nice it feels. Tell me what is written here on the front page."

They said to her, "Your finger is upon the Little White Dove with the olive branch in its mouth, which has beneath it the word 'Patience.'"

"May God give Doctor Dowie patience to send forth the Little White Dove," she said; and God answered that prayer.

The touching story of the prayer of that blind woman, old and weary, who was just slipping away into the world beyond, came to me with power.

She prophesied that LEAVES OF HEALING would be the most wonderful paper in the world.

Constant Demand for Old Issues of "Leaves of Healing."

The first issue was accompanied by salvation, healing, cleansing, and quickening power.

Volume I., No. 1, is sought for still.

I suppose that we have had to reprint it between twenty and thirty times.

We have reprinted practically every number, over and over again.

Does any one want the *American, Examiner, Chronicle*, or *Inter Ocean* of ten years ago reprinted?

Who bothers about them?

Who wants to bother about the reprinting of Methodist or Baptist papers?

But back numbers of LEAVES OF HEALING are called for every day.

What a blank would be in your lives now if there were no more LEAVES OF HEALING!

No more LEAVES OF HEALING!

We rejoice that for ten years God has given us the grace to send forth the literature from Zion.

It all centers around LEAVES OF HEALING; without LEAVES OF HEALING all the rest would be as nothing.

A Letter from India.

A sweet little letter reached me from India this week, written by a young lady of refinement and culture to one of our own girls whose picture had appeared in LEAVES OF HEALING.

The lady wrote, "I liked your face, and I wanted to write to you. I am a young girl; we are coming to Zion City and I want to know you."

Now that young girl in Zion City is in touch with some one in the capital of the great empire of India.

Her face, appearing in LEAVES OF HEALING has attracted the attention of this refined and cultured lady in India, who seeks her friendship.

You people who have your photographs and testimonies published in LEAVES OF HEALING, should say, "O God, I cannot go everywhere, but LEAVES OF HEALING can; bless it to thousands," and then send it out.

Ask God if you are doing your duty in sending out all the LEAVES OF HEALING you can.

Do you not see that I struggle and fight for Zion in all her departments?

I fight for Zion as a Spiritual force, as an Educational force, as a Commercial force, as a Business force, and as a great Political force.

I am doing more of all this through LEAVES OF HEALING than through my voice.

Why do you not ask yourself, "Am I doing all I can in enlisting others that are outside?"

This City would have more inhabitants, more money, and more earnestness if you all did your duty in sending out LEAVES OF HEALING.

Some of you seem to want to stand still.

You will not be allowed to stand still.

I have a "move-on" ordinance, and you have to keep moving on.

Now work.

PRAYER OF CONSECRATION.

My God and Father, help me to support the General Overseer and Zion Printing and Publishing House, by sending forth LEAVES OF HEALING to the uttermost parts of the earth. I cannot go there, so let me send the Message there. For Jesus' sake forgive me if I have not done all my duty. Help me to do it, that none shall perish because I fail. For Jesus' sake. (*All repeat the prayer, clause by clause, after the General Overseer.*)

Hymn No. 234 was sung, after which the General Overseer pronounced the

BENEDICTION.

Beloved, abstain from every form of evil. And may the very God of Peace Himself sanctify you wholly; and I pray God your whole spirit, and soul, and body be preserved entire, without blame, unto the coming of our Lord Jesus, the Christ. Faithful is He that calleth you, who also will do it. The grace of our Lord Jesus, the Christ, the love of God our Father, the fellowship of the Holy Spirit, our Comforter and Guide, one Eternal God, abide in you, bless you, and keep you, and all the Israel of God everywhere, forever. Amen.

GOD'S WAY OF HEALING.

BY THE REV. JOHN ALEX. DOWIE.

God's Way Of Healing Is a Person, Not a Thing.

Jesus said "*I am* the Way, and the Truth, and the Life," and He has ever been revealed to His people in all the ages by the Covenant Name, Jehovah-Rophi, or "*I am* Jehovah that Healeth thee." (John 14:6; Exodus 15:26.)

The Lord Jesus, the Christ, Is Still the Healer.

He cannot change, for "Jesus, the Christ, is the same yesterday and today, yea and forever;" and He is still with us, for He said: "Lo, *I am* with you All the Days, even unto the Consummation of the Age." (Hebrews 13:8; Matthew 28:20.) Because He is Unchangeable, and because He is present, in spirit, just as when in the flesh, He is the Healer of His people.

Divine Healing Rests on the Christ's Atonement.

It was prophesied of Him "Surely He hath borne our griefs (Hebrew, *sickness*), and carried our sorrows: . . . and with His stripes we are healed;" and it is expressly declared that this was fulfilled in His Ministry of Healing, which still continues. (Isaiah 53:4, 5; Matthew 8:17.)

Disease Can Never be God's Will.

It is the Devil's work, consequent upon Sin, and it is impossible for the work of the Devil ever to be the Will of God. The Christ came to "destroy the works of the Devil," and when He was here on earth He healed "all manner of disease and all manner of sickness," and all these sufferers are expressly declared to have been "oppressed of the Devil." (1 John 3:8; Matthew 4:23; Acts 10:38.)

The Gifts of Healings Are Permanent.

It is expressly declared that the "Gifts and the calling of God are without repentance," and the Gifts of Healings are amongst the Nine Gifts of the Spirit to the Church. (Romans 11:29; 1 Corinthians 12:8-11.)

There Are Four Modes of Divine Healing.

The first is the direct prayer of faith; the second, intercessory prayer of two or more; the third, the anointing of the elders, with the prayer of faith; and the fourth, the laying on of hands of those who believe, and whom God has prepared and called to that ministry. (Matthew 8:5-13; Matthew 18:19; James 5:14, 15; Mark 16:18.)

Divine Healing Is Opposed by Diabolical Counterfeits.

Amongst these are Christian Science (falsely so called), Mind Healing, Spiritualism, Trance Evangelism, etc. (1 Timothy 6:20, 21; 1 Timothy 4:1, 2; Isaiah 51:22, 23.)

Multitudes Have Been Healed Through Faith in Jesus.

The writer knows of thousands of cases and has personally laid hands on scores of thousands of persons. Full information can be obtained at the meetings held in the Zion Tabernacles in Chicago, and in Zion City, Illinois, and in many pamphlets which give the experience, in their own words, of many who have been healed in this and other countries, published at Zion Printing and Publishing House, Zion City, Illinois.

"*Belief Cometh of Hearing, and Hearing by the Word of the Christ.*"

You are heartily invited to attend and hear for yourself.

Zion's Bible Class

Conducted by Deacon Daniel Sloan in Shiloh Tabernacle, Zion City, Lord's Day Morning at 11 o'clock, and in Zion Homes and Gatherings throughout the World.

MID-WEEK BIBLE CLASS LESSON, SEPTEMBER 21st or 22d.

What to Testify to in Soul-saving Work.

1. *Testify to assurance of salvation.*—1 Thessalonians 1:2-10.
   Be sure you know that you are saved.
   Have the witness of God within.
   Serve God with a grateful heart.
2. *Testify to blessings received.*—Matthew 5:1-12.
   Speak of the comfort God has given.
   Tell how He has satisfied you.
   Give some reasons for being happy.
3. *Testify to healings received.*—Isaiah 43:8-11.
   Blind eyes are yet opened.
   Deaf ears are unstopped.
   All diseases are healed.
4. *Testify to God's keeping power.*—Philippians 1:19-29.
   Have no fear of the Devil.
   Have no concern about death.
   Live in constant expectation from God.
5. *Testify to redemption from sin.*—Ephesians 1:3-9.
   We are to be redeemed from the love of sin.
   We are to be redeemed from the power of sin.
   We are to be redeemed from the consequences of sin.
6. *Testify to answers to prayer.*—1 Peter 3:8-16.
   When foes have assailed.
   When needs have arisen.
   When temptations have appeared.
7. *Testify to persevering grace and mercy.*—Psalm 136:1-9
   He who has All Power is your Father.
   He created the world by His Word of Power.
   He is so compassionate and kind!
8. *Testify to having all things in the Christ.*—1 Corinthians 3:16-23
   The world is yours.
   The Kingdom is yours.
   The mansion is yours.

The Lord our God is a Disciple-sending God.

SUNDAY BIBLE CLASS LESSON, SEPTEMBER 25th.

The Way to Approach the Unsaved in Personal Work.

1. *Approach with a salutation of peace.*—Luke 10:3-6.
   The Christ's peace must be in you.
   The Christ's peace should never be lost through impatience.
   The Christ's peace is not inconsistent with activity.
2. *Approach with a message of good news.*—Isaiah 52:7-10.
   God is supreme on earth, in heaven, and in hell.
   Sing songs of deliverance.
   The salvation of God has come.
3. *Approach in a friendly spirit.*—Proverbs 18:19-24.
   Do not try to offend people.
   Follow peace with all men.
   Win men, you cannot do them good by driving them.
4. *Approach with sympathetic interest.*—1 Corinthians 9:16-23.
   Do not let them feel that you seek to be lord over them.
   Gain them by manifesting unity of interest with them.
   Are you determined to win the person?
5. *Approach with a sense of obligation.*—Romans 1:13-20.
   How can you excuse yourself?
   You are a debtor to every class.
   Preach the Gospel to every creature.
6. *Approach with a beaming countenance.*—Proverbs 27:11-23
   People read your face.
   Face answers to face, in men.
   Smiles, not frowns, win men.
7. *Approach with the backing of a consistent life.*—Psalm 119:161-168.
   Love God's Word.
   Find in it treasures new and old.
   Do what it says without regard to what others may do.

God's Holy People are a Soul-saving People.

LEAVES OF HEALING.

Two Dollars will bring to you the weekly visits of the Little White Dove for a year; 75 cents will send it to a friend for thirteen weeks, $1.25 will send it for six months; $1.50 will send it to your minister, or to a Y. M. C. A., or to a Public Reading Room for a whole year. We offer no premiums, except the premium of doing good. We receive no advertisements, and print no commercial lies or cheating enticements of unscrupulous thieves. LEAVES OF HEALING is Zion on wings, and we keep out everything that would detract the reader's mind from all except the Extension of the Kingdom of God, for which alone it exists. If we cannot send forth our Little White Dove without soiling its wings with the smoke of the factory and the dirt of the wrangling market-place, or compelling it to utter the screaming cries of the business vultures in the ears of our readers, then we will keep our Dove at home.

OBEYING GOD IN BAPTISM.

"Baptizing Them Into the Name of the Father and of the Son and of the Holy Ghost."

Nineteen Thousand Eight Hundred Thirty-four Baptisms by Triune Immersion Since March 14, 1897.

Nineteen Thousand Eight Hundred Thirty-four Believers have joyfully followed their Lord in the Ordinance of Believer's Baptism by Triune Immersion since the first Baptism in Central Zion Tabernacle on March 14, 1897.

Baptized in Central Zion Tabernacle from March 14, 1897, to December 14, 1901, by the General Overseer,	4754		
Baptized in South Side Zion Tabernacle from January 1, 1902, to June 14, 1903, by the General Overseer.	37		
Baptized at Zion City by the General Overseer........	583		
Baptized by Overseers, Elders, Evangelists and Deacons, at Headquarters (Zion City) and Chicago......	5283		
Total Baptized at Headquarters....................	—		10,657
Baptized in places outside of Headquarters by the General Overseer................................		765	
Baptized in places outside of Headquarters by Overseers, Elders, Evangelists and Deacons............		7796	
Total Baptized outside of Headquarters............		—	8,561
Total Baptized in seven years and three months....			19,218
Baptized since June 14, 1904:			
Baptized in Zion City by the General Overseer........	64		
Baptized in Zion City by Elder Royall...............	16		
Baptized in Zion City by Elder Hammond............	6		
Baptized in Zion City by Overseer Mason............	90		
Baptized in Zion City by Overseer Excell.	87		
Baptized in Zion City by Overseer Piper.............	79		
Baptized in Zion City by Elder Mercer..............	6		
Baptized in Zion City by Elder Dinius..............	4		
Baptized in Zion City by Elder Cossum..............	5		
Baptized in Zion City by Elder Gay.................	2		
Baptized in Chicago by Elder Hoffman	4		
Baptized in Chicago by Elder Cossum	7		
Baptized in Chicago by Elder Keller................	5		
Baptized in Chicago by Elder Hall..................	3		
Baptized in Chicago by Elder Hammond.............	1	379	
Baptized in Canada by Elder Brooks................		6	
Baptized in Canada by Elder Simmons..............		5	
Baptized in California by Elder Taylor		9	
Baptized in England by Overseer Cantel		41	
Baptized in England by Deacon Hall................		1	
Baptized in Illinois by Elder Reed.................		1	
Baptized in Indiana by Elder Osborn................		2	
Baptized in Iowa by Elder Hoy.....................		2	
Baptized in Kansas by Elder Reed		4	
Baptized in Michigan by Elder Reed................		4	
Baptized in Minnesota by Elder Graves.............		5	
Baptized in Minnesota by Elder Simmons............		3	
Baptized in Mississippi by Evangelist Gay..........		1	
Baptized in Mississippi by Elder Hall		3	
Baptized in Missouri by Evangelist Gay		1	
Baptized in Missouri by Elder Brock		9	
Baptized in Missouri by Deacon Robinson...........		1	
Baptized in Nebraska by Elder Hoy.................		7	
Baptized in New York by Overseer Mason............		9	
Baptized in Ohio by Deacon Kelchner...............		3	
Baptized in Ohio by Deacon Arrington		5	
Baptized in Ohio by Deacon Yerger		4	
Baptized in Pennsylvania by Elder Bouck...........		2	
Baptized in South Africa by Overseer Bryant		82	
Baptized in Tennessee by Elder Hall...............		2	
Baptized in Texas by Evangelist Gay		11	
Baptized in Washington by Elder Ernst.............		11	
Baptized in Wisconsin by Elder McClurkin..........		3	237 616
Total Baptized since March 14, 1897...............			19,834

The following-named sixty-four believers were baptized in the Wilge river, Harrismith, Orange River Colony, South Africa, Monday, May 16, 1904, by Overseer Daniel Bryant:

Bhenzu, Eliza, Beaucheff, Harrismith, Orange River Colony, South Africa
Bhenzu, Simon, Beaucheff, Harrismith, Orange River Colony, South Africa
Buchter, Dorothea, Hillside, Harrismith, Orange River Colony, South Africa
Dhlamini, Mantomti, Glen Poal, Harrismith, Orange River Colony, South Africa
Duba, Jumaimah, Hillside, Harrismith, Orange River Colony, South Africa
Duba, Mandhlakazi, Hillside, Harrismith, Orange River Colony, South Africa
Gule, Jennie, Driefontein, Harrismith, Orange River Colony, South Africa
Hlatywako, Judaida, Mill River, Harrismith, Orange, River Colony, South Africa
Kumalo, Edith, Driefontein, Harrismith, Orange River Colony, South Africa
Kumalo, Josephy, Driefontein, Harrismith, Orange River Colony, South Africa
Lutango, Elijah, ..Hopeful, Harrismith, Orange River Colony, South Africa
Lutango, Hannah, Hopeful, Harrismith, Orange River Colony, South Africa
Lutango, Lophy...Hopeful, Harrismith, Orange River Colony, South Africa
Lutango, Martha. Hopeful, Harrismith, Orange River Colony, South Africa
Lutango, Mary Anne, Hillside, Harrismith, Orange River Colony, South Africa
Lutango, Merica...Hillside, Harrismith, Orange River Colony, South Africa
Lutango, Micha...Hopeful, Harrismith, Orange River Colony, South Africa
Lutango, Mitha Elizabeth, Hillside, Harrismith, Orange River Colony, South Africa
Lutango, Rhoda..Hopeful, Harrismith, Orange River Colony, South Africa
Lutango, Samson, Hopeful, Harrismith, Orange River Colony, South Africa
Lutango, Robert..Hillside, Harrismith, Orange River Colony, South Africa
Mabaso, Mbhandalali, The Willows, Harrismith, Orange River Colony, South Africa
Mahlobo, Nomacala, Mill River, Harrismith, Orange River Colony, South Africa
Mahon, Johanna Dorothea, Hillside, Harrismith, Orange River Colony, South Africa
Mazibuku, Cwabile, Reed Spruit, Harrismith, Orange River Colony, South Africa
Mazibuku, Mconzisa, Reed Spruit, Harrismith, Orange River Colony, South Africa
Mazibuku, Nompiz, Reed Spruit, Harrismith, Orange River Colony, South Africa
Mdhlowenz, Dlakala, Velder Beespan, Harrismith, Orange River Colony, South Africa
Mdhlowenz, Macholobela, Velder Beespan, Harrismith, Orange River Colony, South Africa
Mgwena, Johannes, Glen Poal, Harrismith, Orange River Colony, South Africa
Mgwena, Merina, Glen Poal, Harrismith, Orange River Colony, South Africa
Mgwena, Swasi, Glen Poal, Harrismith, Orange River Colony, South Africa
Mkwananzi, Nompi, Velder Beespan, Harrismith, Orange River Colony, South Africa
Msika, Josiah. . Beaucheff, Harrismith, Orange River Colony, South Africa
Msika, Emely...Beaucheff, Harrismith, Orange River Colony, South Africa
Ncola, Citekile, Mill River, Harrismith, Orange River Colony, South Africa
Ncola, Macibise, Mill River, Harrismith, Orange River Colony, South Africa
Ncola, Nompi..Mill River, Harrismith, Orange River Colony, South Africa
Ncongwane, Nokwanda, Welvaart, Harrismith, Orange River Colony, South Africa
Nhlanhla, File.. Welvaart, Harrismith, Orange River Colony, South Africa
Nhlapo, Elijah.. .Hopeful, Harrismith Orange River Colony, South Africa
Nhlapo, Jessie ..Hopeful, Harrismith, Orange River Colony, South Africa
Nhlapo, Msindo ..Hopeful, Harrismith, Orange River Colony, South Africa
Puttrill, John Walter, Beaucheff, Harrismith, Orange River Colony, South Africa
Radebe, Citekile..Hopeful, Harrismith, Orange River Colony, South Africa
Radebe, Matelisa, Hopeful, Harrismith, Orange River Colony, South Africa
Radebe, Nkotasa, Hopeful, Harrismith, Orange River Colony, South Africa
Radebe, Nomgqibelo, Hopeful, Harrismith, Orange River Colony, South Africa
Radebe, Shambu Hopeful, Harrismith, Orange River Colony, South Africa
Shabangu, Nomalanga, Mill River, Harrismith, Orange River Colony, South Africa
Sihuya, Magugu, Glen Poal, Harrismith, Orange River Colony, South Atrica
Sihuya, Mhlalip, Ficksberg, Harrismith, Orange River Colony, South Africa
Sichanga, Mpinda, Mill River, Harrismith, Orange River Colony, South Africa
Sichanga, Mubankwa, Mill River, Harrismith, Orange River Colony, South Africa
Sichanga, Ncbesutu, Mill River, Harrismith, Orange River Colony, South Africa
Sichanga, Nompenzu, Mill River, Harrismith, Orange River Colony, South Africa
Sichanga, Nomshikili, Mill River, Harrismith, Orange River Colony, South Africa
Sichanga, Notywala, Mill River, Harrismith, Orange River Colony, South Africa
Sichanga, Vuso, Mill River, Harrismith, Orange River Colony, South Africa
Tshabalala, Fene, Hillside, Harrismith, Orange River Colony, South Africa
Tshabalala, Jumaimah, Velder Beespan, Harrismith, Orange River Colony, South Africa
Tshabalala, Nomhlolo, Velder Beespan, Harrismith, Orange River Colony, South Africa
Tshabalala, Sawane, Velder Beespan, Harrismith, Orange River Colony, South Africa
Xaba, Nkanise.. Welvaart, Harrismith, Orange River Colony, South Africa

---

The following-named eight believers were baptized in Pretoria, Transvaal, South Africa, Lord's Day, July 24, 1904, by Overseer Daniel Bryant:

Barrett, Susan Magrat.. .4 Dutoit street, Pretoria, Transvaal, South Africa
Horak, William George...P. O. box 606, Pretoria, Transvaal, South Africa
Manneken, Arie.....Bapsfontein, District Pretoria, Transvaal, South Africa
Pullen, Isabella Josepine, P. O. box 13, Krugersdorp, Transvaal, South Africa
Rose, Rachel Elizabeth, 82 Van der Walt St., Pretoria, Transvaal, South Africa
Roos, Francoois Johannes, 53 Koch street, Pretoria, Transvaal, South Africa
Townsend, Frederick..Stellenbosch, Cape Colony, Transvaal, South Africa
Winckworth, Isabella................Middelburg, Transvaal, South Africa

---

The following-named believer was baptized at Jacksonville, Illinois, Tuesday, August 9, 1904, by Elder David A. Reed:

Smith, Andrizza .. ..470 S. East street, Jacksonville, Illinois

---

The following-named believer was baptized at Wakarusa, Kansas, Thursday, August 18, 1904, by Elder David A Reed:

Weaver, Miss Ella Jennie ....Wakarusa, Kansas

The following-named two believers were baptized in Topeka, Kansas, Friday, August 10, 1904, by Elder David A. Reed:
Reed, Allen George............... ...1242 West street, Topeka, Kansas
Reed, Mrs. Mary.......................1242 West street, Topeka, Kansas

The following-named four believers were baptized in Cincinnati, Ohio, Lord's Day, August 21, 1904, by Deacon W. D. Yerger:
Hughes, Miss Daisy Pearl ....Westwood, Cincinnati, Ohio
Hollenkamp, Fred Henry, Jr ....810 Hathaway street, Cincinnati, Ohio
Hollenkamp, Mrs. Mary ....810 Hathaway street, Cincinnati, Ohio
Hollenkamp, Miss Mary Louise .....810 Hathaway street, Cincinnati, Ohio

The following-named believer was baptized at Wakarusa, Kansas, Monday, August 22, 1904, by Elder David A. Reed:
Weaver, James H.... ....Wakarusa, Kansas

The following-named four believers were baptized in Lake Michigan, Zion City, Illinois, Friday, August 26, 1904, by Elder Frank A. S. Mercer:
McDowell, Joseph ....1707 Horeb avenue, Zion City, Illinois
McDowell, Mrs. Minnie.... ....1707 Horeb avenue, Zion City, Illinois
Redmond, Mrs. Martha.......1849 S. Burdick street, Kalamazoo, Michigan
Schemle, Matilda E.............................New Holstein, Wisconsin

The following-named two believers were baptized in Philadelphia, Pennsylvania, Lord's Day, August 28, 1904, by Elder R. N. Bouck:
Deichirt, Mrs. Regena .....545 Venango street, Philadelphia, Pennsylvania
Triemel, Henry Paul......528 Callowhill street, Philadelphia, Pennsylvania

The following-named five believers were baptized in Shiloh Tabernacle, Zion City, Illinois, Wednesday, August 31, 1904, by Elder Frank M. Royall:
Correll, John Monroe ....Edina Hospice, Zion City, Illinois
Godshall, Mrs. Ida ....2810 Ezra avenue, Zion City, Illinois
Miller, Miss Ellen Louise ....Pratt, Kansas
Voorhees, G. W...Zion City, Illinois
Watterson, Walter J......................................Strawn, Illinois

CONSECRATION OF CHILDREN.

The following-named fifty children were consecrated to God, at Harrismith, Orange River Colony, South Africa, Lord's Day, May 15, 1904, by Overseer Daniel Bryant:
Bhengu, Emily Tembalihle, Beaucheff, Harrismith, Orange River Colony, South Africa
Dlamini, Amon, Glen Poal, Harrismith, Orange River Colony, South Africa
Dlamini, Elijah, Glen Poal, Harrismith, Orange River Colony, South Africa
Dlamini, Jeremiah, Glen Poal, Harrismith, Orange River Colony, South Africa
Dlamini, Job . .Glen Poal, Harrismith, Orange River Colony, South Africa
Dube, Dolia......Hillside, Harrismith, Orange River Colony, South Africa
Dube, Phillmon...Hillside, Harrismith, Orange River Colony, South Africa
Dube, William....Hillside, Harrismith, Orange River Colony, South Africa
Hlahywako, William, Mill River, Harrismith, Orange River Colony, South Africa
Kumalo, Nomsa, Drie Fontein, Harrismith, Orange River Colony, South Africa
Kumalo, Constance Nokupana, Drie Fontein, Harrismith, Orange River Colony, South Africa
Kumalo, Ndabezinhle, Drie Fontein, Harrismith, Orange River Colony, South Africa
Lutango, Nomhlolo, Hopeful, Harrismith, Orange River Colony, South Africa
Lutango, Nobesutu, Hopeful, Harrismith, Orange River Colony, South Africa
Lutango, Tabitha, Hopeful, Harrismith, Orange River Colony, South Africa
Lutango, Rosalina, Welvaart, Harrismith, Orange River Colony, South Africa
Lutango, Sityeni..Welvaart, Harrismith, Orange River Colony, South Africa
Lutango, Frank..Welvaart, Harrismith, Orange River Colony, South Africa
Lutango, Dingindawo, Welvaart, Harrismith, Orange River Colony, South Africa
Lutango, Jeu.....Hopeful, Harrismith, Orange River Colony, South Africa
Lutango, Fakazi..Hopeful, Harrismith, Orange River Colony, South Africa
Mahlobo, Mshumayeli, Mill River, Harrismith, Orange River Colony, South Africa
Mahon, Alfred Joseph, Hillside, Harrismith, Orange River Colony, South Africa
Mahon, Evalina Elizabeth, Hillside, Harrismith, Orange River Colony, South Africa
Mahon, Faith Dorothea, Hillside, Harrismith, Orange River Colony, South Africa
Mahon, Grace Johanna, Hillside, Harrismith, Orange River Colony, South Africa
Mahon, Margaretha Hope, Hillside, Harrismith, Orange River Colony, South Africa
Mazibuko, Wyoni, Velder Beespan, Harrismith, Orange River Colony, South Africa
Mazibuko, Ruth, Reed Spruit, Harrismith, Orange River Colony, South Africa
Mazibuko, Zinto, Velder Beespan, Harrismith, Orange River Colony, South Africa
Mdhloweng, Nati, Velder Beespan, Harrismith, Orange River Colony, South Africa
Mdhloweng, Ntutu, Velder Beespan, Harrismith, Orange River Colony, South Africa
Mgwena, Kambul, Glen Poal, Harrismith, Orange River Colony, South Africa
Mgwena, Nomvula, Glen Poal, Harrismith, Orange River Colony, South Africa
Mkwanazi, Toyana, Velder Beespan, Harrismith, Orange River Colony, South Africa
Msika, Lydia ...Beaucheff, Harrismith, Orange River Colony, South Africa
Msika, Philip...Beaucheff, Harrismith, Orange River Colony, South Africa
Nhlapo, Esau ....Hopeful, Harrismith, Orange River Colony, South Africa
Nhlapo, Jacob ...Hopeful, Harrismith, Orange River Colony, South Africa
Nhlapo, Paulos...Hopeful, Harrismith, Orange River Colony, South Africa
Nhlapo, Simon ...Hopeful, Harrismith, Orange River Colony, South Africa
Radebe, Nkululeko, Hopeful, Harrismith, Orange River Colony, South Africa
Shabangu, Mam, Mill River, Harrismith, Orange River Colony, South Africa
Sishanga, Kabonina, Mill River, Harrismith, Orange River Colony, South Africa
Sishanga, Nosikishiwe, Mill River, Harrismith, Orange River Colony, South Africa
Sishanga, Nozinyanga, Mill River, Harrismith, Orange River Colony, South Africa
Sishanga, Zililo, Mill River, Harrismith, Orange River Colony, South Africa
Tshabalala, Bauzeni, Velder Beespan, Harrismith, Orange River Colony, South Africa
Tshabalala, Samsom, Velder Beespan, Harrismith, Orange River Colony, South Africa
Xaba, Dabula...Wilvaart, Harrismith, Orange River Colony, South Africa

The following-named two children were consecrated to God, Tuesday, July 19, 1904, by Elder Eugene Brooks:
Crary, Esther M....................................Trippville, Wisconsin
Crary, Geraldean Monta.............................Trippville, Wisconsin

The following-named child was consecrated to God, at Shelby, Michigan, Lord's Day, July 31, 1904, by Elder David A Reed:
Bowers, Kennith Vivian...............................Shelby, Michigan

The following-named child was consecrated to God, Thursday, August 11, 1904, by Elder David A. Reed:
Sledding, James Saxon.................1428 N., 6th street, Quincy, Illinois

The following-named child was consecrated to God, in Philadelphia, Pennsylvania, Lord's Day, August 14, 1904, by Elder Roland N. Bouck:
Du Mar, Esther Dowie......1713 Bowers street, Philadelphia, Pennsylvania

The following-named two children were consecrated to God, in Zion City, Illinois, Monday, August 29, 1904, by Elder Frank A. S Mercer:
Redmond, Charles Lester. . ...Kalamazoo, Michigan
Redmond, Donald Clarence...........................Kalamazoo, Michigan

Expiration of Subscriptions.

On every subscriber's copy of LEAVES OF HEALING or THE ZION BANNER we attach a yellow label bearing his name, address, and two numbers, the figures referring to the volume and the number with which the subscription will expire.

Thus, should your label number happen to be 16—1, you may know that your subscription expires with Volume XVI, Number 1, which will be October 22, 1904. Also take notice that LEAVES OF HEALING now completes a volume every six months, or twenty-six weeks, that being the number of papers which are put into a bound volume. Earlier in the life of the paper a volume contained fifty-two numbers, as LEAVES OF HEALING had fewer pages in those days.

By making yourselves familiar with these customs and remitting promptly you need never allow your subscription to lapse.

Send money only by Bank Draft, Postoffice or Express Money-order in favor of John Alexander Dowie, and address all letters intended for us to

ZION PRINTING AND PUBLISHING HOUSE,
Zion City, Lake County, Illinois.

TENTH ANNIVERSARY

OF

Zion Printing & Pub. House

WE request that every reader of **LEAVES OF HEALING** pause and try to count the blessings brought to them directly or indirectly by **LEAVES OF HEALING.**

Next examine carefully the reports of the work done since this Printing and Publishing House began, and observe the **phenomenal growth.**

How has all this been accomplished?

By many earnest readers enthusing their friends and neighbors with LEAVES OF HEALING.

Divine Enthusiasm accomplished it. Those who are zealous for good work are needed now to keep the truth ever spreading.

We call for all to double their efforts for the month of September, and to make a record for **LEAVES OF HEALING** that will constitute another landmark in its onward progress. This can be done only by each one's going to work in earnest and keeping it up.

Blätter der Heilung

also should be read by all who understand the German language. It has created a very lively interest and has had a steady and healthy growth; but this is not sufficient. We urge each one who would love his neighbor as himself, to take it upon himself to secure at least one subscription this month. The rates are as follows:

One year (domestic)	50c.	Foreign	75c.
Six months	"	30c.	"	40c.
One copy	"	5c.	"	7c.

Feuilles de Guérison

The **French LEAVES OF HEALING** will soon be published monthly and will contain twenty pages. We are desirous that every person who reads French shall receive this paper regularly. We therefore request every member and friend of Zion, and those who wish to extend the Gospel of Salvation, Healing, and Holy Living, to secure subscriptions, the prices for which are as follows:

One year (domestic)	50c.	Foreign	75c.
Six months "	30c.	"	40c.
One copy "	5c.	"	7c.

WEEKLY PAPER FOR THE EXTENSION OF THE KINGDOM OF GOD
EDITED BY THE REV. JOHN ALEX. DOWIE.

ume XV. No. 21. ZION CITY, SATURDAY, SEPTEMBER 10, 1904. Price Five Cents

;OD'S WITNESSES TO DIVINE HEALING.

JSBAND SAVED AND DELIVERED FROM THE PRACTICE OF MEDICINE, SECRETISM, AND EVIL HABITS—WIFE HEALED OF INFLAMMATORY RHEUMATISM.

'VEN THE CAPTIVES OF THE MIGHTY SHALL BE TAKEN 'AY, AND THE PREY OF THE RRIBLE SHALL BE DELIVERED.

:hovah, our God, gave the Promise.

y the Power of His might it is remed.

y His Right Hand the Captives of the ;hty are taken away.

.nd by His Holy n the Prey of the rible is delivered.

/ho, among all opssors, is mightier 1 Satan?

.nd who is more ible than the Evil :?

1 fetters of error, nger than chains of le steel, he binds his :ives.

aught in the cruel ;s of sinful habits, prey is devoured.

:e tortures his victims with sickness.

:e torments them with fear.

:e crushes them to death.

:e drags them down the dread prisonse of hell.

Shall the prey be taken from the hty?"

:ear the "Sure Word of Prophecy!" Even the Captives of the Mighty shall aken away, and the Prey of the Ter- e shall be delivered."

The same Glorious Promise shines forth from the prophesied words of the Christ: "Jehovah hath anointed Me . . . to proclaim Liberty to the Captives, and the Opening of the Prison to them that are bound." And again God gives a Message of Divine Hope in the words of His apostle: "To this end was the Son

J. H. BLANKS, M. D., WIFE AND FAMILY.

of God manifested, that He might destroy the works of the Devil."

The Devil is the Terrible Captor. Can any doubt the Word of God? Here are "Captives taken from the Mighty," "Prey delivered from the Terrible."

From earliest antiquity the practice of medicine, called "sorcery" in the Word of God, has been a trick of the Devil for taking humanity captive.

It is not only the sick and suffering who seek healing in vain, that thus become the "Prey of the Terrible."

Many good men are drawn into the toils of the "profession" under false conceptions.

Elders of the Church have lost faith in God, and have thus lost the power to pray the Prayer of Faith in accordance with the command:

"Is any among you sick? let him call for the elders of the Church; and let them pray over him, anointing him with oil in the Name of the Lord: and the Prayer of Faith shall save him that is sick, and the Lord shall raise him up."

Faithless elders, called in by the sick, have sought refuge in the false teaching that God now heals through doctors and medicine.

Sorcery has thus been glorified!

It is held up as a "noble profession:"

Many godly young men, deceived by this lie, have been led to enter the profession, little knowing its true nature.

A terrible revelation awaits them.

Many turn back, sick at heart, after a few months in the medical school.

Others, with consciences dulled by the diabolical lie that murder is justified if done "in the name of Science," are drawn deeper into captivity.

When they begin their practice still further revelations horrify them.

Many strive to escape, but the great majority of those whose consciences revolt continue, because they feel that it is their only means of earning a livelihood.

Baal-worshiping Secretism and the heathenism of modern sorcery go hand in hand.

The evil associations of the secret lodges, constant contact with the ghoulish horrors of the Medical school, irregular hours, and exposure drive the young students and practitioners to the use of narcotics and stimulants.

Then, indeed, have they become "Prey of the Terrible."

Hundreds of physicians, annually, in the United States, seek deliverance by suicide.

The husband and father of this beautiful family of Witnesses for God was a practicing physician for twelve years.

Hence it was from the very jaws of the terrible monster of sorcery that he was delivered.

Jehovah God, who, in His Infinite Love and Mercy, anointed His own Son "to proclaim liberty to the Captives" and "to destroy the works of the Devil," has in these Latter Days sent His prophet to restore this glorious truth to His people, that deliverance may come to those who will receive it.

It was through the Messages of that prophet that this Witness was set free.

In August, 1903, he gave up the practice of medicine, and accepted a humble clerkship in Zion City.

In January, 1904, he took the examination of the Illinois State Board of Health, and obtained a state medical license in addition to those of Alabama and Mississippi, which he already held.

He was appointed Acting Commissioner of Health for the City of Zion, July 1, 1904.

His administration has received highest compliments from officials of Chicago and Illinois Boards of Health.

His wife also has a wonderful story of deliverance from the cruel clutches of the Terrible.

Satan had tortured and crippled her with inflammatory rheumatism.

In answer to the Prayer of Faith, God fulfilled His Covenant, "I am Jehovah that Healeth thee," and she became well and strong.

God has also wonderfully answered prayer for her in childbirth.

What a kind, loving and all-powerful Heavenly Father!

What a wonderful Savior, Healer, Cleanser, and Keeper!

We send this little family to all the ends of the earth on the wings of the Little White Dove, to proclaim to the "Captives of the Mighty" and the "Prey of the Terrible," everywhere, that there is deliverance for them through Him. A. W. N.

WRITTEN TESTIMONY OF DR. J. H. BLANKS.

ZION CITY, ILLINOIS, July 4, 1904.

MY DEAR GENERAL OVERSEER:--It is a great joy and pleasure to me to add my testimony to those of the many thousands of others who have been greatly blessed of God in spirit, soul, and body, through the Christ, by heeding your teaching and following your leadership.

Let me say right here, by way of parenthesis, that my faith in you as a leader, teacher, and preacher is such, that I would follow you anywhere, even unto death, if need be, for the sake and service of our dear Lord and Savior, Jesus, the Christ.

It was through the faithful and persistent work of my dear wife, ably assisted by her father, Deacon John A. Lewis, of Meridian, Mississippi, reading of LEAVES OF HEALING, and your prayers, that I was turned Zionward.

When I came to Zion and received the teaching to a small, very small extent, was convinced that Zion was of God, and that the General Overseer was the Prophet of the Restoration, I still had some doubts and fears come to me.

I had studied and practiced medicine for more than fourteen years, and I did not think that I had the skill, or was fitted to do anything else, to earn a livelihood for my family.

I knew that I could not be in Zion and continue the practice of medicine; so the Devil tried hard to lead me off with fear.

I had been in Elijah Hospice, in Zion City, only about five days, however, when I made up my mind to do my duty toward God, serve Him, cast myself upon His promises, and follow the leadership of the General Overseer.

This conclusion was reached one morning when I first awakened, and was silently communing with God.

I called to my wife and asked her if any blank forms of application for membership could be obtained about the Hospice.

I made out the application, was baptized, and oh, how glad I have been ever since!

To enumerate the blessings and deliverances I have had through your prayers, teaching, and leadership, would make a long story.

For more than twelve years prior to July 23, 1903, I had been actively engaged in the practice of medicine.

I belonged to numerous secret organizations, among which were Freemasons, Knights of Pythias, Odd-Fellows, Woodmen of the World, Knights of Honor, Knights and Ladies of Honor, Knights of the Golden Rule, Ancient Order of United Workmen, Independent Order of Heptasophs, Masons' Annuity, and others.

I carried life insurance to the amount of from $5,000 to $15,000, costing from $150 to $500 a year, every cent of which went to swell the big incomes of wicked men at the heads of these organizations, and was taken away from the proper support of my family.

I had been an inveterate user of tobacco the most of my life, much to the detriment of my health and pocketbook.

Twice during these twelve years, through the influence of associates in the medical fraternity and secret societies, I became a tippler to a dangerous degree.

Last, but not least, I had my membership in a rich, aristocratic Methodist church, most of whose members were theatergoers, card-players, punch and wine-drinkers, dancers, etc.

They paid an attractive salary to their pastor, and he had to deliver made-to-order sermons. He fed them on flowery oratory, and tickled their vanity by throwing bouquets at them, but he did not dare preach True Repentance and Salvation to them.

He would never commit the offense that John the Baptist did.

I date my conversion to God back to the age of fourteen years, but through the above-mentioned evil influences I had wandered far away from Him.

I say with absolute certainty, that had it not been for the voice of Elijah the Restorer, calling in thunder tones to just such wine-bibbers, stink-pots, secret society worshipers, medical sorcerers, and seekers after worldly pleasures in general, as I was, to quit their meanness, and come to God to be saved and blessed in spirit, soul, and body, I would soon have been utterly lost.

Yet my former associates in the South are still following in the same paths we were treading so long, and think they are having a good time.

I can tell them now that they are having a mighty hard time serving the Devil. It is so much easier serving God!

Some of my friends in the South, throughout the States of Tennessee, Alabama, Mississippi, and Louisiana, are amazed at me for taking the step I have taken, and think I have gone crazy.

If accepting Zion and being blessed is going crazy, then I pray God to afflict every one of my so-called "friends" with the same kind of "insanity," and do it quickly.

I used to think before I received the teaching and was made to *think*, that the General Overseer was making assertions that he could not prove when he called the doctors such a bad lot, and said that all medicines were poisonous.

I found on reflection, however, that all medicines *are* poisonous, and I promptly quit dispensing them.

But one of the main charges I bring against the medical profession is the same that I bring against secret societies; that is, immorality in drinking and smoking.

It starts, as a rule, when the student first enters a medical college.

Then most of them think it takes two or three drinks and a cigar to brace them up for the ghoulish work of the dissecting-room and for cutting in pieces a fellow human being.

Then when they get out into practice, every city and every community has its medical society, where the members meet once a week or once a month.

They frequently have banquets, and wine always flows freely at these functions.

Now, as to Freemasonry and other secret orders to which I belonged, I was only a "Baby Mason."

I did not go further than the Blue Lodge.

The Name of the Christ is not allowed in the Blue Lodge, and the Masonic Lodge is certainly the parent of all other secret orders.

Hence the Name of the Christ is not allowed in any of them.

The habits I have already mentioned, smoking and drinking, are almost universal in these lodges.

I have been in all classes of lodges.

In sparsely-settled rural districts the form of refreshment is usually a jug of mean whisky, hidden off in the woods in a brush heap, or a tree-top, or a hollow log.

Groups of two to four go occasionally to get a drink, and come back smoking vile pipes.

In the small towns they usually have a keg of beer, ham sandwiches, and cigars.

That is a fine combination!

In the larger cities they often have Masonic Temples in which they have their lodge-rooms, banquet halls, and gilded barrooms.

The whole thing is one mass of rotten corruption and wickedness.

In these lodges many young men get their downward start to hell, and the longer they go the greater momentum they get, until after a few years it is very hard, indeed, for them to stop.

I thank God that through the prayers and leadership of our beloved General Overseer I was freed instantly and permanently from these evil influences.

I was instantly relieved of all desire for tobacco and strong drinks.

I take great pleasure in my work in Zion.

I thank God for Zion City, a place where a man can earn his daily bread working for God, and live a pure life.

In conclusion, I wish to thank God and testify to His Infinite Goodness and Mercies in the wonderful deliverance of my dear wife in her last accouchement, that most trying time of all that mothers are called upon to endure.

It was Saturday afternoon.

I was at home, having a half holiday.

My wife was in the kitchen, baking cake.

The time was five o'clock in the afternoon.

She told me that I had better see Dr. Speicher, and at once.

I did not wait to be told twice.

I saw him, and he prayed to God to give His handmaiden a safe, easy, and speedy delivery.

When I returned home, the nurse, who happened to be in the neighborhood, was there, and by quarter after six o'clock delivery was complete. Afterward there was no trouble with the stomach, bowels, or bladder; all were in perfect order.

Moreover, there was not at any time any fever, nor was there at any time any trouble with the baby. Neither has there been to the present, nine weeks now.

In previous deliveries my wife took chloroform, and in one, morphine as well, and as a result had quite a good deal of nausea, and partial paralysis of bladder, and in one instance the catheter had to be used, which set up a fearful cystitis, and caused a great deal of suffering.

Thank God, we knew His way this time!

I pray God's richest blessings on you and yours, and that you may have abundant strength to keep up this good fight for God and against the Devil.

May I ever be kept faithful to God, to Zion, and to you,

Faithfully, your brother in the Christ's service,

J. H. BLANKS, A. B., M. D.

WRITTEN TESTIMONY OF MRS. IDA BLANKS.

2114 ENOCH AVENUE,
ZION CITY, ILLINOIS, August 12, 1904.

MY DEAR GENERAL OVERSEER:—It is with a heart full of thanksgiving and joy to my Heavenly Father that I confirm my husband's testimony, and tell how thankful I am for our dear General Overseer, who has come to us in the spirit of Elijah the Restorer, and for his wonderful, God-given mission.

I can proclaim with the Psalmist, "Jehovah is my Light and my Salvation; whom shall I fear? Jehovah is the Strength of my life; of whom shall I be afraid?"

I can never relate all the blessings I and all my household have received since coming into Zion.

I was just beginning to recover from an attack of inflammatory rheumatism (through God's mercy to His ignorant but obedient child), which was only one item in my nine years of suffering.

I had exhausted almost everything to be found in an apothecary's shop.

I was just about to have an operation performed, when the Devil tried to kill me with a severe attack of rheumatism.

What a glorious day dawned in my life when God's Way of Healing was pointed out to me through LEAVES OF HEALING!

I became very much interested, for its teachings agreed with my Bible, and then the Light of God beamed forth.

I felt its rays go through my feeble body.

I immediately laid aside my crutches and used a stick.

Then I perceived that that was still trying to aid God, so I laid my stick aside, and then my healing came very rapidly.

I often said to Dr. Blanks, "Oh, if we had only known of Zion and its teaching ten years ago! How much suffering I should have been spared!

I was wonderfully delivered, April 30th, of our little girl, without any trouble at all; and there were no after complications, such as I had always had previously.

Little Marguerite is enjoying perfect health, and I give God all the glory.

What a grand privilege to go to God for everything!

Our little ones trust God as their Healer in all their troubles.

I thank God for a clean, pure City, where we may bring up our children in the nurture and admonition of the Lord, for the extension of His Kingdom, and all to His glory.

The simple childlike faith of the children of Zion is a beautiful example to the world.

I ask your prayers and the prayers of all Zion, that we may be kept and be faithful until He comes.

With love to you, to dear Overseer Jane Dowie, and to your son, I am,

Yours, in the Christ's service,

(MRS.) IDA BLANKS.

IS ANY among you sick? let him call for the Elders of the Church; and let them pray over him, anointing him with oil in the Name of the Lord: And the Prayer of Faith shall save him that is sick, and the Lord shall raise him up; and if he have committed sins, it shall be forgiven him. —*James 5:14, 15.*

MEETINGS IN ZION CITY TABERNACLES.

SHILOH TABERNACLE.

Lord's Day—Early morning service.... 6:30 a. m.
Intermediate Bible Class.. 9:45 a. m.
Bible class, conducted by Deacon Daniel Sloan... 11:00 a. m.
Afternoon service........ 2:30 p. m.
Evening service......... 8:00 p m.

First Lord's Day of Every Month—Communion service.

Third Lord's Day of Every Month—Zion Junior Restoration Host rally.

Third Lord's Day of Every Month—Consecration of children.......................... 10:00 a m.

Monday—Zion Restoration Host rally (Second Monday of every month).... 8:00 p. m.

Tuesday—Divine Healing meeting..... 2:30 p. m.

Tuesday—Adult Choir................ 7:45 p. m.

Wednesday—Baptismal service........ 7:00 p. m.

Wednesday—Citizens' rally............ 8:00 p. m.

Friday—Adult Choir.................. 7:45 p. m.

Friday—Officers of the Christian Catholic Church in Zion........ 8:00 p. m.

Friday—Junior Choir.................. 3:45 p. m.
Meeting in the officers' room.

TWENTY-SIXTH STREET TABERNACLE.

Lord's Day—Junior service............ 9:45 a. m.

Lord's Day—German service.......... 10:30 a. m.

Tuesday—German service............ 8:00 p. m.

TABLE OF FOREIGN SUBSCRIPTION PRICES

LEAVES OF HEALING.

	SINGLE COPY		YEARLY SUBSCRIPTIONS	
	United States Money.	Native Money.	United States Money.	Native Money
Australia	$ 08	4 pence	$3 50	14s. 6d.
Ceylon	08	18c of rupees	3 50	14s. 6d.
India......	08	4 annas	3 50	14s. 6d.
Italy	08	40 centesimi	3 50	18 lira 40c.
Switzerland	08	40 centimes	3 50	18fr. 40c.
France.	08	40 centimes	3 50	18fr. 40c.
Great Britain	08	4 pence	3 50	14s. 6d.

THE ZION BANNER.

	SINGLE COPY		SIX MOS. SUBSCRIPTION	
Australia....	$ 04	2 pence	$ 75	3s. 1½d.
Ceylon..........	04	9c of rupees	75	3s. 1½d.
India.	04	2 annas	75	3s. 1½d.
Italy.	04	20 centesimi	75	4 lira
Switzerland	04	20 centimes	75	4 fr.
France.....	04	20 centimes	75	4 fr.
Great Britain .	04	2 pence	75	3s. 1½d.

Make Remittances by Drafts on London.

A WEEKLY PAPER FOR THE EXTENSION OF THE KINGDOM OF GOD.

EDITED BY THE REV. JOHN ALEX. DOWIE.

Application for entry as Second Class Matter at Zion City, Illinois, pending.

Subscription Rates.		Special Rates.	
One Year	$2.00	100 Copies of One Issue	$3.00
Six Months	1.25	25 Copies of One Issue	1.00
Three Months	75	To Ministers, Y. M. C. A's and Public	
Single Copies	.05	Reading Rooms, per annum	1.50

For foreign subscriptions add $1.50 per year, or three cents per copy for postage.

Subscribers desiring a change of address should give present address, as well as that to which they desire LEAVES OF HEALING sent in the future.

Make Bank Drafts, Express Money or Postoffice Money Orders payable to the order of JOHN ALEX. DOWIE, Zion City, Illinois, U. S. A.

Long Distance Telephone. *Cable Address "Dowie, Zion City."*

All communications upon business must be addressed to
MANAGER ZION PUBLISHING HOUSE,
Zion City, Illinois, U. S. A.

Subscriptions to LEAVES OF HEALING, A VOICE FROM ZION, and the various publications may also be sent to

ZION PUBLISHING HOUSE, 81 EUSTON ROAD, LONDON, N. W., ENGLAND.
ZION PUBLISHING HOUSE, NO. 43 PARK ROAD, ST. KILDA, MELBOURNE, VICTORIA, AUSTRALIA.
ZION PUBLISHING HOUSE, RUE DE MONT, THABOR 1, PARIS, FRANCE
ZIONSHEIM, SCHLOSS LIEBBURG, CANTON THURGAU, BEI ZÜRICH, SWITZERLAND.

ZION CITY, ILLINOIS, SATURDAY, SEPTEMBER 10, 1904.

TABLE OF CONTENTS.

LEAVES OF HEALING, SATURDAY, SEPTEMBER 10, 1904.

GOD'S WAY OF HEALING.

BY THE REV. JOHN ALEX. DOWIE.

God's Way of Healing Is a Person, Not a Thing.

Jesus said "*I am* the Way, and the Truth, and the Life," and He has ever been revealed to His people in all the ages by the Covenant Name, Jehovah-Rophi, or "*I am* Jehovah that Healeth thee." (John 14:6; Exodus 15:26.)

The Lord Jesus, the Christ, is Still the Healer.

He cannot change, for "Jesus, the Christ, is the same yesterday and today, yea and forever;" and He is still with us, for He said: "Lo, *I am* with you All the Days, even unto the Consummation of the Age." (Hebrews 13:8; Matthew 28:20.) Because He is Unchangeable, and because He is present, in spirit, just as when in the flesh, He is the Healer of His people.

Divine Healing Rests on the Christ's Atonement.

It was prophesied of Him, "Surely He hath borne our griefs (Hebrew, *sickness*), and carried our sorrows: . . . and with His stripes we are healed;" and it is expressly declared that this was fulfilled in His Ministry of Healing, which still continues. (Isaiah 53:4, 5; Matthew 8:17.)

Disease Can Never be God's Will.

It is the Devil's work, consequent upon Sin, and it is impossible for the work of the Devil ever to be the Will of God. The Christ came to "destroy the works of the Devil," and when He was here on earth He healed "all manner of disease and all manner of sickness," and all these sufferers are expressly declared to have been "oppressed of the Devil." (1 John 3:8; Matthew 4:23; Acts 10:38.)

The Gifts of Healing Are Permanent.

It is expressly declared that the "Gifts and the calling of God are without repentance," and the Gifts of Healing are amongst the Nine Gifts of the Spirit to the Church. (Romans 11:29; 1 Corinthians 12:8-11.)

There Are Four Modes of Divine Healing.

The first is the direct prayer of faith; the second, intercessory prayer of two or more; the third, the anointing of the elders, with the prayer of faith; and the fourth, the laying on of hands of those who believe, and whom God has prepared and called to that Ministry. (Matthew 8:5-13; Matthew 18:19; James 5:14, 15; Mark 16:18.)

Divine Healing Is Opposed by Diabolical Counterfeits.

Amongst these are Christian Science (falsely so-called), Mind Healing, Spiritualism, Trance Evangelism, etc. (1 Timothy 6:20, 21; 1 Timothy 4:1, 2; Isaiah 51:22, 23.)

Multitudes Have Been Healed Through Faith in Jesus.

The writer knows of thousands of cases and has personally laid hands on scores of thousands of persons. Full information can be obtained at the meetings held in the Zion Tabernacles in Chicago, and in Zion City, Illinois, and in many pamphlets which give the experience, in their own words, of many who have been healed in this and other countries, published at Zion Printing and Publishing House, Zion City, Illinois.

"Belief Cometh of Hearing, and Hearing by the Word of the Christ."

You are heartily invited to attend and hear for yourself.

General Letter from the General Overseer

"Shiloh House,"

Zion City, Lake County, Illinois, U. S. A.,

September 9, 1904.

To the Officers and Members of the Christian Catholic Church in Zion, and of Zion Restoration Host, and to All Who Love Our Lord Jesus, the Christ, in Sincerity, Throughout the World:

Beloved Brothers and Sisters in Jesus, the Christ, Our Lord and Coming King:

Grace to you and Peace,
From Him which Is, and which Was, and which Is to Come;
And from the Seven Spirits which are before His Throne;
And from Jesus, the Christ, who is the Faithful Witness,
The First Born of the dead,
And the Ruler of the Kings of the Earth.

In my General Letter of August 11,1904, published in Leaves of Healing, of August 13th, Volume XV., Number 17, page 544, I wrote these words:

"In another General Letter I will set forth a Plea for the speedy Restoration of the Apostolic Office to the Church, so that she may accomplish her Divine Mission in the establishment of the Kingdom of God upon earth."

In the fulfilment of this promise, I write this letter.

I will not, however, as had been my first intention, set forth herein the Scriptural Argument, the Teaching of the Holy Spirit on the subject of the Restoration of the Apostolic Office; for I have decided to publish in full some important Discussions and Dissertations on this subject, which set forth the whole position far more effectually than I could do it within the confines of this letter.

Hence I will direct your attention to the fact that, with this letter, I send forth in this issue of Leaves of Healing:

(1) Reports of the Preliminary Conferences of January 22, 1896, and of February 4, 1896, and of the Organization of the Christian Catholic Church in Zion, on February 22, 1896. These were published in Leaves of Healing at the time, and have been reprinted in A Voice from Zion, and in pamphlet form, for more than eight years without any alterations, as setting forth officially the facts connected with the Constitution of the Christian Catholic Church in Zion. We have, therefore, reprinted them, after very much consideration; and they will be found, without any alteration whatever, on pages 703 to 732 of this issue.

(2) Reports of Three Conferences of Ordained Officers of the Christian Catholic Church in Zion, on the subject of the Restoration of the Apostolic Office to the Church, held in Shiloh Tabernacle, Zion City, on July 20th, July 23d and July 25th of this year. These reports will be found on pages 733 to 745.

These Reports will give careful readers a clear view of the Evolution of the Christian Catholic Church in Zion, from a little band, in one city, of less than five hundred members, to a World-wide Church, numbering scores of thousands of members, who, with their families and their adherents and active friends, constitute a probable constituency of many hundreds of thousands.

They also trace the Divine Evolution, by the Holy Spirit, of their leader from a Christian Teacher and the Prophet of the Restoration into a Divinely-Commissioned Apostle.

I stood in 1896, when I became the Founder and the General Overseer, under God, of the Christian Catholic Church in Zion, with less than five hundred members, in the bitter winter of 1896, in the city of Chicago.

I stand today amidst the Glory of the Harvest, surrounded by hundreds upon hundreds of educated, experienced people and faithful Officers of all ranks; surrounded by sweet singers in thousands, forming magnificent Zion White-robed Choirs here and in many lands; surrounded by tens and tens of thousands of saved and consecrated members of the Christian Catholic Church in Zion; and surrounded by more than Eight Thousand Messengers of God in the splendid organization known as Zion Restoration Host.

I stand with my hand upon the lever which controls many mighty powers, such as Zion Printing and Publishing House, which I use for God and for humanity.

I stand in the midst of the City of Zion, with its population of many thousands, where every foot of land is God's; and where the people lease from Him, subject to His laws; and where thousands of Zion children and youths throng Zion Schools and College.

I stand as the controller of great Financial, Commercial, and Industrial Institutions which, beyond all question, have been successfully and profitably established; I stand where Purity, Sobriety, and Industry reign; where Vice cannot be endured; and where God rules and the people prosper.

Let every candid mind compare February 22, 1896, with September 10, 1904, and then ask this question:

Have the Christian Catholic Church in Zion, and its Leader, the Seal of God's Approval upon their work?

Surely the Answer "Yes!" is given by the great throngs of those who have been rescued from the Power of the Enemy, and who joyfully testify that Salvation, Healing, and Holy Living through the Faith of God, have come to them through the Ministry of the Christian Catholic Church in Zion.

Therefore, we Go Forward, confident that God has called this Church into existence at this period of the Dispensation of His Grace; and that He has sent us into His vineyard, though at the Eleventh Hour, and also sent us to many high places of the field to take our part in the Great Conflict between the powers of Heaven and Hell, a Host eager and determined to Conquer the World for the Christ, its Redeemer and Rightful Ruler.

To accomplish this end, we must "organize victory" by perfecting our organization.

Like Moses, we must, in doing this, follow the Divine Pattern, as it is written:

Even as Moses is warned of God,
When he is about to make the Tabernacle:
For, See, saith He, that thou make All Things
According to the Pattern that was shown thee in the Mount.

Therefore, I have no desire, and no right, to deviate from the Pattern set forth in the words and example of the Christ in the establishment of His Church, all of which is summed up in the Declaration of Paul the Apostle, in 1st Corinthians, 12th chapter and 28th verse.

God hath set some in the Church,
First Apostles,
Secondly Prophets,
Thirdly Teachers.

These three Offices, and in this order, are the Fundamental Offices of the Church, which our Lord constituted; for the Apostles received from Him, on the Mount, during forty days after His resurrection, and before His reascension to heaven, the details of all that was then necessary. It is written:

He also showed Himself alive after His passion
By many proofs,
Appearing unto them by the space of Forty Days,
And speaking The Things concerning the Kingdom of God.

As the Teacher of the Christian Catholic Church in Zion, I laid down in plain terms, at its organization, certain fundamental and essential requirements, and concerning these I said:

These are the Broad Principles upon which I invite you to come together and form the Christian Catholic Church.

As the Teacher of the Christian Catholic Church in Zion, I continued to develop practically these Principles in my ministry, and God used me to prepare the Church for the Declaration of June 2, 1901.

I then stood forth, before an immense audience, in the Chicago Auditorium, and declared that God had sent me, as John the Baptist had been sent, in the "Spirit and Power of Elijah;" our Lord having said that Elijah would again appear at the end of This Dispensation, as the Prophet of the Restoration of All Things.

As the Teacher and General Overseer of the Christian Catholic Church in Zion, as the Messenger of God's Covenant, and as His Prophet, I have continued to do God's work in these offices all over the world.

I have prepared the Church for the Declaration, which, God permitting, I shall make on Lord's Day afternoon, September 18th, in Shiloh Tabernacle, Zion City, as the *Divinely-Commissioned First Apostle of the Christian Catholic and Apostolic Church in Zion*, with authority to select and to ordain eleven other Apostles, when and where God may direct.

And now, the whole matter is placed before God's people in Zion for prayerful consideration and approval.

A Conference of all members of the Christian Catholic Church in Zion will be held in Shiloh Tabernacle, Zion City, next Wednesday evening, September 14th, and the mind of the entire fellowship then present will be ascertained.

Until that Conference is held, and until my Declaration is made, four days later, I shall reserve all further writing.

But I hope, within a reasonable time after these events, once more to address the Church in a General Letter, after full time for consideration has been given to the words in which I shall make that Declaration.

Further writing upon my part at the present time is not required.

The reports of the Conferences, which cover no less than thirteen pages of this issue of LEAVES OF HEALING, will supply, under the guidance of the Holy Spirit, abundant material for the formation of a Sound and Abiding Conviction concerning this matter.

My direction is that this Letter, and these Reports, *shall be read in all the homes of the City of Zion*, and in the homes of as many members of the Christian Catholic Church in Zion as this shall reach, *during the coming week*.

I desire that the reading shall be prayerful and orderly, and that the entire household, who have reached years of discretion, shall be present without exception at the reading, which will probably take a considerable portion of the mornings and evenings of the entire people during the week.

It is my desire that every man, woman, and child in the Church shall be helped, through these pages, by the Holy Spirit, *to understand where God is leading Zion at this time.*

My humble and earnest cry to all lovers of God, and especially to God's people in the Christian Catholic Church in Zion is, that all should daily, lovingly, and faithfully pray for me, and for those whom God shall, in due time, call to be Apostles, through me, so that as

JOHN ALEXANDER, THE FIRST APOSTLE OF THE CHRISTIAN CATHOLIC AND APOSTOLIC CHURCH IN ZION, AND ELIJAH, THE PROPHET OF THE RESTORATION OF ALL THINGS,

I may be fully prepared for every Service and Sacrifice to which my Lord shall call me.

May the action now being taken hasten that happiest, gladdest of all happy days when our Beloved Savior and our King shall come again to receive from the world His own; and then again to return to this earth, and sit upon the Throne of His Glory, where He shall Rule, and Reign, and Triumph over all the powers of evil, and establish Forever the Rule of God.

Thanking you all for your patient and tender love, which has never failed me in all the toilsome years, as I have pressed on amidst many foes, and tears, and trials, I am,

Faithfully your friend and fellow servant in Jesus, the Christ, our Lord and Coming King,

General Overseer of the Christian Catholic Church in Zion.

Every Reader of Leaves of Healing Should Also Read The Zion Banner.

The cost is too small to be worth mentioning, being fifty cents for six months.

LESS THAN TWO CENTS A WEEK!

If you will put in a few hours' work among your friends, and obtain THREE NEW SUBSCRIBERS TO THE ZION BANNER, we will send you your own copy free.

YOU CAN GET THEM EASILY!

Just give it a trial.

Scarcely any news in THE ZION BANNER is reprinted in LEAVES OF HEALING.

Many people will read THE ZION BANNER who might not be interested in our other publications.

Resolve today that you will do this for the extension of the Kingdom of God.

ZION PRINTING AND PUBLISHING HOUSE,
Zion City, Illinois.

Warning to Subscribers.

Scarcely a week passes that we do not have complaints about money having been sent to us in currency, stamps, or silver, in the open mails, for renewals of subscriptions or for other purposes, WHICH WE HAVE NOT RECEIVED AND WHICH NEVER REACHES US.

Therefore, we desire to warn every member and friend of Zion sending money to us, to always use some safe means, preferably a money-order, or bank-draft on New York or Chicago, or personal check on Zion City Bank.

In conforming to this notice you will save yourselves trouble and expense, and us much annoyance.

ZION PRINTING AND PUBLISHING HOUSE,
Zion City, Illinois.

Street Addresses Are Necessary.

All Zion City Subscribers to *Leaves of Healing*, *The Zion Banner*, *Blätter der Heilung*, and *Voice from Zion*, whose correct street addresses are not positively known to be in our possession should send them to us AT ONCE. Please act upon this notice without delay as it is very important, now that we have postal delivery service, that the exact location of each and every subscriber be known to us. Write your name and address very carefully, designating also to what periodicals you are a subscriber and leave at your very earliest opportunity at our branch Publishing House on Elijah Avenue.

Very Sincerely Yours,
ZION PRINTING AND PUBLISHING HOUSE.

Warning.

I am directed by the General Overseer to warn our members and officers throughout the world against giving money to persons claiming to be members of the Christian Catholic Church in Zion. All benevolence must be given either from Headquarters or under the direction of same. Even though the applicant for benevolence be known to be a member of the Christian Catholic Church in Zion, financial aid must not be given except in extreme cases, and then only in small amounts. Requests for help must be made to the officer-in-charge. In cases where there is no such officer, requests should be made direct to Headquarters, accompanied by recommendations from one or two members of Zion in good standing.

J. G. EXCELL,
General Ecclesiastical Secretary.

Notice to Correspondents.

In writing to Headquarters it is *absolutely essential* that the writer give his full address.

Failure to comply with this request necessitates looking up or referring to the Church Records, which involves much time, and is very frequently fruitless.

Friends and members of the Christian Catholic Church in Zion everywhere will please bear this in mind, especially those in foreign lands.

J. G. EXCELL, General Ecclesiastical Secretary.

Notice to Officers and Members.

Send all newspaper clippings concerning the General Overseer, the Elders, or any department of the work in connection with the Christian Catholic Church in Zion, to Deacon Carl F. Stern, Zion City, Illinois. Send as soon as possible after publication, and carefully mark *name and date of the paper clipped from* on each article. If this is not done, the clippings are absolutely useless.

Zion's Literature Mission

By Evangelist **Sarah E. Hill.**

AND HE SAID, Cast it on the ground. And he cast it on the gound, and it became a serpent; and Moses fled from before it.—*Exodus 4:3.*

IN the wonderful scene before the Burning Bush, where God met Moses and talked to him, Moses stood with his shepherd's rod in his hand as God spake with him.

He was attending to his daily work, as a shepherd, when God met him and told him that He would send him to bring the Israelites out of Egypt, from under their bondage to the flesh, because they had cried to Him for help.

It was through this rod, which Moses used in his daily work, that God performed signs and wonders before the King and the people of Egypt.

The rod suggested the animals in the care of which it was used, and was a good symbol of the animal or human nature of man.

This is like a rod to support man in his journey through life, when held firmly in the grasp of a strong hand.

If it is not controlled and restrained, it grovels on the earth and stings its owner.

Human nature resembles a serpent more than it does any other animal.

When Moses loosened his hold on the rod and threw it on the ground, it became a serpent, and he fled from it.

It is the soul and body in man which constitute his animal being.

Every animal has a soul.

It is the life of the animal, and it is represented by the blood. (Leviticus 17:11, margin. Genesis 1:20, 30, margin.)

The mind of the animal is in the soul, and it was made to understand and deal with material things in the world about us.

Man is not only an animal, but he is much more than an animal, for he has a wonderful spiritual nature, which is capable of communing with God and understanding spiritual things.

Man is a dual being, a crowned animal; crowned with a wonderful crown of life in his spiritual being, which is capable of unfolding in the likeness of God when God reigns in him.

This spiritual being has a spiritual mind, made to deal with spiritual things; just as his material mind was made to deal with material things.

The two are the opposites of each other in their nature and manner of working.

They are made to be united, and to work as one mind; and they do this when the Christ rules in man.

Man's animal being was made to be the servant of his spiritual being, enabling the latter to use the former as an instrument for working with material things.

Man learns about material things through his material mind, which thinks and reasons about the knowledge it gathers through the senses.

He learns about spiritual things through the mind of his spirit, for these are spiritually discerned.

He really learns about spiritual things by obeying God's commands; and as he obeys, the Holy Spirit opens the truth to his spiritual mind through inspiration.

It is by doing the Will of the Father, Jesus says, that we learn the teaching. (John 7:17.)

The mind of the flesh wants to see and think out spiritual truths before it accepts them.

It says seeing is believing.

God says believing is seeing. The apostles were long under the teaching of our Lord before they saw clearly who He was.

They accepted His declaration of His being the Messiah on the authority of His Word.

When our Lord tested the Apostle Peter on this subject, Peter could declare boldly that He was the Christ, the Son of the Living God.

Jesus answered that flesh and blood had not revealed this truth unto him, but His Father which was in heaven. (Matthew 16:15-18.)

Flesh and blood cannot today make any man know surely that Jesus is the Christ of God.

But multitudes have accepted Him by faith, and have within themselves the Holy Spirit, who bears witness with their spirits, that He is the Savior of men.

Multitudes know, too, that He is the Savior of the physical as well as of the spiritual part of man.

The Apostle Paul calls the material mind the "mind of the flesh," the "carnal mind," and the "fleshly mind." (Romans 8:5, 6, 7; Colossians 2:18.)

He tells us that if we are ruled by the mind of the flesh we will be ruled by the things of the flesh; but if we let the mind of our spiritual being rule, we will be ruled by spiritual things.

Christian people make crooked paths, because at times they let the carnal mind rule them.

When this is the case, they want to see and to feel spiritual things, instead of taking them by faith, which is neither seeing nor feeling.

Faith seems like nothing, although it is the power that is able to remove mountains.

It is the most important trait in the Christian character, and it is the one thing which the Devil cannot imitate.

It looks at God's promises, and between it and them there is nothing but "thus saith the Lord," and on that it rests as on a rock, and it cannot be moved.

When God told Moses that He would send him to stand before the king of Egypt and command him to release an army of slaves, Moses looked at his own weakness, the weakness of the flesh, and he felt that the work was too great for him.

The mind of the flesh saw only the mountain of difficulties in the road, and no way over them.

It did not see the strength of God, ready to sweep the mountains aside. Yet God, in presenting Himself to Moses that day in a bush, showed him that if He could use a bush through which to manifest Himself, he could also use a weak man, such as he felt himself to be, through which to manifest Himself to the king and people of Egypt.

Moses was truly a prepared instrument, such as God could use to do a great work; but he did not recognize it himself.

He had not learned the great truth which the Apostle Paul saw when he said, "When I am weak, then am I strong." (2 Cor. 12: 10.)

God has today raised up a Prophet like unto Moses, and has given him a similar work to do.

God promised to send Elijah the Messenger of the Covenant, before the Great and Terrible Day of the Lord.

Jesus tells us that He is to Restore All Things, when He comes. (Malachi 4:5; Matthew 17:10-13.)

John Alexander Dowie is today doing the work which God says Elijah the Messenger of the Covenant, is to do; and He is blessing His work in saving and healing the people.

He is bringing out an army from the bondage of the flesh, and forming them into a nation to be ruled by God.

He needs a multitude of helpers to send over the world the Full Gospel Message of Zion, which is to save and heal the people, and prepare them for the Coming of the Lord.

All may take part in this work—the old and the young, the weak and the strong, the rich and the poor, may send the Message that has such power in bringing out the people from their bondage to the flesh.

Zion Literature Mission invites all to help in sending out Zion's Message.

ELIJAH THE RESTORER.

I affirm that the Church cannot be Christian, and cannot be Catholic, unless it is Apostolic. The Apostolic Office must be declared as belonging to the Church, . . . and it shall be declared to be a Perpetual Office. It is our duty to declare that the Church of God shall eventually, and as speedily as possible, be so organized. We have nothing to do with consequences. God will call His Apostles in His own time and way by the Holy Spirit.

—*The words of John Alex. Dowie in the First General Conference of all believers interested in the organization of the Christian Catholic Church, Zion Tabernacle No. 2, Chicago, Illinois, Wednesday evening, January 22, 1896.*

AN ONWARD MOVEMENT IN THE WORK OF ELIJAH THE RESTORER—BUILDING THE APOSTOLIC "POWER HOUSE."

ZION'S ONWARD MOVEMENT

REPORT OF

THE FIRST GENERAL CONFERENCE

Of all Believers interested in the Organization of

THE CHRISTIAN CATHOLIC CHURCH,

Held in Zion Tabernacle No. 2, Chicago, Wednesday Evening, Jan. 22nd, 1896.

[The weather was the very worst of all the winter. After a general thaw there had been a sudden freeze and the streets were everywhere covered with sheets of ice so that it was difficult to walk and many fell in all parts of the city; and the night was very dark. Nevertheless there were about 700 present.]

THE REV. JOHN ALEX. DOWIE presided, and, in opening the Conference said:—Beloved friends, it seems to me as if we who have been marching together to Zion cannot find a better hymn than

OUR MARCHING SONG

to begin this Conference with. No. 151.

"Come, ye that love the Lord,
And let your joys be known,
Join in a song with sweet accord;
And thus surround the throne."

Oh, there is so much in being in sweet accord, in true communion with God and with each other.

CHO. "We're marching to Zion,
Beautiful, beautiful Zion;
We're marching upward to Zion,
The beautiful City of God.

The hill of Zion yields
A thousand sacred sweets
Before we reach the heavenly fields,
Or walk the golden streets."

I believed in my very heart, while we sang these words that mine eyes shall behold the City, that mine eyes shall see the King in His glory. I heard Charles Spurgeon recite these lines in the Metropolitan Tabernacle, London, twenty-six years ago:—

"My life's a shade,
My days apace to death decline;
My Lord is Life,
He'll raise this dust again, even mine,
Sweet truth to me, I shall arise
And with these eyes my Saviour see."

We shall walk "the golden streets," but meanwhile the hill of Zion "yields a thousand sacred sweets." I am very glad it is a hill, that we have such joy in going upward before we reach those heavenly fields. We have many a lovely experience, as the beauties of God's revelation unfold on every side. Let us sing with a hearty will, let this be a very joyful conference for us.

"Then let our songs abound,
And ev'ry tear be dry,
We're marching thro' Immanuel's ground
To fairer worlds on high."

SCRIPTURE READING AND COMMENTS.

Let us read the 67 Psalm:

"God be merciful unto us, and bless us; and cause His face to shine upon us;

That Thy way may be known upon earth, Thy saving health among all nations."

God's way is not a thing, but a person. Jesus said, "I am the way." Christ is God's way. "That Thy way" (Thy Christ) "may be known upon earth, Thy saving health," (salvation and healing going hand in hand) "among all nations."

"Let the people praise Thee, O God; let all the people praise Thee.

O let the nations be glad and sing for joy: for Thou shalt judge the people righteously, and govern the nations upon earth."

And they need government, and the only rule that men one day will follow on this earth will be the rule of God. (Amen! from the audience.) Not a Democracy, the rule of the people, but a Theocracy, the rule of God, the Kingdom of Heaven on earth.

"O let the nations be glad and sing for joy: for Thou shalt judge the people righteously, and govern the nations upon earth.

Let the people praise Thee, O God; let all the people praise Thee.

Then shall the earth yield her increase; and God, even our own God shall bless us.

God shall bless us; and all the ends of the earth shall fear Him."

Now that is the Word.

We have read it in beginning in many lands a long series of Missions, which with my good wife, I have held, stretching over nearly 20 years since I stepped out of organized ecclesiastical life and consecrated myself afresh to God. And now this Conference may, in the providence of God, be the preliminary step in my returning to organized eccesiastical work. I want God to be greatly glorified: It means more to me than it means to any one here, for in forming the Christian Catholic Church I take a responsibility which, unless God gives me that grace which I believe He will give, will only end in adding one more to the injurious and distressing divisions of Christendom, and that—may God forbid.

I never had any ambition to be the originator, the head, or heart of a petty organization that should be just one more of the innumerable divisions of Christendom. But I have felt with a great, broad, catholic sympathy which God gave me from the beginning, and which God has broadened, and widened, and deepened throughout all the years, that I wanted, if ever I should return to organized church life, to get back to its primitive conditions, where the Church should be catholic, universal, all-embracing, in embracing all who were in communion with God by repentance and faith in our Lord Jesus Christ.

And now I want, beloved friends, that to-night we shall all feel that these first steps in conference shall be all guided by God.

My address has been much thought of, and much prayed over, and I could have written it out much more easily than it will be to speak it without writing; but I felt that the address which I will deliver presently was one that I must leave myself entirely to the guidance of the Holy Ghost in delivering.

I know that to-night I have placed myself in my Heavenly Father's absolute keeping; that by His grace I have absolute confidence in His Son, and that by the power of the Holy Spirit I hope to be able to so guide this Conference, under God, that when we part to-night we shall feel, humble though we are, and few though we be, comparatively, that we are able to claim the Pentecostal Wisdom given to the at least 120 even now, and that from this upper room we shall go down into Chicago with the thought that the Lord is preparing us in His own mighty way for a mightier day than even the first Pentecost.

ABOUT PRAYER.

Now let us pray, and I don't want, when we say "let us pray," that any should feel that this is a sort of opening exercise—one that we have got to get over as quick as we can until we get to what some people call "the business of the meeting." "The business of the meeting" began from the first word of praise to God, and there is no business in this meeting more important than this business of prayer, which we are now going to transact with God upon our knees. Come let us worship and bow down, let us kneel before the Lord our Maker.

I shall ask my good wife and colleague, for she is my fellow-minister, to pray; and then my good brother and colleague, the Rev. Dr. Speicher, to pray; but I want you all to pray in the Spirit with them. Let us be of one mind.

INVOCATION.

Our Father, let the Holy Spirit breathe upon us the spirit of prayer, the grace of a common humiliation, the grace of a common faith and supplication, for Christ's sake.

PRAYER BY MRS. DOWIE.

Our God and Father, we ask Thee for the guidance of Thy Holy Spirit; we thank Thee that we believe that Thou hast guided us and that Thou hast brought us up to this time. We ask Thee, our Father, that in all that is done and said to-night we may be led by Thee, and that we may work good in the unity of the Spirit. Oh, our Father, to-day we ask Thee to help us so that we shall make no mistakes. Give us Thy wisdom, give us knowledge, give us faith, and oh help us to go forward in the name of Jesus. We thank Thee for all Thou hast been doing here; we thank Thee that the people have come in such large numbers to worship Thee, and that they are now believing in Thee as the Saviour from sin, and as the Healer of every sickness and every disease among the people. Oh, our Father, we do thank Thee for this, that there is more faith with the people now than there was a little while ago; that their faith has been growing, and that the people have been coming to see Thee in all Thy blessings. Oh, lead us on, our Father; go before us and show us the way; help us all to work in communion with the Spirit and in communion with Thee, for Jesus' sake. Amen.

DR. SPEICHER'S PRAYER.

Thou knowest, our Father in Heaven, how much we desire to glorify Thee. Thou knowest, O God, how our hearts have been grieved and the sadness that we have felt when we have seen Thy children scattered abroad, without a shepherd, and perplexed on every side because of a divided Church. Oh God, Thou knowest our desire to-night, that we may be made one even as Thou art One. Oh God, we want to be one with Thee and one with Thy people. Oh God, we pray to-night that Thou wilt indeed show us just how this may be done, and we believe that Thou wilt give us the spirit of humiliation and submission to Thy will; that Thou wilt give Thy people the grace to come in willingness of heart, in perfect willingness to obey Thee, and to do Thy will in all things that we may be united, and that Thy Church, Thy people, may gather from all the ends of the earth in one body into the household of faith. May we begin anew, and let the power of Thy Spirit be increased in the world for good. May the little handful here go out and spread the gospel of peace and bring a world of sinners to Jesus. We ask this for Jesus' sake, O God. We believe it will be, we know it in our hearts to-night, for here we have felt Thy Glory. Now, God, bless Thy servant and grant that the message that he may deliver to-night may indeed be through the power and direction of the Holy Spirit. Grant that we may listen as to a message from God Himself, for Jesus' sake. Amen.

After the singing of the hymn, "Beautiful Words of Life," the Rev. John Alex. Dowie delivered the following

ADDRESS ON ORGANIZATION:

Beloved friends, the first part of my address will be to lay down, in the simplest possible language, certain scriptural statements concerning the Church. I shall make no elaborate introduction nor attempt any oratorical display. I am always most effective in my ministry for God, I believe, when I get most directly at my subject.

I AM SIMPLY A BUSINESS MAN IN THE MINISTRY.

That is all. I make a business of my ministry. The Lord Jesus Christ made a business of His ministry. He said when only a child, "Wist ye not that I must be about my Father's business?" I know no separation between this kind of business and that kind of business.

THE ETERNAL GOD IS IN ALL KINDS OF BUSINESS.

He is in the grain business, and He provides corn. He is in the horticultural business, and he provides beautiful flowers. He is in the fishery business, and He has a wonderful fish market in the great ocean. He is in the poultry business. (Laughter.) He is in the meat market. He is in the electrical business, and when the lightnings flash amid the sky you can see what wonderful pyrotechnical displays He sometimes gives. He is in the iron and steel business and in the gas and water business, and provides everything for man; for, after all, man's business is simply to take up and redistribute what He has given. Did you ever reflect that

GOD IS SIMPLY THE EXECUTIVE CENTRE OF THE BUSINESS OF THE UNIVERSE?

In His own Church it is still "His Father's Business" that Christ our Lord pursues, and to-night I speak as one who realizes in a measure that everything that I can use for Christ in the Extension of His Kingdom is my Father's business, and that every one of you who are my brothers and sisters in Christ are in business for the Lord. You good women in your homes, you are keeping house for God, and you men are in business for your God.

So now we will just get to business, and ask God to give us some of

HIS OWN PLAIN, BEAUTIFUL TEACHING CONCERNING THE CHURCH.

Now sometimes you hear the word church as applied to the Jewish Church.

Beloved friends, there was no Jewish Church—there was no Jewish Church. I have, I think, the best Concordance of the Bible here on my desk that has ever been printed in this world, and I always feel so indebted to good Dr. Robert Young of Edinburgh who gave us this remarkable Concordance. Under the heading of the word Church, I was looking over it the other day, the first thing that impressed me was that the word Church does not occur in the whole of the Old Testament. Did you ever notice that?

THERE WAS NO JEWISH CHURCH.

The word Church is a word that Christ Himself first coined. There was no Patriarchal Church. There has never been any Church excepting the Church of the Living God, which Christ Himself founded. And let me tell you that the great distinguishable characteristic of the Jewish economy the dispensation that preceded this dispensation of God as Christ, is the fact that now we have a Church, and then there was none.

ISRAEL WAS CALLED AS A NATION,

and every Israelite was by circumcision a member of the Church, whether good or bad, a member of that nation.

Now I venture to say that the Israelitish Dispensation was formed for the purpose of bringing into existence the Bride of Christ in the shape of His Church. You remember the ancient dispensation was of a very legal, very formal character, and, while there was an inner spiritual life, the greater part of it was ceremonial and legal. Ceremonies so burdensome and numerous and legalities so endless, that the burden was in many respects too hard for any people ever to bear, and the law was a pedagogue, a schoolmaster, to bring God's people to Christ as a Church.

A great many things might be said concerning the thoughts that these facts suggest. I have much more to say than can be said here and now. The mere fact itself that that word Church is not used until Christ first uses it is very remarkable.

THE FIRST TIME THAT CHRIST USES THIS WORD CHURCH IS IN CONNECTION WITH THE REVELATION WHICH GOD, THE FATHER, GAVE TO THE APOSTLE PETER.

Bring your Bibles to these Conferences and a piece of paper and a pencil so that you may all be reporters of these meetings. I want, just in a businesslike way, to bring you into the facts and thoughts connected with the Church.

The first time that this word Church is used is in the 16th chapter of Matthew, and the 18th verse. In some places to-night I will read the revised version, which is by far the best English translation of the scriptures, and I hope that by and by it will come into general use among us for reading, especially the revision of the New Testament. I will ask you to do to-night what our guests do in the Divine Healing Homes. We all read the scriptures together, and if they don't read out I tell them. (Laughter.) Now this is a family gathering to-night to talk over what God says about the organization of His Church. Now if you have got bibles you ought to have them with you, and if you have not got them I cannot help you much. I have several copies here. I can give good Brother Atkins one, he has left his at home.

The 16th chapter of the gospel according to St. Matthew. Now I want you to read with me, because I want you all to be interested in the passage and keep good time. Now we will read the old version and if I see anything altered that I think ought to be mentioned in the new, I am going to tell you. All present read Matthew: 16:13 to 20 as follows:

"When Jesus came into the coasts of Cesarea Phillippi, he asked his disciples saying, Whom do men say that I, the Son of man, am?

And they said, Some *say that Thou art* John the Baptist; some, Elias; and others, Jeremias, or one of the prophets.

He saith unto them, But whom say ye that I am?

And Simon Peter answered and said, Thou art the Christ, the Son of the living God.

And Jesus answered and said unto him, Blessed art thou, Simon Barjona; for flesh and blood hath not revealed *it* unto thee, but my Father which is in heaven.

And I say also unto thee, that thou art Peter, and upon this rock I will build my church; and the gates of hell shall not prevail against it.

And I will give unto thee the keys of the kingdom of heaven; and whatsoever thou shalt bind on earth shall be bound in heaven; and whatsoever thou shalt loose on earth shall be loosed in heaven.

Then charged He His disciples that they should tell no man that He was Jesus the Christ.

I first call your attention to the fact that this revelation of the Church was first of all brought about by the Lord Jesus Christ demanding of His apostles an answer to the question: "Who say ye that I am?"

Now Peter had wonderful spiritual knowledge. He was open, spiritually, on both sides unfortunately, he let in the Devil and he let in God. He was quick to perceive. He was quick to receive, and at this time he was just about as quick to let out as he was to take in. But it was in one of those great flashes of divine inspiration that there came the revelation that Jesus was the Messiah, the Anointed, the Christ, the Son of the Living God," And he saw it at once. Jesus said, "Thou art Petros," (a stone.) That means a chip of a rock, a small stone. "Thou art Petros," that was the name Peter, a stone, "and upon this rock" (petra, a rock) the rock of my own Divinity, of my own Messiahship, "will I build my Church, and the gates of hell shall not prevail against it."

These are the very first words of inspiration concerning the Church; there is the Church, "the pillar and ground of truth."

IN CHRIST, ON CHRIST, CHRIST THE ETERNAL ROCK.

Christ is more than the foundation of the Church. He is the foundation, and much more. He is the rock upon which the foundation was founded. There was a Patriarchal Dispensation. There was a Jewish Dispensation. There is a Christian Dispensation; but the Rock underlay all the dispensations, and we may assuredly say that forever it will underlie everything.

CHRIST HIMSELF THE ROCK OF AGES.

I want to show you the difference just now between Christ as the Rock which is The Foundation upon which all foundations are laid, and the specific "foundation" of the Church of Christ upon that rock.

There is a difference, you will see it presently.

SPECIAL APOSTOLIC POWER.

But before we proceed further, I call your attention to the fact, that in the very same breath that Christ founded the Church, He declared to Peter, that an Apostolic power would be conferred upon him, and not upon him only but upon all the Apostles, as I shall show you presently. Read of the Apostolic power, the 19th verse.

"And I will give unto thee the keys of the kingdom of heaven; and whatsoever thou shalt bind on earth shall be bound in heaven: and whatsoever thou shalt loose on earth shall be loosed in heaven."

The Roman Catholics vainly say that that power is Peter's only, and that, therefore Peter, and his official successors at Rome, are the Unmoving Cathedra or Chair of Certainty in the Church. But it is not so, for, whilst the Lord said these words to Peter, you will please to refer to the 20th chapter of John and the 23rd verse, and you will see that he said that subsequently and on a much more solemn occasion to all the Apostles. The gospel according to St. John, 20th chapter, read together please from the 19th verse.

"Then the same day at evening, being the first *day* of the week, when the doors were shut where the disciples were assembled for fear of the Jews, came Jesus and stood in the midst, and saith unto them, Peace *be* unto you.

And when He had so said, He shewed unto them *His* hands and His side. Then were the disciples glad, when they saw the Lord.

Then said Jesus to them again, Peace *be* unto you; as *my* Father hath sent me, even so send I you.

And when He had said this, He breathed on *them*, and saith unto them, Receive ye the Holy Ghost.

Whosoever sins ye remit, they are remitted unto them; *and* whosesoever *sins* ye retain, they are retained."

Now the word "remit" is equal to "forgive." The revised version in the 23rd verse reads. "Whosesoever sins ye forgive they are forgiven unto them, and whosesoever sins ye retain they are retained."

"RECEIVE YE THE HOLY GHOST."

That word was said to the whole of the Apostles when the door was shut, and Christ stood in the midst. I do not want to make any comment upon this matter just now beyond saying this, that I believe

THIS POWER TO FORGIVE OR REMIT SINS IS THE PREROGATIVE OF GOD ALONE; BUT HE EXERCISES THE PREROGATIVE THROUGH THE ANOINTED AND ORDAINED AND PROPER OFFICERS OF THE CHURCH.

I suppose you know that prerogative means a royal power that is reserved to the monarch alone.

In the British Empire the royal prerogative is the right to step in and suspend the law, to forgive the criminal, to open the gates of the prison, to take away the sentence of death, aud to restore a person to perfect freedom, that is the absolute prerogative of the Queen. But she can delegate that prerogative, and she does, to Viceroys in every province of the British Empire, in India, Australia, the Dominion of Canada, etc. This fact is better understood therefore in a monarchical country than in a republic—the idea of the delegation of the power to forgive.

FEARS OF APPROACHING TO ROME.

Now I know that some may immediately think that this approaches perilously near to Rome.

I do not care a pin; if the Roman Catholic Church has got a truth I am going to say it, and I do not care who takes the other side; if the Greek Church has got a truth I am going to say it; if the Episcopalian Church has got a truth I am going to say it; if the Baptist Church has got a truth I am going to say it; and more than that, I am going to get that truth if I can, into the Christian Catholic Church. (Applause.)

I am going to get every good thing I can get, that God has given, into our organization.

Now the question is this, what does that Power mean?

It means a great deal more than you have supposed. It is repeated over and over again by Christ as a Divine Power lying at the very Foundation of the Organization of the Church.

"THE KEYS OF THE KINGDOM OF HEAVEN,"

Were words not lightly used by Jesus, and mean too much to be ignored without sin.

There is a great deal in a key, is there not?

There are a great many of you here that knew about Divine Healing, but you could not get in at that Door for it seemed to have been locked for centuries, and ministers told you it was shut forever. But God in His infinite goodness and mercy sent me along, and I had "the Key." I had it in my hand; and I said to you, "Look here, this is a divine key, see it, it is the Word of God, it is the key of a divine promise and a divine power, and I put it into the lock. Trembling for deliverance, there stood outside a woman with a cancer whose face was full of sorrow and of pain, and I opened the door with the Key, and said, "You can go in," and she went in. She came out healed, and there she sits amongst you, well and happy. Then there was a poor little boy, lame, and on crutches, and he said, "Can't I get in?" I said now, you watch, and we will open the door, and you can go in; and he went in and came out well. You see that was a key, one of the Keys of the Kingdom of Heaven.

Mr. Calverly: Doctor can I make a remark?

Dr. Dowie: Not just now, brother; you can make any remarks you please afterwards.

I called attention at the outset to this point for the purpose of showing you that when the Lord Jesus founded His Church, the very next thing He said was to dignify the Apostolic Office. But we will go right on.

I have only begun. I don't know when I will get through. I am not going to look at my watch. I have made up my mind not to do it. (Laughter.)

There is only one other reference to the Church by Christ Himself. It is in the 18th chapter of Matthew. Now, then, come along, let us have this, let us read together, please, from the 15th to 20th verse of the 18th chapter of Matthew:

"Moreover if thy brother shall trespass against thee, go and tell him his fault between thee and him alone; if he shall hear thee, thou hast gained thy brother

But if he will not hear thee, then take with thee one or two more, that in the mouth of two or three witnesses every word may be established.

And if he shall neglect to hear them, tell it unto the church; but if he neglect to hear the church, let him be unto thee as a heathen man and a publican

Verily, I say unto you. Whatsoever ye shall bind on earth shall be bound in heaven; and whatsoever ye shall loose on earth shall be loosed in heaven

Again I say unto you, That if two of you shall agree on earth as touching any thing that they shall ask, it shall be done for them of my Father which is in heaven

For where two or three are gathered together in my name, there am I in the midst of them "

Now you see again that the power of binding and loosing is extended in a measure to the whole Church, under Apostolic direction and organization. I could prove that point to you by reading extensively, but I simply mention this point in connection with that. You will see that the Apostle Paul in his Epistles assumes to have a right to this Apostolic power, and gives certain directions to the Church, telling them to purge out "old leaven," to "put away" a wicked man from amongst them, and writing to them and saying in an Epistle "not to keep company with such persons," and so on. He held it was the duty of the Church to obey Apostolic direction. This power was not only conferred upon the Apostles, it was exercised by them, and was recognized by the Church without protest.

THIS APOSTOLIC POWER HAD TO BE DELEGATED,

inasmuch as the Apostles could not be everywhere, and was delegated to bishops or "overseers" in various places.

The remarkable thing is, that in both these cases where Jesus named the Church He adds and links it to this remarkable Power conferred upon the Apostles.

I ask you to notice this because of the importance of what will follow.

PASS FROM THE GOSPELS INTO THE ACTS OF THE APOSTLES.

I will not stop to-night to read with you that first chapter of the Acts of the Apostles, but I will very briefly describe it to you.

"The former treatise have I made, O Theophilus, of all that Jesus began both to do and to teach.

Until the day in which He was taken up, after that he through the Holy Ghost had given commandments unto the apostles whom he had chosen

To whom also He shewed Himself alive after His passion by many infallible proofs, being seen of them forty days, and speaking of the things pertaining to the kingdom of God;

And, being assembled together with them, commanded them that they should not depart from Jerusalem, but wait for the promise of the Father, which, saith He, ye have heard of me.

For John truly baptized with water; but ye shall be baptized with the Holy Ghost not many days hence.

When they therefore were come together, they asked of Him, saying, Lord, wilt thou at this time restore again the kingdom of Israel?

And He said unto them, It is not for you to know the times or the seasons, which the Father hath put in His own hands.

But ye shall receive power, after that the Holy Ghost is come upon you; and ye shall be witnesses unto me both in Jerusalem, and in all Judea, and in Samaria, and unto the uttermost part of the earth

And when He had spoken these things, while they beheld, He was taken up; and a cloud received Him out of their sight.

And while they looked steadfastly toward heaven as He went up, behold, two men stood by them in white apparel,

Which also said, Ye men of Galilee, why stand ye gazing up into heaven? this same Jesus, which is taken up from you into heaven, shall so come in like manner as ye have seen Him go into heaven.

Then returned they unto Jerusalem from the mount called Olivet, which is from Jerusalem a Sabbath day's journey.

And when they were come in, they went up into an upper room, where abode both Peter, and James, and John, and Andrew, Philip, and Thomas, Bartholomew, and Matthew, James the son of Alpheus, and Simon Zelotes, and Judas the brother of James

These all continued with one accord in prayer and supplication, with the women, and Mary the mother of Jesus, and with His brethren.

And in those days Peter stood up in the midst of the disciples, and said, (the number of of names together were about an hundred and twenty,)

Men and brethren, this Scripture must needs have been fulfilled, which the Holy Ghost by the mouth of David spake before concerning Judas, which was guide to them that took Jesus.

For He was numbered with us, and had obtained part of this ministry.

Now this man purchased a field with the reward of iniquity; and falling headlong, he burst asunder in the midst, and all his bowels gushed out.

And it was known unto all the dwellers at Jerusalem, insomuch as that field is called in their proper tongue, Aceldama, that is to say, The field of blood.

For it is written in the book of Psalms, Let his habitation be desolate, and let no man dwell therein; and, His bishoprick let another take.

Wherefore of these men which have companied with us all the time that the Lord Jesus went in and out among us.

Beginning from the baptism of John, unto that same day that He was taken up from us must one be ordained to be a witness with us of His resurrection.

And they appointed two, Joseph called Barsabas, who was surnamed Justus, and Matthias.

And they prayed, and said, Thou, Lord, which knowest the hearts of all men, shew whether of these two Thou has chosen.

That he may take part of this ministry and apostleship, from which Judas by transgression fell, that he might go to his own place.

And they gave forth their lots, and the lot fell upon Matthias; and he was numbered with the eleven apostles."

It is perhaps the most important chapter in that book with reference to church organization. This chapter of the Acts of the Apostles contains an account of nearly six weeks' of Christ's ministry, after He rose from the dead, and before He re-ascended into heaven.

You will remember that the Acts of the Apostles are written by the Evangelist Luke, and that he refers in the first words of the Acts to his Gospel, and says, "The former treatise have I made, O Theophilus." The word Theophilus means a lover of God. "Concerning all that Jesus *began* to do and to teach until the day when He was taken up." Then, continuing the narrative further, he declares that Jesus, after His resurrection from the dead, showed Himself before His re-ascension into Heaven, for forty days, 3d verse, "for forty days, speaking of the things pertaining to the kingdom of God."

That is, He took the eleven Apostles apart and he taught them how to organize the Church of God, because the foundation office in the Church of God was to be the office of Apostle. Apostles were to rule the Church of God.

Therefore He took these eleven men and He told them HOW, and WHAT, and WHY. After six weeks' instruction, all but two days, He told them that they should not depart from Jerusalem but wait for the promise of the Father, the descent of the Holy Ghost, for power would come after that the Holy Ghost had come upon them.

THE FIRST CONFERENCE ON THE ORGANIZATION OF THE CHURCH.

Now that sacred charge was immediately obeyed, and after the Lord ascended into heaven they went into that upper room and after a season, no doubt, of united prayer, they listened to Peter who rose up amidst the 120 in that upper room and told them of a very important appointment which must be made.

That 120 consisted first, of the eleven Apostles, second, in all probability, of the seventy whom Christ had sent out, and who were the next in rank, that made eighty-one; then there were his brothers and sisters, that would account for seven, and his mother would make eighty-nine; and then certain women who are indicated. But of the remaining thirty-one we do not know who they were, except these thirty-one were persons who had been amongst the closest to Jesus, whether men or women. I dare say such a man as Joseph of Aramathea, or Rabbi Jairus, and such women as Mary and Martha; such women as Joanna, the wife of Chusa, Herod's steward, and Susanna, and Mary Magdalene, and others, these might be among the women.

A NEW APOSTLE NEEDED.

In that upper room you have therefore not the whole number of believers, but you have a company of 120 who are divinely chosen, upon whom the Holy Ghost is first to come. When this company is assembled Peter stands up and the first thing he does is to point out that the Church is incomplete in one of its essential offices. There is a link missing, there is an Apostle short; for Judas Iscariot is dead and buried, he has gone to his place, he betrayed the Lord, and the Apostle Peter stands up in their midst and says; "Wherefore of these men which have companied all the time that the Lord Jesus went in and out amongst us, beginning from the Baptism of John, one must be chosen." Judas by transgression fell, and Peter points out that this was prophesied through David long centuries before, "his office should another take." Therefore, said Peter, we must have a new Apostle.

You will please notice that

THE VERY FIRST ACT OF THE CHURCH, ACTING DIRECTLY AFTER RECEIVING CHRIST'S INSTRUCTIONS, WAS TO FILL UP THE APOSTOLIC RANKS.

If Peter had been speaking something that the other Apostles knew was not in accordance with Christ's teaching, why John would have stood up in a minute, or James, or Phillip, the keen Phillip, or the critical Thomas, and said, "Now Peter take care what you are about, you must not mislead the Church, we have lost an Apostle, but let him go;" but Peter puts his hand upon the Word of God and says, "the Holy Ghost prophesies, through David, that this should happen, and that when it did happen a new Apostle should be chosen." Now they knew he had the Word of God for it, he had the command of Christ, he had the consent of his brethren, and as the new Apostle was chosen in this way, it is important to see how it was done.

THE FIRST RECORDED PRAYER IN THE UPPER ROOM.

"And they appointed two, Joseph called Barsabas, who was surnamed Justus, and Matthias, and they prayed and said, 'Thou, Lord, which knowest the hearts of all men, show of these two the one whom Thou hast chosen, that he may take the place in this ministry and Apostleship from which Judas fell away, that he might go to his own place.'" This is the first recorded prayer in the Church after Christ re-ascended and it is a prayer that the Lord shall show them which of these two is His choice to be an Apostle. Well they gave forth their lots and the lot fell upon Matthias and he was numbered with the eleven Apostles.

HE BECAME AN APOSTLE, HE FILLED UP THE APOSTLIC RANKS AND THEN CAME PENTECOST.

Please read the very next words.

"And when the day of Pentecost was fully come, they were all with one accord in one place.

And suddenly there came a sound from heaven as of a rushing mighty wind, and it filled all the house where they were sitting.

And there appeared unto them cloven tongues like as of fire, and it sat upon each of them.

And they were all filled with the Holy Ghost, and began to speak with other tongues, as the Spirit gave them utterance.

And there were dwelling at Jerusalem Jews, devout men. out of every nation under heaven."

Matthias at once took the place of Judas, and the Holy Ghost at once ratified that; for the Holy Ghost came upon the whole assembly, approving their action. We are met in the very beginning of the Church's history by the apostolic office and its importance, even as we meet the office and its especial powers when Christ first speaks of the Church.

Now passing over for the present the history of the Church in the period covered by the Acts of the Apostles, which contains a great many wonderful things, and to which I shall make some references later on: let us come to

THE DECLARATIONS OF THE HOLY SPIRIT CONCERNING THE CHURCH, AS GIVEN THROUGH THE INSPIRED EPISTLES OF THE APOSTLES PAUL, JAMES, PETER, JOHN AND JUDE.

Paul, was above all others the Great Organizing Apostle of the Church.

He possessed in splendid power that great gift, not merely of preaching the gospel and of praying with the sick, and of calling men into fellowship with God; but he possessed that splendid gift of organizing the Church into a thoroughly compact form, so that it might do a thousandfold more good than it could as a disorganized mass, and I pray God to-night that some of that great grace which rested so mightily upon him will rest upon me.

I want it, I need it, and unless God gives it to me I can not be of any use.

I have felt that the organization of the Church demanded the maturest powers, and I may have reached the maturest power I ever can reach on earth in one sense, that is to say I hope to be wiser and better, but I may have reached the strongest period of my physical life. I trust that I shall be spiritually more powerful, but I do not think I can ever expect to be stronger physically than I am now. I do not very well see how I could put more hours into the day. I don't know whether Mrs. Dowie knows how I can; I don't know whether Dr. Speicher knows how I can, because I put in 19 honrs out of the 24 on the average, but I thank God for it. Nobody can rejoice more than I can in the fact that God has given to me this great gift of an unwearied brain and diligence, and almost unwearied power to do work, and I think it is just the time when I ought to do something of the highest order. I humbly ask that these God-given powers may be preserved, and that I may continue on this level for years to come, learning how to make wiser and more effective use of these powers.

PAUL IS BEFORE ALL OTHERS THE GREAT ORGANIZING APOSTLE OF THE CHURCH.

I think we all admit the splendour of the genius of this

man whom God used and set on fire with the Holy Ghost, giving him great keenness of vision and divine power to bring the Church into order.

How does he say the Church is to be ordered?

In the second chapter of his Epistle to the Ephesians we will read from the 19th to the 22nd verse

ABOUT "FOREIGNERS."

This is a very pleasant passage for us to begin on. You know Brother Calverly you and I and many here are called "foreigners" in this country. I fail to see where I am a "foreigner," or as the Boers in Africa would say, an Uitlander. Whatever it may be among ignorant or narrow-minded boors in Africa or America, I want to tell you this, if you are a Christian you are not a foreigner in the Church of God. (Applause.) There is one place you won't be called a stranger or a foreigner, and that will be, God willing, the Christian Catholic Church. I see friends here to-night who are Germans, who are Irish, who are English, who are Scotch, who are Swedish, who are Poles, Bohemians, French and Italians, and I rejoice in the fact. You know we whom they call "foreigners" make up the most of Chicago when we are put together. The so-called Americans are in the minority. The fact of the matter is that you who call yourselves Americans, you are only a hodge podge after all, that is all, we are real, true, pure-blooded lot. That is why we came here to help you. (Applause.) Now for instance we Anglo-Saxons who come here, we are the real old stock, the genuine article. You are all mixed up, and I am very glad to say this, that whilst there are in Chicago under five hundred thousand native born Americans, there are a million and a quarter who have come from all parts of the earth and through them God can bless every land. It is a splendid strategic center for the Christian Catholic Church. That is only by the way, that is only a little prod to you my good American friends to let you know that we do not want to hear the word "foreigners" as applied to brethren, or any such nonsense. Don't you call us "foreigners" any more. Moreover what I want to tell you friends and all whom these words reach all over the world is this, that in the Church of God there are no "strangers." (Applause.)

THE FOUNDATION OF THE CHURCH.

Now where are we? Read the passage together.

"Now therefore ye are no more strangers and foreigners, but fellow-citizens with the saints, and of the household of God

And are built upon the foundation of the apostles and prophets, Jesus Christ Himself being the chief corner *stone*.

In whom all the building fitly framed together groweth unto an holy temple in the Lord·

In whom ye also are builded together for an habitation of God through the Spirit."

THE APOSTLES AND PROPHETS ARE THE FOUNDATION, THEREFORE UPON WHICH THE CHURCH IS BUILT.

WHAT THEN IS JESUS CHRIST?

HE IS THE CHIEF CORNER STONE.

That is, He is the ROCK underneath all the foundations, just as if there was a great rock underneath Chicago and we put separate foundations for our houses upon that. The Rock on whom Apostles and Prophets and Teachers build is the Lord Jesus Christ. But the foundation offices of the Church, are those of Apostles and Prophets, "ye are built upon the Foundation of the Apostles and Prophets." Jesus Christ Himself is the Rock and the Building of the Temple of the Church is built up from that point, then you see the Apostles and Prophets, and then you see the whole building. Paul says, "In whom all the Building fitly framed together, groweth unto an Holy Temple in the Lord."

THE ORGANIZATION OF THE CHURCH.

Read the fourth chapter of the Epistle to the Ephesians verses 1 to 16.

"I therefore, the prisoner of the Lord, beseech you that ye walk worthy of the vocation wherewith ye are called

With all lowliness and meekness, with long-suffering, forbearing one another in love.

Endeavoring to keep the unity of the Spirit in the bond of peace

There is one body, and one Spirit, even as ye are called in one hope of your calling.

One Lord, one Faith, one baptism.

One God and Father of all, who *is* above all, and through all, and in you all.

But unto every one of us is given grace according to the measure of the gift of Christ.

Wherefore he saith, When he ascended up on high, he led captivity captive, and gave gifts unto men.

(Now that he ascended, what is it but that he also descended first into the lower parts of the earth?

He that descended is the same also that ascended up far above all heavens, that he might fill all things)

And he gave some Apostles; and some, prophets; and some, evangelists; and some, pastors and teachers.

For the perfecting of the saints, for the work of the ministry, for the edifying of the body of Christ.

Till we all come in the unity of the faith, and of the knowledge of the Son of God, unto a perfect man, unto the measure of the stature of the fullness of Christ.

That we *henceforth* be no more children, tossed to and fro, and carried about with every wind of doctrine, by the sleight of men, *and* cunning craftiness, whereby they lie in wait to deceive.

But speaking the truth in love, may grow up into Him in all things, which is the head, *even* Christ.

From whom the whole body fitly joined together and compacted by that which every joint supplieth, according to the effectual working in the measure of every part, maketh increase of the body unto the edifying of itself in love"

There are many things in this beautiful passage upon which I should be glad to speak, if we had time, and I commend it to you for private reading, but I ask you to read once more with me especially the 11th verse:

"And He gave some, apostles; and some, prophets; and some, evangelists; and some, pastors and teachers,"

You will see the Divine Order is Apostles, Prophets, etc., in the Organization of the Church.

But the Order of Ministry is not so exactly stated in Ephesians as it is in the first Epistle of Paul to the Corinthians, the 12th chapter:

"Now concerning spiritual gifts, brethren, I would not have you ignorant.

Ye know that ye were Gentiles, carried away unto these dumb idols, even as ye were led.

Wherefore I give you to understand, that no man speaking by the Spirit of God calleth Jesus accursed; and that no man can say that Jesus is the Lord, but by the Holy Ghost.

Now there are diversities of gifts, but the same Spirit.

And there are differences of administration, but the same Lord.

And there are diversities of operations, but it is the same God which worketh all in all.

But the manifestation of the Spirit is given to every man to profit withal.

For to one is given by the Spirit the word of wisdom; to another the word of knowledge by the same Spirit;

To another faith by the same Spirit, to another the gifts of healing by the same Spirit;

To another the working of miracles; to another prophecy; to another discerning of spirits, to another divers kinds of tongues; to another the interpretation of tongues:

But all these worketh that one and the self-same Spirit, dividing to every man severally as he will.

For as the body is one, and hath many members, and all the members of that one body, being many, are one body; so also is Christ.

For by one Spirit are we all baptized into one body, whether we be Jews or Gentiles, whether we be bond or free, and have been all made to drink into one Spirit.

For the body is not one member, but many.

If the foot shall say, Because I am not the hand, I am not of the body; is it therefore not of the body?

And if the ear shall say, Because I am not the eye, I am not of the body; is it therefore not of the body?

If the whole body were an eye, where were the hearing? If the whole were hearing, where were the smelling?

But now hath God set the members every one of them in the body, as it hath pleased Him.

And if they were all one member, where were the body?

But now are they many members, yet but one body.

And the eye cannot say unto the hand, I have no need of thee; nor again the head to the feet, I have no need of you

Nay, much more those members of the body, which seem to be more feeble, are necessary.

And those members of the body, which we think to be less honourable, upon these we bestow more abundant honour; and our uncomely parts have more abundant comeliness.

For our comely parts have no need; but God hath tempered the body together, having given more abundant honor to that part which lacked·

That there should be no schism in the body; but that the members should have the same care one for another.

And whether one member suffer, all the members suffer with it; or one member be honoured, all the members rejoice with it.

Now ye are the body of Christ, and members in particular

And God hath set some in the Church, first apostles, secondarily prophets, thirdly teachers, after that miracles, then gifts of healings, helps, governments, diversities of tongues.

Are all apostles? are all prophets? are all teachers? are all workers of miracles?

Have all the gifts of healing? do all speak with tongues? do all interpret?

But covet earnestly the best gifts, and yet shew I unto you a more excellent way"

THIS IS THE MOST IMPORTANT CHAPTER ON CHURCH ORGANIZATION IN THE BIBLE.

It is also the most neglected.

The first part of this chapter deals with the unity and perfection of God, then with the Nine Gifts of the Spirit, then with the unity of the Body of Christ, and then the Organization of the Body in the 28th verse. Now then read

THE DIVINE ORGANIZATION OF THE BODY.

"And God hath set some in the Church, first apostles, secondarily prophets, thirdly teachers, after that miracles, then gifts of healings, helps, governments, diversities of tongues."

Now then what is the way of perfect wisdom as to the Order of the Church? What is the first office God has established? "Apostles." The second? "Prophets." The third? "Teachers."

Now, then, did God form a Church with these as the first officers? "He did." Is that the Order of the Church of God? "It is." Does the Church of God ever alter? "No." Can the Church of God be acceptable to Christ if it is not organized after His own order? "No."

Now the question arises,

IS THE APOSTOLIC OFFICE A PERPETUAL ONE?

Now that is my contention. You see all the way through reading about the Church you come up against the Apostles from the first mention of the word by Jesus Himself.

The Apostolic Office comes first, the Prophetic Office next, the Teaching Office next. There it is.

I AFFIRM THAT THE CHURCH CANNOT BE CHRISTIAN, AND CANNOT BE CATHOLIC, UNLESS IT IS APOSTOLIC.

The Apostolic Office must be declared as belonging to the Church, if we shall form a Church; and it shall be declared to be a Perpetual Office.

It is our duty to declare that the Church of God shall eventually, and as speedily as possible, be so organized.

We have nothing to do with consequences. God will call His Apostles in His own time and way by the Holy Spirit.

I do not think that I can see any of them yet, but that does not alter the fact that we have got to organize this Church as God did it. It must be upon the pattern that God gave. I shall organize on that pattern, or not at all.

THE ARGUMENT AGAINST THE PERPETUITY OF THE APOSTOLIC OFFICE IS THIS:

(I am a little tired and you will therefore permit me to sit a little while.)

Now follow me.

The argument usually advanced against the continuation of the Apostolic Office is this: that there were only 12 Apostles appointed by Christ, that they all died, and that they have never had any successors.

That is the ordinary argument because you know you go into Roman Catholic Churches and you see statues of the 12 Apostles, and these 12 Apostles are the first 12 Apostles, but instead of Judas Iscariot they put in Paul.

But why didn't they put in Matthias; for he was the first Apostle chosen after the death of Judas?

In order to get over this, and in order to get over the fact that there were more than 12 Apostles, the Roman Catholic and the Greek Catholic Churches, and the Protestant Churches for that matter, have said, that the Apostle Peter made a great mistake when he got the early Church to elect Matthias. That is the argument you know in Ecclesiastical Theology, that Peter made a tremendous blunder and, that it was Paul who should have been elected.

Now that contention is about the most stupid thing possible, for this reason, that Paul was not converted then, and he could not have been chosen as an Apostle. Paul's name at that time was Saul, and instead of being a Christian he was a persecutor of the Church, and he continued so for more than a year. How could he have been elected? Will any man with any sense show me how Paul could have been elected to be an Apostle when he was a Jewish Rabbi at the time, a persecutor and a bitter persecutor? It is ridiculous. But some of them try to get out of it by going around a bit, and they say Peter ought to have waited for a year. (Great Laughter.) That is the new way they have, but that won't do either, because the Holy Ghost did not say that, the Holy Ghost had said from the very beginning that a new Apostle was to be chosen at once, and Peter brought it before the Church, and no doubt they had direction from the Lord, and they did just what came from the Lord. Therefore beloved friends

MATTHIAS WAS PROPERLY ELECTED AND HE WAS THE 13TH APOSTLE.

And the 14th Apostle was not Paul.

In the Epistle to the Galatians Paul writes that after his conversion on the way to Damascus, he went into Arabia and conferred not with flesh and blood, but with God. He came back after three years, to Damascus, and from Damascus he came up to Jerusalem, and when he got to Jerusalem the Christians there were afraid of him for they knew him for the old persecuting Saul and probably the official witness at the martyrdom of Stephen, and they did not want to hear anything about him. They all remembered how he gloated over the death of that innocent saint of God, and the only persons who took any interest in him were Peter and another Apostle. He says, Galatians first, verse nineteen, "But of the other Apostles saw I none, save James, the Lord's brother."

Now James the brother of the Lord was a new Apostle, because in the Apostolic Band there were two James' and neither of them was a son of Mary, because one was James the son of Alpheus, and the other was James the brother of John, and both James and John were sons of Zebedee. Therefore neither of the two James' in the Apostolic Band, while Christ was living, was the brother of the Lord. On the contrary we have the statement in scripture that after he called the first twelve (Mark 3:21) that Jesus' brothers did not believe in Him. He had four brothers, (Mark 6:3) James, Joses, Judas (or Jude), and Simon, sons of Mary, and also sisters. These four brothers of our Lord were not believers in Him, until after His death, apparently, or thereabouts, when they became equally believers in Him and were among His disciples in the upper room on the Day of Pentecost—Acts 1:14.

But you see that Paul comes up to Jerusalem four years after that time and finds that "James, the brother of the Lord" is now an Apostle. Evidently one of the Apostles had died and James, the brother of the Lord, took his place. Now that was four years after Christ's resurrection,

SO THAT THE 14TH APOSTLE IS JAMES THE BROTHER OF THE LORD AND THE 15TH AND 16TH APOSTLES ARE BARNABAS AND SAUL?

In the 13th chapter of the Acts of the Apostles you will read,

"Now there were in the church that was at Antioch certain prophets and teachers; as Barnabas, and Simeon that was called Niger, and Lucius of Cyrene, and Manaen, which had been brought up with Herod the tetrarch, and Saul."

Now what did these five prophets and teachers do? The two following verses tell, "As they ministered to the Lord, and fasted, the Holy Ghost said, Separate me from Barnabas and Saul for the work whereunto I have called them. And when they fasted and prayed, and laid their hands on them, they sent them away." From that moment they became Apostles. They were sent away as Apostles and they are called Apostles throughout the whole of the Acts of the Apostles. Barnabas is called an Apostle just as much as Paul, and Saul's name was changed to Paul. Barnabas and Saul were not elected at Jerusalem to be Apostles, they were chosen by God, and were ordained by Him, through the Prophets and Teachers, eleven years after Christ's resurrection. Saul was only a teacher and prophet for ten years after his conversion, and eleven years after Christ's re-ascension he became an Apostle by the act of the Holy Ghost calling him out from amongst the second and third ranks of the first three offices of the Church, the Prophets and Teachers.

And now we have Matthias, and James the brother of the Lord, and Barnabas and Saul, four new Apostles who took places vacated by death in the Apostlic Order. We have 16 Apostles and we are not through yet.

PAUL DISTINCTLY CALLS APOLLOS AN APOSTLE.

In his first Epistle to the Corinthians, 4th chapter, 6 to 9 he says, "These things, brethren, I have in a figure transferred to myself and to Apollos for your sakes"——and in verse 9, "For I think God hath set forth *us the Apostles*," evidently linking Apollos with himself as an Apostle. He speaks of him as an Apostle, and Apollos was possibly the writer of the Epistle to the Hebrews, for that does not bear Paul's name in any original copy. Paul was the Apostle of the Gentiles, but Apollos was a Jew, specially eloquent in the Scriptures of the Old Testament, and very likely wrote the Epistle to the Hebrews---See Acts 18:24 to 28.

With Apollos, you have 17 Apostles.

In the Epistle to the Romans you have a very remarkable declaration as to two other Apostles in the 16th chapter and 7th verse:---"Salute Andronicus and Junias, my kinsmen, and my fellow prisoners, who are of note among the Apostles, who also were in Christ before me."

Andronicus and Junias were older Christians than Paul, his fellow prisoners, his kinsmen, and they were of note among the Apostles. Now if I should say that Brother Speicher, who is an ordained minister, and Brother Atkin, also an ordained minister were, of "note among the ministers," why I would not mean anything else than that they were ministers.

And if I should say that one of you was "of note among the carpenters," I would mean you were a carpenter; and if I said of another brother that he was "of note among the blacksmiths," I would not mean that you were a woolen merchant, and so on. The meaning is perfectly plain and clear that

ANDRONICUS AND JUNIAS WERE APOSTLES, MAKING NINETEEN APOSTLES.

I will go on aud show you two more Apostles in the New Testament.

In the Epistle of Paul to the Phillipians you will find a reference there to the Apostle Epaphroditus. It is in the second chapter, 25th verse, "But your messenger," but the word messenger in the margin of the revised version is translatad Apostle, and it ought to have been put in the text. The translators had no right to put the word "messenger" there; the word ought to have been put as it is in Greek, Apostolos, but it did not suit the translators, because the translators were mainly Church of England men who wanted to please their fellow Churchmen, and did not want to put anything in there that made it plain that there were other Apostles.

The other Apostle is "Jude, the servant of Jesus Christ, and the brother of James." He is generally considered to be one of the brothers of our Lord, and is the writer of one of the Catholic Epistles in the New Testament, which would have no claim to infallible authority if it were not the writing of an Apostle.

Now I will go back.

How many Apostles have we got? Were there only 12? "No." How many can we count? "Twenty-one."

Now let us tally up.

First there are the first twelve, and then after Christ's Resurrection, we have Matthias, James the brother of the Lord, Barnabas, Paul, Apollos, Andronicus, Junias, Epaphroditus and Jude—nine more, or twenty-one Apostles in all, although there were doubtless 12 in office at one time.

Now what is my point?

My point is this, and I want it to reach the Church of God wherever the report of this Conference will go, and it is this, that in the early Church as fast as an Apostle died another one was selected and put in his place, and man after man stepped in to fill up the Apostolic blanks, and, therefore,

THE APOSTOLIC OFFICE WAS INTENDED TO BE PERPETUAL IN THE CHURCH.

That is my first point.

The organization of the Church is first, Apostles; second, Prophets; third, Teachers, and so on, that is the Divine Order of the Church—who shall dare to deny it? In closing, I have only time to deal briefly with

THE PURPOSE OF GOD IN THE ORGANIZATION OF THE CHURCH.

The purpose is already declared in the passage that we have quoted, "the Unity of the Body of Christ." The bringing together in fact, of the hands and the feet, and the eyes, and the nose, so that I shall have my hand on my body, instead of somewhere else, and instead of my nose being somewhere else I want it on my body, and Christ wants all the various parts of His body together, and therefore He puts them together in the Church, so that the body may be complete. And for what purpose? That the Church of God shall be the divine agency in the building up of the family, the home, the city, the state, the world, the Church of God, until the whole world is redeemed, through faith in Christ by the power of the Holy Spirit working in and through the Church of God.

THE CHURCH IS CATHOLIC FOR IT IS CHRIST'S OWN BRIDE AND THE PURCHASE OF HIS BLOOD; AND THAT CHURCH IS CATHOLIC, BECAUSE IT IS UNIVERSAL.

It is not a mere question of Chicago, but we intend to organize ourselves, God helping us, into a Church upon the primitive model, so that if there is a branch in Joliet, or Rockford, or Ohio, or Iowa, or in Canada, or in England, or Ireland, or Scotland, or Australia, we shall all feel that it is a part of the Christian Catholic Church, which is one Church. More, we shall recognize that our brethren who are apart from us in their various churches, even although they may not recognize the catholicity and unity of the Church of Christ, are also brothers and sisters in Christ with us of the Christian Catholic Church, by the fact that they are Christians. We dare not shut away from the Table of the Lord a single Christian of any kind because the Church of Christ is already formed of all who are in Him. We cannot form it. We simply fall into the form and line that God has already laid down. What we become, we shall be by the grace of God. All the offices in the Church are the recognized call of the Holy Ghost, through duly qualified ministers of the Church, as when Barnabas and Paul were called to be Apostles.

Now I want to ask you to follow me in a very few direct remarks as to

HOW THE CHRISTIAN CATHOLIC CHURCH SHOULD BE FORMED.

I believe, first of all, that *it should be formed of all persons who are willing to come together upon this* BASIS: That (1) they recognize the infallible inspiration and sufficiency of the Holy Scriptures as the rule of faith and practice; that (2) they recognize that no persons can be members of the Church who have not repented of their sins and have not trusted in Christ for salvation; that (3) such persons must also be able to make a good profession, and declare that they do know in their own hearts, that they have truly repented, and are truly trusting Christ, and have the witness, in a measure, of the Holy Spirit; that (4) all other questions of every kind shall be held to be matters of opinion and not matters that are essential to church unity.

Now that is a very Broad Church.

I will show you, therefore, that we cannot be denominational, sectarian, or narrow.

I would refuse to organize a Church which should demand that a man should think exactly as I, or you, or somebody else thinks upon a great many matters that are not essential to salvation.

No matter that they might be true, we have no right to demand of our brethren absolute acquiesence in every line of our experience.

It is impossble to get it and it is not right to try for it, and we have no right to shut anybody out of fellowship who will comply with those essential conditions that I have named; for they belong to God, and are adopted by Christ, and are regenerated by the Holy Ghost and we have no right to shut a man out because he does not follow us in all our opinions and deductions from Scripture.

Now for instance Baptism.

I am a firm believer in Baptism as essential to a full and perfect Obedience, but if you want to make Baptism a test of Christian Fellowship, I decline to be in such a Church, because I was a Christian before I was immersed. I know I was a child of God before I was immersed, and I will never immerse any one who has not become a child of God. Therefore, have I any right to keep a man away from the Lord's Table because of his upbringing or his want of Christian cult- in a matter, or simply because he does not yet see with me on the question of Baptism? The Lord forbid.

Then again Divine Healing.

You know how strong I am about Divine Healing. You know I teach that it is God's will that we should be healed, and I feel that every person who is a Christian ought to rest in Christ for healing, but do you think I would shut out of the Church of God any person simply because he or she was not healed? The Lord forbid. Let them alone. They are in the Church. They are Christ's children, and if they have not yet been able to receive Divine Healing, that is a reason why the Church ought to receive them, and comfort them, and teach them, and educate them, and bring them into the way of Divine Healing. God forbid that I should belong to a Church that should demand of every man that he should see with me exactly even regarding Divine Healing, and would refuse him fellowship, because of his insufficient light.

Then again concerning the Prohibition of the Liquor Traffic.

I suppose there is not a man in this house who does not know how I stand on the question of the liquor traffic. If I could, I would stop at once that accursed traffic so wickedly sanctioned by human law. God forbid that I, or any member of the Christian Catholic Church should ever cast a direct vote on behalf of the saloon. I should ask the Church at once to investigate the Christian character of such a person. I cannot believe in the Christian character of any man when I know that that man has deliberately gone away and cast a vote for the saloon. I do not think he ought to have membership in this Church, and I should suspend him from fellowship and bring the matter before the proper tribunal. I should at once suspend a person who should engage in the tobacco traffic or the liquor traffic and I should ask the Church to dismiss him if he did not repent. I should say that the man who sells the stuff that manufactures whiskey-pots and stink-pots had better be outside the Church. I will say it at once. I shall not have anything to do with a man that manufactures the stuff that makes stink-pots or is a stink-pot. I decline to have him in my house as an intimate friend, and I decline to have him in the Church of God. Such an one has no business in the Church of God, for he is doing the Devil's work. But if a brother should not yet have been able to see with us regarding the voting down of the liquor traffic, in the way we would like to vote it down, do you mean to say that he should be be kept out of the Church of God? That is to say, if he did not vote the Prohibition ticket?

You think it right to vote the Prohibition ticket. Well so do I in a measure; but I tell you this, there are some Prohibitionists that I would no more vote for than I would vote for the Devil. I tell you I have known Prohibitionists that are incarnate devils. I will tell you another thing, I do not take altogether too much stock in the Prohibition Party. I see just as impudent schemers in the Prohibition party as I can in the Republican and Democratic, and the fact of the matter is this, I do not belong to any of your parties and I do not propose to belong to any of them. I have told this to my beloved friend and brother, Professor Samuel Dickie, the Chairman of the Executive Committee of that Party, whom I love very truly. He is a man of God, a statesman, a scholar, a gentleman and a Christian, and I will say this, that very many of the best men in this country are in the Prohibition Party. But I say to you, what I said to him, I am not prepared to say to my people, "You must vote the Prohibition ticket." What right have I got to say that? Has not every man got a right to his independent judgment? I might just as well say to this or that man that he should train his son to be a carpenter or a blacksmith. You have a right to train your sons as you like and to such honorable business as they feel led of God.

Under certain circumstances it might be your duty not to vote for a Prohibitionist.

For instance I know of individuals in the Prohibition Party who are absolute enemies of God, Infidels. I would sooner cut off my right hand than vote for an Infidel. What, shall I put in the House of the Legislature a man who does not fear God? Not a bit of it, not even if he is an Abstainer. I would rather put in a Christian Democrat or a Christian Republican, than a Prohibition Infidel.

Now, listen, I will not have, so far as I am concerned, the Christian Catholic Church committed to any party that is going to make it a part of its political machine. I will not allow the Church of God to be made a political stalking horse. We are independent men and women, and we have a right to vote as God gives us light, and we must do as God gives us light in the various places where we may be placed, and we have no right to impose upon our brethern.

But I want to say at the same time, that when we get to ZION, I know that, by the grace of God, there shall not be a drop of liquor enter into that place. It shall be our purpose in preparing our plans for ZION to prepare not only for a Prohibition ZION, but for a Prohibition District around the town. I omitted to take that precaution in our last land venture, and, therefore, I am going to take another site for ZION because I found among other things, that I could not get a Prohibition Belt around that town large enough to keep the damnable liquor a mile away from it and I intend to do that if I can. You will find me hot enough as regards that matter, but I do not intend for the Church to be committed to any political party at all.

Then again there are other things that I think we must be very clear about, and that is this, for instance, as to Trades Unions.

I am against all Trades Unions of masters or men that are tyranical in their character.

I say that no men have a right to band themselves together to compel another man to work for so much money, and if he won't do that to brand him as a "scab." I say that it is the tyranny of labor and I shall have no part in it. At the same time I recognize the right of men to organize to get a fair day's wage for a fair day's work, and I shall, God helping me, help them to get it. For my part I should say eight hours' labor, eight hours' sleep, and eight hours' recreation make a very good day. (Applause.) A working man has labored hard enough at earthly toil when he has labored eight hours; but I say that nobody shall have a right to say that he shall not work ten hours, if he likes. Then again I do not like an organization to say that every man, no matter what his skill, shall have the same wages. I know some men who are worth two dollars a day, and some who are worth three, and some who are worth four, and some who are worth five, and I know some that are not worth a red cent.

Now let us have some sense about these matters, but so far as the Christian Catholic Church is concerned, I hope it will always be found to be what the Church of God should always be found to be,

A FRIEND OF ALL MEN WHETHER THEY ARE RICH OR WHETHER THEY ARE POOR.

And I tell you this, beloved friends, that the rich men have more need of your prayers than the poor. They are farther from the Kingdom of God. They are deeper in the mire of sin. I would rather take my chances for heaven with the poor fellow who has no education and no piety, than I would with the rich man who is an accursed grinder of the faces of the poor, and goes with outward piety to Church on the Sabbath, and is inwardly an infernal hypocrite. I have no words to say in defense of those who keep back the rightful hire of the laborer, and if this Church will take my counsel, I will tell you what that counsel will be, it will be this:

LET GOD'S PEOPLE GET TOGETHER AND CO-OPERATE.

I trust that our future ZION will have room for the establishment of manufactories, and all sorts of places where we can co-operate together to build up the happiness of homes and the prosperity of the people. My prayer to God is this:— That not a member of the Christian Catholic Church shall ever lack bread; that not a member of it shall ever lack shelter or home; that not a member of it shall ever lack work if he is strong enough to work; but, at the same time, I propose to see that no man shall eat bread that he doesn't work for. It would be a sin for any member of the Christian Catholic Church to be hungry, homeless, or idle, so long as we had a cent left unspent in our pockets.

I can tell you there is nobody in Zion Publishing House, Zion Tabernacles or the Divine Healing Homes who eats bread they don't work for. But I will tell you this, those dear servants, my fellow servants in the Divine Healing Homes, etc., do not need to be lashed to work. Oftentimes when I am in my bed in the early morning, at 5 o'clock, we will hear the maids, all unbidden by their mistress, sweeping out the house long before daylight, and when we come down in the morning everything is nice and clean and proper because they love to do it for God. They don't do it for the dollar, they do it for God, and they put the love of God into their broom, and into their work. May God bring us together as a great company of His children who put God into all their work.

THESE ARE THE BROAD PRINCIPLES UPON WHICH I INVITE YOU TO COME TOGETHER AND FORM THE CHRISTIAN CATHOLIC CHURCH.

PRAYER.

Our Heavenly Father, for Jesus Christ, our dear Lord and Saviour's sake, keep us together a little while longer, and bless, oh Father, by Thy Holy Spirit's power these feeble words that we have spoken. Amen.

REMARKS.

I want, before we close this meeting, to hear a few of you speak. We will all be able to discuss these proposals at our next meeting, for I hope to have the whole of this address in print next week, and you will be able to read it quietly and peacefully in your homes. But if there are any of you who would like to ask me any questions to-night, I am willing to answer them.

QUESTIONS AND OBSERVATIONS.

Mr. Calverly: It was just at the point where you were speaking about the "Keys," Doctor, and I was wondering whether that had any relation to Peter preaching the Gospel on the Day of Pentecost to the Jews, and also when he preached to the Gentiles, and whether that had any reference to the Keys.

Dr. Dowie: I understand the "keys to the kingdom of heaven" to be the Powers, Gifts and Promises of God, bestowed upon whom He wills, as revealed in His Word. For instance, I said in connection with Divine Healing, I put the Key of Knowledge in the door and open it for many. And so the doors of Salvation and Holiness are opened to others.

Rev. Mr. Jones (Logansport, Ind.): Was not a personal knowledge of Christ, a personal acquaintance with Him before His death, a personal knowledge of His resurrection an essential qualification of an Apostle?

Dr. Dowie: There is no statement in scripture that an essential qualification to Apostleship was a previous knowledge of Christ before His death. So far as we know Paul had no such acquaintance, and he was called to the Apostolic Office. But it was distinctly stated that it was essential in the judgment of the Apostle Peter that such a person should be called to take the place of Judas Iscariot. But it is also clear that the mind of Peter and the Church Council in the upper room was not laid down as an essential for future Apostolic calls. It was simply a statement of Peter's for that time, and, I think, a very expedient one at the time. Still every Apostle and true minister of every rank to-day must be a witness of His resurrection. I must be a constant witness of the resurrection of Christ. So must any man that might be called to Apostolic Office. That is to say, we must be a witness to His resurrection You know the word in Greek for Witness is Marturios, or Martyr, that is to say, one that witnesses to the fact that Christ is risen. I witness to Christ's resurrection every time I preach. We must "Know Him and the Power of His Resurrection." Christ is risen, Christ is glorified, He is at the right hand of the Father. That is my understanding of the matter. I may be wrong, but that is my judgment.

A TELEGRAM ON BEHALF OF A SICK CHILD.

Dr. Dowie was here handed a telegram. He said. "There is a dear little child who is very low, and her mother got frightened to-day, and went back to doctors. It is apparently a case of Diphtheria or Scarlet Fever. The dear little child was healed a year ago through my agency of a similar disease. She is a very sweet little child. May we not pray for her on this occasion, just for a moment, that God will spare that little child.

PRAYER FOR THE CHILD.

"Father in Heaven, for our Saviour's sake wilt Thou not stretch forth Thine hand and heal that child? Oh, let not the faithlessness of the father or the mother, if they have been faithless, interfere with the sweet faith of that dear child, but may the child be left now in Thy hands. In Thy hands we know she will be healed; we cannot be sure if she is put in the hands of the doctor. Oh God, make these parents to see that they have no right to change their doctors; that Jesus healed her before when dying. Father, for Jesus' sake, may the Spirit's power descend upon her now. Amen."

[THE PRAYER WAS ANSWERED.

In our Editorial Notes of January 24th in LEAVES OF HEALING, page 242, the following note shows how God answered for this dear child. It is a precious token of His approval:—

"A sweet little story comes to us in a letter this morning concerning a dear little girl for whom we prayed when she lay very low last Wednesday evening. Friends who were at the Conference will remember that the telegram containing the request for prayer was handed to us just before we delivered our address. Her mother had become afraid to trust the little one to God alone, and so she called for a doctor. The child, whose name is Sunshine, refused to take the medicine ordered, having been healed through our agency a year ago when suffering from diphtheria. She said constantly, 'Pray, pray, pray.' 'Her mother,' the letter says, was coaxing Sunshine to take the medicine, when the child raised her hand, and said, 'Ah, you sinner, Why don't you get closer to Jesus?'

The aunt of the little one, who writes the letter says, 'During the evening (after I wired you) she began to grow better, and finally fell into a quiet slumber. This morning she is as well and bright as could be. Praise be to God and to His servant John Alex. Dowie, who prayed with faith. Sunshine is sitting up and dressed. Dr.——pronounced her case to be one of scarlet fever.'"]

QUESTIONS AND OBSERVATIONS CONTINUED.

Mr. O. L. Sprecher: Doctor, I merely want to ask your opinion as to the election of Matthias, whether you think he was elected by a majority, or whether the Holy Ghost inspired the rest of the Apostles to vote for him.

Dr. Dowie: There is no information beyond the words:— "They gave forth their lots; and the lot fell upon Matthias; and he was numbered with the eleven apostles."

ADJOURNMENT.

Now, dear friends, will you agree with me that this conference shall stand adjourned until this day fortnight; Is that your mind? "Yes." On the contrary? Silence.

Thank you. Now I shall give instructions to have these proceedings printed especially for the sake of thousands who cannot be here.

After a few observations from the chair, the Conference was adjourned until Wednesday, February 5th, at 8 p. m.—the Doxology and Benediction closing the proceedings.

GOD'S WAY OF HEALING.

BY THE EDITOR.

God's Way of Healing is a Person, not a Thing.

Jesus said, "*I am* the Way, the Truth and the Life," and He has ever been revealed to His people in all the ages by the Covenant Name, Jehovah-rophi, or "*I am* the Lord that Healeth thee." (John 14:6 and Exodus 15:26).

The Lord Jesus Christ is still the Healer.

He cannot change, for "He is the same, yesterday, to-day, and forever," and He is still with us, for He said, "Lo, *I am* with you always, even unto the end of the world." (Hebrews 13:8 and Matthew 28:20). Because He is Unchangeable, and because He is present, in spirit, just as when in the flesh, He is the Healer of His people.

Divine Healing rests on Christ's Atonement.

It was prophesied of Him, "Surely He hath borne our griefs (Hebrew, *sicknesses*) and carried our sorrows, and with His stripes we are healed," and it is expressly declared that this was fulfilled in His ministry of Healing, which still continues. (Isaiah 53:4, 5 and Matthew 8:17).

Disease can never be God's Will.

It is the Devil's work, consequent upon Sin, and it is impossible for the work of the Devil ever to be the Will of God.

Christ came to "destroy the works of the Devil," and when He was here on earth He "healed every sickness and every disease," and all these diseases are expressly declared to have been the "oppression of the Devil." (1 John 3:8, Matthew 4:23 and Acts 10:38).

The Gifts of Healing are Permanent.

It is expressly declared that the "Gifts and calling of God are without repentance," and the Gifts of Healing are amongst the Nine Gifts of the Spirit to the Church. (Romans 11:29 and 1 Cor. 12:8-11).

There are Four Modes of Divine Healing.

The first is the direct prayer of faith; the second, intercessory prayer of two or more; the third, the anointing of the elders with the prayer of faith; and the fourth, the laying on of hands of those who believe, and whom God has prepared and called to that ministry. (Matthew 8:5-13. Matthew 18:19, James 5:14, 15, Mark 16:18).

Divine Healing is opposed by Diabolical Counterfeits.

Amongst these are Christian Science (falsely so-called), Mind Healing, Spiritualism, Trance Evangelism, etc. (1 Timothy 6:20, 21, 1 Timothy 4:1, 2, Isaiah 51:22, 23).

Multitudes have been healed through Faith in Jesus.

The writer knows of thousands of cases and has personally laid hands on scores of thousands of persons. Full information can be obtained at the meetings held in Zion Tabernacle, 251 E. 62nd St., near Jackson Park, Chicago, and in many pamphlets which give the experience, in their own words, of many who have been healed in this and other countries, published at Zion Publishing House, 6100 Stony Island Ave., Chicago.

"Faith Cometh by Hearing, and Hearing by the Word of God."

You are heartily invited to attend and hear for yourself.

Gottes Weg der Heilung.

Vom Redakteur.

Gottes Weg der Heilung ist eine Person, und kein Ding.

Jesus sagte: „Ich bin der Weg, die Wahrheit und das Leben," und zu allen Zeiten wurde Er stets seinem Volke geoffenbart durch den Vertrags-Namen, Jehovah-rophi, oder „Ich bin der Herr, dein Arzt." (Joh. 14: 6, und 2 Mos. 15:26.)

Der Herr Jesus ist stets der Heiler.

Er kann sich nicht ändern „Er ist stets derselbe, gestern und in alle Ewigkeit" und Er ist stets bei uns, denn Er sagt: „Siehe, Ich bin bei euch alle Tage bis an der Welt Ende" (Hebr. 13: 8 und Math. 28, 20.) Weil Er unveränderlich ist, und weil Er gegenwärtig ist im Geiste, gerade so wie damals im Fleisch, deshalb ist Er der, der sein Volk heilt.

Göttliche Heilung beruht auf Christi Versöhnung.

Es wurde von Ihm prophezeit: „Führwahr Er trug unsere Krankheit und lud auf Sich unsere Schmerzen, und durch seine Wunden sind wir geheilt;" und es wird ausdrücklich erklärt, daß sich dies in Seinem Dienst der Heilung, welcher immer noch fortdauert, erfüllt hat. (Jes. 53 4 u. 5, und Math. 8: 17.)

Krankheit kann Niemals Gottes Wille sein.

Sie ist des Teufels Werk, folgend auf Sünde, und es ist unmöglich daß sie, des Teufels Werk, Gottes Wille ist. Christus kam um „die Werke des Teufels zu zerstören, und, als Er hier auf Erden war, heilte Er allerlei Seuche und Krankheit, und alle diese Krankheiten sind ausdrücklich für die „Überwältigung des Teufels" erklärt worden. (1 Joh. 3: 8, Math. 4: 23, und Apost. 10: 38.)

Die Gaben der Heilung sind fortdauernd.

Es wird ausdrücklich erklärt daß „Gottes Gaben und Berufung Ihn nicht gereuen mögen," und die Gaben der Heilung sind unter den neun Gaben des Geistes an die Kirche zu finden. (Röm. 11: 29, und 1 Cor. 12: 8-14.)

Es giebt vier Arten Göttlicher Heilung.

Die erste Art ist das direkte Gebet des Glaubens, die zweite ist dir Fürbitte von zwei oder mehr Personen; die dritte ist das Salben dee Ältesten mit dem Gebet des Glaubens, und die vierte ist das Handauflegen derjenigen, welche glauben, und welche Gott vorbereitet und zu jenem Dienst berufen hat. (Math. 8: 13, 18, 19; Jac. 5: 14-15, Marc. 16: 18.)

Göttliche Heilung wird von Teuflischen Betrügern bekämpft.

Unter diesen befindet sich die Christliche Wischenschaft (fälschlich so genannt), Geist-Heilung, Spiritualismus, Entzückungs-Evangelismus, u. s. w. (1 Tim. 6: 20-21; 4: 12; Jes. 51: 22-23.)

Tausende sind durch den Glauben an Jesus geheilt worden.

Schreiber dieses sind tausende von Fällen bekannt und er hat persönlich vielen Tausenden Hand aufgelegt. Vollständige Auskunft kann man erhalten in den Versammlungen, welche im Zion Tabernakel No. 2, Ecke 61ste Straße und Stoney Island Avenue, nahe dem Jackson Park, Chicago, abgehalten werden, sowie aus vielen Schriften, welche die Erfahrung von vielen in den eignen Worten enthalten, die in diesen und andern Ländern geheilt worden sind. Diese Schriften werden von dem Zion Publisching House, No. 6100 Stoney Island Ave., Chicago, herausgegeben.

„Der Glaube kommt durch die Predigt und die Predigt durch das Wort Gottes."

Sie sind herzlich eingeladen zu kommen und sich selbst davon zu überzeugen.

ZION'S ONWARD MOVEMENT

REPORT OF

THE SECOND GENERAL CONFERENCE

Of all Believers interested in the Organization of

THE CHRISTIAN CATHOLIC CHURCH,

Held in Zion Tabernacle No. 2, Chicago, Wednesday Evening, Feb. 5th, 1896.

THERE was a very large attendance, and great interest was shown in the proceedings which continued from 8 to 11 p. m.

The Rev. John Alex. Dowie presided, and at once opened the Conference by saying in his bright, quick way:—

I wish you all good evening, and am glad to see you. We will have our marching song, if you please.

"Come, ye that love the Lord,
And let your joys be known,
Join in a song with sweet accord;
And thus surround the throne."

CHO "We're marching to Zion,
Beautiful, beautiful Zion,
We're marching upward to Zion,
The beautiful City of God.

I should imagine that every one among us could sing that without the book. We have got it all in our hearts.

Reading of portions of Epistle to the Ephesians by Dr. Dowie.

Prayer by Rev. Dr. Speicher:—

Our heavenly Father we come to Thee this evening with thanksgiving that Thou hast kept us since we last met here, and that Thou hast given us Thy Spirit and that Thou has instructed us on the way. We thank Thee for this blessed Epistle which has been read in our hearing this evening, for the words of Thine Apostle that were written in the church's beginning, and have been handed down to us for our instruction and guidance. Oh God we pray Thee that Thy Spirit may be with us, that He may guide us in all our deliberations. Oh God we feel the need of this great work, we feel it upon us to-night that there is a great work about to be done. May Thy servant, whom Thou hast chosen and ordained to perform Thy work in this great city, not be disappointed. May the people press forward with him to conquer this great city for Christ. May we realize our union as one body, the Body of the Lord Jesus Christ, the Church of the Living God. We are one in this, and we have only this one desire in our hearts that Thy work may be done as it ought to be done, in faith, in sincerity, in truth. Bless all those who are to speak, and let all be spoken in the spirit of love and truth, for Jesus' sake. Amen.

Dr Dowie:—Father in heaven hear our prayer. Grant unto me this night the spirit of wisdom and of understanding, of knowledge and of the fear of the Lord, that I may be of quick understanding in the fear of God, not judging after the seeing of the eyes or the hearing of the ears. Give unto these my brethren and sisters the wisdom and grace that is needful at this time. Give us a good meeting, and a happy issue to our deliberations; for Jesus' sake. Amen.

OPENING ADDRESS.

Dr. Dowie said:—Beloved friends, that which I had to say has been fully said, twenty closely printed columns of it which have been placed in your hands, and, if you have not read it you ought to have read it. If you have not heard or read it you can not talk about it.

Beloved friends, I feel to-night great love in my heart towards the tens of thousands who have gathered here from time to time and in the Auditorium, from the east and from the west, and from the north and from the south, and towards those who are gathering.

THREE OF THE STRIKING SIGHTS OF EVERY DAY IN OUR LIFE ARE THESE:—

First: Our Mail arriving in great piles, and representing every land beneath the sun, and every state in this union, sometimes to the number of 2,000 letters a week. Second: The wonderful and ever increasing number of requests for prayer which come to us not only in these letters, but in telegrams and cablegrams, from all parts of the world, for there is not now a land beneath the sun with which we are not in constant touch. Third: The spectacle which the Divine Healing Homes present every day, as this morning for instance when more than 80 guests were present, representing, I suppose, well nigh every state in the Union and several parts of Canada. When I look at these facts from day to day, at the ever-widening increasing influence of LEAVES OF HEALING, I am full of joy, hope and faith in God. I hope when this Conference closes to-night to be able to show you the first number of the German Edition, which is now perfected. I say, when I look at these things and consider all that God has wrought, I am filled with love and wonder and praise, and if my good Lord shall only grant unto me the same measure of blessing in the coming two years, that He has in the past, in the same proportion, we shall have a wondrous work: indeed, it is wondrous now.

As thousands upon thousands gather from Sabbath to Sabbath in the Chicago Auditorium, and we increasingly find that through these meetings every part of the United States and distant lands are influenced, we cannot but help feel that it is our duty

BEFORE WE BUILD UP OUR PERMANENT INSTITUTIONS OUTSIDE OF THIS CITY

(as is my positive and fixed intention, God willing) that we shall do our part to more compactly gather a people together and evangelize the city from within its walls, as it were, before our Exodus to Zion. And when we march out to our permanent location, it will only be to organize more perfectly, so that we shall march back again and go in and out in ever continuous Evangelizing Work.

I have not, in my previous address, entered into any of the the detail of intended organization, as regards the application of those principles which I laid down in my first address. I can only say, that

I PROPOSE, IN THE CHRISTIAN CATHOLIC CHURCH, TO CARRY OUT IN THE LETTER AND IN THE SPIRIT THE ORGANIZATION OF THE NEW TESTAMENT.

The organization of the Church as Christ and the Apostles established it.

I PROPOSE TO TRAIN SEVENTIES,

By the grace of God, who two and two, thoroughly understanding the work, and prepared first in our Zion, shall go forth two and two into all parts of the city and do their work from house to house. I shall carry forward the work by deaconesses and deacons and elders; by pastors and teachers and preachers. I propose to carry forward the work upon New Testament lines, by ordaining such persons as I believe God has called and qualified. I propose to carry it forward by training our young people in a very thorough manner in Sabbath and week-day Schools, where they shall not only be taught the letter of the word but its Spirit, and where they shall get a thorough Christian Education from the Kindergarten to the College, and from the very beginning be trained to carry forward the work of God in all parts of the city.

We propose to carry out the principles laid down in the first address, in every possible way and through the Powers that God has given and will give us in this City.

WE SHALL USE THE PRINTING PRESS

extensively, and by books, newspapers and pamphlets and tracts in all the various languages which are spoken in this city, until at least we have something in every language for every person within Chicago; and we shall circulate Bibles in every tongue that is read or spoken in Chicago. We shall care for nothing excepting to be a Practical People as regards God's work, a People who are at it, all at it, always at it, and in all ways at it. (Applause).

In things that are essential we demand Unity, in things that are non-essential we give the fullest Liberty, and we must do all things in Charity.

I do not propose to make my address, in the opening of this second conference, at all lengthy. Some who read my first address may wish to ask some questions, and they are at liberty to do so.

I propose that when we are organized we shall meet together, and I shall tell you what seems to me to be the command of God, and if it is wise and in accordance with the Word of God, I shall expect you to fall into your places in the ranks of the Church and work together in hearty co-operation in that position for which God seems to have qualified you.

That will be a matter of detail, and can only be carried out when we are fully organized, and we will do what we can. May God help us.

And now I earnestly submit to you these remarks, and the ten closely printed pages of my address making in all 20 columns, equal to a little pamphlet of about 40 pages. It has all been placed before you, and has been as carefully revised as I could in the time I had at my disposal. There are a few printers' errors that have escaped me perhaps. Looking at it perhaps I might have arranged it in a different way if I had more time, but I did not want to alter anything I had said, and in every essential particular, the report is a perfect and complete report of the conference that was held on this night, fortnight past, on the 22nd day of January.

I have prepared a very short resolution embracing three points which I shall place in the hands of my friend Dr. Speicher, who has not yet seen it, to read it in due time, and if that resolution meets with your approval, then the action that is indicated in it will be taken.

My address upon Organization, and the Basis of Organization, especially as set forth in the address, are open, not for discussion by those who are not prepared to associate themselves with us, because we have not any time to hear them, but for any intelligent remarks, and for questions, by those who are in sympathy with us, and who have a desire, if they can see with us, to go forward in the organization of this Church.

With that proviso, the meeting is absolutely open. I pray that God the Holy Ghost will guide you, and that none of you will speak excepting in the fear and love of God.

The meeting is open now as a Conference for general discussion upon the basis set forth in my address of January 22nd. Feel perfectly free in the Lord to speak anything that God has given you to say.

CONTINUITY OF THE APOSTOLIC OFFICE.

Rev. Dr. Burns:—I understand that this Church is to be organized after the pattern laid down by the Apostle Paul, and as an essential it will include the Apostles. Now I am in doubt as to how you are going to get the Apostles. It seems to me that the scriptures clearly state that one essential for an Apostle was that he should have been a witness of the facts regarding Christ, both before and after His crucifixion.

Dr. Dowie:—At the last conference, I went into the matter of the question of Apostolic Office, and in answer to the question of the Rev. Dr. Jones, who said:

"Rev. Mr. Jones (Logansport, Ind.): Was not a personal knowledge of Christ, a personal acquaintance with Him before His death, a personal knowledge of His resurrection an essential qualification of an Apostle?

Dr. Dowie:— There is no statement in scripture that an essential qualification to Apostleship was a previous knowledge of Christ before His death. So far as we know Paul had no such acquaintance, and he was called to the Apostolic Office. But it was distinctly stated that it was essential in the judgment of the Apostle Peter that such a person should be called to take the place of Judas Iscariot. But it is also clear that the mind of Peter and the Church Council in the upper room was not laid down as an essential for future Apostolic calls. It was simply a statement of Peter's for that time and, I think, a very expedient one at the time. Still every Apostle and true minister of every rank to-day must be a witness of His resurrection. I must be a constant witness of the resurrection of Christ. So must any man that might be called to Apostolic Office. That is to say, we must be a witness to His resurrection. You know the word in Greek for Witness is Marturios, or Martyr, that is to say, one that witnesses to the fact that Christ is risen. I witness to Christ's resurrection every time I preach We must "Know Him and the Power of His Resurrection." Christ is risen, Christ is glorified, He is at the right hand of the Father. That is my understanding of the matter. I may be wrong, but that is my judgment."

My judgment therefore in the matter is this, that the scriptures do not anywhere state that it is essential to Apostleship that there should be a previous knowledge of Christ before His death, for Paul clearly did not have that knowledge and neither did some others who became Apostles—Apollos certainly.

With regard to the other question, we have simply to deal with the constitution of the Church as laid down in scripture and leave the Holy Ghost in His own time and way to call the Apostles.

CONTINUITY OF THE PROPHETIC OFFICE.

Rev. Mr. Jones:—May I not ask if there were not some other offices in the primitive church, supposing that we grant your position that the Apostolic Office is permanent, is there not at least one more in the primitive church that in the very nature of things must have been limited, that is to say, the Prophetic Office, the second mentioned in the list: "Some Apostles, some Prophets—" Now can there be this office, can it exist now? Giving the power of foretelling future events such as Paul exercised, and also embracing inspiration, empowering one to write what was to be authoritative for the Church, and for the people of God, such as the letters of the Apostles. Now that must have been limited in the very nature of things it seems to me, and if that was limited was not the Apostolic Office also?

Dr Dowie:—The contention of Dr. Jones is not correct. The Prophetic Office is permanent, as is the Apostolic and Teaching Office, it is as permanent as both. The words are very clear in 1 Corinthians 12:28. "And God hath set some in the Church, first apostles, secondarily prophets, thirdly teachers, after that miracles, then gifts of healings, helps, governments, diversities of tongues." There is no limitation there as to the time of the duration of the offices of either Apostles or Prophets or Teachers. The word "set" is "etheto" and it means "to build into," as a permanent part of a permanent organization. As regards our brother's suggestion as to the continuation of the Prophetic Office, I would say, that the suggestion of its temporary nature in not correct, and that the Prophetic Office continued after Christ's resurrection. There were a number of prophets, and a number of Prophetesses. There was Agabus who, it is narrated in Acts 21:10:11, "took Paul's girdle and bound his own hands and feet, and said, Thus saith the Holy Ghost, so shall the Jews at Jerusalem bind the man that owneth this girdle, and shall deliver him into the hands of the Gentiles." At an earlier date this same prophet foretold a world-wide famine "which came to pass in the days of Claudius Caesar," as we read in Acts 11: 27 to 30. Philip the Evangelist, who was also one of the first seven deacons, "had four daughters, virgins, which did prophesy—" Acts 21:8 and 9. Five Prophets are also named in Acts 13:1. These Prophets and Prophetesses in the Primitive Church were valued, and very important members and officers of the Church.

I see no reason whatever why the Gift of Prophecy should be limited, and I believe too that it is in existence. The Prophetic Office was a very large one, and a Prophet might hold other offices, such as that of Teacher, and every Apostle was a Prophet. The Apostolic Power was prophetic as well as apostolic; it was didactic or teaching as well as apostolic. It included all the gifts and it is possible and probable that one of "the signs of an Apostle" was that God used him in the exercise of every one of the gifts set forth in 1 Corinthians 12, the word of wisdom and the word of knowledge and faith, the gifts of healings and the working of miracles, and prophecy, discerning of spirits, tongues and interpretation of tongues.

If my Brother Jones' contention were correct, then we should have to strike out some of the gifts of God as given only for a time whereas the gifts of prophecy and healing are as distinctly given as the gifts of wisdom, and knowledge and faith, and working of miracles, and if you take prophecy out of the nine you have simply denied the Word of God in one of the important points of this teaching, namely, "that the gifts and calling of God are without repentance" Romans 11:29. (Great Applause.) If you admit, as you must, that the Gift of Prophecy is a perpetual gift in the Church, then the office of Prophet must be.

CONTINUITY OF INSPIRATION.

Rev. Mr. Jones:—There is one question, Doctor, in——

Dr. Dowie:—With regard to the question of Inspiration. There is no doubt that Inspiration continues; but such Inspiration must be in perfect accord with the Word of God as it now stands. But I believe that every day that I, or any faithful minister of Christ, utters a word that is from God, it is inspired.

Mr. Marsh:—But it makes no addition to the inspired words of the Bible?

Dr. Dowie:—Precisely so, any man that would add to or take away from the words of the prophecy that are in this book would come under the declaration in Revelation 22:18: 19, which says,

"For I testify unto every man that heareth the words of the prophecy of this book, if any man shall add unto these things, God shall add unto him the plagues that are written in this book.

And if any man shall take away from the words of the book of this prophecy God shall take away his part out of the book of life, and out of the holy city, and from the things which are written in this book."

While I will never allow any man to bring me anything as an addition to the Word, yet the Gift of Prophecy has of necessity a very large place for its exercise within the limits of Divine Revelation as it is now given, and the application of the principles and teachings of the New Testament. The application of these principles to the Church of God gives a tremendously large room for inspiration, in word and teaching and prayer, and in Prophetic Office. Within the bounds of the Constitution of the United States, there is, or ought to be, ample room for the application of every principle of liberty, and so, within the bounds of the Word of God, there is ample room for the explanation and for the application of it to present day conditions; in such a case there must of necessity be a Divine Inspiration in the mind and heart of the man who utters God's message, and this Inspiration is just as much the gift of the Holy Ghost as when Paul got it. If I was not inspired by God to preach my sermon last Lord's Day I ought to have been. If I am not inspired by God to preach my sermon next Sunday I ought to be, and if I am Divinely Commanded to take upon myself as I have been, the responsibility of foretelling an event that will occur I ought to do it: I did it last year. I prophesied Victory! Victory! VICTORY!!! when the sky was dark and everything looked black, for our foes were many and powerful. I did it because God inspired my heart and put that prophetic word in my mouth. Even the secular newspapers said, when I returned last year from my short trip to the east, "Before Dr. Dowie went to the east he 'prophesied' that when he came back he would take the largest building in this city, and that he would prove to his enemies in Chicago that the people of Chicago would hear him, and his prophesy was fulfilled." That was an inspired prophecy. I did not add to the Word of God. Brother Jones' remark is perfectly correct, that no one has the right to add to, nor did the Apostle Paul himself have a right to add to, and he never added to the Gospel. He simply expounded the Gospel.

I find my Gospel inside of the four first books of the New Testament, and if the Apostle Paul had preached something that our Lord Jesus Christ had forbidden I would not consider him inspired. There are points upon which I differ with Paul, if you will discuss that question of inspiration, and there were matters upon which some of the Apostles were not inspired.

Paul sometimes speaks as a man, and sometimes he says, "I say this by permission and not by commandment." A number of things that he said had clearly a limited application to the Church of that day only. His advice, for instance, concerning marriage was distinctly limited and given with very great hesitation, as it was also on some other subjects. The Gift of Prophetic Inspiration is one of the Nine Gifts of the Spirit and since "the gifts and calling of God are without repentance," therefore, the Prophetic Office continues in the Church and prophets will be raised up who shall be able to interpret the mind of God, who enable them to fulfill their blessed office.

QUESTIONING GENERALLY.

Rev. Mr. Jones:—Dr. Dowie you will not consider me a faultfinder, but you are laying foundations and the material should be very solid and enduring, and wisely laid, and points that may be questioned by honest, intelligent and inquisitive minds everywhere should be well discussed.

Dr. Dowie:—That is true; but I do not care what minds outside will say or do. If any friend wants to question our Teaching, question it, if you do not want to do so, leave it; but do not leave an undetermined thought or doubt in the minds of this people. If you want to challenge the perpetuity of the Apostolic Office challenge it; if you want to challenge the perpetuity of the Prophetic Office challenge it; if you want to challenge the perpetuity of the Teaching Office, challenge it. If you want to challenge the perpetuity of any of the Gifts challenge them, then we will know exactly where to place you, but do not throw out doubts without taking a distinct position, and if you can challenge anything successfully by disproving it from the Word of God, I am willing to give it up.

Rev. Mr. Jones:—In regard to writing by Inspiration authoritative scriptures?

Dr. Dowie:—In regard to this I say, that if I am God's minister in this matter, and I write to you something that is in accord with scripture, then you are bound to receive that just as much as if the Apostle Paul wrote it. You will please to observe my qualification. If I write to you something that is in perfect accord with the word of God I have just as much right to write that as the Apostle Paul had to write. Not to add to the Word of God, but to explain it and apply it.

QUESTION AS TO ORGANIZING A NEW CHURCH.

Rev. Dr Burns:—It seems to me as regards the foundation of the Church that we are built upon the foundation of the Apostles and the Prophets, Jesus Christ Himself being the chief corner-stone. It seems to me there can be but one laying of the foundation and the foundation once laid, we cannot build a new church.

Dr. Dowie:—There can never be a *New* Church unless it be a *False* Church. That which is *true*, in regard to Church organization, is not *new*; and that which is *new* is not true. We need the Old Time Christianity of the first century, and therefore, we are seeking for the Old Time Organization of the Church and hope to find it in the Christian Catholic Church. My address is on that line, and it is not a question of opinion. I gave *facts* from the Word of God, not theories, or my own thoughts. You have not shown wherein any statements in that address are not true. It seems to me that we want the Word of God and not attacks in general terms. In this discourse I make the distinct statement that after the Apostle Judas Iscariot died Matthias was called by the Holy Ghost to the Apostolic Office; that after him James, the brother of the Lord was called; that after him Barnabas and Paul were called, and no one has any right to put in a private opinion upon the subject in the face of the historic facts which prove that the Apostolic Office was continued. But you can challenge my statement of facts if you have counter facts, and the Word of God to back you. But your opinions or my opinions are of no value unless they are in accord with the Bible.

Rev. Dr. Burns:—Are we then to understand if there should be some future Apostles, that we are to be built upon them as upon the first Apostles?

Dr. Dowie:—The Church of God in each generation must be a Building whole and complete in itself, and must be such a Building to-day in this 19th century, on the earth, as it was 19 centuries ago. It is as necessary for His work that it shall be just as perfectly equipped and organized to-day as it was then. Since this is clearly true, and since the organization of the Primitive Church was Apostolic and Prophetic and Didactic, and so on, *that same organization* is just as necessary to-day as it was 19 centuries ago. That is the position.

Mr. Marsh:—The trouble with the Church Organization to-day is that they are bringing up a lot of strange things and demand that we have to live up to them and walk in them.

Mr. Murdoch:—I think that the trouble with our churches is that they cannot find material enough to make a good Church, and I think we ought, by the grace of God, to found a Church, like the Primitive Church, and the offices will come all right, if we are willing to obey God and God's servant. I am willing, for one, to do that.

Mr. Marsh:—If we are worthy of the office, the office will come to us and if we are not, it won't.

Dr. Dowie:—I am not claiming any office, no man has heard me claim any office. I am a teacher and have taken no other place. I have not stood here claiming to be recognized as a Prophet; I have not stood here claiming to be recognized as an Apostle, but I have stood here as an authoritative Teacher. If I am a leader, I am a leader; if I am a Teacher, I am a Teacher; if I am a Prophet, I am a Prophet; if I am an Apostle, I am an Apostle. I am so whether you recognise it or not. I am so whether I recognize it or not. I am just what God made me, and at this moment I claim no Prophetic or Apostolic Office Power. I said in my first address, distinctly and positively, that I did not see the Apostles. You have read that if you have been reading the address at all attentively. You will see I uttered these words, on p. 266 of LEAVES OF HEALING.

"Now the question arises,

IS THE APOSTOLIC OFFICE A PERPETUAL ONE?

Now that is my contention. You see all the way through reading about the Church you come up against the Apostles from the first mention of the word by Jesus Himself.

The Apostolic Office comes first, the Prophetic Office next, the Teaching Office next. There it is.

I AFFIRM THAT THE CHURCH CANNOT BE CHRISTIAN, and CANNOT BE CATHOLIC, UNLESS IT IS APOSTOLIC.

The Apostolic Office must be declared as belonging to the Church if we shall form a Church; and it shall be declared to be a Perpetual Office

It is our duty to declare that the Church of God shall eventually, and as speedily as possible, be so organized,

We have nothing to do with consequences God will call His Apostles in His own time and way by the Holy Spirit

I do not think that I can see any of them yet, but that does not alter the fact that we have got to organize this Church as God did it. It must be upon the pattern that God gave. I shall organize on that pattern, or not at all"

Then I go on to speak about the argument against the perpetuity of the Apostolic Office, and I go on to show the perpetuity of the Apostolic office. It is a mere matter of record, if Matthias was an Apostle, and there is no doubt about that, if Barnabas was an Apostle, and there is no doubt about that, if Paul was an Apostle, and there is no doubt about that, if James, the brother of the Lord, was an Apostle, and there is no doubt about that, and there are a number of others whom there is no doubt about; but if these I have mentioned alone were Apostles they would prove the continuity and perpetuity of the Office. And all we have got to do is to leave God to do His own work, and what we have to do is to organize a Church and to declare that the Foundation Office of that Church is Apostolic. If we do not do that we will not organize upon the Primitive Pattern. It is evident that some of the brethren have not fully considered the address.

Mrs. Dowie:—Did you not state that these offices were not made by votes?

Dr. Dowie:—They cannot be made by votes. The Holy Ghost said, "Separate me Barnabas and Saul for the work whereunto I have called them." The Holy Ghost "calls" not the majority of the votes. The Holy Ghost commands "Separate!" and the "prophets and teachers" present were only five in all including Barnabas and Saul.

Three men ordained two Apostles, and the Church was never asked to vote upon the matter. The Apostles ordained Overseers and Elders without asking the opinion of the members of the Church. That was the order Christ established in forming the Church.

Mr. Calverly:—Brethren and Sisters. It seems that we have not kept in our minds, consecutively, the main points of Doctor's address. Individually I don't know whether I am truly orthodox in speaking, for at the outset of this meeting the Doctor said that no man who had not read his address should discuss it. I cannot say that I have read it, but I listened to it at the last meeting here, and I skimmed over the leading points to see that they were there, I had a pretty close recollection of what he put in that address: for I followed him pretty closely, and I must confess that a more conservative and logical address I never heard delivered in my life. We only need to remember the points he established so conclusively and this present discussion will vanish away.

I did not understand the Doctor to say that we were going to build a new foundation, the foundation was laid, and Jesus

Christ was the chief corner-stone, and the Apostles were the next. Those in the churches lost sight of the primitive church, apostacy and consequent declensions detracted from the divine quality of the Church, and the principal divinely established offices vanished away. What we have left has been handed down principally from the Apostate Roman Catholic Church—a miserable institution. The Presbyterians are an offspring from that Church and they brought with them a great number of the evils of that Church. The Episcopalian is another Church that came from them, and they brought with them a lot of the evils. And the Methodists, we rank old Methodists are chips of the Episcopal Church, and we have inherited a lot of their evils too, and a number of others. There is Methodism and Methodism. I came from the very seat of Methodism in England and we have lots of sins we Methodists; but we inherit them, and many of them are evils which we inherited from the Church of Rome.

Well now the idea that the Doctor has, and in his first address advanced is this, that if the perpetuity of these offices was not recognized in Rome, that is no reason why we should not have them. If we are going to have a church like the first church it must be one according to God's will, and these offices must be recognized and they must be filled according to God's will in His own time.

In regard to one point; I remember Dr. Dowie saying in a kind of sad and gloomy way, "I don't know that I can see any of the Apostles yet." But I think I can see one, and I think he is the chief of modern Apostles; (Looking to Dr. Dowie amid great applause.)

I delight in the idea that there is looming in the near future a Church identical with the Primitive Church, that has got within it the inherent forces of the Primitive Church, and the usefulness of the Primitive Church, the exceeding and highly valuable teaching which was in the Primitive Church, which we need so much, and all the Gifts of the Spirit included.

It has been to me a great consolation to reflect upon this Church, remembering that the gifts and calling of God are without repentance."

Now if God has given us these Gifts He has given them to us for our benefit, and for our children's benefit, and for our children's children's benefit, throughout all our generations. Therefore, if we are alive to the situation, we will not see the devil, or any of the modern fanaticisms, rob us of our rights and privileges which we inherit and which are ours in the name of Jesus.

Now in regard to that Inspiration idea, beloved, I am particularly interested in that.

I do not know what your impression has been when you have been listening to the Doctor; but my impression has frequently been that he has been in close touch with that same Power of the Holy Spirit which fell upon Peter on the day of Pentecost, and that same Power is what I understand the Doctor wishes us to understand in regard to the inspiration, as ever present in the Church.

Well now I feel this to be a momentous conference. I felt as I came two weeks ago, that I never attended a more important meeting in all my life, and this is the same conference. I believe that under the Inspiration of God we are to revive the old Primitive Church, and see it founded upon the old primitive basis including the Apostolic Office and the Prophetic Office.

I must confess that I am like the Doctor in many things here, I do not see where they are all going to come from, but that does not concern me very much, for I know Him in whom I have believed and rested. He knows what He wants. What is required in my judgment is a reliance, a perfect trust in Him, so that we shall go according to the Word of the Lord. Let us march in perfect patience, under the direction of the Holy Spirit, and all things will unfold and develop, step by step, as we march along. I know that many other details of an intricate and important nature will arise; but when the time comes, I believe that the way will be opened up.

But the time is going on and I feel that I must not speak too long, and therefore I will close. (Great Applause.)

A PROTEST.

Dr. Dowie:—I have not the slightest idea, not the slightest, but that our dear brother Calverley spoke with that perfect honesty which has always characterised him, and that he would not have been guilty, for a moment, of flattery. I would despise a man who would attempt to flatter me, and I do not imply for a moment but what brother Calverley was perfectly honest in proclaiming me to be an Apostle.

But I too am perfectly honest when with no mock humility I say to you, from my heart, I do not think that I have reached a deep enough depth of true humility, I do not think I have reached a deep enough depth of self-abasement and effacement, for the high office of Apostle, such as he had reached who could say, and mean it too, "I am less than the least of all saints, and not worthy to be called an Apostle." But if my good Lord can ever get me low enough, and deep enough in self-abasement and self-effacement, to be truly what I want to be, and hope in a measure I am," a servant of the servants of the Lord," why then I should be an Apostle by really becoming the servant of all.

No man has ever approximated toward that sacred office without feeling that if ever God called him to it, it would be a call to a cross and perhaps to a martyr's crown.

No man shall ever assume that office in these days, or have it given to him by God, without being willing to take that which, perhaps without an exception, was the reward of every Apostle of whom we read in scripture, that they had to die, that they had to seal with their very life's blood their Apostolic Office.

If I should be called to that office, I feel I should be called, in the depths of my heart, to die. I do not think I am afraid to die for Christ. I live for Him.

But my friends in becoming an Apostle, it is not a question of rising high, it is a question of getting low enough. It is not a question of being a "lord over God's heritage;" but it is a question if a man shall be called to be an Apostle whether he can get low enough, low enough to say from the depths of his heart, to say the words that Paul said when he said, "It is a faithful saying, worthy of all acceptation, that Jesus Christ came into the world to save sinners, of whom," not I was chief, but of whom "I am chief?" Did you ever read that? Did you ever read that the chief of the Apostles had humility enough to say that he was the chief of sinners?

I do not know if any persons here have got a notion in their minds that Apostolic Office means a high pompous position, wearing a tiara, and swaying a scepter, if so they are entirely wrong. It means a high position truly, an authoritative position and power truly, but the power of one who can take the lowest place.

I think some of you have got a very false conception of Power in the Church of God. Power in the Church of God is not like Power in the government of the United States, where a man climbs to the top of a pyramid of his fellows to the acme of his ambition, and there makes it fulfill his personal pride and purpose. Power in the Church of God is shown in this, that a man shall get lower and lower, and lower and lower, until he can put his very spirit, soul and body underneath the miseries and at the feet of a sin-cursed and disease-smitten humanity and live and die for it and for Him who lived and died for it. That is what I understand by Apostolic Office. (Great Applause.)

ACTION NOW REQUIRED.

Rev. Dr. Speicher:—I want to say a few words.

Most of us have been here under the teaching of Dr. Dowie for a long time. Most of us know his mind perfectly. Most of us know just what he has done when we were in great need. We know in just what spirit he has received us. We know what his teaching has been. We know how he has expounded the Word of God, and I feel to-night that this same man, more than any other man, has the right to say how this Church shall be organized, and he said it in that discourse two weeks ago to-night. He has laid down the platform on which this Church shall be organized.

There is no discussion required upon that; there cannot be; for it was laid down upon a scriptural basis, it was all shown to be scriptural; so I would just say before I read this Resolution, that it has my hearty endorsement. The question is whether you will adopt it in sections or as a whole. Please listen carefully.

RESOLVED: That this Conference of Believers interested in the Organization of the CHRISTIAN CATHOLIC CHURCH, hereby declares

FIRST: Their agreement with the general principle of Organization set forth by the Rev. John Alexander Dowie in his address at the Conference held in Zion Tabernacle No. 2 on January 22nd, as printed in the LEAVES OF HEALING for January 31st, pages 260 to 270.

SECOND: That the Basis of Fellowship as set forth on page 267 is hereby accepted, namely:—

> FIRST: That we recognize the infallible inspiration and sufficiency of the Holy Scriptures as the rule of faith and practice.
>
> SECOND: That we recognize that no persons can be members of the Church who have not repented of their sins and have not trusted in Christ for salvation.
>
> THIRD: That such persons must also be able to make a good profession, and declare that they do know in their own hearts, that they have truly repented, and are truly trusting Christ, and have the witness, in a measure, of the Holy Spirit.
>
> FOURTH: That all other questions of every kind shall be held to be matters of opinion and not matters that are essential to church unity.

THIRD: That the Rev. John Alexander Dowie, as the Overseer called by God to that position, shall, it is unanimously agreed, proceed to the enrollment of members.

FOURTH: That the CHRISTIAN CATHOLIC CHURCH shall be fully organized on Saturday, February 22nd, in Zion Tabernacle No. 2.

Dr. Dowie:—If there is any one who yet desires to speak, speak now. I am not desirous of prolonging this meeting an hour or a minute longer than it can be useful. I want no one to vote for that resolution unless they do it heartily.

THE FORGIVENESS OF SINS.

Mr. Palmer:—I would like to know about the forgiveness of sin.

Dr. Dowie:—You have all heard me pray with thousands of penitents every month and you must have noticed that I have for some time taken an important responsibility upon myself.

Again and again in the Tabernacle and in the Auditorium, when the general confession of repentance and of faith in Christ has been uttered by the people I have said, "Do you mean that?" and thousands every week have said "I do."

Then I have said "God means what He said, 'Whosesoever sins ye remit they are remitted, and whosesoever sins ye retain they are retained. Whatsoever ye shall bind on earth shall be bound in heaven, and whatsoever ye shall loose on earth shall be loosed in heaven.' I believe it my duty as a minister, to whom this Power has been given, to say, that if you have truly repented of your sins and trusted in Jesus, *you are forgiven;* for the blood of Jesus Christ, His son, cleanseth us from all sin. Go thy way, sin no more lest a worse thing come unto thee."

What I have said is simply an assurance to a sinner, that if he repents and trusts in the Lord Jesus Christ he is forgiven, and such an assurance coming from authoritative lips is a great comfort, and a great help to the multitudes.

Mr. Palmer. In the Roman Catholic Church the priest claims to forgive sins, and give absolution, thereby taking God's power.

Dr. Dowie:—I do not propose for a moment, brother, to establish a Roman Catholic Confessional in the Christian Catholic Church, nor do I propose to utter the words I have quoted, as if I were an Apostle and with full apostolic authority. But, inasmuch as multitudes do in my ministry publicly confess their sins, then it is for the time being a Public Confessional, and inasmuch as it is my duty to give these penitents a clear assurance of God's mind and will, it is my bounden duty to say to each one who has truly repented and trusted God "You are forgiven," *God says it;* and I say it as an authoritative minister of Christ.

Mr. Palmer:—But they must have the witness first within them that they are forgiven?

Dr. Dowie:—Not at all. That witness of the Spirit follows the exercise of faith. My words being also the words of the Holy Ghost, come with wonderful force to those who have truly repented and trusted, but who are tempted to say "Oh, I wonder if I am forgiven?" I say, "Yes, you are forgiven. Go your way, God will make you victorious over sin, if you will continue to trust Him." Many of you have gone from such a scene as that, and your evil passions, and your bad habits, and your past inclinations, your sins, and sometimes your sicknesses have gone out of you, just at that same moment when I have said these words. Isn't that true brothers? (Loud cries of Yes)

Well that is all. No, Brother Palmer, I have no desire to sit as a priest in a Roman Catholic Confessional.

Mr. Palmer:—I did not mean that in that way. Just as soon as they are forgiven nobody has to tell them, they have a witness within them, don't they?

Dr. Dowie:—There are a great many persons who require, in fact all persons do, authoritative guidance. Brother Marsh you are an old officer in the Customs Department of the United States Government, are you not?

Mr. Marsh:—Yes sir.

Dr. Dowie:— Do you not require in your subordinate office authorative assurances and instructions?

Mr. M:—We have to obey instructions always.

Dr. D:—You need them?

Mr. M:—We need them.

Dr. D:—You have some persons under you?

Mr. M:—I have.

Dr. D:—Do they need instructions?

Mr. M:—Certainly, and without them they cannot proceed to their work.

Dr. Dowie:—That is all. In the Church of God it is the same, there must be authority to give instructions and assurances, and that authority is vested in God's own ministers. If I am sent by God I must have authority to give instructions and assurances to the penitent who are convinced of sin and of Christ's power and will to save. That authority is to tell what the Word of God declares. If you receive it, and believe it, the Holy Ghost witnesses as to whether it is true or not. That is all, Brother Palmer, I do not think there is any difference between us fundamentally.

AN EXPLANATION AND A TRIBUTE FROM AN ABLE PRESBYTERIAN MINISTER.

Rev. Mr. Jones:—I wish to say that I have attended Dr. Dowie's services for a year and a half or more, and I have come nearer to God than at any point I ever did in my life, and I have been widely through the world. I have felt the presence of God here, more perfectly than ever in my life. And yet some of us want some time, and you must not accuse us of being antagonistic to this motion, because we do not at once vote for all its provisions.

I have been a minister of the Presbyterian Church for 40 years and upwards; and if I conclude to bid that church good-bye, I do not want to do anything indecent or hasty, and I should like to leave it in a dignified manner.

I make this statement so that if I should not feel ready to

vote everything to-night you will understand that I want some time to study it over. I am not as quick as some that are younger and I hope that I may not be misunderstood.

I want to say that Dr. Dowie never touched my heart so deeply as he has to-night when he spoke of his need of more humility. Let no man put any hindrance in Dr. Dowie's way. I do not want any personalities, and I do not care who does, I only feel that "Christ is all," and whenever I read those words there on the wall above Dr. Dowie's head as he stands there, I am thrilled with love and admiration. I do not want anybody to stand between me and Christ, and I admire Dr. Dowie's humility, and his apostolic spirit, and Christly love and reverence.

CONCESSION.

Dr. Dowie:—I am very willing to concede all our Brother Jones asks. It is very seldom that a man of the mature years of Brother Jones, is so progressive and so ready and so willing to follow where God leads. If it is the mind of a large number present that this Conference should stand adjourned for another week, for further consideration, I am perfectly willing. Only I would like to know on what points more information is really needed, because the best place to get it is here, and the best time is now.

A CONGREGATIONAL MINISTER'S VIEW

Rev. Mr. Atkins:—It seems that this very hearty meeting might have a little more general expression. I would like very much to see the rank and file of the people here giving utterance. There is a very large number here to-night and I would like to see them to a little larger extent expressing the sentiment of the Conference, and we might say that the Conference up to this time has been something of a discussion by the teachers. It seems to me there is a large number here who have made up their minds and if they spoke at all would give utterance with regard to the great leading idea that was suggested at the opening of the meeting.

Dr. Dowie suggested, if I may put it in my words, that there be an organization here that shall go forward and that shall have a constantly progressive aim, in a word, to better conditions, to save, redeem and cleanse. He suggested an organization for work, and spirited, aggressive, determined kind of work.

Now friends the Doctor in this Conference will want to know whether you are in sympathy with him to *work*, I think that is the very thing, the great thing that you are going to be glad to do, *work*. And I apprehend the Doctor will feel not a little unsatisfied in his mind, if he comes away to-night, and thinks that he has failed to discover whether he has a working body with him or not.

Just a word in regard to that matter of the Apostolic Office and the other offices. I apprehend that most here have not thought of it. Well, dear friends, very few thought a little while ago that the Gift of Healing was still in the Church, until you met Dr. Dowie and got under his influence, and then you thought about it, and expected it; and believed it, and lived and preached it, and prayed it; well now you are convinced of it, that it is a retained Gift. Well, perhaps, after a little more consideration and deliberation, these brethren who have spoken will be persuaded that these other Gifts are here, or will be, and God will make them known in His own good time. But now friends, we would like to have some of you men and women give utterance with regard to the motion, and with regard to the single fundamental idea that is now before the meeting, an organization for Christian Work.

I speak these words out of sympathy and kindness and with the utmost generosity of spirit, and believe that the meeting should not be brought to a close after hearing from say four or five, or half a dozen, and most of those who have spoken are ministers, and I am one of the same class, making, perhaps, too long a speech, for I want to hear others. (Applause.)

Dr. Dowie:—Brother Atkins has not said a word too much, and it would be a very good thing now if a dozen of our strong men and women would speak, and by the way, I have not heard a woman's voice excepting Mrs. Dowie's in the meeting. I am willing to hear the women when they have something to say. I am not of the opinion that some folks think Paul had, that the women were to keep perpetual silence. Paul himself, used them in his ministry and they labored with him in the Gospel. If any woman here has a word to say, or any man, we will be glad to listen. There is one thing I shall say in this Church if I am its Overseer, "He that will not work neither shall he eat." (Great Applause.) And I will make it particularly hot for the fellow that will not work, and on the other hand I am perfectly sure if you do not eat you can not work.

Mrs. S:—With regard to that I am not at all lazy. I feel that the good Lord has intended you for this purpose, and I thank Him for the progress we have come to see. I do not know dear friends how I can praise God enough to-night, for it is something that I have been looking ahead for for the last five years.

I hail Dr. Dowie as one of the leading men for God in this country. I do praise God to-night and I do feel that I am willing to sacrifice all I have, sacrifice my life for Christ's cause. My last drop of blood is His, and my whole life is His.

Mr. E. A. Congdon:—Most of us cold-blooded folks, some are Baptists like myself, have become so deep-rooted in our beliefs that we find it is hard work for us to get on the right track and give up old associations and change to the new. But the light will dawn upon us, brothers and sisters, and we will come straggling in bye-and-bye, sure, every one of us. And I want to say to Brother Atkins, that the primitive ones, the positive ones that he speaks of, are here, and when it comes to a vote their voices will be heard.

Mr. Chas. J. Westwood. I want to say Brethren and Sisters that five years and a half ago the light shone in upon my heart when Dr. Dowie spoke in the First M. E. Church of Chicago, and ever since that I have loved this work and been closely associated with it. As far as my ability has permitted me to do so, I have worked for God along this line, ever since I saw the truth; and to-night I thank God that it is coming to what I have hoped and prayed and longed for right along, a Church organization of some kind, tangible, and I believe that we are ready to have it. I believe with Brother Congdon, who last spoke, that we are almost unanimous upon that point and I believe there are a great many of us ready to work I believe we are working now. I do not believe there is a church anywhere in Chicago, that is working as well as we are as a Mission.

I want to ask to-night about a matter, not for my own enlightenment, because I believe I know Brother Dowie's mind in the matter, I heard of a gentleman when going out of our company inviting two sisters to go and take a little wine; and, when remonstrated with, he spoke of Paul's exhortation to Timothy and said he thought he could do as he liked in regard to it, and he smoked just when he felt like it. Now probably that one is not here to-night, I don't think he is; but being as we are here for enlightenment upon these matters, I mentioned it. I believe we want to be clean people, I know for my own part that is the line I have worked along for the last five and a half years, and I just simply mentioned this fact, and I hope Brother Dowie will define the Church's position very clearly for us on that matter of taking or giving alcoholic liquors.

Dr. Dowie:—If such an act should come to the knowledge of any member of the Christian Catholic Church, when it is formed, that brother or sister would be disloyal to God, to me, and to this Church if he or she did not immediately report that fact.

I would thereupon require that brother, who made the charge, with the party who committed the sin, to come and see me; and if that sin was not at once repented of, and the promise given that it should not be repeated, I should immediately suspend that person from membership, report it to the first Assembly of the Church, and ask the Church to take action by approving the removal of that person from our fellowship. I should not for a moment permit members of this Church to invite their fellow-members to wine-bibbing, or stink-pot manufacturing. (Great Applause.) Such persons as these may be tolerated in other communities, but in a community of men and women, whose motto is "Christ is All.", and who are living for God and who are desiring to keep the temple of their bodies clean, such conduct is simply unbearable and impossible. I say too, that if any Branch of this Church did not see with me on these things, I should disband that Church, as far as I had the power, and I should not continue to be connected with that Church for a moment. (Applause.)

A WORD FROM WHEATON.

Mr. Amos Dresser:—My heart was touched by what brother Jones said regarding the giving up of his Church. I am one of the children of God. I am not in the situation that my brother is, connected with any ecclesiastical body at the present day, the Lord led me out from the Congregational Church two years ago. It has been a glorious privilege to be free, and to come and seek the Lord in Zion Tabernacle. It has been a great privilege to go out to others and tell them how the Lord is working, and I just mention this to show how the Lord is working. We were in Wheaton two weeks ago, and they had three meetings on this line, and one of these meetings was crowded full so that the aisles were full and people were standing at the door, and on next Sunday we expect to have three more meetings of a similar character at Wheaton and Glen Ellyn.

Dr. Dowie:—My heart is with you in that work and you will be a welcome member of the Christian Catholic Church. We expect to have branches of this Church within a year in almost every part of the country. I may say, that already there are scores of ministers and students of Theology who are ready to become ministers of the Christian Catholic Church, and there are thousands of officers and members of all Churches who are weary of the conditions existing in these Churches.

ABOUT SECRET SOCIETIES.

Mr. E. W. Anson:—I did not feel like saying anything at the commencement, but I think I do now. I have to praise the Lord for what He has done for me since I commenced to attend these meetings. Nine years ago I took the Lord for my physician. I think it is the love of God that keeps us from doing anything that displeases Him. I would like to hear the Doctor's opinion in regard to secret societies.

Dr. Dowie:—I am absolutely opposed to secret societies root and branch.

Mr. Anson:—I am glad to hear that. I can not see how one can belong to God and to the Devil at the same time.

Dr. Dowie:—I will not say that a man cannot be a member of the Christian Catholic Church who may be connected with some form of secret society. But I will say that it is my judgment that such a man is sinning against God in belonging to a secret oath-bound organization. Our Lord Jesus distinctly and positively said: "In secret have I done nothing." I cannot understand how any brother, with the clear plain Word of God in his hand can go into secret socities and call men brothers who he believes are going to hell. Secret Society men are like the persons who drink whisky and smoke tobacco, they may be Christans but they consort with devils and I cannot quite see where their Christanity comes in. (Laughter and Applause.)

A WORD FROM OHIO.

Mr. Merchantell, Forest Ohio. I am glad the Star of Bethlehem ever rose, and that it is here, and men from the east as well as the west are coming to worship Christ; everybody. I am here now for my third visit, and I am so happy and glad that the time will come when this man will organize that Church according to his preaching. That is a glorious gospel. I was hunting salvation, I knew nothing about salvation, but Dr. Dowie told me. God send him five lives. He is here to

When I heard the teaching in the Divine Healing Home to-day I thought, What a blessed gospel. Dr. Dowie has risen over all his enemies and he stands to-day victorious, and they are going quickly down to the grave and death.

PURER LOVE AND CLEANER SPIRIT.

Mr. Wilson:—I want to just say to-night that I am surprised at the professed people of God. Sometimes they are so suspicious of Dr. Dowie. They never stop to think what Dr. Dowie has done and is doing, and no man in this city preaches the gospel like he does, and I have heard the leading preachers of this city. My love is purer and my spirit is cleaner, and I thank God that he ever came to Chicago.

Mr. C. G. Ahl:—I had been an officer in the Methodist Church. However, God showed me that that Word contained all the elements that I needed for my salvation. It showed me that there was a forgiveness for sins, healing for the body, sanctification of the spirit. I was taught the doctrine in the Methodist class meeting that the Lord made people sick. I will simply say this, that I had faith to accept Divine Healing before Dr. Dowie came here, through the Word of God and from testimonies I heard in class meeting in this city. I was glad when Dr. Dowie first opened his missions here in Chicago, on Clark and Washington Streets, in the First M. E. Church. When he opened his first Zion Tabernacle down here, I came when he first opened it. I presume there were only 150 people in the place on the first Sunday afternoon, and I thought—I am not saying this out of flattery, because I feel in this matter as Dr. Dowie does himself—as I came into Dr. Dowie's meeting, I felt the Spirit of God upon me, and, I feel compelled to say it, that he looked to me like one of the Apostles. I don't know why it was that I should have that feeling. But I will tell the truth, it don't make any difference who it hits, as they say, and I feel blessed. I have been watching this movement, and I have come here very often, and I feel as if I was glad to go anywhere where the Word of God was preached and the truth was preached according to the Word of God, it don't make any difference where it is preached. Jesus said, "Where two or three are met together in My name, there am I in the midst of them." I have felt His presence here, and have, therefore, come to Dr. Dowie's meetings quite often. On one Sunday afternoon I stood up in the Auditorium and told my experience in regard to secret societies. I belonged to the Knights of Pythias, the Odd Fellows, and the Free Masons, and God took me out of all of them. Should God call upon me to explain the relations of people, with regard to the Free Masons and other secret societies, I believe He will endow me with power to do so, because there are certain facts to be taken into consideration in regard to secret societies that have to be thoroughly discussed from an unprejudiced standpoint, and you must not discuss them if you don't know anything about them. I was not here at the first Conference; but I have read the report of it, and considered it closely, very closely, and I see nothing in there in regard to any plans of Dr. Dowie's or anything that will be done that conflicts with the Word of God as I read it, and as the Spirit of God reveals it to me. Hence I say that it is possible for us to go right ahead. I see God's hand in this movement; and as Dr. Dowie says, he has no business to raise up Apostles, God will do that. All we have got to do is to step in and do our part. I am in hearty sympathy with this movement.

Mr. Schmalgemeier:—I think if a man was a Free Mason he would be glad he was out of it and say nothing about it, as I did.

WORDS OF CHEER FROM A "FRIENDS" MINISTER.

Rev. Dr. Hussey, Mt. Pleasant, Ohio. I am very glad to have an opportunity to express my approbation of this organization, and the foundation principles which have been stated here, and as I have carefully read them, and I believe they are truly apostolic. Since I have heard the words spoken to-night, I am more than pleased with the idea of a Christian Catholic Church and with the principles Dr. Dowie has laid down.

There are so many different sects in the United States that

I have scarcely thought it possible to make any difference in that direction. I think the people are ready to take up the work of God in a great many places with changed conditions: for a great many of these different sects have come away from Christ. And a great many of God's ministers have come away from their sects, because of their unscriptural position. So many are longing to have a wider field of service, and more especially, so many hearts are longing to know Christ in all His fulness and power and come in contact with Him as He is taught by brother Dowie and his co-workers.

I fully realize there is something more in the Gospel, than a mere religion that ordains to work and service without light and power. I am glad that Brother Dowie remembers that in all his teachings.

I am glad also to be a guest in his Home, and wish to speak of the great joy that has come to my heart through the words he has spoken, and the enlightening influence of the Spirit, and of the great many truths that have come into the full light as I have heard him express them. I rejoice that he denounces all sin and all indifference and carelessness among Christians and reproves the world from his paper and from his platform, and I praise him for his works and his way from the depths of my heart, God bless him.

RECOGNITION.

Dr. Dowie:—Permit me to thank Brother Hussey from the depth of my heart. He is not known to many of you perhaps, but he is well-known to me. Although a man of very great modesty, he is known to those who hold advanced views on Divine Healing and True Holiness not only in America but in Europe. Our brother is a member of that sect known as the Friends or Quakers, and a very prominent minister among them. For many long years he has been a steadfastand pre-eminent upholder of higher life teaching in the Church of God, standing side by side in his own Church with such foremost men as David G. Updegraff, Calvin W. Pritchard, Dougan Clark, and.men of that kind. Mr. Hussey stands among them a man in spirit as he is in stature, a giant. I feel the tribute of his approbation very much. Brother Hussey spoke in the great assemblies of the famous International Conference on Healing and Holiness, held in London in 1885, 15 years ago, where I only spoke by letter. I thank Brother Hussey for the love with which he immediately met my communications and my teachings and that he has been my friend from that time. This is not the first time I have had my remarkable brother attend my ministry, for he did me the honor to visit me whilst I was conducting a Mission in Pittsburgh some years ago and we have had his sister and many of his friends from Ohio in our Homes. One of the great privileges of my life, with all its trials, toils, is this exceeding great privilege of receiving God's dear servants from all portions of His Church and from many states and other countries in our Homes. I know that the Christian Catholic Church will have many true friends amongst the servants of God in nearly all denominations. There are more than twelve ministers in this Conference and their presence has been very helpful. I am grateful for the love of the brethren.

WHAT TO DO WHERE THERE IS NO BRANCH OF THE CHRISTIAN CATHOLIC CHURCH.

Mr. C. F. Peters:—I have been cured for a year and a half and was healed when near to death's door. I was given up by the Doctors, but Christ was never so dear to me as when I heard the second lecture of Dr. Dowie, in the Auditorium, the preaching of the true religion as it was 19 centuries ago. I felt that Christ was close, and I felt that I wanted to do all things for God, whether it was in my business or whatever I did. I have been much trouble to my poor mother, I am an only son, and I felt very happy last Christmas when I went to her. Now I am going back to Milwaukee to go in business sometime this Spring. It is hard for me to be where I cannot hear Dr. Dowie, and I do not know what to do. I can not go to another Church for I know they are not speaking the whole truth of God to me, and I do not feel I want to go anywhere else than just to hear Dr. Dowie, for I have been so blessed. There is no one in this room knows how I have been blessed, if they knew what a rascal I was before, they would know how I was blessed. I want to ask your opinion, Doctor, what am I to do as to a Church? You can not preach down there in Milwaukee, and I want to hear the Word of God.

Dr. Dowie:—I would say to my brother that it would be well for him to join the Christian Catholic Church here, and then when he goes to Milwaukee to go to that Church where he can hear the Gospel most earnestly preached, and say to the pastor of that congregation, "I don't want to join your Church, but I would like to be permitted to attend your ministry, to sit at the Lord's Table with you and to help along Christ's cause with my time and money, but I am a member of the Christian Catholic Church. I will co-operate with you if I can retain my membership in the Christian Catholic Church, all right, and if not I can't help it because I am going to stand by the Christian Catholic Church." You will be permitted to co-operate in that way in at least one or two Churches in Milwaukee, I think I can give you a letter to a minister who is in very hearty sympathy with us, and I believe you will find in him a very sympathetic and earnest believer in Divine Healing. You will find in Milwaukee quite a number of our friends who have been healed here, so you can get up a little week-day meeting of members of the Christian Catholic Church amongst yourselves. I will be very glad to give you a note of recommendation to these particular persons who are in fellowship with us, and you can then form the nucleus of a Branch of the Christian Catholic Church in Milwaukee. I will come some day and visit you, and will send you other helpers to aid you in knocking a few of those beer barrels in the head, for which Milwaukee is so infamous, since some of the largest breweries in America are there. (Laughter and Applause.) My friends say that there is not any part of the Uuited States where we cannot draw a very large audience, if it is only for the curiosity of seeing a man who has been arrested a hundred times. So we may reach even besotted Milwaukee, and help God's people who are fighting bravely in that stronghold of the devil.

Dr. Dowie:—Are you prepared to vote?

All answer:—Yes.

Dr. Dowie:—All who are prepared to have the motion again read and submitted say "Aye".

Apparently all answered "Aye."

Dr. Dowie:—Those who are not prepared say "No."

I do not hear any.

I want to say who there are perhaps three parties in this meeting. First, there are those who want the vote; second there may be those who are not antagonistic but who want to be silent; and third, there may be those who are opposed to taking the vote. Therefore I will put the matter again thus:

All who want to take the vote say "Aye."

Apparently all answered "Aye."

All who want to keep silent say "Aye."

None answered.

All who are opposed to taking the vote say "Aye."

None answered.

It is very evident I should not be right if I did not take the vote, for there is nothing but "Aye" on that proposition.

ADOPTION OF RESOLUTION FOR ORGANIZATION.

Dr Speicher:—I move the Resolution which I have already read. (See page 281.)

Mr. John Murdoch:—I heartily second the Resolution.

Dr. Dowie:—Now I will call for the vote, by asking you to stand. All in favor of this resolution stand. (Almost every one in the Tabernacle stands.) Will you please take your seats again.

All those who are opposed to this motion, please to stand.

There are none.

ANNOUNCEMENT OF ACTION TO ORGANIZE.

Beloved friends, the request made to me in this resolution from this Conference requires me to at once proceed to enroll members.

I will print the proceedings of the Conference in the next issue of LEAVES OF HEALING, and I propose to append to the LEAVES OF HEALING a copy of the blank for enrollment, which will be sent therefore to every person throughout the country who has the LEAVES OF HEALING.

I want to get as full particulars of you all as possible for the General Roll of the Christian Catholic Church, so I shall be thoroughly well posted on all that relates to you, and we shall keep our Rolls as perfectly as we can. It will be an interesting record of great present and of future value.

I shall ask you and our friends in distant places to return this slip carefully filled up, and I will then as soon as possible give you private interviews and see your faces, and by direct speaking with you find out about you.

On Saturday, February 22d, Washington's Birthday and a Public Holiday, I shall call you together to spend the day with me in Zion Tabernacle. We shall give the entire morning from 9 to 1 to enrollment and in seeing you individually. In the afternoon at 2:30 p. m. I shall proceed to the Organization of the Church and the reading of the Roll of applicants for membership, and we shall allow none to be present at that meeting except those on the Roll. The Ordinance of the Lord's Supper will be a part of the proceedings.

As to what we will do when we are formed as a Church, that is another matter, and we don't want to discuss that now. Let the Church be first fully formed, and let us proceed carefully as well as rapidly.

All this will involve a great deal of toil, and it will take considerable time to get this new organization fully organized.

I may say that while I have not settled it, the probabilities are strongly in favor of the establishment of our Zion in a central part of the city, and, for a period of years, I am about to acquire control of very valuable properties suitable for a Home, Tabernacle, Publishing House, etc., properties which cost over $500,000. I don't think we can improve upon the name

ZION.

Zion Tabernacle No. 3 will seat, if our present plans are carried out, about 2,000 in the principal auditorium, with an equal space below it, and about five large, very desirable rooms for seeing the sick, and for teaching the seventies, and for holding meetings in connection with the various departments of Zion. We hope to prepare teachers and evangelists and establish a Sabbath School with Bible Classes for young and old. We shall have a larger place for Zion Publishing House and a better position for that work in every way.

Now, all this takes a great deal of money, but the first thing it takes is Faith in God. I propose for the present to go on bearing the financial responsibility and management, as the Church cannot be at first in a condition to undertake these things, and business contracts will be made in my name, etc. I propose to ask you to do your part in placing at my disposal the pecuniary resources that will enable me to make Zion's Onward Movement a glorious success, for it would be impossible to do the work by committees. We have got to proceed carefully, and I will have to bear the burden until the Church has come to a place where it can do a great many things without me. A great many of the details of the work which I do now can be very well relegated to others when they are fitted to do them in the right spirit and in the right way. In the two Homes we have everything arranged in such a way that all runs smoothly, because all our servants are our fellow-servants, and I feel that I am simply the chief of a number of fellow-servants. I will feel the same as

GENERAL OVERSEER OF THE CHRISTIAN CATHOLIC CHURCH.

I want you all to pray that this Church may fulfill the purpose for which it will be organized, viz: The Glory of the Eternal Father through our Lord and Saviour, so that the Holy Ghost may work in the Church, and may enable us to fulfill the great mission for which Christ came to this earth: the Salvation, the Healing, the Cleansing, the Redemption of man from sin and disease and death and hell, and the coming together of the redeemed into one great and glorious Temple for God Himself. That is the one object, and everything must bend to that. I pray that we, ourselves, shall be clean, in spirit, soul and body, and carry the gospel to millions ere we finish our work on earth, and that the proof that God has called this Church into being shall not be in our *numbers*, shall not be in our *material prosperity*, shall not be in our *intellectual advances*, or in our eclessiastical *power and unity*, all of which are good and desirable; but shall be in this *fact*, which no one has been able hitherto to deny, *a fact* that we have been able to glory in as a Mission, that the people will everywhere say,

GOD IS IN THE MIDST OF THEM; AND HE BLESSES THEM IN THE SALVATION AND HEALING OF MULTITUDES.

They may criticise our organization, they may criticise the manner in which we preach, but there is one thing that defies criticism and that is this, when those who are sinners are cleansed from their sins, and when men and women who are sick and dying are healed from their sicknesses, and the Glorious Kingdom of God is extended, then that work is placed in a position where it can defy criticism and prosper in spite of all opposition from the world, the flesh, the devil, and a formal and unspiritual multitude of professors in the denominations.

We are asking God for 100,000 conversions to Him this year in Chicago. Let us ask God to give us that and more.

When we are organized as a Church and feel our Unity, I may say this, I shall feel then a responsibility for you that I have not hitherto felt, that I could not hitherto feel, and I shall ask God to raise up amongst you and send to me men and women whom I can by the grace of God ordain as pastors, elders, deacons, evangelists, etc., who shall help in this work and go in and out amongst you as helpers, taking most of the detail from me and enabling me to give myself more fully "to the Word of God and to Prayer." God grant it.

These things are all in my heart, and you can help me in the doing of them. I desire, my brothers and sisters, that you shall be an active people, working for Christ everywhere, in your office, in your workshop, in all daily labour, in your home, and in every relation of life. Can you all say that is your desire also?

All answer, "IT IS."

Then stand and make consecration to God.

All stood and repeated after Dr. Dowie the following

PRAYER.

"My God and Father, in Jesus' Name I give myself to Thee. Take me as I am; make me what I ought to be, in spirit, soul and body; help me to do right and to help others to do right, that they may find in Christ a perfect Redeemer. For Jesus' sake give me an answer by Thy Spirit. And may the Church now to be formed be such an organization as Thou can'st approve, for Jesus' sake. Amen."

After the singing of the Doxology, the Conference closed with the following

BENEDICTION:

"Beloved, abstain from all appearance of evil. And the very God of Peace Himself sanctify you wholly; and I pray God your whole Spirit, and Soul, and Body, be preserved entire without blame, unto the coming of our Lord Jesus Christ. Faithful is He that calleth you, who also will do it. The Grace of our Lord Jesus, the Love of God, the Eternal Father, the fellowship of the Holy Ghost, the Eternal Comforter, one Eternal God, abide in you, bless you, keep you, and all the Israel of God everywhere, forever. Amen.

ZION'S ONWARD MOVEMENT

Organization of the

CHRISTIAN CATHOLIC CHURCH

In Zion Tabernacle No. 2, Saturday, February 22nd, 1896.

The entire morning from 9 A. M. to 1 P. M. was given to the work of receiving applications, and of examining and filing them in alphabetical order.

Hundreds gathered around the long tables, where volunteer helpers gave every assistance.

At 2 o'clock the Rev. John Alex. Dowie the General Overseer of the Christian Catholic Church, accompanied by many helpers, ascended the platform, and gave out the Marching Song of Zion's Onward Movement.

Come, we that love the Lord,
And let your joys be known,
Join in the song with sweet accord
And thus surround the throne.

CHO:—We're marching to Zion,
Beautiful, beautiful Zion;
We're marching upward to Zion,
The beautiful city of God."

This was sung with great heartiness, and many remarks were made by the General Overseer between the separate verses in his usual interesting way. For instance on the line "The hill of Zion yields a thousand sacred sweets" he remarked, Beloved friends, it is useless to forget, or try for a moment to forget, that we are ascending "a hill" which is far from being easy to climb. The old Reformers used to sing,

"Steep and thorny is the way
Straight to Heaven our Home ascending;
Happy he who every day walks therein for Christ conten
Happier when his conflicts o'er
Conqueror he to Christ shall soar."

As we rise higher and higher in the Divine Life we see more of the great expanse, the wondrous landscape of the divine glory; and as we go still higher and higher, we reach the heights of heavenly hill after heavenly hill, we look on all sides at the glorious prospects, but still see higher hills beyond and upward, until we reach the City of God, and there, from the highest place in the heavens, we shall one day look abroad upon the boundless Universe of God with its unspeakable glories. Now, we are going up the hill of Zion, from the streets of Chicago, and even here we find "a thousand sacred sweets" on the road. There are beautiful things on the road to God, Salvation, Healing and a thousand delights in the King's Highway of Holiness. I have found Life in Christ very, very happy. I do not know that I ever had a happier year than last year. I was so happy amidst all the shameful Persecutions from doctors, devils, the press, the pulpit, and the police, when I was twice arrested on the Lord's Day on this platform, and many times when in the act of praying with God's sick children in this Tabernacle and in the Home; for I was fighting the good fight of faith, and my spirit was very happy with the certain joy of a great victory for God at the end of all.

Again when reading the words

" Then let our joys be known,
And every tear be dry,
We're marching thro' Immanuel's ground,
To fairer worlds on high."

The General Overseer remarked: I always feel that to be true beloved.

I do not feel that any man upon earth owns a single inch of it.

I always feel "the earth is the Lord's." It is Immanuel's ground, and all the fine corner lots in the cities that the wicked have now, and all the fields, and mountains and valleys are going to get into the proper hands. The righteous shall gather here from the realms of glory, and "the meek shall inherit the earth." "We're marching thro' Immanuel's ground to fairer worlds on high." May God help us to march shoulder to shoulder and closer together in heart than ever to countless conflicts with Satan and victories for Christ.

When the hymn had been sung the General Overseer said:—

Beloved friends, I think it well, before we read our roll, to repeat together the beautiful Song of Salvation, of Healing, of Holiness, and of Triumphant Entry into the Zion above, which has been so often, throughout our association as a Mission, an exercise with us. Let it be the beautiful opening exercise now. The 35th of Isaiah, I hope you have all got it in your hearts, and if not read it with us from your books, until you have all got the words in your hearts.

All the people then recited in concert the following words:—

The wilderness and the solitary place shall be glad for them; and the desert shall rejoice, and blossom as the rose.

It shall blossom abundantly, and rejoice even with joy and singing; the glory of Lebanon shall be given unto it, the excellency of Carmel and Sharon. they shall see the glory of the Lord, and the excellency of our God.

Strengthen ye the weak hands, and confirm the feeble knees.

Say to them that are of a fearful heart, Be strong, fear not; behold, your God will come with vengeance, even God with a recompense; he will come and save you.

Then the eyes of the blind shall be opened, and the ears of the deaf shall be unstopped

Then shall the lame man leap as an hart, and the tongue of the dumb sing; for in the wilderness shall waters break out, and streams in the desert.

And the parched ground shall become a pool, and the thirsty land springs of water, in the habitation of dragons, where each lay, shall be grass with reeds and rushes.

And an highway shall be there, and a way, and it shall be called The way of holiness, the unclean shall not pass over it; but it shall be for those: the wayfaring men, though fools, shall not err therein

No lion shall be there, nor any ravenous beast shall go up thereon, it shall not be found there, but the redeemed shall walk there:

And the ransomed of the Lord shall return, and come to Zion with songs and everlasting joy upon their heads: they shall obtain joy and gladness, and sorrow and sighing shall flee away.

ROLL CALL PRAYER BY GENERAL OVERSEER.

Grant unto us, oh God, our heavenly Father, that by Thy Holy Spirit, for Jesus' sake, this Roll Call may be the call of those whose names shall not only be written in the books of Thy Church on earth, but in the Lamb's Book of Life above, so that when earth and seas are fled, and the Great Roll Call is called before Thy Judgment Seat, we may stand before Thee here and hear Thee, Oh Thou Unerring Judge, pronounce our names with blessings on our heads, even as we to-day bless in Thy Name those who enter into fellowship with us. Let Thy blessing abide throughout all our proceedings this day, for Jesus' sake. Amen.

DIRECTION.

The officers at the door will please to listen and attend to this instruction: See that no one enters the door of Zion Tabernacle now unless they have already made application for fellowship, or will do so before they enter this room.

THE GENERAL RECORDER READS THE ROLL.

After ascertaining that there were none present except those who had filled up their forms of application for membership, the General Overseer introduced the Rev. Thomas G. Atteberry as the temporary General Recorder, who at once proceeded to the long task of nearly three hours in reading the Roll.

Hundreds of names in addition to those of the three hundred and seventy present were read by the Recorder. Many of these were engaged in business which they could not leave, and a very large number resided in distant towns and cities, from the Atlantic to the Pacific Oceans. [As the Roll is growing steadily daily we cannot give the exact number of members in the Church, but it will soon be one thousand.]

RECEPTION BY THE GENERAL OVERSEER.

As each one came forward Dr. Dowie received them in the Name of the Lord Jesus Christ into the fellowship of the Christian Catholic Church, adding words of recognition of their special fitness for fellowship from his minute knowledge of each, recalling details connected with their salvation, healing or previous co-operation in Christian service, and invoking God's blessing on each as he gave them the right hand of fellowship.

After this the

ORDINANCE OF THE LORD'S SUPPER

was celebrated. Twelve members of the Church assisted the General Overseer, who presided.

Beloved, at the Lord's Table we gather, for the first time in our history, all who are now together in fellowship.

ZION'S WATCHWORD FOR 1896.

We are among those who at the beginning of the year uttered a midnight vow in this place and repeated Zion's Watchword for the year together. We will all repeat it together now.

All present said: "Come, let us join ourselves to the Lord in a Perpetual Covenant."

There were also four words which we said we would put in our minds, "that shall not be forgotten." And so to-day we have come into Covenant Relations, having joined ourselves to the Lord, we join ourselves together.

You must remember that the few hundreds who are now present are but the advance company of a great company, a great company, for, as you have heard, many are absent, and there has not yet been time to get the enrollment of hundreds, perhaps thousands, of our friends. I have been very much interested in the names that have come in already this week from the country, although they only received the application forms in their LEAVES two or three days ago. We have a number of ministers, as you have heard. Christian people from all parts of the United States are amongst the applicants, and there are many more to be heard from. Had there been time I should liked to have read to you a number of letters that have been received from various brethren and sisters who have desired to come into fellowship with us, but have yet arrangements to make in connection with their churches ere they sever their connection. In some cases whole Churches are considering as to whether they shall not apply for membership in the Christian Catholic Church, and in one case the minister has already applied.

At the Lord's Table we shall now fittingly celebrate our Union. No merely formal words shall be spoken; such words as are spoken will be from the heart. I shall deliver the Charge to the Church at the close of this ordinance. We ant the Lord now to speak. When we have closed the Charge we shall declare the Church formed and make some announcements regarding future movements.

May God our Father now be with us at this Table, and the Lord Jesus Himself, in the power of the Holy Spirit, one Eternal God, be present as we bow in silence, as we come into His presence.

AFTER SILENT PRAYER

the hymn, "Close to Thee," was sung very softly by the whole congregation.

The General Overseer then repeated the words of the Apostle Paul in I. Corinthians, 11th chapter, verses 23 to 32:

"For I have received of the Lord that which also I delivered unto you, that the Lord Jesus the same night in which He was betrayed took bread: And when He had given thanks He brake it, and said, take eat: this is my body, which is broken for you: this do in remembrance of me. For as often as ye eat this bread and drink this cup, ye do show the Lord's death till He come. Wherefore whosoever shall eat this bread and drink this cup of the Lord unworthily, shall be guilty of the body and blood of the Lord. But let a man examine himself and so let him eat of that bread and drink of that cup, for he that eateth and drinketh unworthily eateth and drinketh damnation to himself, not discerning the Lord's body. For this cause many are weak and sickly among you, and many sleep. For if we would judge ourselves we should not be judged. But when we are judged we are chastened of the Lord, that we should not be condemned with the world."

Let us give thanks for this sacred bread, the bread made sacred by the blessed associations of this Table, that God may make, by the Holy Spirit, for Jesus' sake, the eating of it to us a true spiritual communion and partaking of the Blood of Eternal Life, even of the Lord Himself.

THANKS FOR THE BREAD.

We thank Thee our Father in heaven for Christ, the living bread, who came down from heaven, the manna, of which if a man eat he shall never die, and we praise Thee that we are enabled by Thy grace to eat and drink, and to realize that Thy blood and Thy flesh, spiritually, are the portion of this table.

We take this bread remembering that Thy body was broken for us, that we may be an unbroken body in Thee, and we bless Thee this day that by Thy grace we are enabled to believe that we are members of Thine Unbroken Body the Holy Catholic Church which in earth and heaven are forever saved by grace divine. We thank Thee for the great privilege that enables us to come together as a part of Thy glorious universal Church, which, we bless Thee, has been the One Fold of Thy people in all ages. We pray for Thy people in all portions of the visible Churches that they may be blessed and that they may come into Union as One General Assembly and Church of the First Born whose names are written in heaven. Now bless us as we partake of this bread in Jesus' Name, Amen.

The General Overseer then distributed to the elders and deacons, saying, "eat ye all of it. Is it not the communion of the Lord's body?"

When they had partaken he handed a plate of bread to each of the twelve saying, "Distribute in the Name of the Lord."

During the distribution of the bread, he said:—

Jesus said, "I am the Bread of Life which came down from heaven, of which if a man eat he shall never die. Verily, verily I say unto you, he that believeth on me hath everlasting life. I am that bread of life. Your fathers did eat manna in the wilderness and are dead; this is the bread which cometh down from heaven. I am the living bread which came down from heaven. If any man eat of this bread, he shall live forever: and the bread that I will give is my flesh, which I will give for the life of the world. Who so eateth my flesh and drinketh my blood hath eternal life; and I will raise him up at the last day. For my flesh is meat indeed and my blood is drink indeed. He that eateth my flesh, and drinketh my blood dwelleth in me, and I in him. As the living Father hath sent me, and I live by the Father; so he that eateth me even he shall live by me. This is that bread which came down from heaven; not as your fathers did eat manna and and are dead: he that eateth of this bread shall live forever. These things said Jesus in the synagogue as He taught in Capernaum. Many therefore of His disciples, when they had heard this, said, this is an hard saying; who can hear it? When Jesus knew in Himself that His disciples murmered at it, He said unto them, Doth this offend you? What and if ye shall see the son of man ascend up where He was before? It is the spirit that quickeneth; the flesh profiteth nothing; the words that I speak unto you, they are spirit, and they are life."

PRAISE.

Our Father we thank Thee that these words of Thy Son are indeed spirit and life by the Holy Spirit; and we thank Thee for the living power of Thy Word; and bless Thee that it is going forth in triumph through all the earth.

THANKS FOR THE CUP.

We give thanks for this cup, memorial of the blood that was shed for our redemption, precious blood, we are redeemed not with corruptible things, as with silver and gold, but with the precious blood of Jesus, as of a Lamb without spot or blemish. Precious blood, the blood that flowed for us on Calvary, the blood of Jesus, which through faith, hath caused the Fountain of Life to flow to sinful man all these nineteen centuries. We bless Thee for the River of God which has filled us with Thy Holy Spirit, who through Jesus' blessed sacrifice has come and brought blessing to all lands. We receive that blessing to-day in partaking of this cup. Let us take it, and realize that it is the emblem of Thyself the Vine for it is wine unfermented and pure and is for the refreshment of Thy Church. Thou art oh Christ, for us the Living Vine, and as we take this cup may we receive of Thee. Not only may we receive, but may we manifest that fact by living such lives as will make this Church a Living Power, as we tell the story of the redemption of spirit, soul and body, in all our future work for Thee, for Jesus' sake, Amen.

Distribution was made as before by the General Overseer saying, "The cup of blessing which we bless, is it not the communion of the Lord's blood? Drink ye all of it."

During the distribution of the wine to the people, he said:

"And they sang a new song saying. Thou art worthy to take the book, and to open the seals thereof: for thou wast slain and hast redeemed us to God by Thy blood out of every kindred, and tongue. and people, and nation.

And hast made us unto our God kings and priests: and we shall reign on the earth."

"Ye are redeemed not with corruptible things, as with silver and gold, but with the precious blood of Jesus, as of a Lamb without spot or blemish. Without the shedding of blood there is no remission of sins. If we walk in the Light as He is in the Light, we have fellowship one with anolher, and the blood of Jesus Christ, His Son, cleanseth us from all sin. The blood of Christ, who through the eternal Spirit offered Himself without spot to God, shall purge your conscience from dead works to serve the living God."

The ordinance was then closed by singing the hymn "At the Cross."

THE GENERAL OVERSEER'S CHARGE TO THE CHURCH.

INVOCATION.

Let the words of my mouth and the meditation of my heart be inspired by Thy Spirit, and be acceptable in Thy sight, and profitable unto these my brethern and sisters in fellowship now together in this Church, and to all to whom these words shall come, for the sake of Jesus, our Lord, our Strength and our Redeemer.

BASIS OF CHARGE.

I will read to you two portions of the second chapter of the Acts of the Apostles as the basis of this charge to the Christian Catholic Church, now present, and to all its members everywhere. I trust God will Himself inspire my comments thereupon, for which I cast myself upon Him, expecting the guidance of the Holy Spirit, through simple faith in Jesus Christ, in accordance with the will of God, our heavenly Father.

I call your attention first to the words contained in the second chapter of the Acts of the Apostles, following the sermon of the Apostle Peter, on the Day of Pentecost, the 41st verse, "Then they that gladly received His word were baptized, and the same day there were added unto them about three thousand souls."

Now that "*Unto them*" ought not be in the translation because you see the words are there in italics. I do not believe that they were merely "added unto them", I believe that they were first added "unto the Lord."

They "joined themselves to the Lord", and, therefore, we will read it as it ought to be, leaving out those words, "Then they that gladly received His word were baptized, and the same day there were added about three thousand souls."

WHAT DID THEY DO WHEN THEY WERE ADDED?

The forty-second to the forty-seventh verses give the reply.

"And they continued STEDFASTLY in the Apostles' Doctrine, and fellowship, and in breaking of bread, and in prayers.

And fear came upon every soul: and many wonders and signs were done by the Apostles. And all that believed were together, and had all things common. And sold their possessions and goods, and parted them to all men as every man had need. And they, continuing daily with one accord in the temple, and breaking bread from house to house, did eat their meat with gladness and singleness of heart.

Praising God and having favour with all the people. And the Lord added to the Church daily such as should be saved"; or, as the revised version, and the original reads, "And the Lord added together day by day those that were being saved."

I specially call your attention to the words,

"AND THEY CONTINUED STEDFASTLY IN THE APOSTLES' DOCTRINE AND FELLOWSHIP, AND IN BREAKING OF BREAD, AND IN PRAYERS."

Beloved in Christ, I feel to-day that in this upper room, we who are much more in number than the 120 in the upper room in Jerusalem on the Day of Pentecost, we who are the advance guard of this Christian Catholic Church, may well rejoice this day that we have been added to the Lord, and have come together in fellowship in His Name, to extend His kingdom and glory. I cannot therefore speak to you, and to our absent fellow members, and to the thousands who will follow them, from words more appropriate than those concerning the principles of action which guided the Church in the days of its Primitive Purity, Peace, and Power.

STEDFASTNESS IN APOSTOLIC DOCTRINE.

The first thing therefore is to remember, that we, if we are to be strong, are to "continue stedfast in the Apostles' Doctrine."

The doctrine of the first Apostles of Christ was simply the teaching of the Lord Jesus Christ. That Doctrine is mine.

Christ's teaching is not to be fully found in the Four Gospels, and especially His teaching as to the Organization of the Church. Very much had been added to the Gospels, in the remarkable period between Christ's Resurrection and Re-ascension, when for 40 days after He rose from the dead "He spoke to the apostles whom He had chosen of the things pertaining to the Kingdom of God."

He had explained to these men in His risen resurrection life as to how they were to organize and rule the Church, and as to what their position was in connection with His Church.

I feel that I should not be a faithful General Overseer of this Church, unless I lay down this first of all, that if you, my brothers and sisters, are to be strong in the Lord, and in the power of His might," and to be what I have prayed God you may be, or not be at all in existence, I say if you are to be a pure and powerful people, by which the Lord can do the same work that 19 centuries ago was done by and through the Primitive Church,

THEN YOU MUST BE STEDFAST IN HOLDING FAST TO APOSTOLIC TEACHING.

There is no reason why it ought not to be so, I see no reason why in these "Times of Restitution of all things," we should not claim the restoration of every Primitive Power, and ask God to make the Christian Catholic Church in Chicago a Church as full of the Holy Ghost as the Church was in Jerusalem long ago. (Amen.)

And full of the primitive powers and gifts that will make Chicago as it made Jerusalem, to know that Christ was Lord and God. (Amen.)

If that is to be so, let us understand that we must not only *receive* the Apostles' Doctrine, but we must *continue stedfastly* in the Apostles' Doctrine.

Hence it is my duty in this Church to lay before you some of the essential and fundamental requirements of the Apostles' Doctrine, for the first thing that the Holy Ghost impressed upon the Church was the necessity of following in the footsteps of their leaders whom God had called to the Apostolic Office.

REPENTANCE.

Now, beloved friends, the first principles of the gospel laid down by the Apostle Peter, under direct inspiration of the Holy Ghost, in answer to the cry of a conscience-stricken multitude who cried out, "Men and brethren, what shall we do?"

They saw the need to *do* something.

Whenever the heart of a sinful man is awakened to the consciousness of guilt, of separation from God, of violated law, and of impending penalty, doom and damnation, that heart cries out, stung to the quick with grief and shame and sorrow, "What shall I do?"

Now some one must give an authoritative reply, and the first portion of the answer of the Apostle Peter was *Repent.*

THEREFORE, THE FIRST PLANK IN APOSTOLIC DOCTRINE IS REPENTANCE.

It is the first word that must ring out from every pulpit of the Christian Catholic Church, and from my lips as Overseer of this Church, to a world dying in sin, will ever ring out the command, "*Repent!*" To Chicago that lifts itself like Capernaum to heaven, and that is in danger of being cast down into hell, I cry, and this Church must cry, "Repent!" Hell can be found to have a gate in every street, and the great multitudes of this city are flocking through these gates.

A terrible Hell burns in men's bosoms now, and even here the depths of infamy and horrible despair into which sin has plunged them are unspeakably horrible. A future Hell will only be a continuation and aggravation of that Hell in which they are now. Therefore we have to cry "Repent!" to a world in sin, that is in the power of hell, a world with lying tongues, with false lips, with unclean hearts, with diabolical passions run rife in every form. Murder stalks in every street. Crime, hypocricy and iniquity abound. The first word in Apostolic Doctrine is "Repent!"

REMEMBER THAT. IT IS ALSO THE BEGINNING OF THE GOSPEL.

Read with me the first words of the Gospel according to St. Mark:

"The beginning of the Gospel of Jesus Christ, the Son of God; As it is written in the Prophets: Behold I send my messenger before Thy face which shall declare Thy Way before Thee. The Voice of one crying in the wilderness, Prepare ye the way of the Lord, make His paths straight. John did baptize in the wilderness and preach the *Baptism of Repentance* for the remission of sins. And there went out unto him all the land of Judea, and they of Jerusalem, and were all baptized of him in the river of Jordan confessing their sins."

That is the beginning of the gospel, and, therefore, it is the first plank in the Apostles' Doctrine—Repent. The Primitive Church, was blessed by continuing to place Repentance toward God and man in the forefront of its Teaching.

The Christian Catholic Church, therefore, takes issue with the Protestant Churches which, as a whole, cry "Believe!" We shall first command men everywhere to Repent. (Amen.) Let him that stole steal no more, let him that lied lie no more, let him that is filthy be filthy no more, let him that is hypocritical be hypocritical no more.

IT IS THE FIRST PLANK IN CHRIST'S OWN TEACHING.

In the 14th and 15th verses of that first chapter of Mark of which chapter I have quoted the first portion, it is written, "Now after that John was put in prison, Jesus came into Galilee, preaching the gospel of the kingdom of God, and saying: The time is fulfilled, and the kingdom of God is at hand: Repent ye, and Believe the gospel." Repentance first, Faith next.

I scarce need say more; but if I would need any further proof I would call your attention to the whole of Christ's teaching in the Gospels which prove that the Divine Life begins with Repentance. He said: "I am not come to call the righteous but sinners to repentance." "Except ye repent ye shall all likewise perish." And as he sent the twelve and the seventies, two and two, before him into every place and city whither He Himself would go, he said, "As ye go say, Repent ye, for the kingdom of Heaven is at hand."

Let us preach, and by the grace of God, if need be, let us ourselves practice a True Repentance. (Amen.)

PERSONAL CHARGE.

If there is anything yet, beloved, wherein we have sinned, against wife or husband, or child or anyone, let us go and kneel at the feet of God and ask for grace to go humbly to our fellow man and say, Forgive me, I have sinned. Repentance! Repentance ! ! Repentance ! ! ! It is the Door of Salvation in Christ !

BAPTISM.

The very next thing that the Apostle Peter said after he said "Repent" was

"BE BAPTIZED EVERY ONE OF YOU

in the Name of Jesus for the remission of sins."

If a man repents and rests in Christ alone for Salvation, I believe he is saved. But Baptism is essential to a full Obedience and to the indwelling Power of the Holy Ghost in His fullness: for the Apostle adds to the Command a Promise, namely, "And ye shall receive the Gift of the Holy Ghost."

Now, beloved friends, the Apostolic Doctrine then teaches that

THE FIRST THING AFTER REPENTANCE IS OBEDIENCE.

You will notice that the Apostles very emphatically declare that the "Obedience of Faith" is the condition of receiving the Holy Ghost.

Take for instance the Apostolic Doctrine on that matter as set forth by the Apostles themselves a little later when they were brought before the Council which had conspired to crucify Christ. The story in told in the 5th chapter of Acts, verses 12 to 42. After great works were wrought through the Apostles, they were arrested and having been put in prison, from which they were brought forth by the angel of the Lord and commanded to speak in the Temple to the people the Words of Life. The cruel Council sent for the Apostles to the prison, and the messengers found the prison doors shut and no man within. While they were telling this to the Council other messengers came and said, "The men whom ye put in the prison are standing in the Temple and teaching the people." When they were again arrested and brought before the Council the high priest said, "Did we not straitly command you, that ye should not teach in this name? and behold ye have filled Jerusalem with your Doctrine."

How glad we are that we have that fact from the lips of the enemies of the Church and of the Apostles.

That is what we have got to do. We must fill Chicago with the Doctrine of Repentance toward God and Faith in the Lord Jesus Christ. We must declare to Jew and Gentile alike that they are guilty and damned and must repent and look to Christ alone. And we intend to bring "this Man's blood" upon every Jew in Chicago, and upon every Christian who rejects Christ, and make men everywhere to know that the blood of Christ is resting upon them by their rejection of Him.

Peter and the other Apostles answered and said,

"WE OUGHT TO OBEY GOD RATHER THAN MEN.

The God of our fathers raised up Jesus, whom ye slew and hanged on a tree. Him hath God exalted with His right hand for to be a Prince and a Saviour, for to give Repentance to Israel, and forgiveness of sins; and we are His witnesses of these things, and so is also

THE HOLY GHOST, WHOM GOD HATH GIVEN TO THEM THAT OBEY HIM.

REPENTANCE is to be followed by OBEDIENCE, by Baptism for the remission of sins, and that is followed by "Gift of the Holy Ghost."

That is Apostolic Doctrine

Now I want you to repeat the 31st and 32nd verses with me.

All present repeated after the General Overseer, these words:—"Him hath God exalted with His right hand to be a Prince and a Saviour for to give Repentance to Israel, and Forgiveness of sins; and we are Witnesses of these things and so also is the Holy Spirit whom God hath given to them that obey Him."

Brothers and Sisters have you, by the power of the Holy Ghost, repented? What do you say? (All answer Yes!) Are your sins forgiven? (All answer Yes sir!)

Very well. Now then listen. "And we are God's Witnesses of these things." We are to be Witnesses in Chicago of Repentance and of Forgiveness of sin, and of many other things that Christ is exalted to do. And the Holy Ghost is also a Real Witness. Beloved friends if we are the only Witnesses, if the Holy Ghost does not Witness for us and back up our Witness, Where shall we be?

But if the Holy Ghost comes with me to-morrow into the Auditorium and takes my feeble form and my feeble brain, and my feeble spirit, and my feeble words; and if He only gets full power within me, and if He takes possession of me, and gives me the power of God Himself then He will send those feeble words home to the hearts of the people with overwhelming power and the people will know that the Holy Ghost is there.

Now say that again. All repeat:—"And we are His witnesses of these things, and so also is the Holy Ghost whom God hath given to them that obey Him."

Beloved, I therefore say, with divinely imparted authority that Repentance, and the Obedience of Faith, in Baptism and all other Divine Commands, are the first two planks of Apostolic Doctrine.

FAITH IS OBEDIENCE, AND IT ENABLES THE CHURCH TO OBEY GOD IN EVERYTHING.

Faith does not merely say Lord, Lord; but does the things that He says. "Jesus said:—Why call ye me Lord, Lord and do not the things I say?" But the Faith that calls Him Lord in the power of the Spirit, goes and does these things.

Some of the things that God calls us to do and to endure seem to be absolute impossibilities.

Not long ago in this great and wicked city, when I was arrested there was not a single word that was being said in my favor excepting by a comparative few, principally of the dear ones round about me who loved me and had been healed through my agency. You were among these few hundreds, or several thousands at the most, but your voices were lost almost in the roar and the strife of our many adversaries in this great city. Every vile newspaper was crying, "Fraud cheat, impostor, liar, thief, convict, blasphemer, and every evil and false word that could be said. There was a combined attack made by the press, pulpit, police, doctors, drugs, devils, evil men of every kind. The great majority of good men and good women were deceived by the devil's lies, and many professed Christians were clamoring for my extinction, "Get him out, drive him forth," etc., was the cry which rang in the papers.

In the midst of all that some one said to me, "Doctor, I do not see how you are going to get through." I said, "I do not see either, but I am going to get through: for I have the Faith of God in my heart."

"Well, but Doctor, Doctor, exercise some sense in this thing. Do you not think you better give up this fight, or they will kill you sure?"

"Well", I said, "is that all they will do?" "That's all they can do, is it not?" I said, "When my big boy was a little boy, (who is sitting among you to my joy,) he was fond of reading Bunyan's Pilgrim's Progress, (and I would like my people to read that book, and study it; for it is one of the most delighful allegories, and all good men, women, and children love it). He had just come to the part where Christian and Faithful are persecuted in the City of Vanity, and by the people who ran Vanity Fair, which they denounced. At last they are put into prison, and eventually Faithful was put to death for the Name of Christ, and Christian barely escapes with his life and has to go forward on his journey alone. At that point I asked my little boy one day what he thought of Faithful dying for the name of Christ, and as to whether he or Christian had the best of it, and he replied, "Faithful had the best, papa, for he went the quickest way to heaven, did he not?"

"Well now", I said to my friend, "suppose they should kill me, I would get the quickest way to heaven, I should go there at once straight and they could not do me any harm.

But I do not believe they can kill me, I do not believe that all the devils in hell can kill me, and I do not believe that all the devils in Chicago can kill me."

"Well Doctor, "said my friend, "do you not see you are running your head against a stone wall."

I said, "Is it a stone wall? If so, what does the wall consist of?"

He said, "Well, there are the Mayor and the Council, and the newspapers, and the doctors, surgeons and druggists, and there are, as you say, your bad neighbors and the police and the city devils, and in short there is everything evil and powerful in Chicago against you. Isn't that a strong wall?"

I said, "It is not strong. It is weak as the devil: for it is only made out of the corruptions of devils' dirt. But I will tell you what God showed me to-day. I was reading this morning how God had spoken words of comfort to one of His ancient prophets, Ezekiel, when that prophet was cast down because the task that God set before him was so terrific that he quailed before it. He was sent to a rebellious people and he did not see how he could possibly succeed in his task. God then sent him this comforting assurance: 'Behold I have made thy face strong against their faces, and thy forehead strong against their foreheads. *As an Adamant harder than flint* have I made thy forehead: fear them not, neither be dismayed at their looks, though they be a rebellious house.' When I read that I said, 'O God, make my forehead as an adamant *harder than flint*, for there is a wall and you tell me I am to go through it, and I am going through it.' " (Laughter and applause.)

I met my friend a few months later when all our Victories had been won, and he said, "Doctor, you went through that wall baldheaded." And I said, "Yes, look at my head; see how it shines." (Laughter:) I went through. I went on on through, but it was because I obeyed God, and Obedience is Faith.

Now, beloved friends, take the simple analogy.

Here we are, and we are called upon to "obey God rather than man," vile men who sometimes get diabolical wickedness framed into so-called ordinances or laws. There are laws passed that are not laws in any sense, such as the Ordinance of the City of Chicago which we fought and proved upon appeal to be a violation of law and to be unconstitutional. It was so declared by the Supreme Court, but if it had not been so declared it would have been so all the same: for the Lord Jesus Christ had bidden us to go forth and teach and pray and lay hands in His Name upon the sick, and they should be healed. And we are doing it, and we intend to do it, and we shall continue to do it, and we shall teach and we shall preach, and we shall practice a Full Gospel, and we shall live, and if need be, beloved friends, we shall die: for we must obey God rather than man, come what will. (Applause.) (Amen.)

Oh, if God should call us to the glory of a martyr's crown! What a joy and honor! But, beloved friends, I have begun to think it might be best for the martyr's crown to be held back for twenty years. Sometimes I think I would like to fight this battle for twenty years. I don't know how long God will give me breath to live here, but I want to say that I desire to see the Christian Catholic Church, organized this day, spread o'er all the earth, and the Apostolic Doctrine, Repentance and Obedience of Faith, which brings forgiveness of sins, the healing of sickness, and the sanctification of the believer, spirit, soul and body, established from pole to pole in every nation under heaven.

There are a great many other things too in connection with the Apostolic Doctrine, such as the

COMMUNION OF THE LORD'S TABLE IN THE BREAKING OF BREAD.

Beloved friends, I believe that we have not sufficiently realized the glorious privilege of that Ordinance of which we have just partaken.

It is not like the Ordinance of Believer's Baptism, for that can only be once properly administered; but this Ordinance is the continuous feast of the broken sinless body and of the sacred blood of the Lord Jesus. It is the occasion and emblem of Unity. We love to meet together and break this bread and drink this wine and to feel the fellowship of love; and we shall also invite on ordinary occasions in this Christian Catholic Church, not only those that are in immediate fellowship with us, but all God's children, that they may come to their Father's Table, to their Lord's Table, and may rejoice in that Communion, by the Holy Spirit of a Saviour, who is a Real Presence with us alway. But there are times when we must break this bread together as a little company like that 120 when they met in the upper room, and to-day was one of those seasons, sacred to our immediate family.

"They continued stedfastly," not only "in the Apostles' Doctrine" but in their fellowship.

THE APOSTOLIC FELLOWSHIP.

I make no claim to be an Apostle.

Brother Calverly, and many of you in our Conference, and many of my brethren elsewhere have for many years been kind enough to say that Apostolic grace rested upon me. But, if it is so, I do not feel that I dare assume that title or office, and it is not for me at this time to say more than this, that standing as a teacher, standing as a prophet, if you will, I speak to you to-day, and ask you to pray for manifested Apostolic "Fellowship."

I have some of the signs of a Prophet and I know I am a Teacher. The signs of a prophet are set forth by Jesus in the ninth beatitude; "Blessed are ye when men shall revile you and shall persecute you and shall say all manner of evil against you falsely for my sake. Rejoice and be exceeding glad for great is your reward in heaven for so persecuted they the prophets that were before you." Now I think I have had the ninth beatitude for some time, have I not? (Laughter.) And I suppose I may claim therefore to have the signs of a prophet. If there is any malicious invention that they could say against me and did not say it, Joseph Medill of the Chicago Tribune, Joseph Dunlop of the Chicago Dispatch did not know it. But the latter has already been sentenced to pay $2000 fine and to two years' imprisonment for his obscenity in that filthy sheet. This is God's judgment, and, before all Chicago, it is my vindication. (Applause.) God is in the heavens. It is Joseph Dunlop to-day, and it is Joseph Medill on an early to-morrow. Remember I said it; for it will happen just as surely as Dunlop's punishment which I told you would come.

Now, if I were an Apostle to-day, I should desire not merely to teach you Doctrine, but to make you to know that I am in Fellowship with you, and am very really your fellow servant. I am a servant of the servants of God.

Oh how sweet is that word "Fellowship." I want to be in

"FELLOWSHIP" WITH THE LITTLE CHILDREN.

I want them to feel that the General Overseer of their Church loves them, and I want them to feel, in all your homes, that they have now entered into "fellowship" with me. Tell them that I love them, that we all love them, that every member of the Christian Catholic Church loves them, and above all God loves them. I want them all to know that as Christ's servant I love them from the smallest to the largest, from the steadiest to the wayward one that is not very steady, and that I want them to feel that they are in fellowship with me.

I want you all to feel that my time, my talents, the money with which I am entrusted and all the power I can exert for good shall be employed to bring you into, 'Fellowship" with God, and into Fellowship with me. I believe that I can truly say that "our fellowship is with the Father and with His Son Jesus Christ."

Brothers and sisters I am going to give that word Fellowship a very wide meaning before we get through.

I want that you and I shall enter into.

FELLOWSHIP OF SERVICE FOR CHRIST.

That you will follow me when I shall take from amongst you Seventies to go from house to house throughout Chicago, I am going to have you carefully trained, and will ask you to help train yourselves for Christ's service, by searching the Word, by knowing the best means of approaching men, and by knowing how to pray and speak the Word of God so that you may go out two and two and help men to find God. I not only want that, but I want

FELLOWSHIP IN ALL THE GREAT SWEEP OF A GREAT CHURCH'S WORK.

I want fellowship in the visitation of our brothers and sisters and especially when sick and sorrowing. "Brethren if a man be overtaken in a fault, ye which are spiritual restore such an one in the spirit of meekness; considering thyself lest thou also be tempted." Jesus said, "What man of you having a hundred sheep if he lose one of them, doth not leave the ninety and nine in the wilderness, and go after that which is lost, until he find it. ?" We have to go after that erring brother or sister who has got among the sinful, for that brother may have lost his way by a wicked woman, or that woman may have erred because of some wicked man. Go and seek them, and let me help you in seeking them until we find them, and bring them back into the Fold of God. We are never to fail to seek the sheep that goes astray, and the fellowship must extend to our necessities. Is there one amongst us that has become poor, then let us have the Fellowship of Love in helping the poor. The man that is honest and wants to work is sometimes suddenly struck down, in some way that prevents his being able to win bread for his dear ones.

Let us go to him, let us help him, let us pray till he is healed, and let us leave good things in that home, and let there be no lack in these matters. Let us relieve all that we are able to relieve. We must part with some of our own bread if need be, to give bread to others, and we must do without a second coat, if it is needful to give clothing to another. We cannot afford to let our brother lose heart or starve: for how could we do so and face the Great White Throne and Christ thereon on the Judgment Day?

Listen. This is Apostolic Doctrine. "Do good unto all men

as ye have opportunity; but chiefly unto those that are of the Household of Faith."

I see a great deal of evangelization going on for the heathen in distant lands, and I do not complain of that; but the evangelization of the heathen in Africa and Asia for which many are pouring out talents and money is not our first duty, and I see a great deal of neglect of our own sick poor in Chicago. (Applause.) Mothers that have toiled until they can toil no more are left to die of starvation. Not one of you must get into trouble and not let me know. I may not be able personally to go to you, but I have many hands and many feet, and I can send some one if I cannot go myself. I can also go there with my messenger in prayer. I can say "Go there and pray at such a time" and I will be there in spirit. And God hears and answers. We must have a Fellowship of help, money, counsel, and very many other things.

Fellowship with Christ, with the Apostles, and with me, fellowship means that we shall "love one another."

THE CHURCH MUST HAVE A BUSINESS FELLOWSHIP—A FELLOWSHIP IN GETTING MONEY, IN SAVING MONEY, AND IN SPENDING MONEY FOR CHRIST.

Come what will, God helping me, I will spread the truth in these matters. (Applause).

I see in this land, and in all lands, that by means of wicked legislation, and by means of unscrupulous men in the highest places, that there are a favored few who by fraud and falsehood are enabled to acquire many millions, sometimes fifty millions and a hundred millions of dollars, and in one form or another it is stolen out of the earnings of the poor many of whom are at this moment starving to death.

Now I read in my Bible that the Lord Jesus Christ said once: "One is your master even Christ, and all ye are brethren." Say these words. (All repeat them.) "All ye are brethren."

Then the rich man is my brother, then the cultivated man is my brother, if he is a Christian. Now I propose to tell the Christian Catholic Church everywhere that these words must find practical expression. Are you a manufacturer? Yes. Are you rich? Yes. All right then, we need you in Zion. What do you want? Well I want you to bring capital, I want you to bring your machinery, want you to buy up land bye and bye in our Zion, and I want you to stay there and settle there, and use your money, skill, and organizing faculty to build up factories, workshops and stores, on a co-operative basis. I want to see in Zion a condition of things that will enable all who can work to find remunerative work right there.

Do we not all wear boots? I think we do, don't we? I am glad to see you have all got shoes to wear. Don't we all wear coats? Don't we all wear shirts, etc, etc,? Yes. Now there are thousands of us, and I want to know why we cannot make our own boots? I am told there are likely to be soon three thousand members of this church in Chicago alone, and reckoning a family of say four with each that would be a community of 12,000 at once. I want to know why we cannot have a Zion Co-operative Boot Factory. I do not see any reason against it do you? Very well, then I want 10 per cent. of all the profit of that factory for Zion's funds, I want a sufficient return to be given to those who furnish the capital, and I want all the balance of the profit to be divided amongst the workmen in proportion to their salaries.

Now, I want to know whether we who do not drink whisky, and do not drink beer and do not use tobacco, and who do live sober, frugal, temperate and industrious Christian lives, men and women who have strong hands and stout hearts, whether we cannot build up Co-operative Factories and have Fellowship together in Business. How delightful to have a factory where God is honored, and where, when the bell rings in the morning the first thing is "We're Marching to Zion" or some other of the Songs of Zion. Wouldn't that be nice to hear that in the factories? "Beautiful, beautiful Zion, we're marching upward to Zion, the beautiful city of God." It would be nice to have that, and at dinner time to have the boys gather and talk about Zion and the good things of God and man. Can we not have fellowship in Service for Christ, mean Fellowship in Business for Christ? (Yes sir.)

Now that does not mean that everybody is to get the same wages. That is quite another thing. One man is worth a dollar, and there is another who is worth two and there are others who are worth three, four and five; and there is another that is not worth a red cent.

He is lazy or careless and incompetent. There is something wrong with him. We do not propose to starve that man, we shall help him all we can; but I do propose to prod him a little. (Laughter.) And I propose to see whether that man cannot work for his wages, and work so as to improve and get better wages.

I tell you frankly I do not believe in Uniformity of Wages, and I do not believe there is such a thing as Uniformity of Capacity or of Merit. I do not believe God Almighty intended we should all be alike.

I have heard a good many people say we shall all be alike in heaven; but I defy you to find that in the Bible. I have heard people say "as like as two peas in a pod." But I defy you to find two peas in a pod that are just alike. They are all different in size, or in weight, or in shape, every one of them.

Now God has given us great variety, and I propose that we shall cultivate genius by rewarding it. But I will tell you this, the man who gets the most will have to pay the most, because he will have to give 10 per cent. to Zion at least, and that is the lowest. Did you not all agree to give ten per cent., of all we received this year to the Lord? (Yes sir.) Do you mean to keep that vow? (Yes sir.) Then in addition to the ten per cent. of our earnings we have got to give him ten per cent. of our time in spreading the gospel of salvation and healing and holiness through the world. We have got to begin at Chicago and keep pegging away. Let us not only give "tithes" but "offerings', to God's work.

Beloved friends, we are asking God to help us to establish a Christian community upon a sensible and wise business basis, because that is Apostolic Doctrine.

IN PRAYERS.

"Continue steadfastly in the Apostolic Doctrine and fellowship, in breaking of bread, and in *prayers*."

The key to the whole situation is in "prayers."

Oh, my people listen:

If I can teach by the grace of God ten thousand men, a hundred thousand men and women, a million men and women and children to pray "the prayer of faith that saves the sick," the prayer of faith that reaches God and comes down in immediate blessing, what a power that will be in the emancipation of the world, from the slavery, of sin and disease and death and hell, and devils. There is the secret of Power, to know how to pray. That early church was a church of spiritual giants, because they knew how to pray, they knew how to reach God. They touched the springs of Eternal Power every time they prayed. They touched the dynamos in heaven by the wire of prayer, and the heavenly powers came down that drove sin and disease and death and hell before them like chaff before the wind. Friends we need that spirit, we need prayer, prayer, and this Church must be a praying church, a praying church. I think that in our all night prayer meeting at the opening of this year, we learned some lessons about how to pray. One minister of God, who was present, said to me, "Doctor, there was more prayer packed into that meeting inside of two hours than I believe has been put into all the churches in this city in ten years, I believe," he said, "that every prayer went straight to God in heaven". I know not. God alone knows. But we prayed and God answered gloriously.

I CHARGE THE CHRISTIAN CATHOLIC CHURCH TO "CONTINUE STEDFASTLY."

You know there are various ways the devil has of making people give up. Here is Dr. Speicher here. Now, Dr. Speicher, hold on to that chair. (With that Dr. Dowie tried in every way possible to get Dr. Speicher off the chair on which he sat, but was unsuccessful.) Now then the Doctor was stedfast, you see. I did not rehearse that scene at all; I tried to tickle him, and he would not be tickled. But you see the Doctor was steadfast; he knew what I was after, and he held on to that chair. Now won't you be steadfast? Sometimes the devil comes along and he tickles you, and you will let go. There are some people who can't hold on when they are tickled; they let go their hold. There comes along a flatterer, and he says to a young Christian woman, "You are the loveliest creature that ever lived." He is a liar, or if he is not a liar he is a fool. Mrs. Dowie here is very lovely, but I never told her she was the loveliest creature in all the world. I do not believe she would have believed me if I had, and I was not going to lie even to please her. In my eyes she might be the loveliest in the world, and she is; and I have never seen any woman that I cared for so much as I do for her, and I am thankful to God for that. (Applause.)

I love to see husbands think that their wives are just the nicest wives in the world, and their children just the nicest children in the world, and their friends just the nicest friends, and when they are in Fellowship that their pastor is just the best pastor. I want you to feel that way, and stedfastly to believe that the Christian Catholic Church is just the best and nicest Church in the world, and that it shall prove worthy of all our love next to Christ Himself.

Be stedfast. Don't be fooled. Don't let the world win you away from the Church with its offers of money, with its pleasures, with its engagements. When any one comes to visit you on the Lord's Day you have got to be stedfast in the Apostles' Doctrine. It says you are

"NOT TO FORSAKE THE ASSEMBLING OF YOURSELVES TOGETHER."

When company comes on the Sabbath Day, and you know it is time to go to the Church, or to some other Christian work you may be engaged in, do not say, "I can't leave these dear friends," do not neglect duty for the purpose of pleasing men. Perform your duty, and exercise your privileges, no matter who comes. Say "I am going to the House of God," and do not let anybody flatter you or fool you, but go to the House of God. Be honest, be stedfast.

DANGERS AHEAD.

I believe in ten years, if God spares my life, and if we are Faithful, that I shall be at the head, if I continue to be the General Overseer of the Christian Catholic Church, of the strongest and wealthiest Church that the world has ever seen. I believe that. (Applause.) That is a great deal to say.

But just there will come the danger, just there.

John Wesley foresaw it, and he said words in effect as follows: My people now are poor, but I foresee the day when they will be rich, and I fear that when that day comes they will forget God and will place men of wealth in positions of power in the Society, and they will consider elegance and learning more than piety. When that day comes on Ichabod close the doors of the Methodist Society, for the glory will have departed.

That day has come. Men of the world are made Trustees in the Methodist Episcopal Church, and one of these was permitted by his minister to occupy a Methodist Church pulpit, during the World's Fair, that he might plead that the Fair should be open on the Sabbath, and so break one of the Ten Commandments. That was done in a Methodist Church in this city, and the man who was a Trustee and made that speech does not even profess to be a converted Christian. Now that is the condition of the Methodist Church to-day. Wealth and Free Masonry and things of that kind rule many portions of it, and the Holy Spirit is grieved. I tell you that if we do not obey God our very prosperity will be our curse.

EXHORTATIONS.

Listen. Brothers, work and get all you can, not forgetting to reserve a portion of your time for God and your family and your spiritual culture. Give all you can. If you can make ten thousand dollars or a hundred thousand dollars honestly, get it. Save all you can. But give to God and His Church, richly, fully, freely, that millions may be won to Christ. Continue to develop your business; but, in the name of God, give all you can.

Give, and see ere you leave this earth that what God has given to you is put into His work in such permanent forms, in such places, and in such ways that a multitude will go forth as a result of your labors, your faithful prayers, your loving toil. But God forbid that we should grow up to be rich and say, "I have need of nothing," and know not that in God's sight we would then be "miserable and poor and blind and naked."

Brothers, prosperity is a glorious thing if a man uses it for God; but prosperity, even in the Church, as well as in the world, is an unmitigated curse if it means that a man's heart shall be lifted up with pride and if he shall say like Nebuchadnezzar, "This is great Babylon that I have built."

I HOPE TO BUILD A LITTLE CITY TO BE CALLED ZION,

and hope some day to stand upon the dome of a Zion Temple to hold from 10,000 to 20,000 persons, and I hope one day to look abroad over that lovely city and to bring visitors to look upon its beauties, its Homes, Colleges, Schools, etc., and say "This is Zion." But should I stand there with snow white hair, and perhaps with bent back, aged and nearing the end, may I never say, "This is Zion that I have built," but say, as I do to-day, as we start out upon this enterprise, "This is Zion that God has built." (Amen.)

Oh, Friends of Jesus, like our Lord we have no continuing city on earth, but we seek "a City whose builder and maker is God," and into that city we seek to bring sinners saved by Grace from the streets of these cities, from the highways, yea, and the Dark Continents, for ere long I trust away out shall this work stretch into Africa and Asia.

Friends of Jesus, we are seeking to bring from the east and from the west and from the north and from the south a multitude who shall be saved, and healed, and cleansed, and quickened, who shall all sweep on with us, generation after generation, following us in at the beautiful gate of the City of God, the Heavenly Zion.

I want to work with you and your children, and my children, and then I want to pass away, and as the pilgrims come out from all the lands I want to be allowed, if God will let me, to see them come in vast numbers from all the lands, whither our Zion has gone.

Beloved, the day is far spent, the night is at hand, tomorrow is the Lord's Day, and a day of toil is before me, a day of blessed toil; but I could not resist the great joy of telling you some of the things that are in my heart, and of foreshadowing some of the glorious things that I see in the future.

FORESHADOWINGS.

Brothers and sisters, we will pass through great persecutions; we will be tested; we will be tried; we will be abused; we will be passed through the fire; and, because we are gold, God will not permit us to be otherwise than severely tested and tried. But we will go out from these trials purer, we will go out for God. We will walk together in the ways of the Lord, and multitudes shall "ask the way to Zion with their faces thitherward." And they shall inquire the way to Zion from all the lands, yea, they are doing it already.

I MUST NOW CONSTITUTE THIS CHURCH IN THE NAME OF THE LORD.

All present will please to stand. (All stood.) Brothers and sisters, listen.

I CHARGE YOU IN THE SIGHT OF GOD

who preserveth all things that live, and before Jesus Christ, who before Pontius Pilate witnessed the Good Confession, that you keep this Commandment: "Follow after Righteousness, Godliness, Faith, Hope, Love, Patience, Humility and Purity in all things, be faithful to God unto death, continuing stedfastly in the Apostolic Doctrine and fellowship, in the breaking of bread and in prayers; follow Christ fully. I charge you in the Name of the Father and of the Son and of the Holy Ghost.

QUESTIONS.

I ask you in the name of the Lord Jesus Christ, do you promise to obey this Charge as God enables you? Can you say, I do? (All answer, I do.)

PRAYER OF CONSECRATION.

Then kneel and pray with me.

(All kneel whilst the General Overseer uttered this prayer, which the Church repeated after him):

Our God and Father, in Jesus' Name we come to Thee, believing that we are, and that we shall be kept in the Fellowship and in the Love of God, our Father, of God the Son, and of God the Holy Ghost. Give unto us grace to keep us unspotted from the world, united in heart, in tender sympathy, in earnest work for Thy Church, and for the salvation and healing and cleansing and the blessing of multitudes in this city and land and throughout the world, and in the generations to come. Make us faithful as fathers, as mothers, as sons, as daughters, as brethren, as sisters, compassionate, wise, prudent, patient, faithful, loving, true, tender, pure in heart, like unto Jesus, by the power of Thy Spirit. And wherein we differ, let us differ in love from our brothers and sisters in Christ who are in other parts of Thy fold, and bring Thy people into unity that there may be one fold, one flock, with Jesus Christ Thy Son as our One Shepherd.

Give unto Thy servant, the General Overseer of this Church, the grace he needs; keep him humble, faithful, pure, hopeful, loving, wise, and give him the strength in spirit, soul and body that he requires for this work, for Jesus' sake. Amen.

SILENT CONSECRATION.

Still remain on your knees. Let there be silent prayer for needed grace.

DECLARATION OF THE CONSTITUTION OF THE CHURCH.

Admidst profound silence, the General Overseer spoke as follows:

In the Name of the Lord Jesus, in the power of the Holy Spirit, and in accordance with the will of God, our heavenly Father, I believe, and believing that I am thereunto called as the General Overseer of this flock, not only in this place but in all the cities and villages and states and countries where persons have applied or shall apply for fellowship, do now constitute this Church as a gathering of believers under the title of the Christian Catholic Church. I pray that all ye who are now gathered and all who shall yet gather into this Church shall fulfill the great design of our Lord and Saviour, that we may be One as He with the Father is One, and with the Eternal Spirit, that we may be One in Him. May this Church be divinely endowed with the nine Gifts of the Holy Ghost, with the word of Wisdom, the word of Knowledge, Faith, Gifts of Healings, Workings of Miracles, Prophecy, Discernings of Spirits, Divers kinds of Tongues and Interpretation of Tongues, and with that gift of Love which is the crown of all, that precious gift which enables the Church to fulfill all. Oh with that love let these gifts be exercised and this Church go on to the glory of God, the Father, in the Name of the Lord Jesus Christ, and by the power of the Holy Spirit.

Let all the people say Amen. (Amen.)

The hymn, "ONWARD, CHRISTIAN SOLDIERS," was then sung.

"Onward, Christian soldiers,
Marching as to war,
With the Cross of Jesus
Going on before
Christ, the royal Master,
Leads against the foe;
Forward into battle,
See, His banners go.

CHO.—Onward, Christian soldiers,
Marching as to war,
With the Cross of Jesus,
Going on before

Like a mighty army;
Moves the Church of God;
Brothers, we are treading
Where the saints have trod.
We are not divided,
All one body we,
One in hope and doctrine,
One in charity.

Crowns and thrones may perish
Kingdoms rise and wane,
But the Church of Jesus
Constant will remain.
Gates of hell can never
'Gainst that Church prevail;
We have Christ's own promise,
And that cannot fail.

Onward then, ye faithful,
Join our happy throng,
Blend with ours your voices,
In the triumph-song:
Glory, laud, and honor,
Unto Christ the King:
This, thro' countless ages,
Men and angels sing."

(A telegram is handed to Dr. Dowie asking him to pray.)

A telegram has just come from Minnesota asking for prayer. Bow your heads a moment: "Father in heaven for Jesus' sake, by Thy Holy Syirit, bless these dear ones that have asked us to pray for them. Amen."

The General Overseer then pronounced the following

BENEDICTION:

"Beloved, abstain from all appearance of evil. And the very God of Peace Himself sanctify you wholly; and I pray God your whole Spirit, and Soul, and Body, be preserved entire without blame, unto the coming of our Lord Jesus Christ. Faithful is He that calleth you, who also will do it. The Grace of our Lord Jesus, the Love of God, the Eternal Father, the fellowship of the Holy Ghost, the Eternal Comforter, one Eternal God, abide in you, bless you, keep you, and all the Israel of God everywhere, forever. Amen.

"We have thought of Thy loving kindness, O God, in the midst of Thy temple.

According to Thy name, O God, so is Thy praise unto the ends of the earth: Thy right hand is full of righteousness.

Let Mount Zion rejoice, let the daughters of Judah be glad, because of Thy judgments.

Walk about Zion, and go round about her: tell the towers thereof,

Mark ye well her bulwarks, consider her palaces; that ye may tell it to the generation following.

For this God is our God for ever and ever: He will be our guide even unto death."

Special Conference of Officers of the Christian Catholic Church in Zion

Principally Concerning the Organization of the Church on an Apostolic Foundation

REPORTED BY O. L. S. AND A. W. N.

THESE are glorious, terrible times.

It is a glorious privilege to be alive in the "Times of Restoration of All Things, whereof God spake by the mouth of His Holy Prophets which have been since the world began," but it involves a terrible responsibility.

The Age is hastening to its Consummation.

The light of the dawning of the Millennial Glory is already glowing in the eastern sky.

The darkness that covered the earth, and the gross darkness that enveloped the peoples, is fleeing away before the brightness of that rising.

The Voice of the Prophet of these Times has been ringing throughout the earth, waking men, institutions, and nations from their lethargy.

Multitudes are in the Valley of Decision.

But they cannot remain there long; for the time grows short.

Lines are being drawn more and more closely.

Events of eternal importance crowd upon one another's heels.

The valleys are being exalted and the mountains and hills made low.

The crooked is being made straight and the rough places plain.

The Glory of Jehovah is being revealed.

"Behold the Bridegroom cometh."

The Lord is at hand.

The final preparations for the ushering in of the Day of Jehovah—the Thousand Years—are being rapidly made.

There has been no event of greater importance in these Times than the Special Conferences of the Ordained Officers of the Christian Catholic Church in Zion held in Shiloh Tabernacle during Zion's Fourth Feast of Tabernacles in Zion City.

These were held on Wednesday, July 20th, Saturday, July 23d, and Monday, July 25, 1904, and were attended by hundreds of most intensely earnest, thoughtful and prayerful men and women who had been set aside for the ministry of God in this Church.

The subject of these three Conferences was one which was of the most vital and far-reaching importance in connection with the work of the Restoration of All Things; for it dealt with the Restoration of the true Church of God to its primitive Pattern and Power.

Hour after hour was spent in the freest and fullest discussion of all the phases of the momentous questions of the perpetuity of the Apostolic Office in the Church, the fulness and fitness of the present time for the reaffirmation of that Truth, and the Apostolic Commission of John Alexander Dowie, the General Overseer of the Church, already Divinely approved as the Prophet foretold by Moses, the Messenger of God's Covenant, Elijah the Restorer.

It is a noteworthy fact that after the most careful consideration of all the grave issues involved, the officers present, with absolute unanimity answered both these questions in the affirmative.

This conclusion was reached, not only upon Scriptural and historical grounds, and from the known facts, but from a deep conviction of the leading of the Holy Spirit.

Every moment of the many hours spent together seemed to be a season of the most precious and powerful indwelling of that Divine Interpreter, who alone can reveal to man's spirit the hidden riches of the Truth of God.

God has promised most wonderful blessings and victories to His Church in the Last Days, when it has been restored to its proper Foundation.

These blessings and victories will hasten the Coming of the King.

Shiloh Tabernacle, Zion City, Illinois, Wednesday Forenoon, July 20, 1904.

The meeting was opened with Overseer Speicher in the Chair, awaiting the arrival of the General Overseer.

Several hymns were sung.

The Overseer then called for a season of prayer, many of the officers praying most fervently.

The Overseer discussed matters of interest in connection with the meetings of the Feast of Tabernacles, commented upon the presence of some persons of note in attendance at the meetings, and spoke of the work of the Church in foreign fields.

A second season of prayer was then entered into, many of the officers uttering most earnest prayer.

The General Overseer then took the Chair, and led in the recital of the 23d Psalm.

He then prayed as follows:

OPENING PRAYER.

Grant unto us, our Father, that we may realize within all our spirits the guardian care of our Shepherd King; for we are journeying on; and it may be that ere we meet again in a year from now, some of us will have gone down into the valley which looks so dark to those that are not there; and we shall find the word true, "Thou art with me;" and there will be no dark valley.

Meanwhile, therefore, let us realize that we who minister to others must ourselves realize Thy saving, healing, guiding grace; that we who are under-shepherds, may realize the Supremely-tender Shepherd's care. When the day comes that we can no longer care for others, may we cross over the river, and pass up into that City where there shall be no more weakness, no more pain, and no more trouble. Meanwhile, give us grace in this Conference to be of some use to Thy people in all the world. For Jesus' sake. Amen.

General Overseer's Opening Address.

My brethren, I am always glad to meet you as you come up to the Feast from year to year.

The details of the administration of all the Branches and Departments of the Church have been conducted during my absence by Overseer Speicher, the Acting General Ecclesiastical Secretary, and by my large staff.

The business of the General Overseer has been done, I am informed, in a satisfactory way. I hope all the Officers present think so.

OFFICERS—"Yes."

GENERAL OVERSEER—I am sure you all are pleased to recognize, with me, the great ability and capacity which Dr. Speicher has shown as the Overseer-in-charge, and I hope you will all be willing to say Yes to that.

OFFICERS—"Yes."

GENERAL OVERSEER—I find that the good opinion of the people concerning the Overseer is so great that I am not quite sure but that if I went away for a long time it might not be all right. [Overseer Speicher groaned. Laughter.]

I have always had the conviction, and always will have it, that Jehovah has established Zion; and that, no matter whether I, whom God used in the establishment of it, am removed or not, the Christian Catholic Church in Zion will go on.

OFFICERS—"Amen."

The Beginnings of the Church.

GENERAL OVERSEER—Zion has come to stay! The Christian Catholic Church is not the ephemeral growth of a day, although it is only since 1896, about eight and a half years, that the Church has been in existence.

It is wonderful to think that four hundred fifty members, none of them particularly distinguished, should gather around me.

I was the only ordained officer who convened the assembly, and no other was recognized, or could be recognized, until the *Ecclesia* (the Church) was formed.

It seemed a very daring thing to many for me to assume the title of General Overseer when there was so little to see over. [Laughter.]

The Little Wooden Hut.

But I saw a great deal ahead, and I was strong enough to stand the sneers of a Methodist Episcopal Presiding Elder, who one day said that he would give five hundred dollars to put Dr. Dowie in prison and keep him there.

"Why?" he was asked; but he could not tell. At the same time, he talked with the most bitter contempt regarding Zion. "Pooh!" he said. "Its Tabernacle is only a Little Wooden Hut! That's all there is to it!"

What Hath God Wrought?

That "little wooden hut" proved to be the birthplace of a Mighty Movement that is startling all the lands.

The Apostate Churches are everywhere afraid of us; and the paper defenders of monarchies are, in London at least, deeply moved. I smiled a good deal at their agitation, for I had not thought that the British Throne was in such a weak condtion as to be shaken to its foundations by a few words.

It depends, apparently, upon who says the word.

The power of what we said was that it came from the lips of one who claimed that he had the right to speak in the Name of Jehovah, as the Prophet of the Restoration. The enemies of God felt that, but did not like to acknowledge it.

Around-the-World Visitation Leads to an Important Determination.

Now, brethren, I am glad that I made this Reconnaissance Around-the-World; for, among other results, there has come the Divinely-inspired determination to proceed with the fuller Organization of the Church, in view of the terrible, world-wide Apostasies, and the effects of this Apostasy on the Nations.

Never forget the Organization addresses that were delivered before the Church was formed in 1896, and the Principles laid down at that time.

It was impossible, I say, treading a path which had never been trod before, to know just how the Church could be so formed, as to be, first Christian—absolutely obedient to God, in the Christ; and second, have it so broadly Catholic as to leave room for all who, while holding different opinions on minor matters, longed to get together upon fundamentals, and yet have a powerful, active, and effective organization.

I believe the only Organization that can ever be a close and thorough one is one where there is mentally and spiritually a large Liberty.

Zion Is Organized Liberty.

I realize, brethren, that God has called us unto Liberty; only this Liberty must never be used for a cloak for any wrong.

God has called us to Unity. It is my conviction that Zion is organized liberty.

Now get that thought deeply impressed upon your mind, that the Christian Catholic Church in Zion is Organized Christian Liberty.

But, with all this Liberty, I hope that we have no one in our communion who fails to realize that we must have "In things essential, Unity; in things non-essential, Liberty; and, in all things, Charity."

Now, a Unity without Love and Liberty is simply devilry. I cannot think of any other word for it. I want you to see my heart in this matter. Unity of religious thought, upon even a perfectly sound basis, that does not fulfil the Law of Love in every possible, pure, and practical form toward one another and toward all men, is a heartless and base thing.

A unity that can be maintained only by punishing our brothers with a theological lash is not worth having. I warn you all, my brethren in the ministry, that the principles of Christian Unity will never be conserved by the lash.

It is the last thing to use, for the "whip of small cords" used by our Lord and Master upon the backs of those who w the enemies of God, in the Temple at Jerusalem, not upon backs of the children of God.

Our Love must extend to those who do not realize what fundamental principles of unity really are.

We cannot, for instance, allow any one to trifle for a sir moment with the principle of the general Infallibility of Scriptures; and yet at the same time we cannot allow any on define the Infallibility and Inspiration of the Scriptures as rule of faith and practice in such a way as to destroy liberty.

The Prophetic Office in Zion.

When my Declaration of June 2, 1901, as Elijah the Resto was made in the Chicago Auditorium, the Holy Spirit witnes for me in the spirits of that vast audience; and that Decl tion gave expression to no more than what had been the c viction of my people for a long, long time. I think you agree to that.

OFFICERS—"Amen!"

GENERAL OVERSEER—I ask you, has the Holy Spirit contin to witness?

OFFICERS—"He has!"

GENERAL OVERSEER—Because, if He has not, I should co that man my friend who would rise and show me that He not.

No one could better prove his friendship for me than showing that the Holy Spirit is not witnessing to my proph office, if it is not true that He is.

Because, if it is not true, my Declaration must be w drawn and I must go no further.

But in the absence of such proof, I cannot stand still.

Zion must go forward.

The Apostolic Office.

I say now that we must pray very earnestly that God r hasten the day when the organization of the Church shal perfected by the filling of its highest office—the Apostolic.

I do not want to go before the Lord.

I want the Lord to go before me.

But the Christian Catholic Church has only a stop- officer in the General Overseer; he is only a Divinely-C missioned stop-gap for a whole College of Apostles.

I am convinced that we had better get to God in earr prayer, to hasten the day when He shall call out of the Chu those who have been called by the Holy Spirit to the Office Apostle.

The time is coming when no one living man can b the burden that I bear now as General Overseer.

The day has come when the General Overseer himself m see that the Church, ere his departure—should he be cal away before the Rapture, or, whether he tarry till the L come—gets back to the Foundation set forth in 1st Co thians, 12th chapter.

> God hath set some in the Church,
> First, Apostles,
> Secondly, Prophets,
> Thirdly, teachers.

Of course this is no new thing to you, because this was f discussed in the Conferences of 1896, which preceded formation of this Church.

But, beloved friends, it was then a future, but now it is immediate, question.

I would not have dared to enter fully upon my Proph Ministry, in 1896, if I had had any doubt as to my Apost call.

A Conference that Was Moved to Enthusiasm.

Some of you will remember the wave of enthusiasm t passed over the Second Conference, held February 5, 18 when Mr. Calverley rose and demanded that I should be rec nized as an Apostle.

Up they rose, the whole people, and shouted "An Hallelujah! He is!" etc. I had great difficulty in keep them back from declaring me an Apostle, by acclamation.

It was better that I kept the people back.

That night there was a thrill in that Conference that undoubtedly of God; and in my own heart, although I refu to allow myself to be called an Apostle, there was the con tion that I was doing an Apostolic act.

I did not deny the possession of Apostolic Power, but I

unwilling at that time to have the question discussed, or the name assumed.

But I now say that I would not be God's prophet today, if I were not the Christ's Apostle; that is what I believe.

Yet it was needful that I should make my Declaration as Prophet, and first fulfil that ministry.

My prophetic office is really a lesser office than the Apostolic.

The Apostle is a prophet, the Apostle is a teacher, the Apostle is an evangelist; that is to say, the Apostle must combine in himself all the offices, right down to the private member, because he could only become an Apostle as he was, first of all, a member of the Christ's body.

And he must have the signs of the Apostle.

Now, I think there are many things in which I have admitted my Apostolic call, but I have been unwilling prematurely to assume the Apostolic Office; and, if this is not God's time, I am unwilling to do so.

I am not asking this Conference to take any action now.

I shall summon all ordained officers to meet me on Saturday, July 23d, at half past nine o'clock.

Pray, meanwhile.

The Questions Submitted.

I will submit to the adjourned Conference the following questions:

Do we believe, and has the time come for us to reaffirm, that the Apostolic Office should never have been discontinued, and ought to be restored?

Ephesians 2:19, 20; 1 Corinthians 12:28; Matthew 10:2-4; Romans 11:29; Ephesians 4:11-13; Acts 1:23-26; 13:3, 4; 14:14; Matthew 17:11.

Do we recognize John Alexander Dowie, our General Overseer, not only as the Prophet of the Restoration, but as a Divinely-Commissioned Apostle of the Lord Jesus, the Christ?

2 Corinthians 12:12; Matthew 10:7, 8.

Perhaps every one of you at this moment, if I were to put these questions, would answer, "Yes."

But I do not want any hasty affirmation.

If you affirm the first Question, then you must call upon God to appoint some one who shall nominate the first Apostles. That call, or nomination, will have to come through some one who has the Authority to Restore the Church to its Primitive Organization.

Is it, or is it not—the question would arise—a part of the Restoration of All Things which God has promised?

If it is, then it is a part of the duty of Elijah the Restorer.

But that Prophet of the Restoration must act not only as Prophet, but as Teacher and Apostle.

After an earnest discussion by Overseers, Elders, and Evangelists present, the General Overseer offered the closing prayer, as follows:

CLOSING PRAYER.

Father in heaven, by Thy Holy Spirit, follow with Thy blessing the meditations of our own hearts, in the questions to which we have given expression today. Grant that these questions may be the beginning of a period of spiritual enlightenment along those lines which shall prepare us all to give intelligent answers, and enable us, when the answers have been given, to maintain them everywhere.

O God, our Father, the time has come for prophecy to be fulfilled.

But there must come the fulfiller, and no prophecy has ever been fulfilled without the fulfiller.

We know how gloriously our dear Lord Himself fulfilled certain prophecies; and we know that not "one jot or tittle" of the prophetic Word shall pass away until all shall have been fulfilled.

Hasten the fulfilment. The world is so weary, our Father; so sick; so sad; so broken-hearted! The heathen nations are finding, in many thousands, that it is better to die than to live. Hope is fleeing from the hearts of millions, and in the so-called Christian nations numerous suicides occur daily. The people are without hope; for they are without God. O God, quicken us! Revive Thy work in us, and make us better Overseers and Elders; better Evangelists, Deacons, and Deaconesses. Let us do the work of true Evangelists, whatever our other offices may be. Father, guide us in connection with the preparation, in Zion College, of young men and women, and in choosing the right officers and the right time to establish Thy Kingdom in various parts of the earth. Bless Zion's beloved officers all over the world, who would be glad to be with us at these Conferences, and guide them by Thy Spirit. And now be with us between this and Saturday morning; and give me the grace that I need this afternoon. For Jesus' sake. Amen.

BENEDICTION.

The grace of our Lord Jesus, the love of God, the fellowship of the Holy Spirit, be with you all. Amen.

SECOND SPECIAL CONFERENCE OF ORDAINED OFFICERS OF THE CHRISTIAN CATHOLIC CHURCH IN ZION.

REPORTED BY A. C. R., O. L. S., AND I. M. S.

Shiloh Tabernacle, Zion City, Illinois, Saturday Forenoon, July 23, 1904.

The meeting was opened with the singing of Hymn No. 19 in the Program.

The General Overseer then called to the platform Mary Belle Gay and Deaconess Alice J. Lee, who were ordained to the office of Evangelist, and Lydia Saylor, who was ordained a Deaconess in the Christian Catholic Church in Zion.

Evangelist William D. Gay was ordained to the office of Elder.

The General Overseer then asked Overseer Piper to read the questions to be submitted to the adjourned Conference. (See preceding column on this page.)

The General Overseer then said:

I have received a letter from Overseer Speicher, which I will read:

BELOVED GENERAL OVERSEER:—I deeply regret that I shall not be with you in that most important Conference with the Officers of the Christian Catholic Church in Zion, on Saturday, at the time of your propounding these great questions.

On Wednesday, I was intensely interested and greatly blest.

Allow me briefly to set forth what is my firm conviction, directed, as I believe, by the Holy Spirit.

This is the Restoration; therefore, First, as the Church is founded upon the Apostles and Prophets, the Apostolic Office must be restored to the Church, that the Church may fully perform all her functions, and that she may stand before the world in her full dignity and power.

Second, as an Apostle must be one who speaks with authority, and in whom rest various gifts and powers, and as in John Alexander Dowie we find a man who measures up to the standard of the Bible, as no other man in all the earth, to him rightfully belongs the place as the first and principal Apostle in the coming Apostolic College.

[Applause.]

I thought it was only right, beloved, as he was not present, being now on his way to Europe, that he should be allowed to speak for himself.

THE APOSTOLIC ORGANIZATION OF THE CHURCH.

INVOCATION.

Let the words of our mouths and the meditation of our hearts be acceptable in Thy sight, and profitable unto this people, and to all to whom these words shall come. For the sake of Jesus, our Lord, our Strength, and our Redeemer. Amen.

Now, beloved friends, I very earnestly desire to hear what the Conference has to say.

Zion is a Bigger Thing than the Christian Catholic Church.

If it were not, it would be a very small thing.

The Christian Catholic Church is in Zion; but the Christian Catholic Church does not embrace all Zion.

I was in Zion before the Christian Catholic Church was formed; for Zion was in me.

That was true of many of you; but Zion, as the Kingdom of God, had no ecclesiastical expression; that is to say, there was no church, that I could see, that was formed upon lines which would warrant my entering.

I have held, as you know, that the Church is a community of believers, who enter the Church from within the Kingdom; not from the world.

They must enter into the Kingdom of God first, and then pass into the Church; for unless they are born of God they have no place in the Church.

You cannot take worldliness into the Church without its ceasing to be the Church of God.

Hence it is that I want to say very plainly that Apostolic Authority, whether Christians recognize it or not, will extend to the whole Church.

Hence it is that the Prophet of God must declare, and must define, and must of necessity take the first step in the Church's action.

But that Prophet would not be entitled to act in that manner if he were not a man with Apostolic Authority.

He who would set the Church in order must have Divinely-given, Apostolic Authority.

If he does not have Apostolic Authority he has no right to speak; for the Apostle is greater than the Prophet.

Let me here tell you a little story, and read to you the letter in my hand.

A Touching Story.

My departed daughter, Esther, was a very earnest student of her Bible. She was a very profound thinker; and while she was yet a very little child, she would startle us with wise and far-reaching sayings.

The following letter was written over a year ago; but has just been sent me by the writer, a Deaconess in the church:

ZION CITY, ILLINOIS, U. S. A., February 1, 1903.

TO ELIJAH THE RESTORER, THE MESSENGER OF GOD'S COVENANT AND THE PROPHET FORETOLD BY MOSES.

Beloved General Overseer of the Christian Catholic Church in Zion:—God by His Holy Spirit has impressed upon my heart to write to you these words.

In the year of 1897, while I was working in Zion Home, Chicago, Illinois, your dear daughter, Esther, came one day to Room 507, where I was working, and inquired for Mrs. Dowie.

Previously to her coming the thought that you were Elijah occupied my mind.

I then asked her if she realized that you were that prophet, and, in her quick, positive way, she answered, "No. I believe father is an Apostle. His work confirms it."

The positive way in which she said it kept me from saying anything to the contrary.

While I know that later she accepted the General Overseer as Elijah, her acceptance of you as an Apostle and the truth of her saying comes home to me often with great conviction since her departure.

The prophecy of the Christ to His Apostles, "Greater works than these shall ye do; because I go unto My Father," has found and is daily finding its fulfilment in the Prophetic and Apostolic ministry of John Alexander Dowie.

Blessed be God that He has visited His church and people, and through you has reëstablished the Theocratic Rule, which can be maintained only by Apostolic authority.

May God greatly bless you and your faithful companion; may He also bless your son and make him a mighty judge and lawgiver in God's Israel.

Faithfully yours in the Christ, CARRIE W. M. ANDERSON,
Deaconess in Christian Catholic Church in Zion.

I read that for two reasons; first, because, if my daughter had been living in the flesh, she would have been sitting as an Officer in this Conference today, to which she was, no doubt, fully entitled by her devotion to God; therefore I wanted her to speak; and second, it gives me the opportunity of saying that which she could see was really my position, my teaching.

I announced and made the Prophetic Declaration of June 2, 1901, because I knew in my heart that I was an Apostle.

If I had not been convinced of that, I would not have dared to make the Prophetic announcement.

It was one thing to recognize, personally, a certain fact.

It was another thing to make the Declaration that it was true.

For Every Purpose There Is a Time.

One must always remember that Scripture, which says, "For to every purpose there is a time and judgment; because the misery of man is great upon him."

It is because we do not study the times and the purposes, and it is because we fail to get at the right time and to recognize the Divine purpose, that we so often utterly fail in our work.

I saw that many years ago, and I said, I can afford to wait a great deal better than I can afford to make a mistake, and have to retrace my steps; and therefore I was content to be an Evangelist, a Pastor, a Teacher, and a Prophet, before I said anything more.

It was the fact that I had patiently taught these tens and hundreds of thousands of God's people for many years that made it possible for me to move forward with people who were like-minded with me.

Now, you know that the Prophetic Declaration was made without any previous attempt to secure an affirmation of it from any person, persons, Conference, or Church.

Mrs. Dowie, who is now present, will bear me witness that it was absolutely so as applied to her, excepting that I once said a few words in our temporary home in the *Villa mon Desir*, St. Cloud, near Paris, in 1900, when a number of earnest, godly people were discussing the Messenger of the Covenant question.

Significant Incident.

One of them said, "Why, your definition of it would make the Messenger of the Covenant Elijah."

I said, "Certainly."

"Well, then," he replied, "you are Elijah?"

"Exactly so."

"Why," he continued, "you are not going to say that?"

I replied, "I did not say it; *you* have said it."

He said, "I am fighting the Messenger of the Covenant Declaration, and it will be a still more dreadful thing for me to have to fight your saying that you are Elijah."

I answered, "You do not have to fight it."

"Well," he said, "show me."

"No," I said, "I am tired of discussion, brother Arthur Booth-Clibborn. If God Almighty does not show you, I cannot."

And very lovingly we parted and went on our separate ways, and I held no communication with him until some time after God had led him to see it himself.

I do not suppose there is any man in Europe or in America that more earnestly contends for it now than Arthur Booth-Clibborn, who is now an Elder in the Christian Catholic Church in Zion.

A VOICE—"That is right, General Overseer." [Applause.]

GENERAL OVERSEER—And with a very considerable amount of ability, and boldly, and very eloquently does he affirm it.

I knew he was a good man. I saw he was a patient investigator, and I had too much to do to drag theologians about by the hair of their heads.

Doing the Work Is Better than Proclamation.

So I went on; because, after all, the most important thing about this is not, Am I the Prophet, or, Am I the Apostle, but, Am I doing the work?

All I say is, that I picked up the reins of government which had been thrown down for so long, and ventured, by direction of God, to declare certain truths, and to do certain work.

I have the right to prove my right to the place by doing the work.

That is the only way a man ever can prove his right.

And then God's people in vast numbers have believed in me, and have supported me, and are supporting me, to a wonderful extent throughout the world.

But I tell this Conference plainly, what I have said before: that it is only a provisional condition of things; and in my judgment—as the Prophet of God, it is my duty to say so—this Church can never be properly organized without the Restoration of the Apostolic Office, nor can it ever receive the Power which God intends it shall receive, until it is properly organized.

Zion Spiritually a World-Power.

But the question is, Has the time come?

Zion has now become, spiritually, a World Power.

Glory be to God! [Applause. Amen.]

We must rise to the fulfilment of God's purposes, if this is God's time.

You can see by the nature of the questions now in print and in your hands what my conviction is.

These are not for me to answer.

They are questions for you.

The only question in my mind is, Has the time come?

With all respect to you, I should not care a snap whether you cared to affirm or not, if I thought the time had come for me to affirm.

But I have respect for this Church, which is in course of formation.

I have great respect for the opinions of the able ecclesiastical officers who are around me.

These are questions that we shall have to answer before the world, ere long.

I am solemnly inclined to think that if the time has not come, it is not far away; and it is just as well, if the time is not far away, for us to prepare our own minds, and to prepare the Church for the Declaration that will be involved.

The Apostasies Will Howl.

Because, the moment a certain possible declaration is made, there will be another howl, from Dan to Beersheba; and the cry of the Apostasies will arise, *Now he is going to form a Church with Apostolic Authority, and the very next thing he will do as President of the Apostles, will be to put the ban upon us all. And then where shall we be?*

And they will fight.

Well—if they could only see it—*the ban is upon them now*.

I put the ban upon them some time ago; and that was the real bottom of the fight in England.

It was not only the King, but the Archbishop of Canterbury

who was in it; the whole Church of England was in my denunciation.

The Church of Rome has no Apostolic foundation.

The Church of England has no Apostolic foundation.

The Methodist church does not pretend to have any; for its foundations, as an ecclesiastical organization, are in the Masonic Lodge.

The Congregational church has no Apostolic foundation; for its foundations are in an ecclesiastical democratic mob. And so with the Baptists and others.

You cannot find any foundation for the Church of God in the ruling whims of a passing majority. The only true foundation is that on which the Early Church was built, "the Foundation of the Apostles and Prophets, Jesus, the Christ, Himself being the Chief Corner Stone."

As the Prophet of God, I have made this address.

It is of no consequence to me, personally, whether you call me Apostle or General Overseer; it does not alter anything—only that the Apostleship would bring me more work and more responsibility.

But I perceive the time is coming on; and if this is not the time, it is not far distant.

If you say this is the time, I shall give that opinion very earnest consideration.

But I do not press for answers to these questions now.

Let us pray before you speak.

PRAYER.

Father, for Jesus' sake put away words that are very imperfect, and let us not be influenced by the word of man unless it be inspired of God. Give unto my brothers and sisters here, to whom I have submitted these questions, to be able to speak wisely. Our beloved Overseer Speicher has thought well to affirm his assent to all, but we neither asked him for it nor suggested it. Now let each one be fully persuaded in his own mind. For Jesus' sake. Amen.

I will first of all ask my brethren and sisters in the Overseership, that if they have anything to say they will please rise and say it now, in such order as they please. I should like to hear from the Overseership first.

Address by Overseer Mason.

OVERSEER MASON—"General Overseer and brethren and sisters of the Conference:

"Having very prayerfully and carefully considered these questions, I must say that with regard to the first, the Scriptural passages, which as a member of the commission I examined very carefully, leave that question without any possibility of doubt—that the time has come for the reaffirmation.

"Now, as to the second, 'Do we recognize John Alexander Dowie as a Divinely-Commissioned Apostle?' I believe the passage quoted in 2 Corinthians, 12th chapter, is very appropriate.

"I believe with you that the General Overseer is 'not a whit behind the very chiefest Apostles;' and we, with our own eyes, have seen how, in all patience, signs, and wonders, and mighty works have been done.

"I, for one, with deep earnestness and full faith, recognize the General Overseer as a Living Apostle.

"He is much needed now."

Address by Overseer Piper.

OVERSEER PIPER—"Beloved General Overseer:—With reference to the first question, as to whether we believe the time has come to reaffirm that the Apostolic Office should never have been discontinued and ought to be restored, the Scriptures that we have read bear ample testimony to the fact that the Apostolic Office should never have been discontinued. In Ephesians 4:11-13, beginning with the 11th verse, we read:

And He gave some to be Apostles; and some, Prophets; and some, Evangelists; and some, Pastors and Teachers;

For the perfecting of the saints, unto the work of ministering, unto the building up of the body of the Christ:

Till we all attain unto the unity of the faith, and of the knowledge of the Son of God, unto a full-grown man, unto the measure of the stature of the fulness of the Christ.

"The beginning of the 13th verse, 'Till we all attain unto the unity of the faith, and of the knowledge of the Son of God,' shows, in other words, that the Apostolic Office, together with other offices, is to continue 'till we all attain' to the things that are mentioned in the 13th verse.

"We have not, and the church at large has not, yet attained unto these things; and, therefore, the Apostolic Office, together with other offices, must continue until we have attained; therefore, it should be in existence now."

GENERAL OVERSEER—The point is well taken.

OVERSEER PIPER—"Now, as to the second question, as to whether we recognize our General Overseer as an Apostle, the Lord Jesus, the Christ, in sending out His Apostles, mentioned five things that they were to do.

"They were, first of all, to preach the Gospel; they were to heal the sick; they were to raise the dead; they were to cleanse the lepers, and they were to cast out demons.

"I believe a man who can do these things—and the General Overseer has done them, God operating through him—is necessarily an Apostle, no matter who says he is or is not.

"These things have been done by the power of God, through John Alexander Dowie.

"I therefore have no hesitation in saying that which I have believed for some time, that he is an Apostle of the Lord Jesus, the Christ."

GENERAL OVERSEER—Well, I cannot get up a fight on this question at all.

Address by Overseer Jane Dowie.

OVERSEER JANE DOWIE—"We had, some years ago, a good deal of teaching on this subject.

"It is not a new subject to us.

"The General Overseer talked about the Apostolic Office and the Restoration of the Apostolic College quite early in his ministry, after getting out of the Congregational church, before this Church was formed at all, and we thoroughly threshed out the matter, and believed it.

"I answer 'Yes,' to both questions.

"The difficulty has never been about the first Apostle, in my mind.

"Whether it is the right time or not, has always been a question with me, because of the difficulty of finding the other Apostles.

"The General Overseer has held that there were to be Twelve Apostles, and I think it would be a very serious thing to call out Twelve Apostles, and then find that they were not the right ones.

"That is a point that has troubled me in this matter—where the others are to be found?

"If it were only a question of the one Apostle, there would be no difficulty whatever about it, because we have the signs and everything else."

Comment by General Overseer.

GENERAL OVERSEER—There is a saying, "No man is a hero to his valet and seldom to his wife."

I thank Overseer Jane Dowie for her statement; for she is perfectly candid, and just as ready to deny as to affirm, if she thought it right to do so.

I do not know how far this ought to go on, but it seems to me that we are pretty near getting through with these Overseers.

I should like to see whether there is any difficulty.

We have to be careful lest our loving appreciation of each other cause us to assent more quickly than we should.

I can answer the first one; I do not, dare not, answer the second; that is for God and for my brethren to answer, because no man can assume the Presidency of the Apostleship, and the duty of selecting the other Apostles, which would certainly devolve upon one who might be recognized as a Divinely-Commissioned Apostle, without assuming a tremendous responsibility.

I make just this remark in reply to my wife's suggestion—when you remember the men from among whom our Lord Jesus, the Christ, had to select His first apostles, I humbly submit I have just as good material here. [Applause.]

That is all I have to say on that subject.

But then another consideration arises; we must have not only as good, but better; for the Twentieth Century demands the very highest and best.

Overseer Brasefield's Address.

OVERSEER BRASEFIELD—"General Overseer:—There has always been in my thought a great admiration for the Councils of those who occupied this territory hundreds of years ago, because their records show that it was the old men who gave the counsel, and it was the young men who carried it into execution.

"I have hesitated to rise, because, as you have already stated,

I am the youngest among those who have been ordained to the Overseership.

"But, I want to say in passing, that last Wednesday, between the hours of twelve and one, and today, between the hours of ten and twelve, the Christian Catholic Church in Zion passed through two of the most far-reaching periods of its organization and work.

"I class these two meetings with two other meetings in the history of this Church—the meetings that were held in Chicago in January and February, 1896; and the meetings in the Auditorium, and, on the following day, in the Thirteenth Street Building, Chicago, on June 2 and 3, 1901.

"I believe it will not be very long until the Church at large realizes that in these Conferences—the one of last Wednesday, the one of today, and, possibly, another—that that which has been, and will have been done, is most far-reaching in the Work of Restoration.

"Yet, on such occasions, the right to speak does not necessarily connect itself with age; for a man may have had the years and not spent time in thinking on the question that is before this Conference for discussion.

"A man may lack the years and yet have spent much time in thought upon the discussion; and it is with that thought in my heart that I feel that I have some right to speak this morning.

A Christian Church Must Be Controlled by Apostolic Power.

"In 1896, while a student in a Theological Seminary on the Pacific Coast, I made a special study of Church Organization.

"I went into it as deeply as time would allow; and I became thoroughly convinced of that which I afterwards found was being taught in the Christian Catholic Church in Zion—that the organized Christian Church must have Apostles as its Foundation, and that any church that was not controlled by Apostolic Power would have no right to be called a Christian Church.

"I looked all around me.

"I looked into the Presbyterian church. I did not find it there. I found a republic there.

"I looked into the Congregational church. I found a democracy there.

"I looked into the Episcopal church, and found an apostolic succession, so-called, there; but there was nothing to it.

"I looked into the Roman church and the Greek church, and it was nowhere.

"I felt convinced in my heart that if the day ever came in the Twentieth Century, that there should be formed, under the guidance of God, a Church that had the Primitive Church as its model, in that Church, as a Ruling Body, would be found the Apostolic College.

"And when I got Zion Literature, it is needless to say that as soon as I came to see that that was the teaching of our beloved Leader, I was attracted to Zion.

"And I came here today with A VOICE FROM ZION in my hand.

"I believe that teaching, which has gone throughout the world not only in the form of a book, but which has become, throughout the length and breadth of this land, the Voice of Zion in this Church at this time.

Necessity for the Apostolic Office Has Been Declared.

"That is the conviction that is in my spirit this morning; and there are some words that I have found in the Record of the Organization of the Church, that I think we shall do well to consider this morning—words spoken by our Leader at the time of the Conferences of January 22 and February 5, 1896. On page 13:

He [the Christ] took the eleven Apostles apart and taught them how to organize the Church of God; because the foundation office in the Church of God was to be the Office of Apostle.

Apostles were to rule the Church of God.

"And that must come.

"We cannot get away from it.

"God will never let us get away from it.

"Of course, in the submitting of this question, the General Overseer has clearly indicated, in what he said this morning, that he never had any idea of getting away from it.

"But that statement made this morning is just as strong as it was in the time of the Conferences in January, 1896.

Therefore, He took these eleven men and He told them How, and WHAT, and WHY.

After six weeks' instruction, lacking two days, He told them that they should not depart from Jerusalem, but wait for the promise of the Father, the descent of the Holy Ghost; for power would come after that the Holy Ghost had come upon them.

"Then I find another statement, page 20:

I affirm that the Church cannot be Christian, and cannot be Catholic, unless it is Apostolic.

The Apostolic Office must be declared as belonging to the Church, if we shall form a Church; and it shall be declared to be a Perpetual Office.

It is our duty to declare that the Church of God shall eventually, and as speedily as possible, be so organized.

We have nothing to do with consequences. God will call His apostles in His own time and way, by the Holy Spirit. I do not think I can see any of them as yet, but that does not alter the fact that we have to organize this Church as God did it

It must be upon the pattern that God gave. I shall organize on that pattern or not at all.

"Those are very strong words.

"General Overseer, those are your own words, and I think it well for us today to consider them.

"Another statement, page 25:

It is not a mere question of Chicago; but we intend to organize ourselves, God helping us, into a Church upon the primitive model.

A Twentieth Century Church.

"The General Overseer did not say that he intended to organize a First Century Church, for God had called him to organize a Twentieth Century Church; but it was to be upon the primitive model, and the essentials of the First Century Church must be found in the Twentieth Century Church.

"It will not, indeed, be able to do its work; to accomplish that which God has for it to do, until the day has come, until the hour has arrived, when our leader, the Prophet of God, takes the step which God is now calling upon him to take.

"The Church is waiting.

"We heard yesterday that the boom was quiet; that there was a lull on the surface.

"General Overseer, I believe that that is, in a sense, not only true in the business conditions of this Church, but also true of the spiritual conditions; and that the psychological moment has arrived when the Church must be organized as the General Overseer said eight years ago it should be organized.

"And it is not a question of the consequences; it is a question of the first action.

God Will Confirm the Action of His Church.

"And when the First Apostle has issued his call, God by His Spirit, as He did in the primitive Church, will supply the others. [Applause.]

"It may not be twelve, at once.

"It was the Holy Spirit that came to the prophets and the teachers in the Early Church, and laid upon them the obligation that they should separate Paul and Barnabas for the work of the ministry; and at that moment they became Apostles in the church.

"And I believe that God who has founded this work, and who caused our leader to utter these memorable words, in January and February, 1896, is calling now.

"We see it in the words that have been spoken.

"We see it in the questions that have been submitted—God who is calling upon our leader now to take this far-reaching step, will, after we have taken that first step, bring to him the men whom he may need to found that Apostolic College, in His own time and in His own way.

"There are two very striking statements in this narrative of the Organization of the Church, which I read with a good deal of satisfaction.

"I will turn to them:

"Referring to Apostles, he says, 'I do not think that I can see any of them yet,' and in the discussion that followed two weeks after that statement, one who was a member of that Conference said:

In regard to one point, I remember Dr. Dowie's saying, in a kind of sad and gloomy way, "I don't know that I can see any of the Apostles yet."

A Man That Discerned an Apostle.

"This man, in response to that 'sad and gloomy' statement, said:

I think I can see one, and I think he is the chief of modern Apostles.

"As he said it, he looked into the eyes of our leader.

"And I say here, in defining my position on the second question, that from the very first time I looked into his eyes—as he called me into his office, the first day I came to Chicago, when he gave me the privilege, which I never have had since [laughter], of sitting four hours in conference with him—there came into my spirit the conviction that there was sitting before me, talking to me, the man who was to the Twentieth Century Church what the Apostle Paul was to the First Century Church; and I have never doubted the truth of that conviction.

"I can say, too, as the Christ said to Peter, after his affirmation that He was the Christ, that 'flesh and blood' never revealed it to me; it came to me through the ministry of the Spirit of God.

"And when he made the Declaration that he was Elijah the Restorer, it raised a question for which I was not as well prepared as I would have been had he declared that he was an Apostle.

"I was like his own daughter.

"I was better prepared to affirm a Declaration that he was the Apostle for the Century, than to support his claims to the Prophetic Office.

"That was a conviction that had come into my spirit, and that conviction is there yet; it has grown in me.

"So I feel in speaking this morning, General Overseer, that I am not speaking words that express a conviction of a year or two, but one that began in 1896.

An Incident that Was More than a Coincidence.

"While you were announcing in Chicago the fact that this Church was to be organized upon the Primitive model, I was investigating on the Pacific Coast, and getting the same conviction about the organization of the Church.

"I say that that was no mere coincidence.

"The conviction that was in my heart made it necessary, just as surely as a needle must point to a lodestone, that I should find that organization and find my place in it.

"And I thank God today that I found that Church, and that I found my place in it.

"I rejoice in the service it has enabled me to perform for Him, and in the large scope of liberty that we enjoy in its ministry.

"I thank God today for the leader who, I want to say once more, is the Apostle of the Twentieth Century, and I say that God has called him to that work."

Overseer Excell's Address.

OVERSEER EXCELL—"General Overseer and fellow officers in the Christian Catholic Church in Zion:—Those of you who have carefully considered the questions will realize that these are questions of very great moment.

"In the first place, the first question—'Do we believe, and has the time come for us to reaffirm, that the Apostolic Office should never have been discontinued?'

"Jesus said, 'Upon this Rock I will build My Church; and the Gates of Hades shall not prevail against it.'

"That Rock, as the General Overseer has said, is the Rock of the Christ's own Divinity.

"Only those can be built upon the Foundation who believe that Jesus, the Christ, is the Son of God—who have that conviction in their hearts and work it out in their lives.

"Jesus, the Christ, is the Foundation; and, as Paul said, 'Other Foundation can no man lay than that which is laid, which is Jesus, the Christ;' upon this Foundation the whole Church is builded.

"We read also that we are 'built upon the Foundation of the Apostles and Prophets.'

Jesus, the Christ, Is both Foundation and Corner-Stone.

"And He who binds us together, the Chief Corner-Stone, is Jesus, the Christ, or the Foundation-Stone.

"When Jesus, the Christ, built His Church, He first ordained Twelve Apostles.

"He also, at a later time, ordained Prophets, so that the Church was fully organized, fully established, being 'built upon the Foundation of the Apostles and Prophets.'

"That was the perfect organization; that was the true organization; that was the organization which was after God's own mind.

"And you will remember that when one of the Apostles went to the Devil it was necessary that some one should be chosen to fill his place—the place of him who, by transgression, lost that position, and went unto his own place.

"You will remember that not only was Matthias called, but that Barnabas and Paul, then named Saul, were ordained to the Apostolic Office.

"And so on, until we find about twenty-one who were called Apostles.

"We find, therefore, that the Apostolic College is a Perpetual College; else when some one died it would not have been necessary that some one should fill his place.

"The mere fact that they filled the place, and that it was done under the direction of the Holy Spirit, shows that the office was to continue on down through all Time.

The Right Man Will be Called at the Right Time.

"It is said of the Lord Jesus, the Christ, in the 13th chapter of Hebrews, 8th verse, 'Jesus, the Christ, is the same yesterday and today, yea and forever;' and when Jesus, the Christ, was here on earth, He established His Church with Twelve Apostles.

"If Jesus, the Christ, were here today on earth, personally, we should find Him doing the same; for He is the same, yesterday and today, yea and forever.

"He did not select those Twelve Apostles until He had found the men that were qualified.

"Neither will God, in the Christian Catholic Church in Zion, through him whom He has called to select the Apostles, call them until he finds the right men.

"And I say with our beloved Overseer Jane Dowie, that great care should be exercised.

"But has not the General Overseer exercised care?

"In this most important office will he not exercise more care than he has in the lesser offices?

"Verily, yes.

"If Jesus, the Christ, were here He would select twelve Apostles, when He found men qualified, and not until then.

"We find other Apostles ordained to office; not only the twelve, but nine others.

"We find that He is the same Almighty Lord, "I am Jehovah, I change not."

"God manifested Himself through Jesus, the Christ.

"He expressed His wish in the establishment of a Church, which was built upon the foundation of Apostles and Prophets.

"That is God's will.

"His Will is the Eternal Will; His Purpose is the Eternal Purpose; and when He purposes who shall hinder or disannul?

"God's purposes must be carried out at the proper time.

God's Purpose Has Never Been Changed.

"Therefore, we find that it is God's Will; that it is His Purpose, and always has been His Purpose, since the foundation of the Church, since the Church was organized, that it should have this College of Twelve Apostles—that it should also have its Prophets, its Teachers, its Workers of Miracles, and all the Offices of the Spirit, qualified by the Gifts of the Spirit.

"Of this the General Overseer spoke to you in a morning meeting some time ago.

"I say, therefore, we should have at the present time, were it not for the Apostasy of the Church, the College of the Apostles; we should have the prophets and the other officers.

"Now, if we are to get back to the Primitive conditions the Apostolic office must be restored in the Church.

"The question is, Has the time come to reaffirm this in the Church?

"The question does not state distinctly that the time has come to appoint the Twelve Apostles.

"We have nothing to do with that question in this Conference.

"The whole question is, Has the time come to reaffirm in this Church that this office should never have been discontinued?

"I am positive that it is not the General Overseer's mind that the question should imply that the Twelve Apostles should be appointed at this time.

"It does not say that. It asks, Has the time come to reaffirm, that the Apostolic Office ought to be restored to the Church?

"Now, in what times are we living?

"You will all answer at once, 'In the Times of the Restoration of All Things.'

"Do we not believe that?"

VOICES—"Yes."

God Has Promised the Former and the Latter Rain.

OVERSEER EXCELL—"What do we find in the Scriptures, in the 3d chapter of Acts, in connection with the same expression (Acts 3:19-20)? The Apostle Peter speaks of the Times of Refreshing which shall come from the Presence of the Lord —the Times when the Lord shall pour out His Spirit upon the people, the Times spoken of in the Scripture as 'The Latter Rain.'

"You all understand what the 'Former Rain' was.

"You all understand that upon the day of Pentecost God wonderfully poured out His Spirit upon the people, and they spoke with tongues and prophesied, and wonderful things were done.

"But what Church was that?

"That was not the Glorious Church—that was not a Church looking for the Second Coming of the Lord Jesus, the Christ—that was the Primitive Church—that was the Church instituted when the Christ came in His humanity!

"But this Church of today is a Church that is preparing for the time when the Christ shall come in His glory.

"Paul says, in Ephesians 5:27, that it shall be a 'Glorious Church, not having spot, or wrinkle, or any such thing.'

"If the Primitive Church had the Twelve Apostles, shall not this 'Glorious Church' of the Last Days have the Twelve Apostles?

"If it were necessary in those days that the Spirit of God be poured out, and that men be qualified for these different offices, is it not much more necessary in these days?

"It shall be a Glorious Church, 'not having spot or wrinkle.'

The Gifts of the Spirit Will Qualify for the Offices of the Spirit.

"In the 1st chapter of 1 Corinthians, we read that the Church had the Spirit of Prophecy, the testimony of Jesus, and He says 'ye come behind in no Gift; waiting for the revelation of our Lord Jesus, the Christ.'

"Paul there teaches that a Church which is waiting for the Lord Jesus, the Christ, must come behind in no Gift.

"Therefore, since the Gifts of the Spirit prepare the Church for the Coming of the Christ, we must have in the Last Days the Nine Gifts of the Spirit; and these Nine Gifts of the Spirit will qualify for the Nine Offices of the Spirit—the first, the highest, the chief of which is the Office of Apostle; 'for God has set some in the Church, first'—what?"

OFFICERS—"Apostles."

OVERSEER EXCELL—"'Secondly, prophets; thirdly, teachers,' etc.

"The time has come to declare these things unto the people.

"We look at the first Church, and we find that God called one man first, and that man was John the Baptist—that man was Elijah the Preparer, the Forerunner, preparing the way for Jesus, the Christ.

"We come down to our own times, and we find that again God has called a man who is to lead the people—God's people —and prepare them for the Second Coming of the Lord Jesus, the Christ.

The Complete Organization of the Church Necessary for the Full Measure of the Spirit.

"We find that the Lord Jesus, the Christ, chose His Twelve Apostles.

"The Holy Spirit was not poured out until after the Twelve Apostles were chosen. The Apostles had to be ordained and the Church fully organized before Pentecost.

"Let that sink deep into your minds a moment.

"What, then, may we expect in the Last Days?

"Can we expect God to do wonderful things for us until the Church is fully organized?

"It is not fully organized now.

"I have seen that for years.

"I have heard what the General Overseer has said on that point; and I believe it.

"The Church is simply in the process of formation; and we must reach the time when the Church is organized, when the Twelve Apostles are chosen, or at least when one is recognized—when one is pointed out not only to us but to the whole world.

"You will find that people throughout the world, people not in Zion, will recognize what you and I recognize this morning.

"Sometimes we think we are the only people that know anything about it; but we find people outside that know just as much about it as we do; they have recognized it for years.

"We must have the organization of the Twelve Apostles before we can expect that fulness of the Holy Spirit which God has promised.

"In the Book of Joel, He says, you will remember, 'It shall come to pass afterward, that I will pour forth of My Spirit upon all flesh; and your sons and your daughters shall prophesy, your old men shall dream dreams, your young men shall see visions.'

The Day of Pentecost Only a Partial Fulfilment of Prophecy.

"This had its partial fulfilment on the day of Pentecost.

"But is it completely fulfilled?

"No, indeed!

"And the greatest fulfilment, the most wonderful time that the world has known is in our own days, at this time of the 'Latter Rain,' when God shall again pour out His Spirit, not moderately, as He said in Joel.

"'Moderately' had He given the former rain; but He will give the 'Latter Rain' in abundance; as He said in Zechariah, the 'Lord shall make bright clouds, and give them showers of rain.'

"When it thunders and the clouds begin piling up higher and higher, and the lightnings flash, and there is a great sound of thunder, the rain begins to pour down.

"Is not that the time we want?

"How can we expect it, my beloved officers of the Church, until the Church is organized, and until the Church is ready?

"But when the Church is organized, when the Apostles are chosen by God, mark you, not by men, by God Himself, through Him whom He has chosen—who will select, appoint, ordain these Apostles; when that time comes, God will open the Heavens and pour out such a blessing 'that there shall not be room enough to receive it.'

The Church Must Get Ready for the Larger Blessing.

"Pentecost will not be anything compared to the blessings in the Last Days.

"But we must get ready for these things.

"How can we get ready, if we say the time has not come to proclaim to the Church her need of the Apostles?

"I say the time has come.

"Zion has gone on from grace to grace, and from glory to glory.

"The Christian Catholic Church has recognized the Prophet.

"It is time that the Christian Catholic Church should come to the place where it proclaims to the world that we are living in the time when the Church should have the Twelve Apostles.

"Bless your heart, it has been proclaimed!

"The General Overseer has been saying it over and over again; but he wants the men and all the officers to know it, and then he is going to go at it and hit it so hard he will knock something out. [Applause.]

"You know a big storm was raised the last time he said something, and it will be a greater storm this time.

Zion Will Continue to Hit the Devil Harder and Harder.

"It will cause a great commotion.

"Zion can never rest upon her oars.

"Zion can never be satisfied with what she has done in the past.

"She must say, 'Now, we have done one thing by the grace of God, and this time we will hit the Devil harder; we will accomplish more than ever before.'

"That is just what we want to do.

"I believe this Conference is of one mind and one heart in regard to that first question.

"Now, the second question, 'Do we recognize John Alexander Dowie, our General Overseer, not only as the Prophet of the Restoration, but as a Divinely-Commissioned Apostle of the Lord Jesus, the Christ?'

"First, in regard to the point which Overseer Jane Dowie raised; it seems to me that it is not necessary that there should be Twelve Apostles chosen at once. Far from it.

"If we read carefully the New Testament Scriptures, we shall find that the Church did not always have the full number; but it was the Church just the same. God blessed it just the same.

"Let us again see it in the Last Days!

"I call your attention to one Scripture

"You know God called John the Baptist, who was the Messenger of the Covenant in his day.

The General Overseer the Complement of John the Baptist.

"So the General Overseer states, and so I believe, and so I trust you all believe.

"John Alexander Dowie in this day is the complete fulfilment of the prophecies which John the Baptist in his day partially fulfilled.

"Now if you will get that into your heads, it will enable you to get rid of a great many difficulties.

"This man, John Alexander, today, is a man sent from God, just as much as John the Baptist was.

"This man is the Preparer for the Second Coming of the Christ in precisely the same manner as John the Baptist prepared for the First Coming of the Christ.

"This man today is the 'Voice of one crying in the wilderness, Prepare ye the way of the Lord,' just as John in his day was the Voice of one crying in the wilderness.

"But John only in a very small measure fulfilled that prophecy.

"It was not a complete fulfilment of what is foretold in Isaiah 40:5—'And the Glory of Jehovah shall be revealed, and all flesh shall see it together.'

"That was not completely fulfilled in John the Baptist's Day.

"Jesus, the Christ, did not come in glory. He came in humility.

"But in these days He comes in glory.

"In those days 'every eye' did not see him.

"Of the Last Days it is written,

Behold, He cometh with the clouds; and every eye shall see Him, and they which pierced Him; and all the tribes of the earth shall mourn over Him. Even so.

"So, in the Last Days, we have the complete fulfilment of these Scriptures.

"In the Last Days we have one who is the Messenger of the Covenant.

We Can Depend Upon Scripture Testimony.

"The 3d chapter of Malachi has its fulfilment in John Alexander Dowie, 'Behold I send My Messenger, and he shall prepare the way before Me.'

"God says it, the New Testament gives it so; and we can depend upon the New and the Old Testaments.

"God says, 'Behold, I send My Messenger before Thy face (before the face of Jesus) who shall prepare Thy way before Thee.'

"And He also says, 'Jehovah, whom ye seek, shall suddenly come to His Temple.'

"That is the Temple here on earth.

"The Lord Jesus, the Christ, is now above, but He is coming down to this earth, and coming to His Temple.

"Notice, if you please, that the Messenger is sent first. The references say it applied to John the Baptist.

"It is true that it applied to him, but only in a very limited sense.

"But in these days it applies to John Alexander Dowie.

"Now, what do we find?

"You remember that John sent two of His disciples to Jesus to ask Him certain questions, and that Jesus turned to the multitude and spoke concerning John, 'What went ye out for to see?'—what was all this commotion about?

"He said first, 'A reed shaken with the wind?'

"What is the answer? No!

John the Baptist "Much More" Than a Prophet.

"He said that John was more than that. He never was anything of that kind. 'A man clothed in soft raiment?' 'A prophet?' Yes, more than that, 'and I say unto you'—now, what comes next?"

VOICE—"'More than a prophet.'"

OVERSEER EXCELL—"'Much more than a prophet.'

"The trouble with the Church has always been that it has not recognized John the Baptist in his real office.

"It has minimized his office.

"It has not recognized him to be what he really was.

"The Church simply says he was only a prophet, and not 'more than a prophet;' and they do not know whether he was much of a prophet, after all.

"John the Baptist was not a 'little more' than a prophet, but 'much more.'

"You have only to turn to the New Testament to find what one must be to be 'much more' than a prophet.

"God has set in the Church, first, Apostles; secondly, prophets.

"When a man occupies an office that is higher than that of Prophet, what is he?

"He is an Apostle.

"John the Baptist was an Apostle sent of God, and so the Scriptures say, 'There came a man, sent from God.'

"What is an Apostle? A man whom God lays hold upon and sends for a peculiar purpose.

"And that purpose is to overthrow the kingdom of the Devil, and to establish things after God's own pattern.

"That is what John the Baptist did; and if that is not what this man, John Alexander Dowie, is doing, I do not know what is going on. [Applause.]

John Alexander Dowie Is Overturning Things.

"He tells you this morning that his business is to overturn.

"Well, he is turning things over, and over, until even in England they are afraid of the effects of his words upon the Throne.

"And they are afraid to let him speak there.

"They are afraid that the Throne itself will overturn, and that is just what is going to happen.

"If you can understand these things at all you must be able to see that the time will eventually come when the Kingdoms of this world shall become the Kingdom of our Lord and of His Christ.

"Do you think the Kingdoms of this world are going to turn into the Kingdom of our Lord and of His Christ without some overturning?

"There must be some force at work in these kingdoms, and it is the force of Zion—the force of God—through our General Overseer.

"That is what is going on.

"Elijah did it. John the Baptist did it, and John Alexander Dowie is doing the same thing.

"Elijah was a prophet.

"John the Baptist was 'much more than a prophet.'

"Do you think that the prophet of today would be less than the second Elijah?"

VOICES—"No."

John the Baptist an Apostle.

OVERSEER EXCELL—"John the Baptist was an Apostle, sent of God.

"The Greek of the words 'sent forth' in the verse in the first chapter of John, 'There was a man sent forth from God,' is ἀπεσταλμένος.

"Our word 'Apostle' comes from the same Greek root: *apostello* (ἀποστέλλω).

"Put in English it would be *Apostolized*, 'sent out by God;' a man called of God; sent out by God.

"So we have today a man called of God; a man sent out by God to overturn, and overturn, and get things ready for the Second Coming of the Lord Jesus, the Christ.

"I say it would be folly for us to say that the man today was a whit behind the man whom He sent in John the Baptist's day.

"The thing is always getting brighter, and greater, and more glorious; and just as sure as John the Baptist was an Apostle when there were no others, just so surely did the Lord Jesus, the Christ, God the Father, by His Spirit send this man to be an Apostle.

"He is an Apostle, whether you think so or not.

"It does not make a particle of difference.

"I never would have been ordained in the Christian Catholic Church in Zion if I had not believed that he was an Apostle.

"He has been an Apostle for years.

Ordination Must Be in a Church that Has Authority.

"A man to be ordained; to have Authority to lay hands upon the sick; to baptize; and to perform the Ordinances of the Church, must be in a Church that has some Authority and that Authority never was in the prophet; but Authority [illegible] has been in those who were greater than prophets.

"How was it back in Moses' time?

"You remember the Spirit of God came upon the [illegible] and they prophesied; and there were two especially tha[illegible]sied in the camp.

"And Aaron became very much alarmed, and said to Moses 'My lord, tell them to stop.'

"He recognized that, although Moses was a prophet, he was more than a prophet, because he had Authority over the prophets.

"Think of these Scriptures, and they will help you.

"We must have a man in these days who is 'more than a prophet.'

"I believe, with all my heart, that God has called such a man.

"I believed it from the beginning, when the question came to me, 'Who is the Elijah in these days?'

"That question was answered by me to my entire satisfaction before John Alexander Dowie said a word on the subject; before I had heard or read, or any one had spoken to me about it.

"It was clear, in the first place, that John the Baptist was the Elijah in his day.

"But any one can see that Malachi 4:5 was not fulfilled.

"It did not have its complete fulfilment in John the Baptist; and, therefore, there must be a man in these Latter Days who has 'the spirit and power of Elijah.'

"I say our Elijah in these days is not one whit behind the Elijah of John the Baptist's day.

"Look at his works!

"What are the requisites for the Apostleship?

"They have been read in your hearing.

"Do we not find these things in the life of John Alexander Dowie?

God Has Bestowed Authority Upon the General Overseer.

"We find that God has given him Authority.

"We find he is doing the very things that God said His Apostle would do.

"He has said all the time that he had Divine Authority to organize; and we believe it.

"Therefore, the time has come for the Church not only to recognize him as a Prophet, but to recognize in him that which he has been for years—an Apostle.

"For years John Alexander Dowie was only a Teacher; but as he grew in grace and understood more of the Word of God, he became what?

VOICES—"A Prophet."

OVERSEER EXCELL—"He foresaw, and he knew years ago, the very things he is doing today.

"Look back in LEAVES OF HEALING at the things that John Alexander Dowie told you would happen.

"They are the things that are happening; the things that he told you he would do.

"These show you that he was then a prophet.

"But when God called him to organize the Christian Catholic Church in Zion; when He gave him Authority to ordain officers, to overturn the denominations, and to reëstablish His Church, He gave him Apostolic Authority.

"John Alexander Dowie had to be an Apostle before he had the Authority to do the things which he has done; and the mere fact that he has done these things, that he has reëstablished the Christian Church, shows that God then had called him to be an Apostle.

"It is only fitting, my beloved fellow officers in the Christian Catholic Church, that we recognize what the Lord Jesus, the Christ, and what God, the Father, and the Holy Spirit, made manifest years ago, that John Alexander Dowie is an Apostle."

Comments by General Overseer.

GENERAL OVERSEER—It has been said, "No man is a hero to his valet, and very seldom to his wife," but when he is so to the General Ecclesiastical Secretary, a man who has lived with him, gone around the world with him, and ought to know whereof he affirms, it amounts to something.

I thank my brethren and my sister, Overseers in the Christian Catholic Church in Zion, very humbly and very heartily for their kind words.

You have now heard five Overseers.

I do not know whether you know just the number of Overseers there are.

There are ten in the world today, including the General Overseer; and two more would make twelve.

Now, I do not say all the Overseers will be Apostles: that might not be best.

God may show me an Apostle in a very humble position. I cannot tell.

It is one of the strange things in the Church of Rome that a Deacon of the Church may become Pope—that a conclave of cardinals has a right to elect to that office a humble member of the Church.

Rome, with all her faults, has recognized that the highest office may be found in the humblest ranks, just as the Lord Jesus, the Christ, found among the fishermen the Apostles of His time.

It does not follow that, because a man is an Overseer, he has to be an Apostle.

This Conference has gone as far as it can go without throwing out all our arrangements for the afternoon.

I think I can direct you with authority to remain in Zion City until Monday night.

I would like to take the mind of the brethren as to whether they would like the Conference to close today.

Conference Adjourns to July 25th.

The Conference decided that they would adjourn until Monday morning, at ten o'clock.

The General Overseer then adjourned the Conference and pronounced the

BENEDICTION.

Beloved, abstain from every form of evil. And may the very God of Peace Himself sanctify you wholly; and I pray God your whole spirit, and soul, and body be preserved entire, without blame, unto the coming of our Lord Jesus, the Christ. Faithful is He that calleth you, who also will do it. The grace of our Lord Jesus, the Christ, the love of God our Father, the fellowship of the Holy Spirit, our Comforter and Guide, one Eternal God, abide in you, bless you, and keep you, and all the Israel of God everywhere, forever. Amen.

THIRD SPECIAL CONFERENCE OF ORDAINED OFFICERS OF THE CHRISTIAN CATHOLIC CHURCH IN ZION.

REPORTED BY, O. L. S., L. L. H., AND A. C. R.

Shiloh Tabernacle, Zion City, Illinois, Monday Forenoon, July 25, 1904.

The meeting was opened with the singing of No. 29 of the Program.

Prayer was offered by the General Overseer.

Overseer Brasefield read the 3d chapter of the Book of Acts, from the 11th verse to the end of the chapter.

Overseer Brasefield, at the direction of the General Overseer, read a letter from Deacon Charles J. Barnard, who was unable to be present, giving affirmative answers to the questions.

Absolute Liberty of the Conference.

The General Overseer then said:

I have kept my mind open, absolutely so, on this matter. I have refused to allow my mind to come to any definite conclusion as to the time for the Declaration.

I have not asked God to make you see it, or to make you see anything.

I have simply asked God to make you see what was right and true.

I have had no desire, and I know I have none, to impress upon you my will, until we are agreed as to what is the Will of God.

Our conclusions must be reasonable, for God has called us to a reasonable service.

Anything that is contrary to reason cannot be true.

It may be beyond reason; and yet, following the lines of strict logic, nothing that is true can be beyond reason.

If you say that faith is beyond reason, that is scarcely a correct definition, because faith itself is a reasonable thing.

In connection with this there is a great deal to make you pause before you say Yes, finally and absolutely.

You have not only to deal with me, in whom your personal confidence is so loving and so complete, apparently, but with my associates in the Apostleship, in the event of the Apostolic College being formed. You have to deal with the perpetuity of that Apostleship.

You have to remember that these Apostles and the Apostolic College will become the absolute controlling power in the Church, controlling its spiritual, its educational, its commercial, its industrial, and its political interests.

After some further remarks, the General Overseer left the Conference open for discussion.

Address of Elder W. H. Cossum.

ELDER W. H. COSSUM—"General Overseer, beloved brothers and sisters:—If I had been permitted to speak at the close of the First Conference, I should simply have said, 'there is no use trying to paint a bouquet.'

"We had a variety of beautiful utterances on the question of the Scriptural bearing on this Apostolic question, and I felt there was nothing to be added.

"But after the General Overseer said what he did, I felt that possibly it was of some interest to him to hear what was in our hearts.

"I feel that the whole thing could be answered as Deacon Barnard has answered, by saying 'Yes' to these first two questions under discussion. [Reads the first and second questions, and gives an affirmative answer.]

"If the General Overseer had called for a *viva voce* vote I think he would have had a unanimous expression.

Bearing of Divine Healing on Apostolic Question.

"Anything that is dispensational in reference to the question of Divine Healing belongs to us.

"We are in the Church Dispensation.

"Under the Mosaic Dispensation, no matter how apostate the people of God became, whenever a king came along who was willing to wipe the dust off the ark, to dig out the Law, and reread it, give himself to God, and call the people to Repentance, the powers of the Mosaic Dispensation were restored to that king and the people.

"We have discovered, in reference to Divine Healing, that God is just as willing to heal, after the truth has been hidden for centuries in an apostate church, as He was in the beginning of the Dispensation.

"When Jesus was here in the flesh and called His twelve Apostles, and sent them out, that was one thing.

"But when the Elders are called, and the Gifts of the Spirit given to the church, after Pentecost, after Jesus is in heaven, and after the Spirit is out-poured, that is an entirely different thing.

"When we discover, after Jesus has left His Twelve Apostles and has gone up on high, that Apostles are added to the original Twelve, then we have the principle established.

"The Apostolic Office has been placed in this Dispensation, historically and providentially, by the power of God.

"Therefore I affirm that this question ought to be answered in the affirmative. [Reads the question again.]

Ought the Apostolic Office to Be Restored?

"Ought it to be restored?

"Why of course it ought to be restored, for Divine Healing and all these Precious Gifts God has given to His Church, ought to be restored.

"I have the thought that until the Apostolic College is restored, the Latter Rain can never be received.

"God works in an orderly manner, and God will work through His Church as He has established it, but as soon as it is apostate, as soon as it is broken, God will not honor it with a full power.

"I believe that we have been slow, General Overseer, not too fast.

"When my body is sick, and I see no sign of healing, I claim my healing, and God makes me well in the Name of Jesus.

"I believe that, long ago, Edward Irving attempted the restoration of the Apostleship.

"He was thrust aside by the deception of the Devil; but I believe that if the Church had arisen and chosen twelve of the best men it had, and said, 'O God, it is a weak presentation to Thee, but we give to Thee the Apostolic Form. Fill it with Divine Power and the Power of the Holy Spirit,' God would have honored that form.

"We have a man perfectly fitted to fill this place.

"I believe that we have emphasized too much the human side, instead of the Divine.

Humanity Has Never Been Perfect.

"Paul had a quarrel with Barnabas, and they had to move apart; but they continued to be Apostles, and God blessed them.

"The Christ chose a Peter who could swear and deny Him.

"He chose other weak men, and He was patient with them and taught them.

"When the right time for the Early Rain came He filled them with the Holy Spirit.

"When the right time for the Latter Rain comes, God will pour the Holy Spirit upon the Church in its proper form, but not upon an improper form.

"The reason the Y. P. S. C. E., the Y. M. C. A., and other organizations have fallen to pieces is simply because they were not patterned after God's order.

"When Elijah the Restorer restored the Christian Catholic Church, however; when he restored the proper form of the Church, the Tide of Power began to rise.

"I feel like prophesying to our prophet, if he will pardon the presumption.

"I feel like turning back upon the General Overseer the text he gave to us a week ago yesterday, 'Arise, shine; for thy Light is come, and the Glory of Jehovah is risen upon thee. For, behold, darkness shall cover the earth, and gross darkness the peoples: but Jehovah shall arise upon thee, and His Glory shall be seen upon thee.'

"God has given the Glory of His Light and Power to the General Overseer, and all he has to do along Apostolic lines is to rise and shine, for the Glory of Jehovah is arisen upon him.

"That answers the question as to the time.

"I believe that the time has come.

Signs of Apostolic Office.

"In reply to the second question, I do recognize John Alexander Dowie as a Divinely-Commissioned Apostle.

"Why do we recognize Paul as an Apostle?

"People have asked me about this Elijah question: 'Why do you believe that John Alexander Dowie is Elijah the Restorer?'

"'It is in the Scriptures.'

"'Who put it in the Scriptures? Who wrote it? Where do you find it?' they ask.

"Paul testified of himself in the opening sentence of every one of his epistles.

"It was Paul himself who testified to his Apostleship.

"He wrote, 'I will come and show you that I am an Apostle.'

"There is where the man proved his own assertion; over and over again, he said, 'I was called to this office by God, and not by man.'"

GENERAL OVERSEER—John said regarding Diotrephes, "Diotrephes . . . receiveth not us."

ELDER COSSUM—"Yes, and he said he would come and prove it.

"Probably John Alexander Dowie will make the Declaration himself.

"He has made the Declaration of his prophetic office himself.

"Second, the works of an Apostle were shown in Paul.

"Third, you cannot answer such a question with material arguments. The final answer is from the Holy Spirit.

"It is the Spirit of God witnessing with our spirits that he is what he claims to be, and I say Yes to these questions."

Address of Elder John Dietrich.

ELDER DIETRICH—"Dear General Overseer, brothers and sisters in the Conference:—I feel in full accord with what has been spoken by the Overseers and Brother Cossum.

"When the first Conference was held last week, Wednesday, I was in full accord with these thoughts.

"When the questions finally came to my hand, and I had them before me, I sat down with my Bible in hand and studied them over.

"I answer them in the affirmative.

"I have gone back over the last ten years, since these questions came into our hands

"A devoted Christian sister, a member of my parish at that time, said, 'There is a man in Chicago who prays with the sick, and they are healed.'

"'Why,' I said, 'that is strictly Biblical.'

"'Yes,' she said, 'but he prays with the laying on of hands, and all kinds of healings take place.'

"'Why,' I said, 'that is correctly and straight Apostolic, and no other. If we were what we ought to be, strictly Apostolic, the same signs and wonders would follow now.'

"The only question with me is whether a man does the work, and God is with him.

"When Mother Clavadatscher was healed of cancer of the stomach in answer to John Alexander Dowie's prayer, I came to the conclusion that some one was raised up by God who had Apostolic power to pray the Prayer of Faith."

After giving the stories of Miracles of Healing in his own family, in answer to the General Overseer's prayers, Elder Dietrich said, "With all my heart I can say Yes to both these questions.

"May God's richest blessings rest upon our first Apostle!"

GENERAL OVERSEER—Mrs. Dowie desires me to convey to you her love. You heard her expression the other day.

She wishes me to say that she endorsed the speeches she heard here, and could only repeat her own expression of Saturday.

As to Discontinuance of Apostolic Office.

DEACONESS GURNEE—"When was the Apostolic Office discontinued?"

GENERAL OVERSEER—Many of the writings of the early Church were destroyed, and it is exceedingly wonderful that we have as much as we have left.

Nine apostles were chosen after the first twelve, and I do not think that the office was discontinued then; there is no proof of it.

Moreover some of the Apostles were challenged; even some of those that had been appointed by the Christ.

Men rose in the Church like Diotrephes, who disputed even John's Apostleship.

Probably the Apostleship was more or less continued in the second century, by consent of the whole Church; even that is a little problematical.

I do not know that the Church ever got together in Council in such a way as to be able most certainly to give the imprimatur of the whole Church to the Apostles.

But the Apostleship was independent of the imprimatur of the Church; it was really the Apostles that put the imprimatur upon the Church, rather than the Church the imprimatur upon the Apostles.

The probabilities are that the discontinuance took place in the Second Century.

Address of Elder O. L. Tindall.

ELDER TINDALL—"In reference to the first question, I think it is hardly worth discussing at all, because every one that signs the application for membership assents to that when he agrees to the organization of the Church."

Apostles Not to Be Chosen by Lot.

In reference to a point raised by Elder Tindall in his further discussion of this question, the General Overseer said:

I am not of the opinion that it would be a good thing to cast lots for the Apostleship.

I do not say anything against what the Apostles did when they elected Matthias.

I shall never believe that the Apostles should be called into existence by putting our hands into a lucky box.

ELDER TINDALL—"I do not believe that, either.

"My idea is that the Apostles ought to be chosen at once.

"In fact, my idea is that even earlier than this it should have been done, or could have been done. The Authority to do it came with the authority to organize the Church."

A Word as to Time of Declaration of Apostleship.

GENERAL OVERSEER—I would not like much discussion along that line, for this reason; that if I have erred on the side of being slow, I have certainly erred on the right side.

Secondly, I am more than doubtful; I am not convicted that I have erred at all.

I took the lower place of Prophet, when I might have taken the higher place of an Apostle; but I knew that the Prophetic work must be done, and that none but the Prophet of the Restoration could do it.

I had to take the lower place; I had to move in an orderly manner from the office of Teacher to that of Prophet; and then, when both the Church over which I presided and the world generally were compelled more or less to recognize the Prophetic Office, I have been able to move on to the third position.

ELDER TINDALL—"I do not wish to put it in the way I did, General Overseer. That is not a good way of putting it. I will state it the other way. My point is that, with the commission you had from God to restore the Church, He gave you the right to establish it and to organize it."

GENERAL OVERSEER—That is logical, because I had no right to establish the Church if I did not have Apostolic Power. It was Prophetic action based, in my own heart, upon Apostolic power.

ELDER TINDALL—"I have thought of the second question a little differently.

"The commission, and the office, and the work of the General Overseer are very clearly laid down under three heads.

"First, we find in Malachi, that which makes him the Messenger of the Covenant.

"In the next place he is called the Elijah; and under that office and title he is the Restorer of All Things.

"The next is that he is the Prophet foretold by Moses.

"Under that head we find a very strong declaration; so strong that I do not think we can make it any stronger.

"That declaration is:

And it shall come to pass, that every soul, which will not hear that Prophet, shall be utterly destroyed from among the people.

"Those three passages from the Word of God very clearly define his office.

"We believe that he is fulfilling those prophecies; but when we come to the subject of the Apostleship, it is not so clear to me.

"The references that are given here on the paper do not confirm it, in my mind."

GENERAL OVERSEER—But, my brother, you say you recognize my Apostleship.

ELDER TINDALL—"I recognize that you have the powers of the Apostleship."

GENERAL OVERSEER—Very well, that is definitely mentioned in the question, "Apostleship."

ELDER TINDALL—"It seems to me that you are not only an Apostle, but more than an Apostle."

GENERAL OVERSEER—I could not claim to be more than an Apostle, unless I claimed to be the Christ; and that I never will.

If ever I come to believe that, please put me in Kankakee; or please send me over to Ben MacDhui, and put a nice guard around me, until I recover my senses.

Do something, in charity, to keep me quiet; but do not let me ever be so forsaken of my God, and of good sense, as to make any declaration about myself as the Christ; for then I must be God Almighty; and I know of no step between an Apostle and the Christ, in the Church of God.

The Rule of the Church Under the Apostolic College.

I hope it is clear that what the embodiment of the Elijah spirit lacked in organizing power, and in other ways, both in the time of Ahab and in the time of Herod, has been supplied in these Latter Days.

Therefore, as more than a Prophet, I see no other place for me than that of President of the Apostolic College.

As President of that College, I would, of course, control it so far as I should have any right to control it, by the fact that I had been God's Prophet, and that I was still God's Prophet, His Messenger, with all the powers that the beloved brother has said, which I agree are tremendous powers.

It seems to me that the College will be powerless to force upon the Church anything to which the Prophet of the Restoration and President of the College will not agree.

It is quite clear that he who holds the Presidential seal, without which no document would be Apostolic, in the sense of the deliverance of the Apostolic Council, would certainly rule the Church, whether it be I, or another.

Then, you must remember that these Apostles will not be sitting in continual session; these Apostles will be sent out all over the earth.

One or two may be in Africa, perhaps two may be in China, one in Australia, one or two in India, and several in Europe and elsewhere.

The probabilities are that the only man who will be perpetually at the center of power will be the President of the Apostolic College, and he may be away sometimes.

I may be the first and the last President of the Apostolic College.

If this is the Time of the End, the probabilities are that I will be the first and last President, presuming that the Lord will come in my time.

I should insist upon the Apostolic College agreeing upon an Assistant, a Deputy; or agreeing upon my appointing such an one, who would bear the weight of office, and be familiar with the details of the office, in the event of my being suddenly called away.

But I would make a tremendous blunder if I should say to you, "I am not only Elijah, and not only an Apostle, but I stand away up somewhere near the Cherubim and Seraphim."

I am too earthly for that; I am too matter-of-fact. I am too much of a man like yourself for that.

I cannot get away up into the shadows, somewhere, where you cannot find me. I want you to find me.

Address of Elder Gideon Hammond.

ELDER GIDEON HAMMOND—"I have not risen with any idea of adding anything to what has been said. It seems to me that God is forcing us on with a dynamic irresistibility.

"'Do we believe and has the time come for us to reaffirm that the Apostolic Office should never have been discontinued, and ought to be restored?'

"I can say, as far as I know my own spirit, I fully believe it; and that the time has come to reaffirm it.

"I fully believe that the General Overseer is not only the Elijah, but that he goes higher than that, and is the Apostle to take the step, and to continue to run things just as he said.

Address of Elder Gilbert E. Farr.

ELDER FARR—"General Overseer, Brothers and Sisters:—I settled the first two questions in regard to the Apostolic Church, and in my own heart in regard to the General Overseer as the Apostle and Prophet, before I came into Zion.

"Six years ago, after reading a few copies of LEAVES OF HEALING, I saw some tracts and A VOICE FROM ZION advertised.

"I sent to Headquarters for all that were advertised.

"Among those tracts was the "Organization of the Church."

"I read it, and reread it, and studied it.

"From that tract I got the thought of the Apostolic Church; that this was to be organized upon that basis.

"I then began to study on that basis, and settled it in my own mind that that was the thing that should be in the present time—in the Church that is to be restored.

"I became thoroughly convinced that this was the thing to be restored in these times.

"Then I said, 'Who is to be the first Apostle?'

"I saw that the General Overseer was right in his interpretations; I saw that he spoke with Authority, and when I was through I said to myself, 'John Alexander Dowie must be an Apostle of the Lord Jesus, the Christ.'

"A friend of mine asked me, 'where are you to get the Apostolic succession?'

"I said, 'Jesus, the Christ's, arms are long enough to reach to the last early Apostle, and put His hand on him; and to John Alexander Dowie, and lay His hands on him. There we have the Apostolic succession; there is no break."

GENERAL OVERSEER—It is very evident to me that God is wonderfully blessing the Conference.

After some further discussion, the General Overseer began to draw the Conference to a close.

ELDER O. L. TINDALL said—"I do not want to be misunderstood. If you will make the Declaration, that will have more weight with me than anything else, because my idea has always been, that the man that is called of God to do a thing is the man to say it."

GENERAL OVERSEER—Well, have I not said that I recognize my Apostolic Authority?

ELDER TINDALL—"You have said it now; you did not say it before."

GENERAL OVERSEER—Well, I say it.

ELDER TINDALL—"Well, I accept it."

GENERAL OVERSEER—Is it the mind of the Conference that I shall put the questions?

OFFICERS—"Yes."

The Questions Answered Unanimously in the Affirmative.

GENERAL OVERSEER—Do we believe, and has the time come for us to reaffirm, that the Apostolic Office should never have been discontinued, and ought to be restored? All who want to answer that in the affirmative, please stand. [All stand.]

Do you believe, and has the time come for us to reaffirm, that the Apostolic Office should never have been discontinued, and ought to be restored? Will you please say, Yes or No?

OFFICERS—"Yes."

GENERAL OVERSEER—Any one who desires to say No, please say, No. [No answer.]

Will you please read the second question, Overseer Brasefield.

OVERSEER BRASEFIELD—"'Do we recognize John Alexander Dowie, our General Overseer, not only as the Prophet of the Restoration, but as a Divinely-Commissioned Apostle of the Lord Jesus, the Christ?'"

OFFICERS—"Yes."

[No noes.]

GENERAL OVERSEER—I have asked the Overseer to read that, because I would rather he would; and now, these two questions being answered, you have done more than you know.

You have given me—not any authority which I did not possess before, nor any which I do not possess; but you have given me great joy in the intelligent way you have discussed it, and in the final decision to which you have come.

BENEDICTION.

Beloved, abstain from every form of evil. And may the very God of Peace Himself sanctify you wholly; and I pray God your whole spirit, and soul, and body be preserved entire, without blame, unto the coming of our Lord Jesus, the Christ. Faithful is He that calleth you, who also will do it. The Grace of our Lord Jesus, the Christ, the love of God, our Father, the fellowship of the Holy Spirit, our Comforter and Guide, one Eternal God, abide in you, bless you, and keep you, and all the Israel of God everywhere, forever. Amen.

Change of Location in Toronto, Canada.

Zion Gathering in Toronto, Canada, has secured the old Friends' meeting house, 34 Pembroke street, where services will hereafter be conducted. It is easily reached by transferring from any street car line in the city to the Belt Line. Get off at Wilton avenue, and go west one block to Pembroke. Elder Brooks has also changed his residence to No. 360 Parliament street.

Second Anniversary
of
Zion Restoration Host

Lord's Day, Sept. 18, 1904.

A Special General Assembly of the Members of

Will be Held in Shiloh Tabernacle, Zion City, Ill.

Full Procession of Zion White-robed Choir, the Ordained Officers of the Church, and Members of Zion Restoration Host, will begin at 2.30 p. m. All members of Zion Restoration Host will appear in their sashes of Zion Colors.

The Declaration of

John Alexander, First Apostle of the Christian Catholic and Apostolic Church in Zion, and Elijah, the Prophet of the Restoration of all things

Will be Made at this Assembly.

All members of the Christian Catholic Church in Zion within reach are desired to attend. Seats will be reserved for them in the Tabernacle.

Special Excursion Trains will run from the Wells street Chicago and North-Western Station, in Chicago, beginning at 11 o'clock in the morning.

Round Trip Fare, 50 cents. THE CHRIST IS ALL AND IN ALL.

Zion Restoration Host

Elder A. F. LEE, Recorder

IT affords us great pleasure to introduce to the readers of this issue of LEAVES OF HEALING a very interesting group of Zion Restorationists who are doing some faithful work in the great city of London, England, and to give an interesting account of some of their recent work, as reported by Mr. H. Grant, one of their number.

London, England.

Though ye believe not Me, believe the works: . . . They sought again to take Him: and He went forth out of their hand.—*John 10:38, 39.*

The events in the life of the Christ which are described in the account closing with the above words, have been reenacted in the life of His Messenger, who has come to prepare the peoples for the return of Jesus as King of kings.

While in Adelaide some were taking up stones to stone him, Zion in London was preparing the multitudes for the coming of the Prophet of the Restoration by showing them the modern miracle of Restoration manifested in the beautiful City of Zion.

Five lime-light lectures on that City were given by Overseer Cantel in Zion Tabernacle, 81 Euston road, N. W., and five in halls in important outlying centers of the great metropolis.

In carrying the announcements of these lectures, the London Seventy of Zion Restoration Host took an important part.

On Easter Monday, April 4th, a public holiday, we visited Hampstead, a suburb in the north of London, and spent the morning on the heights of the Heath, enjoying a delightful recreation.

At noon, about one hundred members and friends sat down together in an adjacent pavilion for lunch, and the only rain of the day poured down while we were under cover.

During the afternoon the Host visited one thousand one hundred eighty-two homes, and sold about one hundred copies of LEAVES OF HEALING. The previous afternoon four companies had visited this neighborhood, and called at seven hundred ninety homes; and, as the result of their joint labors, five thousand announcement cards were distributed.

Tea was partaken of in the Drill Hall, off the High street, and the lecture was given in the Assembly Room of the same building, the audience numbering about three hundred fifty, so that at least two hundred fifty strangers saw the lime-light views of the beautiful City of Zion, and heard the work of God in Zion described.

The lecture was followed with deepest interest, and at the close several remained to inquire further concerning the way to Zion.

On Wednesday evening, April 20th, a similar lecture was given in the Assembly Rooms at Stoke Newington, a thickly-populated district in the northeast of London.

On the previous Lord's Day the Host had visited one thousand seven hundred homes, sold forty-one copies of LEAVES OF HEALING, and distributed two thousand cards; and during the week had completed their districts by visiting one thousand one hundred ninety homes and giving out three thousand cards.

The result, in part at least, was seen in a splendid audience of about three hundred fifty people, fully three hundred of whom were strangers, and they listened intently to the history and teachings of Zion as the pictures were thrown on the screen. Part of a local paper's report of the lecture reads as follows:

"For nearly an hour we were led, step by step, through the extraordinary work of Dowie and his 'disciples,' as evidenced by one of the most stupendous undertakings, which resulted in 'Zion'—a city unique in plan, with its up-to-date stores *a la* Whiteley; its lace factories, with its agents traversing the States, as the lecturer put it, 'combining religion with business;' its sugar and sweetmeat works, 'nothing but purity guaranteed,' and its parks, palatial dwelling-houses, etc."

The third lecture was delivered on the following Friday week, in the beautiful Town Hall of the Royal Borough of Kensington, which 'Society' people of the West End are wont to frequent.

Again the Restorationists loyally sustained their part, calling at one thousand three hundred seventeen homes on the preceding Lord's Day, selling seventy-three LEAVES OF HEALING, and giving two thousand invitation cards, and during the week visiting one thousand seventy-six more houses, thus completing the distribution of five thousand cards.

In consequence, quite four hundred people gathered in the Town Hall, and listened intently as Overseer Cantel told with much freedom of speech of the work of God in the establishment of a City of Righteousness, while the beautiful views of that City were before them on the seventeen-foot screen.

OVERSEER H. E. CANTEL, ORDAINED OFFICERS, AND A PORTION OF ZION RESTORATION HOST, LONDON, ENGLAND.

The lecture was completed with a powerful call to repentance, and in this manner "they that are rich" had an opportunity of entering into the Kingdom of God.

On the following Lord's Day evening, in Zion Tabernacle, the Overseer commenced a series of five lectures on the life of the Christ.

The titles of some of these lectures were: "The Cradle of Eternity," and "A Cross or a Crown?" and this, together with the announcement that the lectures would be illustrated with colored reproductions from the great masters, drew the attention of the people.

Each week a large poster in front of the Tabernacle announced the lectures to the thousands who pass along Euston road from the various railway termini there.

Week after week the Host went out each Lord's Day afternoon into neighboring districts, and visited six thousand and thirty homes, sold three hundred twenty-two copies of LEAVES OF HEALING, and distributed eleven thousand five hundred cards. Notwithstanding the approach of long twilight evenings, about one hundred strangers, in addition to our own people, gathered each Lord's Day evening.

Each lecture was supplemented with views of Zion City, thus proving from the works of God in Zion in these last days that "Jesus, the Christ, is the same yesterday and today, yea and forever."

At the close of each service the Overseer presented the command for Repentance and Obedience, and thus many were brought into the Kingdom.

About the middle of the month of May preceding the General Overseer's Visitation, Overseer Cantel undertook what proved to be one of the best and most largely attended of these lectures in the outlying centers of London's vast population.

A hall was secured in the Jewish quarter, Stepney, East London—one frequented by the Hebrew people for their weddings and assemblies.

Announcement cards and posters were printed in Yiddish, in addition to those in English; and, during the five days preceding Friday evening, May 13th, the Restorationists cheerfully gave what time they could after their daily occupation and journeyed to the districts assigned them, visiting, in all, two thousand six hundred eighty-one homes, and distributing seven thousand announcement cards.

The service commenced at the beginning of the Jewish Sabbath, and the ground floor of the hall was soon filled with three hundred people, mostly Hebrews, and the gallery was afterwards packed with another two hundred.

A crowd outside could not get in, and one man, who ran two miles from his workroom to see the views of the City of Zion, wept when he found the doors of the hall were closed.

The Overseer spoke to the people with much power concerning the manifestation of Jehovah in the restoration of Zion through the ministry of the promised Elijah, and the great truth that these mighty works had been done in the Name of the rejected Jesus of Nazareth went home to the hearts of his hearers.

After the lecture, many groups waited to inquire further concerning the Zion of the Holy One of Israel.

Into one of these a man came and spoke in Hebrew to one of the Restorationists who was teaching Jesus to the Jewish children.

"What does he say?" the Restorationist asked; and one of the elder girls replied: "He says, 'You are so kind to us.'"

It was just what the children had been saying; and the girl continued, "You must be Jews. The Christians are not kind to us, but you came to our homes with invitation cards and brought us to the meeting."

When the evenings are suitable for the lantern, we shall visit this district again and hold a larger meeting for the Jews, of whom there are more than one hundred thousand in London.

On Whit-Monday, May 23d, a party of Zion members and friends went out to Epping Forest, in the environs of Northeast London.

In the beautiful shade of the forest, near Buckhurst Hill, we enjoyed a morning of refreshing recreation, and took lunch together.

Before the Host workers left by train for their districts we gathered in a group and were photographed, as shown in the print accompanying this report.

During the afternoon the Host visited two thousand five hundred twenty-eight homes in Leyton, a residential suburb of middle-class people in East London, and distributed five thousand invitation cards.

The Town Hall had been secured for the lecture, and although it was a public holiday, when usually the people leave their homes, about four hundred congregated in the beautiful auditorium and enjoyed to the full the views and description of the City of Righteousness.

As it was at all these lectures, the Literature was sold freely to the people as they left the Hall, and opportunity was given after the service to deal with inquirers.

The trains were much overcrowded upon our return home, and we had to protest vigorously to keep free from the stinkpots' invasion of our non-smokers' carriages. We reached the London terminus, and dispersed to our homes in various parts of the city, rejoicing that we had been privileged to take some part in preparing for the release of the captives of this modern Babylon, through the coming of the Restorer.

The total record of Restoration Work done in connection with these ten lectures was, approximately, eighteen thousand five hundred homes visited, seven hundred LEAVES OF HEALING sold, and thirty-eight thousand five hundred announcement cards distributed.

Six hundred posters had also announced the lectures in the outlying centers, and each of these, as well as the announcement cards, showed a beautiful portrait of our General Overseer, whose benignant, prophetic features, as well as his great God-given Mission, are becoming known to earth's remotest bounds.

Following is a statistical report of the work done by the members of Zion Restoration Host throughout the United Kingdom during the quarter ending June 30th.

Town or City.	Houses Called at	Saloons Visited	Leaves Sold: Current	Leaves Sold: Back	Messages and C'rds Given
England—					
London	22930	230	428	729	59930
Ashton-u-Lyne	568	....	60	165	603
Birch	213	....	16	38	208
Bradford	1140	....	203	186	..
Cambridge	1812	....	130	358	....
Chorlton-cum-Hardy	2266	362	268	1097	2945
Crediton	69	....	....	14	54
Doncaster	79	....	91	26	....
East Ardsley	982	.. .	164	333	.. .
Ipswich	1085	14	187	308	642
Kelvedon	275	....	14	131	134
Kilnhurst	620	67	104	24	....
Leeds	4906	103	369	1526	....
Low Fell	1424	....	240	379	986
Morley	3743	....	368	451	...
Ramsgate	415	14	. .	82	495
St. Neots	...	.. .	....	45	115
Southend	17	...	....	146	...
Stanningley	2276	48	192	114	....
Scotland—					
Dundee	341	....	54	89	....
Edinburgh	1095	62	337	284	1217
Kings Kettle	..	1	....	71	139
Ireland—					
Belfast	2322	280	172	992	....
Londonderry	1221	....	. .	314	...
Special Work	1851	...	....	314	943
Total	51650	1181	3397	8216	68411

The Literature reported as sold in London is that sold by the Host only; in the Provinces that sold by the whole Branch.

We know that it will interest our readers to learn also that the little band of Restorationists in Yokohama, Japan, has been organized upon the regular plan, by our faithful brother Tokida, and that most faithful work is being done by them.

In addition to the statistical report for July, which follows, we publish a letter recently received from Mr. Tokida.

JAPAN	No. of Workers	Calls Made	Messages Given	Tracts Given	Tracts Sold
Yokohama	6	700	765	1	13

AUGUST 5, 1904.

REV. A. F. LEE, Recorder of Zion Restoration Host.

Dear Elder:—Peace to thee.

Enclosed please find the report for July.

Brother Uyeki removed to Tokyo in the early part of July, and so now we have no Company D. Company E's work is solely for the prisoners in the penitentiary, and so their report is not included in this report.

We all omitted work on one Lord's Day, on account of a storm.

Company C could go out only twice, for cause.

We have nothing interesting to tell you except that when we went to a house, and told the man that we came to invite him to learn the teachings of the Christ, he coolly put aside the Message and said, "I do not want anything of Christianity, for I have heard that the Christians are all spies of Russia."

There are many who misunderstand Christianity, through the war against Russia, for Russian soldiers in the field treat Japanese captives most cruelly, while the Japanese treat their dead and prisoners most kindly.

The political attitude of so-called Christian nations, is the greatest stumbling-block to our people.

There is no hope for the denominational church missionaries, who have more or less race prejudice.

The only hope is in Zion.

May God lead our people into the True Light through Zion!

Pray for us all.

Yours faithfully in His service, D. TOKIDA.

Reports from Various Points.

Following is a tabulated report of the number of workers and the work done by them during the month of July, 1904, according to reports received to date from the various points named:

UNITED STATES	No. of Workers	No. of Calls	Messages Given	Leaves Sold	Leaves Given
California—					
Fresno	2	233	237	44	38
Haywards	1	10	117	....	12
Los Angeles	6	1650	1569	186	71
San Francisco	12	3500	3500	850	55
Santa Rosa	1	35	70	7	46
St. John	2	90	90	..	122
Colorado—					
Durango	2	132	174	...	14
Trinidad	2	....	5	5	28
Connecticut—					
Meriden	1	3	...	....	19
Illinois—					
Chicago—Southeast Parish	24	1192	1912	125	47
" North Parish	26	628	699	17	135
" North Parish, Ger.	....	90	59	31	8
Highland Park	1	97	987	11	...
Pontiac	2	65	....	....	82
Quincy	2	150	200	30	100
Richmond	1	36	29	4	11
South Holland	2	....	300	....	93
Indiana—					
Albion	1	3	5	..	12
Indianapolis	6	4	600	88	65
Lafayette	4	407	1308	69	92
Linn Grove	1	....	5	....	3
Linton	1	...	200	4	12
Walton	2	10	30	....	26
Iowa—					
Cedar Falls	2	..	20	42	8
Council Bluffs	3	175	325	...	....
Dunkerton	1	48	55	6	6
Elberon	2	72	58	16	33
Forest City	1	2	274	48	4
Laporte City	1	25	22	5	27
Manson	1	32	50	....	6
Marcus	1	....	272	..	211
Newton	2	97	111	....	98
Rock Valley	1	129	412	31	20
Tipton	2	1	....	....	8
Webster City	5	42	600	15	93
Winterset	1	3	....	....	7
Kansas—					
Eskridge	1	80	76	52	8
Manhattan	2	18	112	31	80

UNITED STATES.	No. of Workers	No. of Calls	Messages Given	Leaves Sold	Leaves Given
Kentucky—					
Danville	1	2	309	....	6
Massachusetts—					
Boston	21	4161	2698	1883	306
Lawrence	10	802	1102	275	619
Michigan—					
Ingalls	1	23	23	9	....
Port Huron	5	275	524	114	76
Minnesota—					
Delavan	1	19	38	....	20
Milaca	1	100	170	10	52
Rushford	2	4	135	....	13
Missouri—					
Higginsville	1	103	129	26	19
St. Louis	21	5373	5043	519	8403
Tarkio	1	116	215	1	2
Montana—					
Havre	1	7	10	...	36
Nebraska—					
Falls City	1	2	100	42	50
Inman	1	16	29	....	1
New Hampshire—					
Franklin Falls	1	....	180	4	75
New Jersey—					
Salem	2	3	61	20	25
New York—					
Bluff Point	1	2	14	....	10
Poland	1	1	1	....	..
Syracuse	2	64	154	2	81
North Dakota—					
Denhoff	1	...	....	....	12
Ohio—					
Ada	2	....	26	6	....
Akron	2	184	53	30	122
Alliance	1	18	236	9	10
Bluffton	3	..	..	70	7
Cleveland	22	4319	6561	207	336
Dayton	1	29	76	10	3
Germantown	1	72	118	24	9
Lancaster	1	4	198	10	2
Lebanon	1	222	497	41	4
Mansfield	1	...	48	....	2
Nevada	1	....	5	....	4
Oceola	3	7	91		18
Toledo	2	500	75	129	4
Urbana	2	....	37	....	7
Oregon—					
Union	1	22	9	.	19
Pennsylvania—					
Philadelphia	26	2632*	12844	116	201
Scranton	2	32	122	185	64
West Chester	1	....	120	29	...
South Dakota—					
Alexandria	1	50	224	28	....
Belle	1	...	.	..	60
Brookings	1	250	120	25	28
Centerville	4	60	200	...	44
Summit	1	4	4	2	1
Tennessee—					
Memphis	1	9	134	2	8
Texas—					
Dallas	2	119	109	28	31
Houston	1	6	177	....	45
Virginia—					
Winston	1	10	48	....	15
Washington—					
Easton	2	48	49	7	6
Everett	2	196	202	29	22
Lynden	3	6	...	2	79
Seattle	25	2323	2024	589	246
Spokane	7	925	980	124	90
Tacoma	1	791	856	...	93
Wisconsin—					
Alma	1	31	62	7	19
Columbus	1	80	106	....	....
Kenosha	10	436	685	.	88
Maiden Rock	6	6	83	3	29
Omro	3	96	140	15	22
Racine	6	222	340	116	50
Viroqua	1	14	51	6	3
West Ellis	1	...	11	...	17
Total	359	33819	53189	6471	13314

DOMINION OF CANADA.	No. of Workers	No. of Calls	Messages Given	Leaves Sold	Leaves Given
Canada—					
Berlin	2	..	1352	...	36
Branchton	1	27	32	....	18
Cathcart	1	.	.	30	....
Elmira	2	..	550	....	11
Galt	3	58[illegible]	631	..	31
Ladysmith	1	4	10	.	5
Simcoe	2	66	113	74	4
Toronto	20	2058	4220	240	1212
Vancouver	19	[illegible]	1804	233	463
Victoria	2	[illegible]	270	93	79
Woodstock	1	99	55	20	72
Total	54	[illegible]	9533	[illegible]	1931
Grand Total	413	[illegible]	[illegible]	[illegible]	15245

Notes of Thanksgiving From the Whole World

By Overseer J. G. Excell, General Ecclesiastical Secretary.

Healed of Fractured Limb.

And He took him by the right hand,
And raised him up:
And immediately his feet and his ankle-bones received strength.—*Acts 3:7.*

ZION CITY, ILLINOIS, March 19, 1904.

DEAR GENERAL OVERSEER:—Peace to thee.

I am glad to be able to write my testimony to the wonderful things God has done for me.

About thirty-four years ago my entire right side was paralyzed, so that I could only hobble around the house, and that with great difficulty.

When I went out of doors, I had to have help to get around. I could not use my right hand at all.

I took many different kinds of medicine; also electric baths.

I was treated by many different physicians, but became no better.

But, thanks be to God, shortly after you laid hands on me and prayed, I began to get better. My general health continually improved, so that I was able to do my own housework, until the last day of August, 1903, when I fell down-stairs and broke one of the bones near the ankle in my paralyzed leg. I was also severely bruised in different parts of my body.

I sent for Deacon Sloan who came and prayed, but said that my leg was fractured, and advised me to send for Overseer Speicher.

I did so; he came and prayed. The Lord healed the broken bone without any pain, so that in six weeks I moved to another house.

I continue to improve in my paralyzed side, so that I am now much better than I have been in thirty-four years.

I have been able to do all my housework ever since last Christmas.

I thank God for you, dear General Overseer, for Overseer Jane Dowie, and for the blessed privilege of living in Zion City. I hope to be living here when the Lord comes, although I am now sixty-seven years old.

Faithfully yours, Till Jesus Come,

ALVIRA LAURA BURT.

Prayer for Rain Answered.

But as for me, I would seek unto God,
Who giveth rain upon the earth.—*Job 5:8, 10.*

MILAN, MICHIGAN, June 28, 1904.

DEAR OVERSEER:—Peace to thee.

Your letter received. Your prayer was answered.

We thank God that He did hear and answer the prayers of His children.

On Friday we had two light showers, and the next day a beautiful rain, for which we praise Him "from whom all blessings flow."

Your sister in the Christ,

(MRS.) W. W. KELSEY.

Healed of a Burn.

Then saith He to the man, Stretch forth thy hand.
And he stretched it forth; and it was restored whole, as the other.—*Matthew 12:13.*

401 CENTRAL STREET,
FRANKLIN FALLS, NEW HAMPSHIRE,
April 17, 1904.

DEAR OVERSEER:—I write you with a heart full of gratitude for all that my Heavenly Father has granted unto me since I came to Zion.

I wish to tell you of one healing in particular.

Last week, April 7th, I went to the coffee-pot to get some coffee which was on the stove.

In doing so, I accidentally tipped the content over my hand.

I was severely burned. I suffered great pain a few minutes.

Several people came around me and war to put something on it, but I refused and went the Great Physician, who is ever ready to hea when we call upon Him.

Praise God! He heard and answered.

All the pain left my hand instantly, and it quite cold.

I went up to one lady, showing it to her, she said, "What did you put on it?" I answe "Nothing; I prayed to my Heavenly Father."

She said that it was wonderful.

One would never have known I had recei such a burn.

It is so much better to trust in the Lord tha man!

If people would only accept this truth m readily, how much more happiness there would in the world!

I thank God more and more every day for and for her leader. May God's richest bles rest upon Zion throughout the world.

I trust this little testimony will be a blessin some one.

Yours faithfully, Till Jesus Come.

LIZZIE WEB

Healed of Scrofula and Rickets.

And I will cleanse their blood that I have not cleansed Jehovah dwelleth in Zion.—*Joel 3:21.*

BAKERSFIELD, CALIFORNIA, August 14, 190

DEAR GENERAL OVERSEER:—I wish to add testimony to that of thousands of others, and thank you for the teaching of Jesus, our Savior, is able to save us, spirit, soul, and body.

My little girl had rickets so badly that she not able to go to school, and I had scrofula whi inherited. Nearly every part of my body diseased. Neither of us got any better until E Ernst, of Tacoma, Washington, prayed for us. were received into the Christian Catholic Chur Zion, where I have been an active member since.

I praise the Lord for our leader, and for teaching of Zion.

We have been to Zion City twice, and you prayed for both of us, for which we thank you much.

Yours, Till He Come, (MRS.) ROLP

Delivered in Childbirth.

But she shall be saved through the childbearing.
If they continue in faith and love and sanctification sobriety.—*1 Timothy 2:15.*

EAST ARDSLEY, NEAR WAKEFIELD
YORKSHIRE, ENGLAND.

DEAR GENERAL OVERSEER:—I have plea in testifying to God's goodness and tender me towards me in many ways, especially in the re fulfilment to me of His promise given i Timothy 2:15.

My deliverance was a wonder both to me to the sisters who attended me.

I give God the praise, and am thankful to Deacon and others for their prayers.

Praying that God will bless our dear Gen Overseer, his dear wife, and son. I am,

Yours in the Christ, (MRS.) E. HIL

STIRRING TRUTHS FOR WIDE-AWAKE CHRISTIANS

Present Day Themes of REV. JOHN ALEXANDER DOWIE,
General Overseer of the Christian Catholic Church in Zion

The following list of Pamphlets, Books, and Tracts, supplied on receipt of price by
ZION PRINTING AND PUBLISHING HOUSE
ZION CITY, LAKE COUNTY, ILLINOIS, U. S. A.

Zion, Her Organization, Truths, and Leader.

	Vol.	No.	Price
Zion's Answer to the Messenger of the Nation	3	8	$0.05
Organization of the Christian Catholic Church	2	2	.10
Principles, Practices and Purposes of the Christian Catholic Church in Zion, and The Everlasting Gospel	4	8	.05
Conquests for Christ in America: Past, Present, and to Come	4	5	.05
By What Authority Doest Thou These Things? and The Voice of One Crying in The Wilderness	4	4	.05
Elijah the Restorer and General Letter from the General Overseer	5	7	.05
The Times of Restoration	5	8	.10
The Beatitudes	4	10	.05
The Kingdom of God is Come, Suffering on Behalf of Christ, and Let Not Your Heart be Troubled	4	9	.05
Repentance	3	11	.05
Ye are Come Unto Mount Zion. Will a Man Rob God?	3	2	.05
The Love of God in the Salvation of Man	4	11	.10
The Christian Ordinance of Baptism by Triune Immersion	1	12	.05
The Ordinance of Christian Baptism (18 centuries of proof)	5	10	.05
Organization of Zion Restoration Host	6	12	.05
The City of God; and What Shall This Child Be?	7	2	.05

Zion's Replies to Her Enemies and Critics.

	Vol.	No.	Price
Zion and Her Enemies	3	12	$0.05
Fighting Blackmailers	3	3	.05
Estimates and Realities: Reply to Baptist Ministers	2	11	.05
Reply to D. L. Moody and the *Ram's Horn*	3	10	.05
Reply to *Ram's Horn* of March 3d	4	3	.05
"You Dirty Boy," Reply to Rev. P. S. Henson, D. D.	2	3	.05
Reply to Dr. Hillis	1	3	.05
Christ's Methods of Healing: A Reply to Rev. J. L. Withrow, D. D.	2	5	.05
Reply to Dr. Gray	3	9	.05
Reply to Ingersoll's Lecture on Truth	1	4	.05

The Evils Zion Exposes and Condemns.

	Vol.	No.	Price
Doctors, Drugs, and Devils; or, The Foes of Christ the Healer	1	10	$0.05
Secret Societies: The Foes of God, Home, Church, and State	1	8	.05
Zion's Protest Against Swine's Flesh as a Disease-Producer	2	6	.05
Tobacco, Satan's Consuming Fire	2	7	.05
The Press: The Tree of Good and Evil	2	10	.05
Ethiopia Stretching Out Her Hands to God	1	11	.05
False Christian Science Unmasked	2	8	.05
Christian Science Exposed as an Anti-Christian Imposture	3	5	.05
Diabolical Spiritualism Unmasked	2	12	.05
The Man of Sin Revealed; or, An Exposure of the Blasphemous Claim of the Pope of Rome to be the Infallible Head of the Church of Our Lord Jesus Christ	3	7	.05
Ingersoll Exposed	3	4	.05
Spurious Holiness Exposed	5	3	.05

Divine Healing and Its Truths as Taught in Zion.

	Vol.	No.	Price
Jesus the Healer and Satan the Defiler	4	2	$0.05
Do You Know God's Way of Healing? and He is Just the Same Today	4	1	.05
Reasonings for Inquirers Concerning Divine Healing Teaching	4	7	.05
Divine Healing Vindicated	2	9	.05
Lessons on Divine Healing, from the Story of the Leper	4	12	.05
Job's Boils; or, Objections to Divine Healing Considered	3	6	.05

	Vol.	No.	Price
What Should a Christian Do When Sick?	2	1	$0.05
"I Will"	1	9	.05
Permission and Commission	1	2	.05
How Jesus Heals the Little Ones	5	2	.05
Talks with Ministers	1	6	.05

Prayer and Its Conditions as Realized in Zion.

	Vol.	No.	Price
How to Pray	2	4	$0.05
If It Be Thy Will, Like a Shepherd, and How I Came to Speak for Jesus	4	6	.05
A Woman of Canaan	1	1	.05
The Disciples' Prayer, a series of Morning Discourses at Shiloh Tabernacle	7	3	.10

Zion Standard of Consecration and Sanctified Living.

	Vol.	No.	Price
Sanctification of Spirit, Soul, and Body	1	7	$0.05
The Seal of the Living God	5	4	.05
The Baptism of Fire, and The Cup of Suffering	5	5	.05
Ye are God's Witnesses, and The Power of Passive Faith	5	6	.05
The Chains of Good and Evil, and Sanctification of Triune Man	5	1	.05
Redemption Draweth Nigh	1	5	.05
Zion's First Feast of Tabernacles	5	9	.10
Zion Bible Calendar	3	1	.05
Four Addresses: — Love Fulfils Law; The Zion of the Holy One of Israel; The Wages of Sin; and Seest Thou This Woman?	6	4	.05
The Leaven of the Kingdom	7	4	.05

Devotional and Inspirational Zion Tracts.

Two Cents Each.

How I Came to Speak for Jesus.
If It Be Thy Will.

One Cent Each.

Do You Know God's Way of Healing?
If It Be Thy Will.
Jesus the Healer.
Satan the Defiler.
How I Came to Speak for Jesus.
He is Just the Same Today.

Suitable for enclosing in envelopes.

Special Books.

	Price
Zion's Conflict with Methodist Apostasy	$0.25
Zion's Holy War	.35

Tracts of Zion in Foreign Languages.

	Price
German:	
I Will	$0.05
How to Pray	.05
Permission and Commission	.05
A Woman of Canaan	.05
The Ordinance of Christian Baptism	.05
Organization of the Christian Catholic Church	.10
What Shall a Christian Do When Sick?	.05
Christian Science Exposed as an Anti-Christian Imposture	.05
Reasonings for Inquirers	.05
Sanctification of Spirit, Soul, and Body	.05
How I Came to Speak for Jesus	.02
How Jesus Heals the Little Ones	.05
Do You Know God's Way of Healing?	.01
He Is Just the Same Today	.01
How I Came to Speak for Jesus	.01
Elias	.05
Divine Healing Vindicated	.05
Zion's Protest Against Swine's Flesh	.05
French:	
How I Came to Speak for Jesus	.02
How Jesus Heals the Little Ones	.05
Danish:	
He is Just the Same Today	.02
Do You Know God's Way of Healing	.02
Norwegian:	
If It Be Thy Will	.02
Holland:	
Divine Healing Vindicated	.05

Rates for Quantity Orders.

Charges Prepaid.

Kinds at 35 cents:	$3.75 a dozen.
Kinds at 25 cents:	2.75 a dozen.
Kinds at 10 cents:	1.00 a dozen or $6.00 per 100
Kinds at 5 cents:	.50 a dozen or 3.00 per 100
Kinds at 2 cents:	.75 for 50 or $1.25 per 100.
Kinds at 1 cent:	.60 for 100.

Elijah's Restoration Messages.

	Vol.	No.	Price
Five Messages:—The Purifying Word; Purification by Obedience; The Purifying Water of Life; Purification by the Word of Wisdom; and Purification by Penal Fire	6	1	$0.05
Two Messages:—Christ, the World Conqueror; and Hear What the Unjust Judge Saith	6	2	.05
Five Messages:—Zion's Star of Hope and Peace; Thy God Reigneth; Peace Passing All Understanding; Then Peaceable; Sowing Peace	6	3	.05
Two Messages: — Until Shiloh Come; delivered at the consecration of Shiloh Tabernacle, Zion City, Illinois, March 31, 1902. Theocracy Contrasted with Democracy and Plutocracy, Chicago Auditorium, April 23, 1902.	6	5	.05
Two Messages, at Chicago Auditorium:—Power Belongeth Unto God; The Power and the Wisdom of God	6	6	.05
Two Messages, at Chicago Auditorium:—The Power of Divine Faith; and The Power of Christ's Resurrection	6	7	.05
Two Messages, at Chicago Auditorium:—The Power of a Living Faith; and The Power of the Word of God	6	8	.05
Two Messages, at Chicago Auditorium:—Awake; and The River of God is Full of Water	6	9	.05
Two Messages, at Chicago Auditorium:—The Power of Sacrifice; and Power of the Covenant, and Elijah the Restorer	6	10	.05
Three Messages, at Chicago Auditorium:—On the Purification of The Temple	6	11	.05
One Message, at Chicago Auditorium:—Saved Whole	7	1	.05

Zion's Second Feast of Tabernacles.

A book of over 300 pages, nicely bound in cloth, 30 cents. By mail, 10 cents extra. Should be in the libraries of all Zion people.

Leaves of Healing

A weekly paper for the extension of the Kingdom of God: Containing accounts of Miracles of Healing; Stenographic Reports of Sermons by the Editor; with Testimonials of Blessing realized by God's people through the ministry of the Christian Catholic Church in Zion, of which the Rev. John Alexander Dowie is the General Overseer.

Subscription price, $2 per year; $1.25 for six months; $0.75 for three months. Clubs of ten, $15. To ministers and Public Libraries, $1.50 per year. Foreign subscriptions, $3.50 per year.

Bound Volumes I, II, III, IV, V, VI, VII, VIII, IX, X, XI, XII and XIII, $3.50 per Volume. Three or more Volumes, $3.00 each. Entire set, $32.50. Carriage on bound volumes always to be paid by purchaser.

Blätter der Heilung.

German Edition of LEAVES OF HEALING. Monthly, $0.50 per year. Foreign, $0.75 per year.

The Zion Banner.

A weekly semi-secular paper devoted to the extension of the Kingdom of God and the Elevation of Man, containing the news of Zion City, brightly and interestingly told; the news of the world up to within a few hours of its publication, and editorials on current events from a Zion standpoint. Edited by the Rev. John Alexander Dowie.

Subscription price, $0.50 for six months; $0 30 for three months. Sold for three cents a copy.

A Voice From Zion.

Monthly. Containing leading Sermons by the Rev. John Alexander Dowie. $0.50 per year. Foreign, $0.75 per year.

Bound Volumes I, II, III, IV, V, VI and VII Voice from Zion, may be secured at $1 per Volume; the complete set for $6.10, F. O. B Zion City.

All orders for above publications except those quoted at other prices in the foregoing lists, under 25 copies, 5 cents per copy; exceeding 25 copies, 4 cents per copy; 100 or more copies, 3 cents per copy. If mailed to a foreign address, add 3 cents per copy for additional postage.

Trial subscriptions (new), LEAVES OF HEALING, 10 weeks for 25 cents each; BLÄTTER DER HEILUNG, 10 months for 25 cents each. Foreign 55 cents.

Make All Remittances Payable to the Order of John Alex. Dowie.

Notes of Thanksgiving from the Whole World

By Overseer J. G. Excell, General Ecclesiastical Secretary.

Healed of Catarrh and Extreme Nervousness.

To him that hath no might He increaseth strength.

. . . .

But they that wait upon Jehovah shall renew their strength.—*Isaiah 40:29, 31.*

3000 ELIZABETH AVENUE,
ZION CITY, ILLINOIS, July 7, 1904.

DEAR OVERSEER:—Peace to thee.

I feel that I can no longer remain silent regarding God's wondrous goodness and mercy manifested towards me during the last two or three years, especially during the year that has just passed.

As a child I inherited catarrh and nervousness from my father, and, as I grew older, both these troubles increased until, in 1902, I became so worn and nervous, consequent upon the strain of teaching and studying music at the same time, that I had to give up my studies at the conservatory of music at Toronto.

After the February examination at the conservatory, I was feeling very miserable; and as spring passed and summer advanced, my life became a burden to me.

Often it would seem as if I had gone as far as I could, but God graciously gave me strength to continue my work.

I had severe sinking spells, but as the weather grew cooler, I became stronger.

In the spring of 1903, and also during the summer months, I had to again fight my old enemy; but God again answered prayer in my behalf, and I felt splendidly the following winter.

In December, I came to Zion City and took a position in Zion Milling and Baking Industries, but before I had been there a month the heat and noise of the machinery brought back the old trouble with overwhelming force, and terrible sinking spells would come upon me.

My heart was so weak that even raising my eyes caused it to flutter, and my eyes became so sensitive that I could not look at anything bright without causing them to smart and pain terribly.

For two weeks the sinking spells continued almost daily; and, if I missed them one day, I had a heavier attack the next.

For half or three-quarters of an hour, I would gradually get weaker, until I would lapse into a state of semi-consciousness for about ten minutes; on awakening from this condition, I was so weak that it seemed as if I could scarcely move.

When these spells occurred at night, they were accompanied by night sweats and a terrible smothering sensation.

I would awake in the middle of the night, gasping for breath, which rendered it necessary to raise a window, or open a door.

I could scarcely bear to hear any one move or speak, and if any one touched me, it was all I could do to refrain from screaming.

I attended the Divine healing meeting conducted by Elder Adams, the last Tuesday in February, and when he prayed for me with the laying on of hands, instantly a warm sensation passed down each side of my head, through my ears and round to the back of my neck, and I knew that God had taken away the catarrhal trouble.

My nerves were stronger, although I did not get a complete victory until the following Saturday morning, when I went back to work, determined to conquer.

That afternoon I received a wondrous blessing, as the full significance of what God had done for me began to dawn upon me.

I felt like one raised from the dead.

Ever since then my nerves, heart, and eyes have been stronger, and there is not a vestige of catarrh manifest, except when I have a severe cold in my head.

I feel that I can scarcely praise God enough for the love and care shown to us, and for the many answers to prayer received for many lesser ailments in the home.

Praying that God may bless this testimony to some one, and that He may continue abundantly to bless and prosper Zion, her leader, and all those under him, I am,

Yours in the Master's service,

MURIEL MINNS.

Healed and Blessed in Zion — Blessed in Tithing.

Delight thyself also in Jehovah;
And He shall give thee the desires of thine heart.—*Psalm 37:4.*

2703 EZRA AVENUE, ZION CITY, ILLINOIS,
April 25, 1904.

DEAR GENERAL OVERSEER:—Peace to thee.

It has been upon my heart for some time to tell, in a measure—for the half can never be told—what God has done for me.

During the month of June, 1899, LEAVES OF HEALING came to me.

I thank God that I believed its Message to be true.

When I had doubt as to some portions of it being contrary to God's Word, I searched the Scriptures. Not once did I find any difference.

I praise God that by reading the LEAVES I became interested in the Bible. The more I read the Bible the more I loved it.

I had a similar experience with LEAVES OF HEALING.

My parents, brothers and sisters also became interested in Zion Literature.

In the year 1900, I was baptized by Triune Immersion.

I received great blessing at that time.

The following year I came to Zion City, which place has since been my home.

I am so glad to be here!

I am a member of Zion White-robed Choir and Zion Restoration Host.

God has most wonderfully saved, healed, cleansed, and kept me; for which I praise Him.

I also thank Him for you, dear General Overseer, who have toiled so long and faithfully, preaching the Full Gospel of our Lord Jesus, the Christ, and publishing LEAVES OF HEALING, a paper which has brought much blessing to us all.

When visiting at my home in northern Iowa, where there are no Zion members, I would take copies of LEAVES OF HEALING, and read Dr. Dowie's sermons, which was a great pleasure to me.

I wish to add my testimony to that of many others concerning tithing.

God has fulfilled his promise. Since paying tithes, I get double the salary I got when not paying them.

May Jehovah bless you, and Overseer Jane Dowie and Dr. Gladstone Dowie, and spare you to the ministry many years.

May Jehovah bless you abundantly, till Jesus comes.

Yours in the Master's service,

(MISS) DELLA DORETHA GIBSON.

Healed of Growth in Throat.

The things which are impossible with men are possible with God.—*Luke 18:27.*

937 NORTH ARTESIAN AVENUE,
CHICAGO, April 27, 1904.

BELOVED OVERSEER:—Words cannot express my gratitude toward God and Zion for all I have received in spirit, soul and body.

Five years ago, I began to feel a growth in my throat, which troubled me considerably. It grew very rapidly and distressed me very much.

It alarmed me somewhat, as I also felt sick through my whole body.

On the 15th of April, I went to Deaconess Peetz, who wrote out a request for prayer, asking you to pray for me.

Sunday morning I felt better in my throat, believing in my heart that God would hear and answer your prayer; but I was suffering with a very severe headache.

I went to the Tabernacle in the afternoon, and after the service asked Deaconess Peetz to pray for me. She laid hands on me and prayed.

Twenty minutes later, just as I reached my home, I threw up a piece of some stringy substance about four inches in length covered with fangs or roots.

I have felt a drawing from this growth up to my ear, especially on my right side.

God in His infinite love and mercy has healed me.

I thank you for your prayers, and may God forever bless you in His service.

I also want to add, that my children and myself were healed at different times of different ailments, through the prayers of our beloved General Overseer and Zion.

May God make the General Overseer a mighty power and blessing to all the nations of the earth is our earnest prayer.

Faithfully yours in the Christ,

(MRS.) MATHILDA LUTZ

Healed of Consumption and Heart and Stomach Trouble.

I will cry unto God Most High;
Unto God that performeth all things for me.—*Psalm 57:2*

1410 MISSOURI STREET,
TOLEDO, OHIO, May 11, 1904.

DEAR OVERSEER SPEICHER:—I praise God for His wonderful mercy to me, and for His saving, healing and keeping power.

March 9, 1895, a sweet little girl came to our home; but in a few months I was not able to do my housework and scarcely care for my two children. We were living in Kendallville, Indiana, at that time.

I had always been taught to call for a doctor when sick, instead of doing as God's Word says: "Is any among you sick? let him call for the elders of the church; and let them pray over him."

The doctor I went to told my husband that my lungs were very much affected, that my heart was weak.

My stomach troubled me much of the time.

However, when I think of the swine's flesh we ate, I wonder that my stomach was not more diseased than it was.

I kept taking medicine until I was disgusted, and became no better, but only worse.

In February, 1896, I had the grip and pleurisy.

Thinking I might get better I went to another

doctor. I could hardly walk two blocks, the distance to his office, I had so much pain in my lungs. He said that I was all run down.

I understood my condition. I had inherited consumption from my father, who had died of that terrible disease in 1894.

I also had granulation of the eyelids.

The doctor burned them six times with caustic, until it seemed to me that my eyes would burst.

At this time Rev. Mr. Fletcher, pastor of First Baptist church of Wolcottville, Indiana, of which I was a member, sent LEAVES OF HEALING to me—Volume II., No. 5. It was all new to me.

I read the testimony of Mrs. S. A. Kelly. The Bible became like a new Book. I could see God's promises as I never had seen them before.

I had a great desire to come to Chicago to the Divine Healing Home; but the way was not open for me to do so.

I sent a request for prayer to the General Overseer and Overseer Jane Dowie.

March 9, 1896, I was healed of pleurisy and granulated eyelids.

I grew better slowly, as I knew so little of God's way and sometimes doubted.

We are told in God's Word that we should ask, nothing wavering

Soon after this a Branch of Zion was organized at Wolcottville, Indiana.

I became a member of the Christian Catholic Church in Zion at that time.

I attended a Divine Healing meeting, at Zion Home, Michigan boulevard, Chicago, in October, 1898.

Overseer Speicher led the meeting, and prayed for the sick in the Name of the Lord Jesus. I received a blessing in both spirit and body.

I knew that I was healed. My cough soon left me. I became strong, and did all the work in my home.

I praise God for Zion teaching.

My daily prayer is that God will bless Zion's leader and Zion everywhere.

Yours in the Master's service,

(MRS.) GEORGIA SAWYER

Confirmation of Mrs. Sawyer's Testimony.

ANTIOCH, ILLINOIS, May 26, 1904.

DEAR GENERAL OVERSEER.—I wish to confirm what my sister has said concerning her healing of consumption as being the truth.

It was through your prayer, and God's wonderful mercies, that she was healed.

May God bless you and yours.

Your sister in the Christ,

(MRS.) MARTHA HEIGN.

Healed of Injury Received in Sawmill.

If ye abide in Me,
And My words abide in you,
Ask whatsoever ye will,
And it shall be done unto you.—*John 15:7.*

WEST KORTRIGHT, NEW YORK, March 20, 1904.

DEAR OVERSEER SPEICHER:—Yours of the 8th received, stating that you had prayed for me as requested, and asking for my testimony, which I gladly give, to the glory of God.

While operating a sawmill, I reached over the gage roller frame to turn down a board, and I slipped on the floor, causing almost all of my weight to come on the frame, which is only about one-half an inch wide, with the result that I injured myself about the stomach. Nevertheless, I continued to work until night.

This was on Friday. On Saturday I felt weak, and after eating breakfast went to bed.

I had no appetite until Lord's Day morning.

Towards night on Saturday my head began to ache very hard.

I promised the Lord that if He would deliver me from my headache I would write for prayer, and in a few minutes I went to sleep.

When I awoke, Lord's Day morning, my head had stopped aching, so I wrote to you for prayer for my continued healing. From that time I continued getting better, and am now perfectly healed. Praise the Lord!

He healed my eye in answer to the General Overseer's prayer, my testimony to which appeared in LEAVES OF HEALING, Volume 13, No. 22.

I thank the Lord for His healing and keeping power, and you for your prayer in my behalf.

Yours in the Christ, HOMER L. GREEN.

Healed of Stomach Trouble.

Then shall thy light break forth as the morning, and thy healing shall spring forth speedily: and thy righteousness shall go before thee; the glory of Jehovah shall be thy rearward.—*Isaiah 58:8.*

773 MERCHANT STREET, LOS ANGELES, CALIFORNIA, February 20, 1904.

DEAR GENERAL OVERSEER:—I feel it a duty to God to write a few words as a testimony to His goodness to me since my coming into the Christian Catholic Church in Zion.

It is now almost eight years since I first attended the meetings of Zion.

I was then near the grave.

I thank and praise God for the healing of that awful stomach trouble, through the prayer of the General Overseer.

During the years since, God has healed me many times through the Prayer of Faith by Zion Elders and other officers of the Church.

I also thank God for the spiritual blessing I have received, and I look forward in confidence to more strength and spiritual power to serve Him better in the future, and to more fully aid in the extension of the Heavenly Kingdom.

I give herewith my sincere thanks to you, dear General Overseer, and to the brethren and sisters in Zion, for your faithful prayers in my behalf.

I pray that God may continue to bless you and your family, and all Zion everywhere.

May God grant that Zion shall conquer the world for the Kingdom of God, and be faithful until the Coming of our Lord Jesus, the Christ.

Your brother and servant in the Lord,

LOUIS FISCHER.

Healed of Malaria and Cramps.

I will cry unto God Most High,
Unto God that performeth all things for me.—*Psalm 57:2*

TOLEDO, OHIO, June 4, 1904.

DEAR OVERSEER SPEICHER:—It is with thankfulness that I write my testimony for what God has done for me through Zion's teaching.

God has healed me many times through your prayers.

We sent a request June 22d for prayer for healing of malaria and cramps.

God heard and answered.

Elder Cairns also prayed, with laying on of hands.

I soon was as strong as ever.

We thank God!

Yours in the Master's service,

W. HUGH SAWYER.

Healed of Female Trouble and Bowel Trouble.

I am Jehovah that healeth thee.—*Exodus 15:26.*

773 MERCHANT STREET, LOS ANGELES, CALIFORNIA, February 20, 1904

DEAR GENERAL OVERSEER:—In gratitude to God, and to you, His servant, I write a few words of testimony to the blessings I have received while in Zion.

I praise God and thank Him for the healings I have received in these last eight years.

I was healed of female trouble, of stomach trouble, and of many other sicknesses.

I thank Him for His keeping power and for the spiritual truth He has revealed to me through the teachings of Zion.

I pray that God will keep me faithful to serve Him fully with all the strength He gives me.

I thank you, dear General Overseer, for your kindness in praying for me.

May God bless you and yours abundantly until the coming of our Lord Jesus, the Christ.

Yours in the Christ, (MRS.) MINNIE FISCHER.

God Answers Prayer of Faith for Dumb Animal.

And Jehovah shall sever between the cattle of Israel and the cattle of Egypt, and there shall nothing die of all that belongeth to the children of Israel.—*Exodus 9:4.*

EASTVILLE, NOVA SCOTIA, June 23, 1904.

DEAR GENERAL OVERSEER:—Last winter, while alone, my colt walked into the granary which was near the stable, where he had access to all the grain he could eat.

I felt very badly about it, as he was left in my charge, both my sons being away.

I felt certain that he would die when the wheat had swelled.

In a few hours, just as I expected, he was in terrible agony, growing worse all the time.

No neighbors were near to advise me what to do, and I felt sure they could not do anything if they were.

When I thought he was about to die, I confessed everything that I had done that was wrong, and fully trusted God.

After offering prayer, I went to the stable again.

The colt stood there, the swelling all gone, looking just the same as before touching the wheat.

What a kind and loving Father we have! We should consecrate ourselves and all that we have to Him, and receive His blessing in return.

Yours in love for the truth, (MRS.) E. FISHER.

Healed of Growth on Eye.

Because we have our hope set on the Living God.—*1 Timothy 4:10.*

SAN JOSE, CALIFORNIA, June 15, 1904.

DEAR GENERAL OVERSEER:—I feel it my duty to write of God's goodness to me; of His healing and keeping power.

It is now a year since I was healed of an abscess or growth on one of my eyes, which had been there for eight months. It was very annoying.

I had hoped it would get better, but instead another abscess formed on the same eye.

I then decided to go to a doctor, just to see what he would say about it. He told me that they must be drawn away, and he wanted to perform an operation at once, but because we had friends in Zion, and had heard of others who had been healed, we refused to allow him to operate.

Prayer was offered for me, and the prayer was answered.

My eye is all right now, and has not troubled me since being healed.

Praise God from whom all blessings flow!

Your sister in the Christ,

(MRS.) J. F. BEUTTEL.

Child Healed Through Faith in God.

Whoso putteth his trust in Jehovah shall be safe.—*Proverbs 29:25.*

TOLEDO, OHIO, 1410 MISSOURI STREET.

DEAR OVERSEER SPEICHER:—I praise God for Zion. God has healed me many times in answer to prayer.

May God bless you. EDITH FLOSS SAWYER.

Form of Application for Membership in the Christian Catholic Church in Zion

To all who are desirous of entering into Fellowship with the Christian Catholic Church in Zion.

MY DEAR BROTHERS AND SISTERS:—The Principles of the Christian Catholic Church in Zion have been fully set forth in the Reports of Two Conferences on Organization, held in Zion Tabernacle No. 2, which are fully reported in LEAVES OF HEALING for January 31 and February 7, 1896. The Basis of Fellowship is set forth in the Second Section of the Resolution passed on February 5th (see LEAVES OF HEALING, Volume II, Number 17, Page 267):

First—That we recognize the infallible inspiration and sufficiency of the Holy Scriptures as the rule of faith and practice.

Second—That we recognize that no persons can be members of the Church who have not repented of their sins and have not trusted in Christ for Salvation.

Third—That such persons must also be able to make a good profession, and declare that they do know, in their own hearts, that they have truly repented, and are truly trusting Christ, and have the witness, in a measure, of the Holy Spirit.

Fourth—That all other questions of every kind shall be held to be matters of opinion and not matters that are essential to Church unity.

All who are conscious of fulfilling these conditions, no matter where they may reside, are invited to fill up the following blank and answer all the questions contained therein.

I am, faithfully yours in Jesus,

John Alex. Dowie

General Overseer of the Christian Catholic Church in Zion.

AS FAR AS POSSIBLE THE APPLICANT HIMSELF SHOULD FILL OUT THIS BLANK. WRITE PLAINLY AND WITH INK.

Address..

Date..
PLEASE BE SURE TO FILL IN

TO THE REV. JOHN ALEX. DOWIE, General Overseer of the Christian Catholic Church in Zion,
Zion City, Lake County, Illinois, U.S.A.

I hereby make application to be received as a member of the Christian Catholic Church in Zion, and declare my agreement with the Basis of Fellowship agreed upon at a Conference held February, 5, 1896, as set forth in your Circular Letter of February 7, 1896.

What is your full name?..

Where is your residence?..
PLEASE GIVE FULL POSTOFFICE ADDRESS

What is your age last birthday?..
ALSO GIVE DATE AND YEAR OF BIRTH

Are you married, unmarried, widowed, or divorced?..

How many children have you living?..

What is your occupation, profession, or trade?..

What nationality are you?.................... *Where were you born?*....................

What language or languages do you speak?..

How long have you lived in America (or the country where you are now living)?....................

When and where were you converted to God?..

....

Are you conscious that you are saved through faith in Jesus?..

When and where were you immersed by TRIUNE Immersion?..

By whom were you immersed?..

With what religious organization were you formerly connected?..

Recommended by..

Signature of Applicant..
WRITE VERY PLAINLY

REMARKS

....

....

Extra Copies of this Form will be sent to intending members on application to the General Recorder of the Christian Catholic Church in Zion, Zion City, Lake County, Illinois, U.S.A.

Zion's Bible Class

Conducted by Deacon Daniel Sloan in Shiloh Tabernacle, Zion City, Lord's Day Morning at 11 o'clock, and in Zion Homes and Gatherings throughout the World.

MID-WEEK BIBLE CLASS LESSON, SEPTEMBER 28th or 29th.

Glimpses of Saints.

1. *They are ever right and blameless before God.*—Luke 1:5, 6.
They do right.
They have a clear conscience.
They live by a straight rule.
2. *They live without fear in rich favor with God.*—Luke 1:28-30.
They seek the consolation of God.
They seek God's favor.
They expect only good things from God.
3. *They purpose to live to old age and fall asleep in the Lord without pain.*—Luke 2:25-35.
The Holy Ghost is the spirit of life.
The fruit of the spirit prolongs life.
They live until God gives them sleep.
4. *They are incessant in prayer and thanksgiving.*—Luke 2:36-39.
They know what hinders prayer.
They understand the conditions to be met.
They are looking for better things from God.
5. *They hate every kind of evil but love God's Truth.*—Psalm 1:1-6.
They read God's Word day and night.
They delight in its commands.
They meditate on its righteous statutes.
6. *In all dealings they are ever without just reproach.*—Psalm 15:1-5.
They recompense to no man evil for evil.
They do things honestly in the sight of all.
They have an eye to the end to come.
7. *They are persecuted but know no harm can ever come to them.*—1 Peter 3:10-17.
They love the good and seek peace.
They do not seek trouble.
They do not retaliate under persecution.
8. *They are patient amid trials, knowing that soon the Lord will come.*—James 5:7-12.
While others will make money by any means, they are patient.
Their hearts are fixed on one thing—His appearing.
They know not only the lot but the reward of the godly.
The Lord our God is a High-calling God.

LORD'S DAY BIBLE CLASS LESSON, OCTOBER 2d.

Likenesses of Sinful Man.

1. *He is like a poisonous asp.*—Romans 3:3-16.
He bites and devours his fellows.
He poisons by the sting of his tongue.
He is an enemy to every good.
2. *He resembles a filth-loving sow.*—2 Peter 2:17-22.
He loves sin.
He tries to get satisfaction out of dirty things.
He further pollutes an already sinful nature.
3. *He is worse than a menagerie.*—James 3:5-12.
He is given to things he cannot control.
He is a proud boaster.
One cannot tell when he will go to the Devil.
4. *He is more ungovernable than a horse.*—James 3:1-4.
He does not keep in the narrow way.
His words and thoughts are not few.
He has to be held in check if possible.
5. *He is as selfish and inconsiderate as a swine.*—Matthew 7:1-6
He consumes holy things on his lusts.
He condemns the things he wills to do.
He judges but does not want to be judged.
6. *He is like unto a refuse-seeking dog.*—Revelation 22:10-15.
He runs from one dirty thing to another.
He associates with those as dirty as himself.
He does not want to be under restraint.
7. *He is in nature and habits unclean, and so like the many things which are an abomination.*—Leviticus 11:13-30.
He loves darkness rather than light.
He partakes of the thing he lives on.
He does not have clean associates.
God's Holy People are a Purged People.

LEAVES OF HEALING.

Two Dollars will bring to you the weekly visits of the Little White Dove for a year; 75 cents will send it to a friend for thirteen weeks; $1.25 will send it for six months; $1.50 will send it to your minister, or to a Y. M. C. A., or to a Public Reading Room for a whole year. We offer no premiums, except the premium of doing good. We receive no advertisements, and print no commercial lies or cheating enticements of unscrupulous thieves. LEAVES OF HEALING is Zion on wings, and we keep out everything that would detract the reader's mind from all except the Extension of the Kingdom of God, for which alone it exists. If we cannot send forth our Little White Dove without soiling its wings with the smoke of the factory and the dirt of the wrangling market-place, or compelling it to utter the screaming cries of the business vultures in the ears of our readers, then we will keep our Dove at home.

OBEYING GOD IN BAPTISM.

"Baptizing Them Into the Name of the Father and of the Son and of the Holy Ghost."

Nineteen Thousand Eight Hundred Fifty-five Baptisms by Triune Immersion Since March 14, 1897.

Nineteen Thousand Eight Hundred Fifty-five Believers have joyfully followed their Lord in the Ordinance of Believer's Baptism by Triune Immersion since the first Baptism in Central Zion Tabernacle on March 14, 1897.

Baptized in Central Zion Tabernacle from March 14, 1897, to December 14, 1901, by the General Overseer,	4754			
Baptized in South Side Zion Tabernacle from January 1, 1902, to June 14, 1903, by the General Overseer..	37			
Baptized at Zion City by the General Overseer........	583			
Baptized by Overseers, Elders, Evangelists and Deacons, at Headquarters (Zion City) and Chicago......	5283			
Total Baptized at Headquarters..................	—			10,657
Baptized in places outside of Headquarters by the General Overseer................................		765		
Baptized in places outside of Headquarters by Overseers, Elders, Evangelists and Deacons............		7796		
Total Baptized outside of Headquarters............		—		8,561
Total Baptized in seven years and three months....				19,218
Baptized since June 14, 1904:				
Baptized in Zion City by the General Overseer........	64			
Baptized in Zion City by Elder Royall	16			
Baptized in Zion City by Elder Hammond............	6			
Baptized in Zion City by Overseer Mason............	90			
Baptized in Zion City by Overseer Excell............	87			
Baptized in Zion City by Overseer Piper.............	79			
Baptized in Zion City by Elder Mercer..............	14			
Baptized in Zion City by Elder Dinius..............	4			
Baptized in Zion City by Elder Cossum.............	5			
Baptized in Zion City by Elder Gay.................	2			
Baptized in Chicago by Elder Hoffman...............	4			
Baptized in Chicago by Elder Cossum.	7			
Baptized in Chicago by Elder Keller	5			
Baptized in Chicago by Elder Hall..................	3			
Baptized in Chicago by Elder Hammond.............	1		387	
Baptized in Canada by Elder Brooks................		6		
Baptized in Canada by Elder Simmons............. ..		5		
Baptized in California by Elder Taylor............		9		
Baptized in England by Overseer Cantel............		41		
Baptized in England by Deacon Hall................		1		
Baptized in Illinois by Elder Reed..........		1		
Baptized in Indiana by Elder Osborn...............		2		
Baptized in Iowa by Elder Hoy.....................		2		
Baptized in Kansas by Elder Reed..................		8		
Baptized in Michigan by Elder Reed................		4		
Baptized in Michigan by Elder Cairns...............		1		
Baptized in Minnesota by Elder Graves.............		5		
Baptized in Minnesota by Elder Simmons............		3		
Baptized in Mississippi by Evangelist Gay...........		1		
Baptized in Mississippi by Elder Hall..		3		
Baptized in Missouri by Evangelist Gay.		1		
Baptized in Missouri by Elder Brock................		9		
Baptized in Missouri by Deacon Robinson............		1		
Baptized in Nebraska by Elder Hoy.................		7		
Baptized in New York by Overseer Mason............		9		
Baptized in Ohio by Deacon Kelchner...............		3		
Baptized in Ohio by Deacon Arrington..............		5		
Baptized in Ohio by Deacon Yerger.....		4		
Baptized in Pennsylvania by Elder Bouck...........		2		
Baptized in South Africa by Overseer Bryant		82		
Baptized in Tennessee by Elder Hall................		2		
Baptized in Texas by Evangelist Gay................		11		
Baptized in Washington by Elder Ernst.............		11		
Baptized in Washington by Elder Simmons..........		1		
Baptized in Wisconsin by Elder Gay....		7		
Baptized in Wisconsin by Elder McClurkin..........		3	250	637
Total Baptized since March 14, 1897......				19,855

The following-named believer was baptized at Bellingham, Washington, Friday, August 26, 1904, by Elder R. M. Simmons:

Hewitt, Mrs. Phoebe E........812 Garden street, Bellingham, Washington

The following-named seven believers were baptized at Beloit, Wisconsin, Tuesday, August 30, 1904, by Elder William D. Gay:

Ackroyd, Alice Clara................702 Pleasant street, Beloit, Wisconsin
Ackroyd, Jennie Anna..............702 Pleasant street, Beloit, Wisconsin
Ackroyd, Lilian Louise..............702 Pleasant street, Beloit, Wisconsin
Hamblin, Benjamin Walter ......380 W. Grand avenue, Beloit, Wisconsin
Hopple, Robert ....606 Park avenue, Beloit, Wisconsin
Reynolds, Jacob Henry.............702 Pleasant street, Beloit, Wisconsin
Reynolds, Mrs. Annie Mary.........702 Pleasant street, Beloit, Wisconsin

The following-named believer was baptized in Detroit River, Detroit, Michigan, Wednesday, August 31, 1904, by Elder T. Alexander Cairns:

Cornwall, John Emory............358 St. Aubin avenue, Detroit, Michigan

The following-named four believers were baptized at Wichita, Kansas, Thursday, September 1, 1904, by Elder David A. Reed:

Irish, Isabelle I...................1322 Lewyellan avenue, Wichita, Kansas
Pulver, Mrs. Annie...................1455 Western avenue, Toledo, Ohio
Wilbur, Mrs. Dettie..........1702 South Lawrence street, Wichita, Kansas
Wilbur, Erasmus F..........1702 South Lawrence street, Wichita, Kansas

The following-named eight believers were baptized at Shiloh Tabernacle, Zion City, Illinois, Wednesday, September 7, 1904, by Elder Frank A. S. Mercer.

Burgess, Miss Mabel................2821 Elisha avenue, Zion City, Illinois
Burgess, Miss Myrtle................2821 Elisha avenue, Zion City, Illinois
Burgess, William Henry.............2821 Elisha avenue, Zion City, Illinois
Davidson, Leslie.......................................Midland City, Illinois
Eldridge, Mrs Laura......................711 Center street, Reno, Nevada
Fisher, Walter Henry,...................................Clarksville, Tennessee
Kasten, Mrs. Mary...Wausau, Wisconsin
Linton, Miss Grace.................... Elijah Hospice, Zion City, Illinois

CONSECRATION OF CHILDREN.

The following-named child was consecrated to God, Wednesday, August 10, 1904, by Elder Fred A. Graves:

Fobes, Arnold Henry ....New Lisbon, Wisconsin

The following-named child was consecrated to God, Lord's Day, August 14, 1904, by Elder Fred A. Graves:

Salter, Esther Ina............ ....Chippewa Falls, Wisconsin

The following-named seven children were consecrated to God in Zion City, Illinois, Lord's Day, August 21, 1904, by Overseer J. G. Excell:

Berkshire, Joseph Alex. Royall...3111 Elizabeth avenue, Zion City, Illinois
Brabec, Corcina Albie...............664 West 25th street, Chicago, Illinois
Olsson, Ellen Doretha..............1807 Horeb avenue, Zion City, Illinois
Olsson, Ruth Lilly..................1807 Horeb avenue, Zion City, Illinois
Schafer, Nellie Louisa..............3216 Gilead avenue, Zion City, Illinois
Schafer, Albert......................3216 Gilead avenue, Zion City, Illinois
Schafer, Abaline Elizabeth......... 3216 Gilead avenue, Zion City, Illinois

The following-named child was consecrated to God, Lord's Day, August 21, 1904, by Elder Gideon Hammond:

Strong, Anna May.......................5953 State street, Chicago, Illinois

OFFICIAL REPRESENTATIVES OF ZION

The following addresses of Official Representatives of Zion at important centers throughout the world, are given for the convenience of correspondents:

In the United States

¶ ¶ Overseer George L. Mason, 206 West Eighty-sixth street, New York City.
¶ ¶ Overseer William Hamner Piper, 17 Capin street, New Dorchester, Massachusetts.
¶ ¶ Elder R. N. Bouck, 2129 Mt. Vernon street, Philadelphia, Pennslyvania.
¶ ¶ Elder A. Ernst, 2611 Fourth avenue, Seattle, Washington.
¶ ¶ Elder A. E. Arrington, 501 West Fourth street, Cincinnati, Ohio.
¶ ¶ Elder W. B. Taylor, 1350 East Sixteenth street, Fruitvale, California.
¶ ¶ Elder L. C. Hall, San Antonio, Texas.
¶ ¶ Elder Frank L. Brock, 3401 Morgan street, St. Louis, Missouri.

In Foreign Countries

¶ ¶ Overseer H. E. Cantel, 81 Euston road, London, N. W., England.
¶ ¶ Overseer Wilbur Glenn Voliva, Arlington, 43 Park road, St. Kilda, Melbourne, Victoria, Australia.
¶ ¶ Overseer Daniel Bryant, Box 3074, Johannesburg, Transvaal, South Africa.
¶ ¶ Elder Carl Hodler, 76 Bahnhofstrasse, Zürich, Switzerland.
¶ ¶ Elder Arthur S. Booth-Clibborn, 139 Weesperzijde, Amsterdam, Holland.
¶ ¶ Elder E. B. Kennedy, Zion, Haskell road, Shanghai China.
¶ ¶ Elder R. M. Simmons, 525 Grove Crescent, Vancouver, B. C.
¶ ¶ Elder Eugene Brooks, 360 Parliament street, Toronto, Ontario, Canada.

General Financial Agents

¶ ¶ Deacon N. B. Rideout, Financial Agent for South Africa, Box 3074, Johannesburg, Transvaal, South Africa.
¶ ¶ Elder Percy Clibborn, Financial Agent for Europe, 76 Bahnhofstrasse, Zürich, Switzerland.
¶ ¶ Deacon John W. Innes, Financial Agent for the United Kingdom, 81 Euston Road, London, N. W., England.

"Thy Kingdom Come
Thy Will Be Done"

No more powerful instrument can be used to extend God's Kingdom than

LEAVES OF HEALING

The Will of God is set forth concerning Salvation, Healing, and Holy Living in no other way as in

Leaves of Healing

All who are in the Kingdom and who obey the Father's will should read

LEAVES OF HEALING

The love of everyone for his fellow men may easily be estimated by the effort he makes to reach them with

LEAVES OF HEALING

We are now living to see this prayer, which Our Lord has taught us, and which has been earnestly prayed by hundreds of millions in every century, beginning to be answered in Zion.

Our Prayer to God is that all men may have an opportunity to be saved through

LEAVES OF HEALING

We are expecting to see a hearty endorsement of the teachings in this issue expressed by every reader sending in one or more subscriptions, or at least a remittance for one copy to be sent to some one in need.

**Zion Printing and Publishing House
Zion City
Illinois**

WEEKLY PAPER FOR THE EXTENSION OF THE KINGDOM OF GOD
EDITED BY THE REV. JOHN ALEX. DOWIE.

olume XV. No. 22. ZION CITY, SATURDAY, SEPTEMBER 17, 1904. Price Five Cents

OD'S WITNESSES TO DIVINE HEALING.

NSTANTLY HEALED OF DYSPEPSIA, LIVER TROUBLE, KIDNEY DISEASE, AND OTHER SEVERE AILMENTS IN ANSWER TO THE PRAYER OF FAITH.

RANT UNTO THY SERVANTS TO SPEAK THY WORD WITH LL BOLDNESS, WHILE THOU TRETCHEST FORTH THY HAND O HEAL.

After Pentecost came the ealing of the lame man at the eautiful Gate of the Temple. Salvation and Healing were e two most striking manifestions of the Spirit in the work the first Apostles.

Salvation and Healing went nd in hand in the work of the postles from that time until e Apostolic Office became cant through the Apostasy of e Church.

When the Church lost her postles, she also lost the Gifts Healings.

With the loss of the Apostles d of these Gifts, there came loss of power.

Weaker and weaker has the urch become, until today she the laughing-stock of the orld, the Flesh, and the Devil. She alternately plunges into velry with the World and ands weakly weeping over her potence.

Her beautiful white garments ve been stained and torn.

Her children, driven by false aching from the Tree of Life, whose leaves are for the healing of the peoples, are suffering and dying in the hands of sorcerers who try to counterfeit God's Way of Healing by the use of poisonous drugs and murderous knives. The earth is filled with cries of anguish and watered with tears. God's children are weary, sick, sorrowful. Misery and despair cast their gloom where all should be Joy, and Life, and Light, and abounding Health, and Strength—a full enjoyment of all of God's good Gifts.

MRS. MAGGIE WILLARD.

And the Church, to whom was intrusted the Divine Commission of carrying these good Gifts to men, has lost them and is, herself, miserable and powerless, a servile beggar at the gates of Mammon.

It is time she were restored to her Primitive Beauty, Glory, and Power.

It is time that she resume her God-given work of lifting up the fallen, cheering the faint, healing the sick, and giving liberty to the captives.

God be praised, He is restoring His Church!

In His Infinite Love and Mercy He has sent one with Apostolic Authority and Power to be His instrument in restoring to the Church her Apostles, and with them His Gifts.

He has given to the Church the credentials of that Messenger by stretching forth His hand to heal thousands, in answer to his prayer and by the laying on of his hands.

From all the ends of the earth they come, with songs of praise on their lips and everlasting joy upon their heads.

For years that sublime chorus has grown in volume as the host of the redeemed has increased in number.

Already it rings over land and sea, the opening strains of that Divine oratorio in which all the hosts of heaven and all the saints of all the ages shall join, in the ineffably glorious finale, "The Kingdom of the world is become the Kingdom of our Lord, and of His Christ: and He shall reign for ever and ever."

Where He reigns there can be no sickness and no sorrow.

It was for the establishment of His Rule that the Church was founded.

Here is one who has been delivered from terrible diseases and from the very darkness of the Valley of the Shadow of Death, through the prayers and the laying on of hands of this Apostolic man of God, over eight years ago.

The simple, quiet words in which she has told the wonderful Story of her miraculous deliverance do not begin to tell of all that she suffered from the diseases that tortured her until life seemed all but gone.

Physicians confessed their powerlessness to help her, and pronounced the dread death sentence upon her.

But God was her Father and loved her with a love more tender than that of any earthly parent.

He heard the weak, trembling cry of a spirit that had been cruelly misled by false teaching, so that she even believed that her suffering came from the hand of that Father!

He led her to His Messenger, sent by Him to restore the truth that there is no sickness or any other evil thing in God or in heaven, and that no such curse and calamity can come from One who is Love, Life, Light, and Purity.

When she had repented of her sin in thus believing such a lie about her Heavenly Father, the hands of God's minister were laid upon her, and he prayed for her "in the Name of the Lord Jesus, in the Power of the Holy Spirit, and in accordance with the Will of God, her Heavenly Father," for her healing.

Instantly the promised Healing Virtue of the Spirit of God flowed through her diseased and pain-racked body.

She was made perfectly whole.

That healing is permanent, enduring in its perfection to this day.

Praise God, the Times of the Restoration of All Things have dawned!

The Church is being restored to her primitive Apostolic character and Divine Power! A. W. N.

WRITTEN TESTIMONY OF MRS. MAGGIE WILLARD.

2812 ELIZABETH AVENUE,
ZION CITY, ILLINOIS.

BELOVED GENERAL OVERSEER:—I do thank God for the blessings which have come into my life through the Message brought by you, of Salvation, Healing, and Holy Living through the faith which is of the Son of God.

When very young, I was led to accept Jesus as my Savior from sin, and found Peace and Joy in believing, but was always taught that it was the good hand of God which brought sickness and bereavement.

When my only child died, I said, "Thy Will be done."

I thought it was all according to the wise purposes of God, my Heavenly Father.

Before coming to Zion City, I lived in Chicago over twenty years.

For several years I suffered intensely from dyspepsia and biliousness.

I was attended by two doctors.

One of them was Dr. Coker, of Main street, Chicago, who said I could not live longer than a week.

The pain was so severe that I wished to die; but as a child of God I reproved myself and cried, "O God, give me patience to suffer all Thy Will!"

However, I did not die, but continued using medicine all the time.

In addition to my former troubles, kidney disease and neuralgia set in.

Again I was given up to die.

The doctor told my husband that I had neither stomach nor bowels, and could not possibly live.

Instead of my dying, my husband, after eleven days' sickness, passed away.

My cup of sorrow seemed full; but still I believed that it was all God's way of bringing me closer to Him.

Time wore on, and I continued a weary sufferer.

I went to live with my sister-in-law, who kept a little store.

One day a woman came to the store and told my sister-in-law that she might tell me that there was a man out at the World's Fair who was praying with the sick.

I received the news gladly, and went in search of this man, not even knowing his name.

I found the place, and you, my beloved General Overseer.

One thing especially made a deep impression on me. You said that there were Christians in the meeting who had been blaming God all the time for the work the Devil was doing; that they had lied when they said that God was the one who sent sickness, disease, and death; for the Bible teaches that that is the Devil's work.

I felt so convicted that I heard no more of the teaching.

My heart was very sad at the thought of the wrong I had done to my dear Heavenly Father, whom I was seeking to honor in my life continually.

I left the meeting intending to come again, but I became so sick that I was removed to a hospital.

When I was able to get out again, I went to have you pray for me, but found that you had moved to Zion Tabernacle No. 2, to which I was directed.

I went to the meeting and one of the sisters, seeing that I looked so sick, came forward and spoke to me. As we were a little early, she opened her Bible and quoted some passages relating to Divine Healing.

I said, "Why, these are passages I committed to memory when very young!"

She said, "Don't you see how it means for body as well as spirit?"

The light dawned upon me and I believed that the same God who saved my spirit could and would heal my body.

The sister got me a ticket for the prayer-room.

After the service, I went in to be prayed with, feeling very sick.

My back was bent with pain.

I expected that you would ask all about my trouble and circumstances, and how much I was able to pay, but to my surprise you only put your hands on my head and prayed, saying: "In the Name of the Lord Jesus, in the Power of the Holy Spirit, and according to the Will of God, our Heavenly Father," and immediately my back straightened.

I was healed!

In a very short time I was able to take a situation as cook for a family of eleven.

It is now over eight years since I received this healing, and during these eight years I have found unceasing comfort and joy in Jesus, my Savior, in whose Name I have learned to come to the Father.

I have proved that He is mighty to save, to heal, and to keep.

I have no more use for drugs, having learned to trust in God at all times for spirit, soul, and body.

I thank God that I am a member of the Christian Catholic Church in Zion, having joined when the Church was formed; for the privilege of being a member of Zion Restoration Host; and for the joy of going to New York with the Message of Peace.

I also desire to thank you for bringing the truth to me, and for offering prayer on my behalf, which has been so graciously answered.

My only aim is to live for the glory of God, my Heavenly Father, and to be of some use in the remaining years of my life in the upbuilding of His glorious Kingdom.

Praying God's blessing upon you and your family, I remain yours faithfully in His service,

(MRS.) MAGGIE WILLARD.

IS ANY among you sick? let him call for the Elders of the Church; and let them pray over him, anointing him with oil in the Name of the Lord: And the Prayer of Faith shall save him that is sick, and the Lord shall raise him up; and if he have committed sins, it shall be forgiven him.—*James 5:14, 15.*

MEETINGS IN ZION CITY TABERNACLES.

SHILOH TABERNACLE.

Lord's Day—Early morning service.... 6:30 a. m.
Intermediate Bible Class.. 9:45 a. m.
Bible class, conducted by Deacon Daniel Sloan... 11:00 a. m.
Afternoon service........ 2:30 p. m.
Evening service........ 8:00 p. m.
First Lord's Day of Every Month—Communion service.
Third Lord's Day of Every Month—Zion Junior Restoration Host rally.
Third Lord's Day of Every Month—Consecration of children........................ 10:00 a. m.
Monday—Zion Restoration Host rally (Second Monday of every month).... 8:00 p. m.
Tuesday—Divine Healing meeting..... 2:30 p. m.
Tuesday—Adult Choir............... 7:45 p. m.
Wednesday—Baptismal service........ 7:00 p. m.
Wednesday—Citizens' rally........... 8:00 p. m.
Friday—Adult Choir.................. 7:45 p. m.
Friday—Officers of the Christian Catholic Church in Zion........ 8:00 p. m.
Friday—Junior Choir................. 3:45 p. m.
Meeting in the officers' room.

TWENTY-SIXTH STREET TABERNACLE.

Lord's Day—Junior service............ 9:45 a. m.
Lord's Day—German service.......... 10:30 a. m.
Tuesday—German service............ 8:00 p. m.

ELIJAH THE RESTORER

A WEEKLY PAPER FOR THE EXTENSION OF THE KINGDOM OF GOD.
EDITED BY THE REV. JOHN ALEX. DOWIE.

Application for entry as Second Class Matter at Zion City, Illinois, pending.

Subscription Rates.		**Special Rates.**	
One Year	$2.00	100 Copies of One Issue	$3.00
Six Months	1.25	25 Copies of One Issue	1.00
Three Months	.75	To Ministers, Y. M. C. A's and Public	
Single Copies	.05	Reading Rooms, per annum	1.50

For foreign subscriptions add $1.50 per year, or three cents per copy for postage.
Subscribers desiring a change of address should give present address, as well as that to which they desire LEAVES OF HEALING sent in the future.
Make Bank Drafts, Express Money or Postoffice Money Orders payable to the order of JOHN ALEX. DOWIE, Zion City, Illinois, U. S. A.
Long Distance Telephone. *Cable Address "Dowie, Zion City."*
All communications upon business must be addressed to
MANAGER ZION PUBLISHING HOUSE,
Zion City, Illinois, U. S. A.

Subscriptions to LEAVES OF HEALING, A VOICE FROM ZION, and the various publications may also be sent to
ZION PUBLISHING HOUSE, 81 EUSTON ROAD, LONDON, N. W., ENGLAND.
ZION PUBLISHING HOUSE, No. 43 PARK ROAD, ST. KILDA, VICTORIA, AUSTRALIA.
ZION PUBLISHING HOUSE, 76 BAHNHOFSTRASSE, ZÜRICH, SWITZERLAND.

ZION CITY, ILLINOIS, SATURDAY, SEPTEMBER 17, 1904.

TABLE OF CONTENTS.

LEAVES OF HEALING, SATURDAY, SEPTEMBER 17, 1904.

EDITORIAL NOTES.

"WIST YE NOT THAT I MUST BE ABOUT MY FATHER'S BUSINESS?"

WHEN HE was twelve years old, Jesus, our Savior, our Lord and our King, uttered these words in the Temple of God.

MARY, HIS MOTHER, and Joseph, had taken Him up to Jerusalem, to the Feast of the Passover.

THEY HAD left the city, supposing Him to be in the company.

Not finding Him "among their kinsfolk and acquaintance," in the caravan, "they returned to Jerusalem, seeking for Him."

"AFTER THREE days they found Him in the Temple, sitting in the midst of the Doctors,"—that is, the Teachers—"hearing them, and asking them questions," to the amazement of all, who were astonished "at His understanding and His answers."

Still more astonished were His parents, when they saw Him in such venerable company; but the human mother-love, forgetting for the moment that her Son was also her Lord, rebuked the Christ, saying:

Son, why hast Thou thus dealt with us?
Behold, Thy father and I sought Thee sorrowing!

IT WAS to this question, and to this statement of their agony, that He, by His answer, gently reminded her, and yet severely rebuked her.

SHE KNEW that Joseph was not His father, and that, although He was a son, although He was "the seed of the woman," He was the Son of God who had thus honored the virgin: for He fulfilled His promise, "the Holy Ghost shall come upon Thee, and the Power of the Most High shall overshadow Thee: wherefore also that which is to be Born shall be called Holy, the Son of God."

THEREFORE, HE reminds her that He was in the Temple which was His Father's house, that He was doing His Father's Business; and that, while in the fulfilment of His Father's Will, He was her son, yet, at the same time, He was the Son of God, and her Lord and Savior.

BEAUTIFUL IN disposition, yet majestic in wisdom, He "advanced in wisdom and stature, and in favor with God and men."

AND THE Real Christ is still advancing in favor with God and man.

THAT CHRIST is not the Christ of the Apostasy, as in those churches which have wandered away in the wilderness, and left their catholicity behind them.

In what they vainly call God's House, they have presented as the Christ, either a little baby in a mother's arms, a dead man on a cross, or, worst of all, the shameful lie that the Living Christ can be found in a wafer of flour stamped by a priest.

These foolish and deluded priests have the audacity to declare, contrary to both faith and reason, that they have in their hands, after so-called prayers, a number of wafers, each of which has been divinely transformed into the body, blood, and bones of the Christ of God.

SUCH BUSINESS as that is the Business of the Devil in the Temple of God; for the Living Christ, when He first distributed the bread and wine as His body and His blood, did not do so in a physical sense, inasmuch as He was then sitting among them in His flesh and blood.

In that Body He went from them to the cross, where He poured out His life unto death.

From thence His body was taken to the grave; and, in the Power of the Spirit, He came forth from that tomb in a bloodless body, and ascended into the heavens, where that body now dwells.

In the body He will come again, and in that Body of Glory He will live and reign on earth a Thousand Years, until "the kingdom of the world is become the Kingdom of our Lord, and of His Christ."

IN VIEW of these things, what a pitiful and paltry Business the Apostasy has become, when it can present only a Shameful Lie for the Living Son of God!

WHAT A pitiful business all the varied degrees of the Apostasy are in, when they present to the world a Christ who is either a Christ afar off in the heavens—failing to realize that in Spirit and in Power He is with us "all the days"—or as a being who takes an interest only in speculative theology, or in cold, formal, and lifeless hymns and sermons; or who helps silly people get up bazaars, contemptible theatricals, and silly dances, to "raise money" for His church; or who tells the people that business, and politics, and pleasure are to be divorced from religion; or that the Christ has no longer any sympathy with the carpenter and his workshop, the builder in his toils, the architect in his designs, the manufacturer in his manufactures, or the merchant and mariner in extending the commerce of the world.

HOW PITIFUL that all social, political, commercial, financial, and industrial life is to be carried on, like the Chicago Stock-yards, by brutal packers and brutal strikers who strive for preëminence; gripping each other by the throat, and strangling each other in the effort to obtain supremacy!

BUT THIS is not the real Christ!

The Christ of God was, and is, ever the Friend of man in every relation of life; not only hearing and answering Questions in His Father's house, but in the schoolroom, and at the carpenter's bench in Nazareth.

In every relation in life He was the family Burden-Bearer to the saintly mother, Mary, to the kind foster-father, Joseph, and to the six dear little children who filled the home at Nazareth with the joy of their young lives.

Through it all, the Christ was this for eighteen years in Nazareth, from the time He said in the Temple of God "Wist ye not that I must be about My Father's business?"

All these eighteen years were years of intense interest in all the affairs of the Home, the Business, the Synagogue, and the Nation.

And He is just the Same Today!

JESUS OF NAZARETH, the Messiah of God, was essentially a Business Man in every sense of these words.

HE LOOKED at all human affairs with the Omniscient Eye of God.

Knowing all things concerning the myriads of suns and planets, moons and comets, and asteroids throughout the Universe, He yet concentrated His attention upon this little earth, its little affairs, and its little human beings, whose nature He Himself had condescended to take.

But He also knew that within these bodies were the spirits of which His Father was the Father; "the Offspring of God;" for it was He who said, when He left this earth, "I ascend unto My Father and your Father, and My God and your God."

ALL THROUGH His earthly life, grieved as He was at heart to see that the kingdoms of this earth had become the kingdoms of the Devil and of his servants, He boldly proclaimed the Gospel of the Kingdom of God, and His own ultimate reign and rule.

THIS HE did in His great mission on earth as the Apostle of God; as the High Priest of God; or, to put it in the language of the Letter to the Hebrews, He came as "The Apostle and High Priest of our Confession."

HE SEALED His Testimony with His blood; ended His prophetic mission on earth; ascended into heaven, where He carries on His mission as the "one Mediator between God and men, Himself man, the Christ Jesus."

AND SOON He will come, no longer as Apostle, Prophet, or Priest, but as the "King of kings," "the Ruler of the kings of the Earth;" the "Lord of lords;" the Director of All its Affairs, in the Family, in the City, in the State, in the Nation, and in all the International Affairs of the World.

HIS FLAG must float over all the Lands and all the Seas; over all Halls of Justice and of Legislation; of Education and of Commerce.

WITH THIS view of the present and future, we are about to enter, tomorrow, if God permit, upon the Apostolic Office.

BUT LET there be no misunderstanding, either in the Church or in the world around, as to our laying aside any of the offices which it has been our privilege to exercise during our life in the service of the Christ, our Savior and our King.

"HEIRS OF GOD, and joint heirs with the Christ," we hold that the Church of the Living God, through Him, is the inheritor of All Things, and is the Hope of All Creation; for through His Body, the Church, He comes into touch with all humanity in all its interests.

HENCE, THE First Apostle of our Lord Jesus the Christ in the Christian Catholic and Apostolic Church in Zion, must be not only the Apostle, but the High Priest, the Prophet, the Prophet and the Teacher.

As the Prophet and as the Messenger of God's Covenant, the "Prophet of whom Moses spoke," of whom Malachi spoke, and of whom Jesus Himself spoke, he must be the Elijah of the Restoration; and be, not only, as First Apostle, the earthly head of the Church, but the Restorer "of all things, whereof God spoke by the mouth of His holy prophets which have been since the world began."

WE FEEL that these claims would be idle and foolish words, worthy only of the contempt of humanity and the people of God in all the churches, and of people of God who are in none of the churches, and of all thoughtful and earnest seekers and lovers of God, *were it not that they were true.*

WITHIN OUR mind, and within the minds of thousands and tens of thousands of those who follow the Christ with us, there is no doubt as to their truth.

Were it otherwise, we dare not advance one step.

We would rather be shrouded in our grave-clothes than that we should dishonor our Lord when we stand up tomorrow in Shiloh Tabernacle, before God's people and all the world, in Apostolic robes.

WE ARE in the Times of the Restoration!

The Restoration has begun and is rapidly unfolding and producing the Events now appearing in Zion, which are of more importance than all other events in the world at this time.

MILITARY AND Naval Tyrannies are crushing the vitality of the people, by cruel taxation, by cruelly enforced conscriptions, and by driving the youth of every land in Europe into the army, specially at a time of the year when they should be tilling or gathering in the fruits of the soil.

Cruel wars are being waged where men are fighting with one another, dismembering one another, blowing one another to pieces with murderous shot and shell until the sea runs blood, and the stench of the dead drives the living—as at Liaoyang—from the fortress and the city which they had captured—cruel, needless wars, which only "sow dragon's teeth," and cause more armed men to rise, until the lovely Islands of Japan, the beautiful plains, and peaceful homes of Manchuria, and the homes of Russia, are filled with broken hearts which can never be comforted on earth; for their beloved are thrown as food to the voracious fishes of the deep, as the war vessels sink into the sea, under the rain of missiles of hell, or are left dead upon the plains of Asia for the vultures to pick their flesh to the bones, and pluck out their eyes, or are gathered in gory, rotting heaps to be burned or buried.

HORROR UPON horror! Horror upon horror! War cries for more victims to appease the ambitions of Apostate Churches and cruel Military Tyrannies!

BUT WRITE above it all, "The Christ lives, the Christ of God, who is the Friend of man."

"NO WEAPONS in His hand are seen,
Nor voice of terror heard."

DEPRAVED, INDEED, must be the Christian heart that can listen to the cries of hellish hatred which burn within the breasts of those who are fighting for the supremacy of Czar or Mikado, Slav or Mongolian.

Deluded by false ideas of patriotism, misled by false religions and false priests, they are fighting for the possession of lands which belong to neither; while the great so-called Christian nations of the world look on and say, "Let them fight, and bleed, and die."

They care not that the possibilities of earthly happiness are cut off from hundreds of thousands and even millions of homes in the Islands of the Rising Sun, or on the plains of Asia and Europe.

"*We care not,*" these falsely-called Christian Nations cry, "*for all the bloodshed and misery; for we are ready, if need be, to extend the Empire of Hell: for* 'WAR IS HELL!'"

SHOULD THESE words be a fair interpretation of the facts today, and of the attitude of the world, as we believe they are, then is it not time for all Christian men to say that "War is the Will of Hell," and that "Peace is the Will of God in Heaven?"

PEACE WITH God is War with Sin and Satan!
Peace with Satan is War with God and heaven.

ZION MUST be about her Lord's Business; our Father's Business; for Zion has no other Legitimate Business than that of our Father in Heaven.

IN THIS issue of LEAVES OF HEALING we have directed that the Business of God in Zion shall be attended to, and shall be set forth plainly, in connection with the Commercial, Financial, and Industrial Institutions of Zion.

Interesting and important articles upon these will be found on pages 779 to 783.

These will be continued from time to time.

Articles will also appear in this paper upon the Ecclesiastical, Educational, and Political business of Zion.

IT WILL be our duty to continue to watch over all these interests.

In assuming the Apostleship, we have not laid down the office of General Overseer.

On the contrary, we hold it with a firmer hand since it has been merged in the greater office of Apostle.

We trust to guide all Affairs of Zion in such a manner as shall enable us to extend the Kingdom of God to the myriads of earth who are in darkness and sorrow, sin-stricken, disease-smitten, and politically oppressed, crying for help, looking up to the heavens that seem to them as brass; but are not so.

BUT JOY cometh in the Morning.
"Redemption draweth nigh!"

THE PROPHET Obadiah long ago said, of these times in which we dwell:

But upon Mount Zion shall be Deliverance,
And there shall be Holiness.

THEREFORE WE Go Forward with the Deliverance which the Gospel brings; with the Deliverance which shall be complete when the King reigns.

The Sacred Year has now revolved,
Accepted of the Lord,
When heaven's High Promise is fulfilled,
And Israel is Restored.

Our glad Hosannas, Prince of Peace!
Thy Welcome shall proclaim;
And heaven's exalted arches ring
With Thy most honored Name.

The Beam that shines from Zion's Hill,
Shall lighten every land;
The King who reigns in Salem's Towers
Shall all the world command.

BRETHREN, PRAY FOR US.

Notice to Correspondents.

In writing to Headquarters it is *absolutely essential* that the writer give his full address.

Failure to comply with this request necessitates looking up or referring to the Church Records, which involves much time, and is very frequently fruitless.

Friends and members of the Christian Catholic Church in Zion everywhere will please bear this in mind, especially those in foreign lands.

J. G. EXCELL, General Ecclesiastical Secretary.

Notice to Officers and Members.

Send all newspaper clippings concerning the General Overseer, the Elders, or any department of the work in connection with the Christian Catholic Church in Zion, to Deacon Carl F. Stern, Zion City, Illinois. Send as soon as possible after publication, and carefully mark *name and date of the paper clipped from* on each article. If this is not done, the clippings are absolutely useless.

Notes of Thanksgiving from the Whole World

By Overseer J. G. Excell, General Ecclesiastical Secretary.

Healed of Nervous Prostration.

Thou wilt keep him in perfect peace,
Whose mind is stayed on Thee —*Isaiah 26:3.*

R. R. No. 4, Albion, Indiana,
April 10, 1904.

Dear Overseer Speicher:—I desire to add my testimony to the thousands who witness to God's saving, healing, and keeping power.

It is now almost thirteen years since my first healing, and the trouble has never returned.

Later I suffered for three years from nervous prostration, but on April 16, 1899, I was healed of that trouble in answer to my own prayers, when asking for an evidence that I had done right in leaving the Evangelical Lutheran church and joining the Christian Catholic Church in Zion.

The sweet thrill that passed through my body then will never be forgotten. I gained in strength, and was able to again take up all my work.

I know this healing was complete, as I had never suffered an attack throughout the following years, until April 12, 1903, when through disobedience I again suffered a complete breakdown of the nervous system. Again, on April 16th, God graciously delivered me.

This time, from a human standpoint, it seemed impossible for me to live, and for four days I was most of the time either tossing in uncontrollable nervous agony, or lying in complete exhaustion.

Three telegrams were sent to the General Overseer asking for prayer. Each time God gave relief, although healing did not come until I had confessed my sin to an Elder of the Church, who came in response to the General Overseer's directions.

He showed me the fear in my heart as a sin and a hindrance, and that I must fully claim God's promises. He then prayed with me. I rose from bed and sat up for an hour.

I continued to grow stronger; and now a year has passed and I am strong, and have not had one nervous attack since.

This winter I wrote you asking prayer, that I might be kept from continually taking cold as I have done other winters.

The result is that I have had but two colds this winter, and they were broken up in answer to your prayers.

I thank you and all who have prayed for me, but above all I praise and thank God for His having made it possible for such prayers to be offered and answered. I am,

Sincerely, (Miss) Ella De Camp.

Delivered in Childbirth—Child Healed.

Even so it is not the will of your Father
Which is in heaven,
That one of these little ones should perish —*Matthew 18:14.*

1320 Lippincott Street,
Philadelphia, Pennsylvania,
March 5, 1904.

Dear General Overseer:—Peace to thee.

It is with gratitude to God our Heavenly Father, and to you, that I write this little testimony.

We have learned to trust God and Him alone through your teaching.

My baby was born November 18, 1902. I was safely delivered, in answer to prayer, in a few hours, for which I praise God.

Baby was poor and delicate, and had a projecting navel, and when a few weeks old he was ruptured by hard crying spells.

He cried nearly day and night.

He had about eight screaming spells that lasted from three to four hours, and when sleeping would toss his head from side to side.

He was also oppressed by an evil spirit that caused him to swallow repeatedly, acting as though he were choking when he was nursing.

We thank God that he has been healed and delivered from all, and has grown to be well and strong. He weighs twenty-three pounds.

We have had other healings in our family.

We thank you for your prayers, dear General Overseer, and pray that God will keep you and yours yet many years to preach the Everlasting Gospel.

Yours in the Christ, (Mrs.) Cora Kester.

Confirmation of Testimony.

Beloved General Overseer:—In confirming Sister Kester's testimony, I can say it is true. The half is not told.

It seemed at times as though the demon would crush out the baby's life.

But thanks be unto God, who giveth us the victory through Jesus, the Christ!

The dear little boy is perfectly well, and growing nicely.

Yours in the Christ, Leaanna Hann.

Healed of Weak Eyes and Measles.

If ye then, being evil,
Know how to give good gifts unto your children,
How much more shall your Father which is in Heaven
Give good things to them that ask Him?—*Matthew 7:11.*

Richland Center, Wisconsin,
June 13, 1904.

Dear General Overseer:—I feel it a duty as well as a pleasure to add my testimony to the many already given to God's power and willingness to answer prayer. I hope it may help some one.

A few months ago, I was taken with inflammation of the eyes.

Mrs. Hatch came in and prayed the Prayer of Faith for me.

I slept well that night, and in the morning my eyes were healed.

I have had no trouble with them since.

We had a scourge of measles in our city, and I was exposed to the measles, but did not know it.

I took cold at the time, but knowing God's way of healing I took the Lord for my Physician. I did not suffer as people usually do.

Mrs. Hatch prayed and we had a glorious victory in the Name of the Lord.

Please continue to pray for us, that we may grow in grace and in the knowledge of the Truth as it is in Jesus, the Christ.

I was eleven years old June 10th.

Vera Richards.

Healed of Heart Trouble.

For the Joy of Jehovah is your strength.—*Nehemiah 8:10.*

4 Upper Accommodation Road,
Leeds, Yorkshire, England,
March 30, 1904.

Dear General Overseer:—Peace to thee.

I desire to tell what God has done for me for spirit, soul, and body through Zion teaching.

For twenty years I was a sufferer from heart trouble and nervous debility.

I thought my suffering was God's will, until Leaves of Healing was given to me by a friend.

I have been healed several times through the prayers of Deacon McKell.

I thank God that I am counted worthy to be a member of Zion Restoration Host. I have no desire but to do the Will of God.

I pray that God will bless you, your dear wife, and son, and that you may be kept Till Jesus Come.

Yours in the Master's service,

Selina Hanson.

Healed of Weak Back.

Then shall the lame man leap as an hart.—*Isaiah 35:6*

Haines Falls, Ulster County, R. R. No. 3,
New York, June 19, 1904.

Dear Overseer:—Peace to thee.

I praise God this morning for His healing power.

While attending the meetings of the New York Visitation last fall, on the 21st day of October I went into the prayer-room, and an Elder prayed for me.

I had always had a weak back. The doctor said it was a result of kidney trouble. While the Elder was praying, the pain left me.

When I sat down, the pain came back; but I said, "God will heal me," and, when I left the prayer-room, I experienced no pain.

I thank God I am healed. My back is well and strong. I thank God for Zion teaching.

I am praying for our General Overseer, and all Zion all over the world.

Your sister in the Christ, Emma Wolven.

Healed in Answer to Prayer.

And there was not one feeble person among His tribes.—*Psalm 105:37.*

Orillia, Ontario, Canada, April 11, 1904.

Dear Overseer Speicher:—Your letter of the 18th received. I wrote on the 15th for you to pray for me. God has healed me.

I thank you for your prayers.

I believe that I suffered from kidney trouble.

I have not used any pork or medicine since I first read Leaves of Healing.

I have trusted Jesus for all.

When I could not get answer to my prayers, I wrote to Zion.

The letter was no sooner sent than I got relief.

Your sister in the Christ,

(Mrs.) Mary Quinlan.

ZION'S activities are world-wide.

They also touch human life at every point.

Factories, shops, farms, railroads, stores, picks and shovels, hammers and saws, trowels, stocks and securities, agencies, mines, mills, forests, steamships, cattle, telegraphs and telephones, printing-presses, municipal, state, and national politics; schools, colleges, tabernacles; a host of ecclesiastical and lay workers, and the immortal spirits of hundreds of thousands, aye, millions of men and women, youths and maidens, and children throughout the world, are some of the things with which, and in which, Zion works.

Never has the coördination and remarkable unity of purpose of Zion with reference to all her varied interests been more clearly and succinctly expressed than in the address of the General Overseer in Shiloh Tabernacle, Lord's Day afternoon, August 21, 1904.

The text of the discourse was taken from the words of the rich fool in Luke 12:17, "What Shall I do?" and from the parable of the ten pounds, "Do Business Till I Come."

That is the translation of the words in Luke 19:13, preferred by Dr. Robert Young and many other scholars.

The address was the fitting complement of the two Business Conferences held on July 21st and 22d, during Zion's Fourth Feast of Tabernacles, reports of which were published in full in LEAVES OF HEALING, Volume 15, No. 18.

The address was a remarkable review of the Ecclesiastical, Educational, Commercial, and Political work of Zion, not from the standpoint of statistics, but going deeper.

The man of God dealt with the great, fundamental, Divine principles of which the facts and figures were but the visible manifestation.

Even those who knew Zion, and understood her best, received new light and fresh inspiration from this clear, powerful exposition.

To the many present who were studying Zion, the Message was a revelation, showing Zion's work in its true character and extent.

Those who came to the service out of mere curiosity were also very deeply impressed. The entire audience of about six thousand listened to every word with the most intense interest, many of the visitors sharing in the joyous enthusiasm with which the sermon was received.

Notwithstanding the fact that the day was intensely warm and sultry, threatening the heavy showers that fell during the afternoon and evening, several hundred came out from Chicago on the regular and excursion trains.

Not long after the meeting began the storm broke, heavy rains, accompanied with thunder and lightning, sweeping over the City.

But the elements could not detract attention from the service, which continued with increasing power up to its close.

During the taking of the offering, Zion White-robed Choir, accompanied by Zion Orchestra, gave a very creditable rendering of George W. Garrette's anthem, "Prepare Ye the Way of the Lord," Deacon Conductor Thomas and Deaconess Harriet Ware singing the solos and duet.

Shiloh Tabernacle, Zion City, Illinois, Lord's Day Afternoon, August 21, 1904.

The services were opened by Zion White-robed Choir and Zion Robed Officers entering the Tabernacle singing as they came the words of the

PROCESSIONAL.

Rejoice, ye pure in heart,
  Rejoice, give thanks and sing;
Your festal banner wave on high,
  The Cross of Christ, your King.

REFRAIN—Rejoice, Rejoice,
  Rejoice, give thanks and sing,

Bright youth and snow-crown'd age,
  Strong men and maidens meek,
Raise high your free, exulting song,
  God's wondrous praises speak.

With voice as full and strong
  As Ocean's surging praise,
Send forth the hymns our fathers lov'd,
  The psalms of ancient days.

Yes on, through life's long path,
  Still chanting as we go;
From youth to age, by night and day,
  In gladness and in woe.

Still lift your standard high,
  Still march in firm array,
As warriors through the darkness toil
  Till dawns the golden day.

At last the march shall end
  The wearied ones shall rest,
The pilgrims find their Father's house,
  Jesusalem the blest.

*The following report has not been revised by the General Overseer.

At the close of the Processional the General Overseer came upon the platform, the people rising and standing with bowed heads while he pronounced the

INVOCATION.

God be merciful unto us and bless us,
And cause Thy face to shine upon us;
That Thy Way may be known upon earth,
Thy Saving Health among all the nations,
For the sake of Jesus. Amen.

PRAISE.

The Congregation then joined in singing Hymn No. 231:

Come, Thou Almighty King,
Help us Thy Name to sing,
Help us to praise:
Father! all-glorious,
O'er all victorious.
Come, and reign over us,
Ancient of Days!

The General Overseer then led the Choir and Congregation in the recitation of the Apostles' Creed:

RECITATION OF CREED.

I believe in God, the Father Almighty,
Maker of heaven and earth:
And in Jesus, the Christ, His only Son, our Lord,
Who was conceived by the Holy Ghost:
Born of the Virgin Mary;
Suffered under Pontius Pilate;
Was crucified, dead, and buried:
He descended into hell,
The third day He rose from the dead;
He ascended into heaven,
And sitteth on the right hand of God, the Father Almighty;
From thence He shall come to judge the quick and the dead.
I believe in the Holy Ghost;
The Holy Catholic Church;
The Communion of Saints;
The Forgiveness of Sins;
The Resurrection of the body,
And the Life Everlasting. Amen.

Overseer Excell then led the Congregation in repeating the Commandments; after which the words, "Lord, have mercy upon us, and write all these Thy Laws in our hearts, we beseech Thee," were chanted.

READING OF GOD'S COMMANDMENTS.

I. Thou shalt have no other gods before Me.

II. Thou shalt not make unto thee a graven image, nor the likeness of any form that is in heaven above, or that is in the earth beneath, or that is in the water under the earth; thou shalt not bow down thyself unto them nor serve them; for I, Jehovah, thy God, am a jealous God, visiting the iniquity of the fathers upon the children, upon the third and upon the fourth generation of them that hate Me, and showing mercy unto thousands of them that love Me and keep My commandments.

III. Thou shalt not take the Name of Jehovah thy God in vain; for Jehovah will not hold him guiltless that taketh His Name in vain.

IV. Remember the Sabbath Day, to keep it holy. Six days shalt thou labor and do all thy work; but the seventh day is a Sabbath unto Jehovah thy God: in it thou shalt not do any work; thou, nor thy son, nor thy daughter, thy manservant, nor thy maidservant, nor thy cattle, nor thy stranger that is within thy gates; for in six days Jehovah made heaven and earth, the sea, and all that in them is, and rested the seventh day: wherefore Jehovah blessed the Sabbath Day and hallowed it.

V. Honor thy father and thy mother; that thy days may be long upon the land which Jehovah thy God giveth thee.

VI. Thou shalt do no murder.

VII. Thou shalt not commit adultery.

VIII. Thou shalt not steal.

IX. Thou shalt not bear false witness against thy neighbor.

X. Thou shalt not covet thy neighbor's house, thou shalt not covet thy neighbor's wife, nor his manservant, nor his maidservant, nor his ox, nor his ass, nor anything that is thy neighbor's.

Hear also what our Lord Jesus, the Christ, the Son of God, hath said, which may be called the Eleventh Commandment:

XI. A New Commandment I give unto you, that ye love one another; even as I have loved you, that ye also love one another.

The great Choir then sang the

TE DEUM LAUDAMUS.

We praise Thee, O God; we acknowledge Thee to be the Lord.
All the earth doth worship Thee, the Father Everlasting.
To Thee all Angels cry aloud, the Heavens and all the powers therein.
To Thee Cherubim and Seraphim continually do cry:
Holy, Holy, Holy, Lord God of Sabaoth,
Heaven and earth are full of the majesty of Thy Glory.
The glorious company of the Apostles praise Thee.
The goodly fellowship of the Prophets praise Thee.
The noble army of martyrs praise Thee.
The Holy Church throughout all the world doth acknowledge Thee,
The Father of an Infinite Majesty;
Thine Adorable, True, and Only Son;
Also the Holy Ghost, the Comforter.
Thou art the King of Glory, O Christ;
Thou art the everlasting Son of the Father.
When Thou tookest upon Thee to deliver man,
Thou didst humble Thyself to be born of a Virgin;
When Thou hadst overcome the sharpness of death,
Thou didst open the Kingdom of Heaven to all believers.
Thou sittest at the right hand of God in the Glory of the Father.
We believe that Thou shalt come to be our Judge.
We therefore pray Thee help Thy servants,
Whom Thou hast redeemed with Thy precious blood.
Make them to be numbered with Thy saints in glory everlasting.
O Lord, save Thy people and bless Thine heritage;
Govern them and lift them up forever.
Day by day we magnify Thee;
And we worship Thy Name ever, world without end.
Vouchsafe, O Lord, to keep us this day without sin.
O Lord, have mercy upon us, have mercy upon us.
O Lord, let Thy mercy be upon us as our trust is in Thee.
O Lord, in Thee have I trusted, let me never be confounded.

The General Overseer then read from the Inspired Word of God, the 1st Psalm; also in the 12th chapter of the Gospel according to Saint Luke, verses 13 to 21, inclusive; and in the 19th chapter of the same Gospel, verses 11 to 27, inclusive.

The Choir then sang the Gloria.

The General Overseer announced the receipt of a cablegram from Elder Arthur Booth-Clibborn, which stated that fifty-five persons had been baptized in Holland. He also announced that this was the second baptism that had been conducted by Elder Clibborn.

Elder Cossum led in the general supplication, after which the General Overseer followed with prayer for the Church and people of God everywhere, and for the sick and sorrowing throughout the world, the Congregation uniting at the close in repeating the Disciples' Prayer.

The General Overseer then made the announcements.

The tithes and offerings were received, after which the General Overseer delivered his Message:

"DO BUSINESS TILL I COME."

INVOCATION.

Let the words of my mouth, and the meditation of my heart, be acceptable in Thy sight; be profitable unto this people; and unto all to whom these words shall come, in this and every land, in this and all the coming time, Till Jesus Come.

For my text this afternoon I shall put together two separate passages of Scripture; the first from the 12th Chapter of the Gospel according to Luke, where the rich fool in the parable says, "What shall I do?" and the second, the command of the lord in the parable in the 19th Chapter, "Do business till I come."

I think that it is fitting that at least once a year I preach a Zion business sermon.

In Zion it is all business.

We put religion into our business, and we make a religion of our business.

That is why Zion succeeds.

The Father's Business.

Our Lord Jesus, the Christ, when He was very young, was reproached by Joseph and Mary for discussing with the priests and doctors of the law in the temple.

He said to them, when they expressed sorrow and disappointment that He had grieved them by not coming on with the caravan, "Wist ye not that I must be about My Father's business?"

Even then the little boy Jesus made a business of His religion.

He talked of it as a business.

Religion is a business.

It is God's business.

When you tell me that business and religion are two different things, I know that you are a very ignorant person, and that you know very little about God, for God is in business.

If religion means the worship and service of God, then it is a business.

If God were not in the coal business, I should like to know what we should do.

He made our coal for us.

If God were not in the fish business, I should like to know what we should do.

He certainly attends to that business.

If God were not in the wheat and grain business what should we do?

God is attending to that business also.

All Things Should Be Done in a Business-like Way.

I wish we could make people stop talking nonsense about business.

Every activity that is right is business.

I am quite sure that if you do not make a business of your studies while in school, you will not amount to much in the world.

If you do not make a business of everything you enter into, and go at it in a thorough, business-like manner, you will not make a success of anything

One of the curses of the church are the unbusiness-like ways, both of the ministers and of the people.

We have no difficulty in carrying on the affairs of this Church without ever once appealing to the world.

When did Zion ever go, "cap in hand," to the world, and ask for money?

When?

People—"Never."

General Overseer—When do the churches outside of Zion go?

People—"All the time!"

General Overseer—That is true; they go all the time.

We do not care what kind of fellow it is—Rockefeller or any other kind of "feller;" we do not go after him for money.

A Church that Cannot Raise the Money for Its Own Expenses Ought to Go Out of Business.

It has no right to be in business for God.

I venture to say that we raise more money in one week, in the tithes of this City, than is raised by all the Congregational and Baptist churches in Chicago put together.

I do not hesitate to say that.

I should be inclined to say that you could add the money raised by several more denominations in Chicago, and then you would not equal the weekly tithes of Zion City

That is why Zion's Storehouse has been able, at all times, to care for her poor.

There never has been a time, before this City was built or since, when the poor of Zion have not been cared for.

There never has been a time when, to our knowledge, one member of this Church has been a beneficiary or a dependent upon public funds.

As far as I know, there is not one member of this entire Church throughout the world in a prison or in a poorhouse

I do not know whether this can be said of any other church or not, but I know it can be said of the Christian Catholic Church in Zion, whose banner waves on every continent.

We Have Attended Diligently to God's Business.

We have done it ourselves.

We have not gone outside.

Not only have we attended to the business of God in caring for the poor, and in the service of the Church, but we have been enabled to spend hundreds of thousands of dollars in planting the Gospel on distant shores.

I am so thankful for this!

It is wonderful, that without asking any help from any outside people at any time, or under any circumstances, we have been able to attend to our own affairs and to do our own work.

So before I talk about the workaday business in Zion, I desire to say that the first business to which we have attended has been the business of preaching the Gospel.

When any one makes an accusation against your General Overseer to the effect that he is paying too much attention to worldly business, will you please ask him if he knows of any other minister who preaches as many sermons as he does?

Will you please ask him if he knows of any other minister who has sent forth so many tens of thousands of pages of Christian literature as he has within the last ten years?

Will you please ask him if he knows of any one who has paid more attention to the discipline of his church than he has?

I do not want to give the answer.

You can get it from the man that criticizes, and I do not fear what the answer will be.

Zion's great work is divided into four great Departments.

The first is Spiritual and Ecclesiastical.

The second is Educational.

The third is Commercial, Financial, and Industrial.

The Fourth is Political.

Zion's Spiritual and Ecclesiastical Work.

I will not talk at length this afternoon about the Spiritual and Ecclesiastical work.

It is doing its own talking all over the world.

Today we have a Zion Restoration Host of at least ten thousand members.

It seems to us that if we added a great many that are doing work who are not yet enrolled, we should have many thousands more.

The Recorder, Elder Lee, assents to this.

I know it to be a fact.

Where will you find a church that is only eight years old that has a more thoroughly equipped Episcopacy?

The word *episkopos* means "overseer"—one that oversees.

Where will you find a more thoroughly organized Episcopacy?

Where will you find a more thoroughly organized Eldership?

Where will you find a more thoroughly organized Evangelistic corps?

Where will you find a more thoroughly organized Diaconate?

Where will you find from eight to ten thousand people under vow to go at any moment to any part of the world to do God's work, and who do go the moment they are told?

I told one Deaconess yesterday afternoon that she had to go to Denmark.

She accepted it with joy, and said that she would start the next day if I said so.

So it is all the time.

The other day we sent out eight or ten to Europe, who received their marching orders only a very few days before they sailed.

There is no difficulty in getting obedience in Zion.

I know that you all would go if you were sent.

Every one that would obey if I said, "Go next week," stand. [Almost the entire audience were on their feet in a moment.]

An Organization in which Is Perfect Discipline.

That is good.

Thank God!

That speaks for an organization!

They will not go blindly, nor will they be sent blindly.

This people is being prepared.

I spoke to one young man today and said, "I shall send you to such and such a place. The climate there is the deadliest in the world; perhaps you will die!"

His answer was, "General Overseer, if you send me I will go; and I shall be happy to go. I shall be happy to die if God wants my life."

We defy our critics to find a church that has an equally thorough consecration to God, that has as perfect a discipline, and that will not tolerate sin in its midst.

If sin gets in among us we get it out; there is no allowance made for it.

You cannot break the Ten Commandments and stay in Zion.

You will have to make tracks either for Beer, the city forty-two miles north, or Babel, forty-two miles south—Milwaukee and Chicago.

We are not boasting when we say these things.

They are real, and that is why this City is what it is today.

But the Church throughout the world has the same spirit.

So far as I know, there is not one officer who is unwilling at this moment to give his life for the Christ.

Zion's Educational Work.

Passing over the Ecclesiastical work, and just touching upon the Educational, I will come to the third Department.

Let me say a word or two about the Educational Department.

There will be a Teachers' Institute and Conference this week, beginning, I think, on Wednesday morning.

I desire you to pray for that.

I hope to open that Institute on Wednesday morning.

That is a remarkable work.

In this City alone, in this year 1904, we were educating one thousand nine hundred four persons—exactly the number of the year.

Of all the one thousand nine hundred four children, and young men, and maidens that attended Zion Educational Institutions this year, we lost only four by death, which is a proportion of about two in a thousand.

You will not find, in all the world, another record of such low death rate among children, and youths, and maidens.

I say that without any fear of contradiction.

By the goodness of God we have been able to help our young people to get stronger bodies, clearer minds, purer hearts, and to live holier and happier lives; so that the school and college life of Zion has become a great joy.

Splendid Equipment.

We have a corps of teachers and professors that no one anywhere in the world needs to be ashamed of.

In fact they are capable of doing work far in advance of that which many of them are doing.

We have people teaching in the lower grades who have taught in the higher grades elsewhere; and some who are teaching in the grades have been principals of schools.

It is an exceedingly delightful thing to know that we have such a splendidly equipped Educational Service.

As Overseer Brasefield is not here today, I desire to say that, as my assistant, and as the actual working head of the Educational department, we have in him one of the brightest, most scholarly, and up-to-date men in the world.

He is bright, happy, and splendidly disciplined; and he can play with the boys, too.

Almost the last time I saw him in Zion City he was acting as umpire in a game of baseball.

He and my son, whom I claim to be as well-educated a man as there is in this City, are just as happy with the boys as if they were the humblest of them.

It is very delightful to see how well-behaved, and how splendidly both youths and maidens act while at their games.

Very seldom do we have any trouble with them in any way.

The parents, too, for the most part, are coöperating with us.

There are some exceptions, I am sorry to say; but they are mostly of recent coming, and have not yet got into the right way of doing things.

We are looking forward to a good school year.

It will not be long before Zion College will be a large institution.

We have now in the various schools associated with it several hundred young men and women, and the day is not far distant when we shall see the University of Zion begin to appear.

That will be when our College is thoroughly furnished; then we can bring our pupils up, not only to the gates of the University, but we can do much work in the various departments of the University.

We are, then, doing business in the schools.

Those from Other Countries Carefully Taught the English Language.

In a very remarkable way we are improving the defective education of many that have come from foreign countries—in many cases, however, not so much defective education as a lack of knowledge of the English language.

We have seventy nationalities in this City, and one of the remarkable things is that, except for here and there a little foreign accent in their talk, you would not know it.

The people, although of many nationalities, are one in sentiment.

But we have some people that like to have a German meeting.

Somehow, they seem to think, that God Almighty hears prayer better when it is prayed in German.

Therefore we have German Elders and German meetings in connection with those who can very much better worship God in their own native tongue; especially the older people, who have not learned to pray in English, but who understand us.

They are here today, and always attend these services to listen to my addresses.

They say that somehow they understand my English.

A Belgian lady, who was accused of seeking for Baptism and fellowship when she did not know any English, said, "I do understand!"

"How do you understand Dr. Dowie when he preaches?" she was asked

"I understand him," she replied, "because I know a number of words, such as Jesus, salvation, sin, hell, heaven, death, life, hope, love, joy, and peace; and I watch for these words. Then I watch the Doctor, for he preaches with his whole body."

She was right.

This year we are providing more and more for the Manual Training School, and for the Night School, and for those studies which the young men and women can take up during the long winter nights, partly at home and partly in the College Building

I hope that you will be wise, and take advantage of these opportunities of which hundreds of you took advantage last winter.

We Now Come to the Financial, Commercial, and Industrial Enterprises of Zion.

We have come to the conclusion, as a people, that the banks of the worldly cities should not be allowed to get our money; and that the World, the Flesh, and the Devil shall not be allowed to control it, while we stand by and see it disappear, as some people's money has disappeared.

We do not see why, with the little God-given capacity we have, we cannot use our own money in our own Bank, in buying goods for our own stores, and in manufacturing, at a profit, something that nearly every one wants—articles that are of high grade, and that we have no difficulty in selling.

Zion Largely Engaged in Manufacturing.

We do not see any reason why we should not have our own planing-mill, and make our own doors, and sash, and windows, and various other things.

We see no reason why we should not make our own soap.

We see no reason why we should not make our own baking-powder, especially as we can make the very best in the country.

We see no reason why we should not make our own candy, and thus prevent poisoning our children with mineral coloring and chemical poisons found in candies purchased of outside firms.

There is not an atom of poison in the coloring used in our candies.

We see no reason why, with the capacity we have, we should not continue making the very best lace of its kind in the world; the very best candy of its kind in the world; and the very best soap of its kind in the world; as well as to build our own houses and make our own brick, as we have plenty of good clay.

We do not see why we should be reviled by a lazy church and an envious world for doing that which we have a perfect right to do, and which we can do well.

We must work for our board; and if we can make a profit in our work, why should we hand over the profit to those who spend it for beer and skittles, and for gambling, theaters, and harlots.

Why the General Overseer's Requests Are Granted.

I should like to get several million dollars during the next few weeks; and I have never asked God for a definite thing that I did not get.

I do not ask for unreasonable things, nor do I ask them unseasonably.

I shall get that for which I ask, for several reasons: first, because the Lord has need of it; second, because the City we are building and His people have need of it; and third, because our investments are sound and valuable.

Zion Has Never Been in the Mendicant Business.

I dislike to say this, but I will, nevertheless, namely: that Zion has never gone into the streets and struck a big drum, and then held out a tambourine and said, "Give us money, for if you do not we shall almost starve. We must find money to pay the rent of our hall, and for all our other expenses, and we cannot get a bite to eat until we have paid our expenses."

It is a horrible shame that the General of the Salvation Army should turn that organization into an army of beggars and mendicants.

Shame!

When Zion sends out Elders, Evangelists, Deacons, or Deaconesses, she never tells them to dun the people for money.

We provide them with money for their board and clothing, and for hall rent.

We say to them, "Go and preach the Gospel, and tell these people that you want their hearts for God, and that you do not care a snap whether they give you their money or not; all you want is that they shall do right."

Then these officers go; but not as a band of mendicants.

If we can carry on this work only by making the Christian Catholic Church in Zion a band of mendicants, then it shall be disbanded.

I am no general of a beggar army.

I do not need to beg.

Large Loans from the Outside Refused.

We earn what we have.

We use our own money, and we have been very unwilling to use any one else's.

The heads of the Financial Department will bear me witness that I have frequently refused money—as much as half a million dollars at a time—when it was offered to me at less interest than I was paying my people.

I refused it, because I did not want people outside to have such large interests in any Zion Institution.

These stocks which are now being offered are offered first to our own people.

We could go into the market and get all the money Zion wants for half the interest that will be paid to these stockholders; but I should rather give my people as much as possible of what we earn than to give the world half the sum and let our people invest their money elsewhere.

I tell you today that the people had better hurry up; because there is no excuse for further delay, for there is no question that sufficient time has elapsed to test the capacity of Zion for doing successful business.

Zion Stocks Have Never Decreased in Value, but Are Constantly Increasing.

I call your attention to the Business Conference reports, published in Volume XV., No. 18, of LEAVES OF HEALING.

I will not repeat the statements made therein, but will say briefly that no estate has ever grown in value so steadily, day after day and week after week, with no temporary or permanent decrease in value.

No matter what attacks have been made upon us, Zion stocks have never fallen below par; and today two of them are quoted, and are selling freely, at a premium of ten per cent.

I may tell you frankly that some of them will go up to fifteen and twenty per cent. at the time I have specified in the Editorial Notes in LEAVES OF HEALING of August 20th.

We can easily sell them to the world at that rate.

If some of our stocks were put upon the stock market now they would be quoted very readily at one hundred twenty-five and one hundred thirty.

I determined, from the very beginning, that I would give our own people the full advantages of our united energy, intelligence, and coöperation.

There are no strikes in Zion City.

There cannot be!

If there were a strike it would merely be the people's clinching their fists and striking their own faces.

Everything in this City is designed for the benefit of all.

General Overseer Accepts But Five Per Cent. of Increment of Value as His Portion.

I am sure that none of you doubt for a moment the statement made by our late General Counsel, Mr. Packard, and confirmed by our present General Counsel, that I have provided that, should I depart from this life tonight, ninety-five per cent. of this vast estate would belong absolutely to Zion.

All I have of it is five per cent. of the increment of value.

That was allowed me from the beginning.

My people desired that I should take the tithe; but I said, "No;" and I have been abundantly satisfied with my five per cent. and God's goodness to me throughout the years.

I say again from this platform, that it is an infernal lie that I, John Alexander Dowie, or any of my family, take one penny out of the tithes and offerings; nor have we for years.

Today I could write my check for a very large balance that the bank would owe me if I reckoned my proportion at ten per cent.—the amount allowed the high priest under the Mosaic Law—instead of the five per cent. which I now take.

Any person who talks about my prosperity's being dependent in any degree upon your tithes and offerings is talking nonsense.

Indeed, the tithes and offerings have been insufficient to carry on the work, and I have had the joy of being the largest contributor to that fund.

I say, with great thanksgiving in my heart, that God has richly blessed me.

Many who have died have left their entire estates to me.

Many now living have made wills by which properties, when they have passed away, will be added to my personal estate.

We now have quite a department that takes care of the annuities which I have given under trust deed.

I thank God for the riches which He has poured into my lap; for they have enabled me to do very much good.

Whoever else has envied me, my people never have, at any moment.

Have you?

PEOPLE—"No."

Poverty Not a Blessing, but a Curse.

GENERAL OVERSEER—I do not believe, for a moment, that poverty is a good thing.

It is an abominable lie to say that poverty is a good thing.

You may ask, "When did God say that it was not? Was not the Christ very poor?"

Yes, but He who was rich beyond all human comprehension, became poor for your sakes, "that ye through His poverty might become rich."

He wants us to be rich.

Jesus said, Verily I say unto you, There is no man that hath left house, or brethren, or sisters, or mother, or father, or children, or lands, for My sake, and for the Gospel's sake,

But he shall receive a hundredfold now in this time, houses, and brethren, and sisters, and mothers, and children, and lands, with persecutions; and in the world to come eternal life.

The Steady Increase in Value of Zion's Estate.

Never, in the history of real estate, has there been so steady, so constant, and such an unwavering, onward progress in value as in that of Zion.

God has blessed Zion, so that in point of values we would not think of exchanging this estate for twenty-five million dollars.

We are not talking nonsense, and we have no desire to exaggerate.

If the difficulties were insuperable we would say the same.

Impossible has no meaning in Zion.

All things are possible to him that believeth.

We have never doubted.

We have never taken a crooked path; nor have we ever consciously exaggerated.

In the statements made in the reports of the Business Conferences concerning Zion's position, values were considerably underestimated, and that was done purposely.

We do not profess that they are absolutely correct.

However, if the whole truth were told, it would be better for us; not worse.

In conducting a great industry there are certain reasons why it is not desirable that the profits should be known while the process of securing the business is still going on.

Why Large Profit Is Made in Zion Lace Industries.

I believe that we have reached the point in the manufacture of lace where, with increased capital, we can command a business of from twenty to thirty million dollars a year.

If I told you that all the profit we should make on that would be twenty-five per cent. I should lie, because the profit would be immensely larger.

Twenty-five per cent. on thirty million dollars would be seven and a half million dollars; but we do not intend to work for such a low profit.

We can make a better profit.

We have sixty-five per cent. duty in our favor to start with; and, besides, we can make better lace than the lace makers of Nottingham.

We run our machines by electricity, whereas their machines are run by steam; and we do under one roof what they usually do under four or five.

We will, by the grace of God, win the American trade; then we will cross to England, France, and Australia.

By the grace of God, we have already made our one pound earn more than ten pounds; for the lands of Zion have absolutely increased in average value more than twenty times.

No Pig Raisers Tolerated in Zion.

I say to Zion everywhere, "Come out of these pig-soaked farms. Stop raising pigs and growing tuberculosis, trichinosis, cancer, scrofula, and all kinds of dirt and muck in the form of pig, and then sending them down to market for people to eat."

I wonder that you are not ashamed of yourselves.

How can you be called Christians when you know that you are selling diseased pork, and making a profit out of people's miseries?

You miserable wretches!

I do not want you in Zion—not one of you who will grow pork and sell it for the glory of the Devil and the destruction of humanity.

It is a horrible thing!

I should just as soon preach to a goat as to a man or woman full of pork.

It is a dirty, filthy thing, and breeds every kind of abomination.

If there are any farmers in Zion who have pigs on their farms, who intend to continue to keep them, I ask for their resignations, because God has said,

Their flesh ye shall not eat, and their carcases ye shall not touch; they are unclean unto you.

We do not want growers of that uncleanness to be in Zion.

We have no place for the pig raiser, the whisky maker, the tobacco grower, or the producer of any dirty or unclean thing that defiles humanity.

You farmers cannot make, at the most, an average of over five or six per cent. on your farms, and you see what can be made by putting your money in Zion Investments.

All Can Be Zion Business Messengers.

God helping us, we can do better and better every year, now that the initial expenses have been met and the foundations laid.

I thank God and take courage

Every one of you should be a special Zion business messenger this year; especially in the next few weeks.

I constitute you all Special Zion Business Messengers.

Send out to your friends, far and near, the copy of LEAVES OF HEALING to which I have already referred, and send with it a letter, telling them that you know these things to be true; and thus encourage and help them.

You will not encourage and help them in saying that Zion is going to the dogs, and that every one is leaving,

The fact is, you cannot find a house to rent in the whole City.

That does not look as if it were going to the dogs, does it?

If we begin at once, as we intend doing, to build Shiloah Tabernacle and some other large buildings, we shall certainly have to build more dwelling-houses, for we have no accommodations for more workmen.

I want to kill the lie that has been told all over the world that Zion City went to the dogs while I was away, and that even since my return and after the Feast of Tabernacles people have flocked out of the City so that there were empty houses everywhere.

I have looked for these empty houses, but have not seen them.

The Treatment Future Grumblers Will Receive.

Let us squelch the grumbler.

Let him or her get out as quickly as possible.

I do not propose to help grumblers by paying them a big profit on their properties, nor do I propose to let you help them.

Let Mr. and Mrs. Grumbler, and all the little Grumblers, get as much for their properties as will enable them to leave with the amount of money that they came in with, and no more.

I object to Zion's putting a premium upon grumblers.

We have done too much of this.

We have given the grumbler a great deal of money, and got him out because we needed the property, and could make use of it; but I direct my people to do it no more.

We have not had many grumblers, but they have taken out much more than they put in.

I defy you to find one person that went out with less than he had when he came in; but I can tell you of many who have gone out with more than they had when they came in, and who have lost every dollar since they left.

Those who have not already lost everything are not prospering.

Not one person that has lied about Zion and gone out has prospered, and not one will.

God will take care of that.

Those who have gone out are very few, comparatively; but there is no use in saying that there have not been some.

But not one has gone out fighting against Zion that was not a liar or a hypocrite, and sometimes a thief.

I say to all, far and wide, Take no stock in these grumblers.

Men are to be found that have gone to New York, to Boston, to Vancouver, to Seattle, or elsewhere, who say ugly things about Zion.

Why?

Because they were expelled from Zion for their vices, or for some form of sin.

They lie when they say that they went out of Zion because she had failed.

Let any one in the world demand of those that went, "Did you lose a dollar?" and see if they can truthfully say that they did.

The business of Zion stands upon a strong foundation.

A "Pearl of Great Price."

Our Lord, Jesus, the Christ, in one of His business parables said that "the Kingdom of Heaven is like unto a man that is a merchant seeking goodly pearls: and having found one pearl of great price, he went and sold all that he had, and bought it."

We have those of you in Zion who have been just like that merchantman. You sought something good and you found it in Zion.

Then you sold all that you had, and got as much as you could of the "goodly pearl" in Zion.

I am very thankful that we have the Pearl of a Perfect Salvation, the Pearl of Divine Healing, the Pearl of Holy Living, the Pearl of a Good Education, the Pearl of a Sound Business, and the Pearl, above all things, of a Clean, Sound, Healthy City, where the Devil is kept out as much as possible.

Here it is easy to do right and difficult to do wrong; because the people that want to do wrong in Zion are dealt with very quickly, and if they persist in wrong-doing they must go.

A Boon to All True Parents.

One feature of Zion, to us who are fathers and mothers, is the best of all, namely: we have a City where our children, our youths, and our maidens can go down our streets, and not be insulted by the harlot's invitation, or the whoremonger's suggestion; they never hear blasphemy nor have the stinking tobacco smoke puffed in their faces; nor do they find in our City those who are paid by the World, the Flesh, and the Devil, to drag them to hell.

The filthy billposter has no place in Zion.

The filthy theatrical display has no place in Zion.

We can do without Mephistopheles, the Devil; and Faust, the doctor; and Marguerite, the harlot.

Our young people have become passionately fond of the Holy Inspiration of the Heavenly Music; and I believe we shall have in Zion the most glorious music that the Church in any age has produced.

I am happy about it all.

Zion's Part in Politics.

My last point is that we have done political business in Zion for God.

We belong to neither the Democrats, Republicans, Prohibitionists, nor Populists.

We are Theocrats.

The Prohibition Party does not go far enough for us; it seeks to prohibit the manufacture and sale of alcohol.

We go much farther.

We work to prohibit the manufacture and sale of tobacco, of opium, of morphine, and of cocaine, as well as of every drug that destroys; and, by the grace of God, we are determined to accomplish it.

We do not intend to be linked to any political party; neither do we intend to throw away our votes.

Zion Will Cast Her Vote for Theodore Roosevelt.

When we have the opportunity of electing one of the best men, morally and religiously; one of the bravest and most astute statesmen, who is a warrior in the truest and best sense of the word, and a man of peace, we make the most of that opportunity.

I call upon Zion everywhere to cast their votes this fall for Theodore Roosevelt. [Applause.]

I know what I am talking about.

That other great party is insincere.

They agreed to the gold standard after they had crossed the Rubicon, and found that their candidate would not stand upon any other condition.

In a business sermon I have a right to speak of this.

You cannot trust them with the fiscal policy of the United States of America.

They are a pack of dishonest statesmen.

They are not honest about the tariff.

They are not honest about the gold.

They are not honest about the civil service.

They are not honest about anything.

The only thing they are after is to ride their Democratic donkey into the White House; they want office.

As the Prophet of God, I may as well tell them that they will not get it—not this year. [Applause.]

To cast our vote so as to imperil the return of President Roosevelt, would mean great injury to Zion.

I say this with all respect for hundreds of thousands of excellent Christians who belong to the Democratic party, the Prohibition party, and the Populist party.

I have no quarrel with them.

I desire to say this about Mr. Bryan, to whose fiscal heresies I very much object, he did not wait until all the convention had voted before declaring his policy.

He was a brave man, and outlined his policy to the people before the Democratic convention was held.

Who Is Alton B. Parker?

But this Parker, of whom no one had ever heard, except that he was a successful local lawyer and a good judge, never had any experience in the government of the people.

He has not even been a mayor!

What has he done?

Roosevelt has one of the most brilliant of records.

He served the people as a police commissioner when there was nothing to be gained from it, personally.

He did splendid work in New York.

I recognize the Christianity and the sincerity, as well as the crass ignorance of many Christian people who belong to the Democratic party.

The Apparent Fatuity and Blindness of the South.

I recognize the infatuation of the Southern States, whose people seem to consider that it would be almost an impossibility for them to vote any other than the Democratic ticket.

I am surprised that the far-seeing statesmen of the South do not see that the time has come for the Southern States to become the great manufacturing section of this country, especially in textile fabrics

I am amazed that they should still hold to the policy which compels them to send their raw materials to Europe, when they could send them out manufactured, thus bringing in twenty dollars where they now get one, and successfully competing with other nations that now buy their raw cotton for a few cents a pound.

I am amazed at the fatuity of the people that will not see that the time has come to break with that fiscal heresy, Free Trade.

I am amazed that some of them still hold to the idea of a depreciated currency, and vote for the payment of all public and private debts in dollars that would not be worth more than forty-five cents, if their fiscal heresies were to prevail.

I am amazed at the wilful stupidity and blindness of people that will not face the facts.

I say to Christians of the South, You are no doubt good and sincere people, but you have shut your eyes so long that now you cannot see.

By the grace of God, let them be opened.

President Roosevelt a Man of Peace.

There is no use talking the nonsense of which we have heard so much—about the warlike policy of the President.

I have the honor of a slight personal friendship with, or knowledge of, the President; and I believe that His Excellency would bear with me in making public some parts of a conversation that took place between us when I saw him last November.

I told him that there were many who were afraid that he was too bellicose, personally, and that his policy would be too belligerent and warlike.

I shall never forget the earnestness with which he said, "I thank you for telling me that, and I want to disabuse your mind of the idea.

"I am not bellicose, personally, nor do I want a belligerent policy.

"I want peace in our time.

"I want progress.

"I want prosperity; but I do want to be able to maintain the peace of the world, and especially the peace of America.

"I look upon the navy of the United States as a great naval police, in the interests of all nations, and especially of our own."

These, as far as I can remember them, were the brave, strong words of the President; and I am persuaded that he meant every one of them.

I believe him to be a man of peace, and not a man of war.

But there may yet come a time in this country when he will have to be the Man on Horseback, and put down bloodshed and revolution in our streets.

The day may come when he will have to stand as Commander-in-chief at the head of the Army and put down that Rebellion against all Law and Order, an example of which is, at the present time, being shown in our city of Chicago.

I Speak With Great Kindness Concerning the Strikers.

I am not by any means a friend of the packers.

I believe that many of them are packers of disease, of death, and of damnation.

I believe that they pack that unspeakable hog when they know it is diseased.

I believe that multitudes of people are mourning, because of the horribly-diseased food that is sent out from the Chicago Stockyards.

I believe, too, that for the most part, the packers are without any personal interest in the prosperity, sobriety, and happiness of their employees.

I think that, in some respects, the case made out by Mr. Donnelly was a very strong one, in which he showed that the packers had been accelerating the rate of speed in the killing of the cattle to such an extent that they were destroying the power of the men to work at all, by the tremendous rate at which they were forcing them forward to earn anything.

I have no doubt whatever that much is to be said on the side of the working classes.

Action of the Strikers, which, if Continued, Will Array All Good Powers Against Them.

But this I will say, "impugn it whoso list," that the declaration of unions that men shall not be allowed to work unless they belong to those unions is a declaration that is nothing short of revolution and anarchy.

If it comes to this, that we are to be ruled by trades unions, then the Constitution of the United States must be revised, or some of us will feel that we had better change a flag that makes us dependent upon the whims of a mass of ignorant men, led oftentimes, though not always, by self-seeking, greedy, and unscrupulous leaders.

No one has heard me say, and no one shall hear me say, an unkind word about the men engaged in the struggle that is being carried on at the Chicago Stockyards; but I do say that the murdering of non-union workmen; the maiming, injuring, and insulting of women; and the stealing of cattle, and the boycotting of all business, is the very way to make the strikers lose their cause; as everything that stands for Law and Order must be against them, even if their cause is a good one.

I would censure them, and stop publication.

The next thing I would do would be to clean out all the justice shops of Chicago, and put in men who would give righteous decisions. [Applause.]

Next, I would clean out Mayor Harrison and all his lot, and have a new "stock, lock, and barrel," in the City Hall. [Applause.]

Next, I would close every wholesale and retail liquor shop, and every brewery and distillery in Chicago.

Wouldn't that make an eruption?

Then I would close every tobacco shop.

I would close all those dirty, low, theatrical dives; and I would give the people a complete rest from the theaters.

I would also send out an edict that we would do without the

BIRD'S-EYE VIEW (

I feel deep sympathy for them.

I feel deep sorrow for them.

The greatest foe of the working classes is not their employers; it is themselves.

How Chicago Should Be Renovated.

If I were appointed dictator of that city today, and if I had the power to compel the people to obey, I would have every one at work tomorrow morning, or just as soon thereafter as possible.

I would close, first of all, the newspaper offices [applause], the *American* "*Cesspool*," for instance, which is inciting the people to riot and murder, and which is patting on the back those that have been leading murderous attacks.

I would immediately come down upon such papers.

drug-stores and the doctors, except for sanitary purposes. [Applause.]

Then, with the savings effected from all these things, I would guarantee to feed, clothe, educate, and make as happy as good social conditions could make them, every man, woman, and child in Chicago; and I would not fail in the undertaking. [Applause.]

But I suppose all that is some distance away yet.

But you may now know something of what will happen when the Lord comes and perhaps says, "John Alexander Dowie, go and carry out in Chicago what you said in Shiloh Tabernacle, on the afternoon of August 21, 1904."

I would not ask Him what support He would send with me, for I know that my Lord would never give me a responsibility like that without backing me with all His Divine power.

When the Christ Returns.

It is a good time that is coming, when, after the Christ returns to reign, every city of the world will have a dictator like that, sent out from the King at Jerusalem.

You know that I can do only a limited amount of work while I am in this body; but I am coming back.

How often the press has said of me, "He is gone! He will never come back!"

But every time I answered, "I will come again;" and I came.

I tell the scoffing press, the scoffing pulpit, the scoffing preacher, and such of the scoffing people as still scoff—I tell them all: You may scoff on, but if you hear that my spirit has left this body, to enter the spiritual, celestial, and incorruptible body, do not forget that I am gone only for a little time, and that when Jesus comes back, I hope, Zion Restoration Host and I will come back with Him.

When we come back, we will have better bodies, and purer spirits, and we will be able to do the work that the Lord has for us to do.

Meanwhile, we have to do our work now, and do it as well as we can.

All that are determined to do it, and not grumble, stand and let me see you.

Let us pray.

PRAYER OF CONSECRATION.

My God and Father, in Jesus' Name I come to Thee. Take me as I am. Make me what I ought to be in spirit, in soul, and in body. Give me power to do right, no matter what it costs. Help me to be earnest, to be true-hearted, and to do right in Thy sight, regardless of what men may think, or do, or say, or threaten. Forgive what has been amiss in my life, and give me power now to do my part in Zion. For Jesus' sake.

Did you mean it?

PEOPLE—"Yes."

GENERAL OVERSEER—Then live it.

The Congregation then remained standing while the Choir and Officers marched out singing the Recessional, "The Church's One Foundation."

The General Overseer then pronounced the

BENEDICTION.

Beloved, abstain from every form of evil. And may the very God of Peace Himself sanctify you wholly; and I pray God your whole spirit, and soul, and body be preserved entire, without blame, unto the coming of our Lord Jesus, the Christ. Faithful is He that calleth you, who also will do it.

The grace of our Lord Jesus, the Christ, the love of God our Father, the fellowship of the Holy Spirit, our Comforter and Guide, one Eternal God, abide in you, bless you, and keep you, and all the Israel of God everywhere, forever. Amen.

TY, AUGUST 1, 1904.

RESTORATION MESSAGE NO. 96.

*REPORTED BY S. E. C., O. R., A. C. R., AND A. W. N.

When God's Prophet of the Restoration came on the platform at the close of the Processional Lord's Day afternoon, August 28, 1904, he faced an audience of about five thousand, very many of whom were visitors in the City.

The day was an example of ideal summer weather.

Large numbers of people from Chicago and other nearby

*The following report has not been revised by the General Overseer.

cities had taken advantage of the occasion to visit the City of Zion and to attend the Great General Assembly in Shiloh Tabernacle.

The regular excursion train brought hundreds from Chicago alone, while carriages, automobiles, bicycles, and other trains on the railroad had brought hundreds of others.

The man of God had a Message for them all.

It was a declaration of the Universal and Eternal Supremacy of the Kingdom of God.

It was not an abstract, philosophical discussion of the Power and Authority of God, but, a direct, powerful, simple, Scriptural Proclamation that dealt, in an intensely practical manner, with the Hearts, Homes, Vocations, and Avocations of the people present.

It was not a message to tickle the ears, to please the fancy, to delight by its eloquence, or to excite intellectual admiration and wonder; but a Message, the whole end and aim of which was to get results.

It was clear from the deep earnestness of the speaker that he preached the Gospel of the Kingdom of God for no other purpose than to get men and women into that Kingdom and that Kingdom into them.

This was the reason why those who had come because drawn by mere idle curiosity, simply to see and hear a man of whom they had read much, found that this man had a Message for them personally, and that he was driving that Message home by the power of God's Spirit to their heart of hearts.

This was the reason why they sat with enchained attention throughout the entire service, and why so large a number of them rose with God's people at the close of the Message to express their desire and determination to obey the Rule of God.

But the Message of the afternoon was not alone for strangers and visitors in the City.

The General Overseer had some very important words for the members of the Christian Catholic Church in Zion.

He had already announced that some very important declarations, especially concerning the Apostolic Office in the Church of God, were to be made on Lord's Day, September 18th.

It was with these declarations in view that the man of God spoke some very significant words, during the course of his Message.

The Christ chose His Apostles from among humble fishermen and tax-gatherers, immediately after calling upon His disciples to pray the Lord of the harvest to send forth laborers into His harvest.

Once more the fields are white unto the harvest, and the laborers are few.

It is time for prayer to the Lord of the harvest that He send forth laborers.

There were several incidents of interest and power during the service.

One was a unique, but peculiarly effective, political move by the General Overseer, who is also the leader of the Theocratic party.

As is well known, that party has in the present campaign endorsed the candidacy of Theodore Roosevelt for President of the United States.

All those who would from now until election time pray every day for his election were asked to stand. The response was almost unanimous, even the women and children, who could not aid by their votes, pledging their prayers.

Another incident was at the close of the meeting, when, for the benefit of the visitors present, those who had been healed through faith in Jesus testified to the fact by rising. Probably over four thousand people were on their feet.

Music at this service was worthy of special mention.

While the audience was gathering, Zion City Band rendered a very delightful selection, peculiarly appropriate to a religious service, in a manner that bespoke both musical talent and conscientious training.

While the tithes and offerings were being taken, Zion White-robed Choir showed its excellence in the rendering of "Lovely Appear."

At the close of the service, the audience was deeply touched by the responsive singing of "Art Thou Weary, Art Thou Languid?" by two sections of Zion Junior Choir, seated in the galleries on either side of the platform.

Shiloh Tabernacle, Zion City, Illinois, Lord's Day Afternoon, August 28, 1904.

The service was begun with the Processional, "Crown Him with Many Crowns," and was followed with the usual Invocation, after which Hymn No. 27, from Gospel Hymns, was sung.

The recitation of the Apostles' Creed and the Commandments, and the singing of the Te Deum Laudamus was followed by Scripture reading and exposition.

The General Overseer read from the Inspired Word of God, from the Book of Psalms, 19th chapter, and in the Gospel according to St. Matthew, the 9th chapter, beginning with the 18th verse, and reading through the 21st verse, "For she said within herself, If I do but touch His garment, I shall be made whole," when he paused to say:

Scripture Reading and Exposition.

The margin has a better reading for those last words: "I shall be saved whole."

She knew that her spirit was confident in the Christ, but she wanted healing for her body.

We are composed of more than spirit; we are spirit, soul, and body—a tripartite nature.

She had the intense desire that, while in the flesh, she should be saved whole.

But Jesus turning and seeing her said, Daughter, be of good cheer; thy faith hath made thee whole. And the woman was made whole from that hour.

And when Jesus came into the ruler's house, and saw the flute players, and the crowd making a tumult,

He said, Give place: for the damsel is not dead, but sleepeth. And they laughed Him to scorn.

But when the crowd was put forth,—

The words "put forth" is scarcely strong enough, for *exeblethe* (ἐξεβλήθη) means thrown out; and I believe that the Lord threw them out.

It is the only thing to be done with a certain class of people who would mock at the Message of the Christ Himself, even in the house of mourning.

They were thrown out, and not with a gentle push either. It was a deliberate, strong, powerful hand that threw them out.

This crowd of mockers was put out of the house, and He entered in and took the damsel by the hand, and she rose.

But when the crowd was put forth, He entered in, and took her by the hand; and the damsel arose.

And the fame hereof went forth into all that land.

And as Jesus passed by from thence, two blind men followed Him, crying out, and saying, Have mercy on us, Thou Son of David.

And when He was come into the house, the blind men came to Him: and Jesus saith unto them, Believe ye that I am able to do this? They say unto Him, Yea, Lord.

Then touched He their eyes, saying, According to your faith be it done unto you.

And their eyes were opened. And Jesus strictly charged them,

The marginal reading is "Jesus *sternly* charged them, saying,"

An Unpardonable Sin.

And their eyes were opened. And Jesus strictly charged them saying, See that no man know it.

But they went forth, and spread abroad His fame in all that land.

And as they went forth, behold, there was brought to Him a dumb man possessed with a devil.

And when the devil was cast out, the dumb man spake: and the multitudes marveled, saying, It was never so seen in Israel.

But the Pharisees said, By the prince of the devils casteth He out devils.

It is an unpardonable sin to say that the Lord is possessed with a devil; it is the sin that has no forgiveness.

It is made more clear, perhaps, in the corresponding passage, the 3d chapter of Mark, from the 22d through the 30th verse.

Because they said, He hath an unclean spirit.

To say that the Lord Jesus, the Christ, has an unclean spirit, and to ascribe the works of God to the Prince of Devils, is an unpardonable sin.

And Jesus went about all the cities and villages, teaching in their synagogues, and preaching the Gospel of the Kingdom, and healing all manner of disease and all manner of sickness.

But when He saw the multitudes, He was moved with compassion for them, because they were distressed and scattered, as sheep not having a shepherd.

Then saith He unto His disciples, The harvest truly is plenteous, but the laborers are few.

Pray ye therefore the Lord of the harvest, that He will send forth laborers into His harvest.

And He called unto Him His twelve disciples, and gave them authority over unclean spirits, to cast them out, and to heal all manner of disease and all manner of sickness.

Now the names of the twelve apostles are these: The first, Simon, who is called Peter, and Andrew, his brother; James, the son of Zebedee, and John, his brother;

Philip, and Bartholomew; Thomas, and Matthew, the publican; James, the son of Alphæus, and Thaddæus;

Simon, the Cananæan, and Judas Iscariot, who also betrayed Him.

These twelve Jesus sent forth.

The General Supplication was then offered by Overseer Jane Dowie, after which the General Overseer prayed for the sick and sorrowing, and this was followed with the chanting of the Disciples' Prayer by the Choir and Congregation.

After announcements were made and the tithes and offerings were received, the General Overseer delivered his Message:

THE CALLING OF THE TWELVE.

INVOCATION.

Let the words of my mouth and the meditation of my heart be acceptable in Thy sight, be profitable unto this people, and unto all to whom these words shall come, in this and every land, in this and all the coming time, Till Jesus Come. Amen.

TEXT.

And Jesus went about all the cities and the villages, teaching in their synagogues, and preaching the Gospel of the Kingdom, and healing all manner of disease and all manner of sickness.

But when He saw the multitudes, He was moved with compassion for them, because they were distressed and scattered, as sheep not having a shepherd.

Then saith He unto His disciples, The harvest truly is plenteous, but the laborers are few.

Pray ye therefore the Lord of the harvest, that He send forth laborers into His harvest.

And He called unto Him His twelve disciples, and gave them authority over unclean spirits, to cast them out, and to heal all manner of disease and all manner of sickness.

In the 36th verse, the marginal reading is, "They fainted and were tired, and lay down, because they were distressed and scattered, as sheep not having a shepherd."

Our Lord Jesus, the Christ, carried on His mission on this earth in the most orderly way.

Anything that is Divine can never be disorderly.

That Which Is Disorderly Is Always Devilish.

If there is a disorderly boy or girl; if there is one disorderly member of this Choir; if there is one disorderly member of the Church, can he or she be of God?

Surely not!

Disorder belongs to the Devil.

Disorderly people are always devilish

They are not Divinely led.

God is the Author, not of confusion, but of Divine and Perfect Order.

The strength of our work in Zion is in proportion to its orderly character.

I am pleased that, for the most part, we do have perfect order.

When Jesus, the Christ, went about His ministry, He went about doing three things—teaching, preaching, and healing.

The first in importance is teaching.

Preaching Is of Little Importance Compared With Teaching.

The Christ was first of all a great Teacher, then a great Preacher, and then a great Healer—the Healer of every malady of humanity in spirit, soul, and body.

He went about teaching in their synagogues, and preaching the gospel of the republic? Was that it?

PEOPLE—"The Gospel of the Kingdom of God."

GENERAL OVERSEER—There is no gospel of the republic, or of the autocracy, or democracy.

The only Gospel that the Christ came to preach was the Gospel of the Monarchy of God, the Kingdom of God, the Theocracy, the Rule of God.

He went about teaching in their synagogues and preaching the Gospel of the Kingdom, and healing every sickness and every disease among the people.

He went about doing these things, because He came for the purpose of removing all darkness from the human spirit, the human soul, and the human body.

He desired that all darkness, and sin, and sickness be taken away from all mankind.

Hence His first work was teaching; and that teaching was very fundamental and simple.

The First Truth Taught by the Christ.

The first truth that He taught was that He Himself had the Authority to speak for God.

He made that abundantly plain.

He did not speak as one who was uncertain; He spoke as one having Authority, and not as the scribes.

The scribes and Pharisees of His day were constantly appealing to the Talmud, to the Mishna, to the Gemara, to the tradition of the elders, and to the law of Moses; but He stood superior to them all.

He said regarding Moses:

Ye have heard that it was said, An eye for an eye, and a tooth for a tooth: But I say unto you, Resist not him that is evil: but whosoever smiteth thee on thy right cheek; turn to him the other also.

He said, in effect, "Do not do what Moses tells you, or what Solomon tells you. Solomon said this and that, but a Greater than Solomon is here."

He stood before them as the Teacher of all teachers, putting aside even Moses and Solomon.

Our Lord Jesus, the Christ, claimed to be, and He was, and He is, the Teacher of the Highest, because the Teacher of Divine, Authority.

He, Himself, never taught anything that was authoritative.

He very carefully guarded Himself in that matter.

He said:

The words that I say unto you, I speak not from Myself, but the Father abiding in Me, doeth His works.

He declared that the words that He spoke were all the words of the Eternal God and Father spoken through Him, the Son of Man.

He declared that the works He did were done by God.

The words that I say unto you I speak not from Myself: but the Father abiding in Me, doeth His works.

He came to us with the beautiful words of the Eternal Father—His Father and our Father; His God and our God.

He, the Eternal Son, brought to us the Message of the Eternal Father's Love, and Purity, and Power.

God the Head of All Power and Authority.

He preached a Gospel which declared that God was Supreme in everything; that the rule of His world must be the Rule of God; that God must rule in the heart, in the head, in the feet, in the hand, in the tongue, and in all the members of the body.

He must be the Head of the Home.

He must rule in every room of the house, from the drawing-room to the kitchen.

He must rule in the song that is sung.

He must be preeminent.

No home can ever be right until God rules in every part of it.

God is not invited to take any part in many homes.

Many who call themselves Christians, every day send their wives and families from a prayerless home into a godless world.

Many of those who pretend to be Christians never raise a song of praise in their home; never bow in thanks to God.

These homes are not Christian homes; they are heathen.

They are worse than heathen homes.

The heathen offer libations and make sacrifices at their feasts to some unseen power; some god.

But there are multitudes in Christian lands who call themselves Christians and yet never offer thanks to God.

The Kingdom of God must be established in the heart and in the home.

Nothing Should Be Done that God Cannot Approve.

The song must be one that God can approve.

The story that is told must have in it nothing unclean or improper—nothing that God would not approve.

The laugh may be hearty, but it must be from hearts of Purity.

When you go out into the world, the road you take must be a Divine road.

The words that you speak must be words that God can approve.

You cannot tell lies. You cannot utter words of deceit.

You cannot go into places that are improper.

You cannot enter into business relationships and partnerships with men who are serving the World, the Flesh, and the Devil.

You cannot make companions of young men or women, no matter how amiable or how talented they may be, if they are not Christians; for "what concord hath the Christ with Belial?"

"What Portion Hath a Believer with an Unbeliever?"

How can you be yoked together with an unbeliever and have a happy life? One will pull one way and the other another.

If you are a Christian you must have Christian companionship.

You must do all the good you can for those who are sinful and out of the way, and endeavor to bring them to God; but you must not make companions of them

You must not be companions in sin.

You must not be sympathizers with them in their evil deeds. You must reprove the works of darkness.

Those that follow the Christ cannot go into secret society lodges and listen to the nonsensical, ridiculous, and blasphemous things said there!

They cannot be present at a mock murder, such as that of Hiram Abiff.

They cannot be present at a mock resurrection, such as that in the Masonic Lodge, when King Solomon raises a man from the dead. That is a shameful lie.

Secret Societies No Place for the Christian.

King Solomon never raised any one from the dead.

Before he himself died, he was dead in trespasses and sin—a rotten, disgusting, beastly old king, with seven hundred wives and three hundred concubines, who had led him far from God into the worship of false gods.

He who had been so wise got into these filthy secret society lodges—for heathen worship in every age has been full of secret society mysteries—and went to the Devil.

You cannot get into bad company like that, and do right.

If you walk with the Christ you must walk in the light, and not in the darkness.

You must have no fellowship with the unfruitful works of darkness; you must reprove them.

The Kingdom of God demands that you walk in the light, and be as the Christ who said, in effect, "In secret spake I nothing. I walked in the light; I talked in the light; and My deeds were done in the light."

Those who hate the light, walk in darkness and do not come to the light, lest their deeds should be reproved; for they are not wrought in God.

You have nothing to do with secret society lies and fables.

You cannot be a Christian and stay with them, because that is contrary to God's command: "Come ye out from among them, and be ye separate."

The Kingdom of God must rule everywhere.

It must rule in your social assemblies.

The Rule of the Christ must be supreme. You all know that these secret societies are Christless and Godless.

There is no Christianity in the vaunted "Freemasonry."

There are side issues where they do talk about Him, but in the straight thirty-three degrees of Masonry there is no Christ.

His Name cannot be mentioned, because, they say, "It would offend those who are Mohammedans, Buddhists, Jews, and others; and therefore the Christ cannot be named."

They have a Bible, out of which they have cut the Name of Jesus, the Christ; for in every quotation from the Bible that occurs in their ritual, where the Name of the Christ should appear, it is stricken out.

No one can deny that declaration.

You have never noticed even an address or prayer by a bishop in a Masonic assembly in which occurred the Name of Jesus, the Christ, as our Lord and Master.

He could not without doing that which was contrary to the demands of Masonry.

The Kingdom of God Should Be Within Us.

As Christians, you cannot go into assemblies where the King does not reign; where you cannot recognize the Kingship of our Lord Jesus, the Christ; but you can go and be a child of the Devil.

When the Christ preached the Kingdom of God, He demanded that that Kingdom should be within us—a Kingdom of Righteousness, Peace, and Joy in the Holy Spirit.

He declared of those who did not confess Him before men, but were ashamed of Him, that He should be ashamed of them before the angels in heaven.

Therefore Christianity goes into every activity of life and sees to it that you give sixteen ounces to the pound and thirty-six inches to the yard.

Christianity sees to it that when you contract to give eight hours' labor, you do not skulk and cheat your employer out of about an hour every day.

You are a thief if you do that—a mean, shameful thief!

You have stolen your employer's money just as surely as if you had stolen it from his pocket.

God makes you to carry conscience into everything; not only when you are being watched, but when you cannot be seen.

Nothing that Is Evil Can Ever Belong to the Kingdom of God.

Hence it was that He taught the people that in their hearts, in their homes, in their business, in their politics, and everywhere, God was to be the Ruler, and rule.

If God is not the Supreme Ruler, then this world has gone to the Devil—just in the degree that God does not rule.

The Christ, therefore, came to destroy the works of the Devil, and as He went about doing good and healing all that were oppressed of the Devil, His heart was saddened, for humanity everywhere was sick in spirit, soul, and body.

He healed comparatively few, for Palestine is a little country, and had a comparatively small population.

It is smaller in extent than the State of Illinois, and had at that time a smaller population.

He saw comparatively few people, for He did not go beyond the borders of Palestine in His earthly ministry.

A Picture of the World as the Christ Saw It.

He had been healing large numbers of people, and His heart was sore as He thought of the whole world lying beyond, the hundreds of millions in darkest Africa, and Asia, and Europe; for at that time our parents were in heathen darkness.

At that time the Africans along the Nile were far more civilized than our fathers.

Our fathers were painted savages in the wilds of Europe and Britain.

The Picts and Scots were fighting, murdering, and stealing, and doing everything that was filthy and abominable.

They murdered their own children, and sacrificed them upon the altars of Moloch.

Druidical human sacrifices were being made in Great Britain at the very time when the Christ was teaching the Gospel of the Kingdom.

Let us remember what an unclean set our fathers and mothers were at that time.

As the Christ looked over all the world with His Divine eyes, He was moved with compassion, because He saw the sheep everywhere were tired and fainting, and were lying down in their sickness, and sorrow, and misery; for they were ground down by military oppression and extreme taxation, for the benefit of those who were squandering the revenues of Imperial Rome, and of even the Temple of God, in all kinds of filthy and abominable practices.

The people were laboring, as it were, in the very fire.

They had nothing to show at the end of the year's work except that they had fed the unclean passions of their rulers and of the shamelessly guilty and wicked priests.

The Appointing of the Twelve Apostles.

As the Christ looked at them, His heart was moved with compassion, and it was at that time that He turned to His Twelve Disciples and delivered to them a little discourse concerning the condition of the world; and immediately after that He took the Twelve and ordained them as Apostles.

I desire you to see the direct connection.

In the revision, the 1st verse of the 10th chapter of Matthew forms the last verse of the 9th chapter, and it is correctly placed there.

He delivered to them an address, and I have no doubt that it was of very considerable length.

We have only the text, as it were, of that address, "The harvest truly is plenteous, but the laborers are few. Pray ye therefore the Lord of the harvest, that He send forth laborers into His harvest."

I believe that the moment He said that they began to pray.

I believe that they went at once to prayer, and when they had done praying, He looked around and said, "I will take you."

How Jesus Laid the Foundation of His Church.

He set aside the whole majestic outward ceremonial of the Jewish Dispensation, took these twelve simple men, and ordained them as Apostles.

He set aside High Priests and Temple services, and took fishermen, and an honest tax-gatherer, simple men of Northern Palestine, men of Galilean speech without any learning of the Rabbinical School, and ordained them to be the Twelve Apostles.

That was the way in which He Himself answered the prayer that the Lord of the harvest would send forth laborers into His harvest. He began in the right way.

He laid the foundation of His Church that day.

The Church of God is founded upon the Foundation of the Apostles and Prophets, Jesus, the Christ, Himself being the chief Corner-Stone; and in all the Dispensations, Jewish, Patriarchal, Mosaic, and Christian, and in the Restoration, it will be the same.

It is the Rock of Ages that underlies all systems in all ages.

In the Christian Dispensation the Church is built upon the Apostles and Prophets.

Thus the Christ took these simple people, and made them the Foundation Officers of His Church.

What a wonderful thing it was, as Augustine so beautifully said, that "it pleased God in His infinite wisdom to save philosophers by means of fishermen, and not fishermen by means of philosophers."

It pleased God not to take these men out of great schools of learning, but He took simple men and made them the first Apostles.

All the Apostles Were Not Illiterate Men.

As time went on, it became necessary that men of higher education should become Apostles.

Hence it was that such men as Paul, Barnabas, Apollos, and others became Apostles—men who were not only pious, but of great learning and great eloquence.

These first Apostles set the Church in order, and then laborers were trained in the Church, and sent forth in an orderly manner. It never has been of any use, at any time, to send into the battle soldiers that were not trained.

You never should rest satisfied with your training in warfare.

It would be a perfect farce for Alexander to attempt today to win a campaign with thirty thousand men, with short swords and shields, against a million men, if the million men were equipped as modern armies are.

Long before his phalanx could reach the opposite side they would be mowed down by artillery; they would be blown in pieces by mines, and shot down by long-distance rifles.

We Should Be Prepared to Fight with Long-range Weapons.

One of the striking things in the campaign which is going on now in the far East is the long range at which the Japanese have been able to fire and kill.

On the *Sevastopol*, the battle-ship that was recently dismantled and almost sunk while putting into the German port in China, Admiral Withoft was killed by a shell fired by a vessel of the Japanese fleet, commanded by Admiral Togo.

The shell struck the conning-tower and killed Admiral Withoft, struck the hull twice, and also killed seven or eight of the principal officers.

That shell was fired from the Japanese battleship when she was eight miles away—farther from the vessel than Waukegan is from here.

I have told you this incident to give you an illustration of the accurate and perfect markmanship of today.

If we are to fight the battles of the King, we cannot fight them in the old way.

We must have guns that will fire not only eight miles and do some damage to the Devil, but that will fire a thousand, two thousand, and three thousand miles, and hit the British throne.

Small weapons of the longest range are the ones wanted.

The Apostle Paul knew nothing at all, nor did these first Apostles, of the means that we have at our command today.

For instance, these swift stenographers of mine, who have been working with me for ten years, are taking the words that I am speaking now.

Later they will be typewritten, then revised, and then printed.

One drop of ink has made millions think.

Our Lord Jesus, the Christ, never altered the fundamental office in His Church, and He who laid the foundation of the Apostles intended it to be continued.

You will see much about that in the issue of LEAVES OF HEALING which will be published, God willing, on the 10th day of September; and you will hear much of it in the Declaration of the Restoration of the Apostolic College which I shall make in this place on September 18th, which is the Lord's Day before the Anniversary of Zion Restoration Host, which takes place on the 21st of September.

While we recognize the unchangeableness of the Office and of the Authority, we are glad to know that God expresses Himself now in many ways in which He could not express Himself in the olden times.

The harvest is plenteous.

They are crying out from all the earth.

Men are Crying Out of the Depths of Necessities.

Deep is calling unto deep.

The heart is crying out for the Living God, and men and women are bowing before idol temples in a vain attempt to find God through these heathen institutions.

They are seeking in vain to find God in ordinances that the Christ never established—to find God in a little water that is said to regenerate the human heart; to find God in a bit of bread that is stamped by the priest, and which, after some hocus-pocus in Latin, is transformed, they shamelessly declare, into a bit of the blood and bones of the Living Christ.

It would be a horrible thing, if it were true, to eat the body, blood, and bones of the Living Christ.

There is no such teaching as that, for the Christ Himself, who gave this ordinance, was sitting there in His own body; in His own flesh; in His own blood, when He said, "Take, eat: this is My body, which is broken for you."

After He had supped He gave the cup, but He did not open His veins and give them His blood.

He did not cut off pieces of His body, and offer to one a finger, to another a thumb, and so on.

After He had finished the Sacrament, He was still there in the body, and went to the Cross and died, and ascended into heaven.

The Christ's Body Is Intact, and Remains Intact.

He is the very same Christ, only with a Glorified Body.

It is a shocking blasphemy to talk about body, blood, and bones being eaten, whether you call it a doctrine of consubstantiation or transubstantiation, or any other kind of substantiation; it is an unsubstantial fancy and a shameless lie.

But our Lord Jesus, the Christ, gave us that which is the Animating Power of the Body of Glory; He gave us the Spirit by which He rose from the dead—by which, after His blood had been shed, His body was reanimated.

He gives us all the same Spirit which now fills all things, and which is the Energizing Power of God.

He gives us all His Spirit, and sends us forth into the great harvest field.

"Far, far away," we sing; but near, near at hand, "in heathen darkness dwelling, millions of souls are wandering and lost."

They are scattered; they are distressed; they are tired; they are lying down, and are cursing the cause of their troubles.

They are scattered, as sheep without a shepherd.

These are no shepherds that the poor laboring men are seeking and finding. Poor, miserable men!

Parks, who was one of their great union labor leaders in New York led the procession last year on Labor Day, I understand.

They caught him in the act and convicted him of scores of cases in which he had sold the working men; in which he had trafficked with the union, declaring strikes on and declaring them off just as he pleased.

"Walking delegoat" is the right name for him.

Recently, Weinseimer, a great leader in New York, was caught at the same thing, and he will probably spend Labor Day in prison, if Jerome once gets hold of him.

The World Needs Men of Character and Decision.

Jerome is a fine man; he may make a fine President of the United States some day.

That is the kind of man we want—one who takes these bad people and deals with them properly.

Roosevelt got an important part of his training as Police Commissioner in New York.

He is too strenuous a man, by far, for those who are objecting to him; but may God grant the United States may be worthy of getting him for another term. May God bless him!

Let all the people say, Amen.

PEOPLE—"Amen."

GENERAL OVERSEER—Say it again.

PEOPLE—"Amen."

GENERAL OVERSEER—Every one that will pray every day for the election of President Roosevelt stand. [Almost the entire audience stood.]

I do not hesitate to say that I am in God's order in seeing, so far as I can, to getting upon the seat of power the men who will acknowledge Him; and who will say, "I rule for God."

"Roosevelt has made some blunders," you say.

I know that; but will you please tell me, Have you never made any blunders?

Can you find a man in the world who has never blundered?

There is one Rose only that never had a thorn; only one Lily that never had a spot; only one Sun that is absolutely without spot—the Sun of Righteousness, the Lily of the Valley, and the Rose of Sharon; but there is no other, no perfect man outside of the Perfect Christ.

I am so glad to think that we are living in a time when God wants us to do things in His way!

We are not to slavishly copy old models.

They did many things in those olden times because they had to; because they could not do any better.

It would have been an impossibility to have gathered four, five, or even six thousand people, in Jerusalem, such as are here today in this Tabernacle.

There was no place there, like this, in which they could gather and worship.

We cannot do the work far away until we have done the work at home.

Some one said to me, "Reach Denmark."

I have one now of noble birth working in the capital of Denmark, and I shall send a companion in a week or two; but the way to reach Denmark is to get the Danes here.

How Zion Will Reach the Peoples of the Earth.

The way to reach Sweden is to get the Swedes here.

The way to reach Norway is to get the Norwegians here

The way to reach Russia is to get the Russians here.

The way to reach Finland is to get the Finns here.

The way to reach Poland is to get the Poles here.

The way to get the Jews of the world is to get the Jews here.

The way to reach all the nations of the world is to get them here.

Many from these nations are already here.

There are seventy nationalities represented in this City today.

Let us remember that the way we have reached these nationalities was through those who had been blessed here.

That is the way that others will be blessed.

So it was that the Church radiated from that simple act of the Lord's when He called out those twelve men and set His Church in order.

In these Latter Days let us, upon whom all these responsibilities have come, who have all these hard questions to answer, set His Church in order, as far as is possible.

For many centuries the Jews have said, when anything difficult of solution arises, "Leave that until Elijah comes."

The questions that have been laid aside until Elijah comes have been so many that there is nothing else for him to do but to meet and face these difficulties every day.

In God there is an answer to every difficulty.

There is an answer to these cruel oppressions by capital and by labor.

There is an answer; and the answer is given in our own City.

It is the answer that "one is your Master, even the Christ, and all ye are brethren."

When we are one in the Christ, when capital and labor go together, and when we desire, every one of us, only the happiness and blessing of one another, all the labor troubles, church troubles, and even home troubles, should absolutely disappear. We know nothing about labor troubles here. .

We know nothing about church troubles here.

We have very few broken jars in the homes of Zion, and those are being mended properly.

Only an Apostolic Church Can Be the Right Church.

Let us understand that we have the Key.

I do not hesitate to say what the Lord Himself said, that only an Apostolic Church can be the right Church.

He will commit the keys of the Kingdom of Heaven only to a properly constituted Church.

If we had not had certain Apostolic Commissions, it would not have been possible for us to have opened so many of these gates; but now the time is approaching when very important action must be taken; when we are not only to groan when we see the world's harvest field, but when we are to take pains to see that the Church is better organized and better qualified to send forth men and women into the great harvest field to reap the harvest.

I am very much amazed as I look at the world and see how much is done by the ardent, simple worker.

I shall presently be able to tell you a story, I think, from South Africa, of how more than a thousand members have been brought into the Church and have been baptized.

They are not all baptized yet; but I have the thing in hand, and I expect one of these days to be able to announce to you that a great community has been born in a day, in a very wonderful way.

It is the result of the faithful labor of one faithful man, in whose heart is the Highway of Zion.

We are grateful today for our Master, who has been so patiently teaching us; for the Gospel, which has been so graciously proclaimed, and for the glorious ministration of our God in the Healing of His people.

Shall we not all pray the prayer of those Apostles, Send forth laborers, O Lord of the Harvest, into the Harvest?

If God shall say, "I want you; are you ready to go?" I pray God that you may be.

Let us remember that when this Church is still more perfectly organized you will have to go where you are sent; and you will have to speak what you are told; and you will have to be what you are told to be still more than ever, or else you will have to go to some other church where you can go as you like and do as you please. The Devil has many of those around.

May God help us.

All who are ready to live the Life of God and be prepared for God, stand.

PRAYER OF CONSECRATION.

My God and Father, in Jesus' Name I come to Thee. Take me as I am. Make me what I ought to be, in spirit, in soul, and in body. Give me power to do right, no matter what it may cost; no matter what separations it may involve. Forgive me wherein I have sinned, and help me to restore to my neighbor anything in which I have wronged him, and to confess wherein I have spoken evil. Give me grace to do right, no matter what it costs; truly to repent; simply to believe in Jesus, my Lord, my God, the Lamb of God who taketh away the sin of the world. For His sake, my Father, take away my sins and sicknesses. Give me Thy Spirit that I may get ready and be patient in training for the harvest field. May the children in the homes, and the youths and maidens in the schools, be trained for the work of God in all the Harvest Fields of the World. In Jesus' Name we ask it, and for His sake. Amen.

Do you really mean that?

PEOPLE—"Yes."

GENERAL OVERSEER—You must not say it, and not mean it.

The Congregation then joined in singing the Consecration Hymn, after which the Junior Choir sang, "Art Thou Weary, art Thou Languid."

After the singing of the Recessional, the General Overseer pronounced the

BENEDICTION.

Beloved, abstain from every form of evil. And may the very God of Peace Himself sanctify you wholly; and I pray God your whole spirit, and soul, and body be preserved entire, without blame, unto the coming of our Lord Jesus, the Christ. Faithful is He that calleth you, who also will do it. The grace of our Lord Jesus, the Christ, the love of God, our Father, the fellowship of the Holy Spirit, our Comforter and Guide, one Eternal God, abide in you, bless you, and keep you, and all the Israel of God everywhere, forever. Amen.

Financial, Commercial and Industrial Notes

THE General Overseer of the Christian Catholic Church in Zion, who is the Editor of LEAVES OF HEALING, has given permission for a new department of the paper, which will give an opportunity for those at the heads of the great divisions of Zion's Financial, Commercial, and Industrial Enterprises to make important communications, from time to time, under the above heading.

He has directed Deacon Charles J. Barnard, General Financial Manager of all Zion Institutions and Industries, to compile this matter, and has laid upon us the duty of editing the department.

We feel that we cannot better introduce the business interests of Zion to our readers throughout the world than by reprinting the stirring Editorial Notes, by our editor, which appeared in LEAVES OF HEALING, Volume XV., Number 18, in connection with the reports of Zion Business Conferences, held in Shiloh Tabernacle, during Zion's Fourth Feast of Tabernacles.

We call especial attention to the request made by the General Overseer at the close of these Notes, regarding the sending out of the number of LEAVES OF HEALING referred to. The response, thus far, has been very hearty and encouraging; but we feel that Zion people would double their orders for this number if they knew the wonderful effect that the issue is having.

One shrewd business man, not a member of the Christian Catholic Church in Zion, who had very carefully read this number said: "You will soon have more money for investment than you will know what to do with. That number makes it unmistakably clear that Zion investments are safer than first mortgages on gilt-edge real estate, and the interest is twice as high."

The following are the Notes referred to:

GEN. ASSO. EDITOR.

"Occupy, till I come."

"Trade ye herewith, till I come."

"Do business, till I come."

These three lines are translations of the command given in the Parable of the Ten Pounds. [Luke 19:11-27.]

The first translation is that of the Common Version.

The second is that of the Revised Version.

And the third is that of the eminent Christian scholar, Dr. Robert Young, in his "Translation of the Holy Bible, according to the letters and idioms of the original languages."

We prefer, as a translation, the last of the three:

"Do Business, till I come."

. . . .

Every member of the Christian Catholic Church in Zion is, or ought to be, deeply interested in the progress of Zion City and its Business Institutions.

Constant attacks have been made, from the very beginning, upon the building up of the City and its Business Institutions, and these attacks will possibly never cease until the last hypocrite and liar has gone from this earth to his place in hell.

. . . .

Zion would not be of God if she did not have enemies who are inspired by envy and hatred; for Zion's success is the despair of Satan and his friends.

. . . .

And now we exhort, in the Name of the Lord, the officers and members of the Christian Catholic Church in Zion everywhere, carefully to read and to remember "what God hath wrought," so that they may have answer to give to those who inquire concerning God's Business in Zion.

Zion Lace Industries and Zion City Bank Stock are now at a premium of ten per cent., at which price they are selling freely at the very moment of writing.

These stocks are paying, respectively, ten and nine per cent. per annum.

We are now addressing ourselves to the increase of the capital of both Institutions.

Zion Lace Industries have now been fully established upon a profitable basis, of which we have spoken fully in our address.

Therefore, it will soon be advanced to one hundred fifteen dollars per one hundred dollar share, a premium of fifteen per cent.

The following year it will yield twelve per cent., when the stock will be advanced to a premium of twenty per cent, namely, one hundred twenty dollars for each one-hundred-dollar share.

We now offer ten thousand shares of Zion Lace Industries Stock at the present price of one hundred ten.

When this is subscribed for, we shall probably at once advance the price to one hundred fifteen.

Concerning Zion City Bank Stock, we now offer five thousand shares at the present price of one hundred ten.

When these shares are subscribed for, the bank stock, which yields nine per cent. per annum, will be advanced to one hundred fifteen.

Zion Sugar and Confection Association Stock now earns nine per cent. per annum, and we offer for sale five thousand shares at par—one hundred dollars per share.

When these are subscribed for, the price will at once be advanced to one hundred ten dollars per share.

Zion Building and Manufacturing Association Stock, now earning nine per cent. interest, with contingent benefits as set forth in the agreement, is a stock of great value, which will soon be at a considerable premium.

We now offer twenty-five thousand shares of this stock at twenty dollars per share, par value.

This stock has been very eagerly sought by families; as it can be issued in certificates of one share of twenty dollars each, it furnishes a favorable opportunity for investment for young people who have saved that sum.

Splendid work has already been done by the Association, which there is no doubt can be well continued; and we are justified in speaking of this important stock in the very highest terms.

Zion City General Stores Stock, now earning eight per cent., is a first-class security.

We now offer five thousand shares at the par value of one hundred dollars per share.

It is our intention to begin the construction of new and permanent stores for this great Institution, which is now doing an immense cash business upon a strong and profitable basis.

For the present we shall not offer any stock in Zion Land and Investment Association, which is now an eight per cent. stock.

We are more inclined to retire the balance of the stock, which has always been exchangeable for land, than we are to increase it.

The splendid position which this Association has attained, and the magnificent work which it has done, are well known; which prove that the value of the land in Zion City has increased to *more than twenty times its original cost.*

This is not a mere allegation, but is

proved by the fact that thirty-three and two-thirds acres, which cost us less than five thousand dollars, were sold for one hundred one thousand dollars to the Chicago & Milwaukee Electric Railroad Company.

Lands west of that new line of railway, and further from the present center of population, have already been disposed of, in some cases, at *more than twice that rate of increase*.

All lands already occupied or unoccupied have risen very largely in value.

As the area of the City is limited, it is of the utmost importance to the present holders of Zion Land and Investment Association Stock, that they should exchange their certificates for land.

The exchange will be much more profitable to them than the eight per cent. which they are now receiving on their Stock.

We, therefore, most heartily advise our friends who hold this Stock, to take advantage of the offer contained in a letter, which is about to be issued by Deacon H. Worthington Judd, General Manager and Secretary of Zion Land and Investment Association, which reads as follows:

H. WORTHINGTON JUDD, Secretary and Manager. — Zion City Real Estate and Improvements.

GENERAL OFFICES OF
ZION LAND AND INVESTMENT ASSOCIATION,
JOHN ALEX. DOWIE.
ADMINISTRATION BUILDING,
ZION CITY, ILLINOIS, August 19, 1904.

BELOVED SHAREHOLDER:—It is not expected that any new subdivisions will be placed in the market this year, and understanding that many of our shareholders have delayed making lot selections, in order that they might get the benefit of the ten per cent. discount usually allowed shareholders when new subdivisions are placed on the market, this Association has decided to make a special offer to all original shareholders, which is as follows:

Beginning with September 1, 1904, and extending to November 1, 1904, each shareholder of Stock in this Association will be given the privilege of selecting a lot, or lots, in any of the last three subdivisions made by this Association in Sections 16, 17, 20, and 21, in Zion City, and will be allowed a discount of ten per cent. from the original published rentals.

This is an exceedingly liberal offer, when we consider the fact that the new Chicago & Milwaukee Electric Railroad, now in course of construction, and extending North and South through the center of this City, paid on an average about as much for the leasehold of their right of way as our published lot rental list calls for.

It must be understood that this is not done because of any shrinkage in the rental value of properties in Zion City. On the contrary, we can truthfully say that our Real Estate market was never in a firmer and healthier condition than at this time. Our lots are steadily increasing in value, and must inevitably continue to do so, as the population increases.

These Subdivisions are attractive, high, and well-located, and no better home sites can be found in Zion City; and shareholders in this Association have never had an opportunity to secure a more desirable investment in some of the choicest residence property in Zion City—property which, we are safe in saying, will increase in value at least fifty per cent. within the coming two years.

Rentals of lots adjacent to this new railroad must advance as soon as the line is in operation, and the latter is expected to take place within the next few months. Then it will not be long before the cross-town lines will be constructed and put in operation, bringing all of these lots within from five to ten minutes' ride of the center of the City.

It has already been proved that there are no investments more safe and profitable than the Real Estate investments in Zion City. Hundreds of lot investors realized one hundred per cent. profit on their investments, and some two hundred per cent., within the first year. We again emphasize the fact that there never has been any shrinkage in land values in Zion City, and we have every reason to believe that there never will be. Our General Overseer has declared that this City will, within a few years, have a population of at least one hundred fifty thousand people; that being the case, early investors will easily realize a profit of from three hundred to five hundred per cent. on their investments within that time.

All shareholders in this Association, who are not entirely dependent upon the annual income derived from their stock investments, should take advantage of what we believe to be the best offer that has ever been made by this Association.

Payments for lots can be made as follows: All cash, or one-third of the rental down—the balance, one-third in one year, and one-third in two years, with interest at the rate of six per cent. per annum, payable semi-annually.

The following rules are to be observed in the allotment of shares to shareholders:

First. Shareholders should make a choice of several lots—first choice, second choice, third choice, etc., as indicated on the application accompanying this letter, and sign their name to the application and send it in to this Association.

Second. In order to facilitate matters, Stock Certificates should be assigned to John Alex. Dowie by the shareholder, (see form on back of Certificate), and sent in with the list of lots selected.

Third. The choice of selection will be given to the shareholders according to the date of each application and Certificate of Stock as received, each application being numbered when received by this Association.

Fourth. The Secretary of this Association will act, without compensation, as proxy for any shareholder who desires to accept his services in the selection of desirable lots.

We trust that every shareholder will take advantage of this liberal offer, and thus enable himself or herself to secure most desirable home sites which must prove exceedingly profitable investments, at exceptionally low rentals.

Praying God for the future prosperity of Zion, as well as of every Zion Investor, and believing you will readily see the great advantage of sending in your application at once, I am

Faithfully yours, in the Lord's Service,
H. WORTHINGTON JUDD,
Secretary and Manager.

Copies of the above excellent letter, with the papers referred to therein, will be at once mailed to every Zion Land and Investment Association Shareholder.

We trust that there will be few, if any, who will fail to take advantage of the excellent offer which it contains.

Shareholders in Zion Land and Investment Association, however, do not need to wait for the reception of the official letter, if they desire the general manager to select lands for them in exchange for their Stock.

They may communicate with him at once.

And now we commend this whole matter to God and to His people in Zion.

We have made proposals, which all who are able and who desire to make investments of great value, should at once accept.

The reports of the Conferences, published in this issue, confirm this assertion.

We are sure also, that there is no truthful, competent, and unprejudiced person, who has ever visited Zion City, but will say, that which all such visitors say every day, that "the half has not been told;" and that, far from any exaggeration, the progress of Zion's Business Institutions is even more wonderful than it has been declared to be.

It is self-evident why we are not willing to disclose fully the Large Profits that are now beginning to be made by Zion's Institutions, and which have justified us in paying the large annual interests that we have paid, even when these Institutions were in their infancy.

All that is now needed, both for investors and for Zion generally, is that we shall receive a large and immediate increase to our capital.

In urging this we are not asking for gifts.

We are only asking for that which it is in the interest of those whom we now address to supply.

We ask that they shall quickly realize money by the sale of their properties and stocks in outside Institutions, and invest in Zion City, which God has so abundantly blessed, and where we are so manifestly able to protect and increase the value of our investments.

The security for these investments is not merely the immensely valuable properties now established on Zion City soil, upon which there is not a dollar of mortgage; but they are represented by our own personal estate to the last cent, and by all that we represent as the legal owner and proprietor of the vast Zion estate, here and elsewhere, amounting to many millions of dollars in excess of all liabilities.

Ninety-five per cent. of that vast estate, at our departure from this life, is absolutely *willed in perpetuity*, to the Christian Catholic Church in Zion.

We venture to say that there are no investments better secured than those in Zion.

We therefore confidently expect that our friends all over America and the world, who are in fellowship with us in the Christian Catholic Church in Zion, or who are in active sympathy with us, will quickly subscribe for the Stocks which we have now offered for sale.

Full particulars of forms of agreements between ourselves and our investors, and all necessary papers, can be had immediately upon application to Deacon Fielding H. Wilhite, Manager of Zion Stock and Securities, Administration Building, Zion City, or from our special agents abroad, who are mentioned on page 584 of this issue.

Special Zion financial messengers can also be sent to intending investors, if thought desirable. These messengers will explain the nature and value of Zion's Stocks, and give counsel and help where needed.

And now, in closing these notes, let us remark that the story of the triumph of Zion's Business Institutions over assaults of every kind proves incontestably that *God is with us*.

The blessing of God has been upon us also in the Spiritual and Educational Work of Zion in an extraordinary manner.

Ten years' records, in fifteen large volumes of this paper, LEAVES OF HEALING, have placed the facts, as far as they can be stated, before the world, from week to week.

Only Envy, Malignity, and all Uncharitableness could deny the fact that God has abundantly blessed us in all Zion's Business undertakings.

These are destined, like Zion's Spiritual Operations, to be of a world-wide nature.

But the same conservative, as well as progressive, Spirit which has guided us in the past will continue to guide us in the future.

We are not speculators with God's money, entrusted to us by God's people.

We are, by the grace of God, intelligent and industrious users of every talent thus entrusted to our care.

In this sense of responsibility all our people in Zion City join us.

The Unity, the Love, the Peace, the Purity, and the Energy of Zion City was never greater than it is at the present moment.

We feel that God has not only saved us, and healed us, but that He is cleansing us.

A Powerful and Progressive People have been raised up, and the Banner of Zion is now floating over Zion in many nations and cities on every Continent.

We cannot do without the prayers, and sympathies, and coöperation of our people.

Our very successes call for larger capital and increased production.

We have never made an article that we could not sell.

We are careful to produce only those things that are good and profitable.

It is our delight and our duty to praise God for the wonderful business year through which we have passed.

And this we gratefully, and most sincerely, and humbly do, ascribing unto Him in the Christ our Lord, all the glory, since from Him has been all the power.

Without God's blessing and protection we could have done nothing.

. . . .

May we not ask every one of our friends in Zion to do us a little special personal favor?

We ask that every one will send twenty-five cents to the General Manager of Zion Printing and Publishing House, and a list of ten persons, to whom, for that sum, we may send ten copies of Number 18, Volume XV. LEAVES OF HEALING, which contains the reports of the Business Conferences of Zion, held during Zion's Fourth Feast of Tabernacles.

This will entail an immense amount of work, but we know that we can easily get five hundred of our young men and women to volunteer to address the wrappers and prepare the papers for mailing.

If the papers are for foreign countries, an extra sum of thirty cents for every ten copies must be sent.

Two hundred fifty thousand (250,000) copies of this issue of LEAVES OF HEALING should go forth from Zion City.

We ask as a personal favor that this shall be done.

Some of our friends may be able to send ten or twenty such twenty-five cent subscriptions.

Let them do so.

But, above all things, let **what is done**, be done quickly.

Brethren, Pray for Us.

It is very gratifying to know that the work of our Leader in all Departments of Zion is appreciated by persons not connected with the Christian Catholic Church in Zion, but who are lovers of righteousness and good works.

Scores of letters are received daily, indicating a lively interest in the Spiritual, Ecclesiastical, Commercial, and Political work of Zion. It is no longer a question of results, when within three years ten thousand people have come together determined to live in accordance with God's laws and the laws of America, under the authoritative teaching of God's Prophet.

The following extracts from letters indicate the feelings of our friends:

DAKOTAH, IOWA, September 9, 1904.

I will try and take some more of your Zion Stocks, for I believe they are as good as United States Bonds.

The Lord bless Zion and her business, is my prayer.

CORNING, CALIFORNIA, September 8, 1904.

I assure you that I am in sympathy and heartily wish to be in touch with Dr. Dowie and his people. I believe him to be a noble man, and think his people are mostly intelligent, earnest, and honest.

I have every confidence in Zion City and her various Institutions, and hope some day to own something within her gates.

May God bless you in all things.

It is with grateful hearts that we acknowledge the goodness of God in enabling us to meet Zion's obligations when due. Zion's creditors were paid nearly ninety thousand dollars on September 12th, the day agreed upon between the General Overseer and the Creditors' Committee. This is the third payment made. Two previous payments of ten per cent. and twenty-five per cent. were made several days before due. The balance of forty per cent. will be paid December 12, 1904.

CHARLES J. BARNARD,
General Financial Manager of all Zion's Institutions and Industries.

Soap is one of the most common, and yet one of the most important articles in daily use.

The human skin is a wonderfully delicate covering, and serves as a screen to protect the body. The millions of little pores are constantly being clogged by perspiration and little particles of dirt too small to see with the naked eye.

If these accumulations are permitted to remain they cause decay.

The common agency used to remove dirt, and in some respects the greatest blessing to humanity, is SOAP, of which there are many kinds in the market.

Any kind of animal fat, no matter in what degree of decay, can be made into soap.

Many cases of blood-poisoning can be traced to the use of soap made from FILTHY HOG GREASE, rendered from carcasses of filthy, diseased animals.

When we realize that soap goes into our table linen, towels, and underwear, which is never entirely removed by rinsing, how important it is that we use a soap that we know is clean!

ZION SOAP is made of the purest and best of olive, cocoanut, and palm kernel oils, and clean beef suet from our own meat market.

We believe that a trial of our soap will convince any one that we are in the front rank, and perhaps a little ahead, in the soapmaking business.

The fact that you know you can get an absolutely pure soap from ZION CITY SOAP FACTORY ought to make you a customer at once.

We are making a specialty of a box of assorted soaps for family use containing seven different kinds—about one year's supply for a small family, which would cost at retail Fifteen Dollars.

We will ship to any part of the United States east of the Rocky Mountains, prepaid, for Ten Dollars.

CLEANLINESS IS GODLINESS.

Let all who desire pure, clean soap send orders, or communicate direct with ZION CITY SOAP FACTORY, Zion City, Illinois.

CHARLES A. HANSON,
Manager.

An excellent Christian woman, living in a distant state, tells a pathetic story in a recent letter.

Property had been sold which represented the savings of many weary years of toil and privation by herself and husband. She desired to invest the money in Zion, but the husband was unwilling, and put it in a local bank. Her protests and warnings were unheeded, and even her own personally-earned funds were denied her by the husband, who was fighting Zion.

Shortly afterward the bank failed and all was lost. Now he works on the street for daily support, and the faithful wife must share his bitterness.

Many who read these lines could multiply instances of a similar nature, for it is an old story.

Investments in the world are often unsafe.

God is not in them.

Worldly Stocks and Securities are continually fluctuating through manipulations of unscrupulous men, causing loss to innocent investors of hundreds of millions annually. How significant, then, is the fact that not a dollar of any Zion Investment has ever been lost by any person; and Zion goes forward stronger today than ever before.

Never for an instant have Zion Securities declined in value. On the contrary they are constantly rising.

No investment is dependent for security upon a single enterprise, but each certificate has back of it every Zion Institution, and all that Zion stands for, including a vast, constantly-increasing estate, already rated at many millions of dollars above all liabilities by leading business men of the world.

It is thus easy to understand the growing favor and confidence in which Zion Investments are held.

FIELDING H. WILHITE,
Manager Zion Securities and Investments.

Zion Lace Industries, established by the General Overseer, are destined to be among the largest and finest plants in the world.

The General Overseer has many times said that God has given Zion this beautiful, clean industry, which will furnish means for the evangelization of the world in these Times of Restoration.

In looking back a few years, we joyfully record the amazing success of the undertaking, notwithstanding the terrific assaults and opposition which have been hurled against it.

Four years ago, the first party of lacemakers arrived at Philadelphia, but were held at that port for sixteen days, awaiting the decision of the immigration officials as to their right to land.

The story of this sixteen days' siege, and the legal battles fought and won, would be one of graphic interest to all Zion if there were time and space for it.

This opposition was manifested against each party of Lacemakers that came over, but Zion was victorious in every case, some parties being detained only one or two hours.

Every effort to overthrow the Industries has been made, but Zion everywhere knows that the World, the Flesh, and the Devil have not been able to undermine or destroy this work.

The first machines that were brought to this country for Zion Lace Industries were placed in a frame building in 1901; and the first lace was made and sold at the First Feast of Tabernacles in July of the same year.

This consisted of an eight-inch doily or souvenir, the design, a dove encircled by a wreath—Zion's Emblem of Peace.

These souvenirs were much admired, and were sold in large quantities, being sent all over the world. More than twenty thousand of these were made.

In connection with the making of this first lace, the following quotation, taken from THE ZION BANNER, of July 3, 1901, will be of interest to the readers of LEAVES OF HEALING:

> On Wednesday, July 26th, the General Overseer of the Christian Catholic Church in Zion made his usual visit to the site of Zion City.
>
> Immediately upon arrival at the site, the General Overseer drove to Zion Freight-house, and, after a few minutes' inspection there, he went to Zion Lace Industries' Building.
>
> After a few words of cheerful greeting to those employed near the entrance, he passed to the center of the building, and there, upon one of the large, completed lace machines, he saw the first piece of Lace being manufactured in Zion Lace Industries' building.
>
> This was a moment of great joy and deep gratitude to God.
>
> After months of hard toil in getting Zion Lace Industries into operation, the first signs of reward were before his eyes.
>
> As he stood before that machine, his heart went out to God in thanksgiving, and his voice was lifted in prayer.
>
> With deep reverence those close by bowed their heads and joined in the Prayer of Thanksgiving and Consecration.
>
> Only a few words were spoken, but we are sure God heard, accepted the thanksgiving, and that His blessing will rest upon Zion Lace Industries in the future in still greater measure even than in the months of toil and conflict and victory in the past.

HENRY STEVENSON,
General Manager Zion Lace Industries.

There is a growing demand for our White Dove chocolates, which we confidently believe to be the BEST on the market. It is amusing to watch the expression upon the faces of visitors passing through our factory after tasting some of our chocolates, with a look which says "more." Almost without exception they ask, "Where can we buy those goods in Chicago?"

We find that the people have great confidence in the purity of Zion's confections, and we want to assure all candy-eaters that quality will always be our first consideration.

Very large orders are coming in almost daily, and we are running overtime in every department, and are taxed to our fullest capacity. We can use thirty more girls at once, which would give us more than one hundred employees.

We find no difficulty in selling all the candy we can make. In fact, we could find a market for five times our present output, if we only had facilities for turning out the goods. ROSCOE E. RODDA,
Manager Zion Sugar and Confection Association.

The results of Christian Coöperation are clearly shown in a beautifully illustrated Catalog, of thirty-two pages, just issued by the Mail Order Department of Zion City General Stores.

This Catalog contains numerous illustrations and quotations of some of our latest and most beautiful patterns of Laces and Lace Curtains.

Candy, crackers, soap, shortening, baking powder, flavoring extracts, brooms, tailor-made clothing, and weathered-oak chairs are quoted in detail.

Every member and friend of Zion ought to get one of these Catalogs, as it shows the rapid strides that Zion City has made in her Industrial Institutions.

The General Stores are retail distributors for all of Zion products.

We have facilities for shipping our products to all parts of the world. Distance need be no barrier to any one trading with us.

We have made trading by mail very simple, as will be seen from our catalog. With free delivery established to a large extent throughout the country, and our products so fully described in our catalog, you are enabled to sit in your home, write your order, and mail it to us, feeling assured you are treated with as much consideration as if you were here in person.

Every one interested in the upbuilding of Zion's Institutions ought to be a user of Zion products. Send today for a copy of our Catalog, mailed to any address free.

Address, Mail Order Department, Zion City General Stores, Zion City, Illinois.

W. HURD CLENDINEN,
General Manager.

Letting money or property lie idle and unproductive is as great a sin as personal laziness and uselessness.

When our Lord said: "Wherefore gavest thou not My money into the bank, and I at My coming should have required it with interest?" He taught, not only the figurative, but the literal application of the parable.

His injunction, "Trade ye herewith till I come," applies to the gold and silver which God places in the hands of His people, as well as to "talents" in the commonly-accepted meaning of the word.

"The gold and the silver" are God's.

Unless those whom He has made stewards of these values increase them for Him, they are wicked and unprofitable servants, and for them is reserved the "outer darkness," where there shall be "weeping and gnashing of teeth."

This is especially true in Zion, where God is so richly and so marvelously using the silver and the gold for the building up of His City; for giving employment to thousands of His people in clean, useful, profitable and prosperous Industries; for the building up of great Educational Institutions, from the Kindergarten to the University; for the education, training, and sending forth of Messengers to carry the Everlasting Gospel to all the ends of the earth; for the printing and spread of Zion Literature, bearing Leaves of Healing from the Tree of Life, in all the languages of the world, and in many other ways for the Extension of His Kingdom.

Investing money in the business enterprises of financial institutions controlled for selfish ends by the World, the Flesh, and the Devil, is even worse than letting it lie idle.

In the first place, money invested in the world's business is being used to build up the private fortune of some selfish man or company of men, whose money will do neither them nor the world any good, and is probably doing harm.

In the second place, an investment with the world is either unsafe or brings in a very low percentage of income. There is so much money seeking for safe investment that the rate of interest is very low, unless some element of risk enters in to raise it.

The higher the rate, as a general rule, the greater is the risk.

In case the investment is safe, and the rate high, the Stock Exchange has set a value upon the shares so far above par that interest on the actual investment is small.

In Zion investments this is not the case.

Notwithstanding that the investments are considered so safe, by conservative business men, that he has been offered millions of dollars at an exceedingly low rate of interest, the General Overseer has arbitrarily placed the rate of interest and dividends so high, for the sake of his people, that a comparatively small investment will bring a very comfortable income.

ARTHUR W. NEWCOMB,
General Associate Editor Zion Publications.

Zion Printing and Publishing House has been doing commercial printing since the first of the present year, and in the few months has earned an enviable reputation for the quality of the work and promptness in filling orders, whether by mail or otherwise.

We have recently added to our staff, Joseph B. Coghill, a man of exceptional experience and talent in the printing business, who takes the office of Manager of the Printing Department, with especial oversight of all the commercial job work.

We prefer to do work for the members and friends of Zion as far as possible, and invite all readers of LEAVES OF HEALING who have printing to be done to get our estimates before placing orders.

Our plant is complete in almost every detail, so that we are able to handle every process necessary to the production of first-class work, including designing, engraving, electrotyping, lithography, printing, bookbinding, numbering, indexing and embossing.

We would be glad to place on our files the applications of clean, upright, Christian men and women, experienced in the trades mentioned above, who desire to work in Zion Printing and Publishing House, and live in a clean City.

We have also an Office Specialty and Supplies Department, dealing in everything that is useful in a business office. This department would be glad to receive applications from members of the Christian Catholic Church in Zion who are expeiienced salesmen and would like to travel with Zion City as headquarters.

Zion Printing and Publishing House also desires authentic names and addresses to which to send sample copies of our publications.

ARTHUR W. NEWCOMB,
General Manager.

The beautiful new Elijah Hospice stands on a gentle elevation, affording a magnificent view of Lake Michigan.

It is a three-story building three hundred forty feet long, and one hundred thirty feet wide, having a floor-space of eighty-eight thousand one hundred forty-three square feet, with hall-space of two thousand four hundred feet. The building has three hundred fifty rooms, two hundred sixty-seven of which are bedrooms.

There are five parlors, two lobbies, twenty-two bath-rooms, and twenty-four toilet-rooms.

The dining-room is sixty by ninety feet, having a seating capacity of four hundred.

The lunch-room is thirty-five by thirty-six feet and will seat seventy-five.

There are four large verandas with a combined length of six hundred eighty feet.

A roof-garden, thirty-five by fifty feet, and a tower seventy feet high, afford a view of vast expanse over City and lake. The kitchen is thirty-five by eighty feet, with a six-section Bramhall range twenty-four feet long; two forty-inch boilers; two jacket kettles, capacity seventy-five gallons; two vegetable cookers, capacity fifty gallons; a twenty-two-foot steam-table; and five ten-gallon tea and coffee urns.

The dish-room has a large dishwashing machine, which is propelled by an electric motor.

The engine-room is thirty-five by thirty-six feet, equipped with three large forty-horse-power boilers, one two-thousand-gallon hot water-tank six by six by six, and two pumps. The heating plant has a radiating capacity of one hundred thirty-one thousand one hundred seventy-three feet.

The building is illuminated with one thousand two hundred electric lights.

FRANK W. COTTON,
Manager.

Zion Transportation and Railway Affairs Department is equipped to attend to all matters pertaining to freight and passenger transportation in any part of the world.

Especial attention is paid to the needs of those in distant parts of the United States and in other lands who contemplate removing to Zion City. This department solicits the privilege of aiding all such in reference to the forwarding of household goods, whether by sea or land, and in the purchasing of railway and steamship tickets, as we have unusual facilities for the securing of rates and the economical planning of routes.

Information is cheerfully furnished to all inquirers.

Call at our Office in the Administration Building, Zion City, or write to

JAMES F. PETERS,
Superintendent of Zion Transportation and Railway Affairs.

Notes from Zion's Harvest Field

By Overseer J. G. Excell, General Ecclesiastical Secretary.

South Africa.

The following interesting letter was received from Overseer Daniel Bryant, en route for Johannesburg, his permanent headquarters in South Africa.

The hearty welcome which he received was but an illustration of the love and affection with which the Overseer and his party have been received by the thousands of God's children in that land which has been so wasted by cruel war.

April 30, 1904.

DEAR GENERAL OVERSEER:—"Praise God from whom all blessings flow."

We are just completing our first three weeks' campaign for God in South Africa.

On Tuesday morning, April 12th, the goodly vessel, *Durham Castle*, upon which for three weeks we had been sailing over quiet seas through days of sweet sunshine, came to anchor at Port Elizabeth.

There we were met by the Conductor of the Gathering from Uitenhage, F. A. Magennis, accompanied by H. W. Bates.

Uitenhage is a beautiful town of five thousand inhabitants, twenty miles inland from Port Elizabeth. There we held our first meeting with Zion.

It is impossible to describe the joy which filled these dear people, as well as ourselves, when we stood face to face. For months they had been praying for us, and eagerly awaiting our arrival.

We found them much in need of organization; but with willing, loyal hearts. This made our work easy and rapid.

We remained ten days in Uitenhage, as no vessel upon which we could embark left Port Elizabeth at an earlier date.

Thirteen obeyed God in Baptism, and the work was left in a thorough state of organization, so far as we could see.

We had the pleasure of enrolling among the new members at Uitenhage a Salvation Army worker from Port Elizabeth. He gave up the Salvation Army because of the wicked attack made by its leaders upon our General Overseer, and the failure of General Booth to refute the shameful and false statements that had been made.

So the fire has been kindled in Port Elizabeth, we hope, which bears the proud distinction of being called the "Liverpool of South Africa."

After the ten days of toil we enjoyed the delightful sail of two days on the *Armadale Castle* to Durban.

God's Spirit seemed to burn like fire in every meeting we held in Durban.

We endeavored to conduct a quiet meeting among our own friends, in order to get the work properly organized. It was gratifying to note how wide-spread was the interest. Our Zion Tabernacle was filled on the last service.

We had the joy of receiving into fellowship twenty-one and of baptizing sixteen. A number gave up their sins and found peace with God.

Many touching and gratifying incidents characterized the work in Durban.

One young man, whom God called to Repentance, confessed to having stolen a sum of money. He said to the man from whom he had stolen it, "I know you have the power to put me behind the bars, but I have turned to God, and I want your forgiveness." This was readily granted, and the money will be repaid at the earliest opportunity.

Under the heart-searching of God's Word, it was remarkable how many confessions came to light.

One of the pleasant experiences was the display of Zion lace, and the teaching of the plan and purposes of Zion's Industries.

Many strangers manifested a deep interest in what was said, and openly expressed their admiration for the beautiful lace.

God made it clear in this meeting that no one could be a loyal member of the Christian Catholic Church in Zion and leave his possessions out in the world.

Each meeting at Durban seemed to grow in spiritual power, and the series ended in a climax when we had the joy of administering the Zion Restoration Host Vow to nineteen persons. We shall never forget the sight of their faces. They glowed with fervor and determination to serve God.

We have been able to secure in Durban a beautiful meeting place for our work. This is very important in a city like Durban, which is not overcomplimented in being called "the Garden of South Africa." It is a city of wealth, magnificent buildings, and improvements of every kind.

One can feel the great future which is dawning in South Africa.

Our accommodations while in Durban consisted of a little cottage, all to ourselves, embowered amid lemon and orange trees, banana, plantain, and mango.

Our work in Durban came to a happy close, and we find ourselves on our way to Johannesburg.

It is now April 30th. We are dictating these notes as we ride through the very heart of the war country.

We have just passed through Colenso, Ladysmith, and literally wound about the famous Majuba Hill.

The last station through which we passed bore the familiar name, Zandspruit, where it will be remembered General Joubert rallied the Boer forces and invaded Natal.

Within three miles of Zandspruit is Volksrust. Here, on this morning of the 30th of April, a rally took place of a very different nature.

We have, within a radius of thirty miles surrounding Volksrust, one thousand native Zulus who are obedient to the teaching of Zion.

A number of these, knowing that we were to pass through Volksrust at twelve minutes after nine o'clock in the morning, had gathered to welcome us.

We easily recognized them by their noble, Christian faces, and by the fact that none were smoking.

Their earnest look of expectancy as they came down the train gazing into the different compartments, confirmed our impression of their mission.

We were to stop twenty minutes, and we stepped out of our compartments and were soon surrounded by these people.

The Rev. Mr. le Roux, who has accomplished this great work among these natives, had come all the way from his headquarters at Wakkerstroom to interview us at Durban.

He taught us Zion's beautiful salutation, "Peace to thee," in the Zulu tongue, and as our little party of four stepped out upon the platform at Volksrust into the circle of dark, beaming faces, we were all able to say heartily, "Ukutula!" (Peace to thee.)

"Ukutula akubekuwe!" came back the hearty response.

It was worth days of practice in the pronunciation of these words to witness the delight with which it was received.

We gathered them about us in a circle, and finding one of the number who understood English, through this dear woman as an interpreter, we were able to tell them of Zion City and of our mission to South Africa.

We first told them how the General Overseer loved them, and that he had sent his special love to them.

Their faces beamed with delight.

After speaking a few words on the subject of repentance, we asked all who had given up their sins to lift their hands.

Up went every hand.

We asked all who had been healed through faith in Jesus, the Christ, to lift the hand.

Like a flash the hands went up.

We then spoke a few words upon Baptism, asking how many were ready to obey the command of the Lord Jesus, the Christ.

Eagerly every hand was raised.

In the midst of our talk the signal was given, and we were compelled to tear ourselves away and go to the train.

The table before us is piled up with pineapples, oranges, and bananas with which they loaded us as we were leaving.

They followed the train in a crowd as we moved off, waving their hands and shouting, "Ukutula."

We expect to reach Johannesburg at fifteen minutes past six tonight.

No words can express the joy which fills our hearts.

We are all well, for the Joy of the Lord is our strength.

We are unspeakably happy.

Each day is a day of glad toil to us.

Peace to Zion throughout the world.

DANIEL BRYANT.

Europe.

The following interesting letter was received by Deacon and Deaconess Carl F. Stern, from Evangelist Sophia J. Hertrich, telling of her tour through Switzerland, Germany, Holland, Belgium, England, Scotland, Ireland, and France.

We take pleasure in publishing this letter with the other reports of work being done by Zion in the various parts of the world:

DARLING'S REGENT HOTEL,
20 WATERLOO PLACE,
EDINBURGH, August 25, 1905.

DEAR DEACON AND DEACONESS STERN:—Peace to you.

Deaconess McDuff had several times asked me to come here to visit her; so recently Elder Hodler said that I had better go.

He laid out a route for me and decided upon the places in which I was to visit and hold meetings on my way.

Accordingly on the 25th of July I began my itinerancy.

I first held some meetings in Switzerland, several in Elsas, Germany, and then went to Brussels, Belgium, where I had a nice visit, and held a little evening service in the home of Elders Arthur and Catherine Booth-Clibborn.

Elder Arthur Booth-Clibborn then told me that he had announced a service to be held by me in Rotterdam, Holland.

I did not believe that I could speak through an interpreter, but he assured me that I would be able to do so, and I was surprised to find that I could, and that I understood much of what the Elder said as he translated for me.

I enjoyed both the morning and the evening services, and especially the children's meeting, where between fifty and sixty bright-faced children eagerly drank in the truths of the Full Gospel.

In this meeting I found that Deacon Guttling, also, was a very good translator.

I greatly enjoyed my short stay with these splendid, earnest people.

On Monday, Overseer Cantel met me at the station in London and took me to his home, where I met his wife and Overseer Speicher and his wife and son.

In the evening, I very much surprised Elder Richert and his wife and son, Elder Kosch and his wife, and Deacon Koetz, for they did not know about my coming.

I had a very pleasant day with them all.

The next day I met Deacon Innes and wife, and Deaconess Hurran.

The following day I went to Leeds, where I was met by Evangelist McKell.

I conducted a meeting there in the evening.

The next day we went to Morley, visited Deaconess Westerman, and conducted the evening meeting.

Then I had a nice rest for two days, in the home of Mr. and Mrs. Campbell.

On Sunday there was a rally in Zion Tabernacle, and I had the forenoon and evening meetings, and talked to the Host and once to the children between.

I was very happy to meet so many friends.

On Monday I came on here and was met by Deaconess McDuff, who is in charge of the work here, and who is faithfully doing all she can to advance God's Kingdom.

Last week I spent a very pleasant time in the home of Deaconess Angus and her very courteous husband.

One day I went with Deaconess Angus to St. Andrews, where we sold and gave away fifty copies of LEAVES OF HEALING and two hundred fifty tracts, and had some very interesting conversations with ministers and others.

Some were very frank, and spoke of the churches as having lost their power; and well they might, for the sights I have seen here and in Dundee on Saturday nights, in drunkenness and degradation, exceed all else I have ever seen.

I saw sights that made my heart ache—little children trying to get their drunken parents home, the publican standing at the open door inviting men in, but keeping out those that were already drunk.

After seeing such sights, how thankful we are for the prospect of ten Zion Cities—cities of refuge —where the harlot, the drunkard, and the publican will not be able to carry on their accursed work and ruin the lives of innocent children.

I have been very much interested in reading the testimonies of the heroic Scotch Martyrs.

In company with Deacon Marwick, I visited with much pleasure the Dundee city gate, where George Wishart preached from Psalm 107:20, at a time there was a great plague in the city and the people were healed by God.

But even then the blinded Pharisee stood ready to stab him with a dagger hidden under his priestly garb.

The story is most interesting to those of us who are willing to follow in the Martyrs' train.

It was with a feeling of sadness that I visited the place at St. Andrews, where this fearless preacher was burned at the stake.

Of all the interesting places that I visited at Edinburgh, the home of John Knox was to me the most interesting and inspiring.

I suppose it was on account of the words in the wall, which are so familiar to us all.

We were in St. Giles at a church service. The preaching was very nice, but there was nothing in it calculated to arouse the people.

I was very much surprised to see here in Scotland all the fields divided with stone fences, and most of the houses surrounded with high stone walls; but it seems to me that the great wall of prejudice with which most of the people in this country are surrounded, is the greatest barrier to real success.

But I am so glad to know that, although truth may be barred out for a while, it must conquer in the end.

I expect to leave here on the 5th of September; then, by request of Overseer Cantel, visit Liverpool, Nottingham, and Manchester.

I shall stay in London over Sunday, then go to Paris for a short stay, then back to our much-loved Switzerland.

I shall then have visited more countries and different nationalities, than on any previous trip.

I realize the need of Zion Cities as never before.

With Christian love and greeting to all the co-workers, I am

Yours in the Master's service, Till He Come,

SOPHIA J. HERTRICH.

Omaha, Nebraska, and Council Bluffs, Iowa.

Elder-in-charge, Rev. Charles A. Hoy, Falls City, Nebraska.
Tabernacle, 529 East Broadway, Council Bluffs, Iowa.
Services—Lord's Day, 7:30 p.m.

FALLS CITY, NEBRASKA, April 25, 1904.

DEAR GENERAL OVERSEER:—After holding a meeting in Omaha, March 16th, and visiting the sick who were seeking Divine Healing, I crossed the Missouri River to Council Bluffs, Iowa, which is in close touch with Omaha by trolley connection. I have been impressed that this place would become the open door to establishing thoroughly Zion in the wicked Sodom of Omaha.

After securing a centrally located room as a place of worship and furnishing it, we planned a fifteen days' mission.

We held twenty-one meetings, did much visiting among the sick and others, secured a number of subscriptions for LEAVES OF HEALING, and systematically, with the help of several Omaha members, distributed over ten thousand Messages, cards, and LEAVES OF HEALING.

The attendance, though not large, consisted of those who were inquiring about the Full Gospel; and many were blessed.

We organized a permanent Gathering at the close, appointing Mr. Daniel W. Lehning as the regular Conductor. Meetings are now held every Lord's Day evening by him, and once a month by me, at 529 East Broadway, Henry Delong Mission.

A number of healings occurred during the meetings. We note a few:

On the last Sabbath afternoon of the mission a most interesting testimony meeting was held, at which a number told of the blessing they had received from God:

HENRY W. HOLDER, 14 Voorhis street.—"I am an old soldier. I was wounded in the war.

"I have had thirty-one strokes of paralysis.

"When I received the last stroke, I knew nothing for awhile

"I was in such a miserable condition that all the doctors said that they could do nothing for me.

"I had taken medicines for years, but nothing seemed to benefit me.

"I attended these meetings from the beginning.

"I could not walk as I do now. I tottered and used a cane.

"Since Elder Hoy prayed for me a week ago last Wednesday, I can walk easily without one.

"I could not talk as I am talking now; but, glory to God, I can talk nearly as well as I ever could."

REV. E. A. LOUNSBURY, 1520 South Ninth street.—"I used to be like a great many who thought all that was necessary to be a Christian was to have one's name on a church book.

"I wanted to take the world into partnership, but found the Devil and God did not work together.

"There came a time when I had to clean up everything.

"Through the influence of professing Christians using tobacco, I had formed the habit of using it, but God took all the appetite away from me when I found that it was hurting my body and that I was sinning by using it.

"When Elder Hoy prayed for the healing of my wife, I was healed of a stiff arm, caused by rheumatism, that I could scarcely raise.

"I can now raise it above my head [demonstrating], which I had not been able to do for some time.

"Since Elder Hoy prayed for my wife, who had suffered for years with spinal trouble, she has ceased to complain as she used to do, and is able to get around and do work she had not done for years.

"We all praise God for this, and our hearts are full of joy and gratitude."

MR. J. WILLEFORD, 918 Harmony street, told how thankful he was for the many things Zion's God had done for him and his family, and rejoiced in His saving and keeping power.

He spoke of the joy it gave him to live and work in Zion City for three months last summer.

Many others testified to the saving, healing, and keeping power of God, of which we have no record.

Hundreds studied the many cartoons we had put in the large front windows. They helped attract attention to the Full Gospel.

The unexpected happened when we were able to get our subjects printed in the *Daily News*, and a fair "write up" was given of the meeting and of Zion City and her Leader, our General Overseer.

We sowed the Full Gospel seed and rejoice that there is much sign of its taking deep root.

We praise God for the joy in laboring for Him.

Truly yours, in Jesus' Name,

CHARLES A. HOY.

TABLE OF FOREIGN SUBSCRIPTION PRICES

LEAVES OF HEALING.

	SINGLE COPY		YEARLY SUBSCRIPTIONS	
	United States Money.	Native Money.	United States Money.	Native Money.
Australia	$ 08	4 pence	$3 50	14s. 6d.
Ceylon	08	18c of rupees	3 50	14s. 6d.
India	08	4 annas	3 50	14s. 6d.
Italy	08	40 centesimi	3 50	18 lira 40c.
Switzerland	08	40 centimes	3 50	18fr 40c
France	08	40 centimes	3 50	18fr. 40c.
Great Britain	08	4 pence	3 50	14s. 6d.

THE ZION BANNER.

	SINGLE COPY		SIX MOS. SUBSCRIPTION	
Australia	$ 04	2 pence	$ 75	3s. 1½d.
Ceylon	04	9c of rupees	75	3s. 1½d.
India	04	2 annas	75	3s. 1½d.
Italy	04	20 centesimi	75	4 lira
Switzerland	04	20 centimes	75	4 fr.
France	04	20 centimes	75	4 fr.
Great Britain	04	2 pence	75	3s. 1½d.

Make Remittances by Drafts on London.

Zion's Bible Class

Conducted by Teacher Daniel Sloan in Shiloh Tabernacle, Zion City, Lord's Day Morning at 11 o'clock, and in Zion Homes and Gatherings throughout the World.

MID-WEEK BIBLE CLASS LESSON, OCTOBER 5th or 6th.

Opposing the Word and Work of God.

1. *God is in a work of righteousness which the public clamor against.*—Luke 16:13-18.
People are not permitted to do what they think is right.
Many always try to make wrong appear right.
The Truth of God will not budge.
2. *The fact that everybody is against a thing is no proof that it is wrong.*—Acts 28:22-26.
Some say, "I can't believe that."
The fault lies wholly within themselves.
The Truth must be patiently taught.
3. *Miracles wrought do not convince people that the work is wrought of God.*—Acts 13:13-22.
People will lie to escape convictions that come to them.
They talk for effect—for some personal gain.
If they were to admit a truth they would condemn themselves.
4. *Wonders will never convince a wicked heart.*—Acts 13:38-43.
Men will wonder and sin on.
Some will wonder and blaspheme God.
You cannot get some people to believe.
5. *The thing that lives under persecution is of God.*—Acts 5:33-40.
A man condemned with the truth hates it.
Men want to slay the messenger of God's Message.
God will ride on prosperously over every foe.
6. *God will, as He manifests Himself in different periods, be rejected by the masses.*—Acts 4:5-12.
Men cannot analyze the Power of God.
The Christ is the Power of God.
The few that are saved find Him to be so.
7. *A common-sense look at the Truth and Work wrought must test it.*—Acts 18:7-17.
Man does not like to give up Devil worship.
The Devil also arouses prejudice in men.
Men who follow custom will lose salvation.
8. *Those who oppose God's Truth and Work do not know why they do it.*—Acts 19:30-39.
The Devil is the author of confusion.
Saul could not give God a reason for killing Christians.
The Devil puts in most people a rash spirit which soon becomes frenzied.
The Lord Our God is a Word-performing God.

LORD'S DAY BIBLE CLASS LESSON, OCTOBER 9th.

Being Receptive to New, God-given Truths.

1. *The Spirit of God is ever revealing more truth.*—John 16:12-18.
One must grow in knowledge.
Some things one cannot see until later.
The things to come are greater than all else.
2. *More and more truth will unfold as God's Plans work out.*—Jeremiah 1:11-16.
We come to know if we follow on.
The future will bring good and evil.
No harm can come to those who follow the good.
3. *Some foresee the fulness of time when God will act out His perfect will.*—Habakkuk 2:1-4.
Some are watching for light to arise.
God has a Message to every person.
The set time brings out the clear truth.
4. *Some are not so blind as many who profess to be doing much for God.*—Isaiah 56:9-12.
Some preachers can see only what they were taught.
They do nothing to arouse the world.
They have no flaming torch to make people think.
5. *A God-taught man is always unfolding new things.*—Matthew 13:44-53.
The new things come first.
New light is given to all who seek.
When God speaks man hears and people think.
6. *God has plans reaching beyond these days.*—Daniel 12:5-13.
Some things are for the end of the age.
Some are now sealed to the understanding.
The pure and white shall understand.
7. *Some never believe anything beyond views commonly held.*—Jeremiah 19:3-8.
People do not like to think of the judgment to come.
They wander away from God and disobey Him.
The masses are all wrong.
8. *Vital and lost-sight-of truths, ordinances, and offices must be restored with Divine force and emphasis.*—Isaiah 55:8-13.
God's thoughts never change.
God thought Apostles necessary in the early Church.
God's Word makes it necessary that we should have Apostles now.
God's Holy People are a Believing People.

Second Anniversary
of
Zion Restoration Host

Lord's Day, Sept. 18, 1904.

A Special General Assembly of the Members of

Will be Held in Shiloh Tabernacle, Zion City, Ill.

Full Procession of Zion White-robed Choir, the Ordained Officers of the Church, and Members of Zion Restoration Host, will begin at 2:30 p. m. All members of Zion Restoration Host will appear in their sashes of Zion Colors.

The Declaration of
John Alexander, First Apostle of the Christian Catholic and Apostolic Church in Zion, and Elijah, the Prophet of the Restoration of all things
Will be Made at this Assembly.

All members of the Christian Catholic Church in Zion within reach are desired to attend. Seats will be reserved for them in the Tabernacle.

Special Excursion Trains will run from the Wells street Chicago and North-Western Station, in Chicago, beginning at 11 o'clock in the morning.

Round Trip Fare, 50 cents. THE CHRIST IS ALL AND IN ALL.

OBEYING GOD IN BAPTISM.

"Baptizing Them Into the Name of the Father and of the Son and of the Holy Ghost."

Nineteen Thousand Eight Hundred Ninety-six Baptisms by Triune Immersion Since March 14, 1897.

Nineteen Thousand Eight Hundred Ninety-six Believers have joyfully followed their Lord in the Ordinance of Believer's Baptism by Triune Immersion since the first Baptism in Central Zion Tabernacle on March 14, 1897.

Baptized in Central Zion Tabernacle from March 14, 1897, to December 14, 1901, by the General Overseer,	4754		
Baptized in South Side Zion Tabernacle from January 1, 1902, to June 14, 1903, by the General Overseer..	37		
Baptized at Zion City by the General Overseer........	647		
Baptized by Overseers, Elders, Evangelists and Deacons, at Headquarters (Zion City) and Chicago......	5623		
Total Baptized at Headquarters....................	—		11,061
Baptized in places outside of Headquarters by the General Overseer................................		765	
Baptized in places outside of Headquarters by Overseers, Elders, Evangelists and Deacons............		8,070	
Total Baptized outside of Headquarters............		—	8,835
Total Baptized in seven years and six months......			19,896

The following-named two believers were baptized in Zion Tabernacle, Cleveland, Ohio, Lord's Day, August 21, 1904, by Deacon C. F. Kelchner.

Carrington, E. C. .... Medina, Ohio
Splete, Mrs. Carry.................. 105 Vergennes street, Cleveland, Ohio

The following-named thirteen believers were baptized in the Caledonian Road Baths, N., London, England, Lord's Day, August 28, 1904, by Overseer H. E. Cantel:

Arnold, Thomas Frederick, 117 Harrison street, Gray's Inn road, W. C., London, England
Barth, Miss Elise, 114 Greencroft Gardens, Hampstead, N. W., London, England
Edwards, Mrs. Georgina, Nightingale road, East Molesley, Essex, England
Hughes, Hugh, 79 Charlton street, Euston road, N. W., London, England
Hughes, Mrs. Margaret Ann, 79 Charlton street, Euston road, N. W., London, England
Hull, Joseph Ernest............... ..68 Ross street, Cambridge, England
Lyne, Mrs. Bessie, 35 Droop street, Queen's Park Estate, W., London, England
Sandwell, Miss Adaline, 13 Kenneth Road, W. Kensington, W., London, England
Sandwell, Mrs. Catherine, 13 Kenneth Road, W. Kensington, W., London, England
Scott, William Godfrey, 12 Rupert street, Haymarket, S. W., London, England
Smith, Albert Philip, "Plynlimmon," Salisbury Road, Harrow, Middlesex, England
Smith, Thomas Alexander, "Plynlimmon," Salisbury Road, Harrow, Middlesex, England
Thatcher, Mrs. Emma, 123 Kensal Road, Westbourne Park, W., London, England

The following-named believer was baptized in the Ohio river, at Wellsburg, West Virginia, Lord's Day, September 4, 1904, by Deacon William Splete:

Gracey, Mrs. Lola B........................... Wellsburg, West Virginia

The following-named three believers were baptized at San Francisco, California, Lord's Day, September 4, 1904, by Elder W. D. Taylor.

McDow, Mrs. Mary Etta.............................. Maxwell, California
Phelps, Mrs. Sarah Frances.......................... Maxwell, California
Taylor, Martha Gladys..... 1350 East Sixteenth street, Fruitvale, California

The following-named five believers were baptized at Seattle, Washington, Lord's Day, September 4, 1904, by Elder August Ernst:

Bachman, Friedrika C............... 561 Ward street, Seattle, Washington
Bachman, John .... 561 Ward street, Seattle, Washington
Chase, W. N.................... 2120 Warren avenue, Seattle, Washington
Crisp, John Vivian .... Clinton, Washington
House, Mrs. Jessie M., Summit avenue and Twenty-third street, Everett, Washington

The following-named five believers were baptized in the North Side Zion Tabernacle, Chicago, Illinois, Lord's Day, September 11, 1904, by Elder C. R. Hoffman:

Brasch, Albert Carl Martin........... 1813 Winona street, Chicago, Illinois
Lenz, Mrs. Augusta .... 311 Larrabee street, Chicago, Illinois
Lenz, Mrs. Gertrude Helene Hedwig. 163 Larrabee street, Chicago, Illinois
Vanzandt, A .... 163 Larrabee street, Chicago, Illinois
Vanzandt, Mrs. Eliza......... .... . 163 Larrabee street, Chicago, Illinois

The following-named two believers were baptized in Chicago, Illinois, Lord's Day, September 11, 1904, by Elder Gilbert E. Farr:

Colfax, George R........... 908 South Desplaines street, Chicago, Illinois
Keene, Jesse A............. 384 Washington boulevard, Chicago, Illinois

The following-named six believers were baptized in Lake Michigan, at Zion City, Illinois, Tuesday, September 13, 1904, by Elder W. O. Dinius:

Capp, Miss Margaret M................................ Zion City, Illinois
Hanna, Mrs. Martha Jane............................ Bayard, Nebraska
Heppell, Mrs. Mary................................. Brookfield, Missouri
Hollingsworth, Alfred................ 2803 Elijah avenue, Zion City, Illinois
Mundle, Laura Arabilla............ 2803 Elijah avenue, Zion City, Illinois
Young, Sarah Elizabeth...... ..... 2412 Gideon avenue, Zion City, Illinois

The following-named four believers were baptized in Shiloh Tabernacle, Zion City, Illinois, Wednesday, September 14, 1904, by Elder W. O. Dinius:

Porter, Mrs. Sarah C.................................. Waterman, Illinois
Root, Mrs. Carrie.................. 2202 Ezekiel avenue, Zion City, Illinois
Williams, Daniel Ambrose .... 3008 Eshcol avenue, Zion City, Illinois
Williams, Joseph Benjamin......... 3008 Eshcol avenue, Zion City, Illinois

Every Reader of Leaves of Healing Should Also Read The Zion Banner.

The cost is too small to be worth mentioning, being fifty cents for six months.

LESS THAN TWO CENTS A WEEK!

If you will put in a few hours' work among your friends, and obtain THREE NEW SUBSCRIBERS TO THE ZION BANNER, we will send you your own copy free.

YOU CAN GET THEM EASILY!

Just give it a trial.

Scarcely any news in THE ZION BANNER is reprinted in LEAVES OF HEALING.

Many people will read THE ZION BANNER who might not be interested in our other publications.

Resolve today that you will do this for the extension of the Kingdom of God.

ZION PRINTING AND PUBLISHING HOUSE,
Zion City, Illinois.

Warning to Subscribers.

Scarcely a week passes that we do not have complaints about money having been sent to us in currency, stamps, or silver, in the open mails, for renewals of subscriptions or for other purposes, WHICH WE HAVE NOT RECEIVED AND WHICH NEVER REACHES US.

Therefore, we desire to warn every member and friend of Zion sending money to us, to always use some safe means, preferably a money-order, or bank-draft on New York or Chicago, or personal check on Zion City Bank.

In conforming to this notice you will save yourselves trouble and expense, and us much annoyance.

ZION PRINTING AND PUBLISHING HOUSE,
Zion City, Illinois.

Street Addresses Are Necessary.

All Zion City Subscribers to *Leaves of Healing*, *The Zion Banner*, *Blätter der Heilung*, and *Voice from Zion*, whose correct street addresses are not positively known to be in our possession should send them to us AT ONCE. Please act upon this notice without delay as it is very important, now that we have postal delivery service, that the exact location of each and every subscriber be known to us. Write your name and address very carefully, designating also to what periodicals you are a subscriber and leave at your very earliest opportunity at our branch Publishing House on Elijah Avenue.

Very Sincerely Yours,
ZION PRINTING AND PUBLISHING HOUSE.

ZION'S

FINANCIAL INSTITUTIONS AND INDUSTRIES

JOHN ALEXANDER DOWIE

THE FINANCIAL INTERESTS OF ZION are of vital importance to every member and friend of Zion. Get this on your heart. For when Zion's material work is strengthened, then her ability is increased to carry forward throughout the world the glorious, good tidings of this dispensation — the little leaven which is destined of God to leaven the whole lump.

¶ ¶ Zion has marvelously succeeded in all her business undertakings and operations. Her transactions with her own people, and the business world, have already amounted to hundreds of millions of dollars; and not a dollar has ever been lost by any investor. Within a very few years a vast estate has been created, rapidly increasing in value, and rated at this time by the keenest business firms of Chicago at many millions above all liabilities.

¶ ¶ Such a stewardship finds favor with God, and merits the hearty coöperation of every one who loves our Lord in sincerity, and desires to see His Kingdom extended.

High Class Investments, Secured by the entire estate of Zion, bearing interest at the rate of 9 per cent. and 10 per cent., are now offered to ready investors upon the most liberal terms. Your inquiries are cordially invited.

For information concerning the General Financial or Material Interests of Zion, address
DEACON CHARLES J. BARNARD, General Financial Manager, Zion City, Ill., U. S. A., or
DEACON DANIEL SLOAN Inspector General of Zion, Zion City, Ill., U. S. A.

For information concerning Zion City Bank, or any thing pertaining to the Banking Business, address
DEACON WILLIAM S PECKHAM, Cashier, Zion City Bank, Zion City, Ill., U. S. A.

For information concerning Zion City Real Estate, address
DEACON H. WORTHINGTON JUDD, Secretary and Manager, Zion Land and Investment Association, Zion City, Ill., U. S. A.

For information concerning Zion Securities and Investments, address
DEACON FIELDING H. WILHITE, Manager, Zion Securities and Investments, Zion City, Ill., U. S. A.

Persons living at remote points may find it more convenient to confer with or write to the following special representatives:

ELDER PERCY CLIBBORN, General Financial Agent for the Continent of Europe, No. 76 Bahnhofstrasse, Zurich, Switzerland.

DEACON JOHN W. INNES, General Financial Agent for the United Kingdom. No. 81 Euston Road, London, N. W., England.

DEACON NICHOLAS B. RIDEOUT, General Financial Agent for South Africa, Box 3074, Johannesburg, South Africa.

DEACON GEORGE A. CORLETTE, Manager New York Office, No. 419 Flatiron Building, New York City.

ZION CITY

IS THE ONE SPOT IN GOD'S WORLD that is free from Rum, Tobacco, Drugs, Obscene Literature and Bill Boards, Vulgarity or Profanity and the consequent vice and crime that follows.

¶ ¶ The above may seem incredible, but a personal visit to Zion City by the most skeptical will prove the truth of our assertion.

¶ ¶ Every true lover of God and right living should not fail to visit this clean, beautiful growing City and learn of its plan and purpose.

¶ ¶ Thousands of home sites have already been disposed of and hundreds of homes erected at an outlay of millions of dollars.

¶ ¶ A number of Industries and Commercial enterprises have also been established and are in full operation, employing hundreds of hands.

¶ ¶ Never in the world's history have Christian people been able to secure the clean home life advantages that can be obtained in this City.

¶ ¶ The Educational system of Zion City is complete from the Kindergarten to the College. Students are not only taught to respect and reverence the Word of God, but to study it understandingly.

¶ ¶ Exceptionally fine well-located home sites are now being offered, the value of which must greatly advance within the coming two or three years, with the rapid growth of the City.

¶ ¶ We respectfully solicit a personal interview or correspondence with all honest inquirers or prospective investors, and will gladly furnish copies of our illustrated Booklet, Map of General Design, Plats, Eleven Hundred Year Lease, etc., upon application.

Zion Land and Investment Association, Zion City, Illinois, U. S. A. **H. Worthington Judd, Sec'y. and Mgr.**

WITH ILLUSTRATED SUPPLEMENTS

A WEEKLY PAPER FOR THE EXTENSION OF THE KINGDOM OF GOD

EDITED BY JOHN ALEXANDER, FIRST APOSTLE OF THE LORD JESUS, THE CHRIST, IN THE CHRISTIAN CATHOLIC APOSTOLIC CHURCH IN ZION

Volume XV. No. 23. *ZION CITY, SATURDAY, SEPTEMBER 24, 1904.* *Price Five Cents*

JOHN ALEXANDER, FIRST APOSTLE

OF THE LORD JESUS, THE CHRIST, IN THE CHRISTIAN CATHOLIC APOSTOLIC CHURCH IN ZION

And God hath set some in the Church, first Apostles, secondly Prophets, thirdly Teachers. —I Corinthians 12:28

Ye are fellow-citizens with the Saints, and of the household of God, being built upon the foundation of the Apostles and Prophets, Christ Jesus Himself being the Chief Corner-Stone. —Ephesians 2:19, 20.

A WEEKLY PAPER FOR THE EXTENSION OF THE KINGDOM OF GOD.

EDITED BY

JOHN ALEXANDER, First Apostle of the Lord Jesus, the Christ, in the Christian Catholic Apostolic Church in Zion.

Application for entry as Second Class Matter at Zion City, Illinois, pending.

Subscription Rates.		Special Rates.	
One Year	$2.00	100 Copies of One Issue	$3.00
Six Months	1.25	25 Copies of One Issue	1.00
Three Months	.75	To Ministers, Y. M. C. A's and Public	
Single Copies	.05	Reading Rooms, per annum	1.50

For foreign subscriptions add $1.50 per year, or three cents per copy for postage.

Subscribers desiring a change of address should give present address, as well as that to which they desire LEAVES OF HEALING sent in the future.

Make Bank Drafts, Express Money or Postoffice Money Orders payable to the order of JOHN ALEX. DOWIE. Zion City, Illinois, U. S. A.

Long Distance Telephone. *Cable Address "Dowie, Zion City."*

All communications upon business must be addressed to
MANAGER ZION PUBLISHING HOUSE,
Zion City, Illinois, U. S. A.

Subscriptions to LEAVES OF HEALING, A VOICE FROM ZION, and the various publications may also be sent to
ZION PUBLISHING HOUSE, 81 EUSTON ROAD, LONDON, N. W., ENGLAND.
ZION PUBLISHING HOUSE. NO. 43 PARK ROAD, ST. KILDA, VICTORIA, AUSTRALIA.
ZION PUBLISHING HOUSE, 76 BAHNHOFSTRASSE, ZÜRICH, SWITZERLAND.

ZION CITY, ILLINOIS, SATURDAY, SEPTEMBER 24, 1904.

TABLE OF CONTENTS.

LEAVES OF HEALING, SATURDAY, SEPTEMBER 24, 1904.

LEAVES OF HEALING.

Two Dollars will bring to you the weekly visits of the Little White Dove for a year; 75 cents will send it to a friend for thirteen weeks; $1.25 will send it for six months; $1.50 will send it to your minister, or to a Y. M. C. A., or to a Public Reading Room for a whole year. We offer no premiums, except the premium of doing good. We receive no advertisements, and print no commercial lies or cheating enticements of unscrupulous thieves. LEAVES OF HEALING is Zion on wings, and we keep out everything that would detract the reader's mind from all except the Extension of the Kingdom of God, for which alone it exists. If we cannot send forth our Little White Dove without soiling its wings with the smoke of the factory and the dirt of the wrangling market place, or compelling it to utter the screaming cries of the business vultures in the ears of our readers, then we will keep our Dove at home.

GOD'S WAY OF HEALING.

BY THE REV. JOHN ALEX. DOWIE.

God's Way of Healing Is a Person, Not a Thing.

Jesus said "*I am* the Way, and the Truth, and the Life," and He has ever been revealed to His people in all the ages by the Covenant Name, Jehovah-Rophi, or "*I am* Jehovah that Healeth thee." (John 14:6; Exodus 15:26.)

The Lord Jesus, the Christ, is Still the Healer.

He cannot change, for "Jesus, the Christ, is the same yesterday and today, yea and forever;" and He is still with us, for He said: "Lo, *I am* with you All the Days, even unto the Consummation of the Age." (Hebrews 13:8; Matthew 28:20.) Because He is Unchangeable, and because He is present, in spirit, just as when in the flesh, He is the Healer of His people.

Divine Healing Rests on the Christ's Atonement.

It was prophesied of Him, "Surely He hath borne our griefs (Hebrew, *sickness*), and carried our sorrows: . . . and with His stripes we are healed;" and it is expressly declared that this was fulfilled in His Ministry of Healing, which still continues. (Isaiah 53:4, 5; Matthew 8:17.)

Disease Can Never be God's Will.

It is the Devil's work, consequent upon Sin, and it is impossible for the work of the Devil ever to be the Will of God. The Christ came to "destroy the works of the Devil," and when He was here on earth He healed "all manner of disease and all manner of sickness," and all these sufferers are expressly declared to have been "oppressed of the Devil." (1 John 3:8; Matthew 4:23; Acts 10:38.)

The Gifts of Healing Are Permanent.

It is expressly declared that the "Gifts and the calling of God are without repentance," and the Gifts of Healing are amongst the Nine Gifts of the Spirit to the Church. (Romans 11:29; 1 Corinthians 12:8-11.)

There Are Four Modes of Divine Healing.

The first is the direct prayer of faith; the second, intercessory prayer of two or more; the third, the anointing of the elders, with the prayer of faith; and the fourth, the laying on of hands of those who believe, and whom God has prepared and called to that Ministry. (Matthew 8:5-13; Matthew 18:19; James 5:14, 15; Mark 16:18.)

Divine Healing Is Opposed by Diabolical Counterfeits.

Amongst these are Christian Science (falsely so-called), Mind Healing, Spiritualism, Trance Evangelism, etc. (1 Timothy 6:20, 21; 1 Timothy 4:1, 2; Isaiah 51:22, 23.)

Multitudes Have Been Healed Through Faith in Jesus.

The writer knows of thousands of cases and has personally laid hands on scores of thousands of persons. Full information can be obtained at the meetings held in the Zion Tabernacles in Chicago, and in Zion City, Illinois, and in many pamphlets which give the experience, in their own words, of many who have been healed in this and other countries, published at Zion Printing and Publishing House, Zion City, Illinois.

"Belief Cometh of Hearing, and Hearing by the Word of the Christ."

You are heartily invited to attend and hear for yourself.

By Evangelist **Sarah E. Hill.**

o A GREAT sign was seen in heaven; a woman d with the sun, and the moon under her feet, pon her head a crown of twelve stars.—*ation 12:1.*

VE have here a symbolic picture of God's Zion of these Latter Days sented as a woman arrayed with the ın emblem of the Sun of Righteous-

e Prophet Malachi tells us that He rise again with healing in His wings, the world has for centuries turned from Him as their Healer. (Malachi

is to rise as a result of the teaching ijah, the Messenger of the Covenant. ıchi 3:1; 4:5.)

is is truly a great sign, the sign of ear coming of the Lord and of a le who are to be prepared for Him at coming.

rough the teaching of the Covenant, Christ is to rule in the spirits, souls, bodies of mankind to save, to heal, to enable them to live holy lives. dus 15:26; Malachi 4:4.)

e garments of man, which are his soul body, will be full of life; and light s from life. (Matthew 13:43.)

e establishment of the Kingdom of in man's entire being, is the first step e Restoration of All Things.

r Lord said that Elijah should come estore All Things. (Matthew 17:11.)

n, when he turned from the rule of carried all the earth with him, and ust lead in taking it back to God.

e moon as a satellite of the earth, is od symbol of material things; when rules in man, material things will be after under his feet to help him vard.

on places material things where they g, and uses them to extend God's dom.

on Zion's head the Primitive Apos- Church rests as a crown, representing ority and Rule. The twelve stars sent the Apostolic Office restored to ace in the Church where it belongs.

e Apostle Paul tells us that God set stles and Prophets in the Church as as Teachers, all as different members e Body. (1 Corinthians 12:27, 28.)

storation of the Primitive Apostolic ch as our Lord constituted it, is truly a great sign—the sign of the near coming of the Bridegroom for His Bride.

There is to be born in Zion a people who shall be so united in the Truth through the teaching of the Covenant, that they shall be as one individual. (Verse 5.)

They are to be so strong that they may be compared to a man-child.

They are to realize the wonderful prayer of our Lord for the unity of His people, which has never yet been realized in its fulness when He prayed: "And the glory which Thou hast given Me I have given unto them; that they may be one, even as We are One; I in them, and Thou in Me, that they may be perfected into one; that the world may know that Thou didst send Me, and lovedst them, even as Thou lovedst Me." (John 17:22, 23.)

When this child is being born there is "A Voice of tumult from the city, a Voice from the Temple, a Voice of Jehovah that rendereth recompense to His enemies." (Isaiah 66:6.)

The Voice of tumult from the city we have plainly heard, also the Voice of God that rendereth recompense to His enemies.

How often the enemies of Zion have been overwhelmed, and the plans for her destruction thwarted, because God commanded it so!

The Voice from the Temple is being heard all over the world, and the earth trembles.

It is the Voice that sounded before the Coming of the Lord nineteen centuries ago, saying, "Make ye ready the Way of the Lord, make His paths straight." (Matthew 3:3.)

A nation has been born of Zion, the Theocratic nation, God's Israel, so that the Prophet Isaiah, seeing this in prophetic vision, exclaims in astonishment: "Who hath heard such a thing? who hath seen such things? Shall a land be born in one day? shall a nation be brought forth at once? for as soon as Zion travailed she brought forth her children." (Isaiah 66:8.)

The Prophet saw in a clear vision what has really taken place in Zion: a nation and a land for their possession brought forth in a day.

The exigencies of the times demand this rapid work for the preservation of God's people, and if they live true to Him He will do still more marvelous works for them.

The Apostle saw another sign, a great red dragon, having seven heads and ten horns; and the dragon stood before Zion ready to devour her child. (Revelation 12:3, 4.)

He represents the flesh and all that it loves.

In the beginning of the history of the race, he came as a serpent and induced the woman to turn from the Rule of God to be ruled by the flesh. (2 Corinthians 11:2, 3.)

After having ruled the world for ages he is ready to devour this child of Zion.

John saw also a time of great wo upon the earth, because the Devil had come to it in great wrath, knowing that he had but a short time. (Verse 12.)

It is the Covenant that will enable the people to overcome him through the word of their testimony and the Blood of the Lamb. (Verse 11.)

The teaching of Zion centers around the Covenant, and this must go all over the earth on the pages of Zion Literature to prepare some to go with the Lord when He comes, and others to pass through the world's great Hour of Trial. (Revelation 3:10.)

Never before has the world's need been so great as at the present time.

Never before has there been literature that could meet this need as Zion Literature does today.

"I will cause it to go forth, saith Jehovah of Hosts." (Zechariah 5:4.)

It goes in the transforming power of the Holy Spirit.

You are called to help send it forth.

Will you not help us in this great work?

Zion Literature Sent Out from a Free Distribution Fund Provided by Zion's Guests and the Friends of Zion.

Report for four weeks ending September 17, 1904:

17,611 Rolls to Business Men United States and Canada.

9,809 Rolls to........Hotels in the United States

3,594 Rolls to the Hotels of Europe, Asia, Africa and the Islands of the Sea.

445 Rolls to................Ireland and India

3,052 Rolls to........Various States of the Union

Number of Rolls for four weeks............34,511

Number of Rolls reported to Sep. 17, 1904, 3,375,482

THE FIRST APOSTLE OF THE LORD JESUS, THE CHRIST, IN THE CHRISTIAN CATHOLIC APOSTOLIC CHURCH IN ZION, PUTTING THE CROWN OF ORGANIZATION UPON THE BROW OF ZION.

Declaration of John Alexander

First Apostle of the Lord Jesus, the Christ, in the Christian Catholic Apostolic Church in Zion

REPORTED BY S. E. C., O. L. S., L. M. S., A. C. R., O. R., AND A. W. N.

GOD is at work!

He has put forth the Might of His holy Arm.

He who created the Universe with His Word has sent forth His Spirit with Omnipotent Power to do His Will.

The time is fulfilled.

The long, dark ages of preparation have passed away.

The millenniums of sin and disease, war and bloodshed, poverty, misery, tears, and death are drawing to their close, and the time is at hand when all God's precious promises will be redeemed; when the Final Conflicts will be over; when God shall rule throughout all His infinite Universe, through a glorious Eternity of Life, and Light, and Peace, and Joy.

Holy men of old, kings, prophets, and apostles have longed to see this time.

All through the long ages, men of God have prayed for it.

Ever since the "Former Rain" fell upon the earth at the time of Pentecost, those whose spiritual eyes could pierce the gloom of apostasy and error have been imploring God for the "Latter Rain."

And in these times the Almighty has heard prayer.

He has shown in the heavens the "promised sign," and the clouds have gathered big with blessing.

"The sound of abundance of rain" has filled the whole earth.

Weary, dying humanity is beginning to hear the grateful music of the showers and to feel the refreshing, invigorating breezes of spiritual renewing that tell that the long drouth is broken.

Songs of praises fill all the lands of the earth, for "Redemption draweth nigh."

As in all the ages, God has chosen a man as the instrument in His hands for this work.

Through many years of toil, and trial, and suffering, God has trained him and led him on, step by step.

He saved him, spirit, soul, and body, and filled him with His Holy Spirit.

He made him a Teacher, and clothed him with Prophetic and Apostolic Power.

He led him on in the reorganization of His Church upon its true basis, "upon the foundation of the Apostles and Prophets, Jesus, the Christ, Himself being the Chief Corner-Stone."

He made him the Messenger of His Covenant, and confirmed his office with the works that He did through him.

He led him, by His Spirit, to the Declaration of his prophetic office as Elijah the Restorer of All Things.

His Spirit had already revealed the truth to thousands of His true people, and they praised Him as they saw the dawn of the Times of the Restoration.

The world and the church, sunk in folly, and blinded by the darkness of error, had hated, reviled, persecuted, and attempted, again and again, to kill this mighty man of God.

When the Elijah, or Prophetic, Declaration was made, all these enemies burst in triumphant, scornful laughter.

He, whom they hated, had killed himself by the presumption and folly of his assumption!

It was supremely ridiculous!

But the laughter died on their lips.

The mirth went out of it before it went out of their throats.

God was working.

His mighty arm had been made bare.

It was no time to laugh.

But another step was to be taken.

The Church which had been restored to its Primitive Pattern, must receive its Apostles, that the Primitive Power might return, in even greater measure, "the Latter Rain."

The time was ready.

God was ready with His man, who was to be the First Apostle, and form the Apostolic College, as led by His Spirit.

Once more this same man was led to make the Declaration.

Once more, his people were ready for it; they were eager. They would have proclaimed him an Apostle years before; but the time was not ready.

This time the world did not laugh.

Men everywhere had begun to realize that, whether they liked it or not, whether they would obey or not, God was working out His purposes, in these times, through the man whom He had chosen.

So the momentous Declaration of John Alexander, First Apostle of the Lord Jesus, the Christ, in the Christian Catholic Apostolic Church in Zion, Elijah the Restorer, an epoch-making event in the Times of the Restoration of All Things, was received with the most intense, most earnest, and most respectful interest by practically all the world; for the eyes of the world were on the Apostle.

This Declaration was made Lord's Day afternoon, September 18, 1904, in Shiloh Tabernacle, in the presence of seven thousand two hundred people.

The service was also the Commemoration of the Second Anniversary of Zion Restoration Host.

Under a dull, gray sky, with the first bracing coolness of the early autumn quickening their steps, four thousand members of the Host marched in long lines under the trees of Shiloh Park and into the great Tabernacle.

The scene was one never to be forgotten.

Far off to the west circled one long line, glowing with the beauty of the three Zion colors, gold, white, and blue, which the Restorationists wore as scarfs.

Another line, fully as long, twisted and turned through the oaks to the east until it reached the limits of the park.

Both lines led to the door of the Tabernacle.

Out from the rear of the Tabernacle came two great companies of singers, a striking contrast, in their fluttering robes of white, to the compact masses of Ordained Officers in robes of black.

Above them all the banners of Zion and the flags of a score of nations waved in the fresh breezes.

After escorting the First Apostle and his family from Shiloh House to the Tabernacle, Zion City Band and Colonel Carl F. Stern and his Staff of the First Regiment of Zion Guard, took up their positions at the door of the Tabernacle.

Then the crisp, vigorous music of the band floated out through the park, bringing all steps into unity; and the great company moved forward.

Eight abreast, they moved up the broad walk to the door of the Tabernacle and entered, singing the praises of God.

Section after section of the huge auditorium was filled, and still the tread of thousands of feet was heard.

Zion Guard, Zion City Band, Zion Junior Restoration Host, Zion Restoration Host, Zion White-robed Choir, Officers of the Church, and members of the Church not members of the Host, all marched in and took the places reserved for them.

Then thousands of the general public poured into the building, filling every desirable seat and standing in hundreds until seven thousand two hundred people had entered the place.

Then the music and singing ceased.

The great throng was standing expectant, noting the changed appearance of the platform.

There was the chair for the Apostle in the middle.

At each end there was a chair for a Deacon-attendant. These were occupied by Deacons William S. Peckham and Richard H. Harper.

At one side of the Apostle's chair was a lectern of polished brass surmounted by an eagle.

At the other side was a small altar, a replica of the Altar of Incense in the Ancient Temple of God.

In front of the high platform was a lower platform, upon which were seated Overseers Jane Dowie, John G. Excell, and Harvey D. Brasefield, and Teachers Daniel Sloan and V. V. Barnes, in the robes and hoods of their respective offices.

All these took their respective places facing the great assembly.

Then the First Apostle of the Restored Church came upon the platform.

He was no longer the General Overseer in his episcopal robes.

The robes that he wore were designed by God Himself for His ministers in the Ancient Temple of God.

The Apostleship included the Priesthood, and they were priestly robes that the man of God wore.

On his head was a miter of white, gold, and purple.

The robe that came to his feet was of pure white.

A sleeveless tunic of purple, with a fringe of gold, came to the knees.

Over that, and covering the trunk of the body, was a sleeveless coat of white, richly embroidered with gold, scarlet, and purple, in geometric designs.

Instead of the breastplate with twelve precious stones, was one with a crimson cross, edged with gold.

About the waist was a girdle of white and gold.

The robes were the majestic robes of glory, and most striking in their design and coloring. But there was nothing theatrical about the appearance of their wearer, whose aim was to glorify "the Apostle and High Priest of our Confession, even Jesus."

They befitted him, as did the offices which they symbolized.

The service that followed was the old familiar service of the Christian Catholic Church in Zion, but it had a new power: for the word "Apostolic" had now come into the Church's title—it was not only the *Christian* and the *Catholic*, but it was the *Apostolic*, Church in Zion.

Then followed the Declaration, based on the Word of God, and most simply and humbly made, yet without the slightest trace of fear or doubt.

The people had already in Church Conference accepted their First Apostle, but they publicly, in Special General Assembly, reaffirmed that acceptance with a prayerful, yet joyous, solemnity that showed how deeply they felt its significance.

During the service, Zion White-robed Choir rendered two beautiful and appropriate anthems: "King of Kings" and "Unfold Ye Portals Everlasting."

The intensity of interest in this Declaration was shown by the fact that it took twenty-five extra railway cars to bring the visitors from Chicago, besides several hundred people who came on the regular trains. Over thirteen hundred people were thus brought out to Zion City, and hundreds more came from other places, some from long distances.

Now, Zion prays for the revealing in due season of the rest of the Apostolic College and the outpouring of the "Latter Rain."

God is working.

All the earth shall see His glory in His time.

The Time is come!

The King is at hand!

Shiloh Tabernacle, Zion City, Illinois, Lord's Day Afternoon, September 18, 1904.

The services were opened by Zion White-robed Choir and Zion Robed Officers entering the Tabernacle, singing as they came the words of the three Processionals.

The Church's one Foundation
  Is Jesus Christ our Lord;
She is His new creation,
  By water and the Word;
From Heaven He came and sought her,
  To be His holy bride;
With His own blood He bought her,
  And for her life He died.

Elect from every nation
  Yet One o'er all the earth,
Her charter of salvation,
  One Lord, one faith, one birth;
One holy Name she blesses,
  Partakes one holy food,
And to one hope she presses,
  With every grace endued.

'Mid toil and tribulation,
  And tumult of her war,
She waits the consummation
  Of peace forevermore;
Till with the vision glorious
  Her longing eyes are blest,
And the great Church victorious
  Shall be the Church at rest.

Yet she on earth hath union
  With God the Three in One,
And mystic sweet communion
  With those whose rest is won;
O happy ones and holy!
  Lord, give us grace, that we,
Like them, the meek and lowly,
  On high may dwell with Thee.

Ten thousand times ten thousand
  In sparkling raiment bright,
The armies of the ransom'd saints
  Throng up the steeps of light:
'Tis finished! All is finished!
  Their fight with death and sin:
Fling open wide the golden gates,
  And let the victors in.

What rush of alleluias
  Fills all the earth and sky!
What ringing of a thousand harps
  Bespeaks the triumphs nigh!
Oh, day for which creation
  And all its tribes were made!
Oh, joy, for all its former woes,
  A thousandfold repaid!

Oh, then what raptur'd greetings
  On Canaan's happy shore;
What knitting sever'd friendships up,
  Where partings are no more!
Then eyes with joy shall sparkle,
  That brimm'd with tears of late;
Orphans no longer fatherless,
  Nor widows desolate.

Bring near Thy great Salvation,
  Thou Lamb for sinners slain;
Fill up the roll of Thine elect,
  Then take Thy power, and reign:
Appear, Desire of nations,
  Thine exiles long for home:
Show in the heav'ns Thy promised sign:
  Thou Prince and Savior, come!

Open now Thy gates of beauty,
Zion, let me enter there,
Where my soul in joyful duty
Waits for Him who answers prayer;
Oh, how blessed is this place,
Filled with solace, light, and grace.

Yes, my God, I come before Thee,
Come Thou also down to me;
Where we find Thee and adore Thee,
There a heaven on earth must be.
To my heart, oh, enter Thou,
Let it be Thy temple now.

Here Thy praise is gladly chanted,
Here Thy seed is duly sown;
Let my soul, where it is planted,
Bring forth precious sheaves alone,
So that all I hear may be
Fruitful unto life in me.

Thou my faith increase and quicken,
Let me keep Thy Gift divine,
Howsoe'er temptations thicken;
May Thy Word still o'er me shine,
As my pole-star through my life,
As my comfort in my strife.

Speak, O God, and I will hear Thee,
Let Thy will be done indeed;
May I undisturbed draw near Thee
Whilst Thou dost Thy people feed.
Here of life the fountain flows,
Here is balm for all our woes.

At the beginning of the last Processional, the Overseers present, Jane Dowie, Harvey D. Brasefield, and J. G. Excell, accompanied by two Teachers, Visscher V. Barnes and Daniel Sloan, took their places on the lower platform, followed by the First Apostle, with Deacons Harper and Peckham for Attendants. When he ascended the upper platform, the people rose and stood with bowed heads while he pronounced the

INVOCATION.

God be merciful unto us and bless us,
And cause Thy face to shine upon us;
That Thy Way may be known upon earth,
Thy Saving Health among all the Nations,
For the sake of Jesus. Amen.

PRAISE.

The Congregation then joined in singing Hymn No. 44:

Oh, wondrous Name, by prophets heard
Long years before His birth;
They saw Him coming from afar,
The Prince of Peace on earth.

CHORUS—The Wonderful! The Counsellor!
The Great and Mighty Lord!
The everlasting Prince of Peace!
The King, the Son of God!

Overseer Excell then led the Choir and Congregation in the recitation of the Apostles' Creed:

RECITATION OF CREED.

I believe in God, the Father Almighty,
Maker of heaven and earth:
And in Jesus, the Christ, His only Son, our Lord,
Who was conceived by the Holy Ghost:
Born of the Virgin Mary;
Suffered under Pontius Pilate;
Was crucified, dead, and buried:
He descended into hell,
The third day He rose from the dead;
He ascended into heaven,
And sitteth on the right hand of God, the Father Almighty;
From thence He shall come to judge the quick and the dead.
I believe in the Holy Ghost;
The Holy Catholic Church;
The Communion of Saints;
The Forgiveness of Sins;
The Resurrection of the body,
And the Life Everlasting. Amen.

Overseer Brasefield then led the Congregation in repeating the Commandments; after which the words, "Lord, have mercy upon us, and write all these Thy Laws in our hearts, we beseech Thee," were chanted.

READING OF GOD'S COMMANDMENTS.

I. Thou shalt have no other gods before Me.

II. Thou shalt not make unto thee a graven image, nor the likeness of any form that is in heaven above, or that is in the earth beneath, or that is in the water under the earth; thou shalt not bow down thyself unto them nor serve them: for I, Jehovah, thy God, am a jealous God, visiting the iniquity of the fathers upon the children, upon the third and upon the fourth generation of them that hate Me, and showing mercy unto thousands of them that love Me and keep My commandments.

III. Thou shalt not take the Name of Jehovah thy God in vain; for Jehovah will not hold him guiltless that taketh His Name in vain.

IV. Remember the Sabbath Day, to keep it holy. Six days shalt thou labor and do all thy work; but the seventh day is a Sabbath unto Jehovah thy God: in it thou shalt not do any work, thou, nor thy son, nor thy daughter, thy manservant, nor thy maidservant, nor thy cattle, nor thy stranger that is within thy gates; for in six days Jehovah made heaven and earth, the sea, and all that in them is, and rested the seventh day: wherefore Jehovah blessed the Sabbath Day and hallowed it.

V. Honor thy father and thy mother; that thy days may be long upon the land which Jehovah thy God giveth thee.

VI. Thou shalt do no murder.

VII. Thou shalt not commit adultery.

VIII. Thou shalt not steal.

IX. Thou shalt not bear false witness against thy neighbor.

X. Thou shalt not covet thy neighbor's house, thou shalt not covet thy neighbor's wife, nor his manservant, nor his maidservant, nor his ox, nor his ass, nor anything that is thy neighbor's.

Hear also what our Lord Jesus, the Christ, the Son of God, hath said, which may be called the Eleventh Commandment:

XI. A New Commandment I give unto you, that ye love one another; even as I have loved you, that ye also love one another.

The great Choir then sang the

TE DEUM LAUDAMUS.

We praise Thee, O God; we acknowledge Thee to be the Lord.
All the earth doth worship Thee, the Father Everlasting.
To Thee all Angels cry aloud, the Heavens and all the powers therein.
To Thee Cherubim and Seraphim continually do cry:
Holy, Holy, Holy, Lord God of Sabaoth,
Heaven and earth are full of the majesty of Thy Glory.
The glorious company of the Apostles praise Thee.
The goodly fellowship of the Prophets praise Thee.
The noble army of martyrs praise Thee.
The Holy Church throughout all the world doth acknowledge Thee,
The Father of an Infinite Majesty;
Thine Adorable, True, and Only Son;
Also the Holy Ghost, the Comforter.
Thou art the King of Glory, O Christ;
Thou art the Everlasting Son of the Father.
When Thou tookest upon Thee to deliver man,
Thou didst humble Thyself to be born of a Virgin;
When Thou hadst overcome the sharpness of death,
Thou didst open the Kingdom of Heaven to all believers.
Thou sittest at the right hand of God in the Glory of the Father.
We believe that Thou shalt come to be our Judge.
We therefore pray Thee, help Thy servants,
Whom Thou hast redeemed with Thy precious blood.
Make them to be numbered with Thy saints in glory everlasting.
O Lord, save Thy people and bless Thine heritage;
Govern them and lift them up forever.
Day by day we magnify Thee;
And we worship Thy Name ever, world without end.
Vouchsafe, O Lord, to keep us this day without sin.
O Lord, have mercy upon us, have mercy upon us.
O Lord, let Thy mercy be upon us as our trust is in Thee.
O Lord, in Thee have I trusted, let me never be confounded.

Scripture Reading and Exposition.

The First Apostle then read from the Book of Psalms, the first six verses of the 2d Psalm:

Why do the nations rage,
And the peoples imagine a vain thing?
The kings of the earth set themselves,
And the rulers take counsel together,
Against Jehovah, and against His Anointed, saying,
Let us break their bands asunder,

And cast away their cords from us.
He that sitteth in the heavens shall laugh:
Jehovah shall have them in derision.
Then shall He speak unto them in His wrath,
And vex them in His sore displeasure:
Yet I have set My King
Upon My Holy Hill of Zion.

Turning to the Gospel according to Saint Matthew, he read the first fifteen verses of the 10th chapter:

And He called unto Him His twelve disciples, and gave them authority over unclean spirits, to cast them out, and to heal all manner of disease and all manner of sickness.

Now the names of the twelve Apostles are these: The first, Simon, who is called Peter, and Andrew, his brother; James the son of Zebedee, and John his brother;

Philip, and Bartholomew; Thomas, and Matthew the publican; James the son of Alphæus, and Thaddæus;

Simon the Cananæan, and Judas Iscariot, who also betrayed Him.

These twelve Jesus sent forth, and charged them, saying,

Go not into any way of the Gentiles, and enter not into any city of the Samaritans:

But go rather to the lost sheep of the house of Israel.

And as ye go, preach, saying, The kingdom of heaven is at hand.

Heal the sick, raise the dead, cleanse the lepers, cast out devils: freely ye received, freely give.

Get you no gold, nor silver, nor brass in your purses;

No wallet for your journey, neither two coats, nor shoes, nor staff: for the laborer is worthy of his food.

And into whatsoever city or village ye shall enter, search out who in it is worthy; and there abide till ye go forth.

And as ye enter into the house, salute it.

And if the house be worthy, let your peace come upon it: but if it be not worthy, let your peace return to you.

And whosoever shall not receive you, nor hear your words, as ye go forth out of that house or that city, shake off the dust of your feet.

Verily I say unto you, It shall be more tolerable for the land of Sodom and Gomorrah in the day of judgment, than for that city.

Again, from the Gospel according to Saint Luke the 6th chapter, from the 10th to the 19th verses:

And He looked round about on them all, and said unto him, Stretch forth thy hand. And he did so: and his hand was restored.

But they were filled with madness; and communed one with another what they might do to Jesus.

And it came to pass in these days, that He went out into the mountain to pray; and He continued all night in prayer to God.

And when it was day, He called His disciples: and He chose from them twelve, whom also He named Apostles;

Simon, whom He also named Peter, and Andrew his brother, and James and John, and Philip and Bartholomew, and Matthew and Thomas, and James the son of Alphæus, and Simon which was called the Zealot.

And Judas the son of James, and Judas Iscariot, which was the traitor;

And He came down with them, and stood on a level place, and a great multitude of His disciples, and a great number of the people from all Judæa and Jerusalem, and the sea coast of Tyre and Sidon, which came to hear Him, and to be healed of their diseases;

And they that were troubled with unclean spirits were healed.

And all the multitude sought to touch Him: for power came forth from Him, and healed them all.

Also in the 11th chapter of the same Gospel, the 49th and 50th verses:

Therefore, also said the wisdom of God, I will send unto them Prophets and Apostles; and some of them they shall kill and persecute;

That the blood of all the Prophets, which was shed from the foundation of the world, may be required of this generation;

The final reading was from the Gospel according to Saint Matthew, the 19th chapter from the 28th through the 30th verse:

And Jesus said unto them, Verily I say unto you, that ye which have followed Me, in the regeneration when the Son of man shall sit on the throne of His glory, ye also shall sit upon twelve thrones, judging the twelve tribes of Israel.

And every one that hath left houses, or brethren, or sisters, or father, or mother, or children, or lands, for My Name's sake, shall receive a hundred-fold, and shall inherit eternal life.

But many shall be last that are first; and first that are last.

The Meeting in Jerusalem to Elect the Thirteenth Apostle.

The First Apostle said:

I shall not read to you in detail the passages to which I shall refer in the course of my address in connection with the other Nine Apostles besides the first Twelve, but merely enumerate them.

There were only Twelve at one time, but the Office was perpetual, and ought to have been continued.

The sin of the Church in this matter has been that the Office was not continued.

I shall refer to the fact that in the 1st chapter of the Acts of the Apostles, and the 26th verse, you are told of the Upper Room at Jerusalem, where, before the Holy Spirit came in power upon the Church, the Apostles, in an Assembly of one hundred twenty believers, had met together to elect a new Apostle.

They were acting under the direct instruction of the Lord, with whom they had just spent forty days, and who had spoken to them of the things concerning the Kingdom of Heaven.

They had come back to Jerusalem to put the Church in order.

There was one Apostle lacking, because Judas had fallen by transgression, and had been buried.

Probably Peter, by direction of the Master, called the Assembly's attention to the fact that it had been prophesied long before that one of their number should fall, and that another should take his office.

So Peter announced to the Assembly that they were gathered together for that purpose.

Then they selected Matthias.

The lot lay between him and Joseph; but at last he was selected and ordained.

Matthias made the thirteenth Apostle.

In the 1st chapter of Galatians, and the 18th verse, Paul mentions James, our Lord's brother, as an Apostle, at least three years after Jesus' resurrection and ascension.

James was not an Apostle while the Christ lived, because the brothers of our Lord did not even believe in Him.

That fact is recorded after the calling of the First Twelve.

Our Lord had four brothers and three sisters.

The names of the brothers are given—James, Joses, Simon and Jude.

These were sons of Mary, beside Himself.

He was the Son of God; they were the sons of Mary, by Joseph, her husband.

Thus James makes the second Apostle selected after the first twelve.

The third and fourth Apostles are Barnabas and Saul, as told in the 13th chapter of the Acts of the Apostles, from the 1st to the 3d verse.

They were called by the Holy Spirit from among the prophets at Antioch.

These prophets' names are given in the 1st verse:

Now there were at Antioch, in the Church that was there, prophets and teachers, Barnabas, and Symeon that was called Niger, and Lucius of Cyrene, and Manaen, the foster-brother of Herod the tetrarch, and Saul.

The Holy Spirit came upon these prophets and said "Separate me Barnabas and Saul for the work whereunto I have called them."

They were then prayed with, ordained, and sent forth, and from that time they were called Apostles.

In the 14th chapter, and the 14th verse, they are called Apostles, and Paul claimed that Apostleship in all his letters.

Barnabas and Saul (from that time called Paul) make the third and fourth appointments to the Apostolic Office after the Ascension of Jesus.

Jude, Apollos, Epaphroditus, Andronicus, and Junias Are Named

The fifth Apostle is Jude, the brother of James, the writer of the Epistle of that name, and who is commonly held to be an Apostle. He would be the fifth Apostle.

Without any question an Apostle is mentioned by Paul in the 1st Epistle to the Corinthians, the 4th chapter and the 6th verse, when he says, "Now these things, brethren, I have in figure transferred to myself and Apollos for your sakes."

Apollos makes the sixth Apostle.

Epaphroditus is called an Apostle, in the 2d chapter of Philippians, and the 25th verse.

He makes the seventh Apostle.

The word is translated "messenger," but in the Greek it is "Apostle."

Two very remarkable men are named as Apostles, in the last chapter of Paul's great Epistle to the Romans, where he says

Salute Andronicus and Junias, my kinsmen, and my fellow prisoners, who are of note among the Apostles, who also have been in the Christ before me.

These make the eighth and ninth Apostles.

I take it, therefore, that nine Apostles were ordained after the first Twelve.

There were only twelve at one time; but others were ordained as necessity arose to fill the space in the Apostleship made by martyrdom or natural death.

In the case of the vacancy made by the death of Judas Iscariot, Matthias was selected.

To fill the place of James, the son of Zebedee, who was

slain by Herod, they probably selected Barnabas, Saul no doubt taking the place of another who died about that time.

The continuity of the Apostolic Office would be proved if we had only the election of Matthias, but when in addition to that we have the clear election of James, the Lord's brother, and Barnabas and Saul, even if you were to dispute the rest, it has become an established fact that God made the Apostolic Office a perpetual one, as He did all the other offices in the Church.

May God bless His Word!

The First Apostle then knelt at the Altar of Incense and offered prayer.

PRAYER OF THE FIRST APOSTLE.

Our Father who art in the heavens, as of old the high priest prayed at the Altar of Incense, and as the prayers ascended to Thee and Thou didst hear, hear us today in the Name of our Great High Priest, Jesus, the Christ. Let the power of Thy Holy Spirit rest upon this assembly. Let the record of this afternoon be blessed throughout the world. Bless, we humbly beseech Thee, every Overseer, every Elder, every Evangelist, every Deacon, every Deaconess, and every member of Zion Junior and Senior Restoration Host. Bless the children in all the homes. Bless all the Institutions of Zion—the Ecclesiastical, Educational, Commercial, Industrial, Financial, and Political. Help us to take our part as the people of God in the affairs of men. Hear us as we pray that we may be forgiven wherein we have sinned. Father, the holiest and best have erred and strayed. It is not possible for us always to live with perfect and sinless lives, for we are so ignorant; and we not infrequently sin through ignorance. We plead with Thee, Father, that the atonement of our Apostle and Great High Priest in Heaven may cover all our sins today. Take them all away, and make Thy people pure. Grant unto each of us to carry our religion into the family, into the business, and into the work of God, that everything may be a work for the glory of God and the elevation of man.

PRAYER FOR THE NATION AND ITS GOVERNMENT.

Bless, we humbly pray Thee, the President of the United States and the Administration associated with him in the executive work of the government. Bless the United States Supreme Court, and all the judges and magistrates. Bless the legislative branch of this government—the Congress of the United States and the legislatures and municipal councils of all states and cities. Bless, we pray Thee, all who influence by pen or by voice the opinions and thoughts of the people; and let it be that every man in every place shall one day serve God in all things. We humbly beseech Thee for the wide world. We pray for the dying upon the plains of Manchuria in the horrid and wicked war; and we plead with Thee that Thou wouldst bring about a termination of that war and hasten the coming of peace. Our Father in heaven, we ask that the other nations of the earth shall not be drawn into this war. Keep America out of that maelstrom of blood.

PRAYER THAT THE APOSTOLIC AND PRIESTLY OFFICE MAY BE DISCHARGED WITH WISDOM.

Father in heaven, hear us as we pray for the Holy Catholic Church throughout the world. Grace, mercy, and peace be with all who love our Lord Jesus, the Christ, in sincerity; who are enrolled in the General Assembly and Church of the Firstborn; whose names are enrolled in heaven. Bless Thy people everywhere. Bless the Christian Catholic Apostolic Church in Zion, which Thou hast enabled us to found and establish over all the earth within these last few years. Bless, we pray Thee, the organization of that Church which has now reached the place where we today—having been led thereto by Thy Spirit, and all this Church approving—come before this people to declare our Apostolic Office. Father in heaven, for the sake of Him who is the Apostle of all apostles, the High Priest of all high priests, the Prophet of all prophets, the King Eternal, immortal, and invisible, the Ruler of the kings of the earth, the King of kings and Lord of lords, make this Declaration effective in this Church and in all the world today.

Grant that in due season the other eleven Apostles may be set before the people and endowed by Thee with the grace that they need. Father, we pray Thee, as we take upon ourselves today this Apostolic and High Priestly Office—not after the order of Aaron but after the order of Melchizedek—that we may have, with ever deepening humility, a purer faith, a larger charity, a clearer knowledge, and a greater wisdom, the power needed to discharge this Office. Grant that we may go on until at last we sleep in Jesus, our labor done, and ascend to Thee, to lay whatever crowns Thou hast given us before Thee, and to give an account of our Apostolic and Priestly Office. We pray this in the Name of our Lord Jesus, the Christ, so that Thy Kingdom may be extended, that the poor, the suffering, the needy, and those that walk in darkness and have no light, may be blessed, that the nations may be brought to Thee, and that Thy Rule may be speedily, finally, and eternally established on earth as it is in the Heavens.

PRAYER FOR BLESSING UPON THE CHRISTIAN CATHOLIC APOSTOLIC CHURCH IN ZION THROUGHOUT THE WORLD.

We ask Thee to bless this Church throughout the world today. [Amen]. Bless the Christian Catholic Apostolic Church in Zion throughout America [Amen]; in Asia [Amen]; in Africa [Amen]; in Australasia [Amen]; in Europe [Amen]; and in the Islands of the Sea. We pray for the sick and sorrowing, whose requests are in our hands. We lay them on Thine altar, and cry to Thee, Father, to hear us for them, as in this and all the lands they pray today. May they know that the healing of the Christ's seamless dress is by their beds of pain, and that they may touch Him in life's throng and press and be made whole again. Savior, Healer, Cleanser, Keeper, Thou art pleading for these suppliant sufferers, and, Father, hear and answer them through Thy Son, and for His sake. Amen.

The announcements were made by Overseer Excell, and the tithes and offerings were received.

The First Apostle then delivered his Message:

THE DECLARATION OF JOHN ALEXANDER, FIRST APOSTLE OF THE LORD JESUS, THE CHRIST, IN THE CHRISTIAN CATHOLIC APOSTOLIC CHURCH IN ZION, WHO IS ALSO ELIJAH, THE PROPHET OF THE RESTORATION OF ALL THINGS.

INVOCATION.

Let the words of my mouth and the meditations of my heart be acceptable in Thy sight, and profitable unto this people, and unto all to whom these words shall come, in this and every land, in this and all the coming time, Till Jesus come. Amen.

In front of all the words I have to say to you today, I place the words of Inspiration found in the 3d chapter of Hebrews the 1st verse; the 4th chapter of Ephesians from the 11th to the 16th verse inclusive, and in 1st Corinthians, 12th chapter, from the 28th verse through the 31st.

Wherefore, holy brethren, partakers of a heavenly calling, consider the Apostle and High Priest of our Confession, even Jesus.

. . . .

And He gave some to be Apostles; and some, Prophets; and some, Evangelists; and some, Pastors and Teachers;

For the perfecting of the saints, unto the work of ministering, unto the building up of the body of the Christ:

Till we all attain unto the unity of the faith, and of the knowledge of the Son of God, unto a full-grown man, unto the measure of the stature of the fulness of the Christ:

That we may be no longer children, tossed to and fro and carried about with every wind of doctrine, by the sleight of men, in craftiness, after the wiles of error;

But speaking truth in love, may grow up in all things into Him, which is the Head, even the Christ;

From whom all the body fitly framed and knit together through that which every joint supplieth, according to the working in due measure of each several part, maketh the increase of the body unto the building up of itself in love.

. . . .

And God hath set some in the Church, first Apostles, secondly Prophets, thirdly Teachers, then Miracles, then Gifts of Healings, Helps, Governments, divers kinds of Tongues.

Are all Apostles? are all Prophets? are all Teachers? are all Workers of Miracles?

Have all Gifts of Healings? do all Speak with Tongues? do all Interpret?

But desire earnestly the greater Gifts. And a still more excellent way show I unto you.

If I might reduce my text to a smaller dimension, it would be to give you the words in this form:

TEXT.

Consider the Apostle and High Priest of our Confession, even Jesus.

. . . .

And He gave some to be Apostles; and some, Prophets; and some, Evangelists; and some, Pastors and Teachers.

. . . .

God hath set some in the Church, first Apostles, secondly Prophets, thirdly, Teachers.

Words Are Addressed to the Church Throughout the World.

It is, of course, expected that, at a time like this, I shall speak to the Church throughout the world

I am not speaking merely to the officers and members of the Christian Catholic Apostolic Church in Zion, who at this Special General Assembly are here in thousands today, and to the thousands of friends who have come to be with us and to consider what I say; but I am speaking to that larger audience, the Christian Catholic Apostolic Church in Zion, which is now planted on every continent, in many nations, and in many islands of the sea.

It is my joy and my duty to speak to Zion in its widest signification, to all who are born of the Spirit into the Kingdom of God, and to the true Church of God by whatever name known among men, as far as I can reach it; and to men in all nations everywhere, who are His offspring: for we have all One Father—"the Father of spirits."

We have the great privilege, under God, of sending these words to all the lands through LEAVES OF HEALING, and through what I hope will be fair reports of what I say appearing in the daily secular papers of Chicago, which are so largely represented here to-day.

I am grateful for the opportunity of speaking to you, and for the privilege given me by God of going forward with the organization of the Christian Catholic Apostolic Church in Zion (for that word "Apostolic" will from this time be added).

This would not be possible had not the work been done that has been done.

The work of the past has made it possible for me to stand in this position and make this Declaration today.

God has led me and graciously used me as a Teacher throughout the world for many years.

He has blessed me as His Prophet, Elijah the Restorer.

Now He has given me that which I declared to you eight and one half years ago, when I formed this Church, was the Goal of Ecclesiastical Organization—the Restoration of the Apostolic Office.

Divine Order Is Heaven's First Law.

These are the Times of the Restoration.

The keynote of this discourse is that the Church must get back to its Primitive Order if it would have back its Primitive Power. [Amen.]

It is impossible to get back the Primitive Power without the Primitive Order.

To those who have so little thought of order, let me say that it is Heaven's first law.

This Church was not established to be a disorderly mob of ecclesiastical anarchists and separatists, who go as they like and do as they please.

I am grateful to God for strong, thinking, independent men and women, who have seen with me that there could be no effective work done for God and man in this world until there was an organization in which all individuality was merged, making it one united body.

The True Church is the Body of the Christ, which is knit together by these great and glorious offices.

I did not create the Apostolic Office.

I did not create it any more than I designed these robes.

Perhaps some wonder at the robes.

If you want to find every detail of this robe, save some parts I have omitted and changed, you will find it described in the 28th chapter of the Book of Exodus.

You will find there the pattern which God gave to Moses when the Aaronic Priesthood was established. The omissions and changes are made because the High Priesthood is in the Christ, "after the order of Melchizedek;" for it is written in Hebrews 7:12, "For the Priesthood being changed, there is made of necessity a change also of the law."

There are no apostolic robes, because the Apostle is a Priest, and the First Apostle must be the High Priest on earth of Him who is the First Apostle and High Priest in Heaven, and who is coming back to reign as King.

I ask you, brethren, who have received the heavenly calling, to "consider the Apostle and High Priest of our Confession (not profession but confession), even Jesus."

There Is a Vast Difference Between Confession and Profession.

A great many people make professions who never make any true Confession.

Confession is of great importance.

Repentance begins with confession.

You must be baptized with the Baptism of Repentance, confessing and forsaking your sins, and putting things right with man and God.

That glorious word Confession is the equivalent of martyrdom.

All the early martyrs were called Confessors.

They were not mere professors; they were Confessors.

They confessed the Christ before men, and did what was right, letting the world smile and hate, even though it meant a bloody grave. They did the right, and never feared.

They walked with God, and now they dwell with God.

Hallelujah! Ten thousand times ten thousand the ransomed saints throng up the streets of light from the Church of God, whose one Foundation, underlying the Church of all the ages, is Jesus, the Christ.

He is the Underlying Rock, and upon this Foundation we can build a strong Church.

This Foundation was laid by the Christ Himself as the Great First Apostle and as the First Great High Priest in heaven; and He who has established the Apostolic Office has also established the Priesthood.

The First Apostle Is the High Priest of the Order of Melchizedek on Earth.

Therefore, I stand before you today, leaving out the onyx stones on the shoulders, and the twelve stones which were in the breastplate of the high priest of the Jewish Dispensation, not representing that ancient priesthood, but as the Apostle and High Priest on earth of that glorious priesthood whose Head for ever and ever is Him who is the High Priest forever after the Order of Melchizedek.

This is the priesthood in the Christian Church which offers "spiritual sacrifices" unto God, and may God speedily grant in the Christian Catholic Apostolic Church in Zion a Priesthood of Prevailing Prayer. [Amen.]

I failed to find any Apostolic robe.

It was not until I had finished that sixty-four page issue of LEAVES OF HEALING of September 10th, that the question as to what changes there must be in the order of the Assembly, came up.

Then I saw that, in preparation for a complete Apostleship, every one must take their proper station, and I must take mine.

I, who have ever believed, and believed increasingly as the years have gone on, that God established a Church that in due time should put on its Garments of Beauty, could find nothing but the Aaronic priesthood garb, modified to suit the Melchizedek priesthood.

Therefore, I was not ashamed to wear as my Breastplate the Cross of the Christ.

May God help me to preach it better than ever; to live it better than ever, and to be more compassionate, like unto that Apostle and High Priest of our Confession who was touched with the feeling of our infirmities; who ever loved us and loves us still; and whose touch healed the sick and dying, whose word raised the dead, into whose loving arms mothers put their babes, and into whose loving heart has been poured the sorrows of His Church in all the ages.

For

Now Is Our Salvation Nearer than When We Believed.

Though now exalted up on high,
He bends on earth a brother's eye;
He sympathizes with our grief,
And to the sufferer sends relief.

Where high that heavenly temple stands,
The House of God not made with hands,
A great High Priest our nature wears,
The Guardian of mankind appears.

I thank God today that the Sacred Year has revolved to this important day, and that we can now say that our Salvation and the Salvation of the world is nearer than when we believed.

I think it is nearer because of the work that has been done by the Christian Catholic Church in Zion, and by Zion Restoration Host throughout the world.

I think it is nearer, because, as the whole earth can see, this Church is fearlessly following the Lord, and the patterns which God gave, not only to Moses on the Mount, long ago, but that pattern which He gave when He talked to the disciples on the Mount of Galilee, telling them how to set the Church in order.

I, therefore, say to you that if we would have the Primitive Power of the Primitive Church, we must get back to Primitive Organization, because a Divine Organization is a Divine Power.

Gunpowder is very powerful.

If you put a torch to a great, loose mass of it, it would give a great puff, and noise, and smoke; but nothing more.

But if you ram it into a cannon and then put in a great shell filled with shrapnel it would do something more than make a smoke, a noise, and a flame—it would kill, even when fired many miles away.

The Church Needs Organization as Well as Practice.

It is not only years of practice, but glorious organization, which enables the Church, fully armed, going forth in the conflict with evil, to shoot to kill—to kill or destroy that which is evil, to break down the strongholds of sin and Satan, and to send spiritual bombshells from this platform over land and sea that will amaze all these miserable Kings, emperors, and czars, who are crowned as Heads of the Church and Defenders of the Faith—which they are not.

"The weapons of our warfare are not of the flesh," nor are they made of steel, but they are "mighty before God to the Casting Down of Strongholds; Casting Down Imaginations, and every High Thing that is exalted against the Knowledge of God, and bringing Every Thought into Captivity to the Obedience of the Christ; and being in readiness to Avenge all Disobedience, *when your Obedience shall be fulfilled.*"

The False Priests of False Churches are ready at all times to sing the Te Deum when Military Oppressors send forth their armies to murder each other.

The Te Deum would be sung in France and in Italy, if the soldiers of both nations were rushing into battle with each other.

The Te Deum is sung in Russia, and would be sung in Germany should they battle together.

How many gods are there to hear the Te Deum?

How many gods are there to answer contradictory prayers?

What a sham the whole thing is!

How many Supreme Judges of the Nations are there?

Is there not but one Judge?

VOICES—"Yes."

FIRST APOSTLE—Is there not but one Head of the Church?

VOICES—"Yes."

FIRST APOSTLE—Is there not but one True Organization?

It cannot be organized in the Apostasies, which have neither the Apostolic Power nor Catholicity in them.

"Do you not believe in the Apostolic Succession of the Church of Rome?" you say to me.

I do, with all my heart.

I believe in the Apostolic Succession of the Church of Rome.

I believe that the Pope of Rome is a lineal descendant of Judas Iscariot, who sold his Master for silver and betrayed Him to His death with a kiss, and whose progeny has been ready to shed the blood of the saints for many ages.

The Shame of Romish Pretensions.

What a shame and burning disgrace it is to talk about a church being the Church of the Living God that dares to say that the pope, the cardinals, and the priests of every rank may take a little bit of wet flour and by stamping it and hocus-pocusing it with a little Latin, manufacture the Living God!

They tell you that every one of the wafers they manufacture in this fashion is the body, blood, and bones of Jesus, the Christ, and that, in eating them, you can eat His body, blood, and bones.

What a lie it is! What a shameful lie!

It is only a little more shameful than the lie which is told by apostate churches when they take a little water and sprinkle it upon a baby and declare that by that water and their hocus-pocus that child has been regenerated.

Shame! Shame!

No wonder that the Latins, the Slavs, and other peoples that have been under churches of that kind, hate Christianity, even when they, for political or other purposes, pretend to be faithful Christians.

Although God has waited long, Zion has at last been established!

God in Zion has established the Christian Catholic Apostolic Church in Zion, that is leading a Restoration Host to final victory over the powers of Satan, Sin, Disease, Death, Hell, and all the powers of the Apostasy.

I am very confident that no matter how long or short my life on earth may be, I am today putting, or beginning to put, the Crown of Divine Organization upon the brow of Zion.

God grant that He who in the heavens hears my cry, will hear me as I pray that this act may be followed by the out-pouring of the Holy Spirit upon this Church and upon the whole world. [Amen.]

I thank God this afternoon that there is no need to discuss with this General Assembly of the Christian Catholic Apostolic Church in Zion the question of Apostolic Order which has now been settled, and was settled, in principle, eight and a half years ago, when I organized the Church.

The First Apostle Has Not Hurried the Organization.

I was in no hurry to settle it.

You who know the truth in this matter know that at the very beginning my people desired me to assume the Apostolic Office.

You know that they did so as a result of my teaching.

You know that I set their call aside; not that I did not believe that God had given me a right to assume it, but because the time had not yet come.

The Christ was always the Christ, was He not?

VOICES—"Yes."

FIRST APOSTLE—He was the Christ before He was born.

He was the Christ as a baby.

He was the Christ as a little boy when in the Temple.

He was the Christ in the carpenter's shop at Nazareth.

But He did not assume His Apostolic Office until He had fulfilled all righteousness: for until He was baptized by Elijah the Preparer, John the Baptist, "His Time" had not yet come.

I have not assumed this Apostolate until I have waded to it, metaphorically, almost through seas of blood and fields of death.

It was not the desire of the Sons of Belial in Australia, Great Britain, and America, that I should stand here today.

I have not sought for office, but for Purity, for Peace, and for Power to do the Work of God.

I cared not to assume the Office until God would give me the necessary Purity, Peace, and Power.

Will you pray that He may increase these Gifts and Graces?

I thank God that I am very happy in the assumption of the Office; but if I had an atom of doubt as to my Divine call to this Office, I would rather wear my grave-clothes than that I should dishonor my Lord by wearing these robes of glory.

I thank God today that I have the courage to wear the Apostolic and High-Priestly Robe, and lead this Church with Apostolic Power and Prevailing Prayer into holier living, more glorious contests, and more glorious victories for the Christ, our King.

Declaration.

And now, I solemnly repeat the Declaration which I made before the Conference of this Church, on Wednesday last, September 14th, when the following questions were unanimously answered in the affirmative:

Do we believe, and has the time come for us to reaffirm, that the Apostolic Office should never have been discontinued, and ought to be restored?—*Ephesians 2:19, 20; 1 Corinthians 12:28; Matthew 10:2-4; Romans 11:29; Ephesians 4:11-13; Acts 1:23-26; 13:3, 4; 14:14; Matthew 17:11.*

Do we recognize John Alexander Dowie, our General Overseer, not only as the Prophet of the Restoration, but as a Divinely-Commissioned Apostle of the Lord Jesus, the Christ?—*2 Corinthians 12:12; Matthew 10:7, 8.*

I DECLARE, IN THE NAME OF THE LORD JESUS, THE CHRIST, IN THE POWER OF THE HOLY SPIRIT, IN ACCORDANCE WITH THE WILL OF GOD OUR HEAVENLY FATHER, THAT I AM, IN THESE TIMES OF THE RESTORATION OF ALL THINGS, THE FIRST APOSTLE OF THE LORD JESUS, THE CHRIST, IN THE CHRISTIAN CATHOLIC APOSTOLIC CHURCH IN ZION.

Zion Restoration Host Acknowledges John Alexander as the First Apostle.

Zion Restoration Host, will you please to stand?

Members of Zion Restoration Host, with all my heart I gladly greet you today.

I thank God that, although we have not summoned the Host from far-distant places, it not being desirable at this time, you are here in so many thousands today.

Zion Restoration Host, do you accept me as John Alexander, the First Apostle of our Lord Jesus, the Christ, in the Christian Catholic Apostolic Church in Zion?

ZION RESTORATION HOST—"Yes."

FIRST APOSTLE—Officers and members of the Christian Catholic Apostolic Church in Zion, do you accept me as John Alexander, the First Apostle of our Lord Jesus, the Christ, in the Christian Catholic Apostolic Church in Zion?

MEMBERS AND OFFICERS—"Yes."

FIRST APOSTLE—I thank you.

I do not know that I have anything more to say today than to ask you to pray with me.

I have gone through many weeks and months of great toil in this matter, weakening my body for the first time in my life by long vigils and by earnest prayer, in addition to the constant toils of my many offices and duties.

However, I thank God that today I feel strong and well.

Yet it will be well for me to go apart, and rest a little, and commune with God, and do some things which this Declaration makes immediately necessary.

I ask you now to pray with me that in the little time of retirement I may be able to perform the work that I have to do, and to prepare for the work that is yet to be done here and throughout the world.

Will you follow me as I follow the Apostle and High Priest of our Confession?

PEOPLE—"Yes."

FIRST APOSTLE—Will you pray for me, and by the grace of God hold up my hands, as the days come when they will be feebler in the flesh?

PEOPLE—"Yes."

FIRST APOSTLE—Will you pray for me that I may be guided in the great task that will take months, perhaps years, to accomplish—that of bringing the entire Apostleship into existence?

PEOPLE—"Yes."

FIRST APOSTLE—Let all the people who desire to give themselves wholly to their God stand and tell Him so.

Surely not one will be seated.

Surely none will fail to give themselves to God.

Apparently more than Seven Thousand rose..

Now pray.

PRAYER OF CONSECRATION.

My God and Father, in the Name of Jesus, the Apostle and High Priest of our Confession, the Apostle of all apostles, High Priest of all high priests, the Prophet of all prophets, the Teacher of all teachers, the King of all kings, the Lord of all lords, the Rightful Ruler of all the world, we come to Thee. For His sake, hear us while we pray. Give us True Repentance wherein we may have failed to repent. Give us power by true confession and restoration to put all things right with God and man. Give us faith to live, to love, and to carry the Light of the Everlasting Gospel of the Kingdom of God to all the nations that sit in darkness. Give us a deeper humility, a purer faith, a brighter hope, a larger love, more knowledge, more wisdom, more tenderness for sinners, and more power to help; and when we are done with earth may we enter into heaven through Him who is the Lamb of God that beareth and taketh away the sins of the world. And all this we most humbly ask in His Name. Amen. [*All repeat the prayer, clause by clause, after the First Apostle.*]

Did you mean it?

PEOPLE—"Yes."

FIRST APOSTLE—Will you live it?

PEOPLE—"Yes."

After the Recessional had been sung, the service was closed with the following

APOSTOLIC AND HIGH-PRIESTLY BENEDICTION.

Jehovah bless thee, and keep thee:
Jehovah make His face to shine upon thee, and be gracious unto thee:
Jehovah lift up His countenance upon thee, and give thee Peace.

Beloved, abstain from every form of evil. And may the very God of Peace Himself sanctify you wholly; and I pray God your whole spirit, and soul, and body be preserved entire, without blame, unto the coming of our Lord Jesus, the Christ. Faithful is He that calleth you, who also will do it.

The grace of our Lord Jesus, the Christ, the love of God our Father, the fellowship of the Holy Spirit, our Comforter and Guide, one Eternal God, abide in you, bless you, and keep you, and all the Israel of God everywhere, forever. Amen.

Warning.

I am directed by the General Overseer to warn our members and officers throughout the world against giving money to persons claiming to be members of the Christian Catholic Church in Zion. All benevolence must be given either from Headquarters or under the direction of same. Even though the applicant for benevolence be known to be a member of the Christian Catholic Church in Zion, financial aid must not be given except in extreme cases, and then only in small amounts. Requests for help must be made to the officer-in-charge. In cases where there is no such officer, requests should be made direct to Headquarters, accompanied by recommendations from one or two members of Zion in good standing. J. G EXCELL,

General Ecclesiastical Secretary.

Street Addresses Are Necessary.

All Zion City Subscribers to *Leaves of Healing*, *The Zion Banner*, *Blatter der Heilung*, and *Voice from Zion*, whose correct street addresses are not positively known to be in our possession should send them to us AT ONCE. Please act upon this notice without delay as it is very important, now that we have postal delivery service, that the exact location of each and every subscriber be known to us. Write your name and address very carefully, designating also to what periodicals you are a subscriber and leave at your very earliest opportunity at our branch Publishing House on Elijah Avenue.

Very Sincerely Yours,

ZION PRINTING AND PUBLISHING HOUSE.

DO YOU KNOW GOD'S WAY OF HEALING?

BY THE REV. JOHN ALEX. DOWIE.

Let it be supposed that the following words are a conversation between the reader [A] and the writer [B].

A. What does this question mean? Do you really suppose that God has some one especial way of healing in these days, of which men may know and avail themselves?

B. That is exactly my meaning, and I wish very much that you should know God's Way of Healing, as I have known it for many years.

A. What is the way, in your opinion?

B. You should rather ask, WHO is God's Way? for the way is a Person, not a thing. I will answer your question in His own words, "I am the Way, and the Truth, and the Life: no one cometh unto the Father, but by Me." These words were spoken by our Lord Jesus, the Christ, the Eternal Son of God, who is both our Savior and our Healer. (John 14:6.)

A. But I always thought that these words only referred to Him as the Way of Salvation. How can you be sure that they refer to Him as the Way of Healing also?

B. Because He cannot change. He is "the same yesterday and today, yea, and forever." (Hebrews 13:8.) He said that He came to this earth not only to save us, but to heal us. (Luke 4:18), and He did this when in the flesh on earth. Being unchanged He must be able and willing and desirous to heal now.

A. But is there not this difference, namely, that He is not with us now?

B. No; for He said "Lo, I am with you All the Days, even unto the Consummation of the Age;" and so He is with us now, in spirit, just as much as when He was here in the flesh.

A. But did He not work these miracles of healing when on earth merely to prove that He was the Son of God?

B. No; there was still a greater purpose than that. He healed the sick who trusted in Him in order to show us that He came to die not only for our sins, but for our sicknesses, and to deliver us from both.

A. Then, if that be so, the atonement which He made on the Cross must have been for our sicknesses as well as our sins. Can you prove that is the fact from the Scriptures?

B. Yes, I can, and the passages are very numerous I need quote only two. In Isaiah 53:4, 5, it is written of Him: "Surely He hath borne our griefs (Hebre[illegible], *sicknesses*), and carried our sorrows: . . . . and with His stripes we are healed." Then, in the Gospel according to Matthew, this passage is quoted and directly applied to the work of bodily healing, in the 8th chapter 17th verse: "That it might be fulfilled [illegible]h was spoken by Isaiah the prophet, saying, Himself took our infirmities, and bare our [illegible]seases."

A. But do you not think that sickness is often God's will, and sent for our good, and therefore God may not wish us to be healed?

B. No, that cannot possibly be; for diseases of every kind are the Devil's work, and his work can never be God's will, since the Christ came for the very purpose of destroying "the works of the Devil." (1 John 3:8.)

A. Do you mean to say that all disease is the work of Satan?

B. Yes, for if there had been no sin (which came through Satan) there never would have been any disease, and Jesus never in one single instan[illegible] told any p[illegible]son that sickness was God's work or will, but the very contrary.

A. Can you prove from Scriptures that all forms of sickness and infirmity are the Devil's work?

B. Yes, that can be done very easily. You will see in Matthew 4:23 and 9:35 that when Jesus was here in the flesh He healed "all manner of disease and all manner of sickness among the people." Then if you will refer to Acts 10:38 you will see that the Apostle Peter declares that He (Jesus) "went about doing good, and healing all that were oppressed of the Devil." Notice that all whom He healed, not some, were suffering from Satan's evil power.

A. But does disease never come from God?

B. No, it cannot come from God, for He is pure, and disease is unclean; and it cannot come out of Heaven, for there is no disease there.

A. That is very different from the teachings which I have received all my life from ministers and in the churches. Do you really think that you are right, and that they are all wrong in this matter?

B. It is not a question as between myself and them. The only question is, What does God's Word say? God has said in all the ages, to His Church, "I am Jehovah that healeth thee" (Exodus 15:26), and therefore it would be wicked to say that He is the defiler of His people. All true Christians must believe the Bible, and it is impossible to believe that good and evil, sickness and health, sin and holiness could have a common origin in God. If the Bible really taught that, it would be impossible to believe our Lord Jesus, the Christ, when He says: "A good tree cannot bring forth evil fruit, neither can a corrupt tree bring forth good fruit." (Matthew 7:18.)

A. But even if I agree with all you say, is it not true that the Gifts of Healing were removed from the Church, and are not in it now?

B. No, the "Gifts of Healing" were never withdrawn, and can never be withdrawn, from the true Church of God, for it is written: "The gifts and the calling of God are without repentance." (Romans 11:29.) There are nine gifts of God to the Church (enumerated in 1 Corinthians 12:8-11), and all these are in the Holy Spirit. Therefore, so long as the Holy Spirit is in the Church, all the gifts must be there also. If they are not exercised, that does not prove that they do not exist, but that the faith to exercise them is lacking in God's servants. The gifts are all perfectly preserved; for the Holy Spirit, not the Church, keeps them safely.

A. What should a Christian then do when overtaken with sickness?

B. A Christian should obey God's command, and at once turn to Him for forgiveness of the sin which may have caused the sickness, and for immediate healing. Healing is obtained from God in one of four ways, namely: First, by the direct prayer of faith, without any aid from the officers of the Church, praying as the Centurion did in Matthew 8:5-13; second, by two faithful disciples praying in perfect agreement, in accordance with the Lord's promise in Matthew 18:19; third, by the anointing of the Elders and the prayer of faith, according to the instructions in James 5:14 and 15; and fourth, by the laying on of the hands of them who believe, and whom God calls to that ministry, as the Lord commands in Mark 16:18, and in other places.

A. But are people healed in this way in these days?

B. Yes, in thousands of cases. I have myself laid hands upon many hundreds of thousands of persons, and I have seen the Lord's power manifested in the healing of great numbers, many of whom are living witnesses in many countries, who have testified publicly before thousands, and who are prepared to testify at any time. This ministry is being exercised by devoted Christians in many parts of America, Europe, Australasia, and elsewhere.

A. Is it not the same as Christian Science, Mind Healing, etc.?

B. No. Divine Healing is diametrically opposed to these diabolical counterfeits, which are utterly antichristian. These impostures are only seductive forms of Spiritualism. Trance Evangelism is also a more recent form of this delusion, and it deceives many.

A. But how shall I obtain the necessary faith to receive healing, which faith I am at present conscious that I do not possess?

B. It is written: "Belief cometh of hearing, and hearing by the word of the Christ." (Romans 10:17.) Our Missions are held for the express purpose of teaching fully the Word of God on this matter, and I very heartily invite you to attend the meetings which are announced for Zion Tabernacles in Chicago and other cities, and for Shiloh Tabernacle, Zion City, Illinois. All are welcome and there are no charges of any kind made, for all God's gifts are free gifts. Salvation is the first of these, without which you cannot be healed through faith in Jesus. All the costs of this work are covered by the free-will offerings of the people who attend these meetings, and others whom the Lord leads to help; but the poorest, who have nothing to give, are as heartily welcome as the richest.

A. Do you see the sick and lay hands upon them in this Mission?

B. Yes; after we feel satisfied that they are fully resting in the Lord alone for the healing, we see privately, so far as time permits, those who attend; but under no circumstances do we claim the power to heal any; for "power belongeth unto God."

A. Have you any writings upon this subject which can be purchased?

B. Yes; these can be obtained at the office of Zion Printing and Publishing House, Zion City, Illinois, and at any Zion Tabernacle. But the best book on Divine Healing is the Bible itself, studied prayerfully and earnestly.

We extend to you a hearty invitation to attend the meetings, which are free to all. Our prayer is that you may be led to find in Jesus, the Christ, our Lord and God your present Savior from sin, your Healer from sickness, your Cleanser from all evil, your Keeper in the way to Heaven, your Friend, and your All for Time and Eternity. We pray that these words may help many who read, and that our little conversation may bear fruit in leading many readers to look to Jesus only.

"The Healing of Christ's seamless dress
Is by all beds of pain;
We touch Him in life's throng and press
And we are whole again."

THE Message of the Prophet of the Restoration in Shiloh Tabernacle, Lord's Day afternoon, September 4, 1904, was a strong declaration on the Universal Fatherhood of God and Brotherhood of all Mankind.

These are popular expressions in the religious world of today.

But for the most part they mean nothing.

They glide trippingly from the tongues of pastors in churches where only those with white skins are permitted to rent pews.

They figure in philosophical dissertations by those who maltreat the yellow man, the Jew, and others who do not belong to the same "race" as themselves.

Many grandiloquently and pompously proclaim the Universal Fatherhood of God and Brotherhood of Man who would instantly and indignantly leave a hotel or club where an African was entertained.

This doctrine is a part of the creed of churches which are divided on the "color line," so that we find "African" Baptist, Methodist, and Presbyterian churches.

It is proclaimed in all parts of the earth to men of all nationalities and colors by the many Christian churches, societies, and associations, chief among which is the so-called Young People's Society of Christian Endeavor.

And yet black men, no matter how well educated, how refined, how cultured, or how sincerely Christian they may be, are refused accommodations in a hotel controlled by that society at St. Louis during the World's Fair, and called the "Christian Endeavor" hotel.

With the Prophet of God, however, these words are no mere empty sounds.

The Message of Lord's Day afternoon, September 4th, was made in the presence of an audience of about six thousand people, representing seventy nationalities, among whom were many Chinese, Japanese, and Africans.

There were Africans singing in the Choir, Africans and Chinese wearing the robes of office in the Christian Catholic Church in Zion, and many people with dark-colored skins in all parts of the audience, all of whom were treated with the same respect, courtesy, and brotherly love that was accorded to their white brothers and sisters.

The words of God's Messenger were spoken in a City where every man is treated according to his actual merits, no matter what his birthplace, his parentage, or the color of his skin.

A scholarly and observant man, after a visit to Zion City, wrote for publication the following words:

"And it is a strange thing—which I ask no man to believe until he has seen it, but for which I can personally vouch—that there is a look upon the faces of the colored people in Zion City which I have seen, among their race, nowhere else in the United States—an indefinable something which shows that at last they have come to their own, and are men among men, and know it."

The Universal Fatherhood of God and Brotherhood of Man is a real, genuine, practical actuality with Elijah the Restorer and his people.

The fearless, consistent application of the truth is a portion of the work of the Restoration of All Things.

And that Restoration is begun.

This was the burden of the Message of God's Prophet.

The immediate cause of the General Overseer's dealing with the subject at this particular time was an incident that had occurred at St. Louis during the previous week.

A cultured, well-educated, Christian gentleman from Africa, a member of the Christian Catholic Church in Zion, had been refused accommodations and even a meal at the hotel conducted by the Young People's Society of Christian Endeavor near the World's Fair grounds at St. Louis, Missouri.

In discussing the matter with this gentleman's companion, a young man belonging to the General Overseer's personal staff, the manager of the hotel had wickedly blashemed the Name of the Christ.

It was against this outrage, perpetrated in the name of the Young People's Society of Christian Endeavor, that the man of God, in behalf of all his people, uttered a most solemn and vigorous protest.

But his Message dealt not only with the rights of the black man.

It was of universal application, wherever so-called race prejudice worked its wo.

He warned the white races of the earth against oppression and injustice toward the Mongolian people, who, he pointed out, were so numerous, so powerful, and were acquiring such intelligence and skill in the use of modern methods, that they would have the power within a few years to overrun the earth and enslave the white man, who now despises them.

*The First Apostle has not revised the following report.

This Message was followed with a brief intermission, after which about four thousand earnest, happy Christians gathered about the Lord's Table for the regular monthly Ordinance of Communion.

This was preceded with the General Overseer's giving the right hand of fellowship to several scores of new members of the Christian Catholic Church in Zion.

After a solemn charge, he very heartily and lovingly welcomed each one into the fellowship and communion of the Church, invoking God's blessing with the laying-on of hands.

The Ordinance in remembrance of Him Till He Come, was one of especial spiritual uplift and blessing.

It was followed with a very earnest, loving, and helpful, but brief, "Family Talk" by the leader to his people.

The interest and spiritual power was sustained throughout the entire afternoon's services, which, although four hours long, seemed all too short to the thousands of the children of God who enjoyed them.

An exceptionally large number of visitors from Chicago and other cities was present.

Shiloh Tabernacle, Zion City, Illinois, Lord's Day Afternoon, September 4, 1904

The service was begun with the singing of the Processional "Ten Thousand Times Ten Thousand," which was followed with the usual Invocation and the singing of Hymn No. 63.

The recitation of the Apostles' Creed and of the Commandments, and the singing of the Te Deum Laudamus by the Choir, was followed with

Scripture Reading.

The General Overseer said:

Let us read from the Inspired Word of God, in the 63d chapter of the Book of the Prophet Isaiah, the 15th and 16th verses.

Look down from heaven, and behold from the habitation of Thy holiness and of Thy glory: where is Thy zeal and Thy mighty acts? the yearning of Thy bowels and Thy compassions are restrained toward me.

For Thou art our Father, though Abraham knoweth us not, and Israel doth not acknowledge us: Thou, O Jehovah, art our Father; our Redeemer from Everlasting is Thy Name.

Let us now read in the Book of the Prophet Malachi, the 2d chapter from the 1st to the 10th verse, inclusive:

And now, O ye priests, this commandment is for you.

If ye will not hear, and if ye will not lay it to heart, to give glory unto My Name, saith Jehovah of Hosts, then will I send the curse upon you, and I will curse your blessings: yea, I have cursed them already, because you do not lay it to heart.

Behold, I will rebuke the seed for your sake, and I will spread dung upon your faces: even the dung of your sacrifices; and ye shall be taken away with it.

And ye shall know that I have sent this commandment unto you, that My Covenant might be with Levi, saith Jehovah of Hosts.

My Covenant was with him of Life and Peace; and I gave them to him that he might fear, and he feared Me, and stood in awe of My Name.

The law of truth was in his mouth, and unrighteousness was not found in his lips: he walked with Me in Peace and Uprightness, and did turn many away from iniquity.

For the priest's lips should keep knowledge, and they should seek the law at his mouth: for he is the messenger of Jehovah of Hosts.

But ye are turned aside out of the way; ye have caused many to stumble in the law; ye have corrupted the Covenant of Levi, saith Jehovah of Hosts.

Therefore have I also made you contemptible and base before all the people, according as ye have not kept My ways, but have had respect of persons in the law.

Have we not all one Father? hath not one God created us? why do we deal treacherously every man against his brother, profaning the Covenant of our fathers?

May God bless the reading of His Word.

Overseer John G. Excell led in the general supplication, followed by the General Overseer, who prayed for the sick and sorrowing, and led the Choir and Congregation in chanting the Disciples' Prayer.

The General Overseer made the announcements, after which the tithes and offerings were received.

The General Overseer then delivered his Message:

GOD THE FATHER OF ALL MEN.

INVOCATION.

Let the words of my mouth and the meditation of my heart be acceptable in Thy sight, be profitable unto this people, and unto all to whom these words shall come, in this and every land, in this and all the coming time, Till Jesus Come. Amen.

TEXT.

Have we not all one Father? hath not one God created us? why do we deal treacherously every man against his brother, profaning the Covenant of our fathers?

It would be well for the people of the United States of America to again ask themselves these questions:

"Have we not all one Father?

"Hath not one God created us?"

Or, have the people who have different shades of color in their skin another father, and are there different creators for the different so-called "races" that are upon this earth?

God the Universal Father and Creator.

I speak this afternoon, first, concerning the Universality of the Fatherhood of God; second, regarding the Universality of His Creatorship; for Creator and Father each have a distinct meaning.

To be a Creator is one thing; to be a Father is another.

I speak regarding the Fatherhood and the Creatorship.

I also speak regarding the wickedness of strife between the children of the one common Father and Creator.

God is our Father in a sense essentially different from that which may be applied to any human being, for He is the Father of Spirits.

Our spiritual nature, that which distinguishes us from all other creatures, is that which we get from God only.

There is no essential difference, as regards the construction of the various parts of the body, between a man and an ape.

Man's lungs, and heart, and liver, and kidneys, and all his various organs, do not essentially differ from the animals'; because man, in all these respects, is simply an animal.

Although intelligence in man is greater than in brutes, it is not his superior intelligence that distinguishes man from the brute.

This is the difference: that while man is a triune being, having spirit, soul, and body, all other creatures are dual, having only souls and bodies.

The Spirit and the Soul Are Essentially Different.

Bodies die, and souls die.

Our Lord, in speaking of His own soul, said, "My soul is exceeding sorrowful, even unto death."

The Prophet, in speaking of Him, said that He "poured out His soul unto death."

It is a universal fact that souls die.

The soul, as well as the body of the Christ, died, but His spirit did not die.

That is the difference between the spirit and the soul.

The soul and the body are procreated, as are the souls and bodies of all other creatures; but our spirits come from God.

That which distinguishes us from the brute, the bird, and the fish, is that in God we have a Father, who gave us spirits like His own.

While these bodies and souls will perish, these spirits which God has given us are immortal and eternal, sharing His own essential nature.

"Have we not all one Father?"

Is it not true that the Father of our Spirits is the one God and Father of us all, our Father in heaven?

All America will reply to that question, "Yes, we have one Father."

Then, "Hath not one God created us?"

Is our Creator the God that created the world; that created the birds and the beasts?

Was it some other god that created us, or was it the same Father who gave us our spirits?

Did the God who first of all created Adam and Eve, our first parents, create us?

Is it not true that One is the Father of us all?

PEOPLE—"Yes."

GENERAL OVERSEER—Then is it not true that there is only one Creator?

Are there two races of human beings?

Did the God that made us make three races?

Did He give different spirits to the black race, to the yellow :e, and to the white race—giving the supremacy to the white :e, putting the yellow race a little lower, and the black race ll lower?

Or is it true that there is only one spirit and one race, and at the race of Adam; that all come from Adam and Eve; d that God created all men of one blood to dwell on all the :e of the earth, having determined the bounds of their bitation?

The Earth is the Habitation of One Race.

The earth is the habitation of man.

We have not yet found any power with which to go from inet to planet, from sun to sun.

The bounds of our habitation have been determined.

Did He make more than one race?

If there is more than one race, I want to know it.

I should like to know when these different races were made, d why they were made, and the relative virtue or power of ch race.

I have been somewhat of an anthropologist, and I have been mewhat of a zoölogist.

I am somewhat of an inquirer into all that has ever been itten or spoken upon this matter of so-called racial stinction, and I find that the greatest scientists, even those at are not looked upon as orthodox, men like Wallace and rwin, are compelled to admit that there is a difference tween man and the lower creation, which forbids their ying that man is of the same species.

While those physical and psychical characteristics of soul d body of which I have spoken, are to be found in the ver creation as well as in man, yet the scientists find someing in man that they cannot name, something that they do not derstand, because they have not received the Revelation of od.

Neither have the churches fully received it.

Man Is More than Soul and Body.

Men are continually talking about soul and body, as if that re the whole of man.

Why do you not discriminate and remember that we have irits, souls, and bodies?

If we had only souls and bodies, we would be nothing more an brutes of a higher degree of intelligence.

It is our spiritual nature that distinguishes us from the ute.

Has the God who has given a spirit to the black man, and a irit to the white man, and a spirit to the yellow man, made em in a different way and of different clay?

Did He say that one should stand here, another there, and other in another place, and that each possessed different grees of racial superiority?

If so, then I want to keep to the race to which I belong.

But if there is only one race—the race of Adam—then I nt to mix them all together and get back the primitive an.

I want to see as soon as possible—and Zion will work for it—scegenation in all its fulness.

Do you hear that?

The curse that has come to humanity in this matter is two-d—the curse of color and the curse of different languages.

When the Restoration comes in its fulness (glory be to God, has begun!) then the miscegenation of the races will be mplete.

The spiritual powers of all will blend, and the physical aracteristics which now make each strong while yet apart, en united, will make them far stronger.

The General Overseer's Prophecies Are Being Fulfilled.

Some of you told us that the Mongolian would go down fore the Caucasian; but I told you before the war began that e Caucasian would be humbled beneath the feet of the ongolian.

I told you that the bear, if it put to sea, would find a sword-h there that would stab it to its death.

I told you that even on land the armies of the Japanese were ore than equal to the dissolute armies of the Slav and of the ucasian.

What is the fact today?

Russia has no fleet in Asia.

Their powerful fleets have been swept from the ocean by the Mongolian; and now, with fear and trembling, a poor, puny little fleet has put out from the Baltic Sea.

Where stands their boasted superiority today?

With a hundred million people behind them; with all the resources of a vast empire; with a gold reserve of more than three hundred fifty million dollars, and with vast reserves besides in the treasuries of its church and state—with all this, that army, trained for centuries, has gone down before the armies of the Japanese.

Field-Marshal Oyama, and Generals Kuroki, Oku, and Nodzu, have met the flower of the Caucausian armies, and have steadily driven them north, until at last we hear today that they are in full retreat at Mukden; that more than twenty-five thousand have fallen, and probably thousands more will be captured by the Mongolian race tomorrow.

I know not whether it will be so or not; but one thing is certain, that in all that constitutes what men count the greatest thing in the world, the victorious army and navy in the world is the Mongolian's, and the Caucasian is humbled.

If you do not give the African a chance he will take it by force one of these days.

If you in the South continue to allow him to vote, and mock him by not counting his vote; if you continue to say that there is one law for the white and another law for the black; if you permit countless rapes to be perpetrated by the white man on the black women—the proof of which is the color of one-fourth of the people in the South, which is neither black nor white, but the product of a licentious race that has raped the black woman for centuries—I pray, if you appeal to the sword to settle the racial question, that the great God in the heavens will deal with you scoundrels.

I say plainly, that if it is to be a question of an appeal to force, I will stand with the black man, and fight you incarnate devils who will allow them to live only as you say.

The Time Has Come for this Horrible So-called "Race Prejudice" to Be Wiped Out.

It is being wiped out on the battle-fields of Manchuria in rivers and oceans of blood, and along the shores and in the waters of Asia.

The great God will not tolerate this horrible, disgusting, disgraceful, and utterly unreasonable so-called "race prejudice."

There is only one race; but there are many families.

"Have we not all one Father?

"Hath not one God created us?"

Then why should we "deal treacherously" with one another, and yet demand that brother and sister, no matter what their color, shall be partakers of that Gospel which rests upon the Salvation of Him who "tasted death for every man?"

When I hear people talk about the essential superiority of white people over black, I cannot help smiling.

I cannot help wondering if these learned professors and writers in the South have ever read human history.

Some People Have Poor Memories.

I wonder why it is they do not remember that the brown-black race of Egypt built the pyramids, and gave us the sciences of architecture, sculpture, and languages; and that their laws, that existed eight hundred years before Moses was born, are inscribed on monuments today, showing that they were living in a high state of civilization when our fathers, the white hordes of Europe, were painted savages, roaming the woods, clad in skins, and living very largely upon roots and wild animals.

They were tribes of thieves, always fighting with one another.

That is what our fathers were when the blacks were great and civilized nations, which filled the valley of the Nile with the great pyramids, and temples, and in whose hearts were great thoughts, notwithstanding that they were not Christians.

It was Egypt that trained Moses, the great Law-giver of God.

It was Egypt in which the Son of God Himself received His early training after He was carried, when a babe, out of Palestine.

It was the black man who taught Him.

It was the black man who taught Moses.

It was a black woman whom Moses married, and to whom Miriam so much objected.

She was an Ethiopian woman from the land of the blacks, and Miriam belonged to the "Lily-white Party" of the South.

She did not like her brother's choice, although he was at that time over a hundred years old, and ought to have known his mind.

She thought she could put him right, so she made a rumpus about it; and so did Aaron.

But God Almighty came down and settled that rumpus; for when she came out of the "tent of meeting" she was a leper as white as snow.

Leprosy of Thought May Be the Penalty of Fighting God's Truth.

That is what you get when you fight miscegenation; for the leprosy of the thought that holds a man to be a culprit merely because he has a black skin is that of which every man or woman should be thoroughly ashamed.

I have been very much stirred up in this matter by an incident that occurred during the last week, the details of which I have in my hand, in writing, but which I will not take time to read.

This incident concerns an African gentleman, who had been very industrious amid many difficulties.

Under the equatorial sun, and without any help from his surroundings, he sought for an education, and he got it.

He has in his possession today a certificate which would enable him to teach the English language in that part of Africa, under the governor of one of the British Provinces.

He is a merchant, although quite young in years.

He is a Christian gentleman, and sits in this assembly today.

He writes and speaks good, clear English; and he behaves himself, in all respects, as a gentleman.

He has been a member of this Church for several years; for four, I think.

Three years ago he sent me five thousand dollars for the work of God in Zion, and he has at all times been an earnest supporter of it.

Today he proposes to place in Zion's hands a vast estate.

In order to help him understand certain things in his own country, I sent him, with one of my personal attendants, Mr. Freeman Haehnel, down to St. Louis, to look at certain machinery.

It had not dawned upon them, nor did it upon me, that at a World's Fair, where all the world was asked to come, a man would be shut out of a hotel because of his black skin.

However, they found, upon reaching there, that there was not one white hotel that would receive him, even for one meal.

Hypocrisy of the Christian Endeavor Society.

The quiet, gentlemanly man went with Mr. Haehnel from hotel to hotel, until quite late in the night they reached the Christian Endeavor Hotel, where they thought that they would surely be received.

Miserable, wretched, and hypocritical that pitiable "Try-to-do-it" Society has always been since its inception!

It is an abomination!

It has not helped the church to grow, because the churches that have had this society have not been able to make any considerable increase since the society was formed.

If that statement is false, then their own statistics are false.

This black gentleman—and he is a gentleman, every inch of him—who has dined at my table, lived in Elijah Hospice, and been entertained by our Overseer in London—this gentleman stepped into the Christian Endeavor Hotel, and my attendant inquired at the main office for rooms.

He was told by the head clerk that he could not be received, because he was in company with a colored gentleman.

They were permitted to check their baggage there, because it was quite late, but they were sent on to seek lodging elsewhere.

Returning to town, they were directed by a colored lady to the Douglas Hotel, the largest and most up-to-date colored hotel in St. Louis.

So my attendant, who is a young man with white skin, did what I know all Zion will approve of his doing—he went there at once, with his companion.

They were courteously received, and found the accommodations first-class in every respect.

A Hotel for Colored People Does Not Draw the Color Line.

He then inquired of the manager of the Douglas Hotel, if he, being a white man, would be allowed to remain a few days at their hotel. [Applause.]

He was the only white man that applied, but he received the Christian-like answer ot a Christian gentleman, "Most certainly, sir! You are heartily welcome!"

So they found, as they say in this letter, that the only hotel in St. Louis where they were "treated white" was in a black one.

The next morning they went to the Fair Grounds, and on arriving there made their way to Machinery Hall.

They then tell me how they spent the day.

At six o'clock they returned to the Christian Endeavor Hotel for their baggage, thinking they would take supper there, if possible.

However, they were disappointed; for the clerk informed Mr. Haehnel that he would not be permitted to take the colored man into the dining-room.

The clerk said, "I will get the manager and have him talk with you."

The manager arrived and asked what he wanted.

Mr. Haehnel told him that he was there with a colored gentleman from a certain part of Africa.

The manager answered, "Oh, my, we could not allow a colored man to eat in this place."

Then he said, "Just step here to the door of the dining-room, and I will show you the way our tables are arranged."

He stepped with him to the door of the dining-room (the colored man having to remain at the desk), and the manager said, "Now just look here, this is our dining-room; American tables on one side, *à la carte* on the other If we were to allow that colored man to sit down at one of these tables, why, Jesus Christ! two-thirds of these people would leave the building!"

My attendant said, "What hotel is this?"

He hesitated for a moment, and then replied, "This is the Christian Endeavor Hotel."

A Profane, Drinking Man Runs the Christian Endeavor Hotel.

Mr. Haehnel then asked, "Isn't there some mistake about the name, or at least the 'Christian' part of it? Do you mean to tell me that you are a Christian running this hotel, and yet can talk like that?"

He said, "Oh, I don't belong to the Christian Endeavor Society. I am no Christian myself; I am just hired by these people to run this place. I am ready to take a drink with any one!"

The truthfulness of the latter part of this statement, my young man states, was greatly in evidence; for the fumes of liquor in his breath were so apparent that he could hardly talk with him.

"You see," he continued, "this is the position I am in as manager of this place. Most of our people are Southerners, and if I were to allow you to come in with that colored man it would mean the loss of thousands and thousands of dollars to the Christian Endeavor Society!"

My attendant told him that he had no idea that the color line in the South was drawn so closely; and that he never for a moment dreamed of being turned down in a Christian place.

The manager said that he himself did not uphold them in the position they took.

My attendant said that he thought there could not be much Christianity in a "religion that did not go even skin-deep;" and the manager replied, "That is right!"

He then asked my attendant where he was from, to which he replied "Zion City;" and handed him one of his cards.

The manager exclaimed, "Oh! that's Dowie's place!" [Applause.]

Then he understood.

He said that he had heard me speak, and that he wanted to hear me again.

President Francis E. Clark Has a Duty to Perform.

I pause here to say that Francis Clark, the President of the Young People's Society of Christian Endeavor, had better wipe this disgrace from the Society, or he may hear more about it:

Francis Clark, President of the Christian Endeavor Society, what is the use in your going around the world and telling all the yellow people, all the black people, and all the white people to get together, because God is the Father of them all, and because they are all one in the Christ, and then establishing a hotel and putting it in the hands of a cursing, swearing manager, and turning out a Christian gentleman, because your religion is not "skin-deep?"

"Have we not all one Father?

"Hath not one God created us?"

Are we to discriminate against our brother because of the color of his skin?

Then, my brothers, let us make a solemn protest today against that wretched little Christian "Try-to-do-it" Society! [Applause.]

Big as it may be in numbers, it is exceedingly small in its spirit.

This is the fact concerning Christian people in all the lands.

There is no use in saying that the Englishman is essentially different.

I must say for England, however, that for the most part a man of colored skin can go almost anywhere to a public hotel and get accommodation—unless he belongs to Zion and his name is "Dowie!"

And yet the Englishman in India does not fraternize with the Indian.

He looks upon him with a good deal of contempt, and treats him with a good deal of ignominy.

The Prophet of the Restoration Will Not Be Silent While Evil Exists.

I say to the whole world, as far as my voice can reach, that there is one Christian organization in the world, one Christian teacher, one prophet of God, who, as long as life lasts, will never cease to protest against conduct that makes Christianity a narrow, mean, miserable thing, when it is the glory and joy of Christianity to reëcho the words of the Lord Jesus:

And I, if I be lifted up from the earth, will draw all men unto Myself.

The Apostle Paul said that the Christ "tasted death for every man."

There cannot be Greek and Jew, circumcision and uncircumcision, Barbarian, Scythian, bondman, freeman: but Christ is All, and in All.

The Christ Himself said:

For One is your Teacher, and all ye are brethren.

May God grant us in Zion to maintain this!

It is gross hypocrisy for churches, North, South, East, or West, to send out missionaries to the black and yellow "heathen," as they call them, when they themselves are acting worse than heathen would act.

The heathen would not deny hospitality to you because you are white.

The heathen in Africa and in China are kind, and considerate, and hospitable; and they outnumber us by vast myriads.

Are we to show them the superiority of our race, our family, our religion, and our civilization by making wicked distinctions?

The time has come for us to remember that God appointed to all men this earth for their "habitation;" and that any man has a right to go to any land he pleases, if he is not violently fighting law, or creating disorder, and if he is acting in a proper manner, and lives the Everlasting Gospel.

We contend that "the earth is Jehovah's, and the fulness thereof; the world, and they that dwell therein;" that it has been made by God, our common Father; that all men are made by God, our common Creator; and that, best of all, the spirits that are within us are given to us by God, not made, for "we are His offspring."

He is the Father of our spirits.

Zion Does Not Believe in War.

I protest against war!

I have not said much lately concerning war, but you know that I have always protested against it. I have kept back from saying much regarding the war in the Far East.

However, I believe the statement that has been made, namely, that Japan was forced by Russia to choose between war and giving up her national existence.

It was impossible to evade the issue forced by that most brutal of powers, that gives no tolerance, either civil or religious, notwithstanding every now and then an edict of the Czar, that is usually a promise made to be broken.

The people of Russia must be distinguished from their rulers, and from the cruel, ignorant, and wicked priesthood that rules over them.

Military and ecclesiastical bureaus are the cause of the misery of Russia.

The Russians themselves detest this war.

It is a recorded fact that many of them are driven into battle through fear of being mowed down by artillery on their own side.

This cruel power ought to be broken.

It has had no design upon China except to steal it.

It has had no design upon Japan except to steal it.

It ought to be kept back.

While I hate this war, I must say that it is not the fault of the heathen Japanese.

It is the fault of so-called Christian, but worse than heathen, Russia.

I do not hesitate to say that if I could have offered a prayer to God for victory on either side, it would have been a prayer that Japan would win; but I knew God would permit the humiliation of the Caucasian.

A Warning to the Caucasian Family.

I warn all the families of the earth, that if the Mongolians unite, they will probably compose more than six hundred millions of the human race; perhaps seven hundred million by including China, Korea, Japan, and the other Mongolian states and islands of the seas.

The probabilities are that they will number nearer seven hundred million—one-half of the human race.

These men, now learning to shoot scientifically and straight, will become a great danger to the so-called Christian powers, unless these powers present a very different attitude toward them.

If they were to join hands with the two hundred million Africans, and all the colored races in India, we would have one thousand million of the races of the earth in array against the three hundred million or four hundred million white and partly white.

If it comes to a fight between the so-called races, let the white man everywhere know that what Japan has done to Russia, she can do to England; she can do to Germany; she can do to France; she can do to other powers.

The Japanese, supported by other Mongolian families, can just as quickly turn the other European nations on their heads as they have the Caucasian Russian.

The War Powers Are Facing a Terrific Problem.

Let us take care.

I do not want the war spirit to be stirred up.

I do not want that war to come; but I give you warning.

You, who are the military rulers and despots of the world, take care!

You can see it yourselves, can you not?

You are up against a terrific problem, should the Mongolian races unite.

They understand how to manage ships as almost no other peoples do; they understand how to pull together and scientifically to arm, as you have seen.

Let them, led by the Japanese or the Chinese, enter into a conflict for the supremacy of the world, and I do not hesitate to say that the black and colored peoples of the earth will enslave all of the whites, and the tables will be completely turned.

But this is not the Will of God.

The will and purpose of God is that we, who have obtained the supremacy for the time being, should retain it; and there is no question that the white races of the earth are at the present time supreme.

But we must not be presumptuous or careless.

A people that spends thirteen hundred million dollars a year on liquor, and seven hundred million dollars a year on tobacco, and eats swine's flesh, and is becoming debased, spiritually, morally, and physically, how long will it hold supremacy?

How long is degenerate England going to hold the power of the world?

Cannot all men see how degenerate she has become; how effeminate; how weak; how brutal; ready to cry out for the murder of innocent men in the streets?

Can you not see it?

The time has come for us to say that unless a real Christianity takes possession of this world there is nothing left for it but fire and sword, and perhaps the supremacy of the colored race, and the degradation of the whites.

The whites have degraded themselves so much that there would be very little difficulty, I think, in conquering them.

I have been around the world a number of times, and I am talking of what I know.

The Stronger Peoples Are Those of Colored Skin.

Notwithstanding the skill of the Kaiser, and the splendor of the administration of the military powers of Europe, I do not hesitate to say that it is clear to the mind of the observer who understands the inner facts, that the stronger peoples are those of colored skin.

There is no question about their being far more prolific; for, in this country alone, the Africans of less than four millions have become more than eight millions in thirty-five years.

Let this increase continue in the same proportion and this country will become one-half black, and that very soon.

If you deny the blacks education, and continue to brutalize them in this country, and elsewhere, you will be "sowing dragon's teeth," and they will rise up, as in the olden fable, "armed men."

I pray God to grant that Zion's war may go on.

Zion is at war with war.

Zion is at war with the bloody men who delight in war.

Zion is at war with kingcraft and ecclesiastical brutality and supremacy.

Zion boldly proclaims that the time has come for the Restoration of the Kingdom of God, and the unification of the human race into one great family in God.

All who believe that stand and tell it to God.

Every one who thinks that the yellow man and the black man do not have the same Father and the same Creator keep your seats, and we will pray for your miserable spirits; you need it.

Now, pray.

PRAYER OF CONSECRATION.

My God and Father, in Jesus' Name I come to Thee. Take me as I am. Make me what I ought to be. For Jesus' sake give me a True Repentance for sin, and for all evil talking regarding other peoples. Help me to be patient, to be kind, to pray, and to remember that we all have one Father, one Savior, one Holy Spirit who seeks to lead us into the life and light, into the love and purity of God, and into one great and beautiful heaven. Father, for Jesus' sake, help us to carry forward the Kingdom of God; to extend to Zion all the nations of the earth, and to let them know that the gate of this Church is open wide to men of every clime, and every nation, and every color. For Jesus' sake. Amen. [*All repeat the prayer, clause by clause, after the General Overseer.*]

Did you mean that?

PEOPLE—"Yes."

GENERAL OVERSEER—Will you live it?

PEOPLE—"Yes."

After the Recessional, "Abide with Me," had been sung, the General Overseer pronounced the Benediction, and those who wished retired, the others remaining to the Communion of the Lord's Supper.

COMMUNION OF THE LORD'S SUPPER.

After the singing of Hymn No. 216, the General Overseer received into fellowship several scores of new members of the Christian Catholic Church in Zion.

Before doing so, however, he addressed the candidates, and, among other things, said:

Beloved in the Christ, it is a great joy for me to receive those who are now gathered, seeking fellowship with this Church.

I am glad to know that, increasingly, out of all the lands, from the East, from the West, from the North, and from the South, men of every color are coming into Zion.

I am waiting eagerly to get the news from Africa of nearly a thousand African-born black people coming into our Church.

We have received many hundreds of British and Boers into this Church, and it is a great joy for me to know that Zion in Africa has, like Zion everywhere, no color line.

I am so thankful to see you here today, and to know that we who have come together from all the lands are but a little band that are precursors of a great tide of immigration.

The resources will continue to come with the people.

I believe that Zion can grow in resources only as she grows in good people.

I delight to tell you that on Saturday I received a letter from Overseer Voliva telling me that there are two hundred prepared to come from Australia next March.

May God bless that two hundred. [Amen.]

That which is true of Australia is true regarding Europe.

There are many, many hundreds who, in the early spring of next year, will find their way here.

After the General Overseer, assisted by the officers of the Church, had administered the Ordinance of the Communion of the Lord's Supper, he addressed his people in the regular

Post-communion Family Talk.

We have entered upon the last quarter of this wonderful year

September has always been a month of great power and blessing in the Christian Catholic Church in Zion.

We have many things to do during this month, and we need to call upon God for especial grace.

In some respects, the Declaration that is to be made in this place on this day fortnight, will be one of the most important that has ever yet been made in connection with the onward movement of Zion, and with its organization upon the primitive Foundation of the Apostles and Prophets, Jesus, the Christ, Himself being the Chief Corner-Stone.

I ask your very earnest prayers for the preparation of the Conference Reports, and of the Special Letter, which will accompany this, and which will be published, God willing, in LEAVES OF HEALING, on Saturday, September 10th.

On Lord's Day, September 18th, I will make the Declaration which will be indicated in that Letter.

I thank God for the blessings of last month.

I have not been able to do a tithe of what I longed to do and hoped to do, but I did what I could; and, better than doing, I prepared for better doing.

Foresight and Prearrangement Indispensable to Great Successes.

The most important factor in connection with a campaign is to prearrange every movement, and to see that the army is organized for victory before you begin to fight.

The great power of the Mongolians in this war has been their foresight.

They thoroughly understand the ground upon which they are fighting.

Their topographical surveys are exact.

They knew the possibilities of the whole Russian Empire, and they knew just the place to strike, and to strike effectually.

It is said that every detail of the present campaign was wrought out in Tokyo even before war was declared.

The Russians, on the other hand, had no plan of campaign, and therefore they have been beaten.

The great thing in connection with Zion is not merely to do things, but to do things in a manner that will be effectual and permanent.

We had come to a place where there was much need for care.

I was much concerned, however, regarding the spiritual purification of the Church in the last two months; and I directed the Acting Overseer for Zion City, and those associated with him, in this City, to see to it that every house, every street, and every lane was thoroughly cleansed, spiritually.

The search has been made, and the work has gone on.

Although it will never stop in one sense, for there will always be need for more or less watchfulness and discipline, yet I think that we have reached a place where we can say that there is not a known sin in the City that would defile the people that has not been dealt with or is not being dealt with.

The Root of Things in Zion Lies Deeper than Outward Conformity.

But the root of these things lies deeper.

I say to you, very lovingly, that there are some in whose hearts Zion is not yet deep enough.

You are not yet prepared to make the sacrifices which God demands.

Some of you are not yet prepared to go forward with an Undying Hope and a Confident Faith, never for a moment letting that joy of the Lord be dimmed by any doubt, or fear, or pain, or sorrow.

Within these last two months, I have worked, perhaps, just a little harder than ever before; and the wonder to me is the exceeding goodness of God, which enables me to stand here tonight feeling that I could start the work all over again and do it better.

I do not feel weary.

When I do for a moment or two, I quickly get the strength.

There are times, of course, when I am weary, but these are not very numerous, and then I do not yield to it.

I go right on.

I believe, beloved friends, that change of campaign is what some of you need more than anything else.

This is the time of preparation, and in some things, reconstruction, getting ready for the campaigns that lie before us—campaigns much larger than any of you dream, in connection with the ecclesiastical, educational, commercial, financial, and industrial work of Zion; yes, and taking our part in the political campaign, casting our votes on what we believe to be the best side.

Only God Can Make Human Effort Effectual.

Beloved friends, Paul may plant and Apollos may water, and you and I may work together with indomitable zeal, perseverance, and Purity of spirit, but only God giveth the increase.

Only He can make effectual our labor.

I congratulate the great mass of the people upon their steadfastness, their reliability, their conscientiousness, and their maintaining the standard of Zion as they have.

I know that if we should be called upon for fresh sacrifices, both you and I would not be found wanting in that day.

One thing is certain; the work lies not with me alone, but with you as well.

No matter how powerful the leader may be, it is impossible for the work to be done without the effective support of every member of this Church and Zion Restoration Host.

It is of the utmost importance that you and I remember that we never can lay our armor down.

We must always keep on the Helmet of Salvation, the Breastplate of Righteousness, the Shield of Faith; the loins must be girt about with Truth; our feet must be shod with the preparation of the Gospel of Peace; and we must know how to use the Sword of the Spirit, which is the Word of God.

I desire to thank my people, the children of God, for the very excellent support you give me and those associated with me.

Those who have been troublesome have never been more than an exceedingly small fraction of Zion.

We are apt to make too much of it, only that we do not want evil to spread.

We are keen and quick in detecting evil and in putting things right.

May God keep us all pure, humble, and faithful; make us powerful, and fill us with tender forbearance and love for one another. [Amen.]

May God grant it, for Jesus' sake.

Let us rise and sing, "God Be with You Till We Meet Again."

The Congregation sang the first verse of the hymn, and the General Overseer, as is his custom, sang alone the last verse, the people joining in the chorus.

The service was then closed with the

BENEDICTION.

Beloved, abstain from every form of evil. And may the very God of Peace Himself sanctify you wholly; and I pray God your whole spirit, and soul, and body be preserved entire, without blame, unto the coming of our Lord Jesus, the Christ. Faithful is He that calleth you, who also will do it. The grace of our Lord Jesus, the Christ, the love of God, our Father, the fellowship of the Holy Spirit, our Comforter and Guide, one Eternal God, abide in you, bless you, and keep you, and all the Israel of God everywhere, forever. Amen.

Publisher's Notice.

The remittance must accompany receipt of subscriptions at the Publishing House, no difference by or for whom or for whatever time they may be given, or whether forwarded through Ordained Officers, Branches, or Gatherings of the Christian Catholic Church in Zion. Accounts will be carried with Ordained Officers, Branches, or Gatherings, on quantity orders of periodicals consigned on sale for monthly settlement, but to include only such articles as bear the imprint of Zion. All orders for Bibles, books, buttons, pictures (except prints done by the Publishing House), lace souvenirs, etc., must be sent to the General Stores, Zion City, Lake County, Illinois.

Expiration of Subscriptions.

On every subscriber's copy of LEAVES OF HEALING or THE ZION BANNER we attach a yellow label bearing his name, address, and two numbers, the figures referring to the volume and the number with which the subscription will expire.

Thus, should your label number happen to be 16—1, you may know that your subscription expires with Volume XVI, Number 1, which will be October 22, 1904. Also take notice that LEAVES OF HEALING now completes a volume every six months, or twenty-six weeks, that being the number of papers which are put into a bound volume. Earlier in the life of the paper a volume contained fifty-two numbers, as LEAVES OF HEALING had fewer pages in those days.

By making yourselves familiar with these customs and remitting promptly you need never allow your subscription to lapse.

Send money only by Bank Draft, Postoffice or Express Money-order in favor of John Alexander Dowie, and address all letters intended for us to

ZION PRINTING AND PUBLISHING HOUSE,
Zion City, Lake County, Illinois.

Every Reader of Leaves of Healing Should Also Read The Zion Banner.

The cost is too small to be worth mentioning, being fifty cents for six months.

LESS THAN TWO CENTS A WEEK!

If you will put in a few hours' work among your friends, and obtain THREE NEW SUBSCRIBERS TO THE ZION BANNER, we will send you your own copy free.

YOU CAN GET THEM EASILY!

Just give it a trial.

Scarcely any news in THE ZION BANNER is reprinted in LEAVES OF HEALING.

Many people will read THE ZION BANNER who might not be interested in our other publications.

Resolve today that you will do this for the extension of the Kingdom of God.

ZION PRINTING AND PUBLISHING HOUSE,
Zion City, Illinois.

Warning to Subscribers.

Scarcely a week passes that we do not have complaints about money having been sent to us in currency, stamps, or silver, in the open mails, for renewals of subscriptions or for other purposes, WHICH WE HAVE NOT RECEIVED AND WHICH NEVER REACHES US.

Therefore, we desire to warn every member and friend of Zion sending money to us, to always use some safe means, preferably a money-order, or bank-draft on New York or Chicago, or personal check on Zion City Bank.

In conforming to this notice you will save yourselves trouble and expense, and us much annoyance.

ZION PRINTING AND PUBLISHING HOUSE,
Zion City, Illinois.

Changes in the New York City Branch.

Beginning with Lord's Day, October 2d, the meetings will be removed to the center of New York City, corner of Madison avenue and East One Hundred Twenty-fifth street. Sunday, 11 a. m., 3 p. m., and 8 p. m. Divine Healing Meeting every Thursday, 2:30 p. m. Overseer George L. Mason's new address, No. 4 St. Nicholas Terrace.

Early Morning Meeting in Shiloh Tabernacle

*REPORTED BY S. E. C., O. V. G., AND F. A. F.

WHEN the late Bishop Philips Brooks, of Massachusetts, was about to sail for Europe, having been asked to preach in a celebrated English cathedral, it was reported that some one asked him which sermon he intended to preach.

"Which sermon do I expect to preach?" replied the Bishop, "I have but one sermon—a needy world and a Sympathizing Savior!"

The noble Paul, in going to a certain Church, determined to know nothing among them save Jesus, the Christ, and Him crucified!

The greater the man and his mission, the more definitely and strenuously is everything in his thought and life directed toward one end.

He becomes a diamond point, with a tremendously big body behind it.

The lens—the eye—of the camera is small, but it has a tremendous capacity for seeing; and what it sees, it records; and what it records, all who will may read.

The Reverend John Alexander Dowie, the Prophet of the Restoration, and the Messenger of the Covenant, is the diamond point, the camera's eye, of the mightiest religious movement of the centuries.

No mortal man knows that so well as he.

A knowledge of God and of one's self is the sum of all knowledge.

To know one's self is to be conscious of great need.

To know God is to have that need supplied.

Mankind knows neither the one nor the other.

To the great majority, the body is the principal thing; and to some, "whose God is their belly," the body is all.

The latter-day prophet sees both spirit and body in correct proportion; and it is this to which he had been giving special emphasis in his addresses at the Early Morning Sacrifice of Praise and Prayer.

In his address on Lord's Day morning, August 28, 1904, he emphasized the value of the spirit of men, at the same time exalting the body as the Temple of the spirit.

His continued teaching on the value of embodiment was most enlightening and helpful.

It was an inspiration!

"Even God," said the speaker, "is embodied."

The curse of demons is disembodiment—a curse so great that they have sought to possess themselves of even the meanest forms of animal existence when they could get no other.

The inestimable blessing of a spiritual embodiment that has no limitations is to be obtained only by prayer.

And so God's servant urged his people to pray.

He told them that the greatest faculty of the spirit is that absolute intercourse with God by which one is able to pray and get answers.

Because the nominal church has gone out of business, so far as prayer is concerned, Zion must pray, and put her whole being into it.

Elijah the Restorer has but one sermon.

No one today talks as wisely as he, and no one expresses such a variety of Divine truth; but it is all part of one great, unfinished sermon.

It is a sermon on prayer—teaching the children of God how to so pray that all may become companions of God and habitations of God through the Spirit.

It is a sermon that connects the pitiful need of humanity with the plenteous Grace of God.

It is a sermon that is being heard around the world.

*The First Apostle has not revised the following report.

Shiloh Tabernacle, Zion City, Illinois, Lord's Day Morning, August 28, 1904.

The service was opened with the singing of Hymn No. 103

> Jesus, the very thought of Thee,
> With sweetness fills my breast;
> But sweeter far Thy Face to see,
> And in Thy Presence rest.

Prayer was then offered by the General Overseer, at the close of which he led the Congregation in the chanting of the Disciples' Prayer.

The General Overseer then said:

Let us read together, first in the Epistle of Paul to the Philippians, the 3d chapter.

The General Overseer and Congregation read alternately from the Inspired Word of God, from the 17th verse to the 21st verse, inclusive, of the 3d chapter of the Epistle of Paul to the Philippians.

Scripture Reading and Exposition.

The General Overseer said:

Who shall fashion anew the body of our humiliation, that it may be conformed to the body of His glory, according to the working whereby He is able even to subject all things unto Himself.

"The body of His glory"—the glorified body of the Christ—is, as far as I know, described in only one place: the 1st chapter of the Revelation of Jesus, the Christ.

It is interesting to notice how inconsistent with their contents are the titles of some of the books of the Bible.

The titles are not inspired.

For instance, the last book is headed as you see: "The Revelation of St. John the Divine."

It is not the Revelation of St. John the Divine.

The very first words of the book show whose revelation it is.

Will you all please tell me what you read there?

PEOPLE—"The Revelation of Jesus, the Christ."

GENERAL OVERSEER—It is not the Revelation of St. John; it is the Revelation of Jesus, the Christ, which He gave to His servant John—a totally different thing.

There is even a good deal of controversy as to who really wrote the book.

I am not quite so sure as I used to be that it was written by the Apostle John, although I am still inclined to believe that it was.

It might have been written by another John.

The author is not called Saint John, the Apostle, even in that title, and he nowhere calls himself an Apostle.

However, this wonderful book is the Revelation of Jesus, the Christ, which He gave to His servant, John; it does not matter which John it was.

I have a very learned essay from a noble lady in England who is much interested in our work, and has been a reader of LEAVES OF HEALING for years.

She has given me a very interesting memoir, in which she works out the idea that this was written by John the Baptist.

Whenever you talk about something in the Bible that is human, you get upon controversial ground.

As I looked at that last book this morning, I wished that it had not been called "The Revelation of St. John, the Divine."

The very first words in the book tell you whose the Revelation was: the Revelation of Jesus, the Christ, which God, the Father, gave to Him first, and which He sent and signified by His angel—His messenger—unto His servant, John.

Let us read this with attention.

The Revelation of Jesus, the Christ, which God gave Him—

The Eternal Father gave this to Jesus.

"Oh!" you say, "didn't Jesus know?"

No.

Jesus Himself told you that "of that day or that hour knoweth no one, not even the angels in Heaven, neither the Son, but the Father."

The Father has kept that in His own power.

There were revelations (the Christ Himself is our authority), which had yet to be given to Him as the Son.

I should like to get the fact deeply imprinted on your minds that this is the Revelation of Jesus, the Christ, which God, the Father, gave unto Him, and which He sent and signified by His messenger, His angel, unto His servant, John.

Who bare witness of the Word of God; and of the testimony of Jesus, the Christ, even of all things that He saw.

Blessed is he that readeth, and they that hear the words of the prophecy, and keep the things which are written therein; for the time is at hand.

John to the seven churches which are in Asia: Grace to you, and peace, from Him which is, and which was, and which is to come; and from the seven Spirits which are before His throne.

The Seven Spirits Before the Throne in Heaven.

I wonder how much you or any of us know about the Seven Spirits which are before His throne.

We do not even know their names, yet they must be spirits of surpassing majesty, and power, and dignity, since they are before the throne of Him who is, and was, and is to come.

And from Jesus, the Christ, who is the Faithful Witness, the Firstborn of the Dead, and the Ruler of the kings of the earth. Unto Him that loveth us, and loosed us from our sins by His blood.

I want the rulers and kings of the earth to remember this.

What a fuss they made about it in Australia and in England! One witty paper in Australia put it something like this: "What is all this fuss about? Is it because Dr. Dowie has said that Jesus, the Christ, is a bigger man than Edward VII.?"

That was the whole thing boiled down.

All that trouble was caused by my saying that when the Lord Jesus, the Christ, came, every ruler and potentate on this earth would have to take a back seat, and some of them away low down; that some of them would find it difficult to get in at all; and I was inclined to think that some kings like Edward VII., would get in only by the skin of their teeth.

No one who has a grain of honesty would doubt the truthfulness of what I said.

Neither rulers nor people like to hear that the Christ is the Ruler of the kings and of the peoples of the earth.

He is your Ruler and mine, and we have to toe the line and do just what He tells us.

And from Jesus, the Christ, who is the faithful Witness, the Firstborn of the Dead, and the Ruler of the kings of the earth. Unto Him that loveth us, and loosed us from our sins by His blood;

And He made us to be a kingdom, to be priests unto His God and Father; to Him be the glory and the dominion for ever and ever. Amen.

Members of the Holy Catholic Church a Kingdom.

Notice that the Revision does not read "He has made us to be kings and priests," but "He made us to be *a kingdom*, to be priests unto His God and Father."

Behold, He cometh with the clouds; and every eye shall see Him, and they which pierced Him; and all the tribes of the earth shall mourn over Him. Even so, Amen.

I am the Alpha and the Omega, saith the Lord God which is and which was and which is to come, the Almighty.

I John, your brother and partaker with you in the tribulation and kingdom and patience which are in Jesus, was in the isle that is called Patmos, for the Word of God and the testimony of Jesus.

I was in the Spirit on the Lord's Day, and I heard behind me a great Voice, as of a trumpet saying,

What Thou seest, write in a book, and send it to the seven churches; unto Ephesus, and unto Smyrna, and unto Pergamum, and unto Thyatira, and unto Sardis, and unto Philadelphia, and unto Laodicea.

And I turned to see the Voice which spake with me. And having turned I saw seven golden candlesticks.

I desire you to follow very closely the description of the Glorified Body of the Christ.

And in the midst of the candlesticks—

The Greek says lamp-stands.

No doubt he saw in his vision the seven-branched candelabra of the ancient Temple, symbolizing unity and perfection.

And in the midst of the candlesticks One like unto a son of man.

Some versions say, "the Son of Man," but I give it as the Revision has it.

One like unto a son of man, clothed with a garment down to the foot, and girt about at the breasts with a golden girdle.

And His head and His hair were white as white wool, white as snow; and His eyes were as a flame of fire;

And His feet like unto burnished brass, as if it had been refined in a furnace; and His voice as the voice of many waters.

And He had in His right hand seven stars: and out of His mouth proceeded a sharp two-edged sword: and His countenance was as the sun shineth in his strength.

And when I saw Him, I fell at His feet as one dead. And He laid His right hand upon me, saying, Fear not; I am the First and the Last,

And the Living One; and I was dead, and behold, I am alive for evermore, and I have the keys of Death and of Hades.

Hades is not a Place of Punishment.

The word "Hades," translated "hell" in the Old Version, does not mean a place of punishment for the wicked.

It means the world of unseen spirits, both good and bad.

Hades is not so much a particular location, as the key of the conditions of all spirits: "The keys of Death and of Hades."

Many of the translations in which the word "hell" is used are not good ones; for instance: "Thou wilt not leave My soul in hell, neither wilt Thou suffer Thine Holy One to see corruption."

You cannot imagine for one moment that the Christ's spirit was ever in the condition of those who were punished for sin in Gehenna, the Tartarus, the place of punishment.

His spirit descended into Hades, the world of unseen spirits, both good and bad.

It was He who bridged the gulf.

Abraham said that there was no possibility of going from where he was to the rich man in Hades.

He said, "Between us and you there is a great gulf fixed."

That gives you the idea that in the unseen world there is a place for the good and a place for the evil.

There was a great gulf between them, but it was Jesus, our Lord, who bridged that gulf; and only He could.

Make no mistake about it; that gulf was bridged.

One of the great blunders some people make, is to forget that that gulf was bridged.

What Abraham said was quite true: "Between us and you there is a great gulf fixed, that they which would pass from hence to you may not be able, and that none may cross over from thence to us."

But Jesus, our Lord, descended into Hades, and preached to the spirits in hell, to those who were disobedient in the days of Noah; those wicked, filthy, and abominable antediluvians who were so bad that God saw that every imagination of the thoughts of their hearts were only evil continually.

When the Christ descended to Hades, He went first to the place of the redeemed.

Between His Death and Resurrection the Christ Was in Paradise.

He did not go to heaven when He died.

Paradise is not heaven.

Paradeisos (Παράδεισος) is a Greek word with a different meaning; it is the garden around a great royal palace.

They used to call the gardens around the great palace at Susa, the Oriental palace of great ancient monarchs, *Paradeisos*.

It was called so hundreds of times in secular Greek.

Thus, when the Christ descended into Hades, He went to *Paradeisos* first, the place of the good spirits.

When He was hanging on the Cross He said to the penitent thief, "Today shalt thou be with Me in Paradise."

He did not refer to heaven; because after He rose from the dead He said to Mary: "Touch Me not; for I am not yet ascended unto the Father."

After He had done His work on earth, He went first to Paradise, and then down to the place of the wicked spirits, and preached to those spirits in prison.

You can clearly see two steps.

Get a good grasp of that.

He went to Paradise, not to heaven; but when He ascended He led captivity captive.

He doubtless took multitudes from Paradise to heaven, thus opening heaven to all believers.

Up to that time those who passed away did not go to heaven; they went to Paradise.

But we have a sure and certain hope that when we pass away, and are absent from the body, we shall be present with the Lord; and, as He is in heaven, we shall be there too.

We shall not go to Paradise; we shall go to heaven.

The Restoration Host May Yet Rescue the Lost in Hell.

Paradise must be quite near hell, because Abraham, who was in Paradise, saw the rich man in hell, and communication seemed to be very direct.

I believe that very likely we shall find it to be a place between here and hell, when we go down with Zion Restoration Host some day, to have it out with the Devil.

I have an intense desire that God will, in His infinite mercy, make me so good that I can go to hell and fight it out with the Devil.

I should like to have that task.

I should like to take some part in it anyway.

I do not know whether any of you have ever been ambitious to go to hell—some of you are very ambitious to go to heaven. You are dreadfully lazy, and think, "When we get to heaven we can loaf forever." [Laughter.]

That is the most miserable conception of heaven!

I do not believe that you who think that will ever get to heaven.

I do not believe that this people is looking forward with any very great delight to doing nothing

I like the spirit of this people who desire to be always doing something.

That is right.

Whenever work is dull, get a spade and dig in your back yard.

Do something!

Keep at it!

God did not leave the life of the Christ in Hades.

He did not suffer His Holy One to see corruption in His body.

He raised Him, and gave Him this Body of Glory of which we have just been reading.

It is a wonderful Body!

Write therefore the things which thou sawest, and the things which are, and the things which shall come to pass hereafter;

The mystery of the seven stars which thou sawest in My right hand, and the seven golden candlesticks. The seven stars are the angels of the seven churches: and the seven candlesticks are seven churches.

The Word Angel Means Messenger.

The 2d chapter begins and continues with the Message to the Churches:

To the angel of the Church in Ephesus write—

The word "angel" there means the Messenger of the Church.

All these early Churches had Messengers, who carried the messages from one Church to another.

When Paul would write an epistle to the Romans, it was held as very precious, and copies were made of it, and Messengers were sent with them from the Church in Rome to the Church in Corinth and in Philippi, and so on.

That is how the epistles became known to the Churches.

They had no LEAVES OF HEALING in those days, and they could not send the Messages as we do now.

May God bless the reading of His Word.

Hymn No. 95 was sung, after which the General Overseer delivered his Message:

THE GLORIFIED BODY.

INVOCATION.

Let the words of my mouth, and the meditations of my heart, be acceptable in Thy sight, and profitable unto this people, O Lord, and unto all to whom these words shall come. For the sake of Jesus. Amen.

TEXT.

For our citizenship is in Heaven; from whence also we wait for a Savior, the Lord Jesus, the Christ·

Who shall fashion anew the body of our humiliation,

That it may be conformed to the body of His glory, according to the working whereby He is able even to subject all things unto Himself.—*Philippians 3:20-21.*

The Body of Humiliation and the Body of Glory Widely Differ.

The body of humiliation and the body of glory—of Divine exaltation—what a contrast!

Yet you know that this body is of the very highest value.

We know of no other form that even God Himself has assumed.

God is spirit; so are you; so am I.

God is the Father of our spirits, and we are His offspring; but God is embodied, and so are we.

When Moses stood in the cleft of the rock and God's glory passed by him, he who had asked to see God Himself and was told that he could not see His face and live, saw the back parts of a man—a majestic man!

When the Christ came, it was a Man who came

Why should we shrink from the glorious fact that when God made us He made us in His own image; although this image is now marred by sin and corrupted, and has become a body of death, subject to evil?

Yet, even in its humiliation, it is the same body that God fashioned.

When our Lord Jesus, the Christ, came to this world to preach the Everlasting Gospel, He paid great attention to this body.

His sympathies for humanity were drawn out with intensity; he felt even pathetically painful sympathy as He saw the lepers whose bodies were falling away in decay bit by bit: finger tips rotting, nails falling off, joint after joint falling away, hand falling away, eyebrows going, the flesh eaten away until the eyes dropped out, tongues rotting—horrible!

That is the leper. Not death at once, but the most horrid, slow death.

Man's Body Designed to Be the Temple of God.

But it was the body His Father had made.

It was the Temple that God had designed to be His own dwelling-place, for He made man for Himself—to be a habitation for Himself, through the Spirit.

The apostles never shrank from telling Christians that their bodies were designed to be Temples of God.

So God caused His beloved Son to impress upon humanity the sacredness of the body and the fact that it was to be emancipated.

When the Christ preached that Gospel which God gave Him, He preached the Gospel of Salvation for the Spirit, the Soul, and the Body, and that Gospel has not changed.

Among the letters I received yesterday was one from Calcutta.

Last Wednesday night, you will remember, I told you about having received a letter that day from an officer of the British Army in Calcutta, whose child I had prayed for.

I was talking to you that evening, you will remember, about the fact that in this body we have a spiritual body, which, if we knew how to use the faculties which God has given us, might be projected vast distances.

I told you about the letter I had received from Calcutta—in which the gentleman thanked me very earnestly for praying, in answer to the cablegram he had sent; and I said that I felt very much when I prayed as if I was there with that child.

Do you remember?

PEOPLE—"Yes."

An Interesting and Suggestive Incident.

GENERAL OVERSEER—Only yesterday (Saturday) I received another letter; and I should like to read it to you, because it will illustrate what I shall talk about—a body which is even now growing within our body.

I was very much interested in this child; first, because of the pathetic tone of the cablegram; and also, because I had been greatly disappointed in not being able to visit India in my Around-the-World Visitation.

This is the letter I received yesterday:

6 JHUL ROAD, COSSIPORE, NEAR CALCUTTA, INDIA, July 28, 1904.

DEAR DOCTOR DOWIE:—Mother and I desire to thank you for your prayers. Our hearts are filled with praise and thanksgiving to our Heavenly Father for restoring our little boy to us.

He had been suffering from chronic dysentery.

We tried one medicine after another, and did everything we were told; but nothing did the little fellow any good.

Saturday, July 16th, we all could see that our baby was going fast.

Cramps had set in.

His little body seemed almost like a bag of bones.

We felt powerless to do anything for him, yet we felt we could not let him go.

Saturday afternoon, at two o'clock, my father cabled to you, asking you to pray for him.

Twenty-four hours after we sent the cablegram, the little fellow roused himself and said, "Father! Father! don't you hear Dr. Dowie praying for me? I shall get well now."

From that hour he has been improving, and is now going about.

Praise God!

Praise God for a Healer in Jesus as well as a Savior from sin.

We have known Jesus as a Savior for many, many years, but we thought He only healed when He was here on earth.

My Bible seems a new Book to me, and Jesus is so precious.

I thank God that He has raised you up to give to this poor, sinful, sorrowing world the Full Gospel.

May He spare you and bless you and your family very abundantly.

I am not a member of the Christian Catholic Church in Zion yet.

I am waiting on God to be led, and where He leads I will follow.

Yours truly in Jesus, MURIEL ANGELL SMITH.

The Body of Glory is now Being Fashioned.

I will explain to you why I read this letter.

Last week I said that the Body of Glory, which we shall have, is being fashioned now.

It is the body from heaven; it is the spiritual body. "Not for that we would be unclothed," said the Apostle, "but that we would be clothed upon, that what is mortal may be swallowed up of life."

He did not want to be a disembodied spirit.

Disembodied spirits are devils—devils which are so eager to be embodied that Satan went into a snake, and I do not know that he is out of the snake yet.

It does not seem to me that he is.

Devils went into the pigs, and it does not seem to me that they have gone out of them yet.

Is there anything more filthy than the pig?

Is there anything more like a devil than the dirty, filthy pig?

They love everything that is unclean.

How Christians can eat that dirty, stinking, filthy flesh, of which God Almighty said, "Of their flesh ye shall not eat, and their carcasses ye shall not touch; they are unclean unto you," is more than I can imagine.

There is not much Christianity of a high and holy type in a pig-feeder or a pig-eater.

The negros that feed upon pork, and the white people about them that feed upon pork, are a murderous, filthy lot, always ready to murder each other.

The Eating of Swine's Flesh Promotes Depravity.

I blame pork for a great deal; both for the horrible depravity of the poor negros in the South, and the still more horrible depravity of the white people that torture them to death.

A pig-eating people are a gross, filthy, brutal, murderous people.

The body which we now have is a body in which is being fashioned, in a large degree, the body which is from heaven?

Why?

Because the Holy Spirit, who comes into us, and who is the Transforming Power, is already changing this body of our humiliation into a Body of Glory—a body in which every power glorifies God; a body in which even the thoughts are God's thoughts.

In that body the brain is God's, the heart is God's, the passions and powers are God's, and are used only for Him—the whole being is brought under control for Him.

The greatest faculty that man can possibly have is the faculty of absolute intercourse between himself and God; of absolute, and sure, and certain accord with God's Will in such a manner that prayer is heard and answered.

The church, for the most part, has gone out of business as far as answer to prayer is concerned.

Ministers preach sermons today and say, "O God, give increase to Thy Word. O God, give me a message from Thyself."

Sermons that Do Not Save Men.

Their prayer is a lie, for they have the whole message inside of their coat pocket

They take it out and read it.

They concocted it under the gaslight.

Perhaps they cribbed half of it, and the other half is weaker than the half they cribbed.

Then they read it, and no one upon God Almighty's earth is made better.

The people are yawning and sleepy, but they say, "O God, save the people!"

Then they sing the Doxology and go away, and are greatly surprised if any one is saved.

They never expected it, and they are not disappointed in their expectations.

This is no railing accusation.

For instance, in Australia, the various sections of the Methodist church got together some years ago for a special revival.

That year they lost more members in the cities than they had ever lost before, and at the end of the year, they found that the work of hundreds of ministers and thousands of Sabbath-school teachers and "exhausters" (perhaps I should have said exhorters) had added but one.

That is in their own statistics.

My own opinion is that there was not one.

My own opinion is that a very close examination of the statistics would have shown a loss of very many.

Their own statistics show that hundreds were lost in the cities.

It was only in certain country districts that some godly people were found, and they got in some converts, and managed to let them all escape, with the exception of one.

A Church that Does Not Get Results Should Go out of Business.

If this Church is not filled with men and women who know how to pray and get results, we had better go out of business.

There is no use in maintaining churches where hundreds of ministers, and teachers, and "exhausters" of every kind, work and talk, and spend millions of dollars, and then come out at the end of the year with one additional member.

Christianity is a dead thing if that is all there is to it, and we had better find a religion that has an Active and Living Power.

I am a business man in the ministry, and I would not stay in the business of praying for the sick and caring for them and of winning men to God, if I received no answers to prayer, and accomplished nothing, and won none to God.

I would say, "You can put some one else in this business, Lord, for I am no good. I will dig potatoes or do something else that is honest; but I will not pretend to be a minister, like hundreds of 'exhausters' down there in Australia, and come out at the end of the year with only one convert."

That seems to me to be downright wickedness.

If I were in business and sent out men with capital and large resources to do business for me, and at the end of the year, with all the money I had given them, they did not come back with the twentieth part of one per cent., I would say, "This business must close!"

The Church Must Get to Business and Pray.

Let us get to business; and when we pray, let us pray in the spirit until the whole of our being prays; until the dying can hear our voices thousands of miles away, as the little boy heard mine when he said, "Father, don't you hear Dr. Dowie pray?"

He heard, and he wondered that his father did not.

The little bag of bones rose up in the bed and said, "Father, don't you hear?"

You Elders and Overseers, get to business and pray!

You Evangelists, Deacons, and Deaconesses, you members of Zion Restoration Host, get to business and pray!

Why should you have to ask me to pray for any one in your homes?

Why can you not get to the place where your whole being prays?

When you pray let your whole being go out.

There Will Be No Limitations in the Glorified Body.

The body that we shall have is one in which there will be no limitations.

It will be like the body of the Christ after He rose from the dead, which went in and out of closed doors, and which appeared to disappear, and yet was real.

There was no blood in the Christ's body after He rose from the dead.

He said, "A Spirit hath not flesh and bones, as ye behold Me having."

There is no blood in the body which is in heaven.

That body will be real, having every part and member that we now have; but it will be bloodless.

It will be glorified; and that will make us glorified fathers and glorified mothers in the Millennium, when we come back with the Christ to reign and rule on this earth.

There will be a wonderful difference between these bodies and the red-nosed, beer-soaked, and tobacco-soaked bodies that you find everywhere around you today—bodies that reek and stink with filth and drugs.

This is a City, to a large extent, of people who have clean

faces, clean eyes, clean hearts, clean bodies, and clean spirits.

If it is not, it is because you seek the Devil: for we have done everything we can to make it difficult for you to do wrong and easy for you to do right.

The Spiritual Should Not Be Less than the Material.

May we so live that these mortal bodies shall be quickened and purified.

As we increasingly desire that these bodies shall be Temples of God that He can use, we shall become more and more a people prepared for His work.

Then, when we pray, the little one in the far-away land, will say, "Father, don't you hear? They are praying for me!"

The little fellow knew I was praying.

May God grant that you shall so pray, that God will hear, and that the sick will hear.

Why not?

We have telegraphy that is wireless, and we can throw out a message into the open air.

I was nearing the coast of America last June when, away on the horizon, I saw the smoke of a steamer.

I could not tell which way she was going, but I thought she was coming toward us.

I looked through my glass and, behold, the steamer was coming toward us; but I could see only the top of her funnel.

It was early morning, and every now and then I would take my glass and look.

Presently I saw that which made me think that she was probably a large steamer, for I could see a little of the mast.

While I was standing, intently looking, there came a tap upon my shoulder, and an officer handed me an envelope saying, "Here is a telegram for you, Doctor."

"A telegram?" I said.

"Yes, a wireless telegram."

I opened it.

It was a wireless telegram from the steamer that was approaching, and had been sent before we saw the steamer's smoke.

It came from Deacon Natino, who was on his way to Europe.

The message read: "Peace to thee. I am on my way to Europe. Sorry I shall not see you in New York. Pray for Italy."

That is his native country.

He is a Deacon in this Church, and a very excellent Italian merchant of New York City.

How had the message come?

Was it a fraud?

Not at all.

From the wire at the top of that distant vessel the message, "Peace to thee," had been flung out into the air!

Why "Leaves of Healing" Is Such a Power.

Oh, beloved, can you not fling out your prayer and make it reach some one?

Is not prayer a more wonderful power than wireless telegraphy?

People will know that you are real when you put your whole being into what you say to them.

God knows that you are real when you put your whole being into what you say to Him.

The reason that LEAVES OF HEALING is such a power is because I put my whole being into it.

They reach the poor people in far-away India; not poor, perhaps, in this world's goods or in worldly station, but sorrow-stricken and weary.

One little fellow read LEAVES OF HEALING, and, evidently, before he was sick, he got to know about Doctor Dowie and Divine Healing.

Perhaps he had said, "Send the message."

Have it said by people all over the world, "Don't you hear? We asked God's people in Zion to pray. Don't you hear?"

God hears.

He heard Paul when he got down to business in the street called Straight.

He told Ananias to go and say certain things to Paul, because the prayer had reached heaven.

Paul had prayed many prayers before that time, for he was a great Pharisee, but they never reached heaven as that prayer did. He had got down to business.

The Dying May Hear Our Prayers.

Oh, that God would open your eyes to see His glory, and open your hearts to receive His power! That by and by we might so pray, that all over this world the dying would say, "Father, don't you hear? They are praying!"

Before the vessel of which I told you had come up to us, Deacon Natino had received a message from me in reply, and I saw him and his wife, through my glass, energetically waving to me as the two ships passed.

Can we not be the Messengers of Heaven all over the earth today? God grant it!

May you be so pure that God will help you, that you may help one another.

This is the great aim of Zion.

If these hands are no better than other hands; if this organization is no better than other organizations; then we are no stronger than any one else.

Do not let us make a mock of being a religious community. Let us get out of business and go back into the world and say we belong there, if we have no power with God.

But if we are what God would have us, we shall know how to pray.

My brothers and sisters, let us get down to business.

All who want to get to business for God, stand.

PRAYER OF CONSECRATION.

My God and Father, in Jesus' Name I come to Thee. Take me as I am. Make me what I ought to be in spirit, in soul, and in body. Give me power to do right, that I may be in communion with Thee, purified and made ready for Thy work, so that this people may be a people who can pray and be heard in heaven and on earth. Give us a good day. For Jesus' sake. Amen.

After the singing of the hymn, "I Stand on Zion's Mount," the General Overseer closed the service by pronouncing the

BENEDICTION.

Beloved, abstain from every form of evil. And may the very God of Peace Himself sanctify you wholly; and I pray God your whole spirit, and soul, and body be preserved entire, without blame, unto the coming of our Lord Jesus, the Christ. Faithful is He that calleth you, who also will do it. The grace of our Lord Jesus, the Christ, the love of God, our Father, the fellowship of the Holy Spirit, our Comforter and Guide, one Eternal God, abide in you, bless you, and keep you, and all the Israel of God everywhere, forever. Amen.

EARLY MORNING SACRIFICE OF PRAISE AND PRAYER.

*REPORTED BY O. V. G., A. C. R., AND E. S.

The Early Morning Meeting of Lord's Day, September 18, 1904, was a foreshadowing of that wonderful service of the afternoon, when the man of God publicly declared himself the First Apostle of the Lord Jesus, the Christ, in the Christian Catholic and Apostolic Church in Zion, and assumed the Apostolic Office and its responsibilities.

Out-of-town officers and members of the Church, together with the large influx of visitors, combined to make the attendance probably the largest ever gathered at these early morning meetings.

Although the morning was dark, and the skies overcast with threatening clouds, the people poured into Shiloh Tabernacle until the body of the great building was filled.

The Announcement of the Assumption of the Apostolic Office, so long ardently desired by the Church, had been received with a feeling of intense joy, and a quickening of spiritual life had already appeared.

And now that the day had come which was to mark an onward step in the Church and in the establishment of God's Kingdom on earth, and although fraught with so momentous an import to the world, instead of commotion, a quietness pervaded every home and all the ranks of Zion.

Zion had been listening to God's Voice.

That Voice was unmistakable.

And, as with a Visible Presence, the Holy Spirit bore witness to the truth proclaimed by the man of God in the early morning of the day.

*The First Apostle has not revised the following report.

Shiloh Tabernacle, Zion City, Illinois, Lord's Day Morning, September 18, 1904.

The meeting was opened by the singing of Hymn No. 203.

In the cross of Christ I glory,
Towering o'er the wrecks of time;
All the light of sacred story,
Gathers round its head sublime.

Prayer was offered by the General Overseer after which the Congregation joined in singing Hymn No. 95.

Scripture Reading and Exposition.

The General Overseer then said:

Let us read from the Inspired Word of God in the 1st Epistle of the Apostle Peter, the 5th chapter.

The elders therefore among you I exhort, who am a fellow elder, and a witness of the sufferings of the Christ, who am also a partaker of the glory that shall be revealed:

Tend the flock of God which is among you, exercising the oversight, not of constraint, but willingly, according unto God; nor yet for filthy lucre, but of a ready mind;

Neither as lording it over the charge allotted to you, but making yourselves ensamples to the flock.

And when the Chief Shepherd shall be manifested, ye shall receive the crown of glory that fadeth not away

Likewise, ye younger, be subject unto the elder.

The disobedience of this injunction is one of the saddest things in modern life; not that it is peculiar to modern life, for the insolence of unbridled passion and foolish youth belongs to every age.

However, it does seem sometimes as if there were more of it today than ever; that the younger try to make the elders submit to them.

They have an idea that they are up-to-date, and that the elders are out of date.

I humbly submit that I am up-to-date, and that the younger are quite a little behind.

The most astounding acts of insolence are often to be observed in family life, even where young people have been carefully trained, when, without the slightest respect, they coolly look into the faces of their elders and tell them that they do not know what they are talking about; that if the elders only knew what *they* knew, they would be very different.

They have been to school, and have learned many things that the older people do not know; therefore, they say, it becomes the elders to submit to the younger.

That is a piece of the most astounding insolence!

You little philosophical chicks, who go about airing your philosophy, are like that little chicken in the fable, who asked its mother where it came from, and was told, "Why, you came out of an egg."

"An egg!" the chicken exclaimed, "you cannot make me believe that this beautiful body of mine, with all its feathers and frills, and these beautiful little legs, came out of an egg. You are altogether behind the times!"

Then the philosophic chick began to tell about evolution, and that it was quite impossible for it to have come out of an egg.

Just then the father came along, and gave the chick a vigorous peck, and said, "You little fool, there is a bit of the egg-shell sticking to your back." [Laughter.]

It seems to me, sometimes, that if these philosophic chicks would only stop their talk about evolution, and take a look at themselves in the nearest looking-glass, they might see some of the egg-shell sticking to their backs.

It would become them better to be more humble, and to believe the old mother-hen when she tells them that she hatched them out of an egg.

Deep and Unaffected Humility the Most Beautiful Grace.

That is a very simple illustration, but that which it is intended to illustrate is very important.

On the other hand, I think that older people should admit that their sons and daughters who have been well educated, have learned some things that they do not know.

They should rejoice in the larger knowledge of their children, and encourage them, and be kind to them.

But children should remember that knowledge is not the greatest thing.

Wisdom is the principal thing, and the greatest thing is Love.

With Wisdom and Love, young people should remember that if they know some things that their parents do not know, they owe it to the self-sacrificing love of their parents, who gave them the facilities to obtain the knowledge, and worked hard that they might provide them with the necessary resources.

To me, the most beautiful grace in either a youth or a maiden, a man or a woman, is a deep and unaffected humility; and I pray that God will give us all that.

Likewise, ye younger, be subject unto the elder. Yea, all of you gird yourselves with Humility, to serve one another: for God resisteth the proud, but giveth grace to the humble.

Humble yourselves therefore under the mighty hand of God, that He may exalt you in due time;

Casting all your anxiety upon Him, because He careth for you.

Be sober, be watchful: your adversary, the Devil, as a roaring lion, walketh about, seeking whom he may devour:

Whom withstand steadfast in your Faith, knowing that the same sufferings are accomplished in your brethren who are in the world.

I may say that there is another reading in that passage which I like better:

Whom withstand steadfast in the Faith, knowing that the same sufferings are being accomplished in your brotherhood who are in the world.

And the God of all grace, who called you unto His eternal glory in the Christ, after that ye have suffered a little while, shall Himself perfect, stablish, strengthen you.

To Him be the dominion for ever and ever. Amen.

By Silvanus, our faithful brother, as I account him, I have written unto you briefly, exhorting, and testifying that this is the true grace of God: stand ye fast therein.

She that is in Babylon, elect together with you, saluteth you; and so does Mark my son.

Salute one another with a kiss of love.

Peace be unto you all that are in the Christ.

After the singing of Hymn No. 23, the General Overseer made the announcements, after which he delivered his Message.

HUMILITY.

INVOCATION.

Let the words of my mouth and the meditations of my heart be acceptable in Thy sight, and profitable unto this people, O Lord, my Strength and my Redeemer.

TEXT.

Yea, all of you, gird yourselves with Humility, to serve one another: for God resisteth the proud, but giveth grace to the humble.

The Holy Scriptures say that Moses was the Meekest man on all the earth.

One thing is certain, he was not the Weakest.

Some people have the idea that Meekness and Weakness are synonymous terms; they are not.

He who was Meek and Lowly in heart, who invited all humanity to find rest in Him, was not weak.

He was the Son of God, created with Power, and with Divine Humility.

Meekness and weakness are opposites.

A man that is meek is not weak; and a man that is weak is not meek.

Oftentimes the weakest man is the proudest man.

There are no limits to his good opinion of himself.

I trust that we all shall be clothed and girded with Humility; but Humility does not mean abject groveling.

I never would allow you to grovel at my feet, and I never will grovel at your feet.

Meekness and weakness are opposites.

The man that is meek, is strong in the sight of God.

The man that is weak in the sight of God is proud, and heady, and foolish, and needs humility very much.

It requires greater humility to wield power than to be inactive.

It requires more humility to take an Office such as God imposes upon me today than it would to shun its responsibility, and to seek refuge in the cry that I am too weak for the place.

I believe that I am exceedingly weak.

I believe that I am so weak that I am utterly unsuited to the place, were it not that I will glory in my weakness, that the power of the Christ may rest upon me.

I believe that His grace is sufficient for me.

I believe that I in myself am insufficient for this or any other task.

I never felt sufficient at any time, for my ministry.

The General Overseer First Entered Upon a Lowly Ministry.

I, by my own choice, entered into my ministry in a very humble district with a very little church.

I declined a city church that I might take a church away out in the wilderness, and learn how to take care of sheep that had gone astray, and were scattered.

However, I began lower than that.

I began my ministry in ministering to poor, bed-ridden, dying people.

I would not talk to large assemblies.

I took my Bible, and sat down in the incurable wards of the dying, in hospitals where it was offensive to be.

The bodies of the inmates stank; their minds stank; their lives stank.

They were people who had been filthy and wicked all their lives.

I began my ministry there, and I said that if God, the Almighty, could bless me to some of these old sinners He could bless me anywhere.

Then one day I said to God, "O God, there are people who are worse off than they."

I discovered that as I passed a lunatic asylum.

I went in and said to the superintendent, "Do you know me?"

"Yes, Mr. Dowie," he said, "I know you well."

"May I talk to these insane people?" I asked.

"I should very much like you to try," he answered.

"Well," I said, "I will come down some day; you get them all together."

So one day he got the men and women together, and I began to talk to the lunatics.

I believed that if God could bless me to the miserable, destitute sinners in a lunatic asylvm He could bless me to any one.

I knew also that when I got out into the big world, I would have to preach to many lunatics.

Sometimes I found, in speaking to them, that some of the lunatics knew a good deal.

For instance, there was one woman who would go into fits every time I spoke, and I asked, "Why does she go into fits?"

One of her neighbors said, "I will tell you, Mr. Dowie, why it is. It is only to attract your attention."

I found that was true.

She had the capacity of working herself up into a fit whenever she wanted to.

God Has Honored the Humility of the Lowly.

When I entered upon my ministry I ministered to the most depraved and insane.

Later I talked to public audiences, and I found them more depraved than those in the asylums.

This was especially demonstrated when I went back to Sydney last winter; it seemed to me as though the whole people had gone mad.

However, they are beginning to think it over now, and to wonder why they did it.

The Devil can make great fools of people if they are not careful.

I asked God that if ever I was to be His minister, I should be made strong to help the weak; wise to help the foolish; and kind and considerate to help all men; and that, above all things, I should be girded with humility.

God has given me a high place in His ministry today, but He knows, whatever you may not know, that I started in His work with a desire to serve Him all my life in the lowest place, if He thought it well to keep me there.

I was quite willing to minister to miserable incurables and lunatics all my life.

I was far more willing to minister to them than to assemblies full of hypocrites.

I refused to preach in large churches; and ministers who came to hear me talk to the poor, sick, and destitute, would say, "If you only would deliver that discourse in my church!"

To one of these men I replied, "If I did, I should fill it; but I should like to first get rid of those that are in it now, because your church is full of hypocrisy The day will come when these hypocrites will destroy your church."

That prophecy was fulfilled.

That church, which at that time was filled each Lord's Day with wealthy people, I found when I visited Australia a few months ago, had but thirty people in its largest audience.

I saw the very last of the beloved pastor whom I had known so well.

He had held on to this people that I and others told him were hypocrites.

He was a very charitable man; he could not even find time to fight the Devil.

My opinion is that if he had met the Devil anywhere, he would have stepped out of the way to give him the whole road.

I never felt like that.

If I meet the Devil I like to get into the middle of the road, and say, "You go back where you came from—to hell—that is where you belong!"

If he says, "I will not go back; I will fight you," I say, "Very well, I am willing to fight, too."

I have always taken the middle of the road, and I have not altogether failed.

The General Overseer Less than the Least of All Saints.

I thank God that I have not lost the Humility with which I began my ministry.

I thank God that in entering upon this Apostolic Ministry I am not uttering foolish words when I say that I feel as if I were less than the least of all saints.

Mark that word! Less than the least of all saints.

I do not say less than the least of all people.

You will please remember that Paul did not say, "I am less than the least of all people;" he said, "I am less than the least of all the holy people."

I am less than the least of all the saints in heaven, and, it may be of the saints on earth.

When you find a perfectly holy person on this earth, you will find my superior, because I am not perfectly holy.

I make no pretensions to being perfectly holy.

If you imagine that the First Apostle of the Christian Catholic Apostolic Church in Zion today is a perfectly infallible man, you are mistaken.

I am a fallible man; but, when I speak the Word of the Lord in the Name of the Lord, I am His Apostle, and I must be obeyed.

I am less than the least of all the holy ones; and not worthy to be called an Apostle, but I do not feel that I am a whit behind the chief of the Apostles.

A Little Talk with the Apostle Peter.

If Peter is to be counted the chief, then I shall have a little talk with Peter, and say, "Peter, I never did some of the mean things you did.

"I never denied my Lord with oaths and curses when He was suffering; never!

"Peter, I never laid a burden upon the people of God, such as you laid at Antioch, and for which Paul reproved you.

"Peter, you were a great man, but I have not gone into the sins that you have; and I am thankful that I have not.

"I am not your inferior, Peter; but I love you; you are a mighty man of God.

"I wish that I had had your advantages, and had seen the Lord in the Mount, and had walked and talked with Him.

"Peter, I love Him, not having seen Him. I believed Him, although I had never seen the prints of the nails in His hands.

"I did not see Him when He rose from the grave; but Paul, who also did not see Him, said, 'I reckon that I am not a whit behind the very chiefest Apostles.'

"Jesus said, 'Blessed are they that have not seen, and yet have believed.'

"I have not seen Him, but I believe."

The time has come for some man whom God makes strong to take the First Apostleship.

It has been lost to the Church, and it has been assumed by Apostates.

It has been assumed by those who have been followers of False Prophets.

It has been assumed by those who have no right to the assumption

I would rather be killed now, and be clothed in my grave-clothes before three o'clock this afternoon, than walk up here in my Apostolic robes, if I am not God's First Apostle, in these Times of Restoration.

I would rather my life should end now than that I should take a step that God would not approve

I have no desire to take it for my own part.

The General Overseer Has No Desire for the Apostolic Office.

I have no desire for the office.

I only desire to do the Will of God, and to undertake an

office which, perhaps, no one else in the world, today, is able to undertake.

If I thought otherwise, I should say to that man, "You take that office; you can do it better than I."

I should be glad for him to come here and take it.

But I have not found any one who understood what he was about particularly anxious to be a prophet.

I have not found any one particularly anxious to be a real Apostle.

I find some people very anxious to be apostles, who seem to be proper subjects for one of the wards in a lunatic asylum, and it would be very kind to take care of them for a while.

I am assuming this Office with my mind perfectly clear; but I am not assuming an office that personally I would care to assume at all.

It is only a sense of Divine obligation, and the fact that I believe that I have the right to appeal to God to give me the strength to fulfil the duties of that Office, that would ever give me the power or the right to assume it.

In this matter I am supported, I know, by your convictions and your prayers.

I am supported by the convictions and prayers of a vast number of people throughout the whole world, many of whom are not in Zion.

One of the sweetest letters I have received this week, came from a man living in Prairie avenue, Chicago.

I do not know anything about him except that he is a man of culture and Christian character.

He says that he has been attending my ministry for a number of years, and he frequently attends it out here.

He said, among other things, "I hope that when you stand before your congregation next Lord's Day, you will wear the proper Apostolic vestments."

How Apostolic Vestments Were Suggested.

I had not thought about vestments until after I had finished last week's issue of LEAVES OF HEALING; but the moment that number was finished I saw the necessity for the proper vestments.

I saw the necessity of getting robes as nearly as possible like those worn in Apostolic Times.

I found that there were no Apostolic robes.

All the painters and sculptors differ in their conception of the style of the robes worn by the Apostles.

I had to go back to the robes that God Himself had directed to be made and worn by His High Priests.

I had to come to see that the Priesthood and the Apostolic Office were one.

The question gave me great concern and some sleepless nights —a very rare thing for me.

At last I said, "Lord, I will wear no robes except those that You Yourself designed."

You will find in the 28th chapter of Exodus, that God Himself was the Designer of the robes of the High Priest.

I am not a High Priest of the Aaronic priesthood; I have nothing to do with the Aaronic priesthood.

The Aaronic priesthood has gone.

Nor am I the Christ who is the High Priest forever, after the order of Melchizedek.

I am His Apostle; and, as such today, I shall wear the robes of my Office—robes of beauty and of glory.

The First Apostle Will Wear Robes Designed by God and Made by Zion Women.

One of the things I love about them is that they were designed in Zion after the pattern shown by God to Moses, in the Mount; they were also made by Zion hands, that lovingly labored on them night and day.

I thank God for that, but once more I say, that I would rather lie in my grave-clothes at three o'clock today, than stand in these Apostolic robes, if this were not the Will of God.

I would rather breathe my last breath, and go to my God, than take an office which He has not given to me; and if you will pray that that may be so, I shall be glad.

I am not afraid to say that, because God knows my heart.

Therefore, in entering upon this Office, as I hope and believe I shall, by the grace of God, I want to ask you to pray for me, that I may have the strength and the grace necessary to follow Him who is the Apostle and High Priest of our Confession.

May God grant it!

So far as I follow Him, will you follow me?

PEOPLE—"Yes."

GENERAL OVERSEER—Then rise and tell Him so.

PRAYER OF CONSECRATION.

My God and Father, in Jesus' Name we come to Thee. Take us as we are. Make us what we ought to be. Help us to follow Thee. Help us to follow Thy servant, so far as He follows Thee; to be obedient to Thee; to be obedient to him, so far as He obeys Thee. Give us grace, therefore, to understand our places, his place, and Thy place; and so to fulfil Thy Will that we may all take our places by and by in heaven above. For Jesus' sake. Amen [*All repeat the prayer, clause by clause, after the General Overseer.*]

The service was then closed by the General Overseer's pronouncing the

BENEDICTION.

Beloved, abstain from every form of evil. And may the very God of Peace Himself sanctify you wholly; and I pray God your whole spirit, and soul, and body be preserved entire, without blame, unto the coming of our Lord Jesus, the Christ. Faithful is He that calleth you, who also will do it. The grace of our Lord Jesus, the Christ, the love of God, our Father, the fellowship of the Holy Spirit, our Comforter and Guide, one Eternal God, abide in you, bless you, and keep you, and all the Israel of God everywhere, forever. Amen.

Change of Location in Toronto, Canada.

Zion Gathering in Toronto, Canada, has secured the old Friends' meeting house, 34 Pembroke street, where services will hereafter be conducted. It is easily reached by transferring from any street car line in the city to the Belt Line. Get off at Wilton avenue, and go west one block to Pembroke. Elder Brooks has also changed his residence to No. 360 Parliament street.

OFFICIAL REPRESENTATIVES OF ZION

The following addresses of Official Representatives of Zion at important centers throughout the world, are given for the convenience of correspondents:

In the United States

¶ ¶ Overseer George L. Mason, 206 West Eighty-sixth street, New York City.

¶ ¶ Overseer William Hamner Piper, 17 Capin street, New Dorchester, Massachusetts.

¶ ¶ Elder R. N. Bouck, 2129 Mt. Vernon street, Philadelphia, Pennslyvania.

¶ ¶ Elder A. Ernst, 2611 Fourth avenue, Seattle, Washington.

¶ ¶ Elder A. E. Arrington, 501 West Fourth street, Cincinnati, Ohio.

¶ ¶ Elder W. B. Taylor, 1350 East Sixteenth street, Fruitvale, California.

¶ ¶ Elder L. C. Hall, San Antonio, Texas.

¶ ¶ Elder Frank L. Brock, 3401 Morgan street, St. Louis, Missouri.

In Foreign Countries

¶ ¶ Overseer H. E. Cantel, 81 Euston road, London, N. W., England.

¶ ¶ Overseer Wilbur Glenn Voliva, Arlington, 43 Park road, St. Kilda, Melbourne, Victoria, Australia.

¶ ¶ Overseer Daniel Bryant, Box 3074, Johannesburg, Transvaal, South Africa.

¶ ¶ Elder Carl Hodler, 76 Bahnhofstrasse, Zürich, Switzerland.

¶ ¶ Elder Arthur S. Booth-Clibborn, 139 Weesperzijde, Amsterdam, Holland.

¶ ¶ Elder E. B. Kennedy, Zion, Haskell road, Shanghai China.

¶ ¶ Elder R. M. Simmons, 525 Grove Crescent, Vancouver, B. C.

¶ ¶ Elder Eugene Brooks, 360 Parliament street, Toronto, Ontario, Canada.

General Financial Agents

¶ ¶ Deacon N. B. Rideout, Financial Agent for South Africa, Box 3074, Johannesburg, Transvaal, South Africa.

¶ ¶ Elder Percy Clibborn, Financial Agent for Europe, 76 Bahnhofstrasse, Zürich, Switzerland.

¶ ¶ Deacon John W. Innes, Financial Agent for the United Kingdom, 81 Euston Road, London, N. W., England.

Financial, Commercial and Industrial Notes

ZION LACE INDUSTRIES, after producing the first piece of Lace, the doily mentioned in the last LEAVES OF HEALING, at once began the designing and drafting of Fancy Laces, which has continued up to the present time, with wonderful success.

The laces are made up in sets, consisting of eight and ten widths, ranging from six inches to half an inch; and also all-over nets, which are used for yokes, waists, and lace dresses.

The different styles of Lace produced in Zion Lace Industries are Valenciennes, Normandy, Point de Paris, and Fancy Laces.

The manufacture of these laces continued until the fall of 1902, a period of nearly eighteen months, during which time a very large stock was accumulated. At the time just referred to, the goods were put on the market, and the success of the undertaking was at once confirmed by an unprecedented rush of orders, so that the entire stock was depleted within three months.

The demand for our stock has been continuous, and the salesmen constantly report to us words of high appreciation and praise, for the beauty and originality of Zion Laces, that are given by the best merchants of the country.

HENRY STEVENSON,
General Manager.

Zion City General Stores is one of the attractive features of Zion City.

Its employees are gathered from many parts of this and other lands, and they work together in harmony.

Visitors to the City are interested as they see the neat and attractive appearance of every Department.

In many respects this Institution is unlike other commercial establishments in the same line of trade.

Beginning every morning with prayer and praise, every employee is made conscious of the fact that this is God's business, and that nothing but the best service is acceptable to Him. While we do not claim perfection, yet the standard of business excellence is held very high, and every employee is being trained to this end.

It may surprise many readers of LEAVES OF HEALING to know that patrons of the General Stores are to be found in nearly every state of the Union and in many foreign countries.

We have a thoroughly equipped department which devotes its entire time to looking after the interests of our outside friends.

Among our outside customers are persons who, although not members of the Church, appreciate the privilege of purchasing merchandise from an Institution that does a pure, clean, honest business.

Being headquarters for all Zion Products, we are desirous that members and friends of Zion everywhere shall be users of them.

Full particulars and detailed quotations are given in a new illustrated catalog which we have just issued.

We solicit correspondence with every one interested in this branch of Zion's work.

W. HURD CLENDINEN,
General Manager.

Among our mail received at the Factory last week was a letter from one of our customers, containing the following words: "Thank God, that our beloved Zion, through its newly established Soap Industry, has taken one more long stride away from the *unspeakable hog*."

When I read those words, I said to myself, that would furnish a good text for a sermon on the unclean hog. We are reminded of the words in Leviticus 11:8, "Of their flesh ye shall not eat, and their carcasses ye shall not touch."

I wonder how many of our Zion members realize that when they use soap made in the factories outside of Zion they are taking in their hands and washing their body with an article that is very largely made of the carcass of the filthy *hog*.

Let me tell you, it is not the healthy *hog*, if there is such a thing, that goes into soap, but diseased animals that cannot in any way be used as a food product.

I was told a few days ago of an incident that occurred in Iowa recently.

A young man had left his father's farm and gone to a neighboring state to attend college. His expenses were to be met by the sale of a large herd of hogs that had been raised on the farm. Shortly after entering school he received a letter from his father stating that nearly the entire herd had died of cholera, and that therefore he would have to abandon his school and come home at once.

The son, who was more worldly-wise than the father, sent a telegram containing these words, "Hogs are never a loss; keep their carcasses till I get home and I will dispose of them for cash."

The young man knew of a near-by soap factory, and upon his arrival hauled every hog to the factory and disposed of them for a sufficient sum to pay all the expenses of his college course.

Let all Zion, and all clean people who read these words, use Zion City Pure, Sweet, Clean, Anti-hog Soap.

We will send it to any part of the world, in any quantity desired; but we specially recommend the family box. Address Zion City Soap Factory.

C. A. HANSON,
Manager

Extract from sermon delivered by John Alexander, the First Apostle of the Lord Jesus, the Christ, in the Christian Catholic Apostolic Church in Zion: "We will refuse to allow our country, and our Church, and the people to be ruled over by men who simply crush the people by combines of money, or by combines in the Legislature, or by combines in the press, or by combines in secret society lodges, or by combines in the churches."

One of the basic principles of Christianity is coöperation.

The human messenger, whether he be minister or layman, working in coöperation with the Holy Spirit, is ever striving to bring spiritual fruit into the storehouse of the Kingdom—the Church.

Introducing this same principle of coöperation into the commercial life of the Christian, and carrying it to its logical conclusion, it is readily seen that Christian should deal with Christian. Otherwise the profits of his labor, be it of brain or of muscle, are diverted to the treasury of the Enemy and used to destroy the very Kingdom which he, in his spiritual work, is endeavoring to build up.

The Christian who fails to understand and put in operation this principle is therefore pulling against himself, putting in with one hand while taking out with the other; and oftentimes the hand which takes out is the larger.

The original source of all wealth being the earth, the Christian whose occupation is to cultivate the ground, who is working in coöperation with God—for while he may plant and water, it is God who giveth the increase—should also coöperate with his brother Christian whose necessity calls for the fruits, be they from field, garden, or orchard, which his industry has brought forth. Or should he, like the sons of Jacob, be a "keeper of cattle" then, too, he should coöperate with his brother Christian, whose strength is renewed by the eating of meats.

That Zion City is today the most instructive and practical lesson in Christian coöperation to be found upon the face of the earth, is a self-evident truth. It therefore follows, without ground for contradiction, that Christians outside of Zion City who are producers should coöperate with Christians in Zion City.

G. A. MITCHELL,
Acting Manager Zion Fresh Food Supply.

Recent reports show a large gain in the deposits of both the national and the state banks of Chicago.

This prosperity is shared by Zion City Bank, and we are glad to report a healthy growth in deposits, and also in the number of new accounts opened.

The business of Zion City Bank has increased manifold during this year.

Our facilities for banking by mail are the best We hope each and every member of the Church, no matter where he or she may live, will open an account with us

If all coöperate with us, we will be able to increase the effectiveness of all Zion Institutions.

We will send, free of charge, to all who write for it, the pamphlet, "Saving Money," by Arthur W. Newcomb.

W. S. PECKHAM,
Cashier.

At the present time, United States four per cent. bonds, due 1925, are selling in the New York market at a premium of thirty-one and three-fourths per cent., or at the rate of one hundred thirty-one and seventy-five one-hundredths dollars for each one hundred dollars of interest-bearing investment. Other prominent bonds are now selling as follows:

Illinois Central Railway, rate four per cent., (due 1951), at one hundred fifteen.

Pennsylvania Railway, rate four per cent., (guaranteed first), at one hundred ten and one-quarter.

Wabash Railway, rate five per cent., (first), at one hundred eighteen.

Chicago & North-Western Railway, rate five per cent., (debenture 1933), at one hundred eighteen.

Chicago, Rock Island & Pacific Railway, rate six per cent., (1917), at one hundred twenty-five.

St. Louis & San Francisco Railway, rate six per cent., (general), at one hundred twenty-six.

Chicago, Milwaukee & St. Paul Railway, rate seven per cent. (consolidated 1905), at one hundred seventy-five.

New York Consolidated Gas Company, rate six per cent., at one hundred eighty-seven.

These worldly institutions have outstanding many hundreds of millions of these bonds, and investors are so eager to get them that they are paying premiums of from ten and one-quarter per cent. to eighty-seven per cent. for securities earning only from four per cent. to seven per cent. annually, as above shown.

Zion Lace Industries Shares now yield ten per cent. annually, and will advance to twelve per cent. on July 1, 1906. They are offered at one hundred ten dollars per share.

Zion Candy Shares and Zion Building and Manufacturing Shares are offered at par, although now yielding nine per cent. income, and to advance to ten per cent. next year.

Investors in Zion securities thus have exceptional opportunities, and no one should miss them.

FIELDING H. WILHITE,
Manager Zion Securities and Investments.

The Christian's aim is to glorify God, and to use every talent in His service. The opportunities offered by Zion, in Zion City, free from the vices and contaminating influences of worldly cities, afford the freest exercise of every talent for God. Why, then, should not Christians everywhere rally to the support of the First Apostle of the Lord Jesus, the Christ, in the Christian Catholic Apostolic Church in Zion?

CHARLES J. BARNARD,
General Financial Manager of all Zion's Institutions and Industries.

Zion Sugar and Confection Association is one of the busiest places in Zion City, especially at this season of the year. We now have considerably over one hundred employees—quite a jump from our little tent a little more than two years ago.

The time has come when more sugar and less coloring matter should be used in the manufacture of candy. While our coloring and flavors are the purest that money will buy, still we advocate delicate shades of color, and mild but decided flavors.

We believe we launched our Industry just at the right time. People *will* eat candy, and intelligent people demand *pure* candy. So great has been the demand for Zion's pure candy that the large "Fair Store" in Chicago has given us a counter in their candy department for the exclusive sale of Zion's highest-priced candy, which counter will be in charge of a good Zion woman. We could say very much more that would be of interest to our Zion friends concerning our Industry, but will reserve it until next time.

ROSCOE E. RODDA,
Manager Zion Sugar and Confection Association.

NOTES OF THANKSGIVING FROM THE WHOLE WORLD

By OVERSEER J. G. EXCELL.

Healed of Severe Pain and Soreness.

God also bearing witness with them, both by signs and wonders, and by manifold powers, and by gifts of the Holy Spirit, according to His own will —*Hebrews 2:4*

WAUBAUSHENE, CANADA, July 25, 1904.

DEAR GENERAL OVERSEER:—I feel it my duty to write and testify to God's healing power in answer to your prayers and our own.

On Saturday night, July 9th, I was taken with severe pain and soreness in my right side.

I was so sore that I could not bear to touch my side. I was unable to rest, and the pain became so severe that on Sunday and Sunday night I could not lie down.

My daughter, Mrs. Richard Boyd, stayed up with me until twelve o'clock that night.

I received some relief from the pain and soreness, but I was quite weak, and had pains in my legs and all about my stomach and kidneys.

My daughter sent you a request for prayer Monday, the 11th, and on Wednesday I sat up to the table and ate my meals.

My side was better and the weakness was all gone. I have been gaining ever since.

I am sixty-eight years old.

I thank God for His healing and cleansing power. The answer came the day you replied to my request.

I thank God with all my heart, and you for your prayers for my blessing.

Yours in Jesus, (MRS.) FRANCES L. BAKER.

Eyes Healed in Answer to Prayer.

Jesus of Nazareth, how that God anointed Him with the Holy Ghost and with power: who went about doing good, and healing all that were oppressed of the Devil, for God was with Him.—*Acts 10:38.*

142 NORTH SIXTH STREET,
ELKHART, INDIANA, August 9, 1904.

DEAR OVERSEER SPEICHER:—One year ago this month, when I was visiting in Zion City, I was prayed with for the healing of my eyes.

The healing came two months after I reached home.

I would have been healed in Zion City if I had given up my glasses, but I thought I could not do that, for I had used them so many years.

I have not had a pain in my eyes or head since.

Praise the Lord for His goodness.

Yours in the Master's service.

(MISS) IVAH CONNER.

Baby Healed of Fever.

Every good gift and every perfect boon is from above, coming down from the Father of lights, with whom can be no variation, neither shadow that is cast by turning.—*James 1:17*

VIROQUA, WISCONSIN, August 12, 1904.

DEAR GENERAL OVERSEER:—Peace to thee.

I wish to thank you for your prayers in behalf of my baby. God heard and answered.

The night that I wrote to you for prayer, he began to get better, his fever left to a great extent, and the third day he was entirely healed.

Yours in the Master's service,

(MRS.) NETTIE HAMMOND.

Zion's Bible Class

Conducted by Teacher Daniel Sloan in Shiloh Tabernacle, Zion City, Lord's Day Morning at 11 o'clock, and in Zion Homes and Gatherings throughout the World.

MID-WEEK BIBLE CLASS LESSON, OCTOBER 12th or 13th.

The Christian's High Calling.

1. *We are called to be heirs of God and joint heirs with the Christ.*—Romans 8:9-17.
   To be with Him, we must be like Him.
   We must live for what the Christ lives for.
   We must be in constant prayer.
2. *We are called to be not of the world while yet in it.*—John 17:6-19.
   We are not to imbibe its spirit.
   We are not to follow its customs.
   We are not to seek its ways.
3. *We are called to abstain from all sensual lusts.*—1 Peter 4:1-11.
   Shun that which appeals to the evil eye.
   Abstain from every sensual appetite.
   Guard against excesses.
4. *We are called to live in unbroken fellowship with the Lord.*—John 15:10-16.
   There is joy in obedience.
   There is happiness in forgetting self.
   You can enter into the confidence of God.
5. *We are called to an estate to be inherited only through tribulation.*—1 Peter 1:3-14.
   The end of faith has not yet come.
   The glories beyond reveal no want there.
   There is a Kingdom of Righteousness that is ours.
6. *We are called to go forth to labor, improving every opportunity.*—Luke 9:57-62.
   The Christian cannot sit still; he must go forward.
   He must not make excuses for not going.
   He must never wish he had not started.
7. *We are called to die to all but the Christ.*—Luke 14:25-35.
   You must know no one after the flesh.
   You must know the Christ after the Spirit.
   We must hate the flesh to serve Him in the Spirit.

The Lord Our God is a Life-inspiring God.

LORD'S DAY BIBLE CLASS LESSON, OCTOBER 16th.

What Do Ye More Than Others?

1. *Are you more righteous?*—Matthew 5:17-20.
   What Commandments do you break?
   Which duties do you neglect?
   What principles do you exemplify?
2. *Are you more benevolent?*—Matthew 6:1-4.
   Do you give for the poor?
   Do you help the needy?
   Do you not justify yourself in what you do?
3. *Are you more loving?*—Matthew 5:43-48.
   Do persons have to love you first?
   Which enemy would you help first?
   Show us the list of those you pray for.
4. *Are you less resentful?*—Matthew 5:38-42.
   What do you do when another harms you?
   When provoked, are you kind?
   When wronged, do you retaliate?
5. *Are you more prayerful?*—Matthew 6:5-15.
   What do you know of prayer?
   Who taught you to pray?
   What prayers have been answered?
6. *Are you more forceful?*—Matthew 5:13-16.
   Whom have you saved?
   Have you had any savior?
   Have you ever lighted any one to God?
7. *Are you more devout?*—Matthew 6:16-18.
   Is your religion visible in your face?
   Do you judge a good deal by looks?
   What good comes from your seeming to be religious?
8. *Are you less assertive?*—Matthew 5:33-37.
   Does your affirmation make it true?
   Are you headstrong?
   Do you say from the heart, "If the Lord wills, I will do this or that?"

God's Holy People are a Lowly-Minded People.

OBEYING GOD IN BAPTISM.

"Baptizing Them Into the Name of the Father and of the Son and of the Holy Ghost."

Nineteen Thousand Nine Hundred Twenty-nine Baptisms by Triune Immersion Since March 14, 1897.

Nineteen Thousand Nine Hundred Twenty-nine Believers have joyfully followed their Lord in the Ordinance of Believer's Baptism by Triune Immersion since the first Baptism in Central Zion Tabernacle on March 14, 1897.

Baptized in Central Zion Tabernacle from March 14, 1897, to December 14, 1901, by the General Overseer,	4754			
Baptized in South Side Zion Tabernacle from January 1, 1902, to June 14, 1903, by the General Overseer..	37			
Baptized at Zion City by the General Overseer........	647			
Baptized by Overseers, Elders, Evangelists and Deacons, at Headquarters (Zion City) and Chicago......	5624			
Total Baptized at Headquarters....................	——			11,062
Baptized in places outside of Headquarters by the General Overseer..................................		765		
Baptized in places outside of Headquarters by Overseers, Elders, Evangelists and Deacons............		8,088		
Total Baptized outside of Headquarters............		——		8,853
Total Baptized in seven years and six months......				19,915
Baptized since September 14, 1904:				
Baptized in Zion City by Elder Viking...............	3		3	
Baptized in Illinois by Elder Gay....................		5		
Baptized in Ohio by Deacon Smith....................		1		
Baptized in Pennsylvania by Elder Bouck............		4		
Baptized in Texas by Elder Hall....................		1	11	14
Total Baptized since March 14, 1897...............				19,929

The following-named five believers were baptized near Baltimore City, Maryland, Lord's day, July 3, 1904, by Deacon S. O. Larkins:

James, Harry M., 506 Cold Spring Lane, Roland Park, Baltimore, Maryland
James, Mrs. Rosa K., 506 Cold Spring lane, Roland Park, Baltimore, Maryland
Rochester, Miss Emily..... 1018 North Stricker street, Baltimore, Maryland
Wonderheit, Mrs. Louise........1009 Burgundy alley, Baltimore, Maryland
Waring, Miss Ida..........1018 North Stricker street, Baltimore, Maryland

The following-named believer was baptized in Zion Tabernacle, Vancouver, British Columbia, Thursday, August 11, 1904, by Elder R. M. Simmons:

Pike, Emma...............347 Keefer street, Vancouver, British Columbia

The following-named four believers were baptized near Baltimore, Maryland, Lord's Day, August 14, 1904, by Deacon S. O. Larkins:

Wagner, Mrs. Annie Louise..........................Admiral, Maryland
Wagner, Edward.......................................Admiral, Maryland
Wagner, John August ....Admiral, Maryland
Wagner, Mrs. Louise ....Admiral, Maryland

The following-named seven believers were baptized in the Christian church, Council Bluffs, Iowa, Lord's Day, September 11, 1904, by Elder Charles A. Hoy:

Powell, Charles Elmer. ....500 Harmony street, Council Bluffs, Iowa
Highsmith, Mrs. Laura E.........500 Harmony street, Council Bluffs, Iowa
Lehning, Mrs. Barbara ....4669 Leavenworth street, Omaha, Nebraska
Powell, George Allen............500 Harmony street, Council Bluffs, Iowa
Powell, Miss Gracie Bell.........500 Harmony street, Council Bluffs, Iowa
Willeford, Joseph J.............918 Harmony street, Council Bluffs, Iowa
Willeford, Miss Sena Matilda... 918 Harmony street, Council Bluffs, Iowa

The following-named believer was baptized at San Antonio, Texas, Wednesday, September 14, 1904, by Elder Lemuel C. Hall:

Upchurch, Rev. James T. ....Station A, Dallas, Texas

The following-named five believers were baptized at Kankakee, Illinois, Friday, September 16, 1904, by Elder William D. Gay:

Leach, Miss Elsie Vivian..............219 Court street, Kankakee, Illinois
Peck, Miss Grace Gale ....342 Chicago avenue, Kankakee, Illinois
Peek, Hubert Louis.................342 Chicago avenue, Kankakee, Illinois
Peck, Miss Lulu Olla...............342 Chicago avenue, Kankakee, Illinois
Peck, Miss Mary Jane.............342 Chicago avenue, Kankakee, Illinois

The following-named believer was baptized at Cincinnati, Ohio, Lord's Day, September 18, 1904, by Deacon George W. Smith:

R[illegible]s, Miss Cora Elizabeth.........Wesley Avenue Home, Cincinnati, Ohio

The following-named believer was baptized at San Antonio, Texas, Lord's Day, September 18, 1904, by Elder Lemuel C. Hall:

G[illegible]y, Daniel.........................109 Hood street, San Antonio, Texas

The following-named four believers were baptized at Philadelphia, Pennsylvania, Lord's Day, September 18, 1904, by Elder R. N. Bouck:

Brown, Dora ....1043 South street, Philadelphia, Pennsylvania
Burton, Mrs. Margaret, 215 West Fayette street, West Chester, Pennsylvania
Cairnes, Mrs. Annie ....2955 A street, Philadelphia, Pennsylvania
Nutton, Mrs. Margaret............2955 A street, Philadelphia, Pennsylvania

The following-named three believers were baptized in Shiloh Tabernacle Zion City, Illinois, Wednesday, September 21, 1904, by Elder C. F. Viking:

Coultas, Mrs. Gertrude................................Thawville, Illinois
Hokanson, Mrs. Ellen...................................Hector, Minnesota
Million, Mrs. Annie.................................Royal Center, Indiana

The following name was omitted from the list of names of believers baptized in Shiloh Tabernacle, Zion City, Illinois, Wednesday, September 7, 1904, by Elder Frank A. S. Mercer:

Morse, Mrs. Sarah ....Clinton, Illinois

CONSECRATION OF CHILDREN.

The following-named two children were consecrated to God, at Pretoria, Transvaal, South Africa, Lord's Day, August 14, 1904, by Elder P. L. le Roux:

Standers, Johanna Elizabeth, Rietfontien, Pretoria, Transvaal, South Africa
Standers, Maria Jacoba ......Rietfontien, Pretoria, Transvaal, South Africa

The following-named eight children were consecrated to God at Johannesburg, Transvaal, South Africa, Lord's Day, August 14, by Overseer Daniel Bryant:

Donald, Charles William, 106 Anderson street, Johannesburg, Transvaal, South Africa
Madgwick, William George, 8A Biccard street, Braamfontein, Johannesburg, Transvaal, South Africa
Sheppard, Elizabeth Edith Cabell, 1 Jorissen street, Braamfontein, Johannesburg, Transvaal, South Africa
Sheppard, Irene Agnes Cabell, 1 Jorissen street, Braamfontein, Johannesburg, Transvaal, South Africa
Thomson, Aletta Margareta, Natal Bank, Johannesburg, Transvaal, South Africa
Thomson, Truda Monson, Natal Bank, Johannesburg, Transvaal, South Africa
Van Aswegen, Johannes Jacobus Pienaar, 42 Koch street, Johannesburg, Transvaal, South Africa
Van der Byl, Zoo le Sueur, Stand 222, Richmond street, Johannesburg, Transvaal, South Africa

The following-named two children were consecrated to God, at Council Bluffs, Iowa, Lord's Day, September 11, 1904, by Elder Charles A. Hoy:

Powell, Hazel Marie, ...500 Harmony street, Council Bluffs, Iowa
Powell, James Everett...........500 Harmony street, Council Bluffs, Iowa

The following-named child was consecrated to God at Monee, Illinois, Tuesday, September 13, 1904, by Elder William D. Gay:

Deutsche, Bernice Irene......................................Monee, Illinois

The following-named twenty-seven children were consecrated to God, in Shiloh Tabernacle, Zion City, Illinois, Lord's Day, September 18, 1904, by Overseer H. D. Brasefield:

Angell, Ruby Estella..............2113 Gabriel avenue, Zion City, Illinois
Benckendorf, Harold Henry....................................Streetor, Illinois
Bohl, Bertha Beatrice...............3119 Gideon avenue, Zion City, Illinois
Bohl, Cleo Albert....................3119 Gideon avenue, Zion City, Illinois
Calver, Mary Elizabeth............1806 Hermon avenue, Zion City, Illinois
Edwards, Earl Richard................ ...Zion Farm, Zion City, Illinois
Godshall, Paul Alexander.............2810 Ezra avenue, Zion City, Illinois
Johnson, John Daniel.............2921 Gabriel avenue, Zion City, Illinois
McConnell, Thomas Hugh..............2721 Elim avenue, Zion City, Illinois
McEwen, Evelyn May.............3008 Gabriel avenue, Zion City, Illinois
McEwen, John Alexander..........3008 Gabriel aveuue, Zion City, Illinois
McEwen, Olive Myrtle.............3008 Gabriel avenue, Zion City, Illinois
Mabbett, Truman Gardiner.........2920 Gabriel avenue, Zion City, Illinois
Mabbett, Mildred Wilson...........2920 Gabriel avenue, Zion City, Illinois
Mapes, Phebe Joyce................ 3212 Gilgal avenue, Zion City, Illinois
Meridith, Joy.........................2106 Ezekiel avenue, Zion City, Illinois
Meridith, Edna.......................2106 Ezekiel avenue, Zion City, Illinois
Meridith, Linnie.....................2106 Ezekiel avenue, Zion City, Illinois
Needles, Grace Mabel ....2717 Elizabeth avenue, Zion City, Illinois
Peacock, Paul Harvey..... ......3104 Emmaus avenue, Zion City, Illinois
Petersen, Ruth Margaret..........1904 Hermon avenue, Zion City, Illinois
Populorum, Athlea Louise..........2809 Gabriel avenue, Zion City, Illinois
Porter, Ruth Marion................2608 Elisha avenue, Zion City, Illinois
Shulenberger, Joseph Lloyd ....3014 Gideon avenue, Zion City, Illinois
Smith, Shiloh Tilman ....3211 Gideon avenue, Zion City, Illinois
Wilhite, Joseph Bethel .... 2608 Elim avenue, Zion City, Illinois
Wilson, Edward Henry...............2207 Ezra avenue, Zion City, Illinois

ZION'S

FINANCIAL INSTITUTIONS AND INDUSTRIES

JOHN ALEXANDER DOWIE

THE FINANCIAL INTERESTS OF ZION are of vital importance to every member and friend of Zion. Get this on your heart. For when Zion's material work is strengthened, then her ability is increased to carry forward throughout the world the glorious, good tidings of this dispensation — the little leaven which is destined of God to leaven the whole lump.

¶ ¶ Zion has marvelously succeeded in all her business undertakings and operations. Her transactions with her own people, and the business world, have already amounted to hundreds of millions of dollars; and not a dollar has ever been lost by any investor. Within a very few years a vast estate has been created, rapidly increasing in value, and rated at this time by the keenest business firms of Chicago at many millions above all liabilities.

¶ ¶ Such a stewardship finds favor with God, and merits the hearty coöperation of every one who loves our Lord in sincerity, and desires to see His Kingdom extended.

High Class Investments, Secured by the entire estate of Zion, bearing interest at the rate of 9 per cent. and 10 per cent., are now offered to ready investors upon the most liberal terms. Your inquiries are cordially invited.

For information concerning the General Financial or Material Interests of Zion, address
DEACON CHARLES J. BARNARD, General Financial Manager, Zion City, Ill., U. S. A., or
DEACON DANIEL SLOAN Inspector General of Zion, Zion City, Ill., U. S. A.

For information concerning Zion City Bank, or any thing pertaining to the Banking Business, address
DEACON WILLIAM S. PECKHAM, Cashier, Zion City Bank, Zion City, Ill., U. S. A.

For information concerning Zion City Real Estate, address
DEACON H. WORTHINGTON JUDD, Secretary and Manager, Zion Land and Investment Association, Zion City, Ill., U. S. A.

For information concerning Zion Securities and Investments, address
DEACON FIELDING H. WILHITE, Manager, Zion Securities and Investments, Zion City, Ill., U. S. A.

Persons living at remote points may find it more convenient to confer with or write to the following special representatives:

ELDER PERCY CLIBBORN, General Financial Agent for the Continent of Europe, No. 76 Bahnhofstrasse, Zurich, Switzerland.

DEACON JOHN W. INNES, General Financial Agent for the United Kingdom. No. 81 Euston Road, London, N. W., England.

DEACON NICHOLAS B. RIDEOUT, General Financial Agent for South Africa, Box 3074, Johannesburg, South Africa.

DEACON GEORGE A. CORLETTE, Manager New York Office, No. 419 Flatiron Building, New York City.

Honesty and Quality with Promptness bring Progress

We are especially prepared to make

Fine Catalogs, Brochures, Periodicals and do Bookbinding, Blankbook work & Special Ruling

THIS is the motto which we follow when doing Printing, Designing, Electrotyping, Bookbinding or Blankbook work of any kind for our customers. We notice that many readers of **Leaves of Healing** and **The Zion Banner** are willing that we should do their Printing when they learn that we are doing work for firms at a distance from Zion City. We therefore invite all who have clean and acceptable printing to send copy and get our estimates, as we believe we can make it profitable to you in price, material, and workmanship. We have one of the best Electrotyping plants in the country, and can furnish the best work at prices as low as can be obtained anywhere, and make Electros for every line of clean business.

Zion Printing & Pub. House

Zion City, Illinois.

Our Art Department

is prepared to meet the demands for any kind of designing or drafting that may be required.

CATHOLIC APOSTOLIC CHURCH IN ZION, LORD'S DAY AFTERNOON, SEPTEMBER 18, 1904

A

Vo

(

M

I
T
F

h

n
w
a
u

WEEKLY PAPER FOR THE EXTENSION OF THE KINGDOM OF GOD
EDITED BY JOHN ALEXANDER, FIRST APOSTLE OF THE LORD JESUS, THE CHRIST, IN THE CHRISTIAN CATHOLIC APOSTOLIC CHURCH IN ZION

ıme XV. No. 24. ZION CITY, SATURDAY, OCTOBER 1, 1904. Price Five Cents

›OD'S WITNESSES TO DIVINE HEALING.

RACULOUSLY DELIVERED FROM A TERRIBLE TUMOR AND HEALED OF OTHER DISEASES, WHEN DYING.

EHOLD, I AM JEHOVAH, THE GOD OF ALL FLESH: IS ERE ANY THING TOO HARD R ME?

:ither God is not able to l His children;

)r He is not willing;

)r those Christians who do seek Him for healing are ›ng, and all doctors, drugs, surgical instruments are less.

'here is no alternative.

t is false to say that God ls through doctors, drugs, surgery.

Ie does not.

ˈod is all-wise and un- nging.

'he so-called science of medi- e of today calls the medical of yesterday rot and non- se.

)id God attempt to heal His dren through human rot and ısense yesterday, and is He ay handing His children r to a band of men whom ıorrow's pundits will call ıd experimenters?

:ven if it were true that God d human means, facts would w that He does not *heal* ough them.

Nearly all Christians who die disease die under the treatment of physicians. Which horn of the dilemma will you take, then, you who scoff at Divine Healing? Is it that God is not able to heal His children? Can you say that He who so wonderfully framed the human body in His own image is powerless to heal it? Is there any thing too hard for God? He Himself says that He is "Jehovah, the God of all Flesh."

Even the devils believe it.

Or is He unwilling to heal?

Can you say that He who said, "I am Jehovah that healeth thee," at the waters of Marah, now withholds the boon?

Is it conceivable that He of whom the Psalmist said, "Like as a father pitieth his children, so Jehovah pitieth them that fear Him," would turn a deaf ear to the cry of the humblest and weakest of His little ones?

The answer comes from the woman who touched the hem of His garment, from the man who was born blind, from the man who lay in the sorrow-crowded Porches of Bethesda, from the little daughter of the ruler Jairus, from the leper who heard those wonderful words, "I will; be thou made clean."

It comes from "multitudes" who saw the look of Infinite Love and Compassion in the eyes of Him who "healed them all."

The parable is taken up by the lame man healed at the

MRS. B. J. ALLEN.

Beautiful Gate of the Temple, and by thousands whom God healed through His Apostles.

The answer comes also, in a mighty volume of present-day testimony, that rolls up from all the lands, in this present day, in a tidal wave of truth that forever sweeps away the tissue of fallacy and lies built up to hold it back.

God *is* able to heal.

His Word proclaims it.

Ten thousand times ten thousand joyous witnesses affirm it.

There is naught too hard for Him.

God *is* willing to heal.

The Christ, who spoke the words of the Father, declared it.

A cloud of witnesses answer and say, "It is truth!"

"Let them bring their Witnesses, that they may be justified."

Here is one of them.

What a Miracle of Healing God wrought in her body!

To human eyes, she seemed to be dying.

But her husband's faith failed not; her faith failed not; the faith of God's ministers and people who prayed for and with her failed not.

Theirs was a glorious victory.

Almost instantly, at the time of prayer, she was delivered, miraculously, of a terrible, deadly tumor, and made perfectly whole.

Praise God, it is true! Nothing is too hard for Him!

Do you believe it?

Can you not claim His promises by fulfilling His Divine conditions?

He waits to bless you; for He is your Father, and is no respecter of persons.

A. W. N.

WRITTEN TESTIMONY OF MRS. B. J. ALLEN.

205 BROADWAY,
BENTON HARBOR, MICHIGAN,
September 22, 1904.

DEAR FIRST APOSTLE:—It is with gratitude to my Heavenly Father and for His honor and glory, that I write the following testimony, trusting it may encourage some one to trust God more fully.

The 27th of May, 1903, God gave us a dear, little baby girl

Both before and after her birth, the Devil seemed determined to have my life.

Two weeks before, I was taken quite sick.

I had a very high fever, and it seemed to me that there was not a bone in my body that did not ache.

There was a breaking out all over my body.

For several nights I could not lie down, but sat in a chair, able to sleep but little, for it seemed as though my breath would leave me entirely.

I obeyed the command in James 5:14-15, "Is any sick among you? Let him call for the Elders of the Church; and let them pray over him, anointing him with oil in the Name of the Lord:

"And the Prayer of Faith shall save the sick, and the Lord shall raise him up."

I was then healed by the power of God through the prayers of Elder Adams.

After the birth of our baby I suffered a great deal of pain for five days, not knowing the cause of it.

During this time the Elder and his wife, Evangelist Adams, were very faithful in their ministrations to me.

The Elder came often and encouraged me to trust fully in God, quoting Scripture promises that were of great comfort and help to me.

While God answered prayer for me for other troubles that arose at this time, I was not delivered from this pain, and was growing weaker.

The hemorrhage was very profuse and very unusual.

The night sweats were dreadful.

I could not go to sleep for even a few minutes without dripping with perspiration.

When I felt the worst, those who cared for me would not let me sleep but a few minutes at a time, and then had to work over me for some time, as I had such sinking spells.

I was reported dead at different times.

I realized that unless God gave the deliverance I could not live, but no intimation of my serious condition was even hinted to me.

The Elder seemed to have the assurance given him, as did my husband, that God would deliver me, and was strong in the faith.

The Evangelist said that she knew that I would be healed, for all Zion was praying for me.

Thank God for those who have faith in God and believe He will do what He says, even though it looks impossible to man!

I do praise God for His wonderful love to His children

The fourth day, while in communion with God, I said, "Father in Heaven, if my work in this world is done, well and good. but do not let the Devil take my life before my time comes to go."

On the afternoon of the following day we felt directed to telephone to Overseer Speicher for prayer, you being away.

Overseer Speicher replied to my husband's message thus, "Tell your dear wife to hold on to God. We will pray for her this afternoon. Tell her to expect the blessing."

Immediately after this, Elder Adams came in.

He said that he, too, felt impressed to pray for deliverance that afternoon.

We all united in prayer with Overseer Speicher for this blessing.

I felt God's presence, and He gave me such peace and trust as only He can give.

I expected the blessing—and God wonderfully delivered me from a large growth. Just what it was, I am not prepared to say, and it did not matter to God.

The summer previous to this, I had a growth on my right side.

It seemed several inches long and as large around as my fist.

It hurt me to lie on my right side, feeling like something tearing loose.

At times I suffered much pain from it, through my hips and back.

I suppose this growth from which I was delivered was the same, as I have had nothing of the kind since.

I was also healed of a uterine trouble that I had suffered from for about twenty years.

I have had no return of it.

For all this I can say, "Thanks be to God which giveth us the victory through our Lord Jesus, the Christ."

I do praise God that His power is just the same today as it ever was; that He does not change.

What He has done for one, unworthy as I am, He will do for others.

I thank Overseer Speicher, Elder and Evangelist Adams, and all who helped me by their prayers and words of encouragement.

I also feel thankful for my husband, who did not waver, but was full of courage and hope.

I feel that I owe much, under God, to the Elder's faithfulness in bringing to my mind the Precious Promises of God, and encouraging me to look to Jesus alone, who has taken our infirmities and borne our sicknesses.

My life is given to God, to help in bringing the Full Gospel for spirit, soul, and body, to others.

I feel very thankful for the strength that God has given me to do all my work, and to go out one half day in the week to tell others of this glorious Gospel of Salvation, Healing, and Holy Living.

I hope that this testimony may help some one to look to God alone for healing, even though, "humanly speaking," the way may look dark.

May God bless you and Overseer Jane Dowie and all the faithful ones everywhere.

Yours for the Christ, (MRS.) B. J. ALLEN.

CONFIRMATION BY ELDER JAMES R. ADAMS.

ZION CITY, ILLINOIS.

The healing of this witness is but little short of a raising from the dead.

After the birth of her child, she sank very low through hemorrhages, diaphoresis, and internal disease of some kind.

For several days another birth was expected by the attendants.

On the fifth day we all saw that unless God manifested His power to heal, in a markedly miraculous manner, death would speedily claim its victim

Overseer J. G. Speicher was consulted by telephone and exhorted the witness and her husband to hold on to God, and himself offered earnest prayer for her.

That same afternoon while her husband and the writer were in an adjoining room in prayer, the answer came almost instantly.

The woman was wonderfully freed of a large vascular tumor in a terrible state of decomposition.

The other diseases soon disappeared, and recovery then went on steadily, as the witness truthfully states, until she has reached the condition of comely good health shown in her photograph.

"O Jehovah, ... unto Thy Name give glory."

JAMES R. ADAMS,
Elder in the Christian Catholic Apostolic Church in Zion.

TABLE OF FOREIGN SUBSCRIPTION PRICES

LEAVES OF HEALING.

	SINGLE COPY		YEARLY SUBSCRIPTIONS	
	United States Money.	Native Money.	United States Money.	Native Money.
Australia.........	$ 08	4 pence	$3 50	14s. 6c.
Ceylon	08	18c of rupees	3 50	14s. 6c.
India......	08	4 annas	3 50	14s 6d
Italy	08	40 centesimi	3 50	18 lira 40
Switzerland	08	40 centimes	3 50	18fr 40
France...........	08	40 centimes	3 50	18fr. 40c.
Great Britain . ..	08	4 pence	3 50	14s. 6d.

THE ZION BANNER.

	SINGLE COPY		SIX MOS. SUBSCRIPTION	
Australia........	$ 04	2 pence	$ 75	3s. 1½d.
Ceylon	04	9c of rupees	75	3s. 1½d.
India	04	2 annas	75	3s. 1½d.
Italy..	04	20 centesimi	75	4 lira
Switzerland	04	20 centimes	75	4 fr.
France.	04	20 centimes	75	4 fr
Great Britain ...	04	2 pence	75	3s. 1½d.

Make Remittances by Drafts on London.

John Alexander

First Apostle of the Lord Jesus, the Christ, in the Christian Catholic Apostolic Church in Zion.

A WEEKLY PAPER FOR THE EXTENSION OF THE KINGDOM OF GOD.

EDITED BY

JOHN ALEXANDER, First Apostle of the Lord Jesus, the Christ, in the Christian Catholic Apostolic Church in Zion.

Application for entry as Second Class Matter at Zion City, Illinois, pending.

Subscription Rates.		Special Rates.	
One Year	$2.00	100 Copies of One Issue	$3.00
Six Months	1.25	25 Copies of One Issue	1.00
Three Months	.75	To Ministers, Y. M. C. A's and Public Reading Rooms, per annum	1.50
Single Copies	.05		

For foreign subscriptions add $1.50 per year, or three cents per copy for postage.

Subscribers desiring a change of address should give present address, as well as that to which they desire LEAVES OF HEALING sent in the future.

Make Bank Drafts, Express Money or Postoffice Money Orders payable to the order of JOHN ALEX. DOWIE, Zion City, Illinois, U. S. A.

Long Distance Telephone. *Cable Address "Dowie, Zion City."*

All communications upon business must be addressed to

MANAGER ZION PUBLISHING HOUSE,
Zion City, Illinois, U. S. A.

Subscriptions to LEAVES OF HEALING, A VOICE FROM ZION, and the various publications may also be sent to

ZION PUBLISHING HOUSE, 81 EUSTON ROAD, LONDON, N. W., ENGLAND.
ZION PUBLISHING HOUSE, NO. 43 PARK ROAD, ST. KILDA, VICTORIA, AUSTRALIA.
ZION PUBLISHING HOUSE, 76 BAHNHOFSTRASSE, ZÜRICH, SWITZERLAND.

ZION CITY, ILLINOIS, SATURDAY, OCTOBER 1, 1904.

TABLE OF CONTENTS.

LEAVES OF HEALING, SATURDAY, OCTOBER 1, 1904.

LEAVES OF HEALING.

Two Dollars will bring to you the weekly visits of the Little White Dove for a year; 75 cents will send it to a friend for thirteen weeks; $1.25 will send it for six months; $1.50 will send it to your minister, or to a Y. M. C. A., or to a Public Reading Room for a whole year. We offer no premiums, except the premium of doing good. We receive no advertisements and print no commercial lies or cheating enticements of unscrupulous thieves. LEAVES OF HEALING is Zion on wings, and we keep out everything that would detract the reader's mind from all except the Extension of the Kingdom of God, for which alone it exists. If we cannot send forth our Little White Dove without soiling its wings with the smoke of the factory and the dirt of the wrangling market-place, or compelling it to utter the screaming cries of the business vultures in the ears of our readers, then we will keep our Dove at home.

GOD'S WAY OF HEALING.

BY THE REV. JOHN ALEX. DOWIE.

God's Way of Healing Is a Person, Not a Thing.

Jesus said "*I am* the Way, and the Truth, and the Life," and He has ever been revealed to His people in all the ages by the Covenant Name, Jehovah-Rophi, or "*I am* Jehovah that Healeth thee." (John 14:6; Exodus 15:26.)

The Lord Jesus, the Christ, is Still the Healer.

He cannot change, for "Jesus, the Christ, is the same yesterday and today, yea and forever;" and He is still with us, for He said: "Lo, *I am* with you All the Days, even unto the Consummation of the Age." (Hebrews 13:8; Matthew 28:20.) Because He is Unchangeable, and because He is present, in spirit, just as when in the flesh, He is the Healer of His people.

Divine Healing Rests on the Christ's Atonement.

It was prophesied of Him, "Surely He hath borne our griefs (Hebrew, *sickness*), and carried our sorrows: . . . and with His stripes we are healed;" and it is expressly declared that this was fulfilled in His Ministry of Healing, which still continues. (Isaiah 53:4, 5; Matthew 8:17.)

Disease Can Never be God's Will.

It is the Devil's work, consequent upon Sin, and it is impossible for the work of the Devil ever to be the Will of God. The Christ came to "destroy the works of the Devil," and when He was here on earth He healed "all manner of disease and all manner of sickness," and all these sufferers are expressly declared to have been "oppressed of the Devil." (1 John 3:8; Matthew 4:23; Acts 10:38.)

The Gifts of Healing Are Permanent.

It is expressly declared that the "Gifts and the calling of God are without repentance," and the Gifts of Healing are amongst the Nine Gifts of the Spirit to the Church. (Romans 11:29; 1 Corinthians 12:8-11.)

There Are Four Modes of Divine Healing.

The first is the direct prayer of faith; the second, intercessory prayer of two or more; the third, the anointing of the elders, with the prayer of faith; and the fourth, the laying on of hands of those who believe, and whom God has prepared and called to that Ministry. (Matthew 8:5-13; Matthew 18:19; James 5:14, 15; Mark 16:18.)

Divine Healing Is Opposed by Diabolical Counterfeits.

Amongst these are Christian Science (falsely so-called), Mind Healing, Spiritualism, Trance Evangelism, etc. (1 Timothy 6:20, 21; 1 Timothy 4:1, 2; Isaiah 51:22, 23.)

Multitudes Have Been Healed Through Faith in Jesus.

The writer knows of thousands of cases and has personally laid hands on scores of thousands of persons. Full information can be obtained at the meetings held in the Zion Tabernacles in Chicago, and in Zion City, Illinois, and in many pamphlets which give the experience, in their own words, of many who have been healed in this and other countries, published at Zion Printing and Publishing House, Zion City, Illinois.

"Belief Cometh of Hearing, and Hearing by the Word of the Christ."

You are heartily invited to attend and hear for yourself.

Apostolic and Catholic Letter
To the Church in All the Earth

"Ben MacDhui," White Lake,
Montague, Michigan
U. S. A.,
September 29, 1904.

JOHN ALEXANDER,

First Apostle of Jesus, the Christ, in the Christian Catholic Apostolic Church in Zion,

To the Officers and Members of the Church, to all Lovers of God, and to the Peoples and Rulers of all the Nations:

Grace to you, and Peace,
From Him which is and which was and which is to come;
And from the Seven Spirits which are before His Throne;
And from Jesus, the Christ,
Who is the Faithful Witness,
The Firstborn of the dead,
And the Ruler of the kings of the earth.

Upon the eve of my return to my duties in the City of Zion, I desire to address you, my beloved Brothers and Sisters, concerning my New Relations to you, as the Apostle and High Priest, after the Order of Melchizedec, of Him who is the Divine Apostle of all apostles, the High Priest of all high priests, the "King of kings and Lord of lords."

The World is very dark.

The Signs of the Times betoken impending Great Events.

All Nations and all Classes of people are in great perplexity.

The Children of the Kingdom of God are tired and faint.

The Apostate Church has reached its Laodicean condition. It is neither "cold nor hot." The Christ, as He said He would, is spewing it out of His mouth.

The Apostasy vainly boasts of its riches and sufficiency, while it is "the wretched one, and miserable, and poor, and blind, and naked."

Everywhere the Apostasy compromises with Sin.

Disease, and Death, and Hell hold high carnival in every land.

It is the Eleventh Hour, and the Master has called His chosen in Zion into the Church of the Times of the Restoration of All Things.

Of that Church I am the Teacher, and Prophet, and Apostle.

As such I speak to all mankind, as well as to the Redeemed who have been purchased unto God by the blood of the Christ, out "of every tribe, and tongue, and people, and nation."

The Promise which the Christ gave when on the earth must now be fulfilled; for the Sign of the Son of Man in heaven will soon appear, and "then shall all the tribes of the earth mourn," as they see Him "coming on the clouds of heaven with power and great glory."

He has promised that "He shall send forth His Messengers with a Trumpet of Great Sound."

"They shall gather together His Elect from the four winds, from one end of heaven to the other."

Angels in heaven, angels on earth, angels everywhere—Messengers of Jesus—are going forth from Zion above and Zion on earth with His Message.

The Time of the Great Gathering has begun.

To me has been given that Trumpet, and it must give no uncertain sound; as it is written:

For if the Trumpet give an uncertain voice,
Who shall prepare himself for War?

My voice has already been heard in all the earth, although not by all the people.

But, so far as I can ascertain, the Voice from Zion has been heard by some of nearly all the families of mankind, on every continent, and possibly every nation.

Yet the vast majority of mankind have not heard the Message of God from Zion.

It was not possible hitherto for me to speak with all the Authority that God's people and the Rulers of the Nations rightfully demand.

Clothed by God with Apostolic and Prophetic Authority, I now have a right to speak as the Instructor of the Nations; for it is written:

Out of Zion shall go forth Instructions,
And the Word of Jehovah from Jerusalem.

The fulness of this Instruction can only come when Jehovah, Jesus, speaks in the human form from His Throne at Jerusalem, as the Ruler of the Kings and Peoples of all the earth:

And He shall Judge between the Nations,
And shall Decide concerning many Peoples:
And they shall beat their swords into plowshares,
And their spears into pruninghooks:
Nation shall not lift up sword against Nation,
Neither shall they learn war any more.

In the Name of the Coming King, I COMMAND PEACE!

That Peace must first begin at the House of God.

Never will men obey laws, judicial decisions, international treaties, or maintain any compromise with each other, until God rules.

Authority, not Public Opinion, must decide!

Public Opinion cries "Hosanna" and "Hallelujah" one day, and the day following it cries, "Away with Him! Let Him be crucified!"

The Voice of the People is not the Voice of God!

The Voice of God is not the Voice of the People!

Until Mankind believes and obeys the Voice of God, there can never be Purity, Peace, Progress, and Abiding Prosperity; but all these are the Promise of God.

"In that Day shall the Branch of Jehovah be beautiful and glorious,

"And the fruit of the earth shall be majestic and comely."

I return to Zion City with a very solemn sense of the responsibility which the Apostolic Office imposes.

I shall continue to watch over the manifold interests of Zion in its four great divisions—Ecclesiastical, Educational, Commercial, and Political, aided by the splendid staff of Brethren and Sisters whom God has given to me.

I shall expect, however, to be able to give more attention, than in the past few years, to the Preparation of God's People in Zion, through the Ministerial Training Department of Zion College and through Zion Restoration Host, for service as Zion City Builders and as Messengers of God and Zion in every part of the world.

I am giving much attention to the preparation of Zion Literature in many tongues.

The first issue of Feuilles de Guerison, the French Edition of Leaves of Healing, will appear on Saturday, October 15th.

The German Edition, Blatter der Heilung, has now attained a very large circulation in German-speaking countries; and, as God enables us, we shall continue to send forth, as we now do, large numbers of carefully-prepared Restoration Messages in many languages.

I shall go forward as quickly as possible with the needed alterations in the designs for Shiloah Tabernacle, and expect to be able to utilize the people and the material to be found in Zion City in this great building, in which we are planning to accommodate fully Sixteen Thousand persons.

I shall push with all the Resources and Energy which God gives me every Industry in Zion.

Within the past few weeks I have made, and am still making, arrangements for large extensions of Zion Lace Industries, etc.

But above all, I shall feel it to be my solemn duty to discharge my Spiritual Responsibilities to the Branches of the Christian Catholic Apostolic Church in Zion throughout the world, and to the Evangelization of every country and nation.

I shall deliver, God willing, from week to week, as the Apostle of the Lord Jesus, the Christ, and the Prophet of the Restoration, the Messages which God will give me.

I shall also give such Private and Public Rulings in Doctrine and Discipline as may be required of me as the Teacher and Chief Pastor of the Church.

I can say, gladly, with the Apostle Peter,

> Of a truth I perceive
> That God is no respecter of persons:
> But in every nation, he that feareth Him,
> And worketh Righteousness,
> Is acceptable to Him.

Zion is broader than any church organization, for Zion is the Kingdom of God.

I gladly recognize the fact that there are vast numbers of true-hearted and sincerely earnest Christians in all the earth, both in and out of the Apostate Denominations and so-called "Catholic" Churches of the Greek and Roman communions.

But the Time for Unity in One Body has come.

My conflict is not with "flesh and blood," but with the evil powers, "the world-rulers of this darkness," who have corrupted Christian organizations, and often made them subservient to cruel political and military tyrannies.

With all my heart I cry, "Grace, Mercy, and Peace be with all who love our Lord Jesus, the Christ, in sincerity."

I have besought from God, and I believe that the Answer will speedily be given, Special Tokens of His Favor in the Outpouring of His Spirit upon the Church.

God will "bear us witness," increasingly, by "Signs and Wonders, and by Manifold Powers, and by Gifts of the Holy Ghost, according to His own will."

My earnest desire is that all who read these lines will kindly pray for me, and for all my brethren and sisters associated with me in the ministry, and in every department of Zion's work.

Very earnestly do I lift up my hands to God, in prayer, for all men in all conditions.

I am the Friend of All, and the enemy of none, willing, as God shall will, to be everywhere a "Servant of the Servants of God," and a Helper of All, in the Name of Him who "tasted death for every man."

I am, faithfully yours in the Christ, for Time and for Eternity,

First Apostle of the Christian Catholic Apostolic Church in Zion.

Notes of Thanksgiving from the Whole World

By Overseer J. G. Excell, General Ecclesiastical Secretary.

As I LIVE, saith Jehovah God, I have no pleasure in the death of the wicked; but that the wicked turn from his way and live: turn ye, turn ye from your evil ways; for why will ye die?—*Ezekiel 33:11.*

WHY will ye die?

Turn ye! Ye who have gone into the far country of disobedience and spent your substance in riotous living; ye who have expended your labor for that which satisfieth not, and have reaped in the times of famine the husks of anguish, remorse, and affliction!

Turn ye! Ye who have bartered your eternal birthright for the ephemeral pleasures of an hour, and have cast aside God's blessing of spiritual fellowship, physical quickening, and temporal increase, for carnal companionship, weakened bodies, and poverty!

What though ye have spurned such a royal parentage, rejected such Divine tenderness and holy love, thrown in the mire of sensuality such holy affection, and despised the sacrifice and humiliation of His Son? It is to you who thus, through ignorance of God's Love, suffer the agonies of the sick-room; to you who through sin have the canker eating at your life that the words are spoken, "Come unto Me, all ye that labor and are heavy laden, and I will give you rest."

Turn ye, turn ye! See waiting for you not only the Unsearchable, Ineffable Creator of the Universe and Molder of Infinity, but a Father pleading for His child, arms open for the embrace of acceptance, eyes filled with intense compassion, and lips expressing, with the emotion of Divine Love, the words, "How often would I, ... and ye would not!"

Will ye not come?

Those whose testimonies here appear have come, and have received the touch of Divine favor in their bodies.

God is no respecter of persons.

He is able to heal you.

He is willing.

Return to your Father's house. He will heal you.

Let the reply to the loving entreaty be, "I will arise and go to my Father;" and you will receive the peace and joy which passeth understanding. O. R.

Delivered in Childbirth.

And Jehovah said . . . Surely I will be with thee.—*Judges 6:16.*

HECTOR, MINNESOTA, July 20, 1904.

DEAR OVERSEER:—It is with a full heart of thankfulness to God and to you that I send in my testimony to His many blessings.

I wrote you a request for prayer for my safe delivery in childbirth, and God most wonderfully answered and delivered me without pain.

He gave us a strong, healthy girl, and I was so strong I could have risen the same day. I have not had an hour's illness since.

My daily prayer is that God will bless the dear General Overseer and family, and keep them safe till He comes again.

I thank you for your prayers.

I do not know how to express my gratitude for all the blessings I have received since I became a member of the Christian Catholic Church in Zion.

Your sister in the Christ,

(MRS.) O. F. PETERSON.

Prayer Answered for Abscess in the Throat.

Himself took our infirmities and bare our diseases. *Matthew 8:17.*

2819 EMMAUS AVENUE,
ZION CITY, ILLINOIS, August 18, 1904.

DEAR GENERAL OVERSEER:—I desire to thank God for prayers offered for my wife, who has been wonderfully delivered from a very painful abscess in the throat.

Our Heavenly Father heard and answered, causing it to break last night; and, after a copious discharge of offensive matter, she was enabled to eat and sleep, a blessing not enjoyed for some days.

We give God all the glory, and pray for wisdom so to live that our bodies may be kept pure.

Your servant in the Christ, NEIL STEPHENS.

God Answers Prayer for Rain.

Elijah was a man of like passions with us, . . . And he prayed again, and the heaven gave rain, and the earth brought forth her fruit.—*James 5:17, 18.*

LOWELL, INDIANA, July 23, 1904.

DEAR GENERAL OVERSEER:—With a heart full of thanksgiving to our Father and to you, I write informing you of the answer to your prayer for rain here July 6th.

We had a most delightful rain in answer to your prayer. It rained very gently for twenty-four hours.

We give God the glory and praise for so many blessings.

We are so thankful to live in this time, when we have the Full Gospel preached to us.

I believe that you are Elijah the Restorer, the true Prophet of God.

Praying God's richest blessings upon you and your dear wife and son, I am,

Your sister in Jesus' Name,

(MRS.) M. P. COTTRILL.

Healed of Kidney Trouble and Falling Hair.

I have heard thy prayer, I have seen thy tears: behold, I will heal thee.—*II Kings 20:5.*

ZION CITY, ILLINOIS, July 10, 1904.

DEAR GENERAL OVERSEER:—I rejoice to be able to testify to what God has done for my family and me.

After having been severely ill with kidney trouble, my hair nearly all came out.

I went to see Dr. Speicher, and he prayed for me.

My hair stopped coming out, and now I have a fine head of hair.

We cannot thank God enough for the way He has led us.

We are so happy to be in Zion, where we can hear the true Gospel.

I want to do all I can for the extension of the Kingdom of God.

May God bless you and Mrs. Dowie is my prayer.

Your sister in the Christ,

(MRS.) LYDIA WHITMAN.

Healed of Rheumatism.

But Jesus turning and seeing her said, Daughter, be of good cheer: thy faith hath made thee whole.—*Matthew 9:22.*

SPRINGVILLE, IOWA, July 19, 1904.

DEAR OVERSEER:—I can truly say that I am thankful to God for the blessings He has given me, especially during the last few months.

I thank Him for answering your prayers for me in April.

I thank you very much for your prayers and kind words.

I had an attack of grip, which left me with rheumatism for about two months, when God answered your prayers.

May God's rich blessings be with you in all your work for Him.

Your sister in the Christ,

(MRS.) JANE W. SHELLHAMMER.

Healed of Tuberculosis.

And Jesus went about all the cities and the villages, teaching in their synagogues, and preaching the Gospel of the Kingdom, and healing all manner of disease and all manner of sickness.—*Matthew 9:35.*

Jesus, the Christ, is the same yesterday and today, yea and forever.—*Hebrews 13:8.*

YALE, ILLINOIS, July 8, 1904.

DEAR GENERAL OVERSEER:—My son has written a request for prayer to you, and with it I send a testimony to the answer of the prayer which you offered for me two years ago.

I was wonderfully healed of tuberculosis of the arm, and have not been under the care of doctors since. I thank God for it.

Your follower, in the Christ,

(MRS.) ALICE KIRBY.

Healed of Lung Fever.

Then shall thy light break forth as the morning, and thy healing shall spring forth speedily.—*Isaiah 58:8.*

1723 HOREB AVENUE,
ZION CITY, ILLINOIS, July 6, 1904.

DEAR OVERSEER:—Peace to Thee.

I will write my testimony to the glory of God.

In May I was very sick with lung fever. I did not know anything most of the time.

But I thank God and praise Him for raising me up.

I thank you, dear Overseer, for your prayers and kindness, and others who were so kind.

Praise God for the General Overseer.

May God bless him and all Zion throughout the world.

Your brother in the Christ, G. E. PHILYAW.

Child Healed in Answer to Prayer.

Blessed are all they that put their trust in Him.—*Psalm 2:12.*

WINDOM, MINNESOTA, July 12, 1904.

DEAR OVERSEER:—I am glad to tell you that my little daughter Goldie, for whom you prayed last week is entirely well of that trouble.

To God be all the glory.

Thanking you for your prayers, I am,

Your sister in the Christ,

(MRS.) LETTIE WARD.

THE FIRST APOSTLE OF THE LORD JESUS, THE CHRIST, IN THE CHRISTIAN CATHOLIC APOSTOLIC CHURCH IN ZION REBUKES THE NOMINAL CHRISTIAN FOR HIS SINS IN THE ORIENT.

Message No. 98
SHILOH TABERNACLE
Lord's Day Afternoon,
September 11, 1904

..SUBJECT..
"GOODNESS AND SEVERITY OF GOD."

*REPORTED BY S. E. C., AND A. W. N.

FOOLISH humanity too often fails to see Love in Severity.

Many people forget that He who took the little children in His arms and blessed them, also drove the money-changers from the Temple with a whip of small cords.

They forget that He who said to the erring woman, "Neither do I condemn thee: go thy way; from henceforth sin no more," also heaped upon the wicked scribes and Pharisees the burning words, "Ye hypocrites! . . . Ye offspring of vipers!"

They forget that the eyes that gazed lovingly over Jerusalem and wept for the city, also flashed with Divine anger as He said, "Ye are of your father the Devil, and the lusts of your father it is your will to do!"

They forget that the Lamb of God is also the Lion of the Tribe of Judah.

They are more stupid than little children, who realize love in their parents' severity.

And so they recoil in foolish anger from the severe but loving words of God's Prophet in these Latter Times.

In their folly and ignorance they complain that he shows nothing of the Christ-spirit.

They wilfully shut their eyes and harden their hearts to the truth that it takes more Love to be wisely and justly severe than to be merciful.

To such people meekness means weakness, love means indulgence, mercy means laxness, and sentiment means sentimentality.

The Christ-spirit has nothing in common with a spirit of weak, craven, covering and excusing of sin and sentimental sympathy with the sinner.

Nearly six thousand people in Shiloh Tabernacle, Lord's Day afternoon, September 11, 1904, beheld the lion-like Severity and the lamb-like Gentleness, Love, and Mercy inspired by the Christ-spirit.

They saw that he who could wound and break men's hearts by his terrible denunciations of sin, could weep over the sinners.

He could plead tenderly with them, "It is the Goodness of God that leads you to Repentance."

That was the burden of the Message delivered by God's Prophet on the subject "The Goodness and the Severity of God."

The spirit of the man, the spirit of the Message, and the Holy Spirit of God Himself, were in accord with the subject, and moved upon the audience with mighty power.

*The First Apostle has not revised the following report.

The hearts of many were drawn toward God their Father, who stood revealed to them in a new light by the words of God's Messenger.

It was a deeply sincere and profoundly earnest throng, including nearly every person in that great audience, that responded to the call to Repentance and repeated, after the General Overseer, the Prayer of Consecration.

Lord's Day afternoon service in Shiloh Tabernacle seems to grow more and more attractive, not only to the citizens of Zion City, but also to people everywhere within reach.

The regular Lord's Day morning excursion train from Chicago always brings many hundreds, while the number of those who come on Saturday to spend the Lord's Day in Zion City, and those who come in automobiles, carriages, and other vehicles, is becoming larger and larger.

The delightful September weather on this day made it possible for an especially large number of visitors to attend.

A solo by Deacon Conductor John Thomas, very tenderly and beautifully sung, was a very effective portion of the service.

Shiloh Tabernacle, Zion City, Illinois, Lord's Day Afternoon, September 11, 1904.

The services were opened by Zion White-robed Choir and Zion Robed Officers entering the Tabernacle, singing as they came the words of the

PROCESSIONAL.

All glory, laud, and honor,
To Thee, Redeemer, King,
To whom the lips of children
Made sweet hosannas ring.

Thou art the King of Israel;
Thou David's royal Son,
Who in the Lord's Name comest,
The King and blessed One.

The company of angels
Are praising Thee on high;
And mortal men, and all things
Created, made reply.

The people of the Hebrews
With palms before Thee went;
Our praise and pray'rs and anthems
Before Thee we present.

To Thee, before Thy passion,
They sang their hymns of praise;
To Thee, now high exalted,
Our melody we raise.

Thou didst accept their praises;
Accept the pray'rs we bring.
Who in all good delightest,
Thou good and gracious King.

At the close of the Processional the General Overseer came upon the platform, the people rising and standing with bowed heads while he pronounced the

INVOCATION.

God be merciful unto us and bless us,
And cause Thy face to shine upon us;
That Thy Way may be known upon earth,
Thy Saving Health among all the nations,
For the sake of Jesus. Amen.

PRAISE.

The Congregation then joined in singing Hymn No. 195:

Our Lord is now rejected,
And by the world disowned,
By the many still neglected,
And by the few enthroned;
But soon He'll come in glory,
The hour is drawing nigh,
For the crowning day is coming by and by.

CHORUS—Oh, the crowning day is coming,
Is coming by and by,
When our Lord shall come in "power"
And "glory" from on high.
Oh, the glorious sight will gladden,
Each waiting, watchful eye,
In the crowning day that's coming by and by.

Overseer Excell then led the Choir and Congregation in the recitation of the Apostles' Creed:

RECITATION OF CREED.

I believe in God, the Father Almighty,
Maker of heaven and earth:
And in Jesus, the Christ, His only Son, our Lord,
Who was conceived by the Holy Ghost:
Born of the Virgin Mary;
Suffered under Pontius Pilate;
Was crucified, dead, and buried:
He descended into hell,
The third day He rose from the dead;
He ascended into heaven,
And sitteth on the right hand of God, the Father Almighty;
From thence He shall come to judge the quick and the dead.
I believe in the Holy Ghost;
The Holy Catholic Church;
The Communion of Saints;
The Forgiveness of Sins;
The Resurrection of the body,
And the Life Everlasting. Amen.

Overseer Excell then led the Congregation in repeating the Commandments; after which the words, "Lord, have mercy upon us, and write all these Thy Laws in our hearts, we beseech Thee," were chanted.

READING OF GOD'S COMMANDMENTS.

I. Thou shalt have no other gods before Me.

II. Thou shalt not make unto thee a graven image, nor the likeness of any form that is in heaven above, or that is in the earth beneath, or that is in the water under the earth; thou shalt not bow down thyself unto them nor serve them; for I, Jehovah, thy God, am a jealous God, visiting the iniquity of the fathers upon the children, upon the third and upon the fourth generation of them that hate Me, and showing mercy unto thousands of them that love Me and keep My commandments.

III. Thou shalt not take the Name of Jehovah thy God in vain; for Jehovah will not hold him guiltless that taketh His Name in vain.

IV. Remember the Sabbath Day, to keep it holy. Six days shalt thou labor and do all thy work; but the seventh day is a Sabbath unto Jehovah thy God: in it thou shalt not do any work, thou, nor thy son, nor thy daughter, thy manservant, nor thy maidservant, nor thy cattle, nor thy stranger that is within thy gates; for in six days Jehovah made heaven and earth, the sea, and all that in them is, and rested the seventh day: wherefore Jehovah blessed the Sabbath Day and hallowed it.

V. Honor thy father and thy mother; that thy days may be long upon the land which Jehovah thy God giveth thee.

VI. Thou shalt do no murder.

VII. Thou shalt not commit adultery.

VIII. Thou shalt not steal.

IX. Thou shalt not bear false witness against thy neighbor.

X. Thou shalt not covet thy neighbor's house, thou shalt not covet thy neighbor's wife, nor his manservant, nor his maidservant, nor his ox, nor his ass, nor anything that is thy neighbor's.

Hear also what our Lord Jesus, the Christ, the Son of God, hath said, which may be called the Eleventh Commandment:

XI. A New Commandment I give unto you, that ye love one another; even as I have loved you, that ye also love one another.

The great Choir then sang the

TE DEUM LAUDAMUS.

We praise Thee, O God; we acknowledge Thee to be the Lord.
All the earth doth worship Thee, the Father Everlasting.
To Thee all Angels cry aloud, the Heavens and all the powers therein.
To Thee Cherubim and Seraphim continually do cry:
Holy, Holy, Holy, Lord God of Sabaoth,
Heaven and earth are full of the majesty of Thy Glory.
The glorious company of the Apostles praise Thee.
The goodly fellowship of the Prophets praise Thee.
The noble army of martyrs praise Thee.
The Holy Church throughout all the world doth acknowledge Thee,
The Father of an Infinite Majesty;
Thine Adorable, True, and Only Son;
Also the Holy Ghost, the Comforter.
Thou art the King of Glory, O Christ;
Thou art the everlasting Son of the Father.
When Thou tookest upon Thee to deliver man,
Thou didst humble Thyself to be born of a Virgin;
When Thou hadst overcome the sharpness of death,
Thou didst open the Kingdom of Heaven to all believers.
Thou sittest at the right hand of God in the Glory of the Father.
We believe that Thou shalt come to be our Judge.
We therefore pray Thee help Thy servants,
Whom Thou hast redeemed with Thy precious blood.
Make them to be numbered with Thy saints in glory everlasting.
O Lord, save Thy people and bless Thine heritage;
Govern them and lift them up forever.
Day by day we magnify Thee;
And we worship Thy Name ever, world without end.
Vouchsafe, O Lord, to keep us this day without sin.
O Lord, have mercy upon us, have mercy upon us.
O Lord, let Thy mercy be upon us as our trust is in Thee.
O Lord, in Thee have I trusted, let me never be confounded.

The General Overseer read from the Inspired Word of God in the Epistle of Paul, the Apostle, to the Romans, the 11th chapter.

Elder W. H. Cossum led the people in the general supplications, the General Overseer following with prayer for the sick and sorrowing throughout the world, after which he led the people in the chanting of the Disciples' Prayer.

The tithes and offerings were received, during which Conductor John Thomas sang "Crossing the Bar."

The General Overseer then delivered his Message:

"GOODNESS AND SEVERITY OF GOD."

INVOCATION.

Let the words of my mouth, and the meditation of my heart, be acceptable in Thy sight; be profitable unto this people; and unto all to whom these words shall come, in this and every land, in this and all the coming time, Till Jesus Come.

TEXT.

Or despisest thou the riches of His Goodness and Forbearance and Longsuffering, not knowing that the Goodness of God leadeth thee to Repentance? —*Romans 2:4*.

Behold then the Goodness and Severity of God: toward them that fell, Severity; but toward thee, God's Goodness, if thou continue in His Goodness: otherwise thou also shalt be cut off.—*Romans 11:22*.

"The Goodness and Severity of God" Go Hand in Hand.

I speak to you briefly this afternoon concerning the "Goodness of God," that "leadeth thee to Repentance."

I am so glad that this day has been marked by several incidents that have been particularly interesting to me. Among them is one in which God touched the hearts of several very sinful people who were here this morning, and they have sent me such pathetic letters, showing that "God's Goodness" had led them to Repentance.

I am so glad that "the Goodness and Severity of God" go hand in hand.

Without that "Severity," heaven itself would be a reeking, corrupt mass of impurity.

Had not God cast down from the heavens those angels that rebelled, who would have made anarchy in heaven itself, then heaven would have been a mass of hellish corruption.

Had I not, in the exercise of my Divinely-given Authority, laid down and maintained rules which have been exceedingly severe towards those who wilfully sin, this City, instead of eing today what it is—a home of Happiness, of Blessing, and f Purity, Peace, and Power—would be a seething mass of orruption.

God's Love is expressed more in His Severity than in what e call His Mercy.

If God did not maintain in heaven and here on earth, in ion, a Standard of Purity, we should be in the midst of hellish ondage.

"The Goodness" and "the Severity" of God are expressions f the highest Mercy and intensest Love, that, working together, lead men, by the grace of God, to a true Repentance.

Repentance is a Much Misunderstood Word.

Let me define Repentance.

The word *metanoia* (μετάνοια) signifies a change of mind, a hange of thought.

For instance, when a man is walking with his back to the in, he walks on his own shadow, and sees nothing but his adow in front of him; but when he turns his face to the sun id it shines on him, and the shadow falls behind—that is an lustration of the idea of repentance.

A sinner walks in the darkness of his own sins, and of sinful en and women around him who see no sin.

He walks only in darkness, and has no light.

In his folly, he is going down the dark river of sin, disease, orruption, and death, into a hell on earth and a hell beyond.

He has turned his back upon God.

But when he repents he turns his back upon sin and all its il associations.

He turns his face to God; and the Mercy, and Love, and ight of God flow down upon him.

He walks in the Light as God is in the Light.

That man has repented.

He has turned his back upon Satan, and sin, and rebellion, id disorder of every kind; and now he is walking in the Light ith a great company who are getting nearer and nearer to od every step of their journey.

God is Light, and in Him is no darkness at all.

True Repentance Results in Rightness with God and Man.

True Repentance is, therefore, a real change of mind, companied by a complete change of life, as a result of the ork of the Holy Spirit in the hearts of those who turn from arkness to Light; from Satan to God.

They have been led by the "Goodness of God," who has been eading with them, to find joy in walking in the Light.

Therefore, that change of thought and life is accompanied Fruits meet for Repentance.

Those that have truly repented hasten to put themselves right ith God and with man.

They hasten to confess their sins, and, like the prodigal who me from a "far country," they see the father coming; they eet him in the light, and cry, "Father, I have sinned against aven, and in thy sight: I am no more worthy to be called y son; make me as one of thy hired servants!"

But there is no more darkness for that poor prodigal.

He is not sent into the kitchen.

He is not sent among the slaves.

He is brought in with the cry of the father, "Bring forth ickly the best robe, and put it on him; and put a ring on his nd, and shoes on his feet: and bring the fatted calf, and kill and let us eat, and make merry: for this my son was dead, d is alive again; he was lost, and is found."

There is joy in the presence of the angels!

One sinner has repented; the prodigal has come back.

He repents; and puts things right with God, with his earthly her, with his brothers, with his sisters, with those whom he s defiled and wronged, and with the Church of God.

He is determined to put things right if it costs him his life.

So, humbly and lovingly, he gets free from his sins, the odness of God leading him to Repentance.

God Never Forbids the Thought of Mercy.

Oh, if it were only the "Severity" without Love!

If the Judge were hard and stern, and not in sympathy th us!

If He could not weep over sinners!

While He must banish them from His presence, He makes a y by which His banished may return.

He leaves hope in their poor, sinful, and corrupt hearts.

When God drives the sinner from Eden, He does not forbid the thought of Mercy; and though the Sword of Justice at the Gates of Paradise turned every way when our first parents were driven out, making it impossible to go back, yet it was God who said, "I cannot let you stay in Paradise; go!

"I cannot let you eat of the Fruit of the Tree of Life; Go!

"I cannot let you stay in the place of Purity; Go!" But He added the promise that the Seed of the woman should bruise the head of the serpent.

Weeping they went; but with the Voice of Mercy in their ears, telling them that the day would come when the sinful woman should have a sinless daughter, who should bear a Sinless Son, who should bruise the head of the serpent.

Although that promise was not fulfilled for long centuries, it brought happiness to the hearts of the sinful man and the sinful woman to know that there would be a time when all mankind should get back, not only to Paradise, but to heaven itself.

That is our hope today.

There is Mercy for the Repentant Sinner Even in Hell.

Oh, the depths of the riches of His Grace, who looks beyond the present and immediate future, and sees beyond the dark confines of hell a time when He who "hath shut up all to disobedience," shall have mercy upon the sinner that left this earth impenitent and sinful!

Although a man may have made his bed in hell, still there is mercy for him.

The Christ, who was taken from the cross and laid in the grave, before He ascended, first descended into hell and "preached unto the spirits in prison, which aforetime were disobedient, when the long-suffering of God waited in the days of Noah."

They had been cast out because God saw that man was so wicked, "that every imagination of the thought of his heart was only evil continually."

Yet to those who had been for long centuries in the depths of despair, the Redeemer came and "led captivity captive."

The thought of the Church is the thought of the Restoration, not of Eternal Separation and Damnation.

The true Church of God has a Message of Mercy, even when men have felt the Severity of God and have been driven from His presence.

The Mercy of God has said and written it:

As in Adam all die, so also in the Christ shall all be made alive.

But it is the Goodness of God that is leading you to Repentance.

Oh! what a horrible thing it will be if you are impenitent and go to join the damned in hell; to pass long ages in the darkness, when by repenting and trusting in our Lord Jesus, the Christ, you may find mercy now—mercy that will cover all your sins, purify your heart, and make your life beautiful and happy.

Why not seek it now?

Every saint and sinner who will ask God for mercy to cover his or her sins, and for cleansing and keeping, stand and tell him so.

Now pray.

PRAYER OF CONSECRATION.

My God and Father, we who are Thy children, Thou Father of Spirits, we come to Thee and ask Thee to have mercy upon us. Those of us who have loved Thee best, those of us who have served Thee most, this day say, "Be merciful to me, O God!" We need Thy mercy, for our best love is very imperfect. Oh, forgive our sins of ignorance, even our sins of wilfulness! In Thy Mercy forgive us now. Oh, hear the cry of the prodigal coming back to Thee today and saying unto Thee, "Father, I have sinned!" Bless each one now in Thy presence who is conscious of sin, and through Thy mercy, O God, through faith in Thy Son, bless every one with a true Repentance, with the True Faith, with the Divine Hope, and with that Perfect Love which casts out fear. For Jesus' sake. Amen.

Did you mean it?

PEOPLE—"Yes."

GENERAL OVERSEER—Live it. May God grant it!

The Recessional was then sung, as the Choir and Officers retired, after which the General Overseer pronounced the

BENEDICTION.

Beloved, abstain from every form of evil. And may the very God of Peace Himself sanctify you wholly; and I pray God your whole spirit, and soul, and body be preserved entire, without blame, unto the coming of our Lord Jesus, the Christ. Faithful is He that calleth you, who also will do it. The grace of our Lord Jesus, the Christ, the love of God, our Father, the fellowship of the Holy Spirit, our Comforter and Guide, one Eternal God, abide in you, bless you, and keep you, and all the Israel of God everywhere, forever. Amen.

Early Morning Meeting in Shiloh Tabernacle

*REPORTED BY S. E. C., A. C. R., O. R., O. L. S., AND F. A. F.

GOD'S Word is a Hammer.

"Is not My Word . . . like a Hammer that breaketh the rock in pieces?"

God's Word smashes things!

It smashes the strong hearts of men. It smashes their theories and theologies. It smashes their hollow reputations.

How many beautiful reputations Zion has spoiled!

But God kills that He may make alive. He wounds that He may heal.

As spoken by God's Prophet, in Shiloh Tabernacle, on Lord's Day morning, September 4th, God's Word was a Hammer whose blows will continue to reverberate throughout the world.

While most of the address was necessarily destructive of evil in its purpose and character, there was much of a constructive nature to furnish inspiration and thought to the large and sympathetic audience, which occasionally broke out into spontaneous applause when God's Prophet delivered some especially telling blow.

It was a meeting long to be remembered, and one which sent the people back to their happy homes full of a Holy and Divine Enthusiasm and purpose to support to the end their strong and resourceful leader in his fight against the Hosts of Evil Spirits who are rallying their forces for the Great Armageddon Conflict.

Shiloh Tabernacle, Zion City, Illinois, Lord's Day Morning, September 4, 1904.

The meeting was opened by the singing of Hymn No. 309.

When I shall wake in that fair morn of morns,
After whose dawning never night returns,
And with whose glory day eternal burns,
I shall be satisfied, be satisfied.

REFRAIN—I shall be satisfied,
I shall be satisfied,
When I shall wake in that fair morn of morns.

Prayer was offered by the General Overseer, after which Hymn No. 23 was sung.

Scripture Reading and Exposition.

The General Overseer then said:

Let us read from the Inspired Word of God in the 1st Epistle of Paul to Timothy, the 2d chapter.

I exhort therefore, first of all, that supplications, prayers, intercessions, thanksgivings, be made for all men.

How can people, whether in the South or North, East or West, call themselves Christians, and not pray earnestly in accordance with this inspired instruction?

That injunction is of the first importance, for the Apostle says, "I exhort therefore, first of all."

The supplication is to be for all men, irrespective of color.

Offer thanksgiving for the African, who bore the cross of the Master and has borne it so long.

Offer thanksgiving for the Chinese, who have borne their sorrow through the long night, and are bearing it yet.

Yes, offer thanksgiving for the poor, downtrodden families of the human race; for the Jew who is hated in so-called Christian lands; and yet Salvation is from the Jews.

I offer thanksgiving this morning for my brothers of every color and in every land; do you?

PEOPLE—"Yes."

GENERAL OVERSEER—We thank God that He will bless them all with a full salvation.

Then the people who say that a black man cannot eat in a Christian Try-to-do-it Hotel will feel very small.

May God help us to wipe that miserable, so-called race prejudice off our flag.

Many Families, but Only One Race.

There is only one race, and that is the Adamic race; but there are many families.

It is wicked and infernal prejudice that prevents a man, merely because he has a black skin, from sitting down with a white man.

He can sit down and eat with me.

I had the pleasure of having several black people in my home at my table this week.

There are quite a number of yellow people here today.

They first learned their own language, passed through the high schools of China, and then came to this country.

Now they are young men twenty-five years of age, and have their degrees of LL. B., Ph. D., B. A., and others.

If you do not take care, those other families of the human race will get ahead of us yet.

The Japanese now know how to shoot straighter than we do.

They have turned Russia upside down, and stood her on her head.

They have destroyed the bear, as I said they would.

It is an awful, horrible war, and I hate it; but it was the so-called Christian nation, Russia, that brought it on.

She went into Asia for the purpose of stealing from China.

She wanted to steal everything in sight.

There Is no Color Line in Zion.

However, she is not very much worse than some of the other nations.

May God have mercy on those so-called Christian nations that go to China simply to break it up and take home the pieces.

I almost wish that my skin were black or yellow—I sometimes become so disgusted with the contemptible conduct of the palefaces.

I am heartily ashamed that an excellent African gentleman, who, amid all the darkness of his tribe, sought God, found Him, in a measure, educated himself by his own exertions, can now read and write the English language most creditably, and who entered into Zion years ago and sent me Five Thousand Dollars to extend the work of God, comes to this country, and is not permitted to stay at a Christian Endeavor Hotel.

I thank God that we can receive him in Elijah Hospice.

There is no color line in Elijah Hospice or in Zion City.

I have an excellent organist here who belongs to that shade of color.

If you do not like it, you can stay away.

That wretched, miserable, Christian, try-to-do-it hotel down in St. Louis was guilty of a great sin when it refused our Christian brother entertainment.

I must go back to my subject.

I exhort therefore, first of all, that supplications, prayers, intercessions, thanksgivings, be made for all men;
For kings—

Christians Must Recognize Constituted Authority in the State.

You must recognize the fact that there are kings, although they are not in accordance with the Divine Plan.

Although God should be King, yet certain nations are ruled by earthly Kings, and you must remember that constituted authority must be respected everywhere except where it is so disreputable that it cannot be respected.

For kings and all that are in high place; that we may lead a tranquil and quiet life in all godliness and gravity.
This is good and acceptable in the sight of God our Savior;
Who willeth that all men should be saved, and come to the knowledge of the truth.

That is a good thing, is it not?

---

*The First Apostle has not revised the following reports.

"Who willeth that"—how many men should be saved?

PEOPLE—"All men."

GENERAL OVERSEER—If God wills that "all men" shall be saved, tell me, shall His will be done?

PEOPLE—"Yes."

GENERAL OVERSEER—Can it be frustrated?

PEOPLE—"No."

GENERAL OVERSEER—Can it be possible, if God wills that "all men" shall be saved and come to a knowledge of the truth, that, nevertheless, some men will not be saved throughout eternity, and will never come to a knowledge of the truth?

Can you think that possible?

PEOPLE—"No."

GENERAL OVERSEER—I did not write this. It was written by an Apostle a long time ago.

The Wretched Teaching of Endless Misery.

I hope that you all are willing that "all men" shall be saved.

If you asked that of some high Calvinist he would say, "No! there are vessels of wrath, predestined to eternal misery."

He seems to find great delight in that thought.

Oh, you miserable old wretch!

Is your heart made of granite, like the rocks among which you live?

What a wretched theology, that teaches that the Father of Spirits, who made us, has predestined some to be damned and lost forever!

That wicked Calvinistic doctrine is wittily smitten by Robert Burns in his "Holy Willie's Prayer," in which Holy Willie says:

O, Thou, wha in the heavens dost dwell,
Wha as it pleases best Thysel'
Sends ane to heaven and ten to hell,
A' for Thy glory,
And no for ony good or ill
They've done afore Thee!

Isn't that an old hypocrite's prayer?

I should want to burn my Bible if it taught that.

I should want to fight against a religion that taught the infernal doctrine that God, the Eternal Father, predestined one to heaven and ten to hell; and that they were to be in hell throughout all eternity.

That hell is said to be a place where the wicked are confined, with a lid no doubt, and perhaps the angels sitting on top of it, that the inmates may stew there forever and ever.

What will happen if the lid comes off and they get out again?

Oh! there is something so ludicrous about the whole thing.

If I should talk about it as I think, I should make you laugh too much perhaps.

It seems an awful waste, that God should have made so many millions and millions of people just for the joy of sending them to hell.

It Is God's Will that All Should Be Saved.

Who willeth that *all men* should be saved, and come to the Knowledge of the Truth.

That is clearly His will.

Did not the Christ say, "And I, if I be lifted up from the earth, will draw *all men* unto myself?"

Oh, the depths of the riches of His grace!

For God hath shut up all unto Disobedience, that He might have mercy upon *all*.

. . . .

For as in Adam all die, so also in the Christ shall *all* be made alive.

It is awful to talk about the impossibility of a restoration to God for *all* men.

I know that there are some people who make their bed in hell now, some in the Christian Endeavor Hotel, and in the South, where they want to throw out the black people.

You in the Southland had better take care, or you will create passions that one day will put guns in the hands of the eight million blacks who are there now.

They will not endure forever being trodden under foot.

The land belongs to them as much as to you, and a great deal more than to many of you.

They have been on it for centuries, and have groaned, and toiled, and sweat blood.

But the day of their liberation has come.

Take care! "Have we not all one Father?"

Take care how you treat the black brother, because you may arouse passions that will mean wide-spread murder and massacre.

Jesus, the Christ, Was Man as Well as Son of God.

For there is one God.

Do not forget that.

Some of you talk of God as if there were three Gods.

There are not three Gods, for the Word of God says, "Hear, O Israel, Jehovah our God is one Jehovah."

For there is one God, one Mediator also between God and men, Himself Man, Christ Jesus.

"Oh," you say, "take care! You must always talk of the Christ as God."

I will do no such thing.

I will talk of the Christ as He talked of Himself.

I know that He is the Son of God.

I know that with the Holy Spirit He makes the glorious Triunity, but I shall talk of Him as a Man.

It is my great delight to know that He is a Man.

I could not get along if I did not have a Man in the Christ; if He did not have the body and the passions of a man He could not understand me, for only a man can understand a man.

That Mediator is the Man, Christ Jesus.

He is the man who lay in a virgin's womb; the man who lay on the mother's breast; the man who toddled around the house, often looking up into her face and saying, "Mother, I love you!"

He was the sweet little child, the pure boy, growing up into holy manhood, sympathizing with the sinners, because He knew all the temptations, and powers, and passions of a man.

If He were not a man how could He understand us?

He said, "My Father and your Father; My God and your God."

Where high that Heavenly Temple stands,
That House of God not made with hands,
A great High Priest our nature wears,
The guardian of mankind appears.

Though now exalted up on high,
He bends on earth a brother's eye;
He sympathizes with our grief,
And to the sufferer sends relief.

There Is One God—the God and Father of Us All.

He was "in all points tempted like as we are, yet without sin."

He is a Man.

It is told in Scotland that one day a woman who was carrying an umbrella to shelter herself from the wind and rain, ran against what she thought was a man, and exclaimed apologetically, "O mon, I am so sorry!"

"What! did you call me a mon?" he answered; "I am no mon, I am a meenister."

That was true; he was a minister, but not a man.

It would have been a good thing if he had been a man.

For there is One God, one Mediator also between God and men, Himself Man, Christ Jesus,
Who gave Himself a ransom for *all*.

Oh, no! He gave Himself a ransom only for the Christian Endeavorers!

Oh, no! Only for those who were predestined from all eternity; for the Lord God Almighty intended one for heaven and ten for hell!

Is that true?

He gave Himself a ransom for how many?

PEOPLE—"For all!"

GENERAL OVERSEER—[Continues reading].

The testimony to be born in its own times;
Whereunto I was appointed a preacher, and an Apostle (I speak the truth, I lie not), a teacher of the Gentiles in faith and truth.

I should like you to always read the word "Gentiles," "Nations;" for that is what it means.

The Gentiles included all the nations of the earth with the exception of the Jews.

Barbaric Immodesty, Not Reasonable Adornment, Is Condemned by Paul.

I desire therefore that the men pray in every place, lifting up holy hands, without wrath and disputing.

In like manner, that women adorn themselves in modest apparel, with shamefastness and sobriety; not with braided hair, and gold or pearls or costly raiment.

This does not mean that a woman is never to tie up her hair, or to wear any gold or becoming clothing.

The true meaning is quite clear.

Paul is writing concerning over-adornment and the barbaric immodesty and wastefulness in dress indulged in by the shameful woman of today.

The story is told of a little boy and his very fashionable mamma who had dressed for a dinner party.

His papa said that he would like to see the little boy before he went out that night, so he was sent for.

"Why," said papa, "this little boy is growing tremendously."

"Yes, yes," said his mamma, "he is growing out of his clothes."

Then the little fellow looked at his mamma and said, "Yes, and mamma is growing out of her clothes, too." [Laughter.]

Surely it was never intended that women should wear mere shoulder straps, and leave their arms and chests bare!

I like to see a woman dress neatly and nicely, but let us get a mode of dressing both men and women that is modest, not immodest.

But (which becometh women professing godliness) through good works.

Paul Did Not Deny Women the Right to Teach.

Let a woman learn in quietness with all subjection.
But I permit not a woman to teach, nor to have dominion over a man, but to be in quietness.

Surely that cannot mean what it seems to mean upon the face of it, because he was continually commending Priscilla and Lydia, the seller of purple, of Thyatira, who, with her maidens, spoke the Word of God by the riverside.

The Apostle used to write so affectionately of the women who labored with him in the Gospel.

I have no doubt that he who gave the epistle to the Romans, in which he speaks of Phœbe, a Deaconess of the Church at Cenchrea, taught her what that Gospel meant.

This epistle has been made a magazine of stone-throwing.

I believe that Paul meant that he did not suffer a woman to teach in such a way as to usurp authority over a man.

If any woman teaches in such a way as to usurp authority over a man, she has gone to the Devil.

The man ought to be the head of the house; and if the woman cannot honor him enough to make him the head of her house, then she ought not to have married him.

He has no right to be her husband who has no power to be her head.

Let a woman learn in quietness, with all subjection.

Paul speaks of quietness of spirit.

How splendidly a woman always wins who can hold her peace!

How continually a woman fails who puts in her word against her husband and contradicts him.

A Stupendous and Scientific Piece of Work.

For Adam was first formed, then Eve.

Do not forget that.

Adam was a long time in this world without a wife; so long a time that one of the most stupendous pieces of work that ever was given to man was performed by him before Eve was born.

It was the most scientific piece of work that any man on earth has ever executed.

Do you know what it was?

I will tell you.

God brought every creature, two and two, before man, and he gave to each pair the name which they were to bear.

The name of each animal could be properly given only after considering all the zoölogical facts connected with each particular animal.

Each name indicated the animal's nature.

You can scarcely realize the magnitude of the work, for it took not only months, but probably years and years.

Think of all natural history being grasped by one man!

It was then that man found he had no helpmate.

It was only when he had named all creation, as it passed before him, that he said that he was the only being on earth with no female counterpart.

Then his nature cried out in its need, and God made woman.

Will you women please remember that Adam, the first man, knew all about science before you were made out of one of his ribs?

Man was ahead of you that time. [Laughter.]

I think you got ahead of him later, however, especially in wickedness.

Adam Sinned Knowing That He Was Sharing the Sin and Doom of Eve.

For Adam was first formed, then Eve;
And Adam was not beguiled—

Satan could not beguile Adam.

He had seen both the male serpent and the female serpent.

He had seen all the beasts; he knew that they were beasts.

But the woman was beguiled when the Devil got into the serpent.

"Adam was not beguiled;" he fell through love of woman.

He ate that forbidden fruit with his eyes wide open.

He knew what he was eating.

He knew he was sharing her sin and her doom.

He was not beguiled; he could not plead that.

What a tremendous power that woman had, that she could make him share her sin and her awful doom!

But the woman being beguiled hath fallen into transgression:
But she shall be saved through the child-bearing, if they continue in faith and love and sanctification with sobriety.

Child-bearing, which should have been without pain or apprehension, has been, alas, woman's sorrow.

I believe that now the entail is cut off, if you women will have it so.

You are saved through a Savior who came into this world through a sanctified, sinless woman, who was willing to bear the reproach of the World, the Flesh and the Devil, take her Child from God, and bring Him into this world, pure and holy.

What a wonderful thing it is!

There woman got ahead of man.

Man fell so low, that God could never have brought into this world a Redeemer through a fallen man.

There was not one man in all this world that could procreate a sinless child.

God's glory was to sanctify one woman, making her holy by the power of the Spirit, for, if she had not been holy, the Christ would not have been holy.

She got ahead of every child of humanity, and sometimes I do not wonder that some people worship her.

The Sinless Man Is Greater than the Sinless Woman.

When I was in Europe, I did not wonder, sometimes, at seeing women bowed before her shrine.

They see bad priests and bad men everywhere; but they could think of the pure, holy woman, the sinless mother, the holy, blessed Virgin Mother, and they knew that she could understand a mother's heart.

But they ought to go to the sinless Man, for He is greater than the sinless woman—the Man, Christ Jesus.

But He could not have been a sinless Man without a sinless mother.

Therefore, she had to be saved from sin, sanctified, and made pure and sinless that the conception might be a sinless conception.

It should be so still.

There are some very narrow notions about that.

Many think that anything is permissible in the marital relations, and no longer comes under the name of sin.

Many people get married, and make it a cloak to cover a multitude of sins, and, underneath that cloak of marriage they are worse in their deviltry and filthiness than before.

Oh, if I could just speak it out! Yes, I think I ought to say a great deal more.

Some men marry women and make them beasts.

The woman who is not married would slap your face for one-half the indignity you put upon your wife.

You brutes!

You enslave them with your passions!

There is no freedom for them, you dogs.

Some of you call yourselves Christians, too.

You women are not all angels, but you are far better than the men.

Only a patient, godly woman would bear the brutal slavery of what some call marriage.

It is not marriage at all; it is damning lust! Slavery!

It is not a union in the Lord; it is merely a cloak to cover your brutality.

Criminals Are the Fruit of Lust in the Marriage Relation.

No wonder the world is full of a miserable progeny that has lust stamped upon every feature of its filthy face.

From where do they come—these bandits and brigands that murder in the streets of our large cities?

They are the progeny of brutal mothers and fathers who brought forth children of the Devil.

A woman came to me the other day and said, "What can we do with our son? Oh, how is it that we have such a son, and we are Christians?"

"You, Christians! It is stamped on his face and on his life what you were.

"You were a lustful pair."

Then they confessed.

They are Christians now, but what were they when that child was conceived?

You take a stick sometimes to the children.

You should take a stick to each other.

Remember, it was you who put the hellish passion in that boy and that girl.

Take care, young men and women; if there is to be a godly seed, there must be a godly spirit—purity, self-restraint, wisdom, and love.

There is no real happiness in sin; none at all.

Man was created first and he was greatest.

Woman fell, and she bore the awful burden, until God gave a pure woman.

She got ahead of man then, and gave us the only pure Man that has ever lived.

It is glorious to think that we had one pure Man in the whole world, and that He came from the womb of a pure and holy virgin.

It is glorious to think that that virgin still lives.

I shall not bow down and worship her, but if Mary in heaven will pray for me I shall be glad.

Saints in Heaven Pray for Those on Earth.

If some of my loved ones who have gone to heaven will pray for me I shall be glad.

I know that my mother prays for me.

I shall not worship saints; but if you were to ask me, who, aside from my Lord and Savior, Jesus, the Christ, I should like to have pray for me, I should say, "His mother; let her pray for me."

The mother of the Lord who bore so much sorrow and understood humanity so well!

It is very sweet to think that my daughter prays for me in heaven.

Are you afraid to think of the saints in heaven as praying for you?

You are too thin-skinned, some of you.

You come to saints on earth and ask them to pray for you.

If I were to go to heaven, and you could get at me, I believe that you would send a request to me for prayer even there.

But I should pray without your sending a request.

Are you afraid of becoming too much like Rome in some things, that you do not like to hear of the intercession of saints?

You had better get nearer Rome in some things.

What is it that is poured out of the golden vials?

Is it not the intercession of the saints?

The prayers of the saints are the odors of the incense of heaven.

I am so glad that our Advocate with the Father, our Intercessor, does not wait for us to ask Him to pray.

I like to think of that.

A woman, very sick, once said, "I cannot pray; I cannot even think of Jesus; my mind wanders and I go into a stupor."

She was nearing the heavenly Kingdom, and I knelt by her side.

"Oh," she said, "I am not thinking of Jesus as I ought to."

Then I said, "Do not trouble; Jesus is thinking of you, although you are not thinking of Him.

"He knows your trouble.

"He knows your sorrow.

"He knows your sickness.

"He sees this body of clay falling away and He hears you; and although you are not thinking of Jesus, just remember that Jesus is thinking of you."

HIMSELF MAN.

INVOCATION.

Let the words of my mouth and the meditations of my heart be acceptable in Thy sight, O Lord, my strength and my Redeemer.

TEXT.

One Mediator also between God and men, Himself Man, Christ Jesus.

The Father is Greater than the Son.

There is one God.

That God is our Father.

In the Godhead the supremacy must ever be in the Father.

Jesus said, "The Father is greater than I."

Do not forget that.

Never tell me that the Father is not greater than the Son.

That does not do away with the Divinity of the Son, but it exalts the supremacy of the Father.

The Father is Supreme.

Jesus said, also, "My Father . . . is greater than all."

The Holy Spirit witnesses to that.

The Holy Spirit's great office in our hearts is to teach us to say "Abba, Father."

Do you hear it? Is not that a baby's cry? "Aba-aba-aba-ba-ba-ba!"

Among the Arabs, the Chinese, the Africans, and the Americans, it is the same; it is the first language the child utters.

He says "ba-ba" before he says "ma-ma."

When he is hurt, he cries "Aba-bab-ba."

When the Holy Spirit comes into our hearts we do not know how to talk; we cannot put our thoughts and our wishes into any words, we can only say "Abba."

What am I but "an infant crying in the night; an infant crying for the light; and with no language but a cry?"

We cannot talk.

We come to God "with groanings which cannot be uttered;" but the Spirit at last gets us to say, "Abba, Father."

The first language the Holy Spirit teaches us is "Father."

Jesus taught His Disciples, "When ye pray, say, Father."

The Great Elder Brother Has Taught Us to Pray to His God.

It is so good that the Great Elder Brother has taught us to pray to His God and our God; to His Father and our Father.

The Holy Spirit helps our infirmities and teaches us how to pray.

He is the Intercessor in us for God, and teaches us how to pray.

He reveals to us that we have One in heaven who is praying for us.

If any man sin, we have an Advocate with the Father, Jesus, the Christ, the Righteous.

. . . .

One Mediator also between God and men; Himself Man, Christ Jesus.

I have been talking to you the two previous Lord's Day mornings concerning the two bodies—the body of flesh that will pass away, and the body of glory which Jesus Himself wears, and after which He declares He will fashion our glorified bodies.

He will give us a body like unto His own.

That heavenly body is a body like this, only infinitely better—perfectly pure, clean, sweet, wholesome.

He is pleading with the Father in a glorified body, such as He will give us.

Do you not know that He can show His glory in the bodies we now have?

He can make them Temples of His Spirit.

Then they will shine with His glory, and will be filled with His Spirit, so that out of our bodies shall flow rivers of Living Water.

I want you to remember that He is our Mediator.

You cannot yet be where He is.

Although He is Man, yet by the Eternal Spirit of the Father He is continuously in perfect knowledge of everything.

Our great Intercessor has been given all Authority in the heavens and on the earth.

The Sorrow of Our Intercessor Over the Sins of Earth.

I have been thinking these last few days how He must weep as He sees the children of the common Father rushing into battle to murder and destroy one another upon the plains of Manchuria.

How pitiful it is that the Father's own children, the spirits which came from Him, use their bodies in murdering one another!

Oh, He never made us for that!

But He is pleading with us who stand afar off and see these scenes; and He is saying, "Oh, if you had sent the Gospel to them long ago! If you had done your part, you, who have been squandering each year thirteen hundred million dollars in Liquid Fire and Distilled Damnation, and seven hundred million dollars in Satan's Filthy, Consuming Fire in this so-called Christian country!

"Why did not you who are Christians send them the Gospel instead of sending men to teach them how to fight; instead of building ships with which they murder and destroy one another?

"If you had not sent the fire-water, the vile tobacco, the filthy literature, the demoralizing play!

"But you taught them how to fight, how to sin, and how to lie!"

The Father knows.

The great Elder Brother is not indifferent, and I am sure that out of it all blessing will come to some heart.

General Katsura, the Prime Minister of Japan, and the General that led the Japanese troops in the war with China, said to Bishop McKinn, so Mr. Curtis tells us, "I hate war! Japan does not want war! It was thrust upon us by this so-called Christian power."

It is true!

May God rule in both Russian and Japanese hearts and bring about a speedy peace.

The Father Does Not Need to Be Persuaded to Love Us.

The Father is waiting.

The great Elder Brother is pleading.

He does not plead with the Father for us in the sense that you imagine. The Father is not unwilling.

Do you remember that Jesus once said, "I say not unto you, that I will pray the Father for you; for the Father Himself loveth you?"

You do not need the Lord and Master, the Intercessor, to plead, "Oh, Father, love these poor people."

He loves you with an Everlasting Love.

Our Father does not need to be persuaded to love us; but our Intercessor pleads at the throne of Infinite Justice for the Mercy it would deny if Justice were not satisfied.

He has satisfied the Majesty of heaven, and He has the right to plead for its mercy.

Mercy alone can meet our case, for the best of us have failed to live perfect lives.

I am so glad that my Mediator, your Mediator, the one Mediator between God and men, Himself Man, is pleading for all mankind that all should be saved.

He is working through us, through all that are wholly His, for the salvation and redemption of humanity, and for the obliteration of all differences of color, and clime, and education, bringing us all into one.

The one thing that delights my heart above everything else in Zion, is that here in this little City, seventy nationalities of all shades of color, recognize that One is our Master, One is our Mediator, One is our Father, and "all ye are brethren."

PRAYER OF CONSECRATION.

Our God and Father, in Jesus' Name we come to Thee, recognizing our common brotherhood. We come to Thee in the Name of Him, the one Mediator, "Himself man," between Thee, our Father and men, and ask that by Thy Spirit, Thou wilt help us to call Thee Father and to know it is true; to call Jesus, Lord and Master, Savior, Mediator, and know it to be true; and to turn away from all other, and through Him alone plead for all humanity. May we follow in His footsteps, recognizing the brotherhood of man; and claiming for all men salvation, may we go forward. For Jesus' sake. Amen.

After the singing of the Hymn, "I Stand On Zion's Mount," the General Overseer pronounced the

BENEDICTION.

Beloved, abstain from every form of evil. And may the very God of Peace Himself sanctify you wholly; and I pray God your whole spirit, and soul, and body be preserved entire, without blame, unto the coming of our Lord Jesus, the Christ. Faithful is He that calleth you, who also will do it. The Grace of our Lord Jesus, the Christ, the love of God, our Father, the fellowship of the Holy Spirit, our Comforter and Guide, one Eternal God, abide in you, bless you, and keep you, and all the Israel of God everywhere, forever. Amen.

EARLY MORNING SACRIFICE OF PRAISE AND PRAYER.

REPORTED BY S. E. C., O. L. S., AND E. S.

With an ineffable joy lighting his countenance, the man of God stood before his people Lord's Day morning, September 11, 1904.

A Holy Calm and Peace enveloped him as with a visible garment.

His very presence bespoke Conscious Power.

Yet, strangely at variance with this, there beamed from the eyes an Infinite Love, an Unfathomable Compassion, and the quiet, even voice thrilled with a Vibrant Tenderness. Gentleness sat upon his brow. Goodness enveloped him.

The morning was dark and lowering.

The electric lights inside the building struggled for supremacy with the gray dawn outside.

Yet these externals were all forgotten when the man of God began to speak.

As a living fire the words came; and as by a burning flame the spirits of those present were caught and consumed—yet made alive.

Such is the mystery!

By neither tongue nor pen can it be told; for discernment of Scriptural things comes by the Spirit.

It was all of Joy.

The songs were songs of Joy.

The very spirit of Joy breathed in the petition to God which preceded the words spoken.

Joy unspeakable—a Divine Ecstacy—permeated every utterance of the man of God; yet, side by side, inseparable and never lost, there were the chords of an Infinite Yearning, a very Pathos of Pleading.

Shiloh Tabernacle, Zion City, Illinois, Lord's Day Morning, September 11, 1904.

The service began with the Congregation's singing Hymn No. 128.

Hark, hark! my soul! angelic songs are swelling
O'er earth's green fields and ocean's wave-beat shore;
How sweet the truth those blessed strains are telling,
Of that new life when sin shall be no more,

CHORUS—Angels, sing on! your faithful watches keeping;
Sing us sweet fragments of the songs above,
Till morning's joy shall end the night of weeping,
And life's long shadows break in cloudless love.

The General Overseer led the people in prayer, closing with the Disciples' Prayer.

Scripture Reading and Exposition.

The General Overseer then began the reading of the Scriptures in the 4th chapter of the Epistle of Paul, the Apostle, to the Ephesians.

I therefore, the prisoner in the Lord—

The general and very clear and well-founded conviction of the Church is that this Epistle was written from Rome when Paul was a prisoner, and near the time of his martyrdom.

It, therefore, possesses a wonderfully sacred association.

It may be that he was chained, as was commonly the case, to the Roman soldier who guarded him.

A part of the time he was in "his own hired house," but the rest of the time he was in the prison and chained to his guard.

But it is never dark, no matter how deep the dungeon; it is never dark, no matter how dark the night, to those in whom the Light dwells.

It is always light; for the Light is within.

So the light came from this aged Apostle—"Paul, the aged," as he calls himself.

There are things that suddenly age one, such as sorrow.

Paul was aged in many ways, but perennially young in spirit.

How beautiful, young, hopeful, and sublime in spirit! He was never old!

I therefore, the prisoner in the Lord, beseech you to walk worthily of the calling wherewith ye were called,
With all Lowliness and Meekness, with Long-suffering, forbearing one another in Love;
Giving diligence to keep the Unity of the Spirit, in the Bond of Peace.

Some people imagine that the "Unity of the Spirit" can be better maintained by making a row, and by having a fight with those who love them well and would die for them.

They think it is necessary to maintain the "Unity of the Spirit" in their homes by growling that would be unworthy of an old, stinking bear.

You wretches!

You can never maintain the "Unity of the Spirit" in the bond of grumbling, or the bond of impatience.

I hope that there is not much of this in Zion.

Zion Was Founded that God's Children Might Live in Peace.

Zion was never founded to be a City for the wicked.

It was founded for God's children, that they might live in Peace.

Those who do not want to live in Peace have no business here.

They must go elsewhere, where people think that the "Unity of the Spirit" can be maintained in the bonds of everlasting grumbling, and where they think that another could do better than the one whom God has placed in authority.

You cannot maintain the "Unity of the Spirit," beloved, in any other way than in the "Bond of Peace."

Let our salutation, "Peace to thee!" be a great reality.

Let us all mean it when we say, "Peace to thee be multiplied."

Let Peace be multiplied, and we will have the "Unity of the Spirit in the Bond of Peace."

Giving diligence to keep—

You cannot keep that Unity without Diligence.

You must diligently "keep" it; because, if you are not watchful, Peace will go.

You must be diligent, because the World, the Flesh, and the Devil will try to break it up.

There is one body—

Oh, no! That is a mistake, Paul!

Do you not know, Paul, that there is a Methodist body, a Presbyterian body, a Congregational body, and a Baptist body?

That is the most ridiculous kind of body going; for it has "neither a soul to be saved, nor a body to be kicked."

You cannot find that body anywhere; because it is a body of fragments.

You cannot save it, because it does not exist.

It is no body at all.

Every little backwoods preacher says, "I am a church all to myself. Don't you see?"

He is the whole thing; he and his.

Perfection Is Not Essential to Unity.

Beloved brethren, if we were a company of sinless beings on this earth, we might talk about all understanding things exactly alike; but we cannot, except by coming into the "Unity of the Spirit," and therefore into the organization of the Church, as God established it.

The Apostle, in his last hours, is penning this beautiful letter, not only to that Church, but to all the Churches, and, through them, to us today.

He says, "giving diligence to keep," not the unity of the intellect, the unity of our logic, or the unity of our family prejudices and social status, but "the Unity of the Spirit."

What can bind us together, we are such a discordant people?

PEOPLE—"The Bond of Peace!"

GENERAL OVERSEER—That is beautiful!

You see, we need not break up on "points," because I have many "points" that I have not yet mentioned.

Some one said to me, "I believe that So-and-so is a heretic!"

"Why?" I asked.

"Because he says this, and thus, and so!"

"Is that all? I have a dozen 'points' myself that might make you think me a heretic."

What is the use in talking nonsense like that.

You can make heretics by the hundreds and thousands, if disagreement with your views constitutes heresy.

Then you may get to the place the Roman Catholics reached, where they killed, burned, and tortured people because they were heretics.

It would be ridiculous, if it were not so serious.

The idea of their trying to get doctrine into people by pouring molten lead down their throats, by racking their bodies, and at last by burning them to death.

That is what your trying to make every one see as you do leads to.

It will not do at all.

There is one body, and one spirit, even as also ye were called in one hope of your calling;
One Lord, one Faith, one Baptism.
One God and Father of all.

There Is Unity in the Triunity of God.

"How can you say, 'One God and Father of all,' when there is also Jesus and the Holy Spirit?" you may ask.

Is not Jesus in the Father?

PEOPLE—"Yes."

GENERAL OVERSEER—Is not the Father in Jesus?

PEOPLE—"Yes."

GENERAL OVERSEER—Is not the Spirit in the Father, and the Father in the Spirit?

Can you divide these three?

Can you separate my spirit, and my soul, and my body as I sit here?

Am I three men or one?

PEOPLE—"One."

GENERAL OVERSEER—Get simple thoughts into your mind.

The Spirit is in the Son, and the Son is in the Father; the Father is in the Spirit, and the Father is in the Son.

One God and Father of all, who is over all, and through all, and in all.
But unto each one of us was the grace given according to the measure of the gift of the Christ.
Wherefore He saith,
When He ascended on high, He led captivity captive,
And gave gifts unto men.
(Now this, He ascended, what is it but that He also descended into the lower parts of the earth?
He that descended is the same also that ascended far above all the heavens, that He might fill all things.)

How wonderful that is! That He might fill the material, the psychical, and the spiritual everywhere; that when you cleave the tree, you might find Him in the heart of it.

"What!" you exclaim.

I repeat it: You might find Him in the heart of it.

Do you see that little core—that heart—in the middle?

That was the first of the tree, and He placed it there.

God May Be Seen in Everything.

See that fish swimming so happily!

Catch it and look into its eye!

See! See Him there!

You see Him in the bird, and in the beast; you see Him everywhere!

"O Mamma! I planted a seed; and look, what a beautiful flower! It has eyes! and it looks at me!" said my little daughter.

The flower she spoke of was a pansy; and as the buds burst forth into flowers she came running to her mamma, and said, "Another one has come out; and it has eyes, and is looking at me."

When she was very small, she clapped her hands, and said one day, "Oh, look at the birds, the birds!"

"Where, dear?" her mamma asked. "Oh!" she cried, "there is one!" and it was a fly.

Her eyes saw the beauty of the fly.

Some one else only drove the fly away.

I am afraid that I might have been that person.

But when you get to see what God is, and how He fills "all things," the fly becomes a bird, and you can see its beauty; only I admit that you do not want too many birds about at one time. [Laughter.]

It is beautiful to know that you can find God in all things.

May that truth make us a little more patient, even with the fly.

Beloved, if we are wise we will see God in everything.

Not in vain were the simple lines written,

Sermons in stones;
Books in running brooks;
And God in everything.

Even the Devil Has Some Divine Qualities.

A man once said to me, "You can find no good quality in the Devil."

"Yes, I can," I replied.

"What!" he exclaimed in surprise.

"Yes," I answered, "his perseverance is a magnificent quality. I have a great admiration for the perseverance of the Devil."

The Devil never takes any holiday.

He is at business all the time.

He goes with the holiday people; and they leave all their religion behind; for he is often the leader of the party.

That is not true, however, if we are the children of God, and take God with us everywhere.

It is beautiful just to realize that God is everywhere, and that there is some quality left, even in the Devil, that you can admire.

I do admire his perseverance.

You whip him and whip him hard, and he comes up again smiling, and says, "I will have you yet!"

You whip him again; and he goes back to Chicago, and rubs his head, and says, "Well, I will have you yet!" and he comes back.

Even in the Devil there is some part of the Divine nature left —the spiritual activity that, though perverted, is persistent.

He is oftentimes wiser than the child of light.

Let us be "wise as serpents" and "harmless as doves."

There is so much in the thought that the Christ has "ascended far above all the heavens, that He might fill all things!"

God Has a Place and Work for All.

And He gave some to be Apostles—

Let us pause a moment. Whence do the Apostles come?

Can you educate them?

Can you manufacture them?

Can you ordain them?

Can you make an Apostle?

Is he not a gift? "He *gave* some."

You cannot make them.

And He gave some to be Apostles; and some, Prophets; and some, Evangelists; and some, Pastors and Teachers.

The church has been trying to manufacture preachers.

You might as well try to manufacture a poet as a preacher.

Can you manufacture a poet?

Poeta nascitur, non fit. The poet is born, not made.

Preachers are born; not made.

Artists are born; not made.

Every man, if he could only know it, is born to something.

If he only would not try to be something to which he is not born.

Even if he is born an ass, he is good for something.

Every one of us is good for something.

What that is, we ourselves do not always know; often some-one else knows better than we ourselves.

A good, wise teacher discovers what his scholars are fitted for as their minds unfold.

Can you not see that Bobby is meant to be an artist?

Do you not see that every chance he gets he takes a charred stick and draws a picture?

Do you not notice how often little Bobbie or little Mary comes to you and says, "Now, Mamma, I shall make a horse for you. Now, isn't that like a horse?"

It is no more like a horse than a cow; but she has the genius in her; so do not say, impatiently, "Oh, no! It is not like a horse."

Say to the little child, "Well, dear, it is not very much like a horse, but try it again; you will do it better."

Do you not see that she has the genius?

Then you may hear another little one always humming at first, and then beginning to sing a little.

Watch that!

Do you not see that that child has music in her soul?

How a Little Boy Showed an Aptitude for Preaching.

A little five-year-old boy said the other day, "Papa, are you going to stay home today?"

"Yes, my son," he replied.

"Is Mamma going to church?"

"Yes, Mamma is going to church alone, and I am going to stay and take care of the babies and the home."

"All right, Papa! I shall preach to you when Mamma is gone!"

"Very well, my son."

Then he placed the chairs in order, and said, "Papa, you sit there, and So-and-so, you sit there! Now we will have the service."

Then he got up on the stairs and began.

Papa came in with the baby, who began to cry, and the little fellow said, "Take that baby to the Baby-house! I cannot be disturbed by the baby!" [Laughter.]

That little fellow will make a preacher.

When he was a babe his father asked me what he should name him, and I said, "Name him Paul."

From the time he was consecrated he began to think.

Had his father manifested anger and said, "You little scamp!" he would have been very naughty.

Children should be encouraged in thus giving expression to natural talent.

Every one is not a preacher.

It is not a talker that makes a preacher; he must have authority.

That little fellow thought he had authority.

Was he not conducting a service?

He was in the place where he must have order.

When he comes to the services here, he does not fidget around, because he knows that means the baby-house; and he wants to stay and listen to the service.

Grace Is Needed to Find One's Calling.

Each one of us has a calling.

Some people miss their calling because they are so obstinate.

We see their calling; we, who are older than they.

We try to guide them; and then they break away and try to be something God Almighty never intended them to be.

It is most painful to see a girl who has neither time nor tune in her head sit down to learn to play the piano.

She never learns.

How much better it would be if she spent her time in developing the talent that she has.

God is the Great Master, and by the Spirit, and through a well-organized Church, He ought to be able to lead each of us to find our niche in His own great and beautiful Church, and He will.

This is for the work of the

Perfecting of the saints, unto the work of ministering, unto the building up of the body of the Christ.

"Oh, can the body be built up?" you ask.

Yes, it can be built up; and you can be hands for it, or feet, or fingers, or heart, or something else.

Each one can take his or her place.

The Least Often the Most Honorable in Service.

"My place is such a little place! It is only a little finger" one may say.

That is a most important part of the hand.

"But I am like a man whose fingers are all thumbs."

Well, the thumb is very important.

If I lost my thumb I should lose an important part of my hand.

Another may say, "I am just like a finger nail!"

That is also a good thing.

If I did not have a nail on my finger, I should be in trouble.

Let us not be afraid to take our place in the body, because the body must be built up.

The Church is one body.

Till we all attain unto the Unity of the Faith, and of the Knowledge of the Son of God—

Can Faith ever be a unit?

It can.

We must be a unit in things that are essential; in the things that are not essential there must be Liberty; and in everything, Charity.

But it is fundamental that there be Unity; even where there must be diversity; and in the things you do not understand, there must be Charity.

Till we all attain unto the Unity of the Faith, and of the Knowledge of the Son of God, unto a full-grown man, unto the measure of the stature of the fulness of the Christ:

That we may be no longer children, tossed to and fro, and carried about with every wind of doctrine, by the sleight of men, in craftiness, after the wiles of error;

But speaking truth in love, may grow up in all things into Him, which is the Head, even the Christ.

All Are Needful to the Prosperity of the Whole.

I am so glad that in the Church of God there is only one head, that we may grow up in all things.

Do you not see that it takes all of the things of life to make the Church grow?

The Church must grow in spiritual, in educational, and in business capacity, and in political power, and in family economy, until we grow up "in all things into Him."

Every part of our being, and every occupation of our life will help us to grow up "in all things into Him, which is the Head, even the Christ."

From whom all the body fitly framed--

It is all framed together, united; and every part is a part of every other part.

The Church is to be like the body--every part perfectly united.

From whom all the body fitly framed and knit together through that which every joint supplieth, according to the working in due measure of each several part maketh the increase of the body unto the building up of itself in love

---

"THE UNITY OF THE FAITH."

INVOCATION.

Let the words of my mouth and the meditations of my heart be acceptable in Thy sight, and a blessing to this people, O God, my Strength and my Redeemer.

Long before the morning dawned I realized the presence of God.

When I went to sleep last night I had many thoughts in my mind as to what I should talk to you about this morning.

But there were so many thoughts crowding in upon one another, that I could not come to a decision.

When I awoke this morning the text was in my mind.

It came to me with very great power.

TEXT

Till we all attain unto the Unity of the Faith, and of the Knowledge of the Son of God, unto a full-grown man, unto the measure of the stature of the fulness of the Christ.

A Temple that Has the Capacity of Growth.

The most wonderful thing in all the world is that Temple of God (or it may be a Temple of the Devil)—a wee, little body; just a baby.

When some one says, "There is nothing that is worth the knowing," I say, "Come here! I will show you something worth the knowing;" and I take him to a cot where a little baby lies asleep.

"Look!" I say, "that baby is worth the knowing!"

> There was born a child in that midnight hour,
> It matters not whether in hut or tower.
> We know it but as a child of humanity;
> Heir to its passions, its pains, its vanity,
> And, as changing seasons their flowers unfold
> To bloom in the sunshine, to fade in the cold,
> So that we make a world whose influence may win
> That young life to virtue or drive it to sin.

That is a truth that is worth the knowing.

You can see that Temple grow.

Other temples, made with hands, do not grow.

They are stone, and lime, and brick, and steel.

God made man to be a habitation for Himself, through the Spirit.

Ye are a Temple of God.

The Horrible Possibilities of This Living Temple.

How wonderful it is that this body can grow up and be a Temple of God!

How horrible it is that this body can grow up and be a Temple of the Devil, until the whole being, from the brain to the toes, in every part and every passion, is a Temple, not only of the Devil, but of a thousand devils!

Then the body becomes a Temple of lust, and hate, and murder.

Such a man disciplines himself to shoot, and kill, and murder.

Such a woman trains herself to fascinate, to deceive, and to make herself something that she is not.

The most disgusting and horrible thing in all this world is a woman or a man who has grown up a Temple that is a sham, a horror; a mass of iniquity.

The Church of God is represented as a Human Temple.

God wants this body to be His Temple.

Oh, we have hurt it so!

We have misunderstood what God meant it to be, and have not brought it into subjection, perhaps, to God.

We have not had the liberty and freedom in it that we ought to have had, because we did not know.

Why did we not know?

Because we were in doubt.

Why were we in doubt?

Because the teachers did not go to God for their teaching.

They went to one another.

Many of the people assumed to be teachers who had never had the Divine Seal.

Only God Can Effect Unity in the Christ.

How disunited the Body of the Christ is in the church today!

One says, "I am of Paul;" another, "I am of Apollos;" another, "I am of Cephas;" another, "I am a Baptist;" another, "I will have you know that I am a Methodist;" "I will have you know that I am a Presbyterian;" or, "I am none of these, I am a Disciple."

Was Paul crucified for you?

Was Martin Luther crucified for you?

Was John Calvin crucified for you?

Tell me!

PEOPLE—"No."

GENERAL OVERSEER—Then why do you have this division?

Where is Catholicity?

Where is your Apostolic calling?

Where is your Unity?

The Word of God says, "Till we all attain unto the Unity of the Faith,"—the Unity of the Hope, the Unity of the Love, in the Unity of God.

Only God, who is Triune, can make us One.

That is the hardest thing about it all.

Do you not see that our being wants to strike?

Do you not know that our very selves want to strike?

Our bodies say, "I am the biggest part of you; look after me!"

Our souls say, "Look here, I am the biggest part."

Our spirits sometimes are crushed because we are listening to the soul and the body, and not listening to the spirit.

The spirit itself has no voice.

Then at last we hear God, and He says, "Your spirit is the most important part of you; but I alone can bring you into harmony!"

God Has Promised to Dwell in His People.

"But, who art Thou, Lord? Who art Thou that canst bring my spirit, my soul, and my body into unity, and take every part, every power, and every passion, and make them holy?"

Then comes the answer, "I will dwell in you!"

The General Overseer then led the Congregation in singing:

> I will be within thee
> A Well of Water, a Well of Water,
> Springing up into everlasting life.

Jesus said to the woman of Samaria:

Every one that drinketh of this water shall thirst again:

But whosoever drinketh of the Water that I shall give him shall never thirst; but the Water that I shall give him shall become in him a Well of Water springing up unto eternal life.

"What can make me clean?" you ask.

You are told, "The blood of Jesus."

"Yes, but how?" again you ask. "I cannot go back nineteen centuries and gather up the old blood!

"It rotted!

"It passed away!

"It was never preserved.

"It was blood like my blood; and a soul like my soul."

Ah, but the Christ's body did not pass away!

His body was transformed, and out of that pure, holy, sinless body, there came a body of glory.

How could that poor, sinful woman of Samaria, who was worn-out with her passions; who had had five husbands; who was living in sin and open adultery with a man who was not her husband; a low harlot, a filthy wretch, scarce fit to be left on God Almighty's earth—how could she be made over again?

The water that I shall give him shall become in him a Well of Water springing up unto eternal life.

"Ah! but it will take a long time, Lord," she might have said. "I have been so wicked! I have been so bad! It is all true! I have been a woman of sin, and it will take a long time."

The Transforming Power of the Holy Spirit.

The Christ's answer was, "Whosoever drinketh of the water that I shall give him shall never thirst. Take, O sinful woman, take!"

Did you ever see a drunkard, with his arm hanging inactive by his side, his eyes dull, his whole being in a state of torpor?

What does he want?

He tells you that he wants whisky.

If it is given to him, what do you see?

In a moment he is transformed.

"Ah!" he says, "I feel good. Give me another glass!"

Yes, he has the Devil in him—the Devil in solution.

It is not a well of water; it is a well of abomination.

It is a well of damnation!

He is alive now, ready for any deviltry; and ready for any use you choose to make of him!

Ah! Satan of hell, you can use him now!

You put your water into him, and now he has within him a well of damnation!

Get the other water—the Water of Life!

Get that, and what will happen?

That which happened to the woman at the well!

She did not know it, but she had taken the Water, and that from the hands of the sinless Christ.

He looked so beautiful!

He looked at her as no other man ever had.

He loved her!

He blessed her.

But He was not lustful, and horrible, and filthy.

He was good.

He was sweet.

He was pure; and His words went into her heart.

Sir, give me this Water, that I thirst not!

The Spirit came.

She was asking for the Holy Spirit, and He came.

After a minute or two she passed her hands over her face and eyes, and then questioningly looked at this Man again.

She sees now!

She thought He was a Prophet, but now she says, "I know that Messiah cometh (which is called the Christ): when He is come, He will declare unto us All Things."

"Jesus saith unto her, I that speak unto thee am He!"

How the Living Water Cleansed a Vile Woman.

She looked at Him and saw that it was true.

He was the long-promised Messiah!

He had given her the Living Water, and her heart was made clean!

"What! Clean?" you ask.

Yes, white as snow.

Her mind is clear! Clearer than when she was a sweet maiden and had not yet sinned.

She has had such an eloquent tongue, and with it has led men down to the Devil.

She puts down her water-pot, and goes into the city.

The Living Water is in her body, which is now a Temple of God.

It has been the Temple of the Devil.

Her eyes used to flash with damning lust; now her heart is pure, and she goes to the men and says, "Come, come, and see the Christ!"

They come and see the Christ.

Till we all attain unto the Unity of the Faith.

Do you not see that when the Holy Spirit comes into us with power, then we, the most sinful of us, do not need a long training to be able to bring sinful men and women to the feet of the Teacher, the Christ?

Can we not all do it?

If we have the "Unity of the Faith," of Hope, and of Love, then our little baby Church will grow up "unto the measure of the stature of the fulness of the Christ."

Then each shall have the manly spirit of the Christ; but wh the Church is all put together as one body, then it is a Bri of the Lamb.

The perfected Church is represented as a beautiful a perfect woman.

The Church Is the Body, the Bride, and the Wife of the Christ

The head of the woman is the man; the head of the Chur is the Christ; and the Church is His Bride.

When the Church is perfected she will stand in the similitu of a perfect woman, ready and waiting for her bridegroom, whom she will be taken up out of the wilderness and mad great, glorious, beautiful bride.

Oh, what a beautiful simile!

God means, by that Church and through the Christ to ma Zion not only a bride, but a wife; not only a wife, but a gre glorious, majestic mother.

As soon as she travails, she will bring forth myriads beautiful beings, who will fill all the earth.

There will be no one else left; they will disappear!

And the glorious mother, who is she?

But the Jerusalem that is above is free, which is our mother.

Beloved, we have not seen the Church.

The Christian Catholic Church in Zion has been only process of creation; but she has been growing and w presently be completed.

Then she will be a glorious possibility of Divine Motherho for all the nations.

It is wonderful, what God has done with this Church, ev in its very imperfect state.

How He has brought us together!

How He has brought us out of the "kingdom of Darkne into the "Kingdom of His Son," and then into the fellows of His Church; for there are multitudes in the Kingdom of G that are not in the Church.

The Church Is to Be Without Spot or Wrinkle.

They have not seen a Church at all beautiful or attractive; that has been like the Church that the Scriptures speak "Not having spot or wrinkle or any such thing."

O God, make us a spotless Church! [Amen.]

Recently I read an article about Zion in a paper called *Br* a trade paper published for manufacturers of brick.

It had been placed on my desk marked "Page 117," bu had no time to read it, and I put it aside.

Several times I came across it, and saw the mark, "Pa 117," but I thought, "Perhaps it is some little notice, or a lit skit about me; and I have not time to bother with *Brick*."

But one day I opened it, and found there a long, splen article, with eight beautiful engravings—I shall not say t they were all beautiful, because the first one was an engrav of my own photograph, and I cannot say that that is ve beautiful.

Then I looked at the article, and noticed particularly thing the writer said: "When it was rumored that Zion br was in the market, and was being sold, the writer, as the spe representative of *Brick*, thought it was time to go up and the spotless City!"

The Church Is Now in Her Formative Period.

I looked at those words, and said, "That man said that satire—"The spotless City!"

I stopped and said, "O God, make it spotless; make it pure that what they said in satire will be true."

But as I read on I found that the man did not mean it satire; that to him, as he saw this City, it was spotless.

He did not have sharp enough eyes.

I can see better than that.

I can see that you are not spotless

I can see that you need rubbing off at various places.

I can see that we all need to do much better.

But, as compared with the cities of the world, it is spotle

I want you to ask God to make the Declaration of n week the beginning of a better time.

I want you to ask God to take His poor servant, and to ma him the means and channel by which the Holy Spirit will co into the Church.

I want you to ask God to make the First Apostle of Church the means by which the Living Water can come in, it came into the woman of Sychar, and make her pure.

Will you do it?

PEOPLE—"Yes."

GENERAL OVERSEER—If you do not do it, I would rather not live until next Lord's Day; because, if my Church, the Church of God, the Church which the Christ purchased with His blood, the people whom He has committed to my care, will not be willing to let the Living Water flow through them, what is the use of its flowing through me?

What is the use of my being an Apostle to you, if you will not let the Living Water flow through you?

Did not the Living Water come through those poor, simple fishermen?

Through the lips and hands of Peter, Pentecostal Power and Healing Power came!

Do you want it to come now?

PEOPLE—"Yes."

GENERAL OVERSEER—Do you want to get into the "Unity of the Faith?"

PEOPLE—"Yes."

GENERAL OVERSEER—Are you willing to be one in the Christ, and to follow me as I follow Him?

PEOPLE—"Yes."

GENERAL OVERSEER—Then stand up and tell Him so.

PRAYER OF CONSECRATION.

My God and Father, for Jesus' sake, lead us on; lead Thy servant on; perfect Thy Church. Continue to make it Thine own. Father, we have been growing in the knowledge of the Christ, unto the time when Thou canst give us the Apostleship. Oh, let more spiritual power come with the Apostleship until we all shall be, though sinful, purified and able to go everywhere, telling of the Christ whom we have found at the well—the well of Salvation in the Church of the Living God. Make Zion more and more a well, a fountain, out of which the Living Waters can flow. May the waters flow to all the world from Shiloh today. For Jesus' sake. Amen. [*All repeat the prayer, clause by clause, after the General Overseer.*]

The Congregation then sang the Hymn, "I Will Be Within Thee, a Well of Water," after which the General Overseer pronounced the

BENEDICTION.

Beloved, abstain from every form of evil. And may the very God of Peace Himself sanctify you wholly; and I pray God your whole spirit, and soul, and body be preserved entire, without blame, unto the coming of our Lord Jesus, the Christ. Faithful is He that calleth you, who also will do it. The grace of our Lord Jesus, the Christ, the love of God, our Father, the fellowship of the Holy Spirit, our Comforter and Guide, one Eternal God, abide in you, bless you, and keep you, and all the Israel of God everywhere, forever. Amen.

Zion in California.

Rev. W. D. Taylor, Elder in the Christian Catholic Apostolic Church in Zion, San Francisco, California, will hold religious services as follows:

In Zion Tabernacle, 160 East Santa Clara street, San Jose, California, Monday, October 10th, at 7:30 p. m.; Tuesday, October 11th, at 2:30 and 7:30 p. m., and Wednesday, October 12th, at 2:30 and 7:30 p. m.

At Santa Clara, California, Thursday, October 13th, at 7:30 p. m., and Friday, October 14th, at 2:30 and 7:30 p. m.

At Los Gatos, California, Saturday, October 15th, at 2:30 and 7:30 p. m.

Baptismal services will be held in San Jose.

Publisher's Notice.

The remittance must accompany receipt of subscriptions at the Publishing House, no difference by or for whom or for whatever time they may be given, or whether forwarded through Ordained Officers, Branches, or Gatherings of the Christian Catholic Church in Zion. Accounts will be carried with Ordained Officers, Branches, or Gatherings, on quantity orders of periodicals consigned on sale for monthly settlement, but to include only such articles as bear the imprint of Zion. All orders for Bibles, books, buttons, pictures (except prints done by the Publishing House), lace souvenirs, etc., must be sent to the General Stores, Zion City, Lake County, Illinois.

DO YOU KNOW GOD'S WAY OF HEALING?

BY THE REV. JOHN ALEX. DOWIE.

Let it be supposed that the following words are a conversation between the reader [A] and the writer [B].

A. What does this question mean? Do you really suppose that God has some one especial way of healing in these days, of which men may know and avail themselves?

B. That is exactly my meaning, and I wish very much that you should know God's Way of Healing, as I have known it for many years.

A. What is the way, in your opinion?

B. You should rather ask, WHO is God's Way? for the way is a Person, not a thing. I will answer your question in His own words, "I am the Way, and the Truth, and the Life: no one cometh unto the Father, but by Me." These words were spoken by our Lord Jesus, the Christ, the Eternal Son of God, who is both our Savior and our Healer. (John 14:6.)

A. But I always thought that these words only referred to Him as the Way of Salvation. How can you be sure that they refer to Him as the Way of Healing also?

B. Because He cannot change. He is "the same yesterday and today, yea, and forever." (Hebrews 13:8.) He said that He came to this earth not only to save us but to heal us. (Luke 4:18), and He did this when in the flesh on earth. Being unchanged He must be able and willing and desirous to heal now.

A. But is there not this difference, namely, that He is not with us now?

B. No; for He said "Lo, I am with you All the Days, even unto the Consummation of the Age;" and so He is with us now, in spirit, just as much as when He was here in the flesh.

A. But did He not work these miracles of healing when on earth merely to prove that He was the Son of God?

B. No; there was still a greater purpose than that. He healed the sick who trusted in Him in order to show us that He came to die not only for our sins, but for our sicknesses, and to deliver us from both.

A. Then, if that be so, the atonement which He made on the Cross must have been for our sicknesses as well as our sins. Can you prove that is the fact from the Scriptures?

B. Yes, I can, and the passages are very numerous. I need quote only two. In Isaiah 53:4, 5, it is written of Him: "Surely He hath borne our griefs (Hebrew, *sicknesses*), and carried our sorrows: . . . and with His stripes we are healed." Then, in the Gospel according to Matthew, this passage is quoted and directly applied to the work of bodily healing, in the 8th chapter 17th verse: "That it might be fulfilled which was spoken by Isaiah the prophet, saying, Himself took our infirmities, and bare our diseases."

A. But do you not think that sickness is often God's will, and sent for our good, and therefore God may not wish us to be healed?

B. No, that cannot possibly be; for diseases of every kind are the Devil's work, and his work can never be God's will, since the Christ came for the very purpose of destroying "the works of the Devil." (1 John 3:8.)

A. Do you mean to say that all disease is the work of Satan?

B. Yes, for if there had been no sin (which came through Satan) there never would have been any disease, and Jesus never in one single instance told any person that sickness was God's work or will, but the very contrary.

A. Can you prove from Scriptures that all forms of sickness and infirmity are the Devil's work?

B. Yes, that can be done very easily. You will see in Matthew 4:23 and 9:35 that when Jesus was here in the flesh He healed "all manner of disease and all manner of sickness among the people." Then if you will refer to Acts 10:38 you will see that the Apostle Peter declares that He (Jesus) "went about doing good, and healing all that were oppressed of the Devil." Notice that all whom He healed, not some, were suffering from Satan's evil power.

A. But does disease never come from God?

B. No, it cannot come from God, for He is pure, and disease is unclean; and it cannot come out of Heaven, for there is no disease there.

A. That is very different from the teachings which I have received all my life from ministers and in the churches. Do you really think that you are right, and that they are all wrong in this matter?

B. It is not a question as between myself and them. The only question is, What does God's Word say? God has said in all the ages, to His Church, "I am Jehovah that healeth thee" (Exodus 15:26), and therefore it would be wicked to say that He is the defiler of His people. All true Christians must believe the Bible, and it is impossible to believe that good and evil, sickness and health, sin and holiness could have a common origin in God. If the Bible really taught that, it would be impossible to believe our Lord Jesus, the Christ, when He says: "A good tree cannot bring forth evil fruit, neither can a corrupt tree bring forth good fruit." (Matthew 7:18.)

A. But even if I agree with all you say, is it not true that the Gifts of Healing were removed from the Church, and are not in it now?

B. No, the "Gifts of Healing" were never withdrawn, and can never be withdrawn, from the true Church of God, for it is written: "The gifts and the calling of God are without repentance." (Romans 11:29.) There are nine gifts of God to the Church (enumerated in 1 Corinthians 12:8 11), and all these are in the Holy Spirit. Therefore, so long as the Holy Spirit is in the Church, all the gifts must be there also. If they are not exercised, that does not prove that they do not exist, but that the faith to exercise them is lacking in God's servants. The gifts are all perfectly preserved; for the Holy Spirit, not the Church, keeps them safely.

A. What should a Christian then do when overtaken with sickness?

B. A Christian should obey God's command, and at once turn to Him for forgiveness of the sin which may have caused the sickness, and for immediate healing. Healing is obtained from God in one of four ways, namely: First, by the direct prayer of faith, without any aid from the officers of the Church, praying as the Centurion did in Matthew 8:5 13; second, by two faithful disciples praying in perfect agreement in accordance with the Lord's promise in Matthew 18:19; third, by the anointing of the Elders and the prayer of faith, according to the instructions in James 5:14 and 15; and fourth, by the laying on of the hands of them who believe, and whom God calls to that ministry, as the Lord commands in Mark 16:18, and in other places.

A. But are people healed in this way in these days?

B. Yes, in thousands of cases. I have myself laid hands upon many hundreds of thousands of persons, and I have seen the Lord's power manifested in the healing of great numbers, many of whom are living witnesses in many countries, who have testified publicly before thousands, and who are prepared to testify at any time. This ministry is being exercised by devoted Christians in many parts of America, Europe, Australasia, and elsewhere.

A. Is it not the same as Christian Science, Mind Healing, etc.?

B. No. Divine Healing is diametrically opposed to these diabolical counterfeits which are utterly antichristian. These impostures are only seductive forms of Spiritualism. Trance Evangelism is also a more recent form of this delusion, and it deceives many.

A. But how shall I obtain the necessary faith to receive healing, which faith I am at present conscious that I do not possess?

B. It is written: "Belief cometh of hearing, and hearing by the word of the Christ." (Romans 10:17.) Our Missions are held for the express purpose of teaching fully the Word of God on this matter, and I very heartily invite you to attend the meetings which are announced for Zion Tabernacles in Chicago and other cities, and for Shiloh Tabernacle, Zion City, Illinois. All are welcome and there are no charges of any kind made, for all God's gifts are free gifts. Salvation is the first of these, without which you cannot be healed through faith in Jesus. All the costs of this work are covered by the free-will offerings of the people who attend these meetings, and others whom the Lord leads to help; but the poorest, who have nothing to give, are as heartily welcome as the richest.

A. Do you see the sick and lay hands upon them in this Mission?

B. Yes; after we feel satisfied that they are fully resting in the Lord alone for the healing, we see privately, so far as time permits, those who attend; but under no circumstances do we claim the power to heal any; for "power belongeth unto God."

A. Have you any writings upon this subject which can be purchased?

B. Yes; these can be obtained at the office of Zion Printing and Publishing House, Zion City, Illinois, and at any Zion Tabernacle. But the best book on Divine Healing is the Bible itself, studied prayerfully and earnestly.

We extend to you a hearty invitation to attend the meetings, which are free to all. Our prayer is that you may be led to find in Jesus, the Christ, our Lord and God your present Savior from sin, your Healer from sickness, your Cleanser from all evil, your Keeper in the way to Heaven, your Friend, and your All for Time and Eternity. We pray that these words may help many who read, and that our little conversation may bear fruit in leading many readers to look to Jesus only.

"The Healing of Christ's seamless dress
Is by all beds of pain;
We touch Him in life's throng and press
And we are whole again."

Divine Healing Meeting in Shiloh Tabernacle

*REPORTED BY O. L. S., O. R., AND A. W. N.

THE first Divine Healing Meeting held by God's Prophet, after his return from the Around-the-World Visitation, was that in Shiloh Tabernacle, Tuesday afternoon, July 5, 1904.

It was a memorable meeting to the very large company of people that gathered to hear the words of teaching of him whom God had chosen to restore to His people the truth that He and He alone is their Healer.

It was a delight to hear once more the straightforward, loving, but incisive words of the teacher, and a rich spiritual blessing descended upon all.

Many sick were there, seeking God's Way of Healing.

He—for God's Way is a Person, not a thing—was revealed to them through the Word of God as illuminatingly expounded, and many received the boon that their hearts desired.

Shiloh Tabernacle Zion City, Illinois, Tuesday Afternoon, July 5, 1904.

The service was opened by the Congregation's singing Hymn No. 28.

I know I love Thee better, Lord,
Than any earthly joy;
For Thou has given me the peace,
Which nothing can destroy.

CHORUS—The half has never yet been told,
Of Love, so full and free!
The half has never yet been told,
The Blood—it cleanseth me!

Our Extremity Is God's Opportunity.

The General Overseer then said:

We shall now go to prayer; but before we pray I very earnestly ask that you will pray with me in faith, nothing doubting.

There is no reason why, if you fulfil God's conditions, He should not fulfil His promises.

There is no case so desperate that He cannot save.

There is no case so desperate that He cannot heal.

There is no condition so abject as to be beyond the reach of Divine Power.

Our extremity is always God's opportunity.

I know not how desperate the conditions of some here may be.

It is not always those who look the nearest to death that are nearest to dying.

Some of you here today in apparently good health may be nearer death than any of the sick.

It is often in the midst of life that we meet death.

It is often the unexpected that happens.

You must not be at all affected by the seeing of the eye and the hearing of the ear.

God is just as able to heal the one who is in the greatest straits as the one in whom disease has just begun to work.

There Is Certainty of Healing if We Fulfil God's Conditions.

Get the thought before going to prayer that if you will fulfil God's conditions, He will fulfil His promises.

My purpose this afternoon will be to show you what God's conditions are.

Teaching is of the greatest importance.

Then the work will be done if you fulfil the Divine Conditions.

The General Overseer then led in prayer, after which he said:

From the very beginning of my teaching in connection with Divine Healing I have never got away from the 8th chapter of Matthew.

When I begin a new series of talks, I always go back to that wonderful chapter for my reading, and for the basis of my teaching.

Please open your Bibles to that chapter, because reading and teaching will come together.

And when He was come down from the mountain, great multitudes followed Him.

The question really is, Whom do you follow?

If Peter, and James, and John, and all the apostles and prophets were here, with Jesus in their midst, would you want to follow Isaiah, Jeremiah, Moses, Daniel, Peter, or Paul?

Whom would you want to hear?

PEOPLE—"Jesus."

GENERAL OVERSEER—You cannot blame these people that they followed Jesus.

It would not have mattered if John or Peter had dropped out of the procession; they might have regretted it, but they had their eyes on Jesus.

Never Pray the Prayer of Doubt.

He had been teaching them for many days, no doubt, on that mountainside.

Matthew wrote three chapters, full of His teaching, and no doubt that is only an outline.

When Jesus came down from that mountain, on the last day of the teaching, He must have said something to them which made them to know that He would not speak there again, or at least for some time; so they were all following Him.

And behold, there came to Him a leper and worshiped Him, saying, Lord, if Thou wilt, Thou canst make me clean.

Never pray that prayer.

Because some one else blunders, and the Lord overlooks their blunders and shows them the right way, is that any reason why we should make the same blunder?

Worship Him as that leper did.

See God in Jesus, the Christ.

Believe that in Him the Father and the Spirit dwells; and that He is the Son of God.

That is worshiping.

But do not pray this prayer.

Do not say, "Lord, if Thou wilt, Thou canst."

There is one word in that prayer that I want you to cut out; it is the little word "if."

The Willingness and the Power of the Christ Has Been Declared.

You may ask, "If the leper could pray that prayer, why can't I?"

I will show you.

The leper cried, "Lord, if Thou wilt, Thou canst make me clean;" and Jesus' answer was, "I will."

He stretched forth His hand, and touched him; saying, I will; be thou made clean.

When the Christ said, "I will," would it have been proper for the leper to have continued to pray, "Lord, if Thou wilt?"

When I say to you, "I will," I do not want you to come to me and say again and again, "If thou wilt, If thou wilt, If thou wilt!"

I did not change my purpose to come back all the time I was away from Zion City

I said, "I will come back, by the grace of God, on June 30th," and I came on that date.

I traveled thirty thousand miles after I had set the date for my return, and then reached here on that very date.

I should not have thought very much of my people if they had bothered me with cablegrams and letters, saying, "O Doctor, if thou wilt, please come back upon the date which you have set. If thou wilt! If thou wilt!"

I should have been annoyed.

When the Christ said, "I will," the man came forward, and the Christ touched him; and immediately his leprosy was cleansed.

*The First Apostle has not revised the following report.

Jesus saith unto him, See thou tell no man; but go thy way, shew thyself to the priest, and offer the gift that Moses commanded, for a testimony unto them.

The Efficacy of Testifying to Healing.

He did not obey.

Turn to the Gospel according to St. Mark, the 44th verse of the 1st chapter of that Gospel. Jesus said unto him,

See thou say nothing to any man: but go thy way, shew thyself to the priest, and offer for thy cleansing the things which Moses commanded, for a testimony unto them.

But he did not do what the Christ commanded.

The Christ told him to fulfil the Levitical law, and to show himself to the proper sanitary officer, and to make the proper sacrifice, so that the Priest would proclaim him to be clean, and thus be compelled to witness to all the people that the Lord Jesus, the Christ, had healed the leper.

If the leper had gone to the priest, what a splendid testimony it would have been, for the priest would then have had to declare the healing.

Many people have to learn this lesson.

I have seen people get their healing and then sneak back to their homes and not tell any one about it.

They never testified, and were even afraid to talk much about it, because the minister or the mayor or some one else was against them.

They did not do what the Christ directed.

The church with which they were connected would not listen.

If you cannot testify in your church to your salvation, your healing, or your cleansing, then that is a good church to get out of.

The Scriptures Do Not Warrant the Employment of Doctors.

Are you going to obey God, and not only get the healing but tell it out, so that all the town will know?

PEOPLE—"Yes."

GENERAL OVERSEER—Some of you may have sneaked up here to Zion City and said to your husband or wife, "Don't tell where I have gone!

It would be better to write back to your husband, "Tell the whole town where I have gone."

Some people sneak up here, and then sneak into the room, and then look around to see if any one knows them.

They come to the meetings with fear and trembling.

You will not be healed!

You may as well go back to Jonesville.

You are cowards, and God will not heal cowards!

God has no use for a coward.

It is certain that we have no use for cowards in Zion.

When He was entered into Capernaum, there came unto Him a centurion, beseeching Him,

And saying, Lord, my servant lieth in the house sick of the palsy, grievously tormented.

And He saith unto him, I will come and heal him.

Did He not say, "Go and get the best doctor?"

PEOPLE—"I will come and heal him."

GENERAL OVERSEER—"Give him all that the doctor prescribes?"

PEOPLE—"No; I will come and heal him."

GENERAL OVERSEER—"Pray to Me to bless the medicines?"

PEOPLE—"No."

GENERAL OVERSEER—If you can find a passage in the Scriptures that says that God sent any one to a doctor, tell me.

It is not there.

Jesus did not say, "Go and get a physician for your servant, and give him medicine, and pray to Me, and I will heal him;" but He said, "I will come and heal him."

Self-worthiness Not a Ground of Confidence for Healing.

That is the second time we have found "I will" in this chapter.

If any one said that to you, you would say, "Come on, I will show you where he is."

But the centurion had more faith.

He did not want the Lord to be troubled by coming; he did not think himself worthy, although he had about the best house in Capernaum, for he was the commandant of the garrison, doubtless.

He was a Roman centurion, a man of high rank; probably the representative of the Roman power, not only in Capernaum, but in the province or neighboring district.

He did not think himself worthy that the Christ should come to him, but the Jews thought he was worthy, because another evangelist tells us that the rabbis whom he sent to the Christ said, "He is worthy that Thou shouldest do this for him; for he loveth our nation, and himself built us our synagogue."

Their idea of being worthy was building a church.

But when the Christ approached the centurion's house, he sent friends to say, "Lord, trouble not Thyself: for I am not worthy that Thou shouldest come under my roof: wherefore neither thought I myself worthy to come unto Thee: but say the word, and my servant shall be healed."

Some of you think that you ought to be healed because you are very worthy people!

An Illustration of the Need of Humility.

Some people who come to Zion City bring letters from ministers vouching for their worthiness, saying that they have done a great deal of good, and asking me to receive them because they are worthy.

It makes me sick at heart to get such letters, or to hear such words.

I have received letters from parsons (I used to get them oftener than I do now), saying, "Mrs. Jones is a distinguished member of our church in Jonesville, a woman of great influence in the district, and a good woman, and you will please attend to her, Doctor, for she is very sick."

I can see written upon Mrs. Jones' face that she is boss of the district, and keeps that miserable parson in terror, wondering whether he will have any salary or not.

I once said to such a woman, "Your pastor says that you are a very good woman and very worthy," and she proudly drew herself up.

Then I continued, "Don't you know that that is your condemnation with me! How much faith have you?"

"I have all the faith in the world," she said assuringly.

"Find my photographer," I said to my attendant, "and let him come and take a photograph of a woman that has all the faith in the world! I want to preserve it."

Then I continued, addressing the lady, "My dear madam, why should you come to me? I do not have all the faith that is in the world!

"If you have all the faith in the world, why are you lying there sick? My opinion is, madam, that you are a most unworthy and abominable person!"

"What do you mean, Doctor?" she cried angrily.

"I mean that you are just as full of stinking pride as can be," I said calmly, but firmly.

Personal Presence Not Essential to Healing.

"To my spiritual nostrils it stinks! You are a hateful woman to come here thinking that God Almighty must heal you of that stinking cancer.

"You imagine that what your minister says is true, and that you really are a most worthy person.

"You think that God is under obligation to heal you, because you built a little chapel away down there in that little place where you lorded over every one!"

"I'll go home!" she said.

My reply to her was, "Go!"

But she did not go home, and there came a day when Mrs. Jones repented, and said, "I am so glad you dealt with me like that, Doctor! That is just what I needed!"

She found God and healing.

"I am not worthy!" is what the centurion said.

If you fulfil God's conditions, He must fulfil His promises. [Amen.]

If He does not, then He has failed.

But He never fails!

Blessed be the Lord, there has not failed one word of all His good promises.

That centurion had great faith.

He did not need the Lord to come.

Many of you want me to come.

People write from all over the world, "Oh, come! Your personal presence, your personal touch is what is needed."

I cannot do it.

If Divine Healing is limited to my person, and to the number of people I can touch, then it is a very poor thing.

One of the dangers you have is resting upon my personality.

I am always glad to get away for a while, because it is good for you.

It throws you upon the Lord more than ever.

Some of you come here every Tuesday after you have taken colds by going out into the cold without having properly protected your bodies.

The Highest Form of Faith Does Not Need to See.

You say, "Oh, well, never mind, I have a cold, but I will go to the Tabernacle next Tuesday and have the General Overseer pray; and then I shall be all right."

But that will not do.

That is not right!

God will not have it so.

The highest form of faith is that faith that does not need to see.

The centurion did not need to see Jesus come into his house and touch his servant.

He had some consideration for Jesus.

Jesus was a man, and I dare say He looked a little tired, because He had been at it all day.

Some would have said, "Oh, you must see my servant! Come to the house and touch him."

But the centurion said, "But say the word and my servant shall be healed."

What did Jesus say?

Did He say, "That is very presumptuous of you. I said that I would come and heal him, and you have no right to ask Me to do otherwise?"

He saw the man's motive.

Have you such faith in the Christ as to believe that all the powers of heaven and earth must combine to do His will: and that all the powers of hell must flee before His work?

That is the faith the centurion had.

Larger Conceptions of Jesus' Ability Needed.

You should get a larger conception of what Jesus is able to do.

We see more and more what "a word" means.

Even I can speak a word and it is done.

I can reach men in Africa, in Australia, and in Europe, and the word that I cable under the ocean is obeyed in the Name of the Lord.

If I, who am but a humble servant of His, can move things, surely the Christ Himself, whose Word has "All Power," can accomplish what He wills by that word alone.

It is only through Him that I can approach the Father, and only through faith in Him that I can get any answer.

Then if He who is the Fountain of Power speaks, it must be done.

That centurion's faith was sublime; he said, "but only say the word, and my servant shall be healed."

And when Jesus heard it, He marveled, and said to them that followed, Verily I say unto you, I have not found so great faith, no, not in Israel;

And I say unto you, that many shall come from the east and the west, and shall sit down with Abraham, and Isaac, and Jacob, in the Kingdom of Heaven:

But the sons of the Kingdom shall be cast forth into the outer darkness: there shall be the weeping and gnashing of teeth.

And Jesus said unto the centurion, Go thy way; as thou hast believed, so be it done unto thee. And the servant was healed in that hour.

The Lord is here with us now.

It is not a question of His being visibly present.

If you say to Him, "But only say the word," you may be healed where you sit.

It Is the Devil's Business to Make Men Miserable.

I do not see why you should not.

No one lays hands on me, and yet God has repeatedly healed me of sicknesses that are not allowed to go far.

I go to God and He puts them away.

And when Jesus was come into Peter's house, he saw his wife's mother lying sick of a fever.

And He touched her hand—

It does not say that she said anything.

Do you read any prayer that she made there?

PEOPLE—"No."

GENERAL OVERSEER—This was the home to which Jesus was coming to dinner, and the Devil thought he would make it miserable for them.

That is just like the Devil.

If he can make your dinner miserable tonight he will do it.

This woman had been cooking a hot dinner.

I do not know whether she had fretted herself into a fever over it or not.

Some people fret themselves into a fever.

When the Lord came to Peter's house to dinner, after a hard day's labor, He found the dear old lady of the house, the chief lady, sick.

It is very proper that the mother-in-law should be the chief lady; in the Eastern homes she is.

He touched her hand, and the fever left her; and she arose, and ministered unto Him.

And when even was come, they brought unto Him many possessed with devils; and He cast out the spirits with a word, and healed all that were sick.

There Was Not One of Them that Did Not Have Faith.

Oh, when shall I in this faithless world see meetings where all have faith to be healed?

It is coming.

I have seen meetings in which nearly all were healed.

I once saw a meeting in Ballarat, Victoria, in which there were at least a thousand sick people, and it seemed to me as if every one in that meeting was healed.

It was wonderful!

I had not seen anything like it before, nor have I since.

The power of God came upon that people, and there were wonderful results.

The house doctor of the hospital there believed in Divine Healing and in me, and he sent his patients to the meetings.

They came to the meetings and never went back to the hospital.

He was dismissed from that hospital by the board.

They said that it was most unprofessional conduct to send out the people to be healed.

They saw that if that kind of thing went on there would be no more use for the hospital or the board; and they forced him out.

The people in this meeting had been prepared by teaching and by seeing others healed.

The Word says that the Christ "healed all."

They must have had faith; for "without faith it is impossible to be well-pleasing unto Him."

If you have simple faith in God, and obey Him in the things I shall tell you, you also will receive healing.

That it might be fulfilled which was spoken by Isaiah the Prophet, saying, Himself took our infirmities, and bare our diseases.

I wonder if you really believe that our Lord Jesus, the Christ, by His Atoning Sacrifice, made an Atonement for our sicknesses as well as our sins?

Do you believe it?

PEOPLE—"Yes."

GENERAL OVERSEER—Very well, hold on to that!

What right have you to claim it?

None at all, unless you really have done what I now say.

True Repentance Is a Preparation for Healing.

First, you must repent of your sins.

Repentance does not mean merely saying, "Lord, I repent." It means more than that.

A great many people deliberately and wilfully sin, and think that all they have to do is to come to God and say, "I repent!"

That will not do with God.

You will have to "bring forth . . . fruit worthy of repentance."

I will take no stock in the Repentance of any person who has positively, wilfully, and deliberately sinned, and has brought forth no "fruit worthy of Repentance."

They had better keep outside of Zion City for a while.

There is no place here for unrepentant, disobedient sinners.

You who sin against light and knowledge, deliberately and wilfully, have no right to expect forgiveness and restoration, unless you have brought forth "fruit worthy of Repentance," and you will not get it either.

If you got it, you would be a curse to this City.

You must bring forth "fruit worthy of Repentance" before you can make God believe that you are penitent.

If you are covering up such sins, and say that it is enough that you tell it to God, that will not do; some one else is concerned as well as God.

There is the person against whom you sinned.

There is the person to whom you lied.

You say, "I told it to God;" but that is not enough.

You may ask, "Where does it say that I am to confess to man?"

I will show you.

Turn to James, the 5th chapter, 14th, 15th, and 16th verses.

It is essential to true Repentance, that you shall not only confess your sins to God, but to one another, when some one else is involved in the sin, or when any one else has been lied to or wronged.

Confess therefore your sins one to another, and pray one for another, that ye may be healed. The supplication of a righteous man availeth much in its working.

Elijah was a man of like passions with us, and he prayed fervently that it might not rain; and it rained not on the earth for three years and six months.

And he prayed again; and the heaven gave rain, and the earth brought forth her fruit.

Supplicatory Prayer an Essential Part of the Elijah Ministry.

You see, "supplication" is connected with this incident about Elijah, and it is essentially a part of the Elijah ministry to offer a supplication that availeth much in its working; not only to avail in ways that are spiritual, but in works that are manifest.

My supplication will not avail anything in its working if you do not confess your faults one to another as well as to God, and if you do not put things right with one another as well as with God.

It will not do to say, "I put it right with God, but still I did my neighbor a wrong, and lied to him."

You must make the confession, and ask forgiveness.

Your Repentance must be a reality.

If your Repentance has not been a reality, I cannot see how your Faith can ever be real.

I do not believe that a Real Faith can be built upon a False Repentance.

Your Repentance must be true, if your Faith is to be true

Your Faith will go to pieces upon the foundation of a False Repentance.

You must lay the foundation of Repentance, and lay it well.

If there is anything in the way, tell God this afternoon what it is, and vow that you will put it right.

He may accept your vow.

Perhaps He will say to you, "I will not accept your vow. I will not heal you until you have made the wrong right."

Some people do not receive the healing until they do it.

Why?

I will tell you why.

You have made so many vows to God; He has a record of hundreds of them that are broken.

The Goodness of God leadeth thee to Repentance.

Get your faith established in the Christ and then obey Him.

If a Man Is Thoroughly Penitent, He Obeys.

On the day of Pentecost they cried out, "Brethren, what shall we do?"

What did Peter say?

PEOPLE—"Repent."

GENERAL OVERSEER—What was his first word?

PEOPLE—"Repent!"

GENERAL OVERSEER—What was his next word?

PEOPLE—"Be baptized."

GENERAL OVERSEER—"I was baptized when I was a baby," some object.

But you are told that Repentance should precede Baptism.

Did you repent when you were a baby?

No, you did not repent; and no one could repent for you.

You must be properly baptized into the "Name of the Father and of the Son and of the Holy Spirit."

That is an act of Faith.

Will you obey God in that? Yes or no?

PEOPLE—"Yes."

GENERAL OVERSEER—Get down to business right now.

Are you willing this afternoon to make assurance doubly sure by making a complete and entire confession and consecration?

PEOPLE—"Yes."

GENERAL OVERSEER—Are you willing to obey God, no matter what may follow the obedience?

PEOPLE—"Yes."

GENERAL OVERSEER—That is the kind of people that receive blessing even if they do not receive healing.

Even though you missed it, you would go triumphantly to heaven, because you would be gloriously saved.

I do not like to see people die who have not lived out their lives.

I do not like to see people die who have little children, husbands, or wives that love them, and who might be very useful here.

I do not like to see the Devil score a victory, and steal them away.

Sometimes it is done, and our hearts are made to ache.

Therefore, I say to you, beloved, obey God fully; at this moment tell Him that you will put everything out of the way that hinders your blessing; then you will receive the blessing

But you must be without hypocrisy, with no thought or attempt to get the blessing without obedience.

The Christ taught obedience all the time.

He was obedient Himself.

Though He was a Son, yet learned obedience by the things which He suffered.

. . . .

I delight to do Thy will, O My God;
Yea, Thy law is within My heart.

Rise and make full consecration to God.

Be in earnest about this.

Say it with all your heart.

Speak to God.

PRAYER OF CONSECRATION.

My God and Father, in Jesus' Name I come to Thee. Take me as I am. Make me what I ought to be in spirit, in soul, and in body. Give me power to do right, no matter what it costs. Give me a true Repentance. May I dig deeply into my life, and if I have disobeyed man or disobeyed Thee, in paying tithes and offerings or in any other way, may I repent and restore, and do right in Thy sight, and to my fellow man, no matter what it costs. Father, help me fully to trust in Jesus as the Lamb of God who taketh away the sin of the world. For His sake, take away all my sins, and give me Thy Holy Spirit, that I may do right and serve Thee. Give me healing. Help me to give my body, as well as my soul and my spirit, to Thee. Begin with my spirit, O God, and cleanse me spirit, soul, and body. Cleanse every part of me. If I do not receive the blessing, through ignorance upon my part, or through some failure to obey Thee, help me to persevere until I do get the blessing. Help me to keep asking until I receive; to keep seeking until I find; to keep knocking until it is opened. For Jesus' sake. Amen.

Did you mean it?

PEOPLE—"Yes."

GENERAL OVERSEER—Then, may God bless you.

The General Overseer then pronounced the

BENEDICTION.

Beloved, abstain from every form of evil. And may the very God of Peace Himself sanctify you wholly. And I pray God your whole spirit, and soul, and body be preserved entire, without blame, unto the coming of our Lord Jesus, the Christ. Faithful is He that calleth you, who also will do it. The grace of our Lord Jesus, the Christ, the love of God, our Father, the fellowship of the Holy Spirit, our Comforter and Guide, one Eternal God, abide in you, bless you, and keep you, and all the Israel of God everywhere, forever. Amen.

Expiration of Subscriptions.

On every subscriber's copy of LEAVES OF HEALING or THE ZION BANNER we attach a yellow label bearing his name, address, and two numbers, the figures referring to the volume and the number with which the subscription will expire.

Thus, should your label number happen to be 16—1, you may know that your subscription expires with Volume XVI, Number 1, which will be October 22, 1904. Also take notice that LEAVES OF HEALING now completes a volume every six months, or twenty-six weeks, that being the number of papers which are put into a bound volume. Earlier in the life of the paper a volume contained fifty-two numbers, as LEAVES OF HEALING had fewer pages in those days.

By making yourselves familiar with these customs and remitting promptly you need never allow your subscription to lapse.

Send money only by Bank Draft, Postoffice or Express Money-order in favor of John Alexander Dowie, and address all letters intended for us to

ZION PRINTING AND PUBLISHING HOUSE,
Zion City, Lake County, Illinois.

Zion Restoration Host

Elder A. F. LEE, Recorder

YE SHALL receive power, when the Holy Spirit is come upon you: and ye shall be My witnesses both in Jerusalem, and in all Judea and Samaria, and unto the uttermost part of the earth.—*Acts 1:8.*

DURING the last spring and summer months members of Zion Restoration Host residing in Zion City have been doing faithful work in the towns and country districts adjacent.

Some very interesting experiences are reported by members of Seventy No. 4, who recently engaged a wagonette from Zion City Livery Barn. A team of horses was furnished by one of the Restorationists, who also acted as driver, and the party drove some distance into the country, leaving Literature at the farmhouses in the neighborhood of Wadsworth.

They all finally met at this village, and, after visiting the homes of the people and distributing their Literature, held a street service, and were most kindly received by the people.

Other Seventies have done faithful work in the little cities north and south of Zion City, including Waukegan, Kenosha, and Racine.

Following is a very interesting report received from Deacon William J. Friend, Director of Seventy No. 11:

ZION CITY, ILLINOIS, September 9, 1904.

ELDER A. F. LEE, Recorder of Zion Restoration Host.

Dear Brother in the Christ:—Thinking that perhaps you would be interested to know with what success we met while on our work in Racine, Wisconsin, I herewith submit a report of the work done Saturday night and Lord's Day morning, September 3d and 4th.

The "Red Men" had been holding a carnival all the previous week, and the streets were quite crowded.

We had been informed that we would have no police protection whatever, and that the town was turned over to the Devil; but we thought that perhaps we were just the people to turn it over to God.

We went with a noble band of Restorationists to the work God had sent us to do.

We were delayed some in the evening in getting started for our work, but God most wonderfully blessed us, and kept us from the Evil One.

We had the joy of selling one hundred three copies of LEAVES OF HEALING, and of giving away sixty copies of LEAVES OF HEALING and one thousand Messages, making a total of one thousand one hundred sixty-three pieces of Literature distributed.

We made nine hundred calls.

Not one, to my knowledge refused the Literature with the possible exception of one saloon-keeper, who ordered the Restorationists out of his place of business, then followed them into the next saloon and apologized for his conduct, gave them some money, and invited them back into his saloon, telling them that he knew they could sell fifty cents' worth of Literature.

Some of those we met on our saloon work promised to attend our service, which was a Praise and Testimony service; and we had the joy of seeing them present. They listened very attentively.

We did house-to-house work in the morning, and had a glorious time.

The Restorationists were called in to pray for some who were sick.

One man who met them at the door, when they offered him LEAVES OF HEALING, said, "Yes, I'll buy one. I think it will help my wife. Come in."

They went in and found her suffering very much.

They prayed for her, and she received a blessing.

We found others who had heard of Zion through the children of one of our Restorationists living in Racine.

God gave us the victory over the Evil One in not permitting him to defeat our plans.

Truly "the Seventy returned with joy," not because the demons were subject unto us, but because our names were enrolled in heaven.

We need wisdom and power for God's service. Pray for us.

Faithfully yours in the Christ,

WILLIAM J. FRIEND.

Large numbers of Restorationists have also made most excellent use of the time given them for their vacations during the last few months.

They have traveled from Zion City to the Atlantic and Pacific Oceans, to Manitoba and the Canadian Northwest, and to the Gulf of Mexico on the south. Others have even crossed the waters, but none have gone without first supplying themselves with good Zion ammunition, in the form of Zion Restoration Host Messages and LEAVES OF HEALING.

We publish herewith a letter recently received from Deaconess Lizzie Lee, who, with her companion in the work, had some very pleasant experiences on a trip through the state of Wisconsin.

ZION CITY, ILLINOIS, September 7, 1904.

DEAR ELDER:—Miss Mattausch and I have just returned from our Wisconsin trip.

We have covered the principal parts of two cities, Mondovi and Fairchild, and met with many who were friendly to Zion.

Men crowded around us in the saloons and elsewhere to get the Literature, and sometimes it seemed difficult to get through.

A saloon-keeper asked for the tract on Secret Societies.

A Methodist minister asked if we would please give him some Literature.

He was on his way to conference.

At Foster's large store, in Fairchild, we were very kindly received.

As soon as they saw the Literature, they said, "Oh, we sell Zion lace here, and it is fine lace, too."

They thanked us again and again for LEAVES OF HEALING, and every employee seemed pleased to get it.

I had not realized before how beautifully Zion lace opens the way for Zion Restoration work.

At Mondovi we found that some Roman Catholic sisters had gone to Eau Claire and bought Zion lace.

In the two cities, we found only three who refused the Literature, but two of those took the card of "The Christ Knocking at the Door."

One of the North-Western Railroad officials, after taking a paper, asked me how I had been led to accept Zion teaching.

After telling him the story of how God had led me out of the dead Methodist church, and how I had been blessed and healed under our Leader's ministry, he said, "You are all right. Stay where you are. I am a Methodist, but I, too, am reading along these lines."

During our stay, we gave out over one thousand pieces of Literature, and we know that God will bless it and bless the words which we have spoken in His Name.

Yours in Christian love, LIZZIE LEE.

Vast quantities of Literature are still being distributed among the World's Fair visitors in St. Louis, by members of Zion Restoration Host, as is shown by the following letter recently received from Restorationist John Taylor:

5877 THEODOSIA AVENUE,
ST. LOUIS, MISSOURI, August 19, 1904.

MY DEAR ELDER:—Peace to thee be multiplied.

The four boxes of Literature mentioned in your letter were received and unpacked yesterday, containing four thousand eight hundred copies of LEAVES OF HEALING, three hundred copies of THE ZION BANNER, and three thousand messages.

Brother Sigwalt and I are filled with joy and praise to God, and, together with members of the Host, are counting it a great privilege to continue sowing such precious seed.

Here is an amusing incident: At the St. Louis transfer office I recently had occasion to meet the freight clerk. "Why!" he said, "what stacks of printed matter you are getting. What is it all? Is it political matter?"

"Yes," I replied," it is political, and also very important religious matter of the Christian Catholic Church in Zion."

"Christian Catholic! Christian Catholic!" he repeated very thoughtfully.

"That's it," I said, "and I shall drop in some day and give you a sample of my wares."

"Thank you very much," he continued, "I shall have these boxes delivered the first thing in the morning."

We are very thankful to God, and ask Zion to offer thanks, that we have had no trouble with the railroad or transfer people.

Twenty boxes of Literature from Headquarters and two from Philadelphia have come straight through, were received in good order, and were unpacked and distributed without any trouble.

The seed is being quietly sown, and St. Louis is reading.

The two boxes of BLÄTTER DER HEILUNG were received and opened on Tuesday, and contained three thousand one hundred fifty copies of the paper and two thousand seventy-three Messages. There are a great many German Lutherans and German Roman Catholics in St. Louis.

The World's Fair may be called a whirlpool of iniquity in an ocean of beer. May Zion help to deliver the people!

My companion and I recently met a man who asked us to walk home with him.

He was very drunk.

In that drunkard's home was the sweet wife, who seemed to be almost stupefied by her husband's behavior, and a little, prattling child just beginning to talk.

My companion and I prayed with him and commanded him to repent, and told him that he must exercise the little will power he had left and forsake his sins.

It was a strange scene.

We remained with him for about half an hour, when he retired to his room.

May God save the drunkard and the drunkard's home.

Many tell us the sad story of how they have allowed the drink demon to damn them.

Having received permission from the superintendent of the poorhouse, I held a meeting last Lord's Day morning in the poorhouse chapel.

There were about thirty persons present.

I, myself, led two poor blind men to the chapel.

They earnestly requested that we should come during the week; so we decided to go Friday afternoon at two o'clock.

About four hundred pieces of Literature were distributed.

As I was leaving, the superintendent very kindly inquired how I was progressing.

We expect to continue services there every Lord's Day morning and Friday afternoon, until ordered to stop.

My companion and I have also been able to get LEAVES OF HEALING into two or three more Roman Catholic institutions since last writing.

Praying that God will bless all Zion everywhere, and our beloved Leader, Till Jesus Comes, I am,

Sincerely yours in the Christ, JOHN TAYLOR

Reports from Various Points.

Following is a tabulated report of the number of workers and the work done by them during the month of August, 1904, according to reports received to date from the various points named:

UNITED STATES.	No. of Workers	No. of Calls	Messages Given	Leaves Sold	Leaves Given
California—					
Los Angeles	10	1211	2283	366	88
San Francisco	10	3602	4000	1100	432
Sanger	1	75	140	15	28
Colorado—					
Durango	2	287	390	...	49
Pueblo	2	186	190	21	10
Trinidad	2	210	250	28	16
Connecticut—					
Bethel	1	3	....	....	13
Danbury	1	3	3	...	23
Meriden	1	406	. .	....	5
Illinois—					
Chicago—North Parish	20	2501	2413	38	227
" German Parish	13	335	449	55	100
" Northwest Parish	20	1552	1953	59	440
" West Parish	26	1385	2448	130	333
Geneseo	5	236	497	..	42
Harvey	9	...	513	89	165
Highland Park	....	313	3190	...	16
Lacon	...	7	4	...	9
Mazon	..	..	6	.. .	10
Morris	2	262	387	....	50
Northern	...	2950	....	....	30
Odell	1	22	22	....	17
Richmond	1	26	14	7	12
Waukegan	5	18	70	230	9
Indiana—					
Albion	1	...	5	...	14
Indianapolis	12	203	677	118	54
Lafayette	12	844	2571	142	172
Laotto	1	1	...	...	2
Linn Grove	1	5	....	....	23
Logansport	6	310	439	90	228
Lowell	2	38	69	. .	10
Monon	2	250	278	..	30
Walton	7	196	153	66	59
Iowa—					
Cedar Falls	2	5	38	22	9
Council Bluffs	2	85	252	....	3
Des Moines	1	4	19	....	5
Elberon	4	53	31	23	36
Lake Mills	....	20	175	16	15
Laporte City	1	25	41	4	18
Marcus	....	....	140	....	50
Newton	3	271	438	....	162
Tipton	4	41	31	....	25
Webster City	5	16	444	12	65
Kansas—					
Eldorado	12	402	450	....	50
Erie	1	32	59	....	3
Hoisington	1	2	2	....	5
Industry	1	200	350	....	....
Kansas City	13	358	544	227	164
Manhattan	3	15	27	21	58
Nortonville	1	...	102	....	3
Wichita	13	1026	1123	182	214
Kentucky—					
Danville	3	139	449	37	20
Massachusetts—					
Boston	6	1890	730	1500	800
Michigan—					
Bay City	7	936	519	151	86
Benton Harbor	6	1011	3195	104	738
Detroit	1	2807	3510	202	280
Gladstone	3	180	164	....	28
Ingalls	1	41	36	18	1
Port Huron	5	266	430	119	11
Minnesota—					
Austin	11	10	....	....	8
Delavan	....	24	....	...	27
Minneapolis	7	946	728	49	266
Moorhead	1	9	22	...	....
Rushford	1	3	29	14	....
Tenstrike	1	110	265	16	....
Mississippi—					
Tupelo	....	5	100	12	36
Missouri—					
Higginsville	1	258	274	44	21
Plattsburg	1	200	200	4	3
Springfield	1	140	27	....	...
St. Louis	22	1431	3464	309	2437
Montana—					
Havre	1	49	85	....	30
Libby	1	75	....	....	6
Nebraska—					
Falls City	3	6	38	94	6
Inman	1	16	30	9	3
New Jersey—					
Salem	2	18	28	16	52
New York—					
Bluff Point	1	1	.	....	4
New York City	37	1274	6272	387	735
Syracuse	2	63	142	...	38
Woodmere	1	63	15	....	10
North Dakota—					
Denhoff	1	30	38	.	6
Monango	2	50	34	....	35
Ohio—					
Ada	3	..	6	15	11
Akron	2	125	105	....	6
Bluffton	....	....	..	48	4
Cincinnati	1	110	500	25	.
Cleveland	29	4178	5287	259	338
Dayton	3	58	190	18	14
Fostorio	10	328	325	72	253
Fremont	1	438	112	....	318
Germantown	1	278	180	..	64
Marengo	2	85	127	....	29
Mansfield	1	60	....	.. .	5
Mifflin	2	116	. .	....	15
Nevada	1	3	...	....	5
Oceola	3	4	117	....	17
Oregon—					
Portland	1	279	279	38	20
Union	7	15	...	....	14
Pennsylvania—					
Dubois	1	. ..	15	...	25
New Brighton	1	25	37	...	47
Pittsburg	8	279	130	.	157
Souderton	1	6	69	....	24
Titusville	1	..	1671		348
West Chester	2	395	....	39	...
Philippine Islands—					
Fort McKinley	1	4	20	....	12
South Dakota—					
Alexandria	1	24	97	22	3
Brookings	1	220	115	31	90
Summit	2	29	47	6	2
Tennessee—					
Jackson	1	155	352	...	51
Memphis	1	12	257	....	5
Texas—					
Clarendon	1	25	..	8	5
Dallas	....	128	155	37	32
Houston	1	2	62	...	58
Paris	3	....	134	..	18
Vermont—					
Brattleboro	1	2	....	..	4
Randolph	1	..	...	...	25
Washington—					
Garfield	1	50	227	....	137
Lynden	3	9	....	....	53
Seattle	24	1716	1662	418	165
Spokane	10	1090	1318	161	87
Tacoma	8	551	579	78	66
Wisconsin—					
Alma	3	115	85	7	25
Black Creek	1	196	266	...	8
Brookfield	2	....	....	....	11
Columbus	1	304	73	....	30
Dodgeville	2	...	58	....	13
Kenosha	30	1108	1946	213	230
Maiden Rock	2	33	102	6	58
Milwaukee	8	347	1503	109	48
Mukwonago	3	33	37	..	36
Omro	2	33	110	1	11
Platteville	..	240	176	18	3
Racine	2	25	26	4	5
Viroqua	2	117	502	42	14
Washington	1	28	29	....	32
Wauwatosa	1	....	185	20	1
West Allis	1	79	107	11	20
Total	598	40868	68384	7852	12359

DOMINION OF CANADA AND CONTINENTS.	No. of Workers	No. of Calls	Messages Given	Leaves Sold	Leaves Given
Canada—					
Sarnia	2	75	75	25	....
Simcoe	2	90	195	87	2
Toronto	17	2091	1161	557	1243
Vancouver	19	596	3347	177	263
Victoria	2	280	227	61	43
Waubaushene	1	107	....	1	30
Woodstock	2	60	41	48	52
Switzerland—					
Zürich	....	1901	2187	....	80
Switzerland	....	5779	10971	.. .	163
Total	45	10979	18204	956	876
Grand Total	643	51847	86588	8808	13235

Financial, Commercial and Industrial Notes

IN order to preserve a pure, healthy body as the Temple of a Pure Spirit, it is extremely necessary to use only Pure Food.

No one article enters so largely into the preparation of the food we eat as does the fat of animals. And, alas, it is only too true, and especially so in Christian America, that of all fats used, hog lard takes the lead. But the eyes of the people are being opened, and more and more are they beginning to see the necessity of obeying the command, "Of their flesh we shall not eat, and their carcasses ye shall not touch."

Zion has an excellent substitute for lard in Zion Shortening, made and put up by Zion City Fresh Food Supply.

In the manufacture of Zion Shortening, the Zion City Fresh Food Supply uses only the very best and purest of materials, while great care is taken in mixing and packing.

Zion Shortening is put up in three, five, and ten-pound pails, and in fifty-pound cans, and sent to any part of the world.

G. A. MITCHELL,
Acting Manager Zion City Fresh Food Supply.

Zion Lace Industries has a building which is admitted by many experts to be one of the finest in the world. It has floor space of nearly five acres, and is constructed to give the greatest light and air space possible, the health of the employees having been considered in every particular.

The factory is built so that half the building will contain Lever's lace machines, and half curtain machines. Additional machinery will be introduced from time to time, which, with the present plant, will create work for large numbers of residents of Zion City.

The factory is also one of the most complete in the world, inasmuch as every part of preparing and finishing the lace is done here. In most English lace manufactories, the lace is made, and then sold "in the brown;" that is, just as it comes from the machines, unbleached and unfinished, and the buyer must see to the further processes that will prepare it for the market.

In Zion Lace Industries, on the other hand, the work is all completed under one roof. The yarn, purchased in skeins, passes through the various departments; namely, slip-winding, brass-winding, warping, beaming, etc., preparatory to putting into the machines.

The Lace is then produced in great webs, and mended, ready for the bleachery. At the bleachery, which is very complete and well-equipped, the Lace is washed, bleached, and dressed. It is then brought to the white-room, where it is separated, clipped, scalloped, carded, and finished, ready for the market, and is finally shipped from our own shipping department direct to our customers.

This is one of the many advantages Zion Lace Industries has over the majority of lace manufactories. The expenses which arise from passing a product from hand to hand before it finally reaches the retail market being thus eliminated, makes it possible to offer to the public a better article at a lower price.

HENRY STEVENSON,
General Manager.

The practicability of trading by mail has long been established. No one imagined, when the idea was first conceived, that it would reach such enormous proportions; but today millions of dollars are spent annually by mail order traders.

Everything possible is being done to bring the farmer and those living at distant and remote places into closer touch with the cities. One of the latest and most effective aids in this direction has been the opening of Rural Free Delivery Routes. There is more mail matter delivered to the people of the country today than ever before. This is a great boon to the farmer, as hours of time and miles of travel have been saved him.

Knowing that thousands of people throughout the country have found it very profitable and convenient to do their trading by mail, many unscrupulous individuals have sent forth misleading advertisements, in order to build up a lucrative business at the expense of those who have fallen victims to their deceptions.

In order that the products of Zion shall get into the homes of not only members of Zion, but others who are interested in them, a Mail Order Department has been established to meet these requirements. There is no reason, whatever, why any one desiring to use our products should not get them, for every provision has been made to meet the wishes of our friends in every part of the world.

We make trading by mail so simple and easy that you can write your order, mail it to us, and rest assured that you will be treated with as much consideration and attention as if you were here in person.

The products of Zion are such as enter more or less into the daily needs of every home. By looking through our latest catalog, in which are detailed quotations of everything we manufacture, you will notice that everything has been done to enable you to trade with us successfully.

Great care has been taken in compiling this catalog. Nothing has been written that has the least particle of misrepresentation in it. We have not exaggerated the good qualities of any of our goods. We are prepared to stand by everything printed.

We solicit correspondence with any reader of LEAVES OF HEALING who is interested in this branch of Zion's work, and would like to know something more of our products.

Zion Building and Manufacturing Association is much more than a building department.

The Box Factory, the Bakery, the Lumber and Fuel Departments, the Planing Mill, the Brick-yards, and the Teaming Departments are all included. Also the Power House, without which the Lace Factory would be silent, the Candy Factory would cease to send forth its tons of sweetness, the Printing Machinery would be motionless, and all the Electric Lights in Zion City would refuse to shine.

However, not the least important part of our work is the building of Homes for the people.

That is the common term used, but perhaps we should rather say *houses* than homes; for the home depends, not so much upon the builder or the building as upon the character of the occupants.

A recent writer says:

The men of earth build houses—halls and chambers, roofs and domes—
But the women of the earth—God knows!—the women build the homes.
Eve could not stray from Paradise; for, oh, no matter where
Her gracious presence lit the way, lo! Paradise was there.

We have no objection to offer to the first two lines; they may be largely true. The last two might be true IF — but then we have the highest authority for the assertion that women are *not* all angels.

Careful planning, good material, and skilful workmanship will materially help to make the house a home.

We may have something to say along this line in the future. R. H. HARPER,
General Manager Zion Building and Manufacturing Association.

Zion's Bible Class

Conducted by Teacher Daniel Sloan in Shiloh Tabernacle, Zion City, Lord's Day Morning at 11 o'clock, and in Zion Homes and Gatherings throughout the World.

MID-WEEK BIBLE CLASS LESSON, OCTOBER 19th or 20th.

The First Christian Catholic Apostolic Church.

1. *She had light from God concerning her specific mission.*—Mark 16:15-20.
The preaching of the Gospel involves more than mere talk.
The man of faith gets results.
Miracles always follow the exercise of faith.
2. *She was ceaseless in labor, prayer, and praise.*—1 Corinthians 15:55-58.
She had no fear of death.
She knew her labor was not in vain.
She abounded in the work of faith and labor of love.
3. *She would not tolerate evil-doers.*—Jude 1:17-23.
She separated such from her company.
Such persons became as publicans to them.
She had no pleasure in iniquity.
4. *She was on the watch, lest those who were not Apostles should get into office.*—Philippians 3.15-21.
They followed the mind of the Christ
All were commanded to walk by the same rule and speak the same thing.
Any one who would not do this, even though he were an Apostle, was cut off.
5. *She was patient in well-doing, enduring affliction joyfully.*—Galatians 6:1-10.
She knew it required hardship to sow seed.
She knew she must never weary of God's Work.
She knew work wrought in God would bring joy.
6. *She waned somewhat, and was enticed to deviate from her mission.*—Hebrews 4:7-14.
The temptation to let up is not from God.
The Devil would like to get one each day to listen to him.
We must labor on till the day is done.
7. *She always hated the wicked works of the sects about her.* —2 Timothy 4:1-8.
One must fight for the truth.
People are so prone to turn from it.
They seek teachers with their isms.
8. *She found the Tree of Life in the Christ, who is All, and in All.*—Revelation 22:10-17.
Only the obedient can enjoy the Christ.
He must be All on earth and in heaven.
There is a place even here and now that evil cannot enter.
The Lord our God is a Church-establishing God.

LORD'S DAY BIBLE CLASS LESSON, OCTOBER 23d.

The Gifts of the Spirit are for the Church of God.

1. *When she is worthy of them, they are bestowed.*—Ephesians 4:1-2.
A Christian is called that he may be given Gifts.
First, a person must walk orderly.
Humility, meekness, long-suffering, and forbearance must rule in one.
2. *These Gifts can never come to a Church that is full of discord.*—Ephesians 4:3-6.
God's Spirit is not divided.
The Christ is not divided.
The body cannot be divided.
3. *These Gifts grow out of the indwelling life and resurrection power of the Christ.*—Ephesians 4:7-10.
The Christ, when on earth, did all that the Spirit's Gifts are intended to accomplish.
The Holy Spirit now does the work of the Christ on earth.
The Holy Spirit works through those who obey the Christ and who strive to do as He did.
4. *Without these Gifts, the Church is full of weak and helpless Christians.*—Ephesians 4:11-13.
There can be no perfection for the saints without these Gifts.
The body of the Christ cannot be formed without them.
Many professed Christians are babes when they ought to be full-grown men.
5. *The absence of these Gifts accounts for the multiplied isms.*—Ephesians 4:14-16.
Professed Christians hold to their dogmas.
Men attractively color up a doctrine and people believe it.
Such doctrines do not make people grow.
6. *A church that is powerless, because of the lack of these Gifts, produces worldly Christians.*—Ephesians 4:17-19.
Those who are Christians merely in name, live after the spirit of this world.
They walk, talk, and do as those about them.
Each one is for himself or herself.
7. *The exercise of the Gifts of the Spirit makes the Christ All and in All.*—Ephesians 4:20-24.
One must know the Christ, or be none of His.
One must have His Spirit, or be none of His.
One must have the mind of the Spirit, or be not of the Christ.
8. *The manifestation of these Gifts in the Church incites to Holy Living.*—Ephesians 4:25-32.
Lying ceases when one is full of the Spirit.
Anger is curbed when one is full of the Spirit.
Stealing is at an end if one is mastered by the Spirit.
God's Holy People are a Christ-empowered People.

OBEYING GOD IN BAPTISM.

"Baptizing Them Into the Name of the Father and of the Son and of the Holy Spirit."

Nineteen Thousand Nine Hundred Ninety-nine Baptisms by Triune Immersion Since March 14, 1897.

Nineteen Thousand Nine Hundred Ninety-nine Believers have joyfully followed their Lord in the Ordinance of Believer's Baptism by Triune Immersion since the first Baptism in Central Zion Tabernacle on March 14, 1897.

Baptized in Central Zion Tabernacle from March 14, 1897, to December 14, 1901, by the General Overseer,	4754		
Baptized in South Side Zion Tabernacle from January 1, 1902, to June 14, 1903, by the General Overseer..	37		
Baptized at Zion City by the General Overseer........	647		
Baptized by Overseers, Elders, Evangelists and Deacons, at Headquarters (Zion City) and Chicago......	5626		
Total Baptized at Headquarters....................			11,064
Baptized in places outside of Headquarters by the General Overseer..................................		765	
Baptized in places outside of Headquarters by Overseers, Elders, Evangelists and Deacons............		8,102	
Total Baptized outside of Headquarters............			8,867
Total Baptized in seven years and six months......			19,931
Baptized since September 14, 1904:			
Baptized in Zion City by Elder Viking...............	3		
Baptized in Zion City by Elder Dinius...............	3		
Baptized in Zion City by Elder Royall...............	20		
Baptized in Chicago by Elder Hoffman...............	2		
Baptized in Chicago by Elder Hammond.............	5	33	
Baptized in Illinois by Elder Gay....................		5	
Baptized in Michigan by Deacon Van Woerkom......		1	
Baptized in Missouri by Deacon Robinson............		2	
Baptized in New York by Elder Warszawiak..........		9	
Baptized in New York by Overseer Mason...........		12	
Baptized in Ohio by Deacon Smith..................		1	
Baptized in Pennsylvania by Elder Bouck............		4	
Baptized in Texas by Elder Hall....................		1	35 68
Total Baptized since March 14, 1897...............			19,999

The following-named believer was baptized in Sydney, New South Wales, Australia, Monday, May 23, 1904, by Elder J. Thomas Wilhide:

Slater, John.................................Scarsdale, Victoria, Australia

The following-named seven believers were baptized in Auckland, New Zealand, Lord's Day, May 29, 1904, by Deacon William Johnson:

Cutler, Kate ....Devonport, Auckland, New Zealand
Harrison, Florence Fanny, Wynyard road, Mount Eden, Auckland, New Zealand
Harrison, Annie.....Wynyard road, Mount Eden, Auckland, New Zealand
Harrison, Miss Gladys, Wynyard road, Mount Eden, Auckland, New Zealand
O'Callahan, Elizabeth Constance, Dome Valley, Warkworth, Auckland, New Zealand
Stacey, Mrs. Susannah....Oneill street, Ponsonby, Auckland, New Zealand
Tekua-Whakato, Susannah, Oneill street, Ponsonby, Auckland, New Zealand

The following-named four believers were baptized in Central Zion Tabernacle, Melbourne, Victoria, Australia, Monday, June 13, 1904, by Deacon Charles Moss:

Pearce, William Thomas, 86 Hope street, South Melbourne, Victoria, Australia
Pritchard, Mrs. Nellie.........................Albany, Western Australia
Pritchard, Thomas.............................Albany, Western Australia
Zollinger, Rudolph, 48 Bell street, Glenferrie, Melbourne, Victoria, Australia

The following-named believer was baptized in Melbourne, Victoria, Australia, Wednesday, June 29, 1904, by Deacon Charles Moss:

Daley, John.................................Port Fairy, Victoria, Australia

The following-named believer was baptized in Melbourne, Victoria, Australia, Tuesday, July 26, 1904, by Deacon Charles Moss:

Bracken, George Henry....................Bridgetown, Western Australia

The following-named two believers were baptized in Chicago, Illinois, Lord's Day, September 11, 1904, by Elder W. D. Gay:

Craig, Mrs. Margaret.......271 North Clark street, Flat 4, Chicago, Illinois
Craig, Miss Marion.........271 North Clark street, Flat 4, Chicago, Illinois

The following-named nine believers were baptized in New York City, Lord's Day, September 18, 1904, by Elder Herman Warszawiak:

Bouska, Miss Katie..........138 West Fifty-eighth street, New York City
Geugel, Miss Jean.............170 West Fifty-ninth street, New York City
Hudson, Edwin F..................26 Courtland place, Albany, New York
Nockemann, Charles.......352 South Orange avenue, Newark, New Jersey
Nockemann, Miss Elizabeth..352 South Orange avenue, Newark, New Jersey
Osterberg, Otto C., Eleventh street and Third avenue, College Point, Long Island, New York
Sander, Harry.........................353 Madison street, New York City
Schmidtt, Mrs. Margaret......353 West Forty-fourth street, New York City
Yeomans, Mrs. Emily...........193 Western avenue, Albany, New York

The following-named twelve believers were baptized in New York City, Lord's Day, September 18, 1904, by Overseer G. L. Mason:

Bickel, Mrs. Minnie..............116 Newton street, Newark, New Jersey
Haass, Frank A...............211 East Ninety-eight street, New York City
Hannan, Leslie L.......................131 Third avenue, New York City
Heath, Mrs. M...................140 West Fifteenth street, New York City
Hudson, Mrs. Adeline..............26 Courtland place, Albany, New York
Lang, John...............................301 Third street, New York City
McCosker, Mrs. Louisa.................1192 First avenue, New York City
Morgan, John..114 West One Hundred Thirty-fourth street, New York City
Morgan, Samuel S.............440 West Forty-fifth street, New York City
Nelson, Mrs. Louisa M.......Center street, Newton Centre, Massachusetts
Nockemann, Mrs. Lena.....352 South Orange avenue, Newark, New Jersey
Saltzman, David P.....................9 Columbus avenue, New York City

The following-named believer was baptized at Grand Rapids, Michigan, Lord's Day, September 18, 1904, by Deacon A. Van Woerkom:

Bradley, Willie E..........54 Hogadone avenue, Grand Rapids, Michigan

The following-named two believers were baptized at Plattsburg, Missouri, Saturday, September 24, 1904, by Deacon Charles E. Robinson:

Malm, John. ....Plattsburg, Missouri
Newman, Mrs. Anna Louise...........................Edgerton, Missouri

The following-named five believers were baptized in the South Side Zion Tabernacle, Chicago, Illinois, Lord's Day, September 25, 1904, by Elder Gideon Hammond:

Ferguson, Mrs. Lizzie............4109 Wentworth avenue, Chicago, Illinois
Harbeck, Augusta..........3235 West Forty-fourth street, Chicago, Illinois
Hathaway, Mrs. Louise ...Kankakee avenue, Grant Park, Chicago, Illinois
Paulidis, John ....321 West Sixty-fourth street, Chicago, Illinois
Thompson, Miss Ruth.............6824 Lafayette avenue, Chicago, Illinois

The following-named two believers were baptized in the North Side Zion Tabernacle, Chicago, Illinois, Lord's Day, September 25, 1904, by Elder C. R. Hoffmann:

Bauer, William.........................176 Orchard street, Chicago, Illinois
McKirahan, Josiah ....Buffalo Gap, South Dakota

The following-named three believers were baptized in Lake Michigan, Zion City, Illinois, Monday, September 26, 1904, by Elder W. O. Dinius:

Goodwin, Mrs. Inez Alma ....2914 Elim avenue, Zion City, Illinois
Lyon, Mrs. Ada Lura...................736 Pine street, Trinidad, Colorado
Lyon, Miss Pearl Beulah ....736 Pine street, Trinidad, Colorado

The following-named twenty believers were baptized in Shiloh Tabernacle, Zion City, Illinois, Wednesday, September 28, 1904, by Elder Francis M. Royall:

Andersen, Ludwig A....................Elijah Hospice, Zion City, Illinois
Andersen, Mrs. Sophie ....Elijah Hospice, Zion City, Illinois
Castle, Henry Northrup................109 Waverly place, New York City
Enlow, Grace ....3210 Gideon avenue, Zion City, Illinois
Huston, Miss Beulah ....662 Carmel boulevard, Zion City, Illinois
Huston, Miss Edna...............662 Carmel boulevard, Zion City, Illinois
Julian, Miss Edith Annie...........1811 Hebron avenue, Zion City, Illinois
Pfeiffer, Casper H...................3211 Eshcol avenue, Zion City, Illinois
Rottmayer, Harvey John.............2617 Elim avenue, Zion City, Illinois
Simpson, Mrs. Mary E..Pana, Illinois
Singer, Miss Marie...................2719 Elim avenue, Zion City, Illinois
Singer, Miss Ora.....................2719 Elim avenue, Zion City, Illinois
Stevens, Charles...................................Montesano, Washington
Thorson, Mrs. Lily May ....Edina Hospice, Zion City, Illinois
Tower, Mrs. Emma ....2612 Gilboa avenue, Zion City, Illinois
Tower, Miss Pearl ....2612 Gilboa avenue, Zion City, Illinois
Walker, Alison Alexander...........1728 Horeb avenue, Zion City, Illinois
Wert, Miss Bessie Viola ....3213 Gilboa avenue, Zion City, Illinois
Wert, Miss Dottie ....3213 Gilboa avenue, Zion City, Illinois
Wickham, Miss Julia Maria.........3214 Gideon avenue, Zion City, Illinois

Changes in the New York City Branch.

Beginning with Lord's Day, October 2d, the meetings will be removed to the center of New York City, corner of Madison avenue and East One Hundred Twenty-fifth street. Sunday, 11 a. m., 3 p. m., and 8 p. m. Divine Healing Meeting every Thursday, 2:30 p. m. Overseer George L. Mason's new address, No. is 4 St. Nicholas Terrace.

ZION'S
FINANCIAL INSTITUTIONS AND INDUSTRIES

JOHN ALEXANDER DOWIE

THE FINANCIAL INTERESTS OF ZION are of vital importance to every member and friend of Zion. Get this on your heart. For when Zion's material work is strengthened, then her ability is increased to carry forward throughout the world the glorious, good tidings of this dispensation—the little leaven which is destined of God to leaven the whole lump.

¶ ¶ Zion has marvelously succeeded in all her business undertakings and operations. Her tra. sactions with her own people, and the business world, have already amounted to hundreds of millions of dollars; and not a dollar has ever been lost by any investo·. Within a very few years a vast estate has been created, rapidly increasing in value, and rated at tnis time by the keenest business firms of Chicago at many millions above all liabilities.

¶ ¶ Such a stewardship finds favor with God, and merits the hearty coöperation of every one who loves our Lord in sincerity, and desires to see His Kingdom extended.

High Class Investments, Secured by the entire estate of Zion, bearing interest at the rate of 9 per cent. and 10 per cent., are now offered to ready investors upon the most liberal terms. Your inquiries are cordially invited.

For information concerning the General Financial or Material Interests of Zion, address
DEACON CHARLES J. BARNARD, General Financial Manager, Zion City, Ill., U. S. A., or
DEACON DANIEL SLOAN Inspector General of Zion, Zion City, Ill., U. S. A.

For information concerning Zion City Bank, or any thing pertaining to the Banking Business, address
DEACON WILLIAM S. PECKHAM, Cashier, Zion City Bank, Zion City, Ill., U. S. A.

For information concerning Zion City Real Estate, address
DEACON H. WORTHINGTON JUDD, Secretary and Manager, Zion Land and Investment Association, Zion City, Ill., U. S. A.

For information concerning Zion Securities and Investments, address
DEACON FIELDING H. WILHITE, Manager, Zion Securities and Investments, Zion City, Ill., U. S. A.

Persons living at remote points may find it more convenient to confer with or write to the following special representatives:

ELDER PERCY CLIBBORN, General Financial Agent for the Continent of Europe, No. 76 Bahnhofstrasse, Zurich, Switzerland.

DEACON JOHN W. INNES, General Financial Agent for the United Kingdom. No. 81 Euston Road, London, N. W., England.

DEACON NICHOLAS B. RIDEOUT, General Financial Agent for South Africa, Box 3074, Johannesburg, South Africa.

DEACON GEORGE A. CORLETTE, Manager New York Office, No. 419 Flatiron Building, New York City.

ZION CITY

IS THE ONE SPOT IN GOD'S WORLD that is free from Rum, Tobacco, Drugs, Obscene Literature and Bill Boards, Vulgarity or Profanity and the consequent vice and crime that follows.

¶ ¶ The above may seem incredible, but a personal visit to Zion City by the most skeptical will prove the truth of our assertion.

¶ ¶ Every true lover of God and right living should not fail to visit this clean, beautiful growing City and learn of its plan and purpose.

¶ ¶ Thousands of home sites have already been disposed of and hundreds of homes erected at an outlay of millions of dollars.

¶ ¶ A number of Industries and Commercial enterprises have also been established and are in full operation, employing hundreds of hands.

¶ ¶ Never in the world's history have Christian people been able to secure the clean home life advantages that can be obtained in this City.

¶ ¶ The Educational system of Zion City is complete from the Kindergarten to the College. Students are not only taught to respect and reverence the Word of God, but to study it understandingly.

¶ ¶ Exceptionally fine well-located home sites are now being offered, the value of which must greatly advance within the coming two or three years, with the rapid growth of the City.

¶ ¶ We respectfully solicit a personal interview or correspondence with all honest inquirers or prospective investors, and will gladly furnish copies of our illustrated Booklet, Map of General Design, Plats, Eleven Hundred Year Lease, etc., upon application.

Zion Land and Investment Association, Zion City, Illinois, U. S. A. **H. Worthington Judd, Sec'y. and Mgr.**

A WEEKLY PAPER FOR THE EXTENSION OF THE KINGDOM OF GOD
EDITED BY JOHN ALEXANDER, FIRST APOSTLE OF THE LORD JESUS, THE CHRIST, IN THE CHRISTIAN CATHOLIC APOSTOLIC CHURCH IN ZION

Volume XV. No. 25. *ZION CITY, SATURDAY, OCTOBER 8, 1904.* *Price Five Cents*

ZION AMONG THE ZULUS IN SOUTH AFRICA

A Splendid People Joyfully Receive Restoration Truth and Their Lives Are Transformed Through the Power of the Full Gospel

ETHIOPIA SHALL HASTE TO STRETCH OUT HER HANDS UNTO GOD.

This prophecy is being fulfilled in and through Zion.

The First Apostle and Prophet of the Restoration has, from the beginning, kept it before himself and his people.

It has ever been his belief and practice that the way to have the glorious prophecies of God's Word fulfilled was to set about fulfilling them by God's help.

Hence his Voice has ever been raised fearlessly and effectively in behalf of Ethiopia and her people in all parts of the world.

Wherever and whenever nations, classes, or individuals have wrongfully exercised their power in the oppression of this great family of the human race, this man of God has boldly championed their cause.

His Messages of Repentance, Faith, Hope, Love, Obedience, and Purity have been for them as well as for their brothers and sisters with white skins.

OVERSEER DANIEL BRYANT.

Oppressed, sin-stricken, and disease-smitten Ethiopians in thousands have found a refuge in Zion, and in Zion City they have come into their own rights and privileges as in no other place on earth.

For many years the eyes and heart of God's Messenger have been turned toward the great, dark Continent of Africa, the Scriptural Ethiopia.

Especially has his attention been turned to blood-soaked South Africa.

With prophetic vision he saw, many years ago, that here a "Great Door and Effectual" was being opened and that, although there were "many adversaries," God would give most wonderful victory.

He foresaw how the pure, strong, virile teaching and practice of Zion would appeal powerfully to the spirit of those wearied out with the apostasy and hypocrisy which has cursed that land.

He foresaw how the Everlasting Gospel, proclaimed in its fulness and simplicity, would win the hearts of many thousands of dark-skinned children of God.

His spirit yearned with Divine Love to take South Africa for God.

Military science teaches that one of the most effective ways of capturing a citadel is first to bombard and then assault it.

Zion's Commander began his bombardment on this important citadel several years ago.

The projectiles were more effective than shells of steel filled with dynamite—they were Messages of Truth filled with the Dynamic Power of the Spirit of God.

Month after month, and year after year, he hurled LEAVES OF HEALING and Zion Literature into the strongholds of the enemy.

Great breaches were made in the towering walls of apostasy and prejudice, and the ramparts of error were overthrown.

Even while the horrible fratricidal strife between Briton and Boer was dyeing with blood the plains and hillsides of this great land, Zion's bombardment was also going on.

When the deep-mouthed cannon of carnal warfare ceased to belch forth death, Zion's batteries increased their fire, sending forth Life and Health through the Power of the Spirit of God.

Then came the moment for Zion's assault.

It is now being made.

Stronghold after stronghold has fallen.

There is victory all along the line.

Prophecy is being fulfilled.

Ethiopia is "hastening to stretch out her hands unto God."

In hundreds and in thousands they are forsaking the darkness of heathenism, and the deeper darkness of apostasy, and coming to God in Zion.

They receive the Truths of the Everlasting Gospel as little children.

Therefore it has a mighty power in them, transforming them in spirit, in soul, and in body.

This glorious work is being carried on under the leadership of Overseer Daniel Bryant, and his wife, Elder Emma Dempcy Bryant, of the Christian Catholic Apostolic Church in Zion.

These gifted, earnest, consecrated, and effective servants of God were sent from Zion City on the long journey to their great field of labor by the First Apostle, then the General Overseer of the Christian Catholic Church in Zion, last October.

They were accompanied by Deacon and Mrs. Nicholas B. Rideout, Deacon Rideout going as the Financial Manager of Zion's Institutions and Industries in South Africa.

The little party attended the New York Visitation, spent a few weeks in New York City in temporary charge of the work there, sailed for England in November, spent several weeks in London and other parts of the British Isles, and proceeded to their great field of labor in April of this year.

Since their arrival there, God has given them wonderful blessings and many victories. One most delightful and blessed part of their work has been that among the native Zulus.

ELDER EMMA DEMPCY BRYANT.

It is with praise and thanksgiving to God that we publish an article from the pen of this beloved Overseer concerning his part of the work which God has given him to do, and with it a number of very interesting photo-engravings. A. W. N.

OVERSEER DANIEL BRYANT'S ACCOUNT OF WORK AMONG THE ZULUS.

Having spent two weeks preaching among our native Zulu converts in South Africa, I know Zion throughout the world will rejoice to hear the good news from this part of the world's great harvest field.

The Zulus are the choicest of the Ethiopians in South Africa—intelligent, fearless in war, and magnificent in physique. Many a society belle would give a fortune to be able to walk with the erect, graceful carriage of a Zulu maiden.

We take pleasure in sending the photograph and testimony of Miss Meta Budulwako, whose beautiful figure and pure heart are the work of God's cleansing and healing power.

It is not to be understood that all the Zulus we are winning to Zion are heathen. Many are cultured, and some are well-educated and possess exceptional intellectual power.

The Gospel of Zion is rapidly spreading among them. Large numbers are living its teaching.

Their lives are of such purity and richness of faith that valuable lessons are taught by them to their pale-faced teachers.

When a Zulu accepts Zion he will endure any hardship with patience, and will die before he will prove false in any way.

The character of the results of the missionary work in South Africa has, in the main, been humiliating—impudence, laziness, and beggary having been its chief fruits.

It is a proverb in South Africa that, in choosing a Zulu servant, a raw heathen is preferable to one "spoiled by Christianity."

I cannot pause to contrast this with Zion's success, except to mention the ennobling fact of tithing upon them.

The missionaries went to them with gifts; Zion, with God's law of tithing.

The first made beggars; the second, ready, honest laborers, who love to pay their tithes.

At the close of my meeting at Wakkerstroom, an offering was made for the work.

Quietly they came forward, according to their custom, and laid the money on the table before me.

I was astonished at their liberality and ability to give. Their offering amounted to about five times as much as would have been collected at a denominational church service of like size in America.

Our native Zulu work in the Transvaal, whose headquarters is at Wakkerstroom, is the fruit of the skilful, untirng labor of the Rev. Pieter L. le Roux and wife, whose photograph and testimony appear in this issue.

We had the joy, at the direction of our beloved General Overseer, of ordaining him an Elder, and his wife an Evangelist, in the Christian Catholic Church in Zion, at Pretoria, Lord's Day, July 31, 1904.

In visiting the headquarters of our Zulu work at Wakkerstroom, we were met a mile from the city by the Rev. Pieter L. le Roux, with an escort of Kafir horsemen.

Riding on, we came to the bridge over the Wakkerstroom River leading to the city.

Here the Zulus were assembled in full force to greet us.

They were arrayed in bright colors, their faces radiant with joy.

As we rose and greeted them, through our excellent interpreter, Rev. Peter L. le Roux, three mighty cheers burst from their lips; a procession was then formed which we shall never forget.

Escorted by the horsemen and followed by a line of natives nearly one-eighth of a mile long, we marched through the town, stirring it to its depths.

In little groups on the streets, and from the windows and porches, the white inhabitants gazed at the scene in utter amazement.

We were soon at our place of worship, at the Rev. Pieter L. le Roux's home, and while we richly enjoyed and appreciated our kingly reception (which was truly Zulu in character), we were a little relieved to resume our natural method of life.

Here we remained for several days, ministering to a delighted people, and witnessing with joy the good work wrought by Rev. Pieter L. le Roux and his faithful wife.

We baptized one hundred forty-one out of eight hundred who follow the Faith.

We take pleasure in sending a view of this Baptism, which was one of indescribable beauty.

The Rev. Pieter L. le Roux has three able native evangelists, who give their whole time to the work, besides many whom he sends out upon Restoration work.

Three miles from Wakkerstroom, Daniel Nkonyane has his home and church, located on several acres of ground.

He raises enough to live upon and, assisted by Rev. Pieter L. le Roux, put up his own meeting place.

Among the Zulus he raised the most of five hundred ninety dollars, to pay for seventy acres of land and to erect upon it another house of worship.

The sight of his noble, earnest face impressed me deeply.

We regret that, owing to his absence from Wakkerstroom, we were unable to secure his photograph.

On a little farm twenty miles from the headquarters at Wakkerstroom and near the railroad station at Zandspruit, lives our able Zulu Evangelist, Muneli Ngobese, who is on the right of the two Evangelists in the photograph.

Ngobese is a natural leader and organizer.

On his own farm and with his own hands he erected his house of worship, seating two hundred people.

The native converts to whom he ministers take care of his farm plowing, sowing, and reaping, that their beloved leader may give his full time to the ministry of the Word and to prayer.

They also see to it that the crop is ample, not only for the family of Ngobese, but also to feed the large numbers who from far gather to spend the Lord's Day in worship and praise.

After all-day service, many remain in the sacred spot throughout the night.

My bedroom at Rev. Pieter L. le Roux's home was within forty feet of the church building, and I can personally testify to their singing until morning.

We take pleasure in recording our visit to the native work in the Orange River Colony, the headquarters of which is at Harrismith, on a farm of seven hundred acres, controlled by our conductor, E. H. Mahon.

ZION IN HARRISMITH, O. R. C. SOUTH AFRICA.

His thorough knowledge of the native work, and love for the Zulus, combined with natural power as a leader and deep spirituality, make him invaluable in the work.

He is ably assisted by a devoted wife. Mrs. Mahon is rejoicing in God's gift of another sweet Zion baby, whose name is Daniel Mahon.

Mr. Mahon's farm is worked by natives, whose love for their master is inexhaustible.

On Lord's Day he starts his Evangelists out on horseback upon their respective itineraries.

Knowing the difficulty other farmers have with Zulu labor, I asked Mr. Mahon, who, with a few exceptions, has been used of God in leading all the natives on his farm into Zion, how he got on with Zion native help.

E. H. MAHON, CONDUCTOR OF NATIVE WORK AT HARRISMITH, ORANGE RIVER COLONY, SOUTH AFRICA.

He smiled and said: "I can trust them anywhere, with anything. They work as hard when I am away as when I am with them."

He prays for them, loves them, and teaches them God's Word.

He is rewarded with faithful service, and any one of them would lay down his life for his master.

What a contrast to the slave-driver who hates, and curses, and beats, and who reaps the thorns he sows.

We were taken by surprise at our introduction in the first service, Lord's Day morning, May 15th.

As we entered the house of worship, the audience rose and greeted us in Zulu, "*Ukutula Akubekuwe*," Peace to Thee.

Then a handsome Zulu lad directed the trained Zulu choir.

The choir leader is a natural musician, and the choir sang by note, using the tonic sol-fa system.

We were overcome by the heavenly sweetness of their voices, a number of which, being of such excellence that we have never heard them surpassed, if equalled.

Here at Harrismith we baptized sixty natives within a stone's throw of the place where the Boer General, De Wet, made his terrible Christmas night slaughter of the British, shooting and stabbing to death the sleeping soldiers.

In a quiet stream, amid a network of military trenches, redoubts and blockhouses, where brother slaughtered brother in war, we buried the soldiers of the Cross in Holy Baptism.

Along our ranks no sabres shine,
No blood-red pennons wave;
Our banners bear one single line:
"Our mission is to save!"

We had the joy of baptizing a native Chief, Joseph Kumalo, who presides over a kraal of three thousand natives. We send a photo of Chief Kumalo and wife.

Six years ago, when dying, he was healed, through the prayer of E. H. Mahon. Since this time he has read LEAVES OF HEALING.

He came seventy miles to meet us.

He is a man of magnificent physique, cultured, and kingly in bearing. He is well educated, speaking English with beautiful accuracy.

He has for fourteen years been a local Wesleyan preacher, and a schoolteacher for fifteen years.

It is charming to listen to his oratory when addressing an audience.

Chief Kumalo has six children, the eldest daughter, fourteen years of age, having passed the third class teachers' examination in English.

The Chief has two other well educated native teachers, who are ready to come into Zion.

Chief Kumalo was baptized with great joy of heart, and returned to his people to unfurl the Banner of Zion.

Situated eighteen miles from Harrismith is the farm of Mr. J. W. Putterill. While Mr. Putterill to our knowledge has not yet entered the fellowship of the Christian Catholic Apostolic Church in Zion, he is a man of God and loves the fearless, thorough teaching of the Christian Catholic Apostolic Church in Zion.

At his own expense he has erected a house of worship upon his farm, and supports a native evangelist, Peter Bhengu, who preaches to the Kafirs with great

"ROCKCLIFFE" RESIDENCE OF OVERSEER BRYANT AND DEACON RIDEOUT, 74 HARRISON ST.

power and effect. We take pleasure in sending a photograph of Peter Bhengu, wife and babe. This photograph was taken on the occasion of the baptismal service at Harrismith.

Peter Bhengu speaks the English language, but preaches in the Zulu tongue.

We get some very amusing letters from the States, some of our friends having the idea that we are working among naked savages.

In the native group we publish it will be seen that many are well dressed.

Our personal labors, however, are confined to Europeans, and we publish a little glimpse of Johannesburg and our home, to show that cities and homes in South Africa are like cities and homes "at home."

zing large numbers of both whites and blacks.

We left Johannesburg May 9th, upon an itinerary which embraced the main Zion centers and the largest cities of South Africa.

Our native work is at present largely developed only at two points. And a description of this, our introduction to our dark-skinned brethren, is the object of this letter.

We reached Folksrust at half past four o'clock the following morning.

"Charlie," the big native who acted as interpreter when we first passed through, and a few others, slept in the station all night in order to be there to meet us, and their *ukutulas* (peace to thee) made little warm spots in the cold,

on the brow of a hill; so we looked back and took a photograph of the scattered town and Majuba Hill behind it.

Then on we went, and we enjoyed every minute of that drive.

Autumn had seared the grass, and veldt and mountains showed indescribably beautiful blendings of gold, brown, red, and green.

We saw a few farmhouses; a few herds of cattle, horses, sheep, and goats; a few natives, and an occasional horseman.

Once a solitary bird flew across our path.

We enjoyed the vastness, the solitude, and the restfulness; and we opened our spirits widely to it.

About a mile out of Wakkerstroom Mr. Le Roux, his wife, children, a friend,

OVERSEER DANIEL BRYANT BAPTIZING ONE HUNDRED FORTY-ONE ZULU CHRISTIANS AT WAKKERSTROOM, TRANSVAAL, SOUTH AFRICA, MAY, 1904.

INTERESTING ARTICLE FROM PEN OF ELDER EMMA DEMPCY BRYANT.

From all over South Africa Zion at headquarters has long been receiving pleading letters, which have been referred to the coming Overseer.

The people feel that with the coming of Zion's Messengers light has arisen out of darkness, and they are crying out from every city and town, it seems to us, "Come and baptize us!" "Come and pray for us that we may be healed." "Come and give us the Truth as it is taught and practiced in Zion!"

And we are going, going, night and day, across the veldt and over the mountains, teaching, praying, breaking the bread, and giving the wine, and bapti-

frosty night air as we stepped out into the darkness.

They carried our luggage, and escorted us to the Transvaal Hotel, where we took a bed for a few hours, secured a little sleep, and thawed our chilled limbs.

About nine o'clock we had a good breakfast, and at ten, seated in the mail-cart drawn by six colonial mules—we two the only passengers—we started upon our eighteen miles' drive across the veldt, as happy and bright as possible.

It was a perfect morning. The bright sun had dispelled the chilliness of the previous night, although the high, thin air is always cool and penetrating in winter.

A short distance out our team stopped

and five or six natives on horseback met us.

They gave us most cordial greetings, and took us in.

When we reached the bridge at the entrance of the town, two large companies of native members of Zion awaited us.

As we drew up, they cheered, and waved, and sang. We stood up in the carriage and returned their salutations, then passed on through the town, a triumphal procession, to their hall, where a little service of welcome was to be held.

Our reception was quite spontaneous, except that Mr. Le Roux had announced the service of welcome, and had requested as many as possible to meet us.

Our procession consisted, first, of five or six fine horsemen, who led the way

FRED SUTULI. MUNELI NGOBESE.

and formed an imposing escort; next, the two Cape carts in which we rode; then a long line of dusky men, women and children, all in holiday attire, wearing gay turbans, waists and skirts, rings, bracelets and anklets.

The people of the town were astounded at this, and still more a few days later when they gathered in large numbers to witness the baptism of one hundred forty-one native converts.

We had never witnessed a more beautiful, quiet service.

These were not sudden, emotional converts, but people whom Mr. Le Roux had been teaching for some time. They are *living* the faith.

They have given up drinking, smoking and snuffing, which they practiced almost without exception.

They all trust God for healing, having given up their bones, drugs, and other forms of witchcraft, to which they formerly looked for the cure of disease.

Many of them have been wonderfully healed.

As soon as they see Divine Healing taught in the Bible they unquestioningly accept it.

Many of the people had ridden and walked for miles; but gratifying as was the number present, it represented a small part of Mr. Le Roux's work.

The total number of people ministered to by him and his native helpers is at least one thousand.

One man, hearing that we had passed through a certain point on our way, at the close of his day's work started and walked all night, a distance of eighteen miles, to Wakkerstroom, and reached there just as we were leaving.

His disappointment was pitiful to see.

Especially did he regret missing the Baptism.

Wishing to reward him a little for his long journey, Overseer Bryant gave him a little talk through an interpreter; he then prayed for the man, and looking at him he saw the tears coursing down his cheeks.

Many times have Mr. and Mrs. Le Roux received back a portion of the bread which they have so unceasingly cast upon the waters.

In the early part of their work, their little Josie had convulsions.

There was no minister or church-member in the town who could help them.

Mrs. Le Roux ran to the river, where the native women were washing clothes, and asked them to pray.

For three weeks, during which time the little life seemed to hang by a thread, these faithful people prayed unceasingly, and helped them day and night.

One morning "Charlie" came into the kitchen to inquire after the little sufferer.

Mrs. Le Roux, worn out, was almost discouraged, and told him that she thought Josie could not live.

This humble native looked sternly at her and reminded her how Peter grew fearful and sank when his Lord was close to his side.

They took fresh courage, and shortly after the child was healed.

They then separated themselves entirely from the Dutch church, which they had not done before, although they had been giving their native congregation the teachings of Zion.

After finishing our work at Wakkerstroom, we had another long drive back across the dusty, treeless veldt, occupying another night and half day in reaching Harrismith, in the Orange River Colony.

We are becoming accustomed to traveling long distances, as we have been able to reach very few points without traveling a day and a night—sometimes two nights.

On this particular morning, as the sun rose and revealed the landscape, we found ourselves passing through one of the most picturesque portions of South Africa.

Soon after leaving Ladysmith we began a gradual ascent, which culminated some hours later at the reverse station at Van Runan's Pass.

Here our engine was transferred from the front to the rear of our train, and we found we had climbed to the very crest of a range of great hills.

Below us successively lower ranges extended to the valley.

At Harrismith we were met by Mr. Mahon, conductor of a native work extending over a vast region.

We have no trouble in recognizing our Zion friends.

As we alight at our station we scan the crowd assembled there; then we march straight up to the cleanest, most

REV. J. KUMALO AND WIFE, CHIEF OF KRAAL OF 3000 NATIVES

st and expectant-looking person, rsons, and say, "Peace to thee!"
have made no mistakes as yet.
were soon seated behind Mr. Ma- good span, covering the four miles een the town and his farm.
. Mahon dwells in a typical South an farmhouse of corrugated iron vood.
front of the house the veldt ches away to the west as far as eye ee.
hind are some spurs of the Draken- mountains, and the house and , like mere specks, are situated on opes of one of these.

HARRISON STREET, JOHANNESBURG.

the distance, perhaps seventy away, we can see the main Dra- urg range lifting its glittering snow- ned peaks into the sapphire skies.
. Mahon's native work is of about extent to that which we first vis-

e of the most interesting features is ne choir which he has formed, from g Zulu boys and girls, many of n, only a few months ago, were un- heathen.
has taught them to read music, but aining them has taken care not to their exquisite naturalness and g.

Into their native tongue he has translated some of the grandest old Wesleyan hymns, and these are well suited to the richest, deepest bass voices that we have ever heard.

We could not understand the words as they sang, but we could understand the language of the Holy Spirit who spoke in their earnest faces and thrilling tones.

We baptized several white persons and about sixty natives in the Wilge River.

We drove to the river in great ox carts, each drawn by from five to seven span of great fat oxen.

The scene at the river was one never to be forgotten.

All about us were trenches, redoubts, and block houses.

Near-by was the scene of one of the greatest slaughters of the war, when the Boer General De Wet passed the sleeping, drunken sentinels and stabbed the English soldiers in their tents.

Now an apparent peace is reigning, but in the hearts of those who went down into the baptismal waters there was that "Peace which passeth all understanding."

At Harrismith we bade good-by to our native Zion, and entered upon our ministry to the Africander people. It was with some regret that we left our Zulu friends, for we had been much blessed, spiritually, through our contact with their sweet, earnest faith and childlike spirit of obedience.

WRITTEN TESTIMONY OF THE REV. PIETER L. LE ROUX.

WAKKERSTROOM, TRANSVAAL, SOUTH AFRICA,
August 27, 1904.

THE REV. DANIEL BRYANT, Overseer for South Africa, in the Christian Catholic Apostolic Church in Zion.

Beloved Overseer:—Peace to thee!

At your request, I will tell in a few words, how God has led me into Zion.

My conversion took place in my fifteenth year, and I have been a Christian worker more or less regularly ever since.

The previous year I had left my father's farm to go to a boarding school.

While there, I conceived the idea of being a school teacher, and accordingly went to the normal training school for teachers in Cape Town.

After obtaining the diploma of that institution, I spent two years at college, in Stellenbosch, where the Dutch Reformed church has its theological seminary, and then took charge of a large country school.

Four years later, the Lord called me into mission work, and the Dutch Reformed church sent me to the Zulus, in the southeastern portion of the Transvaal.

Elder and Evangelist P. L. le Roux.

With my dear wife as an earnest coworker, I started in what was practically virgin soil

God blessed us abundantly.

Conversions came right away.

Within the first year about twenty were sprinkled.

Seven years later the Church among the Zulus numbered over two thousand.

The Dutch Reformed church took up the work very heartily.

The Lord sent us good, earnest, native preachers, who came to us from different denominations.

With their help it became possible to extend the work far and wide.

After several years spent in continually going about the country, and seeing the results of our preaching to the Zulus, it became apparent that there was a great lack of real, deep spiritual work.

The conversions appeared to be very shallow, and our converts proved very half-hearted Christians.

They did not give up their native beer, went on defiling their bodies by smoking a strong, poisonous weed, known as *dagga*, and in many other ways showed that their religion had little power to thoroughly change their lives.

It was quite a common thing to hear people say that they would have nothing to do with a Kafir who had been spoiled by religion.

This state of things caused us much grief, and we cried to God to be shown what was wrong.

Meanwhile we had heard of Zion; Leaves of Healing had come into our hands, and had brought new light.

At last we became convinced of the fact that great blessing could not be expected while we were connected with the church to which we belonged.

We gave up the use of drugs, and began to preach Divine Healing to our people. Many at once turned to the Lord and accepted the teaching.

The local authorities of the Dutch church were stirred up over the matter, and would not have this new teaching.

Several conferences, some very stormy, took place, and at last we were threatened with expulsion.

In this perplexity I turned for counsel to some of the ministers of the church.

In answer to my inquiries they all stated that Divine Healing was in the Word of God; it was true, however, at the same time, they said, that it was dangerous ground for public teaching, and would cause trouble.

The one man to whom I especially looked for counsel was my old minister, Andrew Murray.

In his letter he plainly stated that Divine Healing was the teaching of the Word of God—a glorious, Divine Truth.

At the same time, he said that if I insisted on publicly teaching it, I might expect to be put aside, as the church would not allow it in its public ministry of the Word.

It thus became apparent that it was useless to try to convert the church. It only remained to get out of it as soon as possible.

When we came into Zion, many of our people in the Dutch church came with us.

They were so convinced of the truth that no amount of persuasion could move them.

They find no difficulty in accepting the dear General Overseer as the Prophet of the Restoration.

God has richly blessed many of them, not only in healing their bodies, but also in delivering them from evil.

Drink, drugs, and tobacco have long since disappeared from among them.

Personally, I desire to thank God for many blessings to me and my house.

We have been delivered again and again, and now serve Him with a joy we never knew before.

Several years before leaving the Dutch church it had become clear to me that the method of baptizing by sprinkling was utterly unscriptural. I therefore counted it a great privilege, long looked

Meta Budulwako.

forward to, to be baptized by Triune Immersion, in company with my dear wife, on July 11, 1904.

I also desire to thank Him for the blessed privilege of being ordained, with my dear wife, to the ministry of the Christian Catholic Apostolic Church in Zion, and of being associated with the Prophet of the Restoration, our beloved General Overseer, in his great and glorious work for God and humanity.

Faithfully yours for God and Zion,

P. L. LE ROUX,

Elder in the Christian Catholic Apostolic Church in Zion

WRITTEN TESTIMONY OF MISS META BUDULWAKO.

WAKKERSTROOM, TRANSVAAL, SOUTH AFRICA.

THE REV. DANIEL BRYANT, Overseer for South Africa in the Christian Catholic Apostolic Church in Zion.

My Dear Overseer:—Peace to thee.

To the glory of God, I desire to testify of what He has done for me through Zion teaching.

My parents were heathen, and knew nothing of the Word of God.

At about fifteen years of age I went to a Lutheran Mission Station.

There I was taught to read the Bible in my native language, and became a member of the church.

Writing was not taught in the mission school.

Some time after returning home to my people we heard of Zion, but would have nothing to do with it.

In 1900 I went to work in Wakkerstroom, and attended Zion meetings, because there was no other place there where religious services were held.

In this way Zion teaching reached me.

However, being strongly prejudiced, it was a hard struggle to accept the truth and submit to it.

Shortly after this I became very ill. My stomach could not bear any food.

Even a mouthful of water caused severe pain and swelling.

My breath was so short that walking was almost impossible. I also suffered from female trouble.

A Zion family kindly took me into their home, and advised me to ask for prayer.

I was then so ill and weak that they had to prop me up in bed with pillows.

My heart was to some extent in rebellion against the teaching, but as I saw death was near, I consented to having prayer offered for me.

Rev. Pieter le Roux visited me several times and explained the Word, and prayed for me.

I soon improved, became stronger, and walked home to my people, a distance of about five miles.

The full healing, however, did not come at that time.

Later on it became clear that there were things in my life which had to be put right before God could greatly bless me.

The following year I went back to work in Wakkerstroom, and soon my trouble reappeared.

My mistress gave me medicine and brandy. These did not cure me, and I had to give up working.

It now became clear to me that drugs could not cure, and I determined to turn to God with my whole heart, put things right as far as possible, and seek the Lord alone for healing.

Then something occurred which made a very great impression on me, and made me decide to put off doing right no longer.

A woman to whom I was related, and who lived with us, became very ill with pneumonia.

She belonged to Zion, and had given up the use of drugs.

She sent for the minister, and he came and prayed with her, after teaching her and us the Word of God on the subject of Divine Healing.

Some time after he was gone she called us together, and informed us that she could not be healed, as she had to confess some terrible sins, and she would rather die than make the confession.

She suffered terribly for about a week, and then died.

As soon as possible I sought the Zion minister, and made a full confession to him.

I did as he advised me, and God answered prayer for me.

Today it is my privilege and joy to testify to being saved and perfectly healed.

I am strong and happy, and thank God for Zion.

To Him be all the glory!

My people are against me, and so is my master; but I am determined, by the grace of God, to be true to Zion, no matter what others may say or do.

I was baptized by Triune Immersion in April last, during your visit to Wakkerstroom.

May God bless you and Zion in South Africa.

Yours, for God and Zion,

META BUDULWAKO

OVERSEER DANIEL BRYANT'S ACCOUNT OF ARRIVAL IN SOUTH AFRICA.

April 30, 1904.

DEAR GENERAL OVERSEER:—

"Praise God from whom all blessings flow."

We are just completing our first three weeks' campaign for God in South Africa.

On Tuesday morning, April 12th, the goodly vessel, *Durham Castle*, upon which for three weeks we had been sailing over quiet seas through days of sweet sunshine, came to anchor at Port Elizabeth. There we were met by the Conductor of the Gathering from Uitenhage, F. A. Magennis, accompanied by H. W. Bates.

Uitenhage is a beautiful town of five thousand inhabitants, twenty miles inland from Port Elizabeth. There we held our first meeting with Zion.

It is impossible to describe the joy which filled these dear people, as well as ourselves, when we stood face to face. For months they had been praying for us, and eagerly awaiting our arrival.

We found them much in need of organization; but with willing, loyal hearts. This made our work easy and rapid.

We remained ten days in Uitenhage, as no vessel upon which we could embark left Port Elizabeth at an earlier date.

Thirteen obeyed God in Baptism, and the work was left in a thorough state of organization, so far as we could see.

We had the pleasure of enrolling among the new members at Uitenhage a Salvation Army worker from Port Elizabeth. He gave up the Salvation Army because of the wicked attack made by its leaders upon our General Overseer, and the failure of General Booth to refute the shameful and false statements that had been made.

So we hope the fire has been kindled in Port Elizabeth, which bears the proud distinction of being called the "Liverpool of South Africa."

After the ten days of toil we enjoyed the delightful sail of two days on the *Armadale Castle* to Durban.

God's Spirit seemed to burn like fire in every meeting we held in Durban.

We endeavored to conduct a quiet meeting among our own friends, in order to get the work properly organized. It was gratifying to note how wide-spread was the interest. Our Zion Tabernacle was filled at the last service.

We had the joy of receiving into fellowship twenty-one and of baptizing sixteen. A number gave up their sins and found peace with God.

Many touching and gratifying incidents characterized the work in Durban.

One young man, whom God called to Repentance, confessed to having stolen a sum of money.

NATIVE EVANGELIST PETER BHENGU AND WIFE.

He said to the man from whom he had stolen it, "I know you have the power to put me behind the bars, but I have turned to God, and I want your forgiveness." This was readily granted, and the money will be repaid at the earliest opportunity.

Under the heart-searching of God's Word, it was remarkable how many confessions were made.

One of the pleasant experiences was the display of Zion lace, and the teaching of the plan and purposes of Zion's Industries.

Many strangers manifested a deep interest in what was said, and openly expressed their admiration for the beautiful lace.

God made it clear in this meeting that no one could be a loyal member of the Christian Catholic Apostolic Church in Zion and leave his possessions out in the world.

Each meeting at Durban seemed to grow in spiritual power, and the series ended in a climax when we had the joy of administering the Zion Restoration Host Vow to nineteen persons. We shall never forget the sight of their faces. They glowed with fervor and determination to serve God.

We have been able to secure in Durban a beautiful meeting place for our work. This is very important in a city like Durban, which is not over-complimented in being called "The Garden of South Africa." It is a city of wealth, magnificent buildings, and improvements of every kind.

One can feel the great future which is dawning in South Africa.

Our accommodations while in Durban consisted of a little cottage, all to ourselves, embowered amid lemon and orange trees, banana, plantain, and mango.

Our work in Durban came to a happy close, and we find ourselves on our way to Johannesburg.

It is now April 30th. We are dictating these notes as we ride through the very heart of the war country.

We have just passed through Colenso, Ladysmith, and literally wound about the famous Majuba Hill

The last station through which we passed bore the familiar name, Zandspruit, where it will be remembered General Joubert rallied the Boer forces and invaded Natal.

Within three miles of Zandspruit is Volksrust. Here, on this morning of the 30th of April, a rally took place of a very different nature.

We have within a radius of thirty miles surrounding Volksrust, one thousand native Zulus who are obedient to the teaching of Zion.

A number of these, knowing that we were to pass through Volksrust at twelve minutes after nine o'clock in the morning, had gathered to welcome us.

We easily recognized them by their noble, Christian faces, and by the fact that none were smoking.

Their earnest looks of expectancy as they came down the train gazing into the different compartments, confirmed our impression of their mission.

We were to stop twenty minutes, and we stepped out of our compartments and were soon surrounded by these people.

The Rev. Mr. le Roux, who has accomplished this great work among these natives, had come all the way from his headquarters at Wakkerstroom to interview us at Durban.

He taught us Zion's beautiful salutation, "Peace to thee," in the Zulu tongue, and as our little party of four stepped out upon the platform at Volksrust into the circle of dark, beaming faces, we were all able to say heartily, "Ukutula!" (Peace to thee.)

"Ukutula akubekuwe!" came back the hearty response.

It was worth days of practice in the pronunciation of these words to witness the delight with which they were received.

We gathered them about us in a circle, and finding one of the number who understood English, through this dear woman as an interpreter, we were able to tell them of Zion City and of our mission to South Africa.

We first told them how the General Overseer loved them, and that he had sent his special love to them.

Their faces beamed with delight.

After speaking a few words on the subject of repentance, we asked all who had given up their sins to lift their hands.

Up went every hand.

We asked all who had been healed through faith in Jesus, the Christ, to lift the hand.

Like a flash the hands went up.

We then spoke a few words upon Baptism, asking how many were ready to obey the command of the Lord Jesus, the Christ.

Eagerly every hand was raised.

In the midst of our talk the signal was given, and we were compelled to tear ourselves away and go to the train.

The table before us is piled up with pineapples, oranges, and bananas with which they loaded us as we were leaving.

They followed the train in a crowd as we moved off, waving their hands and shouting, "Ukutula."

We expect to reach Johannesburg at fifteen minutes past six tonight.

No words can express the joy which fills our hearts.

We are all well, for the Joy of the Lord is our strength. We are unspeakably happy.

Each day is a day of glad toil to us.

Peace to Zion throughout the world.

DANIEL BRYANT.

Warning.

I am directed by the General Overseer to warn our members and officers throughout the world against giving money to persons claiming to be members of the Christian Catholic Church in Zion. All benevolence must be given either from Headquarters or under the direction of same. Even though the applicant for benevolence be known to be a member of the Christian Catholic Church in Zion, financial aid must not be given except in extreme cases, and then only in small amounts. Requests for help must be made to the officer-in-charge. In cases where there is no such officer, requests should be made direct to Headquarters, accompanied by recommendations from one or two members of Zion in good standing. J. G. EXCELL,
General Ecclesiastical Secretary.

Street Addresses Are Necessary

All Zion City Subscribers to *Leaves of Healing*, *The Zion Banner*, *Blätter der Heilung*, and *Voice from Zion*, whose correct street addresses are not positively known to be in our possession should send them to us AT ONCE. Please act upon this notice without delay as it is very important, now that we have postal delivery service, that the exact location of each and every subscriber be known to us. Write your name and address very carefully, designating also to what periodicals you are a subscriber and leave at your very earliest opportunity at our branch Publishing House on Elijah Avenue.

Very Sincerely Yours,
ZION PRINTING AND PUBLISHING HOUSE.

Warning to Subscribers.

Scarcely a week passes that we do not have complaints about money having been sent to us in currency, stamps, or silver, in the open mails, for renewals of subscriptions or for other purposes, WHICH WE HAVE NOT RECEIVED AND WHICH NEVER REACHES US.

Therefore, we desire to warn every member and friend of Zion sending money to us, to always use some safe means, preferably a money-order, or bank-draft on New York or Chicago, or personal check on Zion City Bank.

In conforming to this notice you will save yourselves trouble and expense, and us much annoyance.

ZION PRINTING AND PUBLISHING HOUSE,
Zion City, Illinois.

Notes from Zion's Harvest Field

By Overseer J. G. Excell, General Ecclesiastical Secretary.

Wichita, Kansas.

Elder-in-charge, Rev. David A. Reed, 509 South Elizabeth avenue.
Tabernacle, 213 South Water street
Services—Lord's Days, 3 and 7:30 p. m.; Wednesday, 7:30 p. m.

DEAR GENERAL OVERSEER:—Peace to thee.

We are going forward in Wichita, encouraged by 2 Corinthians 4:18.

One of the most encouraging parts of our work here is the Junior work.

We know when we start to our Tabernacle for service, no matter what the weather, that the Juniors will be there.

A little Zion boy only two years of age became very sick in the night.

Fear entered the mother's heart, because she could not reach the Elder, as it was too late in the night to get a street-car.

The Devil suggested that the doctor was near, but then the little child began to repeat to his mother the words of that beautiful song, "All power is given unto Me."

Fear left her; and she prayed, and he was soon sitting up, eating and singing over and over that song to his mother.

Mrs. Reed has visited weekly every saloon in the city, with LEAVES OF HEALING and messages.

There are between forty and fifty open saloons here in a "Prohibition State."

Some have said, "There is no use; you do not get them converted."

But it is our business to sow good seed—God will give the increase; and in "due season we shall reap if we faint not."

In the last year we have been able to hold two hundred eighty-eight meetings, make ten thousand nine hundred fifty-nine calls, sell two thousand four hundred copies of LEAVES OF HEALING, and give away twelve hundred copies of LEAVES OF HEALING. We have traveled by railway five thousand two hundred miles, and held meetings in forty-two different places.

Many have given themselves to God.

Many have received healing; have separated themselves from apostate denominations, and have come into Zion.

My family and I spent a week during the holidays at Eldorado with Mr. and Mrs. Mann, who have, by the help of God, sown Good Seed in that community.

We were told that the people all watched them when they moved in there, "to see what kind of people the 'Dowieites' were."

After they had been there some time one man said that no one could truthfully say that they did not live what they preached.

The weather was very cold, but nearly all the neighbors came to the meetings.

We called at nearly every home.

Some threw away their tobacco and gave up the dirty swine's flesh.

When we asked all who would get out from under the dominion of the Devil and come under the rule of the Christ every one in the house rose, and nearly all prayed the Prayer of Repentance and Consecration.

The interest increased every night, and we left the meetings in charge of Mr. Mann and the Junior work with Mrs. Mann, who report a good interest every Lord's Day.

They hold the meetings in a schoolhouse.

I have just returned from holding meetings at Abilene, Junction City, and Manhattan.

At Junction City we found Mr. and Mrs. Krebe waiting for us, with all arrangements made for meetings in the Congregational church.

We called at all the homes for six blocks around the church, inviting the people to the services, and giving them the salutation of Peace with a Message from Elijah the Restorer and a copy of LEAVES OF HEALING.

About thirty persons came. We held three services and the people wanted me to stay longer.

We then went on to Manhattan, where we held six meetings, and many were very eager to ask questions about Zion.

We called on an afflicted brother who is a relative of Mr. W— in Zion City, and a deacon of the Presbyterian church.

He has been reading LEAVES OF HEALING and getting some faith for healing. He very much desires to get to Zion City.

There is great prejudice all over Kansas; but we go on, rejoicing that we have a clean, Full Gospel to bring to the people.

Yours in Christian love and fellowship, Till He Come. DAVID A. REED.

NOTES OF THANKSGIVING FROM THE WHOLE WORLD

Blessed When Obedient to God in Tithing.

Bring ye the whole tithe into the Storehouse,
That there may be meat in Mine house,
And prove Me now herewith,
Saith Jehovah of Hosts,
If I will not open you the windows of Heaven,
And pour you out a blessing,
That there shall not be room enough to receive it.—*Malachi 3:10.*

296 BROOKLINE STREET,
CAMBRIDGE, MASSACHUSETTS,
April 28, 1904

DEAR OVERSEER SPEICHER:—I send to you a copy of part of a letter I received some time ago, believing it may be a blessing to others if published in LEAVES OF HEALING.

I have written to Mrs. Hall, asking her permission, and she replies that she would be glad to have others know of her healing, that they may see the importance of paying tithes faithfully.

HELEN A. SMITH,
Evangelist in the Christian Catholic Apostolic Church in Zion.

COLEBROOK, NEW HAMPSHIRE.

MY DEAR MOTHER IN ZION:—Peace to thee.

I write to let you know that we are now well and trusting in God.

Neglecting to pay tithes was the hindrance to getting the victory sooner.

I was taken very ill with the grip.

As we did not get the answer to our prayers we wrote you.

I received a great blessing at the time you prayed.

This was before we got the pay for the sugar you helped us to sell.

I had a relapse.

My husband's mother came to care for me.

We sent a telegram to the General Overseer, but still I grew worse.

Mr. Hall then wrote to Overseer Dowie, but I received no help.

For five weeks I suffered until I became so weak I could not be raised in bed to take nourishment.

My mother-in-law sent for a doctor who urged me to take medicine.

He said: "You need not expect to get well without medicine; it is as necessary as your food; you cannot gain flesh without eating and you cannot get well without medicine."

My mother thought that I would not live when I refused to take the medicine.

We then sent for you to come to us and you wrote us asking if we had paid tithes on the sugar and if not we had better pray about it.

You believed God would give deliverance without having the expense of your trip, which would be a great deal more than our tithes would be.

Mr. Hall at first thought he need not pay; but after we received your letter, we prayed God to show us what we ought to do.

When we remembered how good God had been to us in giving Mr. Hall health to make the sugar—health such as he had not had for years—we resolved to pay the tithes.

Mr. Hall paid them on the 22d of June, and on the 27th I was out in my kitchen.

It was wonderful how quickly my strength was given back to me.

On the 4th of July my mother left me and I have been able to do the work since.

Before my healing our friends objected greatly to our paying tithes.

Now they advise us to continue if such blessing follows.

We thank you for giving us the teaching and telling us when we made the mistake about the tithes.

We hope some day to be in Zion City.

With love, (MRS.) IVORY HALL.

21 NEWLYN ROAD, BRUCE GROVE,
TOTTENHAM, N., LONDON, ENGLAND.

DEAR GENERAL OVERSEER:—I thank God for wonderfully healing me of a weak heart, from which I suffered greatly.

I used to have these attacks several times, daily.

My dear ones were very much alarmed; so much so that they frequently called in the doctor, for they thought that I was at death's door.

But his efforts were fruitless; his medicine did me no good, and his words describing my critical condition only made me more fearful, for he said that unless I refrained from exertion I was liable to pass away at any moment.

It was not until I came into Zion and there received the gracious light of God's truth, making the Bible a new Book to me, that I grew to know that the Christ is my Healer as well as my Savior.

From my heart I praise God for the great deliverance which He has given me.

When Overseer Cantel prayed for me I was not fully healed at first. I obeyed God in Baptism, and followed that step by coming into fellowship in Zion; and with these steps of obedience came the full deliverance, for which I praise God with all my heart.

(MRS.) EMMA RICHARDSON.

IS ANY among you sick? let him call for the Elders of the Church; and let them pray over him, anointing him with oil in the Name of the Lord: And the Prayer of Faith shall save him that is sick, and the Lord shall raise him up; and if he have committed sins, it shall be forgiven him.—*James 5:14, 15.*

A WEEKLY PAPER FOR THE EXTENSION OF THE KINGDOM OF GOD.

EDITED BY

JOHN ALEXANDER, First Apostle of the Lord Jesus, the Christ, in the Christian Catholic Apostolic Church in Zion.

Application for entry as Second Class Matter at Zion City, Illinois, pending.

Subscription Rates.		Special Rates.	
One Year	$2.00	100 Copies of One Issue	$3.00
Six Months	1.25	25 Copies of One Issue	1.00
Three Months	.75	To Ministers, Y. M. C. A's and Public	
Single Copies	.05	Reading Rooms, per annum	1.50

For foreign subscriptions add $1.50 per year, or three cents per copy for postage.
Subscribers desiring a change of address should give present address, as well as that to which they desire LEAVES OF HEALING sent in the future.
Make Bank Drafts, Express Money or Postoffice Money Orders payable to the order of JOHN ALEX. DOWIE, Zion City, Illinois, U. S. A.

Long Distance Telephone. *Cable Address "Dowie, Zion City."*

All communications upon business must be addressed to
MANAGER ZION PUBLISHING HOUSE,
Zion City, Illinois, U. S. A.

Subscriptions to LEAVES OF HEALING, A VOICE FROM ZION, and the various publications may also be sent to
ZION PUBLISHING HOUSE, 81 EUSTON ROAD, LONDON, N. W., ENGLAND.
ZION PUBLISHING HOUSE, NO. 43 PARK ROAD, ST. KILDA, VICTORIA, AUSTRALIA.
ZION PUBLISHING HOUSE, 76 BAHNHOFSTRASSE, ZÜRICH, SWITZERLAND.

ZION CITY, ILLINOIS, SATURDAY, OCTOBER 8, 1904.

TABLE OF CONTENTS.

LEAVES OF HEALING, SATURDAY, OCTOBER 8, 1904

EDITORIAL NOTES.

"RIGHTEOUSNESS EXALTETH A NATION: BUT SIN IS A REPROACH TO ANY PEOPLE."

OUR READERS will see that Zion has been taking part, in Zion City, during the past week, in the important duties of American Citizenship.

UNDER THE title, a "Theocratic Party Rally," our readers will find on pages 875 to 882 a full report of the proceedings of a Gathering of about Five Thousand persons in Shiloh Tabernacle, on last Wednesday evening, October 5th.

POSSESSING, AS we now do, a very considerable number of votes in Lake County, Illinois, we feel it to be our duty to see that these votes shall be cast for the best available candidates for the County Offices.

BEING ALSO an important part of a State Senatorial District and of the Tenth Illinois National Congressional District, we also felt it was right that we should give our people an opportunity of listening to the very able gentlemen who now represent these districts.

OUR RELATIONS with Lake County officials, at Waukegan, which is the county seat, have been, from the beginning, exceedingly pleasant, and it was an opportunity of showing our friends and neighbors our esteem, and our willingness to coöperate with them in extending the best interests of the community in which our lot is providentially cast.

IT IS a matter for extreme gratitude and thankfulness that, since God enabled us to found Zion City, our relations with all the Representatives of the People in county, state, and nation, from the highest to the humblest, have been, and are of the kindliest nature.

WE ARE indebted to our fellow citizens, and to their official representatives, in all branches of the Judicial, Legislative, and Executive Powers of Government, for more than ordinary courtesy and consideration; and it is a pleasure for us to entertain them in our little City.

WE THANK our people for the hearty and kind reception which they gave, last Wednesday, to our guests and theirs. The evening which was spent was a profitable one.

WE SUPPOSE it is almost without precedent that a Political Gathering of about Five Thousand People should be opened with Praise and Prayer to God and the reading of the Holy Scriptures, and closed with Sacred Song and the Divine Benediction; at least this was the statement of our guests.

The State's Attorney said, "I believe that if our people would arrive at the point where they would demand that meetings of a political character should be opened in that way, corruption would cease to trouble us in our politics, and among people in official positions."

He also said, "I thoroughly appreciate the fact that if the entire population of Lake County were composed of people like these in Zion City there would be no work for a public prosecutor."

OUR FRIENDS must not suppose, although our guests were members of the Republican Party, that Zion is in any way permanently and politically committed to that party.

But for reasons set forth in our addresses, at various times, we have, since 1896 especially, been led of God to give an active and unanimous support to the General National Policies of that Party.

We have, at the same time, regretted that, as yet, the party has not committed itself to many important policies to which it must, soon or late, give earnest heed, or suffer the consequences.

Failure to deal with great vital questions that are, more and more, vehemently demanding a settlement, will bring about the disintegration and destruction of any party.

The choice lies between timely Progression and ultimate Extinction.

WE SHALL soon deal, God willing, with the whole subject of National Righteousness versus Class Lawlessness, and with the Important Duties of the American Voter from the Political Standpoint of Zion, the Rule of God.

WE ACCORDINGLY call attention to the discourse, which, God willing, we shall deliver tomorrow afternoon, in Shiloh Tabernacle, as advertised on page 883, when we shall speak on "THE NATION'S CHOICE OF A PRESIDENT; AND NATIONAL DUTIES AND POLICIES IN THE LIGHT OF THEOCRATIC PRINCIPLES."

OUR MANY duties in connection with the work of God in Zion on every Continent, and in many of the Islands of the Seas, as well as our many local duties, have so engaged our attention during the week now closing, that we have been unable to find time to deal editorially with many matters which we greatly desire to bring before Zion throughout the world.

But, as Americans say, "we shall get there" some day, on these postponed editorials.

WE HAVE pleasure in calling attention to the very excellent article by our General Associate Editor, Overseer Daniel Bryant, and others, on the Work of God in Zion in South Africa, which will be found on pages 853 to 862.

WE SHALL direct our General Associate Editor to prepare a similar article for next week's issue, upon the work of God in Zion in Australasia, which will be illustrated by the pictures of Overseer and Elder Voliva, and many interesting scenes.

WE SHALL also hope, at an early date, to call attention to the Work of Zion in the United Kingdom, and give pictures of Overseer and Elder Cantel and others.

THEREAFTER WE shall give an outline of the Work of God in Zion on the Continent of Europe, with portraits and scenes, and trust that these brief outlines of that which has been, and is being, done in these lands will be of interest to Zion in all the world.

IT IS difficult for even our own people to realize how extensive the work of Zion has become, and how the mere enumeration of all our centers and Branches throughout the world, with a very few words concerning each, would fill many issues of LEAVES OF HEALING.

IT IS an increasing joy to us to know that the "Sun never sets" upon the workers and work of God in Zion-around-the-world.

ZION IS in Australasia, in Northern Europe and North America, and Zion is in the Far East and the Far West. While Zion in one hemisphere is resting and being refreshed in sleep, in the other Zion is wakeful and working. God has watchmen on Zion's towers night and day.

IN ALMOST every zone members of the Christian Catholic Apostolic Church in Zion are to be found carrying God's Message of Peace and Hope, of Light and Life, of Love and Purity to vast multitudes who are crying out of the depths, "deep calling unto deep," for help and deliverance.

BRETHREN, PRAY FOR US.

Apostolic and Prophetic Messages

By......

John Alexander

First Apostle

of the Lord Jesus, the Christ, in the Christian Catholic Apostolic Church in Zion.

MESSAGE NO. I

Shiloh Tabernacle

Lord's Day Afternoon, October 2, 1904.

SUBJECT:

"I Will Come Again."

*REPORTED BY S. E. C., A. C. R., O. L. S., O. R., AND A. W. N.

LORD'S Day, October 2, 1904, began with showers of blessing, brightened to a noontide of Glorious Light, and ended in an evening of Sweetest Peace and Calm under the serene rays of God's stars.

As was the beautiful October day in nature, so was the blessed day in spiritual showers, sunshine, and starlight.

The clouds poured their liquid treasures upon the earth during the early morning meeting, while, in Shiloh Tabernacle, the bounteous rain of spiritual treasures fell upon grateful hearts.

But, before the meeting was over, the rain had ceased, and the clouds were beginning to break and scatter before the bright rays of the autumn sun.

By the time of the Great General Assembly, in the afternoon, the clouds had all fled, and the whole landscape was flooded with light.

It was beauty in the sky; beauty in the lake; beauty in field, forest and meadow; beauty in the clean City; beauty everywhere.

There was a beauty not of this earth in the service.

It was the beauty of the light of the Christ's most precious promise, 'I will come again."

This was most fittingly the theme of the first Message of John Alexander, First Apostle of the Lord Jesus, the Christ, in the Christian Catholic Apostolic Church in Zion; for that Coming Again is the great event toward which the Church tends, and for which it works and prays.

The light of that Blessed Hope illumined not only the future, but the present.

Its warm, cheery rays gave beauty and dignity to the commonest, humblest tasks, and lightened every dark shadow of sorrow, trial, toil, and conflict; for the tasks are done and the trials borne, "Till He Come."

The Prelude to this Message of the Apostle, delivered as an exposition of the Scripture lesson in the 14th chapter of the Gospel according to St. John, was a very lively one; but so logical that there was no escaping the conclusions. One of the matters dealt with most pungently was sin and sickness as the work and property of the Devil.

During the taking of the tithes and offerings, Woodward's beautiful anthem, "The Radiant Morn," was rendered with an expression and power that was an inspiration to hear.

*The First Apostle has not revised the following report.

First Apostolic Communion of the Lord's Supper.

After a brief intermission, the First Apostle returned to th platform, clothed in the Robes of Expiation of ancien Israel, a simple vestment of purest white, except for crimson cross on the breast.

The Sacred Table had been spread, and the Prophet an Apostle of the Restored Church began at once the adminis tration of the First Apostolic Communion.

It was like the old Ordinance that has become so dear t tens of thousands of God's people in all the lands, and yet i was different—there was a new, uplifting power

Zion had gone forward in the month that had elapse since the last celebration of this Ordinance, and will neve again be the same.

The crown of Primitive Organization has been placed upo the brow of the Church by Elijah the Restorer, and sh looks with Clearer Vision for the coming of her King.

The Post-communion "Family Talk" was earnest, joyous confidential; and God blessed it to the four thousand Chris tians who remained at the Lord's Table.

The stars of God were shining when the parting song ha been sung and the Apostolic Benediction had been pro nounced.

And the Stars of Peace, and Joy, and Love, and Hope, an Faith, and Courage, and Humility, and Purity were brighte and clearer as the people went out into the beauteous, silen night.

Shiloh Tabernacle, Zion City, Illinois, Lord's Day Afternoon, October 2, 1904.

The services were opened by Zion White-robed Choi and Zion Robed Officers entering the Tabernacle, singing a they came the words of the

PROCESSIONAL.

A mighty fortress is our God,
  A bulwark never failing;
Our Helper He, amid the flood
  Of mortal ills prevailing.
For still our ancient foe
Doth seek to work his woe;
His craft and power are great,
And armed with cruel hate
  On earth is not his equal.

Did we in our own strength confide,
  Our striving would be losing;
Were not the right Man on our side,
  The man of God's own choosing.
Doth ask who that may be?

Christ Jesus, it is He.
Lord Sabaoth is His name,
From age to age the same;
And He must win the battle.

And tho' this world with demons filled,
Should threaten to undo us,
We will not fear, for God hath willed
His truth to triumph through us
The Prince of darkness grim,
We tremble not for him;
His rage we can endure,
For lo! his doom is sure:
One little word shall fell him.

That word above all earthly pow'rs,
No thanks to them abideth;
The Spirit and the gifts are ours
Thro' Him who with us sideth
Let goods and kindred go,
This mortal life also;
The body they may kill;
God's truth abideth still,
His Kingdom is forever.

At the end of the Processional, the Overseers present, Harvey D. Brasefield and J. G. Excell, accompanied by the two Teachers, Visscher V. Barnes and Daniel Sloan, took their places on the lower platform, followed by the First Apostle, with Deacons Harper and Peckham for Attendants. When he ascended the upper platform, the people rose and stood with bowed heads while he pronounced the

INVOCATION.

God be merciful unto us and bless us,
And cause Thy face to shine upon us;
That Thy Way may be known upon earth,
Thy Saving Health among all the nations,
For the sake of Jesus. Amen.

PRAISE.

The Congregation then joined in singing Hymn No. 348:

Encamped along the hills of light,
Ye Christian soldiers, rise,
And press the battle ere the night
Shall veil the glowing skies.
Against the foe in vales below,
Let all our strength be hurled;
Faith is the victory, we know,
That overcomes the world.

CHORUS—Faith is the victory!
Oh, glorious victory,
That overcomes the world.

Overseer Excell led the Choir and Congregation in the recitation of the Apostles' Creed:

RECITATION OF CREED.

I believe in God, the Father Almighty
Maker of heaven and earth:
And in Jesus, the Christ, His only Son, our Lord,
Who was conceived by the Holy Ghost;
Born of the Virgin Mary:
Suffered under Pontius Pilate;
Was crucified, dead, and buried:
He descended into hell,
The third day He rose from the dead;
He ascended into heaven,
And sitteth on the right hand of God, the Father Almighty;
From thence He shall come to judge the quick and the dead
I believe in the Holy Ghost;
The Holy Catholic Church;
The Communion of Saints;
The Forgiveness of Sins;
The Resurrection of the body,
And the Life Everlasting. Amen.

Overseer Brasefield led the Congregation in repeating the Commandments; after which the words, "Lord, have mercy upon us, and write all these Thy Laws in our hearts, we beseech Thee," were chanted.

READING OF GOD'S COMMANDMENTS.

I. Thou shalt have no other gods before Me.

II. Thou shalt not make unto thee a graven image, nor the likeness of any form that is in heaven above, or that is in the earth beneath, or that is in the water under the earth; thou shalt not bow down thyself unto them nor serve them; for I, Jehovah, thy God, am a jealous God, visiting the iniquity of the fathers upon the children, upon the third and upon the fourth generation of them that hate Me, and showing mercy unto thousands of them that love Me and keep My commandments.

III. Thou shalt not take the Name of Jehovah thy God in vain; for Jehovah will not hold him guiltless that taketh His Name in vain.

IV. Remember the Sabbath Day, to keep it holy. Six days shalt thou labor and do all thy work; but the seventh day is a Sabbath unto Jehovah thy God: in it thou shalt not do any work, thou, nor thy son, nor thy daughter, thy manservant, nor thy maidservant, nor thy cattle, nor thy stranger that is within thy gates; for in six days Jehovah made heaven and earth, the sea, and all that in them is, and rested the seventh day: wherefore Jehovah blessed the Sabbath Day and hallowed it.

V. Honor thy father and thy mother; that thy days may be long upon the land which Jehovah thy God giveth thee.

VI. Thou shalt do no murder.

VII. Thou shalt not commit adultery.

VIII. Thou shalt not steal.

IX. Thou shalt not bear false witness against thy neighbor.

X. Thou shalt not covet thy neighbor's house, thou shalt not covet thy neighbor's wife, nor his manservant, nor his maidservant, nor his ox, nor his ass, nor anything that is thy neighbor's.

Hear also what our Lord Jesus, the Christ, the Son of God, hath said, which may be called the Eleventh Commandment:

XI. A New Commandment I give unto you, that ye love one another; even as I have loved you, that ye also love one another.

The great Choir then sang the

TE DEUM LAUDAMUS.

We praise Thee, O God; we acknowledge Thee to be the Lord.
All the earth doth worship Thee, the Father Everlasting.
To Thee all Angels cry aloud, the Heavens and all the powers therein.
To Thee Cherubim and Seraphim continually do cry:
Holy, Holy, Holy, Lord God of Sabaoth,
Heaven and earth are full of the majesty of Thy Glory.
The glorious company of the Apostles praise Thee.
The goodly fellowship of the Prophets praise Thee.
The noble army of martyrs praise Thee.
The Holy Church throughout all the world doth acknowledge Thee,
The Father of an Infinite Majesty;
Thine Adorable, True, and Only Son;
Also the Holy Ghost, the Comforter.
Thou art the King of Glory, O Christ;
Thou art the everlasting Son of the Father.
When Thou tookest upon Thee to deliver man,
Thou didst humble Thyself to be born of a Virgin;
When Thou hadst overcome the sharpness of death,
Thou didst open the Kingdom of Heaven to all believers.
Thou sittest at the right hand of God in the Glory of the Father.
We believe that Thou shalt come to be our Judge.
We therefore pray Thee help Thy servants,
Whom Thou hast redeemed with Thy precious blood.
Make them to be numbered with Thy saints in glory everlasting.
O Lord, save Thy people and bless Thine heritage;
Govern them and lift them up forever.
Day by day we magnify Thee;
And we worship Thy Name ever, world without end.
Vouchsafe, O Lord, to keep us this day without sin.
O Lord, have mercy upon us, have mercy upon us.
O Lord, let Thy mercy be upon us as our trust is in Thee.
O Lord, in Thee have I trusted, let me never be confounded.

Scripture Reading and Exposition.

The First Apostle then said:

Let us read in the Inspired Word of God, first in the book of the Prophet Isaiah, 12th chapter.

And in that day thou shalt say, I will give thanks unto Thee, O Jehovah; for though Thou wast angry with me, Thine anger is turned away, and Thou comfortest me.

Behold, God is my salvation; I will trust, and will not be afraid: for the Lord Jehovah is my strength and song; and He is become my salvation.

Therefore with joy shall ye draw water out of the Wells of Salvation.

And in that day shall ye say, Give thanks unto Jehovah, call upon His Name, declare His doings among the peoples, make mention that His Name is exalted.

Sing unto Jehovah; for He hath done excellent things: let this be known in all the earth.

Cry aloud and shout, thou inhabitant of Zion: for great is the Holy One of Israel in the midst of thee.

Also in the Gospel according to St. John, the 14th chapter.

The First Apostle read from the 1st to the 16th verse of the 14th chapter of John, pausing to say:

And I will pray the Father, and He shall give you another Comforter—

The word is *Parakla'os* (παράκλητος) and means more than Comforter—Advocate! Intercessor!

He is an Advocate within you, who pleads for God with you.

We have two Advocates; an Advocate with the Father, Jesus, the Christ, the Righteous; and an Advocate within us, the Holy Spirit, making intercession with groanings that cannot be uttered, coming into our hearts and crying "Abba, Father!"

He teaches us how to pray, and makes intercession within us on behalf of God.

How Good It Is to Know that We Have Two Advocates!

These are the offices of the Holy Spirit and of the Son of God.

And I will pray the Father, and He shall give you another Comforter, that He may be with you forever,

Even the Spirit of Truth: whom the world cannot receive—

The Greek words *ou dunatai* (οὐ δύναται) have the meaning, "Is not able to receive."

What?

The world that lies in the Wicked One cannot receive the Spirit of Truth, because it is a world that "lieth,"—not only abides in the Wicked One, but lies in him.

It is a bad, lying world, full of deceit, shame, sham, shoddy, and everything mean.

You must get out of the world into the Kingdom of God before you can receive the Spirit of Truth.

You have no capacity to receive the Spirit of Truth so long as you are in the world, and yield to the flesh and the Devil.

It is not strange that the world lies; it cannot do anything else.

Men have been born, as the Psalmist says, "speaking lies."

Vast multitudes of fathers and mothers lied all the time.

Their very marriage was a lie and a sham.

The Natural Man Cannot Understand the Things of the Spirit.

They lied to each other all the way through their married life.

No wonder that "the natural man receiveth not the things of the Spirit of God: for they are foolishness unto him; and he cannot know them, because they are spiritually judged."

Do not marvel that the world does not understand.

It cannot understand.

It does not have the capacity to understand.

Were I to speak in Greek to you who know nothing about it, would you understand?

Would you understand what I said if I repeated in Greek a part of that beautiful chapter which I am reading?

Μὴ ταρασσέσθω ὑμῶν ἡ καρδία· πιστεύετε εἰς τὸν θεόν, καὶ εἰς ἐμὲ πιστεύετε.
Ἐν τῇ οἰκίᾳ τοῦ πατρός μου μοναὶ πολλαί εἰσιν.

What do you know about that?

It is beautiful to the ear, but you do not understand it.

These are the words in English:

Let not your heart be troubled; ye believe in God, believe also in Me. In My Father's house are many mansions.

You understand now, because that is a language with which you are familiar.

Until you learn the language of heaven and get the Spirit of Truth you do not understand spiritual things.

When the world says, "We do not understand the Apostle," I am not surprised.

I do not expect the world to understand.

How can it?

It does not know the Word of God.

It has never given any attention to the organization of the Church, and it does not know what the Scriptures teach and require.

How Can the World Understand?

It has no spiritual illumination, and no power to interp

But those will understand who enter into the Kingdor God, where the Spirit of God teaches the language of Kingdom of God.

The spiritual illumination will then come.

"Marvel not," said Jesus, "that the world does not un stand you. It hates you. It hated Me also, becaus did not understand Me."

The Light came into the world and the darkness did comprehend the Light, and until you get out of the dark you will not understand us.

You had better free yourselves from the World, the F and the Devil, and get into fellowship with God by Rep ance, Faith, Obedience, and the reception of the I Spirit.

Even the Spirit of Truth: whom the world cannot receive; for it be eth Him not, neither knoweth Him: ye know Him; for He abideth you, and shall be in you.

There is a great difference there.

If I were to abide with you, my beloved Deacon [spea to Deacon Peckham], that might be a help; but if I v right inside of you, and abode in you, you would be a bi man.

That is a simple illustration of what the Lord said to Apostles.

The presence of the Holy Spirit with them did not m them much stronger, although they were happy under influence of that presence; it did not keep Peter from l and being afraid.

The Indwelling Holy Spirit Imparts Power.

But when the Holy Spirit got into him he was a diffe man.

There is a vast difference between the Holy Spi dwelling with you and being in you.

Up to Pentecost the Holy Spirit was not in them.

The Christ said, "He abideth with you and *shall* b you."

There are multitudes of Christians that know that t is a Holy Spirit; and they believe that He is with them, as for any indwelling power, and consciousness of His p ence within them, they have never known anything abou

That is the condition of a vast majority, even of believ

Had you not better get the Holy Spirit in you?

PEOPLE—"Yes."

FIRST APOSTLE—Then pray for that, and open your w being to let God's Spirit in.

When He has entered do not grieve Him with your pe miserable ways of complaining until He says, "This is place for Me. I cannot dwell in a querulous, complain doubting heart."

But if you receive Him, obey Him and let Him con you, then you will have the Power of the Omnipotent within you and you will amount to something.

I will not leave you desolate: I come unto you.

The marginal reading here is better, "I will not le you orphans."

Yet a little while, and the world beholdeth Me no more; but ye be Me: because I live, ye shall live also.

In that day ye shall know that I am in My Father, and ye in Me, and you.

He that hath My commandments, and keepeth them, he it is that lo Me: and he that loveth Me shall be loved of My Father, and I will love and will manifest Myself unto him.

Judas (not Iscariot) saith unto Him, Lord, what is come to pass that wilt manifest Thyself unto us, and not unto the world?

The Christ's answer is very wonderful. I should like all to consider it.

These Apostles did much thinking.

They were on the eve of parting with their Master their Lord.

This was the night of the betrayal, and of the last Sup and Judas said:

Lord, what is come to pass that Thou wilt manifest Thyself unto us, not unto the world?

A Wonderful Promise of the Christ.

This is the answer:

If a man love Me, he will keep My Word: and My Father will love him, and We will come unto him, and make Our abode with him.

That is a wonderful promise. If a man keeps the sayings of the Christ, then not only is he blessed, but the Father and the Son both love him.

The Spirit is in him already, because he could not have kept the Word—guarded the treasure—or obeyed the Christ if he had not had the Spirit.

But there is more.

If he obeys, the Father and the Son both love him, and They come and make Their abode in him.

Thus, as the Holy Spirit is there already, the Triune God comes into a Triune Man, and the Holy Spirit, the Son, and the Father become one with him in his spirit, soul, and body.

That man would then be a pillar of fire.

He would be a mighty man of God.

That is what God wants you all to be.

Jesus answered and said unto him, If a man love Me, he will keep My Word: and My Father will love him, and We will come unto him, and make Our abode with him.

He that loveth Me not keepeth not My Words: and the Word which ye hear is not Mine, but the Father's who sent Me.

These things have I spoken unto you, while yet abiding with you.

But the Comforter, even the Holy Spirit, whom the Father will send in My Name, He shall teach you all things, and bring to your remembrance all that I said unto you.

Peace I leave with you; My peace I give unto you: not as the world giveth, give I unto you. Let not your heart be troubled, neither let it be fearful.

Ye heard how I said to you, I go away, and I come unto you. If ye loved Me ye would have rejoiced, because I go unto the Father: for the Father is greater than I.

The Disciples Mourned Because of Selfish Considerations.

They were mourning because He was going away.

Was that because of love?

If so, what kind of love?

Love for themselves, because they were going to lose His companionship, His help, His sympathy, and His wonderful personality.

It was not because they loved Him.

I once saw a man cry over a horse that had died; but it was not because he loved the horse so much, but because he had lost about one hundred fifty dollars.

I have seen people cry over husbands and wives who had passed away.

"Oh, I loved him so!" the wife wails.

The husband never knew it.

You were very sparing in letting him know how much you loved him, and now you are howling over him.

Yes, but did you love him?

You are thinking of quite a number of things that will be different, now that he is gone.

The Lord Jesus, the Christ, challenged the Disciples' love for Him when they were mourning because He would soon leave them.

He said, "If ye loved Me, ye would have rejoiced."

He asked them why they did not rejoice that He was going to heaven, where He would plead with the Father to send them the Holy Spirit.

To Be Absent from the Body Is to Be Present with the Lord.

They did not feel like rejoicing, and He blamed them for it.

There are multitudes to-day who do not rejoice when their friends go to heaven.

They say that they believe that Nannie went to heaven, but add, "Oh, I am going down to the cemetery to stay for awhile by poor Nannie."

I thought that you believed that Nannie had gone to God.

Is she lying in the grave?

I should not like to think that of any one whom I loved.

I should say that to be absent from the body is to be present with the Lord.

You cannot get me to believe that some day I shall lie down in the cemetery and sleep for several thousand years. (Laughter.).

That is a very poor prospect.

To me, snoring through a thousand years seems a great waste of time.

Some people tell you that you will lie in your grave and sleep until the resurrection morn, and then you will gradually uncoil and get up.

That is awfully stupid!

God is not a being of that kind.

He never made me like that.

I really do not believe that I could sleep that long!

What ridiculous nonsense!

The soul sleeps, does it?

No; the soul dies!

The soul of the Christ died.

Your trouble is that you have never discriminated between the soul and the spirit.

We read in God's Word that "the soul that sinneth, it shall die."

We are told that the Christ "poured out His soul unto death."

The Soul Is the Animal Life, but the Spirit Is Immortal.

You tell me that the soul sleeps.

I will tell you more; the soul dies.

The spirit lives with God.

The dust returns to the earth, and the spirit returns to God who gave it.

You ought to thank God that you are not going to lie and snore for a thousand years.

If ye loved Me, ye would have rejoiced, because I go unto the Father: for the Father is greater than I.

Get that fact into your minds.

I have taught you in this Church, and I teach today with Apostolic Authority, that there is no equality in the Divine Triunity.

The superiority is in the Father.

The Christ himself said, "My Father is greater than I." "My Father is greater than all."

If you say that He is not, then you and the Christ have a controversy.

There were things that the Father knew that the Christ did not know. He told us so.

He said, "Of that day and hour knoweth no one, not even the angels in heaven, neither the Son, but the Father only."

When you talk about equality in the Triunity, you are talking nonsense.

"But how can they be one and yet not equal?" you may ask.

That is easily answered.

You have a spirit, and a soul, and a body, but are they equal?

People—"No."

First Apostle—Is the body as great as the spirit?

People—"No."

First Apostle—Is the soul as great as the spirit?

People—"No."

First Apostle—Which is the greatest?

People—"The spirit."

First Apostle—That lives forever, and yet these three are one.

I stand here to-day, with a spirit, a soul, and a body.

Some day the body will go back to the dust, but the spirit will return to God, who gave it, with whom dwell the spirits of all that have departed in the faith of the Christ.

Ye heard how I said to you, I go away, and I come unto you. If ye loved Me, ye would have rejoiced, because I go unto the Father: for the Father is greater than I.

And now I have told you before it come to pass, that, when it is come to pass, ye may believe.

I will no more speak much with you, for the Prince of the world cometh: and he hath nothing in Me.

The Devil Has a Right to His Own.

Is there anything belonging to the Devil inside of you?

If there is, the Devil has a right to come in and look after his own property.

If I have any goods in your house, have I not a right to come in and get them?

If you have anything belonging to the Devil in you, has he not a right to come in and get his own?

PEOPLE—"Yes."

FIRST APOSTLE—That is the trouble with some of you.

"How has the Devil such power over me?" you ask.

Because he has something inside of you that belongs to him.

Perhaps there is whisky there, and that belongs to him.

That is the Devil in solution.

When you take a glass of whisky or wine, or beer, it has the Devil's alcohol in it, and the Devil comes in to look after his own.

He kicks up a fine row, does he not?

He gets inside of you and makes your tongue wag, and your mind think bad things.

"I have nothing of that kind, but I have a sickness, Doctor," you may say.

That belongs to the Devil, too.

Every disease is his work.

Do you think it is God's?

PEOPLE—"No."

FIRST APOSTLE—Does God send you smallpox?

PEOPLE—"No."

FIRST APOSTLE—Is God the Author of disease?

PEOPLE—"No."

FIRST APOSTLE—If He is, He is a very strange kind of God.

If His hand can impart impurity, the impurity must be in Him.

If you get disease from heaven, there must be a stock of it there.

Where did you get it, if it did not come from God?

Individual Sin Often the Cause of Disease.

Some of you get it from your own sin.

God Almighty gave some of you women a waist o. about thirty-five inches, and you screw it up into twenty-seven, and you wonder why you are sick. [Laughter.]

You have lots of devil in you, because you have displaced the vital organs.

The disordered organs cause inflammation.

This was all brought about because you were foolish.

Some of you went away and danced.

You thought that you could dance to the glory of some one.

Was it God?

Did you say to God before you started, "O God, help me to glorify Thee in this dance to-night?"

For whose glory did you dance?

Your own and the Devil's.

You got a cold.

Later it settled on your lungs, and the Devil began digging them out with consumption.

Did that come from God?

PEOPLE—"No."

FIRST APOSTLE—You got it from the Devil.

The enemy sowed the tares, but you let him in, and helped him do the sowing.

The Devil said to you, "Never mind! Come out and go for another dance!"

You go to another dance; and the disease grows worse.

It Is the Hand of the Devil, Not God, that Afflicts.

At last you become very sick, and are dying. Then some ignorant, foolish parson comes in and says, "Forasmuch as it hath pleased Almighty God in His great mercy to lay His afflicting hand upon you"—

Is it true?

PEOPLE—"No."

FIRST APOSTLE—That is a lie!

It was the hand of the Devil; not the hand of God.

You have a good deal in you that belongs to the Devil, when you have disease.

You had better ask God to take it out; and be quick about it!

If you put in more Devil, by taking drugs and Liquid Fire and Distilled Damnation, and do not turn to God, the Devil will simply finish you up, and send your body to the grave.

Even if your spirit is saved, you will die.

You all know it very well.

No one knows it better than the physicians themselves.

On a recent occasion I entertained several doctors.

I will not say who they were or where it was, but I was their host.

We will call them Doctor "A," Doctor "B," and Doctor "C."

During the course of a conversation I said, "Gentlemen, you are very sensible men, and I should like to ask you, Doctor 'A,' do you give any medicine to your family?"

"You had better believe I don't!" was his emphatic reply

"What!" I ejaculated.

"No, indeed! I have not given a dose of medicine in my family for twenty years!" he answered.

"And yet you have been giving doses to others, you sinner," I said.

"Yes," he said.

"Why?"

Mercenary Conduct of the Medical Profession.

"Well, if I did not do it, Doctor 'B,' over there, would do it, and get all the money."

"Then you do it for money?" I asked.

"I suppose most people labor for that," he answered.

"I have preached without a salary for many years, and do now," I told him.

I will ask Recorder Jensen to confirm that statement now.

Recorder Jensen, do I draw a salary from you?

RECORDER JENSEN—"No, sir."

FIRST APOSTLE—"Did I ever?"

RECORDER JENSEN—"No, sir."

FIRST APOSTLE—Have I ever received a salary from the funds of the Church?

RECORDER JENSEN—"No, sir."

FIRST APOSTLE—He says, "No, sir," and he ought to know, for all the tithes and offerings pass through that man's hands.

I never see them, but I do see that they are properly taken care of and properly used.

To resume my story, Doctor "A" asked, "How do you get on?"

"I get on splendidly," I answered; "better than you!"

"Yes," he said; "I believe you do!"

It Does Not Pay to Be Dishonest.

I said, "It pays to preach for nothing; but it does not pay to give drugs to people, when you would not give them to your own wife or daughter. Why do you not get out and be an honest fellow? You are a clever man; you would make a splendid business man!"

"Well," he said, "I have often thought I should like to."

He was a thoroughly kind gentleman, and very useful in many ways, but he was not honest, and he knew it.

I was at one time an honorary chaplain in Edinburgh Infirmary, while a student at the University; and I had the honor of the friendship of one of the most distinguished surgeons.

This man did me the honor to permit me to attend his clinics.

I once said to him, "Sir James, will you permit me to talk to you perfectly frankly?"

"Certainly," he answered.

"I watched you today by the bedside of Mrs. So-and-so,

s your students made a diagnosis, which you affirmed. ‛he disease was cancer in the uterus.

' When she asked, 'What will you do, Doctor,' you went up o her, put your hand upon her head and said kindly, 'My lear woman, I shall do nothing, only give you all the care hat I can.'

"Then in the most sympathetic way you said, 'My good voman, you must die.'

"At this she burst into tears, and said, 'Oh, I want to live or my children's sake.'

"Then you prayed, 'O God, comfort this woman who must ie.'

A Question that Staggered a Great Physician.

"Doctor, you told me tonight of Her Grace the Duchess of o-and-so, whom you are attending, and that she had a ancer identical in character and in place with that of Irs. ——.

"Doctor, you also told me that for a fee of more than a housand pounds, you would operate upon the Duchess.

"I should like to know why you do not say to the Duchess, My good woman you will die, and it would be torture to cut ou up?'"

He bowed his head in shame, as he said, "I am ashamed hat you should thus expose me, but you are right.

"I wish I were out of this infernal business. I may not erform that operation now."

"If you do," I said, "I shall call you Sir James, the Thief."

"That is terrible," he said.

When there is disease within you it belongs to the Devil, nd it is only God who can take it out.

Deaconess Jennie Paddock, please stand.

How many years ago is it since you had that enormous umor?"

A Wonderful Testimony to Healings.

DEACONESS PADDOCK—"Fourteen years."

FIRST APOSTLE—The horrible signs of decay were there, nd you were dying?

DEACONESS PADDOCK—"Yes."

FIRST APOSTLE—You sent a message to me in Western prings?

DEACONESS PADDOCK—"Yes, sir."

FIRST APOSTLE—I had not seen you. You believed that I prayed you would be healed?

DEACONESS PADDOCK—"Yes, sir."

FIRST APOSTLE—Were you healed?

DEACONESS PADDOCK—"Yes, sir."

FIRST APOSTLE—How many days was it before you got up.

DEACONESS PADDOCK—"I rose the next day."

FIRST APOSTLE—How many days from that time did you ake a carpet?

DEACONESS PADDOCK—"One week."

FIRST APOSTLE—When did you move into another house?

DEACONESS PADDOCK—"In just one week."

FIRST APOSTLE—Have you been working ever since?

DEACONESS PADDOCK—"Yes, and in fourteen years, beoved Apostle, I have had but one day's sickness until the ther day, when I was very sick, and you came and prayed or me."

FIRST APOSTLE—Yes, I found you nearly dead with holera morbus.

God healed you then.

How long did it take?

DEACONESS PADDOCK—"I was healed immediately."

FIRST APOSTLE—Deaconess Paddock has done a splendid ork among God's poor children.

She has worked six years with only about a week's holiday, nd now she shall have a good vacation.

When almost dying she learned that I was teaching that isease was from the Devil.

She believed it.

She let God come in, and He touched her, and the disease ent out.

The Christ Had in Him Nothing that Belonged to the Devil.

The Devil could do nothing inside of Jesus, because there was nothing in His spirit or in His soul that belonged to the Devil.

He said,

The Prince of the world cometh: and he hath nothing in Me.

You had better get out all that belongs to the Devil—both of sin and disease.

Then when the Devil comes and knocks at your heart, you say, "Go away! There is nothing belonging to you here! O God! I appeal to you! Send this Devil away. He has no right to knock at my door! I have nothing belonging to him inside of me."

That would be a good prayer; but I do not know how many of us could pray it!

I am afraid that there are many Christians who have much of the Devil's property inside of them.

Why are you not in earnest about getting it out?

It seems to me that the exposition of this chapter is far more important than any sermon.

The Prince of the world cometh, and he hath nothing in Me;
But that the world may know that I love the Father, and as the Father gave Me commandment, even so I do. Arise, let us go hence.

May God bless His word.

The First Apostle then knelt at the Altar of Incense and offered prayer, at the close of which he led the Choir and congregation in chanting the Disciples' Prayer.

The announcements were made by Overseer John G. Excell, and the tithes and offerings were received.

The First Apostle then delivered his Message:

"I WILL COME AGAIN."

INVOCATION.

Let the words of my mouth, and the meditations of my heart, be acceptable in Thy sight; be profitable unto this people; and unto all to whom these words shall come, in this and every land, in this and all the coming time, Till Jesus Come.

TEXT.

In My Father's house are many abiding-places; if it were not so, I would have told you; for I go to prepare a place for you.
And if I go and prepare a place for you, I come again, and will receive you unto Myself; that where I am, there ye may be also.

In the Father's House There Are Many Abiding-places.

Under the starlit skies our Lord was talking with His Apostles after the Last Supper.

The betrayer had gone out, and the Christ was talking with the eleven.

Looking up to the sky, I fancy, He waved His blessed hand and cried, "In my Father's house are many abiding-places."

Oh, what wonderful abodes there are in these wondrous heavens—below us, above us, around us, beyond all power of eye or telescope to bring within the range of mortal vision.

Many "abiding-places!"

This earth is such a little sphere; it is one of the smallest of the planets.

It is not the hub of the universe; it is just a little speck of light amid worlds, centers, and systems so vast that the proportion of this world, even to the sun itself, would be as a little dot to a vast circle thousands of times larger.

What is that sun as compared with other suns?

What is that center around which our solar system revolves, as compared with the glorious center around which all the suns and all the systems revolve?

The Father's Throne is at the center of the Universe, and every part of it is our Father's dwelling-place.

"There is a hell," you may say.

Yes, but if you make your abode in hell, even there shall His right hand find you, because hell itself is within the circle of His Omnipotence.

Death and Hell will one day be cast into the Lake of Fire

Death and Hell will pass away, "for as in Adam all die, so also in the Christ shall all be made alive."

At last, one attribute, one great Divine and glorious element, the element of Love, will fulfil the one Divine intent to which the whole creation moves, the intent of God in us that nothing that He has made shall be lost; that nothing that has erred or strayed but shall be brought back again.

Strong Son of God, immortal Love,
Whom we, that have not seen Thy face,
By faith, and faith alone, embrace,
Believing where we cannot prove;

Thine are these orbs of light and shade;
Thou madest Life in man and brute;
Thou madest death—

God Did Not Make Death.

Alfred Tennyson was wrong when he said "Thou madest death."

God never made death.

He did not make Satan to be the defiler.

He made him pure.

He did not make man to be a sinner.

If I believed that He made death, I should close my Bible.

I cannot sing with Tennyson:

Thou madest Death; and lo, Thy foot
Is on the skull which Thou hast made.

Oh, no! No! Death is not the foot of God.

Death is the wages of sin.

The Law of Sin and Death is the Devil's own; and sin, and death, and disease are the Devil's work.

The poet continues:

Thou wilt not leave us in the dust:
Thou madest man, he knows not why.

But we do know why.

O Alfred Tennyson, why did you not tell why God made men?

God Himself had told you.

Augustine had told you long before how God revealed it to him when he wrote that sublime sentence, "O God, Thou hast made me for Thyself, and my heart is restless until it finds its rest in Thee."

O Alfred Tennyson, why did you not read your Bible, and learn there that God made man for a habitation for Himself through the Spirit?

Why sing—

Thou madest man, he knows not why.

Man Was Made for a Habitation of God.

We know, because You have told us, our God, why You made us.

You did not make us to trample our skulls beneath Your feet of death, never!

You did not make us to be the victims of disease, and demoralization, and degradation.

You did not make us to be aliens from Thee, and to go away out into the wilderness and then to the swine's trough, and try to feed our immortal spirits on the husks that the swine eat.

You did not make us to be the Devil's plaything—creatures of lust and damning passion, consumed by evil desires and alien from Thee, never!

You did not make us to be the sport of deadly poisons and drugs that kill.

You did not make us to be the dreadful thing that the harlot, and the whoremonger, and the military murderer has made men and women.

Corpses reeking under the forts of Port Arthur!

Blood flowing at Liao-Yang and in the seas around Korea and Manchuria!

You did not make man to hate, and fight, and murder; never!

Thou madest man

And we know why.

We know that we were not made to die.

Our little systems have their day;
They have their day and cease to be:
They are but broken lights of Thee;
And Thou, O Lord, art more than they.

But the dawn is not distant.

The night is not starless.

The Home Above Is Being Prepared for God's People.

It is the Christ who, under the stars, is talking to His Apostles and saying, "If it were not true that there were other lives to live than the present life; if it were not true that there was another and a better dwelling-place than this, I would have told you. I go to prepare a place for you."

Beloved in the Christ, have you ever thought of Him as the City Builder, as the Preparer of Homes in the City above?

Have you ever thought that the loved ones who have gone to glory, who so loved to prepare for you on earth, are being given the lovely task of preparing the home for you?

O beloved, I believe it.

Not only is He preparing, but He is using His loved ones to prepare.

Perhaps He who knows when our life's labor is over, is telling them, "He is coming home to-morrow. Go down to the gates and welcome him. He is coming home tomorrow."

Some day it will be tomorrow.

The gladdest, brightest, most beautiful day of all the days is the day when we lay aside these earthly garments of flesh and receive the heavenly robes.

The bells are ringing, the harps are playing, the song is being sung, and they are happier in heaven in the thought that they who without us cannot be made perfect, will have their happiness completed when we go home "tomorrow."

I go to prepare a place for you.
And if I go and prepare a place for you, I come again.

He Who Has Promised Will Come Again.

How much does the Church of today, for the most part, believe in the return of our Lord Jesus, the Christ?

I do not know of one officer or member of the Christian Catholic Apostolic Church in Zion who doubts for a moment the coming back of the Lord.

Do you believe this?

PEOPLE—"Yes."

FIRST APOSTLE—Do you believe that He who said "I come again" will come?

PEOPLE—"Yes."

FIRST APOSTLE—And that He will receive you unto Himself, that where He is there you may be also?

PEOPLE—"Yes."

FIRST APOSTLE—"Every one that hath this hope set on Him purifieth himself even as He is pure."

Oh, to be purified by the cross of the Christ, that the blood may go into your heart and make it white again—the blood that cleanseth from all unrighteousness!

Had you not better get ready?

They are getting ready in heaven.

Are we getting ready on earth?

He is preparing a place for you.

He is coming again.

Sinning, and sighing, and sorrow shall then cease.

Jesus is coming again to give peace to this warring earth

It may be at morn, when the day is awaking,
When sunlight thro' darkness and shadow is breaking,
That Jesus will come in the fulness of glory,
To receive from the world "His own."

It may be at mid-day, it may be at twilight,
It may be, perchance, that the blackness of midnight
Will burst into light in the blaze of His glory,
When Jesus receives "His own!"

The Thought of the Second Coming Is An Inspiration.

He will not come then to reign; He will come to take those that are ready into the Rapture and the preparation for His descent with His prepared people to reign on earth throughout the glory of the Millennium.

It is not a fancy.

The thought of the Christ's coming again quickens my pulse; makes my blood go faster, and makes me want to get ready and to do the work, although sometimes

Ashes are on my head, and in my lips
Sackcloth, and in my breast a heaviness
And weariness of life, that makes me ready
To say to the dead under us,
"Make room for me." Only I see the dusk
Of evening twilight fast approaching, and have not
Completed half my task; and so at times
The thought of my shortcomings in this life
Falls like a shadow on the life to come.

I want your thoughts to be quickened and you to be quickened in the thought of His coming and in our getting ready.

Are you preparing for everything except His coming?

You would prepare for the coming of a beloved father or mother, wife or husband, sister or brother who was returning after a long absence.

How glad you would be to prepare!

Why do you not get ready for Jesus, your Savior, your Healer, your Cleanser, your Keeper, your Advocate with the Father, the Preparer of heaven for you?

All that want to get ready for Jesus, stand and tell Him so.

[Almost the entire audience rose to make consecration.]

PRAYER OF CONSECRATION.

My God and Father, in Jesus' Name I come to Thee. Take me as I am. Make me what I ought to be, in spirit, in soul, and in body. Give me power to do right. Give me Thy Holy Spirit. Help me to do that which is right in Thy sight, to my fellow men by true repentance, restitution, and confession; by putting my sins into Thy hands, my Father, who in the Christ will take them all away. Help me to put my sicknesses into Thy hands that Thou mayest take them away. Take all the evil away, so that when the Prince of this world cometh he will not find the World, the Flesh, or any Devil within our hearts or homes. Prepare us, O Father, for the return of the King; for the Rapture, and the glory, and the preparation; and for the Millennium. God be with us as we commune at Thy Table. By Thy Spirit help us to realize Thy presence and Thy power. For Jesus' sake. Amen. [*All repeat the prayer, clause by clause, after the First Apostle.*]

FIRST APOSTLE—Did you mean it?

PEOPLE—"Yes."

FIRST APOSTLE—Will you live up to it?

PEOPLE—"Yes."

FIRST APOSTLE—The best preparation we can make today is to sit at the Lord's Table with Him and to receive His blessing there.

Every true Christian here, whether a member of this Church or not, is invited to remain.

After a brief intermission the First Apostle, assisted by the officers of the church, administered the Communion of the Lord's Supper, following which the First Apostle addressed the people in his usual Post-communion Family Talk.

The Congregation then joined in singing "I Stand on Zion's Mount," after which the First Apostle pronounced the

BENEDICTION.

Beloved, abstain from every form of evil. And may the very God of Peace Himself sanctify you wholly; and I pray God your whole spirit, and soul, and body be preserved entire, without blame, unto the coming of our Lord Jesus, the Christ. Faithful is He that calleth you, who also will do it. The grace of our Lord Jesus, the Christ, the love of God, our Father, the fellowship of the Holy Spirit, our Comforter and Guide, one Eternal God, abide in you, bless you, and keep you, and all the Israel of God everywhere, forever. Amen.

Change of Location in Toronto, Canada.

Zion Gathering in Toronto, Canada, has secured the old Friends' meeting house, 34 Pembroke street, where services will hereafter be conducted. It is easily reached by transferring from any street-car line in the city to the Belt Line. Get off at Wilton avenue, and go west one block to Pembroke. Elder Brooks has also changed his residence to No. 360 Parliament street.

Zion in California.

Rev. W. D. Taylor, Elder in the Christian Catholic Apostolic Church in Zion, San Francisco, California, will hold religious services as follows:

In Zion Tabernacle, 160 East Santa Clara street, San Jose, California, Monday, October 10th, at 7:30 p. m.; Tuesday, October 11th, at 2:30 and 7:30 p. m., and Wednesday, October 12th, at 2:30 and 7:30 p. m.

At Santa Clara, California, Thursday, October 13th, at 7:30 p. m., and Friday, October 14th, at 2:30 and 7:30 p. m.

At Los Gatos, California, Saturday, October 15th, at 2:30 and 7:30 p. m.

Baptismal services will be held in San Jose.

Publisher's Notice.

The remittance must accompany receipt of subscriptions at the Publishing House, no difference by or for whom or for whatever time they may be given, or whether forwarded through Ordained Officers, Branches, or Gatherings of the Christian Catholic Church in Zion. Accounts will be carried with Ordained Officers, Branches, or Gatherings, on quantity orders of periodicals consigned on sale for monthly settlement, but to include only such articles as bear the imprint of Zion. All orders for Bibles, books, buttons, pictures (except prints done by the Publishing House), lace souvenirs, etc., must be sent to the General Stores, Zion City, Lake County, Illinois.

Changes in the New York City Branch.

Beginning with Lord's Day, October 2d, the meetings will be removed to the center of New York City, corner of Madison avenue and East One Hundred Twenty-fifth street. Sunday, 11 a. m., 3 p. m., and 8 p. m. Divine Healing Meeting every Thursday, 2:30 p. m. Overseer George L. Mason's new address, is No. 4 St. Nicholas Terrace.

OFFICIAL REPRESENTATIVES OF ZION

The following addresses of Official Representatives of Zion at important centers throughout the world, are given for the convenience of correspondents:

In the United States

Overseer George L. Mason, 4 St. Nicholas Terrace, New York City.

Overseer William Hamner Piper, 17 Capin street, New Dorchester, Massachusetts.

Elder R. N. Bouck, 2129 Mt. Vernon street, Philadelphia, Pennsylvania.

Elder A. Ernst, 2611 Fourth avenue, Seattle, Washington.

Elder A. E. Arrington, 501 West Fourth street, Cincinnati, Ohio.

Elder W. D. Taylor, 1350 East Sixteenth street, Fruitvale, California.

Elder L. C. Hall, San Antonio, Texas.

Elder Frank L. Brock, 3401 Morgan street, St. Louis, Missouri.

In Foreign Countries

Overseer H. E. Cantel, 81 Euston road, London, N. W., England.

Overseer Wilbur Glenn Voliva, Arlington, 43 Park road, St. Kilda, Melbourne, Victoria, Australia.

Overseer Daniel Bryant, Box 3074, Johannesburg, Transvaal, South Africa.

Elder Carl Hodler, 76 Bahnhofstrasse, Zürich, Switzerland.

Elder Arthur S. Booth-Clibborn, 139 Weesperzijde, Amsterdam, Holland.

Elder L. B. Kennedy, Zion, Haskell road, Shanghai China.

Elder R. M. Simmons, 525 Grove Crescent, Vancouver, B. C.

Elder Eugene Brooks, 360 Parliament street, Toronto, Ontario, Canada.

General Financial Agents

Deacon N. B. Rideout, Financial Agent for South Africa, Box 3074, Johannesburg, Transvaal, South Africa.

Elder Percy Clibborn, Financial Agent for Europe, 76 Bahnhofstrasse, Zurich, Switzerland.

Deacon John W. Innes, Financial Agent for the United Kingdom, 81 Euston Road, London, N. W., England.

THE FIRST APOSTLE, AS AN AMERICAN CITIZEN, PLEADING FOR NATIONAL RIGHTEOUSNESS.

Theocratic Party Rally

The First Apostle, Congressman George Edmund Foss, Judge V. V. Barnes, and Lake County Officials and Candidates Address Enthusiastic Gathering.

REPORTED BY O. L. S., A. C. R., L. L. H., S. E. C., O. R., AND A. W. N.

POLITICS in Zion City are joyous, peaceful, clean, but very effective.

There is a blissful "unanimous unanimity" about the political views and acts of her citizens that enables them to enjoy all the happy enthusiasm and high hopes of a political campaign, and not suffer from its bitterness, enmity, and disappointments.

Every citizen of Zion City that runs for office gets elected.

All the voters endorse and defend the same political platform and vote for the same candidates.

Strange as it may seem to many "practical politicians," such unanimity does not cause monotony

When the Theocratic Party—which is the only political party that has any members in the City of Zion—holds a rally, the occasion cannot be beat for high-pressure enthusiasm, with the power of a "whirlwind," and the good order of a regiment of regulars.

And at no other Political Rally is there such splendid music provided—the very best of orchestra, brass band, male chorus, and mixed chorus music, and all combined in one mighty Anthem of Praise to God.

Such a Rally was that held in Shiloh Tabernacle, Wednesday evening, October 5, 1904.

The activities began with a brief, informal reception at Shiloh House by the First Apostle to the Honorable George Edmund Foss, Member of Congress from the Tenth Congressional District of Illinois, and candidate for reëlection on the Republican ticket, and to Messrs. Lewis O. Brockway, Leslie P. Hanna, and A. N. Tiffany, Republican candidates for Circuit Clerk, State's Attorney, and State Senator respectively.

JUDGE V. V. BARNES

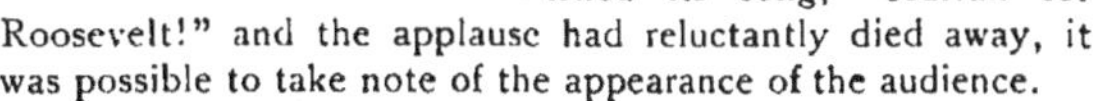

This reception was attended by the members of the National and Local Central Committees of the Theocratic Party, by the City Officials of the City of Zion, and by the resident Overseers in the Christian Catholic Apostolic Church in Zion.

The entire party was escorted to the Tabernacle in carriages by a battalion of the Zion Guard, headed by Colonel Carl F. Stern and Staff, and accompanied by Zion City Band.

As a reminiscence of the old campaigning days, when torchlight processions were an inevitable accompaniment of political excitement, a large number of the Guard were armed with flaming torches, which gave a distinctly political flavor to the march from Shiloh House to Shiloh Tabernacle.

While the people were waiting for the speakers of the evening to appear, they were very delightfully entertained with selections by Zion Orchestra and Zion Male Chorus.

It was while the young men were singing a lively campaign song that the First Apostle and his guests arrived at the Tabernacle and took the platform.

Those who took seats on the platform with the First Apostle, were Honorable George Edmund Foss, Judge V. V. Barnes, Lewis O. Brockway, Circuit Clerk of Lake County and Republican candidate for reëlection; Leslie P. Hanna, State's Attorney for Lake County and Republican candidate for reëlection; State Senator A. N. Tiffany, Republican candidate for reëlection; Judge De Witt L. Jones, County Judge of Lake County; Honorable George R. Lyon, Representative in the Illinois General Assembly; County Treasurer L. C. Price; Honorable George B. Stephens, Chairman of the County Board of Supervisors; Overseers John G. Excell and Harvey D. Brasefield; Deacon Charles J. Barnard, Chairman of the National Central Committee; Deacon William S. Peckham, Chairman of the Local Central Committee; Deacon Jasper H. Depew, Secretary of the National Central Committee; Honorable Richard H. Harper, Mayor of the City of Zion; and Messrs. R. W. L. Ely, A. S. Lasley, John H. Sayrs, W. Hurd Clendinen, and Arthur W. Newcomb, members of the National and Local Central Committees of the Theocratic Party.

When the chorus had finished its song, "Hurrah for Roosevelt!" and the applause had reluctantly died away, it was possible to take note of the appearance of the audience.

The galleries were nearly filled with ladies, looking every bit as much interested as their husbands and brothers.

The Colonel and staff of Zion Guard occupied the first row of seats on the ground floor of the Tabernacle, while the officers and men were massed in the central section.

On the sides of the ground floor were the other hundreds of voters of Zion City, with a very generous admixture of visitors from Waukegan and other cities and towns in the neighorhood.

In all, there were nearly five thousand people present.

After his salutation "Peace to thee," had been very heartily responded to by the people, the First Apostle nominated Judge V. V. Barnes as chairman of the Assembly, National Chairman Barnard seconded the nomination, and it was unanimously affirmed by the gathering.

Shiloh Tabernacle, Zion City, Illinois, Wednesday Evening, October 5, 1904.

Address by Judge V. V. Barnes.

JUDGE V. V. BARNES—"Fellow citizens, Ladies, and Gentlemen: I thank you for the distinguished honor you have conferred upon me this evening in calling me to the chair to preside over this body of voters and other citizens of the City of Zion, in the presence of our distinguished friends who have come here this evening to address us upon the great issues of the day.

"I feel that I can best grace this occasion by remaining silent, for the most part, and giving the time to those whom you all desire to hear.

"We have come together to consider great National Issues, at a time of great importance; at a crisis in American history; and we trust that we are all aware of the duties that rest upon us as voters to go to the polls and vote with integrity and intelligence for the preservation of our institutions, for our national honor, and for the enforcement of good and salutary laws.

"We have to deal tonight with the issues between the great National parties, as well as local issues.

"The candidates before you tonight are those representing the great Republican party of this Nation; and I have no doubt that in your hearing this evening they will go quite extensively into the fundamental principles underlying the platforms of both the great parties.

"You may hear something about the history and the aspirations of the Democratic party.

"It would seem that the history, the career, and the prospects of that party resemble very much the experiences of a man named Washington Smith, who lived in one of the Southern States a few years ago, and who, during a long and severe illness, was nursed by an old colored mammy.

"This man was not very popular in the community—I suppose that most of the people were quite willing that he should drop off.

"However, they had a peculiar curiosity that led them to go daily to inquire as to the condition of Mr. Washington Smith.

"Finally, the old colored woman hit upon the expedient of putting bulletins out upon the veranda, in order that the inquirers might be informed of the condition of her patient.

"These bulletins ran substantially as follows:

"Bulletin No. 1, 'Washington Smith am very sick;' Bulletin No. 2, next day, 'Washington Smith am worse,' Bulletin No. 3, 'Washington Smith am sinking;' and the final Bulletin, No. 4, on the following day read, 'Washington Smith am done sunk.' [Laughter.]

The Exercise of Intelligence Necessary in Casting One's Vote.

"It will be necessary for us, as I said at the outset, to exercise our intelligence.

"Some among us, coming from all parts of the world as we do, may sometimes find it difficult to understand how to use properly the Australian ballot, which has been prescribed by the Legislature of the State of Illinois.

"We may find ourselves doubtful as we listen to the public speakers upon great occasions, before the coming election.

"We will hear one side, and, unless we are careful and on our guard, we will scarcely know what to do; on hearing the other side, we may still be somewhat in a quandary.

"You may, as voters, find yourselves a good deal in the position of a certain judge at the trial of his first case in court.

"After the evidence was all in, and the state's attorney and the lawyer for the defendant had concluded their arguments, it came time for the judge to charge the jury, and he said, 'Gentlemen of the Jury, this is the first case I have ever tried in court.

"'It now becomes my duty to charge the jury in the case.

"'If, gentlemen, you believe what the state's attorney has said about the case, you will bring in a verdict of guilty; but if, on the other hand, you believe what the lawyer for the defendant says, you will bring in a verdict of not guilty.

"'If, like me, you don't believe in either one of them, then I'll be condemned, gentlemen, if I know what you will do. [Laughter.] You may retire, gentlemen, and consider your verdict.'

"But we do not find ourselves in such a position tonight, because we know the distinguished gentlemen who are holding up the banner before the voters of the American people in this great campaign, and we trust that every man will do his duty as a citizen.

"I know that you will profit by what these gentlemen shall say this evening, and I shall take great pleasure in introducing them at the proper time.

"We begin our exercises in Zion decently and in order, remembering always that God is the Author of all government, and at the head of the Theocratic Party.

"We should like all to join in singing 'America.'"

After the singing of the National Hymn, Judge Barnes said:

"We will now listen to the reading of Scripture by Overseer John G. Excell."

Overseer Excell then read the 24th Psalm, after which Overseer Brasefield offered prayer.

After music from Zion City Band, Deacon Willaim S. Peckham, chairman of the local central committee, then read the following platform:

The citizens of the City of Zion, Lake County, State of Illinois, being assembled in their First Convention, held in Zion City, on the night of Monday, April 7, 1902, for the purpose of nominating the first officers of their City, do so on a Theocratic Platform, and desire to set forth their position and their reasons for the formation of this new party in political affairs of the United States of America, in the manner following:

FIRST—We declare our loyalty to the Constitution and Laws of the United States of America.

SECOND—We affirm that both the Constitution and the Laws are capable of amendment and improvement in a Theocratic direction; and we simply propose to advocate the making of such alterations in the manner provided by the Laws of the United States.

THIRD—We declare the motto of our party to be the unalterable and unassailable truth that

WHERE GOD RULES, MAN PROSPERS.

FOURTH—Our object is, therefore, the establishment of the Rule of God in every department of Government, by the free will of the people.

FIFTH—We declare our conviction that the Holy Scriptures, which contain the Ten Commandments, and the inspired Gospel of Jesus, the Christ, the Son of God, constitute the principles of all righteous government for the Individual, for the Nation, and for the whole World.

Judge Barnes then said:

Local Candidates Introduced by the Chairman.

"Fellow citizens, we have with us this evening three of the candidates for election in November.

"I very much regret that the time will not permit of the lengthy speeches which these gentlemen might make for us and to which we would gladly listen, but I desire to introduce them to you that you may make their acquaintance and see them before you cast your ballots.

"I desire to present to you the candidate for circuit court clerk and recorder, Mr. Brockway, of Waukegan." [Cheers.]

LEWIS O. BROCKWAY—"Mr. Chairman, ladies and gentlemen, and citizens of Zion City, I am very glad to meet you this evening

"I have no language with which to express my appreciation of the hearty expressions that we have received here at your hands.

"As we have other speakers to discuss the issues of the evening, I will merely say, Thank you." [Applause.]

JUDGE V. V. BARNES—"Fellow citizens, I desire to present to you Honorable Leslie P. Hanna, candidate for state's attorney for Lake County, and who now occupies the position." [Applause.]

Address by States Attorney for Lake County.

HONORABLE LESLIE P. HANNA—"Ladies and gentlemen, I am indeed very glad to meet you tonight, although I thoroughly appreciate the fact that if the entire population of Lake County were composed of people like these in Zion City there would be no work for a public prosecutor. [Prolonged applause.]

"I am also very glad that I have been given this opportunity of seeing a political meeting opened with the reading of Scriptures and with prayer, and I believe that if our people would arrive at the point where they would demand that meetings of a political character should be opened in that way, corruption would cease to trouble us in our politics and among people in official positions.

"I am also glad to be in a political meeting where there are so many ladies as there are here, because when the ladies come out and look into matters political, they will see that the men vote right. [Applause.]

"But as I was merely to be introduced tonight, I will yield the platform to those who are to make the speeches." [Applause.]

JUDGE V. V. BARNES—"Fellow citizens, I take great pleasure in introducing to you County Treasurer L. C. Price." [Applause.]

Address by Candidate for County Treasurer

L. C. PRICE—"I did not come up here intending to try to make a speech, but I thank you for calling upon me." [Applause.]

JUDGE V. V. BARNES—"Fellow citizens and voters of Lake county: I take pleasure in introducing to you, Senator Tiffany, candidate for state senator the coming term."

Address by Senator Tiffany.

SENATOR A. N. TIFFANY—"Mr. Chairman, Ladies and Gentlemen: I am certainly glad to see such a large audience of people here to listen to the theories of the Republican party.

"I will not try in any way to discuss them, but will leave it to others who are better able than I to do so.

"I merely desire to assure the people of Zion City and vicinity that I have nothing but the kindest feelings toward you, and am glad that we have in our midst an institution that is conducted in the way this is.

"Gentlemen, I thank you. [Applause.]

JUDGE V. V. BARNES—"I take pleasure in introducing to you Chairman Stephens of the county board of supervisors." [Applause.]

Address by Chairman of County Board of Supervisors.

GEORGE B. STEPHENS—"Mr. Chairman, Ladies and Gentlemen: This is a distinguished honor that I never expected to enjoy.

"It is a pleasure for me to meet this people, to see the earnestness in your faces, and your intelligence.

"When I look over this vast audience, I feel assured that if the people were all like these we would have no need, as Mr. Hanna has said, of a prosecuting attorney, or of jails.

"Occupying as I do the position of chairman of the board of supervisors, it certainly has been a wonder to me, in looking over the bills of the various cities along the Lake Shore, to see practically no bills for the support of the poor or the punishment of crime from this great City of Zion.

"Gentlemen, I am not a public speaker; that is not my business.

"I have never attempted to address an audience of this size in my life, and have never expected to.

"I am merely a plain farmer, having been twice elevated to the position of chairman of the county board, and not wholly because of merit, but through the influence of friends as well.

"I feel proud of the ovation you have given to our county officials.

"I can assure you, gentlemen, after a residence of fifty years in this county—my memory dates back thirty-five years—that I have never heard of a scandal connected with a county official in this county. That is a rare record.

"While at the state convention this year, I met many people from various parts.

"When it was learned by some that I came from near Zion City, there was a great curiosity amongst the people to learn what they could about this place.

"It was not a great deal that I could tell, although I knew a little from talking with the people of Zion City.

"When I told them of the care you take of the poor, and your cleanly habits, and the industries you have here, it was a wonder to them.

"A great deal of education is needed along that line.

"It would bring credit to this State, if it would follow the example of the people of Zion City.

"Gentlemen, I thank you." [Applause.]

JUDGE V. V. BARNES—"I desire to have you meet two other gentlemen upon the platform tonight.

"I want you to take another good look at our distinguished friend, Judge Jones, who has not soiled the judicial ermine."

Address by Judge Jones.

HONORABLE DEWITT L. JONES—"I am not here to make a speech to you.

"I have had the pleasure of standing upon this platform and of addressing the people of Zion City before, and it afforded me great pleasure.

"I am glad to meet you again tonight; but I will give way to other speakers.

"I thank you." [Applause.]

JUDGE V. V. BARNES—"I also want to present to you our distinguished friend, the Honorable George R. Lyons, our representative in the Legislature. [Hearty cheers.]

"He is the man who stood by Zion and her institutions and the principles of integrity, and led the State Legislature in that direction." [Hearty applause.]

Address by Honorable G. R. Lyons.

HONORABLE GEORGE R. LYONS—"Mr. Chairman, Ladies, and Gentlemen: This time I am not a candidate for public office.

"Two years ago I was permitted to speak from this platform as a candidate for member of the General Assembly for the fourth term.

"I was elected to that office, and have performed the duties of it to the best of my ability.

"It was a great satisfaction to me when the vote was counted to find that Zion City had given me one thousand one hundred votes.

"I want to take this occasion to publicly thank you, one and all, for the honor you gave me at that time and for that big vote. [Hearty applause.]

"It was certainly appreciated.

"I know that every one of the candidates now on our Republican ticket, most of whom have filled the office for some time, are men of honor and integrity, and should command your votes.

"Our Congressman, Mr. Foss, who has filled the office, I think, for the fifth term, is now at the head of the great Naval Committee of this country.

"No better man ever trod the Halls of Congress than the man who will address you here tonight.

"The Republican party and its achievements constitute some of the brightest pages of our American history.

"The Republican party is right; it is right from every standpoint, and you make no mistake in voting that ticket from top to bottom." [Laughter and applause.]

The male chorus then sang two campaign songs, both of which produced hearty applause.

JUDGE BARNES—"The First Apostle will now introduce the distinguished gentleman whose name has just been celebrated in song." [Laughter.]

Introduction of Mr. Foss by the First Apostle.

John Alexander, First Apostle of the Christian Catho c Apostolic Church in Zion then said:

It would not be right if I did not take this opportunity to express my personal confidence in the Honorable George Edmund Foss, who is now Congressman for this district, and who doubtless will be found to be Congressman when the votes are counted at the next election.

My acquaintance with Mr. Foss covers several years, and every time I have met him I have found him a better man and a growing man.

I am not quite sure that he does not have a bee, the Presidential Bee, buzzing near him sometimes; for it is the opinion of many of Mr. Foss' friends that he will yet show that he is Presidential Timber.

From my own personal knowledge, I can say that he is very highly esteemed in Congress.

I have never heard (perhaps that is not quite to his credit) any one speak against him. [Laughter.]

The work of the United States Congress is done, not upon the floor of the Congressional Hall, but in the committees; and those gentlemen that are chairmen of committees are practically the rulers of the United States, legislatively.

Mr. Foss is Chairman of a Committee which last year spent ninety-eight million dollars.

He is Chairman of the Committee on Naval Affairs and Appropriations; and even President Roosevelt, with his Cabinet, have to speak very kindly to Mr. Foss. I know that he is greatly respected by his Committee and by the House.

Zion Stands for International Police Service.

Zion does not stand for war, and Mr. Foss knows that; but we do stand for an International Police that will keep order in the world, and that will tell these naughty Spanish-American Republics, and even some older nations on other continents, that they must be good and do right.

On the other hand if we are to protect South American Republics from European invasion, they must come nearer to American standards.

Now and then some of the vessels of the navy have had to go down there and tell them that they must do right.

I, myself, approve the action of His Excellency, the President of the United States, and the Committee over which Mr. Foss presides, in sending the fleet to Asiatic waters, to maintain the peace, and to see that the autonomy and integrity of China is maintained.

Russia has paid a very bitter price for breaking faith with the United States, for the Russian government promised to abandon Manchuria, and their failure to fulfil their promise has brought upon them this terrible war.

Mr. Foss is a very good friend of John Alexander Dowie, and of Zion City. [Applause.]

When I went down to Washington (you can always tell what the weight of a man is by his influence with Cabinet Ministers) Mr. Foss was exceedingly kind to me.

His Secretary, Mr. Whitney, of whom I want to speak with great respect and admiration, was exceedingly kind.

And in my visit to the Postmaster-general, in company with Mr. Foss, I saw at once that he was held in very high esteem by the Cabinet, and especially by the gentleman who passed away yesterday, a most lovable, gentle, trustworthy, and clean man—Postmaster-general Payne.

May God comfort his widow! [Amen.]

He has done a good work, and deserves well of his country.

I found in the interview with which I was honored by His Excellency, the President of the United States, on November 9th, last, that Mr. Foss stood very high in Theodore Roosevelt's confidence.

He spoke of him with a kindling eye, and in words of admiration.

I should almost feel that I was breaking confidence if I repeated these words, so I shall only say that he spoke of him as one would speak of a rising young statesman of the highest rank.

We have a clean-cut, broad, statesman-like man in George Edmund Foss, and I desire you to listen to him with the respect to which his utterances are entitled, both from his past, from his present, and, most of all, from his possible future.

May God bless George Edmund Foss!

I hope and believe that when election day comes there will not be a Zion City vote that is not recorded for him. [Applause.]

Address by Honorable George Edmund Foss.

George Edmund Foss—"Fellow citizens, ladies, and gentlemen:

"I desire to thank Doctor Dowie for his exceedingly complimentary introduction. I did not expect it.

"It is true that I have been able to do a little for Zion City in the way of improving her postal facilities now and then, but you more than repaid that two years ago, when you gave me every vote in Zion City. [Applause.]

"Now, that was before I had the pleasure of visiting your City. I wonder if I have made a mistake in coming? [Laughter, and No!]

"I am glad to meet so many of you here tonight.

"I am especially pleased with the music of your excellent male chorus and of your splendid band.

"I do not know when I have attended a political gathering where they were both so good.

"While your male chorus has complimented me, and the distinguished Doctor has complimented me and spoken of something away off in the future, I want you to understand that—I am merely running for Congress; that is all.

"I shall address you for a little while, and only a little while, because you all want to hear from a man who sits behind me, who has weightier matters upon which to talk to you.

"The issues in this campaign—sometimes I think tnat they cannot be seen.

"They were very plain in 1896; they were very plain in 1900, because in those years the Democratic party made paramount issues.

"They said in 1896 that the paramount issue was the free and unlimited coinage of silver, at the ratio of sixteen to one.

"They said in 1900 that the paramount issue was the same, and Mr. Bryant went from one end of the country to the other, saying that we could not have prosperity in this land without the free and unlimited coinage of silver at that ratio.

"They said in 1896 and in 1900 that these were paramount issues; but this year, my friends, they are dodging issues. [Applause.]

"Take up the Democratic Platform of this year; can you see anything on the money question?

"Not one word; and yet, they said that we could not have any very great prosperity in this country until we had the free and unlimited coinage of silver.

"This year they are silent; absolutely silent!

"What, sir, will you give for a party; what, sir, will you give for a man, who, upon the great question which interests you and every citizen of our land, is absolutely silent?

"Infinitely better that a man have convictions, though those convictions be wrong, than that he have no convictions at all.

"That is the position of the Democratic party this year on the money question.

The Democratic Candidate Does Not Commit Himself on the Money Question.

"True, Mr. Parker sent a telegram. Yes, after he had secured the nomination; and that telegram said—what?

"It said that the money question was irrevocably settled.

"He did not say whether it was settled right or wrong.

"He himself voted for Bryan in 1896 and in 1900, but now he says that the question is settled; and if he is elected President of the United States he will be governed accordingly.

"Suppose you wanted to select a man to fill the superintendency in some great business, and two men came before you, and one said, 'I have been a temperate man all my life, and never have taken a glass of liquor.'

"But the other man said, 'I have been a drunkard all my life, but I have just taken the Gold Cure. Will you not take me?' [Laughter.]

"Now this is what Mr. Parker says: 'I admit that I have been a Free Silverite; I admit that I voted for Mr Bryan; but I have just taken the Gold Cure. [Laughter.] Let me have the job. My friends, will you trust me?'

"There was a man in Chicago by the name of Mulcahy who owned a saloon.

"There was another man named O'Leary, who was the bartender in it.

"Mr. Casey went into the saloon one day, and called for a drink, got it, and drank it.

"Then O'Leary, the bartender, stepped back to Mulcahy, the owner of the bar-room, and said, 'Can I trust Casey?'

"Mulcahy scratched his head and said, 'Has he got the whisky?'

"'Yes,' said O'Leary.

"'You can trust him.' [Laughter.]

"Has Parker got the nomination?

"Yes.

"You can trust him. [Laughter.]

"So they are dodging the silver question.

"How are they on the tariff?

You Know Where the Republican Party Stands on the Tariff.

"It stands for Protection of American Industries.

"The Democratic party has ever been the Free Trade party—more often a Free Trade party than anything else.

"Look over its platforms and you will find that to be true; although now and then its platform has come out for a tariff for revenue only—only a phase of free trade.

"This year they say that protection is robbery; but they say, in the second section of their platform, 'We believe in the gradual revision of the tariff.'

"In other words, they say that the protective tariff is a robbery; but they are perfectly willing that this so-called robbery yoke should remain around your necks for a little while, until they can gradually reduce it.

"Mr. Parker goes further and says that there is no likelihood of our being able to reduce the tariff because the Senate of the United States cannot be overturned for at least four years.

"So you see that on the tariff question they are all at sixes and sevens.

"They have no clear-cut opinion on the tariff question, and are trying to dodge it this year in the hope of somehow or other making the people throughout the land think that it does not make very much difference if they do get into power, because they will not be able to overturn anything.

"You know, and I know, and every one who has read the history of this country knows, that it has grown great under protective policies; those policies which have protected American labor, the American market, and the American manufacturer.

"In 1860, the wealth of our country amounted to sixteen billions of dollars.

"What is it today? One hundred billions of dollars, and for the most of that time, except for the last Administration of Grover Cleveland, it has been under these wise protective policies.

"That is why we grow. The Protective Policy is a right policy. [Applause.]

The Alleged Issue of Constitutionalism Against Imperialism.

"Judge Parker says, in his letter of acceptance, published as a Democratic document in this campaign, that the issue is Constitutionalism against Imperialism.

"He says that the President of the United States is overriding the Constitution.

"I have in my pocket tonight the Democratic platform of 1864, which criticises and denounces Abraham Lincoln.

"It says that the Civil War was a failure, and that Abraham Lincoln overrode the Constitution of the United States.

"I can read you tonight the platform of 1872 also, when they said the same thing against Ulysses S. Grant—the same argument they are using against Theodore Roosevelt.

"It is the old Democratic trick, and it will not go down this year. [Applause.]

"The Democratic party will probably be judged this year as any and every party ought to be judged every year—upon its record, rather than upon its platform. You judge men upon their records; upon what they have been in the past and upon what they are today; not so much by what they declare in speech.

"So these two parties will be judged by the thinking men of this country for the next few weeks, until election day, by the records they have made.

"The Democratic party has made a record in recent years.

"They were in power from 1892 to 1896.

"The Republican party has been in power ever since.

"What man in this audience tonight wants to go back to those old times of 1892 and 1896, under the Cleveland administration, when we had soup houses in the city of Chicago, and homeless men by the hundreds were lying in the City Hall, with no other place to lay their heads.

"Oh, you remember those days.

"The Democratic party passed the Wilson Bill that gave us Free Trade.

"They even went farther than that; they gave us no trade at all. [Applause and laughter.]

"The people of this country said that they wanted a change and they got it.

"We took the Democrats on faith, and were bitterly disappointed.

"We got nothing we hoped for and saw more misery than we ever saw before.

A Deacon Who Misquoted Scripture.

"When I think of those old days in 1896, I think of a good old deacon who, it is said, lived up on an old hillside of Vermont, and who knew just enough Scripture to misquote it.

"One night he stood up in a meeting and said, 'Brethren, the disciples of old were the most wonderful persons you ever saw. They made the lame to see, the blind to hear, the deaf to walk, and they cast out the dead and raised the Devil.' [Laughter.]

"My friends, I do not mean to say that that is the mission of the Democratic party; I would not say that.

"The Democratic party is composed of many honorable and honest men.

HONORABLE GEORGE EDMUND FOSS,
Member of Congress for Tenth Congressional District, Illinois.

"I feel very warmly toward the Democratic party.

"Why, the best friend I have on earth is a Democrat.

"I feel as the Frenchman did toward the bed bug. 'I like ze bug, but I do not like ze way ze bug gets his living.' [Applause and laughter.]

"So I would not say that was the mission of the Democratic party, but I do say to my Democratic friends, wherever I meet them, while I do not believe that to be the mission of your party, yet you have produced about that result every time you have run the Government.

"Has the Republican party a mission?

"Yes.

"There were two Irishmen walking up Fifth avenue, in New York City, one Sunday afternoon, and they stopped in front of that great Roman Catholic Cathedral.

"They stood there and gazed at the tall spires that cleft the azure blue of the American sky, when suddenly Pat exclaimed, 'That bates the Devil!' Then Mike turned to Pat and says he, 'That was the original intintion.' [Laughter.]

"When the Republican party came into power on March 4, 1897, it did that very thing.

"You remember that Grover Cleveland issued bonds for two hundred sixty-two million dollars to preserve the gold reserve, and pay the running expenses of the government?

"He added that amount to our national bonded debt.

What the Republican Party Has Done for the Country.

"When the Republican party came into power, it repealed the Wilson Tariff Law and put on the statute books the Dingley Tariff Law, which gave us enough money to pay the running expenses of the government, and has done it ever since.

"The next thing we did was to place the tariff so that it encouraged American industry from one end of the country to the other, and set the wheels going around, and they have been going around ever since. [Applause.]

"Then the Spanish-American War came on, and later we annexed Hawaii, the Cuban Republic, and the Philippines, and accomplished many things of great importance, which I do not have the time tonight to discuss.

"However, through them all, Republican policies have prevailed, and they prevail for the good of the country.

"During the last seven years this nation has had the greatest prosperity we have ever known.

"There have been no other seven years like them in all the history of the country.

"We have refunded all that was possible of our National Debt (five hundred fifty million dollars), on which we are now paying only two per cent. interest, the lowest rate of interest paid by any nation on the globe. That brings the average interest on the entire debt down to a little over two per cent. [Applause.]

"But we did not do that until, against all Democratic opposition, we had first placed the Gold Standard Act upon the statute books of the United States. [Applause.]

"Our average interest charge before that time was four and seven-tenths per cent.

"The actual amount of interest paid on the debt is no longer forty million dollars, but twenty-five million.

"Not only that, but money is circulating now.

Confidence Underlies the Circulation of Money.

"In 1896 we had a billion and a half of dollars, but did not have any confidence.

"You must have the circulation of confidence before you can have the circulation of money, and under the Democratic administration we did not have the circulation of confidence.

"You must have confidence in your fellow men, in the administration of affairs here and in Washington, for confidence underlies the circulation of money, and that is what we did not have from 1892 to 1896; but the moment we got a new administration into power money commenced to circulate.

"We had a billion and a half then; today we have two billion and a half.

"The *per capita* circulation tonight is thirty dollars and eighty cents; whereas back in Cleveland's day it was only twenty-one dollars.

"So much for Republican policy.

"If I had more time I should like to talk about the American Navy

"We have been building up the American Navy, but nowhere in the Democratic Platform do you see this year, nor have you seen any year, anywhere, the statement that it was either a wise policy or a bad policy to build up the American Navy.

"I endorse what Dr. Dowie has said here tonight; we are building it up for peace; but we are also building it up for the protection of the rights of American citizens.

"Not for the kind of peace that means peace at any price, but the kind of peace that never means surrender of national honor, national duty, or national obligation—that kind of peace which is, indeed, American.

"That is the kind of peace Doctor Dowie means, and that we all mean.

How American Authority Was Once Exercised.

"You remember about that American citizen, Ion Perdicaris, who lived up in his country home, above the Bay of Tangier, and who while in his home and surrounded by his family and friends was attacked by Raisuli at the head of a band of bandits.

"They bound him and carried him away up into the mountains of Morocco and demanded of the authorities of Morocco a ransom for his life.

"His friends called upon the United States Government, and we sent Admiral Chadwick over there.

"He took with him the *Brooklyn*, famous in the Santiago fight, also the *Olympia*, Dewey's flag-ship, famous in the Manila conflict.

"He sailed into the Bay of Tangier, and about that time the President of the United States, through his Secretary of State, John Hay, sent a short message to the authorities of Morocco, because we held them responsible for law and order within the realm.

"The message read: 'Perdicaris alive or Raisuli dead!'

"What did that mean?

"It meant that the American citizen wherever he is, in whatever clime, on whatever shore, stands there under the protecting egis of the flag of his country.

"All of our interests; protection of commerce; the backing up of our foreign policy; the defense of the Monroe Doctrine; the guardianship of our Panama Canal, which is no longer a dream, because we have no dreamer in the White House, but a digger; the mighty work we are doing in the Philippines, leading these ten millions of people up the steeps of civilization, into the clear, bright sky of American liberty—all these things demand a navy.

"Yes, a navy is demanded, made of American material, manned and officered by American men, flying aloft the American flag, that will never sail the paths of the Ocean on a mission of duty but that it will carry a message of Peace and Hope.

"The American Navy! May she always stand for Peace. [Applause.]

"May she never be required to fire a single shot.

"War is honorable in the sight of man and justifiable in the sight of God, only after all honorable means of preserving peace have been exhausted.

"So may our navy stand always for Peace. [Applause.]

"Let us go on building it up, so that in every International Conflict, it shall give to our country that calmness and that poise which become a great nation and a great people, 'slow to anger and plenteous in mercy.'

"But when she strikes, if she must strike—pray God that she may never strike—may she not strike in haste, or for vengeance, because 'vengeance belongeth unto the Lord.' [Applause.]

"If she must strike, may she strike for honor, for truth, for justice, for civilization, for liberty, for the eternal verities, and strike as Dewey struck at Manila—always for victory. [Applause.]

A Word About President Roosevelt.

"I wish I had time to say a few words about our President, but I have not.

"You know him.

"He has been in the administration of affairs of this Government for three years.

"He stood in that home in Buffalo, after he had taken the oath of office, and pledged himself to the American people to carry out the policies of William McKinley, and he has done it.

"They say that he is an unsafe man.

"Yes, he is unsafe—to the man who would violate the law.

"He was unsafe as Police Commissioner in the City of New York, when he found policemen loitering on the street, but unsafe only to them.

"He was unsafe as a civil service commissioner when men violated the civil service law; but unsafe only to the violator.

"He was unsafe, when, as assistant secretary of the navy, men came to him to sell old ships at double their value—he was unsafe to them.

"He was unsafe when, as lieutenant colonel, he charged up San Juan Hill, but only to the Spaniard.

"He was unsafe as Governor of New York when men would have used him and his position for some bad end.

"He was unsafe when Colombia would have held us up for blackmail, but only to Colombia.

"He has ever been safe to American honor, to American duty, and to American prosperity, since the hour he went into the Presidential Chair.

"So I urge you to vote for him.

"Vote the good old Republican Ticket.

"My friends, I thank you for your cordial greeting." [Prolonged applause.]

The Choir then sang the "Gloria," from Mozart's Twelfth Mass; after which the Chairman rose and said:

Introduction of the First Apostle by Judge V. V. Barnes.

"I now have the very great pleasure of presenting to you one who needs no introduction, whose name is not only known to you, but to the whole civilized world, and to whose words of instruction and inspiration we are always glad to listen.

"I therefore now turn over the authority and position that has been delegated to me during the proceedings of this meeting, to the First Apostle, who will now take charge, and will address you."

The First Apostle then stepped to the front of the platform and pronounced the

INVOCATION.

Let the words of my mouth, and the meditations of my heart, be acceptable in Thy sight, and profitable unto this people, and unto all to whom these words shall come, in this and every land, in this and all the coming time. Till Jesus Come. Amen.

TEXT.

He that ruleth over men must be just; ruling in the fear of God.

What I shall say tonight will be especially with reference to the presidential candidate.

I desire to speak with the utmost respect of all my fellow citizens in the great American Republic—black, white, North, South, East and West.

May God bless every man, woman, and child in America! [Amen.]

The President of the United States is not the president of a party.

The President of the United States is the President of the Nation and of the whole people, and the moment he assumes the Chief Executive office, party must depart, and he must rule justly and as in the sight of God. [Applause.]

No nation has such a privilege as the American Nation in repairing the mistakes that may have been made by previous generations.

With the exception of the beautiful Swiss Republic—God bless the Swiss Republic! [Applause]—and with the exception of the French Republic—God bless the French Republic and Mr. Combes in his great fight! [Applause]—the nations of Europe and Asia, and largely of Africa (and the curse of Imperialism has extended to Australia and many of the Islands of the Sea) are under monarchical government.

All who know the Word of God know that God said to His Prophet Samuel, when Israel desired a King, "They have not rejected thee, but they have rejected Me, that I should not be King over them."

I am glad that I am in a Republic where there is no man who can claim perpetual power in the chair of the ruler; where no man can send down to posterity a hereditary claim to that chair.

In establishing that claim men have been compelled to fight, and bleed, and die, sometimes for epileptic fools; sometimes for vicious, polluted, dishonored and diseased princes; and sometimes for gamblers.

I am glad that mistakes can be remedied, and that this people, every four years, can reaffirm their confidence in the man and in the principles that he represents, or turn him adrift and put in a better man.

I am for the first time speaking in a presidential campaign as an American citizen; and I am glad to be an American citizen! [Applause.]

But I speak in full sympathy with all my fellow citizens. I have no thought of ridiculing any party or any man.

The First Apostle Reaffirms His Loyalty to Theocracy.

The Democratic party deserves our tenderest sympathy! [Laughter.]

It reminds me, Mr. Lyons, of the time when you, in the Legislature at Springfield, had to do with a number of "Whereasses!" [Laughter.]

The only man who had the manliness to vote for the right when almost the entire legislature went the other way, was Mr. Lyons. [Applause.]

I will not pin my faith to any party in this Republic except to the Theocratic Party, whose platform you have heard read tonight. [Applause.]

I shall back the Republican Party in National Issues as long as I can, and when I cannot longer do it honestly, I shall turn it down.

I desire to give you some reasons tonight why we should support Theodore Roosevelt for President.

I shall speak at greater length on this subject next Lord's Day, when I shall speak about "The Nation's Choice of a President; and National Duties and Policies in the Light of Theocratic Principles."

But this I desire to say tonight.

We have as candidates for the offices of President and Vice-president of this Republic, Theodore Roosevelt and Charles W. Fairbanks, and for this district, the Congressional nominee is Mr. Foss, and I have already shown you some reasons why we should support him unanimously, as you did the last time, for there has been no change.

I ask you, Have you changed, or are you willing to support him at this election? All in favor, say Aye. ["Aye!" in hundreds, and with pronounced emphasis.]

On the contrary, No. [Silence.]

If, after examination, we should find these county officers the right sort, are you willing to say Aye? ["Aye!"] Those to the contrary, No. [Silence.]

We get through things quickly! [Turning to the nominees and visitors sitting on the platform.]

That is why we manage to get things done.

My people and I are one.

I know them and they know me, and we get along all right! [Applause.]

MR. FOSS—"This is unanimous unanimity!"

FIRST APOSTLE—I will guarantee that he has not found elsewhere such 'unanimous unanimity' in all this campaign.

Some Words About the Democratic Presidential Nominee.

On the other side, there is Alton B. Parker, and a gentleman named Davis, an octogenarian.

Beloved friends, as common sense people, on the principle that we don't swap horses when we are crossing a stream, why should we exchange Theodore Roosevelt for Alton B. Parker?

Alton B. Parker has not earned the confidence of this people as a statesman, a legislator, an executive, or a patriot.

Who ever heard of Alton B. Parker in any of these capacities?

Alton B. Parker, no doubt a very respectable gentleman, must have been immensely astonished that he should have been dragged out of judicial obscurity to be the Presidential candidate of the Democratic party.

What has he done to command the interest, enthusiasm, admiration, and confidence of the American voter?

This question of the Executive is a personal one; it is above party.

You are called upon to elect a president of the United States

His power is greater than that of any monarch in the world, as an executive officer.

He is in himself the Government.

He calls to his council board whom he will, utterly irrespective of the opinions of Congress.

He calls to his council and to offices in his Administration gentlemen who have the confidence of the Nation in their respective positions; but he himself is the Executive.

This Government is divided into three parts: First, the Legislative Power; second, the Judicial Power; and third, the Executive Power.

But that Executive Power is strong, as illustrated in Abraham Lincoln's day, when he used the power committed to him by the Constitution; and, utterly regardless of what Congress might say, do, think, or threaten, and utterly regardless of what the Supreme Court and all the Judicial Powers might say, do, think, or threaten, Abraham Lincoln—God forever bless his memory!—signed the Emancipation Proclamation; and showed that upon occasion, the Executive Power was superior to the Legislative and the Judicial.

We place a tremendous weight of responsibility upon Theodore Roosevelt; and you should thank God that there is a man among us who can bear that responsibility, and come out of it with a pure and spotless life. [Applause.]

The First Apostle's Testimony to President Roosevelt's Nobility of Character.

If I had never met the President, if I had never been honored with his kind words and his gracious reception of me in the White House, if I had never known him other than as a public man, I should have honored him, and probably spoken exactly as I am speaking now.

But I speak of the man into whose eyes I have looked; into whose heart I have looked; from whose lips I have heard that which makes me say that of all the statesmen in the world, I do not know a grander and nobler man than Theodore Roosevelt. [Applause.]

I have found, after closely examining his life, that there is a bravery and thoroughness about the man—albeit he does things I would not, and could not do—and a splendid honesty, with a fine underlying sensibility.

With the strength of a giant, he has the tender heart and the modesty of a gentle maiden.

He is polite, gracious; and he can be firm.

He knows how to rule, and he knows how to obey; for I believe from my heart that the best Theocrat I know in public life today, the man who most believes in the Rule of God everywhere, is Theodore Roosevelt! [Applause.]

I could say very much regarding the details of his life and administration, but it is not necessary at this time.

Regarding Mr. Fairbanks, all know that as a senator he has a lily-white reputation.

I have never heard anything against his character or capacity as a man or a statesman of a very high order.

It also happens that I know the Senator a little, personally.

Having had business in Washington a few years ago—long before Mr. Fairbanks was thought of as candidate for the Vice-presidency—Mr. Fairbanks and I sat together at the table, nearly every night, at dinner, in the Arlington Hotel.

I had the pleasure of noticing what a gracious, sweet personality there was sitting there; how perfectly honest and simple he was; and I could not wonder that he had won the friendship of the President and the friendship of the great statesmen in Washington.

If President Roosevelt should pass away during his term of office—which, God forbid—I believe that we would have in Senator Charles W. Fairbanks as Vice-president, a gentleman of patrician dignity and unsullied character.

But turning for a moment to the other side, what have we?

Alton B. Parker Must Take a Back Seat.

How can we have confidence in a man who, as Mr. Foss jocularly suggested, has, after many years of debased silver debauchery, just taken the Gold Cure?

For eight years he fought, tooth and nail, for the supremacy of a debased currency, and the ruin of this country, fiscally and in many other ways, by the advocacy of evil policies.

Now he says that he repents, and the prodigal, coming home from the swine trough of the Silver Party, asks us to make him the chief stone of the corner! [Laughter.]

Verily no, Alton B. Parker. You went into the far country and you tried to fill your belly with the silver husks that the swine did eat, and now you have come home, it would be well for you to take, with all your associates, a very humble place.

We are very glad that you have come into sanity, but we are going to ask you to take a back seat for a few years longer.

I am glad to have around me these gentlemen.

You know that I am not a politician.

I could not say a great many things that they could say; but I shall deal with the great national issues from our Theocratic standpoint next Lord's Day.

I should like to ask a question: All who believe that Theodore Roosevelt and Charles W. Fairbanks should be the next President and Vice-president of the United States, say Aye.

[An enthusiastic and apparently unanimous "Aye."]

Those on the contrary, No. [One solitary "No."]

Deal with him tenderly. [Laughter.]

I think that he must have made a mistake.

Let me thank you very much for this.

The First Apostle then led the people in singing "I Stand on Zion's Mount," after which he pronounced the

BENEDICTION.

Jehovah bless thee, and keep thee:
Jehovah make His face to shine upon thee, and be gracious unto thee:
Jehovah lift up His countenance upon thee, and give thee Peace. Amen.

Notice to Correspondents.

In writing to Headquarters it is *absolutely essential* that the writer give his full address.

Failure to comply with this request necessitates looking up or referring to the Church Records, which involves much time, and is very frequently fruitless.

Friends and members of the Christian Catholic Church in Zion everywhere will please bear this in mind, especially those in foreign lands.

J. G. EXCELL, General Ecclesiastical Secretary.

Notice to Officers and Members.

Send all newspaper clippings concerning the General Overseer, the Elders, or any department of the work in connection with the Christian Catholic Church in Zion, to Deacon Carl F. Stern, Zion City, Illinois. Send as soon as possible after publication, and carefully mark *name and date of the paper clipped from* on each article. If this is not done, the clippings are absolutely useless.

GOD'S WAY OF HEALING.

BY THE REV. JOHN ALEX. DOWIE.

God's Way Of Healing Is a Person, Not a Thing.

Jesus said "*I am* the Way, and the Truth, and the Life," and He has ever been revealed to His people in all the ages by the Covenant Name, Jehovah-Rophi, or "*I am* Jehovah that Healeth thee." (John 14:6; Exodus 15:26.)

The Lord Jesus, the Christ, Is Still the Healer.

He cannot change, for "Jesus, the Christ, is the same yesterday and today, yea and forever;" and He is still with us, for He said: "Lo, *I am* with you All the Days, even unto the Consummation of the Age." (Hebrews 13:8; Matthew 28:20.) Because He is Unchangeable, and because He is present, in spirit, just as when in the flesh, He is the Healer of His people.

Divine Healing Rests on the Christ's Atonement.

It was prophesied of Him "Surely He hath borne our griefs (Hebrew, *sickness*), and carried our sorrows: . . . and with His stripes we are healed;" and it is expressly declared that this was fulfilled in His Ministry of Healing, which still continues. (Isaiah 53:4, 5; Matthew 8:17.)

Disease Can Never be God's Will.

It is the Devil's work, consequent upon Sin, and it is impossible for the work of the Devil ever to be the Will of God. The Christ came to "destroy the works of the Devil," and when He was here on earth He healed "all manner of disease and all manner of sickness," and all these sufferers are expressly declared to have been "oppressed of the Devil." (1 John 3:8; Matthew 4:23; Acts 10:38.)

The Gifts of Healings Are Permanent.

It is expressly declared that the "Gifts and the calling of God are without repentance," and the Gifts of Healings are amongst the Nine Gifts of the Spirit to the Church. (Romans 11:29; 1 Corinthians 12:8-11.)

There Are Four Modes of Divine Healing.

The first is the direct prayer of faith; the second, intercessory prayer of two or more; the third, the anointing of the elders, with the prayer of faith; and the fourth, the laying on of hands of those who believe, and whom God has prepared and called to that ministry. (Matthew 8:5-13; Matthew 18:19; James 5:14, 15; Mark 16:18.)

Divine Healing Is Opposed by Diabolical Counterfeits.

Amongst these are Christian Science (falsely so called), Mind Healing, Spiritualism, Trance Evangelism, etc. (1 Timothy 6:20, 21; 1 Timothy 4:1, 2; Isaiah 51:22, 23.)

Multitudes Have Been Healed Through Faith in Jesus.

The writer knows of thousands of cases and has personally laid hands on scores of thousands of persons. Full information can be obtained at the meetings held in the Zion Tabernacles in Chicago, and in Zion City, Illinois, and in many pamphlets which give the experience, in their own words, of many who have been healed in this and other countries, published at Zion Printing and Publishing House, Zion City, Illinois.

"*Belief Cometh of Hearing, and Hearing by the Word of the Christ.*"

You are heartily invited to attend and hear for yourself.

Zion's Bible Class

Conducted by Teacher Daniel Sloan in Shiloh Tabernacle, Zion City, Lord's Day Morning at 11 o'clock, and in Zion Homes and Gatherings throughout the World.

MID-WEEK BIBLE CLASS LESSON, OCTOBER 26th or 27th.

The Church of God and Its True Work.

1. *She is the body of the Christ.*—Ephesians 1:17-23.
Some must serve in one place and some in another.
Her victory is only in the Christ.
His will must be supreme.
2. *She carries on the work the Christ began.*—John 14:10-14.
If she is like her Lord she will work His works.
If God is within her she will be doing the work of the Christ.
Yea, even greater works are to be wrought.
3. *She is ever to contend that the Faith of the early Church is possible today.*—Jude 1:2-4.
The reason why she may fail in Faith is shown.
The fight of Faith must be fought in all ages.
God delivers the Faith that it may be kept to the end.
4. *She must never swerve from an Apostolic and Prophetic Ministry.*—Ephesians 2:16-22.
The Apostles must do the work of the Christ.
The Prophets must ever arouse and inspire God's people.
A church without these will never grow in power.
5. *Apostles are to be her chief ruling power.*—1 Corinthians 12:27-31.
They are to rule in the Christ's stead.
They are over subordinate officers.
They have the Gift of Wisdom given them.
6. *Examples of Christian conduct must be held forth in teaching, and discipline enforced.*—1 Corinthians 4:10-21.
They first take the lowly places in power.
They are an example to all saints in long-suffering.
They are to rebuke every spirit contrary to God's will.
7. *Persons must not be admitted to office until character and efficiency are proved.*—1 Timothy 3:9-16.
Apostles are to conserve every ordination.
Purity in God's ministry is the first essential.
An officer that does not show Faith and exemplary conduct must be retired.
8. *A watchful oversight of the conduct of all is necessary.*—1 Timothy 5:15-25.
People have a tendency to go back to sinful ways.
The Devil is ever ready to tempt away.
God's work must not be treated with laxity.
The Lord Our God is a Church-commissioning God.

SUNDAY BIBLE CLASS LESSON, OCTOBER 30th.

Apostolic Ministry and Authority.

1. *Apostles must always remember that the Christ is the Head of the Church.*—Luke 9:10-17.
The Christ is the Head of the Household of Faith.
He never sends any away hungry, but fills them.
The ministry of feeding follows healing.
2. *An Apostle is not a Stay-at-home, but a man sent of God to preach, and teach, and heal.*—Luke 9:2-6.
He is sent to tell of God's Kingdom.
He must go full of Faith in God.
He must reckon on a sufficiency in God.
3. *He preaches so plainly that the Devil is stirred to fume and kill.*—Luke 11:45-51.
He condemns sinners who continue in their sins.
He exposes their hypocrisy.
He shows how devilish they are.
4. *He labors in miracle-working power, leading men and women to have faith in God, and get healing mercy.*—Acts 5:12-16.
He has signs of God's favor.
Wonderful healings occur.
He makes people decide for or against God.
5. *He is given to the ministry of God's Word and to prayer, and will not be otherwise occupied.*—Acts 6:1-8.
How to pray is most important.
The Word must be ministered, or no faith is possible.
He has business enough on these two lines.
6. *They are Apostles of the Christ, not of the Church, and go forth in the Christ's stead, whatever the cross may be.*—Matthew 10:32-42.
People receiving them receive the Christ.
They live a self-denying life.
They do things, whether big or little, in the Christ's Name.
7. *A man that cannot pray in faith is no Apostle, and has no key to open or close, or bind or loose.*—Matthew 16:13-23.
He must be Divinely illuminated.
He must know the Christ, the power of God.
He must always pray in faith.
8. *An Apostle is a self-denying, soul-saving, miracle-working, and sin-hating minister of the Christ.*—2 Corinthians 12:10-21.
He must die daily, and forget self.
He must by all means save some.
He must make no compromise with sin.
God's Holy People are a Divinely-led People.

OBEYING GOD IN BAPTISM.

"Baptizing Them Into the Name of the Father and of the Son and of the Holy Spirit."

Twenty Thousand Thirty-three Baptisms by Triune Immersion Since March 14, 1897.

Twenty Thousand Thirty-three Believers have joyfully followed their Lord in the Ordinance of Believer's Baptism by Triune Immersion since the first Baptism in Central Zion Tabernacle on March 14, 1897.

Baptized in Central Zion Tabernacle from March 14, 1897, to December 14, 1901, by the General Overseer,	4754			
Baptized in South Side Zion Tabernacle from January 1, 1902, to June 14, 1903, by the General Overseer..	37			
Baptized at Zion City by the General Overseer........	647			
Baptized by Overseers, Elders, Evangelists and Deacons, at Headquarters (Zion City) and Chicago......	5626			
Total Baptized at Headquarters..............	—			11,064
Baptized in places outside of Headquarters by the General Overseer..................................		765		
Baptized in places outside of Headquarters by Overseers, Elders, Evangelists and Deacons............		8,125		
Total Baptized outside of Headquarters............		—		8,890
Total Baptized in seven years and six months......				19,954
Baptized since September 14, 1904:				
Baptized in Zion City by Elder Viking...............	3			
Baptized in Zion City by Elder Dinius................	3			
Baptized in Zion City by Elder Royall................	20			
Baptized in Chicago by Elder Hoffman..............	2			
Baptized in Chicago by Elder Hammond............	5		33	
Baptized in Illinois by Elder Gay....................		5		
Baptized in Kansas by Elder Reed..................		10		
Baptized in Michigan by Deacon Van Woerkom......		1		
Baptized in Missouri by Deacon Robinson............		2		
Baptized in New York by Elder Warszawiak..........		9		
Baptized in New York by Overseer Mason		12		
Baptized in Ohio by Deacon Smith..................		1		
Baptized in Pennsylvania by Elder Bouck............		4		
Baptized in Texas by Elder Hall....................		1		
Baptized in Washington by Elder Simmons..........		1	46	79
Total Baptized since March 14, 1897..............				20,033

The following-named sixteen believers were baptized in Pretoria, Transvaal, South Africa, Lord's Day, August 21, 1904, by Overseer Daniel Bryant:

Barrett, William Waite....4 Dutoit street, Pretoria, Transvaal, South Africa
Daniel, Ernest Edwin Reuben, 8a Biccard street, Braamfontein, Johannesburg, Transvaal, South Africa
Ford, Sydney Oswald, 18 Von Brandis street, Johannesburg, Transvaal, South Africa
Gardner, William Benjamin, 6 Keizer street, Johannesburg, Transvaal, South Africa
Glenn, Miss Emmy, 82 Van de Wald st., Pretoria, Transvaal, South Africa
Oelofre, Nicolaus Petrus. .....Schweizer-Reneke, Transvaal, South Africa
Schutte, Mrs. Aletta Wilhelemina, Vermeulen street, East Pretoria, Transvaal, South Africa
Schutte, Miss Elizabeth Cornelia, Vermeulen street, East Pretoria, Transvaal, South Africa
Schutte, Miss Hester Helena, Vermeulen street, East Pretoria, Transvaal, South Africa
Schutte, John Francis Jacobus Johan, Vermeulen street, East Pretoria, Transvaal, South Africa
Schutte, Master Nicolaas Jacobus, Vermeulen street, East Pretoria, Transvaal, South Africa
Stander, Hendrik Frederik, Rietfontein West, District Pretoria, Transvaal, South Africa
Townsend, Anna Margaret ....Pretoria, Transvaal, South Africa
Townsend, Frederick.......... ....Pretoria, Transvaal, South Africa
Venter, Jacob............4 Dutoit street, Pretoria, Transvaal, South Africa
Walters, Miss Annie Beatrice Jeanette, 77 Mare street, "The Retreat," Pretoria, Transvaal, South Africa

The following-named six believers were baptized in St. Louis, Missouri, Lord's Day, September 11, 1904, by Elder Frank L. Brock:

Froos, Flortine....................6135 Wilson avenue, St. Louis, Missouri
Froos, Miss Henrietta.............6135 Wilson avenue, St. Louis, Missouri
Froos, John Henry.................6135 Wilson avenue, St. Louis, Missouri
Haenchen, George F............ 1810 De Kalb street, St, Louis, Missouri
Leber, Lena ....2931 South Eighteenth street, St. Louis, Missouri
Morton, Jeannie....................4406 Cottage avenue, St. Louis, Missouri

The following-named believer was baptized at Bellingham, Washington, Thursday, September 29, 1904, by Elder R. M. Simmons:

Jackson, Galland John .... Ferndale, Washington

The following-named believer was baptized at Fort Scott, Kansas, Lord's Day, September 25, 1904, by Elder David A. Reed:

Todd, Mrs. Emma ....R R. Number 2, Fort Scott, Kansas

The following-named two believers were baptized at Yates Center, Kansas, Tuesday, September 27, 1904, by Elder David A. Reed:

Miller, Henry H....................................Yates Center, Kansas
Miller, Mrs. Mary J................ ....Yates Center, Kansas

The following-named believer was baptized at Hammond, Kansas, Lord's Day, September 25, 1904, by Elder David A. Reed:

Woolery, Henry Franklin..............................Hammond, Kansas

The following-named six believers were baptized at Eldorado, Kansas, Lord's Day, October 2, 1904, by Elder David A. Reed:

Neikirk, Ernest O..Eldorado, Kansas
Neikirk, Mrs. Orianna...................................Eldorado, Kansas
Randall, Benjamin T...... ....Eldorado, Kansas
Randall, Mindy B..Eldorado, Kansas
Randall, Sena Cordelia...................................Eldorado, Kansas
Steiner Maurice B ....Eldorado, Kansas

The following name was omitted from the list of names of believers baptized in Pretoria, Transvaal, South Africa, Lord's Day, June 19, 1904, by Overseer Daniel Bryant, and published in LEAVES OF HEALING, issue of August 13, 1904, Volume XV., Number 17:

Roos, Christoffel Johan Wilhelm, Wonderboom Zaid, District of Pretoria, Transvaal, South Africa

CONSECRATION OF CHILDREN.

The following-named two children were consecrated to God, at Pretoria, Transvaal, South Africa, Lord's Day, August 21, 1904, by Overseer Daniel Bryant:

de Jager, Gerrit Jacobus Nickerk, P. O. Box 1180, Pretoria, Transvaal, South Africa
de Jager, Matthy's Johan, P. O. Box 1180, Pretoria, Transvaal, South Africa

The following-named nine children were consecrated to God at Vancouver, British Columbia, Lord's Day, September 25, 1904, by Elder R. M Simmons:

Campbell, Kenneth Victor, 416 East Cordova street, Vancouver, British Columbia
Campbell, Wilfred Wallace, 416 East Cordova street, Vancouver, British Columbia
Campbell, William Clarence, 416 East Cordova street, Vancouver, British Columbia
Carter, Edna Hamley, 828 East Cordova street, Vancouver, British Columbia
Kennedy, Mervin Ewart, 835 East Cordova street, Vancouver, British Columbia
Millar, Elwin George, 14 Seventh avenue East, Vancouver, British Columbia
Morley, Percival Gladstone, 1631 Eighth avenue West, Fairview, Vancouver, British Columbia
Morrison, Alcyone May.........Cedar Cove, Vancouver, British Columbia
Simmons, Beulah Gertrude, 525 Grove Crescent, Vancouver, British Columbia

The following-named child was consecrated to God at Eldorado, Kansas, Lord's Day, October 2, 1904, by Elder David A. Reed:

Mann, Charley Willard ....Eldorado, Kansas

The following-named child was consecrated to God, in Chicago, Illinois, Lord's Day, October 2, 1904, by Elder Gilbert E. Farr:

Johnson, Esther Eva Catherine.......1689 Carroll avenue, Chicago, Illinois

A WEEKLY PAPER FOR THE EXTENSION OF THE KINGDOM OF GOD

EDITED BY JOHN ALEXANDER, FIRST APOSTLE OF THE LORD JESUS, THE CHRIST, IN THE CHRISTIAN CATHOLIC APOSTOLIC CHURCH IN ZION

Volume XV. No. 26. *ZION CITY, SATURDAY, OCTOBER 15, 1904.* *Price Five Cents*

GOD'S WITNESSES TO DIVINE HEALING.

HEALED WHEN DYING OF CONSUMPTION, HEART TROUBLE, AND OTHER DISEASES.

JESUS, THE CHRIST, IS THE SAME YESTERDAY AND TODAY, YEA AND FOREVER.

It was noonday in an eastern city.

The sun beat hot on roof and street.

Between the low, square, white houses the air throbbed and quivered with heat.

The little lake that laved the eastern borders of the town lay smooth as a pool of oil.

Like the gentle breathing of one asleep, a drowsy hum rose and fell, the very echo of stillness.

Sound, motion, and life itself seemed lulled to slumber.

The fishermen dozed among their nets on the beach.

The traders slumbered in the market-places.

Beggars lay inert in their rags along the walls.

On a wayside resting-place sat a woman.

Every line of her limp figure told of weakness and utter weariness.

Her wasted, worn hands, and her much-mended garments, confessed a struggle with poverty by one once accustomed to ease and plenty.

She had been to the market-place and should have been home long ago, but oh, she was so weak, and the way seemed so long! It seemed longer, dustier, and hotter every day, now, and her little basket seemed to grow heavier and heavier. Her pale face was drawn with pain. In her beautiful, dark eyes there was that pathetic cloud of sadness that gathers through years of physical suffering.

Of late there had begun to come into them, at times, that other look, so terrible to see—Despair. In her heart was an anguish even more poignant than that which racked her body.

Hope was gone!

She felt that, after a few more months of growing misery, she must die.

She wanted to live.

The pale, anxious face of her husband rose before her.

How could she leave him now?

She seemed to feel the warm clasp of the tiny, helpless fingers of her children, trying to draw her back from the Dark Valley.

The pain tightened around her heart until she could not bear it, and turned her thoughts to the strange story she had heard in the market-place a few days before.

A young Teacher had been in the city, calling the people to repent of their sins, and healing them of their diseases.

Some of her townspeople had been healed, one of them the servant of the Centurion of the garrison.

These stories had lightened her heart with a gleam of hope.

MRS. IRENA D. JOINER.

If she could but see Him!

But they said that He had gone across the lake.

She had spent her all, in the twelve years of her illness, upon physicians, and could not afford even a few pence for passage across the lake, that she might follow Him.

He might not come back.

Even if He did, she was too weak to seek Him.

She leaned her head against the stones of the wall and closed her eyes.

It was a gesture of exhaustion.

As she waited for the rallying of her little remaining strength her ear caught a strange sound, breaking the noonday stillness.

It swelled in volume and drew nearer.

At first she was too sad and tired to look.

But there seemed to be a crowd coming up the narrow street toward her.

At last she could hear a voice she knew, and slowly she opened her eyes to see what her proud neighbor, the Ruler Jairus, was doing on the street in the midst of a throng, at this hour of the day.

He seemed greatly distressed, and his deep voice broke as he spoke.

But she was so weak that even this unwonted scene did not rouse her, and she was about to close her eyes again, when suddenly she sat erect, all languor gone.

Who was He, that Stranger to whom Jairus was talking?

She forgot Jairus.

She forgot the throng.

She forgot herself and her pains.

She had eyes and thought only for Him.

Who was He?

His elastic step, His powerfully-knit but graceful, erect figure, His clean, steady hands, His resolute chin and perfectly-controlled lips, all betokened unusual strength of physique and character.

His brow was high and broad. His skin, although darkened by exposure, was aglow with the health and vigor of a man of simple diet and clean habits.

But the expression of that face and the unspeakable majesty of the eyes were what had chained her attention.

Was there ever such Purity, Intelligence, Fearlessness, and Nobility of countenance?

Surely many generations of truly royal blood must flow in His veins!

Was there ever such Tenderness, Compassion, Humility, and Love depicted on any human face, or shining out of any human eyes?

He was barely past thirty, but there sat upon Him a quiet dignity that commanded the respect of all in that crowd, of even the proud ruler, Jairus.

And yet there was a genuine friendship and brotherliness that made the throng press close to Him.

In the presence of that Divine Sinlessness, she felt the defilement of her sins, and shrank from His gaze.

Who could He be?

The voices of the multitude fell unheeded on her ears, when suddenly one Name disentangled itself from the confusion with startling clearness.

"Jesus!"

Instantly she started up.

That was the Name she had heard in the market-place—the Name of the Wonder-working Teacher.

Like a revelation, the Truth flashed upon her spirit.

This must be the promised Messiah!

No other than the very Son of God could do such mighty works or show so spotless a character.

"Oh, that I might ask Him to heal me!" she cried.

He had already passed, and she dreaded to delay Him, fearing also the rebukes of the ruler Jairus and the gruff fishermen who accompanied Him.

Yet she *must* get to Him and be healed.

Leaving her basket, she hurriedly pushed her way through the crowd, saying over and over again in her heart, "If I do but touch His garment, I shall be saved whole."

At last she stood in the throng immediately behind Him.

Furtively, timidly, swiftly, she bowed and pressed the blue border of His beautiful, seamless robe to her lips.

A wonderful thing happened!

Instantly she felt an electric thrill in her body and unwonted strength in her limbs.

Her pain was gone!

She stood erect!

The healthful beauty she had known years before again glowed in her face!

Inexpressible joy filled her heart, and she could scarce refrain from shouting aloud.

But her joy was soon turned into panting terror; for she heard a Voice, vibrant with Divine virility and strength, "Who touched Me?"

At first she tried to hide in the crowd, hoping for escape, as she heard Peter, the fisherman, incredulously ask, "Thou seest the multitude thronging Thee and sayest Thou, 'Who touched Me?'"

But His eye was upon her and she saw in it naught but Divine Love.

So, still trembling, she fell down before Him and, in the presence of all the people, declared her miraculous healing.

As she briefly related her story, those wondrous eyes kindled with keenest sympathy, and His Voice grew very tender as He said:

"Daughter,"—it was the Father in Him who had done the work and now spoke—"Daughter, thy Faith hath saved thee whole; go in Peace, and be whole of thy plague."

That was in Capernaum, on the Lake of Galilee, nearly nineteen hundred years ago.

Four years and six months ago, a woman lay dying in San Jose, California.

She, too, had "suffered many things of many physicians, and had been nothing bettered, but rather grew worse."

She, too, longed to live for her beloved children, but was weary, so weary!

She, too, was hopeless, despairing.

To her came messengers of Zion.

Their Message was:

"Jesus, the Christ, is the same yesterday and today, yea and forever.

"His loving heart is moved by the same compassion.

"His Word has still its ancient Power.

"He still longs to heal all those who are weary and heavily laden with pain and sickness."

She believed.

She accepted His promise:

"Lo I am with you all the Days, even unto the Consummation of the Age."

The Healing of His Seamless Dress was by her bed of pain.

She touched its border by the Prayer of Faith.

Instantly she felt the thrill of Healing Virtue flow through her body.

In her heart she heard the loving words:

"Daughter, thy faith hath saved thee whole; go in Peace, and be whole of thy plague."

She now tells the wondrous story to all the world through the pages of LEAVES OF HEALING.

She tells it to you, weary sufferer

Will you learn its lesson? A. W. N.

WRITTEN TESTIMONY OF MRS. IRENA D. JOINER.

837 PREVOST STREET, SAN JOSE, CALIFORNIA, October 3, 1904.

DEAR FIRST APOSTLE:—I gladly send my testimony to the wonderful healing I received in March, 1900, four years and six months ago.

I praise God for raising me out of a bed of disease, despair, and death; also for the Full Gospel of Salvation, Healing, and Holy Living, taught in LEAVES OF HEALING.

In 1886 we lived in South Dakota.

After the birth of my daughter I had an abscess on my left lung. Dr. Peterman said that I must go to a warmer climate if I wanted to live.

We came to National City, California, in 1887.

The change did not help me. I coughed terribly.

We then went to Sacramento, but I became worse, coughing continually, and having severe pains in my heart and lungs. It felt sometimes like the pricking of a needle.

I gave up and went to bed.

Dr. Ewing was called in, who said I had womb trouble and that both of my lungs were diseased.

He said that we must keep my lungs poulticed all winter, and that I must take Scott's Emulsion.

I was in bed two years with this attack.

Dr. Ewing told my family that I had consumption and would not live long, and advised us to go to East Oakland, where the climate was better.

We did so, and I improved for a little while; but when winter came on I had hemorrhages of the lungs.

We were there about a year, when for business reasons we went to San Francisco, California.

We lived there five years.

In 1894, I was stricken down one day with terrible pain.

We called in Dr. Tanner, who lived in the same block. He gave me injections of morphine.

The pain was stopped, but I was thrown into a chill. I was so cold it seemed that I was paralyzed.

When the doctor saw the condition I was in he advised us to send for our family physician, Dr. Miller.

We did so, and he consulted with Dr. McCraith.

I had to undergo the tortures of an operation. I was able to be up and walk about the house after this, but suffered more than I had before.

I took treatment twice a week, but coughed continually.

Words failed to express all I suffered.

Dr. Miller and Dr. McCraith said that I had consumption and catarrh of the womb.

My stomach and heart were very weak.

My breath became so short and I was so weak, I frequently was compelled to sit down to keep from falling.

My pulse seemed to stop. My limbs were swollen, and I had muscular rheumatism.

These doctors had no hope for my recovery, but God spared my life.

We moved to San Jose, California, and the health of my youngest child, which had always been poor, improved, but I grew worse.

I was so ill that we called in Dr. Goss, one of the leading physicians here.

She plainly told me she could do nothing for me. She advised me not to take medicine, saying that it could not reach my case.

She visited me over a year. Then we called in Dr. Habersell.

He treated me from 1898 to 1900. He was very kind, and tried hard to do something for me, but without success.

Four years ago last Christmas, the cough was very heavy, and so violent that I begged for something to relieve me.

Dr. Habersell called in Dr. Goss for consultation. They said they could do nothing for me; the cough was so stubborn that they could not break it up.

They bade me good-by, and left me in despair to die.

I had known for some time that I was not expected to live, and had had my burial clothes made. Still I was not resigned to go and leave my seven children without a mother.

I had not been able to walk across the room or dress myself alone for many months.

I had night sweats, and could not sleep.

I lay there trying to think, my brain aching, and my body racked with pain until it seemed as though I would lose my mind. But, praise God, there was light ahead!

In that dark hour there came a rap on my door. God's messengers had come to tell me, "Jesus, the Christ, is the same yesterday and today, yea and forever."

Zion Seventies had come to give me a knowledge of Salvation, Healing, and Holy Living. They were Mrs. Byler and Mrs. Klein.

Mrs. Byler told me that I need not lie there and suffer; that our God for the Christ's sake would heal me; that I had only a little life left, but that the Christ would give me life abundant, if I would repent and make things right in my life.

It was new to me and very hard to understand at first.

I had belonged to the Methodist Church, and they teach that God afflicts His people to humble them, and draw them closer to Him; but it had not drawn me nearer, for I had gone away from God.

Mrs. Byler told me that disease came from the Devil, and that Jesus came to destroy the works of the Devil.

I did repent; but I thought that I was not good enough to be healed.

They read God's Word and prayed with me, and gave me LEAVES OF HEALING, urging me to read it.

I did so, and there came a gleam of hope into my heart.

Oh, how I prayed that God would spare my life to bring up my children!

I read the Bible with new interest, hunting up all the passages referred to in LEAVES OF HEALING.

My cough was better after the first prayer; but still I had fear in my heart, for I had not obeyed fully.

I had promised to throw out the medicine, but the Devil told me to let it stand on the dresser, and if I was healed, I could then throw it out.

When the sisters came again they asked if I had thrown out the medicine. When I answered "No," they said that I could not get complete victory until I made full surrender.

Then I let go of everything, determined to trust God only.

Mrs. Byler read Mark, 16th chapter, 15th to 20th verse; also Matthew, 18th chapter, 19th to 21st verse. Then they prayed for me.

I asked God to take the fear out of my heart.

I felt the power of God go through my body.

I then lay down and slept sweetly for some hours, the first time I had been able to do so in many months.

I was up a while every day after this; and in two weeks from the first visit of the Zion sisters I was helped into a buggy and taken to the Zion meeting.

Brother Byler, who was Conductor of the Gathering at that time, prayed for and anointed me in the Name of the Lord. Praise God, the Prayer of Faith was answered!

In a short time I was doing the work of our large family—washing, cooking and baking—something I had not been able to do for fifteen years.

At the time of my healing I weighed one hundred seventeen pounds. I now weigh one hundred forty-five pounds.

The year after my healing I camped out in the country with my children, and walked three miles a day, and worked most of the time.

I had not been able to walk more than a block at a time without severe pain and hard breathing for twelve years.

There are hundreds who know that I was raised up from a death-bed.

I have just returned from the fruit-fields where I worked with my children. I rode out seven miles every morning and back at evening.

My healing was recorded in LEAVES OF HEALING, Volume XI., No. 11, July 5, 1902, page 372.

I praise God for restoring my health, and I thank the First Apostle for the teaching we receive in LEAVES OF HEALING.

I trust these words may be a blessing to some poor suffering creature, such as I was.

Yours in the Master's service,

(MRS.) IRENA D. JOINER.

CONFIRMATION OF TESTIMONY BY MRS. MYRA A. CORDER.

978 SOUTH TENTH STREET,
SAN JOSE, CALIFORNIA.

DEAR FIRST APOSTLE:—I wish to confirm the testimony of Mrs. Irena Joiner.

She lived next door to us for some years. She lived there at the time of her healing in 1900.

I visited her daily for some time before her healing.

I know she had Drs. Goss and Habersell treat her. They could do nothing for her. They told her familiy she had consumption, and gave her up to die.

She was discouraged, and had lost all hope, when the Zion sisters visited her.

I know that she was healed when Brother Byler prayed and anointed her.

She has retained her healing four years, for which we praise God.

Yours in His service,

(MRS.) MYRA A. CORDER.

A WEEKLY PAPER FOR THE EXTENSION OF THE KINGDOM OF GOD.

EDITED BY
JOHN ALEXANDER, First Apostle of the Lord Jesus, the Christ, in the Christian Catholic Apostolic Church in Zion.

Application for entry as Second Class Matter at Zion City, Illinois, pending.

Subscription Rates.		Special Rates.	
One Year	$2.00	100 Copies of One Issue	$3.00
Six Months	1.25	25 Copies of One Issue	1.00
Three Months	.75	To Ministers, Y. M. C. A's and Public Reading Rooms, per annum	1.50
Single Copies	.05		

For foreign subscriptions add $1.50 per year, or three cents per copy for postage.
Subscribers desiring a change of address should give present address, as well as that to which they desire LEAVES OF HEALING sent in the future.
Make Bank Drafts, Express Money or Postoffice Money Orders payable to the order of JOHN ALEX. DOWIE, Zion City, Illinois, U. S. A.
Long Distance Telephone. *Cable Address "Dowie, Zion City."*
All communications upon business must be addressed to
MANAGER ZION PUBLISHING HOUSE,
Zion City, Illinois, U. S. A.

Subscriptions to LEAVES OF HEALING, A VOICE FROM ZION, and the various publications may also be sent to
ZION PUBLISHING HOUSE, 81 EUSTON ROAD, LONDON, N. W., ENGLAND.
ZION PUBLISHING HOUSE, NO. 43 PARK ROAD, ST. KILDA, VICTORIA, AUSTRALIA.
ZION PUBLISHING HOUSE, 76 BAHNHOFSTRASSE, ZÜRICH, SWITZERLAND.

ZION CITY, ILLINOIS, SATURDAY, OCTOBER 15, 1904.

TABLE OF CONTENTS.

LEAVES OF HEALING, SATURDAY, OCTOBER 15, 1904.

EDITORIAL NOTES.

"ZION HEARD AND WAS GLAD."

WE HAVE two Announcements to make about Zion in Chicago, which we know will afford much pleasure.

The first is that we have determined to reopen Central Zion Tabernacle, 1621–1633 Michigan Avenue, Chicago.

We have taken another lease of the building which we relinquished on the expiration of our five years' lease, on December 31, 1901.

MANY OF our readers will remember that we reconstructed the interior of the building at a cost of about Thirty Thousand Dollars; filling it with seats from the floor to the roof, thus providing accommodation for over three thousand persons.

LONG BEFORE the expiration of our lease we were crowded out of the building for our General Assemblies on the Lord's Day Afternoons.

We then leased the great Chicago Auditorium, and held the Assemblies there from 1901 to 1903.

BEFORE OUR removal to Zion City, in March, 1902, we moved our Chicago Headquarters to the South Side Zion Tabernacle, which has a capacity of nearly three thousand people, at 6426-6434 Wentworth Avenue.

This building we have found very inconvenient for our Central Ecclesiastical Purposes in Chicago, and have accordingly relinquished our lease of it, in order to resume the occupancy of Central Zion Tabernacle, which is a much superior building, and better adapted as the Center of Zion's Work in Chicago.

LET IT be remembered that, notwithstanding the establishment of Zion City and the erection of Shiloh Tabernacle, which seats over seven thousand, we have never relinquished our work in Chicago.

We have always had a number of large and convenient Zion Tabernacles permanently used for Zion work, on the North, West, and South Sides of the city, besides many Cottage Meetings.

But no building that we ever used in Chicago has more precious memories than Central Zion Tabernacle, where mighty outpourings of the Spirit of God have taken place.

Multitudes have there been saved, and healed, and blessed. Many thousands of our people can say, "I was born there."

IT WILL take some time to renovate both the exterior and the interior of the building and to refurnish it.

The owner has not been able to make any use of it since we relinquished it nearly three years ago, and it has suffered much in consequence.

We shall hope, however, to be able to put it in excellent order, and to reopen it before the end of the year.

WE GIVE a large picture of the exterior of Central Zion Tabernacle, Chicago, on page 911.

We shall keep the matter before our friends, from time to time, in LEAVES OF HEALING.

WE EARNESTLY ask our friends far and near to pray for this Reopening in Chicago.

It will cost many thousands of dollars to reseat, repair, and put the Tabernacle in order. We give this opportunity, to those who have precious memories connected with it especially, to send to us, as the Lord enables them, contributions towards the Reopening Fund.

OUR SECOND ANNOUNCEMENT is that, God willing, we shall reopen Zion Building, corner of Twelfth Street and Michigan Avenue, Chicago.

We had our Headquarters Offices there for nearly eight years.

It was closed only last winter.

AS MANY of our readers know, we own Zion Building, but not the land upon which it is built; of which we took a lease in 1900 for ninety-nine years.

WE SHALL devote the ground floor of Zion Building to the Chicago Offices of our various Industries, and shall also make permanent exhibits there of Zion City manufactures of various kinds.

IT IS our present purpose to let the rest of the Building out as Business Offices to a carefully-selected class of tenants.

IT WILL take some time to repaint the exterior, and to make certain alterations in the interior necessary to adapt it to this purpose.

These changes we hope to be able to complete in a month or two.

WE DIRECT attention to the picture of this Building, which will be found on page 912.

Many glorious memories are connected with its occupancy.

It was used as a Zion Divine Healing Home for a number of years.

Many mighty Miracles of Healing were wrought therein, and many were spiritually blessed.

The Record of many of these Events has appeared during the last eight years in the pages of LEAVES OF HEALING.

THE CONTINUALLY increasing interest in the work of Zion in Chicago, and the intense desire of many thousands to hear us as frequently as possible in that city, has led us to reopen Central Zion Tabernacle.

The officers and members of the Christian Catholic Apostolic Church in Zion will put forth their energies in Chicago more effectually from that point, and it will be especially a center for the work of Zion Restoration Host all over the great city.

IT IS our present intention to go in from Zion City with a number of officers, a portion of our large Choir, Orchestra and Band, and a large number of Restorationists at least once, and possibly twice, in every month.

Occasionally it may be more frequently.

THE DEMAND for Zion Products, and the continual extension of Zion's Business in Chicago, has led to the reopening of Zion Building.

We had been desirous to dispose of it for some time.

It now seems to be the Providence of God which has left the building still in our hands.

WE SHALL, in an early issue, make a number of important announcements concerning Branch Offices in various other parts of Chicago, where Zion Products can now be purchased.

Two important Business Centers have been secured, one on the North Side, and the other in the heart of "the Downtown" district.

WE REJOICE to know that Zion Manufactures are in demand among Chicago merchants and people.

We are doing a trade in Chicago of many thousands of dollars monthly in the attractive and useful productions of Zion Lace Industries, Zion Sugar and Confection Association, and various products of departments of Zion Building and Manufacturing Association.

WE ASK our readers again to pray for us in connection with these important new departures.

DURING THE last few weeks, the Rev. John G. Speicher, Overseer of the Christian Catholic Apostolic Church in Zion for Zion City, has been, as most of our readers are aware, working and resting in Europe.

IN ACCORDANCE with our directions, he has visited many portions of Switzerland, and established the work more permanently in many parts of that Republic.

In Budapest, Hungary, in Berlin, Germany, and in Paris, France, he has installed the Elders and Evangelists who accompanied him from Zion City in July last, and some who were working in Zion Branches in other parts of Europe.

WE SHALL, in due time, publish an Account of the travels of the Overseer, and of the work done by him in Europe during the last few months.

HE HAS also visited Constantinople, the capital of the Turkish Empire.

About the time of his visit there, a servant of the Sultan, that God had blessed through our agency, came to Zion City, to study in Zion College.

OVERSEER SPEICHER will have many interesting items of information to impart in his reports, which have, as yet, been very brief.

ALL ZION will rejoice to know that his beloved wife, Elder Abigail T. Speicher, is in very much better health than when she left America.

God sent to them a dear little Zion daughter, at the "Zionheim," Schloss-Liebburg, Canton Thurgau, Switzerland, on September 29th.

We love to welcome the children.

May God bless this Daughter of Zion born in lovely Switzerland.

EXCELLENT REPORTS continue to reach us from Zion in all parts of the world, and especially from Africa and Australia.

IN THIS connection we desire to say that our General Associate Editor has been unable to prepare the article which we hoped to have published in this issue, upon Zion in Australia, owing to a very great pressure of work.

We hope, however, that he will be able to find time to get the material together at an early date, and that it will be published soon.

THE PRESSURE of Work at Headquarters in Zion City is always so great, and history is being made so rapidly in Zion all over the World, that it is difficult to find time to write up for LEAVES OF HEALING the voluminous record of any particular portion of the work.

Indeed, the Progress is so constant and rapid, that we have considerable difficulty, even at Headquarters, in keeping up to date with the Story of Zion in all lands.

MANY IMPORTANT private conferences have been held by us concerning the important work before us in the construction of Shiloah Tabernacle.

We have taken some important preliminary steps, with a view to setting about the work on improved plans.

IT WILL be readily understood that the construction of so large a building, planned to seat sixteen thousand persons, is a task of considerable magnitude.

It is most important for us to be thoroughly satisfied that we are going about such a work in the best, and yet most economical, manner within our power.

WE HAVE arranged for the construction of a short branch line, or spur, of railway from Zion Printing and Publishing House on Deborah Avenue, Zion City, to the Lake Front, so that we may be able to bring up sand and gravel in very large quantities, and very quickly.

This will be built immediately, and connect with the spur line which was recently constructed from the Main Line of the Chicago & North-Western Railway to the foundations of the New Shiloah Tabernacle, on the northwest side of Shiloh Park.

WE HAVE determined to construct the new Tabernacle, as far as possible, of concrete, and to utilize the beautiful sand and gravel which for two and a half miles lie along the Lake-shore Front of Zion City.

WE DIRECT attention to the important discourse which we delivered on last Lord's Day on "The Nation's Choice of a President, and National Duties and Policies in the Light of Theocratic Principles."

It was listened to by an audience of about Six Thousand persons, with intense interest, and was apparently approved by all present.

LAST LORD'S Day Morning, as will be seen by the report on pages 903 to 907, we began a series of discourses on the 25th chapter of Matthew—the Parables of the Ten Virgins and of the Ten Talents, and the Judgment of All Nations by the Son of Man as King over All.

WE ALSO call attention to the announcement on page 913 of our Apostolic and Prophetic Message for tomorrow afternoon, at the General Assembly in Zion City.

It will, if God permit, be the first of a Series of Messages on the "Responsibilities, Powers, and Duties of the Apostolic Office."

Tomorrow's Message is entitled, "The Exercise of Apostolic Powers Essential to the Establishment of the Rule of God in Church and State."

BRETHREN, PRAY FOR US.

By Evangelist Sarah E. Hill.

GOD SAID: "If thou wilt diligently harken to the Voice of Jehovah thy God, and wilt do that which is right in His eyes, and wilt give ear to His Commandments, and keep all His Statutes, I will [permit to be] put none of the diseases upon thee which I have [permitted to be] put upon the Egyptians: for I am Jehovah that healeth thee."—*Exodus 15:26.*

GOD here tells us how to get healed of diseases, and how to keep healed.

He announces Himself to the world as Jehovah that heals.

This is the Covenant of Salvation, Healing, and Holy Living, which He gave His ancient Israel when He brought them out of Egypt to form them into a Nation to be ruled by Himself—a Theocracy.

A covenant is a compact or agreement between two parties by which one obligates himself to do certain things if the other will fulfil certain conditions

The first requirement which God makes of man is to harken diligently to His Voice.

Man is in a world where there are many voices calling to him to turn aside from the straight and narrow way that leads to Eternal Life.

It is a still, small Voice that speaks to man from the depths of his being, this Voice of God, and unless he listens diligently he may not always hear it when other voices are calling to him from the World, the Flesh, and the Devil.

It is man's spiritual being that is to listen to God's Voice, and, if he listens diligently, the Rule of God will be established in his spirit.

The next requirement is that man shall do what is right in God's eyes.

By nature he loves to do what is right in his own eyes.

It is not sufficient for man to listen to God's Voice; he must *do* what God requires of him.

Many who know what God demands of them refuse to obey.

It is through his body that man is enabled to do; and when he uses his bodily powers in doing what is right, then God will reign in his body.

Then he will not dare defile his body with medicine, alcohol, or tobacco; nor eat food which God has pronounced unclean, because it produces disease. (Deuteronomy 14:8.)

Neither will he defile his body by bad habits, because God declares that it is His Temple and must be kept pure. (1 Corinthians 3:16, 17.)

The third clause in the Covenant requires man to give ear to God's Commandments.

It is the soul of man that uses the outward ear, and through it, it can be taught the Commandments of God.

God will reign in the soul of man when it gives ear to His Commandments.

Children should be taught God's commands.

He commanded His ancient people, saying, "And ye shall teach them your children, talking of them, when thou sittest in thine house, and when thou walkest by the way, and when thou liest down, and when thou risest up." (Deuteronomy 11:19, 21.)

God says, this is to be done "that your days may be multiplied, and the days of your children."

God says His people are destroyed for lack of knowledge.

Yet the knowledge which would save them is in the Scriptures.

We are living in days of great peril, when the most subtle religious teaching and most dangerous practices abound under the cloak of religion

The dangers peculiar to these Latter Days beset our paths on every side.

These are all portrayed in the Scriptures as having great power in these Latter Days.

The teaching of Zion opens our eyes to the knowledge of what will injure spirit, soul, or body.

Zion teaching gives the foundation principles in religious truth, which enables those who live it to discern between error and truth.

Zion Literature is the best Commentary on the Bible, and it is sent forth by God, as He promised centuries ago it should be.

He promised to send it forth to combat the false religious teaching of this Age, and teach the Covenant to the world.

The keeping of the Covenant requires man's whole being.

When God sums up man's part of the Covenant, by demanding that he shall keep all His statutes, that requires man's entire being, and he can be saved, and healed, and enabled to live a holy life through the Christ dwelling in him.

This is the Covenant which Elijah, the Messenger of the Covenant, has been sent by God to teach to the world in these Latter Days. (Malachi 3:1; 4:5.)

It is the first step in the great work of the Restoration of All things, which the Lord said Elijah should come to do. (Matthew 17:10-14.)

He is that Prophet like unto Moses of whom the Apostle Peter said, "And it shall be, that every soul, which shall not harken to that Prophet, shall be utterly destroyed from among the people. (Acts 3:19-24.)

Those who will not harken to him shall be utterly destroyed, because the Covenant which he is sent to teach is the only thing that can preserve the people from destruction in the times which we are entering into.

To get the teaching of Zion into the hands of the nations of the world is the greatest work of the present hour, "the hour of trial, that hour which is to come upon the whole world, to try them that dwell upon the earth." (Revelation 3:10.)

Zion Literature is represented by the Little Book which the Apostle John saw in the hand of the Seventh Angel, or Messenger, and which the Apostle was commanded to take from the hand of the Messenger and eat up. (Revelation 10:2, 8-11.)

When he had eaten the Little Book he found that it was sweet in his mouth, but made his belly bitter.

The world is having this experience with Zion teaching today.

It goes against so much that the flesh has learned to love, that at first in digesting it by living it out, the flesh finds it bitter, but afterwards it yields the peaceable fruits of righteousness, and the bitter becomes so sweet that men are willing to die for the truths in the Full Gospel teaching of Zion.

They obtain such wonderful testimony through the blood of the Lamb that they love not their life even unto death. (Revelation 12:11.)

The teaching of the Covenant is the first step in the great Restoration work which shall finally restore the world and all things in it to their condition, as in the beginning, when they came from the hands of God, and He pronounced everything that He made good, very good.

Will you not take part in this wonderful work of sending Zion Literature over the world?

God calls on you to help.

Accept the Covenant and help others to do the same, if you desire to be blessed.

Zion Literature Sent Out from a Free Distribution Fund Provided by Zion's Guests and the Friends of Zion.

Report for three weeks ending October 8, 1904:

13,600 Rolls to..Business Men in the United States
7,400 Rolls to........................Germany
10,301 Rolls to...........the Hotels of the World
1,800 Rolls to...........the Peerage of Europe
1,382 Rolls to.....................Miscellaneous
Number of Rolls for three weeks...........34,483
Number of Rolls reported to Oct. 8, 1904, 3,409,965

THEODORE ROOSEVELT.

Apostolic and Prophetic Messages

By......

John Alexander

First Apostle

of the Lord Jesus, the Christ, in the Christian Catholic Apostolic Church in Zion.

MESSAGE NO. 2

Shiloh Tabernacle

Lord's Day Afternoon,

October 9, 1904.

SUBJECT:

The Nation's Choice of a Pres...ent; and National Duties and Policies in the Light of Theocratic Principles.

*REPORTED BY O. L. S., A. C. R., S. E. C., AND A. W. N.

"RELIGION must keep out of politics!"

This is the cry of cowards, trimmers, and hypocrites in both politics and religion.

A religion that does not enter the realm of politics is either false or dead, or both.

Politics that is not controlled by True Religion is either corrupt or powerless.

The religion of our Lord Jesus, the Christ, is pure, strong, vigorous, and as broad in its scope as human life itself.

Hence the First Apostle of the Lord Jesus, the Christ, in the Christian Catholic Apostolic Church in Zion, sent of God to lead His people, leads them Politically as well as Ecclesiastically, Educationally, and Commercially.

He teaches them that one of the highest and holiest relations of life is Citizenship.

This, he points out, has been dragged in the mire of inaction and corruption by the weakness, cowardice, and greed of those who whine or bluster that "religion must keep out of politics."

He boldly defies envious and frightened criticism, and makes Good Citizenship essential to Righteousness.

Not an emasculated abstraction, inoffensively couched in trite platitudes!

Not a lazy harmlessness, showing only negative virtues!

His Leadership in this, as in all other things, is intensely practical, definite, positive, and aggressive.

He declares that an important duty of Citizenship is Voting.

He goes further.

He tells his people how to vote, and why.

So important a part of Practical Righteousness does he regard this, that he gave the entire afternoon service on Lord's Day, October 9, 1904, to a discussion of "The Nation's Choice of a President; and National Duties and Policies in the Light of Theocratic Principles."

Like everything Zion does, this was done thoroughly and with a joyous enthusiasm on the part of both speaker and hearers that spoke eloquently of Spiritual Power.

Patriotism as a calm, orderly but happy Christian virtue, was illustrated in the splendid music of Zion City Band and in the stirring spiritual singing of Zion White-robed Choir.

The Message of the First Apostle was clear-cut, witty, charitable toward those who disagreed, but caustically severe with error and hypocrisy, and, above all, convincingly logical.

God's Messenger began with the fundamental Theocratic Principle of the Rule of God, the establishment of which is the political purpose of Zion.

He proceeded with the statement of the position of the Theocratic Party with reference to Prohibition candidates who could not be elected and only took votes away from the better of the other two candidates, one of whom was sure of election.

He demonstrated the Righteousness, Justice, and Economic and Civic Soundness of salient Republican Principles, but declared his independence of the Republican party.

He warned of danger through the political heresies of Democratic candidates.

He closed with a tribute to the character and record of Theodore Roosevelt, the honest, unbiased but loving appreciation of one brave, conscientious man of God for another.

Every word of this important Message was eagerly received by the great audience of about six thousand people, many of whom were visitors in the City from Chicago and other outside places.

At the close of the Message a "straw vote" was taken.

As far as could be seen, it was heartily unanimous in favor of Theodore Roosevelt, the choice of the Republican and Theocratic parties for President of the United States.

Then the entire service was crowned with a ringing, spirited singing of "America," rising to its significant climax in the last two lines—

Protect us by Thy might,
GREAT GOD, OUR KING

Shiloh Tabernacle, Zion City, Illinois, Lord's Day Afternoon, October 9, 1904.

The service was opened by Zion White-robed Choir and Zion Robed Officers entering the Tabernacle, singing as they came the words of the

PROCESSIONAL.

O Zion, haste, thy mission high fulfilling,
To tell to all the world that God is Light;
That He who made all nations is not willing
One soul should perish, lost in shades of night.

REFRAIN—Publish glad tidings, tidings of peace,
Tidings of Jesus, redemption and release.

Behold how many thousands still are lying
Bound in the darksome prison-house of sin,
With none to tell them of the Savior's dying,
Or of the life He died for them to win.

Proclaim to every people, tongue, and nation,
That God, in whom they live and move, is Love:
Tell how He stooped to save His lost creation,
And died on earth that man might live above.

Give of thy sons to bear the Message glorious;
Give of thy wealth to speed them on their way;
Pour out thy soul for them in pray'r victorious;
And all thou spendest Jesus will repay.

He comes again: O Zion, ere thou meet Him,
Make known to every heart His saving grace;
Let none whom He hath ransomed fail to greet Him,
Thro' thy neglect, unfit to see His face.

At the close of the Processional, the First Apostle came upon the platform, the people rising and standing with bowed heads while he pronounced the

INVOCATION.

God be merciful unto us and bless us,
And cause Thy face to shine upon us;
That Thy Way may be known upon earth,
Thy Saving Health among all the Nations,
For the sake of Jesus. Amen.

The Congregation and Choir then sang Hymn No. 116, from Gospel Hymns:

There's a royal banner given for display
To the soldiers of the King;
As an ensign fair we lift it up today,
While as ransomed ones we sing.

CHORUS—Marching on! Marching on!
For Christ count ev'rything but loss;
And to crown Him King, toil and sing,
Beneath the banner of the cross.

Overseer Brasefield then led the people in the recitation of the Apostles' Creed:

RECITATION OF CREED.

I believe in God, the Father Almighty,
Maker of heaven and earth:
And in Jesus, the Christ, His only Son, our Lord,
Who was conceived by the Holy Ghost:
Born of the Virgin Mary;
Suffered under Pontius Pilate;
Was crucified, dead, and buried:
He descended into hell,
The third day He rose from the dead;
He ascended into heaven,
And sitteth on the right hand of God, the Father Almighty;
From thence He shall come to judge the quick and the dead
I believe in the Holy Ghost;
The Holy Catholic Church;
The Communion of Saints;
The Forgiveness of Sins;
The Resurrection of the body,
And the Life Everlasting. Amen.

READING OF GOD'S COMMANDMENTS.

Overseer Excell then led in the recitation of the Commandments, the Choir and Congregation reverently chanting the response, "Lord, have mercy upon us, and incline our hearts to keep this law."

READING OF GOD'S COMMANDMENTS.

I. Thou shalt have no other gods before Me.

II. Thou shalt not make unto thee a graven image, nor the likeness of any form that is in heaven above, or that is in the earth beneath, or that is in the water under the earth; thou shalt not bow down thyself unto them nor serve them: for I, Jehovah, thy God, am a jealous God, visiting the iniquity of the fathers upon the children, upon the third and upon the fourth generation of them that hate Me, and showing mercy unto thousands of them that love Me and keep My Commandments.

III. Thou shalt not take the Name of Jehovah thy God in vain; for Jehovah will not hold him guiltless that taketh His Name in vain.

IV. Remember the Sabbath Day, to keep it holy. Six days shalt thou labor and do all thy work; but the seventh day is a Sabbath unto Jehovah thy God: in it thou shalt not do any work, thou, nor thy son, nor thy daughter, thy manservant, nor thy maidservant, nor thy cattle, nor thy stranger that is within thy gates; for in six days Jehovah made heaven and earth, the sea, and all that in them is, and rested the seventh day: wherefore Jehovah blessed the Sabbath Day and hallowed it.

V. Honor thy father and thy mother; that thy days may be long upon the land which Jehovah thy God giveth thee.

VI. Thou shalt do no murder.

VII. Thou shalt not commit adultery.

VIII. Thou shalt not steal.

IX. Thou shalt not bear false witness against thy neighbor.

X Thou shalt not covet thy neighbor's house, thou shalt not covet thy neighbor's wife, nor his manservant, nor his maidservant, nor his ox, nor his ass, nor anything that is thy neighbor's.

Hear also what our Lord Jesus, the Christ, the Son of God, hath said, which may be called the Eleventh Commandment:

XI. A New Commandment I give unto you, that ye love one another; even as I have loved you, that ye also love one another.

The great Choir then sang the glorious

TE DEUM LAUDAMUS.

We praise Thee, O God; we acknowledge Thee to be the Lord.
All the earth doth worship Thee, the Father Everlasting.
To Thee all Angels cry aloud, the Heavens and all the powers therein.
To Thee Cherubim and Seraphim continually do cry:
Holy, Holy, Holy, Lord God of Sabaoth,
Heaven and earth are full of the majesty of Thy Glory.
The glorious company of the Apostles praise Thee.
The goodly fellowship of the Prophets praise Thee.
The noble army of martyrs praise Thee.
The Holy Church throughout all the world doth acknowledge Thee,
The Father of an Infinite Majesty;
Thine Adorable, True, and Only Son;
Also the Holy Ghost, the Comforter.
Thou art the King of Glory, O Christ;
Thou art the Everlasting Son of the Father.
When Thou tookest upon Thee to deliver man,
Thou didst humble Thyself to be born of a Virgin;
When Thou hadst overcome the sharpness of death,
Thou didst open the Kingdom of Heaven to all believers.
Thou sittest at the right hand of God in the Glory of the Father.
We believe that Thou shalt come to be our Judge.
We therefore pray Thee, help Thy servants,
Whom Thou hast redeemed with Thy precious blood.
Make them to be numbered with Thy saints in glory everlasting.
O Lord, save Thy people and bless Thine heritage;
Govern them and lift them up forever.
Day by day we magnify Thee;
And we worship Thy Name ever, world without end.
Vouchsafe, O Lord, to keep us this day without sin.
O Lord, have mercy upon us, have mercy upon us.
O Lord, let Thy mercy be upon us as our trust is in Thee.
O Lord, in Thee have I trusted, let me never be confounded.

The First Apostle then read the Scripture lesson from the 24th Psalm and the 60th chapter of Isaiah, after which he knelt at the Altar of Incense and offered Prayer, at the close of which he led the Choir and Congregation in chanting the Disciples' Prayer.

Overseer J. G. Excell then made the announcements.

The tithes and offerings were received while the Choir sang an anthem, "The Heavens Resound," after which a second anthem was sung.

THE NATION'S CHOICE OF A PRESIDENT; AND NATIONAL DUTIES AND POLICIES IN THE LIGHT OF THEOCRATIC PRINCIPLES.

The First Apostle then pronounced the

INVOCATION.

Let the words of my mouth and the meditations of my heart be acceptable in Thy sight, be profitable unto this people, in every State of this great Republic, and throughout the world, in every land, in all the coming time, as well as now. Till Jesus come.

The Word Theocratic Means the Rule of God.

In the 2d Book of Samuel, the 23d chapter, the first four verses, we read as follows:

TEXT.

Now these be the last words of David.
David the son of Jesse saith,
And the man who was raised on high saith,
The anointed of the God of Jacob,
And the sweet psalmist of Israel:
The Spirit of Jehovah spake by me,
And His Word was upon my tongue.
The God of Israel said,
The Rock of Israel spake to me:
One that ruleth over men righteously,
That ruleth in the fear of God,
He shall be as the light of the morning, when the sun riseth,
A morning without clouds;
When the tender grass springeth out of the earth,
Through clear shining after rain.

And in the book of Proverbs, the 14th chapter, the 34th verse:

Righteousness exalteth a nation:
But sin is a reproach to any people.

The subject of my address this afternoon is, "The Nation's Choice of a President; and National Duties and Policies in the Light of Theocratic Principles."

The word "Theocratic," to the majority of people, may need definition.

"Democratic" means the rule of the people.

"Autocratic," interpreted in the light of human history, means the rule of one tyrant, one monster, created by military or priestly usurpation, or by foolish law, and invested with absolute power.

But the word "Theocratic" does not seem to be so well understood.

It is the Rule of God.

It is made up of two Greek words—"*Theos*" (θεός) meaning God, and "*crateo*" (κρατέω) signifying to rule.

We speak today concerning the Nation's Choice of a President, and those duties and policies which are essential to the welfare of America at this time, according to the light of Theocratic Principles.

The Responsibility of Persons of Influence at the Present Time.

It is exceedingly important at this time that whoever in any public position has the opportunity and power to influence his fellow men, shall do so in a manner that will be pleasing to God.

Nothing can be more contemptible than talking merely for the exaltation of the talker or of the party for which he talks.

The life of a nation is far too serious a matter to be the subject of barroom chatter, or of a game of political battledore and shuttlecock by professional tricksters.

It is too important to be made the mere pastime of a moment; and the election of officials should not be looked upon as a new shuffle for a deal of cards.

That is how it is looked at by many; and the majority of politicians in all nations have become very much like a pack of cards; they have been very much shuffled.

The more they are shuffled the dirtier they get.

They are willing to be shuffled by the hands of the people; and accept any kind of a deal that the people choose to make.

We are speaking today of politics from the standpoint of those who believe, not in the rule of man, but in the Rule of God in His own world.

I want to attack, in the most vigorous language, the false principle that this nation should be governed in a manner which is commonly described in these words, "Government of the people, by the people, and for the people."

I attack that definition of government as selfish, crude, and wrong in principle.

If I were to say to you that I believe in the government of John Alexander Dowie, by John Alexander Dowie, and for John Alexander Dowie, you would say that John Alexander Dowie was an embodiment of selfishness; and you would be right.

National Selfishness Is Individual Selfishness Multiplied.

What is the difference when seventy or eighty million people say, "We believe in the Government of Ourselves, the people, by Ourselves, and for Ourselves?"

Instead of being one unit of selfishness, it is eighty million times that amount of selfishness.

The Theocratic Principle is not like the Democratic Principle which I have just attacked.

The Theocratic Principle is that we believe in the government of the people by God and for God.

We believe that man was made by God; made for God; and that the people can never be wisely governed so long as they claim the right to govern themselves apart from God and His Laws—to govern themselves, in fact, by Laws passed by a chance majority in the Legislatures.

Majorities in the Congress of the United States have, generation after generation, passed Bad Laws which cost this Nation long weary years of Civil War; and the tears are not yet wiped away, the wounds are not yet healed, which were caused by that bloody strife, ere the Bad Laws which made Slavery legal were expunged from the Statute Book.

How good it would have been had this Nation recognized the Christ's Declaration on the Law of God—"One is your Master, even the Christ, and all ye are Brethren."

This Universe is not governed by any such principle as that which I have denounced.

This Universe is governed by God, in accordance with Eternal Law; and men can never be wise so long as they demand the right to govern themselves by any passing whim, and call that Political Principle.

This is the issue which the Theocratic Party, represented by Zion, places before the whole world, as well as before the nation, today.

We boldly say that "He that ruleth over men must be just; ruling in the Fear of God;" and, therefore, when the people claim the right to elect their own rulers, they themselves must be guided by the Principle which should guide the ruler when elected, namely, the Rule of God.

The Application of the Theocratic Principle Is the Solution of the World's Troubles.

This is a Great Principle, and it will put to flight the selfishness and devilishness which finds expression in the wicked concentration of capital and intelligence for oppression, and in the wicked and diabolical concentration of labor for the purpose of thwarting and crushing capital, and hindering progress.

There can be no solution for the difficulties economic, moral, spiritual, and material—not only of America, but of the whole world today—until the Theocratic Principle is applied to the Individual, to the Home, to the City, to the State, to the Nation, and to all International Relationships.

The Rule of God in God's own world is the most logical rule of which we can conceive.

But the rule of man is too unreasonably stupid to talk about; the rule of man by man; the rule of the masses by the masses.

The masses of the people, even in Free America, today, are dissolute, drunken, and immoral.

They are not governed by God at all.

That is no railing accusation, because you see it before you every day.

You smell it everywhere!

Stinkpots who reek with nicotine poison, whisky, w.ne and beerpots, reeking with alcoholic poison; and all kinds of nasty pots, constitute the Body of Humanity in this sin-stricken and disease-smitten World wherein we mortals exist for a few short years.

The masses today are under the influence of narcotic and other deadly poisons with maddened brains, with beclouded thoughts, and utterly unable to take a calm and dispassionate view of any subject.

One might almost apply to them the words of Defoe, in his "True Born Englishman," when he says:

> Restraint from ill is Freedom to the wise!
> But Englishmen do all restraint despise.
> Slaves to the bottle, drudges to the pots,
> The mob are statesmen, and the statesmen sots;
>
> . . . .
>
> For drunkenness has been the darling of the realm,
> E'er since a Drunken Pilot had the helm.
>
> . . . .
>
> The laboring poor, in spite of double pay,
> Are saucy, mutinous and beggarly;
> So lavish of their money and their time,
> That want of foresight is the nation's crime.
> Good drunken company is their delight;
> And what they get by day they spend by night.

The Masses Are Unfitted to Rule Themselves.

That is not true of all—neither of this nor the English people, nor of our rulers—else the land would go to pieces from very rottenness.

But it is too true of multitudes in both nations.

It is a matter of great gratitude to God that in the Republic of the United States, although good people are in the minority as to numbers, they are always carefully listened to, and regarded with respect by the majority, when it comes to great National Policies and great National Elections; for, with all its faults, this Republic is not prepared to place in the Chair of the Executive an open evil-liver and a shameful infidel who tramples the laws of God beneath his feet.

May the time never come when this Nation shall be ready to put such a man there. [Amen.]

I bring no railing accusation against the majority when I say that the majority of the electors in the United States of America are drinkers of alcoholic liquors, and that a great many of them are drunkards and smokers, who poison their minds and destroy their capacity to think clearly by smoking, chewing,

John Alexander

First Apostle of the Lord Jesus, the Christ, in the Christian Catholic Apostolic Church in Zion.

and spewing nicotine poison, in the form of tobacco, which is a brain poison of the worst kind.

By other evil habits, by their immoralities, by their devotion to pleasure, so-called, the great mass of the people—who are not students, and do not think, and do not strive to understand the great principles of government—are unfitted to rule themselves.

But, after all, I am a citizen of a Republic which is the nearest to a Theocracy that I can find.

While the Theocratic Party declares that it believes the Constitution and Laws of the United States to be capable of amendment in a Theocratic direction, it also declares its loyalty to the Constitution and Laws of the United States.

We only ask the right which all men have under the Constitution, peaceably to agitate, and thus bring about a better condition of things by the education of the people in this righteous direction, and to get them to vote everywhere for God as the King of America. [Amen.]

The last word in our national anthem is "Great God, our King."

That there may be no mistake as to what the Principles of the Theocratic Party are, I will here give you the Platform adopted at the Convention held in Zion City on Monday, April 7, 1902, at which the Party was born:

The citizens of the City of Zion, Lake County, State of Illinois, being assembled in their First Convention, held in Zion City, on the night of Monday, April 7, 1902, for the purpose of nominating the first officers of their City, do so on a Theocratic Platform, and desire to set forth their position and their reasons for the formation of this new party in political affairs of the United States of America, in the manner following:

FIRST—We declare our loyalty to the Constitution and Laws of the United States of America.

SECOND—We affirm that both the Constitution and the Laws are capable of amendment and improvement in a Theocratic direction; and we simply propose to advocate the making of such alterations in the manner provided by the Laws of the United States.

THIRD—We declare the motto of our party to be the unalterable and unassailable truth that

WHERE GOD RULES, MAN PROSPERS.

FOURTH—Our object is, therefore, the establishment of the Rule of God in every department of Government, by the free will of the people.

FIFTH—We declare our conviction that the Holy Scriptures, which contain the Ten Commandments, and the inspired Gospel of Jesus, the Christ, the Son of God, constitute the principles of all righteous government for the individual, for the Nation, and for the whole World.

Zion Is Asking Only that a Recognized Principle be Embodied in Law and Practice.

We are not asking this people to endorse a new principle, but we are asking them to do something more than sing an old one.

We are asking them to act upon it; and to embody it in law and in the constitution of things.

The time will come when the kingdoms of this world and all republics shall become the Kingdom of our God and of His Christ; when the glad "Hallelujah" shall go up from land and sea; and when the angel choirs and the trumpets of heaven shall join with the choirs and trumpets of earth in the great song, "Hallelujah: for the Lord our God, the Almighty, reigneth, . . . and the kingdom of this world is become the Kingdom of our Lord, and of His Christ!"

This is the aim of the Theocratic Party, which I represent today, as its founder, and which finds expression in Zion everywhere.

We are the Party not of Today merely.

We are the Party of Tomorrow, and the Next Day, and of Eternity.

Therefore, no man can truthfully say that I am standing up for the Republican or for any other party, because we choose, as choose we must, to select the better of the two men, one of whom must win in this conflict. We have a right to give reasons for our choice, and if we endorse certain principles which are represented by the Republican party, we have a right to give reasons for that act.

At the same time we have a right to warn that party that we are perfectly independent, and that the very next moment after we have voted for the Republican, we are perfectly consistent, in accordance with our principle, to vote, upon local issues, for either a Democrat or a Prohibitionist, or any one else who will do the work that we believe God wants the man in that position to do. [Amen.]

With these preliminary remarks, I at once enter into the question; because I have a right to assume that the people committed to my care, as the First Apostle of the Christian Catholic Apostolic Church in Zion throughout this Republic, have a right to know how I feel and how I would direct them to exercise their franchise in the coming Presidential Election.

The First Apostle Refuses to Sacrifice the Votes of Zion.

I do not need to contend that there are only two persons who have any chance of being elected to the Presidency of the United States on November 8th next, because all other candidates are simply sacrificial lambs; or some may be better described as sacrificial goats.

I think that they are more goats than lambs.

All things being equal, as you know, I should personally wish to vote for the Prohibition candidate.

I do not know very much about Mr. Swallow, but I should be inclined to swallow him, and a great deal with him, if I thought he had the slightest chance of election.

But Mr. Swallow, and the people who will swallow him at the next election—I mean the people that intend to vote for him—are not wise.

I have been an abstainer from alcohol, and opium, and tobacco all my life; and I have voted them down every chance I could get, and fought for their extinction.

I joined the British League of Juvenile Abstainers in Edinburgh, Scotland, in 1853, if I remember correctly. I lost my first Pledge Card, and signed another in 1856, which I still have. I have kept that Pledge; and "Alcohol, Opium, and Tobacco" have, for more than fifty years, represented Satan in Solution, in Drug, or in Diabolical Fire. I have never compromised with the Devil at any time or in any form."

I have managed, by the grace of God, to found a City in which neither alcohol, opium, nor tobacco can be found so far as we know it; where they cannot be sold; and where they cannot be taken; nor any drug; nor a great many other things.

Mr. Swallow and his party have no right to suppose that I am voting for these things when I vote and direct my people to vote for Theodore Roosevelt and Charles W. Fairbanks.

I say, No!

Those Who Vote the Prohibition Ticket Vote for the Liquor Traffic.

But I say that all who vote the Prohibition ticket this fall will vote straight for the putting of the shackles of the liquor traffic upon this nation.

I do not need to tell you that, although there are many Prohibitionists among the Democrats in some of the Southern States, the "Tammany Tiger" and nearly all its brood, stink of liquor and tobacco in equal proportions, and you cannot have any difficulty in finding Tammany Hall in New York.

Go down into its neighborhood, follow the scent [laughter] and you will find Tammany Hall. [Laughter.]

The great majority of the liquor stores in this country are kept by Democrats; not that there are not a few of them kept by Republicans, and by others who belong to other parties, but the great majority of those that own and control breweries, and whisky manufactories, and saloons are to be found in the Democratic party.

You know one of the Democratic cries everywhere is, "Let the town be wide open."

One of their cries in New York is a demand for this so-called liberty—the liberty to let the "liquid fire and distilled damnation" flow, like a river, down the streets, with its horrid freight of sin, and disease, and death, sweeping multitudes into the Ocean of Despair.

I am very far from saying that the Republican party is the party of total abstinence or prohibition; but I know, and you know, that the Republican party, especially in the Northern States, is usually allied with those who desire to curb and even to destroy the liquor traffic

The First Apostle Believes in and Practices Prohibition.

It is a matter of extreme regret to me that I cannot cast a vote for the Prohibition candidate without imperiling the interests of this Nation, not only in connection with the liquor traffic, but in connection with many matters that are almost as important, if not in some things more important.

I say plainly to my friends who, like me, are prohibitionists, that there is no man in this country who is a more out-and-out prohibitionist than John Alexander, the First Apostle of the Christian Catholic Apostolic Church in Zion.

You cannot point to another place in the United States

where prohibition is wrought into the very soil as it is in Zion City.

I tell you who cast in my face, shamefully and wrongfully, the charge that I am voting and leading my people to vote for the saloons, that the imputation is absolutely false.

You may differ with me on the question of the candidate of my choice at the coming election, but you have no right to make a charge like that.

I know what I am doing.

I know that every vote cast for the Prohibition candidate, on November 8th, will be a vote for the Democratic party, for the whisky-mill, and against protection to American manufactures.

It will be a vote to close the factories all over the United States, to deprive millions of work and wages, and to stab to the heart the industrial, commercial, and financial prosperity of this Nation.

It will be a vote in the direction of a debased currency and a debased government.

I will not advise that course.

I am strong enough and brave enough to take the consequences of my advice and direction, believing I shall, in this matter, stand before God with clean hands.

Zion Does Not Seek for Government Office.

I have no interest, direct or indirect, in the liquor traffic.

I have no interest, direct or indirect, in the political offices which the Republican party may be able to bestow.

I have told the present President, and I told his predecessor, that Zion did not ask official appointments at his hands; for my instruction to my people was to avoid politics, in the way of becoming mere office-holders.

I said that it was my advice to my people to work outside of the Government Crib, and not to eat the Government Oats.

As far as I know, there is not one member of the Christian Catholic Apostolic Church in Zion who holds any municipal office outside of the City of Zion, or any Government office, or who is, in any degree, connected with party politics in any City of the United States.

If the Prohibitionists say that Zion, for some selfish interest, is backing the Republican party, then the Prohibitionists speak that which is not true.

They have no right to say it.

In doing so they break the Ninth Commandment of God, and bear "false witness" against their neighbor

It is false and shamefully false; and it is not the way to get me to favorably consider the Prohibition ticket.

The mere prohibition of the use of alcohol will not make this Nation good

The Mohammedans prohibit its use throughout Turkey, Persia, and a great part of India.

It is absolutely forbidden both by religion and law.

You will find no open saloons in Persia, Turkey, or a great part of India.

Hundreds of millions of men and women never touch intoxicating drinks, but that does not make them good; it does not make them pure, virtuous, or truly righteous, but, instead, more fanatical and more powerful in pushing their fanaticism.

They are without a saving knowledge of God in the Christ, and are the prey of many vices.

Mere Belief in Prohibition Does Not Constitute Fitness to Rule.

I tell you plainly that there are multitudes of men who shoulder the Prohibition banner, and shout for the Prohibition ticket, who are infidels through and through, and who are not to be trusted with the government of the people.

If they want illustrations, they can get them in large numbers.

I repudiate, and I throw back, the shameful insinuation that Zion, because she does not vote the Prohibition ticket, is in alliance with the powers of hell.

We are not; but I will tell you why Zion is advised and directed, as far as I have the power to advise and direct, to vote the Republican Presidential Ticket on November 8, 1904.

First of all, I do not believe in a party's claiming to be capable of ruling this Nation merely because it will prohibit intoxicating liquor.

That does not give it the right to rule the Nation.

There are two wings to that party now.

Am I to be a Silver Prohibitionist or a Gold Prohio...onist?

The fact of the matter is this, that party is not big enough nor broad enough.

The prohibition of intoxicating drink is not to be accomplished by the election—even if you could elect him—of a Prohibition president.

Why talk nonsense?

A President who is a prohibitionist, if he were elected, could not bring in prohibition even in the City of Washington, or in the District of Columbia.

The Presidential Office is not a legislative office nor a judicial office.

It is an Executive Office; and if a prohibitionist were in the Executive Chair, and the law said that people should be licensed to make and sell intoxicating liquor, the prohibitionist president would have to protect those who availed themselves of that law—distillers, brewers, saloon-keepers, etc.

Do you not see it?

No Prohibitionist could be a President of the United States without taking solemn oath that he would administer the laws and constitution of the United States as he found them.

Would he find them anti-liquor?

PEOPLE—"No."

FIRST APOSTLE—Could he alter them?

PEOPLE—"No."

FIRST APOSTLE—Would the mere election of a President who is a Prohibitionist bring in prohibition?

PEOPLE—"No."

FIRST APOSTLE—You know that you must begin lower.

That is the trouble with the Prohibitionist.

That is the trouble with the Woman's Christian Temperance Union, and other temperance organizations.

They aim at the moon, and waste their ammunition.

Zion Begins by Leading to Repentance and Conversion.

In Zion we begin with the people and lead them to see that the use of the deadly poison, alcohol, and of all other poisonous drugs, is sin.

We educated the people to see things as God sees them.

By the grace of God, we have led this people to repentance and conversion, and then there was no need to administer the temperance pledge.

There has never been a temperance pledge administered in Zion.

Yet there is not a member of this Church who is known to take liquor or tobacco.

Something better does it, my Brother Prohibitionist.

We conquer the Spirit of Hell by the Powers of Heaven, by the Holy Spirit of God.

We have a prohibition district and a prohibition City.

We have a little Prohibition Nation.

We have passed no law upon the subject, but we have the Law of God in our hearts.

That shuts our mouth against liquor and tobacco. [Applause]

That is the Maine Law in Zion—the Law of God in the heart.

I do not want to fight my friends, the Prohibitionists.

On the contrary, apart from voting their Presidential ticket, wherever we can do so conscientiously, we help them.

I direct my people throughout this land, that, wherever they have an opportunity to support a good, able, honest, Christian Prohibitionist, not a Democrat, who has a fair chance of getting in, to back him up and vote for him.

I would do the same also, under some circumstances, where the Democratic candidate is a better man than the Republican.

Zion is not wedded to the Republican party, but I do not think you will find the average Democrat a better man than the average Republican.

I warn you upon this matter, however, not to imperil the election of a Republican majority to the State Legislatures or to Congress. The Congress and the President must be in accord, otherwise great national perils are incurred.

However, I must make some modifications to that statement.

I shall not stand in the way of, and I should like to see in the halls of Congress, some able Prohibitionists who are not only true Prohibitionists but true Christians and true Theocrats, and *who are in accord with the fiscal and financial policies of the Republican party.*

Zion Is Always United in Political Action.

We nominate no ticket ourselves, because we will not put up a sacrificial lamb.

When we put up a ticket we shall do as we have always done in Zion, we shall expect to elect it.

Every time we put up a ticket we elect that ticket without a dissentient voice.

We intend, when we put up a ticket anywhere, to win.

We know we shall one day win.

We are acting in accordance with the Divine Principle which tells us that we are to count the cost to see whether we are able with ten thousand to meet the other fellow that comes against us with twenty thousand.

We do not need to go into a fight until we are ready.

The best time to go into a fight with the Devil is when you are ready.

The worst time is when you are not ready; because he is always ready, and is sure to defeat you if you are not.

This is as true in politics as in everything else.

Reasons why Zion in the United States Should Vote for Theodore Roosevelt.

Let me give you reasons why Zion should vote for Theodore Roosevelt rather than for Alton B. Parker.

Beloved friends, I have asked God that I might not say one mean or unkind word regarding the Democratic candidate or the Democratic party.

I have undoubtedly many friends who are Democrats, and "such were some of you," but you have been politically, as well as spiritually, renovated.

You have not left the Democratic party for the Republican party, but you have left the Democratic party for the Theocratic Party; and you have made a very good exchange.

Is that true?

PEOPLE - "Yes."

FIRST APOSTLE—I am glad to hear you reconstructed Democrats say "Yes;" and such were many of you when I first found you.

You were hard fellows to deal with.

You had been riding the "silver goat" for a long time.

You were away out in the political wilderness, trying to feed your bellies with the political husks that the Democratic swine were eating, under Bryan's leadership, in the "far country," and you failed to be satisfied, as Alton B. Parker failed.

He found himself far away from the White House, away out in the wilderness, amid the "wild beasts" of the valleys of political despair, weeping and wailing, and gnashing his teeth.

The more he voted for silver the further he went away into the Wilderness of Anarchy.

Now, under the guidance of a few sane men, safe and solid in regard to fiscal matters, but dangerous guides in other things, he has come back; and I do not see why we should not treat him very kindly.

Gold is the Fiscal Standard of Zion.

We who have fought for the Gold Standard know that, if we had allowed the Silver Standard to win, the Headquarters of Zion would not have been established in the United States.

Zion would not have been established in a country which declared it would pay its debts with a debased currency, offering fifty cents on a dollar in the payment of private, public, and international debts.

It was the most stupid proposal that ever was promulgated as a political principle or a financial proposal.

Gold is the fiscal standard of Zion.

God said, by the Prophet Isaiah, twenty-six hundred years ago,

For Brass I will bring Gold,
And for Iron I will bring Silver,
And for Wood, Brass,
And for Stones, Iron.

That statement is made in that wonderful 60th chapter of Isaiah, and I hold to that as the Promise of God to Zion in the Latter Days, the Consummation of the Age, the Times of the Restoration of All Things, of which I am the prophet.

I am glad that God has made it possible to establish manufactories in this City, and that Zion has attracted capital—gold—in hundreds of thousands of dollars from foreign lands.

Thank God, the gold and the people are continuing to come.

Next spring, to my positive knowledge, between two and four hundred people are coming from Australia.

They are coming in hundreds from many Continents and from all parts of America.

God is bringing in capital as well as labor, which would not have been possible under a Silver Standard.

Any of you who know anything at all about the facts know that.

Alton B. Parker, after he received the nomination of President from the Democratic Convention, declared himself to be in favor of a Gold Standard.

I wonder why he did not do it before.

I wonder why he did not speak out before the delegates had committed themselves to his candidature.

His principles must have been exceedingly—I do not know what color.

I have heard of a color which is called "invisible green." [Laughter.]

I have wondered whether his principles were invisible green.

No one could tell what his principles were until he was nominated, for up to that time they had faded away from "silver into gold," but nobody knew of the change since it had been recorded by "invisible ink" upon "invisible paper" before an "invisible assembly." It took the chemical virtue of a "Nomination" to make these principles appear.

Then he said that there would be no possibility of his accepting the Nomination unless they agreed to consider that the gold question was settled.

When a politically prodigal son, who has gone into a far country and spent his substance in democratic living, and in holding high carnival with the debased political principles of anarchy and repudiation, subsequently repudiates the association and the husks and comes home, I think we ought to welcome him.

May God bless the poor, politically lean, Democrats, who have been endeavoring to feed their souls on silver husks and anarchistic heresies.

They ought to have been blessed by the eight years of Good Government which have been given to this Nation.

They ought to have been fattened again and again on the Prosperity of the country, under Protection and the Gold Standard.

Now they have come home and said that they have repented of all their naughty words about the Gold Bugs, and acknowledged that they were only nasty Silver Goats.

An Impudent Request for Political Preferment.

As Mr. Parker, who acknowledges that for eight years he voted for the Free and Unlimited Coinage of Silver at 16 to 1, returns from the far country, his prayer as a Democratic candidate for the Presidency to the people is, "Oh, my fellow citizens; I have sinned against truth and in thy sight, but I hold myself to be worthy of being your ruler; make me the boss of the ranch." [Laughter.]

That seems to me to be, politically speaking, to lack humility, and in fact to be rather impudent.

The prodigal son, even while he confesses himself to be a political sinner, demands the place of the old man, the elder brother, and every one else.

He wants to run the Government of the Nation.

It will not do.

It is too impudent.

Besides, as one of our Republican friends observed the other night upon this platform, "The drunkard has taken the 'gold-cure,' but you cannot be sure that he will withstand temptation."

The fact of the matter is that, after all, Alton B. Parker has not declared that the Gold Standard is right.

He has simply declared that it has become the policy of the country.

He has not said that it is a right policy.

Who can tell whether he will not go back and lead his party back with him into "the far country."

Eight years ago he voted for a bad policy.

Who can tell that he will not go back to it.

Moreover, he is attacking another policy in which Zion is very much interested, the right Policy of Protection to Industries which must be protected by Customs Duties, especially in their earliest stages.

We invited capital from all the world and put with it our own capital to establish a new industry, because we knew we were protected by sixty-five per cent. duty.

It needed that protection, and it needs it still.

Are we to have Zion Lace Industries ruined?

PEOPLE—"No."

FIRST APOSTLE—Would that be right?

PEOPLE—"No."

FIRST APOSTLE—And yet you have not an iota of consolation in the Democratic Platform, for these Political Prodigals who met last summer in St. Louis told you that if they got into power they would reduce the tariff and practically bring about the ruin of great American Industries, and throw millions of our people into idleness and poverty, with all their attendant miseries.

American Industries Need a Protective Tariff.

What would that mean for all the Industries we have established in Zion City?

It would mean almost ruin.

We should have to fight hard to maintain them

The low price of labor in Europe and the fact that they can make the machinery there that as yet we cannot make here, would enable them to undersell us.

Great quantities of poor lace would be thrown upon the American market, and a new and great American Industry would be injured if not destroyed.

Are you prepared for that?

PEOPLE—"No."

FIRST APOSTLE—It is no selfish motive that makes me say these things.

I asked God to enable me to establish an industry that would give employment to many thousands of good Christian men and women, and make a profit which we could use for the extension of the Kingdom of God.

I always have been a supporter of the protection of new industries in a young country.

It is essential that this policy shall be continued now.

When, under Grover Cleveland, they brought in the Wilson-Gorman Tariff Act, it shut up the factories.

It drove capital out of the country.

No matter how much gold they borrowed to keep up to the standard which was required by law for the reserve in the national treasury, they lost their gold almost as quickly as they got it.

During that period, they saddled this country with a gold-bond debt of two hundred fifty million dollars.

We are not blind,

We are not forgetful.

We know that the policy of the Democratic party, both in regard to money and to manufactories, has been injurious and almost ruinous to this country.

We do not intend to let the prodigal son repeat his political crimes.

Let us understand each other perfectly.

We in Zion have a direct personal interest, as all American manufacturers have, in maintaining a Protective Policy, that we may be able to nurse our factories into stability; and we shall do our best to maintain it.

By and by, when we make our own machinery and grow our own cotton and spin it, I would not mind facing the competition of any country.

But now we have to be fostered and helped.

Only thus can we grow and help this country.

May God help us! [Amen.]

Moreover, we have very great dangers ahead in connection with other policies of the Democratic party, of which they have never openly repented.

Democratic Rule Has Threatened the Independence of the United States Judiciary.

Did they not aim at making the Supreme Court of the United States submissive to Altgeld, and men of that kind?

Did they not aim at destroying that which is one of the greatest bulwarks of liberty in this country, and one of the three great divisions of our Government?

They aimed and did their very best to destroy the Judicial Freedom of the Supreme Court, and they said openly that it was their intention to destroy its independence.

We can not allow that; because the maintenance of that Court in its dignity and in its power to define law is essential to the preservation of the Government.

I have not the slightest doubt that they knew the Supreme Court would have smashed any law that said the indebtedness of this country should be paid in a debased currency; but they intended to get an alteration of such a nature as would make the Supreme Court of the United States a mere tool of the politician, for the time being.

May God prevent that forever, and preserve the independence of the Supreme Court of the United States. [Amen.]

There are many other heresies of which they are guilty, and I do not propose to ask Zion to vote for the prodigal son, and to put him at the head of the ranch.

He may take a back seat for a few more years.

Then it will be time for the Theocratic Party to assume the rule of America. [Applause.]

That good time is coming.

A man who was here the other day said to me, "Doctor, I never cared very much about your religion. I do not know much about it, but I would vote both hands up to make you Dictator of the United States of America, if you could make it one big Zion." [Applause.]

But if I were Dictator, "Babel" (Chicago) would be transformed into Bethel, and "Beer" (Milwaukee) into Beer-lahai-roi.

Think what changes that would entail, and of all the people who would be compelled to do right, or be restrained, and made to work for the public welfare in various penal ways

God will take care of that.

Zion's Reasons for Voting for President Roosevelt.

I shall now give you some reasons why Theodore Roosevelt should be preferred to Alton B. Parker.

The Presidency is a personal matter.

I was glad to see in Dr. Albert Shaw's Introduction to the "Speeches and State Papers of President Roosevelt" the words which I quote, because they are true:

> While the President believes in the utility of the party system, he speaks always as the President of the Whole Country and not merely as the chief of the party.

Thank God for that!

I know it is true.

I know it from his own words to me, personally, and from his words, which are worth reading, in these very plain, simple, outspoken speeches that come from an honest heart and a clear head.

Let me very briefly tell you something about this man.

I have studied him at very short range.

I have talked with him for one hour in the White House, Washington, in a private interview on November 9th last, upon the great policies of this Nation, both domestic and foreign.

I had neither personal nor political interests to serve in that interview; and I was too unimportant a factor in public life to make my support of the President, or the opposite, a matter of any considerable political consequence.

I sought no favors and he promised none. But I thought I was possessed of some important information which might be of value to the Chief Executive of my adopted country, and I imparted it.

I can never forget the President's kindness, and his most interesting, intelligent, thoughtful, far-reaching, powerful and wholesome personality.

I believe that I have your confidence as one who has had large experience with men.

There was no public to applaud what he said to me, and there was nothing very particular to be gained by winning my approval; but the President was speaking freely from his heart, as I think he always speaks when he thinks it is wise to speak at all.

It would be highly improper for me to quote his words, or to commit the President to any policy because of a conversation with me; but I want to say this, that in President Roosevelt you have the most Theocratic statesman that I know of in America.

The man who says from his heart, "I want to rule justly, with God ever before me," is a good man.

That is a very good man to have as President, is he not?

PEOPLE—"Yes"

FIRST APOSTLE—That is the kind of a man you have in Theodore Roosevelt.

Does his career bear out that statement?

It does.

Theodore Roosevelt a Preacher of Righteousness.

I do not know but that I may call him "a preacher of righteousness."

I believe I have a right to say that he is.

He is a preacher of righteousness to the father, the mother, and the family.

He has given much good advice to women, and he is a great upholder of the true rights of women.

He is a man who loves women, and loves them purely; a man who has good and noble desires for a pure and good family life, as a splendid foundation for a great nation.

He is a man who wants to rule in the fear of God, and such a man is a good Theocrat.

So far as I know, a stone was never thrown at his character as a young man.

As a student at Harvard University his career was very creditable.

When he took his degree, although the son of a wealthy man, he did not go and spend his father's wealth on beer and skittles as many do, but he at once devoted himself in his native State to the service of the people of this Nation.

Any one who has read the history of the War of 1812, which was written by him in the year 1882, when he was a young man only twenty-four years of age, would say that he was a student, and especially a student of Anglo-American affairs.

At that very early period of his life he showed himself to be determined to master the history of this people, and to understand its interests.

He immediately offered himself as a representative, and was sent to the legislature at Albany.

There he stood before the people, young, fresh, vigorous—a fine type of the young American citizen.

Then, after being restored more fully to health, through an active life on the Western Prairie, he did not use that health to build up more wealth, but he came back to give himself—his health and his wealth—to his country, which he loves so devotedly, and of which he speaks with a kindling eye, and as a man to whom the word America is one of the sweetest words on earth, as it is to me for I also am, by adoption, an American. [Applause.]

His Excellent Work as Chief Commissioner of Police in New York.

He became the Chief Commissioner of the Civil Service, and righted the wrongs of many who had been in that service, and who had been shamefully wronged.

Then his heart cried out for his native city, and when they wanted him as the Chief Commissioner of Police, although there was no money nor fame in it for him, he took the place, which constantly exposed him to the hatred of corrupt police officers of the Tammany stripe and of those whom they had protected.

Indeed, he was constantly exposed to assassination; for he not only became the Chief Commissioner of Police of New York in name, but in fact.

He went out into the streets at night to see how both his principal and subordinate officers were executing the law; and large numbers of them were found delinquent by the Chief Commissioner himself.

Some of you remember the stories in connection with that experience, how, when he said something to a certain policeman about doing his duty, the policeman turned upon him and was about to club him, when he made himself known; he would have been clubbed, perhaps, had he not been on his guard.

Theodore Roosevelt did one of the greatest services for this Nation in putting the Police Department of New York on a better footing.

When we were in New York, with between three and four thousand of the members of Zion Restoration Host, on our Visitation a year ago, we found that the police of that city under Commissioner Green (and I hope this is true of the police under the present Commissioner, I know nothing to the contrary), were really taken out of the realm of politics, and all who were with me then will bear me witness that we have not found in America or any other part of the world, a better, braver, or a cleaner police force than that of New York City. [Loud applause.]

The credit of that is largely due to Theodore Roosevelt.

New York City is the great gateway of America.

He cleaned America's gateway by working night and day, and continually risking his life.

This man is a true patriot.

Where was Alton B. Parker all that time.

Alton B. Parker was merely an attorney's clerk, or something of that kind, gradually rising higher and higher, until he got on the judicial bench; but he has had no such experience as this man in administrative and legislative work.

His Work as Assistant Secretary of the Navy.

But Theodore Roosevelt did not stop there.

They called him to be Assistant Secretary of the Navy at a time when war with Spain was imminent.

His book, written twenty-two years ago, when a very young man, showed what a grasp he had even then of naval affairs; and he did magnificent service, and saved the United States vast sums of money in the Naval Department.

He put the fleet, with Mr. Long's assistance—for he was really the Acting Secretary of the Navy—in a splendid condition, and was largely instrumental in enabling it to win at Santiago de Cuba and Manila.

When he had done that work—I do not know that I am particularly proud of his next achivement, except from a patriotic point of view—with a sick wife and baby at home, he, with the full consent of his wife, offered his young, brave life to his country, and at San Juan Hill led the charge that settled the whole question as to whether the Spaniard should continue to desolate those beautiful islands off the American coast, and to enslave and oppress their peoples.

He went up that hill at the head of his soldiers, risked his life for his country, and planted the American flag over San Juan.

I say that, from the point of view of the true soldier and true patriot, that was a good thing.

Although I do not like war, I am glad that the Spaniards were cleaned out of the Antilles.

Did he stop there?

He needed rest and wanted his home—no man loves home more than he—but when his State called for him, Theodore Roosevelt answered; and the State, with an immense majority rolled up from every part, even from the Bowery, sweeping the Democrats away for the time, sent him with a great wave of personal love for the brave fellow, into the gubernatorial chair of the State of New York.

And he did splendid work!

It was very clear to all thinking men that, after McKinley's second term was over, he was the logical candidate for the Presidency of the United States in 1904.

"Man Proposes, but God Disposes."

But the politicians of his party thought, it was commonly said, at least, that they would shelve him, by almost compelling him to accept the nomination of Vice-president.

However, "Man proposes, but God disposes."

It was a marvelous Providence that found Theodore Roosevelt Vice-president of the United States when the hand of an assassin, in September, 1901, struck down the President of the United States, and he at last lay low in death.

What was the confidence of this Nation?

What was the confidence of the business men of this Nation?

What was the confidence of foreign nations at the time when Theodore Roosevelt, with a broken heart, lifted up his hand, and over the body of his dead friend and comrade, William McKinley, took the oath of office as President?

What was the feeling in the nations of the world?

Did the securities of the United States fall in the market?

Were the people in foreign countries afraid that their money would be lost, and that the Government could not control the anarchists?

No!

The moment Theodore Roosevelt grasped the Helm of Power, the Nation felt happy; all nations rejoiced; and America stood as strong as if her President had not been assassinated.

Shall we not be thankful to the man who took the office of Vice-president merely because he thought in that way the principles of his party, and the man he loved, William McKinley, would win, although it was at the possible sacrifice of himself?

Gratitude to Theodore Roosevelt Demands His Re-election.

If we do not reëlect him, this country will show its ingratitude for the man whom God raised up to take the Helm of the Ship of State when the hand of the Helmsman was stricken by the blow of an assassin.

When death caused the helm to be dropped from William

McKinley's hand, it was Theodore Roosevelt who seized it, in accordance with the Constitution and Laws of the United States of America; and this country and all countries felt that a man equally as strong, at the least, had taken control of the affairs of this Republic.

I believe that this country is not so ungrateful to the man who three years ago took this position, and who has done so well, as to turn him off when he is unanimously nominated by the party in power for reëlection.

No! No! No!

A thousand times, No!

The Nation has some gratitude:

The policy of the President in regard to home affairs has been a splendid success.

What other President would have dared to risk what he did in endeavoring to settle the coal strike, and in settling it as he did?

That settlement was due to the President's own personal influence.

While he lay in Washington, suffering terrible agony from an injured leg, he sent for all concerned, and, as President of the United States, said that the people had to be considered as well as the mine owners and the miners.

He demanded that they settle the strike in an honorable manner; and he showed them the way.

He made Pierpont Morgan and John Mitchell, men who were far apart, come together, and settle that strike in an honorable manner; for which the Nation is indebted to him.

Are we not?

PEOPLE—"Yes."

FIRST APOSTLE—He showed also what a strong Executive could do in being the Peacemaker.

The President's Attitude Toward Trusts.

It is the fashion of the filthy Hearst papers—these papers which did more to assassinate William McKinley than any other influence—to lie about President Roosevelt.

These papers are likely to fasten the trusts upon us, by lying about them, because no man or system is ever attacked with falsehood without strengthening that which is attacked.

I should like to see these vile papers suppressed by law.

I should like to see it made impossible to print continuously such lies; and such a law will come and be enforced.

Vengeance is God's!

He will repay!

This country will wake up some day and provide a Legislative Muzzle for such wretched papers.

But Theodore Roosevelt dealt with the trusts when Pierpont Morgan, it is said, and Hill, and others, tried, under the New Jersey "Northern Securities Company," to make a merger of the Great Northern Railway and the Northern Pacific Railway, not in the interests of the people, but against the interests of the people.

Then it was that Theodore Roosevelt attacked one of the strongest combinations of capital that this country has ever been able to produce, and he attacked it successfully.

He directed his Attorney General to file a bill at once, and to fight to the finish.

He finished the Northern Securities Company, and knocked out that illegal trust.

Nevertheless some will talk about him as being the supporter of illegal trusts.

He is the destroyer of illegal trusts, and he proved it in that action.

On all these lines he did splendid work.

An Act that Will Never Be Forgotten by God.

There is one work for which, if he were forgotten by every one else, he will not be forgotten by God in the Day when he stands before His Judgment Seat.

He treated the black man as a man, and took him to his table, and ate with him, and did not care what any one said. [Applause.]

I should feel inclined to vote for him for that, if for nothing else.

They talk as if he were the enemy of the South, when his mother was a Southern lady, a Georgian.

He loves the South with all his heart.

Lying and wicked are they that would represent the President as hating the South.

He admires the chivalrous spirit of the best class of the Southland, as also do I; but he says, as I say, that God has "made of one every nation of men for to dwell on all the face of the earth."

We in America, whose fathers wronged the negroes by enslaving them, wronged the negroes still more by demoralizing them.

We, of all people, should raise the Afro-American higher; and, with the assistance of Zion, which is as yet only a little one, we shall assist in putting into power the man who stands for the National Rights of men of every race and color, under the Stars and Stripes.

Do you forget what he did for the oppressed Jew?

Do you not remember that when the streets of Kishinef ran blood, and the Jew was murdered and outraged by the Slav, by the Russian, by the so-called Orthodox Christian, how he addressed a note to the Russian government, demanding the punishment of the guilty and the protection of the Nation from which his Savior and mine came; for Jesus, the Christ, was of the tribe of Judah, and Salvation is from the Jews.

In that day he proved himself to be the great heroic leader of a Christian people, by demanding that the greatest power on earth, next to the American and the British, should do right.

You remember what he said, and you remember, too, what he did.

Russia's Insulting and Treacherous Conduct.

Russia rues the day that she insulted the President of the United States, and that she ever lied to his Secretary of State, the Honorable John Hay; for she not only insulted America and told her to mind her own business, but she lied.

She promised to evacuate Manchuria, and she did not do it; and now she is doing it. [Applause.]

But it is because she is being prodded to do it by the little Japs; and I do not hesitate to express the hope that America and Great Britain will take care that Russia does not get back to Korea and Manchuria.

I trust, and believe, that the government of Theodore Roosevelt will in that matter join hands with the British Empire, and, with Japan and China, will declare to all the nations of the earth, "Hands off; we maintain the autonomy and integrity of the Mongolian Peoples, of China, and of Japan."

What I say from this platform reaches the ear of the Czar; reaches the ear of the Czarina; because there are members of Zion in the Court of Russia who have access to the Czar, who are very frequent readers of LEAVES OF HEALING. [Applause.]

I say to the Czar, who wants to do right and cannot, who wants to do right and is threatened with assassination because of it, "Command peace; retire from Manchuria and Korea, and endeavor to bring your people into harmony with all that is good, and right, and pure, and true; and give to them the liberty that rightfully belongs to every nation—that of being free to serve God as they please."

I call your attention to the Cromwellian splendor of one action of the President.

A miserable African bandit called Raasuli thought he could take an American citizen and hold him for ransom, and that the American Nation would be afraid of him.

I do not know whether Mr. Roosevelt sent that message which is so often quoted, "Perdicaris alive, or Raasuli dead," but I know that he sent the United States war-ships *Olympia* and the *Brooklyn*, and that he said, "Give that man up."

He had to be given up, and that American citizen was living when last heard of in the place from whence the bandits took him.

One word from Theodore Roosevelt settled that question; and may God help us to send back into power the man who can protect the American Citizen, wherever he is. [Applause.]

An Incident of the Time of Cromwell.

It is said that during the time of Cromwell, the Lord-protector of England—that great man who stood for all that was best and noblest, and who has been so shamefully traduced, in reality a great Republican, who had made England great by righteousness—when an Englishman fell into the hands of the Inquisition in a certain Italian city, Cromwell sent a British war-ship with the message that the Englishman must be surrendered instantly or they would clear the decks for action and bombard the city.

The answer of the authorities was that they had no power; that the man was a heretic, and had been handed by the Inquisition over to the civil power, and the civil authorities said they had no power; that the Roman Catholic Inquisition had condemned him to be burned alive for heresy.

Cromwell replied by his captain, Whether it is the Inquisition or the Government, we do not care; the Englishman must be given up, or we will batter you down.

The Englishmen were given up.

This is a Cromwellian man that we have at the head of the Government of the United States of America.

May God keep him there!

If he continues to do as well as he has been doing, I should be inclined to keep him there as long as President Diaz has been President of Mexico.

Did he not come to conclusions with Turkey for her wickedness?

Turkey had wronged some American missionaries, and there had been an award of a large sum of money to restore their ruined churches and colleges.

The Turk in his usual way put it off, and at last sneeringly said he would not do it until he was ready; but Roosevelt sent his fleet to Smyrna, and said that if the Sultan did not mend his ways it would appear in the Bosphorus; and the men of God got their rights.

Thank God again for President Roosevelt!

Once more I say that the policy of President Roosevelt is a Peaceful Policy.

You heard the Chairman of the Committee on Naval Affairs and Naval Appropriations, our friend and Congressman, Mr. Foss, declare from this platform last Wednesday evening, that the American Navy was for Peace.

The white-painted war-ships of America!

How glad we were to see them abroad!

They looked like white doves; and, when we saw the Stars and Stripes floating over these war-ships, our hearts beat faster and higher, and we thanked God for America, and for Theodore Roosevelt, too!

The Blessing of a Just Man Ruling in the Fear of God.

I stand for this man. [Applause.]

I have nothing to gain, personally, except what you all have to gain.

We all gain the blessing of knowing that there is a just man ruling in the fear of God at the head of this Nation.

There is one thing more in my heart which I wish to say regarding Theodore Roosevelt.

His name, Theodore, is, as you know, the combination of two words which mean, "The Gift of God," and I feel that he is especially the Gift of God for this Nation.

I believe he is a man of whom it may be said:

> Wherever Wrong shall Right deny,
> Or suffering spirits urge their plea,
> He is a Voice to smite the lie,
> A Hand to set the captive free.

May God grant us in the Presidential Chair a continuance of such men, till Jesus come. [Amen.]

All who believe that Theodore Roosevelt is such a man, and who desire to pray for him, stand. [*Almost the entire people stood.*]

PRAYER OF CONSECRATION.

My God and Father, in Jesus' Name I come to Thee. Take me as I am. Make me what I ought to be. I thank Thee for Life; for Thy Love; for Thy Salvation, and for Liberty in this American Nation. God bless America. God bless the President. Make us worthy of him. Help him in his toil, in his trials, in his sorrows. Protect him amid the dangers of his position from the hand of the assassin, and from the strife of tongues. God spare him to this Nation. And now be with us in doing our duty. Be with American women in helping their sons and brothers, American men, and those who are about to become Americans. Help them in helping each other. Help them to win the fight for Righteousness and God. Help us to go on until the time shall come when the Theocratic Party shall everywhere contend for the Rule of God; shall win power and rule. We believe that our King, the Christ, shall come, and establish Thy Kingdom from shore to shore. Hear us our Father and help us, for Jesus' sake. [Amen.]

The audience and Choir then joined in singing "America," after which the First Apostle said:

It seems to me that the National Anthem looks forward to a Theocracy, for you see that is the last line of it:

> Protect us by Thy might,
> Great God, our King!"

May God grant that we shall recognize His Kingship.

I do not want to say a harsh word about my Democratic friends.

I desire you to know that, as the President is the President of the whole people, I am the Apostle of the whole people.

May God bless America from one end to the other! [Amen.]

May God bless every man, woman, and child of every political creed and of every color, in it!

May God help us all to get closer together!

The Recessional, "The Shadows of the Evening Hour," was then sung, after which the First Apostle pronounced the

APOSTOLIC AND HIGH-PRIESTLY BENEDICTION.

Jehovah bless thee, and keep thee:
Jehovah make His face to shine upon thee, and be gracious unto thee.
Jehovah lift up His countenance upon thee, and give thee Peace.

Beloved, abstain from every form of evil. And may the very God of Peace Himself sanctify you wholly; and I pray God your whole spirit, and soul, and body be preserved entire, without blame, unto the coming of our Lord Jesus, the Christ. Faithful is He that calleth you, who also will do it. The grace of our Lord Jesus, the Christ, the love of God, our Father, the fellowship of the Holy Spirit, our Comforter and Guide, one Eternal God, abide in you, bless you, and keep you, and all the Israel of God everywhere, forever.

Grace, mercy, and peace from God the Father, Son, and Holy Spirit be with you, and with this Nation, and with all the wide world, forever. Amen.

Notice to Correspondents.

In writing to Headquarters it is *absolutely essential* that the writer give his full address.

Failure to comply with this request necessitates looking up or referring to the Church Records, which involves much time, and is very frequently fruitless.

Friends and members of the Christian Catholic Church in Zion everywhere will please bear this in mind, especially those in foreign lands.

J. G. EXCELL, General Ecclesiastical Secretary.

OFFICIAL REPRESENTATIVES OF ZION

The following addresses of Official Representatives of Zion at important centers throughout the world, are given for the convenience of correspondents:

In the United States

¶ ¶ Overseer George L. Mason, 4 St. Nicholas Terrace, New York City.

¶ ¶ Overseer William Hamner Piper, 17 Capin street, New Dorchester, Massachusetts.

¶ ¶ Elder R. N. Bouck, 2129 Mt. Vernon street, Philadelphia, Pennslyvania.

¶ ¶ Elder A. Ernst, 2611 Fourth avenue, Seattle, Washington.

¶ ¶ Elder A. E. Arrington, 501 West Fourth street, Cincinnati, Ohio.

¶ ¶ Elder W. B. Taylor, 1350 East Sixteenth street, Fruitvale, California.

¶ ¶ Elder L. C. Hall, San Antonio, Texas.

¶ ¶ Elder Frank L. Brock, 3401 Morgan street, St. Louis Missouri.

In Foreign Countries

¶ ¶ Overseer H. E. Cantel, 81 Euston road, London, N. W., England.

¶ ¶ Overseer Wilbur Glenn Voliva, Arlington, 43 Park road, St. Kilda, Melbourne, Victoria, Australia.

¶ ¶ Overseer Daniel Bryant, Box 3074, Johannesburg, Transvaal, South Africa.

¶ ¶ Elder Carl Hodler, 76 Bahnhofstrasse, Zürich, Switzerland.

¶ ¶ Elder Arthur S. Booth-Clibborn, 139 Weesperzijde, Amsterdam, Holland.

¶ ¶ Elder E. B. Kennedy, Zion, Haskell road, Shanghai China.

¶ ¶ Elder R. M. Simmons, 525 Grove Crescent, Vancouver, B. C.

¶ ¶ Elder Eugene Brooks, 360 Parliament street, Toronto, Ontario, Canada.

General Financial Agents

¶ ¶ Deacon N. B. Rideout, Financial Agent for South Africa, Box 3074, Johannesburg, Transvaal, South Africa.

¶ ¶ Elder Percy Clibborn, Financial Agent for Europe, 76 Bahnhofstrasse, Zürich, Switzerland.

¶ ¶ Deacon John W. Innes, Financial Agent for the United Kingdom, 81 Euston Road, London, N. W., England.

Early Morning Meeting in Shiloh Tabernacle

*REPORTED BY O. L. S., A. C. R., S. E. C., AND E. S.

THE Early Morning Meeting, Lord's Day, October 9, 1904, was the first of several which are to be devoted to the unfolding, by the First Apostle and Prophet of the Restoration, of deep truths concerning the Appearing of our Lord, the Rapture, the Reign on Earth of a Thousand Years, and the Final Judgment.

It is peculiarly at such seasons as these, when, speaking with Prophetic Power and Inspired by the Holy Spirit, the man of God gives to his people that Spiritual Insight into God's Holy Word which has made them strong and able to withstand the subtleties of the Evil One in false teachings.

Yet it is not the Discerning alone, but the Believing and the Doing, which make Zion the power she is today.

The three are but radii from one center—the one Fountain-Head—God Himself.

And it is here that the First Apostle begins and ends—always and ever—with God Himself.

Shiloh Tabernacle, Zion City, Illinois, Lord's Day Morning, October 9, 1904.

The service was opened with the Congregational singing of Hymn No. 128, Gospel Hymns 5 and 6.

Hark, hark! my soul! angelic songs are swelling
O'er earth's green fields and ocean's wave-beat shore;
How sweet the truth those blessed strains are telling
Of that new life when sin shall be no more.

CHORUS—Angels sing on! your faithful watches keeping;
Sing us sweet fragments of the songs above,
Till morning's joy shall end the night of weeping,
And life's long shadows break in cloudless love.

The First Apostle then offered prayer, closing with the chanting of the Disciples' Prayer, in which the people united

Scripture Reading and Exposition.

The First Apostle then said:

We will read the 25th chapter of the Gospel according to St. Matthew.

I hope to open this chapter to you on this and the next few Lord's Day mornings, and I want to do so very carefully.

I shall speak to you concerning the parable of the Ten Virgins, the parable of the Ten Talents, and the wondrous revelation concerning the Coming of the Son of Man in His Glory to the Judgment; the three go together.

Very properly, they are all put together in this chapter, although I do not like the division of God's Word into chapters.

I think it would be very much better if we had the Bible divided into sections; the chapter divisions are very misleading.

The arrangement of the Bible is one of the things that ought to have received attention at the time of its revision.

These divisions into chapters are not in the original.

Dear old Stephanus made most of them with a pencil while he was traveling on horseback, just for his own personal help.

I do not believe that dear old Stephanus ever imagined that we were to be saddled with them forever.

Sometimes the chapters begin at the wrong places, and sometimes they end at the wrong places.

Sometimes the verse at the end of a chapter belongs to the following chapter.

But no mistake has been made in this chapter.

I have been thinking much about it; and I have determined to expound it on Lord's Day mornings for some weeks to come.

The contents of this chapter are of great and immediate importance in these Times of the Restoration of All Things—in the time when we are approaching the Final Consummation.

Then shall the Kingdom of Heaven -

We ought always to remember that the word "heaven" there should have been translated in the plural.

The Greek is ἡ βασιλεία τῶν οὐρανῶν (*he basileia ton ouranon*) which means "the Kingdom of the Heavens."

It is Important to Remember that There is More than One Heaven.

Do not forget, beloved, that there is more than one heaven.

One of the greatest blunders we make is to think that there is but one.

Some one said to me recently, "One good thing is that all we Christians are going to one heaven."

"You are mistaken," I said, "some are going to the third heaven; and some to the seventh.

"I do not know to which one you are going; it might be the first, and it might be a long time before your friends came across you, if they were in the sixth or seventh."

I am so thankful that we are going to the right heaven--the one to which we belong.

Paul spoke of the "third heaven" to which he was caught up; and there is "the heaven of heavens," which cannot contain God: for He cannot be limited.

It is a wonderful thought, that we are not all going to one heaven, unless we all belong to one grade.

We shall be sorted out.

Some people will get to the first heaven, and it may be a long time before they will get to the seventh.

They ought to be very glad to get into the first.

I often wonder how some people are going to get into heaven at all.

They are naughty children of God.

There needs to be a sorting out here on earth as well as in the heavens.

Then shall the Kingdom of the Heavens be likened unto Ten Virgins, which took their lamps-

The word "lamps" should have been translated "torches," which gives a truer idea of the original.

These torches had a receiver for oil, and a place for the wick and burner.

Our idea of "lamp" is usually something that we carry in an enclosed frame, or stand upon something in a room, or suspend from a ceiling.

But at a wedding in Palestine bright, flaming torches were carried.

Then shall the Kingdom of the Heavens be likened unto Ten Virgins which took their torches, and went forth to meet the Bridegroom.
And five of them were foolish, and five were wise.

All the Virgins Are Christians.

They were all Virgins; make no mistake about that.

This is not a parable of both the damned and the saved.

To so regard it is the supreme blunder that many people make about this parable.

It is a parable of the Kingdom of the Heavens.

The foolish, as well as the wise, were Virgins.

The idea of spiritual purity and of regeneration is there.

They were born of God, all of them; and they all loved the Bridegroom.

They all went forth to meet Him.

They were all in earnest, in a measure, and all had one purpose.

There are quite a number today who have been told what they should do, and they do not obey.

They are foolish.

They are Christians; but they are foolish in that they do not obey.

There is one essential thing in which they do not obey: and you will see that as we continue the parable.

These Virgins are divided, therefore, into the foolish and the wise.

The Kingdom of God is so divided.

When a man is converted and regenerated his Christian life has only begun.

The Salvation Army idea of instantaneous sanctification and enduement with Divine Wisdom, which lifts the poor, wretched creature, just saved from the gutter, into a condition not only of Salvation and Regeneration, but of perfect Purity, is all nonsense.

It is not in accordance with Divine government, or Divine process, to make a baby grow into a man in an hour or a day.

If you give a baby a man's work, then you soon see how far from being a man the baby is.

It is a screaming farce!

They do not teach that a converted sinner must grow in grace, but that he is to become full-grown in an instant!

That is a heathen myth; it is not Christian teaching.

"Grow in the grace and knowledge of our Lord and Savior Jesus, the Christ."

Even the Holy Spirit's Indwelling Does Not Make One Perfect.

"But if you have Jesus with you, you must become perfect instantaneously!" these people say.

The apostles had the Christ with them, did they not?

PEOPLE—"Yes."

FIRST APOSTLE—And even after three years with the Christ they were very foolish.

"Ah! but when the Holy Spirit gets into you, it is quite different," they might reply.

Peter was filled with the Holy Spirit at Pentecost, but he was very unwise on many occasions after that.

He was perfectly amazed when God told him, in that wonderful vision at Joppa, that he "should not call any man common or unclean."

He was perfectly amazed to learn that God was "no respecter of persons."

It took a vision and a wonderful series of Divine providences to get the truth into Peter's head that God was "no respecter of persons;" and he had received the Holy Spirit for some time.

Twenty-five years after he had received the Holy Spirit, the Apostle Paul had to knock out of him the nonsense that he could be one thing in Jerusalem and another thing in Antioch; that he could be one thing before circumcised Jews came from the Apostle James, and another thing after.

If you imagine that the leading of the Holy Spirit means an entire, infallible Inspiration and Wisdom, you have a dangerous piece of nonsense in your head.

Let us remember that of those who are regenerated and redeemed, and who are right with God as far as their Salvation is concerned, many are foolish, and the others are wise.

Sometimes the wise, like the foolish, slumber.

And five of them were foolish, and five were wise.
For the foolish, when they took their torches, took no oil with them.

They had no reserve.

Large numbers of Christians burn out all the grace they have, in a short time, and have no reserve.

The Wise Take Oil in Their Vessels with Their Torches.

But the wise took oil in their vessels with their torches.
Now while the Bridegroom tarried, they all slumbered and slept.

The wise as well as the foolish slept.

The wise, for the time being, belonged to the category of the fool.

But at midnight there is a cry, Behold the Bridegroom! Come ye forth to meet Him.

Note that in the revision the cry is divided into two distinct parts.

"Behold the Bridegroom!" is the first part, and is quite separate from the second.

The Old Version says, "Go ye out to meet Him."

That is not the correct translation.

It is not "Go ye out," but "Come ye forth."

That is totally different.

It is a cry from the outside, "Come ye forth!"

That is not a cry within the church on earth, but from the descending hosts, "Come ye forth!"

The first cry, "Behold the Bridegroom!" is not necessarily given at the same time as the other.

There is the possibility of a long difference in time between the two.

I do not believe that we have yet heard the cry, "Come ye forth to meet Him."

When we do, we will have to go instantly.

The cry must be instantaneously obeyed; and we shall quit the earth and meet Him in the sky.

I desire to expound this parable more carefully later, but as we read let us get the general outline.

Then all those virgins arose, and trimmed their torches.
And the foolish said unto the wise, Give us of your oil; for our torches are going out.

The Torches of Vast Numbers of Christians Are Going Out.

It should not have been translated "our lamps are *gone out*," but as in the Revision, "Our torches are *going out*."

They were not without light, but it is quite clear that they were spluttering and dim, and the oil was being rapidly exhausted.

It would not be long until the torch would splutter and stink, and be offensive.

You know what an offensive thing a lamp is that is going out.

Just think of that in connection with some Christians whose light is going out.

They splutter, they mutter, and they lie.

They make all kinds of foolish excuses.

They make believe that they are all right.

At last they get to the place where they are compelled to acknowledge that their lamps are going out.

You know very well that that is the condition of vast numbers of Christians in the apostate denominations.

Their torches are going out.

The Methodist torch is going out.

The Baptist torch is going out.

The Episcopalian torch is going out.

There are large numbers of Christians today, whose torches, individually and collectively, are going out.

Every one sees it, except themselves.

They themselves admit it now and then; but let any one outside talk about it, and they make loud objections.

"We are all right!" they say. "We are just as good as you, and even better; and there are more of us, too!"

The Spirit of Criticism Indicates a Lack of Oil.

Whenever you find a man or woman who is beginning, spiritually, to mutter or splutter, you may know that the light is dim, and the torch is going out.

He has no oil.

He is always finding fault with some one else.

Sometimes it is with his leaders, than whom he knows so much more.

The trouble is, he lacks oil, and has a good supply of something that is not oil.

But the wise answered, saying, Peradventure there will not be enough for us and for you: go ye rather to them that sell, and buy for yourselves.
And while they went away to buy, the Bridegroom came; and they that were ready went in with Him to the marriage feast: and the door was shut.

That describes the Rapture very clearly.

That tells of the Reception of the Prepared, which is to take place between the second and the third coming of the Lord.

When He comes the second time He will not come to the earth.

He will come in the clouds and receive from the earth His own, and then after the Rapture will come back with them to reign.

When they go in with Him to the marriage feast, the door is shut.

Afterward come also the other virgins, saying, Lord, Lord, open to us.
But He answered and said, Verily I say unto you, I know you not.

The Unprepared Must Pass Through the Great Tribulation.

He does not say to these people, "I never knew you." There are others to whom He says that.

These are "Virgins;" they have been saved.

Yet He cannot let them in.

They must stay until He comes again, and go through the Great Tribulation, or until they die, because they would not get ready.

They will be left here upon the earth, going up and down the streets, mourning and wailing, "Our dear ones have gone, and we were not ready!"

They will have to pass through the horrible Tribulation; when the Devil will reign and rule for a short time on earth, after all the best are taken out.

I do not want to live here then.

I would rather go home for the Marriage Feast, and then come back.

Watch therefore, for ye know not the day nor the hour.

The expression, "wherein the Son of Man cometh," which is found in the Old Version is not in the Revision; it is not needed there, as I shall show you later.

That is a wonderful parable.

I shall begin the exposition of it this morning.

We Ought to Understand the Things Pertaining to the End.

I desire you to pray about it.

A most important thing is to understand Eschatology—the Science of the Things pertaining to the End.

Let us ask God for wisdom, that I may be wise in speaking, and that you may be wise in hearing.

You must open your ears; not the physical ear, merely, but the spiritual, the inner ear.

Hear, and your soul shall live.

If you do not hear, your soul will die; you will surely be found among the foolish.

I do not say that your spirit will die; because spirits, whether good or bad, do not die.

We are reaching the time when God will clean up things; when there will be very much use for the cemetery.

That time will be upon you before you know it.

In that day, when the wise and the foolish virgins are separated, many will say, "Would God that I had died!"

There are worse things than dying.

If you are left to live throughout the Tribulation, you will wish you had died.

The First Apostle then delivered his Message:

THE PARABLE OF THE TEN VIRGINS.

INVOCATION.

Let the words of my mouth and the meditations of my heart be acceptable in Thy sight, and profitable unto this people, O Jehovah, my strength and my Redeemer.

TEXT.

Then shall the Kingdom of the Heavens be likened unto Ten Virgins.

Will you please remember that it is the Kingdom of the Heavens, and not a Republic.

There is no Republic in the Heavens.

There is no democracy there.

There are no States' Rights there.

There is no differential law nor Inter-state Commissioners.

There is no parliament or congress.

There are no conditions like even the best political conditions under which we live on earth.

He made us to be a Kingdom, to be priests unto His God and Father.

A kingdom necessitates a king.

How many kings are there in a kingdom?

PEOPLE—"One."

FIRST APOSTLE—Do not forget that in the Kingdom of the Heavens there is no king and queen with their house of lords and house of commons.

There is no president with his cabinet, senate, and house of representatives.

It is not the complex thing that we have on earth in our human governments.

If we, who say we are heirs, desire to become inheritors, we must be quite sure as to where we stand.

If we have received the King, we have received "a Kingdom which cannot be shaken."

Many people in Zion are restive because Zion refuses, as she always will refuse, to accommodate herself to their democratic or republican notions.

Zion is not a republic.

The Kingdom of God Is an Absolute Monarchy.

Make no mistake; when you are in the Kingdom, you are not in a republic.

Your position in the Kingdom of God will never depend upon the votes of a church.

When it depends upon the votes of a church, you have gone to the Devil, and have made the Kingdom of God dependent upon thoughtless, inconsiderate, and sometimes scheming, people.

Settle it in your minds once, for all time, whether you are willing to surrender your individuality to the absolute control of the King.

It is easy to say Yes, but it is another thing to obey.

Have you said Yes with a full understanding of what your surrendering implies?

We in Zion hold, and intelligently, I believe, that all human government, even the best, is not only imperfect, but has hitherto failed, absolutely and completely, to solve the problems of humanity.

This is the position that Zion takes.

The Kingdom of God is not merely meat and drink.

It is not food and clothing.

It is true, and forever gloriously true, that while we have need of these things, our Master has said:

Fear not, little flock; for it is your Father's good pleasure to give you the Kingdom.

. . . .

Your Heavenly Father knoweth that ye have need of all these things.

You have need of food and clothing, and a quiet dwelling-place. But the Christ said:

Seek ye first His Kingdom and His righteousness; and all these things shall be added unto you.

The Imperative Need of Seeking First the Kingdom of God.

Let us understand what the first thing is, and let us continue to seek it.

If we do not, we shall certainly be classed among the foolish virgins.

We shall have no Oil in our vessels when the cry is heard, "Come ye forth to meet Him."

We shall find that our Torches are going out, and while we are looking for Oil, the King will come.

The wise will go in, and we shall be left outside, even though we belong to the King and are His Virgins.

The whole thing lies in a proper apprehension and comprehension of the Kingdom, and in having a proper embodiment of it in our lives.

Let us get deeper and deeper into this Divine thought.

There are but two Kingdoms.

Those who say, "We will not have this Man to rule over us," will find that while they are boasting of their freedom, they are in the Kingdom of Darkness and Error, under the rule of Satan.

One day they will find that they are under the rule of the god of this world, the usurper.

Whether they like it or not, they will find that by and by he and his will make laws so oppressive that they will have to decide between their Christianity and his apostasy.

All Will Soon Have to Decide Between the Rule of the Lawless One and the Kingdom of God.

They will have to decide between the Government of the Man of Sin revealed and the Lawless One on the one hand, and that of the Kingdom of God on the other.

Indeed, we have to decide that now.

It is of no use to wait and say, "We will fight that battle when it comes to us. We are strong, and we will come through all right."

You know well that that is what the Russian Empire said in this present war.

The Russians said, "We can afford to carouse, drink, and sin."

As you know, it has been said, and never denied, that their soldiers were doing this when the first battle was fought at Port Arthur, and several ships of the Russian fleet were sunk.

When the first gun was fired from the Japanese ships, the officers of the Russian fleet were at the theater and the circus.

Not one officer of high rank was on board his ship. They had to be brought half drunk from their carousal

So infatuated are they with this kind of thing that recently, it is stated, when they wanted to get the officers together at Liao-Yang, that they were in houses of ill-fame.

They were engaged in all kinds of immoral and shameful conduct, and they could scarcely be aroused to the fact that Kouropatkin had commanded a retreat from Liao-Yang.

They thought they were in winter quarters, and that they could afford to settle down with the harlots and the theaters.

It was with the utmost difficulty that these miserable fellows got it into their heads that there was a great battle being fought, and that they might have to leave Liao-Yang in short order.

You do not get the details of the war in this country. You get rubbish and rumors.

The facts which I have stated are given by a very distinguished resident of Liao-Yang.

He tells the truth regarding the condition of things.

Many Christians Think They Have Gone Into Winter Quarters.

Many Christians think that they have gone into winter quarters and can take things easy.

They think that the Devil will not trouble them.

I do not want to alarm you and tell you that you must scuttle out of Zion City, but it would be much better for you to scuttle out than to imagine that you can get into heaven without a fight.

We will continue to hold Zion City and our Salvation only as we realize that we must exercise continuous watchfulness.

If you or I think that we are saved so completely that we will not need to watch any more, we are mistaken.

If you say, "Hallelujah, I am saved, and on my happy way to heaven, and no one can hurt me," you are a fool.

The Devil may let you alone because he thinks you are not worth bothering about.

He sees exactly where you are going, and he can get you any time.

He is not bothering about some of you.

If I were the Devil I should not bother about some people.

Some of you never did him any damage. Why should he hurt you?

In fact, you are a considerable help to him.

You are one of those lazy dogs who never bark, no matter who comes around.

You say, "If I bark he will know where to hit me."

You never bite, you never fight, and you never give the Devil any difficulty.

You never take the Sword of the Spirit and give him a thrust under the fifth rib.

If I were he I should not bother about you: for you help him.

Earnest Christians Are a Thorn in Satan's Side.

If you are in the Kingdom and have entered into it intelligently, you are a thorn in his side. He does not like you.

Do you imagine that the Devil likes to see Zion City growing and expanding, honored and powerful, lying here between his two great centers, Beer and Babel, Milwaukee and Chicago?

I respect the Devil for one thing, though I do not honor him.

I never heard of his slumbering or sleeping.

Do you ever find the Devil sleeping?

PEOPLE—"No."

FIRST APOSTLE—He is everlastingly at it; yet how often you find the saints sleeping!

That is the thing for which I admire him.

I am never deluded by people who say, "Oh, everything is peaceable now. No possible danger or trouble."

Then I say that it is time to be especially watchful.

The Devil is not asleep, but he is rubbing the wounds received in his last conflict with us and is applying oil of Sodom, and various other anodynes.

He says, "I am getting ready. I have not forgotten the last time that we had a wrestle. Beelzebub, let us get ready for Zion"

That is all right.

I am always pleased to know that the Devil has a particular hatred for Zion, for if he loved Zion then I should be in trouble.

If all men spoke well of me, then I should know that I was a false prophet.

One Praised by All Is the Definition of a False Prophet.

Some of you have great difficulty in understanding what a false prophet is.

When Elder Hawkins spoke to me about it in Australia I said, "Tell our people that the definition for false prophet is, one of whom all men speak well."

That is a fine definition of the majority of the ministers of Australia, for all the people, the press, the Freemasons, and even the saloon-keepers speak well of them.

The Devil in every form speaks well of them.

They never hurt any one.

The Devil says they are very nice people—so quiet.

And then—"Beelzebub, look how they pitch into Dowie!"

The Devil does not have to do much fighting against Zion—the churches and the Masons do it.

Up to this time I have not had any of the signs of a false prophet.

Blessed are ye when men shall reproach you, and persecute you, and say all manner of evil against you falsely, for My sake.

Rejoice and be exceeding glad: for great is your reward in heaven: for so persecuted they the prophets which were before you.

Have you that sign?

Are you persecuted?

Have you had trouble?

If you have no trouble, or have not had any, I cannot see that you are of any account.

I said to a political friend of Zion recently, "When I was in Washington every one spoke well of you, although perhaps that was not to your credit."

He quietly informed me that there were some who did not speak well of him, although I had not met them.

I have no doubt that a man who is determined to do right, will find those who are not friendly; and that his administration will have critics.

All Are Under Either the Absolute Monarchy of Heaven or the Absolute Monarchy of Hell.

Get this thought into your mind at the start and you will make a good beginning.

We who have come out of the Kingdom of Darkness, and Sin, and Satan, and are now in the Kingdom of God—the Kingdom of the Heavens—have exchanged the absolute monarchy of hell for the absolute monarchy of Heaven.

You may imagine that you are in the absolute monarchy of heaven when you are in the absolute monarchy of hell.

You must be under the one or the other.

The foolish virgins will find themselves under the absolute monarchy of hell, when the wise are taken out of this earth at the Rapture to be with the King.

They will find that for the time being, this world is under the absolute monarchy of hell.

The Man of Sin in the church, and the Lawless One in the state, at that time, will combine their forces.

They will be found to be one, as sure as God lives.

That is as clear as anything in the Prophetic Word.

We in Zion have entered—with a clear comprehension of what it means, I trust—into the Kingdom of the Heavens.

Some may say, "Yes, I will obey God, but I will not obey Dowie!"

Well, then, will you please find some other place of refuge?

Will you please find some other leader whom you want to follow?

Will you please go away and see whether you cannot find some better place in which to live?

You will be an awful nuisance here!

As a people you have endorsed, not only today, nor last week, nor week before, but all the way through, this one principle, which from the beginning I never hid from you: that, if I was the Prophet and the Apostle of God, I was, under God, the Ruler of His people.

It Is Necessary that the First Apostle Should Rule With Diligence.

I should be unworthy of the position of Ruler if I did not rule with diligence, with humility, with concentration of purpose; and if I did not see to it that no man should despise my authority.

The moment a Ruler has permitted one to despise his authority, he is gone as the ruler.

If a father in a house permits his wife, his son, his daughter, or his servant to despise him, he had better leave. He is of no more use there.

He has abdicated his Divinely-given authority; and the moment he does that, chaos and confusion must prevail.

That is the danger.

The Kingdom of God is ruled, as all kingdoms are, by those who are appointed by the King.

Rulers are not elected, in an absolute monarchy, by the people.

Human absolute monarchy is a failure, because the king has not been the servant of God.

The theory that a king should be the servant of God and the ruler of the people is a right one.

The practice has been a bad one.

The apostate church has recognized men as kings, and has anointed them as kings, when they knew they were bad; when they knew they were not the servants of God.

Therefore the apostate church has been partaker with the monarchy in its sins.

I do not wonder that Dr. Temple, the late Archbishop of Canterbury, fainted as he anointed King Edward VII.

There was no man who knew better than Dr. Temple that he had been already anointed by the Devil; and that he had been living a life of shameful wickedness, not a life of faith in the Son of God.

Dr. Temple was far too well-informed not to know what kind of man Albert, Prince of Wales, was.

He knew that in consecrating him as the Anointed of Jehovah, and Defender of the Faith, he was simply performing a shocking, shameful lie, and anointing a servant of the Devil.

It Is Imperative that the Truth Shall Be Spoken.

I say that plainly, not caring whether or not I am killed for it.

That would not matter; but that I should speak the truth matters.

It is a very solemn and awful truth.

That is not only true of King Edward VII., but of rulers all over Europe.

No one is under any delusion whatever concerning the real characters of many of the rulers of nations, whom priests and politicians praise, when they should denounce them. But they suit the Apostate Churches.

There is no question at all but that the churches which anoint these men as kings are a mass of hypocrisy.

If they anointed as kings only those who are just, and good, and pure, there would not be many, perhaps not any, anointed in Europe.

The absolute Monarchy of which I speak is the absolute Monarchy of God—of the Christ, the King.

That is the thought which you must get into your minds.

If you are going to get the blessing of the Holy Oil; to be anointed into this Kingdom of God; to be priests that shall offer a spiritual sacrifice, you must know and I must know our own position in this Kingdom, and take it.

If I am not absolutely obedient to God, and you are not absolutely obedient to me, wherein I follow God, then I tell you, you had better go somewhere else, quickly.

You will hinder us and hurt yourself by remaining.

This is the essential truth.

There is no division, in Zion, between the Church and the State.

In Zion it is all Church and all State.

In Zion, the Christ is King, everywhere.

He is King of our spirits, and He is King in our homes; He is King in our business, and He is King in our politics.

Now pray.

PRAYER OF CONSECRATION.

My God and Father, in Jesus' Name I come to Thee. Take me as I am. Make me what I ought to be in spirit, in soul, and in body. Give me power to do right. Give me the liberty wherewith the Christ makes free to serve Thee, with a perfect freedom, a willing service, and an absolute devotion. Help me, my Father, to be truly a Son of the Kingdom—a child of the King. For Jesus' sake. Amen.

The service was then closed by the First Apostle's pronouncing the

APOSTOLIC AND HIGH-PRIESTLY BENEDICTION.

Jehovah bless thee, and keep thee:
Jehovah make His face to shine upon thee, and be gracious unto thee:
Jehovah lift up His countenance upon thee, and give thee Peace.

Beloved, abstain from every form of evil. And may the very God of Peace Himself sanctify you wholly; and I pray God your whole spirit, and soul, and body be preserved entire, without blame, unto the coming of our Lord Jesus, the Christ. Faithful is He that calleth you, who also will do it.

The grace of our Lord Jesus, the Christ, the love of God, our Father, the fellowship of the Holy Spirit, our Comforter and Guide, one Eternal God, abide in you, bless you, and keep you, and all the Israel of God everywhere, forever. Amen.

DO YOU KNOW GOD'S WAY OF HEALING?

BY THE REV. JOHN ALEX. DOWIE.

Let it be supposed that the following words are a conversation between the reader [A] and the writer [B].

A. What does this question mean? Do you really suppose that God has some one especial way of healing in these days, of which men may know and avail themselves?

B. That is exactly my meaning, and I wish very much that you should know God's Way of Healing, as I have known it for many years.

A. What is the way, in your opinion?

B. You should rather ask, WHO is God's Way? for the way is a Person, not a thing. I will answer your question in His own words, "I am the Way, and the Truth, and the Life, no one cometh unto the Father, but by Me." These words were spoken by our Lord Jesus, the Christ, the Eternal Son of God, who is both our Savior and our Healer. (John 14:6.)

A. But I always thought that these words only referred to Him as the Way of Salvation. How can you be sure that they refer to Him as the Way of Healing also?

B. Because He cannot change. He is "the same yesterday and today, yea, and forever." (Hebrews 13:8.) He said that He came to this earth not only to save us but to heal us. (Luke 4:18), and He did this when in the flesh on earth. Being unchanged He must be able and willing and desirous to heal now.

A. But is there not this difference, namely, that He is not with us now?

B. No; for He said "Lo, I am with you All the Days, even unto the Consummation of the Age;" and so He is with us now, in spirit, just as much as when He was here in the flesh.

A. But did He not work these miracles of healing when on earth merely to prove that He was the Son of God?

B. No; there was still a greater purpose than that. He healed the sick who trusted in Him in order to show us that He came to die not only for our sins, but for our sicknesses, and to deliver us from both.

A. Then, if that be so, the atonement which He made on the Cross must have been for our sicknesses as well as our sins. Can you prove that is the fact from the Scriptures?

B. Yes, I can, and the passages are very numerous. I need quote only two. In Isaiah 53:4, 5, it is written of Him: "Surely He hath borne our griefs (Hebrew, *sicknesses*), and carried our sorrows: . . . and with His stripes we are healed." Then, in the Gospel according to Matthew, this passage is quoted and directly applied to the work of bodily healing, in the 8th chapter 17th verse: "That it might be fulfilled which was spoken by Isaiah the prophet, saying, Himself took our infirmities, and bare our diseases."

A. But do you not think that sickness is often God's will, and sent for our good, and therefore God may not wish us to be healed?

B. No, that cannot possibly be; for diseases of every kind are the Devil's work, and his work can never be God's will, since the Christ came for the very purpose of destroying "the works of the Devil." (1 John 3:8.)

A. Do you mean to say that all disease is the work of Satan?

B. Yes, for if there had been no sin (which came through Satan) there never would have been any disease, and Jesus never in one single instance told any person that sickness was God's work or will, but the very contrary.

A. Can you prove from Scriptures that all forms of sickness and infirmity are the Devil's work?

B. Yes, that can be done very easily. You will see in Matthew 4:23 and 9:35 that when Jesus was here in the flesh He healed "all manner of disease and all manner of sickness among the people." Then if you will refer to Acts 10:38 you will see that the Apostle Peter declares that He (Jesus) "went about doing good, and healing all that were oppressed of the Devil." Notice that all whom He healed, not some, were suffering from Satan's evil power.

A. But does disease never come from God?

B. No, it cannot come from God, for He is pure, and disease is unclean; and it cannot come out of Heaven, for there is no disease there.

A. That is very different from the teachings which I have received all my life from ministers and in the churches. Do you really think that you are right, and that they are all wrong in this matter?

B. It is not a question as between myself and them. The only question is, What does God's Word say? God has said in all the ages, to His Church, "I am Jehovah that healeth thee" (Exodus 15:26), and therefore it would be wicked to say that He is the defiler of His people. All true Christians must believe the Bible, and it is impossible to believe that good and evil, sickness and health, sin and holiness could have a common origin in God. If the Bible really taught that, it would be impossible to believe our Lord Jesus, the Christ, when He says: "A good tree cannot bring forth evil fruit, neither can a corrupt tree bring forth good fruit." (Matthew 7:18.)

A. But even if I agree with all you say, is it not true that the Gifts of Healing were removed from the Church, and are not in it now?

B. No, the "Gifts of Healing" were never withdrawn, and can never be withdrawn from the true Church of God, for it is written: "The gifts and the calling of God are without repentance." (Romans 11:29.) There are nine gifts of God to the Church (enumerated in 1 Corinthians 12:8-11), and all these are in the Holy Spirit. Therefore, so long as the Holy Spirit is in the Church, all the gifts must be there also. If they are not exercised that does not prove that they do not exist, but that the faith to exercise them is lacking in God's servants. The gifts are all perfectly preserved; for the Holy Spirit, not the Church, keeps them safely.

A. What should a Christian then do when overtaken with sickness?

B. A Christian should obey God's command, and at once turn to Him for forgiveness of the sin which may have caused the sickness, and for immediate healing. Healing is obtained from God in one of four ways, namely: First, by the direct prayer of faith, without any aid from the officers of the Church, praying as the Centurion did in Matthew 8:5-13; second, by two faithful disciples praying in perfect agreement in accordance with the Lord's promise in Matthew 18:19; third, by the anointing of the Elders and the prayer of faith according to the instructions in James 5:14 and 15; and fourth, by the laying on of the hands of them who believe, and whom God calls to that ministry, as the Lord commands in Mark 16:18, and in other places.

A. But are people healed in this way in these days?

B. Yes, in thousands of cases. I have myself laid hands upon many hundreds of thousands of persons, and I have seen the Lord's power manifested in the healing of great numbers, many of whom are living witnesses in many countries, who have testified publicly before thousands, and who are prepared to testify at any time. This ministry is being exercised by devoted Christians in many parts of America, Europe, Australasia, and elsewhere.

A. Is it not the same as Christian Science, Mind Healing, etc.?

B. No. Divine Healing is diametrically opposed to these diabolical counterfeits which are utterly antichristian. These impostures are only seductive forms of Spiritualism. Trance Evangelism is also a more recent form of this delusion, and it deceives many.

A. But how shall I obtain the necessary faith to receive healing, which faith I am at present conscious that I do not possess?

B. It is written: "Belief cometh of hearing, and hearing by the word of the Christ." (Romans 10:17.) Our Missions are held for the express purpose of teaching fully the Word of God on this matter, and I very heartily invite you to attend the meetings which are announced for Zion Tabernacles in Chicago and other cities, and for Shiloh Tabernacle, Zion City, Illinois. All are welcome and there are no charges of any kind made, for all God's gifts are free gifts. Salvation is the first of these, without which you cannot be healed through faith in Jesus. All the costs of this work are covered by the free-will offerings of the people who attend these meetings, and others whom the Lord leads to help; but the poorest, who have nothing to give, are as heartily welcome as the richest.

A. Do you see the sick and lay hands upon them in this Mission?

B. Yes; after we feel satisfied that they are fully resting in the Lord alone for the blessing, we see privately, so far as time permits, those who attend; but under no circumstances do we claim the power to heal any; for "power belongeth unto God."

A. Have you any writings upon this subject which can be purchased?

B. Yes; these can be obtained at the office of Zion Printing and Publishing House, Zion City, Illinois, and at any Zion Tabernacle. But the best book on Divine Healing is the Bible itself, studied prayerfully and earnestly.

We extend to you a hearty invitation to attend the meetings, which are free to all. Our prayer is that you may be led to find in Jesus, the Christ, our Lord and God your present Savior from sin, your Healer from sickness, your Cleanser from all evil, your Keeper in the way to Heaven, your Friend, and your All for Time and Eternity. We pray that these words may help many who read, and that our little conversation may bear fruit in leading many readers to look to Jesus only.

"The Healing of Christ's seamless dress
Is by all beds of pain;
We touch Him in life's throng and press [illegible]
And we are whole again."

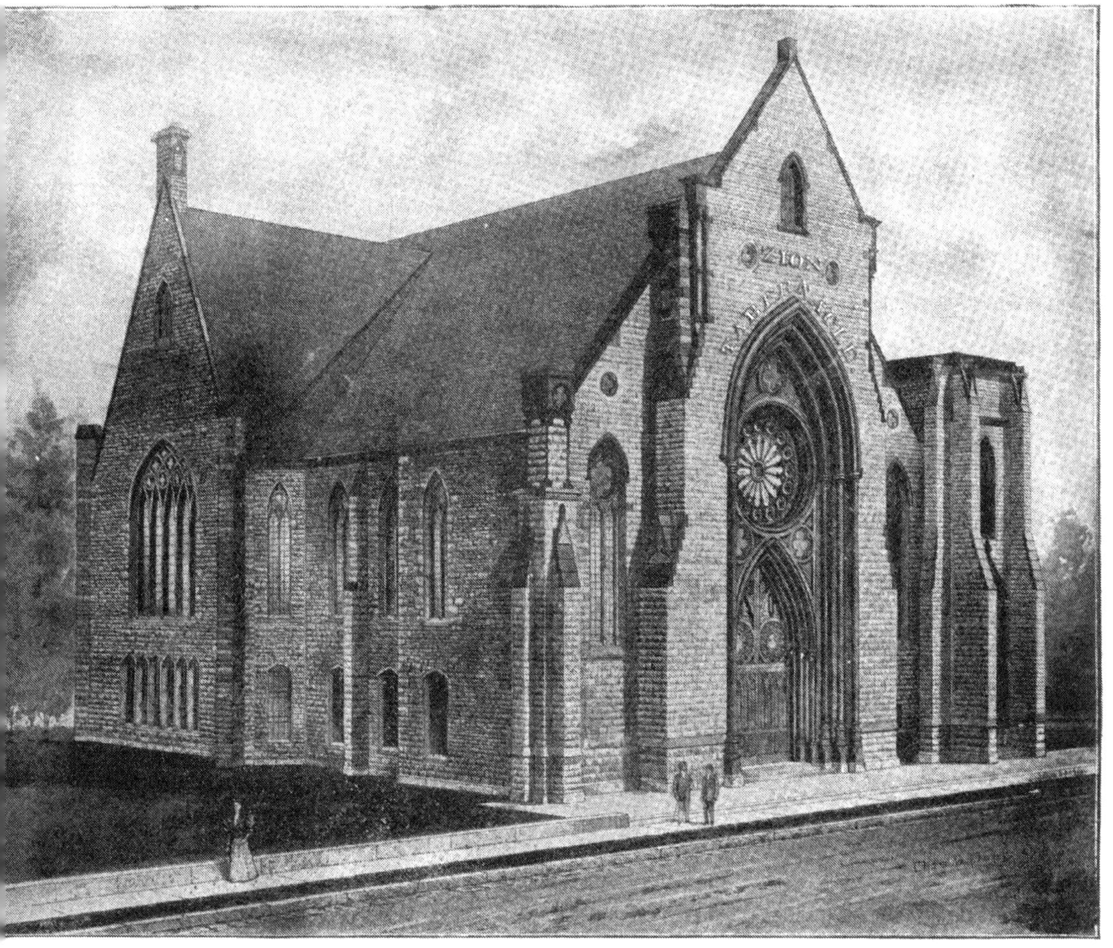

CENTRAL ZION TABERNACLE

1621-1633 Michigan Avenue, Chicago, Illinois

This building was occupied by the Christian Catholic Church in Zion for five years, 1896 to 1901. It was given up at the expiration of the five years' lease on December 31, 1901. Since then it has stood vacant. John Alexander, First Apostle of the Christian Catholic Apostolic Church in Zion has now leased the Tabernacle again, and it will be opened as the Headquarters of his work in Chicago, before the end of the year.

Financial, Commercial and Industrial Notes

THE demand for Zion Pure Soap is constantly increasing. We have orders coming in from every part of the country.

One merchant who sells our soap, and is using it in his home, said last week, "After the people once use your soap they will use no other; it will advertise itself, and is sure to create a large demand."

I said, "Good, then it must be a soap that *talks*." That is the kind of goods we wish to produce—soap that *speaks* for itself.

But we are not satisfied with the present volume of business. The world is big, and it takes tons and tons of soap to wash it and keep it clean; and we want to get our share of the business.

I will tell you how you can help us. There will probably be at least fifty thousand people who will read this article. If each one will buy one bar of soap per week, that will be fifty thousand bars. At a profit of one cent per bar, we would make five hundred dollars per week.

These sales, and what we are now selling, will give employment, at good wages, to at least ten more men. With their families, it would mean a possible increase of twenty-five persons to our population in Zion City.

You may say, "What does my little one bar a week amount to?" But you see, it is the aggregate—the collection of the many little fragments—that constitutes the power to do great good.

Do not be too modest or bashful. If you cannot order a Family Box, send in the small amounts, and help us establish a Great Industry that will make money to be used for the extension of God's Kingdom.

What an opportunity we have before us!

What a Royal Generation God is raising up in Zion!

The boys and girls in our schools today will be men and women in the very near future; and will have their part to perform in the world's work.

There is no place in the world where they can get a training equal to the one offered in Zion City.

God has given us the best of everything, and by His Grace we will make the best of everything He has given.

Remember that Zion Industries have a great part to play in the extension of God's Kingdom, and the Restoration of All Things.

You can help by buying Zion products, and advising others to buy them; and thus indirectly, if not directly, have a part in turning many to righteousness.

The promise is, that they that turn many to righteouness shall shine as the stars forever and ever.

CHARLES A. HANSON,
Manager Zion City Soap Factory.

Zion is actively engaged in the work of the Restoration.

Zion City has been founded for the purpose of training a people for this great work.

Zion's Industries have been established so that Zion everywhere may have a part in the great principle of Christian Coöperation, upon which every Zion Institution is established.

A great responsibility rests upon all Zion in connection with the great business she is doing for the King.

Every resource derived from her Industries is used for His glory in extending the Kingdom of God.

By uniting the efforts of the members and friends of Zion, we shall create a tremendous influence for righteousness in the commercial world.

Every Zion family wants Pure Foodstuffs, free from hog and other adulterations. Our Candies, Crackers and Bakery Goods, Shortening (substitute for lard), etc., are absolutely free from these, and should be used in every Zion household.

Our beautiful Laces and Lace Curtains have attracted the eyes of the public wherever they have been introduced.

We are making the purest Soaps on the market for toilet, bath, and laundry.

Our Box Factory has many beautiful designs of Paper Boxes.

Let Zion everywhere create a demand for our home products.

Speak to your friends and tell them of our goods.

Induce your dealer to carry a line of our products.

CHARLES J. BARNARD,
General Financial Manager.

There are certainly no Investments in all the world so desirable for Christian people as those of Zion. As one compares them with worldly investments their superiority is most strikingly manifest.

Zion Investments have stipulated incomes that are fully double the amounts usually received by investors. Their security does not rest upon the limited capital stock of a single institution, but upon the whole estate of Zion, which is constantly increasing in extent and value, and which has the united support of the most strongly organized community in existence.

Moreover, Zion Investments are clean in every particular. The money is employed in the promotion of none but the most honorable Industries and Institutions, which are essential features of the world's greatest object lesson of practical purity. and righteousness, and Christian coöperation.

Investors in every land have shown great appreciation of Zion Securities; and, as their true worth becomes better understood, there is no doubt that prophecy will be more and more fulfilled, and the wealth of the nations will flow to Zion in an ever-increasing stream.

The world's wealth is greater now than at any other period of its history, and the wealthiest of all the nations is the American Republic.

Some idea of the vast extent and nature of the investments which have been made in American enterprises will be brought to mind in considering the following statement of facts from official sources:

Fifteen of the leading railways of America have a total capitalization of five thousand million dollars, which is double the amount of all the actual money in the nation. Of this amount considerably more than one-half has been borrowed, and is represented by bonds bearing interest at from three to seven per cent. The balance is represented by shares of stock earning a comparatively low rate, and subject to all the prior obligations of the funded debt.

One of these railways is the great Chicago and North-Western, whose main line passes through Zion City. Its funded debt is over one hundred fifty-three million dollars, while its capital stock is less than seventy-one million dollars.

The holders of these bonds have a margin of only one-third in their security, and they receive interest at the rate of not exceeding five per cent. on the face amount of the investment, and to purchase these bonds in the open market must pay premiums as high as nineteen per cent.

Shareholders' dividends depend upon

the uncertain profits of railway operations, after payment of the certain interest upon their overwhelming debt; and the net earnings are comparatively low.

This is sound finance; according to the best standards; and indicates most clearly that the present opportunities of securing Zion's Superior Investments upon such favorable terms will be very brief.

FIELDING H. WILHITE,
Manager Zion Securities and Investments.

It is estimated by the customs authorities that the importation of Laces into the United States amounts to upwards of thirty million dollars a year. This, of course, includes all kinds, styles, and grades, both in real and machine-made Laces.

This enormous demand is supplied largely by the European countries, where for many years Laces have been made and studied—a fact that is recognized by every periodical of note devoted to fancy goods.

With a view to capturing a portion of this great trade, Zion Lace Industries were founded, and have been successfully established, as is known throughout the length and breadth of this country.

The great opening for fine laces, that will correspond with the English manufacture, has been already demonstrated, and there is every encouragement for constantly increasing both the quantity and quality of the output.

The prophetic eye of the founder of the Lace Industries foresaw the demand there would be for an American-made product, and his plans covered all lines of goods in Laces, Curtains, Fancy Trimmings, and Embroideries.

Therefore, Zion Lace Industries will, as soon as possible, make and put on the market such goods as are demanded by the American people in all lines of lace production.

HENRY STEVENSON,
General Manager.

In our mail, a few days ago, we received, accompanied with an order, the following words of appreciation from one of our customers in Montana:

"I sent for an order the last of July, and received everything in good condition. Was so pleased with the Shortening, Soap, and Candy that I do not want to be without them any more, for they are just excellent."

We print these words so that readers of LEAVES OF HEALING may be able to get an idea to what an extent the business of the General Stores has grown.

We are convinced that there are numbers of people throughout the country who would appreciate the privilege of using our Zion products, but are not in a position to send a sufficiently large order to make a profitable freight shipment. To such we wish to say that we have a plan whereby every one wishing to get our Products may do so.

The Products we manufacture are in daily demand in every home. Every thoughtful housewife is always looking for the best and purest foodstuffs she can get. She is also very particular in the kind of soap she uses.

To any reader of LEAVES OF HEALING who has been waiting to send an order until he could make it large enough to make a profitable shipment by freight, we advise him to interest his neighbors and friends, and get them to send an order with his.

This is being done in numbers of cases throughout the country, and has proved very beneficial to those who otherwise would not have been able to profitably send for the goods. By three or four families making up an order between them, and having it shipped to one individual, much will be saved in freight; and by purchasing in larger quantities they would be entitled to lower prices.

We are strongly advocating this plan to our various gatherings throughout the country. We take particular pains with these orders, so that when shipments are received, there is no difficulty whatever in finding the goods you order.

We ask every one who reads these words to consider this matter, and if any other information is needed, we shall be pleased to furnish it.

W. HURD CLENDINEN,
General Manager Zion City General Stores.

The healthy condition of the Candy Business, and the confidence which business men have in it, may be seen by the very few failures and the many new factories which are being started, and by old ones being enlarged. In all parts of the country we see signs of progress and prosperity in the Sugar and Candy business.

The new Sugar Refinery of "The Federal Sugar Refining Company," on the Hudson River, has begun operations with a daily capacity of fifteen hundred barrels, which, we are informed, will soon be increased to four thousand barrels a day.

The concern making the purest and best confections will naturally get the bulk of the most desirable business; hence Zion Sugar and Confection Association will very soon be in the lead, if we are not already there.

Some people boast of being the largest and oldest manufacturers.

Our boast, if we boast at all, is that we make the best and most modern kinds.

The people generally are becoming more convinced of the healthfulness of pure confections, as the following article taken from the *Trade Journal* will show:

"Every one nowadays, owing to the disclosures of scientific investigation, believes that sugar plays a more important part in the dietary than a mere condiment. It is a food and, when judiciously used in combination with other foods, adds much to the value of a ration. The Minnesota Experiment Station, after studying the question, concludes that the addition of five ounces of sugar a day to the ration of the working man proved beneficial. It increased the available energy of the ration twenty-five per cent., and did not affect the digestibility of other foods with which it was combined."

ROSCOE E. RODDA,
Manager Zion Sugar and Confection Association.

Zion City Planing Mills, a department of the Building and Manufacturing Association, one of the chief Industries of Zion City, is making great forward strides in the manufacture of interior finishings for houses, which is a specialty with us.

We make the finest and best Veneered Doors, the highest class of Stairs, beautiful China Closets and Sideboards, beautiful designs in Grille Work and other Wall Ornaments, with hand carvings of Zion Emblems and Mottoes; also Bank and Office Fixtures and Furnishings, all kinds of Desks, Filing Cases, Directors' Tables, etc.

A large number of these are in use in the various Departments of Zion City.

We have orders for hundreds of Small Tables for use in schools, some Bookcases, Pulpits, and various kinds of Desks and equipment for Kindergarten and Junior School work.

Up to the present time we have been unable to supply more than is consumed within the City, with the exception of a few small orders from our neighbors.

We believe that God's people should get what they pay for.

We also believe that they should patronize Institutions that guarantee good, honest, substantial work by honest workmen—work and material that are clean, not made amidst oaths and curses, or saturated with the fumes of tobacco and beer, and bearing the marks of trade unionism and strife, and which carry a curse with them, but that which is made by labor that uses the proceeds in extending the Kingdom of God and establishing clean, pure homes.

As Christian coöperation is the motive and motto of Zion, we expect all to coöperate with us, and thus enable us to increase our capacity, produce larger quantities, and reduce prices.

J. L. OGDEN,
Manager Zion Planing Mill.

ZION BUILDING, CHICAGO, ILLINOIS

1201-1207 MICHIGAN AVENUE

Property of John Alexander, First Apostle of the Christian Catholic Apostolic Church in Zion. To be reopened soon, as the Chicago Headquarters of Zion Institutions and Industries.

Zion's Bible Class

Conducted by Teacher Daniel Sloan in Shiloh Tabernacle, Zion City, Lord's Day Morning at 11 o'clock, and in Zion Homes and Gatherings throughout the World.

MID-WEEK BIBLE CLASS LESSON, NOVEMBER 2d or 3d.

The Wise-hearted.

They are controlled by faith.—Matthew 11:20-27.
They see what the worldly wise do not see.
They see not only the works of God, but God Himself
They accept Kingdom truths as a little child.

They grow in wisdom.—Proverbs 1:1-6.
They believe in knowing more and more.
They heed words of wisdom.
They catch the real meaning of words.

They pray intelligently.—Daniel 2:19-30.
God alone can reveal truth.
They know that all things are in God's hands.
They are discerners of spirits.

They expect to understand fully.—Hosea 14:4-9
They give up all iniquity and folly.
They seek to obey God fully.
They trust God for all and know all.

They use knowledge wisely.—Proverbs 15:2-7
They think before they speak.
They want to do the right thing.
They are not perplexed, because they have a reserve.

This wisdom is in practicable form.—Exodus 31:1-11.
The genius to build comes from Him.
Artistic taste is God-given.
Every man needs God in his business.

They are enabled to discern the signs of the times.—1 Thessalonian 5:1-11.
The wise-hearted live in the light.
The wise-hearted watch, and foresee things.
The wise-hearted do not need to be on exhibition.

They always win many about them to righteousness.—Daniel 12:1-4.
Their lives are not barren of results.
Soul-winners shine forth as bright lights for God.
A man must live rightly before he can do right.
The Lord Our God is a Wisdom-imparting God.

LORD'S DAY BIBLE CLASS LESSON, NOVEMBER 6th.

Unstable Souls.

They twist the Scriptures.—2 Peter 3:11-18
They look at things seen.
They listen to the Devil.
They do not know the Christ.

They follow fables.—1 Timothy 4:
Evil spirits lead them.
They follow vain customs.
They follow foggy notions.

They speak vain words.—2 Peter 2:9-19.
They despise good order and authority.
They will have their way.
They try, and then, with an excuse, give up.

They are never quite sure—2 Timothy 3:1-9.
They doubt, because they sin in other ways.
They make a pretense of this and that.
They have no faith.

They balk at truth—John 6:59-71.
When self-denial is imposed they stop.
They say that truth is too hard to be obeyed.
They say that it is not what they thought.

They do not abide in the doctrine.—2 John 1:6-13.
They obey commandments only when they suit them
They say that this and that is done away with
They establish a creed and a self-made religion.

They cease to listen to exhortation.—Hebrews 3:12-19.
They do not admit that they sin.
They say that they are as good as others.
They do not want to live for God.

They are never fruitful.—Matthew 13:18-23.
They do not receive truth in the heart.
They do good only when they get good.
They cannot stand testing.
God's Holy People are a Steadfast People.

OBEYING GOD IN BAPTISM.

"Baptizing Them Into the Name of the Father and of the Son and of the Holy Spirit."

Twenty Thousand Seventy-nine Baptisms by Triune Immersion Since March 14, 1897.

Twenty Thousand Seventy-nine Believers have joyfully followed their Lord in the Ordinance of Believer's Baptism by Triune Immersion since the first Baptism in Central Zion Tabernacle on March 14, 1897.

Baptized in Central Zion Tabernacle from March 14, 1897, to December 14, 1901, by the General Overseer,	4754			
Baptized in South Side Zion Tabernacle from January 1, 1902, to June 14, 1903, by the General Overseer..	37			
Baptized at Zion City by the General Overseer........	647			
Baptized by Overseers, Elders, Evangelists and Deacons, at Headquarters (Zion City) and Chicago......	5626			
Total Baptized at Headquarters....................	—			11,064
Baptized in places outside of Headquarters by the General Overseer..............................		765		
Baptized in places outside of Headquarters by Overseers, Elders, Evangelists and Deacons............		8,126		
Total Baptized outside of Headquarters............		—		8,891
Total Baptized in seven years and six months......				19,955
Baptized since September 14, 1904:				
Baptized in Zion City by Overseer Excell............	16			
Baptized in Zion City by Elder Viking...............	3			
Baptized in Zion City by Elder Dinius...............	3			
Baptized in Zion City by Elder Royall...............	20			
Baptized in Zion City by Deacon Marpburg............	10			
Baptized in Chicago by Elder Hoffman...............	6			
Baptized in Chicago by Elder Hammond...............	5		63	
Baptized in Illinois by Elder Gay..................		5		
Baptized in Kansas by Elder Reed...................		10		
Baptized in London by Overseer Cantel...............		11		
Baptized in Michigan by Deacon Van Woerkom......		1		
Baptized in Missouri by Deacon Robinson............		2		
Baptized in New York by Elder Warszawiak..........		9		
Baptized in New York by Overseer Mason		12		
Baptized in Ohio by Deacon Smith..................		1		
Baptized in Oregon by Elder Ernst.................		2		
Baptized in Pennsylvania by Elder Bouck............		4		
Baptized in Texas by Elder Hall...................		3		
Baptized in Washington by Elder Simmons...........		1	61	124
Total Baptized since March 14, 1897...............				20,079

The following-named believer was baptized at Chandler, Oklahoma Territory, Thursday, September 8, 1904, by Elder David A. Reed:

Barrows, Mrs. Ellizabeth..................Chandler, Oklahoma Territory

---

The following-named two believers were baptized in Portland, Oregon, Lord's Day, September 25, 1904, by Elder August Ernst:

Grace, Mrs. Tillie...Clarkes, Oregon
Laughlin, Harley Wade...Lagrande, Oregon

The following-named eleven believers were baptized in the Caledonian Road Baths, London, England, Lord's Day, September 25, 1904, by Overseer H. E. Cantel:

Arkell, Horatio James..35 Droop street, Queen's Park, W., London, England
Bryant, Miss Nellie, May Villa, Bellingdon Road, Chesham, Bucks, England
Coles, Mrs. Harriet..67 Charlton street, Marylebone, W., London, England
Dunsdon, Edward John...........7 California, Aylesbury, Bucks, England
Faulkes, George.....35 Droop street, Queen's Park, W., London, England
Lawrence, Thomas..................8 Long Acre, W.C., London, England
Lyne, Mabel ....35 Droop street, Queen's Park, W., London, England
McNicol, Miss Ada, 65 Cleveland street, Fitzroy square, W., London, England
Robertson, Miss Jane Mary........42 Drayton Park, N., London, England
Smith, Mrs. E..........14 Mornington Dwellings, N.W., London, England
Tiernan, Miss M..65 Cleveland street, Fitzroy square, W., London, England

---

The following-named two believers were baptized in San Antonio, Texas, Lord's Day, October 2, 1904, by Elder L. C. Hall:

Robinson, Mrs. Gertrude S..........700 Rio Grande avenue, Austin, Texas
Threadgill, Mrs. Anna Lott..........St. Mary's street, San Antonio, Texas

---

The following-named sixteen believers were baptized in Shiloh Tabernacle, Zion City, Illinois, Lord's Day, October 9, 1904, by Overseer J. G. Excell:

Ayres, Mrs. Ruth....................3012 Gilead avenue, Zion City, Illinois
Ayres, Clarence......................3012 Gilead avenue, Zion City, Illinois
Ayers, Zadock Bowen..... ....3012 Gilead avenue, Zion City, Illinois
Bishop, Floyd...Conklin, Michigan
Burrows, Miss Susan Maria.........3104 Ezekiel avenue, Zion City, Illinois
Cary, Mrs. Frances..Libertyville, Illinois
Cary, Dr. John...Libertyville, Illinois
Collins, Jesse....................2813 Elizabeth avenue, Zion City, Illinois
Cummings, Mrs. Eliza Jane.............................Gaylord, Michigan
Cummings, James L.......................................Gaylord, Michigan
Humbert, Mrs. Lydia Elizabeth.............................Nashua, Iowa
McNally, Miss Margaret............3015 Elisha avenue, Zion City, Illinois
Massuere, Miss Susan.......................................Arcadia, Wisconsin
Parsons, Mrs. Mary.......................................Dimondale, Michigan
Sanford, Mrs. Olinda.......606 East End avenue, Chattanooga, Tennessee
Williams, Stephen H..................3011 Elim avenue, Zion City, Illinois

---

The following-named four believers were baptized in the North Side Zion Tabernacle, Chicago, Illinois, Lord's Day, October 9, 1904, by Elder C. R. Hoffman:

Brasch, Ella M..................1813 West Winona street, Chicago, Illinois
Kresin, Agnes............................365 Homer street, Chicago, Illinois
Kresin, Otto..............................365 Homer street, Chicago, Illinois
Scheel, Louis......................1833 Lawrence avenue, Chicago, Illinois

---

The following-named ten believers were baptized in Shiloh Tabernacle, Zion City, Illinois, Wednesday, October 12, 1904, by Deacon A. E. Marpurg:

Booth, Mrs. Edna ....3004 Gilboa avenue, Zion City, Illinois
Booth, Thomas Ernest..............3004 Gilboa avenue, Zion City, Illinois
Coghill, Eddie T..................2605 Elizabeth avenue, Zion City, Illinois
Coghill, Leroy F..................2605 Elizabeth avenue, Zion City, Illinois
Coghill, Mildred..................2605 Elizabeth avenue, Zion City, Illinois
Dennis, David W...................2112 Emmaus avenue, Zion City, Illinois
Dennis, Miss Ruth.................2112 Emmaus avenue, Zion City, Illinois
Fosner, Ernest Abraham...................................Enterprise, Oregon
Gaug, Andrew...Gibson City, Illinois
Williams, James Roger..............2212 Elisha avenue, Zion City, Illinois

CONSECRATION OF CHILDREN.

The following-named five children were consecrated to God at Pretoria, Transvaal, South Africa, Lord's Day, August 28, 1904, by Overseer Daniel Bryant:

Townsend, Dorothy Cornelia Andrew.....Pretoria, Transvaal, South Africa
Townsend, Edith Sidney Brunt...........Pretoria, Transvaal, South Africa
Townsend, Frances Agnes Margaret.......Pretoria, Transvaal, South Africa
Townsend, Freda Antoinette Catherine...Pretoria, Transvaal, South Africa
Townsend, Lilith Agusta Leonie..........Pretoria, Transvaal, South Africa

---

The following-named child was consecrated to God in Chicago, Illinois, Saturday, September 24, 1904, by Deacon B. W. Brannen:

VanNatta, Harold Edward..........1869 McLean avenue, Chicago, Illinois

---

The following-named child was consecrated to God at Falls City, Nebraska, Monday, October 3, 1904, by Elder C. A. Hoy:

Sperry, Mabel Esther...............................Falls City, Nebraska

---

Changes in the New York City Branch.

Beginning with Lord's Day, October 2d, the meetings will be removed to the center of New York City, corner of Madison avenue and East One Hundred Twenty-fifth street. Sunday, 11 a. m., 3 p. m., and 8 p. m. Divine Healing Meeting every Thursday, 2:30 p. m. Overseer George L. Mason's new address, is No. 4 St. Nicholas Terrace.

Change of Location in Toronto, Canada.

Zion Gathering in Toronto, Canada, has secured the old Friends' meeting house, 34 Pembroke street, where services will hereafter be conducted. It is easily reached by transferring from any street-car line in the city to the Belt Line. Get off at Wilton avenue, and go west one block to Pembroke. Elder Brooks has also changed his residence to No. 360 Parliament street

Publisher's Notice.

The remittance must accompany receipt of subscriptions at the Publishing House, no difference by or for whom or for whatever time they may be given, or whether forwarded through Ordained Officers, Branches, or Gatherings of the Christian Catholic Church in Zion. Accounts will be carried with Ordained Officers, Branches, or Gatherings, on quantity orders of periodicals consigned on sale for monthly settlement, but to include only such articles as bear the imprint of Zion. All orders for Bibles, books, buttons, pictures (except prints done by the Publishing House), lace souvenirs, etc., must be sent to the General Stores, Zion City, Lake County, Illinois.

PUBLICATION DE SION POUR L'EXTENSION DU ROYAUME DE DIEU.

ÉDITÉE PAR LE RÉV. JOHN ALEX. DOWIE.

Matthew 28

18. And Jesus came to them and spake unto them, saying, All authority hath been given unto Me in heaven and on earth.
19. Go ye therefore, and make disciples of all the nations, baptizing them into the Name of the Father and of the Son and of the Holy Ghost:
20. Teaching them to observe all things whatsoever I command you: and lo, I am with you all the days, even unto the Consummation of the Age.

Mark 16

15. And He said unto them, Go ye into all the world, and preach the Gospel to the whole creation.
16. He that believeth and is baptized shall be saved; but he that disbelieveth shall be condemned.
17. And these signs shall follow them that believe: in My Name shall they cast out devils; they shall speak with new tongues.
18. They shall take up serpents, and if they drink any deadly thing, it shall in no wise hurt them; they shall lay hands on the sick, and they shall recover.

A GREAT onward stride in the fulfilment of this command of the Christ is being made by publishing FEUILLES DE GUÉRISON, which is LEAVES OF HEALING in the French language.

The first issue is dated October 15, 1904. The paper will be published monthly, and will contain twenty-four pages the size of LEAVES OF HEALING.

As every advancement made by Zion to carry the full Gospel to every creature is hailed with joy and delight by every true Christian, we are going forward trusting that every reader will enthusiastically do all within his power to provide every French-speaking person he knows with a copy, and, if possible, a year's subscription.

In order that an application for entry as "second class" mail matter may be made, we must have enough subscribers to approximate fifty per cent. of the number of copies regularly issued and circulated.

Therefore, we make this request in order that we may not be limited or restricted in the amount of our issue, or in the extent of our circulation, or be debarred from the privileges of second class rates of postage.

Feeling assured that the French people will give respectful consideration to the words of our beloved First Apostle, John Alexander, we believe that FEUILLES DE GUÉRISON will be cordially welcomed by them, and trust it may win the hearts of this clever people for God and Zion.

The price is 50 cents a year domestic, and 75 cents, or 4 francs, foreign.

May we receive an order from you soon

Zion Printing and Publishing House
Zion City, Ill.

CPSIA information can be obtained
at www.ICGtesting.com
Printed in the USA
LVHW061621040121
675568LV00030BA/1267